University Casebook Series

December, 1979

ACCOUNTING AND THE LAW, Fourth Edition (1978), with Problems Pamphlet (Successor to Dohr, Phillips, Thompson & Warren)

George C. Thompson, Professor, Columbia University Graduate School of Business.
Robert Whitman, Professor of Law, University of Connecticut.
Ellis L. Phillips, Jr., Member of the New York Bar.
William C. Warren, Professor of Law Emeritus, Columbia University.

ACCOUNTING FOR LAWYERS, MATERIALS ON, (1978) (Temporary Edition)

David R. Herwitz, Professor of Law, Harvard University.

ADMINISTRATIVE LAW, Seventh Edition (1979), with 1979 Problems Supplement (edited in association with Paul R. Verkuil, Dean and Professor of Law, Tulane University)

Walter Gellhorn, University Professor, Columbia University.
Clark Byse, Professor of Law, Harvard University.
Peter L. Strauss, Professor of Law, Columbia University.

ADMIRALTY, Second Edition (1978), with Documentary Supplement

Jo Desha Lucas, Professor of Law, University of Chicago.

ADVOCACY, INTRODUCTION TO, Second Edition (1976)

Board of Student Advisers, Harvard Law School.

ADVOCACY, see also Lawyering Process

AGENCY–ASSOCIATIONS–EMPLOYMENT–PARTNERSHIPS, Second Edition (1977)

Reprinted from Conard, Knauss & Siegel's Enterprise Organization.

AGENCY, see also Enterprise Organization

ANTITRUST AND REGULATORY ALTERNATIVES (1977)

Louis B. Schwartz, Professor of Law, University of Pennsylvania.
John J. Flynn, Professor of Law, University of Utah.

ANTITRUST SUPPLEMENT—SELECTED STATUTES AND RELATED MATERIALS (1977)

John J. Flynn, Professor of Law, University of Utah.

BIOGRAPHY OF A LEGAL DISPUTE, THE: An Introduction to American Civil Procedure (1968)

Marc A. Franklin, Professor of Law, Stanford University.

BUSINESS ORGANIZATION, see also Enterprise Organization

BUSINESS PLANNING (1966), with 1979 Problem Supplement

David R. Herwitz, Professor of Law, Harvard University.

UNIVERSITY CASEBOOK SERIES—Continued

CONTRACT LAW, STUDIES IN, Second Edition (1977)

Edward J. Murphy, Professor of Law, University of Notre Dame.
Richard E. Speidel, Professor of Law, University of Virginia.

CONTRACTS, Third Edition (1977)

John P. Dawson, Professor of Law Emeritus, Harvard University, and
William Burnett Harvey, Professor of Law and Political Science, Boston University.

CONTRACTS, Second Edition (1972), with Statutory Supplement

E. Allan Farnsworth, Professor of Law, Columbia University.
William F. Young, Jr., Professor of Law, Columbia University.
Harry W. Jones, Professor of Law, Columbia University.

CONTRACTS, Second Edition (1978), with Statutory and Administrative Law Supplement (1978)

Ian R. Macneil, Professor of Law, Cornell University.

COPYRIGHT, Unfair Competition, and Other Topics Bearing on the Protection of Literary, Musical, and Artistic Works, Third Edition (1978)

Benjamin Kaplan, Professor of Law Emeritus, Harvard University, and
Ralph S. Brown, Jr., Professor of Law, Yale University.

CORPORATE FINANCE, Second Edition (1979)

Victor Brudney, Professor of Law, Harvard University.
Marvin A. Chirelstein, Professor of Law, Yale University.

CORPORATE READJUSTMENTS AND REORGANIZATIONS (1976)

Walter J. Blum, Professor of Law, University of Chicago.
Stanley A. Kaplan, Professor of Law, University of Chicago.

CORPORATION LAW, BASIC, Second Edition (1979), with Documentary Supplement

Detlev F. Vagts, Professor of Law, Harvard University.

CORPORATIONS, Fourth Edition—Unabridged (1969), with 1977 Supplement and 1978 Special Supplement

William L. Cary, Professor of Law, Columbia University.

CORPORATIONS, Fourth Edition—Abridged (1970), with 1977 Supplement and 1978 Special Supplement

William L. Cary, Professor of Law, Columbia University.

CORPORATIONS, THE LAW OF: WHAT CORPORATE LAWYERS DO (1976)

Jan G. Deutsch, Professor of Law, Yale University.
Joseph J. Bianco, Professor of Law, Yeshiva University.

CORPORATIONS COURSE GAME PLAN (1975)

David R. Herwitz, Professor of Law, Harvard University.

CORPORATIONS, see also Enterprise Organization

CREDIT TRANSACTIONS AND CONSUMER PROTECTION (1976)

John Honnold, Professor of Law, University of Pennsylvania.

CREDITORS' RIGHTS, see also Debtor-Creditor Law

CRIMINAL LAW, Second Edition (1979)

Fred E. Inbau, Professor of Law Emeritus, Northwestern University.
James R. Thompson, Professor of Law Emeritus, Northwestern University.
Andre A. Moenssens, Professor of Law, University of Richmond.

CRIMINAL PROCEDURE, CONSTITUTIONAL (1977), with 1980 Supplement

James E. Scarboro, Professor of Law, University of Colorado.
James B. White, Professor of Law, University of Chicago.

CRIMINAL PROCEDURE (1974), with 1977 Supplement

Fred E. Inbau, Professor of Law Emeritus, Northwestern University.
James R. Thompson, Professor of Law Emeritus, Northwestern University.
James B. Haddad, Professor of Law, Northwestern University.
James B. Zagel, Chief, Criminal Justice Division, Office of Attorney General of Illinois.
Gary L. Starkman, Assistant U. S. Attorney, Northern District of Illinois.

CRIMINAL JUSTICE, THE ADMINISTRATION OF, Second Edition (1969)

Francis C. Sullivan, Professor of Law, Louisiana State University.
Paul Hardin III, Professor of Law, Duke University.
John Huston, Professor of Law, University of Washington.
Frank R. Lacy, Professor of Law, University of Oregon.
Daniel E. Murray, Professor of Law, University of Miami.
George W. Pugh, Professor of Law, Louisiana State University.

CRIMINAL JUSTICE ADMINISTRATION AND RELATED PROCESSES, Successor Edition (1976), with 1979 Supplement

Frank W. Miller, Professor of Law, Washington University.
Robert O. Dawson, Professor of Law, University of Texas.
George E. Dix, Professor of Law, University of Texas.
Raymond I. Parnas, Professor of Law, University of California, Davis.

CRIMINAL JUSTICE, LEADING CONSTITUTIONAL CASES ON (1979)

Lloyd L. Weinreb, Professor of Law, Harvard University.

CRIMINAL LAW, Second Edition (1975)

Lloyd L. Weinreb, Professor of Law, Harvard University.

CRIMINAL LAW AND ITS ADMINISTRATION (1940), with 1956 Supplement

The late Jerome Michael, Professor of Law, Columbia University, and
Herbert Wechsler, Professor of Law, Columbia University.

CRIMINAL LAW AND PROCEDURE, Fifth Edition (1977)

Rollin M. Perkins, Professor of Law Emeritus, University of California, Hastings College of the Law.
Ronald N. Boyce, Professor of Law, University of Utah.

CRIMINAL PROCESS, Third Edition (1978), with 1979 Supplement

Lloyd L. Weinreb, Professor of Law, Harvard University.

DAMAGES, Second Edition (1952)

The late Charles T. McCormick, Professor of Law, University of Texas, and
The late William F. Fritz, Professor of Law, University of Texas.

DEBTOR-CREDITOR LAW (1974), with 1978 Case-Statutory Supplement

William D. Warren, Dean of the School of Law, University of California, Los Angeles.
William E. Hogan, Professor of Law, Cornell University.

DECEDENTS' ESTATES (1971)

The late Max Rheinstein, Professor of Law Emeritus, University of Chicago.
Mary Ann Glendon, Professor of Law, Boston College Law School.

DECEDENTS' ESTATES AND TRUSTS, Fifth Edition (1977)

John Ritchie III, Professor of Law Emeritus, University of Virginia.
Neill H. Alford, Jr., Professor of Law, University of Virginia.
Richard W. Effland, Professor of Law, Arizona State University.

DECEDENTS' ESTATES AND TRUSTS (1968)

Howard R. Williams, Professor of Law, Stanford University.

DOMESTIC RELATIONS, Third Edition (1978)

Walter Wadlington, Professor of Law, University of Virginia.
Monrad G. Paulsen, Dean of the Law School, Yeshiva University.

DOMESTIC RELATIONS, see also Family Law

DYNAMICS OF AMERICAN LAW, THE: Courts, the Legal Process and Freedom of Expression (1968)

Marc A. Franklin, Professor of Law, Stanford University.

ELECTRONIC MASS MEDIA, Second Edition (1979)

William K. Jones, Professor of Law, Columbia University.

ENTERPRISE ORGANIZATION, Second Edition (1977), with Statutory and Formulary Supplement (1979)

Alfred F. Conard, Professor of Law, University of Michigan.
Robert L. Knauss, Dean of the School of Law, Vanderbilt University.
Stanley Siegel, Professor of Law, University of California, Los Angeles.

ENVIRONMENTAL PROTECTION, SELECTED LEGAL AND ECONOMIC ASPECTS OF (1971)

Charles J. Meyers, Dean of the Law School, Stanford University.
A. Dan Tarlock, Professor of Law, Indiana University.

EQUITY AND EQUITABLE REMEDIES (1975)

Edward D. Re, Adjunct Professor of Law, St. John's University.

EQUITY, RESTITUTION AND DAMAGES, Second Edition (1974)

The late Robert Childres, Professor of Law, Northwestern University.
William F. Johnson, Jr., Adjunct Professor of Law, New York University.

ESTATE PLANNING PROBLEMS (1973), with 1977 Supplement

David Westfall, Professor of Law, Harvard University.

ETHICS, see Legal Profession, also Professional Responsibility

EVIDENCE, Third Edition (1976)

The late David W. Louisell, Professor of Law, University of California, Berkeley.
John Kaplan, Professor of Law, Stanford University.
Jon R. Waltz, Professor of Law, Northwestern University.

INSTITUTIONAL INVESTORS, 1978

David L. Ratner, Professor of Law, Cornell University.

INSURANCE (1971)

William F. Young, Professor of Law, Columbia University.

INTERNATIONAL LAW, see also Transnational Legal Problems and United Nations Law

INTERNATIONAL LEGAL SYSTEM (1973), with Documentary Supplement

Noyes E. Leech, Professor of Law, University of Pennsylvania.
Covey T. Oliver, Professor of Law, University of Pennsylvania.
Joseph Modeste Sweeney, Professor of Law, Tulane University.

INTERNATIONAL TRADE AND INVESTMENT, REGULATION OF (1970)

The late Carl H. Fulda, Professor of Law, University of Texas.
Warren F. Schwartz, Professor of Law, University of Virginia.

INTERNATIONAL TRANSACTIONS AND RELATIONS (1960)

Milton Katz, Professor of Law, Harvard University, and
Kingman Brewster, Jr., formerly President, Yale University.

INTRODUCTION TO THE STUDY OF LAW (1970)

E. Wayne Thode, Professor of Law, University of Utah.
J. Leon Lebowitz, Professor of Law, University of Texas.
Lester J. Mazor, Professor of Law, Hampshire College.

INTRODUCTION TO LAW, see also Legal Method, also On Law in Courts, also Dynamics of American Law

JUDICIAL CODE: Rules of Procedure in the Federal Courts with Excerpts from the Criminal Code, 1978 Edition

The late Henry M. Hart, Jr., Professor of Law, Harvard University, and
Herbert Wechsler, Professor of Law, Columbia University.

JURISPRUDENCE (Temporary Edition Hard Bound) (1949)

Lon L. Fuller, Professor of Law Emeritus, Harvard University.

JUVENILE COURTS (1967)

Hon. Orman W. Ketcham, Juvenile Court of the District of Columbia.
Monrad G. Paulsen, Dean of the Law School, Yeshiva University.

JUVENILE JUSTICE PROCESS, Second Edition (1976), with 1980 Supplement

Frank W. Miller, Professor of Law, Washington University.
Robert O. Dawson, Professor of Law, University of Texas.
George E. Dix, Professor of Law, University of Texas.
Raymond I. Parnas, Professor of Law, University of California, Davis.

LABOR LAW, Eighth Edition (1977), with Statutory Supplement, and 1979 Case Supplement

Archibald Cox, Professor of Law, Harvard University, and
Derek C. Bok, President, Harvard University.
Robert A. Gorman, Professor of Law, University of Pennsylvania.

LABOR LAW (1968), with Statutory Supplement and 1974 Case Supplement

Clyde W. Summers, Professor of Law, University of Pennsylvania.
Harry H. Wellington, Dean of the Law School, Yale University.

UNIVERSITY CASEBOOK SERIES—Continued

LAND FINANCING, Second Edition (1977)

Norman Penney, Professor of Law, Cornell University.
Richard F. Broude, of the California Bar.

LAW, LANGUAGE AND ETHICS (1972)

William R. Bishin, Professor of Law, University of Southern California.
Christopher D. Stone, Professor of Law, University of Southern California.

LAWYERING PROCESS (1978), with Civil Problem Supplement and Criminal Problem Supplement

Gary Bellow, Professor of Law, Harvard University.
Bea Moulton, Professor of Law, Arizona State University.

LEGAL METHOD, Second Edition (1952)

Noel T. Dowling, late Professor of Law, Columbia University,
The late Edwin W. Patterson, Professor of Law, Columbia University, and
Richard R. B. Powell, Professor of Law, University of California, Hastings
    College of the Law.
Second Edition by Harry W. Jones, Professor of Law, Columbia University.

LEGAL METHODS (1969)

Robert N. Covington, Professor of Law, Vanderbilt University.
The late E. Blythe Stason, Professor of Law, Vanderbilt University.
John W. Wade, Professor of Law, Vanderbilt University.
The late Elliott E. Cheatham, Professor of Law, Vanderbilt University.
Theodore A. Smedley, Professor of Law, Vanderbilt University.

LEGAL PROFESSION (1970)

Samuel D. Thurman, Dean of the College of Law, University of Utah.
Ellis L. Phillips, Jr., Member of the New York Bar.
The late Elliott E. Cheatham, Professor of Law, Vanderbilt University.

LEGISLATIVE AND ADMINISTRATIVE PROCESSES (1976)

Hans A. Linde, Professor of Law, University of Oregon.
George Bunn, Professor of Law, University of Wisconsin.

LEGISLATION, Third Edition (1973)

The late Horace E. Read, Vice President, Dalhousie University.
John W. MacDonald, Professor of Law Emeritus, Cornell Law School.
Jefferson B. Fordham, Professor of Law, University of Utah, and
William J. Pierce, Professor of Law, University of Michigan.

LOCAL GOVERNMENT LAW, Revised Edition (1975)

Jefferson B. Fordham, Professor of Law, University of Utah.

MASS MEDIA LAW (1976), with 1979 Supplement

Marc A. Franklin, Professor of Law, Stanford University.

MENTAL HEALTH PROCESS, Second Edition (1976)

Frank W. Miller, Professor of Law, Washington University.
Robert O. Dawson, Professor of Law, University of Texas.
George E. Dix, Professor of Law, University of Texas.
Raymond I. Parnas, Professor of Law, University of California, Davis.

MUNICIPAL CORPORATIONS, see Local Government Law

NEGOTIABLE INSTRUMENTS, see Commercial Paper

NEW YORK PRACTICE, Fourth Edition (1978)

Herbert Peterfreund, Professor of Law, New York University.
Joseph M. McLaughlin, Dean of the Law School, Fordham University.

OIL AND GAS, Fourth Edition (1979)

Howard R. Williams, Professor of Law, Stanford University,
Richard C. Maxwell, Professor of Law, University of California, Los Angeles, and
Charles J. Meyers, Dean of the Law School, Stanford University.

ON LAW IN COURTS (1965)

Paul J. Mishkin, Professor of Law, University of California, Berkeley.
Clarence Morris, Professor of Law Emeritus, University of Pennsylvania.

OWNERSHIP AND DEVELOPMENT OF LAND (1965)

Jan Krasnowiecki, Professor of Law, University of Pennsylvania.

PARTNERSHIP PLANNING (1970) (Pamphlet)

William L. Cary, Professor of Law, Columbia University.

PERSPECTIVES ON THE LAWYER AS PLANNER (Reprint of Chapters One through Five of Planning by Lawyers) (1978)

Louis M. Brown, Professor of Law, University of Southern California.
Edward A. Dauer, Professor of Law, Yale University.

PLANNING BY LAWYERS, MATERIALS ON A NONADVERSARIAL LEGAL PROCESS (1978)

Louis M. Brown, Professor of Law, University of Southern California.
Edward A. Dauer, Professor of Law, Yale University.

PLEADING AND PROCEDURE, see Procedure, Civil

POLICE FUNCTION (1976) (Pamphlet)

Chapters 1–11 of Miller, Dawson, Dix & Parnas' Criminal Justice Administration, Second Edition.

PREVENTIVE LAW, see also Planning by Lawyers

PROCEDURE—Biography of a Legal Dispute (1968)

Marc A. Franklin, Professor of Law, Stanford University.

PROCEDURE—CIVIL PROCEDURE, Second Edition (1974)

James H. Chadbourn, Professor of Law, Harvard University.
A. Leo Levin, Professor of Law, University of Pennsylvania.
Philip Shuchman, Professor of Law, University of Connecticut.

PROCEDURE—CIVIL PROCEDURE, Fourth Edition (1978), with 1979 Supplement

The late Richard H. Field, Professor of Law, Harvard University.
Benjamin Kaplan, Professor of Law Emeritus, Harvard University.
Kevin M. Clermont, Professor of Law, Cornell University.

PROCEDURE—CIVIL PROCEDURE, Third Edition (1976), with 1978 Supplement

Maurice Rosenberg, Professor of Law, Columbia University.
Jack B. Weinstein, Professor, of Law, Columbia University.
Hans Smit, Professor of Law, Columbia University.
Harold L. Korn, Professor of Law, Columbia University.

UNIVERSITY CASEBOOK SERIES—Continued

PROCEDURE—PLEADING AND PROCEDURE: State and Federal, Fourth Edition (1979)

The late David W. Louisell, Professor of Law, University of California, Berkeley.

Geoffrey C. Hazard, Jr., Professor of Law, Yale University.

PROCEDURE—FEDERAL RULES OF CIVIL PROCEDURE, 1978 Edition

PROCEDURE PORTFOLIO (1962)

James H. Chadbourn, Professor of Law, Harvard University, and
A. Leo Levin, Professor of Law, University of Pennsylvania.

PRODUCTS AND THE CONSUMER: DECEPTIVE PRACTICES (1972)

W. Page Keeton, Professor of Law, University of Texas.
Marshall S. Shapo, Professor of Law, University of Virginia.

PRODUCTS AND THE CONSUMER: DEFECTIVE AND DANGEROUS PRODUCTS (1970)

W. Page Keeton, Professor of Law, University of Texas.
Marshall S. Shapo, Professor of Law, University of Virginia.

PRODUCTS LIABILITY AND SAFETY (1980)

W. Page Keeton, Professor of Law, University of Texas.
David G. Owen, Professor of Law, University of South Carolina.
John E. Montgomery, Professor of Law, University of South Carolina.

PROFESSIONAL RESPONSIBILITY (1976), with 1979 Problems, Cases and Readings, Supplement, 1979 Statutory (National) Supplement, and 1979 Statutory (California) Supplement

Thomas D. Morgan, Professor of Law, University of Illinois.
Ronald D. Rotunda, Professor of Law, University of Illinois.

PROPERTY, Fourth Edition (1978)

John E. Cribbet, Dean of the Law School, University of Illinois.
Corwin W. Johnson, Professor of Law, University of Texas.

PROPERTY—PERSONAL (1953)

The late S. Kenneth Skolfield, Professor of Law Emeritus, Boston University.

PROPERTY—PERSONAL, Third Edition (1954)

The late Everett Fraser, Dean of the Law School Emeritus, University of Minnesota—Third Edition by
Charles W. Taintor II, late Professor of Law, University of Pittsburgh.

PROPERTY—REAL—INTRODUCTION, Third Edition (1954)

The late Everett Fraser, Dean of the Law School Emeritus, University of Minnesota.

PROPERTY—REAL PROPERTY AND CONVEYANCING (1954)

Edward E. Bade, late Professor of Law, University of Minnesota.

PROPERTY, MODERN REAL, FUNDAMENTALS OF (1974), with 1979 Supplement

Edward H. Rabin, Professor of Law, University of California, Davis.

PROPERTY, REAL, PROBLEMS IN (Pamphlet) (1969)

Edward H. Rabin, Professor of Law, University of California, Davis.

PROSECUTION AND ADJUDICATION (1976) (Pamphlet)

Chapters 12–16 of Miller, Dawson, Dix & Parnas' Criminal Justice Administration, Second Edition.

PUBLIC UTILITY LAW, see Free Enterprise, also Regulated Industries

REAL ESTATE PLANNING (1974), with 1978 Supplement

Norton L. Steuben, Professor of Law, University of Colorado.

RECEIVERSHIP AND CORPORATE REORGANIZATION, see Creditors' Rights

REGULATED INDUSTRIES, Second Edition, 1976

William K. Jones, Professor of Law, Columbia University.

RESTITUTION, Second Edition (1966)

John W. Wade, Professor of Law, Vanderbilt University.

SALES (1980)

Marion W. Benfield, Jr., Professor of Law, University of Illinois.
William D. Hawkland, Chancellor, Louisiana State University Law Center.

SALES AND SALES FINANCING, Fourth Edition (1976)

John Honnold, Professor of Law, University of Pennsylvania.

SECURITY, Third Edition (1959)

The late John Hanna, Professor of Law Emeritus, Columbia University.

SECURITIES REGULATION, Fourth Edition (1977), with 1979 Selected Statutes
    Supplement and 1979 Cases and Releases Supplement

Richard W. Jennings, Professor of Law, University of California, Berkeley.
Harold Marsh, Jr., Member of the California Bar.

SENTENCING AND THE CORRECTIONAL PROCESS, Second Edition (1976)

Frank W. Miller, Professor of Law, Washington University.
Robert O. Dawson, Professor of Law, University of Texas.
George E. Dix, Professor of Law, University of Texas.
Raymond I. Parnas, Professor of Law, University of California, Davis.

SOCIAL WELFARE AND THE INDIVIDUAL (1971)

Robert J. Levy, Professor of Law, University of Minnesota.
Thomas P. Lewis, Dean of the College of Law, University of Kentucky.
Peter W. Martin, Professor of Law, Cornell University.

TAX, POLICY ANALYSIS OF THE FEDERAL INCOME (1976)

William A. Klein, Professor of Law, University of California, Los Angeles.

TAXATION, FEDERAL INCOME (1976), with 1979 Supplement

Erwin N. Griswold, Dean Emeritus, Harvard Law School.
Michael J. Graetz, Professor of Law, University of Virginia.

TAXATION, FEDERAL INCOME, Second Edition (1977), with 1979 Supplement

James J. Freeland, Professor of Law, University of Florida.
Stephen A. Lind, Professor of Law, University of Florida.
Richard B. Stephens, Professor of Law Emeritus, University of Florida.

TAXATION, FEDERAL INCOME, Volume I, Personal Tax (1972), with 1979
    Supplement; Volume II, Corporate and Partnership Taxation, Second
    Edition (1980)

Stanley S. Surrey, Professor of Law, Harvard University.
William C. Warren, Professor of Law Emeritus, Columbia University.
Paul R. McDaniel, Professor of Law, Boston College Law School.
Hugh J. Ault, Professor of Law, Boston College Law School.

UNFAIR COMPETITION, see Competitive Process and Business Torts

UNITED NATIONS IN ACTION (1968)

> Louis B. Sohn, Professor of Law, Harvard University.

UNITED NATIONS LAW, Second Edition (1967), with Documentary Supplement (1968)

> Louis B. Sohn, Professor of Law, Harvard University.

WATER RESOURCE MANAGEMENT, Second Edition (1980)

> Charles J. Meyers, Dean of the Law School, Stanford University.
> A. Dan Tarlock, Professor of Law, Indiana University.

WILLS AND ADMINISTRATION, 5th Edition (1961)

> The late Philip Mechem, Professor of Law, University of Pennsylvania, and
> The late Thomas E. Atkinson, Professor of Law, New York University.

WORLD LAW, see United Nations Law

CASES AND COMMENTS

ON

CRIMINAL PROCEDURE

By

FRED E. INBAU

John Henry Wigmore Professor of Law Emeritus,
Northwestern University

JAMES R. THOMPSON

Governor of State of Illinois;
Former United States Attorney, Northern District of Illinois;
and Former Associate Professor of Law,
Northwestern University

JAMES B. HADDAD

Professor of Law, Northwestern University

JAMES B. ZAGEL

Director, Illinois Department of Law Enforcement;
Former Chief, Criminal Division,
Office of Attorney General of Illinois

GARY L. STARKMAN

Counsel to the Governor of Illinois;
Former Assistant United States Attorney,
Northern District of Illinois

SECOND EDITION

Mineola, N. Y.
THE FOUNDATION PRESS, INC.
1980

Library of Congress Cataloging In Publication Data

Main Entry under title:

Cases and comments on criminal procedure.

  (University casebook series)
  Includes index.
  1. Criminal procedure—United States—Cases.
I. Inbau, Fred Edward. II. Series.
KF9618.C38   1980   345.73'05   80–17843

ISBN 0–88277–011–X

Inbau et al.,–Cs.Cr.Proc.2d Ed. UCB

PREFACE

This second (1980) edition of *Cases and Comments on Criminal Procedure* follows, in general, the format of the prior one. However, this edition has been restructured, and, of course, updated with new principal cases and also more extensive notes. We believe and hope that it will serve as an excellent publication for the teaching of criminal procedure to law students. Moreover, it is also a valuable reference source for criminal law practitioners, and for jurists who preside over criminal trials or participate in appellate review.

The present book is divided into two parts. Part I deals with the *Legal Limitations Upon Law Enforcement Practices and Procedures*; Part II is devoted to the *Judicial Process*. As the detailed table of contents will readily reveal, this new edition sets forth the materials for both parts in a logical sequential pattern regarding the procedures involved in a criminal case from beginning to end.

Although containing much factual information, the primary objective of the casebook was to make available for teaching purposes a compilation of provocative and challenging materials for the classical interplay between student and instructor. We believe that objective has been achieved. Furthermore, the student will receive from the materials presented a clear insight into the ways and means by which lawyers and judges dispose of criminal cases.

Part I—*The Legal Limitations Upon Law Enforcement Practices and Procedures*—begins with a major issue, one regarding the permissible police questioning of criminal suspects and the validity of the confessions that may be obtained. At the outset, therefore, the classroom discussion will involve an analysis of a very crucial problem with respect to a highly sensitive police procedure and the ways and means by which the judiciary may secure the rights of individuals suspected or accused of criminal offenses.

Following, in the practical sequence of many investigations, are the also highly important practices employed in the eye-witness viewing of suspected persons. Although an indispensable step, what happens on this level is fraught with high risks to innocent persons.

The casebook then presents a completely reorganized set of Fourth Amendment materials, treating first the concept of probable cause, then searches pursuant to warrants, and searches and seizures without traditional probable cause warrants under ten categories of exceptions to the warrant requirement. "Stop-and-frisk" issues are also explored.

The present edition also offers unified treatment of exclusionary rules, combining materials on standing, derivative evidence, and collateral use of illegally obtained evidence, rather than treating each concept separately in the chapters on confessions, identification, search and seizure, and electronic surveillance. We place our discussion of the exclusionary rule debate after our treatment of substantive controls. This change follows the experiment of one of our authors who has taught *Mapp* as the last Fourth Amendment decision rather than as the first decision to be covered. For the most part we relate the exclusionary rule debate through the contrasting views of Supreme Court justices reflected in recent decisions which, while ostensibly concerned with narrowing or broadening the impact of exclusionary rules, give insights into different views of the purpose and effect of the exclusionary rule itself.

Part II—*The Judicial Process*—covers such matters as bail, preliminary hearings, the grand jury, double jeopardy, speedy trial, and so forth. It also places more emphasis on the trial itself than do most other criminal procedure casebooks. Although a fraction of this trial material may be covered in a course on evidence, students may otherwise never be exposed to much of it in law school unless within the confines of a criminal procedure course or seminar. Matters such as jury instructions, limits on closing arguments, and jury deliberations are among the many topics which we include in that category.

Chapters 9 and 18 reflect additional major organizational changes. In the former we combine treatment of the rights of the indigent in the formal criminal process; in the latter we deal with effective assistance of counsel, conflicts from multiple representation, and ethical issues arising from over-zealousness of prosecutors and defense counsel.

Many of the court opinions in the cases which comprise this casebook have been condensed, and footnotes were either omitted completely or reduced in number. Otherwise the book would be of unmanageable size.

In our textual and note material, whenever "he" and other masculine pronouns are used, they should, in appropriate instances, be considered to mean both females as well as males.

We gratefully acknowledge the research assistance we received from Kaye Reeves and Richard Nogal.

F.E.I.
J.R.T.
J.B.H.
J.B.Z.
G.L.S.

June, 1980

SUMMARY OF CONTENTS

*

TABLE OF CONTENTS

PART 2. THE JUDICIAL PROCESS

TABLE OF CONTENTS

*

TABLE OF CASES

Principal cases are in italic type.   Nonprincipal cases are in roman type.
References are to Pages.

Burdeau v. McDowell, 542
Burkholder v. State, 750
Burks v. United States, 829
Burnett, State v., 1223
Burson, People v., 934
Butera, United States v., 698
Butler, People v., 1404
Byrd v. Wainwright, 1247

Caceres, United States v., 461
Cady v. Dombrowski, 393
Calandra, United States v., 498, 751
California v. Byers, 738
California v. Green, 1180, 1241
California v. Stewart, 48
California Bankers Ass'n V. Shultz, 760
Camara v. Municipal Court of San Francisco, 393, 411
Cardwell v. Lewis, 410, 436
Carroll v. United States, 401
Castaneda v. Partida, 691
Castellanos, United States v., 818
Ceccolini, United States v., 534
Chadwick, United States v., 325
Chaffin v. Stynchcombe, 838
Chambers v. Maroney, 401, 1548
Chambers v. Mississippi, 1197
Chapman v. California, 1380, 1548
Chapman v. United States, 369
Chimel v. California, 326
Chung v. Ogata, 915
Ciucci v. Illinois, 827
Clay v. Riddle, 150
Clewis v. Texas, 535
Coates v. United States, 353
Cobbledick v. United States, 717
Cohen v. United States, 1265
Coleman v. Alabama, 243, 668, 945
Colonnade Catering Corp. v. United States, 419
Colten v. Kentucky, 838
Commonwealth v. _____ (see opposing party)
Connally v. Georgia, 293
Coolidge v. New Hampshire, 292, 371, 372, 406
Cornwall, State v., 1530
County Court of Ulster County v. Allen, 1464
Cowan, United States v., 592
Cozzi, United States v., 864
Crews v. United States, 247, 536
Crist v. Bretz, 810
Crooker v. California, 35
Crosby, United States v., 1407
Cupp v. Murphy, 358, 394
Cupp v. Naughten, 1438

Daley, In re, 739
Dalia v. United States, 448

Daniel v. Louisiana, 1056
Darwin v. Connecticut, 535
Davenport v. United States, 879
Davis v. Alaska, 1226
Davis v. Georgia, 1085
Davis v. Mississippi, 358
Davis v. United States, 705
Dawson v. State, 271
De Diego, United States v., 727
De Luna v. United States, 1241
DeBonis, State v., 667
Decoster, United States v., 1140
Delaware v. Prouse, 421
Dell v. Louisiana, 355
Dellinger, United States v., 1089
Demma, United States v., 569
Dennis, United States v., 1094
Desmond v. United States, 1381
DeStasio, State v., 1529
Di Joseph's Petition, In re, 968
Di Re, United States v., 329, 410
Dickey v. Florida, 851
Dinitz, United States v., 817
Dionisio, United States v., 359, 753
District Court, People ex rel. Van Meveren v., 672
Doherty v. United States, 640
Donovan, United States v., 449
Dotterweich, United States v., 1485
Douglas v. California, 624
Douglas Oil Co. v. Petrol Stops Northwest, 706
Downum v. United States, 810
Doyle v. Ohio, 1289, 1337, 1399
Draper v. United States, 250
Drope v. Missouri, 933
Dukes v. Warden, 1011
Dunaway v. New York, 181, 357, 358, 534
Duncan v. Louisiana, 1034
Dunn v. United States, 1484
Durant, United States v., 657
Duren v. Missouri, 1056
Dutton v. Evans, 1239, 1268
Duvall, United States v., 211

Eaton v. United States, 900
Edelman v. Jordan, 552
Edwards, United States v., 324
Ellis v. Reed, 1484
Ellis v. United States, 738
Elrod, People ex rel. Hemingway v., 789
Erwing, United States v., 795
Estepa, United States v., 745

Falk, United States v., 600
Fare v. Michael C., 135, 138
Fatico, United States v., 1501
Fay v. Noia, 523, 1551
Fisher v. United States, 759

CASES AND COMMENTS

ON

CRIMINAL PROCEDURE

Chapter 1

INTRODUCTION: OUTLINE OF
CRIMINAL PROCEDURE

The procedure followed in a criminal case is not the same for all states, but the differences are rather slight as regards basic concepts and principles. In essential respects there is also very little difference between the procedure of the state courts and that which exists in the federal courts.

The following outline of criminal procedure is here presented for the purpose of familiarizing the beginning law student with the basic procedures that are involved or referred to in the case reports he will be encountering in subsequent chapters.

PRE–ARREST PROCEDURES

In state jurisdictions most prosecutions are initiated by an arrest made before a formal criminal charge has been brought. Sometimes the arrest is made "on the scene," as in the case of a domestic disturbance or a burglary where the offender has been caught within the premises. In other situations, a police investigation precedes the arrest. Sometimes, particularly in the case of crimes without complaining witnesses, such as narcotics and gambling, officers may obtain a search warrant to aid in their pre-arrest investigation. More frequently, however, no legal "process" (e. g., a search warrant, or a grand jury subpoena) is used in the pre-arrest investigation conducted by local authorities.

Even when a period of investigation has preceded an arrest, the typical arrest by state or local authorities, at least in felony cases, is made without an arrest warrant. Once the arrest has been effected, the police often engage in investigative procedures before bringing the arrestee before a judge or magistrate. Generally, they search the suspect's person for evidence and for weapons. In some cases they may interrogate the arrestee in an effort to obtain a confession or an admission. In serious cases, such as armed robbery, the police may present the suspect to witnesses for possible identification, either alone (in a "show-up") or with others (in a "line-up"). Many of the legal issues discussed in Part I of this book arise from police

1

procedures utilized between the arrest and the defendant's first judicial appearance.

If the police decide to go forward with a prosecution, they will formally charge the suspect. Depending upon the law and practice in a particular jurisdiction, sometimes a prosecutor will participate in the decision to charge. In fact, he may have final authority. In other jurisdictions, particularly in less serious cases, the police, unassisted by the prosecutor, may decide what charges, if any, are to be made against the arrestee. Typically, where charges are to be filed, an officer or the victim will sign a preliminary hearing felony complaint or a misdemeanor complaint. In some jurisdictions prosecution is initiated when a district attorney signs a similar document known as an "information."

Another mode of initiating prosecution is used ordinarily in federal prosecutions and occasionally in state prosecutions. A district attorney conducts an investigation, sometimes utilizing the power of a grand jury to compel testimony and to issue subpoenas *duces tecum* for books and records. The prosecutor also may issue directions to investigators from his own office or, as in the federal system, to investigators from other agencies such as the Federal Bureau of Investigation, the Treasury Department, or the Drug Enforcement Administration. In cases of that type, prosecution is initiated by an indictment. An arrest warrant or a summons then issues for the defendant.

PROCEDURE BETWEEN ARREST AND TRIAL

In most states there is a statutory provision to the effect that an arrested person must be taken without unnecessary delay before the nearest judge or magistrate. What happens after presentation to the judge or magistrate will depend upon whether the arrested person is accused of a felony or a misdemeanor. If the charge is a misdemeanor, the judge or magistrate will sometimes have the power and authority to hear the case himself, and he may proceed with the trial unless the accused demands trial by jury or a continuance is requested or ordered for some reason. If the offense charged is a felony, the judge or magistrate before whom the accused is brought will ordinarily lack the constitutional or legislative authority to conduct trials for crimes of that degree of seriousness, and in such instances he only conducts what is known as a "preliminary hearing."

The Right to Bail

After arrest, the first decision made by a court is, frequently, whether the accused is entitled to release on bail. Subject to some exceptions for persons charged with death penalty offenses, persons on parole and others, an accused is entitled to have the court set bail. Bail is fixed at a specific dollar amount. If the accused places cash or property worth that amount with the clerk of court, he will be at liberty pending his trial. If the accused appears at the required proceedings, bail is refunded but failure to appear results in forfeiture of bail. In some states, professional bail bondsmen will, in effect, deposit bail in exchange for a non-refundable fee from the defendant. In other states, a defendant is allowed to deposit a portion of his bail (usually equivalent to the bondsman's fee, i. e., 10%), most of which is refunded if the defendant honors his obligation to appear. More-over, courts generally have the power to allow release without any deposit—merely accepting the defendant's signature on a bond which makes him liable for the amount of bail if he fails to appear. Such defendants, usually thought to be highly likely to appear for trial, are said to be released on "recognizance," "signature," or "individual bond." Finally, an accused has no right to have bail set at an amount he can meet. A number of defendants will fail to "make" bail and re-main in jail pending trial.

Probable Cause to Detain

After a person has been arrested as a suspect by the police or upon authorization of a prosecutor, and remains deprived of his liberty, he is entitled, as a constitutional right, to a prompt, though limited judicial hearing on the question of probable cause *to detain.* At this kind of hearing, normal rules of evidence are not applicable and counsel for the accused is not required. This procedure is akin to that used when, prior to arrest, the prosecutor seeks an arrest war-rant from a court. The accused does not have this right, however, when prosecution has been initiated by arrest warrant or indictment. In such instances an *ex parte* probable cause determination has al-ready been made.

The Right to an Attorney

The Sixth Amendment of the Constitution of the United States provides that "in all criminal prosecutions, the accused shall enjoy the right . . . to have the assistance of Counsel for his defense." And the Supreme Court of the United States has held that where in-carceration may be a consequence of the prosecution the defendant is entitled to appointed counsel in the event he cannot afford one. A "preliminary hearing", of course, is a part of the "criminal prosecu-tion."

Preliminary Hearing

A preliminary hearing is a relatively informal proceeding by means of which a determination is made as to whether there are rea-sonable grounds for believing the accused person committed the of-fense—as to whether it is fair, under the circumstances, to require him to stand a regular trial. If after such a hearing the judge or magistrate decides that the accusation is without probable cause, the accused will be discharged. This discharge, however, will not bar a grand jury indictment if subsequently developed evidence (or the same evidence presented on the preliminary hearing) satisfies the grand jury that the accusation is well founded.

If the preliminary hearing judge or magistrate decides that the accusation is a reasonable one, the accused will be "bound over" to the grand jury—that is, held in jail until the charge against him is presented for grand jury consideration, or, if the offense is a bailable one, the accused may be released after a bond of a certain amount is given to insure his presence until the grand jury has acted in the matter. (The nature and composition of a "grand jury" and the difference between it and a "petit" or "trial jury" is described later in this outline.)

In some jurisdictions, as subsequently detailed, once the magistrate has found probable cause, the prosecutor may bypass the grand jury and file a felony "information" upon which the accused will be tried.

Preliminary hearings are not held if the *initial* charge was by way of indictment. In many federal and in some state jurisdictions, even if the original charge is a preliminary complaint or an information, the prosecution will pre-empt the defendant's right to a preliminary hearing by promptly obtaining a grand jury indictment before the preliminary is conducted. Except in California, post-indictment preliminary hearings ordinarily are not part of the system.

The Habeas Corpus Writ

In the event an arrested person is not formally charged with an offense and is not taken before a judge or other magistrate "without unnecessary delay" he, or rather someone on his behalf, may petition a judge for a "writ of habeas corpus" and thereby attempt to secure his release or at least compel the police to file a specific charge against him, in which latter event he may seek his release on bond. If the court issues the writ, the police or other custodians of the arrested person are required, either immediately or at an early designated time, to bring him into court (that is, "you have the body," which is the literal meaning of the term "habeas corpus"), and, to explain to the court the reason or justification for holding the accused person in custody.

Upon the police showing adequate cause, a court may continue the hearing in order to give the police a little more time to conduct a further investigation before making the formal charge against the arrestee. Many times, however, the police are required to file their charges immediately or release the prisoner. In some jurisdictions the prosecutor makes the decision as to whether the initial charge shall be filed.

Coroner's Inquest

At this point in a discussion of criminal procedure, mention should be made of a proceeding peculiar to homicide cases, which comes into operation soon after a killing or discovered death. This is the "coroner's inquest."

The coroner's inquest is a very old proceeding and its function was and still is to determine "the cause of death." The verdict of the coroner's jury, which is made up, in some states, of six laymen selected by the coroner or one of his deputies, is not binding on the prosecuting attorney, grand jury or court. In effect, it is merely an advisory finding which can be either accepted or completely ignored. For instance, even though a coroner's jury returns a verdict of "accidental death," a grand jury, either upon its own initiative or upon evidence presented by the prosecutor, may find that death resulted because of someone's criminal act and charge that person with the offense.

In some jurisdictions the office of coroner has been replaced by what is known as a medical examiner system. Whereas the coroner is usually an elected official (who may or may not be a physician), a medical examiner must be a physician appointed by a state or county officer or agency; moreover, in many jurisdictions he must be a forensic pathologist, specially trained for the position. He, in turn, has the power of appointing assistants who are physicians already trained for the purpose or at least in the process of receiving such training.

The Grand Jury

Misdemeanors are usually prosecuted upon an "information" filed by the prosecuting attorney after he has received and considered the sworn complaint of the victim or of some other person with knowledge of the facts. As regards felonies, however, many states require that the matter must first be submitted to a "grand jury." Then, after hearing the alleged facts related by the victim or other persons, the grand jury determines whether there are reasonable grounds for proceeding to an actual trial of the person charged.

A grand jury is usually composed of 23 citizen-voters, 16 of whom constitute a quorum. The votes of 12 members are necessary to the return of an "indictment." This indictment is also known as a "true bill."

The Constitution of the United States does not require that state prosecutors use a grand jury to charge felony offenses, and there is an increasing tendency to enact statutes permitting the prosecution to charge felonies by filing an "information." Ordinarily a person charged by information must have a preliminary hearing before he can be tried for the charge. A defendant charged by a grand jury, however, may not have a right to a preliminary hearing since it is thought that his rights are adequately safeguarded by his fellow citizens who serve on the grand jury.

One highly significant and increasing modern purpose of the grand jury is to investigate complex crimes. The grand jury has the right to subpoena witnesses, to ask them questions, and to require the production of books and records. It may exercise these rights before any charge is filed and before the specific crime or its perpetrator is known. Police agencies usually do not possess this authority to compel the production of evidence and it is generally conceded that such a right is required for effective investigation of much financial crime, official corruption, and organized crime.

The consideration of a felony charge by a grand jury is in no sense of the word a trial. Only the state's evidence is presented and considered; the suspected offender is usually not even heard nor is his lawyer present to offer evidence in his behalf. However, some state laws now provide that the suspect has a right to appear before the grand jury if he elects to do so, but very few suspects exercise that option. Other laws provide that a "target" of the grand jury investigation has the right to have counsel with him if he is summoned to appear before the grand jury.

The Arraignment and Plea

Following an indictment, the next step in felony cases is the appearance of the accused person before a judge who is empowered to try felony cases. The indictment is read to the defendant or the essence of its contents is made known to him; in other words, he is advised of the criminal charges made against him. If he pleads guilty, the judge can sentence him immediately or take the matter under advisement for a decision at an early date. If the accused pleads "not guilty," a date is then set for his actual trial.

In some states, and in the federal system, the defendant may enter a plea of "nolo contendere," a plea which has the same effect as a plea of guilty, except that the admission thereby made cannot be used as evidence in any other action.

Pre-trial Motions

After the formal charge has been made against the accused, he may, in advance of trial, seek to terminate the prosecution's case, or at least seek to better prepare his defense, by utilizing a procedure known as making or filing a "motion." A motion is merely a request for a court ruling or order that will afford the defendant the assistance or remedy he is thereby seeking. Some of the more frequently used motions are the following:

Motion to Quash the Indictment. With this motion the defendant may question the legal sufficiency of the indictment. If the court decides that the indictment adequately charges a criminal offense, and that it was obtained in accordance with the prescribed legal procedures, the motion will be overruled; otherwise the indictment will be considered invalid and "quashed." Even after an indictment has been thus rejected and set aside, the prosecutor may nevertheless proceed to obtain another and proper indictment. Moreover, the prosecution is entitled to appeal from a court order quashing an indictment, since at this stage of the proceedings, the defendant has not been placed in jeopardy and consequently a subsequent indictment and trial would not constitute a violation of his constitutional privilege against "double jeopardy."

Motion for a Bill of Particulars. Although the indictment, if valid, will ordinarily contain all the allegations of fact necessary for the defendant to prepare his defense, he may, by a motion for a "bill of particulars," obtain further details respecting the accusation.

In addition to the motion for a bill of particulars, there now exists an expanded right, accorded to both the prosecution and the defense, to learn what evidence the other side intends to use. It is known as a *Motion for Discovery*, whereby both parties seek to learn not only the details of the crime but also the names of the other side's witnesses and what they are expected to say.

Motion for a Change of Venue. A defendant may attempt to avoid trial before a particular judge or in the city, county, or district where the crime occurred by seeking a "change of venue." In instances where this appears to be necessary in order that the defendant may receive a fair trial, the motion for a change of venue will be granted.

Motion to Suppress Evidence. A defendant has the privilege of filing with the court, normally in advance of trial, a "motion to suppress" evidence which he contends has been obtained from him in an unconstitutional manner. The evidence in question may be, on the one hand, a tangible item such as a gun, narcotics, or stolen property or, on the other hand, an intangible item such as a confession or the testimony of eyewitnesses who are expected to identify the accused as the offender. If the court is satisfied that the evidence has been illegally obtained, it will order the evidence suppressed, which means that it cannot be used at the trial. If the court decides that the evidence was lawfully obtained, it is usable against the defendant at the trial.

THE TRIAL

In all states, and in the federal system, the accused is entitled to "a speedy trial." This right to an early trial is guaranteed by the various constitutions, and the constitutional provisions are generally supplemented by legislative enactments particularizing and specifically limiting the pre-trial detention period. In Illinois, for instance, once a person is jailed upon a criminal charge, he must be tried within 120 days, unless the delay has been occasioned by him, or is necessitated by a hearing to determine his mental competency to stand trial. If the accused is out on bail, he can demand trial within 160 days. In either instance, however, if the court determines that the prosecution has exercised, without success, due diligence to obtain evidence material to the case, and that there are reasonable grounds to believe that such evidence will be forthcoming, the time for trial may be extended for another 60 days. Such time limits vary from state to state, but the consistent rule is that unless the accused person is tried within the specified period of time he must be released and is thereafter immune from prosecution for that offense.

The federal courts are governed by the Speedy Trial Act of 1974, which is a statutory scheme providing time periods within which federal trials must begin. Starting July 1, 1980, subject to narrow exceptions, a federal trial must commence within one hundred days from arrest. Not more than seventy days may pass between indictment, or a first judicial appearance, and the commencement of trial. Even under the new federal act, some circumstances permit the accused to waive his right to a trial within the statutory period.

Jury Trial—Trial by Judge Alone

A person accused of a "serious crime", which is considered to be one for which there may be incarceration beyond six months, is entitled to trial by jury, as a matter of constitutional right. However, he may waive this right and elect to be tried by a judge alone. In some jurisdictions the defendant has an absolute right to this waiver (e. g., Illinois); in others (e. g., the federal system) it is conditioned upon the concurrence of the judge and the prosecution.

If the case is tried without a jury, the judge hears the evidence and decides for himself whether the defendant is guilty or not guilty. Where the trial is by a jury, the jury determines the facts and the judge serves more or less as an umpire or referee; it is his function to determine what testimony or evidence is legally "admissible," that is, to decide what should be heard or considered by the jury. But the ultimate decision as to whether the defendant is guilty is one to be made by the jury alone.

Jury Selection

In the selection of the jurors, usually twelve in number, who hear the defendant's case, most states permit his attorney as well as the prosecuting attorney to question a larger number who have been chosen for jury service from the list of registered voters. In the federal system and a growing number of states, however, most trial judges will do practically all of the questioning, with very little opportunity for questioning accorded the prosecutor and defense counsel. Nevertheless, each lawyer has a certain number of "peremptory challenges" which means that he can arbitrarily refuse to accept as jurors a certain number of those who appear as prospective jurors. In some states, by statutory provision, the defendant in larceny cases has ten such challenges and the state has an equal number; in a murder case the defendant and the state each have twenty peremptory challenges; and in minor criminal cases, such as petit larceny, the challenges are five in number for each side. And in all cases, if any prospective juror's answers to the questions of either attorney reveal a prejudice or bias which prevents him from being a fair and impartial juror, the judge, either on his own initiative or at the suggestion of either counsel, will dismiss that person from jury service. Although the desired result is not always achieved, the avowed purpose of this practice of permitting lawyers to question prospective jurors is to obtain twelve jurors who will be fair to both sides of the case.

Opening Statements

After the jury is selected, both the prosecuting attorney and the defense lawyer are entitled to make "opening statements" in which each outlines what he intends to prove. The purpose of this is to acquaint the jurors with each side of the case, so that it will be easier for them to follow the evidence as it is presented.

The Prosecution's Evidence

After the opening statements the prosecuting attorney produces the prosecution's testimony and evidence. He has the burden of proving the state's case "beyond a reasonable doubt." If at the close of the prosecution's case the judge is of the opinion that reasonable jurors could not conclude that the charge against the defendant has been proved, he will "direct a verdict" of acquittal. That ends the matter and the defendant goes free—forever immune from further prosecution for the crime, just the same as if a jury had heard all the evidence and found him "not guilty."

The Defendant's Evidence

If the court does not direct the jury, at the close of the prosecution's case, to find the defendant not guilty, the defendant may, if he wishes, present evidence in refutation. He himself may or may not testify, and if he chooses not to appear as a witness, the prosecuting attorney is not permitted to comment upon that fact to the jury. The basis for this principle, whereby the defendant is not obligated to speak in his own behalf, is the constitutional privilege which protects a person from self-incrimination.

The prosecution is given an opportunity to rebut the defendant's evidence, if any, and the presentation of testimony usually ends at that point. Then, once more, defense counsel will try to persuade the court to "direct a verdict" in favor of the defendant. If the court decides to let the case go to the jury, the prosecuting attorney and defense counsel make their "closing arguments."

The defense and the prosecution have the right to subpoena witnesses and require them to testify at trial or to produce records if such evidence would be of value at trial. It is possible in certain case situations to enforce subpoenas against out-of-state witnesses and, in some instances, against witnesses in foreign countries.

The prosecution has the obligation in most, if not all, cases to notify the defense of any evidence which would be of significance in exculpating the accused or in mitigating his sentence if the prosecution is aware of this evidence.

Closing Arguments

In their closing arguments the prosecutor and defense counsel review and analyze the evidence and attempt to persuade the jury to render a favorable verdict.

Instructions of the Court to the Jury

After the closing arguments are completed, the judge in most jurisdictions will read and give to the jury certain written instructions as to the legal principles which should be applied to the facts of the case as determined by the jury. The judge also gives the jury certain written forms of possible verdicts. The jury then retires to the jury room where they are given an adequate opportunity to deliberate upon the matter, away from everyone, including the judge himself.

Inbau et al.,–Cs.Cr.Proc.2d Ed. UCB—2

The Verdict of the Jury

When the jurors have reached a decision, they advise the bailiff that they have reached a verdict and then return to the court room. The foreman, usually selected by the jurors themselves to serve as their leader and spokesman, announces the verdict of the jury. Insofar as jury participation is concerned, the case is then at an end.

If the verdict is "not guilty" the defendant is free forever from any further prosecution by that particular state or jurisdiction for the crime for which he was tried. If found "guilty," then, in most types of cases and in most jurisdictions, it becomes the function of the trial judge to fix the sentence within the legislatively prescribed limitations.

In the event the jurors are unable to agree upon a verdict—and it must be unanimous in most states—the jury, commonly referred to as a "hung jury," is discharged and a new trial date may be set for a retrial of the case before another jury. The retrial does not constitute a violation of the constitutional protection against double jeopardy—trying a person twice for the same offense—because there actually has not been a first trial; in other words, it has been terminated by the failure of the jury to agree upon a verdict.

The Motion for a New Trial

After a verdict of "guilty" there are still certain opportunities provided the defendant to obtain his freedom. He may file a "motion for a new trial," in which he alleges certain "errors" committed in the course of his trial; and if the trial judge agrees, the conviction is set aside and the defendant may be tried again by a new jury and usually before a different judge. Where this motion for a new trial is "overruled" or "denied," the judge will then proceed to sentence the defendant.

The defendant may also seek a new trial on the grounds of newly discovered evidence favorable to him. Such motions are rarely granted. The defendant must establish that he was not aware of the evidence, that he could not have discovered the evidence by exercising due diligence, and that the evidence would probably change the result of the trial.

The Sentence

In cases tried without a jury, the judge, of course, will determine the sentence to be imposed. In jury cases the practice varies among the states, with most of them following the practice of confining the jury function to a determination of guilt or innocence and permitting the judge to fix the penalty. For the crimes of murder and rape, however, most of the states place both responsibilities upon the jury.

In some states there are statutory provisions which prescribe that upon conviction of a felony the defendant must be sentenced for a specified minimum-maximum term in the penitentiary—for example, 1 year to 10 years for burglary—and the determination of the appropriate time of his release within that period is to be made by a "parole board," whose judgment in that respect is based upon the extent of the convict's rehabilitation, the security risk involved, and similar factors. In many states a judge is permitted to set a minimum-maximum period anywhere within the minimum-maximum term prescribed by the legislature. In other words, the sentence given for grand larceny may be one to ten years, the statutory range, or 1 to 2, 9 to 10, or any other combination between 1 to 10. This minimum-maximum term means that he cannot be released before serving the minimum period, less "time off for good behavior," nor can he be kept in the penitentiary longer than the maximum period, less "time off for good behavior." In between this minimum-maximum period the convict is eligible for "parole," a procedure to be subsequently described.

In instances where imprisonment is fixed at a specified number of years, rather than for an indeterminate period, the law usually provides that the convicted person must serve one-third of the sentence before becoming eligible for parole.

In recent years there has been an increase in two new forms of incarceration. "Work release" allows an inmate to work at a job and return to custody during non-working hours. "Periodic imprisonment" allows an inmate his freedom except for certain specified periods, e. g., weekends.

Recently, some states have adopted a plan which limits the sentencing discretion of judges and the release powers of parole boards, or even the abolition of parole boards. Under this new system the judge is required to set a specific term according to more or less strict guidelines. The sentence may be reduced by "good time" allowance (for "good behavior") in prison, which is calculated by a set formula. When the inmate serves his sentence less "good time" he is automatically released.

PROBATION

In certain types of cases, a judge is empowered, by statute, to grant "probation" to a convicted person. This means that instead of sending the defendant to the penitentiary the court permits him to remain at liberty but upon certain conditions prescribed by law and by the judge. His background must first be investigated by a probation officer for the purpose of determining whether he is the kind of person who may have "learned his lesson" by the mere fact of being caught and convicted, or whether he could be rehabilitated outside of prison better than behind prison walls. In other words, would any useful purpose be served for him or society by sending him to prison?

Among the conditions of a defendant's probation, the court may require him to make restitution of money stolen, or reparations to a person he physically injured. Some state statutes provide that for a period of up to six months in misdemeanor cases, and up to five years in felony cases, a defendant on probation will be subjected to the supervision of a probation officer and, in general, must remain on "good behavior" during the period fixed by the court. A failure to abide by the conditions prescribed by the court will subject the defendant to a sentence in the same manner and form as though he had been denied probation and sentenced immediately after his conviction for the offense.

PAROLE

A penitentiary sentence of a specified term or number of years does not necessarily mean that a convicted person will remain in the penitentiary for that particular period of time. Under certain conditions and circumstances he may be released earlier "on parole," which means a release under supervision until the expiration of his sentence or until the expiration of a period otherwise specified by law. For instance, a person sentenced "for life" is, in some states, eligible for release "on parole" at the end of twenty years, with a subsequent five year period of parole supervision. One sentenced for a fixed number of years, for example 14 years for murder, may be eligible for parole in some states after he has served one-third that period of time. And a person who has been given an indeterminate minimum-maximum sentence, such as to 5 to 10 years for grand larceny, may be eligible for a parole after he has served the 5 year minimum, less time off for good behavior.

The manner of computing time off for good behavior, or "good time," varies among the states. Some states have a system based on yearly credits; under this arrangement, the amount of the credit granted increases as the amount of time served by the obedient prisoner increases. Accordingly, one month off is granted for good behavior in the first year, two months for the second year, and so on up to a maximum of six months off for good behavior in the sixth year and in each succeeding year. The inmate is allowed to accumulate these credits. Thus, under this system, a prisoner who received a minimum-maximum sentence of 3 to 5 years and who served "good time", would be eligible for parole after serving 2 years and 6 months of his sentence.

A violation of the conditions of the parole will subject the parolee to possible return to prison for the remainder of his unexpired sentence.

As previously noted, some states have practically abolished parole by providing mandatory release dates, less time off for good behavior, which means that there can be no parole release prior to that date.

In states maintaining the conventional parole system, revocation of probation or parole cannot be arbitrary. In either case there must be a hearing. The hearing need not be like a full scale trial, i. e., there is no jury, but it must be a fair determination of whether the conditions of probation and parole were violated.

POST–CONVICTION REMEDIES

The Appeal

After sentence has been pronounced, the defendant may appeal his conviction to a reviewing court. The reviewing court will examine all or part of the written record of what happened at the trial, and consider the written and oral arguments of both the defense attorney and the prosecutor. It will then render a written decision and opinion which will either reverse or affirm the trial court conviction and state the reasons for the decision. If the trial court's decision is "reversed and remanded", it means that the defendant's conviction is nullified, although he may be tried over again by another jury. A decision of "reversed" ordinarily means that in addition to an improper trial there appears to be insufficient competent evidence upon which to try the defendant again, and consequently the prosecuting attorney may not make a second attempt to win a conviction.

A decision of the state's highest court affirming a conviction is, in nearly all instances, a final disposition of the case, and there is nothing else the convicted person can do but submit to the judgment of the trial court. But if the appeal involved a *federal* constitutional question or issue the defendant is entitled to seek a review of the state appellate court decision by the Supreme Court of the United States. Such requests, known as petitions for a *writ of certiorari*, are rarely granted, however.

The courts may allow the defendant to remain free on bail pending appeal or they may increase the amount of bail or revoke bail entirely while the case is on appeal.

Whenever a defendant has succeeded in obtaining a reversal of his conviction, he may be retried unless the highest court to review the case has reversed for insufficiency of evidence. The reasons that a second trial after a reversal of a conviction for trial error does not constitute double jeopardy are three-fold, according to the courts which have been confronted with the issue. First of all, by appealing his conviction the accused is considered to "waive" his right not to be tried twice. Secondly, there is a strong societal interest in a final adjudication of the guilt or innocence of the accused. Thirdly, a retrial is in effect a continuation of the original proceeding.

Collateral Attacks

In addition to the appeal itself, nearly all states in recent years have provided additional post-conviction remedies by which a defendant may attack his conviction. Such "collateral" remedies are known, variously, as proceedings in habeas corpus, post-conviction petitions, or by other titles. A defendant may thereby seek a re-litigation, in a trial court, of an issue that had been considered and decided on the direct appeal; or he may attempt to raise an entirely new issue. Moreover, the decision with respect to a collateral attack may be the subject of an appeal to a reviewing court.

Even after a conviction is upheld against collateral attack in the state courts, if a federal constitutional question had been presented, the convicted person has yet another remedy available—the *federal* writ of habeas corpus. The Supreme Court of the United States has held that a state court judgment of conviction resulting from a trial which involved a substantial error of federal constitutional dimension is void, and a prisoner held pursuant to a void judgment is unlawfully confined and subject to release by a federal court upon a writ of habeas corpus. However, the Court has imposed some limitations upon this right. A state prisoner who claims that evidence used against him at trial was obtained in violation of constitutional rules governing arrest, search and seizure, cannot present those claims in a federal habeas corpus proceeding if he had the opportunity to make them in the state court.

In considering a petition for habeas corpus, a federal district court judge may order another "evidentiary hearing." And he has the power to remand the case to the state court for a new trial or for the outright release of the defendant, depending upon the kind of error committed and the evidence still available to the state. But his decision is appealable to higher federal courts.

APPEALS BY THE PROSECUTION

Only the defendant has a right to appeal the result of a trial; to permit the prosecution to appeal from a verdict of acquittal or a trial judge's finding of not guilty has been held to violate the constitutional protection against double jeopardy.

In a growing number of jurisdictions, however, the prosecution is being accorded the right to appeal certain decisions of a pre-trial nature. The Illinois Supreme Court Rules, for example, provide for prosecution appeals from a trial court order dismissing the charge against a defendant, or from an order suppressing a confession or other evidence alleged to have been illegally obtained.

The prosecution generally has the same right of appeal as the defense from an adverse decision of an intermediate appeals court. Many states and the federal government have two kinds of reviewing courts. The first, usually called a court of appeals, hears most appeals. The losing party may then ask the second court, usually called the supreme court, to rehear the appeal. This second court, the highest court, may rehear the appeal and render a final decision or it may simply refuse to rehear the case.

NOTE

A brief comparison, in outline form, between English and American criminal procedure appears in a pamphlet entitled "British Criminal Law," published by the Criminal Law Section of the American Bar Association for use at the Association's London Meeting in 1957, and reproduced in 50 J. Crim.L., C. & P.S. 59 (1959). Also see, for other comparisons between English and American criminal procedure: Fellman, The Defendant's Rights Under English Law (1966), and Karlen, Sawer & Wise, Anglo-American Criminal Justice (1967).

For a brief comparison of criminal procedure in the United States, England, Germany, Italy and Sweden, see Hartshorne, Court Procedure Compared, 41 J.Am.Jud.Soc'y 166 (1958). In his article Judge Hartshorne points out some interesting facts, such as the following: In Sweden, a court will try both the civil and criminal aspects of a case at the same time; in Italy, as is also true in some other countries, there is practically no cross-examination of witnesses, since the lawyers must submit to the judge every question they wish to ask of a witness, whereupon the judge decides whether the question should be modified or perhaps even asked at all; in some of these countries the defendant's past criminal record is before the court for consideration; and in Sweden and Germany there is no jury, as we know it, but a trial body composed of both professional and lay judges who sit as a "jury," deliberate together, and make their findings as a group. After considering a number of differences between American procedure and that of other countries, Judge Hartshorne concludes: "We must not be too sure that simply because we have been accustomed to doing a certain thing in a certain way that that way is the only way it should be done. In fact, the writer discussed many of these Swedish differences in procedure with some of the most estimable and broadminded Swedish citizens, and they were quite as convinced that their system was correct, as an American is that the American system is correct. Naturally, we have a predilection for our own system, because that is what we are used to, and have come to consider to be the only right way to do things. But clearly there are certain advantages in other ways of accomplishing the same result. Whether these advantages outweigh the advantages inhering in our system is another question. But the point is that we must not be hasty in our criticism, before we have considered objectively the merits of older, though to us strange, procedures."

The early English procedures for disposing of criminal accusations by such devices as trial by ordeal, trial by compurgation, and trial by battle, are discussed in 31 Tul.L.Rev. 68 (1956).

As regards Soviet Russia, see Berman, Soviet Criminal Law and Procedure (2d ed. 1972).

A comparative treatment of certain aspects of criminal procedure in the United States, England, Canada, France, Norway, Japan, Germany, and Israel is contained in Sowle (Ed.), Police Power and Individual Freedom (1962), which is a reproduction of a series of articles originally published during 1960 and 1961 in the Journal of Criminal Law, Criminology and Police Science (Vol. 51, 129–188, 385–441; and Vol. 52, 1–74, 245–292).

Among other publications, see Meyer, German Criminal Procedure: The Position of the Defendant in Court, 41 A.B.A.J. 592 (1955); Berg, Criminal Procedure: France, England, and the United States, 8 De Paul L. Rev. 256 (1959); and Abe, Criminal Procedure in Japan, 48 J.Crim.L., C. & P.S. 359 (1957); Pugh, Administration of Criminal Justice in France: An Introductory Analysis, 23 La.L.Rev. 1 (1962); Bratholm, Pagripelse og varetektsfengsel, pp. 379–97 (1957) (summary of law with respect to arrest and detention before trial in Norway, Sweden and Denmark); Robinson, Arrest, Prosecution and Police Power in the Federal Republic of Germany, 4 Duq.U.L.Rev. 225 (1965); Jescheck, Principles of German Criminal Law in Comparison with American Law, 56 Va.L.Rev. 239 (1970); Langbein, Comparative Criminal Procedure: Germany (1977).

For a continuing series of publications in the field of comparative criminal law, see the following (and others to come), under the sponsorship of the Comparative Criminal Law Project of New York University: Mueller (Ed.), Essays in Criminal Science (1961); Mueller & Wise, International Criminal Law (1965); and Andenaes (transl. by Ogle), The General Part of the Criminal Law of Norway (1965). Also see the series under the title The Comparative Study of the Administration of Justice (consisting primarily of reprints from other law journals), edited by Professor Francis C. Sullivan; and The American Series of Foreign Penal Codes, published by F. B. Rothman Co.

PART 1

LIMITATIONS UPON LAW ENFORCEMENT PRACTICES AND PROCEDURES

Chapter 2

CONFESSIONS AND INTERROGATIONS

A. VOLUNTARINESS OF CONFESSIONS

1. STANDARDS OF VOLUNTARINESS

BROWN v. MISSISSIPPI

Supreme Court of the United States, 1936.
297 U.S. 278, 56 S.Ct. 461.

MR. CHIEF JUSTICE HUGHES delivered the opinion of the Court.

* * *

The State is free to regulate the procedure of its courts in accordance with its own conceptions of policy, unless in so doing it "offends some principle of justice so rooted in the traditions and conscience of our people as to be ranked as fundamental." . . . . But the freedom of the State in establishing its policy is the freedom of constitutional government and is limited by the requirement of due process of law. Because a State may dispense with a jury trial, it does not follow that it may substitute trial by ordeal. The rack and torture chamber may not be substituted for the witness stand. The State may not permit an accused to be hurried to conviction under mob domination—where the whole proceeding is but a mask—without supplying corrective process. Moore v. Dempsey, 261 U.S. 86, 91. The State may not deny to the accused the aid of counsel. Powell v. Alabama, 287 U.S. 45. Nor may a State, through the action of its officers, contrive a conviction through the pretense of a trial which in truth is "but used as a means of depriving a defendant of liberty through a deliberate deception of court and jury by the presentation of testimony known to be perjured." Mooney v. Holohan, 294 U.S. 103, 112. And the trial equally is a mere pretense where the state authorities have contrived a conviction resting solely upon confessions obtained by violence. The due process clause requires "that state action, whether through one agency or another, shall be consistent with the fundamental principles of liberty and justice which lie at

16

the base of all our civil and political institutions." Hebert v. Louisiana, 272 U.S. 312, 316. It would be difficult to conceive of methods more revolting to the sense of justice than those taken to procure the confessions of these petitioners, and the use of the confessions thus obtained as the basis for conviction and sentence was clear denial of due process.

* * *

In the instant case, the trial court was fully advised by the undisputed evidence of the way in which the confessions had been procured. The trial court knew that there was no other evidence upon which conviction and sentence could be based. Yet it proceeded to permit conviction and to pronounce sentence. The conviction and sentence were void for want of the essential elements of due process, and the proceeding thus vitiated could be challenged in any appropriate manner. Mooney v. Holohan, supra. It was challenged before the Supreme Court of the State by the express invocation of the Fourteenth Amendment. That court entertained the challenge, considered the federal question thus presented, but declined to enforce petitioners' constitutional right. The court thus denied a federal right fully established and specially set up and claimed and the judgment must be

Reversed.

WATTS v. INDIANA

Supreme Court of the United States, 1949.
338 U.S. 49, 69 S.Ct. 1347.

MR. JUSTICE FRANKFURTER announced the judgment of the Court and an opinion in which MR. JUSTICE MURPHY and MR. JUSTICE RUTLEDGE join.

Although the Constitution puts protection against crime predominantly in the keeping of the States, the Fourteenth Amendment severely restricted the States in their administration of criminal justice. Thus, while the State courts have the responsibility for securing the rudimentary requirements of a civilized order, in discharging that responsibility there hangs over them the reviewing power of this Court.

* * *

This case is here because the Supreme Court of Indiana rejected petitioner's claim that confessions elicited from him were procured under circumstances rendering their admission as evidence against him a denial of due process of law.[1]

* * *

---

1. In the petitioner's statements there was acknowledgment of the possession of an incriminating gun, the existence of which the police independently established. But a coerced confession is inadmissible under the Due Process Clause even though statements in it may be independently established as true. See Lisenba v. California, 314 U.S. 219, 236–237.

On review here of State convictions, all those matters which are usually termed issues of fact are for conclusive determination by the State courts and are not open for reconsideration by this Court. Observance of this restriction in our review of State courts calls for the utmost scruple. But "issue of fact" is a coat of many colors. It does not cover a conclusion drawn from uncontroverted happenings, when that conclusion incorporates standards of conduct or criteria for judgment which in themselves are decisive of constitutional rights. Such standards and criteria, measured against the requirements drawn from constitutional provisions, and their proper applications, are issues for this Court's adjudication.

* * *

[In all the cases where] it was claimed that the admission of coerced confessions vitiated convictions for murder, there has been complete agreement that any conflict in testimony as to what actually led to a contested confession is not this Court's concern. Such conflict comes here authoritatively resolved by the State's adjudication. Therefore only those elements of the events and circumstances in which a confession was involved that are unquestioned in the State's version of what happened are relevant to the constitutional issue here. But if force has been applied, this Court does not leave to local determination whether or not the confession was voluntary. There is torture of mind as well as body; the will is as much affected by fear as by force. And there comes a point where this Court should not be ignorant as judges of what we know as men.

This brings us to the undisputed circumstances which must determine the issue of due process in this case. Thanks to the forthrightness of counsel for Indiana, these circumstances may be briefly stated.

On November 12, 1947, a Wednesday, petitioner was arrested and held as the suspected perpetrator of an alleged criminal assault earlier in the day. Later the same day, in the vicinity of this occurrence, a woman was found dead under conditions suggesting murder in the course of an attempted criminal assault. Suspicion of murder quickly turned towards petitioner and the police began to question him. They took him from the county jail to State Police Headquarters, where he was questioned by officers in relays from about 11:30 that night until sometime between 2:30 and 3 o'clock the following morning. The same procedure of persistent interrogation from about 5:30 in the afternoon until about 3 o'clock the following morning, by a relay of six to eight officers, was pursued on Thursday the 13th, Friday the 14th, Saturday the 15th, Monday the 17th. Sunday was a day of rest from interrogation. About 3 o'clock on Tuesday morning, November 18, the petitioner made an incriminating statement after continuous questioning since 6 o'clock of the preceding evening. The statement did not satisfy the prosecutor who had been called in and he then took petitioner in hand. Petitioner, questioned by an interrogator of twenty years' experience as lawyer, judge and prosecutor, yielded a more incriminating document.

Until his inculpatory statements were secured, the petitioner was a prisoner in the exclusive control of the prosecuting authorities. He was kept for the first two days in solitary confinement in a cell aptly enough called "the hole" in view of its physical conditions as described by the State's witnesses. Apart from the five night sessions, the police intermittently interrogated Watts during the day and on three days drove him around town, hours at a time, with a view to eliciting identifications and other disclosures. Although the law of Indiana required that petitioner be given a prompt preliminary hearing before a magistrate, with all the protection a hearing was intended to give him, the petitioner was not only given no hearing during the entire period of interrogation but was without friendly or professional aid and without advice as to his constitutional rights. Disregard of rudimentary needs of life—opportunities for sleep and a decent allowance of food—are also relevant, not as aggravating elements of petitioner's treatment, but as part of the total situation out of which his confessions came and which stamped their character.

A confession by which life becomes forfeit must be the expression of free choice. A statement to be voluntary of course need not be volunteered. But if it is the product of sustained pressure by the police it does not issue from a free choice. When a suspect speaks because he is overborne, it is immaterial whether he has been subjected to a physical or a mental ordeal. Eventual yielding to questioning under such circumstances is plainly the product of the suction process of interrogation and therefore the reverse of voluntary. We would have to shut our minds to the plain significance of what here transpired to deny that this was a calculated endeavor to secure a confession through the pressure of unrelenting interrogation. The very relentlessness of such interrogation implies that it is better for the prisoner to answer than to persist in the refusal of disclosure which is his constitutional right. To turn the detention of an accused into a process of wrenching from him evidence which could not be extorted in open court with all its safeguards, is so grave an abuse of the power of arrest as to offend the procedural standards of due process.

This is so because it violates the underlying principle in our enforcement of the criminal law. Ours is the accusatorial as opposed to the inquisitorial system. Such has been the characteristic of Anglo-American criminal justice since it freed itself from practices borrowed by the Star Chamber from the Continent whereby an accused was interrogated in secret for hours on end. Under our system society carries the burden of proving its charge against the accused not out of his own mouth. It must establish its case, not by interrogation of the accused even under judicial safeguards, but by evidence independently secured through skillful investigation. "The law will not suffer a prisoner to be made the deluded instrument of his own conviction." The requirement of specific charges, their proof beyond a reasonable doubt, the protection of the accused from confessions extorted through whatever form of police pressures, the right to a prompt hearing before a magistrate, the right to assistance of counsel, to be supplied by government when circumstances make it necessary, the duty to advise an accused of his constitutional rights—these are all characteristics of the accusatorial system and manifestations of its demands. Protracted, systematic and uncontrolled subjection of an accused to interrogation by the police for the purpose of eliciting disclosures or confessions is subversive of the accusatorial system. It is the inquisitorial system without its safeguards. For while under that system the accused is subjected to judicial interrogation, he is protected by the disinterestedness of the judge in the presence of counsel.

In holding that the Due Process Clause bars police procedure which violates the basic notions of our accusatorial mode of prosecuting crime and vitiates a conviction based on the fruits of such procedure, we apply the Due Process Clause to its historic function of assuring appropriate procedure before liberty is curtailed or life is taken. We are deeply mindful of the anguishing problems which the incidence of crime presents to the States. But the history of the criminal law proves overwhelmingly that brutal methods of law enforcement are essentially self-defeating, whatever may be their effect in a particular case. Law triumphs when the natural impulses aroused by a shocking crime yield to the safeguards which our civilization has evolved for an administration of criminal justice at once rational and effective.

We have examined petitioner's other contentions and do not sustain them.

Reversed.

MR. JUSTICE BLACK concurs in the judgment of the Court on the authority of Chambers v. Florida, 309 U.S. 227; Ashcraft v. Tennessee, 322 U.S. 143.

On the record before us and in view of the consideration given to the evidence by the state courts and the conclusion reached, THE CHIEF JUSTICE, MR. JUSTICE REED and MR. JUSTICE BURTON believe that the judgment should be affirmed.

MR. JUSTICE DOUGLAS, concurring.

It would be naive to think that this protective custody was less than the inquisition. The man was held until he broke. Then and only then was he arraigned and given the protection which the law provides all accused. Detention without arraignment is a time-honored method for keeping an accused under the exclusive control of the police. They can then operate at their leisure. The accused is wholly at their mercy. He is without the aid of counsel or friends; and he is denied the protection of the magistrate. We should unequivocally condemn the procedure and stand ready to outlaw, as we did in Malinski v. New York, 324 U.S. 401, and Haley v. Ohio, 332 U.S. 596, any confession obtained during the period of the unlawful detention. The procedure breeds coerced confessions. It is the root of the evil. It is the procedure without which the inquisition could not flourish in the country.

MR. JUSTICE JACKSON concurring in the result [of the Watts case, but dissenting in the other two companion cases of Harris v. South Carolina and Turner v. Pennsylvania].

These three cases, from widely separated states, present essentially the same problem. Its recurrence suggests that it has roots in some condition fundamental and general to our criminal system.

In each case police were confronted with one or more brutal murders which the authorities were under the highest duty to solve. Each of these murders was unwitnessed, and the only positive knowledge on which a solution could be based was possessed by the killer. In each there was reasonable ground to *suspect* an individual but not enough legal evidence to *charge* him with guilt. In each the police attempted to meet the situation by taking the suspect into custody and interrogating him. This extended over varying periods. In each, confessions were made and received in evidence at the trial. Checked with external evidence, they are inherently believable, and were not shaken as to truth by anything that occurred at the trial. Each confessor was convicted by a jury and state courts affirmed. This Court sets all three convictions aside.

The seriousness of the Court's judgment is that no one suggests that any course held promise of solution of these murders other than to take the suspect into custody for questioning. The alternative was to close the books on the crime and forget it, with the suspect at large. This is a grave choice for a society in which two-thirds of the murders already are closed out as insoluble.

A concurring opinion, however, goes to the very limit and seems to declare for outlawing any confession, however freely given, if obtained during a period of custody between arrest and arraignment—which, in practice, means all of them.

Others would strike down these confessions because of conditions which they say make them "involuntary." In this, on only a printed record, they pit their judgment against that of the trial judge and the jury. Both, with the great advantage of hearing and seeing the confessor and also the officers whose conduct and bearing toward him is in question, have found that the confessions were voluntary. In addition, the majority overrule in each case one or more state appellate courts, which have the same limited opportunity to know the truth that we do.

Amid much that is irrelevant or trivial, one serious situation seems to me to stand out in these cases. The suspect neither had nor was advised of his right to get counsel. This presents a real dilemma in a free society. To subject one without counsel to questioning which may and is intended to convict him, is a real peril to individual freedom. To bring in a lawyer means a real peril to solution of the crime, because, under our adversary system, he deems that his sole duty is to protect his client—guilty or innocent—and that in such a capacity he owes no duty whatever to help society solve its crime problem. Under this conception of criminal procedure, any lawyer worth his salt will tell the suspect in no uncertain terms to make no statement to police under any circumstances.

If the State may arrest on suspicion and interrogate without counsel, there is no denying the fact that it largely negates the benefits of the constitutional guaranty of the right to assistance of counsel. Any lawyer who has ever been called into a case after his client has "told all" and turned any evidence he has over to the Government, knows how helpless he is to protect his client against the facts thus disclosed.

I suppose the view one takes will turn on what one thinks should be the right of an accused person against the State. Is it his right to have the judgment on the facts? Or is it his right to have a judgment based on only such evidence as he cannot conceal from the authorities, who cannot compel him to testify in court and also cannot question him before? Our system comes close to the latter by any interpretation, for the defendant is shielded by such safeguards as no system of law except the Anglo-American concedes to him.

Of course, no confession that has been obtained by any form of physical violence to the person is reliable and hence no conviction should rest upon one obtained in that manner. Such treatment not only breaks the will to conceal or lie, but may even break the will to stand by the truth. Nor is it questioned that the same result can sometimes be achieved by threats, promises, or inducements which torture the mind but put no scar on the body. If the opinion of Mr. Justice Frankfurter in the *Watts* case were based solely on the State's admissions as to the treatment of Watts, I should not disagree. But if ultimate quest in a criminal trial is the truth and if the circumstances indicate no violence or threats of it, should society be deprived of the suspect's help in solving a crime merely because he was confined and questioned when uncounseled?

We must not overlook that, in these as in some previous cases, once a confession is obtained it supplies ways of verifying its trustworthiness. In these cases before us the verification is sufficient to leave me in no doubt that the admissions of guilt were genuine and truthful. Such corrobation consists in one case of finding a weapon where the accused has said he hid it, and in others that conditions which could only have been known to one who was implicated correspond with his story. It is possible, but it is rare, that a confession, if repudiated on the trial, standing alone will convict unless there is external proof of its verity.

In all such cases, along with other conditions criticized, the continuity and duration of the questioning is invoked and it is called an "inquiry," "inquest" or "inquisition," depending mainly on the emotional state of the writer. But as in some of the cases here, if interrogation is permissible at all, there are sound reasons for prolonging it—which the opinions here ignore. The suspect at first perhaps makes an effort to exculpate himself by alibis or other statements. These are verified, found false, and he is then confronted with his falsehood. Sometimes (though such cases do not reach us) verification proves them true or credible and the suspect is released. Sometimes, as here, more than one crime is involved. The duration of an interrogation may well depend on the temperament, shrewdness and cunning of the accused and the competence of the examiner. But, assuming a right to examine at all, the right must include what is made reasonably necessary by the facts of the particular case.

If the right of interrogation be admitted, then it seems to me that we must leave it to trial judges and juries and state appellate courts to decide individual cases, unless they show some want of proper standards of decision. I find nothing to indicate that any of the courts below in these cases did not have a correct understanding of the Fourteenth Amendment, unless this Court thinks it means absolute prohibition of interrogation while in custody before arraignment.

I suppose no one would doubt that our Constitution and Bill of Rights, grounded in revolt against the arbitrary measures of George III and in the philosophy of the French Revolution, represent the maximum restrictions upon the power of organized society over the individual that are compatible with the maintenance of organized society itself. They were so intended and should be so interpreted. It cannot be denied that, even if construed as these provisions traditionally have been, they contain an aggregate of restrictions which seriously limit the power of society to solve such crimes as confront us in these cases. Those restrictions we should not for that reason cast aside, but that is good reason for indulging in no unnecessary expansion of them.

I doubt very much if they require us to hold that the State may not take into custody and question one suspected reasonably of an unwitnessed murder. If it does, the people of this country must discipline themselves to seeing their police stand by helplessly while those suspected of murder prowl about unmolested. Is it a necessary price to pay for the fairness which we know as "due process of law"? And if not a necessary one, should it be demanded by this Court? I do not know the ultimate answer to these questions; but, for the present, I should not increase the handicap on society.

PEOPLE v. HESTER

Supreme Court of Illinois, 1968.
39 Ill.2d 489, 237 N.E.2d 466, cert. dismissed as improvidently granted
397 U.S. 660, 90 S.Ct. 1408.

UNDERWOOD, JUSTICE.

The defendant, Lee Arthur Hester, age 14, was found guilty of murder by a jury in the circuit court of Cook County and sentenced to a term of 55 years imprisonment. In this direct appeal the defendant claims 18 instances of reversible error occurred in these proceedings.

About 4:00 P.M., on April 20, 1961, the body of Josephine Keane, a teacher at the Lewis-Champlin Elementary School of Chicago, was discovered in the first floor bookroom of the school. Mrs. Keane had been stabbed repeatedly in the side and chest. Her body was found lying face up with her skirt pushed up over the hips. The crotch of her panties and girdle had been cut as well as the loops that held the garter supports attached to her girdle. The coroner found that spermatazoa were present in the victim's vagina, and the autopsy report fixed the cause of death as hemorrhaging due to multiple stab wounds with death occurring between 8:00 A.M. and noon that day.

On April 21, Detectives Sheldon Teller and Anton Prunkle were assigned to investigate the murder, and arrived at the school before daybreak to conduct a search of the premises. About 7:45 A.M. Hester's gym teacher, Miss Virginia Fritsch, talked with them stating that she had seen Hester alone in the hall on Thursday morning, and that she believed Mrs. Keane was handling a disciplinary case which involved him. Miss Fritsch directed the officers to Mrs. Rita Considine, a clerk in the principal's office, as a possible source of more information. Mrs. Considine informed the policemen that Mrs. Keane had mentioned that a parent had complained about the defendant wanting her son to commit an unnatural act. The detectives then proceeded to the third floor classroom where they met Jean Webster, Hester's fifth grade teacher.

At 8:00 A.M. the defendant arrived in his classroom and Miss Webster directed him to the officers who were waiting outside. The defendant was in the custody of Officers Teller and Prunkle from shortly after 8:00 A.M. until approximately 8:45 A.M. when they turned him over to Sergeant Frank Follis of the youth division. As they were interviewing the defendant outside of his third-floor classroom the detectives noticed what appeared to be bloodstains on Hester's pants and shirt. Detective Teller testified that when the defendant was asked how he acquired the stains on his clothing he gave several answers: that they were due to a fight with another boy; that he had had a nosebleed; that he had cut himself while chopping wood with an ax; and that he cut himself with a saw while sawing wood. Hester testified that as he was being interviewed outside of the classroom Officer Prunkle kicked him in the left shin. This charge was denied by Officers Teller and Prunkle, and their testimony was given support by three school teachers who were present during various portions of the conversation and never saw Hester struck. The defendant did not complain to anyone that morning about being kicked, including a doctor he saw when he was admitted to the Audy Home, a juvenile detention facility.

After questioning Hester on the third floor for approximately fifteen minutes, the detectives took him to the school auditorium where they could use the bright natural sunlight to examine more closely the stains and spots on his clothes. Hester admitted that he knew Mrs. Keane for three semesters or more, but he denied any involvement in the murder. The defendant was then taken to the principal's office and turned over to Sergeant Follis. Hester sat outside the office until 9:00 A.M. when Officers Harold Thomas and Robert Perkins picked him up and transported him by car to the Audy Home. Upon arrival there, the defendant's clothes were turned over to the officers for removal to the crime laboratory and Hester was provided with a robe to wear. The officers left the Audy Home and did not return there until 4:00 in the afternoon. Between 10:00 A.M. and 4:00 P.M. on April 21, Hester was kept in a room in the Audy Home infirmary which he described at his trial as a "dungeon room". The defendant did admit, however, that the room contained a bed with a blanket and clean sheets that he laid upon; he further stated that he was given lunch but claimed he did not eat it. The Audy Home superintendent testified the room was 7 feet 9 inches by 12 feet 8 inches with a 12-foot ceiling, and contained a hospital bed with a 6-inch innerspring mattress, a hospital table and stool, a light fixture, radiator, 28-by-52-inch transom, and 42-by-52-inch barred window.

About 4:00 P.M. Hester was provided with clothes and brought into an interview room at the Audy Home where he was questioned for approximately five minutes by Officers Thomas and Perkins, and Sergeants William Keating and John Killackey. The room where this interview took place was estimated by Officer Perkins to be 15 feet square with a barred window. Sergeant Killackey testified that the four officers began by introducing themselves to Hester, and that the defendant sat next to a wall flanked by Perkins and Thomas while Sergeant Keating sat behind a desk which he (Killackey) was sitting on. Officer Perkins testified that none of the policemen was closer to the defendant than 4½ to 5 feet during this 5-minute period. When Hester denied complicity in the crime he was confronted with the results of the crime laboratory tests which he was told revealed human blood on his clothes, a hair from a Caucasian female and a lipstick smear on his coat, and certain filings from his pocket. The defendant alleges that in addition to this incriminating evidence he was told that his fingerprints were found on the icebox which was in the bookroom. He further claimed that Sergeant Killackey called him a liar when he denied responsibility for the murder and warned him "something was going to happen". The defendant testified that Killackey drew close to him, stuck a pen in his face and spit at him. The allegations of threatening, spitting and telling Hester about his fingerprints being found on the icebox were denied at the trial by all four of the officers who were in the room.

At the end of the 5-minute interview Sergeants Killackey and Keating, both of whom are Caucasian, left Hester in the room with the Negro Officers Perkins and Thomas. According to the defendant, Officer Thomas told him that the two white officers were going to knock his head through the wall if he didn't admit the crime, but that Thomas assured him, "We ain't going to let them knock your head through the wall." Hester testified that he was then promised that if he admitted the murder his mother would bring him some clothes and he would be allowed to go home. The defendant's version of a police "Mutt and Jeff routine" (see Miranda v. State of Arizona, 384 U.S. 436, 452, 86 S.Ct. 1602, 1616), was denied by the officers who testified that Hester was only encouraged "to tell us about it and get it off his chest." Thomas and Perkins testified that after the defendant was given this advice he made an oral admission that an "accident" had occurred which resulted in his stabbing Mrs. Keane. They stated that Hester told them he tripped over some books at the entrance to the bookroom, that this caused a knife which was attached by rubber bands to his wrist to come into his hand, and that he stabbed Mrs. Keane as he fell; that he became scared and stabbed Mrs. Keane several more times, and then proceeded to sexually assault her. In describing his sexual assault, the officers testified that Hester said that he laid on top of her and "squirted", then bent over her to see if her heart was beating, and after he could not hear a heartbeat he locked the bookroom door with keys that he had found, dropped the keys "somewhere", and rejoined a classmate, Sherman Baker, with whom he then returned to Miss Webster's class. After defendant's oral confession to the officers, Perkins testified that he brought photographs of the murder scene into the room and Hester pointed out certain items in the picture which he had mentioned in his statement. The defendant's testimony on this point is directly contradictory to the explanation of the police officers. Hester testified that the photographs of the bookroom were shown to him before and not after he confessed the crime, that he concocted the confession after viewing the pictures of the murder scene, and that the police coached him in portraying the details of the crime.

At approximately 5:00 P.M. Hester was examined by medical personnel at the Audy Home. Following the examination he was taken to the office of the State's Attorney in the Family Court Building which adjoins the Audy Home; and about 6:30 P.M. in the presence of assistant State's Attorney Louis Garripo, a court reporter, and Sergeant Keating, Hester made a confession of the crime which was substantially identical to the statement he had given to Officers Perkins and Thomas. At 8:15 P.M. three typed copies of the confession were returned by the court reporter and Garripo read the statement aloud as Hester followed along by reading a copy with which he had been supplied. Hester testified that the statement was read too fast for him to follow, but the State's witnesses stated that the confession was read slowly with the defendant pointing out several mistakes in the transcript. The copy of the confession admitted into evidence does contain the defendant's initials on each page with his initials appearing at each correction, and his signature on the last page of the statement. The fact that the statement was read aloud to the defendant and initialed by him at several points supports the State's contention that Hester understood what he was signing.

We come now to the defendant's many and varied allegations of error. A primary contention to which defense counsel devoted the bulk of their oral argument is that Hester's constitutional rights were violated by the admission into evidence of a confession elicited by psychological coercion and threats of brutality from a 14-year-old boy of limited mentality who was kept *incommunicado* for over 12 hours before signing a written confession, who was not furnished legal counsel, who was not advised of his constitutional rights, and who, after repeated requests to see his mother was refused the right to see her or any other friend before and during his interrogations. In support of this proposition the defense cites United States Supreme Court cases beginning with Brown v. Mississippi, 297 U.S. 278, 56 S. Ct. 461, and culminating in Miranda v. State of Arizona, 384 U.S. 436, 86 S.Ct. 1602.

The constitutional test governing the admission of a confession by an accused is whether it has been made "freely, voluntarily and without compulsion or inducement of any sort," or whether the defendant's will was overborne at the time he confessed. (Culombe v. Connecticut, 367 U.S. 568, 81 S.Ct. 1860). Compulsion may also include torture of the mind when the will of the suspect succumbs to fear. (Watts v. State of Indiana.) "Determinative factors include not only illegal detention but its duration, the relentlessness of interrogation, disregard of the rudimentary necessities of life, the deprivation of counsel, deception respecting the accused's constitutional rights, the accused's age, education, emotional characteristics, and experience in criminal matters." Since Hester's pre-*Miranda* trial commenced in September, 1961, the standard controlling admission of the defendant's confession is the totality of circumstances test and this requires us to now make an independent review of the factors bearing upon voluntariness of the confession.

A careful review of the extensive record here has led us to the following conclusions: (a) Hester's assertions of physical abuse, threats of impending peril if he did not confess, inducements of leniency if he did confess and fabrications concerning the evidentiary findings of the crime laboratory were controverted by each and every police officer and agent of the State who had contact with the defendant in the 12½-hour period between Hester's arrest and the signing of his written confession. Portions of defendant's testimony as to police brutality appear implausible on their face. In denying the motion to suppress the confession, after a full hearing, the trial judge said, "It is just inconceivable that Officer Prunkle would step up to him in the hallway there and kick him practically the moment when he first saw him . . . ." We note further that the truthfulness of Hester's charge that he was thus kicked was impugned when he stated on cross-examination that he had been kicked in the left leg, but was then shown a newspaper photograph of himself pointing out his right leg as the one that had been kicked. When confronted with this picture the defendant responded "I forgot". In the absence of any evidence whatsoever to corroborate the defendant's somewhat contradictory and implausible testimony, the trial court was free to believe the wholly consistent testimony of the many State witnesses. (b) The defendant was not informed of his constitutional rights, nor was he provided with counsel or other friend to act on his behalf during the relatively brief periods of police interrogation. We have uniformly held, however, that in pre-*Miranda* cases the failure to advise a defendant of his constitutional rights, as well as the absence of an attorney and the unlawful detention of a suspect are only attendant circumstances to be considered in deciding whether a confession was made voluntarily, (People v. Musil, 37 Ill.2d 373, 377–378, 227 N.E.2d 751.) (c) The defendant's allegation that he made several requests to see his mother which were refused was repeatedly denied by the police and agents of the State's Attorney's office with whom he had contact. We find it highly relevant in this regard that Officers Thomas and Perkins went to the home of defendant at approximately 2:45 P.M. on April 21, saw Hester's mother, and apparently told her that defendant was being held by the police, although testimony as to that conversation was largely excluded when objected to on separate occasions by both the State and defense counsel. Defendant's mother agreed the officers called at her home and further testified that she was notified at 2:30 P.M. by a classmate of Hester's that he was in police custody, but she did not attempt to locate her son until approximately 6:00 o'clock that evening; and while no reason appears in the record to explain why Mrs. Hester was unable to see defendant when she arrived at the Audy Home at 9:30 P.M., it is clear that she did see him there at 10:00 A.M the following morning. (d) The defense places heavy reliance on the theory that the confession should not have been admitted into evidence because it was elicited from a 14-year-old boy of subnormal intelligence. Mentality and scholastic achievement-test scores of defendant were admitted into evidence indicating Hester's abilities between November 26, 1958, when he was 11 years, 7 months old, and January 20, 1959. In the November tests Hester's mental age was estimated at 8 years, 8 months, and his IQ was 75. Since defendant was in grade 3–A at the time he was being tested, his reading and arithmetic test scores should have registered at 3.5 to qualify as normal. On the California Achievement Test Hester scored a reading total of 2.0 and a math total of 3.5. The January, 1959, tests registered a mental age of 9 years, 9 months, with an IQ score of 82, which the psychologist testifying for the defense classified as an indication of "a slower than average rate of mental growth." At the time Mrs. Keane was murdered, the defendant was 14 years old; so that based on his lowest test scores and assuming his mental age and academic achievement in English skills continued to lag behind his chronological age at the same rate, defendant's mental age and abilities would have been at least equal to those of a normal 11-year-old child at the time he confessed to the crime. The general rule is that subnormal mentality does not *ipso facto* make a confession involuntary "so long as the subnormality has not deprived the person in question of the capacity to understand the meaning and effect of the confession. But mental subnormality is a factor to be considered in determining the issues of voluntariness and admissibility, and, where accompanied by other factors indicative of an absence of voluntariness, will require that the confession be excluded." In People v. Isby, 30 Cal.2d 879, 186 P.2d 405, the court held admissible a murder confession by a 26-year-old defendant who was near the imbecile classification possessing an IQ of 58 and a mental age of 8 years, 8 months. The court there noted that the defendant did not "dispute the fact that he knew 'the difference between right and wrong', nor [did] he make any claim of insanity . . . . . It was for the trial court to determine the competency of defendant in the light of his ability to 'perceive, and, perceiving, . . . make known [his] perceptions to others' [citation] and his capacity for 'receiving just impressions of the facts . . . or . . . relating them truly' [citation]; and its ruling in favor of defendant Isby's qualification appears from the record to be well within the limits of judicial discretion. The weight and effect to be given his statements by reason of his asserted mental deficiency was then properly left to the jury."

In a more recent case the Supreme Court of California decided that the murder confession of a 17-year-old defendant with a mental age of 10 years, 2 months, and an IQ of 65 to 71 was properly admitted. (People v. Lara, Cal., 62 Cal.Rptr. 586, 432 P.2d 202.) The *Lara* decision concludes that "a minor, even of subnormal mentality, does not lack the capacity as a matter of law to make a voluntary confession without the presence or consent of counsel or other responsible adult . . . the issue is one of fact, to be decided on the 'totality of the circumstances' of each case." A similar holding appears in State v. Watson, 114 Vt. 543, 49 A.2d 174, where the admission into evidence of a confession of a 20-year-old defendant with a mental age between 8 and 9 years was upheld, the court reasoning that "the mere fact that a person is an infant and of low mentality does not render his confession inadmissible as being involuntary, providing he has the mental capacity to commit the crime with which he is charged. The reason for this rule being that if a child has such mental capacity as to render him amenable to the law for the commission of a crime he has sufficient mental capacity to make a confession of guilt."

Similar determinations sustaining the admission into evidence of confessions of minors possessing subnormal intelligence appear in State v. Ordog, 45 N.J. 347, 212 A.2d 370, where one defendant charged with murder had a chronological age of 19 years but the intelligence of a 7-year-old and the judgment of a 6-year-old according to expert opinion, and another 17½-year-old defendant possessed borderline intelligence, was diagnosed as a chronic undifferentiated schizophrenic, and committed to a State mental hospital after committing the murder but before he became a suspect. The admissibility of confessions by minors of subnormal mentality has also been upheld when elicited from a 15-year-old whose IQ was established to be between 61 and 80 (Bean v. State, 234 Md. 432, 199 A.2d 773); where a murder confession was given by a defendant with a chronological age of 15 years but who could not read or write and whose mental age was the equivalent of a 12-year-old (Michaud v. State, 161

Me. 517, 215 A.2d 87); where a 14-year-old Negro defendant with a mental age of 11 years and 4 months and an IQ of 79 confessed to the crime of rape (Johnson v. Commonwealth, 184 Va. 466, 35 S.E.2d 770); and where a defendant under the age of 16 confessed to a murder which he committed 2 days after his escape from a State hospital for the insane. (State v. Ortega, 77 N.M. 7, 419 P.2d 219.) In our own State we have held admissible the confession of a 19-year-old of below normal intelligence who was a confirmed narcotics addict (People v. Townsend, 11 Ill.2d 30, 141 N.E.2d 729, cert. den. 355 U.S. 850, 78 S.Ct. 76), and we have decided that the youthful age of 14, while an important factor bearing on voluntariness, does not alone render a defendant's murder confession inadmissible. (People v. Connolly, 33 Ill.2d 128, 210 N.E.2d 523.) We conclude from the above cases that Lee Arthur Hester's confession was not inadmissible merely because of his youth and below normal mental faculties, and, in the absence of a showing of a coercive atmosphere that would produce an involuntary confession from this defendant we find that Hester's confession was properly admitted.

In alleging that such a coercive atmosphere did in fact exist, defendant relies on such United States Supreme Court cases as Haley v. State of Ohio, 332 U.S. 596, 68 S.Ct. 302; Gallegos v. State of Colorado, 370 U.S. 49, 82 S.Ct. 1209; and Reck v. Pate, 367 U.S. 433, 81 S. Ct. 1541, all of which held that confessions secured from minors through police interrogation were improperly admitted, but we do not believe that those decisions control the outcome of this case. Those factual situations contained certain common elements which amounted to "a totality of coercive circumstances" not here involved. In *Haley* the murder confession of a 15-year-old boy was obtained after 5 or 6 hours of police questioning in relays through the dead of night until approximately 5:00 A.M. when he confessed after being shown alleged statements of two confederates incriminating him. The defendant was then placed in jail and held *incommunicado* for over three days during which time a lawyer retained by his mother was twice refused access to him, and his mother was not allowed to see him until more than five days after his confession, although a newspaper photographer had been admitted to take defendant's picture immediately after he confessed. While it is true that the court in *Haley* notes that a lad of 15 cannot be judged by the more exacting standards of maturity and needs counsel and support if he is not to become the victim of fear and panic, we believe that the reference to the need of such a defendant for "someone on whom to lean lest the overpowering presence of the law, as he knows it, crush him", must be read in the context of the brand of police interrogation there dealt with. And we find the *ratio decidendi* of *Haley* in the following passage: "The age of petitioner, the hours when he was grilled, the duration of his quizzing, the fact that he had no friend or counsel to advise him, the callous attitude of the police towards his rights *combine* to convince us that this was a confession wrung from a child by means which the law should not sanction. Neither man nor child can be allowed to stand condemned by methods which flout constitutional requirements of due process of law." (Emphasis added.)

Turning to Reck v. Pate, we find a concise summary of the salient facts followed by a holding that is clearly framed in the terms of the totality-of-circumstances principle:

> "At the time of his arrest Reck was a nineteen-year-old youth of subnormal intelligence. He had no prior criminal record or experience with the police. He was held nearly eight days without a judicial hearing. Four of those days preceded his first confession. During that period Reck was subjected each day to six- or seven-hour stretches of relentless and incessant interrogation. The questioning was conducted by groups of officers. For the first three days the interrogation ranged over a wide variety of crimes. On the night of the third day of his detention the interrogation turned to the crime for which petitioner stands convicted. During this same four-day period he was shuttled back and forth between police stations and interrogation rooms. In addition, Reck was intermittently placed on public exhibition in 'show-ups.' On the night before his confession, petitioner became ill while on display in such a 'show-up.' He was taken to the hospital, returned to the police station and put back on public display. When he again became ill he was removed from the 'show-up,' but interrogation in the windowless 'handball court' continued relentlessly until he grew faint and vomited blood on the floor. Once more he was taken to the hospital, where he spent the night under the influence of drugs. The next morning he was removed from the hospital in a wheel chair, and intensive interrogation was immediately resumed. Some eight hours later Reck signed his first confession. The next afternoon he signed a second.

> "During the entire period preceding his confessions Reck was without adequate food, without counsel, and without the assistance of family or friends. He was, for all practical purposes, held incommunicado. He was physically weakened and in intense pain. We conclude that this total combination of circumstances 'is so inherently coercive that its very existence is irreconcilable with the possession of mental freedom by a lone suspect against whom its full coercive force is brought to bear.'"

In *Gallegos* the 14-year-old defendant was apprehended by police and immediately confessed to having assaulted and robbed an elderly man who was then hospitalized due to the defendant's beating but who later died as a result thereof. Gallegos was picked up by police on January 1, 1959, when he orally confessed the assault and robbery to the arresting officer. On January 2, the defendant's mother was refused permission to see him at the Juvenile Hall where he was being kept in security. The defendant made a confession to police again on January 2, and signed a full and formal confession on January 7. After a trial in juvenile court on January 16, the defendant was committed to the State Industrial School on the assault charge, but thereafter the robbery victim died and Gallegos was tried criminally, convicted and sentenced to life imprisonment. In reversing the conviction the court notes that while there was no evidence of prolonged questioning, "the five-day detention—during which time the boy's mother unsuccessfully tried to see him and he was cut off from contact with any lawyer or adult advisor—gives this case an ominous cast." The *Gallegos* majority found that the "crucial evidence" introduced at the defendant's murder trial was his formal signed confession, executed after secret inquisitorial processes extending from January 1 to 7, during which time the defendant saw no lawyer, parent or other friendly adult, and the reversal of the murder conviction was predicated on a theory wholly consistent with the prior *Haley* and *Reck* decisions.

Lee Arthur Hester was not held *incommunicado* by the police for over five days (*Haley, Reck* and *Gallegos*), he was not questioned unrelentingly (*Haley* and *Reck*), nor questioned through the dead of night (*Haley*), and he was not reduced to vomiting blood on the floor during interrogation (*Reck*). He was questioned for approximately 45 minutes in the morning and then left virtually alone, though in police custody, from 8:45 A.M. until 4:00 P.M. There is no shred of evidence, besides the defendant's sometimes implausible testimony, that he was treated otherwise than humanely by the law enforcement officials. When Hester was questioned again at 4:00 o'clock it took just over 5 minutes for him to confess the crime, and the officers spent the remainder of the hour listening to the details and confirming the fact that the defendant's description correlated with the physical layout of the murder scene. The hours between 5:00 and 8:15 P.M. were filled with the administrative details of administering a medical examination to the defendant, procuring an assistant State's Attorney and court reporter, recording the defendant's confession, transcribing it into typed copies, rereading it to the defendant, making necessary corrections, and having the defendant initial and sign it. By 10:00 A.M. the next morning the defendant was allowed to see his mother. It is firmly established that this court will not reverse a trial-court determination on the voluntary character of a confession unless it is against the manifest weight of the evidence or amounts to an abuse of discretion (People v. Hall, 38 Ill.2d 308, 231 N.E.2d 416), and we cannot say upon this state of facts that the defendant's confession was coerced.

* * *

Affirmed.

[Dissent of Justice Schaefer omitted.]

NOTE

An interesting case involving the issue of coercive conduct on the part of a private group of citizens in seeking a confession from a young male college student suspected of murdering a female student is Commonwealth v. Mahnke, 368 Mass. 662, 335 N.E.2d 660 (1975). Following unsuccessful police efforts to locate the missing student and their futile efforts to obtain any helpful information from her suspected boyfriend, several citizens abducted the suspect, took him to a cabin in the woods where he was threatened and interrogated for about twenty hours. He ultimately admitted killing the missing girl and told where he had buried the body. Thereupon, all abusive conduct was abandoned, and he willingly directed the police to the location of the body.

Although the statements made in the cabin were considered involuntary, the court held that the subsequent ones as the group proceeded to the grave site were held voluntary and admissible.

2. PERMISSIBLE INTERROGATION TACTICS AND TECHNIQUES

(a) Trickery, Deceit, Promises?

FRAZIER v. CUPP

Supreme Court of the United States, 1969.
394 U.S. 731, 89 S.Ct. 1420.

Mr. Justice Marshall delivered the opinion of the Court.

* * *

Petitioner's second argument concerns the admission into evidence of his own confession. The circumstances under which the confession was obtained can be summarized briefly. Petitioner was arrested about 4:15 p. m. on September 24, 1964. He was taken to headquarters where questioning began at about 5 p. m. The interrogation, which was tape-recorded, ended slightly more than an hour later, and by 6:45 p. m. petitioner had signed a written version of his confession.

After the questioning had begun and after a few routine facts were ascertained, petitioner was questioned briefly about the location of his Marine uniform. He was next asked where he was on the night in question. Although he admitted that he was with his cousin Rawls, he denied being with any third person. Then petitioner was given a somewhat abbreviated description of his constitutional rights. He was told that he could have an attorney if he wanted one and that anything he said could be used against him at trial. Questioning thereafter became somewhat more vigorous, but petitioner continued to deny being with anyone but Rawls. At this point, the officer questioning petitioner told him, falsely, that Rawls had been brought in and that he had confessed. Petitioner still was reluctant to talk, but

after the officer sympathetically suggested that the victim had started a fight by making homosexual advances, petitioner began to spill
out his story. Shortly after he began he again showed signs of reluctance and said, "I think I had better get a lawyer before I talk any
more. I am going to get into trouble more than I am in now." The
officer replied simply, "You can't be in any more trouble than you
are in now," and the questioning session proceeded. A full confession was obtained and, after further warnings, a written version was
signed.

* * *

Petitioner also presses the alternative argument that his confession was involuntary and that it should have been excluded for that
reason. The trial judge, after an evidentiary hearing during which
the tape recording was played, could not agree with this contention,
and our reading of the record does not lead us to a contrary conclusion. Before petitioner made any incriminating statements, he received partial warnings of his constitutional rights; this is, of course,
a circumstance quite relevant to a finding of voluntariness. Davis v.
North Carolina, 384 U.S. 737, 740, 741 (1966). The questioning was
of short duration, and petitioner was a mature individual of normal
intelligence. The fact that the police misrepresented the statements
that Rawls had made is, while relevant, insufficient in our view to
make this otherwise voluntary confession inadmissible. These cases
must be decided by viewing the "totality of the circumstances," see, e.
g., Clewis v. Texas, 386 U.S. 707, 708 (1967), and on the facts of this
case we can find no error in the admission of petitioner's confession.

* * *

Because we find none of petitioner's contentions meritorious, we
affirm the judgment of the Court of Appeals.

Affirmed.

MR. CHIEF JUSTICE WARREN and MR. JUSTICE DOUGLAS concur
in the result.

MR. JUSTICE FORTAS took no part in the consideration or decision
of this case.

NOTES

1. The result reached in *Frazier* is echoed in many other cases. See
People v. Boone, 22 N.Y.2d 476, 293 N.Y.S.2d 287, 239 N.E.2d 885 (1968);
United States ex rel. Caminito v. Murphy, 222 F.2d 698 (2d Cir. 1955) (officers pretended to be witnesses to the crime and then "identified" the accused).

2. Some of the most troublesome cases for the courts are those where
the issue concerns promises or suggestions by an interrogator of some benefit to the suspect as an inducement to confess. The following cases illustrate the problem:

In Bram v. United States, 168 U.S. 532, 554, 18 S.Ct. 183, 191 (1897),
the Court suggested that any inducement "however slight" may be improper. More recently promises of leniency have been treated as just one factor
in the "totality of the circumstances." See Lynumn v. Illinois, 372 U.S.

528, 83 S.Ct. 917 (1963) ("It will go lighter if you cooperate"); Stein v. New York, 346 U.S. 156, 73 S.Ct. 1077 (1953). The decided cases on the question of what is a fatal promise of leniency are not to be reconciled. An exhortation to tell the truth is proper. Crooker v. California, 357 U.S. 433, 437, 78 S.Ct. 1287 (1958). But what of suggestions, even general ones, that things will go better or easier if the truth is told. Compare State v. Pruitt, 286 N.C. 442, 212 S.E.2d 92 (1975) (statement inadmissible where suspect was told it would be better for him if he got it off his chest and would be harder if he did not cooperate) and Dorsciak v. Gladden, 246 Or. 233, 425 P.2d 177 (1967) (improper to say that judge "would be easier on you"), with People v. Hartgraves, 31 Ill.2d 375, 202 N.E.2d 33 (1964) (confession admissible despite statement that "It would go easier in court for you if you made a statement") and Brooks v. State, 229 A.2d 833 (Del.1967) (proper to admit confession where officers said they would see what they could do to help the accused but could not promise anything). Specific promises not to prosecute or not to impose a specific sentence generally render confessions invalid (Grades v. Boles, 398 F.2d 409 (4th Cir. 1968)), but promises to secure bail have not always been so viewed. See United States v. Ferrara, 377 F.2d 16 (2d Cir. 1967); Hickox v. State, 138 Ga.App. 882, 227 S.E.2d 829 (1976).

The exchange of a confession for some consideration is analogous to the plea bargaining process where pleas may be exchanged for rather specific promises not to prosecute or to impose certain sentences. Presumably the difference in judicial tolerance of the guilty plea practice stems from the fact that defendant is represented by counsel who participates in the bargaining. What if, as part of the plea bargain, the accused confesses his part in the crime and then decides to plead not guilty? Is the confession admissible at his trial? Consider the following case:

HUTTO v. ROSS

Supreme Court of the United States, 1977.
429 U.S. 28, 97 S.Ct. 202.

PER CURIAM.

In March 1972, in Johnson County, Ark., respondent was charged by information with the crime of embezzlement. With the assistance of counsel, respondent entered into plea negotiations with the prosecuting attorney, and the parties reached an agreement that respondent would enter a plea of guilty on the understanding that the prosecutor would recommend a 15-year prison sentence, with 10 years suspended. Approximately two weeks later, the prosecuting attorney asked respondent's counsel whether respondent would be willing to make a statement concerning the crimes. Although counsel advised respondent of his Fifth Amendment privilege and informed him that the terms of the negotiated plea bargain were available regardless of his willingness to comply with the prosecuting attorney's request, the respondent agreed to make a statement confessing to the crime charged. The record discloses that the statement was made under oath in the office of respondent's counsel, with counsel present, and after respondent had been advised of his rights under Miranda v. Arizona [infra Section B] . . . . .

Respondent subsequently withdrew from the plea bargain, retained new counsel, and demanded a jury trial. The trial court ruled, after hearing evidence outside the presence of the jury, that respondent had confessed voluntarily. . . .

* * *

. . . The only question in this case is whether a confession is per se inadmissible in a criminal trial because it was made subsequent to an agreed upon plea bargain that did not call for such a confession.[1] We conclude that the Court of Appeals erred when it held that *any* statement made as a result of a plea bargain is inadmissible.

The Court of Appeals reasoned that respondent's confession was involuntary because it was made "as a result of the plea bargain" and would not have been made "but for the plea bargain." But causation in that sense has never been the test of voluntariness. See Brady v. United States, 397 U.S. 742, 749–750, 90 S.Ct. 1463, 1469 (1970). The test is whether the confession was " 'extracted by any sort of threats or violence, [or] obtained by any direct or implied promises, however slight, [or] by the exertion of any improper influence.' " Bram v. United States, 168 U.S. 532, 542–543, 18 S.Ct. 183, 187 (1897). The existence of the bargain may well have entered into respondent's decision to give a statement, but counsel made it clear to respondent that he could enforce the terms of the plea bargain whether or not he confessed. The confession thus does not appear to have been the result of " 'any direct or implied promises' " or any coercion on the part of the prosecution, and was not involuntary.

NOTE

Consider the idea that voluntariness of confessions is enhanced if the accused is fully apprised of the probable consequences of his confession and of the legal significance of each of the facts he admits. The courts have never required such awareness, but where it exists it clearly supports a claim of voluntariness. If this rule is applied, why preclude the police from telling an accused that the fact he has confessed will mitigate his punishment if, in fact, it will? Is the basis for objecting to such police statements that they can never be based on certainty but only probability? Is the basis for objection the belief that the practice may cause an innocent person to confess? See Wigmore, Evidence §§ 824–826, 831–841 (Chadbourn Rev.1970).

---

1. This case does not involve the admissibility at trial of a guilty plea subsequently withdrawn by leave of court. That issue was settled in Kercheval v. United States, 274 U.S. 220, 47 S.Ct. 582 (1927), which held that such pleas could not be used as evidence of guilt at a subsequent trial. Nor does this case involve the admissibility in criminal trials of statements made during the plea negotiation process. See Fed. Rule Crim. Proc. 11(c)(6); Moulder v. State, 154 Ind.App. 248, 289 N.E.2d 522 (1972).

(b) A Summary of Interrogation Practices

Consider the following Table of Contents from the 1967 edition of Criminal Interrogation and Confessions by Inbau and Reid:

TACTICS AND TECHNIQUES FOR THE INTERROGATION OF SUSPECTS WHOSE GUILT IS DEFINITE OR REASONABLY CERTAIN

A.   Display an Air of Confidence in the Subject's Guilt

B.   Point out Some, but by No Means All, of the Circumstantial Evidence Indicative of a Subject's Guilt

C.   Call Attention to the Subject's Physiological and Psychological Symptoms of Guilt

D.   Sympathize with the Subject by Telling Him That Anyone Else under Similar Conditions or Circumstances Might Have Done the Same Thing

E.   Reduce the Subject's Guilt Feelings by Minimizing the Moral Seriousness of the Offense

F.   Suggest a Less Revolting and More Morally Acceptable Motivation or Reason for the Offense Than That Which Is Known or Presumed

G.   Sympathize with the Subject by (1) Condemning His Victim, (2) Condemning His Accomplice, or (3) Condemning Anyone Else Upon Whom Some Degree of Moral Responsibility Might Conceivably Be Placed for the Commission of the Crime in Question

H.   Utilize Displays of Understanding and Sympathy in Urging the Subject to Tell the Truth

I.   Point Out the Possibility of Exaggeration on the Part of the Accuser or Victim or Exaggerate the Nature and Seriousness of the Offense Itself

J.   Have the Subject Place Himself at the Scene of the Crime or in Some Sort of Contact with the Victim or the Occurrence

K.   Seek an Admission of Lying about Some Incidental Aspect of the Occurrence

L.   Appeal to the Subject's Pride by Well-Selected Flattery or by a Challenge to His Honor

M.   Point out the Futility of Resistance to Telling the Truth

N.   Point out to the Subject the Grave Consequences and Futility of a Continuation of His Criminal Behavior

O.   Rather Than Seek a General Admission of Guilt, First Ask the Subject a Question as to Some Detail of the Offense, or Inquire as to the Reason for its Commission

P. When Co-Offenders Are Being Interrogated and the Previously Described Techniques Have Been Ineffective, "Play One Against the Other"

TACTICS AND TECHNIQUES FOR THE INTERROGATION OF SUSPECTS WHOSE GUILT IS UNCERTAIN

Q. Ask the Subject if He Knows Why He is Being Questioned

R. Ask the Subject to Relate All He Knows about the Occurrence, the Victim, and Possible Suspects

S. Obtain from the Subject Detailed Information about His Activities before, at the Time of, and after the Occurrence in Question

T. Where Certain Facts Suggestive of the Subject's Guilt are Known, Ask Him about Them Rather Casually and as Though the Real Facts Were Not Already Known

U. At Various Intervals Ask the Subject Certain Pertinent Questions in a Manner which Implies that the Correct Answers Are Already Known

V. Refer to Some Non-Existing Incriminating Evidence to Determine whether the Subject Will Attempt to Explain It Away; if He Does, That Fact is Suggestive of His Guilt

W. Ask the Subject whether He Ever "Thought" about Committing the Offense in Question or One Similar To It

X. In Theft Cases, if a Suspect Offers to Make Restitution, That Fact Is Indicative of Guilt

Y. Ask the Subject whether He Is Willing to Take a Lie-Detector Test. The Innocent Person Will Almost Always Steadfastly Agree to Take Practically Any Test to Prove His Innocence, whereas the Guilty Person Is More Prone to Refuse to Take the Test or to Find Excuses for not Taking It, or for Backing Out of His Commitment To Take It

Z. A Subject Who Tells the Interrogator, "All Right, I'll Tell You What You Want, but I Didn't Do It", Is, in all Probability, Guilty.

The employment of any of the foregoing techniques, or, indeed of any interrogation whatsoever, of an arrested person, or of one who has been "deprived of his freedom in any significant way" presupposes, of course, the issuance of the warnings prescribed by the Supreme

(c) A Note on the Practical Necessity
for Interrogations

In their book, Criminal Interrogation and Confessions (1st ed. 1962, and 2d ed. 1967), Inbau and Reid expressed the following views (at pp. 213–219) with regard to the practical necessity for the interrogation of criminal suspects and witnesses:

"One completely false assumption accounts for most of the legal restrictions on police interrogations. It is this, and the fallacy is certainly perpetuated to a very considerable extent by mystery writers, the movies, and TV: whenever a crime is committed, if the police will only look carefully at the crime scene they will almost always find some clue that will lead them to the offender and at the same time establish his guilt; and once the offender is located, he will readily confess or disclose his guilt by trying to shoot his way out of the trap. But this is pure fiction; in actuality the situation is quite different. As a matter of fact, the art of criminal investigation has not developed to a point where the search for and the examination of physical evidence will always, or even in most cases, reveal a clue to the identity of the perpetrator or provide the necessary proof of his guilt. In criminal investigations, even of the most efficient type, there are many, many instances where physical clues are entirely absent, and the only approach to a possible solution of the crime is the interrogation of the criminal suspect himself, as well as others who may possess significant information. Moreover, in most instances these interrogations, particularly of the suspect himself, must be conducted under conditions of privacy and for a reasonable period of time; and they frequently require the use of psychological tactics and techniques that could well be classified as 'unethical,' if we are to evaluate them in terms of ordinary, everyday social behavior.

"To protect ourselves from being misunderstood, we want to make it unmistakably clear that we are not advocates of the so-called 'third degree'. We are unalterably opposed to the use of any interrogation tactic or technique that is apt to make an innocent person confess. We are opposed, therefore, to the use of force, threats, or promises of leniency—all of which might well induce an innocent person to confess; but we do approve of such psychological tactics and techniques as trickery and deceit that are not only helpful but frequently necessary in order to secure incriminating information from the guilty, or investigative leads from otherwise uncooperative witnesses or informants.

"Our position, then, is this, and it may be presented in the form of three separate points, each accompanied by case illustrations:

1. MANY CRIMINAL CASES, EVEN WHEN IN-VESTIGATED BY THE BEST QUALIFIED PO-LICE DEPARTMENTS, ARE CAPABLE OF SO-LUTION ONLY BY MEANS OF AN ADMISSION OR CONFESSION FROM THE GUILTY INDI-VIDUAL OR UPON THE BASIS OF INFORMA-TION OBTAINED FROM THE QUESTIONING OF OTHER CRIMINAL SUSPECTS

As to the validity of this statement, we suggest that consideration be given to the situation presented by cases such as these. A man is hit on the head while walking home late at night. He does not see his assail-ant, nor does anyone else. A careful and thorough search of the crime scene reveals no physical clues. Then take the case of a woman who is grabbed on the street at night and dragged into an alley and raped. Here, too, the assailant was unaccommodating enough to avoid leaving his hat or other means of identification at the crime scene, and there are no other physical clues. All the police have to work on is the description of the assailant given by the victim herself. She de-scribes him as about six feet tall, white, and wearing a dark suit. Or consider this case, an actual one in Illi-nois. Three women are vacationing in a wooded resort area. Their bodies are found dead, the result of phys-ical violence, alongside a foot trail, and no physical clues are present.

"In cases of this kind—and they all typify the dif-ficult investigation problem that the police frequently encounter—how else can they be solved, if at all, except by means of the interrogation of suspects or of others who may possess significant information?

"There are times, too, when a police interrogation may result not only in the apprehension and conviction of the guilty, but also in the release of the innocent from well-warranted suspicion. Here is one such actual case within our own professional experience.

"The dead body of a woman was found in her home. Her skull had been crushed, apparently with some blunt instrument. A careful police investigation of the premises did not reveal any clues to the identity of the killer. No fingerprints or other significant evi-dence was located; not even the lethal instrument itself could be found. None of the neighbors could give any helpful information. Although there was some evidence of a slight struggle in the room where the body lay, there were no indications of a forcible entry into the home. The deceased's young daughter was the only other resident of the home, and she had been away in school at the time of the crime. The daughter could not give the police any idea of what, if any, money or property had disap,eared from the home.

"For several reasons the police considered the victim's husband a likely suspect. He was being sued for divorce; he knew his wife had planned on leaving the state and taking their daughter with her; and the neighbors reported that the couple had been having heated arguments, and that the husband was of a violent temper. He also lived conveniently near—in a garage adjoining the home. The police interrogated him and although his alibi was not conclusive his general behavior and the manner in which he answered the interrogator's questions satisfied the police of his innocence. Further investigation then revealed that the deceased's brother-in-law had been financially indebted to the deceased; that he was a frequent gambler; that at a number of social gatherings which he had attended money disappeared from some of the women's purses; that at his place of employment there had been a series of purse thefts; and that on the day of the killing he was absent from work. The police apprehended and questioned him. As the result of a few hours of competent interrogation—unattended by any abusive methods, but yet conducted during a period of delay in presenting the suspect before a committing magistrate as required by state statute—the suspect confessed to the murder. He told of going to the victim's home for the purpose of selling her a radio which she accused him of stealing. An argument ensued and he hit her over the head with a mechanic's wrench he was carrying in his coat pocket. He thereupon located and took some money he found in the home and also a diamond ring. After fleeing from the scene he threw the wrench into a river, changed his clothes, and disposed of the ones he had worn at the time of the killing by throwing them away in various parts of the city. He had hidden the ring in the attic of his mother's home, where it was found by the police after his confession had disclosed its presence there. Much of the stolen money was also recovered or else accounted for by the payment of an overdue loan.

"Without an opportunity for interrogation the police could not have solved this case. The perpetrator of the offense would have remained at liberty, perhaps to repeat his criminal conduct.

2. CRIMINAL OFFENDERS, EXCEPT, OF COURSE, THOSE CAUGHT IN THE COMMISSION OF THEIR CRIMES, ORDINARILY WILL NOT ADMIT THEIR GUILT UNLESS QUESTIONED UNDER CONDITIONS OF PRIVACY, AND FOR A PERIOD OF PERHAPS SEVERAL HOURS

"This point is one which should be readily apparent not only to any person with the least amount of criminal investigative experience, but also to anyone who will reflect momentarily upon the behavior of ordinary law-abiding persons when suspected or accused of nothing more than simple social indiscretions. Self-condemnation and self-destruction not being normal behavior characteristics, human beings ordinarily do not utter unsolicited, spontaneous confessions. They must first be questioned regarding the offense. In some instances, a little bit of information inadvertently given to a competent interrogator by the suspect may suffice to start a line of investigation which might ultimately establish guilt. On other occasions, a full confession, with a revelation of details regarding a body, the loot, or the instruments used in the crime, may be required to prove the case; but whatever the possible consequences may be, it is impractical to expect any but a very few confessions to result from a guilty conscience unprovoked by an interrogation. It is also impractical to expect admissions or confessions to be obtained under circumstances other than privacy. Here again recourse to our everyday experience will support the basic validity of this requirement. For instance, in asking a personal friend to divulge a secret, or embarrassing information, we carefully avoid making the request in the presence of other persons, and seek a time and place when the matter can be discussed in private. The very same psychological factors are involved in a criminal interrogation, and even to a greater extent. For related psychological considerations, if an interrogation is to be had at all, it must be one based upon an unhurried interview, the necessary length of which will in many instances extend to several hours, depending upon various factors, such as the nature of the case situation and the personality of the suspect.

3. IN DEALING WITH CRIMINAL OFFENDERS, AND CONSEQUENTLY ALSO WITH CRIMINAL SUSPECTS WHO MAY ACTUALLY BE INNOCENT, THE INTERROGATOR MUST OF NECESSITY EMPLOY LESS REFINED METHODS THAN ARE CONSIDERED APPROPRIATE FOR

THE TRANSACTION OF ORDINARY, EVERY-DAY AFFAIRS BY AND BETWEEN LAW-ABIDING CITIZENS

"To illustrate this point, let us revert to the previously discussed case of the woman who was murdered by her brother-in-law. His confession was obtained largely by the interrogator's adoption of a friendly attitude in questioning the suspect, when concededly no such genuine feeling existed; by his pretense of sympathizing with the suspect because of his difficult financial situation; by his suggestion that perhaps the victim had done or said something which aroused the suspect's anger and which would have aroused the anger of anyone else similarly situated to such an extent as to provoke a violent reaction; and by his resort to other similar expressions, or even overtures of friendliness and sympathy such as a pat on the suspect's shoulder. In all of this, of course, the interrogation was 'unethical' according to the standards usually set for professional, business, and social conduct, but the pertinent issue in this case was no ordinary, lawful, professional, business, or social matter. It involved the taking of a human life by one who abided by no code of fair play toward his fellow human beings. The killer would not have been moved one bit toward a confession by subjecting him to a reading or lecture regarding the morality of his conduct. It would have been futile merely to give him a pencil and paper and trust that his conscience would impel him to confess. Something more was required—something which was in its essence an 'unethical' practice on the part of the interrogator; but, under the circumstances involved in this case, how else would the murderer's guilt have been established? Moreover, let us bear this thought in mind. From the criminal's point of view, *any* interrogation of him is objectionable. To *him* it may be a 'dirty trick' to be talked into a confession, for surely it was not done for his benefit. Consequently, any interrogation of him might be labeled as deceitful or unethical.

"Of necessity, criminal interrogators must deal with criminal offenders [or suspects] on a somewhat lower moral plane than that upon which ethical, law-abiding citizens are expected to conduct their everyday affairs. That plane, in the interest of innocent suspects, need only be subject to the following restriction: Although both 'fair' and 'unfair' interrogation practices are permissible, nothing shall be done or said to the subject that will be apt to make an innocent person confess.

"If we view this whole problem realistically, we must come to the conclusion that an interrogation opportunity is necessary and that legislative provision ought to be made for a privately conducted police interrogation, covering a reasonable period of time, of suspects who are not unwilling to be interviewed; and that the only tactics or techniques that are to be forbidden are those which are apt to make an innocent person confess.

"There are other ways to guard against abuses in police interrogation short of taking the privilege away from them. Moreover, we could no more afford to do that than we could stand the effect of a law requiring automobile manufacturers to place governors on all cars so that, in order to make the highways safe, no one could go faster than twenty miles an hour."

3. REMEDIES FOR ABUSIVE INTERROGATIONS

It is unmistakably clear that an improperly obtained confession is inadmissible as substantive evidence. As with the exclusion of illegally seized tangible evidence, however, this provides little consolation for the innocent person who is never brought to trial (and hence does not benefit by a suppressed confession), but whose rights and personal dignity were nevertheless violated. There are remedies to which this person can turn, as well as supplemental remedies available to the individual who has already benefited by suppression of illegally obtained evidence. They are discussed in the following sections (a) and (b).

(a) CIVIL REMEDIES

Under recent case law, a federal civil rights action may lie for a person who has been the victim of a coerced confession or even an abusive interrogation. The pertinent federal statute (Tit. 42 U.S.C. § 1983) reads:

Every person who, under color of any statute, ordinance, regulation, custom, or usage, of any State or Territory, subjects, or causes to be subjected, any citizen of the United States or other person within the juisdiction thereof to the deprivation of any rights, privileges, or immunities secured by the Constitution and laws, shall be liable to the party injured in an action at law, suit in equity, or other proper proceeding for redress.

While there is authority which holds that all *Miranda* violations are not actionable per se under this provision, that an illegally obtained confession must be introduced at trial in order to give rise to an action, Ambek v. Clark, 287 F.Supp. 208 (E.D.Penn.1968), and Ransom v. City of Philadelphia, 311 F.Supp. 973 (E.D.Penn.1970), recent decisions have broadened the scope of a § 1983 action in this regard. In Kerr v. City of Chicago, 424 F.2d 1134 (7th Cir. 1970), cert. denied, 400 U.S. 833, 91 S.Ct. 66 (see casenote, 20 De Paul L. Rev. 984 (1971), a complaint alleged that he was illegally detained for 18 hours and a confession was coerced from him through force, threats, and deprivation of food and other necessities of life. The reviewing court reversed the lower court's refusal to admit evidence of the circumstances surrounding the interrogation. The court wrote:

> . . . the jury was entitled to hear the testimony surrounding all the events from the moment Kerr was taken from his home until his indictment by the Grand Jury. All of the acts of commission and omission—the totality of all the circumstances—are of great importance in determining whether plaintiff's confession was coerced in violation of his civil rights and thereby cognizable under 42 U.S.C. § 1983 . . . .

The court further stated:

> . . . in a civil rights action alleging the extraction of an involuntary confession, the issue of guilt or innocence is irrelevant . . .

Since this is an emerging body of law, there are as yet no concrete guidelines to define the kind and quality of constitutional infringement that must be alleged in order to state a cause of action. Consider the court's opinion in Duncan v. Nelson, 466 F.2d 939 (7th Cir. 1972), cert. denied 409 U.S. 894, 93 S.Ct. 116:

> There is no indication from . . . any other case that physical violence need be present to produce the coercion necessary to constitute an involuntary confession cognizable under § 1983 [citation omitted]. In fact, Mr. Justice Harlan in his concurrence in Monroe v. Pape . . . recognized the possibility that psychological coercion leading to a confession would constitute damages under § 1983 . . . .

(b) CRIMINAL SANCTIONS

A civil rights violation which gives rise to a civil suit under 42 U.S.C. § 1983, may also precipitate a criminal indictment against the offending officer(s) under 18 U.S.C. § 242. That provision reads as follows:

> Whoever, under color of any law, statute, ordinance, regulation, or custom, willfully subjects any inhabitant of any State, Territory, or District to the deprivation of any rights, privileges, or immunities secured or protected by the Constitution or laws of the United States, or to different punishments, pains, or penalties, on account of such inhabitant being an alien, or by reason of his color, or race, than are prescribed for the punishment of citizens, shall be fined not more than $1,000 or imprisoned not more than one year, or both; and if death results shall be subject to imprisonment for any term of years or for life.

If two or more persons are involved, the civil rights conspiracy statute may be invoked (18 U.S.C. § 242). That statute provides for a 10 year penalty and a $10,000 fine.

A criminal sanction specifically drafted to encompass the problems under discussion here is the Illinois provision, Ch. 38 § 12–7:

Compelling Confession or Information by Force or Threat

(a) A person who, with intent to obtain a confession, statement or information regarding any offense, inflicts or threatens to inflict physical harm upon the person threatened or upon any other person commits the offense of compelling a confession or information by force or threat.

(b) Sentence.

Compelling a confession or information is a Class 4 felony.

While criminal prosecutions alleging improper interrogation are not requiring prosecutors to work overtime, the recent expansion of the civil side of this question may well lead to an accompanying increase in criminal indictments.

B. MIRANDA v. ARIZONA AND THE INTERPRETATION OF ITS REQUIREMENTS

---

1. MIRANDA v. ARIZONA

MIRANDA v. ARIZONA

VIGNERA v. NEW YORK

WESTOVER v. UNITED STATES

CALIFORNIA v. STEWART

Supreme Court of the United States, 1966.
384 U.S. 436, 86 S.Ct. 1602.

Mr. Chief Justice Warren delivered the opinion of the Court.

The cases before us raise questions which go to the roots of our concepts of American criminal jurisprudence: the restraints society must observe consistent with the Federal Constitution in prosecuting individuals for crime. More specifically, we deal with the admissibility of statements obtained from an individual who is subjected to custodial police interrogation and the necessity for procedures which assure that the individual is accorded his privilege under the Fifth Amendment to the Constitution not to be compelled to incriminate himself.

We dealt with certain phases of this problem recently in Escobedo v. State of Illinois, 378 U.S. 478, 84 S.Ct. 1758 (1964).

There, as in the four cases before us, law enforcement officials took the defendant into custody and interrogated him in a police station for the purpose of obtaining a confession. The police did not effectively advise him of his right to remain silent or of his right to consult with his attorney. Rather, they confronted him with an alleged accomplice who accused him of having perpetrated a murder. When the defendant denied the accusation and said "I didn't shoot Manuel, you did it," they handcuffed him and took him to an interrogation room. There, while handcuffed and standing, he was questioned for four hours until he confessed. During this interrogation, the police denied his request to speak to his attorney, and they prevented his retained attorney, who had come to the police station, from consulting with him. At his trial, the State, over his objection, introduced the confession against him. We held that the statements thus made were constitutionally inadmissible.

This case has been the subject of judicial interpretation and spirited legal debate since it was decided two years ago. Both state and federal courts, in assessing its implications, have arrived at varying conclusions. A wealth of scholarly material has been written tracing its ramifications and underpinnings. Police and prosecutor have speculated on its range and desirability. We granted certiorari in these cases, . . . in order further to explore some facets of the problems, thus exposed, of applying the privilege against self-incrimination to in-custody interrogation, and to give concrete constitutional guidelines for law enforcement agencies and courts to follow.

We start here, as we did in *Escobedo*, with the premise that our holding is not an innovation in our jurisprudence, but is an application of principles long recognized and applied in other settings. We have undertaken a thorough re-examination of the *Escobedo* decision and the principles it announced, and we reaffirm it. That case was but an explication of basic rights that are enshrined in our Constitution—that "No person . . . shall be compelled in any criminal case to be a witness against himself," and that "the accused shall . . . have the Assistance of Counsel"—rights which were put in jeopardy in that case through official overbearing. These precious rights were fixed in our Constitution only after centuries of persecution and struggle. And in the words of Chief Justice Marshall, they were secured "for ages to come, and . . . designed to approach immortality as nearly as human institutions can approach it," . . .

It was necessary in *Escobedo*, as here, to insure that what was proclaimed in the Constitution had not become but a "form of words," . . . in the hands of government officials. And it is in this spirit, consistent with our roles as judges, that we adhere to the principles of *Escobedo* today.

Our holding will be spelled out with some specificity in the pages which follow but briefly stated it is this: the prosecution may not use statements, whether exculpatory or inculpatory, stemming from custodial interrogation of the defendant unless it demonstrates the use of procedural safeguards effective to secure the privilege against self-incrimination. By custodial interrogation, we mean questioning initiated by law enforcement officers after a person has been taken into custody or otherwise deprived of his freedom of action in any significant way.[1] As for the procedural safeguards to be employed, unless other fully effective means are devised to inform accused persons of their right of silence and to assure a continuous opportunity to exercise it, the following measures are required. Prior to any questioning, the person must be warned that he has a right to remain silent, that any statement he does make may be used as evidence against him, and that he has a right to the presence of an attorney, either retained or appointed. The defendant may waive effectuation of these rights, provided the waiver is made voluntarily, knowingly and intelligently. If, however, he indicates in any manner and at any stage of the process that he wishes to consult with an attorney before speaking there can be no questioning. Likewise, if the individual is alone and indicates in any manner that he does not wish to be interrogated, the police may not question him. The mere fact that he may have answered some questions or volunteered some statements on his own does not deprive him of the right to refrain from answering any further inquiries until he has consulted with an attorney and thereafter consents to be questioned.

I.

The constitutional issue we decide in each of these cases is the admissibility of statements obtained from a defendant questioned while in custody or otherwise deprived of his freedom of action in any significant way. In each, the defendant was questioned by police officers, detectives, or a prosecuting attorney in a room in which he was cut off from the outside world. In none of these cases was the defendant given a full and effective warning of his rights at the outset of the interrogation process. In all the cases, the questioning elicited oral admissions, and in three of them, signed statements as well which were admitted at their trials. They all thus share salient features—incommunicado interrogation of individuals in a police-dominated atmosphere, resulting in self-incriminating statements without full warnings of constitutional rights.

An understanding of the nature and setting of this in-custody interrogation is essential to our decisions today. The difficulty in depicting what transpires at such interrogations stems from the fact that in this country they have largely taken place incommunicado. From extensive factual studies undertaken in the early 1930's, . . . it is clear that police violence and the "third degree" flourished at that time. In a series of cases decided by this Court long after these studies, the police resorted to physical brutality—beat-

1. This is what we meant in *Escobedo* when we spoke of an investigation which had focused on an accused.

ings, hanging, whipping—and to sustained and protracted questioning incommunicado in order to extort confessions. The Commission on Civil Rights in 1961 found much evidence to indicate that "some policemen still resort to physical force to obtain confessions." The use of physical brutality and violence is not, unfortunately, relegated to the past or to any part of the country. Only recently in Kings County, New York, the police brutally beat, kicked and placed lighted cigarette butts on the back of a potential witness under interrogation for the purpose of securing a statement incriminating a third party.

The examples given above are undoubtedly the exception now, but they are sufficiently widespread to be the object of concern. Unless a proper limitation upon custodial interrogation is achieved—such as these decisions will advance—there can be no assurance that practices of this nature will be eradicated in the foreseeable future.
. . .

*   *   *

Again we stress that the modern practice of in-custody interrogation is psychologically rather than physically oriented. As we have stated before, . . . "this Court has recognized that coercion can be mental as well as physical, and that the blood of the accused is not the only hallmark of an unconstitutional inquisition." Interrogation still takes place in privacy. Privacy results in secrecy and this in turn results in a gap in our knowledge as to what in fact goes on in the interrogation rooms. A valuable source of information about present police practices, however, may be found in various police manuals and texts which document procedures employed with success in the past, and which recommended various other effective tactics. These texts are used by law enforcement agencies themselves as guides.[2] It should be noted that these texts professedly present the most enlightened and effective means presently used to obtain statements through custodial interrogation. By considering these texts and other data, it is possible to describe procedures observed and noted around the country.

The officers are told by the manuals that the "principal psychological factor contributing to a successful interrogation is privacy—

2. The methods described in Inbau & Reid, Criminal Interrogation and Confessions (1962), are a revision and enlargement of material presented in three prior editions of a predecessor text, Lie Detection and Criminal Interrogation (3d ed. 1953). The authors and their associates are officers of the Chicago Police Scientific Crime Detection Laboratory and have had extensive experience in writing, lecturing and speaking to law enforcement authorities over a 20-year period. They say that the techniques portrayed in their manuals reflect their experiences and are the most effective psychological stratagems to employ during interrogations. Similarly, the techniques described in O'Hara, Fundamentals of Criminal Investigation (1956), were gleaned from long service as observer, lecturer in police science, and work as a federal criminal investigator. All these texts have had rather extensive use among law enforcement agencies and among students of police science, with total sales and circulation of over 44,000.

[Editors' note: Inbau was Director of the Laboratory from 1938–1941; he has had no official connection with it since then. Reid was on the Laboratory staff from 1938 to 1947; he too has had no official connection with it since that time.]

being alone with the person under interrogation." [Inbau and Reid]
The efficacy of this tactic has been explained as follows:

> "If at all practicable, the interrogation should take
> place in the investigator's office or at least in a room of his
> own choice. The subject should be deprived of every psy-
> chological advantage. In his own home he may be confi-
> dent, indignant, or recalcitrant. He is more keenly aware of
> his rights and more reluctant to tell of his indiscretions or
> criminal behavior within the walls of his home. Moreover
> his family and other friends are nearby, their presence lend-
> ing moral support. In his office, the investigator possesses
> all the advantages. The atmosphere suggests the invincibili-
> ty of the forces of the law." [O'Hara]

To highlight the isolation and unfamiliar surroundings, the manuals instruct the police to display an air of confidence in the suspect's
guilt and from outward appearance to maintain only an interest in
confirming certain details. The guilt of the subject is to be posited
as a fact. The interrogator should direct his comments toward the
reasons why the subject committed the act, rather than court failure
by asking the subject whether he did it. Like other men, perhaps the
subject has had a bad family life, had an unhappy childhood, had too
much to drink, had an unrequited desire for women. The officers are
instructed to minimize the moral seriousness of the offense, to cast
blame on the victim or on society. These tactics are designed to put
the subject in a psychological state where his story is but an elaboration of what the police purport to know already—that he is guilty.
Explanations to the contrary are dismissed and discouraged.

The texts thus stress that the major qualities an interrogator
should possess are patience and perseverance. One writer describes
the efficacy of these characteristics in this manner:

> "In the preceding paragraphs emphasis has been placed
> on kindness and strategems. The investigator will, how-
> ever, encounter many situations where the sheer weight of
> his personality will be the deciding factor. Where emotional
> appeals and tricks are employed to no avail, he must rely on
> an oppressive atmosphere of dogged persistence. He must
> interrogate steadily and without relent, leaving the subject
> no prospect of surcease. He must dominate his subject and
> overwhelm him with his inexorable will to obtain the truth.
> He should interrogate for a spell of several hours pausing
> only for the subject's necessities in acknowledgement of the
> need to avoid a charge of duress that can be technically sub-
> stantiated. In a serious case, the interrogation may contin-
> ue for days, with the required intervals for food and sleep,
> but with no respite from the atmosphere of domination. It
> is possible in this way to induce the subject to talk without
> resorting to duress or coercion. The method should be used
> only when the guilt of the subject appears highly probable."
> [O'Hara]

The manuals suggest that the suspect be offered legal excuses for his actions in order to obtain an initial admission of guilt. Where there is a suspected revenge-killing, for example, the interrogator may say:

> "Joe, you probably didn't go out looking for this fellow with the purpose of shooting him. My guess is, however, that you expected something from him and that's why you carried a gun—for your own protection. You knew him for what he was, no good. Then when you met him he probably started using foul, abusive language and he gave some indication that he was about to pull a gun on you, and that's when you had to act to save your own life. That's about it, isn't it, Joe?"   [Inbau & Reid]

Having then obtained the admission of shooting, the interrogator is advised to refer to circumstantial evidence which negates the self-defense explanation. This should enable him to secure the entire story. One text notes that "Even if he fails to do so, the inconsistency between the subject's original denial of the shooting and his present admission of at least doing the shooting will serve to deprive him of a self-defense 'out' at the time of trial."   [Inbau & Reid]

When the techniques described above prove unavailing, the texts recommend they be alternated with a show of some hostility. One ploy often used has been termed the "friendly-unfriendly" or the "Mutt and Jeff" act:

> ".   .   . In this technique, two agents are employed. Mutt, the relentless investigator, who knows the subject is guilty and is not going to waste any time. He's sent a dozen men away for this crime and he's going to send the subject away for the full term. Jeff, on the other hand, is obviously a kindhearted man. He has a family himself. He has a brother who was involved in a little scrape like this. He disapproves of Mutt and his tactics and will arrange to get him off the case if the subject will cooperate. He can't hold Mutt off for very long. The subject would be wise to make a quick decision. The technique is applied by having both investigators present while Mutt acts out his role. Jeff may stand by quietly and demur at some of Mutt's tactics. When Jeff makes his plea for cooperation, Mutt is not present in the room."   [O'Hara]

The interrogators sometimes are instructed to induce a confession out of trickery. The technique here is quite effective in crimes which require identification or which run in series. In the identification situation, the interrogator may take a break in his questioning to place the subject among a group of men in a line-up. "The witness or complainant (previously coached if necessary) studies the line-up and confidently points out the subject as the guilty party." [O'Hara] Then the questioning resumes "as though there were now no doubt about the guilt of the subject." A variation on this technique is called the "reverse line-up":

> "The accused is placed in a line-up, but this time he is identified by several fictitious witnesses or victims who associated him with different offenses. It is expected that the subject will become desperate and confess to the offense under investigation in order to escape from the false accusations." [O'Hara]

The manuals also contain instructions for police on how to handle the individual who refuses to discuss the matter entirely, or who asks for an attorney or relatives. The examiner is to concede him the right to remain silent. "This usually has a very undermining effect. First of all, he is disappointed in his expectation of an unfavorable reaction on the part of the interrogator. Secondly, a concession of this right to remain silent impresses the subject with the apparent fairness of his interrogator." [Inbau & Reid] After this psychological conditioning, however, the officer is told to point out the incriminating significance of the suspect's refusal to talk:

> "Joe, you have a right to remain silent. That's your privilege and I'm the last person in the world who'll try to take it away from you. If that's the way you want to leave this, O.K. But let me ask you this. Suppose you were in my shoes and I were in yours and you called me in to ask me about this and I told you, 'I don't want to answer any of your questions.' You'd think I had something to hide, and you'd probably be right in thinking that. That's exactly what I'll have to think about you, and so will everybody else. So let's sit here and talk this whole thing over." [Inbau & Reid]

Few will persist in their initial refusal to talk, it is said, if this monologue is employed correctly.

In the event that the subject wishes to speak to a relative or an attorney, the following advice is tendered:

> "[T]he interrogator should respond by suggesting that the subject first tell the truth to the interrogator himself rather than get anyone else involved in the matter. If the request is for an attorney, the interrogator may suggest that the subject save himself or his family the expense of any such professional service, particularly if he is innocent of the offense under investigation. The interrogator may also add, 'Joe, I'm only looking for the truth, and if you're telling the truth, that's it. You can handle this by yourself.' " [Inbau & Reid]

From these representative samples of interrogation techniques, the setting prescribed by the manuals and observed in practice becomes clear. In essence, it is this: To be alone with the subject is essential to prevent distraction and to deprive him of any outside sup-

port.   The aura of confidence in his guilt undermines his will to resist.   He merely confirms the preconceived story the police seek to
have him describe.   Patience and persistence, at times relentless
questioning, are employed.   To obtain a confession, the interrogator
must "patiently maneuver himself or his quarry into a position from
which the desired objective may be attained."   When normal procedures fail to produce the needed result, the police may resort to deceptive stratagems such as giving false legal advice.   It is important
to keep the subject off balance, for example, by trading on his insecurity about himself or his surroundings.   The police then persuade,
trick, or cajole him out of exercising his constitutional rights.

    Even without employing brutality, the "third degree" or the spe-
cific stratagems described above, the very fact of custodial interrogation exacts a heavy toll on individual liberty and trades on the weakness of individuals.   This fact may be illustrated simply by referring
to three confession cases decided by this Court in the Term immediately preceding our *Escobedo* decision.   In Townsend v. Sain (1963),
the defendant was a 19-year-old heroin addict, described as a "near
mental defective."   The defendant in Lynumn v. State of Illinois
(1963), was a woman who confessed to the arresting officer after
being importuned to "cooperate" in order to prevent her children
from being taken by relief authorities.   This Court as in those cases
reversed the conviction of a defendant in Haynes v. State of Washington (1963), whose persistent request during his interrogation was
to phone his wife or attorney.   In other settings, these individuals
might have exercised their constitutional rights.   In the incommunicado police-dominated atmosphere, they succumbed.

    In the cases before us today, given this background, we concern
ourselves primarily with this interrogation atmosphere and the evils
it can bring.   In No. 759, Miranda v. Arizona, the police arrested the
defendant and took him to a special interrogation room where they
secured a confession.   In No. 760, Vignera v. New York, the defendant made oral admissions to the police after interrogation in the afternoon, and then signed an inculpatory statement upon being questioned by an assistant district attorney later the same evening.   In
No. 761, Westover v. United States, the defendant was handed over to
the Federal Bureau of Investigation by local authorities after they
had detained and interrogated him for a lengthy period, both at night
and the following morning.   After some two hours of questioning, the
federal officers had obtained signed statements from the defendant.
Lastly, in No. 584, California v. Stewart, the local police held the defendant five days in the station and interrogated him on nine separate occasions before they secured his inculpatory statement.

    In these cases, we might not find the defendants' statements to
have been involuntary in traditional terms.   Our concern for adequate safeguards to protect precious Fifth Amendment rights is, of
course, not lessened in the slightest.   In each of the cases, the defendant was thrust into an unfamiliar atmosphere and run through menacing police interrogation procedures.   The potentiality for compul-

sion is forcefully apparent, for example, in *Miranda,* where the indigent Mexican defendant was a seriously disturbed individual with pronounced sexual fantasies, and in *Stewart,* in which the defendant was an indigent Los Angeles Negro who had dropped out of school in the sixth grade. To be sure the records do not evince over physical coercion or patent psychological ploys. The fact remains that in none of these cases did the officers undertake to afford appropriate safeguards at the outset of the interrogation to insure that the statements were truly the product of free choice.

It is obvious that such an interrogation environment is created for no purpose other than to subjugate the individual to the will of his examiner. This atmosphere carries its own badge of intimidation. To be sure, this is not physical intimidation, but it is equally destructive of human dignity. The current practice of incommunicado interrogation is at odds with one of our Nation's most cherished principles—that the individual may not be compelled to incriminate himself. Unless adequate protective devices are employed to dispel the compulsion inherent in custodial surroundings, no statement obtained from the defendant can truly be the product of his free choice.

From the foregoing, we can readily perceive an intimate connection between the privilege against self-incrimination and police custodial questioning. It is fitting to turn to the Self-Incrimination Clause to determine its applicability in this situation.

II.

* * *

The question in these cases is whether the privilege is fully applicable during a period of custodial interrogation. In this Court, the privilege has consistently been accorded in liberal construction. . . . We are satisfied that all the principles embodied in the privilege apply to informal compulsion exerted by law-enforcement officers during in-custody questioning. An individual swept from familiar surroundings into police custody, surrounded by antagonistic forces, and subjected to the techniques of persuasion described above cannot be otherwise than under compulsion to speak. As a practical matter, the compulsion to speak in the isolated setting of the police station may well be greater than in courts or other official investigations, where there are often impartial observers to guard against intimidation or trickery.

* * *

Our decision in Malloy v. Hogan (1964) necessitates an examination of the scope of the privilege in state cases as well. In *Malloy,* we squarely held the privilege applicable to the States, and held that the substantive standards underlying the privilege applied with full force to state court proceedings. . . . the reasoning in *Malloy* made clear what had already become apparent—that the substantive and procedural safeguards surrounding admissibility of confessions in state cases had become exceedingly exacting, reflecting all the policies embedded in the privilege. The voluntariness doctrine in the state cases, as *Malloy* indicates, encompasses all interrogation practices which are likely to exert such pressure upon an individual as to disable him from making a free and rational choice. The implications of this proposition were elaborated in our decision in Escobedo v. State of Illinois, decided one week after *Malloy* applied the privilege to the States.

Our holding there stressed the fact that the police had not advised the defendant of his constitutional privilege to remain silent at the outset of the interrogation, and we drew attention to that fact at several points in the decision. This was no isolated factor, but an essential ingredient in our decision. The entire thrust of police interrogation there, as in all the cases today, was to put the defendant in such an emotional state as to impair his capacity for rational judgment. The abdication of the constitutional privilege—the choice on his part to speak to the police—was not made knowingly or competently because of the failure to apprise him of his rights; the compelling atmosphere of the in-custody interrogation, and not an independent decision on his part, caused the defendant to speak.

A different phase of the *Escobedo* decision was significant in its attention to the absence of counsel during the questioning. There, as in the cases today, we sought a protective device to dispel the compelling atmosphere of the interrogation. In *Escobedo*, however, the police did not relieve the defendant of the anxieties which they had created in the interrogation rooms. Rather, they denied his request for the assistance of counsel. This heightened his dilemma, and made his later statements the product of this compulsion. The denial of the defendant's request for his attorney thus undermined his ability to exercise the privilege—to remain silent if he chose or to speak without any intimidation, blatant or subtle. The presence of counsel, in all the cases before us today, would be the adequate protective device necessary to make the process of police interrogation conform to the dictates of the privilege. His presence would insure that statements made in the government-established atmosphere are not the product of compulsion.

It was in this manner that *Escobedo* explicated another facet of the pre-trial privilege, noted in many of the Court's prior decisions: the protection of rights at trial. That counsel is present when statements are taken from an individual during interrogation obviously enhances the integrity of the fact-finding processes in court. The presence of an attorney, and the warnings delivered to the individual, enable the defendant under otherwise compelling circumstances to tell his story without fear, effectively, and in a way that eliminates the evils in the interrogation process. Without the protections flowing from adequate warning and the rights of counsel, "all the careful safeguards erected around the giving of testimony, whether by an accused or any other witness, would become empty formalities in a procedure where the most compelling possible evidence of guilt, a confession, would have already been obtained at the unsupervised pleasure of the police." Mapp v. Ohio (1961).

III.

Today, then, there can be no doubt that the Fifth Amendment privilege is available outside of criminal court proceedings and serves to protect persons in all settings in which their freedom of action is curtailed in any significant way from being compelled to incriminate themselves. . . .

It is impossible for us to foresee the potential alternatives for protecting the privilege which might be devised by Congress or the States in the exercise of their creative rule-making capacities. Therefore we cannot say that the Constitution necessarily requires adherence to any particular solution for the inherent compulsions of the interrogation process as it is presently conducted. Our decision in no way creates a constitutional strait-jacket which will handicap sound efforts at reform, nor is it intended to have this effect. We encourage Congress and the States to continue their laudable search for increasingly effective ways of protecting the rights of the individual while promoting efficient enforcement of our criminal laws. However, unless we are shown other procedures which are at least as effective in apprising accused persons of their right of silence and in assuring a continuous opportunity to exercise it, the following safeguards must be observed.

At the outset, if a person in custody is to be subjected to interrogation, he must first be informed in clear and unequivocal terms that he has the right to remain silent. For those unaware of the privilege, the warning is needed simply to make them aware of it—the threshold requirement for an intelligent decision as to its exercise. More important, such a warning is an absolute prerequisite in overcoming the inherent pressures of the interrogation atmosphere. It is not just the subnormal or woefully ignorant who succumb to an interrogator's imprecations, whether implied or expressly stated, that the interrogation will continue until a confession is obtained or that silence in the face of accusation is itself damning and will bode ill when presented to a jury. Further, the warning will show the individual that his interrogators are prepared to recognize his privilege should he choose to exercise it.

The Fifth Amendment privilege is so fundamental to our system of constitutional rule and the expedient of giving an adequate warning as to the availability of the privilege so simple, we will not pause to inquire in individual cases whether the defendant was aware of his rights without a warning being given. Assessments of the knowledge the defendant possessed, based on information as to his age, education, intelligence, or prior contact with authorities, can never be more than speculation; a warning is a clearcut fact. More important, whatever the background of the person interrogated, a warning at the time of the interrogation is indispensable to overcome its pressures and to insure that the individual knows he is free to exercise the privilege at that point in time.

The warning of the right to remain silent must be accompanied by the explanation that anything said can and will be used against the individual in court. This warning is needed in order to make him aware not only of the privilege, but also of the consequences of foregoing it. It is only through an awareness of these consequences that there can be any assurance of real understanding and intelligent exercise of the privilege. Moreover, this warning may serve to make the individual more acutely aware that he is faced with a phase of the adversary system—that he is not in the presence of persons acting solely in his interest.

The circumstances surrounding in-custody interrogation can operate very quickly to overbear the will of one merely made aware of his privilege by his interrogators. Therefore, the right to have counsel present at the interrogation is indispensable to the protection of the Fifth Amendment privilege under the system we delineate today. Our aim is to assure that the individual's right to choose between silence and speech remains unfettered throughout the interrogation process. A once-stated warning, delivered by those who will conduct the interrogation, cannot itself suffice to that end among those who most require knowledge of their rights. A mere warning given by the interrogators is not alone sufficient to accomplish that end. Prosecutors themselves claim that the admonishment of the right to remain silent without more "will benefit only the recidivist and the professional." Brief for the National District Attorneys Association as *amicus curiae*, p. 14. Even preliminary advice given to the accused by his own attorney can be swiftly overcome by the secret interrogation process. Thus, the need for counsel to protect the Fifth Amendment privilege comprehends not merely a right to consult with counsel prior to questioning, but also to have counsel present during any questioning if the defendant so desires.

The presence of counsel at the interrogation may serve several significant subsidiary functions as well. If the accused decides to talk to his interrogators, the assistance of counsel can mitigate the dangers of untrustworthiness. With a lawyer present the likelihood that the police will practice coercion is reduced, and if coercion is nevertheless exercised the lawyer can testify to it in court. The presence of a lawyer can also help to guarantee that the accused gives a fully accurate statement to the police and that the statement is rightly reported by the prosecution at trial. . . . .

An individual need not make a pre-interrogation request for a lawyer. While such request affirmatively secures his right to have one, his failure to ask for a lawyer does not constitute a waiver. No effective waiver of the right to counsel during interrogation can be recognized unless specifically made after the warnings we here delineate have been given. The accused who does not know his rights and therefore does not make a request may be the person who most needs counsel. . . . .

*   *   *

Accordingly we hold that an individual held for interrogation must be clearly informed that he has the right to consult with a lawyer and to have the lawyer with him during interrogation under the system for protecting the privilege we delineate today. As with the warnings of the right to remain silent and that anything stated can be used in evidence against him, this warning is an absolute prerequisite to interrogation. No amount of circumstantial evidence that the person may have been aware of this right will suffice to stand in its stead. Only through such a warning is there ascertainable assurance that the accused was aware of this right.

If an individual indicates that he wishes the assistance of counsel before any interrogation occurs, the authorities cannot rationally ignore or deny his request on the basis that the individual does not have or cannot afford a retained attorney. The financial ability of the individual has no relationship to the scope of the rights involved here. . . .

In order fully to apprise a person interrogated of the extent of his rights under this system then, it is necessary to warn him not only that he has the right to consult with an attorney, but also that if he is indigent a lawyer will be appointed to represent him. . . .

Once warnings have been given, the subsequent procedure is clear. If the individual indicates in any manner, at any time prior to or during questioning, that he wishes to remain silent, the interrogation must cease. At this point he has shown that he intends to exercise his Fifth Amendment privilege; any statement taken after the person invokes his privilege cannot be other than the product of compulsion, subtle or otherwise. Without the right to cut off questioning, the setting of in-custody interrogation operates on the individual to overcome free choice in producing a statement after the privilege has been once invoked. If the individual states that he wants an attorney, the interrogation must cease until an attorney is present. At that time, the individual must have an opportunity to confer with the attorney and to have him present during any subsequent questioning. If the individual cannot obtain an attorney and he indicates that he wants one before speaking to police, they must respect his decision to remain silent.

This does not mean, as some have suggested, that each police station must have a "station house lawyer" present at all times to advise prisoners. It does mean, however, that if police propose to interrogate a person they must make known to him that he is entitled to a lawyer and that if he cannot afford one, a lawyer will be provided for him prior to any interrogation. If authorities conclude that they will not provide counsel during a reasonable period of time in which investigation in the field is carried out, they may refrain from doing so without violating the person's Fifth Amendment privilege so long as they do not question him during that time.

If the interrogation continues without the presence of an attorney and a statement is taken, a heavy burden rests on the government to demonstrate that the defendant knowingly and intelligently waived his privilege against self-incrimination and his right to retained or appointed counsel. . . . Since the State is responsible for establishing the isolated circumstances under which the interrogation takes place and has the only means of making available corroborated evidence of warnings given during incommunicado interrogation, the burden is rightly on its shoulders.

An express statement that the individual is willing to make a statement and does not want an attorney followed closely by a statement could constitute a waiver. But a valid waiver will not be presumed simply from the silence of the accused after warnings are given or simply from the fact that a confession was in fact eventually obtained. . . . Moreover, where in-custody interrogation is involved, there is no room for the contention that the privilege is waived if the individual answers some questions or gives some information on his own prior to invoking his right to remain silent when interrogated. . . .

Whatever the testimony of the authorities as to waiver of rights by an accused, the fact of lengthy interrogation or incommunicado incarceration before a statement is made is strong evidence that the accused did not validly waive his rights. In these circumstances the fact that the individual eventually made a statement is consistent with the conclusion that the compelling influence of the interrogation finally forced him to do so. It is inconsistent with any notion of a voluntary relinquishment of the privilege. Moreover, any evidence that the accused was threatened, tricked, or cajoled into a waiver will, of course, show that the defendant did not voluntarily waive his privilege. The requirement of warnings and waiver of rights is a fundamental with respect to the Fifth Amendment privilege and not simply a preliminary ritual to existing methods of interrogation.

The warnings required and the waiver necessary in accordance with our opinion today are, in the absence of a fully effective equivalent, prerequisites to the admissibility of any statement made by a defendant. No distinction can be drawn between statements which are direct confessions and statements which amount to "admissions" of part or all of an offense. . . . Similarly, for precisely the same reason, no distinction may be drawn between inculpatory statements and statements alleged to be merely "exculpatory." If a statement made were in fact truly exculpatory it would, of course, never be used by the prosecution. In fact, statements merely intended to be exculpatory by the defendant are often used to impeach his testimony at trial or to demonstrate untruths in the statement given under interrogation and thus to prove guilt by implication. These statements are incriminating in any meaningful sense of the word and may not be used without the full warnings and effective waiver required for any other statement. . . .

The principles announced today deal with the protection which must be given to the privilege against self-incrimination when the individual is first subjected to police interrogation while in custody at the station or otherwise deprived of his freedom of action in any significant way. It is at this point that our adversary system of criminal proceedings commences, distinguishing itself at the outset from the inquisitorial system recognized in some countries. Under the system of warnings we delineate today or under any other system which may be devised and found effective, the safeguards to be erected about the privilege must come into play at this point.

Our decision is not intended to hamper the traditional function of police officers in investigating crime. When an individual is in custody on probable cause, the police may, of course, seek out evidence in the field to be used at trial against him. Such investigation may include inquiry of persons not under restraint. General on-the-scene questioning as to facts surrounding a crime or other general questioning of citizens in the fact-finding process is not affected by our holding. It is an act of responsible citizenship for individuals to give whatever information they may have to aid in law enforcement. In such situations the compelling atmosphere inherent in the process of in-custody interrogation is not necessarily present.[3]

In dealing with statements obtained through interrogation, we do not purport to find all confessions inadmissible. Confessions remain a proper element in law enforcement. Any statement given freely and voluntarily without any compelling influences is, of course, admissible in evidence. The fundamental import of the privilege while an individual is in custody is not whether he is allowed to talk to the police without the benefit of warnings and counsel, but whether he can be interrogated. There is no requirement that police stop a person who enters a police station and states that he wishes to confess to a crime, or a person who calls the police to offer a confession or any other statement he desires to make. Volunteered statements of any kind are not barred by the Fifth Amendment and their admissibility is not affected by our holding today.

To summarize, we hold that when an individual is taken into custody or otherwise deprived of his freedom by the authorities in any significant way and is subjected to questioning, the privilege against self-incrimination is jeopardized. Procedural safeguards must be employed to protect the privilege and unless other fully effective means are adopted to notify the person of his right of silence and to assure that the exercise of the right will be scrupulously honored, the following measures are required. He must be warned prior to any

---

3. The distinction and its significance has been aptly described in the opinion of a Scottish court:

"In former times such questioning, if undertaken would be conducted by police officers visiting the house or place of business of the suspect and there questioning him, probably in the presence of a relation or friend. However convenient the modern practice may be, it must normally create a situation very unfavorable to the suspect." Chalmers v. H. M. Advocate, [1954] Sess.Cas. 66, 78 (J.C.).

questioning that he has the right to remain silent, that anything he says can be used against him in a court of law, that he has the right to the presence of an attorney, and that if he cannot afford an attorney one will be appointed for him prior to any questioning if he so desires. Opportunity to exercise these rights must be afforded to him throughout the interrogation. After such warnings have been given, and such opportunity afforded him, the individual may knowingly and intelligently waive these rights and agree to answer questions or make a statement. But unless and until such warnings and waiver are demonstrated by the prosecution at trial, no evidence obtained as a result of interrogation can be used against him.

IV.

A recurrent argument made in these cases is that society's need for interrogation outweighs the privilege. .   .

* * *

In announcing these principles, we are not unmindful of the burdens which law enforcement officials must bear, often under trying circumstances. We also fully recognize the obligation of all citizens to aid in enforcing the criminal laws. This Court, while protecting individual rights, has always given ample latitude to law enforcement agencies in the legitimate exercise of their duties. The limits we have placed on the interrogation process should not constitute an undue interference with a proper system of law enforcement. As we have noted, our decision does not in any way preclude police from carrying out their traditional investigatory functions. Although confessions may play an important role in some convictions, the cases before us present graphic examples of the overstatement of the "need" for confessions. In each case authorities conducted interrogations ranging up to five days in duration despite the presence, through standard investigating practices, of considerable evidence against each defendant.[4]

.   .   .

* * *

Over the years the Federal Bureau of Investigation has compiled an exemplary record of effective law enforcement while advising any suspect or arrested person at the outset of an interview, that he is not required to make a statement, that any statement may be used against him in court, that the individual may obtain the services of an attorney of his own choice and, more recently, that he has a right to free counsel if he is unable to pay. .   .   .

The practice of the FBI can readily be emulated by state and local enforcement agencies. The argument that the FBI deals with different crimes than are dealt with by state authorities does not mitigate the significance of the FBI experience.

---

4. Miranda, Vignera, and Westover were identified by eyewitnesses. Marked bills from the bank robbed were found in Westover's car. Articles stolen from the victim as well as from several other robbery victims were found in Stewart's home at the outset of the investigation.

The experience in some other countries also suggests that the danger to law enforcement in curbs on interrogation is overplayed. . . .

The English procedure since 1912 under the Judges' Rules is significant. As recently strengthened, the Rules require that a cautionary warning be given an accused by a police officer as soon as he has evidence that affords reasonable grounds for suspicion; they also require that any statement made be given by the accused without questioning by police.

The right of the individual to consult with an attorney during this period is expressly recognized.

The safeguards present under Scottish law may be even greater than in England. Scottish judicial decisions bar use in evidence of most confessions obtained through police interrogation. In India, confessions made to police not in the presence of a magistrate have been excluded by rule of evidence since 1872, at a time when it operated under British law. Identical provisions appear in the Evidence Ordinance of Ceylon, enacted in 1895. . . . There appears to have been no marked detrimental effect on criminal law enforcement in these jurisdictions as a result of these rules. Conditions of law enforcement in our country are sufficiently similar to permit reference to this experience as assurance that lawlessness will not result from warning an individual of his rights or allowing him to exercise them. Moreover, it is consistent with our legal system that we give at least as much protection to these rights as is given in the jurisdictions described. We deal in our country with rights grounded in a specific requirement of the Fifth Amendment of the Constitution, whereas other jurisdictions arrived at their conclusions on the basis of principles of justice not so specifically defined.

It is also urged upon us that we withhold decision on this issue until state legislative bodies and advisory groups have had an opportunity to deal with these problems by rule making. . . . We have already pointed out that the Constitution does not require any specific code of procedures for protecting the privilege against self-incrimination during custodial interrogation. Congress and the States are free to develop their own safeguards for the privilege, so long as they are fully as effective as those described above in informing accused persons of their right of silence and in affording a continuous opportunity to exercise it. In any event, however, the issues presented are of constitutional dimensions and must be determined by the courts. The admissibility of a statement in the face of a claim that it was obtained in violation of the defendant's constitutional rights is an issue the resolution of which has long since been undertaken by this Court. . . . Where rights secured by the Constitution are involved, there can be no rule making or legislation which would abrogate them.

* * *

[Miranda reversed; Vignera reversed; Westover reversed; Stewart (state appellate court reversal of conviction) affirmed.]

MR. JUSTICE CLARK, dissenting in Nos. 759, 760, and 761, and concurring in the result in No. 584.

It is with regret that I find it necessary to write in these cases. However, I am unable to join the majority because its opinion goes too far on too little, while my dissenting brethren do not go quite far enough. Nor can I join in the Court's criticism of the present practices of police and investigatory agencies as to custodial interrogation. The materials it refers to as "police manuals" are, as I read them, merely writings in this field by professors and some police officers. Not one is shown by the record here to be the official manual of any police department, much less in universal use in crime detection. Moreover the examples of police brutality mentioned by the Court are rare exceptions to the thousands of cases that appear every year in the law reports. The police agencies—all the way from municipal and state forces to the federal bureaus—are responsible for law enforcement and public safety in this country. I am proud of their efforts, which in my view are not fairly characterized by the Court's opinion.

I.

The *ipse dixit* of the majority has no support in our cases. Indeed, the Court admits that "we might not find the defendants' statements [here] to have been involuntary in traditional terms." In short, the Court has added more to the requirements that the accused is entitled to consult with his lawyer and that he must be given the traditional warning that he may remain silent and that anything that he says may be used against him. Now, the Court fashions a constitutional rule that the police may engage in no custodial interrogation without additionally advising the accused that he has a right under the Fifth Amendment to the presence of counsel during interrogation and that, if he is without funds, counsel will be furnished him. When at any point during an interrogation the accused seeks affirmatively or impliedly to invoke his rights to silence or counsel, interrogation must be forgone or postponed. The Court further holds that failure to follow the new procedures requires inexorably the exclusion of any statement by the accused, as well as the fruits thereof. Such a strict constitutional specific inserted at the nerve center of crime detection may well kill the patient.[5] Since there is at this time a paucity of information and an almost total lack of empirical knowl-

---

5. The Court points to England, Scotland, Ceylon and India as having equally rigid rules. As my Brother Harlan points out, post, . . . the Court is mistaken in this regard, for it overlooks counterbalancing prosecutorial advantages. Moreover, the requirements of the Federal Bureau of Investigation do not appear . . . to be as strict as those imposed today in at least two respects: (1) The offer of counsel is articulated only as "a right to counsel"; nothing is said about a right to have counsel present at the custodial interrogation . . . ; [and (2) the warning issued by the FBI does not indicate that the agent "will secure counsel"].

edge on the practical operation of requirements truly comparable to those announced by the majority, I would be more restrained lest we go too far too fast.

II.

Custodial interrogation has long been recognized as "undoubtedly an essential tool in effective law enforcement." Recognition of this fact should put us on guard against the promulgation of doctrinaire rules. . . . To require all [the warnings and rights] at one gulp should cause the Court to choke over more cases than Crooker v. State of California, (1958), and Cicenia v. La Gay, (1958), which it expressly overrules today.

The rule prior to today . . . depended upon "a totality of circumstances evidencing an involuntary . . . admission of guilt." . . .

III.

I would continue to follow that rule. Under the "totality of circumstances" rule . . . I would consider in each case whether the police officer prior to custodial interrogation added the warning that the suspect might have counsel present at the interrogation and, further, that a court would appoint one at his request if he was too poor to employ counsel. In the absence of warnings, the burden would be on the State to prove that counsel was knowingly and intelligently waived or that in the totality of the circumstances, including the failure to give the necessary warnings, the confession was clearly voluntary.

Rather than employing the arbitrary Fifth Amendment rule which the Court lays down I would follow the more pliable dictates of the Due Process Clauses of the Fifth and Fourteenth Amendments which we are accustomed to administering and which we know from our cases are effective instruments in protecting persons in police custody. In this way we would not be acting in the dark nor in one full sweep changing the traditional rules of custodial interrogation which this Court has for so long recognized as a justifiable and proper tool in balancing individual rights against the rights of society. It will be soon enough to go further when we are able to appraise with somewhat better accuracy the effect of such a holding.

* * *

MR. JUSTICE HARLAN, whom MR. JUSTICE STEWART and MR. JUSTICE WHITE join, dissenting.

I believe the decision of the Court represents poor constitutional law and entails harmful consequences for the country at large. How serious these consequences may prove to be only time can tell. But the basic flaws in the Court's justification seem to me readily apparent now once all sides of the problem are considered.

I. INTRODUCTION

*   *   *

. . . The new rules are not designed to guard against police brutality or other unmistakably banned forms of coercion. Those who use third-degree tactics and deny them in court are equally able and destined to lie as skillfully about warnings and waivers. Rather, the thrust of the new rules is to negate all pressures, to reinforce the nervous or ignorant suspect, and ultimately to discourage any confession at all. The aim in short is toward "voluntariness" in a utopian sense, or to view it from a different angle, voluntariness with a vengeance.

To incorporate this notion into the Constitution requires a strained reading of history and precedent and a disregard of the very pragmatic concerns that alone may on occasion justify such strains.
. . .

II. CONSTITUTIONAL PREMISES

It is most fitting to begin an inquiry into the constitutional precedents by surveying the limits on confessions the Court has evolved under the Due Process Clause . . . because these cases show that there exists a workable and effective means of dealing with confessions in a judicial manner; because the cases are the baseline from which the Court now departs and so serve to measure the actual as opposed to the professed distance it travels; and because examination of them helps reveal how the Court has coasted into its present position.

The earliest confession cases in this Court emerged from federal prosecutions and were settled on a nonconstitutional basis, the Court adopting the common-law rule that the absence of inducements, promises, and threats made a confession voluntary and admissible. Hopt v. People of Territory of Utah [1884]; Pierce v. United States [1896]. While a later case said the Fifth Amendment privilege controlled admissibility, this proposition was not itself developed in subsequent decisions. The Court did, however, heighten the test of admissibility in federal trials to one of voluntariness "in fact," Ziang Sung Wan v. United States [1921], and then by and large left federal judges to apply the same standards the Court began to derive in a string of state court cases.

This new line of decisions, testing admissibility by the Due Process Clause, began in 1936 with Brown v. State of Mississippi, . . . While the voluntariness rubric was repeated . . ., the Court never pinned it down to a single meaning . . . To travel quickly over the main themes, there was an initial emphasis on reliability, e. g., Ward v. State of Texas [1942], supplemented by concern over the legality and fairness of the police practices, e. g., Ashcraft v. State of Tennessee [1944], in an "accusatorial" system of law enforcement, Watts v. State of Indiana [1949], and eventually by close attention to the individual's state of mind and capacity for effective

choice, e. g., Gallegos v. State of Colorado [1962]   .   .   .   The outcome was a continuing re-evaluation on the facts of each case of *how
much* pressure on the suspect was permissible.

Among the criteria often taken into account were threats or imminent danger, e. g., Payne v. State of Arkansas [1958], physical
deprivations such as lack of sleep or food, e. g., Reck v. Pate [1961],
repeated or extended interrogation, e. g., Chambers v. State of Florida [1940], limits on access to counsel or friends, Crooker v. State of
California [1958]; Cicenia v. La Gay [1958], length and illegality of
detention under state law, e. g., Haynes v. State of Washington
[1963], an individual weakness or incapacities, Lynumn v. State of
Illinois [1963].   Apart from direct physical coercion, however, no
single default or fixed combination of defaults guaranteed exclusion,
and synopses of the cases would serve little use because the overall
gauge has been steadily changing, usually in the direction of restricting admissibility.   But to mark just what point had been reached before the Court jumped the rails in Escobedo v. State of Illinois
[1964], it is worth capsulizing the then-recent case of Haynes v.
State of Washington [1963].   There, Haynes had been held some 16
or more hours in violation of state law before signing the disputed
confession, had received no warnings of any kind, and despite requests had been refused access to his wife or to counsel, the police indicating that access would be allowed after a confession.   Emphasizing especially this last inducement and rejecting some contrary indicia of voluntariness, the Court in a 5-to-4 decision held the confession
inadmissible.

There are several relevant lessons to be drawn from this constitutional history.   The first is that with over 25 years of precedent
the Court has developed an elaborate, sophisticated, and sensitive approach to admissibility of confessions.   It is "judicial" in its treatment of one case at a time, see Culombe v. Connecticut [1961], flexible in its ability to respond to the endless mutations of fact presented,
and ever more familiar to the lower courts.   Of course, strict certainty is not obtained in this developing process, but this is often so with
constitutional principles, and disagreement is usually confined to that
borderland of close cases where it matters least.

.   .   .   In practice and from time to time in principle, the
Court has given ample recognition to society's interest in suspect
questioning as an instrument of law enforcement.   Cases countenanc-
ing quite significant pressures can be cited without difficulty, and the
lower courts may often have been yet more tolerant.   Of course the
limitations imposed today were rejected by necessary implication in
case after case, the right to warnings having been explicitly rebuffed
in this Court many years ago.   .   .   .

Finally, the cases disclose that the language in many of the opinions overstates the actual course of decision.   It has been said, for example, that an admissible confession must be made by the suspect "in
the unfettered exercise of his own will," Malloy v. Hogan [1964], and

that "a prisoner is not 'to be made the deluded instrument of his own conviction,'" Culombe v. Connecticut [1961]. Though often repeated, such principles are rarely observed in full measure. Even the word "voluntary" may be deemed somewhat misleading, especially when one considers many of the confessions that have been brought under its umbrella. The tendency to overstate may be laid in part to the flagrant facts often before the Court; but in any event one must recognize how it has tempered attitudes and lent some color of authority to the approach now taken by the Court.

I turn now to the Court's asserted reliance on the Fifth Amendment, an approach which I frankly regard as a *trompe l'oeil*. . . .

The Court's opening contention, that the Fifth Amendment governs police station confessions, is perhaps not an impermissible extension of the law but it has little to commend itself in the present circumstances. Historically, the privilege against self-incrimination did not bear at all on the use of extra-legal confessions, for which distinct standards evolved; indeed, "the *history* of the two principles is wide apart, differing by one hundred years in origin, and derived through separate lines of precedents. . . ." . . . Even those who would readily enlarge the privilege must concede some linguistic difficulties since the Fifth Amendment in terms proscribes only compelling any person "in any criminal case to be a witness against himself." . . .

. . . Certainly the privilege does represent a protective concern for the accused and an emphasis upon accusatorial rather than inquisitorial values in law enforcement, although this is similarly true of other limitations such as the grand jury requirement and the reasonable doubt standard. Accusatorial values, however, have openly been absorbed into the due process standard governing confessions; this indeed is why at present "the kinship of the two rules [governing confessions and self-incrimination] is too apparent for denial." . . . Since extension of the general principle has already occurred, to insist that the privilege applies as such serves only to carry over inapposite historical details and engaging rhetoric and to obscure the policy choices to be made in regulating confessions.

Having decided that the Fifth Amendment privilege does apply in the police station, the Court reveals that the privilege imposes more exacting restrictions than does the Fourteenth Amendment's voluntariness test. It then emerges . . . that the Fifth Amendment requires for an admissible confession that it be given by one distinctly aware of his right not to speak and shielded from "the compelling atmosphere" of interrogation. From these key premises, the Court finally develops the safeguards of warning, counsel, and so forth. I do not believe these premises are sustained by precedents under the Fifth Amendment.

The more important premise is that pressure on the suspect must be eliminated though it be only the subtle influence of the atmosphere and surroundings. The Fifth Amendment, however, has never been thought to forbid *all* pressure to incriminate one's self in the situations covered by it. On the contrary, it has been held that failure to incriminate one's self can result in denial of removal of one's case from state to federal court; in refusal of a military commission; in denial of a discharge in bankruptcy; and in numerous other adverse consequences. This is not to say that short of jail or torture any sanction is permissible in any case; policy and history alike may impose sharp limits. However, the Court's unspoken assumption that *any* pressure violates the privilege is not supported by the precedents and it has failed to show why the Fifth Amendment prohibits that relatively mild pressure the Due Process Clause permits.

The Court appears similarly wrong in thinking that precise knowledge of one's rights is a settled prerequisite under the Fifth Amendment to the loss of its protections. A number of lower federal court cases have held that grand jury witnesses need not always be warned of their privilege, . . . and Wigmore states this to be the better rule for trial witnesses. . . . No Fifth Amendment precedent is cited for the Court's contrary view. . . .

A closing word must be said about the Assistance of Counsel Clause of the Sixth Amendment, which is never expressly relied on by the Court but whose judicial precedents turn out to be linchpins of the confession rules announced today. To support its requirement of a knowing and intelligent waiver, the Court cites [a number of cases which] concerned counsel at trial or on appeal. While the Court finds no pertinent difference between judicial proceedings and police interrogation, I believe the differences are vast . . .

The only attempt in this Court to carry the right to counsel into the station house occurred in *Escobedo* the Court repeating several times that that stage was no less "critical" than trial itself. This is hardly persuasive when we consider that a grand jury inquiry, the filing of a certiorari petition, and certainly the purchase of narcotics by an undercover agent from a prospective defendant may all be equally "critical" yet provision of counsel and advice on the score have never been thought compelled by the Constitution in such cases. The sound reason why this right is so freely extended for a criminal trial is the severe injustice risked by confronting an untrained defendant with a range of technical points of law, evidence, and tactics familiar to the prosecutor but not to himself. This danger shrinks markedly in the police station where indeed the lawyer in fulfilling his professional responsibilities of necessity may become an obstacle to truthfinding.

* * *

III.   POLICY CONSIDERATIONS

. . . Legal history has been stretched before to satisfy deep needs of society. In this instance, however, the Court has not and cannot make the powerful showing that its new rules are plainly desirable in the context of our society, something which is surely demanded before those rules are engrafted onto the Constitution and imposed on every State and county in the land.

Without at all subscribing to the generally black picture of police conduct painted by the Court, I think it must be frankly recognized at the outset that police questioning allowable under due process precedents may inherently entail some pressure on the suspect and may seek advantage in his ignorance or weaknesses. The atmosphere and questioning techniques, proper and fair though they be, can in themselves exert a tug on the suspect to confess, and in this light "[t]o speak of any confessions of crime made after arrest as being 'voluntary' or 'uncoerced' is somewhat inaccurate, although tradition- al. A confession is wholly and incontestably voluntary only if a guilty person gives himself up to the law and become his own accus- er." . . . Until today, the role of the Constitution has been only to sift out *undue* pressure, not to assure spontaneous confessions. . . .

The Court's new rules aim to offset these minor pressures and disadvantages intrinsic to any kind of police interrogation. The rules do not serve due process interests in preventing blatant coercion since, as I noted earlier, they do nothing to contain the policeman who is prepared to lie from the start. The rules work for reliability in confessions almost only in the Pickwickian sense that they can pre- vent some from being given at all.[6] . . .

What the Court largely ignores is that its rules impair, if they will not eventually serve wholly to frustrate, an instrument of law en- forcement that has long and quite reasonably been thought worth the price paid for it. There can be little doubt that the Court's new code would markedly decrease the number of confessions. To warn the suspect that he may remain silent and remind him that his confes- sion be may used in court are minor obstructions. To require also an express waiver by the suspect and an end to questioning whenever he demurs must heavily handicap questioning. And to suggest or provide counsel for the suspect simply invites the end of the interrogation.

How much harm this decision will inflict on law enforcement cannot fairly be predicted with accuracy. Evidence on the role of confessions is notoriously incomplete, and little is added by the Court's reference to the FBI experience and the resources believed wasted in interrogation. We do know that some crimes cannot be solved without confessions, that ample expert testimony attests to their importance in crime control, and that the Court is taking a real risk with society's welfare in imposing its new regime on the country. The social costs of crime are too great to call the new rules anything but a hazardous experimentation.

---

6. The Court's vision of a lawyer "mitigat[ing] the dangers of untrust- worthiness" by witnessing coercion and assisting accuracy in the confes- sion is largely a fancy; for if counsel arrives, there is rarely going to be a police station confession. Watts v. State of Indiana [1949] (separate opinion of Jackson, J.): "[A]ny law- yer worth his salt will tell the sus- pect in no uncertain terms to make no statement to police under any cir- cumstances." . . .

While passing over the costs and risks of its experiment, the Court portrays the evils of normal police questioning in terms which I think are exaggerated. Albeit stringently confined by the due process standards interrogation is no doubt often inconvenient and unpleasant for the suspect. However, it is no less so for a man to be arrested and jailed, to have his house searched, or to stand trial in court, yet all this may properly happen to the most innocent given probable cause, a warrant, or an indictment. Society has always paid a stiff price for law and order, and peaceful interrogation is not one of the dark moments of the law.

. . . it may make the analysis more graphic to consider the actual facts of one of the four cases reversed by the Court. Miranda v. Arizona serves best, being neither the hardest nor easiest of the four under the Court's standards.

On March 3, 1963, an 18-year-old girl was kidnapped and forcibly raped near Phoenix, Arizona. Ten days later, on the morning of March 13, petitioner Miranda was arrested and taken to the police station. At this time Miranda was 23 years old, indigent, and educated to the extent of completing half the ninth grade. He had "an emotional illness" of the schizophrenic type, according to the doctor who eventually examined him; the doctor's report also stated that Miranda was "alert and oriented as to time, place, and person," intelligent within normal limits, competent to stand trial, and came within the legal definition. At the police station, the victim picked Miranda out of a lineup, and two officers then took him into a separate room to interrogate him, starting about 11:30 a. m. Though at first denying his guilt, within a short time Miranda gave a detailed oral confession and then wrote out in his own hand and signed a brief statement admitting and describing the crime. All this was accomplished in two hours or less without any force, threats or promises and—I will assume this though the record is uncertain, without any effective warnings at all.

Miranda's oral and written confessions are now held inadmissible under the Court's new rules. One is entitled to feel astonished that the Constitution can be read to produce this result. These confessions were obtained during brief, daytime questioning conducted by two officers and unmarked by any of the traditional indicia of coercion. They assured a conviction for a brutal and unsettling crime, for which the police had and quite possibly could obtain little evidence other than the victim's identifications, evidence which is frequently unreliable. There was, in sum, a legitimate purpose, no perceptible unfairness, and certainly little risk of injustice in the interrogation. Yet the resulting confessions, and the responsible course of police practice they represent, are to be sacrificed to the Court's own finespun conception of fairness which I seriously doubt is shared by many thinking citizens in this country.

* * *

The Court in closing its general discussion invokes the practice in federal and foreign jurisdictions as lending weight to its new curbs on confessions for all the States. A brief résumé will suffice to show that none of these jurisdictions has struck so one-sided a balance as the Court does today. Heaviest reliance is placed on the FBI practice. Differing circumstances may make this comparison quite untrustworthy, but in any event the FBI falls sensibly short of the Court's formalistic rules. For example, there is no indication that FBI agents must obtain an affirmative "waiver" before they pursue their questioning. Nor is it clear that one invoking his right to silence may not be prevailed upon to change his mind. And the warning as to appointed counsel apparently indicates only that one will be assigned by the judge when the suspect appears before him; the thrust of the Court's rules is to induce the suspect to obtain appointed counsel before continuing the interview. Apparently American military practice, briefly mentioned by the Court, has these same limits and is still less favorable to the suspect than the FBI warning, making no mention of appointed counsel.

The law of the foreign countries described by the Court also reflects a more moderate conception of the rights of the accused as against those of society when other data are considered. Concededly, the English experience is most relevant. In that country, a caution as to silence but not counsel has long been mandated by the "Judges' Rules," which also place other somewhat imprecise limits on police cross-examination suspects. However, in the court's discretion confessions can be and apparently quite frequently are admitted in evidence despite disregard of the Judges' Rules, so long as they are found voluntary under the common-law test. Moreover, the check that exists on the use of pretrial statements in counterbalance by the evident admissibility of fruits of an illegal confession and by the judge's often-used authority to comment adversely on the defendant's failure to testify.

India, Ceylon and Scotland are the other examples chosen by the Court. In India and Ceylon the general ban on police-adduced confessions cited by the Court is subject to a major exception: if evidence is uncovered by police questioning, it is fully admissible at trial along with the confession itself, so far as it relates to the evidence and is not blatantly coerced. Scotland's limits on interrogation do measure up to the Court's; however, restrained comment at trial on the defendant's failure to take the stand is allowed the judge, and in many other respects Scotch law redresses the prosecutor's disadvantage in ways not permitted in this country. The Court ends its survey by imputing added strength to our privilege against self-incrimination since, by contrast to other countries, it is embodied in a written Constitution. Considering the liberties the Court has today taken with constitutional history and precedent, few will find this emphasis persuasive.

* * *

.   .   .   .   Despite the Court's disclaimer, the practical effect of the decision made today must inevitably be to handicap seriously sound efforts at reform, not least by removing options necessary to a just compromise of competing interests.   Of course legislative reform is rarely speedy or unanimous, though this Court has been more patient in the past.   But the legislative reforms when they come would have the vast advantage of empirical data and comprehensive study, they would allow experimentation and use of solutions not open to the courts, and they would restore the initiative in criminal law reform to those forums where it truly belongs.

* * *

In conclusion: Nothing in the letter or the spirit of the Constitution or in the precedents squares with the heavy-handed and one-sided action that is so precipitously taken by the Court in the name of fulfilling its constitutional responsibilities.   The foray which the Court makes today brings to mind the wise and far-sighted words of Mr. Justice Jackson: "This Court is forever adding new stories to the temples of constitutional law, and the temples have a way of collapsing when one story too many is added."

MR. JUSTICE WHITE, with whom MR. JUSTICE HARLAN and MR. JUSTICE STEWART join, dissenting.

* * *

That the Court's holding today is neither compelled nor even strongly suggested by the language of the Fifth Amendment, is at odds with American and English legal history, and involves a departure from a long line of precedent does not prove either that the Court has exceeded its powers or that the Court is wrong or unwise in its present reinterpretation of the Fifth Amendment.   It does, however, underscore the obvious—that the Court has not discovered or found the law in making today's decision, nor has it derived it from some irrefutable sources; what it has done is to make new law and new public policy in much the same way that it has in the course of interpreting other great clauses of the Constitution.   This is what the Court historically has done.   Indeed, it is what it must do and will continue to do until and unless there is some fundamental change in the constitutional distribution of governmental powers.

But if the Court is here and now to announce new and fundamental policy to govern certain aspects of our affairs, it is wholly legitimate to examine the mode of this or any other constitutional decision in this Court and to inquire into the advisability of its end product in terms of the long-range interest of the country.   At the very least, the Court's text and reasoning should withstand analysis and be a fair exposition of the constitutional provision which its opinion interprets.   Decisions like these cannot rest alone on syllogism, metaphysics or some ill-defined notions of natural justice, although each will perhaps play its part.   In proceeding to such constructions as it now announces, the Court should also duly consider all the factors and interests bearing upon the cases, at least insofar as the relevant materials are available;   and if the necessary considerations are not treated in the record or obtainable from some other reliable source, the Court should not proceed to formulate fundamental policies based on speculation alone.

First, we may inquire what are the textual and factual bases of this new fundamental rule. To reach the result announced on the grounds it does, the Court must stay within the confines of the Fifth Amendment, which forbids self-incrimination only if *compelled*. Hence the core of the Court's opinion is that because of the "compulsion inherent in custodial surroundings, no statement obtained from [a] defendant [in custody] can truly be the product of his free choice," absent the use of adequate protective devices as described by the Court. However, the Court does not point to any sudden in-rush of new knowledge requiring the rejection of 70 years' experience. Nor does it assert that its novel conclusion reflects a changing consensus among state courts, see Mapp v. Ohio or that a succession of cases had steadily eroded the old rule and proved it unworkable, . . . Rather than asserting new knowledge, the Court concedes that it cannot truly know what occurs during custodial questioning, because of the innate secrecy of such proceedings. It extrapolates a picture of what it conceives to be the norm from police investigatorial manuals, published in 1959 and 1962 or earlier, without any attempt to allow for adjustments in police practices that may have occurred in the wake of more recent decisions of state appellate tribunals or this Court. But even if the relentless application of the described procedures could lead to involuntary confessions, it most assuredly does not follow that each and every case will disclose this kind of interrogation or this kind of consequence.[7] Insofar as appears from the Court's opinion, it has not examined a single transcript of any police interrogation, let alone the interrogation that took place in any one of these cases which it decides today. Judged by any of the standards for empirical investigation utilized in the social sciences the factual basis for the Court's premise is patently inadequate.

Although in the Court's view in-custody interrogation is inherently coercive, the Court says that the spontaneous product of the coercion of arrest and detention is still to be deemed voluntary. An accused, arrested on probable cause, may blurt out a confession which will be admissible despite the fact that he is alone and in custody, without any showing that he had any notion of his right to remain silent or of the consequences of his admission. Yet, under the Court's rule, if the police ask him a single question such as "Do you have anything to say?" or "Did you kill your wife?" his response, if there

---

7. In fact, the type of sustained interrogation described by the Court appears to be the exception rather than the rule. A survey of 399 cases in one city found that in almost half of the cases the interrogation lasted less than 30 minutes. Barrett, Police Practices and the Law—From Arrest to Release or Charge, 50 Calif.L.Rev. 11, 41–45 (1962). Questioning tends to be confused and sporadic and is usually concentrated on confrontations with witnesses or new items of evidence, as these are obtained by officers conducting the investigation. See generally LaFave, Arrest: The Decision to Take a Suspect into Custody 386 (1965); ALI, A Model Code of Pre-Arraignment Procedure, Commentary § 5.01, at 170, n. 4 (Tent. Draft No. 1, 1966).

is one, has somehow been compelled, even if the accused has been clearly warned of his right to remain silent. Common sense informs us to the contrary. While one may say that the response was "involuntary" in the sense the question provoked or was the occasion for the response and thus the defendant was induced to speak out when he might have remained silent if not arrested and not questioned, it is patently unsound to say the response is compelled.

Today's result would not follow even if it were agreed that to some extent custodial interrogation is inherently coercive. The test has been whether the totality of circumstances deprived the defendant of a "free choice to admit, to deny, or to refuse to answer," and whether physical or psychological coercion was of such a degree that "the defendant's will was overborne at the time he confessed," . . . The duration and nature of incommunicado custody, the presence or absence of advice concerning the defendant's constitutional rights, and the granting or refusal of requests to communicate with lawyers, relatives or friends have all been rightly regarded as important data bearing on the basic inquiry. . . .[8]

But it has never been suggested, until today, that such questioning was so coercive and accused persons so lacking in hardihood that the very first response to the very first question following the commencement of custody must be conclusively presumed to be the product of an overborne will.

If the rule announced today were truly based on a conclusion that all confessions resulting from custodial interrogation are coerced, then it would simply have no rational foundation. . . . *A fortiori* that would be true of the extension of the rule to exculpatory statements, which the Court effects after a brief discussion of why, in the Court's view, they must be deemed incriminatory but without any discussion of why they must be deemed coerced. Even if one were to postulate that the Court's concern is not that all confessions induced by police interrogation are coerced but rather that some such confessions are coerced and present judicial procedures are believed to be inadequate to identify the confessions that are coerced and those that are not, it would still not be essential to impose the rule that the Court has now fashioned. Transcripts or observers could be required, specific time limits, tailored to fit the cause, could be imposed, or other devices could be utilized to reduce the chances that otherwise indiscernible coercion will produce an inadmissible confession.

8. By contrast, the Court indicates that in applying this new rule it "will not pause to inquire in individual cases whether the defendant was aware of his rights without a warning being given." The reason given is that assessment of the knowledge of the defendant based on information as to age, education, intelligence, or prior contact with authorities can never be more than speculation, while a warning is a clear-cut fact. But the officers' claim that they gave the requisite warnings may be disputed, and facts respecting the defendant's prior experience may be undisputed and be of such a nature as to virtually preclude any doubt that the defendant knew of his rights. . . . .

On the other hand, even if one assumed that there was an adequate factual basis for the conclusion that all confessions obtained during in-custody interrogation are the product of compulsion, the rule propounded by the Court will still be irrational, for, apparently, it is only if the accused is also warned of his right to counsel and waives both that right and the right against self-incrimination that the inherent compulsiveness of interrogation disappears. But if the defendant may not answer without a warning a question such as "Where were you last night?" without having his answer be a compelled one, how can the Court ever accept his negative answer to the question of whether he wants to consult his retained counsel or counsel whom the court will appoint? And why if counsel is present and the accused nevertheless confesses, or counsel tells the accused to tell the truth, and that is what the accused does, is the situation any less coercive insofar as the accused is concerned? The Court apparently realizes its dilemma of foreclosing questioning without the necessary warnings but at the same time permitting the accused, sitting in the same chair in front of the same policemen to waive his right to consult an attorney. It expects, however, that the accused will not often waive the right; and if it is claimed that he has, the State faces a severe, if not impossible burden of proof.

All of this makes very little sense in terms of the compulsion which the Fifth Amendment proscribes. That amendment deals with compelling the accused himself. It is his free will that is involved. Confessions and incriminating admissions, as such, are not forbidden evidence; only those which are compelled are banned. I doubt that the Court observes these distinctions today. By considering any answers to any interrogation to be compelled regardless of the content and course of examination and by escalating the requirements to prove waiver, the Court not only prevents the use of compelled confessions but for all practical purposes forbids interrogation except in the presence of counsel. That is, instead of confining itself to protection of the right against compelled self-incrimination the Court has created a limited Fifth Amendment right to counsel—or, as the Court expresses it, a "need for counsel to protect the Fifth Amendment privilege . . . ." The focus then is not on the will of the accused but on the will of counsel and how much influence he can have on the accused. Obviously there is no warrant in the Fifth Amendment for thus installing counsel as the arbiter of the privilege.

In sum, for all the Court's expounding on the menacing atmosphere of police interrogation procedures, it has failed to supply any foundation for the conclusions it draws or the measures it adopts.

Criticism of the Court's opinion, however, cannot stop with a demonstration that the factual and textual bases for the rule it propounds are, at best, less than compelling. Equally relevant is an assessment of the rule's consequences measured against community values. The Court's duty to assess the consequences of its action is not satisfied by the utterance of the truth that a value of our system of criminal justice is "to respect the inviolability of the human personality" and to require government to produce the evidence against the accused by its own independent labors. More than the human dignity of the accused is involved; the human personality of others in the society must also be preserved. Thus the values reflected by the privilege are not the sole desideratum; society's interest in the general security is of equal weight.

The obvious underpinning of the Court's decision is a deep-seated distrust of all confessions. As the Court declares that the accused may not be interrogated without counsel present, absent a waiver of the right to counsel, and as the Court all but admonishes the lawyer to advise the accused to remain silent, the result adds up to a judicial judgment that evidence from the accused should not be used against him in any way, whether compelled or not. This is the not so subtle overtone of the opinion—that it is inherently wrong for the police to gather evidence from the accused himself. And this is precisely the nub of this dissent. I see nothing wrong or immoral, and certainly nothing unconstitutional, in the police's asking a suspect whom they have reasonable cause to arrest whether or not he killed his wife or in confronting him with the evidence on which the arrest was based, at least where he has been plainly advised that he may remain completely silent. Until today, "the admissions or confessions of the prisoner, when voluntarily and freely made, have always ranked high in the scale of incriminating evidence."   . . .   Particularly when corroborated, as where the police have confirmed the accused's disclosure of the hiding place of implements or fruits of the crime, such confessions have the highest reliability and significantly contribute to the certitude with which we may believe the accused is guilty. Moreover, it is by no means certain that the process of confessing is injurious to the accused. To the contrary it may provide psychological relief and enhance the prospects for rehabilitation.

This is not to say that the value of respect for the inviolability of the accused's individual personality should be accorded no weight or that all confessions should be indiscriminately admitted. This Court has long read the Constitution to proscribe compelled confessions, a salutary rule from which there should be no retreat. But I see no sound basis, factual or otherwise, and the Court gives none, for concluding that the present rule against the receipt of coerced confessions is inadequate for the task of sorting out inadmissible evidence and must be replaced by the *per se* rule which is now imposed. Even if the new concept can be said to have advantages of some sort over the present law, they are far outweighed by its likely undesirable impact on other very relevant and important interests.

The most basic function of any government is to provide for the security of the individual and of his property. These ends of society are served by the criminal laws which for the most part are aimed at the prevention of crime. Without the reasonably effective performance of the task of preventing private violence and retaliation, it is idle to talk about human dignity and civilized values.

The modes by which the criminal laws serve the interest in general security are many. First the murderer who has taken the life of another is removed from the streets, deprived of his liberty and thereby prevented from repeating his offense. In view of the statistics on recidivism in this country and of the number of instances in which apprehension occurs only after repeated offenses, no one can sensibly claim that this aspect of the criminal law does not prevent crime or contribute significantly to the personal security of the ordinary citizen.

Secondly, the swift and sure apprehension of those who refuse to respect the personal security and dignity of their neighbor unquestionably has its impact on others who might be similarly tempted. That the criminal law is wholly or partly ineffective with a segment of the population or with many of those who have been apprehended and convicted is a very faulty basis for concluding that it is not effective with respect to the great bulk of our citizens or for thinking that without the criminal laws, or in the absence of their enforcement, there would be no increase in crime. Arguments of this nature are not borne out by any kind of reliable evidence that I have seen to this date.

Thirdly, the law concerns itself with those whom it has confined. The hope and aim of modern penology, fortunately, is as soon as possible to return the convict to society a better and more law-abiding man than when he left. Sometimes there is success, sometimes failure. But at least the effort is made, and it should be made to the very maximum extent of our present and future capabilities.

The rule announced today will measurably weaken the ability of the criminal law to perform these tasks. It is a deliberate calculus to prevent interrogations, to reduce the incidence of confessions and pleas of guilty and to increase the number of trials. Criminal trials, no matter how efficient the police are, are not sure bets for the prosecution, nor should they be if the evidence is not forthcoming. Under the present law, the prosecution fails to prove its case in about 30% of the criminal cases actually tried in the federal courts. But it is something else again to remove from the ordinary criminal case all those confessions which heretofore have been held to be free and voluntary acts of the accused and to thus establish a new constitutional barrier to the ascertainment of truth by the judicial process. There is, in my view, every reason to believe that a good many criminal defendants who otherwise would have been convicted on what this Court has previously thought to be the most satisfactory kind of evidence will now under this new version of the Fifth Amendment, either not be tried at all or will be acquitted if the State's evidence, minus the confession, is put to the test of litigation.

I have no desire whatsoever to share the responsibility for any such impact on the present criminal process.

In some unknown number of cases the Court's rule will return a killer, a rapist or other criminal to the streets and to the environment which produced him, to repeat his crime whenever it pleases him. As a consequence, there will not be a gain, but a loss, in human dignity. The real concern is not the unfortunate consequences of this new decision on the criminal law as an abstract, disembodied series of authoritative proscriptions, but the impact on those who rely on the public authority for protection and who without it can only engage in violent self-help with guns, knives and the help of their neighbors similarly inclined. There is, of course, a saving factor: the next victims are uncertain, unnamed and unrepresented in this case.

Nor can this decision do other than have a corrosive effect on the criminal laws as an effective device to prevent crime. A major component in its effectiveness in this regard is its swift and sure enforcement. The easier it is to get away with rape and murder, the less the deterrent effect on those who are inclined to attempt it. This is still good common sense. If it were not, we should posthaste liquidate the whole law enforcement establishment as a useless, misguided effort to control human conduct.

And what about the accused who has confessed or would confess in response to simple, noncoercive questioning and whose guilt could not otherwise be proved? Is it so clear that release is the best thing for him in every case? Has it so unquestionably been resolved that in each and every case it would be better for him not to confess and to return to his environment with no attempt whatsoever to help him? I think not. It may well be that in many cases it will be no less than a callous disregard for his own welfare as well as for the interests of his next victim.

There is another aspect to the effect of the Court's rule on the person whom the police have arrested on probable cause. The fact is that he may not be guilty at all and may be able to extricate himself quickly and simply if he were told the circumstances of his arrest and were asked to explain. This effort, and his release, must now await the hiring of a lawyer or his appointment by the court, consultation with counsel and then a session with the police or the prosecutor. Similarly, where probable cause exists to arrest several suspects, as where the body of the victim is discovered in a house having several residents, it will often be true that a suspect may be cleared only through the results of interrogation of other suspects. Here too the release of the innocent may be delayed by the Court's rule.

Much of the trouble with the Court's new rule is that it will operate indiscriminately in all criminal cases, regardless of the severity of the crime or the circumstances involved. It applies to every defendant, whether the professional criminal or one committing a crime of momentary passion who is not part and parcel of organized crime. It will slow down the investigation and the apprehension of confederates in those cases where time is of the essence, such as kidnapping, . . . those involving national security . . . and some of those involving organized crime. In the latter context the lawyer who arrives may also be the lawyer for the defendant's colleagues and can be relied upon to insure that no breach of the organization's security takes place even though the accused may feel that the best thing he can do is to cooperate.

At the same time, the Court's *per se* approach may not be justified on the ground that it provides a "bright line" permitting the authorities to judge in advance whether interrogation may safely be pursued without jeopardizing the admissibility of any information obtained as a consequence. Nor can it be claimed that judicial time and effort, assuming that is a relevant consideration, will be conserved because of the ease of application of the new rule. Today's decision leaves open such questions as whether the accused was in custody, whether his statements were spontaneous or the product of interrogation, whether the accused has effectively waived his rights, and whether nontestimonial evidence introduced at trial is the fruit of statements made during a prohibited interrogation, all of which are certain to prove productive of uncertainty during investigation and litigation during prosecution. For all these reasons, if further restrictions on police interrogation are desirable at this time, a more flexible approach makes much more sense than the Court's constitutional straitjacket which forecloses more discriminating treatment by legislative or rule-making pronouncements.

NOTES

1. Assuming the continued employment of the exclusionary rule as a device by which police conduct is conformed to the requirements of substantive law, the question remains, how far should a court—particularly the Supreme Court—go in laying down *specific* rules of police conduct? See Friendly, The Bill of Rights As A Code Of Criminal Procedure, 53 Cal.L. Rev. 929 (1965). What form should such "rules" take? Between the decision in *Escobedo* and that in *Miranda*, one writer suggested that the Supreme Court ought to promulgate rules outside the vehicle of an adjudicated case, and that the Congress, under its power to enforce the Fourteenth Amendment, ought to enact a code of criminal procedure to govern state law enforcement officers. Consider the following materials from Dowling, Escobedo And Beyond: The Need For A Fourteenth Amendment Code Of Criminal Procedure, 56 J.Crim.L., C. & P.S. 143, 153–57 (1965).

"The readily traceable reason for the inaction of Congress and the absence of court rules specially promulgated by the Supreme Court for the area of state-federal criminal procedure is the division of powers between the states and the federal government inherent in our history and emphasized in the ninth and tenth amendments. The reason rested on bedrock when that division existed and where it legitimately continues to exist. But when the reservation of powers of the states in the criminal area is brought into the penumbra of the federal system, it is inefficient, foolhardy and contrary to our form of government to permit the federal-fourteenth amendment part of state-federal criminal procedure to drift forward, backward, or stand still, exclusively on the pages of the *Supreme Court Reports*. Moreover, it is a disservice to make state law enforcement officials and state courts flounder in their duties upon a sea of doubt over which they have no navigable control. If the states are to operate the state-federal criminal system, they ought to be allowed to participate in the full panoply of governmental processes which control that system—which means legislative participation as well as judicial imposition. The resolution of the demands and challenges of the fourteenth amendment to afford fair criminal proceedings against the citizen and on behalf of the state should not be exclusively reposited in the Supreme Court.

"It is, of course, true that the states are left to their own devices in meeting the dictates of the Supreme Court. But obedience, even when it is willing and eager, can be misguided and—when it comes to operating a system of criminal justice within a state—grossly inefficient. . . . I do not suggest that we need to find a way to curb the Court. On the contrary, as to the Court, I suggest that to supplement its present role in making state-federal criminal law on a case-by-case basis, it be encouraged to perform the further function of promulgating rules which would be helpful to the states and lead to greater efficiency in the administration of the state-federal law. The scope of these rules would be within the range of power generally conceded to appellate courts administering laws over which they have jurisdiction.

"Professor Allen's point is sound that many of the problems of fair and decent criminal procedure are, apart from those of the limits of constitutional power, ones of policy and common sense. And legislative initiative on the local level should not preclude legislation *for* the local level by a conglomerate legislature representing thousands of localities and fifty states with *common* local problems under the fourteenth amendment. If the Congress is intelligently advised, perhaps through a Committee on State-Federal Criminal Law with local sub-groups, legislation meeting the demands of decency and efficiency to the citizens prosecuted and the state as law-enforcer could be passed and included in a title to the United States code recognizing and implementing the existing, growing body of state-federal case law under the fourteenth amendment.

"The relationship of the states to the federal government in this area has understandably, but needlessly, been a touchy subject. Fourteenth amendment doctrine has been developed by the Court under a tip-toe method which the states have found leaves the scuff-marks of the big boot. The Supreme Court, while reassuring the states of exclusive jurisdiction in procedural matters concerning the operation of state systems of criminal justice, at the same time dictates requirements under the fourteenth amendment which generally affect the most important aspects of criminal procedure followed within the states. Consider the then thought to be reassuring language of Mr. Justice Burton in Bute v. Illinois, a 1948 decision following the now discarded rule of Betts v. Brady:

> " 'The Fourteenth Amendment . . . does not say that no state shall deprive any person of liberty without following the *federal* process of law as prescribed for the federal courts in comparable federal cases. . . . This *due* process is not an equivalent for the process of the federal courts or for the process of any particular state. It has reference rather to a standard of process that may cover many varieties of processes that are expressive of differing combinations of historical or modern, local or other judicial standards, provided they do not conflict with the 'fundamental principles of liberty and justice which lie at the base of all our civil and political institutions' . . . This clause in the Fourteenth Amendment leaves room for much of the freedom which, under our Constitution of the United States and in accordance with its purposes, was originally reserved to the states for their exercise of their own police powers and for their control over the

procedure to be followed in criminal trials in their respective courts.   .   .   .

"Can it really be said that the problems confronting the California, Oregon, Rhode Island and Illinois Supreme Courts, the New York trial judge, the one from Tennessee and, no doubt, hundreds of other trial judges, are 'local' problems? Are there 'varieties of processes' open to the state courts to be divined out of ther own local, historical or modern settings—the fifty separate precincts—to comport with 'this *due* process' which, it is said, is not an equivalent for federal process or the process of any given state? Is the question whether a man charged with misdemeanor is entitled to appointment of counsel, a question left over from *Gideon*, a 'local' question, assuming the man's indigency? Is whether a man suspected of, say, murder entitled to be provided with a free lawyer if he is poor and wants one during police interrogation, a 'local' question? Is whether *Escobedo* should be made to apply retrospectively subject to 'local' resolution? Or whether we should do away with the voluntary confession altogether? Or what rights a man ought to be told he has before we elicit a confession from him? Or just how to go about 'effectively' telling him about those rights? These questions could be posed for quite some time before one got down to the really 'local' issues: how to charge an offense, as long as one is intelligibly charged; how to provide counsel, as long as counsel is provided; how to provide appellate review of convictions, as long as it is open to all; how to conduct a post-conviction hearing, as long as there is a hearing; and how to conduct a criminal trial, as long as it is conducted fairly. The local and the national procedures can be sorted out for quite some time, and this is the hub of what I propose we do; not just by a majority, but by the fifty states through the Congress.

"Until the Supreme Court of the United States articulates answers to these questions, law enforcement officials will continue to perform their duties as they see them. There is no mysterious process at arriving at the answers that makes the Supreme Court more fit to articulate them than the Congress. There is nothing inherent in our system, other than Congressional lethargy, some lack of imagination, the force of legislative inertia at rest, and the willingness to pass the buck to judicial interpolation, that restricts Congress from legislating fourteenth amendment requirements for state criminal processes.

"We do not have to nationalize the criminal procedure of the several States. But we do have to 'fourteenth amendmentize' their procedure. And the code of fourteenth amendment criminal procedure that we have to start thinking about cannot be thought about in terms of traditional procedural codes. For the code that will have to be worked out with all of the originality that went into drafting the Constitution does not now exist. To be sure, the Congress will have to draw on the best talent in this nation to do the sorting-out and, indeed, the drafting. The statesmen will have to be assembled. For until the job is done, with the full participation of the states, we are going to keep hearing statements like the one of the trial judge from Tennessee, and someone is going to feel the pinches of those statements.

"We do not have to search very far for the answer to the question: does the Congress have authority to enact legislation for the federal part of the state-federal trial that the states are now administering? Section five of the fourteenth amendment states: 'The Congress shall have power to enforce, by appropriate legislation, the provisions of this article.' Mr. Justice

Strong, construing this provision for the Supreme Court of the United States in Ex Parte Virginia, stated:

> " 'It is the power of Congress which has been enlarged. Congress is authorized to *enforce* the prohibitions by appropriate legislation. Some legislation is contemplated to make the amendment fully effective. Whatever legislation is appropriate, that is, adapted to carry out the objects the amendments have in view . . . is brought within the domain of congressional power.

> " 'Nor does it make any difference that such legislation is restrictive of what the State might have done before the constitutional amendment was adopted. The prohibitions of the Fourteenth Amendment are directed to the States, and they are to a degree restrictions of State power. It is these which Congress is empowered to enforce, and to enforce against State action, however put forth, whether that action be executive, legislative, or judicial. Such enforcement is no invasion of State sovereignty. No law can be, which the people of the States have, by the Constitution of the United States, empowered Congress to enact.'

"That the concept of section five of the fourteenth amendment as stated in Ex Parte Virginia still has vitality is borne out by a 1961 decision of the Supreme Court, where Mr. Justice Douglas, speaking for the Court, said:

" 'There can be no doubt at least since Ex Parte Virginia . . . that Congress has the power to enforce provisions of the Fourteenth Amendment.' [Monroe v. Pape, 365 U.S. 167, 81 S.Ct. 473.]

"Assuming Congressional authority to enact a code of fourteenth amendment criminal procedure applicable to state criminal cases, and further assuming a desire on the part of Congress to legislate with a genuine sensitivity to concepts of fairness developed by the Supreme Court and those still being debated in chambers, such a code could contribute substantially to the efficient and sound administration of criminal justice in the United States. Congressional participation potentially offers a greater degree of certainty and predictability for state systems of criminal justice. It offers a wider forum for resolution of important problems confronting the administration of criminal justice, including the opportunity for Congress to solicit the reasoned judgment of members of the state judiciary on important constitutional problems confronting the nation—not just the judiciary.

"Justice Walter V. Schaefer of the Supreme Court of Illinois has said that '[s]uperimposed upon the recency of many of our procedural safeguards is the novelty of federal intervention in the field.' Since Justice Schaefer made that statement in 1956 the 'novelty' has begun to wear off. Nevertheless we remain lulled by the sense of transiency that goes with novelty. The Supreme Court, standing at the summit of our constitutional system, will continue to intervene on a case-by-case basis so long as we—through our Congress—continue to default in our responsibilities to provide uniform machinery to meet the ever-evolving demands and challenges of the fourteenth amendment. But if we use it, there is reason to believe the Court will heed our common sense."

2. The following provision was enacted by Congress as part of Title II of the "Omnibus Crime Control and Safe Streets Act of 1968". Although the statute on its face purports to set forth only a test of "voluntariness", in fact the point of the legislation was to "overrule" the *Miranda* decision.

Does Congress have the power to do so? Would the act be constitutional if it reached *state* trials under the authority of Congress to "implement" the Fourteenth Amendment?

Sec. 701. (a) Chapter 223, title 18, United States Code (relating to witnesses and evidence), is amended by adding at the end thereof the following new sections:

"§ 3501.　Admissibility of Confessions

"(a) In any criminal prosecution brought by the United States or by the District of Columbia, a confession, as defined in subsection (e) hereof, shall be admissible in evidence if it is voluntarily given. Before such confession is received in evidence, the trial judge shall, out of the presence of the jury, determine any issue as to voluntariness. If the trial judge determines that the confession was voluntarily made it shall be admitted in evidence and the trial judge shall permit the jury to hear relevant evidence on the issue of voluntariness and shall instruct the jury to give such weight to the confession as the jury feels it deserves under all the circumstances.

"(b) The trial judge in determining the issue of voluntariness shall take into consideration all the circumstances surrounding the giving of the confession, including (1) the time elapsing between arrest and arraignment of the defendant making the confession, if it was made after arrest and before arraignment, (2) whether such defendant knew the nature of the offense with which he was charged or of which he was suspected at the time of making the confession, (3) whether or not such defendant was advised or knew that he was not required to make any statement and that any such statement could be used against him, (4) whether or not such defendant had been advised prior to questioning of his right to the assistance of counsel; and (5) whether or not such defendant was without the assistance of counsel when questioned and when giving such confession.

"The presence or absence of any of the above-mentioned factors to be taken into consideration by the judge need not be conclusive on the issue of voluntariness of the confession.

"(c) In any criminal prosecution by the United States or by the District of Columbia, a confession made or given by a person who is a defendant therein, while such person was under arrest or other detention in the custody of any law-enforcement officer or law-enforcement agency, shall not be inadmissible solely because of delay in bringing such person before a magistrate or other officer empowered to commit persons charged with offenses against the laws of the United States or of the District of Columbia if such confession is found by the trial judge to have been made voluntarily and if the weight to be given the confession is left to the jury and if such confession was made or given by such person within six hours immediately following his arrest or other detention: *Provided,* That the time limitation contained in this subsection shall not apply in any case in which the delay in bringing such person before such magistrate or other officer beyond such six-hour period is found by the trial judge to be reasonable considering the means of transportation and the distance to be traveled to the nearest available such magistrate or other officer.

"(d) Nothing contained in this section shall bar the admission in evidence of any confession made or given voluntarily by any person to any other person without interrogation by anyone, or at any time at which the person who made or gave such confession was not under arrest or other detention.

"(e) As used in this section, the term 'confession' means any confession of guilt of any criminal offense or any self-incriminating statement made or given orally or in writing."

3. One week after the decision in *Miranda*, the Court held that neither *Escobedo* nor *Miranda* were to apply to cases in which the *trials* were commenced prior to the dates of decision in those cases. Johnson v. New Jersey, 384 U.S. 719, 86 S.Ct. 1772 (1966). In 1969 the Court further limited the effect of *Miranda* by declaring it inapplicable on re-trial of any case where the original trial occurred before *Miranda*, Jenkins v. Delaware, 395 U.S. 213, 89 S.Ct. 1699 (1969).

2. INTERPRETATION OF THE MIRANDA REQUIREMENTS

(a) The Meaning of "Custody" and "Deprivation of Freedom of Action in Any Significant Way"

UNITED STATES v. HALL

United States Court of Appeals, Second Circuit, 1969.
421 F.2d 540, cert. denied 397 U.S. 990, 90 S.Ct. 1123.

FRIENDLY, CIRCUIT JUDGE.

This appeal from a conviction for bank robbery, vindicates the observation by a penetrating scholar: "Probably the most difficult and frequently raised question in the wake of [Miranda v. Arizona] is what constitutes the 'in-custody interrogation' or 'custodial questioning' which must be preceded by the *Miranda* warnings."

. . . At approximately 7:55 A.M. on Thursday, December 12, 1968, Mrs. Richer, the head teller, parked her automobile at the rear of the bank. Approaching it, she sensed she was being followed. A man wearing a stocking mask over his face and carrying a rifle directed her into the bank. He herded Mrs. Richer, Mr. Corbett, the assistant manager, and two other tellers into a vault. There he instructed Mrs. Richer to put the cash, $37,872.44, into a bag and give him the keys to her car. He then made his exit. Later Mrs. Richer saw her car in the parking lot of a bowling alley some 100' away from the back parking lot of the bank.

Unfortunately for the robber, an observant young lady, Barbara Costick, had driven onto the bowling alley parking lot around 7:45 A. M. She saw a maroon or red colored car backed up against the edge of the parking lot and facing the rear of the bank. . . . She noticed that the man in the car was wearing a gray hat and topcoat—a description of the robber's costume generally tallying with Mrs. Richer's. As Miss Costick drove by, the man put his left arm up to the window to shield his face. She was sufficiently struck by this conduct to look at the license plate and, after driving a hundred yards or so and coming to a stop, to write down on a card the number—OA 1587. About five minutes later, Stanley Costick noticed that the red car, which he identified as a Chevrolet, had moved to the other side of the parking lot closer to the bank. Later observation of footprints in the snow by a county sheriff made it evident that the robber had walked from this position up to the bank parking lot and had returned to the same position from Mrs. Richer's car.

The license number was speedily traced . . . a Chevrolet car bearing that number had been assigned to defendant Hall.
. . .

At 4:22 P.M. Special Agent Schaller and two other F.B.I. agents arrived at Hall's apartment in North Tonawanda, N.Y. The apartment, in the rear of the first floor of a three family dwelling, was a small one, with a living room some 12′ × 14′ furnished with a couch and two chairs, a kitchen, a bedroom and bath. After identifying himself and his companions Schaller told Hall they would like to come in and speak to him. He said they were welcome. Schaller related that a bank near Syracuse had been robbed that morning, that a car tallying Hall's in description and license number had then been observed nearby, and that he would like to talk to Hall about the latter's activities during the week of December 9 to 12. [Hall then answered the agent's questions about his car].

. . . After some seventeen minutes Schaller sought permission to search the apartment and the car, and Hall signed waivers and consents. No money was found.

The interview was resumed shortly after 5 P.M. Schaller advised [Hall of his Miranda rights; Hall waived his rights].

The serious question concerns the initial seventeen minutes of questioning which elicited the false exculpatory statement that Hall's car was in front of his apartment at 9:00 A.M. The parties have devoted a large portion of their briefs and arguments to whether during this period Hall had become the "focus" of the investigation. As put the question is unanswerable. Certainly the agents had "focused" on Hall more than on all residents of Cicero or on other residents of North Tonawanda; on the other hand the focus was not so sharp that they had anything approaching certain, indeed even probable cause to believe he was the robber. Furthermore, the "focus" question, derived from Escobedo v. Illinois, is not the appropriate test. The phrase was there used in an effort to define the point when the Sixth Amendment forbids the deprivation of a suspect's access to his lawyer. Moreover, the coming of that point was defined not in terms of "focus" alone but of focus plus. It is well to attend to precisely what the Court said: "We hold, therefore, that where, as here, the investigation is no longer a general inquiry into an unsolved crime but has begun to focus on a particular suspect, the suspect has been taken into police custody, the police carry out a process of interrogations that lends itself to eliciting incriminating statements, the suspect has requested and been denied an opportunity to consult with his lawyer, and the police have not effectively warned him of his absolute constitutional right to remain silent, the accused has been denied 'the Assistance of Counsel' in violation of the Sixth Amendment to the Constitution   .   .   .." "We hold only that when the process shifts from investigatory to accusatory—when its focus is on the accused *and* its purpose is to elicit a confession—our adversary system begins to operate, and, *under the circumstances here*, the accused must be permitted to consult with his lawyer." [Emphasis supplied.] No claim is or could reasonably be made here that the early questioning of Hall violated Sixth Amendment rights.

It is equally plain that "focus" alone does not trigger the need for *Miranda* warnings. As appears from the first *Escobedo* extract we have quoted custody as well as focus and other factors were essential to that decision. Under *Miranda* custody alone suffices. We fail to perceive how one can reason from these two propositions to a conclusion that "focus" alone is enough to bring *Miranda* into play. The only possible basis for such an argument would be that, after limiting *Miranda* to custodial interrogation and defining this as "questioning initiated by law enforcement officers after a person has been taken into custody or otherwise deprived of his freedom of action in any significant way," Chief Justice Warren dropped a footnote:

> This is what we meant in *Escobedo* when we spoke of an investigation which had focused on an accused.

While much dialectic skill has been expended on this footnote, the one thing that is undeniable is that the opinion said that focus means custody, not that custody means focus. As Professor Kamisar has put it, "*Miranda's* use of 'custodial interrogation' actually marks a *fresh start* in describing the point at which the Constitutional protections begin," id.—Fifth Amendment protections, that is.

This still leaves the courts with the far from easy task of determining whether questioning was initiated "after a person has been taken into custody or otherwise deprived of his freedom of action in any significant way." The only two relevant Supreme Court decisions since *Miranda* shed little light. In Mathis v. United States (1968), the person interrogated by a federal revenue agent was in custody under any standard; he was in a state prison serving a sentence for a wholly unrelated crime. If the decision has any significance here, which may be doubtful, it would be that the Court favors a rule-of-thumb approach, assumed to be easily applicable, rather than a detailed inquiry into the coerciveness of the "custody" in the particular case since, as pointed out in Mr. Justice White's dissent, Mathis was not coerced into answering the questions "any more than is the citizen interviewed at home by a revenue agent or interviewed in a Revenue Service office to which citizens are requested to come for interviews." Orozco v. Texas (1969) put beyond doubt that custodial interrogation may take place outside the station-house, as the *Miranda* opinion had rather clearly indicated although none of the four cases there decided had presented the point. But the officers conceded that "from the moment he [Orozco] gave his name . . . petitioner was not free to go where he pleased but was 'under arrest,' " and the decision rested upon that.

Schaller was not asked concerning his intentions about holding Hall during the first stage of the interview, and Hall did not say how he regarded his situation. Doubtless this was just as well. The Court could scarcely have intended the issue whether the person being interrogated had "been taken into custody or otherwise deprived of his liberty in any significant way" to be decided by swearing contests in which officers would regularly maintain their lack of intention to assert power over a suspect save when the circumstances would make such a claim absurd, and defendants would assert with equal regularity that they considered themselves to be significantly deprived of their liberty the minute officers began to inquire of them. Moreover, any formulation making the need for *Miranda* warnings depend upon how each individual being questioned perceived his situation would require a prescience neither the police nor anyone else possesses. On the other hand, a standard hinging on the inner intentions of the police would fail to recognize *Miranda's* concern with the coercive effect of the "atmosphere" from the point of view of the person being questioned.

The test must thus be an objective one. Clearly the Court meant that *something* more than official interrogation must be shown. It is hard to suppose that suspicion alone was thought to constitute that something; almost all official interrogation of persons who later become criminal defendants stems from that very source. While the Court's language in *Miranda* was imprecise, doubtless deliberately so, it conveys a flavor of some affirmative action by the authorities other than polite interrogation. This view is strengthened by the passage at 384 U.S. 478, 86 S.Ct. 1630, where the Chief Justice, after referring to "the compelling atmosphere inherent in the process of in-custody interrogation" and just before a second and slightly altered affirmation of the test, inserted a footnote reading:

> The distinction and its significance has been aptly described in the opinion of a Scottish court [in 1954];
> "In former times such questioning, if undertaken, would be conducted by police officers visiting the house or place of business of the suspect and there questioning him, probably in the presence of a relation or friend. However convenient the modern practice [of interrogation at the police station] may be, it must normally create a situation very unfavourable to the suspect."

Even without the light of *Orozco* we would not have thought this to mean that questioning in the home could never come within the mandate of *Miranda*; we do think it suggests that in the absence of actual arrest something must be said or done by the authorities, either in their manner of approach or in the tone or extent of their questioning, which indicates that they would not have heeded a request to depart or to allow the suspect to do so. This is not to say that the amount of information possessed by the police, and the consequent acuity of their "focus," is irrelevant. The more cause for believing the suspect committed the crime, the greater the tendency to bear down in interrogation and to create the kind of atmosphere of significant restraint that triggers *Miranda*, and *vice versa*. But this is simply one circumstance, to be weighed with all the others.

The *Gibson* case [392 F.2d 373 (4th Cir. 1968)] is closer to this one than any other we have found. There the West Virginia police had received information that Gibson was driving a stolen car with Indiana license plates bearing a designated number. They located the car outside a bar where Gibson was seated. An officer invited him outside and asked whether the car was his; after initial denial, he admitted it was and produced a registration which showed alteration. The police then arrested him and gave the warnings. Writing for the court, Judge Sobeloff did "not read *Miranda* as requiring officers to preface with a warning all non-coercive questioning conducted in the course of a routine investigation as in the circumstances of this case. . . . In the complete absence of the element of coercion, actual or potential, or police dominance of the individual's will, the mild police activity shown here should not prevent the introduction of statements freely made." While the instant case is a bit stronger for the defendant in the restricted size of his quarters, the number of officers present, and the somewhat more extensive questioning, these factors must be weighed against the point that the only piece of information the agents then had was the presence of Hall's car near the scene and at the time of the robbery. Although this was suspicious, it could have been thought susceptible of innocent explanation, especially since Hall's work apparently often took him near Syracuse.

It is altogether too easy to fall into the error of allowing the first seventeen minutes of interrogation to be significantly colored by what developed later. The picture presented to us is one of F.B.I. agents conscientiously interviewing a man, engaged in a respectable occupation, who was under considerable suspicion but whom they knew they could not lawfully arrest, and sedulously abstaining from any threat that they would. We have no reason to believe the agents would not have departed on request or allowed Hall to do so—as indeed they did the next morning when he indicated a desire to see his lawyer—although they might well have kept him under surveillance. It is immaterial that if Hall had attempted to bolt, thereby furnishing added evidence of guilt, the agents would doubtless have restrained him.

BECKWITH v. UNITED STATES

Supreme Court of the United States, 1976.
425 U.S. 341, 96 S.Ct. 1612.

MR. CHIEF JUSTICE BURGER delivered the opinion of the Court.

The important issue presented in this case is whether a special agent of the Internal Revenue Service, investigating potential criminal income tax violations, must, in an interview with a taxpayer, not in custody, give the warnings called for by this Court's decision in Miranda v. Arizona. . . . After a considerable amount of investigation, two special agents of the Intelligence Division of the Internal Revenue Service met with petitioner in a private home where petitioner occasionally stayed. The senior agent testified that they went to see petitioner at this private residence at 8 a. m. in order to spare petitioner the possible embarrassment of being interviewed at his place of employment which opened at 10 a. m. Upon their arrival, they identified themselves to the person answering the door and asked to speak to petitioner. The agents were invited into the house and, when petitioner entered the room where they were waiting, they introduced themselves and, according to the testimony of the senior agent, Beckwith then excused himself for a period in excess of five minutes, to finish dressing. Petitioner then sat down at the dining room table with the agents; they presented their credentials and stated they were attached to the Intelligence Division and that one of their functions was to investigate the possibility of criminal tax fraud. They then informed petitioner that they were assigned to investigate his federal income tax liability for the years 1966 through 1971. The senior agent then read to petitioner from a printed card the following:

> "As a special agent, one of my functions is to investigate the possibility of criminal violations of the Internal Revenue laws, and related offenses.

> "Under the Fifth Amendment to the Constitution of the United States, I cannot compel you to answer any questions or to submit any information if such answers or information might tend to incriminate you in any way. I also advise you that anything which you say and any information which you submit may be used against you in any criminal proceeding which may be undertaken. I advise you further that you may, if you wish, seek the assistance of an attorney before responding."

Petitioner acknowledged that he understood his rights. The agents then interviewed him until about 11 o'clock. The agents described the conversation as "friendly" and "relaxed." The petitioner noted that the agents did not "press" him on any question he could not or chose not to answer.

Prior to the conclusion of the interview, the senior agent requested that petitioner permit the agents to inspect certain records. Petitioner indicated that they were at his place of employment. The agents asked if they could meet him there later. Traveling separately from petitioner the agents met petitioner approximately 45 minutes later and the senior agent advised the petitioner that he was not required to furnish any books or records; petitioner, however, supplied the books to the agents. . . .

. . . The Court of Appeals affirmed the judgment of conviction. 510 F.2d 741 (1975). It noted that the reasoning of *Miranda* was based "in crucial part" on whether the suspect " 'has been taken into custody or otherwise deprived of his freedom in any significant way.' ", and agreed with the District Court that "Beckwith was neither arrested nor detained against his will." We agree with the analysis of the Court of Appeals and, therefore, affirm its judgment.

Petitioner contends that the "entire starting point" for the criminal prosecution brought against him secured from his own statements and disclosures during the interview with the Internal Revenue Agents from the Intelligence Division. He correctly points out that cases are assigned to the Intelligence Division only when there is some indication of criminal fraud and that, especially since tax offenses rarely result in pretrial custody, the taxpayer is clearly the "focus" of a criminal investigation when a matter is assigned to the Intelligence Division. Given the complexity of the tax structure and the confusion on the part of taxpayers between the civil and criminal function of the Internal Revenue Service, such a confrontation, argues petitioner, places the taxpayer under "psychological restraints" which are the functional, and, therefore, the legal equivalent of custody. In short we agree with Chief Judge Bazelon speaking for a unanimous Court of Appeals, that:

> "[t]he major thrust of Beckwith's argument is that the principle of *Miranda* should be extended to cover interrogation in non-custodial circumstances after a police investigation has focused on the suspect."

With the Court of Appeals, we "are not impressed with this argument in the abstract nor as applied to the particular facts of Beckwith's interrogation." Ibid. It goes far beyond the reasons for that holding and such an extension of the *Miranda* requirements would cut this Court's holding in that case completely loose from its own explicitly stated rationale. The narrow issue before the Court in *Miranda* was presented very precisely in the opening paragraph of that opinion—"the admissibility of statements obtained from an individual who is subjected to *custodial* police interrogation." 384 U.S., at 439, 86 S.Ct. at 1609. (Emphasis supplied.) The Court concluded that compulsion "is inherent in custodial surroundings," and, consequently, that special safeguards were required in the case of "incommunicado interrogation of individuals in a police-dominated atmosphere, resulting in self-incrimination statements without full warnings of constitutional rights." In subsequent decisions, the Court specifically stressed that it was the *custodial* nature of the interrogation which triggered the necessity for adherence in the specific requirements of its *Miranda* holding. Orozco v. Texas, 394 U.S. 324, 89 S.Ct. 1095 (1969); Mathis v. United States, 391 U.S. 1, 88 S.Ct. 1503 (1968).

Petitioner's argument that he was placed in the functional and, therefore, legal equivalent of the *Miranda* situation asks us now to ignore completely that *Miranda* was grounded squarely in the Court's explicit and detailed assessment of the peculiar "nature and setting of . . . in-custody interrogation." That courts of appeals have so read *Miranda* is suggested by Chief Judge Lumbard in United States v. Caiello, 420 F.2d 471, 473 (CA2 1969):

> "It was the compulsive aspect of custodial interrogation, and not the strength or content of the government's suspicions at the time the questioning was conducted, which led the court to impose the *Miranda* requirements with regard to custodial questioning."

* * *

An interview with government agents in a situation such as the one shown by this record simply does not present the elements which the *Miranda* Court found so inherently coercive as to require its holding. Although the "focus" of an investigation may indeed have been on Beckwith at the time of the interview in the sense that it was his tax liability which was under scrutiny, he hardly found himself in the custodial situation described by the *Miranda* Court as the basis for its holding. *Miranda* specifically defined "focus," for its purposes, as "questioning initiated by law enforcement officers *after* a person has been taken into custody or otherwise deprived of his freedom of action in any significant way." It may well be true, as petitioner contends that the "starting point" for the criminal prosecution was the information obtained from petitioner and the records exhibited by him. But this amounts to no more than saying that a tax return signed by a taxpayer can be the "starting point" for a prosecution.

We recognize, of course, that non-custodial interrogation might possibly in some situations, by virtue of some special circumstances, be characterized as one where "the behavior of . . . law enforcement officials was such as to overbear petitioner's will to resist and bring about confessions not freely self-determined . . . .." When such a claim is raised, it is the duty of an appellate court, including this Court, "to examine the entire record and make an independent determination of the ultimate issue of voluntariness." Proof that some kind of warnings were given or that none were given would be relevant evidence only on the issue of whether the questioning was in fact coercive. In the present case, however, as Chief Judge Bazelon noted, "[t]he entire interview was free of coercion."

MR. JUSTICE STEVENS took no part in the consideration or decision of this case.

MR. JUSTICE MARSHALL, concurring in the judgment.

While the Internal Revenue Service agents in this case did not give petitioner the full warnings prescribed in *Miranda* they did give him [some] warning before questioning him.

*   *   *

Under the circumstances of this case, in which petitioner was not under arrest and the interview took place in a private home where petitioner occasionally stayed, the warning recited above satisfied the requirements of the Fifth Amendment. If this warning had not been given, however, I would not join the judgment of the Court.

MR. JUSTICE BRENNAN, dissenting.

I respectfully dissent. In my view the District Court should have granted petitioner's motion to suppress all statements made by him to the agents because the agents did not give petitioner the warnings mandated by *Miranda* . . . The fact that Beckwith had not been taken into formal "custody" is not determinative of the question whether the agents were required to give him the *Miranda* warnings. I agree with the Court of Appeals for the Seventh Circuit that the warnings are also mandated when the taxpayer is, as here, interrogated by Intelligence Division agents of the Internal Revenue Service in the surroundings where, as in the case of the subject in "custody," the practical compulsion to respond to questions about his tax returns is comparable to the psychological pressures described in *Miranda*. United States v. Dickerson, 413 F.2d 1111 (1969); United States v. Oliver, 505 F.2d 301 (1974). Interrogation under conditions that have the practical consequence of compelling the taxpayer to make disclosures, and interrogation in "custody" having the same consequence, are in my view peas from the same pod. *Oliver* states the analysis with which I agree and required suppression of Beckwith's statements:

> "The application of *Miranda* does not turn on such a simple axis as whether or not the suspect is in custody when he is being questioned. As the Court repeatedly indicated, the prescribed warnings are required if the defendant is in custody 'or otherwise deprived of his freedom of action in any significant way.' The fact of custody is emphasized in the [*Miranda*] opinion as having the practical consequence of compelling the accused to make disclosures. But the test also differentiates between the questioning of a mere witness and the interrogation of an accused for the purpose of securing his conviction; the test serves the purpose 'of determining when the adversary process has begun, i. e., when the investigative machinery of the government is directed toward the ultimate conviction of a particular individual and when, therefore, a suspect should be advised of his rights.'

> "Since the constitutional protection is expressly applicable to testimony in the criminal case itself, for the purpose

of determining when warnings are required, the *Miranda* analysis treats the adversary proceeding as though it commences when a prospective defendant is taken into custody or otherwise significantly restrained. After that point is reached, it is not unreasonable to treat any compelled disclosure as protected by the Fifth Amendment unless, of course, the constitutional protection has been waived. Adequate warnings, or the advice of counsel, are essential if such a waiver is to be effective.

"The requirement of warnings set forth in *Dickerson* rests on the same underlying rationale. While the commencement of adversary proceedings against Dickerson had not been marked by taking him into custody, the I.R.S., by assigning the matter to the Intelligence Division, had commenced the preparation of its criminal case. When the agents questioned him about his tax return, without clearly explaining their mission, the dual criminal-civil nature of an I.R.S. interrogation created three key misapprehensions for the taxpayer.

" 'Incriminating statements elicited in reliance upon the taxpayer's misapprehension as to *the nature of the inquiry, his obligation to respond,* and *the possible consequences of doing so* must be regarded as equally violative of constitutional protections as a custodial confession extracted without proper warnings.' 413 F.2d at 1116 (emphasis added).

"The practical effect of these misapprehensions during questioning of a taxpayer was to 'compel' him to provide information that could be used to obtain his conviction in a criminal tax fraud proceeding, in much the same way that placing a suspect under physical restraint leads to psychological compulsion. Thus, the misapprehensions are tantamount to the deprivation of the suspect's 'freedom of action in any significant way,' repeatedly referred to in *Miranda*."

I would reverse the judgment of conviction and remand to the District Court for a new trial.

OREGON v. MATHIASON

Supreme Court of the United States, 1977.
429 U.S. 492, 97 S.Ct. 711.

PER CURIAM:

Carl Mathiason was convicted of first-degree burglary after a bench trial in which his confession was critical to the State's case. At trial he moved to suppress the confession as the fruit of questioning by the police not preceded by the warnings required in Miranda v. Arizona (1966). The trial court refused to exclude the confession because it found that Mathiason was not in custody at the time of the confession.

The Oregon Court of Appeals affirmed but on review in the Supreme Court of Oregon that court by a divided vote reversed the conviction. It found that although Mathiason had not been arrested or otherwise formally detained, "the interrogation took place in a 'coercive environment'" of the sort to which Miranda was intended to apply. The court conceded that its holding was contrary to decisions in other jurisdictions, and referred in particular to People v. Yukl, 25 N.Y.2d 585, 256 N.E.2d 172 (1969). We think that court has read Miranda too broadly, and we therefore reverse its judgment.

The Supreme Court of Oregon described the factual situation surrounding the confession as follows:

"An officer of the State Police investigated a theft at a residence near Pendleton. He asked the lady of the house which had been burglarized if she suspected anyone. She replied that the defendant was the only one she could think of. The defendant was a parolee and a 'close associate' of her son. The officer tried to contact defendant on three or four occasions with no success. Finally, about 25 days after the burglary, the officer left his card at defendant's apartment with a note asking him to call because 'I'd like to discuss something with you.' The next afternoon the defendant did call. The officer asked where it would be convenient to meet. The defendant had no preference; so the officer asked if the defendant could meet him at the state patrol office in about an hour and a half, about 5:00 p. m. The patrol office was about two blocks from defendant's apartment. The building housed several state agencies.

"The officer met defendant in the hallway, shook hands and took him into an office. The defendant was told he was not under arrest. The door was closed. The two sat across a desk. The police radio in another room could be heard. The officer told defendant he wanted to talk to him about a burglary and that his truthfulness would possibly be considered by the district attorney or judge. The officer further advised that the police believed defendant was involved in the burglary and [falsely stated that] defendant's fingerprints were found at the scene. The defendant sat for a few minutes and then said he had taken the property. This occurred within five minutes after defendant had come to the office. The officer then advised defendant of his Miranda rights and took a taped confession.

"At the end of the taped conversation the officer told defendant he was not arresting him at this time; he was released to go about his job and return to his family. The officer said he was referring the case to the district attorney for him to determine whether criminal charges would be brought. It was 5:30 p. m. when the defendant left the office.

"The officer gave all the testimony relevant to this issue. The defendant did not take the stand either at the
hearing on the motion to suppress or at the trial."

The Supreme Court of Oregon reasoned from these facts that:

"We hold the interrogation took place in a 'coercive environment.' The parties were in the offices of the State Police; they were alone behind closed doors; the officer informed the defendant he was a suspect in a theft and the
authorities had evidence incriminating him in the crime;
and the defendant was a parolee under supervision. We are
of the opinion that this evidence is not overcome by the evidence that the defendant came to the office in response to a
request and was told he was not under arrest."

Our decision in Miranda set forth rules of police procedure applicable to "custodial interrogation." "By custodial interrogation, we
mean questioning initiated by law enforcement officers after a person
has been taken into custody or otherwise deprived of his freedom of
action in any significant way." Subsequently we have found the Miranda principle applicable to questioning which takes place in a prison setting during a suspect's term of imprisonment on a separate offense. Mathis v. United States, 391 U.S. 1, 88 S.Ct. 1503 (1968), and
to questioning taking place in a suspect's home, after he has been arrested and is no longer free to go where he pleases, Orozco v. Texas,
394 U.S. 324, 89 S.Ct. 1095 (1969).

In the present case, however, there is no indication that the questioning took place in a context where respondent's freedom to depart
was restricted in any way. He came voluntarily to the police station,
where he was immediately informed that he was not under arrest.
At the close of a one half-hour interview respondent did in fact leave
the police station without hindrance. It is clear from these facts that
Mathiason was not in custody "or otherwise deprived of his freedom
of action in any significant way."

Such a noncustodial situation is not converted to one in which
Miranda applies simply because a reviewing court concludes that,
even in the absence of any formal arrest or restraint on freedom of
movement, the questioning took place in a "coercive environment."
Any interview of one suspected of a crime by a police officer will
have coercive aspects to it, simply by virtue of the fact that the police
officer is part of a law enforcement system which may ultimately
cause the suspect to be charged with a crime. But police officers are
not required to administer Miranda warnings to everyone whom they
question. Nor is the requirement of warnings to be imposed simply
because the questioning takes place in the station house, or because
the questioned person is one whom the police suspect. Miranda
warnings are required only where there has been such a restriction
on a person's freedom as to render him "in custody." It was that
sort of coercive environment to which Miranda by its terms was
made applicable, and to which it is limited.

The officer's false statement about having discovered Mathiason's fingerprints at the scene was found by the Supreme Court of Oregon to be another circumstance contributing to the coercive environment which makes the Miranda rationale applicable. Whatever relevance this fact may have to other issues in the case, it has nothing to do with whether respondent was in custody for purposes of the Miranda rule.

The petition for certiorari is granted, the judgment of the Oregon Supreme Court is reversed, and the case is remanded for proceedings not inconsistent with this opinion.

Mr. Justice Brennan would grant the writ but dissents from the summary disposition and would set the case for oral argument.

Mr. Justice Marshall, dissenting.

* * *

. . . I recognize that Miranda is limited to custodial interrogations, but that is because, as we noted last Term, the facts in the Miranda cases raised only this "narrow issue." Beckwith v. United States. The rationale of Miranda, however, is not so easily cabined.

Miranda requires warnings to "combat" a situation in which there are "inherently compelling pressures which work to undermine the individual's will to resist and to compel him to speak where he would not otherwise do so freely." It is of course true, as the Court notes, that "[a]ny interview of one suspected of a crime by a police officer will have coercive aspects to it." But it does not follow that because police "are not required to administer Miranda warnings to everyone whom they question," that they need not administer warnings to *anyone*, unless the factual setting of the Miranda cases is replicated. Rather, faithfulness to Miranda requires us to distinguish situations that resemble the "coercive aspects" of custodial interrogation from those that more nearly resemble "[g]eneral on-the-scene questioning . . . or other general questioning of citizens in the fact-finding process" which Miranda states usually can take place without warnings.

In my view, even if respondent were not in custody, the coercive elements in the instant case were so pervasive as to require Miranda-type warnings.[1] Respondent was interrogated in "privacy" and in "unfamiliar surroundings," factors on which Miranda places great stress. The investigation had focused on respondent. And respondent was subjected to some of the "deceptive stratagems" which called forth the Miranda decision. I therefore agree with the Oregon Supreme Court that to excuse the absence of warnings given these facts is "contrary to the rationale expressed in Miranda."

---

1. I do not rule out the possibility that lesser warnings would suffice when a suspect is not in custody but is subjected to a highly coercive atmosphere. See, e. g., Beckwith v. United States, 425 U.S. 341, 348–349, 96 S.Ct. 1612 (1976) (Marshall, J., concurring in judgment); ALI, Model Code of Pre-Arraignment Procedure § 110.1(2) (Approved Draft 1975) (suspects interrogated at police station must be advised of their right to leave and right to consult with counsel, relatives, or friends).

The privilege against self-incrimination "has always been as 'broad as the mischief against which it seeks to guard.'" Miranda v. Arizona, quoting Counselman v. Hitchcock (1892). Today's decision means, however, that the Fifth Amendment privilege does not provide full protection against mischiefs equivalent to, but different from custodial interrogation. It is therefore important to note that the state courts remain free, in interpreting state constitutions, to guard against the evil clearly identified by this case.

(Dissent of MR. JUSTICE STEVENS omitted.)

NOTES

1. One of the central issues of *Miranda* is the scope of the phrase "custodial interrogation". It is and will always be a complex issue simply because the termination of whether interrogation is "custodial" depends upon a consideration of many circumstances. However, the frequency of cases in which the issue arises has diminished with the passage of time. The issue was of great significance initially because many interrogations conducted prior to *Miranda* were being judged against *Miranda* standards. Since adequate warnings were rarely given, the only issue for the court to consider was whether the interrogation was custodial. In time, as the police established a practice of warning, the issues shifted to the adequacy of warning and waiver. The issue of custody will always be the subject of some opinions, for as often as the police may give warnings, they will not, nor can they be expected to invoke a warning and waiver process lasting from thirty seconds to a minute or more every time and every place they ask a citizen a question.

2. The *Hall* case deals with the intermesh of notions of focus and custody prior to the decisions in *Beckwith* and *Mathiason*. The attention given to the problem has been substantial and the consequences of adopting one or another view has a significant effect on the outcome of cases.

In the leading case of Lowe v. United States, 407 F.2d 1391 (9th Cir. 1969), it was held that the "Court's decision in *Miranda* clearly abandoned 'focus of investigation' as a test to determine when rights attach in confession cases." In essence, the *Lowe* court held that it does not matter what the officer knew about the defendant's guilt or what the officer intended to do with defendant so long as the officer did nothing to make the defendant believe he was in custody.

In line with this reasoning the majority of courts have generally held that (1) the fact an officer knows the suspect committed the crime, or (2) intends to arrest the suspect at the end of the interview, or (3) would not allow the suspect to leave if he tried, does *not* require that *Miranda* warnings be given if the interview is not otherwise custodial. People v. Hazel, 252 Cal.App.2d 412, 60 Cal.Rptr. 437 (1967); People v. Rodney P., 21 N.Y. 2d 1, 286 N.Y.S.2d 225, 233 N.E.2d 255 (1967); State v. Sandoval, 92 Idaho 853, 452 P.2d 350 (1969). In essence, the courts have regarded the intent or knowledge of the officer as irrelevant so long as it is unvoiced, i. e., not stated to the suspect. Allen v. United States, 390 F.2d 476 (D.C.Cir.1968); State v. Crossen, 10 Or.App. 442, 499 P.2d 1357 (1972); United States v. Davis, 259 F.Supp. 496 (1st Cir. 1966) (defendant unaware of arrest warrant in possession of interrogator). In these cases the courts held that intent of the interrogating officer is unimportant. See United States v. Charpentier, 438 F.2d 721 (10th Cir. 1971); United States v. Jaskiewich,

433 F.2d 415 (3rd Cir. 1970); United States v. Squeri, 398 F.2d 785 (2nd Cir. 1968). The most striking example of this interpretation of *Miranda* is People v. Allen, 28 A.D.2d 724, 281 N.Y.S.2d 602 (1967). There an officer with probable cause to arrest and an intention to arrest went to the suspect's home and questioned him in the presence of his family without telling him he was under arrest. After the conversation the suspect was arrested. The court held that warnings were not required.

The courts which adhere generally to the view that the focus concept is to be discarded have formulated an "objective" test of custody, i. e., whether under the circumstances of the case, a reasonable man would believe himself to be in custody. The key phrase is a "reasonable" belief on the part of the "reasonable" suspect. The mere subjective assertion of a suspect that he considered himself under arrest is not enough. Freije v. United States, 408 F.2d 100 (1st Cir 1969); People v. Morse, 70 Cal.2d 711, 76 Cal.Rptr. 391, 452 P.2d 607 (1969). Extraordinary frailties and sensitivities of the individual are not relevant. People v. Rodney P., 21 N.Y.2d 1, 286 N.Y.S.2d 225, 233 N.E.2d 255 (1969) holds that the issue is "not what the defendant thought but rather what a *reasonable man, innocent of any crime*, would have thought had he been in the defendant's position." Also, to the same effect: People v. Yukl, 25 N.Y.2d 585, 589, 307 N.Y.S.2d 857, 859, 256 N.E.2d 172, 174 (1969).

Under the objective test, the court in People v. Arnold, 66 Cal.2d 438, 58 Cal.Rptr. 415, 426 P.2d 515 (1967) refused to accept the simple assertion of a suspect who said she thought she had no alternative but to appear for questioning. The court asked the trial court to consider "the precise language used by the deputy district attorney in summoning Mrs. Arnold to his office, . . . any statements of the deputy not transcribed, made before or after formal interrogation and . . . the physical surroundings . . . the extent to which the authorities confronted defendant with evidence of her guilt, the pressures exerted to detain defendant and any other circumstances which might have led defendant reasonably to believe that she could not leave freely." The application of the objective test was well analyzed in Cummins v. State, 27 Md.App. 361, 341 A.2d 294 (1975).

At the other end of the spectrum are those courts which have used focus as the definitive test. Those courts reasoned that custody arose at the latest when the officer has probable cause to arrest. See Campbell v. Superior Court, 106 Ariz. 542, 479 P.2d 685 (1971) (when officer determines arrest is to be made); People v. Orf, 172 Colo. 253, 472 P.2d 123 (1970) (little doubt in the officer's mind that they had the offender); State v. Kinn, 288 Minn. 31, 178 N.W.2d 888 (1970) (when the officer determines to take the suspect into custody); Windsor v. United States, 389 F.2d 530 (5th Cir. 1968).

Most jurisdictions which initially decided some cases on focus tests have abandoned or modified them with the passage of time. Compare People v. Ridley, 396 Mich. 603, 242 N.W.2d 402 (1976), with People v. Martin, 78 Mich.App. 518, 260 N.W.2d 869 (1977), and see People v. Parada, 188 Colo. 230, 533 P.2d 1121 (1975). Also see State v. Bainch, 109 Ariz. 77, 505 P.2d 248 (1973); McMillian v. United States, 399 F.2d 458 (5th Cir. 1968).

After *Beckwith* and *Mathiason*, few cases have continued to place reliance upon focus as a factor, but see United States v. Del Saccorro Castro De Graulau, 573 F.2d 213 (5th Cir. 1978).

The arguments against a pure focus test were stated in United States v. Hall. The focus cases have also been criticised for ignoring the implication in Hoffa v. United States, 385 U.S. 293, 309–10, 87 S.Ct. 408 (1966), that whether the police have probable cause has no relevance to when the right of a suspect to receive warnings attaches. In *Hoffa,* an informer in Hoffa's group recorded several conversations in which the informer participated and which constituted evidence of jury tampering. In answer to the contention that when the informer and the Government had probable cause to arrest Hoffa, they should have done so instead of continuing to participate in additional conversations, the Court said:

> "Law enforcement officers are under no constitutional duty to call a halt to a criminal investigation the moment they have the minimum evidence to establish probable cause, a quantum of evidence which may fall short of the amount necessary to support a criminal conviction."

Judge Friendly's opinion in the *Hall* case suggests at least one reason why the pure focus test was applied in some cases. He notes that in *Hall* both sides accepted implicitly the focus test and spent their argument on the issue of whether focus was present. It is this dereliction of counsel to apprehend the issues that may account for a good number of judicial opinions which become the subject of criticism with the passage of time.

Does the custody test (and a fair reading of *Miranda*) permit what has been termed a "tactical" interrogation? This is a "designed" noncustodial interview conducted with an individual who is known or suspected of having committed a crime. The purpose of the interview is to secure damaging evidence. In this connection it is worthwhile to consider the words of Chief Justice Weintraub in dealing with a *Miranda* problem, in State v. McKnight, 52 N.J. 35, 52–53, 243 A.2d 240 (1968):

> "There is no right to escape detection. There is no right to commit a perfect crime or to an equal opportunity to that end. The Constitution is not at all offended when a guilty man stubs his toe. On the contrary, it is decent to hope that he will. Nor is it dirty business to use evidence a defendant himself may furnish in the detectional stage. . . . As to the culprit who reveals his guilt unwittingly with no intent to shed his inner burden, it is no more unfair to use the evidence he thereby reveals than it is to turn against him clues at the scene of the crime which a brighter, better informed or more gifted criminal would not have left. . . . It is consonant with good morals and the Constitution to exploit a criminal's ignorance or stupidity in the detectional process."

3. What facts and circumstances are weighed by the courts in determining custody? A summary of the rules follows.

(a) Place of Interrogation

The place of interrogation is a vital, but not conclusive factor. See 31 A.L.R.3d 656. Usually the cases evince a concern with the location of the interrogation but the physical circumstances of the room in which the interrogation takes place is significant. United States v. Lackey, 413 F.2d 655 (7th Cir. 1969) (small room); People v. Bryant, 87 Ill.App.2d 238, 231 N. E.2d 4 (1967) (closed room); State v. Seefeldt, 51 N.J. 472, 242 A.2d 322 (1968) (law library in prosecutor's office).

In all three of the cases decided along with *Miranda*, the suspect was questioned in a police station after arrest, and usually police station interrogation is custodial. Nevertheless, it is clear that interrogation inside what one Court has called "buildings housing law enforcement personnel" (Evans v. United States, 377 F.2d 535 (5th Cir. 1967)) is not necessarily custodial.

Oregon v. Mathiason found a station house interrogation to be non-custodial. Occasionally other courts conclude that a person can legitimately be said to have been invited to the station. Hicks v. United States, 382 F.2d 158 (D.C.Cir.1967); Thompson v. United States, 382 F.2d 390 (9th Cir. 1967). Compare, however, Commonwealth v. Brown, 473 Pa. 562, 375 A.2d 1260 (1977), which rejected the invitation claim upon the particular case facts.

In addition to these kinds of cases the courts have held police station interrogation to be non-custodial when the person questioned is present as a witness. Clark v. United States, 400 F.2d 83 (9th Cir. 1968) (two drivers in an accident; both brought into station for report); People v. Pugliese, 26 N.Y.2d 478, 311 N.Y.S.2d 851, 260 N.E.2d 499 (1970) (defendant was a complainant of whom police were suspicious and who was asked to give an oath). There are cases in which the defendant walks into the station essentially on his own initiative. In People v. Hill, 70 Cal.2d 678, 76 Cal.Rptr. 225, 452 P.2d 329 (1969), the defendant called the police station and volunteered some information concerning a crime; he then offered to and did come to the police station and gave a statement. The questioning was held to be non-custodial. Questioning in police vehicles is also common and where the presence of the person interrogated is clearly a result of invitation the questioning has been held non-custodial. State v. Caha, 184 Neb. 70, 165 N.W.2d 362 (1969); Wussow v. State, 507 S.W.2d 792 (Tex.Cr.App.1974) (a request to sit in a police car does not create custody when the alternative is to stand in a heavy rain). Police car questioning, however, has usually been characterized as custodial. State v. Saunders, 102 Ariz. 565, 435 P.2d 39 (1969); Myers v. State, 3 Md.App. 534, 240 A.2d 288 (1968).

In Mathis v. United States, 391 U.S. 1, 88 S.Ct. 1503 (1968) the Court, by a vote of 5–3, reversed the Fifth Circuit Court and held that one who was incarcerated in a penitentiary for one offense was in custody for purposes of interrogation conducted by I.R.S. agents with respect to another offense. Indeed the general rule is that if the suspect is in jail he is in custody for purposes of any interrogation.

In Commonwealth v. O'Toole, 351 Mass. 627, 223 N.E.2d 87 (1967), aff'd on habeas corpus sub. nom. O'Toole v. Scafati, 386 F.2d 168 (1st Cir. 1968), cert. denied 390 U.S. 385, 88 S.Ct. 1109, the defendant was the City Manager of Revere, Massachusetts. He was the principal suspect in a rather large series of misappropriations of city funds. Defendant was aware of this fact. He was asked to come to the Office of the District Attorney. The Assistant District Attorney asked for an explanation of certain records and disbursements. The defendant's explanations were used against him at his trial. The court held that the failure of the prosecutor to warn O'Toole of his rights was irrelevant. O'Toole was not in custody in the prosecutor's office nor was he brought there under arrest. Under these circumstances the interrogation was held to be non-custodial under *Miranda*. The courts have regarded interrogations in prosecutor's office with a fair degree of willingness to find them non-custodial. State v. Seefeldt, 51 N.J. 472, 242 A.2d 322 (1968).

Ordinarily interrogation in a suspect's home is not custodial, but this principle is not absolute. In Orozco v. Texas, 394 U.S. 324, 89 S.Ct. 1095

(1969), a suspect was questioned at 4 a. m. in his bedroom by four officers, one of whom testified that the suspect was under arrest. The Court held that the suspect was the subject of custodial interrogation even though the questioning was brief and took place in his own bedroom. Of course, the key factors were the time of the interrogation (at 4 a. m., and after the officers were told defendant was asleep), the number of officers, and the evidence of formal arrest (though this is unclear).

Most cases of interrogation at homes involve less severe circumstances, and generally the holding is that questioning a suspect in his own home without arrest is not custodial interrogation. State v. Craney, 381 A.2d 630 (Me.1978); People v. Blovin, 80 Cal.App.3d 269, 145 Cal.Rptr. 701 (1978); United States v. Agy, 374 F.2d 94 (6th Cir. 1967); United States v. Kubik, 266 F.Supp. 501 (S.D.Iowa, 1967) (defendant questioned *several times* at his own home); People v. Allen, 28 App.Div.2d 724, 281 N.Y.S.2d 602 (1967), (defendant questioned at home in the presence of family by officers who intended to arrest him after the interview was over); People v. Rodney P., 21 N.Y.2d 1, 286 N.Y.S.2d 225, 233 N.E.2d 255 (1967) (defendant was questioned in his back yard); People v. Miller, 71 Cal.2d 459, 78 Cal. Rptr. 449, 455 P.2d 377 (1969) (the questioning of defendant in his front yard was non-custodial although the officer suspected the defendant to be involved in what turned out to be a homicide); Virgin Islands v. Berne, 412 F.2d 1055 (3rd Cir. 1969) (officers questioned a man who they strongly suspected committed rape—he was questioned at his home and surrendered some clothes from the trunk of his car—this was held non-custodial). Questioning of a person at his friend's or relative's home is also generally ruled non-custodial. Steigler v. Superior Court, 252 A.2d 300 (Del.1969) (neighbor's home); People v. Rogers, 14 Mich.App. 207, 165 N.W.2d 337 (1968) (grandmother's house). There have been a few, but very few cases in which custodial interrogation was held to have occurred in the suspect's home. These cases have arisen, however, from special circumstances; for instance, People v. Paulin, 61 Misc.2d 289, 305 N.Y.S.2d 607, aff'd 25 N.Y. 2d 445, 306 N.Y.S.2d 929, 255 N.E.2d 164 (1970) ("police dominated" atmosphere).

Interrogation of a suspect in his place of business is usually considered non-custodial. As in the case of homes, the place of business represents a familiar surrounding. United States v. Gallagher, 430 F.2d 1222 (7th Cir. 1970) (suspect's law office); Brown v. State, 278 A.2d 462 (D.C.App.1971) (postal employee questioned at place of employment); People v. Snow, 39 Ill.App.3d 887, 350 N.E.2d 875 (1976) (school employee at school). But see United States v. Nash, 563 F.2d 1166 (5th Cir. 1977) (bank clerk interrogated in bank security office).

The rationale of familiar surroundings applicable to questioning in homes and offices does not invariably apply when the interrogation occurs in a restaurant or bar. However, the usual view in such cases is that the interrogation is not custodial. This result is due to the fact that the suspect is, if not in a completely familiar place, at least in a place of his own choosing. Another significant factor is the lack of isolation from the outside world and the distinct absence of police station atmosphere. See Lucas v. United States, 408 F.2d 835 (9th Cir. 1969) (night club); United States v. Messina, 388 F.2d 393 (2nd Cir. 1968) (park bench and restaurant).

The questioning of persons at government offices presents a situation in which the rationale of familiar surroundings is inapplicable (except for the employees at the office). Nevertheless, the courts have usually construed such questioning as non-custodial. Support for these rulings is found in the fact that the offices in question do not create a "police domi- nated' atmosphere. Often the personnel asking the questions have no pow- er of arrest and the questions asked are few. Further, the decided cases deal with draft resisters and the courts probably tend to view the state- ments of such persons as volunteered in spirit, if not in fact. See United States v. Holmes, 387 F.2d 781 (7th Cir. 1967); Fults v. United States, 395 F.2d 852 (10th Cir. 1968); United States v. Hamlin, 432 F.2d 905 (8th Cir. 1970) (suspect appeared uninvited at a postal inspector's office to discuss his new brochure; the discussion turned to inquiries the postal inspector's office had received; thereafter there were several meetings at which sus- pect was cooperative; *Miranda* held inapplicable).

Questioning of a suspect who is confined in a hospital as a patient, but who is not under arrest, is often held not to be custodial interrogation. State v. District Court, 150 Mont. 128, 432 P.2d 93 (1967) (Sheriff ques- tioned prime suspect in murder who was confined as a private patient in a hospital); People v. Gilbert, 8 Mich.App. 393, 154 N.W.2d 800 (1967) (Po- lice in hospital questioned a defendant walking around the emergency room who was involved in an auto accident and whose breath smelled of liquor); State v. Zucconi, 50 N.J. 361, 235 A.2d 193 (1967) (defendant involved in a fatal auto accident and the principal evidence against him were his admis- sions on two separate occasions to an interrogating State Trooper that he was driving the car; the court said, "defendant never was in the custody of the police nor was he deprived of his freedom by authorities. The question- ing here took place in defendant's hospital room and at his home, surround- ings totally lacking in the compelling atmosphere inherent in the process of in-custody interrogation". On the other hand hospital interviews have of- ten been held custodial in nature. See People v. Braun, 98 Ill.App.2d 5, 241 N.E.2d 25 (1968) (suspect informed that officers had a ticket for him); People v. Tanner, 31 App.Div.2d 148, 295 N.Y.S.2d 709 (1968) (relay ques- tioning); Shedrick v. State, 10 Md.App. 579, 271 A.2d 773 (1970) (suspect at hospital is considered in custody when, aware of the victim's poor condi- tion, he was questioned in a small room by two officers).

Although most cases in which a suspect is questioned in his automobile are usually resolved on the theory that a traffic stop does not constitute custody, there are some cases that emphasize the fact that a suspect in his own car is in familiar surroundings. Under either rationale these cases generally find a lack of custody. Williams v. United States, 381 F.2d 20 (9th Cir. 1967) (defendant stopped his car himself at a border station); Cornish v. State, 6 Md.App. 167, 251 A.2d 23 (1969) (suspect stopped car on his own volition); State v. Miller, 35 Wis.2d 454, 151 N.W.2d 157 (1967) (suspect was driving his car to the police station with a policeman as passenger). Contra: People v. McFall, 259 Cal.App.2d 172, 66 Cal.Rptr. 277 (1968); People v. Ceccone, 260 Cal.App.2d 886, 67 Cal.Rptr. 499 (1968).

In *Miranda* the Court said that its decision was "not intended to ham- per the traditional function of police officers in investigating crime . . . General on-the-scene questioning as to facts surrounding a crime or other general questioning of citizens in the fact finding process is not affected by our holding. It is an act of responsible citizenship for individu- als to give whatever information they may have to aid in law enforcement. In such situations the compelling atmosphere inherent in the process of in- custody interrogation is not necessarily present." Accordingly, questioning of a suspect prior to arrest near the scene of crime is not custodial interrogation: Laury v. State, 260 A.2d 907 (Del.1969) (accosting suspect at robbery scene); Nevels v. State, 216 So.2d 529 (Miss.1968) (at the end of chase and search); People v. Schwartz, 30 App.Div.2d 385, 292 N.Y.S.2d 518 (1968) (two questions of persons leaving scene of reported assault); State v. Largo, 24 Utah 2d 430, 473 P.2d 895 (1970) (interrogation at school of sixty boys concerning incident where some boys invaded a girl's dormitory and raped one girl); Jordan v. Commonwealth, 216 Va. 768, 222 S.E.2d 573 (1976). Several cases have reached the same conclusion with respect to questioning at the scene of an automobile accident. People v. Routt, 100 Ill.App.2d 388, 241 N.E.2d 206 (1968); State v. Desjardins, 110 N.H. 511, 272 A.2d 599 (1970) (inquiry as to who operated vehicle). The most commonly reported instance of on-the-scene questioning involves homicides: Tate v. State, 219 Tenn. 698, 413 S.W.2d 366 (1967) (the defendant shot his boss at the office and his defense at trial was self-defense. Officers testified that they arrived on the scene and asked who did the shooting. In the presence of others, defendant said that he did. The officers asked why and he said because the boss was firing him from his job. This questioning was held to be within the scope of general investigation). See also Bell v. State, 442 S.W.2d 716 (Tex.Crim.App.1969) ("what happened?"); Ison v. State, 281 Ala. 189, 200 So.2d 511 (1967) ("Did you shoot him?"); Weissinger v. State, 218 So.2d 432 (Miss.1969) ("Where is the gun?").

The crime scene situation as well as several others, i. e., street encounters, traffic stops, and stop and frisk often involve an officer who will testify that if the suspect had tried to leave, the officer would have stopped him. This does not usually create a custodial situation so long as such an intent to stop is unvoiced. Can it be argued that, even if the officer at the scene of a crime asks one or more persons to remain at the scene, this should not be thought to establish custody? The Court in *Miranda* referred to deprivation "of freedom of action in any significant way" and declared that its opinion did not apply to "general on-the-scene" interviews, and that "it is an act of responsibile citizenship" for persons to give information to the police. Did the Court envision the brief retention of all potential witnesses at the scene of a crime and exclude this kind of interviewing from *Miranda*? Would an ordinary innocent person directed by an officer not to leave the scene of a crime consider himself in custody or under arrest? See People v. Garrison, 491 P.2d 971 (Colo.1971); Arnold v. United States, 382 F.2d 4 (9th Cir. 1967).

Another form of general on-the-scene questioning occurs when an officer makes inquiries of persons on the public ways under suspicious circumstances. See United States v. Thomas, 396 F.2d 310 (2nd Cir. 1968) (Suspect prowling in railroad yard); United States v. Diaz, 427 F.2d 636 (1st Cir. 1970) (request for identification from a hitchhiker); People v. Cartwright, 26 Mich.App. 687, 182 N.W.2d 811 (1970) (two persons stopped in the vicinity of a break-in); United States v. Owens, 431 F.2d 349 (5th Cir. 1970) (where an officer simply finds someone he is seeking on the street and there makes inquiries of him; the incident is non-custodial in nature); State v. Mitchell, 35 Or.App. 809, 583 P.2d 14 (1978); State v. Webster, 20 Wash.App. 128, 579 P.2d 985 (1978). The basic premise underlying these decisions is that the officers were confronted with suspicious circumstances which could have been resolved with an explanation from the person questioned. The absence of a custodial atmosphere is significant but the investigative nature of the encounter is foremost. Of course, under certain circumstances street and scene encounters may be deemed custodial. See Allen v. United States, 404 F.2d 1335 (D.C.Cir.1968); State v. Shoffner, 31 Wis.

2d 412, 143 N.W.2d 458 (1966); United States v. Ward, 488 F.2d 162 (9th Cir. en banc, 1973).

(b) Time of Interrogation

The intrusion of police in the early morning hours to make inquiries would create serious doubts as to whether an ordinary man would consider himself in custody. (Consider Orozco v. Texas, 394 U.S. 324, 89 S.Ct. 1095 (1969).) Of course, on the scene questioning shortly after the commission of a crime may permissibly take place at odd hours, but seeking out someone some distance away from the scene, as was done in *Orozco*, may create a custodial situation.

(c) The Persons Present at the Interrogation

The language of *Miranda* evinces concern for a suspect "cut off from the outside world". It follows that the presence of friends or neutrals at an interview is a fact of some relevance. Accordingly, several courts have considered the presence of friends as indicative of non-custody. Archer v. United States, 393 F.2d 124 (5th Cir. 1968) (suspect's husband); United States v. Manni, 270 F.Supp. 103 (D.Mass.1967), aff'd 391 F.2d 922 (1st Cir. 1968) (suspect's wife); People v. Butterfield, 258 Cal.App.2d 586, 65 Cal.Rptr. 765 (1968) (suspect's mother); State v. Davis, 157 N.W.2d 907 (Iowa 1968) (doctor and nurses). By the same token the deliberate removal of a suspect from the presence of his family and friends tends to support a finding of custody. Commonwealth v. Sites, 427 Pa. 486, 235 A.2d 387 (1967). Cf. Pemberton v. Peyton, 288 F.Supp. 920 (E.D.Va.1968) (driving a suspect 65 miles to give him a Polygraph, and then interrogation without Polygraph). The "balance of power" may also be significant in cases where the sheer number of police is inferential of police dominated atmosphere. See People v. Paulin, 61 Misc.2d 289, 305 N.Y.S.2d 607 (1969), aff'd 308 N. Y.S.2d 883, 33 App.Div.2d 105 (1969), aff'd 25 N.Y.2d 445, 306 N.Y.S.2d 929, 255 N.E.2d 164 (1969). Presumably the reverse is true and the officer who is significantly outnumbered by suspects or a suspect's friends may be found to have conducted a non-custodial interview. See People v. Robinson, 22 Mich.App. 124, 177 N.W.2d 234 (1970) (single officer). The fact that the interviewer is a uniformed policeman does not render the interview, per se, custodial. State v. Hall, 12 Ariz.App. 147, 468 P.2d 598 (1970); State v. Meunier, 126 Vt. 176, 224 A.2d 922 (1966). Nor does a large number of officers. United States v. Calhoun, 363 A.2d 277 (D.C.App.1976). But the presence of a uniformed officer has been considered as one circumstance supporting a finding of custody. People v. Bliss, 53 Misc.2d 472, 278 N.Y. S.2d 732 (1967).

(d) Indicia of Arrest

The courts have generally recognized that the existence of physical restraint is a significant factor in determining questions of custody. The absence of physical restraint has led several courts to the conclusion that the defendant was not under arrest or in custody. United States v. Fiorillo, 376 F.2d 180 (2nd Cir. 1967) (telephone conversation with suspect); People v. Merchant, 260 Cal.App.2d 875, 67 Cal.Rptr. 459 (1968) (police asked questions from outside locked screen door). But the absence of physical restraint does not automatically require a finding of non-custody. United States v. Bekowies, 432 F.2d 9 (9th Cir. 1970). The existence of physical restraint has almost invariably led to a finding of custody. United States v. Averell, 296 F.Supp. 1004 (S.D.N.Y.1969) (handcuffing); State v. Saunders, 102 Ariz. 565, 435 P.2d 39 (1967) (officer placed his hand on suspect's arm and led him to patrol car). The courts also recognize that in certain cases restraint may be non-physical in nature, but the drawing of lines is not simple. In People v. Gilbert, 21 Mich.App. 442, 175 N.W.2d 547 (1970), a suspect was asked to come to a police car and there informed of an accusation of rape. The court found custody. In Priestly v. State, 446 P.2d 405 (Wyo.1968), custody was found where the officer told the suspect to get into his car. On the other hand, the mere request of an officer to a suspect to step aside does not create a custodial situation. United States v. Arnold, 382 F.2d 4 (9th Cir. 1967); People v. Rodney P., 233 N.E.2d 255 (N.Y. 1967). Nor does a request to step outside a cafe for routine questions create custody. United States v. Gibson, 392 F.2d 373 (4th Cir. 1968). See People v. Pantoja, 28 Mich.App. 681, 184 N.W.2d 762 (1970) (request to step into separate room at tavern did not establish custody). Holding a gun on a suspect clearly creates a custodial situation. State v. Intogna, 101 Ariz. 275, 419 P.2d 59 (1967). The fact that a suspect is himself armed should be weighed strongly against a finding of custody. Yates v. United States, 384 F.2d 586 (5th Cir. 1967); Ison v. State, 281 Ala. 189, 200 So.2d 511 (1967); State v. Paz, 31 Or.App. 851, 572 P.2d 1036 (1977) (en banc) (handcuffs). This sort of situation is not rare; armed felons often make damaging admissions when holding off police. See People v. Tahl, 65 Cal. 2d 719, 56 Cal.Rptr. 318, 423 P.2d 246 (1967). And an officer who arrives at the scene of a shooting may also find that his suspect is armed.

It has been recognized in the earliest cases that the absence of fingerprinting, photographing, and other booking procedures are indicative of the non-custodial interview. Hicks v. United States, 382 F.2d 158 (D.C.Cir. 1967). The use of booking procedures, however, leads to the contrary conclusion. People v. Ellingsen, 258 Cal.App.2d 535, 65 Cal.Rptr. 744 (1968) (fingerprinting and removal of clothes). Similarly, the absence of frisk or search helps to show absence of custody. United States v. Thomas, 396 F. 2d 310 (2nd Cir. 1968). The reverse is true. United States v. Averell, 296 F.Supp. 1004 (S.D.N.Y.1969).

A related problem arises when a suspect is interviewed on premises where the officer is executing a search warrant. A single question to a suspect whose apartment was being searched was held permissible in People v. Cerrato, 24 N.Y.2d 1, 298 N.Y.S.2d 688, 246 N.E.2d 501 (1969), and People v. Fischetti, 47 Ill.2d 92, 264 N.E.2d 191 (1970). Contra: People v. Wilson, 268 Cal.App.2d 581, 74 Cal.Rptr. 131 (1968); United States v. Bekowies, 432 F.2d 8 (9th Cir. 1970). Where the search is illegal the statements may be suppressed as fruits of the poisoned tree. People v. Hendricks, 25 N.Y.2d 129, 303 N.Y.S.2d 33, 250 N.E.2d 323 (1969).

The officer who tells a suspect that he is not under arrest and is free to leave at any time has fairly definitely established that the interview is non-custodial. Lucas v. United States, 408 F.2d 835 (9th Cir. 1969). Exceptions to this rule are rare. See United States v. Di Giacomo, 579 F.2d 1211 (10th Cir. 1978) (suspect given choice between arrest and voluntary appearance next day).

If a suspect is told he is under arrest then, of course, there is custody for *Miranda* purposes. In all such cases a reasonable man would reasonably conclude that he is in custody. It is also clear that custody exists in all cases after formal arrest. There is a scattering of cases relying on what the officer did not say concerning arrest. In State v. Caha, 184 Neb. 70, 165 N.W.2d 362 (1969), the court relied partially on the fact that the suspect had never been told he was under arrest to negate custody. In People v. Ellingsen, 258 Cal.App.2d 535, 65 Cal.Rptr. 744 (1968), the fact that a defendant was never told he was free to go was one circumstance leading to a finding of custody.

Finally, the demeanor of the officer may be significant. The higher the level of courtesy and deference toward the suspect, the more likely a court is to find that the suspect did not reasonably believe he was in custody: State v. Bode, 108 N.J.Super. 363, 261 A.2d 396 (1970) (police chief questioning subordinate with the aim of protecting his fellow officer); Commonwealth v. Willman, 434 Pa. 489, 255 A.2d 534 (1969) (friendly attitude of officers). Where, however, the officer is accusatory and insistently confronts the suspect with evidence of his guilt, the argument that custody existed is strengthened. People v. Arnold, 66 Cal.2d 438, 58 Cal.Rptr. 115, 426 P.2d 515 (1967).

One rather incongruous problem is whether *the giving* of gratuitous warnings establishes the existence of custody. Gratuitous warnings may be given when an individual officer incorrectly believes that warnings are necessary under *Miranda*. One court has held that the fact that warnings are given does not establish the existence of custody. United States v. Owens, 431 F.2d 349 (5th Cir. 1970). It has been held that the giving of unnecessary warnings shows a courteous and respectful attitude on the part of the officer and supports a finding of non-custody. State v. McLam, 82 N.M. 242, 478 P.2d 570 (1970); Cummings v. State, 27 Md.App. 361, 341 A.2d 294 (1975).

(e) The Length and Form of Questions

The length and nature of the interrogation is of considerable significance. Almost all of the cases approving crime scene and street interrogations conducted without warnings rely upon the additional fact that questioning was brief, consuming little time and involving a few, very general inquiries. Brief, routine police inquiries are indicative of a non-custodial interview designed to clarify a questionable situation. In Allen v. United States, 390 F.2d 476 (D.C.Cir.1968), modified in 404 F.2d 1335, an officer stopped a car driven by defendant. There was a passenger in the car who was bleeding and injured. The driver gave some suspicious answers to the officer's questions and the officer asked the passenger if he had been beaten or by whom he had been beaten. The passenger mumbled incoherently and pointed at the driver. The officer asked the driver if he had done it and the driver said "yes". The court held that the officer had to clarify the situation and that he did so properly by asking routine questions. The court found that such questioning was permissible under *Miranda* and pointed out that warnings demean routine police investigation and make cooperative citizens nervous. The courts have generally reached the same result where short, neutral (non-accusatory) inquiries were put, i. e., Who are you?; Where do you live?; What are you doing here?; Where do you come from?; Is this car (or other item) yours?; Where did you get it?; etc.

The existence of lengthy interrogations indicates custody. People v. Ryff, 28 App.Div.2d 1112, 284 N.Y.S.2d 953 (1967); United States v. Kennedy, 573 F.2d 657 (9th Cir. 1978). The use of relay questioning or repeated interviews is highly damaging to a contention of no custody. People v. Tanner, 31 App.Div.2d 148, 295 N.Y.S.2d 709 (1968); Commonwealth v. Banks, 429 Pa. 53, 239 A.2d 416 (1968). The use of accusatory and leading questions, close and persistent questioning, confronting the suspect with evidence against him, and discounting the suspect's denials, are all indicative of custody. United States v. Phelps, 443 F.2d 246 (5th Cir. 1971); United States v. Bekowies, 432 F.2d 8 (9th Cir. 1970). The logic behind the latter cases is fairly sound; confrontation and accusation by the police in many situations would give rise to a reasonable belief of a suspect that he is in custody. Finally those courts that use the concept of focus may approve routine interrogation on the additional grounds that the routine nature of the inquiry tends to show lack of focus.

(f) Summoning the Police and Initiating the Interviews

The fact that a suspect summons the police and/or initiates the interview supports the premise that the interview was non-custodial. The rationale is similar to that underlying the admission of volunteered statements; the element of compulsion is lacking and the statements are not solely the result of police action. It may also be thought that where the suspect initiates contact with the police the police are likely not to assume, at least in the beginning, that he is a guilty party. People v. Lee, 33 App.Div.2d 397, 308 N.Y. S.2d 412 (1970) (defendant flagged down a police car and stated that he shot a would-be robber, who was the true victim). State v. Huson, 73 Wash.2d 660, 440 P.2d 192 (1968) (the defendant arranged for an officer to pick him up at an agreed place; the conversation at the agreed place was held not custodial).

(g) The Lack of Arrest After the Interview

The fact that a suspect was arrested immediately following an interview does not mean the interview was necessarily custodial. In nearly every case dealing with non-custodial interviews the suspect was, in fact, promptly arrested thereafter.

However, the case where a suspect is allowed to go free after the interview is almost certainly one in which the interrogation was non-custodial. United States v. Manglona, 414 F.2d 642 (9th Cir. 1969); United States v. Scully, 415 F.2d 680 (2nd Cir. 1969); Adkins v. Commonwealth, 218 Va. 945, 243 S.E.2d 205 (1978); Matter of V. R., —— S.D. ——, 267 N.W.2d 832 (1978).

(h) Statements Constituting the Crime and Statements to Undercover Agents

Where a suspect in custody attempts to bribe an officer, his statement constitutes a crime in itself and should be admissible even though he may make the bribe offer during a period of custodial interrogation without having received warnings. People v. Ricketson, 129 Ill.App.2d 365, 264 N. E.2d 220 (1970) ("you take the stuff and let us go"—a bribe offer not within *Miranda*).

If a suspect does not know he is speaking to a policeman he can hardly be said to have a reasonable belief that he is in custody. Nevertheless, it has been argued that undercover police should give warnings when the investigation focuses on the particular suspect, but this argument clearly conflicts with Hoffa v. United States, 385 U.S. 293, 87 S.Ct. 408 (1966), and has been rejected by every court that has considered it. Garcia v. United States, 364 F.2d 306 (10th Cir. 1966); United States v. Baker, 373 F.2d 28 (6th Cir. 1967). The ordinary situation involving an undercover agent is clearly non-custodial in all respects. United States v. Viviano, 437 F.2d 295 (2nd Cir. 1971) (no "police compulsion" to meet with supposedly corrupt inspector). There are cases dealing with a jailed suspect who makes a statement to his cellmate who conveys the information to the police. This

has twice been approved.   Holston v. State, 208 So.2d 98 (Fla.1968); State
v. Spence, 271 N.C. 23, 155 S.E.2d 802 (1967).   There is an inherent, subsequently to be discussed, *Massiah* problem involved in such situations however.

(i) Statements After Traffic Stops

Questioning of the driver of a vehicle stopped for traffic violations is
considered non-custodial.   This result is justified by several elements
present in traffic stop cases: (a) the traffic stop is a common everyday occurrence endured by most citizens, one or more times, and is not likely to
create a belief that one is under arrest or in custody; (b) the questions are
usually brief and non-accusatory; (c) the situation seems to fit within the
rubric of "general on-the-scene" investigation; and (d) there is usually no
definite "focus" on the person questioned with respect to a specific crime.
United States v. Balperio, 452 F.2d 389 (9th Cir. 1971); Wilson v. Porter,
361 F.2d 412 (9th Cir. 1966).

(j) Statements During the Course of Stop-and-Frisk

In most jurisdictions having stop-and-frisk procedures, the officer is
usually authorized to ask a few simple questions, i. e., name, address, and
explanation of actions.   People v. Rosemond, 26 N.Y.2d 101, 308 N.Y.S.2d
836, 257 N.E.2d 23 (1970); United States v. Brown, 436 F.2d 702 (9th Cir.
1970) ("There is nothing ipso facto unconstitutional in the brief detention
of citizens for purposes of limited inquiry in the course of routine police investigation even when the circumstances are not such as to justify an arrest").   In People v. Manis, 268 Cal.App.2d 653, 74 Cal.Rptr. 423 (1969),
the court held that a short period of on the street questioning in connection
with a stop-and-frisk does not require *Miranda* warnings.   The California
Court reasoned that a stop-and-frisk, though a deprivation of freedom of
action, was not a *significant* deprivation and thus *Miranda* was inapplicable.
United States v. Thomas, 396 F.2d 310 (2nd Cir. 1968); Utsler v. State, 84
S.D. 360, 171 N.W.2d 739 (1969); State v. Patterson, 59 Hawaii 357, 581
P.2d 752 (1978).   It must be emphasized that the courts sustaining stop-
and-frisk inquiries rely heavily on the brevity and neutrality of the questions.   This suggests that what underlies the opinions is not only the belief
that the situation is not "custodial", but also the belief that what takes
place does not constitute "interrogation" as the Court in *Miranda* used the
word.   See United States v. Ganter, 436 F.2d 369 (7th Cir. 1970).

In People v. Ramos, 17 Mich.App. 515, 170 N.W.2d 189 (1969), the suspect's wife told the officers he had a gun.   They apprehended the suspect
and asked him where the gun was.   He denied having it and was told to
quit kidding and tell where it was.   He pointed to his belt.   The court relied on the right of the officers to protect themselves as justifying the asking of the questions.   Similarly, a court has upheld the actions of an officer
who interrupted his fellow officer, while he was giving the warnings, to ask
where the gun was.   State v. Lane, 77 Wash.2d 860, 467 P.2d 304 (1970).

(b) The Meaning of "Interrogation"

HAIRE v. SARVER

United States Court of Appeals, Eighth Circuit, 1971.
437 F.2d 1262, cert. denied 404 U.S. 910, 92 S.Ct. 235.

Mehaffy, Circuit Judge.

L. V. Haire, defendant, was convicted of second degree murder . . . .

The mother of the deceased reported his disappearance and stated to investigating officers that he was last seen leaving the mother's house in the company of defendant's wife who was subsequently identified and taken into custody. She apparently promptly admitted that the deceased had been murdered and that she and her husband committed the crime. While she was being questioned, defendant appeared voluntarily at the jail and was arrested. Defendant's wife told the officers that the body was in a wheat field on the right side of a county road. She was taken to the area where a search was conducted without success. Defendant was also taken to the scene and when his wife was asked whether she had not told the officers that the body was on the right hand side of the road, defendant, without waiting for her reply, stated, "no, Honey, on the left side." The wife was then asked where the gun was hidden and she replied that it was under the bed at her home. Again, defendant corrected her and stated that the gun was hidden in the fireplace. Defendant had not been given the *Miranda* warnings and was not interrogated. The body was found at the location defendant indicated. The two investigating officers accompanied by defendant's wife went to their house and found the gun where defendant said it was located. It was proven that the gun was the murder weapon from which six bullets had been fired into the body of the deceased. . . .

Defendant argues in brief that in permitting evidence of self-incriminating statements of a person in custody but not in response to a direct question the Arkansas Supreme Court as well as the federal district court engrafted an exception to the *Miranda* rule. It is asserted that such a ruling is not countenanced by the explicit language of the Supreme Court in *Miranda*. We do not agree. Such an interpretation of *Miranda* as suggested would require a broad extension of *Miranda*—one that was not contemplated by the majority of the Supreme Court as clearly reflected by its opinion.

Defendant's argument assumes without record justification that he was interrogated but he was not interrogated at the scene or at any other time. He was under arrest and in custody and was taken to the scene. His wife had previously told the officers the location of the body. They could not find the body so the officers obviously thought that Mrs. Haire might be mistaken as to its location. It was in this light that questions were asked her. No question was put to defendant and his wife jointly, but only to the wife. The answer by defendant was freely, spontaneously and voluntarily given without any semblance of compelling influence. There is no evidence that he was interrogated prior to that time, and indeed there was no need to interrogate him as his wife had apparently immediately admitted that she and her husband had murdered Freddie Jackson. Both the Supreme Court of Arkansas and the federal district court found that the statements by defendant were voluntary and spontaneous and not in response to any interrogation of defendant by the officers. Defendant at no time was asked a single question and at the time he made the voluntary statement both he and his wife apparently were cooperative with the officers. There is no background or atmosphere here in any wise comparable to the four cases in *Miranda*.

In the very first paragraph of Chief Justice Warren's majority opinion in *Miranda*, he stated:

> "More specifically, we deal with the admissibility of statements obtained from an individual who is *subjected to custodial police interrogation.* . . ."

In fact we find that the word "interrogation" is used at least one hundred twenty-nine times in the course of his opinion.

The Chief Justice made quite plain that statements given freely and voluntarily without any compelling influence are admissible and that the fundamental import of the privilege while an individual is in custody is not whether he is allowed to talk to the police without the benefit of warnings and counsel but whether he can be interrogated.

". . . The fundamental import of the privilege while an individual is in custody is not whether he is allowed to talk to the police without the benefit of warnings and counsel, but whether he can be interrogated. There is no requirement that police stop a person who enters a police station and states that he wishes to confess to a crime, or a person who calls the police to offer a confession or any other statement he desires to make. Volunteered statements of any kind are not barred by the Fifth Amendment and their admissibility is not affected by our holding today. . . .

In the case at bar, despite the fact that defendant was in custody for several hours before the statements were made, there is no allegation that he was questioned at all during this period and no evidence of any semblance of pressure or coercion or lack of voluntariness of the statements. "If authorities conclude that they will not provide counsel during a reasonable period of time in which investigation in the field is carried out, they may refrain from doing so without violating the person's Fifth Amendment privilege so long as they do not question him during that time." 384 U.S. at 474, 86 S.Ct. at 1628. We hold that the district court was correct in finding that defendant's statements were spontaneous and voluntary and note that it is not controverted that defendant actually made the statements.

BRIGHT, CIRCUIT JUDGE (dissenting).

Relying upon the testimony of Deputy Sheriff Lewis, and upon his further conclusionary, and somewhat incredible, testimony that the appellant "automatically told us where the body was", the Arkansas courts and the federal district court concluded that appellant's statements were not produced as a result of police interrogation and thus fell outside the dimensions of *Miranda*. Lewis' testimony furnishes but a slender reed to support the conclusion that *Miranda* is inapplicable in this case. On the other hand, the record clearly discloses the following circumstances surrounding the obtaining of appellant's incriminating statements which, considered together, carry their own "badge of intimidation": (1) Sheriff's deputies initially separated Haire from his wife and took her into custody for interrogation; (2) Police arrested Haire and his two friends without a warrant immediately upon their arrival at the jailhouse; (3) Three deputies took Haire's wife to the rural "Bottoms" area to search for the victim's body; (4) Approximately four hours after his arrest, sheriff's deputies brought Haire, then handcuffed, to the "Bottoms" to help find the body; (5) The search took place at night with a search party consisting of five policemen and a friend of one of them; (6) Haire remained in handcuffs throughout this entire nighttime excursion; (7) The sheriff's officers interrogated Mrs. Haire in Haire's presence; and (8) Haire requested permission to join his wife in an automobile immediately after making the incriminating statements.

It is most significant upon the issue of whether Haire spoke voluntarily or under compulsion that the record discloses that upon being advised of his constitutional rights by the prosecuting attorney on the following morning, the accused immediately demanded and received counsel. I think it immaterial that Deputy Sheriff Lewis testified that Haire responded to questions directed at his wife, rather than himself. *Miranda* renders compelled disclosures inadmissible into evidence. . . . Here, questions directed at either one of the beleaguered pair would likely demand responses from either. The circumstances presented in the instant case are easily distinguishable from examples of spontaneous, voluntary statements or confessions to which *Miranda* is inapplicable. . . .

Upon reviewing this record, I believe that the Arkansas courts, as well as the federal district court and the majority, misinterpret the scope of *Miranda*. The issue is not solely whether an accused in custody speaks without responding to a specific question, but whether the inherent pressures of an interrogation atmosphere compelled that response. The circumstances in the instant case constituted the very evil which Chief Justice Warren decried in *Miranda*: "incommunicado interrogation of individuals in a police-dominated atmosphere, resulting in self-incriminating statements without full warnings of constitutional rights." . . . Responses elicited under such pressures are, absent appropriate *Miranda* warnings, excluded from evidence.

In Bosley v. United States, 426 F.2d 1257 (1970), the court enunciated what I believe to be the proper interpretation of *Miranda*:

> [A]t some point in time during the course of the arrest it could no longer be contended that the police were without opportunity to give the *Miranda* warning. We believe that *Miranda* does require the police to warn an arrested suspect of his rights as immediately as practicable after arresting him. A heavy burden rests on the Government to prove any contention that the arrested suspect volunteered a statement without any "interrogation," explicit or implicit, on the part of the police and before he could be warned of his rights.

I would apply that rule to this case. Sheriff's deputies had more than ample opportunity to advise the appellant of his constitutional right as required by *Miranda*, but chose not to do so. Moreover, I am unconvinced that the prosecution has sustained its heavy burden of proving that appellant's incriminating statements were made without any interrogation, either express or implied.

NOTES

1. In Brewer v. Williams (reproduced in Section C—"The Interrogation of Suspects Represented by Counsel"), the Supreme Court found that a detective's statements to a suspect that a ten year old missing girl's body might become covered with expected snow and thereby be deprived of a "Christian burial" unless the body was found soon was tantamount to interrogation. Its effect, if any, on cases like Haire v. Sarver is a subject of contention. Consider, for instance, the opinions in United States v. McCain, 556 F.2d 253 (5th Cir. 1977):

FAY, CIRCUIT JUDGE.

> [Deborah Ann McCain was convicted of importation of 178 grams of cocaine and possession with intent to distribute cocaine.]

* * *

> "The defendant, Deborah Ann McCain, flew into Miami International Airport on January 27, 1976 from Colombia. Upon deplaning, she proceeded to Customs and presented herself and her luggage to Customs Inspector Rollins. Rollins noticed that she appeared very nervous and that her voice cracked. The defendant was wearing tight fitting clothes which revealed a bulge in her abdominal area. Further, the defendant was a young, single female traveling alone, and her duration of stay in Colombia was short. These characteristics are traits which customs inspectors have found to be indicative of drug smugglers. Based upon these indicia, Rollins believed a secondary search was warranted. Rollins informed his supervisor, Inspector Korzeniowski, of the circumstances and Korzeniowski concurred. The defendant was taken to the secondary search room where two female customs inspectors conducted a strip search. This search produced no incriminating evidence. Upon being informed of the unproductive search, Agent Korzeniowski entered the secondary search room and handed the defendant a booklet made up of newspaper clippings reflecting a number of tragedies which had occurred when people had attempt-

ed to hide narcotics in their body cavities.   After reading this booklet, the defendant's bags were removed to a customs enclosure where Inspector Rollins re-inspected the luggage.   The defendant was taken into the supervisor's office, and Inspector Korzeniowski talked to the defendant for some seven or eight minutes while her luggage was being searched.   Korzeniowski testified, and the trial court found in its findings of facts, that the inspector talked to the defendant as 'a father might talk to a daughter, and he told her that these were very serious matters, that she could harm herself seriously, perhaps even cause her death, if she was in fact carrying contraband in her body and if any of these containers ruptured and this narcotic substance was in immediate contact with her body or her internal organs'.   Following this, Agent Korzeniowski testified that the defendant turned white, hung her head down and blurted out that, 'Yes, I do have narcotics in my body.'   The defendant was then allowed to remove the narcotics from her body. The Government argues that even if the defendant was in custody, the statement made by her was voluntary and not in response to any investigation or interrogation, and consequently, *Miranda* warnings were not required.   We do not agree.   The whole purpose of the talk given to the defendant was to persuade the defendant to confess.   This conversation was not unlike the now famous interrogation of Mr. Williams in Brewer v. Williams.   Mr. Justice Stewart, writing for the majority of the Court, condemned that effort by the government to elicit information when he stated:

'There can be no serious doubt, either, that Detective Leaming deliberately and designedly set out to elicit information from Williams just as surely as—and perhaps more effectively than—if he had formally interrogated him.'

We feel that the motive of the government in this case was similar— that is, Inspector Korzeniowski 'deliberately' and 'designedly' set out to elicit from Ms. McCain her admission that she had narcotics within her body.   The fact that the inspector was acting out of concern for the defendant's well-being does not eliminate the requirements of *Miranda*.   We hold, therefore, that the defendant was in custody at the time she made her admission, and that this admission was made in response to the investigatorial or inquisitorial efforts of the government.   The defendant should have been advised of her *Miranda* rights prior to soliciting her admission that she had narcotics within her body, and the failure of the government to do so requires reversal."

GEE, CIRCUIT JUDGE (dissenting):

"I doubt she was interrogated by Agent Korzeniowski.   She was rather warned—granted in a manner most frightening—of the risk she was running by carrying drugs internally.   But the warning called for no response, and she knew when she received it that she had nothing more to fear from a strip search: she had already passed one.   And though the response she made was certainly one not entirely unlikely, it seems to me that a more likely one was that she, having successfully braved the inspection so far, would simply depart and heed Korzeniowski's warning by ridding herself of the contraband as speedily and as carefully as she could.

"As I have said, the question is close, but I entertain grave doubts about extending Brewer v. Williams, a Sixth Amendment case, to this Fifth Amendment problem. My reading of that opinion inclines me to believe that its center of gravity rests on breach of the promise to counsel that his client would not be tampered with in his absence. There was, of course, nothing of that kind done here. Once we begin to equate warnings and environments with interrogation, I fear we have unnecessarily opened another Pandora's Box of case-by-case evaluations.[1] This I am loath to do without some indication from the Court that *Brewer* transcends its Sixth Amendment context."

2. The decided cases may be divided roughly into two categories:

(a) Confronting the Suspect with the Evidence Against Him

Generally speaking, it is proper to confront a suspect with the evidence against him, or with other facts of the case. This has been approved even when the police misstate or falsely represent the state of the evidence, i. e., that an accomplice has confessed. Frazier v. Cupp, 394 U.S. 731, 89 S.Ct. 1420 (1969); Griffith v. Peyton, 284 F.Supp. 650 (D.Va.1968). The issue under *Miranda* is whether confrontation is a form of interrogation. The Courts have divided over the issue. In Howell v. State, 5 Md.App. 337, 247 A.2d 291 (1968) a suspect was told his cohort had confessed after he had refused to talk—the volunteered response of the suspect was held admissible. In State v. Burnett, 429 S.W.2d 239 (Mo.1968) it was held that confronting a person with stolen money was not silent interrogation.

In People v. Sunday, 275 Cal.App.2d 473, 79 Cal.Rptr. 752 (1969), the Court argued that informing the defendant of the evidence against him may be viewed as helpful to him in deciding intelligently whether to waive his rights. In Commonwealth v. Franklin, 438 Pa. 411, 265 A.2d 361 (1970), the suspect volunteered a statement after being told by the officer that his statement was not needed because there were witnesses. The Court found the statements admissible because there was no subterfuge. See also State v. Welch, 4 Or.App. 225, 476 P.2d 822 (1970) (defendant volunteered a statement after confrontation with his co-defendant who identified him).

In People v. Doss, 44 Ill.2d 541, 256 N.E.2d 753 (1970) it was held that confrontation with an accomplice is not a continuation of interrogation; and in Combs v. Commonwealth, 438 S.W.2d 82 (Ky.1969) the Court ruled that confronting a suspect with an adverse ballistics report was not interrogation—over a dissent saying, "the purpose of a question is to get an answer. Anything else that has the same purpose falls in the same category and is susceptible of the same abuses *Miranda* seeks to prevent." Neither the ruling in *Doss* nor that in *Combs* survived federal review on habeas corpus. See United States ex rel. Doss v. Bensinger, 463 F.2d 576 (7th Cir. 1972); Combs v. Wingo, 465 F.2d 96 (6th Cir. 1972). See also United States v. Barnes, 432 F.2d 89 (5th

---

1. Suppose, for example, the booklet of newspaper clippings had simply been lying on a table and had been idly picked up and perused by McCain and that thereafter Korzeniowski had precipitated her admission by merely remarking, "Pretty scary, eh? I hope you aren't doing anything like that." Interrogation? Sadly, the imaginable variations on these themes are legion.

Cir. 1970), holding that a confrontation with an accomplice after the defendant had asserted his right to silence was in violation of *Miranda*. State v. Mills, 6 N.C.App. 347, 170 S.E.2d 189 (1969) (defendant was arrested and warned of his rights. He refused to answer questions. He was then confronted by his co-defendant who confessed and then an officer brought the stolen goods into the interrogation room. The Court did not squarely hold that such conduct constituted interrogation but it found a deliberate effort on the part of the police to break down defendant's refusal to talk). Contra: United States v. Phaester, 544 F.2d 353 (9th Cir. 1976).

All of the cases disapproving confrontation techniques involves suspects who had first asserted their rights and only then were confronted with evidence. Should the result be any different if the suspect is arrested, brought to a police station, never warned of his rights or asked any questions, but is shown, without comment, his accomplice's confession after which he volunteers some admission? This occurred in State v. McClean, 294 N.C. 623, 242 S.E.2d 814 (1978), where the statement was admitted.

Statements volunteered after a line-up identification are usually held admissible. Camacho v. United States, 407 F.2d 39 (9th Cir. 1969); State v. Gallicchio, 51 N.J. 313, 240 A.2d 166 (1968). So too, where a victim accused the defendant at the scene of the crime, the defendant volunteered incriminating statements which were held admissible. Gregg v. State, 446 S.W.2d 630 (Mo.1969).

When the suspect is present at the discovery of some piece of evidence—his volunteered statements are admissible. Diaz v. United States, 264 F.Supp. 937 (1967), aff'd 391 F.2d 932 (5th Cir.); Brown v. State, 226 Ga. 114, 172 S.E.2d 666 (1970) (One officer tells his partner to look at blood on suspect's hand). Similarly, where the suspect learns that the police are undertaking an investigation which he knows will result in the discovery of evidence against him, he may volunteer a statement which will be admissible. United States v. Godfrey, 409 F.2d 1338 (10th Cir. 1969) (suspect was told a check was being run to learn if the car was stolen); People v. Torres, 21 N.Y.2d 49, 286 N.Y.S.2d 264, 233 N.E.2d 282 (1967) (suspect shown search warrant); But see People v. Hendricks, 25 N.Y.2d 129, 303 N.Y.S.2d 33, 250 N.E.2d 323 (1969) (Statement inadmissible if the search is illegal).

(b) Statements in Response to Comments by Police or Other Persons

Closely related to statements volunteered after confrontation with evidence are statements made in response to comments (but not questions) by police officers or other persons. A slightly stronger case for admissibility is present in this situation because, usually, there is no proof of intent to elicit anything from the suspect, and in this respect these cases usually differ from the confrontation ones previously mentioned.

For a very recent case regarding the effects of such comments on confession admissibility, see the subsequent discussion of Rhode Island v. Innis, infra note 4, following Brewer v. Williams, in Section C of this Chapter.

On the other hand in People v. Paulin, 61 Misc.2d 289, 305 N.Y.S. 2d 607 (1969), aff'd 33 App.Div.2d 105, 308 N.Y.S.2d 883, aff'd 25 N.

Y.2d 445, 306 N.Y.S.2d 929, 255 N.E.2d 164, the Court held that remarks concerning the death of the decedent, i. e., "this is a terrible tragedy," "what about funeral arrangements", etc., were a form of subtle interrogation designed to elicit damaging admissions, and were especially impermissible since the suspect had said she wanted to talk to a lawyer and had previously undergone interrogation in a police dominated atmosphere.

3.   In *Miranda* the Court stated that "volunteered statements of any kind are not barred by the Fifth Amendment and their admissibility is not affected by our holding today."   A volunteered statement is one that is *not* made in response to questioning by an officer.   The relative simplicity of this concept makes the determination of whether a statement is volunteered a much easier issue than the question of custody.

Volunteered statements occur when a person simply walks into a police station or talked to a policeman and makes a damaging admission.   See Taylor v. Page, 381 F.2d 717 (10th Cir. 1967); Hammond v. State, 244 Ark. 1113, 428 S.W.2d 639 (1968); People v. Hines, 66 Cal.2d 348, 57 Cal. Rptr. 757, 425 P.2d 557 (1967).   These sorts of volunteered statements are probably also admissible as non-custodial in nature.

Volunteered statements most frequently occur after a suspect has been taken into custody.   Such statements may occur before, during or after actual interrogation so long as they are clearly volunteered.   See Anderson v. United States, 399 F.2d 753 (10th Cir. 1968) (suspect told police that his companion had nothing to do with it); United States v. Maret, 433 F.2d 1064 (8th Cir. 1970) (volunteered during warnings); United States v. McNeil, 433 F.2d 1109 (D.C.Cir.1969) (volunteered after warnings); Wash v. State, 241 So.2d 155 (Miss.1970) (upon arrest defendant asked if the case had to do with a certain victim of crime, when told that it did, defendant stated, "I hope he's dead").

Volunteered statements also occur during interrogation when the suspect makes a damaging admission that is not responsive to the officer's question.   For example, an officer may ask "What is your name?" and the response may be "I'm sorry I killed her".   See Parson v. United States, 387 F.2d 944 (10th Cir. 1968); Cotten v. United States, 371 F.2d 385 (9th Cir. 1967); DeHart v. State, 468 S.W.2d 435 (Tex.1971) ("Do you know your father is dead?"   "I know, I only wish it had been my mother.");   State v. Armstrong, 344 A.2d 42 (Me.1975) ("Do you understand your rights?"— "I killed her and I want to get her out of there.")

On occasion conversations among co-defendants are overheard as are conversations of defendants with relatives, victims and friends.   Admissions made during these conversations are not the product of *Miranda* interrogation.   Caton v. United States, 407 F.2d 367 (8th Cir. 1969);   (Co-defendant);   Soolook v. State, 447 P.2d 555 (Alaska, 1968) (parents);   Edington v. State, 243 Ark. 10, 418 S.W.2d 637 (1967) (girl friend);   Chancellor v. Commonwealth, 438 S.W.2d 783 (Ky.1969) (offer of restitution to victim).

The police have no duty to interrupt a volunteered statement in order to warn a suspect of his rights.   Taylor v. Page, 381 F.2d 717 (10th Cir. 1967);   Ballay v. People, 160 Colo. 309, 419 P.2d 446 (1966).

Finally, a volunteered statement is admissible regardless of when it was made, i. e., while in custody, after indictment, after counsel is retained, etc.   People v. Sunday, 275 Cal.App.2d 473, 79 Cal.Rptr. 752 (1969);   People v. Smith, 173 Colo. 10, 475 P.2d 627 (1970) (after request for counsel);

Dempsey v. State, 238 So.2d 446 (Fla.App.1970) (after request for counsel); Graybeal v. State, 13 Md.App. 557, 284 A.2d 37 (1971) (after assertion of right to silence); State v. Robinson, 198 Neb. 785, 255 N.W.2d 835 (1977) ("The dude died at the hospital, eh?")

4. Apart from the purely volunteered statement the courts have recognized a category which, for want of a better term, may be called noninterrogation questioning. There are four basic types of such questions.

(a) Threshold And Clarifying Questions

The problem of threshold questioning arises because most volunteered admissions are not very detailed. In People v. Savage, 102 Ill.App.2d 477, 242 N.E.2d 446 (1968) a man walked into a police station and said "I done it. I done it. Arrest me. Arrest me." Naturally the officer asked him what he did and when the man said he killed his wife the officer asked him how and he replied, "With an axe, that's all I had." The Court held that this was "threshold questioning" and was permitted by *Miranda*.

The rule is stated in People v. Sunday, 76 Cal.Rptr. 668 and 275 Cal. App.2d 473, 79 Cal.Rptr. 752 (1969), where the defendant, who was in custody, initiated an interview with the police. His statement was largely a monologue but some routine questions were asked. The Court held that a statement is volunteered even if some questions are asked, as long as the questions are neutral, intended to clarify and are not designed to expand the scope of the statement the witness wants to make. See also People v. Superior Court, 3 Cal.App.3d 476, 83 Cal.Rptr. 777 (1970) ("I did it, I am sorry" "What happened?" "Where is the knife?"); Campbell v. State, 4 Md.App. 448, 243 A.2d 642 (1968) ("How much time can I get for this" "For what?" "For robbing that old lady"). But see, People v. Mathews, 264 Cal.App.2d 557, 70 Cal.Rptr. 756 (1968) (exceeded permissible scope of clarification); People v. Connor, 270 Cal.App.2d 630, 75 Cal.Rptr. 905 (1969) (same—32 page transcript of "clarifying" questions.).

(b) Routine Questions And Booking Procedures

The questions asked during booking of suspects by the booking officer are usually held to be non-interrogative. See Toohey v. United States, 404 F.2d 907 (9th Cir. 1968) (information secured in normal booking process is admissible); United States v. Schipani, 414 F.2d 1262 (2nd Cir. 1969) (routine personal history survey in prison is admissible); People v. Hernandez, 263 Cal.App.2d 242, 69 Cal.Rptr. 448 (1968) (age); State v. Rasmussen, 92 Idaho 731, 449 P.2d 837 (1969) (age); Clarke v. State, 3 Md. App. 447, 240 A.2d 291 (1968) (name, address, employment); Contra, Proctor v. United States, 404 F.2d 819 (D.C.Cir.1968) (routine question about employment inadmissible under *Miranda*).

The rationale that brief, routine questions are not interrogation extends to cases beyond the booking procedure. The courts seem to read *Miranda* as directed toward the combination of custody coupled with a series of authoritative demands for answers. See State v. Travis, 250 Or. 213, 441 P.2d 597 (1968). And from this it is concluded that the simple run-of-the-mill question does not constitute interrogation. Further, courts rely heavily in such situations on the lack of focus or intent to incriminate on the part of the officer asking the question. See People v. Ashford, 265 Cal.App.2d 673, 71 Cal.Rptr. 619 (1968) (question from bailiff "How's it going, Ashford?"); Rubey v. City of Fairbanks, 456 P.2d 470 (Alaska 1969) (request for marked money made after arrest).

A most interesting example of non-interrogative questioning is found in State v. Barnes, 54 N.J. 1, 252 A.2d 398 (1969). In that case the defendant was arrested as an escapee pursuant to a warrant. She and her companions were arrested and searched. During a cursory search of their car an officer spotted some checks on the floor of the car. He asked defendant, "Whose stuff is this?" She replied that they were hers. She was in custody. She had not been warned. The officers did not know that the checks were stolen checks nor were they aware that any checks had been recently stolen. After defendant answered the one question, no further questions were asked, and only later did the officers learn the checks were stolen. The Supreme Court of New Jersey affirmed on the grounds that the question was not calculated but was a spontaneous reaction of the officer. Finally, the Court distinguished the prolonged interrogations found in *Miranda* and pointed out that defendant in their case was not suspected of any connection with stolen checks. For a similar case see People v. Stout, 66 Cal. 2d 184, 57 Cal.Rptr. 152, 424 P.2d 704 (1967).

(c) Spontaneous Questions

In People v. Morse, 70 Cal.2d 711, 76 Cal.Rptr. 391, 452 P.2d 607 (1969), a jailer and a guard were called to a cell area where they found one prisoner garroted near death. While tending to this prisoner they asked the defendant, who was also a prisoner, questions about what happened and received incriminating replies. The Court upheld this questioning as not a deliberate effort to elicit damaging evidence but rather general on-the-scene questioning by an "astonished" jailer.

The spontaneity or impulsive nature of questioning depends upon the circumstances in which the question is asked. Though very few courts, of the courts which rely upon the brevity of questions in sustaining the admissibility of the answers explicitly mention the spontaneous nature of the questions, it can be persuasively argued that spontaneity is at least a subliminal factor supporting those judgments. In State v. Barnes, 54 N.J. 1, 252 A.2d 398 (1969) the Court did consider spontaneity. See also United States v. Ganter, 436 F.2d 364 (7th Cir. 1970) (officers made "natural" inquiry concerning the location of the suspect's gun); Dennis v. Commonwealth, 464 S.W.2d 253 (Ky.1971) (after arrest for intoxication defendant who had blood on his arm was asked "What happened?"); Bugg v. State, 267 Ind. 614, 372 N.E.2d 1156 (1978) (police officer went to home of a friend and asked questions out of concern for her health); People v. Huffman, 41 N.Y.2d 29, 390 N.Y.S.2d 843, 359 N.E.2d 353 (1976) (man comes out of the bushes and startled police by asking "What are you doing here?").

(d) Emergency Questions

In the case of search and seizure the police may act in an emergency to protect human life without first securing a warrant. United States v. Barone, 330 F.2d 543 (2nd Cir. 1964). Similarly, where the interest of the police is justifiable self-protection they may ask if the suspect is armed or where his weapon is. See Ballew v. State, 246 Ark. 1191, 441 S.W.2d 453 (1969); Weissinger v. State, 218 So.2d 432 (Miss.1969); People v. Ramos, 17 Mich.App. 515, 170 N.W.2d 189 (1970); State v. Levell, 181 Neb. 401, 149 N.W.2d 46 (1967); State v. Lane, 77 Wash.2d 860, 467 P.2d 304 (1970); Contra: United States v. Pelensky, 300 F.Supp. 976 (Vt.1969).

Where the officer asks the defendant a question about what happened in order to aid the medical treatment of the victim, this has been considered non-interrogative. People v. Paton, 255 Cal.App.2d 347, 62 Cal.Rptr. 865 (1968); People v. Dean, 39 Cal.App.3d 875, 114 Cal.Rptr. 555 (1974) (questions about location of kidnap victim).

(c) THE REQUIRED WARNINGS

UNITED STATES ex rel. WILLIAMS v. TWOMEY

United States Court of Appeals, Seventh Circuit, 1972.
467 F.2d 1248.

DILLIN, DISTRICT JUDGE (by designation).

Appellant . . . appealed, primarily on the grounds that five statements, four oral and one written, were taken in violation of *Miranda* . . .

His state remedies exhausted, appellant petitioned the district court for a writ of habeas corpus, submitting the petition for consideration upon the state court record. That court denied the petition, ruling that the record established that appellant had been adequately warned of his rights under *Miranda* and had voluntarily and knowingly waived them. We likewise rely upon the state court record.

I.

The record reveals that Fleming was killed sometime during the early morning hours of October 15, 1967, in his Chicago apartment. Appellant was first arrested and taken into custody, also in the early morning hours of October 15, 1967, following an automobile accident he had on the Indiana Toll Road while driving Fleming's car. At the accident scene appellant presented Fleming's registration and credit cards to an Indiana State Trooper when asked for identification. The trooper took appellant to a police station to administer a Breathalizer test. Prior to the test the trooper read to appellant the legend printed on a standard form used by the Indiana State Police.[1]

* * *

1. The form reads: "Warning as to Rights:

"Before we ask you any questions, it is our duty as police officers to advise you of your rights and to warn you of the consequences of waiving your rights.

"You have the absolute right to remain silent.

"Anything you say to us can be used against you in court.

"You have the right to talk to an attorney before answering any questions and to have an attorney present with you during questioning.

"You have this same right to the advice and presence of an attorney whether you can afford to hire one or not. We have no way of furnishing you with an attorney, but one will be appointed for you, if you wish, if and when you go to court.

"If you decide to answer questions now without an attorney present, you will still have the right to stop answering at any time. You also have the right to stop answering any time until you talk to an attorney.

"Waiver

"I have read the above statement of my rights, and it has been read to me. I understand what my rights are. I wish to make a voluntary statement, and I do not

Appellant challenges the adequacy of the advice of his right to an attorney, in light of the qualifying language, "We have no way of furnishing you with an attorney, but one will be appointed for you, if you wish, if and when you go to court."

Miranda requires a clear and unequivocal warning to an accused of his constitutional rights, prior to the taking of any statement, whether exculpatory or inculpatory, during interrogation occurring after an accused is taken into custody. One of those rights is, of course, the right to the presence of counsel, hired or appointed. . . .

We hold that the warning given here was not an "effective and express explanation;" to the contrary, it was equivocal and ambiguous. In one breath appellant was informed that he had the right to appointed counsel during questioning. In the next breath, he was told that counsel could not be provided until later. In other words, the statement that no lawyer can be provided at the moment and can only be obtained if and when the accused reaches court substantially restricts the absolute right to counsel previously stated; it conveys the contradictory alternative message that an indigent is first entitled to counsel upon an appearance in court at some unknown, future time. The entire warning is therefore, at best, misleading and confusing and, at worst, constitutes a subtle temptation to the unsophisticated, indigent accused to forego the right to counsel at this critical moment.

The practice of police interrogation of an accused, after informing him that counsel cannot be provided at the present time, is a practice anticipated and expressly prohibited by the *Miranda* decision.

> ". . . if police propose to interrogate a person they must make known to him that he is entitled to a lawyer and that if he cannot afford one, a lawyer will be provided for him prior to any interrogation. If authorities conclude that they will not provide counsel during a reasonable period of time in which investigation in the field is carried out, they may refrain from doing so without violating the person's Fifth Amendment privilege so long as they do not question him during that time." . . .

Consistent with the above, many courts encountering similarly qualified warnings have recognized them as deficient.

We are not unmindful of the fact that a warning identical to that here used by the Indiana trooper has been approved by a divided Supreme Court of Indiana in related cases of Jones v. State, 252 N. E.2d 572 (1969), and Rouse v. State, 266 N.E.2d 209 (1971). As

want an attorney. No force, threats, or promises of any kind or nature have been used by anyone in any way to influence me to waive my rights. I am signing this statement after having been advised of my rights before any questions have been asked of me by the police."

above noted, it was likewise approved by the Appellate Court of Illinois in the appeal of the Illinois conviction here involved. Further, a warning including the phrase that a lawyer would be appointed for the defendant "if and when you go to court," has been given approval by this Court, although the opinion does not set out the entire warning.

In view of the foregoing, we have considered our holding in accordance with the criteria set forth in Stovall v. Denno (1967), and have determined that this decision should be given a prospective application. Our holding, therefore, will apply only to interrogations taking place after the date of this decision.

We reverse the district court order denying the petition for the writ and remand with direction to grant the relief prayed for in the petition unless the Illinois authorities grant Williams a new trial within a reasonable period to be fixed by the district court.

PELL, CIRCUIT JUDGE (dissenting).

While I agree with the majority that its decision should be only prospective, I must respectfully dissent from the holding of the opinion. We have before us a case in which there is little doubt that the defendant committed the homicide with which he was charged, a case in which the conviction was substantially based on his own admissions which were not extracted from him by physical duress and arguably not by psychological stress, but a case in which there is a real possibility that, lacking other independent proof, the defendant may be freed because of noncompliance with an overly technical application of the *Miranda* rule.

My principal point of disagreement with the majority opinion stems from the holding which finds the Indiana State Police warning of October 15, 1967, to be constitutionally deficient. There seems to be no claim that the warning given would not have passed muster if it had not included the words, "[w]e have no way of furnishing you with an attorney, but one will be appointed for you, if you wish, if and when you go to court."

The majority opinion does not purport to overrule United States v. Johnson, yet the issue seems to have been squarely before this court and Judge Kiley stated the following at 1115:

> "Harry Johnson was told that a lawyer would be appointed 'if and when you go to court' and claims this did not fully advise him of his right to have an attorney present during the custodial interrogation. However, he signed a statement which, read as a whole, complied with the *Miranda* requirements. Having signed the written waiver form, without evidence to the contrary, he cannot now contend that he did not understand his rights."

While the *Johnson* case does not set out the entire warning given there, the fair inference seems to be that the remainder of the statement complies with the *Miranda* requirements. Likewise here, as pointed out above, there seems to be no faulting of the balance of the warning statement.

As pointed out in the majority opinion, the inclusion of the "not until court" language in an otherwise proper *Miranda* warning has been held not to be a fatal constitutional defect by the state courts of both Indiana and Illinois.

* * *

While we are not bound by the state court decision, I do not think we should ignore the realistic analysis of the very warning before us given by Judge Burman of the Illinois Appellate Court in *Williams*:

> "The warnings which were read to the defendant informed him (1) that he had a right to remain silent, (2) that anything he said could be used against him in court, (3) that he had a right to talk to a lawyer before and during questioning, (4) that he had a right to a lawyer's advice and presence even if he could not afford to hire one, (5) that a lawyer would be appointed for him, if and when he went to court, and (6) that he had a right to stop answering questions at any time until he talked to a lawyer. The defendant by signing the waiver acknowledged that he had read the warning and that he understood his rights. The above warnings when read in combination, clearly and understandably informed the defendant that he was entitled to appointed counsel prior to questioning."

It seems to me considering the *Miranda* statement here given as a whole that Williams was definitely informed that he did not have to talk without an attorney. He was informed that there were no facilities for getting him an attorney at the time in the jail but it seems nevertheless to me that it was made clear to him that he did not have to talk unless he voluntarily desired to do so. Certainly, the state police had and have no facilities for appointing attorneys and the impact of the majority decision virtually is that the police have to bring in an attorney before they can ever interrogate, irrespective of the warning. Whether this language is in the standard *Miranda* warnings which have been approved or not, it is implicitly there because there is no way of which I am aware by which the police in the initial interrogation of a suspect are able to provide him with counsel at that point. They do have to advise him, however, of his right not to speak without counsel and it seems to me that was adequately done here.

I cannot agree with the correctness of the statement of Lathers v. United States (5th Cir. 1968), that the "*Miranda* warning must effectively convey to the accused that he is entitled to a government-furnished counsel here and now." If "here and now" means the police station, this is just not a realistic statement because police stations do not furnish government counsel. It seems to me that the most that can be said is that, as the *Lathers* court itself said, "[t]he words must asseverate with conviction that any accused can have a lawyer before speaking." With that I cannot disagree. However, if the accused, after being warned, states that he wants a lawyer, either now or later, then while no necessary obligation exists to provide him one "here and now," there is a *Miranda* impediment against further interrogation. If it is contended that the accused, notwithstanding a request for counsel at a time of unavailability of the same, did nevertheless proceed to talk or answer questions on a voluntary basis, there would be indeed a heavy burden upon the state to demonstrate voluntariness. I would not hold, however, that it was an impossible burden.

NOTES

1. The warnings required under *Miranda* are these: (1) Right to silence: "At the outset, if a person in custody is to be subjected to interrogation, he must first be informed in clear and unequivocal terms that he has the right to remain silent." The Court's reasoning is that this warning is needed (a) to assist the uninformed to exercise intelligently this right, (b) to overcome the "inherent pressures of the interrogation atmosphere", and (c) to assure the accused that his interrogators will recognize this right; (2) Courtroom use of the statement: The accused must be given to understand "that anything said can and will be used against the individual in court." In this way the Court states, (a) the accused is made aware of the right that he has to refuse to talk and he is alerted to the consequences that he faces in waiving this right, and (b) he is made to realize "that he is not in the presence of persons acting solely in his interest"; (3) Right to assistance of counsel during interrogation: "An individual held for interrogation must be clearly informed that he has the right to consult with a lawyer and to have the lawyer with him during interrogation under the system for protecting the privilege we delineate today". The accused must be warned "not only that he has the right to consult with an attorney, but also that if he is indigent a lawyer will be appointed to represent him". The Court specifically holds the interrogator to this measure: "If an individual indicates that he wishes the assistance of counsel before any interrogation occurs, the authorities cannot rationally ignore or deny his request on the basis that the individual does not have or cannot afford a retained attorney".

There has been almost no dispute concerning the substance of the *Miranda* warnings. The only contention made with any frequency at all is that the suspect must be warned that anything he says "can and will" be used against him. However, the courts have uniformly rejected the argument holding that it is enough to warn the suspect that what he says "might", "can", or "could" be used against him. United States v. Grady, 423 F.2d 1091 (5th Cir. 1970); United States v. Sanchez, 422 F.2d 1198 (2nd Cir. 1970); Davis v. United States, 425 F.2d 673 (9th Cir. 1970). Peterson v. State, 562 P.2d 1350 (Alaska 1977). One court has held that the warning that a statement could be used "for or against you" is misleading. See Commonwealth v. Singleton, 439 Pa. 185, 266 A.2d 753 (1970). There has been some dispute as to whether additional warnings other than those mentioned should be given. Although suspects are often warned of their right to stop answering questions at any time, Sanchez v. State, 454 S.W.2d 210 (Tex.1970), it has been held that such a warning is not necessary; Commonwealth v. White, — Mass. —, 371 N.E.2d 777 (1978) (reviews decided cases). It is also held that a suspect need not be warned that his refusal to answer questions cannot be used against him nor need he be informed of certain applicable legal rules, i. e., felony murder. State v. McRae, 276 N.C. 308, 172 S.E.2d 37 (1970); Harris v. Riddle, 551 F.2d 936 (4th Cir. 1977) (police need not explain legal rules). The suspect need not be told that he needs or could use the help of a lawyer in deciding to waive his rights. United States v. Hall, 396 F.2d 841 (4th Cir. 1968). The suspect need not specifically be told that oral statements are admissible where the suspect is willing to give an oral statement but not a written one. United States v. Ruth, 394 F.2d 134 (3rd Cir. 1968). But see Frazier v. United States, 419 F.2d 1161 (D.C.Cir.1969).

Some courts require additional admonishment concerning the nature of the charge or subject of investigation. See Commonwealth v. Boykin, 450 Pa. 25, 298 A.2d 258 (1972); State v. Barwick, 94 Idaho 139, 483 P.2d 670 (1971); Schenk v. Ellsworth, 293 F.Supp. 26 (D.Mont.1968). Most courts do not. United States v. Campbell, 431 F.2d 97 (9th Cir. 1970) (suspect need not be warned that he was being investigated for Dyer Act violations); State v. Wilbur, 186 Neb. 306, 192 N.W.2d 906 (1971) (suspect need not be informed of the charges where investigation was in progress); State v. Clough, 259 Iowa 1351, 147 N.W.2d 847 (1967) (suspect need not be informed of charge). Collins v. Brierly, 492 F.2d 735 (3rd Cir. en banc. 1974); People v. Prude, 66 Ill.2d 470, 6 Ill.Dec. 689, 363 N.E.2d 371 (1977). In any event the issue will not arise often because a suspect generally knows the nature of the charge and because local statutes and police procedures usually require such admonishments. Are the cases that do insist that the suspect be fully informed of the charge in conflict with the precedents approving interrogation in homicide cases where the police do not inform the suspect that the victim has died? See Satterfield v. Boles, 297 F.Supp. 609 (D.W.Va.1967) aff'd 408 F.2d 1029 (4th Cir.); Sanchez v. State, 454 S.W.2d 210 (Tex.1970).

2. *Williams v. Twomey* is an example of the most common challenge to the propriety of any given warning. Either the officer merely says the suspect has a right to counsel, or he says counsel will be appointed by the Court, or he informs the suspect that the police have no way of getting counsel for him immediately. To say either of the latter two is to mandate reversal in most cases. See Gilpin v. United States, 415 F.2d 638 (5th Cir. 1969) (no way to give you a lawyer now); Square v. State, 283 Ala. 548, 219 So.2d 377 (1968); People v. Ansley, 18 Mich.App. 659, 171 N.W.2d 649 (1969) (Court will appoint a lawyer); People v. Watts, 35 App.Div.2d 802, 315 N.Y.S.2d 669 (1970) (could not provide counsel on Saturday afternoon). Contra, Steel v. State, 246 Ark. 75, 436 S.W.2d 800 (1969); Bohachef v. State, 50 Wis.2d 694, 185 N.W.2d 339 (1971).

It is understandable that police officers would make these statements —in nearly all cases there is no way they can provide a lawyer immediately. But it is clear from *Miranda* that they must offer the services of a lawyer before interrogation. They need not tender counsel immediately but they must make it clear that, if the suspect wants a lawyer, they will not question him until he has the opportunity to consult with one. Mayzak v. United States, 402 F.2d 152 (5th Cir. 1968).

The rationale for this view was expressed in Mayzak v. United States, 402 F.2d 152, 155 (5th Cir. 1968):

"The fact that the F.B.I. agent truthfully informed Mayzak that the F.B.I. could not furnish a lawyer until federal charges were preferred against him does not vitiate the sufficiency of an otherwise adequate warning. Mayzak knew he could remain silent. He knew he could refuse the interview or terminate it at any point by a simple request. Yet he neither exercised his right of silence nor requested legal counsel.

"We are asked to find that the sufficiency of a *Miranda* warning is diluted or destroyed because the promise of an attorney is not accompanied by a concurrent tender of one. To so hold would be to allow a defendant to use his right to an attorney as a weapon against his custodians. He would simply argue if you will not furnish me an attorney now, even though I am told I can remain silent, I will talk and after talking object to my words going into evidence. This argument is both hollow and specious. The *Miranda* warnings given to Mayzak were constitutionally adequate. That he chose of his own free will to speak without the assistance of counsel should give him no cause for complaint."

See also United States v. Lacy, 446 F.2d 511 (5th Cir. 1971); State v. Blanchey, 75 Wash.2d 926, 454 P.2d 841 (1969). Is *Mayzak* consistent with Williams v. Twomey? Other courts of appeal have rejected the Williams v. Twomey rule. See United States v. Floyd, 496 F.2d 982 (2d Cir. 1974); Wright v. North Carolina, 483 F.2d 405 (4th Cir. 1973).

Would the result in Williams v. Twomey have been different if immediately after making the statement about "an attorney,   .   .   . will be appointed for you   .   .   . when you go to court" the officer had added "and you do not have to say anything until you go to court and talk to your appointed attorney"? Can it be said that Williams v. Twomey requires the police officer to simply say "an attorney will be appointed for you anytime you wish including now". That statement would, of course, be untrue. If the suspect took up the offer of counsel, the consequence would not be the appointment of counsel but rather the cessation of interrogation. Is there anything wrong with this practice? It is clear that the issue with respect to provision of counsel is not whether the police can make good on their offer of counsel but whether the defendant declined the offer and waived his right. See People v. Cooper, 10 Cal.App.3d 96, 88 Cal.Rptr. 919 (1970). On the other hand, if the suspect asks for counsel and it is not provided, may not the suspect become uncertain about the willingness of the police to respect his other rights?

The right to counsel extends to the period prior to questioning and continues during questioning. Failure to make this clear is error. See United States v. Oliver, 421 F.2d 1034 (10th Cir. 1970); United States v. Garcia, 431 F.2d 134 (9th Cir. 1970). But see Klingler v. United States, 409 F.2d 299 (8th Cir. 1969); People v. Gilleylem, 34 Mich.App. 393, 191 N.W.2d 96 (1971) ("before questioning" is sufficient).

One court has sanctioned a less rigorous form of warning for "field interrogation" in two tandem decisions. In both cases the defendants were arrested on the street and given warnings with respect to counsel that were inadequate. In one case defendant was told he had a "right to an attorney"; in the other, that he had a "right to an attorney while making a statement". The court held that both warnings were proper in context and held that they were adequate for on the street interrogation. The court indicated that a more careful warning procedure would be required for a stationhouse interrogation. The dichotomy between street warning and stationhouse warnings was based on the practical differences between the two situations both in terms of police security and custodial atmosphere. See Unit-

ed States v. Lamia, 429 F.2d 373 (2d Cir. 1970); United States v. Cuso-
mano, 429 F.2d 378 (2nd Cir. 1970).

3.   *Miranda* warnings must be given in a clear, unhurried manner—in
such a way that the individual would feel free to claim his rights without
fear.   The warnings should not be given in a perfunctory fashion.   United
States v. Vanterpool, 394 F.2d 697 (2nd Cir. 1968); Lathers v. United
States, 396 F.2d 524 (5th Cir. 1968).   But, "*Miranda* does not require law
enforcement officials to insist upon or to suggest the refusal of cooperation.
As long as the suspect is clearly told and clearly understands that he need
not talk, that he may consult a lawyer before deciding whether or not to
talk, and that he may have one present when he talks, if he decides to talk,
all the requirements of *Miranda* are met".   United States v. Duke, 409 F.2d
669 (4th Cir. 1969).

When warnings are given to an illiterate or subnormal person, "Miranda requires meaningful advice   .   .   .   in language which he can comprehend and on which he can knowingly act.   The crucial test is whether the
words used by the officers, in view of the age, intelligence and demeanor of
the individual being interrogated (conveyed) a clear understanding of all
his rights."   Jenkins v. State, 214 So.2d 470 (Miss.1968).   For an example
of great care in warning one of subnormal intelligence, see Anderson v.
State, 6 Md.App. 688, 253 A.2d 387 (1969).

In dealing with suspects who do not speak English, the warnings, of
course, must be given in a language they understand.   De La Fe v. United
States, 413 F.2d 543 (5th Cir. 1969).   Warnings may be read from a card
(Hammond v. State, 244 Ark. 1113, 428 S.W.2d 639 (1968)) and written
warnings are sufficient where the suspect is literate.   United States v. Lucarz, 430 F.2d 1051 (9th Cir. 1970).

It seems clear that claims arising from an improper manner of admonishment will be settled in trial courts.   If the required warnings are fully
stated it is impossible for anyone but a trier of fact to determine whether
admittedly proper warnings were given in an improper manner.   It is
doubtful that a court of review can effectively deal with such claims.   See
State v. Lay, 427 S.W.2d 394 (Mo.1968) (hollow recitation); People v.
McCottrell, 117 Ill.App.2d 1, 254 N.E.2d 284 (1969) (hurried recitation);
State v. Ortega, 95 Idaho 239, 506 P.2d 466 (1973) (15–20 second warning
is not per se improper).

4.   The warnings must be given at the very beginning of the interrogation, but need not be repeated as the questioning moves from one crime
to another, Heard v. State, 244 Ark. 44, 424 S.W.2d 179 (1968); State v.
Jennings, 448 P.2d 62 (1968); State v. Davidson, 252 Or. 617, 451 P.2d 481
(1969), or after a short break, United States v. Osterburg, 423 F.2d 704
(9th Cir. 1970); United States v. Hopkins, 433 F.2d 1041 (7th Cir. 1970)
(no need to rewarn where there was no significant interval between state
and federal interrogations); Mitchell v. State, 458 S.W.2d 630 (Tenn.Cr.
App.1970) (where warnings with respect to first interrogation concerning
one crime are clearly adequate, interrogation with respect to another crime
the next day need not begin with warnings).   When the questioning is tak-
en over by a new officer, he does not have to rewarn.   Commonwealth v.
Bradley, 449 Pa. 19, 295 A.2d 842 (1972).   It has been held that the warnings must precede only the incriminating question and answer; it need not
precede all questions.   Commonwealth v. Bartlett, 446 Pa. 392, 288 A.2d 796
(1972).   But see People v. Honeycutt, 20 Cal.3d 150, 141 Cal.Rptr. 698, 570

P.2d 1050 (1977) (improper to discuss waiver before giving warnings even where warnings preceded interrogation).

5. The testimony of an officer that he gave the warnings is sufficient. It need not be corroborated even if contradicted by defendant. Neitz v. People, 170 Colo. 428, 462 P.2d 498 (1969); Foreman v. State, 213 So.2d 754 (Fla.App.1968); People v. Lauderdale, 17 Mich.App. 191, 169 N.W.2d 171 (1969); State v. Briggs, 81 N.M. 581, 469 P.2d 730 (1970); State v. Givens, 252 Or. 477, 449 P.2d 151 (1969); Ingram v. State, 1 Tenn.Cr.App. 383, 443 S.W.2d 528 (1969); State v. Bower, 73 Wash.2d 634, 440 P.2d 167 (1968); Bridges v. State, 255 Ind. 201, 263 N.E.2d 368 (1970); Cf. Madkins v. State, 50 Wis.2d 347, 184 N.W.2d 144 (1971) (testimony of two officers not exactly the same). But see Williams v. State, 220 So.2d 325 (Miss.1969) (fact of warnings contradicted, prosecution failed to prove warnings when it did not call second interrogating officer).

The precise nature of the warnings given must be clearly shown in the record. Conclusory testimony that defendant "was given his rights and agreed to talk" is insufficient. (State v. Graham, 240 So.2d 486 (Fla.App. 1970); State v. Seefeldt, 51 N.J. 472, 242 A.2d 322 (1968)), as have signed written warnings, e. g., Searcy v. State, 245 Ark. 159, 431 S.W.2d 477 (1968). However, it is not necessary to tape record warnings, or to have them stenographically reported. People v. Baxter, 7 Cal.App.3d 579, 86 Cal.Rptr. 812 (1970).

The decision in almost all cases is for the trier of fact, and disputes as to the giving of warnings are rarely considered on the merits in a court of review. United States v. Hensley, 374 F.2d 341 (6th Cir. 1967); United States v. Abigando, 439 F.2d 827 (5th Cir. 1971). Often, officers read warnings from a card to be certain they omit nothing. If so, it is essential to either introduce the card into evidence or have it read into evidence. Moll v. United States, 413 F.2d 1233 (5th Cir. 1969); Contra: Tudela v. State, 212 So.2d 387 (Fla.App.1968) (court took judicial notice of the text of the warning card).

Where written or oral warnings are given and one is defective and the other not, the courts have considered the correct warning as reparative of the inadequate one. Brooks v. State, 229 A.2d 833 (Del.1967) (inadequate written warnings); State v. Taggert, 443 S.W.2d 168 (Mo.1969) (inadequate written warnings); People v. Swift, 32 App.Div.2d 183, 300 N.Y.S.2d 639 (1969) (inadequate oral warning). But see United States v. Garcia, 431 F. 2d 134 (9th Cir. 1970) (conflict between two different warnings serves only to confuse.)

(d) THE ADEQUACY OF WAIVER

NORTH CAROLINA v. BUTLER

Supreme Court of the United States, 1979.
441 U.S. 369, 99 S.Ct. 1755.

MR. JUSTICE STEWART delivered the opinion of the Court.

In evident conflict with the present view of every other court that has considered the issue, the North Carolina Supreme Court, has held that Miranda v. Arizona requires that no statement of a per-

son under custodial interrogation may be admitted in evidence
against him unless, at the time the statement was made, he explicitly
waived the right to the presence of a lawyer. We granted certiorari
to consider whether this *per se* rule reflects a proper understanding
of the *Miranda* decision.

The respondent was convicted in a North Carolina trial court of
kidnaping, armed robbery, and felonious assault. The evidence at his
trial showed that he and a man named Elmer Lee had robbed a gas
station in Goldsboro, N.C., in December 1976, and had shot the station attendant as he was attempting to escape. The attendant was
paralyzed, but survived to testify against the respondent.

The prosecution also produced evidence of incriminating statements made by the respondent shortly after his arrest by FBI agents
in the Bronx, N.Y. on the basis of a North Carolina fugitive warrant.
Outside the presence of the jury, FBI Agent Martinez testified that
at the time of the arrest he fully advised the respondent of the rights
delineated in the *Miranda* case. According to the uncontroverted testimony of Martinez, the agents then took the respondent to the FBI
office in nearby New Rochelle, N.Y. There, after the agents determined that the respondent had an 11th grade education and was literate, he was given the Bureau's "Advice of Rights" form which he
read. When asked if he understood his rights, he replied that he did.
The respondent refused to sign the waiver at the bottom of the form.
He was told that he need neither speak nor sign the form, but that
the agents would like him to talk to them. The respondent replied, "I
will talk to you but I am not signing any form." He then made inculpatory statements. Agent Martinez testified that the respondent said
nothing when advised of his right to the assistance of a lawyer. At
no time did the respondent request counsel or attempt to terminate
the agents' questioning.

At the conclusion of this testimony the respondent moved to suppress the evidence of his incriminating statements on the ground that
he had not waived his right to the assistance of counsel at the time
the statements were made. The court denied the motion, finding that

> "the statement made by the defendant, William Thomas
> Butler, to Agent David C. Martinez, was made freely and
> voluntarily to said agent after having been advised of his
> rights as required by the Miranda ruling, including his right
> to an attorney being present at the time of the inquiry and
> that the defendant, Butler, understood his rights; [and]
> that he effectively waived his rights, including the right to
> have an attorney present during the questioning by his indi-
> cation that he was willing to answer questions, having read
> the rights form together with the Waiver of Rights
> . . . ."

The respondent's statements were then admitted into evidence, and
the jury ultimately found the respondent guilty of each offense
charged.

On appeal, the North Carolina Supreme Court reversed the convictions and ordered a new trial. It found that the statements had been admitted in violation of the requirements of the *Miranda* decision, noting that the respondent had refused to waive in writing his right to have counsel present and that there had not been a *specific* oral waiver. As it had in at least two earlier cases, the court read the *Miranda* opinion as

> "provid[ing] in plain language that waiver of the right to counsel during interrogation will not be recognized unless such waiver is 'specifically made' after the *Miranda* warnings have been given."

We conclude that the North Carolina Supreme Court erred in its reading of the *Miranda* opinion. There, this Court said that

> "If the interrogation continues without the presence of an attorney and a statement is taken, a heavy burden rests on the government to demonstrate that the defendant knowingly and intelligently waived his privilege against self-incrimination and his right to retained or appointed counsel."

The Court's opinion went on to say that

> "An express statement that the individual is willing to make a statement and does not want an attorney followed closely by a statement could constitute a waiver. But a valid waiver will not be presumed simply from the silence of the accused after warnings are given or simply from the fact that a confession was in fact eventually obtained."

Thus the Court held that an express statement can constitute a waiver, and that silence alone after such warnings cannot do so. But the Court did not hold that such an express statement is indispensable to a finding of waiver.

An express written or oral statement of waiver of the right to remain silent or of the right to counsel is usually strong proof of the validity of that waiver, but is not inevitably either necessary or sufficient to establish waiver. The question is not one of form, but rather whether the defendant in fact knowingly and voluntarily waived the rights delineated in the *Miranda* case. As was unequivocally said in *Miranda*, mere silence is not enough. That does not mean that the defendant's silence, coupled with an understanding of his rights and a course of conduct indicating waiver, may never support a conclusion that a defendant has waived his rights. The courts must presume that a defendant did not waive his rights; the prosecution's burden is great; but in at least some cases waiver can be clearly inferred from the actions and words of the person interrogated.[1]

---

1. We do not today even remotely question the holding in Carnley v. Cochran, 369 U.S. 506, 82 S.Ct. 884, which was specifically approved in the *Miranda* opinion. In that case, decided before Gideon v. Wainwright, 372 U.S. 335, 83 S.Ct. 792, the Court held that the defendant had a constitutional right to counsel under the Fourteenth Amendment. The Florida

The Court's opinion in *Miranda* explained the reasons for the prophylactic rules it created:

"We have concluded that without proper safeguards the process of in-custody interrogation of persons suspected or accused of crime contains inherently compelling pressures which work to undermine the individual's will to resist and to compel him to speak where he would not otherwise do so freely. In order to combat these pressures and to permit a full opportunity to exercise the privilege against self-incrimination, the accused must be adequately and effectively apprised of his rights and the exercise of those rights must be fully honored."

The *per se* rule that the North Carolina Supreme Court has found in *Miranda* does not speak to these concerns. There is no doubt that this respondent was adequately and effectively apprised of his rights. The only question is whether he waived the exercise of one of those rights, the right to the presence of a lawyer. Neither the state court, nor the respondent has offered any reason why there must be a negative answer to that question in the absence of an *express* waiver. This is not the first criminal case to question whether a defendant waived his constitutional rights. It is an issue with which courts must repeatedly deal. Even when the right so fundamental as that to counsel at trial is involved, the question of waiver must be determined on "the particular facts and circumstances surrounding that case, including the background, experience, and conduct of the accused."

We see no reason to discard that standard and replace it with an inflexible *per se* rule in a case such as this. As stated at the outset of this opinion, it appears that every court that has considered this question has now reached the same conclusion. Ten of the 11 United State Courts of Appeals and the courts of at least 17 States [2] have

Supreme Court had presumed that his right had been waived because there was no evidence in the record that he had requested counsel. The Court refused to allow a presumption of waiver from a silent record. It said "the record must show, or there must be an allegation and evidence which show, that an accused was offered counsel but intelligently and understandingly rejected the offer." This statement is consistent with our decision today, which is merely that a court *may* find an intelligent and understanding rejection of counsel in situations where the defendant did not *expressly* state as much.

2. Sullivan v. State, 351 So.2d 659 (Ala.Cr.App.), cert. denied, 351 So.2d 665 (Ala.Cr.App.1977); State v. Pineda, 110 Ariz. 342, 519 P.2d 41 (1974); State ex rel. Berger v. Superior Court, 109 Ariz. 506, 513 P.2d 935 (1973); People v. Johnson, 70 Cal.2d 541, 75 Cal.Rptr. 401, 450 P.2d 865 (1969) (reversed on other grounds); People v. Weaver, 179 Colo. 331, 500 P.2d 980 (1972); Reed v. People, 171 Colo. 421, 467 P.2d 809 (1970); State v. Craig, 237 So.2d 737 (Fla.1970); Peek v. State, 239 Ga. 422, 238 S.E.2d 12 (1977); People v. Brooks, 51 Ill.2d 156, 281 N.E.2d 326 (1972); State v. Wilson, 215 Kan. 28, 523 P.2d 337 (1974); State v. Hazelton, 330 A.2d 919 (Me.1975); Miller v. State, 251 Md. 362, 247 A.2d 530 (1968); Commonwealth v. Murray, 359 Mass. 541, 269 N.E.2d 641 (1971); State v. Alewine, 474 S.W.2d 848 (Mo.1972); Burnside v. State, 473 S.W.2d 697 (Mo.1971); Shirey v. State, 520 P.2d 701 (Okl.Cr.App.1974); State v. Davidson, 252 Or. 617, 451 P.2d 481 (1969); Commonwealth v. Garnett,

held that an explicit statement of waiver is not invariably necessary to support a finding that the defendant waived the right to remain silent or the right to counsel guaranteed by the *Miranda* case. By creating an inflexible rule that no implicit waiver can ever suffice, the North Carolina Supreme Court has gone beyond the requirements of federal organic law. . . .

MR. JUSTICE POWELL took no part in the consideration or decision of this case.

[MR. JUSTICE BLACKMUN's concurring opinion is omitted.]

MR. JUSTICE BRENNAN, with whom MR. JUSTICE MARSHALL and MR. JUSTICE STEVENS joins, dissenting.

Miranda v. Arizona, held that "[n]o effective waiver of the right to counsel during interrogation can be recognized unless *specifically* made after the warnings we here delineate have been given." (Emphasis added.) Support for this holding was found in Carnley v. Cochran, 369 U.S. 506, 516, 82 S.Ct. 884, 890 (1962), which held that in the absence of an allegation of an "*affirmative* waiver . . . there is no disputed fact question requiring a hearing." (Emphasis added.)

There is no allegation of an affirmative waiver in this case. As the Court concedes, the respondent here refused to sign the waiver form, and "said nothing when advised of his right to the assistance of a lawyer." Thus, there was no "disputed fact question requiring a hearing," and the trial Court erred in holding one. In the absence of an "affirmative waiver" in the form of an express written or oral statement, the Supreme Court of North Carolina correctly granted a new trial. I would, therefore, affirm its decision.

The rule announced by the Court today allows a finding of waiver based upon "inferrence from the actions and words of the person interrogated." The Court thus shrouds in half-light the question of waiver, allowing courts to construct inferences from ambiguous words and gestures. But the very premise of *Miranda* requires that ambiguity be interpreted against the interrogator. That premise is the recognition of the "compulsion inherent in custodial" interrogation, and of its purpose "to subjugate the individual to the will of [the] examiner." Under such conditions, only the most explicit waivers of rights can be considered knowingly and freely given.

The instant case presents a clear example of the need for an express waiver requirement. As the Court acknowledges, there is a disagreement over whether respondent was orally advised of his rights at the time he made his statement. The fact that Butler received a written copy of his rights is deemed by the Court to be sufficient ba-

458 Pa. 4, 326 A.2d 335 (1974); Bowling v. State, 3 Tenn.Cr.App. 176, 458 S.W.2d 639 (1970); State v. Young, 89 Wash.2d 613, 574 P.2d 1171 (1978). See also Aaron v. State, 275 A.2d 791 (Del.1971); State v. Nelson, Minn., 257 N.W.2d 356 (1977); Land v. Commonwealth, 211 Va. 223, 176 S.E.2d 586 (1970) (reversed on other grounds).

sis to resolve the disagreement. But, unfortunately, there is also a dispute over whether Butler could read. And, obviously, if Butler did not have his rights read to him, and could not read them himself, there could be no basis upon which to conclude that he knowingly waived them. Indeed, even if Butler could read there is no reason to believe that his oral statements, which followed a refusal to sign a written waiver form were intended to signify relinquishment of his rights.

Faced with "actions and words" of uncertain meaning, some judges may find waivers where none occurred. Others may fail to find them where they did. In the former case, the defendant's rights will have been violated; in the latter, society's interest in effective law enforcement will have been frustrated. A simple prophylactic rule requiring the police to obtain an express waiver of the right to counsel before proceeding with interrogation eliminates these difficulties. And since the Court agrees that *Miranda* requires the police to obtain some kind of waiver—whether express or implied—the requirement of an express waiver would impose no burden on the police not imposed by the Court's interpretation. It would merely make that burden explicit. Had Agent Martinez simply elicited a clear answer from Willie Butler to the question, "Do you waive your right to a lawyer?," this journey through three courts would not have been necessary.

NOTES

1. The issue of waiver under *Miranda* has become the most dominant issue. And the resolution of waiver issues, as is the case with custody issues, is complex. Where once there were claims of coerced confession there now arise claims of coerced waiver. See Miranda v. Arizona, 384 U.S. at 476, 86 S.Ct. at 1628, 1629; Coyote v. United States, 380 F.2d 305 (10th Cir. 1967); State v. LaFernier, 37 Wis.2d 365, 155 N.W.2d 93 (1967). Indeed, debates over the existence of waiver parallel the old debates over voluntariness because voluntariness of waiver must be determined by the same "totality of the circumstances" that once determined voluntariness of confession. See People v. Hill, 39 Ill.2d 125, 233 N.E.2d 367 (1968).

The use of the term "heavy burden" in *Miranda* may not be particularly helpful. It is often said that no one really understands how heavy is the burden of proof beyond a reasonable doubt or by preponderance of the evidence. These are vague abstractions. Perhaps the Court meant that the prosecution should show unequivocally that there was a waiver. At least the prosecution's case should show waiver clearly if the defendant denies waiver; then the trier of fact decides, but initially the prosecution must be clear in its proof. See United States v. Springer, 460 F.2d 1344 (7th Cir. 1972) (if prosecution shows waiver, then accused has burden of going forward with evidence of involuntariness). And if there is any doubt it must be resolved against the finding of waiver; for example, a case where a suspect is warned, acknowledges his understanding of rights and does not assert his rights, he may say something that muddies the water such as "I should see my lawyer now" but never asks for a lawyer. In such a case, there should be an express waiver of counsel before interrogation continues. Craig v. State, 216 So.2d 19 (Fla.App.1968). For a case in which clarification was carefully made see People v. Smith, 270 Cal.App.2d 715, 76 Cal.Rptr. 53 (1969). On the necessary clarity of the State's proof see Thomas v. State, 458 S.W.2d 817 (Tex. 1970) (warnings given by a judge; confession witnessed by disinterested citizen); Madkins v. State, 50 Wis.2d 347, 184 N.W.2d 144 (1971) (slight variation between testimony of two officers is not fatal to proof of waiver). The court in State v. Davis, 73 Wash.2d 271, 438 P.2d 185 (1971), suggested the use of mechanical devices to record waiver but did not require them. See also People v. Baxter, 7 Cal.App.3d 579, 86 Cal.Rptr. 812 (1970) (tape recording not required).

The courts have singled out certain facts which particularly support findings of waiver. The selective exercise of certain rights, i. e., refusal to answer some questions, tends to show the existence of a deliberate waiver with respect to the questions answered. United States v. Marchildon, 519 F.2d 337 (8th Cir. 1975); United States v. Lovell, 378 F.2d 799 (3rd Cir. 1967); United States v. Barnhill, 429 F.2d 340 (8th Cir. 1970); Mitchess v. United States, 434 F.2d 483 (D.C.Cir.1970) (request for counsel immediately after statement); The existence of a motive to make a statement is supportive of a conscious waiver. State v. Collins, 74 Wash.2d 729, 446 P. 2d 325 (1968) (attempt to secure deal for providing evidence); State v. LaFernier, 37 Wis.2d 365, 155 N.W.2d 93 (1967) (desire to avoid publicity). A suspect's extensive criminal experience will also serve to substantiate existence of a knowing waiver. Mingo v. People, 171 Colo. 474, 468 P.2d 849 (1970).

Finally, the "heavy burden" language of *Miranda* is now subject to some question. Under the decision in Lego v. Twomey, 404 U.S. 477, 92 S. Ct. 619 (1972), the prosecution may introduce a confession upon proof of its voluntariness by a preponderance of the evidence. It can be argued that coercion of a confession is a far more serious matter than violation of *Miranda*. If this is the case, and it obviously is, it may be argued that the prosecution should not bear a greater burden of proof in showing compliance with *Miranda* than it does in establishing voluntariness. Therefore, it can be argued that the language in *Miranda* concerning "heavy burden" is either dictum or has been rendered void in light of *Lego*.

Some courts adopt the preponderance rules in *Miranda* cases. See, for example, Commonwealth v. Sanabria, 478 Pa. 22, 385 A.2d 1292 (1978).

2. Even if there are adequate warnings the question may arise as to whether the suspect was mentally competent to waive his rights. A leading case sustaining waiver is People v. Lara, 67 Cal.2d 365, 62 Cal.Rptr. 586, 432 P.2d 202 (1967). In Dover v. State, 227 So.2d 296 (Miss.1969) a suspect with an I.Q. of 60 with lowered ability in stress situations was held incompetent to waive his right. The question of competency to waive will normally deal with the effect of youth, mental capacity, insanity, drug, alcohol and injury upon the ability to comprehend the rights involved and the gravity of the decision to waive. The decisions on these questions are voluminous.

On the subject of youth, consider: Commonwealth v. Darden, 441 Pa. 41, 271 A.2d 257 (1970) (waiver by 15 year old, mild retarded juvenile upheld); State v. Smith, 192 S.E.2d 870 (S.C.1972) (waiver by 13 year old upheld); In re P., 7 Cal.3d 801, 103 Cal.Rptr. 425, 500 P.2d 1 (1972) (waiver by 14 year old retarded shortly after he was wakened is invalid); Thomas v. North Carolina, 447 F.2d 1320 (4th Cir. 1971) (waiver by 15 year old with I.Q. of 72 invalid after 14 hours in custody). There is no per se rule restricting a juvenile's waiver. Fare v. Michael C., 442 U.S. 707, 99 S.Ct. 2560 (1979).

Insanity or Retardation: Compare United States v. Bush, 466 F.2d 236 (5th Cir. 1972) (waiver by suspect with I.Q. of 68 and mental age of 6 upheld); People v. Stanis, 41 Mich.App. 565, 200 N.W.2d 473 (1972) (waiver by suspect with six year old mind is invalid). Low intelligence does not by itself invalidate a waiver. Commonwealth v. White, 285 N.E.2d 110 (Mass. 1972); State v. Smith, 492 P.2d 317 (Or.App.1971) (waiver upheld where psychiatrist testified that *Miranda* warnings were simply and easily understood); See also Criswell v. State, 86 Nev. 573, 472 P.2d 342 (1970) (waiver by paranoid schizophrenic).

Intoxication: People v. Duke, 63 Misc.2d 407, 311 N.Y.S.2d 312 (1970) (accused cannot challenge waiver on grounds of self-inflicted intoxication); State v. Pease, 129 Vt. 70, 271 A.2d 835 (1970) (intoxication does not invalidate a waiver per se); People v. Moore, 20 Cal.App.3d 444, 97 Cal.Rptr. 601 (1971) (blood alcohol reading of .21 is not sufficient to invalidate waiver); People v. Roy, 49 Ill.2d 113, 273 N.E.2d 363 (1971) (intoxication voids waiver); People v. Gurley, 23 Cal.App.3d 536, 100 Cal.Rptr. 407 (1972) (influence of heroin voids waiver); State v. Hoskins, 292 Minn. 111, 193 N.W.2d 802 (1972) (suspect using tranquilizing medication may validly waive his rights).

Injury: See State v. Pressel, 2 Or.App. 477, 468 P.2d 915 (1970) (wounded suspect may make a valid waiver); State v. Parker, 55 Wis.2d 131, 197 N.W.2d 742 (1972) (suspect with a minor wound may validly waive rights even though wound was thought to be major).

The decision as to competency is usually based on the totality of the circumstances (State v. Smith, 4 Or.App. 130, 476 P.2d 802 (1970), and the trial court's ruling is usually determinative. United States v. Cowley, 452 F.2d 243 (10th Cir. 1971). There has been debate over one suggested per se rule, that is, that to secure a waiver from a juvenile, the juvenile's parents must be present or be notified or that the juvenile must be told of his right to have his parents present. The courts have been severely divided on the issue. See, for examples, State in the Interest of Pino, 359 So.2d 586 (La.1978) (after a complete review of precedents, adult assistance to juveniles was required). Contra: State v. Stewart, 197 Neb. 497, 250 N.W.2d 849 (1977), and State v. Young, 220 Kan. 541, 552 P.2d 905 (1976).

The difficult issue is when waiver may be implied where there is no specific verbal waiver. In State v. Kremens, 52 N.J. 303, 245 A.2d 313 (1968) the court held: "Any clear manifestation of a desire to waive is sufficient. The test is the showing of a knowing intent, not the utterance of a shibboleth. The criterion is not solely the language employed but a combination of that articulation and the surrounding facts and circumstances."

In United States v. Hayes, 385 F.2d 375 (4th Cir. 1967), waiver was implied when after warnings defendant made no acknowledgement but asked to use a phone. He was allowed to do so. After the call he returned to the room and answered questions for a half an hour. He then stopped, asked for a lawyer, and no further questions were put.

In Brown v. State, 3 Md.App. 313, 239 A.2d 761 (1968), a suspect turned himself in and volunteered information. He was warned and made no explicit waiver but promptly answered questions. The Court construed his actions prior to warning as supporting a conclusion of implied waiver. See Commonwealth v. Fisher, 354 Mass. 549, 238 N.E.2d 525 (1968) (Suspect declines use of phone, says he wants to talk, agrees to Polygraph test); People v. Matthews, 22 Mich.App. 619, 178 N.W.2d 94 (1970) (waiver is implied from defendant's initiating conversation).

By the same token a claim of privilege need not be formal in nature, i. e., "Don't bother me" is an assertion of the right to remain silent. State v. Klimczak, 159 Conn. 608, 268 A.2d 372 (1970). But see Commonwealth v. Murray, 269 N.E.2d 641 (Mass.1971). Reeves v. State, 241 Ga. 44, 243 S. E.2d 24 (1978) ("I ain't saying nothing" is not, in context, an assertion of rights). Taylor v. Riddle, 563 F.2d 133 (4th Cir. 1977) ("You done asked me a question I can't answer" is not assertion of right to silence).

4. The courts have rarely dealt with a model *Miranda* waiver, i. e., State v. Ranson, 182 Neb. 243, 153 N.W.2d 916 (1967). The area of waiver is one where "problems do exist". United States v. Corbins, 397 F.2d 790 (7th Cir. 1968). Not the least problem is the indecisive suspect who seems never to quite get to the point of waiving or claiming his rights. State v. Phillips, 563 S.W.2d 47 (Mo.1978). See especially People v. Hiles, 172 Colo. 463, 474 P.2d 153 (1970) (upholding waiver of suspect who refused to acknowledge understanding his rights and refused to waive them but insisted for half an hour that he wanted to talk).

The courts have coped with the problems in the following ways:

> When it is clear that a defendant has been fully informed of his rights any reasonable verbal acknowledgement of understanding or willingness to speak is acceptable. United States v. Boykin, 398 F.2d 483 (3rd Cir. 1968) (after warnings, suspect said "I might as well tell you about it"); Miller v. United States, 396 F.2d 492 (8th Cir. 1968) (acknowledged understanding, stated "I waive" and signed written waiver); People v. Samaniego, 263 Cal.App.2d 804, 69 Cal.Rptr. 904 (1968) (Will you waive? "Yes"); Patrick v. State, 203 So.2d 62 (Fla.App.1967) (after warnings suspect said "I don't need a lawyer"); State v. Brown, 250 La. 1125, 202 So.2d 274 (1967) (after warning, suspect said "I know all that"); State v. Kremens, 52 N.J. 303, 245 A.2d 313 (1968) (after warnings, suspect said "I'll tell you"); State v. Montoya, 78 N.M. 294, 430 P.2d 865 (1967) ("I don't need an attorney. I want to straighten it out"); State v. Lightsey, 6 N.C.App. 745, 171 S.E.2d 27 (1969) (after warnings, suspect said, "I've been in trouble enough to know my rights"); State v. Lipker, 16 Ohio App.2d 21, 241 N.E.2d 171 (1968) (after warning suspect said "I don't want counsel"); People v. Laurant, 131 Ill.App.2d 193, 264 N.E.2d 886 (1970) (after warnings, defendant said, "Yes, of course, I know that" and admitted he understood—adequate waiver); People v. Ruiz, 34 App. Div.2d 908, 311 N.Y.S.2d 336 (1970) ("I know what you said and I'll take you to the car"—adequate waiver); People v. Duke, 63 Misc.2d 407, 311 N.Y.S.2d 312 (1970) (after warnings and inquiry as to waiver defendant said "okay"—adequate waiver).

> The most commonly encountered form of waiver is the acknowledgement that the suspect understands, followed by a statement. It is usually held that once the defendant has been informed of his rights and indicates that he understands those rights, it would seem that his choosing to speak and not requesting a lawyer is sufficient evidence that he knows of his rights and chooses not to exercise them. People v. Johnson, 70 Cal.2d 541, 75 Cal.Rptr. 401, 450 P.2d 865 (1969). This rule is probably valid only if the statement of the defendant follows immediately after he says he understands the warnings. Billings v. People, 171 Colo. 236, 466 P.2d 474 (1970). The cases upholding this rule are le-

gion; e. g., United States v. Osterburg, 423 F.2d 704 (9th Cir. 1970); United States v. Daniel, 441 F.2d 374 (5th Cir. 1971).

In addition, the courts have also approved non-verbal waivers such as nods and shrugs. State v. Flores, 9 Ariz.App. 502, 454 P. 2d 172 (1969) (nodding head); State v. Brammeier, 1 Or.App. 612, 464 P.2d 717 (1970) (shrug); People v. Hurlic, 14 Cal.App.3d 122, 92 Cal.Rptr. 55 (1971) (head shake).

The signing of a written waiver is usually sufficient if the suspect is literate; e. g. Brooks v. United States, 416 F.2d 1044 (5th Cir. 1969); United States v. Chapman, 448 F.2d 1381 (3rd Cir. 1971). The fact that the written acknowledgement of waiver was not made until confession was completed after oral warning and waiver is not crucial. State v. Jones, 257 La. 966, 244 So.2d 849 (1971). Written waivers are not legally necessary. United States v. Crisp, 435 F.2d 354 (7th Cir. 1970); United States v. Jenkins, 440 F.2d 574 (7th Cir. 1970); United States v. McNeil, 433 F.2d 1109 (D.C.Cir. 1969). A written waiver may not always be sufficient. United States v. Hall, 396 F.2d 841 (4th Cir. 1968).

5. A suspect who says that he would talk to an attorney later but presently would answer questions without counsel has waived his right to counsel. State v. Green, 457 P.2d 505 (Hawaii, 1969) (would retain counsel upon release); State v. Capitan, 2 Or.App. 338, 468 P.2d 533 (1970) (wanted no lawyer "at this time"); but see State v. Prossen, 235 So.2d 740 (Fla. App.1970) (sustaining trial court's finding that such language was a request for counsel). A request for counsel made by a suspect to a friend or relative does not have the effect of a request made upon the police even if the police are aware that such a request was made. People v. Smith, 108 Ill.App.2d 172, 246 N.E.2d 689 (1969).

For cases dealing with the effect of an unsuccessful attempt to reach an attorney, see Rouse v. State, 255 Ind. 670, 266 N.E.2d 209 (1971) (valid waiver after failure to reach an attorney); State v. Slobodian, 57 N.J. 18, 268 A.2d 849 (1970) (no right to question after unsuccessful attempt to secure a lawyer); United States v. Coleman, 322 F.Supp. 550 (E.D.Pa.1971) (the fact that after waiver suspect asked to and was allowed to call a lawyer did not operate to retract the waiver); Grimsley v. State, 251 So.2d 671 (Fla.App.1971) (answer to question concerning counsel—"I don't know"— does not vitiate written waiver).

A suspect who requests to see someone other than a lawyer has not asserted his rights under *Miranda*. State v. Franklin, 103 R.I. 715, 241 A.2d 219 (1968); Fare v. Michael C., 442 U.S. 707, 99 S.Ct. 2560 (1979) (request to talk to probation officer). State v. Deardurff, 186 Neb. 92, 180 N.W.2d 890 (1970) (not an assertion of a *Miranda* right). Note, The Right to Non-Legal Counsel During Police Interrogation, 70 Colum.L.Rev. 757 (1970). However, a denial of such a request may lead to a valid challenge on the issue of voluntariness. See Haynes v. Washington, 373 U.S. 503, 83 S.Ct. 1336 (1963).

6. In Frazier v. United States, 419 F.2d 1161 (D.C.Cir. 1969), the suspect objected to the taking of notes. The court held that this inveighed against a finding of waiver because it implied that the suspect thought oral statements could not be used against him. This ruling was made despite the existence of a written waiver. See also United States v. Ramos, 448 F. 2d 398 (5th Cir. 1971) (refusal to sign a written confession militates

against waiver finding); United States v. Van Dusen, 431 F.2d 1278 (1st Cir. 1970) (suggests suspect should be told that refusal to sign the written waiver does not mean he can speak with impunity).

The *Frazier* decision has run contrary to the majority rule. Few state courts have adopted it and most federal courts reject it. Indeed, after remand for additional findings, the court in the *Frazier* case itself upheld *en banc* the waiver, 476 F.2d ⌐91 (D.C.Cir. 1973). The general rule is that refusal to sign a written statement does not impeach the validity of the suspect's waiver with respect to oral statements. Pettyjohn v. United States, 419 F.2d 651 (D.C.Cir. 1969) (refusal to sign acknowledgement of warnings does not constitute non-comprehension of the warnings and such a written acknowledgement is not legally required); United States v. Jenkins, 440 F. 2d 574 (7th Cir. 1971) (must be a clear oral waiver after a refusal to sign a written waiver); United States v. Ellis, 457 F.2d 1204 (8th Cir. 1972) (willing to give oral statements but not to sign without lawyer); United States v. Gardner, 516 F.2d 334 (7th Cir. 1975).

The refusal to answer some particular questions is the right of the suspect; however, a suspect who generally answers some questions, but refuses to answer others and does not indicate that all questioning cease, has not asserted his right to remain silent in the sense that the police must stop all questioning. State v. Adams, 76 Wash.2d 650, 458 P.2d 558 (1969); United States v. Brown, 459 F.2d 319 (5th Cir. 1972); State v. House, 54 Ohio St.2d 297, 376 N.E.2d 588, 8 O.O.3d 282 (1978). Indeed, such events are thought to show clearly a deliberate waiver of rights as to the questions answered. See Note 1, supra.

3. PERMISSIBILITY OF MULTIPLE INTERROGATIONS

MICHIGAN v. MOSLEY

Supreme Court of the United States, 1975.
423 U.S. 96, 96 S.Ct. 321.

MR. JUSTICE STEWART delivered the opinion of the Court.

The respondent, Richard Bert Mosley, was arrested in Detroit, Mich., in the early afternoon of April 8, 1971, in connection with robberies that had recently occurred at the Blue Goose Bar and the White Tower Restaurant on that city's lower east side. The arresting officer, Detective James Cowie of the Armed Robbery Section of the Detroit Police Department, was acting on a tip implicating Mosley and three other men in the robberies. After effecting the arrest, Detective Cowie brought Mosley to the Robbery, Breaking and Entering Bureau of the Police Department, located on the fourth floor of the departmental headquarters building. The officer advised Mosley of his rights under Miranda v. Arizona, and had him read and sign the department's constitutional rights notification certificate. After filling out the necessary arrest papers, Cowie began questioning Mosley about the robbery of the White Tower Restaurant. When Mosley said he did not want to answer any questions about the robberies, Cowie promptly ceased the interrogation. The completion of the arrest papers and the questioning of Mosley together took approximate-

ly 20 minutes.   At no time during the questioning did Mosley indicate
a desire to consult with a lawyer, and there is no claim that the procedures followed to this point did not fully comply with the strictures
of the *Miranda* opinion.   Mosley was then taken to a ninth-floor cell
block.

Shortly after 6 p. m., Detective Hill of the Detroit Police Department Homicide Bureau brought Mosley from the cell block to the
fifth-floor office of the Homicide Bureau for questioning about the
fatal shooting of a man named Leroy Williams.   Williams had been
killed on January 9, 1971, during a holdup attempt outside the 101
Ranch Bar in Detroit.   Mosley had not been arrested on this charge
or interrogated about it by Detective Cowie.   Before questioning
Mosley about this homicide Detective Hill carefully advised him of his
"*Miranda* rights."   Mosley read the notification form both silently
and aloud, and Detective Hill then read and explained the warnings
to him and had him sign the form.   Mosley at first denied any involvement in the Williams murder, but after the officer told him that
Anthony Smith had confessed to participating in the slaying and had
named him as the "shooter," Mosley made a statement implicating
himself in the homicide.   The interrogation by Detective Hill lasted
approximately 15 minutes, and at no time during its course did Mosley ask to consult with a lawyer or indicate that he did not want to
discuss the homicide.   In short, there is no claim that the procedures
followed during Detective Hill's interrogation of Mosley, standing
alone, did not fully comply with the strictures of the *Miranda* opinion.

Mosley was subsequently charged in a one-count information
with first-degree murder.   Before the trial he moved to suppress his
incriminating statement on a number of grounds, among them the
claim that under the doctrine of the *Miranda* case it was constitutionally impermissible for Detective Hill to question him about the Williams murder after he had told Detective Cowie that he did not want
to answer any questions about the robberies.   The trial court denied
the motion to suppress   .   .   .   The jury convicted Mosley of
first-degree murder, and the court imposed a mandatory sentence of
life imprisonment.

On appeal to the Michigan Court of Appeals,   .   .   .   [The appellate court] reversed the judgment of conviction, holding that Detective Hill's interrogation of Mosley had been a *per se* violation of
the *Miranda* doctrine.   .   .   .

* * *

.   .   .   Neither party in the present case challenges the continuing validity of the *Miranda* decision, or of any of the so-called
guidelines it established to protect what the Court there said was a
person's constitutional privilege against compulsory self-incrimination.   The issue in this case, rather, is whether the conduct of the Detroit police that led to Mosley's incriminating statement did in fact
violate the *Miranda* "guidelines," so as to render the statement inad-

missible in evidence against Mosley at his trial. Resolution of the question turns almost entirely on the interpretation of a single passage in the *Miranda* opinion, upon which the Michigan appellate court relied in finding a *per se* violation of *Miranda*:

> "Once warnings have been given, the subsequent procedure is clear. If the individual indicates in any manner, at any time prior to or during questioning, that he wishes to remain silent, the interrogation must cease. At this point he has shown that he intends to exercise his Fifth Amendment privilege; any statement taken after the person invokes his privilege cannot be other than the product of compulsion, subtle or otherwise. Without the right to cut off questioning, the setting of in-custody interrogation operates on the individual to overcome free choice in producing a statement after the privilege has been once invoked."[1]

This passage states that "the interrogation must cease" when the person in custody indicates that "he wishes to remain silent." It does not state under what circumstances, if any, a resumption of questioning is permissible.[2] The passage could be literally read to mean that a person who has invoked his "right to silence" can never again be subjected to custodial interrogation by any police officer at any time or place on any subject. Another possible construction of the passage would characterize "any statement taken after the person in-

---

1. The present case does not involve the procedures to be followed if the person in custody asks to consult with a lawyer, since Mosley made no such request at any time. Those procedures are detailed in the *Miranda* opinion as follows:

    "If the individual states that he wants an attorney, the interrogation must cease until an attorney is present. At that time, the individual must have an opportunity to confer with the attorney and to have him present during any subsequent questioning. If the individual cannot obtain an attorney and he indicates that he wants one before speaking to police, they must respect his decision to remain silent.

    "This does not mean, as some have suggested, that each police station must have a 'station house lawyer' present at all times to advise prisoners. It does mean, however, that if police propose to interrogate a person they must make known to him that he is entitled to a lawyer and that if he cannot afford one, a lawyer will be provided for him, prior to any interrogation. If authorities conclude that they will not provide counsel during a reasonable period of time in which investigation in the field is carried out, they may refrain from doing so without violating the person's Fifth Amendment privilege so long as they do not question him during that time."

2. The Court did state in a footnote:

    "If an individual indicates his desire to remain silent, but has an attorney present, there may be some circumstances in which further questioning would be permissible. In the absence of evidence of overbearing, statements then made in the presence of counsel might be free of the compelling influence of the interrogation process and might fairly be construed as a waiver of the privilege for purposes of these statements."

    This footnote in the *Miranda* opinion is not relevant to the present case, since Mosley did not have an attorney present at the time he declined to answer Detective Cowie's questions, and the officer did not continue to question Mosley but instead ceased the interrogation in compliance with *Miranda's* dictates.

vokes his privilege" as "the product of compulsion" and would therefore mandate its exclusion from evidence, even if it were volunteered by the person in custody without any further interrogation whatever. Or the passage could be interpreted to require only the immediate cessation of questioning, and to permit a resumption of interrogation after a momentary respite.

It is evident that any of these possible literal interpretations would lead to absurd and unintended results. To permit the continuation of custodial interrogation after a monentary cessation would clearly frustrate the purposes of *Miranda* by allowing repeated rounds of questioning to undermine the will of the person being questioned. At the other extreme, a blanket prohibition against the taking of voluntary statements or a permanent immunity from further interrogation, regardless of the circumstances, would transform the *Miranda* safeguards into wholly irrational obstacles to legitimate police investigative activity, and deprive suspects of an opportunity to make informed and intelligent assessments of their interests. Clearly, therefore, neither this passage nor any other passage in the *Miranda* opinion can sensibly be read to create a *per se* proscription of indefinite duration upon any further questioning by any police officer on any subject, once the person in custody has indicated a desire to remain silent.

A reasonable and faithful interpretation of the *Miranda* opinion must rest on the intention of the Court in that case to adopt "fully effective means . . . to notify the person of his right of silence and to assure that the exercise of the right will be scrupulously honored . . .." The critical safeguard identified in the passage at issue is a person's "right to cut off questioning." Through the exercise of his option to terminate questioning he can control the time at which questioning occurs, the subjects discussed, and the duration of the interrogation. The requirement that law enforcement authorities must respect a person's exercise of that option counteracts the coercive pressures of the custodial setting. We therefore conclude that the admissibility of statements obtained after the person in custody has decided to remain silent depends under *Miranda* on whether his "right to cut off questioning" was "scrupulously honored." [3]

A review of the circumstances leading to Mosley's confession reveals that his "right to cut off questioning" was fully respected in this case. Before his initial interrogation, Mosley was carefully advised that he was under no obligation to answer any questions and could remain silent if he wished. He orally acknowledged that he understood the *Miranda* warnings and then signed a printed notifica-

---

3. The dissenting opinion asserts that *Miranda* established a requirement that once a person has indicated a desire to remain silent, questioning may be resumed only when counsel is present. But clearly the Court in *Miranda* imposed no such requirement, for it distinguished between the procedural safeguards triggered by a request to remain silent and a request for an attorney and directed that "the interrogation must cease until an attorney is present" only "[i]f the individual states that he wants an attorney."

tion-of-rights form. When Mosley stated that he did not want to discuss the robberies, Detective Cowie immediately ceased the interrogation and did not try either to resume the questioning or in any way to persuade Mosley to reconsider his position. After an interval of more than two hours, Mosley was questioned by another police officer at another location about an unrelated holdup murder. He was given full and complete *Miranda* warnings at the outset of the second interrogation. He was thus reminded again that he could remain silent and could consult with a lawyer and was carefully given a full and fair opportunity to exercise these options. The subsequent questioning did not undercut Mosley's previous decision not to answer Detective Cowie's inquiries. Detective Hill did not resume the interrogation about the White Tower Restaurant robbery or inquire about the Blue Goose Bar robbery, but instead focused exclusively on the Leroy Williams homicide, a crime different in nature and in time and place of occurrence from the robberies for which Mosley had been arrested and interrogated by Detective Cowie. Although it is not clear from the record how much Detective Hill knew about the earlier interrogation, his questioning of Mosley about an unrelated homicide was quite consistent with a reasonable interpretation of Mosley's earlier refusal to answer any questions about the robberies.

This is not a case, therefore, where the police failed to honor a decision of a person in custody to cut off questioning, either by refusing to discontinue the interrogation upon request or by persisting in repeated efforts to wear down his resistance and make him change his mind. In contrast to such practices, the police here immediately ceased the interrogation, resumed questioning only after the passage of a significant period of time and the provision of a fresh set of warnings, and restricted the second interrogation to a crime that had not been a subject of the earlier interrogation.

The Michigan Court of Appeals viewed this case as factually similar to Westover v. United States, a companion case to *Miranda*. But the controlling facts of the two cases are strikingly different.

In *Westover*, the petitioner was arrested by the Kansas City police at 9:45 p. m. and taken to the police station. Without giving any advisory warnings of any kind to Westover, the police questioned him that night and throughout the next morning about various local robberies. At noon, three FBI agents took over, gave advisory warnings to Westover, and proceeded to question him about two California bank robberies. After two hours of questioning, the petitioner confessed to the California crimes. The Court held that the confession obtained by the FBI was inadmissible because the interrogation leading to the petitioner's statement followed on the heels of prolonged questioning that was commenced and continued by the Kansas City police without preliminary warnings to Westover of any kind. The Court found that "the federal authorities were the beneficiaries of the pressure applied by the local in-custody interrogation" and that the belated warnings given by the federal officers were "not sufficient to protect" Westover because from his point of view "the warnings came at the end of the interrogation process."

Here, by contrast, the police gave full *"Miranda* warnings" to Mosley at the very outset of each interrogation, subjected him to only a brief period of initial questioning, and suspended questioning entirely for a significant period before beginning the interrogation that led to his incriminating statement. The cardinal fact of *Westover*—the failure of the police officers to give any warnings whatever to the person in their custody before embarking on an intense and prolonged interrogation of him—was simply not present in this case. The Michigan Court of Appeals was mistaken, therefore, in believing that Detective Hill's questioning of Mosley was "not permitted" by the *Westover* decision.

For these reasons, we conclude that the admission in evidence of Mosley's incriminating statement did not violate the principles of Miranda v. Arizona.

MR. JUSTICE WHITE, concurring.

I concur in the result and in much of the majority's reasoning. However, it appears to me that in an effort to make only a limited holding in this case, the majority has implied that some custodial confessions will be suppressed even though they follow an informed and voluntary waiver of the defendant's rights. The majority seems to say that a statement obtained within some unspecified time after an assertion by an individual of his "right to silence" is always inadmissible, even if it was the result of an informed and voluntary decision —following, for example, a disclosure to such an individual of a piece of information bearing on his waiver decision which the police had failed to give him prior to his assertion of the privilege but which they give him immediately thereafter. Indeed, the majority characterizes as "absurd" any contrary rule. I disagree. I do not think the majority's conclusion is compelled by Miranda v. Arizona, and I suspect that in the final analysis the majority will adopt voluntariness as a standard by which to judge the waiver of the right to silence by a properly informed defendant. I think the Court should say so now.

* * *

I am no more convinced that *Miranda* was required by the United States Constitution than I was when it was decided. However, there is at least some support in the law both before and after *Miranda* for the proposition that some rights will never be deemed waived unless the defendant is first expressly advised of their existence. There is little support in the law or in common sense for the proposition that an *informed* waiver of a right may be ineffective even where voluntarily made. Indeed, the law is exactly to the contrary. Unless an individual is incompetent, we have in the past rejected any paternalistic rule protecting a defendant from his intelligent and voluntary decisions about his own criminal case. To do so would be to "imprison a man in his privileges," and to disregard " 'that respect for the individual which is the lifeblood of the law.' " I am very reluctant to conclude that *Miranda* stands for such a proposition.

The language of *Miranda* no more compels such a result than does its basic rationale. As the majority points out, the statement in *Mi-*

randa requiring interrogation to *cease* after an assertion of the "right to silence" tells us nothing because it does not indicate how soon this interrogation may resume. The Court showed in the very next paragraph, moreover, that when it wanted to create a *per se* rule against further interrogation after assertion of a right, it knew how to do so. The Court there said "[i]f the individual states that he wants an attorney the interrogation must cease *until an attorney is present.*" However, when the individual indicates that *he* will decide unaided by counsel whether or not to assert his "right to silence" the situation is different. In such a situation, the Court in *Miranda* simply said: "If the interrogation continues without the presence of an attorney and a statement is taken, a heavy burden rests on the government to demonstrate that the defendant knowingly and intelligently waived his privilege against self-incrimination and his right to retained or appointed counsel." Apparently, although placing a heavy burden on the government, *Miranda* intended waiver of the "right to silence" to be tested by the normal standards. In any event, insofar as the *Miranda* decision might be read to require interrogation to cease for some magical and unspecified period of time following an assertion of the "right to silence," and to reject voluntariness as the standard by which to judge informed waivers of that right, it should be disapproved as inconsistent with otherwise uniformly applied legal principles.

In justifying the implication that questioning must inevitably cease for some unspecified period of time following an exercise of the "right to silence," the majority says only that such a requirement would be necessary to avoid "undermining" "the will of the person being questioned." Yet, surely a waiver of the "right to silence" obtained by "undermining the will" of the person being questioned would be considered an involuntary waiver. Thus, in order to achieve the majority's only stated purpose, it is sufficient to exclude all confessions which are the result of involuntary waivers. To exclude any others is to deprive the factfinding process of highly probative information for no reason at all. The "repeated rounds" of questioning following an assertion of the privilege, which the majority is worried about, would, of course, count heavily against the State in any determination of voluntariness—particularly if no reason (such as new facts communicated to the accused or a new incident being inquired about) appeared for repeated questioning. There is no reason, however, to rob the accused of the choice to answer questions voluntarily for some unspecified period of time following his own previous contrary decision. The Court should now so state.

MR. JUSTICE BRENNAN, with whom MR. JUSTICE MARSHALL joins, dissenting.

*   *   *

[The] process of eroding *Miranda* rights, began with Harris v. New York, 401 U.S. 222 (1971), continues with today's holding that police may renew the questioning of a suspect who has once exercised his right to remain silent, provided the suspect's right to cut off questioning has been "scrupulously honored." Today's distortion of *Miranda's* constitutional principles can be viewed only as yet another stop in the erosion and, I suppose, ultimate overruling of *Miranda's* enforcement of the privilege against self-incrimination.

The *Miranda* guidelines were necessitated by the inherently coercive nature of in-custody questioning. . . . To assure safeguards that promised to dispel the "inherently compelling pressures" of in-custody interrogation, a prophylactic rule was fashioned to supplement the traditional determination of voluntariness on the facts of each case. . . . that is, clear, objective standards that might be applied to avoid the vagaries of the traditional voluntariness test.

. . .

As the Court today continues to recognize, under *Miranda,* the cost of assuring voluntariness by procedural tests, independent of any actual inquiry into voluntariness, is that some voluntary statements will be excluded. Thus the consideration in the task confronting the Court is not whether voluntary statements will be excluded, but whether the procedures approved will be sufficient to assure with reasonable certainty that a confession is not obtained under the influence of the compulsion inherent in interrogation and detention. The procedures approved by the Court today fail to provide that assurance.

* * *

In formulating its procedural safeguard, the Court skirts the problem of compulsion and thereby fails to join issue with the dictates of *Miranda.* The language which the Court finds controlling in this case teaches that renewed questioning itself is part of the process which invariably operates to overcome the will of a suspect. That teaching is embodied in the form of a proscription on any further questioning once the suspect has exercised his right to remain silent. Today's decision uncritically abandons that teaching. The Court assumes, contrary to the controlling language, that "scrupulously honoring" an initial exercise of the right to remain silent preserves the efficaciousness of initial and future warnings despite the fact that the suspect has once been subjected to interrogation and then has been detained for a lengthy period of time.

Observing that the suspect can control the circumstances of interrogation "[t]hrough the exercise of his option to terminate questioning," the Court concludes "that the admissibility of statements obtained after the person in custody has decided to remain silent depends . . . on whether his 'right to cut off questioning' was 'scrupulously honored.' " But scrupulously honoring exercises of the right to cut off questioning is only meaningful insofar as the suspect's will to exercise that right remains wholly unfettered. The Court's formulation thus assumes the very matter at issue here: whether renewed questioning following a lengthy period of detention acts to overbear the suspect's will, irrespective of giving the *Miranda* warnings a second time (and scrupulously honoring them), thereby rendering inconsequential any failure to exercise the right to remain silent. For the Court it is enough conclusorily to assert that "[t]he subsequent questioning did not undercut Mosley's previous decision not to answer Detective Cowie's inquiries." Under *Miranda*, however, Mosley's failure to exercise the right upon renewed questioning is presumptively the consequence of an overbearing in which detention and that subsequent questioning played central roles.

I agree that *Miranda* is not to be read, on the one hand, to impose an absolute ban on resumption of questioning "at any time or place on any subject," or on the other hand, "to permit a resumption of interrogation after a momentary respite," *ibid.* But this surely cannot justify adoption of a vague and ineffective procedural standard that falls somewhere between those absurd extremes, for *Miranda* in flat and unambiguous terms requires that questioning "cease" when a suspect exercises the right to remain silent. . . .

The fashioning of guidelines for this case is an easy task. Adequate procedures are readily available. Michigan law requires that the suspect be arraigned before a judicial officer "without unnecessary delay," certainly not a burdensome requirement. Alternatively, a requirement that resumption of questioning should await appointment and arrival of counsel for the suspect would be an acceptable and readily satisfied precondition to resumption. *Miranda* expressly held that "[t]he presence of counsel . . . would be the adequate protective device necessary to make the process of police interrogation conform to the dictates of the privilege [against self-incrimination]." The Court expediently bypasses this alternative in its search for circumstances where renewed questioning would be permissible.

*   *   *

These procedures would be wholly consistent with the Court's rejection of a *"per se* proscription of indefinite duration," a rejection to which I fully subscribe. Today's decision, however, virtually empties *Miranda* of principle, for plainly the decision encourages police asked to cease interrogation to continue the suspect's detention until the police station's coercive atmosphere does its work and the suspect responds to resumed questioning.

*   *   *

In light of today's erosion of *Miranda* standards as a matter of federal constitutional law, it is appropriate to observe that no State is precluded by the decision from adhering to higher standards under state law. Each State has power to impose higher standards governing police practices under state law than is required by the Federal Constitution. See Oregon v. Hass, 420 U.S. 714, 719, 95 S.Ct. 1215, 1219 (1975). . . . Understandably, state courts and legislatures are, as matters of state law, increasingly according protections once provided as federal rights but now increasingly depreciated by decisions of this Court. See, e. g., State v. Santiago, 53 Haw. 254, 492 P. 2d 657 (1971) (rejecting Harris v. New York, 401 U.S. 222, 91 S.Ct. 643 (1971).

NOTES

1. In *Mosley*, the Court approved a second interrogation after an initial assertion of silence. The second interrogation concerned a different crime and different interrogators, but other courts have not found these two factors to be essential. Several courts have simply approved second attempts to interview after an initial refusal with a caveat that successive attempts to interview will be viewed with caution. United States v. Collins, 462 F.2d 792 (2d Cir. 1972) (suspect must be rewarned of *Miranda* rights); State v. Godfrey, 182 Neb. 451, 155 N.W.2d 438 (1968) (warnings repeated before second interrogation); People v. Gary, 31 N.Y.2d 68, 334 N.Y.S.2d 883, 286 N.E.2d 263 (1972) (must be given second warning of *Miranda* rights); Scott v. State, 251 Ark. 918, 475 S.W.2d 699 (1972) (must be rewarned); Franklin v. State, 6 Md.App. 572, 252 A.2d 487 (1969) (usually should give warning at second interrogation); United States v. Crisp, 435 F.2d 354 (7th Cir. 1970) (proper to interrogate where defendant summoned agents and gave statements after new warnings; improper to ask defendant whether he is willing to talk about what occurred before and after the robbery when he declares that he is unwilling to talk about the robbery); McIntyre v. New York, 329 F.Supp. 9 (E.D.N.Y.1971) (permissible where new inquiry occurred after eyewitness identification); Gardner v. State, 10 Md.App. 691, 272 A.2d 410 (1970) (an initial refusal to speak is a heavy factor to be overcome when it is claimed that there was a subsequent waiver); State v. Deardurff, 186 Neb. 92, 180 N.W.2d 890 (1970) (a valid waiver is found where defendant was arrested and warned, after which he asked to see his wife and was told he could not because she was in custody; he then said he did not want to talk and also that he neither knew, could afford nor wished to see a lawyer; on the next day, after being rewarned, defendant made a statement); Brown v. State, 256 Ind. 558, 270 N.E.2d 751 (1971) (heavy burden upon state to show valid waiver).

The opposite conclusion was reached in People v. Fioritto, 68 Cal.2d 714, 68 Cal.Rptr. 817, 441 P.2d 625 (1968) (interrogation must cease after the suspect invokes his right to silence); People v. McIntyre, 31 App.Div.2d 964, 299 N.Y.S.2d 88 (1969) (refusal to be interviewed does not evaporate because the police change the subject of discussion to another offense); United States v. Brown, 466 F.2d 493 (10th Cir. 1972) (repeated attempts are improper); United States v. Hernandez, 574 F.2d 1362 (5th Cir. 1978) (repeated warnings followed by repeated attempts to question may cause suspect to doubt sincerity of warnings).

At least one court has rejected the *Mosley* rule and adopted a more restrictive practice based on the state constitution. People v. Pettingill, 21 Cal.3d 231, 145 Cal.Rptr. 861, 578 P.2d 108 (1978).

All courts tend to approve interrogation after refusal to talk when some of the initiative comes from the defendant. People v. Brockman, 2 Cal.App.3d 1002, 83 Cal.Rptr. 70 (1969) (defendant refused to talk but said he might like to talk about it in a couple of days and police questioned him two days later); State v. Lucia, 74 Wash.2d 819, 447 P.2d 606 (1968) (defendant initiated the second interview); Conway v. State, 7 Md.App. 400, 256 A.2d 178 (1969) (conditional refusal and request for time to think about it does not bar second interrogation where warnings were given); United States v. Jackson, 436 F.2d 39 (9th Cir. 1970) (defendant refused to see a lawyer and said he had something to say later; four days later he was asked about what he had to say and he waived his rights after being re-warned) ; People v. Atkins, 10 Cal.App.3d 1042, 89 Cal.Rptr. 588 (1970) (request to speak to a particular officer).

2. Prior to the decision in *Mosley,* courts were divided on the permissibility of a second interrogation after an assertion of the right to counsel. Compare the following cases in (a) with those in (b) :

    (a) People v. Williams, 131 Ill.App.2d 149, 264 N.E.2d 901 (1970) (during a third interrogation defendant demands a lawyer and interrogation ceases—later defendant says he does not want a lawyer—he is rewarned and waives and his statement is admissible) ; Rouse v. State, 255 Ind. 670, 266 N.E.2d 209 (1971) (proper to secure waiver after the suspect tried and failed to reach his attorney) ; State v. Welch, 4 Or. App. 225, 476 P.2d 822 (1970) (proper to attempt second interrogation with waiver where defendant first refused to make a written statement without his attorney and was then confronted by his co-defendant). State v. Turner, 281 N.C. 118, 187 S.E.2d 750 (1972) (suspect requests attorney and speaks to one who is unable to take the case, suspect may then be questioned after new warnings and explicit waiver of counsel).

    (b) Wakeman v. State, 237 So.2d 61 (Fla.App.1970) (improper to attempt second interrogation while an attorney is on the way) ; State v. Slobodian, 57 N.J. 18, 268 A.2d 849 (1970) (improper to attempt second interrogation after defendant unsuccessfully sought to contact his lawyer) ; People v. Watts, 35 App.Div.2d 802, 315 N.Y.S.2d 669 (1970) (improper to attempt interrogation after indicating on three occasions that counsel could not be provided because of the late hour). Commonwealth v. Nathan, 445 Pa. 470, 285 A.2d 175 (1971) (ignorance of second officer concerning first interrogation is no excuse).

Jurisdictions which prohibit interrogation after a request for counsel probably would not prohibit such interrogation when it is initiated by the suspect. People v. Randall, 1 Cal.3d 948, 83 Cal.Rptr. 658, 464 P.2d 114 (1970) ; and it is clear, from the *Miranda* opinion, that after requesting and consulting with counsel an accused may thereafter consent to be questioned. De La Fe v. United States, 413 F.2d 543 (5th Cir. 1969) ; Coughlan v. United States, 391 F.2d 371 (9th Cir. 1968) ; State v. Sample, 107 Ariz. 407, 489 P.2d 44 (1971) ; Commonwealth v. Jefferson, 445 Pa. 1, 281 A.2d 852 (1971). But see Commonwealth v. Taylor, —— Mass. ——, 374 N. E.2d 81 (1978) (police must give suspect some time to weigh counsel's advice).

3. In some cases, the suspect may waive his rights and submit to interrogation, and after an interval of time he may, of course, be interrogated a second time. Tucker v. United States, 375 F.2d 363 (8th Cir. 1967). The issue is whether warnings must be given before the second interrogation. A few cases require the repetition of warnings. Davis v. State, 44 Ala.App. 145, 204 So.2d 490 (1967) ; Brown v. State, 6 Md.App. 564, 252 A.2d 272 (1969). It is probably the better practice to re-warn. United States v. Thomas, 296 F.2d 310 (2nd Cir. 1968) ; United States v. Brady, 421 F.2d 681 (2nd Cir. 1970). But it is the general rule that the warnings need not be repeated.

4. MIRANDA WARNINGS IN MISDEMEANORS AND TO JUVENILES

(a) MISDEMEANORS

Miranda is not applicable to misdemeanors involving only fines or small jail penalties. State v. Zucconi, 93 N.J.Super. 380, 226 A.2d 16 (N.J.1967); Shumate v. Commonwealth, 207 Va. 877, 153 S.E.2d 243 (1967); State v. Pyle, 19 Ohio St.2d 64, 249 N.E.2d 826 (1969) (Misdemeanors—no more than one year incarceration). See Anno. 25 A.L.R.3rd 1076. *Miranda* is inapplicable even where a three month sentence is mandatory for the offense involved. State v. Macuk, 57 N.J. 1, 268 A.2d 1 (1970). See also Campbell v. Superior Court, 106 Ariz. 542, 479 P.2d 685 (1971) (inapplicable to routine traffic arrests); State v. Neal, 476 S.W.2d 547 (Mo.1972) (motor vehicle case); State v. Gabrielsen, 192 N.W.2d 792 (Iowa 1971) (30 day sentence); County of Dade v. Callahan, 259 So.2d 504 (Fla.App. 1971) (not applicable to drunk driving).

However, where there is a possibility of a substantial term of imprisonment for a misdemeanor—*Miranda* has been held to be applicable. Commonwealth v. Bonser, 215 Pa.Super. 452, 258 A.2d 675 (1969) (drunken driving—maximum of three years imprisonment).

In Clay v. Riddle, 541 F.2d 456 (4th Cir. 1976), the court, without reaching the more general question of *Miranda's* applicability to misdemeanor cases, held that warnings need not be provided to a suspect in a drunk driving case before questioning him about the circumstances of an accident. In *Clay* the suspect was handcuffed at the time of the questioning, having waved a gun at a state trooper. The suspect's answers were held admissible in a *felony* prosecution where Clay was charged with driving a vehicle in violation of an habitual offender provision. The Court concluded that critical factor was that at the time of interrogation the suspect was charged only with drunk driving.

(b) JUVENILES

Miranda's application to juvenile case situations is still in some doubt. See In re Gault, 387 U.S. 85, 87 S.Ct. 1428 (1967). The Supreme Court has shown a wavering reluctance to require full constitutional protections in juvenile proceedings because it is "reluctant to disallow the States to experiment . . . and to seek in new and different ways the elusive answers to the problems of the young." McKeiver v. Pennsylvania, 403 U.S. 528, 547, 91 S.Ct. 1976, 1987 (1971).

Some state jurisdictions have required all or part of the warnings in juvenile cases, either by statute—see Cal.Welf. & Inst.Code, § 625 (West 1972); Colo.Rev.Stat.Ann. § 19–2–102(3)(c)(I) (1974); N.M.Stat.Ann. § 32–1–27 (1978); Okl.Stat.Ann., Tit. 10, § 1109 (Supp.1979); Tex.Fam.Code, § 51.09(b) (Supp.1979); or by court decision—Freeman v. Wilcox, 119 Ga.App. 325, 167 S.E.2d 163 (1969) (but see Riley v. State, 237 Ga. 124, 226 S.E.2d 922 (1976)); People v. Horton, 126 Ill.App.2d 401, 261 N.E.2d 693 (1970); State v. Loyd, 297 Minn. 442, 212 N.W.2d 671 (1973); Lammert v. Parker, 500 S.W. 2d 274 (Mo.App.1973); Forest v. State, 76 Wash.2d 84, 455 P.2d 368 (1969); Theriault v. State, 66 Wis.2d 33, 223 N.W.2d 850 (1974). *Cf.* State v. R. W., 115 N.J.Super. 286, 279 A.2d 709 (1971), aff'd 61 N.J. 118, 293 A.2d 186 (1972). See also People v. Prude, 66 Ill.2d 470, 6 Ill.Dec. 689, 363 N.E.2d 371, cert. denied 434 U.S. 930, 98 S.Ct. 418, 54 L.Ed.2d 291 (1977).

5. MIRANDA AND INTERROGATIONS BY PERSONS OTHER THAN LAW ENFORCEMENT OFFICERS

The case law is very clear that the *Miranda* decision was directed at law enforcement officers, and is not applicable to private citizens, even when questioning persons they have restrained by virtue of a "citizen's arrest." For instance, a store security agent need not give the *Miranda* warnings to a person arrested for shoplifting or an employee arrested for thievery. See, for examples: Schaumberg v. State, 83 Nev. 372, 432 P.2d 500 (1967); People v. Shipp, 96 Ill.App.2d 364, 239 N.E.2d 296 (1968); United States v. Antonelli, 434 F.2d 335 (2nd Cir. 1970); State v. Archuleta, 82 N.M. 378, 482 P.2d 242 (1970); State v. Kelly, 61 N.J. 283, 294 A.2d 41 (1972).

In dealing with private citizen cases, the courts have kept to a precise technical definition of the interrogator's status. In Pratt v. State, 9 Md.App. 220, 263 A.2d 247 (1970) it was held that a private security guard who had been commissioned as a special officer by the Governor was required to give *Miranda* warnings. The same result was reached in a state where parole officers have statutory police powers, State v. Lekas, 201 Kan. 579, 442 P.2d 11 (1968). The mere fact that the private citizen is employed by the state does not require him to give *Miranda* warnings. People v. Wright, 249 Cal.App.2d 692, 57 Cal.Rptr. 781 (1967). The reliance upon the technical status of the interrogator also requires the holding that *Miranda* is inapplicable even if a private citizen falsely represents himself to be a law officer when he questions a suspect. See People v. Vlcek, 114 Ill. App.2d 74, 252 N.E.2d 377 (1969).

Police officers from foreign jurisdictions are not required to give *Miranda* warnings. The theory is that suppression of statements taken in violation of *Miranda* serves to deter future violation by police, but when the police are from Mexico or Canada the deterrent effect is nil. See People v. Helfend, 1 Cal.App.3d 873, 82 Cal.Rptr. 295 (1969); Commonwealth v. Wallace, 356 Mass. 92, 248 N.E.2d 246 (1969); Johnsen v. State, 448 P.2d 266 (Okl.1968); State v. Ford, 108 Ariz. 404, 499 P.2d 699 (1972) (Canadian); United States v. Welch, 455 F.2d 211 (2nd Cir. 1972) (Bahamian); and *Miranda* is inapplicable to American officers in foreign countries—State v. Cranford, 83 N.M. 294, 491 P.2d 511 (1971). But see Cranford v. Rodriguez, 512 F.2d 860 (10th Cir. 1975) (disapproving State v. Cranford).

These generally recognized rules are subject to one universally recognized qualification. That is, the police are forbidden to use private citizens or foreign officers as their agents in order to escape the *Miranda* rule. Nearly every case cited for the proposition that private citizens are not governed by *Miranda* also states that the police may not use the private citizen as an agent. There are cases illustrative of the agency concept.

In State v. Kelly, 439 S.W.2d 487 (Mo.1969), the Court found that while *Miranda* generally was inapplicable to private witnesses it did apply in a case where the defendant was in police custody and has indicated his desire to remain silent. The defendant was in a room with the interrogating officer and the victim. The officer did not question him further but the victim did and soon after the officer joined in the interrogation. The court held that the victim's interrogation was merely a continuation of the police interrogation. In Commonwealth v. Bordner, 432 Pa. 405, 247 A.2d 612 (1968), it was held that the police used the suspect's parents as their agents. Accord: People v. Baugh, 19 Ill.App.3d 448, 311 N.E.2d 607 (1974) (victim's attorney); People v. Jones, 61 A.D.2d 264, 402 N.Y.S.2d 28 (1978) (security officer). Where the suspect asked to speak to the victim and the victim agreed if the suspect were behind bars and the conversation taped, the victim was not a police agent where no questions were suggested by police. People v. Holzer, 25 Cal.App.3d 456, 102 Cal.Rptr. 11 (1972).

As regards an interview by a probation or parole officer with his charge, the general rule is that *Miranda* warnings are not required. See, for example, State v. Davis, 67 N.J. 222, 337 A.2d 33 (1975), which held that only when the charge is in custody are the warnings required.

See also Chapter 6, Section G.

6. MIRANDA AND THE SUSPECT WHO DOES NOT NEED THE WARNINGS

In one apparent pre-*Miranda* case a defendant complained about lack of warnings at his interrogation. The court brushed his complaint aside because the defendant was a judge. Commonwealth v. Schwartz, 210 Pa.Super. 360, 233 A.2d 904 (1967). What of the defendant who is a lawyer or a policeman? The *Miranda* opinion was very clear on this point:

> "We will not pause to inquire in individual cases whether the defendant was aware of his rights without a warning" (on the basis of his education, intelligence and experience); "a warning is a clearcut fact" . . . "More important, whatever the background of the person interrogated, a warning at the time of interrogation is indispensible to overcome its pressures and to insure that the individual knows he is free to exercise his privilege at that point in time".

This clear principle has occasionally been ignored. See State v. Devoe, 430 S.W.2d 164 (Mo.1968) (partial reliance on the prior criminal experience of defendant). United States v. Fayette, 388 F.2d 728 (2nd Cir. 1968).

In Dupont v. United States, 259 A.2d 355 (D.C.1969) a defendant was about to be warned when he said, "I know my rights". The court held that his statement was taken in violation of *Miranda*. When the suspect states that he knows his rights the officer should insist on continuing the warnings. Brown v. Heyd, 277 F.Supp. 899 (D.La.1967); State v. Pressel, 2 Or.App. 477, 468 P.2d 915 (1970) (en banc). Contra, State v. Perez, 182 Neb. 680, 157 N.W.2d 162 (1968) (suspect refused to listen further); State v. Thomas, 16 Wash.App. 1, 553 P.2d 1357 (1976) (court found that one who twice refused to hear warnings had "waived his right to be informed"). One reasonable deviation from the absolute rule is found in Kear v. United States, 369 F.2d 78 (9th Cir. 1966) where it was held unnecessary to warn a defendant of his right to remain silent when he said "I know I don't have to make a statement". In this case it is clear on the face of the record that the defendant knew specifically of his right to remain silent.

The prior criminal experience of the defendant can be used to help establish that the warnings given in the interrogation were understood because they had been given before in other cases. Jordan v. United States, 421 F.2d 493 (9th Cir. 1970); Thessen v. State, 454 P.2d 341 (Alaska 1969); State v. Collins, 74 Wash.2d 729, 446 P.2d 325 (1968). And prior experience may serve to support the validity of a waiver of rights, Heard v. State, 244 Ark. 44, 424 S.W.2d 179 (1968); State v. Miller, 35 Wis.2d 454, 151 N.W.2d 157 (1967).

A different problem is presented by the wealthy defendant. To warn him of his right to the services of a lawyer seems to be enough; the right is made no more meaningful to him if he is told that a lawyer will be appointed if he cannot afford one. For purposes of making a decision to waive his rights, it is enough for him to know he can see a lawyer before interrogation. In essence, the warning concerning appointed counsel is not itself a basic *Miranda* right; rather, it is a safety device designed to protect what is a basic *Miranda* right, the right to counsel. This conclusion is supported by implication in *Miranda*, 384 U.S. at 473 n. 43, 86 S.Ct. at 1627 (n. 43).

There have been various holdings to the effect that a non-indigent need not be warned of his right to appointed counsel, but some courts have required the prosecution to show non-indigency or require that it be apparent to the interrogators that the suspect is not indigent. See, for example, United States v. Messina, 388 F.2d 393 (2nd Cir. 1968).

It has been held that no warnings need be given where the attorney for the defendant contacted the police and said his client wished to make a statement. The court assumed that counsel knew of the interview and did not wish to be present. Dempsey v. State, 225 Ga. 208, 166 S.E.2d 884 (1969); Jones v. State, 47 Wis.2d 642, 178 N.W.

2d 42 (1970). But see Commonwealth v. Goldsmith, 438 Pa. 83, 263 A.2d 322 (1970) (cannot assume suspect knew of his rights because he came to the station with a lawyer). The prudent thing for the police to do, however, is to give the warnings anyway.

C.   INTERROGATION OF COUNSEL REPRESENTED SUSPECTS

MASSIAH v. UNITED STATES

Supreme Court of the United States, 1964.
377 U.S. 201, 84 S.Ct. 1199.

MR. JUSTICE STEWART delivered the opinion of the Court.

The petitioner, a merchant seaman, was in 1958 a member of the crew of the S. S. *Santa Maria*. In April of that year federal customs officials in New York received information that he was going to transport a quantity of narcotics aboard that ship from South America to the United States. As a result of this and other information, the agents searched the *Santa Maria* upon its arrival in New York and found in the afterpeak of the vessel five packages containing about three and a half pounds of cocaine. They also learned of circumstances, not here relevant, tending to connect the petitioner with the cocaine. He was arrested, promptly arraigned, and subsequently indicted for possession of narcotics aboard a United States vessel. In July a superseding indictment was returned, charging the petitioner and a man named Colson with the same substantive offense, and in separate counts charging the petitioner, Colson, and others with having conspired to possess narcotics aboard a United States vessel, and to import, conceal, and facilitate the sale of narcotics. The petitioner, who had retained a lawyer, pleaded not guilty and was released on bail, along with Colson.

A few days later, and quite without the petitioner's knowledge, Colson decided to cooperate with the government agents in their continuing investigation of the narcotics activities in which the petitioner, Colson, and others had allegedly been engaged. Colson permitted an agent named Murphy to install a Schmidt radio transmitter under the front seat of Colson's automobile, by means of which Murphy, equipped with an appropriate receiving device, could overhear from some distance away conversations carried on in Colson's car.

On the evening of November 19, 1959, Colson and the petitioner held a lengthy conversation while sitting in Colson's automobile, parked on a New York street. By prearrangement with Colson, and totally unbeknown to the petitioner, the agent Murphy sat in a car parked out of sight down the street and listened over the radio to the entire conversation. The petitioner made several incriminating statements during the course of this conversation. At the petitioner's trial these incriminating statements were brought before the jury through Murphy's testimony, despite the insistent objection of defense counsel.

* * *

In Spano v. New York, 360 U.S. 315, this Court reversed a state criminal conviction because a confession had been wrongly admitted into evidence against the defendant at his trial. In that case the defendant had already been indicted for first-degree murder at the time he confessed. The Court held that the defendant's conviction could not stand under the Fourteenth Amendment. While the Court's opinion relied upon the totality of the circumstances under which the confession had been obtained, four concurring Justices pointed out that the Constitution required reversal of the conviction upon the sole and specific ground that the confession had been deliberately elicited by the police after the defendant had been indicted, and therefore at a time when he was clearly entitled to a lawyer's help. It was pointed out that under our system of justice the most elemental concepts of due process of law contemplate that an indictment be followed by a trial, "in an orderly courtroom, presided over by a judge, open to the public, and protected by all the procedural safeguards of the law." It was said that a Constitution which guarantees a defendant the aid of counsel at such a trial could surely vouchsafe no less to an indicted defendant under interrogation by the police in a completely extrajudicial proceeding. Anything less, it was said, might deny a defendant "effective representation by counsel at the only stage when legal aid and advice would help him."

Ever since this Court's decision in the *Spano* case, the New York courts have unequivocally followed this constitutional rule. "Any secret interrogation of the defendant, from and after the finding of the indictment, without the protection afforded by the presence of counsel, contravenes the basic dictates of fairness in the conduct of criminal causes and the fundamental rights of persons charged with crime." People v. Waterman, 9 N.Y.2d 561, 565, 175 N.E.2d 445, 448.

This view no more than reflects a constitutional principle established as long ago as Powell v. Alabama, 287 U.S. 45, where the Court noted that ". . . during perhaps the most critical period of the proceedings . . . that is to say, from the time of their arraignment until the beginning of their trial, when consultation, thoroughgoing investigation and preparation [are] vitally important, the defendants . . . [are] as much entitled to such aid [of counsel] during that period as at the trial itself."

Here we deal not with a state court conviction, but with a federal case, where the specific guarantee of the Sixth Amendment directly applies. We hold that the petitioner was denied the basic protections of that guarantee when there was used against him at his trial evidence of his own incriminating words, which federal agents had deliberately elicited from him after he had been indicted and in the absence of his counsel. It is true that in the *Spano* case the defendant was interrogated in a police station, while here the damaging testimony was elicited from the defendant without his knowledge while he was free on bail. But, as Judge Hays pointed out in his dissent in the Court of Appeals, "if such a rule is to have any efficacy it must apply to indirect and surreptitious interrogations as well as those conducted in the jailhouse. In this case, Massiah was more seriously imposed upon . . . because he did not even know that he was under interrogation by a government agent."

The Solicitor General, in his brief and oral argument, has strenuously contended that the federal law enforcement agents had the right, if not indeed the duty, to continue their investigation of the petitioner and his alleged criminal associates even though the petitioner had been indicted. He points out that the Government was continuing its investigation in order to uncover not only the source of narcotics found on the S. S. *Santa Maria,* but also their intended buyer. He says that the quantity of narcotics involved was such as to suggest that the petitioner was part of a large and well-organized ring, and indeed that the continuing investigation confirmed this suspicion, since it resulted in criminal charges against many defendants. Under these circumstances the Solicitor General concludes that the government agents were completely "justified in making use of Colson's cooperation by having Colson continue his normal associations and by surveilling them."

We may accept and, at least for present purposes, completely approve all that this argument implies, Fourth Amendment problems to one side. We do not question that in this case, as in many cases, it was entirely proper to continue an investigation of the suspected criminal activities of the defendant and his alleged confederates, even though the defendant had already been indicted. All that we hold is that the defendant's own incriminating statements, obtained by federal agents under the circumstances here disclosed, could not constitutionally be used by the prosecution as evidence against *him* at his trial.

Reversed.

MR. JUSTICE WHITE, with whom MR. JUSTICE CLARK and MR. JUSTICE HARLAN join, dissenting.

* * *

. . . I am unable to see how this case presents an unconstitutional interference with Massiah's right to counsel. Massiah was not prevented from consulting with counsel as often as he wished. No meetings with counsel were disturbed or spied upon. Preparation for trial was in no way obstructed. It is only a sterile syllogism—an unsound one, besides—to say that because Massiah had a right to counsel's aid before and during the trial, his out-of-court conversations and admissions must be excluded if obtained without counsel's consent or presence. . . .

* * *

[The] Court's newly fashioned exclusionary principle goes far beyond the constitutional privilege against self-incrimination, which neither requires nor suggests the barring of voluntary pretrial admissions. The Fifth Amendment states that no person "shall be compelled in any criminal case to be a witness against himself . . . ." The defendant may thus not be compelled to testify at his trial, but he may if he wishes. Likewise he may not be compelled or coerced into saying anything before trial; but until today he could if he wished to, and if he did, it could be used against him. Whether as a matter of self incrimination or of due process, the proscription is against compulsion—coerced incrimination. Under the prior law, announced in countless cases in this Court, the defendant's pretrial statements were admissible evidence if voluntarily made; inadmissible if not the product of his free will. Hardly any constitutional area has been more carefully patrolled by this Court, and until now the Court has expressly rejected the argument that admissions are to be deemed involuntary if made outside the presence of counsel.

The Court presents no facts, no objective evidence, no reasons to warrant scrapping the voluntary-involuntary test for admissibility in this area. Without such evidence I would retain it in its present form.

This case cannot be analogized to the American Bar Association's rule forbidding an attorney to talk to the opposing party litigant outside the presence of his counsel. Aside from the fact that the Association's canons are not of constitutional dimensions, the specific canon argued is inapposite because it deals with the conduct of lawyers and not with the conduct of investigators. Lawyers are forbidden to interview the opposing party because of the supposed imbalance of legal skill and acumen between the lawyer and the party litigant; the reason for the rule does not apply to nonlawyers and certainly not to Colson, Massiah's codefendant.

Applying the new exclusionary rule is peculiarly inappropriate in this case. At the time of the conversation in question, petitioner was not in custody but free on bail. He was not questioned in what anyone could call an atmosphere of official coercion. What he said was said to his partner in crime who had also been indicted. There was no suggestion or any possibility of coercion. What petitioner did not know was that Colson had decided to report the conversation to the police. Had there been no prior arrangements between Colson and the police, had Colson simply gone to the police after the conversation had occurred, his testimony relating Massiah's statements would be readily admissible at the trial, as would a recording which he might have made of the conversation. In such event, it would simply be said that Massiah risked talking to a friend who decided to disclose what he knew of Massiah's criminal activities. But if, as occurred here, Colson had been cooperating with the police prior to his meeting with Massiah, both his evidence and the recorded conversation are somehow transformed into inadmissible evidence despite the fact that the hazard to Massiah remains precisely the same—the defection of a confederate in crime.

Reporting criminal behavior is expected or even demanded of the ordinary citizen. Friends may be subpoenaed to testify about friends, relatives about relatives and partners about partners. I therefore question the soundness of insulating Massiah from the apostasy of his partner in crime and of furnishing constitutional sanctions for the strict secrecy and discipline of criminal organizations. Neither the ordinary citizen nor the confessed criminal should be discouraged from reporting what he knows to the authorities and from lending his aid to secure evidence of crime. More narrowly, and posed by the precise situation involved here, the question is this: when the police have arrested and released on bail one member of a criminal ring and another member, a confederate, is cooperating with the police, can the confederate be allowed to continue his association with the ring or must he somehow be withdrawn to avoid challenge to trial evidence on the ground that it was acquired after rather than before the arrest, after rather than before the indictment?

Defendants who are out on bail have been known to continue their illicit operations. That an attorney is advising them should not constitutionally immunize their statements made in furtherance of these operations and relevant to the question of their guilt at the pending prosecution. In this very case there is evidence that after indictment defendant Aiken tried to persuade Agent Murphy to go into the narcotics business with him. Under today's decision, Murphy may neither testify as to the content of this conversation nor seize for introduction in evidence any narcotics whose location Aiken may have made known.

Undoubtedly, the evidence excluded in this case would not have been available but for the conduct of Colson in cooperation with Agent Murphy, but is it this kind of conduct which should be forbidden to those charged with law enforcement? . . . Massiah was not being interrogated in a police station, was not surrounded by numerous officers or questioned in relays, and was not forbidden access to others. Law enforcement may have the elements of a contest about it, but it is not a game. Massiah and those like him receive ample protection from the long line of precedents in this Court holding that confessions may not be introduced unless they are voluntary.

. . .

NOTES

1. *Massiah* has not lent itself to uniform interpretation. Some courts read *Massiah* to exclude only statements by defendants which are induced or deliberately elicited by police officers or their agents in the absence of counsel. See United States v. Accardi, 342 F.2d 697 (2d Cir. 1965). This narrower view was adopted, at first, without any consideration of the memorandum decision in McLeod v. Ohio, 381 U.S. 356, 85 S.Ct. 1556 (1966), which reversed State v. McLeod, 203 N.E.2d 349 (Ohio 1965). The Ohio Court had previously adopted the narrow interpretation of *Massiah* to approve admission of a spontaneous, voluntary, oral statement made to government officers after indictment but prior to the appointment of counsel. Further, the narrow interpretation of *Massiah* was adopted in Beatty v. United States, 377 F.2d 181 (5th Cir. 1967), and this opinion, too, was re-

versed in per curiam. Beatty v. United States, 389 U.S. 45, 88 S.Ct. 234 (1967). After these opinions were noted, some courts said that *Massiah* "applies to exclude post-indictment statements of an accused to government agents in the absence of counsel even when not deliberately elicited by interrogation or induced by misapprehension engendered by trickery or deception." Hancock v. White, 378 F.2d 479, 482 (1st Cir. 1967); United States ex rel. O'Connor v. New Jersey, 405 F.2d 632 (3d Cir. 1969).

2. The passage of time has shown courts to be reluctant to extend the *Massiah* rule (which arose in a case of deliberate eliciting of incriminating admissions) to unelicited admissions. See State v. Blizzard, 278 Md. 556, 366 A.2d 1026 (1976) (thorough review of decisions admitting post indictment statements where defendant initiates the interview with a known agent of law enforcement); United States v. Garcia, 377 F.2d 321 (2d Cir. 1967) (volunteered admissions); State v. Goodpaster, 479 S.W.2d 449 (Mo. Sup.Ct.1972) (same). See also State v. Chabonian, 50 Wis.2d 574, 185 N. W.2d 289 (1971) and Chabonian v. Liek, 366 F.Supp. 72 (E.D.Wis.1973).

3. In his dissent, Justice White suggests that *Massiah* would operate to exclude evidence of fresh criminal conduct engaged in by a defendant after his indictment, i. e., Aiken's attempt "to persuade Agent Murphy to go into the Narcotics business with him." The courts generally have not so applied *Massiah*. See Grieco v. Meachum, 533 F.2d 713 (1st Cir. 1976) (indicted prisoner sought to get another inmate to confess to the crime); Deskins v. Commonwealth, 512 S.W.2d 520 (Ky.1974) (indictee recruits informer to steal files from the prosecutor's office). But see United States v. Anderson, 523 F.2d 1192 (5th Cir. 1975) (improper to show that accused sold a drug prescription to undercover agent while under indictment in the trial of that indictment).

4. *Massiah* does not apply when an indictee makes admissions to one who becomes an informer only *after* the admissions are made. United States ex rel. Milani v. Pate, 425 F.2d 6 (7th Cir. 1970); United States ex rel. Baldwin v. Yeager, 314 F.Supp. 10 (D.C.N.J.1969), affirmed 428 F.2d 182 (3d Cir. 1970). See People v. Smith, 5 Ill.App.3d 642, 283 N.E.2d 736 (1972) (admissions to private citizen not precluded by *Massiah*). On the question of whether informer was an agent of the police, see State v. Daugherty, 221 Kan. 612, 562 P.2d 42 (1977), and Gammel v. State, 259 Ark. 96, 531 S.W.2d 474 (1976) (State need not prove absence of agency). One recurring situation is where statements are made to or overheard by an informer in defendant's jail cell. The decisions have hinged on whether or not the informer was deliberately placed in the cell. State v. Killary, 133 Vt. 604, 349 A.2d 216 (1975). United States v. Aloisio, 440 F.2d 705 (7th Cir. 1971) Compare State v. Jensen, 111 Ariz. 408, 531 P.2d 531 (1975) (no placement) with State v. Smith, 107 Ariz. 100, 482 P.2d 863 (1971) (volunteered admissions to informer placed in cell are excluded).

BREWER v. WILLIAMS

Supreme Court of the United States, 1977.
430 U.S. 387, 97 S.Ct. 1232.

Mr. Justice Stewart delivered the opinion of the Court.

An Iowa trial jury found the respondent, Robert Williams, guilty of murder. The judgment of conviction was affirmed in the Iowa Supreme Court by a closely divided vote. In a subsequent habeas corpus proceeding a federal district court ruled that under the United States Constitution Williams is entitled to a new trial, and a divided Court of Appeals for the Eighth Circuit agreed. The question before us is whether the District Court and the Court of Appeals were wrong.

I.

On the afternoon of December 24, 1968, a 10-year-old girl named Pamela Powers went with her family to the YMCA in Des Moines, Iowa, to watch a wrestling tournament in which her brother was participating. When she failed to return from a trip to the washroom, a search for her began. The search was unsuccessful.

Robert Williams, who had recently escaped from a mental hospital, was a resident of the YMCA. Soon after the girl's disappearance Williams was seen in the YMCA lobby carrying some clothing and a large bundle wrapped in a blanket. He obtained help from a 14-year-old boy in opening the street door of the YMCA and the door to his automobile parked outside. When Williams placed the bundle in the front seat of his car the boy "saw two legs in it and they were skinny and white." Before anyone could see what was in the bundle Williams drove away. His abandoned car was found the following day in Davenport, Iowa, roughly 160 miles east of Des Moines. A warrant was then issued in Des Moines for his arrest on a charge of abduction.

On the morning of December 26, a Des Moines lawyer named Henry McKnight went to the Des Moines police station and informed the officers present that he had just received a long distance call from Williams, and that he had advised Williams to turn himself in to the Davenport police. Williams did surrender that morning to the police in Davenport, and they booked him on the charge specified in the arrest warrant and gave him the warnings required by Miranda v. Arizona, 384 U.S. 436, 86 S.Ct. 1602 (1966). The Davenport police then telephoned their counterparts in Des Moines to inform them that Williams had surrendered. McKnight, the lawyer, was still at the Des Moines police headquarters, and Williams conversed with McKnight on the telephone. In the presence of the Des Moines Chief of Police and a Police Detective named Leaming, McKnight advised Williams that Des Moines police officers would be driving to Davenport to pick him up, that the officers would not interrogate him or mistreat him, and that Williams was not to talk to the officers about Pamela Powers until after consulting with McKnight upon his return to Des Moines. As a result of these conversations, it was agreed between McKnight and the Des Moines police officials that Detective Leaming and a fellow officer would drive to Davenport to pick up Williams, that they would bring him directly back to Des Moines, and that they would not question him during the trip.

In the meantime Williams was arraigned before a judge in Davenport on the outstanding arrest warrant. The judge advised him of his *Miranda* rights and committed him to jail. Before leaving the courtroom, Williams conferred with a lawyer named Kelly, who advised him not to make any statements until consulting with McKnight back in Des Moines.

Detective Leaming and his fellow officer arrived in Davenport about noon to pick up Williams and return him to Des Moines. Soon after their arrival they met with Williams and Kelly, who, they understood, was acting as Williams' lawyer. Detective Leaming repeated the *Miranda* warnings, and told Williams:

> ".   .   . we both know that you're being represented here
> by Mr. Kelly and you're being represented by Mr. McKnight
> in Des Moines, and .   .   .   I want you to remember this be-
> cause we"ll be visiting between here and Des Moines."

Williams then conferred again with Kelly alone, and after this conference Kelly reiterated to Detective Leaming that Williams was not to be questioned about the disappearance of Pamela Powers until after he had consulted with McKnight back in Des Moines. When Leaming expressed some reservations, Kelly firmly stated that the agreement with McKnight was to be carried out—that there was to be no interrogation of Williams during the automobile journey to Des Moines. Kelly was denied permission to ride in the police car back to Des Moines with Williams and the two officers.

The two Detectives, with Williams in their charge, then set out on the 160-mile drive. At no time during the trip did Williams express a willingness to be interrogated in the absence of an attorney. Instead, he stated several times that "[w]hen I get to Des Moines and see Mr. McKnight, I am going to tell you the whole story." Detective Leaming knew that Williams was a former mental patient, and knew also that he was deeply religious.

The Detective and his prisoner soon embarked on a wide-ranging conversation covering a variety of topics, including the subject of religion. Then, not long after leaving Davenport and reaching the interstate highway, Detective Leaming delivered what has been referred to in the briefs and oral arguments as the "Christian burial speech." Addressing Williams as "Reverend," the Detective said:

> "I want to give you something to think about while we're
> traveling down the road.   .   .   .   Number one, I want you
> to observe the weather conditions, it's raining, it's sleeting,
> it's freezing, driving is very treacherous, visibility is poor,
> it's going to be dark early this evening. They are predict-
> ing several inches of snow for tonight, and I feel that you
> yourself are the only person that knows where this little
> girl's body is, that you yourself have only been there once,
> and if you get a snow on top of it you yourself may be un-
> able to find it. And, since we will be going right past the
> area on the way into Des Moines, I feel that we could stop
> and locate the body, that the parents of this little girl should
> be entitled to a Christian burial for the little girl who was
> snatched away from them on Christmas Eve and murdered.

And I feel we should stop and locate it on the way in rather than waiting until morning and trying to come back out after a snow storm and possibly not being able to find it at all."

Williams asked Detective Leaming why he thought their route to Des Moines would be taking them past the girl's body, and Leaming responded that he knew the body was in the area of Mitchellville—a town they would be passing on the way to Des Moines.[1] Leaming then stated: "I do not want you to answer me. I don't want to discuss it further. Just think about it as we're riding down the road."

As the car approached Grinnell, a town approximately 100 miles west of Davenport, Williams asked whether the police had found the victim's shoes. When Detective Leaming replied that he was unsure, Williams directed the officers to a service station where he said he had left the shoes; a search for them proved unsuccessful. As they continued towards Des Moines, Williams asked whether the police had found the blanket, and directed the officers to a rest area where he said he had disposed of the blanket. Nothing was found. The car continued towards Des Moines, and as it approached Mitchellville, Williams said that he would show the officers where the body was. He then directed the police to the body of Pamela Powers.

Williams was indicted for first-degree murder. Before trial, his counsel moved to suppress all evidence relating to or resulting from any statements Williams had made during the automobile ride from Davenport to Des Moines. After an evidentiary hearing the trial judge denied the motion. He found that "an agreement was made between defense counsel and the police officials to the effect that the Defendant was not to be questioned on the return trip to Des Moines," and that the evidence in question had been elicited from Williams during "a critical stage in the proceedings requiring the presence of counsel on his request." The judge ruled, however, that Williams had "waived his right to have an attorney present during the giving of such information."

The evidence in question was introduced over counsel's continuing objection at the subsequent trial. The jury found Williams guilty of murder, and the judgment of conviction was affirmed by the Iowa Supreme Court, a bare majority of whose members agreed with the trial court that Williams had "waived his right to the presence of his counsel" on the automobile ride from Davenport to Des Moines. The four dissenting justices expressed the view that "when counsel and police have agreed defendant is not to be questioned until counsel is present and defendant has been advised not to talk and repeatedly has stated he will tell the whole story after he talks with counsel, the state should be required to make a stronger showing of intentional voluntary waiver than was made here."

1. The fact of the matter, of course, was that Detective Leaming possessed no such knowledge.

Williams then petitioned for a writ of habeas corpus in the United States District Court for the Southern District of Iowa. Counsel for the State and for Williams stipulated "that the case would be submitted on the record of facts and proceedings in the trial court, without taking of further testimony." The District Court made findings of fact as summarized above, and concluded as a matter of law that the evidence in question had been wrongly admitted at Williams' trial. This conclusion was based on three alternative and independent grounds: (1) that Williams had been denied his constitutional right to the assistance of counsel; (2) that he had been denied the constitutional protections defined by this Court's decisions in Escobedo v. Illinois and Miranda v. Arizona; and (3) that in any event, his self-incriminatory statements on the automobile trip from Davenport to Des Moines had been involuntarily made. Further, the District Court ruled that there had been no waiver by Williams of the constitutional protections in question.

The Court of Appeals for the Eighth Circuit, with one judge dissenting, affirmed this judgment, and denied a petition for rehearing en banc. We granted certiorari to consider the constitutional issues presented.

* * *

As stated above, the District Court based its judgment in this case on three independent grounds. The Court of Appeals appears to have affirmed the judgment on two of those grounds. We have concluded that only one of them need be considered here.

Specifically, there is no need to review in this case the doctrine of Miranda v. Arizona, supra, a doctrine designed to secure the constitutional privilege against compulsory self-incrimination. It is equally unnecessary to evaluate the ruling of the District Court that Williams' self-incriminating statements were, indeed, involuntarily made. For it is clear that the judgment before us must in any event be affirmed upon the ground that Williams was deprived of a different constitutional right—the right to the assistance of counsel.

* * *

. . . Whatever else it may mean, the right to counsel granted by the Sixth and Fourteenth Amendments means at least that a person is entitled to the help of a lawyer at or after the time that judicial proceedings have been initiated against him—"whether by way of formal charge, preliminary hearing, indictment, information, or arraignment." Kirby v. Illinois. See Powell v. Alabama; Johnson v. Zerbst; Hamilton v. Alabama; Gideon v. Wainwright; White v. Maryland; Massiah v. United States; United States v. Wade; Gilbert v. California; Coleman v. Alabama.

There can be no doubt in the present case that judicial proceedings had been initiated against Williams before the start of the automobile ride from Davenport to Des Moines. A warrant had been issued for his arrest, he had been arraigned on that warrant before a judge in a Davenport courtroom, and he had been committed by the court to confinement in jail. The State does not contend otherwise.

There can be no serious doubt, either, that Detective Leaming deliberately and designedly set out to elicit information from Williams just as surely as—and perhaps more effectively than—if he had formally interrogated him.   Detective Leaming was fully aware before departing for Des Moines that Williams was being represented in Davenport by Kelly and in Des Moines by McKnight.   Yet he purposely sought during Williams' isolation from his lawyers to obtain as much incriminating information as possible.   Indeed, Detective Leaming conceded as much when he testified at Williams' trial:

> "Q.   In fact, Captain, whether he was a mental patient or not, you were trying to get all the information you could before he got to his lawyer, weren't you?

> "A.   I was sure hoping to find out where that little girl was, yes, sir.

> * * *

> "Q.   Well, I'll put it this way: You was hoping to get all the information you could before Williams got back to McKnight, weren't you?

> "A.   Yes, sir." [2]

The state courts clearly proceeded upon the hypothesis that Detective Leaming's "Christian burial speech" had been tantamount to interrogation.   Both courts recognized that Williams had been entitled to the assistance of counsel at the time he made the incriminating statements.   Yet no such constitutional protection would have come into play if there had been no interrogation.

The circumstances of this case are thus constitutionally indistinguishable from those presented in Massiah v. United States.   The petitioner in that case was indicted for violating the federal narcotics law.   He retained a lawyer, pleaded not guilty, and was released on bail.   While he was free on bail a federal agent succeeded by surreptitious means in listening to incriminating statements made by him.   Evidence of these statements was introduced against the petitioner at his trial, and he was convicted.   This Court reversed the conviction, holding "that the petitioner was denied the basic protections of that guarantee [the right to counsel] when there was used against him at his trial evidence of his own incriminating words, which federal agents had deliberately solicited from him after he had been indicted and in the absence of his counsel."

That the incriminating statements were elicited surreptitiously in the Massiah case, and otherwise here, is constitutionally irrelevant.

---

2. Counsel for the State, in the course of oral argument in this Court, acknowledged that the "Christian burial speech" was tantamount to interrogation:

> "Q: But isn't the point, Mr. Attorney General, what you indicated earlier, and that is that the officer wanted to elicit information from Williams—

> "A: Yes, sir.

> "Q: —by whatever techniques he used, I would suppose a lawyer would consider that he were pursuing interrogation.

> "A: It is, but it was very brief."

Rather, the clear rule of *Massiah* is that once adversary proceedings have commenced against an individual, he has a right to legal representation when the government interrogates him. It thus requires no wooden or technical application of the *Massiah* doctrine to conclude that Williams was entitled to the assistance of counsel guaranteed to him by the Sixth and Fourteenth Amendments.

The Iowa courts recognized that Williams had been denied the constitutional right to the assistance of counsel. They held, however, that he had waived that right during the course of the automobile trip from Davenport to Des Moines.

* * *

In the federal habeas corpus proceeding the District Court believing that the issue of waiver was not one of fact but of federal law, held that the Iowa courts had "applied the wrong constitutional standards" in ruling that Williams had waived the protections that were his under the Constitution.   .   .   .   After carefully reviewing the evidence the District Court concluded:

> "[U]nder the proper standards for determining waiver, there simply is no evidence to support a waiver.   .   .   .   [T]here is no affirmative indication   .   .   .   that [Williams] did waive his rights.   .   .   .   [T]he state courts' emphasis on the absence of a demand for counsel was not only legally inappropriate, but factually unsupportable as well, since Detective Leaming himself testified that [Williams], on several occasions during the trip, indicated that he would talk *after* he saw Mr. McKnight. Both these statements and Mr. Kelly's statement to Detective Leaming that [Williams] would talk only after seeing Mr. McKnight in Des Moines certainly were assertions of [Williams'] right or desire not to give information absent the presence of his attorney   .   .   ..   Moreover, the statements were obtained only after Detective Leaming's use of psychology on a person whom he knew to be deeply religious and an escapee from a mental hospital—with the specific intent to elicit incriminating statements. In the face of this evidence, the State has produced no affirmative evidence whatsoever to support its claim of waiver, and, a fortiori, it cannot be said that the State has met its 'heavy burden' of showing a knowing and intelligent waiver of   .   .   .   Sixth Amendment rights." 375 F.Supp. at 182–183 (emphasis in original).

The Court of Appeals approved the reasoning of the District Court:

> "A review of the record here   .   .   .   discloses no facts to support the conclusion of the state court that [Williams] had waived his constitutional rights other than that [he] had made incriminating statements.   .   .   .   The District Court here properly concluded that an incorrect

constitutional standard had been applied by the state court
in determining the issue of waiver. . . .

* * *

"[T]his court recently held that an accused can voluntarily, knowingly and intelligently waive his right to have
counsel present at an interrogation after counsel has been
appointed. . . . The prosecution, however, has the
weighty obligation to show that the waiver was knowingly
and intelligently made. We quite agree with Judge Hanson
that the state here failed to so show." 509 F.2d, at 233.

The District Court and the Court of Appeals were correct in the
view that the question of waiver was not a question of historical fact,
but one which, in the words of Mr. Justice Frankfurter, requires "application of constitutional principles to the facts as found. . . ."
Brown v. Allen, 344 U.S. 443, 507, 73 S.Ct. 397, 446 (separate opinion).

The District Court and the Court of Appeals were also correct in
their understanding of the proper standard to be applied in determining the question of waiver as a matter of federal constitutional law
—that it was incumbent upon the State to prove "an intentional relinquishment or abandonment of a known right or privilege." Johnson v. Zerbst . . .

* * *

We conclude, finally, that the Court of Appeals was correct in
holding that, judged by these standards, the record in this case falls
far short of sustaining the State's burden. It is true that Williams
had been informed of and appeared to understand his right to counsel. But waiver requires not merely comprehension but relinquishment, and Williams' consistent reliance upon the advice of counsel in
dealing with the authorities refutes any suggestion that he waived
that right. He consulted McKnight by long distance telephone before
turning himself in. He spoke with McKnight by telephone again
shortly after being booked. After he was arraigned, Williams sought
out and obtained legal advice from Kelly. Williams again consulted
with Kelly after Detective Leaming and his fellow officer arrived in
Davenport. Throughout, Williams was advised not to make any
statements before seeing McKnight in Des Moines, and was assured
that the police had agreed not to question him. His statements while
in the car that he would tell the whole story *after* seeing McKnight in
Des Moines were the clearest expressions by Williams himself that he
desired the presence of an attorney before any interrogation took
place. But even before making these statements, Williams had effectively asserted his right to counsel by having secured attorneys at
both ends of the automobile trip, both of whom, acting as his agents,
had made clear to the police that no interrogation was to occur during the journey. Williams knew of that agreement and particularly
in view of his consistent reliance on counsel, there is no basis for concluding that he disavowed it.

Despite Williams' express and implicit assertions of his right to counsel, Detective Leaming proceeded to elicit incriminating statements from Williams. Leaming did not preface this effort by telling Williams that he had a right to the presence of a lawyer, and made no effort at all to ascertain whether Williams wished to relinquish that right. The circumstances of record in this case thus provide no reasonable basis for finding that Williams waived his right to the assistance of counsel.

The Court of Appeals did not hold, nor do we, that under the circumstances of this case Williams *could not*, without notice to counsel, have waived his rights under the Sixth and Fourteenth Amendments. It only held, as do we, that he did not.

IV.

The crime of which Williams was convicted was senseless and brutal, calling for swift and energetic action by the police to apprehend the perpetrator and gather evidence with which he could be convicted. No mission of law enforcement officials is more important. Yet "[d]isinterested zeal for the public good does not assure either wisdom or right in the methods it pursues." Haley v. Ohio, 332 U.S. 596, 605, 68 S.Ct. 302. (Frankfurter, J., concurring in the judgment). Although we do not lightly affirm the issuance of a writ of habeas corpus in this case, so clear a violation of the Sixth and Fourteenth Amendments as here occurred cannot be condoned. The pressures on state executive and judicial officers charged with the administration of the criminal law are great, especially when the crime is murder and the victim a small child. But it is precisely the predictability of those pressures that makes imperative a resolute loyalty to the guarantees that the Constitution extends to us all.

The judgment of the Court of Appeals is affirmed.[3]

MR. JUSTICE MARSHALL, concurring. [Opinion omitted.]

MR. JUSTICE POWELL, concurring.

As the dissenting opinion of The Chief Justice sharply illustrates, resolution of the issues in this case turns primarily on one's perception of the facts. There is little difference of opinion, among the several courts (and numerous judges) who have reviewed the

---

3. The District Court stated that its decision "does not touch upon the issue of what evidence, if any, beyond the incriminating statements themselves must be excluded as 'fruit of the poisonous tree.'" 375 F.Supp., at 185. We too have no occasion to address this issue, and in the present posture of the case there is no basis for the view of our dissenting Brethren that any attempt to retry the respondent would probably be futile. While neither Williams' incriminating statements themselves nor any testimony describing his having led the police to the victim's body can constitutionally be admitted into evidence, evidence of where the body was found and of its condition might well be admissible on the theory that the body would have been discovered in any event, even had incriminating statements not been elicited from Williams. Cf. Killough v. United States, 336 F.2d 929 (1964). In the event that a retrial is instituted, it will be for the state courts in the first instance to determine whether particular items of evidence may be admitted.

case, as to the relevant constitutional principles: (i) Williams had the right to assistance of counsel; (ii) once that right attached (it is conceded that it had in this case), the State could not properly interrogate Williams in the absence of counsel unless he voluntarily and knowingly waived the right; and (iii) the burden was on the State to show that Williams in fact had waived the right before the police interrogated him.

The critical factual issue is whether there had been a voluntary waiver, and this turns in large part upon whether there was interrogation. .   .   .

* * *

I join the opinion of the Court which also finds that the efforts of Detective Leaming "to elicit information from Williams," as conceded by counsel for the State at oral argument, were a skillful and effective form of interrogation. Moreover, the entire setting was conducive to the psychological coercion that was successfully exploited. Williams was known by the police to be a young man with quixotic religious convictions and a history of mental disorders. The date was Christmas eve, the weather was ominous, and the setting appropriate for Detective Leaming's talk of snow concealing the body and preventing a "Christian burial." Williams was alone in the automobile with two police officers for several hours. It is clear from the record, as both of the federal courts below found, that there was no evidence of a knowing and voluntary waiver of the right to have counsel present beyond the fact that Williams ultimately confessed. It is settled law that an inferred waiver of a constitutional right is disfavored. I find no basis in the record of this case—or in the dissenting opinions—for disagreeing with the conclusion of the District Court that "the State has produced no affirmative evidence whatever to support its claim of waiver."

The dissenting opinion of The Chief Justice states that the Court's holding today "conclusively presumes a suspect is legally incompetent to change his mind and tell the truth until an attorney is present." I find no justification for this view. On the contrary, the opinion of the Court is explicitly clear that the right to assistance of counsel may be waived, after it has attached, without notice to or consultation with counsel. We would have such a case here if the State had proved that the police officers refrained from coercion and interrogation, as they have agreed, and that Williams freely on his own initiative had confessed the crime.

In discussing the exclusionary rule, the dissenting opinion of The Chief Justice refers to Stone v. Powell, decided last Term. In that case, we held that a federal court need not apply the exclusionary rule on habeas corpus review of a Fourth Amendment claim absent a showing that the state prisoner was denied an opportunity for a full and fair litigation of that claim at trial and on direct review.

This case also involves review on habeas corpus of a state conviction, and the decisions that the Court today affirms held that Williams' incriminating statements should have been excluded. As *Stone* was decided subsequently to these decisions, the courts below had no occasion to consider whether the principle enunciated in *Stone* may have been applicable in this case.   That question has not been presented in the briefs or arguments submitted to us [4] and we therefore have no occasion to consider the possible applicability of *Stone*. The applicability of the rationale of *Stone* in the Fifth and Sixth Amendment context raises a number of unresolved issues.   Many Fifth and Sixth Amendment claims arise in the context of challenges to the fairness of a trial or to the integrity of the factfinding process. In contrast, Fourth Amendment claims uniformly involve evidence that is "typically reliable and often the most probative information bearing on the guilt or innocence of the defendant."   Stone v. Powell. Whether the rationale of *Stone* should be applied to those Fifth and Sixth Amendment claims or classes of claims that more closely parallel claims under the Fourth Amendment is a question as to which I intimate no view, and which should be resolved only after the implications of such a ruling have been fully explored.

MR. JUSTICE STEVENS, concurring.

MR. JUSTICE STEWART, in his opinion for the Court which I join, MR. JUSTICE POWELL and MR. JUSTICE MARSHALL have accurately explained the reasons why the law requires the result we reach today.   Nevertheless, the strong language in the dissenting opinions prompts me to add this brief comment about the Court's function in a case such as this.

Nothing that we write, no matter how well reasoned or forcefully expressed, can bring back the victim of this tragedy or undo the consequences of the official neglect which led to the respondent's escape from a State mental institution.   The emotional aspects of the case make it difficult to decide dispassionately, but do not qualify our obligation to apply the law with an eye to the future as well as with concern for the result in the particular case before us.

Underlying the surface issues in this case is the question whether a fugitive from justice can rely on his lawyer's advice given in connection with a decision to surrender voluntarily.   The defendant placed his trust in an experienced Iowa trial lawyer who in turn trusted the Iowa law enforcement authorities to honor a commitment made during negotiations which led to the apprehension of a potentially dangerous person.   Under any analysis, this was a critical stage of the proceeding in which the participation of an independent professional was of vital importance to the accused and to society. At this stage—as in countless others in which the law profoundly affects the life of the individual—the lawyer is the essential medium

4. The *Stone* issue was not mentioned in any of the briefs, including the State's reply brief filed September 29, 1976—some three months after our decision in *Stone* was announced. The possible relevance of *Stone* was raised by a question from the Bench during oral argument.   This prompted brief comments by counsel for both parties.   But in no meaningful sense can the issue be viewed as having been "argued" in this case.

through which the demands and commitments of the sovereign are communicated to the citizen. If, in the long run, we are seriously concerned about the individual's effective representation by counsel, the State cannot be permitted to dishonor its promise to this lawyer.

MR. CHIEF JUSTICE BURGER, dissenting.

The result reached by the Court in this case ought to be intolerable in any society which purports to call itself an organized society. It continues the court—by the narrowest margin—on the much criticized course of punishing the public for the mistakes and misdeeds of law enforcement officers, instead of punishing the officer directly, if in fact he is guilty of wrongdoing. It mechanically and blindly keeps reliable evidence from juries whether the claimed constitutional violation involves gross police misconduct or honest human error. Williams is guilty of the savage murder of a small child; no Member of the Court contends he is not. While in custody, and after no fewer than *five* warnings of his rights to silence and to counsel, he led police to the place where he had buried the body of his victim. The Court now holds the jury must not be told how the police found the body.

The Court concedes Williams was not threatened or coerced and that he acted voluntarily and with full awareness of his constitutional rights when he guided police to the body. In the face of all this, the Court now holds that because Williams was prompted by the detective's statement—not interrogation but a statement—his disclosure cannot be given to the jury.

The effect of this is to fulfill Justice Cardozo's grim prophecy that someday some court might carry the exclusionary rule to the absurd extent that its operative effect would exclude evidence relating to the body of a murder victim because of the means by which it was found.[5] In so doing the Court regresses to playing a grisly game of "hide and seek," once more exalting the sporting theory of criminal

---

5. "The criminal is to go free because the constable has blundered. . . . A room is searched against the law, and the body of a murdered man is found . . . . The privacy of the home has been infringed, and the murderer goes free." People v. Defore, 242 N.Y. 13, 21, 23–24, 150 N.E. 585, 587, 588 (1926).

The Court protests, that its holding excludes only "Williams' incriminating statements themselves [as well as] any testimony describing his having led the police to the victim's body," thus hinting that successful retrial of this palpably guilty felon is realistically possible. Even if this were all, and the *corpus delicti* could be used to establish the fact and manner of the victim's death, the Court's holding clearly bars all efforts to let the jury know how the police found the body. But the Court's further—and remarkable—statement that "evidence of where the body was found and of its condition" could be admitted *only* "on the theory that the body would have been discovered in any event" makes clear that the Court is determined to keep the truth from the jurors pledged to find the truth. If all use of the *corpus delicti* is to be barred by the Court as "fruit of the poisonous tree" under Wong Sun v. United States, 371 U.S. 471, 83 S. Ct. 407 (1963), except on the unlikely theory suggested by the Court, the Court renders the prospects of doing justice in this case exceedingly remote.

justice which has been experiencing a decline in our jurisprudence. With Justices White and Blackmun, I categorically reject the remarkable notion that the police in this case were guilty of unconstitutional misconduct, or any conduct justifying the bizarre result reached by the Court. Apart from a brief comment on the merits, however, I wish to focus on the irrationality of applying the increasingly discredited exclusionary rule to this case.

* * *

The evidence is uncontradicted that Williams had abundant knowledge of his right to have counsel present and of his right to silence. Since the Court does not question Williams' mental competence, it boggles the mind to suggest that he could not understand that leading police to the child's body would have other than the most serious consequences. All of the elements necessary to make out a valid waiver are shown by the record and, paradoxically, acknowledged by the Court; we thus are left to guess how the Court reached its holding.

One plausible but unarticulated basis for the result reached is that once a suspect has asserted his right not to talk without the presence of an attorney, it becomes legally impossible to waive that right until the suspect has seen an attorney. But constitutional rights are *personal*, and an otherwise valid waiver should not be brushed aside by judges simply because an attorney was not present. The Court's holding operates to "imprison a man in his privileges," Adams v. United States ex rel. McCann, 317 U.S. 269, 280, 63 S.Ct. 236 (1942); it conclusively presumes a suspect is legally incompetent to change his mind and tell the truth until an attorney is present. It denigrates an individual to some sort of nonperson whose free will has become hostage to a lawyer so that until a lawyer consents, the suspect is deprived of any legal right or power to decide for himself that he wishes to make a disclosure. It denies that the rights to counsel and silence are *personal*, nondelegable, and subject to a waiver only by that individual. The opinions in support of the Court's judgment do not enlighten us as to why police conduct—whether good or bad—should operate to suspend Williams' right to change his mind and "tell all" at once rather than waiting until he reached Des Moines.

In his concurring opinion Mr. Justice Powell suggests that the result in this case turns on whether Detective Leaming's remarks constituted "interrogation," as he views them, or whether they were "statements" intended to prick the conscience of the accused. I find it most remarkable that a murder case should turn on judicial interpretation that a statement becomes a question simply because it is followed by an incriminating disclosure from the suspect. The Court seems to be saying that since Williams said he would "tell the whole story" at Des Moines, the police should have been content and waited; of course, that would have been the wiser course, especially in light of the nuances of constitutional jurisprudence applied by the Court, but a murder case ought not turn on such tenuous strands.

In any case, the Court assures us, this is not at all what it intends, and that a valid waiver was *possible* in these circumstances, but was not quite made. Here of course Williams did not confess to the murder in so many words; it was his conduct in guiding police to the body, not his words, which incriminated him. And the record is replete with evidence that Williams knew precisely what he was doing when he guided police to the body. The human urge to confess wrongdoing is, of course, normal in all save hardened, professional criminals, as psychiatrists and analysts have demonstrated. T. Reik, The Compulsion to Confess.

The Exclusionary Rule Should Not Be Applied to
Non-Egregious Police Conduct

Even if there was no waiver, and assuming a technical violation occurred, the Court errs gravely in mechanically applying the exclusionary rule without considering whether that draconian judicial doctrine should be invoked in these circumstances, or indeed whether any of its conceivable goals will be furthered by its application here.

The obvious flaws of the exclusionary rule as a judicial remedy are familiar.

* * *

Against this background, it is striking that the Court fails even to consider whether the benefits secured by application of the exclusionary rule in this case outweigh its obvious social costs. Perhaps the failure is due to the fact that this case arises not under the Fourth Amendment, but under Miranda v. Arizona, 384 U.S. 436, 86 S.Ct. 1602 (1966), and the Sixth Amendment right to counsel. The Court apparently perceives the function of the exclusionary rule to be so different in these varying contexts that it must be mechanically and uncritically applied in all cases arising outside the Fourth Amendment.

But this is demonstrably not the case where police conduct collides with *Miranda's* procedural safeguards rather than with the Fifth Amendment privilege against compulsory self-incrimination. Involuntary and coerced admissions are suppressed because of the inherent unreliability of a confession wrung from an unwilling suspect by threats, brutality, or other coercion. . . . .

* * *

But use of Williams' disclosures and their fruits carries no risk whatever of unreliability, for the body was found where he said it would be found. Moreover, since the Court makes no issue of voluntariness, no dangers are posed to individual dignity or free will. *Miranda's* safeguards are premised on presumed unreliability long associated with confessions extorted by brutality or threats; they are not personal constitutional rights, but are simply judicially created prophylactic measures.

* * *

Thus, in cases where incriminating disclosures are voluntarily made without coercion, and hence not violative of the Fifth Amendment, but are obtained in violation of one of the *Miranda* prophylaxis, suppression is no longer automatic.   . . .

Similarly, the exclusionary rule is not uniformly implicated in the Sixth Amendment, particularly its pretrial aspects. We have held that

> "the core purpose of the counsel guarantee was to assure 'Assistance' at trial, when the accused was confronted with both the intricacies of the law and the advocacy of the public prosecutor."   United States v. Ash (1973).

Thus, the right to counsel is fundamentally a "trial" right necessitated by the legal complexities of a criminal prosecution and the need to offset, to the trier of fact, the power of the State as prosecutor. . . .

As we have seen in the Fifth Amendment setting, violations of prophylactic rules designed to safeguard other constitutional guarantees and deter impermissible police conduct need not call for the automatic suppression of evidence without regard to the purposes served by exclusion; nor do Fourth Amendment violations merit uncritical suppression of evidence.   In other situations we decline to suppress eyewitness identifications which are the products of unnecessarily suggestive lineups or photo displays unless there is a "very substantial likelihood of irreparable misidentification."   Simmons v. United States (1968).   Recognizing that "[i]t is the likelihood of misidentification which violates a defendant's right to due process," Neil v. Biggers (1972), we exclude evidence only when essential to safeguard the integrity of the truth-seeking process.   The test, in short, is the reliability of the evidence.

So too in the Sixth Amendment sphere failure to have counsel in a pretrial setting should not lead to the "knee-jerk" suppression of relevant and reliable evidence.   Just as even uncounselled "critical" pretrial confrontations may often be conducted fairly and not in derogation of Sixth Amendment values, Stovall v. Denno (1967), evidence obtained in such proceedings should be suppressed only when its use would imperil the core values the Amendment was written to protect. Having extended Sixth Amendment concepts originally thought to relate to the trial itself to earlier periods when a criminal investigation is focused on a suspect, application of the drastic bar of exclusion should be approached with caution.

In any event, the fundamental purpose of the Sixth Amendment is to safeguard the fairness of the trial and the integrity of the fact-finding process.   In this case, where the evidence of how the child's body was found is of unquestioned reliability, and since the Court accepts Williams' disclosures as voluntary and uncoerced, there is no issue either of fairness or evidentiary reliability to justify suppression of truth.   It appears suppression is mandated here for no other reason than the Court's general impression that it may have a beneficial effect on future police conduct; indeed, the Court fails to say even that much in defense of its holding.

Thus, whether considered under *Miranda* or the Sixth Amendment, there is no more reason to exclude the evidence in this case than there was in Stone v. Powell; that holding was premised on the utter reliability of evidence sought to be suppressed, the irrelevancy of the constitutional claim to the criminal defendant's factual guilt or innocence, and the minimal deterrent effect of habeas corpus on police misconduct. This case, like Stone v. Powell, comes to us by way of habeas corpus after a fair trial and appeal in the state courts. Relevant factors in this case are thus indistinguishable from those in *Stone*, and from those in other Fourth Amendment cases suggesting a balancing approach toward utilization of the exclusionary sanction. Rather than adopting a formalistic analysis varying with the constitutional provision invoked, we should apply the exclusionary rule on the basis of its benefits and costs, at least in those cases where the police conduct at issue is far from being "outrageous" or "egregious."

. . . the State has directly challenged the applicability of the exclusionary rule to this case, Brief for Petitioner, at 31–32, and has invoked principles of comity and federalism against reversal of the conviction. Moreover, at oral argument—the first opportunity to do so—the State argued that our intervening decision in Stone v. Powell should be extended to this case, just as respondent argued that it should not.

At the least, if our intervening decision in *Stone* makes application of the exclusionary rule in this case an open question which "should be resolved only after the implications of such a ruling have been fully explored," the plainly proper course is to vacate the judgment of the Court of Appeals and remand the case for reconsideration in light of that case. Indeed, only recently we actually applied the intervening decision of Washington v. Davis, 426 U.S. 229, 96 S. Ct. 2040 (1976), to resolve the constitutional issue in Village of Arlington Heights v. Metropolitan Housing Development Corp., 429 U.S. 252, 97 S.Ct. 555 (1977). There, we found no difficulty in applying the intervening holding ourselves without a remand to give the Court of Appeals an opportunity to reconsider its holding; we reached the correct result directly, over Mr. Justice White's dissent urging a remand. Today, the Court declines either to apply the intervening case of Stone v. Powell which Mr. Justice Powell admits may well be controlling, or to remand for reconsideration in light of that case, all the more surprising since Mr. Justice Powell authored Stone v. Powell and today makes the fifth vote for the Court's judgment. . . .

* * *

MR. JUSTICE WHITE, with whom MR. JUSTICE BLACKMUN and MR. JUSTICE REHNQUIST join, dissenting.

The respondent in this case killed a 10-year-old child. The majority sets aside his conviction, holding that certain statements of unquestioned reliability were unconstitutionally obtained from him, and under the circumstances probably makes it impossible to retry him. Because there is nothing in the Constitution or in our previous cases which requires the Court's action, I dissent.

* * *

The strictest test of waiver which might be applied to this case is that set forth in Johnson v. Zerbst and quoted by the majority. In order to show that a right has been waived under this test, the State must prove "an intentional relinquishment or abandonment of a known right or privilege." The majority creates no new rule preventing an accused who has retained a lawyer from waiving his right to the lawyer's presence during questioning. The majority simply finds that no waiver was *proved* in this case. I disagree. That respondent knew of his right not to say anything to the officers without advice and presence of counsel is established on this record to a moral certainty. He was advised of the right by three officials of the State—telling at least one that he understood the right—and by two lawyers. Finally, he further demonstrated his knowledge of the right by informing the police that he would tell them the story in the presence of McKnight when they arrived in Des Moines. The issue in this case, then, is whether respondent relinquished that right intentionally.

Respondent relinquished his right not to talk to the police about his crime when the car approached the place where he had hidden the victim's clothes. Men usually intend to do what they do and there is nothing in the record to support the proposition that respondent's decision to talk was anything but an exercise of his own free will. Apparently, without any prodding from the officers, respondent—who had earlier said that he would tell the whole story when he arrived in Des Moines—spontaneously changed his mind about the timing of his disclosures when the car approached the places where he had hidden the evidence. However, even if his statements were influenced by Detective Leaming's above-quoted statement, respondent's decision to talk in the absence of counsel can hardly be viewed as the product of an overborn will. The statement by Leaming was not coercive; it was accompanied by a request that respondent not respond to it; and it was delivered hours before respondent decided to make any statment. Respondent's waiver was thus knowing and intentional.

* * *

The majority's contrary conclusion seems to rest on the fact that respondent "asserted" his right to counsel by retaining and consulting with one lawyer and by consulting with another. How this supports the conclusion that respondent's later relinquishment of his right not to talk in the absence of counsel was unintentional is a mystery. The fact that respondent consulted with counsel on the question whether he should talk to the police in counsel's absence makes his later decision to talk in counsel's absence *better* informed and, if anything, more intelligent.

The majority recognizes that even after this "assertion" of his right to counsel, it would have found that respondent waived his right not to talk in counsel's absence if his waiver had been expressed

—i. e., if the officers had asked him in the car whether he would be willing to answer questions in counsel's absence and if he had answered "yes." But waiver is not a formalistic concept. Waiver is shown whenever the facts establish that an accused knew of a right and intended to relinquish it. Such waiver, even if not express,[6] was plainly shown here. The only other conceivable basis for the majority's holding is the implicit suggestion that the right involved in Massiah v. United States, as distinguished from the right involved in Miranda v. Arizona, is a right not to be *asked* any questions in counsel's absence rather than a right not to *answer* any questions in counsel's absence, and that the right not to be *asked* questions must be waived *before* the questions are asked. Such wafer-thin distinctions cannot determine whether a guilty murderer should go free. The only conceivable purpose for the presence of counsel during questioning is to protect an accused from making incriminating *answers*. Questions, unanswered, have no significance at all. Absent coercion—no matter how the right involved is defined—an accused is amply protected by a rule requiring waiver before or simultaneously with the giving by him of an answer or the making by him of a statement.

---

6. The Court of Appeals, in administering the rule of Miranda v. Arizona, have not required an express waiver of the rights to silence and to counsel which an accused must be advised about under that case. Waiver has been found where the accused is informed of those rights, understands them, and then proceeds voluntarily to answer questions in the absence of counsel. United States v. Marchildon, 519 F.2d 337, 343 (C.A.8 1975) ("Waiver depends on no form of words, written or oral. It is to be determined from all of the surrounding circumstances. Addressing ourselves to this issue we held in Hughes v. Swenson, 452 F.2d 866, 867–868 (C.A.8 1971), that: 'The thrust of appellant's claim is that a valid waiver cannot be effective absent an expressed declaration to that effect. We are cited to no case which supports appellant's thesis and independent research discloses none. To the contrary, the Fifth, Seventh, Ninth, and Tenth Circuits have held in effect that if the defendant is effectively advised of his rights and intelligently and understandingly declines to exercise them, the waiver is valid' "); United States v. Ganter, 436 F.2d 364, 370 (C.A.7 1970) ("[A]n express statement that the individual does not want a lawyer is not required if it appears that the defendant was effectively advised of his rights and he then intelligently and understandingly declined to exercise them"); United States v. James, 528 F.2d 999, 1019 (C.A.5 1976) (" 'All that the prosecution must show is that the defendant was effectively advised of his rights and that he then intelligently and understandingly declined to exercise them' "); Blackmon v. Blackledge, 541 F.2d 1070, 1072 (C.A.4 1976) ("[H]e was reasonably questioned only after having been fully informed of his rights and permitted to make a telephone call. Under such circumstances, a suspect's submission to questioning without objection and without requesting a lawyer is clearly a waiver of his right to counsel, if, indeed, he understands his rights").

There is absolutely no reason to require an additional question to the already cumbersome Miranda litany just because the majority finds another case —Massiah v. United States—providing exactly the same right to counsel as that involved in Miranda. In either event, the issue is, as the majority recognizes, one of the proofs necessary to establish waiver. If an intentional relinquishment of the right to counsel under Miranda is established by proof that the accused was informed of his right and then voluntarily answered questions in counsel's absence, then similar proof establishes an intentional relinquishment of the Massiah right to counsel.

Mr. Justice Blackmun, with whom Mr. Justice White and Mr. Justice Rehnquist join, dissenting.

The State of Iowa, and 21 States and others, as *amici curiae*, strongly urge that this Court's procedural (as distinguished from constitutional) ruling in Miranda v. Arizona (1966), be re-examined and overruled. I, however, agree with the Court, that this is not now the case in which that issue need be considered.

What the Court chooses to do here, and with which I disagree, is to hold that respondent Williams' situation was in the mold of Massiah v. United States, 377 U.S. 201, 84 S.Ct. 1199 (1964), that is, that it was dominated by a denial to Williams of his Sixth Amendment right to counsel after criminal proceedings had been instituted against him. The Court rules that the Sixth Amendment was violated because Detective Leaming "purposely sought during Williams' isolation from his lawyers to obtain as much incriminating information as possible." I cannot regard that as unconstitutional *per se*.

First, the police did not deliberately seek to isolate Williams from his lawyers so as to deprive him of the assistance of counsel. Cf. Escobedo v. Illinois (1964). The isolation in this case was a necessary incident of transporting Williams to the county where the crime was committed.

Second, Leaming's purpose was not solely to obtain incriminating evidence. The victim had been missing for only two days, and the police could not be certain that she was dead. Leaming, of course, and in accord with his duty, was "hoping to find out where that little girl was," but such motivation does not equate with an intention to evade the Sixth Amendment. Moreover, the Court seems to me to place on undue emphasis, and aspersion on what it and the lower courts have chosen to call the "Christian burial speech," and on Williams' "deeply religious" convictions.

Third, not every attempt to elicit information should be regarded as "tantamount to interrogation." I am not persuaded that Leaming's observations and comments, made as the police car traversed the snowy and slippery miles between Davenport and Des Moines that winter afternoon, were an interrogation, direct or subtle, of Williams. Contrary to this Court's statement, the Iowa Supreme Court appears to me to have thought and held otherwise, and I agree. Williams, after all, was counseled by lawyers, and warned by the arraigning judge in Davenport and by the police, and yet it was he who started the travel conversations and brought up the subject of the criminal investigation. Without further reviewing the circumstances of the trip, I would say it is clear there was no interrogation. . . .

In summary, it seems to me that the Court is holding that *Massiah* is violated whenever police engage in any conduct, in the absence of counsel, with the subjective desire to obtain information from a suspect after arraignment. Such a rule is far too broad. Persons in custody frequently volunteer statements in response to stimuli other than interrogation. . . .

. . . When there is no interrogation, such statements should be admissible as long as they are truly voluntary.

The *Massiah* point thus being of no consequence, I would vacate the judgment of the Court of Appeals and remand the case for consideration of the issue of voluntariness, in the constitutional sense, of Williams' statements, an issue the Court of Appeals did not reach when the case was before it.

One final word: I can understand the discomfiture the Court obviously suffers and expresses in Part IV of its opinion, and the like discomfiture expressed by Justice (now United States District Judge) Stuart of the Iowa Court in the dissent he felt compelled to make by this Court's precedents, 182 N.W.2d, at 406. This was a brutal, tragic, and heinous crime inflicted upon a young girl on the afternoon of the day before Christmas. With the exclusionary rule operating as the Court effectuates it, the decision today probably means that, as a practical matter, no new trial will be possible at this date eight years after the crime, and that this respondent necessarily will go free. That, of course, is not the standard by which a case of this kind strictly is to be judged. But, as Judge Webster in dissent below observed, 509 F.2d, at 237, placing the case in sensible and proper perspective: "The evidence of Williams' guilt was overwhelming. No challenge is made to the reliability of the fact-finding process." I am in full agreement with that observation.

NOTES

1. Would testimony about the little girl's corpse and the cause of death have to be excluded as the fruit of the *Massiah* violation? See Chapter 6, Section E, note 9.

2. Prior to the decision in *Brewer*, the application of *Massiah* had been limited to post-indictment admissions, at least by federal courts. United States ex rel. Forella v. Follette, 405 F.2d 680 (2d Cir. 1969); United States v. Osser, 483 F.2d 727 (3d Cir. 1973); United States v. Lemonakis, 485 F.2d 941 (D.C.Cir.1973); United States v. DeVaughn, 541 F.2d 808 (9th Cir. 1976). Some state courts applied *Massiah* after commencement of any formal proceedings. State v. McCorgary, 218 Kan. 358, 543 P.2d 952 (1975) (complaint and warrant); State v. Darwin, 161 Conn. 413, 288 A.2d 422 (1971).

Brewer v. Williams rather clearly indicates that *Massiah* applies as soon as adversary judicial proceedings have begun and, in *Williams*, that point was the issuance of an arrest warrant. There are few post-*Williams* cases on the question. See People v. Booker, 69 Cal.App.3d 654, 138 Cal. Rptr. 347 (1977) (*Massiah* inapplicable where arrest occurred on out-of-state charges and there was no warrant nor extradition paper). United States v. Brown, 569 F.2d 236 (5th Cir. 1978) (*Massiah* inapplicable to interrogation by federal officers where only state charges had been filed).

Is custody a prerequisite for the application of *Massiah* where the interrogation is conducted by one who identifies himself as a police officer? Compare United States v. Satterfield, 558 F.2d 655 (2d Cir. 1976) (*Massiah* applies despite lack of arrest) with Scaldeferri v. State, 294 So.2d 407 (Fla.App.1974) (post-information, pre-arrest questions not precluded).

3. Brewer v. Williams seemed to answer affirmatively the question of whether rights under *Massiah* could be waived. Courts had so held before. United States v. Crisp, 435 F.2d 354 (7th Cir. 1970); Moore v. Wolff, 495

F.2d 35 (8th Cir. 1974). The principal question is what sort of waiver is valid. In *Williams* it is implied that a specific waiver of counsel is required and other courts have found this to be adequate. United States v. Barone, 467 F.2d 247 (2d Cir. 1972). But in *Williams,* the defendant had explicitly asserted his right to counsel; if this had not occurred would express waiver still be required? Several earlier cases had held that a waiver of *Miranda* rights would also serve to waive *Massiah* rights. Commonwealth v. Hoss, 445 Pa. 98, 283 A.2d 58 (1971); People v. McCrary, 549 P.2d 1320 (Colo.1976). Compare United States ex rel. Lopez v. Zelker, 344 F.Supp. 1050 (S.D.N.Y.1972) with United States v. Diggs, 497 F.2d 391, 393 n. 3 (2d Cir. 1974). The issue is thoughtfully considered in Judge Simpson's dissent in United States v. Brown, 569 F.2d 236 (5th Cir. 1978) (en banc).

4. Although *Brewer* was decided under *Massiah* rather than under *Miranda,* one of the issues discussed in *Brewer* is especially important in the *Miranda* context: What is interrogation? While this casebook was in galley proof, the Supreme Court considered that issue in Rhode Island v. Innis, —— U.S. ——, 100 S.Ct. —— (1980). Following his arrest and after *Miranda* warnings, Innis expressed a desire to talk to a lawyer. Thereafter the officers did not directly question Innis. In the suspect's presence, however, one officer mentioned to another officer his concern that the missing gun might have been left in a place where it posed a danger to handicapped children in the area. Innis then spoke up and directed officers to the weapon. The Court held that the officer's conduct did not constitute interrogation. The Court said that for *Miranda* purposes comments or conduct constitute interrogation if the officer should reasonably know that such conduct or comments are likely to elicit an incriminating response from the suspect. Justices Marshall and Brennan, in dissent, agreed with the standard but rejected the Court's conclusion that, under that test, there had been no interrogation of Innis. Justice Stevens, also dissenting, would have used a test which emphasized the officer's intent rather than what the officer could reasonably foresee.

Massiah and *Miranda* doctrines become intertwined when, prior to charge, a suspect, who is represented by counsel, is questioned.

Technically, *Massiah* is not violated because there has been no adversary judicial proceeding, but it can be argued that the Sixth Amendment rights have been violated. On the other hand, the fact that defendant has retained counsel should make his waiver under *Miranda* of his right to counsel much more persuasive, since he could secure the assistance of counsel with one phone call. Further, if he had the advice of counsel, his decision to waive his rights may be said to be more fully informed. People v. Smith, 42 Ill.2d 479, 248 N.E.2d 68 (1969); State v. Adams, 76 Wash.2d 650, 458 P.2d 558 (1969); White, J. dissenting in Brewer v. Williams.

The majority rule in both pre and post *Miranda* cases is that a voluntary statement made by one who has retained counsel is admissible if he voluntarily elects to speak in the absence of that counsel or waives the right to have counsel present. These holdings are scattered with dissents. In a few cases the courts have alluded to canons of ethics to conclude that such practices are not favored. See Coughlan v. United States, 391 F.2d 371 (9th Cir. 1969); United States v. Fellabaum, 408 F.2d 220 (7th Cir. 1969) (post-*Miranda*); Sabatini v. State, 14 Md.App. 431, 287 A.2d 511 (1972); State v. Moore, 189 Neb. 354, 202 N.W.2d 740 (1972); State v. Adams, 76 Wash.2d 650, 458 P.2d 558 (1969) (en banc).

Other jurisdictions have banned such interrogation outright, or, at least, when it is initiated by police. People v. Vella, 21 N.Y.2d 249, 287 N. Y.S.2d 369, 234 N.E.2d 422 (1967); People v. Arthur, 22 N.Y.2d 325, 292 N.Y.S.2d 663, 239 N.E.2d 537 (1968); United States v. Thomas, 475 F.2d 115 (10th Cir. 1973) (must notify counsel); State v. Witt, 422 S.W.2d 304 (Mo.1967) (relying on *Massiah*); Hart v. State, 484 P.2d 1334 (Okl. 1971) (one ground for exclusion).

There are exceptions even in these jurisdictions. In People v. McKie, 25 N.Y.2d 19, 302 N.Y.S.2d 534, 250 N.E.2d 36 (1969), a defendant, represented by counsel, was followed by police. The defendant then approached the police and initiated an argument during which he made a damaging admission. The court held there was no custody, that the defendant was aware of his rights and initiated the conversation. The conversation is interesting: After the initial foray the defendant said, "You can be killed, too." The officers replied, "You're not dealing with any little old lady now; you weren't so brave when you killed that little old lady". The defendant said, "Sure I did, but you guys can't prove it".

The New York rule is still the most rigid. In one case an investigation was re-opened after a three and a half year delay and, it was held, the police were required to notify counsel who had been previously retained unless they knew he had been discharged. People v. Singer, 44 N.Y.2d 241, 405 N.Y.S.2d 17, 367 N.E.2d 179 (1978). See also People v. Pinzon, 44 N.Y.2d 458, 406 N.Y.S.2d 268, 377 N.E.2d 721 (1978) counsel who called police station and spoke to switchboard operators had "entered" the case and had to be notified.

What of interrogation about unrelated crimes? Prior to *Williams* such interrogation was permitted particularly where the charge that was filed was not a pretext to gain custody and was clearly unrelated. See People v. Stanley, 15 N.Y.2d 30, 255 N.Y.S.2d 74, 203 N.E.2d 475 (1964); United States v. Edwards, 366 F.2d 853 (2d Cir. 1966); State v. Hill, 26 Ariz.App. 37, 545 P.2d 999 (1976). Could the police have questioned Williams about another homicide or a stolen car or his escape from a mental hospital?

5. By implication, Brewer v. Williams dealt with the status of defense counsel instruction to or agreements with police to refrain from interrogating his client. Prior to *Williams*, the courts had divided on the issue. Compare United States v. Wedra, 343 F.Supp. 1183 (S.D.N.Y.1972) with United States v. Moriarity, 375 F.2d 901 (7th Cir. 1967). Since *Williams*, most courts have upheld police interrogations occurring after counsel's contrary instructions or agreements, assuming, of course, the fact of a waiver. Watson v. State, 28 Md. 73, 382 A.2d 574 (1978) (approves waiver despite agreement not to question; three dissents); McPherson v. State, 562 S.W. 2d 210 (Tenn.Crim.App.1977) (attorney requested no interviews but police did not agree; the court said the police "tread on thin ice" when they question a suspect in the face of a request from his attorney that no interrogation occur in his absence); Williams v. State, 566 S.W.2d 919 (Tex. Crim.App.1978) (police disregard attorney's instructions not to question); State v. Jones, 19 Wash.App. 850, 578 P.2d 71 (1978) (suspect may talk despite counsel's instructions but he must be told that his attorney called and instructed police not to question him). But see State v. Weedon, 342 So.2d 642 (La.1977) (improper to violate agreement; three dissents.)

D. VALIDITY OF INTERROGATIONS AFTER AN ILLEGAL ARREST OR DURING "UNNECESSARY DELAY" IN TAKING ARRESTEE BEFORE COMMITTING MAGISTRATE

NOTES

1.   A discussion of the subject matter of the first portion of this section—the validity of interrogations after an illegal arrest—is deferred to a later section (in Chapter 6) dealing with the "exclusionary rule." It is covered in Supreme Court decisions (Brown v. Illinois and Dunaway v. New York), which can be adequately analyzed only after an awareness of cases not yet considered in the casebook. We did feel, however, that the reader should be advised at this point of the existence of the problem and its subsequent treatment. The second portion of this section does fit here appropriately, because it does not require an extensive background for its full understanding. Moreover, the former involves a constitutional issue; the latter is founded upon a utilization of a higher court's "supervisory power" over lower courts within its jurisdiction (or else by legislative enactment). Also, because the subject matter of the latter is more of historical interest than of present day practical significance it will be presented in the form of note material.

2.   In 1943, and again in 1957, the Supreme Court of the United States held, in McNabb v. United States, 318 U.S. 332, 63 S.Ct. 608 (1943), and Mallory v. United States, 354 U.S. 449, 77 S.Ct. 1356 (1957), that where *federal officers* interrogated an arrested person instead of taking him "without unnecessary delay" before a United States commissioner or a federal judge, as required by law, any confession obtained during the period of delay was inadmissible in evidence, regardless of its voluntariness or trustworthiness. This the Court did in the exercise of its "supervisory power" over lower federal courts.

Since the *McNabb-Mallory* rule was not based upon constitutional "due process" considerations, or upon any other provision of the Bill of Rights, the rule was not binding upon the states. Of all the states, Michigan was the first, and for a while the only one, that was inclined to adopt a similar rule. See People v. Hamilton, 359 Mich. 410, 102 N.W.2d 738 (1960), and People v. McCager, 367 Mich. 116, 116 N.W.2d 205 (1962), in which the Michigan Supreme Court said that Michigan was "the first state to adopt the exclusionary rule principle announced in McNabb v. United States". (In *McCager* the confession was made four days after the defendant's arrest.) But within a short time Michigan qualified the application of the rule to such an extent as to effectively discard it. In People v. Farmer, 380 Mich. 198, 156 N.W.2d 504 (1968), the court held that the rule was applicable only where the delay in taking an arrestee before a magistrate was "for the purpose of coercing a confession". In *Farmer* the court found that there were "no circumstances to support a claim of involuntariness" such as appeared in the *Hamilton* case or in the subsequent one of People v. Ubbes, 374 Mich. 571, 132 N.W.2d 669 (1965).

Wisconsin is another state which ventured along a path similar to Michigan's. In a case where there was a delay of 3½ hours for the purpose of interrogating a person arrested *without warrant* the court upheld the admissibility of a confession but stated that a delay for that purpose following an *arrest warrant* would render a confession inadmissible (as a matter of due process). Phillips v. State, 29 Wis.2d 521, 139 N.W.2d 41 (1966).

The Delaware Supreme Court, in Vorhauer v. State, 212 A.2d 886 (Del.1965), held that a confession obtained after the 24 hour limitation set by statute for taking arrestees before a magistrate was inadmissible. The court stated, however, that it was adopting the *McNabb-Mallory* rule "within the framework of the case before us." It then went on to state: "Our ruling is expressly limited to a detention in excess of the 24 hour period" and that "the standard of reasonableness of the detention of less than 24 hours must await another case."

During the last several years, Pennsylvania has been one of the few jurisdictions (until 1977 perhaps the only one) to apply a *per se* rule of inadmissibility to such statements. See Commonwealth v. Williams, 455 Pa. 569, 319 A.2d 419 (1974). Like other states (e. g., Michigan) which once utilized such a rule, Pennsylvania appears to be emasculating the unlawful detention principle. See Commonwealth v. Davenport, 471 Pa. 278, 370 A. 2d 301 (1977) (delay less than six hours does not give rise to *per se* exclusion). Also see the 4–3 decision of the Maryland Court of Appeals in Johnson v. State, 282 Md. 314, 384 A.2d 709 (1978), applying a *per se* exclusionary rule with respect to a confession obtained after a 24 hour delay. *Cf.* the 1980 Maryland case of Kennedy v. State, 26 Cr.L. 2558.

In June, 1968 Congress abolished the *McNabb-Mallory* rule with a provision in the Omnibus Crime Control and Safe Streets Act. The Act specifies a six-hour period as the time limit for presenting an arrestee before a federal magistrate. However, if that limit is transgressed, the delay alone will be only one factor in determining the admissibility (voluntariness) of a confession. (See *supra* note 2 immediately following the report of Miranda v. Arizona for the specific provisions of the Omnibus Act.)

Since the *McNabb-Mallory* rule was not of constitutional dimension, congressional abolition of the rule is constitutionally valid.

3. With respect to the customary statutory requirement as to the disposition of the arrestee, the courts generally hold that "unnecessary delay" means a delay for any reason other than the unavailability of a committing magistrate or circumstances such as distance, lack of ready transportation, etc., which may prevent a quick presentation of the arrestee to a magistrate. Other courts, however, take the view that "unnecessary delay" means only "unreasonable delay" and consequently the police are permitted to hold an arrestee for a "reasonable" length of time, with reasonableness being determined by all the surrounding circumstances and factors in the particular case.[1] As already indicated, of course, some states are specific as to the period of time a person may be held in police custody before presentation to a magistrate.[2]

---

1. For example: Mooradian v. Davis, 302 Mich. 484, 5 N.W.2d 435 (1942); People v. Jackson, 23 Ill.2d 274, 178 N.E.2d 299 (1961).

2. Some states have statutes which require that arrested juveniles be turned over to "youth officers" promptly after their arrest. Typically, statements obtained where the arresting officers have violated this requirement are not for that reason alone rendered inadmissible.

Chapter 3

EYE–WITNESS IDENTIFICATION PROCEDURES

A. THE RIGHT TO PRESENCE OF COUNSEL

UNITED STATES v. WADE

Supreme Court of the United States, 1967.
388 U.S. 218, 87 S.Ct. 1926.

MR. JUSTICE BRENNAN delivered the opinion of the Court.

The question here is whether courtroom identifications of an accused at trial are to be excluded from evidence because the accused was exhibited to the witnesses before trial at a post-indictment lineup conducted for identification purposes without notice to and in the absence of the accused's appointed counsel.

The federally insured bank in Eustace, Texas, was robbed on September 21, 1964. A man with a small strip of tape on each side of his face entered the bank, pointed a pistol at the female cashier and the vice president, the only persons in the bank at the time, and forced them to fill a pillowcase with the bank's money. The man then drove away with an accomplice waiting in a stolen car outside the bank. On March 23, 1965, an indictment was returned against respondent Wade and two others for conspiring to rob the bank, and against Wade and the accomplice for the robbery itself. Wade was arrested on April 2, and counsel was appointed to represent him on April 26. Fifteen days later an FBI agent, without notice to Wade's lawyer, arranged to have the two bank employees observe a lineup made up of Wade and five or six other prisoners and conducted in a courtroom of the local county courthouse. Each person in the line wore strips of tape such as allegedly worn by the robber and upon direction each said something like "put the money in the bag," the words allegedly uttered by the robber. Both bank employees identified Wade in the lineup as the bank robber.

At trial the two employees, when asked on direct examination if the robber was in the courtroom, pointed to Wade. The prior lineup identification was then elicited from both employees on cross-examination. At the close of testimony, Wade's counsel moved for a judgment of acquittal or, alternatively, to strike the bank officials' courtroom identifications on the ground that conduct of the lineup, without notice to and in the absence of his appointed counsel, violated his Fifth Amendment privilege against self-incrimination and his Sixth Amendment right to the assistance of counsel. The motion was denied, and Wade was convicted. The Court of Appeals for the Fifth Circuit reversed the conviction and ordered a new trial at which the in-court identification evidence was to be excluded, holding that, though the lineup did not violate Wade's Fifth Amendment rights, "the lineup, held as it was, in the absence of counsel, already chosen to represent appellant, was a violation of his Sixth Amendment rights. . . ." We granted certiorari and set the case for oral argument with Gilbert v. State of California, and Stovall v. Denno, which present similar questions. We reverse the judgment of the Court of Appeals and remand to that court with direction to enter a new judgment vacating the conviction and remanding the case to the District Court for further proceedings consistent with this opinion.

I.

Neither the lineup itself nor anything shown by this record that Wade was required to do in the lineup violated his privilege against self-incrimination. We have only recently reaffirmed that the privilege "protects an accused only from being compelled to testify against himself, or otherwise provide the State with evidence of a testimonial or communicative nature. . . ." Schmerber v. California, 384 U.S. 757, 86 S.Ct. 1826. We there held that compelling a suspect to submit to a withdrawal of a sample of his blood for analysis for alcohol content and the admission in evidence of the analysis report was not compulsion to those ends. That holding was supported by the opinion in Holt v. United States . . . in which case a question arose as to whether a blouse belonged to the defendant. A witness testified at trial that the defendant put on the blouse and it had fit him. The defendant argued that the admission of the testimony was error because compelling him to put on the blouse was a violation of his privilege. The Court rejected the claim as "an extravagant extension of the Fifth Amendment," Mr. Justice Holmes saying for the Court:

> "[T]he prohibition of compelling a man in a criminal court to be witness against himself is a prohibition of the use of physical or moral compulsion to extort communications from him, not an exclusion of his body as evidence when it may be material."

* * *

We have no doubt that compelling the accused merely to exhibit his person for observation by a prosecution witness prior to trial involves no compulsion of the accused to give evidence having testimonial significance. It is compulsion of the accused to exhibit his physical characteristics, not compulsion to disclose any knowledge he might have. It is no different from compelling Schmerber to provide a blood sample or Holt to wear the blouse, and, as in those instances, is not within the cover of the privilege. Similarly, compelling Wade to speak within hearing distance of the witnesses, even to utter words purportedly uttered by the robber, was not compulsion to utter statements of a "testimonial" nature; he was required to use his voice as an identifying physical characteristic, not to speak his guilt. We held in *Schmerber*, supra, that the distinction to be drawn under the

Fifth Amendment privilege against self-incrimination is one between an accused's "communications" in whatever form, vocal or physical, and "compulsion which makes a suspect or accused the source of 'real or physical evidence,' ". We recognized that "both federal and state courts have usually held that . . . [the privilege] offers no protection against compulsion to submit to fingerprinting, photography, or measurements, to write or speak for identification, to appear in court, to stand, to assume a stance, to walk, or to make a particular gesture." None of these activities becomes testimonial within the scope of the privilege because required of the accused in a pretrial lineup.

Moreover, it deserves emphasis, that this case presents no question of the admissibility in evidence of anything Wade said or did at the lineup which implicates his privilege. The Government offered no such evidence as part of its case, and what came out about the lineup proceedings on Wade's cross-examination of the bank employees involved no violation of Wade's privilege.

II.

The fact that the lineup involved no violation of Wade's privilege against self-incrimination does not, however, dispose of his contention that the court room identifications should have been excluded because the lineup was conducted without notice to and in the absence of his counsel. Our rejection of the right to counsel claim in *Schmerber* rested on our conclusion in that case that "no issue of counsel's ability to assist petitioner in respect of any rights he did possess is presented." In contrast, in this case it is urged that the assistance of counsel at the lineup was indispensable to protect Wade's most basic right as a criminal defendant—his right to a fair trial at which the witnesses against him might be meaningfully cross-examined.

. . . When the Bill of Rights was adopted, there were no organized police forces as we know them today. The accused confronted prosecutor and the witnesses against him, and the evidence was marshalled, largely at the trial itself. In contrast, today's law enforcement machinery involves cirtical confrontations of the accused by the prosecution at pretrial proceedings where the results might well settle the accused's fate and reduce the trial itself to a mere formality. In recognition of these realities of modern criminal prosecution, our cases have construed the Sixth Amendment guarantee to apply to "critical" stages of the proceedings. . . .

. . . It is central to that principle that in addition to counsel's presence at trial, the accused is guaranteed that he need not stand alone against the State at any stage of the prosecution, formal or informal, in court or out, where counsel's absence might derogate the accused's right to a fair trial. . . . The presence of counsel at such critical confrontations, as at the trial itself, operates to assure that the accused's interests will be protected consistently with our adversary theory of criminal prosecution.

In sum, the principle of Powell v. Alabama and succeeding cases requires that we scrutinize *any* pretrial confrontation of the accused to determine whether the presence of his counsel is necessary to preserve the defendant's basic right to a fair trial as affected by his right meaningfully to cross-examine the witnesses against him and to have effective assistance of counsel at the trial itself. It calls upon us to analyze whether potential substantial prejudice to defendant's rights inheres in the particular confrontation and the ability of counsel to help avoid that prejudice.

III.

The Government characterizes the lineup as a mere preparatory step in the gathering of the prosecution's evidence, not different—for Sixth Amendment purposes—from various other preparatory steps, such as systematized or scientific analyses of the accused's fingerprints, blood sample, clothing, hair, and the like. We think there are differences which preclude such stages being characterized as critical stages at which the accused has the right to the presence of his counsel. Knowledge of the techniques of science and technology is sufficiently available, and the variables in techniques few enough, that the accused has the opportunity for a meaningful confrontation of the Government's case at trial through the ordinary processes of cross-examination of the Government's expert witnesses and the presentation of the evidence of his own experts. The denial of a right to have his counsel present at such analyses does not therefore violate the Sixth Amendment; they are not critical stages since there is minimal risk that his counsel's absence at such stages might derogate his right to a fair trial.

IV.

But the confrontation compelled by the State between the accused and the victim or witnesses to a crime to elicit identification evidence is peculiarly riddled with innumerable dangers and variable factors which might seriously, even crucially, derogate from a fair trial. The vagaries of eyewitness identification are well-known; the annals of criminal law are rife with instances of mistaken identification.[1] Mr. Justice Frankfurter once said: "What is the worth of identification testimony even when uncontradicted? The identification of strangers is proverbially untrustworthy. The hazards of such testimony are established by a formidable number of instances in the records of English and American trials. These instances are recent—not due to the brutalities of ancient criminal procedure." The Case of Sacco and Vanzetti 30 (1927). A major factor contributing to the high incidence of miscarriage of justice from

1. Borchard, Convicting the Innocent; Frank & Frank, Not Guilty; Wall, Eyewitness Identification in Criminal Cases, 3 Wigmore, Evidence § 786(a) (3d ed. 1940); Rolph, Personal Identity; Gross, Criminal Investiga- tion 47–54 (Jackson ed. 1962); Williams, Proof of Guilt 83–98 (1952); Wills, Circumstantial Evidence 192–205 (7th ed. 1937); Wigmore, The Science of Judicial Proof §§ 250–253.

mistaken identification has been the degree of suggestion inherent in the manner in which the prosecution presents the suspect to witnesses for pretrial identification. A commentator has observed that "the influence of improper suggestion upon identifying witnesses probably accounts for more miscarriages of justice than any other single factor—perhaps it is responsible for more such errors than all other factors combined." Wall, Eyewitness Identification in Criminal Cases 26. Suggestion can be created intentionally or unintentionally in many subtle ways. And the dangers for the suspect are particularly grave when the witness' opportunity for observation was insubstantial, and thus his susceptibility to suggestion the greatest.

Moreover, "it is a matter of common experience that, once a witness has picked out the accused at the line-up, he is not likely to go back on his word later on, so that in practice the issue of identity may (in the absence of other relevant evidence) for all practical purposes be determined there and then, before the trial." [2]

The pretrial confrontation for purpose of identification may take the form of a lineup, also known as an "identification parade" or "showup," as in the present case, or presentation of the suspect alone to the witness, as in Stovall v. Denno, post. It is obvious that risks of suggestion attend either form of confrontation and increase the dangers inhering in eyewitness identification. But as is the case with secret interrogations, there is serious difficulty in depicting what transpires at lineups and other forms of identification confrontations. "Privacy results in secrecy and this in turn results in a gap in our knowledge as to what in fact goes on . . . ." Miranda v. State of Arizona, supra. For the same reasons, the defense can seldom reconstruct the manner and mode of lineup identification for judge or jury at trial. Those participating in a lineup with the accused may often be police officers; in any event, the participants' names are rarely recorded or divulged at trial.[3] The impediments to an objective observation are increased when the victim is the witness. Lineups are prevalent in rape and robbery prosecutions and present a particular hazard that a victim's understandable outrage may excite vengeful or spiteful motives. In any event, neither witnesses nor lineup participants are apt to be alert for conditions prejudical to the suspect and if they were it would likely be of scant benefit to the suspect since neither witnesses nor lineup participants are likely to be schooled in the detection of suggestive influences.[4] Improper influences may go undetected by a suspect, guilty or not, who experiences

---

2. Williams & Hammelmann, Identification Parades, Part I, [1963] Crim.L. Rev. 479, 482.

3. See Rolph, Personal Identity 50; "The bright burden of identity, at these parades, is lifted from the innocent participants to hover about the suspects, leaving the rest featureless and unknown and without interest."

4. An additional impediment to the detection of such influences by participants, including the suspect, is the physical conditions often surrounding the conduct of the lineup. In many, lights shine on the stage in such a way that the suspect cannot see the witness. In some a one-way mirror is used and what is said on the witness' side cannot be heard.

the emotional tension which we might expect in one being confronted with potential accusers. Even when he does observe abuse, if he has a criminal record he may be reluctant to take the stand and open up the admission of prior convictions. Moreover any protestations by the suspect of the fairness of the lineup made at trial are likely to be in vain; [5] the jury's choice is between the accused's unsupported version and that of the police officers present.[6] In short, the accused's inability effectively to reconstruct at trial any unfairness that occurred at the lineup may deprive him of his only opportunity meaningfully to attack the credibility of the witness' courtroom identification.

What facts have been disclosed in specific cases about the conduct of pretrial confrontations for identification illustrate both the potential for substantial prejudice to the accused at that stage and the need for its revelation at trial. A commentator provides some striking examples:

> "In a Canadian case . . . the defendant had been picked out of a lineup of six men, of which he was the only Oriental. In other cases, a blackhaired suspect was placed upon a group of light-haired persons, tall suspects have been made to stand with short nonsuspects, and, in a case where the perpetrator of the crime was known to be a youth, a suspect under twenty was placed in a lineup with five other persons, all of whom were forty or over."

Similarly state reports, in the course of describing prior identifications admitted as evidence of guilt, reveal numerous instances of

---

5. See In re Groban, 352 U.S. 330, 340, 77 S.Ct. 510, 516 (Black, J., dissenting). The difficult position of defendants in attempting to protest the manner of pretrial identification is illustrated by the many state court cases in which contentions of blatant abuse rested on their unsupportable allegations, usually controverted by the police officers present. . . .
For a striking case in which hardly anyone agreed upon what occurred at the lineup, including who identified whom, see Johnson v. State, 237 Md. 283, 206 A.2d 138 (1965).

6. An instructive example of the defendant's predicament may be found in Proctor v. State, 223 Md. 394, 164 A.2d 708 (1960). A prior identification is admissible in Maryland only under the salutary rule that it cannot have been made "under conditions of unfairness or unreliability." Against the defendant's contention that these conditions had not been met, the Court stated:

"In the instant case, there are no such facts as, in our judgment, would call for a finding that the identification . . . was made under conditions of unfairness or unreliability. The relatively large number of persons put into the room together for [the victim] to look at is one circumstance indicating fairness, and the fact that the police officer was unable to remember the appearances of the others and could not recall if they had physical characteristics similar to [the defendant's] or not is at least suggestive that they were not of any one type or that they all differed markedly in looks from the defendant. There is no evidence that the Police Sergeant gave the complaining witness any indication as to which of the thirteen men was the defendant; the Sergeant's testimony is simply that he asked [the victim] if he could identify [the defendant] after having put the thirteen men in the courtroom."

suggestive procedures, for example, that all in the lineup but the suspect were known to the identifying witness, that the other participants in a lineup were grossly dissimilar in appearance from the suspect, that only the suspect was required to wear distinctive clothing which the culprit allegedly wore, that the witness is told by the police that they have caught the culprit after which the defendant is brought before the witness alone or is viewed in jail, that the suspect is pointed out before or during a lineup, and that the participants in the lineup are asked to try on an article of clothing which fits only the suspect.[7]

The potential for improper influence is illustrated by the circumstances, insofar as they appear, surrounding the prior identifications in the three cases we decide today. In the present case, the testimony of the identifying witnesses elicited on cross-examination revealed that those witnesses were taken to the courthouse and seated in the courtroom to await assembly of the lineup. The courtroom faced on a hallway observable to the witnesses through an open door. The cashier testified that she saw Wade "standing in the hall" within sight of an FBI agent. Five or six other prisoners later appeared in the hall. The vice president testified that he saw a person in the hall in the custody of the agent who "resembled the person that we identified as the one that entered the bank." [8]

The lineup in *Gilbert* was conducted in an auditorium in which some 100 witnesses to several alleged state and federal robberies charged to Gilbert made wholesale identifications of Gilbert as the robber in each others' presence, a procedure said to run counter to the most elemental precepts of the psychology of suggestion. And the vice of suggestion created by the identification in *Stovall* was the presentation to the witness of the suspect alone handcuffed to police officers. It is hard to imagine a situation more clearly conveying the suggestion to the witness that the one presented is believed guilty by the police.

The few cases that have surfaced therefore reveal the existence of a process attended with hazards of serious unfairness to the criminal accused and strongly suggest the plight of the more numerous defendants who are unable to ferret out suggestive influences in the secrecy of the confrontation. We do not assume that these risks are the result of police procedures intentionally designed to prejudice an accused. Rather we assume they derive from the dangers inherent in eyewitness identification and the suggestibility inherent in the context of the pretrial identification. Glanville Williams, in one of the most comprehensive studies of such forms of identification, said

7. [For case citations supporting the foregoing statements, consult original footnotes 18 through 21.]

8. See Wall, supra, n. 7, at 48; Napley, Problems of Effecting the Presentation of the Case for a Defendant, 66 Col.L.Rev. 94, 99 (1966):

"[W]hile many identification parades are conducted by the police with scrupulous regard for fairness, it is not unknown for the identifying witness to be placed in a position where he can see the suspect before the parade forms. . . . ."

"[T]he fact that the police themselves have, in a given case, little or no doubt that the man put up for identification has committed the offense, and that their chief preoccupation is with the problem of getting sufficient proof, because he has not 'come clean,' involves a danger that this persuasion may communicate itself even in a doubtful case to the witness in some way . . . ." Williams & Hammelmann, Identification Parades, Part I, [1963] Crim.L.Rev. 479, 483.

Insofar as the accused's conviction may rest on a courtroom identification in fact the fruit of a suspect pretrial identification which the accused is helpless to subject to effective scrutiny at trial, the accused is deprived of that right of cross-examination which is an essential safeguard to his right to confront the witnesses against him. . . . And even though cross-examination is a precious safeguard to a fair trial, it cannot be viewed as an absolute assurance of accuracy and reliability. Thus in the present context, where so many variables and pitfalls exist, the first line of defense must be the prevention of unfairness and the lessening of the hazards of eyewitness identification at the lineup itself. The trial which might determine the accused's fate may well not be that in the courtroom but that at the pretrial confrontation, with the State aligned against the accused, the witness the sole jury, and the accused unprotected against the overreaching, intentional or unintentional, and with little or no effective appeal from the judgment there rendered by the witness—"that's the man."

Since it appears that there is grave potential for prejudice, intentional or not, in the pretrial lineup, which may not be capable of reconstruction at trial, and since presence of counsel itself can often avert prejudice and assure a meaningful confrontation at trial,[9] there

---

9. One commentator proposes a model statute providing not only for counsel, but other safeguards as well:

"Most if not all, of the attacks on the lineup process could be averted by a uniform statute modeled upon the best features of the civilian codes. Any proposed statute should provide for the right to counsel during any lineup or during any confrontation. Provision should be made that any person, whether a victim or a witness, must give a description of the suspect before he views any arrested person. A written record of this description should be required, and the witness should be made to sign it. This written record would be available for inspection by defense counsel for copying before the trial and for use at the trial in testing the accuracy of the identification made during the lineup and during the trial.

"This ideal statute would require at least six persons in addition to the accused in a lineup, and these persons would have to be of approximately the same height, weight, coloration of hair and skin, and bodily types as the suspect. In addition, all of these men should, as nearly as possible, be dressed alike. If distinctive garb was used during the crime, the suspect should not be forced to wear similar clothing in the lineup unless all of the other persons are similarly garbed. A complete written report of the names, addresses, descriptive details of the other persons in the lineup, and of everything which transpired during the identification would be mandatory. This report would include everything stated by the identifying witness during this step, including any reasons given by him as to what features, etc., have sparked his recognition.

"This statute should permit voice identification tests by having each person in the lineup repeat identical innocuous phrases, and it would

can be little doubt that for Wade the post-indictment lineup was a critical stage of the prosecution at which he was "as much entitled to such aid [of counsel] . . . as at the trial itself." . . . Thus both Wade and his counsel should have been notified of the impending lineup, and counsel's presence should have been a requisite to conduct of the lineup, absent an "intelligent waiver." . . . No substantial countervailing policy considerations have been advanced against the requirement of the presence of counsel. Concern is expressed that the requirement will forestall prompt identifications and result in obstruction of the confrontations. As for the first, we note that in the two cases in which the right to counsel is today held to apply, counsel had already been appointed and no argument is made in either case that notice to counsel would have prejudicially delayed the confrontations. Moreover, we leave open the question whether the presence of substitute counsel might not suffice where notification and presence of the suspect's own counsel would result in prejudicial delay.[10] And to refuse to recognize the right to counsel for fear that counsel will obstruct the course of justice is contrary to the basic assumptions upon which this Court has operated in Sixth Amendment cases. We rejected similar logic in Miranda v. State of Arizona, concerning presence of counsel during custodial interrogation:

> "[A]n attorney is merely exercising the good professional judgment he has been taught. This is not cause for considering the attorney a menace to law enforcement. He is merely carrying out what he is sworn to do under his oath —to protect to the extent of his ability the rights of his client. In fulfilling this responsibility the attorney plays a vital role in the administration of criminal justice under our Constitution."

In our view counsel can hardly impede legitimate law enforcement; on the contrary, for the reasons expressed, law enforcement may be assisted by preventing the infiltration of taint in the prosecution's

---

be impermissible to force the use of words allegedly used during a criminal act.

"The statute would enjoin the police from suggesting to any viewer that one or more persons in the lineup had been arrested as a suspect. If more than one witness is to make an identification, each witness should be required to do so separately and should be forbidden to speak to another witness until all of them have completed the process.

"The statute could require the use of movie cameras and tape recorders to record the lineup process in those states which are financial-

ly able to afford these devices. Finally, the statute should provide that any evidence obtained as the result of a violation of this statute would be inadmissible." Murray, The Criminal Lineup at Home and Abroad, 1966 Utah L.Rev. 610, 627–628.

10. Although the right to counsel usually means a right to the suspect's own counsel, provision for substitute counsel may be justified on the ground that the substitute counsel's presence may eliminate the hazards which render the lineup a critical stage for the presence of the suspect's *own* counsel.

identification evidence.[11]   That result cannot help the guilty avoid conviction but can only help assure that the right man has been brought to justice.[12]

Legislative or other regulations, such as those of local police departments, which eliminate the risks of abuse and unintentional suggestion at lineup proceedings and the impediments to meaningful confrontation at trial may also remove the basis for regarding the stage as "critical." [13] But neither Congress nor the federal authorities has seen fit to provide a solution. What we hold today "in no way creates a constitutional strait-jacket which will handicap sound efforts at reform, nor is it intended to have this effect." . . .

V.

We come now to the question whether the denial of Wade's motion to strike the courtroom identification by the bank witnesses at trial because of the absence of his counsel at the lineup required, as the Court of Appeals held, the grant of a new trial at which such evidence is to be excluded. We do not think this disposition can be justified without first giving the Government the opportunity to establish by clear and convincing evidence that the in-court identifications were based upon observations of the suspect other than the lineup identification. . . . Where, as here, the admissibility of evidence of the lineup identification itself is not involved, a per se rule of exclusion of courtroom identification would be unjustified.

11. Concern is also expressed that the presence of counsel will force divulgence of the identity of government witnesses whose identity the Government may want to conceal. To the extent that this is a valid or significant state interest there are police practices commonly used to effect concealment, for example, masking the face.

12. Most other nations surround the lineup with safeguards against prejudice to the suspect. In England the suspect must be allowed the presence of his solicitor or a friend, Napley, supra, at 98–99; Germany requires the presence of retained counsel; France forbids the confrontation of the suspect in the absence of his counsel; Spain, Mexico, and Italy provide detailed procedures prescribing the conditions under which confrontation must occur under the supervision of a judicial officer who sees to it that the proceedings are officially recorded to assure adequate scrutiny at trial. Murray, The Criminal Lineup at Home and Abroad, 1966 Utah L.Rev. 610, 621–627.

13. Thirty years ago Wigmore suggested a "scientific method" of pretrial identification "to reduce the risk of error hitherto inherent in such proceedings." Wigmore, The Science of Judicial Proof 541 (3d ed. 1937). Under this approach, at least 100 talking films would be prepared of men from various occupations, races, etc. Each would be photographed in a number of stock movements, with and without hat and coat, and would read aloud a standard passage. The suspect would be filmed in the same manner. Some 25 of the films would be shown in succession in a special projection room in which each witness would be provided an electric button which would activate a board backstage when pressed to indicate that the witness had identified a given person. Provision would be made for the degree of hesitancy in the identification to be indicated by the number of presses. Of course, the more systematic and scientific a process or proceeding, including one for purposes of identification, the less the impediment to reconstruction of the conditions bearing upon the reliability of that process or proceeding at trial. . . .

. . . A rule limited solely to the exclusion of testimony concerning identification at the lineup itself, without regard to admissibility of the courtroom identification, would render the right to counsel an empty one. The lineup is most often used, as in the present case, to crystallize the witnesses' identification of the defendant for future reference. We have already noted that the lineup identification will have that effect. The State may then rest upon the witnesses' unequivocal courtroom identification, and not mention the pretrial identification as part of the State's case at trial. Counsel is then in the predicament in which Wade's counsel found himself—realizing that possible unfairness at the lineup may be the sole means of attack upon the unequivocal courtroom identification, and having to probe in the dark in an attempt to discover and reveal unfairness, while bolstering the government witness' courtroom identification by bringing out and dwelling upon his prior identification. Since counsel's presence at the lineup would equip him to attack not only the lineup identification but the courtroom identification as well, limiting the impact of violation of the right to counsel to exclusion of evidence only of identification at the lineup itself disregards a critical element of that right.

We think it follows that the proper test to be applied in these situations is that quoted in Wong Sun v. United States, 371 U.S. 471, 488, 83 S.Ct. 407, 417, "Whether, granting establishment of the primary illegality, the evidence to which instant objection is made has been come at by exploitation of that illegality or instead by means sufficiently distinguishable to be purged of the primary taint." . . . Application of this test in the present context requires consideration of various factors; for example, the prior opportunity to observe the alleged criminal act, the existence of any discrepancy between any pre-lineup description and the defendant's actual description, any identification prior to lineup of another person, the identification by picture of the defendant prior to the lineup, failure to identify the defendant on a prior occasion, and the lapse of time between the alleged act and the lineup identification. It is also relevant to consider those facts which, despite the absence of counsel, are disclosed concerning the conduct of the lineup.

We doubt that the Court of Appeals applied the proper test for exclusion of the in-court identification of the two witnesses. The court stated that "it cannot be said with any certainty that they would have recognized appellant at the time of trial if this intervening lineup had not occurred," and that the testimony of the two witnesses "may well have been colored by the illegal procedure [and] was prejudicial." Moreover, the court was persuaded, in part, by the "compulsory verbal responses made by Wade at the instance of the Special Agent." This implies the erroneous holding that Wade's privilege against self-incrimination was violated so that the denial of counsel required exclusion.

On the record now before us we cannot make the determination whether the in-court identifications had an independent origin. This was not an issue at trial, although there is some evidence relevant to a determination. That inquiry is most properly made in the District Court. We therefore think the appropriate procedure to be followed is to vacate the conviction pending a hearing to determine whether the in-court identifications had an independent source, or whether, in any event, the introduction of the evidence was harmless error, and for the District Court to reinstate the conviction or order a new trial, as may be proper. See United States v. Shotwell Mfg. Co., 355 U.S. 233, 245–246, 78 S.Ct. 245, 253.

The judgment of the Court of Appeals is vacated and the case is remanded to that court with direction to enter a new judgment vacating the conviction and remanding the case to the District Court for further proceedings consistent with this opinion. It is so ordered.

Judgment of Court of Appeals vacated and case remanded with direction.

THE CHIEF JUSTICE joins the opinion of the Court except for Part I, from which he dissents for the reasons expressed in the opinion of MR. JUSTICE FORTAS.

MR. JUSTICE DOUGLAS joins the opinion of the Court except for Part I. On that phase of the case he adheres to the dissenting views in Schmerber v. State of California, that compulsory lineup violates the privilege against self-incrimination contained in the Fifth Amendment.

MR. JUSTICE CLARK, concurring.

With reference to the lineup point involved in this case I cannot, for the life of me, see why a lineup is not a critical stage of the prosecution. Identification of the suspect—a prerequisite to establishment of guilt—occurs at this stage, and with Miranda v. State of Arizona on the books, the requirement of the presence of counsel arises, unless waived by the suspect. I dissented in *Miranda* but I am bound by it now, as we all are. Schmerber v. State of California, precludes petitioner's claim of self-incrimination. I therefore join the opinion of the Court.

MR. JUSTICE BLACK, dissenting in part and concurring in part.

* * *

The Court in Part I of its opinion rejects Wade's Fifth Amendment contention. From that I dissent. In Parts II–IV of its opinion, the Court sustains Wade's claim of denial of right to counsel in the out-of-court lineup, and in that I concur. In Part V, the Court remands the case to the District Court to consider whether the courtroom identification of Wade was the fruit of the illegal lineup, and if it were, to grant him a new trial unless the court concludes that the courtroom identification was harmless error. I would reverse the Court of Appeals' reversal of Wade's conviction, but I would not remand for further proceedings since the prosecution not having used the out-of-court lineup identification against Wade at his trial, I believe the conviction should be affirmed.

I.

In rejecting Wade's claim that his privilege against self-incrimination was violated by compelling him to appear in the lineup wearing the tape and uttering the words given him by the police, the Court relies on the recent holding in Schmerber v. State of California. In that case the Court held that taking blood from a man's body against his will in order to convict him of a crime did not compel him to be a witness against himself. I dissented from that holding, and still dissent. The Court's reason for its holding was that the sample of Schmerber's blood taken in order to convict him of crime was neither "testimonial" nor "communicative" evidence. I think it was both. It seems quite plain to me that the Fifth Amendment's Self-incrimination Clause was designed to bar the Government from forcing any person to supply proof of his own crime, precisely what Schmerber was forced to do when he was forced to supply his blood. The Government simply took his blood against his will and over his counsel's protest for the purpose of convicting him of crime. So here, having Wade in its custody awaiting trial to see if he could or would be convicted of crime, the Government forced him to stand in a lineup, wear strips on his face, and speak certain words, in order to make it possible for government witnesses to identify him as a criminal. Had Wade been compelled to utter these or any other words in open court, it is plain that he would have been entitled to a new trial because of having been compelled to be a witness against himself. Being forced by Government to help convict himself and to supply evidence against himself by talking outside the courtroom is equally violative of his constitutional right not to be compelled to be a witness against himself. Consequently, because of this violation of the Fifth Amendment, and not because of my own personal view that the Government's conduct was "unfair," "prejudicial," or "improper," I would prohibit the prosecution's use of lineup identification at trial.

II.

I agree with the Court, in large part because of the reasons it gives, that failure to notify Wade's counsel that Wade was to be put in a lineup by government officers and to be forced to talk and wear tape on his face denied Wade the right to counsel in violation of the Sixth Amendment. Once again, my reason for this conclusion is solely the Sixth Amendment's guarantee that "the accused shall enjoy the right . . . to have the assistance of counsel for his defence." As this Court's opinion points out, "[t]he plain wording of this guarantee thus encompasses counsel's assistance whenever necessary to assure a meaningful 'defence.'" And I agree with the Court that a lineup is a "critical stage" of the criminal proceedings against an accused, because it is a stage at which the Government makes use of his custody to obtain crucial evidence against him. Besides counsel's presence at the lineup being necessary to protect the defendant's specific constitutional rights to confrontation and the assistance of counsel at the trial itself, the assistance of counsel at the lineup is also necessary to protect the defendant's in-custody assertion of his privilege against self-incrimination, for contrary to the Court, I believe that counsel may advise the defendant not to participate in the lineup or to participate only under certain conditions.

I agree with the Court that counsel's presence at the lineup is necessary to protect the accused's right to a "fair trial," only if by "fair trial" the Court means a trial in accordance with the "law of the land" as specificially set out in the Constitution. But there are implications in the Court's opinion that by a "fair trial" the Court means a trial which a majority of this Court deems to be "fair" and that a lineup is a "critical stage" only because the Court, now assessing the "innumerable dangers" which inhere in it, thinks it is such. That these implications are justified is evidenced by the Court's suggestion that "legislative or other regulations . . . which eliminate the abuse . . . at lineup proceedings . . . may also remove the basis for regarding the stage as 'critical.' " . . . I am wholly unwilling to make the specific constitutional right of counsel dependent on judges' vague and transitory notions of fairness and their equally transitory, though "practical," assessment of the "risk that . . . counsel's absence . . . might derogate from a fair trial." . . .

III.

I would reverse Wade's conviction without further ado had the prosecution at trial made use of his lineup identification either in place of courtroom identification or to bolster in a harmful manner crucial courtroom identification. But the prosecution here did neither of these things. After prosecution witnesses under oath identified Wade in the courtroom, it was the defense, and not the prosecution, which brought out the prior lineup identification. While stating that "a *per se* rule of exclusion of courtroom identification would be unjustified," the Court, nevertheless remands this case for "a hearing to determine whether the in-court identifications had an independent source," or were the tainted fruits of the invalidly conducted lineup. From this holding I dissent.

In the first place, even if this Court has power to establish such a rule of evidence I think the rule fashioned by the Court is unsound. The "taint"-"fruit" determination required by the Court involves more than considerable difficulty. I think it is practically impossible. How is a witness capable of probing the recesses of his mind to draw a sharp line between a courtroom identification due exclusively to an earlier lineup and a courtroom identification due to memory not based on the lineup? What kind of "clear and convincing evidence" can the prosecution offer to prove upon what particular events memories resulting in an in-court identification rest? How long will trials be delayed while judges turn psychologists to probe the subconscious minds of witnesses? All these questions are posed but not answered by the Court's opinion. In my view, the Fifth and Sixth Amendments are satisfied if the prosecution is precluded from using lineup identification as either an alternative to or corroboration of courtroom identification. If the prosecution does neither and its witnesses under oath identify the defendant in the courtroom, then I can find no justification for stopping the trial in midstream to hold a lengthy "taint"-"fruit" hearing. The fact of and circumstances surrounding a prior lineup identification might be used by the defense to impeach the credibility of the in-court identifications, but not to exclude them completely.

But more important, there is no constitutional provision upon which I can rely that directly or by implication gives this Court power to establish what amounts to a constitutional rule of evidence to govern, not only the Federal Government, but the States in their trial of state crimes under state laws in state courts. See Gilbert v. California, post. The Constitution deliberately reposed in States very broad power to create and to try crimes according to their own rules and policies. . . . Before being deprived of this power, the least that they can ask is that we should be able to point to a federal constitutional provision that either by express language or by necessary implication grants us the power to fashion this novel rule of evidence to govern their criminal trials. . . .

Perhaps the Court presumes to write this constitutional rule of evidence on the Fourteenth Amendment's Due Process Clause. This is not the time or place to consider that claim. Suffice it for me to say briefly that I find no such authority in the Due Process Clause. It undoubtedly provides that a person must be tried in accordance with the "Law of the Land." Consequently, it violates due process to try a person in a way prohibited by the Fourth, Fifth, or Sixth Amendments of our written Constitution. But I have never been able to subscribe to the dogma that the Due Process Clause empowers this Court to declare any law, including a rule of evidence, unconstitutional which it believes is contrary to tradition, decency, fundamental justice, or any of the other wide-meaning words used by judges to claim power under the Due Process Clause. . . . I have an abiding idea that if the Framers had wanted to let judges write the Constitution on any such day-to-day beliefs of theirs, they would have said so instead of so carefully defining their grants and prohibitions in a written constitution. With no more authority than the Due Process Clause I am wholly unwilling to tell the state or federal courts that the United States Constitution forbids them to allow courtroom identification without the prosecution first proving that the identification does not rest in whole or in part on an illegal lineup. Should I do so, I would feel that we are deciding what the Constitution is, not from what it says, but from what we think it would have been wise for the Framers to put in it. That to me would be "judicial activism" at its worst. I would leave the States and Federal Government free to decide their own rules of evidence. That, I believe, is their constitutional prerogative.

I would affirm Wade's conviction.

Mr. Justice White, whom Mr. Justice Harlan and Mr. Justice Stewart join, dissenting in part and concurring in part.

The Court has again propounded a broad constitutional rule barring the use of a wide spectrum of relevant and probative evidence, solely because a step in its ascertainment or discovery occurs outside the presence of defense counsel. This was the approach of the Court in Miranda v. State of Arizona. I objected then to what I thought was an uncritical and doctrinaire approach without satisfactory factual foundation. I have much the same view of the present ruling and therefore dissent from the judgment and from Parts II, IV, and V of the Court's opinion.

The Court's opinion is far reaching. It proceeds first by creating a new *per se* rule of constitutional law: a criminal suspect cannot be subjected to a pretrial identification process in the absence of his counsel without violating the Sixth Amendment. If he is, the State may not buttress a later courtroom identification of the witness by any reference to the previous identification. Furthermore, the courtroom identification is not admissible at all unless the State can establish by clear and convincing proof that the testimony is not the fruit of the earlier identification made in the absence of defendant's counsel—admittedly a heavy burden for the State and probably an impossible one. For all intents and purposes, courtroom identifications are barred if pretrial identifications have occurred without counsel being present.

The rule applies to any lineup, to any other techniques employed to produce an identification and *a fortiori* to a face-to-face encounter between the witness and the suspect alone, regardless of when the identification occurs, in time or place, and whether before or after indictment or information. It matters not how well the witness knows the suspect, whether the witness is the suspect's mother, brother, or long-time associate, and no matter how long or well the witness observed the perpetrator at the scene of the crime. The kidnap victim who has lived for days with his abductor is in the same category as the witness who had had only a fleeting glimpse of the criminal. Neither may identify the suspect without defendant's counsel being present. The same strictures apply regardless of the number of other witnesses who positively identify the defendant and regardless of the corroborative evidence showing that it was the defendant who has committed the crime.

The premise for the Court's rule is not the general unreliability of eyewitness identifications nor the difficulties inherent in observation, recall, and recognition. The Court assumes a narrower evil as the basis for its rule—improper police suggestion which contributes to erroneous identifications. The Court apparently believes that improper police procedures are so widespread that a broad prophylactic rule must be laid down, requiring the presence of counsel at all pretrial identifications, in order to detect recurring instances of police misconduct.[1] I do not share this pervasive distrust of all official investigations. None of the materials the Court relies upon supports it.[2] Certainly, I would bow to solid fact, but the Court quite obviously does not have before it any reliable, comprehensive survey of current police practices on which to base its new rule. Until it does, the Court should avoid excluding relevant evidence from state criminal trials.

The Court goes beyond assuming that a great majority of the country's police departments are following improper practices at pretrial identifications. To find the lineup a "critical" stage of the proceeding and to exclude identifications made in the absence of counsel, the Court must also assume that police "suggestion," if it occurs at all, leads to erroneous rather than accurate identifications and that reprehensible police conduct will have an unavoidable and largely undiscoverable impact on the trial. This in turn assumes that there is now no adequate source from which defense counsel can learn about the circumstances of the pretrial identification in order to place before the jury all of the considerations which should enter into an appraisal of courtroom identification evidence. But these are treacherous and unsupported assumptions resting as they do on the notion that the defendant will not be aware, that the police and the witnesses will forget or prevaricate, that defense counsel will be unable to bring out the truth and that neither jury, judge, nor appellate court is a sufficient safeguard against unacceptable police conduct occurring at a pretrial identification procedure. I am unable to share the Court's view of the willingness of the police and the ordinary citizen-witness to dissemble, either with respect to the identification of the defendant or with respect to the circumstances surrounding a pretrial identification.

There are several striking aspects to the Court's holding. First, the rule does not bar courtroom identifications where there have been no previous identifications in the presence of the police, although when identified in the courtroom, the defendant is known to be in custody and charged with the commission of a crime. Second, the Court seems to say that if suitable legislative standards were adopted for the conduct of pretrial identifications, thereby lessening the hazards in such confrontations, it would not insist on the presence of counsel. But if this is true, why does not the Court simply fashion

1. Yet in Stovall in Denno, 388 U.S. 293, 87 S.Ct. 1967, the Court recognizes that improper police conduct in the identification process has not been so widespread as to justify full retroactivity for its new rule.

2. In Miranda v. State of Arizona, the Court noted that O'Hara, Fundamentals of Criminal Investigation (1956) is a text that has enjoyed extensive use among law enforcement agencies and among students of police science. The quality of the work was said to rest on the author's long service as observer, lecturer in police science, and work as a federal crime investigator. O'Hara does not suggest that the police should or do use identification machinery improperly; instead he argues for techniques that would increase the reliability of eyewitness identifications, and there is no reason to suggest that O'Hara's views are not shared and practiced by the majority of police departments throughout the land.

what it deems to be constitutionally acceptable procedures for the authorities to follow? Certainly the Court is correct in suggesting that the new rule will be wholly inapplicable where police departments themselves have established suitable safeguards.

Third, courtroom identification may be barred, absent counsel at a prior identification, regardless of the extent of counsel's information concerning the circumstances of the previous confrontation between witness and defendant—apparently even if there were recordings or sound-movies of the events as they occurred. But if the rule is premised on the defendant's right to have his counsel know, there seems little basis for not accepting other means to inform. A disinterested observer, recordings, photographs—any one of them would seem adequate to furnish the basis for a meaningful cross-examination of the eyewitness who identifies the defendant in the courtroom.

I share the Court's view that the criminal trial, at the very least, should aim at truthful factfinding, including accurate eyewitness identifications. I doubt, however, on the basis of our present information, that the tragic mistakes which have occurred in criminal trials are as much the product of improper police conduct as they are the consequence of the difficulties inherent in eyewitness testimony and in resolving evidentiary conflicts by court or jury. I doubt that the Court's new rule will obviate these difficulties, or that the situation will be measurably improved by inserting defense counsel into the investigative processes of police departments everywhere.

But, it may be asked, what possible state interest militates against requiring the presence of defense counsel at lineups? After all, the argument goes, he *may* do some good, he *may* upgrade the quality of identification evidence in state courts and he can scarcely do any harm. Even if true, this is a feeble foundation for fastening an ironclad constitutional rule upon state criminal procedures. Absent some reliably established constitutional violation, the processes by which the States enforce their criminal laws are their own prerogative. The States *do* have an interest in conducting their own affairs, an interest which cannot be displaced simply by saying that there are no valid arguments with respect to the merits of a federal rule emanating from this Court.

Beyond this, however, requiring counsel at pretrial identifications as an invariable rule trenches on other valid state interests. One of them is its concern with the prompt and efficient enforcement of its criminal laws. Identifications frequently take place after arrest but before indictment or information is filed. The police may have arrested a suspect on probable cause but may still have the wrong man. Both the suspect and the State have every interest in a prompt identification at that stage, the suspect in order to secure his immediate release and the State because prompt and early identification enhances *accurate* identification and because it must know whether it is on the right investigative track. Unavoidably, however, the absolute rule requiring the presence of counsel will cause significant delay and it may very well result in no pretrial identification at all. Counsel must be appointed and a time arranged convenient for him and the witnesses. Meanwhile, it may be necessary to file charges against the suspect who may then be released on bail, in the federal system very often on his own recognizance, with neither the State nor the defendant having the benefit of a properly conducted identification procedure.

Nor do I think the witnesses themselves can be ignored. They will now be required to be present at the convenience of counsel rather than their own. Many may be much less willing to participate if the identification stage is transformed into an adversary proceeding not under the control of a judge. Others may fear for their own safety if their identity is known at an early date, especially when there is no way of knowing until the lineup occurs whether or not the police really have the right man.[3]

Finally, I think the Court's new rule is vulnerable in terms of its own unimpeachable purpose of increasing the reliability of identification testimony.

Law enforcement officers have the obligation to convict the guilty and to make sure they do not convict the innocent. They must be dedicated to making the criminal trial a procedure for the ascertainment of the true facts surrounding the commission of the crime. To this extent, our so-called adversary system is not adversary at all; nor should it be. But defense counsel has no comparable obligation to ascertain or present the truth. Our system assigns him a different mission. He must be and is interested in not convicting the innocent, but, absent a voluntary plea of guilty, we also insist that he defend his client whether he is innocent or guilty. The State has the obligation to present the evidence. Defense counsel need present nothing, even if he knows what the truth is. He need furnish no witnesses to the police, reveal any confidences of his client, nor furnish any other information to help the prosecution's case. If he can confuse a witness, even a truthful one, or make him appear at a disadvantage, unsure or indecisive, that will be his normal course. Our interest in not convicting the innocent permits counsel to put the State to its proof, to put the State's case in the worst possible light regardless of what he thinks or knows to be the truth. Undoubtedly there are some limits which defense counsel must observe but more often than not, defense counsel will cross-examine a prosecution witness, and impeach him if he can, even if he thinks the witness is telling the truth, just as he will attempt to destroy a witness who he thinks is lying. In this respect, as part of our modified adversary system and as part of the duty imposed on the most honorable defense counsel, we countenance or require conduct which in many instances has little, if any, relation to the search for truth.

---

3. I would not have thought that the State's interest regarding its sources of identification is any less than its interest in protecting informants, especially those who may aid in identification but who will not be used as witnesses.

I would not extend this system, at least as it presently operates, to police investigations and would not require counsel's presence at pretrial identification procedures. Counsel's interest is in not having his client placed at the scene of the crime, regardless of his whereabouts. Some counsel may advise their clients to refuse to make any movements or to speak any words in a lineup or even to appear in one. To that extent the impact on truthful factfinding is quite obvious. Others will not only observe what occurs and develop possibilities for later cross-examination but will hover over witnesses and begin their cross-examination then, menacing truthful factfinding as thoroughly as the Court fears the police now do. Certainly there is an implicit invitation to counsel to suggest rules for the lineup and to manage and produce it as best he can. I therefore doubt that the Court's new rule, at least absent some clearly defined limits on counsel's role, will measurably contribute to more reliable pretrial identifications. My fears are that it will have precisely the opposite result. It may well produce fewer convictions, but that is hardly a proper measure of its long-run acceptability. In my view, the State is entitled to investigate and develop its case outside the presence of defense counsel. This includes the right to have private conversations with identification witnesses, just as defense counsel may have his own consultations with these and other witnesses without having the prosecutor present.

Whether today's judgment would be an acceptable exercise of supervisory power over federal courts is another question. But as a constitutional matter, the judgment in this case is erroneous and although I concur in Parts I and III of the Court's opinion I respectfully register this dissent.

Mr. Justice Fortas, with whom The Chief Justice and Mr. Justice Douglas join, concurring in part and dissenting in part.

1. I agree with the Court that the exhibition of the person of the accused at a lineup is not itself a violation of the privilege against self-incrimination. In itself, it is no more subject to constitutional objection than the exhibition of the person of the accused in the courtroom for identification purposes. It is an incident of the State's power to arrest, and a reasonable and justifiable aspect of the State's custody resulting from arrest. It does not require that the accused take affirmative, volitional action, but only that, having been duly arrested he may be seen for identification purposes. It is, however, a "critical stage" in the prosecution, and I agree with the Court that the opportunity to have counsel present must be made available.

2. In my view, however, the accused may not be compelled in a lineup to speak the words uttered by the person who committed the crime. I am confident that it could not be compelled in court. It cannot be compelled in a lineup. It is more than passive, mute assistance to the eyes of the victim or of witnesses. It is the kind of volitional act—the kind of forced cooperation by the accused—which is within the historical perimeter of the privilege against compelled self-incrimination.

Our history and tradition teach and command that an accused may stand mute. The privilege means just that; not less than that. According to the Court, an accused may be jailed—indefinitely—until he is willing to say, for an identifying audience, whatever was said in the course of the commission of the crime. Presumably this would include, "Your money or your life"—or perhaps, words of assault in a rape case. This is intolerable under our constitutional system.

I completely agree that the accused must be advised of and given the right to counsel before a lineup—and I join in that part of the Court's opinion; but this is an empty right unless we mean to insist upon the accused's fundamental constitutional immunities. One of these is that the accused may not be compelled to speak. To compel him to speak would violate the privilege against self-incrimination, which is incorporated in the Fifth Amendment.

* 　 * 　 *

An accused cannot be compelled to utter the words spoken by the criminal in the course of the crime. I thoroughly disagree with the Court's statement that such compulsion does not violate the Fifth Amendment. The Court relies upon Schmerber v. State of California to support this. . . . But *Schmerber* which authorized the .forced extraction of blood from the veins of an unwilling human being, did not compel the person actively to cooperate—to accuse himself by a volitional act which differs only in degree from compelling him to act out the crime, which, I assume, would be rebuffed by the Court. . . .

To permit *Schmerber* to apply in any respect beyond its holding is, in my opinion, indefensible. To permit its insidious doctrine to extend beyond the invasion of the body, which it permits, to compulsion of the will of a man, is to deny and defy a precious part of our historical faith and to discard one of the most profoundly cherished instruments by which we have established the freedom and dignity of the individual. We should not so alter the balance between the rights of the individual and of the state, achieved over centuries of conflict.

3. While the Court holds that the accused must be advised of and given the right to counsel at the lineup, it makes the privilege meaningless in this important respect. Unless counsel has been waived or, being present, has not objected to the accused's utterance of words used in the course of committing the crime, to compel such an utterance is constitutional error.*

Accordingly, while I join the Court in requiring vacating of the judgment below for a determination as to whether the identification of respondent was based upon factors independent of the lineup, I would do so not only because of the failure to offer counsel before the

---

* While it is conceivable that legislation might provide a meticulous lineup procedure which would *satisfy* constitutional requirements, I do not agree with the Court that this would "remove the basis for regarding the [lineup] stage as 'critical.' "

lineup but also because of the violation of respondent's Fifth Amendment rights.

NOTES

1. In Gilbert v. California, 388 U.S. 263, 87 S.Ct. 1951 (1967), the Court elaborated on its several holdings in *Wade*. The Court held that requiring a suspect to give handwriting exemplars in the absence of counsel violated neither Fifth nor Sixth Amendment rights. The Court further held that a lineup conducted without notice to Gilbert's counsel some sixteen days after indictment violated Gilbert's right to counsel. With respect to those witnesses who identified Gilbert at trial, the Court held that Gilbert was entitled to a hearing whether their courtroom identification was untainted by their observations of Gilbert at the illegal lineup. The Court finally held that testimony concerning the pre-trial confrontation introduced by the prosecution was erroneously admitted. Such testimony, according to the Court, was the direct product of illegal law-enforcement conduct and "only a per se exclusionary rule as to such testimony can be an effective sanction to assure that law enforcement authorities will respect the accused's constitutional right to the presence of his counsel at the critical lineup."

2. Can the right to counsel at lineups be waived? Every court that has considered the question has answered in the affirmative. See State v. Taylor, 456 S.W.2d 9 (Mo.1970); Hayes v. State, 46 Wis.2d 93, 175 N.W.2d 625 (1970); Compare State v. Bass, 280 N.C. 435, 186 S.E.2d 384 (1972) with State v. Mems, 281 N.C. 709, 190 S.E.2d 164 (1972). A waiver must be voluntary. Compare Redding v. State, 10 Md.App. 601, 272 A.2d 70 (1971), with Chambers v. State, 46 Ala.App. 247, 240 So.2d 370 (1970) (waiver voluntary when suspect was told he could go home if he was not identified). Warnings of the right to counsel *at the lineup* must be given. The mere giving of Miranda warnings is not sufficient (United States v. Ayers, 426 F.2d 524 (2nd Cir. 1970)) but such warnings may be considered as supplementing other warnings specifically concerning the lineup. See People v. Evans, 16 Cal.App.3d 510, 94 Cal.Rptr. 88 (1971).

KIRBY v. ILLINOIS

Supreme Court of the United States, 1972.
406 U.S. 682, 92 S.Ct. 1877.

MR. JUSTICE STEWART announced the judgment of the Court in an opinion in which THE CHIEF JUSTICE, MR. JUSTICE BLACKMUN, and MR. JUSTICE REHNQUIST join.

. . . In the present case we are asked to extend the *Wade-Gilbert per se* exclusionary rule to identification testimony based upon a police station showup that took place *before* the defendant had been indicted or otherwise formally charged with any criminal offense.

On February 21, 1968, a man named Willie Shard reported to the Chicago police that the previous day two men had robbed him on a Chicago street of a wallet containing, among other things, travellers checks and a Social Security card. On February 22, two police officers stopped the petitioner and a companion, Ralph Bean, on West

Madison Street in Chicago. When asked for identification, the petitioner produced a wallet that contained three travellers checks and a Social Security card, all bearing the name of Willie Shard. Papers with Shard's name on them were also found in Bean's possession. When asked to explain his possession of Shard's property, the petitioner first said that the travellers checks were "play money," and then told the officers that he had won them in a crap game. The officers then arrested the petitioner and Bean and took them to a police station.

Only after arriving at the police station, and checking the records there, did the arresting officers learn of the Shard robbery. A police car was then dispatched to Shard's place of employment, where it picked up Shard and brought him to the police station. Immediately upon entering the room in the police station where the petitioner and Bean were seated at a table, Shard positively identified them as the men who had robbed him two days earlier. No lawyer was present in the room, and neither the petitioner nor Bean had asked for legal assistance, or been advised of any right to the presence of counsel.

. . . A pretrial motion to suppress Shard's identification testimony was denied, and at the trial Shard testified as a witness for the prosecution. In his testimony he described his identification of the two men at the police station on February 22, and identified them again in the courtroom as the men who had robbed him on February 20. He was cross-examined at length regarding the circumstances of his identification of the two defendants. The jury found both defendants guilty, and the petitioner's conviction was affirmed on appeal. The Illinois appellate court held that the admission of Shard's testimony was not error, relying upon an earlier decision of the Illinois Supreme Court, People v. Palmer, 41 Ill.2d 571, 244 N.E.2d 173, holding that the *Wade-Gilbert per se* exclusionary rule is not applicable to preindictment confrontations. We granted certiorari, limited to this question.

I.

We note at the outset that the constitutional privilege against compulsory self-incrimination is in no way implicated here. . . .

It follows that the doctrine of Miranda v. Arizona has no applicability whatever to the issue before us. For the *Miranda* decision was based exclusively upon the Fifth and Fourteenth Amendment privilege against compulsory self-incrimination, upon the theory that custodial *interrogation* is inherently coercive.

The *Wade-Gilbert* exclusionary rule, by contrast, stems from a quite different constitutional guarantee—the guarantee of the right to counsel contained in the Sixth and Fourteenth Amendments. Unless all semblance of principled constitutional adjudication is to be abandoned, therefore, it is to the decisions construing that guarantee that we must look in determining the present controversy.

In a line of constitutional cases in this Court stemming back to the Court's landmark opinion in Powell v. Alabama, 287 U.S. 45, 53 S.Ct. 55, it has been firmly established that a person's Sixth and Fourteenth Amendment right to counsel attaches only at or after the time that adversary judicial proceedings have been initiated against him.

This is not to say that a defendant in a criminal case has a constitutional right to counsel only at the trial itself. The *Powell* case makes clear that the right attaches at the time of arraignment, and the Court has recently held that it exists also at the time of a preliminary hearing. But the point is that, while members of the Court have differed as to existence of the right to counsel in the contexts of some of the above cases, *all* of those cases have involved points of time at or after the initiation of adversary judicial criminal proceedings—whether by way of formal charge, preliminary hearing, indictment, information, or arraignment.

The only seeming deviation from this long line of constitutional decisions, was Escobedo v. Illinois, 378 U.S. 478, 84 S.Ct. 1758. But *Escobedo* is not apposite here for two distinct reasons. First, the Court in retrospect perceived that the "prime purpose" of *Escobedo* was not to vindicate the constitutional right to counsel as such, but, like *Miranda*, "to guarantee full effectuation of the privilege against self-incrimination. . . ." Secondly, and perhaps even more important for purely practical purposes, the Court has limited the holding of *Escobedo* to its own facts, and those facts are not remotely akin to the facts of the case before us.

The initiation of judicial criminal proceedings is far from a mere formalism. It is the starting point of our whole system of adversary criminal justice. For it is only then that the Government has committed itself to prosecute, and only then that the adverse positions of Government and defendant have solidified. It is then that a defendant finds himself faced with the prosecutorial forces of organized society, and immersed in the intricacies of substantive and procedural criminal law. It is this point, therefore, that marks the commencement of the "criminal prosecutions" to which alone the explicit guarantees of the Sixth Amendment are applicable.

In this case we are asked to import into a routine police investigation an absolute constitutional guarantee historically and rationally applicable only after the onset of formal prosecutorial proceedings. We decline to do so. Less than a year after *Wade* and *Gilbert* were decided, the Court explained the rule of those decisions as follows: "The rationale of those cases was that an accused is entitled to counsel at any 'critical stage of the *prosecution*,' and that a post-indictment lineup is such a 'critical stage.' " (Emphasis supplied.) Simmons v. United States, 390 U.S. 377, 382–383, 88 S.Ct. 967, 970. We decline to depart from that rationale today by imposing a *per se* exclusionary rule upon testimony concerning an identification that took place long before the commencement of any prosecution whatever.

II.

What has been said is not to suggest that there may not be occasions during the course of a criminal investigation when the police do abuse identification procedures. Such abuses are not beyond the reach of the Constitution. As the Court pointed out in *Wade* itself, it is always necessary to "scrutinize *any* pretrial confrontation. . . ." The Due Process Clause of the Fifth and Fourteenth Amendments forbids a lineup that is unnecessarily suggestive and conducive to irreparable mistaken identification. When a person has not been formally charged with a criminal offense, *Stovall* strikes the appropriate constitutional balance between the right of a suspect to be protected from prejudicial procedures and the interest of society in the prompt and purposeful investigation of an unsolved crime.

The judgment is affirmed.

MR. CHIEF JUSTICE BURGER, concurring.

I agree that the right to counsel attaches as soon as criminal charges are formally made against an accused and he becomes the subject of a "criminal prosecution." Therefore, I join in the Court's opinion and holding.

MR. JUSTICE POWELL, concurring in the result.

As I would not extend the *Wade-Gilbert per se* exclusionary rule, I concur in the result reached by the Court.

MR. JUSTICE BRENNAN, with whom MR. JUSTICE DOUGLAS and MR. JUSTICE MARSHALL join, dissenting. . . .

While it should go without saying, it appears necessary, in view of the plurality opinion today, to re-emphasize that *Wade* did not require the presence of counsel at pretrial confrontations for identification purposes simply on the basis of an abstract consideration of the words "criminal prosecutions" in the Sixth Amendment. Counsel is required at those confrontations because "the dangers inherent in eyewitness identification and the suggestibility inherent in the context of the pretrial identification," mean that protection must be afforded to the "most basic right [of] a criminal defendant—his right to a fair trial at which the witnesses against him might be meaningfully cross-examined,". Indeed, the Court expressly stated that "[L]egislative or other regulations, such as those of local police departments, which eliminate the risks of abuse and unintentional suggestion at lineup proceedings and the impediments to meaningful confrontation at trial may also remove the basis for regarding the stage as 'critical.'" Hence, "the initiation of adversary judicial criminal proceedings," *ante*, at 1882, is completely irrelevant to whether counsel is necessary at a pretrial confrontation for identification in order to safeguard the accused's constitutional rights to confrontation and the effective assistance of counsel at his trial.

In view of *Wade*, it is plain, and the plurality today does not attempt to dispute it, that there inhere in a confrontation for identification conducted after arrest* the identical hazards to a fair trial that inhere in such a confrontation conducted "after the onset of formal prosecutorial proceedings." The plurality apparently considers an arrest, which for present purposes we must assume to be based upon probable cause to be nothing more than part of "a routine police investigation," ibid., and thus not "the starting point of our whole system of adversary criminal justice,". An arrest, according to the plurality, does not face the accused "with the prosecutorial forces of organized society," nor immerse him "in the intricacies of substantive and procedural criminal law." Those consequences ensue, says the plurality, only with "[t]he initiation of judicial criminal proceedings," "[f]or it is only then that the Government has committed itself to prosecute, and only then that the adverse positions of Government and defendant have solidified." If these propositions do not amount to "mere formalism," ibid., it is difficult to know how to characterize them. An arrest evidences the belief of the police that the perpetrator of a crime has been caught. A post-arrest confrontation for identification is not "a mere preparatory step in the gathering of the prosecution's evidence." A primary, and frequently sole, purpose of the confrontation for identification at that stage is to accumulate proof to buttress the conclusion of the police that they have the offender in hand. The plurality offers no reason, and I can think of none, for concluding that a post-arrest confrontation for identification, unlike a post-charge confrontation is not among those "critical confrontations of the accused by the prosecution at pretrial proceedings where the results might well settle the accused's fate and reduce the trial itself to a mere formality."

The highly suggestive form of confrontation employed in this case underscores the point. This showup was particularly fraught with the peril of mistaken identification. In the setting of a police station squad room where all present except petitioner and Bean were police officers, the danger was quite real that Shard's understandable resentment might lead him too readily to agree with the police that the pair under arrest, and the only persons exhibited to him were indeed the robbers. . . . Shard's testimony itself demonstrates the necessity for such safeguards. On direct examination, Shard identified petitioner and Bean not as the alleged robbers on trial in the courtroom, but as the pair he saw at the police station. . . .

The plurality today "decline[s] to depart from [the] rationale" of *Wade* and *Gilbert*. The plurality discovers that "rationale" not by consulting those decisions themselves, which would seem to be the appropriate course, but by reading one sentence in Simmons v. United States, 390 U.S. 377, 382–383, 88 S.Ct. 967, 970 (1968), where no right to counsel claim was either asserted or considered. The "ra-

---

* This case does not require me to consider confrontations that take place before custody, see e. g., Bratten v. Delaware, 307 F.Supp. 643 (Del. 1969); nor accidental confrontations not arranged by the police, see, e. g., United States v. Pollack, 427 F.2d 1168 (CA5 1970); nor on-the-scene encounters shortly after the crime, see, e. g., Russell v. United States, 408 F.2d 1280 (D.C.Cir.1969).

tionale" the plurality discovers is, apparently, that a post-indictment confrontation for identification is part of the prosecution. The plurality might have discovered a different "rationale" by reading one sentence in Foster v. California, 394 U.S. 440, 442, 89 S.Ct. 1127 (1969), a case decided after *Simmons*, where the Court explained that in *Wade* and *Gilbert* "this Court held that because of the possibility of unfairness to the accused in the way a lineup is conducted, a lineup is a 'critical stage' in the prosecution, at which the accused must be given the opportunity to be represented by counsel." In *Foster*, moreover, although the Court mentioned that the lineups took place after the accused's arrest, it did not say whether they were also after the information was filed against him. Instead, the Court simply pointed out that under Stovall v. Denno, *Wade* and *Gilbert* were "applicable only to lineups conducted after those cases were decided." Similarly, in Coleman v. Alabama, 399 U.S. 1, 90 S.Ct. 1999 (1970), another case involving a pre-*Wade* lineup, no member of the Court saw any significance in whether the accused had been formally charged with a crime before the lineup was held.

* * *

Wade and *Gilbert*, of course, happened to involve post-indictment confrontations. Yet even a cursory perusal of the opinions in those cases reveals that nothing at all turned upon that particular circumstance. In short, it is fair to conclude that rather than "declin[ing] to depart from [the] rationale" of *Wade* and *Gilbert*, the plurality today, albeit purporting to be engaged in "principled constitutional adjudication," refuses even to recognize that "rationale." For my part, I do not agree that we "extend" *Wade* and *Gilbert*, by holding that the principles of those cases apply to confrontations for identification conducted after arrest. Because Shard testified at trial about his identification of petitioner at the police station showup, the exclusionary rule of *Gilbert*, requires reversal.

MR. JUSTICE WHITE, dissenting.

United States v. Wade, and Gilbert v. California, govern this case and compel reversal of the judgment of the Illinois Supreme Court.

NOTES

1. Prior to the *Kirby* decision there were several lines of demarcation. It was held that the right to counsel did not apply to confrontations occurring shortly after the crimes, to accidental confrontations or to confrontations occurring when the suspect was not in custody. Some courts had restricted right to counsel to post-indictment lineups. People v. Palmer, 41 Ill. 2d 571, 244 N.E.2d 173 (1969), but most rejected this limitation, People v. Fowler, 1 Cal.3d 335, 82 Cal.Rptr. 363, 461 P.2d 643 (1969).

Those courts which applied right to counsel more broadly than required by *Kirby* may now reduce the scope of their rules to bring them into conformity with *Kirby*. The Supreme Court of California has done this in People v. Chojnacky, 8 Cal.3d 759, 106 Cal.Rptr. 106, 505 P.2d 530 (1973). See also Commonwealth v. Lopes, 362 Mass. 448, 287 N.E.2d 118 (1972). But see Blue v. State, 558 P.2d 636 (Alaska 1976), holding, as a matter of state constitutional law, the existence of the right to counsel at a lineup or showup conducted before the initiation of judicial proceedings—at least where no exigent circumstances are present.

2. Two serious questions arise with reference to the scope of *Kirby*. First, in some jurisdictions a suspect is brought to a "bond" court shortly after arrest. Does this court appearance, which is limited solely to the setting of bail represent the onset of formal prosecutorial proceedings? Does it make a difference whether a prosecutor appears at the hearing or the police appear without a prosecutor? Second, if the police get an arrest warrant from a court does this signify the commencement of prosecution? Some courts have answered in the affirmative. In United States ex rel. Robinson v. Zelker, 468 F.2d 159 (2d Cir. 1972), the court said:

> "The first question we have is whether 'adversary judicial proceedings' had been 'initiated' within Kirby v. Illinois. . . .
>
> * * *
>
> "Here the arrest warrant itself commanded that appellant be brought forthwith before the Criminal Court 'to answer the said charge, and to be dealt with according to law.' These were formal criminal proceedings, for the warrant had been signed by a judge based on an 'information upon oath' that appellant did commit the crimes of assault, robbery and possession of a dangerous weapon. This being true, *Wade* required counsel at the show-up, for we see no distinction based on the chance fact that the identifying witness was also a police officer. Time was not of the essence, a lineup could have been arranged and there appeared to be no 'substantial countervailing policy considerations' against requiring the presence of counsel as suggested in *Wade*."

In dissent Judge Hayes said:

> "I cannot agree with the majority's conclusion that 'adversary judicial criminal proceedings,' within the meaning of Kirby v. Illinois, had been begun in this case at the time of the pre-trial show-up, entitling Robinson to counsel at that show-up. In *Kirby* the Court said:
>
> > 'The initiation of judicial criminal proceedings is far from a mere formalism. It is the starting point of our whole system of adversary criminal justice. *For it is only then that the Government has committed itself to prosecute, and only then that the adverse positions of Government and defendant have solidified.* It is this point, therefore, that marks the commencement of the "criminal prosecutions" to which alone the explicit guarantees of the Sixth Amendment are applicable.'
>
> "Here the only judicial action taken against Robinson was the issuance of a warrant of arrest. He was not even arraigned until the day after the show-up. . . . It seems clear that such a warrant is not a point at which 'the Government has committed itself to prosecute, and . . . the adverse positions of Government and defendant have solidified' ".

See Arnold v. State, 484 S.W.2d 248 (Mo.1972). See also State v. Earle, 60 N.J. 550, 292 A.2d 2 (1972) (rule does not apply when suspect is in custody on an unrelated charge). Does the answer to the question depend on whether, under local law, a complaint for an arrest warrant, which may only state the facts showing probable cause, is sufficient to meet the formal requirements for complaints charging a crime, i. e., affirmative allegations of each of the elements of the crime, citation to the statute violated, etc.?

Consider the following comments in United States v. Duvall, 537 F.2d 15, at 21–22 (2d Cir. 1976):

> "We see no reason in principle why the filing of a complaint should be deemed to give rise to a right to counsel immediately upon arrest pursuant to warrant. As said in 8 Moore, Federal Practice ¶ 3.02 (Cipes, 1975 rev.), 'The principal function of a complaint "is as a basis for an application for an arrest warrant." ' See Gaither v. United States, 134 U.S.App.D.C. 154, 413 F.2d 1061, 1076 (1969). There is no reason in the nature of things why an arrest warrant should need to be predicated on a complaint rather than simply an affidavit as in the case of a search warrant, F.R. Cr.P. 41; indeed Rule 4 permits the showing of probable cause for arrest to be made either in the complaint or in an affidavit or affidavits filed with the complaint. The requirements of Rule 5 bear equally on 'an officer making an arrest under a warrant issued upon a complaint or any person making an arrest without a warrant.' We perceive no reason why Sixth Amendment rights should accrue sooner in the former instance than in the latter. Furthermore to hold that the accrual of the right to counsel is accelerated by use of the warrant procedure would tend to discourage this whereas the policy should be to encourage it."

Another decision holding that the issuance of an arrest warrant gives rise to the right to counsel at a subsequent lineup is People v. Hinton, 23 Ill.App.3d 369, 319 N.E.2d 313 (1974). The argument that fewer arrest warrants will be issued if the issuance of a warrant creates a right to counsel is not merely puff in an appellate brief. This is precisely what has happened in Cook County, Illinois, where prosecutors are most reluctant to seek an arrest warrant if they know that a lineup will be held after the suspect is captured and if they believe that the suspect will be apprehended within a short period of time.

In People v. Blake, 35 N.Y.2d 331, 361 N.Y.S.2d 881, 320 N.E.2d 625 (1974), the Court held that undue delay between arrest and filing of a formal charge is a suspect circumstance but found a two hour delay to be reasonable. Holland v. Perini, 512 F.2d 99 (6th Cir. 1975) approved a delay of twenty-four hours even though the delay appeared deliberate.

3. An accused who is represented by counsel on another charge does not, for that reason alone, have the right to the presence of that attorney at a lineup conducted for another offense. Boyd v. Henderson, 555 F.2d 52 (2nd Cir. 1977).

4. If the first post-crime confrontation between a witness and the defendant occurs at a preliminary hearing, do *Wade* and *Kirby* require counsel? Must counsel know that this is the first time that the witness has viewed the defendant for the purpose of possible identification? Moore v.

Illinois, 434 U.S. 220, 98 S.Ct. 458 (1977), dealt with the issue in the following way:

"MR. JUSTICE POWELL delivered the opinion of the Court.

"In the instant case, petitioner argues that the preliminary hearing at which the victim identified him marked the initiation of adversary judicial criminal proceedings against him. Hence, under *Wade, Gilbert,* and *Kirby,* he was entitled to the presence of counsel at that confrontation. Moreover, the prosecution introduced evidence of this uncounseled corporeal identification at trial in its case-in-chief. Petitioner contends that under *Gilbert,* this evidence should have been excluded without regard to whether there was an 'independent source' for it.

"The Court of Appeals took a different view of the case. It read *Kirby* as holding that evidence of a corporeal identification conducted in the absence of defense counsel must be excluded only if the identification is made after the defendant is *indicted.* App. 45–46. Such a reading cannot be squared with *Kirby* itself, which held that an accused's rights under *Wade* and *Gilbert* attach to identifications conducted 'at or after the initiation of adversary judicial criminal proceedings,' including proceedings instituted 'by way of formal charge [or] preliminary hearing.' 406 U.S., at 689, 92 S.Ct., at 1882. The prosecution in this case was commenced under Illinois law when the victim's complaint was filed in court. See Ill.Rev.Stat. Ch. 38, § 111 (1970). The purpose of the preliminary hearing was to determine whether there was probable cause to bind petitioner over to the grand jury and to set bail. Id., §§ 109–1, 109–3. Petitioner had the right to oppose the prosecution at that hearing by moving to dismiss the charges and to suppress the evidence against him. Id., § 109–3(e). He faced counsel for the State, who elicited the victim's identification, summarized the State's other evidence against petitioner, and urged that the State be given more time to marshal its evidence. It is plain that '[t]he government ha[d] committed itself to prosecute,' and that petitioner found 'himself faced with the prosecutorial forces of organized society, and immersed in the intricacies of substantive and procedural criminal law.' *Kirby,* supra, at 689, 92 S.Ct., at 1882. The State candidly concedes that this preliminary hearing marked the 'initiation of adversary judicial criminal proceedings' against petitioner, and it hardly could contend otherwise. The Court of Appeals therefore erred in holding that petitioner's rights under *Wade* and *Gilbert* had not yet attached at the time of the preliminary hearing.

"The Court of Appeals also suggested that *Wade* and *Gilbert* did not apply here because the 'in-court identification could hardly be considered a lineup.' The meaning of this statement is not entirely clear. If the court meant that a one-on-one identification procedure, as distinguished from a lineup, is not subject to the counsel requirement, it was mistaken. Although *Wade* and *Gilbert* both involved lineups, *Wade* clearly contemplated that counsel would be required in both situations: 'The pretrial confrontation for purpose of identification may take the form of a lineup . . . or presentation of the suspect alone to the witness. . . . It is obvious that risks of suggestion attend either form of confrontation. . . .' Indeed, a one-on-one confrontation generally is thought to present greater risks of mistaken identification than a lineup. There is no reason, then, to hold that a one-on-one identification procedure is not subject to the same requirements as a lineup.

"If the court believed that petitioner did not have a right to counsel at this identification procedure because it was conducted in the course of a judicial proceeding, we do not agree. The reasons supporting Wade's holding that a corporeal identification is a critical stage of a criminal prosecution for Sixth Amendment purposes apply with equal force to this identification. It is difficult to imagine a more suggestive manner in which to present a suspect to a witness for their critical first confrontation than was employed in this case. The victim, who had seen her assailant for only 10 to 15 seconds, was asked to make her identification after she was told that she was going to view a suspect, after she was told his name and heard it called as he was led before the bench, and after she heard the prosecutor recite the evidence believed to implicate petitioner. Had petitioner been represented by counsel, some or all of this suggestiveness could have been avoided.* Here, petitioner's Sixth Amendment rights were violated by a corporeal identification conducted after the initiation of adversary judicial criminal proceedings and in the absence of counsel. The courts below thought that the victim's testimony at trial that she had identified petitioner at an uncounseled pretrial confrontation was admissible even if petitioner's rights had been violated, because there was an 'independent source' for the victim's identification at the uncounseled confrontation. But Gilbert held that the prosecution cannot buttress its case-in-chief by introducing evidence of a pretrial identification made in violation of the accused's Sixth Amendment rights, even if it can prove that the pretrial identification had an independent source. . . .

"In view of the violation of petitioner's Sixth and Fourteenth Amendment right to counsel at the pretrial corporeal identification, and of the prosecution's exploitation at trial of evidence derived directly from that violation, we reverse the judgment of the

---

* For example, counsel could have requested that the hearing be postponed until a lineup could be arranged at which the victim would view petitioner in a less suggestive setting. See, e. g., United States v. Ravich, 421 F.2d 1196, 1202–1203 (CA2), Mason v. United States, 134 U.S.App.D.C. 280, 283, 414 F.2d 1176, 1179 n. 19 (1969). Short of that, counsel could have asked that the victim be excused from the courtroom while the charges were read and the evidence against petitioner was recited, and that petitioner be seated with other people in the audience when the victim attempted an identification. See Allen v. Rhay, 431 F.2d 1160, 1165 (CA9 1970).

Counsel might have sought to cross-examine the victim to test her identification before it hardened. Cf. Haberstroh v. Montanye, 493 F.2d 483, 485 (CA2 1974); United States ex rel. Riffert v. Rundle, 464 F.2d 1348, 1351 (CA3 1972). Because it is in the prosecution's interest as well as the accused's that witnesses' identifications remain untainted we cannot assume that such requests would have been in vain. Such requests ordinarily are addressed to the sound discretion of the court, see United States v. Ravich, supra, at 1203; we express no opinion as to whether the preliminary hearing court would have been required to grant any such requests.

Court of Appeals and remand for a determination of whether the failure to exclude that evidence was harmless constitutional error."

5. The question of right to counsel has also arisen in connection with identification from photographs. Without exception every court considering the question has held that there is no right to counsel when police show photographs of suspects who are not in custody. What is the basis for this holding? The same result has been reached by the majority of courts when the Sixth Amendment claim was made on behalf of a suspect in custody.

In United States v. Ash, 413 U.S. 300, 93 S.Ct. 2568 (1973), the Court resolved the question, as appears in the following excerpts from the opinion.

"MR. JUSTICE BLACKMUN delivered the opinion of the Court.

"In this case the Court is called upon to decide whether the Sixth Amendment grants an accused the right to have counsel present whenever the Government conducts a post-indictment photographic display, containing a picture of the accused, for the purpose of allowing a witness to attempt an identification of the offender. The United States Court of Appeals for the District of Columbia Circuit, sitting *en banc*, held, by a 5-to-4 vote, that the accused possesses this right to counsel. The court's holding is inconsistent with decisions of the court of appeals of nine other circuits.

I.

"On the morning of August 26, 1965, a man with a stocking mask entered a bank in Washington, D.C., and began waving a pistol. He ordered an employee to hang up the telephone and instructed all others present not to move. Seconds later a second man, also wearing a stocking mask, entered the bank, scooped up money from tellers' drawers into a bag, and left. The gunman followed, and both men escaped through an alley. The robbery lasted three or four minutes.

"A Government informer, Clarence McFarland, told authorities that he had discussed the robbery with Charles J. Ash, Jr., the respondent here. Acting on this information, an FBI agent, in February 1966, showed five black-and-white mug shots, of Negro males of generally the same age, height, and weight, one of which was of Ash, to four witnesses. All four made uncertain identifications of Ash's picture. At this time Ash was not in custody and had not been charged. On April 1, 1966, an indictment was returned charging Ash and a codefendant, John L. Bailey, in five counts related to this bank robbery, in violation of D.C.Code § 22–2901 and 18 U.S.C. § 2113(a).

"Trial was finally set for May 1968, almost three years after the crime. In preparing for trial, the prosecutor decided to use a photographic display to determine whether the witnesses he planned to call would be able to make in-court identifications. Shortly before the trial, an FBI agent and the prosecutor showed five color photographs to the four witnesses who previously had tentatively identified the black-and-white photograph of Ash. Three of the witnesses selected the picture of Ash, but one was unable to make any selection. None of the witnesses selected the picture of Bailey which was in the group. This post-indictment identification provides the basis for respondent Ash's claim that he was denied the right to counsel at a 'critical stage' of the prosecution. . . .

"At trial, the three witnesses who had been inside the bank identified Ash as the gunman, but they were unwilling to state that they were certain of their identifications. None of these made an in-court identification of Bailey. The fourth witness, who had been in a car outside the bank and who had seen the fleeing robbers after they had removed their masks, made positive in-court identifications of both Ash and Bailey. Bailey's counsel then sought to impeach this in-court identification by calling the FBI agent who had shown the color photographs to the witnesses immediately before trial. Bailey's counsel demonstrated that the witness who had identified Bailey in court had failed to identify a color photograph of Bailey. During the course of the examination, Bailey's counsel also, before the jury, brought out the fact that this witness had selected another man as one of the robbers. At this point the prosecutor became concerned that the jury might believe that the witness had selected a third person when, in fact, the witness had selected a photograph of Ash. After a conference at the bench, the trial judge ruled that all five color photographs would be admitted into evidence. The Court of Appeals held that this constituted the introduction of a post-indictment identification at the prosecutor's request and over the objection of defense counsel.

"McFarland testified as a Government witness. He said he had discussed plans for the robbery with Ash before the event and, later, had discussed the results of the robbery with Ash in the presence of Bailey. McFarland was shown to possess an extensive crminal record and a history as an informer.

"The jury convicted Ash on all counts. It was unable to reach a verdict on the charges against Bailey and his motion for acquittal was granted. . . .

II.

"The Court of Appeals relied exclusively on that portion of the Sixth Amendment providing, 'In all criminal prosecutions, the accused shall enjoy the right . . . to have the Assistance of Counsel for his defence.' The right to counsel in Anglo-American law has a rich historical heritage, and this Court has regularly drawn on that history in construing the counsel guarantee of the Sixth Amendment. . . .

"This historical background suggests that the core purpose of the counsel guarantee was to assure 'Assistance' at trial, when the accused was confronted with both the intricacies of the law and the advocacy of the public prosecutor. Later developments have led this Court to recognize that 'Assistance' would be less than meaningful if it were limited to the formal trial itself.

"This extension of the right to counsel to events before trial has resulted from changing patterns of criminal procedure and investigation that have tended to generate pretrial events that might appropriately be considered to be parts of the trial itself. At these newly emerging and significant events, the accused was confronted, just as at trial, by the procedural system, or by his expert adversary, or by both. . . .

"The Court consistently has applied an historical interpretation of the guarantee, and has expanded the constitutional right to counsel only when new contexts appear presenting the same dangers that gave birth initially to the right itself.

"Recent cases demonstrate the historical method of this expansion. In Hamilton v. Alabama (1961), and in White v. Maryland (1963), the accused was confronted with the procedural system and was required, with definite consequences, to enter a plea. In Massiah v. United States (1964), the accused was confronted by prosecuting authorities who obtained, by ruse and in the absence of defense counsel, incriminating statements. In Coleman v. Alabama (1970), the accused was confronted by his adversary at a 'critical stage' preliminary hearing at which the uncounseled accused could not hope to obtain so much benefit as could his skilled adversary.

"The analogy between the unrepresented accused at the pretrial confrontation and the unrepresented defendant at trial, implicit in the cases mentioned above, was explicitly drawn in *Wade*:

> 'The trial which might determine the accused's fate may well not be that in the courtroom but that at the pretrial confrontation, with the State aligned against the accused, the witness the sole jury, and the accused unprotected against the overreaching, intentional or unintentional, and with little or no effective appeal from the judgment there rendered by the witness—"that's the man." '

"Throughout this expansion of the counsel guarantee to trial-like confrontations, the function of the lawyer has remained essentially the same as his function at trial. In all cases considered by the Court, counsel has continued to act as a spokesman for, or advisor to, the accused. The accused's right to the 'Assistance of Counsel' has meant just that, namely, the right of the accused to have counsel acting as his assistant. In *Hamilton* and *White*, for example, the Court envisioned the lawyer as advising the accused on available defenses in order to allow him to plead intelligently. In *Massiah* counsel could have advised his client on the benefits of the Fifth Amendment and could have sheltered him from the overreaching of the prosecution. In *Coleman* the skill of the lawyer in examining witnesses, probing for evidence, and making legal arguments was relied upon by the Court to demonstrate that, in the light of the purpose of the preliminary hearing under Alabama law, the accused required 'Assistance' at that hearing.

"The function of counsel in rendering 'Assistance' continued at the lineup under consideration in *Wade* and its companion cases. Although the accused was not confronted there with legal questions, the lineup offered opportunities for prosecuting authorities to take advantage of the accused. Counsel was seen by the Court as being more sensitive to, and aware of, suggestive influences than the accused himself, and as better able to reconstruct the events at trial. Counsel present at lineup would be able to remove disabilities of the accused in precisely the same fashion that counsel compensated for the disabilities of the layman at trial. Thus the Court mentioned that the accused's memory might be dimmed by 'emotional tension,' that the accused's credibility at trial would be diminished by his status as defendant, and that the accused might be unable to present his version effectively without giving up his privilege against compulsory self-incrimination. It was in order to compensate for these deficiencies that the Court found the need for the assistance of counsel.

"This review of the history and expansion of the Sixth Amendment counsel guarantee demonstrates that the test utilized by the Court has called for examination of the event in order to determine whether the accused required aid in coping with legal problems or assistance in meeting his adversary. Against the background of this traditional test, we now consider the opinion of the Court of Appeals.

III.

*   *   *

"After the Court in *Wade* held that a lineup constituted a trial-like confrontation requiring counsel, a more difficult issue remained in the case for consideration. The same changes in law enforcement that led to lineups and pretrial hearings also generated other events at which the accused was confronted by the prosecution. The Government had argued in *Wade* that if counsel was required at a lineup, the same forceful considerations would mandate counsel at other preparatory steps in the 'gathering of the prosecution's evidence,' such as, for particular example, the taking of fingerprints or blood samples.

"The Court concluded that there were differences. Rather than distinguishing these situations from the lineup in terms of the need for counsel to assure an equal confrontation at the time, the Court recognized that there were times when the subsequent trial would cure a one-sided confrontation between prosecuting authorities and the uncounseled defendant. In other words, such stages were not 'critical.' Referring to fingerprints, hair, clothing, and other blood samples, the Court explained:

> 'Knowledge of the techniques of science and technology is sufficiently available, and the variables in techniques few enough, that the accused has the opportunity for a meaningful confrontation of the Government's case at trial through the ordinary processes of cross-examination of the Government's expert witnesses and the presentation of the evidence of his own experts.'

"The structure of *Wade*, viewed in light of the careful limitation of the Court's language to 'confrontations,' makes it clear that lack of scientific precision and inability to reconstruct an event are not the tests for requiring counsel in the first instance. These are, instead, the tests to determine whether confrontation with counsel at trial can serve as a substitute for counsel at the pretrial confrontation. If accurate reconstruction is possible, the risks inherent in any confrontation still remain, but the opportunity to cure defects at trial causes the confrontation to cease to be 'critical.'

.   .   .

"The Court of Appeals considered its analysis complete after it decided that a photographic display lacks scientific precision and ease of accurate reconstruction at trial. That analysis, under *Wade*, however, merely carries one to the point where one must establish that the trial itself can provide no substitute for counsel if a pretrial confrontation is conducted in the absence of counsel. Judge Friendly, writing for the Second Circuit in United States v. Bennett, 409 F.2d 888 (1969), recognized that the 'criticality' test of *Wade*, if applied outside the confrontation context, would result in drastic expansion of the right to counsel:

> 'None of the classical analyses of the assistance to be given by counsel, Justice Sutherland's in Powell v. Alabama . . . and Justice Black's in Johnson v. Zerbst . . . and Gideon v. Wainwright . . . suggests that counsel must be present when the prosecution is interrogating witnesses in the defendant's absence even when, as here, the defendant is under arrest; counsel is rather to be provided to prevent the defendant himself from falling into traps devised by a lawyer on the other side and to see to it that all available defenses are proffered. Many other aspects of

the prosecution's interviews with a victim or a witness to a crime afford just as much opportunity for undue suggestion as the display of photographs; so, too, do the defense's interviews, notably with alibi witnesses'.

We now undertake the threshold analysis that must be addressed.

IV.

"A substantial departure from the historical test would be necessary if the Sixth Amendment were interpreted to give Ash a right to counsel at the photographic identification in this case. Since the accused himself is not present at the time of the photographic display, and asserts no right to be present, Brief for the Respondent 40, no possibility arises that the accused might be misled by his lack of familiarity with the law or overpowered by his professional adversary. Similarly, the counsel guarantee would not be used to produce equality in a trial-like adversary confrontation. Rather, the guarantee was used by the Court of Appeals to produce confrontation at an event that previously was not analogous to an adversary trial.

"Even if we were willing to view the counsel guarantee in broad terms as a generalized protection of the adversary process, we would be unwilling to go so far as to extend the right to a portion of the prosecutor's trial-preparation interviews with witnesses. Although photography is relatively new, the interviewing of witnesses before trial is a procedure that predates the Sixth Amendment. In England in the 16th and 17th centuries counsel regularly interviewed witnesses before trial. The traditional counterbalance in the American adversary system for these interviews arises from the equal ability of defense counsel to seek and interview witnesses himself.

"That adversary mechanism remains as effective for a photographic display as for other parts of pretrial interviews. No greater limitations are placed on defense counsel in constructing displays, seeking witnesses, and conducting photographic identifications than those applicable to the prosecution. Selection of the picture of a person other than the accused, or the inability of a witness to make any selection, will be useful to the defense in precisely the same manner that the selection of a picture of the defendant would be useful to the prosecution. In this very case, for example, the initial tender of the photographic display was by Bailey's counsel, who sought to demonstrate that the witness had failed to make a photographic identification. Although we do not suggest that equality of access to photographs removes all potential for abuse, it does remove any inequality in the adversary process itself and thereby fully satisfies the historical spirit of the Sixth Amendment's counsel guarantee.

"The argument has been advanced that requiring counsel might compel the police to observe more scientific procedures or might encourage them to utilize corporeal rather than photographic displays. This Court has recognized that improved procedures can minimize the dangers of suggestion. Simmons v. United States (1968). Commentators have also proposed more accurate techniques.

"Pretrial photographic identifications, however, are hardly unique in offering possibilities for the actions of the prosecutor unfairly to prejudice the accused. Evidence favorable to the accused may be withheld; testimony of witnesses may be manipulated; the results of laboratory tests may be contrived. In many ways the prosecutor, by accident or by design, may improperly subvert the trial. The primary safeguard against abuses of this kind is the ethical responsibility of the prosecutor, who, as so often has been said, may 'strike hard blows' but not 'foul ones.' If that safeguard fails, review remains available under due process standards. These same safeguards apply to misuse of photographs. See Simmons v. United States.

"We are not persuaded that the risks inherent in the use of photographic displays are so pernicious that an extraordinary system of safeguards is required.

"We hold, then, that the Sixth Amendment does not grant the right to counsel at photographic displays conducted by the Government for the purpose of allowing a witness to attempt an identification of the offender. . . . .

"Reversed and remanded."

"MR. JUSTICE STEWART concurring in the judgment.

* * *

"A photographic identification is quite different from a lineup, for there are substantially fewer possibilities of impermissible suggestion when photographs are used, and those unfair influences can be readily reconstructed at trial. It is true that the defendant's photograph may be markedly different from the others displayed, but this unfairness can be demonstrated at trial from an actual comparison of the photographs used or from the witness' description of the display. Similarly, it is possible that the photographs could be arranged in a suggestive manner, or that by comment or gesture the prosecuting authorities might single out the defendant's picture. But these are the kinds of overt influence that a witness can easily recount and that would serve to impeach the identification testimony. In short, there are few possibilities for unfair suggestiveness—and those rather blatant and easily reconstructed. Accordingly, an accused would not be foreclosed from an effective cross-examination of an identification witness simply because his counsel was not present at the photographic display. For this reason, a photographic display cannot fairly be considered a 'critical stage' of the prosecution. . . . .

"Preparing witnesses for trial by checking their identification testimony against a photographic display is little different, in my view, from the prosecutor's other interviews with the victim or other witnesses before trial. While these procedures can be improperly conducted, the possibility of irretrievable prejudice is remote, since any unfairness that does occur can usually be flushed out at trial through cross-examination of the prosecution witnesses. The presence of defense counsel at such pretrial preparatory sessions is neither appropriate nor necessary under our adversary system of justice 'to preserve the defendant's basic right to a fair trial as affected by his right meaningfully to cross-examine the witnesses against him and to have effective assistance of counsel at the trial itself.'

"MR. JUSTICE BRENNAN, with whom MR. JUSTICE DOUGLAS and MR. JUSTICE MARSHALL join, dissenting.

* * *

"In my view, today's decision is wholly unsupportable in terms of such considerations as logic, consistency and, indeed, fairness. As a result, I must reluctantly conclude that today's decision marks simply another step towards the complete evisceration of the fundamental constitutional principles established by this Court, only six years ago, in United States v. Wade. I dissent.

* * *

III.

"As the Court of Appeals recognized, 'the dangers of mistaken identification . . . set forth in *Wade* are applicable in large measure to photographic as well as corporeal identifications.' To the extent that misidentification may be attributable to a witness' faulty memory or perception, or inadequate opportunity for detailed observation during the crime, the risks are obviously as great at a photographic display as at a lineup. But '[b]ecause of the inherent limitations of photography, which presents its subject in two dimensions rather than the three dimensions of reality, . . . a photographic identification, even when properly obtained, is clearly inferior to a properly obtained corporeal identification.' P. Wall, Eye-Witness Identification in Criminal Cases 70 (1965). Indeed, noting 'the hazards of initial identification by photograph,' we have expressly recognized that 'a corporeal identification . . . is normally more accurate' than a photographic identification. Thus, in this sense at least, the dangers of misidentification are even greater at a photographic display than at a lineup.

"Moreover, as in the lineup situation, the possibilities for impermissible suggestion in the context of a photographic display are manifold. Such suggestion, intentional or unintentional, may derive from three possible sources. First, the photographs themselves might tend to suggest which of the pictures is that of the suspect. For example, differences in age, pose, or other physical characteristics of the persons represented, and variations in the mounting, background, lighting or markings of the photographs all might have the effect of singling out the accused.

"Second, impermissible suggestion may inhere in the manner in which the photographs are displayed to the witness. The danger of misidentification is, of course, 'increased if the police display to the witness . . . the pictures of several persons among which the photograph of a single such individual recurs or is in some way emphasized.' Simmons v. United States, 88 S.Ct., at 971. And if the photographs are arranged in an asymmetrical pattern, or if they are displayed in a time sequence that tends to emphasize a particular photograph, 'any identification of the photograph which stands out from the rest is no more reliable than an identification of a single photograph, exhibited alone.' P. Wall, supra, at 81.

"Third, gestures or comments of the prosecutor at the time of the display may lead an otherwise uncertain witness to select the 'correct' photograph. For example, the prosecutor might 'indicate to the witness that [he has] other evidence that one of the persons pictured committed the crime,' and might even point to a particular photograph and ask whether the person pictured 'looks familiar.' More subtly, the prosecutor's inflection, facial expressions, physical motions and myriad other almost imperceptible means of communication might tend, intentionally or unintentionally, to compromise the witness' objectivity. Thus, as is the case with lineups, '[i]mproper photographic identification procedures, . . . by exerting a suggestive influence upon the witnesses, can often lead to an erroneous identification . . . .' P. Wall, supra, at 89. And '[r]egardless of how the initial misidentification comes about, the witness thereafter is apt to retain in his memory the image of the photograph rather than of the person actually seen. . . . ' Simmons v. United States, supra. As a result, 'the issue of identity may (in the absence of other relevant evidence) for all practical purposes be determined there and then, before the trial.'

"Moreover, as with lineups, the defense can 'seldom reconstruct' at trial the mode and manner of photographic identification. It is true, of course, that the photographs used at the pretrial display might be preserved for examination at trial. But 'it may also be said that a photograph can preserve the record of a lineup; yet this does not justify a lineup without counsel.' Indeed, in reality, preservation of the photographs affords little protection to the unrepresented accused. For although retention of the photographs may mitigate the dangers of misidentification due to the suggestiveness of the photographs themselves, it cannot in any sense reveal to defense counsel the more subtle, and therefore more dangerous, suggestiveness that might derive from the manner in which the photographs were displayed or any accompanying comments or gestures. Moreover, the accused cannot rely upon the witnesses themselves to expose these latter sources of suggestion, for the witnesses are not 'apt to be alert for conditions prejudicial to the suspect. And if they were, it would be of scant benefit to the suspect' since the witnesses are hardly 'likely to be schooled in the detection of suggestive influences.'

"Finally, and *unlike* the lineup situation, the accused himself is not even present at the photographic identification, thereby reducing the likelihood that irregularities in the procedures will ever come to light. . . .

* * *

IV.

"Ironically, the Court does not seriously challenge the proposition that presence of counsel at a pretrial photographic display is essential to preserve the accused's right to a fair trial on the issue of identification. Rather, in what I can only characterize a triumph of form over substance, the Court seeks to justify its result by engrafting a wholly unprecedented—and wholly unsupportable—limitation on the Sixth Amendment right of 'the accused . . . to have the Assistance of Counsel for his defense.' Although apparently conceding that the right to counsel attaches, not only at the trial itself, but at all 'critical stages' of the prosecution, the Court holds today that, in order to be deemed 'critical,' the particular 'stage of the prosecution' under consideration must, at the very least, involve the physical 'presence of the accused,' at a 'trial-like confrontation' with the Government, at which the accused requires the 'guiding hand of counsel.' A pretrial photographic identification does not, of course, meet these criteria. . . .

"The fundamental premise underlying *all* of this Court's decisions holding the right to counsel applicable at 'critical' pretrial proceedings, is that a 'stage' of the prosecution must be deemed 'critical' for the purposes of the Sixth Amendment if it is one at which the presence of counsel is necessary to protect the fairness of *the trial itself*.

"This established conception of the Sixth Amendment guarantee is, of course, in no sense dependent upon the physical 'presence of the accused,' at a 'trial-like confrontation' with the Government, at which the accused requires the 'guiding hand of counsel.' On the contrary, in Powell v. Alabama (1932), the seminal decision in this area, we explicitly held the right to counsel applicable at a stage of the pretrial proceedings involving *none* of the three criteria set forth by the Court today. In *Powell*, the defendants in a State felony prosecution were not appointed counsel until the very eve of trial. This Court held, in no uncertain terms, that such an appointment could not satisfy the demands of the Sixth Amendment, for '[i]t is vain

. . . to guarantee [the accused] counsel without giving the latter any opportunity to acquaint himself with the facts or law of the case.' In other words, *Powell* made clear that, in order to preserve the accused's right to a fair trial and to 'effective and substantial' assistance of counsel at that trial, the Sixth Amendment guarantee necessarily encompasses a reasonable period of time before trial during which counsel might prepare the defense. Yet it can hardly be said that this preparatory period of research and investigation involves the physical 'presence of the accused,' at a 'trial-like confrontation' with the Government, at which the accused requires the 'guiding hand of counsel.' . . .

"Thus, contrary to the suggestion of the Court, the conclusion in *Wade* that a pretrial lineup is a 'critical stage' of the prosecution did not in any sense turn on the fact that a lineup involves the physical 'presence of the accused' at a 'trial-like confrontation' with the Government. And that conclusion most certainly did not turn on the notion that presence of counsel was necessary so that counsel could offer legal advice or 'guidance' to the accused at the lineup. On the contrary, *Wade* envisioned counsel's function at the lineup to be primarily that of a trained observer, able to detect the existence of any suggestive influences and capable of understanding the legal implications of the events that transpire. Having witnessed the proceedings, counsel would then be in a position effectively to reconstruct at trial any unfairness that occurred at the lineup, thereby preserving the accused's fundamental right to a fair trial on the issue of identification.

"There is something ironic about the Court's conclusion today that a pretrial lineup identification is a 'critical stage' of the prosecution because counsel's presence can help to compensate for the accused's deficiencies as an observer, but that a pretrial photographic identification is not a 'critical stage' of the prosecution because the accused is not able to observe at all. In my view, there simply is no meaningful difference, in terms of the need for attendance of counsel, between corporeal and photographic identifications. And applying established and well-reasoned Sixth Amendment principles, I can only conclude that a pretrial photographic display, like a pretrial lineup, is a 'critical stage' of the prosecution at which the accused is constitutionally entitled to the presence of counsel."

6. After the decision in *Ash*, one court, the Supreme Court of Michigan, held that the right to counsel at a photographic identification was required under its own state constitution. People v. Jackson, 391 Mich. 323, 217 N.W.2d 22 (1974). Other state courts have not. For example: State v. Malani, 59 Hawaii 167, 578 P.2d 236 (1978).

7. Assuming that counsel has no right to be present when the police talk to a witness shortly before a lineup, must counsel be permitted to be present when the police interview the witness immediately after the witness views the lineup? Consider United States v. Tolliver, 569 F.2d 724 (2d Cir. 1978):

"The Line-Up Procedure

"We consider first the line-up procedure. The issue posed is whether the exclusion of counsel from the room where Zima made his identification was an unconstitutional deprivation of appellant's right to counsel at a 'crucial stage of the proceeding' and whether this should not have compelled the suppression of the Zima in-court identification.

"The Supreme Court has not yet passed on the precise question. In *Wade*, the Court held that a post-indictment line-up was a 'critical' stage in a criminal proceeding and that the Sixth Amendment right of confrontation required the presence of counsel at the line-up. The Court said nothing about when a line-up ends, so that counsel need no longer be present. Cf. Fed.R.Crim.P. 44(a). It can be argued that a line-up is not finished until the witness has declared whether or not he can identify a particular person as the perpetrator of the crime. People v. Williams, 3 Cal.3d 853, 856, 92 Cal.Rptr. 6, 8–9, 478 P.2d 942, 944–45 (1971) (4 to 3). On the other hand, it can be maintained that the purpose for which counsel must be present is essentially to see that the line-up procedure is itself adequate to avoid improper suggestion, such as the wearing of differentiating clothes, or a disparity in appearance between the other persons in the line-up and the suspect himself.

"The Fourth, Fifth and Ninth Circuits have held that the 'confrontation' ends when the defendant is no longer in the presence of the identifying witness, and that his identification may, therefore, be revealed in private to the prosecution, at least in the first instance, without the presence of defense counsel.

"In [the Fourth Circuit case of United States v. Cummingham, 423 F.2d 1269 (1970)], Judge Winter reasoned that '[t]he rationale of these cases is the potential intentional or unintentional suggestion inherent in the actual confrontation and the difficulty of establishing at trial by objective evidence the circumstances under which the line-up proceeded.'

"We now join our sister circuits in holding that the actual identification from a *line-up* (as well as a photographic spread), if made outside the presence of the defendant, is constitutionally valid, since the actual confrontation is the only 'critical stage' requiring the presence of counsel.

"We note, however, that the verbatim recording of the identification or failure of identification is so easy to achieve that it should be considered as an extension of the line-up, even though the 'confrontation' feature ends when the defendant no longer faces the witness. There is no reason why the statement of the witness, even if not made immediately available to the defendant, should not be preserved and made available to defense counsel in time for a pretrial suppression hearing. See ALI, A Model Code of Pre-Arraignment Procedures § 160.4 (May 20, 1975). And even when videotape is not available, a tape recording machine is generally procurable without difficulty.

"No recording was made here. We think this was error, but, in the circumstances of this case, harmless error.

"Our problem on this appeal goes beyond the problem faced by the Fourth, Fifth and Ninth Circuits. Those cases did not deal with a refusal by the prosecution to let the defense know who the identifying witness was, nor did they involve a denial of access to him for pretrial interview, as was the case here.

"On the contrary, part of the rationale for holding that defense counsel need not be present at the moment of identification has been thought to be that the witness was made available to defense counsel for interview thereafter and, in any event, before the trial began. In this case, the opposite procedure was followed. The witness was told not to say anything during the line-up while defense counsel was present, and defense counsel was not permitted to learn the identity of the witness until it was flushed out by means of the motion to suppress.

"Discovery of evidence in criminal prosecutions is, inevitably, more restricted than discovery in civil cases. . . . In strict logic one may, of course, ask why, if the object of discovery is truth, it is not even more important to allow full discovery to a criminal defendant whose liberty is at stake. The conventional answers, which have stood the test of time, are that there is more likelihood of the subornation of perjury by bribery or threat in criminal cases, and that where certain defendants who have been committed to a life of violence are involved, the danger to the safety of the witness outweighs total discovery as a *preliminary* requirement of fair trial. Cross-examination at the trial assisted by such modern aids as the Jencks Act, 18 U.S.C. § 3500, and the limited discovery provided by the Federal Rules of Criminal Procedure, have been thought to be weapons strong enough to prevent miscarriages of justice.

"There is, to be sure, no way to prove the thesis. We may in fact, admit that the prevalence of violence in our social order has led to some weakening of the procedures available to defendants charged with crimes. In consequence, the pervasive fear for the safety of witnesses must, in some respects, adversely affect even the docile type of criminal defendant who would harm no one by physical violence. . . .

* * *

"Even if a constitutional principle were involved, however, we could hardly suggest a neutral principle that separates the potentially violent defendant from others. It has always been the burden of the non-violent criminal to suffer from some of the restrictions imposed for fear of harm from the violent. Here the defendant was a participant in an armed robbery and escape. The third man was unapprehended and at large. We can make no special rule for such a case, but the wisdom, indeed the necessity, for protecting identifying witnesses from harm must be a paramount consideration. We, accordingly, hold that the prosecution may withhold the identity of witnesses on identification, subject to the rules applicable to disclosure of prosecutorial evidence, and, generally, only if the interview after the line-up is recorded and preserved. We believe, moreover, that, before such withholding of identity by the prosecution upon a post-indictment line-up, a direction to permit such procedure should be obtained from the judge *ex parte* as a means of resolving the conflict between a defendant's need for evidence and the Government's claim of privilege based on a finding that the public security requires the withholding. While such a direction was not obtained from Judge Dooling, and the identification interviews were not recorded, the error was harmless here. There can be no doubt that Tolliver was, indeed, the driver of the Cadillac, and the only exculpating evidence presented was defendant's pretrial statement that he was not involved in the robbery, which the jury declined to credit. There was no constitutional or other error in the line-up procedure followed, and even if the refusal to disclose the identity of Zima should be held to be error of constitutional magnitude, it would be 'harmless constitutional error.' "

8. The cases decided after *Wade* and *Gilbert* have held the essential purpose served by counsel at the lineup is that of a witness or observer. Counsel cannot stop a lineup simply by walking away. See Vernen v. State, 12 Md.App. 430, 278 A.2d 609 (1971). There are some inherent problems for defense counsel who appears at a lineup for his client. Does he have a duty to make suggestions about how to make the lineup fairer? If he does make suggestions, should they be designed to produce a fair lineup or one weighted as heavily as possible in favor of his client? A searching criticism of the use of counsel to correct lineup abuses is found in Read, Lawyers at Lineups, Constitutional Necessity or Avoidable Extravagance?, 17 U.C.L.A.L.Rev. 339 (1969). Consider these excerpts:

"(a) *Those Participating May Be Police Officers.* How will a lawyer's presence change this and is this an evil in and of itself? It must be remembered that the purpose of a lineup is to aid the police in investigating a crime. Certainly it must be conceded that police should be able to participate in their own investigative techniques.

"(b) *The Participants' Names Are Rarely Divulged.* The obvious remedy is to require the names to be divulged. In the District of Columbia a 'sheet' is routinely kept, listing the names of those participating in the lineup and the names of the conducting officers. The sheet is available to the defense.

"(c) *The Victim Is Not an Effective Witness as to What Occured.* Neither is the defendant's lawyer. Audio and visual recording devices, photographs, and the like are much more effective. Even a lay observer, in the absence of such devices, would probably make a better witness than the defendant's lawyer. It is my view the jury would be much more likely to believe an independent observer than an accused's own attorney testifying on behalf of his client.

"(d) *The Victim's Outrage May Excite 'Vengeful or Spiteful Motives' and the Victim Will Not Be Alert to Conditions Prejudicial to the Suspect.* A lawyer's presence will not change this. Only regularized lineup procedures that are faithfully followed can minimize suggestive procedures that may point the victim's outrage at the wrong person.

"(e) *Neither Witnesses Nor Lineup Participants Are Alert for Conditions 'Prejudicial' to the Suspect or Schooled in the Detection of Suggestive Influence.* A lawyer is not necessarily 'schooled' in detecting suggestive influences either. A psychologist might be better equipped for the task. Even assuming the lawyer spots such conditions, what can he do about them except prepare himself to be a witness at trial? Certainly any impartial observer, acquainted with the problem and given examples of what to look for, could do as well as any lawyer. Better yet, since the purpose of a lawyer's presence is to acquaint judge and jury with what occurred, photographs, videotapes, or recordings would do this much more vividly. And adoption of regularized procedures might avoid suggestive conditions in the first place.

"(f) *Jury Will Not Believe a Suspect's Version of What Occurred.* Will it be much more likely to believe the suspect's lawyer's version of what occurred? Probably not. Therefore, objective reproduction by mechanical devices again will better counter this evil."

Professor Read studied one jurisdiction (District of Columbia) in which efforts were made to provide counsel at lineups. His finding:

"Legal Aid seems to concede that under present conditions there is no real reason for defense counsel to appear at the lineup. First, except for minor alterations, the police will not change their set procedures. Second, there is no one there to record any objection that might be made. Legal Aid personnel seem generally to be of the opinion that the presence of an attorney at a lineup is simply not necessary if the attorney is to take a limited role.

* * *

"Experienced police officers and prosecuting attorneys are convinced that any discovery of a witness' name by some defense attorneys is tantamount to disclosure of that name to that lawyer's client. These same police officers and prosecuting attorneys feel that many prospective witnesses are refusing to participate in lineup procedures because of real fear of retaliation from the accused or friends of the accused once a witness' identity is discovered. A particularly sensitive situation evidently exists in the District of Columbia. It was reported that fear of physical intimidation seems especially acute among many Negro witnesses and victims of crime who are asked to cooperate with the police. Police officers charged that the real problem with the lineups is not that witnesses are too susceptible to suggestion but, on the contrary, witnesses are too reluctant to participate freely in the process. Several defense attorneys conceded that a serious problem of witness intimidation does exist and that Wade's command that a lawyer be present at lineups may have exacerbated the situation.

"Another vigorously raised complaint of police and prosecution attorneys relates to the conduct of defense counsel in altering the appearance of their clients prior to their client's participation in a lineup. For example, a young defendant may be arrested while sporting a mustache, an 'Afro haircut' and very bright clothing. When he shows up for the lineup, his Afro haircut is removed, his mustache is shaved off, and he is wearing a suit and tie. An extreme example of this occurred when a female impersonator was arrested in his feminine disguise and then showed up for the lineup in typical male attire. The United States Attorney's Office thus feels that intimidation and disguise of suspects by defense lawyers is the 'other side of the coin' from the suggestive influence problem."

[Ed. Note. The incident of changed appearance cited by Professor Read is quite similar to that which occurred in United States v. Jackson, 476 F.2d 249 (7th Cir. 1973)]

"My observations and conversations with police, prosecuting attorneys and defense attorneys have convinced me that the lineup is a necessary tool in the arsenal of investigatory techniques available to the police. However, it is also my view that the presence of defense counsel at a lineup is simply not necessary to insure the fairness of the procedure. His passive role renders him basically impotent; he is unable to change the slightest detail in any way unless the police decide to cooperate; he is unable to make and have recorded any objections he may have; and he has no way of preserving what occurred except through his own notes and memory.

"Not only is the defense lawyer's presence only minimally effective in preventing unfairness and preserving a record of what occurred, his presence, in certain cases, can actually hinder the administration of criminal justice. Some lawyers have turned the lineup, a police investigatory technique, into a discovery proceeding. A serious danger of intimidation exists in many cases when the identity of witnesses is discovered and disclosed to defendants. Furthermore, by drastically altering the appearance of defendants, defense counsel can actually nullify the usefulness of the lineup process as an investigatory tool. Wade was intended to protect an accused from suggestive lineup procedures; however, in certain cases, the real effect of the Wade remedy is to destroy the utility of the lineup procedure and to make intimidation of witnesses easier."

9. In *Wade* it was suggested that "Legislative or other regulations, such as those of local police departments, which eliminate the risk of abuse and unintentional suggestion at lineup proceedings and the impediments to meaningful confrontation at trial may also remove the basis for regarding the stage as 'critical' ", United States v. Wade, 388 U.S. at 239. Yet, that language was explicitly disavowed by four of six Justices joining in the opinion. (Black, J. and Fortas, J. joined by Warren, C.J., and Douglas, J.). A fifth Justice implicitly rejected the proposition. (Clark, J.).

The only attempt to rely on the suggestion that regulations might obviate the right to counsel has been rebuffed with the reasoning that such regulations would be adequate only if they succeeded in elevating eyewitness identification procedures to the level of reliability present in procedures for analyzing fingerprints, blood samples and hair. See People v. Fowler, 1 Cal.3d 355, 461 P.2d 643, 652 (1969). If this is the standard to be met by legislation or regulation, then is acceptable regulation possible? Is this the appropriate standard by which to judge lineup regulations?

10. In 1968 Congress enacted the following provision as part of the "Omnibus Crime Control And Safe Streets Act of 1968":

§ *3502. Admissibility in evidence of eye witness testimony*

The testimony of a witness that he saw the accused commit or participate in the commission of the crime for which the accused is being tried shall be admissible in evidence in a criminal prosecution in any trial court ordained and established under Article III of the Constitution of the United States.

Is this provision constitutional?

B. SUGGESTIVENESS IN IDENTIFICATION PROCEDURES

MANSON v. BRATHWAITE

Supreme Court of the United States, 1977.
432 U.S. 98, 97 S.Ct. 2243.

MR. JUSTICE BLACKMUN delivered the opinion of the Court.

This case presents the issue as to whether the Due Process Clause of the Fourteenth Amendment compels the exclusion, in a state criminal trial, apart from any consideration of reliability, of pretrial identification evidence obtained by a police procedure that was both suggestive and unnecessary. This Court's decisions in Stovall v. Denno, 388 U.S. 293, 87 S.Ct. 1967 (1967), and Neil v. Biggers, 409 U.S. 188, 93 S.Ct. 375 (1972), are particularly implicated.

I.

Jimmy D. Glover, a full-time trooper of the Connecticut State Police, in 1970 was assigned to the Narcotics Division in an undercover capacity. On May 5 of that year, about 7:45 p. m. E.D.T. and while there was still daylight, Glover and Henry Alton Brown, an informant, went to an apartment building at 201 Westland, in Hartford, for the purpose of purchasing narcotics from "Dickie Boy" Cicero, a known narcotics dealer. Cicero, it was thought, lived on the third floor of that apartment building. Glover and Brown entered the building, observed by back-up Officers D'Onofrio and Gaffey, and proceeded by stairs to the third floor. Glover knocked at the door of one of the two apartments served by the stairway. The area was illuminated by natural light from a window in the third floor hallway. The door was opened 12 to 18 inches in response to the knock. Glover observed a man standing at the door and, behind him, a woman. Brown identified himself. Glover then asked for "two things" of narcotics. The man at the door held out his hand, and Glover gave him two $10 bills. The door closed. Soon the man returned and handed Glover two glassine bags. While the door was open Glover stood within two feet of the person from whom he made the purchase and observed his face. Five to seven minutes elapsed from the time the door first opened until it closed the second time.

Glover and Brown then left the building. This was about eight minutes after their arrival. Glover drove to headquarters where he described the seller to D'Onofrio and Gaffey. Glover at that time did not know the identity of the seller. He described him as being "a colored man, approximately five feet eleven inches tall, dark complexion, black hair, short Afro style, and having high cheekbones, and of heavy build. He was wearing at the time blue pants and a plaid shirt." D'Onofrio, suspecting from this description that respondent might be the seller, obtained a photograph of respondent from the Records Division of the Hartford Police Department. He left it at

Glover's office. D'Onofrio was not acquainted with respondent personally, but did know him by sight and had seen him "[s]everal times" prior to May 5. Glover, when alone, viewed the photograph for the first time upon his return to headquarters on May 7; he identified the person shown as the one from whom he had purchased the narcotics.

The toxicological report on the contents of the glassine bags revealed the presence of heroin. The report was dated July 16, 1970.

Respondent was arrested on July 27 while visiting at the apartment of a Mrs. Ramsey on the third floor of 201 Westland, This was the apartment at which the narcotics sale had taken place on May 5.

Respondent was charged, in a two-count information, with possession and sale of heroin. At his trial in January 1971, the photograph from which Glover had identified respondent was received in evidence without objection on the part of the defense. Glover also testified that, although he had not seen respondent in the eight months that had elapsed since the sale, "there [was] no doubt whatsoever" in his mind that the person shown on the photograph was respondent. Glover also made a positive in-court identification without objection.

No explanation was offered by the prosecution for the failure to utilize a photographic array or to conduct a lineup. .   .   .

The jury found respondent guilty on both counts of the information. He received a sentence of not less than six nor more than nine years. His conviction was affirmed *per curiam* by the Supreme Court of Connecticut.

Fourteen months later, respondent filed a petition for habeas corpus in the United States District Court for the District of Connecticut. He alleged that the admission of the identification testimony at his state trial deprived him of due process of law to which he was entitled under the Fourteenth Amendment. The District Court, by an unreported written opinion based on the court's review of the state trial transcript, dismissed respondent's petition. On appeal, the United States Court of Appeals for the Second Circuit reversed . .   . .[1]

In brief summary, the court felt that evidence as to the photograph should have been excluded, regardless of reliability, because the examination of the single photograph was unnecessary and suggestive. And, in the court's view, the evidence was unreliable in any event. We granted certiorari.

---

1. Although no objection was made in the state trial to the admission of the identification testimony and the photograph, the issue of their propriety as evidence was raised on the appeal to the Supreme Court of Connecticut. Petitioner has asserted no claims related to the failure of the respondent either to exhaust state remedies or to make contemporaneous objections. The District Court and the Court of Appeals, each for a somewhat different reason, concluded that the merits were properly before them. We are not inclined now to rule otherwise.

II.

Stovall v. Denno, supra, concerned a petitioner who had been convicted in a New York court of murder. He was arrested the day following the crime and was taken by the police to a hospital where the victim's wife, also wounded in the assault, was a patient. After observing Stovall and hearing him speak, she identified him as the murderer. She later made an in-court identification. On federal habeas, Stovall claimed the identification testimony violated his Fifth, Sixth, and Fourteenth Amendment rights. The District Court dismissed the petition, and the Court of Appeals, en banc, affirmed. This Court also affirmed. On the identification issue, the Court reviewed the practice of showing a suspect singly for purposes of identification, and the claim that this was so unnecessarily suggestive and conducive to irreparable mistaken identification that it constituted a denial of due process of law. The Court noted that the practice "has been widely condemned," but it concluded that "a claimed violation of due process of law in the conduct of a confrontation depends on the totality of the circumstances surrounding it." In that case, showing Stovall to the victim's spouse "was imperative." The Court then quoted the observations of the Court of Appeals, to the effect that the spouse was the only person who could possibly exonerate the accused; that the hospital was not far from the courthouse and jail; that no one knew how long she might live; that she was not able to visit the jail; and that taking Stovall to the hospital room was the only feasible procedure, and, under the circumstances, " 'the usual police station line-up   .   .   . was out of the question.' "

Neil v. Biggers, supra, concerned a respondent who had been convicted in a Tennessee court of rape, on evidence consisting in part of the victim's visual and voice identification of Biggers at a stationhouse showup seven months after the crime. The victim had been in her assailant's presence for some time and had directly observed him indoors and under a full moon outdoors. She testified that she had "no doubt" that Biggers was her assailant. She previously had given the police a description of the assailant. She had made no identification of others presented at previous showups, lineups, or through photographs. On federal habeas, the District Court held that the confrontation was so suggestive as to violate due process. The Court of Appeals affirmed. This Court reversed on that issue, and held that the evidence properly had been allowed to go to the jury. The Court reviewed Stovall and certain later cases where it had considered the scope of due process protection against the admission of evidence derived from suggestive identification procedures, namely, Simmons v. United States, 390 U.S. 377, 88 S.Ct. 967 (1968); Foster v. California, 394 U.S. 440, 89 S.Ct. 1127 (1969); and Coleman v. Alabama, 399 U.S. 1, 90 S.Ct. 1999 (1970).[2] The Court concluded that

2. Simmons involved photographs, mostly group ones, shown to bankteller victims who made in-court identifications. The Court discussed the "chance of misidentification," declined to prohibit the procedure "either in the exercise of our supervisory power or, still less, as a matter

general guidelines emerged from these cases "as to the relationship between suggestiveness and misidentification." The "admission of evidence of a showup without more does not violate due process." The Court expressed concern about the lapse of seven months between the crime and the confrontation and observed that this "would be a seriously negative factor in most cases." The "central question," however, was "whether under the 'totality of the circumstances' the identification was reliable even though the confrontation procedure was suggestive." Applying that test, the Court found "no substantial likelihood of misidentification. The evidence was properly allowed to go to the jury."

* * *

Biggers well might be seen to provide an unambiguous answer to the question before us: the admission of testimony concerning a suggestive and unnecessary identification procedure does not violate due process so long as the identification possesses sufficient aspects of reliability.[3] In one passage, however, the Court observed that the

of constitutional requirement," and held that each case must be considered on its facts and that a conviction would be set aside only if the identification procedure "was so impermissibly suggestive as to give rise to a very substantial likelihood of irreparable misidentification." The out-of-court identification was not offered. Mr. Justice Black would have denied Simmons' due process claim as frivolous.

Foster concerned repeated confrontations between a suspect and the manager of an office that had been robbed. At a second lineup, but not at the first and not at a personal one-to-one confrontation, the manager identified the suspect. At trial he testified as to this and made an in-court identification. The Court reaffirmed the Stovall standard and then concluded that the repeated confrontations were so suggestive as to violate due process. The case was remanded for the state courts to consider the question of harmless error.

In Coleman a plurality of the Court was of the view that the trial court did not err when it found that the victim's in-court identifications did not stem from a lineup procedure so impermissibly suggestive as to give rise to a substantial likelihood of misidentification.

3. Mr. Justice Marshall argues in dissent that our cases have "established two different due process tests for

two very different situations." Pretrial identifications are to be covered by Stovall, which is said to require exclusion of evidence concerning unnecessarily suggestive pretrial identifications without regard to reliability. In-court identifications, on the other hand, are to be governed by Simmons and admissibility turns on reliability. The Court's cases are sorted into one category or the other. Biggers, which clearly adopts the reliability of the identification as the guiding factor in the admissibility of both pretrial and in-court identifications, is condemned for mixing the two lines and for adopting a uniform rule.

Although it must be acknowledged that our cases are not uniform in their emphasis, they hardly suggest the formal structure the dissent would impose on them. If our cases truly established two different rules, one might expect at some point at least passing reference to the fact. There is none. And if Biggers departed so grievously from the past cases, it is surprising that there was not at least some mention of the point in Mr. Justice Brennan's dissent. In fact, the cases are not so readily sorted as the dissent suggests. Although Foster involved both in-court and out-of-court identifications, the Court seemed to apply only a single standard for both. And although Coleman involved only an in-court identification, the plurality cited Stovall for the guiding rule that the claim was to be assessed on the "totality of

challenged procedure occurred pre-*Stovall* and that a strict rule would make little sense with regard to a confrontation that preceded the Court's first indication that a suggestive procedure might lead to the exclusion of evidence. One perhaps might argue that, by implication, the Court suggested that a different rule could apply post-*Stovall*. The question before us, then, is simply whether the *Biggers* analysis applies to post-*Stovall* confrontations as well as to those pre-*Stovall*.

III.

In the present case the District Court observed that the "sole evidence tying Brathwaite to the possession and sale of the heroin consisted in his identifications by the police undercover agent, Jimmy Glover."

* * *

IV.

The State at the outset acknowledges that "the procedure in the instant case was suggestive [because only one photograph was used] and unnecessary" [because there was no emergency or exigent circumstance]. The respondent, in agreement with the Court of Appeals, proposes a *per se* rule of exclusion that he claims is dictated by the demands of the Fourteenth Amendment's guarantee of due process. He rightly observes that this is the first case in which this Court has had occasion to rule upon strictly post-*Stovall* out-of-court identification evidence of the challenged kind.

Since the decision in *Biggers*, the courts of appeals appear to have developed at least two approaches to such evidence. The first, or *per se* approach, employed by the Second Circuit in the present case, focuses on the procedures employed and requires exclusion of the out-of-court identification evidence, without regard to reliability, whenever it has been obtained through unnecessarily suggested confrontation procedures.[4] The justifications advanced are the elimination of evidence of uncertain reliability, deterrence of the police and prosecutors, and the stated "fair assurance against the awful risks of misidentification."

The second, or more lenient, approach is one that continues to rely on the totality of the circumstances. It permits the admission of the confrontation evidence if, despite the suggestive aspect, the out-of-court identification possesses certain features of reliability. Its adherents feel that the *per se* approach is not mandated by the Due Process Clause of the Fourteenth Amendment. This second ap-

the surrounding circumstances." Thus, Biggers is not properly seen as a departure from the past cases, but as a synthesis of them.

4. Although the *per se* approach demands the exclusion of testimony concerning unnecessarily suggestive identifications, it does permit the admission of testimony concerning a subsequent identification, including an in-court identification, if the subsequent identification is determined to be reliable. The totality approach, in contrast, is simpler: if the challenged identification is reliable, then testimony as to it and any identification in its wake is admissible.

proach, in contrast to the other, is *ad hoc* and serves to limit the societal costs imposed by a sanction that excludes relevant evidence from consideration and evaluation by the trier of fact.

The respondent here stresses the need for deterrence of improper identification practice, a factor he regards as pre-eminent. Photographic identification, it is said, continues to be needlessly employed. He notes that the legislative regulation "the Court hoped *Wade* would engender" has not been forthcoming. He argues that a totality rule cannot be expected to have a significant deterrent impact; only a strict rule of exclusion will have direct and immediate impact on law enforcement agents. Identification evidence is so convincing to the jury that sweeping exclusionary rules are required. Fairness of the trial is threatened by suggestive confrontation evidence, and thus, it is said, an exclusionary rule has an established constitutional predicate.

There are, of course, several interests to be considered and taken into account . . . . *Wade* and its companion cases reflect the concern that the jury not hear eyewitness testimony unless that evidence has aspects of reliability. It must be observed that both approaches before us are responsive to this concern. The *per se* rule, however, goes too far since its application automatically and peremptorily, and without consideration of alleviating factors, keeps evidence from the jury that is reliable and relevant.

The second factor is deterrence. Although the *per se* approach has the more significant deterrent effect, the totality approach also has an influence on police behavior. The police will guard against unnecessarily suggestive procedures under the totality rule, as well as the *per se* one, for fear that their actions will lead to the exclusion of identifications as unreliable.

The third factor is the effect on the administration of justice. Here the *per se* approach suffers serious drawbacks. Since it denies the trier reliable evidence, it may result, on occasion, in the guilty going free. Also, because of its rigidity, the *per se* approach may make error by the trial judge more likely than the totality approach. And in those cases in which the admission of identification evidence is error under the *per se* approach but not under the totality approach—cases in which the identification is reliable despite an unnecessarily suggestive identification procedure—reversal is a draconian sanction. Certainly, inflexible rules of exclusion, that may frustrate rather than promote justice, have not been viewed recently by this Court with unlimited enthusiasm.

* * *

The standard, after all, is that of fairness as required by the Due Process Clause of the Fourteenth Amendment.

We therefore conclude that reliability is the linchpin in determining the admissibility of identification testimony for both pre-and post-*Stovall* confrontations. The factors to be considered are set out in *Biggers*. These include the opportunity of the witness to view the criminal at the time of the crime, the witness' degree of attention, the accuracy of his prior description of the criminal, the level of certainty demonstrated at the confrontation, and the time between the crime and the confrontation. Against these factors is to be weighed the corrupting effect of the suggestive identification itself.

V.

We turn, then, to the facts of this case and apply the analysis:

1. The opportunity to view. Glover testified that for two to three minutes he stood at the apartment door, within two feet of the respondent. The door opened twice, and each time the man stood at the door. The moments passed, the conversation took place, and payment was made. Glover looked directly at his vendor. It was near sunset, to be sure, but the sun had not yet set, so it was not dark or even dusk or twilight. Natural light from outside entered the hallway through a window. There was natural light, as well, from inside the apartment.

2. The degree of attention. Glover was not a casual or passing observer, as is so often the case with eyewitness identification. Trooper Glover was a trained police officer on duty— and specialized and dangerous duty—when he called at the third floor of 201 Westland in Hartford on May 5, 1970. Glover himself was a Negro and unlikely to perceive only general features of "hundreds of Hartford black males," as the Court of Appeals stated. It is true that Glover's duty was that of ferreting out narcotics offenders and that he would be expected in his work to produce results. But it is also true that, as a specially trained, assigned, and experienced officer, he could be expected to pay scrupulous attention to detail, for he knew that subsequently he would have to find and arrest his vendor. In addition, he knew that his claimed observations would be subject later to close scrutiny and examination at any trial.

3. The accuracy of the description. Glover's description was given to D'Onofrio within minutes after the transaction. It included the vendor's race, his height, his build, the color and style of his hair, and the high cheekbone facial feature. It also included clothing the vendor wore. No claim has been made that respondent did not possess the physical characteristics so described. D'Onofrio reacted positively at once. Two days later, when Glover was alone, he viewed the photograph D'Onofrio produced and identified its subject as the narcotics seller.

4. The witness' level of certainty. There is no dispute that the photograph in question was that of respondent. Glover, in response to a question whether the photograph was that of the person from whom he made the purchase, testified: "There is no question whatsoever." This positive assurance was repeated.

5. The time between the crime and the confrontation. Glover's description of his vendor was given to D'Onofrio within minutes of the crime. The photographic identification took place only two days later. We do not have here the passage of weeks or months between the crime and the viewing of the photograph.

These indicators of Glover's ability to make an accurate identification are hardly outweighed by the corrupting effect of the challenged identification itself. Although identifications arising from single-photograph displays may be viewed in general with suspicion, we find in the instant case little pressure on the witness to acquiesce in the suggestion that such a display entails. D'Onofrio had left the photograph at Glover's office and was not present when Glover first viewed it two days after the event. There thus was little urgency and Glover could view the photograph at his leisure. And since Glover examined the photograph alone, there was no coercive pressure to make an identification arising from the presence of another. The identification was made in circumstances allowing care and reflection.

*   *   *

Surely, we cannot say that under all the circumstances of this case there is "a very substantial likelihood of irreparable misidentification." Simmons v. United States. Short of that point, such evidence is for the jury to weigh. We are content to rely upon the good sense and judgment of American juries, for evidence with some element of untrustworthiness is customary grist for the jury mill. Juries are not so susceptible that they cannot measure intelligently the weight of identification testimony that has some questionable feature.

We conclude that the criteria laid down in *Biggers* are to be applied in determining the admissibility of evidence offered by the prosecution concerning a post-*Stovall* identification, and that those criteria are satisfactorily met and complied with here.

The judgment of the Court of Appeals is reversed.

Mr. Justice Stevens, concurring.

While I join the Court's opinion, I would emphasize two points.

First, as I indicated in my opinion in United States ex rel. Kirby v. Sturges, 510 F.2d 397, 405–406 (7th Cir. 1975), the arguments in favor of fashioning new rules to minimize the danger of convicting the innocent on the basis of unreliable eyewitness testimony carry substantial force. Nevertheless, for the reasons stated in that opinion, as well as those stated by the Court today, I am persuaded that this rulemaking function can be performed "more effectively by the legislative process than by a somewhat clumsy judicial fiat," and that the Federal Constitution does not foreclose experimentation by the States in the development of such rules.

Second, in evaluating the admissibility of particular identification testimony it is sometimes difficult to put other evidence of guilt entirely to one side.[5]

MR. JUSTICE BLACKMUN's opinion for the Court carefully avoids this pitfall and correctly relies only on appropriate indicia of the reliability of the identification itself. Although I consider the factual question in this case extremely close, I am persuaded that the Court has resolved it properly.

MR. JUSTICE MARSHALL, with whom MR. JUSTICE BRENNAN joins, dissenting.

Today's decision can come as no surprise to those who have been watching the Court dismantle the protections against mistaken eye-witness testimony erected a decade ago in *Wade, Gilbert,* and Stovall v. Denno. But it is still distressing to see the Court virtually ignore the teaching of experience embodied in those decisions and blindly uphold the conviction of a defendant who may well be innocent.

The development of due process protections against mistaken identification evidence, begun in *Stovall,* was continued in Simmons v. United States (1968). There, the Court developed a different rule to deal with the admission of in-court identification testimony that the accused claimed had been fatally tainted by a previous suggestive confrontation. In *Simmons,* the exclusionary effect of *Stovall* had already been accomplished, since the prosecution made no use of the suggestive confrontation. *Simmons,* therefore, did not deal with the constitutionality of the pretrial identification procedure. The only question was the impact of the Due Process Clause on an in-court identification that was not itself unnecessarily suggestive. *Simmons* held that due process was violated by the later identification if the pretrial procedure had been "so impermissibly suggestive as to give rise to a very substantial likelihood of irreparable misidentification." This test focused not on the necessity for the challenged pretrial procedure, but on the degree of suggestiveness that it entailed. In applying this test, the Court understandably considered the circumstances surrounding the witnesses' initial opportunity to view the crime. Finding that any suggestion in the pretrial confrontation had not affected the fairness of the in-court identification, *Simmons* rejected petitioner's due process attack on his conviction.

Again, comparison with the *Wade* cases is instructive. The inquiry mandated by *Simmons* is similar to the independent source test used in *Wade* where an in-court identification is sought following an

---

5. In this case, for example, the fact that the defendant was a regular visitor to the apartment where the drug transaction occurred tends to confirm his guilt. In the *Kirby* case, supra, where the conviction was for robbery, the fact that papers from the victim's wallet were found in the possession of the defendant made it difficult to question the reliability of the identification. These facts should not, however, be considered to support the admissibility of eyewitness testimony when applying the criteria identified in *Biggers.* Properly analyzed, however, such facts would be relevant to a question whether error, if any, in admitting identification testimony was harmless.

uncounseled lineup. In both cases, the issue is whether the witness is identifying the defendant solely on the basis of his memory of events at the time of the crime, or whether he is merely remembering the person he picked out in a pretrial procedure. Accordingly, in both situations, the relevant inquiry includes factors bearing on the accuracy of the witness' identification, including his opportunity to view the crime.

Thus, *Stovall* and *Simmons* established two different due process tests for two very different situations. Where the prosecution sought to use evidence of a questionable pretrial identification, *Stovall* required its exclusion, because due process had been violated by the confrontation, unless the necessity for the unduly suggestive procedure outweighed its potential for generating an irreparably mistaken identification. The *Simmons* test, on the other hand, was directed to ascertaining due process violations in the introduction of in-court identification testimony that the defendant claimed was tainted by pretrial procedures. In the latter situation, a court could consider the reliability of the identification under all the circumstances.

* * *

The Court inexplicably seemed to erase the distinction between *Stovall* and *Simmons* situations in Neil v. Biggers.

* * *

Apparently, the Court does not consider *Biggers* controlling in this case. I entirely agree, since I believe that *Biggers* was wrongly decided. The Court, however, concludes that *Biggers* is distinguishable because it, like the identification decisions that preceded it, involved a pre-*Stovall* confrontation, and because a paragraph in *Biggers* itself seems to distinguish between pre- and post-*Stovall* confrontations. Accordingly, in determining the admissibility of the post-*Stovall* identification in this case, the Court considers two alternatives, a *per se* exclusionary rule and a totality of the circumstances approach. The Court weighs three factors in deciding that the totality approach, which is essentially the test used in *Biggers*, should be applied. In my view, the Court wrongly evaluates the impact of these factors.

First, the Court acknowledges that one of the factors, deterrence of police use of unnecessarily suggestive identification procedures, favors the *per se* rule. Indeed, it does so heavily, for such a rule would make it unquestionably clear to the police they must never use a suggestive procedure when a fairer alternative is available. I have no doubt that conduct would quickly conform to the rule.

Second, the Court gives passing consideration to the dangers of eyewitness identification recognized in the *Wade* trilogy. It concludes, however, that the grave risk of error does not justify adoption of the *per se* approach because that would too often result in exclusion of relevant evidence. In my view, this conclusion totally ignores the lessons of *Wade*. The dangers of mistaken identification are, as *Stovall* held, simply too great to permit unnecessarily suggestive identifications. Neither *Biggers* nor the Court's opinion today point to any contrary empirical evidence. Studies since *Wade* have only reinforced the validity of its assessment of the dangers of identification testimony. While the Court is "content to rely on the good sense and judgment of American juries," the impetus for *Stovall* and *Wade* was repeated miscarriages of justice resulting from juries' willingness to credit inaccurate eyewitness testimony.

Finally, the Court errs in its assessment of the relative impact of the two approaches on the administration of justice. The Court relies most heavily on this factor finding that "reversal is a draconian sanction" in cases where the identification is reliable despite an unnecessarily suggestive procedure used to obtain it. Relying on little more than a strong distaste for "inflexible rules of exclusion," the Court rejects the *per se* test. In so doing, the Court disregards two significant distinctions between the *per se* rule advocated in this case and the exclusionary remedies for certain other constitutional violations.

First, the *per se* rule here is not "inflexible." Where evidence is suppressed, for example, as the fruit of an unlawful search, it may well be forever lost to the prosecution. Identification evidence, however, can by its very nature be readily and effectively reproduced. The in-court identification, permitted under *Wade* and *Simmons* if it has a source independent of an uncounseled or suggestive procedure, is one example. Similarly, when a prosecuting attorney learns that there has been a suggestive confrontation, he can easily arrange another lineup conducted under scrupulously fair conditions. Since the same factors are evaluated in applying both the Court's totality test and the *Wade-Simmons* independent source inquiry, any identification which is "reliable" under the Court's test will support admission of evidence concerning such a fairly conducted lineup. The evidence of an additional, properly conducted confrontation will be more persuasive to a jury, thereby increasing the chance of a justified conviction where a reliable identification was tainted by a suggestive confrontation. At the same time, however, the effect of an unnecessarily suggestive identification—which has no value whatsoever in the law enforcement process—will be completely eliminated.

Second, other exclusionary rules have been criticized for preventing jury consideration of relevant and usually reliable evidence in order to serve interests unrelated to guilt or innocence, such as discouraging illegal searches or denial of counsel. Suggestively obtained eyewitness testimony is excluded, in contrast, precisely because of its unreliability and concomitant irrelevance. Its exclusion both protects the integrity of the truth-seeking function of the trial and discourages police use of needlessly inaccurate and ineffective investigatory methods.

Indeed, impermissibly suggestive identifications are not merely worthless law enforcement tools. They pose a grave threat to society at large in a more direct way than most governmental disobedience of the law. For if the police and the public erroneously conclude, on the basis of an unnecessarily suggestive confrontation, that the right man has been caught and convicted, the real outlaw must still remain at large. Law enforcement has failed in its primary function and has left society unprotected from the depredations of an active criminal.

For these reasons, I conclude that adoption of the *per se* rule would enhance, rather than detract from, the effective administration of justice. In my view, the Court's totality test will allow seriously unreliable and misleading evidence to be put before juries. Equally important, it will allow dangerous criminals to remain on the streets while citizens assume that police action has given them protection. According to my calculus, all three of the factors upon which the Court relies point to acceptance of the *per se* approach.

Even more disturbing than the Court's reliance on the totality test, however, is the analysis it uses, which suggests a reinterpretation of the concept of due process of law in criminal cases. The decision suggests that due process violations in identification procedures may not be measured by whether the Government employed procedures violating standards of fundamental fairness. By relying on the probable accuracy of a challenged identification, instead of the necessity for its use, the Court seems to be ascertaining whether the defendant was probably guilty. Until today, I had thought that "Equal justice under law" meant that the existence of constitutional violations did not depend on the race, sex, religion, nationality or likely guilt of the accused. The Due Process Clause requires adherence to the same high standard of fundamental fairness in dealing with every criminal defendant, whatever his personal characteristics and irrespective of the strength of the State's case against him. Strong evidence that the defendant is guilty should be relevant only to the determination whether an error of constitutional magnitude was nevertheless harmless beyond a reasonable doubt. See Chapman v. California (1967). By importing the question of guilt into the initial determination of whether there was a constitutional violation, the apparent effect of the Court's decision is to undermine the protection afforded by the Due Process Clause. It is therefore important to note that the state courts remain free, in interpreting state constitutions, to guard against the evil clearly identified by this case.

* * *

Despite my strong disagreement with the Court over the proper standards to be applied in this case, I am pleased that its application of the totality test does recognize the continuing vitality of *Stovall*. In assessing the reliability of the identification, the Court mandates weighing "the corrupting effect of the challenged identification itself" against the "indicators of [a witness'] ability to make an accurate identification." The Court holds, as Neil v. Biggers failed to, that a due process identification inquiry must take account of the suggestiveness of a confrontation and the likelihood that it led to misidentification, as recognized in *Stovall* and *Wade*. Thus, even if a witness did have an otherwise adequate opportunity to view a criminal, the later use of a highly suggestive identification procedure can render his testimony inadmissible. Indeed, it is my view that, assuming applicability of the totality test enunciated by the Court, the facts of the present case require that result.

*   *   *

NOTES

1. The testimony of an eyewitness is subject to a complex set of exclusionary rules. Evidence of pre-trial identification (testimony by the witness on direct examination that he attended a lineup and picked out the defendant as the offender) is subject to one per se rule of exclusion. If the pre-trial confrontation is conducted in violation of the right to counsel (Wade-Gilbert), evidence of the pre-trial confrontation is excluded. A similar per se rule of exclusion for cases involving unnecessarily suggestive confrontations was rejected in Manson v. Brathwaite. Rather, the Court adopted a rule admitting evidence of suggestive confrontations if the identification possesses sufficient aspects of reliability; to exclude there must be "a very substantial likelihood of irreparable mistaken identification." Evidence of in-court identification (i. e. testimony by the witness that the offender is the defendant sitting in the courtroom) is subject to derivative exclusionary rules. If, and only if, the Court has found that the pre-trial confrontation violates one (or both) of the per se exclusionary rules, will there be suppression of evidence of in-court identification. People v. Rodriguez, 10 Cal.App.3d 18, 88 Cal.Rptr. 789 (1970). However, if the prosecution can prove by clear and convincing evidence that the in-court identification has a source independent of the illegal pre-trial confrontation, then evidence of the in-court identification is admissible.

In determining whether there was an independent source of an in-court identification, several factors are considered. The most common of these are:

> (1) prior opportunity of witnesses to observe the criminal act, (2) existence of a discrepancy between any pre-lineup description and the actual appearance of the accused, (3) any identification of another person prior to the lineup, (4) failure to identify the accused on a prior occasion, (5) lapse of time between the criminal act and the lineup identification, (6) prior photographic identification from a large group of photographs, (7) the presence of distinctive physical characteristics in defendant, (8) prior acquaintance of witness with the suspect, (9) ability and training at identification, (10) the exercise of unusual care to make observations, (11) prompt identification at first confrontation.

See United States ex rel. Geralds v. Deegan, 292 F.Supp. 968 (S.D.N.Y. 1968) and 307 F.Supp. 56 (S.D.N.Y.1969), and People v. Kacher, 400 Mich. 78, 252 N.W.2d 807 (1977).

If the trial court decides to suppress evidence of pre-trial confrontation but refuses to suppress evidence of in-court identification, the defense has the option to bring the pre-trial confrontation out at trial if it is thought helpful to a defense attack on the courtroom identification. Davis v. State, 467 P.2d 521 (Okl.Cr.App.1970). If the defense brings out some of the facts concerning the pre-trial confrontation, the state may bring out the rest of the circumstances. Commonwealth v. Redmond, 357 Mass. 475, 258 N.E.2d 287 (1970).

An error in the admission of identification evidence does not constitute automatic reversible error. Such errors may be harmless. See Gilbert v. California, 388 U.S. 263, 274, 87 S.Ct. 1951 (1967); United States v. Wade, 388 U.S. 218, 242, 87 S.Ct. 1926 (1967).

2. There are two important questions about the functional effect of the exclusion rules:

(a) Can it be said from the point of view of the prosecutor that *Stovall* and *Brathwaite* are far more significant than *Wade* because, as a practical matter, only the application of *Stovall* and *Brathwaite* can cause the loss of the entire testimony of a witness, and that the worst consequence of a violation of *Wade-Gilbert* is the suppression of evidence of a pre-trial identification by a witness?

Assume a case arising where a defendant is placed in a post-indictment lineup without waiving counsel. *Wade-Gilbert* has been violated. But assume that the lineup is perfectly fair, consisting of seven men of the same height, hair color, race and general appearance, all similarly dressed. If the victim identifies the defendant, the victim will not be able to testify concerning the lineup. But the witness will be able to make a courtroom identification because it is clear that a perfectly fair lineup could not have tainted the courtroom identification. See Nielsen v. State, 456 S.W.2d 928 (Tex.1970). Indeed, the fairness of the lineup itself, coupled with a positive identification, is clear and convincing evidence that the witness had a strong basis for identification prior to the lineup. The ease with which a court can sustain an identification when the pre-trial procedures have been exemplary is found in Butler v. State, 226 Ga. 56, 172 S.E.2d 399 (1970). . . . A *Stovall-Brathwaite* violation is of far greater potential consequence than a *Wade-Gilbert* violation. The former tends to impugn the integrity of the witness' courtroom identification while the latter does not. In those jurisdictions where the prosecution is prohibited from showing that a witness made a prior identification the effect of *Wade-Gilbert* alone is negligible. See 4 Wigmore, Evidence, Sec. 1130 (3rd Ed. 1940); 71 A. L.R.2d 449.

In those jurisdictions where evidence of pre-trial identification is admissible what value does this evidence have? See United States v. Williams, 421 F.2d 1166 (D.C.Cir.1970). In an urban jurisdiction a jury may hear evidence of an in-court identification a year or more after the date of the crime. Could the absence of evidence of pre-trial identification affect their verdict?

(b) Again, as a practical matter, will there be a case where a pre-trial confrontation is deemed unreliable under *Brathwaite* but the in-court identification is properly admitted as untainted? When a court determines reliability of a pre-trial confrontation under the guidelines announced in *Brathwaite*, is it not considering precisely the same factors it must consider when determining whether an in-court identification has a source independent of a pre-trial confrontation?

3. As an alternative to exclusionary rules, would a careful jury instruction on the subject of eye-witness identification strike directly at the problem? Jurisdictions vary widely with respect to their jury-instruction policy in this area. See the elaborate instruction required in United States v. Holley, 502 F.2d 273 (4th Cir. 1974). The Illinois Pattern Jury Instructions on the other hand, recommend that no special instruction be given on

the subject, leaving the matter covered only by a general instruction relating to the credibility of the witnesses and suggesting that the arguments of counsel can focus on the circumstances of identification. Illinois I.P.I. (Criminal) 3.15. For a more extensive treatment of this topic, see Chapter 20, C–3.

4. The due process clause condemns confrontations which are "unnecessarily suggestive and conducive to irreparable mistaken identification." Stovall v. Denno, supra, which announced this rule, also upheld a confrontation with a witness thought to be near death because the procedure was *necessarily* suggestive.

Are there any other forms of necessarily suggestive confrontations? Consider the 6′ 10″ or the 4′ 10″ suspect, or the suspect with prominent scars or tattoos. See State v. Mallette, 159 Conn. 143, 267 A.2d 438 (1970) ; People v. Faulkner, 28 Cal.App.3d 625, 104 Cal.Rptr. 625 (1972). Consider also the suspect who engages in conduct which attracts attention, i. e., protests his arrest, buries his head in his hands, etc. See United States v. Holsey, 437 F.2d 250 (10th Cir. 1970) ; People v. Nelson, 40 Ill.2d 146, 238 N. E.2d 378 (1968). What value has the notion that in difficult cases the police ought to use photographic identification procedures? Is the notion based on the assumption that eyewitness identification is based exclusively on facial characteristics? If so, is that a valid assumption? Is photographic identification as reliable as corporeal identification? In the last analysis does the presence of unusual physical characteristics make identification more or less reliable? If a suspect is so unusual that he cannot be placed in an adequate line-up, is it fairer to use a one to one "showup"?

5. The first test by which a line-up or a photographic display is judged is whether it is suggestive. The question of necessity need be reached only if there is suggestiveness.

Suggestiveness is tested by looking at what the witness sees and then asking which of the persons in the line-up stands out. A line-up must also be weighed in terms of the individual witnesses. For example, a line-up may include several fairly similar men all wearing eyeglasses only one of which has horn rim frames. If the witness described the criminal as wearing eyeglasses, the line-up may be perfectly valid. If the witness specifically described the criminal's glasses as hornrimmed, a different view of the line-up might be taken. Generally speaking, a few objective standards for fair line-ups can be definitely established but the courts have not had great difficulty making the determination on a case by case basis. Sometimes, however, the judgment is difficult to make at the trial level. Both court and counsel are familiar with what the defendant looks like, and in a line-up photograph, the defendant will stand out. Whether the defendant would stand out to the eyes of a witness who had observed only the crime is another question and, of course, the only question that has to be answered.

One interesting method to test suggestiveness would be to form a street corner poll, by presenting a picture of a line-up to a group of strangers and inquiring whether they can tell which person is the one suspected by the police. This was tried in People v. Suleski, 58 App.Div.2d 1023, 397 N.Y.S.2d 280 (1977), but the results (seven out of ten picked the defendant) did not persuade the court to condemn the line-up.

6. Suggestiveness may also inhere in circumstances occurring outside the limited sphere of what the witness sees at a line-up. The police may indirectly tell a witness that a particular man is their candidate for prosecu-

tion, i. e., "Take a good look at the third man from the left." The fact that the police say that they have a suspect in custody does not constitute a suggestive practice so long as no particular suspect is pointed out by police. See People v. Wooley, 127 Ill.App.2d 249, 262 N.E.2d 237 (1967) ; State v. McClure, 107 Ariz. 351, 488 P.2d 971 (1971). The reasoning of these courts is that any witness who is asked to view a line-up will obviously conclude that the police have a suspect. See Coleman v. Alabama, 399 U.S. 1, 6, 90 S.Ct. 1999, 2001 (1970).

7. In *Stovall* the Supreme Court specifically noted that "The practice of showing suspects singly to persons for the purpose of identification, and not as part of a line-up has been widely condemned." Yet an exception to this rule has been found in cases involving confrontations occurring shortly after the crime. A discussion of one-man showups is contained in Bates v. United States, 405 F.2d 1104 (D.C.Cir. 1968), which involved a pre-*Wade* confrontation. In affirming, the Court (Burger, C. J.) said:

> "There is no prohibition against a view of a suspect alone in what is called a 'one-man show-up' when this occurs near the time of the alleged criminal act; such a course does not tend to bring about misidentification but rather tends under some circumstances to insure accuracy. The rationale underlying this is in some respects not unlike that which the law relies on to make an exception to the hearsay rule, allowing spontaneous utterances a standing which they would not be given if uttered at a later point in time. An early identification is not in error. Of course, proof of infirmities and subjective factors, such as hysteria of a witness, can be explored on cross-examination and in argument. Prudent police work would confine these on-the-spot identifications to situations in which possible doubts as to identification needed to be resolved promptly; absent such need the conventional line-up viewing is the appropriate procedure.

> ". . . [T]he police action in returning the suspect to the vicinity of the crime for immediate identification fosters the desirable objective of fresh, accurate identification which in some instances may lead to the immediate release of an innocent suspect and at the same time enable the police to resume the search for the fleeing culprit while the trial is fresh".

How prompt must a confrontation be in order to come within this exception? The usual case involves an identification made no more than two or three hours after the offense. See Virgin Islands v. Callwood, 440 F.2d 1206 (3rd Cir. 1971) ; State v. Sears, 182 Neb. 384, 155 N.W.2d 332 (1967).

A similar doctrine has arisen when a witness accidentally encounters a suspect as in the case where both are injured and brought to the same emergency room. In such a case *Stovall* is not likely to affect admissibility. This conclusion rests on two factors: (a) there is no deliberate misconduct by the police, see Coleman v. Alabama, 399 U.S. 1, 90 S.Ct. 1999 (1970), and, (b) if the confrontation is truly accidental then there is likely to have been no suggestive aspect leading to an unreliable identification. See United States v. Johnson, 448 F.2d 963 (9th Cir. 1971) ; United States v. Pollack, 427 F.2d 1168 (5th Cir. 1970) (court building) ; State v. Dutton, 112 N.J.Super. 402, 271 A.2d 593 (1970) (at hospital—victim on a stretcher) ; Commonwealth v. Leaster, 362 Mass. 407, 287 N.E.2d 122 (1972).

8. The exclusionary rule of *Stovall* and *Brathwaite* has not been thought to affect the validity of normal courtroom identification procedures. It is completely within the discretion of the trial court whether to grant a defense or prosecution request for a lineup in the courtroom to test witness identification. See People ex rel. Blassick v. Callahan, 50 Ill.2d 330, 279 N.E.2d 1 (1972) (thorough citation of cases on point). Consider the comments of the court in United States v. Hamilton, 469 F.2d 880 (9th Cir. 1972):

> "It might well be argued that the deeply-rooted practice of allowing witnesses to identify the defendant in open court is no less a suggestive show-up than those condemned by *Stovall* and *Foster*. But we decline to take the giant step of holding in-court identifications inadmissible. It is sufficient safeguard that the accused be allowed to question the weight to be given the 'in-court' identification considering the length of time the witness saw the perpetrator of the crime, the elapsed time between the act and the trial, and the fact that the witness had made no other identification of the defendant."

In Moore v. Illinois, note 4 following Kirby v. Illinois, Section A, supra, the Supreme Court took note of some procedures designed to diminish courtroom suggestiveness but did not assert that they were required. Perhaps the basis for accepting a traditional courtroom identification rests on the assumption that it will have been preceded by a less suggestive identification procedure. The broader question of the significance of a suggestive procedure which follows a valid identification is discussed in Patterson v. United States, 384 A.2d 663 (D.C.Ct.App.1978):

FERREN, ASSOCIATE JUDGE:

> "Just after 11:00 p. m. on September 6, 1975, Raymond Holmes set out for a local bar . . .. As he approached the corner . . . Mr. Holmes spotted two men standing on the opposite side of the street. As he was waiting at the corner for a vehicle to pass, one of the men approached him, grabbed him from behind, and, pressing a hard object into his back, demanded his money. When Mr. Holmes turned and discovered that he was being threatened at 'Coke-bottle-point,' he started to scuffle with the assailant. At that point the second individual whom he had observed across the street approached, struck him on the head with a bottle, and removed his watch. After some further scuffling, during the course of which Mr. Holmes observed the facial features of the attackers, the robbers took flight amidst a shower of hard objects (stones, bottles, etc.) thrown by Mr. Holmes. The entire incident lasted approximately five minutes.

> "Mr. Holmes hailed a passing policewoman and reported the incident; she summoned another officer by radio. The police transported Mr. Holmes around the vicinity for a while, hoping that he might spot the attackers. After approximately one-half hour of unsuccessful searching, they returned him to his home.

> "Before long, Mr. Holmes set out once again for the bar. Sometime between 12:30 and 12:45 a. m. on September 7, as he neared the same corner at which he was robbed, he saw the individual who had first grabbed him coming down Buchanan Street.

Mr. Holmes called the police, pointed out the assailant to Officer Belisle (who had responded to the call), and rode with the officer down the block to the robber's location. As he observed Officer Belisle arresting the first attacker (later identified as appellant Witherspoon), Mr. Holmes saw the other assailant (appellant Patterson) standing among the onlookers. He apprised Officer Thornes who was standing nearby, whereupon Officer Thornes arrested Mr. Patterson.

"The grand jury indicted Messrs. Patterson and Witherspoon, each on one count of robbery (D.C.Code 1973, § 22–2901), on December 1, 1975. On the morning set for trial, April 1, 1976, the Assistant United States Attorney assigned to the case displayed "mug shot" photographs of the defendants to Mr. Holmes to be certain that he could identify them at trial. To the prosecutor's surprise, Mr. Holmes first stated that the individuals in the photographs did not look like his assailants—that the men in the pictures looked older, more mature. Only after more viewing and reflection did Mr. Holmes decide that the photographs depicted the likenesses of the robbers.

"The prosecutor informed defense counsel and the court about these events. The court then entertained defense motions to suppress prospective in-court identifications.

"In the present case, the trial judge implicitly found suggestiveness; he then . . . found . . . a basis for identification that makes it nonetheless reliable. His suggestiveness determination unquestionably was correct. The prosecutor, in his office on the morning of the day originally set for trial, had handed mug shot photographs of the two defendants to Mr. Holmes and asked if they were the men who had robbed him. Such single-photo displays are inherently suggestive.

"Ordinarily, once unnecessary suggestiveness is found, its conduciveness to "irreparable misidentification" is obvious. The court accordingly proceeds . . . to . . . the assessment of whether the identification is nonetheless reliable, based on the various factors enumerated in *Manson* . . . .. The present case is of a rare breed, however, for although the single-photo displays were unnecessarily suggestive, they were not conducive to irreparable misidentification. Thus . . . we do not leave the first stage of the inquiry; reliability does not become an issue in the same sense that it typically does following a suggested identification.

"In the more common case of a challenged identification, a suspect is apprehended based on a police lookout, after which a complaining witness is asked to identify the suspect at a highly suggestive showup or at an arguably skewed or otherwise suggestive photographic array or lineup. From the very first identification, therefore, suggestiveness is inherent in the process; there is a risk of initial misidentification. Here, however, the first identifications occurred when Mr. Holmes sighted the suspects (who had robbed him merely an hour and a half before) and pointed them out to the officers. He led the police to the appellants; the police did not bring them to Mr. Holmes. Thus, the initial identifications to the authorities unmistakably were based on observation without suggestion.

"It may well be true that the lapse of time between robbery and trial dimmed Mr. Holmes' memory of the suspects and that the single-photo displays helped bring his memory back. Nevertheless, as recent Supreme Court cases have made clear, these suggestive showings could not have created a "very substantial likelihood of irreparable *misidentification*." At worst, the "refresher" photos produced a misleadingly current, positive identification derived from a previously untainted one. Just as a procedure devoid of suggestion cannot yield the 'primary evil' of misidentification, id., a procedure that includes suggestive elements *subsequent* to an unequivocal, unsuggested identification does not pose an unconstitutional risk of misidentification—of trying and convicting the wrong person.

"The D.C. Circuit Court of Appeals has so held in United States v. Hines, 147 U.S.App.D.C. 249, 262–63, 455 F.2d 1317, 1330–31, which concerned the display of refresher photographs of the defendant to the complaining witness before trial but *after* the witness had identified the defendant at a valid showup and lineup. The court stated:

".   .   . *We do not believe that once an eyewitness has made a positive identification, counsel's attempt to review that identification through the use of photographs in a preparatory session falls within the bounds of that case. Such an identification is neither 'initial' nor is it likely to lead to a misidentification, since the witness has already identified the suspect in a constitutionally acceptable manner.* [Emphasis added.]

"In summary, we conclude that when there has been an unequivocal, unsuggested, and otherwise constitutionally acceptable identification, subsequent identifications—even 'refreshed' ones in open court, such as Mr. Holmes'—are not conducive to irreparable misidentification, in violation of due process. For admissibility, therefore, such subsequent identifications need not be justified by the comprehensive 'reliability' (or 'independent source') analysis required when an initial identification has been tainted. Under such circumstances it will be defense counsel's responsibility during cross-examination to expose weaknesses of the identifications which follow suggestive procedures employed by the government to refresh recollection.

"In the present case, the circumstances surrounding the refresher photograph, line-up, and in-court identifications were thoroughly examined at trial. Defense counsel relied heavily on the suggestiveness of the photo display, on Mr. Holmes' unexpected, initially negative responses, and on the various contradictions and confusion betrayed by his testimony describing the assailants. In the circumstances of this case, where positive on-sight identifications were made, the ambiguity and confusion which followed the photographic showing could only redound to the defendant's benefit. The credibility of Mr. Holmes' on-the-scene identifications could well have been damaged and his subsequent identifications devalued by his hesitation and inaccuracy at the photographic display. Appellants took full advantage of this development in their presentations before the jury.

"On the facts of this case, therefore, we hold, after making the first-stage inquiry, that the unnecessarily suggestive single-photo displays were *not* conducive to irreparable misidentification, because there had been a prior unequivocal, unsuggested, and otherwise constitutionally acceptable identification. No further inquiry is required. We affirm appellants' convictions.

"In so holding, however, we caution that the invocation of the principles of this opinion will be justified only when the constitutionally acceptable identification which precedes the challenged suggestive procedures has been *unequivocal and unsuggested.*"

9. Another possible basis for excluding eye-witness identifications, either out-of-court or in-court, might be that the initial identification took place after an unlawful arrest or during an unlawful detention. See People v. Bean, 121 Ill.App.2d 332, 257 N.E.2d 562 (1970), approving such exclusion, and United States v. Young, 512 F.2d 321 (4th Cir. 1975), disapproving such exclusion. See also Baker v. State, 39 Md.App. 133, 383 A.2d 698 (1978) excluding such evidence only when the arrest was not made in reasonable good faith. This topic is discussed further in Chapter 6, Section E, infra, which also discusses the very recent case in this area, Crews v. United States, —— U.S. ——, 100 S.Ct. —— (1980). See also Johnson v. Louisiana, 406 U.S. 356, 92 S.Ct. 1620 (1972), where the Supreme Court found that a suspect's appearance before a magistrate, after an alleged unlawful arrest but before a lineup, purged the lineup of the taint of Fourth Amendment illegality.

Chapter 4

THE LAW OF ARREST, SEARCH AND SEIZURE

A. INTRODUCTION: THE THEORETICAL FRAMEWORK

The Fourth Amendment regulates governmental searches and seizures. Although the Amendment does not use the word "arrest," arrests and other involuntary detentions of the person are seizures within the meaning of the Fourth Amendment.

The Amendment has two clauses. The first requires that governmental searches and seizures be reasonable: *"The right of the people to be secure in their persons, houses, papers, and effects, against unreasonable searches and seizures, shall not be violated. . . ."* This "reasonableness clause" is the source of many Fourth Amendment doctrines. Among the most important questions that call for an interpretation of the reasonableness requirement are: (1) What kind and quantum of data is necessary to make reasonable a particular search or seizure?, and (2) Is a warrant essential to make reasonable a particular search or seizure?

The second clause of the Fourth Amendment specifies that ". . . *no warrant shall issue, but upon probable cause, supported by oath or affirmation, and particularly describing the place to be searched, and the persons or things to be seized."* The warrant clause does not govern the question of *when* a warrant is essential to satisfy the Fourth Amendment. That issue requires an interpretation of the reasonableness clause. Moreover, the Fourth Amendment's warrant clause specifies certain requirements for the warrant *if* a warrant is utilized: probable cause, oath or affirmation, and specificity.

Although the term "probable cause" appears only in the warrant clause, the requirements of probable cause are important to an interpretation of both clauses of the Fourth Amendment. Some (though not all) warrantless searches and seizures—for example, warrantless arrests—are deemed reasonable only if supported by probable cause. Thus we must know the meaning of "probable cause" to determine whether the reasonableness clause of the Fourth Amendment was satisfied in the case of a particular warrantless arrest. So, too, we must know the meaning of "probable cause" to determine whether a particular search warrant conformed to the dictates of the warrant clause of the Fourth Amendment.

This chapter begins with a treatment of the probable cause concept because of its importance to litigation under both clauses of the Amendment. Next it turns to the issuance and execution of search warrants. In practice, warrantless searches and seizures occur more frequently than searches and seizures under the command of a warrant. Nevertheless, the Supreme Court has frequently interpreted the reasonableness clause of the Fourth Amendment so as to make searches under warrants the rule and warrantless searches the exception; in other words, "searches conducted outside the judicial process, without prior judicial approval, are *per se* unreasonable under the Fourth Amendment—subject only to a few specially established and well delineated exceptions." [1]

The validity of the issuance of warrants turns largely upon the requirements of the warrant clause: probable cause, oath or affirmation, and specificity. In theory, however, a search warrant which satisfied these requirements of the warrant clause could still fail to satisfy the reasonableness requirements of the Fourth Amendment. For example, a warrant commanding the seizure of a bullet from the body of an innocent third party (or even a suspect) through a life endangering operation might satisfy the warrant clause but still fail to satisfy the reasonableness clause absent certain additional safeguards.[2]

Requirements for the execution of search warrants arise from the reasonableness clause of the Fourth Amendment. Thus, for example, this chapter treats questions concerning notice of authority and purpose, and the use of force and trickery, in the execution of search warrants. So, also, the question of when a search warrant may constitutionally be executed requires an interpretation of the reasonableness clause.

The chapter then turns to the major exceptions to the requirement that searches and seizures be made under the authority of a search warrant. Perhaps the oldest recognized exception, and certainly among the most important, is the doctrine which permits a warrantless search incident to a valid arrest. Because an essential predicate for this exception is a valid arrest, the chapter's section on the "search-incident" doctrine includes treatment of the requirements, under both state law and the Fourth Amendment, for a valid arrest. In criminal cases the question of the legality of an arrest arises most frequently during a motion to suppress evidence seized without a search warrant where the prosecutor claims the seizure was made during the search of the defendant incident to his valid arrest.

Among the various other exceptions to the search warrant requirement are consent searches, emergency searches, searches of vehicles stopped in transit, seizures under the plain view doctrine, searches and seizures in open fields, and seizures of abandoned property. This chapter treats the scope and the limits of each of these warrantless search and seizure doctrines.

So-called administrative searches, which have as their main justification something other than the catching of criminals and the seizure of criminal evidence, are placed near the end of the chapter be-

---

1. Katz v. United States, 389 U.S. 347, 357, 88 S.Ct. 507, 514 (1967).

2. United States v. Crowder, 543 F.2d 312 (D.C.Cir.1976), cert. denied 429 U.S. 1062, 97 S.Ct. 788 (1977).

cause they require re-thinking of Fourth Amendment theory. Absent an emergency or consent, some administrative searches, such as governmental health and safety inspections of homes or of the workplace, are deemed reasonable only if authorized in advance by a judicial officer. The judicial order or "search warrant" in such cases, however, can be issued upon a showing of something other than the traditional probable cause needed for the issuance of a valid search warrant in quest of criminal evidence. Phrased another way, such administrative warrants can be issued without probable cause to believe that a crime has been committed and that evidence of the offense will be found in the place to be searched.

Finally, the chapter ends where other authors might have begun. In our treatment of "The Borderlands of the Fourth Amendment" we inquire "What is a search or a seizure?" and "What constitutes Fourth Amendment activity?" If there is no search and no seizure, the Fourth Amendment provides no limits upon governmental activity. There can be no "unreasonable" search proscribed by the Fourth Amendment unless there is first a search. We deliberately leave this question to the end so that the student will have some experience in dealing with what everyone agrees are searches and seizures before being called upon to consider the borderline cases. We also have chosen to end with this topic because it constitutes a natural introduction to the electronic surveillance topic in the next chapter. In the *Katz* case on such surveillance, the Supreme Court considered whether non-trespassory wiretapping constituted Fourth Amendment activity, and in United States v. White [3] it considered whether governmental overhearing and recording of a conversation with the consent of one party constituted Fourth Amendment activity.

B.   PROBABLE CAUSE

DRAPER v. UNITED STATES

Supreme Court of the United States, 1959.
358 U.S. 307, 79 S.Ct. 329.

MR. JUSTICE WHITTAKER delivered the opinion of the Court.

*   *   *

The evidence offered at the hearing on the motion to suppress was not substantially disputed. It established that one Marsh, a federal narcotic agent with 29 years' experience, was stationed at Denver; that one Hereford had been engaged as a "special employee" of the Bureau of Narcotics at Denver for about six months, and from time to time gave information to Marsh regarding violations of the narcotic laws, for which Hereford was paid small sums of money, and that Marsh had always found the information given by Hereford to

3.   401 U.S. 745, 91 S.Ct. 1122 (1971).

be accurate and reliable. On September 3, 1956, Hereford told Marsh that James Draper (petitioner) recently had taken up abode at a stated address in Denver and "was peddling narcotics to several addicts" in that city. Four days later, on September 7, Hereford told Marsh "that Draper had gone to Chicago the day before [September 6] by train [and] that he was going to bring back three ounces of heroin [and] that he would return to Denver either on the morning of the 8th of September or the morning of the 9th of September also by train." Hereford also gave Marsh a detailed physical description of Draper and of the clothing he was wearing, and said that he would be carrying "a tan zipper bag," and habitually "walked real fast."

On the morning of September 8, Marsh and a Denver police officer went to the Denver Union Station and kept watch over all incoming trains from Chicago, but they did not see anyone fitting the description that Hereford had given. Repeating the process on the morning of September 9, they saw a person, having the exact physical attributes and wearing the precise clothing described by Hereford, alight from an incoming Chicago train and start walking "fast" toward the exit. He was carring a tan zipper bag in his right hand and the left was thrust in his raincoat pocket. Marsh, accompanied by the police officer, overtook, stopped and arrested him. They then searched him and found the two "envelopes containing heroin" clutched in his left hand in his raincoat pocket, and found the syringe in the tan zipper bag. Marsh then took him (petitioner) into custody. Hereford died four days after the arrest and therefore did not testify at the hearing on the motion.

26 U.S.C. (Supp. V) § 7607, added by § 101(a) of the Narcotic Control Act of 1956, 70 Stat. 570, 26 U.S.C.A. § 7607, provides, in pertinent part:

> "The Commissioner . . . and agents, of the Bureau of Narcotics . . . may—
>
> * * *
>
> "(2) Make arrests without warrant for violations of any law of the United States relating to narcotic drugs . . . where the violation is committed in the presence of the person making the arrest or where such person has reasonable grounds to believe that the person to be arrested has committed or is committing such violation."

The crucial question for us then is whether knowledge of the related facts and circumstances gave Marsh "probable cause" within the meaning of the Fourth Amendment, and "reasonable grounds" within the meaning of § 104(a), supra, to believe that petitioner had committed or was committing a violation of the narcotic laws. If it did, the arrest, though without a warrant, was lawful. . . .

Petitioner . . . contends (1) that the information given by Hereford to Marsh was "hearsay" and, because hearsay is not legally competent evidence in a criminal trial, could not legally have been considered, but should have been put out of mind, by Marsh in assessing whether he had "probable cause" and "reasonable grounds" to arrest petitioner without a warrant, and (2) that, even if hearsay could lawfully have been considered, Marsh's information should be held insufficient to show "probable cause" and "reasonable grounds" to believe that petitioner had violated or was violating the narcotic laws and to justify his arrest without a warrant.

Considering the first contention, we find petitioner entirely in error. Brinegar v. United States, 338 U.S. 160, 172–173, 69 S.Ct. 1302, 1309, has settled the question the other way. There, in a similar situation, the convict contended "that the factors relating to inadmissibility of the evidence [for] *purposes of proving guilt at the trial,* deprive[d] the evidence as a whole of sufficiency to show probable cause for the search. . . ." (Emphasis added.) But this Court, rejecting that contention, said: "[T]he so-called distinction places a wholly unwarranted emphasis upon the criterion of admissibility in evidence, to prove the accused's guilt, of facts relied upon to show probable cause. The emphasis, we think, goes much too far in confusing and disregarding the difference between what is required to prove guilt in a criminal case and what is required to show probable cause for arrest or search. It approaches requiring (if it does not in practical effect require) proof sufficient to establish guilt in order to substantiate the existence of probable cause. There is a large difference between the two things to be proved [guilt and probable cause], as well as between the tribunals which determine them, and therefore a like difference in the *quanta* and modes of proof required to establish them." . . .

Nor can we agree with petitioner's second contention that Marsh's information was insufficient to show probable cause and reasonable grounds to believe that petitioner had violated or was violating the narcotic laws and to justify his arrest without a warrant. The information given to narcotic agent Marsh by "special employee" Hereford may have been hearsay to Marsh, but coming from one employed for that purpose and whose information had always been found accurate and reliable, it is clear that Marsh would have been derelict in his duties had he not pursued it. And when, in pursuing that information, he saw a man, having the exact physical attributes and wearing the precise clothing and carrying the tan zipper bag that Hereford had described, alight from one of the very trains from the very place stated by Hereford and start to walk at a "fast" pace toward the station exit, Marsh had personally verified every facet of the information given him by Hereford except whether petitioner had accomplished his mission and had the three ounces of heroin on his person or in his bag. And surely, with every other bit of Hereford's information being thus personally verified, Marsh had "reasonable grounds" to believe that the remaining unverified bit of Hereford's information—that Draper would have the heroin with him—was likewise true.

"In dealing with probable cause . . . as the very name implies, we deal with probabilities. These are not technical; they are the factual and practical considerations of everyday life on which reasonable and prudent men, not legal technicians, act." Brinegar v. United States. Probable cause exists where "the facts and circumstances within their [the arresting officer's] knowledge and of which they had reasonably trustworthy information [are] sufficient in themselves to warrant a man of reasonable caution in the belief that" an offense has been or is being committed. Carroll v. United States, 267 U.S. 132, 162, 45 S.Ct. 280, 288. . . .

We believe that, under the facts and circumstances here, Marsh had probable cause and reasonable grounds to believe that petitioner was committing a violation of the laws of the United States relating to narcotic drugs at the time he arrested him. The arrest was therefore lawful, and the subsequent search and seizure, having been made incident to that lawful arrest, were likewise valid. It follows that petitioner's motion to suppress was properly denied and that the seized heroin was competent evidence lawfully received at the trial.

Affirmed.

THE CHIEF JUSTICE and MR. JUSTICE FRANKFURTER took no part in the consideration or decision of this case.

MR. JUSTICE DOUGLAS, dissenting.

Of course, the education we receive from mystery stories and television shows teaches that what happened in this case is efficient police work. The police are tipped off that a man carrying narcotics will step off the morning train. A man meeting the precise description does alight from the train. No warrant for his arrest has been —or as I see it, could then be—obtained. Yet he is arrested; and narcotics are found in his pocket and a syringe in the bag he carried. This is the familiar pattern of crime detection which has been dinned into public consciousness as the correct and efficient one. It is however, a distorted reflection of the constitutional system under which we are supposed to live.

With all due deference, the arrest made here on the mere word of an informer violated the spirit of the Fourth Amendment and the requirement of the law, . . . governing arrests in narcotics cases. If an arrest is made without a warrant, the offense must be committed in the presence of the officer or the officer must have "reasonable grounds to believe that the person to be arrested has committed or is committing" a violation of the narcotics law. The arresting officers did not have a bit of evidence, known to them and as to which they could take an oath had they gone to a magistrate for a warrant, that petitioner had committed any crime. The arresting officers did not know the grounds on which the informer based his conclusion; nor did they seek to find out what they were. They acted solely on the informer's word. In my view that was not enough.

. . . Lord Chief Justice Pratt in Wilkes v. Wood, condemned not only the odious general warrant, in which the name of the citizen to be arrested was left blank, but the whole scheme of seizures and searches under "a discretionary power" of law officers to act "wherever their suspicions may chance to fall"—a practice which he denounced as "totally subversive of the liberty of the subject." See III May, Constitutional History of England, c. XI. Wilkes had written in 1762, "To take any man into custody, and deprive him of his liberty, without having some seeming foundation at least, on which to justify such a step, is inconsistent with wisdom and sound policy." The Life and Political Writings of John Wilkes, p. 372.

George III in 1777 pressed for a bill which would allow arrests on suspicion of treason committed in America. The words were "suspected of" treason and it was to these words that Wilkes addressed himself in Parliament. "There is not a syllable in the Bill of the degree of probability attending the suspicion. . . . Is it possible, Sir, to give more despotic powers to a bashaw of the Turkish empire? What security is left for the devoted objects of this Bill against the malice of a prejudiced individual, a wicked magistrate . . . ?" The Speeches of Mr. Wilkes, p. 102.

These words and the complaints against which they were directed were well known on this side of the water. Hamilton wrote about "the practice of arbitrary imprisonments" which he denounced as "the favorite and most formidable instruments of tyranny." Federalist No. 84. The writs of assistance, against which James Otis proclaimed, were vicious in the same way as the general warrants, since they required no showing of "probable cause" before a magistrate, and since they allowed the police to search on suspicion and without "reasonable grounds" for believing that a crime had been or was being committed. Otis' protest was eloquent; but he lost the case. His speech, however, rallied public opinion. "Then and there," wrote John Adams, "the child Independence was born." 10 Life and Works of John Adams (1856), p. 248. . . .

The Court is quite correct in saying that proof of "reasonable grounds" for believing a crime was being committed need not be proof admissible at the trial. It could be inferences from suspicious acts, e. g., consort with known peddlers, the surreptitious passing of a package, an intercepted message suggesting criminal activities, or any number of such events coming to the knowledge of the officer. . . . But, if he takes the law into his own hands and does not seek the protection of a warrant, he must act on some evidence known to him. This important requirement should be strictly enforced, lest the whole process of arrest revert once more to whispered accusations by people. When we lower the guards as we do today, we risk making the role of the informer—odious in our history—once more supreme. . . .

Here the officers had no evidence—apart from the mere word of an informer—that petitioner was committing a crime. The fact that petitioner walked fast and carried a tan zipper bag was not evidence of any crime. The officers knew nothing except what they had been told by the informer. If they went to a magistrate to get a warrant of arrest and relied solely on the report of the informer, it is not conceivable to me that one would be granted. For they could not present to the magistrate any of the facts which the informer may have had. They could swear only to the fact that the informer had made the accusation. They could swear to no evidence that lay in their own knowledge. They could present, on information and belief, no facts which the informer disclosed. No magistrate could issue a warrant on the mere word of an officer, without more. We are not justified in lowering the standard when an arrest is made without a warrant and allowing the officers more leeway than we grant the magistrate.

With all deference I think we break with tradition when we sustain this arrest. . . .

BECK v. OHIO

Supreme Court of the United States, 1964.
379 U.S. 89, 85 S.Ct. 223.

MR. JUSTICE STEWART delivered the opinion of the Court.

On the afternoon of November 10, 1961, the petitioner, William Beck, was driving his automobile in the vicinity of East 115th Street and Beulah Avenue in Cleveland, Ohio. Cleveland police officers accosted him, identified themselves, and ordered him to pull over to the curb. The officers possessed neither an arrest warrant nor a search warrant. Placing him under arrest, they searched his car but found nothing of interest. They then took him to a nearby police station where they searched his person and found an envelope containing a number of clearing house slips "beneath the sock of his leg." The petitioner was subsequently charged in the Cleveland Municipal Court with possession of clearing house slips in violation of a state criminal statute. He filed a motion to suppress as evidence the clearing house slips in question, upon the ground that the police had obtained them by means of an unreasonable search and seizure in violation of the Fourth and Fourteenth Amendments. After a hearing the motion was overruled, the clearing house slips were admitted in evidence, and the petitioner was convicted. His conviction was affirmed by an Ohio Court of Appeals, and ultimately by the Supreme Court of Ohio, with two judges dissenting. We granted certiorari to consider the petitioner's claim that, under the rule of Mapp v. Ohio, the clearing house slips were wrongly admitted in evidence against him because they had been seized by the Cleveland police in violation of the Fourth and Fourteenth Amendments.

Although the police officers did not obtain a warrant before arresting the petitioner and searching his automobile and his person, the Supreme Court of Ohio found the search nonetheless constitutionally valid as a search incident to a lawful arrest. And it is upon that basis that the Ohio decision has been supported by the respondent here. See Draper v. United States; Ker v. California, 374 U.S. 23, 83 S.Ct. 1623.

There are limits to the permissible scope of a warrantless search incident to a lawful arrest, but we proceed on the premise that, if the arrest itself was lawful, those limits were not exceeded here. The constitutional validity of the search in this case, then, must depend upon the constitutional validity of the petitioner's arrest. Whether that arrest was constitutionally valid depends in turn upon whether, at the moment the arrest was made, the officers had probable cause to make it—whether at that moment the facts and circumstances within their knowledge and of which they had reasonably trustworthy information were sufficient to warrant a prudent man in believing that the petitioner had committed or was committing an offense. Brinegar v. United States, 338 U.S. 160, 175–176, 69 S.Ct. 1302, 1310–1311; Henry v. United States, 361 U.S. 98, 102, 80 S.Ct. 168, 171. "The rule of probable cause is a practical, nontechnical conception affording the best compromise that has been found for accommodating . . . often opposing interests. Requiring more would unduly hamper law enforcement. To allow less would be to leave law-abiding citizens at the mercy of the officers' whim or caprice." Brinegar v. United States, supra. . . .

The trial court made no findings of fact in this case. The trial judge simply made a conclusory statement: "A lawful arrest has been made, and this was a search incidental to that lawful arrest." The Court of Appeals merely found "no error prejudicial to the appellant." In the Supreme Court of Ohio, Judge Zimmerman's opinion contained a narrative recital which is accurately excerpted in the dissenting opinions filed today. But, putting aside the question of whether this opinon can fairly be called the opinion of the court, such a recital in an appellate opinion is hardly the equivalent of findings made by the trier of the facts. In any event, after giving full scope to the flexibility demanded by "a recognition that conditions and circumstances vary just as do investigative and enforcement techniques," we hold that the arrest of the petitioner cannot on the record before us be squared with the demands of the Fourth and Fourteenth Amendments.

The record is meager, consisting only of the testimony of one of the arresting officers, given at the hearing on the motion to suppress. As to the officer's own knowledge of the petitioner before the arrest, the record shows no more than that the officer "had a police picture of him and knew what he looked like," and that the officer knew that the petitioner had "a record in connection with clearing house and scheme of chance." Beyond that, the officer testified only that he had "information" that he had "heard reports," that "someone specifically did relate that information," and that he "knew who that person was." There is nowhere in the record any indication of what "information" or "reports" the officer had received, or, beyond what has been set out above, from what source the "information" and "reports" had come. The officer testified that when he left the station house, "I had in mind looking for [the petitioner] in the area of East 115th Street and Beulah, stopping him if I did see him make a stop in that area." But the officer testified to nothing that would indicate that any informer had said that the petitioner could be found at that time and place. Cf. Draper v. United States. And the record does not show that the officers saw the petitioner "stop" before they arrested him, or that they saw, heard, smelled, or otherwise perceived anything else to give them ground for belief that the petitioner had acted or was then acting unlawfully.

No decision of this Court has upheld the constitutional validity of a warrantless arrest with support so scant as this record presents. The respondent relies upon Draper v. United States. But in that case the record showed that a named special employee of narcotics agents who had on numerous occasions given reliable information had told the arresting officer that the defendant, whom he described minutely, had taken up residence at a stated address and was selling narcotics to addicts in Denver. The informer further had told the officer that the defendant was going to Chicago to obtain narcotics and would be returning to Denver on one of two trains from Chicago, which event in fact took place. In complete contrast, the record in this case does not contain a single objective fact to support a belief by the officers that the petitioner was engaged in criminal activity at the time they arrested him.

An arrest without a warrant bypasses the safeguards provided by an objective predetermination of probable cause, and substitutes instead the far less reliable procedure of an after-the-event justification for the arrest or search, too likely to be subtly influenced by the familiar shortcomings of hindsight judgment. "Whether or not the requirements of reliability and particularity of the information on which an officer may act are more stringent where an arrest warrant is absent, they surely cannot be less stringent than where an arrest warrant is obtained. Otherwise, a principal incentive now existing for the procurement of arrest warrants would be destroyed." Wong Sun v. United States, 371 U.S. 471, 479–480, 83 S.Ct. 407, 413. Yet even in cases where warrants were obtained, the Court has held that the Constitution demands a greater showing of probable cause than can be found in the present record.

When the constitutional validity of an arrest is challenged, it is the function of a court to determine whether the facts available to the officers at the moment of the arrest would "warrant a man of reasonable caution in the belief" that an offense has been committed. Carroll v. United States, 267 U.S. 132, 162, 45 S.Ct. 280, 288. If the court is not informed of the facts upon which the arresting officers acted, it cannot properly discharge that function. All that the trial court was told in this case was that the officers knew what the petitioner looked like and knew that he had a previous record of arrests or convictions for violations of the clearing house law. Beyond that, the arresting officer who testified said no more than that someone (he did not say who) had told him something (he did not say what) about the petitioner. We do not hold that the officer's knowledge of the petitioner's physical appearance and previous record was either inadmissible or entirely inrrelevant upon the issue of probable cause. See Brinegar v. United States, 338 U.S. 160, 172–174, 69 S.Ct. 1302,

1309–1310. But to hold that knowledge of either or both of these facts constituted probable cause would be to hold that anyone with a previous criminal record could be arrested at will.

It is possible that an informer did in fact relate information to the police officer in this case which constituted probable cause for the petitioner's arrest. But when the constitutional validity of that arrest was challenged, it was incumbent upon the prosecution to show with considerably more specificity than was shown in this case what the informer actually said, and why the officer thought the information was credible. We may assume that the officers acted in good faith in arresting the petitioner. But "good faith on the part of the arresting officers is not enough." Henry v. United States. If subjective good faith alone were the test, the protections of the Fourth Amendment would evaporate, and the people would be "secure in their persons, houses, papers, and effects," only in the discretion of the police.

Reversed.   .   .   .

[The dissenting opinions of Justices Black, Clark and Harlan have been omitted. They were of the view that the facts found by the Ohio Supreme Court, and the inferences drawn from the testimony of the prosecution's witnesses satisfied the probable cause element.]

SPINELLI v. UNITED STATES

Supreme Court of the United States, 1969.
393 U.S. 410, 89 S.Ct. 584.

MR. JUSTICE HARLAN delivered the opinion of the Court.

William Spinelli was convicted under 18 U.S.C. § 1952 of traveling to St. Louis, Missouri, from a nearby Illinois suburb with the intention of conducting gambling activities proscribed by Missouri law. .   .   .   At every appropriate stage in the proceedings in the lower courts, the petitioner challenged the constitutionality of the warrant which authorized the FBI search that uncovered the evidence necessary for his conviction. .   .   .

Believing it desirable that the principles of [Aguilar v. Texas, 378 U.S. 108, 84 S.Ct. 1509 (1964)] should be further explicated, we granted certiorari, our writ being later limited to the question of the constitutional validity of the search and seizure. For reasons that follow we reverse.

In Aguilar, a search warrant had issued upon an affidavit of police officers who swore only that they had "received reliable information from a credible person and do believe" that narcotics were being illegally stored on the described premises. While recognizing that the constitutional requirement of probable cause can be satisfied by hearsay information, this Court held the affidavit inadequate for two reasons. First, the application failed to set forth any of the "underlying circumstances" necessary to enable the magistrate independently to judge of the validity of the informant's conclusion that the narcotics were where he said they were. Second, the affiant-officers did not attempt to support their claim that their informant was " 'credible' or his information 'reliable.' " The Government is, however, quite right in saying that the FBI affidavit in the present case is more ample than that in *Aguilar*. Not only does it contain a report from an anonymous informant, but it also contains a report of an independent FBI investigation which is said to corroborate the informant's tip. We are, then, required to delineate the manner in which *Aguilar's* two-pronged test should be applied in these circumstances.

In essence, the affidavit, reproduced in full in the Appendix to this opinion, contained the following allegations:

    1.   The FBI had kept track of Spinelli's movements on five days during the month of August 1965. On four of these occasions, Spinelli was seen crossing one of two bridges leading from Illinois into St. Louis, Missouri, between 11 a. m. and 12:15 p. m. On four of the five days, Spinelli was also seen parking his car in a lot used by residents of an apartment house at 1108 Indian Circle Drive in St. Louis, between 3:30 p. m. and 4:45 p. m. On one day, Spinelli was followed further and seen to enter a particular apartment in the building.

    2.   An FBI check with the telephone company revealed that this apartment contained two telephones listed under the name of Grace P. Hagen, and carrying the numbers WYdown 4–0029 and WYdown 4–0136.

    3.   The application stated that "William Spinelli is know to this affiant and to federal law enforcement agents and local law enforcement agents as a bookmaker, an associate of bookmakers, a gambler, and an associate of gamblers."

    4.   Finally it was stated that the FBI "has been informed by a confidential reliable informant that William Spinelli is operating a handbook and accepting wagers and disseminating wagering information by means of the telephones which have been assigned the numbers WYdown 4–0029 and WYdown 4–0136."

There can be no question that the last item mentioned, detailing the informant's tip, has a fundamental place in this warrant application. Without it, probable cause could not be established. The first two items reflect only innocent-seeming activity and data. Spinelli's travels to and from the apartment building and his entry into a particular apartment on one occasion could hardly be taken as bespeaking gambling activity; and there is surely nothing unusual about an apartment containing two separate telephones. Many a householder indulges himself in this petty luxury. Finally, the allegation that Spinelli was "known" to the affiant and to other federal and local law enforcement officers as a gambler and an associate of gamblers is but a bald and unilluminating assertion of suspicion that is entitled to no weight in appraising the magistrate's decision. Nathanson v. United States, 290 U.S. 41, 46, 54 S.Ct. 11, 12 (1933).

So much indeed the Government does not deny. Rather, following the reasoning of the Court of Appeals, the Government claims that the informant's tip gives a suspicious color to the FBI's reports detailing Spinelli's innocent-seeming conduct and that, conversely, the FBI's surveillance corroborates the informant's tip, thereby entitling it to more weight. It is true, of course, that the magistrate is obligated to render a judgment based upon a commonsense reading of the entire affidavit. United States v. Ventresca, 380 U.S. 102, 108, 85 S.Ct. 741, 745 (1964). We believe, however, that the "totality of circumstances" approach taken by the Court of Appeals paints with too broad a brush. Where, as here, the informer's tip is a necessary element in a finding of probable cause its proper weight must be determined by a more precise analysis.

The informer's report must first be measured against *Aguilar's* standards so that its probative value can be assessed. If the tip is found inadequate under *Aguilar*, the other allegations which corroborate the information contained in the hearsay report should then be considered. At this stage as well, however, the standards enunciated in *Aguilar* must inform the magistrate's decision. He must ask: Can it fairly be said that the tip, even when certain parts of it have been corroborated by independent sources, is as trustworthy as a tip which would pass *Aguilar's* tests without independent corroboration? *Aguilar* is relevant at this stage of the inquiry as well because the tests it establishes were designed to implement the long-standing principle that probable cause must be determined by a "neutral and detached magistrate," and not by "the officer engaged in the often competitive enterprise of ferreting out crime." A magistrate cannot be said to have properly discharged his constitutional duty if he relies on an informer's tip which—even when partially corroborated—is not as reliable as one which passes *Aguilar's* requirements when standing alone.

Applying these principles to the present case, we first consider the weight to be given the informer's tip when it is considered apart from the rest of the affidavit. It is clear that a Commissioner could not credit it without abdicating his constitutional function. Though the affiant swore that his confidant was "reliable," he offered the magistrate no reason in support of this conclusion. Perhaps even more important is the fact that *Aguilar's* other test has not been satisfied. The tip does not contain a sufficient statement of the underlying circumstances from which the informer concluded that Spinelli was running a bookmaking operation. We are not told how the FBI's source received his information—it is not alleged that the informant personally observed Spinelli at work or that he had ever placed a bet with him. Moreover, if the informant came by the information indirectly, he did not explain why his sources were reliable. Compare Jaben v. United States, 381 U.S. 214, 85 S.Ct. 1365 (1965). In the absence of a statement detailing the manner in which the information was gathered, it is especially important that the tip describe the accused's criminal activity in sufficient detail so that the magistrate may know that he is relying on something more substantial than a casual rumor circulating in the underworld or an accusation based merely on an individual's general reputation.

The detail provided by the informant in Draper v. United States, 358 U.S. 307, 79 S.Ct. 329 (1959), provides a suitable benchmark. While Hereford, the FBI's informer in that case did not state the way in which he had obtained his information he reported that Draper had gone to Chicago the day before by train and that he would return to Denver by train with three ounces of heroin on one of two specified mornings. Moreover Hereford went on to describe with minute particularity the clothes that Draper would be wearing upon his arrival at the Denver station. A magistrate, when confronted with such detail, could reasonably infer that the informant had gained his information in a reliable way. Such an inference cannot be made in the present case. Here, the only facts supplied were that Spinelli was using two specified telephones and that these phones were being used in gambling operations. This meager report could easily have been obtained from an offhand remark heard at a neighborhood bar.

Nor do we believe that the patent doubts *Aguilar* raises as to the report's reliability are adequately resolved by a consideration of the allegations detailing the FBI's independent investigative efforts. At most, these allegations indicated that Spinelli could have used the telephones specified by the informant for some purpose. This cannot by itself be said to support both the inference that the informer was generally trustworthy and that he had made his charge against Spinelli on the basis of information obtained in a reliable way. Once again, *Draper* provides a relevant comparison. Independent police work in that case corroborated much more than one small detail that had been provided by the informant. There, the police, upon greeting the inbound Denver train on the second morning specified by informer Hereford, saw a man whose dress corresponded precisely to Hereford's detailed description. It was then apparent that the informant had not been fabricating his report out of whole cloth; since the report was of the sort which in common experience may be recognized as having been obtained in a reliable way, it was perfectly clear that probable cause had been established.

We conclude, then, that in the present case the informant's tip— even when corroborated to the extent indicated—was not sufficient to provide the basis for a finding of probable cause. This is not to say that the tip was so insubstantial that it could not properly have counted in the magistrate's determination. Rather, it needed some further support. When we look to the other parts of the application, however, we find nothing alleged which would permit the suspicions engendered by the informant's report to ripen into a judgment that a crime was probably being committed. As we have already seen, the allegations detailing the FBI's surveillance of Spinelli and its investigation of the telephone company records contain no suggestion of criminal conduct when taken by themselves—and they are not endowed with an aura of suspicion by virtue of the informer's tip. Nor do we find that the FBI's reports take on a sinister color when read in light of common knowledge that bookmaking is often carried on over the telephone and from premises ostensibly used by others for perfectly normal purposes. Such an argument would carry weight in a situation in which the premises contain an unusual number of telephones or abnormal activity is observed, cf. McCray v. Illinois, 386 U.S. 300, 302, 87 S.Ct. 1056, 1057 (1967), but it does not fit this case where neither of these factors is present. All that remains to be considered is the flat statement that Spinelli was "known" to the FBI and others as a gambler. But just as a simple assertion of police suspicion is not itself a sufficient basis for a magistrate's finding of probable cause, we do not believe it may be used to give additional weight to allegations that would otherwise be insufficient.

The affidavit, then, falls short of the standards set forth in *Aguilar, Draper,* and our other decisions that give content to the notion of probable cause. In holding as we have done, we do not retreat from the established propositions that only the probability, and not a prima facie showing, of criminal activity is the standard of probable cause, Beck v. Ohio, 379 U.S. 89, 96, 85 S.Ct. 223, 228 (1964); that affidavits of probable cause are tested by much less rigorous standards than those governing the admissibility of evidence at trial. McCray v. Illinois, 386 U.S. 300, 311, 87 S.Ct. 1056, 1062 (1967); that in judging probable cause issuing magistrates are not to be confined by niggardly limitations or by restrictions on the use of their common sense. United States v. Ventresca, 380 U.S. 102, 108, 85 S. Ct. 741, 745 (1964); and that their determination of probable cause should be paid great deference by reviewing courts, Jones v. United States, 362 U.S. 257, 270–271, 80 S.Ct. 725, 735–736 (1960). But we cannot sustain this warrant without diluting important safeguards that assure that the judgment of a disinterested judicial officer will interpose itself between the police and the citizenry.

The judgment of the Court of Appeals is reversed and the case is remanded to that court for further proceedings consistent with this opinion.

It is so ordered.

Reversed and remanded.

MR. JUSTICE MARSHALL took no part in the consideration or decision of this case.

APPENDIX

Affidavit in Support of Search Warrant

I, Robert L. Bender, being duly sworn, depose and say that I am a Special Agent of the Federal Bureau of Investigation, and as such am authorized to make searches and seizures.

That on August 6, 1965, at approximately 11:44 a. m., William Spinelli was observed by an Agent of the Federal Bureau of Investigation driving a 1964 Ford convertible, Missouri license HC3–649, onto the Eastern approach of the Veterans Bridge leading from East St. Louis, Illinois, to St. Louis, Missouri.

That on August 11, 1965, at approximately 11:16 a. m., William Spinelli was observed by an Agent of the Federal Bureau of Investigation driving a 1964 Ford convertible, Missouri license HC3–649, onto the Eastern approach of the Eads Bridge leading from East St. Louis, Illinois, to St. Louis, Missouri.

Further, at approximately 11:18 a. m. on August 11, 1965, I observed William Spinelli driving the aforesaid Ford convertible from the Western approach of the Eads Bridge into St. Louis, Missouri.

Further, at approximately 4:40 p. m. on August 11, 1965, I observed the aforesaid Ford convertible, bearing Missouri license HC3–649, parked in a parking lot used by residents of The Chieftain Manor Apartments, approximately one block east of 1108 Indian Circle Drive.

On August 12, 1965, at approximately 12:07 p. m. William Spinelli was observed by an Agent of the Federal Bureau of Investigation driving the aforesaid 1964 Ford convertible onto the Eastern approach of the Veterans Bridge from East St. Louis, Illinois, in the direction of St. Louis, Missouri.

Further, on August 12, 1965, at approximately 3:46 p. m., I observed William Spinelli driving the aforesaid 1964 Ford convertible onto the parking lot used by the residents of The Chieftain Manor Apartments approximately one block east of 1108 Indian Circle Drive.

Further, on August 12, 1965, at approximately 3:49 p. m., William Spinelli was observed by an Agent of the Federal Bureau of Investigation entering the front entrance of the two-story apartment building located at 1108 Indian Circle Drive, this building being one of The Chieftain Manor Apartments.

On August 13, 1965, at approximately 11:08 a. m., William Spinelli was observed by an Agent of the Federal Bureau of Investigation driving the aforesaid Ford convertible onto the Eastern approach of the Eads Bridge from East St. Louis, Illinois, heading towards St. Louis, Missouri.

Further, on August 13, 1965 at approximately 11:11 a. m., I observed William Spinelli driving the aforesaid Ford convertible from the Western approach of the Eads Bridge into St. Louis, Missouri.

Further, on August 13, 1965, at approximately 3:45 p. m., I observed William Spinelli driving the aforesaid 1964 Ford convertible onto the parking area used by residents of The Chieftain Manor Apartments, said parking area being approximately one block from 1108 Indian Circle Drive.

Further, on August 13, 1965, at approximately 3:55 p. m., William Spinelli was observed by an Agent of the Federal Bureau of Investigation entering the corner apartment located on the second floor in the southwest corner, known as Apartment F, of the two-story apartment building known and numbered as 1108 Indian Circle Drive.

On August 16, 1965, at approximately 3:22 p. m., I observed William Spinelli driving the aforesaid Ford convertible onto the parking lot used by the residents of The Chieftain Manor Apartments approximately one block east of 1108 Indian Circle Drive.

Further, an Agent of the F.B.I. observed William Spinelli alight from the aforesaid Ford convertible and walk toward the apartment building located at 1108 Indian Circle Drive.

The records of the Southwestern Bell Telephone Company reflect that there are two telephones located in the southwest corner apartment on the second floor of the apartment building located at 1108 Indian Circle Drive under the name of Grace P. Hagen. The numbers listed in the Southwestern Bell Telephone Company records for the aforesaid telephones are WYdown 4–0029 and WYdown 4–0136.

William Spinelli is known to this affiant and to federal law enforcement agents and local law enforcement agents as a bookmaker, an associate of bookmakers, a gambler, and an associate of gamblers.

The Federal Bureau of Investigation has been informed by a confidential reliable informant that William Spinelli is operating a handbook and accepting wagers and disseminating wagering information by means of the telephones which have been assigned the numbers WYdown 4–0029 and WYdown 4–0136.

> /s/ Robert L. Bender,
> Robert L. Bender,
>
> Special Agent Federal Bureau of Investigation.

Subscribed and sworn to before me this 18th day of August, 1965, at St. Louis, Missouri.

> /s/ William R. O'Toole.

MR. JUSTICE WHITE, concurring.

An investigator's affidavit that he has seen gambling equipment being moved into a house at a specified address will support the issuance of a search warrant. The oath affirms the honesty of the statement and negatives the lie or imagination. Personal observation attests to the facts asserted—that there is gambling equipment on the premises at the named address.

But if the officer simply avers, without more, that there is gambling paraphernalia on certain premises, the warrant should not issue, even though the belief of the officer is an honest one, as evidenced by his oath, and even though the magistrate knows him to be an experienced, intelligent officer who has been reliable in the past. This much was settled in Nathanson v. United States, 290 U.S. 41, 54 S.Ct. 11 (1933), where the Court held insufficient an officer's affidavit swearing he had cause to believe that there was illegal liquor on the premises for which the warrant was sought. The unsupported assertion or belief of the officer does not satisfy the requirement of probable cause.

What is missing in *Nathanson* and like cases is a statement of the basis for the affiant's believing the facts contained in the affidavit—the good "cause" which the officer in *Nathanson* said he had. If an officer swears that there is gambling equipment at a certain address, the possibilities are (1) that he has seen the equipment; (2) that he has observed or perceived facts from which the presence of the equipment may reasonably be inferred; and (3) that he has obtained the information from someone else. If (1) is true, the affidavit is good. But in (2), the affidavit is insufficient unless the perceived facts are given, for it is the magistrate, not the officer, who is to judge the existence of probable cause. With respect to (3), where the officer's information is hearsay, no warrant should issue absent good cause for crediting that hearsay. Because an affidavit asserting, without more, the location of gambling equipment at a particular address does not claim personal observation of any of the facts by the officer, and because of the likelihood that the information came from an unidentified third party, affidavits of this type are unacceptable.

Neither should the warrant issue if the officer states that there is gambling equipment in a particular apartment and that his information comes from an informant, named or unnamed, since the honesty of the informant and the basis for his report are unknown. Nor would the missing elements be completely supplied by the officer's oath that the informant has often furnished reliable information in the past. This attests to the honesty of the informant, but Aguilar v. Texas, supra, requires something more—did the information come from observation, or did the informant in turn receive it from another? Absent additional facts for believing the informant's report, his assertion stands no better than the oath of the officer to the same effect. Indeed, if the affidavit of an officer, known by the magistrate to be honest and experienced, stating that gambling equipment is located in a certain building is unacceptable, it would be quixotic if a similar statement from an honest informant were found to furnish probable cause. A strong argument can be made that both should be acceptable under the Fourth Amendment, but under our cases neither is. The past reliability of the informant can no more furnish probable cause for believing his current report than can previous experience with the officer himself.

If the affidavit rests on hearsay—an informant's report—what is necessary under *Aguilar* is one of two things: the informant must declare either (1) that he has himself seen or perceived the fact or facts asserted; or (2) that his information is hearsay, but there is good reason for believing it—perhaps one of the usual grounds for crediting hearsay information. The first presents few problems: since the report, although hearsay, purports to be first-hand observation, remaining doubt centers on the honesty of the informant, and that worry is dissipated by the officer's previous experience with the informant. The other basis for accepting the informant's report is more complicated. But if, for example, the informer's hearsay comes from one of the actors in the crime in the nature of admission against interest, the affidavit giving this information should be held sufficient.

I am inclined to agree with the majority that there are limited special circumstances in which an "honest" informant's report, if sufficiently detailed, will in effect verify itself—that is, the magistrate when confronted with such detail could reasonably infer that the informant had gained his information in a reliable way. Detailed information may sometimes imply that the informant himself has observed the facts. Suppose an informant with whom an officer has had satisfactory experience states that there is gambling equipment in the living room of a specified apartment and describes in detail not only the equipment itself but the appointments and furnishings in the apartment. Detail like this, if true at all must rest on personal observation of either the informant or of someone else. If the latter, we know nothing of the third person's honesty or sources; he may be fabricating a wholly false report. But it is arguable that on these facts it was the informant himself who has perceived the facts, for the information reported is not usually the subject of casual day-to-day conversation. Because the informant is honest and it is probable that he has viewed the facts, there is probable cause for the issuance of a warrant.

So too in the special circumstances of Draper v. United States, 358 U.S. 307, 79 S.Ct. 329 (1959), the kind of information related by the informant is not generally sent ahead of a person's arrival in a city except to those who are intimately connected with making careful arrangements for meeting him. The informant, posited as honest, somehow had the reported facts, very likely from one of the actors in the plan, or as one of them himself. The majority's suggestion is that a warrant could have been obtained based only on the informer's report. I am inclined to agree, although it seems quite plain that if it may be so easily inferred from the affidavit that the informant has himself observed the facts or has them from an actor in the event, no possible harm could come from requiring a statement to that effect, thereby removing the difficult and recurring questions which arise in such situations.

Of course, *Draper* itself did not proceed on this basis. Instead the Court pointed out that when the officer saw a person getting off the train at the specified time, dressed and conducting himself precisely as the informant had predicted, all but the critical fact with respect to possessing narcotics had then been verified and for that reason the officer had "reasonable grounds" to believe also that Draper was carrying narcotics. Unquestionably, verification of arrival time, dress and gait reenforced the honesty of the informant—he had not reported a made up story. But if what *Draper* stands for is that the existence of the tenth and critical fact is made sufficiently probable to justify the issuance of a warrant by verifying nine other facts coming from the same source, I have my doubts about that case.

In the first place, the proposition is not that the tenth fact may be logically inferred from the other nine or that the tenth fact is usually found in conjunction with the other nine. No one would suggest that just anyone getting off the 10:30 train dressed as Draper was, with a brisk walk and carrying a zipper bag, should be arrested for carrying narcotics. The thrust of *Draper* is not that the verified facts have independent significance with respect to proof of the tenth. The argument instead relates to the reliability of the source: because an informant is right about some things, he is more probably right about other facts, usually the critical, unverified facts.

But the Court's cases have already rejected for Fourth Amendment purposes the notion that the past reliability of an officer is sufficient reason for believing his current assertions. Nor would it suffice. I suppose, if a reliable informant states there is gambling equipment in Apartment 607 and then proceeds to describe in detail Apartment 201, a description which is verified before applying for the warrant. He was right about 201, but that hardly makes him more believable about the equipment in 607. But what if he states that there are narctoics locked in a safe in Apartment 300, which is described in detail, and the apartment manager verifies everything but the contents of the safe? I doubt that the report about the narcotics is made appreciably more believable by the verification. The informant could still have gotten his information concerning the safe from others about whom nothing is known or could have inferred the presence of narcotics from circumstances which a magistrate would find unacceptable.

The tension between *Draper* and the *Nathanson-Aguilar* line of cases is evident from the course followed by the majority opinion. First, it is held that the report from a reliable informant that Spinelli is using two telephones with specified numbers to conduct a gambling business plus Spinelli's reputation in police circles as a gambler does not add up to probable cause. This is wholly consistent with *Aguilar* and *Nathanson*: the informant did not reveal whether he had personally observed the facts or heard them from another, and if the latter, no basis for crediting the hearsay was presented. Nor were the facts, as Mr. Justice Harlan says, of such a nature that they normally would be obtainable only by the personal observation of the informant himself. The police, however, did not stop with the informant's report. Independently, they established the existence of two phones having the given numbers and located them in an apartment house which Spinelli was regularly frequenting away from his home. There remained little question but that Spinelli was using the phones, and it was a fair inference that the use was not for domestic but for business purposes. The informant had claimed the business involved gambling. Since his specific information about Spinelli using two phones with particular numbers had been verified, did not his allegation about gambling thereby become sufficiently more believable if the *Draper* principle is to be given any scope at all? I would think so, particularly since information from the informant which was verified was not neutral, irrelevant information but was material to proving the gambling allegation: two phones with different numbers in an apartment used away from home indicates a business use in an operation, like bookmaking, where multiple phones are needed. The *Draper* approach would reasonably justify the issuance of a warrant in this case, particularly since the police had some awareness of Spinelli's past activities. The majority, however, while seemingly embracing *Draper*, confines that case to its own facts. Pending full scale reconsideration of that case, on the one hand, or of the *Nathanson-Aguilar* cases on the other, I join the opinion of the Court and the judgment of reversal, especially since a vote to affirm would produce an equally divided Court.

MR. JUSTICE BLACK, dissenting.

In my view, this Court's decision in Aguilar v. Texas, 378 U.S. 108, 84 S.Ct. 1509 (1964) was bad enough. That decision went very far toward elevating the magistrate's hearing for issuance of a search warrant to a full-fledged trial, where witnesses must be brought forward to attest personally to all the facts alleged. But not content with this, the Court today expands *Aguilar* to almost unbelievable proportions. Of course, it would strengthen the probable cause presentation if eyewitnesses could testify that they saw the defendant commit the crime. It would be stronger still if these witnesses could explain in detail the nature of the sensual perceptions on which they based their "conclusion" that the person they had seen was the defendant and that he was responsible for the events they observed. Nothing in our Constitution, however, requires that the facts be established with that degree of certainty and with such elaborate specificity before a policeman can be authorized by a disinterested magistrate to conduct a carefully limited search.

The Fourth Amendment provides that "no warrants shall issue but upon probable cause, supported by oath or affirmation, and particularly describing the place to be searched, and the persons or things to be seized." In this case a search warrant was issued supported by an oath and particularly describing the place to be searched and the things to be seized. The supporting oath was three printed pages and the full text of it is included in an Appendix to the Court's opinion. The magistrate, I think properly, held the information set forth sufficient facts to show "probable cause" that the defendant was violating the law. Six members of the Court of Appeals also agreed that the affidavit was sufficient to show probable cause. A majority of this Court today holds, however, that the magistrate and all of these judges were wrong. In doing so, they substitute their own opinion for that of the local magistrate and the circuit judges, and reject the *en banc* factual conclusion of the Eighth Circuit and reverse the judgment based upon that factual conclusion. I cannot join in any such disposition of an issue so vital to the administration of justice, and dissent as vigorously as I can.

I repeat my belief that the affidavit given the magistrate was more than ample to show probable cause of the defendant's guilt. The affidavit meticulously set out facts sufficient to show the following:

1.   The defendant had been shown going to and coming from a room in an apartment which contained two telephones listed under the name of another person.   Nothing in the record indicates that the apartment was of that large and luxurious type which could only be occupied by a person to whom it would be a "petty luxury" to have two separate telephones, with different numbers, both listed under the name of a person who did not live there.

2.   The defendant's car had been observed parked in the apartment's parking lot.   This fact was, of course, highly relevant in showing that the defendant was extremely interested in some enterprise which was located in the apartment.

3.   The FBI had been informed by a reliable informant that the defendant was accepting wagering information by telephones —the particular telephones located in the apartment the defendant had been repeatedly visiting.   Unless the Court, going beyond the requirements of the Fourth Amendment, wishes to require magistrates to hold trials before issuing warrants, it is not necessary—as the Court holds—to have the affiant explain "the underlying circumstances from which the informer concluded that Spinelli was running a bookmaking operation."

4.   The defendant was known by federal and local law enforcement agents as a bookmaker and an associate of gamblers. I cannot agree with the Court that this knowledge was only a "bald and unilluminating assertion of suspicion that is entitled to no weight in appraising the magistrate's decision."   Although the statement is hearsay that might not be admissible in a regular trial, everyone knows, unless he shuts his eyes to the realities of life, that this is a relevant fact which together with other circumstances, might indicate a factual probability that gambling is taking place.

The foregoing facts should be enough to constitute probable cause for anyone who does not believe that the only way to obtain a search warrant is to prove beyond a reasonable doubt that a defendant is guilty.   Even *Aguilar*, on which the Court relies, cannot support the contrary result, at least as that decision was written before today's massive escalation of it.   .   .   .

[The dissenting opinions of MR. JUSTICE FORTAS and MR. JUSTICE STEWART are omitted.]

NOTE

The Supreme Court's major post-*Spinelli* treatment of the probable cause issue is in United States v. Harris, 403 U.S. 573, 91 S.Ct. 2075 (1971), in which the Court sustained a search warrant based upon the following affidavit.

"Roosevelt Harris has had a reputation with me for over 4 years as being a trafficker of nontaxpaid distilled spirits, and over this period I have received numerous information [*sic*] from all types of persons as to his activities. Constable Howard Johnson located a sizeable stash of illicit whiskey in an abandoned house under Harris' control during this period of time. This date, I have received information from a person who fears for their [sic] life and property should their name be revealed. I have interviewed this person, found this person to be a prudent person, and have, under a sworn verbal statement, gained the following information: This person has personal knowledge of and has purchased illicit whiskey from within the residence described, for a period of more than 2 years, and most recently within the past two weeks, has knowledge of a person who purchased illicit whiskey within the past two days from the house, has personal knowledge that the illicit whiskey is consumed by purchasers in the out-building known as and utilized as the 'dance hall,' and has seen Roosevelt Harris go to the other outbuilding located about 50 yards from the residence, on numerous occasions, to obtain the whiskey for this person and other persons."

The Court was not in agreement why the warrant was valid. Four members of the Court (Burger, Black, Stewart and Blackmun) held that the personal and recent observations of the informant distinguished the case from Spinelli and the allegation that the informer was "prudent" presents adequate probable cause.

Four members of the Court (Burger, Black, White and Blackmun) ruled that there was a special basis for crediting the informer's tip since the informer made an admission against his own interest i. e., he admitted personal participation in the crime. "People do not lightly admit a crime and place critical evidence in the hands of the police in the form of their own admissions. Admissions of crime . . . carry their own indicia of credibility—sufficient at least to support a finding of probable cause to search".

Three members of the Court (Burger, Black and Blackmun) ruled that it was not necessary for a warrant to allege that the informant had previously given correct information and that Spinelli was wrong when it held that a magistrate could not rely upon a suspect's prior reputation for involvement in criminal activities.

Four members of the Court (Harlan, Douglas, Brennan and Marshall) dissented. The dissenters conceded that the information given by the informer was, if credible, sufficient to establish probable cause. The dissenters thought that there was insufficient grounds to establish the informer's credibility. First, the vague allegation the informer was "prudent" is not enough to establish credibility. Second the mere fact that personal knowledge is claimed is not sufficient and, although information given to the police may be so thoroughly detailed as to support a finding of reliability, the information in this case is not so detailed.* Third, the informer who makes a declaration against interest should not be deemed reliable for that reason alone. Fourth, the dissenters reiterated the *Spinelli* rule against consider-

---

* An example of reliance upon extensive detail to establish credibility is found in State v. Perry, 59 N.J. 383, 283 A.2d 330 (1971). An additional example is in Judge Moylan's thoughtful opinion in Soles v. State, 16 Md.App. 656, 299 A.2d 502 (1973), to the effect that the richness of detail may indicate that the source came upon his information "in a reliable way."

ing a suspect's reputation. The dissenters suggested that it would be better practice for the government to bring the informer to the magistrate who could assess his credibility for himself while still maintaining the secrecy of his identity. Alternatively, the dissenters suggested that the agent should tell the magistrate of the informer's general background, employment, personal attributes that enable him to observe and relate accurately, position in the community, reputation with others, personal connection with the suspect, or any other circumstances which suggest the probable absence of any motivation to falsify, the apparent motivation for supplying the information, the presence or absence of a criminal record or association with known criminals, and the like.

DAWSON v. STATE

Court of Special Appeals of Maryland, 1971.
11 Md.App. 694, 276 A.2d 680.

MOYLAN, JUDGE.

The appellants, Donald Lee Dawson and Frances M. Dawson, husband and wife were convicted . . . of unlawfully maintaining a premises for the purpose of selling lottery tickets. . . .

On this appeal, they [contend] that the search warrant for their home was issued and executed without adequate probable cause having been shown to justify its issuance. . . .

The Dual Analysis of Probable Cause

The existence of probable cause to justify the issuance of either a search and seizure warrant or an arrest warrant may be predicated upon either or both of two broad categories of information—1) the direct observation of the affiant applying for the warrant (or of the affiants on supporting affidavits . . . or 2) hearsay information furnished to the affiant by someone else and then recited by the affiant in his affidavit. It is axiomatic that probable cause may be based upon the direct observation of the affiant himself. * * * It is equally well-established that probable cause may be based upon hearsay information alone and need not reflect the direct personal observation of the affiant. . . . It follows that probable cause may also be based upon a combination of direct observation and hearsay information.

Confusion somehow manages to creep into the cases, however, where the affidavit offered to support probable cause is based upon the mixed predicate of both direct observation and hearsay information. That confusion is engendered by the failure to grasp the unifying principle—to appreciate that both of the broad categories of information are evaluated by the same general standards of measurement. The apparent difference in the standards is simply one of surface application and not of theoretical significance.

Whether the information being evaluated is the direct observation of the affiant or is hearsay information, the issuing magistrate is required to perform the same intellectual surgery. In determining the existence *vel non* of probable cause, the magistrate must make two distinct determinations. The number and the nature of these determinations do not vary, whether the specimen being analyzed is direct observation or hearsay information. He must:

(1) Evaluate the truthfulness of the source of the information; and

(2) Evaluate the adequacy of the factual premises furnished by that source, to support the validity of the source's conclusion.

In the first instance, he is judging the integrity of a person. In the second instance, he is judging the logic of a proposition. . . .

In evaluating the truthfulness of the source of the information, the magistrate is presented with no problem in dealing with the affiant-observer. "The oath affirms the honesty of the statement and negatives the lie or imagination." *Spinelli*, 393 U.S. at 423, 89 S.Ct. at 592 (concurring opinion by White, J.). The oath, as a trustworthiness device, establishes, *per se*, the credibility of the affiant-source and, thereby, the reliability of his directly observed information. Where the source of the information, however, is an absent, non-swearing declarant (an informant), the pathway to the establishment of that source's credibility is more circuitous. The issuing magistrate must have, as a substitute for the oath, some other reason to be persuaded of the credibility of the source of the information.

In deciding whether he is so persuaded, the magistrate must perform the same analysis whether the non-swearing source is named or unnamed.

His evaluation, in theory, will be the same in either case. The practical distinction is that in dealing with a named source, the very naming of the source and the relationship of the source to the observed information may go a long way (or even be sufficient unto itself), under the facts of a particular case, to establish the credibility of that source or the reliability of his information. * * *

Where the source of the information is unnamed, however, the method of persuading the magistrate is more involved. He must be furnished sufficient background information for him to judge for himself the credibility of the unnamed source and/or the reliability of that source's information. . . . The credibility of the person and the reliability of the information are but alternative aspects of the same trustworthiness phenomenon. To conclude that trustworthiness is probably present, the magistrate must be convinced either (1) that the source himself, as a person, is inherently honest and credible, or (2) in the absence of such proof of character of the man, that the information is furnished by that source under circumstances redolent with insurances of trustworthiness. Credibility and reliability may operate alternatively or in combination to establish probable trustworthiness.

In evaluating the credibility of different types of sources, the practical applications may vary, but the common denominator of all such decisions is that the issuing magistrate must have before him enough circumstances to be able to judge for himself the honesty of the source of the information, whether that source be an affiant, a named non-swearing informant or an unnamed non-swearing informant. The magistrate may no more accept an affiant's assertion that his source (named or unnamed) is credible in lieu of a recitation of facts from which the magistrate may draw that conclusion for himself than he may accept an affiant's assertion that the affiant himself is credible as a substitute for the affiant's taking of the oath. The concluding, in either case, is only for the magistrate.

Once the magistrate has decided that the information is trustworthy, he has still only half completed his ultimate determination. He must still decide what the information is worth. He has decided that the source is not lying; but he has not yet decided whether the source is mistaken. The magistrate's second function is now to evaluate the information which he is accepting as true and to see what probabilities emerge from that available data. Again, he may not accept the conclusion of either the affiant-observer or the non-swearing informant. He must take from either of those sources his facts and then arrive at his own conclusion as to the significance of those facts. . . .

In the case of the affiant-observer, the magistrate cannot accept the affiant's mere conclusion that "A probably committed a crime" or that "B probably contains contraband." The magistrate needs to know what the observations were so that he can conclude for himself whether that observed data persuades him that "A probably committed a crime" or that "B probably contains contraband." . . . By the same logic, the magistrate may not accept the nonsworn hearsay conclusion of even a credible informant any more than he may accept the sworn conclusion of a credible affiant-observer. . . . Again, he needs to know just what the informant saw and just what the informant heard to warrant the informant's conclusion.[1] At issue here is not the informant's credibility but the informant's thinking process—not his integrity but his ratiocination. In applying then these tools of analysis to an application based upon a mixed predicate of direct observation and hearsay information, the issuing magistrate may, after evaluating both the trustworthiness of the source of the

1. If the informant himself is offering not direct observation but hearsay twice compounded, the entire evaluation process must begin again at a second level of remoteness. The primary informant must then pass along sufficient data in sufficient detail so that the magistrate may again judge for himself (1) the credibility of the secondary informant and (2) the worth of that secondary informant's information. If, in some extreme hypothetical situation, the secondary informant should be a mere conduit for hearsay thrice compounded from a tertiary informant, the evaluation process is escalated to yet another level of remoteness and so on ad infinitum. Ultimately, the magistrate must have the benefit of someone's firsthand observation in order to evaluate the worth of the information and must have also satisfactory proof of the credibility of every person involved in the chain of transmission of the information from the initial observer to the magistrate himself.

information and the weight and worth of the information itself, reach one of four conclusions:

(1) That the direct observation is adequate unto itself to establish probable cause; . . .

(2) That the hearsay information is adequate unto itself to establish probable cause; . . .

(3) That neither the direct observation nor the hearsay information, standing alone, is adequate to establish probable cause but that the two combined do add up to the establishment of such probable cause; . . .

(4) That even the sum total of the direct observation plus the hearsay information does not establish probable cause.

The most logical procedure to follow in evaluating a warrant application is to look first at the hearsay information. If the affiant has furnished the issuing magistrate enough of the underlying circumstances to persuade the magistrate (1) that the informant is credible or his information otherwise reliable and (2) that the informant's conclusion was validly arrived at, probable cause is established. What *Spinelli* refers to as "*Aguilar's* two-pronged test" has been met. If, on the other hand, the information furnished about the informant and the information furnished from the informant fail to pass muster by either or both of *Aguilar's* prongs, the informant's information is still not rendered valueless. "Rather, it need[s] some further support."

In search of that "further support," the magistrate may then look to the direct observation recounted by the affiant. That direct observation may serve a dual function. As substance in its own right, it bears directly on the question of probable cause. It may also serve the ancillary and concomitant function of corroborating or verifying the hearsay information. Initially, the trustworthiness of an informant's information may not have been adequately established intrinsically because either 1) the magistrate was not persuaded that the informant was, by proven past performance or testimonials as to character, or otherwise, inherently credible or 2) the magistrate was not persuaded that the information was otherwise reliable by virtue of having been furnished under circumstances reasonably insuring trustworthiness.

The necessary trustworthiness may then be established extrinsically by the independent verification of the affiant's direct observation. If some of the significant details of the informant's story are shown to be, in fact, true that encourages the magistrate to believe that all of the story is probably true. The Supreme Court outlined this procedure in *Spinelli*:

"The informer's report must first be measured against *Aguilar's* standards so that its probative value can be assessed. If the tip is found inadequate under *Aguilar,* the other allegations which corroborate the information contained in the hearsay report should then be considered. At this stage as well, however, the standards enunciated in *Aguilar* must inform the magistrate's decision. He must ask: Can it fairly be said that the tip, even when certain parts of it have been corroborated by independent sources, is as trustworthy as a tip which would pass *Aguilar's* tests without independent corroboration?"

The Warrant in this Case

The substance of the affidavit of Detective Fyfe in support of the application for the search and seizure warrant consists of nine paragraphs. The first paragraph lists the investigative experience of Detective Fyfe and ends with his conclusion that gambling activities are being conducted at the suspected premises. Paragraphs three through nine contain the direct observations of Detective Fyfe himself. Only the second paragraph deals with the hearsay information. That paragraph contains not simply Detective Fyfe's description of the confidential informant but also the information furnished to Detective Fyfe by the confidential informant. The paragraph recites:

> "That on Thursday April 17, 1969 your affiant interviewed a confidential source of information who has given reliable information in the past relating to illegal gambling activities which has resulted in the arrest and conviction of persons arrested for illegal gambling activities and that the source is personally known to your affiant. That this source related that there was illegal gambling activities taking place at 8103 Legation Road, Hyattsville Prince George's County, Maryland by a one Donald Lee Dawson. That the source further related that the source would call telephone #577–5197 and place horse and number bets with Donald Lee Dawson."

A moment's analysis reveals that the first sentence relates to the "credibility reliability" prong of the *Aguilar* test and that the second and third sentences relate to the "conclusionary validity" prong of the *Aguilar* test.

In looking at the "conclusionary validity" prong first, *Aguilar* is satisfied by the recitation in this case. It is clear that the confidential informant is not passing on mere hearsay or idle rumor that he has picked up from some secondary source. He has related that he has personally called telephone number 577–5197 and has personally placed horse and number bets with the appellant. His knowledge is first hand. His facts support his conclusion. With respect to meeting this prong of the *Aguilar* test, the hearsay recitation in the case at bar is diametrically contrary to that found to be inadequate in *Spinelli*.

The information furnished by the affiant about his confidential source is more borderline, however, in meeting the "credibility/reliability" prong of the *Aguilar* test. In that the recitation includes the assertion that the informant's information in the

past has resulted in the "conviction of persons arrested for illegal
gambling activities," the circumstances go further to establish credibility than they did in *Spinelli,* wherein the confidential source was
simply described as "a confidential reliable informant," with no further recitation cataloging any results flowing from that source's information, even in vague, general terms. . . . It may well be
that the facts here recited are enough to establish the credibility of
the informant. In view of the strong independent verification hereinafter to be discussed, however, it is unnecessary for the State to
rely exclusively on such recitation.

Even were we to assume, arguendo, that the trustworthiness of
the confidential information has not been directly established because
(1) the circumstances furnished to support the informant's credibility have been not quite adequate and (2) no circumstances have been
furnished to show that the information is otherwise reliable, we must
now explore the third avenue to trustworthiness. We must look to
the direct observations of the affiant and see whether enough verification of parts of the informant's story exists to foster the conclusion
that the whole story is probably true. Our analysis of the direct observations leads us to conclude that ample verification does exist;
that the confidential information is sufficiently corroborated to be as
trustworthy as that information would need to be to "pass *Aguilar's*
tests without independent corroboration." In looking at "the other
parts of the application," we find ample allegations "which would
permit the suspicions engendered by the informant's report to ripen
into a judgment that a crime was probably being committed."

A discreet surveillance was conducted on the appellant's movements for six consecutive working days—Friday, April 18, 1969,
through Thursday, April 24, 1969, excluding only the intervening
Sunday. The pattern of conduct that emerged strongly suggested
that the appellant was a middle-echelon executive in the gambling
business—a business that can conveniently accommodate both bets on
the horses and bets on the day's winning number, since both wagering activities are geared to the same hourly schedule and both look to
the same sporting events for the winning and losing results.

The appellant urges strongly that not one of his observed activities could not easily have been engaged in by an innocent man. That
is true. It is also beside the point. What the appellant ignores is
that probable cause emerges not from any single constituent activity
but, rather, from the overall pattern of activities. Each fragment of
conduct may communicate nothing of significance, but the broad
mosaic portrays a great deal. The whole may, indeed, be greater
than the sum of its parts.

In the gambling business particularly, with its sophisticated pyr-
amidal structure, only the lower-level operatives—the street writers
—are vulnerable to surveillance that may yield directly-observed illicit transactions. The management level of the gambling syndicate is
generally isolated from compromising contact with the better. Even
at the management level, however, each echelon of command has its

own telltale pattern of activity. The patterns are distinct. One does not expect the backer, the layoff man or the office manager—except when he is careless—to carry brown paper bags or to engage in overheard conversation about a three digit number, anymore than one expects the president of a bank to stand at a teller's cage. The office manager does not behave as does the pick-up man; the backer does not behave as does the writer. If the law, in its wisdom, were not to realize this—that different levels of the pyramid display different behavioral characteristics—it would be condemning law enforcement to the frustrating and never-ending futility of merely annoying the syndicate by reeling in occasionally its little fish—the low-level attrition that is little more than a license to do business to multi-million-dollar-a-year underworld cartels.

The affiant ascertained that the appellant, less than three years before the current observations, had been arrested and convicted of gambling violations. In interpreting otherwise ambiguous conduct, a man's history of criminal activity may well be of probative force. Although as we observed in Silbert v. State, 10 Md.App. 56, 65, 267 A.2d 770, a convicted gambler does not forever after walk through life "enveloped in probable cause," he, nevertheless, is burdened by a history that does at least lend interpretative color to otherwise ambiguous activity.

The appellant seeks to equate the sworn fact of his criminal conviction for gambling in the present affidavit with the assertion condemned in *Spinelli*, that Spinelli was "known" to the affiant there as a "bookmaker." The appellant misreads *Spinelli*. The fact that a man is "known" as a gambler could be highly relevant where a proper factual foundation is laid for either the affiant's or the informant's conclusion. What was there condemned was not the probative force and relevance of a suspect being a known gambler, but simply the bald conclusory assertion of that fact with no factual basis furnished to the magistrate in support of the assertion. The court there said:

> "All that remains to be considered is the flat statement that Spinelli was 'known' to the FBI and others as a gambler. But just as a simple assertion of police suspicion is not itself a sufficient basis for a magistrate's finding of probable cause, we do not believe it may be used to give additional weight to allegations that would otherwise be insufficient."

The unsubstantiated assertion in *Spinelli* is, therefore, in no way analogous to the sworn recitation of the appellant's criminal record in the case at bar.

The appellant—an able-bodied adult male—was observed over portions of two work weeks to be engaged in no apparent legitimate employment. There are, of course, possible innocent hypotheses to explain this. There is also the hypothesis that there was no time for other employment because the gambling business is a full-time job that permits of little or no moonlighting in the legitimate sector. The appellant's history is a relevant factor in weighing the conflicting hypotheses which might account for this, otherwise unexplained, occupational inactivity in mid-April.

The affiant ascertained that the appellant had two telephones in his residence—not two instruments but two separate lines. This is not at all unusual. Neither, however, is it the norm. The affiant also ascertained that both of those telephone lines had silent listings. This is not highly unusual; it is, nevertheless, unusual. There are again, of course, possible innocent hypotheses. In weighing the hypotheses, however, the circumstances surrounding the telephones are not to be viewed in a vacuum. When the normal telephonic capacity of a house is doubled when steps are taken both to cloak the phones at least partially in secrecy and to keep unwanted callers off the lines and when a man who has been convicted of gambling in the past and is currently manifesting no means of legitimate livelihood is at home in close proximity to those phones during the busy hours of a bookmaking operation—an operation carried on in large measure by telephone—a pattern begins to emerge.

Another factor was added to the equation when the affiant observed that one of the appellant's silent listings—577–5197—was picked up in the course of a September, 1966, raid on a lottery operation in College Park. It is axiomatic that different outposts of a gambling operation need to know how to establish communication with each other.

On each day of observation, the appellant was observed to purchase an Armstrong Scratch Sheet, which gives information about horses running at various tracks that day. The purchase of an Armstrong Scratch Sheet is not, of itself, illegal. It, nevertheless, reveals to the prudent and reasonable mind that the purchaser has some interest in horseraces. That interest, of course, might be simply that of a bettor. It might, on the other hand, be that of a receiver or transmitter of bets. In weighing the relative probabilities, the reasonable mind cannot ignore the number and the privacy of the appellant's telephones, the time when the appellant is near those telephones, the appellant's criminal history and the appellant's apparent lack of legitimate employment.

On each morning of observation, the appellant was observed to leave his house between 9:02 and 10:20—to wit, at 9:02, 10:00, 10:20, 9:30, 10:00 and 9:30, respectively. On each day of observation, the appellant was observed to return to his house between 11:20 a. m. and 12:06 p. m.—to wit, at 11:50, 11:20, 11:53, 12:06, 11:55 and 11:48, respectively. On each day of observation, the appellant was observed, once he had returned to his house, to remain steadfastly in that house until after 6 p. m. The affiant, whose experience and expertise in gambling investigations was amply set out in the first paragraph of the affidavit, averred that the hours between noon and 6 p. m. are those when horse and number bets can be placed and when the results of the betting become available.

On each day of observation, the appellant was observed, during his morning rounds, to stop at a number of places, including liquor stores and restaurants, for periods of no more than several minutes in duration. Except for the Armstrong Scratch Sheets, he was never observed to purchase anything from any of the stores he visited. He was never observed to eat or drink anything at any of the restaurants he visited. The conduct of the appellant on these regular morning rounds is not viewed by the prudent and reasonable mind in a vacuum, but, rather, in meaningful conjunction with all of the other known data about him recounted in the application. The brevity and the frequency of the stops and the methodical regularity of the daily regimen are classic characteristics of the pick-up man phase of a gambling operation. He picks up the "action" (money and/or lists of bets) from the previous day or evening from prearranged locations —"drops." At the same time, he delivers cash to the appropriate locations for the pay-off of yesterday's successful players.

On one of the days of observation, the appellant was observed in close association during all of the day's activities—both upon the morning rounds and in the appellant's house throughout the afternoon—with a William Abdo, who was known by the affiant to have been arrested in 1966 along with the appellant for alleged gambling violations. It is not to permit "guilt by association" to reason that one's association may, at least, lend interpretive color to otherwise ambiguous activity.

In reviewing the observations, the ultimate question for the magistrate must be What is revealed by the whole pattern of activity? In the case at bar, the various strands of observation, insubstantial unto themselves, together weave a strong web of probable guilt.

The appellant seeks to equate the independent verification in this case to that in *Spinelli*. The two situations could not be in greater contrast. On five days, Spinelli was observed to drive across a Mississippi bridge from Illinois to St. Louis, Missouri, at between 11 a. m. and 12:15 p. m. On four occasions, Spinelli was observed to arrive at a parking lot near a suspected premises at between 3:30 p. m. and 4:45 p. m. No account at all was given of his activities in the St. Louis area during the approximate four-hour interval between crossing the bridge and arriving at the parking lot. On one occasion, Spinelli was observed to enter the apartment listed to a Grace Hagen. As in the instant case, two telephones were in the Hagen apartment. Unlike the instant case the telephones were not unlisted. In *Spinelli*, there were no observations placing Spinelli in close proximity to the telephones throughout the rush-hour period of a bookmaking operation.

In *Spinelli*, unlike the case at bar, there were no observations of the "pick-up man"—type of activity, whatsoever. In *Spinelli*, unlike the case at bar, there was no observed association with a previously arrested gambler. In *Spinelli*, unlike the case at bar, there was no daily purchase of an Armstrong Scratch Sheet to evidence some daily interest in horseraces. In *Spinelli*, unlike the case at bar, neither Spinelli's telephone number nor Grace Hagen's telephone number had been picked up in a raided gambling headquarters. In *Spinelli*, unlike the case at bar, Spinelli was not a convicted gambler. The affiant's conclusion there that he was a "known" gambler failed to merit consideration because of the absence of any factual basis for that conclusion.

Finally, the confidential hearsay information in *Spinelli* was so inadequate, under *Aquilar*, as to lend no interpretative color to the direct observations. In contrast, the confidential hearsay information was very substantial and would lend significant interpretative color to the direct observations here, if any further interpretative color, indeed, were needed. The hearsay information may, of course, reinforce the direct observation just as the direct observation may reinforce the hearsay information. There is no one-way street from direct observation to hearsay information. Rather, each may simultaneously cross-fertilize and enrich the other.

The direct observation in the case at bar may well be adequate unto itself to establish probable cause for the issuance of the search warrant. It is unnecessary to decide that question, however, since the direct observation amply verified the already significant confidential hearsay information and boosted it above *Aguilar's* threshold. The trustworthiness of the informant's assertion that he placed racing bets with the appellant over one of the unlisted telephone numbers—577–5197—was clearly extrinsically established. That the combination then of (1) the verified hearsay information and (2) the direct observation, as substance in its own right, served to establish probable cause is patent. . . . .

Affirmed.

[The author of the *Dawson* opinion further developed his explanation of probable cause in Stanley v. State, 19 Md.App. 507, 313 A.2d 847 (1974). See also the excellent article, Moylan, Hearsay and Probable Cause: An Aguilar and Spinelli Primer, 25 Mercer L.Rev. 741 (1974).]

NOTES

1. Probable Cause in Both Warrant and Warrantless Cases

For an arrest warrant or a search warrant to be valid under the Fourth Amendment, data establishing probable cause must appear within the four corners of the warrant or, at least, must be communicated under oath to the magistrate *before* issuance of the warrant. Data known to the police but not communicated to the magistrate is "wasted" for the purposes of establishing the warrant's validity. Hignut v. State, 17 Md.App. 399, 303 A.2d 173 (1973). Some jurisdictions, as a matter of state law, will not even accept sworn *oral* data, but insist upon the use of affidavits. Others require that any oral testimony presented to the issuing magistrate be contemporaneously recorded, lest a dispute later arise as to what was communicated under oath to the issuing magistrate. State v. O'Brien, 22 Ariz.App. 425, 528 P.2d 176 (1974), petition for review denied 112 Ariz. 41, 537 P.2d 28 (1975).

In a case where a valid warrant was not essential to establish the reasonableness of the police conduct (e. g., where the police made a warrantless felony arrest in a public place), probable cause may be established at a hearing on a motion to suppress. The student may be helped by thinking of the testimony presented at such a hearing in a warrantless arrest case (as in *Beck* and *Draper*) as akin to an affidavit for a search warrant or for an arrest warrant. Probable cause must be established through sworn testimony at such a hearing. The probable cause determination in a warrantless arrest hearing looks back to what was known at the moment of arrest. Just as it is possible for an ineptly drawn affidavit to omit known information which could establish probable cause, so also poorly presented testimony at a motion to suppress in a warrantless arrest case may omit facts which were known to the officer and which, if brought out at the hearing, would establish that probable cause existed. Is this what happened in *Beck*? Did the officer have more facts when he made the arrest than those which he communicated at the hearing on the motion to suppress?

2. Non-Hearsay and Hearsay Bases

A large percentage of warrant cases, and many warrantless arrest cases, involve secondary or hearsay sources. Frequently such sources are professional tipsters from the criminal milieu, particularly in areas such as gambling and narcotics, where citizen-complainants are not likely to come forward with information. Concentration on such situations (as in *Draper*, *Spinelli*, and *Dawson*), however, should not blur the fact that sometimes probable cause is developed without hearsay sources, and that, in other cases, the hearsay sources are of types that have a presumptive reliability not attributed to professional tipsters.

(a) Non-Hearsay Sources

In a warrant situation, the issuing magistrate may be asked to conclude that probable cause exists based entirely upon the claimed personal observations of the affiant. Similarly, in warrantless arrest cases, the judge may be asked to conclude that probable cause existed, based solely on observations made by the arresting officer and later recounted in his courtroom testimony.

In either of the foregoing non-hearsay situations, the reliability of the person who made the observations and tells of them under oath need not be established mechanically. The judicial officer can assess the credibility of this person who appears before him under oath.

The judge's opportunity to personally evaluate the credibility of the source who claims he made the observations distinguishes non-hearsay cases from hearsay situations. Even if the affiant is a professional tipster, it is unnecessary that the affidavit contain data establishing a record of reliability. The issuing magistrate can assess credibility by scrutinizing the demeanor of the affiant and, if he chooses, by requiring the affiant orally respond to questions under oath before determining whether to issue the warrant.

Once the magistrate decides that the affiant is credible, then he need only decide whether the non-hearsay affiant's observations add up to probable cause. In the words of *Dawson*, what is left to evaluate is the "logic of a proposition." Case opinions which explain the difference between hearsay probable cause and non-hearsay probable cause include People v. O'Neal, 40 Ill.App.3d 448, 352 N.E.2d 282 (1976); State v. Collins, 317 So.2d 846 (Fla.App.1975) cert. denied 330 So.2d 16 (Fla.1976), and Skelton v. Superior Court, 1 Cal.3d 144, 81 Cal.Rptr. 613, 460 P.2d 485 (1969).

Suppose that a professional tipster contacts the police and alleges that he saw certain specified occurrences which, if they really happened, would provide probable cause. Suppose further that the tipster has no past record of reliability. Also, to avoid problems with one prong of the *Aguilar* test, the officers avoid the use of hearsay, have the tipster sign the affidavit, and allow the issuing magistrate to decide whether the tipster is credible; to protect the source's identity, however, the tipster merely signs the affidavit "John Doe." Is there anything constitutionally impermissible about this? Compare United States ex rel. Pugh v. Pate, 401 F.2d 6 (7th Cir. 1968), with People v. Stansberry, 47 Ill.2d 541, 268 N.E.2d 431 (1971). Is use of the "John Doe" affidavit—where the source personally appears before the magistrate—a greater threat to liberty and privacy than the use of unnamed hearsay sources in affidavits? Do any dangers exist in the latter case that do not exist in the former?

(b) Hearsay Sources

The Professional Tipster. If a police officer is to make an arrest based upon the claimed observations of a professional tipster, such as an addict-informant, *facts* known to the police must establish the reliability of the tipster. Similarly, if a warrant is to issue based upon such a tipster's alleged firsthand information, and if the tipster is not the affiant but rather is a hearsay declarant, *facts* made known to the magistrate must demonstrate the tipster's reliability. Granted that the affiant's sworn declaration that the tipster is "reliable" will not suffice, how much more is necessary? Will an assertion that the source "gave reliable information in the past" suffice? Compare People v. Parker, 42 Ill.2d 42, 245 N.E.2d 487 (1968), with State v. Ebron, 61 N.J. 207, 294 A.2d 1 (1972).

Reliability of a tipster is often established by an allegation in the affidavit that on a specified number of occasions the tipster gave information to the police about criminal activity, which information the police investigated and found to be true. Is a source who has proved his reliability in one area of criminal activity reliable for probable cause purposes when he gives information in another area? See State v. Comeau, 114 N.H. 431, 321 A.2d 590 (1974).

The Citizen Informant. A different rationale exists for establishing the reliability of named "citizen-informers" as opposed to the traditional idea of unnamed police contacts or informers who usually themselves are criminals. Information supplied to officers by the traditional police informer is not given in the spirit of a concerned citizen, but often is given in exchange for some concession, payment, or simply out of revenge against the subject. The nature of these persons and the information which they supply convey a certain impression of unreliability, and it is proper to demand that some evidence of their credibility and reliability be shown. One practical way of making such a showing is to point to accurate information which they have supplied in the past.

However, an ordinary citizen who reports a crime which has been committed in his presence, or that a crime is being or will be committed, stands on much different ground that a police informer. He is a witness to criminal activity who acts with an intent to aid the police in law enforcement because of his concern for society or for his own safety. He does not expect any gain or concession in exchange for his information. An informer of this type usually would not have more than one opportunity to supply information to the police, thereby precluding proof of his reliability by pointing to previous accurate information which he has supplied.

It would be unreasonable to demand the same showing of prior reliability in the case of such an informer as in the case of a "traditional police informer." Rather, the reliability of such a person should be evaluated from the nature of his report, his opportunity to hear and see the matters reported, and the extent to which it can be verified by independent police investigation. State v. Paszek, 50 Wis.2d 619, 184 N.W.2d 836 (1971). See also United States v. Mahler, 442 F.2d 1172, 1174–75 (9th Cir. 1971) (crime victim is presumed reliable).

Consult Thompson and Starkman, The Citizen Informant Rule, 64 J. Crim.L. & C. 163 (1973).

Named and Anonymous Sources. In *Dawson* Judge Moylan distinguished named hearsay sources from unnamed sources and noted that naming a source may go a long way toward establishing reliability. Actually there may be several categories of sources in such a classification system. A source's identity may be unknown to the police, as in the case of an anonymous telephone caller. Such a person's word is not presumed reliable. If the police ever are justified in acting upon the tip of such a source, it is because in some situations emergency action may obviate the need for full probable cause. See, e. g., In re Boykin, 39 Ill.2d 617, 237 N.E.2d 460 (1968).

Information may be personally conveyed to an officer by someone whose name is unknown to the officer and who quickly disappears. Alternatively, the name of a source may be known to the officer but kept secret from the judicial officer, as in the typical unnamed hearsay-declarant affidavit, or in a hearing following a warrantless arrest where the prosecutor invokes the informer privilege. Finally, the identity of the hearsay source may be revealed in the affidavit or, following a warrantless arrest, may be revealed at the motion to suppress. The presumption of reliability is increased in this progression of examples. See State v. Northness, 20 Wash. App. 551, 582 P.2d 546 (1978).

If the name of the hearsay source is to be revealed in the affidavit, would it make more sense if the police had the source serve as the affiant so as to eliminate the need to establish the reliability of a hearsay source? Consider the case of People v. Lindner, 24 Ill.App.3d 995, 322 N.E.2d 229 (1975), where the court held that the naming of a certain prisoner as the source of certain information was insufficient to establish the prisoner's reliability. If the prisoner had appeared before a magistrate, had sworn to the truth of his allegations, and had been believed by the magistrate, a valid warrant could have issued.

The Fellow Officer. Officer X is safe in relying upon the claimed personal observations of Officer Y as long as those observations, if true, add up to probable cause. When the hearsay source is a fellow officer, there is a presumption of reliability. See Brooks v. United States, 416 F.2d 1044 (5th Cir. 1969).

The Declarant Against Interest. If A confesses to a known burglary and states that the proceeds are in his own garage, the police may relate A's confession to a magistrate through an officer's affidavit and thereby establish probable cause. The law presumes that A will not falsely make declarations against his own interest. Many cases extend the presumption of reliability to the portion of A's confession which implicates an alleged accomplice. Thus B may be arrested based upon A's unsworn confession implicating both A and B in an offense. See United States v. Long, 449 F.2d 288 (8th Cir. 1971).

Sometimes declarations against interest are made to government agents unwittingly. Thus if conspirator A, in his conversations with an undercover government agent, reveals that conspirator B has the weapons to be used in a bank robbery, A's declarations may be presumed to be reliable, either as declarations against interest or as declarations of a conspirator in furtherance of a conspiracy. See Thompson v. State, 16 Md.App. 560, 298 A.2d 458 (1973). The Supreme Court gave support to the declaration-against-interest theory of reliability in probable cause determinations when, in United States v. Harris, 403 U.S. 573, 91 S.Ct. 2075 (1971), it extended the concept quite far. See also United States v. Matlock, 415 U.S. 164, 94 S.Ct. 988 (1974).

When a person is caught with contraband, admits guilt and alleges that X was his supplier, do authorities have probable cause to arrest X? Does either the declaration against interest theory or anything else suggest that the accusation is trustworthy? See Commonwealth v. Reisinger, 252 Pa.Super. 1, 380 A.2d 1250 (1977). Compare State v. Appleton, 297 A.2d 363 (Me.1972).

Computers and Other Non-Human Sources. The reliability of a computer obviously depends upon the reliability of the data input. Frequently police officers rely upon computers in either making warrantless arrests or in applying for arrest or search warrants. The real issue in such cases is how extensive must the information, presented under oath to the judicial officer, be in an individual case before the reliability of a computer is established. If a car rental company's computer indicates that a particular car rented by X is thirty days' overdue, can that information be relied upon in a car theft-investigation without a showing as to when or by whom the information was placed in the computer? Are certain standard law enforcement data banks presumptively reliable? See United States v. Wilson, 479 F.2d 936 (7th Cir. 1973) (en banc), and United States v. Williams, 459 F.2d 44 (9th Cir. 1972).

If a police officer relied upon radar or a "speed gun" in deciding that a driver violated a traffic law, and if the validity of the arrest is at issue, must the prosecutor at the probable cause hearing demonstrate the reliability of the equipment? See People v. Leverenz, 55 Ill.App.3d 146, 12 Ill. Dec. 866, 370 N.E.2d 670 (1977). If a drug enforcement officer used a specially trained dog to sniff out marijuana, to what extent must the dog's training and experience be established by data presented under oath before the dog will be considered a reliable source for probable cause purposes? See United States v. Venema, 563 F.2d 1003 (10th Cir. 1977).

3. Additional Probable Cause Issues

(a) Probable Cause for What?

"Probable cause for arrest" refers to the probability that a crime has been committed—*crime probable cause*—and the probability that the particular suspect committed it—*offender probable cause*. "Probable cause for a search warrant" refers to the probability that a crime has been committed (crime probable cause)—and the probability that evidence of that crime is located at the place to be searched—*search probable cause*. In other situations, for example, as to plain view seizures, to be subsequently discussed in Section H of the chapter, probable cause refers to the probability that an item to be seized is either contraband or constitutes evidence of a crime—*seizure probable cause*. This classification system for the various types of probable cause is explored in Haddad, Well-Delineated Exceptions,

Claims of Sham, and Fourfold Probable Cause, 68 J.C.L. & Crim. 198, 214–224 (1977).

(b) A Special Problem Concerning "Crime Probable Cause"

Can the police ever have probable cause to believe that a crime has been committed without having knowledge of a specific offense or a particular victim? Consider the following from People v. Georgev, 38 Ill.2d 165, 230 N.E.2d 851 (1967):

> "We deem that the circumstances here reasonably indicated to the lone officer who stopped the defendant's car that he had probable cause to believe he was confronted with a crime other than the simple automobile regulatory violations. The auto the accused occupied was 'running with fictitious plates,' as the officer testified. The defendant and Cantu each claimed to have been the driver of the auto. The defendant did not have any driver's license and Cantu did not have a valid one. The officer observed rolls of coins on the floor of the auto and an adding machine on the rear seat of the car, partially covered by a coat. It was 2:00 A.M. Considering all of the circumstances surrounding the officer's encounter with the defendant and Cantu, the officer as a reasonably prudent person was justified in the belief that a crime, such as auto theft, burglary or knowing possession of stolen property, had been committed and that evidence confirming such belief could be found in the auto occupied by the defendant and Cantu. The search's validity was not impaired by the fact that the officer did not know of the specific offense that the search might disclose."

(c) Special Problems Concerning "Search Probable Cause"

For a valid search warrant to issue, there must be probable cause to believe that evidence named in the warrant is present at the place to be searched. Similarly, because search probable cause is required under the warrantless vehicle search doctrine (treated subsequently in Section L of this chapter), there must be a probability that contraband or evidence of the crime will be discovered. The probabilities will vary from factual situation to factual situation, but some patterns recur.

An affidavit may recite facts that demonstrate the reliability of a hearsay source and then recite the source's claimed personal observations but neglect to say when the source claimed that these observations occurred. If the source saw certain criminal evidence in an apartment an hour before the affidavit was presented to the magistrate, search probable cause will exist. If the observations were three years ago, there most likely is no probable cause to believe that the items are now in the place to be searched. The affidavit just does not say. Should there be a presumption that the information is fresh? See Dean v. State, 46 Ala.App. 365, 242 So.2d 411 (1970); Commonwealth v. Simmons, 450 Pa. 624, 301 A.2d 819 (1973). Compare State v. Boudreaux, 304 So.2d 343 (La.1974).

Ordinarily the date of the observations will be stated in the affidavit. Then the question is whether the passage of time between the observation of the criminal evidence and the issuance of the warrant will raise the question as to whether probable cause still existed at the time of issuance. This may depend on a variety of factors. Obviously, a single observation of a small quantity of marijuana in an apartment will be insufficient to create a probability that marijuana will be there a month later. On the other hand, repeated observations of the use in a business of certain stolen machines may create a probability that such machines are still in the same place many months after the latest observation.

Sometimes no source will have claimed that he saw criminal evidence in the place to be searched. The issue then is whether circumstantial evidence creates probable cause. For example, police officers may have probable cause to believe that *A* committed a burglary, that several valuable pieces of jewelry were taken and that *A* resides at a certain address. Do they have probable cause to believe that the stolen articles are hidden or kept in *A's home*? Most courts adopt the principle that a suspect's own home may be searched, and also accept the principle that "evidence of [a suspect's] continued presence or, at least, of frequent visits [will mark] the premises as a logical target for a search warrant, despite . . . lack of a possessory interest in the premises". Commonwealth v. DeMasi, 362 Mass. 53, 283 N.E. 2d 845 (1972). Some courts reject this principle. See United States v. Flanigan, 423 F.2d 745 (5th Cir. 1970). The issue is not fully settled. In United States v. Bailey, 458 F.2d 408 (9th Cir. 1972) the court was faced with this problem: In writing for the majority, Judge Hufstedler held:

> "The affidavit in support of the search of the house is no better than the affidavit for the automobile warrant. The affidavit simply discloses that Bailey had been seen at the house and that Cochran was arrested there. No facts are recited from which it could be inferred that Bailey and Cochran were other than casual social guests at the residence. At the trial, there was evidence that Bailey and Cochran had leased the house, but that fact was not before the issuing magistrate.

> " 'All data necessary to show probable cause for the issuance of a search warrant must be contained within the four corners of a written affidavit given under oath.'

> "In short, there is nothing but conjecture to sustain the conclusion that the house contained the objects of the search. As we observed in United States v. Lucarz (9th Cir. 1970) 430 F.2d 1051, 1055:

> " '[Simply from the existence of probable cause to believe a suspect guilty, [it does not follow in all cases] that there is also probable cause to search his residence. If that were so, there would be no reason to distinguish search warrants from arrest warrants, and cases like Chimel v. California, . . . would make little sense.' "

In dissent, Judge Kilkenny wrote:

> "The affidavit supporting the issuance of the warrant for the search of the home reveals that appellant's female co-conspirator in the bank robbery, the lady who used the large brown manila envelope to carry the money obtained in the robbery, was arrested at 2256 E. Prince Road, Tucson, Arizona. The affidavit reveals that the home had been under surveillance for some time and that appellant was observed in the premises on April 23, 1971, and at other subsequent times prior to the arrest. The affidavit clearly sets forth the joint activities of appellant and the female co-conspirator immediately prior to and at the time of the robbery. From the facts stated in the affidavit, the Magistrate could reasonably infer: (1) that appellant or his co-conspirator, or both, were occupy-

ing the premises; (2) that as occupants, they might well have concealed on the premises a portion of the fruits of the robbery or the clothing which they wore at the time; and (3) probable cause existed for the issuance of the warrant. The logic employed by our court in *Lucarz,* supra, is here of particular significance. I quote from the opinion:

> " 'The affidavit demonstrated the theft of the sort of materials that one would expect to be hidden at appellant's place of residence, both because of their value and bulk.'

> "The affidavit should be interpreted in a common sense and realistic manner, United States v. Ventresca, and the warrant should issue when a man of reasonable caution would be of the belief that the items to be seized were in a particular location."

Sometimes the facts will include both (1) a passage of time between the reported criminal activity, and (2) no claim that anyone ever actually saw the particular evidence in the known offender's home. Again the ultimate test is whether at the time of the issuance of the warrant (or, if no warrant is required, at the time of the search) there was probable cause to believe that evidence was at the place to be searched. For a remarkable case, see People v. Mason, 15 Ill.App.3d 404, 304 N.E.2d 466 (1973), where the court held that 107 days after the last observation there was still probable cause to search the offender's home for a stolen credit card even though no one had actually ever seen such in his home.

Offender probable cause is not essential for the issuance of a search warrant. A person not suspected of a crime may have his privacy invaded if there is probable cause to believe that a crime has been committed and that evidence of that crime is on his property. Zurcher v. Stanford Daily, 436 U.S. 547, 98 S.Ct. 1970 (1978). However, cases like *Mason* suggest that where there is offender probable cause, some courts will be quicker to approve a search under a warrant for evidence of the suspect's offense.

One search probable cause question arises when an officer, following a traffic stop, smells the odor of burned marijuana. Does this, by itself, create a probability that a search of the vehicle will yield contraband or evidence of a crime? See State v. Schoendaller, —— Mont. ——, 578 P.2d 730 (1978), expressing what is probably a minority viewpoint, that probable cause to search is not present under these circumstances, absent additional data. Compare State v. Ruzicka, 202 Neb. 257, 274 N.W.2d 873 (1979).

Another search probable question is whether a warrant can issue where there is probable cause to believe that at some future time evidence will be at a specified place. (Anticipatory warrants will be subsequently discussed in Section C of this chapter).

(d) Imputed Knowledge

Sometimes Officer *A* will act at the direction of Officer *B* without pausing to learn what data *B* has in his or her possession. The classic example is a patrol officer's response to a directive received over a police radio. From *A*'s point of view, it may seem reasonable to do what he is told without pausing to learn of the underlying data. However, when the matter is litigated, as for example at a hearing on a motion to suppress following a warrantless arrest by *A,* the prosecution must prove that within the knowledge of someone in the police department were data personally observed by an officer or information from a credible source which added up to probable cause. Sometimes courts say that what is known to one officer is, for probable cause purposes, known by all under the doctrine of "imputed knowledge."

If Officer *C* happens to know something which would help establish probable cause to arrest *X* but never communicates that information to anyone and never directs or requests any action, can such data be used to support probable cause following Officer *D*'s warrantless arrest of *X*? Should *C*'s knowledge be imputed to *D* in such a case? See State v. Mickelson, 18 Or.App. 647, 526 P.2d 583 (1974); Commonwealth v. Hawkins, 361 Mass. 384, 280 N.E.2d 665 (1972). Compare State v. Pruitt, 479 S.W.2d 785 (Mo.1972).

Sometimes the imputed knowledge doctrine is invoked where an officer in one jurisdiction acts at the direction of an officer in another jurisdiction. But, again, the underlying probable cause data must be brought out at the hearing on the motion to suppress. Police Department # 1 cannot insulate an arrest from probable cause scrutiny by asserting that it acted at the direction of Department # 2. Whiteley v. Warden, 401 U.S. 560, 91 S. Ct. 1031 (1971), may be viewed an example of the failure to prove up probable cause data in an imputed knowledge case, although that issue was not the focus of the decision.

4. The Probable Cause Standard

Both of the foregoing principal cases of *Draper* and *Beck* refer to the general standard by which the existence of probable cause is judged. Consider in connection with those cases the following additional observations in Browne v. State, 24 Wis.2d 491, 129 N.W.2d 175, 180 (1964):

> "Probable cause to arrest refers to the quantum of evidence which would lead a reasonable man to believe that the defendant probably committed a crime. While the standard is objective . . . it is not necessary that the evidence be sufficient to prove ultimate guilt beyond a reasonable doubt or even that it be sufficient to prove that guilt is more probable than not. It is only necessary that the information lead a reasonable officer to believe that guilt is more than a possibility."

Also consider this judicial language:

> "Probable cause . . . is to be viewed from the vantage point of a prudent, reasonable, cautious police officer on the scene at the time of the arrest guided by his experience and training. . . . It is 'a plastic concept whose existence depends on the facts and circumstances of the particular case' . . . Because of the kaleidoscopic myriad that goes into the probable cause mix 'seldom does a decision in one case handily dispose of the next' . . . It is however, the totality of these facts and circumstances which is the relevant consideration. . . . Viewed singly these factors may not be dispositive, yet when viewed in unison the puzzle may fit." United States v. Davis, 458 F.2d 819, 821 (D.C.Cir. 1972).

See Davis v. United States, 409 F.2d 458, 460 (D.C.Cir. 1969), cert. denied 395 U.S. 949, 89 S.Ct. 2031 (1969). ("conduct innocent in the eyes of the untrained may carry entirely different 'messages' to the experienced or trained observer").

See also Houser v. Geary, 465 F.2d 193, 196 (9th Cir. 1972) (with respect to mistaken inferences as the basis for police action, the Court held "The inferences might be wrong in fact, but they are . . . more reasonable than not and that is enough for probable cause").

In Hill v. California, 401 U.S. 797, 91 S.Ct. 1106 (1971), the Supreme Court dealt with a mistaken identity arrest (in a robbery case):

> "Based on our own examination of the record, we find no reason to disturb either the findings of the California courts that the police had probable cause to arrest Hill and that the arresting officers had a reasonable, good faith belief that the arrestee Miller was in fact Hill, or the conclusion that '[w]hen the police have probable cause to arrest one party, and when they reasonably mistake a second party for the first party, then the arrest of the second party is a valid arrest.' The police unquestionably had probable cause to arrest Hill; they also had his address and a verified description. The mailbox at the indicated address listed Hill as the occupant of the apartment. Upon gaining entry to the apartment, they were confronted with one who fit the description of Hill received from various sources. That person claimed he was Miller, not Hill. But aliases and false identifications are not uncommon. Moreover, there was a lock on the door and Miller's explanation for his mode of entry was not convincing. He also denied knowledge of firearms in the apartment although a pistol and loaded ammunition clip were in plain view in the room. The upshot was that the officers in good faith believed Miller was Hill and arrested him. They were quite wrong as it turned out, and subjective good-faith belief would not in itself justify either the arrest or the subsequent search. But sufficient probability, not certainty, is the touchstone of reasonableness under the Fourth Amendment and on the record before us the officers' mistake was understandable and the arrest a reasonable response to the situation facing them at the time.
>
> "Nor can we agree with petitioner that however valid the arrest of Miller, the subsequent search violated the Fourth Amendment. It is true that Miller was not Hill; nor did Miller have authority or control over the premises, although at the very least he was Hill's guest. But the question is not what evidence would have been admissible against Hill (or against Miller for that matter) if the police, with probable cause to arrest Miller, had arrested him in Hill's apartment and then carried out the search at issue. Here there was probable cause to arrest Hill and the police arrested Miller in Hill's apartment reasonably believing him to be Hill. In these circumstances the police were entitled to do what the law would have allowed them to do if Miller had in fact been Hill, that is, to search incident to arrest and to seize evidence of the crime the police had probable cause to believe Hill had committed. When judged in accordance with 'the factual and practical considerations of everyday life on which reasonable and prudent men, not legal technicians, act' the arrest and subsequent search were reasonable and valid under the Fourth Amendment."

Suppose that a police officer, because of his erroneous understanding of a particular penal statute, believes that certain facts known to him constitute a violation of the law. Does he have probable cause to arrest? See People v. Teresinski, 78 Cal.App.3d 322, 144 Cal.Rptr. 257 (1978), for a decision which favors the prosecution in this situation. Suppose that the facts known to constitute a violation of the statute, but long after the officer makes the arrest, the penal statute is held to be unconstitutional. Was the arrest based on probable cause? Michigan v. De Fillippo, 443 U.S. 31, 99 S.Ct. 2627 (1979), answered that question affirmatively.

5. Miscellaneous Probable Cause Factors

Hundreds of decisions assign greater or lesser weight to certain factors frequently relied upon to establish probable cause, particularly in warrantless arrest cases: flight, furtive gestures, presence in the company of a known offender at or near the time of his offense, false or contradictory answers to police questions and the like. For every case giving weight to such a factor, there is likely to be another cautioning against according too much weight to such a factor. For example, the Supreme Court in Wong Sun v. United States, 371 U.S. 471, 83 S.Ct. 407 (1963), deprecated the value of flight (at the sight of a police officer) in the probable cause calculation although hundreds of decisions, including a few Supreme Court cases, have used flight as a factor helping to establish probable cause. The following factual situations are cited as examples of courts' efforts to assign proper weight to various factors.

Assuming that it is permissible for the police to *ask* questions of citizens, United States v. Brown, 436 F.2d 702 (9th Cir. 1970), it is clear that the citizen does not have to *answer* them. Loyd v. Douglas, 313 F.Supp. 1364 (S.D.Iowa 1970). A citizen's refusal to answer does not give rise to probable cause to arrest, but if he does answer and his answers are evasive, contradictory or patently false they may be considered as elements contributing to the existence of probable cause. In *Hill*, the Court thought the suspect's evasive answers helped the police to establish probable cause to arrest. Consider the following situation in People v. Rosemond, 26 N.Y.2d 101, 257 N.E.2d 23 (1970):

"On January 4, 1966, while on a motor patrol, a policeman observed defendant and another man enter, empty-handed, an apartment building at 102 Patchen Avenue, Brooklyn. This was at 12:10 p. m. The patrol continued around the block and came back to the Patchen Avenue address a short time later.

"At this time the officer saw defendant and his companion coming out of the building, one carrying a plaid zippered suitcase, the other a plaid plastic shopping bag. The officer followed them until they started to enter a hallway around the corner from the place where they were first seen.

"The officer testified: 'At that time . . . I approached them. I asked the defendant, Rosemond, what did he have in the package. He said he didn't know.'

* * *

"The police can and should find out about unusual situations they see, as well as suspicious ones. It is unwise, and perhaps futile, to codify them or to prescribe them precisely in advance as a rule of law. To a very large extent what is unusual enough to call for inquiry must rest in the professional experience of the police.

"But reasonable ground to suspect a felony goes forward should not be the sole criterion on which inquiry may be activated. Nor is inquiry interdicted even though most of what it elicits may be quite innocent.

"For example, men carrying a cash register out of a grocery store may very well be taking it out for repair; but they may not; and under conditions of manner and attitude difficult to lay down categorically, police would be quite warranted in finding out by asking questions.

* * *

"In the background of what the police had observed immediately before the answers given would have made it perfectly manifest to anyone that a criminal enterprise was afoot.

* * *

"From the moment the defendant Rosemond made the highly suggestive sort of answer that he did not know what he had in the bag he had just carried out of the house, there was reasonable ground to arrest him and his companion at least for larceny, since then the situation became clear and a larceny was probable."

See also Commonwealth v. DeFlemingue, 450 Pa. 163, 299 A.2d 246 (1973).

If a suspect may refuse to answer questions and his refusal to respond cannot be used to establish probable cause for arrest, what can be said of the situation of a suspect who flees when he sees the police? Consider and compare the following cases:

(a) In re Harvey, 222 Pa.Super. 222, 295 A.2d 93, 94–95 (1972):

"On January 3, 1972, Officers Roberts and Stevenson were patrolling the area of Woodstock and Norris Streets in an unmarked police vehicle. According to Officer Roberts' testimony, the officers were assigned to that area '. . . specifically to try to curb the number of gang shootings which had taken place in the area, and also the shooting of residents and bystanders to these gang activities.' At approximately 8:55 p. m. the officers were proceeding west on Norris Street, approaching Woodstock Street, when they observed three young males, including appellant, going north on Woodstock from Norris. Officer Roberts testified that the police vehicle was brought to a stop and both officers approached the three males on foot 'for investigation.' The officer then stated that 'the defendant appeared to move away from the other two boys.' The officer then called to appellant, and when appellant approached the officer, appellant was pulled by his coat and belt. The officer stated that he felt an object inside appellant's left coat pocket. Officer Roberts then 'frisked' appellant and seized a revolver.

* * *

"In the instant case the police officers, when seizing appellant, had no information that he was committing any illegal acts, or that he was armed and dangerous. The officers had no information that either appellant or his companions were members of a gang or were involved in a gang incident. At the time appellant was seized, there was nothing in appellant's conduct from which the officer could reasonably infer that criminal activity was afoot and that appellant was armed. Appellant's failure to immediately heed the officer's command to stop was not sufficient to justify the officer's touching and holding of appellant."

(b) People v. Siegenthaler, 7 Cal.3d 465, 499 P.2d 499, 500–02 (1972):

"The record . . . discloses that at 2:45 a. m. officers in a marked police vehicle stopped at an intersection in Los Angeles. One of the officers observed three men on foot who after looking in the direction of the vehicle, immediately ran off in the opposite direction. The officers were in a commercial area where there had been many burglaries of business establishments although they were not aware that any particular burglary had recently taken place. They nevertheless pursued the men and saw some discard objects which on examination proved to be a business-type checkbook and a checkwriter. The officers continued the pursuit and apprehended the three men, one of whom was defendant.

"The abandoned checkbook bore the name of the Ideal Brush Company at a nearby address. An investigation at that address was conducted by other officers who reported that the premises appeared to have been recently burglarized.

"Defendant was observed late at night in a commercial area where there had been a high incidence of burglaries. His only inducement to flee, insofar as appears, was the appearance of a marked police vehicle and police officers who took notice of defendant and his companions. In no way could defendant claim that the officers infringed any right which induced defendant's actions. . . . Nevertheless he fled and in doing so discarded evidence which, together with the flight and other circumstances, would necessarily lead a prudent man to conscientiously entertain a strong suspicion that defendant and his companions had committed a burglary . . . the officers were thus armed with probable cause for his arrest. . . ."

C. THE ISSUANCE OF WARRANTS

For a warrant to be valid there must be compliance with the second clause of the Fourth Amendment: " . . . no warrants shall issue, but upon probable cause, supported by oath or affirmation and particularly describing the place to be searched, and the person or things to be seized." Most doctrines governing the issuance of warrants are derived from this clause, although occasionally the requirement of "reasonableness" from the Amendment's first clause might be invoked to limit the issuance of search warrants.

We have already considered the probable cause requirement in the preceding Section B; now we shall consider some of the other requirements and limitations upon the issuance of search warrants.

NOTES

1. The Issuance Requirements

(a) Neutral Judicial Officer

Warrants may be issued only by neutral judicial officers. The centrality of the warrant requirement is premised upon the belief that the right of citizens to be free from unreasonable searches will be better protected if the assessment of probable cause is made by a judicial officer who is not in the competitive business of enforcing the criminal law. Thus, in Coolidge v. New Hampshire, 403 U.S. 443, 91 S.Ct. 2022 (1971), to be discussed in Section H, the Court invalidated a warrant issued by the state Attorney General (in his capacity as an *ex officio* justice of the peace), in a case where the Attorney General himself had directed the investigation. Similarly in Lo-Ji Sales, Inc. v. New York, 442 U.S. 319, 99 S.Ct. 2319 (1979), a magistrate who went to the scene of the search and performed as if he were the supervising investigative officer was held not be be sufficiently detached. The problem often arises in the armed services, where company commanders have the power to issue warrants. If such commanders play the role of "police officer" in the investigation, they are not sufficiently neutral. United States v. Ezell, 6 M.J. 307 (C.M.A.1979). On the other hand, if neutrality is preserved, the "judicial officer" need not be a judge or magistrate. He can be a court clerk. Shadwick v. City of Tampa, 407 U.S. 345, 92 S.Ct. 2119 (1972). The latter case, contrasted with *Coolidge*, demonstrates that "detachment," not learnedness in the law, underlies the neutral judicial officer requirement. See also Connally v. Georgia, 429 U.S. 245, 97 S.Ct. 546 (1977), where neutrality was lacking because the officer received a fee if he issued the warrant, received no fee if he issued no warrant, and he had issued thousands of warrants without ever refusing to issue one.

A major premise of the neutrality requirement (and of the law's preference for the use of warrants) is that the judicial officer will *not* simply defer to the judgment of the law enforcement officer who presents the complaint for a warrant, together with the proposed warrant for the magistrate's signature. Rather, the magistrate will carefully review the affidavits or sworn oral testimony and will make an independent assessment of probable cause.

Perhaps because there are few empirical studies, little about actual practice is reflected in reported cases, even though many lawyers believe that the magistrate who carefully reviews a warrant application is the exception rather than the rule. Occasionally claims are raised that in the particular case the magistrate did not even read the supporting affidavits. See State v. Dudick, —— W.Va. ——, 213 S.E.2d 458 (1975); Rooker v. Commonwealth, 508 S.W.2d 570 (Ky.App.1974), both of which suggest that the warrant is invalid if such an allegation is proved. Compare Clodfelter v. Commonwealth, 218 Va. 98, 235 S.E.2d 340 (1977), which suggested that a two-minute review is not presumptively inadequate. Usually the only witnesses to the issuance of a search warrant are a law enforcement officer and the issuing magistrate. (A few empirical studies are cited in LaFave, Search and Seizure, § 4.2 (1978).)

(b) Oral or Written Sworn Probable Cause Data: Personal Appearance of Affiant?

As indicated in the preceding Section B, probable cause data must be presented under oath to the issuing magistrate before issuance of a warrant. Although the Fourth Amendment has been interpreted to allow the use of sworn oral data, the normal practice is to use affidavits in applying for a search warrant.

Some jurisdictions have special procedures for the use of telephonic applications for search warrants. Fed.R.Crim.Pro. 41 now allows such a procedure. Other such provisions are found in the laws of certain states. Consider, for example:

Arizona Rev.Stat., § 13–3914

    A. The migistrate may, before issuing the warrant, examine on oath the person or persons, seeking the warrant, and any witnesses produced, and must take his affidavit, or their affidavits, in writing, and cause the same to be subscribed by the party or parties making the affidavit. The magistrate may also, before issuing the warrant, examine any other sworn affidavit submitted to him which sets forth facts tending to establish probable cause for the issuance of the warrant.

B.   The affidavit or affidavits must set forth the facts ending to establish the grounds of the application, or probable cause for believing they exist.

C.   In lieu of, or in addition to, a written affidavit, or affidavits, as provided in subsection A, the magistrate may take an oral statement under oath which shall be recorded on tape, wire, or other comparable method. This statement may be given in person to the magistrate, or by telephone, radio, or other means of electronic communication. This statement shall be deemed to be an affidavit for the purposes of issuance of a search warrant. In such cases if a recording of the sworn statement has been made, the magistrate shall direct that the statement be transcribed and certified by the magistrate and filed with the court.

Arizona Rev.Stat., § 13–3915(c)

C.   The magistrate may orally authorize a peace officer to sign the magistrate's name on a search warrant if the peace officer applying for the warrant is not in the actual physical presence of the magistrate. This warrant shall be called a duplicate original search warrant and shall be deemed a search warrant for the purposes of this chapter. In such cases, the magistrate shall cause to be made an original warrant and shall enter the exact time of issuance of the duplicate original warrant on the face of the original warrant. Upon the return of the duplicate original warrant, the magistrate shall cause the original warrant and the duplicate original warrant to be filed as provided for in § 13–3923.

When affidavits are used, the magistrate must make a judgment about the credibility of the affiant, as pointed out in the proceeding Section B. This suggests that the affiant must appear before the issuing magistrate (or at least communicate telephonically with the magistrate). Nevertheless, Federal Rule 41 allows, but does not require, the magistrate to insist upon the appearance of the affiant. Suppose that the police use a professional tipster as the affiant rather than a hearsay source, thus avoiding the need to establish within the affidavit itself the reliability of the tipster. How can the magistrate make a credibility judgment in such a situation without the opportunity to scrutinize the demeanor of the tipster-affiant?

(c) Fictitious Name Signatures

Reconsider the problem, already discussed in the preceeding Section B, of the affiant who uses an admittedly fictitious signature.

(d) Anticipatory Warrants

When reliable information indicates that contraband or criminal evidence is likely to be transported to a particular place in the near future, officers may wish to secure a search warrant for that place, to be executed after arrival of the evidence. To wait until the goods arrive may be too late, particularly if the criminals plan to quickly transport the goods elsewhere (as would be true in a common narcotics transaction). The law's preference for prior judicial evaluation of probable cause data has led *some* jurisdictions to approve use of anticipatory warrants based upon a kind of "future" search probable cause: a probability that evidence of a crime will soon be in the place to be searched. See F.R.Crim.P. 41. See also United States v. Lowe, 575 F.2d 1193 (6th Cir. 1978); People v. Wyatt, 60 A.D.2d 958, 401 N.Y.S.2d 890 (1978); State v. Mier, 147 N.J.Super. 17, 370 A.2d

515 (1977). Some warrant statutes, however, may be too narrow to permit issuance of a warrant absent a probability that criminal evidence *presently* is at the place to be searched.

2. Form of Warrant

Even when telephonic applications are used, the warrant itself is almost always a written instrument, which can serve as a notice to a property owner of the authority under which a search is to be made. But see State v. Cymerman, 135 N.J.Super. 591, 343 A.2d 825 (1975). A warrant may command a search to be made by a particular law enforcement agency or officer or, under different state law or custom, it may be directed to all peace officers in the county or state.

3. Specificity as to Place to Be Searched and Items to Be Seized

The place to be searched must be described with particularity. In the case of a single family residence this is usually done by giving the street address. In rural areas a rural route address may be given. In some cases a map may be incorporated into the warrant or a legal description (which is the surveyor's official description) of the property may be given. See United States v. Ortiz, 311 F.Supp. 880 (D.Colo.1970). Problems arise in cases involving multiple dwellings at a specific address. See People v. Avery, 173 Colo. 315, 478 P.2d 310 (1970). Often apartments do not have numbers and they should be described by location. Even this technique presents problems, for the police may not be able to secure an accurate description of the manner in which apartments are distributed. See United States v. Higgins, 428 F.2d 232 (7th Cir. 1970) (warrant for basement apartment in a building with three basement apartments). It may be advisable for officers to identify apartments by the name of the occupant if it is known, as well as apartment number or location.

Occasionally deficiencies occur in warrant descriptions. When the affidavit or complaint for the warrant contains a complete description the courts will contrue the warrant and the affidavit together as one document and sustain the warrant. Moore v. United States, 461 F.2d 1236 (D.C.Cir. 1972) (warrant for entire second floor with several apartments is saved by the affidavit which mentioned a specific apartment). But see Giles v. State, 10 Md.App. 593, 271 A.2d 766 (1970). Some law enforcement officers will draft a warrant adding the specific statement that the material contained in the affidavit is incorporated in the warrant and made a part of the warrant.

Minor errors in street address are not always fatal, if the court can conclude that only one particular place is obviously referred to in the warrant and that the officers (who may well have conducted a surveillance of the place) could not have possibly been confused about the place to be searched. State v. Bisaccia, 58 N.J. 586, 279 A.2d 675 (1971); People v. Burrell, 8 Ill.App.3d 14, 288 N.E.2d 889 (1972); United States v. Sklaroff, 323 F.Supp. 296 (S.D.Fla.1971).

A warrant must specifically describe the items to be seized. A general warrant is constitutionally prohibited and a warrant which simply authorizes a search of a certain premises without specifying what is to be seized is invalid.

In determining what kind of description is sufficient, a rule of reason applies. "Gaming apparatus" may be sufficient, People v. Reid, 315 Ill. 597, 146 N.E. 504 (1925), while "stolen tires" may be insufficient, People v.

Prall, 314 Ill. 518, 145 N.E. 610 (1924), because the tires clearly can be described by reference to a brand name or perhaps even serial number. "Narcotics paraphernalia" is generally good enough. People v. Henry, 173 Colo. 523, 482 P.2d 357 (1971), but see State v. Stewart, 129 Vt. 175, 274 A.2d 500 (1971) (inadequate to authorize seizure of "contraband, to wit: regulated drugs"). Contraband generally need not be described in great detail. Steele v. United States, 267 U.S. 498, 45 S.Ct. 414 (1925); United States v. Sultan, 463 F.2d 1066 (2nd Cir. 1972) (warrant description of "various merchandise and assets of Sultan, Inc." is adequate).

On the other hand, when a case has First Amendment overtones, e. g., when allegedly obscene magazines are to be seized, a high degree of specificity is required. Marcus v. Search Warrant, 367 U.S. 717, 81 S.Ct. 1708 (1961).

Warrants commanding the seizure of personal or business documents, in the absence of enforcement of a stringent specificity requirement, may allow for a complete rummaging through papers. See McKenna, The Constitutional Protection of Private Papers: The Role of the Hierarchical Fourth Amendment, 53 Ind.L.J. 55 (1977). Nevertheless, in Andresen v. Maryland, infra Note 5, the Court refused to require particular exactitude in a warrant commanding the seizure of certain business records.

The specificity requirement is related to the probable cause requirement: there must be probable cause to believe that the particularly described item (not just some unspecified evidence of a particular crime) is at the place to be searched. This can be a problem in a case where the police have reason to believe that some clues, they know not what, may be found at the scene of a homicide. For cases which give the prosecution great leeway in this regard, see In re Search Warrant, 61 Ill.App.3d 99, 18 Ill.Dec. 437, 377 N.E.2d 1073 (1978), and People ex rel. Carey v. Covelli, 61 Ill.2d 394, 336 N.E.2d 759 (1975). The latter decision, in upholding the search of a safe at the home of the victim in quest of unspecified clues to his murder (over the objections of his survivors) seemed to read the specificity requirement out of the Fourth Amendment. It treated the more general question of whether it was "reasonable" to search the safe under all of the known circumstances.

4. Consequences of Overbreadth; Severability

Sometimes the command of the warrant clause may be divisible. For instance, the warrant commands the search of the house (for which there is probable cause) and the barn (for which there is not probable cause); or the warrant specifies designated items (which is proper) and then adds "and other items too numerous to mention." Does the overbreadth invalidate the entire warrant in such a case, or are searches and seizures within the confines of the "good" part of the warrant valid? Some decisions tend to uphold such searches. See People v. Holton, 326 Ill. 481, 158 N.E. 134 (1927); People v. Hellemeyer, 28 Ill.App.3d 491, 328 N.E.2d 626 (1975). In effect, these decisions proceed as if there were two warrants, one good and one bad. They uphold searches within the confines of the "good" warrant, and they strike down the "bad" warrant as surplusage, particularly where no search was made under its purported authority.

Most of the cases, unlike People v. Hicks, 49 Ill.App.3d 421, 7 Ill.Dec. 279, 364 N.E.2d 440 (1977), limit use of the severability principle to instances where the warrant is severable on its face: e. g., a warrant to search X and Y or a warrant to search Apartment 10 and Apartment 11, or to seize item A and all other evidence. To use the doctrine where the description is unitary, e. g., "the building at 10 Elm Street," is to leave the specificity requirement of the Fourth Amendment with very little vitality.

Leading cases on severability include People v. Hansen, 38 N.Y.2d 17, 339 N.E.2d 873 (1975); Aday v. Superior Court, 55 Cal.2d 789, 362 P.2d 47, 13 Cal.Rptr. 415 (1961). See also People v. Mangialino, 75 Misc.2d 698, 348 N.Y.S.2d 327 (1973); People v. Hass, 55 App.Div.2d 683, 390 N.Y.S.2d 202 (1976); State v. DeGraw, 26 Ariz.App. 595, 550 P.2d 641 (1976). Compare United States v. 63,250 Gallons of Beer, 13 F.2d 242 (D.Mass. 1926). As these cases indicate, some courts which recognize the principle of severability have developed elaborate tests for determining when the principle should be invoked.

5.   Items Which May Be Named for Seizure

Older warrant statutes sometimes specify items which can be named for seizure if there is probable cause, e. g., guns, narcotic paraphernalia, gambling instruments, etc. More modern statutes merely state that any evidence of a crime may be seized. Sometimes even under modern statutes a question arises as to whether a search warrant statute is broad enough to permit a search of a place in quest of a kidnap victim or an illegal alien. These are questions of state law without federal constitutional overtones. Nevertheless, from time to time certain constitutional issues have arisen concerning what may be named for seizure.

Once there was a constitutional principle which prohibited the use of search warrants to seize "mere evidence": items which were neither contraband, nor fruits of a crime, nor an instrumentality of a crime. The limitation was severely criticized by academic writers and, in actual practice, was eviscerated by courts which stretched the concept of "instrumentality" to great lengths in order to avoid the "mere evidence" prohibition. This limitation finally was eliminated in Warden v. Hayden, 387 U.S. 294, 87 S. Ct. 1642 (1967). Now "mere evidence" can be seized except in those jurisdictions whose warrant statutes are not broad enough to allow such seizures.

Occasionally a search warrant will issue for something even "lower" in status than "mere evidence." Exemplars (e. g., handwriting samples) may have no connection with a crime and yet could serve as evidence of guilt. Many search warrant statutes would appear to authorize their seizure. If authorities had made no effort to secure exemplars through other channels, however, would it be reasonable to issue a search warrant for a home upon a showing that such items, with potential evidentiary value, probably could be located in a suspect's home? If so, in a vast number of cases, under the guise of seeking exemplars, a prosecutor under a warrant could search many a suspect's home at almost any time.

Before Andresen v. Maryland, 427 U.S. 463, 96 S.Ct. 2737 (1976), courts were divided over whether documents could be seized under a search warrant if those same documents would be protected by a Fifth Amendment claim in the event that a subpoena duces tecum issued. The question was phrased: can the government get by warrant what it cannot get by subpoena? In *Andresen* the Supreme Court answered "Yes." The Fifth Amendment protection is not violated because no testimonial compulsion takes place when a search warrant issues. The documents in *Andresen* were not personal, such as a diary. This distinction was once deemed important by some courts. See Romanelli v. Commission, 466 F.2d 872 (7th Cir. 1972).

The rationale of *Andresen*, however, is not easily limited to business documents. Some courts have applied *Andresen* in cases involving personal papers. See People v. Superior Court, 137 Cal.Rptr. 391 (Cal.App.1977).

In Zurcher v. Stanford Daily, 436 U.S. 547, 98 S.Ct. 1970 (1978), the court held that there is no blanket immunity from seizure under a warrant for photographs (or presumably reporters' notes or other records) in the possession of a newspaper. Of course, the requirements of probable cause and specificity must be met. The court noted that the reasonableness requirement of the Fourth Amendment still might set some limits upon the issuance of such warrants. The *Zurcher* decision did not resolve the question of what effect a state shield law would have on the issuance of such a warrant. Under many shield laws, probable cause to believe that the material constitutes evidence of a crime will leave the material unprotected. Does a shield law, however, with its procedural safeguards, provide the exclusive means of securing evidence in a newspaper's possession? In many communities the issue is purely academic. No subpoena (much less a search warrant) has been directed at a media member, without his or her prior approval, by Cook County prosecutors in the last six years. Publicly elected prosecutors—who in many jurisdictions review warrant applications before the police officer goes before the magistrate—are usually not eager to offend the news media. Nevertheless, some states have already enacted statutes to limit the use of search warrants directed at media premises.

Could a warrant issue for documents which were protected under state law by a testimonial privilege? Consider this hypothetical. A client has written a letter to an attorney hired to defend him against possible charges arising out of a past business transaction. The letter details the client's role in the transaction and includes facts which, if true, make the client guilty. If the prosecutor could somehow establish the existence of such a letter in the lawyer's files, could a search warrant be issued for the letter?

6. Docketing the Warrant

Sometimes it is suggested that there should be a system of keeping track of unproductive warrants. One way of developing insights into our probable cause standards is to study statistics reflecting success and failure in the execution of search warrants. Some persons assert that the statutory obligation of the officer to fill a "return" will not be enough to accomplish the purpose. An officer may have little incentive to file a return if the search proves fruitless. Thus it is suggested that some numbering system be used which would account for all warrants within a fixed period of time after execution. The federal wiretap statute provides for such a system. See 18 U.S.C. §§ 2518(8)(b), (d), 2519. One court has rejected an argument that the reasonableness requirement of the Fourth Amendment requires such a system of docketing search warrants. See People v. Stansberry, 47 Ill.2d 541, 268 N.E.2d 431 (1971); People v. Price, 46 Ill.2d 209, 263 N.E.2d 484 (1970).

7. Additional Cross-References

Many doctrines pertaining to the issuance of search warrants are equally applicable to the issuance of arrest warrants. See infra Section E–3, note 4.

Concerning challenges to the truthfulness of facts stated in an affidavit in support of an application for a search warrant, see infra Ch. 13, Section H.

D.　THE EXECUTION OF SEARCH WARRANTS

The prohibition against unreasonable searches and seizures contained in the first clause of the Fourth Amendment places limits upon the manner of execution of search warrants. Added restrictions are sometimes found in the statutes or court rules of a particular jurisdiction.

NOTES

1.　Time Limits for Execution

The warrant itself will usually not contain specific requirements that a warrant be executed at any particular time. There are time limits applicable to warrants, but these limits are usually prescribed by statute or court rule and vary from jurisdiction to jurisdiction. See Rule 41(c), Fed.R. Crim.P. (10 days); Texas Crim.Proc. Code Ant. 18.07 (Vernon, 1977) (3 whole days exclusive of dates of issuance and execution); N.Y.Crim.Pro. Law, § 690.30 (McKinney 1971) (10 days); Ill.Rev.Stats., ch. 38, § 108–6 (96 hours).

Some jurisdictions have no express time limit other than a period which is "reasonable" under all the circumstances. Whether the named items can be expected to still be at the place to be searched is a factor in deciding whether a delay is reasonable. (Note the similarity to the "search probable cause" issue when a warrant is issued based upon dated information. See preceding Section B–3.) However, such factors as weather or road conditions and the need to prevent danger to an undercover agent have also been cited as relevant to the calculation of the reasonableness of the delay. See, e. g., United States v. Bedford, 519 F.2d 650 (3d Cir. 1975); Cabble v. State, 347 So.2d 546 (Ala.Crim.App.1977). Compare People v. Wiedeman, 324 Ill. 66, 154 N.E. 432 (1926); People v. Fetsko, 332 Ill. 110, 163 N.E. 359 (1928).

In theory a delay that does not exeed an express statutory period could still be unreasonable for Fourth Amendment purposes. See House v. United States, 411 F.2d 725 (D.C.Cir. 1969); United States v. Nepstead, 424 F. 2d 269 (9th Cir. 1970).

2.　Nighttime Execution

Some jurisdictions require that warrants be executed only in daylight hours unless special procedures are followed and the warrant specifies that nighttime execution is permissible. Among the special procedures are requirements of securing the signatures of two magistrates, of showing a need for prompt execution of the warrant, or of producing "positive" affidavits. The restrictive nighttime search rule is purely a matter of local or statutory law. However in his dissent in Gooding v. United States, 416 U. S. 430, 94 S.Ct. 1780 (1974), Mr. Justice Marshall suggested that the reasonableness requirement of the Fourth Amendment should be read to place limits upon the execution of warrants at night.

3.　Notice and "No-Knock"

The United States Supreme Court has never decided whether the Fourth Amendment requires notice of authority and purpose before an officer enters a building to execute a search warrant. Conversely, it has never said under what circumstances notice could be excused. The cases it has decided either interpret federal statutes or rules (Sabbath v. United States, 391 U.S. 585, 88 S.Ct. 1755 (1968); and Miller v. United States, 357 U.S. 301, 78 S.Ct. 1190 (1958)), or concern entry of a dwelling to effect a warrantless arrest. Ker v. California, 374 U.S. 23, 83 S.Ct. 1623 (1963). A 5-to-4 decision allowing a no-knock entry under exigent circumstances, *Ker* is not the definitive word on no-knock entries in the execution of search warrants.

Most jurisdictions, either by statute, court rule, or judicial decision do require that, absent exigent circumstances, the officer knock, allow adequate time for response, and properly identify himself and the purpose for which he has come. Special circumstances may excuse the use of "knock and announce" procedures. The real debate is over what circumstances should warrant a "no knock" entry. A majority of courts have held that the mere destructibility of evidence (heroin, gambling slips etc.) does not justify a no-knock entry. See Heaton v. Commonwealth, 215 Va. 137, 207 S.E.2d 829 (1974); People v. Gastelo, 67 Cal.2d 586, 63 Cal.Rptr. 10, 432 P.2d 706 (1967). More objective factors suggesting that on this particular occasion destruction is likely are required. United States v. Marshall, 488 F.2d 1169 (9th Cir. 1974).

The debate over no-knock procedures is impassioned. On the one hand, a no-knock entry into a home, particularly at night, is a gross intrusion on personal privacy. It also can cause confusion and generate violence. On the other hand, advanced warning of entry (particularly in the execution of narcotic warrants) has sometimes led to the death or the wounding of law enforcement officers. It is one thing for a court to mandate a procedure which makes it more difficult to catch criminals or recover evidence; it is another to mandate a procedure which officers perceive as endangering their lives.

In the last decade Congress passed and then *repealed* the following statute for use in the District of Columbia, which repeal reflected a belief that the "no knock" procedures themselves, as well as potential and actual abuses, threatened the privacy and security of the citizenry beyond anything justified by legitimate law enforcement needs:

Title 23, District of Columbia Code, Section 23–591

(a) Any officer authorized by law to make arrests, or to execute search warrants, or any person aiding such an officer, may break and enter any premises, any outer or inner door or window of a dwelling house or other building, or any part thereof, any vehicle, or anything within such dwelling house, building or vehicle, or otherwise enter to execute search or arrest warrants, to make an arrest where authorized by law without a warrant, or where authorized by law without a warrant, or where necessary to liberate himself or a person aiding him in the execution of such warrant or in making such arrest.

(b) Breaking and entry shall not be made until after such officer or person makes an announcement of his identity and purpose and the officer reasonably believes that admittance to the dwelling house or other building or vehicle is being denied or unreasonably delayed.

(c) An announcement of identity and purpose shall not be required prior to such breaking and entry—

(1) if the warrant expressly authorizes breaking and entry without such a prior announcement, or

(2) if circumstances known to such officer or person at the time of breaking and entry, but, in the case of the execution of a warrant, unknown to the applicant when applying for such warrant, give him probable cause to believe that—

(A) such notice is likely to result in the evidence subject to seizure being easily and quickly destroyed or disposed of,

(B) such notice is likely to endanger the life or safety of the officer or another person,

(C) such notice is likely to enable the party to be arrested to escape, or

(D) such notice would be a useless gesture.

(d) Whoever, after notice is given under subsection (b) or after entry where such notice is unnecessary under subsection (c), destroys, conceals, disposes of, or attempts to destroy, conceal, or dispose of, or otherwise prevents or attempts to prevent the seizure of, evidence subject to seizure shall be fined not more than $5,000 or imprisoned for not more than 5 years, or both.

(e) As used in this section and in subchapter II and IV, the terms "break and enter" and "breaking and entering" include any use of physical force or violence or other unauthorized entry but do not include entry obtained by trick or strategem.

4. Trickery and Force

Most jurisdictions provide that all necessary force can be used in the execution of a search warrant or an arrest warrant. Where the police have the right to enter under the authority of a warrant (and thus do not need consent), entering through use of a passkey or by means of trickery (avoiding actual force) is also permitted. State v. Valentine, 264 Or. 54, 504 P.2d 84 (1972); People v. Troy, 70 Misc.2d 799, 334 N.Y.S.2d 953 (1972); State v. Sardo, 112 Ariz. 509, 543 P.2d 1138 (1975).

5. Places and Persons Subject to Search, and Seizable Items

The executing officers can search any place which falls within the description in the warrant. Thus when the search of an apartment is authorized for a small item, a purse in the apartment may be searched. State v. White, 538 P.2d 860 (Wash.App.1975). They cannot, however, go beyond the decribed area. A further limitation upon a search is that once on property to be searched, an officer can look only in a place where the item could possibly turn up. Thus, if the named item is a gun, the pages of a diary could not be perused under the authority of the warrant. If the item is a piano a search of a drawer would be improper, unless some *other* theory (e. g., search incident to arrest of suspect standing near drawer) is available. Nor can one look for a television in a small drawer. State v. James, 579 P. 2d 1257 (N.M.App.1978) (dictum). Nor in a search for wheels and tires is a close inspection of a closet shelf proper when the items are obviously not there. United States v. Chadwell, 427 F.Supp. 692 (D.Del.1977).

If an individual is specifically named by the warrant as a person to be searched (not just as the occupant of the place to be searched), then obviously that person can be searched. A much more difficult question is whether a person who is found on the premises during the execution of a warrant, or one who arrives during the execution, can be searched even though he or she is not named in the warrant as a person to be searched. Some jurisdictions have prohibited searches of persons not designated in a search warrant or else require some showing that such persons very possibly are concealing the evidence. See Ferguson v. State ex rel. Biggers, 250 So.2d 634 (Miss.1971); Walker v. United States, 327 F.2d 597 (D.C.Cir. 1963); Clay v. United States, 246 F.2d 298 (5th Cir. 1957). Illinois, on the other hand, allowed the search of anyone who is found on the premises at the time the warrant is executed. Ill.Rev.Stat.Ch. 38, § 108–9. In Ybarra v. Illinois, —— U.S. ——, 100 S.Ct. 338 (1979), the Supreme Court considered execution of an Illinois warrant which commanded the search of a certain tavern in quest of narcotics. The officers frisked the nine to thirteen patrons of the tavern without any particular reason to believe that any one of them was armed or dangerous. The Court held that absent an indication that a patron was armed and dangerous within the meaning of Terry v. Ohio, Section F infra, the frisk was unlawful. The Court further stated that the quest for evidence named in a warrant does not justify either a search or a frisk of any person who happens to be in a public place which is named in a warrant. The Court did not say what quantum of evidence would be required to justify such a search of the person. Nor did it consider whether the case would be different if the place searched was a private home or if the person had a greater nexus with the place, as for example, as lessee.

An officer can seize any item named in the warrant. Under normal plain view principles (and subject to limitations on plain view principles), he or she may also seize items not named in the warrant if the officer discovers such items while looking in a place where the officer has a right to search under the warrant and if there is probable cause to believe that such items constitute evidence of a crime. (See infra Section H.)

E.   THE LAW OF ARREST AND OF SEARCH INCIDENT TO ARREST

1.   DEFINITION OF "ARREST" AND REPRESENTATIVE STATUTES

"An arrest is the taking of another into custody for the actual or purported purpose of bringing the other before a court, body or official, or of otherwise securing the administration of the law.   .   .   .

"Mere words will not constitute an arrest, while on the other hand no actual physical touching is essential.   .   .   . an assertion of authority and purpose to arrest followed by submission of the arrestee constitutes an arrest. There can be no arrest without either touching or submission." Perkins, Elements of Police Science 223, 227 (1942).

"Arrest is the taking of a person into custody in order that he may be forthcoming to answer for the commission of an offense." Sec. 18, Code of Criminal Procedure, American Law Institute.

———————

" 'Arrest' means the taking of a person into custody." Sec. 102–5 of the 1963 Illinois Code of Criminal Procedure. "An arrest is made by an actual restraint of the person or by his submission to custody." Sec. 107–5, ibid.

———————

At the present time, the arrest rights of police officers and of private citizens are usually prescribed by legislative enactments, and they vary to a considerable extent, from jurisdiction to jurisdiction, as will be observed from the following selections:

STATUTES AND CODE PROVISIONS

California

Penal Code (Part 2 of Criminal Procedure);

§ 836

A peace officer may make an arrest in obedience to a warrant, or may . . . without a warrant, arrest a person:

1. Whenever he has reasonable cause to believe that the person to be arrested has committed a public offense in his presence.

2. When a person arrested has committed a felony, although not in his presence.

3. Whenever he has reasonable cause to believe that the person to be arrested has committed a felony, whether or not a felony has in fact been committed.

§ 837

A private person may arrest another:

1. For a public offense committed or attempted in his presence.

2. When the person arrested has committed a felony, although not in his presence.

3. When a felony has been in fact committed, and he has reasonable cause for believing the person arrested to have committed it.

(According to § 16, "crimes and public offenses" include "felonies", "misdemeanors", and "infractions". § 17 provides: "A felony is a crime which is punishable with death or by imprisonment in the state prison. Every other crime or public offense is a misdemeanor except offenses that are classified as infractions.")

Illinois

Code of Criminal Procedure:

§ 107–2. Arrest by Peace Officer

A peace officer may arrest a person when:

(a) He has a warrant commanding that such person be arrested; or

(b) He has reasonable grounds to believe that a warrant for the person's arrest has been issued in this State or in another jurisdiction; or

(c) He has reasonable grounds to believe that the person is committing or has committed an offense [defined in § 102–15 as "a violation of any penal statute of this State"].

§ 107–3. Arrest by Private Person

Any person may arrest another when he has reasonable grounds to believe that an offense other than an ordinance violation is being committed.

§ 107–4. Arrest by Peace Officer from Other Jurisdiction

(a) As used in this Section:

(1) "State" means any State of the United States and the District of Columbia.

(2) "Peace Officer" means any peace officer or member of any duly organized State, County, or Municipal peace unit or police force of another State.

(3) "Fresh pursuit" means the immediate pursuit of a person who is endeavoring to avoid arrest.

(b) Any peace officer of another State who enters this State in fresh pursuit and continues within this State in fresh pursuit of a person in order to arrest him on the ground that he has committed an offense in the other State has the same authority to arrest and hold the person in custody as peace officers of this State have to arrest and hold a person in custody on the ground that he has committed an offense in this State.

(c) If an arrest is made in this State by a peace officer of another State in accordance with the provisions of this Section he shall without unnecessary delay take the person arrested before the circuit court of the county in which the arrest was made. Such court shall conduct a hearing for the purpose of determining the lawfulness of the arrest. If the court determines that the arrest was lawful it shall commit the person arrested, to await for a reasonable time the issuance of an extradition warrant by the Governor of this State, or admit him to bail for such purpose. If the court determines that the arrest was unlawful it shall discharge the person arrested.

[In addition to the citizen arrest power in § 107–3, the Code, in § 107–8, also imposes an obligation upon persons over the age of 18 to aid a police officer in making an arrest if such aid is requested.]

New York

Criminal Procedure Law:

§ 140.10

1. Subject to the provisions of subdivision two, a police officer may arrest a person for:

(a) Any offense when he has reasonable cause to believe that such person has committed such offense in his presence; and

(b) A crime when he has reasonable cause to believe that such person has committed such crime, whether in his presence or otherwise.

2. A police officer may arrest a person for a petty offense, pursuant to subdivision one, only when:

(a) Such offense was committed or believed by him to have been committed within the geographical area of such police officer's employment; and

(b) Such arrest is made in the county in which such offense was committed or believed to have been committed or in an adjoining county; except that the police officer may follow such person in continuous close pursuit, commencing either in the county in which the offense was or is believed to have been committed or in an adjoining county, in and through any county of the state, and may arrest him in any county in which he apprehends him.

3. A police officer may arrest a person for a crime, pursuant to subdivision one, whether or not such crime was committed within the geographical area of such police officer's employment, and he may make such arrest within the state, regardless of the situs of the commission of the crime. In addition, he may, if necessary, pursue such person outside the state and may arrest him in any state the laws of which contain provisions equivalent [to New York law].

§ 140.30

1. Subject to the provisions of subdivision two, any person may arrest another person (a) for a felony when the latter has in fact committed such felony, and (b) for any of-

fense when the latter has in fact committed such offense in his presence.

2. Such an arrest, if for a felony, may be made anywhere in the state. If the arrest is for an offense other than a felony, it may be made only in the county in which such offense was committed.

[When an arrest is made in accordance with this provision, according to § 140.35, the arrester "must inform the person whom he is arresting of the reason for such arrest unless he encounters physical resistance, flight or other factors rendering such procedure impractical".]

———

According to § 10.00 of the Penal Code, the words "offense" and "crime" are differentiated as follows:

"Offense" means conduct for which a sentence to a term of imprisonment or to a fine is provided by any law of this state or by any law, local law or ordinance of a political subdivision of this state, or by any order, rule or regulation of any governmental instrumentality authorized by law to adopt the same.

"Crime" means a misdemeanor or a felony.

And in New York (also in § 10.00), the distinction between "misdemeanor" and "felony" is set out in the following terms:

"Misdemeanor" means an offense, other than a "traffic infraction," for which a sentence to a term of imprisonment in excess of fifteen days may be imposed, but for which a sentence to a term of imprisonment in excess of one year cannot be imposed.

"Felony" means an offense for which a sentence to a term of imprisonment in excess of one year may be imposed.

Federal

There is no single act regarding the arrest powers of federal officers generally. The matter is dealt with by separate statutes pertaining to particular groups of officers. For instance, there is a separate provision for FBI agents, and it authorizes an arrest, without warrant, for any offense against the United States committed in their presence, or for any felony cognizable under the laws of the United States if they have reasonable grounds to believe that the person to be arrested has committed or is committing such felony (18 U.S.C.A. § 3052.) Another statute confers a similar power upon marshals and their deputies. (18 U.S. C.A. § 3053.)

Separate statutes provide similar arrest powers for offenses that are the province of the Secret Service (18 U.S. C.A. § 3056), the Drug Enforcement Administration as successor to the Bureau of Narcotics and Dangerous Drugs (21 U.S.C.A. § 878), the Postal Personnel (18 U.S.C.A. § 3061), Officers of the Customs Service (26 U.S.C.A. § 7607), and the I.R.S. enforcement agents (26 U.S.C.A. § 7608). Bureau of Prisons enforcement personnel may make warrantless arrests for specified offenses only if they have "reasonable grounds to believe that the arrested person is guilty of such offense, and if there is likelihood of his escaping before a warrant can be obtained for his arrest." (18 U.S.C.A. § 3050).

The District of Columbia, however, has its own provisions with regard to arrest powers. They are found in the District of Columbia Code. (D.C. Code, §§ 23–581, 582.)

ORDINANCES

In addition to the arrest rights covered by state statutes, there are, in some jurisdictions, city and county ordinances dealing with the subject. Although such ordinances seldom differ from or exceed the arrest rights set forth in the statutes themselves, there are instances where they are broader. For example, note the following with respect to the State of Illinois and the City of Chicago:

Although the Criminal Code, as previously noted, provides that a peace officer may arrest a person when he has reasonable grounds to believe that the person is committing or has committed an offense (meaning a violation of any penal statute of the state), Section 11–25 of the Municipal Code of Chicago grants to members of its police department the power

"(1) to arrest or cause to be arrested, with or without process, all persons who break the peace, or are found violating any municipal ordinance or any criminal law of the State; (2) to commit arrested persons for examination; (3) if necessary, to detain arrested persons in custody overnight or Sunday in any safe place, or until they can be brought before the proper court; and (4) to exercise all other powers as conservators of the peace as are provided in this code."

This ordinance was enacted pursuant to authorization conferred by the Illinois legislature upon Illinois municipalities to prescribe the duties and powers of police officers. Ch. 24, §§ 11–1–1, 11–1–2, Ill.Rev.Stats.

THE MEANING OF "REASONABLE GROUNDS" FOR AN ARREST

The "reasonable grounds" requirement for an arrest to be valid under typical state statutes is almost always treated synonymously with the "probable cause" requirement under the Fourth Amendment. People v. Wright, 56 Ill.2d 523, 309 N.E.2d 537 (1974). Thus the probable cause materials in Section B of this chapter have relevance for determining the validity of an arrest under both state and federal standards.

2. ARREST IMMUNITY

Certain individuals may be exempt from arrest on a temporary or permanent basis, depending upon the nature of the arrest, and the person's occupation and activities. The exemption in some cases is common law, but generally it is pursuant to statute. The exemption from civil arrest is far more common than one for criminal detention.

The broadest arrest immunity is conferred upon diplomats of a foreign nation, their families and staffs. These individuals are not subject to the criminal laws of the host country.

Statutory immunity from civil arrest has been conferred upon public officials in the performance of their official duties, military personnel, and officers of the court while attending or traveling to and from court. This latter privilege arose from the common law.

Article 1, § 6 of the United States Constitution provides that Senators and Representatives "shall in all cases, except Treason, Felony and Breach of the Peace, be privileged from arrest during their attendance at the session of their respective Houses, and in going to and returning from the same". This phrase removes criminal offenses from the Congressional arrest immunity.

3. ARRESTS IN PUBLIC PLACES: WARRANT REQUIRED?

UNITED STATES v. WATSON

Supreme Court of the United States, 1976.
423 U.S. 411, 96 S.Ct. 820.

[On August 17, 1972, an informant of proven reliability delivered a stolen credit card to federal postal inspectors, alleging that he had received the card from Henry Watson, who had instructed the informant to purchase airline tickets with it. Although authorities had probable cause to arrest Watson, they neither arrested him immediately nor applied for an arrest warrant. Instead they arranged for a meeting between the informant and Watson to be held on August 22. The meeting was postponed until August 23, at which time the informant signalled to postal inspectors that Watson had indicated that he presently had additional stolen credit cards in his possession. The inspectors entered the restaurant where the meeting had taken place, arrested Watson without a warrant, and searched his person, finding nothing. Watson, however, consented to a search of his near-by car; that search yielded stolen credit cards. These cards were admitted at trial, at which Watson was acquitted of the August 17 charge and convicted of August 23 charges. The United States Court of Appeals for the Ninth Circuit reversed the convictions, holding that the arrest was illegal for want of a warrant, and that the illegal arrest fatally tainted the consent to search. The Ninth Circuit held that an arrest warrant must be obtained even for a felony arrest in a public place, unless emergency circumstances necessitate an immediate arrest.]

MR. JUSTICE WHITE delivered the opinion of the Court.

* * *

Contrary to the Court of Appeals' view, Watson's arrest was not invalid because executed without a warrant. Section 3061(a) of Title 18 U.S.C. expressly empowers the Board of Governors of the Postal Service to authorize Postal Service officers and employees "performing duties related to the inspection of postal matters" to

"(3) make arrests without warrant for felonies cognizable under the laws of the United States if they have reasonable grounds to believe that the person to be arrested has committed or is committing such a felony."

. . . [T]he Board of Governors has exercised that power and authorized warrantless arrests. There being probable cause in this case to believe that Watson had violated § 1708, the inspector and his subordinates, in arresting Watson, were acting strictly in accordance with the governing statute and regulations. The effect of the judgment of the Court of Appeals was to invalidate the statute as applied in this case and as applied to all the situations where a court fails to find exigent circumstances justifying a warrantless arrest. We reverse that judgment.

Under the Fourth Amendment, the people are to be "secure in their persons, houses, papers, and effects, against unreasonable searches and seizures, . . . and no Warrants shall issue, but upon probable cause . . . ." Section 3061 represents a judgment by Congress that it is not unreasonable under the Fourth Amendment for postal inspectors to arrest without a warrant provided they have probable cause to do so. This was not an isolated or quixotic judgment of the legislative branch. Other federal law enforcement officers have been expressly authorized by statute for many years to make felony arrests on probable cause but without a warrant. This is true of United States Marshals, 18 U.S.C. § 3053, and of agents of the Federal Bureau of Investigation, 18 U.S.C. § 3052; the Drug Enforcement Administration, 84 Stat. 1273, 21 U.S.C. § 878; the Secret Service, 18 U.S.C. § 3056(a); and the Customs Service, 26 U.S.C. § 7607.

. . . Moreover, there is nothing in the Court's prior cases indicating that under the Fourth Amendment a warrant is required to make a valid arrest for a felony. Indeed, the relevant prior decisions are uniformly to the contrary.

"The usual rule is that a police officer may arrest without warrant one believed by the officer upon reasonable cause to have been guilty of a felony . . . ." Carroll v. United States, 267 U.S. 132, 156, 45 S.Ct. 280, 286 (1925). In Henry v. United States, 361 U.S. 98, 80 S.Ct. 168 (1959), the Court dealt with an FBI agent's warrantless arrest under 18 U.S.C. § 3052 which authorizes a warrantless arrest where there are reasonable grounds to believe that the person to be arrested has committed a felony. The Court declared that "[t]he statute states the constitutional standard . . . ." . . . . The necessary inquiry, therefore, was not whether there was a warrant or whether there was time to get one but whether there was probable cause for the arrest. . . . Just last Term, while recognizing that maximum protection of individual rights could be assured by requiring a magistrate's review of the factual justification prior to any arrest, we stated that "such a requirement would constitute an intolerable handicap for legitimate law enforcement" and noted that the Court "has never invalidated an arrest supported by probable cause solely because the officers failed to secure a warrant." Gerstein v. Pugh, ...

The cases construing the Fourth Amendment thus reflect the ancient common-law rule that a peace officer was permitted to arrest without a warrant for a misdemeanor or felony committed in his presence as well as for a felony not committed in his presence if there was reasonable grounds for making the arrest. 10 Halsbury's Laws of England 344–345 (3d ed. 1955); 4 Blackstone's Commentaries 292–293 (Lewis ed. 1902); 1 J. Stephen, A History of the Criminal Law of England 193 (1883) . . . . This has also been the prevailing rule under state constitutions and statutes. . . .

In Rohan v. Sawin, 59 Mass. (5 Cush.) 281 (1851), a false-arrest case, the Supreme Judicial Court of Massachusetts held that the common-law rule obtained in that State. Given probable cause to arrest, "[t]he authority of the constable to arrest without warrant, in cases of felony, is most fully established by the elementary books, and adjudicated cases." . . . In reaching this judgment the court observed:

> "It has been sometimes contended, that an arrest of this character, without a warrant, was a violation of the great fundamental principles of our national and state constitutions, forbidding unreasonable searches and arrests, except by warrant founded upon a complaint made under oath. Those provisions doubtless had another and different purpose, being in restraint of general warrants to make searches, and requiring warrants to issue only upon a complaint made under oath. They do not conflict with the authority of constables or other peace-officers, or private persons under proper limitations, to arrest without warrant those who have committed felonies. The public safety, and the due ap-

prehension of criminals, charged with heinous offenses, imperiously require that such arrests should be made without warrant by officers of the law." . . .

Also rejected . . . was the trial court's view that to justify a warrantless arrest, the State must show "an immediate necessity therefor, arising from the danger, that the plaintiff would otherwise escape, or secrete the stolen property, before a warrant could be procured against him." The Supreme Judicial Court ruled that there was no "authority for thus restricting a constable in the exercise of his authority to arrest for a felony without a warrant." . . .

* * *

The balance struck by the common law in generally authorizing felony arrests on probable cause, but without warrant, has survived substantially intact. It appears in almost all of the States in the form of express statutory authorization. . . .

This is the rule Congress has long directed its principal law enforcement officers to follow. Congress has plainly decided against conditioning warrantless arrest power on proof of exigent circumstances. Law enforcement officers may find it wise to seek arrest warrants where practicable to do so, and their judgments about probable cause may be more readily accepted where backed by a warrant issued by a magistrate. See United States v. Ventresca, 380 U.S. 102, 106, 85 S.Ct. 741, 744–745 (1965) . . . . But we decline to transform this judicial preference into a constitutional rule when the judgment of the Nation and the Congress has for so long been to authorize warrantless public arrests on probable cause rather than to encumber criminal prosecutions with endless litigation with respect to the existence of exigent circumstances, whether it was practicable to get a warrant, whether the suspect was about to flee, and the like.

Watson's arrest did not violate the Fourth Amendment, and the Court of Appeals erred in holding to the contrary.

* * *

MR. JUSTICE POWELL, concurring.

On its face, our decision today creates a certain anomaly. There is no more basic constitutional rule in the Fourth Amendment area than that which makes a warrantless search unreasonable except in a few "jealously and carefully drawn" exceptional circumstances. . . . On more than one occasion this Court has rejected an argument that a law enforcement officer's own probable cause to search a private place for contraband or evidence of crime should excuse his otherwise unexplained failure to procure a warrant beforehand. . . .

Since the Fourth Amendment speaks equally to both searches and seizures, and since an arrest, the taking hold of one's person is quintessentially, a seizure, it would seem that the constitutional provision should impose the same limitations upon arrests that it does upon searches. Indeed, as an abstract matter an argument can be made that the restrictions upon arrest perhaps should be greater. A search may cause only annoyance and temporary inconvenience to the law-abiding citizen, assuming more serious dimension only when it turns up evidence of criminality. An arrest, however, is a serious personal intrusion regardless of whether the person seized is guilty or innocent. Although an arrestee cannot be held for a significant period without some neutral determination that there are grounds to do so, no decision that he should go free can come quickly enough to erase the invasion of his privacy that already will have occurred. . . . Logic therefore would seem to dictate that arrests be subject to the warrant requirement at least to the same extent as searches.

But logic sometimes must defer to history and experience. The Court's opinion emphasizes the historical sanction accorded warrantless felony arrests. . . .

The historical momentum for acceptance of warrantless arrests, already strong at the adoption of the Fourth Amendment, has gained strength during the ensuing two centuries. Both the judiciary and the legislative bodies of this Nation repeatedly have placed their imprimaturs upon the practice and, as the Government emphasizes, law enforcement agencies have developed their investigative and arrest procedures upon an assumption that warrantless arrests were valid so long as based upon probable cause. The decision of the Court of Appeals in this case was virtually unprecedented. Of course, no practice that is inconsistent with constitutional protections can be saved merely by appeal to previous uncritical acceptance. But the warrantless felony arrest, long preferred at common law and unimpeached at the passage of the Fourth Amendment, is not such a practice. Given the revolutionary implications of such a holding, a declaration at this late date that warrantless felony arrests are constitutionally infirm would have to rest upon reasons more substantial than a desire to harmonize the rules for arrest with those governing searches.

Moreover, a constitutional rule permitting felony arrests only with a warrant or in exigent circumstances could severely hamper effective law enforcement. Good police practice often requires postponing an arrest, even after probable cause has been established, in order to place the suspect under surveillance or otherwise develop further evidence necessary to prove guilt to a jury. Under the holding of the Court of Appeals such additional investigative work could imperil the entire prosecution. Should the officers fail to obtain a warrant initially, and later be required by unforeseen circumstances to arrest immediately with no chance to procure a last-minute warrant, they would ask a court decision that the subsequent exigency did not excuse their failure to get a warrant in the interim since they first developed probable cause. If the officers attempted to meet such a contingency by procuring a warrant as soon as they had probable cause and then merely held it during their subsequent investigation, they would risk a court decision that the warrant had grown stale by the time it was used. Law enforcement personnel caught in this squeeze could ensure validity of their arrests only be obtaining a warrant and arresting as soon as probable cause existed, thereby foreclosing the possibility of gathering vital additional evidence from the suspect's continued actions.

In sum, the historical and policy reasons sketched above fully justify the Court's sustaining of a warrantless arrest upon probable cause, despite the resulting divergence between the constitutional rule governing searches and that now held applicable to seizures, of the person.

* * *

[STEWART, J., concurring.]

The arrest in this case was made upon probable cause in a public place in broad daylight. The Court holds that this arrest did not violate the Fourth Amendment, and I agree. The Court does *not* decide, nor could it decide in this case, whether or under what circumstances an officer must obtain a warrant before he may lawfully enter a private place to effect an arrest. . . .

* * *

[MR. JUSTICE MARSHALL, dissenting.]

* * *

. . . . The Court reaches its conclusion that a warrant is not necessary for a police officer to make an arrest in a public place, so long as he has probable cause to believe a felony has been committed, on the basis of its views of precedent and history. . . . None of the cases cited by the Court squarely confronted the issue decided today. Moreover, an examination of the history relied on by the Court shows that it does not support the conclusion laid upon it.

* * *

[MR. JUSTICE MARSHALL then engaged in a thorough analysis of historical developments, from which he concluded that at common law only the most serious offenses were called "felonies," and that many crimes presently deemed felonies were considered misdemeanors at common law.]

* * *

Thus the lesson of the common law, and those courts in this country that have accepted its rule, is an ambiguous one. Applied in its original context, the common-law rule would allow the warrantless arrest of some, but not all, of those we call felons today. Accordingly, the Court is simply historically wrong when it tells us that "[t]he balance struck by the common law in generally authorizing felony arrests on probable cause, but without a warrant, has survived substantially intact." . . . Indeed, the only clear lesson of history is contrary to the one the Court draws: the common law considered the arrest warrant far more important than today's decision leaves it.

I do not mean by this that a modern warrant requirement should apply only to arrests precisely analogous to common-law misdemeanors, and be inapplicable to analogues of common-law felonies.

Rather, the point is simply that the Court's unblinking literalism cannot replace analysis of the constitutional interests involved. While we can learn from the common law, the ancient rule does not provide a simple answer directly transferable to our system. Thus, in considering the applicability of the common-law rule to our present constitutional scheme, we must consider *both* of the rule's two opposing constructs: the presumption favoring warrants, as well as the exception allowing immediate arrests of the most dangerous criminals. The Court's failure to do so, indeed its failure to recognize any tension in the common-law rule at all, drains all validity from its historical analysis.

* * *

The Court has typically engaged in a two-part analysis in deciding whether the presumption favoring a warrant should be given effect in situations where a warrant has not previously been clearly required. Utilizing that approach we must now consider (1) whether the privacy of our citizens will be better protected by ordinarily requiring a warrant to be issued before they may be arrested; and (2) whether a warrant requirement would unduly burden legitimate governmental interests. . . .

The first question is easily answered. Of course the privacy of our citizens will be better protected by a warrant requirement. We have recognized that "the Fourth Amendment protects people, not places." Katz v. United States . . . [Casebook, ch. 13–F]. Indeed, the privacy guaranteed by the Fourth Amendment is quintessentially personal. . . . Thus a warrant is required in search situations not because of some high regard for property, but because of our regard for the individual, and *his* interest in his possessions and person. . . .

Not only is the Fourth Amendment directly addressed to the privacy of our citizens, but it speaks in indistinguishable terms about the freedom of both persons and property from unreasonable seizures. A warrant is required in the search situation to protect the privacy of the individual, but there can be no less invasion of privacy when the individual himself, rather than his property, is searched and seized. Indeed, an unjustified arrest that forces the individual temporarily to forfeit his right to control his person and movements and interrupts the course of his daily business may be more intrusive than an unjustified search. . . .

A warrant requirement for arrests would, of course, minimize the possibility that such an intrusion into the individual's sacred sphere of personal privacy would occur on less than probable cause. Primarily for this reason, a warrant is required for searches. Surely there is no reason to place greater trust in the partisan assessment of a police officer that there is probable cause for an arrest than in his determination that probable cause exists for a search. . . .

We come then to the second part of the warrant test: whether a warrant requirement would unduly burden legitimate law enforcement interests. . . .

The Government's assertion that a warrant requirement would impose an intolerable burden stems, in large part, from the specious supposition that procurement of an arrest warrant would be necessary as soon as probable cause ripens. Brief for the United States, 22–24. There is no requirement that a search warrant be obtained the moment police have probable cause to search. The rule is only that present probable cause be shown and a warrant obtained before a search is undertaken. Fed.Rule Crim.Proc. 41. . . . The same rule should obtain for arrest warrants, where it may even make more sense. Certainly, there is less need for prompt procurement of a warrant in the arrest situation. Unlike probable cause to search, probable cause to arrest, once formed will continue to exist for the indefinite future, at least if no intervening exculpatory facts come to light. . . .

This sensible approach obviates most of the difficulties that have been suggested with an arrest warrant rule. Police would not have to cut their investigation short the moment they obtain probable cause to arrest, nor would undercover agents be forced suddenly to terminate their work and forfeit their covers. . . . Moreover, if in the course of the continued police investigation exigent circumstances develop that demand an immediate arrest, the arrest may be made without fear of unconstitutionality, so long as the exigency was unanticipated and not used to avoid the arrest warrant requirement. . . . Likewise, if in the course of the continued investigation police uncover evidence tying the suspect to another crime, they may immediately arrest him for that crime if exigency demands it, and still be in full conformity with the warrant rule. . . . Other than where police attempt to evade the warrant requirement, the rule would invalidate an arrest only in the obvious situation: where police, with probable cause but without exigent circumstances, set out to arrest a suspect. Such an arrest must be void, even if exigency develops in the course of the arrest that would ordinarily validate it; otherwise the warrant requirement would be reduced to a toothless prescription.

In sum, the requirement that officers about to arrest a suspect ordinarily obtain a warrant before they do so does not seem unduly burdensome, at least no more burdensome than any other requirement that law enforcement officials undertake a new procedure in order to comply with the dictates of the Constitution. . . .

It is suggested, however, that even if application of this rule does not require police to secure a warrant as soon as they obtain probable cause, the confused officer would nonetheless be prone to do so. If so, police "would risk a court decision that the warrant had grown stale by the time it was used." . . . (Powell, J., concurring) . . . . This fear is groundless. First, as suggested above, the requirement that police procure a warrant before an arrest is made is rather simple of application. Thus, there is no need for the police to find themselves in this "squeeze." Second, the "squeeze" is nonexistent. Just as it is virtually impossible for probable cause for an arrest to grow stale between the time of formation and the time a warrant is procured, it is virtually impossible for probable cause to become stale between procurement and arrest. Delay by law enforcement officers in executing an arrest warrant does not ordinarily affect the legality of the arrest. .   .   .

* * *

NOTES

1. The "failure" to obtain an arrest warrant for Henry Watson between August 17 and August 23 may be readily explained. The purpose of an arrest warrant is to initiate prosecution. An Assistant United States Attorney should not permit application for a warrant unless he or she has a prosecutable case. Until August 23, when the informant signalled that additional evidence was at hand, the only evidence authorities had linking Watson to the August 17 possession of a stolen credit card was the uncorroborated word of the informant. This was adequate for probable cause but was hardly sufficient to persuade a federal prosecutor to bring a charge. Even after the August 23 corroborative evidence was presented to the jury, Watson was acquitted of the August 17 charge. He was convicted of the August 23 charges on the basis of the federal inspectors' testimony concerning the discovery of cards in Watson's glove compartment on August 23.

2. Five months after *Watson*, the Supreme Court decided United States v. Santana, 427 U.S. 38, 96 S.Ct. 2406 (1976). Police officers had probable cause to arrest Santana. As they approached her home, they observed her on its threshold. The police entered onto her property. Santana retreated into her home. The police followed her through the open door. They arrested her within, and discovered incriminating evidence incident to the arrest. In a 7–2 decision, the Court found the warrantless arrest valid and offered the following rationale:

"While it may be true that under the common law of property the threshold of one's dwelling is 'private,' as is the yard surrounding the house, it is nonetheless clear that under the cases interpreting the Fourth Amendment Santana was in a 'public' place. She was not in an area where she had any expectation of privacy. 'What a person knowingly exposes to the public, even in his own house or office, is not a subject of Fourth Amendment protection.' Katz v. United States (1967). She was not merely visible to the public but as exposed to public view, speech, hearing and touch as if she had been standing completely outside her house. Hester v. United States, 265 U.S. 57, 59, 44 S.Ct. 445, 446 (1924). Thus, when the police, who concededly had probable cause to do so, sought to arrest her, they merely intended to perform a function which we have approved in *Watson*.

"The only remaining question is whether her act of retreating into her house could thwart an otherwise proper arrest. We hold that it could not. In Warden v. Hayden, 387 U.S. 294, 87 S.Ct. 1642 (1967), we recognized the right of police, who had probable cause to believe that an armed robber had entered a house a few minutes before, to make a warrantless entry to arrest the robber and to search for weapons. This case, involving a true 'hot pursuit,' is clearly governed by *Warden*; the need to act quickly here

is even greater than in that case while the intrusion is much less.
. . . The fact that the pursuit here ended almost as soon as it
began did not render it any the less a 'hot pursuit' sufficient to
justify the warrantless entry into Santana's house. Once Santana
saw the police, there was likewise a realistic expectation that any
delay would result in destruction of evidence. See Vale v. Louisiana, 379 U.S. 30, 35, 90 S.Ct. 1969, 1972 (1970). Once she had
been arrested the search, incident to that arrest, which produced
the drugs and money was clearly justified. . . .

"We thus conclude that a suspect may not defeat an arrest
which has been set in motion in a public place, and is therefore
proper under *Watson*, by the expedient of escaping to a private
place. . . ."

3. In view of the significant role that the *Watson* court gave to the
common law in interpreting Fourth Amendment limits upon arrest powers,
are there serious constitutional questions about the validity of statutes in
some states which permit an officer, upon probable cause, to make a warrantless arrest for a misdemeanor offense *not* committed in his or her presence (see, e. g., the Illinois statute in Section E–1, supra.

4. Even if an arrest warrant were never required by the Fourth
Amendment, there still could be concern about whether a particular arrest
warrant were valid for purposes of the Fourth Amendment. Suppose that a
federal agent obtains an arrest warrant and then makes the arrest in a public place and finds evidence on the arrestee's person in a search incident to
arrest. If in order to justify the arrest, the prosecutor relies solely upon
the arrest warrant and makes no effort to prove through live testimony
that there was probable cause for the arrest, then the validity of the arrest
(and of the search incident to arrest) will depend upon the validity of the
arrest warrant. This is true even though the Fourth Amendment did not
mandate that an arrest warrant be obtained.

As with search warrants, arrest warrants, to pass the test of the
Fourth Amendment, must be supported by sworn data establishing probable
cause and presented to the magistrate before issuance. Whiteley v. Warden, 401 U.S. 560, 91 S.Ct. 1031 (1971); Giordenello v. United States, 357
U.S. 480, 78 S.Ct. 1245 (1958). (In many jurisdictions sworn oral testimony rather than affidavits are used to support applications for arrest warrants). Only a neutral judicial officer can issue a constitutionally valid arrest warrant. The arrestee must be named or described with particularity.
In other words, many of the doctrines discussed earlier in this chapter are
applicable in arrest warrant cases.

In many jurisdictions arrest warrants are frequently issued upon the
basis of conclusory allegations that a particular person has committed a
crime. These warrants are invalid for Fourth Amendment purposes. The
significance of their invalidity often is not great, however. As *Watson*, and
the other previous material indicates, frequently arrest warrants are not
constitutionally required. Faced with an invalid warrant, a prosecutor can
proceed as if no warrant existed at all. If the arrest is challenged in such a
case, the prosecutor need only prove through live testimony that there was
probable cause for arrest. Then, too, if the arrest yielded no evidence, ordinarily the legality of the arrest will be irrelevant to the outcome of the
criminal case. See Section E–6.

5.   Some jurisdictions, as a matter of state law, apparently require arrest warrants to be used to effect non-emergency felony arrests, even in a public place, if the offense has not been committed in the officer's presence. See People v. Hoinville, —— Colo. ——, 553 P.2d 777 (1976); Colo.Rev.Stat. § 16–3–102.

4.   ENTRY TO ARREST

(a) Is a Warrant Required?   On April 15, 1980, as this casebook was in galley proof form, the Supreme Court of the United States held, by a 6–3 decision, that a warrant is required for a non-consensual, non-emergency entry made for the purpose of arresting a suspect within his home.   Payton v. New York, —— U.S. ——, —— S.Ct. ——.

(b) Must There Be Probable Cause to Believe Suspect Is Home? Police obviously cannot use an entry-to-arrest justification for entering an apartment if they have positive knowledge that the suspect is not inside.   But must they have probable cause to believe that he is at home?   Compare United States v. Phillips, 497 F.2d 1131 (9th Cir. 1974), with People v. Sprovieri, 43 Ill.2d 223, 252 N.E.2d 531 (1969). In deciding what reasons to believe that the suspect is at home will suffice to justify entry, should the answer depend upon whether or not the police have an arrest warrant?

(c) Method of Entry.   Problems concerning no-knock entries and the use of force and trickery arise in the case of entries to arrest (with or without a warrant), just as they do in the case of entries to execute a search warrant.   See Section D (3–4), supra.   The Supreme Court in Ker v. California, 374 U.S. 23, 83 S.Ct. 1623 (1963), a five-to-four decision, permitted a no-knock entry with a passkey to effect an arrest under emergency circumstances.

5.   THE DOCTRINE OF SEARCH INCIDENT TO ARREST

(a) RIGHT TO SEARCH

UNITED STATES v. ROBINSON

Supreme Court of the United States, 1973.
414 U.S. 218, 94 S.Ct. 467.

MR. JUSTICE REHNQUIST delivered the opinion of the Court.

Respondent Robinson was convicted in United States District Court for the District of Columbia of the possession and facilitation of concealment of heroin . . . On his appeal . . . the Court of Appeals *en banc* reversed the judgment of conviction, holding that the heroin introduced in evidence against respondent had been obtained as a result of a search which violated the Fourth Amendment to the United States Constitution. . . .

On April 23, 1968, at approximately 11 o'clock p. m., Officer Richard Jenks, a 15-year veteran of the District of Columbia Metropolitan Police Department, observed the respondent driving a 1965 Cadillac near the intersection of 8th and C Streets, Southeast, in the District of Columbia. Jenks, as a result of previous investigation following a check of respondent's operator's permit four days earlier, determined there was reason to believe that respondent was operating a motor vehicle after the revocation of his operator's permit. This is an offense defined by statute in the District of Columbia which carries a mandatory minimum jail term, a mandatory minimum fine, or both.

Jenks signaled respondent to stop the automobile, which respondent did, and all three of the occupants emerged from the car. At that point Jenks informed respondent that he was under arrest for "operating after revocation and obtaining a permit by misrepresentation." It was assumed by the majority of the Court of Appeals, and is conceded by the respondent here, that Jenks had probable cause to arrest respondent, and that he effected a full custody arrest.

In accordance with procedures prescribed in Police Department instructions, Jenks then began to search respondent. He explained at a subsequent hearing that he was "face to face" with the respondent, and "placed [his] hands on [the respondent], my right hand to his left breast like this (demonstrating) and proceeded to pat him down thus (with the right hand)." During this patdown, Jenks felt an object in the left breast pocket of the heavy coat respondent was wearing, but testified that he "couldn't tell what it was" and also that he "couldn't actually tell the size of it." Jenks then reached into the pocket and pulled out the object, which turned out to be a "crumpled up cigarette package." Jenks testified that at this point he still did not know what was in the package:

> "As I felt the package I could feel objects in the package but I couldn't tell what they were . . . I knew they weren't cigarettes."

The officer then opened the cigarette pack and found 14 gelatin capsules of white powder which he thought to be, and which later analysis proved to be, heroin. Jenks then continued his search of respondent to completion, feeling around his waist and trouser legs, and examining the remaining pockets. The heroin seized from the respondent was admitted into evidence at the trial which resulted in his conviction in the District Court. . . .

It is well settled that a search incident to a lawful arrest is a traditional exception to the warrant requirement of the Fourth Amendment. This general exception has historically been formulated into two distinct propositions. The first is that a search may be made of the *person* of the arrestee by virtue of the lawful arrest. The second is that a search may be made of the area within the control of the arrestee.

Examination of this Court's decisions in the area show that these two propositions have been treated quite differently. The validity of the search of a person incident to a lawful arrest has been regarded as settled from its first enunciation, and has remained virtually unchallenged until the present case. The validity of the second proposition, while likewise conceded in principle, has been subject to differing interpretations as to the extent of the area which may be searched.

Because the rule requiring exclusion of evidence obtained in violation of the Fourth Amendment was first enunciated in Weeks v. United States, 232 U.S. 383 (1914), it is understandable that virtually all of this Court's search and seizure law has been developed since that time. . . .

* * *

In its decision of this case, the majority of the Court of Appeals decided that even after a police officer lawfully places a suspect under arrest for the purpose of taking him into custody, he may not ordinarily proceed to fully search the prisoner. He must instead conduct a limited frisk of the outer clothing and remove such weapons that he may, as a result of that limited frisk, reasonably believe the suspect has in his possession. While recognizing that Terry v. Ohio, 392 U.S. 1 (1968) [to be reported in a subsequent chapter of this casebook], dealt with a permissible "frisk" incident to an investigative stop based on less than probable cause to arrest, the Court of Appeals felt that the principles of that case should be carried over to this probable cause arrest for driving while one's license is revoked. Since there would be no further evidence of such a crime to be obtained in a search of the arrestee, the Court held that only a search for weapons could be justified.

Terry v. Ohio did not involve an arrest for probable cause, and it made quite clear that the "protective frisk" for weapons which it approved might be conducted without probable cause. The Court's opinion explicitly recognized that there is a "distinction in purpose, character, and extent between a search incident to an arrest and a limited search for weapons" . . .

* * *

[Although] earlier authorities are sketchy, they tend to support the broad statement of the authority to search incident to arrest found in the successive decisions of this Court, rather than the restrictive one which was applied by the Court of Appeals in this case. The scarcity of case law before Weeks is doubtless due in part to the fact that the exclusionary rule there enunciated had been first adopted only 11 years earlier in Iowa; but it would seem to be also due in part to the fact that the issue was regarded as well-settled.

The Court of Appeals in effect determined that the only reason supporting the authority for a full search incident to lawful arrest was the possibility of discovery of evidence or fruits. Concluding that there could be no evidence or fruits in the case of an offense such as that with which respondent was charged, it held that any protective search would have to be limited by the conditions laid down in *Terry* for a search upon less than probable cause to arrest. Quite apart from the fact that *Terry* clearly recognized the distinction between the two types of searches, and that a different rule governed one than governed the other, we find additional reason to disagree with the Court of Appeals.

The justification or reason for the authority to search incident to a lawfull arrest rests quite as much on the need to disarm the suspect in order to take him into custody as it does on the need to preserve evidence on his person for later use at trial. The standards traditionally governing a search incident to lawful arrest are not, therefore, commuted to the stricter *Terry* standards by the absence of probable fruits or further evidence of the particular crime for which the arrest is made.

Nor are we inclined, on the basis of what seems to us to be a rather speculative judgment, to qualify the breadth of the general authority to search incident to a lawful custodial arrest on an assumption that persons arrested for the offense of driving while their license has been revoked are less likely to be possessed of dangerous weapons than are those arrested for other crimes.[1] It is scarcely open to doubt that the danger to an officer is far greater in the case of the extended exposure which follows the taking of a suspect into custody and transporting him to the police station than in the case of the relatively fleeting contact resulting from the typical *Terry*-type stop. This is an adequate basis for treating all custodial arrests alike for purposes of search justification.

But quite apart from these distinctions, our more fundamental disagreement with the Court of Appeals arises from its suggestion that there must be litigated in each case the issue of whether or not there was present one of the reasons supporting the authority for a search of the person incident to a lawful arrest. We do not think the long line of authorities of this Court dating back to *Weeks,* nor what we can glean from the history of practice in this country and in England, requires such a case by case adjudication. A police officer's determination as to how and where to search the person of a suspect whom he has arrested is necessarily a quick *ad hoc* judgment which the Fourth Amendment does not require to be broken down in each

---

1. Such an assumption appears at least questionable in light of the available statistical data concerning assaults on police officers who are in the course of making arrests. The danger to the police officer flows from the fact of the arrest, and its attendant proximity, stress and uncertainty, and not from the grounds for arrest. One study concludes that approximately 30% of the shootings of police officers occur when the officer approaches a person seated in a car. Bristow Police Officer Shootings—A Factual Evaluation, 54 J.Crim.L.C. & P.S. 93 (1963), cited in Adams v. Williams, 407 U.S. 143, 148 (1972). The Government in its brief notes that the Uniform Crime Reports, prepared by the Federal Bureau of Investigation, indicate that a significant percentage of police officer murders occur when the officers are making traffic stops. Those reports indicate that during January–March, 1973, 35 police officers were murdered; 11 of those officers were killed while engaged in traffic stops.

instance into an analysis of each step in the search. The authority to search the person incident to a lawful custodial arrest while based upon the need to disarm and to discover evidence, does not depend on what a court may later decide was the probability in a particular arrest situation that weapons or evidence would in fact be found upon the person of the suspect. A custodial arrest of a suspect based on probable cause is a reasonable intrusion under the Fourth Amendment; that intrusion being lawful, a search incident to the arrest requires no additional justification. It is the fact of the lawful arrest which establishes the authority to search, and we hold that in the case of a lawful custodial arrest a full search of the person is not only an exception to the warrant requirement of the Fourth Amendment, but is also a "reasonable" search under that Amendment.

* * *

[MR. JUSTICE POWELL's concurring opinion is omitted.]

MR. JUSTICE MARSHALL, with whom MR. JUSTICE DOUGLAS and MR. JUSTICE BRENNAN join, dissenting.

Certain fundamental principles have characterized this Court's Fourth Amendment jurisprudence over the years. Perhaps the most basic of these was expressed by Mr. Justice Butler, speaking for a unanimous Court in Go-Bart Co. v. United States, 282 U.S. 344 (1931): "There is no formula for the determination of reasonableness. Each case is to be decided on its own facts and circumstances." As we recently held, "The constitutional validity of a warrantless search is preeminently the sort of question which can only be decided in the concrete factual context of the individual case." Sibron v. New York, 392 U.S. 40, 59 (1968). And the intensive, at times painstaking, case by case analysis characteristic of our Fourth Amendment decisions bespeaks our "jealous regard for maintaining the integrity of individual rights." Mapp v. Ohio, 367 U.S. 643, 647 (1961).

In the present case, however, the majority turns its back on these principles, holding that "the fact of the lawful arrest" always establishes the authority to conduct a full search of the arrestee's person, regardless of whether in a particular case "there was present one of the reasons supporting the authority for a search of the person incident to a lawful arrest." The majority's approach represents a clear and marked departure from our long tradition of case-by-case adjudication of the reasonableness of searches and seizures under the Fourth Amendment. I continue to believe that "[t]he scheme of the Fourth Amendment becomes meaningful only when it is assured that at some point the conduct of those charged with enforcing the laws can be subjected to the more detached, neutral scrutiny of a judge who must evaluate the reasonableness of a particular search or seizure in light of the particular circumstances." Terry v. Ohio. Because I find the majority's reasoning to be at odds with these fundamental principles, I must respectfully dissent.

* * *

The majority's attempt to avoid case-by-case adjudication of Fourth Amendment issues is not only misguided as a matter of principle, but is also doomed to fail as a matter of practical application. As the majority itself is well aware, the powers granted the police in this case are strong ones, subject to potential abuse. Although, in this particular case. Officer Jenks was required by Police Department regulation to make an in-custody arrest rather than to issue a citation, in most jurisdictions and for most traffic offenses the determination of whether to issue a citation or effect a full arrest is discretionary with the officer. There is always the possibility that a police officer, lacking probable cause to obtain a search warrant, will use a traffic arrest as a pretext to conduct a search. I suggest this possibility not to impugn the integrity of our police, but merely to point out that case-by-case adjudication will always be necessary to determine whether a full arrest was effected for purely legitimate reasons or, rather, as a pretext for searching the arrestee. . . .

* * *

NOTES

1. In the companion case of Gustafson v. Florida, 414 U.S. 260, 94 S. Ct. 488 (1973), the Supreme Court issued the following ruling (with the same three Justices dissenting as in *Robinson*):

> We hold that upon arresting petitioner for the offense of driving his automobile without a valid operator's license, and taking him into custody, Smith was entitled to make a full search of petitioner's person incident to that lawful arrest. Since it is the fact of custodial arrest which gives rise to the authority to search, it is of no moment that Smith did not indicate any subjective fear of the petitioner or that he did not himself suspect that the petitioner was armed. Having in the course of his lawful search come upon the box of cigarettes, Smith was entitled to inspect it; and when his inspection revealed the homemade cigarettes which he believed to contain an unlawful substance, he was entitled to seize them as "fruits, instrumentalities or contraband" probative of criminal conduct.

2. Several state courts, utilizing state constitutions, have invalidated *on state grounds* searches which under *Robinson* comport with the Fourth Amendment. They have done so in traffic cases and in cases involving other minor offenses, where a search of the arrestee is unlikely to produce "fruits" or evidence of the offense. Such state decisions also frequently involve a situation where, although the arrest is "custodial," the suspect will be able to secure his release pending trial without ever going through complete "booking" procedures or being confined in a lock-up or jail. See e.g., People v. Brisendine, 13 Cal.3d 528, 119 Cal.Rptr. 315, 531 P.2d 1099 (1975); Zehrung v. State, 569 P.2d 189 (Alaska 1977).

(b) REQUIREMENT OF PROXIMITY TO ARREST

Search Before Arrest. A search incident to arrest must, in time and place, be substantially proximate to arrest. If a search precedes the arrest by any significant span of time, it cannot be considered incident thereto. However, as long as probable cause to arrest exists before the search, the search, in the interest of the officer's safety, may slightly precede the formal arrest. See the concurring opinion of Justice Harlan in Sibron v. New York, 392 U.S. 40, 88 S.Ct. 1889 (1968). See also United States v. Collins, 439 F.2d 610 (D.C. Cir. 1971) ; People v. Simon, 45 Cal.2d 645, 290 P.2d 531 (1955). As was said in Holt v. Simpson, 340 F.2d 853, 856 (7th Cir. 1965) :

> "When probable cause for an arrest exists independent-
> ly of what the search produces, the fact that the search pre-
> cedes the formal arrest is immaterial when the search and
> arrest are nearly simultaneous and constitute for all practi-
> cal purposes but one transaction. To hold differently would
> be to allow a technical formality of time to control when
> there had been no real interference with the substantive
> rights of a defendant."

However, even if probable cause to arrest existed before the search, and even if the arrest immediately followed the search, if the officer did not intend to make an arrest unless the search proved fruitful, then, according to some courts, the search cannot be considered to be incident to the arrest. See, e.g., State v. Baker, 112 N.J. Super. 351, 271 A.2d 435 (1970) ; People v. Cox, 49 Ill.2d 245, 274 N.E.2d 45 (1971). This limitation could be very important in traffic cases. If an officer has a right to take a driver into custody following a traffic offense, but does not decide to make a custodial arrest until a search of the driver yields evidence of a more serious offense, the search cannot be justified as incident to the arrest. State v. Cotterman, 544 S.W.2d 322 (Mo.App.1976).

Search After Arrest: Delayed and Second Searches. As discussed in the next subsection, searches incident to arrest include (a) searches of the arrestee's person, and (b) searches of the place within his reaching distance at the time of his arrest. With respect to the first type of search, the requirement that the search be substantially contemporaneous with the arrest has not been applied rigorously. Thus searches of the suspect conducted while he is being transported to the police station have been upheld, as have been searches of the arrestee at the police station, even when such searches are "second searches." See generally State v. Wiley, 522 S.W.2d 281 (Mo.1975); People v. Garrett, 49 Ill. App.2d 296, 200 N.E.2d 7 (1964). Compare People v. Dixon, 392 Mich. 691, 222 N.W.2d 749 (1974); People v. Bowen, 29 Ill.2d 349, 194 N.E.2d 316 (1963).

In United States v. Edwards, 415 U.S. 800, 94 S.Ct. 1234 (1974), a suspect's clothes were confiscated 12 hours after his arrest at a time when he was in jail. The Supreme Court upheld this procedure. One way of looking at the decision is to say that the requirement of contemporaneity has been made meaningless. A different view is that the court did not use the traditional search-incident analysis, but instead, concluded that the search was reasonable under all the circumstances even if no well recognized category precisely fit the case.

After an arrestee has been removed from a place, search of that place ordinarily may not be justified as incident to the arrest. Preston v. United States, 376 U.S. 364, 84 S.Ct. 881 (1964). Thus removing a suspect from his home may terminate an officer's right to search even the area of the home which could have been properly searched within the spatial limits of _Chimel,_ discussed in the next subsection.

(c) Scope and Intensity of the Search

The Arrestee's Person and His Immediate Effects. A person who is subjected to a lawful arrest can be thoroughly searched. The permissible intensity is illustrated by a few decisions. State v. Riley, 226 N.W.2d 907 (Minn.1975) (inspection of penis of alleged rapist); State v. Wood, 262 La. 259, 263 So.2d 28 (1972) (mouth); United States v. Sanders, 477 F.2d 112 (5th Cir.1973) (fingerprints); Gaddis v. State, 497 P.2d 1087 (Okl.Cr.App.1972) (pubic hairs); United States v. Klein, 522 F.2d 296 (1st Cir. 1975) (strip search and rectum inspection). However, the requirement of reasonableness under the Fourth Amendment and general due process considerations prohibit methods of searching which would shock the conscience. See, e. g., United States ex rel. Guy v. McCauley, 385 F.Supp. 193 (E.D. Wis.1974), concerning body cavity searches by persons without medical training. An excellent analysis of older cases involving thorough searches of the person is found in McIntyre and Chabraja, The Intensive Search of a Suspect's Body and Clothing, 58 J.Crim.L., C., & P.S. 18 (1967).

Following the Supreme Court's decisions in the cases of _Robinson_ and _Gustafson,_ reported in supra 5(a), many courts held that officers could search not only the arrestee's person but also could inspect containers carried by the arrestee (or within his reach), such as briefcases and suitcases. Doubt was cast upon these decisions, however, by United States v. Chadwick, 433 U.S. 1, 97 S.Ct. 2476 (1977). There federal agents seized a locked trunk which was in the possession of persons whom they arrested at a railway station. More than an hour later, the agents, back at their office, opened the trunk without a search warrant. The Court refused to uphold the search as incident to arrest because the search took place long after the arrest. It added: "Once law enforcement officers have reduced luggage or other personal property not immediately associated with the person of the arrestee to their exclusive possession and there is no longer any danger that the arrestee might gain access to the property to seize a weapon or destroy evidence, a search of that property is no longer an incident of the arrest." This language has led *some* courts to hold that a suitcase removed from the arrestee cannot be searched without a warrant even if there is no passage of time between arrest and search. See United States v. Berry, 560 F.2d 861 (7th Cir. 1977); Sanders v. State, 262 Ark. 595, 559 S.W.2d 704 (1977); United States v. Ester, 442 F.Supp. 736 (S.D.N.Y.1977); State v. Dean, 2 Kan. App.2d 64, 574 P.2d 572 (1978); State v. Dudley, 561 S.W.2d 403 (Mo.App.1977).

Other courts indicate that if a search of the container is made immediately or at the first practical time, the dictates of *Chadwick* are not violated. See People v. De Santis, 46 N.Y.2d 82, 412 N.Y.S. 2d 838, 385 N.E.2d 577 (1978).

Although Arkansas v. Sanders, 442 U.S. 753, 99 S.Ct. 2586 (1979), Section L, infra, which involved a prompt search of a suitcase found in a car, discusses *Chadwick*, because the State was not relying on the search-incident doctrine in *Sanders*, that case offers no guidance as to the limits placed by *Chadwick* upon searches incident to arrest. In Dawson v. State, 40 Md.App. 640, 395 A.2d 160 (1978), the Court held that items "immediately associated" with the arrestee's person could be taken and searched without a warrant. See also Middleton v. State, 577 P.2d 1050 (Alaska 1978) (opening of folded paper in wallet).

Beyond the Arrestee's Person. As the Supreme Court held in Chimel v. California, 395 U.S. 752, 89 S.Ct. 2034 (1969), a search incident to arrest may not exceed the area within reach of the arrestee. This limitation was said to be consonant with the rationale of the doctrine of search incident to arrest: the need to prevent the arrestee from obtaining a weapon to use against the arrestee and the need to prevent him from destroying evidence. By looking to the rationale of the rule, the Court finally resolved an issue which had seen the Court reverse its position no less than five times concerning the proper scope of a search incident to arrest. The reversals of position are treated candidly in *Chimel* and also are the subject of an excellent discussion in Moylan, The Plain View Doctrine: Unexpected Child of the Great "Search Incident," Geography Battle, 26 Mercer L.Rev. 1047 (1975). *Chimel* worked a radical change in the law because in the era immediately preceding that decision, following the Supreme Court lead, lower courts routinely deemed "reasonable," searches, for example, of the entire house in which a person was arrested.

Naturally some fine lines are drawn in determining the perimeter of searches permitted by *Chimel*. Concerning search of an area to which the suspect might possibly "lunge," see Application of Kiser, 419 F.2d 1134 (8th Cir. 1969), and compare United States v. Mapp, 476 F.2d 67 (2d Cir. 1973). Suppose that the danger of an arrestee's reaching out for a weapon or evidence has been limited by the hand-cuffing of the arrestee. Has the officer lost the right to search the area which was within reach at the time of the arrest? See United States v. Ciotti, 469 F.2d 1204 (3d Cir. 1972), United States v. Mehciz, 437 F.2d 145 (9th Cir. 1971), and State v. Shane, 255 N.W.2d 324 (Iowa 1977) (no). Compare People v. Robbins, 54 Ill.App.3d 298, 12 Ill.Dec. 80, 369 N.E.2d 577 (1977) (yes).

The police cannot move the suspect from place to place within a home to broaden the area of the permissible search under *Chimel*. United States v. Griffith, 537 F.2d 900 (7th Cir. 1976). Decision which permit the police to allow or direct the arrestee to go from place to place to gather clothing or identification preparatory to the trip to the station seem to lay the groundwork for rather crude tactics designed to broaden the area which is "within reach" of the arrestee. Naturally, however, the officer can follow the arrestee as the arrestee looks in closets or drawers. See People v. Surles, 29 Mich. App. 132, 185 N.W.2d 126 (1970); United States v. Di Stefano, 555 F.2d 1094 (2d Cir. 1977); United States v. Titus, 445 F.2d 577 (2d Cir. 1971); United States v. Holmes, 452 F.2d 249 (7th Cir. 1971); People v. Mancl, 55 Ill.App.3d 41, 12 Ill.Dec. 860, 370 N.E.2d 664 (1977).

Frequently when officers make an arrest in a home, they will claim that the possible presence of third persons elsewhere in the house justifies at least a "protective sweep" through other rooms to ensure that a third person neither poses a danger to the officers nor is in a position to destroy evidence. In *Chimel* itself, however, the arrestee's wife was at home. The Court discussed and apparently rejected, as a basis for broadening the search beyond the area within the arrestee's reach, the possibility that a third person, alerted by the arrest, might destroy evidence elsewhere in the house. The Court reasoned that the police could not create their own exigencies by arresting a suspect at his home and then relying on an emergency theory to justify a warrantless search of all the rooms. Nevertheless, a large number of lower court decisions permit officers to enter other rooms (though not to search them intensely) on the theory that third persons who pose a danger might be present. The usual scenario sees the officer enter a room (out of the arrestee's reach) ostensibly to look for dangerous third persons. Following entry he spots and seizes evidence in plain view. (See Section H, infra.) Although the cases are not uniform, the more objective data suggesting (a) that someone else is present and (b) that such person is dangerous, the more likely is a court to permit the protective sweep. See United States v. Hobson, 519 F.2d 765 (9th Cir. 1975); United States v. Christophe, 470 F.2d 865 (2d Cir. 1972); United States v. Looney, 481 F.2d 31 (5th Cir. 1973). However, concerns about the officer's safety, without more, sometimes have been deemed inadequate to justify a protective sweep. State v. Ranker, 343 So.2d 189 (La.1977); State v. Peterson, 525 S.W.2d 599 (Mo.App.1975); United States v. Gamble, 473 F.2d 1274 (7th Cir. 1973).

Frisks and Searches of Arrestee's Companions. If *A* is arrested in *B's* presence *B* can be frisked for weapons if there is independent justification for such a frisk under Terry v. Ohio (Section F, infra). Some courts, however, seem to hold that such frisks are proper even though the criteria of *Terry* are not satisfied. Consider the following from United States v. Berryhill, 445 F.2d 1189 (9th Cir. 1971):

> "The postal inspectors had obtained a warrant for the arrest of defendant for the Kawa check theft and were looking for him. The arresting officers had knowledge of defendant's prior arrest history, including information that he usually had weapons close to him. Defendant and his wife, the former driving, the latter a front-seat passenger, were located in an automobile and were stopped to effectuate the

arrest at a busy intersection. The arrest was made with drawn pistols covering both occupants of the car, defendant was required to disembark and spread-eagle against the car where he was searched for weapons, handcuffed and taken to the officer's car by Inspector Loffler. Inspector Michaelson observed that Mrs. Berryhill was clutching a handbag with a paper sack protruding from the top. The paper sack was too small for its contents and in the top of the sack, the officer saw what appeared to be several envelopes. Michaelson, covering Mrs. Berryhill with his firearm, searched the handbag for weapons and found the mail matter which is the subject of Counts VI and XIII. On interrogation, defendant said, 'Look here, officer, the mail in her purse is mine. I told her to put it in there and she does what I say because she is my wife.'

"We are here concerned with the right to search another occupant of the vehicle, Mrs. Clarice Berryhill, who was clutching the handbag in which the stolen mail matter described in Counts VI and XIII was found. The fact that envelopes were observed protruding from the top of the paper sack might arguably have supported the reasonableness of the search, but the arresting officer described it as purely a search for weapons. And the lawful arrest of Berryhill cannot legalize a personal search of a companion for evidence against her simply because she was there. United States v. Di Re, 332 U.S. 581, 68 S.Ct. 222 (1948). The Supreme Court, however, has clarified the right of peace officers to protect themselves from the reasonably anticipated possibility of assault. In Terry v. Ohio, 392 U.S. 1, 88 S.Ct. 1868 (1967), the Court affirmed the right of a limited search 'to assure * * * that the person with whom he is dealing is not armed with a weapon that could unexpectedly and fatally be used against him' despite the absence of probable cause for an arrest. We think that *Terry* recognizes and common sense dictates that the legality of such a limited intrusion into a citizen's personal privacy extends to a criminal's companions at the time of arrest. It is inconceivable that a peace officer effecting a lawful arrest of an occupant of a vehicle must expose himself to a shot in the back from defendant's associate because he cannot, on the spot, make the nice distinction between whether the other is a companion in crime or a social acquaintance. All companions of the arrestee within the immediate vicinity, capable of accomplishing a harmful assault on the officer, are constitutionally subjected to the cursory 'pat-down' reasonably necessary to give assurance that they are unarmed."

Also consider United States v. Simmons, 567 F.2d 314 (7th Cir. 1977), which held that under narrowly defined circumstances, *B* may be searched incident to the arrest of *A*. On the other hand, routine frisks or searches of companions of arrestees have been condemned on occasion. United States v. Di Re, 332 U.S. 581, 68 S.Ct. 222 (1948); People v. Johnson, 14 Ill.App.3d 254, 302 N.E.2d 430 (1973).

(d) Limitations Upon Power to Seize

Although under United States v. Robinson, supra 5(a), the right to search a person who has been subject to a lawful custodial arrest does not depend upon the probability that something will turn up, the right to take and carry away the arrestee's property *may* depend upon a probability that such property (discovered within a proper search incident to arrest) is contraband or constitutes evidence of a crime. Suppose, for example, that within reach of the arrestee on his dresser is a bottle of pills. Can the police take and carry it away absent seizure probable cause? State v. Elkins, 245 Or. 279, 422 P.2d 250 (1966), suggests not. See also Justice Harlan's concurring opinion in Von Cleef v. New Jersey, 395 U.S. 814, 89 S.Ct. 2051 (1969), discussing Kremen v. United States, 353 U.S. 346, 77 U.S. 828 (1957). Compare the clear requirement of seizure probable cause in plain view cases, covered in Section H, note 7, infra.

Another limitation upon seizures incident to arrest is found in Roaden v. Kentucky, 413 U.S. 496, 93 S.Ct. 2796 (1973), which held that obscene films within reach of an arrestee cannot be seized. Because of First Amendment implications, issuance of a search warrant by a neutral judicial officer is required. Possibly *Roaden* would apply also to seizures of *multiple* copies of allegedly obscene printed matter incident to an arrest. The danger is the same: possible suppression of speech without any probable cause decision by a judicial officer.

6. EFFECT OF UNLAWFUL ARREST UPON POWER TO PROSECUTE

Although lawyers frequently speak of "quashing an arrest," the fact that an arrest is illegal does not deprive the court of jurisdiction. An illegally arrested defendant—even one who has been improperly returned to the state or country where the crime was committed— may still be subjected to trial. For instance, in the case of Adolph Eichmann, the chief executioner of millions of Jews during the Nazi regime in Germany, the Supreme Court of Israel relied heavily upon American case law to justify its right to try Eichmann, who had been kidnapped in Argentina and flown to Israel for trial. See Pearlman, The Capture and Trial of Adolph Eichmann (1963) 112. To the same effect are the cases of Frisbie v. Collins, 342 U.S. 519, 72 S.Ct. 509 (1952); United States v. Sobel, 142 F.Supp. 515 (D.C.N.Y.1956); People v. Griffith, 130 Colo. 475, 276 P.2d 559 (1954).

Against the weight of hundreds of precedents, a very few recent decisions hold that when a suspect is returned to a jurisdiction by flagrantly unlawful means, due process requires that he be released, although the re-filing of charges is not necessarily barred. See United States v. Toscanino, 500 F.2d 267 (2d Cir. 1974), which, however, was sharply limited to its particular by several subsequent Second Circuit cases. In *Toscanino* the defendant had been kidnapped, drugged, and tortured. Nevertheless, one state Supreme Court applied the *Toscanino* doctrine: Benally v. Marcum, 89 N.M. 463, 553 P.2d 1270 (1976).

The law varies from jurisdiction to jurisdiction as to whether the illegality of an arrest prevents the prosecution from securing a conviction for resisting arrest and whether force used against an officer in resisting an unlawful arrest can be deemed justified when the arrestee is faced with a charge such as battery against the officer. What policy arguments are most persuasive in resolving these questions?

Concerning the suppression of evidence derived from an illegal arrest, see Chapter 6, Section E, infra.

F. STOP–AND–FRISK AND OTHER LIMITED INVESTIGATIVE DETENTIONS

TERRY v. OHIO

Supreme Court of the United States, 1968.
392 U.S. 1, 88 S.Ct. 1868.

MR. CHIEF JUSTICE WARREN delivered the opinion of the Court.

This case presents serious questions concerning the role of the Fourth Amendment in the confrontation on the street between the citizen and the policeman investigating suspicious circumstances.

Petitioner Terry was convicted of carrying a concealed weapon. Following the denial of a pretrial motion to suppress, the prosecution introduced in evidence two revolvers and a number of bullets seized from Terry and a codefendant, Richard Chilton, by Cleveland Police Detective Martin McFadden. At the hearing on the motion to suppress this evidence, Officer McFadden testified that while he was patrolling in plain clothes in downtown Cleveland at approximately 2:30 in the afternoon of October 31, 1963, his attention was attracted by two men, Chilton and Terry, standing on the corner of Huron Road and Euclid Avenue. He had never seen the two men before, and he was unable to say precisely what first drew his eye to them. However, he testified that he had been a policeman for 39 years and a detective for 35 and that he had been assigned to patrol this vicinity of downtown Cleveland for shoplifters and pickpockets for 30 years. He explained that he had developed routine habits of observation over the years and that he would "stand and watch people or walk and watch people at many intervals of the day." He added: "Now, in this case when I looked over they didn't look right to me at the time."

His interest aroused, Officer McFadden took up a post of observation in the entrance to a store 300 to 400 feet away from the two men. "I get more purpose to watch them when I seen their movements," he testified. He saw one of the men leave the other one and walk southwest on Huron Road, past some stores. The man paused for a moment and looked in a store window, then walked on a short distance, turned around and walked back toward the corner, pausing once again to look in the same store window. He rejoined his companion at the corner, and the two conferred briefly. Then the second man went through the same series of motions, strolling down Huron Road, looking in the same window, walking on a short distance, turning back, peering in the store window again, and returning to confer with the first man at the corner. The two men repeated this ritual alternately between five and six times apiece—in all, roughly a dozen trips. At one point, while the two were standing together on the corner, a third man approached them and engaged them briefly in conversation. This man then left the two others and walked west on Euclid Avenue. Chilton and Terry resumed their measured pacing, peering, and conferring. After this had gone on for 10 to 12 minutes, the two men walked off together, heading west on Euclid Avenue, following the path taken earlier by the third man.

By this time Officer McFadden had become thoroughly suspicious. He testified that after observing their elaborately casual and oft-repeated reconnaissance of the store window on Huron Road, he suspected the two men of "casing a job, a stick-up," and that he considered it his duty as a police officer to investigate further. He added that he feared "they may have a gun." Thus, Officer McFadden followed Chilton and Terry and saw them stop in front of Zucker's store to talk to the same man who had conferred with them earlier on the street corner. Deciding that the situation was ripe for direct action, Officer McFadden approached the three men, identified himself as a police officer and asked for their names. At this point his knowledge was confined to what he had observed. He was not acquainted with any of the three men by name or by sight, and he had received no information concerning them from any other source. When the men "mumbled something" in response to his inquiries, Officer McFadden grabbed petitioner Terry, spun him around so that they were facing the other two, with Terry between McFadden and the others, and patted down the outside of his clothing. In the left breast pocket of Terry's overcoat Officer McFadden felt a pistol. He reached inside the overcoat pocket, but was unable to remove the gun. At this point, keeping Terry between himself and the others, the officer ordered all three men to enter Zucker's store. As they went in, he removed Terry's overcoat completely, retrieved a .38 caliber revolver from the pocket and ordered all three men to face the wall with their hands raised. Officer McFadden proceeded to pat down the outer clothing of Chilton and the third man, Katz. He discovered another revolver in the outer pocket of Chilton's overcoat, but no weapons were found on Katz. The officer testified that he only patted the men down to see whether they had weapons, and that he did not put his hands beneath the outer garments of either Terry or Chilton until he felt their guns. So far as appears from the record, he never placed his hands beneath Katz's outer garments. Officer Mc-

Fadden seized Chilton's gun, asked the proprietor of the store to call a police wagon, and took all three men to the station, where Chilton and Terry were formally charged with carrying concealed weapons.

On the motion to suppress the guns the prosecution took the position that they had been seized following a search incident to a lawful arrest. The trial court rejected this theory, stating that it "would be stretching the facts beyond reasonable comprehension" to find that Officer McFadden had had probable cause to arrest the men before he patted them down for weapons. However, the court denied the defendants' motion on the ground that Officer McFadden, on the basis of his experience, "had reasonable cause to believe . . . that the defendants were conducting themselves suspiciously, and some interrogation should be made of their action." Purely for his own protection, the court held, the officer had the right to pat down the outer clothing of these men, whom he had reasonable cause to believe might be armed. The court distinguished between an investigatory "stop" and an arrest, and between a "frisk" of the outer clothing for weapons and a full-blown search for evidence of crime. The frisk, it held, was essential to the proper performance of the officer's investigatory duties, for without it "the answer to the police officer may be a bullet, and a loaded pistol discovered during the frisk is admissible."

After the court denied their motion to suppress, Chilton and Terry waived jury trial and pleaded not guilty. The court adjudged them guilty. . . . .

I.

The Fourth Amendment provides that "the right of the people to be secure in their persons, houses, papers, and effects, against unreasonable searches and seizures, shall not be violated . . . .." This inestimable right of personal security belongs as much to the citizen on the streets of our great cities as to the homeowner closeted in his study to dispose of his secret affairs. * * *

Unquestionably petitioner was entitled to the protection of the Fourth Amendment as he walked down the street in Cleveland. The question is whether in all the circumstances of this on-the-street encounter, his right to personal security was violated by an unreasonable search and seizure.

We would be less than candid if we did not acknowledge that this question thrusts to the fore difficult and troublesome issues regarding a sensitive area of police activity—issues which have never before been squarely presented to this Court. Reflective of the tensions involved are the practical and constitutional arguments pressed with great vigor on both sides of the public debate over the power of the police to "stop and frisk"—as it is sometimes euphemistically termed —suspicious persons.

On the one hand, it is frequently argued that in dealing with the rapidly unfolding and often dangerous situations on city streets the police are in need of an escalating set of flexible responses, graduated in relation to the amount of information they possess. For this purpose it is urged that distinctions should be made between a "stop" and an "arrest" (or a "seizure" of a person), and between a "frisk" and a "search." Thus, it is argued, the police should be allowed to "stop" a person and detain him briefly for questioning upon suspicion that he may be connected with criminal activity. Upon suspicion that the person may be armed, the police should have the power to "frisk" him for weapons. If the "stop" and the "frisk" give rise to probable cause to believe that the suspect has committed a crime, then the police should be empowered to make a formal "arrest," and a full incident "search" of the person. This scheme is justified in part upon the notion that a "stop" and a "frisk" amount to a mere "minor inconvenience and petty indignity," which can properly be imposed upon the citizen in the interest of effective law enforcement on the basis of a police officer's suspicion.[1]

On the other side the argument is made that the authority of the police must be strictly circumscribed by the law of arrest and search as it has developed to date in the traditional jurisprudence of the Fourth Amendment. It is contended with some force that there is not—and cannot be—a variety of police activity which does not depend solely upon the voluntary cooperation of the citizen and yet which stops short of an arrest based upon probable cause to make such an arrest. The heart of the Fourth Amendment, the argument runs, is a severe requirement of specific justification for any intrusion upon protected personal security, coupled with a highly developed system of judicial controls to enforce upon the agents of the State the commands of the Constitution. Acquiescence by the courts in the compulsion inherent in the field interrogation practices at issue here, it is urged, would constitute an abdication of judicial control over, and indeed an encouragement of, substantial interference with liberty and personal security by police officers whose judgment is necessarily colored by their primary involvement in "the often competitive enterprise of ferreting out crime." Johnson v. United States, 333 U.S. 10, 14, 68 S.Ct. 367, 369 (1948). This, it is argued, can only serve to exacerbate police-community tensions in the crowded centers of our Nation's cities.

1. ". . . [T]he evidence needed to make the inquiry is not of the same degree or conclusiveness as that required for an arrest. The stopping of the individual to inquire is not an arrest and the ground upon which the police may make the inquiry may be less incriminating than the ground for an arrest for a crime known to have been committed. . . .
"And as the right to stop and inquire is to be justified for a cause less conclusive than that which would sustain an arrest, so the right to frisk may be justified as an incident to inquiry upon grounds of elemental safety and precaution which might not initially sustain a search. Ultimately the validity of the frisk narrows down to whether there is or is not a right by the police to touch the person questioned. The sense of exterior touch here involved is not very far different from the sense of sight or hearing—senses upon which police customarily act." People v. Rivera, 14 N.Y.2d 441, 445, 447, 201 N.E.2d 32, 34, 35, 252 N.Y.S.2d 458, 461, 463 (1964), cert. denied, 379 U.S. 978, 85 S.Ct. 679 (1965).

In this context we approach the issues in this case mindful of the limitations of the judicial function in controlling the myriad daily situations in which policemen and citizens confront each other on the street. The State has characterized the issue here as "the right of a police officer . . . to make an on-the-street stop, interrogate and pat down for weapons (known in the street vernacular as 'stop and frisk')." But this is only partly accurate. For the issue is not the abstract propriety of the police conduct, but the admissibility against petitioner of the evidence uncovered by the search and seizure. Ever since its inception, the rule excluding evidence seized in violation of the Fourth Amendment has been recognized as a principal mode of discouraging lawless police conduct. Thus its major thrust is a deterrent one, and experience has taught that it is the only effective deterrent to police misconduct in the criminal context, and that without it the constitutional guarantee against unreasonable searches and seizures would be a mere "form of words." The rule also serves another vital function—"the imperative of judicial integrity." Courts which sit under our Constitution cannot and will not be made party to lawless invasions of the constitutional rights of citizens by permitting unhindered governmental use of the fruits of such invasions. Thus in our system evidentiary rulings provide the context in which the judicial process of inclusion and exclusion approves some conduct as comporting with constitutional guarantees and disapproves other actions by state agents. A ruling admitting evidence in a criminal trial, we recognize, has the necessary effect of legitimizing the conduct which produced the evidence, while an application of the exclusionary rule withholds the constitutional imprimatur.

The exclusionary rule has its limitations, however, as a tool of judicial control. It cannot properly be invoked to exclude the products of legitimate police investigative techniques on the ground that much conduct which is closely similar involves unwarranted intrusions upon constitutional protections. Moreover, in some contexts the rule is ineffective as a deterrent. Street encounters between citizens and police officers are incredibly rich in diversity. They range from wholly friendly exchanges of pleasantries or mutually useful information to hostile confrontations of armed men involving arrests, or injuries, or loss of life. Moreover, hostile confrontations are not all of a piece. Some of them begin in a friendly enough manner, only to take a different turn upon the injection of some unexpected element into the conversation. Encounters are initiated by the police for a wide variety of purposes, some of which are wholly unrelated to a desire to prosecute for crime.[2] Doubtless some police "field interrogation"

2. See Tiffany, McIntyre & Rotenberg, Detection of Crime: Stopping and Questioning, Search and Seizure, Encouragement and Entrapment 18–56 (1967). This sort of police conduct may, for example, be designed simply to help an intoxicated person find his way home, with no intention of arresting him unless he becomes obstreperous. Or the police may be seeking to mediate a domestic quarrel which threatens to erupt into violence. They may accost a woman in an area known for prostitution as part of a harassment campaign designed to drive prostitutes away without the considerable difficulty involved in prosecuting them. Or they

conduct violates the Fourth Amendment. But a stern refusal by this Court to condone such activity does not necessarily render it responsive to the exclusionary rule. Regardless of how effective the rule may be where obtaining convictions is an important objective of the police, it is powerless to deter invasions of constitutionally guaranteed rights where the police either have no interest in prosecuting or are willing to forego successful prosecution in the interest of serving some other goal.

Proper adjudication of cases in which the exclusionary rule is invoked demands a constant awareness of these limitations. The wholesale harassment by certain elements of the police community, of which minority groups, particularly Negroes, frequently complain,[3] will not be stopped by the exclusion of any evidence from any criminal trial. Yet a rigid and unthinking application of the exclusionary rule, in futile protest against practices which it can never be used effectively to control, may exact a high toll in human injury and frustration of efforts to prevent crime. No judicial opinion can comprehend the protean variety of the street encounter, and we can only judge the facts of the case before us. Nothing we say today is to be taken as indicating approval of police conduct outside the legitimate investigative sphere. Under our decision, courts still retain their traditional responsibility to guard against police conduct which is overbearing or harassing, or which trenches upon personal security without the objective evidentiary justification which the Constitution requires. When such conduct is identified, it must be condemned by the judiciary and its fruits must be excluded from evidence in criminal trials. And, of course, our approval of legitimate and restrained investigative conduct undertaken on the basis of ample factual justification should in no way discourage the employment of other remedies than the exclusionary rule to curtail abuses for which that sanction may prove inappropriate.

---

may be conducting a dragnet search of all teenagers in a particular section of the city for weapons because they have heard rumors of an impending gang fight.

3. The President's Commission on Law Enforcement and Administration of Justice found that "in many communities, field interrogations are a major source of friction between the police and minority groups." President's Commission on Law Enforcement and Administration of Justice, Task Force Report: The Police 183 (1967). It was reported that the friction caused by "misuse of field interrogations" increases "as more police departments adopt 'aggressive partol' in which officers are encouraged routinely to stop and question persons on the street who are unknown to them, who are suspicious, or whose purpose for being abroad is not readily evident." Id., at 184. While the frequency with which "frisking" forms a part of field interrogation practice varies tremendously with the locale, the objective of the interrogation, and the particular officer, see Tiffany, McIntyre & Rotenberg, supra, n. 9, at 47–48, it cannot help but be a severely exacerbating factor in police-community tensions. This is particularly true in situations where the "stop and frisk" of youths or minority group members is "motivated by the officers' perceived need to maintain the power image of the beat officer, an aim sometimes accomplished by humiliating anyone who attempts to undermine police control of the streets." Id., at 47–48.

Having thus roughly sketched the perimeters of the constitutional debate over the limits on police investigative conduct in general and the background against which this case presents itself, we turn our attention to the quite narrow question posed by the facts before us: whether it is always unreasonable for a policeman to seize a person and subject him to a limited search for weapons unless there is probable cause for an arrest. Given the narrowness of this question, we have no occasion to canvass in detail the constitutional limitations upon the scope of a policeman's power when he confronts a citizen without probable cause to arrest him.

II.

Our first task is to establish at what point in this encounter the Fourth Amendment becomes relevant. That is, we must decide whether and when Officer McFadden "seized" Terry and whether and when he conducted a "search." There is some suggestion in the use of such terms as "stop" and "frisk" that such police conduct is outside the purview of the Fourth Amendment because neither action rises to the level of a "search" or "seizure" within the meaning of the Constitution. We emphatically reject this notion. It is quite plain that the Fourth Amendment governs "seizures" of the person which do not eventuate in a trip to the station house and prosecution for crime—"arrests" in traditional terminology. It must be recognized that whenever a police officer accosts an individual and restrains his freedom to walk away, he has "seized" that person. And it is nothing less than sheer torture of the English language to suggest that a careful exploration of the outer surfaces of a person's clothing all over his or her body in an attempt to find weapons is not a "search." Moreover, it is simply fantastic to urge that such a procedure performed in public by a policeman while the citizen stands helpless, perhaps facing a wall with his hands raised, is a "petty indignity." [4] It is a serious intrusion upon the sanctity of the person, which may inflict great indignity and arouse strong resentment, and it is not to be undertaken lightly.[5]

The danger in the logic which proceeds upon distinctions between a "stop" and an "arrest," or "seizure" of the person, and between a "frisk" and a "search" is two-fold. It seeks to isolate from

---

4. Consider the following apt description:

"[T]he officer must feel with sensitive fingers every portion of the prisoner's body. A thorough search must be made of the prisoner's arms and armpits, waistline and back, the groin and area about the testicles, and entire surface of the legs down to the feet." Priar & Martin, Searching and Disarming Criminals, 45 J.Crim., L.C. & P.S. 481 (1954).

5. We have noted that the abusive practices which play a major, though by no means exclusive, role in creating this friction are not susceptible of control by means of the exclusionary rule, and cannot properly dictate our decision with respect to the powers of the police in genuine investigative and preventive stiuations. However, the degree of community resentment aroused by particular practices is clearly relevant to an assessment of the quality of the intrusion upon reasonable expectations of personal security caused by those practices.

constitutional scrutiny the initial stages of the contact between the policeman and the citizen. And by suggesting a rigid all-or-nothing model of justification and regulation under the Amendment, it obscures the utility of limitations upon the scope, as well as the initiation, of police action as a means of constitutional regulation. This Court has held in the past that a search which is reasonable at its inception may violate the Fourth Amendment by virtue of its intolerable intensity and scope. The scope of the search must be "strictly tied to and justified by" the circumstances which rendered its initiation permissible. Warden v. Hayden, 387 U.S. 294, 310, 87 S.Ct. 1642, 1651, 1652 (1967) (Mr. Justice Fortas, concurring).

The distinctions of classical "stop-and-frisk" theory thus serve to divert attention from the central inquiry under the Fourth Amendment—the reasonableness in all the circumstances of the particular governmental invasion of a citizen's personal security. "Search" and "seizure" are not talismans. We therefore reject the notions that the Fourth Amendment does not come into play at all as a limitation upon police conduct if the officers stop short of something called a "technical arrest" or a "full-blown search."

In this case there can be no question, then, that Officer McFadden "seized" petitioner and subjected him to a "search" when he took hold of him and patted down the outer surfaces of his clothing. We must decide whether at that point it was reasonable for Officer McFadden to have interfered with petitioner's personal security as he did.[6] And in determining whether the seizure and search were "unreasonable" our inquiry is a dual one—whether the officer's action was justified at its inception, and whether it was reasonably related in scope to the circumstances which justified the interference in the first place.

III.

If this case involved police conduct subject to the Warrant Clause of the Fourth Amendment, we would have to ascertain whether "probable cause" existed to justify the search and seizure which took place. However, that is not the case. We do not retreat from our holdings that the police must, whenever practicable, obtain advance judicial approval of searches and seizures through the warrant procedure . . . or that in most instances failure to comply with the warrant requirement can only be excused by exigent circumstances. But we deal here with an entire rubric of police conduct—

---

6. We thus decide nothing today concerning the constitutional propriety of an investigative "seizure" upon less than probable cause for purposes of "detention" and/or interrogation. Obviously, not all personal intercourse between policemen and citizens involves "seizures" of persons. Only when the officer, by means of physical force or show of authority, has in some way restrained the liberty of a citizen may we conclude that a "seizure" has occurred. We cannot tell with any certainty upon this record whether any such "seizure" took place here prior to Officer McFadden's initiation of physical contact for purposes of searching Terry for weapons, and we thus may assume that up to that point no intrusion upon constitutionally protected rights had occurred.

necessarily swift action predicated upon the on-the-spot observations of the officer on the beat—which historically has not been, and as a practical matter could not be, subjected to the warrant procedure. Instead, the conduct involved in this case must be tested by the Fourth Amendment's general proscription against unreasonable searches and seizures.

Nonetheless, the notions which underlie both the warrant procedure and the requirement of probable cause remain fully relevant in this context. In order to assess the reasonableness of Officer McFadden's conduct as a general proposition, it is necessary "first to focus upon the governmental interest which allegedly justifies official intrusion upon the constitutionally protected interests of the private citizen," for there is "no ready test for determining reasonableness other than by balancing the need to search [or seize] against the invasion which the search [or seizure] entails." Camara v. Municipal Court, 387 U.S. 523, 534, 536–537, 87 S.Ct. 1727, 1733–1735 (1967). And in justifying the particular intrusion the police officer must be able to point to specific and articulable facts which, taken together with rational inferences from those facts, reasonably warrant that intrusion. The scheme of the Fourth Amendment becomes meaningful only when it is assured that at some point the conduct of those charged with enforcing the laws can be subjected to the more detached, neutral scrutiny of a judge who must evaluate the reasonableness of a particular search or seizure in light of the particular circumstances. And in making that assessment it is imperative that the facts be judged against an objective standard: would the facts available to the officer at the moment of the seizure or the search "warrant a man of reasonable caution in the belief" that the action taken was appropriate? Anything less would invite intrusions upon constitutionally guaranteed rights based on nothing more substantial than inarticulate hunches, a result this Court has consistently refused to sanction. And simple " 'good faith on the part of the arresting officer is not enough.' . . . If subjective good faith alone were the test, the protections of the Fourth Amendment would evaporate, and the people would be 'secure in their persons, houses, papers, and effects,' only in the discretion of the police."

Applying these principles to this case, we consider first the nature and extent of the governmental interests involved. One general interest is of course that of effective crime prevention and detection; it is this interest which underlies the recognition that a police officer may in appropriate circumstances and in an appropriate manner approach a person for purposes of investigating possibly criminal behavior even though there is no probable cause to make an arrest. It was this legitimate investigative function Officer McFadden was discharging when he decided to approach petitioner and his companions. He had observed Terry, Chilton, and Katz go through a series of acts, each of them perhaps innocent in itself, but which taken together warranted further investigation. There is nothing unusual in two men standing together on a street corner, perhaps waiting for someone. Nor is there anything suspicious about people in such circumstances strolling up and down the street, singly or in pairs. Store windows, moreover, are made to be looked in. But the story is quite different where, as here, two men hover about a street corner for an extended period of time, at the end of which it becomes apparent that they are not waiting for anyone or anything; where these men pace alternately along an identical route, pausing to stare in the same store window roughly 24 times; where each completion of this route is followed immediately by a conference between the two men on the corner; where they are joined in one of these conferences by a third man who leaves swiftly; and where the two men finally follow the third and rejoin him a couple of blocks away. It would have been poor police work indeed for an officer of 30 years' experience in the detection of thievery from stores in this same neighborhood to have failed to investigate this behavior further.

The crux of this case, however, is not the propriety of Officer McFadden's taking steps to investigate petitioner's suspicious behavior, but rather, whether there was justification for McFadden's invasion of Terry's personal security by searching him for weapons in the course of that investigation. We are now concerned with more than the governmental interest in investigating crime; in addition, there is the more immediate interest of the police officer in taking steps to assure himself that the person with whom he is dealing is not armed with a weapon that could unexpectedly and fatally be used against him. Certainly it would be unreasonable to require that police officers take unnecessary risks in the performance of their duties. American criminals have a long tradition of armed violence, and every year in this country many law enforcement officers are killed in the line of duty, and thousands more are wounded. Virtually all of these deaths and a substantial portion of the injuries are inflicted with guns and knives.

In view of these facts, we cannot blind ourselves to the need for law enforcement officers to protect themselves and other prospective victims of violence in situations where they may lack probable cause for an arrest. When an officer is justified in believing that the individual whose suspicious behavior he is investigating at close range is armed and presently dangerous to the officer or to others, it would appear to be clearly unreasonable to deny the officer the power to take necessary measures to determine whether the person is in fact carrying a weapon and to neutralize the threat of physical harm.

We must still consider, however, the nature and quality of the intrusion on individual rights which must be accepted if police officers are to be conceded the right to search for weapons in situations where probable cause to arrest for crime is lacking. Even a limited search of the outer clothing for weapons constitutes a severe, though brief, intrusion upon cherished personal security, and it must surely be an annoying, frightening, and perhaps humiliating experience. Petitioner contends that such an intrusion is permissible only incident to a lawful arrest, either for a crime involving the possession of weapons or for a crime the commission of which led the officer to investigate in the first place. However, this argument must be closely examined.

Petitioner does not argue that a police officer should refrain from making any investigation of suspicious circumstances until such time as he has probable cause to make an arrest; nor does he deny that police officers in properly discharging their investigative function may find themselves confronting persons who might well be armed and dangerous. Moreover, he does not say that an officer is always unjustified in searching a suspect to discover weapons. Rather, he says it is unreasonable for the policeman to take that step until such time as the situation evolves to a point where there is probable cause to make an arrest. When that point has been reached, petitioner would concede the officer's right to conduct a search of the suspect for weapons, fruits or instrumentalities of the crime, or "mere" evidence, incident to the arrest.

There are two weaknesses in this line of reasoning, however. First, it fails to take account of traditional limitations upon the scope of searches, and thus recognizes no distinction in purpose, character, and extent between a search incident to an arrest and a limited search for weapons. The former, although justified in part by the acknowledged necessity to protect the arresting officer from assault with a concealed weapon, Preston v. United States, 376 U.S. 364, 367, 84 S.Ct. 881, 883 (1964), is also justified on other grounds, ibid., and can therefore involve a relatively extensive exploration of the person. A search for weapons in the absence of probable cause to arrest, however, must, like any other search, be strictly circumscribed by the exigencies which justify its initiation. Warden v. Hayden, 387 U.S. 294, 310, 87 S.Ct. 1642, 1651, 1652 (1967) (Mr. Justice Fortas, concurring). Thus it must be limited to that which is necessary for the discovery of weapons which might be used to harm the officer or others nearby, and may realistically be characterized as something less than a "full" search, even though it remains a serious intrusion.

A second, and related, objection to petitioner's argument is that it assumes that the law of arrest has already worked out the balance between the particular interests involved here—the neutralization of danger to the policeman in the investigative circumstance and the sanctity of the individual. But this is not so. An arrest is a wholly different kind of intrusion upon individual freedom from a limited search for weapons, and the interests each is designed to serve are likewise quite different. An arrest is the initial stage of a criminal prosecution. It is intended to vindicate society's interest in having its laws obeyed, and it is inevitably accompanied by future interference with the individual's freedom of movement, whether or not trial or conviction ultimately follows. The protective search for weapons, on the other hand, constitutes a brief, though far from inconsiderable, intrusion upon the sanctity of the person. It does not follow that because an officer may lawfully arrest a person only when he is apprised of facts sufficient to warrant a belief that the person has committed or is committing a crime, the officer is equally unjustified, absent that kind of evidence, in making any intrusions short of an arrest. Moreover, a perfectly reasonable apprehension of danger may arise long before the officer is possessed of adequate information to justify taking a person into custody for the purpose of prosecuting him for a crime. Petitioner's reliance on cases which have worked out standards of reasonableness with regard to "seizures" constituting arrests and searches incident thereto is thus misplaced. It assumes that the interests sought to be vindicated and the invasions of personal security may be equated in the two cases, and thereby ignores a vital aspect of the analysis of the reasonableness of particular types of conduct under the Fourth Amendment. See Camara v. Municipal Court, supra.

Our evaluation of the proper balance that has to be struck in this type of case leads us to conclude that there must be a narrowly drawn authority to permit a reasonable search for weapons for the protection of the police officer, where he has reason to believe that he is dealing with an armed and dangerous individual, regardless of whether he has probable cause to arrest the individual for a crime. The officer need not be absolutely certain that the individual is armed; the issue is whether a reasonably prudent man in the circumstances would be warranted in the belief that his safety or that of others was in danger. And in determining whether the officer acted reasonably in such circumstances, due weight must be given, not to his inchoate and unparticularized suspicion or "hunch," but to the specific reasonable inferences which he is entitled to draw from the facts in light of his experience. Cf. Brinegar v. United States, supra.

IV.

We must now examine the conduct of Officer McFadden in this case to determine whether his search and seizure of petitioner were reasonable, both at their inception and as conducted. He had observed Terry, together with Chilton and another man, acting in a manner he took to be preface to a "stick-up." We think on the facts and circumstances Officer McFadden detailed before the trial judge a reasonably prudent man would have been warranted in believing petitioner was armed and thus presented a threat to the officer's safety while he was investigating his suspicious behavior. The actions of Terry and Chilton were consistent with McFadden's hypothesis that these men were contemplating a daylight robbery—which, it is reasonable to assume, would be likely to involve the use of weapons—and nothing in their conduct from the time he first noticed them until the time he confronted them and identified himself as a police officer gave him sufficient reason to negate that hypothesis. Although the trio had departed the original scene, there was nothing to indicate abandonment of an intent to commit a robbery at some point. Thus, when Officer McFadden approached the three men gathered before the display window at Zucker's store he had observed enough to make it quite reasonable to fear that they were armed; and nothing in their response to his hailing them, identifying himself as a police officer, and asking their names served to dispel that reasonable belief. We cannot say his decision at that point to seize Terry and pat his clothing for weapons was the product of a volatile or inventive imagination, or was undertaken simply as an act of harassment; the record evidences the tempered act of a policeman who in the course of an investigation had to make a quick decision as to how to protect himself and others from possible danger, and took limited steps to do so.

The manner in which the seizure and search were conducted is, of course, as vital a part of the inquiry as whether they were warranted at all. The Fourth Amendment proceeds as much by limitations upon the scope of governmental action as by imposing preconditions upon its initiation. The entire deterrent purpose of the rule excluding evidence seized in violation of the Fourth Amendment rests on the assumption that "limitations upon the fruit to be gathered tend to limit the quest itself." United States v. Poller, 43 F.2d 911, 914 (C.A.2d Cir. 1930). Thus, evidence may not be introduced if it was discovered by means of a seizure and search which were not reasonably related in scope to the justification for their initiation.

We need not develop at length in this case, however, the limitations which the Fourth Amendment places upon a protective seizure and search for weapons. These limitations will have to be developed in the concrete factual circumstances of individual cases. See Sibron v. New York, decided today. Suffice it to note that such a search, unlike a search without a warrant incident to a lawful arrest, is not justified by any need to prevent the disappearance or destruction of evidence of crime. The sole justification of the search in the present situation is the protection of the police officer and others nearby, and it must therefore be confined in scope to an intrusion reasonably designed to discover guns, knives, clubs, or other hidden instruments for the assault of the police officer.

The scope of the search in this case presents no serious problem in light of these standards. Officer McFadden patted down the outer clothing of petitioner and his two companions. He did not place his hands in their pockets or under the outer surface of their garments until he had felt weapons, and then he merely reached for and removed the guns. He never did invade Katz's person beyond the outer surfaces of his clothes, since he discovered nothing in his pat down which might have been a weapon. Officer McFadden confined his search strictly to what was minimally necessary to learn whether the men were armed and to disarm them once he discovered the weapons. He did not conduct a general exploratory search for whatever evidence of criminal activity he might find.

V.

We conclude that the revolver seized from Terry was properly admitted in evidence against him. At the time he seized petitioner and searched him for weapons, Officer McFadden had reasonable grounds to believe that petitioner was armed and dangerous, and it was necessary for the protection of himself and others to take swift measures to discover the true facts and neutralize the threat of harm if it materialized. The policeman carefully restricted his search to what was appropriate to the discovery of the particular items which he sought. Each case of this sort will, of course, have to be decided on its own facts. We merely hold today that where a police officer observes unusual conduct which leads him reasonably to conclude in light of his experience that criminal activity may be afoot and that the persons with whom he is dealing may be armed and presently dangerous; where in the course of investigating this behavior he identifies himself as a policeman and makes reasonable inquiries; and where nothing in the initial stages of the encounter serves to dispel his reasonable fear for his own or others' safety, he is entitled for the protection of himself and others in the area to conduct a carefully limited search of the outer clothing of such persons in an attempt to discover weapons which might be used to assault him. Such a search is a reasonable search under the Fourth Amendment, and any weapons seized may properly be introduced in evidence against the person from whom they were taken.

Affirmed.

* * *

Mr. Justice Harlan, concurring.

While I unreservedly agree with the Court's ultimate holding in this case, I am constrained to fill in a few gaps, as I see them, in its opinion. I do this because what is said by this Court today will serve as initial guidelines for law enforcement authorities and courts throughout the land as this important new field of law develops. . . . .

If the State of Ohio were to provide that police officers could, on articulable suspicion less than probable cause, forcibly frisk and disarm persons thought to be carrying concealed weapons, I would have little doubt that action taken pursuant to such authority could be constitutionally reasonable. Concealed weapons create an immediate and severe danger to the public, and though that danger might not warrant routine general weapons checks, it could well warrant action on less than a "probability." I mention this line of analysis because I think it vital to point out that it cannot be applied in this case. On the record before us Ohio has not clothed its policemen with routine authority to frisk and disarm on suspicion; in the absence of state authority, policemen have no more right to "pat down" the outer clothing of passers-by, or of persons to whom they address casual questions, than does any other citizen. . . . .

The state courts held, instead, that when an officer is lawfully confronting a possibly hostile person in the line of duty he has a right, springing only from the necessity of the situation and not from any broader right to disarm, to frisk for his own protection. This holding, with which I agree and with which I think the Court agrees, offers the only satisfactory basis I can think of for affirming this conviction. The holding has, however, two logical corollaries that I do not think the Court has fully expressed.

In the first place, if the frisk is justified in order to protect the officer during an encounter with a citizen, the officer must first have constitutional grounds to insist on an encounter, to make a *forcible* stop. Any person, including a policeman, is at liberty to avoid a person he considers dangerous. If and when a policeman has a right instead to disarm such a person for his own protection, he must first have a right not to avoid him but to be in his presence. That right must be more than the liberty (again, possessed by every citizen) to address questions to other persons, for ordinarily the person addressed has an equal right to ignore his interrogator and walk away; he certainly need not submit to a frisk for the questioner's protection. I would make it perfectly clear that the right to frisk in this case depends upon the reasonableness of a forcible stop to investigate a suspected crime.

Where such a stop is reasonable, however, the right to frisk must be immediate and automatic if the reason for the stop is, as here, an articulable suspicion of a crime of violence. Just as a full search incident to a lawful arrest requires no additional justification, a limited frisk incident to a lawful stop must often be rapid and routine. There is no reason why an officer, rightfully but forcibly confronting a person suspected of a serious crime, should have to ask one question and take the risk that the answer might be a bullet.

The facts of this case are illustrative of a proper stop and an incident frisk. Officer McFadden had no probable cause to arrest Terry for anything, but he had observed circumstances that would reasonably lead an experienced, prudent policeman to suspect that Terry was about to engage in burglary or robbery. His justifiable suspicion afforded a proper constitutional basis for accosting Terry, restraining his liberty of movement briefly, and addressing questions to him, and Officer McFadden did so. When he did, he had no reason whatever to suppose that Terry might be armed, apart from the fact that he suspected him of planning a violent crime. McFadden asked Terry his name, to which Terry "mumbled something." Whereupon McFadden, without asking Terry to speak louder and without giving him any chance to explain his presence or his actions, forcibly frisked him.

I would affirm this conviction for what I believe to be the same reasons the Court relies on. I would, however, make explicit what I think is implicit in affirmance on the present facts. Officer McFadden's right to interrupt Terry's freedom of movement and invade his privacy arose only because circumstances warranted forcing an encounter with Terry in an effort to prevent or investigate a crime. Once that forced encounter was justified, however, the officer's right to take suitable measures for his own safety followed automatically.

Upon the foregoing premises, I join the opinion of the Court.

MR. JUSTICE WHITE, concurring.

I join the opinion of the Court, reserving judgment, however, on some of the Court's general remarks about the scope and purpose of the exclusionary rule which the Court has fashioned in the process of enforcing the Fourth Amendment.

Also, although the Court puts the matter aside in the context of this case, I think an additional word is in order concerning the matter of interrogation during an investigative stop. There is nothing in the Constitution which prevents a policeman from addressing questions to anyone on the streets. Absent special circumstances, the person approached may not be detained or frisked but may refuse to cooperate and go on his way. However, given the proper circumstances, such as those in this case, it seems to me the person may be briefly detained against his will while pertinent questions are directed to him. Of course, the person stopped is not obliged to answer, answers may not be compelled, and refusal to answer furnishes no basis for an arrest, although it may alert the officer to the need for continued observation. In my view, it is temporary detention, warranted by the circumstances, which chiefly justifies the protective frisk for weapons. Perhaps the frisk itself, where proper, will have beneficial results whether questions are asked or not. If weapons are found, an arrest will follow. If none are found, the frisk may nevertheless serve preventive ends because of its unmistakable message that suspicion has been aroused. But if the investigative stop is sustainable at all, constitutional rights are not necessarily violated if pertinent questions are asked and the person is restrained briefly in the process.

MR. JUSTICE DOUGLAS, dissenting.

I agree that petitioner was "seized" within the meaning of the Fourth Amendment. I also agree that frisking petitioner and his companions for guns was a "search." But it is a mystery how that "search" and that "seizure" can be constitutional by Fourth Amendment standards, unless there was "probable cause" to believe that (1) a crime had been committed or (2) a crime was in the process of being committed or (3) a crime was about to be committed.

The opinion of the Court disclaims the existence of "probable cause." If loitering were an issue and that was the offense charged, there would be "probable cause" shown. But the crime here is carrying concealed weapons; and there is no basis for concluding that the officer had "probable cause" for believing that crime was being committed. Had a warrant been sought, a magistrate would, therefore, have been unauthorized to issue one, for he can act only if there is a showing of "probable cause." We hold today that the police have greater authority to make a "seizure" and conduct a "search" than a judge has to authorize such action. We have said precisely the opposite over and over again.

In other words, police officers, up to today have been permitted to effect arrests or searches without warrants only when the facts within their personal knowledge would satisfy the constitutional standard of *probable cause*. At the time of their "seizure" without a warrant they must possess facts concerning the person arrested that would have satisfied a magistrate that "probable cause" was indeed present. The term "probable cause" rings a bell of certainty that is not sounded by phrases such as "reasonable suspicion." Moreover, the meaning of "probable cause" is deeply imbedded in our constitutional history. As we stated in Henry v. United States, 361 U.S. 98, 100–102, 80 S.Ct. 168, 171.

"The requirement of probable cause has roots that are deep in our history. The general warrant, in which the name of the person to be arrested was left blank, and the writs of assistance, against which James Otis inveighed, both perpetuated the oppressive practice of allowing the police to arrest and search on suspicion. Police control took the place of judicial control, since no showing of 'probable cause' before a magistrate was required.

* * *

"That philosophy [rebelling against these practices] later was reflected in the Fourth Amendment. And as the early American decisions both before and immediately after its adoption show, common rumor or report, suspicion, or even 'strong reason to suspect' was not adequate to support a warrant for arrest. And that principle has survived to this day.

* * *

"It is important, we think, that this requirement [of probable cause] be strictly enforced, for the standard set by the Constitution protects both the officer and the citizen. If the officer acts with probable cause, he is protected even though it turns out that the citizen is innocent . . . And while a search without a warrant is, within limits, permissible if incident to a lawful arrest, if an arrest without a warrant is to support an incidental search, it must be made with probable cause . . . This immunity of officers cannot fairly be enlarged without jeopardizing the privacy or security of the citizen."

The infringement on personal liberty of any "seizure" of a person can only be "reasonable" under the Fourth Amendment if we require the police to possess "probable cause" before they seize him. Only that line draws a meaningful distinction between an officer's mere inkling and the presence of facts within the officer's personal knowledge which would convince a reasonable man that the person seized has committed, is committing, or is about to commit a particular crime. "In dealing with probable cause, . . . as the very name implies, we deal with probabilities. These are not technical; they are the factual and practical considerations of everyday life on which reasonable and prudent men, not legal technicians, act." Brinegar v. United States, 338 U.S. 160, 175, 69 S.Ct. 1302, 1310.

To give the police greater power than a magistrate is to take a long step down the totalitarian path. Perhaps such a step is desirable to cope with modern forms of lawlessness. But if it is taken, it should be the deliberate choice of the people through a constitutional amendment.

NOTES

1. *Terry's Companion Decision.* In a decision handed down on the same day as *Terry*, the Supreme Court ruled on two other police-citizen encounters sub nom. Sibron v. New York, 392 U.S. 40, 88 S.Ct. 1889 (1968) and Peters v. New York (same citation). As to *Sibron*, the Court found that there was not probable cause for an arrest. Assuming there were *Terry*-type grounds for a stop, the Court found that there was not sufficient reason to believe that Sibron, a narcotics suspect, was armed and dangerous. Moreover, the officer's search was more intrusive than the limited pat down for a weapon permitted by *Terry*. Justice Harlan, concurring in *Sibron*, believed that the stop itself was improper for want of reasonable suspicion. As to the other appellant (Peters), a majority of the Court upheld the inspection as incident to a proper arrest. Justices Harlan and White concurring, believed that although there was no probable cause, there were grounds for a *Terry*-type stop of Peters. They further noted that the evidence was discovered not in a full search but rather within the confines of a proper frisk under *Terry*.

2. *Stop-and-Frisk Statutes.* Although stop-and-frisk has frequently been debated in legislative halls, courts generally have upheld such procedures, if within *Terry* limits, without regard to the existence or non-existence of a statute or ordinance affirmatively authorizing stop-and-frisk, and without regard to the wording of a particular stop-and-frisk statute. See e. g., People v. Lee, 48 Ill.2d 272, 269 N.E.2d 488 (1971); State v. Hetland, 366 So.2d 831 (Fla.App.1979). When is a state statute affirmatively authorizing an intrusion essential to a determination that the intrusion is reasonable under the Fourth Amendment? Contrast the significance of the absence of an "investigative detention" statute discussed in note B–3 of Section F, infra.

ADAMS v. WILLIAMS

Supreme Court of the United States, 1972.
407 U.S. 143, 92 S.Ct. 1921.

MR. JUSTICE REHNQUIST delivered the opinion of the Court.

Respondent Robert Williams was convicted in a Connecticut state court of illegal possession of a handgun found during a "stop and frisk," as well as possession of heroin that was found during a full search incident to his weapons arrest.

Police Sgt. John Connolly was alone early in the morning on car patrol duty in a high crime area of Bridgeport, Connecticut. At approximately 2:15 a. m. a person known to Sgt. Connolly approached his cruiser and informed him that an individual seated in a nearby vehicle was carrying narcotics and had a gun at his waist.

After calling for assistance on his car radio, Sgt. Connolly approached the vehicle to investigate the informant's report. Connolly tapped on the car window and asked the occupant, Robert Williams to open the door. When Williams rolled down the window instead, the sergeant reached into the car and removed a fully loaded revolver from Williams' waistband. The gun had not been visible to Connolly from outside the car, but it was in precisely the place indicated by the informant. Williams was then arrested by Connolly for unlawful possession of the pistol. A search incident to that arrest was conducted after other officers arrived. They found substantial quantities of heroin on Williams' person and in the car, and they found a machete and a second revolver hidden in the automobile.

Respondent contends that the initial seizure of his pistol, upon which rested the later search and seizure of other weapons and narcotics, was not justified by the informant's tip to Sgt. Connolly. He claims that absent a more reliable informant, or some corroboration of the tip, the policeman's actions were unreasonable under the standards set forth in Terry v. Ohio, supra.

After respondent's conviction was affirmed by the Supreme Court of Connecticut, State v. Williams, 157 Conn. 114, 249 A.2d 245 (1968), Williams' petition for federal habeas corpus relief was denied by the District Court and by a divided panel of the Second Circuit, 436 F.2d 30 (1970), but on rehearing *en banc* the Court of Appeals granted relief. 441 F.2d 394 (1971). That court held that evidence introduced at Williams' trial had been obtained by an unlawful search of his person and car, and thus the state court judgments of conviction should be set aside. Since we conclude that the policeman's actions here conformed to the standards this Court laid down in Terry v. Ohio, we reverse.

In *Terry* this Court recognized that "a police officer may in appropriate circumstances and in an appropriate manner approach a person for purposes of investigating possibly criminal behavior even though there is no probable cause to make an arrest." The Fourth Amendment does not require a policeman who lacks the precise level of information necessary for probable cause to arrest to simply shrug his shoulders and allow a crime to occur or a criminal to escape. On the contrary, *Terry* recognizes that it may be the essence of good police work to adopt an intermediate response. A brief stop of a suspicious individual, in order to determine his identity or to maintain the status quo momentarily while obtaining more information, may be most reasonable in light of the facts known to the officer at the time.

The Court recognized in *Terry* that the policeman making a reasonable investigatory stop should not be denied the opportunity to protect himself from attack by a hostile suspect. "When an officer is justified in believing that the individual whose suspicious behavior he is investigating at close range is armed and presently dangerous to the officer or to others," he may conduct a limited protective search for concealed weapons. The purpose of this limited search is not to discover evidence of crime, but to allow the officer to pursue his investigation without fear of violence, and thus the frisk for weapons might be equally necessary and reasonable whether or not carrying a concealed weapon violated any applicable state law. So long as the officer is entitled to make a forcible stop and has reason to believe that the suspect is armed and dangerous, he may conduct a weapons search limited in scope to this protective purpose.

Applying these principles to the present case we believe that Sgt. Connolly acted justifiably in responding to his informant's tip. The informant was known to him personally and had provided him with information in the past. This is a stronger case than obtains in the case of an anonymous telephone tip. The informant here came forward personally to give information that was immediately verifiable at the scene. Indeed, under Connecticut law, the informant herself might have been subject to immediate arrest for making a false complaint had Sgt. Connolly's investigation proven the tip incorrect [for false reporting of a crime]. Thus, while the Court's decisions indicate that this informant's unverified tip may have been insufficient for a narcotics arrest or search warrant, the information carried enough indicia of reliability to justify the officer's forcible stop of Williams.

In reaching this conclusion, we reject respondent's argument that reasonable cause for a stop and frisk can only be based on the officer's personal observation, rather than on information supplied by another person. Informants' tips, like all other clues and evidence coming to a policeman on the scene, may vary greatly in their value and reliability. One simple rule will not cover every situation. Some tips, completely lacking in indicia of reliability, would either warrant no police response or require further investigation before a forcible stop of a suspect would be authorized. But in some situations—for example, when the victim of a street crime seeks immediate police aid and gives a description of his assailant, or when a credible informant warns of a specific impending crime—the subtleties of the hearsay rule should not thwart an appropriate police response.

While properly investigating the activity of a person who was reported to be carrying narcotics and a concealed weapon and who was sitting alone in a car in a high crime area at 2:15 in the morning, Sgt. Connolly had ample reason to fear for his safety.[1] When Williams rolled down his window, rather than complying with the policeman's request to step out of the car so that his movements could more easily be seen, the revolver allegedly at Williams' waist became an even greater threat. Under these circumstances the policeman's action in reaching to the spot where the gun was thought to be hidden constituted a limited intrusion designed to insure his safety, and we conclude that it was reasonable. The loaded gun seized as a result

---

1. Figures reported by the Federal Bureau of Investigation indicate that 125 policemen were murdered in 1971, with all but five of them having been killed by gunshot wounds. Federal Bureau of Investigation Law Enforcement Bulletin, February 1972, p. 33. According to one study, approximately 30% of police shootings occurred when a police officer approached a suspect seated in an automobile. Bristow, Police Officer Shootings—A Tactical Evaluation, 54 J. Crim.L.C. & P.S. 93 (1963).

of this intrusion was therefore admissible at Williams' trial. Terry v. Ohio.

Once Sgt. Connolly had found the gun precisely where the informant had predicted, probable cause existed to arrest Williams for unlawful possession of the weapon. Probable cause to arrest depends "upon whether, at the moment the arrest was made . . . the facts and circumstances within [the arresting officers'] knowledge and of which they had reasonably trustworthy information were sufficient to warrant a prudent man in believing that the [suspect] had committed or was committing an offense." Beck v. Ohio. In the present case the policeman found Williams in possession of a gun in precisely the place predicted by the informant. This tended to corroborate the reliability of the informant's further report of narcotics, and together with the surrounding circumstances certainly suggested no lawful explanation for possession of the gun. Probable cause does not require the same type of specific evidence of each element of the offense as would be needed to support a conviction. See Draper v. United States. Rather, the court will evaluate generally the circumstances at the time of the arrest to decide if the officer had probable cause for his action:

> "In dealing with probable cause, however, as the very name applies, we deal with probabilities. These are not technical; they are the factual and practical considerations of everyday life on which reasonable and prudent men, not legal technicians, act." Brinegar v. United States, 338 U.S. 160, 175, 69 S.Ct. 1302, 1310, 93 L.Ed. 1879 (1949).

See also id., at 177. Under the circumstances surrounding Williams' possession of the gun seized by Sgt. Connolly, the arrest on the weapons charge was supported by probable cause, and the search of his person and of the car incident to that arrest was lawful. The fruits of the search were therefore properly admitted at Williams' trial.

MR. JUSTICE DOUGLAS, with whom MR. JUSTICE MARSHALL concurs, dissenting.

My views have been stated in substance by Judge Friendly in the Court of Appeals. 436 F.2d 30, 35. Connecticut allows its citizens to carry weapons, concealed or otherwise, at will, provided they have a permit. Conn.Gen.Stat. §§ 29–35, 29–38. Connecticut law gives its police no authority to frisk a person for a permit. Yet the arrest was for illegal possession of a gun. The only basis for that arrest was the informer's tip on the narcotics. Can it be said that a man in possession of narcotics will not have a permit for his gun? Is that why the arrest for possession of a gun in the free-and-easy State of Connecticut becomes constitutional?

The police problem is an acute one not because of the Fourth Amendment, but because of the ease with which anyone can acquire a pistol. A powerful lobby dins into the ears of our citizenry that these gun purchases are constitutional rights protected by the Second Amendment which reads, "A well regulated Militia, being necessary to the security of a free State, the right of the people to keep and bear Arms, shall not be infringed."

There is under our decisions no reason why stiff state laws governing the purchase and possession of pistols may not be enacted. There is no reason why pistols may not be barred from anyone with a police record. There is no reason why a State may not require a purchaser of a pistol to pass a psychiatric test. There is no reason why all pistols should not be barred to everyone except the police.

Critics say that proposals like this water down the Second Amendment. Our decisions belie that argument, for the Second Amendment, as noted, was designed to keep alive the militia. But if watering-down is the mood of the day, I would prefer to water down the Second rather than the Fourth Amendment.

MR. JUSTICE BRENNAN, dissenting.

The crucial question on which this case turns, as the Court concedes, is whether, there being no contention that Williams acted voluntarily in rolling down the window of his car, the State had shown sufficient cause to justify Officer Connolly's "forcible" stop. I would affirm, believing, for the following reasons stated by Judge, now Chief Judge, Friendly, 436 F.2d at 38–39, that the State did not make that showing: I would not find the combination of Officer Connolly's almost meaningless observation and the tip in this case to be sufficient justification for the intrusion. The tip suffered from a three-fold defect, with each fold compounding the others. The informer was unnamed, he was not shown to have been reliable with respect to guns or narcotics, and he gave no information which demonstrated personal knowledge or—what is worse—could not readily have been manfactured by the officer after the event. To my mind, it has not been sufficiently recognized that the difference between this sort of tip and the accurate prediction of an unusual event is as important on the latter score as on the former. [In Draper v. United States], Narcotics Agent Marsh would hardly have been at the Denver Station at the exact moment of the arrival of the train Draper had taken from Chicago unless *someone* had told him *something* important, although the agent might later have embroidered the details to fit the observed facts. . . . There is no such guarantee of a patrolling officer's veracity when he testifies to a "tip" from an unnamed informer saying no more than that the officer will find a gun and narcotics on a man across the street, as he later does. If the state wishes to rely on a tip of that nature to validate a stop and frisk, revelation of the name of the informer or demonstration that his name is unknown and could not reasonably have been ascertained should be the price.

Terry v. Ohio was intended to free a police officer from the rigidity of a rule that would prevent his doing anything to a man reasonably suspected of being about to commit or having just committed a crime of violence, no matter how grave the problem or impelling the need for swift action, unless the officer had what a court would later determine to be probable cause for arrest. It was meant for the serious cases of imminent danger or of harm recently perpetrated to persons or property, not the conventional ones of possessory offenses. If it is to be extended to the latter at all, this should be only where observation by the officer himself or well authenticated information shows "that criminal activity may be afoot." I greatly fear that if the [contrary view] should be followed, *Terry* will have opened the sluicegates for serious and unintended erosion of the protection of the Fourth Amendment.

MR. JUSTICE MARSHALL, with whom MR. JUSTICE DOUGLAS joins, dissenting.

Terry did not hold that whenever a policeman has a hunch that a citizen is engaging in criminal activity, he may engage in a stop and frisk. It held that if police officers want to stop and frisk, they must have specific facts from which they can reasonably infer that an individual is engaged in criminal activity and is armed and dangerous. It was central to our decision in *Terry* that the police officer acted on the basis of his own personal observations and that he carefully scrutinized the conduct of his suspects before interfering with them in any way. When we legitimated the conduct of the officer in *Terry* we did so because of the substantial *reliability* of the information on which the officer based his decision to act.

If the Court does not ignore the care with which we examined the knowledge possessed by the officer in *Terry* when he acted, then I cannot see how the actions of the officer in this case can be upheld. The Court explains what the officer knew about respondent before accosting him. But what is more significant is what he did not know. With respect to the scene generally, the officer had no idea how long respondent had been in the car, how long the car had been parked, or to whom the car belonged. With respect to the gun [1] the officer did not know if or when the informant had ever seen the gun, or whether the gun was carried legally, as Connecticut law permitted, or illegally. And with respect to the narcotics, the officer did not know what kind of narcotics respondent allegedly had, whether they were legally or illegally possessed, what the basis of the informant's knowledge was, or even whether the informant was capable of distinguishing narcotics from other substances.

Unable to answer any of these questions, the officer nevertheless determined that it was necessary to intrude on respondent's liberty. I believe that his determination was totally unreasonable. As I read *Terry*, an officer may act on the basis of *reliable* information short of probable cause to make a stop, and ultimately a frisk, if necessary; but, the officer may not use unreliable, unsubstantiated, conclusory hearsay to justify an invasion of liberty. *Terry* never meant to approve the kind of knee-jerk police reaction that we have before us in this case.

Even assuming that the officer had some legitimate reason for relying on the informant, *Terry* requires, before any stop and frisk is

1. The fact that the respondent carried his gun in a high crime area is irrelevant. In such areas it is more probable than not that citizens would be more likely to carry weapons authorized by the State to protect themselves.

made, that the reliable information in the officer's possession demonstrate that the suspect is both armed and *dangerous*. The fact remains that Connecticut specifically authorizes persons to carry guns
so long as they have a permit. Thus, there was no reason for the officer to infer from anything that the informant said that the respondent was dangerous. His frisk was, therefore, illegal under *Terry*.

Even if I could agree with the Court that the stop and frisk in
this case was proper, I could not go further and sustain the arrest,
and the subsequent searches. It takes probable cause to justify an
arrest and search and seizure incident thereto. Probable cause
means that the "facts and circumstances before the officer are such
as to warrant a man of prudence and caution in believing that the offense has been committed. . . ."

Once the officer seized the gun from respondent, it is uncontradicted that he did not ask whether respondent had a license to carry
it, or whether respondent carried it for any other legal reason under
Connecticut law. Rather, the officer placed him under arrest immediately and hastened to search his person. Since Connecticut has not
made it illegal for private citizens to carry guns, there is nothing in
the facts of this case to warrant a man "of prudence and caution" to
believe that any offense had been committed merely because respondent had a gun on his person. Any implication that respondent's silence was some sort of a tacit admission of guilt would be utterly absurd.

It is simply not reasonable to expect someone to protest that he
is not acting illegally before he is told that he is suspected of criminal
activity. It would have been a simple matter for the officer to ask
whether respondent had a permit, but he chose not to do so. In making this choice, he clearly violated the Fourth Amendment.

NOTES

A. Stop-and-Frisk

1. *When Does a "Stop" Become a Seizure?* Some confrontations between police officers and citizens, including confrontations in which police
officers ask questions, are not "seizures" for the purpose of the Fourth
Amendment. Thus, they may need *no* justification to be deemed constitutional: not probable cause (as needed for arrest); not reasonable suspicion
(as needed for a *Terry* stop); not *anything*. The officer who asks, "How
are you this morning?" needs no justification for his question because he
has not seized the citizen to whom he has addressed the inquiry. See People v. Osman, 51 Ill.App.3d 333, 366 N.E.2d 1012 (1977), for a good statement recognizing three categories of police activity: (1) no seizure within
the meaning of the Fourth Amendment; (2) *Terry* stops; and (3) full arrests.

Defining the point at which a Fourth Amendment seizure occurs is difficult. In Coates v. United States, 413 F.2d 371 (D.C.Cir. 1969), a case
which Illinois courts have cited, Judge Warren Burger, citing footnote 16 in
Terry, said that no seizure occurs when there is no physical force, no show
of authority, and no implied restraint.

An excellent decision distinguishing between "contacts" (no Fourth Amendment activity, therefore no justification needed) and *Terry* stops (requiring reasonable suspicion), is United States v. Wylie, 569 F.2d 62 (D.C.Cir. 1977) ("Sir, may I talk to you a moment?" held to be a mere contact). Compare United States v. Coleman, 450 F.Supp. 433 (E.D.Mich. 1978), where, noting the social pressure which inhibits a citizen from walking away from a police officer, a district judge used a standard under which police activity would more frequently be classified as a seizure within the meaning of *Terry*.

If the police conduct amounts to a seizure for Fourth Amendment purposes, then it must be justified as reasonable under the Fourth Amendment. In the street stop setting, this means that the reasonable suspicion required under *Terry* must have existed *before* the stop became a Fourth Amendment seizure.

The issue is relevant in criminal litigation where the stop yielded some evidence: a narcotics "drop," a blurted out incriminatory statement, or the like. In the typical case, the defense will argue that the seizure occurred at an early stage (when the police were less likely to have reasonable suspicion). The prosecutor will argue that the seizure occurred late, after the citizen had already dropped the narcotics or blurted out the statement. Thus, the prosecution will argue that the evidence was not the product of an unreasonable seizure of the person because no seizure had occurred before the evidence was yielded.

2. The Court in *Terry* summarizes its holding by referring to a reasonable belief "that criminal activity may be afoot." One possible reading is that the decision approves certain conduct only with regard to suspects who have just completed a crime, or are presently engaging in one, or are about to commit one. In other words, nothing in *Terry* would justify involuntary street stops to question persons suspected of crimes which occurred several days ago. The "real thrust of *Terry* is directed at instances in which there is reasonable suspicion that someone is about to commit or has just committed a crime." Anderson v. State, 281 Md. 701, 387 A.2d 281, 284 (1978). Nevertheless, courts have generally assumed that upon reasonable suspicion all suspects can be involuntarily detained for brief questioning even if criminal activity is not presently "afoot." See, *e.g.*, People v. Williams, 37 Ill.App.3d 151, 345 N.E.2d 705 (1976) (stop made five days after crime). In People v. Moore, 55 Ill.App.3d 706, 371 N.E.2d 194 (1977), moreover, the court apparently was presented with and rejected an argument that a *Terry* stop is improper where the suspected criminal activity took place weeks earlier and, therefore, was not "afoot."

Perhaps the availability of limited investigative detentions discussed later in Note B, infra, minimizes the importance of whether such a belated stop technically falls within *Terry*.

3. In order to stop and frisk, the officer does not have to establish that he personally feared the suspect. The validity of the stop and frisk is not based on the existence of actual fear but rather on whether a hypothetical reasonable officer could have reasonably been suspicious. See Brown v. State, 295 A.2d 575 (Del.1972). But see United States v. Green, 465 F.2d 620 (D.C.Cir. 1972). Also see United States v. Thorpe, 536 F.2d 1098 (5th Cir. 1976).

4. The requirement that the suspect reasonably be believed to be armed and dangerous must be fulfilled before a frisk is lawful, even though the suspect was properly stopped. Are certain persons, suspected of presently

being involved in criminal activity, *presumptively* armed and dangerous? See Whitten v. United States, 396 A.2d 208 (D.C.App.1978) (shoplifter, no); People v. McGowan, 69 Ill.2d 73, 12 Ill.Dec. 733, 370 N.E.2d 537 (1977) (burglar, yes); Sibron v. New York, 392 U.S. 40, 88 S.Ct. 1889 (1968), Harlan, J. concurring (narcotics dealer, question left open).

5.　During a stop and frisk, prying into places which could not contain a weapon or exploration of soft bulges is not permitted. Tinney v. Wilson, 408 F.2d 912 (9th Cir. 1969); United States v. Gonzalez, 319 F.Supp. 563 (D.Conn.1970); State v. Washington, 82 N.M. 284, 480 P.2d 174 (1971); People v. McKelvy, 23 Cal.App.3d 1027, 100 Cal.Rptr. 661 (1972). Other cases in which the frisk went beyond proper *Terry* limits include State v. Post, 98 Idaho 834, 573 P.2d 153 (1978), and Meeks v. State, 356 So.2d 45 (Fla.App.1978).

However, if an officer does no more than is necessary to accomplish a frisk and discovers seizable material that is not a weapon, he may seize it. Worthy v. United States, 409 F.2d 1105 (D.C.Cir. 1968) ("The need to seize weapons and the potential instruments of crime, thus indicated as relevant to the scope of a search, does not limit its admissible fruit to weapons if conducted consistently with a proper search for weapons").

Some commentators have argued for a use-exclusion rule which would allow police officers to use stop-and-frisk procedures, but which would exclude any evidence other than a weapon which was discovered through the frisk, even if the frisk did not exceed proper limits. See Amsterdam, Perspectives on the Fourth Amendment, 58 Minn.L.Rev. 349, 434 (1974). For an argument against use-exclusion, see Haddad, Well-Delineated Exceptions, Claims of Sham, and Fourfold Probable Cause, 68 J.C.L. & Crim. 198, 204–214 (1977).

6.　The properly conducted stop and frisk, as in Terry v. Ohio and Adams v. Williams, may escalate into situations allowing broader searches. One example of this is Dell v. Louisiana, 468 F.2d 324 (5th Cir. 1972):

> "At 2:30 a. m. on December 16, 1969, the attendant of a gas station reported to the police that he had just been held up by an armed black man with a paper bag mask over his head. He reported that the robber has escaped with two rolls of wrapped nickels, an ESSO envelope containing loose change and bills, and a .25 caliber automatic belonging to the station manager. Shortly thereafter, a police officer responding to the call noticed a car driving very slowly past the gas station. In the car were two black men who were staring intently at the gas station. The police officer summoned the car to the curb and the driver, petitioner in this case, ignored the command until the officer lifted his shotgun, at which time petitioner pulled over. The police officer asked petitioner to step out of the car and display his identification. When the door opened, the officer could plainly see a .25 caliber automatic on the front floorboard and an ESSO envelope, identical to the one taken from the gas station, on the rear floorboard. When petitioner failed to produce his driver's license, he was placed under arrest for driving without a license. See La.Stat.Ann.-Rev.Stat. 32:427. The search of petitioner's person pursuant to this initial arrest produced a roll of wrapped nickels. When the other occupant of the car stepped out to show his identification, a second officer who had arrived on the scene noticed a revolver and two paper bags on the floor of the car. At that point petitioner was

placed in the back seat of the police car and the envelope, paper bags and guns which had been observed in the automobile were removed by the officers.

"The general rule is that a police officer may stop a vehicle and request the production of a driver's license with somewhat less than probable cause as a requisite. E. g., United States v. Marlow, 5 Cir. 1970, 423 F.2d 1064. See La.Stat.Ann.-Rev.Stat. 32:411(D). Here the initial stopping took place at 2:30 a. m., under suspicious circumstances, and we are not prepared to say that merely requesting the production of a driver's license under such conditions was unreasonable.

* * *

"The initial arrest for driving without a license did not take place until after petitioner admitted he had no license; therefore, probable cause clearly existed for the initial arrest. The search of petitioner's person pursuant to this initial arrest was a valid search incident to the arrest, therefore, the discovery and seizure of the roll of nickels from his person was clearly lawful. At the point in time when the nickels were seized and prior to the seizure from the car, the officer was cognizant of the following: the stolen nickels found on petitioner's person, the guns, envelope, and masks lying in plain view in the car and petitioner's suspicious behavior, including the fact that he was driving without a license at 2:30 a. m. at the scene of the robbery moments after the robbery. In sum, it is indisputable that probable cause to arrest petitioner for the further crime of armed robbery existed prior to the time the items were seized from the car."

7. Besides *Terry* and its companion decisions, and Adams v. Williams, the only other United States Supreme Court decision in the area of stop-and-frisk of pedestrians is Brown v. Texas, 443 U.S. 47, 99 S.Ct. 2637 (1979). Brown was convicted under a statute which made it a crime to refuse to give one's name and address "to a peace officer who has lawfully stopped him and requested the information." Without determining the validity of the statute, the Court found on the facts that the stop was unlawful under the Fourth Amendment for want of reasonable suspicion. The officer had been unable to articulate the basis of his conclusion that Brown "looked suspicious" as he entered an alley. When a "stop is not based on objective criteria, the risk of arbitrary and abusive police practice exceeds tolerable limits," wrote Chief Justice Burger for a unanimous court.

B. Investigative Detentions Longer than "Stops"

1. *Terry* referred to a "protean" variety of street encounters between police officers and citizens, and it suggested a balancing test to determine the reasonableness of the police conduct in each instance. Frequently the police will wish to go beyond the limited detention for questioning upon reasonable suspicion approved in *Terry*. For example, authorities may wish to:

Detain a suspect while the police determine whether there are reports of recent burglary;

Detain a suspect while the police determine whether a warrant is outstanding for his arrest;

Return a suspect to the scene of a crime for a prompt show-up;

Detain a suspect, perhaps at a police station, for more than the brief interrogation contemplated under stop and frisk procedures;

Secure a suspect's fingerprints or voiceprints, fingernail scrapings, a sample of his blood, his hair, or his handwriting;

Require a suspect to stand in a lineup;

Stop vehicles passing the scene of a hit-and-run accident which occurred on some prior day.

Following *Terry* a number of cases allowed extended detentions and some even approved the transporting of suspects back to the scene on less than probable cause. See People v. Gatch, 56 Cal.App.3d 505, 128 Cal.Rptr. 481 (1976); In re Lynette G., 54 Cal.App.3d 1087, 126 Cal.Rptr. 898 (1976); State v. Isham, 70 Wis.2d 718, 235 N.W.2d 506 (1975); State v. Byers, 85 Wash.2d 783, 539 P.2d 833 (1975), all involving transportation of suspects. Compare People v. Harris, 15 Cal.3d 384, 124 Cal.Rptr. 536, 540 P.2d 632 (1975). See also State v. Wronko, 26 Ariz.App. 263, 547 P.2d 1063 (1976); State v. Clark, 13 Wash.App. 21, 533 P.2d 387 (1975); People v. Rosenfeld, 16 Cal.App.3d 619, 94 Cal.Rptr. 380 (1971). Compare United States v. Jennings, 468 F.2d 111 (9th Cir. 1972).

"Aggravated" Street Stops. A case of some significance is Goldsmith v. United States, 277 F.2d 335, 344–345 (D.C.Cir. 1960), where Judge Warren Burger expressed the notion that the required quantum of probability will vary depending upon the intensity of the intrusion. The thought is that taking a person back to the scene for an identification procedure should not require the same level of probability as would arresting, charging, booking and placing the suspect in a jail cell.

Some decisions make the point that shows of force (such as a drawing of the officer's gun), necessary to preserve the status quo, do not transform a stop (requiring reasonable suspicion) into an arrest (requiring probable cause). See People v. Attaway, 41 Ill.App.3d 837, 354 N.E.2d 448 (1976); People v. Gatheright, 43 Ill.App.3d 922, 2 Ill.Dec. 430, 357 N.E.2d 597, (1976). Contrast People v. Tebedo, 81 Mich.App. 535, 265 N.W.2d 406 (1978) (placing suspect on ground in handcuffs constitutes an arrest), and United States v. Miller, 546 F.2d 251 (8th Cir. 1976) (ten-minute detention goes beyond what is justified by reasonable suspicion under *Terry*.

These decisions may have to be reconsidered in light of Dunaway v. New York, 442 U.S. 200, 99 S.Ct. 2248 (1979). The narrow holding of *Dunaway* is that absent a suspect's consent, the police may not take a suspect to the police station for interrogation if they lack probable cause for an arrest. Except in the State of New York, this is not new law. Broad language in *Dunaway*, however, suggests that there are only three categories of police-citizen encounters: (1) encounters which are not seizures within the meaning of the Fourth Amendment and which require no justification; (2) *Terry* stops which require reasonable suspicion; and (3) seizures which are arrests or their equivalent and thus demand full probable cause. The majority places great emphasis on the need for certainty and suggests that a sliding-scale or balancing test will not suffice to prevent the erosion of Fourth Amendment freedoms. Justice Brennan wrote for the majority:

> "In effect, respondents urge us to adopt a multifactor balancing test of 'reasonable police conduct under the circumstances' to cover all seizures that do not amount to technical arrests. But the protections intended by the Framers could all too easily disappear in the consideration and balancing of the multifarious circumstances presented by different cases, especially when that balancing may be done in the first instance by police officers engaged in the 'often competitive enterprise of ferreting out crime.' Johnson

v. United States (1948). A single, familiar standard is essential to guide police officers, who have only limited time and expertise to reflect on and balance the social and individual interests involved in the specific circumstances they confront. Indeed, our recognition of these dangers, and our consequent reluctance to depart from the proven protections afforded by the general rule, is reflected in the narrow limitations emphasized in the cases employing the balancing test. For all but those narrowly defined intrusions, the requisite 'balancing' has been performed in centuries of precedent and is embodied in the principle that seizures are 'reasonable' only if supported by probable cause."

Just three weeks later, for the unanimous court in Brown v. Texas, supra note 7, however, the Chief Justice wrote this dictum: "The reasonableness of seizures that are less intrusive than a traditional arrest . . . depends on 'a balance between the public interest and the individual's right to personal security free from arbitrary interference by law officers.' Pennsylvania v. Mimms (1977); United States v. Brignoni-Ponce (1975). Consideration of the constitutionality of such seizures involves a weighing of the gravity of the public concerns served by the seizure, the degree to which the seizure advances the public interest, and the severity of the interference with individual liberty."

2. *Seizure of Identification Characteristics.* Sometimes law enforcement officials will want to do something more than interrogate a suspect or hold a suspect pending further investigation. They will wish to take from his person evidence of physical characteristics which might link him to a crime: a hair sample, a blood sample, fingerprints or the like. Or they may wish to place him in a lineup. Here we assume that the search-incident method is unavailable because there is no probable cause to arrest. We also assume that there is no probable cause to issue a search warrant. Finally, we assume that the situation is not an emergency in which the evanescent nature of the evidence might allow an emergency search on something less than probable cause to believe that a search will prove fruitful. See Cupp v. Murphy, 412 U.S. 291, 93 S.Ct. 2000 (1973).

3. *Warrants Issued Upon Less Than Probable Cause.* Davis v. Mississippi, 394 U.S. 721, 89 S.Ct. 1394, (1969), held that the warrantless detention of a citizen without probable cause for the purpose of securing fingerprints is a violation of the Fourth Amendment. Dictum in *Davis* suggested that such a limited-purpose detention could be justified if prior judicial approval was secured based upon a showing of reasonableness. That showing might be sufficient even if it fell somewhat short of probable cause.

Based upon the dictum in *Davis*, a number of jurisdictions have enacted statutes which permit courts to issue warrants or orders for lineups or the seizure of evidence of identifying physical characteristics. Typically such statutes permit judicial authorization for such procedures where there is (1) probable cause to believe that a crime has been committed; (2) some degree of probability, less than probable cause, that the intrusion against the named person will yield evidence of the crime; and (3) reasonable limitations upon the methods and scope of the intrusion (as to time, place, etc.). See Colorado Supreme Court Rule 41.1; Arizona Rev. Stat. 13–3931.

Two caveats are required. Most states have no warrant or court order procedure similar to that in Arizona and Colorado. The typical warrant statute in most jurisdictions requires full probable cause and cannot be adapted, unless amended, to fit the *Davis* dictum. Second, Dunaway v. New York, supra, must be considered. The *Dunaway* court placed great emphasis upon the lack of probable cause in *Davis*, not the lack of a warrant. In indicating that a detention which goes beyond a *Terry* stop requires probable cause for arrest, the Court ignored the *Davis* dictum that had suggested that some detentions on less than probable cause (other than *Terry* stops) would be proper if done under prior judicial approval.

4. *The Grand Jury Alternative.* An alternative method of securing at least some evidence of identifying physical characteristics is utilization of the grand jury. A grand jury can command the giving of a handwriting exemplar or a voice exemplar, apparently without any showing of the likelihood that the ordered intrusion will prove fruitful. See United States v. Dionisio, 410 U.S. 1, 93 S.Ct. 764 (1973); United States v. Mara, 410 U.S. 19, 93 S.Ct. 774 (1973) (see Chapter 11, F-4). Whether in the case of more intensive intrusions, such as the taking of blood samples, the grand jury procedure could be utilized without a showing of reasonable grounds or probable cause has not been decided by the United States Supreme Court. Two decisions have upheld grand-jury ordered line up appearances. In re Toon, 364 A.2d 1177 (D.C.App.1976); In re Melvin, 546 F.2d 1 (1st Cir. 1976).

Even if the grand jury procedure satisfies the Fourth Amendment, some state law questions may remain. For example, under state law is it clear that a grand jury has the power to compel evidence of a non-testimonial nature (i. e., evidence other than the testimony of witnesses and books and records)? See the dissent of Justice Marshall in *Dionisio*. Assuming the power, how shall it be exercised? Can the prosecutor direct the grand jury foreman to issue the order? Does the power lie with the foreman? Must the grand jurors vote on the issue? Just as defense lawyers ought not overlook state law questions, prosecutors should be careful not to use procedures which make the grand jury simply the alter ego of the district attorney.

5. *Use of Discovery Rules.* In some jurisdictions, once a suspect has been charged (or perhaps indicted or held to trial on a felony information), discovery rules may provide another route for securing evidence of physical characteristics. Even if the state discovery rules on their face require no particular showing before a defendant can be compelled to give a blood sample, a hair sample, or fingerprints or be compelled to stand in a lineup, the safer course of conduct is for the prosecutor to support his or her discovery request by an affidavit detailing the reasons for the request. See People v. Jones, 30 Ill.App. 3d 562, 333 N.E.2d 725 (1975). The indictment (or a finding of probable cause on an information) may suffice to provide probable cause to believe that a crime has been committed and that the defendant committed it. However, it does not provide probable cause to believe that the proposed procedure will yield evidence (search probable cause). If such is required, by analogy to search warrant requirements, an affidavit should be used.

6. *Order Under Inherent Order of Court.* Some jurisdictions have no criminal discovery rules which can be utilized to compel a defendant to yield evidence of identifying physical characteristics. Additionally, in many jurisdictions, criminal discovery rules cannot be invoked until after indictment. In such cases can a court issue orders for lineups or the seizure of evidence of identifying physical characteristics upon a showing of something less than probable cause? Few decisions resolve the question of whether a court has the inherent authority to issue such an order. As to lineups, see In re Alphonso C., 50 A.D.2d 97, 376 N.Y.S.2d 126 (1975), and compare Wise v. Murphy, 275 A.2d 205 (D.C.App.1971) (en banc). Because of the broad investigative powers of the grand jury, a grand-jury ordered lineup

or seizure of evidence is more likely to be upheld than a court order whose only basis is a court's inherent authority.

G.   CONSENT SEARCHES AND SEIZURES

If a search of property is made by law enforcement officers under the voluntary consent of a person who has sufficient authority over the property, such a search is deemed reasonable under the Fourth Amendment even if the police have neither a warrant nor probable cause. Normally a consent to search is not so broad as to authorize the police to take and carry away any item which they come upon. If, however, looking in a place which they have a right to inspect under the authority of the consent to search, officers come upon an item which they have probable cause to believe is contraband or evidence of a crime, the officers can seize the item. The seizure in such an instance can be justified under plain view principles (discussed in the following Section H), rather under the doctrine of consent.

Much of consent search litigation focuses upon two questions: (1) was there, in fact, a voluntary consent?, and (2) did the consenting party have sufficient authority to make it reasonable for the officers to search based upon his or her consent? We begin with the first question.

SCHNECKLOTH v. BUSTAMONTE

Supreme Court of the United States, 1973.
412 U.S. 218, 93 S.Ct. 2041.

MR. JUSTICE STEWART delivered the opinion of the Court.

* * *

While on routine patrol in Sunnyvale, California, at approximately 2:40 in the morning, Police Officer James Rand stopped an automobile when he observed that one headlight and its license plate light were burned out. Six men were in the vehicle. Joe Alcala and the respondent, Robert Bustamonte, were in the front seat with Joe Gonzales, the driver. Three older men were seated in the rear. When, in response to the policeman's question, Gonzales could not produce a driver's license, Officer Rand asked if any of the other five had any evidence of identification. Only Alcala produced a license, and he explained that the car was his brother's. After the six occupants had stepped out of the car at the officer's request and after two additional policemen had arrived, Officer Rand asked Alcala if he could search the car. Alcala replied, "Sure, go ahead." Prior to the search no one was threatened with arrest and, according to Officer Rand's uncontradicted testimony, it "was all very congenial at this time." Gonzales testified that Alcala actually helped in the search of the car, by opening the trunk and glove compartment. In Gonzales' words: "[T]he police officer asked Joe [Alcala], he goes, 'Does the trunk open?' And Joe said, 'Yes.' He went to the car and got the keys and opened up the trunk." Wadded up under the left rear seat, the police officers found three checks that had previously been stolen from a car wash.

The trial judge denied the motion to suppress, and the checks in question were admitted in evidence at Bustamonte's trial. On the basis of this and other evidence he was convicted, and the California Court of Appeal for the First Appellate District affirmed the conviction. [The California Supreme Court denied further review; Bustamonte then filed a federal habeas corpus petition which was denied by the district court. The Ninth Circuit Court of Appeals reversed and remanded for a hearing whether Joe Alcala knew he had a right to refuse to consent. The State's (Warden's) petition for certiorari was granted.]

The precise question in this case, then, is what must the prosecution prove to demonstrate that a consent was "voluntarily" given. And upon that question there is a square conflict of views between the state and federal courts that have reviewed the search involved in the case before us. The Court of Appeals for the Ninth Circuit concluded that it is an essential part of the State's initial burden to prove that a person knows he has a right to refuse consent. The California courts have followed the rule that voluntariness is a question of fact to be determined from the totality of all the circumstances, and that the state of a defendant's knowledge is only one factor to be taken into account in assessing the voluntariness of a consent.

The most extensive judicial exposition of the meaning of "voluntariness" has been developed in those cases in which the Court has had to determine the "voluntariness" of a defendant's confession for purposes of the Fourteenth Amendment. . . .

* * *

The significant fact about all of these decisions is that none of them turned on the presence or absence of a single controlling criterion; each reflected a careful scrutiny of all the surrounding circumstances. In none of them did the Court rule that the Due Process Clause required the prosecution to prove as part of its initial burden that the defendant knew he had a right to refuse to answer the questions that were put. While the state of the accused's mind, and the failure of the police to advise the accused of his rights, were certainly factors to be evaluated in assessing the "voluntariness" of an accused's responses, they were not in and of themselves determinative.

Similar considerations lead us to agree with the courts of California that the question whether a consent to a search was in fact "voluntary" or was the product of duress or coercion, express or implied, is a question of fact to be determined from the totality of all the circumstances. While knowledge of the right to refuse consent is one factor to be taken into account, the government need not establish such knowledge as the *sine qua non* of an effective consent. As with police questioning, two competing concerns must be accommodated in determining the meaning of a "voluntary" consent—the le-

gitimate need for such searches and the equally important requirement of assuring the absence of coercion.

* * *

.   .   .   But the Fourth and Fourteenth Amendments require
that a consent not be coerced, by explicit or implicit means, by implied threat or covert force. For, no matter how subtly the coercion
was applied, the resulting "consent" would be no more than a pretext
for the unjustified police intrusion against which the Fourth Amendment is directed. .   .   .

* * *

The problem of reconciling the recognized legitimacy of consent
searches with the requirement that they be free from any aspect of
official coercion cannot be resolved by any infallible touchstone. To
approve such searches without the most careful scrutiny would sanction the possibility of official coercion; to place artificial restrictions
upon such searches would jeopardize their basic validity. Just as
was true with confessions, the requirement of a "voluntary" consent
reflects a fair accommodation of the constitutional requirements involved. In examining all the surrounding circumstances to determine
if in fact the consent to search was coerced, account must be taken of
subtly coercive police questions, as well as the possibly vulnerable
subjective state of the person who consents. Those searches that are
the product of police coercion can thus be filtered out without undermining the continuing validity of consent searches. In sum, there is
no reason for us to depart in the area of consent searches, from the
traditional definition of "voluntariness."

The approach of the Court of Appeals for the Ninth Circuit
finds no support in any of our decisions that have attempted to define the meaning of "voluntariness." Its ruling, that the State must
affirmatively prove that the subject of the search knew that he had a
right to refuse consent, would, in practice, create serious doubt
whether consent searches could continue to be conducted. There
might be rare cases where it could be proved from the record that a
person in fact affirmatively knew of his right to refuse—such as a
case where he announced to the police that if he didn't sign the consent form, "you [police] are going to get a search warrant;" or a
case where by prior experience and training a person had clearly and
convincingly demonstrated such knowledge. But more commonly
where there was no evidence of any coercion, explicit or implicit, the
prosecution would nevertheless be unable to demonstrate that the subject of the search in fact had known of his right to refuse consent.

* * *

One alternative that would go far toward proving that the subject of a search did know he had a right to refuse consent would be to
advise him of that right before eliciting his consent. That, however,
is a suggestion that has been almost universally repudiated by both
federal and state courts, and, we think, rightly so. For it would be
thoroughly impractical to impose on the normal consent search the
detailed requirements of an effective warning. Consent searches are

part of the standard investigatory techniques of law enforcement agencies. They normally occur on the highway, or in a person's home or office, and under informal and unstructured conditions. The circumstances that prompt the initial request to search may develop quickly or be a logical extension of investigative police questioning. The police may seek to investigate further suspicious circumstances or to follow up leads developed in questioning persons at the scene of a crime. These situations are a far cry from the structured atmosphere of a trial where, assisted by counsel if he chooses, a defendant is informed of his trial rights. And, while surely a closer question, these situations are still immeasurably, far removed from "custodial interrogation" where, in Miranda v. Arizona, we found that the Constitution required certain now familiar warnings as a prerequisite to police interrogation. Indeed, in language applicable to the typical consent search, we refused to extend the need for warnings:

> "Our decision is not intended to hamper the traditional function of police officers in investigating crime. . . .
> When an individual is in custody on probable cause, the police may, of course, seek out evidence in the field to be used at trial against him. Such investigation may include inquiry of persons not under restraint. General on-the-scene questioning as to facts surrounding a crime or other general questioning of citizens in the fact-finding process is not affected by our holding. It is an act of responsible citizenship for individuals to give whatever information they may have to aid in law enforcement."

Consequently, we cannot accept the position of the Court of Appeals in this case that proof of knowledge of the right to refuse consent is a necessary prerequisite to demonstrating a "voluntary" consent. Rather it is only by analyzing all the circumstances of an individual consent that it can be ascertained whether in fact it was voluntary or coerced. It is this careful sifting of the unique facts and circumstances of each case that is evidenced in our prior decisions involving consent searches.

* * *

It is said, however, that a "consent" is a "waiver" of a person's rights under the Fourth and Fourteenth Amendments. The argument is that by allowing the police to conduct a search, a person "waives" whatever right he had to prevent the police from searching. It is argued that under the doctrine of Johnson v. Zerbst, 304 U.S. 458, 464, 58 S.Ct. 1019, 1023, to establish such a "waiver" the State must demonstrate "an intentional relinquishment or abandonment of a known right or privilege."

But these standards were enunciated in *Johnson* in the context of the safeguards of a fair criminal trial. Our cases do not reflect an uncritical demand for a knowing and intelligent waiver in every situation where a person has failed to invoke a constitutional protection. As Mr. Justice Black once observed for the Court: " 'Waiver' is a vague term used for a great variety of purposes, good and bad, in the law." With respect to procedural due process, for example, the Court has acknowledged that waiver is possible, while explicitly leaving open the question whether a "knowing and intelligent" waiver need be shown.

The requirement of a "knowing" and "intelligent" waiver was articulated in a case involving the validity of a defendant's decision to forego a right constitutionally guaranteed to protect a fair trial and the reliability of the truth-determining process. Johnson v. Zerbst, supra, dealt with the denial of counsel in a federal criminal trial. There the Court held that under the Sixth Amendment a criminal defendant is entitled to the assistance of counsel, and that if he lacks sufficient funds to retain counsel, it is the Government's obligation to furnish him with a lawyer. As Mr. Justice Black wrote for the Court: "The Sixth Amendment stands as a constant admonition that if the constitutional safeguards it provides be lost, justice will not 'still be done.' It embodies a realistic recognition of the obvious truth that the average defendant does not have the professional legal skill to protect himself when brought before a tribunal with power to take his life or liberty, wherein the prosecution is presented by experienced and learned counsel. That which is simple, orderly, and necessary to the lawyer—to the untrained layman may appear intricate, complex and mysterious." To preserve the fairness of the trial process the Court established an appropriately heavy burden on the Government before waiver could be found—"an intentional relinquishment or abandonment of a known right or privilege."

Almost without exception, the requirement of a knowing and intelligent waiver has been applied only to those rights which the Constitution guarantees to a criminal defendant in order to preserve a fair trial. Hence, and hardly surprisingly in view of the facts of *Johnson* itself, the standard of a knowing and intelligent waiver has most often been applied to test the validity of a waiver of counsel, either at trial, or upon a guilty plea. And the Court has also applied the *Johnson* criteria to assess the effectiveness of a waiver of other trial rights such as the right to confrontation, to a jury trial, and to a speedy trial, and the right to be free from twice being placed in jeopardy. Guilty pleas have been carefully scrutinized to determine whether the accused knew and understood all the rights to which he would be entitled at trial, and that he had intentionally chosen to forgo them. And the Court has evaluated the knowing and intelligent nature of the waiver of trial rights in trial-type situations, such as the waiver of the privilege against compulsory self-incrimination before an administrative agency or a congressional committee, or the waiver of counsel in a juvenile proceeding.

The guarantees afforded a criminal defendant at trial also protect him at certain stages before the actual trial, and any alleged waiver must meet the strict standard of an intentional relinquishment of a "known" right. But the "trial" guarantees that have been applied to the "pretrial" stage of the criminal process are similarly designed to protect the fairness of the trial itself.

Hence, in United States v. Wade (1967) and Gilbert v. California (1967), the Court held "that a post-indictment pre-trial lineup at which the accused is exhibited to identifying witnesses is a critical stage of the criminal prosecution; that police conduct of such a line-up without notice to and in the absence of his counsel denies the accused his Sixth [and Fourteenth] Amendment right to counsel. . . ." Accordingly, the Court indicated that the standard of a knowing and intelligent waiver must be applied to test the waiver of counsel at such a lineup. The Court stressed the necessary interrelationship between the presence of counsel at a post-indictment lineup before trial and the protection of the trial process itself. . . .

And in Miranda v. Arizona (1966) the Court found that *custodial* interrogation by the police was inherently coercive, and consequently held that detailed warnings were required to protect the privilege against compulsory self-incrimination. The Court made it clear that the basis for decision was the need to protect the fairness of the trial itself. . . .

The standards of *Johnson* were, therefore, found to be a necessary prerequisite to a finding of a valid waiver.

There is a vast difference between those rights that protect a fair criminal trial and the rights guaranteed under the Fourth Amendment. Nothing, either in the purposes behind requiring a "knowing" and "intelligent" waiver of trial rights, or in the practical application of such a requirement suggests that it ought to be extended to the constitutional guarantee against unreasonable searches and seizures.

A strict standard of waiver has been applied to those rights guaranteed to a criminal defendant to insure that he will be accorded the greatest possible opportunity to utilize every facet of the constitutional model of a fair criminal trial. Any trial conducted in derogation of that model leaves open the possibility that the trial reached an unfair result precisely because all the protections specified in the Constitution were not provided. A prime example is the right to counsel. For without that right, a wholly innocent accused faces the real and substantial danger that simply because of his lack of legal expertise he may be convicted. As Mr. Justice Harlan once wrote: "The sound reason why [the right to counsel] is so freely extended for a criminal trial is the severe injustice risked by confronting an untrained defendant with a range of technical points of law, evidence, and tactics familiar to the prosecutor but not to himself." Miranda v. Arizona (dissenting opinion). The Constitution requires that every effort be made to see to it that a defendant in a criminal case has not unknowingly relinquished the basic protections that the Framers thought indispensable to a fair trial.

The protections of the Fourth Amendment are of a wholly different order, and have nothing whatever to do with promoting the fair ascertainment of truth at a criminal trial. . . .

Those cases that have dealt with the application of the Johnson v. Zerbst rule make clear that it would be next to impossible to apply to a consent search the standard of "an intentional relinquishment or abandonment of a known right or privilege." To be true to *Johnson* and its progeny, there must be examination into the knowing and understanding nature of the waiver, an examination that was designed for a trial judge in the structured atmosphere of a courtroom. . . . .

* * *

It would be unrealistic to expect that in the informal, unstructured context of a consent search, a policeman, upon pain of tainting the evidence obtained, could make the detailed type of examination demanded by *Johnson*. And, if for this reason a diluted form of "waiver" were found acceptable, that would itself be ample recognition of the fact that there is no universal standard that must be applied in every situation where a person foregoes a constitutional right.

* * *

Our decision today is a narrow one. We hold only that when the subject of a search is not in custody and the State attempts to justify a search on the basis of his consent, the Fourth and Fourteenth Amendments require that it demonstrate that the consent was in fact voluntarily given, and not the result of duress or coercion, express or implied. Voluntariness is a question of fact to be determined from all the circumstances, and while the subject's knowledge of a right to refuse is a factor to be taken into account, the prosecution is not required to demonstrate such knowledge as a prerequisite to establishing a voluntary consent. Because the California court followed these principles in affirming the respondent's conviction, and because the Court of Appeals for the Ninth Circuit in remanding for an evidentiary hearing required more, its judgment must be reversed.

It is so ordered.

Judgment of Court of Appeals reversed.

[Justice Blackmun concurred. In a separate concurring opinion, Justice Powell, joined by Chief Justice Burger and Justice Rehnquist agreed as to the consent search question. The thrust of Powell's opinion, however, was that the use of federal habeas corpus to litigate Fourth Amendment claims should be sharply limited. This suggestion was later accepted in Stone v. Powell, Chapter 6, Section C. Justice Douglas dissented, arguing that a hearing should be held to determine whether Alcala knew his rights and suggesting that the issue would be moot if he did. Justice Brennan wrote a brief dissent, asserting: "It wholly escapes me how our citizens meaningfully can be said to have waived something as precious as a constitutional guarantee without ever being aware of its existence." Justice Marshall wrote a dissent calling for a requirement of a knowing consent and indicating that appropriate Fourth Amendment warnings would prima facie satisfy the prosecution's burden.]

NOTES

1. In United States v. Watson, 423 U.S. 411, 96 S.Ct. 820 (1976), the United States Supreme Court held that Fourth Amendment warnings were

not essential even where the consenting party was in police custody. In *Watson*, while there was custody, there was not *police station* custody with its inherently coercive atmosphere.

Many courts have upheld consent searches, in the absence of warnings, even when the consenting individual was in custody at a police station. However, where a suspect is in custody, the absence of warnings may be given significant weight in determining whether a consent is voluntary under the totality of the circumstances. United States v. Heimforth, 493 F.2d 970 (9th Cir. 1974); United States v. De Marco, 488 F.2d 828 (2d Cir. 1973).

2. In preliminary remarks in a perceptive article concerning involuntary confessions, Professor Joseph Grano points out that voluntariness, under the Supreme Court decisions, means different things in different contexts. In insisting upon voluntariness in consent search case, Grano notes, the Court has assigned little weight to the cognitive aspect: a person can voluntarily consent without knowing his rights. However, the Court has suggested "that even 'implied' or subtle coercion will render the consent involuntary." On the other hand, Grano notes, in the cases in which the Court has considered guilty pleas (see Chapter 16), the Court has insisted that the accused know his rights but has de-emphasized the volitional aspect of voluntariness by permitting significant pressures in the plea-bargaining process to influence the accused's determination of whether to plead guilty. See Grano, Voluntariness, Free Will, and The Law of Confessions, 65 Va. L.Rev. 859 (1979).

3. When the prosecution relies upon a consent search theory, it has the burden of establishing that the consent was voluntary. Bumper v. North Carolina, 391 U.S. 543, 88 S.Ct. 1788 (1968). A false assertion that officers have the present right to search will vitiate the consent. *Bumper*, supra (claim that officers had a warrant; warrant never produced); United States v. J. B. Kramer Grocery Co., 418 F.2d 987 (8th Cir. 1969) (false assertion of right to make an administrative inspection). However, the mere threat to get a warrant (especially if probable cause sufficed to get a warrant) does not render a consent involuntary. State v. Davis, 26 N.C. App. 696, 217 S.E.2d 131 (1975); Barlow v. State, 280 A.2d 703 (Del. 1971); State v. Douglas, 260 Or. 60, 488 P.2d 1366 (1971). Compare Herriott v. State, 337 So.2d 165 (Ala.Crim.App.1976) (police lacked probable cause and could not have obtained a warrant). Threats or violence are likely to invalidate a consent. Waldron v. United States, 219 F.2d 37 (D.C.Cir. 1955) (police told young expectant mother that they could not be responsible for the conditions of the house if they had to get a warrant); United States v. Kampbell, 574 F.2d 962 (8th Cir. 1978) (threat to trash the house).

Deception may vitiate consent. Compare Commonwealth v. Brown, 437 Pa. 1, 261 A.2d 879 (1970) (officer told defendant he would sell gun and instead had a ballistics test run) with Graves v. Beto, 424 F.2d 524 (5th Cir. 1970) (defendant told blood sample was for alcohol test but it was used to type his blood for comparison with blood stains in rape case). When a government agent uses deception to gain entry to a home or other place not open to the public, the entry is illegal if the right to enter depends upon consent (and not, for example upon a valid search warrant), and if the deception consists of an assertion that the agent has come to engage in some lawful, non-law enforcement activity. Thus, posing as a meter reader will invalidate a consent. People v. Dalpe, 371 Ill. 607, 21 N.E.2d 756 (1939)

("It is the houseman . . . .") On the other hand, if the government agent through deception secures an invitation to do *unlawful* business, the entry is valid. On Lee v. United States, 343 U.S. 747, 72 S.Ct. 967 (1952); Lewis v. United States, 385 U.S. 206, 87 S.Ct. 424 (1966).

Individual characteristics of the consenting person may be relevant to a determination of voluntariness. United States v. Elrod, 441 F.2d 353 (5th Cir. 1971) (incompetent individual); United States v. Williams, 544 F.2d 807 (5th Cir. 1777), and White v. State, 261 Ark. 23, 545 S.W.2d 641 (1977) (intoxicated individual); Laasch v. State, 84 Wis.2d 587, 267 N.W.2d 278 (1978) (consent to enter granted by five-year old is invalid).

The illegality of an arrest preceding a consent is one factor (sometimes a heavy factor) in determining involuntariness. State v. Mitchell, 360 So. 2d 189 (La.1978); United States v. Bazinet, 462 F.2d 982 (8th Cir. 1972); State v. Ruud, 90 N.M. 647, 567 P.2d 496 (1977) (illegal stop).

4. A person who consents to a search may limit the scope of the search and those limitations must be respected. United States v. Dichiarinte, 445 F.2d 126 (7th Cir. 1971) (consent to search for narcotics does not confer authority to search for papers). See the excellent discussion in State v. Koucoules, 343 A.2d 860 (Me.1974). A consent to enter does not authorize a search. Gouled v. United States, 255 U.S. 298, 41 S.Ct. 261 (1921).

5. In third-party consent cases, if Officer *A* obtains an involuntary consent from *B* to search the joint property of *B* and *C*, the search is illegal even as to *C*. The question of standing is not involved. Absent the voluntary consent of *someone* who had sufficient authority, the search of the property is illegal as to all persons who have an interest in the property. In *Bumper*, note 3, supra, the search and seizure was illegal as to the cotenant grandson even though it was the grandmother whose consent was deemed involuntary. The foregoing principal case of *Schneckloth* also involved the voluntariness of consent by a third party.

6. The question as to who can consent usually arises where a defendant challenges the reasonableness of a search made under the purported authority of a consent granted by someone else. Rarely will a defendant claim that he himself had no authority to consent. Ordinarily, if he had an insufficient relationship to the property to authorize a consent search then he will have an insufficient relationship to the property to merit standing. In one case where the defendant attacked his own authority to consent, the court invoked an estoppel theory to defeat his claim. State v. Cole, 337 So. 2d 1067 (La.1976). When the question as to who can consent is posed, an examination is made of the person's relationship to the property to determine whether it was reasonable to conduct a search under his consent. One approach to third-party consent cases is to inquire whether *A* had the right to waive *B*'s rights. Usually this is a defense-oriented phrasing of the issue, although the Court in Amos v. United States, 255 U.S. 313, 41 S.Ct. 266 (1921), phrased the issue in precisely those terms. A more modern and, at the same time, more neutral posing of the issue asks whether *A* himself had a sufficient relationship to the property to make his consent effective. See United States v. Matlock, 415 U.S. 164, 94 S.Ct. 988 (1974), and Frazier v. Cupp, 394 U.S. 731, 89 S.Ct. 1420 (1969). Under this phrasing *A* is exercising his own rights over the property by consenting, not waiving someone else's rights.

Another analytical approach raises the question whether *B* had such a reasonable expectation of privacy in the property as to render *A*'s consent ineffective. A number of consent search cases utilize the reasonable expectation of privacy concept, borrowed from Katz v. United States, 389 U.S. 347, 88 S.Ct. 507 (1967) (see Ch. 5). Typical is People v. Nunn, 55 Ill.2d 344, 304 N.E.2d 81 (1973). The Supreme Court of the United States, however, has never taken this approach to consent searches. Indeed, in Mancusi v. DeForte, 392 U.S. 364, 88 S.Ct. 2120 (1968), the Court noted that even though the accused had a sufficient reasonable expectation of privacy to merit standing, this expectation would not necessarily preclude a valid third-party consent. Later, in *Matlock*, the Court again avoided injecting *Katz* notions into consent search cases. Subsequently, the Illinois Supreme Court followed suit in People v. Stacey, 58 Ill.2d 83, 317 N.E.2d 24 (1974), where it sharply limited *Nunn* and the significance attributed to *Katz* in consent cases. For now, then, it is probably safe to analyze third-party consent cases in traditional terms and without reference to *Katz*.

Following is a summary of the various categories of the consent issue which the courts have considered:

(a) A landlord cannot consent to search of tenant's apartment. Chapman v. United States, 365 U.S. 610, 81 S.Ct. 776 (1961). The landlord may consent if it appears that the tenant has vacated the premises. See United States v. Kress, 446 F.2d 358 (9th Cir. 1971); Eisentrager v. Hocker, 450 F.2d 490 (9th Cir. 1971). A landlord may consent to search of common areas. Gillars v. United States, 182 F.2d 962 (D.C.Cir.1950); State v. Bazella, 522 S.W.2d 57 (Mo.App.1975).

(b) Generally a university official cannot consent to a search of a student's dormitory room. United States v. Kress, 446 F.2d 358 (9th Cir. 1971); Commonwealth v. McCloskey, 217 Pa.Super. 432, 272 A.2d 271 (1970); Piazzola v. Watkins, 442 F.2d 284 (5th Cir. 1971).

(c) Co-tenants can consent to search of property they share with each other. Frazier v. Cupp, 394 U.S. 731, 89 S.Ct. 1420 (1969); United States v. Matlock, 415 U.S. 164, 94 S.Ct. 988 (1974).

(d) A spouse who is a co-tenant can consent to search of jointly occupied premises, Commonwealth v. Martin, 358 Mass. 282, 264 N.E. 2d 366 (1970), even if parties are antagonistic, State v. McCarthy, 23 Ohio St.2d 87, 269 N.E.2d 424 (1971); People v. Koshiol, 45 Ill.2d 573, 262 N.E.2d 446 (1970). A lover may also consent to the search if he or she has jointly occupied the premises for a period of time. White v. United States, 444 F.2d 724 (10th Cir. 1971); United States v. Wilson, 447 F.2d 1 (9th Cir. 1971). However, some jurisdictions recognize some limits upon the authority for a particular seizure. Hawaii v. Evans, 45 Hawaii 622, 372 P.2d 365 (1962) (wife cannot consent to search of husband's possessions); United States ex rel. Cabey v. Mazurkiewicz, 431 F.2d 839 (3rd Cir. 1970) (wife cannot consent to search of garage where husband is sole lessee and has only key); People v. Elders, 63 Ill.App.3d 554, 20 Ill.Dec. 333, 380 N.E.2d 10 (1978) (one spouse had exclusive control of car).

(e) Consent by parents or children pose knotty problems. Some courts hold that a parent can consent to the search of a child's room. State v. Schotl, 289 Minn. 175, 182 N.W.2d 878 (1971) (twenty-two-year-old son); Jones v. State, 13 Md.App. 309, 283 A.2d 184 (1971); People v. Daniels, 16 Cal.App.3d 36, 93 Cal.Rptr. 628 (1971) (adult son present in next room). However, where the son or daughter has exclusive use of a particular room, other courts have invalidated parental consent. Reeves v. Warden, 346 F.2d 915 (4th Cir. 1965). See People

v. Daniels, supra (mother cannot consent to search of son's suitcase). Other relatives may have a right to consent under some circumstances. Consent by adult, married sister to search of home owned by the parents of her and her defendant brother has been held proper in Garr v. Commonwealth, 463 S.W.2d 109 (Ky.App.1971). See also State v. Boyle, 207 Kan. 833, 486 P.2d 849 (1971) (consent by defendant's older brother in parent's absence). However, the "exclusive use" doctrine may limit the scope of the search in these cases also. Thus in Shorry v. Warden, 401 F.2d 474 (4th Cir. 1968), a sister who owned a home was said not to be authorized to consent to the search of her brother's bedroom in her home. In People v. Overall, 7 Mich.App. 153, 151 N.W. 2d 225 (1967), a grandmother was held not authorized to consent to the search of a room occupied by her grandson.

(f) A host may permit the search of the guest's room but not the search of closed recesses and the seizure of the guest's personal property. United States v. Block, 590 F.2d 535 (4th Cir. 1978) (footlocker); People v. Laursen, 22 Cal.App.3d 1033, 99 Cal.Rptr. 841, affirmed, 8 Cal.3d 192, 104 Cal. Rptr. 425, 501 P.2d 1145 (1972). The exclusive use limitation may also be applied in these cases. Burge v. United States, 333 F.2d 210 (9th Cir. 1964). The right to clean a room of a paying or a nonpaying guest may not authorize a host to consent to a search or a seizure. Purvis v. Wiseman, 298 F.Supp. 761 (D.Ore.1969).

(g) The area of employer-employee authority to consent is not well settled. See United States v. Blok, 188 F.2d 1019 (D.C.Cir.1951) (employer's consent to search of employee's desk invalid); Braddock v. State, 127 Ga.App. 313, 194 S.E.2d 317 (1972) (truck owner may consent to search of his truck even though evidence discovered is used against employee-driver); People v. Smith, 204 N.W.2d 308 (Mich. App.1972) (employee cannot consent to police inspection of calculator owned by employer). More recent decisions include United States v. Speights, 557 F.2d 362 (3d Cir. 1977) (chief of police cannot consent to search of officer's locker); United States v. Bunkers, 521 F.2d 1217 (9th Cir. 1975) (postal employee locker search upheld). Cases in which government itself is the consenting party probably lend themselves to a reasonable expectation of privacy analysis better than do cases in which a private third-party grants the consent.

(h) Consent by bailee with whom a man leaves his property depends upon particular facts of bailment and extent to which bailor has relinquished control. See Pielow v. United States, 8 F.2d 492 (9th Cir. 1925); Von Eichelberger v. United States, 252 F.2d 184 (9th Cir. 1958).

Can a common carrier grant an effective consent? Compare United States v. Kelly, 529 F.2d 1365 (8th Cir. 1976), with State v. Pacheco, 121 Ariz. 88, 588 P.2d 830 (1978). Can a hospital nurse consent to inspection of a patient's clothing? Compare State v. Smith, 88 Wash.2d 127, 559 P. 2d 970 (1977), with Commonwealth v. Silo, 480 Pa. 15, 389 A.2d 62 (1978).

7. A situation analogous to third party consent occurs when, instead of consenting to a search, the third party seizes the evidence and brings it to the police. No question of the legality of the seizure will be raised in the criminal trial because no motion to suppress lies where the search was conducted by a private citizen acting on his own. Barnes v. United States, 373 F.2d 517 (5th Cir. 1967) (motel owner); People v. Hively, 173 Colo. 485, 480 P.2d 558 (1971) (airline official); Cash v. Williams, 455 F.2d

1227 (6th Cir. 1972) (owner of private garage where police towed vehicle); People v. Morton, 23 Cal.App.3d 172, 98 Cal.Rptr. 261 (1971) (hospital employee). Whenever the private citizen acts in concert with the police, state action will be found. Stapleton v. Superior Court, 70 Cal.2d 97, 73 Cal. Rptr. 575, 447 P.2d 967 (1969). Consider in this connection part III–B of the majority opinion in Coolidge v. New Hampshire, reported in the following Section H, where the majority held that there was no search because Coolidge's wife, without being asked, voluntarily turned over to the police certain weapons.

8. If it ordinarily would be reasonable to conduct a search under the authority of *A*'s consent, even though *B* also has an interest, *A*'s consent might not be enough to make the search reasonable if *B* has previously refused consent, particularly when *B* is present at the time of the search. See Padron v. State, 328 So.2d 216 (Fla.App.1976); People v. Reynolds, 55 Cal.App.3d 357, 127 Cal.Rptr. 561 (1976); United States v. Elrod, 441 F.2d 353 (5th Cir. 1971). See also Silva v. State, 344 So.2d 559 (Fla.1977) (alternate holding).

9. Sometimes a law enforcement officer will conduct a search pursuant to the consent of a person who, from all the facts known to the officer, clearly appears to have authority over property, but who, as it turns out, has no such authority. Is such a search reasonable? The true property owner may ask, "How can an officer derive the right to search my property from someone who had no authority over my property?" The officer might respond, "How can I be accused of making an unreasonable search when in good faith I reasonably concluded that the consenting party was the owner?" In Stoner v. California, 376 U.S. 483, 84 S.Ct. 889 (1964), the Court stated that the Fourth Amendment could not be eroded by "unrealistic doctrines of apparent authority." It did not state whether all doctrines of apparent authority are per se unrealistic, and in United States v. Matlock, 415 U.S. 164, 94 S.Ct. 988 (1974), the Court specifically treated "apparent authority" consents as an open question.

Some lower courts have treated as invalid any search under the consent of a person who had no actual authority. A "textbook" case of an apparent authority consent search led to exclusion in People v. Miller, 40 Ill.2d 154, 238 N.E.2d 407 (1968). On the other hand former Chief Justice Traynor of the California Supreme Court made a strong case for upholding certain apparent-authority consents. See Traynor, Mapp v. Ohio at Large in the Fifty States, 1962 Duke L.J. 319; People v. Gorg, 45 Cal.2d 776, 291 P.2d 469 (1955). See also Hayes v. Cady, 500 F.2d 1212 (7th Cir. 1974); United States v. Peterson, 524 F.2d 167 (4th Cir. 1975).

Questions of "apparent authority" arise in various Fourth Amendment contexts, and some have been treated earlier in this chapter. For one effort to provide a uniform solution to apparent authority questions, see Haddad, Arrest, Search and Seizure: Six Unexamined Issues in Illinois Law, 26 De Paul L.Rev. 492, 501–505 (1977). The other apparent authority questions there considered are:

(1) An officer honestly but erroneously believes that a hotel clerk can consent to a search of the guest's room (the situation in *Stoner*);

(2) An officer executes a search warrant which turns out to have been invalidly issued;

(3) An officer conducts a search expressly or arguably authorized by a statute which later is declared violative of the Fourth Amendment or is construed not to authorize the conduct;

(4) An officer conducts a search incident to an arrest under a penal provision which later is held to violate the First Amendment;

(5) An officer executes an arrest warrant which, unknown to him, has just been withdrawn by the issuing judge;

(6) An officer arrests *A*, reasonably believing him to be *B*, for whom a valid arrest warrant is outstanding. The officer then searches *A* incident to the mistaken-identity arrest.

H. PLAIN VIEW SEIZURES

[Editor's Note: The following decision is important in connection with plain view seizures and automobile searches (Section L, infra). It also touches upon the area of consent searches. The authors have placed the entire edited decision here rather than placing fragments of the decision at different places in the casebook.]

COOLIDGE v. NEW HAMPSHIRE

Supreme Court of the United States, 1971.
403 U.S. 443, 91 S.Ct. 2022, rehearing denied 404 U.S. 874, 92 S.Ct. 26.

MR. JUSTICE STEWART delivered the opinion of the Court.

We are called upon in this case to decide issues under the Fourth and Fourteenth Amendments arising in the context of a state criminal trial for the commission of a particularly brutal murder. As in every case, our single duty is to determine the issues presented in accord with the Constitution and the law.

Pamela Mason, a 14-year-old girl, left her home in Manchester, New Hampshire on the evening of January 13, 1964, during a heavy snowstorm, apparently in response to a man's telephone call for a babysitter. Eight days later, after a thaw, her body was found by the side of a major north-south highway several miles away. She had been murdered. The event created great alarm in the area, and the police immediately began a massive investigation.

On January 28, having learned from a neighbor that the petitioner, Edward Coolidge, had been away from home on the evening of the girl's disappearance, the police went to his house to question him. They asked him, among other things, if he owned any guns, and he produced three, two shotguns and a rifle. They also asked whether he would take a lie detector test concerning his account of his activities on the night of the disappearance. He agreed to do so on the following Sunday, his day off. The police later described his attitude on the occasion of this visit as fully "cooperative." His wife was in the house throughout the interview.

On the following Sunday a policeman called Coolidge early in the morning and asked him to come down to the police station for the trip to Concord, New Hampshire, where the lie detector test was to be administered. That evening, two plain clothes policemen arrived at the Coolidge house, where Mrs. Coolidge was waiting with her mother-in-law for her husband's return.   These two policemen were not the two who had visited the house earlier in the week, and they apparently did not know that Coolidge had displayed three guns for inspection during the earlier visit.   The plainclothesmen told Mrs. Coolidge that her husband was in "serious trouble" and probably would not be home that night.   They asked Coolidge's mother to leave, and proceeded to question Mrs. Coolidge.   During the course of the interview they obtained from her four guns belonging to Coolidge, and some clothes that Mrs. Coolidge thought her husband might have been wearing on the evening of Pamela Mason's disappearance.

Coolidge was held in jail on an unrelated charge that night, but he was released the next day.   During the ensuing two and a half weeks, the State accumulated a quantity of evidence to support the theory that it was he who had killed Pamela Mason.   .   .   .

[On February 19 a warrant was issued for the search of a 1951 Pontiac sedan owned by Coolidge.   The Supreme Court held the warrant invalid because it was not issued by a neutral judicial officer, but rather by the State Attorney General, who himself had been directing the investigation.   (This issue was earlier discussed in the casebook, Ch. 4, Section C, Note 1(a).)]

The police arrested Coolidge in his house on the day the warrant issued.   Mrs. Coolidge asked whether she might remain in the house with her small child, but was told that she must stay elsewhere, apparently in part because the police believed that she would be harassed by reporters if she were accessible to them.   When she asked whether she might take her car, she was told that both cars had been "impounded," and that the police would provide transportation for her.   Some time later, the police called a towing company, and about two and a half hours after Coolidge had been taken into custody the cars were towed to the police station.   It appears that at the time of the arrest the cars were parked in the Coolidge driveway, and that although dark had fallen they were plainly visible both from the street and from inside the house where Coolidge was actually arrested.   The 1951 Pontiac was searched and vacuumed on February 21, two days after it was seized, again a year later, in January 1965. and a third time in April, 1965.

At Coolidge's subsequent jury trial on the charge of murder, vacuum sweepings, including particles of gun powder, taken from the Pontiac were introduced in evidence against him, as part of an attempt by the State to show by microscopic analysis that it was highly probable that Pamela Mason had been in Coolidge's car.   Also introduced in evidence was one of the guns taken by the police on their Sunday evening visit to the Coolidge house—a .22 calibre Mossberg rifle, which the prosecution claimed was the murder weapon.   Conflicting ballistics testimony was offered on the question whether the bullets found in Pamela Mason's body had been fired from this rifle.   Finally, the prosecution introduced vacuum sweepings of the clothes taken from the Coolidge house that same Sunday evening, and attempted to show through microscopic analysis that there was a high probability that the clothes had been in contact with Pamela Mason's body. . . .

II.

The State proposes three distinct theories to bring the facts of this case within one or another of the exceptions to the warrant requirement. . . .

[T]he most basic constitutional rule in this area is that "searches conducted outside the judicial process, without prior approval by judge or magistrate, are *per se* unreasonable under the Fourth Amendment—subject only to a few specifically established and well-delineated exceptions." The exceptions are "jealously and carefully drawn," and there must be "a showing by those who seek exemption . . . that the exigencies of the situation made that course imperative." "[T]he burden is on those seeking the exemption to show the need for it." In times of unrest, whether caused by crime or racial conflict or fear of internal subversion, this basic law and the values that it represents may appear unrealistic or "extravagant" to some. But the values were those of the authors of our fundamental constitutional concepts. In times not altogether unlike our own they won—by legal and constitutional means in England, and by revolution on this continent—a right of personal security against arbitrary intrusions by official power. If times have changed, reducing every man's scope to do as he pleases in an urban and industrial world, the changes have made the values served by the Fourth Amendment more, not less, important.

A

The State's first theory is that the seizure and subsequent search of Coolidge's Pontiac on February 19 were "incident" to a valid arrest. We assume that the arrest of Coolidge inside his house was valid, so that the first condition of a warrantless "search incident" is met. And since the events in issue took place in 1964, we assess the State's argument in terms of the law as it existed before Chimel v. California, 395 U.S. 752, which substantially restricted the "search incident" exception to the warrant requirement, but did so only prospectively. Williams v. United States, 401 U.S. 646. But even under pre-*Chimel* law, the State's position is untenable.

* * *

B

The second theory put forward by the State to justify a warrantless seizure and search of the Pontiac car is that under Carroll v. United States, 267 U.S. 132, the police may make a warrantless search of an automobile whenever they have probable cause to do so, and, under our decision last Term in Chambers v. Maroney, 399 U.S. 42, whenever the police may make a legal contemporaneous search under *Carroll*, they may also seize the car, take it to the police station, and search it there. But even granting that the police had probable cause to search the car, the application of the *Carroll* case to these facts would extend it far beyond its original rationale.

Carroll did indeed hold that "contraband goods concealed and illegally transported in an automobile or other vehicle may be searched for without a warrant," provided that "the seizing officer shall have reasonable or probable cause for believing that the automobile which he stops and seizes has contraband liquor therein which is being illegally transported." Such searches had been explicitly authorized by Congress, and, as we have pointed out elsewhere, in the conditions of the time "[a]n automobile . . . was an almost indispensable instrumentality in large-scale violation of the National Prohibition Act, and the car itself therefore was treated somewhat as an offender and became contraband." In two later cases, each involving an occupied automobile stopped on the open highway and searched for contraband liquor, the Court followed and reaffirmed *Carroll*. And last Term in *Chambers*, supra, we did so again.

The underlying rationale of *Carroll* and of all the cases which have followed it is that there is

> "a necessary difference between a search of a store, dwelling house or other structure in respect of which a proper official warrant readily may be obtained, and a search of a ship, motor boat, wagon or automobile, for contraband goods, where *it is not practicable to secure a warrant* because the vehicle can be quickly moved out of the locality or jurisdiction in which the warrant must be sought." 267 U. S., at 153. (Emphasis supplied.)

As we said in *Chambers*, "exigent circumstances" justify the warrantless search of "an automobile *stopped on the highway*," where there is probable cause, because the car is "movable, the occupants are alerted, and the car's contents may never be found again if a warrant must be obtained." "[T]he opportunity to search is fleeting . . . ." (Emphasis supplied.)

In this case, the police had known for some time of the probable role of the Pontiac car in the crime. Coolidge was aware that he was a suspect in the Mason murder, but he had been extremely cooperative throughout the investigation, and there was no indication that he meant to flee. He had already had ample opportunity to destroy any evidence he thought incriminating. There is no suggestion that, on the night in question, the car was being used for any illegal purpose, and it was regularly parked in the driveway of his house. The opportunity for search was thus hardly "fleeting." The objects which the police are assumed to have had probable cause to search for in the car were neither stolen nor contraband nor dangerous.

When the police arrived at the Coolidge house to arrest him, two officers were sent to guard the back door while the main party approached from the front. Coolidge was arrested inside the house, without resistance of any kind on his part, after he had voluntarily admitted the officers at both front and back doors. There was no way in which he could conceivably have gained access to the automobile after the police arrived on his property. When Coolidge had been taken away, the police informed Mrs. Coolidge, the only other adult occupant of the house, that she and her baby must spend the night elsewhere and that she could not use either of the Coolidge cars. Two police officers then drove her in a police car to the house of a relative in another town, and they stayed with her there until around midnight, long after the police had had the Pontiac towed to the station house. The Coolidge premises were guarded throughout the night by two policemen.[1]

The word "automobile" is not a talisman in whose presence the Fourth Amendment fades away and disappears. And surely there is nothing in this case to invoke the meaning and purpose of the rule of Carroll v. United States—no alerted criminal bent on flight, no fleeting opportunity on an open highway after a hazardous chase, no contraband or stolen goods or weapons, no confederates waiting to move the evidence, not even the inconvenience of a special police detail to guard the immobilized automobile. In short, by no possible stretch of the legal imagination can this be made into a case where "it is not practicable to secure a warrant," *Carroll*, supra, at 153, and the "automobile exception," despite its label, is simply irrelevant.

Since *Carroll* would not have justified a warrantless search of the Pontiac at the time Coolidge was arrested, the later search at the station house was plainly illegal, at least so far as the automobile exception is concerned. *Chambers*, supra, is of no help to the State, since that case held only that, where the police may stop and search an automobile under *Carroll*, they may also seize it and search it later at the police station. Rather, this case is controlled by Dyke v. Taylor Implement Mfg. Co. There the police lacked probable cause to seize or search the defendant's automobile at the time of his arrest, and this was enough by itself to condemn the subsequent search at the station house. Here there was probable cause, but no exigent cir-

---

1. It is frequently said that occupied automobiles stopped on the open highway may be searched without a warrant because they are "mobile," or "movable." No other basis appears for Mr. Justice White's suggestion in his dissenting opinion that we should "treat searches of automobiles as we do the arrest of a person." In this case, it is of course true that even though Coolidge was in jail, his wife was miles away in the company of two plainclothesmen, and the Coolidge property was under the guard of two other officers, the automobile was in a literal sense "mobile." A person who had the keys and could slip by the guard could drive it away. We attach no constitutional significance to this sort of mobility.

First, a good number of the containers which the police might discover on a person's property and want to search are equally movable, e. g., trunks, suitcases, boxes, briefcases, and bags. How are such objects to be distinguished from an unoccupied automobile—not then being used for any illegal purpose—sitting on the owner's property? It is true that the automobile has wheels and its own locomotive power. But given the virtually universal availability of automobiles in our society there is little difference between driving the container itself away and driving it away in a vehicle brought to the scene for that purpose. Of course if there is a criminal suspect close enough to the automobile so that he might get a weapon from it or destroy evidence within it, the police may make a search of appropriately limited scope. Chimel v. California, 395 U.S. 752. But if Carroll v. United States, 267 U.S. 132, permits a warrantless search of an unoccupied vehicle, on private property and beyond the scope of a valid search incident to an arrest, then it would permit as well a warrantless search of a suitcase or a box. We have found no case that suggests such an extension of *Carroll*.

cumstances justified the police in proceeding without a warrant. As in *Dyke*, the later search at the station house was therefore illegal.

C

The State's third theory in support of the warrantless seizure and search of the Pontiac car is that the car itself was an "instrumentality of the crime," and as such might be seized by the police on Coolidge's property because it was in plain view. Supposing the seizure to be thus lawful, the case of Cooper v. California, 386 U.S. 58, is said to support a subsequent warrantless search at the station house, with or without probable cause. Of course, the distinction between an "instrumentality of crime" and "mere evidence" was done away with by Warden v. Hayden, 387 U.S. 294, and we may assume that the police had probable cause to seize the automobile. But, for the reasons that follow, we hold that the "plain view" exception to the warrant requirement is inapplicable to this case. Since the seizure was therefore illegal, it is unnecessary to consider the applicability of *Cooper*, supra, to the subsequent search.

It is well established that under certain circumstances the police may seize evidence in plain view without a warrant. But it is important to keep in mind that, in the vast majority of cases, *any* evidence seized by the police will be in plain view, at least at the moment of seizure. The problem with the "plain view" doctrine has been to identify the circumstances in which plain view has legal significance rather than being simply the normal concomitant of any search, legal or illegal.

An example of the applicability of the "plain view" doctrine is the situation in which the police have a warrant to search a given area for specified objects, and in the course of the search come across some other article of incriminating character. Where the initial intrusion which brings the police within plain view of such an article is supported not by a warrant, but by one of the recognized exceptions to the warrant requirement, the seizure is also legitimate. Thus the police may inadvertently come across evidence while in "hot pursuit" of a fleeing suspect. Warden v. Hayden, supra. Cf. Hester v. United States, 265 U.S. 57. And an object which comes into view during a search incident to arrest that is appropriately limited in scope under existing law may be seized without a warrant. Chimel v. California, 395 U.S. 752, 762–763. Finally, the "plain view" doctrine has been applied where a police officer is not searching for evidence against the accused, but nonetheless inadvertently comes across an incriminating object. Harris v. United States, 390 U.S. 234; Frazier v. Cupp, 394 U.S. 731; Ker v. California, 374 U.S. 23, 43. Cf. Lewis v. United States, 385 U.S. 206.

What the "plain view" cases have in common is that the police officer in each of them had a prior justification for an intrusion in the course of which he came inadvertently across a piece of evidence incriminating the accused. The doctrine serves to supplement the prior justification—whether it be a warrant for another object, hot pursuit, search incident to lawful arrest, or some other legitimate reason for being present unconnected with a search directed against the accused—and permits the warrantless seizure. Of course, the extension of the original justification is legitimate only where it is immediately apparent to the police that they have evidence before them; the "plain view" doctrine may not be used to extend a general exploratory search from one object to another until something incriminating at last emerges. Cf. Stanley v. Georgia, supra, 571–572 (Stewart, J., concurring).

The rationale for the "plain view" exception is evident if we keep in mind the two distinct constitutional protections served by the warrant requirement. First, the magistrate's scrutiny is intended to eliminate altogether searches not based on probable cause. The premise here is that *any* intrusion in the way of search or seizure is an evil, so that no intrusion at all is justified without a careful prior determination of necessity. The second, distinct objective is that those searches deemed necessary should be as limited as possible. Here, the specific evil is the "general warrant" abhorred by the colonists, and the problem is not that of intrusion *per se*, but of a general, exploratory rummaging in a person's belongings. The warrant accomplishes this second objective by requiring a "particular description" of the things to be seized.

The "plain view" doctrine is not in conflict with the first objective because plain view does not occur until a search is in progress. In each case, this initial intrusion is justified by a warrant or by an exception such as "hot pursuit" or search incident to a lawful arrest, or by an extraneous valid reason for the officer's presence. And given the initial intrusion, the seizure of an object in plain view is consistent with the second objective, since it does not convert the search into a general or exploratory one. As against the minor peril to Fourth Amendment protections, there is a major gain in effective law enforcement. Where, once an otherwise lawful search is in progress, the police inadvertently come upon a piece of evidence, it would often be a needless inconvenience, and sometimes dangerous—to the evidence or to the police themselves—to require them to ignore it until they have obtained a warrant particularly describing it.

The limits on the doctrine are implicit in the statement of its rationale. The first of these is that plain view *alone* is never enough to justify the warrantless seizure of evidence. This is simply a corollary of the familiar principle discussed above, that no amount of probable cause can justify a warrantless search or seizure absent "exigent circumstances." Incontrovertible testimony of the senses that an incriminating object is on premises belonging to a criminal suspect may establish the fullest possible measure of probable cause. But even where the object is contraband, this Court has repeatedly stated and enforced the basic rule that the police may not enter and make a warrantless seizure.

The second limitation is that the discovery of evidence in plain view must be inadvertent. The rationale of the exception to the warrant requirement, as just stated, is that a plain view seizure will not turn an initially valid (and therefore limited) search into a "general," one, while the inconvenience of procuring a warrant to cover an inadvertent discovery is great. But where the discovery is anticipated, where the police know in advance the location of the evidence and intend to seize it, the situation is altogether different. The requirement of a warrant to seize imposes no inconvenience whatever, or at least none which is constitutionally cognizable in a legal system that regards warrantless searches as "per se unreasonable" in the absence of "exigent circumstances."

If the initial intrusion is bottomed upon a warrant which fails to mention a particular object, though the police know its location and intend to seize it, then there is a violation of the express constitutional requirement of "warrants . . . particularly describing . . . [the] things to be seized." The initial intrusion may, of course, be legitimated not by a warrant but by one of the exceptions to the warrant requirement, such as hot pursuit or search incident to lawful arrest. But to extend the scope of such an intrusion to the seizure of objects—not contraband nor stolen nor dangerous in themselves—which the police know in advance they will find in plain view and intend to seize, would fly in the face of the basic rule that no amount of probable cause can justify a warrantless seizure.

In the light of what has been said, it is apparent that the "plain view" exception cannot justify the police seizure of the Pontiac car in this case. The police had ample opportunity to obtain a valid warrant; they knew the automobile's exact description and location well in advance; they intended to seize it when they came upon Coolidge's property. And this is not a case involving contraband or stolen goods or objects dangerous in themselves.

The seizure was therefore unconstitutional, and so was the subsequent search at the station house. Since evidence obtained in the course of the search was admitted at Coolidge's trial, the judgment must be reversed and the case remanded to the New Hampshire Supreme Court. . . .

III.

The petitioner contends that when the police obtained a rifle and articles of his clothing from his home on the night of Sunday, February 2, 1964, while he was being interrogated at the police station, they engaged in a search and seizure violative of the Constitution. . . .

A

The lie detector test administered to Coolidge in Concord on the afternoon of the 2d was inconclusive as to his activities on the night of Pamela Mason's disappearance, but during the course of the test Coolidge confessed to stealing $375 from his employer. After the group returned from Concord to Manchester, the interrogation about Coolidge's movements on the night of the disappearance continued, and Coolidge apparently made a number of statements which the police immediately checked out as best they could. The decision to send two officers to the Coolidge house to speak with Mrs. Coolidge was apparently motivated in part by a desire to check his story against whatever she might say, and in part by the need for some corroboration of his admission to the theft from his employer. The trial judge found as a fact, and the record supports him, that at the time of the visit the police knew very little about the weapon that had killed Pamela Mason. The bullet that had been retrieved was of small calibre, but the police were unsure whether the weapon was a rifle or a pistol. During the extensive investigation following the discovery of the body, the police had made it a practice to ask all those questioned whether they owned any guns, and to ask the owners for permission to run tests on those which met the very general description of the murder weapon. The trial judge found as a fact that when the police visited Mrs. Coolidge on the night of the 2d, they were unaware of the previous visit during which Coolidge had shown other officers three guns, and that they were not motivated by a desire to find the murder weapon.

The two plainclothesmen asked Mrs. Coolidge whether her husband had been at home on the night of the murder victim's disappearance, and she replied that he had not. They then asked her if her husband owned any guns. According to her testimony at the pretrial suppression hearing, she replied, "Yes, I will get them in the bedroom." One of the officers replied, "We will come with you." The three went into the bedroom where Mrs. Coolidge took all four guns out of the closet. Her account continued:

> "A. I believe I asked if they wanted the guns. One gentleman said, 'No;' then the other gentleman turned around and said, 'We might as well take them.' I said, 'If you would like them, you may take them.'
>
> "Q. Did you go further and say, 'We have nothing to hide.'?
>
> "A. I can't recall if I said that then or before. I don't recall.
>
> "Q. But at some time you indicated to them that as far as you were concerned you had nothing to hide, and they might take what they wanted?
>
> "A. That was it.
>
> *   *   *   *   *   *   *   *   *   *
>
> "Q. Did you feel at that time that you had something to hide?
>
> "A. No."

The two policemen also asked Mrs. Coolidge what her husband had been wearing on the night of the disappearance. She then produced four pairs of trousers and indicated that her husband had probably worn either of two of them on that evening. She also brought out a hunting jacket. The police gave her a receipt for the guns and the clothing, and, after a search of the Coolidge cars not here in issue, took the various articles to the police station.

B

The first branch of the petitioner's argument is that when Mrs. Coolidge brought out the guns and clothing and then handed them over to the police, she was acting as an "instrument" of the officials, complying with a "demand" made by them. Consequently, it is argued, Coolidge was the victim of a search and seizure within the constitutional meaning of those terms. Since we cannot accept this interpretation of the facts, we need not consider the petitioner's further argument that Mrs. Coolidge could not or did not "waive" her husband's constitutional protection against unreasonable searches and seizures.

Had Mrs. Coolidge, wholly on her own initiative, sought out her husband's guns and clothing and then taken them to the police station to be used as evidence against him, there can be no doubt under existing law that the articles would later have been admissible in evidence. The question presented here is whether the conduct of the police officers at the Coolidge house was such as to make her actions their actions for purposes of the Fourth and Fourteenth Amendments and their attendant exclusionary rules. The test as the petitioner's argument suggests, is whether Mrs. Coolidge, in light of all the circumstances of the case, must be regarded as having acted as an "instrument" or agent of the state when she produced her husband's belongings.

*   *   *

Yet it cannot be said that the police should have obtained a warrant for the guns and clothing before they set out to visit Mrs. Coolidge, since they had no intention of rummaging around among Coolidge's effects or of dispossessing him of any of his property. Nor can it be said that they should have obtained Coolidge's permission for a seizure they did not intend to make. There was nothing to compel them to announce to the suspect that they intended to question his wife about his movements on the night of the disappearance or about the theft from his employer. Once Mrs. Coolidge had admitted them, the policemen were surely acting normally and properly when they asked her, as they had asked those questioned earlier in the investigation, including Coolidge himself, about any guns there might be in the house. The question concerning the clothes Coolidge had been wearing on the night of the disappearance was logical and in no way coercive. Indeed, one might doubt the competence of the officers involved had they not asked exactly the questions they did ask. And surely when Mrs. Coolidge of her own accord produced the guns and clothes for inspection, rather than simply describing them, it was not incumbent on the police to stop her or avert their eyes.

The crux of the petitioner's argument must be that when Mrs. Coolidge asked the policemen whether they wanted the guns, they should have replied that they could not take them, or have first telephoned Coolidge at the police station and asked his permission to take them, or have asked her whether she had been authorized by her husband to release them. Instead, after one policeman had declined the offer, the other turned and said, "We might as well take them," to which Mrs. Coolidge replied, "If you would like them, you may have them."

In assessing the claim that this course of conduct amounted to a search and seizure, it is well to keep in mind that Mrs. Coolidge described her own motive as that of clearing her husband, and that she believed that she had nothing to hide. She had seen her husband himself produce his guns for two other policemen earlier in the week, and there is nothing to indicate that she realized that he had offered only three of them for inspection on that occasion. The two officers who questioned her behaved, as her own testimony shows, with perfect courtesy. There is not the slightest implication of an attempt on their part to coerce or dominate her, or, for that matter, to direct her actions by the more subtle techniques of suggestion that are available to officials in circumstances like these. To hold that the conduct of the police here was a search and seizure would be to hold, in effect, that a criminal suspect has constitutional protection against the adverse consequences of a spontaneous, good-faith effort by his wife to clear him of suspicion.

The judgment is reversed and the case is remanded to the Supreme Court of New Hampshire for further proceedings not inconsistent with this opinion.

[Opinion of JUSTICE HARLAN, concurring, omitted.]

[Opinion of JUSTICE BLACK, concurring and dissenting, omitted.]

MR. JUSTICE WHITE, with whom THE CHIEF JUSTICE joins, concurring and dissenting.

I would affirm the judgment. In my view, Coolidge's Pontiac was lawfully seized as evidence of the crime in plain sight and thereafter was lawfully searched under Cooper v. California, 386 U.S. 58 (1967). I am therefore in substantial disagreement with Parts II–C and II–D of the Court's opinion. Neither do I agree with Part II–B, and I can concur only in the result as to Part III.

II.

In the case before us, the officers had probable cause both to arrest Coolidge and to seize his car. In order to effect his arrest, they went to his home—perhaps the most obvious place in which to look for him. They also may have hoped to find his car at home and, in fact, when they arrived on the property to make the arrest, they did find the 1951 Pontiac there. Thus, even assuming that the Fourth Amendment protects against warrantless seizures outside the house, but see Hester v. United States, supra, at 59, the fact remains that the officers had legally entered Coolidge's property to effect an arrest and that they seized the car only after they observed it in plain view before them. The Court, however, would invalidate this seizure on the premise that officers should not be permitted to seize effects in plain sight when they have anticipated they will see them.

Even accepting this premise of the Court, seizure of the car was not invalid. The majority makes an assumption that, when the police went to Coolidge's house to arrest him, they anticipated that they would also find the 1951 Pontiac there. In my own reading of the record, however, I have found no evidence to support this assumption. For all the record shows, the police, although they may have hoped to find the Pontiac at Coolidge's home, did not know its exact location when they went to make the arrest, and their observation of it in Coolidge's driveway was truly inadvertent. Of course, they did have probable cause to seize the car, and, if they had had a valid warrant as well, they would have been justified in looking for it in Coolidge's driveway—a likely place for it to be. But if the fact of probable cause bars this seizure, it would also bar seizures not only of cars found at a house, but also of cars parked in a parking lot, hidden in some secluded spot, or delivered to the police by a third party at the police station. This would simply be a rule that the existence of probable cause bars all warrantless seizures.

It is evident on the facts of this case that Coolidge's Pontiac was subject to seizure if proper procedures were employed. It is also apparent that the Pontiac was in plain view of the officers who had legally entered Coolidge's property to effect his arrest. I am satisfied that it was properly seized whether or not the officers expected that it would be found where it was. And, since the Pontiac was legally seized as evidence of the crime for which Coolidge was arrested, . . . authorizes its warrantless search while in lawful custody of the police. "It would be unreasonable to hold that the police, having to retain the car in their custody for such a length of time, had no right, even for their own protection, to search it. It is no answer to say that the police could have obtained a search warrant, for '[t]he relevant test is not whether it is reasonable to procure a search warrant, but whether the search was reasonable.' . . . Under the circumstances of this case, we cannot hold unreasonable under the Fourth Amendment the examination or search of a car validly held by officers for use as evidence. . . ." Cooper v. California, supra, at 62.

III.

Given the foregoing views, it is perhaps unnecessary to deal with the other grounds offered to sustain the search of Coolidge's car. Nonetheless, it may be helpful to explain my reasons for relying on the plain-sight rule rather than on Chambers v. Maroney, 399 U.S. 42 (1970), to validate this search.

Chambers upheld the seizure and subsequent search of automobiles at the station house rather than require the police to search cars immediately at the places where they are found. But *Chambers* did not authorize indefinite detention of automobiles so seized; it contemplated some expedition in completing the searches so that automobiles could be released and returned to their owners. In the present case, however, Coolidge's Pontiac was not released quickly but was retained in police custody for more than a year and was searched not only immediately after seizure but also on two other occasions: one of them 11 months and the other 14 months after seizure. Since fruits of the later searches as well as the earlier one were apparently introduced in evidence, I cannot look to *Chambers* and would invalidate the later searches but for the fact that the police had a right to seize and detain the car not because it was a car, but because it was itself evidence of crime. It is only because of the long detention of the car that I find *Chambers* inapplicable, however, and I disagree strongly with the majority's reasoning for refusing to apply it.

As recounted earlier, arrest and search of the person on probable cause but without a warrant is the prevailing constitutional and legislative rule, without regard to whether on the particular facts there was opportunity to secure a warrant. Apparently, exigent circumstances are so often present in arrest situations that it has been deemed improvident to litigate the issue in every case.

In similar fashion, "practically since the beginning of the Government," Congress and the Court have recognized "a necessary difference between a search of a store, dwelling house or other structure in respect of which a proper official warrant readily may be obtained, and a search of a ship, motor boat, wagon or automobile, for contraband goods, where it is not practicable to secure a warrant because the vehicle can be quickly moved out of the locality or jurisdiction in which the warrant must be sought." Carroll v. United States, 267 U.S. 132, 153 (1925). As in the case of an arrest and accompanying search of a person, searches of vehicles on probable cause but without a warrant have been deemed reasonable within the meaning of the Fourth Amendment without requiring proof of exigent circumstances beyond the fact that a movable vehicle is involved. The rule has been consistently recognized, see Cooper v. California, supra; Brinegar v. United States, 338 U.S. 160 (1949); Harris v. United States, supra, at 168 (dissenting opinion); Davis v. United States, 328 U.S. 582, 609 (1946) (dissenting opinion); Scher v. United States, 305 U.S. 251 (1938); Husty v. United States, 282 U.S. 694 (1931); United States v. Lee, supra; and was reaffirmed less than a year ago in Chambers v. Maroney, supra, where a vehicle was stopped on the highway but was searched at the police station, there being probable cause but no warrant.

The majority now approves warrantless searches of vehicles in motion when seized. On the other hand, warrantless, probable-cause searches of parked but movable vehicles in some situations would be valid only upon proof of exigent circumstances justifying the search. Although I am not sure, it would seem that, when police discover a parked car that they have probable cause to search, they may not immediately search but must seek a warrant. But if before the warrant arrives, the car is put in motion by its owner or others, it may be stopped and searched on the spot or elsewhere. In the case before us, Coolidge's car, parked at his house, could not be searched without a valid warrant, although if Coolidge had been arrested as he drove away from his home, immediate seizure and subsequent search of the car would have been reasonable under the Fourth Amendment.

I find nothing in the language or the underlying rationale of the line of cases from *Carroll* to *Chambers* limiting vehicle searches as the Court now limits them in situations such as the one before us. Although each of those cases may, as the Court argues, have involved vehicles or vessels in motion prior to their being stopped and searched, each of them approved the search of a vehicle that was no longer moving and, with the occupants in custody, no more likely to move than the unattended but movable vehicle parked on the street or in the driveway of a person's house. In both situations the probability of movement at the instance of family or friends is equally real, and hence the result should be the same whether the car is at rest or in motion when it is discovered.

In Husty v. United States, supra, the police had learned from a reliable informant that Husty had two loads of liquor in automobiles of particular make and description parked at described locations. The officers found one of the cars parked and unattended at the indicated spot. Later, as officers watched, Husty and others entered and started to drive away. The car was stopped after having moved no more than a foot or two; immediate search of the car produced contraband. Husty was then arrested. The Court, in a unanimous opinion, sustained denial of a motion to suppress the fruits of the search, saying that "[t]he Fourth Amendment does not prohibit the search, without warrant, of an automobile, for liquor illegally transported or possessed, if the search is upon probable cause . . . ." Id., at 700. Further, "[t]he search was not unreasonable because, as petitioners argue, sufficient time elapsed between the receipt by the officer of the information and the search of the car to have enabled him to procure a search warrant. He could not know when Husty would come to the car or how soon it would be removed. In such circumstances we do not think the officers should be required to speculate upon the chances of successfully carrying out the search, after the delay and withdrawal from the scene of one or more officers which would have been necessary to procure a warrant. The search was, therefore, on probable cause, and not unreasonable. . . ." Id., at 701.

The Court apparently cites *Husty* with approval as involving a car in motion on the highway. But it was obviously irrelevant to the Court that the officers could have obtained a warrant before Husty attempted to drive the car away. Equally immaterial was the fact that the car had moved one or two feet at the time it was stopped. The search would have been approved even if it had occurred before Husty's arrival or after his arrival but before he had put the car in motion. The Court's attempt to distinguish *Husty* on the basis of the car's negligible movement prior to its being stopped is without force.

The Court states flatly, however, that this case is not ruled by the *Carroll-Chambers* line of cases but by Dyke v. Taylor Implement Mfg. Co., 391 U.S. 216 (1968). There the car was properly stopped and the occupants arrested for reckless driving, but the subsequent search at the station house could not be justified as incident to the arrest. See Preston v. United States, 376 U.S. 364 (1964). Nor could the car itself be seized and later searched, as it was, absent probable cause to believe it contained evidence of crime. In *Dyke,* it was pointed out that probable cause did not exist at the time of the search, and we expressly rested our holding on this fact, noting that "[s]ince the search was not shown to have been based upon sufficient cause," it was not necessary to reach other grounds urged for invalidating it. 391 U.S., at 222. Given probable cause, however, we would have upheld the search in *Dyke.*

For Fourth Amendment purposes, the difference between a moving and movable vehicle is tenuous at best. It is a metaphysical distinction without roots in the commonsense standard of reasonableness governing search and seizure cases. Distinguishing the case before us from the *Carroll-Chambers* line of cases further enmeshes Fourth Amendment law in litigation breeding refinements having little relation to reality. I suggest that in the interest of coherence and credibility we either overrule our prior cases and treat automobiles precisely as we do houses or apply those cases to readily movable as well as moving vehicles and thus treat searches of automobiles as we do the arrest of a person. By either course we might bring some modicum of certainty to Fourth Amendment law and give the law enforcement officers some slight guidance in how they are to conduct themselves.

I accordingly dissent from Parts II–B, II–C, and II–D of the Court's opinion. I concur, however, in the result reached in Part III of the opinion. I would therefore affirm the judgment of the New Hampshire Supreme Court.

[Dissenting opinion of CHIEF JUSTICE BURGER, omitted.

NOTES

1. The statement that plain view by itself does not justify a seizure has several implications. (a) It means that plain view observations and seizures are unlawful if the vantage point for the observations was gained through an intrusion which violated the Fourth Amendment. (b) It means that although plain view observations may be lawful, if a further intrusion (e. g., entering a home) is necessary before the items can be seized, the plain view doctrine does not justify the intrusion. Some other justification is required. (c) The statement means that items spotted in plain view cannot be seized and carried away absent probable cause to believe that the items are contraband or evidence of a crime. (d) The statement also suggests that plain view observations and seizures are impermissible if the original viewing violated a reasonable expectation of privacy even if there was no trespass (the *Katz* limitation). (e) Finally the statement may mean that, subject to qualifications, plain view seizures are impermissible unless the discovery of evidence was inadvertent (the *Coolidge* limitation). Each of these meanings is explored in the notes which follow.

2. Under the traditional (pre-*Katz*) view, observations made from a place where the officer has a right to be are lawful plain view observations. Such observations sometimes are made from a vantage point gained without any prior Fourth Amendment intrusion; for example, from a public sidewalk or from that part of a store or a tavern or a hotel which is open to the public. Occasionally the question of what is a public area is a close one. What about the common hall of a large apartment building or the garage of

a building which houses many condominium units? See State v. Bazella, 522 S.W.2d 57 (Mo.App.1975); United States v. Cruz Pagan, 537 F.2d 554 (1st Cir. 1976). Compare People v. Killebrew, 76 Mich.App. 215, 256 N.W. 2d 581 (1977). A most interesting case is People v. Abrams, 48 Ill.2d 446, 271 N.E.2d 37 (1971), where a home was open to general members of the public who made a small "donation" to attend an anti-war meeting. According to the court, the nature of the place changed when the hosts indicated that police officers were not welcome. If an undercover police agent attends a meeting of citizens, open to the general public, called to discuss police brutality, has he violated the Fourth Amendment? Or is this a problem which calls for First Amendment analysis? The issue will arise in the context of a criminal case only if the police see or hear evidence of a crime, as in *Abrams*, where liquor law violations were observed.

3. Even if a police officer gains his vantage point without trespassing against a suspect's property, under the post-*Katz* approach, his observations still may violate the Fourth Amendment if the observations violated a "reasonable expectation of privacy." See e. g., State v. Kaaheena, 59 Hawaii 23, 575 P.2d 462 (1978) (officer peeked over top of curtain). See also, People v. Triggs, 8 Cal.3d 884, 106 Cal.Rptr, 408, 506 P.2d 232 (1973) (officer peeked into stall in public washroom). An officer who with his unaided ear overhears conversations inside a motel room while stationed in the hallway or in an adjacent room probably violates no *reasonable* expectation of privacy. United States v. Jackson, 588 F.2d 1046 (5th Cir. 1979); State v. Moses, 367 So.2d 800 (La.1979). Nor does an officer who looks through an undraped window while standing in a parking lot. Gil v. Beto, 440 F.2d 666 (5th Cir. 1971).

If, while standing in a place where he has a right to be, an officer looks into private property with the aid of a mechanical device, a court is more likely to find a violation of a reasonable expectation of privacy, particularly if the device is highly sophisticated like the high-power telescope in People v. Kender, — Hawaii —, 588 P.2d 447 (1979). On the other hand, numerous cases have upheld the use of flashlights, including Walker v. Beto, 437 F.2d 1018 (5th Cir. 1971). Observations made through the use of binoculars may present a close question which turns upon the individual circumstances. See People v. Ciochon, 23 Ill.App.3d 363, 319 N.E.2d 332, (1974). What if the police use a "startron" to look through an undraped window and make observations of activity in a dark room? See Commonwealth v. Williams, — Pa. —, 396 A.2d 1286 (1978). Suppose they fly over property in a helicopter at a low altitude? See People v. Sneed, 32 Cal.App.3d 535, 108 Cal.Rptr. 146 (1973). In an airplane at 2400 feet? See People v. Lashmett, 71 Ill.App.3d 429, 27 Ill.Dec. 657, 389 N.E.2d 888 (1979).

4. Sometimes the vantage point will be gained only through some prior intrusion, for example, after entry to arrest, after a "civil emergency" entry (see Section I), or during the execution of a search warrant which names item *A* but does not name item *B* (the plain view evidence). For the observations and any subsequent seizure to be valid under plain view doctrines, the original entry must have been made without violating the defendant's Fourth Amendment rights. Thus the legality will turn upon application of some doctrine other than plain view. For example, a plain view seizure made after entry to arrest is proper only if the police had the right to enter for that purpose. See People v. Sprovieri, 43 Ill.2d 223, 252 N.E.2d 531 (1969). Plain view seizures following a consent to enter will be invalid if the consent was involuntary.

5. Consider the following hypotheticals. An officer walking down the street looks into a window and spots what he has probable cause to believe is a large quantity of marijuana resting on a kitchen table. Can he enter without a warrant? If so, on what theory? Plain view by itself does not permit an entry to seize evidence. Does it make a difference if someone is sitting at the table? What theory would justify the entry in such a case? Suppose instead the marijuana is spotted in an unoccupied car parked on a public street. Consider this hypothetical again in connection with the material in Section L.

6. The "inadvertency" limitation of *Coolidge* has not had the major impact on plain view seizures that one might have expected. Some courts have refused to recognize it as the law of the land, noting that only four of the nine participating justices adopted the doctrine. North v. Superior Court of Riverside County, 8 Cal.3d 301, 104 Cal.Rptr. 833, 502 P.2d 1305 (1972); State v. Pontier, 95 Idaho 707, 518 P.2d 969 (1974). Other courts have decided that unless the police have probable cause sufficient to obtain a search warrant before they came upon the scene, they cannot be faulted for not getting a warrant; and thus the inadvertency doctrine has no application absent pre-existing probable cause. State v. Davenport, 510 P.2d 78 (Alaska 1973); United States v. Hare, 589 F.2d 1291 (6th Cir. 1979). This puts defense counsel in the awkward position of arguing that there *was* probable cause if the defense wishes to rely upon the inadvertency doctrine. Additionally, if the doctrine has no application to items which are not "contraband nor stolen nor dangerous in themselves," many plain view seizures fall outside its borders.

The inadvertency doctrine raises other questions. Does it bar testimony about observations which were expected to be made, or only physical evidence which was seized? See People v. Spinelli, 35 N.Y.2d 77, 358 N.Y.S. 2d 743, 315 N.E.2d 792 (1974). In *Coolidge* the Court suggested that the initial intrusion, an entry to arrest, although lawful, might have been used as a guise to place the officers in a position where they could seize plain view evidence. Does the inadvertency limitation, created as a response to that possibility, apply without regard to the nature of the original intrusion? Suppose the police have probable cause to search for item X and item Y at a specified apartment, but get a warrant to seize only X. Is the seizure of Y impermissible? See Chambers v. State, 508 S.W.2d 348 (Tex.Crim.App.1974); State v. Davenport, supra. Suppose the police obtain consent to enter an apartment to talk to a suspect and see, in plain view, evidence in the form of bloody clothing which they expected would be somewhere in the apartment. Is its seizure improper? Or suppose the police obtain consent to search an automobile trunk, but not consent to take anything (see Section G, supra). If they come across evidence which they expected to find, is seizure impermissible because the discovery was not inadvertent?

7. The plain view doctrine operates on the premise that there is no "search". There is, however, a seizure and there must be probable cause to seize.

Assume police officers were executing a valid search warrant which authorizes the seizure of marijuana. In the course of the search one officer discovered several United States savings bonds bearing names and addresses different from that of the suspect. The officer took the bonds to a different room of the residence and gave them to another officer. That officer telephoned one of the persons whose names were on the bonds. That person told the police that the bonds were stolen. Until the call was made the officers had no knowledge that the bonds were stolen. Was the police conduct proper? Consider the views of the court deciding the case. Commonwealth v. Hawkins, 280 N.E.2d 665 (Mass.1972):

Tauro, C. J. . . .

Articles not named in a search warrant, except weapons or contraband, may be seized only if the police have probable cause to believe that they were stolen. . . .

In the instant case the police admitted they had no actual knowledge that the bonds had been stolen until after investigating their ownership. The mere fact that the names on the bonds were different from that of the defendant was insufficient to provide probable cause for their seizure. . . .

In the circumstances of this case it might appear to some that the defendant is being given unwarranted protection. However, if the situation in the instant case were transposed to a different setting, for example, to the home of a person of wealth, it would appear irrational to argue that United States government bonds could be taken from his possession, even momentarily, in order to establish their ownership. It is fundamental in our concept of justice that the denial of constitutional protection to the worst of men effectively serves to deny the same protection to the best of men.

Braucher, J. (dissenting)

I agree that the police did not have probable cause to believe that the bonds had been stolen. They acquired such probable cause only after they made a telephone call to an owner named on one of the bonds.

I also agree that the police had a right to look into the brown envelope in their search for drugs. But they were under a duty to keep the defendant's belongings in order and were therefore justified in noting that the articles were United States savings bonds with names and addresses different from that of the defendant. Such bonds are not transferable. 31 U.S.C. § 757c(a) (1970). 31 C.F.R. (1971) § 315.15. McDonald v. Hanahan, 328 Mass. 539, 540, 105 N.E.2d 240. Their presence in a small apartment being searched for narcotics warranted a further threshold inquiry. . . .

If a threshold inquiry is unreasonably extended, there is danger to the security guaranteed by the Fourth Amendment. . . . But in the present case the police made a telephone call which could have taken only a few minutes. There is no indication that it prolonged the concurrent search for narcotics. The telephone call was likely to produce a less serious invasion of an innocent defendant's privacy than the alternative of sending an officer out to investigate and to bring back a new warrant.

The record indicates that the police took the bonds from one room to another before they had probable cause. It does not indicate a definitive "seizure" until afterwards.

I do not believe that it is proper for either the police or this court to base a judgment on the assumed wealth or poverty of the defendant. If police, acting lawfully in searching a millionaire's mansion, found in a bureau drawer in his bedroom United States savings bonds bearing the names of several other people, they would have solid reason for making further inquiry. Millionaires have no more right to steal than anyone else.

8. The *Hawkins* decision in the preceding note raises the issue of how close an examination the police may make of an item whose incriminating nature is not immediately apparent before their activities constitute an impermissible warrantless search rather than plain view observations. Can they pick up and inspect shoes spotted in plain view? State v. Holloman, 197 Neb. 139, 248 N.W.2d 15 (1976). Can they smell a pipe? Gardner v. State, 32 Md.App. 629, 363 A.2d 616 (1976). Can they, in the absence of probable cause, record serial numbers of television sets or securities? Compare State v. Wilson, 279 Md. 189, 367 A.2d 1223 (1977); United States v. Clark, 531 F.2d 928 (8th Cir. 1976). What about holding slides to a light? See Anderson v. State, 555 P.2d 251 (Alaska, 1976). Many of the "close look" decisions are discussed in Commonwealth v. Bond, —— Mass. ——, 375 N.E.2d 1214 (1978).

I. EMERGENCY SEARCHES

PATRICK v. STATE

Supreme Court of Delaware, 1967.
227 A.2d 486.

The defendant appeals from his conviction of murder in the second degree on the grounds . . . that evidence introduced at trial was illegally obtained.

The pertinent threshold facts are undisputed:

Ernest R. Patrick, the defendant, lived with Joseph Woods and Beverly Goodwyn. Beverly was Woods' mistress but she was also intimate with Patrick on occasion. On the night before the killing, Beverly and Woods had an altercation, over her leaving the house without him, during which Woods struck Beverly, drawing blood, and she attempted to cut him with a razor blade. Beverly and Patrick spent the next day and evening together. After some drinking, they returned to the Woods apartment about 11:00 P.M. En route, Beverly expressed fear of what Woods might do when they arrived. The door of the apartment was open; they entered the living room; and Beverly asked Patrick if Woods was in the bedroom. Patrick went to the bedroom and returned, saying that Woods was there.

Against this background, the jury heard Beverly, called by the State, testify as follows:

That after returning to the living room, Patrick stated that he was going to kill Woods; that Patrick picked up a brick supporting the sofa, entered the hallway, and turned toward the bedroom. Beverly testified that she heard noises which sounded like a brick hitting the bed and like Woods choking; that it did not sound like the brick was hitting Woods. Beverly testified that Patrick returned to the living room with blood on his hands, saying Woods was dead, and then went to the bathroom to wash his hands; that she went into the bedroom and saw Woods' bloody body on the bed; that, in response to her question, Patrick repeated that Woods was dead; that she and

Patrick immediately left the apartment and returned to her sister's home where they spent the balance of the night.

Patrick, testifying in his own defense, stated that it was Beverly who took the brick from under the sofa, went to the bedroom, and killed Woods; that it was he in the living room, not Beverly, who heard the thuds of the blows.

Admitted in evidence was the shirt worn by Patrick on the night in question, bearing stains of Group A blood—Woods' blood type but not Patrick's. Also admitted were pieces of brick, stained with Group A blood, found on the bed and headboard, bloodstained bed clothing, and other items taken by the police from the room in which Woods' body was found. The State proved that the cause of Woods' death was depressed fracture of the skull. Patrick was indicted for murder in the second degree and was found guilty. He appeals.

. . .

The defendant claims that articles introduced in evidence against him were obtained by the police by unlawful search and seizure. The facts pertinent to this issue are as follows:

Woods' body was discovered by his employer, W. A. Larrimore, on the morning after the killing. Larrimore found Woods in bed, a bloody "mess", with his head "beaten in with a brick." Larrimore, "panicked"; he could not tell whether Woods was dead or alive. He immediately called the police and, upon their arrival, stated that Woods had a head wound and might be dead. The police officers immediately entered the premises. They found Woods dead, with fragments of brick "five to six inches from his left ear"; and on the headboard of the bed they found half a brick bearing apparent blood stains. The police took photographs in the room, had the body removed, and took into custody the brick pieces, the bed clothing, Woods' clothing, and a wire cord. All items taken were open to view in the room in which the body was found. The police had no search warrant when they entered the premises.

The contention is now made that, absent a warrant, the articles were taken in violation of . . . the defendant's constitutional guaranties against unreasonable search and seizure; that the admission in evidence of such articles requires reversal of the conviction.

The basic question is whether the police were in the Woods apartment lawfully. That this question must be answered in the affirmative is obvious.

The general rules governing searches and seizures are subject to the exception of emergency situations, sometimes called the "exigency rule." The reasonableness of an entry by the police upon private property is measured by the circumstances then existing. The right of police to enter and investigate in an emergency, without an accompanying intent either to seize or arrest, is inherent in the very nature of their duties as peace officers, and derives from the common law. United States v. Barone (C.A.2) 330 F.2d 543 (1964). The preservation of human life is paramount to the right of privacy protected by

search and seizure laws and constitutional guaranties; it is an overriding justification for what otherwise may be an illegal entry. It
follows that a search warrant is not required to legalize an entry by
police for the purpose of bringing emergency aid to an injured person. Frequently, the report of a death proves inaccurate and a spark
of life remains, sufficient to respond to emergency police aid. As a
general rule, we think, an emergency may be said to exist, within the
meaning of the "exigency" rule, whenever the police have credible information that an unnatural death has, or may have, occurred. And
the criterion is the reasonableness of the belief of the police as to the
existence of an emergency, not the existence of an emergency in fact.
Wayne v. United States, 115 U.S.App.D.C. 234, 318 F.2d 205 (1963);
Davis v. State, 236 Md. 389, 204 A.2d 76 (1964); compare Miller v.
United States, 357 U.S. 301, 78 S.Ct. 1190, 1200 (1958).

Applying these tenets to the instant case, we have no doubt that
the entry of the police was reasonable under the circumstances. The
officers were informed by Larrimore that Woods was dead or dying
from a head wound. Clearly, the police had good reason to believe
that a life was in balance and that emergency aid might be needed.
Under the circumstances, it was the duty of the police to act forthwith
upon the report of the emergency—not to speculate upon the accuracy of the report or upon legal technicalities regarding search warrants. It follows that the entry by the police was reasonable and
lawful.

After the entry, there was no further search by the officers. All
articles taken were in open view in the room in which the body was
found. The seizure of evidence in open view upon a lawful entry violates no right of privacy. Wayne v. United States, supra. That
which is in open view is not the product of a search. United States
v. Barone, supra; Ker v. State of California, 374 U.S. 23, 36–37, 83
S.Ct. 1623, 1635 (1963).

Accordingly, we conclude that there was no violation of statute
or constitutional guaranty as to the evidence here in question.
. . .

NOTES

1. *Patrick* exemplifies Fourth Amendment intrusions which are justified on a "civil" emergency theory, that is, by the need to preserve life,
health, or property from imminent danger. The reasonableness of such
intrusions depends upon a weighing of various factors, including (1) the basis for believing that an emergency exists; (2) the gravity of the situation; (3) the extent of the intrusion; (4) the availability of less intrusive
alternatives; and (5) the chances that the intrusion will prove successful.
See People v. Mitchell, 39 N.Y.2d 173, 383 N.Y.S.2d 246, 347 N.E.2d 607
(1976). As *Mitchell* indicates, close scrutiny is justified where authorities
appeared motivated to secure criminal evidence, and where the civil emergency theory appears as a prosecutor's afterthought. On the other hand, as
Judge Burger noted in Wayne v. United States, 318 F.2d 205 (D.C.Cir.
1963), courts are reluctant to hold officers to a fine standard of probabilities if such officers were facing a now-or-never situation in which they had
to make a quick assessment of the facts.

2.   Civil emergency theories have been mentioned in several Supreme Court opinions.   In Cady v. Dombrowski, 413 U.S. 433, 93 S.Ct. 2523 (1977), the Court upheld the warrantless search of the trunk of a car owned by an out-of-state police officer who had been arrested while intoxicated.   One theory used to justify the search was that the trunk might have contained the officer's service revolver, vandals might have broken into the locked trunk, obtained the weapon, and endangered the community.   In the small town where Dombrowski had been arrested, alternative means of securing the vehicle were impractical.

In Michigan v. Tyler, 436 U.S. 499, 98 S.Ct. 1942 (1978), the Court, in dictum, stated that even after a fire is extinguished, officials may remain or *promptly* reenter to determine the fire's origin so as to prevent its recurrence.   Dictum in Camara v. Municipal Court, 387 U.S. 523, 87 S.Ct. 1727 (1967) (Section M), spoke of emergency health situations (rather than routine inspections) which would justify a warrantless entry.   The Court cited other examples of bona fide emergency action, such as the warrantless seizure and destruction of diseased cattle.

3.   The need to protect persons from being victimized by imminent criminal violence also justifies emergency intrusions.   The typical case involves entry after the officer hears screams.   United States v. Barone, 330 F.2d 543 (2d Cir. 1964); State v. Hills, 283 So.2d 220 (La.1973).   People v. Sirhan, 7 Cal.3d 710, 102 Cal.Rptr. 385, 497 P.2d 1121 (1972), stretched the "thwarting crime" theory to its outer limits.   In *Sirhan* the court upheld an entry into an offender's home and an exploratory search because a police officer theorized that the shooting of Senator Robert Kennedy might have been the first in a conspiracy to kill several national figures.   Prompt action to learn the details was deemed proper to save other intended victims.

4.   "Hot pursuit" entry into a home in search of a fleeing felon is another example of a warrantless emergency intrusion.   One such entry was upheld in Warden v. Hayden, 387 U.S. 294, 87 S.Ct. 1642 (1967), where the Court permitted inspection of all areas of the house where the fleeing felon could have been hiding or where he might have stashed a weapon to aid his escape.   Particularly where the home is the suspect's—and not that of some innocent third person—warrantless entries into a home for arrest purposes are not always limited to true "hot pursuit" situations.   See Section E–4, supra.   Thus Warden v. Hayden, although thought of as the prime example of emergency doctrine, is more important for general theory than for its "hot pursuit" holding.

5.   Several United States Supreme Court cases suggest that under some circumstances even a home might be entered without a warrant to prevent the imminent destruction of evidence of a crime.   The Court, however, has not spelled out the limits of such a doctrine.   Lower courts, however, occasionally have upheld such entries, where the threat of destruction by natural causes, by a suspect, or by a third party was very substantial and where the officers did not deliberately create the emergency which made the immediate entry necessary to prevent the destruction.   Representative cases include People v. Clark, 37 Colo.App. 188, 547 P.2d 267 (1976); United States v. Blake, 484 F.2d 50 (8th Cir. 1973); United States v. Rubin, 474 F.2d 262 (3rd Cir. 1973).   For a good summary of the Supreme Court dicta and a catalogue of lower court decisions, see Warrantless Residential Searches to Prevent the Destruction of Evidence: A Need for Strict Standards, 70 J.C.L. & Crim. 255 (1979).

Assuming that emergency entries are sometimes permissible to prevent the destruction of evidence, must the police, if they are able, "freeze" the scene after making the emergency entry and then apply for a warrant? See generally People v. Freeny, 37 Cal.App.3d 20, 112 Cal.Rptr. 33 (1974); United States v. Hand, 516 F.2d 472 (5th Cir. 1975).

6. In the years preceding Mincey v. Arizona, 437 U.S. 385, 98 S.Ct. 2408 (1978), a number of lower courts began to recognize a "homicide scene" search exception to the warrant requirement, allowing warrantless inspections of the scene of a homicide even after the victim and the suspect had been removed from the suspect's home. Decisions of this type from several jurisdictions were discussed in Haddad, Arrest, Search, and Seizure, Six Unexamined Issues in Illinois Law, 26 De Paul L.Rev. 492, 505–510 (1977). In *Mincey* the Court held that there was no such exception. To justify a warrantless search of a homicide scene, law enforcement officers must show an actual "evidence emergency." Alternatively, they must obtain consent or confine their activities within the limits of one of the other recognized exceptions (e. g., search incident to arrest or plain view seizure). Concerning difficulties of obtaining a warrant to search a homicide scene because of the specificity requirement, see Section C–3, supra.

7. Warrantless emergency intrusions against the person have been upheld in Schmerber v. California, 384 U.S. 757, 86 S.Ct. 1826 (1966), where officers took a blood sample for use in a blood-alcohol test and in Cupp v. Murphy, 412 U.S. 291, 93 S.Ct. 2000 (1973), where the police took a fingernail scraping from a homicide suspect. *Cupp* is probably more significant to emergency theory than is *Schmerber* because (1) in *Cupp*, unlike *Schmerber*, the doctrine of search incident to arrest could not be utilized because the suspect was not arrested; and (2) in *Cupp*, unlike *Schmerber*, it is not clear that there was full probable cause to believe that the search would yield evidence. On the other hand, in upholding the procedure in *Cupp*, the Court emphasized that the intensity of the intrusion was not as great as in *Schmerber*.

J. SEARCHES OF OPEN FIELDS AND OTHER LAND EXPOSED TO PUBLIC VIEW

In a single brief paragraph, relying on common law precedent, Justice Holmes in Hester v. United States, 265 U.S. 57, 44 S.Ct. 445 (1924), recognized an "open-fields" doctrine. According to this doctrine, government agents who trespass against open fields commit no violation against the Fourth Amendment. The area outside of the curtilage (that is, the area beyond the courtyard or equivalent space which surrounds the dwelling house) is not an area protected by the Fourth Amendment. Thus neither a warrant nor probable cause is required. Although the Supreme Court did not consider another open fields case during the half-century after *Hester*, some lower courts developed the doctrine to the point that even buildings not within the curtilage of a dwelling were unprotected by the Fourth Amendment. See LaFave, Search and Seizure: The Course of True Law . . . Has Not . . . Run Smooth, 1966 U.Ill.L.F. 255, 334, 338–340. Certainly even fenced areas posted with "No Trespass" signs were considered as open fields under this doctrine.

With Katz v. United States, 389 U.S. 347, 88 S.Ct. 507 (1967), the rejection of the notion of "protected areas," and recognition of the concept that the Fourth Amendment protects "people not places," some commentators concluded that the open-fields doctrine would not survive. However, in Air Pollution Variance Control Bd. v. Western Alfalfa Corp., 416 U.S. 861, 94 S.Ct. 2114 (1974), the Court, through Justice Douglas, invoked the *Hester* open-fields precedent and made no reference to *Katz*. In *Western Alfalfa* the Court found that the Fourth Amendment had not been violated by a trespassory entry onto land by inspectors who took a smoke reading.

Lower courts have divided over the continuing vitality of *Hester*. In some cases intensive warrantless searches (e. g., digging for a buried body) have been upheld under the open-fields doctrine. See generally United States ex rel. Saiken v. Bensinger, 489 F.2d 865 (7th Cir. 1973), aff'd, after remand, 546 F.2d 1292 (1976); Conrad v. State, 63 Wis.2d 616, 218 N.W.2d 252 (1974); Norman v. State, 362 So.2d 444 (Fla.App.1978). Other cases read *Katz* to sharply modify the open-fields doctrine, suggesting that a person could have a protected reasonable expectation of privacy even on land outside the curtilage. State v. Stanton, 7 Or.App. 286, 490 P.2d 1274 (1971); State v. Wert, 550 S.W.2d 1 (Tenn.Cr.App.1977); State v. Byers, 359 So.2d 84 (La. 1978). An intermediate view is that although *Katz* must be considered, an individual is less likely to have a reasonable expectation of privacy in open fields than in other places. United States v. Williams, 581 F.2d 451 (5th Cir. 1978).

Katz can be read as expanding the open-fields doctrine so as to include certain areas within the curtilage of a home. For instance, suppose that a homeowner leaves criminal evidence within a fenced yard immediately adjacent to his home. Suppose further that the evidence is visible from a public way. A police officer makes a trespassory entry to reach the evidence. (Recall that plain view by itself does *not* justify the intrusion necessary to reach the evidence—Section H.) Some courts would hold that the trespassory entry did not violate the Fourth Amendment because the homeowner had no reasonable expectation of privacy as to what he exposed to public view, even though the property was on his land. City of Decatur v. Kushmer, 43 Ill.2d 334, 253 N.E.2d 425 (1969); People v. George, 49 Ill.2d 372, 274 N.E.2d 26 (1971); People v. Stein, 51 Ill.App.3d 421, 9 Ill. Dec. 372, 366 N.E.2d 629 (Ill.App.1977). Other courts would disagree, asserting that *Katz* does not justify a warrantless entry onto land to seize evidence any more than it permits entry into a home to seize evidence which is visible from a public way. See State v. O'Herron, 153 N.J.Super. 570, 380 A.2d 728 (1977).

K. ABANDONED PROPERTY

When a person has abandoned his property, the police can search or seize that property without violating his Fourth Amendment rights. Neither a warrant nor probable cause is required. In Hester v. United States, 265 U.S. 57, 44 S.Ct. 445 (1924), the Supreme Court referred to certain jugs of moonshine liquor as "abandoned," but it provided no legal analysis of the doctrine. It did suggest that if in order to reach goods which X had abandoned, the police committed a Fourth Amendment intrusion in violation of X's rights, X could complain that the seizure of the goods violated his Fourth Amendment rights. In Abel v. United States, 362 U.S. 217, 80 S.Ct. 683 (1960), a Soviet agent, arrested by immigration officials in his hotel room, checked out of the room and departed with the officials, leaving behind incriminating evidence in the room's wastebasket. The Court stated that nothing was wrong with the "Government's appropriation of such abandoned property." As far as the Court was concerned, the Fourth Amendment was not implicated because the items were "bona vacantia" (goods without a claimant). Finally in Rios v. United States, 364 U.S. 253, 80 S.Ct. 1431 (1960), the Court stated that property which a taxi passenger sought to conceal on the cab floor when police approached could not be considered abandoned. Again, there was no discussion of the elements of abandonment.

Lower courts generally agree that property can be considered abandoned for Fourth Amendment purposes even though a person retains an interest which the law of property might recognize. The key seems to be an intent to abandon, that is, to make no return to claim the property. Thus a lessee can "abandon" an apartment by fleeing the jurisdiction before his lease expires. Bloodworth v. State, 233 Ga. 589, 212 S.E.2d 774 (1975). So, also, a person who ditches his car in flight from a robbery which he has committed, under some circumstances, may have abandoned the car although he retains legal title. Sometimes the requisite intent to abandon may be absent even though a person has been separated from his property. See People v. Dorney, 17 Ill.App.3d 785, 308 N.E.2d 646 (1976) (mobile home gutted by fire causing occupants to find quarters elsewhere). For another decision concerning the meaning of "abandonment", see United States v. Robinson, 430 F.2d 1141 (6th Cir. 1970).

After Katz v. United States (see Section N), some defendants argued that even if they had manifested an intent to lay no further claims to certain goods, a search and seizure of such goods could, under some circumstances, constitute an intrusion against a reasonable expectation of privacy. Thus the Fourth Amendment is implicated and a warrantless search or seizure without probable cause violates the Fourth Amendment. The argument was made most frequently in "trash" cases, largely because of a favorable decision in 1971 from the California Supreme Court in People v. Krivda, 5 Cal.3d 357, 96 Cal.Rptr. 62, 486 P.2d 1262 (1971), vacated and remanded 409 U.S. 33, 93 S.Ct. 32 (1972), affirmed 8 Cal.3d 623, 105 Cal.Rptr. 521, 504 P.2d 457 (1973). Excerpts from the first *Krivda* opinion by the California Supreme Court follow:

> "Burke, J.
>
> "The question presented by this appeal is whether a householder who places contraband in trash barrels and subsequently places the barrels adjacent to the street for pickup

by the rubbish collector may be deemed to have abandoned the trash at that location and to have forsaken any reasonable expectation of privacy with respect thereto.

"The People urge that the placement of the barrels near the sidewalk for collection constituted an abandonment of their contents. Indeed, had defendants simply cast their trash onto the sidewalk for anyone to pick over and cart away, we would have no difficulty finding that defendants had thereby forsaken any reasonable expectation of privacy with respect thereto.

"The placement of one's trash barrels onto the sidewalk for collection is not, however, necessarily an abandonment of one's trash to the police or general public. To the contrary, many municipalities have enacted ordinances which restrict the right to collect and haul away trash to licensed collectors whose activities are carefully regulated. (See, e. g., Los Angeles County Ord. No. 5860, ch. IX, §§ 1611–1622, 1681–1691.) Moreover, these ordinances commonly prohibit unauthorized persons from tampering with trash containers. The provisions of these ordinances would appear to refute the view that the contents of one's trash barrels become public property when placed on the sidewalk for collection.

"Aside from municipal ordinances, there may exist an additional element of expected privacy whenever one consigns his property to the trash can, to be dumped, destroyed and forgotten. As stated in *Edwards*, 'The marijuana itself was not visible without "rummaging" in the receptacle. So far as appears defendants alone resided at the house. In the light of the combined facts and circumstances it appears that defendants exhibited an expectation of privacy, and we believe that expectation was reasonable under the circumstances of the case. We can readily ascribe many reasons why residents would not want their castaway clothing, letters, medicine bottles or other telltale refuse and trash to be examined by neighbors, or others, *at least not until the trash had lost its identity and meaning by becoming part of a large conglomeration of trash elsewhere.* Half truths leading to rumor and gossip may readily flow from an attempt to "read" the contents of another's trash.' (People v. Edwards, 71 Cal.2d 1096, 1104, 458 P.2d 713, 718.)

"Similarly, in the instant case the contraband was concealed in paper sacks within the barrels, and was not visible without emptying or searching through the barrels' contents. The fact that the officers did not examine the contents until the trash had been placed into the well of the refuse truck does not distinguish *Edwards*, for at no time did defendants' trash lose its 'identity' by being mixed and combined with the 'conglomeration' of trash previously placed in the truck. Under such circumstances, we hold

that defendants had a reasonable expectation that their
trash would not be rummaged through and picked over by
police officers acting without a search warrant.   .   .   .

"We should hesitate to encourage a practice whereby
our citizens' trash cans could be made the subject of police
inspection without the protection of applying for and securing a search warrant.

"WRIGHT, C. J. (dissenting) :

"I do not agree that the area protected by the Fourth
Amendment proscription of unreasonable searches and seizures encompasses parkways immediately adjacent to public
thoroughfares or pedestrian walkways or that the police action enlisting the assistance of the authorized trash collectors in separately picking up trash placed at the curb for
pickup transmuted the collection into an unreasonable seizure. Moreover, in my view, a householder has neither a
reasonable expectation of privacy as to his curbside trash,
nor a right to expect that his trash will be commingled with
that of others before it is subject to examination, governmental or otherwise. Whatever his hope may be as to the
ultimate disposition of his trash, it does not, in my view,
rise to a 'reasonable expectation of privacy'."

The *Krivda* case was the subject of a fair amount of ridicule, and
it was often cited by opponents of the exclusionary rule as an example
of the extremes to which courts had gone to free the guilty. The California Attorney General was unsuccessful in his efforts to have the
United States Supreme Court reconsider the exclusionary rule in the
Krivda context. Most courts, however, have rejected the *Krivda* result, either refusing to inject *Katz* notions into abandonment cases, or
holding that no reasonable expectation of privacy exists in garbage
left for the trash collector. See e. g., United States v. Alden, 576 F.2d
772 (8th Cir. 1978); United States v. Shelby, 573 F.2d 971 (7th Cir.
1978). In California the *Krivda* case has been "distinguished" when
the government agent testified that he found the item in question *on
top* of the pile without rummaging through the trash. People v. Sirhan, 7 Cal.3d 710, 102 Cal.Rptr. 385, 497 P.2d 1121 (1972).

Many abandoned property cases are also plain view cases. The
difference is that property which is abandoned can be seized even
without seizure probable cause. Property spotted in plain view, if it
has not been abandoned, can be seized only if its incriminating nature
is immediately apparent, that is, only if there is probable cause to believe that it is contraband or evidence of a crime. One decision
which makes this distinction is People v. Hermesch, 49 A.D.2d 587,
370 N.Y.S.2d 152 (1975).

A great majority of courts hold that when a suspect drops property in response to unlawful police activity (an illegal arrest, an improper *Terry* stop, etc.), the property cannot be viewed as abandoned.
Instead, it must be considered to be the fruit of the improper police

conduct and inadmissible in a criminal prosecution. Commonwealth v. Barnett, 484 Pa. 211, 398 A.2d 1019 (1979) (property dropped after unlawful stop); People v. Severson, — Colo.App. —, 561 P.2d 373 (1977) (property dropped after illegal arrest). As the conflicting views in the following excerpts from State v. Smithers, 256 Ind. 512, 269 N.E.2d 874 (1971), indicate, there is not universal agreement concerning this limitation upon abandonment doctrine:

"DE BRULER, J.

"The State appeals on a reserved question of law alleging that the trial court erred in suppressing the evidence.

"Sergeant Mastin testified that he was called by Officers McKinney and Connors to the scene of a stopped car at around 12:45 a. m. on October 17th. Upon arrival at the scene Mastin was given the following information by the two officers: The officers thought there were juveniles in the car out after 11:00 p. m. curfew and they stopped the car to check the occupants to see if they were juveniles. When the car was stopped Connors observed the defendant, riding in the right front seat, put his arm out the car door and drop a brown manila envelope. Connors picked it up and asked defendant about it but he denied having possession of it. Mastin testified that after his arrival at the scene he looked in the envelope and found a substance that could have been marijuana. Mastin talked to the defendant who denied ever having the envelope. Mastin then permitted the car with defendant in it to proceed on its way.

"Appellant contends that the police legally obtained the envelope containing marijuana because the defendant had abandoned it. It is true that the police may legally seize abandoned property. Hardin v. State, 257 N.E.2d 671 (Ind.1970). However, where police action triggers the abandonment, that action must be lawful or the evidence will be considered obtained in an illegal search and seizure within the meaning of the Fourth Amendment. Rios v. United States, 364 U.S. 253, 80 S.Ct. 1431 (1960). For purposes of the Fourth Amendment, there is no real abandonment if there is no lawful arrest or detention in the first instance because the 'primary illegality would taint the abandonment and, as such, the abandonment could not justify the admission of the evidence.' People v. Baldwin, 25 N.Y.2d 66, 250 N.E.2d 62 (1969). Therefore, the crucial issue is whether the police action in stopping the car, which precipitated the abandonment of the envelope, was lawful. If the police were justified in stopping the car then there was a 'true abandonment' of the envelope by defendant, the evidence contained in the envelope was admissible in evidence and the trial court erred in suppressing it.

[The Court then held that under Indiana law, the arrests were illegal and the evidence was properly suppressed].

"ARTERBURN, C. J. (dissenting).

"I disagree with the majority opinion for the reason that no search is involved in this case, and there is nothing in the Constitution which prevents an officer or anyone else from picking up something from the street that has been abandoned or thrown away by a defendant or any third party. I go further and state that this includes articles thrown away in the act of excitement or fear, whatever the cause may be. In Von Hauger v. State, 266 N.E.2d 197 (Ind. 1971), the defendant dropped a package containing hypodermic needles and other apparatus used in drug injections and walked away when he saw the law enforcement officers. We held that the evidence so obtained was admissible.

"The defendant in this case was not searched nor seized. He was merely asked for his identification and driver's license. I think a police officer, and particularly a traffic officer, has not only the right, but at times the duty, to ask for the driver's license. In particular, I am thinking about road blocks that are necessary to be set up for the apprehension of fleeing criminals. Anything abandoned by fleeing persons is entirely open to seizure by anyone including police officers. The majority opinion is an unnecessary restriction upon law enforcement activities where a guilty conscience causes the party to flee or abandon articles which are incriminating. Again, I say there is no constitutional prohibition against the entry of the evidence which the appellant threw away or discarded in his case. It is an uncalled for stretching of the prohibition against unreasonable searches."

For a dispute similar to the one in the foregoing case, see People v. Boodle, 47 N.Y.2d 398, 418 N.Y.S.2d 352, 391 N.E.2d 1329 (1979), where the majority held that under the circumstances the "drop" could not be considered the product of the police illegality.

There is no disagreement among the courts as to whether even without probable cause, the police can lawfully seize property which was abandoned as an officer approached, as long as the police officer had done nothing unlawful. There is skepticism, however, about the frequency with which police officers claim that suspects dropped property. Some skeptics assert that officers who have found evidence during a course of a search frequently testify that the suspect dropped the property. By perjuriously testifying that no search took place, the officers can avoid the necessity of justifying the search. See People v. Quinones, 61 A.D.2d 765, 402 N.Y.S.2d 196 (1978).

L. MOTOR VEHICLE SEARCHES

Various theories are used to justify warrantless searches of motor vehicles. One of these, commonly known as the "automobile exception" or the "*Carroll* doctrine," (after Carroll v. United States, 267 U.S. 132, 45 S.Ct. 280 (1925), is especially tailored for motor vehicles. The authors also refer to this doctrine as "moving vehicle" exception to the warrant requirement because that term adequately describes the limitation placed upon the *Carroll* doctrine by the *Coolidge* decision, (Section H, supra). Other theories of general applicability may come into play in automobile search and seizure cases (*e. g.*, abandonment or search incident to arrest). We begin with treatment of the *Carroll* doctrine.

CHAMBERS v. MARONEY

Supreme Court of the United States, 1970.
399 U.S. 42, 90 S.Ct. 1975.

MR. JUSTICE WHITE delivered the opinion of the Court.

The principal question in this case concerns the admissibility of evidence seized from an automobile, in which petitioner was riding at the time of his arrest, after the automobile was taken to a police station and was there thoroughly searched without a warrant. The Court of Appeals for the Third Circuit found no violation of petitioner's Fourth Amendment rights. We affirm.

I.

During the night of May 20, 1963, a Gulf service station in North Braddock, Pennsylvania, was robbed by two men each of whom carried and displayed a gun. The robbers took the currency from the cash register; the service station attendant, one Stephen Kovacich, was directed to place the coins in his right hand glove, which was then taken by the robbers. Two teen-agers, who had earlier noticed a blue compact station wagon circling the block in the vicinity of the Gulf station, then saw the station wagon speed away from a parking lot close to the Gulf station; about the same time, they learned that the Gulf station had been robbed. They reported to police, who arrived immediately, that four men were in the station wagon and one was wearing a green sweater. Kovacich told the police that one of the men who robbed him was wearing a green sweater and the other wearing a trench coat. A description of the car and the two robbers was broadcast over the police radio. Within an hour, a light blue compact station wagon answering the description and carrying four men was stopped by the police about two miles from the Gulf station. Petitioner was one of the men in the station wagon. He was wearing a green sweater and there was a trench coat in the car. The occupants were arrested and the car was driven to the police station. In the course of a thorough search of the car at the station, the police found concealed in a compartment under the dashboard two .38 caliber revolvers (one loaded with dumdum bullets), a right hand glove containing small change, and certain cards bearing the name of Raymond Havicon, the attendant at a Boron service station in McKeesport, Pennsylvania, who had been robbed at gun point on May 13, 1963. In the course of a warrant-authorized search of petitioner's home the day after petitioner's arrest, police found and seized certain .38 caliber ammunition, including some dumdum bullets similar to those found in one of the guns taken from the station wagon.

Petitioner was indicted for both robberies. His first trial ended in a mistrial but he was convicted of both robberies at the second trial. Both Kovacich and Havicon identified petitioner as one of the robbers. The materials taken from the station wagon were introduced into evidence, Kovacich identifying his glove and Havicon the cards taken in the May 13 robbery. The bullets seized at petitioner's house were also introduced over objections of petitioner's counsel. Petitioner was sentenced to a term of four to eight years' imprisonment for the May 13 robbery and to a term of two to seven years' imprisonment for the May 20 robbery, the sentences to run consecutively. Petitioner did not take a direct appeal from these convictions. In 1965, petitioner sought a writ of habeas corpus in the state court, which denied the writ after a brief evidentiary hearing; the denial of the writ was affirmed on appeal in the Pennsylvania appellate courts. Habeas corpus proceedings were then commenced in the United States District Court for the Western District of Pennsylvania. An order to show cause was issued. Based on the State's response and the state court record, the petition for habeas corpus was denied without a hearing. The Court of Appeals for the Third Circuit affirmed, . . . and we granted certiorari.

II.

We pass quickly the claim that the search of the automobile was the fruit of an unlawful arrest. Both the courts below thought the arresting officers had probable cause to make the arrest. We agree. Having talked to the teen-age observers and to the victim Kovacich, the police had ample cause to stop a light blue compact station wagon carrying four men and to arrest the occupants, one of whom was wearing a green sweater and one of whom had a trench coat with him in the car.[1]

Even so, the search which produced the incriminating evidence was made at the police station some time after the arrest and cannot be justified as a search incident to an arrest: "Once an accused is under arrest and in custody, then a search made at another place, without a warrant, is simply not incident to the arrest." Preston v. United States, 376 U.S. 364, 367, 84 S.Ct. 881, 883 (1964). Dyke v. Tay-

---

1. In any event, as we point out below, the validity of an arrest is not necessarily determinative of the right to search a car if there is probable cause to make the search. Here, as will be true in many cases, the circumstances justifying the arrest are also those furnishing probable cause for the search.

lor Implement Mfg. Co., 391 U.S. 216, 88 S.Ct. 1472 (1968), is to the same effect; the reasons which have been thought sufficient to justify warrantless searches carried out in connection with an arrest no longer obtain when the accused is safely in custody at the station house.

There are, however, alternative grounds arguably justifying the search of the car in this case. In *Preston,* supra, the arrest was for vagrancy; it was apparent that the officers had no cause to believe that evidence of crime was concealed in the auto. In *Dyke,* supra, the Court expressly rejected the suggestion that there was probable cause to search the car. Here the situation is different, for the police had probable cause to believe that the robbers, carrying guns and the fruits of the crime, had fled the scene in a light blue compact station wagon which would be carrying four men, one wearing a green sweater and another wearing a trench coat. As the state courts correctly held, there was probable cause to arrest the occupants of the station wagon that the officers stopped; just as obviously was there probable cause to search the car for guns and stolen money.

In terms of the circumstances justifying a warrantless search, the Court has long distinguished between an automobile and a home or office. In Carroll v. United States, 267 U.S. 132, 45 S.Ct. 280 (1925), the issue was the admissibility in evidence of contraband liquor seized in a warrantless search of a car on the highway. After surveying the law from the time of the adoption of the Fourth Amendment onward, the Court held that automobiles and other conveyances may be searched without a warrant in circumstances which would not justify the search without a warrant of a house or an office, provided that there is probable cause to believe that the car contains articles that the officers are entitled to seize. The Court expressed its holding as follows:

> "We have made a somewhat extended reference to these statutes to show that the guaranty of freedom from unreasonable searches and seizures by the Fourth Amendment has been construed, practically since the beginning of the government, as recognizing a necessary difference between a search of a store, dwelling house, or other structure in respect of which a proper official warrant readily may be obtained and a search of a ship, motor boat, wagon, or automobile for contraband goods, where it is not practicable to secure a warrant, because the vehicle can be quickly moved out of the locality or jurisdiction in which the warrant must be sought.

> "Having thus established that contraband goods concealed and illegally transported in an automobile or other vehicle may be searched for without a warrant, we come now to consider under what circumstances such search may be made. . . . [T]hose lawfully within the country, entitled to use the public highways, have a right to free passage without interruption or search unless there is known to

a competent official, authorized to search, probable cause for believing that their vehicles are carrying contraband or illegal merchandise.

* * *

"The measure of legality of such a seizure is, therefore, that the seizing officer shall have reasonable or probable cause for believing that the automobile which he stops and seizes has contraband liquor therein which is being illegally transported." 267 U.S., at 153–154, 155–156, 45 S.Ct. at 285–286.

The Court also noted that the search of an auto on probable cause proceeds on a theory wholly different from that justifying the search incident to an arrest:

"The right to search and the validity of the seizure are not dependent on the right to arrest. They are dependent on the reasonable cause the seizing officer has for belief that the contents of the automobile offend against the law." 267 U.S., at 158–159, 45 S.Ct. at 287.

Finding that there was probable cause for the search and seizure at issue before it, the Court affirmed the convictions.

Carroll was followed and applied in Husty v. United States, 282 U.S. 694, 51 S.Ct. 240 (1931), and Scher v. United States, 305 U.S. 251, 59 S.Ct. 174 (1938). It was reaffirmed and followed in Brinegar v. United States, 338 U.S. 160, 69 S.Ct. 1302 (1949). In 1964, the opinion in *Preston*, supra, cited both *Brinegar* and *Carroll* with approval. In Cooper v. California, 386 U.S. 58, 87 S.Ct. 788 (1967),[2] the Court read *Preston* as dealing primarily with a search incident to arrest and cited that case for the proposition that the mobility of a car may make the search of a car without a warrant reasonable "although the result might be the opposite in a search of a home, a store, or other fixed piece of property." The Court's opinion in *Dyke*, recognized that "[a]utomobiles, because of their mobility, may be searched without a warrant upon facts not justifying a warrantless search of a residence or office," citing *Brinegar* and *Carroll*, supra. However, because there was insufficient reason to search the car involved in the *Dyke* case, the Court did not reach the question of whether those cases "extend to a warrantless search, based upon probable cause, of an automobile which, having been stopped original-

---

2. *Cooper* involved the warrantless search of a car held for forfeiture under state law. Evidence seized from the car in that search was held admissible. In the case before us no claim is made that state law authorized that the station wagon be held as evidence or as an instrumentality of the crime; nor was the station wagon an abandoned or stolen vehicle. The question here is whether probable cause justifies a warrantless search in the circumstances presented.

ly on a highway, is parked outside a courthouse." 391 U.S., at 222, 88 S.Ct. at 1476.[3]

Neither *Carroll*, supra, nor other cases in this Court require or suggest that in every conceivable circumstance the search of an auto even with probable cause may be made without the extra protection for privacy which a warrant affords. But the circumstances which furnish probable cause to search a particular auto for particular articles are most often unforeseeable; moreover, the opportunity to search is fleeting since a car is readily movable. Where this is true, as in *Carroll* and the case before us now, if an effective search is to be made at any time, either the search must be made immediately without a warrant or the car itself must be seized and held without a warrant for whatever period is necessary to obtain a warrant for the search.[4]

In enforcing the Fourth Amendment's prohibition against unreasonable searches and seizures, the Court has insisted upon probable cause as a minimum requirement for a reasonable search permitted by the Constitution. As a general rule, it has also required the judgment of a magistrate on the probable cause issue and the issuance of a warrant before a search is made. Only in exigent circumstances will the judgment of the police as to probable cause serve as a sufficient authorization for a search. *Carroll*, supra, holds a search warrant unnecessary where there is probable cause to search an automobile stopped on the highway; the car is movable, the occupants are alerted, and the car's contents may never be found again if a warrant must be obtained. Hence, an immediate search is constitutionally permissible.

Arguably, because of the preference for a magistrate's judgment, only the immobilization of the car should be permitted until a search warrant is obtained; arguably, only the "lesser" intrusion is permissible until the magistrate authorizes the "greater." But which is the "greater" and which the "lesser" intrusion is itself a debatable question and the answer may depend on a variety of circumstances. For constitutional purposes, we see no difference between on the one hand seizing and holding a car before presenting the probable cause issue to a magistrate and on the other hand carrying out an immediate

3. Nothing said last term in Chimel v. California, 395 U.S. 752, 89 S.Ct. 2034 (1969), purported to modify or affect the rationale of *Carroll*. As the Court noted:

"Our holding today is of course entirely consistent with the recognized principle that, assuming the existence of probable cause, automobiles and other vehicles may be searched without warrants 'where it is not practicable to secure a warrant, because the vehicle can be quickly moved out of the locality or jurisdiction in which the warrant must be sought.' Carroll v. United States, 267 U.S. 132, 153, 45 S.Ct. 280, 285, 69 L.Ed. 543; see Brinegar v. United States, 338 U.S. 160, 69 S.Ct. 1302, 93 L.Ed. 1879." 395 U.S., at 764 n. 9, 89 S.Ct. at 2040.

4. Following the car until a warrant can be obtained seems an impractical alternative since, among other things, the car may be taken out of the jurisdiction. Tracing the car and searching it hours or days later would of course permit instruments or fruits of crime to be removed from the car before the search.

search without a warrant. Given probable cause to search, either course is reasonable under the Fourth Amendment.

On the facts before us, the blue station wagon could have been searched on the spot when it was stopped since there was probable cause to search and it was a fleeting target for a search. The probable cause factor still obtained at the station house and so did the mobility of the car unless the Fourth Amendment permits a warrantless seizure of the car and the denial of its use to anyone until a warrant is secured. In that event there is little to choose in terms of practical consequences between an immediate search without a warrant and the car's immobilization until a warrant is obtained.[5] The same consequences may not follow where there is unforeseeable cause to search a house. But as *Carroll*, supra, held, for the purposes of the Fourth Amendment there is a constitutional difference between houses and cars. . . .

Affirmed.

MR. JUSTICE BLACKMUN took no part in the consideration or decision of this case.

(The concurring opinion of MR. JUSTICE STEWART is omitted.)

[MR. JUSTICE HARLAN concurred in part and dissented in part. Opinion omitted.]

[Ed. Note: For another important case regarding automobile searches, Coolidge v. New Hampshire, supra Section H.]

NOTES

1. *Prerequisites for a Carroll Search.* The *Carroll* doctrine applies only to motor vehicles. Sometimes this raises a definitional issue. Is a mobile home more like a home or more like a car for purposes of the *Carroll* doctrine? Does the rationale of *Carroll* apply if a mobile home is stopped in transit? See State v. Million, 120 Ariz. 10, 583 P.2d 897 (1978); People v. Uselding, 39 Ill.App.3d 677, 350 N.E.2d 283 (1976). The doctrine does not apply to other portable chattels. United States v. Chadwick, 433 U.S. 1, 97 S.Ct. 2476 (1977). As *Coolidge* indicates, the *Carroll* doctrine does not apply unless the car is stopped in transit. What about a "getaway" car parked near the scene of a robbery? See People v. Powell, 9 Ill.App.3d 54, 291 N.E.2d 669 (1972). The issue may not be critical because even if the *Carroll* doctrine does not apply, a theory of *particularized* exigent circumstances (see note 5, *infra*) may be available to justify the search.

If a car is unlawfully stopped while in transit the search is unlawful. The *Carroll* doctrine itself may justify the stop, that is the stop can be

---

5. It was not unreasonable in this case to take the car to the station house. All occupants in the car were arrested in a dark parking lot in the middle of the night. A careful search at that point was impractical and perhaps not safe for the officers, and it would serve the owner's convenience and the safety of his car to have the vehicle and the keys together at the station house.

made if there is probable cause to believe that the vehicle contains contraband or criminal evidence. Alternatively, the stop preceding the *Carroll* search sometimes is justified on some other theory (e. g., reasonable suspicion for a *Terry* stop). If following a lawful stop (on whatever theory) probable cause for a search develops, then the search can be made under the *Carroll* doctrine. In every case, probable cause to believe that contraband or criminal evidence is in the vehicle is a prerequisite for a valid *Carroll* search. On the other hand, the validity of the search does not depend upon a probability that somebody in the car has committed an offense. People v. Henry, 48 Ill.App.3d 606, 363 N.E.2d 112 (1977).

2. *No Requirement of an Actual Emergency.* If a car is lawfully stopped while in transit, and if there is probable cause for a search, under *Carroll* a warrant is unnecessary even if there is no actual emergency. This was apparent from *Chambers* and from the majority per curiam opinion in the following case of Texas v. White, 423 U.S. 67, 96 S.Ct. 304 (1975):

> "Respondent was arrested at 1:30 p. m. by Amarillo, Tex., police officers while attempting to pass fraudulent checks at a drive-in window of the First National Bank of Amarillo. Only 10 minutes earlier, the officers had been informed by another bank that a man answering respondent's description and driving an automobile exactly matching that of respondent had tried to negotiate four checks drawn on a non-existent account. Upon arrival at the First National Bank pursuant to a telephone call from that bank the officers obtained from the drive-in teller other checks that respondent had attempted to pass there. The officers directed respondent to park his automobile at the curb. While parking the car, respondent was observed by a bank employee and one of the officers attempting to 'stuff' something between the seats. Respondent was arrested and one officer drove him to the station house while the other drove respondent's car there. At the station house, the officers questioned respondent for 30 to 45 minutes and, pursuant to their normal procedure, requested consent to search the automobile. Respondent refused to consent to the search. The officers then proceeded to search the automobile anyway. During the search, an officer discovered four wrinkled checks that corresponded to those respondent had attempted to pass at the first bank. The trial judge, relying on Chambers v. Maroney (1970), admitted over respondent's objection the four checks seized during the search of respondent's automobile at the station house. The judge expressly found probable cause both for the arrest and for the search of the vehicle, either at the scene or at the station house. Respondent was convicted after a jury trial of knowingly attempting to pass a forged instrument. The Texas Court of Criminal Appeals, in a 3–2 decision, reversed respondent's conviction on the ground that the four wrinkled checks used in evidence were obtained without a warrant in violation of respondent's Fourth Amendment rights. We reverse.

> "In Chambers v. Maroney we held that police officers with probable cause to search an automobile at the scene where it was stopped could constitutionally do so later at the station house without first obtaining a warrant. There, as here, '[t]he probable-cause factor' that developed at the scene 'still obtained at the station house.' The Court of Criminal Appeals erroneously exclud-

ed the evidence seized from the search at the station house in light of the trial judge's finding, undisturbed by the appellate court, that there was probable cause to search respondent's car.

"The petition for certiorari and the motion of respondent to proceed *in forma pauperis* are granted, the judgment of the Court of Criminal Appeals is reversed, and the case is remanded to that court for further proceedings not inconsistent with this opinion.

"It is so ordered.   Reversed and remanded.

MR. JUSTICE MARSHALL, with whom MR. JUSTICE BRENNAN concurs, dissenting.

"Only by misstating the holding of *Chambers v. Maroney* (1970), can the Court make that case appear dispositive of this one.   The Court in its brief *per curiam* opinion today extends *Chambers* to a clearly distinguishable factual setting, without having afforded the opportunity for full briefing and oral argument. I respectfully dissent.

"*Chambers* did not hold, as the Court suggests, that 'police officers with probable cause to search an automobile at the scene where it was stopped could constitutionally do so later at the station house without first obtaining a warrant.'   *Chambers* simply held that to be the rule when it is reasonable to take the car to the station house in the first place.

"In *Chambers* the Court took as its departure point this Court's holding in *Carroll v. United States*, (1925):

'*Carroll* . . . holds a search warrant unnecessary where there is probable cause to search an automobile stopped on the highway; the car is movable, the occupants are alerted, and the car's contents may never be found again if a warrant must be obtained.   Hence an immediate search is constitutionally permissible.'

Carroll, however, did not dispose of *Chambers*, for in *Chambers*, as in this case, the police did not conduct an 'immediate search,' but rather seized the car and took it to the station house before searching it.   The Court in *Chambers* went on to hold that once the car was legitimately at the station house a prompt search could be conducted.   But in recognition of the need to justify the seizure and removal of the car to the station house, the Court added:

'It was not unreasonable in this case to take the car to the station house.   All occupants in the car were arrested in a dark parking lot in the middle of the night.   A careful search at that point was impractical and perhaps not safe for the officers, and it would serve the owner's convenience and the safety of his car to have the vehicle and the keys together at the station house.'

"In this case, the arrest took place at 1:30 in the afternoon, and there is no indication that an immediate search would have been either impractical or unsafe for the arresting officers.   It may be, of course, that respondent preferred to have his car brought to the station house, but if his convenience was the concern of the police they should have consulted with him.   Surely a seizure cannot be justified on the sole ground that a citizen might have consented to it as a matter of convenience.   Since, then, there was no apparent justification for the warrantless removal of respondent's car, it is clear that this is a different case from *Chambers*.

* * *

"In short, the basic premise of *Chambers'* conclusion that seizures pending the seeking of a warrant are not constitutionally preferred to warrantless searches was that temporary seizures are themselves intrusive. That same premise suggests that the seizure and removal of respondent's car in this case were quite apart from the subsequent search, an intrusion of constitutional dimension that must be independently justified. The seizure and removal here were not for the purpose of immobilizing the car until a warrant could be secured, nor were they for the purpose of facilitating a safe and thorough search of the car. In the absence of any other justification, I would hold the seizure of petitioner's car unlawful and exclude the evidence seized in the subsequent search.

"I would have denied the petition for certiorari, but now that the writ has been granted I would affirm the judgment of the Court of Criminal Appeals, or at least set the case for oral argument. In any event, it should be clear to the court below that nothing this Court does today precludes it from reaching the result it did under applicable state law. See Oregon v. Hass (1975)."

The Supreme Court has previously acknowledged that under its application of the *Carroll-Chambers* doctrine warrantless searches were to be upheld even though "the possibilities of the vehicle's being removed or evidence in it destroyed were remote, if not non-existent." Cady v. Dombrowski, 413 U.S. 433, 93 S.Ct. 2523 (1973). Despite *Chambers*, *White*, and *Dombrowski*, however, at least one court has seemingly held that absent an actual emergency, a vehicle stopped in transit cannot be searched without a warrant. See State v. Colvin, 358 So.2d 1250 (La.1978).

3. *The Carroll Search: Where and When?* Under *Chambers* and *White*, the *Carroll* search can take place either at the scene of the stop or at a place to which the car has been transported. What if the search is delayed for several hours? Several days? Is the rationale expressed in *Chambers* inconsistent with such a delay? Compare People v. White, 68 Mich.App. 348, 242 N.W.2d 579 (Mich.App.1976), with People v. Emert, 1 Ill.App.3d 993, 274 N.E.2d 364 (1971).

4. *What and Who Can Be Searched Under the Carroll Doctrine?* If there is probable cause to believe that evidence is in a vehicle which has been stopped in transit, can the entire car be searched under *Carroll*? Many decisions assume so, but recently some courts have considered the car as composed of divisible units. Thus probable cause to believe that there is marijuana in the interior of a vehicle may not suffice to justify a search of the trunk. See State v. Astalos, 160 N.J.Super. 407, 390 A.2d 144 (1978) for a good summary of cases which consider this issue. See also People v. Fraijo, 78 Cal.App.3d 977, 144 Cal.Rptr. 424 (1978).

What if a container, such as a briefcase, is found in a car which has been lawfully stopped under the *Carroll* doctrine. Can it be searched? In Arkansas v. Sanders, 442 U.S. 753, 99 S.Ct. 2586 (1979), the Court considered a situation in which officers had probable cause to believe that a particular suitcase, being conveyed in a vehicle, contained contraband. They did not have probable cause to believe that the car contained contraband or evidence other than that in the suitcase. The Court held that the stop was proper under *Carroll*, but that the warrantless search of the suitcase was improper; the authorities should have impounded the suitcase and applied for a warrant. Is this consistent with the rationale of *Chambers*? The Court in *Sanders* did not say whether a search of a suitcase would be proper if the officers had probable cause to search the vehicle but did not know precisely where in the car the contraband could be located. Nor in *Sanders* did the Court say whether an immediate warrantless search of the suitcase would have been proper under a "search-incident" theory if the suitcase had been within reach of the driver or a passenger at the time of his arrest. (See Section E–5(c) supra, and note 6 infra.)

If there is probable cause to believe that somewhere in a car there is contraband or evidence, is it proper to search each person in the vehicle without a particular reason to believe that the person has the evidence? United States v. Di Re, 332 U.S. 581, 68 S.Ct. 222 (1948), indicated not; but that opinion did not state what would be required. The issue is somewhat analogous to the question of which occupants can be searched when a warrant commands the search of a certain apartment. (See Section D–5.)

5. *Particularized Exigent Circumstances. Coolidge* indicated that under *Carroll* a parked car cannot be searched without a warrant even if there is probable cause to believe that a search will yield evidence. However, sometimes particular exigent circumstances justify such a search. The difference is that if a car is lawfully stopped while in transit, and if there is probable cause, the car can be searched without any particular showing of exigency; whereas if the car is parked, a particular showing of exigency must be made.

Courts have been rather quick to justify warrantless entries into parked cars on an emergency theory, certainly much more quick than in the case of warrantless emergency entries into homes. Courts will say, for example, that a relative of an arrestee might enter the car or that someone might break in and take a weapon lying in plain view in the car. See Haefeli v. Chernoff, 526 F.2d 1314 (1st Cir. 1975); United States v. Gaultney, 581 F.2d 1137 (5th Cir. 1978); United States v. Alden, 576 F.2d 772 (8th Cir. 1978); People v. Peter, 55 Ill.2d 443, 303 N.E.2d 398 (1973). The alternative of posting a guard at the car and applying for a warrant has not been required. One way of viewing cases like these is to say that *Coolidge* has been totally eviscerated by lower courts. A different view is that *Coolidge* truly was "one of a kind." The circumstances in *Coolidge* indicated, despite the inherent mobility of a vehicle, there was absolutely no emergency. Thus the court in United States v. Bowles, 304 A.2d 277 (D.C.App. 1973), called *Coolidge* "sui generis." See also Bailey v. State, 16 Md.App. 83, 294 A.2d 123 (1972), where Judge Moylan noted that *Coolidge* was the only case in Supreme Court history where, despite the existence of probable cause to search a vehicle, the Court invalidated the search for want of exigent circumstances. The prevailing plurality opinion in Cardwell v. Lewis, 417 U.S. 583, 94 S.Ct. 2464 (1974), also gave a narrow interpretation to *Coolidge*. On the other hand, some lower courts have invalidated warrantless searches of parked cars for want of exigent circumstances. See, e. g., Commonwealth v. Ball, 254 Pa.Super. 148, 385 A.2d 568 (1978); United States v. Kelly, 547 F.2d 82 (8th Cir. 1977); State v. Miles, 97 Idaho 396, 545 P.2d 484 (1976).

6. *Other Theories.* Sometimes theories other than the ones just discussed must be considered when a warrantless search of a car is made. For example, when a driver is lawfully arrested, there is not always probable cause to believe that evidence is in the car. Thus the *Carroll* theory may be

unavailable. On the other hand, the "search-incident" theory may be invoked. Under this theory, however, only the area where the arrestee could reach can be searched. Thus, ordinarily a car trunk cannot be searched under a "search-incident" theory. Additionally, which parts of the interior of the vehicle can be searched will depend upon where the driver is standing or sitting at the moment of arrest. See Jacobs v. United States, 374 A.2d 850 (D.C.App.1977) (vehicle cannot be searched when arrestee is a distance from his car).

Students should also reflect upon how other doctrines may apply to cases involving motor vehicles. Among the doctrines which should be considered are "stop-and-frisk" (Section F); inventory search (Section M); plain view search (Section H); license-regulation stop (Section M); consent search (Section G); and abandonment (Section K).

M.   ADMINISTRATIVE SEARCHES

Fourth Amendment intrusions which are categorized as "administrative searches" are intended to serve some governmental regulatory purpose other than the capture of criminals or the discovery and seizure of evidence for use in a criminal trial. Thus their reasonableness must be judged by a standard different from traditional probable cause to believe that evidence of a crime will be found in the place to be searched. Even though traditional probable cause is not required, the reasonableness requirement of the Fourth Amendment *sometimes* demands that administrative searches be carried out only after prior judicial approval. As the following case of Camara v. Municipal Court of San Francisco indicates, the notion that judges can issue warrants or judicial orders approving searches in the absence of traditional probable cause calls for reflection upon the interrelationship of the "reasonableness clause" and the "warrant clause" of the Fourth Amendment.

CAMARA v. MUNICIPAL COURT OF SAN FRANCISCO

Supreme Court of the United States, 1967.
387 U.S. 523, 87 S.Ct. 1727.

MR. JUSTICE WHITE delivered the opinion of the Court.

On November 6, 1963, an inspector of the Division of Housing Inspection of the San Francisco Department of Public Health entered an apartment building to make a routine annual inspection for possible violations of the city's Housing Code. The building's manager informed the inspector that appellant, lessee of the ground floor, was using the rear of his leasehold as a personal residence. Claiming that the building's occupancy permit did not allow residential use of the ground floor, the inspector confronted appellant and demanded that he permit an inspection of the premises. Appellant refused to allow the inspection because the inspector lacked a search warrant.

The inspector returned on November 8, again without a warrant, and appellant again refused to allow an inspection. A citation was then mailed ordering appellant to appear at the district attorney's office. When appellant failed to appear, two inspectors returned to his apartment on November 22. They informed appellant that he was required by law to permit an inspection under § 503 of the Housing Code:

> "Sec. 503. RIGHT TO ENTER BUILDING. Authorized employees of the City departments or City agencies, so far as may be necessary for the performance of their duties, shall, upon presentation of proper credentials, have the right to enter, at reasonable times, any building, structure, or premises in the City to perform any duty imposed upon them by the Municipal Code."

Appellant nevertheless refused the inspectors access to his apartment without a search warrant. Thereafter, a complaint was filed charging him with refusing to permit a lawful inspection in violation of § 507 of the Code.

In Frank v. State of Maryland, [359 U.S. 360, 79 S.Ct. 804] this Court upheld the conviction of one who refused to permit a warrantless inspection of private premises for the purposes of locating and abating a suspected public nuisance. . . . the *Frank* opinion has generally been interpreted as carving out an additional exception to the rule that warrantless searches are unreasonable under the Fourth Amendment.

To the *Frank* majority, municipal fire, health, and housing inspection programs "touch at most upon the periphery of the important interests safeguarded by the Fourteenth Amendment's protection against official intrusions," because the inspections are merely to determine whether physical conditions exist which do not comply with minimum standards prescribed in local regulatory ordinances.

We may agree that a routine inspection of the physical condition of private property is a less hostile intrusion than the typical policeman's search for the fruits and instrumentalities of crime. . . . But we cannot agree that the Fourth Amendment interests at stake in these inspection cases are merely "peripheral." It is surely anomalous to say that the individual and his private property are fully protected by the Fourth Amendment only when the individual is suspected of criminal behavior. For instance, even the most law-abiding citizen has a very tangible interest in limiting the circumstances under which the sanctity of his home may be broken by official authority, for the possibility of criminal entry under the guise of official sanction is a serious threat to personal and family security. And even accepting Frank's rather remarkable premise, inspections of the kind we are here considering do in fact jeopardize "self protection" interests of the property owner. Like most regulatory laws, fire, health, and housing codes are enforced by criminal processes. . . .

The *Frank* majority suggested, and appellee reasserts, two other justifications for permitting administrative health and safety inspections without a warrant. First, it is argued that these inspections are "designed to make the least possible demand on the individual occupant." The ordinances authorizing inspections are hedged with safeguards, and at any rate the inspector's particular decision to enter must comply with the constitutional standard of reasonableness even if he may enter without a warrant. In addition, the argument proceeds, the warrant process could not function effectively in this field. The decision to inspect an entire municipal area is based upon legislative or administrative assessment of broad factors such as the area's age and condition. Unless the magistrate is to review such policy matters, he must issue a "rubber stamp" warrant which provides no protection at all to the property owner.

In our opinion, these arguments unduly discount the purposes behind the warrant machinery contemplated by the Fourth Amendment. Under the present system, when the inspector demands entry, the occupant has no way of knowing whether enforcement of the municipal code involved requires inspection of his premises, no way of knowing the lawful limits of the inspector's power to search, and no way of knowing whether the inspector himself is acting under proper authorization. These are questions which may be reviewed by a neutral magistrate without any reassessment of the basic agency decision to canvass an area. Yet, only by refusing entry and risking a criminal conviction can the occupant at present challenge the inspector's decision to search. And even if the occupant possesses sufficient fortitude to take this risk, as appellant did here, he may never learn any more about the reason for the inspection than that the law generally allows housing inspectors to gain entry. The practical effect of this system is to leave the occupant subject to the discretion of the official in the field. This is precisely the discretion to invade private property which we have consistently circumscribed by a requirement that a disinterested party warrant the need to search.

The final justification suggested for warrantless administrative searches is that the public interest demands such a rule: it is vigorously argued that the health and safety of entire urban populations is dependent upon enforcement of minimum fire, housing, and sanitation standards, and that the only effective means of enforcing such codes is by routine systematized inspection of all physical structures. Of course, in applying any reasonableness standard, including one of constitutional dimension, an argument that the public interest demands a particular rule must receive careful consideration. But we think this argument misses the mark. The question is not, at this stage at least, whether these inspections may be made, but whether they may be made without a warrant. . . .

It has nowhere been urged that fire, health, and housing code inspection programs could not achieve their goals within the confines of a reasonable search warrant requirement. Thus, we do not find the public need argument dispositive.

In summary, we hold that administrative searches of the kind at issue here are significant intrusions upon the interests protected by

the Fourth Amendment, that such searches when authorized and conducted without a warrant procedure lack the traditional safeguards
which the Fourth Amendment guarantees to the individual   .   .   .
Because of the nature of the municipal programs under consideration,
however, these conclusions must be the beginning, not the end of our
inquiry.   The *Frank* majority gave recognition to the unique character of these inspection programs by refusing to require search warrants; to reject that disposition does not justify ignoring the question whether some other accommodation between public need and individual rights is essential.

II.

The Fourth Amendment provides that, "no Warrants shall issue
but upon probable cause." Borrowing from more typical Fourth
Amendment cases, appellant argues not only that code enforcement
inspection programs must be circumscribed by a warrant procedure,
but also that warrants should issue only when the inspector possesses
probable cause to believe that a particular dwelling contains violations of the minimum standards prescribed by the code being enforced.   We disagree.

Unlike the search pursuant to a criminal investigation, the
inspection programs at issue here are aimed at securing city-wide
compliance with minimum physical standards for private property.
The primary governmental interest at stake is to prevent even the
unintentional development of conditions which are hazardous to public health and safety. Because fires and epidemics may ravage large
urban areas, because unsightly conditions adversely affect the economic values of neighboring structures, numerous courts have upheld
the police power of municipalities to impose and enforce such minimum standards even upon existing structures. In determining
whether a particular inspection is reasonable—and thus in determining whether there is probable cause to issue a warrant for that
inspection—the need for the inspection must be weighed in terms of
these reasonable goals of code enforcement.

There is unanimous agreement among those most familiar with
this field that the only effective way to seek universal compliance
with the minimum standards required by municipal codes is through
routine periodic inspections of all structures. It is here that the
probable cause debate is focused, for the agency's decision to conduct
an area inspection is unavoidably based on its appraisal of conditions
in the area as a whole, not on its knowledge of conditions in each particular building. Appellee contends that, if the probable cause standard urged by appellant is adopted, the area inspection will be eliminated as a means of seeking compliance with code standards and the
reasonable goals of code enforcement will be dealt a crushing blow.

In meeting this contention, appellant argues first, that his probable cause standard would not jeopardize area inspection programs because only a minute portion of the population will refuse to consent
to such inspections, and second, that individual privacy in any event

should be given preference to the public interest in conducting such inspections. The first argument, even if true, is irrelevant to the question whether the area inspection is reasonable within the meaning of the Fourth Amendment. The second argument is in effect an assertion that the area inspection is an unreasonable search. Unfortunately, there can be no ready test for determining reasonableness other than by balancing the need to search against the invasion which the search entails. But we think that a number of persuasive factors combine to support the reasonableness of code enforcement area inspections. First, such programs have a long history of judicial and public acceptance. Second, the public interest demands that all dangerous conditions be prevented or abated, yet it is doubtful that any other canvassing technique would achieve acceptable results. Many such conditions—faulty wiring is an obvious example—are not observable from outside the building and indeed may not be apparent to the inexpert occupant himself. Finally, because the inspections are neither personal in nature nor aimed at the discovery of evidence of crime, they involve a relatively limited invasion of the urban citizen's privacy. . . .

* * *

Having concluded that the area inspection is a "reasonable" search of private property within the meaning of the Fourth Amendment, it is obvious that "probable cause" to issue a warrant to inspect must exist if reasonable legislative or administrative standards for conducting an area inspection are satisfied with respect to a particular dwelling. Such standards, which will vary with the municipal program being enforced, may be based upon the passage of time, the nature of the building (e. g., a multi-family apartment house), or the condition of the entire area, but they will not necessarily depend upon specific knowledge of the condition of the particular dwelling. It has been suggested that so to vary the probable cause test from the standard applied in criminal cases would be to authorize a "synthetic search warrant" and thereby to lessen the overall protections of the Fourth Amendment. But we do not agree. The warrant procedure is designed to guarantee that a decision to search private property is justified by a reasonable governmental interest. But reasonableness is still the ultimate standard. If a valid public interest justifies the intrusion contemplated, then there is probable cause to issue a suitably restricted search warrant. . . . Such an approach neither endangers time-honored doctrines applicable to criminal investigations nor makes a nullity of the probable cause requirement in this area. It merely gives full recognition to the competing public and private interests here at stake and, in so doing, best fulfills the historic purpose behind the constitutional right to be free from unreasonable government invasions of privacy. . . .

III.

Since our holding emphasizes the controlling standard of reasonableness, nothing we say today is intended to foreclose prompt inspections, even without a warrant, that the law has traditionally upheld in emergency situations. See North American Cold Storage Co. v. City of Chicago, 211 U.S. 306, 29 S.Ct. 101 (seizure of unwholesome food); Jacobson v. Commonwealth of Massachusetts, 197 U.S. 11, 25 S.Ct. 358 (compulsory smallpox vaccination); Compagnie Francaise de Navigation à Vapeur v. Louisiana State Board of Health, 186 U.S. 380, 22 S.Ct. 811 (health quarantine); Kroplin v. Truax, 119 Ohio St. 610, 165 N.E. 498 (summary destruction of tubercular cattle). On the other hand, in the case of most routine area inspections, there is no compelling urgency to inspect at a particular time or on a particular day. Moreover, most citizens allow inspections of their property without a warrant. Thus, as a practical matter and in light of the Fourth Amendment's requirement that a warrant specify the property to be searched, it seems likely that warrants should normally be sought only after entry is refused unless there has been a citizen complaint or there is other satisfactory reason for securing immediate entry. . . .

SEE v. CITY OF SEATTLE

Supreme Court of the United States, 1967.
387 U.S. 541, 87 S.Ct. 1737.

MR. JUSTICE WHITE delivered the opinion of the Court.

Appellant seeks reversal of his conviction for refusing to permit a representative of the City of Seattle Fire Department to enter and inspect appellant's locked commercial warehouse without a warrant and without probable cause to believe that a violation of any municipal ordinance existed therein. The inspection was conducted as part of a routine, periodic city-wide canvass to obtain compliance with Seattle's Fire Code.

* * *

We therefore conclude that administrative entry, without consent, upon the portions of commercial premises which are not open to the public may only be compelled through prosecution or physical force within the framework of a warrant procedure. We do not in any way imply that business premises may not reasonably be inspected in many more situations than private homes, nor do we question such accepted regulatory techniques as licensing programs which require inspections prior to operating a business or marketing a product. Any constitutional challenge to such programs can only be resolved, as many have been in the past, on a case-by-case basis under the general Fourth Amendment standard of reasonableness.

[Dissenting opinion in both *Camara* and *See*:]

MR. JUSTICE CLARK with whom MR. JUSTICE HARLAN and MR. JUSTICE STEWART join, dissenting.

Eight years ago my Brother Frankfurter wisely wrote in Frank v. State of Maryland . . . . :

"Time and experience have forcefully taught that the power to inspect dwelling places, either as a matter of systematic area-by-area search or, as here, to treat a specific problem, is of indispensable importance to the maintenance of community health; a power that would be greatly hobbled by the blanket requirement of the safeguards necessary for a search of evidence of criminal acts. The need for preventive action is great, and city after city has seen this need and granted the power of inspection to its health officials; and these inspections are apparently welcomed by all but an insignificant few."

Today the Court renders this municipal experience, which dates back to Colonial days, for naught by overruling Frank v. State of Maryland and by striking down hundreds of city ordinances throughout the country and jeopardizing thereby the health, welfare, and safety of literally millions of people.

But this is not all. It prostitutes the command of the Fourth Amendment that "no Warrants shall issue, but upon probable cause" and sets up in the health and safety codes area inspection a new-fangled "warrant" system that is entirely foreign to Fourth Amendment standards. It is regrettable that the Court wipes out such a long and widely accepted practice and creates in its place such enormous confusion in all of our towns and metropolitan cities in one fell swoop. I dissent.

The great need for health and safety inspection is emphasized by the experience of San Francisco, a metropolitan area known for its cleanliness and safety ever since it suffered earthquake and fire back in 1908. For the fiscal year ending June 30, 1965, over 16,000 dwelling structures were inspected, of which over 5,600 required some type of compliance action in order to meet code requirements. . . .

In the larger metropolitan cities such as Los Angeles, over 300,000 inspections (health and fire) revealed over 28,000 hazardous violations. In Chicago during the period November 1965 to December 1966, over 18,000 buildings were found to be rodent infested out of some 46,000 inspections. . . . And in New York City the problem is even more acute. A grand jury in Brooklyn conducted a housing survey of 15 square blocks in three different areas and found over 12,000 hazardous violations of code restrictions in those areas alone. Prior to this test there were only 567 violations reported in the entire area. The pressing need for inspection is shown by the fact that some 12,000 additional violations were actually present at that very time.

An even more disastrous effect will be suffered in plumbing violations. These are not only more frequent but also the more dangerous to the community. Defective plumbing causes back siphonage of sewage and other household wastes. Chicago's disastrous amoebic dysentery epidemic is an example. Over 100 deaths resulted. Fire code violations also often cause many conflagrations. Indeed, if the fire inspection attempted in District of Columbia v. Little, 339 U.S. 1, 70 S.Ct. 468 (1950), had been permitted a two-year-old child's death resulting from a fire that gutted the home involved there on August 6, 1964, might well have been prevented.

Inspections also play a vital role in urban redevelopment and slum clearance. Statistics indicate that slums constitute 20% of the residential area of the average American city, still they produce 35% of the fires, 45% of the major crimes, and 50% of the disease. Today's decision will play havoc with the many programs now designed to aid in the improvement of these areas. We should remember the admonition of Mr. Justice Douglas in Berman v. Parker:

> "Miserable and disreputable housing conditions may do more than spread disease and crime and immorality. They may also suffocate the spirit by reducing those who live there to the status of cattle. They may indeed make living an almost insufferable burden."

The majority propose two answers to this admittedly pressing problem of need for constant inspection of premises for fire, health, and safety infractions of municipal codes. First, they say that there will be few refusals of entry to inspect. Unlike the attitude of householders as to codes requiring entry for inspection, we have few empirical statistics on attitudes where consent must be obtained. It is true that in the required entry to inspect situations most occupants welcome the periodic visits of municipal inspectors. In my view this will not be true when consent is necessary. The City of Portland, Oregon, has a voluntary home inspection program. The 1966 record shows that out of 16,171 calls where the occupant was at home, entry was refused in 2,540 cases—approximately one out of six. This is a large percentage and would place an intolerable burden on the inspection service when required to secure warrants. What is more important is that out of the houses inspected 4,515 hazardous conditions were found! Hence, on the same percentage, there would be approximately 800 hazardous situations in the 2,540 in which inspection was refused in Portland. . . .

The majority seems to hold that warrants may be obtained after a refusal of initial entry; I can find no such constitutional distinction or command. This boxcar warrant will be identical as to every dwelling in the area, save the street number itself. I daresay they will be printed up in pads of a thousand or more—with space for the street number to be inserted—and issued by magistrates in broadcast fashion as a matter of course.

I ask: Why go through such an exercise, such a pretense? As the same essentials are being followed under the present procedures, I ask: Why the ceremony, the delay, the expense, the abuse of the search warrant? In my view this will not only destroy its integrity but will degrade the magistrate issuing them and soon bring disrepute not only upon the practice but upon the judicial process. It will be very costly to the city in paperwork incident to the issuance of the paper warrants, in loss of time of inspectors and waste of the time of magistrates and will result in more annoyance to the public. . . .

NOTES

1. Following *Camara* and *See* the Court considered several regulatory schemes which the government sought to justify under the "licensing" power referred to in the *See* opinion:

(a) In Colonnade Catering Corp. v. United States, 397 U.S. 72, 90 S.Ct. 774 (1970) the Court excluded evidence seized by federal agents who had, without a warrant, forcibly entered a locked storeroom on the premises of a federally licensed dealer in alcoholic beverages. The Court decided that the Act of Congress which authorized inspection of such premises did not authorize forcible entry. The statute took the alternative position of making it a criminal offense to refuse admission to the inspectors.

Many state statutory schemes under which a driver as a condition of his or her license is required, under specified circumstances, to take a breathalyzer or other blood-alcohol test are of the *Colonnade* type. If the driver refuses to take the test, in many jurisdictions he cannot be commanded or forced to take the test; the penalty for a refusal, however, is a suspension or revocation of the license.

(b) In United States v. Biswell, 406 U.S. 311, 92 S.Ct. 1593 (1972), the Court approved a federal agent's inspection of a federally licensed gun dealer's storeroom. The gun dealer objected to the inspection but acquiesced upon being shown a copy of the federal statute specifically authorizing such inspections during business hours. The court distinguished *Colonnade* by asserting the absence of forcible entry and holding that submission by the dealer to *lawful* authority rather than risking a criminal charge by refusing entry is a valid basis for the inspector's entry into the storeroom. The Court also said:

> "In See v. Seattle, supra, the mission of the inspection system was to discover and correct violations of the building code, conditions that were relatively difficult to conceal or to correct in a short time. Periodic inspection sufficed, and inspection warrants could be required and privacy given a measure of protection with little if any threat to the effectiveness of the inspection system there at issue. We expressly refrained in that case from questioning a warrantless regulatory search such as that authorized by § 923 of the Gun Control Act. Here, if inspection is to be effective and serve as a credible deterrent, unannounced, even frequent, inspections are essential. In this context, the prerequisite of a warrant could easily frustrate inspection; and if the necessary flexibility as to time, scope and frequency is to be preserved, the protections afforded by a warrant would be negligible."

(c) In Marshall v. Barlow's, Inc., 436 U.S. 307, 98 S.Ct. 1816 (1978), it became apparent that the power of government to regulate various human enterprises does not give the government the right to condition a person's or corporation's participation in those activities upon a willingness to submit to whatever Fourth Amendment intrusions the government deems appropriate. At issue in that case was the right of federal agents to inspect the work area of places of employment governed by the 1970 Occupational Safety and Health Act. Writing for the majority, Justice White noted that use of implied-consent regulatory schemes had been approved only in the case of "closely regulated industry of the type involved in *Colonnade* and *Biswell*." Efforts to expand this approach to justify warrantless inspections or searches in every type of industry in interstate commerce were deemed constitutionally impermissible: "The clear import of our cases is that the closely regulated industry . . . is the exception. The Secretary (of Labor) would make it the rule." The Court then decided that under the balancing test of *Camara* the legitimate governmental purpose of promoting safety in the work place could be safeguarded by an administrative warrant procedure available for use in cases in which the employer refused to consent to an inspection. Under this scheme, "Probable cause in the criminal sense is not required. . . . A warrant showing that a specific business has been chosen for an OSHA search on the basis of a general administrative plan for the enforcement of the Act derived from neutral sources such as, for example, dispersion of employees in various types of industries across a given area, and the desired frequency of searches in any of the lesser divisions of the area, would protect an employer's Fourth Amendment rights."

In his dissent in *Barlow's*, Justice Stevens asserted that the majority had provided no clear guidelines for determining which industries can be subjected to warrantless inspections of the *Biswell* type. Is it the longevity of the regulatory program that matters, he asked, noting that the *Biswell* regulatory scheme had been enacted in 1968 and asserting that the "recent vintage" of congressional concern for safety in the workplace ought not be determinative of the validity of the warrantless inspection scheme.

2. In his dissent in *Camara* and *See*, Justice Clark, spoke of destroying the integrity of the warrant clause by permitting the issuance of warrants without traditional probable cause to believe that criminal evidence is in the place to be searched. In his dissent in Marshall v. Barlow's, Inc., Justice Stevens made a similar argument. He said that the "Court's approach disregards the plain language of the Warrant Clause and is unfaithful to the balance struck by the Framers of the Fourth Amendment. . . . ." He made the point that historically the concern of the drafters was primarily the use of general warrants absent probable cause and not the warrantless search. (Compare T. Taylor, Two Studies in Constitutional Interpretation, 21–43, with Amsterdam, Perspectives on the Fourth Amendment, 58 Minn.L.Rev. 349, 398–400.) Interestingly, Justice Stewart, who had joined in Justice Clark's attack on "new-fangled" warrants in *Camara* and *See*, sided with the majority in Marshall v. Barlow's, Inc.

Does not the Clark-Stevens position put a straitjacket upon the Court in deciding what can be required as a condition of reasonableness? If it can deem certain intrusions reasonable without either traditional probable cause or a warrant (e. g., the inspections approved in *Biswell* and *Colonnade Catering*), why can it not, as a condition of reasonableness, excuse traditional probable cause but require prior judicial approval? If a traditional warrant cannot issue for want of probable cause, would not Clark and Stevens force courts into a position of approving more searches without any prior judicial approval? On the other hand, does not the warrant clause become superfluous under the majority opinions in *See* and *Marshall*? Why could not the reasonableness clause be utilized to support any result in any Fourth Amendment case previously studied, including probable cause-warrant cases like *Spinelli* (Section B, supra).

3. *Welfare Home Visits.* In Wyman v. James, 400 U.S. 309, 91 S.Ct. 381 (1971) the Court approved a state law which required welfare recipi-

ents to admit caseworkers into their homes or else face termination of benefits. The Court based its holding on several factors: the caseworkers are
reasonably attempting to determine if aid is properly given to dependent
children, the refusal to permit entry is not made a criminal offense, written
notice of visits must be made several days in advance, forcible entry or entry under false pretenses is prohibited, visits must occur during normal
working hours, the essential information secured by home visits is not
available from other sources and the visit is not conducted by a law-enforcement officer looking for criminal violations. Thus, although *Camara* indicated that the Fourth Amendment protects all persons, not just those suspected of criminal activity, the "benign" purpose of the governmental intrusion was deemed relevant in *James* to the determination of reasonableness
under the Fourth Amendment.

4. *License Check Stops.* Even in areas in which governmental regulation is lengthy and pervasive, the power to regulate and to license does not
protect government from scrutiny of the reasonableness of its warrantless
inspection schemes. In Delaware v. Prouse, 440 U.S. 648, 99 S.Ct. 1391
(1979), the Court framed the issue: "The question is whether it is an unreasonable seizure under the Fourth and Fourteenth Amendments to stop an
automobile, for the purpose of checking the driving license of the operator
and the registration of the car, where there is neither probable cause to believe nor reasonable suspicion that the car is being driven contrary to the
laws governing the operation of motor vehicles or that either the car or any
of its occupants is subject to seizure or detention in connection with the violation of any other applicable law." The Court held that such random
stops violate the Fourth Amendment. The Court stated that an individual
who drives a car—engaging in a "basic, pervasive, and often necessary
mode of transportation"—cannot be deemed to have yielded all Fourth
Amendment protections. The question is resolved, said the Court, by a balancing of the intensity of the intrusion against governmental necessity.
Here the Court decided the marginal contribution which a random license
inspection would make to safety did not justify the intrusion involved, particularly in light of the "grave danger of abuse of discretion." The Court
added that its holding did not preclude the States "from developing methods
for spot checks that involve less intrusion or that do not involve the unconstrained exercise of discretion. Questioning of all oncoming traffic at roadblock-type stops is one possible alternative."

5. *Border Searches.* When a person is crossing into the United States
at a border, he can be searched and his goods inspected. The supposed purpose of such searches is not simply to enforce the penal laws, but also to
prohibit the entry into the country of substances which violate health standards. No warrant is required. Nor must the authorities possess any data
suggesting that a particular person is carrying contraband before they can
search such persons. According to lower court decisions, however, if the intensity of the search goes beyond the "ordinary" search—as, for example, it
escalates to a strip search and then to an intrusion into body cavities—an
increasing amount of objective data focusing suspicion on the person is required. See, e. g., United States v. Smith, 557 F.2d 1206 (5th Cir. 1977);
United States v. Mastberg, 503 F.2d 465 (9th Cir. 1974). The United
States Supreme Court has never directly ruled on any case involving a
search of a person at the border, so that it has not had occasion to pass
judgment on lower court distinctions as to "ordinary" searches and strip
searches and body cavity searches, and as to lower court standards such as
"real suspicion," "reasonable suspicion," and "clear indication." In United

States v. Ramsey, 431 U.S. 606, 97 S.Ct. 1972 (1977), the Court did uphold warrantless inspection of mail which is crossing into the United States from another country. It is generally agreed that border search doctrines are also applicable at first points of entry by airplane, known as "functional equivalents." See United States v. Brown, 499 F.2d 829 (7th Cir. 1974) (international gate at Chicago's O'Hare Airport).

6. *"Border Vicinity" Searches.* The Supreme Court has been very active in ruling on the validity of (1) stops and (2) searches of vehicles (3) at fixed checkpoints or (4) by roving patrols perhaps ten, twenty, or fifty miles distant from a border. In United States v. Martinez-Fuerte, 428 U.S. 543, 96 S.Ct. 3074 (1976), the Court summarized some earlier holdings. That summary is paraphrased here:

> In Almeida-Sanchez v. United States (1973), the question was whether a roving-patrol unit constitutionally could search a vehicle for illegal aliens simply because it was in the general vicinity of the border. The Court held that searches by roving patrols could be conducted without consent only if there was probable cause to believe that a car contained illegal aliens, at least in the absence of a judicial warrant authorizing random stops by roving patrols in a given area. The Court held in United States v. Ortiz, (1975) that the same limitations were applied to vehicle searches conducted at a permanent checkpoint.

> In United States v. Brignoni-Ponce (1975), however, the Court recognized that other traffic-checking practices involve a different balance of public and private interest and appropriately are subject to less stringent constitutional safeguards. The question there was under what circumstances a roving patrol could stop motorists in the general area of the border for inquiry into their residence status. The Court said that a roving-patrol stop need not be justified by probable cause and may be undertaken if the stopping officer is "aware of specific articulable facts, together with rational inferences from those facts, that reasonably warrant suspicion" that a vehicle contains illegal aliens.

The Court in *Martinez-Fuerte* held that even without reasonable suspicion, vehicles may be stopped at fixed checkpoints in the vicinity of a border and the occupants briefly questioned. It rejected the argument that, at a minimum, such detentions for questioning could be considered reasonable only if done under the authority of an "area warrant" issued upon a judicial determination that it was reasonable to stop cars, in accord with certain guidelines, at that particular checkpoint. Questions thus arise as to what is a "fixed" checkpoint. Such issues are of critical importance in many drug prosecutions in certain border states.

7. *Urban I.N.S. Stops.* The procedures of the Immigration and Naturalization Service also give rise to Fourth Amendment issues in the context of the "urban stop" in quest of illegal aliens. See Illinois Migrant Council v. Pilliod, 540 F.2d 1062 (7th Cir. 1976), mod. in 548 F.2d 715 (7th Cir. 1977); Lee v. Immigration and Naturalization Service, 590 F.2d 497 (3d Cir. 1979).

8. *Inventory Searches.* Sometimes, as, for example, when a driver is intoxicated or becomes ill, or when an arrestee is to be placed in a jail cell, law enforcement officials may become temporary custodians of a citizen's property. In such cases they have claimed the right to conduct a warrant-

less "inventory search" of the property. The stated rationale is to safeguard the property, to protect against false claims of theft, and, occasionally, to prevent danger to the officers. Despite a growing trend by state and lower federal courts to limit the use of the inventory search, the United States Supreme Court gave broad approval to the inventory search doctrine in South Dakota v. Opperman, 428 U.S. 364, 96 S.Ct. 3092 (1976), a 5 to 4 decision, with Justices Marshall, Brennan, White, and Stewart dissenting. The Court held that when vehicles are lawfully impounded, routine inventorying of the vehicle, including locked components, is permissible. In *Opperman* there was no suggestion that the inventory was a pretext to find evidence of a crime. The car had been towed in connection with parking ordinance violations.

In *Prouse*, supra note 4, the Court obviously was concerned that the police would use the license-check stop to put themselves in a position to spot plain view evidence in a car which, for want of reasonable suspicion, they could not otherwise stop. Opponents of the inventory search claim that the doctrine often is used to justify warrantless searches of an arrestee's car which, for want of search probable cause, could not otherwise be searched. However, in *Opperman* the Court was apparently less impressed by the danger of abuse of inventory searches than by the danger of abuse of license check stops.

Since *Opperman* many lower courts have adopted doctrines which have limited the use of the inventory search doctrine. If the car is not in *lawful* custody (i. e., if the police had no right to take it), then the inventory is unlawful. G. B. v. State, 339 So.2d 696 (Fla.App.1976). The inventory cannot be a pretext for an investigation of a crime, but must be to protect property, prevent danger, or discourage false claims of theft. Commonwealth v. Brandt, 244 Pa.Super. 154, 366 A.2d 1238 (1976). See also State v. Creel, 142 Ga. 158, 235 S.E.2d 628 (1977); United States v. Hellman, 556 F.2d 442 (9th Cir. 1977) (need for proof that inventory was routine practice); State v. Hudson, 390 A.2d 509 (Me.1978) (similar). Some "inventories" are so intensive that it is obvious that the officers were going beyond the legitimate purpose of an inventory. See People v. Rutovic, —— Colo. ——, 566 P.2d 705 (1977). A number of courts have held that where available alternatives exist to taking the property into police custody (e. g., a friend who is willing to take the vehicle), authorities must allow this to be done. See Session v. State, 353 So.2d 854 (Fla.App.1977); Arrington v. United States, 382 A.2d 14 (D.C.App.1978); People v. Hamilton, 56 Ill. App.3d 196, 14 Ill.Dec. 181, 371 N.E.2d 1234 (1978); State v. Goodrich, 256 N.W.2d 506 (Minn.1977); State v. Hardman, 17 Wash.App. 910, 567 P.2d 238 (1977). See also State v. Ludvicek, 147 Ga.App. 784, 250 S.E.2d 503 (1978); State v. Ercolano, 79 N.J. 25, 397 A.2d 1062 (1979). Some states use state grounds to limit inventory searches. State v. Opperman, —— S.D. ——, 247 N.W.2d 673 (1976); State v. Sawyer, —— Mont. ——, 571 P.2d 1131 (1977).

9. *Searches of Prisoners, Probationers, and Parolees.* In Bell v. Wolfish, 441 U.S. 520, 99 S.Ct. 1961 (1979), the Supreme Court approved intensive searches of prisoners (including pre-trial detainees) even where no particular suspicion focused on a prisoner and even where other security measures had pretty well limited the opportunity of prisoners to obtain contraband items. Searches of the persons, houses, cars, and other effects of probationers and parolees have also been upheld on an administrative search theory: the need to make sure that the probationer or parolee is following

the prescribed regimen. Sometimes an implied-consent theory is used. However, some decisions have limited this type of search. Compare, e. g., People v. Keller, 76 Cal.App.3d 827, 143 Cal.Rptr. 184 (1978); United States ex rel. Santos v. New York State Bd. of Parole, 441 F.2d 1216 (2d Cir. 1971); Tamez v. State, 534 S.W.2d 686 (Tex.Cr.App.1976); United States v. Consuelo-Gonzalez, 521 F.2d 259 (9th Cir. 1975). It is generally agreed that parole agents cannot use their search powers if they are merely acting as agents of the police in quest of evidence of a new crime. People v. Candelaria, 63 A.D.2d 85, 406 N.Y.S.2d 783 (1978).

10. *Air Passenger Searches.* Anti-hijacking measures at airports provide another example of administrative searches. Some decisions emphasize an implied consent theory, which raises the issue of whether a person about to be searched can avoid the search by choosing not to board. See, e. g., United States v. Edwards, 498 F.2d 496 (2d Cir. 1974). To some extent a "balancing" test is used. As the intensity of the search escalates from magnetometer to pat down to full search, objective data focusing suspicion may have to be present and to increase. Less intrusive measures may have to be exhausted before more intrusive ones are used. United States v. Albarado, 495 F.2d 799 (2d Cir. 1974).

11. *Courthouses and Other Public Buildings.* Judges appear more willing to approve searches and inspections of citizens entering "public" courthouses and governmental office buildings than they are to approve inspections at public arenas where rock concerts are being held. See Downing v. Kunzig, 454 F.2d 1230 (6th Cir. 1972) (building where Sixth Circuit sat), and compare State v. Carter, 267 N.W.2d 385 (Iowa, 1978), and Gaioni v. Folmar, 460 F.Supp. 10 (M.D.Ala.1978). If it is improper to frisk a pedestrian for weapons in a high crime area absent "reasonable suspicion," how can it be reasonable to inspect purses at the entrance to a public courts complex simply because of a generalized concern for safety of the building's occupants? See Jesmore, The Courthouse Search, 21 U.C.L.A.L.Rev. 797 (1974).

12. *Fire Scene Inspections.* In Michigan v. Tyler, 436 U.S. 488, 98 S. Ct. 1942 (1978), the Court placed limits upon the rights of fire inspectors, absent consent, to make warrantless searches, recognizing three distinct categories of fire inspection searches:

(1) A warrantless entry is permissible to extinguish a fire. Even after the blaze is out, officials may remain or reenter to promptly determine the fire's origin so as to prevent recurrence and to prevent intentional or accidental destruction of evidence. Evidence found in a place where officials have a right to look may be seized during this period.

(2) Subsequent entries to determine the cause of the fire, however, after a "reasonable time" for the initial investigation, necessitate, at a minimum, an administrative warrant. Traditional probable cause is not required. Rather the magistrate must balance several factors to determine the reasonableness of the proposed search: the "number of prior entries, the scope of the search, the time of day when it is proposed to be made, the lapse of time since the fire, the continued use of the building, and the owner's efforts to secure it against intruders might all be relevant factors."

(3) Once the purpose of the investigation becomes a quest for evidence of arson for use in a criminal prosecution, however, rather than the discovery of the cause of the fire as to prevent such fires from re-

curring, then a search is proper only upon traditional probable cause, i. e., probable cause to believe that a crime has been committed and that evidence of the crime will be found in the place to be searched. Apparently this third stage—when a traditional warrant is necessary—is reached no later than when earlier investigations have yielded probable cause to believe that a crime has been committed.

As a practical matter, probable cause to believe that arson has been committed frequently will be found during the first segment of the investigation. Apparently, under such circumstances—once the immediate danger has clearly been abated—officials would be required to apply for a traditional search warrant. Thus use of the administrative warrant provided for in time-segment two will often be bypassed.

N. FOURTH AMENDMENT BORDERLANDS: WHAT CONSTITUTES A SEARCH OR SEIZURE

In previous sections of this chapter, we have generally assumed that the governmental conduct under scrutiny was subject to the Fourth Amendment's requirement of reasonableness because such conduct was a search or a seizure within the meaning of the amendment. Thus, for example, although a police officer's spotting evidence in plain view might not be a search, his taking and carrying away the evidence is a seizure which requires justification to satisfy the reasonableness requirement of the first clause of the Fourth Amendment.

We now consider borderline cases where an essential preliminary question is whether the governmental conduct constitutes Fourth Amendment activity. If the answer is negative, the Fourth Amendment analysis need go no further. There can be no *unreasonable* search or seizure unless, to begin with, there is a search or a seizure. In the absence of a search or a seizure, those who would limit governmental intrusions upon liberty and privacy must look elsewhere in the law, beyond the Fourth Amendment, for a source of protection.

KATZ v. UNITED STATES

Supreme Court of the United States, 1967.
389 U.S. 347, 88 S.Ct. 507.

MR. JUSTICE STEWART delivered the opinion of the Court.

The petitioner was convicted in the District Court for the Southern District of California under an eight-count indictment charging him with transmitting wagering information by telephone from Los Angeles to Miami and Boston in violation of a federal statute. At trial the Government was permitted, over the petitioner's objection, to introduce evidence of the petitioner's end of telephone conversations, overheard by FBI agents who had attached an electronic listening and recording device to the outside of the public telephone booth from which he had placed his calls. In affirming his conviction, the Court of Appeals rejected the contention that the recordings had been obtained in violation of the Fourth Amendment, because "[t]here was no physical entrance into the area occupied by, [the petitioner]." We granted certiorari in order to consider the constitutional questions thus presented.

The petitioner has phrased those questions as follows:

"A.   Whether a public telephone booth is a constitutionally protected area so that evidence obtained by attaching an electronic listening recording device to the top of such a booth is obtained in violation of the right to privacy of the user of the booth.

"B.   Whether physical penetration of a constitutionally protected area is necessary before a search and seizure can be said to be violative of the Fourth Amendment to the United States Constitution."

We decline to adopt this formulation of the issues.   In the first place the correct solution of Fourth Amendment problems is not necessarily promoted by incantation of the phrase "constitutionally protected area."   Secondly, the Fourth Amendment cannot be translated into a general constitutional "right to privacy."   That Amendment protects individual privacy against certain kinds of governmental intrusion, but its protections go further, and often have nothing to do with privacy at all.   Other provisions of the Constitution protect personal privacy from other forms of governmental invasion.   But the protection of a person's *general* right to privacy—his right to be let alone by other people—is, like the protection of his property and of his very life, left largely to the law of the individual States.

Because of the misleading way the issues have been formulated, the parties have attached great significance to the characterization of the telephone booth from which the petitioner placed his calls.   The petitioner has strenuously argued that the booth was a "constitutionally protected area."   The Government has maintained with equal vigor that it was not.   But this effort to decide whether or not a given "area," viewed in the abstract, is "constitutionally protected" deflects attention from the problem presented by this case.   For the Fourth Amendment protects people, not places.   What a person knowingly exposes to the public, even in his own home or office, is not a subject of Fourth Amendment protection.   But what he seeks to preserve as private, even in an area accessible to the public may be constitutionally protected.

The Government stresses the fact that the telephone booth from which the petitioner made his calls was constructed partly of glass, so that he was as visible after he entered it as he would have been if he had remained outside.   But what he sought to exclude when he entered the booth was not the intruding eye—it was the uninvited ear. He did not shed his right to do so simply because he made his calls from a place where he might be seen.   No less than an individual in a business office, in a friend's apartment, or in a taxicab, a person in a telephone booth may rely upon the protection of the Fourth Amendment. One who occupies it, shuts the door behind him, and pays the toll that permits him to place a call, is surely entitled to assume that the words he utters into the mouthpiece will not be broadcast to the world. To read the Constitution more narrowly is to ignore the vital role that the public telephone has come to play in private communication.

The Government contends, however, that the activities of its agents in this case should not be tested by Fourth Amendment requirements, for the surveillance technique they employed involved no physical penetration of the telephone booth from which the petitioner placed his calls. It is true that the absence of such penetration was at one time thought to foreclose further Fourth Amendment inquiry, although a closely divided Court supposed in Olmstead v. United States (1928) that surveillance without any trespass and without the seizure of any material object fell outside the ambit of the Constitution, we have since departed from the narrow view on which that decision rested. Indeed, we have expressly held that the Fourth Amendment governs not only the seizure of tangible items, but extends as well to the recording of oral statements overheard without any "technical trespass under   .   .   .   local property law." Once this much is acknowledged, and once it is recognized that the Fourth Amendment protects people—and not simply "areas"—against unreasonable searches and seizures it becomes clear that the reach of that Amendment cannot turn upon the presence or absence of a physical intrusion into any given enclosure.

We conclude that the underpinnings of Olmstead v. United States and Goldman v. United States (1940) have been so eroded by our subsequent decisions that the "trespass" doctrine there enunciated can no longer be regarded as controlling. The Government's activities in electronically listening to and recording the petitioner's words violated the privacy upon which he justifiably relied while using the telephone booth and thus constituted a "search and seizure" within the meaning of the Fourth Amendment. The fact that the electronic device employed to achieve that end did not happen to penetrate the wall of the booth can have no constitutional significance.

The question remaining for decision, then, is whether the search and seizure conducted in this case complied with constitutional standards. In that regard, the Government's position is that its agents acted in an entirely defensible manner: They did not begin their electronic surveillance until investigation of the petitioner's activities had established a strong probability that he was using the telephone in question to transmit gambling information to persons in other States, in violation of federal law. Moreover, the surveillance was limited, both in scope and in duration, to the specific purpose of establishing the contents of the petitioner's unlawful telephonic communications. The agents confined their surveillance to the brief periods during which he used the telephone booth, and they took great care to overhear only the conversations of the petitioner himself.

Accepting this account of the Government's actions as accurate, it is clear that this surveillance was so narrowly circumscribed that a

duly authorized magistrate, properly notified of the need for such investigation, specifically informed of the basis on which it was to proceed, and clearly apprised of the precise intrusion it would entail,
could constitutionally have authorized, with appropriate safeguards,
the very limited search and seizure that the Government asserts in
fact took place.   Only last Term we sustain the validity of such an
authorization, holding that, under sufficiently "precise and discriminate circumstances," a federal court may empower government
agents to employ a concealed electronic device "for the narrow and
particularized purpose of ascertaining the truth of the . . . allegations" of a "detailed factual affidavit alleging the commission of
a specific criminal offense."   Osborn v. United States (1966).   Discussing that holding, the Court in Berger v. State of New York,
. . . said that "the order authorizing the use of the electronic
device" in *Osborn* "afforded similar protections to those . . . of
conventional warrants authorizing the seizure of tangible evidence."
Through those protections, "no greater invasion of privacy was permitted than was necessary under the circumstances."   Here, too, a
similar judicial order could have accommodated "the legitimate needs
of law enforcement" by authorizing the carefully limited use of electronic surveillance.

The Government urges that, because its agents relied upon the
decisions in *Olmstead* and *Goldman*, and because they did no more
here than they might properly have done with prior judicial sanction,
we should retroactively validate their conduct.   That we cannot do.
It is apparent that the agents in this case acted with restraint.   Yet
the inescapable fact is that this restraint was imposed by the agents
themselves, not by a judicial officer.   They were not required, before
commencing the search, to present their estimate of probable cause
for detached scrutiny by a neutral magistrate.   They were not compelled, during the conduct of the search itself, to observe precise limits established in advance by a specific court order.   Nor were they
directed, after the search had been completed, to notify the authorizing magistrate in detail of all that had been seized.   In the absence of
such safeguards, this Court has never sustained a search upon the
sole ground that officers reasonably expected to find evidence of a
particular crime and voluntarily confined their activities to the least
intrusive means consistent with that end.   *   *   *

[The government argues that] that surveillance of a telephone
booth should be exempted from the usual requirement of advance authorization by a magistrate upon a showing of probable cause.   We
cannot agree.   Omission of such authorization

> "bypasses the safeguards provided by an objective predeter-
> mination of probable cause, and substitutes instead the far
> less reliable procedure of an after-the-event justification for
> the . . . search, too likely to be subtly influenced by
> the familiar shortcomings of hindsight judgment."

And bypassing a neutral predetermination of the *scope* of a search leaves individuals secure from Fourth Amendment violations "only in the discretion of the police."

These considerations do not vanish when the search in question is transferred from the setting of a home, an office, or a hotel room, to that of a telephone booth. Wherever a man may be, he is entitled to know that he will remain free from unreasonable searches and seizures. The government agents here ignored "the procedure of antecedent justification . . . that is central to the Fourth Amendment," a procedure that we hold to be a constitutional precondition of the kind of electronic surveillance involved in this case. Because the surveillance here failed to meet that condition, and because it led to the petitioner's conviction, the judgment must be reversed.

It is so ordered.

Judgment reversed.

MR. JUSTICE MARSHALL took no part in the consideration or decision of this case.

MR. JUSTICE DOUGLAS, with whom MR. JUSTICE BRENNAN joins, concurring.

While I join the opinion of the Court, I feel compelled to reply to the separate concurring opinion of my BROTHER WHITE, which I view as a wholly unwarranted green light for the Executive Branch to resort to electronic eavesdropping without a warrant in cases which the Executive Branch itself labels "national security" matters.

Neither the President nor the Attorney General is a magistrate. In matters where they believe national security may be involved they are not detached, disinterested, and neutral as a court or magistrate must be. Under the separation of powers created by the Constitution, the Executive Branch is not supposed to be neutral and disinterested. Rather it should vigorously investigate and prevent breaches of national security and prosecute those who violate the pertinent federal laws. The President and Attorney General are properly interested parties, cast in the role of adversary, in national security cases. They may even be the intended victims of subversive action. Since spies and saboteurs are as entitled to the protection of the Fourth Amendment as suspected gamblers like petitioner, I cannot agree that where spies and saboteurs are involved adequate protection of Fourth Amendment rights is assured when the President and Attorney General assume both the position of adversary-and-prosecutor and disinterested, neutral magistrate.

There is, so far as I understand constitutional history, no distinction under the Fourth Amendment between types of crimes. Article III, § 3, gives "treason" a very narrow definition and puts restrictions on its proof. But the Fourth Amendment draws no lines between various substantive offenses. The arrests in cases of "hot pursuit," the arrests on visible or other evidence of probable cause cut across the boards and are not peculiar to any kind of crime.

I would respect the present lines of distinction and not improvise because a particular crime seems particularly heinous. When the Framers took that step, as they did with treason, the worst crime of all, they made their purpose manifest.

MR. JUSTICE HARLAN, cncurring.

I join the opinion of the Court, which I read to hold only (a) that an enclosed telephone booth is an area where, like a home, a person has a constitutionally protected reasonable expectation of privacy; (b) that electronic as well as physical intrusion into a place that is in this sense private may constitute a violation of the Fourth Amendment; and (c) that the invasion of a constitutionally protected area by federal authorities is, as the Court has long held, presumptively unreasonable in the absence of a search warrant.

As the Court's opinion states, "The Fourth Amendment protects people, not places." The question, however, is what protection it affords to those people. Generally, as here, the answer to that question requires reference to a "place." My understanding of the rule that has emerged from prior decisions is that there is a twofold requirement, first that a person have exhibited an actual (subjective) expectation of privacy, and, second, that the expectation be one that society is prepared to recognize as "reasonable." Thus a man's home is, for most purposes, a place where he expects privacy, but objects, activities, or statements that he exposes to the "plain view" of outsiders are not "protected" because no intention to keep them to himself has been exhibited. On the other hand, conversations in the open would not be protected against being overheard, for the expectation of privacy under the circumstances would be unreasonable.

The critical fact in this case is that "[o]ne who occupies it, [a telephone booth] shuts the door behind him, and pays the toll that permits him to place a call, is surely entitled to assume" that his conversation is not being intercepted. The point is not that the booth is "accessible to the public" at other times, but that it is a temporarily private place whose momentary occupants' expectations of freedom from intrusion are recognized as reasonable.

In Silverman v. United States (1961) we held that eavesdropping accomplished by means of an electronic device that penetrated the premises occupied by petitioner was a violation of the Fourth Amendment. That case established that interception of conversations reasonably intended to be private could constitute a "search and seizure," and that the examination or taking of physical property was not required. This view of the Fourth Amendment was followed in Wong Sun v. United States, and Berger v. State of New York. Also compare Osborne v. United States. In *Silverman* we found it unnecessary to re-examine Goldman v. United States, which had held that electronic surveillance accomplished without the physical penetration of petitioner's premises by a tangible object did not violate the Fourth Amendment. This case requires us to reconsider *Goldman*, and I agree that it should now be overruled. Its limitation on Fourth Amendment protection is, in the present day, bad physics as well as bad law, for resonable expectations of privacy may be defeated by electronic as well as physical invasion.

Finally, I do not read the Court's opinion to declare that no interception of a conversation one-half of which occurs in a public telephone booth can be reasonable in the absence of a warrant. As elsewhere under the Fourth Amendment, warrants are the general rule, to which the legitimate needs of law enforcement may demand specific exceptions. It will be time enough to consider any such exceptions when an appropriate occasion presents itself, and I agree with the Court that this is not one.

MR. JUSTICE WHITE, concurring.

I agree that the official surveillance of petitioner's telephone conversations in a public booth must be subjected to the test of reasonableness under the Fourth Amendment and that on the record now before us the particular surveillance undertaken was unreasonable absent a warrant properly authorizing it. This application of the Fourth Amendment need not interfere with legitimate needs of law enforcement.*

In joining the Court's opinion, I note the Court's acknowledgment that there are circumstances in which it is reasonable to search without a warrant. In this connection, the Court points out that today's decision does not reach national security cases. Wiretapping to protect the security of the Nation has been authorized by successive Presidents. The present Administration would apparently save national security cases from restrictions against wiretapping. We should not require the warrant procedure and the magistrate's judgment if the President of the United States or his chief legal officer, the Attorney General, has considered the requirements of national security and authorized electronic surveillance as reasonable.

MR. JUSTICE BLACK, dissenting.

If I could agree with the Court that eavesdropping carried on by electronic means (equivalent to wiretapping) constitutes a "search"

---

* In previous cases, which are undisturbed by today's decision, the Court has upheld, as reasonable under the Fourth Amendment, admission at trial of evidence obtained (1) by an undercover police agent to whom a defendant speaks without knowledge that he is in the employ of the police, Hoffa v. United States, (2) by a recording device hidden on the person of such an informant, Lopez v. United States, Osborn v. United States, and (3) by a policeman listening to the secret micro-wave transmissions of an agent conversing with the defendant in another location, On Lee v. United States. When one man speaks to another he takes all the risks ordinarily inherent in so doing, including the risk that the man to whom he speaks will make public what he has heard. The Fourth Amendment does not protect against unreliable (or law-abiding) associates. Hoffa v. United States, supra. It is but a logical and reasonable extension of this principle that a man take the risk that his hearer, free to memorize what he hears for later verbatim repetitions, is instead recording it or transmitting it to another. The present case deals with an entirely different situation, for as the Court emphasizes the petitioner "sought to exclude . . . the uninvited ear," and spoke under circumstances in which a reasonable person would assume that uninvited ears were not listening.

or "seizure," I would be happy to join the Court's opinion. For on that premise my BROTHER STEWART sets out methods in accord with the Fourth Amendment to guide States in the enactment and enforcement of laws passed to regulate wiretapping by government. In this respect today's opinion differs sharply from Berger v. State of New York, decided last Term, which held void on its face a New York statute authorizing wiretapping on warrants issued by magistrates on showings of probable causes. The *Berger* case also set up what appeared to be insuperable obstacles to the valid passage of such wiretapping laws by States. The Court's opinion in this case, however, removes the doubts about state power in this field and abates to a large extent the confusion and near paralyzing effect of the *Berger* holding. Notwithstanding these good efforts of the Court, I am still unable to agree with its interpretation of the Fourth Amendment.

My basic objection is twofold: (1) I do not believe that the words of the Amendment will bear the meaning given them by today's decision, and (2) I do not believe that it is the proper role of this Court to rewrite the Amendment in order "to bring it into harmony with the times" and thus reach a result that many people believe to be desirable.

While I realize that an argument based on the meaning of words lacks the scope, and no doubt the appeal, of broad policy discussions and philosophical discourses on such nebulous subjects as privacy, for me the language of the Amendment is the crucial place to look in construing a written document such as our Constitution. The Fourth Amendment says that

> "The right of the people to be secure in their persons, houses, papers, and effects, against unreasonable searches and seizures, shall not be violated, and no Warrants shall issue, but upon probable cause, supported by Oath or affirmation, and particularly describing the place to be searched, and the persons or things to be seized."

The first clause protects "persons, houses, papers, and effects, against unreasonable searches and seizures . . . ." These words connote the idea of tangible things with size, form, and weight, things capable of being searched, seized, or both. The second clause of the Amendment still further establishes its Framers' purpose to limit its protection to tangible things by providing that no warrants shall issue but those "particularly describing the place to be searched and the person or things to be seized." A conversation overheard by eavesdropping whether by plain snooping or wiretapping, is not tangible and, under the normally accepted meanings of the words, can neither be searched nor seized. In addition the language of the second clause indicates that the Amendment refers to something not only tangible so it can be seized but to something already in existence so it can be described. Yet the Court's interpretation would have the Amendment apply to overhearing future conversations which by their very nature are nonexistent until they take place. How can one "describe" a future conversation, and if not, how can a magistrate issue a warrant to eavesdrop one in the future? It is argued that information showing what is expected to be said is sufficient to limit the boundaries of what later can be admitted into evidence; but does such general information really meet the specific language of the Amendment which says "particularly describing"? Rather than using language in a completely artificial way, I must conclude that the Fourth Amendment simply does not apply to eavesdropping.

Tapping telephone wires, of course, was an unknown possibility at the time the Fourth Amendment was adopted. But eavesdropping (and wiretapping is nothing more than eavesdropping by telephone) was, as even the majority opinion in *Berger,* supra, recognized, "an ancient practice which at common law was condemned as a nuisance. IV Blackstone, Commentaries § 168. In those days the eavesdropper listened by naked ear under the eaves of houses or their windows, or beyond their walls seeking out private discourse." 388 U.S., at 45, 87 S.Ct., at 1876. There can be no doubt that the Framers were aware of this practice, and if they had desired to outlaw or restrict the use of evidence obtained by eavesdropping, I believe that they would have used the appropriate language to do so in the Fourth Amendment. They certainly would not have left such a task to the ingenuity of language-stretching judges. No one, it seems to me, can read the debates on the Bill of Rights without reaching the conclusion that its Framers and critics well knew the meaning of the words they used, what they would be understood to mean by others, their scope and their limitations. Under these circumstances it strikes me as a charge against their scholarship, their common sense and their candor to give to the Fourth Amendment's language the eavesdropping meaning the Court imputes to it today.

I do not deny that common sense requires and that this Court often has said that the Bill of Rights' safeguards should be given a liberal construction. This principle, however, does not justify construing the search and seizure amendment as applying to eavesdropping or the "seizure" of conversations. The Fourth Amendment was aimed directly at the abhorred practice of breaking in, ransacking and seaching homes and other buildings and seizing peoples' personal belongings without warrants issued by magistrates. The Amendment deserves, and this Court has given it, a liberal construction in order to protect against warrantless searches of buildings and seizures of tangible personal effects. But until today this Court has refused to say that eavesdropping comes within the ambit of Fourth Amendment restrictions. . . .

Goldman v. United States, is an example of this Court's traditional refusal to consider eavesdropping as being covered by the Fourth Amendment. There federal agents used a detectaphone, which was placed on the wall of an adjoining room, to listen to the conversation of a defendant carried on in his private office and intended to be confined within the four walls of the room. This Court, referring to *Olmstead,* found no Fourth Amendment violation.

It should be noted that the Court in *Olmstead* based its decision squarely on the fact that wiretapping or eavesdropping does not violate the Fourth Amendment. As shown, supra, in the cited quotation from the case, the Court went to great pains to examine the actual language of the Amendment and found that the words used simply could not be stretched to cover eavesdropping. That there was no trespass was not the determinative factor, and indeed the Court in citing Hester v. United States, indicated that even where there was a trespass the Fourth Amendment does not automatically apply to evidence obtained by "hearing or sight." The *Olmstead* majority characterized *Hester* as holding "that the testimony of two officers of the law who trespassed on the defendant's land, concealed themselves 100 yards away from his house, and saw him come out and hand a bottle of whiskey to another, was not inadmissible. While there was a trespass, there was no search of person, house, papers, or effects." Thus the clear holding of the *Olmstead* and *Goldman* cases, undiluted by any question of trespass, is that eavesdropping, in both its original and modern forms, is not violative of the Fourth Amendment. . . . .

Thus, I think that although the Court attempts to convey the impression that for some reason today *Olmstead* and *Goldman* are no longer good law, it must face up to the fact that these cases have never been overruled or even "eroded." It is the Court's opinions in this case and *Berger* which for the first time since 1790, when the Fourth Amendment was adopted, have declared that eavesdropping is subject to Fourth Amendment restrictions and that conversation can be "seized." I must align myself with all those judges who up to this year have never been able to impute such a meaning to the words of the Amendment.

Since I see no way in which the words of the Fourth Amendment can be construed to apply to eavesdropping, that closes the matter for me. In interpreting the Bill of Rights, I willingly go as far as a liberal construction of the language takes me, but I simply cannot in good conscience give a meaning to words which they have never before been thought to have and which they certainly do not have in common ordinary usage. I will not distort the words of the Amendment in order to "keep the Constitution up to date" or "to bring it into harmony with the times." It was never meant for this Court to have such power, which in effect would make us a continuously functioning constitutional convention.

With this decision the Court has completed, I hope, its rewriting of the Fourth Amendment, which started only recently when the Court began referring incessantly to the Fourth Amendment not so much as a law against *unreasonable* searches and seizures as one to protect an individual's privacy. By clever word juggling the Court finds it plausible to argue that language aimed specifically at searches and seizures of things that can be searched and seized may, to protect privacy, be applied to eavesdropped evidence of conversations that can neither be searched nor seized. Few things happen to an individual that do not affect his privacy in one way or another. Thus, by arbitrarily substituting the Court's language, designed to protect privacy, for the Constitution's language, designed to protect against unreasonable searches and seizures, the Court has made the Fourth Amendment its vehicle for holding all laws violative of the Constitution which offend the Court's broadest concept of privacy. As I said in Griswold v. State of Connecticut, "The Court talks about a constitutional 'right of privacy' as though there is some constitutional provision or provisions forbidding any law ever to be passed which might abridge the 'privacy' of individuals. But there is not." I made clear in that dissent my fear of the dangers involved when this Court uses the "broad, abstract and ambiguous concept" of "privacy" as a "comprehensive substitute for the Fourth Amendment's guarantee against 'unreasonable searches and seizures.' "

The Fourth Amendment protects privacy only to the extent that it prohibits unreasonable searches and seizures of "persons, houses, papers and effects." No general right is created by the Amendment so as to give this Court the unlimited power to hold unconstitutional everything which affects privacy. Certainly the Framers, well acquainted as they were with the excesses of governmental power, did not intend to grant this Court such omnipotent lawmaking authority as that. The history of governments proves that it is dangerous to freedom to repose such powers in courts.

For these reasons I respectfully dissent.

NOTES

1. Many courts have used Justice Harlan's concurring opinion in *Katz* as if it expressed the majority viewpoint. Thus they have stated that the Fourth Amendment offers protection when an individual has (1) an actual (subjective) expectation of privacy, and when (2) that expectation is "reasonable." Even Justice Stewart, who wrote the *Katz* majority opinion, has occasionally paraphrased the *Katz* analysis by referring to Harlan's formulation. Today the Supreme Court sometimes substitutes the word "legitimate" in place of the word "reasonable" to indicate that the Fourth Amendment is implicated only if society makes a value judgment that an expectation of privacy is worthy of protection.

2. To say that government has intruded upon a reasonable expectation of privacy is not to say that it has violated the Fourth Amendment. Rather it is merely to say that the government has engaged in a search or a seizure within the meaning of the amendment. The remaining issue, then, is whether such conduct was reasonable. Sometimes, however, courts will use the term "violation of a reasonable expectation of privacy" to indicate that the government has engaged in a search or seizure *and* that such Fourth Amendment activity was unreasonable.

3. With the demise of a "trespass" as an essential element of a search or a seizure, new challenges to government conduct may now be brought under the Fourth Amendment. Consider again *Katz*-inspired modification of the doctrines of plain view (Section H), abandonment (Section K) and open fields (Section J).

Conversely, with emphasis upon privacy rather than property, government lawyers sometimes argue that no search or seizure has occurred in cases in which, before *Katz*, all would have characterized the government's

actions as a search or a seizure and the only issue would have been its reasonableness.   Thus in Marshall v. Barlows' (Section M) the government argued that its inspection of factories and other workplaces—including places
closed to the general public—did not constitute a search because the employer knowingly exposed to its employees the areas which were to be inspected.
The *Barlow* Court rejected the argument, reasoning that vis-à-vis members
of the public and inspectors, the employer retained a reasonable expectation
of privacy.

4.   In United States v. Miller, 425 U.S. 435, 96 S.Ct. 1619 (1976), a
federal prosecutor utilized the grand jury to subpoena records from two
banks pertaining to Miller's accounts. The Court stated that one who engages in commercial transactions utilizing banking facilities has no reasonable expectation of privacy in the papers, so that he can make no claim under the Fourth Amendment. The "depositor takes the risk, in revealing his
affairs to another, that the information will be conveyed by that person to
the government."   The Court attributed no legal significance to the fact
that it is the government itself, under the new Bank Secrecy Act, upheld in
California Bankers Assn. v. Shultz, 416 U.S. 21, 94 S.Ct. 1494 (1974), which
requires the bank to keep the records. "Many banks traditionally kept permanent records of their depositors' accounts" even before the Bank Secrecy
Act compelled that practice.

The result in *Miller* is in accord with the result in the typical state case
where the target of an investigation seeks to quash a grand jury subpoena
duces tecum issued to his bank or some other third party. Such a person
typically is told that he has no standing to complain about the breadth of
the subpoena or any other alleged irregularity.

In Rakas v. Illinois, Chapter 6, the Court emphasized that whether a
person has "standing" depends upon whether he has a reasonable expectation of privacy. Under this view the *Miller* approach to the bank records
issue is not different from a "standing to object" approach.

5.   Consider application of the *Katz* formulation to the following situations to determine whether a search or a seizure has taken place. Remember that in doing so an affirmative response does not necessarily mean that
either prior judicial approval or full probable cause or both is required.
Some Fourth Amendment intrusions may be so minimal, and the benefit to
society so great, that the intrusion could be deemed reasonable without
prior judicial approval and upon a relatively small quantity of data.

(a) An officer places a "tracking beeper" on the underside of a car
and is thus able to electronically monitor the whereabouts of the vehicle,
without overhearing or recording any conversation.

(b) An officer conducts visual surveillance of a vehicle by "tailing" the
car in his own unmarked police vehicle. Or he uses a helicopter to keep
watch on the suspect's movements.

(c) An officer takes a small paint scraping from a car parked on a
public street. See Cardwell v. Lewis, 417 U.S. 583, 94 S.Ct. 2464 (1974).

(d) As part of an investigation, an officer places a key in the lock of a
door and turns the key to determine that it fits. He then withdraws the
key without pushing the door open. See United States v. Portillo-Reyes,
529 F.2d 844 (9th Cir. 1975). Compare Thomas v. State, 145 Ga.App. 69,
243 S.E.2d 250 (1978); People v. Trull, 64 Ill.App.3d 385, 20 Ill.Dec. 960,
380 N.E.2d 1169 (1978).

(e) A federal agent at an airport uses a specially trained dog to sniff luggage in order to detect the presence of marijuana.

(f) An undercover agent attends a meeting, held in a private home, but open to the public, the subject of which is police spying.

(g) Postal authorities, before delivering a citizen's mail, copy return addresses, postmarks, and other identifying features.

For decisions on these and related topics, consult Volume 1 of LaFave, Search and Seizure (1978), particularly §§ 2.2 and 2.7.

6.   The question of whether electronic recording of a conversation with one-party consent is a search or seizure is treated in United States v. White (Chapter 5, infra).   The same issue with respect to pen registers is also treated in Chapter 5.

7.   In the welfare home visit decision, Wyman v. James (Section M, note 3, supra), an alternative basis for the holding was that the caseworker's conduct did not constitute a search within the meaning of the Fourth Amendment.   Over a strong dissent, the Court suggested that the purpose of the governmental conduct is relevant to the threshold question, "What is a search?"   How can it possibly be said that certain non-consensual governmental entries into a home do not constitute activity which is subject to the Fourth Amendment requirement of reasonableness?

Chapter 5

WIRETAPPING AND ELECTRONIC SURVEILLANCE

A. AN OVERVIEW

This chapter concerns electronic surveillance and recording of conversations. Wiretapping is the prime example of electronic surveillance conducted without the consent of any party to the conversation. Such non-consensual interception of communications sometimes is accomplished without a trespass against the property of any party to the conversation. At other times a trespass is made to place a "bug" or monitoring device on the telephone itself. Such a device can also be placed in a home or a business to effectuate the non-consensual overhearing and recording of non-telephonic conversations within the premises. Katz v. United States, ch. 4, Sec. N, provides an example of non-consensual electronic surveillance.

Distinguished from non-consensual surveillance is the electronic auditing and recording of a conversation with the consent of one party to the conversation, typified by United States v. White (Section C, infra). Usually the consenting party is "wired for sound," so that the conversation can be overheard and recorded by third-parties (often by law enforcement agents with whom the consenting party is working). Sometimes the consenting party carries the transmitter, hidden on his person, onto the property of the suspect and there activates the device to broadcast or record conversations between himself and the suspect.

In Olmstead v. United States, 277 U.S. 438, 48 S.Ct. 564 (1928), the Supreme Court held that wiretapping which was accomplished without a trespass was neither a search nor a seizure within the meaning of the Fourth Amendment. Over a strong and now famous dissent of Justice Brandeis, the five-man majority refused to exclude the fruits of such federal non-trespassory wiretapping from a federal prosecution even though it assumed that such wiretapping violated state penal laws. Thereafter, as noted in *Katz*, the fruits of non-consensual overhearing were excluded on Fourth Amendment grounds only if effectuated by a trespass (however slight) against property.

Through the Federal Communcations Act of 1934, in 47 U.S.C. 605, Congress prohibited interception and divulgence of certain communications. The statute was interpreted to apply to both interstate and intrastate telephonic communications. The Supreme Court engrafted upon it an exclusionary rule so as to prevent use of such communications as evidence in federal courts. However, not until 1968 did violation of this federal statute by state agents result in the exclusion of evidence in state courts. The history of this statute is told in Lee v. Florida, 392 U.S. 378, 88 S.Ct. 2096 (1968), and in Carr, The Law of Electronic Surveillance § 1.02 (1977).

Many states prohibited wiretapping, and some utilized an exclusionary rule to enforce this state prohibition. New York prohibited wiretapping except by court order. In Berger v. New York, 388 U.S. 41, 87 S.Ct. 1873 (1967), a case which involved trespassory wiretapping, (and, therefore, was within the ambit of the Fourth Amendment even before the *Katz* revolution), the United States Supreme Court invalidated the New York statute. The Court noted several defects in the statute: (1) The statute did not require a showing that any *particular* offense was being committed and it did not mandate that the conversation to be seized must be described with specificity. (2) There were inadequate limits upon the duration of the execution of the warrant. On a single showing of probable cause, conversations could be seized, within the discretion of the officer, over a sixty-day period, without even a requirement that the wiretapping cease after the evidence sought had been obtained. (3) The warrant could be renewed without a showing that probable cause still existed. (4) The statute did not require that notice be given to the monitored party even *after* the conversation was seized, and it did not require a showing as to why the decision not to give notice in an individual case was justified. (5) The statute did not provide for the filing of a "return" with the court indicating what conversations had been overheard.

Although *Berger* was soon eclipsed by *Katz* and by new federal wiretapping legislation (Section B2, infra) it remains important in so far as courts must judge claimed deficiencies of the 1968 federal legislation against the standards articulated in *Berger*.

NOTES

In the decades before adoption of Title III of the 1968 Omnibus Crime Act, Section B2, infra, much of the debate over proposed statutes which provided for court-authorized wiretapping focused upon the experience in the State of New York. Until *Berger*, supra, invalidated the New York law, court-authorized electronic surveillance was used in New York for many years. Consider the following views of the New York experience.

1. Justice William O. Douglas of the United States Supreme Court, in his book "An Almanac of Liberty" (1954), stated (at p. 355):

"During 1952, there were in New York City alone at least 58,000 orders issued which allowed wire tapping—over 150 a day every day in the year. The New York system has in practice been oppressive; it has been used as the means whereby police have obtained guarded confidences of people and used the information for corrupt purposes."

". . . wire tapping is a blight on the civil liberties of the citizen."

Mr. Edward S. Silver, District Attorney of Kings County, New York, in an appearance before a Judiciary Committee of the House of Representatives (on April 19, 1955), made the following reply to Justice Douglas' accusations:

"I made a check and here are the actual facts: For the year 1952, there was a total of 480 wiretaps in the city of New York.

Not 58,000, but 480. . . . If there were 58,000 orders procured in the city of New York or any other comparable area, I would be for taking the right away from everybody. Order or no order, if there was such an abuse, but it is not so." [1]

In an effort to ascertain the true facts, Justice Douglas was asked whether he would be willing to appear before the House Committee and reveal the source of his information. In response, Justice Douglas wrote a letter to the Committee in which he said, in part:

"The person who made the New York City study for me is Sidney M. Davis, Esq., 1501 Broadway, New York City. . . . Mr. Davis is an exceedingly competent person in whom I had and still have great confidence. . . . The report . . . seemed to me to be a conservative one. And I am sure it was obtained from competent and reliable sources." [2]

What were Mr. Davis' sources? Here is what he himself told the committee a few days later, when questioned by the chairman of the Committee, Emanuel Cellar, and by Representatives Keating and Scott:

Mr. Davis:

". . . approximately 3 years ago . . . Justice Douglas' office called me in New York where I was practicing law and asked me to make some inquiries as to the extent of wire tapping in New York. I believe it was in connection with getting some material together for a speech which the Justice was then going to make. I took some time off and went around to see some people and talk to them . . . people whom I regarded as responsible, reliable, and well informed people in this field. I recollect seeing some police officials, some people in a number of offices of the various clerks of the county courts, or supreme courts, and speaking to some members of the bar, and I received a number of estimates from them. . . . I was told variously, that there were anywhere from 1000 to somewhat in excess of that, wiretaps a week going on in New York City at that time . . . and I was given an estimate of 58,000 wiretaps for that year in New York City."

The Chairman:

"When you say 'wiretaps' does that mean legal wiretaps, as well as illegal wiretaps, or do you mean legal wiretaps?"

Mr. Davis:

"To the best of my recollection, sir, and it is a few years back, that meant wiretaps, in general."

Mr. Chairman:

"That is, it took in all types of wiretaps, those with court orders as well as those without a court order?"

Mr. Davis:

"Yes, sir". * * *

---

1. See Hearings before Subcommittee 5 of the Committee on the Judiciary of the 84th Congress (April 19, 1955), pp. 99–100.

2. P. 144, Hearings.

Mr. Keating:

"Who were these people you saw? Can you identify any of them?"

Mr. Davis:

"Well, it is about 3 years back, Congressman, and I can't at the moment remember exactly who I talked to. . . ."

Mr. Keating:

"You mentioned police officials. Could you identify any police officials with whom you talked?"

Mr. Davis:

"No, I can't." * * *

Mr. Keating:

"How much time did you take off to do this assignment?"

Mr. Davis:

"I would guess about a day or two."

Mr. Keating:

"You said you spoke to members of the bar. Could you identify any of those members of the bar with whom you discussed it?"

Mr. Davis:

"No, Congressman." * * *

Mr. Scott:

"How many people did you talk to, altogether?"

Mr. Davis:

"I would guess somewhere between 6 people and 10 people, sir."

Mr. Scott:

"And yet you can't remember, though it has been only 3 years, a single person with whom you talked?"

Mr. Davis:

"No, Congressman; I can't." [3]

Mr. Frank S. Hogan, District Attorney of New York County commented upon this matter, as follows, in his appearance at a public hearing conducted by the New York State Commission of Investigation on April 5, 1960 (p. 7 of transcript):

"When you get a United States Supreme Court Justice making such an unsupported and ridiculous statement—and mind you, he hasn't retracted it to this day—and his figures are off by at least 10,000 per cent, it is well to examine carefully the promiscuous, hearsay contentions of lesser personages who find that this kind of mathematical shocker readily attracts the ear of the community. * * *

". . . A statewide survey by the New York District Attorneys' Association, conducted some years ago, revealed about 500 legal wiretaps annually in the entire state. With respect to the alleged illegal wiretaps by law enforcement personnel, I can only say

3. Pp. 202–208, Hearings.

Inbau et al.,–Cs.Cr.Proc.2d Ed. UCB—11

that in my 18 years of experience as District Attorney I have never received any evidence or even a complaint that a police officer has used this information for corrupt, extorsive or coercive reasons, and there wouldn't be any other reason for using it illegally."

2. Consider the following comment by Mr. Edward S. Silver, District Attorney, Kings County, N.Y., in his article "Wiretapping and Electronic Surveillance" in 55 J.Crim.L., C. & P.S. 114 (1964):

"In *Olmstead*, the 'great dissenter,' Justice Holmes, was absolutely right when he said that officers of the law should not violate the law in fighting crime. Nobody should dispute this. But the principle announced in *Olmstead* has no bearing on a situation such as exists under the laws of New York State and other similar statutes of other states, as well as in proposed federal legislation presently under consideration by Congress. *Olmstead* has no application where a state constitution or a state statute *authorizes* district attorneys and high ranking police officials to tap wires under specified conditions and with *meaningful* safeguards to our liberties."

B. NON–CONSENSUAL WIRETAPPING AND ELECTRONIC SURVEILLANCE

1. THE CONSTITUTION

KATZ v. UNITED STATES

Supreme Court of the United States, 1967.
389 U.S. 347, 88 S.Ct. 507.

[There should be a reconsideration of this case, the text of which is in Chapter 4, Section N.]

2. THE FEDERAL STATUTE

The "Omnibus Crime Control and Safe Streets Act of 1968" contained provisions for the control and authorization of wiretapping and electronic surveillance (18 U.S.C. §§ 2510–2520). Congress prohibited these activities in the absence of judicial authorization and provided fines and imprisonment for violation of the prohibitions. The Act exempts from its prohibitions the interception or surveillance of communications when one party to the conversation consents to the recording or overhearing.

The Act specifically provides, in part, as follows:

"§ 2512. **Manufacture, distribution, possession, and advertising of wire or oral communication intercepting devices prohibited**

[Text omitted.]

"§ 2513.   Confiscation of wire or oral communication intercepting devices

[Text omitted.]

"§ 2514.   Immunity of witnesses

[Subsequent to enactment, this section was amended so that immunity is now granted pursuant to the general federal immunity statute, 18 U.S.C. § 6002.]

"§ 2515.   Prohibition of use as evidence of intercepted wire or oral communications

"Whenever any wire or oral communication has been intercepted, no part of the contents of such communication and no evidence derived therefrom may be received in evidence in any trial, hearing, or other proceeding in or before any court, grand jury, department, officer, agency, regulatory body, legislative committee, or other authority of the United States, a State, or a political subdivision thereof if the disclosure of that information would be in violation of this chapter.

Authorization for interception of wire or oral communication and for disclosure and use of its fruits may be sought only on the authority of the Attorney General or a specially designated assistant. Use of the electronic overhearing is limited to specified crimes.

The statute further provides:

"§ 2518.   Procedure for interception of wire or oral communications

"(1) Each application for an order authorizing or approving the interception of a wire or oral communication shall be made in writing upon oath or affirmation to a judge of competent jurisdiction and shall state the applicant's authority to make such application. Each application shall include the following information:

"(a) the identity of the investigative or law enforcement officer making the application, and the officer authorizing the application;

"(b) a full and complete statement of facts and circumstances relied upon by the applicant, to justify his belief that an order should be issued, including (i) details as to the particular offense that has been, is being, or is about to be committed, (ii) a particular description of the nature and location of the facilities from which or the place where the communication is to be intercepted, (iii) a particular description of the type of communications sought to be intercepted, (iv) the identity of the person, if known, committing the offense and whose communications are to be intercepted;

"(c) a full and complete statement as to whether or not other investigative procedures have been tried and failed or why they reasonably appear to be unlikely to succeed if tried or to be too dangerous;

"(d) a statement of the period of time for which the interception is required to be maintained. If the nature of the investigation is such that the authorization for interception should not automatically terminate when the described type of communication has been first obtained, a particular description of facts establishing probable cause to believe that additional communications of the same type will occur thereafter;

"(e) a full and complete statement of the facts concerning all previous applications known to the individual authorizing and making the application, made to any judge for authorization to intercept, or for approval of interceptions of, wire or oral communications involving any of the same persons, facilities or places specified in the application, and the action taken by the judge on each such application; and

"(f) where the application is for the extension of an order, a statement setting forth the results thus far obtained from the interception, or a reasonable explanation of the failure to obtain such results.

"(2) The judge may require the applicant to furnish additional testimony or documentary evidence in support of the application.

"(3) Upon such application the judge may enter an ex parte order, as requested or as modified, authorizing or approving interception of wire or oral communications within the territorial jurisdiction of the court in which the judge is sitting, if the judge determines on the basis of the facts submitted by the applicant that—

"(a) there is probable cause for belief that an individual is committing, has committed, or is about to commit a particular offense enumerated in section 2516 of this chapter;

"(b) there is probable cause for belief that particular communications concerning that offense will be obtained through such interception;

"(c) normal investigative procedures have been tried and have failed or reasonably appear to be unlikely to succeed if tried or to be too dangerous;

"(d) there is probable cause for belief that the facilities from which, or the place where, the wire or oral communications are to be intercepted are being used, or are about to be used, in connection with the commission of such offense, or are leased to, listed in the name of, or commonly used by such person.

"(4) Each order authorizing or approving the interception of any wire or oral communication shall specify—

"(a) the identity of the person, if known, whose communications are to be intercepted;

"(b) the nature and location of the communications facilities as to which, or the place where, authority to intercept is granted;

"(c) a particular description of the type of communication sought to be intercepted, and a statement of the particular offense to which it relates;

"(d) the identity of the agency authorized to intercept the communications, and of the person authorizing the application; and

"(e) the period of time during which such interception is authorized, including a statement as to whether or not the interception shall automatically terminate when the described communication has been first obtained. An order authorizing the interception of a wire or oral communication under this chapter shall, upon request of the applicant, direct that a communication common carrier, landlord, custodian or other person shall furnish the applicant forthwith all information, facilities, and technical assistance necessary to accomplish the interception unobtrusively and with a minimum of interference with the services that such carrier, landlord, custodian, or person is according the person whose communications are to be intercepted. Any communication common carrier, landlord, custodian or other person furnishing such facilities or technical assistance shall be compensated therefor by the applicant at the prevailing rates.

"(5) No order entered under this section may authorize or approve the interception of any wire or oral communication for any period longer than is necessary to achieve the objective of the authorization, nor in any event longer than thirty days. Extensions of an order may be granted, but only upon application for an extension made in accordance with subsection (1) of this section and the court making the findings required by subsection (3) of this section. The period of extension shall be no longer than the authorizing judge deems necessary to achieve the purposes for which it was granted and in no event for longer than thirty days. Every order and extension thereof shall contain a provision that the authorization to intercept shall be executed as soon as practicable, shall be conducted in such a way as to minimize the interception of communications not otherwise subject to interception under this chapter, and must terminate upon attainment of the authorized objective, or in any event in thirty days.

"(6) Whenever an order authorizing interception is entered pursuant to this chapter, the order may require reports to be made to the judge who issued the order showing what progress has been made toward achievement of the authorized objective and the need for continued interception. Such reports shall be made at such intervals as the judge may require.

The Act contains provisions for emergencies in national security and organized crime cases which allow interceptions without judicial authorization where such authorization is sought within forty-eight hours of the beginning of interception.

Recording must be done in a manner to protect against editing and alteration and the recordings must be sealed under judicial supervision. Preservation of applications, orders and recordings is required. Persons who are subjects of overhearings are to be notified of that fact but this requirement may be excused by the court. A similar notification requirement exists with respect to persons against whom applications are filed and denied. Pre-trial (ten days) discovery of the application and court order is required. Anyone whose statements were overheard and anyone against whom the overhearing was directed is granted standing to suppress the intercepted communications at any kind of proceeding.

Civil damages for violations of the Act are specified. The Act also provides a mechanism for gathering appropriate statistical information on both state and federal overhearings.

NOTES

1. In United States v. Giordano, 416 U.S. 505, 94 S.Ct. 1820 (1974), the Supreme Court ruled that only the Attorney General or a specially designated assistant attorney general could authorize a federal wiretap application. Attorney General Mitchell's Executive Assistant was not an assistant attorney general, and hence in those cases in which he authorized the application without Mitchell's approval, the wiretap was unlawful. Dozens of hearings have been held around the country to determine whether Mitchell personally approved particular applications. See also United States v. Chavez, 416 U.S. 562, 94 S.Ct. 1849 (1974), which holds that the form of the consent is not controlling if the Attorney General or a specially designated assistant attorney general actually approved the application.

2. The broad range of issues arising under the federal statute are discussed and resolved in United States v. Baynes, 400 F.Supp. 285 (E.D.Pa. 1975), aff'd 517 F.2d 1399 (3d Cir. 1975). The district court opinion is a good starting point for research of statutory issues which commonly arise.

3. The federal wiretap and electronic surveillance statute has been construed and upheld by several federal courts. State courts have upheld similar state statutes. See Commonwealth v. Vitello, 327 N.E.2d 819 (Mass.1975). Many states, however, have not adopted laws in conformity with the federal legislation, so that, many states do not permit any electronic interception of communications but instead require the consent of one party to record a conversation. See Section C, Note 5, infra.

4. Suppose a state law prohibits warrantless electronic recording of conversations absent the consent of *every* party. Does a federal prosecutor or agent violate state law when he or she arranges a recording with one-party consent? 18 U.S.C.A. § 2511(2)(c) states that it is not unlawful "under this chapter for a person acting under color of law to intercept a wire or oral communication where such person is a party to the communication or one of the parties to the communication has given prior consent to such interception." One court, emphasizing the language "under this chapter" has held that § 2511 does not affirmatively authorize such conduct so as to pre-empt state laws, saying, "It is not clear, therefore, that Congress showed an intention to displace more rigorous requirements found in state laws." United States v. Keen, 508 F.2d 986 (9th Cir. 1974).

Most federal cases, however, have held that even if federal overhearings and recordings violate state laws, no exclusionary rule is necessary where there was no violation of federal statutes or the United States Constitution. See, e. g., United States v. Infelice, 506 F.2d 1358 (7th Cir. 1974); Olmstead v. United States, 277 U.S. 438, 48 S.Ct. 564 (1928).

Although no exclusionary rule need be applied in the federal courts for violation of state electronic eavesdropping laws, could a federal officer be charged with a violation of state law if he acted in contravention of a state electronic eavesdropping statute? The *Olmstead* decision, supra, left this issue open. Presumably such a state prosecution would be removed to federal court and the United States District Court would make the decision.

5. All records arising from *illegal* eavesdropping or wiretapping concerning which a criminal defendant has standing to object must be disclosed to him. Neither grounds of national security nor the protection of third parties justifies the withholding of such materials, although the court may place defendants and counsel under protective orders against unwarranted disclosure of the records. See Alderman v. United States, 394 U.S. 165, 89 S.Ct. 961 (1969). The Justice Department, on several occasions where illegal wiretapping occurred, has dismissed prosecutions rather than disclosing wiretap materials to defendants. (It is difficult to know how many of these dismissals were truly based upon "national security," and how many simply served to keep from public light either gross illegalities or other conduct which might prove embarrassing to law enforcement officials or to other members of the executive branch.)

A defendant is not entitled to disclosure until *after* it is established that he was a victim of illegal wiretapping. To make such a determination, a judge may conduct an *in camera* inspection of wiretap tapes and logs without disclosing such data to the accused. See Taglianetti v. United States, 394 U.S. 316, 89 S.Ct. 1099 (1969). Thus, an *in camera* inspection (without defendant's participation) is thought adequate to determine whether he was the victim of illegal wiretapping; but once that is shown, the accused must be allowed to inspect the materials to determine what part, if any, the illegality may have played in the building of the case against him.

6. Before the Act was amended in late 1978, the power of the President to authorize warrantless wiretapping for national security was left for the courts to decide. Section 2511 (3) stated that the "constitutional power of the president" to take such measures was not limited by the Act. In United States v. United States District Court, 407 U.S. 297, 92 S.Ct. 2125 (1972), the government sought to justify warrantless eavesdropping on the grounds that domestic security was involved. The Court held that the pro-

vision in 18 U.S.C. § 2511(3) that nothing in the chapter was deemed to limit the constitutional power of the President to take such action as necessary to protect the United States against overthrow of the Government was only a congressional disclaimer and an expression of neutrality. It did not grant authority. "[T]he statute is not a measure of the executive authority exercised in this case." The constitutional powers of the President are not found to override the requirements of the Fourth Amendment.

The Court also rejected the argument that internal security matters are too subtle and complex for judicial evaluation.

The Court emphasized the scope of its decision by pointing out it has expressed no opinion with respect to activities of foreign powers or their agents. Further, it recognized that Title Three of the Omnibus Crime Control and Safe Streets Act of 1968 does not apply to presidential action to meet domestic threats to national security and that there may be some changes by Congress so as to provide a lesser standard in dealing with domestic security surveillance. "Different standards may be compatible with the Fourth Amendment if they are reasonable both in relation to the legitimate need of Government for intelligence information and the protected rights of our citizens."

Congress subsequently passed and President Carter signed the Foreign Intelligence Surveillance Act of 1978, 50 U.S.C. §§ 1801–1811. A special warrant procedure is established for the interception, within the United States, of conversations to which a "United States person" is a party, where there is a probability that foreign intelligence, not available through other means, can be obtained. Executive certification of the necessity for such a wiretap is required. A special panel of judges, selected by the Chief Justice, is available to rule on requests for such wiretaps.

7. Pen registers are devices which record the telephone numbers which are dialed from a particular phone. They do not overhear or record conversations and do not indicate whether a call was completed. Their use does not involve any physical trespass against the property of the subscriber. According to the Supreme Court, governmental employment of such a device, without a warrant, violates neither Title III nor the Fourth Amendment. In Smith v. Maryland, 442 U.S. 735, 99 S.Ct. 2577 (1979), the Court held that a subscriber can have no "reasonable" or "legitimate" expectation of privacy as to the numbers dialed. Great emphasis was placed upon the widely known fact that telephone companies have and utilize devices which indicate what numbers are dialed from specifed telephones. Subscribers voluntarily expose to the telephone company the numbers dialed, just as they did in former days when they had to tell an operator what number to dial. They have "assumed the risk" that the telephone company will convey this information to the government. Justices Stewart, Marshall, and Brennan dissented in *Smith*. In United States v. New York Telephone Co., 434 U.S. 159, 98 S.Ct. 364 (1977), the Court held that a telephone company could be compelled to assist the government in the installation of pen registers, and also held that use of such devices does not violate the Act.

8. In Dalia v. United States, 441 U.S. 238, 99 S.Ct. 1682 (1979), the Court held that a judge or magistrate who issues a wiretap authorization under Title III can also authorize covert entry upon a person's property for the purpose of installing the monitoring device. The Court also held that explicit authorization for such entry need not appear in the wiretap order: "(W)e would promote empty formalism were we to require magistrates to

make explicit what unquestionably is implicit in bugging authorizations: that a covert entry, with its attendant interference with Fourth Amendment interest, may be necessary for the installation of surveillance equipment." Four justices dissented. (Today the Justice Department usually seeks express authorization for covert entries necessary for installation of surveillance equipment.)

UNITED STATES v. DONOVAN

Supreme Court of the United States, 1977.
429 U.S. 413, 97 S.Ct. 658.

MR. JUSTICE POWELL delivered the opinion of the Court.

*   *   *

. . . Pursuant to the Government's request, the District Court authorized for a period of 15 days the interception of gambling-related wire communications of Kotoch, Spaganlo, Florea, three named individuals other than the respondents, and "others as yet unknown," to and from the four listed telephones.

During the course of the wiretap, the Government learned that respondents Donovan, Robbins, and Buzzaco were discussing illegal gambling activities with the named subjects. On December 26, 1972, the Government applied for an extension of the initial intercept order. This time it sought authorization to intercept gambling-related conversations of Kotoch, Spaganlo, Florea, two other named individuals, and "others as yet unknown," but it did not identify respondents Donovan, Buzzaco, and Robbins in this second application. The District Court again authorized interception of gambling-related conversations for a maximum of 15 days.

On February 21, 1973, the Government submitted to the District Court a proposed order giving notice of the interceptions to 37 persons, a group which the Government apparently thought included all individuals who could be identified as having discussed gambling over the monitored telephones. The District Court signed the proposed order, and an inventory notice was served on the listed persons, including respondents Donovan, Buzzaco, and Robbins. On September 11, 1973, after the Government submitted the names of two additional persons whose identities allegedly had been omittted inadvertently from the initial list, the District Court entered an amended order giving notice to those individuals. As a result of what the Government labels "administrative oversight," respondents Merlo and Lauer were not included in either list of names and were never served with inventory notice.

. . . With respect to Merlo and Lauer, who were not known to the Government until after the December 26 application, the District Court suppressed all evidence derived from both intercept orders on the ground that they had not been served with inventory notice.

We turn first to the identification requirements of § 2518(1)(b)(iv). That provision requires a wiretap application to specify "the identity of the person, if known, committing the offense and whose communications are to be intercepted." In construing that language, this Court already has ruled that the Government is not required to identify an individual in the application unless it has probable cause to believe (i) that the individual is engaged in the criminal activity under investigation and (ii) that the individual's conversations will be intercepted over the target telephone. United States v. Kahn, 415 U.S. 143, 94 S.Ct. 977 (1974). The question at issue here is whether the Government is required to name *all* such individuals.

The United States argues that the most reasonable interpretation of the plain language of the statute is that the application must identify only the principal target of the investigation, who "will almost always be the individual whose phone is monitored." Brief for the United States, at 18. Under this interpretation, if the Government has reason to believe that an individual will use the target telephone to place or receive calls, and the Government has probable cause to believe that the individual is engaged in the criminal activity under investigation, the individual qualifies as a principal target and must be named in the wiretap application. On the other hand, an individual who uses a different telephone to place calls to or receive calls from the target telephone is not a principal target even if the Government has probable cause to believe that the individual is engaged in the criminal activity under investigation. In other words, whether one is a principal target of the investigation depends on whether one operates the target telephone to place or receive calls.

Whatever the merits of such a statutory scheme, we find little support for it in the language and structure of Title III or in the legislative history. The statutory language itself refers only to "the person, if known, committing the offense and whose communications are to be intercepted." That description is as applicable to a suspect placing calls to the target telephone as it is to a suspect placing calls from that telephone. . . . But nothing on the face of the statute suggests that Congress intended to remove from the identification requirement those suspects whose intercepted communications originated on a telephone other than that listed in the wiretap application.

Nor can we find support in the legislative history for the "principal target" interpretation. . . .

* * *

. . . . Congress included an identification requirement which on its face draws no distinction based on the telephone one uses, and the United States points to no evidence in the legislative history that supports such a distinction. Indeed, the legislative materials apparently contain no use of the term "principal target" or any discussion of a different treatment based on the telephone from which a suspect speaks. We therefore conclude that a wiretap application must name an individual if the Government has probable cause to believe that the individual is engaged in the criminal activity under investigation and expects to intercept the individual's conversations over the target telephone.

The other statutory provision at issue in this case is 18 U.S.C. § 2518(8)(d), which provides that the judge shall cause to be served on the persons named in the order or application an inventory, which must give notice of the entry of the order or application, state the disposition of the application, and indicate whether communications were intercepted. Although the statute mandates inventory notice only for persons named in the application or the order, the statute also provides that the judge may order similar notice to other parties to intercepted communications if he concludes that such action is in the interest of justice. Observing that this notice provision does not expressly require law enforcement authorities routinely to supply the judge with specific information upon which to exercise his discretion, the United States contends that it would be inappropriate to read such a requirement into the statute since the judge has the option of asking the law enforcement authorities for whatever information he requires.

Our reading of the legislative history of the discretionary notice provision in light of the purposes of Title III leads us to reject the Government's interpretation. As reported from the Judiciary Committee, section 2518(8)(d) contained only a provision mandating notice to the persons named in the application or the order; the discretionary notice provison was added by amendment on the floor of the Senate. In introducing that amendment, Senator Hart explained its purpose:

> "The amendment would give the judge who issued the order discretion to require notice to be served on other parties to intercepted conversations, even though such parties are not specifically named in the court order. The Berger and Katz decisions established that notice of surveillance is a constitutional requirement of any surveillance statute. It may be that the required notice must be served on all parties to intercepted communications. Since legitimate interests of privacy may make such notice to all parties undesirable, the amendment leaves the final determination to the judge."

In deciding whether legitimate privacy interests justify withholding inventory notice from parties to intercepted conversations, a judge is likely to require information and assistance beyond that contained in the application papers and the recordings of intercepted conversations made available by law enforcement authorities. No purpose is served by holding that those authorities have no routine duty to supply the judge with relevant information. The Court of Appeals for the Ninth Circuit recently confronted this problem of dual responsibility, and we adopt the balanced construction that court placed on § 2518(8)(d):

> "To discharge this obligation the judicial officer must have, at a minimum, knowledge of the particular categories into which fall all the individuals whose conversations have been intercepted. Thus, while precise identification of each party to an intercepted conversation is not required, a description

of the general class, or classes, which they comprise is essential to enable the judge to determine whether additional information is necessary for a proper evaluation of the interests of the various parties. Furthermore, although the judicial officer has the duty to cause the filing of the inventory [notice], it is abundantly clear that the prosecution has greater access to and familiarity with the intercepted communications. Therefore we feel justified in imposing upon the latter the duty to classify all those whose conversations have been intercepted, and to transmit this information to the judge. Should the judge desire more information regarding these classes in order to exercise his statutory § 2518(8)(d) discretion, . . . the government is also required to furnish such information as is available to it." **United States v. Chun, 503 F.2d 533, 540 (9th Cir. 1974).**

We agree with the Ninth Circuit that this allegation of responsibility best serves the purposes of Title III.

Currently, the policy of the Justice Department is to provide the issuing judge with the name of every person who has been overheard as to whom there is any reasonable possibility of indictment. Because it fails to assure that the necessary range of information will be before the issuing judge, this policy does not meet the test set out in *Chun.* Moreover, where, as here, the Government chooses to supply the issuing judge with a list of all identifiable persons rather than a description of the classes into which those persons fall, the list must be complete. Applying these principles, we find that the Government did not comply adequately with § 2518(8)(d), since the names of respondents Merlo and Lauer were not included on the purportedly complete list of identifiable persons submitted to the issuing judge.

We turn now to the question whether the District Court properly suppressed evidence derived from the wiretaps at issue solely because of the failure of the law enforcement authorities to comply fully with the provisions of §§ 2518(1)(b)(iv) and 2518(8)(d). Section 2515 expressly prohibits the use at trial, and at certain other proceedings, of the contents of any intercepted wire communication or any evidence derived therefrom "if the disclosure of that information would be in violation of this chapter." The circumstances that trigger suppression under § 2515 are in turn enumerated in § 2518(10)(a):

"(i) the communication was unlawfully intercepted;

"(ii) the order of authorization or approval under which it was intercepted is insufficient on its face; or

"(iii) the interception was not made in conformity with the order of authorization or approval."

There is no basis on the facts of this case to suggest that the authorization orders are facially insufficient, or that the interception was not conducted in conformity with the orders. Thus, only § 2518(10)(a)(i) is relevant: were the communications "unlawfully intercepted" given the violations of §§ 2518(1)(b)(iv) and 2518(8)(d)?

Resolution of that question must begin with United States v. Giordano (1974) and United States v. Chavez (1974). Those cases hold that "[not] every failure to comply fully with any requirement provided in Title III would render the interception of wire or oral communications 'unlawful.'" United States v. Chavez. To the contrary, suppression is required only for a "failure to satisfy any of those statutory requirements that directly and substantially implement the congressional intention to limit the use of intercept procedures to those situations clearly calling for the employment of this extraordinary device." United States v. Giordano.

* * *

As to § 2518(1)(b)(iv), the issue is whether the identification in an intercept application of all those likely to be overheard in incriminating conversations plays a "substantive role" with respect to judicial authorization of intercept orders and consequently imposes a limitation on the use of intercept procedures. The statute provides that the issuing judge may approve an intercept application if he determines that normal investigative techniques have failed or are unlikely to succeed and there is probable cause to believe that: (i) an individual is engaged in criminal activity; (ii) particular communications concerning the offense will be obtained through interception; and (iii) the target facilities are being used in connection with the specified criminal activity. That determination is based on the "full and complete statement" of relevant facts supplied by law enforcement authorities. If, after evaluating the statutorily enumerated factors in light of the information contained in the application, the judge concludes that the wiretap order should issue, the failure to identify additional persons who are likely to be overheard engaging in incriminating conversations could hardly invalidate an otherwise lawful judicial authorization. The intercept order may issue only if the issuing judge determines that the statutory factors are present, and the failure to name additional targets in no way detracts from the sufficiency of those factors.

This case is unlike *Giordano*, where failure to satisfy the statutory requirement of prior approval by specified Justice Department officials bypassed a congressionally imposed limitation on the use of the intercept procedure. The Court there noted that it was reasonable to believe that requiring prior approval from senior officials in the Justice Department "would inevitably foreclose resort to wiretapping in various situations where investigative personnel would otherwise seek intercept authority from the court and the court would very likely authorize its use." Here, however, the statutorily imposed preconditions to judicial authorization were satisfied, and the issuing judge was simply unaware that additional persons might be overheard engaging in incriminating conversations. In no meaningful sense can it be said that the presence of that information as to additional targets would have precluded judicial authorization of the intercept. Rather, this case resembles *Chavez*, where we held that a wiretap was not unlawful simply because the issuing judge was incorrectly informed as to which designated official had authorized the application. The *Chavez* intercept was lawful because the Justice Department had performed its task of prior approval, and the instant intercept is lawful because the application provided sufficient information to enable the issuing judge to determine that the statutory preconditions were satisfied.

Finally, we note that nothing in the legislative history suggests that Congress intended this broad identification requirement to play "a central, or even functional, role in guarding against unwarranted use of wiretapping or electronic surveillance." . . .

* * *

The floor discussion concerning the amendment adding the provision for discretionary notice merely indicates an intent to provide notice to such additional persons as may be constitutionally required.

Nothing in the structure of the Act or this legislative history suggests that incriminating conversations are "unlawfully intercepted" whenever parties to those conversations do not receive discretionary inventory notice as a result of the Government's failure to inform the District Court of their identities. At the time inventory notice was served on the other identifiable persons, the intercept had been completed and the conversations had been "seized" under a valid intercept order. The fact that discretionary notice reached 39 rather than 41 identifiable persons does not in itself mean that the conversations were unlawfully intercepted.

The legislative history indicates that postintercept notice was designed instead to assure the community that the wiretap technique is reasonably employed. But even recognizing that Congress placed considerable emphasis on that aspect of the overall statutory scheme, we do not think that postintercept notice was intended to serve as an independent restraint on resort to the wiretap procedure.

Although the Government was required to identify respondents Donovan, Robbins, and Buzzaco in the December 26 application for an extension of the initial intercept, failure to do so in the circumstances here presented did not warrant suppression under § 2518(10)(a)(i). Nor was suppression justified with respect to respondents Merlo and Lauer simply because the Government inadvertently omitted their names from the comprehensive list of all identifiable persons whose conversations had been overheard. We hold that this is the correct result under the provisions of Title III, but we re-emphasize the suggestion we made in United States v. Chavez, that "strict adherence by the Government to the provisions of Title III would nonetheless be more in keeping with the responsibilities Congress has imposed upon it when authority to engage in wiretapping or electronic surveillance is sought."

The order of the Court of Appeals is reversed and the case is remanded to that court for further proceedings in accord with this opinion.

MR. CHIEF JUSTICE BURGER, concurring in part and concurring in the judgment. [opinion omitted.]

MR. JUSTICE STEVENS, concurring in part and dissenting in part. [opinion omitted.]

MR. JUSTICE MARSHALL, with whom MR. JUSTICE BRENNAN joins, dissenting in part.

*   *   *

I continue to adhere to the position, expressed for four Members of the Court by Mr. Justice Douglas in his dissent in United States v. Chavez (1974), that Title III does not authorize "the courts to pick and choose among various statutory provisions, suppressing evidence only when they determine that a provision is 'substantive,' 'central,' or 'directly and substantially' related to the congressional scheme." The Court has rejected that argument, however, and nothing is to be gained by renewing it here. But even under the standard set forth in *Giordano* and *Chavez* and reaffirmed by the Court today, the evidence at issue here should be suppressed.

*   *   *

The Court's opinion implies that if the violations of Title III considered here had been intentional, the result would be different. This must be so, for surely this Court would not tolerate the Government's intentional disregard of duties imposed on it by Congress. I also assume that if the Government fails to establish procedures which offer reasonable assurance that it will strictly adhere to the statutory requirements, resulting failures to comply will be recognized as intentional. There is, therefore, reason to hope that the Court's admonition that the Government should obey the law will have some effect in the future.

But that hope is a poor substitute for certainty that the Government will make every effort to fulfill its responsibilities under Title III. We can obtain that certainty only by according full recognition to the role of the naming and notice requirements in the statutory scheme created by Congress. I respectfully dissent from the Court's failure to do so.

NOTE

One other question of great concern is the extent to which authorities must "minimize" the overhearing and recording of conversations "not otherwise subject to interception." 18 U.S.C. § 2518(5). In Scott v. United States, 436 U.S. 128, 98 S.Ct. 1717 (1978), the government received authorization for a wiretap in connection with a narcotics investigation. Of the conversations intercepted only "40% of them were shown to be narcotics related." The Court held that the agents actions, not their motives nor their good faith or bad faith, were relevant to the minimization issue. The percentage of innocent calls is not dispositive. Following are the Court's comments upon the issue:

" . . . when the investigation is focusing on what is thought to be a widespread conspiracy more extensive surveillance may be justified in an attempt to determine the precise scope of the enterprise. And it is possible that many more of the conversations will be permissibly interceptable because they will involve one or more of the co-conspirators. The type of use to which the telephone is normally put may also have some bearing on the extent of minimization required. For example, if the agents are permitted to tap a public telephone because one individual is thought to be placing bets over the phone, substantial doubts as to minimization may arise if the agents listen to every call which goes out over that phone regardless of who places the call. On the other hand, if the phone is located in the residence of a person who is thought to be the head of a major drug ring, a contrary conclusion may be indicated.

"Other factors may also play a significant part in a particular case. For example, it may be important to determine at exactly what point during the authorized period the interception was made. During the early stages of surveillance the agents may be forced to intercept all calls to establish categories of nonpertinent calls which will not be intercepted thereafter. Interception of those same types of calls might be unreasonable later on, however, once the nonpertinent categories have been established and it is clear that this particular conversation is of that type. Other situations may arise where patterns of nonpertinent calls do not appear. In these circumstances it may not be unreasonable to intercept almost every short conversation because the determination of relevancy cannot be made before the call is completed."

Applying these standards, the Court held that the requirement of minimization had not been violated. Justices Brennan and Marshall dissented, noting that the agents had monitored every call and had made no effort to "minimize" the interception of innocent conversations.

C. INTERCEPTIONS WITH ONE–PARTY'S CONSENT

As is pointed out in the opinion of the Supreme Court in the following case, the factual events occurred before the enactment of the Congressional enactment in 1968 which specifically provided that electronic interceptions when one party to the conversation has given consent are not prohibited by that act. The case is presented here, nevertheless, because the analysis of the Fourth Amendment problem affords an instructive classroom discussion.

UNITED STATES v. WHITE

Supreme Court of the United States, 1971.
401 U.S. 745, 91 S.Ct. 1122.

MR. JUSTICE WHITE announced the judgment of the Court and an opinion in which The Chief Justice, Mr. Justice Stewart, and Mr. Justice Blackmun join.

In 1966, respondent James A. White was tried and convicted under two consolidated indictments charging various illegal transactions in narcotics violative of 26 U.S.C. § 4705(a) and 21 U.S.C. § 174. He was fined and sentenced as a second offender to 25-year concurrent sentences. The issue before us is whether the Fourth Amendment bars from evidence the testimony of governmental agents who related certain conversations which had occurred between defendant White and a government informant, Harvey Jackson, and which the agents overheard by monitoring the frequency of a radio transmitter carried by Jackson and concealed on his person. On four occasions the conversations took place in Jackson's home; each of these conversations was overheard by an agent concealed in a kitchen closet with Jackson's consent and by a second agent outside the house using a radio receiver. Four other conversations—one in respondent's home, one in a restaurant, and two in Jackson's car—were overheard by the use of radio equipment. The prosecution was unable to locate and produce Jackson at the trial and the trial court overruled objections to the testimony of the agents who conducted the electronic surveillance. The jury returned a guilty verdict and defendant appealed.

The Court of Appeals read Katz v. United States (1967), as overruling On Lee v. United States (1952), and interpreting the Fourth Amendment to forbid the introduction of the agents' testimony in the circumstances of this case. Accordingly, the court reversed but without adverting to the fact that the transactions at issue here had occurred before *Katz* was decided in this Court. In our view, the Court of Appeals misinterpreted both the *Katz* case and the Fourth Amendment and in any event erred in applying the *Katz* case to events that occurred before that decision was rendered by this Court.

* * *

The Court of Appeals understood *Katz* to render inadmissible against White the agents' testimony concerning conversations that Jackson broadcast to them. We cannot agree. *Katz* involved no revelation to the Government by a party to conversations with the defendant nor did the Court indicate in any way that a defendant has a justifiable and constitutionally protected expectation that a person with whom he is conversing will not then or later reveal the conversation to the police.

* * *

To reach this result it was necessary for the Court of Appeals to hold that On Lee v. United States was no longer good law. In that case, which involved facts very similar to the case before us, the Court first rejected claims of a Fourth Amendment violation because the informer had not trespassed when he entered the defendant's premises and conversed with him. To this extent the Court's rationale cannot survive *Katz*. But the Court announced a second and independent ground for its decision; for it went on to say that overruling *Olmstead* and *Goldman* would be of no aid to On Lee since he "was talking confidentially and indiscreetly with one he trusted, and he was overheard. . . . It would be a dubious service to the genuine liberties protected by the Fourth Amendment to make them bedfellows with spurious liberties improvised by farfetched analogies which would liken eavesdropping on a conversation, with the connivance of one of the parties, to an unreasonable search or seizure. We find no violation of the Fourth Amendment here." We see no indication in *Katz* that the Court meant to disturb that understanding of the Fourth Amendment or to disturb the result reached in the *On Lee* case, nor are we now inclined to overturn this view of the Fourth Amendment.

Concededly a police agent who conceals his police connections may write down for official use his conversations with a defendant and testify concerning them, without a warrant authorizing his encounters with the defendant and without otherwise violating the latter's Fourth Amendment rights. Hoffa v. United States. For constitutional purposes, no different result is required if the agent instead of immediately reporting and transcribing his conversations with defendant, either (1) simultaneously records them with electronic equipment which he is carrying on his person, Lopez v. United States, supra; (2) or carries radio equipment which simultaneously transmits the conversations either to recording equipment located elsewhere or to other agents monitoring the transmitting frequency. If the conduct and revelations of an agent operating without electronic equipment do not invade the defendant's constitutionally justifiable expectations of privacy, neither does a simultaneous recording of the same conversations made by the agent or by others from transmissions received from the agent to whom the defendant is talking and whose trustworthiness the defendant necessarily risks.

Our problem is not what the privacy expectations of particular defendants in particular situations may be or the extent to which they may in fact have relied on the discretion of their companions. Very probably, individual defendants neither know nor suspect that their colleagues have gone or will go to the police or are carrying recorders or transmitters. Otherwise, conversation would cease and our problem with these encounters would be nonexistent or far different from those now before us. Our problem, in terms of the principles announced in *Katz*, is what expectations of privacy are constitutionally "justifiable"—what expectations the Fourth Amendment will protect in the absence of a warrant. So far, the law permits the frustration of actual expectations of privacy by permitting authorities to use the testimony of those associates who for one reason or another have determined to turn to the police, as well as by authorizing the use of informants in the manner exemplified by *Hoffa* and *Lewis*. If the law gives no protection to the wrongdoer whose trusted accomplice is or becomes a police agent, neither should it protect him when that same agent has recorded or transmitted the conversations which are later offered in evidence to prove the State's case. See Lopez v. United States (1963).

Inescapably, one contemplating illegal activities must realize and risk that his companions may be reporting to the police. If he sufficiently doubts their trustworthiness, the association will very probably end or never materialize. But if he has no doubts, or allays them, or risks what doubt he has, the risk is his. In terms of what his course will be, what he will or will not do or say, we are unpersuaded that he would distinguish between probable informers on the one hand and probable informers with transmitters on the other. Given the possibility or probability that one of his colleagues is cooperating with the police, it is only speculation to assert that the defendant's utterances would be substantially different or his sense of security any less if he also thought it possible that the suspected colleague is wired for sound. At least there is no persuasive evidence that the difference in this respect between the electronically equipped and the unequipped agent is substantial enough to require discrete constitutional recognition, particularly under the Fourth Amendment which is ruled by fluid concepts of "reasonableness."

Nor should we be too ready to erect constitutional barriers to relevant and probative evidence which is also accurate and reliable. An electronic recording will many times produce a more reliable rendition of what a defendant has said than will the unaided memory of a police agent. It may also be that with the recording in existence it is less likely that the informant will change his mind, less chance that threat or injury will suppress unfavorable evidence and less chance that cross-examination will confound the testimony. Considerations like these obviously do not favor the defendant, but we are not prepared to hold that a defendant who has no constitutional right to exclude the informer's unaided testimony nevertheless has a Fourth Amendment privilege against a more accurate version of the events in question.

It is thus untenable to consider the activities and reports of the police agent himself, though acting without a warrant, to be a "reasonable" investigative effort and lawful under the Fourth Amendment but to view the same agent with a recorder or transmitter as conducting an "unreasonable" and unconstitutional search and seizure. Our opinion is currently shared by Congress and the Executive Branch, Title III, Omnibus Crime Control and Safe Streets Act of 1968, 82 Stat. 212, 18 U.S.C. §§ 2510 et. seq. (1964 ed, Supp V), and the American Bar Association. Project on Standards for Criminal Justice, Electronics Surveillance § 4.1 (Approved Draft 1971). It is also the result reached by prior cases in this Court.

*   *   *

Hoffa v. United States (1966), which was left undisturbed by *Katz,* held that however strongly a defendant may trust an apparent colleague, his expectations in this respect are not protected by the Fourth Amendment when it turns out that the colleague is a government agent regularly communicating with the authorities. In these circumstances, "no interest legitimately protected by the Fourth Amendment is involved," for that amendment affords no protection to "a wrongdoer's misplaced belief that a person to whom he voluntarily confides his wrongdoing will not reveal it." No warrant to "search and seize" is required in such circumstances, nor is it when the Government sends to defendant's home a secret agent who conceals his identity and makes a purchase of narcotics from the accused, Lewis v. United States (1966), or when the same agent, unbeknown to the defendant, carries electronic equipment to record the defendant's words and the evidence so gathered is later offered in evidence. Lopez v. United States (1963).

Conceding that *Hoffa*, *Lewis*, and *Lopez* remained unaffected by *Katz*, the Court of Appeals nevertheless read both *Katz* and the Fourth Amendment to require a different result if the agent not only records his conversations with the defendant but instantaneously transmits them electronically to other agents equipped with radio receivers. Where this occurs, the Court of Appeals held, the Fourth Amendment is violated and the testimony of the listening agents must be excluded from evidence.

* * *

No different result should obtain where, as in *On Lee* and the instant case, the informer disappears and is unavailable at trial; for the issue of whether specified events on a certain day violate the Fourth Amendment should not be determined by what later happens to the informer. His unavailability at trial and proffering the testimony of other agents may raise evidentiary problems or pose issues of prosecutorial misconduct with respect to the informer's disappearance, but they do not appear critical to deciding whether prior events invaded the defendant's Fourth Amendment rights.

II.

The Court of Appeals was in error for another reason. In Desist v. United States (1969), we held that our decision in Katz v. United States applied only to those electronic surveillances that occurred subsequent to the date of that decision. Here the events in question took place in late 1965 and early 1966, long prior to Katz. The court should have judged this case by the pre-*Katz* law and under that law, as *On Lee* clearly holds, the electronic surveillance here involved did not violate White's rights to be free from unreasonable searches and seizures.

The judgment of the Court of Appeals is reversed.

It is so ordered.

[The brief concurring opinion of Justice Black is omitted, and so is the "concurrence in the result" of Justice Brennan, and the dissenting opinion of Justice Douglas.]

NOTES

1. Justice Black, citing his views in *Katz*, provided the fifth vote needed by the Government for reversal of the Court of Appeals in *White*. Justice Brennan concurred because of his view that *Katz* should not be applied retroactively. He argued, however, that *Katz* would require a different result if the challenged conduct took place after the date of the *Katz* decision: "(I)t is my view that current Fourth Amendment jurisprudence interposes a warrant requirement not only in cases of third-party electronic monitoring (the situation in *On Lee* and in this case) but also in cases of electronic recording by a government agent of a face-to-face conversation with a criminal suspect, which was the situation in Lopez."

Justice Douglas dissented. He argued that *On Lee* and *Lopez* were "of a vintage opposed to *Berger* and *Katz* . . . products of the old common-law notions of trespass." He contended that monitoring "kills free disclosure" and suggested that the practice may run afoul of the First and Fifth Amendment, as well as the Fourth. Douglas reasserted his view that *Katz* and every other decision of federal constitutional dimension should be applied retroactively.

Justice Harlan also dissented, arguing that affirmance of the Court of Appeals was proper even if *Katz* be denied retroactive effect (a decision with which he disagreed as to cases still pending on direct review at the time *Katz* was announced).

[Justice Marshall wrote a short dissent expressing agreement with the positions of Justices Douglas and Harlan.]

2. In United States v. Caceres, 440 U.S. 741, 99 S.Ct. 1465 (1979), the Court was confronted with violation of certain internal administrative regulations of the Internal Revenue Service concerning the use of one-party consensual electronic surveillance. Even though the agent who recorded the conversation had not secured the approval of Justice Department officials as required by the regulations, the Court refused to utilize an exclusionary sanction to exclude the recordings from use as evidence in a criminal prosecution. *Caceres* also implicity upheld *White* and *Lopez*, with only Justices Brennan and Marshall dissenting.

3. In the aftermath of the "Nixon tapes" episode, various Congressional proposals to limit one-party consensual recordings have been made. To date, none has passed. How should that experience be interpreted? Was the value of having accurate versions of important conversations for use in criminal prosecutions against Watergate co-conspirators outweighed by the invasion of privacy involved in recording conversations without the knowledge or the consent of the co-conspirators and of innocent persons as well?

4. Justice Harlan stated that the choice in *White* was not between recording and not recording, but between recording with a warrant and recording without a warrant. Often this is true. A probable cause requirement, however, will decrease the use of one-party consensual recordings. Such has been the case in Cook County, Illinois since the adoption of a probable cause requirement. Many "wired" informers are individuals from the criminal milieu whose credibility might not suffice to establish probable cause for the issuance of a warrant.

5. On state constitutional grounds some state high courts have rejected the result reached in *White*. See, for example, People v. Beavors, 393 Mich. 554, 227 N.W.2d 511 (1975). Others, however, have upheld statutes similar to the federal one. See Commonwealth v. Vitello, 367 Mass. 224, 327 N.E.2d 819 (1975).

Many states have not adopted laws in conformity with the federal legislation. Moreover, a few prohibit all electronic interceptions of communications. Others require the consent of all parties, or at least one of them. As regards one-party consent situations, Illinois has, perhaps, the most stringent restriction. A 1976 statute prohibits electronic overhearing and recording done without the consent of *all* parties, unless with the consent of one party, but then only upon a court order, the application for which must be approved by the prosecutor. Provision is made, however, for emergency situations, but subject to post-event court sanction. Ill.Rev.Stats., Ch. 38, Arts. 14 and 108A.

Chapter 6

EXCLUSIONARY PRINCIPLES AND ALTERNATIVE REMEDIES FOR UNLAWFUL INVESTIGATIVE PRACTICES

A.   AN OVERVIEW OF EXCLUSIONARY PRINCIPLES

In previous chapters we have considered limitations, primarily of a federal constitutional dimension, upon police and prosecutorial powers to investigate crime and to effect arrests.   Our attention now turns to the consequences of violations of those restrictions, particularly as they may limit the prosecution's use of evidence in a criminal trial.

The impact of exclusionary rules is narrowed by the requirement of "standing," the principle which permits only those whose rights have been violated to obtain exclusion against them of evidence derived from unlawful police conduct.   The exclusionary rule is also restricted when the law permits the use of illegally obtained evidence in certain phases of a criminal proceeding (for example, in the grand jury or at a sentencing hearing) and in other "non-criminal" proceedings (for example, at a parole revocation hearing or at a hearing to revoke a business license).

The denial of retroactive application of certain new constitutional decisions also narrows the impact of exclusionary rules, as does the admission of evidence which has been secured through the wrongdoing of private citizens without governmental participation.   On the other hand, the concept of derivative evidence (the notion that suppression is proper even for evidence *remotely* derived from exploitation of a police illegality) expands the impact of exclusionary rules.

The debate over these subsidiary principles—such as standing, collateral use of illegally seized evidence, and derivative evidence—requires an understanding of the rationale for exclusionary rules, and thus the cases involving these subsidiary doctrines provide insight into a court's view of exclusionary rules themselves.   One's attitude toward each of the concepts discussed in the present chapter reflects his attitude toward the exclusionary rule itself.

We begin with Mapp v. Ohio, then work through decisions involving the subsidiary principles (as applied to violations of all the types of constitutional restrictions treated in earlier chapters), and then return to a final consideration of the Fourth Amendment exclusionary rule and to suggested alternative remedies.

B.   AN INTRODUCTION TO THE EXCLUSIONARY RULE

MAPP v. OHIO

Supreme Court of the United States, 1961.
367 U.S. 643, 81 S.Ct. 1684.

MR. JUSTICE CLARK delivered the opinion of the Court.

Appellant stands convicted of knowingly having had in her possession and under her control certain lewd and lascivious books, pictures, and photographs in violation of § 2905.34 of Ohio's Revised Code. As officially stated in the syllabus to its opinion, the Supreme Court of Ohio found that her conviction was valid though "based primarily upon the introduction in evidence of lewd and lascivious books and pictures unlawfully seized during an unlawful search of defendant's home. . . . "

On May 23, 1957, three Cleveland police officers arrived at appellant's residence in that city pursuant to information that "a person [was] hiding out in the home, who was wanted for questioning in connection with a recent bombing, and that there was a large amount of policy paraphernalia being hidden in the home." Miss Mapp and her daughter by a former marriage lived on the top floor of the two-family dwelling. Upon their arrival at that house, the officers knocked on the door and demanded entrance but appellant, after telephoning her attorney, refused to admit them without a search warrant. They advised their headquarters of the situation and undertook a surveillance of the house.

The officers again sought entrance some three hours later when four or more additional officers arrived on the scene. When Miss Mapp did not come to the door immediately, at least one of the several doors to the house was forcibly opened and the policemen gained admittance. Meanwhile Miss Mapp's attorney arrived, but the officers, having secured their own entry, and continuing in their defiance of the law, would permit him neither to see Miss Mapp nor to enter the house. It appears that Miss Mapp was halfway down the stairs from the upper floor to the front door when the officers, in this high-handed manner, broke into the hall. She demanded to see the search warrant. A paper, claimed to be a warrant, was held up by one of the officers. She grabbed the "warrant" and placed it in her bosom. A struggle ensued in which the officers recovered the piece of paper and as a result of which they handcuffed appellant because she had been "belligerent" in resisting their official rescue of the "warrant" from her person. Running roughshod over appellant, a policeman "grabbed" her, "twisted [her] hand," and she "yelled [and] pleaded with him" because "it was hurting." Appellant, in handcuffs, was then forcibly taken upstairs to her bedroom where the officers searched a dresser, a chest of drawers, a closet and some suitcases. They also looked into a photo album and through personal papers belonging to the appellant. The search spread to the rest of the second floor including the child's bedroom, the living room, the kitchen and a dinette. The basement of the building and a trunk found therein were also searched. The obscene materials for possession of which she was ultimately convicted were discovered in the course of that widespread search.

At the trial no search warrant was produced by the prosecution, nor was the failure to produce one explained or accounted for. At best, "There is, in the record, considerable doubt as to whether there ever was any warrant for the search of defendant's home." The Ohio Supreme Court believed a "reasonable argument" could be made that the conviction should be reversed "because the 'methods' employed to obtain the [evidence] were such as to 'offend "a sense of justice," ' " but the court found determinative the fact that the evidence had not been taken "from defendant's person by the use of brutal or offensive physical force against defendant   .   .   ."

The State says that even if the search were made without authority, or otherwise unreasonably, it is not prevented from using the unconstitutionally seized evidence at trial, citing Wolf v. People of State of Colorado, 1949, 338 U.S. 25, 69 S.Ct. 1359, in which this Court did indeed hold "that in a prosecution in a State court for a State crime the Fourteenth Amendment does not forbid the admission of evidence obtained by an unreasonable search and seizure." On this appeal, of which we have noted probable jurisdiction, it is urged once again that we review that holding.

I.

Seventy-five years ago, in Boyd v. United States, 1886, 116 U.S. 616, 630, 6 S.Ct. 524, 532, considering the Fourth and Fifth Amendments as running "almost into each other" on the facts before it, this Court held that the doctrines of those Amendments

"apply to all invasions on the part of the government and its employes of the sanctity of a man's home and the privacies of life. It is not the breaking of his doors, and the rummaging of his drawers, that constitutes the essence of the offence; but it is the invasion of his indefeasible right of personal security, personal liberty and private property .   .   .. Breaking into a house and opening boxes and drawers are circumstances of aggravation; but any forcible and compulsory extortion of a man's own testimony or of his private papers to be used as evidence to convict him of crime or to forfeit his goods, is within the condemnation .   .   . [of those Amendments]."

The Court noted that

"constitutional provisions for the security of person and property should be liberally construed.   .   .   . It is the duty of courts to be watchful for the constitutional rights of the citizen, and against any stealthy encroachments thereon."

Less than 30 years after Boyd, this Court, in Weeks v. United States, 1914, 232 U.S. 383, 34 S.Ct. 341, . . . stated that

> "the 4th Amendment . . . put the courts of the United States and Federal officials, in the exercise of their power and authority, under limitations and restraints [and] . . . forever secure[d] the people, their persons, houses, papers, and effects, against all unreasonable searches and seizures under the guise of law . . . and the duty of giving to it force and effect is obligatory upon all entrusted under our Federal system with the enforcement of the laws."

Specifically dealing with the use of the evidence unconstitutionally seized, the Court concluded:

> "If letters and private documents can thus be seized and held and used in evidence against a citizen accused of an offense, the protection of the Fourth Amendment declaring his right to be secure against such searches and seizures is of no value, and, so far as those thus placed are concerned, might as well be stricken from the Constitution. The efforts of the courts and their officials to bring the guilty to punishment, praiseworthy as they are, are not to be aided by the sacrifice of those great principles established by years of endeavor and suffering which have resulted in their embodiment in the fundamental law of the land."

Finally, the Court in that case clearly stated that use of the seized evidence involved "a denial of the constitutional rights of the accused." Thus, in the year 1914, in the Weeks case, this Court "for the first time" held that "in a federal prosecution the Fourth Amendment barred the use of evidence secured through an illegal search and seizure." Wolf v. People of State of Colorado, supra. This Court has ever since required of federal law officers a strict adherence to that command which this Court has held to be a clear, specific, and constitutionally required—even if judicially implied—deterrent safeguard without insistence upon which the Fourth Amendment would have been reduced to "a form of words." Holmes, J., Silverthorne Lumber Co. v. United States, 1920, 251 U.S. 385, 392, 40 S.Ct. 182, 183. It meant, quite simply, that "conviction by means of unlawful seizures and enforced confessions . . . should find no sanction in the judgments of the courts . . .," Weeks v. United States, supra, and that such evidence "shall not be used at all." Silverthorne Lumber Co. v. United States, supra.

There are in the cases of this Court some passing references to the Weeks rule as being one of evidence. But the plain and unequivocal language of Weeks—and its later paraphrase in Wolf—to the effect that the Weeks rule is of constitutional origin, remains entirely undisturbed. In Byars v. United States, 1927, a unanimous Court declared that "the doctrine [cannot] . . . be tolerated *under our constitutional system*, that evidences of crime discovered by a federal officer in making a search without lawful warrant may be used against the victim of the unlawful search where a timely challenge has been interposed." (Emphasis added.) The Court, in Olmstead v. United States, 1928, 277 U.S. 438, at page 462, 48 S.Ct. 564, 567, 72 L.Ed. 944, in unmistakable language restated the Weeks rule:

> "The striking outcome of the Weeks case and those which followed it was the sweeping declaration that the Fourth Amendment, although not referring to or limiting the use of evidence in court, really forbade its introduction if obtained by government officers through a violation of the amendment." . . .

II.

In 1949, 35 years after Weeks was announced, this Court, in Wolf v. People of State of Colorado, supra, again for the first time, discussed the effect of the Fourth Amendment upon the States through the operation of the Due Process Clause of the Fourteenth Amendment. It said:

> "[W]e have no hesitation in saying that were a State affirmatively to sanction such police incursion into privacy it would run counter to the guaranty of the Fourteenth Amendment."

Nevertheless, after declaring that the "security of one's privacy against arbitrary intrusion by the police" is "implicit in 'the concept of ordered liberty' and as such enforceable against the States through the Due Process Clause," and announcing that it "stoutly adhere[d]" to the Weeks decision, the Court decided that the Weeks exclusionary rule would not then be imposed upon the States as "an essential ingredient of the right." . . . The Court's reasons for not considering essential to the right to privacy, as a curb imposed upon the States by the Due Process Clause, that which decades before had been posited as part and parcel of the Fourth Amendment's limitation upon federal encroachment of individual privacy, were bottomed on factual considerations.

While they are not basically relevant to a decision that the exclusionary rule is an essential ingredient of the Fourth Amendment as the right it embodies is vouchsafed against the States by the Due Process Clause, we will consider the current validity of the factual grounds upon which Wolf was based.

The Court in Wolf first stated that "[t]he contrariety of views of the States" on the adoption of the exclusionary rule of Weeks was "particularly impressive" . . . ; and, in this connection, that it could not "brush aside the experience of States which deem the incidence of such conduct by the police too slight to call for a deterrent remedy . . . by overriding the [States'] relevant rules of evidence." . . . While in 1949, prior to the Wolf case, almost two-thirds of the States were opposed to the use of the exclusionary rule, now, despite the Wolf case, more than half of those since passing upon it, by their own legislative or judicial decision, have wholly or partly adopted or adhered to the Weeks rule. . . . Significantly, among those now following the rule is California, which, according to its highest court, was "compelled to reach that conclusion because other remedies have completely failed to secure compliance with the constitutional provisions . . . ." People v. Cahan, 1955, . . . In connection with this California case, we note that the second basis elaborated in Wolf in support of its failure to enforce the exclusionary doctrine against the States was that "other means of protection" have been afforded "the right to privacy." . . . The experience of California that such other remedies have been worthless and futile is buttressed by the experience of other States. The obvious futility of relegating the Fourth Amendment to the protection of other remedies has, moreover, been recognized by this Court since Wolf. See Irvine v. People of State of California, 1954, . . .

Likewise, time has set its face against what Wolf called the "weighty testimony" of People v. Defore, 1926, 242 N.Y. 13, 150 N.E. 585. There Justice (then Judge) Cardozo, rejecting adoption of the Weeks exclusionary rule in New York, had said that "[t]he Federal rule as it stands is either too strict or too lax." However, the force of that reasoning has been largely vitiated by later decisions of this Court. These include the recent discarding of the "silver platter" doctrine which allowed federal judicial use of evidence seized in violation of the Constitution by state agents, Elkins v. United States, [364 U.S. 206, 80 S.Ct. 1437]; the relaxation of the formerly strict requirements as to standing to challenge the use of evidence thus seized, so that now the procedure of exclusion, "ultimately referable to constitutional safeguards," is available to anyone even "legitimately on [the] premises" unlawfully searched, Jones v. United States, 1960; and finally, the formulation of a method to prevent state use of evidence unconstitutionally seized by federal agents, Rea v. United States, 1956. Because there can be no fixed formula, we are admittedly met with "recurring questions of the reasonableness of searches," but less is not to be expected when dealing with a Constitution, and, at any rate, "[r]easonableness is in the first instance for the [trial court] to determine." . . .

It, therefore, plainly appears that the factual considerations supporting the failure of the Wolf Court to include the Weeks exclusionary rule when it recognized the enforceability of the right to privacy against the States in 1949, while not basically relevant to the constitutional consideration, could not, in any analysis, now be deemed controlling.

III.

[Omitted]

IV.

Since the Fourth Amendment's right of privacy has been declared enforceable against the States through the Due Process Clause of the Fourteenth, it is enforceable against them by the same sanction of exclusion as is used against the Federal Government. Were it otherwise, then just as without the Weeks rule the assurance against unreasonable federal searches and seizures would be "a form of words", valueless and undeserving of mention in a perpetual charter of inestimable human liberties, so too, without that rule the freedom from state invasions of privacy would be so ephemeral and so neatly severed from its conceptual nexus with the freedom from all brutish means of coercing evidence as not to merit this Court's high regard as a freedom "implicit in 'the concept of ordered liberty.'" At the time that the Court held in Wolf that the Amendment was applicable to the States through the Due Process Clause, the cases of this Court, as we have seen, had steadfastly held that as to federal officers the Fourth Amendment included the exclusion of the evidence seized in violation of its provisions. Even Wolf "stoutly adhered" to that proposition. The right to privacy, when conceded operatively enforceable against the States, was not susceptible of destruction by avulsion of the sanction upon which its protection and enjoyment had always been deemed dependent under the Boyd, Weeks and Silverthorne cases. Therefore, in extending the substantive protections of due process to all constitutionally unreasonable searches—state or federal—it was logically and constitutionally necessary that the exclusion doctrine—an essential part of the right to privacy—be also insisted upon as an essential ingredient of the right newly recognized by the Wolf case. In short, the admission of the new constitutional right by Wolf could not consistently tolerate denial of its most important constitutional privilege, namely, the exclusion of the evidence which an accused had been forced to give by reason of the unlawful seizure. To hold otherwise is to grant the right but in reality to withhold its privilege and enjoyment. Only last year the Court itself recognized that the purpose of the exclusionary rule "is to deter—to compel respect for the constitutional guaranty in the only effectively available way—by removing the incentive to disregard it."

Indeed, we are aware of no restraint, similar to that rejected today, conditioning the enforcement of any other basic constitutional right. The right to privacy, no less important than any other right carefully and particularly reserved to the people, would stand in marked contrast to all other rights declared as "basic to a free society." Wolf v. People of State of Colorado, supra, . . . This Court has not hesitated to enforce as strictly against the States as it does against the Federal Government the rights of free speech and of a free press, the rights to notice and to a fair, public trial, including, as it does, the right not to be convicted by use of a coerced confession, however logically relevant it be, and without regard to its reliability. And nothing could be more certain than that when a coerced confession is involved, "the relevant rules of evidence" are overridden without regard to "the incidence of such conduct by the police," slight or frequent. Why should not the same rule apply to what is tantamount to coerced testimony by way of unconstitutional seizure of goods, papers, effects, documents, etc.? We find that, as to the Federal Government, the Fourth and Fifth Amendments and, as to the States, the freedom from unconscionable invasions of privacy and the freedom from convictions based upon coerced confessions do enjoy an "intimate relation" in their perpetuation of "principles of humanity and civil liberty [secured] . . . only after years of struggle." Bram v. United States, 1897. They express "supplementing phases of the same constitutional purpose—to maintain inviolate large areas of personal privacy." Feldman v. United States, 1944. The philosophy of each Amendment and of each freedom is complementary to, although not dependent upon, that of the other in its sphere of influence—the very least that together they assure in either sphere is that no man is to be convicted on unconstitutional evidence. . . .

V.

Moreover, our holding that the exclusionary rule is an essential part of both the Fourth and Fourteenth Amendments is not only the logical dictate of prior cases, but it also makes very good sense. There is no war between the Constitution and common sense. Presently, a federal prosecutor may make no use of evidence illegally seized, but a State's attorney across the street may, although he supposedly is operating under the enforceable prohibitions of the same Amendment. Thus the State, by admitting evidence unlawfully seized, serves to encourage disobedience to the Federal Constitution which it is bound to uphold. Moreover, as was said in Elkins, "[t]he very essence of a healthy federalism depends upon the avoidance of needless conflict between state and federal courts." Such a conflict, hereafter needless, arose this very Term, in Wilson v. Schnettler, 1961, in which, and in spite of the promise made by Rea, we gave full recognition to our practice in this regard by refusing to restrain a federal officer from testifying in a state court as to evidence unconstitutionally seized by him in the performance of his duties. Yet the double standard recognized until today hardly put such a thesis into practice. In non-exclusionary States, federal officers, being human, were by it invited to and did, as our cases indicate, step across the street to the State's attorney with their unconstitutionally seized evidence. Prosecution on the basis of that evidence was then had in a state court in utter disregard of the enforceable Fourth Amendment. If the fruits of an unconstitutional search had been inadmissible in both state and federal courts, this inducement to evasion would have been sooner eliminated. There would be no need to reconcile such cases as Rea and Schnettler, each pointing up the hazardous uncertainties of our heretofore ambivalent approach.

Federal-state cooperation in the solution of crime under constitutional standards will be promoted, if only by recognition of their now mutual obligation to respect the same fundamental criteria in their approaches. "However much in a particular case insistence upon such rules may appear as a technicality that inures to the benefit of a guilty person, the history of the criminal law proves that tolerance of shortcut methods in law enforcement impairs its enduring effectiveness." Denying shortcuts to only one of two cooperating law enforcement agencies tends naturally to breed legitimate suspicion of "working arrangements" whose results are equally tainted. . . .

There are those who say, as did Justice (then Judge) Cardozo, that under our constitutional exclusionary doctrine "[t]he criminal is to go free because the constable has blundered." People v. Defore [supra]. In some cases this will undoubtedly be the result. But, as was said in Elkins, "there is another consideration—the imperative of judicial integrity." . . . The criminal goes free, if he must, but it is the law that sets him free. Nothing can destroy a government more quickly than its failure to observe its own laws, or worse, its disregard of the charter of its own existence. As Mr. Justice Brandeis, dissenting, said in Olmstead v. United States, 1928, 277 U. S. 438, 485, 48 S.Ct. 564, 575: "Our government is the potent, the omnipresent teacher. For good or for ill, it teaches the whole people by its example. . . . If the government becomes a lawbreaker, it breeds contempt for law; it invites every man to become a law unto himself; it invites anarchy." Nor can it lightly be assumed that, as a practical matter, adoption of the exclusionary rule fetters law enforcement. Only last year this Court expressly considered that contention and found that "pragmatic evidence of a sort" to the contrary was not wanting. Elkins v. United States, supra. The Court noted that

> "The federal courts themselves have operated under the exclusionary rule of Weeks for almost half a century; yet it has not been suggested either that the Federal Bureau of Investigation has thereby been rendered ineffective, or that the administration of criminal justice in the federal courts has thereby been disrupted. Moreover, the experience of the states is impressive . . . . The movement towards the rule of exclusion has been halting but seemingly inexorable." . . .

The ignoble shortcut to conviction left open to the State tends to destroy the entire system of constitutional restraints on which the liberties of the people rest. Having once recognized that the right to privacy embodied in the Fourth Amendment is enforceable against the States, and that the right to be secure against rude invasions of privacy by state officers is, therefore, constitutional in origin, we can no longer permit that right to remain an empty promise. Because it is enforceable in the same manner and to like effect as other basic rights secured by the Due Process Clause, we can no longer permit it to be revocable at the whim of any police officer who, in the name of law enforcement itself, chooses to suspend its enjoyment. Our decision, founded on reason and truth, gives to the individual no more than that which the Constitution guarantees him, to the police officer no less than that to which honest law enforcement is entitled, and, to the courts, that judicial integrity so necessary in the true administration of justice.

The judgment of the Supreme Court of Ohio is reversed and the cause remanded for further proceedings not inconsistent with this opinion.

Reversed and remanded.

MR. JUSTICE BLACK, concurring.

* * *

I am still not persuaded that the Fourth Amendment, standing alone, would be enough to bar the introduction into evidence against an accused of papers and effects seized from him in violation of its commands. For the Fourth Amendment does not itself contain any provision expressly precluding the use of such evidence, and I am extremely doubtful that such a provision could properly be inferred from nothing more than the basic command against unreasonable searches and seizures. Reflection of the problem however, in the light of cases coming before the Court since Wolf, has led me to conclude that when the Fourth Amendment's ban against unreasonable searches and seizures is considered together with the Fifth Amendment's ban against compelled self-incrimination, a constitutional basis emerges which not only justifies but actually requires the exclusionary rule.

The close interrelationship between the Fourth and Fifth Amendments, as they apply to this problem, has long been recognized and, indeed, was expressly made the ground for this Court's holding in Boyd v. United States. There the Court fully discussed this relationship and declared itself "unable to perceive that the seizure of a man's private books and papers to be used in evidence against him is substantially different from compelling him to be a witness against himself." . . . In the final analysis, it seems to me that the Boyd doctrine, though perhaps not required by the express language of the Constitution strictly construed, is amply justified from an historical standpoint, soundly based in reason, and entirely consistent with what I regard to be the proper approach to interpretation of our Bill of Rights—an approach well set out by Mr. Justice Bradley in the Boyd case:

> "[C]onstitutional provisions for the security of person and property should be liberally construed. A close and literal construction deprives them of half their efficacy, and leads to gradual depreciation of the right, as if it existed more in sound than in substance. It is the duty of [the] courts to be watchful for the constitutional rights of the citizen, and against any stealthy encroachments thereon."

. . . As I understand the Court's opinion in this case, we . . . set aside this state conviction in reliance upon the precise, intelligible and more predictable constitutional doctrine enunciated in the Boyd case. I fully agree with Mr. Justice Bradley's opinion that the two Amendments upon which the Boyd doctrine rests are of vital importance in our constitutional scheme of liberty and that both are entitled to a liberal rather than a niggardly interpretation. The courts of the country are entitled to know with as much certainty as possible what scope they cover. The Court's opinion, in my judgment, dissipates the doubt and uncertainty in this field of constitutional law and I am persuaded, for this and other reasons stated, to depart from my prior views, to accept the Boyd doctrine as controlling in this state case and to join the Court's judgment and opinion which are in accordance with that constitutional doctrine.

[MR. JUSTICE DOUGLAS' concurring opinion is omitted.]

[The Memorandum of MR. JUSTICE STEWART is omitted.]

MR. JUSTICE HARLAN, whom MR. JUSTICE FRANKFURTER and MR. JUSTICE WHITTAKER join, dissenting.

In overruling the Wolf case the Court, in my opinion, has forgotten the sense of judicial restraint which, with due regard for *stare decisis*, is one element that should enter into deciding whether a past decision of this Court should be overruled. Apart from that I also believe that the Wolf rule represents sounder Constitutional doctrine than the new rule which now replaces it.

I.

From the Court's statement of the case one would gather that the central, if not controlling, issue on this appeal is whether illegally state-seized evidence is Constitutionally admissible in a state prosecution, an issue which would of course face us with the need for re-examining Wolf. However, such is not the situation. For, although that question was indeed raised here and below among appellant's subordinate points, the new and pivotal issue brought to the Court by this appeal is whether § 2905.34 of the Ohio Revised Code making criminal the *mere* knowing possession or control of obscene material, and under which appellant has been convicted, is consistent with the rights of free thought and expression assured against state action by the Fourteenth Amendment. That was the principal issue which was decided by the Ohio Supreme Court, which was tendered by appellant's Jurisdictional Statement, and which was briefed and argued in this Court.

In this posture of things, I think it fair to say that five members of this Court have simply "reached out" to overrule Wolf. With all respect for the views of the majority, and recognizing that *stare decisis* carries different weight in Constitutional adjudication than it does in nonconstitutional decision, I can perceive no justification for regarding this case as an appropriate occasion for re-examining Wolf.

Since the demands of the case before us do not require us to reach the question of the validity of Wolf, I think this case furnishes a singularly inappropriate occasion for reconsideration of that decision, if reconsideration is indeed warranted. Even the most cursory examination will reveal that the doctrine of the Wolf case has been of continuing importance in the administration of state criminal law. Indeed, certainly as regards its "nonexclusionary" aspect, Wolf did no more than articulate the then existing assumption among the States that the federal cases enforcing the exclusionary rule "do not bind [the States], for they construe provisions of the federal Constitution, the Fourth and Fifth Amendments, not applicable to the states." Though, of course, not reflecting the full measure of this continuing reliance, I find that during the last three Terms, for instance, the issue of the inadmissibility of illegally state-obtained evidence appears on an average of about fifteen times per Term just in the *in forma pauperis* cases summarily disposed of by us. This would indicate both that the issue which is now being decided may well have untoward practical ramifications respecting state cases long since disposed of in reliance on Wolf, and that were we determined to re-examine that doctrine we would not lack future opportunity.

The occasion which the Court has taken here is in the context of a case where the question was briefed not at all and argued only extremely tangentially. The unwisdom of overruling Wolf without full-dress argument is aggravated by the circumstance that that decision is a comparatively recent one (1949) to which three members of the present majority have at one time or other expressly subscribed, one to be sure with explicit misgivings. I would think that our obligation to the States, on whom we impose this new rule, as well as the obligation of orderly adherence to our own processes would demand that we seek that aid which adequate briefing and argument lends to the determination of an important issue. It certainly has never been a postulate of judicial power that mere altered disposition, or subsequent membership on the Court, is sufficient warrant for overturning a deliberately decided rule of Constitutional law. . . .

I am bound to say that what has been done is not likely to promote respect either for the Court's adjudicatory process or for the stability of its decisions. Having been unable, however, to persuade any of the majority to a different procedural course, I now turn to the merits of the present decision.

II.

Essential to the majority's argument against Wolf is the proposition that the rule of Weeks v. United States, [supra] excluding in federal criminal trials the use of evidence obtained in violation of the Fourth Amendment, derives not from the "supervisory power" of this Court over the federal judicial system, but from Constitutional requirement. This is so because no one, I suppose, would suggest that this Court possesses any general supervisory power over the state courts. Although I entertain considerable doubt as to the soundness of this foundational proposition of the majority, . . . I shall assume, for present purposes, that the Weeks rule "is of constitutional origin."

At the heart of the majority's opinion in this case is the following syllogism: (1) the rule excluding in federal criminal trials evidence which is the product of an illegal search and seizure is a "part and parcel" of the Fourth Amendment; (2) Wolf held that the "privacy" assured against federal action by the Fourth Amendment is also protected against state action by the Fourteenth Amendment; and (3) it is therefore "logically and constitutionally necessary" that the Weeks exclusionary rule should also be enforced against the States.

This reasoning ultimately rests on the unsound premise that because Wolf carried into the States, as part of "the concept of ordered liberty" embodied in the Fourteenth Amendment, the principle of "privacy" underlying the Fourth Amendment . . ., it must follow that whatever configurations of the Fourth Amendment have been developed in the particularizing federal precedents are likewise to be deemed a part of "ordered liberty," and as such are enforceable against the States. For me, this does not follow at all.

It cannot be too much emphasized that what was recognized in Wolf was not that the Fourth Amendment *as such* is enforceable against the States as a facet of due process, a view of the Fourteenth Amendment which, as Wolf itself pointed out . . ., has long since been discredited, but the principle of privacy "which is at the core of the Fourth Amendment." . . . It would not be proper to expect or impose any precise equivalence, either as regards the scope of the right or the means of its implementation, between the requirements of the Fourth and Fourteenth Amendments. For the Fourth, unlike what was said in Wolf of the Fourteenth, does not state a general principle only; it is a particular command, having its setting in a pre-existing legal context on which both interpreting decisions and enabling statutes must at least build.

Thus, even in a case which presented simply the question of whether a particular search and seizure was constitutionally "unreasonable"—say in a tort action against state officers—we would not be true to the Fourteenth Amendment were we merely to stretch the general principle of individual privacy on a Procrustean bed of federal precedents under the Fourth Amendment. But in this instance more than that is involved, for here we are reviewing not a determination that what the state police did was Constitutionally permissible (since the state court quite evidently assumed that it was not), but a determination that appellant was properly found guilty of conduct which, for present purposes, it is to be assumed the State could Constitutionally punish. Since there is not the slightest suggestion that Ohio's policy is "affirmatively to sanction . . . police incursion into privacy," what the Court is now doing is to impose upon the States not only federal substantive standards of "search and seizure" but also the basic federal remedy for violation of those standards. For I think it entirely clear that the Weeks exclusionary rule is but a remedy which, by penalizing past official misconduct, is aimed at deterring such conduct in the future.

I would not impose upon the States this federal exclusionary remedy. The reasons given by the majority for now suddenly turning its back on Wolf seem to me notably unconvincing.

First, it is said that "the factual grounds upon which Wolf was based" have since changed, in that more States now follow the Weeks exclusionary rule than was so at the time Wolf was decided. While that is true, a recent survey indicates that at present one-half of the States still adhere to the common-law non-exclusionary rule, and one, Maryland, retains the rule as to felonies. Berman and Oberst, Admissibility of Evidence Obtained by an Unconstitutional Search and Seizure, 55 N.W.L.Rev. 525, 532–533. But in any case surely all this is beside the point, as the majority itself indeed seems to recognize. Our concern here, as it was in Wolf, is not with the desirability of that rule but only with the question whether the States are Constitutionally free to follow it or not as they may themselves determine, and the relevance of the disparity of views among the States on this point lies simply in the fact that the judgment involved is a debatable one. Moreover, the very fact on which the majority relies, instead of lending support to what is now being done, points away from the need of replacing voluntary state action with federal compulsion.

The preservation of a proper balance between state and federal responsibility in the administration of criminal justice demands patience on the part of those who might like to see things move faster among the States in this respect. Problems of criminal law enforcement vary widely from State to State. One State, in considering the totality of its legal picture, may conclude that the need for embracing the Weeks rule is pressing because other remedies are unavailable or inadequate to secure compliance with the substantive Constitutional principle involved. Another, though equally solicitous of Constitutional rights, may choose to pursue one purpose at a time, allowing all evidence relevant to guilt to be brought into a criminal trial, and dealing with Constitutional infractions by other means. Still another may consider the exclusionary rule too rough-and-ready a remedy, in that it reaches only unconstitutional intrusions which eventuate in criminal prosecution of the victims. Further, a State after experimenting with the Weeks rule for a time may, because of unsatisfactory experience with it, decide to revert to a non-exclusionary rule. And so on. From the standpoint of Constitutional permissibility in pointing a State in one direction or another, I do not see at all why "time has set its face against" the considerations which led Mr. Justice Cardozo, then chief judge of the New York Court of Appeals, to reject for New York in People v. Defore, [supra], the Weeks exclusionary rule. For us the question remains, as it has always been, one of state power, not one of passing judgment on the wisdom of one state course or another. In my view this Court should continue to forbear from fettering the States with an adamant rule which may embarrass them in coping with their own peculiar problems in criminal law enforcement.

Further, we are told that imposition of the Weeks rule on the States makes "very good sense," in that it will promote recognition by state and federal officials of their "mutual obligation to respect the same fundamental criteria" in their approach to law enforcement, and will avoid " 'needless conflict between state and federal courts.' "

Indeed the majority now finds an incongruity in Wolf's discriminating perception between the demands of "ordered liberty" as respects the basic right of "privacy" and the means of securing it among the States. That perception, resting both on a sensitive regard for our federal system and a sound recognition of this Court's remoteness from particular state problems, is for me the strength of that decision.

An approach which regards the issue as one of achieving procedural symmetry or of serving administrative convenience surely disfigures the boundaries of this Court's functions in relation to the state and federal courts. Our role in promulgating the Weeks rule and its extensions in such cases as Rea, Elkins, and Rios was quite a different one than it is here. There, in implementing the Fourth Amendment, we occupied the position of a tribunal having the ultimate responsibility for developing the standards and procedures of judicial administration within the judicial system over which it presides. Here we review state procedures whose measure is to be taken not against the specific substantive commands of the Fourth Amendment but under the flexible contours of the Due Process Clause. I do not believe that the Fourteenth Amendment empowers this Court to mould state remedies effectuating the right to freedom from "arbitrary intrusion by the police" to suit its own notions of how things should be done, as, for instance, the California Supreme Court did in People v. Cahan, . . . with reference to procedures in the California courts or as this Court did in Weeks for the lower federal courts.

A state conviction comes to us as the complete product of a sovereign judicial system. Typically a case will have been tried in a trial court, tested in some final appellate court, and will go no further. In the comparatively rare instance when a conviction is reviewed by us on due process grounds we deal then with a finished product in the creation of which we are allowed no hand, and our task, far from being one of over-all supervision, is, speaking generally, restricted to a determination of whether the prosecution was Constitutionally fair. The specifics of trial procedure, which in every mature legal system will vary greatly in detail, are within the sole competence of the States. I do not see how it can be said that a trial becomes unfair simply because a State determines that evidence may be considered by the trier of fact, regardless of how it was obtained, if it is relevant to the one issue with which the trial is concerned, the guilt or innocence of the accused. Of course, a court may use its procedures as an incidental means of pursuing other ends than the correct resolution of the controversies before it. Such indeed is the Weeks rule, but if a State does not choose to use its courts in this way, I do not believe that this Court is empowered to impose this much-debated procedure on local courts, however efficacious we may consider the Weeks rule to be as a means of securing Constitutional rights.

Finally, it is said that the overruling of Wolf is supported by the established doctrine that the admission in evidence of an involuntary confession renders a state conviction Constitutionally invalid. Since such a confession may often be entirely reliable, and therefore of the greatest relevance to the issue of the trial, the argument continues, this doctrine is ample warrant in precedent that the way evidence was obtained, and not just its relevance, is Constitutionally significant to the fairness of a trial. I believe this analogy is not a true one. The "coerced confession" rule is certainly not a rule that any illegally obtained statements may not be used in evidence. I would suppose that a statement which is procured during a period of illegal detention is, as much as unlawfully seized evidence, illegally obtained, but this Court has consistently refused to reverse state convictions resting on the use of such statements. Indeed it would seem the Court laid at rest the very argument now made by the majority when in Lisenba v. People of State of California, a state-coerced confession case, it said:

> "It may be assumed [that the] treatment of the petitioner [by the police] . . . deprived him of his liberty without due process and that the petitioner would have been afforded preventive relief if he could have gained access to a court to seek it.

> "But illegal acts, as such, committed in the course of obtaining a confession . . . do not furnish an answer to the constitutional question we must decide. . . . The gravamen of his complaint is the unfairness of the *use* of his confessions, and what occurred in their procurement is relevant only as it bears on that issue." (Emphasis supplied.)

The point, then, must be that in requiring exclusion of an involuntary statement of an accused, we are concerned not with an appropriate remedy for what the police have done, but with something which is regarded as going to the heart of our concepts of fairness in judicial procedure. The operative assumption of our procedural system is that "Ours is the accusatorial as opposed to the inquisitorial system. Such has been the characteristic of Anglo-American criminal justice since it freed itself from practices borrowed by the Star Chamber from the Continent whereby an accused was interrogated in secret for hours on end." . . . The pressures brought to bear against an accused leading to a confession, unlike an unconstitutional violation of privacy, do not, apart from the use of the confession at trial, necessarily involve independent Constitutional violations. What is crucial is that the trial defense to which an accused is entitled should not be rendered an empty formality by reason of statements wrung from him, for then "a prisoner . . . [has been] made the deluded instrument of his own conviction." 2 Hawkins, Pleas of the Crown (8th ed., 1824), c. 46, § 34. That this is a *procedural right*, and that its violation occurs at the time his improperly obtained statement is admitted at trial, is manifest. For without this right all the careful safeguards erected around the giving of testimony, whether by an accused or any other witness, would become empty formalities in a procedure where the most compelling possible evidence of guilt, a confession, would have already been obtained at the unsupervised pleasure of the police.

This, and not the disciplining of the police, as with illegally seized evidence, is surely the true basis for excluding a statement of the accused which was unconstitutionally obtained. In sum, I think the coerced confession analogy works strongly *against* what the Court does today.

In conclusion, it should be noted that the majority opinion in this case is in fact an opinion only for the *judgment* overruling Wolf, and not for the basic rationale by which four members of the majority have reached that result. For my Brother Black is unwilling to subscribe to their view that the Weeks exclusionary rule derives from the Fourth Amendment itself, but joins the majority opinion on the premise that its end result can be achieved by bringing the Fifth Amendment to the aid of the Fourth. On that score I need only say that whatever the validity of the "Fourth-Fifth Amendment" correlation which the Boyd case [supra] found, we have only very recently again reiterated the long-established doctrine of this Court that the Fifth Amendment privilege against self-incrimination is not applicable to the States. . . .

I regret that I find so unwise in principle and so inexpedient in policy a decision motivated by the high purpose of increasing respect for Constitutional rights. But in the last analysis I think this Court can increase respect for the Constitution only if it rigidly respects the limitations which the Constitution places upon it, and respects as well the principles inherent in its own processes. In the present case I think we exceed both, and that our voice becomes only a voice of power, not of reason.

NOTES

1. As the following materials will illustrate, a court's view of the purpose of the exclusionary rule may determine its attitude toward preserving or abolishing the rule, or toward broadening or narrowing its impact. To the extent that the rule's purpose and justification is to deter police misconduct, the empirical question as to its impact is of utmost importance. To the extent to which the rule's purpose has to do with the "imperative of the judicial integrity," the advocates of exclusion need not rest their case upon an empirical base. What purpose is emphasized in *Mapp*? For a view that not until *Wolf*, thirty-five years after *Weeks*, was deterrence offered as a justification for the exclusionary rule, see McKay, Mapp v. Ohio, The Exclusionary Rule and The Right of Privacy, 15 Ariz.L.Rev. 327 (1973).

2. Statutes which prohibit the possession of obscene materials intended for personal use—such as the one under which Mrs. Mapp was sentenced to seven years—were held to violate the First Amendment in Stanley v. Georgia, 394 U.S. 557, 89 S.Ct. 1243 (1969). For very light reading which provides some background about Mrs. Mapp, the police "investigation" in her case, and her later encounters with the law, see L. Stevens, Trespass! (1977).

3. The exclusionary rule and proposed alternatives are further discussed at the conclusion of the present chapter.

4. For a recent attack upon *Mapp* and its progeny, see the dissenting opinion of Justice Rehnquist, joined by Chief Justice Burger, in California v. Minjares, —— U.S. ——, 100 S.Ct. 9 (1979). In a concurring opinion in Gannett Co., Inc. v. DePasquale, —— U.S. ——, 99 S.Ct. 2898 (1979), Chief Justice Burger advanced another reason for abolishing the exclusionary rule: Pre-trial hearings on motions to suppress, necessitated by the rule, generate problems of pre-trial publicity.

C. "STANDING" TO OBTAIN EXCLUSION OF EVIDENCE

---

1. DEBATE OVER THE "STANDING" REQUIREMENT

PEOPLE v. MARTIN

Supreme Court of California, 1955.
45 Cal.2d 755, 290 P.2d 855.

MR. JUSTICE TRAYNOR delivered the opinion of the Court:

By information defendant was charged with two counts of horse-race bookmaking, and two counts of keeping and occupying premises for the purposes of such bookmaking. The trial court granted defendant's motion to set the information aside on the ground that all of the evidence against him had been obtained by illegal searches and seizures in violation of his constitutional rights. The People appeal.

Two of the counts were based on defendant's activities that were discovered by the arresting officers on April 20, 1955, at an office on Ventura Boulevard in Los Angeles.

*   *   *

The other two counts were based on defendant's activities that were discovered by the arresting officers six days later at another small office building on Ventura Boulevard. . . .

The Attorney General contends that since defendant disclaimed any interest in the premises searched and the property seized, his constitutional rights could not have been violated and that therefore he has no standing to challenge the legality of the searches and seizures.

*   *   *

We cannot agree with this contention.

It is true that in Goldstein v. United States, 316 U.S. 114, 62 S. Ct. 1000, the United States Supreme Court recognized that the rule is well established in the lower federal courts that only those whose constitutional rights have been violated may object to the introduction of illegally obtained evidence against them.

Thus, the rule of the lower federal courts is based on the theory that the evidence is excluded to provide a remedy for a wrong done to the defendant, and that accordingly, if the defendant has not been wronged he is entitled to no remedy. In adopting the exclusionary rule, however, this court recognized that it could not be justified on that theory, People v. Cahan, 44 Cal.2d 434, 443, 282 P.2d 905, and based its decision on the ground that "other remedies have completely failed to secure compliance with the constitutional provisions on the part of police officers with the attendant result that the courts under the old rule have been constantly required to participate in, and in effect condone, the lawless activities of law enforcement officers." This result occurs whenever the government is allowed to profit by its own wrong by basing a conviction on illegally obtained evidence, and if law enforcement officers are allowed to evade the exclusionary rule by obtaining evidence in violation of the rights of third parties, its deterrent effect is to that extent nullified. Moreover, such a limitation virtually invites law enforcement officers to violate the rights of third parties and to trade the escape of a criminal whose rights are violated for the conviction of others by the use of the evidence illegally obtained against them.

The United States Supreme Court has clearly recognized that the purpose of the exclusionary rule is not to provide redress or punishment for a past wrong, but to deter lawless enforcement of the law. "The Government cannot violate the Fourth Amendment . . . and use the fruits of such unlawful conduct to secure a conviction. Nor can the Government make indirect use of such evidence for its case, or support a conviction on evidence obtained through leads from the unlawfully obtained evidence. All these methods are outlawed, and convictions obtained by means of them are invalidated, because they encourage the kind of society that is obnoxious to free men." Walder v. United States, 347 U.S. 62, 64–65, 74 S.Ct. 354, 356.

*   *   *

Since all of the reasons that compelled us to adopt the exclusionary rule are applicable whenever evidence is obtained in violation of constitutional guarantees, such evidence is inadmissible whether or not it was obtained in violation of the particular defendant's constitutional rights. Accordingly, it must be determined whether the evidence was illegally obtained in this case.

[After reviewing the merits, the court found that the seizures made in this case were lawful.]

The order is reversed.

NOTES

1. *Martin* is very much a minority decision. Only Louisiana, through Article 1, Section 5 of its 1974 constitution, has joined California in permitting a defendant at his or her criminal trial to secure exclusion of evidence derived from a violation of another person's constitutional rights. Louisiana courts have not been expansive in their interpretation of the state constitution's abolition of the standing requirement. See State v. Roach, 338 So.2d 621 (La.1976).

Martin is presented here as a good statement of the argument against the standing requirement as applied to Fourth Amendment cases and as a background for *Alderman*, the next principal case in this book, which considered and rejected this argument.

2. If the police, in possession of data which fell short of justifying an emergency entry, unlawfully entered *A's* house and found *B* in the process of burglarizing that house, under *Martin* could *B* secure the exclusion of (1) *B's* burglary tools which the officers found within and (2) the observations of *B* going through drawers, which observations the officers made after illegally entering *A's* house? For a decision according "standing" to a *burglar*, see People v. Solario, 64 Cal.App.3d 532, 184 Cal.Rptr. 563 (1976). However, the California Supreme Court reversed, 19 Cal.3d 760, 139 Cal.Rptr. 725, 566 P.2d 627 (1977), but, finding the police conduct lawful, avoided the broad issue as to whether a burglar has "standing" to object to the use against him of evidence secured in violation of his victim's Fourth Amendment rights.

ALDERMAN v. UNITED STATES

Supreme Court of the United States, 1969.
394 U.S. 165, 89 S.Ct. 961.

[Under the above case title the Supreme Court consolidated several wiretapping cases arising out of unrelated investigations and prosecutions. In one case the Attorney General conceded that an unlawful tap had occurred. In other cases the Court assumed, without deciding that the police conduct was unlawful. In each of the cases the Government argued that certain of the petitioners lacked standing to secure exclusion of evidence derived from the allegedly improper wiretapping.]

MR. JUSTICE WHITE delivered the opinion of the Court:

*   *   *

The exclusionary rule fashioned in Weeks v. United States (1914) and Mapp v. Ohio (1961), excludes from a criminal trial any evidence seized from the defendant in violation of his Fourth Amendment rights. Fruits of such evidence are excluded as well. Silverthorne Lumber Co. v. United States (1920). Because the Amendment now affords protection against the uninvited ear, oral statements, if illegally overheard, and their fruits are also subject to suppression. Silverman v. United States (1967).

In *Mapp* and *Weeks* the defendant against whom the evidence was held to be inadmissible was the victim of the search. However, in the cases before us each petitioner demands retrial if any of the evidence used to convict him was the product of unauthorized surveillance, regardless of whose Fourth Amendment rights the surveillance violated. At the very least, it is urged that if evidence is inadmissible against one defendant or conspirator, because tainted by electronic surveillance illegal as to him, it is also inadmissible against his codefendant or coconspirator.

This expansive reading of the Fourth Amendment and of the exclusionary rule fashioned to enforce it is admittedly inconsistent with prior cases, and we reject it. The established principle is that suppression of the product of a Fourth Amendment violation can be successfully urged only by those whose rights were violated by the search itself, not by those who are aggrieved solely by the introduction of damaging evidence. Coconspirators and codefendants have been accorded no special standing.

Thus in Goldstein v. United States, testimony induced by disclosing to witnesses their own telephonic communications intercepted by the Government contrary to 47 U.S.C. § 605 was held admissible against their coconspirators. The Court equated the rule under § 605 with the exclusionary rule under the Fourth Amendment. Wong Sun v. United States (1963) came to like conclusions. There, two defendants were tried together; narcotics seized from a third party were held inadmissible against one defendant because they were the product of statements made by him at the time of his unlawful arrest. But the same narcotics were found to be admissible against the codefendant because "[t]he seizure of this heroin invaded no right of privacy of person or premises which would entitle [him] to object to its use at his trial.

The rule is stated in Jones v. United States (1960):

> "In order to qualify as a 'person aggrieved by an unlawful search and seizure' one must have been a victim of a search or seizure, one against whom the search was directed, as distinguished from one who claims prejudice only through the use of evidence gathered as a consequence of a search or seizure directed at someone else. . . .
>
> "Ordinarily, then, it is entirely proper to require of one who seeks to challenge the legality of a search as the basis for suppressing relevant evidence that he allege, and if the allegation be disputed that he establish, that he himself was the victim of an invasion of privacy." [1]

* * *

We adhere to these cases and to the general rule that Fourth Amendment rights are personal rights which, like some other constitutional rights, may not be vicariously asserted. None of the special circumstances which prompted NAACP v. Alabama, 357 U.S. 449, 78 S.Ct. 1163 (1958), and Barrows v. Jackson, 346 U.S. 249, 73 S. Ct. 1031 (1953), are present here. There is no necessity to exclude evidence against one defendant in order to protect the rights of another. No rights of the victim of an illegal search are at stake when the evidence is offered against some other party. The victim can and very probably will object for himself when and if it becomes important for him to do so.

---

1. The "person aggrieved" language is from Fed.Rule Crim.Proc. 41(e). *Jones* thus makes clear that Rule 41 conforms to the general standard and is no broader than the constitutional rule.

McDonald v. United States, 335 U.S. 451, 69 S.Ct. 191 (1948), is not authority to the contrary. It is not at all clear that the *McDonald* opinion would automatically extend standing to a codefendant. Two of the five Justices joining the majority opinion did not read the opinion to do so and found the basis for the codefendant's standing to be the fact that he was a guest on the premises searched. "But even a guest may expect the shelter of the rooftree he is under against criminal intrusion."

What petitioners appear to assert is an independent constitutional right of their own to exclude relevant and probative evidence because it was seized from another in violation of the Fourth Amendment. But we think there is a substantial difference for constitutional purposes between preventing the incrimination of a defendant through the very evidence illegally seized from him and suppressing evidence on the motion of a party who cannot claim this predicate for exclusion.

The necessity for that predicate was not eliminated by recognizing and acknowledging the deterrent aim of the rule. See Linkletter v. Walker (1965); Elkins v. United States (1960). Neither those cases nor any others hold that anything which deters illegal searches is thereby commanded by the Fourth Amendment. The deterrent values of preventing the incrimination of those whose rights the police have violated have been considered sufficient to justify the suppression of probative evidence even though the case against the defendant is weakened or destroyed. We adhere to that judgment. But we are not convinced that the additional benefits of extending the exclusionary rule to other defendants would justify further encroachment upon the public interest in prosecuting those accused of crime and having them acquitted or convicted on the basis of all the evidence which exposes the truth.

We do not deprecate Fourth Amendment rights. The security of persons and property remains a fundamental value which law enforcement officers must respect. Nor should those who flout the rules escape unscathed. In this respect we are mindful that there is now a comprehensive statute making unauthorized electronic surveillance a serious crime. The general rule under the statute is that official eavesdropping and wiretapping are permitted only with probable cause and a warrant. Without experience showing the contrary, we should not assume that this new statute will be cavalierly disregarded or will not be enforced against transgressors.

Of course, Congress or state legislatures may extend the exclusionary rule and provide that illegally seized evidence is inadmissible against anyone for any purpose. But for constitutional purposes, we are not now inclined to expand the existing rule that unlawful wiretapping or eavesdropping, whether deliberate or negligent, can produce nothing usable against the person aggrieved by the invasion.

In these cases, therefore, any petitioner would be entitled to the suppression of government evidence originating in electronic surveillance violative of his own Fourth Amendment right to be free of unreasonable searches and seizures. Such violation would occur if the United States unlawfully overheard conversations of a petitioner himself or conversations occurring on his premises, whether or not he was present or participated in those conversations.

* * *

NOTES

1. In *Alderman* Chief Justice Warren, Justice Brennan, and Justice Black joined in the dissenting opinion of Justice Marshall, who argued that

any "target" of the investigation should have standing. This theory was later discussed and rejected in Rakas v. Illinois, Section C–2, infra. Justice Harlan joined by Justice Stewart argued for a narrower standing rule in wiretap cases, so that only persons whose conversational privacy was violated could secure exclusion of illegally obtained wiretap evidence. Under the view of these justices, even if a physical trespass was made against a homeowner's property to install the electronic device (as apparently was true in the *Alderman* and consolidated cases), he would have no standing to object to the seizure of a conversation to which he was not a party. Thus, under the views of Harlan and Stewart, if the law of evidence permitted the use against the homeowner of such conversations (under the coconspirator exception to the hearsay rule), he could not secure exclusion of evidence derived from illegal wiretaps even if the conversations occurred on his property and had been overheard through a trespass to that property.

Suppose that an unlawful wiretap occurs without any trespass. Should the homeowner who was not present when the conversation occurred on a telephone in his home be accorded standing to object to admission of the conversations to which he was not a party? To what was said by each party or only to what was said by the party who was using the homeowner's phone?

The dispute as to a nonparticipant's standing to object to admission of a conversation occurring on his premises should be reconsidered in light of *Rakas*.

2. Under the standing requirement which was reaffirmed in *Alderman*, would standing be denied no matter how egregious the Fourth Amendment violation? Suppose that police officers, in non-emergency circumstances, without a warrant, and without knocking and announcing, broke down the door to *A's* apartment in the middle of the night, forced her children into the winter's cold, and ransacked the entire apartment, hoping to secure evidence against *B*, who lacked standing to complain of the search of *A's* apartment. Should *B* have standing even if he does not allege and prove an interest in the items seized? Should there be a "bad faith" exception to the standing requirement of *Alderman*?

2. "STANDING" CONCEPTS IN FOURTH AMENDMENT CASES

RAKAS v. ILLINOIS

Supreme Court of the United States, 1978.
439 U.S. 128, 99 S.Ct. 421.

MR. JUSTICE REHNQUIST delivered the opinion of the Court.

Petitioners were convicted of armed robbery in the Circuit Court of Kankakee County, Ill., and their convictions were affirmed on appeal. At their trial, the prosecution offered into evidence a sawed-off rifle and rifle shells that had been seized by police during a search of an automobile in which petitioners had been passengers. Neither petitioner is the owner of the automobile and neither has ever asserted that he owned the rifle or shells seized. The Illinois Appellate Court held that petitioners lacked standing to object to the allegedly unlawful search and seizure and denied their motion to suppress the evidence. We granted certiorari in light of the obvious importance of the issues raised to the administration of criminal justice.

I.

Because we are not here concerned with the issue of probable cause, a brief description of the events leading to the search of the automobile will suffice. A police officer on a routine patrol received a radio call notifying him of a robbery of a clothing store in Bourbonnais, Ill., and describing the getaway car. Shortly thereafter, the officer spotted an automobile which he thought might be the getaway car. After following the car for some time and after the arrival of assistance, he and several other officers stopped the vehicle. The occupants of the automobile, petitioners and two female companions, were ordered out of the car and after the occupants had left the car, two officers searched the interior of the vehicle. They discovered a box of rifle shells in the glove compartment, which had been locked, and a sawed-off rifle under the front passenger seat. After discovering the rifle and the shells, the officers took petitioners to the station and placed them under arrest.

Before trial petitioners moved to suppress the rifle and shells seized from the car on the ground that the search violated the Fourth and Fourteenth Amendments. They conceded that they did not own the automobile and were simply passengers; the owner of the car had been the driver of the vehicle at the time of the search. Nor did they assert that they owned the rifle or the shells seized. The prosecutor challenged petitioners' standing to object to the lawfulness of the search of the car because neither the car, the shells nor the rifle belonged to them. The trial court agreed that petitioners lacked standing and denied the motion to suppress the evidence. In view of this holding, the court did not determine whether there was probable cause for the search and seizure. On appeal after petitioners' conviction, the Appellate Court of Illinois, Third Judicial District, affirmed the trial court's denial of petitioners' motion to suppress because it held that "without a proprietary or other similar interest in an automobile, a mere passenger therein lacks standing to challenge the legality of the search of the vehicle." The court stated:

"We believe that defendants failed to establish any prejudice to their own constitutional rights because they were not persons aggrieved by the unlawful search and seizure. . . . They wrongly seek to establish prejudice only through the use of evidence gathered as a consequence of a search and seizure directed at someone else and fail to prove an invasion of their own privacy. The Illinois Supreme Court denied petitioners leave to appeal.

II.

Petitioners first urge us to relax or broaden the rule of standing enunciated in *Jones v. United States* (1960), so that any criminal defendant at whom a search was "directed" would have standing to contest the legality of that search and object to the admission at trial of evidence obtained as a result of the search. Alternatively, petitioners argue that they have standing to object to the search under *Jones* because they were "legitimately on [the] premises" at the time of the search.

*   *   *

We decline to extend the rule of standing in Fourth Amendment cases in the manner suggested by petitioners. As we stated in Alderman v. United States (1969), "Fourth Amendment rights are personal rights which, like some other constitutional rights, may not be vicariously asserted." A person who is aggrieved by an illegal search and seizure only through the introduction of damaging evidence secured by a search of a third person's premises or property has not had any of his Fourth Amendment rights infringed. And since the exclusionary rule is an attempt to effectuate the guaranties of the Fourth Amendment, United States v. Calandra, 414 U.S. 338, 347, 94 S.Ct. 613, 619 (1974), it is proper to permit only defendants whose Fourth Amendment rights have been violated to benefit from the rule's protections.[1] See Simmons v. United States, supra, 390 U.S., at 389, 88 S.Ct., at 973. There is no reason to think that a party whose rights have been infringed will not, if evidence is used against him, have ample motivation to move to suppress it. Even if such a person is not a defendant in the action, he may be able to recover damages for the violation of his Fourth Amendment rights, or seek redress under state law for invasion of privacy or trespass.

In support of their target theory, petitioners rely on the following quotation from *Jones*:

> "In order to qualify as a 'person aggrieved by an unlawful search and seizure' one must have been a victim of a search or seizure, *one against whom the search was directed*, as distinguished from one who claims prejudice only through the use of evidence gathered as a consequence of a search or seizure directed at someone else."

The above-quoted statement from *Jones* suggests that the italicized language was meant merely as a parenthetical equivalent of the previous phrase "a victim of a search or seizure." To the extent that the language might be read more broadly, it is dictum which was impliedly repudiated in Alderman v. United States (1969), and which we now expressly reject. In *Jones*, the Court set forth two alternative holdings: it established a rule of "automatic" standing to contest an allegedly illegal search where the same possession needed to establish standing is an essential element of the offense charged;[2] and

---

1. The necessity for a showing of a violation of personal rights is not obviated by recognizing the deterrent purpose of the exclusionary rule. Despite the deterrent aim of the exclusionary rule, we never have held that unlawfully seized evidence is inadmissible in all proceedings or against all persons. See, e. g., United States v. Ceccolini (1978); Stone v. Powell (1976); United States v. Calandra (1974). "[T]he application of the rule has been restricted to those areas where its remedial objectives are thought most efficaciously served."

2. We have not yet had occasion to decide whether the automatic standing rule of Jones survives our decision in Simmons v. United States

second, it stated that "anyone legitimately on premises where a search occurs may challenge its legality by way of a motion to suppress." Had the Court intended to adopt the target theory now put forth by petitioners, neither of the above two holdings would have been necessary since Jones was the "target" of the police search in that case.   .   .   .

In *Alderman*, Mr. Justice Fortas, in a concurring and dissenting opinion, argued that the Court should "include within the category of those who may object to the introduction of illegal evidence 'one against whom the search was directed.' " The Court did not directly comment on Mr. Justice Fortas' suggestion, but it left no doubt that it rejected this theory by holding that persons who were not parties to unlawfully overheard conversations or who did not own the premises on which such conversations took place did not have standing to contest the legality of the surveillance, regardless of whether or not they were the "targets" of the surveillance. Mr. Justice Harlan, concurring and dissenting, did squarely address Mr. Justice Fortas' arguments and declined to accept them. He identified administrative problems posed by the target theory:

> "[T]he [target] rule would entail very substantial administrative difficulties. In the majority of cases, I would imagine that the police plant a bug with the expectation that it may well produce leads to a large number of crimes. A lengthy hearing would, then, appear to be necessary in order to determine whether the police knew of an accused's criminal activity at the time the bug was planted and whether the police decision to plant a bug was motivated by an effort to obtain information against the accused or some other individual. I do not believe that this administrative burden is justified in any substantial degree by the hypothesized marginal increase in Fourth Amendment protection."

When we are urged to grant standing to a criminal defendant to assert a violation, not of his own constitutional rights but of someone else's, we cannot but give weight to practical difficulties such as those foreseen by Mr. Justice Harlan in the quoted language.

Conferring standing to raise vicarious Fourth Amendment claims would necessarily mean a more widespread invocation of the exclusionary rule during criminal trials. . . . Each time the exclusionary rule is applied it exacts a substantial social cost for the vindication of Fourth Amendment rights. Relevant and reliable evidence is kept from the trier of fact and the search for truth at trial is deflected. Since our cases generally have held that one whose Fourth Amendment rights are violated may successfully suppress evidence obtained in the course of an illegal search and seizure, misgivings as to the benefit of enlarging the class of persons who may invoke that

(1968). See Brown v. United States, 411 (1973). Such a rule is, or course, one which may allow a defendant to   assert the Fourth Amendment rights of another.

rule are properly considered when deciding whether to expand standing to assert Fourth Amendment violations.

* * *

. . . . This Court's long history of insistence that Fourth Amendment rights are personal in nature has already answered many of these traditional standing inquiries, and we think that definition of those rights is more properly placed within the purview of substantive Fourth Amendment law than within that of standing.[3]

* * *

Analyzed in these terms, the question is whether the challenged search or seizure violated the Fourth Amendment rights of a criminal defendant who seeks to exclude the evidence obtained during it. That inquiry in turn requires a determination of whether the disputed search and seizure has infringed an interest of the defendant which the Fourth Amendment was designed to protect. We are under no illusion that by dispensing with the rubric of standing used in *Jones* we have rendered any simpler the determination of whether the proponent of a motion to suppress is entitled to contest the legality of a search and seizure. But by frankly recognizing that this aspect of the analysis belongs more properly under the heading of substantive Fourth Amendment doctrine than under the heading of standing, we think the decision of this issue will rest on sounder logical footing.

Here petitioners, who were passengers occupying a car which they neither owned nor leased, seek to analogize their position to that of the defendant in Jones v. United States (1960). In *Jones*, petitioner was present at the time of the search of an apartment which was owned by a friend. The friend had given Jones permission to use the apartment and a key to it, with which Jones had admitted himself on the day of the search.[4] . . . He had a suit and shirt at the apartment and had slept there "maybe a night," but his home was elsewhere. At the time of the search, Jones was the only occupant of the apartment because the lessee was away for a period of several days. Id., at 259, 80 S.Ct., at 730. Under these circumstances, this Court stated that while one wrongfully on the premises could not move to suppress evidence obtained as a result of searching them, "anyone legitimately on premises where a search occurs may

---

3. This approach is consonant with that which the Court already has taken with respect to the Fifth Amendment privilege against self-incrimination, which also is a purely personal right.

4. The Court in *Jones* was quite careful to note that "wrongful" presence at the scene of a search would not enable a defendant to object to the legality of the search. The Court stated: "No just interest of the Government in the effective and rigorous enforcement of the criminal law will be hampered by recognizing that anyone legitimately on premises where a search occurs may challenge its legality by way of a motion to suppress, when its fruits are proposed to be used against him. *This would of course not avail those who, by virtue of their wrongful presence, cannot invoke the privacy of the premises searched.*" (emphasis added). Despite this clear statement in *Jones*, several lower courts inexplicably have held that a person present in a stolen automobile at the time of a search may object to the lawfulness of the search of the automobile. See, e. g., Cotton v. United States, 371 F. 2d 385 (CA9 1967); Simpson v. United States, 346 F.2d 291 (CA10 1965).

challenge its legality." 362 U.S., at 267, 80 S.Ct., at 734. Petitioners argue that their occupancy of the automobile in question was comparable to that of Jones in the apartment and that they therefore have standing to contest the legality of the search—or as we have rephrased the inquiry, that they, like Jones, had their Fourth Amendment rights violated by the search.

We do not question the conclusion in *Jones* that the defendant in that case suffered a violation of his personal Fourth Amendment rights if the search in question were unlawful. Nonetheless, we believe that the phrase "legitimately on premises" coined in *Jones* creates too broad a gauge for measurement of Fourth Amendment rights.[5] For example, applied literally, this statement would permit a casual visitor who has never seen, or been permitted to visit the basement of another's house to object to a search of the basement if the visitor happened to be in the kitchen of the house at the time of the search. Likewise, a casual visitor who walks into a house one minute before a search of the house commences and leaves one minute after the search ends would be able to contest the legality of the search. The first visitor would have absolutely no interest or legitimate expectation of privacy in the basement, the second would have none in the house, and it advances no purpose served by the Fourth Amendment to permit either of them to object to the lawfulness of the search.[6]

We think that *Jones* on its facts merely stands for the unremarkable proposition that a person can have a legally sufficient interest in a place other than his own home so that the Fourth Amendment protects him from unreasonable governmental intrusion into that place. In defining the scope of that interest, we adhere to the view expressed in *Jones* and echoed in later cases that arcane distinctions developed in property and tort law between guests, licensees, invitees, and the like, ought not to control. . . .

* * *

. . . the holding in *Jones* can best be explained by the fact that Jones had a legitimate expectation of privacy in the premises he was using and therefore could claim the protection of the Fourth

---

5. The Court in Mancusi v. DeForte, 392 U.S. 364, 88 S.Ct. 2120, 20 L.Ed. 2d 1154 (1968), also must have been unsatisfied with the "legitimately on premises" statement in *Jones*. DeForte was legitimately in his office at the time of the search and if the *Mancusi* Court had literally applied the statement from *Jones*, DeForte's standing to object to the search should have been obvious. Instead, to determine whether DeForte possessed standing to object to the search, the Court inquired into whether DeForte's office was an "area was one in which there was a reasonable expectation of freedom from governmental intrusion."

Unfortunately, with few exceptions, lower courts have literally applied this language from *Jones* and have held that anyone legitimately on premises at the time of the search may contest its legality. See, e. g., Garza-Fuentes v. United States, 400 F.2d 219 (CA5 1968); State v. Bresolin, 13 Wash.App. 386, 534 P.2d 1394 (1975).

6. This is not to say that such visitors could not contest the lawfulness of the seizure of evidence or the search if their own property were seized during the search.

Amendment with respect to a governmental invasion of those premises, even though his "interest" in those premises might not have been a recognized property interest at common law.[7]

*   *   *

. . . *Katz* held that capacity to claim the protection of the Fourth Amendment depends not upon a property right in the invaded place but upon whether the person who claims the protection of the Amendment has a legitimate expectation of privacy in the invaded place.

Our Brother White in dissent expresses the view that by rejecting the phrase "legitimately on [the] premises" as the appropriate measure of Fourth Amendment rights, we are abandoning a thoroughly workable, "bright line" test in favor of a less certain analysis of whether the facts of a particular case give rise to a legitimate expectation of privacy. If "legitimately on premises" were the successful litmus test of Fourth Amendment rights that he assumes it is, his approach would have at least the merit of easy application, whatever it lacked in fidelity to the history and purposes of the Fourth Amendment. But a reading of lower court cases that have applied the phrase "legitimately on premises," and of the dissent itself, reveals that this expression is not a shorthand summary for a bright line rule which somehow encapsulates the "core" of the Fourth Amendment's protections.

*   *   *

7. Obviously, however, a "legitimate" expectation of privacy by definition means more than a subjective expectation of not being discovered. A burglar plying his trade in a summer cabin during the off season may have a thoroughly justified subjective expectation of privacy, but it is not one which the law recognizes as "legitimate." His presence, in the words of *Jones*, is "wrongful"; his expectation is not "one that society is prepared to recognize as 'reasonable.'" Katz v. United States (1967) (Harlan, J., concurring). And it would, of course, be merely tautological to fall back on the notion that those expectations of privacy which are legitimate depend primarily on cases deciding exclusionary rule issues in criminal cases. Legitimation of expectations of privacy by law must have a source outside of the Fourth Amendment, either by reference to concepts of real or personal property law or to understandings that are recognized and permitted by society. One of the main rights attaching to property is the right to exclude others, see W. Blackstone, Commentaries, Book II, Ch. I, and one who owns or lawfully possesses or controls property will in all likelihood have a legitimate expectation of privacy by virtue of this right to exclude. Expectations of privacy protected by the Fourth Amendment, of course, need not be based on a common-law interest in real or personal property, or on the invasion of such an interest. These ideas were rejected both in *Jones*, supra, and *Katz*, supra. But by focusing on legitimate expectations of privacy in Fourth Amendment jurisprudence, the Court has not altogether abandoned use of property concepts in determining the presence or absence of the privacy interests protected by that Amendment. No better demonstration of this proposition exists than the decision in Alderman v. United States (1969), where the Court held that an individual's property interest in his own home was so great as to allow him to object to electronic surveillance of conversations emanating from his home, even though he himself was not a party to the conversations. On the other hand, even a property interest in premises may not be sufficient to establish a legitimate expectation of privacy with respect to particular items located on the premises or activity conducted thereon.

Our disagreement with the dissent is not that it leaves these questions unanswered, or that the questions are necessarily irrelevant in the context of the analysis contained in this opinion. Our disagreement is rather with the dissent's bland and self-refuting assumption that there will not be fine lines to be drawn in Fourth Amendment cases as in other areas of the law, and that its rubric, rather than a meaningful exegesis of Fourth Amendment doctrine, is more desirable or more easily resolves Fourth Amendment cases. In abandoning "legitimately on premises" for the doctrine that we announce today, we are not forsaking a time-tested and workable rule, which has produced consistent results when applied, solely for the sake of fidelity to the values underlying the Fourth Amendment. We also are rejecting blind adherence to a phrase which at most has superficial clarity and which conceals underneath that thin veneer all of the problems of line drawing which must be faced in any conscientious effort to apply the Fourth Amendment. Where the factual premises for a rule are so generally prevalent that little would be lost and much would be gained by abandoning case-by-case analysis, we have not hesitated to do so. See United States v. Robinson, 414 U.S. 218, 235, 94 S.Ct. 467, 476 (1973). But the phrase "legitimately on premises" has not shown to be an easily applicable measure of Fourth Amendment rights so much as it has proved to be simply a label placed by the courts on results which have not been subjected to careful analysis. We would not wish to be understood as saying that legitimate presence on the premises is irrelevant to one's expectation of privacy, but it cannot be deemed controlling.

Judged by the foregoing analysis, petitioners' claims must fail. They asserted neither a property nor a possessory interest in the automobile, nor an interest in the property seized. And as we have previously indicated, the fact that they were "legitimately on [the] premises" in the sense that they were in the car with the permission of its owner is not determinative of whether they had a legitimate expectation of privacy in the particular areas of the automobile searched. It is unnecessary for us to decide here whether the same expectations of privacy are warranted in a car as would be justified in a dwelling place in analogous circumstances. We have on numerous occasions pointed out that cars are not to be treated identically with houses or Apartments for Fourth Amendment purposes.[8] But here petitioners' claim is one which would fail even in an analogous situation in a dwelling place since they made no showing that they had any legitimate expectation of privacy in the glove compartment or area under the seat of the car in which they were merely passengers. Like the trunk of an automobile, these are areas in which a passenger *qua* passenger simply would not normally have a legitimate expectation of privacy.

. . . Katz and Jones could legitimately expect privacy in the areas which were the subject of the search and seizure they sought to

---

8. As we noted in *Martinez-Fuerte*, "[O]ne's expectation of privacy in an automobile and of freedom in its operation are significantly different from the traditional expectation of privacy and freedom in one's residence."

contest. No such showing was made by these petitioners with respect to those portions of the automobile which were searched and from which incriminating evidence was seized.

The Illinois courts were therefore correct in concluding that it was unnecessary to decide whether the search of the car might have violated the rights secured to someone else by the Fourth and Fourteenth Amendments to the United States Constitution. Since it did not violate any rights of these petitioners, their judgment of conviction is

Affirmed.

MR. JUSTICE POWELL, with whom THE CHIEF JUSTICE joins, concurring.

I concur in the opinion of the Court, and add these thoughts. I do not believe my dissenting Brethren correctly characterize the rationale of the Court's opinion when they assert that it ties "the application of the Fourth Amendment . . . to property law concepts." On the contrary, I read the Court's opinion as focusing on whether there was a *legitimate* expectation of privacy protected by the Fourth Amendment.

The petitioners do not challenge the constitutionality of the police action in stopping the automobile in which they were riding; nor do they complain of being made to get out of the vehicle. Rather, petitioners assert that their constitutionally protected interest in privacy was violated when the police, after stopping the automobile and making them get out, searched the vehicle's interior, where they discovered a sawed-off rifle under the front seat and rifle shells in the locked glove compartment. The question before the Court, therefore, is a narrow one: Did the search of their friend's automobile after they had left it violate any Fourth Amendment right of the petitioners?

The ultimate question, therefore, is whether one's claim to privacy from government intrusion is reasonable in light of all the surrounding circumstances. As the dissenting opinion states, this standard "will not provide law enforcement officials with a bright line between the protected and the unprotected." See post, at 443. Whatever the application of this standard may lack in ready administration, it is more faithful to the purposes of the Fourth Amendment than a test focusing solely or primarily on whether the defendant was legitimately present during the search.[9]

*   *   *

9. Allowing anyone who is legitimately on the premises searched to invoke the exclusionary rule extends the rule far beyond the proper scope of Fourth Amendment protections, as not all who are legitimately present invariably have a reasonable expectation of privacy. And, as the Court points out, the dissenters' standard lacks even the advantage of easy application.

I do not share the dissenters' concern that the Court's ruling will "invite[ ] police to engage in patently unreasonable searches every time an automobile contains more than one occupant." A police officer observing an automobile carrying several passengers will not know the circumstances surrounding each occupant's presence in the automobile, and certainly will not know whether an occupant will

MR. JUSTICE WHITE, with whom MR. JUSTICE BRENNAN, MR. JUSTICE MARSHALL, and MR. JUSTICE STEVENS join, dissenting.

The Court today holds that the Fourth Amendment protects property, not people, and specifically that a legitimate occupant of an automobile may not invoke the exclusionary rule and challenge a search of that vehicle unless he happens to own or have a possessory interest in it. Though professing to acknowledge that the primary purpose of the Fourth Amendment's prohibition of unreasonable searches is the protection or privacy—not property—the Court nonetheless effectively ties the application of the Fourth Amendment and the exclusionary rule in this situation to property law concepts. Insofar as passengers are concerned, the Court's opinion today declares an "open season" on automobiles. However unlawful stopping and searching a car may be, absent a possessory or ownership interest, no "mere" passenger may object, regardless of his relationship to the owner.

* * *

The Court's holding is contrary not only to our past decisions and the logic of the Fourth Amendment, but also to the everyday expectations of privacy that we all share. Because of that, it is unworkable in all the various situations that arise in real life. If the owner of the car had not only invited petitioners to join her but had said to them "I give you a temporary possessory interest in my vehicle so that you will share the right to privacy that the Supreme Court says that I own," then apparently the majority would reverse. But people seldom say such things, though they may mean their invitation to encompass them if only they had thought of the problem. If the nonowner were the spouse or child of the owner, would the Court recognize a sufficient interest? If so, would distant relatives somehow have more of an expectation of privacy than close friends? What if the nonowner were driving with the owner's permission? Would nonowning drivers have more of an expectation of privacy than mere passengers? What about a passenger in a taxicab? *Katz* expressly recognized protection for such passengers. Why should Fourth Amendment rights be present when one pays a cabdriver for a ride but be absent when one is given a ride by a friend?

The distinctions the Court would draw are based on relationships between private parties, but the Fourth Amendment is concerned with the relationship of one of those parties to the government. Divorced as it is from the purpose of the Fourth Amendment, the Court's essentially property-based rationale can satisfactorily answer none of the questions posed above. That is reason enough to reject it. The *Jones* rule is relatively easily applied by police and courts; the rule announced today will not provide law enforcement officials

be able to establish that he had a reasonable expectation of privacy. Thus, there will continue to be a significant incentive for the police to comply with the requirements of the Fourth Amendment, lest otherwise valid prosecutions be voided. Moreover, any marginal diminution in this incentive that might result from the Court's decision today is more than justified by society's interest in restricting the scope of the exclusionary rule to those cases where in fact there was a reasonable expectation of privacy.

with a bright line between the protected and the unprotected. Only rarely will police know whether one private party has or has not been granted a sufficient possessory or other interest by another private party. Surely in this case the officers had no such knowledge. The Court's rule will ensnare defendants and police in needless litigation over factors that should not be determinative of Fourth Amendment rights.

More importantly, the ruling today undercuts the force of the exclusionary rule in the one area in which its use is most certainly justified—the deterrence of bad-faith violations of the Fourth Amendment. See *Stone v. Powell* (WHITE, J., dissenting). This decision invites police to engage in patently unreasonable searches every time an automobile contains more than one occupant. Should something be found, only the owner of the vehicle, or of the item, will have standing to seek suppression, and the evidence will presumably be usable against the other occupants. The danger of such bad faith is especially high in cases such as this one where the officers are only after the passengers and can usually infer accurately that the driver is the owner. The suppression remedy for those owners in whose vehicles something is found and who are charged with crime is small consolation for all those owners *and* occupants whose privacy will be needlessly invaded by officers following mistaken hunches not rising to the level of probable cause but operated on in the knowledge that someone in a crowded car will probably be unprotected if contraband or incriminating evidence happens to be found. After this decision, police will have little to lose by unreasonably searching vehicles occupied by more than one person.

Of course, most police officers will decline the Court's invitation and will continue to do their jobs as best they can in accord with the Fourth Amendment. But the very purpose of the Bill of Rights was to answer the justified fear that governmental agents cannot be left totally to their own devices, and the Bill of Rights is enforceable in the courts because human experience teaches that not all such officials will otherwise adhere to the stated precepts. Some policemen simply do act in bad faith, even if for understandable ends, and some deterrent is needed. In the rush to limit the applicability of the exclusionary rule somewhere, anywhere, the Court ignores precedent, logic, and common sense to exclude the rule's operation from situations in which, paradoxically, it is justified and needed.

NOTES

1. After *Rakas*, can standing be decided as a preliminary matter before the merits of a search and seizure claim are explored, or must an evidentiary hearing "on the merits" always be held where the accused alleges a violation of a reasonable expectation of privacy? See Pollard v. State, —— Ind. ——, 388 N.E.2d 496 (1979); Rawlings v. Commonwealth, 581 S.W.2d 348 (Ky.1979).

2. Under what circumstances, if not those in *Rakas*, would a passenger have a reasonable expectation of privacy in portions of the vehicle?

3. Does *Rakas* apply to homes? Let us suppose that *B* is present as a guest in *A's* home when the police make an illegal, warrantless entry of *A's* home and search *A's* bedroom closet. *B* may have no reasonable expectation of privacy in *A's* closet, but can all the evidence be viewed as the fruit of the illegal entry of the home? Does *B* have a reasonable expectation of privacy vis-á-vis entry into *A's* home?

4. Normally, a person who is in possession of a stolen vehicle has no standing to complain about the unlawful search of the vehicle. See Palmer v. State, 14 Md.App. 159, 286 A.2d 572 (1972); People v. Henenberg, 55 Ill. 2d 5, 302 N.E.2d 27 (1973). Suppose, however, that the original stop of the car is unlawful. Can the thief-driver complain that all evidence discovered was the product of his unlawful detention and must be suppressed as the fruit of a violation of *his* rights? Could a passenger in a stolen vehicle make a similar argument following an unlawful stop? Could a passenger lawfully present in a vehicle complain about a search of the car's trunk following an unlawful stop? Did Rakas advance such an argument, contending that the items discovered should be viewed as the product of *his* unlawful detention? How significant is the statement in the *Rakas* concurring opinion indicating that the passengers did not claim that the stop of the car was illegal?

5. As noted in *Rakas*, an alternative holding in Jones v. United States (1960) provided for "automatic standing" in a certain class of cases. In that class of cases (generally interpreted as "possession" cases), a defendant did *not* have to allege or prove an interest in the place searched or the items seized. The Court said that it was unfair for the Government to assert the contradictory position that (a) the defendant was guilty because of his possession of certain items, but that (b) the defendant did not have sufficient interest in the place searched or the items seized so as to obtain standing. The Court also held that it was unfair to require a defendant, in order to urge a Fourth Amendment violation, to incriminate himself by testifying that he possessed or controlled the place searched or the items seized because such testimony was tantamount to a confession. Thereafter, in Simmons v. United States, 390 U.S. 377, 88 S.Ct. 967 (1968) the Court held that such testimony given by the defendant on a motion to suppress as was essential to acquire standing could *not* be used against the defendant at trial. In Brown v. United States, 411 U.S. 223, 93 S.Ct. 1565 (1973), the government argued that this "use-exclusion" rule of *Simmons* had removed any unfairness in requiring the defendant to allege and prove facts essential to acquire standing. The *Brown* Court did not pass judgment upon this argument, but it refused to extend automatic standing beyond cases where the defendant is "charged with an offense which includes, as an essential element of the offense charged, possession of the seized evidence at the time of the contested search and seizure."

6. Does *Brown* afford automatic standing in all cases where possession is an element of the offense? Suppose that in an allegedly illegal search of *A's* home, *A* is found in illegal possession of narcotics. The government's theory is that *B* is also guilty of possession, under principles of accountability, in that he and *A* obtained the narcotics for resale and stored them at *A's* home. *B* was not present at the search and, unless he is afforded "automatic" standing, he will not be able to prevent use of the narcotics against *B* unless he alleges and proves that the narcotics were his. Would elimination of automatic standing be fair to *B*? Would the government be taking inconsistent positions if it insisted that absent proof of ownership of the items seized, *B* should be denied standing? See United

States v. Jones, 518 F.2d 64 (9th Cir. 1975); United States v. Hunter, 550 F.2d 1066 (6th Cir. 1977). Compare United States v. Galante, 547 F.2d 733 (2d Cir. 1976); United States v. Boston, 510 F.2d 35 (9th Cir. 1974). The issue could be resolved in United States v. Salvucci, 599 F.2d 1094 (5th Cir. 1979), cert. granted — U.S. —, 100 S.Ct. 519.

7. Occasionally government attorneys have argued that automatic standing should be totally abolished because the defendant's testimony, offered to acquire standing, cannot be used against him at trial (at least in the government's case-in-chief, see Section D2, Note 7, infra.) Some courts have held that the "use-exclusion" rule is not adequate. See United States v. Cobb, 432 F.2d 716 (4th Cir. 1970); United States v. Anderson, 552 F.2d 1296 (8th Cir. 1977). What the Fifth Amendment prohibits the government from doing is (1) compelling a person to give testimonial evidence against himself *and* (2) making evidentiary use of compelled testimony. *Normally*, absent a formal grant of immunity, we do *not* say that it is permissible to compel incriminating testimony as long as the testimony is not used against the compelled person. See Chapter 11, Section E, note 2 following Gardner v. Broderick.

8. If "automatic" standing is left for use in possession cases, what about situations where possession, although not an element, is highly probative of guilt, as for example, in a case where the jury is instructed that an inference of guilt in a burglary case arises from a defendant's recent, unexplained possession of the proceeds of the burglary. *Brown* would disallow automatic standing in such a situation, but can one logically defend automatic standing in a possession case while denying it in the hypothetical burglary case? See Duncan v. State, 276 Md. 715, 351 A.2d 144 (1976). Compare People v. McNeil, 53 Ill.2d 187, 290 N.E.2d 602 (1972). Was *Jones* itself a case where possession was an *element* of the offense?

9. As *Alderman* indicates in a footnote, *B* is not accorded standing simply because he is on trial with codefendant *A*, whose rights were violated, although at one time, in lower federal courts at least, the *McDonald* decision cited in the *Alderman* note was read to create a co-defendant standing rule. If very damning evidence is inadmissible against *A* but admissible against *B* for want of standing, in some circumstances *A* may be entitled to a separate trial if the case is to be tried before a jury.

---

3.   "STANDING" CONCEPTS RESPECTING THE FRUITS OF UN-LAWFUL INTERROGATION AND EYE–WITNESS IDENTIFICATION PROCEDURES

Most standing questions arise in the context of Fourth Amendment claims. Confession cases do not give rise to as many standing issues because hearsay rules normally prevent use of *A's* confession as substantive evidence against *B*. What *A* says on a relevant subject is admissible against *A* as an admission of a party opponent. As to *B*, however, *A's* confession is inadmissible hearsay. Where derivative evidence questions are involved, however, standing issues can arise in a confession case. Generally, *Miranda* rights are considered personal and cannot be vicariously asserted. If a gun is discovered through custodial interrogation of *A* without warnings or waiver, the gun can be used against *B* if relevant and otherwise admissible. Similarly, if *B* is arrested as a result of *A's* confession, *B* cannot com-

plain that probable cause data was acquired through a violation of
A's Miranda rights. See People v. Denham, 41 Ill.2d 1, 241 N.E.2d
415 (1968). This is true even in California, where Fourth Amendment rights can be vicariously asserted (see Section C–1, *supra*). In
People v. Varnum, 66 Cal.2d 808, 59 Cal.Rptr. 108, 427 P.2d 772
(1967), the court reasoned that until the prosecutor offers *A's* confession (or evidence derived therefrom) against *A*, there is no violation of *A's* Miranda rights. In this view, although a constitutional
violation occurs when *A's* house is illegally searched to obtain evidence against *B*, no constitutional violation occurs when *A* is subjected to custodial interrogation without warnings to secure information
which may lead to evidence against *B*.

Suppose that the police obtain an involuntary confession from *A*
and are led by it to physical evidence which helps establish *B's* guilt.
Should *B* be allowed to obtain exclusion based upon a violation of *A's*
rights? Or suppose *A* testifies as a defense witness for *B* and the
prosecution seek to impeach *A* by reference to *A's* involuntary confession. Should the standing concept bar *B* from raising a challenge to
this use of *A's* confession? Should all involuntary confessions be excluded in this situation or just confessions which are, in fact, unreliable? Consider these issues in connection with the materials on impeachment use of involuntary confessions, Section D–2, note 5, infra.

An identification of *A* as one of the bank robbers may tend to
prove *B's* guilt if *B* is proved to be an associate of *A* and to have been
in *A's* company shortly before and shortly after the robbery. If the
in-court identification and proof of the out-of-court identification of
A are ruled to be inadmissible against *A* under *Stovall* and Manson v.
Brathwaite (Chapter 3, Section B, supra), should not they also be inadmissible against *B* even though not the product of a violation of *B's*
rights? Is not the court under *Manson* saying that such evidence is
unreliable? Should unreliable evidence ever be utilized? Would different reasoning apply to an out-of-court identification excluded under *Gilbert* because of a violation of *A's* right to counsel? Only a
few decisions treat standing questions as they relate to eyewitness
identification. Compare Burton v. State, 442 S.W.2d 354 (Tex.Crim.
App.1969), with State v. Isaacs, 24 Ohio App.2d 115, 265 N.E.2d 327,
53 O.O.2d 331 (1970). See also People v. Bisogni, 4 Cal.3d 582, 94
Cal.Rptr. 164, 483 P.2d 780 (1971), and United States v. Bruton, 416
F.2d 310 (8th Cir. 1969).

D.   COLLATERAL USE OF ILLEGALLY OBTAINED EVIDENCE

1.   COLLATERAL PROCEEDINGS USAGE

UNITED STATES v. CALANDRA

Supreme Court of the United States, 1974.
414 U.S. 338, 94 S.Ct. 613.

[Federal agents executed a search warrant at Calandra's place of business and seized an alleged loansharking record bearing the name of a Dr. Loveland. Calandra was subpoenaed before a federal grand jury, and the government petitioned the district court to grant Calandra transactional immunity. Calandra received a postponement of a hearing on the immunity petition. He then filed a motion to suppress under Rule 41(e) of the Federal Rules of Criminal Procedure and asked that the seized items be returned and that he not be required to answer before the grand jury questions based upon illegally seized evidence. The district court found that the search warrant had been issued without probable cause and that the seizure exceeded the scope of the warrant. The district court prohibited questions based on the illegally seized evidence. The Sixth Circuit Court of Appeals affirmed. The Supreme Court granted certiorari.]

MR. JUSTICE POWELL delivered the opinion of the Court.

This case presents the question whether a witness summoned to appear and testify before a grand jury may refuse to answer questions on the ground that they are based on evidence obtained from an unlawful search and seizure. The issue is of considerable importance to the administration of criminal justice.

* * *

The institution of the grand jury is deeply rooted in Anglo-American history. In England, the grand jury served for centuries both as a body of accusers sworn to discover and present for trial persons suspected of criminal wrongdoing and as a protector of citizens against arbitrary and oppressive governmental action. In this country the Founders thought the grand jury so essential to basic liberties that they provided in the Fifth Amendment that federal prosecution for serious crimes can only be instituted by "a presentment or indictment of a Grand Jury." Cf. Costello v. United States . . . (1956). The grand jury's historic functions survive to this day. Its responsibilities continue to include both the determination whether there is probable cause to believe a crime has been committed and the protection of citizens against unfounded criminal prosecutions. Branzburg v. Hayes . . . (1972).

Traditionally the grand jury has been accorded wide latitude to inquire into violations of criminal law. No judge presides to monitor its proceedings. It deliberates in secret and may determine alone the course of its inquiry. The grand jury may compel the production of evidence or the testimony of witnesses as it considers appropriate, and its operation generally is unrestrained by the technical procedural and evidentiary rules governing the conduct of criminal trials. "It is a grand inquest, a body with powers of investigation and inquisition, the scope of whose inquiries is not to be limited narrowly by questions of propriety or forecasts of the probable result of the investigation, or by doubts whether any particular individual will be found properly subject to an accusation of crime." Blair v. United States . . . (1919).

The scope of the grand jury's powers reflects its special role in insuring fair and effective law enforcement. A grand jury proceeding is not an adversary hearing in which the guilt or innocence of the accused is adjudicated. Rather, it is an ex parte investigation to determine whether a crime has been committed and whether criminal proceedings should be instituted against any person. The grand jury's investigative power must be broad if its public responsibility is adequately to be discharged. Branzburg v. Hayes, supra. . . .

* * *

Of course, the grand jury's subpoena power is not unlimited.[1] It may consider incompetent evidence, but it may not itself violate a valid privilege, whether established by the Constitution, statutes, or the common law. . . . Although, for example, an indictment based on evidence obtained in violation of a defendant's Fifth Amendment privilege is nevertheless valid, Lawn v. United States, supra, the grand jury may not force a witness to answer questions in violation of that constitutional guarantee. Rather, the grand jury may override a Fifth Amendment claim only if the witness is granted immunity co-extensive with the privilege against self-incrimination. Kastigar v. United States, supra. Similarly, a grand jury may not compel a person to produce books and papers that would incriminate him. Boyd v. United States . . . (1886). Cf. Couch v. United States . . . (1973). The grand jury is also without power to invade a legitimate privacy interest protected by the Fourth Amendment. A grand jury's subpoena duces tecum will be disallowed if it is "far too sweeping in its terms to be regarded as reasonable" under the Fourth Amendment. Hale v. Henkel . . . (1906). Judicial supervision is properly exercised in such cases to prevent the wrong before it occurs.

In the instant case, the Court of Appeals held that the exclusionary rule of the Fourth Amendment limits the grand jury's power to

---

1. The grand jury is subject to the court's supervision in several respects. See Brown v. United States . . . (1959); Fed.Rules Crim. Proc. 6 and 17; 1 L. Orfield, Criminal Procedure Under the Federal Rules § 6:108, pp. 475–477 (1966). In particular, the grand jury must rely on the court to compel production of books, papers, documents. and the testimony of witness, and the court may quash or modify a subpoena on motion if compliance would be "unreasonable or oppressive." Fed.Rule Crim.Proc. 17(c).

compel a witness to answer questions based on evidence obtained from a prior unlawful search and seizure. . . .

The purpose of the exclusionary rule is not to redress the injury to the privacy of the search victim:

> "[T]he ruptured privacy of the victims' homes and effects cannot be restored. Reparation comes too late." Linkletter v. Walker . . . (1965).

Instead, the rule's prime purpose is to deter future unlawful police conduct and thereby effectuate the guarantee of the Fourth Amendment against unreasonable search and seizures:

> "The rule is calculated to prevent, not to repair. Its purpose is to deter—to compel respect for the constitutional guaranty in the only effectively available way—by removing the incentive to disregard it." Elkins v. United States . . . (1960).

Accord, Mapp v. Ohio, 367 U.S. 643, at 656; Tehan v. Shott . . . (1966); Terry v. Ohio . . . (1968). In sum, the rule is a judicially created remedy designed to safeguard Fourth Amendment rights generally through its deterrent effect, rather than a personal constitutional right of the party aggrieved.

Despite its broad deterrent purpose, the exclusionary rule has never been interpreted to proscribe the use of illegally seized evidence in all proceedings or against all persons. As with any remedial device, the application of the rule has been restricted to those areas where its remedial objectives are thought most efficaciously served. The balancing process implicit in this approach is expressed in the contours of the standing requirement. Thus, standing to invoke the exclusionary rule has been confined to situations where the Government seeks to use such evidence to incriminate the victim of the unlawful search. Brown v. United States . . . (1973); Alderman v. United States . . . (1969); Wong Sun v. United States, supra; Jones v. United States . . . (1960). This standing rule is premised on a recognition that the need for deterrence and hence the rationale for excluding the evidence are strongest where the Government's unlawful conduct would result in imposition of a criminal sanction on the victim of the search.[2]

In deciding whether to extend the exclusionary rule to grand jury proceedings, we must weigh the potential injury to the historic role and functions of the grand jury against the potential benefits of the rule as applied in this context. It is evident that this extension

---

2. The Court of Appeals also found that the government's offer of immunity under 18 U.S.C.A. § 2514 was irrelevant to respondent's standing to invoke the exclusionary rule. . . . We agree with that determination. . . .

The force of this argument is well illustrated by the facts of the present case. As of the date of this decision, almost two and one-half years will have elapsed since respondent was summoned to appear and testify before the grand jury. If respondent's testimony was vital to the grand jury's investigation in August 1971 of extortionate credit transactions, it is possible that this particular investigation has been completely frustrated.

of the exclusionary rule would seriously impede the grand jury. Because the grand jury does not finally adjudicate guilt or innocence, it has traditionally been allowed to pursue its investigative and accusatorial functions unimpeded by the evidentiary and procedural restrictions applicable to a criminal trial. Permitting witnesses to invoke the exclusionary rule before a grand jury would precipitate adjudication of issues hitherto reserved for the trial on the merits and would delay and disrupt grand jury proceedings. Suppression hearings would halt the orderly progress of an investigation and might necessitate extended litigation of issues only tangentially related to the grand jury's primary objective.[3] The probable result would be "protracted interruption of grand jury proceedings," Gelbard v. United States . . . (1972) (White, J., concurring), effectively transforming them into preliminary trials on the merits. In some cases the delay might be fatal to the enforcement of the criminal law. Just last Term we reaffirmed our disinclination to allow litigious interference with grand jury proceedings:

> "Any holding that would saddle a grand jury with minitrials and preliminary showings would assuredly impede its investigation and frustrate the public's interest in the fair and expeditious administration of the criminal laws." United States v. Dionisio . . . (1973).

In sum, we believe that allowing a grand jury witness to invoke the exclusionary rule would unduly interfere with the effective and expeditious discharge of the grand jury's duties.

Against this potential damage to the role and functions of the grand jury, we must weigh the benefits to be derived from this proposed extension of the exclusionary rule. Suppression of the use of illegally seized evidence against the search victim in a criminal trial is thought to be an important method of effectuating the Fourth Amendment. But it does not follow that the Fourth Amendment requires adoption of every proposal that might deter police misconduct. In Alderman v. United States . . . for example, this Court declined to extend the exclusionary rule to one who was not the victim of the unlawful search:

> "The deterrent values of preventing the incrimination of those whose rights the police have violated have been considered sufficient to justify the suppression of probative evidence even though the case against the defendant is weakened or destroyed. We adhere to that judgment. But we

---

3. In holding that the respondent had standing to invoke the exclusionary rule in a grand jury proceeding, the Court of Appeals relied on Fed.Rule Crim.Proc. 41(e). . . . Rule 41(e) provides, in relevant part, that "[a] person aggrieved by an unlawful search and seizure may move the district court . . . for the return of the property and to suppress for the use as evidence anything so obtained . . . ." It further states that "[t]he motion shall be made before trial or hearing . . . ." We have recognized that Rule 41(e) is "no broader than the constitutional rule." Alderman v. United States . . . (1969). Jones v. United States . . . (1960). Rule 41(e), therefore, does not constitute a statutory expansion of the exclusionary rule.

are not convinced that the additional benefits of extending the exclusionary rule to other defendants would justify further encroachment upon the public interest in prosecuting those accused of crime and having them acquitted or convicted on the basis of all the evidence which exposes the truth."

We think this observation equally applicable in the present context.

Any incremental deterrent effect which might be achieved by extending the rule to grand jury proceedings is uncertain at best. Whatever deterrence of police misconduct may result from the exclusion of illegally seized evidence from criminal trials, it is unrealistic to assume that application of the rule to grand jury proceedings would significantly further that goal. Such an extension would deter only police investigation consciously directed toward the discovery of evidence solely for use in a grand jury investigation. The incentive to disregard the requirement of the Fourth Amendment solely to obtain an indictment from a grand jury is substantially negated by the inadmissibility of the illegally seized evidence in a subsequent criminal prosecution of the search victim. For the most part, a prosecutor would be unlikely to request an indictment where a conviction could not be obtained. We therefore decline to embrace a view that would achieve a speculative and undoubtedly minimal advance in the deterrence of police misconduct at the expense of substantially impeding the role of the grand jury. . . .

Questions based on illegally obtained evidence are only a derivative use of the product of a past unlawful search and seizure. They work no new Fourth Amendment wrong. Whether such derivative use of illegally obtained evidence by a grand jury should be proscribed presents a question, not of rights, but of remedies.

In the usual context of a criminal trial, the defendant is entitled to the suppression of, not only the evidence obtained through an unlawful search and seizure, but also any derivative use of that evidence. The prohibition of the exclusionary rule must reach such derivative use if it is to fulfill its function of deterring police misconduct. In the context of a grand jury proceeding, we believe that the damage to that institution from the unprecedented extension of the exclusionary rule urged by respondent outweighs the benefit of any possible incremental deterrent effect. Our conclusion necessarily controls both the evidence seized during the course of an unlawful search and seizure and any question or evidence derived therefrom (the fruits of the unlawful search).[4] The same considerations of log-

---

4. It should be noted that, even absent the exclusionary rule, a grand jury witness may have other remedies to redress the injury to his privacy and to prevent a further invasion in the future. He may be entitled to maintain a cause of action for damages against the officers who conducted the unlawful search. Bivens v. Six Unknown Federal Narcotics Agents . . . (1971). He may also seek return of the illegally seized property, and exlusion of the property and its fruits from being used as evidence against him in a criminal trial. Go-Bart Importing Co. v. United States . . . (1931). In these circumstances, we cannot say that such a witness is necessarily left remediless in the face of an unlawful search and seizure.

ic and policy apply to both the fruits of an unlawful search and seizure and derivative use of that evidence, and we do not distinguish between them.[5]

The judgment of the Court of Appeals is

Reversed.

MR. JUSTICE BRENNAN, with whom MR. JUSTICE DOUGLAS and MR. JUSTICE MARSHALL join, dissenting.

* * *

This downgrading of the exclusionary rule to a determination whether its application in a particular type of proceeding furthers deterrence of future police misconduct reflects a startling misconception, unless it is a purposeful rejection, of the historical objective and purpose of the rule.

It is true that deterrence was a prominent consideration in the determination whether Mapp v. Ohio . . . (1961), which applied the exclusionary rule to the States, should be given retrospective effect. Linkletter v. Walker . . . (1965). But that lends no support to today's holding that the application of the exclusionary rule depends solely upon whether its invocation in a particular type of proceeding will significantly further the goal of deterrence. The emphasis upon deterrence in Linkletter must be understood in the light of the crucial fact that the States had justifiably relied from 1949 to 1961 upon Wolf v. Colorado . . . (1949), and consequently, that application of Mapp would have required the wholesale release of innumerable convicted prisoners, few of whom could have been successfully retried. In that circumstance, Linkletter held not only that retrospective application of Mapp would not further the goal of deterrence but also that it would not further "the administration of justice and the integrity of the judicial process."

---

5. The dissent's reliance on Gelbard v. United States . . . (1972) is misplaced. There, the Court construed 18 U.S.C.A. § 2515, the evidentiary prohibition of Tit. III of the Omnibus Crime Control and Safe Streets Act of 1968, . . . as amended. . . . It held that § 2515 could be invoked by a grand jury witness as a defense to a contempt charge brought for refusal to answer questions based on information obtained from the witness' communications alleged to have been unlawfully intercepted through wiretapping and electronic surveillance. The Court's holding rested exclusively on an interpretation of Tit. III, which represented a congressional effort to afford special safeguards against the unique problems posed by misuse of wiretapping and electronic surveillance. There was no indication, in either Gelbard or the legislative history, that Tit. III was regarded as a restatement of existing law with respect to grand jury proceedings. As Mr. Justice White noted in his concurring opinion in Gelbard, Tit. III "unquestionably works a change in the law with respect to the rights of grand jury witnesses . . . ."

The dissent also voices concern that today's decision will betray " 'the imperative of judicial integrity,' " sanction "illegal government conduct," and even "imperil the very foundation of our people's trust in their Government." . . . There is no basis for this alarm. "Illegal conduct" is hardly sanctioned, nor are the foundations of the Republic imperiled, by declining to make an unprecedented extension of the exclusionary rule to grand jury proceedings where the rule's objectives would not be effectively served and where other important and historic values would be unduly prejudiced.

Thus, the Court seriously errs in describing the exclusionary rule as merely "a judicially created remedy designed to safeguard Fourth Amendment rights generally through its deterrent effect . . . ." . . . Rather, the exclusionary rule is "part and parcel of the Fourth Amendment's limitation upon [governmental] encroachment of individual privacy," Mapp v. Ohio, supra, . . . and "an essential part of both the Fourth and Fourteenth Amendments," . . . that "gives to the individual no more than that which the Constitution guarantees him, to the police officer no less than that to which honest law enforcement is entitled, and, to the courts, that judicial integrity so necessary in the true administration of justice."

It is no answer, to suggest as the Court does, that the grand jury witnesses' Fourth Amendment rights will be sufficiently protected "by the inadmissibility of the illegally seized evidence in a subsequent criminal prosecution of the search victim." . . . This, of course, is no alternative for Calandra, since he was granted transactional immunity and cannot be criminally prosecuted. . . .

To be sure, the exclusionary rule does not "provide that illegally seized evidence is inadmissible against anyone for any purpose." Alderman v. United States . . . (1969). But clearly there is a crucial distinction between withholding its cover from individuals whose Fourth Amendment rights have not been violated—as has been done in the "standing" cases, Alderman v. United States, supra, Jones v. United States . . . (1960)—and withdrawing its cover from persons whose Fourth Amendment rights have in fact been abridged.

Respondent does not seek vicariously to assert another's Fourth Amendment rights. He himself has been the victim of an illegal search and desires "to mend no one's privacy [but his] own." Gelbard v. United States, supra . . . (Douglas, J., concurring). Respondent is told that he must look to damages to redress the concededly unconstitutional invasion of his privacy. In other words, officialdom may profit from its lawlessness if it is willing to pay a price.

In Mapp, the Court thought it had "close[d] the only courtroom door remaining open to evidence secured by official lawlessness" in violation of Fourth Amendment rights. . . . The door is again ajar. As a consequence, I am left with the uneasy feeling that today's decision may signal that a majority of my colleagues have positioned themselves to reopen the door still further and abandon altogether the exclusionary rule in search-and-seizure cases; for surely they cannot believe that application of the exclusionary rule at trial furthers the goal of deterrence, but that its application in grand jury proceedings will not "significantly" do so. Unless we are to shut our eyes to the evidence that crosses our desks every day, we must concede that official lawlessness has not abated and that no empirical data distinguishes trials from grand jury proceedings. I thus fear that when next we confront a case of a conviction rested on illegally seized evidence, today's decision will be invoked to sustain the conclusion in that case also that "it is unrealistic to assume" that application of the rule at trial would "significantly further" the goal of deterrence—though, if the police are presently undeterred, it is difficult to see how removal of the sanction of exclusion will induce more lawful official conduct.

The exclusionary rule gave life to Madison's prediction that "independent tribunals of justice . . . will be naturally led to resist every encroachment upon rights expressly stipulated for in the Constitution by the declaration of rights." 1 Annals of Cong. 439 (1789). We betray the trust upon which that prediction rested by today's long step toward abandonment of the exclusionary rule. The observations of a recent commentator highlight the grievous error of the majority's retreat:

> "If constitutional rights are to be anything more than pious pronouncements, then some measurable consequence must be attached to their violation. It would be intolerable if the guarantee against unreasonable search and seizure could be violated without practical consequence. It is likewise imperative to have a practical procedure by which courts can review alleged violations of constitutional rights and articulate the meaning of those rights. The advantage of the exclusionary rule—entirely apart from any direct deterrent effect—is that it provides an occasion for judicial review, and it gives credibility to the constitutional guarantees. By demonstrating that society will attach serious consequences to the violation of constitutional rights, the exclusionary rule invokes and magnifies the moral and educative force of the law. Over the long term this may integrate some fourth amendment ideals into the value system or norms of behavior of law enforcement agencies." Oaks, Studying the Exclusionary Rule in Search and Seizure, 37 U.Chi.L.Rev. 665, 756 (1970). . . .

I dissent and would affirm the judgment of the Court of Appeals.

NOTES

1. The use of illegally seized evidence before a grand jury may be the focus of a dispute in different contexts. A target defendant might seek an order preventing presentation to the grand jury of evidence secured in violation of his rights. Alternatively, a witness might seek a suppression order prohibiting any questioning based upon data secured in violation of the rights of the witness. Or the witness might refuse to answer questions and then, in response to a contempt allegation, might assert the *defense* that the questioning was based upon illegally obtained data. Finally, a defendant might seek dismissal of an indictment because illegally obtained evidence was presented to the grand jury. Are different policies involved in each of these situations? Does the reasoning of *Calandra* apply to each?

2. Because of certain *statutory* provisions, the Supreme Court in Gelbard v. United States, 408 U.S. 41, 92 S.Ct. 2537 (1972), held that a grand jury witness accused of contempt can defend on the grounds that the questions he refused to answer in the grand jury were based upon information

acquired by illegal interceptions of communications. Mr. Justice White, who made the majority with his concurrence, added a significant proviso to his opinion:

> "Where the Government produces a court order for the interception, however, and the witness nevertheless demands a full blown suppression hearing to determine the legality of the order, there may be room for striking a different accommodation between the due functioning of the grand jury system and the federal wiretap statute. . . . It is well, therefore, that the Court has left this issue open for consideration by the District Court on remand. . . . Of course, where the Government officially denies the fact of electronic surveillance of the witness, the matter is at an end and the witness must answer."

See Chapter 11, Section F.

3. Does the nature of the transgression make any difference as to the use of illegally obtained evidence before a grand jury? Suppose that the only evidence connecting a suspect to a crime is an involuntary confession. Should the target defendant have a pre-indictment remedy to the presentation of that confession to the grand jury?

4. The use of illegally obtained evidence in proceedings other than the guilt-innocence phase of a criminal trial arises in many contexts in addition to the grand jury context. Normally, courts weigh various policy considerations against what they perceive to be the policies underlying the exclusionary rule. In some instances the government is allowed to have the benefit of the fruits of official wrongdoing; in other instances courts have required adherence to exclusionary principles:

(a) *Preliminary Hearings.* In some jurisdictions illegally obtained evidence is excluded at preliminary hearings in felony cases. Other jurisdictions, including federal courts (see F.R.Crim.P. 5.1), do not allow motions to suppress at this stage. Where such motions are heard, courts differ as to whether principles of res judicata make the preliminary hearing ruling binding when the motion to suppress is renewed before the trial judge.

(b) *Probation Revocation Hearings.* There is a split of authority as to whether illegally seized evidence can be used to revoke probation. Compare United States v. Workman, 585 F.2d 1205 (4th Cir. 1978), and Michaud v. State, 505 P.2d 1399 (Okl.Crim.1973), with United States v. Hill, 447 F.2d 817 (7th Cir. 1971), and Stone v. Shea, 113 N. H. 174, 304 A.2d 647 (1973). Some jurisdictions allow for suppressions only where there is a showing of harassment of the probationer or bad faith on the part of governmental officials. See People v. Atencio, 186 Colo. 76, 525 P.2d 461 (1974); State v. Sears, 553 P.2d 907 (Alaska 1976). The issue of admissibility of illegally seized evidence at probation revocation hearings should be distinguished from the question of the legality of warrantless searches of probationer by probation officers. See Chapter 4, Section N, supra. Presumably an involuntary confession or at least one which is, in fact, unreliable should not be used at a probation revocation hearing. People v. Peterson, 74 Ill.2d 478, 23 Ill.Dec. 554, 384 N.E.2d 348 (1978).

(c) *Sentencing Hearings.* Some courts permit illegally seized evidence to be used at sentencing hearings. See United States v. Schipani, 435 F.2d 26 (2d Cir. 1970); United States v. Lee, 540 F.2d 1205

(4th Cir. 1976).   Compare Verdugo v. United States, 402 F.2d 599 (9th Cir. 1968).

(d) *Forfeiture Proceedings.*   In cases where the crime in which property was used is relatively minor compared to the value of the property subject to forfeiture, illegally seized evidence is not admissible at a forfeiture hearing.   One 1958 Plymouth v. Pennsylvania, 380 U.S. 693, 85 S.Ct. 1246 (1965).   Such a hearing, like a criminal trial itself, is viewed as penal in nature.

(e) *License Revocation Proceedings.*   License hearings have a purpose of protecting the public in a manner which is more direct than forfeiture proceedings or criminal trials.   License revocations are not simply penal.   Thus some courts permit the use of illegally seized evidence at hearings to revoke licenses as long as the evidence is relevant. See Daley v. Berzanskis, 47 Ill.2d 395, 269 N.E.2d 716 (1971); but compare Liquor Control Bd. v. Mottola's Tavern, 37 Pa.Cmwlth. 234, 389 A.2d 1213 (1978).

(f) *Civil Cases.*   Normally the methods by which evidence was secured—whether by private parties or by government agents—does not affect its admissibility in a civil case.   Indeed, early opponents of the exclusionary rule rested their case on the evidentiary principle that prohibited interruption of a civil case for a collateral inquiry into the source of evidence.   See Wigmore, Vol. 8, § 2183 (Third Ed. 1940). Thus, under some decisions, even the wrongdoer may use in a civil case the evidence which he has wrongfully obtained.   See, e. g., Sackler v. Sackler, 15 N.Y.2d 40, 255 N.Y.S.2d 83, 203 N.E.2d 481 (1964), involving the not infrequent divorce litigation scenario of one spouse using unlawful investigative methods to acquire evidence against the other. However, where government is both the wrongdoer and a party, the policy considerations may be different.   The issue arises most frequently in the context of civil tax litigation.   For instance, in Pizzarello v. United States, 408 F.2d 579 (2d Cir. 1969), evidence illegally seized by federal Treasury Department Agents was held inadmissible in a federal civil tax proceeding.   In United States v. Janis, 428 U.S. 433, 96 S.Ct. 3021 (1976), however, the Supreme Court held that evidence illegally seized by *state* agents could be used by the federal government in a federal tax proceeding.   This decision has caused some courts to consider whether evidence impermissibly seized by federal agents could be used in a federal tax proceeding, even though *Janis* clearly did not reach that issue.   See Ryan v. Commissioner of Internal Revenue, 568 F.2d 531 (7th Cir. 1977).

(g) *Parole Revocations.*   It is generally agreed that illegally seized evidence is admissible at a parole revocation hearing.   See United States ex rel. Sperling v. Fitzpatrick, 426 F.2d 1161 (2d Cir. 1970); Reeves v. Turner, 28 Utah 2d 310, 501 P.2d 1212 (1972).   See, however, Picarillo v. New York State Bd. of Parole, 48 N.Y.2d 76, 421 N. Y.S.2d 842, 397 N.E.2d 354 (1979).   Parole revocation hearings, unlike probation revocation hearings, ordinarily are conducted by administrative officials rather than judges.   Does the "imperative of the judicial integrity" have application in parole revocation proceedings?   Is it far-fetched that a police officer would deliberately ignore Fourth Amendment restrictions, knowing that a parolee can be recommitted without regard to the method by which the evidence has been secured?

2. IMPEACHMENT AND REBUTTAL USAGE OF ILLEGALLY OBTAINED EVIDENCE

HARRIS v. NEW YORK

Supreme Court of the United States, 1971.
401 U.S. 222, 91 S.Ct. 643.

MR. CHIEF JUSTICE BURGER delivered the opinion of the Court.

We granted the writ in this case to consider petitioner's claim that a statement made by him to police under circumstances rendering it inadmissible to establish the prosecution's case in chief under Miranda v. Arizona (1966), may not be used to impeach his credibility.

The State of New York charged petitioner in a two-count indictment with twice selling heroin to an undercover police officer. At a subsequent jury trial the officer was the State's chief witness, and he testified as to details of the two sales. A second officer verified collateral details of the sales, and a third offered testimony about the chemical analysis of the heroin.

Petitioner took the stand in his own defense. He admitted knowing the undercover police officer but denied a sale on January 4, 1966. He admitted making a sale of contents of a glassine bag to the officer on January 6 but claimed it was baking powder and part of a scheme to defraud the purchaser.

On cross-examination petitioner was asked seriatim whether he had made specified statements to the police immediately following his arrest on January 7—statements that partially contradicted petitioner's direct testimony at trial. In response to the cross-examination, petitioner testified that he could not remember virtually any of the questions or answers recited by the prosecutor. At the request of petitioner's counsel the written statement from which the prosecutor had read questions and answers in his impeaching process was placed in the record for possible use on appeal; the statement was not shown to the jury.

The trial judge instructed the jury that the statements attributed to petitioner by the prosecution could be considered only in passing on petitioner's credibility and not as evidence of guilt. In closing summations both counsel argued the substance of the impeaching statements. The jury then found petitioner guilty on the second count of the indictment.

At trial the prosecution made no effort in its case in chief to use the statements allegedly made by petitioner, conceding that they were inadmissible under Miranda v. Arizona. The transcript of the interrogation used in the impeachment, but not given to the jury, shows that no warning of a right to appointed counsel was given before questions were put to petitioner when he was taken into custody. Petitioner makes no claim that the statements made to the police were coerced or involuntary.

Some comments in the *Miranda* opinion can indeed be read as indicating a bar to use of an uncounseled statement for any purpose, but discussion of that issue was not at all necessary to the Court's holding and cannot be regarded as controlling. *Miranda* barred the prosecution from making its case with statements of an accused made while in custody prior to having or effectively waiving counsel. It does not follow from *Miranda* that evidence inadmissible against an accused in the prosecution's case in chief is barred for all purposes, provided of course that the trustworthiness of the evidence satisfies legal standards.

In Walder v. United States (1954), the Court permitted physical evidence, inadmissible in the case in chief, to be used for impeachment purposes.

> "It is one thing to say that the Government cannot make an affirmative use of evidence unlawfully obtained. It is quite another to say that the defendant can turn the illegal method by which evidence in the Government's possession was obtained to his own advantage, and provide himself with a shield against contradiction of his untruths. Such an extension of the *Weeks* doctrine would be a perversion of the Fourth Amendment.

> "[T]here is hardly justification for letting the defendant affirmatively resort to perjurious testimony in reliance on the Government's disability to challenge his credibility."

It is true that Walder was impeached as to collateral matters included in his direct examination, whereas petitioner here was impeached as to testimony bearing more directly on the crimes charged. We are not persuaded that there is a difference in principle that warrants a result different from that reached by the Court in *Walder*. Petitioner's testimony in his own behalf concerning the events of January 7 contrasted sharply with what he told the police shortly after his arrest. The impeachment process here undoubtedly provided valuable aid to the jury in assessing petitioner's credibility, and the benefits of this process should not be lost, in our view, because of the speculative possibility that impermissible police conduct will be encouraged thereby. Assuming that the exclusionary rule has a deterrent effect on proscribed police conduct, sufficient deterrence flows when the evidence in question is made unavailable to the prosecution in its case in chief.

Every criminal defendant is privilged to testify in his own defense, or to refuse to do so. But that privilege cannot be construed to include the right to commit perjury. Having voluntarily taken the stand, petitioner was under an obligation to speak truthfully and accurately, and the prosecution here did no more than utilize the traditional truth-testing devices of the adversary process.[1] Had inconsist-

1. If, for example, an accused confessed fully to a homicide and led the police to the body of the victim under circumstances making his confession inadmissible, the petitioner would have us allow that accused to take the stand and blandly deny every fact disclosed to the police or

ent statements been made by the accused to some third person, it could hardly be contended that the conflict could not be laid before the jury by way of cross-examination and impeachment.

The shield provided by *Miranda* cannot be perverted into a license to use perjury by way of a defense, free from the risk of confrontation with prior inconsistent utterances. We hold, therefore, that petitioner's credibility was appropriately impeached by use of his earlier conflicting statements.

Affirmed.

MR. JUSTICE BLACK dissents.

MR. JUSTICE BRENNAN, with whom MR. JUSTICE DOUGLAS and MR. JUSTICE MARSHALL, join, dissenting.

* * *

The State's case against Harris depended upon the jury's belief of the testimony of the undercover agent that petitioner "sold" the officer heroin on January 4 and again on January 6. Petitioner took the stand and flatly denied having sold anything to the officer on January 4. He countered the officer's testimony as to the January 6 sale with testimony that he had sold the officer two glassine bags containing what appeared to be heroin, but that actually the bags contained only baking powder intended to deceive the officer in order to obtain $12. The statement contradicted petitioner's direct testimony as to the events of both days. The statement's version of the events on January 4 was that the officer had used petitioner as a middleman to buy some heroin from a third person with money furnished by the officer. The version of the events on January 6 was that petitioner had again acted for the officer in buying two bags of heroin from a third person for which petitioner received $12 and a part of the heroin. Thus, it is clear that the statement was used to impeach petitioner's direct testimony not on collateral matters but on matters directly related to the crimes for which he was on trial.

* * *

From this recital of facts it is clear that the evidence used for impeachment in *Walder* was related to the earlier 1950 prosecution and had no direct bearing on "the elements of the case" being tried in 1952. The evidence tended solely to impeach the credibility of the defendant's direct testimony that he had never in his life possessed heroin. But that evidence was completely unrelated to the indictment on trial and did not in any way interfere with his freedom to deny all elements of that case against him. In contrast, here, the evidence used for impeachment, a statement concerning the details of the very sales alleged in the indictment, was directly related to the case against petitioner.

While *Walder* did not identify the constitutional specifics that guarantee "a defendant the fullest opportunity to meet the accusation

discovered as a "fruit" of his confession, free from confrontation with his prior statements and acts. The voluntariness of the confession would, on this thesis, be totally irrelevant. We reject such an extravagant extension of the Constitution.

against him . . . [and permit him to] be free to deny all the elements of the case against him," in my view Miranda v. Arizona identified the Fifth Amendment's privilege against self-incrimination as one of those specifics. It is fulfilled only when an accused is guaranteed the right "to remain silent unless he chooses to speak in the *unfettered* exercise of his own will," (emphasis added). The choice of whether to testify in one's own defense must therefore be "unfettered," since that choice is an exercise of the constitutional privilege, Griffin v. California. *Griffin* held that comment by the prosecution upon the accused's failure to take the stand or a court instruction that such silence is evidence of guilt is impermissible because it "fetters" that choice—"[i]t cuts down on the privilege by making its assertion costly." For precisely the same reason the constitutional guarantee forbids the prosecution to use a tainted statement to impeach the accused who takes the stand: The prosecution's use of the tainted statement "cuts down on the privilege by making its assertion costly."

Ibid. Thus, the accused is denied an "unfettered" choice when the decision whether to take the stand is burdened by the risk that an illegally obtained prior statement may be introduced to impeach his direct testimony denying complicity in the crime charged against him.

* * *

The objective of deterring improper police conduct is only part of the larger objective of safeguarding the integrity of our adversary system. The "essential mainstay" of that system, Miranda v. Arizona, 384 U.S., at 460, 86 S.Ct. 1602, is the privilege against self-incrimination, which for that reason has occupied a central place in our jurisprudence since before the Nation's birth. Moreover, "we may view the historical development of the privilege as one which groped for the proper scope of governmental power over the citizen. . . . All these policies point to one overriding thought: the constitutional foundation underlying the privilege is the respect a government . . . must accord to the dignity and integrity of its citizens." Ibid. These values are plainly jeopardized if an exception against admission of tainted statements is made for those used for impeachment purposes. Moreover, it is monstrous that courts should aid or abet the law-breaking police officer. It is abiding truth that "[n]othing can destroy a government more quickly than its failure to observe its own laws, or worse, its disregard of the charter of its own existence." Mapp v. Ohio. Thus even to the extent that *Miranda* was aimed at deterring police practices in disregard of the Constitution, I fear that today's holding will seriously undermine the achievement of that objective. The Court today tells the police that they may freely interrogate an accused incommunicado and without counsel and know that although any statement they obtain in violation of *Miranda* cannot be used on the State's direct case, it may be introduced if the defendant has the temerity to testify in his own defense. This goes far toward undoing much of the progress made in conforming police methods to the Constitution. I dissent.

NOTES

1. The dissent in *Harris* implicitly assumes that the decision is an invitation to the police to violate *Miranda*. Is it? Would a police officer ordinarily know at the time he first questions a suspect whether he has a legally sufficient case against the suspect and will only need the suspect's admissions for possible impeachment? Would a police officer ordinarily know that his other evidence, i. e. physical evidence and eyewitness identification will not be subject to exclusion? In short, is it likely an officer will know at the interrogation that he does not need the statements for the state's case in chief?

2. Oregon v. Hass, 420 U.S. 714, 95 S.Ct. 1215 (1975), also approved the use for impeachment purposes of a *Miranda*-violative statement. In that case the violation had occurred when the officer continued interrogation after the suspect had indicated a desire to consult with counsel. The majority held that *Harris* controlled. In dissent Justice Brennan wrote:

> "The Court's decision today goes beyond *Harris* in undermining *Miranda*. Even after *Harris*, police had some incentive for following *Miranda* by warning an accused of his right to remain silent and his right to counsel. If the warnings were given, the accused might still make a statement which could be used in the prosecution's case-in-chief. Under today's holding, however, once the warnings are given, police have almost no incentive for following *Miranda's* requirement that '[i]f the individual states that he wants an attorney, the interrogation must cease until an attorney is present.' If the requirement is followed there will almost surely be no statement since the attorney will advise the accused to remain silent. If, however, the requirement is disobeyed, the police may obtain a statement which can be used for impeachment if the accused has the temerity to testify in his own defense. Thus, after today's decision, if an individual states that he wants an attorney, police interrogation will doubtless now be vigorously pressed to obtain statements before the attorney arrives. I am unwilling to join this fundamental erosion of Fifth and Sixth Amendment rights and therefore dissent. . . ."

3. Some state courts have rejected the *Harris* rule, in the exercise of their option to adopt a stricter state standard than the federal one. People v. Disbrow, 16 Cal.3d 101, 127 Cal.Rptr. 360, 545 P.2d 272 (1976).

4. The question of impeachment use of illegally obtained evidence can come up in different contexts. The defendant can create the issue by testifying on direct examination (or by volunteering an unresponsive answer on cross-exam) to a fact which is not relevant to innocence or guilt. Sometimes such testimony is admitted without objection or, erroneously, over the prosecutor's objection. This is what happened in *Walder*. Under the rules of evidence of most jurisdictions, the prosecutor can pursue this matter on cross-examination by confronting the defendant with questions about the contradictory evidence. Wholly apart from constitutional considerations, the rules of evidence in some jurisdictions prohibit prosecution pursuit of this "collateral" material through rebuttal testimony. The cross-examiner must "take" the response he gets on this collateral issue. See Wigmore, Vol. 3A, § 1007 (Chadbourne rev. 1970). Compare United States v. Jansen, 475 F.2d 312 (7th Cir. 1973). When the impeachment material, as in *Walder*, includes evidence of criminal conduct for which the defendant is not

presently on trial, a substantial issue arises under Federal Rule of Evidence 608(b) as to whether the prosecutor can pursue the matter by offering extrinsic evidence or whether he must "take" the answer he gets on cross-examination. Some persons argue that Rule 608(b), wholly apart from constitutional provisions, would prohibit use of rebuttal evidence in a case factually identical to *Walder*. The differing views are expressed in United States v. Batts, 558 F.2d 513 (9th Cir. 1977), mod. in 573 F.2d 599 (9th Cir. 1978).

In a second situation the prosecutor seeks to impeach testimony which the defendant gave on direct (or volunteered on cross), where the testimony sought to be contradicted is directly relevant to innocence or guilt. Such was the case in *Harris*.

In a third situation the defendant testifies on direct but says nothing which is contradictory to the evidence which the police obtained unlawfully. The prosecution is not allowed to "open the door" in this situation by confronting the defendant with the illegally obtained evidence. Agnello v. United States, 269 U.S. 20, 46 S.Ct. 4 (1925). Many cases turn on whether the accused has so carefully confined his direct testimony as to prevent cross-examination (and, if otherwise permitted, rebuttal testimony) based upon the illegally obtained evidence. See United States v. Mariani, 539 F. 2d 915 (2d Cir. 1976); compare People v. Doss, 26 Ill.App.3d 1, 324 N.E.2d 210 (1975); People v. Brown, 40 Ill.App.3d 1003, 353 N.E.2d 244 (1976). On November 26, 1979, the Supreme Court granted certiorari from United States v. Havens, 592 F.2d 848 (5th Cir. 1979), a case in which the Fifth Circuit found a violation of the *Agnello* principle. In *Havens* the Government has argued that when a defendant testifies he opens himself to cross-examination concerning details other than those which he has mentioned on direct examination. Therefore, the Government contends, the *Walder* rule should permit the use of illegally obtained evidence in cross-examination and rebuttal even if such material is not directly contrary to answers given on direct examination. The only limit, under the Government's theory, would be the evidentiary principle that some inquiries are beyond the scope of proper cross-examination.

5. After *Harris* the question remained whether there was a prohibition against impeaching a defendant through the use of any involuntary confession or only through the use of confessions which were in fact unreliable. In Mincey v. Arizona, 437 U.S. 385, 98 S.Ct. 2408 (1978), however, the Court seemed to say that *no* involuntary confession could be used for impeachment purposes.

6. Concerning impeachment by reference to a defendant's silence following *Miranda* warnings, see Doyle v. Ohio, Ch. 19, Section E-2, infra.

7. When, in order to establish standing to raise a Fourth Amendment claim, a defendant gives testimony which is incriminating on the issue of guilt, the prosecution is prevented by Simmons v. United States, 390 U.S. 377, 88 S.Ct. 967 (1968), from using such testimony in its case-in-chief at trial. See Section C-2, notes 5 et seq., supra. The Supreme Court has not expressly resolved the question of whether a defendant's pre-trial testimony given to establish standing can be used to impeach a defendant who testifies differently at trial. One court, relying on *Harris* and *Walder,* has approved impeachment use of such testimony. See People v. Sturgis, 58 Ill.2d 211, 317 N.E.2d 545 (1974).

3. ILLEGALLY OBTAINED EVIDENCE AND FEDERAL HABEAS CORPUS RELIEF

STONE v. POWELL

WOLFF v. RICE

Supreme Court of the United States, 1976.
428 U.S. 465, 96 S.Ct. 3037.

MR. JUSTICE POWELL delivered the opinion of the Court.

Respondents in these cases were convicted of criminal offenses in state courts, and their convictions were affirmed on appeal. The prosecution in each case relied upon evidence obtained by searches and seizures alleged by respondents to have been unlawful. Each respondent subsequently sought relief in a federal district court by filing a petition for a writ of federal habeas corpus under 28 U.S.C. § 2254. The question presented is whether a federal court should consider, in ruling on a petition for habeas corpus relief filed by a state prisoner, a claim that evidence obtained by an unconstitutional search or seizure was introduced at his trial, when he has previously been afforded an opportunity for full and fair litigation of his claim in the state courts. The issue is of considerable importance to the administration of criminal justice.

I.

We summarize first the relevant facts and procedural history of these cases.

A

Respondent Lloyd Powell was convicted of murder in June 1968 after trial in a California state court. At about midnight on February 17, 1968, he and three companions entered the Bonanza Liquor Store in San Bernardino, Cal., where Powell became involved in an altercation with Gerald Parsons, the store manager, over the theft of a bottle of wine. In the scuffling that followed Powell shot and killed Parson's wife. Ten hours later an officer of the Henderson, Nev., Police Department arrested Powell for violation of the Henderson vagrancy ordinance,[1] and in the search incident to the arrest discovered a .38 caliber revolver with six expended cartridges in the cylinder.

Powell was extradited to California and convicted of second-degree murder in the Superior Court of San Bernardino County. Parsons and Powell's accomplices at the liquor store testified against

---

1. The ordinance provides:
    "Every person is a vagrant who:
    "[1] Loiters or wanders upon the streets or from place to place without apparent reason or business and [2] who refuses to identify himself and to account for his presence when asked by any police officer to do so [3] if surrounding circumstances are such as to indicate to a reasonable man that the public safety demands such identification."

him. A criminologist testified that the revolver found on Powell was the gun that killed Parsons' wife. The trial court rejected Powell's contention that testimony by the Henderson police officer as to the search and the discovery of the revolver should have been excluded because the vagrancy ordinance was unconstitutional. In October 1969, the conviction was affirmed by a California District Court of Appeal. Although the issue was duly presented, that court found it unnecessary to pass upon the legality of the arrest and search because it concluded that the error, if any, in admitting the testimony of the Henderson officer was harmless beyond a reasonable doubt under Chapman v. California, 386 U.S. 18 (1967). The Supreme Court of California denied Powell's petition for habeas corpus relief.

In August 1971 Powell filed an amended petition for a writ of federal habeas corpus under 28 U.S.C. § 2254 in the United States District Court for the Northern District of California, contending that the testimony concerning the .38 caliber revolver should have been excluded as the fruit of an illegal search. He argued that his arrest had been unlawful because the Henderson vagrancy ordinance was unconstitutionally vague, and that the arresting officer lacked probable cause to believe that he was violating it. The District Court concluded that the arresting officer had probable cause and held that even if the vagrancy ordinance was unconstitutional, the deterrent purpose of the exclusionary rule does not require that it be applied to bar admission of the fruits of a search incident to an otherwise valid arrest. In the alternative, that court agreed with the California District Court of Appeal that the admission of the evidence concerning Powell's arrest, if error, was harmless beyond a reasonable doubt.

In December 1974, the Court of Appeals for the Ninth Circuit reversed. . . .   The Court concluded that the vagrancy ordinance was unconstitutionally vague,[2] that Powell's arrest was therefore illegal, and that although exclusion of the evidence would serve no deterrent purpose with regard to police officers who were enforcing statutes in good faith, exclusion would serve the public interest by deterring legislators from enacting unconstitutional statutes. . . .   After an independent review of the evidence the court concluded that the admission of the evidence was not harmless error since it supported the testimony of Parsons and Powell's accomplices.
. . .

B

Respondent David Rice was convicted of murder in April 1971 after trial in a Nebraska state court. At 2:05 a. m. on August 17, 1970, Omaha police received a telephone call that a woman had been heard screaming at 2867 Ohio Street. As one of the officers sent to that address examined a suitcase lying in the doorway, it exploded, killing him instantly. By August 22 the investigation of the murder centered on Duane Peak, a 15-year-old member of the National Committee to Combat Fascism ("NCCF"), and that afternoon a warrant

---

2. . . .   Petitioner Stone challenges these conclusions, but in view of our disposition of the case we need not consider this issue.

was issued for Peak's arrest. The investigation also focused on other known members of the NCCF, including Rice, some of whom were believed to be planning to kill Peak before he could incriminate them. In their search for Peak, the police went to Rice's home at 10:30 p. m. that night and found lights and a television on, but there was no response to their repeated knocking. While some officers remained to watch the premises, a warrant was obtained to search for explosives and illegal weapons believed to be in Rice's possession. Peak was not in the house but upon entering the police discovered, in plain view, dynamite, blasting caps, and other materials useful in the construction of explosive devices. Peak subsequently was arrested, and on August 27, Rice voluntarily surrendered. The clothes Rice was wearing at that time were subjected to chemical analysis, disclosing dynamite particles.

Rice was tried for first-degree murder in the District Court of Douglas County. At trial Peak admitted planting the suitcase and making the telephone call, and implicated Rice in the bombing plot. As corroborative evidence the State introduced items seized during the search, as well as the results of the chemical analysis of Rice's clothing. The Court denied Rice's motion to suppress this evidence. On appeal the Supreme Court of Nebraska affirmed the conviction, holding that the search of Rice's home had been pursuant to a valid search warrant. . . .

In September 1972 Rice filed a petition for a writ of habeas corpus in the United States District Court for Nebraska. Rice's sole contention was that his incarceration was unlawful because the evidence underlying his conviction had been discovered as the result of an illegal search of his home. The District Court concluded that the search warrant was invalid, as the supporting affidavit was defective under Spinelli v. United States, 393 U.S. 410 (1969), and Aguilar v. Texas, 378 U.S. 108 (1964).[3] . . . The court also rejected the State's contention that even if the warrant was invalid the search was justified because of the valid arrest warrant for Peak and because of the exigent circumstances of the situation—danger to Peak

---

3. The sole evidence presented to the magistrate was the affidavit in support of the warrant application. It indicated that the police believed explosives and illegal weapons were present in Rice's home because (1) Rice was an official of the NCCF, (2) a violent killing of an officer had occurred and it appeared that the NCCF was involved, and (3) police had received information in the past that Rice possessed weapons and explosives, which he had said should be used against the police. . . . In concluding that there existed probable cause for issuance of the warrant, although the Nebraska Supreme Court found the affidavit alone sufficient, it also referred to information contained in testimony adduced at

the suppression hearing but not included in the affidavit. . . . The District Court limited its probable cause inquiry to the face of the affidavit, see Spinelli v. United States, 393 U.S. 410, 413 n. 3 (1969); Aguilar v. Texas, 378 U.S. 108, 109 n. 1 (1964), and concluded probable cause was lacking. Petitioner Wolff contends that police should be permitted to supplement the information contained in an affidavit for a search warrant at the hearing on a motion to suppress, a contention that we have several times rejected. see, e. g., Whitely v. Warden, 401 U.S. 560, 565 n. 8 (1971), Aguilar v. Texas, supra, at 109 n. 1, and need not reach again here.

and search for bombs and explosives believed in possession of NCCF. The court reasoned that the arrest warrant did not justify the entry as the police lacked probable cause to believe Peak was in the house, and further concluded that the circumstances were not sufficiently exigent to justify an immediate warrantless search.[4] . . . The Court of Appeals for the Eighth Circuit affirmed, substantially for the reasons stated by the District Court. . . .

Petitioners Stone and Wolff, the wardens of the respective state prisons where Powell and Rice are incarcerated, petitioned for review of these decisions, raising questions concerning the scope of federal habeas corpus and the role of the exclusionary rule upon collateral review of cases involving Fourth Amendment claims. We granted their petitions for certiorari. . . . We now reverse.

II.

The authority of federal courts to issue the writ of *habeas corpus ad subjiciendum* was included in the first grant of federal court jurisdiction, made by the Judiciary Act of 1789, c. 20, § 14, 1 Stat. 81, with the limitation that the writ extend only to prisoners held in custody by the United States. The original statutory authorization did not define the substantive reach of the writ. It merely stated that the courts of the United States "shall have power to issue writs of . . . *habeas corpus*. . . ." Ibid. The courts defined the scope of the writ in accordance with the common law and limited it to an inquiry as to the jurisdiction of the sentencing tribunal. . . .

In 1867 the writ was extended to state prisoners. . . . Under the 1867 Act federal courts were authorized to give relief in "all cases where any person may be restrained of his or her liberty in violation of the constitution, or of any treaty or law of the United States. . . ." But the limitation of federal habeas corpus jurisdiction to consideration of the jurisdiction of the sentencing court persisted. . . . And, although the concept of "jurisdiction" was subjected to considerable strain as the substantive scope of the writ was expanded, this expansion was limited to only a few classes of cases until Frank v. Mangum, 237 U.S. 309, in 1915. In *Frank*, the prisoner had claimed in the state courts that the proceedings which resulted in his conviction for murder had been dominated by a mob. After the state supreme court rejected his contentions, Frank unsuccessfully sought habeas corpus relief in the federal district court. This Court affirmed the denial of relief because Frank's federal claims had been considered by a competent and unbiased state tribunal. The Court recognized, however, that if a habeas corpus court found that the State had failed to provide adequate "corrective process" for the full and fair litigation of federal claims, whether or not

---

4. The District Court further held that the evidence of dynamite particles found on Rice's clothing should have been suppressed as the tainted fruit of an arrest warrant that would not have been issued but for the unlawful search of his home. . . . See Wong Sun v. United States, 371 U.S. 471 (1963); Silverthorne Lumber Co., Inc. v. United States, 251 U.S. 385 (1920).

"jurisdictional," the court could inquire into the merits to determine whether a detention was lawful.   .   .   .

In the landmark decisions in Brown v. Allen, 344 U.S. 443 (1953), and Daniels v. Allen, 344 U.S., at 482–487, the scope of the writ was expanded still further.   In these cases state prisoners applied for federal habeas corpus relief claiming that the trial courts had erred in failing to quash their indictments due to alleged discrimination in the selection of grand jurors and in ruling certain confessions admissible.   In *Brown*, the highest court of the State had rejected these claims on direct appeal,   .   .   .   and this Court had denied certiorari   .   .   ..   Despite the apparent adequacy of the state corrective process, the Court reviewed the denial of the writ of habeas corpus and held that Brown was entitled to a full reconsideration of these constitutional claims, including, if appropriate, a hearing in the Federal District Court.   In *Daniels*, however, the state supreme court on direct review had refused to consider the appeal because the papers were filed out of time.   This Court held that since the state court judgment rested on a reasonable application of the State's legitimate procedural rules, a ground that would have barred direct review of his federal claims by this Court, the District Court lacked authority to grant habeas corpus relief.   .   .   .

This final barrier to broad collateral re-examination of state criminal convictions in federal habeas corpus proceedings was removed in Fay v. Noia, 372 U.S. 391 (1963).   Noia and two codefendants had been convicted of felony murder.   The sole evidence against each defendant was a signed confession.   Noia's codefendants, but not Noia himself, appealed their convictions.   Although their appeals were unsuccessful, in subsequent state proceedings they were able to establish that their confessions had been coerced and their convictions therefore procured in violation of the Constitution.   In a subsequent federal habeas corpus proceeding, it was stipulated that Noia's confession also had been coerced, but the District Court followed *Daniels* in holding that Noia's failure to appeal barred habeas corpus review.   .   .   .   The Court of Appeals reversed, ordering that Noia's conviction be set aside and that he be released from custody or a new trial be granted.   This Court affirmed the grant of the writ, narrowly restricting the circumstances in which a federal court may refuse to consider the merits of federal constitutional claims.

* * *

III.

* * *

The exclusionary rule was a judicially created means of effectuating the rights secured by the Fourth Amendment.   .   .   .

Decisions prior to *Mapp* advanced two principal reasons for application of the rule in federal trials.   The Court in *Elkins*, for example, in the context of its special supervisory role over the lower federal courts, referred to the "imperative of judicial integrity," suggesting that exclusion of illegally seized evidence prevents contamination of the judicial process. . . . But even in that context a more pragmatic ground was emphasized:

> "The rule is calculated to prevent, not to repair. Its purpose is to deter—to compel respect for the constitutional guaranty in the only effectively available way—by removing the incentive to disregard it." . . .

The *Mapp* majority justified the application of the rule to the States on several grounds, but relied principally upon the belief that exclusion would deter future unlawful police conduct. . . .

Although our decisions often have alluded to the "imperative of judicial integrity," . . . they demonstrate the limited role of this justification in the determination whether to apply the rule in a particular context. Logically extended this justification would require that courts exclude unconstitutionally seized evidence despite lack of objection by the defendant, or even over his assent. . . . It also would require abandonment of the standing limitations on who may object to the introduction of unconstitutionally seized evidence, . . . and retreat from the proposition that judicial proceedings need not abate when the defendant's person is unconstitutionally seized . . . . Similarly, the interest in promoting judicial integrity does not prevent the use of illegally seized evidence in grand jury proceedings. . . . Nor does it require that the trial court exclude such evidence from use for impeachment of a defendant, even though its introduction is certain to result in convictions in some cases. . . . While courts, of course, must ever be concerned with preserving the integrity of the judicial process, this concern has limited force as a justification for the exclusion of highly probative evidence.[5] The force of this justification becomes minimal where federal habeas corpus relief is sought by a prisoner who previously has been afforded the opportunity for full and fair consideration of his search-and-seizure claim at trial and on direct review.

The primary justification for the exclusionary rule then is the deterrence of police conduct that violates Fourth Amendment rights. Post-*Mapp* decisions have established that the rule is not a personal constitutional right. It is not calculated to redress the injury to the privacy of the victim of the search or seizure, for any "[r]eparation comes too late." Linkletter v. Walker, 381 U.S. 618, 637 (1965). Instead,

> "the rule is a judicially created remedy designed to safeguard Fourth Amendment rights generally through its deterrent effect . . . ." United States v. Calandra . . . .

---

5. As we recognized last Term, judicial integrity is "not offended if law enforcement officials reasonably believed in good faith that their conduct was in accordance with the law even if decisions subsequent to the search and seizure have held that conduct of the type engaged in by the law enforcement officials is not permitted by the Constitution." United States v. Peltier, 422 U.S. 531, 538 (1975) (emphasis omitted).

. . . But despite the broad deterrent purpose of the exclusionary rule, it has never been interpreted to proscribe the introduction of illegally seized evidence in all proceedings or against all persons. As in the case of any remedial device, "the application of the rule has been restricted to those areas where its remedial objectives are thought most efficaciously served." United States v. Calandra
. . . .[6]

* * *

IV.

We turn now to the specific question presented by these cases. Respondents allege violations of Fourth Amendment rights guaranteed them through the Fourteenth Amendment. The question is whether state prisoners—who have been afforded the opportunity for full and fair consideration of their reliance upon the exclusionary rule with respect to seized evidence by the state courts at trial and on direct review—may invoke their claim again on federal habeas corpus review. The answer is to be found by weighing the utility of the exclusionary rule against the costs of extending it to collateral review of Fourth Amendment claims.

The costs of applying the exclusionary rule even at trial and on direct review are well known: the focus of the trial, and the attention of the participants therein, is diverted from the ultimate question of guilt or innocence that should be the central concern in a criminal proceeding. Moreover, the physical evidence sought to be excluded is typically reliable and often the most probative information bearing on the guilt or innocence of the defendant. . . . Application of the rule thus deflects the truthfinding process and often frees the guilty. The disparity in particular cases between the error committed by the police officer and the windfall afforded a guilty defendant by application of the rule is contrary to the idea of proportionality that is essential to the concept of justice.[7] Thus, al-

---

6. As Professor Amsterdam has observed:

"The rule is unsupportable as reparation or compensatory dispensation to the injured criminal; its sole rational justification is the experience of its indispensability in 'exert[ing] general legal pressures to secure obedience to the Fourth Amendment on the part of . . . law-enforcing officers.' As it serves this function, the rule is a needed, but grudgingly [sic] taken, medicament; no more should be swallowed than is needed to combat the disease. Granted that so many criminals must go free as will deter the constables from blundering, pursuance of this policy of liberation beyond the confines of necessity inflicts gratuitous harm on the public interest . . . ." Amsterdam Search, Seizure, and Section 2255: A Comment, 112 U.Pa.L.Rev. 378, 388–389 (1964).

7. Many of the proposals for modification of the scope of the exclusionary rule recognize at least implicitly the role of proportionality in the criminal justice system and the potential value of establishing a direct relationship between the nature of the violation and the decision whether to invoke the rule. See A.L.I., A Model Code of Pre-arraignment Procedure, May 20, 1975, § 290.2, at 181–183 ("substantial violations"); H. Friendly, Benchmarks 260–262 (1967) (even at trial, exclusion should be limited to "the fruit of activity intentionally or flagrantly illegal."): Wigmore, supra, n. 27 at 52–53.

though the rule is thought to deter unlawful police activity in part through the nurturing of respect for Fourth Amendment values, if applied indiscriminately it may well have the opposite effect of generating disrespect for the law and administration of justice. These long-recognized costs of the rule persist when a criminal conviction is sought to be overturned on collateral review on the ground that a search-and-seizure claim was erroneously rejected by two or more tiers of state courts.[8]

Evidence obtained by police officers in violation of the Fourth Amendment is excluded at trial in the hope that the frequency of future violations will decrease. Despite the absence of supportive empirical evidence,[9] we have assumed that the immediate effect of exclusion will be to discourage law enforcement officials from violating the Fourth Amendment by removing the incentive to disregard it. More importantly, over the long term, this demonstration that our society attaches serious consequences to violation of constitutional rights is thought to encourage those who formulate law enforcement policies, and the officers who implement them, to incorporate Fourth Amendment ideals into their value system.

We adhere to the view that these considerations support the implementation of the exclusionary rule at trial and its enforcement on direct appeal of state court convictions. But the additional contribution, if any, of the consideration of search-and-seizure claims of state prisoners on collateral review is small in relation to the costs. To be sure, each case in which such claim is considered may add marginally to an awareness of the values protected by the Fourth Amendment. There is no reason to believe, however, that the overall educative effect of the exclusionary rule would be appreciably diminished if search-and-seizure claims could not be raised in federal habeas corpus review of state convictions. Nor is there reason to assume that any specific disincentive already created by the risk of exclusion of evidence at trial or the reversal of convictions on direct review would be enhanced if there were the further risk that a conviction obtained in

---

8. Resort to habeas corpus, especially for purposes other than to assure that no innocent person suffers an unconstitutional loss of liberty, results in serious intrusions on values important to our system of government. They include "(i) the most effective utilization of limited judicial resources, (ii) the necessity of finality in criminal trials, (iii) the minimization of friction between our federal and state systems of justice, and (iv) the maintenance of the constitutional balance upon which the doctrine of federalism is founded." Schneckloth v. Bustamonte, 412 U.S., at 259 (Powell, J., concurring). . . .

We nevertheless afford broad habeas corpus relief, recognizing the need in a free society for an additional safeguard against compelling an innocent

man to suffer an unconstitutional loss of liberty. The Court in Fay v. Noia, supra, described habeas corpus as a remedy for "whatever society deems to be intolerable restraints," and recognized that those to whom the writ should be granted "are persons whom society has grieviously wronged." . . . But in the case of a typical Fourth Amendment claim, asserted on collateral attack, a convicted defendant is usually asking society to redetermine an issue that has no bearing on the basic justice of his incarceration.

9. The efficacy of the exclusionary rule has long been the subject of sharp debate. Until recently, scholarly empirical research was unavailable. . . .

state court and affirmed on direct review might be overturned in collateral proceedings often occurring years after the incarceration of the defendant. The view that the deterrence of Fourth Amendment violations would be furthered rests on the dubious assumption that law enforcement authorities would fear that federal habeas review might reveal flaws in a search or seizure that went undetected at trial and on appeal. Even if one rationally could assume that some additional incremental deterrent effect would be present in isolated cases, the resulting advance of the legitimate goal of furthering Fourth Amendment rights would be outweighed by the acknowledged costs to other values vital to a rational system of criminal justice.

In sum, we conclude that where the State has provided an opportunity for full and fair litigation of a Fourth Amendment claim, a state prisoner may not be granted federal habeas corpus relief on the ground that evidence obtained in an unconstitutional search or seizure was introduced at his trial.[10] In this context the contribution of the exclusionary rule, if any, to the effectuation of the Fourth Amendment is minimal and the substantial societal costs of application of the rule persist with special force.

Accordingly, the judgments of the Courts of Appeals are reversed.

10. The policy arguments that respondents marshal in support of the view that federal habeas corpus review is necessary to effectuate the Fourth Amendment stem from a basic mistrust of the state courts as fair and competent forums for the adjudication of federal constitutional rights. The argument is that state courts cannot be trusted to effectuate Fourth Amendment values through fair application of the rule, and the oversight jurisdiction of this Court on certiorari is an inadequate safeguard. The principal rationale for this view emphasizes the broad differences in the respective institutional setting within which federal judges and state judges operate. Despite differences in institutional environment and the unsympathetic attitude to federal constitutional claims of some state judges in years past, we are unwilling to assume that there now exists a general lack of appropriate sensitivity to constitutional rights in the trial and appellate courts of the several States. State courts, like federal courts, have a constitutional obligation to safeguard personal liberties and to uphold federal law. . . . Moreover, the argument that federal judges are more expert in applying federal constitutional law is especially unpersuasive in the context of search-and-seizure claims, since they are dealt with on a daily basis by trial level judges in both systems. . . .

With all respect, the hyperbole of the dissenting opinion is misdirected. Our decision today is *not* concerned with the scope of the habeas corpus statute as authority for litigating constitutional claims generally. We do reaffirm that the exclusionary rule is a judicially created remedy rather than a personal constitutional right, . . . and we emphasize the minimal utility of the rule when sought to be applied to Fourth Amendment claims in a habeas corpus proceeding. . . . In sum, we hold only that a federal court need not apply the exclusionary rule on habeas review of a Fourth Amendment claim absent a showing that the state prisoner was denied an opportunity for a full and fair litigation of that claim at trial and on direct review. Our decision does not mean that the federal court lacks jurisdiction over such a claim, but only that the application of the rule is limited to cases in which there has been both such a showing and a Fourth Amendment violation.

[Concurring and dissenting opinions are omitted here, but they are summarized briefly in the notes which follow.]

NOTES

1. In a concurring opinion in *Stone* Chief Justice Burger stated that the reach of the exclusionary rule should be modified, "even if it is retained for a small and limited category of cases." He contended that the true purpose of the exclusionary rule is deterrence and argued that empirical evidence fails to demonstrate a deterrent effect. He noted that the requirement of standing is inconsistent with the notion that the "imperative of the judicial integrity" underlies the exclusionary rule. Moreover, he asserted other common law countries, including Canada and England, uphold the integrity of the judicial system without utilizing the exclusionary rule. He concluded that the rule, by excluding relevant evidence, had become too costly and that its very existence might dissuade legislators from experimenting with more meaningful remedies for Fourth Amendment violations.

Justice White dissented, asserting that Congressional amendments to the federal habeas corpus statute following Fay v. Noia provided for federal relief to state prisoners whose convictions were secured in violation of any federal constitutional rights, drawing no such distinction as did the *Stone* majority opinion. He stated that he would be willing to join in an opinion which generally limited the applicability of the exclusionary rule, one in which the good faith of the officer would be relevant. He stated, however, that as long as the rule stood in its present form, he could not approve denial of habeas corpus relief to state prisoners whose convictions were secured through the use of evidence seized in violation of their Fourth Amendment rights.

Justice Brennan, joined by Justice Marshall, strongly dissented. He stated that state prisoners convicted on the basis of evidence secured in violation of their Fourth Amendment rights are in custody in violation of the Constitution and thus are entitled to relief under the plain language of 28 U.S.C. § 2254. Much of Justice Brennan's opinion concerned the interpretation of the federal habeas corpus statute, which, he asserted, like Fay v. Noia, draws no distinction between rights which are related to the integrity of the fact-finding process and other constitutional rights. He reaffirmed the principle set forth in *Fay* and companion decisions that federal habeas corpus should be available to state prisoners as an alternative to certiorari. He emphasized the importance of those federal constitutional rights which are not necessarily designed to improve the fact-finding process. Justice Brennan cited Wolff v. Rice as demonstrating the need for federal habeas corpus to review search and seizure claims. In *Rice*, he said, although the affidavit for the warrant was "clearly deficient," the search was upheld by the Nebraska Supreme Court, which, contrary to established precedent, permitted the prosecutor to sustain the warrant by proving facts which had not been presented to the issuing magistrate. Justice Brennan also suggested that, to his great regret, "the groundwork is being laid today for a drastic withdrawal of federal habeas jurisdiction, if not for all grounds of alleged unconstitutional detention, then at least for claims—for example, of double jeopardy, entrapment, self-incrimination, Miranda violations, and use of invalid identification procedures—that this Court later decides are not 'guilt-related.' "

2. If defense trial counsel did not seek suppression of the evidence in the state court, is there any method by which, despite *Stone*, the issue can be heard in the federal court? See Sallie v. North Carolina, 587 F.2d 636 (4th Cir. 1978), and compare United States ex. rel. Maxey v. Morris, 591 F.2d 386 (7th Cir. 1979).

3. Suppose that a particular issue of law has been resolved one way by the highest court of a state and a different way by a federal circuit. If binding state precedent ensures an adverse rule for a defendant in state court, has he been afforded the opportunity for a full and fair hearing? Two decisions suggest that he has, even though if he could get the federal district court to reach the merits of the claim, he would be entitled to relief under applicable federal Court of Appeals Fourth Amendment precedents. See Maxey, supra note 2; United States ex rel. Petillo v. New Jersey, 562 F. 2d 903 (3d Cir. 1977). Certiorari from an adverse state rule seems the only possible remedy for such a defendant.

E. DERIVATIVE EVIDENCE PRINCIPLES AND LIMITATIONS

Carried to their logical conclusion, exclusionary rules would deprive the prosecution of any benefit from a violation of the defendant's constitutional rights. Courts would exclude not only the immediate product of an unlawful search or of *Miranda*-violative interrogation, but also evidence more remotely derived from the constitutional transgression. Although all evidence obtained, directly or remotely, as a result of violations can be considered "derivative," frequently the term "derivative evidence" is used to describe the fruits of police illegality which are not the immediate product of the misconduct.

Let us begin with an example. An officer engages in custodial interrogation of a suspect without providing *Miranda* warnings. He obtains a confession in which the suspect indicates that he buried the murder weapon at a certain spot in a forest dozens of miles from both the suspect's home and the murder scene. Pursuant to that lead, officers find the weapon, which bears the suspect's fingerprints and which, through expert firearms identification testimony, is established as the gun which was used to fire the fatal bullet. In this hypothetical, the immediate product of the improper interrogation is the confession. Derivative evidence includes the gun and the testimony of the experts about the fingerprints and the class and individual characteristics of the gun. Relying on cases which date to Silverthorne Lumber Co. v. United States, 251 U.S. 385, 40 S.Ct. 182 (1920), where the Supreme Court said that unlawfully acquired evidence "shall not be used at all," the defendant will seek to have both the confession and the derivative evidence excluded from his criminal trial.

Absent application of one of the doctrines discussed below, if the requirement is merely a chain of causality, whether short or long, the defendant should prevail.

If, however, he is questioning the merits of the exclusionary rule, an opponent might argue that any deterrent effect is adequately achieved by exclusion of the confession.   Exclusion of more remotely derived evidence will serve no added deterrent function.

For the most part, the Supreme Court has excluded even remotely derived evidence.   One exception came in Michigan v. Tucker, 417 U.S. 433, 94 S.Ct. 2357 (1974), where derivative evidence secured in good faith before *Miranda* was permitted to be used in a post-*Miranda* trial, even though the confession itself could not be used.   See note 8, p. 537.

Most disputes concern whether certain evidence should be considered to be the product of the original illegality.   If the evidence is discovered independently, without any exploitation of the illegality, then the exclusionary rule need not be applied because of the "independent source" or "independent origin" limitation upon derivative evidence principles.   Thus in our original hypothetical if an officer, with no knowledge of the suspect's confession, and not acting in a chain of command originating from someone who knew of the confession, found the gun on his own and linked it to the suspect, the gun, together with the expert testimony, could be received at trial.

A second commonly recognized exception—though not one universally accepted—is the principle of inevitable discovery.   Let us suppose that following a suspect's lawful arrest, the police legally seize the murder weapon from his person.   They then subject him to *Miranda*-violative interrogation and learn the name of the retailer from whom he had purchased the weapon two weeks earlier.   To aid in proof of premeditation, the prosecution seeks to use the testimony of the dealer, who remembers the transaction.   In fact the dealer has been discovered through exploitation of a violation of the defendant's *Miranda* rights.   However, the prosecution can show that the dealer could have been easily located through readily available manufacturer's records discoverable through the serial number on the weapon, which the police had lawfully seized.   Thus the prosecution claims that even without the illegal procedure the police inevitably would have discovered the retailer.

Those who reject the doctrine of inevitable discovery argue that, whatever might have been, the police *did* exploit the illegality and exclusion will both effectuate deterrence of future police misconduct and uphold the imperative of judicial integrity.   Those who accept the doctrine are left to determine the burden which the prosecution must sustain in order to rely upon the doctrine.   How certain must it be that the police could have or would have discovered the evidence through means wholly independent of the unlawful procedure?   For one view see People v. Payton, 45 N.Y.2d 300, 408 N.Y.S.2d 395, 380 N.E.2d 224 (1978), reversed on other grounds —— U.S. ——, 100 S.Ct. —— (1980), which suggests that the test is a "very high degree of probability."

One caveat is necessary.   The doctrine of inevitable discovery does not depend upon the notion that the police could have lawfully performed the very procedure which they in fact unlawfully performed and could thereby have lawfully discovered the evidence.   The doctrine does not mean that because the officers easily could have secured a search warrant, therefore they will be permitted to use evidence derived from an unlawful warrantless search. Rather it means that the evidence is admissible because even apart from the challenged search (or interrogation or wiretap) the police through *other* available investigative techniques would inevitably have come upon the same evidence which, as it happened, was discovered, somewhat remotely, through exploitation of the challenged investigative procedure.

A third doctrine, "attenuation," serves to limit exclusionary principles. This limitation is treated in the materials which follow.

BROWN v. ILLINOIS

Supreme Court of the United States, 1975.
422 U.S. 590, 95 S.Ct. 2254.

MR. JUSTICE BLACKMUN delivered the opinion of the Court.

This case lies at the crossroads of the Fourth and the Fifth Amendments. Petitioner was arrested without probable cause and without a warrant. He was given, in full, the warnings prescribed by Miranda v. Arizona. Thereafter, while in custody, he made two inculpatory statements. The issue is whether evidence of those statements was properly admitted, or should have been excluded, in petitioner's subsequent trial for murder in state court. Expressed another way, the issue is whether the statements were to be excluded as the fruit of the illegal arrest, or were admissible because the giving of the *Miranda* warnings sufficiently attenuated the taint of the arrest. See Wong Sun v. United States, 371 U.S. 471 (1963). The Fourth Amendment, of course, has been held to be applicable to the States through the Fourteenth Amendment.

I.

As petitioner Richard Brown was climbing the last of the stairs leading to the rear entrance of his Chicago apartment in the early evening of May 13, 1968, he happened to glance at the window near the door. He saw, pointed at him through the window, a revolver held by a stranger who was inside the apartment. The man said, "Don't move, you are under arrest." Another man, also with a gun, came up behind Brown and repeated the statement that he was under arrest. It was about 7:45 p. m. The two men turned out to be detectives William Nolan and William Lenz of the Chicago police force. It is not clear from the record exactly when they advised Brown of their identity, but it is not disputed that they broke into his apartment, searched it, and then arrested Brown, all without probable cause and without any warrant, when he arrived. They later testified that they made the arrest for the purpose of questioning Brown as part of their investigation of the murder of a man named Roger Corpus.

Corpus was murdered one week earlier, on May 6, with a .38 caliber revolver in his Chicago West Side second floor apartment.

Shortly thereafter, Officer Lenz obtained petitioner's name, among others, from Corpus' brother. Petitioner and the others were identified as acquaintances of the victim, not as suspects.

On the day of petitioner's arrest, detectives Lenz and Nolan, armed with a photograph of Brown, and another officer arrived at petitioner's apartment about 5 p. m. While the third officer covered the front entrance downstairs, the two detectives broke into Brown's apartment and searched it. Lenz then positioned himself near the rear door and watched through the adjacent window which opened onto the back porch. Nolan sat near the front door. He described the situation at the later suppression hearing:

> "After we were there for awhile, Detective Lenz told me that somebody was coming up the back stairs. I walked out the front door through the hall and around the corner, and I stayed there behind a door leading on to the back porch. At this time I heard Detective Lenz say, 'Don't move, you are under arrest.' I looked out. I saw Mr. Brown backing away from the window. I walked up behind him, I told him he is under arrest, come back inside the apartment with us."

As both officers held him at gunpoint, the three entered the apartment. Brown was ordered to stand against the wall and was searched. No weapon was found. He was asked his name. When he denied being Richard Brown, Officer Lenz showed him the photograph, informed him that he was under arrest for the murder of Roger Corpus, handcuffed him, and escorted him to the squad car.

The two detectives took petitioner to the Maxwell Street police station. During the 20-minute drive Nolan again asked Brown, who then was sitting with him in the back seat of the car, whether his name was Richard Brown and whether he owned a 1966 Oldsmobile. Brown alternately evaded these questions or answered them falsely. Upon arrival at the station house Brown was placed in the second floor central interrogation room. The room was bare, except for a table and four chairs. He was left alone, apparently without handcuffs, for some minutes while the officers obtained the file on the Corpus homicide. They returned with the file, sat down at the table, one across from Brown and the other to his left, and spread the file on the table in front of him.

The officers warned Brown of his rights under *Miranda*.[1] They then informed him that they knew of an incident that had occurred in a poolroom on May 5, when Brown, angry at having been cheated at dice, fired a shot from a revolver into the ceiling. Brown answered, "Oh, you know about that." Lenz informed him that a bullet had been obtained from the ceiling of the poolroom and had been taken to the crime laboratory to be compared with bullets taken from Corpus' body. Brown responded, "Oh, you know that, too." At this point—it was about 8:45 p. m.—Lenz asked Brown whether he wanted to talk about the Corpus homicide. Petitioner answered that

---

1. There is no assertion here that he did not understand those rights.

he did. For the next 20 to 25 minutes Brown answered questions put to him by Nolan, as Lenz typed.

This questioning produced a two-page statement in which Brown acknowledged that he and a man named Jimmy Claggett visited Corpus on the evening of May 6; that the three for some time sat drinking and smoking marijuana; that Claggett ordered him at gunpoint to bind Corpus' hands and feet with cord from the headphone of a stereo set; and that Claggett, using a .38 caliber revolver sold to him by Brown, shot Corpus three times through a pillow. The statement was signed by Brown.

About 9:30 p. m. the two detectives and Brown left the station house to look for Claggett in an area of Chicago Brown knew him to frequent. They made a tour of that area but did not locate their quarry. They then went to police headquarters where they endeavored, without success, to obtain a photograph of Claggett. They resumed their search—it was now about 11 p. m.—and they finally observed Claggett crossing at an intersection. Lenz and Nolan arrested him. All four, the two detectives and the two arrested men, returned to the Maxwell Street station about 12:15 a. m.

Brown was again placed in the interrogation room. He was given coffee and was left alone, for the most part, until 2 a. m. when Assistant State's Attorney Crilly arrived.

Crilly, too, informed Brown of his *Miranda* rights. After a half hour's conversation, a court reporter appeared. Once again the *Miranda* warnings were given: "I read him the card." Crilly told him that he "was sure he would be charged with murder." Brown gave a second statement, providing a factual account of the murder substantially in accord with his first statement, but containing factual inaccuracies with respect to his personal background. When the statement was completed, at about 3 a. m., Brown refused to sign it. An hour later he made a phone call to his mother. At 9:30 that morning, about 14 hours after his arrest, he was taken before a magistrate.

On June 20 Brown and Claggett were jointly indicted by a Cook County grand jury for Corpus' murder. Prior to trial, petitioner moved to suppress the two statements he had made. He alleged that his arrest and detention had been illegal and that the statements were taken from him in violation of his constitutional rights. After a hearing, the motion was denied.

The case proceeded to trial. The State introduced evidence of both statements. Officer Nolan testified as to the contents of the first, but the writing itself was not placed in evidence. The second statement was introduced and was read to the jury in full. Brown was 23 at the time of the trial.

The jury found petitioner guilty of murder. He was sentenced to imprisonment for not less than 15 years nor more than 30 years.

On appeal, the Supreme Court of Illinois affirmed the judgment of conviction. The court refused to accept the State's argument that Brown's arrest was lawful. "Upon review of the record, we conclude that the testimony fails to show that at the time of his apprehension there was probable cause for defendant's arrest, [and] that his arrest was, therefore, unlawful." But it went on to hold in two significant and unembellished sentences:

> "[W]e conclude that the giving of the *Miranda* warnings, in the first instance by the police officer and in the second by the assistant State's Attorney, served to break, the causal connection between the illegal arrest and the giving of the statements, and that defendant's act in making the statements was 'sufficiently an act of free will to purge the primary taint of the unlawful invasion' Wong Sun v. United States. We hold, therefore, that the circuit court did not err in admitting the statements into evidence."

Aside from its reliance upon the presence of the *Miranda* warnings, no specific aspect of the record or of the circumstances was cited by the court in support of its conclusion. The court, in other words, appears to have held that the *Miranda* warnings in and of themselves broke the causal chain so that any subsequent statement, even one induced by the continuing effects of unconstitutional custody, was admissible so long as, in the traditional sense, it was voluntary and not coerced in violation of the Fifth and Fourteenth Amendments.

Because of our concern about the implication of our holding in Wong Sun v. United States, to the facts of Brown's case, we granted certiorari.

II.

In *Wong Sun*, the Court pronounced the principles to be applied where the issue is whether statements and other evidence obtained after an illegal arrest or search should be excluded. In that case, federal agents elicited an oral statement from defendant Toy after forcing entry at 6 a. m. into his laundry at the back of which he had his living quarters. The agents had followed Toy down the hall to the bedroom and there had placed him under arrest. The Court of Appeals found that there was no probable cause for the arrest. This Court concluded that that finding was "amply justified by the facts clearly shown on this record." Toy's statement, which bore upon his participation in the sale of narcotics, led the agents to question another person, Johnny Yee, who actually possessed narcotics. Yee stated that heroin had been brought to him earlier by Toy and another Chinese known to him only as "Sea Dog." Under questioning, Toy said that "Sea Dog" was Wong Sun. Toy led agents to a multi-family dwelling where, he said, Wong Sun lived. Gaining admittance to the building through a bell and buzzer, the agents climbed the stairs and entered the apartment. One went into the back room and brought Wong Sun out in handcuffs. After arraignment, Wong Sun was released on his own recognizance. Several days later, he returned voluntarily to give an unsigned confession.

This Court ruled that Toy's declarations and the contraband taken from Yee were the fruits of the agents' illegal action and should not have been admitted as evidence against Toy. It held that the statement did not result from "an intervening independent act of a free will," and that it was not "sufficiently an act of free will to purge the primary taint of the unlawful invasion." With respect to Wong Sun's confession, however, the Court held that in the light of his lawful arraignment and release on his own recognizance, and of his return voluntarily several days later to make the statement, the connection between his unlawful arrest and the statement "had 'become so attenuated as to dissipate the taint.' Nardone v. United States, 308 U.S. 338, 341." The Court said:

> "We need not hold that all evidence is 'fruit of the poisonous tree' simply because it would not have come to light but for the illegal actions of the police. Rather, the more apt question in such a case is 'whether, granting establishment of the primary illegality, the evidence to which instant objection is made has been come at by exploitation of that illegality or instead by means sufficiently distinguishable to be purged of the primary taint.' Maguire, Evidence of Guilt, 221 (1959)."

The exclusionary rule thus was applied in *Wong Sun primarily* to protect Fourth Amendment rights. Protection of the Fifth Amendment right against self-incrimination was not the Court's paramount concern there. To the extent that the question whether Toy's statement was voluntary was considered, it was only to judge whether it "was *sufficiently* an act of free will to purge the primary taint of the unlawful invasion."

The Court in *Wong Sun*, as is customary, emphasized that application of the exclusionary rule on Toy's behalf protected Fourth Amendment guarantees in two respects: "in terms of deterring lawless conduct by federal officers," and by "closing the doors of the federal courts to any use of evidence unconstitutionally obtained." These considerations of deterrence and of judicial integrity, by now, have become rather commonplace in the Court's cases. See, e. g., United States v. Peltier, 422 U.S. 531, 535–538 (1975); United States v. Calandra, 414 U.S. 338, 347 (1974); Terry v. Ohio, 392 U.S. 1, 12–13, 28–29 (1968). "The rule is calculated to prevent, not to repair. Its purpose is to deter—to compel respect for the constitutional guarantee in the only effectively available way—by removing the incentive to disregard it." Elkins v. United States, 364 U.S. 206, 217 (1960). But "[d]espite its broad deterrent purpose, the exclusionary rule has never been interpreted to proscribe the use of illegally seized evidence in all proceedings or against all persons." United States v. Calandra, 414 U.S. at 348. See also Michigan v. Tucker, 417 U.S. 433, 446–447 (1974).[2]

2. Members of the Court on occasion have indicated disenchantment with the rule. See, e. g., Coolidge v. New Hampshire, 403 U.S. 443, 490, 492, 493, 510 (1971) (concurring and dissenting opinions); Bivens v. Six Unknown Federal Narcotics Agents, 403 U.S. 388, 411 (1971) (dissenting opinion). Its efficacy has been subject to some dispute. United States v. Calandra, 414 U.S. 338, 348, n. 5 (1974). See Elkins v. United States, 364 U.S. 206, 218 (1960).

III.

The Illinois courts refrained from resolving the question, as apt here as it was in *Wong Sun*, whether Brown's statements were obtained by exploitation of the illegality of his arrest. They assumed that the *Miranda* warnings, by themselves, assured that the statements (verbal acts, as contrasted with physical evidence) were of sufficient free will as to purge the primary taint of the unlawful arrest. *Wong Sun*, of course, preceded *Miranda*.

This Court has described the *Miranda* warnings as a "prophylactic rule," Michigan v. Payne, 412 U.S. 47, 53 (1973), and as a "procedural safeguard," Miranda v. Arizona, 384 U.S., at 457, 478, employed to protect Fifth Amendment rights against "the compulsion inherent in custodial surroundings." The function of the warnings relates to the Fifth Amendment's guarantee against coerced self-incrimination, and the exclusion of a statement made in the absence of the warnings, it is said, serves to deter the taking of an incriminating statement without first informing the individual of his Fifth Amendment rights.

Although, almost 90 years ago, the Court observed that the Fifth Amendment is in "intimate relation" with the Fourth, Boyd v. United States (1886), the *Miranda* warnings thus far have not been regarded as a means either of remedying or deterring violations of Fourth Amendment rights. Frequently, as here, rights under the two Amendments may appear to coalesce since "the 'unreasonable searches and seizures' condemned in the Fourth Amendment are almost always made for the purpose of compelling a man to give evidence against himself, which in criminal cases is condemned in the Fifth Amendment." The exclusionary rule, however, when utilized to effectuate the Fourth Amendment, serves interests and policies that are distinct from those it serves under the Fifth. It is directed at all unlawful searches and seizures, and not merely those that happen to produce incriminating material or testimony as fruits. In short, exclusion of a confession made without *Miranda* warnings might be regarded as necessary to effectuate the Fifth Amendment, but it would not be sufficient fully to protect the Fourth. *Miranda* warnings, and the exclusion of a confession made without them, do not alone sufficiently deter a Fourth Amendment violation.[3]

Thus, even if the statements in this case were found to be voluntary under the Fifth Amendment, the Fourth Amendment issue remains. In order for the causal chain, between the illegal arrest and the statements made subsequent thereto, to be broken, *Wong Sun* requires not merely that the statement meet the Fifth Amendment standard of voluntariness but that it be "sufficiently an act of free will to purge the primary taint." *Wong Sun* thus mandates consideration of a statement's admissibility in light of the distinct policies and interests of the Fourth Amendment.

3. The *Miranda* warnings in no way inform a person of his Fourth Amendment rights, including his right to be released from unlawful custody following an arrest made without a warrant or without probable cause.

If *Miranda* warnings, by themselves, were held to attenuate the taint of an unconstitutional arrest, regardless of how wanton and purposeful the Fourth Amendment violation, the effect of the exclusionary rule would be substantially diluted. See Davis v. Mississippi, 394 U.S. 721, 726–727 (1969). Arrests made without warrant or without probable cause, for questioning or "investigation," would be encouraged by the knowledge that evidence derived therefrom hopefully could be made admissible at trial by the simple expedient of giving *Miranda* warnings. Any incentive to avoid Fourth Amendment violations would be eviscerated by making the warnings, in effect, a "cure-all," and the constitutional guarantee against unlawful searches and seizures could be said to be reduced to "a form of words."

It is entirely possible, of course, as the State here argues, that persons arrested illegally frequently may decide to confess, as an act of free will unaffected by the initial illegality. But the *Miranda* warnings, *alone* and *per se*, cannot always make the act sufficiently a product of free will to break, for Fourth Amendment purposes, the causal connection between the illegality and the confession. They cannot assure in every case that the Fourth Amendment violation has not been unduly exploited.

While we therefore reject the *per se* rule which the Illinois courts appear to have accepted, we also decline to adopt any alternative *per se* or "but for" rule. The petitioner himself professes not to demand so much. The question whether a confession is the product of a free will under *Wong Sun* must be answered on the facts of each case. No single fact is dispositive. The workings of the human mind are too complex, and the possibilities of misconduct too diverse, to permit protection of the Fourth Amendment to turn on such a talismanic test. The *Miranda* warnings are an important factor, to be sure, in determining whether the confession is obtained by exploitation of an illegal arrest. But they are not the only factor to be considered. The temporal proximity of the arrest and the confession, the presence of intervening circumstances, see Johnson v. Louisiana, 406 U.S. 356, 365 (1972), and, particularly, the purpose and flagrancy of the official misconduct are all relevant. See Wong Sun v. United States. The voluntariness of the statement is a threshold requirement. And the burden of showing admissibility rests, of course, on the prosecution.

IV.

Although the Illinois courts failed to undertake the inquiry mandated by *Wong Sun* to evaluate the circumstances of this case in the light of the policy served by the exclusionary rule, the trial resulted in a record of amply sufficient detail and depth from which the determination may be made. We therefore decline the suggestion of the United States, as *amicus curiae*, see Morales v. New York, 396 U. S. 102 (1969), to remand the case for further factual findings. We conclude that the State failed to sustain the burden of showing that the evidence in question was admissible under *Wong Sun*.

Brown's first statement was separated from his illegal arrest by less than two hours, and there was no intervening event of significance whatsoever. In its essentials, his situation is remarkably like that of James Wah Toy in *Wong Sun*. We could hold Brown's first statement admissible only if we overrule *Wong Sun*. We decline to do so. And the second statement was clearly the result and the fruit of the first.[4]

The illegality here, moreover, had a quality of purposefulness. The impropriety of the arrest was obvious; awareness of that fact was virtually conceded by the two detectives when they repeatedly acknowledged, in their testimony, that the purpose of their action was "for investigation" or for "questioning." The arrest, both in design and in execution, was investigatory. The detectives embarked upon this expedition for evidence in the hope that something might turn up. The manner in which Brown's arrest was affected gives the appearance of having been calculated to cause surprise, fright, and confusion.

We emphasize that our holding is a limited one. We decide only that the Illinois courts were in error in assuming that the *Miranda* warnings, by themselves, under *Wong Sun* always purge the taint of an illegal arrest.

The judgment of the Supreme Court of Illinois is reversed and the case is remanded for further proceedings not inconsistent with this opinion.

It is so ordered.

———

MR. JUSTICE WHITE, concurring in the judgment.

Insofar as the Court holds (1) that despite *Miranda* warnings the Fourth and Fourteenth Amendments require the exclusion from evidence of statements obtained as the fruit of an arrest which the arresting officers knew or should have known was without probable cause and unconstitutional, and (2) that the statements obtained in this case were in this category, I am in agreement and therefore concur in the judgment.

MR. JUSTICE POWELL, with whom MR. JUSTICE REHNQUIST joins, concurring in part.

I join the Court insofar as it holds that the *per se* rule adopted by the Illinois Supreme Court for determining the admissibility of petitioner's two statements inadequately accommodates the diverse interests underlying the Fourth Amendment exclusionary rule. I would, however, remand the case for reconsideration under the general standards articulated in the Court's opinion and elaborated herein.

*   *   *

4. The fact that Brown had made one statement, believed by him to be admissible, and his cooperation with the arresting and interrogating officers in the search for Claggett, with his anticipation for leniency, bolstered the pressures for him to give the second, or at least vitiated any incentive on his part to avoid self-incrimination. Cf. Fahy v. Connecticut, 375 U.S. 85 (1963).

NOTES

1. If the effort is to decide whether, in some psychological sense, the illegal police conduct "caused" the confession, what difference does it make whether the question of probable cause was close or not? Consider the statement of Justice Stevens, concurring in Dunaway v. New York, 442 U.S. 200, 99 S.Ct. 2248 (1979), a decision which applied *Brown* and held inadmissible a confession following an illegal arrest:

> "The flagrancy of the official misconduct is relevant, in my judgment, only insofar as it has a tendency to motivate the defendant. A midnight arrest with drawn guns will be equally frightening whether the police acted recklessly or in good faith. Conversely, a courteous command has the same effect on the arrestee whether the officer thinks he has probable cause or not."

When the law considers the flagrancy of the police conduct in determining the admissibility of derivative evidence, has it abandoned any pretext of searching for "causality" and determined that where certain facts are present, the police conduct will be deemed to be the "legal cause" of a confession? Does causality in *Brown* have any more scientific or philosophical meaning than does the term "proximate cause" in tort law?

2. Does *Brown* signal that a "good faith" exception to the exclusionary rule is likely to be adopted in the near future?

3. In United States v. Ceccolini, 435 U.S. 268, 98 S.Ct. 1054 (1978), a government agent, through the unlawful inspection of an envelope belonging to Ceccolini, discovered that Lois Hennessey, though perhaps not herself implicated, might have knowledge bearing upon Ceccolini's gambling activities. Four months later authorities interviewed Hennessey concerning her knowledge. She said she "was studying police science and would be willing to help." Later Ceccolini was indicted for perjury in connection with his sworn denials of gambling. Three years after the original search, the government called Hennessey to testify against Ceccolini. The Supreme Court approved admission of her testimony. Relevant criteria included (a) the willingness of the witness to testify, (b) the passage of time between the search and the first witness contact, on the one hand, and the date of her trial testimony on the other hand, and (c) the fact that the officer who conducted the original search had not been investigating Ceccolini or gambling activity when, in his unlawful snooping, he examined the envelope. The Court indicated that a per se rule of exclusion ought not be adopted lest a willing witness who might have come forward anyway be forever barred from testifying. Post-*Ceccolini* cases where the testimony of a witness discovered through unlawful means was suppressed include United States v. Cruz, 581 F.2d 535 (5th Cir. 1978), and United States v. Scios, 590 F.2d 956 (D.C.Cir.1978).

4. In Harrison v. United States, 392 U.S. 219, 88 S.Ct. 2008 (1968), the Supreme Court indicated that even a defendant's own trial testimony sometimes must be viewed as the fruit of improper police investigative procedures. There a statement in which the suspect admitted a killing was secured in violation of the principles of the *McNabb-Mallory* rule. After the erroneous denial of a motion to suppress, the defendant testified in his own behalf, admitted the killing, but claimed that it was accident. The Supreme Court held that at the retrial the prosecution could not offer Harrison's testimony because it had not established by clear and convincing evidence that Harrison would have admitted the killing absent the erroneous admission of

his post-arrest statement. Compare McMann v. Richardson, 397 U.S. 759, 90 S.Ct. 1441 (1970), where the Supreme Court held that, if a defendant had competent trial counsel, a plea of guilty will not be vacated where the defendant later claims that the reason that he entered his plea was that the police had through unconstitutional means secured evidence which the prosecution hoped to use at trial. One difference between *Harrison* and *Mc-Mann* is that in the later case the defendant made no motion to suppress, while in the former case the trial judge erroneously denied a motion to suppress. See generally Chapter 16, Section B, note 2 following North Carolina v. Alford.

5. Some of the oldest derivative evidence cases involve situations where the police have improperly secured a statement from the accused and then, hours or days later, secured a second statement. See United States v. Bayer, 331 U.S. 532, 67 S.Ct. 1394 (1947); Darwin v. Connecticut, 391 U.S. 346, 88 S.Ct. 1488 (1968) (Harlan, J., concurring); Beecher v. Alabama, 389 U.S. 35, 88 S.Ct. 189 (1967). In Clewis v. Texas, 386 U.S. 707, 87 S.Ct. 1338 (1967), a nine day spread between the first statement and the second was deemed an inadequate break in the stream of events to render the second statement admissible. Decisions treating the admissibility of a statement given after proper *Miranda* warnings where an earlier statement had been obtained in violation of *Miranda* include State v. Michael, 103 Ariz. 46, 436 P.2d 595 (1968); Evans v. United States, 375 F.2d 355 (8th Cir. 1967); United States ex rel. Williams v. Twomey, 467 F.2d 1248 (7th Cir. 1972). Typical is United States v. Pierce, 397 F.2d 128 (4th Cir. 1968): "The F.B.I. agent entered the fray armed with defendant's earlier admissions to the Williamson police, and it is most probable that the defendant was aware of this fact. . . . The decision to respond under such circumstances can hardly be termed voluntary . . . The F.B.I. agent had the advantage of all that Chief Bucci knew. Warning after the admission is too late."

After a statement is improperly secured, what intervening circumstances can render a second statement admissible? Suppose a prosecutor in interrogating a suspect tells him that he should assume that what he has previously told the police will be inadmissible and that the suspect should decide anew whether he wishes to talk. Would that purge the taint of an earlier *Miranda* violation? Would consultation with a defense lawyer after the first statement adequately purge the taint if the defendant gives a subsequent statement?

6. Derivative evidence theories are as unbounded as a defense lawyer's imagination. Consider a statement made by a suspect who has been confronted with physical evidence seized in violation of his Fourth Amendment rights. And what about an incriminating statement blurted out by a suspect following a lineup identification at a proceeding which violates the principles of *Stovall* or of *Wade-Gilbert*? Or a warrant issued based upon probable cause data obtained in violation of the defendant's rights under *Miranda* or under the Fourth Amendment? Or the product of a search incident to a warrantless arrest when the arrest was based upon probable cause data which had been observed in an earlier unlawful search of the suspect's home? Reported decisions supporting each of these derivative evidence theories are readily available. The task of the defense lawyer is to determine in what fashion the evidence which the prosecutor seeks to offer— whether physical evidence, the defendant's statements, in-court or out-of-court identifications, or other testimony of prosecution witnesses—can be traced to the alleged police wrongdoing at the investigative stage. This is true whether the alleged illegality relates to arrest, search and seizure,

wiretapping, *Stovall* or *Wade-Gilbert* identification principles, or *Miranda* or one of the other principles limiting police interrogation practices.

7.   The most ordinary consequence of an unlawful arrest, in the context of the arrestee's criminal case, is the suppression of physical evidence derived from the arrest. If the arrest is unlawful, the prosecution is deprived of an essential predicate of the doctrine of search incident to arrest. See Chapter 4, Section E, supra. Beck v. Ohio, Chapter 4, Section B, supra, illustrates this phenomenon. An illegal arrest may also be one factor in determining the voluntariness of a consent to search granted by the arrestee. See Chapter 4, Section G, supra.

In Crews v. United States, —— U.S. —— (1980), the government appealed from a decision of the District of Columbia Appellate Court reported at 389 A.2d 277 (D.C.App.1978). The Appellate Court had suppressed proof on an out-of-court identification made from a photograph taken of a suspect following his arrest without probable cause. The government did not challenge that order. In dictum three of the eight participating Supreme Court justices said that this suppression order was mandated by the Fourth Amendment. The other justices made no comment on that part of the Appellate Court order.

All eight justices voted to overturn the Appellate Court order suppressing the in-court identification. Five justices, in several different opinions, seemed to say that an in-court identification of a defendant generally should not be suppressed as the fruit of an illegal arrest of the defendant. They reasoned that where, as here, the authorities' knowledge of the witness is not derived from the illegal arrest, and where the witness's knowledge of the offender's looks is not derived from the arrest, the witness will be in court prepared to make an identification. They further reasoned that an illegal arrest does not deprive the court of jurisdiction, and they asserted that it followed that the accused cannot make any Fourth Amendment claim related to his presence at trial. They concluded that, therefore, the in-court identification cannot be deemed the product of an unlawful arrest.

Three justices would have left the broader question open. They emphasized that the authorities here knew the identity of the suspect before the arrest was made. They apparently reasoned that the confrontation between witness and suspect was inevitable, *perhaps* because the suspect could have been compelled to appear in a lineup. They concluded that this in-court identification ought not be suppressed.

8.   When a statement taken in violation of *Miranda* leads to incriminating physical evidence does the fruit of the poisoned tree doctrine operate to exclude this derivative evidence? The answer would seem to be yes from indications in the text of *Miranda*, 384 U.S. at 479, 86 S.Ct. 1602 and Orozco v. Texas, 394 U.S. 324, 89 S.Ct. 1095 (1969). However, the issue is not completely clear and it can be argued that a statement taken in violation only of *Miranda* is not serious enough to warrant application of the poisoned tree rule. Keister v. Cox, 307 F.Supp. 1173 (W.D.Va.1969). See George, "The Fruits of Miranda: Scope of the Exclusionary Rule", 39 U. Colo.L.Rev. 478 (1967).

Many courts, however, have held or assumed that the derivative evidence rule applies. Sullins v. United States, 389 F.2d 985 (10th Cir. 1968); United States v. Cassell, 452 F.2d 533 (7th Cir. 1971); People v. Oramus, 25 N.Y.2d 825, 303 N.Y.S.2d 679, 250 N.E.2d 723 (1969); State v. Mitchell, 270 N.C. 753, 155 S.E.2d 96 (1967); Commonwealth v. Leaming, 432 Pa. 326, 247 A.2d 590 (1968); Shannon v. State, 427 S.W.2d 26 (Tex.1968).

The Supreme Court addressed the issue in Michigan v. Tucker, 417 U. S. 433, 94 S.Ct. 2357 (1974):

"Mr. Justice Rehnquist delivered the opinion of the Court.

"This case presents the question whether the testimony of a witness in respondent's state court trial for rape must be excluded simply because police had learned the identity of the witness by questioning respondent at a time when he was in custody as a suspect, but had not been advised that counsel would be appointed for him if he was indigent. The questioning took place before this Court's decision in *Miranda*, but respondent's trial, at which he was convicted, took place afterwards. Therefore, *Miranda* is applicable to this case.

"A comparison of the facts in this case with the historical circumstances underlying the privilege against compulsory self-incrimination strongly indicates that the police conduct here did not deprive respondent of his privilege against compulsory self-incrimination as such, but rather failed to make available to him the full measure of procedural safeguards associated with that right since *Miranda*. Certainly no one could contend that the interrogation faced by respondent bore any resemblance to the historical practices at which the right against compulsory self-incrimination was aimed. The District Court in this case noted that the police had 'warned [respondent] that he had the right to remain silent,' 352 F.Supp. 266, 267 (1972), and the record in this case clearly shows that respondent was informed that any evidence taken could be used against him. The record is also clear that respondent was asked whether he wanted an attorney and that he replied that he did not. Thus, his statements could hardly be termed involuntary as that term has been defined in the decisions of this Court. Additionally, there were no legal sanctions, such as the threat of contempt, which could have been applied to respondent had he chosen to remain silent. He was simply not exposed to 'the cruel trilemma of self-accusation, perjury or contempt.' Murphy v. Waterfront Comm'n, 378 U.S., at 55, 84 S.Ct., at 1596.

"Our determination that the interrogation in this case involved no compulsion sufficient to breach the right against compulsory self-incrimination does not mean there was not a disregard, albeit an inadvertent disregard, of the procedural rules later established in *Miranda*. The question for decision is how sweeping the judicially imposed consequences of this disregard shall be. This Court said in *Miranda* that statements taken in violation of the *Miranda* principles must not be used to prove the prosecution's case at trial. That requirement was fully complied with by the state court here: respondent's statements, claiming that he was with Henderson and then asleep during the time period of the crime were not admitted against him at trial. This Court has also said, in Wong Sun v. United States, 371 U.S. 471, 83 S.Ct. 407, (1963), that the 'fruits' of police conduct which actually infringed a defendant's Fourth Amendment rights must be suppressed. But we have already concluded that the police conduct at issue here did not abridge respondent's constitutional privilege against compulsory self-incrimination, but departed only from the prophylactic standards later laid down by this Court in *Miranda* to safeguard that privilege. . . .

"Just as the law does not require that a defendant receive a perfect trial, only a fair one, it cannot realistically require that policemen investigating serious crimes make no errors whatsoever. The pressures of law enforcement and the vagaries of human nature would make such an expectation unrealistic. Before we penalize police error, therefore, we must consider whether the sanction serves a valid and useful purpose.

* * *

"The deterrent purpose of the exclusionary rule necessarily assumes that the police have engaged in willful, or at the very least negligent, conduct which has deprived the defendant of some right. By refusing to admit evidence gained as a result of such conduct, the courts hope to instill in those particular investigating officers, or in their future counterparts, a greater degree of care toward the rights of an accused. Where the official action was pursued in complete good faith, however, the deterrence rationale loses much of its force.

"We consider it significant to our decision in this case that the officers' failure to advise respondent of his right to appointed counsel occurred prior to the decision in *Miranda*. Although we have been urged to resolve the broad question of whether evidence derived from statements taken in violation of the *Miranda* rules must be excluded regardless of when the interrogation took place, we instead place our holding on a narrower ground. For at the time respondent was questioned these police officers were guided, quite rightly, by the principles established in Escobedo v. Illinois, 378 U.S. 478, 84 S.Ct. 1758, (1964), particularly focusing on the suspect's oportunity to have retained counsel with him during the interrogation if he chose to do so. Thus, the police asked respondent if he wanted counsel, and he answered that he did not. The statements actually made by respondent to the police, as we have observed, were excluded at trial . . . Whatever deterrent effect on future police conduct the exclusion of those statements may have had, we do not believe it would be significantly augmented by excluding the testimony of the witness Henderson as well."

* * *

One Court has extended the rule in *Tucker* to a case involving a post-Miranda interrogation. United States ex rel. Hudson v. Cannon, 529 F.2d 890 (7th Cir. 1976).

9. A similar problem concerning the admissibility of physical evidence discovered through the exploitation of a *Massiah* violation arose in the aftermath of Brewer v. Williams, Chapter 2, Section C, supra. On remand the trial judge admitted testimony concerning the little girl's corpse, which the police had discovered through a violation of the suspect's right to counsel. The Iowa Supreme Court following re-conviction upheld the admission of such testimony on the theory that the body would inevitably have been discovered. State v. Williams, 285 N.W.2d 248 (Iowa 1979).

10. The question is somewhat different when the problem involved a second statement taken in adherence to *Miranda* but taken after the suspect gave a first statement without warnings. The Court in *Miranda* recognized that the taint of the first statement in one of the cases (*Westover*) might be deemed removed if the second statement were given at a time and place remote from the time and place of original statement. Ultimately, the issue will be resolved on the facts of each individual case.

Compare United States ex rel. B. v. Shelly, 430 F.2d 215 (2nd Cir. 1970) (also relying on youth and inexperience of the suspect), and State v. Dickson, 82 N.M. 408, 482 P.2d 916 (1971) (illegality of second confession presumed unless clearly rebutted), People v. Chapple, 38 N.Y.2d 112, 378 N.Y.S.2d 682, 341 N.E.2d 243 (1975); with People v. Young, 131 Ill.App.2d 113, 266 N.E.2d 160 (1970) (removed in time and place, warned twice and questioned by an officer who did not know of the first confession); Klamant v. Cupp, 437 F.2d 1153 (9th Cir. 1970) (second statement voluntered); Williams v. Commonwealth, 211 Va. 609, 179 S.E.2d 512 (1971) (second statement made in response to stepmother's question). State v. McDonald, 195 Neb. 625, 240 N.W.2d 8 (1976). In United States v. Trabucco, 424 F.2d 1311 (5th Cir. 1970), it was held that when an initial inadmissible statement is exculpatory the "cat has not been let out of the bag" and there is little compulsion to give a second statement admitting the crime. The court also held that being caught in a lie in the first statement is not a sufficient cause to believe the second statement flowed from the first inadmissible one.

11. Of course, the prosecution has the option of showing that the evidence was discoverable by means completely independent of the tainted statement. This option exists in any derivative evidence case. United States v. Nagelberg, 434 F.2d 585 (2nd Cir. 1970); United States v. De Marce, 513 F.2d 755 (8th Cir. 1975).

12. The final question arising when *Miranda* is considered in relation to the fruit of the poisoned tree doctrine is whether the giving of *Miranda* warnings operates to dissipate the taint of some earlier illegality. This rather abstract issue has some very practical consequences. In a 1969 case, People v. Johnson, 70 Cal.2d 541, 75 Cal.Rptr. 401, 450 P.2d 865 (1969), the California Supreme Court considered the following circumstances: The police illegally entered the co-defendant's apartment and seized a stolen T.V. Shortly after this the co-defendant was arrested. He was shown the illegally seized T.V. He was given *Miranda* warnings. He was asked about the T.V. and confessed also implicating defendant. Defendant was arrested and warned of his rights. He was then confronted by co-defendant. Both were again warned of their rights. Co-defendant confessed and then the defendant confessed. Defendant claimed that his confession was the product of co-defendant's confession and that the co-defendant's confession was the product of an illegal search, i. e., his confession was fruit of a poisoned tree. In a 4–3 decision the court held that *Miranda* warnings, while helpful in attenuating taint, are not sufficient to do so alone and that they did not do so in the present case. A dissent argued that the chain of illegality leading to defendant's confession was weak to begin with and that the majority opinion, by implication, treats the *Miranda* warnings as a trivial incident in the process of interrogation. The question of whether *Miranda* warnings can serve to break the taint of an earlier illegality is considered in Brown v. Illinois, supra.

F. NON–RETROACTIVITY

In Linkletter v. Walker, 381 U.S. 618, 85 S.Ct. 1731 (1965), the Supreme Court for the first time approved the practice of denying retroactive effect to new decisions, such as *Mapp*, which had broadened the federal constitutional rights of the accused. In so doing it relied largely upon precedents from civil cases, where the use of the "prospective only" technique was fairly well established. (For example, in abolishing sovereign tort immunity, state courts, in deference to the reliance which governmental bodies, in deciding not to obtain accident insurance, had placed upon older decisions, typically applied their new decision, except for the case at hand, only to torts occurring after the date of the new decision.) The general rule from civil cases was that as long as the older rule did not itself violate the Constitution, it was not constitutionally impermissible for a court to apply the old rule to cases arising before the new decision. See Great Northern Railway Co. v. Sunburst Oil and Refining Co., 287 U.S. 358, 53 S.Ct. 145 (1932).

Application of this technique to deny criminal defendants the benefit of a new decision of federal constitutional dimension was not free of controversy. Justices Black and Douglas consistently refused to recognize the legitimacy of the technique. Justice Fortas commented that the practice rewarded states which acted only under Supreme Court compulsion and placed a "dunce cap" on those which moved on their own in reforming their systems. Eventually Justice Harlan, an early supporter of non-retroactivity, became one of its strong critics.

As Professor Beytagh has written, however, non-retroactivity seems to be so well established now that concern should be not over the legitimacy of the technique, but the manner in which it is utilized. See Beytagh, Ten Years of Non-Retroactivity: A Critique and a Proposal, 61 Va.L.Rev. 1557 (1975). In *Linkletter* and subsequent decisions the Court indicated that three criteria should determine whether a new constitutional decision is to be denied retroactive effect: (1) the extent to which the new decision has as its purpose the implementation of a value other than improvement of the integrity of the fact-finding process; (2) the extent to which government justifiably relied upon the now overruled decision; and (3) the extent to which the orderly administration of justice would be impaired by retroactive application of the new decision. Most critics believe that the Court has not been true to these criteria in ruling on retroactivity questions.

For an extensive list of cases in which retroactivity questions have been resolved, see W. LaFave, Search and Seizure § 11.5. Among the previously studied decisions which have not been given full retroactive effect are *Mapp, Miranda, Wade-Gilbert,* and *Katz. Mapp* applied to cases which were still alive at the trial level or on appeal on the date of the *Mapp* decision. However, prisoners whose conviction had become final before *Mapp,* and who then sought collateral review through federal habeas corpus or state post-conviction remedies, were denied the benefit of *Mapp. Miranda* affected cases in which confessions had been secured before the date of the *Miranda* decisions, but only if the *trial* commenced after *Miranda* had been decided. *Wade–Gilbert* applied only to lineups held after the date of those decisions. *Katz* applied only to non-trespassory electronic surveillance which took place after *Katz* was decided.

Thus non-retroactivity has had the effect of narrowing the impact of exclusionary rules.

NOTE

In United States v. Peltier, 422 U.S. 531, 95 S.Ct. 2313 (1975), the Supreme Court denied retroactive effect to Almeida-Sanchez v. United States, 413 U.S. 266 (1973). The Government in *Peltier* urged that the law enforcement officers acted in accordance with administrative regulations of the United States Department of Immigration, which had been promulgated pursuant to authority granted by Congress. *Almeida-Sanchez* struck down these regulations. In denying retroactive effect to *Almeida-Sanchez* and in permitting the evidence seized to be admitted in *Peltier*, Mr. Justice Rehnquist wrote for the majority:

> We think that these cases tell us a great deal about the nature of the exclusionary rule, as well as something about the nature of retroactivity analysis . . . The teaching of these retroactivity cases is that if the law enforcement officers reasonably believed that the evidence they had seized was admissible at trial, the "imperative of judicial integrity" is not offended by the introduction into evidence of that material even if decisions subsequent to the search or seizure have broadened the exclusionary rule to encompass evidence seized in that manner.

Mr. Justice Brennan responded for the minority:

> The Court's opinion depends upon an entirely new understanding of the exclusionary rule in Fourth Amendment cases, one which, if the vague contours outlined today are filled in as I fear they will be, forecasts the complete demise of the exclusionary rule as fashioned by this Court in over 61 years of Fourth Amendment jurisprudence. An analysis of the Court's unsuccessfully veiled reformulation demonstrates that its apparent rush to discard 61 years of constitutional development has produced a formula difficult to comprehend and, on any understanding of its meaning, impossible to justify.
>
> The Court signals its new approach in these words: "If the purpose of the exclusionary rule is to deter unlawful police conduct, then evidence obtained from a search should be suppressed only if it can be said that the law enforcement officer had knowledge, or may properly be charged with knowledge, that the search was unconstitutional under the Fourth Amendment." True, the Court does not state in so many words that this formulation of the exclusionary rule is to be applied beyond the present retroactivity context. But the proposition is stated generally and, particularly in view of the concomitant expansion of prospectivity announced today, I have no confidence that the new formulation is to be confined to putative retroactivity cases. Rather, I suspect that when a suitable opportunity arises, today's revision of the exclusionary rule will be pronounced applicable to all search and seizure cases. I therefore register my strong disagreement now.
>
> The new formulation obviously removes the very foundation of the exclusionary rule as it has been expressed in countless decisions. Until now the rule in federal criminal cases decided on direct review has been that suppression is necessarily the sanction to be applied when it is determined that the evidence was in fact illegally acquired. The revision unveiled today suggests that instead

of that single inquiry, district judges may also have to probe the subjective knowledge of the official who orders the search, and the inferences from existing law that official should have drawn. The decision whether or not to order suppression would then turn upon whether, based on that expanded inquiry, suppression would comport with either the deterrence rationale of the exclusionary rule or the imperative of judicial integrity.

G. NON–GOVERNMENTAL CONDUCT

As with private citizen interrogations (e. g., by private security officers), for which *Miranda* warnings are generally held not to be required (Ch. 2, B–5), the courts have generally held that non-governmental illegal seizures of physical evidence do not invoke the exclusionary rule. The first case so holding is Burdeau v. McDowell, 256 U.S. 465, 41 S.Ct. 574 (1921). Representative later cases to the same effect are: Barnes v. United States, 373 F.2d 517 (5th Cir. 1967); United States v. Mekjian, 505 F.2d 1320 (5th Cir. 1975).

There are four categories of cases, however, in which the exclusionary rule may be applied to illegal private citizen searches. First, where private security officers have been accorded full police powers, the exclusionary rule may become applicable. People v. Eastway, 67 Mich.App. 464, 241 N.W.2d 249 (1976). Contra: People v. Toliver, 60 Ill.App.3d 650, 18 Ill.Dec. 54, 377 N.E.2d 207 (1978). Second, where a private person acts in concert with or as an agent for the police (or where he is a "moonlighting" law enforcement officer), his illegal seizures are subject to the exclusionary rule. Machlan v. State, 248 Ind. 218, 225 N.E.2d 762 (1967); United States v. Newton, 510 F.2d 1149 (7th Cir. 1975). Third, if the searcher is a public employee (e. g., a school principal), the public employee status alone has been held to subject him to Fourth Amendment controls and the exclusionary rule sanction. People v. Scott D., 34 N.Y.2d 483, 315 N.E. 2d 466 (1974). Fourth, even where a private security officer is empowered by statute to search a person he has arrested, the search is limited to a search for a weapon or the retrieval of stolen items; if the search extends beyond that (e. g., the seizure of heroin in a shoplifter's purse containing a stolen blouse) such evidence will be excluded. People v. Zelinski, 24 Cal.3d 357, 155 Cal.Rptr. 575, 594 P. 2d 1000 (1979).

H. ALTERNATIVE REMEDIES

1. ADMINISTRATIVE REMEDY PROPOSAL

BIVENS v. SIX UNKNOWN NAMED AGENTS OF FEDERAL BUREAU OF NARCOTICS

Supreme Court of the United States, 1971.
403 U.S. 388, 91 S.Ct. 1999.

*   *   *

MR. CHIEF JUSTICE BURGER, dissenting.

*   *   *

This case has significance far beyond its facts and its holding. For more than 55 years this Court has enforced a rule under which evidence of undoubted reliability and probative value has been suppressed and excluded from criminal cases whenever it was obtained in violation of the Fourth Amendment. The rule has rested on a theory that suppression of evidence in these circumstances was imperative to deter law enforcement authorities from using improper methods to obtain evidence.

The deterrence theory underlying the suppression doctrine, or exclusionary rule, has a certain appeal in spite of the high price society pays for such a drastic remedy. . . .

The plurality opinion in Irvine v. California, 347 U.S. 128, 136, 74 S.Ct. 381, 385 (1954), catalogued the doctrine's defects:

> "Rejection of the evidence does nothing to punish the wrong-doing official, while it may, and likely will, release the wrong-doing defendant. It deprives society of its remedy against one lawbreaker because he has been pursued by another. It protects one against whom incriminating evidence is discovered, but does nothing to protect innocent persons who are the victims of illegal but fruitless searches."

From time to time members of the Court, recognizing the validity of these protests, have articulated varying alternative justifications for the suppression of important evidence in a criminal trial. Under one of these alternative theories the rule's foundation is shifted to the "sporting contest" thesis that the government must "play the game fairly" and cannot be allowed to profit from its own illegal acts. But the exclusionary rule does not ineluctably flow from a desire to ensure that government plays the "game" according to the rules. If an effective alternative remedy is available, concern for official observance of the law does not require adherence to the exclusionary rule. Nor is it easy to understand how a court can be thought to endorse a violation of the Fourth Amendment by allowing illegally seized evidence to be introduced against a defendant if an effective remedy is provided against the government.

The exclusionary rule has also been justified on the theory that the relationship between the Self-Incrimination Clause of the Fifth Amendment and the Fourth Amendment requires the suppression of evidence seized in violation of the latter.

Even ignoring, however, the decisions of this Court that have held that the Fifth Amendment applies only to "testimonial" disclosures, it seems clear that the Self-Incrimination Clause does not protect a person from the seizure of evidence that is incriminating. It protects a person only from being the conduit by which the police acquire evidence. Mr. Justice Holmes, once put it succinctly, "A party is privileged from producing the evidence, but not from its production." Johnson v. United States, 228 U.S. 457, 458, 33 S.Ct. 572 (1913).

It is clear, however, that neither of these theories undergirds the decided cases in this Court. Rather the exclusionary rule has rested on the deterrent rationale—the hope that law enforcement officials would be deterred from unlawful searches and seizures if the illegally seized, albeit trustworthy, evidence was suppressed often enough and the courts persistently enough deprived them of any benefits they might have gained from their illegal conduct.

This evidentiary rule is unique to American jurisprudence. Although the English and Canadian legal systems are highly regarded, neither has adopted our rule. See Martin, The Exclusionary Rule Under Foreign Law—Canada, 52 J.Crim.L.C. & P.S. 271, 272 (1961); Williams, The Exclusionary Rule Under Foreign Law—England, 52 J.Crim.L.C. & P.S. 272 (1961).

I do not question the need for some remedy to give meaning and teeth to the constitutional guarantees against unlawful conduct by government officials. Without some effective sanction, these protections would constitute little more than rhetoric. Beyond doubt the conduct of some officials requires sanctions. . . . But the hope that this objective could be accomplished by the exclusion of reliable evidence from criminal trials was hardly more than a wistful dream. Although I would hesitate to abandon it until some meaningful substitute is developed, the history of the suppression doctrine demonstrates that it is both conceptually sterile and practically ineffective in accomplishing its stated objective. . . .

Some clear demonstration of the benefits and effectiveness of the exclusionary rule is required to justify it in view of the high price it extracts from society—the release of countless guilty criminals. . . . But there is no empirical evidence to support the claim that the rule actually deters illegal conduct of law enforcement officials. . . .

There are several reasons for this failure. The rule does not apply any direct sanction to the individual official whose illegal conduct results in the exclusion of evidence in a criminal trial. With rare exceptions law enforcement agencies do not impose direct sanctions on the individual officer responsible for a particular judicial application of the suppression doctrine. Thus there is virtually nothing done to bring about a change in his practices. The immediate sanction triggered by the application of the rule is visited upon the prosecutor whose case against a criminal is either weakened or destroyed. The doctrine deprives the police in no real sense; except that apprehending wrongdoers is their business, police have no more stake in successful prosecutions than prosecutors or the public.

The suppression doctrine vaguely assumes that law enforcement is a monolithic governmental enterprise. For example, the dissenters in Wolf v. Colorado, supra, 338 U.S., at 44, 69 S.Ct., at 1370, argued that:

> "Only by exclusion can we impress upon the zealous *prosecutor* that violation of the Constitution will do him no good. And only when that point is driven home can the *prosecutor* be expected to emphasize the importance of observing the constitutional demands in *his instructions to the police.*" (Emphasis added.)

But the prosecutor who loses his case because of police misconduct is not an official in the police department; he can rarely set in motion any corrective action or administrative penalties. Moreover, he does not have control or direction over police procedures or police actions that lead to the exclusion of evidence. It is the rare exception when a prosecutor takes part in arrests, searches, or seizures so that he can guide police action.

Whatever educational effect the rule conceivably might have in theory is greatly diminished in fact by the realities of law enforcement work. Policemen do not have the time, inclination, or training to read and grasp the nuances of the appellate opinions that ultimately define the standards of conduct they are to follow. The issues that these decisions resolve often admit of neither easy nor obvious answers, as sharply divided courts on what is or is not "reasonable" amply demonstrate. Nor can judges, in all candor, forget that opinions sometimes lack helpful clarity.

The presumed educational effect of judicial opinions is also reduced by the long time lapse—often several years—between the original police action and its final judicial evaluation. Given a policeman's pressing responsibilities, it would be surprising if he ever becomes aware of the final result after such a delay. Finally, the exclusionary rule's deterrent impact is diluted by the fact that there are large areas of police activity that do not result in criminal prosecutions—hence the rule has virtually no applicability and no effect in such situations. . . .

Although unfortunately ineffective, the exclusionary rule has increasingly been characterized by a single, monolithic, and drastic judicial response to all official violations of legal norms. Inadvertent errors of judgment that do not work any grave injustice will inevitably occur under the pressure of police work. These honest mistakes have been treated in the same way as deliberate and flagrant *Irvine*-type violations of the Fourth Amendment.

* * *

Freeing either a tiger or a mouse in a schoolroom is an illegal act, but no rational person would suggest that these two acts should be punished in the same way. From time to time judges have occasion to pass on regulations governing police procedures. I wonder what would be the judicial response to a police order authorizing "shoot to kill" with respect to every fugitive. It is easy to predict our collective wrath and outrage. We, in common with all rational minds, would say that the police response must relate to the gravity and need; that a "shoot" order might conceivably be tolerable to prevent the escape of a convicted killer but surely not for a car thief, a pickpocket or a shoplifter.

I submit that society has at least as much right to expect rationally graded responses from judges in place of the universal "capital punishment" we inflict on all evidence when police error is shown in its acquisition. See ALI, Model Code of Pre-Arraignment Procedure § SS 8.02(2), p. 23 (Tent. Draft No. 4, 1971), reprinted in the Appendix to this opinion. Yet for over 55 years, and with increasing scope and intensity our legal system has treated vastly dissimilar cases as if they were the same.

Instead of continuing to enforce the suppression doctrine inflexibly, rigidly, and mechanically, we should view it as one of the experimental steps in the great tradition of the common law and acknowledge its shortcomings. But in the same spirit we should be prepared to discontinue what the experience of over half a century has shown neither deters errant officers nor affords a remedy to the totally innocent victims of official misconduct.

I do not propose, however, that we abandon the suppression doctrine until some meaningful alternative can be developed. In a sense our legal system has become the captive of its own creation. To overrule *Weeks* and *Mapp*, even assuming the Court was now prepared to take that step, could raise yet new problems. Obviously the public interest would be poorly served if law enforcement officials were suddenly to gain the impression, however erroneous, that all constitutional restraints on police had somehow been removed—that as open season on "criminals" had been declared. I am concerned lest some such mistaken impression might be fostered by a flat overruling of the suppression doctrine cases. For years we have relied upon it as the exclusive remedy for unlawful official conduct; in a sense we are in a situation akin to the narcotics addict whose dependence on drugs precludes any drastic or immediate withdrawal of the supposed prop, regardless of how futile its continued use may be.

Reasonable and effective substitutes can be formulated if Congress would take the lead, as it did for example in 1946 in the Federal Tort Claims Act. I see no insuperable obstacle to the elimination of the suppression doctrine if Congress would provide some meaningful and effective remedy against unlawful conduct by government officials.

The problems of both error and deliberate misconduct by law enforcement officials call for a workable remedy. Private damage actions against individual police officers concededly have not adequately met this requirement. . . . There is some validity to the claims that juries will not return verdicts against individual officers except in those unusual cases where the violation has been flagrant or where the error has been complete, as in the arrest of the wrong person or the search of the wrong house. There is surely serious doubt, for example, that a drug peddler caught packing his wares will be able to arouse much sympathy in a jury on the ground that the police officer did not announce his identity and purpose fully . . . Jurors may well refuse to penalize a police officer at the behest of a person they believe to be a "criminal" and probably will not punish an officer for honest errors of judgment. In any event an actual recovery depends on finding nonexempt assets of the police officer from which a judgment can be satisfied.

I conclude, therefore, that an entirely different remedy is necessary but it is one that in my view is as much beyond judicial power as the step the Court takes today. Congress should develop an administrative or quasi-judicial remedy against the government itself to afford compensation and restitution for persons whose Fourth Amendment rights have been violated. The venerable doctrine of *respondeat superior* in our tort law provides an entirely appropriate conceptual basis for this remedy. If, for example, a security guard privately employed by a department store commits an assault or other tort on a customer such as an improper search, the victim has a simple and obvious remedy—an action for money damages against the guard's employer, the department store. W. Prosser, The Law of Torts § 68, pp. 470–480 (3d ed., 1964). Such a statutory scheme would have the added advantage of providing some remedy to the completely innocent persons who are sometimes the victims of illegal police conduct—something that the suppression doctrine, of course, can never accomplish.

A simple structure would suffice. For example, Congress could enact a statute along the following lines:

(a) a waiver of sovereign immunity as to the illegal acts of law enforcement officials committed in the performance of assigned duties;

(b) the creation of a cause of action for damages sustained by any person aggrieved by conduct of governmental agents in violation of the Fourth Amendment or statutes regulating official conduct;

(c) the creation of a tribunal, quasi-judicial in nature or perhaps patterned after the United States Court of Claims to adjudicate all claims under the statute;

(d) a provision that this statutory remedy is in lieu of the exclusion of evidence secured for use in criminal cases in violation of the Fourth Amendment; and

(e) a provision directing that no evidence, otherwise admissible, shall be excluded from any criminal proceeding because of violation of the Fourth Amendment.

I doubt that lawyers serving on such a tribunal would be swayed either by undue sympathy for officers or by the prejudice against "criminals" that has sometimes moved lay jurors to deny claims. In addition to awarding damages, the record of the police conduct that is condemned would undoubtedly become a relevant part of an officer's personnel file so that the need for additional training or disciplinary action could be identified or his future usefulness as a public official evaluated. Finally, appellate judicial review could be made available on much the same basis that it is now provided as to district courts and regulatory agencies. This would leave to the courts the ultimate responsibility for determining and articulating standards.

Once the constitutional validity of such a statute is established, it can reasonably be assumed that the States would develop their own remedial systems on the federal model. Indeed there is nothing to prevent a State from enacting a comparable statutory scheme without waiting for the Congress. Steps along these lines would move our system toward more responsible law enforcement on the one hand and away from the irrational and drastic results of the suppression doctrine on the other. Independent of the alternative embraced in this dissenting opinion, I believe the time has come to re-examine the scope of the exclusionary rule and consider at least some narrowing of its thrust so as to eliminate the anomalies it has produced.

In a country that prides itself on innovation, inventive genius, and willingness to experiment, it is a paradox that we should cling for more than a half century to a legal mechanism that was poorly designed and never really worked. I can only hope now that the Congress will manifest a willingness to view realistically the hard evidence of the half-century history of the suppression doctrine revealing thousands of cases in which the criminal was set free because the constable blundered and virtually no evidence that innocent victims of police error—such as petitioner claims to be—have been afforded meaningful redress.

----

2. CIVIL REMEDIES

In some instances in which law enforcement officers have violated the constitutional rights of a citizen or other resident, a cause of action may be present under state tort law. Typical is the action against a police officer for false arrest when the officer lacked reasonable grounds to believe that the arrestee had committed an offense. The liability of the officer's governmental employer—for example, the city, county or state—will turn upon state law. For example, the governmental employer may not be automatically liable for the officer's conduct under the principle of respondeat superior. Plaintiff may be required to show that the government was negligent in hiring or training or that the officer acted in accordance with official policy. Moreover state law may either (1) retain governmental immunity from actions for money damages or (2) set a limit upon the amount of such recoveries. Additionally an action against the state or other governmental entity (again depending upon state law) may have to be brought in a special state court such as a legislative "court of claims" where the right to trial by jury does not exist. On the other hand, many government employers make it a practice of either reimbursing the officer or paying the money judgment when an action against an individual officer is successful. Is this wise policy? What limits, if any, should be placed upon such a practice?

A cause of action may also lie against the officer under the federal civil rights act of 1871. Consider the following decision.

MONROE v. PAPE

Supreme Court of the United States, 1961.
365 U.S. 167, 81 S.Ct. 473.

MR. JUSTICE DOUGLAS delivered the opinion of the Court.

This case presents important questions concerning the construction of R.S. § 1979, 42 U.S.C. § 1983, which reads as follows:

> "Every person who, under color of any statute, ordinance, regulation, custom, or usage, of any State or Territory, subjects, or causes to be subjected, any citizen of the United States or other person within the jurisdiction thereof to the deprivation of any rights, privileges, or immunities secured by the Constitution and laws, shall be liable to the party injured in an action at law, suit in equity, or other proper proceeding for redress."

The complaint alleges that 13 Chicago police officers broke into petitioners' home in the early morning, routed them from bed, made them stand naked in the living room, and ransacked every room, emptying drawers and ripping mattress covers. It further alleges that Mr. Monroe was then taken to the police station and detained on "open" charges for 10 hours, while he was interrogated about a two-day-old murder, that he was not taken before a magistrate, though one was accessible, that he was not permitted to call his family or attorney, that he was subsequently released without criminal charges being preferred against him. It is alleged that the officers had no search warrant and no arrest warrant and that they acted "under color of the statutes, ordinances, regulations, customs and usages" of Illinois and of the City of Chicago. . . .

The City of Chicago moved to dismiss the complaint on the ground that it is not liable under the Civil Rights Acts nor for acts committed in performance of its governmental functions. All defendants moved to dismiss, alleging that the complaint alleged no cause of action under those Acts or under the Federal Constitution. The District Court dismissed the complaint. The Court of Appeals affirmed.
. . . .

I.

Petitioners claim that the invasion of their home and the subsequent search without a warrant and the arrest and detention of Mr. Monroe without a warrant and without arraignment constituted a deprivation of their "rights, privileges, or immunities secured by the Constitution" within the meaning of R.S. § 1979. It has been said that when 18 U.S.C. § 241 made criminal a conspiracy "to injure, oppress, threaten, or intimidate any citizen in the free exercise or enjoyment of any right or privilege secured to him by the Constitution," it embraced only rights that an individual has by reason of his relation to the central government, not to state governments. United States v. Williams, 341 U.S. 70, 71 S.Ct. 581. But the history of the section of the Civil Rights Act presently involved does not permit such a narrow interpretation.

Section 1979 came onto the books as § 1 of the Ku Klux Act of April 20, 1871. It was one of the means whereby Congress exercised the power vested in it by § 5 of the Fourteenth Amendment to enforce the provisions of that Amendment. . . . Allegation of facts constituting a deprivation under color of state authority of a right guaranteed by the Fourteenth Amendment satisfies to that extent the requirement of R.S. § 1979. See Douglas v. Jeannette, 319 U.S. 157, 161–162, 63 S.Ct. 877, 880. So far petitioners are on solid ground. For the guarantee against unreasonable searches and seizures contained in the Fourth Amendment has been made applicable to the States by reason of the Due Process Clause of the Fourteenth Amendment. . . .

II.

There can be no doubt at least since Ex parte Virginia, 100 U.S. 339, 346–347, that Congress has the power to enforce provisions of the Fourteenth Amendment against those who carry a badge of authority of a State and represent it in some capacity, whether they act in accordance with their authority or misuse it. See Home Tel. & Tel. Co. v. Los Angeles, 227 U.S. 278, 287–296, 33 S.Ct. 312, 314, 318. The question with which we now deal is the narrower one of whether Congress, in enacting § 1979, meant to give a remedy to parties deprived of constitutional rights, privileges and immunities by an official's abuse of his position.

We conclude that it did so intend.

* * *

We had before us in United States v. Classic, infra, § 20 of the Criminal Code, 18 U.S.C. § 242, which provides a criminal punishment for anyone who "under color of any law, statute, ordinance, regulation, or custom" subjects any inhabitant of a State to the deprivation of "any rights, privileges, or immunities secured or protected by the Constitution or laws of the United States." . . . The right involved in the *Classic* case was the right of voters in a primary to have their votes counted. The laws of Louisiana required the defendants "to count the ballots, to record the result of the count, and to certify the result of the election." United States v. Classic, supra, 313 U.S. 325–326, 61 S.Ct. 1043. But according to the indictment they did not perform their duty. In an opinion written by Mr. Justice (later Chief Justice) Stone, in which Mr. Justice Roberts, Mr. Justice Reed, and Mr. Justice Frankfurter joined, the Court ruled, "Misuse of power, possessed by virtue of state law and made possible only because the wrongdoer is clothed with the authority of state law, is action taken 'under color of' state law." There was a dissenting opinion; but the ruling as to the meaning of "under color of" state law was not questioned.

That view of the meaning of the words "under color of" state law, 18 U.S.C. § 242, was reaffirmed in Screws v. United States. The acts there complained of were committed by state officers in performance of their duties, viz., making an arrest effective. It was urged there, as it is here, that "under color of" state law should not be construed to duplicate in federal law what was an offense under state law (dissenting opinion). It was said there, as it is here, that the ruling in the *Classic* case as to the meaning of "under color of" state law was not in focus and was ill-advised (dissenting opinion). It was argued there, as it is here, that "under color of" state law included only action taken by officials pursuant to state law (dissenting opinion). We rejected that view. . . . it is beyond doubt that this phrase should be accorded the same construction in both statutes —in § 1979 and in 18 U.S.C. § 242.

Since the *Screws* and *Williams* decisions, Congress has had several pieces of civil rights legislation before it.

If the results of our construction of "under color of" law were as horrendous as now claimed, if they were as disruptive of our federal scheme as now urged, if they were such an unwarranted invasion of States' rights as pretended, surely the voice of the opposition would have been heard in Committee reports. Their silence and the new uses to which "under color of" law have recently been given reinforce our conclusion that our prior decisions were correct on this matter of construction.

We conclude that the meaning given "under color of" law in the *Classic* case and in the *Screws* and *Williams* cases was the correct one; and we adhere to it.

In the *Screws* case we dealt with a statute that imposed criminal penalties for acts "wilfully" done. We construed that word in its setting to mean the doing of an act with "a specific intent to deprive a person of a federal right." We do not think that gloss should be placed on § 1979 which we have here. The word "wilfully" does not appear in § 1979. Moreover, § 1979 provides a civil remedy, while in the *Screws* case we dealt with a criminal law challenged on the ground of vagueness. Section 1979 should be read against the background of tort liability that makes a man responsible for the natural consequences of his actions.

So far, then, the complaint states a cause of action. There remains to consider only a defense peculiar to the City of Chicago.

* * *

[The concurring opinion of MR. JUSTICE HARLAN, joined by MR. JUSTICE STEWART, is omitted.]

MR. JUSTICE FRANKFURTER, dissenting.

* * *

[All] the evidence converges to the conclusion that Congress by § 1979 created a civil liability enforceable in the federal courts only in instances of injury for which redress was barred in the state courts because some "statute, ordinance, regulation, custom, or usage" sanctioned the grievance complained of. . . . The jurisdiction which Article III of the Constitution conferred on the national judiciary reflected the assumption that the state courts, not the federal courts, would remain the primary guardians of that fundamental security of person and property which the long evolution of the common law had secured to one individual as against other individuals. The Fourteenth Amendment did not alter this basic aspect of our federalism.

* * *

NOTES

1. In *Monroe* the Court held that the employer of the offending police officers was not liable under 42 U.S.C. § 1983 because a city was not a "person" within the meaning of that statute. However, in Monell v. Dep't of Social Services, 436 U.S. 658, 98 S.Ct. 2018 (1978), the Court overturned that aspect of *Monroe* and held that a municipality was a person within the meaning of the act. The Court indicated that a city would not be automatically liable for the constitutional violations of its officers under the principle of respondeat superior. Rather some additional conduct on the part of the employer—not yet well defined—is required. If the employer is *state* government, wholly apart from the question of whether a state is a "person" within the meaning of § 1983, the state, absent a waiver, may have immunity under the Eleventh Amendment from an action for money damages. See Edelman v. Jordan, 415 U.S. 651, 94 S.Ct. 1347 (1974).

2. Suppose that an officer obtains and executes a search warrant, but later a court rules that, although the question is a close one, insufficient probable cause data existed to justify the issuance of the search warrant. Should the officer be liable under § 1983 because he engaged in a search which was unlawful under the Fourth Amendment? On the other hand, should the officer be automatically exempt from liability when the underlying legal question was a close one? When a magistrate by issuing an arrest warrant or a search warrant gave prior authorization for the officer's conduct? Even if the probable cause data was woefully inadequate? In Pierson v. Ray, 386 U.S. 547, 87 S.Ct. 1213 (1967), the Court held "that the defense of good faith and probable cause, which the Court of Appeals found available to the officers in the common-law action for false arrest and imprisonment, is also available to them in the action under § 1983." Lower courts have differed widely on the interpretation of the phrase "good faith *and* probable cause," but it is generally agreed that "probable cause" here means something different from probable cause as used earlier in the case-

book. *Pierson* must also be read in light of subsequent § 1983 decisions with respect to the liability of governmental officers and employees, other than law enforcement officers. Decisions such as Wood v. Strickland, 420 U.S. 308, 95 S.Ct. 992 (1975), although important to the issue of "good faith," are beyond the scope of a criminal procedure book.

3. For a thoughtful criticism of the defense of "good faith" in § 1983 actions against police officers, see an article authored by an expert in the law of torts: Theis, "Good Faith" as a Defense to Suits for Police Deprivations of Individual Rights, 59 Minn.L.Rev. 991 (1975).

4. Does a defense of "good faith" in a civil rights action make more sense than use of a "good faith" exception to the exclusionary rule? Recall that in his dissent in Stone v. Powell, Section D–3, supra, Justice White argued that the civil rights defense of good faith should be imported into the administration of the exclusionary rule. On this topic, see Comment, The Proposed Good Faith Test for Fourth Amendment Exclusion Compared to the § 1983 Good Faith Defense: Problems and Prospects, 20 Ariz.L.Rev. 915 (1978).

5. In Bivens v. Six Unknown Named Agents of Federal Bureau of Narcotics, 403 U.S. 388, 91 S.Ct. 1999 (1971), the petitioner claimed that federal agents had unconstitutionally forced their way into his house, arrested him, manacled him in front of his wife and children, threatened arrest of the entire family, searched his home exhaustively, and transported him to a courthouse where he was interrogated, booked and strip searched. Section 1983 applies only to persons acting under color of state law and not to federal officers, although the Court held that a civil remedy could be based upon a Fourth Amendment violation. A federal cause of action is inherent in the Amendment and does not require Congressional action. Three dissenters (Burger, C.J., Black and Blackmun, JJ.) all agreed that only Congress could create the remedy envisioned by the Court. The Court did not deal with the claim of immunity but on remand the immunity argument was rejected. See 456 F.2d 1339 (2nd Cir. 1972).

6. For a summary of the debate over the exclusionary rule and alternative remedies, see the series of articles in Volume 62 of Judicature: Judge Malcolm Wilkey's article at p. 215, Professor Yale Kamisar's response at p. 337, and comments by Canon and Schlesinger on empirical studies at p. 398. Rather than attempt to summarize the arguments, we strongly urge that students interested in the topic begin their further study by reading these articles.

3. OTHER REMEDIES

Among other proposed "remedies" for investigative misconduct are criminal prosecutions under the federal civil rights law, as discussed in *Monroe*, or under state law. Concerning disciplinary actions against police officers, see Burger, Who Will Watch the Watchman?, 14 Am.U.L.Rev. 1 (1964). As to possible use of contempt of court, see McNear v. Rhay, 65 Wash.2d 530, 398 P.2d 732 (1965). Concerning "self-help," that is, resisting unlawful police conduct, see W. LaFave, Search and Seizure, § 1.11, and also see § 1.10 of the same volume concerning injunctions against unlawful police conduct.

Chapter 7

POLICE ENTRAPMENT

SHERMAN v. UNITED STATES

Supreme Court of the United States, 1958.
356 U.S. 369, 78 S.Ct. 819.

MR. CHIEF JUSTICE WARREN delivered the opinion of the Court.

The issue before us is whether petitioner's conviction should be set aside on the ground that as a matter of law the defense of entrapment was established. Petitioner was convicted under an indictment charging three sales of narcotics in violation of 21 U.S.C. § 174, 21 U.S.C.A. § 174. A previous conviction had been reversed on account of improper instructions as to the issue of entrapment. In the second trial, as in the first, petitioner's defense was a claim of entrapment: an agent of the Federal Government induced him to take part in illegal transactions when otherwise he would not have done so.

In late August 1951, Kalchinian, a government informer, first met petitioner at a doctor's office where apparently both were being treated to be cured of narcotics addiction. Several accidental meetings followed, either at the doctor's office or at the pharmacy where both filled their prescriptions from the doctor. From mere greetings, conversation progressed to a discussion of mutual experiences and problems, including their attempts to overcome addiction to narcotics. Finally Kalchinian asked petitioner if he knew of a good source of narcotics. He asked petitioner to supply him with a source because he was not responding to treatment. From the first, petitioner tried to avoid the issue. Not until after a number of repetitions of the request, predicated on Kalchinian's presumed suffering, did petitioner finally acquiesce. Several times thereafter he obtained a quantity of narcotics which he shared with Kalchinian. Each time petitioner told Kalchinian that the total cost of narcotics he obtained was twenty-five dollars and that Kalchinian owed him fifteen dollars. The informer thus bore the cost of his share of the narcotics plus the taxi and other expenses necessary to obtain the drug. After several such sales Kalchinian informed agents of the Bureau of Narcotics that he had another seller for them. On three occasions during November 1951, government agents observed petitioner give narcotics to Kalchinian in return for money supplied by the Government.

At the trial the factual issue was whether the informer had convinced an otherwise unwilling person to commit a criminal act or whether petitioner was already predisposed to commit the act and exhibited only the natural hesitancy of one acquainted with the narcotic trade. The issue of entrapment went to the jury, and a conviction resulted. Petitioner was sentenced to imprisonment for ten years. The Court of Appeals for the Second Circuit affirmed. We granted certiorari.

554

In Sorrells v. United States, 287 U.S. 435, 53 S.Ct. 210, this Court firmly recognized the defense of entrapment in the federal courts. The intervening years have in no way detracted from the principles underlying that decision. The function of law enforcement is the prevention of crime and the apprehension of criminals. Manifestly, that function does not include the manufacturing of crime. Criminal activity is such that stealth and strategy are necessary weapons in the arsenal of the police officer. However, "A different question is presented when the criminal design originates with the officials of the Government, and they implant in the mind of an innocent person the disposition to commit the alleged offense and induce its commission in order that they may prosecute." Then stealth and strategy become as objectionable police methods as the coerced confession and the unlawful search. Congress could not have intended that its statutes were to be enforced by tempting innocent persons into violations.

However, the fact that government agents "merely afford opportunities or facilities for the commission of the offense does not" constitute entrapment. Entrapment occurs only when the criminal conduct was "the product of the *creative* activity" of law-enforcement officials. (Emphasis supplied.) To determine whether entrapment has been established, a line must be drawn between the trap for the unwary innocent and the trap for the unwary criminal. The principles by which the courts are to make this determination were outlined in *Sorrells*. On the one hand, at trial the accused may examine the conduct of the government agent; and on the other hand, the accused will be subjected to an "appropriate and searching inquiry into his own conduct and predisposition" as bearing on his claim of innocence.

We conclude from the evidence that entrapment was established as a matter of law. In so holding, we are not choosing between conflicting witnesses, nor judging credibility. Aside from recalling Kalchinian, who was the Government's witness, the defense called no witnesses. We reach our conclusion from the undisputed testimony of the prosecution's witnesses.

It is patently clear that petitioner was induced by Kalchinian. The informer himself testified that, believing petitioner to be undergoing a cure for narcotics addiction, he nonetheless sought to persuade petitioner to obtain for him a source of narcotics. In Kalchinian's own words we are told of the accidental, yet recurring, meetings, the ensuing conversations concerning mutual experiences in regard to narcotics addiction, and then of Kalchinian's resort to sympathy. One request was not enough, for Kalchinian tells us that additional ones were necessary to overcome, first, petitioner's refusal, then his evasiveness, and then his hesitancy in order to achieve capitulation. Kalchinian not only procured a source of narcotics but apparently also induced petitioner to return to the habit. Finally, assured of a catch, Kalchinian informed the authorities so that they could close the net. The Government cannot disown Kalchinian and insist it is not responsible for his actions. Although he was not being paid, Kalchinian was an active government informer who had but recently been the instigator of at least two other prosecutions. Undoubtedly the impetus for such achievements was the fact that in 1951 Kalchinian was himself under criminal charges for illegally selling narcotics and had not yet been sentenced. It makes no difference that the sales for which petitioner was convicted occurred after a series of sales. They were not independent acts subsequent to the inducement but part of a course of conduct which was the product of the inducement. In his testimony the federal agent in charge of the case admitted that he never bothered to question Kalchinian about the way he had made contact with petitioner. The Government cannot make such use of an informer and then claim disassociation through ignorance.

The Government sought to overcome the defense of entrapment by claiming that petitioner evinced a "ready complaisance" to accede to Kalchinian's request. Aside from a record of past convictions, which we discuss in the following paragraph, the Government's case is unsupported. There is no evidence that petitioner himself was in the trade. When his apartment was searched after arrest, no narcotics were found. There is no significant evidence that petitioner even made a profit on any sale to Kalchinian. The Government's characterization of petitioner's hesitancy to Kalchinian's request as the natural wariness of the criminal cannot fill the evidentiary void.

The Government's additional evidence in the second trial to show that petitioner was ready and willing to sell narcotics should the opportunity present itself was petitioner's record of two past narcotics convictions. In 1942 petitioner was convicted of illegally selling narcotics; in 1946 he was convicted of illegally possessing them. However, a nine-year-old sales conviction and a five-year-old possession conviction are insufficient to prove petitioner had a readiness to sell narcotics at the time Kalchinian approached him, particularly when we must assume from the record he was trying to overcome the narcotics habit at the time.

The case at bar illustrates an evil which the defense of entrapment is designed to overcome. The government informer entices someone attempting to avoid narcotics not only into carrying out an illegal sale but also into returning to the habit of use. Selecting the proper time, the informer then tells the government agent. The set-up is accepted by the agent without even a question as to the manner in which the informer encountered the seller. Thus the Government plays on the weaknesses of an innocent party and beguiles him into committing crimes which he otherwise would not have attempted. Law enforcement does not require methods such as this.

It has been suggested that in overturning this conviction we should reassess the doctrine of entrapment according to principles announced in the separate opinion of Mr. Justice Roberts in Sorrells v. United States, 287 U.S. 435, 453, 53 S.Ct. 210, 217. To do so would be to decide the case on grounds rejected by the majority in *Sorrells* and, so far as the record shows, not raised here or below by the parties before us. We do not ordinarily decide issues not presented by the parties and there is good reason not to vary that practice in this case.

At least two important issues of law enforcement and trial procedure would have to be decided without the benefit of argument by the parties, one party being the Government. Mr. Justice Roberts asserted that although the defendant could claim that the Government had induced him to commit the crime, the Government could not reply by showing that the defendant's criminal conduct was due to his own readiness and not to the persuasion of government agents. The handicap thus placed on the prosecution is obvious. Furthermore, it was the position of Mr. Justice Roberts that the factual issue of entrapment—now limited to the question of what the government agents did—should be decided by the judge, not the jury. Not only was this rejected by the Court in *Sorrells*, but where the issue has been presented to them, the Courts of Appeals have since *Sorrells* unanimously concluded that unless it can be decided as a matter of law, the issue of whether a defendant has been entrapped is for the jury as part of its function of determining the guilt or innocence of the accused.

To dispose of this case on the ground suggested would entail both overruling a leading decision of this Court and brushing aside the possibility that we would be creating more problems than we would supposedly be solving.

The judgment of the Court of Appeals is reversed and the case is remanded to the District Court with instructions to dismiss the indictment.

Reversed and remanded.

MR. JUSTICE FRANKFURTER, whom MR. JUSTICE DOUGLAS, MR. JUSTICE HARLAN, and MR. JUSTICE BRENNAN join, concurring in the result.

Although agreeing with the Court that the undisputed facts show entrapment as a matter of law, I reach this result by a route different from the Court's.

Today's [ruling] fails to give the doctrine of entrapment the solid foundation that the decisions of the lower courts and criticism of learned writers have clearly shown is needed. Instead it accepts without re-examination the theory espoused in Sorrells v. United States, 287 U.S. 435, 53 S.Ct. 210, over strong protest by Mr. Justice Roberts, speaking for Brandeis and Stone, JJ., as well as himself. The fact that since the *Sorrells* case the lower courts have either ignored its theory and continued to rest decision on the narrow facts of each case, or have failed after penetrating effort to define a satisfactory generalization is proof that the prevailing theory of the *Sorrells* case ought not to be deemed the last word. In a matter of this kind the Court should not rest on the first attempt at an explanation for what sound instinct counsels. It should not forego re-examination to achieve clarity of thought, because confused and inadequate analysis is too apt gradually to lead to a course of decisions that diverges from the true ends to be pursued.

It is surely sheer fiction to suggest that a conviction cannot be had when a defendant has been entrapped by government officers or informers because "Congress could not have intended that its statutes were to be enforced by tempting innocent persons into violations." In these cases raising claims of entrapment, the only legislative intention that can with any show of reason be extracted from the statute is the intention to make criminal precisely the conduct in which the defendant has engaged. That conduct includes all the elements necessary to constitute criminality. Without compulsion and "knowingly," where that is requisite, the defendant has violated the statutory command. If he is to be relieved from the usual punitive consequences, it is on no account because he is innocent of the offense described. In these circumstances, conduct is not less criminal because the result of temptation, whether the tempter is a private person or a government agent or informer.

The courts refuse to convict an entrapped defendant, not because his conduct falls outside the proscription of the statute, but because, even if his guilt be admitted, the methods employed on behalf of the Government to bring about conviction cannot be countenanced. As Mr. Justice Holmes said in Olmstead v. United States, 277 U.S. 438, 470, 48 S.Ct. 564, 575 (dissenting), in another connection, "It is desirable that criminals should be detected, and to that end that all available evidence should be used. It also is desirable that the Government should not itself foster and pay for other crimes, when they are the means by which the evidence is to be obtained. . . . [F]or my part I think it a less evil that some criminals should escape than that the Government should play an ignoble part." Insofar as they are used as instrumentalities in the administration of criminal justice, the federal courts have an obligation to set their face against enforcement of the law by lawless means or means that violate rationally vindicated standards of justice, and to refuse to sustain such methods by effectuating them. They do this in the exercise of a recognized jurisdiction to formulate and apply "proper standards for the enforcement of the federal criminal law in the federal courts," an obligation that goes beyond the conviction of the particular defendant before the court. Public confidence in the fair and honorable administration of justice, upon which ultimately depends the rule of law, is the transcending value at stake.

The formulation of these standards does not in any way conflict with the statute the defendant has violated, or involve the initiation of a judicial policy disregarding or qualifying that framed by Congress. A false choice is put when it is said that either the defendant's conduct does not fall within the statute or he must be convicted. The statute is wholly directed to defining and prohibiting the substantive offense concerned and expresses no purpose, either permissive or prohibitory, regarding the police conduct that will be tolerated in the detection of crime. A statute prohibiting the sale of narcotics is as silent on the question of entrapment as it is on the admissibility of illegally obtained evidence. It is enacted, however, on the basis of certain presuppositions concerning the established legal order and the role of the courts within that system in formulating standards for the administration of criminal justice when Congress itself has not specifically legislated to that end. Specific statutes are to be fitted into an antecedent legal system.

It might be thought that it is largely an academic question whether the court's finding a bar to conviction derives from the statute or from a supervisory jurisdiction over the administration of criminal justice; under either theory substantially the same considerations will determine whether the defense of entrapment is sustained. But to look to a statute for guidance in the application of a policy not remotely within the contemplation of Congress at the time of its enactment is to distort analysis. It is to run the risk, furthermore, that the court will shirk the responsibility that is necessarily in its keeping, if Congress is truly silent, to accommodate the dangers of overzealous law enforcement and civilized methods adequate to counter the ingenuity of modern criminals. The reasons that actually underlie the defense of entrapment can too easily be lost sight of in the pursuit of a wholly fictitious congressional intent.

The crucial question, not easy to answer, to which the court must direct itself is whether the police conduct revealed in the particular case falls below standards, to which common feelings respond, for the proper use of governmental power. For answer it is wholly irrelevant to ask if the "intention" to commit the crime originated with the defendant or government officers, or if the criminal conduct was the product of "the creative activity" of law-enforcement officials. Yet in the present case the Court repeats and purports to apply these unrevealing tests. Of course in every case of this kind the intention that the particular crime be committed originates with the police, and without their inducement the crime would not have occurred. But . . . where the police in effect simply furnished the opportunity for the commission of the crime, . . . this is not enough to enable the defendant to escape conviction.

The intention referred to, therefore, must be a general intention or predisposition to commit, whenever the opportunity should arise, crimes of the kind solicited, and in proof of such a predisposition evidence has often been admitted to show the defendant's reputation, criminal activities, and prior disposition. The danger of prejudice in such a situation, particularly if the issue of entrapment must be submitted to the jury and disposed of by a general verdict of guilty or innocent, is evident. The defendant must either forego the claim of entrapment or run the substantial risk that, in spite of instructions, the jury will allow a criminal record or bad reputation to weigh in its determination of guilt of the specific offense of which he stands charged. Furthermore, a test that looks to the character and predisposition of the defendant rather than the conduct of the police loses sight of the underlying reason for the defense of entrapment. No matter what the defendant's past record and present inclinations to criminality, or the depths to which he has sunk in the estimation of society, certain police conduct to ensnare him into further crime is not to be tolerated by an advanced society. And in the present case it is clear that the Court in fact reverses the conviction because of the conduct of the informer Kalchinian, and not because the Government has failed to draw a convincing picture of petitioner's past criminal conduct. Permissible police activity does not vary according to the particular defendant concerned; surely if two suspects have been solicited at the same time in the same manner, one should not go to jail simply because he has been convicted before and is said to have a criminal disposition. No more does it vary according to the suspicions, reasonable or unreasonable, of the police concerning the defendant's activities. Appeals to sympathy, friendship, the possibility of exorbitant gain, and so forth, can no more be tolerated when directed against a past offender than against an ordinary law-abiding citizen. A contrary view runs afoul of fundamental principles of equality under law, and would espouse the notion that when dealing with the criminal classes anything goes. The possibility that no matter what his past crimes and general disposition the defendant might not have committed the particular crime unless confronted with inordinate inducements, must not be ignored. Past crimes do not forever outlaw the criminal and open him to police practices, aimed at securing his repeated conviction, from which the ordinary citizen is protected. The whole ameliorative hopes of modern penology and prison administration strongly counsel against such a view.

This does not mean that the police may not act so as to detect those engaged in criminal conduct and ready and willing to commit further crimes should the occasion arise. Such indeed is their obligation. It does mean that in holding out inducements they should act in such a manner as is likely to induce to the commission of crime only these persons and not others who would normally avoid crime and through self-struggle resist ordinary temptations. This test shifts attention from the record and predisposition of the particular defendant to the conduct of the police and the likelihood, objectively considered, that it would entrap only those ready and willing to commit crime. It is as objective a test as the subject matter permits, and will give guidance in regulating police conduct that is lacking when the reasonableness of police suspicions must be judged or the criminal disposition of the defendant retrospectively appraised. It draws directly on the fundamental intuition that led in the first instance to the outlawing of "entrapment" as a prosecutorial instrument. The power of government is abused and directed to an end for which it was not constituted when employed to promote rather than detect crime and to bring about the downfall of those who, left to themselves, might well have obeyed the law. Human nature is weak enough and sufficiently beset by temptations without government adding to them and generating crime.

What police conduct is to be condemned, because likely to induce those not otherwise ready and willing to commit crime, must be picked out from case to case as new situations arise involving different crimes and new methods of detection. The *Sorrells* case involved persistent solicitation in the face of obvious reluctance, and appeals to sentiments aroused by reminiscences of experiences as companions in arms in the World War. Particularly reprehensible in the present case was the use of repeated requests to overcome petitioner's hesitancy, coupled with appeals to sympathy based on mutual experiences with narcotics addiction. Evidence of the setting in which the inducement took place is of course highly relevant in judging its likely effect, and the court should also consider the nature of the crime involved, its secrecy and difficulty of detection, and the manner in which the particular criminal business is usually carried on.

As Mr. Justice Roberts convincingly urged in the *Sorrells* case, such a judgment, aimed at blocking off areas of impermissible police conduct, is appropriate for the court and not the jury. "The protection of its own functions and the preservation of the purity of its own temple belongs only to the court. It is the province of the court and of the court alone to protect itself and the government from such prostitution of the criminal law. The violation of the principles of justice by the entrapment of the unwary into crime should be dealt with by the court no matter by whom or at what stage of the proceedings the facts are brought to its attention." 287 U.S., at 457, 53 S.Ct., at 218 (separate opinion). Equally important is the consideration that a jury verdict, although it may settle the issue of entrapment in the particular case, cannot give significant guidance for official conduct for the future. Only the court, through the gradual evolution of explicit standards in accumulated precedents, can do this with the degree of certainty that the wise administration of criminal justice demands.

KADIS v. UNITED STATES

United States Court of Appeals, 1st Cir. 1967.
373 F.2d 370.

ALDRICH, CHIEF JUDGE.

Defendants, the Walnut Drug Corp. and two individual pharmacists, were convicted of violating 21 U.S.C. § 331(k) by refilling prescriptions for two drugs, librium and dexedrine, without obtaining authorization from the prescriber. They appeal on the ground that the two pharmacists were entrapped by agents of the Food and Drug Administration.

The facts are largely undisputed. In September 1964 the FDA office in Boston received a telephone call from a person who identified himself as Wilfred Chagnon, the treasurer of the Massachusetts Pharmacy Association. The caller said that the Walnut Drug Corp. was refilling librium and other drugs without authorization. Two agents were assigned to investigate. One obtained a medical prescription for librium, the other for dexedrine. Neither prescription referred to refills. Each agent went in plain clothes to the Walnut

Pharmacy and had his prescription filled. Thereafter, over a period of about three months, the agents returned to the pharmacy a number of times and successfully asked for refills. The transactions are typically reflected by the following testimony of one of the agents.

> "[Kadis] came to the cash register in front of me, placed a prescription envelope on the counter in front of me. He said, 'Does the doctor want you to keep on taking these?' I said, 'I don't know.' He said, 'Of course you have been in to see him, and he probably said to continue.' I looked at him and said, 'I have not been back to see him since I got the prescription.' At that time I handed him a ten dollar bill.
>
> "He said, 'You will be going back to see him pretty soon, won't you?'
>
> "I said, 'I suppose I should' I replied, 'It is one of those things,' and he said 'We are supposed to keep track of how many tablets you take. It is just a technicality.'
>
> "I nodded my head. He handed me my change."

The defendants' principal claim is that they were entrapped as a matter of law because the government agents had inadequate grounds to seek them out.

The doctrine of entrapment as developed by the courts is far from simple, and has led to a number of misunderstandings. Thirty-five years ago, in Sorrells v. United States, the Court said, "[T]he question whether it [entrapment] precludes prosecution or affords a ground of defense, and, if so, upon what theory, has given rise to conflicting opinions." Unhappily, this statement is no less true today. We believe that one reason for the confusion is that there may not be general agreement about "the true ends to be pursued." In *Sorrells*, the Court said, "[Entrapment occurs] when the criminal design originates with the officials of the government, and they implant in the mind of an innocent person the disposition to commit the alleged offense and induce its commission in order that they may prosecute." See also Sherman v. United States. It can be argued that this definition suggests two different objectives: to prevent prosecution of persons who were innocent until corrupted by government agents, and to preclude certain police conduct whether the particular defendant was innocent or not.[1]

In the original *Sherman* appeal, Judge Learned Hand divided the issue of entrapment into two subsidiary questions: whether the police had induced the crime, and whether the defendant was predisposed, that is, whether the inducement had been directed towards an innocent man, or one already corrupt. The court placed the burden as to the first issue on the defendant, and the burden as to the second on the government. This separation has given rise to an increasing

---

1. In both *Sorrells* and *Sherman* concurring minorities contended that the sole proper purpose of the doctrine of entrapment was to prevent certain police activities. In both cases the Court rejected this view.

number of problems. We believe the time has come to review not only the problems, but the rationale underlying the division itself.

Although Judge Hand placed the burden of showing inducement upon the defendant, he did not define the quantum of burden. Subsequently, in United States v. Pugliese, the court reversed a conviction as plain error because the district court had failed to make clear to the jury that this burden was only to prove inducement by a fair preponderance, and not beyond a reasonable doubt. [We, too, have] held that the defendant's evidence must merely preponderate. Later, however, since it was clear that the government must show the predisposition of the defendant beyond a reasonable doubt, and since we were troubled by the potential confusion introduced by requiring the jury to be instructed on two different burdens, we held that there is no burden of proof on the defendant even as to inducement. All that we [then] required was that there be some evidence indicating that the defendant was induced.

Consideration of inducement as a separate issue has encouraged the previously mentioned thought, that one of the "ends" to be achieved by the doctrine of entrapment is to police the police, to prevent certain antisocial police conduct—no matter how corrupt the defendant may, in fact, have been. There are really two claims. The first, which is advanced in the case at bar in its most extreme form, is that no inducement of any kind is justified unless the police had prior grounds warranting the initiation of their activity. We rejected this contention in Whiting v. United States, 321 F.2d 72 (1963). So have a number of other circuits. We adhere to that view.

At the other end of the spectrum, it is argued that extreme forms of inducement are socially offensive, and should defeat any prosecution based thereon. We see no purpose in debating the wisdom of such a principle, for there is a more ready answer. Extreme police tactics, for example, of badgering, or making massive appeals to the sympathy of an obviously reluctant person, will mean that as a matter of law the government cannot be found to have sustained its burden of proving that it did not corrupt an innocent or unwilling man. No situation suggests itself in which such police behavior, if conceded or found, would not necessarily create a reasonable doubt that the defendant was ready and willing to commit the crime when he was approached. Since an acquittal would thereby be required, we see no reason for making ethical appraisals of the police behavior.

We find, in sum, that consideration of inducement as a separate issue serves no useful purpose, and we believe it to be a mistake. We will no longer bifurcate entrapment into sub-issues of inducement and predisposition, . . . Henceforth we will look, singly, at the ultimate question of entrapment. If the defendant shows, through government witnesses or otherwise, some indication that a government agent corrupted him, the burden of disproving entrapment will be on the government; but such a showing is not made simply by evidence of a solicitation. There must be some evidence tending to show unreadiness.

While this conclusion modifies our prior decisions, we do not feel it to be at variance with the position thus far taken by the Supreme Court, which has never distinguished between the issues of inducement and predisposition, nor condemned the act of inducement apart from its effect on an innocent man. In Sherman v. United States, 1958, 356 U.S. 369, 78 S.Ct. 819, very forceful, what might well be described as offensive, inducement resulted in a directed acquittal not by virtue of singling out the acts of inducement for criticism, but because the Court held that in the face of such massive inducement the government could not sustain the burden of proving that the defendant had not been corrupted. More recently, in Osborn v. United States, 1966, 385 U.S. 323, 87 S.Ct. 429, in a situation in which inducement, as such, could have raised interesting questions, the Court made no mention of it. There a government agent who managed to gain employment with an attorney defending a criminal case remarked that one of the prospective jurors was his cousin. The attorney "jumped up" and said, "Let's go outside and talk about it," and immediately suggested the possibility of offering a bribe. It is difficult to say that the agent's remark did not induce the offense in the broad sense of the word. The Court's sole observation, however, was "At [most, the] statement afforded the petitioner 'opportunities or facilities' for the commission of a criminal offense, and that is a far cry from entrapment."

One question remains: when has the defendant shown "some evidence" of entrapment, viz., when is the burden placed upon the government to show that the defendant was not in fact corrupted by the government agent. The amount need not be so substantial as to require, if uncontroverted, a directed verdict of acquittal, but it must be more than a mere scintilla. It cannot be enough, for example, where the defendant readily agreed to engage in a criminal act, to show that he enjoys a good reputation. However, any evidence, whether introduced by the defense or by the prosecution, that the government agents went beyond a simple request and pleaded or argued with the defendant, should be enough. Evidence that the defendant resisted the criminal suggestion raises the question whether his hesitation exhibited the conscience of the upright, or merely the circumspection of the criminal. Evidence that on other occasions the defendant refused to engage in acts similar to those with which he is charged tends to prove that he was not ready and willing, and equally creates a jury issue. On the other hand, evidence, as in the case at bar, of unwillingness to commit much more serious or otherwise noncomparable crimes, would seem insufficient.

Whether in the present case there was enough evidence, we need not determine. The court in fact submitted the question to the jury with clear and accurate instructions, and fully explained the burden that was upon the government. Defendants have shown no prejudicial error.

Affirmed.

NOTES

1. In United States v. Russell, 411 U.S. 423, 93 S.Ct. 1637 (1973), an undercover agent provided a difficult to obtain but legal chemical essential to manufacturing the illegal drug which was the basis of the conviction. The Court refused to vacate conviction solely because the undercover agent "supplied an indispensable means to the commission of the crime."

In People v. Strong, 21 Ill.2d 320, 172 N.E.2d 765 (1961), the Illinois Supreme Court made the following ruling:

> While we are sympathetic to the problems of enforcement agencies in controlling the narcotics traffic, and their use of informers to that end, we cannot condone the action of one acting for the government in supplying the very narcotics that gave rise to the alleged offense. . . . This is more than mere inducement. In reality the government is supplying the *sine qua non* of the offense.

In Hampton v. United States, 425 U.S. 484, 96 S.Ct. 1646 (1976), the defendant sought a jury instruction stating that if the government informer had originally supplied the narcotics, the defendant must be acquitted without regard to the defendant's predisposition. In a 5 to 3 opinion the United States Supreme Court upheld the refusal to give such an instruction. Two members of the majority, in a concurring opinion, left open the possibility that some governmental conduct could be so shocking as to entitle a defendant to acquittal because of entrapment without regard to the defendant's predisposition or lack of predisposition to criminal activity.

Cases like *Hampton* and *Strong* frequently involve maneuvers designed to require the prosecution to produce an informer at trial. Typically, after introduction to the defendant by an informer, an undercover agent makes a hand-to-hand purchase from the defendant in the absence of the informer. The prosecution thus hopes to try the case without producing the informer at trial; but the defendant testifies that the informer, out of the presence of the undercover agent, originally left the packet of narcotics with the defendant. If this is a good defense, then the prosecution will have to produce the informer at trial to rebut the allegation.

Even in more traditional entrapment defenses, often the defense testimony requires the prosecution to produce the informer even though he was not present at the actual sale—for instance, to deny that he begged and pleaded with the defendant to secure drugs to satisfy the informer's habit. Generally an informer need only be produced at trial if he has knowledge relevant to innocence or guilt, so that the effort on the defense part is to make the informer's knowledge relevant even though the informer was not present at the sale.

Even after *Russell* and *Hampton*, some jurisdictions, as a matter of state law, continue to apply a rule like that announced in *Strong*: a defendant cannot be convicted of a narcotics offense if the government informer originally supplied the substance in question to the defendant. See State v. Talbot, 71 N.J. 160, 364 A.2d 9 (1976); People v. Stanley, 68 Mich.App. 559, 243 N.W.2d 684 (1976). As this book went to press, however, Illinois reversed its position and rejected the rule that it had announced in *Strong*. See People v. Cross, 77 Ill.2d 396, 33 Ill.Dec. 285, 396 N.E.2d 812 (1979).

2. In People v. Moran, 1 Cal.3d 755, 83 Cal.Rptr. 411, 463 P.2d 763 (1970), the majority of the trial court adhered to the viewpoint that the issue of entrapment was one for the jury, but three of the justices expressed

the view that the same rule should prevail as the one used in determining the admissibility of confessions and of other evidence alleged to have been illegally acquired; in other words, the matter should be left to the trial judge because "A jury verdict of guilty or not guilty tells the police nothing about the jury's evaluation of the police conduct".

In State v. Grilli, 230 N.W.2d 445 (Minn.1975), the Minnesota Supreme Court declared that the accused should have the option, in a jury trial, of having either the judge or the jury decide the entrapment issue. In a bifurcated proceeding, the accused would present evidence to the judge alone on the entrapment issue. The jury would hear evidence related to whether the accused did the acts alleged.

3. The California Supreme Court has adopted an unusual approach to entrapment defenses. See People v. Barraza, 23 Cal.3d 675, 153 Cal.Rptr. 459, 591 P.2d 947 (1979):

"Mosk, J.

* * *

"The principle currently applied in California represents a hybrid position, fusing elements of both the subjective and objective theories of entrapment. In People v. Benford (1959) 53 Cal.2d 1, 9, 345 P.2d 928, this court unanimously embraced the public policy/deterrence rationale that Justices Roberts and Frankfurter had so persuasively urged. In doing so, we ruled inadmissible on the issue of entrapment the most prejudicial inquiries that are allowed under the subjective theory, i. e., evidence that the defendant 'had previously committed similar crimes or had the reputation of being engaged in the commission of such crimes or was suspected by the police of criminal activities . . . .' Despite the lessons of *Benford*, however, this court has continued to maintain that entrapment depends upon where the intent to commit the crime originated. People v. Moran (1970) 1 Cal.3d 755, 760, 83 Cal.Rptr. 411, 463 P.2d 763.

"Chief Justice Traynor, dissenting in *Moran*, in an opinion joined by two other justices of this court, recognized that in thus departing from the rationale adopted in *Benford*, we have seriously undermined the deterrent effect of the entrapment defense on impermissible police conduct. He reasoned that attempts to fix the origin of intent or determine the defendant's criminal predisposition divert the court's attention from the only proper subject of focus in the entrapment defense: the dubious police conduct which the court must deter. The success of an entrapment defense should not turn on differences among defendants; we are not concerned with who first conceived or who willingly, or reluctantly, acquiesced in a criminal project. What we do care about is how much and what manner of persuasion, pressure, and cajoling are brought to bear by law enforcement officials to induce persons to commit crimes. Even though California courts do not permit introduction of the highly prejudicial evidence of subjective predisposition allowed in jurisdictions following the federal rule, our more limited focus on the character and intent of the accused is still misplaced and impairs our courts in their task of assuring the lawfulness of law enforcement activity.

"Commentators on the subject have overwhelmingly favored judicial decision of the issue by application of a test which looks only to the nature and extent of police activity in the criminal enterprise. . . . In recent years several state courts (see Grossman v. State (Alaska 1969) 457 P.2d 226; People v. Turner (1973) 390 Mich. 7, 210 N.W.2d 336; State v. Mullen (Iowa 1974) supra, 216 N.W.2d 375) and legislatures (see N.D.Cent.Code, § 12.-1–05–11 (1976); N.H.Rev.Stat.Ann., § 626:5 (1974); Pa.Cons. Stat.Ann., tit. 18, § 313 (Purdon 1973); Haw.Rev.Stat., § 702–237) have recognized that such a test is more consistent with and better promotes the underlying purpose of the entrapment defense. Such support for the position no doubt derives from a developing awareness that 'entrapment is a facet of a broader problem. Along with illegal search and seizures, wiretapping, false arrest, illegal detention and the third degree, it is a type of lawless law enforcement. They all spring from common motivations. Each is a substitute for skillful and scientific investigation. Each is condoned by the sinister sophism that the end, when dealing with known criminals or the "criminal classes," justifies the employment of illegal means.' (Donnelly, Judicial Control of Informants, Spies, Stool Pigeons, and Agent Provocateurs (1951) 60 Yale L.J. 1091, 1111.)

"For all the foregoing reasons we hold that the proper test of entrapment in California is the following: was the conduct of the law enforcement agent likely to induce a normally law-abiding person to commit the offense? For the purposes of this test, we presume that such a person would normally resist the temptation to commit a crime presented by the simple opportunity to act unlawfully. Official conduct that does no more than offer that opportunity to the suspect—for example, a decoy program—is therefore permissible; but it is impermissible for the police or their agents to pressure the suspect by overbearing conduct such as badgering, cajoling, importuning, or other affirmative acts likely to induce a normally law-abiding person to commit the crime.

"Although the determination of what police conduct is impermissible must to some extent proceed on an ad hoc basis, guidance will generally be found in the application of one or both of two principles. First, if the actions of the law enforcement agent would generate in a normally law-abiding person a motive for the crime other than ordinary criminal intent, entrapment will be established. An example of such conduct would be an appeal by the police that would induce such a person to commit the act because of friendship or sympathy, instead of a desire for personal gain or other typical criminal purpose. Second, affirmative police conduct that would make commission of the crime unusually attractive to a normally law-abiding person will likewise constitute entrapment. Such conduct would include, for example, a guarantee that the act is not illegal or the offense will go undetected, an offer of exorbitant consideration or any similar enticement.

"Finally, while the inquiry must focus primarily on the conduct of the law enforcement agent, that conduct is not to be viewed in a vacuum; it should also be judged by the effect it would have on a normally law-abiding person situated in the circumstances of the case at hand. Among the circumstances that may be relevant for this purpose, for example, are the transactions preceding the offense, the suspect's response to the inducements of the officer, the gravity of the crime, and the difficulty of detecting instances of its commission. We reiterate, however, that under this test such matters as the character of the suspect, his predisposition to commit the offense, and his subjective intent are irrelevant.

"Richardson, J.

"I respectfully dissent, . . . from that portion of the majority's opinion which establishes a new test for the defense of entrapment.

"As the majority concedes, in determining the existence of an entrapment, the United States Supreme Court has consistently rejected the 'objective' ('hypothetical person') test which the majority adopts in favor of the 'subjective' ('origin of intent') test.

"In Sorrells v. United States (1932) 287 U.S. 435, 53 S.Ct. 210, Sherman v. United States (1958) 356 U.S. 369, 78 S.Ct. 819, and recently in United States v. Russell (1973) 411 U.S. 423, 93 S. Ct. 1637, the high court has approved and reapproved the 'subjective' test. Following this lead, the federal courts and the courts of the overwhelming majority of states, including California, apply the 'subjective' test, thereby keeping attention properly focused on the unique interrelationship of the police and the particular defendant who is asserting the defense of entrapment.

"The majority now proposes to ban consideration of the particular defendant and replace him with a hypothetical 'normally law-abiding person' who is described as 'a person [who] would normally resist the temptation to commit a crime presented by the simple opportunity to act unlawfully.' The briefest reflection reveals the difficulties inherent in this definition. The individual who has *never* committed a criminal act can safely be categorized as a 'normally law-abiding person' since presumably his unblemished record is proof of his ability to resist temptation. However, what of the individual who has transgressed in the past either once or several times? Is he no longer '*normally* law-abiding'? Is 'normally' synonymous with 'generally'? If it may be drawn at all, the line between 'normally law-abiding' individuals and 'others' is not so easily fixed as the majority suggests.

"The fallacy underlying the majority's thesis, of course, is that in the very real world of criminal conduct there are no hypothetical people. To attempt to judge police conduct in a vacuum is to engage in a futile and meaningless exercise in semantics. It is the recognition of this precise fact that has restrained the United States Supreme Court from discarding the subjective test whereby attention is pointed at the particular defendant rather than on some imaginary or fictitious person. The majority abandons the actual for the hypothetical. It thereby substitutes the unreal for the real, with unnecessary complications that inevitably result therefrom.

"Further, by adopting an 'objective' test, the majority does not really eliminate the 'subjective' test. Even if the jury makes a finding adverse to the defendant pursuant to the 'objective' test, the defendant may still presumably argue entrapment to the jury using the 'subjective' standard to negate intent. The question of what the defendant intended is always relevant. Indeed, in the present case defendant admitted commission of the act. He denied only the requisite intent. The majority ignores entirely this problem of the double assertion of the entrapment defense.

"The issue of entrapment is a factual matter, the determination of which is of critical importance to both parties. Regardless of any salutary effect which a trial court opinion might have on police administration, the matter is properly entrusted to the jury and should remain within its province."

4. May entrapment be interposed as a defense in a case where the defendant denies having committed the act charged against him? In United States v. Demma, 523 F.2d 981 (9th Cir. 1975), the court overturned its longstanding rule precluding the entrapment defense where the crime is denied. The court said:

"It is well established that a defendant in a criminal prosecution may assert inconsistent defenses. The rule in favor of inconsistent defenses reflects the belief of modern criminal jurisprudence that a criminal defendant should be accorded every reasonable protection in defending himself against governmental prosecution. That established policy bespeaks a healthy regard for circumscribing the Government's opportunities for invoking the criminal sanction.

"The inconsistency theory [in Eastman v. United States, 212 F.2d 320 (9th Cir. 1954)] is an exception to the rule in favor of inconsistent defenses. But it is an exception without any justification. There is no conceivable reason for permitting a defendant to assert inconsistent defenses in other contexts but denying him that right in the context of entrapment. Indeed, there is a compelling reason for not making an exception of the entrapment defense. The primary function of entrapment is to safeguard the integrity of the law enforcement and prosecution process. In light of this important public function, we conclude that the rule in favor of inconsistent defenses must extend to the defense of entrapment.

"Of course, it is very unlikely that the defendant will be able to prove entrapment without testifying and, in the course of testifying, without admitting that he did the acts charged. Unless the Government's case-in-chief discloses entrapment as a matter of law (an unusual phenomenon), the defendant must come forward with evidence of his non-predisposition and of governmental inducement. A defendant can rarely produce such evidence without taking the stand—as did both defendants in the case at bar—and admitting that he did the acts to which the Government's witnesses attested. When he takes the stand, the defendant forfeits his right to remain silent, subjects himself to all the rigors of cross-examination, including impeachment, and exposes himself to prosecution for perjury. Inconsistent testimony by the defendant seriously impairs and potentially destroys his credibility. While we hold that a defendant may both deny the acts and other elements necessary to constitute the crime charged and at the same time claim entrapment, the high risks to him make it unlikely as a strategic matter that he will choose to do so."

In California the accused may assert entrapment and at the same time deny the acts charged (People v. Perez, 62 Cal.2d 769, 44 Cal.Rptr. 326, 401 P.2d 934 (1965)), but the accused bears the burden of proving entrapment. People v. Moran, 1 Cal.3d 755, 83 Cal.Rptr. 411, 463 P.2d 763 (1970).

Many jurisdictions adhere to the rule requiring admissions before permitting entrapment to be raised. Consider the interesting comments from the court in United States v. Shameia, 464 F.2d 629 (6th Cir. 1972):

> "We deem it unnecessary in this case to take an absolute position that there are no circumstances where the defense of entrapment will be unavailable because of the failure of the defendant to take the witness stand and admit the facts constituting the offense in question. It may well be that as suggested in Sendejas v. United States, 428 F.2d 1040 (9th Cir. 1970), the Government's proofs will establish entrapment as a matter of law. Under such circumstances the defense of entrapment would be available to the defendant. It could be said that by asserting such defense the defendant admits the facts without taking the witness stand.

> * * *

> ". . . The defendant here took the witness stand and absolutely denied that he did any of the acts necessary to constitute the crimes charged. In the course of his testimony he did state that he *would have been* unwilling to commit any of these crimes while denying that he did any of the acts. We, therefore, hold that the defendant may not absolutely deny every act necessary to constitute the offense and then claim entrapment on the part of the Government agents."

5. For an excellent overview of entrapment issues, see Park, The Entrapment Controversy, 60 Minn.L.Rev. 163 (1976). Professor Park has thought through the implications of alternative approaches to entrapment in various factual situations and has offered some original insights.

PEOPLE v. ISAACSON

Court of Appeals of New York, 1978.
44 N.Y.2d 511, 378 N.E.2d 78.

COOKE, JUDGE.

We reverse and dismiss the indictment against defendant; we so hold for the fundamental reason that due process compels it.

This case concerns fortunately rare, and inexplicable, police misconduct. Involved is reprehensible police action, including violence and deception, culminating in the further deceitful luring of a Pennsylvania resident into New York solely to make a sale of cocaine, for which he was convicted and sentenced to 15 years to life at Attica. At the time of trial, defendant was in his mid-twenties and was a graduate student and teacher at Penn State University, on the brink of receiving his doctoral degree in plant physiology and biochemistry. He resided at State College, Pennsylvania. Although he admitted to having used three controlled substances on very few occasions, he had no prior criminal record.

The events leading to defendant's conviction trace back to December 5, 1974 when J. D. Breniman, a young man with an unsavory drug history, was arrested by the New York State Police in Steuben County for possession of a controlled substance in the second degree, a class A–2 felony punishable by a 15-year to life term. At the time of his apprehension, Breniman was on bail pending an appeal from a 1973 conviction, based on a guilty plea for possession of a dangerous drug in the fourth degree, for which he had been sentenced to an indeterminate term of zero to three years at the New York Correctional Facility at Attica.

Breniman, who at defendant's trial admitted to being an inveterate user of drugs, including amphetamines, sedatives, hallucinogens, marihuana and heroin, and a seller for profit to maintain his habit, was interviewed after his arrest on December 5, 1974 at the New York State Police substation at Painted Post. As found as a matter of fact by the trial court, during this questioning, an investigator of the New York State Police struck Breniman with such force as to knock him out of a chair, then kicked him, resulting in a cutting of his mouth and forehead, and shortly thereafter threatened to shoot him. Breniman testified that this abuse was administered because he refused to answer a question, that when struck his glasses flew off, that he was kicked in the ribs when down, that a chair was thrown at him, that he was also threatened with being hurled down a flight of steps, and that one of two uniformed State troopers who witnessed these events said, "I [Breniman] may as well forget about it. They would swear that I fell coming in the substation on the steps."

Following his seizure on December 5, 1974, Breniman was held without bail at the Steuben County Jail until December 24, when he was released. By December 23, one of the officers involved in his case had received a lab report showing that the capsules found on Breniman, which were the basis for his class A–2 felony charge and which had been purchased from defendant, were not controlled substances at all. Rather than being amphetamines of a type referred to on the street as "Black Beauties", they were in fact nothing more pernicious than caffeine. However, Breniman was not told of this until some time later, at the trial of this matter—after he had been used by the police as an informant in this case.

Upon the advice of his attorney, and while suffering under the contrived delusion that he was still facing a long prison incarceration if found guilty of the A–2 felony on top of his previous conviction, Breniman agreed to assist the State Police as an informant. Although not specifically promised that his aid to the police would result in a lesser sentence, his attorney advised that this would provide him with a bargaining position with respect to the charges against him. The violence and threats of the investigator were not the reason for his co-operation, so he stated. Nevertheless, the trial court found that Breniman testified he would not have aided the police were it not for the fact that they deceived him by not revealing that the charges relating to the December 5 arrest would not stand up in court.

Breniman began his informant activities by telephoning various persons indiscriminately for the purpose of setting up drug sales in which the police would arrest the sellers. He made "collect" calls and one of the individuals contacted was defendant, whom he had known for two years through a mutual friend at State College. Defendant's version of the conversations is that Breniman cried and sobbed on the phone, relating that he was facing 15 years to life in Attica, that his parents had effectively cast him from the family home, that he was running out of friends, and that he was looking for ways to make money to hire a decent lawyer. Breniman's recollection was that he had not made the remarks in the manner described by defendant, but he otherwise corroborated defendant's version. He admitted telling defendant that he was in trouble, that the police had beaten him, that he feared going to Attica, and that he needed a "score" or "deal" so that he could hire an attorney and "make" bail.

Between December 24, 1974 and January 4, 1975, Breniman made seven phone calls to defendant before finally arranging a sale. Initially, he sought to buy heroin, but defendant flatly refused. As to cocaine, defendant tried to put him off by saying that there was nothing worthwhile, but Breniman persisted in his efforts to get defendant to make a sale.

At the time of Breniman's calls, defendant was living in an apartment in State College with Denise Marcon, a legal secretary, who admitted that she was a daily user of drugs including marihuana, cocaine, LSD, amphetamines and depressants. She testified that in October and November of 1974 defendant had sold one-gram quantities of cocaine which he kept at the apartment, and this was confirmed by Breniman who alleged that he made two purchases of small amounts of cocaine from defendant during these months. Although Marcon had not herself spoken to Breniman about a sale, defendant discussed with her at length Breniman's request.

Defendant's studies and his teaching responsibilities required him to work 12 to 14 hours a day. He did not have access to someone who could supply him with the cocaine—the two ounces worth $3,800 which Breniman was seeking—but Denise Marcon did. She called a girl friend who gave her a number at which to contact a man known as "Zorch". Although Marcon testified that defendant indicated that a sale of this magnitude to Breniman was worth $1,000 to them, she also confirmed that a desire to help Breniman was defendant's motivation for entering into the transaction.

The sale was scheduled for January 4, 1975. The State Police claimed no knowledge of Breniman's prior negotiations, but had spoken to Breniman concerning the sale in general. The investigator, who had previously struck Breniman, detailed the specifications to his victim-turned-informant. Breniman said he might be able to get an ounce of cocaine, but the investigator told him to get two because it was his experience that one never gets exactly what is asked for and he wanted a sale of at least one ounce to obtain a conviction for a higher grade of crime. Defendant feared New York's drug laws and did not want to enter the State, but the investigator instructed Breniman that the transaction must take place in New York where he had authority to make an arrest.

To cause defendant to sell drugs in this State, Breniman cleverly kept changing the destination, progressively northward, culminating in an arrangement by which defendant would make a three- or four-hour trip to meet at a place near the Pennsylvania-New York border, at a spot where it would be difficult for defendant to ascertain his location. Initially, defendant agreed to meet in Williamsport, Pennsylvania, one and a half hours distant from State College. Breniman then succeeded in inducing defendant to commit himself to journey to Mansfield, a point near Williamsport and also in the Quaker State. Finally, he acceded to drive another 15 miles north from Mansfield to Lawrenceville, Pennsylvania, which is just south of the State boundary.

The meeting place finally settled upon was the Whiffle Tree Bar, which Breniman told defendant was in Lawrenceville. What Breniman did know, and defendant did not, was that the bar was actually in the Town of Lindley, Steuben County, New York. Traveling north on Route 15 in Pennsylvania toward Lawrenceville, the only clear indication a motorist might have that he is leaving Pennsylvania is a sign adjacent to the southerly approach of a bridge spanning the Cowanesque River and welcoming the traveler to New York State. Actually, the State line is several hundred yards southerly of the bridge and is designated by a stone marker, which at the time of defendant's visit had crumbled and was obscured in the vegetation alongside the road. The Whiffle Tree Bar is situate between the hidden stone marker and the bridge sign and thus is located in the Town of Lindley in New York State, rather than in Lawrenceville, Pennsylvania, as defendant had been led to believe. Although Breniman devised the scheme for bringing defendant into this State, it was the State Police investigator who independently determined that the proposed location was within his jurisdiction.

Defendant engaged in a rather elaborate method of delivering the cocaine, including an arrangement to have Denise Marcon drive along in a separate vehicle conveying the contraband and the toting beneath his shirt of a plastic bag containing a nonnarcotic substance with a cocaine appearance to be turned over in the event of a "rip-off". He testified these precautions were suggested by Zorch, the supplier. The Appellate Division majority and trial court inferred that defendant's use of these methods showed he was not unskilled but was knowledgeable and wary. This evaluation is belied by the ease with which he was enticed into New York.

Defendant's precautions notwithstanding, he was arrested in the course of the transaction outside of the Whiffle Tree Bar. Breniman was called as a material witness. So was defendant's former paramour, Denise Marcon, who testified for the prosecution in return for a promise of life-time probation for her part in the sale.

Following a trial, without a jury, at which defendant raised the defense of entrapment and urged that his due process rights were violated, the County Judge found him guilty of criminal sale of a controlled substance in the first degree in violation of section 220.43 of the Penal Law, and imposed sentence. The Appellate Division affirmed, but two Justices vigorously dissented. For reasons which follow, we reverse and dismiss the indictment.

In holding that this prosecution should be barred, we find it unnecessary to examine in detail the question of whether this defendant was predisposed to commit the crime (see Penal Law, § 40.05). County Court found as a matter of law and fact that defendant did not prove by a preponderance of the evidence the defense of entrapment and the Appellate Division majority in turn held that the record amply supports the determination that defendant was predisposed to commit the offense for which he was charged. Even though defendant did not sustain his burden as to this affirmative defense (see Penal Law, § 25.00, subd. 2), the police conduct, when tested by due process standards, was so egregious and deprivative as to impose upon us an obligation to dismiss.

Recent cases show greater recognition of due process as a check on police misconduct. In United States v. Russell, based on a finding that defendant was predisposed to commit the crime, the Supreme Court rejected an entrapment defense even though a government agent supplied him with a chemical ingredient used by him to manufacture drugs illegally. However, while adhering to the test enunciated in Sorrells v. United States, the court envisioned: "[W]e may some day be presented with a situation in which the conduct of law enforcement agents is so outrageous that due process principles would absolutely bar the government from invoking judicial processes to obtain a conviction. In a later case, however, the meaning of *Russell* divided the majority of the court, which upheld a conviction where the government supplied contraband to a defendant later prosecuted for trafficking in the same (Hampton v. United States, 425 U.S. 484, 96 S.Ct. 1646). Referring to *Russell*, the plurality stated: "We ruled out the possibility that the defense of entrapment could ever be based upon governmental misconduct in a case, such as this one, where the predisposition of the defendant to commit the crime was established". Two Justices concurred, on the basis that they were "unwilling to join the plurality in concluding that, no matter what the circumstances, neither due process principles nor our supervisory power could support a bar to conviction in any case where the Government is able to prove predisposition". Therefore, in light of the concurrence and the dissent of three Justices in *Hampton*, a dismissal on due process grounds in the context of an insufficient entrapment defense has not been ruled out by the Supreme Court.

Of course, under our own State due process clause this court may impose higher standards than those held to be necessary by the Supreme Court under the corresponding Federal constitutional provision. . . . We therefore decide this case under our own State Constitution.

* * *

Where the police obtain evidence by brutalizing a defendant, a conviction resulting from such methods offends due process. And, as noted, even where a defense of entrapment is not made out because of the predisposition of the defendant to commit the crime, police misconduct may warrant dismissal on due process grounds. Moreover, the type of conduct which mandates the barring of prosecution ought not to be limited to situations involving police brutality. To prevent improper and unwarranted police solicitation of crime, there is a need for courts to recognize and to uphold principles of due process. This is a case that demands the application of these principles.

While due process is a flexible doctrine, certain types of police action manifest a disregard for cherished principle of law and order. . . . Each instance in which a deprivation is asserted requires its own testing in the light of fundamental and necessarily general but pliant postulates. All components of the complained of conduct must be scrutinized but certain aspects of the action are likely to be indicative.

Illustrative of factors to be considered are: (1) whether the police manufactured a crime which otherwise would not likely have occurred, or merely involved themselves in an ongoing criminal activity; (2) whether the police themselves engaged in criminal or improper conduct repugnant to a sense of justice; (3) whether the defendant's reluctance to commit the crime is overcome by appeals to humanitarian instincts such as sympathy or past friendship, by temptation of exorbitant gain, or by persistent solicitation in the face of unwillingness; and (4) whether the record reveals simply a desire to obtain a conviction with no reading that the police motive is to prevent further crime or protect the populace. No one of these submitted factors is in itself determinative but each should be viewed in combination with all pertinent aspects and in the context of proper law enforcement objectives—the prevention of crime and the apprehension of violators, rather than the encouragement of and participation in sheer lawlessness. As a bare minimum, there should be a purposeful eschewal of illegality or egregious foul play. A prosecution conceived in or nurtured by such conduct, as exemplified in these guidelines, so as to cast aside and mock "that fundamental fairness essential to the very concept of justice" should be forbidden under traditional due process principles.

Applying these factors to this case, first we find the manufacture and creation of crime. At most, and over his denial, the record shows that defendant had made small and rather casual sales of drugs. Indeed, it was established that he did not himself have access to the quantity of drugs sought by Breniman and for which he was arrested but was only directed to the source by one who testified against him. Doubtless, a crime of this magnitude would not have occurred without active and insistent encouragement and instigation by the police and their agent.

Turning to the second component, serious police misconduct repugnant to a sense of justice is revealed. Initially, there was conceded abuse of Breniman at the substation. While this harm was visited upon a third party, it cannot be overlooked, for to do so would be to accept police brutality as long as it was not pointed directly at defendant himself. Not only does the end not justify the means, but one should not be permitted to accomplish by indirection that which is prohibited by direction. More importantly, these actions set the pattern for further disregard of Breniman's rights in failing to reveal to him that the material he possessed on December 5 would not subject him to criminal charges. This was deceptive, dishonest and improper; it displayed a lawless attitude and, if countenanced, would suggest that the police are not bound by traditional notions of justice and fair play.

The third factor embraces a persistent effort to overcome defendant's reluctance to commit the crime. Breniman, as informant, played upon defendant's sympathy, their past relationship, and persevered in his requests despite defendant's obvious unwillingness. Moreover, even if defendant was motivated by expectation of profit, the lure of exorbitant gain is not a proper basis to create crime for the purpose of obtaining convictions. With resistance so undermined, even a person not predisposed to crime may be enticed to violate the law.

Finally, there is the overriding police desire for a conviction of any individual. In this respect, one is immediately shocked by an incredible geographical shell game—a deceit which effected defendant's unknowing and unintended passage across the border into this State. While this outright fraud was ostensibly accomplished by an informant, he was acting at the behest of the police, who emphasized that the sale must take place in New York, and thus are chargeable with the tactics employed by their agent. Of course, in a particular case, it may be necessary for the police to apprehend a criminal who operates outside our borders, but this is not such a situation. There is no suggestion that defendant had previously sold great quantities of cocaine. In short, the police wanted a conviction and simply set two specifications—a large amount of the substance to denote a high grade of crime and a situs of sale in New York. There was no indication of any desire to prevent crime by cutting off the source and, thus, the conviction obtained became little more than a statistic.

In sum, this case exposes the ugliness of police brutality, upon which was imposed a cunning subterfuge employed to enlist the services of an informant who, deceived into thinking he was facing a stiff prison sentence, desperately sought out any individual he could to satisfy the police thirst for a conviction, even of a resident of another State possessed of no intention to enter our confines. Separately considered, the items of conduct may not rise to a level justifying dismissal but viewed in totality they reveal a brazen and continuing pattern in disregard of fundamental rights.

As expected, the argument is advanced that the police are to be condemned, but the criminal should still be punished. Indeed, defendant's conviction was allowed despite the castigation of police conduct as "improper" and "reprehensible". Whether conduct is so outrageous is a question of degree to be answered by sound judgment, but "there comes a time when enough is more than enough—it is just too much." In this case, the police have simply gone too far. This court would be paying mere lip service to the principle of due process if it sanctioned the continuance of a prosecution in the face of the revelations of this record.

Certain comments in the dissent warrant discussion. Although stated elsewhere in this opinion, it appears to be necessary to emphasize our recognition that defendant has not established the defense of entrapment. That defense is not the issue in this case and no attempt has been made to interfere with or disturb the factfinding powers of other courts. Analysis is not advanced by disputes over the extent of defendant's predisposition. To be sure, he was predisposed to commit the crime, and for that reason the defense of entrapment failed. However, the proper focus is on whether, regardless of defendant's inclinations or criminal intent, due process mandates dismissal of his indictment.

Presented for our legal evaluation are undisputed facts and findings of the trial court that the police engaged in serious misconduct, which even the dissent characterizes as "devious" and "inexcusable". The dissent would overlook this conduct because the defendant was not "a direct victim of police misfeasance". The point is, however, that while the informant was the victim of the trickery and beating, these actions were indeed directed at defendant. This misbehavior set the pattern for an investigation in which the informant was maliciously used as a pawn to obtain a conviction of any individual. The dissent apparently finds nothing wrong with this technique. Tactics here employed, if not checked, are certain to encourage lawlessness and destroy cherished freedoms. A defendant charged with the most heinous of crimes is still entitled to the fundamental fairness we conceive under the notion of due process.

The undisputed facts and the express findings of the trial court provide the pivot on which this case turns and the basis from which this opinion is reasoned. A standard must be set somewhere and the line should be drawn here.

To be sure, "[c]riminal activity is such that stealth and strategy are necessary weapons in the arsenal of the police officer". However, while Justice Frankfurter's view was not adopted in the analysis of the entrapment defense, we now apply it in a due process context, thereby affirming this fundamental principle: "No matter what the defendant's past record and present inclinations to criminality, or the depths to which he has sunk in the estimation of society, certain police conduct to ensnare him into further crime is not to be tolerated by an advanced society". There may be those who fear that dismissal of convictions on due process grounds may portend an unmanageable subjectivity. Such apprehension is unjustified for courts by their very nature are constantly called upon to make judgments and, though differences of opinion often surround human institutions, this is the nature of the judicial process. Circumscribed by a sizeable body of constitutional and common law pronounced and steeped in traditions of Anglo-Saxon jurisprudence, due process is our most fundamental principle of law and must be applied here. The administration of justice must be above reproach. We therefore hold that this prosecution should be barred.

Accordingly, the order of the Appellate Division should be reversed, and the indictment dismissed.

GABRIELLI, JUDGE (dissenting).

I cannot agree that due process either as urged by the defendant or as expostulated by the majority mandates a reversal of defendant's conviction and a dismissal of the charges against him. Accordingly, I vote to affirm the order appealed from and sustain the conviction.

While it may well be that under certain egregious circumstances due process might mandate dimissal in an entrapment situation although the defendant is in fact predisposed to commit the crime of which he stands accused, this is not that case. My disagreement with the majority today lies more in the court's unwarranted assessment of the facts than in its enunciation of basic principles. The defendant has been convicted, and that conviction has been affirmed by the Appellate Division. The testimony at trial, both as to defendant's prior involvement in the drug subculture, and as to the details of the sale with respect to which he was convicted, was conflicting to say the least. The defendant, according to his own testimony which has been implicitly, and improperly, credited by the majority of this court, was a veritable innocent: an occasional user of marihuana, who agreed to sell cocaine in this case only because he wanted to help his friend, Breniman (whom he had met casually only three times before); a man who did not even know that the woman he was living with was a regular drug user.

Other witnesses, however, describe a completely different man. Breniman, the police informant, testified that he had on three prior occasions purchased varying amounts of marihuana, cocaine, and phenocyclidine from defendant. Denise Marcon, who shared an apartment with defendant, testified that defendant had been involved in several cocaine sales in the two or three months immediately preceding his arrest. She declared that on at least five occasions cocaine had been delivered to their apartment; that defendant took that cocaine to his laboratory, where he weighed it and broke it down into grams for easier sale; that he subsequently delivered it to several different people. As a perusal of the trial transcript indicates, someone at defendant's trial took certain liberties with the truth. As we have stated on many prior occasions, the trial court was in the best position to assess the testimony, and that court believed the prosecution witnesses; indeed the experienced Trial Judge concluded that some of defendant's testimony was incredible. These conclusions were not disturbed by the Appellate Division, and I cannot agree that it is proper for this court to supplant the conclusions of the original trier of fact with its own speculations absent clear error as a matter of law.

The majority has wisely chosen not to decide this case on the statutory entrapment defense issue, since a reversal on that ground would require that the court explicitly disturb the factual finding that defendant was predisposed to commit the crime of which he stands convicted. Unfortunately, it has fallen into the same difficulty in its due process analysis, for although the court admits that the defendant was in fact predisposed to commit the crime, it nonetheless then finds itself in the troublesome position of having to show that defendant's character is such that he would not have committed this crime had he not been lured into it by Breniman. The distinction is tenuous at best. As I have noted, it is not for this court to set aside the factual determination of credibility made by the lower courts. Indeed, the majority concedes that defendant was previously involved in drug sales, but dismisses that impertinent fact by characterizing those sales as at most "small and rather casual sales". Whatever the wisdom of our drug laws, it is for the courts to apply them, not demean them. Although the amount of drugs involved in a sale may lessen the degree of liability which attaches, the sale itself remains a criminal act, be it casual or the result of ten years' planning. In the present case, at any rate, the testimony of Marcon tends to belie the lack of professionalism implied by the majority. I find it difficult to reconcile this evidence with the portrait of entrapped innocence drawn by the court.

Turning then to the police misbehavior which the majority posits as proof that defendant has been deprived of his basic right to fair treatment at the hands of the government, I agree, of course, that the beating of Breniman was inexcusable, as were the devious means used to convince him to work for the police. These actions, however, had no significant connection with defendant, and in no way violated any of *defendant's* constitutional rights. While police misbehavior is not to be condoned, neither should the punishment for such activity be lightly visited upon society as a whole. Had defendant been a direct victim of police malfeasance, the situation would be quite different. As it is, however, the beating and the trickery were directed solely toward Breniman. To free this defendant, a confirmed drug dealer, simply because the police had mistreated the man who was later to inform on him, makes as little sense as would invalidating *all* arrests made by a policeman who has mistreated one suspect.

Apart from the mistreatment of Breniman, there has been no other police misbehavior shown in this case. The majority would castigate the police for the "deceitful luring of a Pennsylvania resident into New York solely to make a sale of cocaine". I do not agree that the actions which are so characterized constitute misconduct under the facts of this case. Proper analysis is furthered by separate consideration of the two discrete aspects of this alleged police misbehavior; the "luring" into New York, and the "entrapment" into the sale in the first place. Assuming that there was no real element of entrapment in this case, as I will discuss below, then surely there is no wrong in "luring" into the confines of New York State a man who would breach our laws with impunity from the far side of the border. Are not the people of this State entitled to some protection from criminal conduct outside the State which is intended to have a harmful effect inside the State? Defendant knew that Breniman intended to resell the cocaine in New York, and he had absolutely no compunction about that. His avowed reason for not wishing to enter New York had nothing to do with any desire not to commit a crime, for he had already agreed to do that by agreeing to sell the cocaine to Breniman. Rather, he did not wish to complete the sale in New York because he was afraid of our strict drug laws. In a situation such as this, involving someone who is selling contraband with the knowledge that it will be resold in New York, I see no problem in "luring" that person into our State for the purpose of obtaining criminal jurisdiction over him.

With respect to the nature of the incidents and communications which led to the sale itself, my differences with the majority are in large part based on our interpretations of the record. I find myself compelled to accept that version of the facts which has been accepted by the trial court and left undisturbed by the Appellate Division. So should the majority. As was discussed above, the testimony of Breniman and Marcon, the two other participants in the sale, indicates that the defendant was deeply involved in the drug subculture, and was in fact a seller of cocaine on a fairly regular basis. He had sold cocaine, as well as other illicit drugs, to Breniman on several prior occasions, and obviously had no compunctions about entering into subsequent transactions with Breniman. Although he did not wish to become involved in heroin, he clearly was already involved in the sale of cocaine.

The majority emphasizes that it took some time and several phone calls to set up the deal, and suggests that this is indicative of a disinclination upon the part of defendant to enter into the sale. I would note that the delay was due to the fact that these events transpired over the Christmas-New Year recess, during which time the campus was empty and defendant's normal source of cocaine doubtless was temporarily curtailed. Thus, he was forced to delay until he could locate a new supply, which he eventually did, purchasing the drugs from a friend of a friend of Marcon.

In light of defendant's prior sales, both to Breniman and to others, it is clear that this was not the type of manufactured crime which would never have taken place had it not been for the police, and with respect to which society might not wish to impose criminal liability. This is simply not a case in which an innocent man is seduced into criminal activity by police agents solely in order to obtain another conviction. Any reluctance upon defendant's part came not from a disinclination to sell drugs, but from a temporary disruption of his supply lines and from a disinclination to travel into this State to complete the sale. It is simply not the type of reluctance relevant to either the statutory defense of entrapment or a due process based quasi-entrapment doctrine.

In conclusion, I would note that the police conduct in this case is much less offensive than that in Hampton v. United States [supra note 1]. There, the Supreme Court held that due process was not violated, and a prima facie entrapment defense was not available to a defendant who was predisposed to commit the crime, in a situation in which defendant alleged that not only had a police agent talked him into becoming involved in a heroin sale, but that it had in fact been the police agent who supplied the heroin.

Accordingly, I am compelled to vote to affirm the order appealed from .

BREITEL, C. J., and JONES, WACHTLER and FUCHSBERG, JJ., concur with COOKE, J.

GABRIELLI, J., dissents and votes to affirm in a separate opinion in which JASEN, J., concurs.

NOTE

Isaacson represents a fairly unique application of due process theory to police conduct in arranging the commission of crime. The dissent takes little issue with the basic rule of law found by the majority. But some questions must be considered:

(1) The majority states: "There may be those who fear that dismissal of convictions on due process grounds may portend an unmanageable subjectivity. Such apprehension is unjustified for courts by their very nature are constantly called upon to make judgments". Is the stated objection adequately answered by the court?

(2) Entrapment is a defense to a criminal charge and the issue of entrapment is tried when the case is tried on the merits. A due process claim for dismissal may be resolved in a pre-trial hearing. Does *Isaacson* allow the defendant to seek a pre-trial hearing of his claim? In *Isaacson* such a hearing would have required presentation of nearly all the evidence in the case at the pre-trial hearing. If the defendant loses his motion, all the witnesses must be recalled at trial. Should a pre-trial hearing of such claims be permitted?

(3) Is *Isaacson* consistent with principles of "standing" discussed earlier in Chapter 6, Section C which deny defendants the right to exclude evidence obtained by virtue of violating the rights of a third party?

PART 2

THE JUDICIAL PROCESS

Chapter 8

PROSECUTORIAL DISCRETION

A. THE EXERCISE OF DISCRETION

The prosecutor is the single most powerful officer in the criminal justice system. This quality of his office stems from two factors: the influence he exercises upon the actions of other agencies within the system; and his freedom from review—except in the most extraordinary circumstances—of the decisions he makes as to whether or not to prosecute.

More than any other agency, the influence of a prosecutor's office is felt at every stage of the proceedings within the system. He is usually an advisor to, and sometimes a supervisor of, the police or other investigative agencies. His views, therefore, may influence the course of investigations directly; or, even if unsupervised in a particular area, the police may tailor their actions to accommodate the known preferences or prejudices of their local prosecutor. After verdict, the prosecutor's relationship to the judge, or the prosecutor's standing in the community, may influence the decision of the judge in the imposition of sentence. On appeal, the prosecutor, by virtue of his power to concede issues or, in some jurisdictions, to press a cross-appeal, may continue to shape the case even after it has been decided in the trial court.

After the defendant has been incarcerated, the influence of the prosecutor is still felt. Prison authorities may accept his view of the kind of custodial care which is required in individual cases. In many jurisdictions it is commonplace for the prosecutor to send a letter to the prison authorities giving his views of the nature of the charge, the evidence presented, and the character of the defendant. When parole or executive clemency is at issue, the view of the prosecutor, especially if vigorously and publicly pressed, may well be the controlling factor in determining whether the prisoner wins release or is continued in custody.

Thus, the prosecutor occupies the most powerful position in the system by virtue of his control over who is prosecuted and who is not, and the fact that the influence of his office is felt at every stage from arrest to parole and pardon.

The most important factor contributing to the power of the prosecutor is his almost unbridled right, both formal and informal, to make the decision either to prosecute or not to prosecute a particular defendant. This right is largely a product of the separation of powers within our system rather than a studied determination by legislatures; and generations of acceptance by legislatures as well as the courts have endowed it with an almost unquestioned character which prosecutors are anxious to see unchanged.

This immense prosecutorial power becomes even more apparent when contrasted with that possessed by other agencies of government involved in the law enforcement process and the administration of criminal justice—the legislatures, the police, and the courts.

In contrast to the prosecutor's almost complete freedom from review by other persons or agencies, even the power of the legislature to define offenses and set punishment is subject to some controls by the executive branch of government, whose police may not arrest offenders and whose prosecutors may not initiate prosecutions. Moreover, the validity of legislative enactments is subject to judicial scrutiny.

Although the actions of the police are subject to the control of the executive branch which governs them, their power to make arrests, searches and seizures, and engage in other investigative procedures may come to naught if the prosecutor declines to process their cases through the prosecution stage. Moreover, trial judges, and later on, appellate judges may nullify as evidence the results of police investigative efforts. Then, too, there are always legislative initiatives to confine the investigative and apprehension powers and practices of the police.

Trial judges in the federal system are subject to review by federal courts of appeal as well as by the Supreme Court. The decisions of state trial judges must withstand the scrutiny, not only of the appellate courts within the state system, but, where federal constitutional rights are involved, federal trial and appellate courts are able to review the conclusions of state trial and appellate judges through federal collateral relief.

Even prison and parole authorities, historically insulated by the concept of "discretion", now find themselves checked by the recent willingness of judges, especially federal judges, to set minimum standards of prison housekeeping and disciplinary procedures within the context of civil rights or damage actions. Moreover, parole authorities, long undisputed guardians of their own procedures for determining eligibility for parole, have now been told that there are minimum due process rights with which their procedures must comply.

The prosecutor's broad discretionary power is subject to one fairly remote restriction. Under our system of checks and balances, the prosecutor may always risk rejection by the electorate at the next election or, if he holds office by appointment, removal for misfeasance. Removal for abuse of prosecutorial discretion is rare, however.

Control of a prosecutor's budget by the legislative authority may conceivably act as a brake in curbing prosecutorial zeal in pursuing

particular cases, but the ability of the prosecutor to shift his resources may neutralize such a control attempt; moreover, power over
the budget cannot compel the prosecutor to act affirmatively with regard to particular case situations.

Finally, judicial control over the prosecutor is felt only with regard to those matters which the prosecutor chooses to place within
the system by initiating a prosecution. Even this control is largely
negative, in the sense that it operates only to curb prosecutorial misbehavior in the gathering of evidence or during the trial of a case.

From this perspective, then, we turn to a discussion of the factors which may influence the decision of the prosecutor to proceed
with, or decline to bring, criminal prosecutions.

1. The Prosecutor and His Office

Who and what the prosecutor is must be taken into account in
assessing how and why he makes his decisions. A federal prosecutor,
for example, is normally subject to the control only of the President
and the Attorney General. He may be a powerful political figure in
his own right or he may be politically weak and thus dependent upon
the favor of the senior Senator of the President's party, who traditionally recommends both prosecutorial and judicial nominees within
the federal system. On the other hand, a state prosecutor and the attorney general of a state, may be elected or appointed by the governor.
A county prosecutor may be elected or appointed by the Governor or
the Attorney General.

The area in which the prosecutor operates may also influence his
decisions to some degree. Thus the problems faced by the rural prosecutor are much different than those faced by the urban or suburban
prosecutor. Since his priorities of law enforcement are bound to be
different, so too are his decisions to prosecute or not to prosecute.
For example, prosecutors in rural or suburban areas tend to regard
commercial offenses such as embezzlement, forgery, check "kiting",
and petty theft with more seriousness than their urban counterparts
who must cope with a much larger number of such offenses and who
may not have such close personal relationships with community mer-
chants.

Discretion is also affected by the quality of assistant prosecutors
and the method of their selection and retention. If the office is regarded as a political stepping-stone, and if appointments are made as
part of a political patronage system, political factors or favors may
weigh in the balance. Sensitivity to community opinion (more precisely, the prosecutor's conception of community opinion) may be
more influential. If the prosecutor, even an elected one, has served
for a long time, and his assistants are chosen from outside the political system, or are civil service employees, less concern may be shown
in this regard.

The stage of the principal prosecutor's career may also be important. If the prosecutor is young and at the beginning of a legal or
political career, he may tend to caution in investigations and prosecu-

tions to lessen the chances of mistakes which will adversely affect that career. Or, if the political balance is such, he may assume the role of the "white knight" who charges forth in an aggressive manner to joust with the established order or political hierarchy. A career prosecutor will tend to steer a more even, balanced course. And an older prosecutor, perhaps one to whom a small community has turned because of the shortage of lawyers, may be less concerned with community opinion.

The size of the office is also important. In small offices discretion will remain largely with the principal prosecutor since control of the assistants and their decisions is more easily attained. In larger offices, with 50 or 100 assistants or more, control is more structured, with fewer decisions flowing to the top. The result is that initial, and often controlling, discretion rests largely with assistants who may be new, inexperienced or who do not share, to the same degree, the philosophy of enforcement of the principal prosecutor. His discretion is thus supervisory, rather than original, and his control of decisions depends heavily upon the ability of his supervisory staff and the formal structure of office authority. Thus, discretion in a large prosecutor's office may be that of many persons, rather than one, with review often hurried or haphazard. As a result discretion may be exercised in an internally inconsistent manner.

2. General Factors Influencing Discretion

Before examining those considerations which may influence the discretion to prosecute or decline in a particular case, some mention of *general* factors which shape a prosecutor's discretion should be made.

The first decision to be made is whether a criminal statute should be enforced at all. Though the statutory duty of prosecutors is often cast in mandatory terms, selective enforcement or nonenforcement of particular statutes is not uncommon in practice. Whether due to the personal predilections of the prosecutor, the tolerance of the local community, or the antiquity or irrationality of the statute, some laws are enforced only *pro forma* or sporadically in response to media pressure, and some laws are not enforced at all.

The second problem faced is how many criminal offenders are to be prosecuted if all cannot be. For example, if a federal prosecutor in a large urban area decided to prosecute all thefts from the mail, or all forgeries of government instruments, or all false statements on government employment applications, or all interstate auto thefts, he would be able to prosecute nothing else.

Third, if a particular offender has committed more than one offense, a question is raised as to whether he should be prosecuted for *all* crimes or only for the most serious. The decision on other offenses can be reserved until the disposition of the first offense charged. If one serious offense may be charged, the prosecutor may also consider filing a less serious one—an "included" or "reduced" offense.

A prosecutor must also consider the views of the police agencies with which he works. Some police agencies, whose abilities to win appropriations depends upon the statistics they are able to present to a budget director or a legislative body, exert pressures upon a prosecutor to maintain a high level of prosecutions in selected areas within their jurisdiction. Under other circumstances, the desires of the investigative agencies may have little effect upon the decision to prosecute, except within the framework of a prosecutor's desire to maintain "good relations". Some prosecutors, when dealing with agencies which are especially cooperative on a regular basis, may, in return, prosecute more of that agencies' cases, or go on borderline cases where the agency has a particular interest in proceeding.

The decision may also turn upon what alternative remedies are open to the prosecutor and the administrative or investigative agency. For example, if a federal prosecutor declines to prosecute a theft from interstate shipment, no alternative (other than state prosecution) is available to satisfy the FBI. But if he declines to prosecute a case of fraud on the Social Security Administration, the agency may recoup lost monies from future payments. The failure to prosecute food stamp violations ferreted out by agents from the Department of Agriculture does not preclude the imposition of administrative sanctions by the agency. On occasion there may be pressure from a police agency to at least initiate prosecution to protect agents from the threat of civil litigation in cases where the arrest or search techniques were questionable. And, in a related area, there may be occasional industry pressures to proceed with a weak case against an employee—a theft case against a truck driver—to forestall union demands for reinstatement in the face of management's desire to discharge the errant employee.

The kind of offense under consideration may also affect the decision to prosecute or decline. A county prosecutor, for example, would rarely decline to prosecute a crime of violence or a narcotics charge, except for insufficiency of evidence or unlawful police practices which would result in suppression and consequent acquittal. Discretion in these instances is limited to legal assessments of these two potential problems. On the other hand, when considering whether to prosecute low level visibility offenses not involving threats to life or safety, and not particularly outrageous from society's standpoint, guilt is not, ordinarily, in issue and the decision to prosecute turns upon other factors. It is, of course, a truism that the lower the visibility of the offense and the lower the visibility of the prosecution, the easier it is to exercise discretion in deciding whether to prosecute.

The particular deterrence rationale involved may also be a factor. The prosecution of a particular offense may be likely to produce a fairly effective deterrent to the commission of crimes by *others* if prosecuted vigorously and notoriously. Tax evasion, embezzlement, and other crimes involving substantial periods of contemplation and planning are viewed as offenses within this classification. On the other hand, the offense may be one which often is the product of a momentary aberration, not likely to be repeated. In such a case, the deterrence of others is of little moment. The primary concern is safeguarding society from a repetition of the acts by the *same* offender. This would be true in reckless homicide and certain marital batteries. Or the offense may simply not respond well to the criminal process: drunken and disorderly conduct, gambling, prostitution, and other crimes without complainants.

A prosecutor must also consider what kind of office he wants to conduct, for almost every prosecutor's office reflects the personal philosophies and priorities of the principal prosecutor. He may strive for a statistical result such as a high "conviction rate"; if so, he will be inclined to be cautious and refuse to proceed with cases which are doubtful or risky. The type of community credibility he seeks to attain is another important consideration. If the office is used as a political lance, the prosecutor will probably seek to be aggressive, though hopefully not reckless. If he deliberately seeks community recognition in certain high visibility areas of prosecution—public corruption, narcotics, financial frauds, civil rights, or pollution—he will probably be keenly aware of the difference between merely "winning" and "not losing".

Finally, the stage of the prosecution at which the decision is being made is a factor to consider in the exercise of prosecutorial discretion. Is the prosecutor being called upon to decide whether to proceed before arrest? Or after the decision to arrest has been made by the police without his concurrence, but before a complaint has been filed? Should a case in which a complaint has been filed be taken through the grand jury process? Should the case be reassessed after indictment but before trial? Is there any reason, after conviction, to aquiesce in a motion for new trial? If a case is reversed on appeal some period of time after commission of the offense, the decision to reprosecute is often made after consideration of totally different factors than those which made up the initial decision to proceed; the current state of the evidence, the current climate of community opinion, a possible change in prosecutors, the expense of a retrial, a sentence mostly served awaiting appeal, and similar considerations.

3.   The Specific Factors of Discretion

We turn then to a consideration of some of the *specific* factors which may enter into a prosecutor's decision of whether to proceed with a charge of a criminal offense. We assume, for these purposes, the sufficiency of the evidence.

Not all of these factors may enter into the decision in every case. And a prosecutor may not consciously be aware that he is even considering some of those that do enter into the case, for, depending upon his experience, his ability to analyze summaries of evidence and the time devoted to such analysis, he may conclude very quickly that a case is worth prosecuting or it is not.

The first question to be considered is whether the case fits within the prosecution priorities of the office. Especially in large offices, many cases in which the guilt of the accused is clear are not prosecuted simply because the office resources are not sufficient to proceed in every instance. For example, in a large office, small cases of theft, embezzlement, marijuana possession and the like may be declined in order to allow the prosecutor to proceed with more serious offenses. Sometimes the potential defendants are placed in a status of "probation without conviction", which, if successfully completed, results in eventual dismissal of the charge. The federal prosecutor may decline in favor of local prosecution. If the offender is a member of the armed forces, he may be returned to the processes of military justice. A juvenile may be turned over to local juvenile authorities. Or the case may simply be declined, especially where restitution (in theft or fraud cases) has been made before the prosecutor must exercise his discretion.

In some cases, a prosecutor will decide that the arrest and temporary incarceration before release on bail was a sufficient sanction to promote deterrence. For example, the drunken business man who makes threatening remarks aboard an aircraft, and who spends the night in jail before release, is unlikely to need the additional sanction of actual prosecution to carry home the gravity of the offense. Care must be exercised in these cases, however, to prevent the concept of "trial" or "punishment" by arrest or incarceration from becoming a stated concept of law enforcement, especially one to be engaged in by investigative agencies in their discretion.

The defendant's background is also important. Prosecuting authorities tend to be more lenient with youthful and elderly offenders, with persons who have led disadvantaged lives, with people who have wretched family situations which may have been contributing factors in the commission of the offense, with defendants who have many children or whose earnings are near the poverty level, with defendants who have creditable military service records, with people who have no prior arrest or conviction records, and with defendants who have been ill or who have mental problems not amounting to insanity. Sometimes these factors may have little or nothing to do with the commission of the offense, but, since prosecutors may feel a natural sympathy for the disadvantaged, the factors weigh in the balance when the decision to prosecute or decline is made. If a prosecutor receives 100 small embezzlement cases a year and has the resources to prosecute only twenty, it is likely that he will look for extenuating factors as an excuse to rationalize his declination of the eighty on grounds other than lack of resources.

The defendant's record of embroilment with the law on collateral charges is also important. If a defendant has just been convicted of another offense in the same or a sister jurisdiction, the likelihood is that a presently pending charge will not go forward, particularly if the prosecutor suspects that conviction of a second offense will simply result in the imposition of a concurrent sentence. On the other hand, if the defendant has just been acquitted of another charge, particularly in a sister jurisdiction, and there is reason to believe that the acquittal was not based upon the merits, if crucial evidence was suppressed, or, assuming conviction, if the sentence for the other offense is thought to be too lenient, the decision may well be to proceed with the pending offense.

Even though guilt of the offense is clear, the quality of the prosecution's case must be constantly scrutinized. This is especially true when the prosecutor deals with a witness to a succession of offenses, such as an accomplice in a number of prosecutions against different hijackers or "fences." While the state of the evidence in earlier prosecutions may have been convincing and convictions may have been obtained, witnesses who testify repeatedly sometimes "wear out", and their testimony may become less credible either because they or the prosecutor become careless by reason of earlier successes, or continued trials may furnish additional impeaching material. If the string of victories ends, and the prosecutor suffers several setbacks, he may well reconsider prosecuting the balance of the cases which looked promising a year earlier, when the indictments were obtained. On the other hand, a prior loss with the same key witness does not necessarily foreclose prosecution of a case in a new jurisdiction. The new prosecutors, jurors, community opinion, and differences in corroborating evidence may justify proceeding with an indictment in one jurisdiction even though the case is based substantially upon the testimony of a witness who has previously testified in a losing prosecution in another jurisdiction.

The age of a case may also persuade a prosecutor not to proceed. The case may be old when the offense is discovered, or the case may have lain dormant too long within the police agency or through trial delay, and the evidence may now be stale. This factor is particularly important when, following reversal for reasons other than the sufficiency of the evidence, a decision whether a case should be retried must be made. Here, the factors of cost and manpower, which may not have been considered when the initial decision to prosecute was made, may outweigh the advantages of finally achieving a verdict of guilty. This is often true when the controversial nature of a case may have stretched a trial for a lesser offense beyond the limits which ordinarily would be reached.

Even though legal guilt is clear, a prosecutor who has set prosecution goals or wishes to maintain a community posture of invincibility in priority areas may closely weigh the "winability" of a case. If there are factors upon which a jury might rest a verdict of acquittal despite the evidence of guilt, a prosecutor may fear the harmful effect of that acquittal upon the deterrence which a previous string of victories has presumably generated among potential offenders and decide that the prosecution is not worth the risk. In an analogous area, a prosecutor may also decide to delay the institution of a prosecution, even though the offense is complete at that point and there is sufficient evidence of guilt, because the case may have more "jury appeal" if subsequent conditions change. For example, if a defendant has obtained a large number of loans by means of false financial statements submitted to various lending institutions, he may be guilty of several offenses and the evidence may be sufficient to indict. But if all the loans are current and there are no losses to the banks, the case may not have the "jury appeal" necessary to obtain a conviction. Delay in the institution of prosecution until the loans go bad may appear to be a more discrete course of action of the part of the cautious prosecutor.

Prosecutors may also exercise their discretion to punish or reward defendants and, sometimes, their lawyers. Prosecution may be foregone as part of an agreement to obtain the defendant's cooperation against others. Or a case that, by application of routine standards might be declined, is pressed when a defendant refuses to cooperate with investigating or prosecuting authorities.

Occasionally, the fortuitous choice of a lawyer may work to the advantage of a defendant in his invocation of the prosecutor's discretion. If a lawyer has established a close relationship with a prosecutor, and if he has been of material assistance in other cases, persuading guilty clients not only to plead, but to testify against others, the prosecutor may be more inclined to deal leniently with a current client. Conversely, if a lawyer is employed who has an antagonistic relationship with the principal prosecutor or his assistants, the current client may find that his borderline case is decided in favor of prosecution.

The decision to make "new law" by instituting a criminal prosecution for the first time under a statute not previously utilized is one of the most difficult for a prosecutor. Many criminal statutes—particularly in the regulatory area—are broadly drawn and when their breadth is teamed with a prosecutor's ingenuity, practices close to the line—particularly in the business community—may be swept within the net of criminal prosecution.

When the application of the statute is clear enough, and only a new or more vigorous program of enforcement is in issue, the question is relatively easy. For example, upon the imposition of wage and price controls, the government, in order to achieve national uniformity and maximum compliance, will prosecute, with maximum public exposure, all cases brought by the investigative agency, whether large or small. When the enforcement program is well under way and a sufficient compliance has been obtained, the prosecutor will invoke his discretion only in those cases which will clear doubtful areas of the law or which, because of the visibility of the offense or the offender, will presumably serve special deterrent purposes.

When the statute has been in force for some time and the question of whether certain conduct is violative of the act is without precedent, the issues which the prosecutor must confront are somewhat different. If the conduct in question is asserted to have some claim to legitimacy—either by widespread or long time acceptance in the business community or by the assertion of industry leaders—it may well be the fairer course to publicly announce a prosecutorial conclusion that the conduct in question is viewed as unlawful. If the conduct ceases, the objectives of criminal prosecution have been accomplished. If offenders persist, then at least they have had fair warning.

Finally, a prosecutor always takes account of how a prosecution will be perceived by the defendant and his associates, by the press and public, by the court, by the investigative agency and by fellow lawyers. A case which is otherwise perfectly ripe for prosecution may be declined if, for example, a United States Attorney believes it is not "worthy" of being brought in a federal court, or, at least, suspects that a federal judge would think so. Or a case may be declined if the press or public would consider a prosecutor's priorities out of kilter if he brought it: the theft of a pair of shoes from a hospital supply room by a patient. And if cases too close to the borderline are prosecuted with sudden regularity, the investigative agencies might legitimately conclude that the prosecutor's standards have undergone unspoken adjustment and readjust their investigative priorities without consultation with the prosecutor.

Perhaps the qualities which an individual must possess in order to combine these discretionary factors into a correct and meaningful decision were best described by Mr. Justice Jackson when he was Attorney General of the United States:

> "The qualities of a good prosecutor are as elusive and as impossible to define as those which mark a gentleman. And those who need to be told would not understand it anyway. A sensitiveness to fair play and sportsmanship is perhaps the best protection against the abuse of power, and the citizen's safety lies in the prosecutor who tempers zeal with human kindness, who seeks truth and not victims, who serves the law and not factional purposes, and who approaches his task with humility." [1]

NOTES

Compare the following from the ABA Standards Relating to the Prosecution Function:

3.9 Discretion in the charging decision

(a) In addressing himself to the decision whether to charge, the prosecutor should first determine whether there is evidence which would support a conviction.

(b) The prosecutor is not obliged to present all charges which the evidence might support. The prosecutor may in some circumstances and for good cause consistent with the public interest decline to prosecute, notwithstanding that evidence exists which would support a conviction. Illustrative of the factors which the prosecutor may properly consider in exercising his discretion are:

(i) the prosecutor's reasonable doubt that the accused is in fact guilty;

1. Jackson, The Federal Prosecutor, 31 J.Crim.L., C. & P.S. 3, 6 (1940). See, also Friedman, The Prosecutor: A   Model for Role and Function, 1978 Wash.L.Q. 109.

(ii) the extent of the harm caused by the offense;

(iii) the disproportion of the authorized punishment in relation to the particular offense or the offender;

(iv) possible improper motives of a complainant;

(v) prolonged non-enforcement of a statute, with community acquiescence;

(vi) reluctance of the victim to testify;

(vii) cooperation of the accused in the apprehension or conviction of others;

(viii) availability and likelihood of prosecution by another jurisdiction.

(c) In making the decision to prosecute, the prosecutor should give no weight to the personal or political advantages or disadvantages which might be involved or to a desire to enhance his record of convictions.

(d) In cases which involve a serious threat to the community, the prosecutor should not be deterred from prosecution by the fact that in his jurisdiction juries have tended to acquit persons accused of the particular kind of criminal act in question.

(e) The prosecutor should not bring or seek charges greater in number or degree than he can reasonably support with evidence at trial.

UNITED STATES v. COWAN

United States Court of Appeals, Fifth Circuit, 1975.
524 F.2d 504.

MURRAH, CIRCUIT JUDGE: *

The first sentence of Rule 48(a) Fed.R.Crim.P. provides that "The Attorney General or the United States attorney may by leave of court file a dismissal of an indictment, information or complaint and the prosecution shall thereupon terminate." In our case the trial judge, the Honorable Robert M. Hill, denied the United States Attorney's motion under Rule 48(a) to dismiss pending criminal proceedings in the Northern District of Texas, and upon formal declination of the government to proceed, appointed private, special prosecutors to continue the prosecution of the case. The government took a timely appeal from the order appointing the special prosecutors. . . .

* * *

In February of 1974, a federal grand jury in the Northern District of Texas returned a seven-count indictment against Jake Jacobsen. Six of the counts charged Jacobsen and Roy Cowan with the fraudulent misapplication of funds of a federally insured savings and loan association in San Angelo, Texas. A seventh count charged Jacobsen alone with knowingly making a false statement under oath to

---

* Senior Circuit Judge of the Tenth Circuit, sitting by designation. This opinion was concurred in prior to Judge Murrah's death on October 30, 1975. See Coca Cola Co. v. Federal Trade Comm., 5 Cir. 1973, 475 F.2d 299, 301.

the grand jury. The indictment was signed by the United States Attorney for the district. After rather extensive motion practice resulting in a pretrial order in April, the case was set for trial in July. On joint motion of the parties the case was continued until a day in September due to the unavailability of a government witness.

Meanwhile and in May of the same year, the Watergate Special Prosecution Force and Jacobsen's Washington counsel negotiated an agreement whereunder Jacobsen agreed to plead guilty to a one-count charge to be filed in the District of Columbia alleging violation of 18 U.S.C. § 201(f) (bribing a public official) and make a full and truthful disclosure of all relevant information and documents within Jacobsen's knowledge and possession concerning matters then under investigation by the Watergate Special Prosecution Force, and if required, be a witness on any charges arising out of any such investigation. The Special Prosecution Force agreed not to press any potential charges against Jacobsen in the District of Columbia arising out of the relevant investigation. It was also a part of the plea agreement that the government would dismiss the Texas indictment.

Apparently Jacobsen appeared before a grand jury in the District of Columbia in May giving testimony incriminating himself and others. In any event, in July the grand jury returned an indictment in the District of Columbia charging Jacobsen in one count with violation of 18 U.S.C. § 201(f) and as an unindicted co-conspirator in a conspiracy count against former Secretary of the Treasury John Connally. In August Jacobsen entered a guilty plea to the bribery count (18 U.S.C. § 201(f)). The plea was accepted and the sentence postponed. At the same time the plea agreement was filed with the clerk of the court.

In accordance with the plea agreement, the United States Attorney for the Northern District of Texas moved under Rule 48(a) to dismiss the indictment set for trial in September. A copy of the plea agreement was attached to the motion. The motion to dismiss recited that the Office of the Special Prosecutor and the Attorney General believed that Jacobsen's testimony was necessary to the investigation and prosecution of the indictment in the District of Columbia; that if it did not enter into the plea agreement, the testimony of Jacobsen in that case, or any other case in which his testimony is relevant, would be lost; that the motion to dismiss the Texas charges was made in good faith, in accordance with the plea agreement and not for purposes of harassment; and that the interest of justice will be best served by disposing of the charges against Jacobsen in this manner. A memorandum of law supporting the Attorney General's absolute discretion to dismiss the indictment even without leave of court was filed with the motion. Jacobsen's Texas counsel joined in the United States Attorney's motion to dismiss. The motion was submitted in open court without further argument or testimony. On the same day and pursuant to another plea agreement, Judge Hill accepted a guilty plea by co-defendant Cowan to two counts of the Texas indictment and the United States Attorney agreed to move to dismiss the remaining counts after sentencing. Thus, all charges against Jacobsen and Cowan not disposed of by guilty pleas were made the subject of motions to dismiss by the government with consent of the defendants in accordance with the two plea agreements.

In an exhaustive opinion, the trial court asserted its discretionary power under Rule 48(a) to grant or deny the motion for leave to dismiss the Texas indictment against Jacobsen. Upon denial of the motion to dismiss, the United States Attorney filed its notice of intention not to prosecute. Whereupon, the court, asserting its inherent power to protect the public interest in these extraordinary circumstances, appointed private special prosecutors "with full authority to control the course of investigation and litigation related to the offenses charged in the indictment and to handle all aspects of the case to the same extent as the United States Attorney in any criminal prosecution."

The Attorney General stakes his claim to absolute power to dismiss the proceedings even without "leave of court" squarely upon the Doctrine of Separation of Powers as derived from the provisions of the Constitution establishing three separate, but co-equal branches of government, each supreme in its own sphere; and more particularly upon Article II, Section 3 which provides in material part that the President "shall take Care that the Laws be faithfully executed" and upon 28 U.S.C. §§ 516, 519, empowering the Attorney General as surrogate of the President to conduct or supervise all litigation in which the government is a party. The court-appointed prosecutors counter that the Doctrine of Separation of Powers implied in the Constitution does not cast the three branches of our government into water-tight compartments; that room is left for some commingling of responsibilities in the orderly administration of governmental affairs; that by the promulgation of Rule 48(a) as part of the Rules of Criminal Procedure, Congress intended to vest in the courts a shared responsibility for the dismissal of prosecutions once lodged in the court; and that the power to grant leave to dismiss a criminal prosecution carries with it the correlative power to exercise a discretion to deny leave to dismiss and, if necessary, to effectuate such denial by the appointment of private prosecutors.

To sustain the asserted absolute power to dismiss the proceedings without "leave of court," the Attorney General relies heavily on United States v. Cox, 342 F.2d 167 (5th Cir. 1965) and its progeny. That case involved the power of the district court to require the United States Attorney, under penalty of contempt, to sign an indictment or true bill as presented by the grand jury in accordance with Rule 7(c) Fed.R.Crim.P., which provides that an indictment "shall be signed by the attorney for the government." A majority of the en banc court sustained the government's petition to prohibit the trial judge from enforcing its contempt order and from asserting jurisdiction to require the Attorney General of the United States or the United States Attorney "to institute criminal prosecution or to take any steps in regard thereto."

After delineating the powers of the Judicial Department under Article III and of the Executive Department under Article II, Section

1 of the Constitution, Judge Jones speaking for the majority of the en banc court declared:

> "Although as a member of the bar, the attorney for the United States is an officer of the court, he is nevertheless an executive official of the Government, and it is as an officer of the executive department that he exercises a discretion as to whether or not there shall be a prosecution in a particular case. It follows, as an incident of the constitutional separation of powers, that the courts are not to interfere with the free exercise of the discretionary powers of the attorneys of the United States in their control over criminal prosecutions. The provision of Rule 7, requiring the signing of the indictment by the attorney for the Government, is a recognition of the power of the Government counsel to permit or not to permit the bringing of an indictment. . . . ." United States v. Cox, supra at 171.

This succinct and forthright statement has been quoted and applied, quite correctly we think, in a variety of situations under differing circumstances, all involving the Executive's power and authority to initiate a criminal prosecution or the power of the court to dismiss on its own motion a pending prosecution.

* * *

Though the Rule was not at issue in *Cox*, it came under the scrutiny of the court in connection with the interpretation of Rule 7(c). The majority was apparently of the view that without the discretionary power given to the United States Attorney to prevent an indictment under 7(c) by withholding his signature, the constitutionality of Rule 48(a) would be doubtful. The court accordingly justified the Rule with the observation that it was intended solely to authorize the court to protect a defendant from harassment by successive filings and dismissals. Chief Judge Brown specially concurring agreed that 48(a) "vests the unfettered discretion in the District Attorney to determine whether a prosecution is to be maintained or dismissed." He was careful, however, to acknowledge that the interpretation of 48(a) had not been directly presented and that there was no assurance the rule "might not ultimately be construed [to reserve] considerable power to the District Judge himself in determining whether to enter a dismissal on the Government's motion." See *Cox* at 183 n. 6. Judge Wisdom specially concurring was sure that "the district attorney has absolute control over criminal prosecutions [with power to] dismiss or refuse to prosecute . . . [t]he responsibility is wholly his."

* * *

The holding in *Cox* is doubtless the law on its facts, and nothing we say here is intended to derogate from it. But ours is not a *Cox* case. *Cox* involved a challenge to the power of the court to direct the commencement of a prosecution, under Rule 7(c). We are concerned with the power of the court to supervise the termination of a prosecution in being, under Rule 48(a). While the dicta in all the opinions in the *Cox* case provide a formidable preface to our inquiry, this dicta is inconclusive here because that court was not called upon to distinguish between the power to initiate and the power to terminate prosecutions.

The absolute power and discretion of the Attorney General or his subordinates to institute prosecution is conceded, as it must also be conceded that no federal appellate court has come face to face with the asserted power of the district court under 48(a) to grant or withhold leave to dismiss a criminal prosecution once begun. The question is squarely presented here for the first time as a controversy between the Executive and Judicial Branches of government involving opposing asserted powers under the Rule.

* * *

In situations like these history has its claims, and we think it is appropriate to review it. Before the adoption of 48(a), more than thirty states had, by statute or judicial decision, modified the common law to give courts a responsible role in the dismissal of a pending criminal proceeding by requiring an "order" or "leave" or "consent" of court. The state case law interpreting this change is sparse, but what there is of it consistently affirms the power and duty of the court to exercise discretion to grant or withhold leave to dimiss pending criminal prosecutions in "the public interest."

* * *

[The Advisory Committee created to propose Federal Rules of Criminal Procedure Submitted a Draft Rule to the Supreme Court which read: "The Attorney General or the United States Attorney may file a dismissal of the indictment or information with a statement of the reasons therefor and the prosecution shall thereupon terminate."]

The Supreme Court deleted the phrase "with a statement of the reasons therefor," and, in lieu thereof, inserted the phrase "by leave of court." As thus amended, 48(a) was submitted to Congress and adopted. It seems manifest that the Supreme Court intended to make a significant change in the common law rule by vesting in the courts the power and the duty to exercise a discretion for the protection of the public interest.

* * *

It seems to us that the history of the Rule belies the notion that its only scope and purpose is the protection of the defendant. . . . Viewed in this light, we think it manifestly clear that the Supreme Court intended to clothe the federal courts with a discretion broad enough to protect the public interest in the fair administration of criminal justice. It is against this background that we consider the overpowering effect of the Doctrine of Separation of Powers.

In the resolution of this question, we think United States v. Nixon, [418 U.S. 683, 94 S.Ct. 3090 (1974)], both pertinent and authoritative. In that case the Chief Executive asserted the unqualified privilege of an immunity from judicial process under all circumstances as a derivative of the Doctrine of Separation of Powers. Chief Justice Burger responded:

> "The impediment that an absolute unqualified privilege would place in the way of the primary constitutional duty of the Judicial Branch to do justice in criminal prosecutions would plainly conflict with the function of the courts under Art. III. In designing the structure of our Government and dividing and allocating the sovereign power among three coequal branches, the Framers of the Constitution sought to provide a comprehensive system, but the separate powers were not intended to operate with absolute independence.
>
> > " 'While the Constitution diffuses power the better to secure liberty, it also contemplates that practice will integrate the dispersed powers into a workable government. It enjoins upon its branches separateness but interdependence, autonomy but reciprocity.' Youngstown Sheet & Tube Co. v. Sawyer, 343 U.S. 579, 635 [72 S.Ct. 863, 870] (1952) (Jackson, J., concurring)."
>
> United States v. Nixon, supra at 707, 94 S.Ct. at 3107.

The Chief Justice, speaking for a unanimous court, went on to conclude that the legitimate needs of the judicial process may very well outweigh Executive privilege; and that it is necessary to resolve these competing interests in a manner that preserves the essential function of the Executive Branch by according high respect to its claim of privilege. Ultimately, the Court sustained the power to subpoena Executive material pertaining to the fair administration of criminal justice without affecting the national security.

That authoritative reasoning should be our guide here. We think the rule should and can be construed to preserve the essential judicial function of protecting the public interest in the evenhanded administration of criminal justice without encroaching on the primary duty of the Executive to take care that the laws are faithfully executed. The resulting balance of power is precisely what the Framers intended. As Judge Wisdom put it, quoting Montesquieu, " 'To prevent the abuse of power, it is necessary that by the very disposition of things, power should be a check to power' . . . [thus] the framers wove a web of checks and balances designed to prevent abuse of power" and "were too sophisticated to believe that the three branches of government were absolutely separate, air-tight departments." United States v. Cox, supra at 190. From this, it seems altogether proper to say that the phrase "by leave of court" in Rule 48(a) was intended to modify and condition the absolute power of the Executive, consistently with the Framer's concept of Separation of Powers, by erecting a check on the abuse of Executive prerogatives. But this is not to say that the Rule was intended to confer on the Judiciary the power and authority to usurp or interfere with the good faith exercise of the Executive power to take care that the laws are faithfully executed. The rule was not promulgated to shift absolute power from the Executive to the Judicial Branch. Rather, it was intended as a power to check power. The Executive remains the absolute judge of whether a prosecution should be initiated and the first and presumptively the best judge of whether a pending prosecution should be terminated. The exercise of its discretion with respect to the termination of pending prosecutions should not be judicially disturbed unless clearly contrary to manifest public interest. In this way, the essential function of each branch is synchronized to achieve a balance that serves both practical and constitutional values.

Judge Hill was undoubtedly clothed with a discretion to determine whether the dismissal of these charges was clearly contrary to the public interest. But it is a judicial discretion subject to appellate review. And since that discretion is constitutionally sensitive, we feel bound to a closer scrutiny than in the ordinary case where such practical considerations as finality of decision, judicial economy, and trial judge's closeness to the evidentiary process dictate greater appellate court deference. If upon appraisal of all the relevant factors, the appellate court has a definite and firm conviction that the trial court committed a clear error of judgment in the conclusion it reached, the judgment must be reversed.

* * *

Judge Hill was "unable to perceive how the best interest of justice could be served by dismissing serious charges with a potential penalty of thirty-five years imprisonment and a $70,000 fine in exchange for a guilty plea in an unrelated case carrying a maximum penalty of two years and a $10,000 fine." He also referred to the fact that "the investigatory material developed by [Texas] state and federal agencies was turned over to the federal officials with the understanding that the federal government would initiate and pursue appropriate prosecution"; that the government's "bare assertion" of reasons for dismissal was unaccompanied by factual evidence. In these circumstances, he concluded, "the interest of justice would not be served by a dismissal of this case." The brief of the court-appointed prosecutors seems to impugn the good faith of the government by suggesting that the motion to continue the trial, filed jointly by the prosecution and both defendants in June 1974, was calculated to facilitate the surreptitious performance of the plea agreement negotiated one month earlier between Jacobsen and the Watergate Special Prosecution Force, and thus dispense with the trial of the Texas case.

We think this appraisal of the whole matter misapprehends the relative roles of the Executive and the Judiciary under 48(a). The considerations which prompted Judge Hill to overrule the motion to dismiss are, in our judgment, legally insufficient to overcome the presumption of the government's good faith and establish its betrayal of the public interest. We do not think the plea negotiations between the two prosecutorial arms of the government and counsel for both defendants were improper, even though not disclosed to the sentencing judges until consummation. It is not suggested that the facts recited in the joint motion for continuance were untrue, or that they were inadequate grounds for a continuance. In this situation, we can hardly say that the motion was a sham or a deception. It was not incumbent upon the government to inform the sentencing judges of the plea negotiations until after they had been consummated. The result of these negotiations was finally placed before both sentencing courts in the form of plea agreements, which themselves have a legitimate and desirable function in the effective administration of criminal justice. Nor was it clearly contrary to the public interest for the government to accept in these plea agreements a reduction in the maximum possible sentence of Cowan and Jacobsen, when, as stated in the government's motion, it served to further an investigation by an especially created and wholly autonomous arm of the Executive. We cannot agree with Judge Hill's view that this motion lacked specificity of evidentiary proof. The representations in the motion and the supporting memorandum were not merely conclusory; they specified the investigation being pursued in the District of Columbia and the necessity of obtaining Jacobsen's cooperation under the plea agreement calling for dismissal of the Texas charges. We are convinced that this is legally sufficient to justify leave of court to dismiss the Texas charges against Jacobsen in consideration of his guilty plea in the District of Columbia.

In sum, it was within the province of the two prosecutorial arms of the government to weigh the relative importance of two separate prosecutions in two separate districts and dispose of them as practical considerations seemed to dictate. Nothing in this record overcomes the presumption that they did so in good faith for substantial reasons sufficiently articulated in the motion to dismiss. As to the interest of the State of Texas in these charges, we can perceive no reason why the dismissal would bar or prejudice a state prosecution on substantially the same Texas charges. In the first place, Jacobsen was never put in jeopardy on the Texas charges. Moreover, a prosecution by one sovereign is no bar to a prosecution by another sovereign arising out of the same facts. . . .

Having concluded that the trial court exceeded the bounds of its discretion under Rule 48(a) in denying the government's motion to dismiss, we have no cause to consider the propriety of its order effectuating that denial by appointing special prosecutors. The case is reversed and remanded with directions to sustain the motion to dismiss.

NOTES

1. The authority of the prosecutor to refuse to bring a case is almost unlimited; and the authority of a court to compel a prosecution is barred by the separation of powers. In Inmates of Attica v. Rockefeller, 477 F.2d 375 (2d Cir. 1973), the inmates of a prison sought to compel the United States Attorney to prosecute persons who had allegedly violated certain federal and state statutes in connection with the treatment of the inmates during and following a prison uprising. Upholding prosecutorial discretion to initiate proceedings, the court observed that "the problems inherent in the task of supervising prosecutorial decisions do not lend themselves to resolution by the judiciary." Similarly, in Powell v. Katzenbach, 359 F.2d 234 (D.C.Cir. 1965), the court upheld the trial judge's dismissal of a mandamus action to require the Attorney General to initiate a criminal prosecution

against a national bank and its officers on the ground that the statute relied upon disclosed no congressional intent to alter the Executive's exclusive discretion to initiate a prosecution.

2.   May a judge compel the prosecutor to treat defendants equally with respect to plea-bargaining?   In Newman v. United States, 382 F.2d 479 (D.C.Cir. 1967), defendant claimed that the United States Attorney violated his constitutional rights by allowing a codefendant to plead guilty to a lesser included offense under the indictment while refusing to consent to the same plea for the appellant.   Chief Justice (then Judge) Burger, speaking for the court, affirmed the absolute discretion of the United States Attorney as an executive official as to whether or not there shall be a prosecution in a particular case as an incident of the constitutional separation of powers.

3.   In many federal cases, individual counts of an indictment may be drawn for each resort to the federal jurisdictional element.   Thus, in a mail fraud case, for example, each mailing in furtherance of a scheme to defraud may be charged as a separate offense, although the underlying scheme is the event of concern for purposes of the criminal law.   In some instances, the prosecutor will proliferate counts in the hope that, at a minimum, he will force a jury compromise.   Does this kind of conduct exceed the prosecutor's power to initiate case?   In United States v. Olson, 504 F.2d 1222 (9th Cir. 1974), the court held that the district court was powerless to require the United States Attorney to elect which valid count of a multi-count indictment the government would try, and upon failure to elect, to dismiss any of the valid counts in the indictment.   Do multi-count indictments of this nature represent sound prosecutorial policy?   Are there other remedies available to the court to restrict this kind of practice?

4.   When criminal conduct is prohibited by two separate statutes, must the prosecution proceed on the one that carries the lesser penalty?   In United States v. Batchelder, 442 U.S. 114, 99 S.Ct. 2198 (1979), the Court held that, in the absence of discrimination against a class of individuals, the prosecutor is free to elect the more severe of two overlapping statutes in bringing an indictment.

B.   RESTRICTIONS UPON DISCRETION

UNITED STATES v. FALK

United States Court of Appeals, Seventh Circuit, 1973.
479 F.2d 616.

Before SWYGERT, CHIEF JUDGE, HASTINGS, SENIOR CIRCUIT JUDGE, KILEY, FAIRCHILD, CUMMINGS, PELL, and SPRECHER, CIRCUIT JUDGES.

SPRECHER, CIRCUIT JUDGE.   This appeal reheard *en banc* requires us to focus closely upon the dividing line between presumptive regularity in the enforcement of penal laws and impermissible prosecutorial selectivity.

Jeffrey Falk was charged in a four-count indictment with refusing to submit to induction into the Armed Forces and with failure to possess a registration card or his 1968 and 1969 I–A classification cards, all in violation of 50 U.S.C.App. § 462. The defendant filed a pretrial motion to dismiss those counts of the indictment charging him with failure to possess the proper cards on the ground that the prosecution sought the indictment for the improper purpose of chilling the exercise of rights guaranteed by the First Amendment and to punish him for participation in a draft counseling organization. The trial judge denied the motion without holding an evidentiary hearing. At trial, an offer of proof based on the same contention was similarly rejected. A jury found Falk guilty on all four counts, but the district court granted a post-trial motion for acquittal on count one on the ground that there had been no basis in fact for denying Falk classification as a conscientious objector. He received three consecutive one year sentences on the card-carrying counts.

On appeal, a panel of this court affirmed Falk's conviction, one judge dissenting. A petition for rehearing *en banc* was granted, in which the principal issue was the alleged discriminatory prosecutorial purpose in seeking the indictment. We have concluded that Falk is entitled to a hearing on his charge of an improper purpose. We accordingly reverse.

The Fourteenth Amendment prohibits any state from taking action which would "deny to any person within its jurisdiction the equal protection of the laws." This admonition is applicable to the federal government through the Fifth Amendment. The promise of equal protection of the laws is not limited to the enactment of fair and impartial legislation, but necessarily extends to the application of these laws. The basic principle was stated long ago in Yick Wo v. Hopkins, 118 U.S. 356, 373–74 (1886) :

> "Though the law itself be fair on its face and impartial in appearance, yet, if it is applied and administered by public authority with an evil eye and an unequal hand, so as practically to make unjust and illegal discriminations between persons in similar circumstances, material to their rights, the denial of equal justice is still within the prohibition of the Constitution."

The city ordinance for which violation Yick Wo was convicted made it unlawful for any person to maintain a laundry in the city of San Francisco without first obtaining the permission of the board of supervisors unless the laundry were located in a building constructed of brick or stone. Although the statute was, on its face, a fair and reasonable exercise of the police power, the facts showed that principally Chinese were refused permission to continue using wooden facilities. The Supreme Court held that criminal enforcement of the law was therefore illegal.

Yick Wo was concerned with an abuse of discretion in the administration of a public ordinance by a city licensing board, and not with the activities of law enforcement officials who presumably prosecuted all Chinese who violated the commands of the licensing board. The underlying principle has nevertheless been properly held to apply to the actions of prosecutors and police officials.

Despite the seemingly undeniable application of *Yick Wo* to discriminatory prosecutions, [1] two questions have troubled various courts and appear to be the source of the disagreement between the majority and dissenters on this court. The first of these arises from the decision in Oyler v. Boles, 368 U.S. 448, 456 (1962), in which the Court noted that the "conscious exercise of some selectivity in enforcement is not in itself a federal constitutional violation," and went on to state that since it had not been alleged "that the selection was deliberately based upon an unjustifiable standard such as race, religion, or other arbitrary classification" there were no grounds to support a finding that the equal protection clause had been violated. From this it is argued that a person attempting to defend against the discriminatory enforcement of a law must show that he is a member of a class against which the law is being selectively enforced. . . . [We conclude that] *Oyler* does not preclude the granting of relief against intentional or purposeful discrimination against an individual. No intentional discrimination against the petitioner as an individual was alleged by Oyler and he merely attempted to show, by statistical evidence, that fewer than all multiple offenders were given heavier sentences. In the present case intentional discrimination is alleged.

Falk's allegations indicate that he was singled out for selective and discriminatory treatment on the basis of activities which form an unjustifiable standard for selectivity in prosecution. Falk was an active member of a draft counseling organization known as the Chicago Area Draft Resisters. In his pretrial motion and again in his offer of proof he asserted that the prosecution against him for violation of the card-carrying requirements was brought not because he had violated the statute but to punish him for and stifle his and others' participation in protected First Amendment activities in opposition to the draft in the war in Vietnam. There can be no doubt but that the expression of views opposing this country's foreign policy with regard to Vietnam is protected by the First Amendment. And, just as discrimination on the basis of religion or race is forbidden by the Constitution, so is discrimination on the basis of the exercise of protected First Amendment activities, whether done as an individual or, as in this case, as a member of a group unpopular with the government.

* * *

The second source of disagreement among some courts and within this court concerns the problem of proof. Certainly, the prospect of government prosecutors being called to the stand by every criminal defendant for cross-examination as to their motives in seeking an in-

---

1. There are decisions which deny the applicability of *Yick Wo* to allegedly discriminatory prosecutions. Those courts denying its applicability (generally in earlier cases) have given various reasons, such as that there is no right to commit a crime, that failure to prosecute all violators should not nullify a valid penal law and that there is a distinction between acts which are *malum prohibitum* and *malum in se.* See Comment, "The Right to Nondiscriminatory Enforcement of State Penal Laws," 61 Colum.L.Rev. 1103, 1106–1107 (1961).

dictment is to be avoided. That does not mean that a criminal defendant is never to be afforded an opportunity to prove that the prosecution stems from an improper prosecutorial design or that he may never question a prosecutor under oath. The presumption is always that a prosecution for violation of a criminal law is undertaken in good faith and in nondiscriminatory fashion for the purpose of fulfilling a duty to bring violators to justice. However, when a defendant alleges intentional, purposeful discrimination and presents facts sufficient to raise a reasonable doubt about the prosecutor's purpose, we think a different question is raised.

Defendant in this case twice attempted to present evidence which would have shown an impermissible prosecutorial purpose. In his pretrial motion for dismissal of those counts of the indictment charging violations of the card possession requirements, the defendant expressed his belief that over 25,000 Selective Service registrants had dispossessed themselves of their draft cards without criminal sanction, and sought an evidentiary hearing at which he would submit evidence in proof of his allegations. In his motion for acquittal at the close of the government's case, Falk again attempted to show that the government was aware of many violations and that others were not being prosecuted. . . .

* * *

The particular circumstances of this case which we believe compelled the government to accept the burden of proving nondiscriminatory enforcement of the law are several. Falk was, as noted earlier, actively involved in advising others on methods of legally avoiding military service and in protesting American actions in Vietnam. Similar circumstances, in which a vocal dissenter appeared to have been singled out for prosecution, led the court in United States v. Steele, [461 F.2d 1148 (9th Cir. (1972)] to hold that "[a]n enforcement procedure that focuses upon the vocal offender is inherently suspect, since it is vulnerable to the charge that those chosen for prosecution are being punished for their expression of ideas, a constitutionally protected right." In the present case there are several indications that this was exactly the purpose of the prosecution. At the close of the trial Falk's attorney asked that the Assistant United States Attorney who tried the case be called as a witness, and offered to prove that the Assistant United States Attorney had told Falk's attorney at a meeting in December, 1970, that he knew of defendant's draft counseling activities, that a good deal of their trouble in enforcing the draft laws came from people such as Falk, that few indictments were brought for non-possession of draft cards, that defendant's draft-counseling activity was one of the reasons why the prosecution for non-possession of draft cards was brought, and that the government would not dismiss the card-carrying counts of the indictment even though Falk agreed to carry the cards in the future. The court refused the offer of proof but did allow the Assistant United States Attorney to make a reply. We think the unsolicited reply is itself some evidence that Falk was singled out for special prosecution.

Apparently in an effort to show that his own participation in the process of deciding to prosecute was inconsequential, the Assistant noted that the indictment against Falk was approved not only by him, but also by the Chief of the Criminal Division of the United States Attorney's Office, the First Assistant United States Attorney, the United States Attorney and the Department of Justice in Washington. It is difficult to believe that the usual course of proceedings in a draft case requires such careful consideration by such a distinguished succession of officials prior to a formal decision to prosecute.

The particular circumstances of this case which overcome the initial presumption of legal regularity in enforcement of penal laws also includes the lengthy delay in bringing the indictment. Falk returned his registration card to the Department of Justice on December 4, 1967, mailed his I–A classification notice to Federal District Judge Hubert Will in October, 1968 and sent a later notice of classification to his draft board in May, 1969. The government therefore had notice of his violations of the regulations from December, 1967. Yet the indictment charging violations of the card possession requirements was not returned until almost three years had passed, in October of 1970, following Falk's refusal to submit to induction in May of that year. Some explanation for the delay in prosecution for the earlier offenses may be found in a statement of policy by the Director of the Selective Service System:

> "Selective Service Regulations are designed to delay the prosecution of a violator of the law until after he has failed to report for or refused to submit to induction or assigned civilian work. This is to prevent, wherever possible, prosecutions for minor infractions of rules during his selective service processing, thereby reducing the number of cases that reach the courts and also giving the registrant, before being prosecuted, an opportunity to report for service in the armed forces. Since the purpose of the law is to provide men for the military establishment rather than for the penitentiaries, *it would seem that when a registrant is willing to be inducted, he should not be prosecuted for minor offenses committed during his processing.* The result of this procedure is that the great majority of prosecutions involve the failure to report for or refusal to submit to induction or assigned civilian work." *Legal Aspects of Selective Service, supra,* 46–47. (Emphasis added.)

Although this statement would seem to provide a valid, and even in some cases benevolent, explanation for a delay of up to three years in bringing the indictment, it also adds forceful weight to defendant's contention that the prosecution in this case was for the purpose of punishing Falk for his exercise of First Amendment rights. According to this statement, it is government policy to prosecute only a portion of those who commit "minor infractions of rules;" whether a violator is one of those prosecuted depends upon whether he accepts or refuses induction. We may assume, at least for purposes of this case, that a general decision to prosecute those who refuse induction on grounds which will support a conviction to the exclusion of those who agree to cooperate with the Selective Service in the future is within the prosecutor's discretion.   The problem in this case, however, is that Falk was found to have been justified in refusing induction in that he was entitled to classification as a conscientious objector.   The result is that he faces three years' imprisonment because his local draft board arbitrarily and without grounds to so act refused his claim as a conscientious objector and he was forced to refuse induction in order to assert a valid claim, thereby also incurring prosecution for prior "minor infractions."   The conclusion would seem to be compelling that, in the admitted policy of the Selective Service officials and apart from whether Falk's draft counseling activities were involved in the decision to prosecute, he was indicted and prosecuted for violation of the card possession requirements only because he exercised his First Amendment privilege to claim a statutory right as a conscientious objector.   But "[i]t is clearly unconstitutional to enable a public official to determine which expressions of view will be permitted and which will not or to engage in invidious discrimination among persons or groups .   .   .   by selective enforcement of an extremely broad prohibitory statute."

Punishment of Falk, however valid otherwise, only because he chose to assert his right as a conscientious objector, is very similar to the conduct of city officials who reinstated criminal charges for alleged traffic violations following the defendant's action in filing an official complaint charging police misconduct in Dixon v. District of Columbia, 394 F.2d 966, 968 (D.C.Cir. 1968).   Chief Judge Bazelon, in reversing the defendant's conviction on those charges, stated:

> "The Government may not prosecute for the purpose of deterring people from exercising their right to protest official misconduct and petition for redress of grievances.   Moreover, a prosecution under such circumstances would be barred by the equal protection clause, since the Government employs an impermissible classification when it punishes those who complain against police misconduct and excuses those who do not."

Similarly, the government is not free to punish those who refuse to acquiesce in a local draft board's irrational refusal to give a conscientious objector his proper classification while it excuses those who, however much their decision may conflict with moral principles, agree to submit to induction.

To summarize, the combination in this case of the published government policy not to prosecute violators of the card possession regulations, Falk's status as an active and vocal dissenter to United States policy with regard to the draft and the Vietnam War, the Assistant United States Attorney's statement that officials ranging from an Assistant Attorney to the Department of Justice in Washington participated in the decision to prosecute Falk, the untimely delay in bringing the indictment and the government's stated policy to prosecute only those who refuse induction while absolving those who submit to the will of the authorities, lead us to conclude that the district court erred in refusing a hearing on the offer of proof. The unrebutted evidence before the court, including the admission of the Assistant United States Attorney and the two published statements by the Selective Service officials which contradict the propriety of the action taken in this case, made out at least a *prima facie* case of improper discrimination in enforcing the law. We will therefore remand the case, to a different judge, for a hearing at which time Falk may question the Assistant United States Attorney as to the content of his previous statements to defendant's counsel [2] and present any additional evidence he wishes on the issue of other alleged violators and the government's lack of general enforcement. In accordance with our holding that a *prima facie* case has already been presented, . . . however, the burden of going forward with proof of nondiscrimination will then rest on the government. Particularly with regard to the seemingly inherent discrimination against Falk in prosecuting him for insisting on his claim as a conscientious objector, we think the government will be required to present compelling evidence to the contrary if its burden is to be met. If the district court finds that the prosecution was not the result of a purpose to punish Falk for exercising First Amendment rights as a draft counselor and Vietnam protestor and is also satisfied that the government has not made an invidious discrimination between violators who acquiesce to the power of the Selective Service System and those who continue to assert their rights to be classified as conscientious objectors, the conviction will stand. If the court finds that Falk would not have been prosecuted for violation of the card possession requirements except for his assertion of a conscientious objector claim or his draft counseling and lawful protest activities, the indictment must be dismissed.

* * *

Judgment of conviction vacated and cause remanded.

[The concurring opinion of Judge Fairchild is omitted.]

CUMMINGS, CIRCUIT JUDGE, with whom HASTINGS, SENIOR CIRCUIT JUDGE, and PELL, CIRCUIT JUDGE, join, dissenting.

* * *

The majority holds that on the strength of the allegations in the pre-trial motion to dismiss, defendant was entitled to an evidentiary hearing. If this be so, Senior Judge Campbell's observation that in criminal cases "[w]e now have eight trials to replace the original one!" is outdated. In this Circuit there are now nine! For there are few criminal defendants who will be unable to make assertions as bald and unspecific as defendant's, and naturally there is now incentive to make them. If the magic in defendant's allegations is thought

---

2. . . . [T]his is not a case in which the motives of a prosecuting attorney are being probed. He is simply being asked to relate the content of a prior alleged admission regarding the government's purpose in bringing the prosecution.

to lie in the assertion that defendant exercised his First Amendment rights, it is hard to imagine a criminal who cannot search his past to find that he too has exercised his right of free speech. Since defendant's draft-counseling work took place after his commission of the crimes, a criminal need only speak out after he has broken the law. Perhaps the magic is defendant's alleged espousal of viewpoints unpopular with the incumbent Administration. Thus if they have not already done so, criminals would be well advised to criticize some policy of the Government which may indict them. Finally, the mere assertion that over 25,000 violators were not indicted lends no support whatever to an allegation of invidiously discriminatory prosecutorial selectivity, as will be demonstrated below. Any defendant could make a comparably meaningless allegation by stating that during some unspecified period of time he believed that, in absolute terms, an apparently large number of violators, not stated to be similarly situated, were not prosecuted.

I.

Defendant alleged both that he believed over 25,000 Selective Service registrants had dispossessed themselves of their draft cards and had not been indicted and that his indictment had been brought for the purpose of punishing him for and chilling him in the exercise of the First Amendment rights. He claims that these allegations would support an unequal protection finding and that without more he is entitled to a hearing on his claim. The difficulty with this contention is obvious. If defendant were to prove exactly what he alleged concerning over 25,000 other registrants, he would not demonstrate anything of probative value to show that a line has been drawn between those who exercised their First Amendment rights and those who did not.

* * *

If the class of persons not prosecuted was not situated similarly to defendant   .   .   ., his equal protection violation claim must fail. Likewise if the class of persons not prosecuted was situated similarly to defendant but also voiced opposition to the war and the draft, etc., any claim that defendant was comparatively disadvantaged on the basis of his engagement in protected First Amendment activities would be unsustainable. Without these crucial allegations defendant's claim at best is that he was prosecuted for a crime which was routinely handled administratively until ten months prior to his indictment because he possessed a certain characteristic and that a large number of men (who may or may not have possessed that characteristic) were not prosecuted at some unspecified time in the past. If this unspecific and misleading allegation deserved a hearing to determine whether a defendant's prosecution violated equal protection, then it is inescapable that practically any defendant can precipitate such a hearing.

Perhaps this result would be tolerable if defendant were required at the outset to show that the 25,000 persons were different from him only in respect to the alleged impermissible selection factor. But it is apparent that defendant never intended to establish that the effect of the Government's prosecutive policy was to prosecute a card-dispossessing registrant only if he vocally opposed governmental war policy, and the majority does not require him to do so. Rather, defendant wants, and now receives, a hearing to determine whether in his particular case the decision to prosecute was made for an invidious purpose—to punish him for and chill him in the exercise of his First Amendment rights. Let there be no mistake about this: the hearing is to determine the actual motive of the Government attorneys responsible for defendant's indictment principally through their own testimony.

* * *

The common thread running through [decisions on which the majority relies] was an allegation and a showing that the effect of the administrative or prosecutive policy was a division between persons otherwise similarly situated according to whether or not they possessed a certain characteristic. But again, defendant never alleged or offered to prove, or at any time during the course of these proceedings took the position that those registrants who turned in their draft cards and were not prosecuted were similarly situated to defendant except that they had not engaged in protected First Amendment activities. Unless the impact or effect of challenged governmental action is actually to discriminate between persons or classes according to an impermissible basis of selection, no denial of equal protection can be made out. Thus although defendant contends his prosecution violated equal protection, his claim lacks the essential stuff of an equal protection violation.

Defendant's case, then, comes to this: without making any effort to establish that the effect of the Government's prosecution is to differentiate between him and others on an impermissible basis, he would have a court inquire into the actual motivation behind the Government's indictment and rule his prosecution unconstitutional solely on the basis of a wrongful prosecutorial purpose. But the "purpose" of the executive, as Falk uses the term, is not a basis for declaring this otherwise valid prosecution unconstitutional.

* * *

. . . In the case at bar, Falk's indictment was drafted by someone in the United States Attorney's Office in Chicago, approved by the Chief of its Criminal Division, by the First Assistant United States Attorney, by the United States Attorney, and by the Department of Justice in Washington. Whose motivation is supposed to be decisive of the Government's purpose in prosecuting Falk? And doubtless any evil purpose will be coincident with a purpose to enforce the law. Indeed, in his offer of proof defense counsel stated he expected an Assistant United States Attorney to testify that "one of the reasons" defendant was prosecuted was his draft-counseling activities. As explained later, I do not believe that to be an impermissible reason, but if a court feels otherwise, is it to engage in the guesswork of trying to determine the "dominant" purpose? . . . Unless a judge has made an indefensible *a priori* determination, this type of judicial inquiry must only lead to an assumption. And it is simply not the function of the judiciary within our constitutional scheme to void otherwise valid governmental acts solely on the basis of such an assumption.

* * *

II.

* * *

But putting to one side these basic infirmities of the majority's unprecedented approach, if indeed Falk's draft counseling activity was one of the reasons why the prosecution was brought, that is hardly an impermissible reason for prosecution. Quite the contrary. As stated in the panel decision, "select enforcement of a law against someone in a position to influence others is unquestionably a legitimate prosecutorial scheme to secure general compliance with the law." Nowhere does the majority choose to dispute that proposition. Instead it quotes from United States v. Steele, 461 F.2d 1148, 1152 (9th Cir. 1972), to the effect that "[a]n enforcement procedure that focuses upon the vocal offender is inherently suspect, since it is vulnerable to the charge that those chosen for prosecution are being punished for their expression of ideas, a constitutionally protected right." As a general proposition, and certainly under the circumstances of this case, I cannot subscribe to that view. Though such a procedure may be vulnerable to that charge, at least in cases such as this, where it is ridiculous to expect prosecution of all violators, it is likewise consistent with the sensible enforcement scheme of securing general compliance through prosecution of those who defiantly violate the law in the public eye. It is well within the realm of prosecutorial discretion to take into account the personal characteristics of the defendant, and among those his visibility and influence over others may quite properly weigh heavily in the decision whether to prosecute.

* * *

Certainly no one would expect Federal prosecutors to expend their limited resources on indicting and trying all Selective Service registrants who have violated the card possession requirements. In the fall of 1970, when Falk was indicted, recourse to the usual administrative procedure for dealing with draft card delinquencies was no longer open, and prosecution was the only means available for enforcing the regulations. That the United States Attorney's Office would want carefully to consider proposals for indicting registrants in order to insure that the prosecutions had sufficient potential for effecting deterrence and securing general compliance to justify the expenditure of limited resources is a reasonable approach indeed. And, as I have said before, unquestionably it is a sound enforcement technique to prosecute the notorious violator or counselor, to whom others look, in order to deter would-be violators and promote general compliance. Furthermore, if all violators cannot be prosecuted, the United States

Attorney's Office has an interest in carefully reviewing proposals to prosecute in order to insure decisional uniformity as a matter of fairness to the registrants.

The Justice Department, at a time when a large prosecutorial responsibility had just been created as a result of Supreme Court decisions, must have had similar concerns in obtaining maximum enforcement without needless expenditure of resources better spent elsewhere, if possible, and also in insuring a nationwide uniformity among the various United States Attorneys' Offices' decisions to prosecute these violators. Consequently, if the multi-leveled approval procedure was used in Falk's case, it is beside the point that it is not the usual course of proceedings in the universe of all draft cases, and it hardly follows that defendant was singled out according to an impermissible selection factor. Finally, the multi-leveled approval procedure is inconsistent with any governmental purpose to punish defendant for being a draft counselor and opposing the war unless one is willing to assume that even the Justice Department was so petty as to approve the indictment out of a small-minded animus against one Jeffrey Stuart Falk. I would view the several approvals involved here as a prophylactic against arbitrariness on the part of a low level prosecutor as well as against non-uniform treatment and wastefulness.

* * *

To summarize, the principal points of my disagreement with the majority are as follows: First, the bare-boned and conclusionary allegations in defendant's motion to dismiss did not deserve a hearing. Second, defendant's allegations were facially insufficient to sustain a claim that he was denied equal protection of the laws. Third, the "purpose" of his prosecution, as defendant uses the term, is not a basis for declaring that prosecution unconstitutional. Fourth, it is not permissible for a defendant to call a prosecuting attorney for the United States or his superiors to the witness stand for interrogation as to the Government's motive for prosecuting him. Fifth, assuming the propriety of the majority's approach and the truth of everything defendant alleged and offered to prove, defendant did not make out a *prima facie* case that his prosecution was impermissibly brought, much less that he was denied equal protection.

Finally, I could hardly take issue with the proposition that "[t]he judiciary has always borne the basic responsibility for protecting individuals against unconstitutional invasions of their rights by all branches of the Government." Stamler v. Willis, 415 F.2d 1365, 1369–1370 (7th Cir. 1969), certiorari denied 399 U.S. 929. However, the judiciary can only exercise that responsibility within the confines of its institutional competence in our constitutional system. Even if it is conceded that the executive acted lawlessly in prosecuting the defendant out of an evil animus, this Court likewise acts lawlessly when it undertakes to right a wrong it has no competence to right. Unless the Court suggests that its purposes or motives may be inquired into and their nobility balanced against the baseness of the executive's, I fail to see how the Court's action can be any less lawless than the executive's. As noted previously, the Supreme Court stated in McCray v. United States, 195 U.S. 27, 55:

> "It is, of course, true, as suggested, that if there be no authority in the judiciary to restrain a lawful exercise of power by another department of the government, where a wrong motive or purpose has impelled to the exertion of the power, that abuses of a power conferred may be temporarily effectual. The remedy for this, however, lies not in the abuse by the judiciary of its functions, but in the people, upon whom, after all, under our institutions, reliance must be placed for the correction of abuses committed in the exercise of a lawful power."

I respectfully dissent.

PELL, CIRCUIT JUDGE, dissenting. [Opinion omitted.]

NOTES

1. On remand in *Falk*, with the cooperation of the district judge, the parties struck a compromise which reduced the defendant's sentence to probation and avoided an evidentiary hearing on the selective-prosecution claim. What, if anything, does this disposition say about the issues in *Falk*. Was such a compromise a just result?

2. While the *Falk* decision did not articulate extensive procedures for dealing with discriminatory-prosecution motions, subsequent federal decisions have addressed these issues.

A mere allegation of selective prosecution does not require the government to disclose the contents of its files. United States v. Cammisano, 546 F.2d 238, 241 (8th Cir. 1976); State v. Mitchell, 164 N.J.Super. 198, 395 A. 2d 1257 (1978). Rather, the defendant must produce "some evidence tending to show the existence of the essential elements of the defense and that the documents in the government's possession would indeed be probative of these elements." United States v. Berrios, 501 F.2d 1207, 1211–12 (2d Cir. 1974).

A hearing is required only when the motion alleges facts (United States v. Erne, 576 F.2d 212 (9th Cir. 1978); United States v. Oaks, 508 F.2d 1403, 1404 (9th Cir. 1974)), and raises a reasonable doubt as to the prosecutor's purpose. United States v. Peskin, 527 F.2d 71, 86 (7th Cir. 1975). In the absence of such a showing, the criminal prosecution is presumed to have been undertaken in good faith. United States v. Ojala, 544 F.2d 940, 943 (8th Cir. 1976).

To establish a prima facie discriminatory prosecution case, a defendant must demonstrate "intentional and purposeful discrimination." That is accomplished only upon a showing that (1) he has been singled out for prosecution while others similarly situated have not been prosecuted for conduct similar to that for which he was prosecuted; and (2) the government's discriminatory selection of him for prosecution was based upon an impermissible ground, such as race, religion or his exercise of his first amendment right to free speech. United States v. Swanson, 509 F.2d 1205, 1208–09 (8th Cir. 1975).

3. As indicated, discriminatory prosecution motions may be based upon race, religion, and the exercise of first amendment rights. Does the motion also lie for allegations of discrimination based upon sex? See City of Minneapolis v. Buschette, 307 Minn. 60, 240 N.W.2d 500 (1976), regarding the issue created by the larger number of arrests and prosecutions of females than males on charges of prostitution. The court held that this fact alone did not amount to discriminatory enforcement.

Chapter 9

THE RIGHTS OF INDIGENTS IN FORMAL CRIMINAL PROCEEDINGS

A. APPELLATE ASSISTANCE: THE EQUAL PROTECTION AND DUE PROCESS APPROACHES

At various stages of formal criminal proceedings, the accused who lacks financial resources could be disadvantaged in litigating against the prosecutor, who draws upon the resources of government. By comparison to a person of wealth, an indigent defendant, caught up in the criminal process, could have the odds stacked against him unless government were to minimize some of the consequences which flow from a disparity of wealth.

Various legal theories have been invoked to lessen the economic-based inequities within the criminal justice system. They include the right to counsel under the sixth amendment, the due process clauses of the fifth and the fourteenth amendments, and the equal protection clause of the fourteenth amendment.

In our treatment of the rights of indigents within the criminal justice system we begin by considering the rights of the indigent on appeal. If this appears strange, it can be explained by the fact that the Supreme Court's first broad-sweeping pronouncements about indigents in the formal criminal process came in a decision which treated a claim that an indigent had a right to a free transcript to assist in an appeal of his felony conviction. Griffin v. Illinois, infra. Even today it is arguable that an indigent's right to counsel in certain minor criminal cases is broader on appeal than at trial, as the materials which follow may suggest.

GRIFFIN v. ILLINOIS

Supreme Court of the United States, 1956.
351 U.S. 12, 76 S.Ct. 585.

MR. JUSTICE BLACK announced the judgment of the Court and an opinion in which THE CHIEF JUSTICE, MR. JUSTICE DOUGLAS, and MR. JUSTICE CLARK, join.

Illinois law provides that "Writs of error in all criminal cases are writs of right and shall be issued of course." The question presented here is whether Illinois may, consistent with the Due Process and Equal Protection Clauses of the Fourteenth Amendment, administer this statute so as to deny adequate appellate review to the poor while granting such review to all others.

The petitioners Griffin and Crenshaw were tried together and convicted of armed robbery in the Criminal Court of Cook County, Illinois. Immediately after their conviction they filed a motion in the trial court asking that a certified copy of the entire record, including a stenographic transcript of the proceedings, be furnished them without cost. They alleged that they were "poor persons with no means of paying the necessary fees to acquire the Transcript and Court Records needed to prosecute an appeal . . . ." These allegations were not denied. Under Illinois law in order to get full direct appellate review of alleged errors by a writ of error it is necessary for the defendant to furnish the appellate court with a bill of exceptions or report of proceedings at the trial certified by the trial judge.[1] As Illinois concedes, it is sometimes impossible to prepare such bills of exceptions [2] or reports without a stenographic transcript of the trial proceedings.[3] Indigent defendants sentenced to death are provided with a free transcript at the expense of the county where convicted. In all other criminal cases defendants needing a transcript, whether indigent or not, must themselves buy it. The petitioners contended in their motion before the trial court that failure to provide them with the needed transcript would violate the Due Process and Equal Protection Clauses of the Fourteenth Amendment. The trial court denied the motion without a hearing.

Griffin and Crenshaw then filed a petition under the Illinois Post-Conviction Hearing Act. Only questions arising under the Illinois or Federal Constitution may be raised in proceedings under this Act. A companion state act provides that indigent petitioners under the Post-Conviction Act may, under some circumstances, obtain a free transcript. The effect is that indigents may obtain a free transcript

---

1. Ill.Rev.Stat., 1953, c. 110, § 259.70A (Supreme Court Rule 70A), now Ill. Rev.Stat., 1955, c. 110, § 101.65 (Supreme Court Rule 65). A writ of error may also be prosecuted on a "mandatory record" kept by the clerk, consisting of the indictment, arraignment, plea, verdict and sentence. The "mandatory record" can be obtained free of charge by an indigent defendant. In such instances review is limited to errors on the face of the mandatory record, and there is no review of trial errors such as an erroneous ruling on the admission of evidence. See People v. Loftus, 400 Ill. 432, 81 N.E.2d 495. See also Cullen v. Stevens, 389 Ill. 35, 58 N.E.2d 456; A Study of the Illinois Supreme Court, 15 U. of Chi.L.Rev. 107, 125.

2. "A complete bill of exceptions consists of all proceedings in the case from the time of the convening of the court until the termination of the trial. It includes all of the motions and rulings of the trial court, evidence heard, instructions and other matters which do not come within the clerk's mandatory record." Peo-

ple ex rel. Iasello v. McKinlay, 409 Ill. 120, 124–125, 98 N.E.2d 728, 730.

3. In oral argument counsel for Illinois stated:

    "With respect to the so-called bystanders' bill of exceptions or the bill of exceptions prepared from someone's memory in condensed and narrative form and certified to by the trial judge—as to whether that's available in Illinois I can say that everybody out there understands that it is but nobody has heard of its ever being actually used in a criminal case in Illinois in recent years. I think if you went back before the days of court reporting you would find them but none today. And I will say that Illinois has not suggested in the brief that such a narrative transcript would necessarily or even generally be the equivalent of a verbatim transcript of all of the trial.

    * * *

    "There isn't any way that an Illinois convicted person in a noncapital case can obtain a bill of exceptions without paying for it."

to obtain appellate review of constitutional questions but not of other alleged trial errors such as admissibility and sufficiency of evidence. In their Post-Conviction proceeding petitioners alleged that there were manifest nonconstitutional errors in the trial which entitled them to have their convictions set aside on appeal and that the only impediment to full appellate review was their lack of funds to buy a transcript. These allegations have not been denied. Petitioners repeated their charge that refusal to afford full appellate review solely because of poverty was a denial of due process and equal protection. This petition like the first was dismissed without hearing any evidence. The Illinois Supreme Court affirmed the dismissal solely on the ground that the charges raised no substantial state or federal constitutional questions—the only kind of questions which may be raised in Post-Conviction proceedings.

Counsel for Illinois concedes that these petitioners needed a transcript in order to get adequate appellate review of their alleged trial errors. There is no contention that petitioners were dilatory in their efforts to get appellate review, or that the Illinois Supreme Court denied review on the ground that the allegations of trial error were insufficient. We must therefore assume for purposes of this decision that errors were committed in the trial which would merit reversal, but that the petitioners could not get appellate review of those errors solely because they were too poor to buy a stenographic transcript. Counsel for Illinois denies that this violates either the Due Process or the Equal Protection Clause, but states that if it does, the Illinois Post-Conviction statute entitles petitioners to a free transcript. The sole question for us to decide, therefore, is whether due process or equal protection has been violated.

Providing equal justice for poor and rich, weak and powerful alike is an age-old problem. People have never ceased to hope and strive to move closer to that goal. This hope, at least in part, brought about in 1215 the royal concessions of Magna Charta: "To no one will we sell, to no one will we refuse, or delay, right or justice. . . . No free man shall be taken or imprisoned, or disseised, or outlawed, or exiled, or any wise destroyed; nor shall we go upon him nor send upon him, but by the lawful judgment of his peers or by the law of the land." These pledges were unquestionably steps toward a fairer and more nearly equal application of criminal justice. In this tradition, our own constitutional guaranties of due process and equal protection both call for procedures in criminal trials which allow no invidious discriminations between persons and different groups of persons. Both equal protection and due process emphasize the central aim of our entire judicial system—all people charged with crime must, so far as the law is concerned, "stand on an equality before the bar of justice in every American court."

Surely no one would contend that either a State or the Federal Government could constitutionally provide that defendants unable to pay court costs in advance should be denied the right to plead not guilty or to defend themselves in court. Such a law would make the constitutional promise of a fair trial a worthless thing. Notice, the right to be heard, and the right to counsel would under such circumstances be meaningless promises to the poor. In criminal trials a State can no more discriminate on account of poverty than on account of religion, race, or color. Plainly the ability to pay costs in advance bears no rational relationship to a defendant's guilt or innocence and could not be used as an excuse to deprive a defendant of a fair trial. Indeed, a provision in the Constitution of Illinois of 1818 provided that every person in Illinois "ought to obtain right and justice freely, and without being obliged to purchase it, completely and without denial, promptly and without delay, conformably to the laws."

There is no meaningful distinction between a rule which would deny the poor the right to defend themselves in a trial court and one which effectively denies the poor an adequate appellate review accorded to all who have money enough to pay the costs in advance. It is true that a State is not required by the Federal Constitution to provide appellate courts or a right to appellate review at all. But that is not to say that a State that does grant appellate review can do so in a way that discriminates against some convicted defendants on account of their poverty. Appellate review has now become an integral part of the Illinois trial system for finally adjudicating the guilt or innocence of a defendant. Consequently at all stages of the proceedings the Due Process and Equal Protection Clauses protect persons like petitioners from invidious discriminations.

All of the States now provide some method of appeal from criminal convictions, recognizing the importance of appellate review to a correct adjudication of guilt or innocence. Statistics show that a substantial proportion of criminal convictions are reversed by state appellate courts. Thus to deny adequate review to the poor means that many of them may lose their life, liberty or property because of unjust convictions which appellate courts would set aside. Many States have recognized this and provided aid for convicted defendants who have a right to appeal and need a transcript but are unable to pay for it. A few have not. Such a denial is a misfit in a country dedicated to affording equal justice to all and special privileges to none in the administration of its criminal law. There can be no equal justice where the kind of trial a man gets depends on the amount of money he has. Destitute defendants must be afforded as adequate appellate review as defendants who have money enough to buy transcripts.

The Illinois Supreme Court denied these petitioners relief under the Post-Conviction Act because of its holding that no constitutional rights were violated. In view of our holding to the contrary the State Supreme Court may decide that petitioners are now entitled to a transcript, as the State's brief suggests. We do not hold, however, that Illinois must purchase a stenographer's transcript in every case where a defendant cannot buy it. The Supreme Court may find other means of affording adequate and effective appellate review to indigent defendants. For example, it may be that bystanders' bills of exceptions or other methods of reporting trial proceedings could be used in some cases. The Illinois Supreme Court appears to have broad power to promulgate rules of procedure and appellate practice. We are confident that the State will provide corrective rules to meet the problem which this case lays bare.

The judgment of the Supreme Court of Illinois is vacated and the cause is remanded to that court for further action not inconsistent with the foregoing paragraph. Mr. Justice Frankfurter joins in this disposition of the case.

Vacated and remanded.

MR. JUSTICE FRANKFURTER, concurring in the judgment.

The admonition of de Tocqueville not to confuse the familiar with the necessary has vivid application to appeals in criminal cases. The right to an appeal from a conviction for crime is today so established that this leads to the easy assumption that it is fundamental to the protection of life and liberty and therefore a necessary ingredient of due process of law. "Due process" is, perhaps, the least frozen concept of our law—the least confined to history and the most absorptive of powerful social standards of a progressive society. But neither the unfolding content of "due process" nor the particularized safeguards of the Bill of Rights disregard procedural ways that reflect a national historic policy. It is significant that no appeals from convictions in the federal courts were afforded (with roundabout exceptions negligible for present purposes) for nearly a hundred years; and, despite the civilized standards of criminal justice in modern England, there was no appeal from convictions (again with exceptions not now pertinent) until 1907. Thus, it is now settled that due process of law does not require a State to afford review of criminal judgments.

Nor does the equal protection of the laws deny a State the right to make classifications in law when such classifications are rooted in reason.

* * *

But neither the fact that a State may deny the right of appeal altogether nor the right of a State to make an appropriate classification, based on differences in crimes and their punishment, nor the right of a State to lay down conditions it deems appropriate for criminal appeals, sanctions differentiations by a State that have no relation to a rational policy of criminal appeal or authorizes the imposition of conditions that offend the deepest presuppositions of our society. Surely it would not need argument to conclude that a State could not, within its wide scope of discretion in these matters, allow an appeal for persons convicted of crimes punishable by imprisonment of a year or more, only on payment of a fee of $500. Illinois, of course, has done nothing so crude as that. But Illinois has said, in effect, that the Supreme Court of Illinois can consider alleged errors occurring in a criminal trial only if the basis for determining whether there were errors is brought before it by a bill of exceptions and not otherwise. From this it follows that Illinois has decreed that only defendants who can afford to pay for the stenographic minutes of a trial may have trial errors reviewed on appeal by the Illinois Supreme Court. It has thereby shut off means of appellate review for indigent defendants.

This Court would have to be willfully blind not to know that there have in the past been prejudicial trial errors which called for reversal of convictions of indigent defendants, and that the number of those who have not had the means for paying for the cost of a bill of exceptions is not so negligible as to invoke whatever truth there may be in the maxim *de minimis*.

Law addresses itself to actualities. It does not face actuality to suggest that Illinois affords every convicted person, financially competent or not, the opportunity to take an appeal, and that it is not Illinois that is responsible for disparity in material circumstances. Of course a State need not equalize economic conditions. A man of means may be able to afford the retention of an expensive, able counsel not within reach of a poor man's purse. Those are contingencies of life which are hardly within the power, let alone the duty, of a State to correct or cushion. But when a State deems it wise and just that convictions be susceptible to review by an appellate court, it cannot by force of its exactions draw a line which precludes convicted indigent persons, forsooth erroneously convicted, from securing such a review merely by disabling them from bringing to the notice of an appellate tribunal errors of the trial court which would upset the conviction were practical opportunity for review not foreclosed.

To sanction such a ruthless consequence, inevitably resulting from a money hurdle erected by a State, would justify a latter-day Anatole France to add one more item to his ironic comments on the "majestic equality" of the law. "The law, in its majestic equality, forbids the rich as well as the poor to sleep under bridges, to beg in the streets, and to steal bread." John Cournos, A Modern Plutarch, p. 27.

The State is not free to produce such a squalid discrimination. If it has a general policy of allowing criminal appeals, it cannot make lack of means an effective bar to the exercise of this opportunity. The State cannot keep the word of promise to the ear of those illegally convicted and break it to their hope. But in order to avoid or minimize abuse and waste, a State may appropriately hedge about the opportunity to prove a conviction wrong. When a State not only gives leave for appellate correction of trial errors but must pay for the cost of its exercise by the indigent, it may protect itself so that frivolous appeals are not subsidized and public moneys not needlessly spent. The growing experience of reforms in appellate procedure and sensible, economic modes for securing review still to be devised, may be drawn upon to the end that the State will neither bolt the door to equal justice nor support a wasteful abuse of the appellate process.

* * *

[JUSTICE FRANKFURTER suggested that the Court's holding be denied retroactive effect as to prisoners whose time for appeal had expired.]

MR. JUSTICE BURTON and MR. JUSTICE MINTON, whom MR. JUSTICE REED and MR. JUSTICE HARLAN join, dissenting. [Omitted.]

MR. JUSTICE HARLAN, dissenting.

* * *

The record contains nothing more definite than the allegation that "petitioners are poor persons with no means of paying the necessary fees to acquire the Transcript and Court Records needed to prosecute an appeal from their convictions." For my part I cannot tell whether petitioners' claim is that a transcript was "needed" because (a) under Illinois *law* a transcript is a prerequisite to appellate review of trial errors, or (b) as a *factual* matter petitioners could not prepare an adequate bill of exceptions short of having a transcript.

If the claim is that a transcript was *legally* necessary, it is based on an erroneous view of Illinois law. The Illinois cases cited by the petitioners establish only that trial errors cannot be reviewed in the absence of a bill of exceptions, and not that a transcript is essential to the preparation of such a bill. To the contrary, an unbroken line of Illinois cases establishes that a bill of exceptions may consist simply of a narrative account of the trial proceedings prepared from any available sources—for example, from the notes or memory of the trial judge, counsel, the defendant, or bystanders—and that the trial judge must either certify such a bill as accurate or point out the corrections to be made. Viewed in the light of these cases, the only constitutional question presented by petitioners' bare allegation that they were unable to purchase a transcript would be: Is an indigent defendant, who has not shown that he is unable to obtain full appellate review of his conviction by a narrative bill of exceptions, constitutionally entitled to the added advantage of a free transcript of the trial proceedings for use as a bill of exceptions? I need hardly pause to suggest that such a claim would present no substantial constitutional question.

* * *

. . . . The record does not even disclose whether petitioners were incarcerated during the period in which the bill of exceptions had to be filed, or whether they were represented by counsel at the trial. We are left to speculate on the nature of the alleged trial errors and the scope of the bill of exceptions needed to present them. Who can say that if we knew the facts we might not have before us a much narrower constitutional question than the one decided today, or perhaps no such question at all.

* * *

According to petitioners' tabulation, no more than 29 States provide free transcripts as of right to indigents convicted of non-capital crimes. Thus the sweeping constitutional pronouncement made by the Court today will touch the laws of at least 19 States and will create a host of problems affecting the status of an unknown multitude of indigent convicts. A decision having such wide impact should not be made upon a record as obscure as this, especially where there are means ready at hand to have clarified the issue sought to be presented.

However, since I stand alone in my view that the Court should refrain from deciding the broad question urged upon us until the necessity for such a decision becomes manifest, I deem it appropriate also to note my disagreement with the Court's decision of that question. Inasmuch as the Court's decision is not—and on this record cannot be—based on any facts peculiar to this case, I consider that question to be: Is an indigent defendant who "needs" a transcript in order to appeal constitutionally entitled, regardless of the nature of the circumstances producing that need, to have the State either furnish a free transcript or take some other action to assure that he does in fact obtain full appellate review?

Equal Protection. In finding an answer to that question in the Equal Protection Clause, the Court has painted with a broad brush. It is said that a State cannot discriminate between the "rich" and the "poor" in its system of criminal appeals. That statement of course commands support, but it hardly sheds light on the true character of the problem confronting us here. Illinois has not imposed any arbitrary conditions upon the exercise of the right of appeal nor any requirements unnecessary to the effective working of its appellate system. Trial errors cannot be reviewed without an appropriate record of the proceedings below; if a transcript is used, it is surely not unreasonable to require the appellant to bear its cost; and Illinois has not foreclosed any other feasible means of preparing such a record. Nor is this a case where the State's own action has prevented a defendant from appealing. All that Illinois has done is to fail to alleviate the consequences of differences in economic circumstances that exist wholly apart from any state action.

The Court thus holds that, at least in this area of criminal appeals, the Equal Protection Clause imposes on the States an affirmative duty to lift the handicaps flowing from differences in economic circumstances. That holding produces the anomalous result that a constitutional admonition to the States to treat all persons equally means in this instance that Illinois must give to some what it requires others to pay for. Granting that such a classification would be reasonable, it does not follow that a State's failure to make it can be regarded as discrimination. It may as accurately be said that the real issue in this case is not whether Illinois *has* discriminated but whether it has a duty *to* discriminate.

I do not understand the Court to dispute either the necessity for a bill of exceptions or the reasonableness of the general requirement that the trial transcript, if used in its preparation, be paid for by the appealing party. The Court finds in the operation of these requirements, however, an invidious classification between the "rich" and the "poor." But no economic burden attendant upon the exercise of a privilege bears equally upon all, and in other circumstances the resulting differentiation is not treated as an individuous classification by the State, even though discrimination against "indigents" by name would be unconstitutional. Thus, while the exclusion of "indigents" from a free state university would deny them equal protection, requiring the payment of tuition fees surely would not, despite the resulting exclusion of those who could not afford to pay the fees. And if imposing a condition of payment is not the equivalent of a classification by the State in one case, I fail to see why it should be so regarded in another. Thus if requiring defendants in felony cases to pay for a transcript constitutes a discriminatory denial to indigents of the right of appeal available to others, why is it not a similar denial in misdemeanor cases or, for that matter, civil cases?

It is no answer to say that equal protection is not an absolute, and that in other than criminal cases the differentiation is "reasonable." The resulting *classification* would be invidious in all cases, and an invidious classification offends equal protection regardless of the seriousness of the consequences. Hence it must be that the differences are "reasonable" in other cases not because the "classification" is reasonable but simply because it is not unreasonable in those cases for the State to fail to relieve indigents of the economic burden. That is, the issue here is not the typical equal protection question of the reasonableness of a "classification" on the basis of which the State has imposed legal disabilities, but rather the reasonableness of the State's failure to remove natural disabilities. The Court holds that the failure of the State to do so is constitutionally unreasonable in this case although it might not be in others. I submit that the basis for that holding is simply an unarticulated conclusion that it violates "fundamental fairness" for a State which provides for appellate review, and thus apparently considers such review necessary to assure justice, not to see to it that such appeals are in fact available to those it would imprison for serious crimes. That of course is the traditional language of due process and I see no reason to import new substance into the concept of equal protection to dispose of the case, especially when to do so gives rise to the all-too-easy opportunity to ignore the real issue and solve the problem simply by labeling the Illinois practice as invidious "discrimination."

Due Process. Has there been a violation of the Due Process Clause? The majority of the Court concedes that the Fourteenth Amendment does not require the States to provide for any kind of appellate review. Nevertheless, Illinois, in the forefront among the States, established writs of error in criminal cases as early as 1827. In 1887, it provided for offical court reporters, thereby relieving defendants of the burden of hiring reporters in order to obtain a transcript. In 1927, it provided that for indigents sentenced to death "all necessary costs and expenses" incident to a writ of error, including the cost of a transcript, would be paid by the counties. And in 1953, free transcripts were authorized for the presentation of constitutional claims. Thus Illinois has steadily expanded the protection afforded defendants in criminal cases, and in recent years has made substantial strides towards alleviating the natural disadvantages of indigents. Can it be that, while it was not unconstitutional for Illinois to afford no appeals, its steady progress in increasing the safeguards against erroneous convictions has resulted in a constitutional decline?

Of couse the fact that appeals are not constitutionally required does not mean that a State is free of constitutional restraints in establishing the terms upon which appeals will be allowed. It does mean, however, that there is no "right" to an appeal in the same sense that there is a right to a trial. Rather the constitutional right under the Due Process Clause is simply the right not to be denied an appeal for arbitrary or capricious reasons. Nothing of that kind, however, can be found in any of the steps by which Illinois has established its appellate system.

We are all agreed that no objection of substance can be made to the provisions for free transcripts in capital and constitutional cases. The due process challenge must therefore be directed to the basic step of permitting appeals at all without also providing an *in forma pauperis* procedure. But whatever else may be said of Illinois' reluctance to expend public funds in perfecting appeals for indigents, it can hardly be said to be arbitrary. A policy of economy may be unenlightened, but it is certainly not capricious. And that it has never generally been so regarded is evidenced by the fact that our attention has been called to no State in which *in forma pauperis* appeals were established contemporaneously with the right of appeal. I can find nothing in the past decisions of this Court justifying a holding that the Fourteenth Amendment confines the States to a choice between allowing no appeals at all or undertaking to bear the cost of appeals for indigents, which is what the Court in effect now holds.

It is argued finally that, even if it cannot be said to be "arbitrary," the failure of Illinois to provide petitioners with the means of exercising the right of appeal that others are able to exercise is simply so "unfair" as to be a denial of due process. I have some question whether the non-arbitrary denial of a right that the State may withhold altogether could ever be so characterized. In any event, however, to so hold it is not enough that we consider free transcripts for indigents to be a desirable policy or that we would weigh the competing social values in favor of such a policy were it our function to distribute Illinois' public funds among alternative uses. Rather the question is whether some method of assuring that an indigent is able to exercise his right of appeal is "implicit in the concept of ordered liberty," Palko v. Connecticut, 302 U.S. 319, 325, 58 S.Ct. 149, 152, 82 L.Ed. 288, so that the failure of a State so to provide constitutes a "denial of fundamental fairness, shocking to the universal sense of justice," Betts v. Brady, supra [316 U.S. 462, 62 S.Ct. 1256]. Such an equivalence between persons in the means with which to exercise a right of appeal has not, however, traditionally been regarded as an essential of "fundamental fairness," and the reforms extending such aid to indigents have only recently gained widespread acceptance.

Indeed, it was not until an Act of Congress in 1944 that defendants in federal criminal cases became entitled to free transcripts, and to date approximately one-third of the States still have not taken that step. With due regard for the constitutional limitations upon the power of this Court to intervene in State matters, I am unable to bring myself to say that Illinois' failure to furnish free transcripts to indigents in all criminal cases is "shocking to the universal sense of justice."

As I view this case, it contains none of the elements hitherto regarded as essential to justify action by this Court under the Fourteenth Amendment. In truth what we have here is but the failure of Illinois to adopt as promptly as other States a desirable reform in its criminal procedure. Whatever might be said were this a question of procedure in the federal courts, regard for our system of federalism requires that matters such as this be left to the States. However strong may be one's inclination to hasten the day when *in forma pauperis* criminal procedures will be universal among the States, I think it is beyond the province of this Court to tell Illinois that it must provide such procedures.

NOTES

1. At one time some commentators believed that the United States Supreme Court would use the *Griffin* equal protection-due process rationale to alleviate many of the consequences of economic disparity which confront the poor as they go through life. As San Antonio Independent School District v. Rodriguez, 411 U.S. 1, 93 S.Ct. 1278 (1973), indicates, however, the *Griffin* approach has largely been limited to addressing the consequences of poverty insofar as they affect the criminally accused. With one exception, the Court has even permitted civil litigants to be denied *access* to avenues of redress simply because of an inability to pay a filing fee. See United States v. Kras, 409 U.S. 434, 93 S.Ct. 631 (1973) (bankruptcy filing fee); Ortwein v. Schwab, 410 U.S. 656, 93 S.Ct. 1172 (1973) (administrative appeal concerning public assistance rights).

Only in Boddie v. Connecticut, 401 U.S. 371, 91 S.Ct. 780 (1971), where the Court held that lack of a filing fee could not bar access to divorce court, has the Supreme Court extended *Griffin* beyond the formal criminal process. Rejecting equal protection analysis and using a generalized due process approach, Justice Harlan wrote the majority opinion in *Boddie*. Justice Black, criticizing this due process approach to the extension of rights, drew a sharp distinction between the obligation of courts to remove the consequences of economic inequality in criminal cases and the obligation of courts as to other areas.

2. Justice Black's distinction between economic disparity in the criminal process and other disparities finds support in the 1963 Report of the Attorney General's Committee on Poverty and the Administration of Criminal Justice, chaired by Professor Francis Allen:

> ". . . governmental obligation to deal effectively with problems of poverty in the administration of criminal justice does not rest or depend upon some hypothetical obligation of government to indulge in acts of public charity. It does not presuppose a general commitment on the part of the federal government to re-

lieve impoverished persons of the consequences of limited means, whenever or however manifested. It does not even presuppose that government is always required to take into account the means of the citizen when dealing directly with its citizens. . . . The essential point is that the problems of poverty with which this report is concerned arise in a process initiated by government for the achievement of basic governmental purposes. It is, moreover, a process that has as one of its consequences the imposition of severe disabilities on the persons proceeded against. Duties arise from action. When a course of conduct, however legitimate, entails the possibility of serious injury to persons, a duty on the actor to avoid the reasonably avoidable injuries is ordinarily recognized. When government chooses to exert its powers in the criminal area, its obligation is surely no less than that of taking reasonable measures to eliminate those factors that are irrelevant to just administration of the law but which, nevertheless, may occasionally affect determinations of the accused's liability or penalty. While government may not be required to relieve the accused of his poverty, it may properly be required to minimize the influence of poverty on its administration of justice. . . ."

Is this view consonant with the philosophy underlying American government today? Would it make sense for government to take no action while an individual, because of poverty, is denied educational and vocational opportunities, and while he suffers from inadequate nutrition and health care, but then to become concerned about the effects of economic disparity if and when the individual gets caught up in the criminal process?

3. Commonly by court rule, custom, or statute, indigents are permitted to proceed *in forma pauperis* in civil litigation in many jurisdictions. Although through federally funded Legal Services Corporation offices, and through other legal aid agencies, the indigent also may be able to obtain legal counseling and representation in civil matters, it is a rare situation in which an indigent has a statutory *right* to such services even in a matter of such significance as divorce litigation.

DOUGLAS v. CALIFORNIA

Supreme Court of California, 1963.
372 U.S. 353, 83 S.Ct. 814.

MR. JUSTICE DOUGLAS delivered the opinion of the Court.

Petitioners, Bennie Will Meyes and William Douglas, were jointly tried and convicted in a California court on an information charging them with 13 felonies. A single public defender was appointed to represent them. At the commencement of the trial, the defender moved for a continuance, stating that the case was very complicated, that he was not as prepared as he felt he should be because he was handling a different defense every day, and that there was a conflict of interest between the petitioners requiring the appointment of separate counsel for each of them. This motion was denied. Thereafter, petitioners dismissed the defender, claiming he was unprepared, and again renewed motions for separate counsel and for a continuance. These motions also were denied, and petitioners were ultimately convicted by a jury of all 13 felonies, which included robbery, assault with a deadly weapon, and assault with intent to commit murder. Both were given prison terms. Both appealed as of right to the California District Court of Appeal. That court affirmed their convictions. Both Meyes and Douglas then petitioned for further discretionary review in the California Supreme Court, but their petitions were denied without a hearing. . . . We granted certiorari. . . .

Although several questions are presented in the petition for certiorari, we address ourselves to only one of them. The record shows that petitioners requested, and were denied, the assistance of counsel on appeal, even though it plainly appeared they were indigents. In denying petitioners' requests, the California District Court of Appeal stated that it had "gone through" the record and had come to the conclusion that "no good whatever could be served by appointment of counsel." . . . The District Court of Appeal was acting in accordance with a California rule of criminal procedure which provides that state appellate courts, upon the request of an indigent for counsel, may make "an independent investigation of the record and determine whether it would be of advantage to the defendant or helpful to the appellate court to have counsel appointed. . . . After such investigation, appellate courts should appoint counsel if in their opinion it would be helpful to the defendant or the court, and should deny the appointment of counsel only if in their judgment such appointment would be of no value to either the defendant or the court." People v. Hyde, 51 Cal.2d 152, 154, 331 P.2d 42, 43.

We agree, however, with Justice Traynor of the California Supreme Court, who said that the "[d]enial of counsel on appeal [to an indigent] would seem to be a discrimination at least as invidious as that condemned in Griffin v. People of State of Illinois . . . ." In Griffin v. Illinois, 351 U.S. 12, 76 S.Ct. 585, we held that a State may not grant appellate review in such a way as to discriminate against some convicted defendants on account of their poverty. There, as in Draper v. Washington, 372 U.S. 487, 83 S.Ct. 774, the right to a free transcript on appeal was in issue. Here the issue is whether or not an indigent shall be denied the assistance of counsel on appeal. In either case the evil is the same: discrimination against the indigent. For there can be no equal justice where the kind of an appeal a man enjoys "depends on the amount of money he has."

In spite of California's forward treatment of indigents, under its present practice the type of an appeal a person is afforded in the District Court of Appeals hinges upon whether or not he can pay for the assistance of counsel. If he can the appellate court passes on the merits of his case only after having the full benefit of written briefs and oral argument by counsel. If he cannot the appellate court is forced to prejudge the merits before it can even determine whether counsel should be provided. At this state in the proceedings only the barren record speaks for the indigent, and, unless the printed pages show that an injustice has been committed, he is forced to go without a champion on appeal. Any real chance he may have had of showing that his appeal has hidden merit is deprived him when the court decides on an *ex parte* examination of the record that the assistance of counsel is not required.

We are not here concerned with problems that might arise from the denial of counsel for the preparation of a petition for discretionary or mandatory review beyond the stage in the appellate process at which the claims have once been presented by a lawyer and passed upon by an appellate court. We are dealing only with the first appeal, granted as a matter of right to rich and poor alike (Cal.Penal Code §§ 1235, 1237), from a criminal conviction. We need not now decide whether California would have to provide counsel for an indigent seeking a discretionary hearing from the California Supreme Court after the District Court of Appeals had sustained his conviction, or whether counsel must be appointed for an indigent seeking review of an appellate affirmance of his conviction in this Court by appeal as of right or by petition for a writ of certiorari which lies within the Court's discretion. But it is appropriate to observe that a State can, consistently with the Fourteenth Amendment, provide for differences so long as the result does not amount to a denial of due process or an "invidious discrimination." . . . Absolute equality is not required; lines can be and are drawn and we often sustain them . . . . But where the merits of the one and only appeal an indigent has as of right are decided without benefit of counsel, we think an unconstitutional line has been drawn between rich and poor.

When an indigent is forced to run this gauntlet of a preliminary showing of merit, the right to appeal does not comport with fair procedure. In the federal courts, on the other hand, an indigent must be afforded counsel on appeal whenever he challenges a certification that the appeal is not taken in good faith. Johnson v. United States, 352 U.S. 565, 77 S.Ct. 550. The federal courts must honor his request for counsel regardless of what they think the merits of the case may be; and, "representation in the role of an advocate is required." Ellis v. United States, 356 U.S. 674, 675, 78 S.Ct. 974, 975. In California, however, once the court has "gone through" the record and denied counsel, the indigent has no recourse but to prosecute his appeal on his own, as best he can, no matter how meritorious his case may turn out to be. The present case, where counsel was denied petitioners on appeal, shows that the discrimination is not between "possibly good and obviously bad cases," but between cases where the rich man can require the court to listen to argument of counsel before deciding on the merits, but a poor man cannot. There is lacking that equality demanded by the Fourteenth Amendment where the rich man, who appeals as of right, enjoys the benefit of counsel's examination into the record, research of the law, and marshalling of arguments on his behalf, while the indigent, already burdened by a preliminary determination that his case is without merit, is forced to shift for himself. The indigent, where the record is unclear or the errors are hidden, has only the right to a meaningless ritual, while the rich man has a meaningful appeal.

We vacate the judgment of the District Court of Appeals and remand the case to that court for further proceedings not inconsistent with this opinion. It is so ordered.

Judgment of the District Court of Appeal vacated and case remanded.

MR. JUSTICE CLARK, dissenting.

I adhere to my vote in Griffin v. Illinois [supra], but, as I have always understood that case, it does not control here. It had to do with the State's obligation to furnish a record to an indigent on appeal. There we took pains to point out that the State was free to "find other means of affording adequate and effective appellate review to indigent defendants." . . . Here California has done just that in its procedure for furnishing attorneys for indigents on appeal. We all know that the overwhelming percentage of *in forma pauperis* appeals are frivolous. Statistics of this Court show that over 96% of the petitions filed here are of this variety.[1] California in the light of a like experience, has provided that upon the filing of an application for the appointment of counsel the District Court of Appeal shall make "an independent investigation of the record and determine whether it would be of advantage to the defendant or helpful to the appellate court to have counsel appointed." California's courts did that here and after examining the record certified that such an appointment would be neither advantageous to the petitioners nor helpful to the court. It, therefore, refused to go through the useless gesture of appointing an attorney. In my view neither the Equal Protection Clause nor the Due Process Clause requires more. I cannot understand why the Court says that this procedure afforded petitioners "a meaningless ritual." To appoint an attorney would not only have been utter extravagance and a waste of the State's funds but as surely "meaningless" to petitioners.

With this new fetish for indigency the Court piles an intolerable burden on the State's judicial machinery. Indeed, if the Court is correct it may be that we should first clean up our own house. We have afforded indigent litigants much less protection than has California. Last Term we received over 1,200 *in forma pauperis* applications in none of which had we appointed attorneys or required a record. Some were appeals of right. Still we denied the petitions or dismissed the appeals on the moving papers alone. At the same time we had hundreds of paid cases in which we permitted petitions or appeals to be filed with not only records but briefs by counsel, after which they were disposed of in due course. On the other hand, California furnishes the indigent a complete record and if counsel is requested requires its appellate courts either to (1) appoint counsel or (2) make an independndent investigation of that record and determine whether it would be of advantage to the defendant or helpful to the

---

1. Statistics from the office of the Clerk of this Court reveal that in the 1961 Term only 38 of 1093 *in forma pauperis* petitions for certiorari were granted (3.4%). Of 44 *in forma pauperis* appeals, all but one were summarily dismissed (2.3%).

court to have counsel appointed. Unlike Lane v. Brown, 372 U.S. 477, 83 S.Ct. 768, decision in these matters is not placed in the unreviewable discretion of the Public Defender or appointed counsel but is made by the appellate court, itself.

California's concern for the rights of indigents is clearly revealed in People v. Hyde, supra. There, although the Public Defender had not undertaken the prosecution of the appeal the District Court of Appeal nevertheless referred the application for counsel and the record to the Los Angeles Bar Association. One of its members reviewed these papers, after which he certified that no meritorious ground for appeal was disclosed. Despite this the California District Court of Appeal made its own independent examination of the record.

There is an old adage which my good Mother used to quote to me, i. e., "People who live in glass houses had best not throw stones." I dissent.

[The dissenting opinion of JUSTICES HARLAN and STEWART is omitted.]

MAYER v. CITY OF CHICAGO

Supreme Court of the United States, 1971.
404 U.S. 189, 92 S.Ct. 410.

MR. JUSTICE BRENNAN delivered the opinion of the Court.

A jury in the Circuit Court of Cook County, Illinois, convicted appellant on nonfelony charges of disorderly conduct and interference with a police officer in violation of ordinances of the city of Chicago. He was sentenced to a $250 fine on each offense; violation of each ordinance carried a maximum penalty of $500. Desiring to appeal, he petitioned the Circuit Court for a free transcript of the proceedings of his trial to support his grounds of appeal that the evidence was insufficient for conviction and that misconduct of the prosecutor denied him a fair trial.[1] The Circuit Court found that he was indigent, but denied his application, stating "that defendant was found guilty of ordinance violations and . . . rule 607 of the Supreme Court applies to felony cases." The reference was to Illinois Supreme Court Rule 607(b), which in pertinent part provided: "In any

---

1. A court reporter was provided at appellant's trial pursuant to the State Court Reporters Act, Ill.Rev.Stat., c. 37, § 651 et seq. (1969). It was estimated that the cost of preparing a transcript would be $300. The record refers in some places to a two-day trial and in other places to a three-day trial.

Under Illinois law at the time of appellant's convictions an appeal lay as of right either to the Illinois Supreme Court or to the Illinois Appellate Court, depending upon the nature of the case or the contentions raised. See Constitution of Illinois 1870, Art. 6, §§ 5, 7. If a case was erroneously appealed to the wrong court, it was transferred to the proper court without any loss of rights. Illinois Supreme Court Rule 365, Ill. Rev.Stat., c. 110A, § 365 (1969). Of course, whether an appeal is discretionary or as of right does not affect an indigent's right to a transcript, since "[i]ndigents must . . . have the same opportunities to invoke the discretion of the" court as those who can afford the costs. Burns v. Ohio, 360 U.S. 252, 258 (1959).

case in which the defendant is convicted of a *felony*, he may petition
the court in which he was convicted for a report of proceedings at his
trial." (Emphasis supplied.) Other Illinois Supreme Court rules,
Rules 323(c) and 323(d), provided for alternatives to a transcript in
the form of a "Settled Statement" or an "Agreed Statement of
Facts." [2] Without resorting to either alternative, appellant made a
motion in the Illinois Supreme Court for an order that he be furnished a transcript of proceedings without cost. The Supreme Court
denied the motion in an unreported order without filing an opinion.
We noted probable jurisdiction of appellant's appeal challenging the
constitutionality of the limitation of Rule 607(b) to felony cases. 401
U.S. 906 (1971).

I.

Griffin v. Illinois, 351 U.S. 12 (1956), is the watershed of our
transcript decisions. We held there that "[d]estitute defendants
must be afforded an adequate appellate review as defendants who
have money enough to buy transcripts." This holding rested on the
"constitutional guaranties of due process and equal protection both
[of which] call for procedures in criminal trials which allow no invidious discriminations between persons and different groups of persons." We said that "[p]lainly the ability to pay costs in advance
bears no rational relationship to a defendant's guilt or innocence
. . . ," and concluded that "[t]here can be no equal justice where
the kind of trial a man gets depends on the amount of money he has."
Appellee city of Chicago urges that we re-examine *Griffin*. We decline to do so. For "it is now fundamental that, once established
. . . avenues [of appellate review] must be kept free of unreasoned distinctions that can only impede open and equal access to the
courts." Rinaldi v. Yeager, 384 U.S. 305, 310 (1966).[3] Therefore,

2. These rules, Ill.Rev.Stat., c. 110A, §
   323(c) and (d) (1969), provided:
   "(c) Procedure If No Verbatim
   Transcript Is Available. If no verbatim transcript of the evidence or
   proceedings is obtainable the appellant may prepare a proposed report of proceedings from the best
   available sources, including recollection. It shall be served within sev-
   en days after the notice of appeal
   is filed. Within 21 days after the
   notice of appeal is filed, any other
   party may serve proposed amendments or his proposed report of proceedings. Within seven days thereafter, the appellant shall, upon notice, present the proposed report or
   reports and any proposed amendments to the trial court for settlement and approval. The court,
   holding hearings if necessary, shall
   promptly settle, certify, and order
   filed an accurate report of proceedings.
   "(d) Agreed Statement of Facts.
   The parties by written stipulation

may agree upon a statement of the
facts material to the controversy
and file it in lieu of and within the
time for filing a report of proceedings."

These rules were also amended effective July 1, 1971, but not in ways
material to this case. See 1971 Illinois Legislative Service, No. 5, p.
1690. Despite the provision limiting use of a "Settled" statement to
cases where no verbatim transcript
is "available" or "obtainable," the
procedure of subsection (c) evidently is permissible even though the
court reporter's notes are available
for transcription. See Tone, New
Supreme Court Rule on Expeditious and Inexpensive Appeals, 53
Ill.B.J. 18, 20 (1964).

3. Our decisions on the question of
   free transcripts for indigents include:
   Wade v. Wilson, 396 U.S. 282 (1970)
   . . . . .

"[i]n all cases the duty of the State is to provide the indigent as adequate and effective an appellate review as that given appellants with funds . . . ." Draper v. Washington, 372 U.S. 487, 496 (1963). In terms of a trial record, this means that the State must afford the indigent a " 'record of sufficient completeness' to permit proper consideration of [his] claims."

A "record of sufficient completeness" does not translate automatically into a complete verbatim transcript. We said in *Griffin* that a State "may find other means [than providing stenographic transcripts for] affording adequate and effective appellate review to indigent defendants." 351 U.S., at 20. We considered this more fully in Draper v. Washington:

> "Alternative methods of reporting trial proceedings are permissible if they place before the appellate court an equivalent report of the events at trial from which the appellant's contentions arise. A statement of facts agreed to by both sides, a full narrative statement based perhaps on the trial judge's minutes taken during trial or on the court reporter's untranscribed notes, or a bystander's bill of exceptions might all be adequate substitutes, equally as good as a transcript. Moreover, part or all of the stenographic transcript in certain cases will not be germane to consideration of the appeal, and a State will not be required to expend its funds unnecessarily in such circumstances. If, for instance, the points urged relate only to the validity of the statute or the sufficiency of the indictment upon which conviction was predicated, the transcript is irrelevant and need not be provided. If the assignments of error go only to rulings on evidence or to its sufficiency, the transcript provided might well be limited to the portions relevant to such issues. Even as to this kind of issue, however, it is unnecessary to afford a record of the proceedings pertaining to an alleged failure of proof on a point which is irrelevant as a matter of law to the elements of the crime for which the defendant has been convicted. In the examples given, the fact that an appellant with funds may choose to waste his money by unnecessarily including in the record all of the transcript does not mean that the State must waste its funds by providing what is unnecessary for adequate appellate review."

We emphasize, however, that the State must provide a full verbatim record where that is necessary to assure the indigent as effective an appeal as would be available to the defendant with resources to pay his own way. Moreover, where the grounds of appeal, as in this case, make out a colorable need for a complete transcript, the burden is on the State to show that only a portion of the transcript or an "alternative" will suffice for an effective appeal on those grounds. This rationale underlies our statement in *Draper*, that:

> "[T]he State could have endeavored to show that a narrative statement or only a portion of the transcript would be

adequate and available for appellate consideration of petitioners' contentions. The trial judge would have complied with . . . the constitutional mandate . . . in limiting the grant accordingly on the basis of such a showing by the State."

II.

The distinction between felony and nonfelony offenses drawn by Rule 607(b) can no more satisfy the requirements of the Fourteenth Amendment than could the like distinction in the Wisconsin law, held invalid in Groppi v. Wisconsin, 400 U.S. 505 (1971), which permitted a change of venue in felony but not in misdemeanor trials. The size of the defendant's pocketbook bears no more relationship to his guilt or innocence in a nonfelony than in a felony case. The distinction drawn by Rule 607(b) is, therefore, an "unreasoned distinction" proscribed by the Fourteenth Amendment. That conclusion follows directly from our decision in Williams v. Oklahoma City, 395 U.S. 458, 459 (1969), rejecting the argument " 'that an indigent person, convicted for a violation of a city ordinance, quasi criminal in nature and often referred to as a petty offense, is [not] entitled to a casemade or transcript at city expense in order to perfect an appeal . . . .' " 4

III.

The city of Chicago urges another distinction to set this case apart from *Griffin* and its progeny. The city notes that the defendants in all the transcript cases previously decided by this Court were sentenced to some term of confinement. Where the accused, as here, is not subject to imprisonment, but only a fine, the city suggests that his interest in a transcript is outweighed by the State's fiscal and other interests in not burdening the appellate process. This argument misconceives the principle of *Griffin* no less than does the line that Rule 607(b) expressly draws. *Griffin* does not represent a balance between the needs of the accused and the interests of society; its principle is a flat prohibition against pricing indigent defendants out of as effective an appeal as would be available to others able to pay their own way. The invidiousness of the discrimination that exists when criminal procedures are made available only to those who can pay is not erased by any differences in the sentences that may be imposed. The State's fiscal interest is, therefore, irrelevant.

We add that even approaching the problem in the terms the city suggests hardly yields the answer the city tenders. The practical effects of conviction of even petty offenses of the kind involved here are not to be minimized. A fine may bear as heavily on an indigent accused as forced confinement. The collateral consequences of con-

---

4. It is true, as the city of Chicago argues, that in *Williams* the defendant was effectively denied any right of appeal, whereas here a transcript was not a condition precedent for appeal. The constitutional infirmity in Rule 607(b) is not the less for that reason. The indigent defendant must be afforded as effective an appeal as the defendant who can pay.

viction may be even more serious, as when (as was apparently a possibility in this case) the impecunious medical student finds himself barred from the practice of medicine because of a conviction he is unable to appeal for lack of funds. Moreover, the State's long-term interest would not appear to lie in making access to appellate processes from even its most inferior courts depend upon the defendant's ability to pay. It has been aptly said:

> "[F]ew citizens ever have contact with the higher courts. In the main, it is the police and the lower court Bench and Bar that convey the essence of our democracy to the people.
>
> "Justice, if it can be measured, must be measured by the experience the average citizen has with the police and the lower courts." [5]

Arbitrary denial of appellate review of proceedings of the State's lowest trial courts may save the State some dollars and cents, but only at the substantial risk of generating frustration and hostility toward its courts among the most numerous consumers of justice.

IV.

We conclude that appellant cannot be denied a "record of sufficient completeness" to permit proper consideration of his claims. We repeat that this does not mean that he is automatically entitled to a full verbatim transcript. He urges that his claims of insufficiency of the evidence and prejudicial prosecutorial misconduct cannot be fairly judged without recourse to the trial record. *Draper* suggests that these are indeed the kinds of claims that require provision of a verbatim transcript. In *Draper*, however, the State of Washington did not undertake to carry its burden of showing that something less than a complete transcript would suffice. Here the City of Chicago urges that the Illinois procedures for a "Settled" or "Agreed" statement may provide adequate alternatives. The city also argues that even if a verbatim record is required, less than a complete transcript may assure fair appellate review. We cannot address these questions, since the record before us contains only the parties' conflicting assertions; so far as appears, neither of the Illinois courts below regarded resolution of the dispute to be relevant in light of Rule 607(b). That this was the view of the Circuit Court is clear. The order of the Supreme Court, however, may not have been based on the rule, but on the ground that appellant had the burden of showing that the alternatives of a "Settled" or "Agreed" statement were inadequate. We hold today that a denial of appellant's motion, either on the basis of the rule, or, in the context of his grounds of appeal, on the basis that he did not meet the burden of showing the inadequacy of the alternatives, would constitute constitutional error.

We are informed that appellant's appeal from his conviction has been docketed in the Illinois Supreme Court and that its disposition

5. Murphy, The Role of the Police in Our Modern Society, 26 The Record of the Association of the Bar of the City of New York 292, 293 (1971).

has been deferred pending our decision of this case. We therefore vacate the order of the Illinois Supreme Court and remand the case to that court for further proceedings not inconsistent with this opinion.

It is so ordered.

MR. CHIEF JUSTICE BURGER, concurring.

I join the Court's opinion but add these observations chiefly to underscore that there are alternatives in the majority of cases to a full verbatim transcript of an entire trial. The references to what was said in Draper v. Washington [supra] emphasize the duty of counsel as officers of the court to seek only what is needed. In most cases, unlike this one, the essential facts are not in dispute on appeal, or if there is dispute it centers on certain limited aspects of the case. One need only examine briefs in appeals to see that at the appellate stage the area of conflict on the facts is generally narrow.

Every busy court is plagued with excessive demands for free transcripts in criminal cases. My own experience over the years indicates that privately employed counsel are usually spartan in their demands because the client must pay his own costs. Unfortunately one consequence of the advent of the Criminal Justice Act and state counterparts is that when costs are paid by the public, counsel are sometimes profligate in their demands, or yield their professional judgment to the client's desires. This is more than a matter of costs. An affluent society ought not be miserly in support of justice, for economy is not an objective of the system; the real vice is the resulting delay in securing transcripts and hence determining the appeal. When excessive demands are made by an appellant in order to postpone the day when the appeal is finally determined, because, for example, he is at liberty pending appeal, a lawyer who cooperates is guilty of unprofessional conduct.

I quite agree with MR. JUSTICE BRENNAN that "a full verbatim record where that is necessary . . ." should be provided but judges and lawyers have a duty to avoid abuses that promote delays.

[JUSTICE BLACKMUN's concurring opinion is omitted.]

NOTES

1. After *Griffin, Douglas,* and *Mayer,* can there be any doubt that an indigent convicted of a "fine-only" offense has a right to appointed counsel on appeal if appellate review of such convictions is permitted under state law? Consider the question again after reading the *Argersinger* and *Scott* cases which follow in Section B of this chapter.

2. If counsel appointed for the first appeal concludes that the appeal is wholly without merit, he or she still must submit a brief discussing the arguable issues and defending the decision not to file a brief on the merits. Anders v. California, 386 U.S. 738, 87 S.Ct. 1396 (1967). One career public defender shortly after the *Anders* decision argued that *Anders* would place upon appointed counsel the "quixotic" requirement of "trying to find support for an appeal which he has already concluded to be without any merit whatsoever. . . ." He concluded that *Anders* would encourage mediocrity, contribute to a backlog of unreviewed convictions, and impair the ef-

fectiveness of the *in forma pauperis* bar. Doherty, Wolf! Wolf!—The Ramifications of Frivolous Appeals, 59 J.Crim.L., C. & P.S. 1 (1968). The underlying premise of Doherty's argument was that appointed counsel, if required to file a brief, would choose to make frivolous arguments rather than briefing the case against their clients. In point of fact, the use of *Anders* briefs has varied widely from jurisdiction to jurisdiction.

3. Another issue is whether a convicted defendant must be admonished of his appellate rights, including the rights of the indigent to a free transcript and appointed counsel. In some instances a state or rule of court may require such admonitions. Are such warnings constitutionally required? See United States ex rel. Singleton v. Woods, 440 F.2d 835 (7th Cir. 1971), for one viewpoint.

4. Consider the implications of Justice Brennan's statement that fiscal consequences are irrelevant to an equal protection approach. Should a legislature have no say in whether available resources go to increase the standard of living of welfare recipients or instead go to purchase free transcripts for indigents who have been convicted of fine-only ordinance violations? Under *Mayer* do the "needs" of defendants in the criminal justice system, no matter how petty their case, take economic precedence over the needs of other citizens, no matter how worthy their cause?

5. In People v. Hopping, 60 Ill.2d 246, 326 N.E.2d 395 (1975), an "official" court reporter was not present at the indigent's plea of guilty to a misdemeanor charge. Presumably a wealthy defendant could have hired a court reporter to record and transcribe the proceeding. (This is the practice in civil cases in many parts of the country. The parties, not the court, supply the reporter.) The Illinois Supreme Court rejected a claim of equal protection in *Hopping*. It declared that the bystander bill provisions of Illinois Supreme Court Rule 323 were sufficient to provide a record to be utilized in determining whether the plea admonition and waiver procedures had been adequate.

ROSS v. MOFFITT

Supreme Court of the United States, 1974.
417 U.S. 600, 94 S.Ct. 2437.

MR. JUSTICE REHNQUIST delivered the opinion of the Court.

We are asked in this case to decide whether Douglas v. California (1963), which requires appointment of counsel for indigent state defendants on their first appeal as of right, should be extended to require counsel for discretionary state appeals and for applications for review in this Court.

* * *

The case now before us has resulted from consolidation of two separate cases, North Carolina criminal prosecutions brought in the respective Superior Courts for the counties of Mecklenburg and Guilford. In both cases respondent pleaded not guilty to charges of forgery and uttering a forged instrument, and because of his indigency was represented at trial by court-appointed counsel. He then took separate appeals to the North Carolina Court of Appeals, where he was again represented by court-appointed counsel, and his convictions were affirmed. At this point the procedural histories of the two cases diverge.

* * *

The Court of Appeals reversed the two District Court judgments, holding that respondent was entitled to the assistance of counsel at state expense both on his petition for review in the North Carolina Supreme Court and on his petition for certiorari in this Court. Reviewing the procedures of the North Carolina appellate system and the possible benefits that counsel would provide for indigents seeking review in that system, the court stated:

> "As long as the state provides such procedures and allows other convicted felons to seek access to the higher court with the help of retained counsel, there is a marked absence of fairness in denying an indigent the assistance of counsel as he seeks access to the same court."

This principle was held equally applicable to petitions for certiorari in this Court. For, said the Court of Appeals, "[t]he same concepts of fairness and equality, which require counsel in a first appeal of right, require counsel in other and subsequent discretionary appeals. . . . ."

* * *

The precise rationale for the Griffin and Douglas lines of cases has never been explicitly stated, some support being derived from the Equal Protection Clause of the Fourteenth Amendment, and some from the Due Process Clause of that Amendment. Neither clause by itself provides an entirely satisfactory basis for the result reached, each depending on a different inquiry which emphasizes different factors. "Due process" emphasizes fairness between the State and the individual dealing with the State, regardless of how other individuals in the same situation may be treated. "Equal protection," on the other hand, emphasizes disparity in treatment by a State between classes of individuals whose situations are arguably indistinguishable. We will address these issues separately in the succeeding sections.

Recognition of the due process rationale in Douglas is found both in the Court's opinion and in the dissenting opinion of Mr. Justice Harlan. The Court in Douglas stated that "[w]hen an individual is forced to run this gantlet of a preliminary showing of merit, the right to appeal does not comport with fair procedure." Mr. Justice Harlan thought that the due process issue in Douglas was the only one worthy of extended consideration, remarking: "The real question in this case, I submit, and the only one that permits of satisfactory analysis, is whether or not the state rule, as applied in this case, is consistent with the requirements of fair procedure guaranteed by the Due Process Clause."

We do not believe that the Due Process Clause requires North Carolina to provide respondent with counsel on his discretionary appeal to the State Supreme Court. At the trial stage of a criminal proceeding, the right of an indigent defendant to counsel at his trial is fundamental and binding upon the States by virtue of the Sixth and Fourteenth Amendments. But there are significant differences between the trial and appellate stages of a criminal proceeding. The purpose of the trial stage from the State's point of view is to convert a criminal defendant from a person presumed innocent to one found guilty beyond a reasonable doubt. To accomplish this purpose, the State employs a prosecuting attorney who presents evidence to the court, challenges any witnesses offered by the defendant, argues rulings of the court, and makes direct arguments to the court or jury seeking to persuade them of the defendant's guilt. . . .

By contrast, it is ordinarily the defendant, rather than the State, who initiates the appellate process, seeking not to fend off the efforts of the State's prosecutor but rather to overturn a finding of guilt made by a judge or jury below. The defendant needs an attorney on appeal not as a shield to protect him against being "haled into court" by the State and stripped of his presumption of innocence, but rather as a sword to upset the prior determination of guilt. This difference is significant for, while no one would agree that the State may simply dispense with the trial stage of proceedings without a criminal defendant's consent, it is clear that the State need not provide any appeal at all. McKane v. Durston, supra. The fact that an appeal *has* been provided does not automatically mean that a State then acts unfairly by refusing to provide counsel to indigent defendants at every stage of the way. Douglas v. California, supra. Unfairness results only if indigents are singled out by the State and denied meaningful access to that system because of their poverty. That question is more profitably considered under an equal protection analysis.

Language invoking equal protection notions is prominent both in Douglas and in other cases treating the rights of indigents on appeal.

* * *

Despite the tendency of all rights "to declare themselves absolute to their logical extreme," there are obviously limits beyond which the equal protection analysis may not be pressed without doing violence to principles recognized in other decisions of this Court. The Fourteenth Amendment "does not require absolute equality or precisely equal advantages," San Antonio Independent School District v. Rodriquez (1973), nor does it require the State to "equalize economic conditions." Griffin v. Illinois (Frankfurter, J., concurring). It does require that the state appellate system be "free of unreasoned distinctions." Rinaldi v. Yaeger (1966), and that indigents have an adequate opportunity to present their claims fairly within the adversarial system. Griffin v. Illinois, supra; Draper v. Washington, supra. The State cannot adopt procedures which leave an indigent defendant "entirely cut off from any appeal at all," by virtue of his indigency, Lane v. Brown, supra, or extend to such indigent defendants merely a "meaningless ritual" while others in better economic circumstances have a "meaningful appeal." Douglas v. California, supra. The question is not one of absolutes, but one of degrees. In this case we do not believe that the Equal Protection Clause, when interpreted in the context of these cases, requires North Carolina to provide free counsel for indigent defendants seeking to take discretionary appeals to the North Carolina Supreme Court, or to file petitions for certiorari in this Court.

* * *

The facts show that respondent, in connection with his Mecklenburg County conviction, received the benefit of counsel in examining the record of his trial and in preparing an appellate brief on his behalf for the state Court of Appeals. Thus, prior to his seeking discretionary review in the State Supreme Court, his claims "had once been presented by a lawyer and passed upon by an appellate court." Douglas v. California, supra. We do not believe that it can be said, therefore, that a defendant in respondent's circumstances is denied meaningful access to the North Carolina Supreme Court simply because the State does not appoint counsel to aid him in seeking review in that court. At that stage he will have, at the very least, a transcript or other record of trial proceedings, a brief on his behalf in the Court of Appeals setting forth his claims of error, and in many cases an opinion by the Court of Appeals disposing of his case. These materials, supplemented by whatever submission respondent may make pro se, would appear to provide the Supreme Court of North Carolina with an adequate basis on which to base its decision to grant or deny review.

We are fortified in this conclusion by our understanding of the function served by discretionary review in the North Carolina Supreme Court. The critical issue in that court, as we perceive it, is not whether there has been "a correct adjudication of guilt" in every individual case, see Griffin v. Illinois, but rather whether "the subject matter of the appeal has significant public interest," whether "the cause involves legal principles of major significance to the jurisprudence of the state," or whether the decision below is in probable conflict with a decision of the Supreme Court. The Supreme Court may deny certiorari even though it believes that the decision of the Court of Appeals was incorrect, since a decision which appears incorrect may nevertheless fail to satisfy any of the criteria discussed above. Once a defendant's claims of error are organized and presented in a lawyer-like fashion to the Court of Appeals, the justices of the Supreme Court of North Carolina who make the decision to grant or deny discretionary review should be able to ascertain whether his case satisfies the standards established by the legislature for such review.

This is not to say, of course, that a skilled lawyer, particularly one trained in the somewhat arcane art of preparing petitions for discretionary review, would not prove helpful to any litigant able to employ him. An indigent defendant seeking review in the Supreme Court of North Carolina is therefore somewhat handicapped in comparison with a wealthy defendant who has counsel assisting him in every conceivable manner at every stage in the proceeding. But both the opportunity to have counsel prepare an initial brief in the Court of Appeals and the nature of discretionary review in the Supreme Court of North Carolina make this relative handicap far less that the handicap borne by the indigent defendant denied counsel on his initial appeal as of right in Douglas. And the fact that a particular service might be of benefit to an indigent defendant does not mean that the service is constitutionally required. The duty of the State under our cases is not to duplicate the legal arsenal that may be privately retained by a criminal defendant in a continuing effort to reverse his conviction, but only to assure the indigent defendant an adequate opportunity to present his claims fairly in the context of the State's appellate process. We think respondent was given that opportunity under the existing North Carolina system.

Much of the discussion in the preceding section is equally relevant to the question of whether a State must provide counsel for a defendant seeking review of his conviction in this Court. North Carolina will have provided counsel for a convicted defendant's only appeal as of right, and the brief prepared by that counsel together with one and perhaps two North Carolina appellate opinions will be available to this Court in order that it may decide whether or not to grant certiorari. This Court's review, much like that of the Supreme Court of North Carolina, is discretionary and depends on numerous factors other than the perceived correctness of the judgment we are asked to review.

* * *

The suggestion that a State is responsible for providing counsel to one petitioning this Court simply because it initiated the prosecution which led to the judgment sought to be reviewed is unsupported by either reason or authority. It would be quite as logical under the rationale of Douglas and Griffin, and indeed perhaps more so, to require that the Federal Government or this Court furnish and compensate counsel for petitioners who seek certiorari here to review state judgments of conviction. Yet this Court has followed a consistent policy of denying applications for appointment of counsel by persons seeking to file jurisdictional statements or petitions for certiorari in this Court.

* * *

Reversed.

MR. JUSTICE DOUGLAS, with whom MR. JUSTICE BRENNAN and MR. JUSTICE MARSHALL concur, dissenting.

I would affirm the judgment below because I am in agreement with the opinion of Chief Judge Haynsworth for a unanimous panel in the Court of Appeals.

In Douglas v. California we considered the necessity for appointed counsel on the first appeal as of right, the only issue before us. We did not deal with the appointment of counsel for later levels of discretionary review, either to the higher state courts or to this Court, but we noted that "there can be no equal justice where the kind of appeal a man enjoys 'depends on the amount of money he has.' "

Judge Haynsworth could find "no logical basis for differentiation between appeals of right and permissive review procedures in the context of the Constitution and the right to counsel." More familiar with the functioning of the North Carolina criminal justice system than are we, he concluded that "in the context of constitutional questions arising in criminal prosecutions, permissive review in the state's highest court may be predictably the most meaningful review the conviction will receive." Ibid. The North Carolina Court of Appeals, for example, will be constrained in diverging from an earlier opinion of the State Supreme Court, even if subsequent developments have rendered the earlier Supreme Court decision suspect. "[T]he state's highest court remains the ultimate arbiter of the rights of its citizens."

Judge Haynsworth also correctly observed that the indigent defendant, proceeding without counsel, is at a substantial disadvantage relative to wealthy defendants represented by counsel when he is forced to fend for himself in seeking discretionary review from the State Supreme Court or from this Court. It may well not be enough to allege error in the courts below in layman's terms; a more sophisticated approach may be demanded:[1]

> "An indigent defendant is as much in need of the assistance of a lawyer in preparing and filing a petition for certiorari as he is in the handling of an appeal as of right. In many appeals, an articulate defendant could file an effective brief by telling his story in simple language without legalisms, but the technical requirement for applications for writs of certiorari are hazards which one untrained in the law could hardly be expected to negotiate.
>
> " 'Certiorari proceedings constitute a highly specialized aspect of appellate work. The factors which [a court] deems important in connection with deciding whether to grant certiorari are certainly not within the normal knowl-

---

1. An indigent defendant proceeding without the assistance of counsel would be attempting to satisfy one of the three statutory standards for review when seeking certiorari from the North Carolina Supreme Court:

"(1) The subject matter of the appeal has significant public interest, or

"(2) The cause involves legal principles of major significance to the jurisprudence of the State, or

"(3) The decision of the Court of Appeals appears likely to be in conflict with a decision of the Supreme Court."

N.C.Gen.Stat. § 7A–31(c). It seems likely that only the third would have been explored in a brief on the merits before the Court of Appeals, and the indigent defendant would draw little assistance from that brief in attempting to satisfy either of the first two standards.

Rule 19 of this Court provides some guidelines for the exercise of our certiorari jurisdiction, including decisions by a state court on federal questions not previously decided by this Court; but it may not be enough simply to assert that there was error in the decision of the court below. Cf. Magnum Co. v. Coty, 262 U.S. 159, 163, 43 S.Ct. 531. Moreover, this Court is greatly aided by briefs prepared with accuracy, brevity, and clarity in its determination of whether certiorari should be granted. See Furness, Withy & Co. v. Yang-Tsze Insurance Assn., 242 U.S. 430, 434, 37 S.Ct. 141.

edge of an indigent appellant. Boskey, The Right to Counsel in Appellate Proceedings, 45 Minn.L.Rev. 783, 797 (1961).'"

Furthermore, the lawyer who handled the first appeal in a case would be familiar with the facts and legal issues involved in the case. It would be a relatively easy matter for the attorney to apply his expertise in filing a petition for discretionary review to a higher court, or to advise his client that such a petition would have no chance of succeeding.

Douglas v. California was grounded on concepts of fairness and equality. The right to discretionary review is a substantial one, and one where a lawyer can be of significant assistance to an indigent defendant. It was correctly perceived below that the "same concepts of fairness and equality, which require counsel in a first appeal of right, require counsel in other and subsequent discretionary appeals."

NOTES

1. *Ross* seemed to approve "line-drawing" in determining at what point in the criminal justice system the State no longer is required to alleviate the consequences of economic disparity. Can the decision be squared with *Mayer*? After *Ross* do fiscal considerations, always relevant to a due process approach, become relevant again? What is left of an equal protection approach after *Ross*? Has the view that due process analysis is more appropriate (expressed by Justice Harlan in *Griffin*) finally prevailed?

2. Would *Ross* hold true where appellant was under a sentence of death? See Carey v. Garrison, 403 F.Supp. 395 (W.D.N.C.1975). Compare Graham v. State, 372 So.2d 1363 (Fla.1979).

In the federal appellate system, a convicted federal defendant represented before the Court of Appeals on direct review by an attorney appointed under the Federal Criminal Justice Act can require his attorney to file a petition for certiorari. See Doherty v. United States, 404 U.S. 28, 92 S.Ct. 175 (1971) (Douglas, J., concurring); Wilkins v. United States, 441 U.S. 468, 99 S.Ct. 1829 (1979).

B.   TRIAL COUNSEL: THE SIXTH AMENDMENT APPROACH

GIDEON v. WAINWRIGHT

Supreme Court of the United States, 1963.
372 U.S. 335, 83 S.Ct. 792.

MR. JUSTICE BLACK delivered the opinion of the Court.

Petitioner was charged in a Florida state court with having broken and entered a poolroom with intent to commit a misdemeanor. This offense is a felony under Florida law. Appearing in court without funds and without a lawyer, petitioner asked the court to appoint counsel for him, whereupon the following colloquy took place:

"The Court: Mr. Gideon, I am sorry, but I cannot appoint Counsel to represent you in this case. Under the laws
of the State of Florida, the only time the Court can appoint
Counsel to represent a Defendant is when that person is
charged with a capital offense. I am sorry, but I will have
to deny your request to appoint Counsel to defend you in
this case.

"The Defendant: The United States Supreme Court
says I am entitled to be represented by Counsel."

Put to trial before a jury, Gideon conducted his defense about as well
as could be expected from a layman. He made an opening statement
to the jury, cross-examined the State's witnesses, presented witnesses
in his own defense, declined to testify himself, and made a short argument "emphasizing his innocence to the charge contained in the Information filed in this case." The jury returned a verdict of guilty,
and petitioner was sentenced to serve five years in the state prison.
Later, petitioner filed in the Florida Supreme Court this habeas corpus petition attacking his conviction and sentence on the ground that
the trial court's refusal to appoint counsel for him denied him rights
"guaranteed by the Constitution and the Bill of Rights by the United
States Government." Treating the petition for habeas corpus as
properly before it, the State Supreme Court, "upon consideration
thereof" but without an opinion, denied all relief. Since 1942, when
Betts v. Brady, 316 U.S. 455, 62 S.Ct. 1252, 86 L.Ed. 1595, was decided by a divided Court, the problem of a defendant's federal constitutional right to counsel in a state court has been a continuing source of
controversy and litigation in both state and federal courts. To give
this problem another review here, we granted certiorari. . . .
Since Gideon was proceeding *in forma pauperis*, we appointed counsel
to represent him and requested both sides to discuss in their briefs
and oral arguments the following: "Should this Court's holding in
Betts v. Brady, . . . be reconsidered?"

I.

The facts upon which Betts claimed that he had been unconstitutionally denied the right to have counsel appointed to assist him are
strikingly like the facts upon which Gideon here bases his federal
constitutional claim. Betts was indicted for robbery in a Maryland
state court. On arraignment, he told the trial judge of his lack of
funds to hire a lawyer and asked the court to appoint one for him.
Betts was advised that it was not the practice in that county to appoint counsel for indigent defendants except in murder and rape cases. He then pleaded not guilty, had witnesses summoned, cross-examined the State's witnesses, examined his own, and chose not to testify himself. He was found guilty by the judge, sitting without a
jury, and sentenced to eight years in prison. Like Gideon, Betts
sought release by habeas corpus, alleging that he had been denied the
right to assistance of counsel in violation of the Fourteenth Amendment. Betts was denied any relief, and on review this Court af-

firmed. It was held that a refusal to appoint counsel for an indigent defendant charged with a felony did not necessarily violate the Due Process Clause of the Fourteenth Amendment, which for reasons given the Court deemed to be the only applicable federal constitutional provision. The Court said:

> "Asserted denial [of due process] is to be tested by an appraisal of the totality of facts in a given case. That which may, in one setting, constitute a denial of fundamental fairness, shocking to the universal sense of justice, may, in other circumstances, and in the light of other considerations, fall short of such denial." . . .

Treating due process as "a concept less rigid and more fluid than those envisaged in other specific and particular provisions of the Bill of Rights," the Court held that refusal to appoint counsel under the particular facts and circumstances in the Betts case was not so "offensive to the common and fundamental ideas of fairness" as to amount to a denial of due process. Since the facts and circumstances of the two cases are so nearly indistinguishable, we think the Betts v. Brady holding if left standing would require us to reject Gideon's claim that the Constitution guarantees him the assistance of counsel. Upon full reconsideration we conclude that Betts v. Brady should be overruled.

II.

The Sixth Amendment provides, "In all criminal prosecutions, the accused shall enjoy the right . . . to have the Assistance of Counsel for his defence." We have construed this to mean that in federal courts counsel must be provided for defendants unable to employ counsel unless the right is competently and intelligently waived. Betts argued that this right is extended to indigent defendants in state courts by the Fourteenth Amendment. In response the Court stated that, while the Sixth Amendment laid down "no rule for the conduct of the states, the question recurs whether the constraint laid by the amendment upon the national courts expresses a rule so fundamental and essential to a fair trial, and so, to due process of law, that it is made obligatory upon the states by the Fourteenth Amendment." . . . In order to decide whether the Sixth Amendment's guarantee of counsel is of this fundamental nature, the Court in Betts set out and considered "[r]elevant data on the subject . . . afforded by constitutional and statutory provisions subsisting in the colonies and the states prior to the inclusion of the Bill of Rights in the national Constitution, and in the constitutional, legislative, and judicial history of the states to the present date." . . . On the basis of this historical data the Court concluded that "appointment of counsel is not a fundamental right, essential to a fair trial." . . . It was for this reason the Betts Court refused to accept the contention that the Sixth Amendment's guarantee of counsel for indigent federal defendants was extended to or, in the words of that Court, "made obligatory upon the states by the Fourteenth Amendment". Plainly, had the Court concluded that appointment of counsel for an indigent criminal defendant was "a fundamental right, essential to a fair trial," it would have held that the Fourteenth Amendment requires appointment of counsel in a state court, just as the Sixth Amendment requires in a federal court.

We think the Court in Betts had ample precedent for acknowledging that those guarantees of the Bill of Rights which are fundamental safeguards of liberty immune from federal abridgment are equally protected against state invasion by the Due Process Clause of the Fourteenth Amendment. This same principle was recognized, explained, and applied in Powell v. Alabama, 287 U.S. 45, 53 S.Ct. 55 (1932), a case upholding the right of counsel, where the Court held that despite sweeping language to the contrary in Hurtado v. California, 110 U.S. 516, 4 S.Ct. 292 (1884), the Fourteenth Amendment "embraced" those " 'fundamental principles of liberty and justice which lie at the base of all our civil and political institutions,' " even though they had been "specifically dealt with in another part of the Federal Constitution." 287 U.S., at 67, 53 S.Ct., at 63. In many cases other than Powell and Betts, this Court has looked to the fundamental nature of original Bill of Rights guarantees to decide whether the Fourteenth Amendment makes them obligatory on the States. Explicitly recognized to be of this "fundamental nature" and therefore made immune from state invasion by the Fourteenth, or some part of it, are the First Amendment's freedoms of speech, press, religion, assembly, association, and petition for redress of grievances. For the same reason, though not always in precisely the same terminology, the Court has made obligatory on the States the Fifth Amendment's command that private property shall not be taken for public use without just compensation, the Fourth Amendment's prohibition of unreasonable searches and seizures, and the Eighth's ban on cruel and unusual punishment. On the other hand, this Court in Palko v. Connecticut, 302 U.S. 319, 58 S.Ct. 149 (1937), refused to hold that the Fourteenth Amendment made the double jeopardy provision of the Fifth Amendment obligatory on the States. In so refusing, however, the Court, speaking through Mr. Justice Cardozo, was careful to emphasize that "immunities that are valid as against the federal government by force of the specific pledges of particular amendments have been found to be implicit in the concept of ordered liberty, and thus, through the Fourteenth Amendment, become valid as against the states" and that guarantees "in their origin .   .   . effective against the federal government alone" had by prior cases "been taken over from the earlier articles of the Federal Bill of Rights and brought within the Fourteenth Amendment by a process of absorption."

We accept Betts v. Brady's assumption, based as it was on our prior cases, that a provision of the Bill of Rights which is "fundamental and essential to a fair trial" is made obligatory upon the States by the Fourteenth Amendment. We think the Court in Betts was wrong, however, in concluding that the Sixth Amendment's guarantee of counsel is not one of these fundamental rights. Ten years before Betts v. Brady, this Court, after full consideration of all the historical data examined in Betts, had unequivocally declared that "the right to the aid of counsel is of this fundamental character." Powell v. Alabama, 287 U.S. 45, 68, 53 S.Ct. 55, 63 (1932). While the Court at the close of its Powell opinion did by its language, as this Court frequently does, limit its holding to the particular facts and circumstances of that case, its conclusions about the fundamental nature of the right to counsel are unmistakable. Several years later, in 1936 [and in 1938], the Court re-emphasized what it had said about the fundamental nature of the right to counsel . . .

In light of these and many other prior decisions of this Court, it is not surprising that the Betts Court, when faced with the contention that "one charged with crime, who is unable to obtain counsel, must be furnished counsel by the state," conceded that "[e]xpressions in the opinions of this court lend color to the argument . . ." The fact is that in deciding as it did—that "appointment of counsel is not a fundamental right, essential to a fair trial"—the Court in Betts v. Brady made an abrupt break with its own well-considered precedents. In returning to these old precedents, sounder we believe than the new, we but restore constitutional principles established to achieve a fair system of justice. Not only these precedents but also reason and reflection require us to recognize that in our adversary system of criminal justice, any person haled into court, who is too poor to hire a lawyer, cannot be assured a fair trial unless counsel is provided for him. This seems to us to be an obvious truth. Governments, both state and federal, quite properly spend vast sums of money to establish machinery to try defendants accused of crime. Lawyers to prosecute are everywhere deemed essential to protect the public's interest in an orderly society. Similarly, there are few defendants charged with crime, few indeed, who fail to hire the best lawyers they can get to prepare and present their defenses. That government hires lawyers to prosecute and defendants who have the money hire lawyers to defend are the strongest indications of the widespread belief that lawyers in criminal courts are necessities, not luxuries. The right of one charged with crime to counsel may not be deemed fundamental and essential to fair trials in some countries, but it is in ours. From the very beginning, our state and national constitutions and laws have laid great emphasis on procedural and substantive safeguards designed to assure fair trials before impartial tribunals in which every defendant stands equal before the law. This noble ideal cannot be realized if the poor man charged with crime has to face his accusers without a lawyer to assist him. A defendant's need for a lawyer is nowhere better stated than in the moving words of Mr. Justice Sutherland in Powell v. Alabama:

> "The right to be heard would be, in many cases, of little avail if it did not comprehend the right to be heard by counsel. Even the intelligent and educated layman has small and sometimes no skill in the science of law. If charged with crime, he is incapable, generally, of determining for

himself whether the indictment is good or bad. He is unfamiliar with the rules of evidence. Left without the aid of counsel he may be put on trial without a proper charge, and convicted upon incompetent evidence, or evidence irrelevant to the issue or otherwise inadmissible. He lacks both the skill and knowledge adequately to prepare his defense, even though he have a perfect one. He requires the guiding hand of counsel at every step in the proceedings against him. Without it, though he be not guilty, he faces the danger of conviction because he does not know how to establish his innocence."

The Court in Betts v. Brady departed from the sound wisdom upon which the Court's holding in Powell v. Alabama rested. Florida, supported by two other States, has asked that Betts v. Brady be left intact. Twenty-two States, as friends of the Court, argue that Betts was "an anachronism when handed down" and that it should now be overruled. We agree.

The judgment is reversed and the cause is remanded to the Supreme Court of Florida for further action not inconsistent with this opinion.

Reversed.

[The concurring opinion of JUSTICES DOUGLAS and CLARK are omitted.]

[MR. JUSTICE HARLAN's concurring opinion is omitted.]

ARGERSINGER v. HAMLIN

Supreme Court of the United States, 1972.
407 U.S. 25, 92 S.Ct. 2006.

MR. JUSTICE DOUGLAS delivered the opinion of the Court.

Petitioner, an indigent, was charged in Florida with carrying a concealed weapon, an offense punishable by imprisonment up to six months and a $1,000 fine. The trial was to a judge and petitioner was unrepresented by counsel. He was sentenced to serve 90 days in jail and brought this habeas corpus action in the Florida Supreme Court, alleging that, being deprived of his right to counsel, he was unable as an indigent layman properly to raise and present to the trial court good and sufficient defenses to the charges for which he stands convicted. The Florida Supreme Court by a four-to-three decision, in ruling on the right to counsel, followed the line we marked out in Duncan v. Louisiana (1968) as respects the right to trial by jury and held that the right to court-appointed counsel extends only to trials "for nonpetty offenses punishable by more than six months imprisonment." [1]

* * *

1. Nineteen States provide for the appointment of counsel in most misdemeanor cases. Id., pp. 124–133. One of these is Oregon whose Supreme Court said in Application of Stevenson, 254 Or. 94, 458 P.2d 414, 418, "If our objective is to insure a fair trial in every criminal prosecution, the

The Sixth Amendment, which in enumerated situations has been made applicable to the States by reason of the Fourteenth Amendment . . . provides specified standards for "all criminal prosecutions."

One is the requirement of a "public trial." In re Oliver (1948), held that the right to a "public trial" was applicable to a state proceeding even though only a 60-day sentence was involved.

Another guarantee is the right to be informed of the nature and cause of the accusation. Still another, the right of confrontation. Pointer v. Texas (1965). And another, compulsory process for obtaining witnesses in one's favor. Washington v. Texas (1967). We have never limited these rights to felonies nor to lesser but serious offenses.

* * *

The right to trial by jury, also guaranteed by the Sixth Amendment by reason of the Fourteenth, was limited by Duncan v. Louisiana, supra, to trials where the potential punishment was imprisonment for six months or more. But, as the various opinions in Baldwin v. New York, 399 U.S. 66, 90 S.Ct. 1886, 26 L.Ed.2d 437, make plain, the right to trial by jury has a different genealogy and is brigaded with a system of trial to a judge alone. As stated in *Duncan*:

> "Providing an accused with the right to be tried by a jury of his peers gave him an inestimable safeguard against the corrupt or overzealous prosecutor and against the compliant, biased, or eccentric judge. If the defendant preferred the common-sense judgment of a jury to the more tutored but perhaps less sympathetic reaction of the single judge, he was to have it. Beyond this, the jury trial provisions in the Federal and State Constitutions reflect a fundamental decision about the exercise of official power—a reluctance to entrust plenary powers over the life and liberty of the citizen to one judge or to a group of judges. Fear of unchecked power, so typical of our State and Federal Governments in other respects, found expression in the criminal law in this insistence upon community participation in the determination of guilt or innocence. The deep commitment of the Nation to the right of jury trial in serious criminal cases as a defense against arbitrary law enforcement qualifies for protection under the Due Process Clause of the Fourteenth Amendment, and must therefore be respected by the States."

need for counsel is not determined by the seriousness of the crime. The assistance of counsel will best avoid conviction of the innocent—an objective as important in the municipal court as in a court of general jurisdiction."
California's requirement extends to traffic violations. Blake v. Municipal Court, 242 Cal.App.2d 731, 51 Cal. Rptr. 771.

Overall, 31 States have now extended the right to defendants charged with crimes less serious than felonies. Comment, Right to Counsel, *supra*, at 134.

While there is historical support for limiting the "deep commitment" to trial by jury to "serious criminal cases," there is no such support for a similar limitation on the right to assistance of counsel:

> "Originally, in England, a person charged with treason or felony was denied the aid of counsel, except in respect of legal questions which the accused himself might suggest. At the same time parties in civil cases and persons accused of misdemeanors were entitled to the full assistance of counsel. . . . [It] appears that in at least twelve of the thirteen colonies the rule of the English common law, in the respect now under consideration, had been definitively rejected and the right to counsel fully recognized in all criminal prosecutions, save that in one or two instances the right was limited to capital offenses or to the more serious crimes . . . ." Powell v. Alabama (1932).

The Sixth Amendment thus extended the right to counsel beyond its common-law dimensions. But there is nothing in the language of the Amendment, its history, or in the decisions of this Court, to indicate that it was intended to embody a retraction of the right in petty offenses wherein the common law previously did require that counsel be provided.

We reject, therefore, the premise that since prosecutions for crimes punishable by imprisonment for less than six months may be tried without a jury, they may always be tried without a lawyer.

The assistance of counsel is often a requisite to the very existence of a fair trial.

*   *   *

Both *Powell* and *Gideon* involved felonies. But their rationale has relevance to any criminal trial, where an accused is deprived of his liberty. *Powell* and *Gideon* suggest that there are certain fundamental rights applicable to all such criminal prosecutions, even those, such as In re Oliver, *supra,* where the penalty is 60 days' imprisonment:

> "A person's right to reasonable notice of a charge against him, and an opportunity to be heard in his defense —a right to his day in court—are basic in our system of jurisprudence; and these rights included, as a minimum, a right to examine the witnesses against him, to offer testimony, *and to be represented by counsel.*" 333 U.S., at 273, 68 S.Ct., at 507 (emphasis supplied).

The requirement of counsel may well be necessary for a fair trial even in a petty offense prosecution. We are by no means convinced that legal and constitutional questions involved in a case that actually leads to imprisonment even for a brief period are any less complex than when a person can be sent off for six months or more.

*   *   *

The trial of vagrancy cases in illustrative. While only brief sentences of imprisonment may be imposed, the cases often bristle with thorny constitutional questions.

*   *   *

Beyond the problem of trials and appeals is that of the guilty plea, a problem which looms large in misdemeanor as well as in felony cases. Counsel is needed so that the accused may know precisely what he is doing, so that he is fully aware of the prospect of going to jail or prison, and so that he is treated fairly by the prosecution.

In addition, the volume of misdemeanor cases, far greater in number than felony prosecutions, may create an obsession for speedy dispositions, regardless of the fairness of the result. . . .

* * *

"The misdemeanor trial is characterized by insufficient and frequently irresponsible preparation on the part of the defense, the prosecution, and the court. Everything is rush, rush." Hellerstein, The Importance of the Misdemeanor Case on Trial and Appeal, 38 The Legal Aid Brief Case 151, 152 (1970).

There is evidence of the prejudice which results to misdemeanor defendants from this "assembly-line justice." One study concluded that "Misdemeanants represented by attorneys are five times as likely to emerge from police court with all charges dismissed as are defendants who face similar charges without counsel." ACLU, Legal Counsel for Misdemeanants, Preliminary Report, 1 (1970).

We must conclude, therefore, that the problems associated with misdemeanor and petty offenses often require the presence of counsel to insure the accused a fair trial. Mr. Justice Powell suggests that these problems are raised even in situations where there is no prospect of imprisonment. We need not consider the requirements of the Sixth Amendment as regards the right to counsel where loss of liberty is not involved, however, for here petitioner was in fact sentenced to jail. And, as we said in Baldwin v. New York (1970): "[T]he prospect of imprisonment for however short a time will seldom be viewed by the accused as a trivial or 'petty' matter and may well result in quite serious repercussions affecting his career and his reputation."

We hold, therefore, that absent a knowing and intelligent waiver, no person may be imprisoned for any offense, whether classified as petty, misdemeanor, or felony, unless he was represented by counsel at his trial.

* * *

Under the rule we announce today, every judge will know when the trial of a misdemeanor starts that no imprisonment may be imposed, even though local law permits it, unless the accused is represented by counsel. He will have a measure of the seriousness and gravity of the offense and therefore know when to name a lawyer to represent the accused before the trial starts.

The run of misdemeanors will not be affected by today's ruling. But in those that end up in the actual deprivation of a person's liberty, the accused will receive the benefit of "the guiding hand of counsel" so necessary when one's liberty is in jeopardy.

Reversed.

Mr. Chief Justice Burger, concurring in the result.

I agree with much of the analysis in the opinion of the Court and with Mr. Justice Powell's appraisal of the problems. Were I able to confine my focus solely to the burden that the States will have to bear in providing counsel, I would be inclined, at this stage of the development of the constitutional right to counsel, to conclude that there is much to commend drawing the line at penalties in excess of six months' confinement. Yet several cogent factors suggest the infirmities in any approach that allows confinement for any period without the aid of counsel at trial; any deprivation of liberty is a serious matter. The issues that must be dealt with in a trial for a petty offense or a misdemeanor may often be simpler than those involved in a felony trial and yet be beyond the capability of a layman, especially when he is opposed by a law-trained prosecutor. There is little ground, therefore, to assume that a defendant, unaided by counsel, will be any more able adequately to defend himself against the lesser charges that may involve confinement than more serious charges. Appeal from a conviction after an uncounseled trial is not likely to be of much help to a defendant since the die is usually cast when judgment is entered on an uncounseled trial record.

Trial judges sitting in petty and misdemeanor cases—and prosecutors—should recognize exactly what will be required by today's decision. Because no individual can be imprisoned unless he is represented by counsel, the trial judge and the prosecutor will have to engage in a predictive evaluation of each case to determine whether there is a significant likelihood that, if the defendant is convicted, the trial judge will sentence him to a jail term. The judge can preserve the option of a jail sentence only by offering counsel to any defendant unable to retain counsel on his own. This need to predict will place a new load on courts already overburdened and already compelled to deal with far more cases in one day than is reasonable and proper. Yet the prediction is not one beyond the capacity of an experienced judge, aided as he should be by the prosecuting officer. As to jury cases, the latter should be prepared to inform the judge as to any prior record of the accused, the general nature of the case against the accused, including any use of violence, the severity of harm to the victim, the impact on the community and the other factors relevant to the sentencing process. Since the judge ought to have some degree of such information after judgment of guilt is determined, ways can be found in the more serious misdemeanor cases when jury trial is not waived to make it available to the judge before trial. This will not mean a full "presentence" report on every defendant in every case before the jury passes on guilt, but a prosecutor should know before trial whether he intends to urge a jail sentence and if he does he should be prepared to aid the court with the factual and legal basis for his view on that score.

This will mean not only that more defense counsel must be provided, but also additional prosecutors and better facilities for securing information about the accused as it bears on the probability of a decision to confine.

* * *

MR. JUSTICE BRENNAN, with whom MR. JUSTICE DOUGLAS and MR. JUSTICE STEWART join, concurring.

I join the opinion of the Court and add only an observation upon its discussion of legal resources, *ante* at 2012, n. 7. Law students as well as practicing attorneys may provide an important source of legal representation for the indigent. The Council on Legal Education for Professional Responsibility (CLEPR) informs us that more than 125 of the country's 147 accredited law schools have established clinical programs in which faculty-supervised students aid clients in a variety of civil and criminal matters. CLEPR Newsletter, May 1972, at 2. These programs supplement practice rules enacted in 38 States authorizing students to practice law under prescribed conditions. Like the American Bar Association's Model Student Practice Rule (1969), most of these regulations permit students to make supervised court appearances as defense counsel in criminal cases. CLEPR, State Rules Permitting the Student Practice of Law: Comparisons and Comments 13 (1971). Given the huge increase in law school enrollments over the past few years, see Ruud, That Burgeoning Law School Enrollment, 58 A.B.A.J. 146 (1972), I think it plain that law students can be looked to to make a significant contribution, quantitatively and qualitatively, to the representation of the poor in many areas, including cases reached by today's decision.

[Other opinions omitted.]

NOTES

1. In Scott v. Illinois, 440 U.S. 367, 99 S.Ct. 1158 (1979), petitioner had been convicted of theft under $150, a misdemeanor which carried a possible punishment of one year in jail and a fine of $500. After a bench trial without defense counsel, Scott was convicted and sentenced to a fine of $50. By a vote of five-to-four, the Supreme Court held that Illinois was not required to provide Scott with court-appointed counsel. Writing for himself and three other justices, Justice Rehnquist suggested that in *Argersinger* the Court had drawn the line in misdemeanor trials at "actual imprisonment" and had not left the question open as petitioner contended:

> "Although the intentions of the Argersinger Court are not unmistakably clear from its opinion, we conclude today that Argersinger did indeed delimit the constitutional right to appointed counsel in state criminal proceedings. Even were the matter res nova, we believe that the central premise of Argersinger—that actual imprisonment is a penalty different in kind from fines or the mere threat of imprisonment—is eminently sound and warrants adoption of actual imprisonment as the line defining the constitutional right to appointment of counsel. Argersinger has proved reasonably workable, whereas any extension would create confusion and impose unpredictable, but necessarily substantial, costs on 50 quite diverse States. We therefore hold that the Sixth and Fourteenth Amendments to the United States Constitution require only that no indigent criminal defendant be sentenced to a term of imprison-
> **ment unless the State has afforded him the right to assistance**

of appointed counsel in his defense. The judgment of the Supreme Court of Illinois is accordingly affirmed."

In a concurring opinion Mr. Justice Powell provided the fifth vote for affirmance:

"For the reasons stated in my opinion in Argersinger v. Hamlin (1972), I do not think the rule adopted by the Court in that case is required by the Constitution. Moreover, the drawing of a line based on whether there is imprisonment (even for overnight) can have the practical effect of precluding provision of counsel in other types of cases in which conviction can have more serious consequences. The Argersinger rule also tends to impair the proper functioning of the criminal justice system in that trial judges, in advance of hearing any evidence and before knowing anything about the case except the charge, all too often will be compelled to forego the legislatively granted option to impose a sentence of imprisonment upon conviction. Preserving this option by providing counsel often will be impossible or impracticable—particularly in congested urban courts where scores of cases are heard in a single setting, and in small and rural communities where lawyers may not be available.

"Despite my continuing reservations about the Argersinger rule, it was approved by the Court in the 1972 opinion and four Justices have reaffirmed it today. It is important that this Court provide clear guidance to the hundreds of courts across the country that confront this problem daily. Accordingly, and mindful of stare decisis, I join the opinion of the Court. I do so, however, with the hope that in due time a majority will recognize that a more flexible rule is consistent with due process and will better serve the cause of justice."

Justice Brennan authored a dissent, joined by Justices Stevens and Marshall. He argued that in *Argersinger* all assumed that counsel is required in any case where the possible statutory punishment exceeds six months. He noted that Justice Powell (whose vote for affirmance was necessary in *Scott*) had argued in *Argersinger* that the "right-to-counsel line must be drawn so that an indigent has a right to appointed counsel in all cases in which there is a due process right to jury trial." Brennan noted that, as a result of *Scott*, the right to trial by jury attaches in some cases in which an indigent defendant has no right to appointed counsel. He also argued that the authorized imprisonment standard is the traditional test for measuring the seriousness of the offense. He said that, as a result of *Scott*, courts, as a means of avoiding counsel, will negate the legislative judgment as to what offenses merit imprisonment. Brennan also challenged the assumption that the fiscal impact of a decision contrary to *Scott* would be intolerable. He added that "This Court's role in enforcing constitutional guarantees for criminal defendants cannot be made dependent on the budgetary decisions of state governments." Even Brennan's views left open the possibility that some "regulatory" offenses (including traffic cases), if no imprisonment is to be imposed, could be exempted from the requirement of counsel. He asserted, however, that theft, with its moral stigma, is not such an offense.

Justice Blackmun also dissented. He argued that counsel must be provided for the indigent in any case in which the statutory punishment exceeds six months *or* the actual punishment includes any period of incarceration.

2. In Baldasar v. Illinois, —— U.S. ——, 100 S.Ct. —— (1980), the defendant previously had been convicted of misdemeanor theft. At his trial, although indigent, he was not represented by counsel and was not offered appointed counsel. He received a fine but no prison sentence. Subsequently he was tried on a felony charge of "second theft" under an enhancement provision whereby a misdemeanor theft rose to the felony level by virtue of the prior theft conviction. The Supreme Court held that under these circumstances the prior conviction, obtained at a trial where the defendant neither had nor waived counsel, could not be used to enhance the offense even though the original trial comported with the principles of *Argersinger* and *Scott*. The felony sentence of not less than one year nor more than three years was invalidated in favor of a misdemeanor sentence of not more than 364 days.

C. OTHER ASSISTANCE FOR THE INDIGENT

PEOPLE v. WATSON

Supreme Court of Illinois, 1966.
36 Ill.2d 228, 221 N.E.2d 645.

SOLFISBURG, JUSTICE. The defendant was indicted in Winnebago County for attempt to commit the offense of forgery. A jury trial resulted in a guilty verdict and the defendant was sentenced to a term of one to five years in the penitentiary. He has appealed directly to this court on the grounds that a question has arisen under the sixth and fourteenth amendments to the United States constitution and under section 9 of article II of the constitution of Illinois, S. H.A. Specifically defendant, an indigent, contends that the trial judge's refusal to provide him with funds with which to obtain the services of a questioned document examiner deprived the defendant of due process in that he was not allowed to call witnesses in his favor. . . .

In August, 1965, Stanwood Trein purchased some $50 worth of American Express traveler's checks. Later on the day of the purchase, Trein picked up a stranger in his automobile and gave him a ride from Rockford to Dixon, Illinois. When Trein arrived home, he noticed that $30 or $40 of the traveler's checks were missing. Some days thereafter a person entered a Rockford tavern and asked the bartender to cash a ten-dollar traveler's check. The person presenting the check signed it in the bartender's presence, but since the name signed was not the same as that on the top of the check, the bartender called the manager who inquired about the disparity of signatures. After a short conversation, the person attempting to cash the check left the tavern, leaving the check behind. The manager then called the police.

The following day two police officers brought the defendant to the Rockford tavern and at that time both the bartender and the manager identified the defendant as the person who had tried to cash the check the day before. During the trial, the defendant was also identified as the person who had ridden in the Trein car from Rockford to Dixon and the check was identified as one of those purchased by Trein.

Prior to trial the defendant, through his court-appointed attorney, filed a motion requesting the court to provide him with funds, because of his indigency, in order to obtain the services of a questioned document examiner. Attached to the motion was an affidavit of defense counsel stating, in substance, that the charge was attempted forgery of an American Express traveler's check, that the State would produce a witness who will testify that the check was signed by the defendant in his presence, that the State has not obtained the opinion of an expert as to whether defendant signed the check or whether his fingerprints appear thereon, that an examination of the check by a qualified expert will show that defendant did not sign it and that his fingerprints do not appear thereon, and that in his opinion the testimony of such an expert is essential to provide defendant with an adequate defense and to establish his innocence. The State contended, in urging the motion be denied, that since the charge against the defendant was attempt to commit forgery by delivery of a forged check, the handwriting of the defendant was not in issue. Furthermore, the State contended that the motion should be denied since there is no statutory authority for appointment of expert witnesses in noncapital cases. After arguments, the court denied the motion.

* * *

It has long been a major goal of our entire judicial system to see that all persons charged with a crime "stand on an equality before the bar of justice in every American court." (Chambers v. State of Florida, 309 U.S. 227, 241, 60 S.Ct. 472, 479.) Such cases as Gideon v. Wainwright, 372 U.S. 335, 83 S.Ct. 792, and Griffin v. People of State of Illinois, 351 U.S. 12, 76 S.Ct. 585, have gone far to achieve this goal by assuring indigent defendants, even in noncapital cases, the right to counsel and to appellate review. The problem now facing the court concerns the production of witnesses on behalf of indigents. The Illinois constitution provides, in section 9 of article II, that in criminal prosecutions the accused is entitled to have process to compel the attendance of witnesses in his behalf. In almost identical language the sixth amendment to the United States constitution provides that the accused in criminal cases is entitled to have compulsory process for obtaining witnesses in his favor. Thus it is at once apparent that the right to summon witnesses is fundamental to our legal system. It is defendant's contention that a right so fundamental should not be made to depend upon the financial circumstances of the defendant. We share this view.

The court recognizes that there is a distinction between the right to call witnesses and the right to have these witnesses paid for by the government, but in certain instances involving indigents, the lack of funds with which to pay for the witness will often preclude him from calling that witness and occasionally prevent him from offering a defense. Thus, although the defendant is afforded the shadow of the right to call witnesses, he is deprived of the substance.

The value of an expert witness's testimony lies in his experience and, more particularly, in his preparation. Although a *subpoena* would suffice to compel his appearance at trial, this appearance by itself would be of no value unless he had been able to make findings upon which to base his testimony. It is the cost of making these preparatory findings which the defendant feels should be borne by the government.

Indeed, the State legislature has taken a similar view but only in certain instances, the most pertinent of these being in capital cases where the court is allowed to order the county treasurer to pay a reasonable fee, not to exceed $250 for each defendant for expert witnesses in support of the accused. (Ill.Rev.Stat.1965, chap. 38, par. 113–3(e).) While we commend this legislative policy, we are of the opinion that in certain instances this policy should be extended to noncapital felonies. The constitutional provisions for compelling the attendance of witnesses make no distinction between capital and noncapital cases and neither should the safeguards for a fair trial.

Whether it is necessary to subpoena expert witnesses in order to assure a fair trial will depend upon the facts in each case. There are instances in noncapital cases where an expert might be necessary to establish a defense. Here a handwriting expert could give a professional opinion as to whether the defendant signed the check he is accused of attempting to deliver, and could compare the signature on that check with the signature on the check which was signed and delivered while defendant was in custody. If it is his opinion that defendant could not have signed it, then the jury could be permitted to draw the conclusion that defendant is innocent. Despite the language of the indictment, the issue of handwriting goes to the heart of the defense. The opinion of a handwriting expert in this case then may have been crucial, and defendant's lack of funds prevented him from presenting to the jury evidence which may have established his innocence. We hold that under the facts presented in this case defendant was entitled to a reasonable fee for the purposes of hiring a questioned document examiner. Recognizing that the payment of expert witness fees is an appropriate subject for the legislature, as is the payment of legal costs and fees, we trust the General Assembly will consider the expansion of section 113–3(e) to include noncapital cases where expert testimony is deemed by the trial judge to be crucial to a proper defense. Such a step has been taken by the California legislature, and appears to have met with satisfactory results. In view of our decision regarding the admissibility of the subsequently presented check and the defendant's right to an expert witness, this cause must be remanded for a new trial.

HOUSE, JUSTICE (specially concurring). I concur with the holding that defendant under the circumstances of this case was entitled to have an expert witness examine the questioned document, but I do believe that the majority has gone too far when it apparently equates the legislative pronouncement in section 113–3(e) of the Code of Criminal Procedure, with the requirements of due process. I feel that the defendant in this case had the right to have the check examined by handwriting and fingerprint experts, but I do not think he is "entitled to a reasonable fee for the purposes of hiring a questioned-document examiner".

Section 113–3(e) provides, "In capital cases, in addition to counsel, if the court determines that the defendant is indigent the court may, upon the filing with the court of a verified statement of services rendered, order the county treasurer of the county of trial to pay necessary expert witnesses for defendant reasonable compensation stated in the order not to exceed $250 for each defendant." The legislature has seen fit to limit this provision to capital cases. To expand the philosophy and force of this section to cover this case is to legislate by judicial metaphysics.

We have held on several occasions that the refusal to furnish an indigent defendant with an expert witness or witnesses in addition to those already produced by the People on the same issue does not constitute a denial of due process in the absence of a showing that the People's expert witness or witnesses gave other than their honest and unprejudiced opinion based upon their special knowledge and examination. People v. Carpenter, 13 Ill.2d 470, 150 N.E.2d 100 (psychiatrist); People v. Myers, 35 Ill.2d 311, 220 N.E.2d 297 (psychiatrist); People v. Nash, No. 39002 (ballistics), 36 Ill.2d 275, 222 N.E.2d 473.

In this case the People produced no expert testimony as to whether defendant signed the check or whether his fingerprints appeared on it. Under the facts of this case, we have decided that there is a reasonable doubt of defendant's guilt and that such opinion evidence is necessary in order to convict defendant. It seems to me our opinion should go no further than this. To hold that defendant should hire a questioned-document examiner is in effect asking him to prove himself innocent. If the People do produce such testimony, then the rulings in *Carpenter, Myers* and *Nash* become operative.

For still another reason, I think that the majority opinion has gone beyond the requirements of due process of law. It holds that the indigent defendant should be provided with funds to hire a questioned-document examiner. This is in sharp contrast with the constitutional provision guaranteeing the right to counsel, which has never been construed to mean that funds should be paid to an indigent defendant with which to pay counsel of his choice. The legislature in section 113–3(b) has provided that the trial court shall appoint an attorney for an indigent defendant and not that the court furnish funds with which an indigent may retain counsel.

I think this court should go no further than to state that defendant was not proved guilty beyond a reasonable doubt and reverse and remand the cause for a new trial. In my opinion, the majority has exceeded the bounds of judicial restraint in ordering the county treasurer to pay the fees of an expert witness hired by defendant.

UNDERWOOD, JUSTICE (concurring in part and dissenting in part):

I agree that this case must be remanded for a new trial because of the trial court's error in precluding defendant from offering evidence that a similar traveler's check was forged and cashed after defendant was in custody, but I cannot agree with the extension of the defendant's right to the assistance of expert witnesses which is accomplished by the majority opinion.

*   *   *

I do not quarrel with the majority premise that the bare right to subpoena expert witnesses is of little value, for without an opportunity for pre-trial preparation the value of the expert's testimony would be, in all likelihood, substantially reduced. And, while an expert may undoubtedly be subpoenaed and compelled to appear, it seems to me there are substantial constitutional questions (deprivation of property without due process) as to whether a court may compel him to expend his time and apply his expertise to pretrial examination of documents without compensating him therefor. But these factors do not invalidate the legislative limitation upon the type of case in which expert assistance shall be available to indigent defendants unless the right thereto is constitutional in dimension. There are, in fact, compelling reasons for such limitations. It would be unrealistic to assume that the holding in the majority opinion that there are "instances in noncapital cases" where experts must be furnished indigent defendants will result in other than a request for such assistance by such defendants in most cases involving issues upon which an expert could conceivably be employed. We are aware, from the substantial number of records coming before us, that the trial courts frequently refer defendants to clinics or private physicians for the purpose of pretrial competency examinations. In all of such cases, presumably, the indigent defendant will now also be entitled to examination by his own psychiatrist or psychologist or both. Cases involving signatures, finger prints, chemical analyses and ballistics, to mention only a few, will automatically qualify as may every case in which an expert in any field appears for the State either as a witness or assists in pretrial investigative or preparatory activities.

While it is not my intention to make an *ad terrorem* presentation, it seems proper to point out the substantial arguments against the result reached by the majority without any constitutionally imposed necessity for so doing, and in the face of legislative decision to the contrary.

I would abide by our earlier indications in *Nash, Myers* and *Carpenter* and uphold the trial court's action in denying defendant's request for expert assistance.

NOTES

1. For an interesting decision which demonstrates that *Watson* has not been read expansively, see People v. Nichols, 70 Ill.App.3d 748, 27 Ill.Dec. 21, 388 N.E.2d 984 (1979).

2. Except for decisions concerning an indigent defendant's right at trial to counsel and to a transcript of testimony given in an earlier proceeding (to be discussed subsequently in Note 4), the Supreme Court has generally avoided indigents' claims concerning the right to assistance at the trial level. Lower courts have frequently dealt with such issues. Generally they have refused to rule that the indigent is entitled to assistance which is the

same as (or just as good as) what the defendant with funds could purchase. Normally courts have required quite a specific showing of necessity, even though the non-indigent might purchase the services in a case where necessity is not manifest. See generally State v. Sahlie, —— S.D. ——, 245 N.W. 2d 476 (1976), setting forth criteria for the granting of an indigent's request for trial assistance. The cases can be grouped according to type of service:

(a) *Investigators.* Although commissions and agencies which promulgate standards for defender offices always include an investigative component, the indigent defendant, represented by appointed counsel, has not often succeeded in overturning a trial judge's denial of funds for investigative assistance or a judge's denial of the appointment of an investigator. See Mason v. Arizona, 504 F.2d 1345 (9th Cir. 1974); United States v. Harris, 542 F.2d 1283 (7th Cir. 1976); Watson v. State, 64 Wis.2d 264, 219 N.W.2d 398 (1974).

(b) *Experts.* Absent statutory authority, an indigent defendant who has been denied the existence of an expert, even after *Watson*, rarely succeeds in overturning a conviction on that basis. State v. Williams, 263 S.C. 290, 210 S.E.2d 298 (1974) (pathologist); Patterson v. State, 239 Ga. 409, 238 S.E.2d 2 (1977) (firearms identification expert); Bright v. State, 293 So.2d 818 (Miss.1974), and State v. Clemons, 168 Conn. 395, 363 A.2d 33 (1975) (chemist or toxicologist for drug analysis); Knapp v. Hardy, 111 Ariz. 107, 523 P.2d 1308 (1974) (arson expert). Frequently courts emphasize that there was no suggestion that the prosecutor's expert was biased or incompetent. Alexander v. State, 257 Ark. 343, 516 S.W.2d 368 (1974). But see People v. Gunnerson, 74 Cal.App.3d 370, 141 Cal.Rptr. 488 (1977) (sufficient showing of uncertainty as to cause of death to require that defendant be permitted the services of a cardiologist); People v. Hatterson, 63 A.D.2d 736, 405 N.Y.S.2d 297 (1978) (defense right to services of a psychiatrist where prosecution psychotherapist had been permitted to testify that the alleged rape victim had a "compliant" or "obedient" personality). A defendant's claim of insanity may more frequently result in the appointment of an expert or in expenditure of funds for tests. See United States v. Hartfield, 513 F.2d 254 (9th Cir. 1975).

(c) *Interpreters.* Courts often have held that an indigent who speaks no English is entitled to the services of an interpreter. Ex parte Nanes, 558 S.W.2d 893 (Tex.Cr.App.1977); State v. Rios, 112 Ariz. 143, 539 P.2d 900 (1975). The trial judge's assessment of the necessity for appointment of an interpreter is not likely to be overturned, however. Flores v. State, 509 S.W.2d 580 (Tex.Cr.App.1974) (defendant's English deemed good enough). The common practice of using an interpreter from the police department or the prosecutor's office (which should be avoided in court, if possible, even when the non-English speaking person is a prosecution witness), always should be avoided when it is the defendant who faces the language barrier. See Gonzales v. State, 372 A.2d 191 (Del.1977).

The appellate decisions, as is often the case, may tell only half of the story. Presumably in many instances an indigent's request for the expenditure of funds in his defense is granted, and the prosecution does not challenge the order in a higher court.

3. In United States v. Durant, 545 F.2d 823 (2d Cir. 1976), the Court held that the federal district judge had erred under the Criminal Justice

Act, 18 U.S.C. § 3006A (1970), in denying a fingerprint expert in a case where fingerprint evidence was crucial to the defense theory of the case. As this case demonstrates, some statutory rights to trial-level assistance may be broader than an indigent's rights under the Constitution. Consider again the various possible rationales for defense services: due process, equal protection, statutory right, supervisory powers, right to counsel, right to compulsory process. What rationale prevailed in *Watson*?

4. When a prosecution witness has testified on the same subject in a former proceeding (e. g., at a preliminary hearing, a trial which resulted in a hung jury, or a co-defendant's trial), a defendant may have a constitutional right, under the *Griffin* line of cases, to a transcript of the earlier testimony if no alternative is available which would permit defense counsel to learn the content of such testimony (so as to be able to use it for discovery or impeachment purposes). See generally Roberts v. LaVallee, 389 U.S. 40, 88 S.Ct. 194 (1967); Britt v. North Carolina, 404 U.S. 226, 92 S.Ct. 431 (1971).

WILLIAMS v. ILLINOIS

Supreme Court of the United States, 1970.
399 U.S. 235, 90 S.Ct. 2018.

MR. CHIEF JUSTICE BURGER delivered the opinion of the Court.

This appeal from Illinois presents an important question involving a claim of discriminatory treatment based upon financial inability to pay a fine and court costs imposed in a criminal case. The narrow issue raised is whether an indigent may be continued in confinement beyond the maximum term specified by statute because of his failure to satisfy the monetary provisions of the sentence. . . .

On August 16, 1967, appellant was convicted of petty theft and received the maximum sentence provided by state law: one year imprisonment and a $500 fine. Appellant was also taxed $5 in court costs. The judgment directed, as permitted by statute, that if appellant was in default of the payment of the fine and court costs at the expiration of the one-year sentence, he should remain in jail pursuant to § 1–7(k) of the Ill.Crim.Code to "work off" the monetary obligations at the rate of $5 per day.[1] Thus, whereas the maximum term of imprisonment for petty theft was one year, the effect of the sentence imposed here required appellant to be confined for 101 days beyond the maximum period of confinement fixed by the statute since he could not pay the fine and costs of $505.

On November 29, 1967, appellant, while still an inmate in the county jail, petitioned the sentencing judge to vacate that portion of

1. Section 1–7(k) of the Criminal Code of 1961 provides:
   "Working out Fines.
   "A judgment of a fine imposed upon an offender may be enforced in the same manner as a judgment entered in a civil action; provided, however, that in such judgment imposing the fine the court may fur-
   ther order that upon nonpayment of such fine, the offender may be imprisoned until the fine is paid, or satisfied at the rate of $5.00 per day of imprisonment; provided, further, however, that no person shall be imprisoned under the first proviso hereof for a longer period than 6 months."

the order requiring that he remain imprisoned upon expiration of his one year sentence because of nonpayment of the fine and court costs. Appellant alleged that he was indigent at all stages of the proceedings, was without funds or property to satisfy the money portion of the sentence and that he would "be able to get a job and earn funds to pay the fine and costs if . . . released from jail upon expiration of his one year sentence." The State did not dispute the factual allegations and the trial court granted the State's motion to dismiss the petition ". . . for the reason that [appellant] was not legally entitled at that time to the relief requested . . . because he still has time to serve on his jail sentence and when that sentence has been served financial ability to pay a fine might not be the same as it was on the date [of sentencing]."

Appeal was taken directly to the Supreme Court of Illinois, which appears to have rejected any suggestion by the trial court that the petition was premature and went on to decide appellant's constitutional claim on the merits. It held that "there is no denial of equal protection of the law when an indigent defendant is imprisoned to satisfy payment of the fine." People v. Williams, 41 Ill.2d 511, 517, 244 N.E.2d 197, 200 (1969).

In addition to renewing the constitutional argument rejected by the state courts, appellant advances a host of other claims [2] which, in light of our disposition, we find unnecessary to reach or decide. Appellant challenges the constitutionality of § 1–7(k) of the Illinois Criminal Code and argues primarily that the Equal Protection Clause of the Fourteenth Amendment prohibits imprisonment of an indigent beyond the maximum term authorized by the statute governing the substantive offense when that imprisonment flows directly from his present inability to pay a fine and court costs. In response the State asserts its interest in the collection of revenues produced by payment of fines and contends that a "work off" system, as provided by § 1–7(k), is a rational means of implementing that policy. That interest is substantial and legitimate but for present purposes it is not unlike the State's interest in collecting a fine from an indigent person in circumstances where no imprisonment is included in the judgment. The State argues further that the statute is not constitutionally infirm simply because the legislature could have achieved the same result by some other means. With that general proposition we have no quarrel but that generality does not resolve the issue.

As noted earlier, appellant's incarceration beyond the statutory maximum stems from separate albeit related reasons: nonpayment of a fine and nonpayment of court costs. We find that neither of those grounds can constitutionally support the type of imprisonment imposed here, but we treat the fine and costs together because disposition of the claim on fines governs our disposition on costs.

---

2. Appellant also argues that every instance of default imprisonment violates either the Equal Protection and/or Due Process Clause(s) of the Fourteenth Amendment. He also asserts that the $5.00 per diem figure is unreasonable and irrational.

The custom of imprisoning a convicted defendant for nonpayment of fines dates back to medieval England and has long been practiced in this country. At the present time all States and the Federal Government have statutes authorizing incarceration under such circumstances. Most States permit imprisonment beyond the maximum term allowed by law, and in some there is no limit on the length of time one may serve for nonpayment.[3] While neither the antiquity of a practice nor the fact of steadfast legislative and judicial adherence to it through the centuries insulates it from constitutional attack, these factors should be weighed in the balance.[4] Indeed, in prior cases this Court seems to have tacitly approved incarceration to "work off" unpaid fines. See Hill v. United States ex rel. Wampler, 298 U. S. 460, 56 S.Ct. 760 (1936); Ex parte Jackson, 96 U.S. 727 (1878).[5]

The need to be open to reassessment of ancient practices other than those explicitly mandated by the Constitution is illustrated by the present case since the greatly increased use of fines as a criminal sanction has made nonpayment a major cause of incarceration in this country. Default imprisonment has traditionally been justified on the grounds it is a coercive device to ensure obedience to the judgment of the court. Thus, commitment for failure to pay has not been viewed as a part of the punishment or as an increase in the penalty; rather, it has been viewed as a means of enabling the court to enforce collection of money which a convicted defendant was obligated by the sentence to pay. The additional imprisonment, it has been said, may always be avoided by payment of the fine.

We conclude that when the aggregate imprisonment exceeds the maximum period fixed by the statute and results directly from an involuntary nonpayment of a fine or court costs we are confronted with an impermissible discrimination which rests on ability to pay, and accordingly, we reverse.

Griffin v. Illinois, 351 U.S. 12, 76 S.Ct. 585 (1956), marked a significant effort to alleviate discrimination against those who are unable to meet the costs of litigation in the administration of criminal justice. In holding the failure to provide an indigent criminal defendant with a trial transcript at public expense in order to prosecute an appeal was a violation of the Equal Protection Clause, this Court

---

3. The National Legal Aid and Defender Association, as Amicus Curiae, has filed a brief containing an extensive appendix which includes all the state statutes with helpful annotations. We have reproduced this portion of their brief as an appendix to this opinion. The corresponding federal statutes are 18 U.S.C. §§ 3565, 3569 (1964). See also Note, The Equal Protection Clause and Imprisonment of the Indigent for Nonpayment of Fines, 64 Mich.L.Rev. 938 (1968).

4. See Walz v. Tax Comm'n of New York City decided May 4, 1970, 397 U.S. 664, 90 S.Ct. 1409, 1420, where we noted that "nearly 50 years ago Mr. Justice Holmes stated:
" '[I]f a thing has been practised for two hundred years by common consent, it will need a strong case for the Fourteenth Amendment to affect it.' Jackman v. Rosenbaum, 260 U.S. 22, 31, 43 S.Ct. 9, 10 (1922)."

5. We note, however, that neither in those cases, nor at any other time, were the constitutional issues flowing from lack of funds presented to this Court for resolution.

declared that "[t]here can be no equal justice where the kind of trial a man gets depends on the amount of money he has." In the years since the *Griffin* case the Court has had frequent occasion to reaffirm allegiance to the basic command that justice be applied equally to all persons. Subsequent decisions of this Court have pointedly demonstrated that the passage of time has heightened rather than weakened the attempts to mitigate the disparate treatment of indigents in the criminal process.[6] Applying the teaching of the *Griffin* case here, we conclude that an indigent criminal defendant may not be imprisoned in default of payment of a fine beyond the maximum authorized by the statute regulating the substantive offense.

A State has wide latitude in fixing the punishment for state crimes. Thus, appellant does not assert that Illinois could not have appropriately fixed the penalty, in the first instance, at one year and 101 days. Nor has the claim been advanced that the sentence imposed was excessive in light of the circumstances of the commission of this particular offense. However, once the State has defined the outer limits of incarceration necessary to satisfy its penological interests and policies, it may not then subject a certain class of convicted defendants to a period of imprisonment beyond the statutory maximum solely by reason of their indigency.

It is clear, of course, that the sentence was not imposed upon appellant because of his indigency but because he had committed a crime. And the Illinois statutory scheme does not distinguish between defendants on the basis of ability to pay fines. But, as we said in Griffin v. Illinois, supra, "a law nondiscriminatory on its face may be grossly discriminatory in its operation." Here the Illinois statute as applied to Williams works an invidious discrimination solely because he is unable to pay the fine. On its face the statute extends to all defendants an apparently equal opportunity for limiting confinement to the statutory maximum simply by satisfying a money judgment. In fact, this is an illusory choice for Williams or any indigent who, by definition, is without funds. Since only a convicted person with access to funds can avoid the increased imprisonment the Illinois statute in operative effect exposes only indigents to the risk of imprisonment beyond the statutory maximum. By making the maximum confinement contingent upon one's ability to pay, the State has visited different consequences on two categories of persons since the result is to make incarceration in excess of the statutory maximum applicable only to those without the requisite resources to satisfy the money portion of the judgment.[7]

The mere fact that an indigent in a particular case may be imprisoned for a longer time than is a non-indigent convicted of the

6. See, e. g., Rinaldi v. Yeager, 384 U. S. 305, 86 S.Ct. 1497 (1966); Douglas v. California, 372 U.S. 353, 83 S.Ct. 814 (1962); Smith v. Bennett, 365 U. S. 708, 81 S.Ct. 895 (1961).

7. We wish to make clear that nothing in our decision today precludes imprisonment for willful refusal to pay a fine or court costs. See Ex parte Smith, 97 Utah 280, 92 P.2d 1098 (1939). Cf. Illinois v. Allen, 397 U.S. 337, 90 S.Ct. 1057 (1970).

same offense does not, of course, give rise to a violation of the Equal Protection Clause. Sentencing judges are vested with wide discretion in the exceedingly difficult task of determining the appropriate punishment in the countless variety of situations which appear. The Constitution permits qualitative differences in meting punishment and there is no requirement that two persons convicted of the same offense receive identical sentences. Thus it was that in Williams v. New York, 337 U.S. 241, 248, 69 S.Ct. 1079, 1083 (1949), we said "The belief no longer prevails that every offense in a like legal category calls for an identical punishment without regard to the past life and habits of a particular offender."

Nothing in today's decision curtails the sentencing prerogative of a judge because, as noted previously, the sovereign's purpose in confining an indigent beyond the statutory maximum is to provide a coercive means of collecting or "working out" a fine. After having taken into consideration the wide range of factors underlying the exercise of his sentencing function, nothing we now hold precludes a judge from imposing on an indigent, as on any defendant, the maximum penalty prescribed by law.

It bears emphasis that our holding does not deal with a judgment of confinement for nonpayment of a fine in the familiar pattern of an alternative sentence of "$30 or 30 days." We hold only that a State may not constitutionally imprison beyond the maximum duration fixed by statute a defendant who is financially unable to pay a fine. A statute permitting a sentence of both imprisonment and fine cannot be parlayed into a longer term of imprisonment than is fixed by the statute since to do so would be to accomplish indirectly as to an indigent that which cannot be done directly. We have no occasion to reach the question whether a State is precluded in any other circumstances from holding an indigent accountable for a fine by use of penal sanction. We hold only that the Equal Protection Clause of the Fourteenth Amendment requires that the statutory ceiling placed on imprisonment for any substantive offense be the same for all defendants irrespective of their economic status.[8]

The State is not powerless to enforce judgments against those financially unable to pay a fine; indeed, a different result would amount to inverse discrimination since it would enable an indigent to avoid both the fine and imprisonment for nonpayment whereas other defendants must always suffer one or the other conviction.

---

8. What we have said regarding imprisonment for involuntary nonpayment of fines applies with equal force to imprisonment for involuntary nonpayment of court costs. Although the actual amounts prescribed for fines and court costs reflect quite different considerations, see generally, Litigation Costs: The Hidden Barrier to the Indigent, 56 Geo.L.J. 516 (1968), the purpose of incarceration appears to be the same in both instances: ensuring compliance with a judgment. Thus inability to pay court costs cannot justify imprisoning an indigent beyond the maximum statutory term since the Equal Protection Clause prohibits expanding the maximum term specified by the statute simply because of inability to pay.

It is unnecessary for us to canvass the numerous alternatives to which the State by legislative enactment—or judges within the scope of their authority—may resort in order to avoid imprisoning an indigent beyond the statutory maximum for involuntary nonpayment of a fine or court costs. Appellant has suggested several plans, some of which are already utilized in some States, while others resemble those proposed by various studies.[9] The State is free to choose from among the variety of solutions already proposed and, of course, it may devise new ones.

We are not unaware that today's holding may place a further burden on States in administering criminal justice. Perhaps a fairer and more accurate statement would be that new cases expose old infirmities which apathy or absence of challenge have permitted to stand. But the constitutional imperatives of the Equal Protection Clause must have priority over the comfortable convenience of the status quo. "Any supposed administrative inconvenience would be minimal, since . . . [the unpaid portion of the judgment] could be reached through the ordinary processes of garnishment in the event of default." Rinaldi v. Yeager, 384 U.S. 305, 310, 86 S.Ct. 1497, 1500 (1966).

Nothing we hold today limits the power of the sentencing judge to impose alternative sanctions permitted by Illinois law; the definition of such alternatives, if any, lies with the Illinois courts. We therefore vacate the judgment appealed from and remand to the Supreme Court of Illinois for further proceedings not inconsistent with this opinion.

It is so ordered.

Judgment vacated and case remanded.

MR. JUSTICE BLACKMUN took no part in the consideration or decision of this case.

MR. JUSTICE HARLAN, concurring in the result.

I concur in today's judgment, but in doing so wish to dissociate myself from the "equal protection" rationale employed by the Court to justify its conclusions.

The "equal protection" analysis of the Court is, I submit, a "wolf in a sheep's clothing," for that rationale is no more than a masquerade of a supposedly objective standard for *subjective* judicial judgment as to what state legislation offends notions of "fundamental

---

9. Appellant has suggested that the fine and costs could be collected through an installment plan as is currently used in several States. E. g., Cal.Pen.Code § 1205; Mich.Stats. Ann., M.C.L.A. § 769.3, (1948); Pa. Stat.Ann. tit. 19, §§ 953–956 (1964). See also A.B.A. Minimum Standards for Criminal Justice, Sentencing Alternatives and Procedures (Approved Draft, 1968) § 2.7(b), pp. 117–123.

Appellant also suggests that the trial judge could impose a parole requirement on an indigent that he do specified work during the day to satisfy the fine. Cf. 50 U.S.C.App. 456.

See also Model Penal Code § 7.02(3)(a). (Proposed Official Draft 1962).

fairness." Under the rubric of "equal protection" this Court has in recent times effectively substituted its own "enlightened" social philosophy or that of the legislature no less than did in the older days the judicial adherents of the now discredited doctrine of "substantive" due process. I, for one, would prefer to judge the legislation before us in this case in terms of due process, that is to determine whether it arbitrarily infringes a constitutionally protected interest of this petitioner. . . .

An analysis under due process standards, correctly understood is, in my view, more conducive to judicial restraint than an approach couched in slogans and ringing phrases, such as "suspect" classification or "invidious" distinctions, or "compelling" state interest, that blur analysis by shifting the focus away from the nature of the individual interest affected, the extent to which it is affected, the rationality of the connection between legislative means and purpose, the existence of alternative means for effectuating the purpose, and the degree of confidence we may have that the statute reflects the legislative concern for the purpose that would legitimately support the means chosen. Accordingly, I turn to the case at hand.

* * *

The State by this statute, or any other statute fixing a penalty of a fine, has declared its penological interest—deterrence, retribution and rehabilitation—satisfied by a monetary payment, and disclaimed, as serving any penological purpose in such cases, a term in jail. While there can be no question that the State has a legitimate concern with punishing an individual who cannot pay the fine, there is serious question in my mind whether, having declared itself indifferent to fine and jail, it can consistently with due process refrain from offering some alternative for payment on the installment plan.

There are two conceivable justifications for not doing so. The most obvious and likely justification for the present statute is administrative convenience. Given the interest of the individual affected, I do not think a State may after declaring itself indifferent between a fine and jail, rely on the convenience of the latter as a constitutionally acceptable means for enforcing its interest, given the existence of less restrictive alternatives.

The second conceivable justification is that the jail alternative serves a penological purpose that cannot be served by collection of a fine over time. It is clear that having declared itself satisfied by a fine, the alternative of jail to a fine serves neither a rehabilitative or retributive interest. The question is, then, whether the requirement of a lump-sum payment can be sustained as a rational legislative determination that deterrence is effective only when a fine is exacted at once after sentence and by lump sum, rather than over a term. This is a highly doubtful proposition, since, apart from the mere fact of conviction and the humiliation associated with it and the token of punishment evidenced by the forfeiture, the deterrent effect of a fine is apt to derive more from its pinch on the purse than the time of payment.

That the Illinois statutes represent a considered judgment, evincing the belief that jail is a rational and necessary trade-off to punish the individual who possesses no accumulated assets seems most unlikely, since that substitute sentence provision, phrased in terms of a judgment collection statute, does not impose a discretionary jail term as an alternative sentence, but rather equates days in jail with a fixed sum. Thus, given that the only conceivable justification for this statute that would satisfy due process—that a lump-sum fine is a better deterrent than one payable over a period of time—is the one that is least likely to represent a considered legislative judgment, I would hold these statutes invalid.

The conclusion I reach is only that when a State declares its penal interest may be satisfied by a fine or a forfeiture in combination with a jail term the administrative inconvenience in a judgment collection procedure does not, as a matter of due process, justify sending to jail or extending the jail term of individuals who possess no accumulated assets. I would reserve the question as to whether a considered legislative judgment that a lump-sum fine is the only effective kind of forfeiture for deterrence and that the alternative must be jail. It follows, *a fortiori*, that no conclusion reached herein casts any doubt on the conventional "$30 or 30 days" if the legislature decides that should be the *penalty* for the crime. Note, Discriminations Against the Poor and the Fourteenth Amendment, 81 Harv.L.Rev. 435 (1967). Such a statute evinces the perfectly rational determination that some individuals will be adequately punished by a money fine, and others, indifferent to money—whether by virtue of indigency or other reasons—can only be punished by a jail term. Still more patently nothing said herein precludes the State from punishing ultimately by jail individuals who fail to pay fines or imprisoning immediately individuals who, in the judgment of a court, will not undertake to pay their fines.

On these premises I join the Court's judgment vacating appellant's sentence and remanding to the Supreme Court of Illinois to afford it an opportunity to instruct the sentencing judge as to any permissible alternatives under Illinois law. It may be that Illinois courts have the power to fashion a procedure pending further consideration of this problem by the state legislature.

NOTES

1. Can the reach of the Court's opinion in *Williams* logically stop with the case of the defendant who has been imprisoned for the maximum term? Or does the Court's rationale apply as well to one who has received less than the maximum sentence of imprisonment or who has simply been fined? What impact does the *Williams* opinion have upon the question of bail and the indigent? Given the presence of other factors which make the risk of flight unlikely, may a money bail be required of an indigent accused after *Williams*? See Chapter 12.

2. In Tate v. Short, 401 U.S. 395, 91 S.Ct. 668 (1971), the maximum statutory penalty for a certain traffic offense was a fine only. Imprisonment was not a possible punishment. The Supreme Court held that requir-

ing a defendant to work out his fine at five dollars per day ran afoul of the principles of *Williams.*

3. In Morris v. Schoonfield, 399 U.S. 508, 90 S.Ct. 2232 (1970), the Supreme Court vacated and remanded in light of *Williams* in a situation where (a) both a fine and imprisonment were possible penalties, (b) a fine was imposed, and (c) working out of the fine did *not*, as in *Williams*, extend the period of incarceration beyond the maximum allowed by such statute. Four of the justices, concurring, expressed the view that the incarceration for inability to pay a fine was impermissible under these circumstances, arguing that: the same constitutional defect condemned in *Williams* also inheres in jailing an indigent for failing to make immediate payment of any fine, whether or not the jail term of the indigent extends beyond the maximum term that may be imposed on a person willing and able to pay a fine.

Interestingly, the majority in *Tate*, note 2, cited the opinion of the four justices in *Morris*, even though *Tate* presented a narrower issue than did *Morris.*

4. Consider the propriety of the following periods of incarceration under (a) the narrow holding of *Williams*, (b) the narrow holding of *Tate*, and (c) the view of the four justices in *Morris.*

	Statutory Penalty	Penalty Imposed	Time Served
a.	6 months and $500	6 months and $500	9 months, 10 days
b.	6 months and $500	4 months and $500	7 months, 10 days
c.	6 months and $500	2 months and $100	2 months, 20 days
d.	6 months and $500	$150 or 1 month	1 month
e.	$500	$50	10 days
f.	6 months and $500	$30 or 30 days	30 days
g.	6 months or $500	6 months	6 months

When the legislature has provided incarceration as a possible sentence, what is to prevent a judge from imposing a jail sentence upon an indigent in a case where, if the accused had funds, the judge would impose a fine? Will a judge who does this violate the spirit of *Williams*? Of *Tate*? Ought he be condemned for violating an indigent's constitutional rights in a way which ordinarily will not be subject to review if he is careful enough not to articulate his thought process for the trial record?

5. If incarceration in lieu of a fine is still permitted in some circumstances, is there any constitutionally mandated minimum dollar figure which must be assigned to a day of incarceration? See People v. Saffore, 18 N.Y.2d 101, 218 N.E.2d 686 (1966), for one view. At the time of Williams, Illinois, with its $5 and its maximum "working out" period of 6 months was probably as progressive as most states. Today incarceration for failure to pay a fine is flatly prohibited by the Illinois Constitution, Article 1, Section 14. An Illinois defendant with funds who wilfully refuses to pay a fine is punished for contempt (and, unlike the situation in some jurisdictions), receives no credit toward the fine for the days he is incarcerated. Ill.Rev.Stat. ch. 38, § 1005–9–3 (1979).

6. The concept of "working out" a fine may still have meaning when a defendant is incarcerated before trial but upon conviction receives only a fine. He may be entitled to credit toward his fine, at a statutory rate, for each day of pre-trial incarceration. See Ill.Rev.Stat. ch. 38, § 110–14 (1979).

If state law does not provide such credit, has the United States Constitution been violated?

7.   The *Williams-Tate* line of decisions has had considerable impact. In State v. DeBonis, 58 N.J. 182, 276 A.2d 137 (1971), the court examined the alternatives available to the sentencing court when the defendant was unable to pay fine immediately.   Unable to pay a lump sum fine, defendant there offered to pay in installments.   The trial court refused the offer and ordered him to jail at the statutory rate of five dollars a day.   After studying several methods of payment, the New Jersey Supreme Court concluded that the installment system was the most practical alternative and that the defendant was therefore entitled to it by right.

Justice Blackmun, concurring in *Tate*, suggested that an alternative to fines, fair to all, would be a "jail only" policy.   The Hawaii Supreme Court, in State v. Tackett, 483 P.2d 191, 52 Haw. 601 (1971), rejected this idea because it would reduce sentencing flexibility and would work an inverse discrimination against "the employed man with funds".

Because of the high administrative cost involved in collecting small fines, will *Tate*, as a practical matter, force judges to impose short jail sentences rather than fines?   Is this a desirable result?

Chapter 10

THE PRELIMINARY HEARING

A. THE NATURE AND PURPOSE OF THE HEARING

COLEMAN v. ALABAMA

Supreme Court of the United States, 1970.
399 U.S. 1, 90 S.Ct. 1999, conformed to 46 Ala.App. 737, 239 So.2d 223.

MR. JUSTICE BRENNAN announced the judgment of the Court and delivered the following opinion.

Petitioners were convicted in an Alabama Circuit Court of assault with intent to murder in the shooting of one Reynolds after he and his wife parked their car on an Alabama highway to change a flat tire.

* * *

This Court has held that a person accused of crime "requires the guiding hand of counsel at every step in the proceedings against him," Powell v. Alabama, 287 U.S. 45, 69 (1932), and that that constitutional principle is not limited to the presence of counsel at trial. "It is central to that principle that in addition to counsel's presence at trial, the accused is guaranteed that he need not stand alone against the State at any stage of the prosecution, formal or informal, in court or out, where counsel's absence might derogate from the accused's right to a fair trial." United States v. Wade [388 U.S. 218, 226, 87 S.Ct. 1926, 1932 (1967)]. Accordingly, "the principle of Powell v. Alabama and succeeding cases requires that we scrutinize *any* pretrial confrontation of the accused to determine whether the presence of his counsel is necessary to preserve the defendant's basic right to a fair trial as affected by his right meaningfully to cross-examine the witnesses against him and to have effective assistance of counsel at the trial itself. It calls upon us to analyze whether potential substantial prejudice to defendant's rights inheres in the particular confrontation and the ability of counsel to help avoid that prejudice." Id., at 227. Applying this test, the Court has held that "critical stages" include the pretrial type of arraignment where certain rights may be sacrificed or lost, Hamilton v. Alabama, 368 U.S. 52, 54, 82 S.Ct. 157, 158–159 (1961), see White v. Maryland, 373 U.S. 59, 83 S.Ct. 1050 (1963), and the pretrial lineup, United States v. Wade, supra; Gilbert v. California [388 U.S. 263, 87 S.Ct. 1951 (1967)]. Cf. Miranda v. Arizona, 384 U.S. 436, 86 S.Ct. 1602 (1966), where the Court held that the privilege against compulsory self-incrimination includes a right to counsel at a pretrial custodial interrogation. See also Massiah v. United States, 377 U.S. 201, 84 S.Ct. 1199 (1964).

The preliminary hearing is not a required step in an Alabama prosecution. The prosecutor may seek an indictment directly from the grand jury without a preliminary hearing. Ex parte Campbell, 278 Ala. 114, 176 So.2d 242 (1965). The opinion of the Alabama Court of Appeals in this case instructs us that under Alabama law the sole purposes of a preliminary hearing are to determine whether there is sufficient evidence against the accused to warrant presenting his case to the grand jury, and if so to fix bail if the offense is bailable. 44 Ala.App., at 433; 211 So.2d, at 920. See Code of Alabama, Tit. 15, §§ 139, 140, 151.[1] The court continued:

> "At the preliminary hearing . . . the accused is not required to advance any defenses, and failure to do so does not preclude him from availing himself of every defense he may have upon the trial of the case. Also Pointer v. State of Texas [380 U.S. 400 (1965)] bars the admission of testimony given at a pre-trial proceeding where the accused did not have the benefit of cross-examination by and through counsel. Thus, nothing occurring at the preliminary hearing in the absence of counsel can substantially prejudice the rights of the accused on trial." 44 Ala.App., at 433; 211 So.2d at 921.

This Court is of course bound by this construction of the governing Alabama law. However, from the fact that in cases where the accused has no lawyer at the hearing the Alabama courts prohibit the State's use at trial of anything that occurred at the hearing, it does not follow that the Alabama preliminary hearing is not a "critical stage" of the State's criminal process. The determination whether the hearing is a "critical stage" requiring the provision of counsel depends, as noted, upon an analysis "whether potential substantial prejudice to defendant's rights inheres in the . . . confrontation and the ability of counsel to help avoid that prejudice." United States v. Wade, supra, at 227, 87 S.Ct. at 1932. Plainly the guiding hand of counsel at the preliminary hearing is essential to protect the indigent accused against an erroneous or improper prosecution. First, the lawyer's skilled examination and cross-examination of witnesses may expose fatal weaknesses in the State's case, that may lead the magistrate to refuse to bind the accused over. Second, in any

---

1. A textbook, "Criminal Procedure in Alabama," by M. Clinton McGee (University of Alabama Press 1954), at p. 41, states:
"A preliminary hearing or examination is not a trial in its ordinary sense nor is it a final determination of guilt. It is a proceeding whereby an accused is discharged or held to answer, as the facts warrant. It seeks to determine whether there is probable cause for believing that a crime has been committed and whether the accused is probably guilty, in order that he may be informed of the nature of such charge and to allow the state to take the necessary steps to bring him to trial. Such hearing also serves to perpetuate evidence and to keep the necessary witnesses within the control of the state. It also safeguards the accused against groundless and vindictive prosecutions, and avoids for both the accused and the state the expense and inconvenience of a public trial."

event, the skilled interrogation of witnesses by an experienced lawyer can fashion a vital impeachment tool for use in cross-examination of the State's witnesses at the trial, or preserve testimony favorable to the accused of a witness who does not appear at the trial. Third, trained counsel can more effectively discover the case the State has against his client and make possible the preparation of a proper defense to meet that case at the trial. Fourth, counsel can also be influential at the preliminary hearing in making effective arguments for the accused on such matters as the necessity for an early psychiatric examination or bail.

The inability of the indigent accused on his own to realize these advantages of a lawyer's assistance compels the conclusion that the Alabama preliminary hearing is a "critical stage" of the State's criminal process at which the accused is "as much entitled to such aid [of counsel] . . . as at the trial itself." Powell v. Alabama, supra, at 57, 53 S.Ct. at 60.

There remains, then, the question of the relief to which petitioners are entitled. The trial transcript indicates that the prohibition against use by the State at trial of anything that occurred at the preliminary hearing was scrupulously observed. Cf. White v. Maryland, supra. But on the record it cannot be said whether or not petitioners were otherwise prejudiced by the absence of counsel at the preliminary hearing. That inquiry in the first instance should more properly be made by the Alabama courts. The test to be applied is whether the denial of counsel at the preliminary hearing was harmless error under Chapman v. California, 386 U.S. 18, 87 S.Ct. 824 (1967).

We accordingly vacate the petitioners' convictions and remand the case to the Alabama courts for such proceedings not inconsistent with this opinion as they may deem appropriate to determine whether such denial of counsel was harmless error, see Gilbert v. California, supra, at 272, 87 S.Ct. at 1956, and therefore whether the convictions should be reinstated or a new trial ordered.

It is so ordered.

[Omitted are the concurring opinions of Justices White and Black, the dissenting opinions of Chief Justice Burger and Justice Stewart, the separate opinion of Justice Douglas, concurring, and the dissenting opinion of Justice Harlan.]

MAESTAS v. DISTRICT COURT

Supreme Court of Colorado, 1975.
189 Colo. 443, 541 P.2d 889.

ERICKSON, JUSTICE.

* * *

Maestas was charged in a three-count information with attempted robbery and with two enhancement of punishment counts under the Habitual Criminal Statute. He was represented by a public defender who filed a timely motion for a preliminary hearing in the county court.   At this hearing, the prosecution relied solely on the testimony of one witness, a detective, whose testimony consisted of a hearsay account of a telephone conversation with the alleged victim, coupled with hearsay information the detective had gleaned from the police file.

The defendant moved to strike the detective's testimony at the preliminary hearing on the ground that it was 100% hearsay and effectively denied him the right to confront his accusers.

* * *

The purpose of a preliminary hearing is to determine whether probable cause exists to support the prosecution's charge that the accused committed a particular crime.   .   .   .   The preliminary hearing serves as a screening device to test the sufficiency of the prosecution's case before an impartial judge and to weed out the fatally weak case.   .   .   .

"The holding of a preliminary hearing is of value to the prosecution in that it offers a method for testing the complaints of prosecuting witnesses, and eliminating prosecutions actuated by prejudice or motives inconsistent with a fair administration of the criminal law. A preliminary hearing accords the defendant an opportunity to correct any misconceptions which may have arisen with respect to his conduct.   An innocent defendant may be spared the ignominy resulting from a trial.   (Orfield, Criminal Procedure from Arrest to Appeal pps. 72–73 (1947))."   T. Borrillo, Colorado Practice, Criminal Practice and Procedure § 82.

The preliminary hearing, however, is not a mini trial, and the rules of evidence may be tempered in accordance with the sound discretion of the trial judge.   .   .   .   The prosecution is thus granted greater evidentiary latitude in proving the existence of probable cause.   To that end, this court has held that "[h]earsay evidence, and other evidence, which would be incompetent if offered at the time of trial, may well be the bulk of the evidence at the preliminary hearing."

The parameters of [this doctrine], however, should not be extended beyond their original design.   As demonstrated by the preliminary hearing in this case, the prosecution presented the testimony of peripheral, if not extraneous, witnesses who recited in a narrative fashion what others had seen, heard, or done.   .   .   .   Neither the key witness in this case nor the arresting officers were produced at the hearing.   Instead, the sole testimony of a nonperceiving witness relating second-hand information was relied upon to establish probable cause.   A minimum investment of time and talent characterized this hearing.   The perfunctory fashion in which it was held belies the fact that the preliminary hearing is a critical stage in the administration of criminal justice.   Coleman v. Alabama (1970)   .   .   . .

The preliminary hearing is not a "judicial rubber stamp for prosecutorial discretion."   See, K. Graham and L. Letwin, The Preliminary Hearings in Los Angeles: Some Field Findings and Legal-

Policy Observations, 18 U.C.L.A.L.Rev. 636 (1971). The full potential and purpose of the preliminary hearing is only realized when it is utilized as a check on the power of the prosecution. That check assumes significance where, as in the instant case, the prosecution attempts to establish probable cause on the basis of second-hand hearsay testimony.

Where the prosecution exploits the use of hearsay on hearsay and establishes probable cause solely on the basis of second-half information, the historical function of the preliminary hearing is vitiated—that being to place before the judge evidence which establishes that probable cause exists to prove that the defendant did commit the crime charged. . . . By our holding here, we seek fair play and substantial justice at the preliminary hearing.

We reaffirm our previous holding that hearsay evidence is admissible at a preliminary hearing, but we admonish the courts to beware of the excessive use of hearsay in the presentation of government cases. The inordinate use of hearsay, as in the present case, foils the protective defense against unwarranted prosecutions that preliminary hearings are designed to afford to the innocent. . . .

Unsubstantiated complaints can only be detected if a means exists by which their shaky foundations may be disclosed. . . . We do not require that the prosecution produce all, or even the best, witnesses at a preliminary hearing. But the evidence presented at the preliminary hearing must have some semblance of a factual foundation and must show probable cause. The process is best served when at least one witness is called whose direct perception of the criminal episode is subject to evaluation by the judge at the preliminary hearing. Establishing probable cause on the basis of hearsay alone should only be resorted to when the testimony of a perceiving witness is unavailable or when "it is demonstrably inconvenient to summon witnesses able to testify to facts from personal knowledge." . . . Better prosecutorial practice entails the presentation of a residuum of competent, non-hearsay evidence at the preliminary hearing to support probable cause. . . .

On the basis of the foregoing, we remand with the direction that the defendant be granted a new preliminary hearing in accordance with the views expressed in this opinion.

PEOPLE ex rel. VAN MEVEREN v. DISTRICT COURT

Supreme Court of Colorado, 1978.
—— Colo. ——, 575 P.2d 405.

HODGES, JUSTICE.

. . . The [district attorney] maintains that the respondent judge abused his discretion when he dismissed a first-degree sexual assault charge against one Waheeb Esam Ismail at the conclusion of a preliminary hearing.

The respondent district judge grounded the dismissal on findings that the evidence presented by the district attorney was entirely hearsay and there was insufficient evidence to establish the element of physical force or violence required to prove the crime. . . .

The officer who investigated the case was the only witness produced by the prosecution at the preliminary hearing. He testified as to statements made to him by the complaining witness, the defendant and other witnesses. He also testified regarding the appearance and behavior of the complaining witness when she made her complaint to him.

The following story emerged from the officer's testimony. The complaining witness was hitchhiking and accepted a ride from the defendant and his friend. She voluntarily spent the next six hours in the defendant's company, doing her laundry at his apartment complex, going out to dinner, and watching television at the defendant's apartment with him and his friends. She voluntarily entered the defendant's bedroom, and he began to make sexual overtures, which she resisted. Some time later, she accepted the defendant's offer to spend the night in the apartment, but she insisted upon sleeping on the floor. The alleged assault occurred around 3:00 a.m. in the following manner, as quoted from the officer's testimony:

> "She told me that he grabbed her breasts, held on to her breasts very tightly and he reached up under her dress and removed her Kotex and threw it to the side and that he had sexual intercourse with her against her will."

The officer testified that the complaining witness was taken to a hospital for examination, and the doctor's report indicated bruises on her breasts.

In dismissing the charge, the respondent judge stated that all the evidence tending to show probable cause was hearsay and further, that there was inadequate evidence of physical force, violence, threats or intimidation of the alleged victim. We disagree with these conclusions as a matter of law.

I.

In support of dismissal because the evidence consisted entirely of hearsay testimony, the respondent judge alluded to the case of Maestas v. Dist. Ct., Colo., 541 P.2d 889 (1975). That case does not support dismissal here. In *Maestas*, the only witness for the prosecution was a detective who was, at most, peripherally involved in the investigation of the case. He was neither a key witness nor the arresting officer and all of the testimony he gave was totally hearsay and consisted mostly of information he obtained from police files. We held that such testimony could not support the prosecutor's case in a preliminary hearing, and we observed that the inordinate use of hearsay "foils the protective defense against unwarranted prosecutions that preliminary hearings are designed to afford to the innocent." In *Maestas*, the witness was so unfamiliar with the case that an effective cross-examination could not be afforded the defendant, and the screening function of the preliminary hearing was rendered meaningless.

On the contrary, in this case the prosecution witness is the investigating officer of the case who had knowledge and information about many of the aspects of the alleged crime. Although much of his testimony was hearsay, he also testified concerning his observations of the alleged victim when she made her complaint to him. Also, he personally interviewed the defendant and witnesses whose statements he related. The transcript reflects that defendant's counsel comprehensively cross-examinined the witness here.

II.

The second reason assigned by the respondent district judge for dismissing the charge was that the prosecution produced insufficient evidence of force, violence, threats or intimidation. . . . According to the officer's testimony, one instance of the application of physical force or violence was the grabbing of the complaining witness' breasts in the manner she described to the officer. We must determine whether this evidence was sufficient to support a finding of probable cause as to the element of "the actual application of physical force."

We recently, in People v. Treat, Colo., 568 P.2d 473 (1977), defined the probable cause standard for preliminary hearings as follows:

> "The probable cause standard requires evidence sufficient to induce a person of ordinary prudence and caution conscientiously to entertain a reasonable belief *that the defendant may have committed the crimes charged."* (Emphasis added.)

Considering the evidence in the light most favorable to the prosecution, it is convincingly clear that an ordinarily prudent person could conscientiously believe that the defendant here may have committed the crime of first-degree sexual assault. The complaining witness' allegation that the defendant grabbed her breasts and held them very tightly is certainly evidence of the "actual application of physical force." This is buttressed by the doctor's report in evidence.

III.

In their answer to the rule to show cause, the respondents assert that the judge's order to dismiss was properly based on a determination that the alleged victim's statements were incredible as a matter of law. The judge's statements in the record make no mention of this consideration, but if this was his hidden reason for dismissing the case, he abused his discretion.

It is not the function of the presiding judge at a preliminary hearing to weigh the credibility of a witness' statement, unless the testimony is "implausible or incredible as a matter of law."   The respondent judge made no such finding in this case.

[Justice Carrigan's dissenting opinion omitted.]

NOTES

1.   In most jurisdictions hearsay is admissible at preliminary hearings, although frequently limitations are placed upon the use of hearsay in actual practice.   See People v. Beasley, 250 Cal.App.2d 71, 58 Cal.Rptr. 485 (1967); Wolke v. Fleming, 24 Wis.2d 606, 129 N.W.2d 841 (1964); United States v. Catino, 403 F.2d 491 (2d Cir. 1968).

Concerning the question of whether illegally obtained evidence may be admitted at a preliminary hearing, see Chapter 6, Section D–1, Note 4(a) of this casebook.

2.   In United States v. Wilkins, 422 F.Supp. 1371 (E.D.Pa.), aff'd at 547 F.2d 1166 (3d Cir. 1976), and Coleman v. Burnett, 477 F.2d 1187 (D.C.Cir. 1973), the courts upheld the right of a magistrate to restrict cross-examination of witnesses designed to secure discovery of the prosecution's case rather than to refute the assertion of probable cause.   The courts declared that discovery may be a byproduct of the process of demonstrating probable cause, but declared that is is not a legitimate end into itself.

3.   If counsel for the accused is present at a preliminary hearing, under the law of some jurisdictions preliminary hearing testimony may be used as substantive evidence if a witness is unavailable at the time of trial. See Chapter 19, Section A, including the discussion in California v. Green.

4.   Judicial review of preliminary hearings is often difficult to secure under the laws or the practice of many jurisdictions.   In many jurisdictions a preliminary hearing finding of probable cause is not an appealable order and an extraordinary remedy by way of writs of mandamus, prohibition, or habeas corpus is difficult, if not impossible, to secure.   Similarly, review of evidentiary issues which arise at a preliminary hearing may be difficult to secure by direct appeal or by writ.

B.   SCOPE OF THE HEARING REQUIREMENT

GERSTEIN v. PUGH

Supreme Court of the United States, 1975.
420 U.S. 103, 95 S.Ct. 854.

Mr. Justice Powell delivered the opinion of the Court.

The issue in this case is whether a person arrested under a prosecutor's information is constitutionally entitled to a judicial determination of probable cause for pretrial restraint of liberty.

I.

In March 1971 respondents Pugh and Henderson were arrested in Dade County, Florida.   Each was charged with several offenses under a prosecutor's information.   Pugh was denied bail because one of the charges against him carried a potential life sentence, and Henderson remained in custody because he was unable to post a $4,500 bond.

In Florida, indictments are required only for prosecution of capital offenses. Prosecutors may charge all other crimes by information, without a prior preliminary hearing and without obtaining leave of court. . . . The only possible methods for obtaining a judicial determination of probable cause were a special statute allowing a preliminary hearing after 30 days, and arraignment, which the District Court found was often delayed a month or more after arrest. . . . As a result, a person charged by information could be detained for a substantial period solely on the decision of a prosecutor.

Respondents Pugh and Henderson filed a class action against Dade County officials in the Federal District Court, claiming a constitutional right to a judicial hearing on the issue of probable cause and requesting declaratory and injunctive relief. Respondents Turner and Faulk, also in custody under informations, subsequently intervened. Petitioner Gerstein, the State Attorney for Dade County, was one of several defendants. . . . The District Court granted the relief sought. . . . The court certified the case as a class action under Fed.Rule Civ.Proc. 23(b)(2), and held that the Fourth and Fourteenth Amendments give all arrested persons charged by information a right to a judicial hearing on the question of probable cause. . . . Before the District Court issued its findings, however, the Florida Supreme Court amended the procedural rules governing preliminary hearings statewide, and the parties agreed that the District Court should direct its inquiry to the new rules rather than the Dade County procedures.

Under the amended rules every arrested person must be taken before a judicial officer within 24 hours. Fla.Rule Crim.Proc. 3.-130(b). This "first appearance" is similar to the "first appearance hearing" ordered by the District Court in all respects but the crucial one: the magistrate does not make a determination of probable cause. The rule amendments also changed the procedure for preliminary hearings, restricting them to felony charges and codifying the rule that no hearings are available to persons charged by information or indictment. Rule 3.131; see In re Rule 3.131(b), Florida Rules of Criminal Procedure, 289 So.2d 3 (Fla.1974).

In a supplemental opinion the District Court held that the amended rules had not answered the basic constitutional objection, since a defendant charged by information still could be detained pending trial without a judicial determination of probable cause. . . . Reaffirming its original ruling, the District Court declared that the continuation of this practice was unconstitutional. The Court of Appeals affirmed, . . . modifying the District Court's decree in minor particulars and suggesting that the form of preliminary hearing provided by the amended Florida rules would be acceptable, as long as it was provided to all defendants in custody pending trial. . . .

State Attorney Gerstein petitioned for review, and we granted certiorari because of the importance of the issue.[1] . . . We affirm in part and reverse in part.

II.

As framed by the proceedings below, this case presents two issues: whether a person arrested and held for trial on an information is entitled to a judicial determination of probable cause for detention, and if so, whether the adversary hearing ordered by the District Court and approved by the Court of Appeals is required by the Constitution.

A

Both the standards and procedures for arrest and detention have been derived from the Fourth Amendment and its common-law antecedents. The standard for arrest is probable cause, defined in terms of facts and circumstances "sufficient to warrant a prudent man in believing that the [suspect] had committed or was committing an offense." Beck v. Ohio (1964) [Supra casebook, Chapter 4, Section B] . . . This standard, like those for searches and seizures, represents a necessary accommodation between the individual's right to liberty and the State's duty to control crime. . . .

To implement the Fourth Amendment's protection against unfounded invasions of liberty and privacy, the Court has required that the existence of probable cause be decided by a neutral and detached magistrate whenever possible. The classic statement of this principle appears in Johnson v. United States, 333 U.S. 10, 13–14, 68 S.Ct. 367, 369 (1948):

> "The point of the Fourth Amendment, which often is not grasped by zealous officers, is not that it denies law enforcement the support of the usual inferences which reasonable men draw from evidence. Its protection consists in requiring that those inferences be drawn by a neutral and detached magistrate instead of being judged by the officer engaged in the often competitive enterprise of ferreting out crime."

See also Terry v. Ohio (1968) [Supra casebook, Chapter 4, Section F.] [2]

---

1. At oral argument counsel informed us that the named respondents have been convicted. Their pretrial detention therefore has ended. This case belongs, however, to that narrow class of cases in which the termination of a class representative's claim does not moot the claims of the unnamed members of the class. See Sosna v. Iowa, 419 U.S. 393, 95 S.Ct. 553 (1975).

2. We reiterated this principle in United States v. United States District Court, 407 U.S. 297, 92 S.Ct. 2125 (1972). In terms that apply equally to arrests, we described the "very heart of the Fourth Amendment directive" as a requirement that "where practical, a governmental search and seizure should represent both the efforts of the officer to gather evidence of wrongful acts and

Maximum protection of individual rights could be assured by requiring a magistrate's review of the factual justification prior to any arrest, but such a requirement would constitute an intolerable handicap for legitimate law enforcement. Thus, while the Court has expressed a preference for the use of arrest warrants when feasible, Beck v. Ohio, supra, it has never invalidated an arrest supported by probable cause solely because the officers failed to secure a warrant.[3]

Under this practical compromise, a policeman's on-the-scene assessment of probable cause provides legal justification for arresting a person suspected of crime, and for a brief period of detention to take the administrative steps incident to arrest. Once the suspect is in custody, however, the reasons that justify dispensing with the magistrate's neutral judgment evaporate. There no longer is any danger that the suspect will escape or commit further crimes while the police submit their evidence to a magistrate. And, while the State's reasons for taking summary action subside, the suspect's need for a neutral determination of probable cause increases significantly. The consequences of prolonged detention may be more serious than the interference occasioned by arrest. Pretrial confinement may imperil the suspect's job, interrupt his source of income, and impair his family relationships. See R. Goldfarb, Ransom 32–91 (1965); L. Katz, Justice Is the Crime 51–62 (1972). Even pretrial release may be accompanied by burdensome conditions that effect a significant restraint on liberty. See, e. g., 18 U.S.C. § 3146(a)(2), (5). When the stakes are this high, the detached judgment of a neutral magistrate is essential if the Fourth Amendment is to furnish meaningful protection from unfounded interference with liberty. Accordingly, we hold that the Fourth Amendment requires a judicial determination of probable cause as a prerequisite to extended restraint on liberty following arrest.

This result has historical support in the common law that has guided interpretation of the Fourth Amendment. . . . At common law it was customary, if not obligatory, for an arrested person to be brought before a justice of the peace shortly after arrest. . . . The justice of the peace would "examine" the prisoner and the witnesses to determine whether there was reason to believe the prisoner had committed a crime. If there was, the suspect would be committed to jail or bailed pending trial. If not, he would be discharged from custody.[4] The initial determination of probable cause

the judgment of the magistrate that the collected evidence is sufficient to justify invasion of a citizen's private premises or conversation." Id., at 316, 92 S.Ct., at 2136. See also Terry v. Ohio . . . (1968).

3. The issue of warrantless arrest that has generated the most controversy, and which remains unsettled, is whether and under what circumstances an officer may enter a suspect's home to make a warrantless arrest.

4. The examination of the prisoner was inquisitorial, and the witnesses were questioned outside the prisoner's presence. Although this method of proceeding was considered quite harsh, . . . it was well established that the prisoner was entitled to be discharged if the investigation turned up insufficient evidence of his guilt. . . .

also could be reviewed by higher courts on a writ of habeas corpus.
.   .   . This practice furnished the model for criminal procedure in
America immediately following the adoption of the Fourth Amend-
ment,   .   .   . and there are indications that the Framers of the
Bill of Rights regarded it as a model for a "reasonable" seizure.

B

Under the Florida procedures challenged here, a person arrested
without a warrant and charged by information may be jailed or subjected to other restraints pending trial without any opportunity for a
probable cause determination. Petitioner defends this practice on the
ground that the prosecutor's decision to file an information is itself a
determination of probable cause that furnishes sufficient reason to
detain a defendant pending trial. Although a conscientious decision
that the evidence warrants prosecution affords a measure of protection against unfounded detention, we do not think prosecutorial judgment standing alone meets the requirements of the Fourth Amendment. Indeed, we think the Court's previous decisions compel disapproval of the Florida procedure. In Albrecht v. United States
.   .   . (1927), the Court held that an arrest warrant issued solely
upon a United States Attorney's information was invalid because the
accompanying affidavits were defective. Although the Court's opinion did not explicitly state that the prosecutor's official oath could
not furnish probable cause, that conclusion was implicit in the judgment that the arrest was illegal under the Fourth Amendment.[5]
More recently, in Coolidge v. New Hampshire, 403 U.S. 43, 449–453,
91 S.Ct. 2022, 2029–2031, 29 L.Ed.2d 564 (1971), the Court held that
a prosecutor's responsibility to law enforcement is inconsistent with
the constitutional role of a neutral and detached magistrate.   .   .   .

In holding that the prosecutor's assessment of probable cause is
not sufficient alone to justify restraint on liberty pending trial, we do
not imply that the accused is entitled to judicial oversight or review
of the decision to prosecute. Instead, we adhere to the Court's prior
holding that a judicial hearing is not prerequisite to prosecution by
information. Beck v. Washington   .   .   . (1962); Lem Woon v.
Oregon   .   .   . (1913). Nor do we retreat from the established
rule that illegal arrest or detention does not void a subsequent conviction. Frisbie v. Collins   .   .   . (1952).   .   .   . Thus, as the
Court of Appeals noted below, although a suspect who is presently detained may challenge the probable cause for that confinement, a conviction will not be vacated on the ground that the defendant was detained pending trial without a determination of probable cause.

---

5. By contrast, the Court has held that
an indictment, "fair upon its face,"
and returned by a "properly constituted grand jury" conclusively determines the existence of probable cause
and requires issuance of an arrest
warrant without further inquiry.
.   .   . The willingness to let a
grand jury's judgment substitute for
that of a neutral and detached magistrate is attributable to the grand
jury's relationship to the courts and
its historical role of protecting individuals from unjust prosecution. See
United States v. Calandra   .   .   .
(1974).

III.

Both the District Court and the Court of Appeals held that the determination of probable cause must be accompanied by the full panoply of adversary safeguards—counsel, confrontation, cross-examination, and compulsory process for witnesses. A full preliminary hearing of this sort is modeled after the procedure used in many States to determine whether the evidence justifies going to trial under an information or presenting the case to a grand jury. . . . The standard of proof required of the prosecution is usually referred to as "probable cause," but in some jurisdictions it may approach a prima facie case of guilt. A.L.I. Model Code of Pre-arraignment Procedure Commentary on Article 330, at 90–91 (Tent. Draft No. 5, 1972). When the hearing takes this form, adversary procedures are customarily employed. The importance of the issue to both the State and the accused justifies the presentation of witnesses and full exploration of their testimony on cross-examination. This kind of hearing also requires appointment of counsel for indigent defendants. And, as the hearing assumes increased importance and the procedures become more complex, the likelihood that it can be held promptly after arrest diminishes. . . .

These adversary safeguards are not essential for the probable cause determination required by the Fourth Amendment. The sole issue is whether there is probable cause for detaining the arrested person pending further proceedings. This issue can be determined reliably without an adversary hearing. The standard is the same as that for arrest.[6] That standard—probable cause to believe the suspect has committed a crime—traditionally has been decided by a magistrate in a nonadversary proceeding on hearsay and written testimony, and the Court has approved these informal modes of proof.

The use of an informal procedure is justified not only by the lesser consequences of a probable cause determination but also by the nature of the determination itself. It does not require the fine resolution of conflicting evidence that a reasonable-doubt or even a preponderance standard demands, and credibility determinations are seldom crucial in deciding whether the evidence supports a reasonable belief in guilt. See F. Miller, Prosecution: The Decision to Charge a Suspect with a Crime 64–109 (1969). This is not to say that confrontation and cross-examination might not enhance the reliability of probable cause determinations in some cases. In most cases, however, their value would be too slight to justify holding, as a matter of constitutional principle, that these formalities and safeguards de-

---

6. Because the standards are identical, ordinarily there is no need for further investigation before the probable cause determination can be made.

"Presumably, whomever the police arrest they must arrest on 'probable cause.' It is not the function of the police to arrest, as it were at large and to use an interrogating process at police headquarters in order to determine whom they should charge before a committing magistrate on 'probable cause.'" Mallory v. United States . . . (1957).

signed for trial must also be employed in making the Fourth Amendment determination of probable cause.[7]

Because of its limited function and its nonadversary character, the probable cause determination is not a "critical stage" in the prosecution that would require appointed counsel. The Court has identified as "critical stages" those pretrial procedures that would impair defense on the merits if the accused is required to proceed without counsel. In Coleman v. Alabama, where the Court held that a preliminary hearing was a critical stage of an Alabama prosecution, the majority and concurring opinions identified two critical factors that distinguish the Alabama preliminary hearing from the probable cause determination required by the Fourth Amendment. First, under Alabama law the function of the preliminary hearing was to determine whether the evidence justified charging the suspect with an offense. A finding of no probable cause could mean that he would not be tried at all. The Fourth Amendment probable cause determination is addressed only to pretrial custody. To be sure, pretrial custody may affect to some extent the defendant's ability to assist in preparation of his defense, but this does not present the high probability of substantial harm identified as controlling in *Wade* and *Coleman*. Second, Alabama allowed the suspect to confront and cross-examine prosecution witnesses at the preliminary hearing. The Court noted that the suspect's defense on the merits could be compromised if he had no legal assistance for exploring or preserving the witnesses' testimony. This consideration does not apply when the prosecution is not required to produce witnesses for cross-examination.

Although we conclude that the Constitution does not require an adversary determination of probable cause, we recognize that state systems of criminal procedure vary widely. There is no single preferred pretrial procedure, and the nature of the probable cause determination usually will be shaped to accord with a State's pretrial procedure viewed as a whole. While we limit our holding to the precise requirement of the Fourth Amendment, we recognize the desirability of flexibility and experimentation by the States. It may be found desirable, for example, to make the probable cause determination at the suspect's first appearance before a judicial officer, see McNabb v. United States, 318 U.S. 332, 342–344, 63 S.Ct. 608, 613–614, 87 L.Ed. 819 (1943), or the determination may be incorporated into the procedure for setting bail or fixing other conditions of pretrial release. In some States, existing procedures may satisfy the requirement of the Fourth Amendment. Others may require only minor adjustment such as acceleration of existing preliminary hearings.   .   .   . Whatever procedure a State may adopt, it must provide a fair and re-

---

7. Criminal justice is already overburdened by the volume of cases and the complexities of our system. The processing of misdemeanors, in particular, and the early stages of prosecution generally are marked by delays that can seriously affect the quality of justice. A constitutional doctrine requiring adversary hearings for all persons detained pending trial could exacerbate the problem of pretrial delay.

liable determination of probable cause as a condition for any significant pretrial restraint on liberty,[8] and this determination must be made by a judicial officer either before or promptly after arrest.

IV.

We agree with the Court of Appeals that the Fourth Amendment requires a timely judicial determination of probable cause as a prerequisite to detention, and we accordingly affirm that much of the judgment. As we do not agree that the Fourth Amendment requires the adversary hearing outlined in the District Court's decree, we reverse in part and remand to the Court of Appeals for further proceedings consistent with this opinion.

Affirmed in part, reversed in part, and remanded.

MR. JUSTICE STEWART, with whom MR. JUSTICE DOUGLAS, MR. JUSTICE BRENNAN, and MR. JUSTICE MARSHALL join, concurring.

I concur in Parts I and II of the Court's opinion, since the Constitution clearly requires at least a timely judicial determination of probable cause as a prerequisite to pretrial detention. Because Florida does not provide all defendants in custody pending trial with a fair and reliable determination of probable cause for their detention, the respondents and the members of the class they represent are entitled to declaratory and injunctive relief.

Having determined that Florida's current pretrial detention procedures are constitutionally inadequate, I think it is unnecessary to go further by way of dicta. In particular, I would not, in the abstract, attempt to specify those procedural protections that constitutionally need *not* be accorded incarcerated suspects awaiting trial.

Specifically, I see no need in this case for the Court to say that the Constitution extends less procedural protection to an imprisoned human being than is required to test the propriety of garnisheeing a commercial bank account, the custody of a refrigerator, . . ., the temporary suspension of a public school student, . . . or the suspension of a driver's license. . . . Although it may be true that the Fourth Amendment's "balance between individual and public interests always has been thought to define the 'process that is due' for seizures of person or property in criminal cases," . . ., this case does not involve an initial arrest, but rather the continuing incarceration of a presumptively innocent person. Accordingly, I cannot join the Court's effort to foreclose any claim that the traditional

---

8. Because the probable cause determination is not a constitutional prerequisite to the charging decision, it is required only for those suspects who suffer restraints on liberty other than the condition that they appear for trial. There are many kinds of pretrial release and many degrees of conditional liberty. See 18 U.S.C. § 3146; ABA Standards Relating to the Administration of Criminal Justice, Pretrial Release § 5.2 (1974); Uniform Rules of Criminal Procedure, Rule 341 (Proposed Final Draft 1974). We cannot define specifically those that would require a prior probable cause determination, but the key factor is significant restraint on liberty.

requirements of constitutional due process are applicable in the context of pretrial detention.

* * *

NOTES

1. Does *Gerstein* affect cases where prosecution is initiated by a complaint signed by a citizen? If, before the complaint is filed, the citizen appears before a magistrate for examination under oath, does the magistrate's decision to permit leave to file satisfy the requirement of a judicial hearing under *Gerstein* even if no warrant issues because the suspect has already been arrested without a warrant?

2. What kinds of restraints besides custody did the court have in mind in *Gerstein* when it stated that significant restraint would trigger the right to a judicial determination of probable cause?

3. Without benefit of a formal survey, some persons believe that the impact of *Gerstein* probably has not been overwhelming. In many jurisdictions, persons who have been arrested without a warrant and who have been unable to post bond quite regularly do not receive the prompt judicial determination of probable cause hearing contemplated by *Gerstein*. Under *Gerstein*, once a defendant is tried (or, perhaps, once a probable cause hearing is eventually held), the improper initial delay would seem to have no legal impact on the criminal case, and, thus, typically would not be litigated in reviewing courts. The *Gerstein* constitutionally-mandated hearing by definition serves such a limited purpose that denial of a prompt *Gerstein* hearing could not be said to prejudice the merits of the defense at trial. See United States v. Kabat, 586 F.2d 325 (4th Cir. 1978) ("an accused has no constitutional right to a preliminary hearing, so long as he receives some form of 'judicial determination of probable cause as a prerequisite to extended restraint of liberty following arrest.' ") See also McKinstry, System Impact in Gerstein v. Pugh, 7 Loyola (Chi.) U.L.Rev. 901 (1976).

4. *Gerstein*, fully implemented, could affect misdemeanor proceedings more radically than felony proceedings. This is because in misdemeanor cases, in most jurisdictions, there is no statutory provision for a preliminary hearing. The alleged misdemeanant is arrested, bond is set, bond is either made or it is not, and the matter eventually goes to trial without the intermediate step of a preliminary hearing. The leading decision applying *Gerstein* to misdemeanors is In re Walters, 15 Cal.3d 738, 126 Cal.Rptr. 239, 543 P.2d 607 (1975). In other jurisdictions *Gerstein* typically has not been implemented so as to alter misdemeanor procedures which are inconsistent with *Gerstein*.

5. At a preliminary hearing, a defendant receives more than a probable cause determination. He has the right to counsel, to confront and cross-examine witnesses, and to obtain early discovery. A grand jury indictment offers the defendant no similar "rights." In light of this, may a defendant indicted by a grand jury claim that he is denied equal protection compared to a similarly situated defendant prosecuted by information? If so, what is the appropriate remedy?

6. A footnote in *Gerstein* indicated that the return of a grand jury indictment provides sufficient cause to justify a restraint on liberty. It is the equivalent of a judicial determination of probable cause, made either upon the issuance of an arrest warrant or, in compliance with *Gerstein*, at an ex parte hearing following a warrantless arrest. From your knowledge of

grand jury proceedings, do you believe that a grand jury determination of probable cause should be deemed the equivalent of a judicial determination? See Thompson, The Fourth Amendment Function of the Grand Jury, 37 Ohio State L.J. 727 (1976).

HAWKINS v. SUPERIOR COURT

Supreme Court of California, 1975.
22 Cal.3d 584, 150 Cal.Rptr. 435, 586 P.2d 916.

MOSK, JUSTICE.

In this proceeding we consider the constitutionality of present California procedures for prosecution by grand jury indictment. Defendants were charged, in a multiple-count indictment returned by the San Francisco Grand Jury, with conspiracy and grand theft; in addition, some of the defendants were individually charged with other offenses.

Defendants were arraigned, and each pleaded not guilty to all counts. Their motion for a dismissal or in the alternative for a post-indictment preliminary hearing was in due course denied. Defendants seek a writ of mandate, asserting a right . . . to an adversarial preliminary hearing.

* * *

I.

It is undeniable that there is a considerable disparity in the procedural rights afforded defendants charged by the prosecutor by means of an information and defendants charged by the grand jury in an indictment. The defendant accused by information "immediately becomes entitled to an impressive array of procedural rights, including a preliminary hearing before a neutral and legally knowledgeable magistrate, representation by retained or appointed counsel, the confrontation and cross-examination of hostile witnesses, and the opportunity to personally appear and affirmatively present exculpatory evidence. . . .

In vivid contrast, the indictment procedure omits *all* the above safeguards: the defendant has no right to appear or be represented by counsel, and consequently may not confront and cross-examine the witnesses against him, object to evidence introduced by the prosecutor, make legal arguments, or present evidence to explain or contradict the charge. . . . If he is called to testify, the defendant has no right to the presence of counsel, even though, because of the absolute secrecy surrounding grand jury proceedings, he may be completely unaware of the subject of inquiry or his position as a target witness. This remarkable lack of even the most basic rights is compounded by the absence from the grand jury room of a neutral and detached magistrate, trained in the law, to rule on the admissibility of evidence and insure that the grand jury exercises its indicting function with proper regard for the independence and objectivity so necessary if it is to fulfill its purported role of protecting innocent citizens from unfounded accusations, even as it proceeds against those who it has probable cause to believe have committed offenses.

*   *   *

II.

Under the traditional two-tier test of equal protection, a discriminatory legislative classification that impairs fundamental rights will be subjected to strict scrutiny by the courts, and the state will be required to bear the heavy burden of proving not only that it has a compelling interest which justifies the classification but also that the discrimination is necessary to promote that interest.

The Attorney General fails to discharge his burden of proof under this test. His sole attempt to do so is to list in his brief a few tactical advantages gained by the prosecutor who chooses to use the indictment procedure.[1] But none of these reasons amounts to a constitutionally "compelling" state interest that justifies depriving an indicted defendant of the above-discussed fundamental rights guaranteed to him in a preliminary hearing. Nor, indeed, does the Attorney General make any effort to show that this discrimination is constitutionally "necessary" to preserve any such advantages.

We conclude that the denial of a postindictment preliminary hearing deprived defendants herein of equal protection of the laws guaranteed by article I, section 7, of the California Constitution.[2]

III.

The appropriate remedy for the constitutionally infirm treatment of indicted defendants is not to eliminate or alter radically the general indicting function of the grand jury; indeed, that function is explicitly sanctioned in the California Constitution and specifically implemented by the Legislature. Until such time as the Legislature may prescribe other appropriate procedures, the remedy most consistent with the state Constitution as a whole and least intrusive on the Legislature's prerogative is simply to permit the indictment process to continue precisely as it has, but to recognize the right of indicted

---

1. "A prosecutor may proceed by indictment for valid reasons: the prospective defendant cannot be found; witnesses may fear testifying in court; the case may have potential for prejudicial pretrial publicity; publicity may jeopardize a continuing investigation; a preliminary examination may involve prolonged delay because of the number of defendants or the complexity of the case."

2. While we held to the contrary in People v. Sirhan (1972) 7 Cal.3d 710, 746–747, 102 Cal.Rptr. 385, 497 P.2d 1121, the issue was treated cursorily and was neither argued nor decided in relation to the California Constitution. As we have previously stated, "[I]n criminal actions, where life or liberty is at stake, courts should not adhere to precedents unjust to the accused. It is never too late to mend.'" (People v. Aranda (1965) 63 Cal.2d 518, 530, 47 Cal.Rptr. 353, 360, 407 P.2d 265, 272, quoting from United States v. Delli Paoli (2d Cir. 1956) 229 F.2d 319, 323 (dis. opn. of Frank, J.).) To the extent it is contrary to the views herein expressed, *Sirhan* is overruled.

defendants to demand a postindictment preliminary hearing prior to or at the time of entering a plea. If the defendant makes a timely request for such a preliminary hearing, at the direction of the court the prosecuting attorney shall refile the indictment as a complaint, thus activating the procedures set forth in the Penal Code.

The state constitutional provision recognizing the grand jury's indicting function—article I, section 14—is no bar to our holding herein. It provides, "Felonies shall be prosecuted as provided by law, either by indictment or, after examination and commitment by a magistrate, by information." The term "law," of course, encompasses judicial decisions as well as legislative enactments. Thus, while the Constitution authorizes the use of grand juries to indict criminal defendants, it leaves to the Legislature and the courts the task of developing procedures, consistent with other state constitutional provisions, for implementing that mode of initiating prosecutions.

Because of previous reliance by the bench and bar on the validity of current postindictment procedures, the rule announced herein shall apply only to the present case and to those indicted defendants who have not entered a plea at the time this opinion becomes final. ⸱

Let a peremptory writ of mandate issue directing the trial court to proceed in accordance with the views expressed herein.

[Omitted are the concurring opinions of Justice Mosk, who, although the author of the majority opinion, added a scholarly and noval exposition of his views on equal protection as a separate statement, and of Chief Justice Bird.]

[Justice Richardson's dissenting opinion is omitted.]

NOTES

1. *Hawkins* stands alone in holding that an indicted defendant is entitled to a preliminary hearing. See Seim v. State, —— Nev. ——, 590 P.2d 1152 (1979), where the court, rejecting *Hawkins*, held that "the existence of statutory and other procedural safeguards, coupled with the availability of extraordinary relief in our district courts . . . are adequate to protect an accused from discriminatory treatment and unfounded allegations." However, some judges feel that *Hawkins* represents the better view. See Commonwealth v. Bestwick, —— Pa.Super. ——, 396 A.2d 1311 (1978) (Spaeth, J., concurring):

> The rights lost by indicted defendants through being denied a postindictment preliminary hearing are fundamental, and thus the strict scrutiny tier of equal protection analysis is applicable. The few tactical advantages gained by the prosecutor by using the indictment procedure do not amount to a constitutionally compelling state interest that justifies depriving an indicted defendant of these fundamental rights. Nor does the Attorney General make any effort to show that this discrimination is constitutionally necessary to preserve these advantages.

2. Is the hearing mandated by *Hawkins* simply another needless minitrial which will further clog the system and delay trials? Does the hearing provide important protection to the defendant? Can a California pros-

ecutor who wins an indictment but loses a post-indictment preliminary hearing seek a second indictment of the defendant on the same charges?

3.   A finding of no probable cause at a pre-indictment preliminary hearing ordinarily requires that the accused be released from custody or from the requirements of bond.   It does not, however, ordinarily bar a subsequent prosecution or in any way constitute "jeopardy" so as to prevent return of an indictment.   See People v. Kent, 54 Ill.2d 161, 295 N.E.2d 710 (1972).   What would happen if at a post-indictment preliminary hearing held in accordance with *Hawkins*, the prosecutor called one witness, asked her her name, and then rested, in effect consenting to a finding of no probable cause?   Would prosecution be barred?   Would the pending indictment be dismissed, subject to the possibility of re-indictment?   Would the indictment remain despite the finding of no probable cause at the preliminary hearing?

Chapter 11

GRAND JURY PROCEEDINGS

A. HISTORICAL ROLE

The evolution of the Grand Jury from its English antecedents to its contemporary function in the American criminal process was described by Justice Mosk, a critic of the use of Grand Juries, in Johnson v. Superior Court, 15 Cal.3d 248, 124 Cal.Rptr. 32, 539 P.2d 792 (1975) (concurring opinion):

".   .   . Most authorities date the origin of the grand jury to the Assize of Clarendon (1166) in the reign of Henry II. (2 Pollock & Maitland, The History of English Law (2d ed. 1909) p. 642 (hereinafter Pollock & Maitland); 1 Holdsworth, A History of English Law (1903) pp. 147–148 (hereinafter Holdsworth); 4 Blackstone, Commentaries, p. 301.) It was there provided that 12 knights or 'good and lawful men' of every hundred and four were to declare under oath the identities of those in the community suspected of public offenses. All persons thus "presented" were then tried by ordeal (Edwards, The Grand Jury (1906) p. 7 (hereinafter Edwards)), a method undeniably more barbaric than the present ordeal of trial. Failure to demonstrate innocence at the ordeal resulted in banishment and the loss of a hand and a foot; success at the ordeal was rewarded by mere banishment. (Id. at p. 9.)[1]

" 'Slowly the character of the institution changed. Originally an important instrument of the Crown, it gradually became instead a strong independent power guarding the rights of the English people.' (Younger, The People's Panel: The Grand Jury in the United States, 1634–1941 (1963) p. 2 (hereinafter Younger).) By 1352 the panel that accused no longer assumed responsibility for the trial itself, and the first seeds of the present bifurcated system of grand and petit jury were sown. (2 Pollock & Maitland, p. 649.) As the age of royal absolutism developed, this body of freemen became a singularly effective deterrent to politically motivated prosecution by the crown. The return by one famous grand jury of a bill of 'ignoramus' in the attempted prosecution of the Earl of Shaftesbury in 1681 is frequently cited as demonstrating the evolution of the institution from a prosecutorial arm into an agency responsible for protecting the individual from officially sanctioned oppression.[2]

---

1. "There is a technical difference between an indictment and a presentment. A presentment is an accusation made by the grand jury itself, flowing from the knowledge and personal observation of the members. An indictment comes to the grand jury as a charge from without, usually from a prosecutor or the king's officer, to which the grand jury either returns a true bill or a bill of 'ignoramus.' "

2. "Thus Edwards states: 'So far as we have considered it, we have found it to be an arm of the government,

688

"The establishment of British hegemony in the American colonies resulted in the exportation to our shores of British legal institutions, including the grand jury. While certain of the colonies, particularly the theocracies, altered the institution to conform to religious or social predilections, the colonists themselves continued to regard the grand jury as a fundamental feature of a civilized state. Thus when in 1683 the inhabitants of New York forced the Duke of York to permit the colonial assembly to pass a 'Charter of Libertyes and Priviledges,' there was included the protection 'That in all Cases Capitall or Criminall there shall be a grand Inquest who shall first present the offence and then twelve men of the neighborhood to try the Offender who after his plea to the Indictment shall be allowed his reasonable Challenges.' (1 Schwartz, The Bill of Rights: A Documentary History (1971) p. 383.)

" 'By the end of the Colonial period the grand jury had become an indispensable part of government in each of the American colonies. Grand juries served as more than panels of public accusers. They acted as local representative assemblies ready to make known the wishes of the people. They proposed new laws, protested against abuses in government, and performed many administrative tasks. They wielded tremendous authority in their power to determine who should and who should not face trial. They enforced or refused to enforce laws as they saw fit and stood guard against indiscriminate prosecution by royal officials.' (Younger, p. 26.)

"It is thus clear that a functional revolution in the grand jury occurred in the six centuries between the Assize of Clarendon and the adoption of the Fifth Amendment to the United States Constitution. By the time of the latter, the institution had evolved to its purest form: a citizen's tribunal, set resolutely between the state and the individual. Unhappily, the contemporary grand jury no longer serves that historic role and has regressed to little more than a convenient prosecutorial tool.

*   *   *

". . . the indicting function of the grand jury has not changed in character or procedure in centuries. By contrast, in England, the country of its origin, there is no longer a need to consider reforming the grand jury to comport with modern notions of justice and due process, because the British deemed the shortcomings of the whole grand jury system compelling enough to abolish the institution in 1933.[3]

acting as a public prosecutor for the purpose of ferreting out all crime, the members of the inquest being at all times bound to inform the court either singly or collectively their reasons for arriving at their verdict and the evidence upon which it was based. The seed, however, had been sown in Bracton's time, which was destined to change the grand jury from a mere instrument of the crown to a strong independent power which stood steadfast between the crown and the people in the defence of the liberty of the citizen.' (Edwards, p. 27.)"

3. "Some writers contend that the abolition of the grand jury in England was an economic decision (Whyte, Is the Grand Jury Necessary? (1959) 45 Va.L.Rev. 461, 483; Younger, The Grand Jury Under Attack (1955) 46 J.Crim.L. 214, 217–220.) However,

"By contrast, California clings steadfastly to the anachronistic rules of the discarded English past. . . . In this state there remains the legally tenable possibility that an individual may be compelled to undergo the trauma of a felony trial based on an ex parte proceeding from which he and all his evidence are statutorily excluded."

* * *

Despite conclusions of this nature, the Supreme Court of the United States has repeatedly stressed that the modern Grand Jury is intended to fulfill its "Historic role as a protective bulwark standing solidly between the ordinary citizen and an overzealous prosecutor." In United States v. Dionisio, 410 U.S. 1, 17, 93 S.Ct. 764, 773 (1973), the Court said:

"Under the ancient English system . . . the most valuable function of the grand jury was not only to examine into the commission of crimes, but to stand between the prosecutor and the accused, and to determine whether the charge was founded on credible testimony or dictated by malice or personal ill will." Hale v. Henkel, 201 U.S. 43, 59, 26 S.Ct. 370, 373 (1906); see also Hoffman v. United States, 341 U.S. 479, 71 S.Ct. 814 (1951)."

Nonetheless, those who have urged the abolition of the grand jury have focused upon the dominant role played by the prosecutor in the proceedings. For example, Judge Frankel has concluded that the "contemporary grand jury investigates only those whom the prosecutor asks to be investigated, and by and large indicts those whom the prosecutor wants to be indicted." Frankel & Naftalis, The Grand Jury: An Institution on Trial 100 (1977). And Judge Campbell, long a critic of the grand jury, has bluntly stated in Campbell, Eliminate the Grand Jury, 64 J.Crim.L. & C. 174 (1973):

"Today, the grand jury is the total captive of the prosecutor who, if he is candid, will concede that he can indict anybody, at any time, for almost anything, before any grand jury."

Thus, the movement for abolishing the grand jury process springs from the notion expressed in *Dionisio*, supra, that:

"It is, indeed, common knowledge that the grand jury, having been conceived as a bulwark between the citizen and the Government, is now a tool of the Executive."

In this fashion, the critical commentary has abounded. See, e. g., Antell, The Modern Grand Jury: Benighted Supergovernment, 51 A.B.A.J. 153 (1965); Comment, Grand Jury Proceedings: The Prosecutor, The Trial Judge and Undue Influence, 39 U.Chi.L.Rev. 761

the reason for this economic decision was the fact that the grand jury's indicting function was no longer deemed necessary in view of the de- velopment of the information and preliminary examination. Similar sentiments were being voiced at the same time in the United States."

(1972); Boudin, The Federal Grand Jury, 61 Geo.L.J. 1 (1972); Shannon, The Grand Jury: True Tribunal of the People or Administrative Agency of the Prosecutor?, 2 N.M.L.Rev. 141 (1972); Foster, Grand Jury Practice in the 1970's, 32 Ohio St.L.J. 701 (1971); Schwartz, Demythologizing the Historic Role of the Grand Jury, 10 Am.Crim.L.Rev. 701 (1972).

This criticism notwithstanding, the grand jury is firmly rooted in our history as a democratic institution; and, because it remains an important part of our criminal justice system, it is necessary to understand the law surrounding grand jury practice. However, it is precisely because of the criticism that the lawyer's role in the grand jury proceeding is currently emerging. Claims of overbearing prosecutorial grand jury tactics—particularly those designed to harass political dissent in the mid-1960s—coupled with an increased reliance on immunized testimony have sensitized the courts into a reconsideration of some of the legal issues involved in grand jury procedures. Because of these developments, "counsel should regard representation of a grand jury witness as requiring the same sort of thought, research and preparation as would be devoted to defending a person charged under a new, untested criminal statute." Grand Jury Manual 3 (Seventh Federal Circuit Bar Association 1975).

[Ed. Note: For a further treatment of the historical role of the Grand Jury, see United States v. Calandra, Ch. 6, Sec. D.]

B.   GRAND JURY COMPOSITION

CASTANEDA v. PARTIDA

Supreme Court of the United States, 1977.
430 U.S. 482, 97 S.Ct. 1272.

MR. JUSTICE BLACKMUN delivered the opinion of the Court.

The sole issue presented in this case is whether the State of Texas, in the person of petitioner, the Sheriff of Hidalgo County, successfully rebutted respondent-prisoner's prima facie showing of discrimination against Mexican-Americans in the state grand jury selection process. In his brief, petitioner, in claiming effective rebuttal, asserts:

> "This list [of the grand jurors that indicted respondent] indicates that 50 percent of the names appearing thereon were Spanish. The record indicates that 3 of the 5 jury commissioners, 5 of the grand jurors who returned the indictment, 7 of the petit jurors, the judge presiding at the trial, and the Sheriff who served notice on the grand jurors to appear had Spanish surnames."

*   *   *

Texas employs the "key man" system, which relies on jury commissioners to select prospective grand jurors from the community at large.[1] The procedure begins with the state district judge's appointment of from three to five persons to serve as jury commissioners. The commissioners then "shall select not less than 15 nor more than 20 persons from the citizens of different portions of the county" to comprise the list from which the actual grand jury will be drawn. When at least 12 of the persons on the list appear in court pursuant to summons, the district judge proceeds to "test their qualifications." [A] grand juror must be a citizen of Texas and of the county, be a qualified voter in the county, be "of sound mind and good moral character," be literate, have no prior felony conviction, and be under no pending indictment "or other legal accusation for theft or of any felony." Interrogation under oath is the method specified for testing the prospective juror's qualifications. . . . After the court finds 12 jurors who meet the statutory qualifications, they are impaneled as the grand jury.

Respondent, Rodrigo Partida, was indicted in March 1972 by the grand jury of the 92d District Court of Hidalgo County for the crime of burglary of a private residence at night with intent to rape. Hidalgo is one of the border counties of southern Texas. After a trial before a petit jury, respondent was convicted and sentenced to eight years in the custody of the Texas Department of Corrections. He first raised his claim of discrimination in the grand jury selection process on a motion for new trial in the state district court. In support of his motion, respondent testified about the general existence of discrimination against Mexican-Americans in that area of Texas and introduced statistics from the 1970 Census and the Hidalgo County grand jury records. The census figures show that in 1970, the population of Hidalgo County was 181,535. Persons of Spanish language or Spanish surname totaled 143,611. On the assumption that all the persons of Spanish language or Spanish surname were Mexican-Americans, these figures show that 79.1% of the county's population was Mexican-American.

Respondent's data compiled from the Hidalgo County grand jury records from 1962 to 1972 showed that over that period, the average percentage of Spanish-surnamed grand jurors was 39.0%. In the two and one-half year period during which the district judge who impanelled the jury that indicted respondent was in charge, the average percentage was 45.5%. On the list from which the grand jury that indicted respondent was selected, 50% were Spanish-surnamed. The last set of data that respondent introduced, again from the 1970 Census, illustrated a number of ways in which Mexican-Americans tend to be underprivileged, including poverty level incomes, less desirable jobs, substandard housing and lower levels of education. The State offered no evidence at all either attacking respondent's allegations of discrimination or demonstrating that his statistics were unreliable in

1. The other principal state mode of juror selection is a random method similar to that used in the federal system. See 28 U.S.C. § 1864. See generally Sperlich and Jaspovice, Grand Juries, Grand Jurors and the Constitution, 1 Hastings Const.L.Q. 63, 68 (1974).

any way. The state district court, nevertheless, denied the motion for a new trial.

On appeal, the Texas Court of Criminal Appeals affirmed the conviction. Reaching the merits of the claim of grand jury discrimination, the court held that respondent had failed to make out a prima facie case. In the court's view, he should have shown how many of the females who served on the grand juries were Mexican-Americans married to men with Anglo-American surnames, how many Mexican-Americans were excused for reasons of age, health, or other legal reasons, and how many of those listed by the Census would not have met the statutory qualifications of citizenship, literacy, sound mind, moral character, and lack of criminal record or accusation. Quite beyond the uncertainties in the statistics, the court found it impossible to believe that discrimination could have been directed against a Mexican-American, in light of the many elective positions held by Mexican-Americans in the county and the substantial representation of Mexican-Americans on recent grand juries. In essence, the court refused to presume that Mexican-Americans would discriminate against their own kind.

After exhausting his state remedies, respondent filed his petition for habeas corpus in the Federal District Court, alleging a denial of due process and equal protection, guaranteed by the Fourteenth Amendment, because of gross under-representation of Mexican-Americans on the Hidalgo County grand juries. At a hearing at which the state transcript was introduced, petitioner presented the testimony of the state judge who selected the jury commissioners who had compiled the list from which respondent's grand jury was taken. The judge first reviewed the State's grand jury selection process. In selecting the jury commissioners, the judge stated that he tried to appoint a greater number of Mexican-Americans than members of other ethnic groups. He testified that he instructed the commissioners about the qualifications of a grand juror and the exemptions provided by law. The record is silent, however, with regard to instructions dealing with the potential problem of discrimination directed against any identifiable group. The judge admitted that the actual results of the selection process had not produced grand jury lists that were "representative of the ethnic balance in the community." The jury commissioners themselves, who were the only ones in a position to explain the apparent substantial under-representation of Mexican-Americans and to provide information on the actual operation of the selection process, were never called.

On the basis of the evidence before it, the court concluded that respondent had made out a *"bare prima facie* case" of invidious discrimination with his proof of "a long continued disproportion in the composition of the grand juries in Hidalgo County." (emphasis in original). Based on an examination of the reliability of the statistics offered by respondent, however, despite the lack of evidence in the record justifying such an inquiry, the court stated that the prima facie case was weak. The court believed that the census statistics did not reflect the true situation accurately, because of recent changes in the Hidalgo County area and the court's own impression of the demographic characteristics of the Mexican-American community. On the other hand, the court recognized that the Texas key man system of grand jury selection was highly subjective, and was "archaic and inefficient," and that this was a factor arguing for less tolerance in the percentage differences. On balance, the court's doubts about the reliability of the statistics, coupled with its opinion that Mexican-Americans constituted a "governing majority" in the county, caused it to conclude that the prima facie case was rebutted. The "governing majority" theory distinguished respondent's case from all preceding cases involving similar disparities. On the basis of those findings, the court dismissed the petition.

The United States Court of Appeals for the Fifth Circuit reversed. It agreed with the District Court that respondent had succeeded in making out a prima facie case. It found, however, that the State had failed to rebut that showing. The "governing majority" theory contributed little to the State's case in the absence of specific proof to explain the disparity. In light of the State's abdication of its responsibility to introduce controverting evidence, the court held that respondent was entitled to prevail.

We granted certiorari to consider whether the existence of a "governing majority" in itself can rebut a prima facie case of discrimination in grand jury selection, and, if not, whether the State otherwise met its burden of proof.

*   *   *

[In] order to show that an equal protection violation has occurred in the context of grand jury selection, the defendant must show that the procedure employed resulted in substantial under-representation of his race or of the identifiable group to which he belongs. The first step is to establish that the group is one that is a recognizable, distinct class, singled out for different treatment under the laws, as written or as applied. Next, the degree of under-representation must be proved, by comparing the proportion of the group in the total population to the proportion called to serve as grand jurors, over a significant period of time. This method of proof, sometimes called the "'rule of exclusion," has been held to be available as a method of proving discrimination in jury selection against a delineated class. Finally, as noted above, a selection procedure that is susceptible to abuse or not racially neutral supports the presumption of discrimination raised by the statistical showing. Once the defendant has shown substantial under-representation of his group, he has made out a prima facie case of discriminatory purpose, and the burden then shifts to the State to rebut that case.

In this case, it is no longer open to dispute that Mexican-Americans are a clearly identifiable class. The statistics introduced by respondent from the 1970 Census illustrate disadvantages to which the group has been subject. Additionally, as in Alexander v. Louisiana (1972), the selection procedure is not racially neutral with respect to Mexican-Americans; Spanish surnames are just as easily identifiable as race was from the questionnaires in *Alexander* or the notations and card colors in Whitus v. Georgia (1967) and in Avery v. Georgia (1953).

The disparity proved by the 1970 Census statistics showed that the population of the county was 79.1% Mexican-American, but that, over an 11-year period, only 39% of the persons summoned for grand jury service were Mexican-American. This difference of 40% is greater than that found significant in Turner v. Fouche (1970) (60% Negroes in the general population, 37% on the grand jury lists). Since the State presented no evidence showing why the 11-year period was not reliable, we take it as the relevant base for comparison. The mathematical disparities that have been accepted by this Court as adequate for a prima facie case have all been within the range presented here. For example, in Whitus v. Georgia (1967), the number of Negroes listed on the tax digest amounted to 27.1% of the population, but only 9.1% of those on the grand jury venire. The disparity was held to be sufficient to make out a prima facie case of discrimination. See Sims v. Georgia (1967) (24.4% on tax lists, 4.7% on grand jury lists); Jones v. Georgia (1967) (19.4% on tax lists, 5.-0% on jury list). We agree with the District Court and the Court of Appeals that the proof in this case was enough to establish a prima facie case of discrimination against the Mexican-Americans in the Hidalgo County grand jury selection.

Supporting this conclusion is the fact that the Texas system of selecting grand jurors is highly subjective. The facial constitutionality of the key man system, of course, has been accepted by this Court. Nevertheless, the Court has noted that the system is susceptible to abuse as applied. Additionally, as noted, persons with Spanish surnames are readily identifiable.

The showing made by respondent therefore shifted the burden of proof to the State to dispel the inference of intentional discrimination. Inexplicably, the State introduced practically no evidence. The testimony of the state district judge dealt principally with the selection of the jury commissioners and the instructions given to them. The commissioners themselves were not called to testify. . . .

* * *

. . . . Without some testimony from the grand jury commissioners about the method by which they determined the other qualifications for grand jurors prior to the statutory time for testing qualifications, it is impossible to draw any inference about literacy, sound mind and moral character, and criminal record from the statistics about the population as a whole. These are questions of disputed fact that present problems not amenable to resolution by an appellate court. We emphasize, however, that we are not saying that the statistical disparities proved here could never be explained in another case; we are simply saying that the State did not do so in this case.

In light of our holding that respondent proved a prima facie case of discrimination that was not rebutted by any of the evidence presently in the record, we have only to consider whether the District Court's "governing majority" theory filled the evidentiary gap. In our view, it did not dispel the presumption of purposeful discrimination in the circumstances of this case. Because of the many facets of human motivation, it would be unwise to presume as a matter of law that human beings of one definable group will not discriminate against other members of their group. Indeed, even the dissent of Mr. Justice Powell does not suggest that such a presumption would be appropriate. The problem is a complex one, about which widely differing views can be held, and, as such, it would be somewhat precipitous to take judicial notice of one view over another on the basis of a record as barren as this.

* * *

Rather than relying on an approach to the jury discrimination question that is as faintly defined as the "governing majority" theory is on this record, we prefer to look at all the facts that bear on the issue, such as the statistical disparities, the method of selection, and any other relevant testimony as to the manner in which the selection process was implemented. Under this standard, the proof offered by respondent was sufficient to demonstrate a prima facie case of discrimination in grand jury selection. Since the State failed to rebut the presumption of purposeful discrimination by competent testimony, despite two opportunities to do so, we affirm the Court of Appeals' holding of a denial of equal protection of the law in the grand jury selection process in respondent's case.

MR. JUSTICE MARSHALL, concurring. [opinion omitted.]

MR. CHIEF JUSTICE BURGER, with whom MR. JUSTICE POWELL and MR. JUSTICE REHNQUIST join, dissenting. [opinion omitted.]

MR. JUSTICE STEWART, dissenting. [opinion omitted.]

MR. JUSTICE POWELL, with whom THE CHIEF JUSTICE and MR. JUSTICE REHNQUIST join, dissenting.

* * *

The Court holds that a criminal defendant may demonstrate a violation of the Equal Protection Clause merely by showing that the procedure for selecting grand jurors "resulted in substantial underrepresentation of his race or the identifiable group to which he belongs." By so holding, the Court blurs the traditional constitutional distinctions between the grand and petit juries, and misapplies the equal protection analysis mandated by our most recent decisions.

The Fifth Amendment right to a grand jury does not apply to a state prosecution. Hurtado v. California (1884). A state defendant cannot complain if the State foregoes the institution of the grand jury and proceeds against him instead through prosecutorial information, as many States prefer to do. See Gerstein v. Pugh (1975). Nevertheless, if a State chooses to proceed by grand jury it must proceed within the constraints imposed by the Equal Protection Clause of the Fourteenth Amendment. . . .

* * *

But a state defendant has no right to a grand jury that reflects a fair cross-section of the community. The right to a "representative" grand jury is a federal right that derives not from the requirement of equal protection but from the Fifth Amendment's explicit requirement of a grand jury. That right is similar to the right—applicable to state proceedings—to a representative petit jury under the Sixth Amendment. See Taylor v. Louisiana (1975). To the extent that the Fifth and Sixth Amendments are applicable, a defendant need only show that the jury selection procedure "systematically exclude[s] distinctive groups in the community and thereby fail[s] to be reasonably representative thereof." But in a state case in which the challenge is to the grand jury, only the Fourteenth Amendment applies, and the defendant has the burden of proving a violation of the Equal Protection Clause.

Proof of discriminatory intent in such a case was explicitly mandated in our recent decisions in Washington v. Davis, 426 U.S. 229 (1976), and Arlington Heights v. Metropolitan Housing Development Corp., 429 U.S. 252, 97 S.Ct. 555 (1977). In *Arlington Heights* we said:

> "Our decision last Term in Washington v. Davis, made it clear that official action will not be held unconstitutional solely because it results in a racially disproportionate impact. 'Disproportionate impact is not irrelevant, but it is not the sole touchstone of an invidious racial discrimination.' Proof of racially discriminatory intent or purpose is required to show a violation of the Equal Protection Clause. . . . ."

* * *

In this case, the following critical facts are beyond dispute: the judge who appointed the jury commissioners and later presided over respondent's trial was Mexican-American; three of the five jury commissioners were Mexican-American; 10 of the 20 members of the grand jury array were Mexican-American; five of the 12 grand jurors who returned the indictment, including the foreman, were Mexican-American, and seven of the 12 petit jurors who returned the verdict of guilt were Mexican-American. In the year in which respondent was indicted, 52.5% of the persons on the grand jury list were Mexican-American. In addition, a majority of the elected officials in Hidalgo County were Mexican-American, as were a majority of the judges. That these positions of power and influence were so held is not surprising in a community where 80% of the population is Mexican-American. As was emphasized by District Judge Garza, the able Mexican-American jurist who presided over the habeas proceedings in the District Court, this case *is* unique. Every other jury discrimination case reaching this Court has involved a situation where the governing majority, and the resulting power over the jury selection process, was held by a white electorate and white officials.

The most significant fact in this case, all but ignored in the Court's opinion, is that a majority of the jury commissioners were Mexican-American. The jury commission is the body vested by Texas law with the authority to select grand jurors. Under the Texas selection system, as noted by the Court, the jury commission has the opportunity to identify in advance those potential jurors who have Spanish surnames. In these circumstances, where Mexican-Americans control both the selection of jurors and the political process, rational inferences from the most basic facts in a democratic society render improbable respondent's claim of an intent to discriminate against him and other Mexican-Americans. As Judge Garza observed, "If people in charge can choose whom they want, it is unlikely they will discriminate against themselves."

* * *

There is for me a sense of unreality when Justices here in Washington decide solely on the basis of inferences from statistics that the Mexican-Americans who control the levers of power in this remote border county are manipulating them to discriminate "against themselves." In contrast, the judges on the scene, the state judge who appointed the jury commissioners and presided over respondent's trial and the United States District Judge—both Mexican-Americans and familiar with the community—perceived no basis for respondent's claim of invidious discrimination.

It seems to me that the Court today, in rejecting the District Court's finding that no such discrimination took place, has erred grievously. I would reinstate the judgment of the District Court.

UNITED STATES v. BUTERA

United States Court of Appeals, First Circuit, 1970.
420 F.2d 564.

[The defendant was indicted for attempted income tax evasion by the federal grand jury for the southern division of Maine. He filed a motion to dismiss the indictment, alleging that it had been returned by a grand jury drawn from an improperly constituted jury pool. The motion was denied; he was convicted; and he now contests the denial of his motion.]

COFFIN, CIRCUIT JUDGE.

[Defendant] claims underrepresentation of (1) the young and the very old, (2) women, (3) the less educated, and (4) people of certain Maine counties. He concedes that proportional representation is not required; he also concedes that the disparities did not arise from any purposeful or deliberate discrimination in the sense that the jury pool selection system was administered with a lack of good faith. He claims simply that the system used in Maine resulted in unconstitutional discrimination against members of what he claims are legally cognizable groups.

The Constitutional Mandate

This contention necessitates a determination of what the Constitution requires concerning the selection of juries. The Supreme Court has consistently required that jury selection systems draw their jurors from a fair cross section of the community. It has been suggested that such non-discriminatory jury selection is an essential aspect of our democratic form of government. However, the Court has long recognized that fair and reasonable qualifications for jury service eligibility can be imposed even though they detract from a cross section in the actual jury pools.[1] Moreover, the Court has recognized that it is neither possible nor necessary—in order to assure an impartial jury—that there be a fair cross section of the community on each individual grand and petit jury. In particular, Hoyt v. Florida (1961), demonstrates the Court's conviction that an impartial jury can be assured even though members of one's class are not present either on the jury or in the jury pool. In that case, despite the fact that the defendant—who had killed her husband with a baseball bat—was tried by an all-male jury drawn from a virtually all-male jury pool, the Court upheld the conviction because there had been no impermissible discrimination against women in the operation of the jury system.

We conclude from these cases that the Supreme Court has focused on whether the alleged underrepresentation in the jury pool is the result of discrimination in the juror selection system. Concededly, most of the jury exclusion cases have involved alleged *state* discrimination and thus the application of the Fourteenth Amendment's assurance of equal protection. Here we deal with a federal jury and can exercise our supervisory power in addition to the Constitutional requirements. However, even in exercising this supervisory power, the Supreme Court has focused on discriminatory selection practices. We therefore understand the Constitutional mandate to be for a jury selection system free of discrimination.

In carrying out this mandate, the Supreme Court has normally imposed on the defendant the initial burden of demonstrating, prima facie, the existence of purposeful discrimination. However, the exact meaning of "purposeful discrimination" has been elusive at best.

---

1. Rawlins v. Georgia, 201 U.S. 638, 26 S.Ct. 560 (1906) (approving statutory exemption for lawyers, ministers, doctors, and railroad engineers); Fay v. New York, 332 U.S. 261, 67 S.Ct. 1613 (1947) (approving "blue ribbon" juries for certain cases); Hoyt v. Florida, 368 U.S. 57, 82 S.Ct. 159 (1961) (approving statutory exemption for women unless affirmative request to serve); Carter v. Jury Commission of Greene County, 396 U.S. 320, 90 S.Ct. 518 (1970) (approving statutory limitation of jurors to those "generally reputed to be honest and intelligent and esteemed in the community for their integrity, good character and sound judgment").

[Editors' note: in 1955 the New York legislature abolished the "blue ribbon" grand jury system referred to in the *Fay* case above cited.]

Such discrimination has been found when the jury commissioners limited their selections to acquaintances or certain lists of persons which necessarily resulted in discrimination against a class of persons not falling within either category. It has been found when Negroes were underrepresented and the list or method used indicated each prospective juror's race, thereby providing the opportunity for discrimination. Sometimes it has been found when complete exclusion or significant disparities existed which could not be adequately explained or justified by the responsible officials. At other times it has been found when jury commissioners, albeit completely well-intended, deliberately excluded certain groups.

Thus, while "purposeful discrimination" may connote an element of bad faith in ordinary usage, the term has not been so limited by the Supreme Court; rather, the breadth with which the term has been used by the Court indicates that purposeful discrimination exists whenever significant unexplained disparities exist. In other words, it is not the significant disparities themselves which are unconstitutional; they only raise the inference of discrimination. Once that inference has been raised, it is the government's failure or inability to demonstrate that the disparities are not the product of discrimination which confirms the inference and invalidates the jury pool. Finally, our reading of the cases indicates that underrepresentation of the more sociologically distinct groups in our country necessitates a more compelling demonstration by the government to overcome the inference of discrimination.

Defendant's Prima Facie Case

Defendant has the burden of showing, prima facie, discriminatory selection practices. Equally important, he has to show such discrimination against "distinct" groups in the general population. We think he has disclosed sufficient disparities, in three cognizable groups, to raise a reasonable inference of discrimination which the government should come forth to dispel.

Defendant's first claim relates to age; he insists that the young and very old were not adequately represented on the jury pool. Obviously there are some significant disparities in the age groups as defendant has classified them. Equally obvious, we think, is the problem of deciding what age groups are cognizable for purposes of defendant's prima facie case. We do not believe that that question can be given a definitive answer which will be satisfactory for all cases; rather, we think that age groupings must be viewed from several perspectives in order to give a fair view of the significance of any disparity.

We take defendant's breakdown of age groups as one acceptable perspective. More importantly, we note that there were only 148 persons under age 40 when defendant's "true cross section" indicated 335, and that there were only 20 persons under age 30 when the "true cross section" indicated 147. Below age 35, defendant's three age groupings show minimal representation of the jury pool; above age

35, the representation appears satisfactory and raises no inference of discrimination. These observations, when taken together, indicate to us a sufficient disparity to infer—in the absence of some explanation and justification—some discrimination against young adults. Moreover, the government has not directed our attention to any jury qualification or exemption which would *on its face* adequately explain this underrepresentation of young adults.[2]

Finally, we are satisfied that young adults constitute a cognizable—though admittedly ill-defined—group for purposes of defendant's prima facie case. We cannot allow the requirement of a "distinct" group to be applied so stringently with regard to age grouping that possible discrimination against a large class of persons—in our case, those between 21 and 34—will be insulated from attack. Nor can we close our eyes to the contemporary national preoccupation with a "generation gap," which creates the impression that the attitudes of young adults are in some sense distinct from those of older adults. That apparent distinctness is sufficient for us to say that neither class could be excluded from jury pools without some justification. Accordingly, we find the "significant disparity" with regard to age which raises the inference of discrimination and shifts the burden of explanation to the government.

Defendant's second claim relates to an alleged discrimination according to sex; his figures indicate that the actual jury pool was only 36 per cent female when the "true cross section" was about 52 per cent female. While this class poses no problem of definite identification, the disparity is not so great as it was with regard to age. However, a 30 percent underrepresentation of so large and important a group as women cannot lightly be dismissed; it at least raises an inference of discrimination. Unlike the situation in Hoyt v. Florida (1961), there is no statutory provision to explain the disparity. That males and females can have sufficiently different points of view to be considered legally cognizable groups for purposes of defendant's prima facie case should not require [citation of] authority.

Defendant's third claim relates to educational attainment; he insists that his statistics indicate an impermissible underrepresentation of the less educated. Expressed in another manner, they indicate that 83.6 per cent of the actual jury pool had at least a high school diploma, while only 43.2 per cent of the general population of Maine over age 25 did; 18.1 per cent of the actual jury pool had at least a college degree, compared with 5.5 per cent of the general population.

It seems clear that these disparities give rise to an inference of discrimination against the less educated, despite the difficulty, similar to that encountered with regard to age groupings, of defining any

---

2. Defendant has *not* complained about the total exclusion of persons under 21. If he had, an adequate response would have been the statute limiting jury service to persons 21 and over. Thus, a defendant would have to demonstrate the invalidity of that statute before he could complain of the exclusion of persons under 21. But see United States v. Tantash, 409 F.2d 227, 228 (9th Cir. 1969), cert. denied, 395 U.S. 968, 89 S.Ct. 2115 (1969) (statute limiting jury service to those 21 and over held valid).

precise group to be termed "less educated". Again, to require a more precise definition would introduce unnecessary and unrealistic inflexibility and might effectively preclude anyone from ever showing a "distinct" class in terms of educational attainment. Moreover we think the statutory requirement of literacy *on its face* explains only a part of the variance; there is no statutory provision for "blue ribbon" juries which might explain the remainder. Fay v. New York [f.n. 2]. Finally, we are convinced that the less educated are a sufficiently large group with sufficiently distinct views and attitudes that its diluted presence on the actual jury pool requires some explanation by the government.

Defendant's fourth contention gives us more difficulty. His figures indicate some disparities between the actual jury pool and the general population of southern Maine in terms of county residence. First of all, these are generally not as serious discrepancies as those which have appeared above. Secondly, we note that the relevant statute provides that jurors can be selected with regard to their distance from the courthouse, 28 U.S.C. § 1865(a) (1964), the validity of which has not been attacked by defendant. At least part of these rather minor disparities may be attributable to this statute. More importantly, however, we are not aware that residents of counties can be said to hold views and attitudes which are in any way "distinct" from those of their neighbors in nearby counties, nor has defendant given us any evidence of such distinctness. While common experience tells us that people's attitudes differ to some degree along lines of age, sex and extent of education, we are not aware that they differ along county lines. We have been willing above to give a broad meaning to the requisite "distinctness" of classes but in each instance we could point to some indication that the groups isolated by defendant—at least in a general sense—possessed the essential element of distinctness. That term would have no meaning at all were we to say —in the absence of any supporting evidence—that residents of some counties have views and attitudes genuinely distinct from those of nearby counties. Cf. Krause v. Chartier, 406 F.2d 898, 901 (1st Cir. 1968) (drawing of jurors from last names T–Z not unconstitutional).

The defendant having raised an inference of discrimination against young adults, women, and the less educated, the burden shifts to the government to dispel that inference. It should be remembered at the outset that, while a true cross section is the ultimate ideal, it is by no means the Constitutional mandate. What is required is a jury selection system free of discrimination against properly cognizable groups.

The Government's Explanation

The government offered the testimony of one of the Jury Commissioners—the other having died prior to the hearing—as well as various documents evidencing the manner in which the "key man" system was administered in Maine during the 1960's. Briefly, the two Jury Commissioners, working in conjunction with the district court, first determined that about 900 persons were needed for the jury pool in the Southern Division. They then determined how many of those 900 should be drawn from each community by ascertaining the total number of registered voters in southern Maine, dividing that number by 900, finding that about one of every 275 registered voters would be needed, and then allocating a rough quota to each local community based on that proportion. Thereafter, they obtained through the Maine Register the names of several hundred "key men", most of whom were local town officials. These key men were asked by letter to send the names of four or five potential jurors to the Jury Commissioners, who then sent questionnaires to the persons recommended. After receiving the completed questionnaires, the Jury Commissioners struck nearly half for reasons of statutory ineligibility or apparent hardship and placed the remaining names in the jury pool for selection at random of a grand jury.

Defendant concedes that the key man system is *not* per se invalid. From the evidence adduced before the district court, it appears that the Jury Commissioners acted at all times in good faith—defendant concedes that—and in conscientious accordance with the applicable statutes and the suggestions gleaned from the 1960 Judicial Conference Report, 26 F.R.D. 409 (1960); indeed, the defendant relied exclusively on his statistical analysis and challenged no particular aspect of the administration of the system.

It has become well-established that voter registration lists are appropriate for use in jury selection systems. Thus, there can be no objection to the fact that such lists were used here to determine how many persons should be taken from each community. There was no claim that the key men were selected in a discriminatory manner; indeed, the evidence adduced would belie such a claim. The letter which the Commissioners sent to the key men did not suggest that they confine their selections to persons of fair education, intelligence or esteem. Moreover, there was no reason to suspect that the key men would not be acquainted either personally or by reputation with a fair cross section of their local communities in Maine. Thus, we are satisfied that the persons recommended to the Commissioners as potential jurors were selected in a non-discriminatory manner.

There is, however, the question concerning the Commissioner's exclusion of nearly half the persons recommended, in order to get down to the 900 persons needed for the jury pool. Part of that exclusion can be attributed to the fact that some key men sent too many names; when this occurred, the extra names were struck. Secondly, the Commissioner testified that some young adults who had been recommended were struck because they were out of the state for reasons relating to their education and were thus either ineligible under the uncontested qualifications for jury service—residence for one year— or were so far away that jury service would have posed a substantial hardship. Surely military service by some young men might put them in this same category. Thirdly, some young adults—particularly women, apparently—were excused from jury service when their questionnaires indicated that such service would be a hardship because of employment or the presence of young children at home. Finally, the Commissioner has indicated that almost 10 per cent of the recommended jurors were found unqualified for jury service for mental or physical reasons.

Defendant has not contended that such individual excuses from jury service for hardship or disqualification were improperly granted. Importantly it appears that members of the classes in question were excused only upon request or clear evidence from the questionnaire that excusable hardship did exist and not simply as a matter of course. That such exclusions were made by the Jury Commissioners rather than the district judge is not fatal.

We of course acknowledge that a system which persistently produced substantial and recognized underrepresentations of sociologically distinct groups would not be insulated from attack simply because it was fair on its face. Moreover, mere protestations or even evidence of subjective good faith would not dispel the inference that those who administer the system had purposed the results which they knew the system was producing. Here, however, the system was operated substantially in accordance with the 1960 Judicial Conference suggestions; the principle governing the selection of the several hundred key men was a neutral one; the letters from the Jury Commissioners to the key men were unexceptionable, as were the questionnaires sent to prospective jurors; there was no suggestion that the Commissioners applied improper standards in disqualifying or excusing individual jurors; the Commissioners made an effort to retain persons whose groups might otherwise be depleted; and, so far as we have reason to believe, this case—directed to the representation of groups of varying degrees of distinctness—is the first occasion that such protests have formally been brought to the attention of the Jury Commissioners.

We therefore conclude that this key man system was reasonably designed to obtain a fair cross section for the jury pools in southern Maine and that it has been administered in an effort to effectuate this design without discernible discrimination against any group. The Constitution's mandate for a non-discriminatory jury selection system is not frustrated simply by the existence of certain inadvertent disparities arising from an otherwise fair system. As we said at the outset, it would be virtually impossible to assure a full representation of every cognizable group in every jury pool; all the Constitution requires in this regard is a jury selection system completely free of discrimination. This one was.

The sole remaining question is whether this case presents any need for us to exercise our supervisory power over the federal jury selection systems within our purview. We think not. As we observed in our discussion, there were some aspects of the system which could be improved to provide greater assurance of full representation for all cognizable groups. But Congress perceived these imperfections before they were brought to our attention; in 1968, Congress amended the existing federal jury system to provide that jury pools are to be chosen at random from a fair cross section of those eligible in the community. Accordingly, there is no need for us to offer any supervisory suggestions for improvements of the key man system.

Affirmed.

NOTES

1. In Rose v. Mitchell, —— U.S. ——, 99 S.Ct. 2993 (1979), defendants sought to quash their Tennessee murder indictments on the ground that the foreman of the grand jury which indicted them was selected in a racially discriminatory manner. To support their contention, defendants, at a hearing on the issue, called, among other witnesses, two former foremen who testified that they had never heard of a black grand jury foreman in the county and the current grand jury foreman who testified that he had no knowledge of whether a black had ever served as foreman. The Court held that claims of racial discrimination in the selection of state grand jury members are cognizable in federal habeas corpus proceedings even though the trial jury was untainted and guilt was established. However, although acknowledging that grand jury exclusion based on race was constitutionally impermissible, the Court concluded that, on the facts before it, defendants failed to make a prima facie case of improper exclusion. "Absent evidence as to the total number of foremen appointed by the judges in the county during the critical period of time, it is difficult to say that the number of Negroes appointed foreman, even if zero, is statistically so significant as to make out a case of discrimination under the 'rule of exclusion.' "

2. The states are accorded substantial discretion in developing the proper mechanism for producing the grand jury pool. See United States v. Leonetti, 291 F.Supp. 261 (S.D.N.Y.1968). While the grand jury need not represent a mirror image of the community, the discriminatory exclusion of identifiable groups is prohibited. See United States v. Gast, 457 F.2d 141 (7th Cir.), cert. denied, 406 U.S. 969, 92 S.Ct. 2426 (1972) (while residency requirements are constitutionally suspect, one year requirement to qualify for grand jury service does not constitute discriminatory exclusion); United States v. Dellinger, 472 F.2d 340 (7th Cir. 1972), cert. denied 410 U.S. 970, 93 S.Ct. 1443 (1973) ("young alienated" not cognizable group); Foster v. Sparks, 506 F.2d 805 (5th Cir. 1975) (identifying *Butera* as a "judicial rarity" in finding "young adults" to be a cognizable group).

3. Many jurisdictions permit various classes of individuals to be excused from grand jury service upon request. Some examples include senior citizens, women with young children, law enforcement officers, firemen, attorneys, clergymen, school teachers, doctors, nurses, and sole proprietors of business. Do exclusions of this nature rise to the level of a constitutional violation? See United States v. Grey, 355 F.Supp. 529 (W.D.Okla.1973).

4. Objections to the composition of the grand jury are generally made in the form of a motion to dismiss the indictment. However, if the statute of limitations has not run, a successful motion will not bar reindictment by another grand jury. Since reindictment is permissible, what advantages are there to a client in challenging the grand jury's composition?

5. Ordinarily a challenge to grand jury composition is waived if not raised by a pre-trial motion. Tollett v. Henderson, 411 U.S. 258, 93 S.Ct. 1602 (1973); Davis v. United States, 411 U.S. 233, 93 S.Ct. 1577 (1973).

C.   SECRECY OF THE GRAND JURY

DOUGLAS OIL CO. v. PETROL STOPS NORTHWEST

Supreme Court of the United States, 1979.
441 U.S. 211, 99 S.Ct. 1667.

MR. JUSTICE POWELL delivered the opinion of the Court.

[Two independant gasoline retailers filed antitrust actions in the District of Arizona against a number of large oil companies. They claimed that there had been a sharp reduction in the amount of gasoline offered for sale by the large companies because of a conspiracy to restrain trade. As a part of civil discovery, the retailers requested, through interrogatories, whether the companies had any communication with their competitors concerning the price of gasoline. The companies responded that there were no such communications.

In the meantime, representatives of some of the large oil companies testified before a grand jury in the Central District of California which was investigating criminal antitrust violations. The large companies were eventually indicted, and, during the course of criminal discovery, obtained copies of the grand jury testimony. Thereafter, each company pled nolo contendere and was fined $50,000.

As discovery proceeded in the civil antitrust case, the retailers sought to obtain the relevant grand jury transcripts, but the companies objected. Rather than seeking to compel production in the District of Arizona, the retailers sought the grand jury materials from the court in California. Ultimately, the district judge in California permitted the release of the grand jury materials subject to several protective conditions. The release was upheld by the Ninth Circuit on Appeal.]

*   *   *

We consistently have recognized that the proper functioning of our grand jury system depends upon the secrecy of grand jury proceedings. See, e. g., United States v. Procter & Gamble, 356 U.S. 677 (1958).[1] In particular, we have noted several distinct interests

---

1. Since the 17th century, grand jury proceedings have been closed to the public, and records of such proceedings have been kept from the public eye. See Calkins, Grand Jury Secrecy, 63 Mich.L.Rev. 455, 457 (1965). The rule of grand jury secrecy was imported into our federal common law and is an integral part of our criminal justice system. Rule 6(e) of the Federal Rules of Criminal Procedure codifies the requirement that grand jury activities generally be kept secret, by providing that,
"A grand juror, an interpreter, a stenographer, an operator of a recording device, a typist who transcribes recorded testimony, [or] an attorney for the Government . . . shall not disclose matters occurring before the grand jury, except as otherwise provided for in these rules. . . . A knowing violation of rule 6 may be punished as a contempt of court."

Although the purpose for grand jury secrecy originally was protection of the criminally accused against an overreaching Crown, see Calkins, Grand Jury Secrecy, *supra*, with time it came to be viewed as necessary for the proper functioning of the grand jury.

served by safeguarding the confidentiality of grand jury proceedings. First, if preindictment proceedings were made public, many prospective witnesses would be hesitant to come forward voluntarily, knowing that those against whom they testify would be aware of that testimony. Moreover, witnesses who appeared before the grand jury would be less likely to testify fully and frankly, as they would be open to retribution as well as to inducements. There also would be the risk that those about to be indicted would flee, or would try to influence individual grand jurors to vote against indictment. Finally, by preserving the secrecy of the proceedings, we assure that persons who are accused but found innocent by the grand jury will not be held up to public ridicule.[2]

For all of these reasons, courts have been reluctant to lift unnecessarily the veil of secrecy from the grand jury. At the same time, it has been recognized that in some situations justice may demand that discrete portions of transcripts be made available for use in subsequent proceedings. Indeed, recognition of the occasional need for litigants to have access to grand jury transcripts led to the provision in Fed.Rule Crim.Proc. 6(e)(2)(C)(i) that disclosure of grand jury transcripts may be made "when so directed by a court preliminarily to or in connection with a judicial proceeding."[3]

* * *

2. In United States v. Procter & Gamble, 356 U.S. 677, 681–682, n. 6 (1958), we said that the reasons for grand jury secrecy had been summarized correctly in United States v. Rose, 215 F.2d 617, 628–629 (CA3 1954):

"(1) To prevent the escape of those whose indictment may be contemplated; (2) to insure the utmost freedom to the grand jury in its deliberations, and to prevent persons subject to indictment or their friends from importuning the grand jurors; (3) to prevent subornation of perjury or tampering with the witnesses who may testify before the grand jury and later appear at the trial of those indicted by it; (4) to encourage free and untrammeled disclosures by persons who have information with respect to the commission of crimes; (5) to protect innocent accused who is exonerated from disclosure of the fact that he has been under investigation, and from the expense of standing trial where there was no probability of guilt."

3. Fed.Rule Crim.Proc. 6(e) provides in full:

"(e) Secrecy of Proceedings and Disclosure.—

"(1) *General Rule.* A grand juror, an interpreter, a stenographer, an operator of a recording device, a typist who transcribes recorded testimony, an attorney for the Government, or any person to whom disclosure is made under paragraph (2)(A)(ii) of this subdivision shall not disclose matters occurring before the grand jury, except as otherwise provided for in these rules. No obligation of secrecy may be imposed on any person except in accordance with this rule. A knowing violation of rule 6 may be punished as a contempt of court.

"(2) *Exceptions.*—

"(A) Disclosure otherwise prohibited by this rule of matters occurring before the grand jury, other than its deliberations and the vote of any grand juror, may be made to—

"(i) an attorney for the government for use in the performance of such attorney's duty; and

"(ii) such government personnel as are deemed necessary by an attorney for the government to assist an attorney for the government in the performance of such attorney's duty to enforce Federal criminal law.

From *Procter & Gamble* and *Dennis v. United States*, 384 U.S. 855 (1966), emerges the standard for determining when the traditional secrecy of the grand jury may be broken: Parties seeking grand jury transcripts under Rule 6(e) must show that the material they seek is needed to avoid a possible injustice in another judicial proceeding, that the need for disclosure is greater than the need for continued secrecy, and that their request is structured to cover only material so needed.[4] Such a showing must be made even when the grand jury whose transcripts are sought has concluded its operations, as it had in *Dennis*. For in considering the effects of disclosure on grand jury proceedings, the courts must consider not only the immediate effects upon a particular grand jury, but also the possible effect upon the functioning of future grand juries. Persons called upon to testify will consider the likelihood that their testimony may one day be disclosed to outside parties. Fear of future retribution or social stigma may act as powerful deterrents to those who would come forward and aid the grand jury in the performance of its duties. Concern as to the future consequences of frank and full testimony is heightened where the witness is an employee of a company under investigation. Thus, the interests in grand jury secrecy, although reduced, are not eliminated merely because the grand jury has ended its activities.

"(B) Any person to whom matters are disclosed under subparagraph (A)(ii) of this paragraph shall not utilize that grand jury material for any purpose other than assisting the attorney for the government in the performance of such attorney's duty to enforce Federal criminal law. An attorney for the government shall promptly provide the district court, before which was impaneled the grand jury whose material has been so disclosed, with the names of the persons to whom such disclosure has been made.

"(C) Disclosure otherwise prohibited by this rule of matters occurring before the grand jury may also be made—

"(i) when so directed by a court preliminarily to or in connection with a judicial proceeding; or

"(ii) when permitted by a court at the request of the defendant, upon a showing that grounds may exist for a motion to dismiss the indictment because of matters occurring before the grand jury.

"(3) *Sealed Indictments.* The Federal magistrate to whom an indictment is returned may direct that the indictment be kept secret until the defendant is in custody or has been released pending trial. Thereupon the clerk shall seal the indictment and no person shall disclose the return of the indictment except when necessary for the issuance and execution of a warrant or summons."

Although Fed.Rule Crim.Proc. 6(e) was amended in 1977, all parties agree that the changes do not bear upon the issues in the present case.

4. As noted in United States v. Procter & Gamble, 356 U.S. 677, 683 (1958), the typical showing of particularized need arises when a litigant seeks to use "the grand jury transcript at the trial to impeach a witness to refresh his recollection, to test his credibility and the like." Such use is necessary to avoid misleading the trier of fact. Moreover, disclosure can be limited strictly to those portions of a particular witness' testimony that bear upon some aspect of his direct testimony at trial.

It is clear from *Procter & Gamble* and *Dennis* that disclosure is appropriate only in those cases where the need for it outweighs the public interest in secrecy, and that the burden of demonstrating this balance rests upon the private party seeking disclosure. It is equally clear that as the considerations justifying secrecy become less relevant, a party asserting a need for grand jury transcripts will have a lesser burden in showing justification. . . . In sum, as so often is the situation in our jurisprudence, the court's duty in a case of this kind is to weigh carefully the competing interests in light of the relevant circumstances and the standards announced by this Court. And if disclosure is ordered, the court may include protective limitations on the use of the disclosed material, as did the District Court in this case. Moreover, we emphasize that a court called upon to determine whether grand jury transcripts should be released necessarily is infused with substantial discretion.

Applying these principles to the present case, we conclude that neither the District Court nor the Court of Appeals erred in the standard by which it assessed the request for disclosure under Rule 6(e). The District Court made clear that the question before it was whether a particularized need for disclosure outweighed the interest in continued grand jury secrecy. Similarly, the Court of Appeals correctly understood that the standard enunciated in *Procter & Gamble* requires a court to examine the extent of the need for continuing grand jury secrecy, the need for disclosure, and the extent to which the request was limited to that material directly pertinent to the need for disclosure.

* * *

In the present case, the District Court for the Central District of California was called upon to make an evaluation entirely beyond its expertise. The District Judge readily conceded that he had no knowledge of the civil proceedings pending several hundred miles away in Arizona. Nonetheless, he was asked to rule whether there was a "particularized need" for disclosure of portions of the grand jury transcript and whether this need outweighed the need for continued grand-jury secrecy. Generally we leave it to the considered discretion of the District Court to determine the proper response to requests for disclosure under Rule 6(e). See *Pittsburgh Plate Glass Co. v. United States*, 360 U.S. 395, 399 (1959). We have a duty, however, to guide the exercise of discretion by district courts, and when necessary to overturn discretionary decisions under Rule 6(e). . . .

We find that the District Court here abused its discretion in releasing directly to [the retailers] the grand jury minutes they requested. Appreciating that is was largely ignorant of the Arizona civil suits, the court nonetheless made a judgment concerning the relative needs for secrecy and disclosure. The court based its decision largely upon the unsupported assertions of counsel during oral argument before it, supplemented only by the criminal indictment returned by the grand jury, the civil complaints, and [the companies'] response to a single interrogatory that appeared to be inconsistent with petitioners' *nolo contendere* plea in the criminal case. Even the court's comparison of the criminal indictment and the civil complaints did not indicate unambiguously what, if any, portions of the grand jury transcripts would be pertinent to the subject of the Arizona actions, as only some of the same parties were named and only some of the same territory was covered.

The possibility of an unnecessary breach of grand jury secrecy in situations such as this is not insignificant. A court more familiar with the course of the antitrust litigation might have seen important differences between the allegations of the indictment and the contours of the conspiracy respondents sought to prove in their civil actions—differences indicating that disclosure would likely be of little value to respondents, save perhaps as a mechanism for general discovery. Alternatively, the courts where the civil proceedings were pending might have considered disclosure at that point in the litigation to be premature; if there were to be conflicts between petitioners' statements and their actions in the criminal proceedings, the court might have preferred to wait until they ripened at depositions or even during testimony at trial.

Under these circumstances, the better practice would have been for the District Court, after making a written evaluation of the need for continued grand jury secrecy and a determination that the limited evidence before it showed that disclosure might be appropriate, to have sent the requested materials to the courts where the civil cases were pending. The Arizona court, armed with their special knowledge of the status of the civil actions, then could have considered the requests for disclosure in light of the California court's evalution of the need for continued grand jury secrecy. In this way, both the need for continued secrecy and the need for disclosure could have been evaluated by the courts in the best position to make the respective evaluations.

We do not suggest, of course, that such a procedure would be required in every case arising under Rule 6(e). Circumstances that dictate the need for cooperative action between the courts of different districts will vary, and procedures to deal with the many variations are best left to the rulemaking procedures established by Congress. Undoubtedly there will be cases in which the court to whom the Rule 6(e) request is directed will be able intelligently on the basis of limited knowledge to decide that disclosure plainly is inappropriate or that justice requires immediate disclosure to the requesting party, without reference of the matter to any other court. Our decision today therefore is restricted to situations, such as that presented by this case, in which the District Court having custody of the grand jury records is unlikely to have dependable knowledge of the status of, and the needs of the parties in, the civil suit in which the desired transcripts are to be used.

The judgment of the Court of Appeals is reversed, and the case remanded for further proceedings consistent with this opinion.

[The concurring opinion of Mr. Justice Rehnquist and the dissenting opinion of Mr. Justice Stevens, joined by Chief Justice Burger and Mr. Justice Stewart, are omitted.]

NOTES

1.　Does a grand jury witness have the right to a transcript of his own testimony?　See In re Russo, 53 F.R.D. 564 (C.D.Cal.1971).　Although *Russo* contains an excellent discussion of the secrecy issue, most courts require a greater showing before they will provide a witness with his testimony.　The general rule is that a witness "is not automatically entitled to a transcript of his testimony before a federal grand jury and may only contain it upon a showing of a particularized need."　Bast v. United States, 542 F.2d 893, 896 (4th Cir. 1976); In re Bianchi, 542 F.2d 98 (1st Cir. 1976).

* * *

2.　The preservation of grand jury secrecy is, of course, one of the reasons for excluding all other persons than those enumerated in either the federal rules or state statutes.　The court in United States v. Isaacs, 347 F. Supp. 743 (N.D.Ill.1972), considered the avoidance of undue influence upon the jury as the major reason for the rule.　See United States v. Bowdach, 324 F.Supp. 123 (S.D.Fla.1971) (indictment invalidated because an FBI agent was present in the grand jury room to operate a tape recorder); United States v. Borys, 169 F.Supp. 366 (D.Alaska 1959) (indictment invalid because a 7 year old witness' mother remained in the grand jury room).

3.　Does a grand jury witness have the right, during the course of his testimony before the jury, to confer with counsel outside the jury room? Consider the following from the opinion of the New York Court of Appeals in People v. Ianniello, 21 N.Y.2d 418, 288 N.Y.S.2d 462, 235 N.E.2d 439 (1968):

> .　.　.　It is, of course, a familiar proposition that the lawyer for a witness is not entitled to be present in the Grand Jury room　.　.　.　This rule rests upon the statutory exclusion of all except certain authorized persons before the Grand Jury and the need to preserve the secrecy of Grand Jury proceedings.　There remains, however, the further question whether the witness should not be entitled to leave the Grand Jury room to consult with his lawyer　.　.　.　Such conduct by the witness does not violate the statutory policy of secrecy, for it has always been understood that the witness is at all times free to discuss his testimony outside the Grand Jury room.　Whether and to what extent the witness ought to have a right to consult with his lawyer depends upon an analysis of the proper role of counsel in these circumstances, and the need to avoid procedural strictures which would impair the effectiveness of Grand Jury investigation.
>
> Since a Grand Jury proceeding is properly an investigation rather than a prosecution directed against the witness, the witness has no right to be "represented" by counsel, in the technical sense. However, in light of current recognition of the importance of counsel in providing effective notice of rights, it is difficult to maintain that the witness is not entitled to the advice of his lawyer. As a matter of fairness, government ought not compel individuals to make binding decisions concerning their legal rights in the enforced absence of counsel.　.　.　.　Courts have a particular re-

sponsibility to prevent unfairness in Grand Jury proceedings, for the Grand Jury is an "arm of the court".

The legal rights which may be critically affected before the Grand Jury, and concerning which the witness should be entitled to consult with his lawyer, are several. First, the witness may be put in a position of determining whether to assert or waive his privilege against self incrimination. When the witness is a "target" of the investigation, his statements and any evidence derived from them ("fruits") cannot be used in a prosecution against him for a previous substantive offense unless he expressly waives the privilege. Even he, however, must make a legally significant choice in answering or claiming his privilege; unless he claims his privilege he does not receive immunity. . . . The witness who is not a target of the inquiry faces an even more critical decision for, unless he claims his privilege and thereby invokes immunity, his statements can be used against him substantively. Faced with a confusing variety of rules concerning the existence and scope of his privileges, a witness should not be required to make these choices unaided by his lawyer.

A second legal right which may be affected before the Grand Jury is the witness' right to refuse to answer questions having no bearing on the subject of the investigation. To prevent unwarranted intrusion into the witness' privacy, he ought to be allowed to consult with his lawyer concerning the propriety of Grand Jury questioning. Finally, where a question may involve a testimonial privilege enjoyed by the witness or to which he may be subject—for example, between attorney and client, doctor and patient or husband and wife—the witness should be permitted to consult with counsel.

Whenever a witness demands to see his lawyer for counselling concerning his legal rights (as opposed to mere strategic advice), he should be given an opportunity to do so. If his right is denied, however, he does not have license to commit perjury or contempt. Rather, he must persist in his refusal to answer, thus forcing the prosecutor to take the matter into open court for a ruling. By requiring the matter to be taken to the presiding Justice, the proceeding is expedited and the danger of stalling tactics reduced. The judge can rule on questions of pertinency, after argument of counsel. He can determine whether a colorable claim of testimonial privilege is presented, and can inform the defendant of the extent of his immunity from prosecution for prior offenses. Where a witness persists in raising objections which are palpably not in good faith, the judge may compel him to desist from this course under the sanction of contempt proceedings.

Compare United States v. George, 444 F.2d 310 (6th Cir. 1971) (witness had the right to consult with his attorney outside the jury room after every question was asked him) with Commonwealth v. McCloskey, 443 Pa. 117, 277 A.2d 764, cert. denied 404 U.S. 1000, 92 S.Ct. 559 (1971) ("to allow a witness to leave the grand jury room and consult with his attorney at the door prior to responding to every question would cause undue delay and all but terminate the institution of the investigating grand jury procedure . . . [and] an invitation to evasive and stalling tactics").

Some states now permit the "target" of the investigation to have his attorney with him in the grand jury room. The attorney is permitted to advise the witness, but the attorney is not otherwise allowed to participate in the proceedings. See, for example, Ch. 38, § 112–6 (1979), Ill.Rev. Stats.

4. Despite the overwhelming concern for secrecy, the courts have authorized disclosure of grand jury evidence in a number of instances. See In re April 1956 Term Grand Jury, 239 F.2d 263 (7th Cir. 1956) (to another agency preparing a civil case); Doe v. Rosenberry, 255 F.2d 118 (2d Cir. 1958) (to a bar association grievance committee); In re Petition for Disclosure of Evidence Before the October, 1959 Grand Jury, 184 F.Supp. 38 (E.D.Va.1960) (to state prosecutor). Do these exceptions to the secrecy rule raise some question of its value? The traditional policy of grand jury secrecy was held to be so sacrosanct in State v. Terrebone, 256 La. 385, 236 So.2d 773 (1970), that a grand jury transcript was found to be inadmissible for purposes of impeachment. The court wrote, however, that this prohibition would not disallow the use of a grand jury transcript in a perjury prosecution arising out of the grand jury proceedings themselves.

5. When a suspect provides evidence to a grand jury as part of a broad investigation but is not thereafter indicted, may he object to disclosure of that evidence to another person who is indicted by the same grand jury and seeks the evidence through trial discovery? The issue is particularly important in criminal antitrust cases because the disclosure of documents under subpoena may affect the competitive balance between companies. In N L Industries, Inc. v. Snyder, 599 F.2d 1183 (3d Cir. 1979), the court held that an unindicted firm's objection to the disclosure of materials provided to the grand jury should make a court require the party seeking the evidence to show why it is material and why traditional secrecy policies should not prohibit disclosure. The court expressed the following view:

> Grand jury witnesses ought to be able to rely, generally, upon Rule 6(e) secrecy, with the reasonable assurance that matters not material to the Government's case or to the defense will not be disclosed in connection with the trial of an indictment. If such disclosure is actually necessary it must of course occur, but only with appropriate safeguards taken in the interest of preserving property rights in confidential business information. If the material is claimed to be confidential, and is in fact immaterial, the secrecy policies of Rule 6(e) ought to prevail.

D.　SUBPOENAS

IN THE MATTER OF THE GRAND JURY INVESTIGATION (GENERAL MOTORS CORP.)

United States District Court, S.D.N.Y.1959.
174 F.Supp. 393.

McGohey, District Judge.

General Motors has moved to quash a subpoena duces tecum which was caused to be issued by Government attorneys commanding the corporation to appear before a grand jury in this district to testi-

fy and give evidence in regard to "an alleged violation of the federal
anti-trust law"; and to produce "documents and items" described in
an attached schedule. The latter covers 13 legal size pages and consists of 16 numbered paragraphs most of which are subdivided into
sub-paragraphs ranging in number from 2 to 18.

The motion is granted.

Whether, as counsel for the corporation asserts, a subpoena
duces tecum of such scope as this is without precedent in antitrust litigation need not be decided. But certainly it is unprecedented in the
experience of the writer. What is demanded is a vast volume of records covering in minute detail practically every internal and external aspect of the corporation's widespread activities except labor relations, for varying periods of which the shortest is 11 years and the
longest is 30 years; and in addition extensive detailed data as to the
production, financial standing and "profitability and prospects" of
unidentified "competitors in each product field."

Among the papers called for are what are designated as "policy
documents," a term which is defined in the subpoena as follows:

" 'Policy Documents' are all originals, copies, micro-
films, tape recordings, and reproductions of any kind of:

"1. Minutes and records of the Board of Directors
and all committees and subcommittees thereof and all
reports, minutes, recommendations, surveys, studies, financial records and communications and records of any
kind going to, coming from or retained by such Board,
or by any of its committees or subcommittees, or by any
members thereof.

"2. All reports, minutes, memoranda, recommendations, surveys, studies, financial records and communications of any kind received by, prepared by, for, or
on behalf of, or transmitted by or on behalf of the general manager or president, as the case may be, of any
division or subsidiary of the Corporation, the committees and subcommittees of each such division or subsidiary and the members thereof.

"3. All reports, memoranda, recommendations,
surveys, studies, financial records and communications
and records of any kind received by, prepared by, for,
or on behalf of, or transmitted by or on behalf of any
officer of the Corporation who functions on behalf of
the Corporation as a whole or who is a group executive."

On Argument, the Government's attorney consented to modify
the foregoing by eliminating "members thereof" from paragraphs 1
and 2. It developed on argument that a "policy document" is every
piece of paper, however informal, relating to any activity covered by
the subpoena, which ever came to the attention of any member of the
boards or committees or any of the officials named in the definition,

without regard to whether the contents of the paper were approved or rejected. The corporation has 44 operating divisions and subsidiaries. Each of these has its own hierarchy of managing officials who from time to time serve on various standing or special committees formed to study matters of business policy and practice in their own or other divisions. The corporation's board of directors likewise work largely through several committees made up of board members and numerous corporate officers who are not directors.

The subpoena itself must be read and studied to appreciate the extraordinary breadth of the demand for "policy documents." It includes, for example, those relating to "products" produced by the corporation or purchased by it from others. The corporation's "products" range from small mechanical parts such as screws, bolts and nuts, through a wide range of machine tools to the following "products" and each of their multitudinous parts: engines, passenger cars, trucks, railroad locomotives, earth moving machinery, refrigerators and other electrical household appliances. The corporation's general counsel asserts under oath that, to secure the "policy documents" demanded for the specified period from its Pontiac Motor Division alone would require a search by responsible personnel of 30,000 file drawers. This assertion is not denied by Government counsel. They merely argue that they "hardly believe" top management officials would concern themselves with any but "major" products, a term they do not define. This argument, however, is contradicted by the subpoena which these same counsel have caused to be issued. That is not limited to "major" products. It includes all. I accept the sworn statement of the corporation's general counsel and find accordingly. It is a fair inference that searches of proportionate magnitude would be required in the other numerous divisions of the corporation, and I so find.

As appears from the subpoena, copies of many of the demanded documents have heretofore been produced in prior and even presently pending litigations. The Government, however, does not specify which of these are now excluded from the demand but puts on the corporation the burden of determining that.

It is settled law that a demand for production of documents by subpoena must be reasonable.[1] I hold that this subpoena which requires production of practically every paper outside of routine correspondence relating to every phase of the corporation's affairs, in an unlimited exploratory investigation such as is here frankly proposed, "whose purposes and limits can be determined only as it proceeds,"[2] is unreasonable. It will be quashed.[3]

* * *

1. Boyd v. United States, 116 U.S. 616, 6 S.Ct. 524, 29 L.Ed. 746; Hale v. Henkel, 201 U.S. 43, 26 S.Ct. 370.

2. See McMann v. Securities and Exchange Commission, 2 Cir., 87 F.2d 377, 379, 109 A.L.R. 1445.

3. See In re United Shoe Machinery Corporation, D.C., 6 F.R.D. 347.

Government counsel assert they have received recent complaints of possibly illegal practices by the corporation in certain specified areas of business. The grand jury, of course, may investigate these as well as any other possible criminal violations. But surely it is not inevitably necessary in such investigations or for the prosecution of any criminal charges that may result, that proof of conduct 30 years ago be produced. There is, after all, a statute of limitations for criminal offenses against the antitrust laws. Moreover it is never necessary in order to prove a course of conduct, to show each and every act in one's history. This, of course, is as true of an antitrust prosecution as of any other.

*   *   *

The motion is granted and the instant subpoena is quashed.

So Ordered.

NOTES

1. The grand jury's power to subpoena witnesses derives from its investigative function and its standing as an "arm of the court." Blair v. United States, 250 U.S. 273, 39 S.Ct. 468 (1919). Subpoenas are generally prepared in blank under the seal of the relevant court clerk and filled in by the prosecutor. A subpoena may require testimony (subpoena ad testificandum) or the production of documents (subpoena duces tecum). Testimonial subpoenas may be challenged on privilege grounds, and documentary subpoenas may be contested for privilege, overbreadth or hardship, although few subpoenas call for the kind of documentation sought in *General Motors*.

2. Because a presumption of regularity attaches to grand jury proceedings, one who attempts to quash or modify a subpoena carries a heavy burden. However, some courts have indicated that an appropriate challenge will compel the prosecution to show, at least by affidavit, that the testimony or documents sought are relevant to the investigation. Compare In re Grand Jury Proceedings (Universal Mfg. Co. v. United States), 508 F.2d 684 (8th Cir. 1975) with In re Grand Jury Proceedings (Schofield), 486 F. 2d 85 (3d Cir. 1973).

3. The fact that a subpoena need not disclose the subject or direction of the investigation, Hale v. Henkel, 201 U.S. 43, 65, 26 S.Ct. 370, 375, (1905), makes it difficult to ascertain the scope of the grand jury's concern. However, because a grand jury cannot investigate matters beyond the jurisdiction of the court, it is conceivable that a subpoena can be quashed when counsel is able to determine that testimony is sought in relation to an area beyond the grand jury's jurisdiction. Compare Brown v. United States, 245 F.2d 549 (8th Cir. 1957) (reversal of perjury conviction when grand jury investigating matters that could not have constituted crimes within district) with United States v. Nickels, 502 F.2d 1173 (7th Cir. 1974) (perjury conviction upheld although questioning related to matters on which statute of limitations had run).

4. When the subject of a subpoena refuses to appear, he or she may be arrested as a material witness. Does this power extend to a situation in which the appearance before the grand jury has not yet occurred, but potential for flight is demonstrated? See Bacon v. United States, 449 F.2d 933 (9th Cir. 1971).

5. The denial of a motion to quash a subpoena is not a final, appealable order. Thus, ordinarily, a witness will have to refuse to obey the subpoena and be held in contempt in order to obtain the decision of a reviewing court. Cobbledick v. United States, 309 U.S. 323, 60 S.Ct. 540 (1940).

E. IMMUNIZED TESTIMONY

KASTIGAR v. UNITED STATES

Supreme Court of the United States, 1972.
406 U.S. 441, 92 S.Ct. 1653.

MR. JUSTICE POWELL delivered the opinion of the Court.

This case presents the question whether the United States Government may compel testimony from an unwilling witness, who invokes the Fifth Amendment privilege against compulsory self-incrimination, by conferring on the witness immunity from use of the compelled testimony in subsequent criminal proceedings, as well as immunity from use of evidence derived from the testimony.

Petitioners were subpoenaed to appear before a United States grand jury in the Central District of California on February 4, 1971. The Government believed that petitioners were likely to assert their Fifth Amendment privilege. Prior to the scheduled appearances, the Government applied to the District Court for an order directing petitioners to answer questions and produce evidence before the grand jury under a grant of immunity conferred pursuant to 18 U.S.C. §§ 6002, 6003. Petitioners opposed issuance of the order, contending primarily that the scope of the immunity provided by the statute was not coextensive with the scope of the privilege against self-incrimination, and therefore was not sufficient to supplant the privilege and compel their testimony. The District Court rejected this contention, and ordered petitioners to appear before the grand jury and answer its questions under the grant of immunity.

Petitioners appeared but refused to answer questions, asserting their privilege against compulsory self-incrimination. They were brought before the District Court, and each persisted in his refusal to answer the grand jury's questions, notwithstanding the grant of immunity. The court found both in contempt, and committed them to the custody of the Attorney General until either they answered the grand jury's questions or the term of the grand jury expired. The Court of Appeals for the Ninth Circuit affirmed. This Court granted certiorari to resolve the important question whether testimony may be compelled by granting immunity from the use of the compelled testimony and evidence derived therefrom ("use and derivative use" immunity), or whether it is necessary to grant immunity from prosecution for offenses to which compelled testimony relates ("transactional" immunity).

I.

The power of government to compel persons to testify in court or before grand juries and other governmental agencies is firmly established in Anglo-American jurisprudence. The power with respect to courts was established by statute in England as early as 1562, and Lord Bacon observed in 1612 that all subjects owed the King their "knowledge and discovery." While it is not clear when grand juries first resorted to compulsory process to secure the attendance and testimony of witnesses, the general common law principle that "the public has a right to every man's evidence" was considered an "indubitable certainty" which "cannot be denied" by 1742. The power to compel testimony, and the corresponding duty to testify, are recognized in the Sixth Amendment requirements that an accused be confronted with the witnesses against him, and have compulsory process for obtaining witnesses in his favor. The first Congress recognized the testimonial duty in the Judiciary Act of 1789, which provided for compulsory attendance of witnesses in the federal courts. Mr. Justice White noted the importance of this essential power of government in his concurring opinion in Murphy v. Waterfront Comm'n, 378 U.S. 52, 93–94, 84 S.Ct. 1594, 1611 (1964):

> "Among the necessary and most important of the powers of the States as well as the Federal Government to assure the effective functioning of government in an ordered society is the broad power to compel residents to testify in court or before grand juries or agencies. Such testimony constitutes one of the Government's primary sources of information."

But the power to compel testimony is not absolute. There are a number of exemptions from the testimonial duty, the most important of which is the Fifth Amendment privilege against compulsory self-incrimination. The privilege reflects a complex of our fundamental values and aspirations, and marks an important advance in the development of our liberty. It can be asserted in any proceeding, civil or criminal, administrative or judicial, investigatory or adjudicatory; and it protects against any disclosures which the witness reasonably believes could be used in a criminal prosecution or could lead to other evidence that might be so used. This Court has been zealous to safeguard the values which underlie the privilege.

Immunity statutes, which have historical roots deep in Anglo-American jurisprudence, are not incompatible with these values. Rather they seek a rational accommodation between the imperatives of the privilege and the legitimate demands of government to compel citizens to testify. The existence of these statutes reflects the importance of testimony, and the fact that many offenses are of such a character that the only persons capable of giving useful testimony are those implicated in the crime. Indeed, their origins were in the context of such offenses, and their primary use has been to investigate such offenses. Congress included immunity statutes in many of the regulatory measures adopted in the first half of this century. Indeed, prior to the enactment of the statute under consideration in this case, there were in force over 50 federal immunity statutes. In addition, every State in the Union, as well as the District of Columbia and Puerto Rico, has one or more such statutes. The commentators, and this Court on several occasions, have characterized immunity statutes as essential to the effective enforcement of various criminal statutes. As Mr. Justice Frankfurter observed, such statutes have "become part of our constitutional fabric."

II.

Petitioners contend first that the Fifth Amendment's privilege against compulsory self-incrimination, which is that "no person . . . shall be compelled in any criminal case to be a witness against himself," deprives Congress of power to enact laws which compel self-incrimination, even if complete immunity from prosecution is granted prior to the compulsion of the incriminatory testimony. In other words, petitioners assert that no immunity statute, however drawn, can afford a lawful basis for compelling incriminatory testimony. They ask us to reconsider and overrule Brown v. Walker, 161 U.S. 591, 16 S.Ct. 644 (1896), and Ullmann v. United States, 350 U.S. 422, 76 S.Ct. 497 (1956), decisions which uphold the constitutionality of immunity statutes. We find no merit to this contention and reaffirm the decisions in *Brown* and *Ullmann*.

III.

Petitioners' second contention is that the scope of immunity provided by the federal witness immunity statute, 18 U.S.C. § 6002, is not coextensive with the scope of the Fifth Amendment privilege against compulsory self-incrimination, and therefore is not sufficient to supplant the privilege and compel testimony over a claim of the privilege. The statute provides that when a witness is compelled by district court order to testify over a claim of the privilege:

> "the witness may not refuse to comply with the order on the basis of his privilege against self-incrimination; but no testimony or other information compelled under the order (or any information directly or indirectly derived from such testimony or other information) may be used against the witness in any criminal case, except a prosecution for perjury, giving a false statement, or otherwise failing to comply with the order."

The constitutional inquiry, rooted in logic and history, as well as in the decisions of this Court, is whether the immunity granted under this statute is coextensive with the scope of the privilege. If so, petitioners' refusals to answer based on the privilege were unjustified, and the judgments of contempt were proper, for the grant of immunity has removed the dangers against which the privilege protects. If, on the other hand, the immunity granted is not as comprehensive as the protection afforded by the privilege, petitioners were justified in refusing to answer, and the judgments of contempt must be vacated.

Petitioners draw a distinction between statutes which provide transactional immunity and those which provide, as does the statute before us, immunity from use and derivative use. They contend that a statute must at a minimum grant full transactional immunity in order to be coextensive with the scope of the privilege. In support of this contention, they rely on Counselman v. Hitchcock, 142 U.S. 547, 12 S.Ct. 195 (1892), the first case in which this Court considered a constitutional challenge to an immunity statute. The statute, a reenactment of the Immunity Act of 1868, provided that no "evidence obtained from a party or witness by means of a judicial proceeding . . . shall be given in evidence, or in any manner used against him . . . in any court of the United States. . . ." Notwithstanding a grant of immunity and order to testify under the revised 1868 Act, the witness, asserting his privilege against compulsory self-incrimination, refused to testify before a federal grand jury. He was consequently adjudged in contempt of court. On appeal, this Court construed the statute as affording a witness protection only against the use of the specific testimony compelled from him under the grant of immunity. This construction meant that the statute "could not, and would not, prevent the use of his testimony to search out other testimony to be used in evidence against him." Since the revised 1868 Act, as construed by the Court, would permit the use against the immunized witness of evidence derived from his compelled testimony, it did not protect the witness to the same extent that a claim of the privilege would protect him. Accordingly, under the principle that a grant of immunity cannot supplant the privilege, and is not sufficient to compel testimony over a claim of the privilege, unless the scope of the grant of immunity is coextensive with the scope of the privilege, the witness' refusal to testify was held proper. In the course of its opinion, the Court made the following statement, on which petitioners heavily rely:

> "We are clearly of opinion that no statute which leaves the party or witness subject to prosecution after he answers the criminating question put to him, can have the effect of supplanting the privilege conferred by the Constitution of the United States. [The immunity statute under consideration] does not supply a complete protection from all the perils against which the constitutional prohibition was designed to guard, and is not a full substitute for that prohibition. In view of the constitutional provision, a statutory enactment, to be valid, must afford absolute immunity against future prosecution for the offence to which the question relates."

Sixteen days after the Counselman decision, a new immunity bill was introduced by Senator Cullom, who urged that enforcement of the Interstate Commerce Act would be impossible in the absence of an effective immunity statute. The bill, which became the Compulsory Testimony Act of 1893, was drafted specifically to meet the broad language in *Counselman* set forth above. The new Act removed the privilege against self-incrimination in hearings before the Interstate Commerce Commission and provided that:

> "no person shall be prosecuted or subjected to any penalty or forfeiture for or on account of any transaction, matter or thing, concerning which he may testify, or produce evidence, documentary or otherwise. . . ."

This transactional immunity statute became the basic form for the numerous federal immunity statutes until 1970, when, after re-examining applicable constitutional principles and the adequacy of existing law, Congress enacted the statute here under consideration. The new statute, which does not "afford [the] absolute immunity against future prosecution" referred to in *Counselman*, was drafted to meet what Congress judged to be the conceptual basis of *Counselman*, as elaborated in subsequent decisions of the Court, namely, that immunity from the use of compelled testimony and evidence derived therefrom is coextensive with the scope of the privilege.

The statute's explicit proscription of the use in any criminal case of "testimony or other information compelled under the order (or any information directly or indirectly derived from such testimony or other information)" is consonant with Fifth Amendment standards. We hold that such immunity from use and derivative use is coextensive with the scope of the privilege against self-incrimination, and therefore is sufficient to compel testimony over a claim of the privilege. While a grant of immunity must afford protection commensurate with that afforded by the privilege, it need not be broader. Transactional immunity, which accords full immunity from prosecution for the offense to which the compelled testimony relates, affords the witness considerably broader protection than does the Fifth Amendment privilege. The privilege has never been construed to mean that one who invokes it cannot subsequently be prosecuted. Its sole concern is to afford protection against being "forced to give testimony leading to the infliction of 'penalties affixed to . . . criminal acts.'" Immunity from the use of compelled testimony and evidence derived directly and indirectly thereform affords this protection. It prohibits the prosecutorial authorities from using the compelled testimony in *any* respect, and it therefore insures that the testimony cannot lead to the infliction of criminal penalties on the witness.

Our holding is consistent with the conceptual basis of *Counselman*. The *Counselman* statute, as construed by the Court, was plainly deficient in its failure to prohibit the use against the immunized witness of evidence derived from his compelled testimony. The Court repeatedly emphasized this deficiency, noting that the statute:

> "could not, and would not, prevent the use of his testimony to search out other testimony to be used in evidence against him or his property, in a criminal proceeding . . .",

that it:

> "could not prevent the obtaining and the use of witnesses and evidence which should be attributable directly to the tes-

timony he might give under compulsion and on which he might be convicted, when otherwise, and if he had refused to answer, he could not possibly have been convicted",

and that it:

"affords no protection against that use of compelled testimony which consists in gaining therefrom a knowledge of the details of a crime, and of sources of information which may supply other means of convicting the witness or party".

The basis of the Court's decision was recognized in Ullmann v. United States (1956), in which the Court reiterated that the *Counselman* statute was insufficient:

"because the immunity granted was incomplete, in that it merely forbade the use of the testimony given and failed to protect a witness from future prosecution *based on knowledge and sources of information obtained from the compelled testimony.*" (Emphasis supplied.)

The broad language in *Counselman* relied upon by petitioners was unnecessary to the Court's decision, and cannot be considered binding authority.

In Murphy v. Waterfront Comm'n, 378 U.S. 52, 84 S.Ct. 1594 (1964), the Court carefully considered immunity from use of compelled testimony and evidence derived therefrom. The *Murphy* petitioners were subpoenaed to testify at a hearing conducted by the Waterfront Commission of New York Harbor. After refusing to answer certain questions on the ground that the answers might tend to incriminate them, petitioners were granted immunity from prosecution under the laws of New Jersey and New York. They continued to refuse to testify, however, on the ground that their answers might tend to incriminate them under federal law, to which the immunity did not purport to extend. They were adjudged in civil contempt, and that judgment was affirmed by the New Jersey Supreme Court.

The issue before the Court in *Murphy* was whether New Jersey and New York could compel the witnesses, whom these States had immunized from prosecution under their laws, to give testimony which might then be used to convict them of a federal crime. Since New Jersey and New York had not purported to confer immunity from federal prosecution, the Court was faced with the question what limitations the Fifth Amendment privilege imposed on the prosecutorial powers of the Federal Government, a nonimmunizing sovereign. After undertaking an examination of the policies and purposes of the privilege, the Court overturned the rule that one jurisdiction within our federal structure may compel a witness to give testimony which could be used to convict him of a crime in another jurisdiction. The Court held that the privilege protects state witnesses against incrimination under federal as well as state law, and federal witnesses against incrimination under state as well as federal law. Applying this principle to the state immunity legislation before it, the Court held the constitutional rule to be that:

"a state witness may not be compelled to give testimony
which may be incriminating under federal law unless the
compelled testimony and its fruits cannot be used in any
manner by federal officials in connection with a criminal
prosecution against him. We conclude, moreover, that in order to implement this constitutional rule and accommodate
the interests of the State and Federal Government in investigating and prosecuting crime, the Federal Government
must be prohibited from making any such use of compelled
testimony and its fruits."

The Court emphasized that this rule left the state witness and the
Federal Government, against which the witness had immunity only
from the *use* of the compelled testimony and evidence derived therefrom, "in substantially the same position as if the witness had
claimed his privilege in the absence of a state grant of immunity."

* * *

IV.

Petitioners argue that use and derivative use immunity will not
adequately protect a witness from various possible incriminating uses
of the compelled testimony: for example, the prosecutor or other law
enforcement officials may obtain leads, names of witnesses, or other
information not otherwise available which might result in a prosecution. It will be difficult and perhaps impossible, the argument goes,
to identify, by testimony or cross-examination the subtle ways in
which the compelled testimony may disadvantage a witness, especially
in the jurisdiction granting the immunity.

This argument presupposes that the statute's prohibition will
prove impossible to enforce. The statute provides a sweeping proscription of any use, direct or indirect, of the compelled testimony
and any information derived therefrom:

"no testimony or other information, compelled under the order (or any information directly or indirectly derived from
such testimony or other information) may be used against
the witness in any criminal case. . . . ." 18 U.S.C. §
6002.

This total prohibition on use provides a comprehensive safeguard
barring the use of compelled testimony as an "investigatory lead,"
and also barring the use of any evidence obtained by focusing investigation on a witness as a result of his compelled disclosures.

A person accorded this immunity under 18 U.S.C. § 6002, and
subsequently prosecuted, is not dependent for the preservation of his
rights upon the integrity and good faith of the prosecuting authorities. As stated in *Murphy:*

"Once a defendant demonstrates that he has testified, under
a state grant of immunity, to matters related to the federal
prosecution, the federal authorities have the burden of
showing that their evidence is not tainted by establishing

that they had an independent, legitimate source for the disputed evidence."

This burden of proof, which we reaffirm as appropriate, is not limited to a negation of taint; rather, it imposes on the prosecution the
affirmative duty to prove that the evidence it proposes to use is derived from a legitimate source wholly independent of the compelled
testimony.

This is very substantial protection, commensurate with that resulting from invoking the privilege itself. The privilege assures that
a citizen is not compelled to incriminate himself by his own testimony. It usually operates to allow a citizen to remain silent when asked
a question requiring an incriminatory answer. This statute, which
operates after a witness has given incriminatory testimony, affords
the same protection by assuring that the compelled testimony can in
no way lead to the infliction of criminal penalties. The statute, like
the Fifth Amendment, grants neither pardon nor amnesty. Both the
statute and the Fifth Amendment allow the government to prosecute
using evidence from legitimate independent sources.

The statutory proscription is analogous to the Fifth Amendment
requirement in cases of coerced confessions. A coerced confession, as
revealing of leads as testimony given in exchange for immunity, is inadmissible in a criminal trial, but it does not bar prosecution. Moreover, a defendant against whom incriminating evidence has been obtained through a grant of immunity may be in a stronger position at
trial than a defendant who asserts a Fifth Amendment coerced confession claim. One raising a claim under this statute need only show
that he testified under a grant of immunity in order to shift to the
government the heavy burden of proving that all of the evidence it
proposes to use was derived from legitimate independent sources. On
the other hand, a defendant raising a coerced confession claim under
the Fifth Amendment must first prevail in a voluntariness hearing
before his confession and evidence derived from it become inadmissible.

There can be no justification in reason or policy for holding that
the Constitution requires an amnesty grant where, acting pursuant to
statute and accompanying safeguards, testimony is compelled in exchange for immunity from use and derivative use when no such amnesty is required where the government, acting without colorable
right, coerces a defendant into incriminating himself.

We conclude that the immunity provided by 18 U.S.C. § 6002
leaves the witness and the prosecutorial authorities in substantially
the same position as if the witness had claimed the Fifth Amendment
privilege. The immunity therefore is coextensive with the privilege
and suffices to supplant it.   .   .   .

Affirmed.

MR. JUSTICE BRENNAN and MR. JUSTICE REHNQUIST took no part
in the consideration or decision of this case.

Mr. Justice Douglas, dissenting.

The Self-Incrimination Clause says "No person   .   .   .   shall be compelled in any criminal case to be a witness against himself."   I see no answer to the proposition that he is such a witness when only "use" immunity is granted.

* * *

This Court, however, apparently believes that *Counselman* and its progeny were overruled, *sub silentio*, in Murphy v. Waterfront Commission.

I would adhere to Counselman v. Hitchcock and hold that this attempt to dilute the Self-Incrimination Clause is unconstitutional.

Mr. Justice Marshall, dissenting.

Today the Court holds that the United States may compel a witness to give incriminating testimony, and subsequently prosecute him for crimes to which that testimony relates.   I cannot believe the Fifth Amendment permits that result.

The Fifth Amendment gives a witness an absolute right to resist interrogation, if the testimony sought would tend to incriminate him. A grant of immunity may strip the witness of the right to refuse to testify, but only if it is broad enough to eliminate all possibility that the testimony will in fact operate to incriminate him.   It must put him in precisely the same position, *vis-à-vis* the government that has compelled his testimony, as he would have been in had he remained silent in reliance on the privilege.   .   .   .   I cannot agree that a ban on use will in practice be total, if it remains open for the Government to convict the witness on the basis of evidence derived from a legitimate independent source.   The Court asserts that the witness is adequately protected by a rule imposing on the Government a heavy burden of proof it it would establish the independent character of evidence to be used against the witness.   But in light of the inevitable uncertainties of the fact-finding process, a greater margin of protection is required in order to provide a reliable guarantee that the witness is in exactly the same position as if he had not testified.   That margin can be provided only by immunity from prosecution for the offenses to which the testimony relates, i. e., transactional immunity.

I do not see how it can suffice merely to put the burden of proof on the Government.   First, contrary to the Court's assertion, the Court's rule does leave the witness "dependent for the preservation of his rights upon the integrity and good faith of the prosecuting authorities."   For the information relevant to the question of taint is uniquely within the knowledge of the prosecuting authorities.   They alone are in a position to trace the chains of information and investigation that lead to the evidence to be used in a criminal prosecution. A witness who suspects that his compelled testimony was used to develop a lead will be hard pressed indeed to ferret out the evidence necessary to prove it.   And of course it is no answer to say he need not prove it, for though the Court puts the burden of proof on the Government, the Government will have no difficulty in meeting its burden by mere assertion if the witness produces no contrary evidence. The good faith of the prosecuting authorities is thus the sole safeguard of the witness' rights. Second, even their good faith is not a sufficient safeguard. For the paths of information through the investigative bureaucracy may well be long and winding, and even a prosecutor acting in the best of faith cannot be certain that somewhere in the depths of his investigative apparatus, often including hundreds of employees, there was not some prohibited use of the compelled testimony. The Court today sets out a loose net to trap tainted evidence and prevent its use against the witness, but it accepts an intolerably great risk that tainted evidence will in fact slip through that net.

In my view the Court turns reason on its head when it compares a statutory grant of immunity to the "immunity" that is inadvertently conferrred by an unconstitutional interrogation. The exclusionary rule of evidence that applies in that situation has nothing whatever to do with this case. Evidence obtained through a coercive interrogation, like evidence obtained through an illegal search, is excluded at trial because the Constitution prohibits such methods of gathering evidence. The exclusionary rules provide a partial and inadequate remedy to some victims of illegal police conduct, and a similarly partial and inadequate deterrent to police officers. An immunity statute, on the other hand, is much more ambitious than any exclusionary rule. It does not merely attempt to provide a remedy for past police misconduct, which never should have occurred. An immunity statute operates in advance of the event, and it authorizes—even encourages—interrogation which would otherwise be prohibited by the Fifth Amendment. An immunity statute thus differs from an exclusionary rule of evidence in at least two critical respects.

First, because an immunity statute gives constitutional approval to the resulting interrogation, the Government is under an obligation here to remove the danger of incrimination completely and absolutely, whereas in the case of the exclusionary rules it may be sufficient to shield the witness from the fruits of the illegal search or interrogation in a partial and reasonably adequate manner. For when illegal police conduct has occurred, the exclusion of evidence does not purport to purge the conduct of its unconstitutional character. The constitutional violation remains, and may provide the basis for other relief, such as a damage action, or a criminal prosecution of the responsible officers. The Constitution does not authorize police officers to coerce confessions or to invade privacy without cause, so long as no use is made of the evidence they obtain. But this Court has held that the Constitution does authorize the Government to compel a witness to give potentially incriminating testimony, so long as no incriminating use is made of the resulting evidence. Before the Government puts its seal of approval on such an interrogation, it must provide an absolutely reliable guarantee that it will not use the testimony in any way at all in aid of prosecution of the witness. The only way to provide that guarantee is to give the witness immunity from prosecution for crimes to which his testimony relates.

Second, because an immunity statute operates in advance of the interrogation, there is room to require a broad grant of transactional immunity without imperiling large numbers of otherwise valid convictions. An exclusionary rule comes into play after the interrogation or search has occurred; and the decision to question or to search is often made in haste, under pressure, by an officer who is not a lawyer. If an unconstitutional interrogation or search were held to create transactional immunity, that might well be regarded as an excessively high price to pay for the "constable's blunder." An immunity statute, on the other hand, creates a framework in which the prosecuting attorney can make a calm and reasoned decision whether to compel testimony and suffer the resulting ban on prosecution, or to forgo the testimony.

For both these reasons it is clear to me that an immunity statute must be tested by a standard far more demanding than that appropriate for an exclusionary rule fashioned to deal with past constitutional violations. Measured by that standard, the statute approved today by the Court fails miserably. I respectfully dissent.

NOTES

1. In the companion case to *Kastigar*, Zicarelli v. New Jersey State Commission of Investigation, 406 U.S. 472, 92 S.Ct. 1670 (1972), the Supreme Court upheld the validity of the New Jersey use immunity statute. The Court also held that the statutory condition of a "responsive answer" (inserted as a safeguard against a witness giving himself a complete "immunity bath" beyond the subject matter of the investigation) was not unconstitutionally vague since the phrase "responsive answer" has a clearly understood meaning, and, moreover, the person examined has the right to counsel before the Commission who could "secure clarification of vague and ambiguous questions in advance of a response by the witness".

2. Some persons, particularly prosecutors, say that there is little difference between use immunity and transactional, except where multiple jurisdictions are interested in the same matter. This is because of the difficulty of demonstrating that a prosecution is based entirely upon evidence derived independently of the immunized testimony.

The case of the Watergate figure Gordon Strachan is often cited as an example. Strachan acquired use immunity but later was indicted. The Government special prosecutor abandoned the case against Strachan, however, because of the difficulties of proving independent origins, and because of the time and effort which evidentiary hearings on the point would have demanded. The *Strachan* case is noted in United States v. De Diego, 511 F.2d 818 (D.C.Cir.1975), but is apparently not itself the subject of a reported opinion even though it was a court order suggesting enormous difficulties ahead which led to the dismissal. *De Diego* like *Strachan*, does demonstrate that some people who have acquired use immunity do get indicted. See also United States v. Hinton, 543 F.2d 1002 (2d Cir. 1976). Gordon Strachan's wife has analyzed her husband's case in developing an interesting rationale upon which she advocates a return to transactional immunity. See Strachan, Self-Incrimination, Immunity and Watergate, 56 Texas L. Rev. 791 (1978).

If the prosecutor intends to indict at the time use immunity is granted, and if he has foreknowledge of the immunity order, he can "seal" his evidence, as was done by the special prosecutor to preserve evidence against John Dean in the Watergate case.

3. Consider the following scenario: The government, fully aware that it has enough evidence to indict a suspect, presents all of its evidence to the grand jury. Instead of seeking an indictment, the government subpoenas the suspect to the grand jury. When the suspect refuses to testify on fifth amendment grounds, the government "seals" its evidence—to protect it from becoming tainted by immunized testimony—and obtains an order immunizing the suspect. At this point, the suspect has three choices: he can refuse to testify and be jailed for contempt; he can confess; or he can testify in a manner that is inconsistent with the government's evidence. If he takes the latter course, the government can continue to use the grand jury to learn the suspect's story, add a perjury count to his indictment, or do both. Under circumstances such as this, is use immunity consistent with the fifth amendment privilege? Does *Kastigar* authorize the government to use immunity in this manner? In United States v. Hinton, 543 F.2d 1002 (2d Cir. 1976), the court held that a non-perjury indictment cannot be returned against a person who testifies before it under a grant of immunity. Compare United States v. Anzalone, 560 F.2d 492 (2d Cir. 1977).

In New Jersey v. Portash, 440 U.S. 450, 99 S.Ct. 1292 (1979), the Supreme Court held that testimony which was given under a grant of immunity cannot be used to impeach the witness who at trial tells a version of events different from that included in his immunized testimony. The Court held that immunized testimony is coerced in a "classical" sense and upon that basis distinguished the use for impeachment purposes of a Miranda-violative statement. Compare Harris v. New York, Chapter 6, Section D–2, supra. Of course a defendant who changes his story from the version he gave under immunity may be setting himself up for a perjury indictment.

4. While the court must issue the immunity order, this function has been described as "ministerial". The court may not review the prosecutor's decision to grant immunity; the primary purpose of a hearing on the question is to permit technical objections to compliance requirements. See In re Lochiatto, 497 F.2d 803 (1st Cir. 1974). Moreover, a defendant has no standing to object to the granting of immunity to a witness against him. United States v. Braasch, 505 F.2d 139, 146 (7th Cir. 1974); United States v. Lewis, 456 F.2d 404 (3d Cir. 1972).

5. A corporation has no Fifth Amendment privilege against self-incrimination. Therefore, it cannot invoke the privilege as a defense to a subpoena for corporate records. Is there ever a justification, then, for granting a corporation immunity? What practical considerations might lead a prosecutor to apply for such an immunity order? Should the law deem such reasons legitimate?

6. If a witness has perjured himself in one proceeding and then later testifies under a grant of immunity in another proceeding, in a use-immunity jurisdiction his immunized testimony cannot be used against him in a prosecution for the perjury committed in the first proceeding. (In a transactional immunity jurisdiction, he could not be prosecuted at all for the original perjury.) Of course, false testimony given under a grant of immunity can be the subject of a perjury charge. In some jurisdictions, ordinarily proof of two materially inconsistent statements made under oath by an individual is sufficient to establish a prima facie case of perjury. However, where the second statement is given under a grant of immunity and the prosecutor charges that such a statement was perjurious, the prosecu-

tion is denied benefit of the ordinary presumption arising from inconsistent sworn statements. See United States v. Patrick, 542 F.2d 381 (7th Cir. 1976).

GARRITY v. NEW JERSEY

Supreme Court of the United States, 1967.
385 U.S. 493, 87 S.Ct. 616.

Mr. Justice Douglas delivered the opinion of the Court.

Appellants were police officers in certain New Jersey boroughs. The Supreme Court of New Jersey ordered that alleged irregularities in handling cases in the municipal courts of those boroughs be investigated by the Attorney General, invested him with broad powers of inquiry and investigation, and directed him to make a report to the court. The matters investigated concerned alleged fixing of traffic tickets.

Before being questioned each appellant was warned (1) that anything he said might be used against him in any state criminal proceeding; (2) that he had the privilege to refuse to answer if the disclosure would tend to incriminate him; but (3) that if he refused to answer he would be subject to removal from office.[1]

Appellants answered the questions. No immunity was granted, as there is no immunity statute applicable in these circumstances. Over their objections, some of the answers given were used in a subsequent prosecution for conspiracy to obstruct the administration of the traffic laws. Appellants were convicted and their conviction was sustained over their protests that their statements were coerced,[2] by reason of the fact that, if they refused to answer, they could lose their positions with the police department.

1. "Any person holding or who has held any elective or appointive public office, position or employment (whether State, county, or municipal), who refuses to testify upon matters relating to the office, position or employment in any criminal proceeding wherein he is a defendant or is called as a witness on behalf of the prosecution, upon the ground that his answer may tend to incriminate him or compel him to be a witness against himself or refuses to waive immunity when called by a grand jury to testify thereon or who willfully refuses or fails to appear before any court, commission or body of this state which has the right to inquire under oath upon matters relating to the office, position or employment of such person or who, having been sworn, refuses to testify or to answer any material question upon the ground that his answer may tend to incriminate him or compel him to be a witness against himself, shall, if holding elec-

tive or public office, position or employment, be removed therefrom or shall thereby forfeit his office, position or employment and any vested or future right of tenure or pension granted to him by any law of this State provided the inquiry relates to a matter which occurred or arose within the preceding five years. Any person so forfeiting his office, position or employment shall not thereafter be eligible for election or appointment to any public office, position or employment in this State." N.J.Rev. Stat. § 2A:81–17.1 (Supp.1965), N.J.S. A.

2. At the trial the court excused the jury and conducted a hearing to determine whether, *inter alia*, the statements were voluntary. The State offered witnesses who testified as to the manner in which the statements were taken; the appellants did not testify at that hearing. The court held the statements to be voluntary.

We postponed the question of jurisdiction to a hearing on the merits. The statute whose validity was sought to be "drawn in question," 28 U.S.C. § 1257(2), was the forfeiture statute. But the New Jersey Supreme Court refused to reach that question, deeming the voluntariness of the statements as the only issue presented. The statute is therefore too tangentially involved to satisfy 28 U.S.C. § 1257(2), for the only bearing it had was whether, valid or not, the fear of being discharged under it for refusal to answer on the one hand and the fear of self-incrimination on the other was "a choice between the rock and the whirlpool" which made the statements products of coercion in violation of the Fourteenth Amendment. We therefore dismiss the appeal, treat the papers as a petition for certiorari, grant the petition and proceed to the merits.

We agree with the New Jersey Supreme Court that the forfeiture of office statute is relevant here only for the bearing it has on the voluntary character of the statements used to convict appellants in their criminal prosecutions.

The choice imposed on appellants was one between self-incrimination or job forfeiture. Coercion that vitiates a confession under Chambers v. State of Florida, 309 U.S. 227, 60 S.Ct. 472, and related cases can be "mental as well as physical"; "the blood of the accused is not the only hallmark of an unconstitutional inquisition." Subtle pressures may be as telling as coarse and vulgar ones. The question is whether the accused was deprived of his "free choice to admit, to deny, or to refuse to answer."

We adhere to Boyd v. United States, 116 U.S. 616, 6 S.Ct. 524, a civil forfeiture action against property. A statute offered the owner an election between producing a document or forfeiture of the goods at issue in the proceeding. This was held to be a form of compulsion in violation of both the Fifth Amendment and the Fourth Amendment.

The choice given appellants was either to forfeit their jobs or to incriminate themselves. The option to lose their means of livelihood or to pay the penalty of self-incrimination is the antithesis of free choice to speak out or to remain silent. That practice, like interrogation practices we reviewed in Miranda v. State of Arizona, is "likely to exert such pressure upon an individual as to disable him from making a free and rational choice." We think the confessions were infected by the coercion inherent in this scheme of questioning and cannot be sustained as voluntary under our prior decisions.

It is said that there was a "waiver." That, however, is a federal question for us to decide. . . .

Where the choice is "between the rock and the whirlpool," duress is inherent in deciding to "waive" one or the other. . . .

Mr. Justice Holmes, in McAuliffe v. New Bedford, 155 Mass. 216, 29 N.E. 517, stated a dictum on which New Jersey heavily relies:

> "The petitioner may have a constitutional right to talk politics, but he has no constitutional right to be a policeman.

There are few employments for hire in which the servant does not agree to suspend his constitutional right of free speech as well as of idleness by the implied terms of his contract. The servant cannot complain, as he takes the employment on the terms which are offered him. On the same principle the city may impose any reasonable condition upon holding offices within its control."

The question in this case, however, is not cognizable in those terms. Our question is whether the Government, contrary to the requirement of the Fourteenth Amendment, can use the threat of discharge to secure incriminatory evidence against an employee.

We held in Slochower v. Board of Education, 350 U.S. 551, 76 S. Ct. 637, that a public school teacher could not be discharged merely because he had invoked the Fifth Amendment privilege against self-incrimination when questioned by a congressional committee:

"The privilege against self-incrimination would be reduced to a hollow mockery if its exercise could be taken as equivalent either to a confession of guilt or a conclusive presumption of perjury. . . . The privilege serves to protect the innocent who otherwise might be ensnared by ambiguous circumstances."

We conclude that policemen, like teachers and lawyers, are not relegated to a watered-down version of constitutional rights.

There are rights of constitutional stature whose exercise a State may not condition by the exaction of a price. . . . We now hold the protection of the individual under the Fourteenth Amendment against coerced confessions prohibits use in subsequent criminal proceedings of confessions obtained under threat of removal from office, and that it extends to all, whether they are policemen or other members of our body politic.

Reversed.

MR. JUSTICE HARLAN, whom MR. JUSTICE CLARK and MR. JUSTICE STEWART join, dissenting.

*   *   *

I.

I turn first to the suggestion that these statements were involuntary in fact. An assessment of the voluntariness of the various statements in issue here requires a more comprehensive examination of the pertinent circumstances than the majority has undertaken.

The petitioners were at all material times policemen in the boroughs of Bellmawr and Barrington, New Jersey. Garrity was Bellmawr's chief of police and Virtue one of its police officers; Holroyd, Elwell, and Murray were police officers in Barrington. Another defendant below, Mrs. Naglee, the clerk of Bellmawr's municipal court, has since died. In June 1961 the New Jersey Supreme Court *sua sponte* directed the State's Attorney General to investigate reports of traffic ticket fixing in Bellmawr and Barrington. Subsequent investigations produced evidence that the petitioners, in separate conspiracies, had falsified municipal court records, altered traffic tickets, and diverted moneys produced from bail and fines to unauthorized purposes. In the course of these investigations the State obtained two sworn statements from each of the petitioners; portions of those statements were admitted at trial. The petitioners were convicted in two separate trials of conspiracy to obstruct the proper administration of the state motor traffic laws, the cases being now consolidated for purposes of our review. The Supreme Court of New Jersey affirmed all the convictions.

The first statements were taken from the petitioners by the State's Deputy Attorney General in August and November 1961. All of the usual indicia of duress are wholly absent. As the state court noted, there was "no physical coercion, no overbearing tactics of psychological persuasion, no lengthy incommunicado detention, or efforts to humiliate or ridicule the defendants." The state court found no evidence that any of the petitioners were reluctant to offer statements, and concluded that the interrogations were conducted with a "high degree of civility and restraint."

These conclusions are fully substantiated by the record. The statements of the Bellmawr petitioners were taken in a room in the local firehouse, for which Chief Garrity himself had made arrangements. None of the petitioners were in custody before or after the depositions were taken; each apparently continued to pursue his ordinary duties as a public official of the community. The statements were recorded by a court stenographer, who testified that he witnessed no indications of unwillingness or even significant hesitation on the part of any of the petitioners. The Bellmawr petitioners did not have counsel present, but the Deputy Attorney General testified without contradiction that Garrity had informed him as they strolled between Garrity's office and the firehouse that he had arranged for counsel, but thought that none would be required at that stage. The interrogations were not excessively lengthy, and reasonable efforts were made to assure the physical comfort of the witnesses. Mrs. Naglee, the clerk of the Bellmawr municipal court, who was known to suffer from a heart ailment, was assured that questioning would cease if she felt any discomfort.

The circumstances in which the depositions of the Barrington petitioners were taken are less certain, for the New Jersey Supreme Court found that there was an informal agreement at the Barrington trial that the defendants would argue simply that the possibility of dismissal made the statements "involuntary as a matter of law." The defense did not contend that the statements were the result of physical or mental coercion, or that the wills of the Barrington petitioners were overborne. Accordingly, the State was never obliged to offer evidence of the voluntariness in fact of the statements. We are, however, informed that the three Barrington petitioners had counsel present as their depositions were taken. Insofar as the majority suggests that the Barrington statements are involuntary in fact, in the fashion of *Chambers* or *Haynes*, it has introduced a factual contention never urged by the Barrington petitioners and never considered by the courts of New Jersey.

As interrogation commenced, each of the petitioners was sworn, carefully informed that he need not give any information, reminded that any information given might be used in a subsequent criminal prosecution, and warned that as a police officer he was subject to a proceeding to discharge him if he failed to provide information relevant to his public responsibilities. The cautionary statements varied slightly, but all, except that given to Mrs. Naglee, included each of the three warnings.* Mrs. Naglee was not told that she could be removed from her position at the court if she failed to give information pertinent to the discharge of her duties. All of the petitioners consented to give statements, none displayed any significant hesitation, and none suggested that the decision to offer information was motivated by the possibility of discharge.

A second statement was obtained from each of the petitioners in September and December 1962. These statements were not materially different in content or circumstances from the first. The only significant distinction was that the interrogator did not advert even obliquely to any possibility of dismissal. All the petitioners were cautioned that they were entitled to remain silent, and there was no evidence whatever of physical or mental coercion.

All of the petitioners testified at trial, and gave evidence essentially consistent with the statements taken from them. At a preliminary hearing conducted at the Bellmawr trial to determine the voluntariness of the statements, the Bellmawr petitioners offered no evidence beyond proof of the warning given them.

The standards employed by the Court to assess the voluntariness of an accused's statements have reflected a number of values, and thus have emphasized a variety of factual criteria. The criteria employed have included threats of imminent danger, physical deprivations, repeated or extended interrogation, limits on access to counsel

---

* The warning given to Chief Garrity is typical. "I want to advise you that anything you say must be said of your own free will and accord without any threats or promises or coercion and anything you say may be, of course, used against you or any other person in any subsequent criminal proceedings in the courts of our state.
"You do have, under our law, as you probably know, a privilege to refuse to make any disclosure which may tend to incriminate you. If you make a disclosure with knowledge of this right or privilege, voluntarily, you thereby waive that right or privilege in relation to any other questions which I might put to you relevant to such disclosure in this investigation.

"This right or privilege which you have is somewhat limited to the extent that you as a police officer under the laws of our state . . . may be subjected to a proceeding to have you removed from office if you refuse to answer a question put to you under oath pertaining to your office or your function within that office. It doesn't mean, however, you can't exercise that right. You do have the right."

A. "No, I will cooperate."

Q. "Understanding this, are you willing to proceed at this time and answer any questions?"

A. "Yes."

or friends, length and illegality of detention under state law, Haynes v. State of Washington, individual weakness or incapacities, Lynumn v. State of Illinois, and the adequacy of warnings of constitutional rights. Whatever the criteria employed, the duty of the Court has been "to examine the entire record," and thereby to determine whether the accused's will "was overborne by the sustained pressures upon him."

It would be difficult to imagine interrogations to which these criteria of duress were more completely inapplicable, or in which the requirements which have subsequently been imposed by this Court on police questioning were more thoroughly satisfied. Each of the petitioners received a complete and explicit reminder of his constitutional privilege. Three of the petitioners had counsel present; at least a fourth had consulted counsel but freely determined that his presence was unnecessary. These petitioners were not in any fashion "swept from familiar surroundings into police custody, surrounded by antagonistic forces, and subjected to the techniques of persuasion . . . ." Miranda v. State of Arizona. I think it manifest that, under the standards developed by this Court to assess voluntariness, there is no basis for saying that any of these statements were made involuntarily.

The issue remaining is whether the statements were inadmissible because they were "involuntary as a matter of law," in that they were given after a warning that New Jersey policemen may be discharged for failure to provide information pertinent to their public responsibilities. What is really involved on this score, however, is not in truth a question of "voluntariness" at all, but rather whether the condition imposed by the State on the exercise of the privilege against self-incrimination, namely dismissal from office, in this instance serves in itself to render the statements inadmissible. Absent evidence of involuntariness in fact, the admissibility of these statements thus hinges on the validity of the consequence which the State acknowledged might have resulted if the statements had not been given. If the consequence is constitutionally permissible, there can surely be no objection if the State cautions the witness that it may follow if he remains silent. If both the consequence and the warning are constitutionally permissible, a witness is obliged, in order to prevent the use of his statements against him in a criminal prosecution, to prove under the standards established since Brown v. State of Mississippi that as a matter of fact the statements were involuntarily made. The central issues here are therefore identical to those presented in Spevack v. Klein, whether consequences may properly be permitted to result to a claimant after his invocation of the constitutional privilege, and if so, whether the consequence in question is permissible. For reasons which I have stated in Spevack v. Klein, in my view nothing in the logic or purposes of the privilege demands that all consequences which may result from a witness' silence be forbidden merely because that silence is privileged. The validity of a consequence depends both upon the hazards, if any, it presents to the integrity of the privilege and upon the urgency of the public interests it is designed to protect.

* * *

I would affirm the judgments of the Supreme Court of New Jersey.

GARDNER v. BRODERICK

Supreme Court of the United States, 1968.
392 U.S. 273, 88 S.Ct. 1913.

Mr. Justice Fortas delivered the opinion of the Court.

Appellant brought this action in the Supreme Court of the State of New York seeking reinstatement as a New York City patrolman and back pay. He claimed he was unlawfully dismissed because he refused to waive his privilege against self-incrimination. In August 1965, pursuant to subpoena, appellant appeared before a New York County grand jury which was investigating alleged bribery and corruption of police officers in connection with unlawful gambling operations. He was advised that the grand jury proposed to examine him concerning the performance of his official duties. He was advised of his privilege against self-incrimination [1] but he was asked to sign a "waiver of immunity" after being told that he would be fired if he did not sign. [2] Following his refusal, he was given an administrative hearing and was discharged solely for this refusal, pursuant to § 1123 of the New York City Charter.

The New York Supreme Court dismissed his petition for reinstatement, 27 A.D.2d 800, 279 N.Y.S.2d 150 (1967), and the New

---

1. The Assistant District Attorney said to appellant:
    "You understand . . . that under the Constitution of the United States, as well as the Constitution of New York, no one can be compelled to testify against himself, and that he has a right, the absolute right to refuse to answer any questions that would tend to incriminate him?"

2. Appellant was told:
    "You understand . . . that under the Constitution of the United States, as the Charter of the City of New York, . . . a public officer, which includes a police officer, when called before a Grand Jury to answer questions concerning the conduct of his public office and the performance of his duties is required to sign a waiver of immunity if he wishes to retain that public office?"

The document appellant was asked to sign was phrased as follows:
    "I . . . do hereby waive all benefits, privileges, rights and immunity which I would otherwise obtain from indictment, prosecution, and punishment for or on account of, regarding or relating to any matter, transaction or things, concerning the conduct of my office or the performance of my official duties, or the property, government or affairs of the State of New York or of any county included within its territorial limits, or the nomination, election, appointment or official conduct of any officer of the city or of any such county, concerning any of which matters, transactions or things I may testify or produce evidence documentary or otherwise, before the [blank] Grand Jury in the County of New York in the investigation being conducted by said Grand Jury."

York Court of Appeals affirmed.   20 N.Y.2d 227, 282 N.Y.S.2d 487, 229 N.E.2d 184 (1967).   We noted probable jurisdiction.

Our decisions establish beyond dispute the breadth of the privilege to refuse to respond to questions when the result may be self-incriminatory and the need fully to implement its guaranty.   .   .   . The privilege is applicable to state as well as federal proceedings. .   .   .   The privilege may be waived in appropriate circumstances if the waiver is knowingly and voluntarily made.   Answers may be compelled regardless of the privilege if there is immunity from federal and state use of the compelled testimony or its fruits in connection with a criminal prosecution against the person testifying.   .   .   .

The question presented in the present case is whether a policeman who refuses to waive the protections which the privilege gives him may be dismissed from office because of that refusal.

About a year and a half after New York City discharged petitioner for his refusal to waive this immunity, we decided Garrity v. State of New Jersey, 385 U.S. 493, 87 S.Ct. 616 (1967).   .   .   .

The New York Court of Appeals considered that *Garrity* did not control the present case.   It is true that *Garrity* related to the attempted use of compelled testimony.   It did not involve the precise question which is presented here: namely, whether a State may discharge an officer for refusing to waive a right which the Constitution guarantees to him.   The New York Court of Appeals also distinguished our post-*Garrity* decision in Spevack v. Klein, 385 U.S. 511, 87 S.Ct. 625.   In *Spevack*, we ruled that a lawyer could not be disbarred solely because he refused to testify at a disciplinary proceeding on the ground that his testimony would tend to incriminate him. The Court of Appeals concluded that *Spevack* does not control the present case because different considerations apply in the case of a public official such as a policeman.   A lawyer, it stated, although licensed by the state is not an employee.   This distinction is now urged upon us.   It is argued that although a lawyer could not constitutionally be confronted with Hobson's choice between self-incrimination and forfeiting his means of livelihood, the same principle should not protect a policeman.   Unlike the lawyer, he is directly, immediately, and entirely responsible to the city or State which is his employer. He owes his entire loyalty to it.   He has no other "client" or principal.   He is a trustee of the public interest, bearing the burden of great and total responsibility to his public employer.   Unlike the lawyer who is directly responsible to his client, the policeman is either responsible to the State or to no one.

We agree that these factors differentiate the situations.   If appellant, a policeman, had refused to answer questions specifically, directly, and narrowly relating to the performance of his official duties, without being required to waive his immunity with respect to the use of his answers or the fruits thereof in a criminal prosecution of himself,   .   .   .   the privilege against self-incrimination would not have been a bar to his dismissal.

The facts of this case, however, do not present this issue. Here, petitioner was summoned to testify before a grand jury in an investigation of alleged criminal conduct. He was discharged from office, not for failure to answer relevant questions about his official duties, but for refusal to waive a constitutional right. He was dismissed for failure to relinquish the protections of the privilege against self-incrimination. The Constitution of New York State and the City Charter both expressly provided that his failure to do so, as well as his failure to testify, would result in dismissal from his job. He was dismissed solely for his refusal to waive the immunity to which he is entitled if he is required to testify despite his constitutional privilege.

We need not speculate whether, if appellant had executed the waiver of immunity in the circumstances, the effect of our subsequent decision in Garrity v. State of New Jersey, supra, would have been to nullify the effect of the waiver. New York City discharged him for refusal to execute a document purporting to waive his constitutional rights and to permit prosecution of himself on the basis of his compelled testimony. Petitioner could not have assumed—and certainly he was not required to assume—that he was being asked to do an idle act of no legal effect. In any event, the mandate of the great privilege against self-incrimination does not tolerate the attempt, regardless of its ultimate effectiveness, to coerce a waiver of the immunity it confers on penalty of the loss of employment. It is clear that petitioner's testimony was demanded before the grand jury in part so that it might be used to prosecute him, and not solely for the purpose of securing an accounting of his performance of his public trust. If the latter had been the only purpose, there would have been no reason to seek to compel petitioner to waive his immunity. Proper regard for the history and meaning of the privilege against self-incrimination, ... dictate the conclusion that the provision of the New York City Charter pursuant to which petitioner was dismissed cannot stand. Accordingly, the judgment is reversed.

Reversed.

Mr. Justice Black concurs in the result.

NOTES

1. Does Gardner v. Broderick permit a police department to immunize its officers from criminal prosecution by requiring them to answer questions concerning their conduct while on duty—for instance, a case involving the questionable shooting of a citizen? Granted that after Kastigar the immunity provided in such a situation would probably be use immunity rather than transactional immunity, the burden would still be on the prosecution to show that none of its evidence is derived from the "compelled" testimony given by the officer under threat of loss of job if the self-incrimination privilege is invoked in an official police internal investigation. Would the prosecution do better to refuse to examine the internal investigation reports for fear of tainting a criminal prosecution? Is this solution practical?

2. The Gardner solution to a difficult Fifth Amendment problem, permitting the compulsion of testimony upon the promise that it may not be

used, is one example of the "use exclusion" doctrine which had its origins in Murphy v. Waterfront Commissioner, 378 U.S. 52, 84 S.Ct. 1594 (1964). There a state investigative agency granted a witness immunity from state prosecution. The witness claimed that he still had a right to invoke the Fifth Amendment because his answers could subject him to prosecution under federal law. In upholding the statute, the Court prohibited the subsequent use by federal authorities of the testimony thus compelled.

In *Murphy* a state authority was, in effect, permitted to give use-immunity in federal prosecutions. In *Gardner* police administrators were empowered to give police officers use-immunity by requiring the officers to cooperate with internal investigations. Carried to absurdity, the use-exclusion doctrine would permit any judge to order a witness to testify over Fifth Amendment objections on the theory that testimony given under such an order, and evidence derived from such testimony, could not be used against him in any future prosecution. The fallacy is that the procedure would permit a grant of immunity without specific statutory authorization and, in many instances, without any prosecutorial participation in the decision to grant immunity. See Ellis v. United States, 416 F.2d 791 (D.C.Cir. 1969), where the reviewing court held that a district judge who compelled testimony using such reasoning created "a circular self-fulfilling prophecy." The Court said that such compulsion "can only be viewed as a grant of immunity." It further declared that, absent a statute authorizing immunity and absent a prosecutorial request, the district court's order compelling testimony was "outside the scope of judicial authority."

3. Historically grants of immunity have been given only where (1) a statute specifically authorizing immunity exists, and (2) the prosecutor of the jurisdiction in question has exercised his discretion to seek judicial approval of a grant of immunity.

Use-exclusion is often proposed as a method of upholding statutory schemes which arguably compel a person to give testimony against himself. In California v. Byers, 402 U.S. 424, 91 S.Ct. 1535 (1971), a "stop and report" law applicable to motorists involved in auto accidents was challenged. One possible solution was to uphold enforcement of the statute but to prohibit use in any criminal case of evidence derived from compliance by a motorist. The Supreme Court rejected this solution, finding no Fifth Amendment violation. Nothing in the statute suggested that the California legislature had intended to make enforcement of penal provisions of its traffic code more difficult by granting use immunity to motorists who complied with the "stop and report" provision. See also Marchetti v. United States, 390 U.S. 39, 88 S.Ct. 697 (1968), where, in striking down certain gambling registration requirements, the Court refused to "save" the federal statute by creating a use immunity doctrine which would have made state gambling prosecutions more difficult. The statute was intended to do just the opposite. Thus in both *Byers*, where the statute was upheld, and in *Marchetti*, where the statute was struck down, the Court avoided the tempting middle ground of use-immunity and made the hard decision whether the statute violated the Fifth Amendment privilege. To have done otherwise would have been to create a situation where use immunity might be acquired absent specific statutory authority and absent any prosecutorial participation in the decision to grant immunity.

4. In Lefkowitz v. Turley, 414 U.S. 70, 94 S.Ct. 316 (1973), the Supreme Court voided a statute which prohibited any person who refused to waive immunity in a grand jury investigation from obtaining public con-

tracts for a period of five years. A majority of the court suggested that the statute would have been proper if it provided use immunity for the contractor who raised a Fifth Amendment claim before the grand jury.

How is a statute like the one in *Turley* affected by the proposition that a corporation has no protection against self-incrimination under the Fifth and Fourteenth Amendments?

In Lefkowitz v. Cunningham, 431 U.S. 801, 97 S.Ct. 2132 (1977), the Supreme Court invalidated a New York statute which provided for forfeiture of political party office by officeholders who invoked the fifth amendment privilege during a grand jury investigation related to their conduct in office. Again the Court suggested that such forfeiture would be permissible if the statutory scheme provided use-immunity for the party officeholder who is compelled to testify.

5. If an individual receives a formal grant of immunity, or if he acquires use immunity by yielding to governmental requirements that he cooperate in an investigation, his protection extends only to criminal prosecution. His immunized testimony can be used against him in a civil matter. See In re Schwarz, 51 Ill.2d 334, 282 N.E.2d 689 (1972), where a lawyer testified against a defendant in a criminal trial and then was disbarred on the basis of the testimony which he had given under a grant of immunity. Sometimes prosecutors claim that immunity from prosecution is not enough to persuade certain witnesses to cooperate in an investigation. Should a judge be permitted to enter an order protecting a witness from loss of a liquor license or disbarment in return for testimony? Would this infringe upon the authority of other agencies? See In re Daley, 549 F.2d 469 (7th Cir. 1977), where the reviewing court held that federal immunity statutes do not authorize entry of an order protecting an immunized attorney from use of his immunized testimony against him in a disbarment proceeding.

F. EVIDENCE BEFORE THE GRAND JURY

1. WARNINGS

UNITED STATES v. MANDUJANO

Supreme Court of the United States, 1976.
425 U.S. 564, 96 S.Ct. 1768.

MR. CHIEF JUSTICE BURGER announced the judgment of the Court in an opinion in which MR. JUSTICE WHITE, MR. JUSTICE POWELL, and MR. JUSTICE REHNQUIST join.

This case presents the question whether the warnings called for by Miranda v. Arizona, 384 U.S. 436 (1966), must be given to a grand jury witness who is called to testify about criminal activities in which he may have been personally involved; and whether, absent such warnings, false statements made to the grand jury must be suppressed in a prosecution for perjury based on those statements.

* * *

Under settled principles, the Fifth Amendment does not confer an absolute right to decline to respond in a grand jury inquiry; the privilege does not negate the duty to testify but simply conditions that duty. The privilege cannot, for example, be asserted by a witness to protect others from possible criminal prosecution. Nor can it be invoked simply to protect the witness' interest in privacy. . . .

The very availability of the Fifth Amendment privilege to grand jury witnesses, recognized by this Court in Counselman v. Hitchcock, 142 U.S. 547 (1892), suggests that occasions will often arise when potentially incriminating questions will be asked in the ordinary course of the jury's investigation. Probing questions to all types of witnesses is the stuff that grand jury investigations are made of; the grand jury's mission is, after all, to determine whether to make a presentment or return an indictment. "The basic purpose of the English grand jury was to provide a fair method for instituting criminal proceedings against persons believed to have committed crimes." Costello v. United States, supra, at 362.

It is in keeping with the grand jury's historic function as a shield against arbitrary accusations to call before it persons suspected of criminal activity, so that the investigation can be complete. This is true whether the grand jury embarks upon an inquiry focused upon individuals suspected of wrongdoing, or is directed at persons suspected of no misconduct but who may be able to provide links in a chain of evidence relating to criminal conduct of others, or is centered upon broader problems of concern to society. It is entirely appropriate—indeed imperative—to summon individuals who may be able to illuminate the shadowy precincts of corruption and crime. Since the subject matter of the inquiry is crime, and often organized, systematic crime—as is true with drug traffic—it is unrealistic to assume that all of the witnesses capable of providing useful information will be pristine pillars of the community untainted by criminality.

*   *   *

Accordingly, the witness, though possibly engaged in some criminal enterprise, can be required to answer before a grand jury, so long as there is no compulsion to answer questions that are self-incriminating; the witness can, of course, stand on the privilege, assured that its protection "is as broad as the mischief against which it seeks to guard." Counselman v. Hitchcock, 142 U.S., at 562. The witness must invoke the privilege, however, as the "Constitution does not forbid the asking of criminative questions." United States v. Monia, 317 U.S., at 433 (Frankfurter, J., dissenting):

> "The [Fifth] Amendment speaks of compulsion. It does not preclude a witness from testifying voluntarily in matters which may incriminate him. If, therefore, he desires the protection of the privilege, he must claim it or he will not be considered to have been 'compelled' within the meaning of the Amendment."

Absent a claim of the privilege, the duty to give testimony remains absolute.

The stage is therefore set when the question is asked. If the witness interposes his privilege, the grand jury has two choices. If the desired testimony is of marginal value, the grand jury can pursue other avenues of inquiry; if the testimony is thought sufficiently important, the grand jury can seek a judicial determination as to the bona fides of the witness' Fifth Amendment claim, in which case the witness must satisfy the presiding judge that the claim of privilege is not a subterfuge. If in fact " 'there is reasonable ground to apprehend danger to the witness from his being compelled to answer,' " the prosecutor must then determine whether the answer is of such overriding importance as to justify a grant of immunity to the witness.

If immunity is sought by the prosecutor and granted by the presiding judge, the witness can then be compelled to answer, on pain of contempt, even though the testimony would implicate the witness in criminal activity. The reason for this is not hard to divine; Mr. Justice Frankfurter indicated as much in observing that immunity is the *quid pro quo* for securing an answer from the witness: "Immunity displaces the danger." Ullmann v. United States, 350 U.S. 422, 439 (1956) . . . . .

* * *

In this constitutional process of securing a witness' testimony, perjury simply has no place whatever. Perjured testimony is an obvious and flagrant affront to the basic concepts of judicial proceedings. Effective restraints against this type of egregious offense are therefore imperative. The power of subpoena, broad as it is, and the power of contempt for refusing to answer, drastic as that is—and even the solemnity of the oath—cannot insure truthful answers. Hence, Congress has made the giving of false answers a criminal act punishable by severe penalties; in no other way can criminal conduct be flushed into the open where the law can deal with it.

Similarly, our cases have consistently—indeed without exception —allowed sanctions for false statements or perjury; they have done so even in instances where the perjurer complained that the Government exceeded its constitutional powers in making the inquiry.

* * *

In this case, the Court of Appeals required the suppression of perjured testimony given by respondent, as a witness under oath, lawfully summoned before an investigative grand jury and questioned about matters directly related to the grand jury's inquiry. The court reached this result because the prosecutor failed to give *Miranda* warnings at the outset of Mandujano's interrogation. Those warnings were required, in the Court of Appeals' view, because Mandujano was a "virtual" or "putative" defendant—that is, the prosecutor had specific information concerning Mandujano's participation in an attempted sale of heroin and the focus of the grand jury interrogation, as evidenced by the prosecutor's questions, centered on Mandujano's involvement in narcotics traffic. The fundamental error of the prosecutor, in the court's view, was to treat respondent in such a way as to " 'smack' of entrapment"; as a consequence, the court concluded that "elemental fairness" required the perjured testimony to be suppressed. . . .

The court's analysis, premised upon the prosecutor's failure to give *Miranda* warnings, erroneously applied the standards fashioned by this Court in *Miranda*. Those warnings were aimed at the evils seen by the Court as endemic to police interrogation of a person in custody. *Miranda* addressed extrajudicial confessions or admissions procured in a hostile, unfamiliar environment which lacked procedural safeguards. The decision expressly rested on the privilege against compulsory self-incrimination; the prescribed warnings sought to negate the "compulsion" thought to be inherent in police station interrogation. But the *Miranda* Court simply did not perceive judicial inquiries and custodial interrogation as equivalents: "[T]he compulsion to speak in the isolated setting of the police station may well be greater than in courts or other official investigations, where there are often impartial observers to guard against intimidation or trickery."

The Court thus recognized that many official investigations, such as grand jury questioning, take place in a setting wholly different from custodial police interrogation. Indeed, the Court's opinion in *Miranda* reveals a focus on what was seen by the Court as police "coercion" derived from "factual studies [relating to] police violence and the 'third degree' . . . physical brutality—beating, hanging, whipping—and to sustained and protracted questioning incommunicado in order to extort confessions. . . ." Id., at 445–446. To extend these concepts to questioning before a grand jury inquiring into criminal activity under the guidance of a judge is an extravagant expansion never remotely contemplated by this Court in *Miranda*; the dynamics of constitutional interpretation do not compel constant extension of every doctrine announced by the Court.

* * *

The warnings volunteered by the prosecutor to respondent in this case were more than sufficient to inform him of his rights—and his responsibilities—and particularly of the consequences of perjury. To extend the concepts of *Miranda*, as contemplated by the Court of Appeals, would require that the witness be told that there was an absolute right to silence, and obviously any such warning would be incorrect, for there is no such right before a grand jury. Under *Miranda*, a person in police custody has, of course, an absolute right to decline to answer any question, incriminating or innocuous, whereas a grand jury witness, on the contrary, has an absolute duty to answer all questions, subject only to a valid Fifth Amendment claim. And even when the grand jury witness asserts the privilege, questioning need not cease, except as to the particular subject to which the privilege has been addressed. Other lines of inquiry may properly be pursued.

Respondent was also informed that if he desired he could have the assistance of counsel, but that counsel could not be inside the grand jury room. That statement was plainly a correct recital of the law. No criminal proceedings had been instituted against respondent, hence the Sixth Amendment right to counsel had not come into play. A witness "before a grand jury cannot insist, as a matter of constitutional right, on being represented by his counsel. . . ." Under settled principles the witness may not insist upon the presence of his attorney in the grand jury room.

Respondent, by way of further explanation, was also warned that he could be prosecuted for perjury if he testified falsely. Since respondent was already under oath to testify truthfully, this explanation was redundant; it served simply to emphasize the obligation already imposed by the oath.

* * *

In any event, a witness sworn to tell the truth before a duly constituted grand jury will not be heard to call for suppression of false statements made to that jury, any more than would be the case with false testimony before a petit jury or other duly constituted tribunal. In another context, this Court has refused to permit a witness to protect perjured testimony by proving a *Miranda* violation. In Harris v. New York, 401 U.S. 222 (1971), the Court held that notwithstanding a *Miranda* violation:

> "[The Fifth Amendment] privilege cannot be construed to include the right to commit perjury." Id., at 225.

More recently, the Court reaffirmed this salutary principle:

> "[T]he shield provided by *Miranda* is not to be perverted to a license to testify inconsistently, or even perjuriously, free from the risk of confrontation with prior inconsistent utterances." Oregon v. Hass, 420 U.S. 714, 722 (1975).

* * *

The judgment of the Court of Appeals is therefore reversed, and the cause is remanded for further proceedings consistent with this opinion.

Reversed and remanded.

MR. JUSTICE STEVENS took no part in the consideration or decision of this case.

MR. JUSTICE BRENNAN, with whom MR. JUSTICE MARSHALL joins, concurring in the judgment. [Opinion omitted.]

MR. JUSTICE STEWART, with whom MR. JUSTICE BLACKMUN joins, concurring in the judgment. [Opinion omitted.]

NOTES

1. Only four justices joined in the Court's opinion in *Mandujano*. The other four participating justices concurred on the narrow ground that the failure of the prosecutor to secure an express waiver of Fifth Amendment rights was not a defense to a charge of perjury. Justices Marshall and Brennan specifically indicated that if the prosecution has probable cause

to believe that a suspect has committed a crime, it cannot subpoena him before a grand jury, elicit testimony absent a knowing and intelligent waiver (such as would follow from the giving of warnings), and then use such testimony against him later at a trial on the substantive charges on which the grand jury indicted him. *Mandujano* asserts that an appearance before the grand jury is not a custodial situation under *Miranda*. See Chapter 2, Section B. Does the fact that the witness appears under the compulsion of a subpoena contain a custodial element? What about the witness who refuses to comply with a subpoena and is arrested under a material witness warrant and brought to the grand jury?

2. Is the false testimony of a witness subject to suppression when that witness is brought before a grand jury while under investigation for criminal conduct, given no effective warning of the right to silence, and later indicted for perjury? In United States v. Wong (1977), the Court held that the same general considerations applicable to a prospective witness, as identified in *Mandujano,* are applicable to a potential defendant.

3. When the prosecutor has cause to believe that a person has committed a crime, must he warn that person of his potential indictment before the grand jury in order to use the witness' testimony against him in a later trial on a substantive offense? In United States v. Washington, 431 U.S. 181, 97 S.Ct. 1814 (1977), the plurality of the Court held:

> "Because target witness status neither enlarges nor diminishes the constitutional protection against compelled self-incrimination, potential defendant warnings add nothing of value to protection of Fifth Amendment rights."

Consistent with his position in *Mandujano,* Justice Brennan, joined by Justice Marshall, dissented:

> "I would hold that a failure to warn the witness that he is a potential defendant is fatal to an indictment of him when it is made unmistakably to appear, as here, that the grand jury inquiry became an investigation directed against the witness and was pursued with the purpose of compelling him to give self-incriminating testimony upon which to indict him. I would further hold that without such prior warning and the witness' subsequent voluntary waiver of his privilege, there is such gross encroachment upon the witness' privilege as to render worthless the values protected by it unless the self-incriminating testimony is unavailable to the Government for use at any trial brought pursuant to even a valid indictment."

4. Does the *Mandujano-Wong-Washington* trilogy allow the police and the prosecutor to circumvent *Miranda* by bringing a prospective defendant before the grand jury? When the grand jury inquiry is in fact a proceeding against a witness, are there situations in which the encroachment upon the witness' fifth amendment privilege—in the absence of warnings—justify suppression of his testimony? See Newman, The Suspect and the Grand Jury: A Need for Constitutional Protection, 11 U.Rich.L.Rev. 1 (1976); Comment, The Grand Jury Witness' Privilege Against Self-Incrimination, 62 Nw.U.L.Rev. 207, 223 (1967).

2. HEARSAY

UNITED STATES v. ESTEPA

United States Court of Appeals, Second Circuit, 1972.
471 F.2d 1132.

FRIENDLY, CHIEF JUDGE.

Charles Estepa and Francis Vasquez appeal from their conviction, after a bench trial before Judge Brieant in the District Court for the Southern District of New York, on four counts of an indictment charging them, along with Jaime Vasquez, Rafael Perez and Jose Luis Dones, with distributing heroin, possessing it with an intent to distribute, and conspiring to do so, in violation of 21 U.S.C. §§ 812, 841 and 846. Although Estepa challenges the sufficiency of the evidence and Vasquez raises some other points, it is unnecessary to consider these since we hold dismissal of the indictment to be required because of the nature of the presentation to the grand jury.

For purposes of this opinion we can adopt the statement of facts in the Government's brief on Vasquez' appeal:

> In the late afternoon of October 14, 1971, Patrolman Jose Guzman of the New York Joint Task Force, acting in an undercover capacity, met with defendant Jaime Vasquez at approximately 5:30 p. m., at 878 Southern Boulevard, Bronx, New York, where they discussed the possibility of Patrolman Guzman purchasing one-eighth of a kilogram of heroin. When Vasquez suggested they see "Joe and Frank," referring to his brother, defendant Francis Vasquez, they proceeded to a house on Longfellow Avenue in the Bronx.

> At that location, Patrolman Guzman met Francis Vasquez who told him he could sell him an eighth of heroin for $3100. Shortly thereafter, defendant Dones joined the conversation and was told by the Vasquez brothers that Patrolman Guzman was looking for some cocaine. Dones responded that for $700[0] he could supply him with one-half a kilogram of cocaine. Patrolman Guzman was then told to return later that evening.

> That evening, Guzman returned to 878 Southern Boulevard where he met Jaime Vasquez and showed him a roll of money which he then placed in the trunk of his automobile. A short time later, Frank Vasquez and Dones arrived in a Volkswagen. Jaime Vasquez had a short conversation with his brother and Dones after which he instructed Guzman to follow the Volkswagen. The two cars proceeded to Longwood Avenue where Dones exited his automobile, came over to Guzman's car and told the undercover patrolman that he would return in ten minutes with the "stuff". While Jaime Vasquez remained with Guzman, Dones returned to his auto-

mobile and was driven by Frank Vasquez to 149th Street where he and Vasquez entered a social club. A short time later, Dones and Vasquez left the club accompanied by defendant Charles Estepa, but did not enter the Volkswagen which Vasquez had left double-parked in front of the club, proceeding instead on foot to 150th Street.

Approximately twenty-five minutes later, a blue Ford containing Dones, Frank Vasquez, Estepa (in the front passenger's seat) and driven by an unknown male, returned to Longwood Avenue and parked opposite Patrolman Guzman's automobile. Dones exited the Ford and told Guzman and Jaime Vasquez that he would return in thirty minutes. Approximately one hour later, the same Ford returned with the same passengers, passed Guzman's parked car, hesitating as it did so, and parked around the corner. A few minutes later, Dones arrived alone on foot, entered Guzman's car and handed Guzman a tin foil package inside of which was a plastic bag containing 128.73 grams of heroin hydrochloride. Guzman went to the trunk of his car where he had placed the money and dropped his keys as a signal to the surveillance agents. Dones and Jaime Vasquez, who had remained with Guzman during the evening, were then placed under arrest.

A few blocks away, other agents, who had kept the Ford containing Estepa and the unidentified driver under surveillance, received word of the arrest by radio. As the surveillance agents pulled alongside the Ford and identified themselves by showing their badges, the Ford made a quick U-turn and sped off. A high speed chase ensued. At the intersection of Garrison and Whorten Avenues, two packages were thrown out the front window of the Ford on the passenger side where Estepa was sitting. These packages were later retrieved and found to contain a total of 17.27 grams of heroin hydrochloride. The agents then pulled alongside the Ford and again ordered the car to stop after identifying themselves. The Ford, however, sped up, swerved to avoid a truck and at 156th Street made a right turn, a maneuver the agents were unable to negotiate because of the speed of their automobile. The Ford stopped on 156th Street, and both occupants, Estepa and the driver, alighted. The driver escaped on foot and Estepa was placed under arrest. A search of the automobile revealed a packet containing 10.94 grams of heroin hydrochloride on the floor of the passenger side of the front seat where Estepa had been sitting.

Although the Ford in question was officially registered to one Joseph M. Medina, Estepa referred to the car after his arrest as "my car", and was in possession of the automobile's registration.

It is plain from this recitation that, except for the individuals named in the indictment, the person, and the only person, who was in a position to inform the grand jury of just what occurred up to the point of the arrest of Dones and Jamie Vasquez was Patrolman Guzman. Examination of the trial records shows that the persons (other than the defendants) in the best position to inform the grand jury of what occurred thereafter were Narcotics Agent Finnerty and New York City Policeman Walpole, and, with respect to Estepa's post-arrest statement, New York City Policeman Miller. None of these men was called. The sole witness before the grand jury was New York City Policeman Twohill, whose observations of the appellants were both limited and remote. When we inquired at argument why Patrolman Guzman was not called to testify before the grand jury, we were told he was in the field doing other work that day; when we asked what reason prevented postponement of the presentation for a day or two, we were told there was none.

Despite Policeman Twohill's extremely limited personal knowledge, he spoke to the grand jury at length and in detail. He began with an incident on September 13, 1971, a month before the substantive crime with which the two appellants were charged. He testified that Perez passed a package, later analyzed by the laboratory of the Bureau of Narcotics and Dangerous Drugs, to Jaime Vasquez who then passed it on to Patrolman Guzman, who paid $150. On this occasion the Assistant United States Attorney interjected "you didn't observe the actual pass, but you did observe the meeting, is that correct?", to which Twohill responded "I did." Twohill then testified that, on September 27, Jaime Vasquez passed a package, later determined to contain heroin, to Patrolman Guzman who paid $120. This time the Assistant did nothing to alert the grand jury to any limitations on Twohill's knowledge. Moving on to the transaction on October 14, 1971, which constituted Counts IV, V and VI against these defendants (and also the principal—in Estepa's case the sole—basis for the conspiracy count), Twohill testified that Guzman requested Jaime Vasquez to furnish a one-eighth kilo of heroin and some cocaine and that Jaime Vasquez told Guzman to drive to Dones' home on Longfellow Avenue. Even if we assume that Twohill had witnessed this meeting from afar, there was nothing in his testimony or in the questions of the Assistant to inform the grand jury that he had not and could not have heard any such request or answer. He recounted to the grand jury what took place at Dones' house and a conversation between Frank Vasquez and Guzman in connection with the sale of a one-eighth kilo of heroin for $3100, a conversation between Dones and Guzman for the sale of a half kilo of cocaine for $7,000, and an instruction by Frank Vasquez to Guzman to meet near Jaime Vasquez' home. Here again, even if we assume, perhaps overgenerously, so far as the record goes, that Twohill saw something, he clearly heard nothing, but the grand jurors were not told this. There followed testimony about Guzman's having driven Jaime Vasquez back to his home, returning there, and showing him a roll of money, which Twohill might well have observed. He next described the meeting of the Vasquez brothers, Dones and Guzman. Here he failed to follow the script and said that Guzman, rather than Jaime Vasquez, directed that they follow Dones' car. The error was natural since, as we are aware but the grand jury was not, he had no personal knowledge whatever. Twohill then testified that Vasquez and Guzman, followed by Dones and his passengers, proceeded to a location on Longwood Avenue in the Bronx where Vasquez spoke with the individuals in Dones' car. Next came testimony of the arrival at and departure from the social club, which Twohill had in fact observed. He then proceeded to testify to the arrival of Dones, Frank Vasquez and Estepa in the blue Ford and to Guzman's being told to wait for half an hour for the defendants' return with the narcotics; nothing informed the grand jury that Twohill had not heard anything of the sort. Finally, and most egregiously, after relating the return of the blue Ford, the signal and the arrest, he described the chase, the throwing of the packets out of the Ford, the arrest of Estepa, and the discovery of a package under the front seat of the Ford, which he had not observed at all since, as he testified at trial, he had remained at the scene of the arrest.

We have previously condemned the casual attitude with respect to the presentation of evidence to a grand jury manifested by the decision of the Assistant United States Attorney to rely on testimony of the law enforcement officer who knew least, rather than subject the other officers, or himself, to some minor inconvenience, . . . When the framers of the Bill of Rights directed in the Fifth Amendment that "No person shall be held to answer for a capital, or otherwise infamous crime, unless on a presentment or indictment of a Grand Jury," they were not engaging in a mere verbal exercise. The importance of avoiding undue reliance upon hearsay before a grand jury is heightened by this circuit's view that an indictment constitutes a finding of probable cause and avoids the need for a preliminary hearing. We have not gone so far as to apply to grand juries the proposal in the American Law Institute's Model Code of Pre-Arraignment Procedure §§ 330.4(4) and 340.5 (Tent. Draft No. 5, 1972), that hearsay may be received at a preliminary hearing or by a grand jury only "if the court determines that it would impose an unreasonable burden on one of the parties or on a witness to require that the primary source of the evidence be produced at the hearing, and if the witness furnishes information bearing on the informant's reliability and, as far as possible, the means by which the information was obtained," see also ABA Standards Relating to the Prosecution Function and the Defense Function § 3.6 (Approved Draft 1971), although . . . we do not believe Costello v. United States, 350 U.S. 359 (1956), would prevent this exercise of our supervisory powers should we deem it wise. But we have insisted that, even though "[t]here is no affirmative duty to tell the grand jury *in haec verba* that it is listening to hearsay," United States v. Malofsky, 388 F.2d 288 (2 Cir.), cert. denied 390 U.S. 1017 (1968), the grand jury must not be "misled into thinking it is getting eye-witness testimony from the agent whereas it is actually being given an account

whose hearsay nature is concealed . . . ." United States v. Lei-
bowitz, 420 F.2d 39, 42 (2 Cir. 1969). That was what happened here.

The Government argues that the prosecutor discharged his obligation to enlighten the grand jury by bringing out that Twohill did
not see "the actual pass" from Perez to Jaime Vasquez to Guzman on
September 13, 1971, and by two other statements noted in the margin. But grand jurors cannot be supposed to possess sufficient as-
tuteness to infer that, because Twohill on one occasion made clear the
limited degree of his knowledge of a transaction occurring more than
a month before the events of October 14, this carried through to all;
indeed, the contrary inference would be quite as reasonable. The
Government contends more broadly that, since Twohill never stated
he was acting in an undercover capacity, the grand jurors should
have known he was only a surveilling agent who could not have seen
or heard the details of the occurrences and conversations to which he
testified with such specificity. Grand jurors do not have this degree
of familiarity with law enforcement techniques, and it would have
been so easy for the Assistant United States Attorney to tell them
what they are now claimed to have known. Moreover, this explanation does not at all explain Twohill's testimony about the chase, the
throwing of the packets, and Estepa's arrest. This was something a
surveilling agent could well have observed, yet the fact, presumably
known to the Assistant, was that Twohill had not witnessed it at all.

The many opinions in which we have affirmed convictions despite the Government's needless reliance on hearsay before the grand
jury show how loathe we have been to open up a new road for attacking convictions on grounds unrelated to the merits. We have been
willing to allow ample, many doubtless think too ample, latitude in
the needless use of hearsay, subject to only two provisos—that the
prosecutor does not deceive grand jurors as to "the shoddy merchandise they are getting so they can seek something better if they wish,"
or that the case does not involve "a high probability that with eyewitness rather than hearsay testimony the grand jury would not have indicted." We had hoped that, with the clear warnings we have given
to prosecutors, going back to . . . 1966, and the assurances giv-
en by United States Attorneys, a reversal for improper use of
hearsay before the grand jury would not be required. Here the Assistant United States Attorney, whether wittingly or unwittingly—
we prefer to think the latter, clearly violated the first of these provisos. We cannot, with proper respect for the discharge of our duties,
content ourselves with yet another admonition; a reversal with instructions to dismiss the indictment may help to translate the assurances of the United States Attorneys into consistent performance by
their assistants. As Judge Medina [once said], "This would not let
appellants go scot free, as there would be time to reindict them and
have their guilt or innocence passed upon again on a record not tainted with irregularity."

The judgments of conviction are reversed, with instructions to
dismiss the indictment.

NOTES

1. A prosecutor who provides the grand jury with nothing but hearsay evidence may have a number of reasons for so doing. He may desire to protect his witness from potential impeachment resulting from disclosure of a transcript of the witnesses' grand jury testimony when the case goes to trial. He may not have had sufficient time to develop—or find evidence to corroborate—the details of the witnesses' testimony at the grand jury stage. He may want to save the taxpayers the expense of bringing in witnesses from distant locations. He may simply want to refrain from imposing a burden on the witness who would otherwise have to miss work, come "downtown", and appear before the grand jury. Are any of these reasons sufficient to justify the exclusive use of hearsay?

2. The *Estepa* doctrine has rarely been followed. In Burkholder v. State, 491 P.2d 754 (Alaska 1971), an indictment charging the sale of depressant, stimulant, or hallucinogenic drugs was returned solely on the basis of the testimony of a police officer who related to the grand jury the sale of drugs by the defendant to a police informant. The name of the informant, the nature and extent of his relationship with the police and the accused, and the circumstances relating to the sale of the contraband were not revealed to the grand jury. The reviewing court concluded "In this case the hearsay presented was so devoid of persuasive force as to fail to furnish a logical basis to justify an indictment. The indictment must be dismissed." In People v. Cunningham, 88 Misc.2d 1065, 390 N.Y.S.2d 547 (1976), the court concluded that an indictment could not be based upon evidence consisting of tapes of intercepted conversations in which witnesses and others had engaged in cynical gossip and suspicious speculations. Other decisions from the same jurisdictions support the *Estepa* Rule. See State v. Gieffels, 554 P.2d 460 (Alaska 1976); People v. Bishop, 64 Misc.2d 147, 314 N.Y.S.2d 419 (1970).

3. Some courts have rejected *Estepa* outright. In United States v. Barone, 584 F.2d 118, 125 (6th Cir. 1978), the court rejected *Estepa*, saying "we are not inclined to adopt [*Estepa*]. The strong historical policy considerations [surrounding grand jury practices] persuade us that this is the correct result. We are especially reluctant to see the trial of criminal cases further attenuated by preliminary trials concerning the adequacy of the grand jury proceeding . . ."

In United States v. Chanen, 549 F.2d 1306 (9th Cir. 1977), the court declined to follow *Estepa* when transcripts of witness' testimony were presented to the grand jury in the place of actual appearances.

4. Most courts take the position that *Estepa* does not apply unless there is a deliberate attempt by the prosecution to mislead the grand jury. Since that type of situation is rare, *Estepa* has been found readily distinguishable. See, e. g., United States v. Fife, 573 F.2d 369 (6th Cir. 1978); United States v. Smith, 552 F.2d 257 (8th Cir. 1977); United States v. Jett, 491 F.2d 1078 (1st Cir. 1974); United States v. Pray, 452 F.Supp. 788 (M.D.Pa.1978).

3. ILLEGALLY SEIZED EVIDENCE

UNITED STATES v. CALANDRA

Supreme Court of the United States, 1974.
414 U.S. 338, 94 S.Ct. 613.

[The opinion in this case, which should be reviewed here, appears in Chapter 6, Section D, supra.]

NOTES

1. The rationale for the reluctance of the courts to inquire into the quality of the evidence presented to grand juries is well-stated in West v. United States, 359 F.2d 50 (8th Cir. 1966), a case involving grand jury use of illegally seized evidence:

> If we adopted appellant's position we would be faced with two alternatives. We could leave the essential nature of the grand jury proceeding unchanged. The government would then be forced to make an ex parte determination of the legality of the offered evidence without the guidance of opposition or ruling from judicial authority. The penalty for a mistake in judgment would be the striking down of the entire grand jury proceeding. We could, on the other hand, change the nature of the grand jury investigation, making it into an adversary system. The exclusionary rule could then be enforced by a case-by-case judicial determination. Such a change, however, would add an additional burden to judicial time, completely alter our judicial system, and seriously cripple the supposedly investigative purpose of the grand jury. We do not believe such a move is warranted or wise and consequently hold that the exclusionary rule does not apply to grand jury proceedings.

2. Although the Supreme Court in *Calandra* repeated its statements from prior decisions that the Constitution does not require a showing of good cause for the issuance of a grand jury subpoena, one federal court has utilized its "supervisory" powers to impose such a requirement. See In re Grand Jury Proceedings, 486 F.2d 85 (3d Cir. 1974), and In re Grand Jury Proceedings, 507 F.2d 963 (3d Cir. 1975).

3. The legislature, by statute, can avoid the effect of *Calandra* and prohibit the use of illegally seized evidence before the grand jury. The federal wire tapping statute contains a provision which the Supreme Court has construed to prohibit punishment for contempt of a witness who defends his refusal to respond to questions by asserting that the questions are the product of a violation of the rights of the witness to be free from unlawful wiretaps.

In Gelbard v. United States, 408 U.S. 41, 92 S.Ct. 2357 (1972), the Court considered the right of a grand jury witness to invoke this prohibition:

> "The purposes of [the statute] as a whole would be subverted were the plain command of [this section] ignored when the victim of an illegal interception is called as a witness before a grand jury and asked questions based upon that interception. . . . Contrary to the Government's assertion that the invasion of privacy is

over and done with, to compel the testimony of these witnesses compounds the statutorily proscribed invasion of their privacy by adding to the injury of the interception the insult of compelled disclosure. . . . Hence, if the prohibition of [the section] is not available as a defense to the contempt charge, disclosure through compelled testimony makes the witness the victim, once again, of a federal crime. Finally, recognition of [the section] as a defense "relieves judges of the anomalous duty of finding a person in civil contempt for failing to cooperate with the prosecutor in a course of conduct which, if pursued unchecked, could subject the prosecutor himself to heavy civil and criminal penalties."

* * *

In their dissent in *Gelbard*, Chief Justice Burger and Justices Rehnquist, Blackmun, and Powell, had this to say:

". . . what was presented to the trial court in this proceeding was not a neatly stipulated question of law, but a demand by the petitioners that they be permitted to roam at will among the prosecutor's records in order to see whether they might be able to turn up any evidence indicating that the Government's overhearing of their conversations had been unauthorized by statute. In order to determine whether this particular type of remedy is open to these petitioners at this particular stage of potential criminal proceedings it is not enough to recite, as the Court does, that [the statute] prohibits the use of illegally overheard wire communications before grand juries as well as before other governmental bodies. This proposition is not disputed. The far more difficult inquiry posed by these facts is whether the granting to these petitioners at this particular stage of these proceedings of sweeping discovery as a prelude to a full hearing on the issue of alleged unlawful surveillance can fairly be inferred from the enactment. . . .

* * *

"It seems to me to be clear beyond cavil from [our prior decisions] that prior to the enactment of the Omnibus Crime and Safe Streets Act of 1968, a hearing such as that which the Court awards these petitioners was not only unauthorized by law, but completely contrary to the ingrained principles which have long governed the functioning of the grand jury."

Gelbard does not hold that a target defendant can enjoin the government from presenting evidence to the grand jury through the testimony of government agents or other witnesses even though such testimony was derived from a violation of the target's right to be free of unlawful wiretaps. Nor does it hold that an indictment based upon evidence derived from a violation of the accused's rights must be dismissed. These issues are analytically distinct. See Chapter 6, Section D, note 1, supra, Congress could have prohibited grand jury use of the fruits of illegal wiretaps. Whether it did so, however, would turn upon an interpretation of statutory provisions other than those upon which the *Gelbard* decision vacated the contempt finding.

4. NON–TESTIMONIAL EVIDENCE

UNITED STATES v. DIONISIO

Supreme Court of the United States, 1973.
410 U.S. 1, 93 S.Ct. 764.

Mr. Justice Stewart delivered the opinion of the Court.

A special grand jury was convened in the Northern District of Illinois in February 1971, to investigate possible violations of federal criminal statutes relating to gambling. In the course of its investigation the grand jury received in evidence certain voice recordings that had been obtained pursuant to court orders.[1]

The grand jury subpoenaed approximately 20 persons, including the respondent Dionisio, seeking to obtain from them voice exemplars for comparison with the recorded conversations that had been received in evidence. Each witness was advised that he was a potential defendant in a criminal prosecution. Each was asked to examine a transcript of an intercepted conversation, and to go to a nearby office of the United States Attorney to read the transcript into a recording device. The witnesses were advised that they would be allowed to have their attorneys present when they read the transcripts. Dionisio and other witnesses refused to furnish the voice exemplars, asserting that these disclosures would violate their rights under the Fourth and Fifth Amendments.

The Government then filed separate petitions in the United States District Court to compel Dionisio and the other witnesses to furnish the voice exemplars to the grand jury. The petitions stated that the exemplars were "essential and necessary" to the grand jury investigation, and that they would "be used solely as a standard of comparison in order to determine whether or not the witness is the person whose voice was intercepted. . . ."

Following a hearing, the district judge rejected the witnesses' constitutional arguments and ordered them to comply with the grand jury's request.

* * *

When Dionisio persisted in his refusal to respond to the grand jury's directive, the District Court adjudged him in civil contempt

---

1. The court orders were issued pursuant to 18 U.S.C. § 2518, a statute authorizing the interception of wire communications upon a judicial determination that "(a) there is probable cause for belief that an individual is committing, has committed, or is about to commit a particular offense enumerated in section 2516 of this chapter [including the transmission of wagering information]; (b) there is probable cause for belief that particular communications concerning that offense will be obtained through such interception; (c) normal investigative procedures have been tried and have failed or reasonably appear to be unlikely to succeed if tried or to be too dangerous; (d) there is probable cause for belief that the facilities from which, or the place where, the wire or oral communications are to be intercepted are being used, or are about to be used, in connection with the commission of such offense, or are leased to, listed in the name of, or commonly used by such person."

and ordered him committed to custody until he obeyed the court order, or until the expiration of 18 months.[2]

The Court of Appeals for the Seventh Circuit reversed. 442 F. 2d 276. It agreed with the District Court in rejecting the Fifth Amendment claims, but concluded that to compel the voice recordings would violate the Fourth Amendment. In the Court's view, the grand jury was "seeking to obtain the voice exemplars of the witnesses by the use of its subpoena powers because probable cause did not exist for their arrest or for some other, less unusual method of compelling the production of the exemplars." The Court found that the Fourth Amendment applied to grand jury process, and that "under the fourth amendment law enforcement officials may not compel the production of physical evidence absent a showing of the reasonableness of the seizure. Davis v. Mississippi, 394 U.S. 721, 89 S.Ct. 1394 . . . . ."

In *Davis* this Court held that it was error to admit the petitioner's fingerprints into evidence at his trial for rape, because they had been obtained during a police detention following a lawless wholesale roundup of the petitioner and more than 20 other youths. Equating the procedures followed by the grand jury in the present case to the fingerprint detentions in *Davis*, the Court of Appeals reasoned that "[t]he dragnet effect here, where approximately twenty persons were subpoenaed for purposes of identification, has the same invidious effect on fourth amendment rights as the practice condemned in *Davis*."

* * *

I.

The Court of Appeals correctly rejected the contention that the compelled production of the voice exemplars would violate the Fifth Amendment. It has long been held that the compelled display of identifiable physical characteristics infringes no interest protected by the privilege against compulsory self-incrimination. In Holt v. United States, 218 U.S. 245, 252, 31 S.Ct. 2, 6, Mr. Justice Holmes, writing for the Court, dismissed as an "extravagant extension of the Fifth Amendment" the argument that it violated the privilege to require a defendant to put on a blouse for identification purposes. He explained that "the prohibition of compelling a man in a criminal court to be witness against himself is a prohibition of the use of physical or moral compulsion to extort communications from him, not an exclusion of his body as evidence when it may be material."

More recently, in Schmerber v. California, 384 U.S. 757, 86 S.Ct. 1826, we relied on *Holt*, and noted that "both federal and state courts have usually held that [the privilege] it offers no protection against compulsion to submit to fingerprinting, photographing, or measurements, to write or speak for identification, to appear in court, to stand, to assume a stance, to walk, or to make a particular gesture.

2. The life of the special grand jury was 18 months, but could be extended for an additional 18 months. 18 U.S.C. § 3331.

The distinction which has emerged often expressed in different ways, is that the privilege is a bar against compelling 'communications' or 'testimony,' but that compulsion which makes a suspect or accused the source of 'real or physical evidence' does not violate it."

The Court held that the extraction and chemical analysis of a blood sample involved no "shadow of testimonial compulsion upon or enforced communication by the accused."

These cases led us to conclude in Gilbert v. California, 388 U.S. 263, 87 S.Ct. 1951, that handwriting exemplars were not protected by the privilege against compulsory self-incrimination. While "[o]ne's voice and handwriting are, of course, means of communication," we held that a "mere handwriting exemplar, in contrast to the content of what is written, like the voice or body itself, is an identifying physical characteristic outside its protection." And similarly in United States v. Wade, 388 U.S. 218, 87 S.Ct. 1926, we found no error in compelling a defendant accused of bank robbery to utter in a line-up words that had allegedly been spoken by the robber. The accused there was "required to use his voice as an identifying physical characteristic, not to speak his guilt."

Wade and Gilbert definitively refute any contention that the compelled production of the voice exemplars in this case would violate the Fifth Amendment. The voice recordings were to be used solely to measure the physical properties of the witnesses' voices, not for the testimonial or communicative content of what was to be said.

II.

The Court of Appeals held that the Fourth Amendment required a preliminary showing of reasonableness before a grand jury witness could be compelled to furnish a voice exemplar, and that in this case the proposed "seizures" of the voice exemplars would be unreasonable because of the large number of witnesses summoned by the grand jury and directed to produce such exemplars. We disagree.

The Fourth Amendment guarantees that all people shall be "secure in their persons, houses, papers, and effects, against unreasonable searches and seizures . . . ." Any Fourth Amendment violation in the present setting must rest on a lawless governmental intrusion upon the privacy of "persons" rather than on interference with "property relationships or private papers." Schmerber v. California, 384 U.S. 757, 767, 86 S.Ct. 1826, 1833; see United States v. Doe, (Schwartz), 2 Cir., 457 F.2d 895, 897. In Terry v. Ohio, 392 U.S. 1, 88 S.Ct. 1868, the Court explained the protection afforded to "persons" in terms of the statement in Katz v. United States, 389 U.S. 347, 88 S.Ct. 507, that "the Fourth Amendment protects people, not places," and concluded that "wherever an individual may harbor a reasonable 'expectation of privacy,' . . . he is entitled to be free from unreasonable governmental intrusion."

As the Court made clear in Schmerber, supra, the obtaining of physical evidence from a person involves a potential Fourth Amendment violation at two different levels—the "seizure" of the "person" necessary to bring him into contact with government agents, see Davis v. Mississippi, 394 U.S. 721, 89 S.Ct. 1394, and the subsequent search for and seizure of the evidence. In *Schmerber* we found the initial seizure of the accused justified as a lawful arrest, and the subsequent seizure of the blood sample from his body reasonable in light of the exigent circumstances. And in *Terry*, we concluded that neither the initial seizure of the person, an investigatory "stop" by a policeman, nor the subsequent search, a pat down of his outer clothing for weapons, constituted a violation of the Fourth and Fourteenth Amendments. The constitutionality of the compulsory production of exemplars from a grand jury witness necessarily turns on the same dual inquiry—whether either the initial compulsion of the person to appear before the grand jury, or the subsequent directive to make a voice recording is an unreasonable "seizure" within the meaning of the Fourth Amendment.

It is clear that a subpoena to appear before a grand jury is not a "seizure" in the Fourth Amendment sense, even though that summons may be inconvenient or burdensome. . . .

* * *

This is not to say that a grand jury subpoena is some talisman that dissolves all constitutional protections. The grand jury cannot require a witness to testify against himself. It cannot require the production by a person of private books and records that would incriminate him. The Fourth Amendment provides protection against a grand jury subpoena *duces tecum* too sweeping in its terms "to be regarded as reasonable."

But we are here faced with no such constitutional infirmities in the subpoena to appear before the grand jury or in the order to make the voice recordings. There is, as we have said, no valid Fifth Amendment claim. There was no order to produce private books and papers, and no sweeping subpoena *duces tecum*. And . . . there is still no indication in this case of the kind of harassment . . .

But the conclusion that Dionisio's compulsory appearance before the grand jury was not an unreasonable "seizure" is the answer to only the first part of the Fourth Amendment inquiry here. Dionisio argues that the grand jury's subsequent directive to make the voice recording was itself an infringement of his rights under the Fourth Amendment. We cannot accept that argument.

In Katz v. United States, supra, we said that the Fourth Amendment provides no protection for what "a person knowingly exposes to the public, even in his own home or office. . . ." The physical characteristics of a person's voice, its tone and manner, as opposed to the content of a specific conversation, are constantly exposed to the public. Like a man's facial characteristics, or handwriting, his voice is repeatedly produced for others to hear. No person can have a reasonable expectation that others will not know the sound of his voice, any more than he can reasonably expect that his face will be a mystery to the world. As the Court of Appeals for the Second Circuit stated:

"Except for the rare recluse who chooses to live his life in complete solitude, in our daily lives we constantly speak and write, and while the content of a communication is entitled to Fourth Amendment protection, . . . the underlying identifying characteristics—the constant factor throughout both public and private communications—are open for all to see or hear. There is no basis for constructing a wall of privacy against the grand jury which does not exist in casual contacts with strangers. Hence no intrusion into an individual's privacy results from compelled execution of handwriting or voice exemplars; nothing is being exposed to the grand jury that has not previously been exposed to the public at large." United States v. Doe (Schwartz), 2 Cir., 457 F.2d 895, 898–899.

The required disclosure of a person's voice is thus immeasurably further removed from the Fourth Amendment protection than was the intrusion into the body effected by the blood extraction in *Schmerber*. "The interests in human dignity and privacy which the Fourth Amendment protects forbid any such intrusions on the mere chance that desired evidence might be obtained." Schmerber v. California, 384 U.S. 757, 769–770, 86 S.Ct. 1826, 1835. Similarly, a seizure of voice exemplars does not involve the "severe, though brief, intrusion upon cherished personal security," effected by the "pat down" in *Terry*—"surely . . . an annoying, frightening, and perhaps humiliating experience." Terry v. Ohio, 392 U.S. 1, 24–25, 88 S.Ct. 1868, 1882. Rather, this is like the fingerprinting in *Davis*, where, though the initial dragnet detentions were constitutionally impermissible, we noted that the fingerprinting itself, "involves none of the probing into an individual's private life and thoughts that marks an interrogation or search."

Since neither the summons to appear before the grand jury, nor its directive to make a voice recording infringed upon any interest protected by the Fourth Amendment, there was no justification for requiring the grand jury to satisfy even the minimal requirement of "reasonableness" imposed by the Court of Appeals. A grand jury has broad investigative powers to determine whether a crime has been committed and who has committed it. The jurors may act on tips, rumors, evidence offered by the prosecutor, or their own personal knowledge. No grand jury witness is "entitled to set limits to the investigation that the grand jury may conduct." And a sufficient basis for an indictment may only emerge at the end of the investigation when all the evidence has been received. . . . Since Dionisio raised no valid Fourth Amendment claim, there is no more reason to require a preliminary showing of reasonableness here than there would be in the case of any witness who, despite the lack of any constitutional or statutory privilege, declined to answer a question or comply with a grand jury request. Neither the Constitution nor our prior cases justify any such interference with grand jury proceedings.

The Fifth Amendment guarantees that no civilian may be brought to trial for an infamous crime "unless on a presentment or indictment of a Grand Jury." This constitutional guarantee presupposes an investigative body "acting independently of either prosecuting attorney or judge," Stirone v. United States, 361 U.S. 212, 218, 80 S.Ct. 270, 273, whose mission is to clear the innocent, no less than to bring to trial those who may be guilty. Any holding that would saddle a grand jury with mini-trials and preliminary showings would assuredly impede its investigation and frustrate the public's interest in the fair and expeditious administration of the criminal laws. The grand jury may not always serve its historic role as a protective bulwark standing solidly between the ordinary citizen and an overzealous prosecutor, but if it is even to approach the proper performance of its constitutional mission, it must be free to pursue its investigations unhindered by external influence or supervision so long as it does not trench upon the legitimate rights of any witness called before it.

Since the Court of Appeals found an unreasonable search and seizure where none existed, and imposed a preliminary showing of reasonableness where none was required, its judgment is reversed and this case is remanded to that Court for further proceedings consistent with this opinion.

It is so ordered.

Judgment reversed and case remanded.

[The opinion of Justices Brennan (concurring and dissenting) and the dissenting opinions of Justices Douglas and Marshall are omitted.]

NOTES

1. Notwithstanding *Dionisio*, In re Grand Jury Proceedings (Schofield II), 507 F.2d 963 (3d Cir. 1975), held "it reasonable that the Government be required to make some preliminary showing by affidavit that each item is at least relevant to an investigation being conducted by the grand jury and properly within its jurisdiction, and is not sought primarily for another purpose." This position was rejected in United States v. McLean, 565 F.2d 318 (5th Cir. 1977):

> "The Third Circuit made it clear that the guidelines it set were to be the law in that circuit and not required by the Constitution or the Supreme Court. We are not prepared to make such the law in the Fifth. As noted by the Supreme Court: 'Any holding that would saddle a grand jury with mini-trials and preliminary showings would assuredly impede its investigation and frustrate the public's interest in the fair and expeditious administration of the criminal laws.'"

2. The eye-witness identification cases discussed in Chapter 3 provide further examples of the courts' attempts to deal with the problems on non-testimonial evidence.

3. Are there any limits upon the grand jury's power to compel "non-testimonial" evidence without a showing of probable cause? Can a grand jury order a suspect to stand in a lineup? See In the Matter of Toon, 364 A.2d 1177 (D.C.App.1976), and In re Melvin, 546 F.2d 1 (1st Cir. 1976). Could a grand jury order a suspect to yield a hair sample? What about a

blood specimen? Presumably, the greater the intrusion, the weaker is the argument that *Dionisio* is the controlling precedent.

4. In Fisher v. United States, 425 U.S. 391, 96 S.Ct. 1569 (1976), a taxpayer had turned over to his attorney certain papers which had been prepared by the taxpayer's accountant. A subpoena issued to compel the attorney to produce the papers. The Supreme Court declared that a subpoena which does not compel the client (as distinguished from his or her attorney) to do anything does not violate the client's Fifth Amendment rights. The Court went on to determine whether the subpoena violated the attorney-client privilege. It recognized that if papers which were protected by the Fifth Amendment in the hands of the client were turned over to the attorney within the scope of the attorney-client relationship, a subpoena against the attorney could violate the attorney-client privilege. On the other hand, the Court reasoned, if the papers were not privileged in the hands of the client (and therefore could be reached by a subpoena to the client), the attorney-client privilege was not violated. The Court then considered whether the papers would have been privileged in the hands of the taxpayer. It held that the papers would not have been protected by the Fifth Amendment if a subpoena had issued against the taxpayer himself while the papers were still in his hands, reasoning that the taxpayer had not been compelled to create the papers in the first instance but rather did so voluntarily. It added that the papers were actually created by the accountant and not by the client.

The Court reserved the question of whether a different result would follow if the records had been personal writings or other documents personally created by the taxpayer. Finally, the Court noted that although the act of producing papers in response to a subpoena in a sense has testimonial aspects (in that the taxpayer is admitting the existence of the papers), those aspects do not seem to be significant enough to be within the Fifth Amendment protection against testimonial compulsion. The Court especially noted that the government did not intend to rely upon the act of producing the records as a means of "authenticating" the records for use at trial.

The *Fisher* decision is significant in that the Supreme Court expressly rejected broad language in Boyd v. United States, 116 U.S. 616, 6 S.Ct. 524 (1886), which has provided a Fifth Amendment defense to the production of records in response to a subpoena duces tecum. The Court left for another day the issue of what records or other writings if any, will remain protected by the Fifth Amendment.

5. In Andresen v. Maryland, 427 U.S. 463, 96 S.Ct. 2737 (1976), decided shortly after *Fisher*, the Supreme Court held that authorities could seize records through a valid search warrant even if those same records would be protected by the Fifth Amendment if a subpoena duces tecum had been issued. Again the Court reasoned that testimonial compulsion was not present under such circumstances. When records are seized under a search warrant, their owner is not compelled to do anything of an affirmative nature. He is "not asked to do or say anything," and, therefore, is not testimonially compelled.

6. In United States v. Miller, 425 U.S. 435, 96 S.Ct. 1619 (1976), a federal prosecutor utilized the grand jury to subpoena records from two banks pertaining to Miller's accounts. Without utilizing the word, the Court, in effect, held that Miller had no "standing" to complain about alleged irregularities in the issuance of the subpoena. The Court stated that one who engages in commercial transactions utilizing banking facilities has

no reasonable expectation of privacy in the papers, so that he can make no claim under the Fourth Amendment. The "depositor takes the risk, in revealing his affairs to another, that the information will be conveyed by that person to the government." The Court attributed no legal significance to the fact that it is the government itself, under the new Bank Secrecy Act, upheld in California Bankers Assn. v. Shultz, 416 U.S. 21, 94 S.Ct. 1494 (1974), which requires the bank to keep the records. "Many banks traditionally kept permanent records of their depositors' accounts" even before the Bank Secrecy Act compelled that practice.

The result in *Miller* is in accord with the result in the typical state case where the target of an investigation seeks to quash a grand jury subpoena duces tecum issued to his bank or some other third party. Such a person typically is told that he has no standing to complain about the breadth of the subpoena or any other alleged irregularity. See also Chapter 4, Section N, note 4.

G. ABUSE OF THE GRAND JURY PROCESS

UNITED STATES v. BASURTO

United States Court of Appeals, Ninth Circuit, 1974.
497 F.2d 781.

FERGUSON,[*] DISTRICT JUDGE.

Appellants and 14 others were charged in a one-count indictment with conspiring to import and distribute marijuana . . . . The conspiracy was alleged to . . . have involved smuggling marijuana from Mexico into the United States by airplane. Following the denial of motions to suppress evidence and to dismiss the indictment, appellants were convicted of the charged offense after a jury trial. We reverse.

* * *

Perjury by a Witness Before the Grand Jury

William Barron was named in the indictment as a co-conspirator but not a defendant. He testified as to appellants' activities in the conspiracy before the grand jury which brought the indictment. Prior to the commencement of trial, Barron informed the Assistant United States Attorney prosecuting the case that he had committed perjury before the grand jury in important respects. In particular, he told the prosecutor that all his grand jury testimony relating to his knowledge of appellants' activities in the conspiracy prior to May 1, 1971, was untrue. That date is significant, because effective then [the statute on which the indictment was based] was repealed. Persons convicted of narcotics offenses under [that statute] were subject to a mandatory minimum sentence of five years, while those convicted under the new statute were not subject to such inflexible sentencing.

---

[*] Honorable Warren J. Ferguson, United States District Judge, Central District of California, sitting by designation.

The only witness other than Barron to testify before the grand jury as to appellants' activities in connection with the conspiracy prior to May 1, 1971, was Thomas Waddill, a Customs agent. Both Barron's and Waddill's testimony was unrecorded. The parties dispute whether Agent Waddill, at the time of his grand jury appearance, had any knowledge of appellants' activities prior to May 1, 1971, other than what Barron had told Waddill.[1]

Upon learning of Barron's perjured grand jury testimony, the prosecuting attorney informed opposing counsel. He did not, however, notify the court or the grand jury. In his opening statement at trial, he made reference to Barron's perjury before the grand jury, but sought to minimize its scope and importance:

> "Mr. Barron did testify at the Grand Jury, but part of his testimony was a lie. Mr. Barron will take the stand and tell you that today, or excuse me, when he takes the stand. He will tell you he lied about where he met [one of the defendants]. He will tell you that the reason he told this lie is he was protecting a friend of his in Seattle, Washington. He will tell you that other than minute details which he has since recalled, such as a change in a date or a change in possibly who was present at exactly a particular moment, other than those details this is the only material lie that he told before the Grand Jury, but it was a lie. He will tell you that when he takes the stand in this trial he will tell the truth."

The conduct of the prosecutor in this case reinforces the expression by Professor Moore that, over the years, the government prosecutor has gained substantial influence over the grand jury, and subsequently that institution has lost much of its former independence. See 8 J. Moore, Federal Practice, ¶ 6.02[1].

The Fifth Amendment provides that "[n]o person shall be held to answer for a capital, or otherwise infamous crime, unless on a presentment or indictment of a Grand Jury." The purpose of that requirement is to limit a person's jeopardy to offenses charged by a group of his fellow citizens acting independently of either the prosecutor or the judge.

It is clear, however, that when a duly constituted grand jury returns an indictment valid on its face, no independent inquiry may be made to determine the kind of evidence considered by the grand jury in making its decision. To do so would further invade the independence of the grand jury. The holding reached by this court does not affect that established rule.

Today, the grand jury relies upon the prosecutor to initiate and prepare criminal cases and investigate which come before it. The

---

1. It is not necessary that the dispute be resolved, since it does not affect the holding of this court. The issue here is not one relating to the sufficiency of evidence before a grand jury to sustain an indictment, but rather, the duty of a prosecutor when he becomes aware that perjury as to a material matter has been committed.

prosecutor is present while the grand jury hears testimony; he calls and questions the witnesses and draws the indictment. With that great power and authority there is a correlative duty, and that is not to permit a person to stand trial when he knows that perjury permeates the indictment.

At the point at which he learned of the perjury before the grand jury, the prosecuting attorney was under a duty to notify the court and the grand jury, to correct the cancer of justice that had become apparent to him. To permit the appellants to stand trial when the prosecutor knew of the perjury before the grand jury only allowed the cancer to grow.

As we have noted above, the perjury before the grand jury was material because of the change in the law; all of Barron's grand jury testimony relating to the appellants' activities before May 1, 1971 was perjured. The grand jury, if it returned an indictment, might have done so under the [new statute] had it known of the perjury.

We also note that jeopardy had not attached at the time the prosecutor learned of the perjured testimony, nor had the statute of limitations for the offenses charged run. If the prosecutor had brought the perjury to the court's attention before the trial commenced and the indictments had been dismissed, the Double Jeopardy Clause of the Fifth Amendment would not have barred trial under a new indictment.

We hold that the Due Process Clause of the Fifth Amendment is violated when a defendant has to stand trial on an indictment which the government knows is based partially on perjured testimony, when the perjured testimony is material, and when jeopardy has not attached. Whenever the prosecutor learns of any perjury committed before the grand jury, he is under a duty to immediately inform the court and opposing counsel—and, if the perjury may be material, also the grand jury—in order that appropriate action may be taken.

We base our decision on a long line of cases which recognize the existence of a duty of good faith on the part of the prosecutor with respect to the court, the grand jury, and the defendant.

* * *

.   .   . Permitting a defendant to stand trial on an indictment which the government knows is based on perjured testimony cannot comport with [what the Supreme Court has described as a] "fastidious regard for the honor of the administration of justice."

* * *

The judgments of convictions are reversed.

HUFSTEDLER, Circuit Judge (concurring specially):

I concur in the result reached by the majority, but I find unsatisfactory the constitutional theory it advances to support its conclusion that the prosecutor had a duty to inform the grand jury of Barron's perjured testimony.   .   .   .

.   .   . [T]he prosecutor in the case at bench notified both defense counsel and the trial court upon learning of the perjured testimony.   I do not believe that the prosecutor's failure additionally to inform the grand jury was such a breach of his constitutional duty of good faith as to constitute a violation of defendants' due process rights.

Although the majority's constitutional analysis is not persuasive, it would be an appropriate exercise of our power to supervise the administration of criminal justice in the federal courts to impose upon federal prosecutors the duty to notify the grand jury described by the majority.   An important function of our supervisory power is to guarantee that federal prosecutors act with due regard for the integrity of the administration of justice.

The grand jury serves important public interests not only through its examination into the commission of crimes but also by its ability "to stand between the prosecutor and the accused, and to determine whether the charge was founded on credible testimony or was dictated by malice or personal ill will."   .   .   .   By failing to inform the grand jury of Barron's perjured testimony and thus precluding the opportunity to reconsider the indictment in light of the corrected version of the defendants' activities, the prosecutor effectively frustrated this vital function.   A supervisory rule requiring a prosecutor who learns before trial that an indictment is based in some material way on perjured testimony to seek dismissal of the tainted indictment would safeguard the grand jury's role as mediator between prosecutor and potential defendant.   Such a supervisory rule would also help insure that the prosecutor fulfills his responsibility to deal with the grand jury in a way that promotes the wise exercise of its investigatory and indictment powers.   Even though breach of that prosecutorial duty may not constitute a violation of defendant's constitutional rights, the prosecutor is nevertheless responsible to the court for conduct that is potentially detrimental to the integrity of the judicial system.

*   *   *

NOTES

1.   It is improper to use a grand jury solely or dominantly to develop evidence for use at the trial of an already indicted defendant.   See United States v. Doss, 563 F.2d 265 (6th Cir. 1977).   In State v. Burri, 87 Wash.2d 175, 550 P.2d 507 (1976), the court upheld the dismissal of an indictment when the prosecutor, following notice of an alibi defense, convened a special inquiry proceeding in order to examine the alibi witnesses in the absence of the defendant.   The court found that the action of the prosecutor was "government misconduct or arbitrary action of the type historically regarded by this court as sufficient to support a dismissal of a criminal charge."

Courts are reluctant, however, to inquire into the nature and course of the grand jury's investigation to determine whether it embraces a pending indictment.   In United States v. Doe, 455 F.2d 1270 (1st Cir. 1972), a defendant who had been indicted in California sought a protective order banning a grand jury in Massachusetts from gathering evidence which would be relevant to the California prosecution.   Although the government was represented by the same attorneys in both proceedings, the court would go only so far as to rule that the prosecutors must make available to the District Court in California the transcript of any witness who is both examined before the grand jury in Massachusetts and called to testify at the trial in California. The California court could then determine if the Government was using the Boston grand jury as a discovery device. In United States v. Braasch, 505 F.2d 139, 147 (7th Cir. 1974), the court went even further, holding that "the government has every right to interrogate witnesses on subjects relevant to a continuing grand jury investigation when the evidence received may also relate to a pending indictment."

2. Other abuses of the grand jury concern prosecutorial misconduct of the type condemned by the ABA standards. See, e. g., United States v. Calvert, 523 F.2d 895 (8th Cir. 1975) ("leaking" items under grand jury investigation to the media); United States v. Sweig, 316 F.Supp. 1148 (S.D.N.Y.1970) (generation of adverse publicity); Bursey v. United States, 466 F.2d 1059 (9th Cir. 1972) (coaxing perjury); Brown v. United States, 245 F.2d 549 (8th Cir. 1957) (altering the location of the investigation); United States v. Ryan, 455 F.2d 728 (9th Cir. 1972) (using the grand jury to collect intelligence information).

H. INDICTMENTS

1. SUFFICIENCY OF THE CHARGE

UNITED STATES v. ZOLLI

United States District Court, E.D.N.Y.1970.
51 F.R.D. 522.

MISHLER, CHIEF JUDGE.   *   *   *

The first ground upon which the motion to dismiss is made is that the indictment fails to charge defendants with knowledge or notice that John Hodges was to be a witness. In ascertaining the standard by which to test the sufficiency of the indictment, it must be observed that the older cases have held indictments to a quite strict standard. In Pettibone v. United States, 148 U.S. 197, 202, 13 S.Ct. 542, 545 (1893), for example, the Supreme Court enunciated the following strict standard:

> The general rule in reference to an indictment is that all the
> material facts and circumstances embraced in the definition
> of the offense must be stated, and that, if any essential ele-
> ment of the crime is omitted, such omission cannot be sup-
> plied by intendment or implication.

Under the *Pettibone* standard, an indictment under a predecessor of section 1503 was quashed for failure to adequately charge that the defendant knew there was a pending proceeding.

More recent cases, however, have indicated that the standard to which pleaders were held in the *Pettibone* era would no longer be applicable. The Supreme Court noted the evolution in pleading theory in its 1932 decision in Hagner v. United States, . . . the courts should overlook minor and technical defects in the drafting of an indictment so long as it is not violative of minimum constitutional standards and so long as it can be said to fairly apprise a defendant of the charge and allow him to prepare his defense. Hence courts have upheld indictments attacked on the ground of failure to allege a purpose or intention to obstruct the administration of justice, Holland v. United States, 245 F.2d 341 (5th Cir. 1957); failure to allege that the defendant had knowledge that there was a case pending, Anderson v. United States, 215 F.2d 84 (6th Cir. 1954) (indictment charged that defendants "did corruptly endeavor to impede the due administration of justice; that is to say, [defendants] did agree and promise to [a named defendant in a pending case] that they would alter the testimony of [witnesses in the pending case] and did by this means corruptly endeavor to impede the due administration of justice)"; and failure to allege that the endeavor was corrupt, Seawright v. United States, 224 F.2d 482 (6th Cir.) (1955) (indictment charged that the defendants did "wilfully endeavor to influence, intimidate and impede [name], a witness . . . endeavoring to influence, obstruct, and impede the due administration of justice.").

* * *

The language of the indictment charges the defendants "corruptly by force and by threats did endeavor to influence, intimidate and impede . . . ." The word "corruptly" has been held to mean with "an improper motive." Martin v. United States, 166 F.2d 76 (4th Cir. 1948). The word "endeavor" is defined: "To exert physical and intellectual strength toward the attainment of an object; a systematic or continuous effort." Black's Law Dictionary 621 (4th Ed. 1957). In view of the above definitions, it can be fairly said that the use of the words "corruptly endeavored" does charge the defendants with committing an intentional and knowing act, and such use in the indictment renders it sufficient.

The defendants' object that the first and second counts of the indictment are duplicitous. The Federal Rules of Criminal Procedure, Rule 8(a), requires that each separate and distinct offense be pleaded in a separate count. Failure to so plead will render an indictment subject to attack on grounds of duplicity. "Duplicity" may therefore be defined as "the charging of two or more separate and distinct offenses in one count, not the charging of a single offense into which several related acts enter as ways and means of accomplishing the purpose." Travis v. United States, . . . Therefore an indictment which in a single count joins two or more distinct and separate offenses will violate the rule against duplicity, and is subject to a successful motion for dismissal.

The crux of the problem hence is what allegations in an indictment will render it duplicitous. In Crain v. United States (1896), the United States Supreme Court had the opportunity to expound upon permissible drafting of an indictment at a time when the strict and technical rules of pleading under *Pettibone* were in effect. The *Crain* court examined the statute and noted that

[t]he statute was directed against certain defined modes for accomplishing a general object, and declared that the doing of either one of several specified things, each having reference to that object, should be punished * * *. We perceive no sound reason why the doing of the prohibited thing in each and all of the prohibited modes may not be charged in one count, so that there may be a verdict of guilty upon proof that the accused had done any one of the things constituting a substantive crime under the statute.

The Court thus made clear that an indictment will not be duplicitous merely because drafted in conjunctive allegations closely paralleling the statutory framework.

* * *

The first count of the indictment, which the defendants challenge as duplicitous, reads as follows:

On or about the 20th day of September, 1970, within the Eastern District of New York, the defendant Richard Zolli, the defendant Rocco Surace, and the defendant Angelo Winchell corruptly by force and by threats did endeavor to influence, intimidate and impede one John Hodges, a witness in a case pending before the United States District Court for the Eastern District of New York, and did corruptly by force and by threats endeavor to influence, obstruct and impede the due administration of justice. (Title 18 United States Code, § 1503; Title 18 United States Code, § 2.)

The alleged duplicity is that defendants are charged with endeavoring to (1) "influence, intimidate and impede one John Hodges, a witness in a case pending . . ."; and (2) "influence, obstruct, and impede the due administration of justice." Such language, it is argued, charges two separate crimes.

The language of the statute, which the defendants are charged with violating in the first count, reads in pertinent part:

Whoever corruptly, or by threats or force . . . endeavors to influence, intimidate, or impede any witness, in any court of the United States . . . or injures any party or witness in his person or property on account of his . . . testifying or having testified to any matter pending therein . . . or corruptly or by threats or force . . . influences, obstructs, or impedes, or endeavors to influence, obstruct, or impede, the due administration of justice . . .

18 U.S.C. § 1503 (1966).

It can readily be observed that the indictment is framed in the same language as that of the statute. Under the case law, this alone would be sufficient to sustain the indictment from the attack made by the defendants.

However, the defendants allege that the language "influence, obstruct, or impede the due administration of justice" creates a crime which is separate and distinct from endeavoring to "influence, intimidate, or impede any witness, in any court of the United States." That such contention is erroneous becomes clear with even the most casual perusal of the construction doctrines. Under the doctrine of *noscitur a sociis*, the clauses in question must be construed in the context of the other clauses in the statute which define the proscribed conduct. Under the principle of *ejusdem generis*, such clause can be construed only to include conduct similar to that specifically proscribed in the preceding clauses. Indeed, in Haili v. United States (1958), the clause in question was held "to embrace only acts similar in nature to those acts enumerated by the preceding specific words." Such clause was included to cover those means of interference as to which the draftsmen of the statute were not sufficiently prescient to enumerate. Consequently the attack upon the indictment cannot be sustained on the ground alleged.

* * *

The defendants mount a similar attack upon count 2. Count 2 reads:

> On or about the 20th day of September 1970, within the Eastern District of New York, the defendant Richard Zolli, the defendant Rocco Surace, and the defendant Angelo Winchell wilfully did endeavor by means of intimidation, force and threats thereof, to obstruct, delay and prevent the communication of information relating to a violation of a criminal statute of the United States by one John Hodges to a criminal investigator of the United States, and did injure the aforementioned John Hodges in his person on account of the giving by John Hodges of such information. (Title 18 United States Code, § 1510(a); Title 18 United States Code, § 2.)

The defendants alleged that such count is duplicitous because it charged the defendants with: "(1) wilfully endeavoring to obstruct the future communication of information and (2) with injuring John Hodges because he had already given information."

* * *

The language of the statute, the violation of which the defendants are charged in the first count, reads in pertinent part:

> (a) Whoever wilfully endeavors by means of . . . intimidation or force, or threats thereof to obstruct, delay, or prevent the communication of information relating to a violation of any criminal statute of the United States by any person to a criminal investigator; or

> Whoever injures any person in his person or property on account of the giving by such person . . . of any such information to any criminal investigator . . . . . .

18 U.S.C. § 1510(a) (Supp.1970).

The second count, just as the first, is framed in the language of the statute. Similarly, such framing would, under the case law, be sufficient to sustain the indictment. . . .

The defendants [also] attack the first and second counts as being multiplicitous. Multiplicity is defined as charging a single offense in multiple counts. The indictment charges intimidating a witness in a pending case in count 1, a violation of 18 U.S.C. § 1503 (1966), and intimidating an informant giving information in a pending investigation, in violation of 18 U.S.C. § 1510(a) (Supp.1970).

The test for determining whether offenses charged in one or more counts are identical was set forth in Bozel v. United States (1943). The inquiry to be made is "whether the facts alleged in one, if offered in support of the other would sustain a conviction." 139 F.2d at 155. Hence, if one count requires proof of facts which another count does not require, the offenses therein alleged are not identical.

The indictment in the instant case requires proof of differing facts to support a conviction on each count in question. Count 1, for example, requires proof, among other things, that John Hodges was to be a witness in a pending case, whereas count 2 would instead require a showing that John Hodges was giving information in a pending investigation. Certainly then under the *Bozel* test, there are two separate and distinct offenses alleged in this indictment. The mere fact that a single act or transaction is involved cannot preclude the possibility that such conduct may be violative of two criminal statutes.

For the reasons stated, the motions are in all respects denied.

PEOPLE v. AUD

Supreme Court of Illinois, 1972.
52 Ill.2d 368, 288 N.E.2d 453.

MR. JUSTICE SCHAEFER delivered the opinion of the court:

The circuit court of Gallatin County dismissed indictments for perjury against appellees George Aud and Cecelia Aud. The Appellate Court affirmed and we allowed leave to appeal.

The substance of both indictments was identical. The pertinent part of that against George Aud charged ". . . that on the 30th day of November, 1970, in the City of Shawneetown, Illinois, at and within said County, George Aud committed the offense of Perjury, in that he under oath, before Judge Don A. Foster of the Circuit Court of the County of Gallatin in the Second District of the State of Illinois in a proceeding entitled: The People of the State of Illinois v. George Kilmer, Defendant, Case Number 70–CM–25, charging the Defendant with the offense of selling and delivering alcoholic liquor to a person under the age of 21 years, did make false statements material to the issue or point in question which he does [sic] not believe to be true. In violation of Section 32–3, Chapter 38, Illinois Revised Statutes, 1969 . . . ."

The indictments contain details of time and place but they do not allege either the exact content or the substance of the false statements which are the subject of the charge. The State argues that "[a]ny additional information required for preparation of a defense could have been obtained by resort to a motion for a Bill of Particulars as provided in Paragraph 111–6." This argument does not bear upon the problem in this case, which concerns the legal sufficiency of the indictment to charge an offense, rather than the amount of information necessary for preparation of a defense. In People v. Patrick (1967) we noted that "[t]he office of a bill of particulars is to provide more specificity of detail to supplement a *sufficient indictment* so as to enable an accused better to understand the nature of the charge against him or better to prepare his defense." (Emphasis added.) But it has long been settled that "a bill of particulars cannot be used to cure a void charge."

The general rule governing the sufficiency of indictments was reiterated in People v. Grieco (1970): "[A]n indictment phrased in the language of the statute creating the crime is sufficiently certain where the words of the statute so particularize the offense as by their use alone to notify the accused of the precise offense charged against him. [Citations.] But where the statute does not specifically define the crime, or does so only in general terms, some act showing an alleged violation of the statute must be averred."

We have been referred to no decision of any court which has sustained an indictment for perjury that did not set forth the alleged false statement, either verbatim or in its substance. We have found no such case. That is because the offense of perjury can be committed only by the use of words; the words used are both the offense and the means by which the offense is committed. Perjury thus differs from burglary, for example, in which the validity of the indictment does not depend on whether the unlawful entry was through the front door, the rear door or a window, and from murder, in which the validity of the indictment does not depend on whether the victim was killed by strangulation, by stabbing or by shooting. Those offenses are adequately charged by an indictment that uses the language of the statute creating the crime. But where the means used are integral parts of the offense, as is the case in an indictment for perjury, they must be stated.

The judgment of the appellate court in the consolidated case is affirmed.

UNITED STATES v. ARCHAMBAULT

United States Court of Appeals, Tenth Circuit, 1971.
441 F.2d 281, cert. denied 404 U.S. 843, 92 S.Ct. 140.

HILL, CIRCUIT JUDGE.

Appellant Archambault was a bank teller at a national bank in Denver, Colorado. On a two-count indictment she was charged with embezzling, abstracting, purloining or misapplying the bank's money, funds or credits with intent to injure or defraud the bank in violation of 18 U.S.C. § 656. . . . [On] direct appeal, appellant contends that the indictment was fatally defective because it was insufficient to apprise her of the nature of the accusation with reasonable certainty.

"The traditional criteria by which the legal sufficiency of an indictment is determined is whether it contains the elements of the offense charged and apprises the accused of the nature of the charge, so as to enable [her] to prepare a defense and to plead the judgment in bar." Mims v. United States (1964). Appellant does not appear to suggest that the indictment, insofar as it charged embezzlement, was too general to apprise her of what she must defend against. It is settled that an indictment following the wording of § 656 which charges embezzlement of bank funds is sufficient to charge a violation of the federal criminal statute. . . . In the main appellant's contention is that the words "abstract, purloin, or misapply" are generic terms which did not sufficiently particularize the species of the charged offense, making it impossible for appellant to prepare a defense.

While generic terms cannot properly be used without more to allege an offense, we cannot for that reason find fault with the indictment brought against appellant. The terminology used in the indictment followed the wording of the statute. The word "abstract" has long been a term of certain, simple and unambiguous meaning. When the word is coupled in an indictment with an allegation of intent to injure or defraud a bank, as in the instant case, there can be no misunderstanding of the true meaning of the allegation and the offense is well charged.

Turning to the portion of the indictment which charged purloining, we have found no cases deciding whether such a charge sufficiently apprises an accused of the alleged offense which he must defend against. Apparently either purloining never has been charged in an indictment before, or no one before appellant has seriously felt that such terminology in an indictment was inadequate to inform of the charge to be met. In any event, we are not convinced that "purloin" is a generic term requiring particularization. In the only federal cases found which discuss the crime of purloining, albeit with reference to other criminal statutes, it is demonstrated that "to purloin" encompasses a narrow criminal offense. The cases elaborate that purloin is a species of larceny and was developed in modern pleading to fill the gap between the sometimes doubtful common law definition of larceny and the modern criminal code definition of larceny. Suffice it to say with respect to the charge of purloining, we believe that appellant was clearly informed of that with which she was accused and was enabled to prepare a defense and to plead the judgment in bar of any further prosecutions for the same offense.

The adequacy of the term "misapply" to advise appellant of her alleged offenses poses a more difficult question. We find that, "[T]he statutory concept of misapplication is not a vague word of such uncertain application as to require a dismissal of the indictment." We have not overlooked the fact that the indictment against appellant did not contain an allegation that she converted the bank's money, funds or credits to her own use. Moreover, we are aware of the reasoning of United States v. Quinn, 365 F.2d 256 (7th Cir. 1966), that when the charge of willful misapplication is made there must be an accompanying allegation that the bank's money, funds or credits were converted to the use of the accused or to some party other than the bank. However, in view of the fact that the total charge in the indictment against appellant Archambault was embezzlement, abstraction, purloining or misapplication, it is unmistakably inherent in the indictment that appellant stood accused of converting the alleged sums to her own use. .   . . .

In concluding that the indictment was legally sufficient to apprise appellant of the charges, we only add that, "In a prosecution under 18 U.S.C. § 656, where the offense is set out in the language of the statute, the omission of the means by which the offense was committed does not render the indictment insufficient."

NOTES

1. On the question of the sufficiency of indictments, see Russell v. United States, 369 U.S. 749, 82 S.Ct. 1038 (1962) and Note, Indictment Sufficiency, 70 Colum.L.Rev. 876 (1970).

2. The range of potential problems with pleading by indictment is quite broad. There are technical requirements pertaining to the return and filing of the indictment, the loss or destruction of indictments, the return of successive or superseding indictments. The form of the indictment is governed by detailed requirements concerning the caption, the form of accusation, the allegation of venue, the conclusion, i. e., "against the peace and dignity of the people", and other such statements, the citation of statutes violated, the signature of the prosecutor or the grand jury foreman or both, the endorsement of the phrase "a true bill", and the names of witnesses. There are occasional problems arising from mistakes in grammar or spelling, and erasures and interlineations. None of these technical concerns have a significant impact on criminal procedure. Compliance with required details usually becomes routine and, even if errors occur, few courts regard them as substantial enough to require reversal.

3. There are questions of more that technical significance, not covered by the principal cases, which are worthy of a brief mention:

(a) The accused is frequently identified in an indictment by one name and several aliases. Some courts have concluded that such a practice needlessly prejudices an accused unless the aliases are relevant to the facts of the case and will be proved.

(b) The usual practice in alleging the time and place of the offense is to state the day when, and the county or district where, the offense occurred. This is generally deemed sufficient, but the accused may be entitled to a bill of particulars giving the specific time of day and the street address of the occurrence in question. See People v. Blanchett, 33 Ill.2d 527, 212 N.E.2d 97 (1965); Sparks v. State, 273 So.2d 74 (Fla.1973) ("on or about" a certain date is proper).

(c) The indictment usually does not have to negative or deny the existence of exceptions or provisos in the statute which will exempt the accused from liability. There are many instances where the general rule does not apply. Some exceptions are so deeply incorporated in the description of the offense, e. g., "Whoever, without lawful justification, kills another, etc." that the indictment will have to negate the existence of the exception.

(d) The jurisdictions adopt different approaches to surplus allegations in a charge. For example, it may not be necessary to allege that murder was committed by strangulation but, if it is alleged, must it be proved? The courts split on the answer.

(e) It is generally not necessary to allege a lesser included offense in an indictment, but some jurisdictions require it under certain circumstances.

2. VARIANCE AND AMENDMENT

STIRONE v. UNITED STATES

Supreme Court of the United States, 1960.
361 U.S. 212, 80 S.Ct. 270.

MR. JUSTICE BLACK delivered the opinion of the Court.

Petitioner Nicholas Stirone was indicted and convicted in a federal court for unlawfully interfering with interstate commerce in violation of the Hobbs Act. The crucial question here is whether he was convicted of an offense not charged in the indictment.

So far as relevant to this question the indictment charged the following:

From 1951 until 1953, a man by the name of William G. Rider had a contract to supply ready-mixed concrete from his plant in Pennsylvania to be used for the erection of a steel-processing plant at Allenport, Pennsylvania. For the purpose of performing this contract Rider

> "caused supplies and materials [sand] to move in interstate commerce between various points in the United States and the site of his plant for the manufacture or mixing of ready mixed concrete, and more particularly, from outside the State of Pennsylvania into the State of Pennsylvania."

The indictment went on to charge that Stirone, using his influential union position,

> "did . . . unlawfully obstruct, delay [and] affect interstate commerce between the several states of the United States and the movement of the aforesaid materials and supplies in such commerce, by extortion . . . of $31,274.-13 . . . induced by fear and by the wrongful use of threats of labor disputes and threats of the loss of, and obstruction and prevention of, performance of his contract to supply ready mixed concrete."

The district judge, over petitioner's objection as to its materiality and relevancy, permitted the Government to offer evidence of an effect on interstate commerce not only in sand brought into Pennsylvania from other States but also in interference with steel shipments from the steel plant in Pennsylvania into Michigan and Kentucky. Again over petitioner's objection the trial judge charged the jury that so far as the interstate commerce aspect of the case was concerned, Stirone's guilt could be rested either on a finding that (1) sand used to make the concrete "had been shipped from another state into Pennsylvania" or (2) "Mr. Rider's concrete was used for constructing a mill which would manufacture articles of steel to be shipped in interstate commerce　. . ." from Pennsylvania into other States. . . .

We agree with the Court of Appeals that Rider's dependence on shipments of sand from outside Pennsylvania to carry on his ready-mixed concrete business entitled him to the Hobbs Act's protection against interruption or stoppage of his commerce in sand by extortion of the kind that the jury found the petitioner had committed here. That Act speaks in broad language, manifesting a purpose to use all the constitutional power Congress has to punish interference with interstate commerce by extortion, robbery or physical violence. The Act outlaws such interference "in any way or degree." 18 U.S. C. § 1951(a), 18 U.S.C.A. § 1951(a). Had Rider's business been hindered or destroyed, interstate movements of sand to him would have slackened or stopped. The trial jury was entitled to find that commerce was saved from such a blockage by Rider's compliance with Stirone's coercive and illegal demands. It was to free commerce from such destructive burdens that the Hobbs Act was passed. United States v. Green, 350 U.S. 415, 420, 76 S.Ct. 522, 525.

Whether prospective steel shipments from the new steel mills would be enough, alone, to bring this transaction under the Act is a more difficult question. We need not decide this, however, since we agree　. . .　that it was error to submit that question to the jury and that the error cannot be dismissed as merely an insignificant variance between allegation and proof and thus harmless error as in Berger v. United States, 295 U.S. 78, 55 S.Ct. 629. The crime charged here is a felony and the Fifth Amendment requires that prosecution be begun by indictment.

Ever since Ex parte Bain, 121 U.S. 1, 7 S.Ct. 781, was decided in 1887, it has been the rule that after an indictment has been returned its charges may not be broadened through amendment except by the grand jury itself.

* * *

The *Bain* case which has never been disapproved, stands for the rule that a court cannot permit a defendant to be tried on charges that are not made in the indictment against him. Yet the court did permit that in this case. The indictment here cannot fairly be read as charging interference with movements of steel from Pennsylvania to other States nor does the Court of Appeals appear to have so read it. The grand jury which found this indictment was satisfied to charge that Stirone's conduct interfered with interstate importation of sand. But neither this nor any other court can know that the grand jury would have been willing to charge that Stirone's conduct would interfere with interstate exportation of steel from a mill later to be built with Rider's concrete. And it cannot be said with certainty that with a new basis for conviction added, Stirone was convicted solely on the charge made in the indictment the grand jury returned. Although the trial court did not permit a formal amendment of the indictment, the effect of what it did was the same. And the addition charging interference with steel exports here is neither trivial, useless, nor innocuous. While there was a variance in the sense of a variation between pleading and proof, that variation here destroyed the defendant's substantial right to be tried only on charges presented in an indictment returned by a grand jury. Deprivation of such a basic right is far too serious to be treated as nothing more than a variance and then dismissed as harmless error.

Here, as the trial court charged the jury, there are two essential elements of a Hobbs Act crime: interference with commerce, and extortion. Both elements have to be charged. Neither is surplusage and neither can be treated as surplusage. The charge that interstate commerce is affected is critical since the Federal Government's jurisdiction of this crime rests only on that interference. It follows that when only one particular kind of commerce is charged to have been burdened a conviction must rest on that charge and not another, even though it be assumed that under an indictment drawn in general terms a conviction might rest upon a showing that commerce of one kind or another had been burdened. The right to have the grand jury make the charge on its own judgment is a substantial right which cannot be taken away with or without court amendment. Here, as in the *Bain* case, we cannot know whether the grand jury would have included in its indictment a charge that commerce in steel from a nonexistent steel mill had been interfered with. Yet because of the court's admission of evidence and under its charge this might have been the basis upon which the trial jury convicted petitioner. If so, he was convicted on a charge the grand jury never made against him. This was fatal error.

Reversed.

NOTE

Variance is often found harmless. See Jacobs v. United States, 395 F. 2d 469 (8th Cir. 1968) (variance between dates alleged and those proved not fatal); United States v. Williams, 254 F.Supp. 199 (D.Mont.1966) (it is not necessary to prove exact date alleged and proof of crime on another date is proper if the date proved is within the statute of limitations and prior to indictment); Gray v. United States, 314 F.2d 838 (5th Cir. 1963) (allegation that offense occurred in Miami, proof that it occurred in Miami Beach is not prejudicial); Rathban v. United States, 236 F.2d 514 (10th Cir. 1956) (extortion of 100,000 shares of stock claimed, proper to prove extortion of 120,000 shares). But see United States v. Russano, 257 F.2d 712 (2nd Cir. 1958) (allegation of continuing conspiracy is improperly at variance with proof of separate conspiracies); United States v. Varelli, 407 F.2d 735 (7th Cir. 1969) (same).

The problems of variance are of far less significance in jurisdictions which permit prosecution by complaint or information. Both forms of charge are subject to amendment usually up until the time of verdict. The Fifth Amendment precludes any Congressional authorization to allow federal felony prosecution by information, but the grand jury requirement in the Fifth Amendment has never been thought to apply to state prosecutions.

PEOPLE v. JONES

Supreme Court of Illinois, 1973.
53 Ill.2d 460, 292 N.E.2d 361.

UNDERWOOD, CHIEF JUSTICE.

James Jones was convicted of armed robbery following a jury trial in Macon County on November 16, 1970, and sentenced to imprisonment for a term of eight to twenty-four years. Claiming that he had been denied his constitutional right to be indicted by a grand jury, defendant appealed to the Appellate Court. That court reversed his conviction, and we granted the State's petition for leave to appeal.

On October 7, 1970, the Macon County grand jury returned an indictment charging defendant Jones and Michael Anderson with armed robbery. Its relevant portions are:

> "The Grand Jurors . . . present, that Michael Anderson and James J. Jones, . . . the twenty-fourth day of September in the year of our Lord One Thousand Nine Hundred and Seventy, at and in the County of Macon aforesaid, in the State of Illinois, aforesaid, at 406 East Cantrell Street, City of Decatur, committed the offense of armed robbery, in violation of Chapter 38, Section 18–2, Ill. Rev.Stat., 1969, in that they knowingly took an indeterminate amount of United States currency from the person and presence of Charles Mundy, by threatening the imminent use of force, while armed with a dangerous weapon, to-wit: a Winchester, single-barrel, sawed-off shotgun . . . ."

On the morning of trial, November 16, 1970, the State's Attorney moved to amend the indictment by substituting the name "Delbert R. Mundy" for "Charles Mundy"; the motion was granted over defendant's objection. Testimony at trial established that Charles Mundy was Delbert R. Mundy's son. Defendant was found guilty of armed robbery under the amended indictment.

The sole issue before us is whether the misnomer of the armed-robbery victim in this case constituted a formal defect under our amendment statute, section 111–5 of the Code of Criminal Procedure, which provides:

> "An indictment, information or complaint which charges the commission of an offense in accordance with Section 111–3 of this Code shall not be dismissed and may be amended on motion by the

State's Attorney or defendant at any time because of formal defects, including:

    (a) Any miswriting, misspelling or grammatical error;

    (b) Any misjoinder of the parties defendant;

    (c) Any misjoinder of the offense charged;

    (d) The presence of any unnecessary allegation;

    (e) The failure to negative any exception, any excuse or proviso contained in the statute defining the offense; or

    (f) The use of alternative or disjunctive allegations as to the acts, means, intents or results charged."

It is, of course, clear from a reading of the statute that its enumeration of certain defects as "formal" is not intended to be exclusive.

The State contends that proof of the armed-robbery victim's name is not an essential element of the crime charged and that an indictment would be sufficient without it. If this is so, they urge that such an error in pleading must be formal and may be properly amended before trial. In support of this position, the State cites the *Crouch* and *Adams* cases in which we held that the identities of "victims" in forgery and sale-of-narcotics cases were unnecessary allegations in indictments charging those offenses.

In *Crouch* we said that "[t]he gist of the offense of forgery is the intent to defraud involved in the making of a forged instrument or knowingly uttering the same." Similarly, in *Adams* we noted: "The statute creating the offense makes no reference to the purchaser of the drug and his identity is not an element of the crime. The gravamen of the offense is the unlawful sale itself."

Those cases are clearly distinguishable from the offense of armed robbery, which requires the taking of property from the person or presence of another by the use or threat of force, while armed with a dangerous weapon. Armed robbery is one of those crimes whose impact is focused more directly upon an individual victim than upon society generally. Danger to the person, as well as the taking of property, is the essence of the crime. We believe the law to be well stated in People v. Walker (1955): "Where an indictment charges an offense either against persons or property, the name of the person or property injured, if known, must be stated, and the allegation must be proved as alleged." The opinion in *Walker* continued. "Proof of the Christian name is unnecessary, however, where the facts in evidence leave no doubt as to the identity of the person."

A holding that the identity of an armed-robbery victim is an essential allegation of an indictment charging that offense is, however, not dispositive of the issue of whether the misstatement of identity is a formal or substantial defect. We have examined with care the authorities from other States cited to us and find a nearly even split among those jurisdictions which have considered this question. Those cases which permitted the amendment of a victim's identity through a change of first name tend to be more persuasive, however, because of their greater currency. [Cases from other jurisdictions cited.] This trend away from the formalism which characterized criminal pleading in the past is embodied in our section 111–5, as disclosed by the chief draftsman's commentary: "The committee felt that the practical limitations should overcome the conceptual ones and provided for the efficient amendment of formal defects."

The liberalization of criminal pleading also reflects a lessening in importance of the indictment's secondary functions. The indictment as a means of informing defendants of particulars concerning the case is now far overshadowed by the array of discovery procedures available to the defense. Similarly, the time when an indictment defined the limits of jeopardy has passed and a prior prosecution on the same facts may be proved by resort to the record. The primary safeguard of indictment by grand jury which remains secured to criminal defendants, is to protect individuals from the caprice of the public prosecutor. "The very purpose of the requirement that a man be indicted by grand jury is to limit his jeopardy to offenses charged by a group of his fellow citizens acting independently of either prosecuting attorney or judge."

We believe that this constitutionally required protection has been afforded this defendant and that the particular facts in this case demonstrate the amendment of the victim's first name to be a mere formality. Where, as here, no hint of surprise or prejudice to the defendant is shown, allowance of such an amendment is not error.

The judgment of the Appellate Court for the Fourth District is reversed and the judgment of the circuit court of Macon County is affirmed.

Appellate court reversed; circuit court affirmed.

NOTE

The bill of particulars is a device of substantial vintage, yet there is no consistent theory concerning either its purpose or its necessity. The bill of particulars is not intended to be a discovery device, yet its purpose is to provide the accused with information about the details of the charge so that he may prepare his defense and proceed to trial without the risk of unfair surprise. Anything that gives a party information about the case is a discovery device of some kind. The bill of particulars may not be ordered solely for discovery purposes; in any event, the scope of a bill is quite narrow. The principal use of the bill is to secure a declaration of the precise date and time and place of the occurrences the government will prove. In a burglary case, this would mean the time of day and the street address of the burglarized premises; in a conspiracy case, the date, time and address of the meetings of the conspirators, and the names of the persons at the meeting. Occasionally the bill concerns the names of the persons present at the occurrence. For example, in narcotics sale cases, the name of the purchaser is not in most jurisdictions, a necessary allegation, and bills are often granted to secure this name. In cases prosecuted under accountability theories, the particular acts which the government will prove in order to establish accountability for the conduct of other persons are the subjects of bills. The bill cannot be used to discover the names of the witnesses the prosecution will call or the evidence it will use, since an accusation of crime can be made sufficiently complete without resort to such matters.

The granting of a bill of particulars is purely discretionary and for nearly every decision allowing a bill in regard to certain items, a decision denying it as to the same items can be found. A bill of particulars may be amended at any time, but substantial variances between the bill and the proof at trial are improper.

Chapter 12

THE RIGHT TO BAIL

A. THE BAIL SYSTEM

THE BAIL REFORM ACT OF 1966

(18 U.S.C.A. §§ 3146–50.)

§ 3146.   **Release in noncapital cases prior to trial**

(a) Any person charged with an offense, other than an offense punishable by death, shall, at his appearance before a judicial officer, be ordered released pending trial on his personal recognizance or upon the execution of an unsecured appearance bond in an amount specified by the judicial officer, unless the officer determines, in the exercise of his discretion, that such a release will not reasonably assure the appearance of the person as required.   When such a determination is made, the judicial officer shall, either in lieu of or in addition to the above methods of release, impose the first of the following conditions of release which will reasonably assure the appearance of the person for trial or, if no single condition gives that assurance, any combination of the following conditions:

(1) place the person in the custody of a designated person or organization agreeing to supervise him;

(2) place restrictions on the travel, association, or place of abode of the person during the period of release;

(3) require the execution of an appearance bond in a specified amount and the deposit in the registry of the court, in cash or other security as directed, of a sum not to exceed 10 per centum of the amount of the bond, such deposit to be returned upon the performance of the conditions of release;

(4) require the execution of a bail bond with sufficient solvent sureties, or the deposit of cash in lieu thereof; or

(5) impose any other condition deemed reasonably necessary to assure appearance as required, including a condition requiring that the person return to custody after specified hours.

(b) In determining which conditions of release will reasonably assure appearance, the judicial officer shall, on the basis of available information, take into account the nature and circumstances of the offense charged, the weight of the evidence against the accused, the accused's family ties, employment, financial resources, character and mental condition, the length of his residence in the community, his record of convictions, and his record of appearance at court proceedings

779

or of flight to avoid prosecution or failure to appear at court proceedings.

(c) A judicial officer authorizing the release of a person under this section shall issue an appropriate order containing a statement of the conditions imposed, if any, shall inform such person of the penalties applicable to violations of the conditions of his release and shall advise him that a warrant for his arrest will be issued immediately upon any such violation.

(d) A person for whom conditions of release are imposed and who after twenty-four hours from the time of the release hearing continues to be detained as a result of his inability to meet the conditions of release, shall, upon application, be entitled to have the conditions reviewed by the judicial officer who imposed them. Unless the conditions of release are amended and the person is thereupon released, the judicial officer shall set forth in writing the reasons for requiring the conditions imposed. A person who is ordered released on a condition which requires that he return to custody after specified hours shall, upon application, be entitled to a review by the judicial officer who imposed the condition. Unless the requirement is removed and the person is thereupon released on another condition, the judicial officer shall set forth in writing the reasons for continuing the requirement. In the event that the judicial officer who imposed conditions of release is not available, any other judicial officer in the district may review such conditions.

(e) A judicial officer ordering the release of a person on any condition specified in this section may at any time amend his order to impose additional or different conditions of release: *Provided,* That if the imposition of such addition or different conditions results in the detention of the person as a result of his inability to meet such conditions or in the release of the person on a condition requiring him to return to custody after specified hours, the provisions of subsection (d) shall apply.

(f) Information stated in, or offered in connection with, any order entered pursuant to this section need not conform to the rules pertaining to the admissibility of evidence in a court of law.

(g) Nothing contained in this section shall be construed to prevent the disposition of any case or class of cases by forfeiture of collateral security where such disposition is authorized by the court.

§ 3147. Appeal from conditions of release

(a) A person who is detained, or whose release on a condition requiring him to return to custody after specified hours is continued, after review of his application pursuant to section 3146(d) or section 3146(e) by a judicial officer, other than a judge of the court having original jurisdiction over the offense with which he is charged or a judge of a United States court of appeals or a Justice of the Supreme Court, may move the court having original jurisdiction over the offense with which he is charged to amend the order. Said motion shall be determined promptly.

(b) In any case in which a person is detained after (1) a court denies a motion under subsection (a) to amend an order imposing conditions of release, or (2) conditions of release have been imposed or amended by a judge of the court having original jurisdiction over the offense charged, an appeal may be taken to the court having appellate jurisdiction over such court. Any order so appealed shall be affirmed if it is supported by the proceedings below. If the order is not so supported, the court may remand the case for a further hearing, or may, with or without additional evidence, order the person released pursuant to section 3146(a). The appeal shall be determined promptly.

§ 3148.   Release in capital cases or after conviction

A person (1) who is charged with an offense punishable by death, or (2) who has been convicted of an offense and is either awaiting sentence or sentence review .   .   .   or has filed an appeal or a petition for a writ of certiorari, shall be treated in accordance with the provisions of section 3146 unless the court or judge has reason to believe that no one or more conditions of release will reasonably assure that the person will not flee or pose a danger to any other person or to the community. If such a risk of flight or danger is believed to exist, or if it appears that an appeal is frivolous or taken for delay, the person may be ordered detained. The provisions of section 3147 shall not apply to persons described in this section: *Provided*, That other rights to judicial review of conditions of release or orders of detention shall not be affected.

§ 3150.   Penalties for failure to appear

Whoever, having been released pursuant to his chapter, willfully fails to appear before any court or judicial officer as required, shall, subject to the provisions of the Federal Rules of Criminal Procedure, incur a forfeiture of any security which was given or pledged for his release, and, in addition, shall, (1) if he was released in connection with a charge of felony, or while awaiting sentence or pending appeal or certiorari after conviction of any offense, be fined not more than $5,000 or imprisoned not more than five years, or both, or (2) if he was released in connection with a charge of misdemeanor, be fined not more than the maximum provided for such misdemeanor or imprisoned for not more than one year, or both, or (3) if he was released for appearance as a material witness, shall be fined not more than $1,000 or imprisoned for not more than one year, or both.

NOTES

1.   The question of bail first arises on the accused's initial appearance before a judicial officer. In some instances, where minor offenses such as traffic tickets are involved, a scheduled amount may be posted for bail without resort to an immediate court appearance. In that connection, there has been an increasing trend, particularly in large metropolitan areas, toward the use of a summons for traditional petty offenses to simply notify the accused of his responsibility to appear in court at a particular time.

2. The administration of the Bail Reform Act was viewed as follows in a Report to Congress: The Federal Bail Process Fosters Inequities 17–18 (Comptroller General 1978):

> "Because judicial officers do not have the guidance and information they need to make sound bail decisions, the Bail Reform Act has been inconsistently applied. On occasion, defendants have been treated unfairly or society has been exposed to unnecessary risks. Judicial officers need information and guidance on the purposes of bail and in understanding and evaluating how the criteria listed in the act relate to determining the bail conditions which will reasonably assure a defendant's appearance. They also need complete and accurate personal information on defendants to help them in making bail decisions. Once judicial officers are supplied with this information, they should be in a better position to establish a defendant's risk of nonappearance. In addition, the use of blanket conditions of release imposed without regard to the defendant's danger of flight and excessive reliance on financial conditions of release need to be eliminated.

> "Because the bail process dramatically affects the lives and families of defendants and society, concerted efforts are needed to better assure that this process is carried out as uniformly and as fairly as possible."

3. Following the Bail Reform Act of 1966, many states made major changes in their bail laws. Even before then, Illinois had enacted a law which allowed the alleged offender to deposit 10 per cent of the amount set for bail to gain release. Upon disposition of the charge, one per cent of the bail was retained by the clerk for administrative costs and the remainder was returned. Does the one per cent retention charge violate equal protection? Can it result in a cost assessed against a not guilty person? In Schilb v. Kuebel, 404 U.S. 357, 92 S.Ct. 479 (1971), the Court rejected a bailed defendant's arguments, noting:

> "We are compelled to note preliminarily that the attack on the Illinois bail statutes, in a very distinct sense, is paradoxical. The benefits of the new system, as compared with the old, are conceded. And the appellants recognize that under the [old] system Schilb's particular bail bond cost would have been 10% of his bail, or $75; that this premium price for his pretrial freedom, once paid, was irretrievable; and that, if he could not raise the $75, he would have been consigned to jail until his trial. Thus, under the old system the cost of Schilb's pretrial freedom was $75, but under the new it was only $7.50. While acknowledging this obvious benefit of the statutory reform, Schilb and his co-appellants decry the classification the statutes make and present the usual argument that the legislation must be struck down because it does not reform enough.

> * * *

> "We refrain from nullifying this Illinois statute that, with its companion sections, has brought reform and needed relief to the State's bail system."

4. Once the trial judge resolves to admit a defendant to bail, the person so admitted must execute an appearance bond. The bond must be signed by a surety who binds himself to pay the face amount of the bond if the defendant fails to appear pursuant to the orders of the court. General-

ly, sureties can be divided into two classes: individual sureties and professional bondsmen. Individual sureties must go through a procedure termed justification whereby an affidavit is submitted disclosing the extent of the surety's property used to secure the bond in question. While justification is generally dispensed with where approved corporate sureties are involved, it is necessary, in the case of smaller, independent sureties, to insure that the same property is not pledged to secure a great number of individual bonds. See United States v. Nebbia, 357 F.2d 303 (2d Cir. 1966) ("if the court lacks confidence in a surety's purpose or ability to secure the appearance of a bail defendant, it may refuse its approval of a bond even though the financial standing of bail is beyond question"); United States v. Melville, 309 F.Supp. 822 (S.D.N.Y.1970) (trial judge has discretion to require justification even in the case of a professional surety).

5. The professional bail bondsman is usually an agent of a surety company who has authority from the company to write bonds up to a certain amount. See generally D. Freed & P. Wald, Bail in the United States (1964). The regulation of bondsmen is a matter left exclusively to state control and the licensing considerations vary substantially among the states. There is substantial weight to the argument that "the bail bond business [is] a pattern of institutionalized corruption", 8A J. Moore, Moore's Federal Practice § 46.12 [3], at 46–69 (Cipes ed. 1972). Some of the arguments amassed by Professor Moore in deprecating the bail bond system are: (1) the intimate relationship of bail bondsmen to the organized crime syndicate; (2) the fact that bondsmen usually have initial contact with an arrested person puts them in a unique position to act as ombudsmen for particular defense attorneys; (3) the fact that bondsmen often use illegal tactics in recapturing defendants who jump bail; and (4) statistics demonstrate that bail jumping is not very high to begin with. In light of these problems, are professional bondsmen of any value to the administration of the bail system? Can public agencies sufficiently administer the bail system in the absence of bondsmen?

6. Recent modernizations of the state bail systems carry few practical implications other than to suggest that counsel should be sensitive to undue pretrial incarceration. It is only natural for the prosecutor to argue for high bail in a case in which he firmly believes that guilt is apparent. And excessive bail can almost invariably be classified as harmless error when the merits of a conviction are reviewed. See Whitty v. State, 34 Wis.2d 278, 149 N.W.2d 557 (1967). However, where the defendant has ties to the community—and the risk of danger through a repeated offense is negligible —vociferous arguments against bail tend to diminish the prosecutor's credibility. On the other hand, arguments clearly delineating a risk of flight, coupled with a danger to the community, are appropriate in certain cases. Issues of importance are: (1) the defendant's proclivity toward crime through his past record; (2) the danger which he presents because of the manner in which he is alleged to have committed the offense; and (3) the high risk of flight because of either minimal ties to the community or the severity of the potential penalty. Where a defendant has previously jumped bail, that factor may clearly be taken into account. See Babb v. United States, 414 F.2d 719 (10th Cir. 1968).

7. Upon breach of the conditions of release, the bond may be forfeited. In instances where a forfeiture is ordered, trial judges, in most jurisdictions, retain the power to set aside the forfeiture before judgment is entered. See United States v. Kirkman, 426 F.2d 747 (4th Cir. 1970); United States v. Egan, 394 F.2d 262 (2d Cir. 1968). A defendant who "jumps"

bail subjects himself to the prosecution for such conduct; but a motion to forfeit bail is not necessarily a requirement to initiation of a subsequent charge for bail jumping. See United States v. DePugh, 434 F.2d 548 (8th Cir. 1970). Where a defendant returns after an interim period of bail jumping, he may be remitted to bail under the same or new conditions of release. However, because a defendant who has once jumped bail obviously evidences a prospensity toward flight, the trial judge can reconsider the conditions of bond.

B. BAIL UPON CHARGE

STACK v. BOYLE

Supreme Court of the United States, 1951.
342 U.S. 1, 72 S.Ct. 1.

MR. CHIEF JUSTICE VINSON delivered the opinion of the Court.

Indictments have been returned in the Southern District of California charging the twelve petitioners with conspiring to violate the Smith Act. Upon their arrest, bail was fixed for each petitioner in the widely varying amounts of $2,500, $7,500, $75,000 and $100,000. On motion of petitioner Schneiderman following arrest in the Southern District of New York, his bail was reduced to $50,000 before his removal to California. On motion of the Government to increase bail in the case of other petitioners, and after several intermediate procedural steps not material to the issues presented here, bail was fixed in the District Court for the Southern District of California in the uniform amount of $50,000 for each petitioner.

Petitioners moved to reduce bail on the ground that bail as fixed was excessive under the Eighth Amendment. In support of their motion, petitioners submitted statements as to their financial resources, family relationships, health, prior criminal records, and other information. The only evidence offered by the Government was a certified record showing that four persons previously convicted under the Smith Act in the Southern District of New York had forfeited bail. No evidence was produced relating those four persons to the petitioners in this case. At a hearing on the motion, petitioners were examined by the District Judge and cross-examined by an attorney for the Government. Petitioners' factual statements stand uncontroverted.

After their motion to reduce bail was denied, petitioners filed applications for habeas corpus in the same District Court. Upon consideration of the record on the motion to reduce bail, the writs were denied. The Court of Appeals for the Ninth Circuit affirmed. Prior to filing their petition for certiorari in this Court, petitioners filed with MR. JUSTICE DOUGLAS an application for bail and an alternative application for habeas corpus seeking interim relief. Both applications were referred to the Court and the matter was set down for argument on specific questions covering the issues raised by this case.

Relief in this type of case must be speedy if it is to be effective. The petition for certiorari and the full record are now before the Court and, since the questions presented by the petition have been fully briefed and argued, we consider it appropriate to dispose of the petition for certiorari at this time. Accordingly, the petition for certiorari is granted for review of questions important to the administration of criminal justice.[1]

First. From the passage of the Judiciary Act of 1789, 1 Stat. 73, 91, to the present Federal Rules of Criminal Procedure, Rule 46(a)(1), federal law has unequivocally provided that a person arrested for a non-capital offense *shall* be admitted to bail. This traditional right to freedom before conviction permits the unhampered preparation of a defense, and serves to prevent the infliction of punishment prior to conviction. See Hudson v. Parker, 156 U.S. 277, 285, 15 S.Ct. 450, 453 (1895). Unless this right to bail before trial is preserved, the presumption of innocence, secured only after centuries of struggle, would lose its meaning.

The right to release before trial is conditioned upon the accused's giving adequate assurance that he will stand trial and submit to sentence if found guilty. Ex parte Milburn, 9 Pet. 704, 710 (1835). Like the ancient practice of securing the oaths of responsible persons to stand as sureties for the accused, the modern practice of requiring a bail bond or the deposit of a sum of money subject to forfeiture serves as additional assurance of the presence of an accused. Bail set at a figure higher than an amount reasonably calculated to fulfill this purpose is "excessive" under the Eighth Amendment. . . .

Since the function of bail is limited, the fixing of bail for any individual defendant must be based upon standards relevant to the purpose of assuring the presence of that defendant. The traditional standards as expressed in the Federal Rules of Criminal Procedure[2] are to be applied in each case to each defendant. In this case petitioners are charged with offenses under the Smith Act and, if found guilty, their convictions are subject to review with the scrupulous care demanded by our Constitution. Upon final judgment of conviction, petitioners face imprisonment of not more than five years and a fine of not more than $10,000. It is not denied that bail for each petitioner has been fixed in a sum much higher than that usually imposed for offenses with like penalties and yet there has been no factual showing to justify such action in this case. The Government asks the courts to depart from the norm by assuming, without the introduction of evidence, that each petitioner is a pawn in a conspiracy and will, in obedience to a superior, flee the jurisdiction. To infer

1. In view of our action in granting and making final disposition of the petition for certiorari, we have no occasion to determine the power of a single Justice or Circuit Justice to fix bail pending disposition of a petition for certiorari in a case of this kind.

2. Rule 46(c). "Amount. If the defendant is admitted to bail, the amount thereof shall be such as in the judgment of the commissioner or court or judge or justice will insure the presence of the defendant, having regard to the nature and circumstances of the offense charged, the weight of the evidence against him, the financial ability of the defendant to give bail and the character of the defendant."

from the fact of indictment alone a need for bail in an unusually high amount is an arbitrary act. Such conduct would inject into our own system of government the very principles of totalitarianism which Congress was seeking to guard against in passing the statute under which petitioners have been indicted.

If bail in an amount greater than that usually fixed for serious charges of crimes is required in the case of any of the petitioners, that is a matter to which evidence should be directed in a hearing so that the constitutional rights of each petitioner may be preserved. In the absence of such a showing, we are of the opinion that the fixing of bail before trial in these cases cannot be squared with the statutory and constitutional standards for admission to bail. .   .   .

MR. JUSTICE MINTON took no part in the consideration or decision of this case.

By MR. JUSTICE JACKSON, whom MR. JUSTICE FRANKFURTER joins.

I think the principles governing allowance of bail have been misunderstood or too casually applied in these cases and that they should be returned to the Circuit Justice or the District Courts for reconsideration in the light of standards which it is our function to determine. We have heard the parties on only four specific questions relating to bail before conviction—two involving considerations of law and of fact which should determine the amount of bail, and two relating to the procedure for correcting any departure therefrom. I consider first the principles which govern release of accused persons upon bail pending their trial.

The practice of admission to bail, as it has evolved in Anglo-American law, is not a device for keeping persons in jail upon mere accusation until it is found convenient to give them a trial. On the contrary, the spirit of the procedure is to enable them to stay out of jail until a trial has found them guilty. Without this conditional privilege, even those wrongly accused are punished by a period of imprisonment while awaiting trial and are handicapped in consulting counsel, searching for evidence and witnesses, and preparing a defense. To open a way of escape from this handicap and possible injustice, Congress commands allowance of bail for one under charge of any offense not punishable by death, Fed.Rules Crim.Proc. 46(a)(1) providing: "A person arrested for an offense not punishable by death shall be admitted to bail .   .   ." before conviction.

Admission to bail always involves a risk that the accused will take flight. That is a calculated risk which the law takes as the price of our system of justice. We know that Congress anticipated that bail would enable some escapes, because it provided a procedure for dealing with them. Fed.Rules Crim.Proc., 46(f).

In allowance of bail, the duty of the judge is to reduce the risk by fixing an amount reasonably calculated to hold the accused available for trial and its consequence. Fed.Rules Crim.Proc., 46(c). But the judge is not free to make the sky the limit, because the Eighth

Amendment to the Constitution says: "Excessive bail shall not be required   .   .   .."

Congress has reduced this generality in providing more precise standards, stating that ".   .   . the amount thereof shall be such as in the judgment of the commissioner or court or judge or justice will insure the presence of the defendant, having regard to the nature and circumstances of the offense charged, the weight of the evidence against him, the financial ability of the defendant to give bail and the character of the defendant." Fed.Rules Crim.Proc., 46(c).

These statutory standards are not challenged as unconstitutional, rather the amounts of bail established for these petitioners are alleged to exceed these standards. We submitted no constitutional questions to argument by the parties, and it is our duty to avoid constitutional issues if possible. For me, the record is inadequate to say what amounts would be reasonable in any particular one of these cases and I regard it as not the function of this Court to do so. Furthermore, the whole Court agrees that the remedy pursued in the circumstances of this case is inappropraite to test the question and bring it here. But I do think there is a fair showing that these congressionally enacted standards have not been correctly applied.

It is complained that the District Court fixed a uniform blanket bail chiefly by consideration of the nature of the accusation and did not take into account the difference in circumstances between different defendants. If this occurred, it is a clear violation of Rule 46(c). Each defendant stands before the bar of justice as an individual. Even on a conspiracy charge defendants do not lose their separateness or identity. While it might be possible that these defendants are identical in financial ability, character and relation to the charge—elements Congress has directed to be regarded in fixing bail—I think it violates the law of probabilities. Each accused is entitled to any benefits due to his good record, and misdeeds or a bad record should prejudice only those who are guilty of them. The question when application for bail is made relates to each one's trustworthiness to appear for trial and what security will supply reasonable assurance of his appearance.

Complaint further is made that the courts below have been unduly influenced by recommendations of very high bail made by the grand jury. It is not the function of the grand jury to fix bail, and its volunteered advice is not governing. Since the grand jury is a secret body, ordinarily hearing no evidence but the prosecution's, attended by no counsel except the prosecuting attorneys, it is obvious that it is not in a position to make an impartial recommendation. Its suggestion may indicate that those who have heard the evidence for the prosecution regard it as strongly indicative that the accused may be guilty of the crime charged. It could not mean more than that without hearing the defense, and it adds nothing to the inference from the fact of indictment. Such recommendations are better left unmade and if made should be given no weight.

But the protest charges, and the defect in the proceedings below appears to be, that, provoked by the flight of certain Communists after conviction, the Government demands and public opinion supports a use of the bail power to keep Communist defendants in jail before conviction. Thus, the amount is said to have been fixed not as a reasonable assurance of their presence at the trial but also as an assurance they would remain in jail. There seems reason to believe that this may have been the spirit to which the courts below have yielded, and it is contrary to the whole policy and philosophy of bail. This is not to say that every defendant is entitled to such bail as he can provide, but he is entitled to an opportunity to make it in a reasonable amount. I think the whole matter should be reconsidered by the appropriate judges in the traditional spirit of bail procedure.

The other questions we have heard argued relate to the remedy appropriate when the standards for amount of bail are misapplied. Of course, procedural rights so vital cannot be without means of vindication. In view of the nature of the writ of habeas corpus, we should be reluctant to say that under no circumstances would it be appropriate. But that writ will best serve its purpose and be best protected from discrediting abuse if it is reserved for cases in which no other procedure will present the issues to the courts. Its use as a substitute for appeals or as an optional alternative to other remedies is not to be encouraged. Habeas corpus is not, in the absence of extraordinary circumstances, the procedure to test reasonableness of bail. . . .

NOTES

1. Given the Bail Reform Act's favoritism for unsecured pretrial release, the magistrate or trial judge who passes on the bail question must, in order to impose more restrictive conditions, make a factual finding that such conditions are essential to secure the appearance of the defendant. Although the practice among the various jurisdictions with regard to the fact finding process upon bail application is substantially diverse, both the prosecution and defense attorneys are obligated to bring to the court's attention a feasible plan for release if one can be devised on the particular facts involved. See United States v. Alston, 420 F.2d 171 (D.C.Cir. 1969); Vauss v. United States, 365 F.2d 956 (D.C.Cir. 1966).

In the federal courts, detailed findings of fact are necessary to assure informed appellate review of the issuing officer's determination of bail. Fed.R.App.P. 9(b); Febre v. United States, 400 U.S. 1225, 91 S.Ct. 40 (1969). In the state courts, where the violent crime caseloads are much greater, the requirements are not as strict. But see In re Podesto, 15 Cal. 3d 921, 127 Cal.Rptr. 97, 544 P.2d 1297 (1976) (requiring brief statement of reasons for denying bail through supervisory power over state criminal procedure).

2. While the court may consider hearsay in deciding whether to grant bail, it cannot take evidence outside the defendant and his counsel. United States v. Wind, 527 F.2d 672 (6th Cir. 1975).

3. In cases considering whether the conditions imposed provide reasonable assurance that the accused will appear for trial, indigency alone does not automatically prohibit the court from imposing financial conditions

on release. See United States v. Bronson, 433 F.2d 537 (D.C.Cir. 1970); United States v. Cook, 442 F.2d 723 (D.C.Cir. 1970).

4. The concept of preventive detention, running counter to the philosophy of the Bail Reform Act of 1966, is that the community is entitled to protection from dangerous offenders and, therefore, the bail system should be employed to detain alleged offenders where the risk that they will commit additional offenses if released is substantial. Now codified in the District of Columbia, D.C. Code Encycl. Ann. § 23–1321–32, the doctrine of preventive detention has generated a great deal of argument with regard to its constitutionality under the eighth amendment. See Hickey, Preventive Detention and the Crime of Being Dangerous, 58 Geo.L.Rev. 287 (1969); Comment, Pretrial Detention in the District of Columbia: A Common Law Approach, 62 J.Crim.L.C. & P.S. 194 (1971); Comment, Constitutional Limitations on the Conditions of Pretrial Detention, 79 Yale L.J. 941 (1970). In essence, the District of Columbia pretrial detention law stands as a partial repeal of the federal statute making bail mandatory in non-capital cases by granting a limited power to deny bail before trial. Under the Act, the offender is entitled to an adversary hearing to determine whether any conditions of release would reasonably assure the safety of the community. The hearing must result in a finding that there exists a substantial probability that the defendant committed the offense for which he is charged. Immediate appellate review is available; and limitations on the time of pretrial incarceration exist to provide some degree of procedural protection. Is such a provision constitutional under the eighth amendment excessive bail limitation? Does preventive detention trench upon the presumption of innocence?

5. Many states have different constitutional and statutory bail provisions for capital cases. Thus, a person charged with an offense for which death is a possible penalty has a heavy burden to demonstrate that he is entitled to bail. What happens in the case of a person who is alleged to have committed an offense which had been punishable by death *before* a court or legislative act nullified the death penalty or prohibited its use in a situation in which death had previously been a permissible sentence? See People ex rel. Hemingway v. Elrod, 60 Ill.2d 74, 322 N.E.2d 837 (1975), for a discussion of two conflicting approaches to this issue. For a decision which reached the opposite result, see Hudson v. McAdory, 268 So.2d 916 (Miss. 1972) (fact that death penalty is unenforceable does not nullify statutory exemption of right to bail in capital cases).

6. Consider Ill.Rev.Stat., Ch. 38, § 110–6 (1977), which was enacted in response to dictum in *Hemingway,* note 5, supra:

110—6. Grant, reduction, increase, or denial of bail]

§ 110–6. (a) Upon application by the State or the defendant the court before which the proceeding is pending may increase or reduce the amount of bail or may alter the conditions of the bail bond or grant bail where it has been previously revoked.

(b) Violation of the conditions of paragraph (a)(4) of Section 110—10 of this Code [committing a crime] shall constitute grounds for the court to increase the amount of bail, or otherwise alter the conditions of bail, or, where the alleged offense committed on bail is a forcible felony, revoke bail pursuant to the appropriate provisions of subsection (e) of this section.

(c) Reasonable notice of such application by the defendant shall be given to the State.

(d) Reasonable notice of such application by the State shall be given to the defendant, except as provided in subsection (e).

(e) Upon verified application by the State stating facts or circumstances constituting a breach or a threatened breach of any of the conditions of the bail bond the court may issue a warrant commanding any peace officer to bring the defendant without unnecessary delay before the court for a hearing on the matters set forth in the application. At the conclusion of the hearing the court may enter an order authorized by subsection (a). Where the alleged breach consists of the violation of one or more felony statutes of any jurisdiction which would be a forcible felony in Illinois and the defendant is on bail for the alleged commission of a forcible felony, the court shall revoke bail in accordance with the provisions of this subsection (e):

(1) The court shall hold the defendant without bail pending the hearing on the alleged breach; however, if the defendant is not admitted to bail the hearing shall be commenced within 10 days from the date the defendant is taken into custody or the defendant may not be held any longer without bail, unless delay is occasioned by the defendant. Where defendant occasions the delay, the running of the 10 day period is temporarily suspended and resumes at the termination of the period of delay. Where defendant occasions the delay with 5 or fewer days remaining in the 10 day period, the court may grant a period of up to 5 additional days to the State for good cause shown. The State, however, shall retain the right to proceed to hearing on the alleged violation at any time, upon reasonable notice to the defendant and the court.

(2) At a hearing on the alleged violation the State has the burden of going forward and proving the violation by clear and convincing evidence. The evidence shall be presented in open court with the right of confrontation, cross-examination, and representation by counsel. The rules of evidence applicable in criminal trials in this State shall govern the admissibility of evidence at such hearing.

(3) Upon a finding by the court that the State has established by clear and convincing evidence that the defendant has committed a forcible felony while admitted to bail, the court shall revoke the bail of the defendant and hold the defendant for trial without bail. Neither the finding of the court nor any transcript or other record of the hearing shall be admissible in evidence against the defendant in the trial of the offense for which the violation was found, and no reference of any kind whatsoever shall be made during that trial to the hearing or any evidence or the court's finding therein.

(4) If the bail of any defendant is revoked pursuant to paragraph (e)(3) of this Section, the defendant may demand and shall be entitled to be brought to trial on the offense with respect to which he was formerly released on bail within 60 days after the date on which his bail was revoked. If the defendant is not brought to trial within the 60 day period required by the preceding sentence, he shall not be held longer without bail. In computing the 60 day period, the court shall omit any

period of delay resulting from a continuance granted at the request of the defendant.

Does this statute provide for preventive detention in some instances?

7. In *Hemingway*, note 5, supra, the court indicated that where the conditions of bail are violated, the trial judge can order the defendant to be held in custody pending the disposition of his case. Under the *Hemingway* dictum, the judge can revoke bail rather than merely forfeiting the previously posted bond and setting bond in a higher amount. For a contrasting view, see the dissent of Justice Doris in Mello v. Superior Court, 117 R.I. 578, 370 A.2d 1262 (1977). Justice Doris argued that except in cases in which bail may be denied altogether, a trial judge must always set bail in some amount even if the defendant has violated the conditions of a previous bond. Is the distinction of any importance? Can very high bonds be used to achieve preventive detention even in the absence of a preventive detention statute or rule? Is such use of high bonds worthy of praise or of condemnation?

8. Appellate review of pre-trial bond is not sought in the typical case where the accused is unable to post the amount set. Often the only method of high-court review is through habeas corpus. Direct appeal is unavailable in many jurisdictions. In many states, a petition for a writ of habeas corpus can be filed in a court of review only after the reviewing court exercises its discretion to grant leave to file. The procedure can be cumbersome, and pretrial bond issues can become moot before the reviewing court acts. Even in jurisdictions which have streamlined procedures for appellate review of pre-trial bond (see, e. g., Ill.Rev.Stat., Ch. 110A, § 604(c), Supreme Court Rule 604(c) (1975)), appellate opinions on bond matters are rarely published. As a result, there are very few reviewing-court opinions on the very important subject of bail.

"Review" of pre-trial bond usually comes in the form of a motion to reduce bond filed in the trial court. As cases get older, and as they are passed from one judge to another in the course of the proceedings, trial court reduction of bail is not unusual.

C. BAIL DURING TRIAL

BITTER v. UNITED STATES

Supreme Court of the United States, 1967.
389 U.S. 15, 88 S.Ct. 6.

PER CURIAM.

Petitioner was tried on 18 counts of violating the mail fraud statute and one count of using an assumed name. On the third day of trial, the Government rested its case. This was earlier than it had announced or than petitioner had anticipated. At recess time petitioner sought leave of the court to go to his office in order to gather additional evidence for the defense. Permission for this was granted. Forty-five minutes were allotted for the recess.

Petitioner, who had previously appeared promptly at every session of the trial, was this time tardy by 37 minutes in returning to court. Without warning, hearing, or explanation the trial judge ordered petitioner into custody for the balance of the trial. Attempts by petitioner's counsel to offer explanations for petitioner's lateness were to no avail.

Defense counsel was then advised that petitioner would be kept in custody in a county jail located some 18 miles from the court. In fact, petitioner was taken about 40 miles distant, to a different jail. Counsel's endeavors throughout the trial to obtain petitioner's release proved fruitless. Petitioner remained in custody for the duration of the trial. He was convicted on seven counts of mail fraud. . . .

Petitioner contended that his incarceration was unjustified and that it materially interfered with his right to counsel and severely impeded his defense. . . .

A trial judge indisputably has broad powers to ensure the orderly and expeditious progress of a trial. For this purpose, he has the power to revoke bail and to remit the defendant to custody. But this power must be exercised with circumspection. It may be invoked only when and to the extent justified by danger which the defendant's conduct presents or by danger of significant interference with the progress or order of the trial.[1] See Fernandez v. United States, 365 U.S. 397, 81 S.Ct. 642 (1961) (memorandum of Mr. Justice Harlan in chambers); Carbo v. United States, 288 F.2d 282 (C.A.9th Cir. 1961); Christoffel v. United States, 89 U.S.App.D.C. 341, 196 F.2d 560 (1951).

The record in this case shows only a single, brief incident of tardiness, resulting in commitment of the defendant to custody for the balance of the trial in a jail 40 miles distant from the courtroom. In these circumstances, the trial judge's order of commitment, made without hearing or statement of reasons, had the appearance and effect of punishment rather than of an order designed solely to facilitate the trial. Punishment may not be so inflicted. We therefore hold that the order was unjustified and that it constituted an unwarranted burden upon defendant and his counsel in the conduct of the case.

Accordingly, we grant certiorari and reverse the judgment.

Judgment reversed.

MR. JUSTICE MARSHALL took no part in the consideration or decision of this case.

NOTES

1. A defendant released prior to trial generally continues on bail during trial unless the trial judge, in his discretion, determines that a revision of the terms of the bail is necessary to assure presence during trial or the expeditious progress of the trial. There are two general categories of misconduct by the defendant that will warrant revocation of bail during trial. The first is his obstructive misconduct during the course of trial. See United States v. Bentena, 288 F.2d 442 (2d Cir. 1961), aff'd sub nom., Fer-

---

1. It does not appear whether defendant was at large on bail at the time of the order remitting him to custody. But the same principle would apply if he had been at liberty on his own recognizance. Cf. Bail Reform Act of 1966, 18 U.S.C. § 3146.

nandez v. United States, 81 S.Ct. 642 (1961) (Harlan, J., in chambers). *Fernandez* was relied upon by the United States Court of Appeals for the Seventh Circuit in upholding the revocation of bail of a defendant who, after exhibiting contemptuous tendencies throughout the trial, responded to a government witness' answer with the comment: "Oh, bull shit. That's a lie." The Court's opinion is unreported; and the contempt citation resulting from this and other misconduct during the trial was remanded for further proceedings. In re Dellinger, 461 F.2d 389 (7th Cir. 1972).

2. The second category of bail revocation during trial arises where threats to government witnesses are made by a particular defendant. See Carbo v. United States, 288 F.2d 686 (9th Cir. 1961). However, the defendant is entitled to an adequate hearing on the issue of whether such threats were made. Therefore, where the conduct is not within the observation of the trial judge, it is apparent that he cannot revoke bail absent a hearing on the merits. Cf. United States v. Gilbert, 425 F.2d 490 (D.C. Cir. 1969).

D. BAIL PENDING APPEAL

HARRIS v. UNITED STATES

On Application to Mr. Justice Douglas as Circuit Justice, 1971.
404 U.S. 1232, 92 S.Ct. 10.

MR. JUSTICE DOUGLAS, CIRCUIT JUSTICE.

This is an application for bail pending appeal to the Ninth Circuit of Appeals. Both the District Court and the Court of Appeals have previously denied similar applications, and their action is entitled to great deference. Reynolds v. United States, 80 S.Ct. 30 (1959). Nevertheless, "where the reasons for the action below clearly appear, a Circuit Justice has a non-delegable responsibility to make an independent determination of the merits of the application." Fed.Rule Crim.Proc. 46(a)(2); 18 U.S.C. §§ 3146, 3148. Accord, Sellers v. United States, 89 S.Ct. 36 (1968). While there is no automatic right to bail after convictions, Bowman v. United States, 85 S. Ct. 232 (1964), "The command of the Eighth Amendment that 'Excessive bail shall not be required * * *' *at the very least* obligates judges passing on the right to bail to deny such relief only for the strongest of reasons." The Bail Reform Act of 1966, 18 U.S.C. §§ 3146, 3148, further limits the discretion of a court or judge to deny bail, as it provides that a person *shall* be entitled to bail pending appeal, if that appeal is not frivolous or taken for delay, or "unless the court or judge has reason to believe that no one or more conditions of release will reasonably assure that the person will not flee or pose a danger to any other person or to the community."

Applying these principles, my examination of the papers submitted by applicant and by the Solicitor General in opposition persuade me that the Government has not met its burden of showing that bail should be denied.

The primary ground upon which the Solicitor General opposes bail is that "[t]here are no substantial questions raised" by the appeal. It is true that the questions raised relate primarily to evidentiary matters. It is settled however, that these are within the purview of review of an application of this kind, and that they may raise nonfrivolous—indeed, even "substantial"—questions. See, e. g., Wolcher v. United States, 76 S.Ct. 254 (1955).

Applicant principally argues that there was no evidence in the record from which an inference is permissible that he knew that a truck guided by him and a codefendant, in a separate vehicle, from one location in Los Angeles to another location in that city contained unlawfully imported narcotics. It is beyond question, of course, that a conviction based on a record lacking any relevant evidence as to a crucial element of the offense charged would violate due process.

* * *

Applicant cites a case from the Ninth Circuit as a factually similar example in which a conviction for a narcotics offense was reversed for lack of proof of knowledge that another possessed the contraband. While I express no opinion on the merits of the analogy, Circuit Justices have granted bail pending appeal based in part on similar claims of failure of proof. See, e. g., Brussel v. United States, 396 U.S. 1229, 90 S.Ct. 2 (1969).

* * *

Where an appeal is not frivolous or taken for delay, bail "is to be denied only in cases in which, from substantial evidence, it seems clear that the right to bail may be abused or the community may be threatened by the applicant's release." According to the Solicitor General, the District Judge denied bail in part because "there was reason to believe that defendant, who had no employment, would not respond to required future appearances and would be a danger to the community." Applicant's Bail Reform Act form indicates, however, that he is a self-employed auto mechanic making $150 per week, that he has lived in Los Angeles for the past eight years, that he has several relatives, including his mother and a sister, living there, and that he has never failed to make a required court appearance while on bail. The moving papers further indicate that applicant was at liberty after sentencing, pursuant to a stay of execution granted by the Court of Appeals, and that he voluntarily submitted to the authorities upon the expiration of the stay. There is not such "substantial evidence" in this record to justify denying bail on the ground that applicant is a flight risk.

Furthermore, a far stronger showing of danger to the community must be made than is apparent from this record to justify a denial of bail on that ground. Accordingly, bail should be granted pending disposition of the appeal in this case, pursuant to the standards set forth in the Bail Reform Act. It is so ordered.

Application granted.

NOTES

1. Bail pending appeal is not an absolute right, but in the federal system and in some states, it is ordinarily granted when the defendant abided

by the conditions of bail during the course of trial. It is rarely granted, however, where no bail was allowed during trial. The criterion normally applied is whether the appeal is frivolous or taken for delay; but even if it is not, bail may be denied if there is a risk of flight or a likelihood that the appellant will present a danger to the community. See Note, Bail Pending Appeal in the Federal Courts, 32 N.Y.U.L.Rev. 557 (1957). That the release of an appellant will present a danger to the community or that he is likely to flee are not things that will be assumed, but must be shown by concrete facts. See Hung v. United States, 439 U.S. 1326, 99 S.Ct. 16 (1978) (Brennan, J., in chambers); Sellers v. United States, 89 S.Ct. 36 (1968); Chambers v. Mississippi, 405 U.S. 1205, 92 S.Ct. 754 (1972) (Powell, J., in chambers).

2. The mere threat that an appellant on bail will again commit the same kind of act for which he stands convicted, will not generally permit the court to revoke appellate bail. Roth v. United States, 77 S.Ct. 17, 18 (1956) (Harlan, J., in chambers):

> And although I should regard it as most ill-advised were the petitioner to continue, pending the final disposition of his case, the activities for which he has been convicted, I am inclined to think that the possibility that he may do so is not a proper circumstance to be taken into account where the constitutionality of the statute itself may be at stake.

Where the repeated offense comes about, revocation of appellate bail is likely—United States v. Erwing, 268 F.Supp. 879 (N.D.Cal.1967):

> After sentencing defendant to concurrent fifteen year terms of imprisonment for conviction on three counts of an indictment charging the sale of heroin, a narcotic drug, the Court fixed bail on appeal at $20,000. The government made an ex parte motion to set aside bail on appeal because defendant had been arrested and complaints were filed against him charging the concealment of heroin. . . .
>
> *   *   *
>
> The government urges as the sole ground for revocation of bail that the defendant, because of his continuing association in the narcotic traffic, poses a real danger to the safety of the community. The defendant, in opposition to this motion, asserts that the terms used in the new legislation were not intended to apply to non-violent narcotic offenders, but are limited only to those cases where there is a threat of physical violence to a person or to the community at large and are inapplicable here.
>
> *   *   *
>
> At the time this Court allowed defendant to be released on bail pending his appeal, it was made perfectly clear to him that he must forego all associations with the narcotics traffic, and the Court received assurances from him that he would do so. It is not the function of this Court to find that defendant has or has not committed the new offenses charged. However, the Court cannot ignore the fact that there is reasonable cause to believe that the defendant is still engaged in his nefarious business. When this fact is placed alongside defendant's history of narcotics peddling then there is every reason to believe that if bail were not revoked the defendant would resume his harmful calling.

The community must be protected from violations of the law which prey on the weakness of mankind. A wholesale drug peddler, such as the defendant, exploits this weakness and, in doing so, certainly poses a danger to the welfare of the community.

For these reasons, and in light of the known character and conduct of the defendant, the Court in the exercise of its discretion believes that he should not be entitled to bail pending his appeal.

Chapter 13
PRE–TRIAL MOTIONS

The modern concept of pretrial motions evolved from common law concept of pleading to a criminal charge. Although, with the exception of the plea of guilty or not guilty, "pleadings" are generally associated with civil cases, they are particularly important to criminal cases in the pretrial setting. At common law, there were five basic challenges available to a criminal defendant:

(1) a plea to jurisdiction. See United States v. Thomas, 151 U. S. 577 (1894) (jurisdiction over Indians); (2) a plea in abatement, challenging the technical sufficiency of the indictment because of some defect in the grand jury process. See United States v. Storrs, 272 U.S. 652 (1926); (3) a motion to quash, raising defects of both form and substance in the indictment itself. See United States v. Rosenburgh, 74 U.S. (7 Wall.) 580 (1868); (4) demur to the indictment for its failure to allege an offense. Demurrers were extremely rare since they admitted the facts alleged in the indictment and the objections raised by demurrer could be argued by plea in abatement or motion to quash. See United States v. Cook, 84 U.S. (17 Wall.) 168 (1872); and (5) Pleas in bar, raising claims prohibiting the action such as double jeopardy and statute of limitations concerns. See Heike v. United States, 217 U.S. 423 (1910). See generally Chitty, Criminal Law 434 (2d ed. 1826); 2 Bishop, New Criminal Procedure § 746 (4th ed. 1895).

The propriety of granting a motion to dismiss an indictment prior to trial is contingent upon whether the alleged infirmity is a question of law or involves the determination of facts. If a question of law is involved, consideration of the motion is generally proper. See United States v. Korn, 557 F.2d 1089 (5th Cir. 1977). However, trial courts may make preliminary findings of fact necessary to decide questions of law. The facts may be developed at a pretrial hearing, but the court's findings on the motion cannot invade the province of the ultimate fact-finder. United States v. Jones, 542 F.2d 661 (6th Cir. 1976).

As a general matter, the motions discussed in this chapter must be raised prior to trial or they will be deemed waived, and relief from waiver will not be granted in the absence of a strong showing of good cause and actual prejudice. United States v. Kaplan, 554 F.2d 958 (9th Cir. 1977); United States v. Williams, 544 F.2d 1215 (4th Cir. 1976). In the rare case when a trial judge refuses to consider a properly filed pretrial motion, the waiver doctrine is inapplicable. See United States v. Appawoo, 553 F.2d 1242 (10th Cir. 1977).

The following sections dealing with specific pretrial motions is not intended to be an exhaustive list of available remedies. Certain very basic motions, such as those for discovery, bill of particulars, and grand jury challenges, are dealt with in other sections of this book. It should be noted, however, that pretrial motions range from the relatively standard, as those discussed in the following sections, to the very esoteric as that analyzed in Comment, Removal of State Court Criminal Prosecutions to Federal Court Under 42 U.S.C. § 1443, 64 J.Crim.L. & C. 76 (1973).

With regard to the subject generally, consider Rule 12 of the Federal Rules of Criminal Procedure:

PLEADINGS AND MOTIONS BEFORE TRIAL; DEFENSES AND OBJECTIONS

(a) Pleadings and Motions. Pleadings in criminal proceedings shall be the indictment and the information, and the pleas of not guilty, guilty and nolo contendere. All other pleas, and demurrers and motions to quash are abolished, and defenses and objections raised before trial which heretofore could have been raised by one or more of them shall be raised only by motion to dismiss or to grant appropriate relief, as provided in these rules.

(b) Pretrial Motions. Any defense, objection, or request which is capable of determination without the trial of the general issue may be raised before trial by motion. Motions may be written or oral at the discretion of the judge. The following must be raised prior to trial:

     (1) Defenses and objections based on defects in the institution of the prosecution; or

     (2) Defenses and objections based on defects in the indictment or information (other than that it fails to show jurisdiction in the court or to charge an offense which objections shall be noticed by the court at any time during the pendency of the proceedings); or

     (3) Motions to suppress evidence; or

     (4) Requests for discovery . . . ; or

     (5) Requests for a severance of charges or defendants . . . .

(c) Motion Date. Unless otherwise provided by local rule, the court may, at the time of the arraignment or as soon thereafter as practicable, set a time for the making of pretrial motions or requests and, if required, a later date of hearing.

(d) Notice by the Government of the Intention to Use Evidence. (1) *At the Discretion of the Government.* At the arraignment or as soon thereafter as is practicable, the government may give notice to the defendant of its intention to use specified evidence at trial in order to afford the defendant an opportunity to raise objections to such evidence prior to trial under subdivision (b)(3) of this rule.

     (2) *At the Request of the Defendant.* At the arraignment or as soon thereafter as is practicable the defendant may, in order to afford an opportunity to move to suppress evidence under subdivision (b)(3) of this rule, request notice of the government's intention to use (in its evidence in chief at trial) any evidence which the defend-

ant may be entitled to discover under [the federal rules] subject to any relevant limitations prescribed [therein].

(e) Ruling on Motion. A motion made before trial shall be determined before trial unless the court, for good cause, orders that it be deferred for determination at the trial of the general issue or until after verdict, but no such determination shall be deferred if a party's right to appeal is adversely affected. Where factual issues are involved in determining a motion, the court shall state its essential findings on the record.

(f) Effect of Failure to Raise Defenses or Objections. Failure by a party to raise defenses or objections or to make requests which must be made prior to trial, at the time set by the court pursuant to subdivision (c), or prior to any extension thereof made by the court, shall constitute waiver thereof, but the court for cause shown may grant relief from the waiver.

(g) Records. A verbatim record shall be made of all proceedings at the hearing, including such findings of fact and conclusions of law as are made orally.

(h) Effect of Determination. If the court grants a motion based on a defect in the institution of the prosecution or in the indictment or information, it may also order that the defendant be continued in custody or that his bail be continued for a specified time pending the filing of a new indictment or information. Nothing in this rule shall be deemed to affect the provisions of any Act of Congress relating to periods of limitations.

A. DISMISSAL FOR DOUBLE JEOPARDY AND RELATED PRINCIPLES

1. GENERAL INTRODUCTION

The Fifth Amendment to the United States Constitution provides, in part: "nor shall any person be subject for the same offense to be twice put in jeopardy of life or limb." As interpreted by our courts, a multiplicity of values underlies this prohibition, including: (1) reduction of the possibility that an innocent person might be convicted through multiple trials; (2) limitation of the period in which an accused must suffer anxiety over the possibility of facing criminal sanctions; (3) control upon the time and money an accused must expend in defending himself, particularly where prosecutorial harassment is a possibility; and (4) elimination of multiple punishment for a single offense.

On the other hand, other values militate against an expansive reading of the double jeopardy prohibition. Prominent among these is the societal interest in providing the prosecutor a single, *fair* opportunity to establish the accused's guilt.

Knowledge of the diverse policy considerations which underlie the double jeopardy clause and those which underlie efforts to limit its application, while helpful, will not always aid us in predicting how the clause will be interpreted in a concrete situation. Although the student ought not abandon the effort to achieve a unified theory of double jeopardy, he or she should realize that no single theory is compatible with the various black-letter rules which now govern double jeopardy claims. Among the most difficult cases to reconcile are those which sometimes permit but sometimes prohibit the commencement of a new trial after an earlier proceeding had passed the point where jeopardy had "attached" for purposes of the Fifth Amendment. These cases are treated in subsections 3–6, infra. Theories with labels such as "waiver" or "continuing jeopardy" have been advanced, but none is entirely satisfactory.

PALKO v. CONNECTICUT

Supreme Court of the United States, 1937.
302 U.S. 319, 58 S.Ct. 149.

[Palko was charged with first degree murder, but was convicted by a jury of the lesser included offense of second-degree murder. Connecticut law permitted the prosecution to appeal to raise errors "of law." The state Supreme Court of Error reversed for a new trial on the charge of first degree murder, finding that the trial court improperly excluded a confession of the defendant and certain evidence designed to impeach the defendant's trial testimony. The reviewing court also found that the judge had erred against the prosecution in the jury instructions concerning the difference between first degree murder and second degree murder. Over objections that double jeopardy concepts barred a retrial, the defendant was retried and convicted, and that conviction was affirmed. Defendant appealed to the United States Supreme Court.]

MR. JUSTICE CARDOZO delivered the opinion of the Court.

* * *

We have said that in appellant's view the Fourteenth Amendment is to be taken as embodying the prohibitions of the Fifth. His thesis is even broader. Whatever would be a violation of the original bill of rights (Amendments 1 to 8) if done by the federal government is now equally unlawful by force of the Fourteenth Amendment if done by a state. There is no such general rule.

* * *

. . . The right to trial by jury and the immunity from prosecution except as the result of an indictment may have value and importance. Even so, they are not of the very essence of a scheme of ordered liberty. To abolish them is not to violate a "principle of justice so rooted in the traditions and conscience of our people as to be ranked as fundamental." Snyder v. Massachusetts, 291 U.S. 97, 105, 54 S.Ct. 330, 332. Few would be so narrow or provincial as to maintain that a fair and enlightened system of justice would be impossible without them. What is true of jury trials and indictments is true also, as the cases show, of the immunity from compulsory self-incrimination. This too might be lost, and justice still be done. Indeed, today as in the past there are students of our penal system who look upon the immunity as a mischief rather than a benefit, and who would limit its scope, or destroy it altogether. No doubt, there would remain the need to give protection against torture, physical or mental. Justice, however, would not perish if the accused were subject to a duty to respond to orderly inquiry. The exclusion of these immunities and privileges from the privileges and immunities protected against the action of the States has not been arbitrary or casual. It has been dictated by a study and appreciation of the meaning, the essential implications, of liberty itself.

We reach a different plane of social and moral values when we pass to the privileges and immunities that have been taken over from the earlier articles of the Federal Bill of Rights and brought within the Fourteenth Amendment by a process of absorption. These in their origin were effective against the federal government alone. If the Fourteenth Amendment has absorbed them, the process of absorption has had its source in the belief that neither liberty nor justice would exist if they were sacrificed. This is true, for illustration, of freedom of thought and speech. Of that freedom one may say that it is the matrix, the indispensable condition, of nearly every other form of freedom. With rare aberrations a pervasive recognition of that truth can be traced in our history, political and legal. So it has come about that the domain of liberty, withdrawn by the Fourteenth Amendment from encroachment by the states, has been enlarged by latter-day judgments to include liberty of the mind as well as liberty of action. The extension became, indeed, a logical imperative when once it was recognized, as long ago it was that liberty is something more than exemption from physical restraint, and that even in the field of substantive rights and duties the legislative judgment, if oppressive and arbitrary, may be overridden by the courts. Fundamental too in the concept of due process, and so in that of liberty, is the thought that condemnation shall be rendered only after trial. The hearing, moreover, must be a real one, not a sham or a pretense. For that reason, ignorant defendants in a capital case were held to have been condemned unlawfully when in truth, though not in form, they were refused the aid of counsel. Powell v. Alabama. The decision did not turn upon the fact that the benefit of counsel would have been guaranteed to the defendants by the provisions of the Sixth Amendment if they had been prosecuted in a federal court. The decision turned upon the fact that in the particular situation laid before us in the evidence the benefit of counsel was essential to the substance of a hearing.

Our survey of the cases serves, we think, to justify the statement that the dividing line between them, if not unfaltering throughout its course, has been true for the most part to a unifying principle. On which side of the line the case made out by the appellant has appropriate location must be the next inquiry and the final one. Is that kind of double jeopardy to which the statute has subjected him a hardship so acute and shocking that our polity will not endure it? Does it violate those "fundamental principles of liberty and justice which lie at the base of all our civil and political institutions"? The answer surely must be "no." What the answer would have to be if the state were permitted after a trial free from error to try the accused over again or to bring another case against him, we have no occasion to consider. We deal with the statute before us and no other. The state is not attempting to wear the accused out by a multitude of cases with accumulated trials. It asks no more than this, that the case against him shall go on until there shall be a trial free from the corrosion of substantial legal error. This is not cruelty at all, nor even vexation in any immoderate degree. If the trial had been infected with error adverse to the accused, there might have been review at his instance, and as often as necessary to purge the vicious taint. A reciprocal privilege, subject at all times to the discretion of the presiding judge (State v. Carabetta, 106 Conn. 114, 137 A. 394), has now been granted to the state. There is here no seismic innovation. The edifice of justice stands, its symmetry, to many, greater than before.

* * *

The judgment is affirmed.

MR. JUSTICE BUTLER dissents.

BENTON v. MARYLAND

Supreme Court of the United States, 1969.
395 U.S. 784, 89 S.Ct. 2056.

MR. JUSTICE MARSHALL delivered the opinion of the Court.

In August 1965, petitioner was tried in a Maryland state court on charges of burglary and larceny. The jury found petitioner not guilty of larceny but convicted him on the burglary count. He was sentenced to 10 years in prison. Shortly after his notice of appeal was filed in the Maryland Court of Appeals, that court handed down its decision in the case of Schowgurow v. State, 240 Md. 121, 213 A. 2d 475 (1965). In *Schowgurow* the Maryland Court of Appeals struck down a section of the state constitution which required jurors to swear their belief in the existence of God. As a result of this decision, petitioner's case was remanded to the trial court. Because both the grand and petit juries in petitioner's case had been selected under the invalid constitutional provision, petitioner was given the option of demanding re-indictment and retrial. He chose to have his conviction set aside, and a new indictment and new trial followed. At this second trial, petitioner was again charged with both larceny and burglary. Petitioner objected to retrial on the larceny count, arguing that because the first jury had found him not guilty of larceny, retrial would violate the constitutional prohibition against subjecting persons to double jeopardy for the same offense. The trial judge denied petitioner's motion to dismiss the larceny charge, and petitioner was tried for both larceny and burglary. This time the jury found petitioner guilty of both offenses, and the judge sentenced him to 15 years on the burglary count and 5 years for larceny, the sentences to run concurrently. On appeal to the newly created Maryland Court of Special Appeals, petitioner's double jeopardy claim was rejected on the merits. The Court of Appeals denied discretionary review.

*   *   *

After consideration of all the questions before us, we find no bar to our decision of the double jeopardy issue. On the merits, we hold that the Double Jeopardy Clause of the Fifth Amendment is applicable to the States through the Fourteenth Amendment, and we reverse petitioner's conviction for larceny.

*   *   *

Palko represented an approach to basic constitutional rights which this Court's recent decisions have rejected. It was cut of the same cloth as Betts v. Brady, 316 U.S. 455, 62 S.Ct. 1252 (1942), the case which held that a criminal defendant's right to counsel was to be determined by deciding in each case whether the denial of that right was "shocking to the universal sense of justice." It relied upon Twining v. New Jersey (1908), which held that the right against compulsory self-incrimination was not an element of Fourteenth Amendment due process. Betts was overruled by Gideon v. Wainwright (1963); *Twining*, by Malloy v. Hogan (1964). Our recent cases have thoroughly rejected the *Palko* notion that basic constitutional rights can be denied by the States as long as the totality of the circumstances does not disclose a denial of "fundamental fairness." Once it is decided that a particular Bill of Rights guarantee is "fundamental to the American scheme of justice," Duncan v. Louisiana, 88 S.Ct., at 1447, the same constitutional standards apply against both the State and Federal Governments. *Palko*'s roots had thus been cut away years ago. We today only recognize the inevitable.

The fundamental nature of the guarantee against double jeopardy can hardly be doubted. Its origins can be traced to Greek and Roman times, and it became established in the common law of England long before this Nation's independence. See Bartkus v. Illinois, 359 U.S. 121, 151–155, 79 S.Ct. 676, 697 (1959) (Black, J., dissenting). As with many other elements of the common law, it was carried into the jurisprudence of this Country through the medium of Blackstone, who codified the doctrine in his Commentaries. "[T]he plea of *autrefoits acquit*, or a former acquittal," he wrote, "is grounded on this universal maxim of the common law of England, that no man is to be brought into jeopardy of his life more than once for the same offence." Today, every State incorporates some form of the prohibition in its constitution or common law. As this Court put it in Green v. United States, 355 U.S. 184, 187–188, 78 S.Ct. 221, 223 (1957), "[t]he underlying idea, one that is deeply ingrained in at least the Anglo-American system of jurisprudence, is that the State with all its resources and power should not be allowed to make repeated attempts to convict an individual for an alleged offense, thereby subjecting him to embarrassment, expense and ordeal and compelling him to live in a continuing state of anxiety and insecurity, as well as enhancing the possibility that even though innocent he may be found guilty." This underlying notion has from the very beginning been part of our constitutional tradition. Like the right to trial by jury, it is clearly "fundamental to the American scheme of justice." The validity of petitioner's larceny conviction must be judged, not by the watered-down standard enunciated in *Palko*, but under this Court's interpretations of the Fifth Amendment double jeopardy provision.

It is clear that petitioner's larceny conviction cannot stand once federal double jeopardy standards are applied. Petitioner was acquitted of larceny in his first trial. Because he decided to appeal his burglary conviction, he is forced to suffer retrial on the larceny count as well. As this Court held in Green v. United States, "[c]onditioning an appeal of one offense on a coerced surrender of a valid plea of former jeopardy on another offense exacts a forfeiture in plain conflict with the constitutional bar against double jeopardy."

Judgment vacated and case remanded.

[Omitted are the concurring opinion of Justice White and the dissenting opinion of Justice Harlan, joined by Justice Stewart.]

NOTES

1. At the time of *Palko* the overwhelming majority of state constitutions contained a prohibition against double jeopardy. Even in Connecticut a double jeopardy prohibition of some sort was embodied in the state's common law. No reported Connecticut decision entertained a prosecutor's claim that the jury's verdict of acquittal was manifestly against the weight of the evidence. This form of review (on what might be called a mixed question of law and fact) was apparently not available to the prosecution even in Connecticut. Contrast, however, the situation in most jurisdictions where, under limited circumstances, a reviewing court will overturn a jury's verdict in *civil* litigation when that verdict is contrary to the evidence.

2. *Palko* assumed that under the Fifth Amendment the federal government could not appeal following a jury's verdict of acquittal even if its claims related solely to errors of law which may have contributed to the verdict. This interpretation of the Fifth Amendment still prevails, although through the decades it has had its critics, including Justice Holmes, who, dissenting in Kepner v. United States, 195 U.S. 100, 24 S.Ct. 797 (1904), advanced a theory of "continuing jeopardy" which would have permitted the government an appeal so as to assure a single, error-free trial. Appeal following acquittal is treated further in subsection 5, infra.

3. One recent effort to offer a unified theory—though not one which purports to be consistent with what the Supreme Court has done in all the various cases—is Westen and Drubel, Toward a General Theory of Double Jeopardy, 1979 Supreme Court Review 81.

2. WHEN DOES JEOPARDY ATTACH?

SERFASS v. ·UNITED STATES

Supreme Court of the United States, 1975.
420 U.S. 377, 95 S.Ct. 1055.

MR. CHIEF JUSTICE BURGER delivered the opinion of the Court.

We granted certiorari to decide whether a court of appeals has jurisdiction of an appeal by the United States from a pretrial order dismissing an indictment based on a legal ruling made by the District Court after an examination of records and an affidavit setting forth evidence to be adduced at trial.

I.

* * *

A grand jury returned an indictment charging petitioner with willfully failing to report for and submit to induction into the Armed Forces, in violation of 50 U.S.C.A.App. § 462(a) (1970). At petitioner's arraignment he pleaded not guilty and demanded a jury trial. The trial date was set for January 9, 1973. Prior to that time, petitioner filed a motion to dismiss the indictment on the ground that the Local Board did not state adequate reasons for its refusal to reopen his file. Attached to the motion was an affidavit of petitioner stating merely that he had applied for conscientious objector status and that the Local Board's letter was the only communication concerning his claim which he had received. At the same time, petitioner moved "to postpone the trial of the within matter which is now scheduled for January 9, 1973, for the reason that a Motion to Dismiss has been simultaneously filed and the expeditious administration of justice will be served best by considering the Motion prior to trial."

. . . Briefs were submitted, and after hearing oral argument, the District Court entered an order directing the parties to submit a copy of petitioner's Selective Service file. On July 16, 1973, it ordered that the indictment be dismissed. In its memorandum, the court noted that the material facts were derived from petitioner's affidavit, from his Selective Service file, and from the oral stipulation of counsel at the argument "that the information which Serfass submitted to the Board establishes a prima facie claim for conscientious objector status based upon late crystallization." The District Court held that dismissal of the indictment was appropriate because petitioner was "entitled to full consideration of his claim prior to assignment to combatant training and service," and because the Local Board's statement of reasons for refusing to reopen his Selective Service file was "sufficiently ambiguous to be reasonably construed as a rejection on the merits, thereby prejudicing his right to in-service review."

The United States appealed to the United States Court of Appeals for the Third Circuit, asserting jurisdiction under the Criminal

Appeals Act, 18 U.S.C. § 3731, as amended by the Omnibus Crime Control and Safe Streets Act of 1970, 84 Stat. § 1890.[1] In a "Motion to Quash Appeal for Lack of Jurisdiction" and in his brief, petitioner contended that the Court of Appeals lacked jurisdiction because further prosecution was prohibited by the Double Jeopardy Clause of the United States Constitution. The Court of Appeals rejected that contention. It concluded that, although no appeal would have been possible in this case under the Criminal Appeals Act as it existed prior to the 1970 amendments,[2] those amendments were "clearly intended to enlarge the Government's right to appeal to include all cases in which such an appeal would be constitutionally permissible." Relying on its earlier opinion in United States v. Pecora, 484 F.2d 1289 (C.A.3d, 1973), the Court of Appeals held that since petitioner had not waived his right to a jury trial and no jury had been empaneled and sworn at the time the District Court ruled on his motion to dismiss the indictment, jeopardy had not attached and the dismissal was an appealable order. *Pecora* had held appealable, under the present version of § 3731, a pretrial dismissal of an indictment based on a stipulation of the facts upon which the indictment was based. In this case the Court of Appeals saw "no significant constitutional difference" arising from the fact that "the instant dismissal was based upon the trial court's finding that the defendant had established a defense as a matter of law, rather than upon the finding, as in *Pecora*, that there were insufficient facts as a matter of law to support a conviction." In both cases "the pretrial motion of dismissal was based upon undisputed facts raising a legal issue and the defendant did not waive his right to a jury trial," and in both denial of the motion to dismiss "[would have] entitled the defendant to the jury trial which he ha[d] not waived."

As to the merits, the Court of Appeals concluded that in Musser v. United States . . . (1973), this Court had "placed an abrupt end to [the] line of cases" on which the District Court relied. It held that *Musser* should be applied retroactively to registrants such as petitioner who refused induction before the case was decided, and that since petitioner's Local Board was without power to rule on the mer-

---

1. 18 U.S.C.A. § 3731 (1970) provides in pertinent part:
"In a criminal case an appeal by the United States shall lie to a court of appeals from a decision, judgment or order of a district court dismissing an indictment or information as to any one or more counts, except that no appeal shall lie where the double jeopardy clause of the United States Constitution prohibits further prosecution.

* * *

"The provisions of this section shall be liberally construed to effectuate its purposes."
2. Prior to the 1970 amendments, which were effective January 2, 1971,

18 U.S.C.A. § 3731 authorized an appeal by the United States to a court of appeals in all criminal cases "[f]rom a decision or judgment setting aside, or dismissing any indictment or information, or any count thereof, except where a direct appeal to the Supreme Court is provided by this section." Under this provision, the Court of Appeals concluded, appeals "were permissible only if the dismissal of an indictment was based on a defect in the indictment or in the institution of the prosecution, rather than upon evidentiary facts outside the face of the indictment which would possibly constitute a defense at trial."

its of a post-induction order conscientious objector claim, his right to in-service review was not prejudiced. Accordingly, it reversed the order of the District Court and remanded the case for trial or other proceedings consistent with its opinion.

Because of an apparent conflict among the courts of appeals concerning the question whether the Double Jeopardy Clause permits an appeal under § 3731 from a pretrial order dismissing an indictment in these circumstances, we granted certiorari. Petitioner did not seek review of, and we express no opinion with respect to, the holding of the Court of Appeals on the merits.

II.

Prior to 1971, appeals by the United States in criminal cases were restricted by 18 U.S.C. § 3731 to categories descriptive of the action taken by a district court, and they were divided between this Court and the courts of appeals. In United States v. Sisson .   .   . (1970), Mr. Justice Harlan aptly described the situation obtaining under the statute as it then read:

> "Clarity is to be desired in any statute, but in matters of jurisdiction it is especially important. Otherwise the courts and the parties must expend great energy, not on the merits of dispute settlement, but on simply deciding whether a court has the power to hear a case. When judged in these terms, the Criminal Appeals Act is a failure. Born of compromise, and reflecting no coherent allocation of appellate responsibility, the Criminal Appeals Act proved a most unruly child that has not improved with age. The statute's roots are grounded in pleading distinctions that existed at common law but which, in most instances, fail to coincide with the procedural categories of the Federal Rules of Criminal Procedure. Not only does the statute create uncertainty by its requirement that one analyze the nature of the decision of the district court in order to determine whether it falls within the class of common law distinctions for which an appeal is authorized, but it has also engendered confusion over the court, to which an appealable decision should be brought." .   .   .

In light of the language of the present version of § 3731, including the admonition that its provisions "shall be liberally construed to effectuate its purposes," and of its legislative history, it is clear to us that Congress intended to authorize an appeal to a court of appeals in this case so long as further prosecution would not be barred by the Double Jeopardy Clause. We turn to that inquiry.

III.

Although articulated in different ways by this Court, the purposes of, and the policies which animate, the Double Jeopardy Clause in this context are clear. "The constitutional prohibition against 'double jeopardy' was designed to protect an individual from being subjected to the hazards of trial and possible conviction more than once for an alleged offense. . . . The underlying idea, one that is deeply ingrained in at least the Anglo-American system of jurisprudence, is that the State with all its resources and power should not be allowed to make repeated attempts to convict an individual for an alleged offense, thereby subjecting him to embarrassment, expense and ordeal and compelling him to live in a continuing state of anxiety and insecurity, as well as enhancing the possibility that even though innocent he may be found guilty." Green v. United States . . . (1957) . . .

As an aid to the decision of cases in which the prohibition of the Double Jeopardy Clause has been invoked, the courts have found it useful to define a point in criminal proceedings at which the constitutional purposes and policies are implicated by resort to the concept of "attachment of jeopardy." . . . In the case of a jury trial, jeopardy attaches when a jury is empaneled and sworn. . . . In a nonjury trial, jeopardy attaches when the court begins to hear evidence. . . . The Court has consistently adhered to the view that jeopardy does not attach and the constitutional prohibition can have no application, until a defendant is "put to trial before the trier of facts, whether the trier be a jury or a judge." United States v. Jorn, 400 U.S., at 479, 91 S.Ct., at 554. . . .

Under our cases jeopardy had not yet attached when the District Court granted petitioner's motion to dismiss the indictment. Petitioner was not then, nor has he ever been, "put to trial before the trier of facts." The proceedings were initiated by his motion to dismiss the indictment. Petitioner had not waived his right to a jury trial, and, of course, a jury trial could not be waived by him without the consent of the Government and of the court. Fed.Rule Crim. Proc. 23(a). . . . In such circumstances, the District Court was without power to make any determination regarding petitioner's guilt or innocence. Petitioner's defense was raised before trial precisely because "trial of the facts surrounding the commission of the alleged offense would be of no assistance in determining" its validity. United States v. Covington . . . (1969). See Fed.Rule Crim.Proc. 12(b)(1). His motion to postpone the trial was premised on the belief that "the expeditious administration of justice will be served best by considering the Motion [to dismiss the indictment] prior to trial." At no time during or following the hearing on petitioner's motion to dismiss the indictment did the District Court have jurisdiction to do more than grant or deny that motion, and neither before nor after the ruling did jeopardy attach.

IV.

Petitioner acknowledges that "formal or technical jeopardy had not attached" at the time the District Court ruled on his motion to dismiss the indictment. However, he argues that because that ruling was based on " 'evidentiary facts outside of the indictment, which facts would constitute a defense on the merits at trial,' United States v. Brewster, . . . (1972)," it was the "functional equivalent of an acquittal on the merits" and "constructively jeopardy had attached." The argument is grounded on two basic and interrelated premises. First, petitioner argues that the Court has admonished against the use of "technicalities" in interpreting the Double Jeopardy Clause, and he contends that the normal rule as to the attachment of jeopardy is merely a presumption which is rebuttable in cases where an analysis of the respective interests of the Government and the accused indicates that the policies of the Double Jeopardy Clause would be frustrated by further prosecution. . . . Second, petitioner maintains that the disposition of his motion to dismiss the indictment was, in the circumstances of this case, the "functional equivalent of an acquittal on the merits," and he concludes that the policies of the Double Jeopardy Clause would in fact be frustrated by further prosecution. . . . We disagree with both of petitioner's premises and with his conclusion.

It is true that we have disparaged "rigid, mechanical" rules in the interpretation of the Double Jeopardy Clause. Illinois v. Somerville . . . (1973). However, we also observed in that case that "the conclusion that jeopardy has attached begins, rather than ends, the inquiry as to whether the Double Jeopardy Clause bars retrial." Ibid. Cf. United States v. Sisson . . . (1971). Implicit in the latter statement is the premise that the "constitutional policies underpinning the Fifth Amendment's guarantee" are not implicated before that point in the proceedings at which "jeopardy attaches." United States v. Jorn . . . (1971). As we have noted above, the Court has consistently adhered to the view that jeopardy does not attach until a defendant is "put to trial before the trier of facts, whether the trier be a jury or a judge." . . . This is by no means a mere technicality, nor is it a "rigid, mechanical" rule. It is, of course, like most legal rules, an attempt to impart content to an abstraction.

When a criminal prosecution is terminated prior to trial, an accused is often spared much of the expense, delay, strain, and embarrassment which attend a trial. See Green v. United States . . . (1957); United States v. Jorn . . . . Although an accused may raise defenses or objections before trial which are "capable of determination without the trial of the general issue," Fed.Rule Crim. Proc. 12(b)(1), and although he must raise certain other defenses or objections before trial, Fed.Rule Crim.Proc. 12(b)(2), in neither case is he "subjected to the hazards of trial and possible conviction." . . . Moreover, in neither case would an appeal by the United States "allow the prosecutor to seek to persuade a second trier of fact of the defendant's guilt after having failed with the first." United States v. Wilson, 95 S.Ct. at 1026. See United States v. Jorn, 400 U. S., at 484, 91 S.Ct., at 556. Both the history of the Double Jeopardy Clause and its terms demonstrate that it does not come into play until a proceeding begins before a trier "having jurisdiction to try the question of the guilt or innocence of the accused." Kepner v. United States, 195 U.S. 100, 133 . . . (1904) . . . Without risk of a determination of guilt, jeopardy does not attach, and neither an appeal nor further prosecution constitutes double jeopardy.

Petitioner's second premise, that the disposition of his motion to dismiss the indictment was the "functional equivalent of an acquittal on the merits," and his conclusion that the policies of the Double Jeopardy Clause would be frustrated by further prosecution in his case need not, in light of the conclusion we reach above, long detain us. It is, of course, settled that "a verdict of acquittal . . . is a bar to a subsequent prosecution for the same offense." United States v. Ball . . . (1896). But the language of cases in which we have held that there can be no appeal from, or further prosecution after, an "acquittal" cannot be divorced from the procedural context in which the action so characterized was taken. See United States v. Wilson, 95 S.Ct. at 1023–1024. The word itself has no talismanic quality for purposes of the Double Jeopardy Clause. In particular, it has no significance in this context unless jeopardy has once attached and an accused has been subjected to the risk of conviction.

* * *

V.

In holding that the Court of Appeals correctly determined that it had jurisdiction of the United States' appeal in this case under 18 U. S.C. § 3731, we of course express no opinion on the question whether a similar ruling by the District Court after jeopardy had attached would have been appealable. Nor do we intimate any view concerning the case put by the Solicitor General, of "a defendant who is afforded an opportunity to obtain a determination of a legal defense prior to the trial and nevertheless knowingly allows himself to be placed in jeopardy before raising the defense." We hold only that the Double Jeopardy Clause does not bar an appeal by the United States under 18 U.S.C. § 3731 with respect to a criminal defendant who has not been "put to trial before the trier of facts, whether the trier be a jury or a judge." United States v. Jorn. . . . .

Affirmed.

Mr. Justice Douglas dissents, being of the view that the ruling of the District Court was based on evidence which could constitute a defense on the merits and therefore cause jeopardy to attach.

NOTE

In Downum v. United States, 372 U.S. 734, 83 S.Ct. 1033 (1963), the Court held that in a federal jury trial jeopardy attaches when the jury is empaneled and sworn and, unlike a bench trial, it does not require the commencement of the testimony of the first witness. In Crist v. Bretz, 437 U. S. 28, 98 S.Ct. 2156 (1978), the Court considered the validity of the Montana rule under which, despite the swearing of the jury, jeopardy did not attach until the commencement of the evidence. Through Justice Stewart the Court struck down the Montana rule on the following grounds:

"The reason for holding that jeopardy attaches when the jury is empaneled and sworn lies in the need to protect the interest of an accused in retaining a chosen jury. That interest was described in Wade v. Hunter, supra, as a defendant's 'valued right to have his trial completed by a particular tribunal.' 336 U.S., at 689,

69 S.Ct. 834, 93 L.Ed. 974. It is an interest with roots deep in the historic development of trial by jury in the Anglo-American system of criminal justice. Throughout that history there ran a strong tradition that once banded together a jury should not be discharged until it had completed its solemn tasks of announcing a verdict.

"Regardless of its historic origin, however, the defendant's 'valued right to have his trial completed by a particular tribunal' is now within the protection of the constitutional guarantee against double jeopardy, since it is that 'right' that lies at the foundation of the federal rule that jeopardy attaches when the jury is empaneled and sworn."

Joined by Chief Justice Burger and Justice Rehnquist, Justice Powell dissented:

"The rule that jeopardy attaches in a jury trial at the moment the jury is sworn is not mandated by the Constitution. It is the product of historical accident, embodied in a Court decision without the slightest consideration of the policies it purports to serve. Because these policies would be served equally well by a rule fixing the attachment of jeopardy at the swearing of the first witness, I would uphold the Montana statute. Even if one assumed that the Fifth Amendment now requires the attachment of jeopardy at the swearing of the jury, I would view that rule as incidental to the purpose of the Double Jeopardy Clause and hence not incorporated through the Due Process Clause of the Fourteenth Amendment and not applicable to the States. I therefore dissent.

* * *

". . . The federal rule of attachment in jury trials offers no basis for a double jeopardy claim if the prosecutor—dissatisfied by the jury selection process—is successful in dismissing the prosecution before the last juror is seated, or indeed before the whole panel is sworn. A defendant's protection against denial or abuse of his rights in this respect lies in the Due Process Clause."

[Similarly, Justice Powell argued, Due Process would protect against deliberate prosecution misconduct after the swearing in of the jury, but before any evidence was heard.]

3. RETRIAL WHERE TRIAL IS TERMINATED WITHOUT VERDICT

UNITED STATES v. JORN

Supreme Court of the United States, 1971.
400 U.S. 470, 91 S.Ct. 547.

Mr. Justice Harlan announced the judgment of the Court in an opinion joined by The Chief Justice, Mr. Justice Douglas, and Mr. Justice Marshall.

The Government directly appeals the order of the United States District Court for the District of Utah dismissing, on the ground of former jeopardy, an information charging the defendant-appellee with willfully assisting in the preparation of fraudulent income tax returns, in violation of 26 U.S.C. § 7206(2).

Appellee was originally charged in February 1968 with 25 counts of violating § 7206(2). He was brought to trial before Chief Judge Ritter on August 27, 1968. After the jury was chosen and sworn, 14 of the counts were dismissed on the Government's motion. The trial then commenced, the Government calling as its first witness an Internal Revenue Service agent in order to put in evidence the remaining 11 allegedly fraudulent income tax returns the defendant was charged with helping to prepare. At the trial judge's suggestion, these exhibits were stipulated to and introduced in evidence without objection.

The Government's five remaining witnesses were taxpayers whom the defendant allegedly had aided in preparation of these returns.

After the first of these witnesses was called, but prior to the commencement of direct examination, defense counsel suggested that these witnesses be warned of their constitutional rights. The trial court agreed, and proceeded, in careful detail, to spell out the witness' right not to say anything that might be used in a subsequent criminal prosecution against him and his right, in the event of such a prosecution, to be represented by an attorney. The first witness expressed a willingness to testify and stated that he had been warned of his constitutional rights when the Internal Revenue Service first contacted him. The trial judge indicated, however, that he did not believe the witness had been given any warning at the time he was first contacted by the IRS, and refused to permit him to testify until he had consulted an attorney.

The trial judge then asked the prosecuting attorney if his remaining four witnesses were similarly situated. The prosecutor responded that they had been warned of their rights by the IRS upon initial contact. The judge, expressing the view that any warnings that might have been given were probably inadequate, proceeded to discharge the jury; he then called all the taxpayers into court, and informed them of their constitutional rights and of the considerable dangers of unwittingly making damaging admissions in these factual circumstances. Finally, he aborted the trial so the witnesses could consult with attorneys.

The case was set for retrial before another jury, but on pretrial motion by the defendant, Judge Ritter dismissed the information on the ground of former jeopardy. The Government filed a direct appeal to this Court, and we noted probable jurisdiction.

* * *

But it is also true that a criminal trial is, even in the best of circumstances, a complicated affair to manage. The proceedings are dependent in the first instance on the most elementary sort of considerations, e. g., the health of the various witnesses, parties, attorneys, jurors, etc., all of whom must be prepared to arrive at the courthouse at set times. And when one adds the scheduling problems arising from case overloads, and the Sixth Amendment's requirement that the single trial to which the double jeopardy provision restricts the Government be conducted speedily, it becomes readily apparent that a mechanical rule prohibiting retrial whenever circumstances compel the discharge of a jury without the defendant's consent would be too high a price to pay for the added assurance of personal security and freedom from governmental harassment which such a mechanical rule would provide. As the Court noted in Wade v. Hunter, 69 S.Ct., at 837 "a defendant's valued right to have his trial completed by a particular tribunal must in some instances be subordinated to the public's interest in fair trials designed to end in just judgments."

Thus the conclusion that "jeopardy attaches" when the trial commences expresses a judgment that the constitutional policies underpinning the Fifth Amendment's guarantee are implicated at that point in the proceedings. The question remains, however, in what circumstances retrial is to be precluded when the intitial proceedings are aborted prior to verdict without the defendant's consent.

In dealing with that question, this Court has, for the most part, explicitly declined the invitation of litigants to formulate rules based on categories of circumstances which will permit or preclude retrial. Thus, in United States v. Perez (1824), this Court held that a defendant in a capital case might be retried after the trial judge, had, without the defendant's consent, discharged a jury that reported itself unable to agree. Mr. Justice Story's opinion for the Court in *Perez* expressed the following thoughts on the problem of reprosecution after a mistrial had been declared without the consent of the defendant:

> "We think, that in all cases of this nature, the law has invested Courts of justice with the authority to discharge a jury from giving any verdict, whenever, in their opinion, taking all the circumstances into consideration, there is a manifest necessity for the act, or the ends of public justice would otherwise be defeated. They are to exercise a sound discretion on the subject; and it is impossible to define all the circumstances, which would render it proper to interfere. To be sure, the power ought to be used with the greatest caution, under urgent circumstances, and for very plain and obvious causes; and, in capital cases especially, Courts should be extremely careful how they interfere with any of the chances of life, in favour of the prisoner. But, after all, they have the right to order the discharge; and the security which the public have for the faithful, sound, and conscientious exercise of this discretion, rests, in this, as in other cases, upon the responsibility of the Judges, under their oaths of office."

The *Perez* case has since been applied by this Court as a standard of appellate review for testing the trial judge's exercise of his discretion in declaring a mistrial without the defendant's consent. E. g., Simmons v. United States (1891) (reprosecution not barred where mistrial declared because letter published in newspaper rendered juror's impartiality doubtful); Logan v. United States (1892) (reprosecution not barred where jury discharged after 40 hours of deliberation for inability to reach a verdict); Thompson v. United States (1894) (reprosecution not barred where jury discharged because one juror had served on grand jury indicting defendant); Wade v. Hunter, 336 U.S. 684, 69 S.Ct. 834 (1949) (retrial not barred where military courtmartial discharged due to tactical necessity in the field).

But a more recent case—Gori v. United States (1961)—while adhering in the main to the *Perez* theme of a "manifest necessity" standard of appellate review—does suggest the possibility of a variation on that theme according to a determination by the appellate court as to which party to the case was the beneficiary of the mistrial ruling. In *Gori*, the Court was called upon to review the action of a trial judge in discharging the jury when it appeared to the judge that the prosecution's questioning of a witness might lead to the introduction of evidence of prior crimes. We upheld reprosecution after the mistrial in an opinion which, while applying the principle of *Perez*, appears to tie the judgment that there was no abuse of discretion in these circumstances to the fact that the judge was acting "in the sole interest of the defendant."

In the instant case, the Government, relying principally on *Gori* contends that even if we conclude the trial judge here abused his discretion, reprosecution should be permitted because the judge's ruling "benefited" the defendant and also clearly was not compelled by bad-faith prosecutorial conduct aimed at triggering a mistrial in order to get another day in court. If the judgment as to who was "benefited" by the mistrial ruling turns on the appellate court's conclusion concerning which party the trial judge was, in point of personal motivation, trying to protect from prejudice, it seems reasonably clear from the trial record here that the judge's insistence on stopping the trial until the witnesses were properly warned was motivated by the desire to protect the witnesses rather than the defendant. But the Government appears to view the question of "benefit" as turning on an appellate court's *post hoc* assessment as to which party would in fact have been aided in the hypothetical event that the witnesses had been called to the stand after consulting with their own attorneys on the course of conduct that would best serve to insulate them personally from criminal and civil liability for the fraudulent tax returns. That conception of benefit, however, involves nothing more than an exercise in pure speculation. In sum, we are unable to conclude on this record that this is a case of a mistrial made "in the sole interest of the defendant." See Gori v. United States, supra.

Further, we think that a limitation on the abuse-of-discretion principle based on an appellate court's assessment of which side benefited from the mistrial ruling does not adequately satisfy the policies underpinning the double jeopardy provision. Reprosecution after a mistrial has unnecessarily been declared by the trial court obviously subjects the defendant to the same personal strain and insecurity regardless of the motivation underlying the trial judge's action.

* * *

. . . For the crucial difference between reprosecution after appeal by the defendant and reprosecution after a *sua sponte* judicial mistrial declaration is that in the first situation the defendant has not been deprived of his option to go to the first jury and, perhaps, end the dispute then and there with an acquittal. On the other hand, where the judge, acting without the defendant's consent, aborts the proceeding, the defendant has been deprived of his "valued right to have his trial completed by a particular tribunal."

* * *

In sum, counsel for both sides perform in an imperfect world; in this area, bright-line rules based on either the source of the problem or the intended beneficiary of the ruling would only disserve the vital competing interests of the Government and the defendant. The trial judge must recognize that lack of preparedness by the Government to continue the trial directly implicates policies underpinning both the double jeopardy provision and the speedy trial guarantee. Alternatively, the judge must bear in mind the potential risks of abuse by the defendant of society's unwillingness to unnecessarily subject him to repeated prosecutions. Yet, in the final analysis, the judge must always temper the decision whether or not to abort the trial by considering the importance to the defendant of being able, once and for all, to conclude his confrontation with society through the verdict of a tribunal he might believe to be favorably disposed to his fate.

Applying these considerations to the record in this case, we must conclude that the trial judge here abused his discretion in discharging the jury. Despite assurances by both the first witness and the prosecuting attorney that the five taxpayers involved in the litigation had all been warned of their constitutional rights, the judge refused to permit them to testify, first expressing his disbelief that they were warned at all, and then expressing his views that any warnings that might have been given would be inadequate. In probing the assumed inadequacy of the warnings that might have been given, the prosecutor was asked if he really intended to try a case for willfully aiding in the preparation of fraudulent returns on a theory that would not incriminate the taxpayers. When the prosecutor started to answer that he intended to do just that, the judge cut him off in midstream and immediately discharged the jury. It is apparent from the record that no consideration was given to the possibility of a trial continuance; indeed, the trial judge acted so abruptly in discharging the jury that, had the prosecutor been disposed to suggest a continuance, or the defendant to object to the discharge of the jury, there would have been no opportunity to do so. When one examines the circumstances surrounding the discharge of this jury, it seems abundantly apparent that the trial judge made no effort to exercise a sound discretion to assure that, taking all the circumstances into account, there was a manifest necessity for the *sua sponte* declaration of this mistrial. Therefore, we must conclude that in the circumstances of this case, appellee's reprosecution would violate the double jeopardy provision of the Fifth Amendment.

Affirmed.

MR. CHIEF JUSTICE BURGER, concurring.

I join in the plurality opinion and in the judgement of the Court not without some reluctance, however, since the case represents a plain frustration of the right to have this case tried, attributable solely to the conduct of the trial judge. If the accused had brought about the erroneous mistrial ruling we would have a different case, but this record shows nothing to take appellee's claims outside the classic mold of being twice placed in jeopardy for the same offense.

[Omitted are the concurring opinion of Justices Black and Brennan and the dissenting opinion of Justice Stewart which was joined by Justices White and Blackmun.]

NOTES

1. The determination as to when manifest necessity permits termination of a trial and commencement of a new trial continued to pose problems after *Jorn*. In Illinois v. Somerville, 410 U.S. 458, 93 S.Ct. 1066 (1973), the jury had been sworn and jeopardy had attached when, before the commencement of trial, the prosecutor discovered a defect in the indictment which was "nonwaivable" and which deprived the trial court of jurisdiction. Over defense objection, the indictment was dismissed and the jury discharged. The grand jury returned a new indictment and the defendants were tried and convicted. The state appellate court rejected a double jeopardy claim as did the Seventh Circuit, following a federal habeas corpus application. The Supreme Court granted certiorari and directed the Seventh Circuit to reconsider in light of *Jorn*. The Seventh Circuit reversed its original decision and held that under *Jorn* double jeopardy principles had been violated. The Supreme Court granted certiorari on the state's petition and, by a vote of 5 to 4, held that the retrial had been proper and that *Jorn* required no contrary conclusion. The reasons given were:

"While virtually all of the cases turn on the particular facts and thus escape meaningful categorization, it is possible to distill from them a general approach, to situations such as that presented by this case. A trial judge properly exercises his discretion to declare a mistrial if an impartial verdict cannot be reached, or if a verdict of conviction could be reached but would have to be reversed on appeal due to an obvious procedural error in the trial. If an error would make reversal on appeal a certainty, it would not serve 'the ends of public justice' to require that the Government proceed with its proof when, if it succeeded before the jury, it would automatically be stripped of that success by an appellate court. While the declaration of a mistrial on the basis of a rule or a defective procedure that lent itself to prosecutorial manipulation would involve an entirely different question, such was not the situation in the above cases or in the instant case."

The dissenters responded:

"Although recognizing that 'a criminal trial is, even in the best of circumstances, a complicated affair to manage,' the Court has not thought prosecutorial error sufficient excuse for not applying the Double Jeopardy Clause. . . .

"Here, the prosecutorial error, not the independent operation of a state procedural rule, necessitated the mistrial . . . the inability to amend an indictment does not come into play, and a mistrial is not necessitated, unless an error on the part of the State in the framing of the indictment is committed. Only when the indictment is defective—only when the State has failed to properly execute its responsibility to frame a proper indictment—does the State's procedural framework necessitate a mistrial."

2. The *Somerville* principle was extended in Lee v. United States, 432 U.S. 33, 97 S.Ct. 2141 (1977). There, after the prosecutor's opening statement in a nonjury trial, defense counsel moved to dismiss the information because of omission of a material element. The judge, without objection, denied the motion subject to reconsideration after time for study. He then heard all the evidence in a two-hour period and commented that the accused had been proved guilty beyond a reasonable doubt. He nevertheless dismissed the indictment because of its material defect. Finding no "bad faith" on the part of the prosecutor in drafting the indictment nor on the part of the judge in not immediately granting the motion to dismiss before evidence was presented, the Court held that a second trial was permissible.

3. In United States v. Dinitz, 424 U.S. 600, 96 S.Ct. 1075 (1976), the Supreme Court stated that where a defendant asks for a mistrial or consents to a mistrial, the case can be tried anew. However, the Court, in *dictum*, recognized that deliberate bad-faith conduct by the prosecutor designed to provoke a mistrial, so as to improve the prosecution's chances at a subsequent trial, would bar a new trial. In *Dinitz* the problem arose from defense counsel's misconduct which was so serious that the trial court excluded counsel from the trial.

4. In Arizona v. Washington, 434 U.S. 497, 98 S.Ct. 824 (1978), the prosecutor sought a mistrial because of the defense lawyer's misconduct in putting before the jury through opening statements inadmissible matter which cast the prosecutor in a bad light. Before granting the mistrial, the trial judge reminded the prosecutor that if termination of the trial over a defense objection were later deemed to be improper, jeopardy principles would forever prevent attainment of a valid conviction. (For this reason prosecutors rarely seek a mistrial. Some follow the wise policy of always seeking the detached opinion of colleagues who have not participated in the particular trial before taking the gamble entailed by a mistrial granted over defense objection.) Writing for the majority, Justice Stevens said that the requisite "high degree" of necessity for a mistrial under the "manifest necessity" test had been met. Justice Marshall dissented, arguing that perhaps a remedy short of a mistrial would have sufficed to permit the prosecution a fair trial. He noted that the trial judge had specifically not declared that a new trial was manifestly necessary.

5. Suppose that an indigent defendant's misdemeanor trial begins without either appointment of counsel or a knowing waiver. Midway through the prosecution's case the trial judge concludes that the facts are aggravated enough so that, if the defendant is found guilty, a jail sentence would be appropriate. May the judge terminate the trial, appoint counsel, and start anew? Would "manifest necessity" be present? Would it make a difference if the *pro se* defendant made no objection to the termination? Suppose the court, without explaining about *Argersinger* or *Scott* Chapter 9, (Section B) or double jeopardy principles, obtained an affirmative response to the following offer: "This is a serious matter. You need a lawyer. How about if we start all over and I appoint counsel to represent you in a new trial?"

6. In United States v. Jenkins, 420 U.S. 358, 95 S.Ct. 1006 (1975), a case decided one week before *Serfass*, the trial judge had dismissed an indictment at the conclusion of a bench trial. The government appealed, arguing that the dismissal was based upon an erroneous theory of law. The Supreme Court noted that even if the trial judge had applied the correct theory of law, he still would have been required to make further factual determinations before deciding the question of innocence or guilt under the proper legal standard. Thus, if the case were to be remanded, further evidentiary proceedings would be required. Under these circumstances, the Supreme Court held that the Double Jeopardy clause of the Fifth Amendment barred a government appeal.

In United States v. Scott, 437 U.S. 82, 98 S.Ct. 2187 (1978), however, the Court expressly overruled *Jenkins*. In *Scott*, both before and after jeopardy had attached, the defendant sought dismissal of the indictment because of alleged prejudicial pre-indictment delay. At the close of all the evidence, before submitting the case to the jury, the court (as to the count in question) granted the motion to dismiss. The government appealed and the Court had to consider whether, assuming the trial judge had erred in granting the motion to dismiss, the Double Jeopardy clause prohibited remanding for a new trial. The Court held that even though a new trial would require new evidence—and this would run afoul of *Jenkins*—a new trial was permissible. The Court emphasized that the *defendant* had sought to terminate the trial on "grounds unrelated to guilt or innocence." While rejecting a "waiver" analysis, the Court held that the "Double Jeopardy Clause, which guards against oppression, does not relieve a defendant from the consequences of his voluntary choice." It added that under the circumstances the defendant cannot be said to be "deprived" of his "valued right to go the first jury; only the public has been deprived of its valued right to 'one complete opportunity to convict those who have violated its laws.'" Four Justices dissented, arguing that *Jenkins* should not be overruled.

7. When a jury fails to reach agreement, the trial judge may declare a mistrial and allow the prosecution to begin anew. A retrial following a hung jury has been held not to violate the double jeopardy clause. This principle appears well settled. United States v. Sanford, 429 U.S. 14, 97 S. Ct. 20 (1976). Consider, however, the policies underlying the double jeopardy prohibition. Is retrial after a hung jury likely to increase the chances of convicting an innocent person? What about concerns for the time, money, and anxiety of the defendant. On the other hand, what policies militate against permitting a single juror to, in effect, acquit the accused? Are there any limits on how many "hung juries" the accused must suffer through before reprosecution is barred. For one view see United States v. Castellanos, 349 F.Supp. 720 (E.D.N.Y.1972), rev'd 478 F.2d 749 (2d Cir. 1973). As this decision indicates, in the federal system the trial judge has the option, following a hung jury, of entering an acquittal rather than permitting a new trial. See Section A–4, infra, concerning the effect of such an order.

8. Suppose that a defendant makes a Fourth Amendment motion to suppress after jeopardy has attached but before verdict. If he wins, may the prosecution, consistent with the Double Jeopardy clause, have the jury discharged, take an interlocutory appeal, and then begin trial anew following the appellate decision? Is this the issue left open in *Serfass* of "a defendant who is afforded an opportunity to obtain a determination of a legal defense prior to trial and nevertheless knowingly allows himself to be placed in jeopardy before raising the defense"? Suppose that a defendant is al-

lowed to make the belated, mid-trial motion to suppress only when, for some reason, he was not at fault in failing to make the motion earlier. Could state law still permit the prosecution an interlocutory review of an adverse decision? Some courts have permitted termination of the trial to allow the prosecution interlocutory review of a mid-trial suppression order; but they have not always fully explored the jeopardy issue. See, e. g., People v. Young, 60 Ill.App.3d 49, 17 Ill.Dec. 566, 376 N.E.2d 712 (1978).

4. RETRIAL FOLLOWING INITIAL ACQUITTAL

As already discussed, when the *initial* verdict of a jury is "not guilty" or the initial judgment of the court in a bench trial is "not guilty," the defendant cannot be tried again for the offense of which he was acquitted. Fed.R.Crim.P. 29(c) permits a district court judge to enter a judgment of acquittal after a jury has been unable to reach a verdict. In United States v. Martin Linen Supply Co., 430 U.S. 564, 97 S.Ct. 1349 (1977), the Court held that the Double Jeopardy prohibition prevents the Government from appealing such a judgment. It held that such a judgment was an acquittal in substance as well as in form. It further noted that the consequences of a successful government appeal would be a requirement that the defendant go through another trial. This, the Court found, is forbidden. The acquittal under Fed.R.Crim.P. 29(c) contemplates an end to litigation as much as does a judgment of acquittal (the federal equivalent of a directed verdict) for the defendant before the case is submitted to the jury.

Retrial following an *initial* verdict of acquittal should be carefully distinguished from the situation in which the judge or jury initially finds the defendant guilty, but the judge then vacates that finding. The latter situation is treated in subsection 5, infra.

Most "retrial following acquittal" cases involve convictions of lesser included offenses followed by retrial for the greater offense. When the jury's verdict has either expressly or impliedly acquitted the defendant of the greater offense, he can never be validly convicted of that greater offense. (Ordinarily under state law conviction of the lesser included charge is an implied acquittal of the greater charge.) In Price v. Georgia, 398 U.S. 323, 90 S.Ct. 1757 (1970), defendant was charged with murder but found guilty of voluntary manslaughter. He obtained a new trial because of error which infected the first trial. The prosecution was permitted to try him again for murder. Again Price was found guilty of manslaughter. The Supreme Court held that double jeopardy barred the new trial for murder and that, although he was convicted of manslaughter, trial of the greater charge may have affected the jury's deliberation of the manslaughter charge. It reversed the second conviction and dictated that if Price were to be tried again, it be solely on the charge of manslaughter.

Somewhat different issues arise when the defendant is tried for an offense different from (and not included in) a closely related offense of which he was previously acquitted. This raises the question of "collateral estoppel," which is the subject of the next decision.

ASHE v. SWENSON

Supreme Court of the United States, 1970.
397 U.S. 436, 90 S.Ct. 1189.

MR. JUSTICE STEWART delivered the opinion of the Court.

In Benton v. Maryland, 395 U.S. 784, 89 S.Ct. 2056, the Court held that the Fifth Amendment guarantee against double jeopardy is enforceable against the States through the Fourteenth Amendment. The question in this case is whether the State of Missouri violated that guarantee when it prosecuted the petitioner a second time for armed robbery in the circumstances here presented.

Sometime in the early hours of the morning of January 10, 1960, six men were engaged in a poker game in the basement of the home of John Gladson at Lee's Summit, Missouri. Suddenly three or four masked men, armed with a shotgun and pistols, broke into the basement and robbed each of the poker players of money and various articles of personal property. The robbers—and it has never been clear whether there were three or four of them—then fled in a car belonging to one of the victims of the robbery. Shortly thereafter the stolen car was discovered in a field, and later that morning three men were arrested by a state trooper while they were walking on a highway not far from where the abandoned car had been found. The petitioner was arrested by another officer some distance away.

The four were subsequently charged with seven separate offenses—the armed robbery of each of the six poker players and the theft of the car. In May 1960 the petitioner went to trial on the charge of robbing Donald Knight, one of the participants in the poker game. At the trial the State called Knight and three of his fellow poker players as prosecution witnesses. Each of them described the circumstances of the holdup and itemized his own individual losses. The proof that an armed robbery had occurred and that personal property had been taken from Knight was unassailable. But the State's evidence that the petitioner had been one of the robbers was weak. Two of the witnesses thought that there had been only three robbers altogether, and could not identify the petitioner as one of them. Another of the victims, who was the petitioner's uncle by marriage, said that at the "patrol station" he had positively identified each of the other three men accused of the holdup, but could say only that the petitioner's voice "sounded very much like" that of one of the robbers. The fourth participant in the poker game did identify the petitioner, but only by his "size and height, and his actions."

The cross-examination of these witnesses was brief, and it was aimed primarily at exposing the weakness of their identification testimony. . . .

The defense offered no testimony and waived final argument.

The trial judge instructed the jury that if it found that the petitioner was one of the participants in the armed robbery, the theft of "any money" from Knight would sustain a conviction. He also instructed the jury that if the petitioner was one of the robbers, he was guilty under the law even if he had not personally robbed Knight. The jury—though not instructed to elaborate upon its verdict—found the petitioner "not guilty due to insufficient evidence."

Six weeks later the petitioner was brought to trial again, this time for the robbery of another participant in the poker game, a man named Roberts. The petitioner filed a motion to dismiss, based on his previous acquittal. The motion was overruled, and the second trial began. The witnesses were for the most part the same, though this time their testimony was substantially stronger on the issue of the petitioner's identity. For example, two witnesses who at the first trial had been wholly unable to identify the petitioner as one of the robbers, now testified that his features, size, and mannerisms matched those of one of their assailants. Another witness who before had identified the petitioner only by his size and actions now also remembered him by the unusual sound of his voice. The State further refined its case at the second trial by declining to call one of the participants in the poker game whose identification testimony at the first trial had been conspicuously negative. The case went to the jury on instructions virtually identical to those given at the first trial. This time the jury found the petitioner guilty, and he was sentenced to a 35-year term in the state penitentiary. The operative facts here are virtually identical to those of Hoag v. New Jersey, [356 U.S. 464, 78 S.Ct. 829]. In that case the defendant was tried for the armed robbery of three men who, along with others, had been held up in a tavern. The proof of the robbery was clear, but the evidence identifying the defendant as one of the robbers was weak, and the defendant interposed an alibi defense. The jury brought in a verdict of not guilty. The defendant was then brought to trial again, on an indictment charging the robbery of a fourth victim of the tavern holdup. This time the jury found him guilty.

Viewing the question presented solely in terms of Fourteenth Amendment due process—whether the course that New Jersey had pursued had "led to fundamental unfairness,"—this Court declined to reverse the judgment of conviction, because "in the circumstances shown by this record, we cannot say that petitioner's later prosecution and conviction violated due process." The Court found it unnecessary to decide whether "collateral estoppel"—the principle that bars relitigation between the same parties of issues actually determined at a previous trial—is a due process requirement in a state criminal trial, since it accepted New Jersey's determination that the petitioner's previous acquittal did not in any event give rise to such an estoppel.

The doctrine of Benton v. Maryland, puts the issues in a perspective quite different from that in Hoag v. New Jersey. The question is no longer whether collateral estoppel is a requirement of due process, but whether it is a part of the Fifth Amendment's guarantee against double jeopardy. And if collateral estoppel is embodied in that guarantee, then its applicability in a particular case is no longer a matter to be left for state court determination within the broad bounds of "fundamental fairness," but a matter of constitutional fact we must decide through an examination of the entire record.

"Collateral estoppel" is an awkward phrase, but it stands for an extremely important principle in our adversary system of justice. It means simply that when an issue of ultimate fact has once been determined by a valid and final judgment, that issue cannot again be litigated between the same parties in any future lawsuit. Although first developed in civil litigation, collateral estoppel has been an established rule of federal criminal law at least since this Court's decision more than 50 years ago in United States v. Oppenheimer, 242 U. S. 85, 37 S.Ct. 68.

The federal decisions have made clear that the rule of collateral estoppel in criminal cases is not to be applied with the hypertechnical and archaic approach of a 19th century pleading book, but with realism and rationality. Where a previous judgment of acquittal was based upon a general verdict, as is usually the case, this approach requires a court to "examine the record of a prior proceeding, taking into account the pleadings, evidence, charge, and other relevant matter, and conclude whether a rational jury could have grounded its verdict upon an issue other than that which the defendant seeks to foreclose from consideration." The inquiry "must be set in a practical frame and viewed with an eye to all the circumstances of the proceedings." Sealfon v. United States, 332 U.S. 575, 579, 68 S.Ct. 237, 240. Any test more technically restrictive would, of course, simply amount to a rejection of the rule of collateral estoppel in criminal proceedings, at least in every case where the first judgment was based upon a general verdict of acquittal.

Straightforward application of the federal rule to the present case can lead to but one conclusion. For the record is utterly devoid of any indication that the first jury could rationally have found that an armed robbery had not occurred, or that Knight had not been a victim of that robbery. The single rationally conceivable issue in dispute before the jury was whether the petitioner had been one of the robbers. And the jury by its verdict found that he had not. The federal rule of law, therefore, would make a second prosecution for the robbery of Roberts wholly impermissible.

The ultimate question to be determined, then, in the light of Benton v. Maryland, supra, is whether this established rule of federal law is embodied in the Fifth Amendment guarantee against double jeopardy. We do not hestitate to hold that it is. For whatever else that constitutional guarantee may embrace, it surely protects a man who has been acquitted from having to "run the gantlet" a second time.

The question is not whether Missouri could validly charge the petitioner with six separate offenses for the robbery of the six poker players. It is not whether he could have received a total of six punishments if he had been convicted in a single trial of robbing the six victims. It is simply whether, after a jury determined by its verdict that the petitioner was not one of the robbers, the State could constitutionally hale him before a new jury to litigate that issue again.

After the first jury had acquitted the petitioner of robbing Knight, Missouri could certainly not have brought him to trial again upon that charge. Once a jury had determined upon conflicting testimony that there was at least a reasonable doubt that the petitioner was one of the robbers, the State could not present the same or different identification evidence in a second prosecution for the robbery of Knight in the hope that a different jury might find that evidence more convincing. The situation is constitutionally no different here, even though the second trial related to another victim of the same robbery. For the name of the victim, in the circumstances of this case, had no bearing whatever upon the issue of whether the petitioner was one of the robbers.

In this case the State in its brief has frankly conceded that following the petitioner's acquittal, it treated the first trial as no more than a dry run for the second prosecution: "No doubt the prosecutor felt the state had a provable case on the first charge and, when he lost, he did what every good attorney would do—he refined his presentation in light of the turn of events at the first trial." But this is precisely what the constitutional guarantee forbids.

MR. JUSTICE BLACK, concurring. [omitted]

MR. JUSTICE HARLAN, concurring. [omitted]

MR. JUSTICE BRENNAN, whom MR. JUSTICE DOUGLAS and MR. JUSTICE MARSHALL join, concurring.

I agree that the Double Jeopardy Clause incorporates collateral estoppel as a constitutional requirement and therefore join the Court's opinion. However, even if the rule of collateral estoppel had been inapplicable to the facts of this case, it is my view that the Double Jeopardy Clause nevertheless bars the prosecution of petitioner a second time for armed robbery. The two prosecutions, the first for the robbery of Knight and the second for the robbery of Roberts, grew out of one criminal episode, and therefore I think it clear on the facts of this case that the Double Jeopardy Clause prohibited Missouri from prosecuting petitioner for each robbery at a different trial.

* * *

In my view, the Double Jeopardy Clause requires the prosecution, except in most limited circumstances, to join at one trial all the charges against a defendant that grow out of a single criminal act, occurrence, episode, or transaction. This "same transaction" test of "same offence" not only enforces the ancient prohibition against vexatious multiple prosecutions embodied in the Double Jeopardy Clause, but responds as well to the increasingly widespread recognition that the consolidation in one lawsuit of all issues arising out of a single transaction or occurrence best promotes justice, economy, and convenience. Modern rules of criminal and civil procedure reflect this recognition.

* * *

Mr. Chief Justice Burger, dissenting.

The Fifth Amendment to the Constitution of the United States provides in part: "nor shall any person be subject for the same offence to be twice put in jeopardy of life or limb . . . ." Nothing in the language or gloss previously placed on this provision of the Fifth Amendment remotely justifies the treatment that the Court today accords to the collateral-estoppel doctrine. The concept of double jeopardy and our firm constitutional commitment is against repeated trials "for the *same offence*." This Court, like most American jurisdictions, has expanded that part of the Constitution into a "same evidence" test. For example, in Blockburger v. United States, 284 U.S. 299, 304, 52 S.Ct. 180, 182, (1932), it was stated, so far as here relevant, that

> "the test to be applied to determine whether there are two offenses or only one is whether each provision [i. e., each charge] requires *proof of a fact which the other does not.*" (Emphasis added).

Clearly and beyond dispute the charge against Ashe in the second trial required proof of a fact—robbery of Roberts—which the charge involving Knight did not. The Court, therefore, has had to reach out far beyond the accepted offense-defining rule to reach its decision in this case. What it has done is to superimpose on the same-evidence test a new and novel collateral-estoppel gloss.

The collateral-estoppel concept—originally a product only of civil litigation—is a strange mutant as it is transformed to control this criminal case. In civil cases the doctrine was justified as conserving judicial resources as well as those of the parties to the actions and additionally as providing the finality needed to plan for the future. It ordinarily applies to parties on each side of the litigation who have the same interest as or who are identical with the parties in the initial litigation. Here the complainant in the second trial is not the same as in the first even though the State is a party in both cases. Very properly, in criminal cases, finality and conservation of private, public, and judicial resources are lesser values than in civil litigation. Also, courts that have applied the collateral-estoppel concept to criminal actions would certainly not apply it to *both* parties, as is true in civil cases, i. e., here, if Ashe had been convicted at the first trial, presumably no court would then hold that he was thereby foreclosed from litigating the identification issue at the second trial.

Perhaps, then, it comes as no surprise to find that the only expressed rationale for the majority's decision is that Ashe has "run the gantlet" once before. This is not a doctrine of the law or legal reasoning but a colorful and graphic phrase, which, as used originally in an opinion of the Court written by Mr. Justice Black, was intended to mean something entirely different. The full phrase is "run the gantlet once *on that charge* . . . ." (emphasis added); it is to be found in Green v. United States, 355 U.S. 184, 190, 78 S.Ct. 221, 225 (1957).

Today's step in this area of constitutional law ought not be taken on no more basis than casual reliance on the "gantlet" phrase lifted out of the context in which it was originally used. This is decision by slogan.

Some commentators have concluded that the harassment inherent in standing trial a second time is a sufficient reason for use of collateral estoppel in criminal trials. If the Court is today relying on a harassment concept to superimpose a new brand of collateral-estoppel gloss on the "same evidence" test, there is a short answer; this case does not remotely suggest harassment of an accused who robbed six victims and the harassment aspect does not rise to constitutional levels. Finally, the majority's opinion tells us "that the rule of collateral estoppel in criminal cases is not to be applied with the hypertechnical and archaic approach of a 19th century pleading book, but with realism and rationality." With deference I am bound to pose the question: what is reasonable and rational about holding that an acquittal of Ashe for robbing Knight bars a trial for robbing Roberts? To borrow a phrase from the Court's opinion, what could conceivably be more "hypertechnical and archaic" and more like the stilted formalisms of 17th and 18th century common-law England, than to stretch jeopardy for robbing Knight into jeopardy for robbing Roberts?

After examining the facts of this case the Court concludes that the first jury must have concluded that Ashe was not one of the robbers—that he was not present at the time. Also, since the second jury necessarily reached its decision by finding he was present, the collateral-estoppel doctrine applies. But the majority's analysis of the facts completely disregards the confusion injected into the case by the robbery of Mrs. Gladson [in the upstairs bedroom]. To me, if we are to psychoanalyze the jury, the evidence adduced at the first trial could more reasonably be construed as indicating that Ashe had been at the Gladson home with the other three men but was not one of those involved in the basement robbery. Certainly, the evidence at the first trial was equivocal as to whether there were three or four robbers, whether the man who robbed Mrs. Gladson was one of the three who robbed the six male victims, and whether a man other than the three had robbed Mrs. Gladson. Then, since the jury could have thought that the "acting together" instruction given by the trial court in both trials only applied to the actual taking from the six card players, and not to Mrs. Gladson, the jury could well have acquitted Ashe but yet believed that he was present in the Gladson home. On the other hand, the evidence adduced at the second trial resolved issues other than identity that may have troubled the first jury. If believed, that evidence indicated that a fourth robber, Johnson, not Ashe, was with Mrs. Gladson when Ashe, Larson, and Brown were robbing the male victims. Johnson did go to the basement where the male victims were located, but only after the other three had already taken the stolen items and when the robbers were preparing for their departure in a car to be stolen from Roberts.

Accordingly, even the facts in this case, which the Court's opinion considers to "lead to but one conclusion," are susceptible of an interpretation that the first jury did not base its acquittal on the identity ground which the Court finds so compelling. The Court bases its holding on sheer "guesswork," which should have no place particularly in our review of state convictions by way of habeas corpus.

* * *

The essence of MR. JUSTICE BRENNAN's concurrence is that this was all one transaction, one episode, or, if I may so characterize it, one frolic, and, hence, only one crime. His approach, like that taken by the Court, totally overlooks the significance of there being *six entirely separate charges of robbery* against six individuals.

This "single frolic" concept is not a novel notion; it has been urged in various courts including this Court. One of the theses underlying the "single frolic" notion is that the criminal episode is "indivisible." The short answer to that is that to the victims, the criminal conduct is readily divisible and intensely personal; each offense is an offense against *a person*. For me it demeans the dignity of the human personality and individuality to talk of "a single transaction" in the context of six separate assaults on six individuals.

No court that elevates the individual rights and human dignity of the accused to a high place—as we should—ought to be so casual as to treat the victims as a single homogenized lump of human clay. I would grant the dignity of individual status to the victims as much as to those accused, not more but surely no less.

If it be suggested that multiple crimes can be separately punished but must be collectively tried, one can point to the firm trend in the law to allow severance of defendants and offenses into separate trials so as to avoid possible prejudice of one criminal act or of the conduct of one defendant to "spill over" on another.

What the Court holds today must be related to its impact on crimes more serious than ordinary housebreaking, followed by physical assault on six men and robbery of all of them. To understand its full impact we must view the holding in the context of four men who break and enter, rob, and then kill six victims. The concurrence tells us that unless all the crimes are joined in one trial the alleged killers cannot be tried for more than one of the killings even if the evidence is that they personally killed two, three, or more of the victims. Or alter the crime to four men breaking into a college dormitory and assaulting six girls. What the Court is holding is, in effect, that the second and third and fourth criminal acts are "free," unless the accused is tried for the multiple crimes in a single trial—something defendants frantically use every legal device to avoid, and often succeed in avoiding. This is the reality of what the Court holds today; it does not make good sense and it cannot make good law.

NOTE

In Harris v. Washington, 404 U.S. 55, 92 S.Ct. 183 (1971), the defendant allegedly sent a bomb through the mail which exploded, killing his infant son and injuring his estranged wife. He was tried for the murder of his son and acquitted. At a subsequent trial for assaulting his wife, he pleaded double jeopardy and collateral estoppel. The court rejected his defense because a threatening letter to his wife, excluded at the first trial, was admitted at the second and, thereby, the issues relating to identity had not been fully litigated so as to give rise to estoppel. The Supreme Court reversed, holding that a prior acquittal on the "ultimate issue" bars a second trial irrespective of the State's good faith in bringing successive prosecutions.

5. RETRIAL FOLLOWING CONVICTION

Several situations may give rise to a retrial following a conviction. One occurs when a defendant has been convicted of one offense and then is prosecuted for another offense arising out of the same transaction. As indicated in his separate opinion in *Ashe*, supra, Justice Brennan believes that absent a defense request for severance, the prosecution should be required to proceed in a single trial on all charges which arise from a single transaction. Although he and Justice Marshall have repeatedly taken the position, a majority of the Court has never concurred. Why would a prosecutor wish to try a defendant several times rather than once? Does the possibility of collateral estoppel under *Ashe* diminish the advantages which "holding" back certain charges might otherwise provide to a prosecutor? Are there any legitimate policy reasons justifying separate prosecutions for closely related offenses when defendant is not arguing for separate trials? What problems would arise in defining "same transaction" for purposes of the Brennan approach? How should it be defined?

One of the most unusual multiple prosecutions cases to reach the Supreme Court was decided before *Benton* made the Double Jeopardy Clause applicable to the States. In Ciucci v. Illinois, 356 U.S. 571, 78 S.Ct. 839 (1958), the defendant was charged in four separate indictments with murdering his wife and three children, all of whom, with bullet wounds in their heads, were found dead in a burning building. In three successive trials, the defendant was found guilty. At each trial the prosecution introduced into evidence the details of all four deaths. At the first two trials, involving the death of the wife and one of the children, the jury fixed the penalty at 20 and 45 years respectively. At the third trial, involving the death of a second child, the penalty was fixed at death. The Supreme Court held that this third trial did not violate due process: "The State was constitutionally entitled to prosecute these individual offenses singly at separate trials, and to utilize therein all relevant evidence, in the absense of proof establishing that such a course of action entailed fundamental unfairness."

The Ciucci dissenters considered the multiple prosecutions as "an instance of the prosecution being allowed to harass the accused with repeated trials and convictions on the same evidence, until it achieves its desired result of a capital verdict." The prosecution's efforts were viewed as an "unseemly and oppressive use of a criminal trial that violates the concept of due process contained in the Fourteenth Amendment   .   .   .."

Although four justices in *Ciucci* dissented and two others referred to the possibility of other remedies, Vincent Ciucci was electrocuted.   In 1961 the Illinois legislature adopted Ill.Rev.Stat. Ch. 38, § 3–3, which bars separate multiple prosecutions for offenses "if they are based on the same act," and if they are known to the proper prosecuting authority at the time prosecution is commenced.   Would the "same act" language bar multiple prosecutions in a multiple murder case like *Ciucci*?   What statutory language would you use if you wished to prohibit what was done in *Ciucci*?   "Same conduct"? "Same transaction"?   Suppose that a sniper kills eight people over a twenty-hour period.   What language would bar separate multiple prosecutions in such a case?   Should a homicide during flight from an armed robbery have to be prosecuted along with the armed robbery charge?

In a 1980 case in the Circuit Court of Cook County, Illinois, the defendant, John Gacy, was convicted of murdering thirty-three individuals over the course of several years and burying most of the bodies beneath his house.   The defense of insanity was raised as to each killing.   Suppose that the prosecution had wished to proceed separately on each charge.   Would a "same transaction" test have barred separate prosecutions?   Often in multiple offense cases the prosecution may seek consolidation, in which case no jeopardy claim will arise.   If the defense resists joinder, then the issue is akin to the severance of counts issue discussed in Chapter 13, Section E, infra.

As this casebook goes to press the United States Supreme Court is considering Vitale v. Illinois.   In that case the Illinois Supreme Court held that a juvenile prosecution for vehicular homicide was barred by an earlier prosecution on a state traffic charge arising out of the same conduct which culminated in the vehicular homicide. The United States Supreme Court has granted the State's petition for certiorari.

In United States v. Wilson, 420 U.S. 332, 95 S.Ct. 1013 (1975), the trial judge had dismissed an indictment after a finding of guilty. The government appealed.   The Supreme Court noted that if the government was correct in its argument that an erroneous interpretation of law underlay the dismissal, the error could be corrected by a reinstatement of the verdict of guilty without the necessity for a further evidentiary hearing.   Under these circumstances the Court held that the government could appeal.

Many states do not permit the prosecution to appeal in situations where after a verdict of guilty the trial judge has ordered a new trial or has directed an acquittal.   This remains true even though under *Wilson* the Double Jeopardy clause would seem to allow such appeals in any situation where a reversal would lead to reinstatement of the guilty verdict without any further hearing.

Retrial may occur when at the defendant's request, a reviewing court determines that error occurred in the first trial.   One possible exception occurs where the prosecutor in bad faith injected the error. See People v. Pendleton, 75 Ill.App.3d 580, 31 Ill.Dec. 294, 394 N.E.2d 496 (1979), and *Dinitz*, Section A–3, Note 3, supra.

When a reviewing court determines that the evidence was insufficient to sustain a conviction, a remand for a new trial is barred by the Double Jeopardy Clause. See Burks v. United States, 437 U.S. 1, 98 S.Ct. 2141 (1978); Greene v. Massey, 437 U.S. 19, 98 S.Ct. 2151 (1978). These decisions, however, very probably do not bar the highest reviewing court of a state from reversing an intermediate appellate court's decision that the evidence failed to sustain a conviction. In such a case, the high court would reinstate the conviction and no further evidentiary proceeding would be required. Nor do *Burks* and *Greene* decide whether following a conviction at a trial in which significant prosecution evidence was erroneously excluded, a new trial would be permitted even though the evidence which was admitted at the first trial was too slight to sustain the guilty verdict.

In Brown v. Ohio, 432 U.S. 161, 97 S.Ct. 2221 (1977), the Supreme Court held that Double Jeopardy prohibits trial of a defendant for the greater offense after he has been convicted of a lesser "included" offense even if he has not been previously tried for the greater offense. If proof of the greater offense necessarily would establish every element of the lesser, then the lesser offense is "included" in the greater. In Jeffers v. United States, 432 U.S. 137, 97 S.Ct. 2207 (1977), however, the Court held that where the prosecution separately charges both the greater offense and the lesser included offense, and where the defendant obtains a severance of the charges, he has waived his right to prevent trial on the greater charge after conviction of the lesser included offense.

Suppose that pursuant to a plea bargaining agreement the defendant is convicted of a lesser included offense. Later he is allowed to withdraw his guilty plea or successfully attacks the plea on appeal or in a post-conviction proceeding. Can he now be prosecuted for the greater offense? Consider this situation in connection with Chapter 16, Section C, Note 6, infra.

Consider this hypothetical. Under the laws of State X a defendant can be sentenced to death only if the *same* jury which convicted signs a death verdict after a separate sentencing hearing. After the jury signs a death verdict and is discharged, a reviewing court finds that no error occurred in the guilt-innocence phase, but finds that error occurred in the sentencing proceeding. Could the defendant be forced to endure a whole new trial so that the prosecutor could have the possibility of obtaining a death verdict? Would this clearly violate the Double Jeopardy prohibition? Would any theory of "waiver" be available to the prosecution? Suppose that under state law *no* sentence could be imposed except by the same jury which found the defendant guilty. Would a new trial following error in a sentencing proceeding violate the Fifth Amendment even if death was not a possible sentence?

Consider also Ludwig v. Massachusetts, 427 U.S. 618, 96 S.Ct. 2781 (1976), upholding a statutory scheme which seemingly institutionalized multiple prosecutions. There the defendant was first tried in a proceeding in which no jury was available. An acquittal in that bench trial would be final. On the other hand, upon conviction defendant could automatically exercise the right to trial *de novo* before a jury. He could not, however, bypass the first proceedings and immediately obtain a jury trial. Although the defendant was required to undergo the time and expense of two trials in order to exercise his constitutional right to trial by jury, a majority of the Court upheld the procedure. The plurality opinion emphasized a waiver theory, asserting that it was defendant who elected the second trial. The dissenters found that the procedure violated the Sixth Amendment trial by jury right and did not dwell upon the double jeopardy claim.

6. JEOPARDY, DUE PROCESS, AND SENTENCING

The Double Jeopardy clause prohibits not only multiple trials for the same offense but also multiple convictions and multiple sentences. Ex parte Lange, 85 U.S. (18 Wall.) 163 (1873); United States v. Benz, 282 U.S. 304, 51 S.Ct. 113 (1931). The limitation, however, is quite narrow. "(T)he test to be applied to determine whether there are two offenses (thus avoiding the Double Jeopardy prohibition) or one is whether each requires proof of a fact which the other does not." Blockburger v. United States, 284 U.S. 299, 52 S.Ct. 180 (1932). Thus a single act of reckless driving can result in multiple convictions and multiple sentences if the act causes death: proof of the offense of vehicular homicide requires proof of a death, which proof is not required for a conviction of reckless driving. Similarly a person who through a single act of arson kills eight people could receive eight sentences for felony-murder. The offense of murdering X requires proof of something not required for the offense of murdering Y, namely the death of X.

Some states have placed limits upon multiple punishments beyond those required by *Blockburger*, particularly as to sentences which are consecutive rather than concurrent. See, e. g., Ill.Rev.Stat. Ch. 38, § 1005–8–4 (1979), which, subject to certain exceptions, prohibits consecutive sentences "for offenses which were committed as part of a single course of conduct during which there was no substantial change in the nature of the criminal objective." See, also, Whalen v. United States, —— U.S. ——, 27 Cr.L.R. 3064 (1980), which interpreted Congressional intent to preclude imposition of consecutive sentences in federal cases for felony-murder and the underlying felony.

The problem of multiple punishments for closely related offenses should be distinguished from the problem of separate trials for closely related offenses.

Based upon Stroud v. United States, 251 U.S. 15, 40 S.Ct. 50 (1919), it was generally assumed that when a defendant through his appeal received a new trial because of trial error, the slate was wiped clean. If he was convicted at a second trial, any punishment permitted by statute could be imposed, including one which was greater than that imposed after the first trial. A "waiver" theory was invoked to reach this result. Thus a capital defendant who, like Stroud, had avoided a death sentence could be sentenced to death following a successful appeal, retrial, and a new conviction. Some persons chose not to appeal for this reason. See Fay v. Noia, 372 U.S. 391, 83 S.Ct. 822 (1963).

Increased sentences following retrial were made especially visible after *Gideon*, Chapter 9, Section B. Some defendants who won reversals because they had been denied counsel at their first trial received much more severe punishments following retrials. One who had been sentenced to two years, and who had won a reversal, was sentenced to ten years following reconviction. As indicated in the next case, the continuing vitality of *Stroud* was challenged, but the Supreme Court reached a solution on grounds other than the Double Jeopardy clause.

NORTH CAROLINA v. PEARCE

Supreme Court of the United States, 1969.
395 U.S. 711, 89 S.Ct. 2072.

MR. JUSTICE STEWART delivered the opinion of the Court.

When at the behest of the defendant a criminal conviction has been set aside and a new trial ordered, to what extent does the Constitution limit the imposition of a harsher sentence after conviction upon retrial? That is the question presented by these two cases.

Pearce was convicted in a North Carolina court upon a charge of assault with intent to commit rape. The trial judge sentenced him to prison for a term of 12 to 15 years. Several years later he initiated a state post-conviction proceeding which culminated in the reversal of his conviction.

.   .   . He was retried, convicted, and sentenced by the trial judge to an eight-year prison term, which, when added to the time Pearce had already spent in prison, the parties agree amounted to a longer total sentence than that originally imposed. The United States District Court held that the longer sentence imposed upon retrial was "unconstitutional and void." .   .   . This order was affirmed by the United States Court of Appeals for the Fourth Circuit.

*   *   *

The respondent Rice pleaded guilty in an Alabama trial court to four separate charges of second-degree burglary. He was sentenced to prison terms aggregating 10 years. Two and one-half years later the judgments were set aside in a state *coram nobis* proceeding.
.   .   . He was retried upon three of the charges, convicted, and sentenced to prison terms aggregating 25 years. No credit was given for the time he had spent in prison on the original judgments. He then brought this habeas corpus proceeding alleging that the state trial court had acted unconstitutionally in failing to give him credit

for the time he had already served in prison, and in imposing grossly harsher sentences upon retrial. Judge Johnson agreed with both contentions. While stating that he did "not believe that it is constitutionally impermissible to impose a harsher sentence upon retrial if there is recorded in the court record some legal justification for it," Judge Johnson found that Rice had been denied due process of law, because "[u]nder the evidence in this case, the conclusion is inescapable that the State of Alabama is punishing petitioner Rice for his having exercised his post-conviction right of review and for having the original sentences declared unconstitutional." 274 F.Supp. 116, 121, 122. The judgment of the District Court was affirmed by the United States Court of Appeals for the Fifth Circuit.

The problem before us involves two related but analytically separate issues. One concerns the constitutional limitations upon the imposition of a more severe punishment after conviction for the same offense upon retrial. The other is the more limited question whether, in computing the new sentence, the Constitution requires that credit must be given for that part of the original sentence already served. The second question is not presented in *Pearce*, for in North Carolina it appears to be the law that a defendant must be given full credit for all time served under the previous sentence. Alabama law, however, seems to reflect a different view. And respondent Rice, upon being resentenced, was given no credit at all for the two and one-half years he had already spent in prison.

We turn first to the more limited aspect of the question before us—whether the Constitution requires that, in computing the sentence imposed after conviction upon retrial, credit must be given for time served under the original sentence. We then consider the broader question of what constitutional limitations there may be upon the imposition of a more severe sentence after reconviction.

I.

. . . The Fifth Amendment guarantee against double jeopardy has been said to consist of three separate constitutional protections. It protects against a second prosecution for the same offense after acquittal. It protects against a second prosecution for the same offense after conviction. And it protects against multiple punishments for the same offense.

* * *

We think it is clear that this basic constitutional guarantee is violated when punishment already exacted for an offense is not fully "credited" in imposing sentence upon a new conviction for the same offense. The constitutional violation is flagrantly apparent in a case involving the imposition of a maximum sentence after reconviction. Suppose, for example, in a jurisdiction where the maximum allowable sentence for larceny is 10 years' imprisonment, a man succeeds in getting his larceny conviction set aside after serving three years in prison. If, upon reconviction, he is given a 10-year sentence, then, quite clearly, he will have received multiple punishments for the same offense. For he will have been compelled to serve separate prison terms of three years and 10 years, although the maximum single punishment for the offense is 10 years' imprisonment. Though not so dramatically evident, the same principle obviously holds true whenever punishment already endured is not fully subtracted from any new sentence imposed.

We hold that the constitutional guarantee against multiple punishments for the same offense absolutely requires that punishment already exacted must be fully "credited" in imposing sentence upon a new conviction for the same offense. If, upon a new trial, the defendant is acquitted, there is no way the years he spent in prison can be returned to him. But if he is reconvicted, those years can and must be returned—by subtracting them from whatever new sentence is imposed.

II.

To hold that the second sentence must be reduced by the time served under the first is, however, to give but a partial answer to the question before us. We turn, therefore, to consideration of the broader problem of what constitutional limitations there may be upon the general power of a judge to impose upon reconviction a longer prison sentence than the defendant originally received.

A

Long-established constitutional doctrine makes clear that, beyond the requirement already discussed, the guarantee against double jeopardy imposes no restrictions upon the length of a sentence imposed upon reconviction.

. . . at least since 1919, when Stroud v. United States, 251 U.S. 15, 40 S.Ct. 50, was decided, it has been settled that a corollary of the power to retry a defendant is the power, upon the defendant's reconviction, to impose whatever sentence may be legally authorized, whether or not it is greater than the sentence imposed after the first conviction.

* * *

Although the rationale for this "well-established part of our constitutional jurisprudence" has been variously verbalized, it rests ultimately upon the premise that the original conviction has, at the defendant's behest, been wholly nullified and the slate wiped clean. As to whatever punishment has actually been suffered under the first conviction, that premise is, of course, an unmitigated fiction, as we have recognized in Part I of this opinion. But, so far as the conviction itself goes, and that part of the sentence that has not yet been served, it is no more than a simple statement of fact to say that the slate *has* been wiped clean. The conviction *has* been set aside and the unexpired portion of the original sentence will never be served. A new trial may result in an acquittal. But if it does result in a conviction, we cannot say that the constitutional guarantee against double jeopardy of its own weight restricts the imposition of an otherwise lawful single punishment for the offense in question. To hold to the contrary would be to cast doubt upon the whole validity of the basic principle and upon the unbroken line of decisions that have followed that principle for almost 75 years. We think those decisions are entirely sound, and we decline to depart from the concept they reflect.

B

The other argument advanced in support of the proposition that the Constitution absolutely forbids the imposition of a more severe sentence upon retrial is grounded upon the Equal Protection Clause of the Fourteenth Amendment. The theory advanced is that, since convicts who do not seek new trials cannot have their sentences increased, it creates an invidious classification to impose that risk only upon those who succeed in getting their original convictions set aside. The argument, while not lacking in ingenuity, cannot withstand close examination. In the first place, we deal here, not with increases in existing sentences, but with the imposition of wholly new sentences after wholly new trials. Putting that conceptual nicety to one side, however, the problem before us simply cannot be rationally dealt with in terms of "classifications." A man who is retried after his first conviction has been set aside may be acquitted. If convicted, he may receive a shorter sentence, he may receive the same sentence, or he may receive a longer sentence than the one originally imposed. The result may depend upon a particular combination of infinite variables peculiar to each individual trial. It simply cannot be said that a State has invidiously "classified" those who successfully seek new trials, any more than that the State has invidiously "classified" those prisoners whose convictions are *not* set aside by denying the members of that group the opportunity to be acquitted. To fit the problem of this case into an equal protection framework is a task too Procrustean to be rationally accomplished.

C

We hold, therefore, that neither the double jeopardy provision nor the Equal Protection Clause imposes an absolute bar to a more severe sentence upon reconviction. A trial judge is not constitutionally precluded, in other words, from imposing a new sentence, whether greater or less than the original sentence, in the light of events subsequent to the first trial that may have thrown new light upon the defendant's "life, health, habits, conduct, and mental and moral propensities." Williams v. New York, 337 U.S. 241, 245, 69 S.Ct. 1079, 1082. Such information may come to the judge's attention from evidence adduced at the second trial itself, from a new presentence investigation, from the defendant's prison record, or possibly from other sources. The freedom of a sentencing judge to consider the defendant's conduct subsequent to the first conviction in imposing a new sentence is no more than consonant with the principle that a State may adopt the "prevalent modern philosophy of penology that the punishment should fit the offender and not merely the crime."

To say that there exists no absolute constitutional bar to the imposition of a more severe sentence upon retrial is not, however, to end the inquiry. There remains for consideration the impact of the Due Process Clause of the Fourteenth Amendment.

It can hardly be doubted that it would be a flagrant violation of the Fourteenth Amendment for a state trial court to follow an announced practice of imposing a heavier sentence upon every reconvicted defendant for the explicit purpose of punishing the defendant for his having succeeded in getting his original conviction set aside. Where, as in each of the cases before us, the original conviction has been set aside because of a constitutional error, the imposition of such a punishment, "penalizing those who choose to exercise" constitutional rights, "would be patently unconstitutional." And the very threat inherent in the existence of such a punitive policy would, with respect to those still in prison, serve to "chill the exercise of basic constitutional rights." But even if the first conviction has been set aside for nonconstitutional error, the imposition of a penalty upon the defendant for having successfully pursued a statutory right of appeal or collateral remedy would be no less a violation of due process of law. "A new sentence, with enhanced punishment, based upon such a reason, would be a flagrant violation of the rights of the defendant." Nichols v. United States, 106 F. 672, 679. A court is "without right to .   .   . put a price on an appeal. A defendant's exercise of a right of appeal must be free and unfettered. .   .   . [I]t is unfair to use the great power given to the court to determine sentence to place a defendant in the dilemma of making an unfree choice."

Due process of law, then, requires that vindictiveness against a defendant for having successfully attacked his first conviction must play no part in the sentence he receives after a new trial. And since the fear of such vindictiveness may unconstitutionally deter a defendant's exercise of the right to appeal or collaterally attack his first conviction, due process also requires that a defendant be freed of apprehension of such a retaliatory motivation on the part of the sentencing judge.

In order to assure the absence of such a motivation, we have concluded that whenever a judge imposes a more severe sentence upon a defendant after a new trial, the reasons for his doing so must affirmatively appear. Those reasons must be based upon objective information concerning identifiable conduct on the part of the defendant occurring after the time of the original sentencing proceeding. And the factual data upon which the increased sentence is based must be made part of the record, so that the constitutional legitimacy of the increased sentence may be fully reviewed on appeal.

We dispose of the two cases before us in the light of [the fact] that .   .   . "the State of Alabama offers no evidence attempting to justify the increase in Rice's original sentences" [and] that neither at the time the increased sentence was imposed upon Pearce, nor at any stage in this habeas corpus proceeding, has the State offered any reason or justification for that sentence beyond the naked power to impose it. We conclude that in each of the cases before us, the judgment should be affirmed.

MR. JUSTICE BLACK, concurring in part and dissenting in part.

* * *

. . . Punishment based on the impermissible motivation described by the Court is, as I have said, clearly unconstitutional, and courts must of course set aside the punishment if they find, by the normal judicial process of fact-finding, that such a motivation exists. But, beyond this, the courts are not vested with any general power to prescribe particular devices "[i]n order to assure the absence of such a motivation."

* * *

Apart from this, the possibility that judicial action will be prompted by impermissible motives is a particularly poor reason for holding that detailed rules of procedure are constitutionally binding in every state and federal prosecution. The danger of improper motivation is of course ever present. A judge *might* impose a specially severe penalty solely because of a defendant's race, religion, or political views. He *might* impose a specially severe penalty because a defendant exercised his right to counsel, or insisted on a trial by jury, or even because the defendant refused to admit this guilt and insisted on any particular kind of trial. In all these instances any additional punishment would of course be, for the reasons I have stated, flagrantly unconstitutional. But it has never previously been suggested by this Court that "[i]n order to assure the absence of such a motivation," this Court could, as a matter of constitutional law, direct all trial judges to spell out in detail their reasons for setting a particular sentence, making their reasons "affirmatively appear," and basing these reasons on "objective information concerning identifiable conduct." Nor has this Court ever previously suggested in connection with sentencing that "the factual data . . . must be made part of the record." On the contrary, we spelled out in some detail in Williams v. New York, 337 U.S. 241, 69 S.Ct. 1079 (1949), our reasons for refusing to subject the sentencing process to any such limitations, which might hamstring modern penological reforms, and the Court has, until today, continued to reaffirm that decision.

* * *

MR. JUSTICE HARLAN, concurring in part and dissenting in part.

. . . The Court today, in Benton v. Maryland, 395 U.S. 784, 89 S.Ct. 2056, has held, over my dissent, that the Double Jeopardy Clause of the Fifth Amendment is made applicable to the States by the Fourteenth Amendment Due Process Clause. . . .

Given *Benton*, it is my view that the decision of this Court in Green v. United States, 355 U.S. 184, 78 S.Ct. 221 (1957), from which I dissented at the time, points strongly to the conclusion that the Double Jeopardy Clause of the Fifth Amendment governs *both* issues presently decided by the Court. Accordingly, I join in Part I of the Court's opinion, and concur in the result reached in Part II.

Green held in effect that a defendant who is convicted of a lesser offense included in that charged in the original indictment, and who thereafter secures reversal, may be retried only for the lesser included offense. Mr. Justice Frankfurter observed, in a dissent which I joined, that:

> "As a practical matter, and on any basis of human values, it is scarcely possible to distinguish a case in which the defendant is convicted of a greater offense from one in which he is convicted of an offense that has the same name as that of which he was previously convicted but carries a significantly [increased] . . . punishment . . . ."

Further reflection a decade later has not changed my view that the two situations cannot be meaningfully distinguished.

Every consideration enunciated by the Court in support of the decision in *Green* applies with equal force to the situation at bar. In each instance, the defendant was once subjected to the risk of receiving a maximum punishment, but it was determined by legal process that he should receive only a specified punishment less than the maximum. See id., 355 U.S., at 190, 78 S.Ct., at 225. And the concept or fiction of an "implicit acquittal" of the greater offense, ibid., applies equally to the greater sentence: in each case it was determined at the former trial that the defendant or his offense was of a certain limited degree of "badness" or gravity only, and therefore merited only a certain limited punishment. Most significantly, perhaps, in each case a contrary rule would place the defendant considering whether to appeal his conviction in the same "incredible dilemma" and confront him with the same "desperate" choice. Id., at 193, 78 S.Ct., at 227. His decision whether or not to appeal would be burdened by the consideration that success, followed by retrial and conviction, might place him in a far worse position than if he remained silent and suffered what seemed to him an unjust punishment. In terms of *Green*, that the imposition of a more severe sentence on retrial is a matter of pure *chance*, rather than the result of purposeful retaliation for having taken an appeal, renders the choice no less "desperate."

I therefore conclude that, consistent with the Fifth Amendment, a defendant who has once been convicted and sentenced to a particular punishment may not on retrial be placed again in jeopardy of receiving a greater punishment than was first imposed. . . .

MR. JUSTICE WHITE, concurring in part.

I join the Court's opinion except that in my view Part II-C should authorize an increased sentence on retrial based on any objective, identifiable factual data not known to the trial judge at the time of the original sentencing proceeding.

MR. JUSTICE DOUGLAS, whom MR. JUSTICE MARSHALL joins, concurring. The governing principle has thus developed that a convicted man may be retried after a successful appeal; that he may run the risk, on retrial, of receiving a sentence as severe as that previously imposed; and that he may run the risk of being tried for a separate offense. But with all deference, I submit that the State does not, because of prior error, have a second chance to obtain an enlarged sentence.

Where a man successfully attacks a sentence that he has already "fully served," the State cannot create an additional sentence and send him back to prison. Similarly, where a defendant successfully attacks a sentence that he has begun to serve, the State cannot impose an added sentence by sending him to prison for a greater term.

* * *

NOTES

1. In Chaffin v. Stynchcombe, 412 U.S. 17, 93 S.Ct. 1977 (1973), on retrial, after a reversal for error and reconviction, a *jury* sentenced the accused to a higher sentence than the one which had been imposed after the first trial. The Court held that the rule of *Pearce* was not offended because the possibility of vindictiveness in such a case was "*de minimis.*" In such a retrial the jury ordinarily does not know what sentence had previously been imposed. It may not even know that a prior trial had resulted in a guilty verdict. Moreover, "the jury, unlike the judge who has been reversed, will have no personal stake in the prior conviction and no motivation to engage in self-vindication. Similarly, the jury is unlikely to be sensitive to the institutional interests that might occasion higher sentences by a judge desirous of discouraging what he regards as meritless appeals."

2. In Colten v. Kentucky, 407 U.S. 104, 92 S.Ct. 1953 (1972), the Court was faced with a claim that a two-tier trial system violated the dictates of North Carolina v. Pearce. The system in question provided for the trial of misdemeanors in an inferior court. After conviction or a plea of guilty, the accused could secure as a matter of right a new trial in the superior court. Upon conviction in the higher court a more severe sentence might be imposed. From this conviction and sentence the accused could take a conventional appeal. The Court (with one dissent) held:

> ". . . [T]he court which conducted Colten's trial and imposed the final sentence was not the court with whose work Colten was sufficiently dissatisfied to seek a different result on appeal; and it is not the court that is asked to do over what it thought it had already done correctly. Nor is the *de novo* court even asked to find error in another court's work. . . . It would also appear that however understandably a court of general jurisdiction might feel that the defendant who has had a due process trial ought to be satisfied with it, the *de novo* court in the two-tier system is much more likely to reflect the attitude of the Kentucky Court of Appeals in this case when it stated that 'the inferior courts are not designed or equipped to conduct error-free trials, or to insure full recognition of constitutional freedoms. They are courts of convenience, to provide speedy and inexpensive means of disposition of charges of minor offenses.'
>
> "It is suggested, however, that the sentencing strictures imposed by *Pearce* are essential in order to minimize an asserted unfairness to criminal defendants who must endure a trial in an inferior court with less-than-adequate protections in order to secure a trial comporting completely with constitutional guarantees. We are not persuaded, however, that the Kentucky arrangement for dealing with the less serious offenses disadvantages defendants

any more or any less than trials conducted in a court of general jurisdiction in the first instance, as long as the latter are always available. Proceedings in the inferior courts are simple and speedy, and, if the results in Colten's case are any evidence, the penalty is not characteristically severe. Such proceedings offer a defendant the opportunity to learn about the prosecution's case and, if he chooses, he need not reveal his own. He may also plead guilty without a trial and promptly secure a *de novo* trial in a court of general criminal jurisdiction. He cannot, and will not, face the realistic threat of a prison sentence in the inferior court without having the help of counsel, whose advice will also be available in determining whether to seek a new trial, with the slate wiped clean, or to accept the penalty imposed by the inferior court. The State has no such options. Should it not prevail in the lower court, the case is terminated, whereas the defendant has the choice of beginning anew. In reality his choices are to accept the decision of the judge and the sentence imposed in the inferior court or to reject what in effect is no more than an offer in settlement of his case and seek the judgment of judge or jury in the superior court, with sentence to be determined by the full record made in that court. We cannot say that the Kentucky trial *de novo* system, as such, is unconstitutional or that it presents hazards warranting the restraints called for in North Carolina v. Pearce, particularly since such restraints might, to the detriment of both defendant and State, diminish the likelihood that inferior courts would impose lenient sentences whose effect would be to limit the discretion of a superior court judge or jury if the defendant is retried and found guilty."

3. In Blackledge v. Perry, 417 U.S. 21, 94 S.Ct. 2098 (1974), the Supreme Court held that a prosecutor may not bring a more serious charge based upon the same conduct after a defendant has exercised his right to a trial de novo following his conviction on a less serious charge. (This case is discussed further in Bordenkircher v. Hayes, Chapter 16.)

4. What justifies a higher sentence after retrial? Compare the following viewpoints:

In United States v. Sanders, 435 F.2d 165 (9th Cir. 1970), the court said:

When resentencing Sanders the district court judge restated the comments he had made after the second trial, noting that:

"(1) Sanders had committed a serious crime;

"(2) Sanders had an extremely poor record as a citizen;

"(3) Sanders had obviously fabricated his defense and testified falsely at his trial, thus committing a further crime of perjury; and

"(4) It was apparent to me after studying the presentence report provided to me by the Probation Officer that Sanders had regressed rather than progressed toward rehabilitation during the time that he was in prison. I was aware of only the first two of these things at the time that I pronounced the initial sentence of fifteen years."

The stated reasons fully comply with the requirements of *Pearce*. It was appropriate for the district court judge to take

Sanders' perjury into account in resentencing, Williams v. New York, 337 U.S. 241, 69 S.Ct. 1079 (1949) and the fact that he had not been favorably considered for parole.

In United States v. Saletko, 452 F.2d 193 (7th Cir. 1971), the court said:

> In attempting to follow the dictates of *Pearce*, the trial judge set forth in the record the factual basis which he believed justified the longer sentence. Essentially, two factors were relied upon: first, that the defendant was impeached by his testimony at the previous trial and, second, that his testimony concerning Schang's solicitation of perjury was a fabrication on the part of the defendant. With respect to the impeachment of the defendant, we do not believe that sufficient discrepancies were revealed to warrant the additional sentence. The second trial occurred three years after the first and it is understandable that defendant was unable to recall the events in the same detail as he had at the first trial. When the defendant was confronted with his prior testimony, he acknowledged that his memory of the details was not good but admitted that if he had testified to something in the prior trial, it was correct. Similarly, the defendant's allegation of Schang's solicitation, even if perjurious, constituted no new fact upon which a more severe sentence could be predicated since that same testimony was given at the first trial. No, "identifiable conduct," subsequent to the first sentencing having been found upon which the increased sentence could be based, the mandate of *Pearce* was not complied with.

7. DUAL SOVEREIGNTY PROBLEMS

In situations where former jeopardy would bar a new trial (under any of the circumstances described in subsections 3–5, supra), additional considerations arise when the prosecuting entity is different from the governmental entity which brought the former prosecution. Consider the following:

In Bartkus v. Illinois, 359 U.S. 121, 79 S.Ct. 676 (1959), the Court upheld a state conviction for bank robbery after an unsuccessful federal prosecution for the same offense. In Abbate v. United States, 359 U.S. 187, 79 S.Ct. 666 (1959), the Court upheld a federal conviction after a state conviction. These decisions were based upon a dual sovereignty theory which states that a citizen owes allegiance to both the United States and the state in which he resides and, if principles of federalism are to remain undisturbed, he may be prosecuted by both jurisdictions for the act. This concept has been heavily criticized. See Fisher, Double Jeopardy, Two Sovereignties, and the Intruding Constitution, 28 U. of Chi.L.R. 591 (1961); Comment, Successive State and Federal Prosecutions for the Same Offense: Bartkus v. Illinois Revisited, 62 J.Crim.L., C., & P.S. 29 (1971).

Nevertheless, in United States v. Wheeler, 435 U.S. 313, 98 S.Ct. 1079 (1978), a case involving successive prosecutions before an Indian tribal court and the United States District Court, the continuing vitality of *Bartkus* and *Abbate* was reaffirmed without extended discussion. Those who had previously distinguished these cases on the ground they had been decided before *Benton* (Section A–1, supra) made the Double Jeopardy clause applicable to the States were disappointed. Of course, through legislation or through interpretations of state constitutions, the individual States remain free to prohibit prosecution in their own jurisdiction following a federal prosecution based upon the same conduct. See Ill.Rev.Stat. Ch. 38, § 3–4 (1979), a post-*Bartkus* statute which would prohibit what had been done in *Bartkus*.

Do you agree with the result in *Bartkus*? Suppose that a police officer, accused of homicide, is convicted but given probation in a state court. Should he remain subject to a federal civil rights prosecution? What about the federal civil rights prosecution of Collie Lee Wilkins following his acquittal by a Loundes County, Alabama jury in connection with the 1965 slaying of civil rights worker, Viola Liuzzo? Should federal prosecution have been barred?

Can any test be defined to indicate when the interest of the second sovereign truly is distinct so that the *Bartkus* result could be reversed without prohibiting all "same conduct" prosecutions by the second sovereign?

Following *Abbate*, under the so-called "Petite" policy, the United States Justice Department prohibited United States Attorneys from prosecuting federally after a state prosecution except under the prior authority of Justice Department officials in Washington. Such permission was granted infrequently. When such prosecutions went forward without permission and resulted in convictions, the Justice Department, after the matter was brought to its attention, prevailed upon federal courts to vacate such perfectly valid convictions in order to implement the Petite policy. See the discussion in Rinaldi v. United States, 434 U.S. 22, 98 S.Ct. 81 (1970).

In Waller v. Florida, 397 U.S. 387, 90 S.Ct. 1184 (1970), Chief Justice Burger, for a unanimous Court, held that successive state and municipal prosecutions were barred by the double jeopardy clause. The theory is that because the city is a creature of the state, for double jeopardy purposes it must be thought of as the same sovereign. As in many multiple jurisdiction situations, the problem may be complicated because the elements of the state offense may be slightly different from those under the city ordinance. *Waller* does not on its face reach such a situation even if both prosecutions resulted from the same course of conduct. Arguably (except in the included offense situation, Section A–4, supra), a single sovereign could bring successive prosecutions where the elements are different. Thus successive city-state prosecutions may be permitted. In the case of an acquittal on the city charge, however, a combination of *Waller* and the collateral estoppel principles of *Ashe* (Section A–6, supra) may benefit the accused if the state subsequently prosecutes for a different but closely related offense.

8. JEOPARDY AND PROCEDURAL PROBLEMS

With respect to the issue of waiver, until Blackledge v. Perry, 417 U.S. 21, 94 S.Ct. 2098 (1974), it was generally agreed that a pretrial motion to dismiss was required in order to preserve a claim of former jeopardy. Such a motion might be entitled a "plea in bar" or, if common-law pleas be preserved, *"autrefois acquit"* or *"autrefois convict."* See, e. g. United States v. Hill, 473 F.2d 759 (9th Cir. 1972); Haddad v. United States, 349 F.2d 511 (9th Cir. 1965). *Blackledge,* however, indicated that if a defendant entered a plea of guilty without raising a claim of former jeopardy, he still could attack the plea through federal habeas corpus, and his prior procedural default would not bar a decision on the merits of his claim. See, also, Menna v. New York, 423 U.S. 61, 96 S.Ct. 241 (1975). Although *Blackledge* did not require that *state* courts entertain belated claims of former jeopardy when the issue was not raised by pre-trial motion, some state courts, noting that a federal decision on the merits lies ahead, may decide to abandon their former strict rule of forfeiture in double jeopardy matters.

It is not altogether clear that *Blackledge* would make federal habeas corpus available to a defendant who entered a plea of *not* guilty, put the state through a full trial, was convicted, and thereafter, for the first time raised a claim that the trial should have been barred because of former jeopardy. For a rather heated controversy over the meaning of *Blackledge* and other "waiver" or forfeiture decisions, see Westen, Forfeiture By Guilty Pleas—A Reply, 76 Mich.L.Rev. 1308 (1978), the earlier article by Westen, and the response by Professor Saltzburg, both cited in Westen's reply.

As to interlocutory appeals, consider the following:

In Abney v. United States, 431 U.S. 651, 97 S.Ct. 2034 (1977), the Supreme Court held that in the federal system, under 28 U.S.C. § 1291, an order denying the accused's motion to dismiss on double jeopardy grounds is a final decision and therefore immediately appealable. "[T]he rights conferred on a criminal accused by the Double Jeopardy Clause would be significantly undermined if appellate review of double jeopardy claims were postponed until after conviction and sentence. . . . It is a guarantee against being twice put to *trial* for the same offense."

Reasoning that if a criminal defendant who has been convicted has no *constitutional* right to an appeal—as the Supreme Court has often said—one state court has concluded that there can be no federal constitutional right to an interlocutory appeal. As long as the trial judge rules on the former jeopardy motion before trial, the Constitution is not offended, according to the Supreme Court of Illinois. *Abney,* it said, in requiring interlocutory review, applies only to the federal system and is not of federal constitutional dimension. The same court, however, promised to make interlocutory review available when a substantial claim of former jeopardy has been rejected by a trial judge. People ex rel. Mosley v. Carey, 74 Ill.2d 527, 25 Ill.Dec. 669, 387 N.E.2d 325 (1979).

B. DISMISSAL FOR PLEADING DEFECTS

Concerning defective indictments, informations, and complaints, re-consider Chapter 11, Section H.

C. DISMISSAL FOR LACK OF SPEEDY (EARLY) TRIAL

BARKER v. WINGO

Supreme Court of the United States, 1972.
407 U.S. 514, 92 S.Ct. 2182.

MR. JUSTICE POWELL delivered the opinion of the Court.

Although a speedy trial is guaranteed the accused by the Sixth Amendment to the Constitution, this Court has dealt with that right on frequent occasions. . . . The Court's opinion in Klopfer v. North Carolina, 386 U.S. 213, 87 S.Ct. 988 (1967), established that the right to speedy trial is "fundamental" and is imposed by the Due Process Clause of the Fourteenth Amendment on the States. See Smith v. Hooey, 393 U.S. 374, 89 S.Ct. 575 (1969); Dickey v. Florida, 398 U.S. 30, 90 S.Ct. 1564 (1970). As Mr. Justice Brennan pointed out in his concurring opinion in *Dickey*, in none of these cases have we attempted to set out the criteria by which the speedy trial right is to be judged. This case compels us to make such an attempt.

I.

On July 20, 1958, in Christian County, Kentucky, an elderly couple was beaten to death by intruders wielding an iron tire tool. Two suspects, Silas Manning and Willie Barker, the petitioner, were arrested shortly thereafter. The grand jury indicted them on September 15. Counsel was appointed on September 17, and Barker's trial was set for October 21. The Commonwealth had a stronger case against Manning, and it believed that Barker could not be convicted unless Manning testified against him. Manning was naturally unwilling to incriminate himself. Accordingly, on October 23, the day Silas Manning was brought to trial, the Commonwealth sought and obtained the first of what was to be a series of 16 continuances of Barker's trial. Barker made no objection. By first convicting Manning, the Commonwealth would remove possible problems of self-incrimination and would be able to assure his testimony against Barker.

The Commonwealth encountered more than a few difficulties in its prosecution of Manning. The first trial ended in a hung jury. A second trial resulted in a conviction, but the Kentucky Court of Appeals reversed because of the admission of evidence obtained by an illegal search. At his third trial, Manning was again convicted, and the Court of Appeals again reversed because the trial court had not granted a change of venue. A fourth trial resulted in a hung jury. Finally, after five trials, Manning was convicted, in March 1962, of murdering one victim, and after a sixth trial, in December 1962, he was convicted of murdering the other.[1]

The Christian County Circuit Court holds three terms each year —in February, June, and September. Barker's initial trial was to take place in the September term of 1958. The first continuance postponed it until the February 1959 term. The second continuance was granted for one month only. Every term thereafter for as long as the Manning prosecutions were in process, the Commonwealth routinely moved to continue Barker's case to the next term. When the case was continued from the June 1959 term until the following September, Barker, having spent 10 months in jail, obtained his release by posting a $5,000 bond. He thereafter remained free in the community until his trial. Barker made no objection, through his counsel, to the first 11 continuances.

When on February 12, 1962, the Commonwealth moved for the twelfth time to continue the case until the following term, Barker's counsel filed a motion to dismiss the indictment. The motion to dismiss was denied two weeks later, and the State's motion for a continuance was granted. The State was granted further continuances in June 1962 and September 1962, to which Barker did not object.

In February 1963, the first term of court following Manning's final conviction, the Commonwealth moved to set Barker's trial for March 19. But on the day scheduled for trial, it again moved for a continuance until the June term. It gave as its reason the illness of the ex-sheriff who was the chief investigating officer in the case. To this continuance, Barker objected unsuccessfully.

The witness was still unable to testify in June, and the trial, which had been set for June 19, was continued again until the September term over Barker's objection. This time the court announced that the case would be dismissed for lack of prosecution if it were not tried during the next term. The final trial date was set for October 9, 1963. On that date, Barker again moved to dismiss the indictment, and this time specified that his right to a speedy trial had been violated. The motion was denied; the trial commenced with Manning as the chief prosecution witness; Barker was convicted and given a life sentence.

Barker appealed his conviction to the Kentucky Court of Appeals, relying in part on his speedy trial claim. The court affirmed. Barker petitioned for habeas corpus [and] the United States District Court for the Western District of Kentucky rejected the petition without holding a hearing. . . . On appeal, the Court of Appeals for the Sixth Circuit affirmed the District Court. 442 F.2d 1141 (CA6 1971).

* * *

1. Apparently Manning chose not to appeal these final two convictions.

II.

The right to a speedy trial is generically different from any of the other rights enshrined in the Constitution for the protection of the accused.   In addition to the general concern that all accused persons be treated according to decent and fair procedures, there is a societal interest in providing a speedy trial which exists separate from and at times in opposition to the interests of the accused.   The inability of courts to provide a prompt trial has contributed to a large backlog of cases in urban courts which, among other things, enables defendants to negotiate more effectively for pleas of guilty to lesser offenses and otherwise manipulate the system.   In addition, persons released on bond for lengthy periods awaiting trial have an opportunity to commit other crimes.[2]   It must be of little comfort to the residents of Christian County, Kentucky, to know that Barker was at large on bail for over four years while accused of a vicious and brutal murder of which he was ultimately convicted.   Moreover, the longer an accused is free awaiting trial, the more tempting becomes his opportunity to jump bail and escape.   Finally, delay between arrest and punishment may have a detrimental effect on rehabilitation.

If an accused cannot make bail, he is generally confined, as was Barker for 10 months, in a local jail.   This contributes to the overcrowding and generally deplorable state of those institutions.   Lengthy exposure to these conditions "has a destructive effect on human character and makes the rehabilitation of the individual offender much more difficult."   At times the result may even be violent rioting.   Finally, lengthy pretrial detention is costly.   The cost of maintaining a prisoner in jail varies from $3 to $9 per day, and this amounts to millions across the Nation.   In addition, society loses wages which might have been earned, and it must often support families of incarcerated breadwinners.

A second difference between the right to speedy trial and the accused's other constitutional rights is that deprivation of the right may work to the accused's advantage.   Delay is not an uncommon defense tactic.   As the time between the commission of the crime and trial lengthens, witnesses may become unavailable or their memories may fade.   If the witnesses support the prosecution, its case will be weakened, sometimes seriously so.   And it is the prosecution which carries the burden of proof.   Thus, unlike the right to counsel or the right to be free from compelled self-incrimination, deprivation of the right to speedy trial does not *per se* prejudice the accused's ability to defend himself.

Finally, and perhaps most importantly, the right to speedy trial is a more vague concept than other procedural rights.   It is, for example, impossible to determine with precision when the right has been denied.   We cannot definitely say how long is too long in a sys-

---

2. In Washington, D.C., in 1968, 70.1% of the persons arrested for robbery and released prior to trial were rearrested while on bail.   Mitchell, Bail Reform and the Constitutionality of Pretrial Detention, 55 Va.L.Rev. 1223, 1236 (1969).

tem where justice is supposed to be swift but deliberate.[3] As a consequence, there is no fixed point in the criminal process when the State can put the defendant to the choice of either exercising or waiving the right to a speedy trial. If, for example, the State moves for a 60-day continuance, granting that continuance is not a violation of the right to speedy trial unless the circumstances of the case are such that further delay would endanger the values the right protects. It is impossible to do more than generalize about when those circumstances exist. There is nothing comparable to the point in the process when a defendant exercises or waives his right to counsel or his right to a jury trial. Thus, in any inquiry into a speedy trial claim necessitates a functional analysis of the right in the particular context of the case.

* * *

The amorphous quality of the right also leads to the unsatisfactorily severe remedy of dismissal of the indictment when the right has been deprived. This is indeed a serious consequence because it means that a defendant who may be guilty of a serious crime will go free, without having been tried. Such a remedy is more serious than an exclusionary rule or a reversal for a new trial, but it is the only possible remedy.

III.

Perhaps because the speedy trial right is so slippery, two rigid approaches are urged upon us as ways of eliminating some of the uncertainty which courts experience in protecting the right. The first suggestion is that we hold that the Constitution requires a criminal defendant to be offered a trial within a specified time period. The result of such a ruling would have the virtue of clarifying when the right is infringed and of simplifying courts' application of it. Recognizing this, some legislatures have enacted laws, and some courts have adopted procedural rules which more narrowly define the right.

* * *

But such a result would require this Court to engage in legislative or rulemaking activity, rather than in the adjudicative process to which we should confine our efforts. We do not establish procedural rules for the States, except when mandated by the Constitution. We find no constitutional basis for holding that the speedy trial right can be quantified into a specified number of days or months. The States, of course, are free to prescribe a reasonable period consistent with constitutional standards, but our approach must be less precise.

The second suggested alternative would restrict consideration of the right to those cases in which the accused has demanded a speedy trial. Most States have recognized what is loosely referred to as the

3. "[I]n large measure because of the many procedural safeguards provided an accused, the ordinary procedures for criminal prosecution are designed to move at a deliberate pace. A requirement of unreasonable speed would have a deleterious effect both upon the rights of the accused and upon the ability of society to protect itself." United States v. Ewell, 383 U.S. 116, 120, 86 S.Ct. 773, 776 (1966).

"demand rule," although eight States reject it. It is not clear, however, precisely what is meant by that term. Although every Federal Court of Appeals that has considered the question has endorsed some kind of demand rule, some have regarded the rule within the concept of waiver, whereas others have viewed it as a factor to be weighed in assessing whether there has been a deprivation of the speedy trial right. We shall refer to the former approach as the demand-waiver doctrine. The demand-waiver doctrine provides that a defendant waives any consideration of his right to speedy trial for any period prior to which he has not demanded a trial. Under this rigid approach, a prior demand is a necessary condition to the consideration of the speedy trial right.

Such an approach, by presuming waiver of a fundamental right from inaction, is inconsistent with this Court's pronouncements on waiver of constitutional rights. The Court has defined waiver as "an intentional relinquishment or abandonment of a known right or privilege." Courts should "indulge every reasonable presumption against waiver," and they should "not presume acquiescence in the loss of fundamental rights."

* * *

In excepting the right to speedy trial from the rule of waiver we have applied to other fundamental rights, courts that have applied the demand-waiver rule have relied on the assumption that delay usually works for the benefit of the accused and on the absence of any readily ascertainable time in the criminal process for a defendant to be given the choice of exercising or waiving his right. But it is not necessarily true that delay benefits the defendant. There are cases in which delay appreciably harms the defendant's ability to defend himself. Moreover, a defendant confined to jail prior to trial is obviously disadvantaged by delay as is a defendant released on bail but unable to lead a normal life because of community suspicion and his own anxiety.

The nature of the speedy-trial right does make it impossible to pinpoint a precise time in the process when the right must be asserted or waived, but that fact does not argue for placing the burden of protecting the right solely on defendants. Moreover, for the reasons earlier expressed society has a particular interest in bringing swift prosecutions, and society's representatives are the ones who should protect that interest.

It is also noteworthy that such a rigid view of the demand rule places defense counsel in an awkward position. Unless he demands a trial early and often, he is in danger of frustrating his client's right. If counsel is willing to tolerate some delay because he finds it reasonable and helpful in preparing his own case, he may be unable to obtain a speedy trial for his client at the end of that time. Since under the demand-waiver rule no time runs until the demand is made, the government will have whatever time is otherwise reasonable to bring the defendant to trial after a demand has been made. Thus, if the first demand is made three months after arrest in a jurisdiction which prescribes a six months rule, the prosecution will have a total of nine months—which may be wholly unreasonable under the circumstances. The result in practice is likely to be either an automatic, *pro forma* demand made immediately after appointment of counsel or delays which, but for the demand-waiver rule, would not be tolerated. Such a result is not consistent with the interests of defendants, society, or the Constitution.

We reject, therefore, the rule that a defendant who fails to demand a speedy trial forever waives his right. This does not mean, however, that the defendant has no responsibility to assert his right. We think the better rule is that the defendant's assertion of or failure to assert his right to a speedy trial is one of the factors to be considered in an inquiry into the deprivation of the right. Such a formulation avoids the rigidities of the demand-waiver rule and the resulting possible unfairness in its application. It allows the trial court to exercise a judicial discretion based on the circumstances, including due consideration of any applicable formal procedural rule. It would permit, for example, a court to attach a different weight to a situation in which the defendant knowingly fails to object from a situation in which his attorney acquiesces in long delay without adequately informing his client or from a situation in which no counsel is appointed. It would also allow a court to weigh the frequency and force of the objections as opposed to attaching significant weight to a purely *pro forma* objection.

* * *

We, therefore, reject both of the inflexible approaches—the fixed time period because it goes further than the Constitution requires; the demand-waiver rule because it is insensitive to a right which we have deemed fundamental. The approach we accept is a balancing test, in which the conduct of both the prosecution and the defendant are weighed.[4]

IV.

A balancing test necessarily compels courts to approach speedy-trial cases on an *ad hoc* basis. We can do little more than identify some of the factors which courts should assess in determining whether a particular defendant has been deprived of his right. Though some might express them in different ways, we identify four such factors: Length of delay, the reason for the delay, the defendant's assertion of his right, and prejudice to the defendant.

The length of the delay is to some extent a triggering mechanism. Until there is some delay which is presumptively prejudicial, there is no necessity for inquiry into the other factors that go into the balance. Nevertheless, because of the imprecision of the right to speedy trial, the length of delay that will provoke such an inquiry is necessarily dependent upon the peculiar circumstances of the case.[5]

---

4. Nothing we have said should be interpreted as disapproving a presumptive rule adopted by a court in the exercise of its supervisory powers which establishes a fixed time period within which cases must normally be brought.

5. For example, the First Circuit thought a delay of nine months over-

To take but one example, the delay that can be tolerated for an ordinary street crime is considerably less than for a serious, complex conspiracy charge.

Closely related to length of delay is the reason the government assigns to justify the delay. Here, too, different weights should be assigned to different reasons. A deliberate attempt to delay the trial in order to hamper the defense should be weighed heavily against the government.[6] A more neutral reason such as negligence or overcrowded courts should be weighed less heavily but nevertheless should be considered since the ultimate responsibility for such circumstances must rest with the government rather than with the defendant. Finally, a valid reason, such as a missing witness, should serve to justify appropriate delay.

We have already discussed the third factor, the defendant's responsibility to assert his right. Whether and how a defendant asserts his right is closely related to the other factors we have mentioned. The strength of his efforts will be affected by the length of the delay, to some extent by the reason for the delay, and most particularly by the personal prejudice, which is not always readily identifiable, that he experiences. The more serious the deprivation, the more likely a defendant is to complain. The defendant's assertion of his speedy trial right, then, is entitled to strong evidentiary weight in determining whether the right is being deprived. We emphasize that failure to assert the right will make it difficult for a defendant to prove that he was denied a speedy trial.

A fourth factor is prejudice to the defendant. Prejudice, of course, should be assessed in the light of the interests of defendants which the speedy trial right was designed to protect. This Court has identified three such interests: (i) to prevent oppressive pretrial incarceration; (ii) to minimize anxiety and concern of the accused; and (iii) to limit the possibility that the defense will be impaired.[7] Of these, the most serious is the last, because the inability of a defendant adequately to prepare his case skews the fairness of the entire system. If witnesses die or disappear during a delay, the prejudice is obvious. There is also prejudice if defense witnesses are unable to recall accurately events of the distant past. Loss of memory, however, is not always reflected in the record because what has been forgotten can rarely be shown.

We have discussed previously the societal disadvantages of lengthy pretrial incarceration, but obviously the disadvantages for

ly long, absent a good reason, in a case that depended on eyewitness testimony. United States v. Butler (C.A.1 1970).

6. We have indicated on previous occasions that it is improper for the prosecution intentionally to delay "to gain some tactical advantage over [defendants] or to harass them." United States v. Marion (1971).

7. In Klopfer v. North Carolina (1967), we indicated that a defendant awaiting trial on bond might be subjected to public scorn, deprived of employment, and chilled in the exercise of his right to speak for, associate with, and participate in unpopular political causes.

the accused who cannot obtain his release are even more serious. The time spent in jail awaiting trial has a detrimental impact on the individual. It often means loss of a job; it disrupts family life; and it enforces idleness. Most jails offer little or no recreational or rehabilitative programs. The time spent in jail is simply dead time. Moreover, if a defendant is locked up, he is hindered in his ability to gather evidence, contact witnesses, or otherwise prepare his defense. Imposing those consequences on anyone who has not yet been convicted is serious. It is especially unfortunate to impose them on those persons who are ultimately found to be innocent. Finally, even if an accused is not incarcerated prior to trial, he is still disadvantaged by restraints on his liberty and by living under a cloud of anxiety, suspicion, and often hostility.

We regard none of the four factors identified above as either a necessary or sufficient condition to the finding of a deprivation of the right of speedy trial. Rather, they are related factors and must be considered together with such other circumstances as may be relevant. In sum, these factors have no talismanic qualities; courts must still engage in a difficult and sensitive balancing process. But, because we are dealing with a fundamental right of the accused, this process must be carried out with full recognition that the accused's interest in a speedy trial is specifically affirmed in the Constitution.

V.

The difficulty of the task of balancing these factors is illustrated by this case, which we consider to be close. It is clear that the length of delay between arrest and trial—well over five years—was extraordinary. Only seven months of that period can be attributed to a strong excuse, the illness of the ex-sheriff who was in charge of the investigation. Perhaps some delay would have been permissible under ordinary circumstances, so that Manning could be utilized as a witness in Barker's trial, but more than four years was too long a period, particularly since a good part of that period was attributable to the Commonwealth's failure or inability to try Manning under circumstances that comported with due process.

Two counter-balancing factors, however, outweigh these deficiencies. The first is that prejudice was minimal. Of course, Barker was prejudiced to some extent by living for over four years under a cloud of suspicion and anxiety. Moreover, although he was released on bond for most of the period, he did spend 10 months in jail before trial. But there is no claim that any of Barker's witnesses died or otherwise became unavailable owing to the delay. The trial transcript indicates only two very minor lapses of memory—one on the part of a prosecution witness—which were in no way significant to the outcome.

More important than the absence of serious prejudice, is the fact that Barker did not want a speedy trial. Counsel was appointed for Barker immediately after his indictment and represented him throughout the period. Despite the fact that counsel had notice of the motions for continuances, the record shows no action whatever taken between October 21, 1958, and February 12, 1962, that could be construed as the assertion of the speedy-trial right. On the latter date, in response to another motion for continuance, Barker moved to dismiss the indictment. The record does not show on what ground this motion was based, although it is clear that no alternative motion was made for an immediate trial. Instead the record strongly suggests that while he hoped to take advantage of the delay in which he had acquiesced, and thereby obtain a dismissal of the charges, he definitely did not want to be tried.   . . .   The probable reason for Barker's attitude was that he was gambling on Manning's acquittal. The evidence was not terribly strong against Manning, as the reversals and hung juries suggest, and Barker undoubtedly thought that if Manning were acquitted, he would never be tried.   . . .   It was not until March 1963, after Manning's convictions were final, that Barker, having lost his gamble, began to object to further continuances. At that time, the Commonwealth's excuse was the illness of the ex-sheriff, which Barker has conceded justified the further delay.

We do not hold that there may never be a situation in which an indictment may be dismissed on speedy-trial grounds where the defendant has failed to object to continuances. There may be a situation in which the defendant was represented by incompetent counsel, was severely prejudiced, or even cases in which the continuances were granted *ex parte*. But barring extraordinary circumstances, we would be reluctant indeed to rule that a defendant was denied this constitutional right on a record that strongly indicates, as does this one, that the defendant did not want a speedy trial. We hold, therefore, that Barker was not deprived of his due process right to a speedy trial.

Affirmed.

MR. JUSTICE WHITE, with whom MR. JUSTICE BRENNAN joins, concurring in the judgment and opinion of the Court. [Opinion omitted.]

NOTES

1. Prior to *Wingo*, the Court had considered many of the ancillary aspects of the speedy trial guarantee, but had never genuinely defined its contours. See Dickey v. Florida, 398 U.S. 30, 90 S.Ct. 1564 (1970) (defendant incarcerated for one crime has right to demand speedy trial on another pending charge); Smith v. Hooey, 393 U.S. 374, 89 S.Ct. 575 (1969) (state has obligation to attempt to bring federal prisoner to trial on state charge); Klopfer v. North Carolina, 386 U.S. 213, 87 S.Ct. 988 (1967) (Sixth Amendment speedy trial guarantee applicable to states through due process clause of Fourteenth Amendment).

2. In Strunk v. United States, 412 U.S. 434, 93 S.Ct. 2260 (1973), the lower court found that, although a speedy trial violation occurred, the fact that the defendant had received a sentence concurrent to a then pending state sentence was sufficient to relieve him of the prejudice suffered from the violation. The Supreme Court reversed, holding that outright dismissal of the indictment was the only relief available to one deprived of a speedy trial.

3.   In United States v. Marion, 404 U.S. 307, 92 S.Ct. 455 (1971), the Court held that the Sixth Amendment right to a speedy trial did not extend to delays prior to indictment when the defendant was not incarcerated. Some lower courts interpreted this to mean that pre-indictment delay is not to be counted for Sixth Amendment purposes absent an actual showing of prejudice.   However, in Dillingham v. United States, 423 U.S. 64, 96 S.Ct. 303 (1975), the Court held that for purposes of determining whether the *constitutional* right to a speedy trial has been violated, the time must be calculated from the date of arrest rather than from the date of a subsequent indictment or arraignment upon the indictment.

Marion also held out the possibility that an indictment might be dismissed upon Fifth or Fourteenth Amendment "due process" grounds (rather than Sixth Amendment "speedy trial" grounds) when an unjustified delay occurred *before* charges were brought, if the defendant was prejudiced by the delay—even though the statute of limitations had not run.   Under what circumstances would delay before any charge is brought sufficiently prejudice a defendant to require dismissal of his indictment on due process grounds; for instance, the death of his witnesses?   A concession by the prosecutor that the delay yielded no additional evidence?

UNITED STATES v. LOVASCO

Supreme Court of the United States, 1977.
431 U.S. 783, 97 S.Ct. 2044.

MR. JUSTICE MARSHALL delivered the opinion of the Court.

We granted certiorari in this case to consider the circumstances in which the Constitution requires that an indictment be dismissed because of delay between the commission of an offense and the initiation of prosecution.

I.

On March 6, 1975, respondent was indicted for possessing eight firearms stolen from the United States mail, and for dealing in firearms without a license.   The offenses were alleged to have occurred between July 25 and August 31, 1973, more than 18 months before the indictment was filed.   Respondent moved to dismiss the indictment due to the delay.

The District Court conducted a hearing on respondent's motion at which the respondent sought to prove that the delay was unnecessary and that it had prejudiced his defense.   In an effort to establish the former proposition, respondent presented a Postal Inspector's report on his investigation that was prepared one month after the crimes were committed, and a stipulation concerning the post-report progress of the probe.   The report stated, in brief, that within the first month of the investigation respondent had admitted to Government agents that he had possessed and then sold five of the stolen guns, and that the agents had developed strong evidence linking respondent to the remaining three weapons.[1]   The report also stated,

----

1.   The report indicated that the person to whom respondent admitted selling five guns had told Government agents that respondent had actually

however, that the agents had been unable to confirm or refute respondent's claim that he had found the guns in his car when he returned to it after visiting his son, a mail handler, at work.   The stipulation into which the Assistant United States Attorney entered indicated that little additional information concerning the crimes was uncovered in the 17 months following the preparation of the Inspector's report.[2]

To establish prejudice to the defense, respondent testified that he had lost the testimony of two material witnesses due to the delay. The first witness, Tom Stewart, died more than a year after the alleged crimes occurred.   At the hearing respondent claimed that Stewart had been his source for two or three of the guns.   The second witness, respondent's brother, died in April 1974, nine months after the crimes were completed.   Respondent testified that his brother was present when respondent called Stewart to secure the guns, and witnessed all of respondent's sales.   Respondent did not state how the witnesses would have aided the defense had they been willing to testify.

The Government made no systematic effort in the District Court to explain its long delay.   The Assistant United States Attorney did expressly disagree, however, with defense counsel's suggestion that the investigation had ended after the Postal Inspector's Report was prepared.   The prosecutor also stated that it was the Government's theory that respondent's son, who had access to the mail at the railroad terminal from which the guns were "possibly stolen," was responsible for the thefts.   Finally, the prosecutor elicited somewhat cryptic testimony from the Postal Inspector indicating that the case "as to these particular weapons involves other individuals"; that information had been presented to a grand jury "in regard to this case other than . . . [on] the day of the indictment itself"; and that he had spoken to the prosecutors about the case on four or five occasions.

Following the hearing, the District Court found that by October 2, 1973, the date of the postal inspector's report, "The Government had all the information relating to defendant's alleged commission of the offense charged against him," and that the 17-month delay before the case was presented to the grand jury "had not been explained or

---

sold him eight guns which he, in turn, had sold to one Martin Koehnken.   The report also indicated that Koehnken had sold three of these guns to undercover federal agents and that a search of his house had uncovered four others.   Finally the report stated that the eighth gun was sold by one David Northdruft to Government agents, and that Northdruft claimed Koehnken had sold him the gun.

At the hearing on the motion to dismiss, respondent for the first time admitted that he had possessed and sold eight guns.

2.   In March 1975, the Inspector learned of another person who claimed to have purchased a gun from respondent.   At the hearing the parties disagreed as to whether this evidence would have been admissible since it did not involve any of the guns to which the indictment related. In any event, the Assistant United States Attorney stated that the decision to prosecute was made before this additional piece of evidence was received.

justified" and was "unnecessary and unreasonable." The Court also found that "[a]s a result of the delay defendant has been prejudiced by reason of the death of Tom Stewart, a material witness on his behalf." Accordingly, the court dismissed the indictment.

* * *

II.

In United States v. Marion, 404 U.S. 307, 92 S.Ct. 455 (1971), this Court considered the significance, for constitutional purposes, of a lengthy preindictment delay. We held that as far as the Speedy Trial Clause of the Sixth Amendment is concerned, such delay is wholly irrelevant, since our analysis of the language, history and purposes of the Clause persuaded us that only "a formal indictment or information or else the actual restraints imposed by arrest and holding to answer a criminal charge . . . engage the particular protections" of that provision. We went on to note that statutes of limitations which provide predictable, legislatively enacted limits on prosecutorial delay, provide "the primary guarantee, against bringing overly stale criminal charges." But we did acknowledge that the "statute of limitations does not fully define [defendants'] rights with respect to the events occurring prior to indictment," and that the Due Process Clause has a limited role to play in protecting against oppressive delay.

Respondent seems to argue that due process bars prosecution, whenever a defendant suffers prejudice as a result of preindictment delay. To support that proposition respondent relies on the concluding sentence of the Court's opinion in *Marion* where, in remanding the case, we stated that "[e]vents of the trial may demonstrate actual prejudice, but at the present time appellees' due process claims are speculative and premature." But the quoted sentence establishes only that proof of actual prejudice makes a due process claim concrete and ripe for adjudication, not that it makes the claim automatically valid. Indeed, two pages earlier in the opinion we expressly rejected the argument respondent advances here:

"[W]e need not . . . determine when and in what circumstances actual prejudice resulting from preaccusation delay requires the dismissal of the prosecution. Actual prejudice to the defense of a criminal case may result from the shortest and most necessary delay; and no one suggests that every delay-caused detriment to a defendant's case should abort a criminal prosecution."

Thus *Marion* makes clear that proof of prejudice is generally a necessary but not sufficient element of a due process claim, and that the due process inquiry must consider the reasons for the delay as well as the prejudice to the accused.

. . . [T]he Due Process Clause does not permit courts to abort criminal prosecutions simply because they disagree with a prosecutor's judgment as to when to seek an indictment. Judges are not free, in defining "due process," to impose on law enforcement officials our "personal and private notions" of fairness and to "disregard the limits that bind judges in their judicial function."   Rochin v. California, 342 U.S. 165, 170, 72 S.Ct. 205, 209 (1952).   Our task is more circumscribed.   We are to determine only whether the actions complained of—here, compelling respondent to stand trial after the Government delayed indictment to investigate further—violates those "fundamental conceptions of justice which lie at the base of our civil and political institutions." . . .

It requires no extended argument to establish that prosecutors do not deviate from "fundamental conceptions of justice" when they defer seeking indictments until they have probable cause to believe an accused is guilty; indeed it is unprofessional conduct for a prosecutor to recommend an indictment on less than probable cause.   It should be equally obvious that prosecutors are under no duty to file charges as soon as probable cause exists but before they are satisfied they will be able to establish the suspect's guilt beyond a reasonable doubt. To impose such a duty "would have a deleterious effect both upon the rights of the accused and upon the ability of society to protect itself." From the perspective of potential defendants, requiring prosecutions to commence when probable cause is established is undesirable because it would increase the likelihood of unwarranted charges being filed, and would add to the time during which defendants stand accused but untried.[3]   These costs are by no means insubstantial since, as we recognized in *Marion*, a formal accusation may "interfere with the defendant's liberty, . . .   disrupt his employment, drain his financial resources, curtail his associations, subject him to public obloquy, and create anxiety in him, his family and his friends."   From the perspective of law enforcement officials, a requirement of immediate prosecution upon probable cause is equally unacceptable because it could make obtaining proof of guilt beyond a reasonable doubt impossible by causing potentially fruitful sources of information to evaporate before they are fully exploited.   And from the standpoint of the courts, such a requirement is unwise because it would cause scarce resources to be consumed on cases that prove to be insubstantial, or that involve only some of the responsible parties or some of the criminal acts.[4]   Thus, no one's interests would be well served by compelling prosecutors to initiate prosecutions as soon as they are legally entitled to do so.

---

3. To the extent that the period between accusation and trial has been strictly limited by legislative action, see, e. g., Speedy Trial Act of 1974, 88 Stat. 2076, 18 U.S.C. § 3161 et seq. (Supp. V 1975), compelling immediate prosecutions upon probable cause would not add to the time during which defendants stand accused, but would create a risk of guilty persons escaping punishment simply because the Government was unable to move from probable cause to guilt beyond a reasonable doubt in the short time available to it.   Even absent a statute, of course, the Speedy Trial Clause of the Sixth Amendment imposes restraints on the length of post-accusation delay.

4. Defendants also would be adversely affected by trials involving less than all of the criminal acts for which they are responsible, since they likely would be subjected to multiple trials growing out of the same transaction or occurrence.

It might be argued that once the Government has assembled sufficient evidence to prove guilt beyond a reasonable doubt, it should be constitutionally required to file charges promptly, even if its investigation of the entire criminal transaction is not complete. Adopting such a rule, however, would have many of the same consequences as adopting a rule requiring immediate prosecution upon probable cause.

First, compelling a prosecutor to file public charges as soon as the requisite proof has been developed against one participant on one charge would cause numerous problems in those cases in which a criminal transaction involves more than one person or more than one illegal act. In some instances, an immediate arrest or indictment would impair the prosecutor's ability to continue his investigation, thereby preventing society from bringing lawbreakers to justice. In other cases, the prosecutor would be able to obtain additional indictments despite an early prosecution, but the necessary result would be multiple trials involving a single set of facts. Such trials place needless burdens on defendants, law enforcement officials, and courts.

Second, insisting on immediate prosecution once sufficient evidence is developed to obtain a conviction would pressure prosecutors into resolving doubtful cases in favor of early—and possibly unwarranted—prosecutions. The determination of when the evidence available to the prosecution is sufficient to obtain a conviction is seldom clear-cut, and reasonable persons often will reach conflicting conclusions. In the instant case, for example, since respondent admitted possessing at least five of the firearms, the primary factual issue in dispute was whether respondent knew the guns were stolen. Not surprisingly, the Postal Inspector's report contained no direct evidence bearing on this issue. The decision whether to prosecute, therefore, required a necessarily subjective evaluation of the strength of the circumstantial evidence available and the credibility of respondent's denial. Even if a prosecutor concluded that the case was weak and further investigation appropriate, he would have no assurance that a reviewing court would agree. To avoid the risk that a subsequent indictment would be dismissed for preindictment delay, the prosecutor might feel constrained to file premature charges, with all the disadvantages that entails.[5]

Finally, requiring the Government to make charging decisions immediately upon assembling evidence sufficient to establish guilt would preclude the Government from giving full consideration to the desirability of not prosecuting in particular cases. The decision to file criminal charges, with the awesome consequences it entails, requires consideration of a wide range of factors in addition to the strength of the Government's case, in order to determine whether prosecution would be in the public interest. Prosecutors often need more information than proof of a suspect's guilt, therefore, before de-

---

5. In addition, if courts were required to decide in every case when the prosecution should have commenced, it would be necessary for them to trace the day-by-day progress of each investigation. Maintaining daily records would impose an administrative burden on prosecutors, and reviewing them would place an even greater burden on the courts. . . .

ciding whether to seek an indictment. Again the instant case provides a useful illustration. Although proof of the identity of the mail thieves was not necessary to convict respondent of the possessory crimes with which he was charged, it might have been crucial in assessing respondent's culpability, as distinguished from his legal guilt. If, for example, further investigation were to show that respondent had no role in or advance knowledge of the theft and simply agreed, out of paternal loyalty, to help his son dispose of the guns once respondent discovered his son had stolen them, the United States Attorney might have decided not to prosecute, especially since at the time of the crime respondent was over 60 years old and had no prior criminal record.[6] Requiring prosecution once the evidence of guilt is clear, however, could prevent a prosecutor from awaiting the information necessary for such a decision.

We would be most reluctant to adopt a rule which would have these consequences absent a clear constitutional command to do so. We can find no such command in the Due Process Clause of the Fifth Amendment. In our view, investigative delay is fundamentally unlike delay undertaken by the Government solely "to gain tactical advantage over the accused," United States v. Marion, supra, 404 U.S., at 324, 92 S.Ct., at 465, precisely because investigative delay is not so one-sided.[7] Rather than deviating from elementary standards of "fair play and decency," a prosecutor abides by them if he refuses to seek indictments until he is completely satisfied that he should prosecute and will be able promptly to establish guilt beyond a reasonable doubt. * * * We therefore hold that to prosecute a defendant following investigative delay does not deprive him of due process, even if his defense might have been somewhat prejudiced by the lapse of time.

* * *

III.

In *Marion* we conceded that we could not determine in the abstract the circumstances in which preaccusation delay would require dismissing prosecutions. 404 U.S., at 324, 92 S.Ct., at 465. More than five years later, that statement remains true. Indeed, in the intervening years so few defendants have established that they were prejudiced by delay that neither this Court nor any lower court has had a sustained opportunity to consider the constitutional signifi-

---

6. Of course, in this case further investigation proved unavailing and the United States Attorney ultimately decided to prosecute based solely on the Inspector's report. But this fortuity cannot transform an otherwise permissible delay into an impermissible one.

7. In *Marion* we noted with approval that the Government conceded that a "tactical" delay would violate the Due Process Clause. The Govern-

ment renews that concession here, and expands it somewhat by stating that "A due process violation might also be made out upon a showing of prosecutorial delay incurred in reckless disregard of circumstances, known to the prosecution, suggesting that there existed an appreciable risk that delay would impair the ability to mount an effective defense." As the Government notes, however, there is no evidence of recklessness here.

cance of various reasons for delay.[8] We therefore leave to the lower courts, in the first instance, the task of applying the settled principles of due process that we have discussed to the particular circumstances of individual cases. We simply hold that in this case the lower courts erred in dismissing the indictment.

Reversed.

[Mr. Justice Stevens' dissenting opinion omitted.]

NOTES

1. The Federal Speedy Trial Act of 1974, 18 U.S.C. § 3161, as amended in 1979, provides a statutory scheme dictating the time periods within which federal trials must begin. Congress intended the Act "to assist in reducing crime and the danger of recidivism by requiring speedy trials . . . ." 1974 U.S. Code & Cong'l & Adm. News, 93d Cong., 2d Sess. 7401. See Frase, The Speedy Trial Act of 1974, 43 U.Chi.L.Rev. 667 (1976).

After July 1, 1980, a federal defendant must be indicted within 30 days of arrest, and brought to trial within 70 days of his first judicial appearance, or his indictment, whichever comes last. Section 3161(h), identifying periods of time which may be excluded in computing the time limit, exempts periods of delay resulting from: (1) other proceedings concerning the defendant, such as a hearing on mental competency; (2) an agreement between the parties, approved by the court, permitting the defendant to demonstrate his good conduct; (3) the absence or unavailability of the defendant or an essential witness; (4) the defendant's mental or physical inability to stand trial; (5) the treatment of defendant for drug rehabilitation; (6) the time between dismissal of an indictment and reindictment; (7) a reasonable period beyond the limit for a defendant joined for trial with another person against whom the time limit has not run; and (8) the delay resulting from a continuance at the request of the defendant or, if the ends of justice are served, at the government's request. Are there any other exemptions which should be added to the list?

8. Professor Amsterdam has catalogued some of the noninvestigative reasons for delay:

"[P]roof of the offense may depend upon the testimony of an undercover informer who maintains his 'cover' for a period of time before surfacing to file charges against one or more persons with whom he has dealt while disguised. . . .

[I]f there is more than one possible charge against a suspect, some of them may be held back pending the disposition of others in order to avoid the burden upon the prosecutor's office of handling charges that may turn out to be unnecessary to obtain the degree of punishment that the prosecutor seeks. There are many other motives for delay, of course, including sinister ones, such as a desire to postpone the beginning of defense investigation, or the wish to hold a 'club' over the defendant.

"Additional reasons for delay may be partly or completely beyond the control of the prosecuting authorities. Offenses may not be immediately reported; investigation may not immediately identify the offender; an identified offender may not be immediately apprehendable. . . . [A]n indictment may be delayed for weeks or even months until the impaneling of the next grand jury. It is customary to think of these delays as natural and inevitable . . . but various prosecutorial decisions —such as the assignment of manpower and priorities among investigations of known offenses—may also affect the length of such delays." Amsterdam, Speedy Criminal Trial: Rights and Remedies, 27 Stan.L.Rev. 525, 527–728 (1975).
. . . .

2.   During the phase-in period of the Act, a defendant in custody must be brought to trial within 90 days or released pending trial.   In United States v. Tirasso, 532 F.2d 1298 (9th Cir. 1976), the court held that the exemptions listed above do not apply to this provision and, unless the defendant occasions the delay, he must be released.   Other courts have found the exemptions applicable.   See United States v. Corley, 548 F.2d 1043 (D.C. Cir. 1976); United States v. Masko, 415 F.Supp. 1317 (W.D.Wis.1976). District Courts which face congested calendars may, with Court of Appeals' approval, further delay full implementation of the act until July 1, 1981.

3.   When does a trial "commence" for purposes of a speedy trial act statute?   In Commonwealth v. Griffin, 257 Pa.Super. 153, 390 A.2d 758 (1978), the state argued that an indictment should have not been dismissed under the Pennsylvania rule because the defendant received a suppression hearing within the relevant time period.   Acknowledging that, in some instances, a suppression hearing could mark the commencement of trial, the fact that there was a 62 day delay between the hearing and trial justified dismissal.

4.   It seems clear that the courts are not enamored of the Speedy Trial Act.   In *Tirasso* (discussed in note 2), the Court said:

"In light of these facts, the wisdom of the result Congress has decreed is questionable.   We release a man alleged to be the head of a foreign criminal organization dedicated to the smuggling of large quantities of illegal drugs, so that he may quickly cross the border and resume operating his business.   We are also releasing his alleged right-hand man, as if to make certain that the enterprise continues to operate at top efficiency.   But this result is the only one open to us under the plain terms of the statute.

"It is discouraging that our highly refined and complex system of criminal justice is suddenly faced with implementing a statute that is so inartfully drawn as this one.   But this is the law, and we are bound to give it effect."

In United States v. Howard, 440 F.Supp. 1106 (D.C.Md.1977), the court went even farther and declared the federal act unconstitutional:

"Regardless of the proper construction of the Speedy Trial Act, its commands cannot be given effect because they are an unconstitutional legislative encroachment on the judiciary.   The constitutional principle of the separation of powers is implicit in the basic structure of the Constitution.   The doctrine has been recognized from the earliest days of our constitutional history.

* * *

"Courts have occasionally acquiesced in legislative action over procedural rule-making.   But there must be a line beyond which legislative action directed to the administration of judicial procedures becomes legislative control, and, as such, an unwarranted intrusion into the judicial system.

* * *

"The deficiencies of the Speedy Trial Act are more than theoretical.   Its practical impact triggers the operation of the doctrine of the separation of powers.   The burden which the time limits place on the federal district courts is heavy and the disruption severe.   The limits of § 3161 and § 3164 may, in various contexts, be too short, and thus interfere with the quality of justice.

* * *

".   .   .   This Court, on two occasions in the last twelve months has granted separate trials in lengthy conspiracy cases to accommodate the Speedy Trial requirements. Further reflection now causes this Court to reject the unwarranted congressional intrusion into the internal functions of the judicial process.

"Interference with judicial business caused by the congressionally imposed deadlines for criminal cases also results when the civil docket is unduly disrupted.

* * *

"The Court is cognizant of the defendants' right to a speedy trial, just as it is cognizant of all their rights under the Constitution, and it is satisfied that the evenhanded scrutiny of the appellate courts will not only preserve those rights but will do it without legislative interference. The dictates of Barker v. Wingo, and Rules 48(b) and 50(b) of the Federal Rules of Criminal Procedure adequately protect a defendant's right to a speedy trial, which must by its very being remain a 'relative concept.' Under these principles there is no valid reason requiring that this indictment should be dismissed or that the defendants should be released."

Is the Speedy Trial Act an unconstitutional intrusion upon the separation of powers? Is legislation of this nature wise from a policy standpoint?

5.   Are the time limits established by the Act realistic? Consider the following newspaper editorial (Chicago Tribune, June 16, 1979) advocating an extended period of time between indictment and trial:

"This seemingly well-meaning legislation—which requires that criminal cases go to trial within 70 days after indictment—has triggered petitions for emergency relief from federal judges around the country on grounds that they face impossible caseloads and that strict enforcement would lead to dismissal of many cases. A Justice Department study shows that had the time limits been in effect for the fiscal year ending last June 30, 5,174 criminal cases —17 per cent of the crimes brought to federal court during that period—would have been thrown out for failure to meet the 70-day requirement.

"Many cases would go to trial without proper preparation if prosecutors were forced to meet the new deadlines. Sometimes the defendant has been involved in a chain of offenses, and tracing the evidence and interviewing potential witnesses takes time. Getting laboratory reports from chemists and other experts routinely takes weeks.

"Civil cases would face longer delays as judges try to meet the time constraints for criminal cases. Plea bargaining could become more widespread, and arrests of dangerous criminals could be postponed to delay the beginning of the 70-day period as long as possible."

In light of the enormous practical problems involved, does it make sense to have limits at all? Does the Speedy Trial Act require more judges and prosecutors in order to be workable? Is the potential benefit to society **worth the cost?**

D. REQUEST FOR CONTINUANCE

AVERY v. ALABAMA

Supreme Court of the United States, 1940.
308 U.S. 444, 60 S.Ct. 321.

MR. JUSTICE BLACK delivered the opinion of the Court.

Petitioner was convicted of murder in Alabama; he was sentenced to death and the State Supreme Court affirmed. The sole question presented is whether in violation of the Fourteenth Amendment, "petitioner was denied the right of counsel, with the accustomed incidents of consultation and opportunity of preparation for trial", because after competent counsel were duly appointed their motion for continuance was denied. Vigilant concern for the maintenance of the constitutional right of an accused to assistance of counsel led us to grant certiorari.

* * *

Since the Constitution nowhere specifies any period which must intervene between the required appointment of counsel and trial, the fact, standing alone, that a continuance has been denied, does not constitute a denial of the constitutional right to assistance of counsel. In the course of trial, after due appointment of competent counsel, many procedural questions necessarily arise which must be decided by the trial judge in the light of facts then presented and conditions then existing. Disposition of a request for continuance is of this nature and is made in the discretion of the trial judge, the exercise of which will ordinarily not be reviewed.

But the denial of opportunity for appointed counsel to confer, to consult with the accused and to prepare his defense, could convert the appointment of counsel into a sham and nothing more than a formal compliance with the Constitution's requirement that an accused be given the assistance of counsel. The Constitution's guarantee of assistance of counsel cannot be satisfied by mere formal appointment.

* * *

The record shows—

Petitioner was convicted on an indictment filed in the Bibb County Circuit Court for murder alleged to have occurred in 1932. He was found and arrested in Pittsburg, Pennsylvania, shortly before March 21, 1938. On that date, Monday, he was arraigned at a regular term of the Court; two practicing attorneys of the local bar were appointed to defend him; pleas of not guilty and not guilty by reason of insanity were entered and the presiding judge set his trial for Wednesday, March 23. The case was not reached Wednesday, but was called Thursday, the 24th, at which time his attorneys filed a motion for continuance, on the ground that they had not had sufficient time and opportunity since their appointment to investigate and prepare his defense. Affidavits of both attorneys accompanied the motion.

One attorney's affidavit alleged that he had not had time to investigate and prepare the defense because he had been actually engaged in another trial from the time of his appointment at 2 P.M., Monday, until 9 P.M. that evening; his presence had been required in the court room on Tuesday, March 22, due to employment in other cases set, but not actually tried; he had been detained in court Wednesday, March 23, waiting for petitioner's case to be called; but after his appointment he had talked with petitioner and "had serious doubts as to his sanity."

The affidavit by the other attorney stated that he too had not had proper time and opportunity to investigate petitioner's case because of his employment in other pending cases, some of which were not disposed of until Tuesday at 4:30 P.M.

No ruling on the motion for continuance appears in the record, but on Thursday, the 24th, the trial proceeded before a jury.

*   *   *

The jury returned a verdict of guilty with the death penalty. On the same day, the 24th, petitioner's counsel moved for a new trial, setting up error in the failure to grant the requested continuance. This motion for new trial was continued from time to time until June 30. In the interim, a third attorney had been employed by petitioner's sister, and on June 30, petitioner's three lawyers filed an amendment to the motion for new trial, specifically setting out that the denial of a continuance had deprived petitioner of the equal protection of the laws and due process of law guaranteed by the Fourteenth Amendment, by denying him "the right of counsel, with the accustomed incidents of consultation and opportunity of preparation for trial."

When the motion for new trial was heard the only witnesses were petitioner's three attorneys. The third attorney, employed by petitioner's sister, testified only that he had been employed after the trial and verdict. The two attorneys who had represented petitioner at the trial substantially repeated what they had set out in their original affidavits. In some detail they testified that: they had conferred with petitioner after their appointment on Monday, March 21, but he gave them no helpful information available as a defense or names of any witnesses; between their appointment and the trial they made inquiries of people who lived in the community in which the petitioner had lived prior to the crime with which he was charged and in which the killing occurred and none of those questioned, including a brother of petitioner, could offer information or assistance helpful to the defense; they (the attorneys) had not prior to the trial conferred with local doctors, of whom there were four, as to petitioner's mental condition, had neither summoned any medical experts or other witnesses nor asked for compulsory process. And in response to inquiries made by the trial judge they stated that they had not made any request for leave of absence from the court to make further inquiry or investigation.

The motion for new trial was overruled.

* * *

Under the particular circumstances appearing in this record, we do not think petitioner has been denied the benefit of assistance of counsel guaranteed to him by the Fourteenth Amendment. His appointed counsel, as the Supreme Court of Alabama recognized, have performed their "full duty intelligently and well." Not only did they present petitioner's defense in the trial court, but in conjunction with counsel later employed, they carried an appeal to the State Supreme Court, and then brought the matter here for our review. Their appointment and the representation rendered under it were not mere formalities, but petitioner's counsel have—as was their solemn duty —contested every step of the way leading to final disposition of the case. Petitioner has thus been afforded the assistance of zealous and earnest counsel from arraignment to final argument in this Court.

The offense for which petitioner was convicted occurred in a County largely rural. The County seat, where court was held, has a population of less than a thousand. Indictments in the Bibb County Circuit Court, as in most rural Counties throughout the Nation, are most frequently returned and trials had during fixed terms or sessions of court. And these rural "Court Weeks" traditionally bring grand and petit jurors, witnesses, interested persons and spectators from every part of the County into the County seat for court. Unlike metropolitan centers, people in these rural Counties know each other, and information concerning witnesses and events is more widespread and more generally known than in large cities. Because this was so, petitioner's attorneys were able to make the inquiries during Court Week at the County seat, to which they testified, and that they apparently withdrew the plea of insanity after this inquiry is significant. That the examination and preparation of the case, in the time permitted by the trial judge, had been adequate for counsel to exhaust its every angle is illuminated by the absence of any indication, on the motion and hearing for new trial, that they could have done more had additional time been granted.

Under the circumstances of this case we cannot say that the trial judge, who concluded a fairly conducted trial by carefully safeguarding petitioner's rights in a clear and fair charge, deprived petitioner of his constitutional right to assistance of counsel. The Supreme Court of Alabama having found that petitioner was afforded that right, its judgment is

Affirmed.

NOTES

1. Because the parties to an action are entitled to a prompt disposition on the merits, unreasonable delay caused by a motion for continuance is generally unwarranted. While extreme circumstances preclude a court's insistence upon expedience in the face of a justifiable request for a continuance, the determination of a continuance is within the sound discretion of the trial court. See Ungar v. Sarafite, 376 U.S. 575, 589, 84 S.Ct. 841 (1964); United States v. Arlen, 252 F.2d 491, 495 (2nd Cir. 1958); United

States ex rel. Gallo v. Follette, 270 F.Supp. 507, 511 (S.D.N.Y.1967). Abuse of discretion is subject to no mechanical test, but is measured by the facts and circumstances of each case. Compare United States ex rel. Davis v. McMann, 386 F.2d 611 (2nd Cir. 1967), cert. denied 390 U.S. 958, 88 S. Ct. 1049 (1968) (one hour for counsel to prepare case held inadequate) with Goforth v. United States, 314 F.2d 868 (10th Cir.), cert. denied 374 U.S. 812, 83 S.Ct. 1703 (1963) (no continuance required where defendant had only fifteen minutes to confer with counsel). Absent a clear abuse of discretion, the denial of a continuance affords no deprivation of the right to counsel. Upon review, an alleged abuse of discretion must be subjected to a stringent test measuring the action of the trial court against the reasons disclosed to it at the time the motion was made and not on the basis of a more elaborate argument tendered on appeal. See United States v. Bryan, 534 F.2d 205 (9th Cir. 1976). On the other hand, the denial of a motion for continuance may be so arbitrary and fundamentally unfair as to rise to a constitutional deprivation. Shirley v. North Carolina, 528 F.2d 819 (4th Cir. 1975).

2. Most continuances arise in the context of a claim that, by refusing to grant the motion, the court infringed upon defendant's right to counsel.

In Kobey v. United States, 208 F.2d 583 (9th Cir. 1953), local counsel who had filed an appearance was required to proceed when chosen counsel complained that he represented only one defendant and was merely an assistant to the other counsel. The court held that a failure to grant a continuance until chosen counsel had recovered was not an abuse of discretion. Lias v. United States, 51 F.2d 215 (4th Cir.), aff'd. mem. 284 U.S. 584 (1931), held that the illness of "leading" counsel did not warrant a continuance where two members of the same firm were present in court.

In United States v. Vrilium Products Co., 185 F.2d 3 (7th Cir. 1950), cert. denied 340 U.S. 947, 71 S.Ct. 531 (1951), a continuance was sought on the eve of trial because one of counsel of record had suffered a heart attack and would have been unable to proceed for two weeks. Although co-counsel claimed that because of his age he had refrained from trial practice for several years, the court recognized the ability to proceed to trial on the basis of co-counsel's several appearances in the case. Similarly, in United States v. Cozzi, 354 F.2d 637 (7th Cir. 1965), cert. denied 383 U.S. 911, 86 S.Ct. 896 (1966), original counsel moved for a continuance alleging a conflict of interest. The trial court, noting that the defendant had adequate representation of record, expressly refused to question the defendant as to his preferred choice of counsel and ordered the case to proceed. The court found no conflict of interest and held that the refusal to grant a continuance was a sound exercise of discretion. Judge Castle, announcing the opinion, observed that an attempt to substitute counsel "merely as a matter of preference" does not justify an attendant delay in the trial: "Absent justifiable basis therefor there is no constitutional right to make a new choice of counsel, with attendant necessity for a continuance because thereof, at the time the trial is scheduled to commence." See also United States v. Burton, 584 F.2d 485 (D.C.Cir. 1978).

Consequently, the right to counsel of choice does not support a concomitant right to a continuance where other counsel of record is present, where the motion is made close to the trial date, where an extended period for preparation has been allowed and where the trial promises to be of long duration. This is especially true where available counsel is highly competent and other counsel is sought merely as a matter of preference.

3.   Only in extreme circumstances where co-counsel is not associated with the case, has a conflict of interest, or is not given adequate opportunity to prepare will the refusal to grant a continuance constitute error. See, e. g., Glasser v. United States, 315 U.S. 60, 62 S.Ct. 457 (1942) (appointed counsel's conflict of interest was discernible from the record); United States ex rel. Davis v. McMann, 386 F.2d 611 (2nd Cir. 1967), cert. denied 390 U.S. 958, 88 S.Ct. 1049 (1968) (inadequate time to prepare); McConnell v. United States, 375 F.2d 905 (5th Cir. 1967) (request for appointed counsel was refused forcing defendant to trial without counsel); United States v. Gougis, 374 F.2d 758 (7th Cir. 1967) (appointed counsel had conflict of interest); United States v. Mitchell, 354 F.2d 767 (2nd Cir. 1966) (inadequate time to prepare); Releford v. United States, 288 F.2d 298 (9th Cir. 1961) (counsel who merely shared office space with unavailable chosen counsel forced to represent defendant); United States v. Bergamo, 154 F.2d 31 (3rd Cir. 1946) (counsel not adequately prepared).

4.   An excellent survey of the case law in the area, and a variety of examples of the frequency with which the continuance issue is raised, is contained in United States v. Uptain, 531 F.2d 1281 (5th Cir. 1976):

"The reasons for a continuance which were timely asserted in this case fall into two categories. First, Uptain through his attorney claimed that the interval between arraignment and trial was insufficient to allow proper time to prepare motions, to consult concerning the case, and to properly interview potential witnesses and subpoena them for appearance at trial. Second, counsel for Uptain asserted at trial that he could no longer represent his client as a result of conflicts of strategy and because of nonpayment for services; because no other counsel was present, withdrawal would have necessitated a continuance.

"None of these justifications for a continuance is new to this court. To the contrary, the cases are so numerous and involve such varying factual contexts and bases for decision that merely cataloging them is a task of significant proportion. We have deemed the following factors highly relevant in assessing claims of inadequate preparation time: the quantum of time available for preparation, the likelihood of prejudice from denial, the accused's role in shortening the effective preparation time, the degree of complexity of the case, and the availability of discovery from the prosecution. We have also explicitly considered the adequacy of the defense actually provided at trial, the skill and experience of the attorney, any pre-appointment or pre-retention experience of the attorney with the accused or the alleged crime, and any representation of the defendant by other attorneys that accrues to his benefit.

"Within this general category of cases, a particularly common claim is that a continuance was necessary to interview and subpoena potential witnesses. The panels of this court that have ruled on such claims have considered the diligence of the defense in interviewing witnesses and procuring their presence, the probability of procuring their testimony within a reasonable time, the specificity with which the defense is able to describe their expected knowledge or testimony, the degree to which such testimony is expected to be favorable to the accused, and the unique or cumulative nature of the testimony. A general rule recently has emerged:

'A movant must show that due diligence has been exercised to obtain the attendance of the witness, that substantial favorable testimony would be tendered by the witness, that the witness is available and willing to testify, and that the denial of a continuance would materially prejudice the defendant.'
United States v. Miller, 513 F.2d 791, 793 (5 Cir. 1975). . . .

"Turning to the facts of this case, we find that Uptain's claim, to the extent that it is based upon an inability to interview and procure the presence of witnesses, fails to meet the rather stringent standards enunciated by this court in United States v. Miller. First, it can be doubted that 'due diligence' in interviewing and subpoenaing witnesses was exercised. Given the number and location of the witnesses, it obviously was impossible to do a thorough job in this regard, but the court was entitled to expect initial steps in that direction to have been taken.

* * *

"The claim that the general lack of preparation time rendered the denial of a continuance an abuse of discretion must also be rejected. Although there was considerable time pressure on him, [counsel] in fact was able to prepare adequate pre-trial motions and received favorable consideration on the majority of them. Uptain has failed to point out to us what other motions might have been made that could have materially aided his cause, and we are inclined to believe that there are none. Similarly, we are unable to see how more preparation would have significantly changed the course of the trial. The essence of the case against Uptain was the testimony of the co-conspirators. They were effectively cross-examined and their testimony rebutted by Uptain. The jury apparently believed the co-conspirators. Nothing has been suggested to us that would indicate the possibility of a different outcome had a continuance been granted. Accordingly we find that a great number of the factors previously considered significant—likelihood or prejudice, degree of complexity of the case, the adequacy of the defense at trial, and the pre-appointment experience of the attorney with the accused and the crime—coalesce to counsel upholding the district court.

"A different issue is presented by [counsel's] attempt to withdraw from the representation of Uptain at trial. Because no other attorney was present and prepared to carry on, this necessarily would have involved a continuance as well. It too, however, is not an unfamiliar phenomenon to this court. . . . In each of [the cases] which involved attempts by the defendant to change attorneys, the court noted that the freedom to have counsel of one's own choosing may not be used for the purposes of delay. . . . The courts noted in each case that there was prior opportunity to bring to the court's attention any conflicts between client and counsel and that the timing of the motion gave reason to believe that it might have been imposed for purposes of delay.

"The circumstances of this case depart from these previous cases in two important particulars. First, it is not clear here that conflicts between Uptain and [his attorney] could have been brought out earlier. To the extent that the conflicts were matters of trial strategy only, it may be that they developed only in the few days prior to trial or on the first day of trial itself. Second, as well as the existence of conflict between the two, [counsel] contended that Uptain's check to him had not been honored, thus putting him in uncertainty as to whether he would be paid for his services at trial.

"We rather reluctantly conclude again that these circumstances do not warrant a finding of abuse of discretion. Here again, counsel did not specify to a significant degree the nature of any strategy conflicts which arose, and the fact that the objection was raised only on the third and last day of trial, after repeated attempts to obtain a continuance on other grounds had failed, gave some basis for a belief that the asserted conflict either was fabricated or was not a serious problem. Finally, to the extent that any specific attorney-client conflict was mentioned, the only statement made by [counsel] concerned his association with Uptain's corporation as counsel and investor. If this was the origin of the conflict, then the court properly could have concluded that it should have been discovered and brought to the attention of the court sooner, if indeed the representation of Uptain by [this attorney] should have been undertaken at all. At the least, and regardless of the origin of the conflict, the court had a right to expect [counsel] to have his co-counsel present when he sought to withdraw from the case.

"By the same token, the claim of nonpayment of services did not compel a continuance. In the first place, [counsel] did not claim that he would not eventually be paid, but only that one of Uptain's checks had been dishonored . . . . The fact that a single check was worthless would not alone justify an indefinite suspension of the trial, particularly with the government's case already complete and the defendant on the stand. The trial judge was entitled to take into account both the opportunity, that counsel did not take advantage of, to obtain earlier payment from Uptain, and the prejudice to Uptain in the eyes of the jury that might result if the attorney who began his direct examination suddenly disappeared. . . . We therefore are unable to conclude that the court's refusal to allow withdrawal of counsel at the beginning of the second day of trial, pending arrival of co-counsel, was an abuse of discretion.

"Several lessons to defense lawyers should emerge from this case. The first is that, in cases where there is a substantial basis for a continuance, the attorney should present the claim as early as possible. Second, the attorney should exercise all reasonable diligence to prepare for trial despite the time constraints confronting him. Finally, such claims should be advanced with all the specificity and detail that is feasible under the circumstances. While some of these 'lessons' are rules of law under *Miller* with respect to continuances to interview and subpoena witnesses, they are counsels of wisdom in any continuance situation. Only with detailed information as to counsel's efforts and the legitimate justifications for extra time can the court conclude that the motion is made for reasons other than delay. Only then can it be expected to subordinate the very legitimate needs of both the criminal justice system and the defendant for speedy and economical justice.

"Finally, and without in any way disparaging the trial court, whose actions we today uphold, we must reiterate that a scheduled trial date should never become such an overarching end that it results in the erosion of the defendant's right to a fair trial. If forcing a defendant to an early trial date substantially impairs his ability to effectively present evidence to rebut the prosecution's case or to establish defenses, then pursuit of the goal of expeditiousness is far more detrimental to our common purposes in the criminal justice system than the delay of a few days or weeks that may be sought. The district courts to whom these difficult and inexact judgments are committed have, in the majority of cases, made them with a proper consideration of the rights of defendants to due process of law as well as the demands of judicial economy. Where, as here, it is possible to see how a denial of continuance resulted from a reasonable resolution of the various factors confronting a court, we will uphold its action, even if it may seem somewhat harsh."

E. REQUEST FOR SEVERANCE

UNITED STATES v. BARRETT

United States Court of Appeals, Seventh Circuit, 1974.
505 F.2d 1091.

[The government alleged that, without disclosure of his interest, Barrett shared in the commissions on insurance premiums paid by Cook County to Arthur J. Gallagher & Co. to insure all Cook County voting machines from 1968 through 1970. At that time Barrett had substantial responsibility in the awarding of these insurance contracts. The government proved its case through the use of books and records and through the testimony of associates of Barrett whose credibility the defendant did not seriously challenge. The defense was a legal one, with the factual dispute confined primarily to the defendant's state of mind. The mail fraud conviction was based upon these insurance transactions.

The government also alleged that Barrett received kickbacks on the purchase of certain new voting machines from 1967 through 1970 at a time when he had major responsibility for the County's purchase of such machines. The government's case rested largely upon the credibility of an immunized witness who had also received a favorable compromise of a civil tax dispute. Defendant attacked the credibility of this witness and suggested that this witness had kept the alleged kickback money for himself. This kickback scheme was the basis of the Travel Act and the tax fraud convictions.]

JUDGE SPRECHER delivered the Court's opinion:

* * *

Defendant's pre-trial motion to sever the mail fraud charges from the bribery and tax evasion charges under Rules 8(a) and 14, Fed.R.Crim.P., was denied.

The government's theory of joinder is that the bribery scheme and the insurance commission scheme were two transactions connected by Barrett's use of his public office for private gain.

In Finnegan v. United States, 204 F.2d 105 (8th Cir.), cert. denied, 346 U.S. 821, 74 S.Ct. 36 (1953), defendant was an I.R.S. employee charged with three counts of representing private clients and two counts of bribery. He was acquitted of bribery and one of the representation counts. The court held joinder of the five counts was proper under Rule 8(a): . . .

> All five of the offenses charged in this indictment were for violations of statutes designed to protect the government. The charge in each of the counts was the acceptance of money either for representing an interest adverse to the government or as a bribe to perform some act adverse to the interest of the government, the defendant being a trusted public official. All the offenses in effect charged a government official with taking the part of private interest in matters in which the government was a party. . . .

In Egan v. United States, . . . 287 F. 958 (1923), defendant was a public official charged with representing a private party and with taking money to influence his official decisions. The court said the two crimes belonged to the same class.

In United States v. Weber, 437 F.2d 327 (3d Cir. 1970), cert. denied, 402 U.S. 932, 91 S.Ct. 1524 (1971), defendant was a union official charged with Taft-Hartley and Hobbs Act violations. The court upheld the joinder under Rule 8(a) because the violations were connected by defendant's scheme to accept money from New Jersey contractors who employed members of his union.

In the Kerner case, Kerner asked for a severance under Rule 8(a) only of the perjury charge from all the other charges. The court held that the perjury and other charges were "all connected with, or arose out of, a common plan to corruptly influence the regulation of horse racing." United States v. Isaacs, 493 F.2d 1124, 1159 (7th Cir. 1974), cert. denied, 417 U.S. 976, 94 S.Ct. 3184, 41 L.Ed.2d 1146 (1974).

These cases support the government's position that here "[t]wo or more offenses may be charged in the same indictment . . . if the offenses charged . . . are . . . two or more acts or transactions connected together . . . ."

A more difficult question arises under Rule 14, which looks to the prejudice caused a defendant by a joinder of offenses. Obviously any adding of offenses to others is prejudicial to some extent. However, "[w]hether a severance of related offenses should be granted must remain largely within the discretion of the trial judge upon consideration of the circumstances of the individual case." American Bar Association Project on Standards For Criminal Justice, Standards Relating to Joinder and Severance, § 2.2(b) Commentary, p. 32 (1968).[1]

Reversal of a conviction on the ground of abuse of discretion for failure to sever an offense under Rule 14 is almost non-existent. Recently such a reversal occurred in this circuit in United States v. Pacente, 490 F.2d 661 (7th Cir. 1973), but on rehearing en banc the conviction was affirmed, 503 F.2d 543, 546 (7th Cir. 1974), where this court said:

> The grant or denial of severance or separate trials under Rule 14 is discretionary. . . . Denial of relief will produce reversal only if abuse of discretion is shown. . . .

We cannot say that the district judge abused his discretion in this case.

JUDGE STEVENS, dissenting:

* * *

The joinder of two separate offenses was highly prejudicial to the defendant and, in my opinion, not authorized by Rule 8(a).

Unquestionably the jury's knowledge that for several years Barrett had been accepting secret insurance commissions on County business enhanced the likelihood that they would credit Meyers' testimony about secret cash bribes. Consider the impact of the prosecutor's argument:

> "See, it wasn't enough for Edward Barrett to receive $180,000 in bribes. After he got the machines he got a little hungrier and he wanted some more money, and so he went ahead and worked out an agreement where he could insure the machines, something he was required to do under the terms of his job, and then get a kickback in the form of a broker's commission." . . .

In its brief in this court the government argued that the insurance arrangement which originated as early as 1961, and the bribery in connection with the purchase of machines in 1967 and thereafter, were "parts of a common scheme or plan." The evidence affords no support at all for that contention and, quite properly, it is not accepted by the majority here. The two arrangements were made with entirely different sets of persons, at different times, and neither was in any way dependent upon the other. As the government states in its brief,

---

1. The A.B.A. Standards Commentary also states in regard to joinder: "The joinder together for one trial of two or more offenses of the same or similar character when the offenses are not part of a single scheme or plan has been subjected to severe criticism over the years. . . . Such joinder is allowed under Federal Rule 8. . . ." Section 2.2(a) Commentary, pp. 29–30.

"other than with regard to background information, no one
witness testified to events underlying both the bribery and
the mail fraud offenses."[2]

Thus, considerations of trial convenience do not support this joinder.

The theory on which the joinder is upheld is that the two crimes
were "connected" because they both involved a breach of Barrett's
public trust. No special significance is, or should be, attached to the
fact that they both involved voting machines. In my judgment that
"connection" is too tenuous to justify such a prejudicial joinder. Indeed, I believe the result is foreclosed by both branches of our decision on the severance issue in the *Quinn* case. [365 F.2d 256 (7th Cir.
1966)]. There the fact that the unlawful disbursement of funds on
April 3, 1963, and again on July 8, 1963, both involved a breach of
Quinn's fiduciary obligation to the depositors and shareholders of the
Beverly Savings & Loan Association was insufficient to justify the
joinder. Moreover, the similarity between the two transactions in
the *Quinn* case, both of which involved the same institution, the same
source of funds, and an appropriation of a large sum for the defendant's own benefit, was much more marked than the fact, present
here, that two different illegal schemes both happened to relate to
voting machines. Frankly, I have some doubt about the validity of
the *Quinn* holding, but even if it were to be rejected, I would disapprove of this joinder. Certainly if *Quinn* is viable today, prejudicial
error was committed in this case.

ROBINSON v. UNITED STATES

United States Court of Appeals, District of Columbia Circuit, 1972.
459 F.2d 847.

SPOTTSWOOD W. ROBINSON III, CIRCUIT JUDGE.

[Appellant was tried upon a twelve count indictment, stating
three separate offenses for each of four distinct narcotics sales. Although he conceded that original joinder was proper, he filed a pretrial motion for severance on the ground that the joinder was prejudicial. He asserts that the trial judge's denial of this motion was reversible error].

* * *

2. Government's Brief at p. 43. The
statement is made in support of the
government's position, which I accept, that there was no significant
risk that the joinder would tend to
confuse the jury. The possibility of
confusion, however, is not the source
of prejudice which troubles me about
this joinder. Rather, it is the vice of
using evidence of one crime to prove
the defendant's disposition to commit
another. I think the government is
correct in suggesting that Judge
Hand's analysis in United States v.
Lotsch, 102 F.2d 35, 36 (2d Cir. 1939),
would lead to approval of this joinder. I believe, however, that prevailing opinion favors the views expressed long ago in Kidwell v. United
States, 38 App.D.C. 566, at 570
(1912), as follows:

"It is doubtful whether separate
and distinct felonies, involving different parties, not arising out of
the same transaction or dependent
upon the same proof, should ever
be consolidated. But it should not
be permitted where the crimes
charged are of such a nature that
the jury might regard one as corroborative of the other, when, in
fact, no corroboration exists."

We have recognized that the trial of multiple counts jointly, though conducive to economy and expedition in criminal litigation, may in particular instances breed prejudice to the accused. One danger is that "the jury may use the evidence of one of the crimes charged to infer a criminal disposition on the part of the defendant from which is found his guilt of the other crime or crimes charged." Another danger is that "the jury may cumulate the evidence of the various crimes charged and find guilt when, if considered separately, it would not so find." Still another may be "a latent feeling of hostility engendered by the charging of several crimes as distinct from only one." [1]

At the same time, we have acknowledged that separate trials offer no panacea where evidence of each joined offense is admissible as to each of the others, for in that event the accused could fare no better from a severance and trial of the severed counts independently. We also have "found no prejudicial effect from joinder when the evidence of each crime is simple and distinct, even though such evidence might not have been admissible in separate trials" since, "with a proper charge, the jury can easily keep such evidence separate in their deliberations and, therefore, the danger of the jury's cumulating the evidence is substantially reduced." Thus, by our standard, no severance is required if "evidence of the joined offenses would be mutually admissible, or if not, the evidence is sufficiently 'simple and distinct' to mitigate the danger of cumulation." And "in any given case the court must weigh prejudice to the defendant caused by the joinder against the obviously important considerations of economy and expedition in judicial administration." We think that upon a separate trial of either of the four drug transactions alleged in the indictment,[2] evidence relating to the other three transactions would have become admissible, and that in any event the evidence was so uninvolved and so readily referable to the several offenses as to reduce the hazard of cumulation to the point of insubstantiality. We accordingly conclude that the trial judge did not err in favoring the needs of trial administration by denying the sought-after severance.

---

1. We have also recognized that the accused "may become embarrassed or confounded in presenting separate defenses," as where the accused desires to testify but to limit his testimony to less than all of the joined counts. In the case before us, appellant's boilerplate pretrial motion for severance stated that he might wish to do just that, but the thought seemingly perished before trial was reached. At the hearing on the motion, just prior to the commencement of trial, defense counsel made no mention of such a possibility, and at the trial appellant denied complicity in any of the narcotics transactions and attempted to set up an alibi for each. Moreover, at no time did appellant make the informational proffer which our decisions require "to satisfy the court that the claim of prejudice is genuine and to enable it intelligently to weigh the considerations of 'economy and expedition in judicial administration' against the defendant's interest in having a free choice with respect to testifying."

2. Appellant's motion did not specify just what sort of a severance he desired. We think a severance of counts by the four transactions alleged in the indictment would have marked the practical limit since for each transaction proved three independent offenses separately punishable would emerge.

To be sure, evidence indicating the accused's commission of an offense not on trial, because of its potential for prejudice, is generally to be excluded. There are, however, situations wherein evidence having such a tendency would serve "some substantial, legitimate purpose" in the case on trial, and thus may summon an exception to the general rule. One established exception obtains where the other-offense evidence bears significantly upon the identity of the perpetrator of the offense being tried, in which event it may properly be let in although it also associates the accused with other crime. Just such an occasion, we believe, was presented here.

* * *

In such distinctive circumstances, we believe that upon a separate trial of the counts relating to any one of the four drug transactions, these details from the other three would promise real assistance in the jury's evaluation of Officer James' identification of appellant. We believe, too, that in this milieu the probative values of such evidence would suffice to serve "a substantial, legitimate purpose" warranting admission. And since upon any separate trial some testimonial items from the transactions not on trial would have become admissible, we find no prejudice stemming from the denial of the motion for severance.

There is yet another consideration lending support to our conclusion that the trial judge's refusal to sever did not operate to enhance other-crimes prejudice to appellant. As we have observed, a severance of counts is not required where the evidence, even when not mutually admissible in separate trials, is so simple that the jury should encounter no substantial difficulty in properly confining its treatment within zones of relevance. "[T]he very essence of this rule is that the evidence be such that the jury is unlikely to be confused by it or misuse it," and that, we believe, was clearly so here. The four narcotics sales for which appellant was blamed were not only uncomplicated transactions but were so markedly similar that each was virtually a duplicate of all the rest. Moreover, the single factual issue arising with respect to the four was identity, with one witness for the Government affirming and one witness for the defense denying that appellant was the seller, and the jury's principal task was a credibility resolution. We are unable to perceive any significant probability that the jury could have become confused by the evidentiary presentation on either side. We need not decide whether this case would qualify under the "simple and distinct" principle in the absence of the mutual admissibility of the four drug sales which we have already found. We do say, however, that on the balance of probative value and harm to the accused, the situation before us is of a piece with those which our previous decisions have held to present inadequate claims of resulting prejudice.

In upholding the declination to sever in this case, we disclaim once again any thought "that every item having some tendency to show identity is automatically to be made available to the jury."

* * *

We caution then, that our decision herein is not to be taken as a license for admission of evidence tending to show merely that an identification witness on some other occasion saw the accused engaging in other criminal conduct. In the case at bar there was much more than just another occasion for observation; the number of such occasions, their duration, the opportunities for scrutinizing they afforded, the imperative reason for scrutiny, and the recordation of descriptive details all combined to add peculiar value to Officer James' identification of appellant. In sum, we sustain the ruling denying appellant's motion for severance because we find such a plus-quality in evidentiary items emanating from each of the four drug transactions as to warrant mutual admissibility, and too little likelihood of jurors' misunderstanding of the evidence to override the husbandry of a single trial.

The judgment of appellant's conviction is

Affirmed.

FAHY, SENIOR CIRCUIT JUDGE (dissenting):

The trial was on a twelve count indictment involving four alleged sales of narcotics on four different dates, each sale leading to charges of three separate offenses under the narcotics laws. Prior to trial, appellant moved for relief from prejudicial joinder. The motion was denied. This I think was reversible error.

I do not understand the court to conclude that there was no prejudice in lumping in one trial the evidence in support of all twelve charges growing out of the four sales of narcotics. The dangers arising from a joint trial of multiple crimes is pointed out by the court. Nevertheless the court, as I understand, holds that the obvious prejudice to the defendant which accompanies such a joint trial must be accepted because were a separate trial had for each of the four sales evidence of the other sales would be admissible to support the testimony of Officer James identifying defendant as the one who made the sale involved in the separate trial. Additionally, the court relies on a rule which in some circumstances permits joint trial of offenses when evidence of each is simple and distinct, even though all the evidence of one would not be admissible in a separate trial of the other.

First. I agree that in a separate trial involving any one of the four sales, in turn involving the decisive issue of identity of the alleged offender, evidence of other encounters of Officer James with the accused would be admissible as tending to verify the correctness of the officer's identification of the accused. I do not agree, however, that the right to introduce evidence of other encounters in aid of identification also carries with it a right of the prosecution on direct examination to adduce from the officer evidence that the encounters involved other sales of narcotics in violation of the laws. If it be said that the added detail of criminal circumstances enhanced the credibility of the identification by underscoring for the jury the reason why Officer James remembered defendant, for the same reasons such detail increased unnecessarily the prejudice to the accused.

* * *

Second. As indicated above, the court also seeks support in the rule permitting joint trial of offenses when the evidence of each is sufficiently simple and distinct to avoid prejudice because "the jury is unlikely to be confused" or to "misuse" the evidence of one in considering the others. In the first place, the court's conclusion that the evidence of each transaction was simple and distinct is not borne out by the record. Both the Government's argument to the jury and the District Court's instructions treated the evidence relating to defendant's identification as if a single issue were involved—whether he was the party to all four transactions. To conclude that the jury did not misuse the evidence—that is, did not cumulate the identifying testimony as to each of the four transactions to reinforce the identifying testimony as to the others—is to me incredible.

* * *

Third. The court refers to the discretion which it attributes to the trial judge in "weigh[ing] prejudice to the defendant caused by the joinder against the obviously important considerations of economy and expedition in judicial administration."

* * *

I think we must move away from considering that prejudice to the right of the individual to a fair trial must be permitted in aid of economy and expedition in the administration of justice. The courts should pursue attainment of those ends by other means available.

The simple fact is that as a matter of common sense no abstract evidentiary rule obscures the prejudice that attached to the use in each offense of the evidence of the four offenses in the joint trial. This prejudice is not offset by any acceptable rationale which justifies imposing upon the defendant an exception to the rule which excludes at trial for one crime evidence of a different one. . . . Moreover, no case controls another. The issue is always one of preserving the fairness of the trial, a judgment to be exercised on the facts of each case.

I respectfully dissent from affirmance for the reasons stated.

NOTES

1. If the prosecution improperly connects a number of counts against one defendant or a variety of defendants in one indictment, a motion for improper joinder or severance to divide the matters for separate trials may be filed. Improper joinder and severance are two different concepts; the former compels mandatory severance while the latter applies where the joinder of counts or defendants, although originally proper, may be so prejudicial as to warrant the court, in its discretion, to grant a severance. Both doctrines are applicable in situations involving multiple counts against one defendant and multiple defendants.

Joinder and severance are governed by statutory rules in all jurisdictions. Some states leave the decision of whether to be tried on multiple counts to the defendant (e. g. 15 Ala.Code § 319; Ga.Code Ann. § 918.02), while others specify the kinds of offenses that may be joined in a single indictment. (e. g. Ark.Stat.Ann. § 43–1010; Iowa Code Ann. § 773.37). Provisions comparable to, or specifically adopting, the Federal Rule have been enacted in a number of states. (e. g. Alaska R.Crim.P. 8; Del.R. Crim.P. 8; Ill.Rev.Stat., ch. 38, § 38, § 111–4; Ky.R.Crim.P. 6.20; Md.R.P. 716).

Fed.R.Crim.P. 8 provides:

(a) Joinder of Offenses. Two or more offenses may be charged in the same indictment or information in a separate count for each offense if the offenses charged, whether felonies or misdemeanors or both, are of the same or similar character or are based on the same act or transaction or on two or more acts or transactions connected together or constituting parts of a common scheme or plan.

(b) Joinder of Defendants. Two or more defendants may be charged in the same indictment or information if they are alleged to have participated in the same act or transaction or in the same series of acts or transactions constituting an offense or offenses. Such defendants may be charged in one or more counts together or separately and all of the defendants need not be charged in each count.

2. There is a great deal of confusion with regard to the scope of application of the respective subdivisions of Rule 8. However, "[i]t is firmly established in the case law that the propriety of joinder in cases where there are multiple defendants must be tested by Rule 8(b) alone and that Rule 8(a) has no application." 1 C. Wright, Federal Practice and Procedure § 144, at 318 (1969). See also Williams v. United States, 415 F.2d 1064, 1068 (8th Cir. 1969); Cupo v. United States, 123 U.S.App.D.C. 324, 359 F. 2d 990, 992 (1966), cert denied 385 U.S. 1013, 87 S.Ct. 723 (1967). Thus, under the law of joinder, satisfaction of the demands of Rule 8(b) in multi-defendant cases renders unnecessary a determination that all counts against each single defendant are joined within the meaning of 8(a). "Rule 8(a) relates only to cases in which there is only one defendant. It would seem to follow that all other cases of joinder are governed by Rule 8(b)." 1 L. Orfield, Criminal Procedure Under the Federal Rules § 38:47, at 801 (1966). See also United States v. Welsh, 14 F.R.D. 189, 190 (D.D.C.1953). Such a reading is consistent with the Advisory Committee notes on Rule 8 which suggested that the two subdivisions were "mutually exclusive." 8 J. Moore, Federal Practice ¶ 8.06[1], at 8–23 n. 2 (Cipes ed. 1970). In United States v. Friedman, 445 F.2d 1076, 1082–83 (9th Cir. 1971), defendant contended that separate counts of perjury and influencing witnesses were improperly joined under 8(a) with substantive and conspiracy counts relating to the possession of unreleased grand jury transcript. Rejecting this contention, the court found Rule 8(a)'s demand that separate counts against a single defendant be "of the same or similar character" inapplicable in cases involving multiple defendants:

Preliminarily, it does not matter that the offenses charged [in the two counts alleged to be improperly joined] are not "of the same or similar character" as those charged in the other counts. We covered that ground thoroughly in Roselli v. United States, [432 F.2d 879, 898 (9th Cir. 1970), cert. denied 401 U.S. 924, 91 S.Ct. 883, (1971)] where we said that "even dissimilar charges may be joined against multiple defendants if they arise out of the same series of transactions constituting an offense or offenses."

In *Roselli*, cited in the *Friedman* case, two defendants argued under Rule 8(a) that tax counts were improperly joined with substantive and conspiracy counts against each of them. Judge Browning's scholarly opinion disposed of this contention:

> We set aside appellants argument that joinder was improper because the tax charges were not similar in character to the [other charges in the indictment]. Joinder of charges against multiple defendants is controlled by Rule 8(b), not by Rule 8(a). Under Rule 8(b), the sole basis for joinder of charges against multiple defendants is that the defendants "are alleged to have participated in the same act or transaction or in the same series of acts or transactions constituting an offense or offenses." It is irrelevant that Rule 8(a) permits charges "of the same or similar character" to be joined against a single defendant, even though they do not arise out of the same or connected transactions. Charges against multiple defendants may not be joined merely because they are similar in character; and even dissimilar charges may be joined against multiple defendants if they arise out of the same series of transactions constituting an offense or offenses. Except for this difference, the test for joinder under the two provisions is the same.

Therefore, it is clear that the multiple charges against a single defendant and indictments involving more than one defendant must be considered separately.

3. Where a single defendant is involved in a multiple count indictment, Fed.R.Crim.P. 8(a) operates to the exclusion of the provisions governing multidefendant trials set forth in Rule 8(b). The cases uniformly support joinder of several counts against a single defendant where the offenses charged arise out of a series of connected transactions forming elements of one overall scheme or plan. For example, in United States v. Baker, 131 U.S.App.D.C. 7, 401 F.2d 958 (1968), cert. denied 400 U.S. 965, 91 S.Ct. 367 (1971), a decision that has apparently become the leading case on Rule 8(a) single defendant joinder, the court concluded that separate counts charging tax evasion and interstate transportation of fraudulently obtained funds were connected to the same series of transactions and could, therefore, be properly joined:

> In determining whether offenses are based on acts or transactions connected together, the predominant consideration is whether joinder would serve the goals of trial economy and convenience; the primary purpose of this kind of joinder is to insure that a given transaction need only be proved once.

Pursuant to these guidelines, the courts have approved the joinder of offenses arising out of the same series of transactions no matter how diverse the crimes involved. See, e. g., United States v. Lee, 428 F.2d 917, 920 (6th Cir. 1970) (transportation of gun by felon and possession of counterfeit money); United States v. Bourassa, 411 F.2d 69, 74 (10th Cir. 1969), cert. denied 396 U.S. 915 (1970) (bail jumping and counterfeiting); Blunt v. United States, 131 U.S.App.D.C. 306, 404 F.2d 1283, 1288 (1969), cert. denied 394 U.S. 909, 89 S.Ct. 1021 (1969) (forgery and robbery). Compare United States v. Quinn, 365 F.2d 256 (7th Cir. 1966). In *Quinn*, the defendant, a savings and loan officer, was indicted in four counts for two independent, fraudulent transactions between the financial institution he represented and companies that he personally controlled. Because no relationship between the transactions other than the identity of the defendant and the savings and loan existed, the government argued on appeal that joinder was justified because the offenses were of the same or similar character. The court found the transactions to be different in character and unconnected and the evidence to be so complex that "the most optimistic seer would hesitate to endanger his reputation by claiming that the jury could separate the proof relevant to different counts". 365 F.2d at 265. Therefore, it held that before multiple counts could be joined against a single defendant, each count had to be connected to every other count in some evidentiary manner.

4.   Fed.R.Crim.P. 8(b)'s "series of transactions" test does not mean that factually unrelated charges against some defendants can be joined for trial because all of the defendants are charged with one common offense or joined in a common count. See United States v. Nettles, 570 F.2d 547 (5th Cir. 1978) (three defendants charged with operating three separate gambling establishments and bribing police for protection against raids); United States v. Eagleston, 417 F.2d 11, 14 (10th Cir. 1969) (joinder of two defendants in two common counts does not justify joinder of unrelated count against one codefendant); Chubert v. United States, 414 F.2d 1018, 1019 (8th Cir. 1969) (one defendant common to six counts does not justify joinder of unrelated counts against other defendants). Accord, King v. United States, 355 F.2d 700, 703–04 (1st Cir. 1966); United States v. Spector, 346 F.2d 345, 349–50 (7th Cir. 1963). Nor will 8(b) be satisfied by joining defendants who commit similar but unrelated crimes. McElroy v. United States, 164 U.S. 76, 81 (1896); Ingram v. United States, 272 F.2d 567 (4th Cir. 1959). Thus, while counts of "the same or similar character" may be joined against a single defendant under Rule 8(a), the more restrictive language of Rule 8(b) demands that each count arise out of the "same series of acts or transactions constituting an offense or offenses."

Where the conduct upon which each count is based represents one segment of a series of factually related transactions in which all defendants, at some point, participated, the charges are properly joined although the various offenses are distinct and all defendants are not charged in each count. United States v. Amick, 439 F.2d 351, 360 (7th Cir. 1971); United States v. Scott, 413 F.2d 932, 935 (7th Cir. 1969), cert. denied 396 U.S. 1006, 90 S.Ct. 560 (1970).

"Participation," as used in Rule 8(b), does not mean that each defendant must have engaged in all transactions of the series, but that all defendants must have involved themselves in a connected course of conduct out of which separate crimes arose. See, e. g., Haggard v. United States, 369 F.2d 968, 973 (8th Cir. 1966) (twelve count indictment: one count charging conspiracy between A, B, and C; three counts of embezzlement against A with B aiding and abetting, and eight counts of false entry by A, three alone, three with C aiding and abetting, one with D aiding and one with D and E aiding); Scheve v. United States, 184 F.2d 695, 696–97 (D. C.Cir. 1970) (separate counts of keeping a gaming table against several defendants and aggravated assault against one).

A conspiracy allegation in an indictment, if charged in good faith, serves as a "connecting link" between unrelated transactions and justifies the joinder of those who participated. See Gordon v. United States, 438 F. 2d 858, 878 (5th Cir. 1971); United States v. Bryant, 364 F.2d 598, 603 (4th Cir. 1966); United States v. Wright, 309 F.2d 735, 739 (7th Cir. 1962), cert. denied 372 U.S. 929, 83 S.Ct. 873 (1963).

5. Based upon the principles of judicial economy, efficiency and speed and the public interest in avoiding multiple trials, it has become axiomatic that defendants jointly indicted should be tried together except for the most compelling reasons. Parker v. United States, 404 F.2d 1193 (9th Cir. 1968), cert. denied 394 U.S. 1004, 89 S.Ct. 1602 (1969); Brown v. United States, 126 U.S.App.D.C. 134, 375 F.2d 310, 315, cert. denied 388 U.S. 915, 87 S.Ct. 2133 (1967); Golliher v. United States, 352 F.2d 594, 603 (8th Cir. 1966). This is particularly true where a conspiracy is alleged; and, therefore, an exceptionally strong demonstration of likely prejudice is a prerequisite for severance. United States v. Kahn, 381 F.2d 824, 838–39 (7th Cir.), cert. denied 389 U.S. 1015, 88 S.Ct. 591 (1967); Davenport v. United States, 260 F.2d 591 (9th Cir. 1958).

Thus a severance will be granted for only the most cogent reasons; the "moving party must show prejudice, that he will be unable to obtain a fair trial without severance, not merely that a separate trial will offer a better chance of acquittal." United States v. Blue, 440 F.2d 300, 302 (7th Cir. 1971). The decision as to whether a joint trial will deprive a defendant of the right to a fair trial is resolved by determining whether it is within the jury's capacity to follow the trial judge's instructions to limit and separate the evidence against each defendant:

> The ultimate test is whether the jury can follow admonitory instructions of the court and appraise independent evidence against each defendant solely upon the defendant's own acts, statements and conduct.

United States v. Turner, 274 F.Supp. 412, 416 (E.D.Tenn.1967). Accord, United States v. Kahn, 381 F.2d 824, 839 (7th Cir.), cert. denied 389 U.S. 1015, 88 S.Ct. 591 (1967). The determination of severance motions rests exclusively "within the sound discretion of the trial judge. . . ." Opper v. United States, 348 U.S. 84, 95, 75 S.Ct. 158, 165 (1954).

6. The severance issue is often linked to an evidentiary issue. If evidence of crime A would be admissible in the trial of crime B under an exception to the general prohibition against "other crime" evidence (e. g., to show motive, intent, common scheme, *modus operandi*, etc.), then the reason for holding separate trials is diminished. Conversely, if evidence of crime A would be inadmissible in the trial of crime B if that case were tried separately, then the argument for severance is stronger. See United States v. Foutz, 540 F.2d 733 (4th Cir. 1976), for a good demonstration of the interrelationship of the severance issue and the "other crime" evidence issue. (See material in Chapter 19, Section D, for a treatment of evidence of other crimes.)

7. The mere fact that several defendants and offenses are combined in one indictment does not constitute a basis for severance. Where the defendants are all charged with having participated in the same series of transactions, the proof of separate charges may be largely dependent upon evidence applicable to all defendants. If it is, potential jury confusion regarding evidence applicable to only one defendant can be obviated by appropriate instructions from the bench. See Butler v. United States, 317 F.2d 249, 264 (8th Cir.), cert. denied 375 U.S. 836, 84 S.Ct. 67 (1963); United States v. Garrison, 265 F.Supp. 108, 112 (M.D.Ga.1967). As the court said in Hanger v. United States, 398 F.2d 91, 100 (8th Cir. 1968), cert. denied 393 U.S. 1119, 89 S.Ct. 995 (1969):

> The feature of certain evidence being evidence against one defendant but not against another defendant is usually present in every

joint trial. It is well settled that the fact that in a joint trial there will be evidence against one defendant which is not evidence against another defendant does not require separate trials.

However, severances have been sought on a wide variety of imaginative grounds. See, e. g. United States v. Cohen, 145 F.2d 82 (2d Cir. 1944) (defendant sought severance alleging that he was only a minor participant in a conspiracy); United States v. Myers, 406 F.2d 746 (4th Cir. 1969) (unsavory character of codefendant); United States v. Hoffa, 367 F.2d 698, 709 (7th Cir. 1966), rev'd on other grounds, 387 U.S. 231, 87 S.Ct. 1583 (1967) (antagonistic personality of codefendant); United States v. Turner, 274 F. Supp. 412, 419 (E.D.Tenn.1967) (fact that one defendant is a police officer and his codefendants have prior criminal records).

8. It has been contended that it is unfair to try a defendant on a substantive count and a grand jury perjury count arising out of the defendant's testimony during the course of the investigation which led to the substantive count. What arguments support this contention? See United States v. Pacente, 503 F.2d 543 (7th Cir. 1974) (en banc), which rejected the contention, overturning a panel opinion which had accepted the theory. See Comment, Joinder of Substantive Offenses and Perjury in One Indictment, 66 J.Crim.L. & C. 44 (1975).

9. A defendant, named in more than one indictment, who wants to avoid the expense, aggravation and delay involved in separate proceedings may move to consolidate the indictments for trial. See Fed.R.Crim.P. 13. The operative rules regarding consolidation are the same concepts governing original joinder. If the separate charges could have been joined in the first instance, the court, in its discretion, may consolidate them for trial. See United States v. Escobedo, 430 F.2d 14 (7th Cir. 1970); Dunaway v. United States, 205 F.2d 23 (D.C.Cir. 1953). To avoid forum shopping and venue problems, consolidation is not available to indictments brought in separate jurisdictions.

10. An excellent collection of the governing authorities may be found in Decker, Joinder and Severence in Federal Criminal Cases: An Examination of Judicial Interpretation of the Federal Rules, 53 Notre Dame L.Rev. 147 (1977).

11. Concerning severance of co-defendants' cases when one or more defendant confessed, see Bruton v. United States, Ch. 19, Section B, infra, and notes thereafter.

F. REQUEST FOR CHANGE OF PLACE OF TRIAL

---

1. THE PROBLEMS OF INNATE COMMUNITY PREJUDICE AND PREJUDICIAL NEWS MEDIA PUBLICITY

MAINE v. SUPERIOR COURT

Supreme Court of California, 1968.
68 Cal.2d 375, 66 Cal.Rptr. 724, 438 P.2d 372.

MOSK, JUSTICE.

Petitioners, Leonard E. Maine and Thomas E. Braun, seek writs of mandate directed to the Superior Court of the County of Mendocino. By grand jury indictment they are each accused of murder, two counts of kidnaping, forcible rape, and assault with intent to commit murder. Petitioners each filed a timely motion under section 1033 of the Penal Code for a change of venue on the ground that a fair and impartial trial could not be had in Mendocino County. The trial court found there could be a fair and impartial trial and denied the motions.

* * *

The People contend that petitioners Maine and Braun have an adequate remedy at law in that the trial court denied their motion for a change of venue without prejudice to its renewal "if the facts should so warrant." It has long been the practice, sanctioned in the decisions of this court to permit the trial court to defer its final ruling on a motion for a change of venue until the jury is empaneled. The trial court can thereby take into consideration any unanticipated difficulties encountered during *voir dire* examination of prospective jurors.

Experience shows, however, that trial courts are often reluctant to order a venue change after a jury has been empaneled. Defense counsel, moreover, is placed in an unnecessarily awkward position: unless he exhausts all his peremptory challenges he cannot claim on appeal, in the absence of a specific showing of prejudice, that the jury was not impartial. Yet, convinced that he must go to trial because his motion for a venue change was at first denied and in all likelihood will not ultimately prevail, he may fail to use every peremptory challenge sensing that the jurors he has examined may be comparatively less biased than others who might be seated were his peremptory challenges exhausted. In an antagonistic atmosphere "there will remain the problem of obtaining accurate answers on *voir dire*—is the juror consciously or subconsciously harboring prejudice against the accused resulting from widespread news coverage in the community." We can only conclude that the naked right to renew the motion for change of venue is not an adequate remedy at law to require denial of a mandamus petition.

Although we have reversed judgments of conviction on but four occasions [out of 66 cases in which the issue was raised] many cases have presented serious constitutional issues arising out of prejudicial newspaper publicity which either caused or reflected widespread hostility to a defendant in the community. .   .   .   In such cases the offenses committed were often bestial and heinous, and the discovery of the crimes as well as the unfolding of subsequent events inevitably received abundant attention in the communications media. .   .   .
In many cases that are the focus of unusual public attention, the effect of prejudicial pretrial disclosures or widespread community antagonism can be substantially overcome by a change of venue.
.   .   .

After long study the American Bar Association has tendered proposals for judicial consideration which should contribute toward freeing criminal trials from the taint of partiality.

* * *

Section 3.2(c), entitled "Standards for granting the motion," provides: "A motion for change of venue or continuance shall be granted whenever it is determined that because of the dissemination of potentially prejudicial material, there is a reasonable likelihood that in the absence of such relief, a fair trial cannot be had. This determination may be based on such evidence as qualified public opinion surveys or opinion testimony offered by individuals, or on the court's own evaluation of the nature, frequency, and timing of the material involved. A showing of actual prejudice shall not be required."

* * *

In the case at bench petitioners are accused of crimes of the gravest consequence. They are strangers to Ukiah, a small community where they have been held for trial. On the other hand, the two victims, a popular teen-age couple from respected families in the area, were assaulted under circumstances that would compel any community's shock and indignation. Since the case has not progressed beyond the pretrial stage it would be inappropriate for us to comment on the evidence that may unfold at the trial. We confine our discussion to a few uncontradicted illustrations which demonstrate a reasonable likelihood that petitioners cannot receive a fair trial in Mendocino County.

One of the victims, the girl, was discovered on a public road nearly unconscious with bullet wounds about her neck and head. Her condition was critical and several complicated operations were performed to save her life. Local citizens immediately organized a fund to help the girl's parents defray the medical expenses, and the Ukiah Daily Journal, the local newspaper, urged every citizen to contribute. It is no small measure of the community's laudable warmth and generosity that a substantial sum was quickly raised, mostly in modest contributions. We do not hold it to be an invariable rule that sympathy for a victim demonstrates antipathy to the alleged perpetrators of an offense. But such pervasive civic involvement in the fate of a victim, particularly when the events all transpire in a relatively small community, [Ukiah (9,900); Mendocino County (51,200)] is a strong indication that the venue should be changed.

We recognize that from the outset of the investigation the local law enforcement authorities scrupulously avoided divulging any details of the crime. Both the Ukiah Daily Journal and the Santa Rosa Press Democrat, which extensively reported the case to residents of Mendocino County and vicinity, noted that the sheriff and district attorney were "extremely close-mouthed on any details." Their commendable efforts in this regard, however, were frustrated by other authorities who talked freely with representatives of the press and other news media about the crime. Principally at fault appears to be an official of the State of Washington, where petitioners are also charged with murder, who revealed that one of the petitioners had confessed and placed full responsibility on the other for the crimes. This disclosure received substantial attention in the local newspaper, and it is undoubted that the existence of a confession is now common knowledge in the community. The admissibility of the confession into evidence has not been tested in a judicial hearing, however and its premature release must be regarded as potentially prejudicial to petitioners. When such a disclosure occurs in a small community, the only effective remedy, if the defense so requests, is to change the venue. Indeed, failure to seek a change of venue may suggest to a reviewing court on appeal that no prejudice was suffered by the defendant.

Finally, this case has to some extent become involved in county politics. The district attorney disqualified Judge Winslow, an experienced trial judge, whom he is opposing on the June 1968 election ballot. The People do not deny that political factors might have influenced the district attorney's decision, but contend that since a judge from outside the county has now been assigned to hear the case, petitioners' right to a fair trial will not be infringed. The People also note that counsel for one of the petitioners has announced his candidacy for the same judgeship, but assert their belief that the assigned trial judge can exercise effective control over both the district attorney and the defense counsel. Under these circumstances, nevertheless, we harbor a gnawing fear that the campaign competition between two election adversaries might inadvertently intrude during the course of a proceeding in which they are also trial adversaries. Political factors have no place in a criminal proceeding, and when they are likely to appear, as here, they constitute an independent reason for a venue change.

. . .

The People insist that sufficient time has now elapsed since the date of petitioners' arrest that any prejudice they might have suffered has been dissipated. Under the circumstances of the case at bench this position is not persuasive. While a lengthy continuance might sufficiently protect the accused in some cases, it does not do so here. Delays may be an efficacious antidote to publicity in medium-size and large cities, but in small communities, where a major crime becomes embedded in the public consciousness, their effectiveness is greatly diminished. . . .

We do not assert categorically that each individual circumstance here, isolated and alone, would compel a change of venue. It may do so, or may not, depending upon the extent of the hostility engendered toward a defendant, and to some extent upon the sophistication of the community. Generally no single indicium is available as a barometer of the public mind.

We hold that where, as here, the defendants are friendless in the community, the victims prominent, the occurrence of the crime probably fortuitous as to locale, community-wide interest and generosity are expressed on behalf of the victim, newspaper publicity includes accounts of a purported confession, and two opposing counsel are also election opponents, a change of venue is clearly necessary to assure a fair trial to the defendants.

It is now incumbent upon the parties to suggest a convenient site for a fair trial. In a case of this nature it would probably be prudent to transfer the cause to a metropolitan area where comparatively little difficulty will be encountered in empaneling a jury free from any kind of prejudgment.

PAMPLIN v. MASON

United States Court of Appeals, Fifth Circuit, 1966.
364 F.2d 1.

WISDOM, CIRCUIT JUDGE.

In August 1963 Alexander Mason, a Negro minister active in the civil rights movement, led a sit-in demonstration in "white" restaurants in Marlin, the county-seat of Falls County, Texas. This was the first racial demonstration in the community. Shortly after, he was arrested for contributing to the delinquency of a minor. He and, presumably, the minor, had refused to leave a sit-in demonstration in an all-white restaurant in Marlin.

When he was taken to jail for the sit-in violation, Mason asked to use the telephone. The Sheriff agreed, and several deputy sheriffs accompanied Mason to their office where he made his call. After completing the call, he lay down on the office floor and refused to return to his cell. The deputies carried Mason bodily back to the third floor of the jail where they set him down. At this point, Mason seized the bars outside a cell and refused to move. Witnesses for the State testified that when the jailer, a deputy sheriff, attempted to pull Mason into the cell, Mason broke loose. He swung at one of the deputies and pushed him onto a cell bunk, knocking off his glasses and bloodying his nose.

Mason's assault case came to trial eleven days later August 23, 1963. Before presenting his case, the petitioner moved for a change of venue, stating under oath that prejudice against him prevented his obtaining a fair trial in Falls County. The court denied the motion. The court overruled petitioner's request that the jurors be examined individually and qualified them as a group. In the voir dire, the prospective jurors answered, together, that they did not know petitioner; had formed no opinions in the case; and had no prejudices against the Negro race or against a Negro acting as counsel for petitioner. After a one-day trial, the jury found Mason guilty.

The federal district court, in granting the writ of habeas corpus, found that the state court's denial of venue change, in "the totality of the surrounding facts", amounted to the possibility of the denial of a fair and impartial trial. The court based its decision on Irvin v. Dowd, 1961, 366 U.S. 717, 81 S.Ct. 1639, and its progeny. "[T]he right to jury trial guarantees to the criminally accused a fair trial by a panel of impartial, 'indifferent' jurors."

Irvin v. Dowd was a habeas proceeding to test the validity of the petitioner's conviction for murder in an Indiana county where intensive publicity had aroused great indignation before the trial. Indiana law allowed only a single change of venue. Since the defendant had already made one transfer, the trial judge denied any further change. The county where the trial was held had 30,000 inhabitants. Justice Clark, for the Supreme Court, found the evidence of prejudice against the defendant "clear and convincing": extensive newspaper stories of the defendant's previous criminal record, police line-up identification, lie detector test, negotiations with the prosecutor, and confessions to similar crimes. The trial court had permitted individual examination of prospective jurors; on voir dire, eight of the panel finally selected expressed the opinion that the petitioner was guilty. The Court concluded that the record showed a pattern of deep and bitter prejudice had existed in the community and *that a clear nexus existed between the community prejudice and the possibility of jury prejudice.* The Court reversed and remanded for a new trial.

More recent Supreme Court cases hold that evidence of pervasive community prejudice is enough for reversal, *even without the showing of a clear nexus between community feeling and jury feeling.* In Rideau v. Louisiana, 1963, 373 U.S. 723, 83 S.Ct. 1417, the facts were similar to *Irvin.* The alleged pattern of prejudice in *Rideau* was generated in large part by the defendant's confessions on a televised interview with the sheriff. The trial court denied a change of venue and challenge for cause of three members of the jury who had seen and heard the damning interview. The Court held that the nationwide spectacle of the defendant's personally confessing in detail over television to the crimes with which he was later to be charged was in itself sufficient to void his conviction. The Court found it unnecessary to determine from the voir dire transcript whether opinionated jurors actually found their way into the jury box. "[D]ue process of law in this case required a trial before a jury drawn from a community of people who had not seen and heard Rideau's televised 'interview'." [In] Estes v. Texas, 1965, 381 U.S. 532, 85 S.Ct. 1628, Justice Clark held that televising portions of a state criminal trial *in itself* constitutes a denial of due process.

Justice Clark noted that *Estes,* like *Rideau,* marks a departure from Irvin v. Dowd, in which the Court had made a careful examination of the facts to determine whether actual jury prejudice resulted. In *Estes,* as in *Rideau,* the Court found the probability of prejudice inherent in the obnoxious practice: "the circumstances were held to be inherently suspect." As we read the Supreme Court cases, the test is: Where outside influences affecting the community's climate of opinion as to a defendant are inherently suspect, the resulting probability of unfairness requires suitable procedural safeguards, such as a change of venue, to assure a fair and impartial trial.

The record is inadequate to judge the intensity of feeling about the petitioner in Falls County prior to his trial. However, there is sufficient evidence to show that the state court's denial of a pre-trial hearing was in itself a denial of due process. We know that Mason was a civil rights leader in Falls County at the time of his trial. He offered to produce witnesses at a hearing for change of venue who would testify to the generally hostile atmosphere of the community. The jury assessed the maximum statutory penalty, and under Texas law the severity of the penalty itself may indicate existence of prejudice against the defendant. Falls County has just about the same population as the community in *Irvin* (less than 30,000). There are enough danger signals to warrant reversal for a hearing under the venue procedure.

It is immaterial that the voir dire did not demonstrate community prejudice. It is unnecessary to prove that local prejudice actually entered the jury box. Moreover, Justice Clark has warned that in this type situation we must suspect the response of prospective jurors even on individual examination: "No doubt each juror was sincere when he said that he would be fair and impartial to petitioner, but psychological impact requiring such a declaration before one's fellows is often its father." Irvin v. Dowd, 366 U.S. at 728, 81 S.Ct. at 1645. The Supreme Court's emphasis on the feeling in the community rather than the transcript of the voir dire finds ample justification in this case. Where racial feeling may be strong, the voir dire, let alone the group examination to which this defendant was restricted, can hardly be expected to reveal the shades of prejudice that may influence a verdict. Due process of law requires a trial before a jury drawn from a community of people free from inherently suspect circumstances of racial prejudice against a particular defendant.

We do not decide whether the petitioner is entitled to a change of venue. The primary responsibility for that determination rests with the Texas courts. The district court was satisfied that there was sufficient possibility of prejudice lurking in the background to warrant reversal for new trial. We agree that no remedy short of a new trial, with the possibility of a change of venue if necessary, would provide adequate correction of the constitutional error in the petitioner's original trial.

The judgment and order of the district court must be

Affirmed.

NOTES

1. There are few reported cases other than Maine v. Superior Court which deal strictly with the pre-trial showing required to secure a change of place of trial. Ordinarily, if the motion is allowed, the issue is not reviewed on appeal. If the motion is denied, then trial proceeds and on review, the appeal court will consider not only the pre-trial showing but the actual voir dire of the jury to determine whether the accused was prejudiced. In a situation much like *Maine*, the court issued another mandate to require a change of place of trial. Frazier v. Superior Court, 5 Cal.3d 321, 486 P.2d 694 (1972). Frazier was accused of the murder of a local physician, his wife, secretary and two small sons. The accused was generally described as a "hippie" and the court took notice of local antipathy toward hippies. The court praised the law enforcement officers for exceptional restraint in releasing news but held that "No amount of self-restraint or judicial caution . . . could change . . . the case. This was not an 'ordinary' homicide . . . as all too often occurs in . . . a robbery . . . or . . . family dispute; we entertain no doubt the de-

fendants in these cases can receive unbiased trials in Santa Cruz County. Rather we deal here with an alienated member of an unpopular subculture accused of a bizarre and senseless mass murder of prominent citizens of a small community."

Quaere: Where does "an alienated member of an unpopular subculture accused of a bizarre and senseless mass murder" get a fair trial? What if hostile public sentiment and wide publicity extend throughout an entire state?

The court in People v. Speck, 41 Ill.2d 177, 242 N.E.2d 208 (1968), was faced with such a problem and so was the court in State v. Thompson, 273 Minn. 1, 139 N.W.2d 490 (1966). Thompson was a lawyer, "quite successful . . . in the fields of personal injury, domestic relations and criminal law" who also did some teaching in law school. He hired men to kill his wife which they did in a particularly brutal way. The court held:

"On an application by defendant for mandamus, we required a change of venue. In so doing, we noted:

> ' * * * Probably no case in the memory of anyone in this locality has aroused so much interest and so much discussion as this one. Over a period of several months hardly a day has elapsed when something has not been said or written in a news medium of one kind or another.'

> "Ordinarily a defendant on motion for change of venue does not have a right to select a particular county for his trial, but it is left to the trial court to choose a county in which a fair trial can be obtained. In this case, however, defendant was granted a change to Hennepin County at his request. It cannot be denied that the case was given an unusual amount of publicity, much of which could better have been omitted. The day may come when in this country we find a way to strike a fair balance between the constitutional guaranty of a free press and the constitutional right to a fair trial. It seems that we have not yet found a solution to that problem.

> "It is doubtful in this case that a more fair trial could have been obtained elsewhere in this state. The same news coverage extended throughout the state as in Ramsey and Hennepin Counties. The case was one of public interest everywhere. We do not have a record of the voir dire examination of the jurors but are willing to accept counsel's statement that of some 112 jurors examined 67 expressed actual bias. That does not mean, however, that the 12 accepted were also biased. On the record before us we cannot say he was denied a fair trial, nor are we convinced that a more fair trial could have been obtained elsewhere in the state. Criminal cases must be tried somewhere and, having gone as far as we did in this case in permitting the defendant to choose his own county, we do not know what more we could have done."

2. On the question of publicity affecting the grand jury, see United States v. Anselmo, 319 F.Supp. 1106 (E.D.La.1970):

> "The third alleged basis of grand jury bias is that preindictment publicity was so intense that (a) the publicity was inherently prejudicial, (b) the grand jurors felt compelled to return an indictment or (c) in any event, the rights of the defendants were substantially prejudiced and violated.

"In the instant case, all the defendants especially Jack P. F. Gremillion, the Attorney General of Louisiana, have been thrust upon the public eye almost daily in newspaper headlines, pictures, editorials, editorial cartoons and stories from July 1968 to the date of indictment. The local TV stations have small libraries of tapes concerning the financial collapse of LL&T and the resultant Board of Ethics, legislative and federal grand jury investigations.

"The cases which have considered the question of preindictment publicity and its effect on the grand jury, rather than holding that preindictment publicity is inherently prejudicial and cause for dismissal of the indictment, have held that the defendant must show specifically that such publicity caused prejudice and bias in the grand jurors and that the indictment returned was the result of essential unfairness. Beck v. Washington, 369 U.S. 541, 82 S. Ct. 955 (1962).

"There appears to be a lingering doubt whether one is entitled to an impartial grand jury. Judge Holtzoff, in United States v. Knowles, 147 F.Supp. 19 (D.D.C.1957), writes:

'The basic theory of the functions of a grand jury does not require that grand jurors should be impartial and unbiased. In this respect, their position is entirely different from that of petit jurors. The Sixth Amendment to the Constitution of the United States expressly provides that the trial jury in a criminal case must be "impartial." No such requirement in respect to grand juries is found in the Fifth Amendment, which contains the guaranty against prosecutions for infamous crimes unless on a presentment or indictment of a grand jury.'

"Judge Thornberry, in a concurring opinion in Martin v. Beto, 397 F.2d 741 (5th Cir. 1968), after wrestling with this question of preindictment prejudicial publicity concluded, reluctantly, that 'the rule today is that the grand jury is an accusatory body which does not have to be impartial and that we depend on a fair trial . . . .'

"This Court, judging this case on its particular merits, adopts the view expressed by Justice Douglas in his dissenting opinion in Beck v. Washington, 369 U.S. 541, 82 S.Ct. 955 (1967):

'The question is not whether one who receives large-scale adverse publicity can escape grand jury investigation nor whether the hue and cry attendant on adverse publicity must have died down before the grand jury can make its investigation. This case shows the need to make as sure as is humanly possible that one after whom the mob and public passion are in full pursuit is treated fairly, that the grand jury stands between him and an aroused public . . . .'

"Therefore, this Court rejects the contention that the inherently prejudicial rule, proper at the trial level, is applicable to grand jury procedures because such a rule could prevent or postpone grand jury investigations. This Court adheres to the requirement of specific showing of prejudice, with an admonition to the prosecution that it maintain the necesssary procedures to insure dispassionate consideration by the grand jurors of the charges presented."

MURPHY v. FLORIDA

Supreme Court of the United States, 1975.
421 U.S. 794, 95 S.Ct. 2031.

MR. JUSTICE MARSHALL delivered the opinion of the Court.

* * *

Petitioner was convicted in the Dade County, Fla., Criminal Court in 1970 of breaking and entering a home, while armed, with intent to commit robbery, and of assault with intent to commit robbery. The charges stemmed from the January 1968 robbery of a Miami Beach home and petitioner's apprehension, with three others, while fleeing from the scene.

The robbery and petitioner's arrest received extensive press coverage because petitioner had been much in the news before. He had first made himself notorious for his part in the 1964 theft of the Star of India sapphire from a museum in New York. His flamboyant lifestyle made him a continuing subject of press interest; he was generally referred to—at least in the media—as "Murph the Surf."

Before the date set for petitioner's trial on the instant charges, he was indicted on two counts of murder in Broward County, Fla. Thereafter the Dade County court declared petitioner mentally incompetent to stand trial; he was committed to a hospital and the prosecutor *nolle prossed* the robbery indictment. In August 1968 he was indicted by a federal grand jury for conspiring to transport stolen securities in interstate commerce. After petitioner was adjudged competent for trial, he was convicted on one count of murder in Broward County (March 1969) and pleaded guilty to one count of the federal indictment involving stolen securities (December 1969). The indictment for robbery was refiled in August 1969 and came to trial one year later.

The events of 1968 and 1969 drew extensive press coverage. Each new case against petitioner was considered newsworthy, not only in Dade County but elsewhere as well. The record in this case contains scores of articles reporting on petitioner's trials and tribulations during this period; many purportedly relate statements that petitioner or his attorney made to reporters.

Jury selection in the present case began in August 1970. Seventy-eight jurors were questioned. Of these, 30 were excused for miscellaneous personal reasons; 20 were excused peremptorily by the defense or prosecution; 20 were excused by the court as having prejudged petitioner; and the remaining eight served as the jury and two alternates. Petitioner's motions to dismiss the chosen jurors, on the ground that they were aware that he had previously been convicted of either the 1964 Star of India theft or the Broward County murder, were denied, as was his renewed motion for a change of venue based on allegedly prejudicial pretrial publicity.

At trial, petitioner did not testify or put in any evidence; assertedly in protest of the selected jury, he did not cross-examine any of the State's witnesses. He was convicted on both counts, ...

*   *   *

Petitioner relies principally upon Irvin v. Dowd, 366 U.S. 717, 81 S.Ct. 1639 (1961), Rideau v. Louisiana, 373 U.S. 723, 83 S.Ct. 1417 (1963), Estes v. Texas, 381 U.S. 532, 85 S.Ct. 1628 (1965), and Sheppard v. Maxwell, 384 U.S. 333, 86 S.Ct. 1507 (1966). In each of these cases, this Court overturned a state-court conviction obtained in a trial atmosphere that had been utterly corrupted by press coverage.

In Irvin v. Dowd the rural community in which the trial was held had been subjected to a barrage of inflammatory publicity immediately prior to trial, including information on the defendant's prior convictions, his confession to 24 burglaries and six murders including the one for which he was tried, and his unaccepted offer to plead guilty in order to avoid the death sentence. As a result, eight of the 12 jurors had formed an opinion that the defendant was guilty before the trial began; some went "so far as to say that it would take evidence to overcome their belief" in his guilt. In these circumstances, the Court readily found actual prejudice against the petitioner to a degree that rendered a fair trial impossible.

Prejudice was presumed in the circumstances under which the trials in *Rideau, Estes,* and *Sheppard* were held. In those cases the influence of the news media, either in the community at large or in the courtroom itself, pervaded the proceedings. In *Rideau* the defendant had "confessed" under police interrogation to the murder of which he stood convicted. A 20-minute film of his confession was broadcast three times by a television station in the community where the crime and the trial took place. In reversing, the Court did not examine the *voir dire* for evidence of actual prejudice because it considered the trial under review "but a hollow formality"—the real trial had occurred when tens of thousands of people, in a community of 150,000 had seen and heard the defendant admit his guilt before the cameras.

The trial in *Estes* had been conducted in a circus atmosphere, due in large part to the intrusions of the press, which was allowed to sit within the bar of the court and to overrun it with television equipment. Similarly, *Sheppard* arose from a trial infected not only by a background of extremely inflammatory publicity but also by a courthouse given over to accommodate the public appetite for carnival. The proceedings in these cases were entirely lacking in the solemnity and sobriety to which a defendant is entitled in a system that subscribes to any notion of fairness and rejects the verdict of a mob. They cannot be made to stand for the proposition that juror exposure to information about a state defendant's prior convictions or to news accounts of the crime with which he is charged alone presumptively deprives the defendant of due process. To resolve this case, we must turn, therefore, to any indications in the totality of circumstances **that petitioner's trial was not fundamentally fair.**

The constitutional standard of fairness requires that a defendant have "a panel of impartial, 'indifferent' jurors." Qualified jurors need not, however, be totally ignorant of the facts and issues involved.

> "To hold that the mere existence of any preconceived notion as to the guilt or innocence of an accused, without more, is sufficient to rebut the presumption of a prospective juror's impartiality would be to establish an impossible standard. It is sufficient if the juror can lay aside his impression or opinion and render a verdict based on the evidence presented in court."

At the same time, the juror's assurances that he is equal to this task cannot be dispositive of the accused's rights, and it remains open to the defendant to demonstrate "the actual existence of such an opinion in the mind of the juror as will raise the presumption of partiality."

The *voir dire* in this case indicates no such hostility to petitioner by the jurors who served in his trial as to suggest a partiality that could not be laid aside. Some of the jurors had a vague recollection of the robbery with which petitioner was charged and each had some knowledge of petitioner's past crimes, but none betrayed any belief in the relevance of petitioner's past to the present case.[1] Indeed, four of the six jurors volunteered their views of its irrelevance, and one suggested that people who have been in trouble before are too often singled out for suspicion of each new crime—a predisposition that could only operate in petitioner's favor.

In the entire *voir dire* transcript furnished to us, there is only one colloquy on which petitioner can base even a colorable claim of partiality by a juror. In response to a leading and hypothetical question, presupposing a two- or three-week presentation of evidence against petitioner and his failure to put on any defense, one juror conceded that his prior impression of petitioner would dispose him to convict. We cannot attach great significance to this statement, however, in light of the leading nature of counsel's questions and the juror's other testimony indicating that he had no deep impression of petitioner at all.

The juror testified that he did not keep up with current events and, in fact, had never heard of petitioner until he arrived in the room for prospective jurors where some veniremen were discussing him. He did not know that petitioner was "a convicted jewel thief" even then; it was petitioner's counsel who informed him of this fact. And he volunteered that petitioner's murder conviction, of which he

1. We must distinguish between mere familiarity with petitioner or his past and an actual predisposition against him, just as we have in the past distinguished largely factual publicity from that which is invidious or inflammatory. E. g., Beck v. Washington, 369 U.S. 541, 556, 82 S.Ct. 955, 963 (1962). To ignore the real differences in the potential for prejudice would not advance the cause of fundamental fairness, but only make impossible the timely prosecution of persons who are well known in the community, whether they be notorious or merely prominent.

had just heard, would not be relevant to his guilt or innocence in the present case, since "[w]e are not trying him for murder."

Even these indicia of impartiality might be disregarded in a case where the general atmosphere in the community or courtroom is sufficiently inflammatory, but the circumstances surrounding petitioner's trial are not at all of that variety. Petitioner attempts to portray them as inflammatory by reference to the publicity to which the community was exposed. . . . However, the news articles concerning petitioner had appeared almost entirely during the period between December 1967 and January 1969, the latter date being seven months before the jury in this case was selected. They were, moreover, largely factual in nature.

The length to which the trial court must go in order to select jurors who appear to be impartial is another factor relevant in evaluating those jurors' assurances of impartiality. In a community where most veniremen will admit to a disqualifying prejudice, the reliability of the others' protestations may be drawn into question; for it is then more probable that they are part of a community deeply hostile to the accused, and more likely that they may unwittingly have been influenced by it. In Irvin v. Dowd, for example, the Court noted that 90% of those examined on the point were inclined to believe in the accused's guilt, and the court had excused for this cause 268 of the 430 veniremen. In the present case, by contrast, 20 of the 78 persons questioned were excused because they indicated an opinion as to petitioner's guilt. This may indeed be 20 more than would occur in the trial of a totally obscure person, but it by no means suggests a community with sentiment so poisoned against petitioner as to impeach the indifference of jurors who displayed no animus of their own.

In sum, we are unable to conclude, in the circumstances presented in this case, that petitioner did not receive a fair trial. Petitioner has failed to show that the setting of the trial was inherently prejudicial or that the jury-selection process of which he complains permits an inference of actual prejudice. The judgment of the Court of Appeals must therefore be affirmed.

Judgment affirmed.

MR. CHIEF JUSTICE BURGER, concurring in the judgment.

I agree with MR. JUSTICE BRENNAN that the trial judge was woefully remiss in failing to insulate prospective jurors from the bizarre media coverage of this case and in not taking steps to prevent pretrial discussion of the case among them. Although I would not hesitate to reverse petitioner's conviction in the exercise of our supervisory powers, were this a federal case, I agree with the Court that the circumstances of petitioner's trial did not rise to the level of a violation of the Due Process Clause of the Fourteenth Amendment.

MR. JUSTICE BRENNAN, dissenting. [Opinion omitted.]

NOTE

The problems of prejudicial publicity do not abate with jury selection. With respect to the trial judge's function when claims of mid-trial publicity arise, see Margoles v. United States, 407 F.2d 727 (7th Cir.), cert. denied 396 U.S. 833, 90 S.Ct. 89 (1969). That substantial deference will be paid a trial judge's findings with respect to the ability to proceed in light of mid-trial publicity is evidenced by United States v. Persico, 425 F.2d 1375 (2d Cir. 1970). There, the government called noted crime syndicate inform- ant Joseph Valachi as a surprise witness. The trial judge found that, not- withstanding the literal flood of publicity accompanying Valachi's appear- ance, a mistrial was unwarranted. His decision was affirmed. The court said, at p. 1380:

> "The publicity to which the jurors were exposed did not deal with the issues of appellants' guilt, as in Sheppard v. Maxwell, 384 U.S. 333, 86 S.Ct. 1507 (1966), and Rideau v. Louisiana, 373 U.S. 723, 83 S.Ct. 1417 (1963), but involved background information. Most of the material, save the reference to Cosa Nostra which we believe to have been dealt with effectively, was brought out at trial as competent evidence.
>
> "The three weeks that passed before the jury was called upon to make its decision also served to blunt much of the adverse effect of the publicity.
>
> "Appellants moved for a mistrial on the ground that the pub- licity prejudiced the jury, making it impossible for them to receive a fair trial. The trial judge took prompt and effective corrective action. He held a separate voir dire of each juror, frankly and candidly discussing the problems caused by the publicity. He cor- rectly isolated the reference to the Cosa Nostra as the most poten- tially prejudicial aspect of the publicity and placed that element in its proper perspective by instructing each juror that it was com- pletely irrelevant to the case. After completing this process and carefully considering the problem, Judge Dooling concluded that, although the publicity was prejudicial, the jurors remained capable of giving the appellants a fair trial.
>
> * * *
>
> "We think this determination was correct both because the publicity objectively viewed in the setting of the trial was not so prejudicial to Persico or to his co-defendants that declaring a mis- trial was the only avenue open to the trial judge, and because prop- er corrective procedures were employed.
>
> "The issue of whether the nature of prejudicial publicity is such that a fair trial cannot be had is always difficult and 'each case must turn on its special facts.' The trial judge has broad dis- cretion in determining whether prejudice has resulted.
>
> "Since the publicity was not inherently prejudicial, considera- tion of its effect upon each juror is crucial. The essential ques- tion which had to be answered was whether the jurors retained the requisite impartiality. Judge Dooling was in the best position to make this difficult evaluation. We attach great weight to his de- termination that the publicity did not prevent a fair trial."

But compare United States v. Thomas, 463 F.2d 1061 (7th Cir. 1972), where the Court, in a questionable split decision, reversed the trial court's determination that a newspaper article, allegedly used by the jury during deliberations, could not have affected the verdict.

2. RESTRAINTS AND CONTROLS OVER PREJUDICIAL NEWS MEDIA REPORTING

Publicity about a case can be controlled by direct means, i. e., a rule prohibiting publication by news media; however, the First Amendment leaves our courts without significant power to do so. See Craig v. Harney, 331 U.S. 367, 67 S.Ct. 1249 (1947). In Nebraska Press Association v. Stuart, 427 U.S. 539, 96 S.Ct. 2791 (1976) a state court, acting on a joint motion by prosecution and defense restrained news media from publishing or broadcasting accounts of accused's confessions or admissions and other facts "strongly implicative" of the accused. The Court, while not prohibiting per se such restraint, held that the order was invalid. Despite the certainty of intense and pervasive publicity about the accusation of the accused murdering six members of one family, the Court found that the impact of the publicity on the jury was speculative; that there was no finding that measures short of restraint would be inadequate and, in any event, where the offense occurred in a small community rapidly spreading rumors would nullify the effect of any restraint on publication. Moreover, the Court found improper any prohibition of reporting on what occurred at open hearings and found the restriction on reporting facts "strongly implicative" to be too vague and too broad. Brennan, Stewart, and Marshall, JJ. would have found publication restrictions to be impermissible under any circumstances and a fourth Justice (White) wrote that he had "grave doubt" whether such orders would ever be justifiable. Mr. Justice Powell would sustain restraining orders only on the extraordinary showing that:

> "(i) there is a clear threat to the fairness of trial, (ii) such a threat is posed by the actual publicity to be restrained, and (iii) no less restrictive alternatives are available. Notwithstanding such a showing, a restraint may not issue unless it also is shown that previous publicity or publicity from unrestrained sources will not render the restraint inefficacious."

The indirect control of publicity is achieved by closing off the sources of information about cases. In Gannett Co. v. De Pasquale, —— U.S. ——, 99 S.Ct. 2898 (1979) the accuseds moved to exclude press and public from a pretrial hearing on the admissibility of confessions and the trial judge granted the motion. The Court approved, finding that publicity concerning pretrial suppression hearings has particularly high potential to influence public opinion and to inform prospective jurors of damaging, inadmissible evidence. The majority rejected the press claim that it had a Sixth Amendment right to attend trials and, in the alternative, found that even if such a right existed, it was overcome by the accuseds' right to a fair trial, particularly in light of the fact that the denial of access was temporary, because a transcript would be provided presumably after a jury was selected and sequestered. The Court's ruling is, on its face, limited to closure of pretrial hearings.

In 1968, the American Bar Association recommended the use of indirect controls of pretrial publicity. First, the A.B.A. endorsed closure of preliminary hearings and motions and, second, the A.B.A. advocated restrictions on the right of lawyers, judges, police officers and court personnel to release information. A.B.A., Fair Trial and Free Press. The A.B.A. evinced particular concern with information about prior criminal records, confessions, refusal to make statements, the results of tests or examinations, the identity, testimony, or credibility of prospective witnesses and possible plea bargaining. The A.B.A. position was criticized as unduly restrictive of the First Amendment rights of lawyers. See Chicago Council of Lawyers v. Bauer, 522 F.2d 242 (7th Cir. 1975) cert. denied 427 U.S. 912, 96 S.Ct. 3201 (1976). In 1978, the A.B.A. moved toward modification of its position. The basic format of its rules and procedures remains the same, but the range of applicability is narrowed. In 1968 the prohibitions applied to dissemination of information "if there is a reasonable likelihood that such dissemination will interfere with a fair trial or otherwise prejudice the due administration of justice" (Section 1.1). Ten years later dissemination must "pose a clear and present danger to the fairness of the trial" A.B.A., Fair Trial and Free Press (2nd Ed. Tent. Draft 1978). In Gannett Co. v. De Pasquale, the Court upheld the closure of the pretrial hearing because an open hearing would pose a "reasonable probability of prejudice to [the] defendants".

G. REQUEST FOR CHANGE OF JUDGE

UNITED STATES v. GARRISON

United States District Court, E.D.La.1972.
340 F.Supp. 952.

CHRISTENBERRY, DISTRICT JUDGE. * * *

A special federal grand jury . . . returned a true bill indicting Jim Garrison and nine other persons "for conspiracy to obstruct state or local law enforcement." As part of the conspiracy it was alleged that defendant Garrison "would receive protection bribe monies contributed by the defendants who would operate the illegal gambling businesses, to permit these businesses to operate free of any substantial law enforcement interference." As a further part of the alleged conspiracy the indictment states that:

> "Perishing Gervais, a former New Orleans Police Officer and former Chief Investigator for the Orleans Parish District Attorney's Office, would receive the protection bribe monies from the principals of the illegal gambling businesses and deliver it to the District Attorney Jim Garrison."

On the same day as the indictment was returned, December 3, 1971, the case was allotted to the Honorable Lansing L. Mitchell of this court. Judge Mitchell thereupon recused himself because "this case is one which involves parties with whom the Judge was formerly associated in the practice of law . . . ." On reallotment the case fell to this section of the court.

In accordance with the requirements of Title 28 U.S.C. § 144 (1970),[1] the instant motion was accompanied by defendant Garrison's affidavit with allegations to support the motion and a certificate of his local counsel, Louis B. Merhige, stating that the defendant's affidavit was made in good faith. Because it is the focal point of this opinion, the affidavit is set forth:

> "In the latter part of 1966, my office received information which convinced me that a conspiracy to kill President John F. Kennedy was formulated in Orleans Parish. With this information in hand, I felt duty bound to conduct an investigation. As a result of this investigation, I ordered the arrest of Clay L. Shaw, for conspiracy, with others, to kill President Kennedy.

> "Because of the seriousness of the charge, I asked that a preliminary hearing be held in the case. This hearing resulted in all three State judges unanimously finding probable cause to bind the defendant over for trial. Still mindful of the awesome gravity of the charge, I presented the state's evidence to the Orleans Parish grand jury. After hearing the evidence, the grand jury returned an indictment against Shaw. This indictment, after much delay occasioned by defense pleadings, was finally tried. On March 1, 1969, the petit jury acquitted the defendant.

> "A review of the testimony in the case convinced me that Shaw had committed perjury. Consequently, a bill of information was filed against him for violating the state's perjury statute. As in the conspiracy case, the defendant sought refuge in the federal court. Shaw sought an injunction preventing the state from proceeding with its perjury case, citing claimed prosecutorial bad faith as his grounds for relief.

> "An evidentiary hearing was held on his complaint by this honorable court. I, members of my staff and certain

1. "Section 144. Bias or prejudice of judge

    "Whenever a party to any proceeding in a district court makes and files a timely and sufficient affidavit that the judge before whom the matter is pending has a personal bias or prejudice either against him or in favor of any adverse party, such judge shall proceed no further therein, but another judge shall be assigned to hear such proceeding.

    "The affidavit shall state the facts and the reasons for the belief that bias or prejudice exists, and shall be filed not less than ten days before the beginning of the term at which the proceeding is to be heard, or good cause shall be shown for failure to file it within such time. A party may file only one such affidavit in any case. It shall be accompanied by a certificate of counsel of record stating that it is made in good faith."

state and defense witnesses on the conspiracy trial were heard. On May 27, 1971, the court rendered its decision granting the relief sought. In the course of its opinion, a copy of which is attached hereto as exhibit 'A' and made a part of this affidavit, the court launched a personal attack upon me. The opinion stated that I wrongfully used certain esoteric methods to 'implant' an otherwise untrue story in the mind of a state witness, that our prosecution was conducted in bad faith and that my sole interest in the case was financial. These conclusions, in my judgment, were totally unsupported by any evidence adduced at the hearing nor were they supportable by any form of objective reasoning.

"Feeling strongly in the matter, I caused to be issued a press release denouncing your honor's findings. A copy of this press release is annexed hereto as exhibit 'B' and made a part of this affidavit.

"Given the personal character of the court's remarks in its opinion and my equally personal remarks in my press release, it is submitted that this court cannot sit in fair judgment of me. The bias of the court, conscious or otherwise, is patent.

"/s/ Jim Garrison"

The case alluded to by Mr. Garrison, the affiant, is Shaw v. Garrison, 328 F.Supp. 390 (E.D.La.1971). As defendant states, it is this decision, rendered in the normal course of the performance of this court's judicial duties, that forms his first basis for recusal. As a second ground, Mr. Garrison asks that I recuse myself because he "issued a press release denouncing [my] findings."

Defendant Garrison's press release, which he candidly admits to having authored, represents certainly an unusual statement for an attorney to have transmitted to the media. Attorneys traditionally, occasionally pursuant to a judicial admonition, try their law suits in courts of law and not the market place. To do otherwise can be a serious reflection on a counselor's sense of propriety and, of course, can result in a finding of contempt of court. In this instance, however, nothing has transpired which would affect this court's ability to accord all litigants a fair and impartial trial. Were there any reason, apparent or otherwise, why this court could not feel assured that justice would be applied evenhandedly, then on its own volition the court would recuse itself. Affiant's contention reduces itself to the proposition that he can avoid being tried before any particular judge if he has publicly voiced disapproval of that judge or that judge's work. All the more so, affiant contends, if that judge has previously decided a case adverse to the defendant. That simply is not the law and the idea of it is counter to this court's policy against allowing a defendant to select the judge who will preside over his trial. The policy rather is that all cases should be allotted on a random basis. It should never be of any moment to a judge as to whether or not he sits on a particular case. "The court is not a party. There is nothing that affects the judges in their own persons. Their concern is only that the law should be obeyed and enforced, and their interest is no other than that they represent in every case." United States v. Shipp, 203 U.S. 563, 574, 27 S.Ct. 165, 167 (1906) (Holmes, J.). Similarly, a litigant's case must stand on its own merits and not depend on being heard by any particular judge.

In passing upon a motion to recuse on the grounds of bias or prejudice the facts alleged in the affidavit are taken as true, Berger v. United States, 255 U.S. 22, 33–35, 41 S.Ct. 230, 233 (1921), and the judge to whom the motion is presented determines only the legal sufficiency and timeliness of the affidavit and the certificate of counsel. . . . Where the affidavit and certificate pass the dual tests of sufficiency and timeliness the motion to recuse must be granted though the judge knows for a certainty that the allegations of prejudice and bias are false. . . . The affidavit, however, is strictly construed against the affiant, for a judge is presumed to be impartial. . . .

The affidavit and certificate of counsel were timely filed on February 14, 1972, within the delay permitted by this court for the filing of special pleadings. The sufficiency of the affidavit, however, is quite another matter. Section 144 requires a "sufficient affidavit that the judge before whom the matter is pending has a *personal* bias or prejudice . . . ." Personal bias is defined as an attitude of extrajudicial origin. Neither prior judicial exposure to a defendant nor prior judicial rulings adverse to a defendant constitute bias or prejudice on the part of the judge sufficient to cause his recusal. . . .

It follows then that Garrison's allegation of bias or prejudice founded upon the opinion in Shaw v. Garrison is insufficient as a matter of law.

Movant's second ground alleged to support the motion for recusal —his own press release denouncing the federal judiciary and this court's opinion in the *Shaw* case—is similarly inadequate. It is well settled that prior written attacks upon a judge are legally insufficient to support a charge of bias or prejudice on the part of the judge toward the author of such a statement. . . .

The reasoning behind these decisions is not difficult to ascertain. As one jurist in a similar case stated:

> "Only a psychic pleader could allege that because a defendant has published uncomplimentary statements concerning a judge, the latter will be unable to give his critic a fair and impartial trial. If such a fantastic procedure were permitted, a defendant could get rid of a judge by the simple expedient of publishing a scurrilous article, *truthfully* alleging that the article was published, and clinching the matter by asserting the bald conclusion that, since the article was uncomplimentary, the judge must of necessity be prejudiced against the publisher."

United States v. Fujimoto, [101 F.Supp. 293, 296 (D.Hawaii 1951)]. The mere fact that a defendant has made derogatory remarks about a judge is insufficient to convince a sane and reasonable mind that the attacked judge is biased or prejudiced, the standard used to test the sufficiency of an affidavit for recusal under section 144. To allow prior derogatory remarks about a judge to cause the latter's compulsory recusal would enable any defendant to cause the recusal of any judge merely by making disparaging statements about him. Such a bizarre result clearly is not contemplated in section 144.

The denial of a motion to recuse under these circumstances is in accord with the oft-stated principle that courts should not only be fair and impartial but should also appear to be fair and impartial. Indeed, the majority of circuit courts hold that it is the duty of a judge not to recuse himself where the statutory standards are not met.

* * *

Having found the reasons given in the recusal affidavit to lack the requisite legal sufficiency, the motion of defendant Jim Garrison for the recusal of this court must be and it is denied. It is so ordered.

NOTES

1. Compare the following rulings:

(a) Defendant, Musgrave, and Bryant were jointly indicted for their conduct in connection with loans from federally insured institutions. Defendant's trial was severed because of his ill health. Musgrave and Bryant were tried and convicted. Prior to the defendant's subsequent trial before the same judge he filed an affidavit seeking the judge's disqualification, which was denied. Following a trial and conviction the defendant successfully appealed. The court of appeals, in United States v. Womack, 454 F.2d 1337 (5th Cir. 1972) said:

> Because of the disruption and delay of the judicial processes that can be caused by the disqualification of a trial judge, affidavits of disqualification are strictly scrutinized for form, timeliness, and sufficiency. In the instant case, the form is not challenged, but the timeliness and sufficiency are. The Government urges that the affidavit was untimely because filed more than a year after appellant's plea of not guilty, eleven months after the trial judge first ruled on a series of appellant's pretrial motions, and two months after the transcript of the Musgrave trial, which provided the basis for the first affidavit, became a public record.
>
> We do not agree that the first affidavit was untimely. Appellant had no reason to believe the trial judge would be biased against him until word reached his counsel through the legal grapevine of comments by the judge during the Musgrave trial. Counsel for appellant was under no duty to sit in on the Musgrave trial or read the transcript of that trial the day it became a public record. There is no indication in the record that once appellant learned of the judge's derogatory comments about him and obtained the Musgrave trial transcript he did not file his affidavit promptly.

We now turn to the sufficiency of the affidavits. The law on this question is extensive but we need not belabor its breadth or nuances to decide this case in which the allegations of the affidavits are clearly sufficient. During the Musgrave trial the judge referred to appellant as a man "who everybody admits was certainly a shady character," and told the jury: "If you find that Musgrave did this there is no question but that Womack was working with him hand in glove . . . . he would be as culpable."

The genesis of appellant's supplemental affidavit of disqualification was a June 15, 1970 pretrial conference. When appellant moved for a continuance because of his alleged ill health following a heart attack, the judge replied that appellant should have taken care of his health problems earlier and would go to trial even if he had to have a doctor in court to hold his hand. In response to appellant's motion for a change of venue to Fort Worth to put him closer to his heart specialist, the judge replied that appellant would be tried in Pecos because the judge had heard all the evidence in the Musgrave case, the Pecos jury had convicted Musgrave and Bryant, and the court was convinced appellant was guilty and would be so found by a Pecos jury. The judge said further that appellant could expect favorable treatment at his hands only if appellant saved the Government money in the trial of the cause. The motion for change of venue for convenience was denied.

Appellant's affidavits of disqualification setting forth these remarks of the trial judge were in proper form, timely, and legally sufficient. The judge erred in not withdrawing from the case.

(b) Petitioners in Eaton v. United States, 458 F.2d 704 (7th Cir. 1972), alleged that the sentencing judge had not been impartial, contending that he had said before the change of plea that petitioners were "shooting craps with the government only to come out losers." The record shows that the remark actually made was addressed to counsel, after inquiring as to the theory of the defense.

The judge went on:

"I am curious as to what the theory of the defense is in the case. It doesn't mean you have to have one. You can stand trial without one. Just shoot craps with justice if you want to. That is part of your constitutional right, but I have always assumed counsel had a responsibility to advise clients that shooting craps with justice is not likely to be a profitable way to deal with a problem; that there was some theory, at least, on which the defense is predicated."

This colloquy occurred at the motion to suppress, a considerable time before the change of plea. In our opinion neither the remark quoted nor anything else in the record shows bias; certainly it does not show such probability of bias that the judge was obligated to disqualify himself from decision thereof.

2. An excellent discussion of the subject of judicial disqualification appears in Laird v. Tatum, 409 U.S. 824, 93 S.Ct. 7 (1972). (Memorandum of Mr. Justice Rehnquist).

3. When a judge sets bond, he may often be required to make findings about the character of the accused. Setting high bonds or adjudging that an accused is a threat to the community do not require disqualification.

United States v. Roca-Alvarez, 451 F.2d 843 (5th Cir. 1972). Nor do adverse rulings and improper judicial demeanor, even though they may suffice for reversal of a conviction. See United States v. Anderson, 433 F.2d 856 (8th Cir. 1970).

4. The subject of judicial bias is dealt with in two comprehensive articles: Frank, "Disqualification of Judges: In Support of the Bayh Bill" 35 Law and Contemp.Prob. 43 (1970), and Frank, "Disqualification of Judges" 56 Yale L.J. 605 (1947). Excerpts from the latter article follow:

> Each state has some statutory or constitutional law on the subject, but all shadings of view on particular grounds for disqualification are discovered. The traditional grounds of disqualification for interest, for relationship, or for bias, set a general framework for most states; but within that framework there is room for wide variety.
>
> The divergencies stem from two fundamentally different policies which govern the field. All courts want justice done, but the conflict of values comes over method: if disqualification of judges is too easy, both the cost and the delay of justice go out of bounds. If disqualification is too hard, cases may be decided quickly, but unfairly.
>
> * * *
>
> The polar views are expressed thus:
>
> By New Mexico, an "easy" disqualification state:
>
> "Our Legislature in effect has said that a judge, even though blessed with all of the virtues any judge ever possessed, shall not be permitted to exercise judicial power to determine the fact of his own disqualifications, not because the judge in doing so would attempt to act otherwise than conscientiously, but because in their legislative judgment it is not fitting for him to make such an attempt, and it is better that the courts shall maintain the confidence of the people than that the rights of judge and litigant in a particular case be served."
>
> By Pennsylvania, a "hard" disqualification state:
>
> "Due consideration should be given by him [the judge] to the fact that the administration of justice should be beyond the appearance of unfairness. But while the mediation of courts is based upon the principal of judicial impartiality, disinterestedness, and fairness pervading the whole system of judicature, so that courts may as near as possible be above suspicion, there is, on the other side, an important issue at stake; that is, that causes may not be unfairly prejudiced, unduly delayed, or discontent created through unfounded charges of prejudice or unfairness made against the judge in the trial of a cause."
>
> The cases and statutes reflect, as might be expected, a mixture of these two views. All jurisdictions have some disqualifications and all draw a line where they believe the privilege of disqualification may be abused.
>
> * * *
>
> Although in many states a party cannot charge "bias" and thereby have another judge assigned to hear a case, the develop-

ment is toward that end in the trial courts. This tendency is exemplified by the increasing popularity of two basic statutory devices. The first is an extension of the usual statutory grounds for disqualification to include additional situations where, in the opinion of the legislature, a likelihood of judicial partiality exists. The second is in the form of disqualification by affidavit, which amounts simply to mandatory change of venue at the request of either party. Affidavit statutes sometimes require the party requesting the change to establish grounds indicating bias, while in others a simple affidavit without supporting evidence is sufficient to effect a transfer of the case. Although some affidavit statutes have been held unconstitutional as encroachments upon judicial power, they are generally accepted without question.

The more significant situations involving possibility of judicial bias may, for convenience of analysis, be classified into those arising from the judge's "attorney contacts" his "party contacts" and his "government contacts."

* * *

A judge's former "government contacts" present a possibility of grounds for bias. The young lawyer with political ambitions follows a familiar path to fame: a prosecuting attorney to begin with, election to the legislature or Congress, perhaps a stopover in the executive branch of the state or federal government, and finally a judgeship.

* * *

A judge might disqualify himself for bias because of his government experience (1) if he participated personally as a government lawyer in the case under consideration; (2) if the case is presented by his former government associates; (3) if he participated in formulating the policy which the case involves; and (4) if he is a former legislator and the case involves construction of a statute he supported.

That the same man should not assume the roles of prosecutor and judge at different hearings of the same case needs hardly to be said. The impropriety is obvious, and prosecutors who become judges almost invariably disqualify themselves in these situations. The case of the Tennessee prosecutor who after his election as trial judge, sat on the retrial of an action originally instituted by him is exceptional, and reversal in that case was swift. But there is no impropriety where the judge's role as prosecutor has been largely formal, as in the case of Attorneys General, who have only theoretical responsibility for minor cases in their departments.

H. REQUEST FOR SUPPRESSION OF EVIDENCE

JACKSON v. DENNO

Supreme Court of the United States, 1964.
378 U.S. 368, 84 S.Ct. 1774.

MR. JUSTICE WHITE delivered the opinion of the Court.

* * *

I.

On June 14, 1960, at about 1 a. m., petitioner, Jackson, and Nora Elliott entered a Brooklyn hotel where Miss Elliott registered for both of them. After telling Miss Elliott to leave, which she did, Jackson drew a gun and took money from the room clerk. He ordered the clerk and several other people into an upstairs room and left the hotel, only to encounter Miss Elliott and later a policeman on the street. A struggle with the latter followed, in the course of which both men drew guns. The policeman was fatally wounded and petitioner was shot twice in the body. He managed to hail a cab, however, which took him to the hospital.

A detective questioned Jackson at about 2 a. m., soon after his arrival at the hospital. Jackson, when asked for his name, said, "Nathan Jackson, I shot the colored cop. I got the drop on him." He also admitted the robbery at the hotel. According to the detective, Jackson was in "strong" condition despite his wounds.

Jackson was given 50 milligrams of demerol and 1/50 of a grain of scopolamine at 3:55 a. m. Immediately thereafter an Assistant District Attorney, in the presence of police officers and hospital personnel, questioned Jackson, the interrogation being recorded by a stenographer. Jackson, who had been shot in the liver and lung, had by this time lost about 500 cc. of blood. Jackson again admitted the robbery in the hotel, and then said "Look, I can't go on." But in response to further questions he admitted shooting the policeman and having fired the first shot. The interview was completed at 4 a. m. An operation upon petitioner was begun at 5 a. m. and completed at 8 a. m.

Jackson and Miss Elliott were indicted for murder in the first degree and were tried together. The statements made by Jackson, both at 2 and 3:55 a. m., were introduced in evidence without objection by Jackson's counsel. Jackson took the stand in his own defense. His account of the robbery and of the shooting of the policeman differed in some important respects from his confession. According to Jackson's testimony, there was a substantial interval of time between his leaving the hotel and the shooting, and the policeman attempted to draw his gun first and fired the first shot. As to the questioning at the hospital, Jackson recalled that he was in pain and gasping for breath at the time and was refused water and told he would not be let alone until the police had the answers they wanted. He knew that he had been interrogated but could remember neither the questions nor the answers.

To counter Jackson's suggestion that he had been pressured into answering questions, the State offered the testimony of the attending physician and of several other persons. They agreed that Jackson was refused water, but because of the impending operation rather than his refusal to answer questions. On cross-examination of the doctor, Jackson's counsel, with the help of the hospital records, elicited the fact that demerol and scopolamine were administered to Jackson immediately before his interrogation. But any effect of these drugs on Jackson during the interrogation was denied.

Although Jackson's counsel did not specifically object to the admission of the confession initially, the trial court indicated its awareness that Jackson's counsel was questioning the circumstances under which Jackson was interrogated.

In his closing argument, Jackson's counsel did not ask for an acquittal but for a verdict of second-degree murder or manslaughter. Counsel's main effort was to negative the premeditation and intent necessary to first-degree murder and to separate the robbery felony from the killing. He made much of the testimony tending to show a substantial interval between leaving the hotel and the beginning of the struggle with the policeman. The details of that struggle and the testimony indicating the policeman fired the first shot were also stressed.

Consistent with the New York practice where a question has been raised about the voluntariness of a confession, the trial court submitted that issue to the jury along with the other issues in the case. The jury was told that if it found the confession involuntary, it was to disregard it entirely, and determine guilt or innocence solely from the other evidence in the case; alternatively, if it found the confession voluntary, it was to determine its truth or reliability and afford it weight accordingly.

The jury found Jackson guilty of murder in the first degree, Miss Elliott of manslaughter in the first degree.

II.

In our view, the New York procedure employed in this case did not afford a reliable determination of the voluntariness of the confession offered in evidence at the trial, did not adequately protect Jackson's right to be free of a conviction based upon a coerced confession and therefore cannot withstand constitutional attack under the Due Process Clause of the Fourteenth Amendment. We therefore reverse the judgment below denying the writ of habeas corpus.

III.

Under the New York rule, the trial judge must make a preliminary determination regarding a confession offered by the prosecution and exclude it if in no circumstances could the confession be deemed voluntary. But if the evidence presents a fair question as to its voluntariness, as where certain facts bearing on the issue are in dispute or where reasonable men could differ over the inferences to be drawn from undisputed facts, the judge "must receive the confession and leave to the jury, under proper instructions, the ultimate determination of its voluntary character and also its truthfulness." Stein v. New York, 346 U.S. 156, 172, 73 S.Ct. 1077, 1086. If an issue of coercion is presented, the judge may not resolve conflicting evidence or arrive at his independent appraisal of the voluntariness of the confession, one way or the other. These matters he must leave to the jury.

This procedure has a significant impact upon the defendant's Fourteenth Amendment rights. In jurisdictions following the orthodox rule, under which the judge himself solely and finally determines the voluntariness of the confession, or those following the Massachusetts procedure,[1] under which the jury passes on voluntariness only after the judge has fully and independently resolved the issue against the accused, the judge's conclusions are clearly evident from the record since he either admits the confession into evidence if it is voluntary or rejects it if involuntary. Moreover, his findings upon disputed issues of fact are expressly stated or may be ascertainable from the record. In contrast, the New York jury returns only a general verdict upon the ultimate question of guilt or innocence. It is impossible to discover whether the jury found the confession voluntary and relied upon it, or involuntary and supposedly ignored it. Nor is there any indication of how the jury resolved disputes in the evidence concerning the critical facts underlying the coercion issue. Indeed, there is nothing to show that these matters were resolved at all, one way or the other. . . .

A defendant objecting to the admission of a confession is entitled to a fair hearing in which both the underlying factual issues and the voluntariness of his confession are actually and reliably determined.

---

1. We raise no question here concerning the Massachusetts procedure. In jurisdictions following this rule, the judge hears the confession evidence, himself resolves evidentiary conflicts and gives his own answer to the coercion issue, rejecting confessions he deems involuntary and admitting only those he believes voluntary. It is only the latter confessions that are heard by the jury, which may then, under this procedure, disagree with the judge, find the confession involuntary and ignore it. Given the intergrity of the preliminary proceedings before the judge, the Massachusetts procedure does not, in our opinion, pose hazards to the rights of a defendant. While no more will be known about the views of the jury than under the New York rule, the jury does not hear all confessions where there is a fair question of voluntariness, but only those which a judge actually and independently determines to be voluntary, based upon all of the evidence. The judge's consideration of voluntariness is carried out separate and aside from issues of the reliability of the confession and the guilt or innocence of the accused and without regard to the fact the issue may again be raised before the jury if decided against the defendant. The record will show the judge's conclusions in this regard and his findings upon the underlying facts may be express or ascertainable from the record.

Once the confession is properly found to be voluntary by the judge, reconsideration of this issue by the jury does not, of course, improperly affect the jury's determination of the credibility or probativeness of the confession or its ultimate determination of guilt or innocence.

But did the jury in Jackson's case make these critical determinations, and if it did, what were these determinations?

Notwithstanding these acknowledged difficulties inherent in the New York procedure, the Court in Stein v. New York, found no constitutional deprivation to the defendant. The Court proceeded to this conclusion on the basis of alternative assumptions regarding the manner in which the jury might have resolved the coercion issue. Either the jury determined the disputed issues of fact against the accused, found the confession voluntary and therefore properly relied upon it; or it found the contested facts in favor of the accused and deemed the confession involuntary, in which event it disregarded the confession in accordance with its instructions and adjudicated guilt based solely on the other evidence. On either assumption the Court found no error in the judgment of the state court.

We disagree with the Court in Stein; for in addition to sweeping aside its own express doubts that the jury acted at all in the confession matter the Court, we think, failed to take proper account of the dangers to an accused's rights under either of the alternative assumptions.

On the assumption that the jury found the confession voluntary, the Court concluded that it could properly do so. But this judgment was arrived at only on the further assumptions that the jury had actually found the disputed issues of fact against the accused and that these findings were reliably arrived at in accordance with considerations that are permissible and proper under federal law. These additional assumptions, in our view, were unsound.

The New York jury is at once given both the evidence going to voluntariness and all of the corroborating evidence showing that the confession is true and that the defendant committed the crime. The jury may therefore believe the confession and believe that the defendant has committed the very act with which he is charged, a circumstance which may seriously distort judgment of the credibility of the accused and assessment of the testimony concerning the critical facts surrounding his confession.

In those cases where without the confession the evidence is insufficient, the defendant should not be convicted if the jury believes the confession but finds it to be involuntary. The jury, however, may find it difficult to understand the policy forbidding reliance upon a coerced, but true, confession, a policy which has divided this Court in the past, see Stein v. New York, supra, and an issue which may be reargued in the jury room. That a trustworthy confession must also be voluntary if it is to be used at all, generates natural and potent pressure to find it voluntary. Otherwise the guilty defendant goes free. Objective consideration of the conflicting evidence concerning the circumstances of the confession becomes difficult and the implicit findings become suspect.

The danger that matters pertaining to the defendant's guilt will infect the jury's findings of fact bearing upon voluntariness, as well as its conclusion upon that issue itself, is sufficiently serious to preclude their unqualified acceptance upon review in this Court, regardless of whether there is or is not sufficient other evidence to sustain a finding of guilt.   In Jackson's case, he confessed to having fired the first shot, a matter very relevant to the charge of first degree murder.   The jury also heard the evidence of eyewitnesses to the shooting.   Jackson's testimony going to his physical and mental condition when he confessed and to the events which took place at that time, bearing upon the issue of voluntariness, was disputed by the prosecution.   The obvious and serious danger is that the jury disregarded or disbelieved Jackson's testimony pertaining to the confession because it believed he had done precisely what he was charged with doing.

The failure to inquire into the reliability of the jury's resolution of disputed factual considerations underlying its conclusion as to voluntariness—findings which were afforded decisive weight by the Court in Stein—was not a mere oversight but stemmed from the premise underlying the Stein opinion that the exclusion of involuntary confessions is constitutionally required solely because of the inherent untrustworthiness of a coerced confession.   It followed from this premise that a reliable or true confession need not be rejected as involuntary and that evidence corroborating the truth or falsity of the confession and the guilt or innocence of the accused is indeed pertinent to the determination of the coercion issue.

*   *   *

It is now inescapably clear that the Fourteenth Amendment forbids the use of involuntary confessions not only because of the probable unreliability of confessions that are obtained in a manner deemed coercive, but also because of the "strongly felt attitude of our society that important human values are sacrificed where an agency of the government, in the course of securing a conviction, wrings a confession out of an accused against his will," and because of "the deep-rooted feeling that the police must obey the law while enforcing the law; that in the end life and liberty can be as much endangered from illegal methods used to convict those thought to be criminals as from the actual criminals themselves."   Because it did not recognize this "complex of values" underlying the exclusion of involuntary confessions, Stein also ignored the pitfalls in giving decisive weight to the jury's assumed determination of the facts surrounding the disputed confession.

Under the New York procedure, the evidence given the jury inevitably injects irrelevant and impermissible considerations of truthfulness of the confession into the assessment of voluntariness.   Indeed the jury is told to determine the truthfulness of the confession in assessing its probative value.   As a consequence, it cannot be assumed, as the Stein Court assumed, that the jury reliably found the facts against the accused.   This unsound assumption undermines Stein's authority as a precedent and its view on the constitutionality of the New York procedure.   The admixture of reliability and voluntariness in the considerations of the jury would itself entitle a defendant to further proceedings in any case in which the essential **facts are disputed,** for we cannot determine how the jury resolved these issues and will not assume that they were reliably and properly resolved against the accused. And it is only a reliable determination on the voluntariness issue which satisfies the constitutional rights of the defendant and which would permit the jury to consider the confession in adjudicating guilt or innocence.

But we do not rest on this ground alone, for the other alternative hypothesized in Stein—that the jury found the confession involuntary and disregarded it—is equally unacceptable. Under the New York procedure, the fact of a defendant's confession is solidly implanted in the jury's mind, for it has not only heard the confession, but it has been instructed to consider and judge its voluntariness and is in position to assess whether it is true or false. If it finds the confession involuntary, does the jury—indeed, can it—then disregard the confession in accordance with its instructions? If there are lingering doubts about the sufficiency of the other evidence, does the jury unconsciously lay them to rest by resort to the confession? Will uncertainty about the sufficiency of the other evidence to prove guilt beyond a reasonable doubt actually result in acquittal when the jury knows the defendant has given a truthful confession?

It is difficult, if not impossible, to prove that a confession which a jury has found to be involuntary has nevertheless influenced the verdict or that its finding of voluntariness, if this is the course it took, was affected by the other evidence showing the confession was true. But the New York procedure poses substantial threats to a defendant's constitutional rights to have an involuntary confession entirely disregarded and to have the coercion issue fairly and reliably determined. These hazards we cannot ignore.[2]

* * *

Expanded concepts of fairness in obtaining confessions have been accompanied by a correspondingly greater complexity in determining whether an accused's will has been overborne—facts are frequently disputed, questions of credibility are often crucial, and inferences to be drawn from established facts are often determinative. The overall determination of the voluntariness of a confession has thus become an exceedingly sensitive task, one that requires facing the issue squarely, in illuminating isolation and unbeclouded by other issues and the effect of extraneous but prejudicial evidence. Where pure factual considerations are an important ingredient, which is true in the usual case, appellate review in this Court is, as a practical matter,

---

2. Further obstacles to a reliable and fair determination of voluntariness under the New York procedure result from the ordinary rules relating to cross-examination, both of whose Although not the case here, an accused may well be deterred from testifying on the voluntariness issue when the jury is present because of his vulnerability to impeachment by proof of prior convictions and broad **cross-examination and impeachment.** prejudicial effects are familiar. The fear of such impeachment and extensive cross-examination in the presence of the jury that is to pass on guilt or innocence as well as voluntariness may induce a defendant to remain silent, although he is perhaps the only source of testimony on the facts underlying the claim of coercion. Where this occurs the determination of voluntariness is made upon less than all of the relevant evidence.

an inadequate substitute for a full and reliable determination of the voluntariness issue in the trial court and the trial court's determination, *pro tanto*, takes on an increasing finality. The procedures used in the trial court to arrive at its conclusions on the coercion issue progressively take on added significance as the actual measure of the protection afforded a defendant under the Due Process Clause of the Fourteenth Amendment against the use of involuntary confessions. These procedures must, therefore, be fully adequate to insure a reliable and clear-cut determination of the voluntariness of the confession, including the resolution of disputed facts upon which the voluntariness issue may depend. In our view, the New York procedure falls short of satisfying these constitutional requirements. Stein v. New York is overruled.

IV.

We turn to consideration of the disposition of this case. Since Jackson has not been given an adequate hearing upon the voluntariness of his confession he must be given one, the remaining inquiry being the scope of that hearing and the court which should provide it.

This is not a case where the facts concerning the circumstances surrounding the confession are undisputed and the task is only to judge the voluntariness of the confession based upon the clearly established facts and in accordance with proper consitutional standards. Here there are substantial facts in dispute: . . . Whether Jackson is entitled to relief depends upon how these facts are resolved, for if the State is to be believed we cannot say that Jackson's confession was involuntary, whereas if Jackson's version of the facts is accepted the confession was involuntary and inadmissible.

As we have already said, Jackson is entitled to a reliable resolution of these evidentiary conflicts. If this case were here upon direct review of Jackson's conviction, we could not proceed with review on the assumption that these disputes had been resolved in favor of the State for as we have held we are not only unable to tell how the jury resolved these matters but, even if the jury did resolve them against Jackson, its findings were infected with impermissible considerations and accordingly cannot be controlling here. Likewise, a federal habeas corpus court, in the face of the unreliable state court procedure, would not be justified in disposing of the petition solely upon the basis of the undisputed portions of the record. At the very least, Townsend v. Sain, 372 U.S. 293, 83 S.Ct. 745, would require a full evidentiary hearing to determine the factual context in which Jackson's confession was given.

However, we think that the further proceedings to which Jackson is entitled should occur initially in the state courts rather than in the federal habeas corpus court. Jackson's trial did not comport with constitutional standards and he is entitled to a determination of the voluntariness of his confession in the state courts in accordance with valid state procedures; the State is also entitled to make this determination before this Court considers the case on direct review or a

petition for habeas corpus is filed in a Federal District Court.
. . . .

It is New York therefore, not the federal habeas corpus court,
which should first provide Jackson with that which he has not yet
had and to which he is constitutionally entitled—an adequate evidentiary hearing productive of reliable results concerning the voluntariness of his confession. It does not follow, however, that Jackson is
automatically entitled to a complete new trial including a retrial of
the issue of guilt or innocence. . . . If at the conclusion of such
an evidentiary hearing in the state court on the coercion issue, it is
determined that Jackson's confession was voluntarily given, admissible in evidence, and properly to be considered by the jury, we see no
constitutional necessity at that point for proceeding with a new trial,
for Jackson has already been tried by a jury with the confession
placed before it and has been found guilty. True, the jury in the
first trial was permitted to deal with the issue of voluntariness and
we do not know whether the conviction rested upon the confession;
but if it did, there is no constitutional prejudice to Jackson from the
New York procedure if the confession is now properly found to be
voluntary and therefore admissible. If the jury relied upon it, it was
entitled to do so. Of course, if the state court, at an evidentiary
hearing, redetermines the facts and decides that Jackson's confession
was involuntary, there must be a new trial on guilt or innocence
without the confession's being admitted in evidence.

Obviously, the State is free to give Jackson a new trial if it so
chooses, but for us to impose this requirement before the outcome of
the new hearing on voluntariness is known would not comport with
the interests of sound judicial administration and the proper relationship between federal and state courts. . . . Accordingly, the
judgment denying petitioner's writ of habeas corpus is reversed and
the case is remanded to the District Court to allow the State a reasonable time to afford Jackson a hearing or a new trial, failing which
Jackson is entitled to his release.

Reversed and remanded.

MR. JUSTICE BLACK, with whom MR. JUSTICE CLARK joins as to
Part I of this opinion, dissenting in part and concurring in part.
[Opinion omitted.]

[MR. JUSTICE CLARK's dissenting opinion is omitted]

MR. JUSTICE HARLAN, whom MR. JUSTICE CLARK and MR. JUS-
TICE STEWART join, dissenting. [Opinion omitted.]

NOTES

1. Did Jackson v. Denno indicate that the independent determination
of the voluntariness had to be made upon a hearing conducted by the trial
judge *outside* the presence of the jury? That was the contention made in
Pinto v. Pierce, 389 U.S. 31, 88 S.Ct. 192 (1967), but it was rejected by the
Court in a per curiam opinion in which the Court said:

"The petition for certiorari is granted and the judgment is reversed. This Court has never ruled that all voluntariness hearings

must be held outside the presence of the jury, regardless of the circumstances. Jackson v. Denno held that a defendant's constitutional rights are violated when his challenged confession is introduced without a determination by the trial judge of its voluntariness after an adequate hearing. A confession by the defendant found to be involuntary by the trial judge is not to be heard by the jury which determines his guilt or innocence. Hence, because a disputed confession may be found involuntary and inadmissible by the judge, it would seem prudent to hold voluntariness hearings outside the presence of the jury. In this case, however, the confession was held voluntary and admitted as evidence suitable for consideration by the jury. In addition, there is no claim that because the hearing was held in the presence of the jury it was inadequate or had any other unfair consequences for the respondent."

2. The so-called "orthodox" rule under which the Court but not the jury considers the voluntariness of confessions is now the rule in federal trials. See 18 U.S.C. § 3501(a). A list of the states and the rules they follow is found in the appendices to the opinions in Jackson v. Denno. Since Jackson the majority of jurisdictions seem to favor the orthodox rule. See Anno. 1 A.L.R.3d 1251. Some courts adopt the Massachusetts procedure and permit the jury to reconsider voluntariness after the court finds the confession to be voluntary. See People v. Huntley, 15 N.Y.2d 72, 255 N.Y.S.2d 838, 204 N.E.2d 179 (1965). What of the other rules of suppression? Should a jury be allowed to consider Miranda compliance? The admissibility of eyewitness testimony? The legality of a search? The settled law is that search and seizure issues do not go to the jury. Can reassigned distinctions be drawn between the various types of suppressable evidence for purposes of submitting the issue to the jury? In jurisdictions where questions like these can be reargued before the jury, should the jury be told that the court has found the evidence admissible or that the lineup was not suggestive, etc.? Submission to the jury of suppression issues is not constitutionally mandated in any case. See United States v. Panepinto, 430 F.2d 613, 617–18 (3rd Cir. 1970).

3. The Court which hears motions to suppress must make findings. These need not be specific findings of fact. See Sims v. Georgia, 385 U.S. 538, 87 S.Ct. 639 (1967). Commonly the trial court will say "the motion to suppress is denied" or "I find the confession voluntary" or "the defendant waived his Miranda rights" or "the identification is legal". The Courts will sustain such rulings if there is evidence to support it. United States v. Montos, 421 F.2d 215 (5th Cir. 1970); La Vallee v. Delle Rose, 410 U.S. 690, 93 S.Ct. 1203 (1973); Dempsey v. Wainwright, 471 F.2d 604 (5th Cir. 1973). The general ruling on a motion to suppress usually presents no problem when the hearing involves contradictory testimony by witnesses. The general finding is sometimes less than helpful when there is agreement on the facts but not upon their interpretation. Compare Mora v. People, 481 P.2d 729 (Colo.1971), with State v. Thompson, 465 S.W.2d 590 (Mo. 1971). Formal and detailed findings of fact should be made in complex cases, but it is doubtful that the failure to do so is grounds for reversal on appeal. Recent cases have required specific findings on certain narrow issues. E. g., People v. Brake, —— Colo. ——, 553 P.2d 763 (1976) (whether accused requested counsel); United States v. Brown, 575 F.2d 746 (9th Cir. 1978) (whether accused was intoxicated).

4. The motion to suppress is ordinarily made in advance of trial. Fed.R.Crim.P.Rule 41; Ill.Rev.Stat., Ch. 38, Secs. 114–11 and 114–12. The

American Bar Association Standards Relating to Discovery and Procedure
Before Trial (1970) adopt a policy of encouraging pre-trial litigation of
suppression issues. See also State v. Maloney, 300 A.2d 259 (R.I.1973).
The pre-trial motion is usually required regardless of the kind of evidence
at issue. Some jurisdictions still do not provide for or require pre-trial
suppression motions. The cases on both sides are collected in Annot. 50 A.
L.R.2d 531. The policy arguments are difficult to resolve by logic alone.
The use of pre-trial motions will enable the trial of the case to proceed
smoothly without interruptions and delay when the jury leaves the courtroom so the judge may hear the evidence concerning admissibility. If evidence is suppressed prior to trial the prosecution may be spared the use of
scarce resources in preparing for trial and the court may not have to
waste time impaneling a jury, hearing opening statements and various witnesses before ending the case by suppressing evidence. On the other hand,
a pretrial motion to suppress takes as much time, i. e., delay, as a motion
to suppress at any other time. Further, counsel may cause more delay by
stringing out a series of suppression motions. The court will hear the evidence in the case in a piecemeal fashion. Witnesses may also be inconven-
ienced by having to come to court two or three times rather than once. It
should be observed that a trial judge may, and they often do, set motions to
suppress for a given day and then set the trial for the day following resolution of the motions. In many cases, motions may be heard in the morning
and trial may start in the afternoon. The prosecution will have a strong
interest to have suppression issues resolved before trial if it has the right
to appeal from adverse rulings.

Consider the comments in State v. Broxton, 49 N.J. 373, 230 A.2d 489
(1967):

> There are obvious advantages and disadvantages in a separate
> hearing either before or at trial. . . . It may be well for the
> State and defense to know before trial whether the confessions will
> come in, and in some cases it may be desirable to permit interlocu-
> tory review. But on the other hand, when the issue is tried out-
> side the presence of the jury, the issue must then be retried before
> the jury both under the orthodox and the Massachusetts rules. A
> replay is rarely as satisfactory, for there is absent the freshness of
> the first cross-examination. Moreover, the burden upon all con-
> cerned, principals and witnesses, is substantial, to say nothing of
> the burden on the judicial process which already moves at a snail's
> pace in criminal matters. In the case before us, the trial of the is-
> sue of voluntariness covers some 650 pages of transcript. Realisti-
> cally, most confessions are admissible, and to encumber all cases
> with two trials of the same issue because of the danger of a mis-
> trial in a few may be too heavy a price to exact from all concerned.
> Moreover, several trials of the same issue may present difficult
> questions. If in testifying in the absence of the jury, the defend-
> ant makes damaging admissions with respect to voluntariness, may
> the State prove them on the re-run before the jury? If not, the
> jury will be using a record different from the one the trial judge
> used. And what should be done if a defendant who does not testi-
> fy on the preliminary hearing decides to testify before the jury, or
> if he offers before the jury other evidence not submitted to the
> trial judge alone?

Where a pre-trial suppression motion is allowed, it is often required as
well. That is, failure to file a pre-trial motion operates as a waiver of the

claim. Commonwealth v. Underwood, 265 N.E.2d 577 (Mass.1970); State v. Levesque, 281 A.2d 570 (Me.1971). The validity of this waiver rule has been the subject of much debate. Compare Empire State v. Macon, 57 N.J. 325, 273 A.2d 1 (1971), with State v. Lemme, 244 A.2d 585, 104 R.I. 416 (1968). The constitutional validity of waiver rules generally is subject to debate. Compare Henry v. Mississippi, 379 U.S. 443, 85 S.Ct. 564 (1965) with Davis v. United States, 411 U.S. 233, 93 S.Ct. 1577 (1973); Tollett v. Henderson, 411 U.S. 258, 93 S.Ct. 1602 (1973). Regardless of the debate over the abstract question of waiver, the waiver rule is applied in the overwhelming number of cases, state and federal. The corollaries to the rule requiring pre-trial suppression motions are two: (a) the ruling at the pre-trial motion is final in the absence of newly discovered evidence and the issue cannot be relitigated at trial, (b) the filing of a pre-trial motion to suppress and the ruling thereon preserve the question for review and the defense need not object at trial. Some jurisdictions of course accept only one one of these rules and others accept neither.

5. Apart from suppression of constitutionally inadmissible evidence, may a party seek pre-trial suppression of damaging evidence rendered inadmissible by ordinary rules of evidence? The right to do this may be crucial, more crucial than suppression of illegally seized evidence. Assume (and it is a fair assumption) that neither reversals on appeal nor mistrials are easy to procure even when one side acting in either good or bad faith gets inadmissible evidence before the jury. The only relief is to seek some advance ruling on the issue of admissibility at least prior to opposing counsel's opening statement. Probably every jurisdiction would permit the court discretion to entertain such a pre-trial motion (variously called motion to exclude, motion to limit proof, motion in limine, etc.). Are such motions common? Should they be and should the courts entertain them? What are the arguments for and against pre-trial motions on ordinary (as opposed to constitutional) objections to evidence and argument?

6. Consider the relevant provisions of Rule 104, Fed.R.Evid.:

Preliminary Questions

(a) **Questions of Admissibility Generally.** Preliminary questions concerning the qualification of a person to be a witness, the existence of a privilege, or the admissibility of evidence shall be determined by the judge, subject to the provisions of subdivision (b). In making his determination he is not bound by the rules of evidence except those with respect to privileges.

(b) **Relevancy Conditioned on Fact.** When the relevancy of evidence depends upon the fulfillment of a condition of fact, the judge shall admit it upon, or subject to, the introduction of evidence sufficient to support a finding of the fulfillment of the condition.

(c) **Hearing of Jury.** Hearings on the admissibility of confessions shall in all cases be conducted out of the hearing of the jury. Hearings on other preliminary matters shall be so conducted when the interests of justice require or, when an accused is a witness, if he so requests.

* * *

(e) **Weight and credibility.** This rule does not limit the right of a party to introduce before the jury evidence relevant to weight or credibility.

7. An increasing number of states allow the prosecution to appeal orders suppressing evidence. The new federal rule has been construed to allow prosecution appeal from any order suppressing evidence except those entered during trial. See United States v. Calandra, 455 F.2d 770 (6th Cir. 1972). Could a statute provide for state appeal of an order entered during trial? See People v. Shipp, 96 Ill.App.2d 364, 239 N.E.2d 296 (1968) (allowing appeal from order entered in the course of a bench trial and effectively blocking entire prosecution—trial court had suspended trial). Would it be theoretically possible, practically feasible or desirable to allow suspension of jury trials for state appeals? See Ill.Rev.Stat., 1971, Ch. 38, Secs. 114–11, 114–12 (providing for termination of trial when suppression occurs during trial and the state elects to appeal). See Casebook, Ch. 13, § A–3, note 8, concerning double jeopardy problems when a trial is terminated in order to permit the prosecution to appeal a suppression ruling.

The President's Crime Commission advocated the prosecution's right to appeal suppression orders. The Commission asserted the injustice to the state caused by an improper exclusion of evidence and said, "But the importance of allowing the government to appeal goes beyond the significance of any particular prosecution. The rules on search and seizure and confessions are today characterized by a high degree of uncertainty. If lower court rulings restricting police conduct cannot be appealed and if inconsistent lower court decisions can be resolved only on an appeal by a defendant, it is most difficult to formulate law enforcement policies. When the prosecution is not permitted to appeal, . . . officials faced with a restrictive ruling which they feel is erroneous have two choices: they may follow the lower court decision and abandon the practice, in which case an authoritative decision by an appellate court may never be obtained, or they may continue the practice, hoping that in a future case a trial court will sustain it and that the defendant will appeal. The first course results in the abandonment of what may be a legitimate police practice solely because of the lack of any vehicle for testing it in the appellate courts. The second course puts the police in the undesirable position of deciding which lower court decisions they will accept and which they will not." Task Force Report: *The Courts* 47 (1967).

Considering the rationale offered by the Commission, would it be proper for a court to hear appeals when the order does not arise from the illegal acquisition of evidence, e. g., an order excluding evidence for failure to comply with discovery rules, or an order excluding allegedly inflammatory evidence pursuant to a motion *in limine*? See People v. Schmidt, 8 Ill.App.3d 1024, 291 N.E.2d 225 (1972) (allowing appeal from exclusion of evidence for failure to comply with discovery orders).

When the state appeals, should the defendant be entitled to bail without security? Should the defendant even be required to post a recognizance bond?

The suppression appeal is the newest of the state appeals. See, generally, Casebook, ch. 23, § A–3. Several jurisdictions have allowed the state to appeal from orders dismissing indictments or granting new trials. See generally, Kronenberg, Right of a State to Appeal in Criminal Cases, 49 J.Crim.L.C. & P.S. 473 (1959). The government appeal is purely statutory, it does not exist at common law. Some states, i. e., California, allow the use of petitions for the extraordinary writs of mandamus (by the prosecution to compel admission of evidence) and prohibition (by defense to forbid its admission) to provide for appellate review of suppression orders. Most jurisdictions do not follow this practice. The Supreme Court of

Hawaii has held that the absence of another remedy does not, by itself, justify the use of the extraordinary writ:

> "The Legislature is vested with power to determine whether a ruling of an inferior court shall be reviewed. If it fails to provide for such review and this court, in its discretion, refuses, as we have in this case, to assume jurisdiction by granting extraordinary relief in the form of a writ of prohibition, the rights of the parties involved are finally settled by the ruling of the inferior court. The result may appear harsh, particularly in a criminal case where the prosecution seeks relief from a pretrial order. But this does not present an unusual situation in criminal jurisprudence. .   .   .   The prosecution is certainly no more disadvantaged by an erroneous ruling before trial than during trial when such ruling leads to acquittal."

See Chung v. Ogata, 54 Haw. 146, 504 P.2d 868 (1972).

LEGO v. TWOMEY

Supreme Court of the United States, 1972.
404 U.S. 477, 92 S.Ct. 619.

MR. JUSTICE WHITE delivered the opinion of the Court.

Lego was convicted of armed robbery in 1961 after a jury trial. The court sentenced him to prison for 25 to 50 years. The evidence introduced against Lego at trial included a confession he had made to police after arrest and while in custody at the station house. Prior to trial Lego sought to have the confession suppressed. He did not deny making it but did challenge that he had done so voluntarily. The trial judge conducted a hearing, out of the presence of the jury, at which Lego testified that police had beaten him about the head and neck with a gun butt. His explanation of this treatment was that the local police chief, a neighbor and former classmate of the robbery victim, had sought revenge upon him. Lego introduced into evidence a photograph which had been taken of him at the county jail on the day after his arrest. The photograph showed that petitioner's face had been swollen and had traces of blood on it. Lego admitted that his face had been scratched in a scuffle with the robbery victim but maintained that the encounter did not explain the condition shown in the photograph. The police chief and four officers also testified. They denied either beating or threatening petitioner and disclaimed knowledge that any other officer had done so. The trial judge resolved this credibility problem in favor of the police and ruled the confession admissible. At trial, Lego testified in his own behalf. Although he did not dispute the truth of the confession directly, he did tell his version of the events which had transpired at the police station. The trial judge instructed the jury as to the prosecution's burden of proving guilt. He did not instruct that the jury was required to find the confession voluntary before it could be used in judging guilt or innocence. On direct appeal the Illinois Supreme Court affirmed the conviction. .   .   .

Four years later petitioner challenged his conviction by seeking a writ of habeas corpus in the United States District Court. He maintained that the trial judge should have found the confession voluntary beyond a reasonable doubt before admitting it into evidence. Although the judge had made no mention of the standard he used, Illinois law provided that a confession challenged as involuntary could be admitted into evidence if, at a hearing outside the presence of the jury, the judge found it voluntary by a preponderance of the evidence. In the alternative petitioner argued that the voluntariness question should also have been submitted to the jury for its separate consideration. [T]he District Court denied relief on the merits. The Court of Appeals affirmed.

I.

Petitioner challenges the judgment of the Court of Appeals on three grounds. The first is that he was not proved guilty beyond a reasonable doubt as required by In re Winship, 397 U.S. 358, 90 S.Ct. 1068 (1970), because the confession used against him at his trial had been proved voluntary only by preponderance of the evidence. Implicit in the claim is an assumption that a voluntariness hearing is designed to enhance the reliability of jury verdicts. To judge whether that is so we must return to Jackson v. Denno, 378 U.S. 368, 84 S. Ct. 1774 (1964).

* * *

We did not think it necessary, or even appropriate, in *Jackson* to announce that prosecutors would be required to meet a particular burden of proof in a *Jackson* hearing held before the trial judge. Indeed, the then-established duty to determine voluntariness had not been framed in terms of a burden of proof, nor has it been since *Jackson* was decided. We could fairly assume then, as we can now, that a judge would admit into evidence only those confessions which he reliably found, at least by a preponderance of the evidence, had been made voluntarily.

We noted in *Jackson* that there may be a relationship between the involuntariness of a confession and its unreliability. But our decision was not based in the slightest on the fear that juries might misjudge the accuracy of confessions and arrive at erroneous determinations of guilt or innocence. That case was not aimed at reducing the possibility of convicting innocent men.

Quite the contrary, we feared that the reliability and truthfulness of even coerced confessions could impermissibly influence a jury's judgment as to voluntariness. The use of coerced confessions, whether true or false, is forbidden because the method used to extract them offends constitutional principles. The procedure we established in *Jackson* was designed to safeguard the right of an individual, entirely apart from his guilt or innocence, not to be compelled to condemn himself by his own utterances. Nothing in *Jackson* questioned the province or capacity of juries to assess the truthfulness of confessions. Nothing in that opinion took from the jury any evidence relating to the accuracy or weight of confessions admitted into evidence.

A defendant has been as free since *Jackson* as he was before to familiarize a jury with circumstances which attend the taking of his confession, including facts bearing upon its weight and voluntariness. In like measure, of course, juries have been at liberty to disregard confessions which are insufficiently corroborated or otherwise deemed unworthy of belief.

Since the purpose that a voluntariness hearing is designed to serve has nothing whatever to do with improving the reliability of jury verdicts, we cannot accept the charge that judging the admissibility of a confession by a preponderance of the evidence undermines the mandate of In re Winship, 397 U.S. 358, 90 S.Ct. 1068 (1970). Our decision in *Winship* was not concerned with standards for determining the admissibility of evidence or with the prosecution's burden of proof at a suppression hearing when evidence is challenged on constitutional grounds. *Winship* went no further than to confirm the fundamental right that protects "the accused against conviction except upon proof beyond a reasonable doubt of every fact necessary to constitute the crime with which he is charged." A high standard of proof is necessary, we said, to ensure against unjust convictions by giving substance to the presumption of innocence. A guilty verdict is not rendered less reliable or less consonant with *Winship* simply because the admissibility of a confession is determined by a less stringent standard. Petitioner does not maintain that either his confession or its voluntariness is an element of the crime with which he was charged. He does not challenge the constitutionality of the standard by which the jury was instructed to decide his guilt or innocence; nor does he question the sufficiency of the evidence which reached the jury to satisfy the proper standard of proof. Petitioner's rights under *Winship* have not been violated.[1]

II.

Even conceding that *Winship* is inapplicable because the purpose of a voluntariness hearing is not to implement the presumption of innocence, petitioner presses for reversal on the alternative ground that evidence offered against a defendant at a criminal trial and challenged on constitutional grounds must be determined admissible beyond a reasonable doubt in order to give adequate protection to those values which exclusionary rules are designed to serve. Jackson v. Denno requires judicial rulings on voluntariness prior to admitting confessions. Miranda v. Arizona, excludes confessions flowing from custodial interrogations unless adequate warnings were administered and a waiver was obtained. Weeks v. United States and Mapp v.

---

1. Nothing is to be gained from restating the constitutional rule as requiring proof of guilt beyond a reasonable doubt on the basis of constitutionally obtained evidence and then arguing that rights under *Winship* are diluted unless admissibility is governed by a high standard. Transparently, this assumes the question at issue, which is whether a confession is admissible if found voluntary by a preponderance of the evidence. United States v. Schipani, 289 F.Supp. 43 (E.D.N.Y.1968), aff'd 414 F.2d 1262 (C.A.2 1969), followed this unsatisfactory course in a Fourth Amendment case but stopped short of basing the decision on the Constitution.

Ohio make impermissible the introduction of evidence obtained in violation of a defendant's Fourth Amendment rights.   In each instance, and without regard to its probative value, evidence is kept from the trier of guilt or innocence for reasons wholly apart from enhancing the reliability of verdicts.   These independent values, it is urged, themselves require a stricter standard of proof in judging admissibility.

The argument is straightforward and has appeal.   But we are unconvinced that merely emphasizing the importance of the values served by exclusionary rules is itself sufficient demonstration that the Constitution also requires admissibility to be proved beyond reasonable doubt.[2]   Evidence obtained in violation of the Fourth Amendment has been excluded from federal criminal trials for many years.   The same is true of coerced confessions offered in either federal or state trials.   But, from our experience over this period of time no substantial evidence has accumulated that federal rights have suffered from determining admissibility by a preponderance of the evidence.   Petitioner offers nothing to suggest that admissibility rulings have been unreliable or otherwise wanting in quality because not based on some higher standard.   Without good cause, we are unwilling to expand currently applicable exclusionary rules by erecting additional barriers to placing truthful and probative evidence before state juries and by revising the standards applicable in collateral proceedings.   Sound reason for moving further in this direction has not been offered here nor do we discern any at the present time.   This is particularly true since the exclusionary rules are very much aimed at deterring lawless conduct by police and prosecution and it is very doubtful that escalating the prosecution's burden of proof in Fourth and Fifth Amendment suppression hearings would be sufficiently productive in this respect to outweigh the public interest in placing probative evidence before juries for the purpose of arriving at truthful decisions about guilt or innocence.

To reiterate what we said in *Jackson*: when a confession challenged as involuntary is sought to be used against a criminal defendant at his trial, he is entitled to a reliable and clear-cut determination that the confession was in fact voluntarily rendered.   Thus, the prosecution must prove at least by a preponderance of the evidence that the confession was voluntary.   Of course, the States are free, pursuant to their own law, to adopt a higher standard.   They may indeed differ as to the appropriate resolution of the values they find at stake.

III.

We also reject petitioner's final contention that, even though the trial judge ruled on his coercion claim, he was entitled to have the

---

2. It is no more persuasive to impose the stricter standard of proof as an exercise of supervisory power rather than as a constitutional rule.   Cf. Ralph v. Warden, 438 F.2d 786, 793 (C.A.4 1970), clarifying United States v. Inman, 352 F.2d 954 (C.A.4 1965); Pea v. United States, 130 U.S.App.D. C. 66, 397 F.2d 627 (1968).

jury decide the claim anew.   To the extent this argument asserts that the judge's determination was insufficiently reliable, it is no more persuasive than petitioner's other contentions.   To the extent the position assumes that a jury is better suited than a judge to determine voluntariness, it questions the basic assumptions of Jackson v. Denno; it also ignores that *Jackson* neither raised any question about the constitutional validity of the so-called orthodox rule for judging the admissibility of confessions nor even suggested that the Constitution requires submission of voluntariness claims to a jury as well as a judge. Finally, Duncan v. Louisiana, 391 U.S. 145, 88 S.Ct. 1444 (1968), which made the Sixth Amendment right to trial by jury applicable to the States, did not purport to change the normal rule that the admissibility of evidence is a question for the court rather than the jury. Nor did that decision require that both judge and jury pass upon the admissibility of evidence when constitutional grounds are asserted for excluding it.   We are not disposed to impose as a constitutional requirement a procedure we have found wanting merely to afford petitioner a second forum for litigating his claim.

The decision of the Court of Appeals is affirmed.

Affirmed.

MR. JUSTICE POWELL and MR. JUSTICE REHNQUIST took no part in the consideration or decision of this case.

MR. JUSTICE BRENNAN, with whom MR. JUSTICE DOUGLAS and MR. JUSTICE MARSHALL join, dissenting.   [Opinion omitted.]

NOTES

1.   Prior to Lego v. Twomey, the bare majority of jurisdictions had adopted a less than reasonable doubt standard for admitting confessions. Many jurisdictions never specifically deal with burden of proof but it is clear that the standard is less than reasonable doubt.   A substantial minority had adopted a reasonable doubt standard.

After Lego v. Twomey, the federal courts will apply the preponderance standard.   So will some of the state courts which adopted the reasonable doubt standard because they believed the United States Supreme Court would eventually require it.   State v. Wajda, 296 Minn. 29, 206 N.W.2d 1 (1973).   But such state courts are free to retain the heavier burden of proof and one jurisdiction has done so.   See State v. Collins, 297 A.2d 620 (Me. 1972).

2.   Lego v. Twomey disapproved the rule stated in United States v. Schipani, 289 F.Supp. 43 (E.D.N.Y.1968) which promulgated a doctrine that the government must prove beyond a reasonable doubt the admissibility of all suppressable evidence.   Nevertheless, students may find interesting Judge Weinstein's mathematical approach in *Schipani*.

3.   The rules relating to burdens of proof in motions to suppress are fitted as parts in a patchwork quilt.   A summary follows:

Under Bumper v. North Carolina, 391 U.S. 543, 548, 88 S.Ct. 1788 (1968), the prosecution bears the burden of persuasion when it relies on consent to justify a search.   However, under federal rules, the defendant bears the burden of proving the illegality of a seizure of evidence pursuant to warrant and the prosecution bears the burden of proof only when the search is warrantless. See United States v. Thompson, 421 F.2d 373, 377 (5th Cir. 1970); United States v. Cleaver, 402 F.2d 148 (9th Cir. 1968); Irby v. United States, 314 F.2d 251, 253 (D.C.Cir. 1963).

There are several federal cases seemingly holding that the burden of proof is upon defendant to establish the illegality of any challenged seizure but these cases do not seem to represent the prevailing federal rule. See United States v. Morin, 378 F.2d 472, 475 (2nd Cir. 1967); Wilson v. United States, 218 F.2d 754, 757 (10th Cir. 1955); Jarabo v. United States, 158 F.2d 509, 513 n. 3 (1st Cir. 1946). Under federal rules the defendant must prove that he has standing to object to an illegal seizure. United States v. Sacco, 436 F.2d 780, 784 (2nd Cir. 1971); Fullbright v. United States, 392 F.2d 432, 435-36 (10th Cir. 1968), cert. denied 393 U.S. 830. A federal defendant must prove that wiretapping was unlawfully employed against him in order to secure suppression of wiretap evidence. Nardone v. United States, 308 U.S. 338, 341 (1939); Nolan v. United States, 423 F.2d 1031, 1041 (10th Cir. 1970). A defendant claiming abuse of civil summons must prove that no proper civil purpose underlay the summons. United States v. Ferrone, 438 F.2d 381, 387-88 (3rd Cir. 1971). Where the prosecution bears the burden on motions to suppress physical evidence, the burden is not that of reasonable doubt. Manuel v. United States, 355 F.2d 344, 346 (5th Cir. 1966).

Although the federal rule is widely followed, many states provide that on motions to suppress seized evidence the burden of proving illegal seizure is, in all cases, except consent search, borne by the defendant. See People v. Berrios, 28 N.Y.2d 361, 270 N.E. 2d 709, 712-14 (1971); People v. Wright, 42 Ill.2d 457, 248 N.E.2d 78 (1969); People v. Ferguson, 376 Mich. 90, 135 N.W.2d 537 (1965); State v. Holt, 415 S.W.2d 761, 764-65 (Mo.1967); State v. Freese, 166 N.W.2d 785, 787 (Iowa 1969); State v. Towles, 155 Conn. 516, 235 A.2d 639, 640 (1967); Moore v. State, 244 Ark. 1197, 429 S.W.2d 122, 125 (1968); State v. Merrill, 82 S.D. 609, 152 N.W.2d 349, 351 (1967); State v. Pokini, 45 Haw. 295, 367 P. 2d 499, 505 (1961); Booze v. State, 390 P.2d 261, 265-66 (Okla. 1964); State v. Hall, 1 Ohio App.2d 297, 204 N.E.2d 557, 559-60 (1964).

When the suppression of eyewitness identification is sought, the basic rule seems to place upon the defendant the burden of proving that his rights were violated. In other words, the defendant must prove the primary illegality, i. e., denial of counsel or unnecessarily suggestive confrontation. People v. Caruso, 68 Cal.2d 183, 184; 436 P.2d 336 (1968); People v. Rodriguez, 10 Cal.App. 3d 18, 88 Cal.Rptr. 789, 796 (1970); People v. Nelson, 40 Ill.2d 146, 238 N.E.2d 378 (1968); People v. Johnson, 45 Ill.2d 38, 257 N.E.2d 3 (1970). See also People v. Rahming, 26 N.Y.2d 411, 311 N.Y.S.2d 292, 259 N.E.2d 727 (1970); People v. Young, 21 Mich. App. 684, 176 N.W.2d 420 (1970). But see United States v. Gaines, 439 F.2d 525 (D.C.Cir. 1970). If the defendant carries his burden the prosecution, if it wishes to use in court identification evidence, bears the burden of establishing by "clear and convincing evidence that the in court identifications were based upon observations of the suspect other than the line-up identification". United States v. Wade, 388 U.S. 218, 240, 87 S.Ct. 1926 (1967).

Finally, Lego v. Twomey arose in a jurisdiction where the prosecution by state law bore the burden of proof in confession questions. This is the rule in nearly every jurisdiction. Would it be constitutional to place upon the accused the burden of proof in confession cases? See Sims v. Georgia, 389 U.S. 404, 88 S.Ct. 523 (1967).

Of what significance is the burden of proof in suppression motions? It has been suggested that there is a high risk of perjury by some police officers in certain suppression hearings (a risk which is often cited by prosecutors as a ground for believing the exclusionary rule is pointless). It is then argued that placing the burden of proof on the prosecution (or placing a higher burden if the burden is already on the prosecutor) will diminish the profit in such perjury. Will it? If a police officer and an accused give diametrically opposed testimony about the seizure of evidence, the trial court must ordinarily decide to believe one or the other. This judgment does not depend upon the burden of proof but upon the credibility of the witnesses. See generally People v. Benios, 28 N. Y.2d 361, 270 N.E.2d 709 (1971). When the trier of fact chooses between two different versions of events, does it matter which burden of proof theory is applied? Doesn't the court have to decide in favor of the witness he believes in direct credibility contest cases? If the police officer (or the accused) is a successful perjurer, will he not win regardless of the burden? If he is an unsuccessful perjurer, will he not lose? Can it be argued that burden of proof assumes practical significance only in circumstantial evidence cases?

FRANKS v. DELAWARE

Supreme Court of the United States, 1978.
438 U.S. 154, 98 S.Ct. 2674.

Mr. Justice Blackmun delivered the opinion of the Court.

This case presents an important and long-standing issue of Fourth Amendment law. Does a defendant in a criminal proceeding ever have the right, under the Fourth and Fourteen Amendments, subsequent to the *ex parte* issuance of a search warrant, to challenge the truthfulness of factual statements made in an affidavit supporting the warrant?

In the present case the Supreme Court of Delaware held, as a matter of first impression for it, that a defendant under *no* circumstances may so challenge the veracity of a sworn statement used by police to procure a search warrant. We reverse, and we hold that, where the defendant makes a substantial preliminary showing that a false statement knowingly and intentionally, or with reckless disregard for the truth, was included by the affiant in the warrant affidavit, and if the allegedly false statement is necessary to the finding of probable cause, the Fourth Amendment requires that a hearing be held at the defendant's request. In the event that at that hearing the allegation of perjury or reckless disregard is established by the defendant by a preponderance of the evidence, and, with the affidavit's false material set to one side, the affidavit's remaining content is insufficient to establish probable cause, the search warrant must be voided and the fruits of the search excluded to the same extent as if probable cause was lacking on the face of the affidavit.

The controversy over the veracity of the search warrant affidavit in this case arose in connection with petitioner Jerome Franks' state conviction for rape, kidnaping, and burglary. On Friday, March 5, 1976, Mrs. Cynthia Bailey told police in Dover, Delaware, that she had been confronted in her home earlier that morning by a man with a knife, and that he had sexually assaulted her. She described her assailant's age, race, height, build, and facial hair, and gave a detailed description of his clothing as consisting of a white thermal undershirt, black pants with a silver or gold buckle, a brown leather three-quarter length coat, and a dark knit cap that he wore pulled down around his eyes.

That same day, petitioner Franks coincidentally was taken into custody for an assault involving a 15-year-old girl, Brenda B. _____, six days earlier. After his formal arrest, and while awaiting a bail hearing in Family Court, petitioner allegedly stated to Robert Mc-Clements, the youth officer accompanying him, that he was surprised the bail hearing was "about Brenda B. _____. I know her. I thought you said Bailey. I don't know her." . . .

On the following Monday, March 8, officer McClements happened to mention the courthouse incident to a detective, Ronald R. Brooks, who was working on the *Bailey* case. On March 9, detective Brooks and detective Larry D. Gray submitted a sworn affidavit to a justice of the peace in Dover, in support of a warrant to search petitioner's apartment. In paragraph 8 of the affidavit's "probable cause page" mention was made of petitioner's statement to Mc-Clements. In paragraph 10, it was noted that the description of the assailant given to the police by Mrs. Bailey included the above-mentioned clothing. Finally, the affidavit also described the attempt made by police to confirm that petitioner's typical outfit matched that of the assailant. Paragraph 15 recited: "On Tuesday, 3/9/76, your affiant contacted Mr. James Williams and Mr. Wesley Lucas of the Delaware Youth Center where Jerome Franks is employed and did have personal conversation with both these people." Paragraphs 16 and 17 respectively stated: "Mr. James Williams revealed to your affiant that the normal dress of Jerome Franks does consist of a white knit thermal undershirt and a brown leather jacket," and "Mr. Wesley Lucas revealed to your affiant that in addition to the thermal undershirt and jacket, Jerome Franks often wears a large green knit hat."

The warrant was issued on the basis of this affidavit. Pursuant to the warrant, police searched petitioner's apartment and found a white thermal undershirt, a knit hat, dark pants, and a leather jacket, and, on petitioner's kitchen table, a single-blade knife. All these ultimately were introduced in evidence at trial.

Prior to the trial, however, petitioner's counsel filed a written motion to suppress the clothing and the knife found in the search; this motion alleged that the warrant on its face did not show probable cause and that the search and seizure were in violation of the Fourth and Fourteenth Amendments. At the hearing on the motion to suppress, defense counsel orally amended the challenge to include an attack on the veracity of the warrant affidavit; he also specifically requested the right to call as witnesses detective Brooks, Wesley Lucas of the Youth Center, and James D. Morrison, formerly of the Youth Center. Counsel asserted that Lucas and Morrison would testify that neither had been personally interviewed by the warrant affiants, and that, although they might have talked to another police officer, any information given by them to that officer was "somewhat different" from what was recited in the affidavit. Defense counsel charged that the misstatements were included in the affidavit not inadvertently, but in "bad faith." Counsel also sought permission to call officer McClements and petitioner as witnesses, to seek to establish that petitioner's courthouse statement to police had been obtained in violation of petitioner's *Miranda* rights, and that the search warrant was thereby tainted as the fruit of an illegally obtained confession.

In rebuttal, the State's attorney argued in detail, (a) that Del. Code Ann., Tit. 11, §§ 2306 and 2307 (1974), contemplated that any challenge to a search warrant was to be limited to questions of sufficiency based on the face of the affidavit; (b) that, purportedly, a majority of the States whose practice was not dictated by statute observed such a rule. . . . The State objected to petitioner's "going behind [the warrant affidavit] in any way," and argued that the court must decide petitioner's motion "on the four corners" of the affidavit.

The trial court sustained the State's objection to petitioner's proposed evidence. . . .

On appeal, the Supreme Court of Delaware affirmed. 373 A.2d 578 (1977). It agreed with what it deemed to be the "majority rule" that no attack upon the veracity of a warrant affidavit could be made:

> "We agree with the majority rule for two reasons. First, it is the function of the issuing magistrate to determine the reliability of information and credibility of affiants in deciding whether the requirement of probable cause has been met. There has been no need demonstrated for interfering with this function. Second, neither the probable cause nor suppression hearings are adjudications of guilt or innocence; the matters asserted by defendant are more properly considered in a trial on the merits."

* * *

Whether the Fourth and Fourteenth Amendments, and the derivative exclusionary rule made applicable to the States under Mapp v. Ohio, 367 U.S. 643, 81 S.Ct. 1684 (1961), ever mandate that a defendant be permitted to attack the veracity of a warrant affidavit after the warrant has been issued and executed, is a question that encounters conflicting values. The bulwark of Fourth Amendment protection, of course, is the Warrant Clause, requiring that, absent certain exceptions, police obtain a warrant from a neutral and disinterested magistrate before embarking upon a search. In deciding today that, in certain circumstances, a challenge to a warrant's veracity must be permitted, we derive our ground from language of the Warrant Clause itself, which surely takes the affiant's good faith as its premise: "[N]o warrants shall issue, but upon probable cause, supported by Oath or affirmation . . . ." Judge Frankel, in United States v. Halsey, 257 F.Supp. 1002, 1005 (S.D.N.Y.1966), put the matter simply: "[W]hen the Fourth Amendment demands a factual showing sufficient to comprise 'probable cause,' the obvious assumption is that there will be a *truthful* showing" (emphasis in original). This does not mean "truthful" in the sense that every fact recited in the warrant affidavit is necessarily correct, for probable cause may be founded upon hearsay and upon information received from informants, as well as upon information within the affiant's own knowledge that sometimes must be garnered hastily. But surely it is to be "truthful" in the sense that the information put forth is believed or appropriately accepted by the affiant as true. It is established law that a warrant affidavit must set forth particular facts and circumstances underlying the existence of probable cause, so as to allow the magistrate to make an independent evaluation of the matter. If an informant's tip is the source of information, the affidavit must recite "some of the underlying circumstances from which the informant concluded" that relevant evidence might be discovered, and "some of the underlying circumstances from which the officer concluded that the informant, whose identity need not be disclosed, . . . was 'credible' or his information 'reliable.' " Because it is the magistrate who must determine independently whether there is probable cause, it would be an unthinkable imposition upon his authority if a warrant affidavit, revealed after the fact to contain a deliberately or reckless false statement, were to stand beyond impeachment.

In saying this, however, one must give cognizance to competing values that lead us to impose limitations. They perhaps can best be addressed by noting the arguments of respondent and others against allowing veracity challenges. The arguments are several:

First, respondent argues that the exclusionary rule, created in Weeks v. United States, 232 U.S. 383, 34 S.Ct. 341 (1914), is not a personal constitutional right, but only a judicially created remedy extended where its benefit as a deterrent promises to outweigh the societal cost of its use; that the Court has declined to apply the exclusionary rule when illegally seized evidence is used to impeach the credibility of a defendant's testimony, Walder v. United States, 347 U.S. 62, 74 S.Ct. 354 (1954), is used in a grand jury proceeding, United States v. Calandra, 414 U.S. 338, 94 S.Ct. 613 (1974), or is used in a civil trial, United States v. Janis, 428 U.S. 433, 96 S.Ct.

3021 (1976); and that the Court similarly has restricted application of the Fourth Amendment exclusionary rule in federal habeas corpus review of a state conviction.   See Stone v. Powell, 428 U.S. 465, 96 S.Ct. 3037 (1976).   Respondent argues that applying the exclusionary rule to another situation—the deterrence of deliberate or reckless untruthfulness in a warrant affidavit—is not justified for many of the same reasons that led to the above restrictions; interfering with a criminal conviction in order to deter official misconduct is a burden too great to impose on society.

Second, respondent argues that a citizen's privacy interests are adequately protected by a requirement that applicants for a warrant submit a sworn affidavit and by the magistrate's independent determination of sufficiency based on the face of the affidavit.   Applying the exclusionary rule to attacks upon veracity would weed out a minimal number of perjurious government statements, says respondent, but would overlap unnecessarily with existing penalties against perjury, including criminal prosecutions, departmental discipline for misconduct, contempt of court, and civil actions.

Third, it is argued that the magistrate already is equipped to conduct a fairly vigorous inquiry into the accuracy of the factual affidavit supporting a warrant application.   He may question the affiant, or summon other persons to give testimony at the warrant proceeding.   The incremental gain from a post-search adversary proceeding, it is said, would not be great.

Fourth, it is argued that it would unwisely diminish the solemnity and moment of the magistrate's proceeding to make his inquiry into probable cause reviewable in regard to veracity.   The less final, and less deference paid to, the magistrate's determination of veracity, the less initiative will he use in that task.   Denigration of the magistrate's function would be imprudent insofar as his scrutiny is the last bulwark preventing any particular invasion of primacy before it happens.

Fifth, it is argued that permitting a post-search evidentiary hearing on issues of veracity would confuse the pressing issue of guilt or innocence with the collateral question as to whether there had been official misconduct in the drafting of the affidavit.   The weight of criminal dockets, and the need to prevent diversion of attention from the main issue of guilt or innocence, militate against such an added burden on the trial courts.   And if such hearings were conducted routinely, it is said, they would be misused by defendants as a convenient source of discovery.   Defendants might even use the hearings in an attempt to force revelation of the identity of informants.

Sixth and finally, it is argued that a post-search veracity challenge is inappropriate because the accuracy of an affidavit in large part is beyond the control of the affiant.   An affidavit may properly be based on hearsay, on fleeting observations, and on tips received from unnamed informants whose identity often will be properly protected from revelation under McCray v. Illinois, 386 U.S. 300, 87 S. Ct. 1056 (1967).

None of these considerations is trivial. Indeed, because of them, the rule announced today has a limited scope, both in regard to when exclusion of the seized evidence is mandated, and when a hearing on allegations of misstatements must be accorded. But neither do the considerations cited by respondent and others have a fully controlling weight; we conclude that they are insufficient to justify an *absolute* ban on post-search impeachment of veracity. On this side of the balance, also, there are pressing considerations:

First, a flat ban on impeachment of veracity could denude the probable cause requirement of all real meaning. The requirement that a warrant not issue "but upon probable cause, supported by Oath or affirmation," would be reduced to a nullity if a police officer was able to use deliberately falsified allegations to demonstrate probable cause, and, having misled the magistrate, then was able to remain confident that the ploy was worthwhile. It is this specter of intentional falsification that, we think, has evoked such widespread opposition to the flat nonimpeachment rule from the commentators, from the American Law Institute in its Model Code of Pre-Arraignment Procedure, § SS290.3(1), from the federal courts of appeals, and from state courts. On occasion, of course, an instance of deliberate falsity will be exposed and confirmed without a special inquiry either at trial or at a hearing on the sufficiency of the affidavit. A flat nonimpeachment rule would bar re-examination of the warrant even in these cases.

Second, the hearing before the magistrate not always will suffice to discourage lawless or reckless misconduct. The presearch proceeding is necessarily *ex parte*, since the subject of the search cannot be tipped off to the application for a warrant lest he destroy or remove evidence. The usual reliance of our legal system on adversary proceedings itself should be an indication that an *ex parte* inquiry is likely to be less vigorous. The magistrate has no acquaintance with the information that may contradict the good faith and reasonable basis of the affiant's allegations. The presearch proceeding will frequently be marked by haste, because of the understandable desire to act before the evidence disappears; this urgency will not always permit the magistrate to make an extended independent examination of the affiant or other witnesses.

Third, the alternative sanctions of a perjury prosecution, administrative discipline, contempt, or a civil suit are not likely to fill the gap. Mapp v. Ohio, supra, implicitly rejected the adequacy of these alternatives. Mr. Justice Douglas noted this in his concurrence in *Mapp*: " 'Self-scrutiny is a lofty ideal, but its exaltation reaches new heights if we expect a District Attorney to prosecute himself or his associates for well-meaning violations of the search and seizure clause during a raid the District Attorney or his associates have ordered.' "

Fourth, allowing an evidentiary hearing, after a suitable preliminary proffer of material falsity, would not diminish the importance and solemnity of the warrant-issuing process. It is the *ex parte* nature of the initial hearing, rather than the magistrate's capacity, that is the reason for the review. A magistrate's determination is presently subject to review before trial as to *sufficiency* without any undue interference with the dignity of the magistrate's function. Our reluctance today to extend the rule of exclusion beyond instances of deliberate misstatements, and those of reckless disregard, leaves a broad field where the magistrate is the sole protection of a citizen's Fourth Amendment rights, namely, in instances where police have been merely negligent in checking or recording the facts relevant to a probable cause determination.

Fifth, the claim that a post-search hearing will confuse the issue of the defendant's guilt with the issue of the State's possible misbehavior is footless. The hearing will not be in the presence of the jury. An issue extraneous to guilt already is examined in any probable cause determination or review of probable cause. Nor, if a sensible threshold showing is required and sensible substantive requirements for suppression are maintained, need there be any new large-scale commitment of judicial resources; many claims will wash out at an early stage, and the more substantial ones in any event would require judicial resources for vindication if the suggested alternative sanctions were truly to be effective. The requirement of a substantial preliminary showing would suffice to prevent the misuse of a veracity hearing for purposes of discovery or obstruction. And because we are faced today with only the question of the integrity of the affiant's representations as to his own activities, we need not decide, and we in no way predetermine, the difficult question whether a reviewing court must ever require the revelation of the identity of an informant once a substantial preliminary showing of falsity has been made. *McCray v. Illinois*, the Court's earlier disquisition in this area, concluded only that the Due Process Clause of the Fourteenth Amendment did not require the State to expose an informant's identity routinely, upon a defendant's mere demand, when there was ample evidence in the probable cause hearing to show that the informant was reliable and his information credible.

Sixth and finally, as to the argument that the exclusionary rule should not be extended to a "new" area, we cannot regard any such extension really to be at issue here. Despite the deep skepticism of Members of this Court as to the wisdom of extending the exclusionary rule to collateral areas, such as civil or grand jury proceedings, the Court has not questioned, in the absence of a more efficacious sanction, the continued application of the rule to suppress evidence from the State's case where a Fourth Amendment violation has been substantial and deliberate. We see no principled basis for distinguishing between the question of the sufficiency of an affidavit, which also is subject to a post-search re-examination, and the question of its integrity.

In sum, and to repeat with some embellishment what we stated at the beginning of this opinion: There is, of course, a presumption of validity with respect to the affidavit supporting the search warrant. To mandate an evidentiary hearing, the challenger's attack must be more than conclusory and must be supported by more than a mere desire to cross-examine. There must be allegations of deliberate falsehood or of reckless disregard for the truth, and those allegations must be accompanied by an offer of proof. They should point out specifically the portion of the warrant affidavit that is claimed to be false; and they should be accompanied by a statement of supporting reasons. Affidavits or sworn or otherwise reliable statements of witnesses should be furnished, or their absence satisfactorily explained. Allegations of negligence or innocent mistake are insufficient. The deliberate falsity or reckless disregard whose impeachment is permitted today is only that of the affiant, not of any nongovernmental informant. Finally, if these requirements are met, and if, when material that is the subject of the alleged falsity or reckless disregard is set to one side, there remains sufficient content in the warrant affidavit to support a finding of probable cause, no hearing is required. On the other hand, if the remaining content is insufficient, the defendant is entitled, under the Fourth Amendment, to his hearing. Whether he will prevail at that hearing is, of course, another issue.

Because of Delaware's absolute rule, its courts did not have occasion to consider the proffer put forward by petitioner Franks. Since the framing of suitable rules to govern proffers is a matter properly left to the States, we decline ourselves to pass on petitioner's proffer. The judgment of the Supreme Court of Delaware is reversed, and the case is remanded for further proceedings not inconsistent with this opinion.

It is so ordered.   [Appendix omitted.]

MR. JUSTICE REHNQUIST, with whom The Chief Justice joins, dissenting.

The Court's opinion in this case carefully identifies the factors which militate against the result which it reaches, and emphasizes their weight in attempting to limit the circumstances under which an affidavit supporting a search warrant may be impeached. I am not ultimately persuaded, however, that the Court is correct as a matter of constitutional law that the impeachment of such an affidavit must be permitted under the circumstances described by the Court, and I am thoroughly persuaded that the barriers which the Court believes that it is erecting against misuse of the impeachment process are frail indeed.

I.

* * *

The notion that there may be incorrect or even deliberately falsified information presented to a magistrate in the course of an effort to obtain a search warrant does not render the proceeding before a magistrate any different from any other factfinding procedure known to the law. The Court here says that "it would be an unthinkable imposition upon [the magistrate's] authority if a warrant affidavit, revealed after the fact to contain a deliberately or recklessly false statement, were to stand beyond impeachment." I do not believe that this flat statement survives careful analysis.

If the function of the warrant requirement is to obtain the determination of a neutral magistrate as to whether sufficient grounds have been urged to support the issuance of a warrant, that function is fulfilled at the time the magistrate concludes that the requirement has been met. Like any other determination of a magistrate, of a court, or of countless other factfinding tribunals, the decision may be incorrect as a matter of law. Even if correct, some inaccurate or falsified information may have gone into the making of the determination. But unless we are to exalt as the *ne plus ultra* of our system of criminal justice the absolute correctness of every factual determination made along the tortuous route from the filing of the complaint or the issuance of an indictment to the final determination that a judgment of conviction was properly obtained, we shall lose perspective as to the purposes of the system as well as of the warrant requirement of the Fourth and Fourteenth Amendments. . . .

* * *

I am quite confident that if our system of justice were not administered by judges who were once lawyers, it might well be less satisfactory than it now is. But I am equally confident that one improvement which would manifest itself as a result of such a change would be a willingness, reflected in almost all callings in our society except lawyers, to refrain from constant relitigation, whether in the form of collateral attack, appeal, retrial, or whatever, of issues that have originally been decided by a competent authority.

It would be extraordinary troubling in any system of criminal justice if a verdict or finding of guilt, later conclusively shown to be based on false testimony, were to result in the incarceration of the accused notwithstanding this fact. But the Court's reference to the "unthinkable imposition" of not allowing the impeachment of an affiant's testimony in support of a search warrant is a horse of quite another color. Particularly in view of the many hurdles which the prosecution must surmount to ultimately obtain and retain a finding of guilt in the light of the many constitutional safeguards which surround a criminal accused, it is essential to understand the role of a search warrant in the process which may lead to the conviction of such an accused. The warrant issued on impeachable testimony has, by hypothesis, turned up incriminating and admissible evidence to be considered by the jury at the trial. The fact that it was obtained by reason of an impeachable warrant bears not at all on the innocence or guilt of the accused. The only conceivable harm done by such evidence is to the accused's rights under the Fourth and Fourteenth Amendments, which have nothing to do with his guilt or innocence of the crime with which he is charged.

. . . it seems to me it would be quite reasonable for this Court, consistently with the Fourth and Fourteenth Amendments, to adopt any one of three positions with respect to the impeachability of a search warrant which had been in fact issued by a neutral magistrate who satisfied the requirements of Shadwick v. City of Tampa, 407 U.S. 345, 92 S.Ct. 2119 (1972).

First, it could decide that the warrant requirement was satisfied when such a magistrate had been persuaded, and allow no further collateral attack on the warrant. . . . [The Court for more than a decade has] rejected the first possible stopping place in judicial re-examination of affidavits in support of warrants, and held that the legal determination as to probable cause was subject to collateral attack. While this conclusion does not seem to me to flow inexorably from the Fourth Amendment, I think that it makes a good deal of sense in light of the fact that a magistrate need not be a trained lawyer, see *Shadwick*, supra, and therefore may not be versed in the latest nuances of what is or what is not "probable cause" for purposes of the Fourth Amendment.

But to allow collateral examination of an affidavit in support of a warrant on a legal ground such as that is quite different from the rejection of the second possible stopping place as the Court does today. Magistrates need not be lawyers, but lawyers have no monoply on determining whether or not an affiant who appears before them is or is not telling the truth. Indeed, a magistrate whose time may be principally spent in conducting preliminary hearings and trying petty offenses may have every bit as good a feel for the veracity of a particular witness as a judge of a court of general jurisdiction.

True, a warrant is issued *ex parte*, without an opportunity for the person whose effects are to be seized to impeach the testimony of the affiant. The proceeding leading to the issuance of a warrant is, therefore, obviously less reliable and less likely to be a search inquiry into the truth of the affiant's statements than is a full dress adversary proceeding. But it is at this point that I part company with the Court in its underlying assumption that somehow a full dress adversary proceeding will virtually guarantee a truthful answer to the question of whether or not the affiant seeking the warrant falsified his testimony. A full dress adversary proceeding is undoubtedly a better vehicle than an *ex parte* proceeding for arriving at the truth of any particular inquiry, but it is scarcely a guarantee of truth. Mr. Justice Jackson in his concurring opinion in Brown v. Allen, 344 U.S. 443, 73 S.Ct. 397 (1953), observed with respect to purely legal issues decided by this Court:

> "However, reversal by a higher court is not proof that justice is thereby better done. There is no doubt that if there were a super-Supreme Court, a substantial proportion of our reversals of state courts would also be reversed. We are not final because we are infallible, but we are infallible only because we are final."

The same is surely true of a judge's review of the factual determinations of a magistrate; a larger percentage of the judge's findings as to the truth of an affiant's statement may be objectively correct than the percentage of the magistrate's determinations which are, but neither one is going to be one hundred per cent. Since once the warrant is issued and the search is made, the privacy interest protected by the Fourth and Fourteenth Amendments is breached, a subsequent determination that it was wrongfully breached cannot possibly restore the privacy interest. Since the evidence obtained pursuant to the warrant is by hypothesis relevant and admissible on the issue of guilt, the only purpose served by suppression of such evidence is deterrence of falsified testimony on the part of affiant in the future. Without attempting to summarize the many cases in which this Court has discussed the balance to be struck in such situations, I simply do not think the game is worth the candle in this situation.

* * *

II.

The Court has commendably, in my opinion, surrounded the right to impeach the affidavit relied upon to support the issuance of a warrant with numerous limitations. My fear, and I do not think it an unjustified one, is that these limitations will quickly be subverted in actual practice. The Court states that:

> "Nor, if a sensible threshold showing is required and sensible substantive requirements for suppression are maintained, need there be any new large-scale commitment of judicial resources; many claims will wash out at an early stage, and the more substantial ones in any event would require judicial resources for vindication if the suggested alternative sanctions were truly to be effective. The requirement of a substantial preliminary showing should suffice to prevent the misuse of a veracity hearing for purposes of discovery or obstruction."

I greatly fear that this generalized language will afford insufficient protection against the natural tendency of ingenious lawyers charged with representing their client's cause to ceaselessly undermine the limitations which the Court has placed on impeachment of the affidavit offered in support of a search warrant. I am sure that the Court is sincere in its expressed hope that the doctrine which it adopts will not lead to "any new large-scale commitment of judicial resources," but in the end I am led once more to echo the observation contained in another opinion of Mr. Justice Jackson:

> "The case which irresistibly comes to mind as the most fitting precedent is that of Julia who, according to Byron's reports, 'whispering "I will ne'er consent."—consented.'"
> Everson v. Board of Education, 330 U.S. 1, 19, 67 S.Ct. 504, 513 (Jackson, J., dissenting).

Since I would not "consent" even to the extent that the Court does in its opinion, I dissent from that opinion and would affirm the judgment of the Supreme Court of Delaware.

NOTE

To what extent may the suppression motion be used for discovery purposes? Consider that most of the facts which are developed in motions to suppress are not particularly relevant to guilt or innocence. The existence or sufficiency of a warrant and the method of executing a search will have little relation to the ultimate issue in the case. Only in jurisdictions offering very little formal discovery will the motions to suppress be useful discovery devices. There may be two exceptions to this rule, one minor and one major. The minor exception involves cases in which the crime is unlawful possession of some prohibited thing and the possession in question is that which the officer witnessed as he discovered the narcotics or weapon, etc. In such a case the testimony on a motion to suppress will include nearly everything the prosecution will prove at trial. However, the evidence in these cases is not ordinarily difficult to discover in any event and is fairly predictable. The major exception involves motions to suppress eyewitness identification. This is particularly true when the defense does establish primary illegality and the hearing turns to admissibility of in court identification. Then the defense may gain the benefit of a searching, sworn and recorded interview with the eyewitness, who may refuse to speak with defense counsel except while on the stand. The suppression hearing may not be used solely for discovery purposes and a court may limit examination. See State v. Bishop, 289 Minn. 188, 183 N.W.2d 536 (1971); Cefalo v. Fitzpatrick, 434 F.2d 187 (1st Cir. 1970). It is difficult to see precisely where the line may be drawn and several courts have continued to permit trial judges to allow full development of the facts. People v. Robinson, 46 Ill.2d 229, 263 N.E.2d 57 (1970).

What opportunity does the prosecution have for discovery? The answer depends largely on the degree to which the defense must offer evidence to make a case in the motion. Even so, the prosecutor is generally limited in two ways. Like the defense, he cannot examine witnesses (particularly the defendant) concerning issues outside the scope of the hearing. Rule 104(d), Fed.R.Evid. states the general rule:

> (d) Testimony by accused. The accused does not, by testifying upon a preliminary matter, subject himself to cross-examination as to other issues in the case.

Within those limits, the prosecution may get some idea of the impending defense. Apart from this, if the accused makes damaging admissions on the motion to suppress, may the prosecutor use these admissions at trial. Simmons v. United States, 390 U.S. 377, 88 S.Ct. 966 (1968) held that the admissions were inadmissible (at least in the prosecution's case-in-chief). May they be used to impeach trial testimony? Compare Woody v. United States, 379 F.2d 130 (D.C.Cir.1967), and People v. Sturgis, 58 Ill.2d 211, 317 N.E.2d 545 (1974) (allowing impeachment) with People v. Luna, 37 Ill.2d 299, 226 N.E.2d 586 (1967) (forbidding impeachment). Consider the effect of Harris v. New York, 401 U.S. 222, 91 S.Ct. 644 (1971).

Both prosecution and defense do make one valuable discovery at motions to suppress; they learn a good deal about the courtroom demeanor and intelligence of the witnesses who do testify.

Chapter 14

COMPETENCY TO STAND TRIAL

A. SUBSTANTIVE STANDARDS AND PROCEDURES FOR DETERMINING COMPETENCY

DROPE v. MISSOURI

Supreme Court of the United States, 1975.
420 U.S. 162, 95 S.Ct. 896.

MR. CHIEF JUSTICE BURGER delivered the opinion of the Court.

[The issue was whether, because of certain facts which came to the attention of the trial judge before and during trial, the United States Constitution required him to conduct an evidentiary hearing to determine whether the defendant was competent to stand trial.]

* * *

It has long been accepted that a person whose mental condition is such that he lacks the capacity to understand the nature and object of the proceedings against him, to consult with counsel, and to assist in preparing his defense may not be subjected to a trial. Thus, Blackstone wrote that one who became "mad" after the commission of an offense should not be arraigned for it "because he is not able to plead to it with that advice and caution that he ought." Similarly, if he became "mad" after pleading, he should not be tried, "for how can he make his defense?" 4 W. Blackstone Commentaries, 24. See Youtsey v. United States, 97 F. 937, 940–946 (CA6 1899). Some have viewed the common-law prohibition "as a by-product of the ban against trials *in absentia*; the mentally incompetent defendant, though physically present in the courtroom, is in reality afforded no opportunity to defend himself."

* * *

. . . For our purposes, it suffices to note that the prohibition is fundamental to an adversary system of justice. Accordingly, as to federal cases, we have approved a test of incompetence which seeks to ascertain whether a criminal defendant " 'has sufficient present ability to consult with his lawyer with a reasonable degree of rational understanding—and whether he has a rational as well as factual understanding of the proceedings against him.' " Dusky v. United States, 362 U.S., at 402, 80 S.Ct. 788.

[The unamimous Court concluded that the trial judge erred in not holding a competency hearing either before or during trial.]

* * *

The question remains whether petitioner's due process rights would be adequately protected by remanding the case now for a psychiatric examination aimed at establishing whether petitioner was in fact competent to stand trial in 1969. Given the inherent difficulties of such a *nunc pro tunc* determination under the most favorable circumstances, see Pate v. Robinson, 383 U.S., at 386–387, 86 S.Ct. 836, 842–843; Dusky v. United States, 362 U.S., at 403, 80 S.Ct. at 789, we cannot conclude that such a procedure would be adequate here. The State is free to retry petitioner, assuming, of course, that at the time of such trial he is competent to be tried.

The judgment is reversed, and the cause is remanded for proceedings not inconsistent with this opinion.

Reversed and remanded.

———

PEOPLE v. BURSON

Supreme Court of Illinois, 1957.
11 Ill.2d 360, 143 N.E.2d 239.

DAVIS, JUSTICE.

After trial by jury in the circuit court of Kane County, Robert Burson was convicted of murder and sentenced to death. He sued out writ of error to review the judgment. . . .

* * *

Before the trial began, defendant's appointed counsel . . . sought a continuance on the ground that they had not had sufficient time to prepare the case because, except for the last four days, defendant had refused to talk to them. The public defender advised the court that the defendant, by virtue of his experience with [an imposter attorney], was distrustful of all counsel and people generally; and that counsel believed that they now had his confidence and co-operation and could prepare his defense if given time. The defendant then told the court that, when he had previously stated that he had counsel, he was referring to spiritual counsel; that he had been preparing to try his own case; and that if he did not get an attorney, he would still reject appointed counsel. An argument then ensued between the court and the defendant as to his right to reject counsel, one of whom then sought to withdraw from the case. The court denied the request and told the defendant that his rejection of counsel would not be accepted; that the court had appointed competent counsel and they would have to serve. The court denied the motion for continuance, whereupon the defendant asked the court whether he believed in God, and said "I will say that when the day of reckoning comes, you people who have shown me no leniency, shall also be shown none on reckoning day by God."

The defendant participated in the *voir dire* examination of the jurors and inquired at length as to their religious beliefs and experiences. Typical examples of the questions asked were: "Do you believe in God?" "Do you believe in the inspired word as written in the Bible?" "Have you read the Old Testament?" "Have you read the New Testament?" "Do you believe in Jesus Christ as the son of

God?" "Have you ever been born again?" Many of the jurors, obviously perplexed by this interrogation, asked for his interpretation of being "born again." The defendant then explained his conception of salvation by quotations from the Bible, to which objections were sustained; and he frequently became argumentative.

The possible insanity of the defendant was first mentioned by one of his counsel in opening argument. The State's Attorney immediately objected on the ground that such defense had not been specially pleaded, and a lengthy argument then took place in chambers as to the manner in which the issue of insanity might be presented. The record indicates that neither court nor counsel differentiated between the question of insanity at the time of the alleged offense and at the time of trial. During this discussion, one of the defendant's counsel stated that they had the right "to have a prior hearing on the issue whether insanity does exist, not only preliminary to assigning it on the issues, but whether this man is able to go ahead with the defense." The State's Attorney then argued that the defense of insanity had to be properly raised prior to trial. The court remarked that, if petition had been filed prior to trial, it would have been his duty to first determine the issue of sanity before trying the defendant on the indictment, but "We are now embarked on the trial of the indictment to determine the guilt or innocence of the defendant," and the court ruled that the defendant was entitled to raise any defense he saw fit on the trial, including the defense of insanity at the time of the commission of the offense. The defendant, who was present during this colloquy, protested vigorously that he was sane and stated that in no case would he plead any type of insanity to the charge.
. . .

Throughout the two-week trial, defendant persisted in arguing with the court, the State's Attorney and his appointed counsel in the presence of the jury. He characterized the court's adverse rulings on evidence as efforts on the part of the court to conceal the true facts and to aid the prosecution. His distrust of his appointed counsel increased as the trial progressed, even though the record reflects a conscientious effort on their part to properly represent him. The climax came when the defendant called his attorneys, as witnesses, to prove that they failed to give him their full support because of bargaining, collusion, prejudice and political pressure, and that he had objected to their representation throughout the trial. He examined both of them at length in a highly insulting manner. After the defendant had examined attorney Heimdal, public defender Galvin objected to being called as a witness on the ground that the tactics being pursued would damage the defendant's case before the jury, but the court compelled him to testify. At one point in the interrogation, the defendant said: "Speak up, Mr. Galvin, if you have any guts," and in conclusion stated: "I have only one thing further to say, Mr. Galvin, that I would rather be in my shoes 100 times over than be in your shoes."

Defendant made his own closing argument to the jury. It was, for the most part, a long and rambling dissertation covering his own religious beliefs, the sinfulness of man's nature, the need for salvation and his opinions on the theory of evolution. In closing he told the jury that he was innocent, but if they found him guilty he wanted the extreme penalty of death in the electric chair. He objected to all instructions tendered by his counsel, both during conferences thereon and later, on the ground that he had neither approved nor read them. His counsel offered two instructions on the subject of insanity, to which defendant offered particular objection, and, the court, in refusing these instructions, stated it was acting in accordance with defendant's wishes. However, the court gave other instructions tendered by defense counsel to which the defendant had likewise objected. . . .

The trial, adjudication, sentence, or execution of a person charged with a criminal offense, while insane, is a violation of due process of law . . . and is expressly prohibited by . . . the Criminal Code. . . . The statute providing for a sanity hearing does not, and was not intended to, abrogate the common-law rule that no person should be compelled to stand trial while insane. . . . A formal petition for such hearing prior to trial is unnecessary to afford a defendant the protection of the statute and his rights at common law. We have decided that the question may be raised by oral suggestions of counsel during the trial, and if made in good faith, it becomes the duty of the court to conduct a hearing before a jury upon the issue, and the denial thereof is a violation of due process. . . . These views are in accord with the rule in other jurisdictions. In 14 Am.Jur. sec. 44, page 801, it is stated: "The rule at common law and by statute in many jurisdictions is well settled that a person while insane cannot be tried, sentenced, or executed. It is obvious that if tried while insane, his insanity may disable him from making a rational defense. Hence, both at common law and by statute in many jurisdictions, if, at any time while criminal proceedings are pending against a person accused of a crime, whether before, during, or after the trial, the trial court, either from observation or upon the suggestion of counsel, has facts brought to its attention which raise a doubt of the sanity of the defendant, the question should be settled before further steps are taken."

When the question of sanity at the time of trial is raised, the issue presented is whether the defendant has the capacity to make a rational defense. . . . He should be capable of understanding the nature and object of the proceedings against him, his own condition in reference to such proceedings, and have sufficient mind to conduct his defense in a rational and reasonable manner, although upon other subjects his mind may be unsound or deranged. . . . In order to conduct his defense in a rational and reasonable manner, he should be capable of co-operating with his counsel to the end that any available defenses may be interposed. . . .

The record in this case raises serious doubt concerning the defendant's sanity at the time of his trial. He appears to have been possessed of a persecution complex pertaining to his relation with man, and of delusions of grandeur in connection with his identification with God. In view of his exalted beliefs and irrational conduct, it must have become apparent to his counsel, the State, and the court, before and as the trial progressed, that he was neither capable of cooperating with his counsel, of giving them the assistance necessary to a proper defense, nor of defending himself. When such facts became evident, the issue of sanity was raised, and it was the duty of counsel for defendant and the State to request a determination of the defendant's sanity. We believe that the suggestion of insanity by defense counsel, the defendant's departure from the general rules governing human conduct, and his exalted beliefs raised the sanity issue; and that the court abused its discretion in refusing to direct a sanity hearing pursuant to statute. The court did not discharge its duty under the statute by taking the defendant's word as to his sanity, or by substituting its judgment for that of a jury. .   .   .   When, before or during the trial, facts are brought to the attention of the court, either by suggestion of counsel or the State, or by its own observation, which raise a *bona fide* doubt of the defendant's present sanity, a duty devolves upon the court to then cause a sanity hearing to be held as provided by law.

In the motion for new trial, after verdict and before judgment, the court was again advised that counsel believed that defendant had been insane during his trial and was then insane. It was then the duty of the court under section 13 of division II of the Criminal Code (Ill.Rev.Stat.1955, chap. 38, par. 593), to conduct a jury trial upon the issue before pronouncing judgment. The fact that the issue was presented by a motion for a new trial rather than by a formal petition for such a hearing is immaterial. .   .   .   The failure of the court to afford the defendant a hearing on the question of his sanity during the trial and after verdict was a denial of due process.

We recognize that counsel for defendant did not present or argue this point; and that the general rule is that where a question is not raised or reserved in the trial court, or where, though raised in the lower court, it is not urged or argued on appeal, it will not be considered and will be deemed to have been waived. However, this is a rule of administration and not of jurisdiction or power, and it will not operate to deprive an accused of his constitutional rights of due process. "The court may, as a matter of grace, in a case involving deprivation of life or liberty, take notice of errors appearing upon the record which deprived the accused of substantial means of enjoying a fair and impartial trial, although no exceptions were preserved or the question is imperfectly presented." .   .   .

Reversed and remanded.

PATE v. ROBINSON

Supreme Court of the United States, 1966.
383 U.S. 375, 86 S.Ct. 836.

MR. JUSTICE CLARK delivered the opinion of the Court.

In 1959 respondent Robinson was convicted of the murder of his common-law wife, Flossie May Ward, and was sentenced to imprisonment for life. Being an indigent he was defended by court-appointed counsel. It was conceded at trial that Robinson shot and killed Flossie May, but his counsel claimed that he was insane at the time of the shooting and raised the issue of his incompetence to stand trial. On writ of error to the Supreme Court of Illinois it was asserted that the trial court's rejection of these contentions deprived Robinson of due process of law under the Fourteenth Amendment. His conviction was affirmed, the court finding that no hearing on mental capacity to stand trial had been requested, that the evidence failed to raise sufficient doubt as to his competence to require the trial court to conduct a hearing on its own motion, and further that the evidence did not raise a "reasonable doubt" as to his sanity at the time of the offense. We denied certiorari. Thereupon, Robinson filed this petition for habeas corpus, which was denied without a hearing by the United States District Court for the Northern District of Illinois. [The Court of Appeals reversed and remanded the case on several grounds.]

. . . The Court of Appeals directed that the District Court should also determine upon the hearing whether Robinson was denied due process by the state court's failure to conduct a hearing upon his competence to stand trial; and, if it were found his rights had been violated in this respect, that Robinson "should be ordered released, but such release may be delayed for a reasonable time . . . to permit the State of Illinois to grant Robinson a new trial." We granted certiorari to resolve the difficult questions of state-federal relations posed by these rulings. We have concluded that Robinson was constitutionally entitled to a hearing on the issue of his competence to stand trial. Since we do not think there could be a meaningful hearing on that issue at this late date, we direct that the District Court, after affording the State another opportunity to put Robinson to trial on its charges within a reasonable time, order him discharged. Accordingly, we affirm the decision of the Court of Appeals in this respect, except insofar as it contemplated a hearing in the District Court on Robinson's competence. Our disposition makes it unnecessary to reach the other reasons given by the Court of Appeals for reversal.

The State concedes that the conviction of an accused person while he is legally incompetent violates due process, Bishop v. United States, 350 U.S. 961, 76 S.Ct. 440 (1956), and that state procedures must be adequate to protect this right. It insists, however, that Robinson intelligently waived this issue by his failure to request a hearing on his competence at the trial; and further, that on the basis of the evidence before the trial judge no duty rested upon him to order a hearing *sua sponte*. A determination of these claims necessitates a detailed discussion of the conduct of the trial and the evidence touching upon the question of Robinson's competence at that time.

[The Court then reviewed the indications in the record which it believed suggested a bona fide doubt about the competency of the accused. Accurately summarized in the dissent which follows, the relevant data was found in the testimony of defense witnesses, presented as part of an insanity defense, that the accused over a period of years had behaved in an irrational manner. The Court also emphasized the testimony of witnesses who believed Robinson was insane at the time of the crime and the assertion by defense counsel that Robinson was "presently insane." (Under then existing Illinois law, if a judge or jury found the defendant not guilty by reason of insanity, the trier of fact also had to decide whether the accused was "presently insane" in which case he would be committed for mental treatment. Ordinarily defense counsel urged that the client was presently insane lest the judge or jury be faced with the option of either convicting or letting the accused go free.]

* * *

The State insists that Robinson deliberately waived the defense of his competence to stand trial by failing to demand a sanity hearing as provided by Illinois law. But it is contradictory to argue that a defendant may be incompetent, and yet knowingly or intelligently "waive" his right to have the court determine his capacity to stand trial. See Taylor v. United States, 282 F.2d 16, 23 (C.A. 8th Cir. 1960). In any event, the record shows that counsel throughout the proceedings insisted that Robinson's present sanity was very much in issue. He made a point to elicit Mrs. Robinson's opinion of Robinson's "present sanity." And in his argument to the judge, he asserted that Robinson "should be found not guilty and presently insane on the basis of the testimony that we have heard." Moreover, the prosecutor himself suggested at trial that "we should have Dr. Haines' testimony as to his opinion whether this man is sane or insane." With this record we cannot say that Robinson waived the defense of incompetence to stand trial.[1]

1. Although defense counsel phrased his questions and argument in terms of Robinson's present insanity, we interpret his language as necessarily placing in issue the question of Robinson's mental competence to stand trial. Counsel was simply borrowing the terminology of the relevant Illinois statutes and decisions. The state law in effect at the time of Robinson's trial differentiated between lack of criminal responsibility and competence to stand trial, but used "insanity" to describe both concepts. Ill.Rev.Stat., c. 38, §§ 592, 593 (1963). The judges likewise phrased their decisions only in terms of sanity and insanity. See, e. g., People v. Baker, 26 Ill.2d 484, 187 N.E.2d 227 (1962). The statutory provisions and terminology in this field have now been clarified by the enactment of an article dealing with the "competency of accused." Ill.Rev.Stat., c. 38, §§ 104-1 to 104-3 (1963), as amended by the Code of Criminal Procedure of 1963. Even if counsel may also have meant to refer to the statutory provisions dealing with commitment for present insanity, Ill.Rev.Stat., c. 38, § 592 (1963), this fact would not affect the determination that counsel's words raised a question as to competence that the trial judge should have considered.

We believe that the evidence introduced on Robinson's behalf entitled him to a hearing on this issue. The court's failure to make such inquiry thus deprived Robinson of his constitutional right to a fair trial. See Thomas v. Cunningham, 313 F.2d 934 (C.A. 4th Cir. 1963). Illinois jealously guards this right. Where the evidence raises a *"bona fide* doubt" as to a defendant's competence to stand trial, the judge on his own motion must impanel a jury and conduct a sanity hearing pursuant to Ill.Rev.Stat., c. 38, § 104–2 (1963). People v. Shrake, 25 Ill.2d 141, 182 N.E.2d 754 (1962). The Supreme Court of Illinois held that the evidence here was not sufficient to require a hearing in light of the mental alertness and understanding displayed in Robinson's "colloquies" with the trial judge. 22 Ill.2d, at 168, 174 N.E.2d, at 823. But this reasoning offers no justification for ignoring the uncontradicted testimony of Robinson's history of pronounced irrational behavior. While Robinson's demeanor at trial might be relevant to the ultimate decision as to his sanity, it cannot be relied upon to dispense with a hearing on that very issue. . . .

Having determined that Robinson's constitutional rights were abridged by his failure to receive an adequate hearing on his competence to stand trial, we direct that the writ of habeas corpus must issue and Robinson be discharged, unless the State gives him a new trial within a reasonable time.

*   *   *

It has been pressed upon us that it would be sufficient for the state court to hold a limited hearing as to Robinson's mental competence at the time he was tried in 1959. If he were found competent, the judgment against him would stand. But we have previously emphasized the difficulty of retrospectively determining an accused's competence to stand trial. Dusky v. United States (1960). The jury would not be able to observe the subject of their inquiry, and expert witnesses would have to testify solely from information contained in the printed record. That Robinson's hearing would be held six years after the fact aggravates these difficulties. This need for concurrent determination distinguishes the present case from Jackson v. Denno (1964), where we held that on remand the State could discharge its constitutional obligation by giving the accused a separate hearing on the voluntariness of his confession.

If the State elects to retry Robinson, it will of course be open to him to raise the question of his competence to stand trial at that time and to request a special hearing thereon. In the event a sufficient doubt exists as to his present competence such a hearing must be held. If found competent to stand trial, Robinson would have the usual defenses available to an accused.

The case is remanded to the District Court for action consistent with this opinion. It is so ordered.

Case remanded to District Court with directions.

MR. JUSTICE HARLAN, whom MR. JUSTICE BLACK joins, dissenting.

The facts now canvassed by this Court to support its constitutional holding were fully sifted by the Illinois Supreme Court. I cannot agree that the state court's unanimous appraisal was erroneous and still less that it was error of constitutional proportions.

The Court appears to hold that a defendant's present incompetence may become sufficiently manifest during a trial that it denies him due process for the trial court to fail to conduct a hearing on that question on its own initiative. I do not dissent from this very general proposition, and I agree also that such an error is not "waived" by failure to raise it and that it may entitle the defendant to a new trial without further proof. Waiver is not an apposite concept where we premise a defendant so deranged that he cannot oversee his lawyers. Since our further premise is that the trial judge should and could have avoided the error, a new trial seems not too drastic an exaction in view of the proof problems arising after a significant lapse of time. However, I do not believe the facts known to the trial judge in this case suggested Robinson's incompetence at time of trial with anything like the force necessary to make out a violation of due process in the failure to pursue the question.

Before turning to the facts, it is pertinent to consider the quality of the incompetence they are supposed to indicate. In federal courts —and I assume no more is asked of state courts—the test of incompetence that warrants postponing the trial is reasonably well settled. In language this Court adopted on the one occasion it faced the issue, "the 'test must be whether . . . [the defendant] has sufficient present ability to consult with his lawyer with a reasonable degree of rational understanding—and whether he has a rational as well as factual understanding of the proceedings against him.' " . . . In short, emphasis is on capacity to consult with counsel and to comprehend the proceedings, and lower courts have recognized that this is by no means the same test as those which determine criminal responsibility at the time of the crime. The question, then, is not whether the facts before the trial judge suggested that Robinson's crime was an insane act but whether they suggested he was incompetent to stand trial.

The Court's affirmative answer seemingly rests on two kinds of evidence, principally adduced by Robinson to prove an insanity defense after the State rested its main case. First, there was evidence of a number of episodes of severe irrationality in Robinson's past. Among them were the slaying of his infant son, his attempted suicide, his efforts to burn his wife's clothing, his fits of temper and of abstraction, and his seven week incarceration in a state hospital eight years before the trial. This evidence may be tempered by the State's counterarguments, for example, that Robinson was found guilty of his son's killing and that alcoholism may explain his hospitalization, but it cannot be written off entirely. The difficulty remains that while this testimony may suggest that Flossie May Ward's killing was just one more irrational act, I cannot say as a matter of common knowledge that it evidences incapacity during the trial. Indeed, the pattern revealed may best indicate that Robinson did function adequately during most of his life interrupted by periods of severe derangement that would have been quite apparent had they occurred at trial. The second class of data pertinent to the Court's theory, remarks by witnesses and counsel that Robinson was "presently insane," deserves little comment. I think it apparent that these statements were addressed to Robinson's responsibility for the killing, that is, his ability to do insane acts, and not to his general competency to stand trial.

Whatever mild doubts this evidence may stir are surely allayed by positive indications of Robinson's competence at the trial. Foremost is his own behavior in the courtroom. The record reveals colloquies between Robinson and the trial judge which undoubtedly permitted a reasonable inference that Robinson was quite cognizant of the proceedings and able to assist counsel in his defense. Turning from lay impressions to those of an expert, it was stipulated at trial that a Dr. Haines, Director of the Behavior Clinic of the Criminal Court of Cook County, had examined Robinson several months earlier and, if called, would testify that Robinson "knows the nature of the charge and is able to co-operate with his counsel." The conclusive factor is that Robinson's own lawyers, the two men who apparently had the closest contact with the defendant during the proceedings, never suggested he was incompetent to stand trial and never moved to have him examined on incompetency grounds during trial; indeed, counsel's remarks to the jury seem best read as an affirmation of Robinson's present "lucidity" which would be highly peculiar if Robinson had been unable to assist properly in his defense.

Thus, I cannot agree with the Court that the requirements of due process were violated by the failure of the trial judge, who had opportunities for personal observation of the defendant that we do not possess to halt the trial and hold a competency hearing on his own motion.

NOTES

1. Competency to stand trial presents a different issue than insanity at the time of the crime, although courts still sometimes use the word "insanity" when speaking of incompetency. This is a vestige of the common law prohibition against trying persons who at the time of trial were "insane". See generally La Fave and Scott, Criminal Law, 295–304 (1972). In cases where the issue on appeal is whether indicia of incompetency before the trial judge were sufficient to mandate a competency hearing, evidence of bizarre conduct presented as part of an insanity defense often is given weight by appellate courts on the competency question. For examples of this phenomenon see the full text of Drope and Pate v. Robinson, supra. Some courts, however, believe that evidence of insanity at the time of the crime, without other data which call into question competency to stand trial, may not, by itself, suffice to require that a hearing be held to determine competency. In other words evidence that the accused was insane at the time of the alleged offense does not, by itself, create a bona fide doubt as to the defendant's ability to understand the charge or to assist in his defense. In Bryant v. State, 563 S.W.2d 37 (Mo.1978), the court held that the

trial judge need not, sua sponte, hold a hearing to determine competency when a psychiatric report submitted to the judge indicates the psychiatrist's conclusion that the defendant is competent to stand trial but at the time of the crime suffered a mental disease or defect.

When a hearing is held and the defendant found competent to stand trial, appellate reversals of this determination are rare. Relief is much more likely to be granted where no hearing was held and defense counsel on appeal argues that the record contains data indicating a bona fide doubt about the accused's competency.

2. As a practical matter, the question of competency is frequently resolved without an evidentiary hearing. At the suggestion of counsel for either side, or on its own, the court may order a psychiatric evaluation of the accused. (Not infrequently where a defense of insanity is raised, the psychiatrist may examine the accused to form an opinion as to both sanity and competency.) If a psychiatric report indicates that the accused is competent, the court may declare that there is no bona fide doubt as to competency and dispense with a hearing. Such a procedure is contemplated by 18 U.S.C. § 4244, the statute governing federal competency proceedings. See Pizzi, Competency to Stand Trial in Federal Courts: Conceptual and Constitutional Problems, 45 U.Chi.L.Rev. 21–71 (1977).

3. Should departures from the norm automatically trigger a psychiatric evaluation of a defendant for the purpose of determining competency? In some jurisdictions defendants who are clearly homosexual, transsexual, or transvestite are routinely subjected to competency inquiries. So, too, are persons who manifest religious beliefs substantially different from those prevalent in the community. Even if a trial judge does not believe that unorthodoxy is a sign of incompetency, he or she must be concerned about how a reviewing court will view the record. See People v. Thomas, 43 Ill.2d 328, 253 N.E.2d 431 (1969), one of a series of decisions in which the defendants, although deemed by a psychiatrist to be capable of cooperating with counsel, in fact were uncooperative with appointed counsel, stating that their attorney was "El-elohe, the Lord God of Israel."

4. Because the law of evidence raises questions as to the competency of witnesses who either at the time of the event or at the time of trial were under the influence of narcotics, some trial judges are reluctant to permit a defendant to stand trial while he is undergoing treatment through the use of psychopharmacological drugs. Reviewing courts, however, have frequently held that an individual who is able to understand the charges and assist in his defense while under medication may stand trial if, in the absence of the drugs, he would be incompetent. See, e. g., State v. Law, 270 S.C. 664, 244 S.E.2d 302 (1978); State v. Stacey, 556 S.W.2d 552 (Tenn. Cr.App.1977). See also Haddox, Gross and Pollack, Mental Competency to Stand Trial While Under the Influence of Drugs, 7 Loyola (L.A.) L.Rev. 425 (1974).

5. As *Pate* and *Drope* indicate, the failure to hold a competency hearing when a bona fide doubt exists often cannot be rectified by an appellate court remand to determine whether the defendant, at trial several years earlier, was, in fact, competent to stand trial. To avoid a retrial for want of a competency hearing, some trial judges, often at the suggestion of a prosecutor, will hold competency hearings even when everybody seems to agree that the accused is competent to stand trial.

Most courts agree with *Drope* and *Pate* that a determination of someone's competency cannot be validly made years after the trial. See Hayden

v. Commonwealth, 563 S.W.2d 720 (Ky.1978); Roach v. Bennett, 319 F.
Supp. 79 (S.D.Iowa 1970); United States v. Burgin, 440 F.2d 1092 (4th Cir.
1971). However, under certain limited circumstances the courts have approved such determinations. See Arnold v. United States, 432 F.2d 871
(10th Cir. 1970); Barefield v. New Mexico, 434 F.2d 307 (10th Cir. 1970).
See especially Carroll v. Beto, 330 F.Supp. 71 (N.D.Texas 1971) aff'd 446
F.2d 648 (5th Cir. 1971). See also State v. Wagner, 114 Ariz. 459, 561 P.2d
1231 (1977) (competency hearing ordered fourteen years after trial).

6. Does entry of a plea of guilty require a higher degree of competency than does standing trial following a plea of not guilty? Compare Siel-
ing v. Eyman, 478 F.2d 211 (9th Cir. 1973), with People v. Heral, 62 Ill.2d
329, 342 N.E.2d 34 (1976). Does the standard change if the question of
competency arises after trial has commenced? For one view see State v.
Wright, 19 Wash.App. 381, 575 P.2d 740 (1978).

7. In some jurisdictions, including United States District Courts, competency hearings are conducted by the trial judge sitting without a jury.
In other jurisdictions, absent a waiver, a jury (different than the one
trying the question of innocence or guilt), will decide the issue. Because
there is no federal constitutional right to a jury trial on this issue, jurisdictions which provide for jury trials sometimes do allow the allegedly incompetent defendant to waive trial by jury. See People v. Brown, 43 Ill.2d 79,
250 N.E.2d 647 (1969). Does this make sense?

The burden of proof may be allocated differently in different jurisdictions, the United States Supreme Court not having dictated a federal constitutional standard. Compare State v. Aumann, 265 N.W.2d 316 (Iowa 1978)
(burden on defendant), with People v. McCullum, 66 Ill.2d 306, 5 Ill.Dec.
836, 362 N.E.2d 307 (1977) (statute held unconstitutional in so far as it
placed burden on the accused when the defense raised the issue). Where
juries are used to determine competency, sometimes directed verdicts are
entered on the issue as in civil cases. See People v. Speck, 41 Ill.2d 177,
242 N.E.2d 208 (1968).

8. Psychiatrists often are key witnesses in competency hearings, although some psychiatrists insist that the defense lawyer, whose job it is to
communicate with the defendant, is in a better position to assist the court
in determining competency. In People v. Parney, 74 Mich.App. 173, 253 N.
W.2d 698 (1977), the court held that a "forensic" social worker was unqualified to express an opinion on competency for want of medical training.
Does this decision make sense? See Hattaway and Pothyress, A Mental
Health Critique of People v. Parney: Medical and Non-Medical Expertise
on Competency to Stand Trial, 56 Mich.St.B.J. 784 (1977).

In addition to the witnesses already discussed in connection with the
insanity defense, the arresting officers and jail personnel are particularly
helpful in competency cases. See Lingo v. State, 224 Ga. 333, 162 S.E.2d 1
(1968); People v. Herrera, 12 Mich.App. 67, 162 N.W.2d 330 (1968).

It may also be permissible to require or permit the testimony of defense counsel so long as his testimony does not repeat what his client has
told him. If defense counsel testifies solely concerning his observations of
defendant's conduct and ability to communicate and cooperate, and does not
reveal the substance of the communications, the privilege is not violated.
Tanner v. United States, 434 F.2d 260 (10th Cir. 1970); Howell v. United
States, 282 F.Supp. 246 (N.D.Ill.1968); United States v. Tom, 340 F.2d 127
(2nd Cir. 1965); United States v. Kendrick, 331 F.2d 110 (4th Cir. 1964).
But see Gunther v. United States, 230 F.2d 222 (D.C.Cir.1966).

One jurisdiction has sought to give statutory guidance to the sort of questions to be considered in competency hearings. See Ill.Rev.Stats., Ch. 38, Sec. 1005–2–1(E) (1977):

> Subject to the rules of evidence, matters admissible on the question of the defendant's fitness to stand trial or be sentenced may include, but shall not be limited to, the following items:
>
> > (1) the defendant's social behavior or abilities; orientation as to time and place; recognition and correlation of persons, places and things; performance of motor processes; and behavioral functions, habits, and practices;
> >
> > (2) the defendant's knowledge and understanding of the nature of the charge; of the nature of the proceedings; of the consequences of a finding, judgment or sentence; of the courtroom facilities and personnel; and of the functions of the participants in the trial process;
> >
> > (3) the defendant's abilities before and during trial to observe, recollect, consider, correlate and narrate occurrences, especially those concerning his own past and those concerning the incidents alleged; to communicate with counsel; and to reason and make judgments concerning questions and suggestions of counsel before trial and in the trial process.

9.   For reasons of administrative convenience, many jurisdictions postpone the determination of competency in felony trials until after there has been a finding of probable cause. A hearing is held only after an indictment is returned or after there has been a probable cause finding on an information. If a particular state has a full-blown preliminary hearing, as in Coleman v. Alabama (Casebook, Ch. 10, Sec. A), is not the accused denied Sixth Amendment rights if he is incompetent at that critical stage? See Hale v. Superior Court, 15 Cal.3d 221, 124 Cal.Rptr. 57, 539 P.2d 817 (1975), where the practice of postponing the determination of competency was upheld.

10.   When the need for a hearing to determine competency does not appear until mid-trial, administrative convenience might suggest completing the trial and, if the defendant is found guilty, immediately thereafter holding the competency hearing. *Drope* commented favorably upon such a procedure. But see People v. Burnside, 52 Ill.App.3d 524, 10 Ill.Dec. 280, 367 N. E.2d 733 (1977). Of course, a defendant must be competent not only at plea and trial but also at sentencing. See Wojtowicz v. United States, 550 F.2d 786 (2d Cir. 1977).

11.   In some jurisdictions the accused cannot appeal a finding of incompetency to stand trial, his remedy being a "restoration" hearing in the trial court to determine whether he has regained competency. When the accused's condition is "stable" and the only issue is whether in that state he is competent, appellate review seems appropriate even if a finding of incompetency is not a "final order." See Jolley v. State, 282 Md. 353, 384 A.2d 91 (1978). To some extent, a state's failure to provide an appellate remedy has a less drastic effect because of the limits placed by Jackson v. Indiana (treated in the next section) upon holding an accused in custody solely by virtue of a finding of incompetence.

B. LONG–TERM OR PERMANENT INCOMPETENCE TO STAND TRIAL

JACKSON v. INDIANA

Supreme Court of the United States, 1972.
406 U.S. 715, 92 S.Ct. 1845.

MR. JUSTICE BLACKMUN delivered the opinion of the Court.

We are here concerned with the constitutionality of certain aspects of Indiana's system for pretrial commitment of one accused of crime.

Petitioner, Theon Jackson, is a mentally defective deaf mute with a mental level of a pre-school child. He cannot read, write, or otherwise communicate except through limited sign language. In May 1968, at age 27, he was charged in the Criminal Court of Marion County, Indiana, with separate robberies of two women. The offenses were alleged to have occurred the preceding July. The first involved property (a purse and its contents) of the value of four dollars. The second concerned five dollars in money. The record sheds no light on these charges since, upon receipt of not-guilty pleas from Jackson, the trial court set in motion the Indiana procedures for determining his competency to stand trial.

As the statute requires, the court appointed two psychiatrists to examine Jackson. A competency hearing was subsequently held at which petitioner was represented by counsel. The court received the examining doctors' joint written report and oral testimony from them and from a deaf-school interpreter through whom they had attempted to communicate with petitioner. The report concluded that Jackson's almost nonexistent communication skill, together with his lack of hearing and his mental deficiency, left him unable to understand the nature of the charges against him or to participate in his defense. One doctor testified that it was extremely unlikely that petitioner could ever learn to read or write and questioned whether petitioner even had the ability to develop any proficiency in sign language. He believed that the interpreter had not been able to communicate with petitioner to any great extent and testified that petitioner's "prognosis appears rather dim." The other doctor testified that even if Jackson were not a deaf mute, he would be incompetent to stand trial, and doubted whether petitioner had sufficient intelligence ever to develop the necessary communication skills. The interpreter testified that Indiana had no facilities that could help someone as badly off as Jackson to learn minimal communication skills.

On this evidence, the trial court found that Jackson "lack[ed] comprehension sufficient to make his defense," and ordered him committed to the Indiana Department of Mental Health until such time as that Department should certify to the court that "the defendant is sane."

Petitioner's counsel then filed a motion for a new trial, contending that there was no evidence that Jackson was "insane," or that he would ever attain a status which the court might regard as "sane" in the sense of competency to stand trial. Counsel argued that Jackson's commitment under these circumstances amounted to a "life sentence" without his ever having been convicted of a crime, and that the commitment therefore deprived Jackson of his Fourteenth Amendment rights to due process and equal protection, and constituted cruel and unusual punishment under the Eighth Amendment made applicable to the States through the Fourteenth. The trial court denied the motion. On appeal the Supreme Court of Indiana affirmed, with one judge dissenting. Rehearing was denied with two judges dissenting. We granted certiorari.

For the reasons set forth below, we conclude that, on the record before us, Indiana cannot constitutionally commit the petitioner for an indefinite period simply on account of his incompetency to stand trial on the charges filed against him. Accordingly, we reverse.

* * *

Petitioner's central contention is that the State, in seeking in effect to commit him to a mental institution indefinitely, should have been required to invoke the standards and procedures of Ind.Ann. Stat. § 22–1907, now Ind.Code 16–15–1–3 (1971), governing commitment of "feeble-minded" persons. That section provides that upon application of a "reputable citizen of the county" and accompanying certificate of a reputable physician that a person is "feeble-minded and is *not insane* or epileptic" (emphasis supplied), a circuit court judge shall appoint two physicians to examine such person. After notice, a hearing is held at which the patient is entitled to be represented by counsel. If the judge determines that the individual is indeed "feeble-minded," he enters an order of commitment and directs the clerk of the court to apply for the person's admission "to the superintendent of the institution for feeble-minded persons located in the district in which said county is situated." A person committed under this section may be released "at any time," provided that "in the judgment of the superintendent, the mental and physical condition of the patient justifies it." The statutes do not define either "feeble-mindedness" or "insanity". But a statute establishing a special institution for care of such persons refers to the duty of the State to provide care for its citizens who are "feeble-minded, and are therefore unable properly to care for themselves." These provisions evidently afford the State a vehicle for commitment of persons in need of custodial care who are "not insane" and therefore do not qualify as "mentally ill" under the State's general involuntary civil commitment scheme.

* * *

Scant attention was paid this general civil commitment law by the Indiana courts in the present case. An understanding of it, however, is essential to a full airing of the equal protection claims raised by petitioner.   Section 22–1201(1) defines a "mentally ill person" as one who

> "is afflicted with a psychiatric disorder which substantially impairs his mental health; and, because of such psychiatric disorder, requires care, treatment, training or detenion in the interest of the welfare of such person or the welfare of others of the community in which such person resides."

Because the evidence established little likelihood of improvement in petitioner's condition, he argues that commitment under § 9–1706a in his case amounted to a commitment for life.   This deprived him of equal protection, he contends, because, absent the criminal charges pending against him, the State would have had to proceed under other statutes generally applicable to all other citizens: either the commitment procedures for feeble-minded persons, or those for mentally ill persons.   He argues that under these other statutes (1) the decision whether to commit would have been made according to a different standard, (2) if commitment were warranted, applicable standards for release would have been more lenient, (3) if committed under § 22–1907, he could have been assigned to a special institution affording appropriate care, and (4) he would then have been entitled to certain privileges not now available to him.

* * *

In Baxstrom v. Herold, 383 U.S. 107, 86 S.Ct. 760 (1966), the Court held that a state prisoner civilly committed at the end of his prison sentence on the finding of a surrogate was denied equal protection when he was deprived of a jury trial that the State made generally available to all other persons civilly committed.   Rejecting the State's argument that Baxstrom's conviction and sentence constituted adequate justification for the difference in procedures, the Court said that "there is no conceivable basis for distinguishing the commitment of a person who is nearing the end of a penal term from all other civil commitments."   383 U.S., at 111–112, 86 S.Ct., at 763; see United States ex rel. Schuster v. Herold, 410 F.2d 1071 (CA2), cert. denied, 396 U.S. 847, 90 S.Ct. 81 (1969).   The Court also held that Baxstrom was denied equal protection by commitment to an institution maintained by the state corrections department for "dangerously mentally ill" persons, without a judicial determination of his "dangerous propensities" afforded all others so committed.

If criminal conviction and imposition of sentence are insufficient to justify less procedural and substantive protection against indefinite commitment than that generally available to all others, the mere filing of criminal charges surely cannot suffice.   This was the precise holding of the Massachusetts Court in Commonwealth v. Druken, 356 Mass. 503, 507, 254 N.E.2d 779, 781 (1969).   The *Baxstrom* principle also has been extended to commitment following an insanity acquittal, Bolton v. Harris, 130 U.S.App.D.C. 1, 395 F.2d 642 (1968);   Cameron v. Mullen, 128 U.S.App.D.C. 235, 387 F.2d 193 (1967);   People v. Lally, 19 N.Y.2d 27, 277 N.Y.S.2d 654, 224 N.E.2d 87 (1966), and to commitment in lieu of sentence following conviction as a sex offender. Humphrey v. Cady, 405 U.S. 504, 92 S.Ct. 1048 (1972).

Respondent argues, however, that because the record fails to establish affirmatively that Jackson will never improve, his commitment "until sane" is not really an indeterminate one. It is only temporary, pending possible change in his condition. Thus, presumably, it cannot be judged against commitments under other state statutes that are truly indeterminate. The State relies on the lack of "exactitude" with which psychiatry can predict the future course of mental illness, and on the Court's decision in what is claimed to be "a fact situation similar to the case at hand" in Greenwood v. United States, 350 U.S. 366, 76 S.Ct. 410 (1956).

Were the State's factual premise that Jackson's commitment is only temporary a valid one, this might well be a different case. But the record does not support that premise. One of the doctors testified that in his view Jackson would be unable to acquire the substantially improved communication skills that would be necessary for him to participate in any defense. The prognosis for petitioner's developing such skills, he testified, appeared "rather dim." In answer to a question whether Jackson would ever be able to comprehend the charges or participate in his defense, even after commitment and treatment, the doctor said, "I doubt it, I don't believe so." The other psychiatrist testified that even if Jackson were able to develop such skills, he would *still* be unable to comprehend the proceedings or aid counsel due to his mental deficiency. The interpreter, a supervising teacher at the state school for the deaf, said that he would not be able to serve as an interpreter for Jackson or aid him in participating in a trial, and that the State had no facilities that could, "after a length of time," aid Jackson in so participating. The court also heard petitioner's mother testify that Jackson already had undergone rudimentary out-patient training communications skills from the deaf and dumb School in Indianapolis over a period of three years without noticeable success. There is nothing in the record that even points to any possibility that Jackson's present condition can be remedied at any future time.

We note also that neither the Indiana statute nor state practice makes the likelihood of the defendant's improvement a relevant factor. The State did not seek to make any such showing, and the record clearly establishes that the chances of Jackson's ever meeting the competency standards of § 9–1706a are at best minimal, if not nonexistent. The record also rebuts any contention that the commitment could contribute to Jackson's improvement. Jackson's § 9–1706a commitment is permanent in practical effect.

We therefore must turn to the question whether, because of the pendency of the criminal charges that triggered the State's invocation of § 9–1706a, Jackson was deprived of substantial rights to which he would have been entitled under either of the other two state commitment statutes. *Baxstrom* held that the State cannot withhold from a few the procedural protections or the substantive requirements for commitment that are available to all others. In this case commitment procedures under all three statutes appear substantially similar: notice, examination by two doctors, and a full judicial hearing at which the individual is represented by counsel and can cross-examine witnesses and introduce evidence. Under each of the three statutes, the commitment determination is made by the court alone, and appellate review is available.

In contrast, however, what the State must show to commit a defendant under § 9–1706a, and the circumstances under which an individual so committed may be released, are substantially different from the standards under the other two statutes.

Under § 9–1706a, the State needed to show only Jackson's inability to stand trial. We are unable to say that, on the record before us, Indiana could have civilly committed him as mentally ill under § 22–1209 or committed him as feeble-minded under § 22–1907. The former requires at least (1) a showing of mental illness and (2) a showing that the individual is in need of "care, treatment, training or detention." § 22–1201(1). Whether Jackson's mental deficiency would meet the first test is unclear; neither examining physician addressed himself to this. Furthermore, it is problematical whether commitment for "treatment" or "training" would be appropriate since the record establishes that none is available for Jackson's condition at any state institution. The record also fails to establish that Jackson is in need of custodial care or "detention." He has been employed at times, and there is no evidence that the care he long received at home has become inadequate. The statute appears to require an independent showing of dangerousness ("requires . . . detention in the interest of the welfare of such person or . . . others . . ."). Insofar as it may require such a showing, the pending criminal charges are insufficient to establish it, and no other supporting evidence was introduced. For the same reasons, we cannot say that this record would support a feeble-mindedness commitment under § 22–1907 on the ground that Jackson is "unable properly to care for [himself]."[1] § 22–1801.

More important, an individual committed as feeble-minded is eligible for release when his condition "justifies it," § 22–1814, and an individual civilly committed as mentally ill when the "superintendent or administrator shall discharge such person *or* [when] cured of such illness." § 22–1223 (emphasis supplied). Thus, in either case release is appropriate when the individual no longer requires the custodial care or treatment or detention that occasioned the commitment, or when the department of mental health believes release would be in

---

1. Perhaps some confusion on this point is engendered by the fact that Jackson's counsel, far from asserting that the State could *not* commit him as feeble-minded under § 22–1907, actively sought such a commitment in the hope that Jackson would be assured assignment to a special institution. The Indiana Supreme Court thought this concern unnecessary. In any event, we do not suggest that a feeble-mindedness commitment would be inappropriate. We not only that there is nothing in *this* record to establish the need for custodial care that such a commitment seems to require under §§ 22–1907 and 22–1801.

his best interests. The evidence available concerning Jackson's past employment and home care strongly suggests that under these standards he might be eligible for release at almost any time, even if he did not improve. On the other hand, by the terms of his present § 9–1706a commitment, he will not be entitled to release at all, absent an unlikely substantial change for the better in his condition.[2]

Baxstrom did not deal with the standard for release, but its rationale is applicable here. The harm to the individual is just as great if the State, without reasonable justification, can apply standards making his commitment a permanent one when standards generally applicable to all others afford him a substantial opportunity for early release.

As we noted above, we cannot conclude that pending criminal charges provide a greater justification for different treatment than conviction and sentence. Consequently, we hold that by subjecting Jackson to a more lenient commitment standard and to a more stringent standard of release than those generally applicable to all others not charged with offenses, and by thus condemning him in effect to permanent institutionalization without the showing required for commitment or the opportunity for release afforded by § 22–1209 or § 22–1907, Indiana deprived petitioner of equal protection of the laws under the Fourteenth Amendment.

For reasons closely related to those discussed in Part II above, we also hold that Indiana's indefinite commitment of a criminal defendant solely on account of his incompetency to stand trial does not square with the Fourteenth Amendment's guarantee of due process.

A. *The Federal System.* In the federal criminal system, the constitutional issue posed here has not been encountered precisely because the federal statutes have been construed to require that a mentally incompetent defendant must also be found "dangerous" before he can be committed indefinitely. But the decisions have uniformly articulated the constitutional problems compelling this statutory interpretation.

The federal statute, 18 U.S.C. §§ 4244 to 4246, is not dissimilar to the Indiana law. It provides that a defendant found incompetent to stand trial may be committed "until the accused shall be mentally competent to stand trial or until the pending charges against him are disposed of according to law." § 4246. Section 4247, applicable on its face only to convicted criminals whose federal sentences are about

---

2. Respondent argues that Jackson would not in fact be eligible for release under § 22–1907 or § 22–1223 if he did not improve since, if the authorities could not communicate with him, they could not decide whether his condition "justified" release. Respondent further argues that because no state court has ever construed the release provisions of any of the statutes, we are barred from relying upon any differences between them. **This line of reasoning is unpersua-**sive. The plain language of the provisions, when applied to Jackson's particular history and condition, dictates different results. No state court has held that an Indiana defendant committed as incompetent is eligible for release when he no longer needs custodial care or treatment. The commitment order here clearly makes release dependent upon Jackson's regaining competency to stand trial.

to expire, permits commitment if the prisoner is (1) "insane or mentally incompetent" and (2) "will probably endanger the safety of the officers, the property, or other interests of the United States, and . . . suitable arrangements for the custody and care of the prisoner are not otherwise available," that is, in a state facility. See Greenwood v. United States, 350 U.S., at 373–374, 76 S.Ct., at 414–415. One committed under this section, however, is entitled to release when any of the three conditions no longer obtains, "whichever event shall first occur." § 4248. Thus, a person committed under § 4247 must be released when he no longer is "dangerous."

In *Greenwood*, the Court upheld the pretrial commitment of a defendant who met all three conditions of § 4247, even though there was little likelihood that he would ever become competent to stand trial. Since Greenwood had not yet stood trial, his commitment was ostensibly under § 4244. By the related release provision, § 4246, he could not have been released until he became competent. But the District Court had in fact applied § 4247, and found specifically that Greenwood would be dangerous if not committed. This Court approved that approach, holding § 4247 applicable before trial as well as to those about to be released from sentence. 350 U.S., at 374, 76 S.Ct., at 414. Accordingly, Greenwood was entitled to release when no longer dangerous, § 4248, even if he did not become competent to stand trial and thus did not meet the requirement of § 4246. Under these circumstances, the Court found the commitment constitutional.

Since *Greenwood*, federal courts without exception have found improper any straightforward application of §§ 4244 and 4246 to a defendant whose chance of attaining competency to stand trial is slim, thus effecting an indefinite commitment on the ground of incompetency alone. The holding in each of these cases was grounded in an expressed substantial doubt that §§ 4244 and 4246 could survive constitutional scrutiny if interpreted to authorize indefinite commitment.

These decisions have imposed a "rule of reasonableness" upon §§ 4244 and 4246. Without a finding of dangerousness, one committed thereunder can be held only for a "reasonable period of time" necessary to determine whether there is a substantial chance of his attaining the capacity to stand trial in the foreseeable future. If the chances are slight, or if the defendant does not in fact improve, then he must be released or granted a §§ 4247–4248 hearing.

B. *The States.* Some States appear to commit indefinitely a defendant found incompetent to stand trial until he recovers competency. Other States require a finding of dangerousness to support such a commitment or provide forms of parole. New York has recently enacted legislation mandating release of incompetent defendants charged with misdemeanors after 90 days of commitment, and release and dismissal of charges against those accused of felonies after they have been committed for two-thirds of the maximum potential prison sentence. The practice of automatic commitment with release conditioned solely upon attainment of competence has been decried on both policy and constitutional grounds. Recommendations for changes made by commentators and study committees have included incorporation into pretrial commitment procedures of the equivalent of the federal "rule of reason," a requirement of a finding of dangerousness or of full-scale civil commitment, periodic review by court or mental health administrative personnel of the defendant's condition and progress, and provisions for ultimately dropping charges if the defendant does not improve. One source of this criticism is undoubtedly the empirical data available which tend to show that many defendants committed before trial are never tried, and that those defendants committed pursuant to ordinary civil proceedings are, on the average, released sooner than defendants automatically committed solely on account of their incapacity to stand trial.[3] Related to these statistics are substantial doubts about whether the rationale for pretrial commitment––that care or treatment will aid the accused in attaining competency—is empirically valid given the state of most of our mental institutions.[4] However, very few courts appear to have addressed the problem directly in the state context.

In United States ex rel. Wolfersdorf v. Johnston, 317 F.Supp. 66 (S.D.N.Y.1970), an 86-year-old defendant committed for nearly 20 years as incompetent to stand trial on state murder and kidnapping charges applied for federal habeas corpus. He had been found "not dangerous," and suitable for civil commitment. The District Court granted relief. It held that petitioner's incarceration in an institution for the criminally insane constituted cruel and unusual punishment, and that the "shocking circumstances" of his commitment violated the Due Process Clause. The court quoted approvingly the language of Cook v. Ciccone, 312 F.Supp., at 824, concerning the "substantial injustice in keeping an unconvicted person in . . . custody to await trial where it is plainly evident his mental condition will not permit trial within a reasonable period of time."

In a 1970 case virtually indistinguishable from the one before us, the Illinois Supreme Court granted relief to an illiterate deaf mute who had been indicted for murder four years previously but found incompetent to stand trial on account of his inability to communicate, and committed. People ex rel. Myers v. Briggs, 46 Ill.2d 281, 263 N. E.2d 109 (1970). The institution where petitioner was confined had determined, "[I]t now appears that [petitioner] will never acquire the necessary communication skills needed to participate and cooperate in his trial." Petitioner, however, was found to be functioning at a "nearly normal level of performance in areas other than communication." The State contended petitioner should not be released until

---

3. See Matthews, Mental Disability and the Criminal Law 138–140 (American Bar Foundation 1970); Morris, The Confusion of Confinement Syndrome: An Analysis of the Confinement of Mentally Ill Criminals and Ex-Criminals by the Department of Correction of the State of New York, 17 Buffalo L.Rev. 651 (1968); McGarry & Bendt, Criminal vs. Civil Commitment of Psychotic Offenders: A Seven-Year Follow-Up, 125 Am.J. Psychiatry 1387, 1391 (1969); D.C.Report 50–52.

4. Note, supra, 81 Harv.L.Rev., at 472–473; American Bar Foundation, The Mentally Disabled and the Law 415–418 (rev.ed.1971) (hereafter ABF Study); N.Y.Report 72–77, 102–105, 186–190.

his competency was restored. The Illinois Supreme Court disagreed. It held:

> "This court is of the opinion that this defendant, handicapped as he is and facing an indefinite commitment because of the pending indictment against him, should be given an opportunity to obtain a trial to determine whether or not he is guilty as charged or should be released."

C. *This Case.* Respondent relies heavily on *Greenwood* to support Jackson's commitment. That decision is distinguishable. It upheld only the initial commitment without considering directly its duration or the standards for release. It justified the commitment by treating it as if accomplished under allied statutory provisions relating directly to the individual's "insanity" and society's interest in his indefinite commitment, factors not considered in Jackson's case. And it sustained commitment only upon the finding of dangerousness. As Part A, *supra,* shows, all these elements subsequently have been held not simply sufficient, but necessary, to sustain a commitment like the one involved here.

The States have traditionally exercised broad power to commit persons found to be mentally ill. The substantive limitations on the exercise of this power and the procedures for invoking it vary drastically among the States. The particular fashion in which the power is exercised—for instance, through various forms of civil commitment, defective delinquency laws, sexual psychopath laws, commitment of persons acquitted by reason of insanity—reflects different combinations of distinct bases for commitment sought to be vindicated. The bases that have been articulated include dangerousness to self, dangerousness to others, and the need for care or treatment or training. Considering the number of persons affected, it is perhaps remarkable that the substantive constitutional limitations on this power have not been more frequently litigated.

We need not address these broad questions here. It is clear that Jackson's commitment rests on proceedings that did not purport to bring into play, indeed did not even consider relevant, *any* of the articulated bases for exercise of Indiana's power of indefinite commitment. The state statutes contain at least two alternative methods for invoking this power. But Jackson was not afforded any "formal commitment proceedings addressed to [his] ability to function in society," or to society's interest in his restraint, or to the State's ability to aid him in attaining competency through custodial care or compulsory treatment, the ostensible purpose of the commitment. At the least, due process requires that the nature and duration of commitment bear some reasonable relation to the purpose for which the individual is committed.

We hold, consequently, that a person charged by a State with a criminal offense who is committed solely on account of his incapacity to proceed to trial cannot be held more than the reasonable period of time necessary to determine whether there is a substantial probability that he will attain that capacity in the foreseeable future. If it is determined that this is not the case, then the State must either institute the customary civil commitment proceeding that would be required to commit indefinitely any other citizen, or release the defendant. Furthermore, even if it is determined that the defendant probably soon will be able to stand trial, his continued commitment must be justified by progress toward that goal. In light of differing state facilities and procedures and a lack of evidence in this record, we do not think it appropriate for us to attempt to prescribe arbitrary time limits. We note, however, that petitioner Jackson has now been confined for three and one-half years on a record that sufficiently establishes the lack of a substantial probability that he will ever be able to participate fully in a trial.

These conclusions make it unnecessary for us to reach petitioner's Eighth-Fourteenth Amendment claim.

Petitioner also urges that fundamental fairness requires that the charges against him now be dismissed. The thrust of his argument is that the record amply establishes his lack of criminal responsibility at the time the crimes are alleged to have been committed. The Indiana court did not discuss this question. Apparently it believed that by reason of Jackson's incompetency commitment the State was entitled to hold the charges pending indefinitely. On this record, Jackson's claim is a substantial one. For a number of reasons, however, we believe the issue is not sufficiently ripe for ultimate decision by us at this time.

DISPOSITION OF THE CHARGES

A. Petitioner argues that he has already made out a complete insanity defense. Jackson's criminal responsibility at the time of the alleged offenses, however, is a distinct issue from his competency to stand trial. The competency hearing below was not directed to criminal responsibility, and evidence relevant to it was presented only incidentally. Thus, in any event, we would have to remand for further consideration of Jackson's condition in the light of Indiana's law of criminal responsibility.

B. Dismissal of charges against an incompetent accused has usually been thought to be justified on grounds not squarely presented here: particularly, the Sixth-Fourteenth Amendment right to a speedy trial, or the denial of due process inherent in holding pending criminal charges indefinitely over the head of one who will never have a chance to prove his innocence. Jackson did not present the Sixth-Fourteenth Amendment issue to the state courts. Nor did the highest state court rule on the due process issue, if indeed it was presented to that court in precisely the above-described form. We think, in light of our holdings in Parts II and III, that the Indiana courts should have the first opportunity to determine these issues.

C. Both courts and commentators have noted the desirability of permitting some proceedings to go forward despite the defendant's incompetency.[5]   For instance, § 4.06(3) of the Model Penal Code would permit an incompetent accused's attorney to contest any issue "susceptible of fair determination prior to trial and without the personal participation of the defendant."   An alternative draft of § 4.-06(4) of the Model Penal Code would also permit an evidentiary hearing at which certain defenses, not including lack of criminal responsibility, could be raised by defense counsel on the basis of which the court might quash the indictment.   Some States have statutory provisions permitting pretrial motions to be made or even allowing the incompetent defendant a trial at which to establish his innocence, without permitting a conviction.[6]   We do not read this Court's previous decisions to preclude the States from allowing, at a minimum, an incompetent defendant to raise certain defenses such as insufficiency of the indictment, or make certain pretrial motions through counsel.   Of course, if the Indiana courts conclude that Jackson was almost certainly not capable of criminal responsibility when the offenses were committed, dismissal of the charges might be warranted. But even if this is not the case, Jackson may have other good defenses that could sustain dismissal or acquittal and that might now be asserted.   We do not know if Indiana would approve procedures such as those mentioned here, but these possibilities will be open on remand.

Reversed and remanded.

MR. JUSTICE POWELL and MR. JUSTICE REHNQUIST took no part in the consideration or decision of this case.

NOTES

1.   If an accused who is found incompetent to stand trial is committed under a state's civil commitment statutes, the narrow holding of Jackson v. Indiana has no impact.   The defendant can be kept in custody on the same basis as any other civilly committed person.   Problems may arise when the defendant is treated differently from other civilly committed persons.   For example, the mental health authorities may, at some point, believe that a home-visit or a furlough is in the best interest of their patient.   Should such furloughs be denied to patients who have murder or rape charges pending, on which they have been adjudicated incompetent to stand trial? The rights of the "mittimus patient" (one who has pending criminal charges) are often the subject of a classical institutional conflict between the mental health authorities, with paramount concern for their patient, and prosecutors, with an obligation to protect the public.   Few things are as likely to generate public concern as an act of violence by an accused killer during a home-visit following a determination of incompetence to stand trial.

5. People ex rel. Myers v. Briggs, supra, 46 Ill.2d, at 288, 263 N.E.2d, at 113; Neely v. Hogan, 62 Misc.2d 1056, 310 N.Y.S.2d 63 (1970); N.Y.Report 115–123 (Recommendation No. 13); D.C. Report 143–144 (Recommendation No. 15); Foote, supra, n. 14, at 841–845; Model Penal Code § 4.06 (alternative subsections 3, 4) (Proposed Official Draft 1962); ABF **Study 423.**

6. Wis.Stat.Ann. § 971.14(6) (1971); N.Y.Crim.Proc.Law § 730.60(5) (1971); Mass.Gen.Laws, c. 123, § 17 (Supp. 1972); Mont.Rev.Code Ann. § 95–506(c) (1969); Md.Ann.Code, Art. 59, § 24(a) (1972). See Reg. v. Roberts, [1953] 3 W.L.R. 178, [1953] 2 All.E.R. 340 (Devlin, J.).

2. If the incompetent defendant is civilly committed, the holding of *Jackson* does not mandate the dismissal of charges. Even if the accused is not civilly committed, as long as he is not in custody, *Jackson* does not mandate the dropping of charges against a permanently incompetent accused. Consider, for example, a defendant on bond who suffers a permanent physical disability which renders him incompetent to stand trial. Can charges against him remain until his death, or does the right of a speedy trial at some point mandate dismissal of charges even though the state is not to be blamed for denying the accused a speedy trial? Some states mandate the termination of criminal proceedings once an incompetent accused has been in custody longer than the maximum period to which he could have been sentenced if found guilty. See Ill.Rev.Stat. ch 38, § 1005–2–2 (1977). Such a provision benefits neither an incompetent defendant who is on bond nor one charged with a crime for which either life or any number of years is a possible sentence.

3. How long may an accused be held in custody by virtue of a finding of incompetency if he is not civilly committed? See State ex rel. Matalik v. Schubert, 57 Wis.2d 315, 204 N.W.2d 13 (1973) (suggesting a six month limitation); In re Harmon, 425 F.2d 916 (1st Cir. 1970); United States v. Jackson, 306 F.Supp. 4 (N.D.Cal.1969); State ex rel. Haskins v. County Court, 62 Wis.2d 250, 214 N.W.2d 575 (1974).

Let us suppose that if it appears that a defendant may regain competency, he can be held in custody a maximum of one year by virtue of (a) an unproved criminal charge, (b) a finding of incompetency, and (c) the possibility that within a year he will gain competency. Let us further suppose that a court in our jurisdiction has declared that such a person must be released from custody at the end of one year unless he is civilly committed. Further suppose that the legislature then enacts a statutory procedure which permits the accused to advance "defenses" to the crime which, if successful, will result in his discharge on the criminal charge even though he has never been in jeopardy of a finding of guilty. (The *Jackson* Court noted that such "innocent only" trials are provided for incompetent defendants in a few jurisdictions.) Would the possibility of discharge on the indictment through an "innocent only" trial lengthen the period for which the state can hold the incompetent accused if such an accused is unsuccessful in winning discharge at his innocent only trial? In other words if the accused is afforded such a procedure and the government has proved the likelihood of conviction, is there now justification for holding the accused for longer than one year to see if he will regain competency to stand trial at a regular trial in which he would be in jeopardy of conviction? The Illinois legislature apparently believes so. As this book went to press, it enacted a law which provides for an "innocent only" trial but allows a person who is found "not innocent" of murder to be held for as long as five years in an effort to make him competent. See Ill.Rev.Stat. ch. 38, § 104–25 (1979), (1980 Supp.)

4. The most difficult dilemma is posed by persons who are neither competent to stand trial nor civilly committable. If state law provides for commitment of those who, because of a mental disease, are dangerous to themselves or others, some incompetent defendants may escape commitment because they have no mental disease, even though dangerous, or because their dangerousness cannot be proved. What happens to such persons after the outer limits of *Jackson* are reached? Must such persons be returned to society without ever standing trial?

In many jurisdictions the category of persons who are neither competent nor civilly committable, but nevertheless are thought dangerous by the public, is not small. Donald Lang, a deaf mute mentioned in *Jackson,* falls into that category. Although the origin of his incompetency is atypical, the problems illustrated by his case are not atypical of problems posed by persons who are neither competent nor civilly committable. Lang was accused of murdering an alleged prostitute. Because of his inability to communicate, he was found incompetent to stand trial. For many years (before *Jackson*) he was held in custody in a facility for the criminally insane. Then (before *Drope*) the Supreme Court of Illinois, on defense counsel's motion, ordered that he be tried despite his incompetency. By then, however, essential prosecution witnesses were missing and the charges were dropped. Lang was released. Within a year Lang was charged with the recent murder of a second alleged prostitute. The trial judge, believing that Lang must be tried, whether competent or not, according to the prior Illinois Supreme Court case, ordered a trial. Lang was convicted of murder on proof that was largely circumstantial. The Appellate Court reversed because the trial judge had not held a competency hearing. On remand the defendant was found to be incompetent. He was also found not to be within the civil mental commitment statute, thus creating the "limbo" status that poses the great dilemma. Should he be released without trial? The story of Donald Lang is told in a book entitled *Dummy* by Ernest Tidyman. The problem his situation has posed to the Illinois courts is updated in the latest opinion, People v. Lang, 76 Ill.2d 311, 29 Ill.Dec. 87, 391 N.E.2d 350 (1979).

5. Does the discussion of federal practice in *Jackson* suggest that a defendant can be held permanently upon a finding of incompetency and a "special finding of dangerousness"? Under this system, although a state has no general provision for locking up citizens on the grounds of "dangerousness," a citizen who was charged with a crime and found incompetent could be held if found to be dangerous. Would this approach violate equal protection? The Illinois Supreme Court although indirectly, seems to have approved such an approach in its most recent decision in *Lang*, note 4. There the court found that a defendant who has been found unfit to stand trial (for any reason other than a purely physical one) is, by that very fact, mentally ill for the purposes of the Illinois civil commitment statute. To subject such a person to the civil commitment statute the government need only show that because of his condition the person is a danger to himself or another. In other words, incompetency to stand trial plus dangerousness can justify commitment even though the accused does not have a "mental disease" as psychiatrists might define that term.

6. It is difficult to generalize about the fate of persons who are neither competent nor civilly committable. Some probably have been released on bond, perhaps subject to the requirement of treatment designed to make them competent. Others have been shuttled between the mental health system and the correctional system without obtaining their freedom. Once found incompetent, they are given a civil commitment hearing. Once found not committable, they are given another competency hearing. Should courts reinterpret civil commitment standards to make it easier to civilly commit persons who are incompetent?

7. Should we consider the possibility of trying the permanently incompetent accused, affording him whatever special procedures may be available in an effort to remedy disadvantages which flow from incompetency? Such a solution was proposed in Burt & Morris, A Proposal for the Abolition of the Incompetency Plea, 40 U.Chi.L.Rev. 66 (1972). This proposal is

different from the "innocent only" procedure which, according to *Jackson*, is used in some states. (See note 4, supra.) Under the Morris-Burt proposal the result of a trial of the incompetent accused could be a finding of guilty. The proponents of the approach, however, would make it easier to vacate such a conviction based upon newly discovered evidence than is normally possible in criminal cases. In light of the subsequent *Drope* decision, must we conclude that such a scheme would be unconstitutional?

8. Consider the prosecutor's problem where a defendant is found incompetent to stand trial. Is there any way a prosecutor can preserve the testimony of witnesses who may not be available to testify when the defendant many years later is found competent to stand trial? If a defendant is not competent to participate in his own trial, can evidence depositions be taken at a time when he is incompetent? If legal representation is not sufficient to permit an incompetent defendant to be tried, would the defendant's lawyers presence and participation at depositions be adequate?

9. Another kind of permanent incompetency—at least some would argue—occurs in the case of an accused who suffers permanent retrograde amnesia as a result of which he has no recollection of the time period or events alleged in the indictments. Wilson v. United States, 391 F.2d 460 (D.C.Cir. 1968), is among the leading decisions confronting this problem. There Judge Wright set forth six factors for the trial court to consider in determining whether such a person is presently able to consult with counsel and to understand the charges so to be able to obtain a fair trial:

(1) The extent to which the amnesia affected the defendant's ability to consult with and assist his lawyer.

(2) The extent to which the amnesia affected the defendant's ability to testify in his own behalf.

(3) The extent to which the evidence in suit could be extrinsically reconstructed in view of the defendant's amnesia. Such evidence would include evidence relating to the crime itself as well as any reasonably possible alibi.

(4) The extent to which the Government assisted the defendant and his counsel in that reconstruction.

(5) The strength of the prosecution's case. Most important here will be whether the Government's case is such as to negate all reasonable hypotheses of innocence. If there is any substantial possibility that the accused could, but for his amnesia, establish an alibi or other defense, it should be presumed that he would have been able to do so.

(6) Any other facts and circumstances which would indicate whether or not the defendant had a fair trial.

Under Wright's opinion, charges must be dismissed if the unfairness of trying the amnesiac defendant cannot be overcome.

More recent decisions include Thompson v. State, 364 So.2d 683 (Ala. App.1978); United States v. Swanson, 572 F.2d 523 (5th Cir. 1978); Commonwealth v. Barky, 383 A.2d 526 (Pa.1978). See also Commonwealth v. Lombardi, —— Mass. ——, 393 N.E.2d 346 (1979).

Chapter 15

DISCLOSURE AND DISCOVERY

A. THE PROSECUTION'S CONSTITUTIONAL OBLIGATION TO DISCLOSE

UNITED STATES v. AGURS

Supreme Court of the United States, 1976.
427 U.S. 97, 96 S.Ct. 2392.

MR. JUSTICE STEVENS delivered the opinion of the Court.

After a brief interlude in an inexpensive motel room, respondent repeatedly stabbed James Sewell, causing his death. She was convicted of second-degree murder. The question before us is whether the prosecutor's failure to provide defense counsel with certain background information about Sewell, which would have tended to support the argument that respondent acted in self-defense, deprived her of a fair trial under the rule of Brady v. Maryland, 373 U.S. 83, 83 S.Ct. 1194 [1962].

The answer to the question depends on (1) a review of the facts, (2) the significance of the failure of defense counsel to request the material, and (3) the standard by which the prosecution's failure to volunteer exculpatory material should be judged.

I.

At about 4:30 p. m. on September 24, 1971, respondent, who had been there before, and Sewell, registered in a motel as man and wife. They were assigned a room without a bath. Sewell was wearing a bowie knife in a sheath, and carried another knife in his pocket. Less than two hours earlier, according to the testimony of his estranged wife, he had had $360 in cash on his person.

About 15 minutes later three motel employees heard respondent screaming for help. A forced entry into their room disclosed Sewell on top of respondent struggling for possession of the bowie knife. She was holding the knife; his bleeding hand grasped the blade; according to one witness he was trying to jam the blade into her chest. The employees separated the two and summoned the authorities. Respondent departed without comment before they arrived. Sewell was dead on arrival at the hospital. Circumstantial evidence indicated that the parties had completed an act of intercourse, that Sewell had then gone to the bathroom down the hall, and that the struggle occurred upon his return. The contents of his pockets were in disarray on the dresser and no money was found; the jury may have inferred that respondent took Sewell's money and that the fight started when Sewell re-entered the room and saw what she was doing.

On the following morning respondent surrendered to the police. She was given a physical examination which revealed no cuts or bruises of any kind, except needle marks on her upper arm. An autopsy of Sewell disclosed that he had several deep stab wounds in his chest and abdomen, and a number of slashes on his arms and hands, characterized by the pathologist as "defensive wounds."

Respondent offered no evidence. Her sole defense was the argument made by her attorney that Sewell had initially attacked her with the knife, and that her actions had all been directed toward saving her own life. The support for this self-defense theory was based on the fact that she had screamed for help. Sewell was on top of her when help arrived, and his possession of two knives indicated that he was a violence-prone person. It took the jury about 25 minutes to elect a foreman and return a verdict.

Three months later defense counsel filed a motion for a new trial asserting that he had discovered (1) that Sewell had a prior criminal record that would have further evidenced his violent character; (2) that the prosecutor had failed to disclose this information to the defense; and (3) that a recent opinion of the United States Court of Appeals for the District of Columbia Circuit made it clear that such evidence was admissible even if not known to the defendant. Sewell's prior record included a plea of guilty to a charge of assault and carrying a deadly weapon in 1963, and another guilty plea to a charge of carrying a deadly weapon in 1971. Apparently both weapons were knives.

The Government opposed the motion, arguing that there was no duty to tender Sewell's prior record to the defense in the absence of an appropriate request; that the evidence was readily discoverable in advance of trial and hence was not the kind of "newly discovered" evidence justifying a new trial; and that, in all events, it was not material.

The District Court denied the motion. .   .   .

The Court of Appeals reversed. The court found no lack of diligence on the part of the defense and no misconduct by the prosecutor in this case. It held, however, that the evidence was material, and that its nondisclosure required a new trial because the jury might have returned a different verdict if the evidence had been received.

The decision of the Court of Appeals represents a significant departure from this Court's prior holding; because we believe that that court has incorrectly interpreted the constitutional requirement of due process, we reverse.

II.

The rule of Brady v. Maryland arguably applies in three quite different situations. Each involves the discovery, after trial of information which had been known to the prosecution but unknown to the defense.

In the first situation, typified by Mooney v. Holohan, 294 U.S. 103, 55 S.Ct. 340, the undisclosed evidence demonstrates that the prosecution's case includes perjured testimony and that the prosecution knew, or should have known, of the perjury. In a series of subsequent cases, the Court has consistently held that a conviction obtained by the knowing use of perjured testimony is fundamentally unfair, and must be set aside if there is any reasonable likelihood that the false testimony could have affected the judgment of the jury. It is this line of cases on which the Court of Appeals placed primary reliance. In those cases the Court has applied a strict standard of materiality, not just because they involve prosecutorial misconduct, but more importantly because they involve a corruption of the truth-seeking function of the trial process. Since this case involves no misconduct, and since there is no reason to question the veracity of any of the prosecution witnesses, the test of materiality followed in the *Mooney* line of cases is not necessarily applicable to this case.

The second situation, illustrated by the *Brady* case itself, is characterized by a pretrial request for specific evidence. In that case defense counsel had requested the extrajudicial statements made by Brady's accomplice, one Boblit. This Court held that the suppression of one of Boblit's statements deprived Brady of due process, noting specifically that the statement had been requested and that it was "material." A fair analysis of the holding in *Brady* indicates that implicit in the requirement of materiality is a concern that the suppressed evidence might have affected the outcome of the trial.

Brady was found guilty of murder in the first degree. Since the jury did not add the words "without capital punishment" to the verdict, he was sentenced to death. At his trial Brady did not deny his involvement in the deliberate killing, but testified that it was his accomplice, Boblit, rather than he, who had actually strangled the decedent. This version of the event was corroborated by one of several confessions made by Boblit but not given to Brady's counsel despite an admittedly adequate request.

After his conviction and sentence had been affirmed on appeal, Brady filed a motion to set aside the judgment, and later a post-conviction proceeding, in which he alleged that the State had violated his constitutional rights by suppressing the Boblit confession. The trial judge denied relief largely because he felt that Boblit's confession would have been inadmissible at Brady's trial. The Maryland Court of Appeals disagreed; it ordered a new trial on the issue of punishment. It held that the withholding of material evidence, even "without guile," was a denial of due process and that there were valid theories on which the confession might have been admissible in Brady's defense.

This Court granted certiorari to consider Brady's contention that the violation of his constitutional right to a fair trial vitiated the entire proceeding. The holding that the suppression of exculpatory evidence violated Brady's right to due process was affirmed, as was the separate holding that he should receive a new trial on the issue of punishment but not on the issue of guilt or innocence. The Court interpreted the Maryland Court of Appeals opinion as ruling that the confession was inadmissible on that issue. For that reason, the confession could not have affected the outcome on the issue of guilt but could have affected Brady's punishment. It was material on the latter issue but not the former. And since it was not material on the issue of guilt, the entire trial was not lacking in due process.

The test of materiality in a case like *Brady* in which specific information has been requested by the defense is not necessarily the same as in a case in which no such request has been made. Indeed, this Court has not yet decided whether the prosecutor has any obligation to provide defense counsel with exculpatory information when no request has been made. Before addressing that question, a brief comment on the function of the request is appropriate.

In *Brady* the request was specific. It gave the prosecutor notice of exactly what the defense desired. Although there is, of course, no duty to provide defense counsel with unlimited discovery of everything known by the prosecutor, if the subject matter of such a request is material, or indeed if a substantial basis for claiming materiality exists, it is reasonable to require the prosecutor to respond either by furnishing the information or by submitting the problem to the trial judge. When the prosecutor receives a specific and relevant request, the failure to make any response is seldom, if ever, excusable.

In many cases, however, exculpatory information in the possession of the prosecutor may be unknown to defense counsel. In such a situation he may make no request at all, or possibly ask for "all *Brady* material" or for "anything exculpatory." Such a request really gives the prosecutor no better notice than if no request is made. If there is a duty to respond to a general request of that kind, it must derive from the obviously exculpatory character of certain evidence in the hands of the prosecutor. But if the evidence is so clearly supportive of a claim of innocence that it gives the prosecution notice of a duty to produce, that duty should equally arise even if no request is made. Whether we focus on the desirability of a precise definition of the prosecutor's duty or on the potential harm to the defendant, we conclude that there is no significant difference between cases in which there has been merely a general request for exculpatory matter and cases, like the one we must now decide, in which there has been no request at all. The third situation in which the *Brady* rule arguably applies, typified by this case, therefore embraces the case in which only a general request for "*Brady* material" has been made.

We now consider whether the prosecutor has any constitutional duty to volunteer exculpatory matter to the defense, and if so, what standard of materiality gives rise to that duty.

III.

We are not considering the scope of discovery authorized by the Federal Rules of Criminal Procedure, or the wisdom of amending those Rules to enlarge the defendant's discovery rights. We are dealing with the defendant's right to a fair trial mandated by the Due Process Clause of the Fifth Amendment to the Constitution. Our construction of that Clause will apply equally to the comparable Clause in the Fourteenth Amendment applicable to trials in state courts.

The problem arises in two principal contexts. First, in advance of trial, and perhaps during the course of a trial as well, the prosecutor must decide what, if anything, he should voluntarily submit to defense counsel. Second, after trial a judge may be required to decide whether a nondisclosure deprived the defendant of his right to due process. Logically the same standard must apply at both times. For unless the omission deprived the defendant of a fair trial, there was no constitutional violation requiring that the verdict be set aside; and absent a constitutional violation, there was no breach of the prosecutor's constitutional duty to disclose.

Nevertheless, there is a significant practical difference between the pretrial decision of the prosecutor and the post-trial decision of the judge. Because we are dealing with an inevitably imprecise standard, and because the significance of an item of evidence can seldom be predicted accurately until the entire record is complete, the prudent prosecutor will resolve doubtful questions in favor of disclosure. But to reiterate a critical point, the prosecutor will not have violated his constitutional duty of disclosure unless his omission is of sufficient significance to result in the denial of the defendant's right to a fair trial.

The Court of Appeals appears to have assumed that the prosecutor has a constitutional obligation to disclose any information that might affect the jury's verdict. That statement of a constitutional standard of materiality approaches the "sporting theory of justice" which the Court expressly rejected in *Brady*. For a jury's appraisal of a case "might" be affected by an improper or trivial consideration as well as by evidence giving rise to a legitimate doubt on the issue of guilt. If everything that might influence a jury must be disclosed, the only way a prosecutor could discharge his constitutional duty would be to allow complete discovery of his files as a matter of routine practice.

Whether or not procedural rules authorizing such broad discovery might be desirable, the Constitution surely does not demand that much. While expressing the opinion that representatives of the State may not "suppress substantial material evidence," former Chief Justice Traynor of the California Supreme Court has pointed out that "they are under no duty to report sua sponte to the defendant all that they learn about the case and about their witnesses." In re Imbler, 60 Cal.2d 554, 569, 35 Cal.Rptr. 293, 301, 387 P.2d 6, 14 (1963). And this Court recently noted that there is "no constitutional requirement that the prosecution make a complete and detailed accounting to the defense of all police investigatory work on a case." Moore v. Illinois, 408 U.S. 786, 795, 92 S.Ct. 2562, 2568. The mere possibility that an item of undisclosed information might have helped the defense, or might have affected the outcome of the trial, does not establish "materiality" in the constitutional sense.

Nor do we believe the constitutional obligation is measured by the moral culpability, or the willfulness, of the prosecutor. If evidence highly probative of innocence is in his file, he should be presumed to recognize its significance even if he has actually overlooked it. Conversely, if evidence actually has no probative significance at all, no purpose would be served by requiring a new trial simply because an inept prosecutor incorrectly believed he was suppressing a fact that would be vital to the defense. If the suppression of evidence results in constitutional error, it is because of the character of the evidence, not the character of the prosecutor.

As the District Court recognized in this case, there are situations in which evidence is obviously of such substantial value to the defense that elementary fairness requires it to be disclosed even without a specific request. For though the attorney for the sovereign must prosecute the accused with earnestness and vigor, he must always be faithful to his client's overriding interest that "justice shall be done." He is the "servant of the law, the twofold aim of which is that guilt shall not escape or innocence suffer." Berger v. United States, 295 U.S. 78, 88, 55 S.Ct. 629, 633. This description of the prosecutor's duty illuminates the standard of materiality that governs his obligation to disclose exculpatory evidence.

On the one hand, the fact that such evidence was available to the prosecutor and not submitted to the defense places it in a different category than if it had simply been discovered from a neutral source after trial. For that reason the defendant should not have to satisfy the severe burden of demonstrating that newly discovered evidence probably would have resulted in acquittal. If the standard applied to the usual motion for a new trial based on newly discovered evidence were the same when the evidence was in the State's possession as when it was found in a neutral source, there would be no special significance to the prosecutor's obligation to serve the cause of justice.

On the other hand, since we have rejected the suggestion that the prosecutor has a constitutional duty routinely to deliver his entire file to defense counsel, we cannot consistently treat every nondisclosure as though it were error. It necessarily follows that the judge should not order a new trial every time he is unable to characterize a nondisclosure as harmless under the customary harmless-error standard. Under that standard when error is present in the record, the reviewing judge must set aside the verdict and judgment unless his "conviction is sure that the error did not influence the jury, or had but very slight effect." Kotteakos v. United States, 328 U.S. 750, 764, 66 S.Ct. 1239, 1248. Unless every nondisclosure is regarded as automatic error, the constitutional standard of materiality must impose a higher burden on the defendant.

The proper standard of materiality must reflect our overriding concern with the justice of the finding of guilt. Such a finding is permissible only if supported by evidence establishing guilt beyond a reasonable doubt. It necessarily follows that if the omitted evidence creates a reasonable doubt that did not otherwise exist, constitutional error has been committed. This means that the omission must be evaluated in the context of the entire record. If there is no reasonable doubt about guilt whether or not the additional evidence is considered, there is no justification for a new trial. On the other hand, if the verdict is already of questionable validity, additional evidence of relatively minor importance might be sufficient to create a reasonable doubt.

This statement of the standard of materiality describes the test which courts appear to have applied in actual cases although the standard has been phrased in different language. It is also the standard which the trial judge applied in this case. He evaluated the significance of Sewell's prior criminal record in the context of the full trial which he recalled in detail. Stressing in particular the incongruity of a claim that Sewell was the aggressor with the evidence of his multiple wounds and respondent's unscathed condition, the trial judge indicated his unqualified opinion that respondent was guilty. He noted that Sewell's prior record did not contradict any evidence offered by the prosecutor, and was largely cumulative of the evidence that Sewell was wearing a bowie knife in a sheath and carrying a second knife in his pocket when he registered at the motel.

Since the arrest record was not requested and did not even arguably give rise to any inference of perjury, since after considering it in the context of the entire record the trial judge remained convinced of respondent's guilt beyond a reasonable doubt, and since we are satisfied that his firsthand appraisal of the record was thorough and entirely reasonable, we hold that the prosecutor's failure to tender Sewell's record to the defense did not deprive respondent of a fair trial as guaranteed by the Due Process Clause of the Fifth Amendment. Accordingly, the judgment of the Court of Appeals is

Reversed.

MR. JUSTICE MARSHALL, with whom MR. JUSTICE BRENNAN joins, dissenting.

*   *   *

Under today's ruling, if the prosecution has not made knowing use of perjury, and if the defense has not made a specific request for an item of information, the defendant is entitled to a new trial only if the withheld evidence actually creates a reasonable doubt as to guilt in the judge's mind. With all respect, this rule is completely at odds with the overriding interest in assuring that evidence tending to show innocence is brought to the jury's attention. The rule creates little, if any, incentive for the prosecutor conscientiously to determine whether his files contain evidence helpful to the defense. Indeed, the rule reinforces the natural tendency of the prosecutor to overlook evidence favorable to the defense, and creates an incentive for the prosecutor to resolve close questions of disclosure in favor of concealment.

More fundamentally, the Court's rule usurps the function of the jury as the trier of fact in a criminal case. The Court's rule explicitly establishes the judge as the trier of fact with respect to evidence withheld by the prosecution. The defendant's fate is sealed so long as the evidence does not create a reasonable doubt as to guilt in the judge's mind, regardless of whether the evidence is such that reasonable men could disagree as to its import—regardless, in other words, of how "close" the case may be.

* * *

The Court approves—but only for a limited category of cases—a standard virtually identical to the one I have described as reflecting the prevailing view. In cases in which "the undisclosed evidence demonstrates that the prosecution's case includes perjured testimony and that the prosecution knew, or should have known, of the perjury," the judgment of conviction must be set aside "if there is any reasonable likelihood that the false testimony could have affected the judgment of the jury." This lesser burden on the defendant is appropriate, the Court states, primarily because the withholding of evidence contradicting testimony offered by witnesses called by the prosecution "involve[s] a corruption of the truth-seeking function of the trial process." But surely the truth-seeking process is corrupted by the withholding of evidence favorable to the defense, regardless of whether the evidence is directly contradictory to evidence offered by the prosecution. . . . The suppression of the information unquestionably corrupts the truth-seeking process, and the burden on the defendant in establishing his entitlement to a new trial ought be no different from the burden he would face if related testimony had been elicited by the prosecution.

* * *

NOTES

1. Where defendant negotiates for an agreed disposition on a plea of guilty and eventually does plead guilty, has the prosecutor violated his duty by failing to disclose that the complaining witness died four days before the plea was agreed to and entered? Does the fact that the witness has died constitute exculpatory evidence? Is there an obligation to disclose information which is material to the tactical considerations which attend a determination to plead guilty? Would it make a difference if the prosecutor had affirmatively, and falsely, told defense counsel that the witness was available to testify at trial? What if the defendant gave a full, inculpatory statement at the time of his plea? What if the defendant asserts at the time of the plea that he is innocent but, in light of his assessment of the strength of the evidence against him, desires to enter a plea to a lesser offense rather than risk conviction on the greater offense? See People v. Jones, 44 N.Y.2d 76, 404 N.Y.S.2d 85, 375 N.E.2d 41 (1978).

2. For a good treatment of the development of the law concerning the prosecutor's duty to disclose favorable evidence, and for a discussion of some issues arising under *Agurs*, see Comment, The Prosecutor's Duty to Disclose. From *Brady* to *Agurs* and Beyond, 69 J.C.L. & C. 197 (1978).

B. PRE–TRIAL DISCOVERY

IN RE DI JOSEPH'S PETITION

Supreme Court of Pennsylvania, 1958.
394 Pa. 19, 145 A.2d 187.

[In a murder case the trial court required the prosecution to make available to the defendant, before trial, the gun which the prosecution alleged to be the gun used in the murder, photographs of fingerprints, if any, on the gun, the defendant's bloodstained clothing, photographs of the bedroom which was the scene of the killing, and articles of bedroom furniture seized by the police. Upon a hearing of the prosecutor's petition for a writ of prohibition regarding the order, the Supreme Court of Pennsylvania, in a per curiam opinion, affirmed the trial court's ruling except as regards the photographs of fingerprints. It was held that the prosecutor need not make the photographs available for inspection by the defendant and her counsel. Following are the concurring and dissenting opinions.]

CHARLES ALVIN JONES, CHIEF JUSTICE (concurring).

It is the rule in this State that a defendant in a criminal case has no absolute right to examine and inspect, prior to trial, evidence in the possession of the Commonwealth. Counsel for the present accused so conceded at bar and the Attorney General, as *amicus curiae*, so argued both orally and by brief. However, a trial court having jurisdiction of an alleged offender possesses discretionary power to permit a defendant, in appropriate circumstances, to examine and inspect in advance of trial physical or documentary evidence in the hands of the prosecution. And, this court's current action so confirms.

* * *

In [an earlier] case, we said with respect to the question of an accused being allowed to examine and inspect before trial evidence in the possession of the prosecution " .   .   .   the better view is that .   .   .   of the Court of Appeals of Maryland in State v. Haas, 188 Md. 63, 75–76, 51 A.2d 647, 653, as follows: "There can be no doubt that the recognition of the right in a trial court to permit the defendant to examine his confession in advance of the trial was not recognized at common law. But law is a growth and a great many matters, commonplace to us now, were not thought of many years ago. .   .   .   the tendency in the courts of this country is to permit discretion in the trial judge. The argument made against any such discretion is based upon a fear that the State, which is charged with the prosecution of crime, may be hampered in its duty by the disclosure of its evidence to those charged with offenses. Whatever merit that argument has as applied to a situation where it is contended that the accused has a *right* to inspect the evidence, it has no application, we think, to a situation where the trial judge in each case and on each application, determines what should be done in the interest of justice.

There are cases in which it would be clearly unjust to deny such an application and, on the other hand, cases are conceivable in which it might improperly hamper the prosecution to grant such an application. We do not understand that the court below decided that the appellees were entitled to this disclosure as a matter of right."

Likewise in the instant case, the trial court did not hold that the petitioning defendant was entitled *as a matter of right* to the disclosure ordered. And, this court in its *pro tanto* approval of the order entered by the court below is not laying down a new rule. Chief Justice Stern's quotation in Commonwealth v. Wable, 382 Pa. 80, 86, 114 A.2d 334, 338, from Wharton's Criminal Evidence that "The general rule is that the accused has no right to the inspection or disclosure before trial of evidence in the possession of the prosecution" continues to be the rule in Pennsylvania. The matter of permitting a defendant to examine and inspect evidence in the keeping of the Commonwealth depends upon an exercise of judicial discretion in any instance and our trial courts can be trusted to exercise it wisely. The justification for the discretion so reposed lies, in part, in the concept expressed by Judge Hoban in Commonwealth v. Stepper, 54 Lack.Jur. 205, 212–213,—"We would rather remove any obstacle to a fair trial, before the trial, rather than have it removed later and double the expense of difficult and protracted proceedings to the Commonwealth." Like the court in State v. Haas, supra, "We are not impressed by the fear of the prosecuting attorneys that the exercise of such discretion will change the whole practice of criminal law in this State, or will make the securing of proper convictions more difficult to obtain. It has not apparently had that effect elsewhere and we see no reason why it should have it here."

The only question before us, then, is whether the court below properly exercised its discretion. The court *en banc*, composed of the four judges of the Court of Common Pleas of Montgomery County, after reciting that it had reviewed all the evidence at its command, unanimously concluded that ". . . the Commonwealth has impeded and hampered defense counsel's investigation and preparation for trial by unrestrained and arbitrary power without fair co-operation and is therefore depriving the accused of that due process of law commanded by the 14th Amendment to the Constitution of the United States." Neither the record, the printed briefs, nor the oral argument has presented anything that would justify us in holding that the foregoing considered conclusion of the court below was false. Consequently, it necessarily follows that the court below, acting for the purpose of vitiating the indicated harm, exercised a sound discretion by the entry of its order as restricted by the limitation now put upon it by this court.

For my own part, I would have refused the writ of prohibition, for which the district attorney has petitioned, without imposing on the order of the court below the limitation with respect to the photographs of fingerprints, if any, in the hands of the district attorney.

MUSMANNO, JUSTICE (concurring).

I concur in the order entered by the majority of this Court. I believe that a person who asserts his innocence of a crime of which he stands accused is entitled to examine prosecution exhibits which are reasonably associated with the theory of guilt and of which he probably may be unaware. However, where an exhibit is one of which the accused is entirely cognizant and *already knows* whether it could or could not be an item of incrimination against him, he is not entitled to its inspection if such inspection would hamper the Commonwealth in proceeding with its case. . . .

We have affirmed the action of the lower Court with regard to inspection of the weapon but have refused to the defendant an inspection of the photographs of fingerprints, if any. I believe this action to be eminently just and in no way handicaps the defendant in the preparation of her case. She is one person who knows whether she used the weapon or not and, therefore, she is not being denied anything which she needs in the ascertainment of truth. . . .

I believe the prosecution here might find itself impeded in preparing for trial if it were required to announce to the world what it found on the 38-calibre revolver discovered in the culvert. . . .

BELL, JUSTICE (dissenting). I dissent from the majority's order which requires the Commonwealth to make available to this defendant before trial, the gun which the Commonwealth alleges is the gun used in the murder, defendant's bloodstained clothing, photographs of their bedroom which was the scene of the crime, and articles of bedroom furniture which were seized by the police. This disastrous precedent-shattering decision breaches one of the few barriers which are left to protect peaceable communities and law-abiding citizens from murderers and dangerous criminals. While the order directs the Commonwealth merely to turn over to defendant for examination before trial nearly all of its physical evidence, I believe that *the effect* of the order will be to compel the Commonwealth in the near future to turn over or disclose to a defendant in advance of trial *all* of its evidence. That this is no idle fear is clearly demonstrated by the contention of the Attorney General of Pennsylvania, who personally appeared in opposition to the Trial District Attorney and to the District Attorneys' Association of Pennsylvania.

The Attorney General orally argued that a criminal case was just like a civil case, and consequently the Commonwealth, in the interest of justice, should give or disclose to the defendant before trial *all* its evidence. It is difficult to imagine a more untenable argument or a more far-fetched analogy. A criminal trial is as different from a civil trial as day is from night. In civil trials there is pre-trial discovery and a *mutual* exchange of evidence. In a criminal trial the defendant does not have to inform the Commonwealth before or during trial or at any time his defense or any of his evidence; he does not have to take the witness stand and no unfavorable inference can be drawn therefrom; he can be convicted only if the Commonwealth proves his guilt beyond a reasonable doubt, which is defined to be a doubt which would restrain a reasonable man from acting in a matter of importance to himself; he is presumed to be innocent no matter how many terrible crimes he may have committed; if he has never been convicted of crime he can place in evidence his good reputation and that alone can be sufficient to justify his acquittal; and finally, he cannot be convicted unless all twelve of the jurors unanimously find him guilty beyond a reasonable doubt.

If we descend from ethereal theorism to the world of reality, we know that if Courts require the Commonwealth to inform each defendant of or permit him to examine its evidence, it will enable a person who commits a murder or a felony to devise, fabricate and manufacture his defense before trial—alibi, "blackout", insanity, self-defense or perpetration of the crime by someone else—and determine whether he should take the witness stand or introduce any evidence and if so, what kind. .　.　. At the very least, a defendant should be required to present exceptional circumstances and compelling reasons to justify an exception to the general rule. No such exceptional circumstances or compelling reasons were presented by the defendant in this case. Furthermore, the contention of the Attorney General flies in the teeth of and would require us to overrule Commonwealth v. Wable and abrogate a rule which for the protection of society has existed for centuries.

In recent years the Supreme Court of the United States and this Court, in their zeal to assure a fair trial to persons accused or convicted of crime, have, in my judgment, too often forgotten that law-abiding citizens and communities likewise possess certain fundamental inalienable rights. One of these rights is that their life and property shall be protected by the State against murderers and criminals. Justice is not a one-way street—law-abiding citizens are entitled to the protection of the law, and to justice just as much as (if not more so than) criminals.

The present order goes further than this Court or, we believe, the Supreme Court of the United States, has ever gone. It permits fishing expeditions by a defendant; it sets a precedent which will make fabrication of defenses easy, and consequently (although of course unintentionally) it will make the protection of society and the conviction of dangerous criminals far more difficult than ever before. In the interest and for the protection of all law-abiding people in Pennsylvania I register this protest and dissent.

WILLIAMS v. FLORIDA

Supreme Court of the United States, 1970.
399 U.S. 78, 90 S.Ct. 1893.

MR. JUSTICE WHITE delivered the opinion of the Court.

Prior to his trial for robbery in the State of Florida, petitioner filed a "Motion for a Protective Order," seeking to be excused from the requirements of Rule 1.200 of the Florida Rules of Criminal Procedure, 33 F.S.A. That rule requires a defendant, on written demand of the prosecuting attorney, to give notice in advance of trial if the defendant intends to claim an alibi, and to furnish the prosecuting attorney with information as to the place where he claims to have been and with the names and addresses of the alibi witnesses he intends to use. In his motion petitioner openly declared his intent to claim an alibi, but objected to the further disclosure requirements on the ground that the rule "compels the Defendant in a criminal case to be a witness against himself" in violation of his Fifth and Fourteenth Amendment rights. The motion was denied.

Florida's notice-of-alibi rule is in essence a requirement that a defendant submit to a limited form of pretrial discovery by the State whenever he intends to rely at trial on the defense of alibi. In exchange for the defendant's disclosure of the witnesses he proposes to use to establish that defense, the State in turn is required to notify the defendant of any witnesses it proposes to offer in rebuttal to that defense. Both sides are under a continuing duty promptly to disclose the names and addresses of additional witnesses bearing on the alibi as they become available. The threatened sanction for failure to comply is the exclusion at trial of the defendant's alibi evidence—except for his own testimony—or, in the case of the State, the exclusion of the State's evidence offered in rebuttal of the alibi.

In this case, following the denial of his Motion for a Protective Order, petitioner complied with the alibi rule and gave the State the name and address of one Mary Scotty. Mrs. Scotty was summoned to the office of the State Attorney on the morning of the trial, where she gave pretrial testimony. At the trial itself, Mrs. Scotty, petitioner, and petitioner's wife all testified that the three of them had been in Mrs. Scotty's apartment during the time of the robbery. On two occasions during cross-examination of Mrs. Scotty, the prosecuting attorney confronted her with her earlier deposition in which she had given dates and times that in some respects did not correspond with the dates and times given at trial. Mrs. Scotty adhered to her trial story, insisting that she had been mistaken in her earlier testimony. The State also offered in rebuttal the testimony of one of the officers investigating the robbery who claimed that Mrs. Scotty had asked him for directions on the afternoon in question during the time when she claimed to have been in her apartment with petitioner and his wife.

We need not linger over the suggestion that the discovery permitted the State against petitioner in this case deprived him of "due process" or a "fair trial." Florida law provides for liberal discovery by the defendant against the State, and the notice-of-alibi rule is itself carefully hedged with reciprocal duties requiring state disclosure to the defendant. Given the ease with which an alibi can be fabricated, the State's interest in protecting itself against an eleventh hour defense is both obvious and legitimate. Reflecting this interest, notice-of-alibi provisions, dating at least from 1927, are now in existence in a substantial number of States. The adversary system of trial is hardly an end in itself; it is not yet a poker game in which players enjoy an absolute right always to conceal their cards until played.

We find ample room in that system, at least as far as "due process" is concerned, for the instant Florida rule, which is designed to enhance the search for truth in the criminal trial by insuring both the defendant and the State ample opportunity to investigate certain facts crucial to the determination of guilt or innocence.

Petitioner's major contention is that he was "compelled . . . to be a witness against himself" contrary to the commands of the Fifth and Fourteenth Amendments because the notice-of-alibi rule required him to give the State the name and address of Mrs. Scotty in advance of trial and thus to furnish the State with information useful in convicting him. No pretrial statement of petitioner was introduced at trial; but armed with Mrs. Scotty's name and address and the knowledge that she was to be petitioner's alibi witness, the State was able to take her deposition in advance of trial and to find rebuttal testimony. Also, requiring him to reveal the elements of his defense is claimed to have interfered with his right to wait until after the State had presented its case to decide how to defend against it. We conclude, however, as has apparently every other court that has considered the issue, that the privilege against self-incrimination is not violated by a requirement that the defendant give notice of an alibi defense and disclose his alibi witnesses.

The defendant in a criminal trial is frequently forced to testify himself and to call other witnesses in an effort to reduce the risk of conviction. When he presents his witnesses, he must reveal their identity and submit them to cross-examination which in itself may prove incriminating or which may furnish the State with leads to incriminating rebuttal evidence. That the defendant faces such a dilemma demanding a choice between complete silence and presenting a defense has never been thought an invasion of the privilege against compelled self-incrimination. The pressures generated by the State's evidence may be severe but they do not vitiate the defendant's choice to present an alibi defense and witnesses to prove it, even though the attempted defense ends in catastrophe for the defendant. However "testimonial" or "incriminating" the alibi defense proves to be, it cannot be considered "compelled" within the meaning of the Fifth and Fourteenth Amendments.

Very similar constraints operate on the defendant when the State requires pretrial notice of alibi and the naming of alibi witnesses. Nothing in such a rule requires the defendant to rely on an alibi or prevents him from abandoning the defense; these matters are left to his unfettered choice. That choice must be made, but the pressures that bear on his pretrial decision are of the same nature as those that would induce him to call alibi witnesses at the trial: the force of historical fact beyond both his and the State's control and the strength of the State's case built on these facts. Response to that kind of pressure by offering evidence or testimony is not compelled self-incrimination transgressing the Fifth and Fourteenth Amendments.

In the case before us, the notice-of-alibi rule by itself in no way affected petitioner's crucial decision to call alibi witnesses or added to the legitimate pressures leading to that course of action. At most, the rule only compelled petitioner to accelerate the timing of his disclosure, forcing him to divulge at an earlier date information that the petitioner from the beginning planned to divulge at trial. Nothing in the Fifth Amendment privilege entitles a defendant as a matter of constitutional right to await the end of the State's case before announcing the nature of his defense, any more than it entitles him to await the jury's verdict on the State's case-in-chief before deciding whether or not to take the stand himself.

Petitioner concedes that absent the notice-of-alibi rule the Constitution would raise no bar to the court's granting the State a continuance at trial on the ground of surprise as soon as the alibi witness is called. Nor would there be self-incrimination problems if, during that continuance, the State was permitted to do precisely what it did here prior to trial: take the deposition of the witness and find rebuttal evidence. But if so utilizing a continuance is permissible under the Fifth and Fourteenth Amendments, then surely the same result may be accomplished through pretrial discovery, as it was here, avoiding the necessity of a disrupted trial. We decline to hold that the privilege against compulsory self-incrimination guarantees the defendant the right to surprise the State with an alibi defense.

MR. CHIEF JUSTICE BURGER, concurring.

I join fully in MR. JUSTICE WHITE's opinion for the Court. I see an added benefit to the notice-of-alibi rule in that it will serve important functions by way of disposing of cases without trial in appropriate circumstances—a matter of considerable importance when courts, prosecution offices, and legal aid and defender agencies are vastly overworked. The prosecutor upon receiving notice will, of course, investigate prospective alibi witnesses. If he finds them reliable and unimpeachable he will doubtless re-examine his entire case and this process would very likely lead to dismissal of the charges. In turn he might be obliged to determine why false charges were instituted and where the breakdown occurred in the examination of evidence that led to a charge.

On the other hand, inquiry into a claimed alibi defense may reveal it to be contrived and fabricated and the witnesses accordingly subject to impeachment or other attack. In this situation defense counsel would be obliged to re-examine his case and, if he found his client has proposed the use of false testimony, either seek to withdraw from the case or try to persuade his client to enter a plea of guilty, possibly by plea discussions which could lead to disposition on a lesser charge.

In either case the ends of justice will have been served and the processes expedited. These are the likely consequences of an enlarged and truly reciprocal pretrial disclosure of evidence and the move away from the "sporting contest" idea of criminal justice.

Mr. Justice Black, with whom Mr. Justice Douglas joins, dissenting.

* * *

. . . the Fifth Amendment itself clearly provides that "[n]o person . . . shall be compelled in any criminal case to be a witness against himself." If words are to be given their plain and obvious meaning, that provision, in my opinion, states that a criminal defendant cannot be required to give evidence, testimony, or any other assistance to the State to aid it in convicting him of crime. The Florida notice-of-alibi rule in my opinion is a patent violation of that constitutional provision because it requires a defendant to disclose information to the State so that the State can use that information to destroy him. It seems to me at least slightly incredible to suggest that this procedure may have some beneficial effects for defendants. There is no need to encourage defendants to take actions they think will help them. The fear of conviction and the substantial cost or inconvenience resulting from criminal prosecutions are more than sufficient incentives to make defendants want to help themselves. If a defendant thinks that making disclosure of an alibi before trial is in his best interest, he will obviously do so. And the only time the State needs the compulsion provided by this procedure is when the defendant has decided that such disclosure is likely to hurt his case.

It is no answer to this argument to suggest that the Fifth Amendment as so interpreted would give the defendant an unfair element of surprise, turning a trial into a "poker game" or "sporting contest," for that tactical advantage to the defendant is inherent in the type of trial required by our Bill of Rights. The Framers were well aware of the awesome investigative and prosecutorial powers of government and it was in order to limit those powers that they spelled out in detail in the Constitution the procedure to be followed in criminal trials. A defendant, they said, is entitled to notice of the charges against him, trial by jury, the right to counsel for his defense, the right to confront and cross-examine witnesses, the right to call witnesses in his own behalf, and the right not to be a witness against himself. All of these rights are designed to shield the defendant against state power. None are designed to make convictions easier and taken together they clearly indicate that in our system the entire burden of proving criminal activity rests on the State. The defendant, under our Constitution, need not do anything at all to defend himself, and certainly he cannot be required to help convict himself. Rather he has an absolute, unqualified right to compel the State to investigate its own case, find its own witnesses, prove its own facts, and convince the jury through its own resources. Throughout the process the defendant has a fundamental right to remain silent, in effect challenging the State at every point to: "Prove it!"

The Bill of Rights thus sets out the type of constitutionally required system that the State must follow in order to convict individuals of crime. That system requires that the State itself must bear the entire burden without any assistance from the defendant. This requirement is clearly indicated in the Fifth Amendment itself, but it is equally apparent when all the specific provisions of the Bill of Rights relating to criminal prosecutions are considered together. And when a question concerning the constitutionality of some aspect of criminal procedure arises, this Court must consider all those provisions and interpret them together. The Fifth Amendment prohibition against compelling a defendant to be a witness against himself is not an isolated, distinct provision. It is part of a system of constitutionally required procedures, and its true meaning can be seen only in light of all those provisions. "Strict construction" of the words of the Constitution does not mean that the Court can look only to one phrase, clause, or sentence in the Constitution and expect to find the right answer. Each provision has clear and definite meaning, and various provisions considered together may have an equally clear and definite meaning. It is only through sensitive attention to the specific words, the context in which they are used, and the history surrounding the adoption of those provisions that the true meaning of the Constitution can be discerned.

This constitutional right to remain absolutely silent cannot be avoided by superficially attractive analogies to any so-called "compulsion" inherent in the trial itself that may lead a defendant to put on evidence in his own defense. Obviously the Constitution contemplates that a defendant can be "compelled" to stand trial, and obviously there will be times when the trial process itself will require the defendant to do something in order to try to avoid a conviction. But nothing in the Constitution permits the State to add to the natural consequences of a trial and compel the defendant in advance of trial to participate in any way in the State's attempt to condemn him.

A criminal trial is in part a search for truth. But it is also a system designed to protect "freedom" by insuring that no one is criminally punished unless the State has first succeeded in the admittedly difficult task of convincing a jury that the defendant is guilty. That task is made more difficult by the Bill of Rights, and the Fifth Amendment may be one of the most difficult of the barriers to surmount. The Framers decided that the benefits to be derived from the kind of trial required by the Bill of Rights were well worth any loss in "efficiency" that resulted. Their decision constitutes the final word on the subject, absent some constitutional amendment. That decision should not be set aside as the Court does today.

II.

On the surface this case involves only a notice-of-alibi provisions, but in effect the decision opens the way for a profound change in one of the most important traditional safeguards of a criminal defendant. The rationale of today's decision is in no way limited to alibi defenses, or any other type or classification of evidence. The theory advanced goes at least so far as to permit the State to obtain under threat of sanction complete disclosure by the defendant in advance of trial of all evidence, testimony, and tactics he plans to use at that trial. In each case the justification will be that the rule affects only the "timing" of the disclosure, and not the substantive decision itself. This inevitability is clearly revealed by the citation to Jones v. Superior Court, 58 Cal.2d 56, 22 Cal.Rptr. 879, 372 P.2d 919 (1962). The prosecutor [there] successfully obtained an order compelling the defendant to reveal the names and addresses of any doctors he consulted and the medical reports of any examinations relating to the claimed incapacity [impotency in a rape case]. The majority found no barrier to the judicial creation of pretrial discovery by the State against the defendant, least of all a barrier raised by any constitutional prohibition on compelling the defendant to be a witness against himself.

The dangerous implications of the *Jones* rationale adopted today are not, however, limited to the disclosure of evidence that the defendant has already decided he will use at trial. In State v. Grove, 65 Wash.2d 525, 398 P.2d 170 (1965), the Washington Supreme Court, relying on *Jones,* held that a defendant in a murder trial could be compelled to produce a letter he had written his wife about the alleged crime, even though he had no thought at all of using that evidence in his own behalf. These cases are sufficient evidence of the inch-by-inch, case-by-case process by which the rationale of today's decision can be used to transform radically our system of criminal justice into a process requiring the defendant to assist the State in convicting him, or be punished for failing to do so.

. . . In spite of the history of oppression that produced the Bill of Rights and the strong reluctance of our governments to compel a criminal defendant to assist in his own conviction, the Court today reaches out to embrace and sanctify at the first opportunity a most dangerous departure from the Constitution and the traditional safeguards afforded persons accused of crime. I cannot accept such a result and must express my most emphatic disagreement and dissent.

MR. JUSTICE MARSHALL, dissenting in part. [Opinion omitted.]

NOTES

1. Williams v. Florida left open the question of whether alibi evidence could be excluded if the defense failed to comply with discovery orders. Other courts have upheld the exclusion of such evidence. See State v. Nunn, 113 N.J.Super. 161, 273 A.2d 366 (1971). Rider v. Crouse, 357 F.2d 317 (10th Cir. 1966).

In Wardius v. Oregon, 412 U.S. 470, 93 S.Ct. 2208 (1973) the Court dealt with the issue of reciprocal discovery as follows:

MR. JUSTICE MARSHALL delivered the opinion of the Court.

This case involves important questions concerning the right of a defendant forced to comply with a "notice of alibi" rule to reciprocal discovery.

*   *   *

We hold that the Due Process Clause of the Fourteenth Amendment forbids enforcement of alibi rules unless reciprocal discovery rights are given to criminal defendants. Since the Oregon statute did not provide for reciprocal discovery, it was error for the court below to enforce it against petitioner, and his conviction must be reversed.

On May 22, 1970, petitioner was indicted for unlawful sale of narcotics. The sale allegedly occurred the previous day. At trial, after the State had concluded its case, petitioner called one Colleen McFadden who testified that on the night in question, she had been with petitioner at a drive-in movie. The prosecutor thereupon brought to the judge's attention petitioner's failure to file a notice of alibi, and after hearing argument the trial judge granted the State's motion to strike McFadden's testimony because of this failure. Petitioner himself then took the stand and attempted to testify that he was at the drive-in with McFadden at the time when the State alleged the sale occurred. Once again, however, the State objected and the trial judge again refused to permit the evidence.

Petitioner was convicted as charged and sentenced to 18 months imprisonment. On appeal, the Oregon Court of Appeals rejected petitioner's contentions that the Oregon statute was unconstitutional in the absence of reciprocal discovery rights and that the exclusion sanction abridged his right to testify in his own behalf and his right to compulsory process.

Notice of alibi rules, now in use in a large and growing number of States, are based on the proposition that the ends of justice will best be served by a system of liberal discovery which gives both parties the maximum possible amount of information with which to prepare their cases and thereby reduces the possibility of surprise at trial.

* * *

The growth of such discovery devices is a salutary development which, by increasing the evidence available to both parties, enhances the fairness of the adversary system. As we recognized in [Williams v. Florida], nothing in the Due Process Clause precludes States from experimenting with systems of broad discovery designed to achieve these goals.

* * *

But although the Due Process Clause has little to say regarding the amount of discovery which the parties must be afforded, it does speak to the balance of forces between the accused and his accuser. The *Williams* court was therefore careful to note that "Florida law provides for liberal discovery by the defendant against the State, and the notice-of-alibi rule is itself carefully hedged with reciprocal duties requiring state disclosure to the defendant." The same cannot be said of Oregon law. As the State conceded at oral argument, Oregon grants no discovery rights to criminal defendants, and, indeed, does not even provide defendants with bills of particulars. More significantly, Oregon, unlike Florida, has no provision which requires the State to reveal the names and addresses of witnesses it plans to use to refute an alibi defense.

We do not suggest that the Due Process Clause of its own force requires Oregon to adopt such provisions. But we do hold that in the absence of a strong showing of state interests to the contrary, discovery must be a two-way street. The State may not insist that trials be run as a "search for truth" so far as defense witnesses are concerned, while maintaining "poker game" secrecy for its own witnesses. It is fundamentally unfair to require a defendant to divulge the details of his own case while at the same time subjecting him to the hazard of surprise concerning refutation of the very pieces of evidence which he disclosed to the State.

*   *   *

2. A statute requiring discovery of insanity and, self-defense as well as alibi evidence was upheld in Radford v. Stewart, 320 F.Supp. 826 (D. Mont.1970); State ex rel. Sikora v. District Court, 154 Mont. 241, 462 P.2d 897 (1969) (over a dissent stating that insanity and self-defense claims required admission of some of the elements of the charge and discovery of these defenses could not be allowed).

3. One state court has found overwhelming barriers to discovery of defense materials. See Allen v. Superior Court, 18 Cal.3d 520, 134 Cal.Rptr. 774, 557 P.2d 65 (1976).

4. Pre-trial discovery has been extremely limited in federal criminal cases, especially when compared to that available in a state such as Illinois.

The amended Fed.R.Crim.P. 16, in final form, became effective December 1, 1975:

FEDERAL RULES OF CRIMINAL PROCEDURE

RULE 16.   DISCOVERY AND INSPECTION

(a) **Disclosure of Evidence by the Government.**

(1) **Information Subject to Disclosure.**

(A) Statement of Defendant. Upon request of a defendant the government shall permit the defendant to inspect and copy or photograph: any relevant written or recorded statements made by the defendant, or copies thereof, within the possession, custody or control of the government, the existence of which is known, or by the exercise of due diligence may become known, to the attorney for the government; the substance of any oral statement which the government intends to offer in evidence at the trial made by the defendant whether before or after arrest in response to interrogation by any person then known to the defendant to be a government agent; and recorded testimony of the defendant before a grand jury which relates to the offense charged. Where the defendant is a corporation, partnership, association or labor union, the court may grant the defendant upon its motion, discovery of relevant recorded testimony of any witness before a grand jury who (1) was, at the time of his testimony so situated as an officer or employee as to have been able legally to bind the defendant in respect to conduct constituting the offense, or (2) was at the time of the offense, personally involved in the alleged conduct constituting the offense and so situated as an officer or employee as to have been able legally to bind the defendant in respect to that alleged conduct in which he was involved.

(B) Defendant's Prior Record. Upon request of the defendant, the government shall furnish to the defendant such copy of his

prior criminal record, if any, as is within the possession, custody, or control of the government, the existence of which is known, or by the exercise of due diligence may become known, to the attorney for the government.

(C) Documents and Tangible Objects. Upon request of the defendant the government shall permit the defendant to inspect and copy or photograph books, papers, documents, photographs, tangible objects, buildings or places, or copies or portions thereof, which are within the possession, custody or control of the government, and which are material to the preparation of his defense or are intended for use by the government as evidence in chief at the trial, or were obtained from or belong to the defendant.

(D) Reports of Examinations and Test. Upon request of a defendant the government shall permit the defendant to inspect and copy or photograph any results or reports of physical or mental examinations, and of scientific tests or experiments, or copies thereof, which are within the possession, custody, or control of the government, the existence of which is known, or by the exercise of due diligence may become known, to the attorney for the government, and which are material to the preparation of the defense or are intended for use by the government as evidence in chief at the trial.

(2) Information Not Subject to Disclosure. Except as provided in paragraphs (A), (B), and (D) of subdivision (a)(1), this rule does not authorize the discovery or inspection of reports, memoranda, or other internal government documents made by the attorney for the government or other government agents in connection with the investigation or prosecution of the case, or of statements made by government witnesses or prospective government witnesses except as provided in 18 U.S.C. § 3500.

(3) Grand Jury Transcripts. Except as provided in Rule 6 and subdivision (a)(1)(A) of this rule, these rules do not relate to discovery or inspection of recorded proceedings of a grand jury.

(b) Disclosure of Evidence by the Defendant.

(1) Information Subject to Disclosure.

(A) Documents and Tangible Objects. If the defendant requests disclosure under subdivision (a)(1)(C) or (D) of this rule, upon compliance with such request by the government, the defendant, on request of the government, shall permit the government to inspect and copy or photograph books, papers, documents, photographs, tangible objects, or copies or portions thereof, which are within the possession, custody, or control of the defendant and which the defendant intends to introduce as evidence in chief at the trial.

(B) Reports of Examinations and Tests. If the defendant requests disclosure under subdivision (a)(1)(C) or (D) of this rule, upon compliance with such request by the government, the defendant, on request of the government, shall permit the government to inspect and copy or photograph any results or reports of physical or mental examinations and of scientific tests or experiments made in connection with the particular case, or copies thereof, within the possession or control of the defendant, which the defendant intends

to introduce as evidence in chief at the trial or which were prepared by a witness whom the defendant intends to call at the trial when the results or reports relate to his testimony.

(2) Information Not Subject to Disclosure. Except as to scientific or medical reports, this subdivision does not authorize the discovery or inspection of reports, memoranda, or other internal defense documents made by the defendant, or his attorneys or agents in connection with the investigation or defense of the case, or of statements made by the defendant, or by government or defense witnesses, or by prospective government or defense witnesses, to the defendant, his agents or attorneys.

(c) Continuing Duty to Disclose. If, prior to or during trial, a party discovers additional evidence or material previously requested or ordered, which is subject to discovery or inspection under this rule, he shall promptly notify the other party or his attorney or the court of the existence of the additional evidence or material.

(d) Regulation of Discovery.

(1) Protective and Modifying Orders. Upon a sufficient showing the court may at any time order that the discovery or inspection be denied, restricted, or deferred, or make such other order as is appropriate. Upon motion by a party, the court may permit the party to make such showing, in whole or in part, in the form of a written statement to be inspected by the judge alone. If the court enters an order granting relief following such an ex parte showing, the entire text of the party's statement shall be sealed and preserved in the records of the court to be made available to the appellate court in the event of an appeal.

(2) Failure to Comply With a Request. If at any time during the course of the proceeding it is brought to the attention of the court that a party has failed to comply with this rule, the court may order such party to permit the discovery or inspection, grant a continuance, or prohibit the party from introducing evidence not disclosed, or it may enter such other order as it deems just under the circumstances. The court may specify the time, place and manner of making the discovery and inspection and may prescribe such terms and conditions as are just.

(e) Alibi Witnesses. Discovery of alibi witnesses is governed by Rule 12.1.

5. The arguments over discovery have been exceptionally vigorous in recent years and the law has undergone extensive development. Some observations on the debate and development of the law are found in Zagel and Carr, State Criminal Discovery And The New Illinois Rules, 1971 Ill.L.F. 557 (1972):

> "The arguments for both sides over criminal discovery can be summarized in a few paragraphs. The proponents of criminal discovery argue generally that pretrial discovery serves justice by ensuring that all relevant facts will be presented to the court and that the unseemly use of surprise tactics will be eliminated. These same arguments persuaded lawmakers to adopt discovery in civil cases.

"Furthermore, proponents argue that several specific aspects of the criminal process itself support the institution of discovery. First, it is only fair to give an accused, who stands to lose his liberty, the same rights given to a civil defendant. Second, the prosecution has a superior investigative force that has usually begun to act before the accused has counsel or an opportunity to commence the preparation of a defense. Third, the accused has often given the state a statement or confession. Fourth, adequate investigation by the accused may be precluded by investigating officers who usually refuse to discuss the case with defense counsel. Fifth, the late start given the accused may present defense counsel with witnesses whose memory has dimmed. Sixth, scientific evidence cannot be met effectively at trial without discovery. Finally, the accused is presumed innocent and consequently, presumed to know nothing of the crime charged.

"The opponents of discovery argue that the severity of the criminal sanction increases the likelihood that the accused will use discovery to help devise effective perjury and better fabrications in his defense. Furthermore, discovery will result in the increased intimidation of witnesses. Eventually, witnesses would be reluctant to step forward and sources of information would wither away. Discovery in criminal cases would be a one way street since the fifth amendment protects the accused from giving discovery of his case. Moreover, the defendant already has so many rights including the presumption of innocence, the right to insist on proof beyond a reasonable doubt, and the benefit of the exclusionary rule, that any additional rights would serve only to prevent the effective and just enforcement of the criminal law.

"Finally, except in rare cases, the only person who definitely knows the truth of the charge is the accused. Therefore, the most valuable source of information belongs exclusively to the defense after counsel is appointed. Indeed, if an accused consistently refuses to speak to the police, this vital source of information is totally unavailable to the prosecution.

"The advocates of discovery answer these arguments by contending that perjury is committed without discovery. With hardened criminals, the risk of intimidation exists with or without discovery, and ordinary criminals do not indulge in intimidation. Intimidation problems can be solved by provisions for protective orders. Furthermore, in the absence of discovery there is an unjustified disparity between the wealthy accused or the professional criminal, both of whom have the means to secure discovery through legitimate investigation or irregular methods, and the ordinary defendant who does not have these resources or abilities. The reply to the 'one way street' argument is that the prosecution has marvelous investigative facilities—the modern police force, the right to seize evidence and the investigative grand jury. [This argument, often cited as decisive, is only make-weight to state prosecutors in urban communities whose police forces are occupied with patrol and not investigation, and whose grand juries are of necessity used only to charge and not to investigate.] In any event, discovery against the defense is no longer the forbidden road it was once thought to be.

"The recent United States Supreme Court decision allowing prior inconsistent statements to be used as substantive evidence [California v. Green, discussed later] serves to reduce the incentive to intimidate witnesses. If the prior statement is admissible for its truth, an accused has little to gain by intimidation (short of killing the witness), since the prosecution will usually be able to use the witness' statement to prove its case. Furthermore, the change in the witness' testimony may lead to an adverse inference against the defendant.

"Some arguments for discovery do not rest on the merits of discovery itself, but rather emphasize the considerable collateral benefits thought to flow from discovery. These arguments, like most others, meet with significant replies.

"Brady v. Maryland requires the prosecution to produce material evidence favorable to the accused on the issues of guilt and punishment. *Brady* is not thought to require pretrial disclosure of such evidence, but arguably complete pretrial discovery would ensure both fulfillment of the prosecution's obligation under *Brady* and production of favorable evidence in time for the defense to make effective use of it. A prosecutor acting in good faith, however, will comply with *Brady* even without discovery. If the prosecutor is not acting in good faith, he can hide the evidence even if there is discovery. Compliance with *Brady* cannot be secured by courtroom procedure alone; ultimately complianc? will depend upon the good faith of law enforcement personnel.

"Discovery will be valuable, it is argued, when the favorable evidence is so unobvious that even the fairest prosecutor might overlook it. This argument, however, basically supports discovery against the defense. Only when the court knows the theories of the defense can it decide what seemingly immaterial facts are relevant, material, and producible under *Brady*.

"The final argument for discovery is based on a concern for efficiency, orderliness, and finality in criminal cases. The profusion of collateral attacks upon convictions may be a direct result of the lack of discovery. Without complete discovery, a court, upon collateral review, cannot be sure that all the relevant constitutional questions were either resolved or knowingly waived at the original trial or plea of guilty. Complete discovery would help ensure the completeness of the original trial record and reveal that an adequate basis existed for a guilty plea. On the other hand, the existence of complete discovery against the prosecution may encourage defense counsel not to make an independent investigation. If this occurs, and it obviously will in some cases, courts conducting collateral proceedings will still face serious allegations which cannot be resolved on the basis of the original trial record.

* * *

"The summary of the arguments on discovery shows clearly that there are compelling arguments on both sides which cannot be satisfactorily reconciled. As Professor Wright has said: 'The arguments for each point of view may be put in balanced fashion. This is plainly an issue on which highly responsible and experienced people disagree.' [1 C. Wright, Federal Practice and Procedure § 252, at 500 (1969).] Professor Wright is also correct in that regardless of the merits of the arguments those who favor discovery are gaining support with the courts. Several jurisdictions have adopted what purport to be comprehensive discovery provisions for criminal cases.

"The new criminal discovery procedures disclose a desire to codify and clarify discovery practices. Although the new rules vary widely in substance, each one represents an expansion of criminal discovery within its own jurisdiction. Several reasons may lie behind this trend.

"Pretrial discovery never has been held to be constitutionally required. The United States Supreme Court has never gone further than to say that 'in some circumstances it may be a denial of due process for a defendant to be refused any [pretrial] discovery of his statements to the police.' Neither Jencks v. United States, nor Brady v. Maryland require pretrial discovery. *Jencks* was decided specifically on nonconstitutional grounds, and the Court later approved legislation which both codified and limited the *Jencks* rule.

"*Jencks* is clearly limited to impeachment situations. The Court refused to require the states to provide pretrial discovery even of the defendant's own confession. [Clewis v. Texas, 386 U. S. 707, 87 S.Ct. 1338 (1967).] Recently the Court reaffirmed its position that the '*Jencks* decision and the Jencks Act were not cast in constitutional terms.' [United States v. Augenblick, 393 U.S. 348, 89 S.Ct. 528 (1969).] Furthermore, it cannot be said that the arguments favoring discovery indisputably outweigh the arguments against it.

"The expansion of discovery is the specific consequence of a more general condition—the wholesale dissatisfaction with the criminal process in this country. The present day administration of criminal justice satisfies no one. Justice for both society and the defendant in many cases is achieved by accident rather than by design.

"The civil law countries appear to do a better job of combining the search for truth with humane treatment of the accused. Significantly, discovery in criminal cases is present in nearly all civil law countries. But it is not admiration for continental systems of criminal law that moves us to broaden discovery. Few American lawyers have more than a passing acquaintance with these systems. Those that do realize that there are substantial cultural and social conditions essential to the success of those systems that do not exist here. [Some would argue that there are substantial constitutional barriers to the institution of continental systems in the United States. This is true, but the barriers are not as high or permanent as might be argued. Under the original test of due process, notice, and a fair hearing, the civil law systems would be acceptable. Even later developments do not preclude these systems. Modifications far short of total abandonment of the exclusionary rule of Mapp v. Ohio, 367 U.S. 643, 81 S.Ct. 1684 (1961) and similar state cases, and overruling Griffin v. California, 380 U.S. 609, 85 S.Ct. 1229 (1965) and similar state cases, might well be sufficient to allow development of a continental system here. This matter is subject for an essay in itself.]

"In the final analysis, discovery is developing in this country because of two underlying assumptions. The first is that nearly all prosecutors and defense counsel are honest men who will fully comply with the discovery rules finally approved by the courts. Thus, surprise and trickery will be drastically reduced and the courts will be far more certain that the facts of the case are being fairly presented. The second, and perhaps equally important underlying assumption, is that discovery will improve a sorry state of affairs and can hardly worsen it."

6. In the federal system a defendant has had no absolute right to learn before trial the names of the government witnesses. United States v. Payseur, 501 F.2d 966 (9th Cir. 1974). Most federal courts, however, have held that the district judge has discretion to order the government to supply such a list. See, e. g., United States v. Jackson, 508 F.2d 1001 (7th Cir. 1975).

Amendments to Federal Rule of Criminal Procedure 16, which had been scheduled to take effect on August 1, 1975, would have provided for lists of witnesses. Just before that date, however, Congress deleted these provisions from the new version of Rule 16. The Conference report declared:

A majority of the Conferees believe it is not in the interest of the effective administration of criminal justice to require that the government or the defendant be forced to reveal the names and addresses of its witnesses before trial. Discouragement of witnesses and improper contacts directed at influencing their testimony were deemed paramount concerns in the formulation of this policy.

H.R.Rep.No. 94–414, 94th Cong., 1st Sec. 12 (1975).

Consider the following from Haddad, Criminal Procedure and Habeas Corpus, Seventh Circuit Review, 52 Chi.–K.L.R. 294, 305 (1975):

If Congress intended to forbid a judge from ever ordering a list of witnesses, it may have created a serious sixth amendment question . . . even though (the sixth amendment) has rarely been used as a basis for developing the law of criminal discovery.

Considering the denial of mid-trial discovery (the true name of a witness), the Supreme Court in Smith v. Illinois, 390 U.S. 129, 131 in 1968 declared: "The witness' name and address open countless avenues of in-court examination and out-of-court investigation. To forbid this most rudimentary inquiry at the threshold is effectively to emasculate the right of cross-examination itself."

In the real world where efficient administration is a valued goal, mid-trial continuances are almost never granted. Accordingly, the kind of out-of-court investigation contemplated by the *Smith* decision is impossible absent a list of witnesses before trial.

The amended Fed.R.Crim.P. 16, in final form, became effective December 1, 1975. Even before the Amendment became effective, the court in United States v. Cannone, 528 F.2d 296 (2d Cir. 1975), anticipated and rejected the argument that federal district courts no longer have the discretion to order the government to disclose the names of its witnesses in advance of trial.

ILLINOIS SUPREME COURT RULES
OF CRIMINAL DISCOVERY

Rule 411.　Applicability

These rules shall be applied in all criminal cases wherein the accused is charged with an offense for which, upon conviction, he might be imprisoned in the penitentiary. They shall become applicable following indictment or information and shall not be operative prior to or in the course of any preliminary hearing.

Rule 412.　Disclosure to Accused

(a) Except as is otherwise provided in these rules as to matters not subject to disclosure and protective orders, the State shall, upon written motion of defense counsel, disclose to defense counsel the following material and information within its possession or control:

(i) the names and last known addresses of persons whom the State intends to call as witnesses, together with their relevant written or recorded statements, memoranda containing substantially verbatim reports of their oral statements, and a list of memoranda reporting or summarizing their oral statements. Upon written motion of defense counsel memoranda reporting or summarizing oral statements shall be examined by the court *in camera* and if found to be substantially verbatim reports of oral statements shall be disclosed to defense counsel;

(ii) any written or recorded statements and the substance of any oral statements made by the accused or by a codefendant, and a list of witnesses to the making and acknowledgment of such statements;

(iii) a transcript of those portions of grand jury minutes containing testimony of the accused and relevant testimony of persons whom the prosecuting attorney intends to call as witnesses at the hearing or trial;

(iv) any reports or statements of experts made in connection with the particular case, including results of physical or mental examinations and of scientific tests, experiments, or comparisons;

(v) any books, papers, documents, photographs or tangible objects which the prosecuting attorney intends to use in the hearing or trial or which were obtained from or belong to the accused; and

(vi) any record of prior criminal convictions, which may be used for impeachment, of persons whom the State intends to call as witnesses at the hearing or trial.

If the State has obtained from the defendant pursuant to Rule 413(d) information regarding defenses the defendant intends to make, it shall provide to defendant not less than 7 days before the date set for the hearing or trial, or at such other time as the court may direct, the names and addresses of witnesses the state intends to call in rebuttal, together with the information required to be disclosed in connection with other witnesses by subdivisions (i), (iii), and (vi), above, and a specific statement as to the substance of the testimony such witnesses will give at the trial of the cause.

(b) The State shall inform defense counsel if there has been any electronic surveillance (including wiretapping) of conversations to which the accused was a party, or of his premises.

(c) Except as is otherwise provided in these rules as to protective orders, the State shall disclose to defense counsel any material or information within its possession or control which tends to negate the guilt of the accused as to the offense charged or would tend to reduce his punishment therefor.

(d) The State shall perform its obligations under this rule as soon as practicable following the filing of a motion by defense counsel.

(e) The State may perform these obligations in any manner mutually agreeable to itself and defense counsel or by:

(i) notifying defense counsel that material and information, described in general terms, may be inspected, obtained, tested, copied or photographed, during specified reasonable times; and

(ii) making available to defense counsel at the time specified such material and information, and suitable facilities or other arrangements for inspection, testing, copying, and photographing of such material and information.

(f) The State should ensure that a flow of information is maintained between the various investigative personnel and its office sufficient to place within its possession or control of material and information relevant to the accused and the offense charged.

(g) Upon defense counsel's request and designation of material or information which would be discoverable if in the possession or control of the State and which is in the possession or control of other governmental personnel, the State shall use diligent good faith efforts to cause such material to be made available to defense counsel; and if the State's efforts are unsuccessful and such material or other governmental personnel are subject to the jurisdiction of the court, the court shall issue suitable subpoenas or orders to cause such material to be made available to defense counsel.

(h) *Discretionary Disclosures.* Upon a showing of materiality to the preparation of the defense, and if the request is reasonable, the court in its discretion may require disclosure to defense counsel of relevant material and information not covered by this rule.

(i) *Denial of Disclosure.* The court may deny disclosure authorized by this rule and Rule 413 if it finds that there is a substantial risk to any person of physical harm, intimidation, bribery, economic reprisals, or unnecessary annoyance or embarrassment resulting from such disclosure which outweighs any usefulness of the disclosure to counsel.

(j) *Matters Not Subject to Disclosure.*

(i) **Work Product.** Disclosure under this rule and Rule 413 shall not be required of legal research or of records, correspondence, reports or memoranda to the extent that they contain the opinions, theories or conclusions of the State or members of its legal or investigative staffs, or of defense counsel or his staff.

(ii) **Informants.** Disclosure of an informant's identity shall not be required where his identity is a prosecution secret and a failure to disclose will not infringe the constitutional rights of the accused. Disclosure shall not be denied hereunder of the identity of witnesses to be produced at a hearing or trial.

(iii) **National Security.** Disclosure shall not be required where it involves a substantial risk of grave prejudice to national security and where a failure to disclose will not infringe the constitutional rights of the accused. Disclosure shall not thus be denied hereunder regarding witnesses or material to be produced at a hearing or trial.

Rule 413. Disclosure to Prosecution

(a) *The Person of the Accused.* Notwithstanding the initiation of judicial proceedings, and subject to constitutional limitations, a judicial officer may require the accused, among other things, to:

(i) appear in a line-up;

(ii) speak for identification by witnesses to an offense;

(iii) be fingerprinted;

(iv) pose for photographs not involving reenactment of a scene;

(v) try on articles of clothing;

(vi) permit the taking of specimens of material under his fingernails;

(vii) permit the taking of samples of his blood, hair and other materials of his body which involve no unreasonable intrusion thereof;

(viii) provide a sample of his handwriting; and

(ix) submit to a reasonable physical or medical inspection of his body.

(b) Whenever the personal appearance of the accused is required for the foregoing purposes, reasonable notice of the time and place of such appearance shall be given by the State to the accused and his counsel, who shall have the right to be present. Provision may be made for appearances for such purposes in an order admitting the accused to bail or providing for his release.

(c) *Medical and Scientific Reports.* Subject to constitutional limitations, the trial court shall, on written motion, require that the State be informed of, and permitted to inspect and copy or photograph, any reports or results, or testimony relative thereto, of physical or mental examinations or of scientific tests, experiments or comparisons, or any other reports or statements of experts which defense counsel has in his possession or control, except that those portions of reports containing statements made by the defendant may be withheld if defense counsel does not intend to use any of the material contained in the report at a hearing or trial.

(d) *Defenses.* Subject to constitutional limitations and within a reasonable time after the filing of a written motion by the State, defense counsel shall inform the State of any defenses which he intends to make at a hearing or trial and shall furnish the State

(i) The names and last known addresses of persons he intends to call as witnesses together with their relevant written or recorded statements, including memoranda reporting or summarizing their oral statements, any record of prior criminal convictions known to him; and

(ii) any books, papers, documents, photographs, or tangible objects he intends to use as evidence or for impeachment at a hearing or trial;

(iii) and if the defendant intends to prove an alibi, specific information as to the place where he maintains he was at the time of the alleged offense.

(e) *Additional Disclosure.* Upon a showing of materiality, and if the request is reasonable, the court in its discretion may require disclosure to the State of relevant material and information not covered by this rule.

Rule 414. Evidence Depositions

(a) If it appears to the court in which a criminal charge is pending that the deposition of any person other than the defendant is necessary for the preservation of relevant testimony because of the substantial possibility it would be unavailable at the time of hearing or trial, the court may, upon motion and notice to both parties and their counsel, order the taking of such person's deposition under oral examination or written questions for use as evidence at a hearing or trial.

(b) The taking of depositions shall be in accordance with rules providing for the taking of depositions in civil cases, and the order for the taking of a deposition may provide that any designated books, papers, documents or tangible objects, not privileged, be produced at the same time and place.

(c) If a witness is committed for failure to execute a recognizance to appear to testify at a hearing or trial, the court on written motion of the witness and upon notice to the State and defense counsel may order that his deposition be taken, and after the deposition has been subscribed, the court may discharge the witness.

(d) Rule 207—Signing and Filing Depositions—shall apply to the signing and filing of depositions taken pursuant to this rule.

(e) The defendant and defense counsel shall have the right to confront and cross-examine any witness whose deposition is taken.

The defendant and defense counsel may waive such right in writing, filed with the clerk of the court.

(f) If the defendant is indigent, all costs of taking depositions shall be paid by the county wherein the criminal charge is initiated. If the defendant is not indigent the costs shall be allocated as in civil cases.

Rule 415. Regulation of Discovery

(a) *Investigations Not to Be Impeded.* Except as is otherwise provided as to matters not subject to disclosure and protective orders, neither the counsel for the parties nor other prosecution or defense personnel shall advise persons having relevant material or information (except the accused) to refrain from discussing the case with opposing counsel or showing opposing counsel any relevant material, nor shall they otherwise impede opposing counsel's investigation of the case.

(b) *Continuing Duty to Disclose.* If, subsequent to compliance with the rules or orders pursuant thereto, a party discovers additional material or information which is subject to disclosure, he shall promptly notify the other party or his counsel of the existence of such additional material, and if the additional material or information is discovered during trial, the court shall also be notified.

(c) *Custody of Materials.* Any materials furnished to an attorney pursuant to these rules shall remain in his exclusive custody and be used only for the purposes of conducting his side of the case, and shall be subject to such other terms and conditions as the court may provide.

(d) *Protective Orders.* Upon a showing of cause, the court may at any time order that specified disclosures be restricted or deferred, or make such other order as is appropriate provided that all material and information to which a party is entitled must be disclosed in time to permit counsel to make beneficial use thereof.

(e) *Excision.* When some parts of certain material are discoverable under these rules, and other parts not discoverable, as much of the material should be disclosed as is consistent with the rules. Excision of certain material and disclosure of the balance is preferable to witholding the whole. Material excised pursuant to judicial order shall be sealed, impounded and preserved in the records of the court, to be made available to the reviewing court in the event of an appeal.

(f) *In Camera Proceedings.* Upon request of any person, the court may permit any showing of cause for denial or regulation of disclosures, or portion of such showing, to be made *in camera.* A record shall be made of such proceedings. If the court enters an order granting relief following a showing *in camera,* the entire record of such showing shall be sealed, impounded, and preserved in the records of the court, to be made available to the reviewing court in the event of an appeal.

(g) *Sanctions.*

(i) If at any time during the course of the proceedings it is brought to the attention of the court that a party has failed to comply with an applicable discovery rule or an order issued pursuant thereto, the court may order such party to permit the discovery of material and information not previously disclosed, grant a continuance, exclude such evidence, or enter such other order as it deems just under the circumstances.

(ii) Wilful violation by counsel of an applicable discovery rule or an order issued pursuant thereto may subject counsel to appropriate sanctions by the court.

NOTES

1. The Illinois rules are used as an example of a unified modern code of discovery for several reasons. The rules are comprehensive, expansive, and are one of the most recently adopted set of procedures. Further, though there are important differences, the rules follow closely the pattern and substance of the American Bar Association Standards Relating To Discovery And Procedure Before Trial (1970), and the A.B.A. Standards have become a focal point of debate throughout the nation over the question of discovery. (Somewhat revised standards were approved in 1978.) It should be noted that Florida (Fla.R.Crim.P. 1.220) New Jersey (N.J.Ct.R. 3–11, 3–12, 3–13) and the United States (F.R.Crim.P. 16, 12.1, 12.2) have adopted new discovery procedures though none are as extensive as those in Illinois. An exhaustive table of each state's discovery provisions as well as discussions of California, Florida, Illinois, New Jersey, New York, Pennsylvania, Texas and federal procedures is found in Zagel and Carr, State Criminal Discovery And The New Illinois Rules, 1971 Ill.L.F. 557 (1972).

2. One distinguishing feature of the Illinois rules is the elimination of nearly all judicial discretion. Discretion in the discovery process causes two problems. First, there is a substantial difficulty in resolving questions of materiality and reasonableness of discovery requests. If "showings" by the moving party are required, much court time will be consumed in adjudicating the issues. Second, there is a tendency in discretionary systems leading to the uneven administration of discovery rules. Variations may exist from courtroom to courtroom depending on individual judicial predilections on discovery policy. Is the elimination of discretion wise? Is the means by which mandatory discretion can be restricted, i. e., the protective order, sufficient to meet objections to excessive discovery? Are better techniques available?

3. Consider the following questions in connection with the Illinois Rules:

(a) Discovery practice is initiated by motion. The A.B.A. Standards suggest the use of informal meetings between counsel. The Illinois practice leads to preservation of the record of the discovery process in each case. Does this justify requiring an essentially pointless filing of a formal motion which, without court action, requires the other party to give discovery?

(b) The defense is allowed the pre-trial discovery of a witness' written statements. The A.B.A. recommends this but most other jurisdictions expressly forbid it. Is it wise to permit such discovery? What are the arguments on either side? The prosecution has a similar right of discovery of defense witness statements. Would this include the defendant's statement to his lawyer? Would the defense counsel ordinarily take written statements from his witnesses? Would prosecutors and police and defense counsel begin to cease taking written statements or writing verbatim reports of oral statements simply to avoid discovery or to avoid creating potentially impeaching statements?

The Rules require production of prosecution memoranda of oral statements only if they are substantially verbatim reports. The Rules require production of defense documents including memoranda "summarizing . . . oral statements". What accounts for the difference? Is the danger attendant upon production of "summaries", i. e., the improper attempt to contradict a witness with a prior statement he did not actually make, sufficient to justify exempting the summary from production? Would a protective order work as well? Would it make any difference if the witness had made a written statement which was produced or it there was no producible statement ever made by the witness? When the Rules are administered, the prosecution will tender a list of "summaries" which they don't intend to produce and the defense is entitled to have the court inspect them. Will this procedure strengthen or erode the limitation on production? Is it possible or likely that an overburdened trial court will simply order production of all memoranda and reserve ruling on the propriety of use at the time of trial? Discovery of witnesses and witness' statements are limited to three witnesses the party intends to call to trial. How about witnesses not to be called? Should the prosecution or defense be required to give a list of all persons they talked to or at least of all persons who were present at the time of the crime (potential occurrence witnesses)?

(c) The Illinois Rules provided for evidence depositions but not discovery depositions. A few jurisdictions have provisions for discovery depositions. See Fla.R.Crim.P. 3.220(d) (deposition allowed if witness will not give written statement to counsel); Tex.Code Crim.Proc. Ann., Art. 39.02 (1979) (depositions in discretion of court upon showing good cause); Vt.R.Crim.P. 15 (depositions mandatory if testimony may be material or relevant on the trial or of assistance in the preparation of the case).

The Vermont experience has been favorable. See Langrock, Vermont's Experience In Criminal Discovery, 53 A.B.A.J. 732 (1967). An ad hoc committee appointed by the New Jersey Supreme Court to study the question decided against discovery depositions for the following reasons:

(1) Depositions are time consuming and costly. (2) Impartial witnesses might be unduly harassed. (3) Constitutional problems would be created by prosecutors reciprocal right to depose defense witnesses. (4) The indigent defendant might insist upon exercising his right to depose as a matter of course, apart from indications of need.

Are these the only problems with depositions? Ordinarily in civil matters, depositions are taken by a lawyer who summons the witness to his office. Would such a procedure be appropriate with the witnesses to (or victims of) serious crimes of violence? Could a reasonable deposition procedure be devised to meet the objections? Would it be best to provide for depositions on motions to be granted in the discretion of the court?

(d) Counsel are prohibited from telling or instructing a witness not to talk to the other party but may an attorney advise a witness that he has a right to talk or refuse to talk to opposing counsel as he sees fit? The witness does, of course, have this personal right but if he hears the advice from a lawyer he may infer that the lawyer does not want him to talk to opposing counsel. If the witness is to testify for one party he may think he is on that party's "team" and be unwilling to do anything against the "coach's" (lawyer's) wishes. On the other hand, how could a court today hold that an individual citizen cannot or should not be advised of his rights? Will the amount of discovery of witness statements reduce the need for personal interviews by opposing counsel?

(e) The rules adopt the exclusion sanction among others and provide an open-ended option to devise other sanctions. What of allowing counsel to prove that the opposing party failed to comply with discovery and argue unfavorable inferences from this to the jury? See, e. g., Higgins v. Wainwright, 424 F.2d 177 (5th Cir. 1970) (comment on refusal to participate in lineup); United States v. Parhms, 424 F.2d 152 (9th Cir. 1970) (same); People v. Hess, 10 Cal.App.3d 1071, 90 Cal.Rptr. 268 (1970) (comment on refusal to give a handwriting exemplar after court order); State v. Huson, 66 Wash.2d 660, 440 P.2d 192 (1968) (comment on refusal to participate in court-ordered mental examination).

Would this be an effective sanction? Would it be so effective as to render exclusion of evidence unnecessary except in extreme cases?

(f) Will extensive discovery provisions force attorneys on both sides to pay serious attention to their cases at an earlier stage and formulate theories of prosecution and defense? Will police be more careful in writing reports when they know that the reports are discoverable? Would such changes benefit the administration of criminal justice?

4. Apart from formal discovery procedures what of the use of preliminary hearings and suppression hearings to gain discovery? The purpose of such hearings is not discovery, but a collateral benefit is often a substantial degree of discovery. Do both prosecution and defense benefit equally in the sense of gaining discovery from such hearings? Consider the materials in this book on preliminary and suppression hearings in this light. Is it proper for defense counsel to file knowingly meritless suppression motion to gain discovery?

5. May the defense or the prosecution use the civil process for discovery? For example, may the defendant file a civil action for malicious prosecution or violation of civil rights and depose the prosecutor and subpoena his records? If the immunity doctrine is a barrier, may the defendant sue the individual witnesses and seek depositions from them? How do you think a court would react to such suits? May the government use civil suits to gain discovery? In United States v. Kordel, 397 U.S. 1, 90 S.Ct. 763 (1970), the government filed both criminal charges and civil proceedings against a violator of the Food and Drug Act. Information derived from civil interrogatories was used in the criminal case. The Court held that individual corporate officers could have declined to answer interrogatories on

Fifth Amendment grounds and their failure to do so waives any claim of error. Further, the Court assumed that a trial court had power to order civil discovery postponed until the end of the criminal action.

6. The privilege issue was considered in the following two recent cases:

(a) State v. Mingo, 77 N.J. 576, 392 A.2d 590 (1978), excerpts of which are:

> ". . . While in police custody, Mingo, at the instruction of the police, furnished handwriting exemplars in the exact words which had been handwritten by the rapist. Several of the exemplars were rendered on small pieces of paper from a note pad. Prior to trial, Mingo's attorney sought to compel the State's production of the note allegedly written by the assailant for the purpose of having it examined and analyzed by a handwriting expert retained by the defense attorney to aid in the preparation of a defense. Over objection, the judge conditioned his grant of this request on defense counsel's agreeing to furnish the prosecutor with a copy of any reports concerning the handwriting on the note rendered by the expert irrespective of whether the defense intended to use the expert as a witness at trial. The expert concluded that the same person had written each and gave a report to that effect to defense counsel. The defense attorney accordingly determined that he would not use the expert as a witness at trial, since the expert's conclusion effectively precluded any attack based on the identity of that document's author.

> "Over defense counsel's strenuous objection that testimony by the expert would violate the attorney-client privilege, he was allowed to testify in the State's case-in-chief.

> ". . . To safeguard the defense attorney's ability to provide the effective assistance guaranteed by these constitutional provisions, it is essential that he be permitted full investigative latitude in developing a meritorious defense on his client's behalf. This latitude will be circumscribed if defense counsel must risk a potentially crippling revelation to the State of information discovered in the course of investigation which he chooses not to use at trial.

> "We think it makes no difference whether the principle calling for vindication in such a situation is to be denominated the effective representation by counsel or the attorney-client privilege. We regard them as related, and basically subserving the right of a criminal defendant to be effectively represented by counsel. We believe that right to be clearly subverted if an expert report obtained for defense purposes by defendant's counsel is to be made discoverable to the State and utilizable by it, directly or indirectly, at trial, unless a defendant signifies his intention to use the expert evidence at trial or in fact does so.

> ". . . Our holding here is confined to reports of opinions of expert witnesses and is not intended in any way to bear upon the question of discovery or utilization at trial of information of any other nature assembled by the defense.

> "[As we have indicated], the immunity from discovery by the State of defense experts reports is subject to waiver in the event

the defense intends to use the substance of those reports at the trial. However, should the defense elect not to present the expert as a witness after previously indicating to the contrary, the fact that his otherwise confidential reports have been disclosed to the prosecution does not entitle the State to call the expert as its witness over objection by the defense. The testimony of a defense consultant concerning the substance of expert services he has performed for the defense is exclusively available to the defense."

(b) United States v. Pipkins, 528 F.2d 559 (5th Cir. 1976):

". . . In preparing Pipkins' defense, the Public Defender's Office retained a handwriting expert, Albert Somerford. At the direction of defense counsel, Somerford met with Pipkins at the Public Defender's Office. A representative of the United States Attorney's office hand delivered the forged check and the handwriting samples that Pipkins had given to the government. . . . Somerford's analysis incriminated Pipkins, and the defense decided not to call the expert at trial. . . .

"At trial the *government* called Somerford as an expert witness. Outside the presence of the jury defense counsel objected to the government's calling of Somerford. Defense counsel argued that Somerford was an agent of defense counsel and that the attorney-client privilege applied to his testimony.

". . . The privilege does not embrace everything that arises out of the existence of an attorney-client relationship. By the same token,

> '[n]othing in the policy of the privilege suggests that attorneys, simply by placing accountants, scientists or investigators on their payrolls and maintaining them in their offices, should be able to invest all communications by clients to such persons with a privilege the law has not seen fit to extend when the latter are operating under their own steam.'

United States v. Kovel, 296 F.2d at 921.

". . . Pipkins failed to establish that the handwriting samples that he gave Somerford were confidential. One's style of handwriting is not an intrinsically confidential attribute; and there is nothing in the record that indicates that Pipkins subjectively intended his style of handwriting to be confidential. . . . Moreover, even assuming, *arguendo*, that the samples of handwriting that Pipkins gave Somerford were privileged communications, there was no error in admitting the expert's testimony. Somerford was asked to compare the handwriting on two government exhibits; he was not questioned about either the subsequent samples or the results of the test conducted at the behest of defense counsel. Consequently, the questions propounded Somerford did not call for the revelation of the substance of a confidential communication; his testimony was confined to nonconfidential matters. Somerford stated that he would be able to form his opinion without any reference to the subsequent samples. Therefore, Somerford's opinion about the handwriting on the government exhibits was not 'inextricably intertwined with communications which passed between him and his client.' "

C. DISCOVERY AT TRIAL

The Jencks Act (18 U.S.C. § 3500) reads:

"Demands for production of statements and reports of witnesses.

"(a) In any criminal prosecution brought by the United States, no statement or report in the possession of the United States which was made by a Government witness or prospective Government witness (other than the defendant) shall be the subject of subpena, discovery, or inspection until said witness has testified on direct examination in the trial of the case.

"(b) After a witness called by the United States has testified on direct examination, the court shall, on motion of the defendant, order the United States to produce any statement (as hereinafter defined) of the witness in the possession of the United States which relates to the subject matter as to which the witness has testified. If the entire contents of any such statement relate to the subject matter of the testimony of the witness, the court shall order it to be delivered directly to the defendant for his examination and use.

"(c) If the United States claims that any statement ordered to be produced under this section contains matter which does not relate to the subject matter of the testimony of the witness, the court shall order the United States to deliver such statement for the inspection of the court in camera. Upon such delivery the court shall excise the portions of such statement which do not relate to the subject matter of the testimony of the witness. With such material excised, the court shall then direct delivery of such statement to the defendant for his use. If, pursuant to such procedure, any portion of such statement is withheld from the defendant and the defendant objects to such withholding, and the trial is continued to an adjudication of the guilt of the defendant, the entire text of such statement shall be preserved by the United States and, in the event the defendant appeals, shall be made available to the appellate court for the purpose of determining the correctness of the ruling of the trial judge. Whenever any statement is delivered to a defendant pursuant to this section, the court in its discretion, upon application of said defendant, may recess proceedings in the trial for such time as it may determine to be reasonably required for the examination of such statement by said defendant and his preparation for its use in the trial.

"(d) If the United States elects not to comply with an order of the court under subsection (b) or (c) hereof to deliver to the defendant any such statement, or such portion thereof as the court may direct, the court shall strike from the record the testimony of the witness, and the trial shall proceed unless the court in its discretion shall determine that the interests of justice require that a mistrial be declared.

"(e) The term 'statement,' as used in subsections (b), (c), and (d) of this section in relation to any witness called by the United States, means—

"(1) a written statement made by said witness and signed or otherwise adopted or approved by him; or

"(2) a stenographic, mechanical, electrical, or other recording, or a transcription thereof, which is a substantially verbatim recital of an oral statement made by said witness and recorded contemporaneously with the making of such oral statement.

"(3) a statement, however taken or recorded, or a transcription thereof, if any, made by said witness to a grand jury."

NOTES

1. The rights created by the Jencks Act are not constitutional in scope. See United States v. Augenblick, 393 U.S. 348, 89 S.Ct. 528 (1969). Would a violation of the Jencks Act always constitute a violation of the prosecution's duty under United States v. Agurs, supra? If not, could it constitute a violation? If so, under what circumstances would this occur?

In United States v. Nobles, 422 U.S. 225, 95 S.Ct. 2160 (1975), the Supreme Court held that a trial judge has the inherent authority to require the defense to tender statements made to a defense investigator by persons other than the defendant if the defense calls such persons as witnesses at the trial. The Court rejected claims of attorney-client and Fifth Amendment privileges because such statements do not involve client communications. The Court also narrowly construed the "work product" privilege and held that once the defense witness testified, such a privilege would not bar disclosure of his substantially verbatim statements.

In Goldberg v. United States, 425 U.S. 94, 96 S.Ct. 1338 (1976), the Supreme Court held that a statement made to a prosecutor and reduced to writing is not exempt from production after the witness has testified at trial. The Court stated that there is no "work product" exception to the Jencks Act. Any statement otherwise within the Jencks Act must be produced even though it was a lawyer rather than an investigator who took the statement.

In 1979, the Supreme Court approved, subject to Congressional veto, a general "Jencks Rule" applicable to both parties. Rule 26.2(a), F.R.Crim.P. provides:

"After a witness other than the defendant has testified on direct examination, the court, on motion of a party who did not call the witness, shall order the attorney for the government or the defendant and his attorney, as the case may be, to produce, for the examination and use of the moving party, any statement of the witness that is in their possession and that relates to the subject matter concerning which the witness has testified."

2. Consider the tactical problem created by the dictates of the Jencks Act described in United States v. Gardin, 352 F.2d 601 (2d Cir. 1967):

ANDERSON, J. . . .

The appellant further objects to the fact that his trial counsel was not permitted to make his request for Jencks Act material relating to Agent Jensen's testimony outside of the presence of the jury, although he made the request at the trial.

The Court of Appeals for the District of Columbia Circuit, in a divided panel, has held it to be reversible error for the trial judge to direct that Jencks Act material be sought in the presence of the jury. The court reasoned that the production of such material in the presence of the jury, followed by a failure to use it in cross-examining the Government's witness, implied to the jury that the witness had made prior consistent statements, which are generally not admissible.

While we are not entirely in accord with the conclusion that allowing circumstances to arise at a trial which create the possibility that a jury may draw the inference of a past consistent statement, of itself, constitutes reversible error, we are of the opinion that the fair and just administration of criminal prosecutions might well be better served if the proceeding for the production of Jencks Act statements or reports were to take place out of the presence of the jury when the defendant requests that this be done.

It is, of course, entirely possible, if not probable, that members of a jury may draw an inference or gain impressions scarcely helpful to a defendant who in their presence has pressed a motion for production of a statement or report made by the witness to the Government and who, after gaining possession of it, examines it with care and then makes no use of it. As this court said in United States v. Annunziato, 293 F.2d 373, 382 (2d Cir.):

> "Had we been defense counsel, we would have bitterly regretted receiving it, [the witness' statement producible under the Jencks Act] since its production would have presented the dilemma, which trial lawyers strive desperately to avoid, that examination of the report would only reinforce the witness' testimony whereas failure to use it would do the same."

The Government on the other hand argues that it is entitled to have the jury know if material, made available under the Jencks Act, is used by the defense, that it has been provided by the Government. While the possible prejudice to the Government's witness resulting from nondisclosure of the statement's source is somewhat more subtle, there is no very cogent reason against letting it be known.

The procedure to be followed should be left to the discretion of the trial judge. While we therefore lay down no hard and fast rule, we do suggest the following which generally may meet the positions of both parties. After the completion of the witness' direct testimony and before cross-examination has been concluded, the defendant will state that he requests leave to make a motion in the absence of the jury; the trial judge will then excuse the jury, and, in its absence, the defendant will move for disclosure of Jencks Act material. Thereafter all steps through the delivery to the defendant of the statement or report, or the portions thereof, to which the defendant is found to be entitled, and including the allowance of a reasonable time to the defendant to examine the material, will take place while the jury is still absent. If, thereafter, the defendant decides to make use of any of the material for cross-examination of the witness, he will be permitted to do so only upon condition that he state preliminarily to the court and jury that he is about to question the witness on the basis of a written statement or report which the Government has made available to the defendant as required by law. This is to negative any inference that the Government had been covering something up and will precede compliance with the general rule of evidence for the protection of the witness which requires the laying of a proper foundation for the introduction of a past contradictory statement.

MOORE, CIRCUIT JUDGE [concurring opinion omitted.]

3. The issue of discovery at trial is not a minor one. Most states do not allow much pre-trial discovery. In one state whose discovery rules are of recent vintage, there is a specific prohibition on pre-trial discovery of the written statements of witnesses. See Pa.R.Crim.P. 310. See also Kan. Stats. § 22–3213 (1974) Ky.R.Crim.P. 7.25.

4. On the question of "lost" evidence see United States v. Bryant, 439 F.2d 642 (D.C.Cir. 1971). In *Bryant* the court held that sanctions for nondisclosure based on loss of evidence will be invoked in the future unless the Government can show that it has promulgated, enforced and attempted in good faith to follow rigorous and systematic procedures designed to preserve *all* discoverable evidence gathered in the course of a criminal investigation.

The court then went on to say:

"The burden, of course, is on the Government to make this showing. Negligent failure to comply with the required procedures will provide no excuse. Although we leave it up to the various investigative agencies to draft rules suited to their own method of operation, all such rules will be subject to review of their adequacy to the assigned task.

"A more amorphous definition of 'earnest efforts' would be difficult to administer and would inevitably deal less evenhandedly with individual defendants. A right so crucial as that of disclosure ought not to be built on such shifting sands. It ought, rather, to be protected by rules, systematically applied and systematically enforced. By requiring that the discretionary authority of investigative agents be controlled by regular procedures for preserving evidence, we intend to ensure that rights recognized at one stage of the criminal process will not be undercut at other, less visible, stages."

Chapter 16

PLEAS

One of the Federal Rules of Criminal Procedure provides:

Rule 11. Pleas

(a) *Alternatives.* A defendant may plead not guilty, guilty, or nolo contendere. If a defendant refuses to plead or if a defendant corporation fails to appear, the court shall enter a plea of not guilty.

(b) *Nolo Contendere.* A defendant may plead nolo contendere only with the consent of the court. Such a plea shall be accepted by the court only after due consideration of the views of the parties and the interest of the public in the effective administration of justice.

(c) *Advice to Defendant.* Before accepting a plea of guilty or nolo contendere, the court must address the defendant personally in open court and inform him of, and determine that he understands, the following:

(1) the nature of the charge to which the plea is offered, the mandatory minimum penalty provided by law, if any, and the maximum possible penalty provided by law; and

(2) if the defendant is not represented by an attorney, that he has the right to be represented by an attorney at every stage of the proceeding against him and, if necessary, one will be appointed to represent him; and

(3) that he has the right to plead not guilty or to persist in that plea if it has already been made, and that he has the right to be tried by a jury and at that trial has the right to the assistance of counsel, the right to confront and cross-examine witnesses against him, and the right not to be compelled to incriminate himself; and

(4) that if he pleads guilty or nolo contendere there will not be a further trial of any kind, so that by pleading guilty or nolo contendere he waives the right to a trial; and

(5) that if he pleads guilty or nolo contendere, the court may ask him questions about the offense to which he has pleaded, and if he answers these questions under oath, on the record, and in the presence of counsel, his answers may later be used against him in a prosecution for perjury or false statement.

(d) *Insuring That the Plea is Voluntary.* The court shall not accept a plea of guilty or nolo contendere without first, by addressing the defendant personally in open court, determining that the plea is voluntary and not the result of force or threats or of promises apart from a plea agreement. The court shall also inquire as to whether the defendant's willingness to plead guilty or nolo contendere results from prior discussions between the attorney for the government and the defendant or his attorney.

(e) *Plea Agreement Procedure.*

(1) In General. The attorney for the government and the attorney for the defendant or the defendant when acting pro se may engage in discussions with a view toward reaching an agreement that, upon the entering of a plea of guilty or nolo contendere to a charged offense or to a lesser or related offense, the attorney for the government will do any of the following:

(A) move for dismissal of other charges; or

(B) make a recommendation, or agree not to oppose the defendant's request, for a particular sentence, with the understanding that such recommendation or request shall not be binding upon the court; or

(C) agree that a specific sentence is the appropriate disposition of the case.

The court shall not participate in any such discussions.

(2) Notice of Such Agreement. If a plea agreement has been reached by the parties, the court shall, on the record, require the disclosure of the agreement in open court or, on a showing of good cause, in camera, at the time the plea is offered. If the agreement is of the type specified in subdivision (e)(1)(A) or (C), the court may accept or reject the agreement, or may defer its decision as to the acceptance or rejection until there has been an opportunity to consider the presentence report. If the agreement is of the type specified in subdivision (e)(1)(B), the court shall advise the defendant that if the court does not accept the recommendation or request, the defendant nevertheless has no right to withdraw the plea.

(3) Acceptance of a Plea Agreement. If the court accepts the plea agreement, the court shall inform the defendant that it will embody in the judgment and sentence the disposition provided for in the plea agreement.

(4) Rejection of a Plea Agreement. If the court rejects the plea agreement, the court shall, on the record, inform the parties of this fact, advise the defendant personally in open court or, on a showing of good cause, in camera, that the court is not bound by the plea agreement, afford the defendant the opportunity to then withdraw his plea, and advise the defendant that if he persists in his guilty plea or plea of nolo contendere the disposition of the case may be less favorable to the defendant than that contemplated by the plea agreement.

(5) **Time of Plea Agreement Procedure.** Except for good cause shown, notification to the court of the existence of a plea agreement shall be given at the arraignment or at such other time, prior to trial, as may be fixed by the court.

(6) **Inadmissibility of Pleas, Offers of Pleas, and Related Statements.** Except as otherwise provided in this paragraph, evidence of a plea of guilty, later withdrawn, or a plea of nolo contendere, or of an offer to plead guilty or nolo contendere to the crime charged or any other crime, or of statements made in connection with, and relevant to, any of the foregoing pleas or offers, is not admissible in any civil or criminal proceeding against the person who made the plea or offer. However, evidence of a statement made in connection with, and relevant to, a plea of guilty, later withdrawn, a plea of nolo contendere, or an offer to plead guilty or nolo contendere to the crime charged or any other crime, is admissible in a criminal proceeding for perjury or false statement if the statement was made by the defendant under oath, on the record, and in the presence of counsel.

(f) *Determining Accuracy of Plea.* Notwithstanding the acceptance of a plea of guilty, the court should not enter a judgment upon such plea without making such inquiry as shall satisfy it that there is a factual basis for the plea.

(g) *Record of Proceedings.* A verbatim record of the proceedings at which the defendant enters a plea shall be made and, if there is a plea of guilty or nolo contendere, the record shall include, without limitation, the court's advice to the defendant, the inquiry into the voluntariness of the plea including any plea agreement, and the inquiry into the accuracy of a guilty plea.

A.   ADVICE TO THE DEFENDANT

BOYKIN v. ALABAMA

Supreme Court of the United States, 1969.
395 U.S. 238, 89 S.Ct. 1709.

MR. JUSTICE DOUGLAS delivered the opinion of the Court.

In the spring of 1966, within the period of a fortnight, a series of armed robberies occurred in Mobile, Alabama. The victims, in each case, were local shopkeepers open at night who were forced by a gunman to hand over money. While robbing one grocery store, the assailant fired his gun once, sending a bullet through a door into the ceiling. A few days earlier in a drug store, the robber had allowed his gun to discharge in such a way that the bullet, on ricochet from the floor, struck a customer in the leg. Shortly thereafter, a local grand jury returned five indictments against petitioner, a 27-year-old Negro, for common-law robbery—an offense punishable in Alabama by death.

Before the matter came to trial, the court determined that petitioner was indigent and appointed counsel to represent him. Three days later, at his arraignment, petitioner pleaded guilty to all five indictments. So far as the record shows, the judge asked no questions of petitioner concerning his plea, and petitioner did not address the court.

Trial strategy may of course make a plea of guilty seem the desirable course. But the record is wholly silent on that point and throws no light on it.

Alabama provides that when a defendant pleads guilty, "the court must cause the punishment to be determined by a jury" (except where it is required to be fixed by the court) and may "cause witnesses to be examined, to ascertain the character of the offense." Ala.Code Tit. 15, § 277 (1958). In the present case a trial of that dimension was held, the prosecution presenting its case largely through eyewitness testimony. Although counsel for petitioner engaged in cursory cross-examination, petitioner neither testified himself nor presented testimony concerning his character and background. There was nothing to indicate that he had a prior criminal record.

In instructing the jury, the judge stressed that petitioner had pleaded guilty in five cases of robbery, defined as "the felonious taking of money . . . from another against his will . . . by violence or by putting him in fear . . . [carrying] from ten years minimum in the penitentiary to the supreme penalty of death by electrocution." The jury, upon deliberation, found petitioner guilty and sentenced him severally to die on each of the five indictments.

Taking an [appeal, petitioner argued] that a sentence of death for common-law robbery was cruel and unusual punishment within the meaning of the Federal Constitution, a suggestion which that court unanimously rejected. 281 Ala. 659, 207 So.2d 412. On their own motion, however, four of the seven justices discussed the constitutionality of the process by which the trial judge had accepted petitioner's guilty plea. From the order affirming the trial court, three justices dissented on the ground that the record was inadequate to show that petitioner had intelligently and knowingly pleaded guilty. The fourth member concurred separately, conceding that "a trial judge should not accept a guilty plea unless he has determined that such a plea was voluntarily and knowingly entered by the defendant," but refusing "[f]or aught appearing" "to presume that the trial judge failed to do his duty." 281 Ala., at 662, 663, 207 So.2d, at 414, 415.

Respondent does not suggest that we lack jurisdiction to review the voluntary character of petitioner's guilty plea because he failed to raise that federal question below and the state court failed to pass upon it. But the question was raised on oral argument and we conclude that it is properly presented. The very Alabama statute (Ala. Code, Tit. 15, § 382(10) (1958)) that provides automatic appeal in capital cases also requires the reviewing court to comb the record for "any error prejudicial to the appellant, even though not called to our attention in brief of counsel." Lee v. State, 265 Ala. 623, 630, 93 So. 2d 757, 763. The automatic appeal statute "is the only provision under the Plain Error doctrine of which we are aware in Alabama criminal appellate review." Douglas v. State, 42 Ala.App. 314, 331, n. 6, 163 So.2d 477, 494, n. 6. In the words of the Alabama Supreme Court:

> "Perhaps it is well to note that in reviewing a death case under the automatic appeal statute, . . . we may consider any testimony that was seriously prejudicial to the rights of the appellant and may reverse thereon, even though no lawful objection or exception was made thereto. [Citations omitted.] Our review is not limited to the matters brought to our attention in brief of counsel." Duncan v. State, 278 Ala. 145, 157, 176 So.2d 840, 851.

It was error, plain on the face of the record, for the trial judge to accept petitioner's guilty plea without an affirmative showing that it was intelligent and voluntary. That error, under Alabama procedure, was properly before the court below and considered explicitly by a majority of the justices and is properly before us on review.

A plea of guilty is more than a confession which admits that the accused did various acts; it is itself a conviction; nothing remains but to give judgment and determine punishment. See Kercheval v. United States, 274 U.S. 220, 223, 47 S.Ct. 582, 583. Admissibility of a confession must be based on a "reliable determination on the voluntariness issue which satisfies the constitutional rights of the defendant." Jackson v. Denno, 378 U.S. 368, 387, 84 S.Ct. 1774, 1786. The requirement that the prosecution spread on the record the prerequisites of a valid waiver is no constitutional innovation. In Carnley v.

Cochran, 369 U.S. 506, 516, 82 S.Ct. 884, 890, we dealt with a problem of waiver of the right to counsel, a Sixth Amendment right. We held: "Presuming waiver from a silent record is impermissible. The record must show, or there must be an allegation and evidence which show, that an accused was offered counsel but intelligently and understandingly rejected the offer. Anything less is not waiver."

We think that the same standard must be applied to determining whether a guilty plea is voluntarily made. For, as we have said, a plea of guilty is more than an admission of conduct; it is a conviction. Ignorance, incomprehension, coercion, terror, inducements, subtle or blatant threats might be a perfect cover-up of unconstitutionality. The question of an effective waiver of a federal constitutional right in a proceeding is of course governed by federal standards. Douglas v. Alabama, 380 U.S. 415, 422, 85 S.Ct. 1074, 1078.

Several federal constitutional rights are involved in a waiver that takes place when a plea of guilty is entered in a state criminal trial. First, is the privilege against compulsory self-incrimination guaranteed by the Fifth Amendment and applicable to the States by reason of the Fourteenth. Malloy v. Hogan, 378 U.S. 1, 84 S.Ct. 1489. Second, is the right to trial by jury. Duncan v. Louisiana, 391 U.S. 145, 88 S.Ct. 1444. Third, is the right to confront one's accusers. Pointer v. Texas, 380 U.S. 400, 85 S.Ct. 1065. We cannot presume a waiver of these three important federal rights from a silent record.

What is at stake for an accused facing death or imprisonment demands the utmost solicitude of which courts are capable in canvassing the matter with the accused to make sure he has a full understanding of what the plea connotes and of its consequence. When the judge discharges that function, he leaves a record adequate for any review that may be later sought (Garner v. Louisiana, 368 U.S. 157, 173, 82 S.Ct. 248, 256; Specht v. Patterson, 386 U.S. 605, 610, 87 S. Ct. 1209, 1212, and forestalls the spin-off of collateral proceedings that seek to probe murky memories.[1]

The three dissenting justices in the Alabama Supreme Court stated the law accurately when they concluded that there was reversible error "because the record does not disclose that the defendant voluntarily and understandingly entered his pleas of guilty." 281 Ala., at 663, 207 So.2d, at 415.

Reversed.

---

1. "A majority of criminal convictions are obtained after a plea of guilty. If these convictions are to be insulated from attack, the trial court is best advised to conduct an on the record examination of the defendant which should include, inter alia, an attempt to satisfy itself that the defendant understands the nature of the charges, his right to a jury trial, the acts sufficient to constitute the offenses for which he is charged and the permissible range of sentences." Commonwealth ex rel. West v. Rundle, 428 Pa. 102, 105–106, 237 A.2d 196, 197–198 (1968).

MR. JUSTICE HARLAN, whom MR. JUSTICE BLACK joins, dissenting.

The Court today holds that petitioner Boykin was denied due process of law, and that his robbery convictions must be reversed outright, solely, because "the record [is] inadequate to show that petitioner . . . intelligently and knowingly pleaded guilty." Ante, at 1711. The Court thus in effect fastens upon the States, as a matter of federal constitutional law, the rigid prophylactic requirements of Rule 11 of the Federal Rules of Criminal Procedure. It does so in circumstances where the Court itself has only very recently held application of Rule 11 to be unnecessary in the federal courts. See Halliday v. United States, 394 U.S. 831, 89 S.Ct. 1498 (1969). Moreover, the Court does all this at the behest of a petitioner who has never at any time alleged that his guilty plea was involuntary or made without knowledge of the consequences. I cannot possibly subscribe to so bizarre a result.

In June 1966, an Alabama grand jury returned five indictments against petitioner Boykin, on five separate charges of common-law robbery. He was determined to be indigent, and on July 11 an attorney was appointed to represent him. Petitioner was arraigned three days later. At that time, in open court and in the presence of his attorney, petitioner pleaded guilty to all five indictments. The record does not show what inquiries were made by the arraigning judge to confirm that the plea was made voluntarily and knowingly.

Petitioner was not sentenced immediately after the acceptance of his plea. Instead, pursuant to an Alabama statute, the court ordered that "witnesses . . . be examined, to ascertain the character of the offense," in the presence of a jury which would then fix petitioner's sentence. See Ala.Code, Tit. 14, § 415 (1958); Tit. 15, § 277. That proceeding occurred some two months after petitioner pleaded guilty. During that period, petitioner made no attempt to withdraw his plea. Petitioner was present in court with his attorney when the witnesses were examined. Petitioner heard the judge state the elements of common-law robbery and heard him announce that petitioner had pleaded guilty to that offense and might be sentenced to death. Again, petitioner made no effort to withdraw his plea.

On his appeal to the Alabama Supreme Court, petitioner did not claim that his guilty plea was made involuntarily or without full knowledge of the consequences. In fact, petitioner raised no questions at all concerning the plea. In his petition and brief in this Court, and in oral argument by counsel, petitioner has never asserted that the plea was coerced or made in ignorance of the consequences.

Against this background, the Court holds that the Due Process Clause of the Fourteenth Amendment requires the outright reversal of petitioner's conviction. This result is wholly unprecedented. There are past holdings of this Court to the effect that a federal habeas corpus petitioner who makes sufficiently credible allegations that his state guilty plea was involuntary is entitled to a hearing as to the truth of those allegations. See, e. g., Waley v. Johnston, 316

U.S. 101, 62 S.Ct. 964 (1942); cf. Machibroda v. United States, 368 U.S. 487, 82 S.Ct. 510 (1962). These holdings suggest that if equally convincing allegations were made in a petition for certiorari on direct review, the petitioner might in some circumstances be entitled to have a judgment of affirmance vacated and the case remanded for a state hearing on voluntariness. Cf. Jackson v. Denno, 378 U.S. 368, 393–394, 84 S.Ct. 1774, 1789–1790 (1964). However, as has been noted, this petitioner makes no allegations of actual involuntariness.

The Court's reversal is therefore predicated entirely upon the failure of the arraigning state judge to make an "adequate" record. In holding that this is a ground for reversal, the Court quotes copiously from McCarthy v. United States, 394 U.S. 459, 89 S.Ct. 1166 (1969), in which we held earlier this Term that when a *federal* district judge fails to comply in every respect with the procedure for accepting a guilty plea which is prescribed in Rule 11 of the Federal Rules of Criminal Procedure, the plea must be set aside and the defendant permitted to replead, regardless of lower-court findings that the plea was in fact voluntary. What the Court omits to mention is that in *McCarthy* we stated that our decision was based "solely upon our construction of Rule 11," and explicitly disavowed any reliance upon the Constitution. Id., at 464, 89 S.Ct., at 1169. Thus *McCarthy* can provide no support whatever for today's constitutional edict.

So far as one can make out from the Court's opinion, what is now in effect being held is that the prophylactic procedures of Criminal Rule 11 are substantially applicable to the States as a matter of federal constitutional due process. If this is the basis upon which Boykin's conviction is being reversed, then the Court's disposition is plainly out of keeping with a sequel case to *McCarthy*, decided only last month. For the Court held in Halliday v. United States, 394 U. S. 831, 89 S.Ct. 1498 (1969), that "in view of the large number of constitutionally valid convictions that may have been obtained without full compliance with Rule 11, we decline to apply *McCarthy* retroactively."

The Court quite evidently found Halliday's conviction to be "constitutionally valid," for it affirmed the conviction even though Halliday's guilty plea was accepted in 1954 without any explicit inquiry into whether it was knowingly and understandingly made, as now required by present Rule 11. In justification, the Court noted that two lower courts had found in collateral proceedings that the plea was voluntary. The Court declared that:

> "[A] defendant whose plea has been accepted without full compliance with Rule 11 may still resort to appropriate post-conviction remedies to attack his plea's voluntariness. Thus, if his plea was accepted prior to our decision in *McCarthy*, he is not without a remedy to correct constitutional defects in his conviction." Id., at 833, 89 S.Ct., at 1499.

It seems elementary that the Fifth Amendment due process to which petitioner Halliday was entitled must be at least as demanding as the Fourteenth Amendment process due petitioner Boykin. Yet petitioner Halliday's federal conviction has been affirmed as "constitutionally valid," despite the omission of any judicial inquiry of record at the time of his plea, because he initiated collateral proceedings which revealed that the plea was actually voluntary. Petitioner Boykin, on the other hand, today has his Alabama conviction reversed because of exactly the same omission, even though he too "may . . . resort to appropriate post-conviction remedies to attack his plea's voluntariness" and thus "is not without a remedy to correct constitutional defects in his conviction." In short, I find it utterly impossible to square today's holding with what the Court has so recently done.

I would hold that petitioner Boykin is not entitled to outright reversal of his conviction simply because of the "inadequacy" of the record pertaining to his guilty plea. Further, I would not vacate the judgment below and remand for a state-court hearing on voluntariness. For even if it is assumed for the sake of argument that petitioner would be entitled to such a hearing if he had alleged that the plea was involuntary, a matter which I find it unnecessary to decide, the fact is that he has never made any such claim. Hence, I consider that petitioner's present arguments relating to his guilty plea entitle him to no federal relief.

NOTES

1. In McCarthy v. United States, 394 U.S. 459, 89 S.Ct. 1166 (1969), the Court held that Fed.R.Crim.P. 11 required the court to personally address the defendant to ascertain the voluntariness and basis of the plea and the defendant's understanding of its consequences. Acceptance of pleas upon the assurance of counsel that the defendant had been admonished was held to be improper. The Court did not indicate any dissatisfaction with the guidelines for admonitions contained in Rule 11. The purpose of direct inquiry is to make the court "better able to ascertain the plea's voluntariness and also to develop a more complete record to support his determination in a subsequent post-conviction attack." The holding in *McCarthy* was applicable only to federal cases, and in Halliday v. United States, 394 U.S. 831, 89 S.Ct. 1498 (1969), the Court refused to apply its requirements retroactively.

2. When *McCarthy* was decided, Rule 11 required the court to determine that the plea was made with "understanding of the nature of the charge and the consequences of the plea." In 1975, the Rule was amended to codify the requirements of *Boykin*. The amended Rule is designed to permit some flexibility in determining whether the defendant understands the nature of the charge. In most cases, it is sufficient for the court to read or summarize the indictment and explain the elements of the offense. However, the nature of the court's explanation must vary on the basis of the complexity of the circumstances and the sophistication of the particular defendant.

3. It is clear that the specific requirements of Rule 11 are inapplicable to guilty pleas in state courts. See Roddy v. Black, 516 F.2d 1380 (6th Cir. 1975); State v. Storbakken, 246 N.W.2d 78 (N.D.1976); State v. Ricks, 48 Ohio App.2d 128, 356 N.E.2d 312 (1976). However, the fact that the Court did not delineate a precise procedure for the states to follow in *Boykin* has

led to two different results. Some states have concluded that the admonitions set forth in *Boykin* must be specifically followed. See Nachtigall v. Erickson, 85 S.D. 122, 178 N.W.2d 198 (1970); Bailey v. State, 277 A.2d 246 (M.D.App.1971); Cooper v. State, 47 Ala.App. 178, 252 So.2d 104 (1971); State ex rel. Jackson v. Henderson, 260 La. 90, 255 So.2d 85 (1971); In re Sutherland, 6 Cal.3d 666, 100 Cal.Rptr. 129, 493 P.2d 857 (1972); Brown v. Warden, 494 P.2d 959 (Nev.1972). The possibility that this theory may be valid has led several courts to hold that *Boykin* applies only prospectively. Green v. Turner, 443 F.2d 832 (10th Cir. 1971). The second theory is that *Boykin* stands for the principle that an adequate record must be made in state guilty plea cases but does not prescribe specific admonitions. See Hansen v. Matthews, 424 F.2d 1025 (7th Cir. 1970): "In *Boykin* the Supreme Court held only that there must be evidence in the trial record showing that a guilty plea was knowingly and intelligently entered. Procedures similar to Fed.R.Crim.P. 11 were not suggested by the Court and are not required by its decision." See also People v. Ferguson, 383 Mich. 645, 178 N.W.2d 490 (1970); Kelly v. State, 254 So.2d 22 (Fla.App. 1971); State v. Laurino, 106 Ariz. 586, 480 P.2d 342 (1971); State v. Turner, 183 N.W.2d 763 (Neb.1971); State v. White, 5 Wash.App. 615, 489 P.2d 934 (1971).

In order to assure that a precise procedure is followed in accepting pleas, several states have devised specific and detailed rules for pleas of guilty in response to *Boykin*. See Rule 402, Rules of the Supreme Court of Illinois; People v. Williams, 386 Mich. 277, 192 N.W.2d 466 (1971).

4.   What must the record reflect in order for the plea to be acceptable? The defendant must plead with knowledge of the charge and its basic elements. Examples of the minimum acceptable explanation are set forth in United States v. Coronado, 554 F.2d 166 (5th Cir. 1977), and United States v. Journet, 544 F.2d 633 (2d Cir. 1976). There is some difference of opinion as to the degree that the record must reflect detailed discussion of specific elements. Compare People v. Rosado, 2 Ill.App.3d 231, 276 N.E.2d 473 (1971) (receipt of indictment and a general verbal statement of the charge is sufficient) with People v. Randolph, 488 P.2d 203 (Colo.1971); People v. Riney, 489 P.2d 1304 (Colo.1971); People v. Mason, 491 P.2d 1383 (Colo. 1971) (requiring detailed admonition). See also Belgarde v. Turner, 421 F.2d 1395 (10th Cir. 1970) (daytime vs. nighttime burglary); United States v. Davis, 212 F.2d 264 (7th Cir. 1954) (conspiracy vs. substantive offense); United States ex rel. Williams v. Follette, 408 F.2d 658 (2nd Cir. 1969) (felony vs. misdemeanor); United States v. Hegecoe, 420 F.2d 458 (4th Cir. 1970) (scienter).

5.   In Henderson v. Morgan, 426 U.S. 637, 96 S.Ct. 2253 (1976), the Supreme Court deemed involuntary a state court defendant's plea to second-degree murder. Defendant had been charged with first-degree murder. As is often the case, no separate charge of second-degree murder was filed. Thus the accused had no written notice of the elements of that offense. The trial court did not explain the elements of second-degree murder. Neither the defendant nor his counsel stipulated that the defendant had the necessary intent. The plurality opinion held:

> "We assume, as [the state] argues, that the prosecutor had overwhelming evidence of guilt available. We also accept [the State's] characterization of the competence of respondent's counsel and of the wisdom of their advice to plead guilty to a charge of second-degree murder. Nevertheless, such a plea cannot support a

judgment of guilt unless it was voluntary in a constitutional sense. And clearly the plea could not be voluntary in the sense that it constituted an intelligent admission that he committed the offense unless the defendant received 'real notice of the true nature of the charge against him, the first and most universally recognized requirement of due process.'

"The charge of second-degree murder was never formally made. Had it been made, it necessarily would have included a charge that respondent's assault was 'committed with a design to effect the death of the person killed.' That element of the offense might have been proved by the objective evidence even if respondent's actual state of mind was consistent with innocence or manslaughter. But even if such a design to effect death would almost inevitably have been inferred from evidence that respondent repeatedly stabbed [the victim], it is nevertheless also true that a jury would not have been required to draw that inference. The jury would have been entitled to accept defense counsel's appraisal of the incident as involving only manslaughter in the first degree. Therefore, an admission by respondent that he killed [the victim] does not necessarily also admit that he was guilty of second-degree murder.

"There is nothing in this record that can serve as a substitute for either a finding after trial, or a voluntary admission, that respondent had the requisite intent. Defense counsel did not purport to stipulate to that fact; they did not explain to him that his plea would be an admission of that fact; and he made no factual statement or admission necessarily implying that he had such intent. In these circumstances it is impossible to conclude that his plea to the unexplained charge of second-degree murder was voluntary."

6. The degree to which the direct or collateral consequences of a plea must be explained has generated substantial confusion. Compare Durant v. United States, 410 F.2d 689 (1st Cir. 1969) (parole ineligibility must be stated) with Trujillo v. United States, 377 F.2d 266 (5th Cir. 1967) (advice concerning parole eligibility not required). As a result, the amendment to Rule 11 requires the court to advise the defendant of any minimum sentence which *must* be imposed and any maximum which *may* be imposed. Advice on matters such as parole eligibility and other collateral issues is left to the court's discretion, to be given only when it is felt that a particular consequence of a plea is of real significance to the particular defendant. However, the admonition should be given in plain language, such as, "any number of years such as fifty or one hundred years" rather than "an indeterminate number of years". See People v. McCracken, 3 Ill.App.3d 759, 279 N. E.2d 183 (1972).

As a general rule, consequences positively required by statute should be explained, see People v. Holland, 1 Ill.App.2d 885, 275 N.E.2d 190 (1971); State v. Young, 106 Ariz. 589, 480 P.2d 345 (1971) (mandatory consecutive sentences). On the other hand, possible consequences may not require an explanation. See Faulisi v. Daggett, 527 F.2d 305 (7th Cir. 1975) (no explanation required when a federal sentence may run consecutive to a pending state sentence); Bunker v. Wise, 550 F.2d 1155 (9th Cir. 1977) (need not advise defendant of when he will be eligible for parole).

In United States v. Timmreck, 441 U.S. 780, 99 S.Ct. 2085 (1979), the Court held that a technical violation of Rule 11—a trial court's failure to mention a mandatory special parole term—does not provide a basis for setting aside the plea on collateral attack. Compare Note, Rule 11 and Collateral Attacks on Guilty Pleas, 86 Yale L.J. 1395 (1977).

7. The fact that a defendant is aware of the available defenses is significant and contributes to the finding of a valid plea. See United States ex rel. McDonald v. Pennsylvania, 343 F.2d 447 (3rd Cir. 1965); Young v. Brewer, 190 N.W.2d 434 (Iowa 1971). In one case a court found that an absolute defense to the charge was known to the defendant and nevertheless waived by his plea of guilty. See Quijada-Gaxiola v. United States, 435 F. 2d 264 (9th Cir. 1970). Compare United States v. Lucia, 416 F.2d 920 (5th Cir. 1969).

8. The defendant must respond affirmatively to the various judicial admonitions concerning the charge, the various waivers of rights, the desire to plead guilty, and, where appropriate, the nature of the agreement which is the basis of the plea. The failure or refusal of the defendant to respond for the record renders the plea invalid.

While the defendant is not required to state, in his own words, the facts of the offense and his detailed understanding of each consequence of the plea, United States. v. Madrigal, 518 F.2d 166 (7th Cir. 1975), he must acknowledge the court's admonitions. Thus, a defendant who remains mute throughout the plea procedure cannot be said to have pleaded guilty. See Williams v. State, 473 S.W.2d 97 (Mo.1971). Moreover, when co-defendants plead guilty at the same time the court must address each individually to assure that he understands his rights and the consequences of the plea. United States v. Fels, 599 F.2d 142 (7th Cir. 1979).

A clear showing of awareness of the rights must appear from the responses of the accused though express language such as "I waive this right" is not required. An acknowledgement that the admonitions are understood should be sufficient. See People v. Kirkpatrick, 22 Cal.App.3d 420, 99 Cal. Rptr. 207 (1971). Where the record shows a waiver, it will prevail over the accused's denials of waiver. See State v. Barlow, 193 N.W.2d 455 (N.D. 1971).

9. Where defendant is not represented by counsel and pleads guilty, there must be both a valid waiver of counsel and an adequate plea procedure. See Smith v. United States, 238 F.2d 925 (5th Cir. 1956); Ford v. United States, 412 F.2d 499 (4th Cir. 1969); Malignaro v. Smith, 408 F.2d 795 (5th Cir. 1969).

The presence of counsel does not give rise to presumption that a proper plea procedure was followed. See Gomez v. United States, 396 F.2d 323 (9th Cir. 1968); United States v. Diggs, 304 F.2d 929 (6th Cir. 1969); Stetson v. United States, 417 F.2d 1250 (7th Cir. 1969). However, the presence of counsel may justify an inference that the plea was entered voluntarily. McMann v. Richardson, 397 U.S. 759, 90 S.Ct. 441 (1970); Brady v. United States, 397 U.S. 742, 90 S.Ct. 1463 (1970); Parker v. North Carolina, 397 U.S. 790, 90 S.Ct. 1458 (1970). But that inference can be overcome by other facts of record. See Henderson v. Morgan, 426 U.S. 637, 96 S.Ct. 2253 (1976).

Defense counsel at a plea of guilty owes the same duty to his client as he would during a trial of the cause. His representation must be free from any conflict of interest. See Dukes v. Warden, 406 U.S. 250, 92 S.Ct. 1551 (1972).

10. One of the major reasons for the detailed inquiry necessary to support a guilty plea is the fact that the defendant waives not only his basic right to a trial, but also many of the legal issues which attended the proceeding to the point of the plea. In Tollett v. Henderson, 411 U.S. 258, 267, 93 S.Ct. 1602, 1608 (1973), the court said: "A guilty plea represents a break in the chain of events which has preceded it in the criminal process. When a criminal defendant has solemnly admitted in open court that he is in fact guilty of the offense with which he is charged, he may not thereafter raise independent claims relating to the deprivation of constitutional rights that occurred prior to the entry of the guilty plea."

May a defendant plead guilty and reserve the right to appeal on a non-jurisdictional issue such as an adverse ruling following a suppression hearing? Compare United States v. Sepe, 486 F.2d 1044 (5th Cir. 1973) (en banc) (disapproving of the practice of a reserved right to appeal), with United States v. Brown, 499 F.2d 829 (7th Cir. 1974) (considering merits of issue when court accepted a conditional plea). An alternative to this procedure is to stipulate to the facts, allow the court to enter judgment, and appeal the issue. Under this procedure, however, the guilty plea admonitions are not required. See United States v. Terrack, 515 F.2d 558 (9th Cir. 1975).

B. VOLUNTARINESS OF THE PLEA

NORTH CAROLINA v. ALFORD

Supreme Court of the United States, 1970.
400 U.S. 25, 91 S.Ct. 160.

MR. JUSTICE WHITE delivered the opinion of the Court.

On December 2, 1963, Alford was indicted for first-degree murder, a capital offense under North Carolina law.[1] The court appointed an attorney to represent him, and this attorney questioned all but one of the various witnesses who appellee said would substantiate his claim of innocence. The witnesses, however, did not support Alford's story but gave statements that strongly indicated his guilt. Faced with strong evidence of guilt and no substantial evidentiary support for the claim of innocence, Alford's attorney recommended that he plead guilty, but left the ultimate decision to Alford himself. The prosecutor agreed to accept a plea of guilty to a charge of second-degree murder, and on December 10, 1963, Alford pleaded guilty to the reduced charge.

Before the plea was finally accepted by the trial court, the court heard the sworn testimony of a police officer who summarized the

---

1. At the time Alford pleaded guilty, North Carolina law provided that if a guilty plea to a charge of first-degree murder was accepted by the prosecution and the court, the penalty would be life imprisonment rather than death. The provision permitting guilty pleas in capital cases was re- pealed in 1969. Though under present North Carolina law it is not possible for a defendant to plead guilty to a capital charge, it seemingly remains possible for a person charged with a capital offense to plead guilty to a lesser charge.

State's case. Two other witnesses besides Alford were also heard. Although there was no eyewitnesses to the crime, the testimony indicated that shortly before the killing Alford took his gun from his house, stated his intention to kill the victim, and returned home with the declaration that he had carried out the killing. After the summary presentation of the State's case, Alford took the stand and testified that he had not committed the murder but that he was pleading guilty because he faced the threat of the death penalty if he did not do so.[2] In response to the questions of his counsel, he acknowledged that his counsel had informed him of the difference between second- and first-degree murder and of his rights in case he chose to go to trial.[3] The trial court then asked appellee if, in light of his denial of guilt, he still desired to plead guilty to second-degree murder and appellee answered, "Yes, sir. I plead guilty on—from the circumstances that he [Alford's attorney] told me." After eliciting information about Alford's prior criminal record, which was a long one,[4] the trial court sentenced him to 30 years' imprisonment, the maximum penalty for second-degree murder.

Alford sought post-conviction relief in the state court. Among the claims raised was the claim that his plea of guilty was invalid because it was the product of fear and coercion. After a hearing, the state court in 1965 found that the plea was "willingly, knowingly, and understandingly" made on the advice of competent counsel and in the face of a strong prosecution case. Subsequently, Alford petitioned for a writ of habeas corpus [which was denied], on the basis of the

2. After giving his version of the events of the night of the murder, Alford stated:

"I pleaded guilty on second degree murder because they said there is too much evidence, but I ain't shot no man, but I take the fault for the other man. We never had an argument in our life and I just pleaded guilty because they said if I didn't they would gas me for it, and that is all."

In response to questions from his attorney, Alford affirmed that he had consulted several times with his attorney and with members of his family and had been informed of his rights if he chose to plead not guilty. Alford then reaffirmed his decision to plead guilty to second-degree murder:

"Q. [by Alford's attorney]. And you authorized me to tender a plea of guilty to second degree murder before the court?

"A. Yes, sir.

"Q. And in doing that, that you have again affirmed your decision on that point?

"A. Well, I'm still pleading that you all got me to plead guilty. I plead the other way, circumstantial evidence; that the jury will prosecute me on—on the second. You told me to plead guilty, right. I don't—I'm not guilty but I plead guilty."

3. At the state court hearing on post-conviction relief, the testimony confirmed that Alford had been fully informed by his attorney as to his rights on a plea of not guilty and as to the consequences of a plea of guilty. Since the record in this case affirmatively indicates that Alford was aware of the consequences of his plea of guilty and of the rights waived by the plea, no issues of substance under Boykin v. Alabama, 395 U.S. 238, 89 S.Ct. 1709 (1969), would be presented even if that case was held applicable to the events here in question.

4. Before Alford was sentenced, the trial judge asked Alford about prior convictions. Alford answered that, among other things, he had served six years of a ten-year sentence for murder, had been convicted nine times for armed robbery, and had been convicted for transporting stolen goods, forgery, and carring a concealed weapon.

state court's findings that Alford voluntarily and knowingly agreed to plead guilty. In 1967, Alford again petitioned for a writ of habeas corpus in the [Federal] District Court. That court, without an evidentiary hearing, again denied relief on the grounds that the guilty plea was voluntary and waived all defenses and nonjurisdictional defects in any prior stage of the proceedings and that the findings of the state court in 1965 clearly required rejection of Alford's claim that he was denied effective assistance of counsel prior to pleading guilty. On appeal, a divided panel of the Court of Appeals for the Fourth Circuit reversed on the ground that Alford's guilty plea was made involuntarily. 405 F.2d 340 (1968). In reaching its conclusion, the Court of Appeals relied heavily on United States v. Jackson, 390 U.S. 570, 88 S.Ct. 1209 (1968), which the court read to require invalidation of the North Carolina statutory framework for the imposition of the death penalty because North Carolina statutes encouraged defendants to waive constitutional rights by the promise of no more than life imprisonment if a guilty plea was offered and accepted. Conceding that *Jackson* did not require the automatic invalidation of pleas of guilty entered under the North Carolina statutes, the Court of Appeals ruled that Alford's guilty plea was involuntary because its principal motivation was fear of the death penalty. By this standard, even if both the judge and the jury had possessed the power to impose the death penalty for first-degree murder or if guilty pleas to capital charges had not been permitted, Alford's plea of guilty to second-degree murder should still have been rejected because impermissibly induced by his desire to eliminate the possibility of a death sentence. . . . We vacate the judgment of the Court of Appeals and remand the case for further proceedings.

We held in Brady v. United States, 397 U.S. 742, 90 S.Ct. 1463 (1970), that a plea of guilty which would not have been entered except for the defendant's desire to avoid a possible death penalty and to limit the maximum penalty to life imprisonment or a term of years was not for that reason compelled within the meaning of the Fifth Amendment. *Jackson* established no new test for determining the validity of guilty pleas. The standard was and remains whether the plea represents a voluntary and intelligent choice among the alternative courses of action open to the defendant. . . .

That he would not have pleaded except for the opportunity to limit the possible penalty does not necessarily demonstrate that the plea of guilty was not the product of a free and rational choice, especially where the defendant was represented by competent counsel whose advice was that the plea would be to the defendant's advantage. The standard fashioned and applied by the Court of Appeals was therefore erroneous.

* * *

As previously recounted after Alford's plea of guilty was offered and the State's case was placed before the judge, Alford denied that he had committed the murder but reaffirmed his desire to plead guilty to avoid a possible death sentence and to limit the penalty to the 30-year maximum provided for second-degree murder. Ordinarily, a judgment of conviction resting on a plea of guilty is justified by the defendant's admission that he committed the crime charged against him and his consent that judgment be entered without a trial of any kind. The plea usually subsumes both elements, and justifiably so, even though there is no separate, express admission by the defendant that he committed the particular acts claimed to constitute the crime charged in the indictment. . . . Here Alford entered his plea but accompanied it with the statement that he had not shot the victim.

If Alford's statements were to be credited as sincere assertions of his innocence, there obviously existed a factual and legal dispute between him and the State. Without more, it might be argued that the conviction entered on his guilty plea was invalid, since his assertion of innocence negatived any admission of guilt, which, as we observed in *Brady*, is normally "[c]entral to the plea and the foundation for entering judgment against the defendant . . . ." 397 U.S., at 748, 90 S.Ct., at 1468.

In addition to Alford's statement, however, the court had heard an account of the events on the night of the murder, including information from Alford's acquaintances that he had departed from his home with his gun stating his intention to kill and that he had later declared that he had carried out his intention. Nor had Alford wavered in his desire to have trial court determine his guilt without a jury trial. Although denying the charge against him, he nevertheless preferred the dispute between him and the State to be settled by the judge in the context of a guilty plea proceeding rather than by a formal trial. Thereupon, with the State's telling evidence and Alford's denial before it, the trial court proceeded to convict and sentence Alford for second-degree murder.

State and lower federal courts are divided upon whether a guilty plea can be accepted when it is accompanied by protestations of innocence and hence contains only a waiver of trial but no admission of guilt. Some courts . . . require that trial judges reject such pleas. But others have concluded that they should not "force any defense on a defendant in a criminal case," particularly when advancement of the defense might "end in disaster . . . ." They have argued that, since "guilt, or the degree of guilt, is at times uncertain and elusive," "[a]n accused, though believing in or entertaining doubts respecting his innocence, might reasonably conclude a jury would be convinced of his guilt and that he would fare better in the sentence by pleading guilty . . . ." As one state court observed nearly a century ago, "[r]easons other than the fact that he is guilty may induce a defendant to so plead, . . . [and] [h]e must be permitted to judge for himself in this respect." [5] . . .

---

5. A third approach has been to decline to rule definitively that a trial judge must either accept or reject an otherwise valid plea containing a protestation of innocence, but to leave that decision to his sound discretion. See Maxwell v. United States, 368 F. 2d 735, 738–739 (C.A.9 1966).

This Court has not confronted this precise issue, but prior decisions do yield relevant principles. In Lynch v. Overholser, 369 U.S. 705, 82 S.Ct. 1063 (1962), . . . the Court expressly refused to rule that Lynch had an absolute right to have his guilty plea accepted, but implied that there would have been no constitutional error had his plea been accepted even though evidence before the judge indicated that there was a valid defense.

The issue in Hudson v. United States, 272 U.S. 451, 47 S.Ct. 127 (1926), was whether a federal court has power to impose a prison sentence after accepting a plea of *nolo contendere*, a plea by which a defendant does not expressly admit his guilt, but nonetheless waives his right to a trial and authorizes the court for purposes of the case to treat him as if he were guilty.[6] The Court held that a trial court does have such power, and the federal courts have uniformly followed this rule, even in cases involving moral turpitude. . . . Implicit in the *nolo contendere* cases is a recognition that the Constitution does not bar imposition of a prison sentence upon an accused who is unwilling expressly to admit his guilt but who, faced with grim alternatives, is willing to waive his trial and accept the sentence.

These cases would be directly in point if Alford had simply insisted on his plea but refused to admit the crime. The fact that his plea was denominated a plea of guilty rather than a plea of *nolo contendere* is of no constitutional significance with respect to the issue now before us, for the Constitution is concerned with the practical consequences, not the formal categorizations, of state law. . . . Thus, while most pleas of guilty consist of both a waiver of trial and an express admission of guilt, the latter element is not a constitutional requisite to the imposition of criminal penalty. An individual accused of crime may voluntarily, knowingly, and understandingly consent to the imposition of a prison sentence even if he is unwilling or unable to admit his participation in the acts constituting the crime.

Nor can we perceive any material difference between a plea that refuses to admit commission of the criminal act and a plea containing

---

6. Courts have defined the plea of *nolo contendere* in a variety of different ways, describing it, on the one hand, as "in effect, a plea of guilty," and on the other, as a query directed to the court to determine the defendant's guilt. See generally Lott v. United States, 367 U.S. 421, 426–427, 81 S.Ct. 1563, 1566–1567 (1961). As a result, it is impossible to state precisely what a defendant does admit when he enters a *nolo* plea in a way that will consistently fit all the cases.

* * *

The plea may have originated in the early medieval practice by which defendants wishing to avoid imprisonment would seek to made an end of the matter (*finem facere*) by offering to pay a sum of money to the king.

See 2 F. Pollock & F. Maitland, The History of English Law 517 (2d ed. 1909).

* * *

Throughout its history, that is, the plea of *nolo contendere* has been viewed not as an express admission of guilt but as a consent by the defendant that he may be punished as if he were guilty and a prayer for leniency. Fed.Rule Crim.Proc. 11 preserves this distinction in its requirement that a court cannot accept a guilty plea "unless it is satisfied that there is a factual basis for the plea"; there is no similar requirement for pleas of *nolo contendere*, since it was thought desirable to permit defendants to plead *nolo* without making any inquiry into their actual guilt.

a protestation of innocence when, as in the instant case, a defendant intelligently concludes that his interests require entry of a guilty plea and the record before the judge contains strong evidence of actual guilt. Here the State had a strong case of first-degree murder against Alford. Whether he realized or disbelieved his guilt, he insisted on his plea because in his view he had absolutely nothing to gain by a trial and much to gain by pleading. Because of the overwhelming evidence against him, a trial was precisely what neither Alford nor his attorney desired. Confronted with the choice between a trial for first-degree murder, on the one hand, and a plea of guilty to second-degree murder, on the other, Alford quite reasonably chose the latter and thereby limited the maximum penalty to a 30-year term. When his plea is viewed in light of the evidence against him, which substantially negated his claim of innocence and which further provided a means by which the judge could test whether the plea was being intelligently entered, see McCarthy v. United States, supra, 394 U.S., at 466–467, 89 S.Ct., at 1170–1171 (1969),[7] its validity cannot be seriously questioned. In view of the strong factual basis for the plea demonstrated by the State and Alford's clearly expressed desire to enter it despite his professed belief in his innocence, we hold that the trial judge did not commit constitutional error in accepting it.[8]

Relying in United States v. Jackson, supra, Alford now argues in effect that the State should not have allowed him this choice but should have insisted on proving him guilty of murder in the first degree. The States in their wisdom may take this course by statute or otherwise and may prohibit the practice of accepting pleas to lesser included offenses under any circumstances. But this is not the mandate of the Fourteenth Amendment and the Bill of Rights. The prohibitions against involuntary or unintelligent pleas should not be re-

---

7. Because of the importance of protecting the innocent and of insuring that guilty pleas are a product of free and intelligent choice, various state and federal court decisions properly caution that pleas coupled with claims of innocence should not be accepted unless there is a factual basis for the plea, see, e. g., Griffin v. United States, 132 U.S.App.D.C. 108, 110, 405 F.2d 1378, 1380 (1968); Bruce v. United States, supra, 126 U.S.App.D.C., at 342, 379 F.2d, at 119 (1967); Commonwealth v. Cottrell, 433 Pa. 177, 249 A.2d 294 (1969); and until the judge taking the plea has inquired into and sought to resolve the conflict between the waiver of trial and the claim of innocence. See, e. g., People v. Serrano, 15 N.Y.2d 304, 308–309, 258 N.Y.S.2d 386, 388–389, 206 N.E.2d 330, 332 (1965); State v. Branner, 149 N.C. 559, 563, 63 S.E. 169, 171 (1908). See also Kreuter v. United States, 201 F.2d 33, 36 (C.A.10 1952).

In the federal courts, Fed.Rule Crim. Proc. 11 expressly provides that a court "shall not enter a judgment upon a plea of guilty unless it is satisfied that there is a factual basis for the plea."

8. Our holding does not mean that a trial judge must accept every constitutionally valid guilty plea merely because a defendant wishes so to plead. A criminal defendant does not have an absolute right under the Constitution to have his guilty plea accepted by the court, although the States may by statute or otherwise confer such a right. Likewise, the States may bar their courts from accepting guilty pleas from any defendants who assert their innocence. Cf. Fed.Rule Crim.Proc. 11, which gives a trial judge discretion to "refuse to accept a plea of guilty . . . ." We need not now delineate the scope of that discretion.

laxed, but neither should an exercise in arid logic render those constitutional guarantees counterproductive and put in jeopardy the very human values they were meant to preserve.

The Court of Appeals for the Fourth Circuit was in error to find Alford's plea of guilty invalid because it was made to avoid the possibility of the death penalty. That court's judgment directing the issuance of the writ of habeas corpus is vacated and the case is remanded to the Court of Appeals for further proceedings consistent with this opinion.

It is so ordered.

Vacated and remanded.

MR. JUSTICE BLACK, while adhering to his belief that United States v. Jackson, 390 U.S. 570, 88 S.Ct. 1209, was wrongly decided, concurs in the judgment and in substantially all of the opinion in this case.

MR. JUSTICE BRENNAN, with whom MR. JUSTICE DOUGLAS and MR. JUSTICE MARSHALL join, dissenting.

Last Term, this Court held, over my dissent, that a plea of guilty may validly be induced by an unconstitutional threat to subject the defendant to the risk of death, so long as the plea is entered in open court and the defendant is represented by competent counsel who is aware of the threat, albeit not of its unconstitutionality. Brady v. United States, 397 U.S. 742, 745–758, 90 S.Ct. 1463, 1467–1474 (1970); Parker v. North Carolina, 397 U.S. 790, 795, 90 S.Ct. 1458, 1461 (1970). Today the Court makes clear that its previous holding was intended to apply even when the record demonstrates that the actual effect of the unconstitutional threat was to induce a guilty plea from a defendant who was unwilling to admit his guilt.

I adhere to the view that, in any given case, the influence of such an unconstitutional threat "must necessarily be given weight in determining the voluntariness of a plea." Parker v. North Carolina, 397 U.S. at 805, 90 S.Ct., at 1458 (dissent). And, without reaching the question whether due process permits the entry of judgment upon a plea of guilty accompanied by a contemporaneous denial of acts constituting the crime, I believe that at the very least such a denial of guilt is also a relevant factor in determining whether the plea was voluntarily and intelligently made. With these factors in mind, it is sufficient in my view to state that the facts set out in the majority opinion demonstrate that Alford was "so gripped by fear of the death penalty" that his decision to plead guilty was not voluntary but was "the product of duress as much so as choice reflecting physical constraint." Accordingly, I would affirm the judgment of the Court of Appeals.

NOTES

1. What kind of showing must the record reflect to establish guilt and to justify the court's belief that defendant was guilty? See Edwards v. State, 51 Wis.2d 231, 186 N.W.2d 193 (1971) and State v. Miller, 15 Ariz.

App. 327, 488 P.2d 683 (1971) on the nature of the showing. When there is either a showing that the state could prove guilt or an admission of guilt by the defendant, the plea is valid. Oaks v. Wainwright, 445 F.2d 1062 (5th Cir. 1971). The defendant's refusal to admit guilt will not require that the plea be vacated when a factual basis has been shown. United States v. Gaskins, 485 F.2d 1046 (D.C.Cir. 1973). A guilty plea may be properly accepted even though the defendant, while persisting in his plea, denies guilt where the judge determines from the prosecutor's recital of the evidence that proof of guilt is strong. United States v. Davis, 516 F.2d 574 (7th Cir. 1975). Thus, a plea may be accepted even though the defendant disclaims knowledge or intent to commit the crime. United States v. Navedo, 516 F.2d 293 (2d Cir. 1975).

It should be noted that some state rules or decisions might be contrary to *Alford* and still require a personal admission of guilt before acceptance of a plea. People v. Coates, 32 Mich.App. 52, 188 N.W.2d 265 (1971); People v. Thomas, 36 Mich.App. 589, 194 N.W.2d 88 (1971).

As a practical matter, it might be best to have key witnesses testify or make a statement or to stipulate to their testimony even where the defendant says he is guilty. This may be of value where the defendant seeks to withdraw his plea after a period of time when he learns that key witnesses are no longer available. See United States v. DeCavalcante, 449 F.2d 139 (3d Cir. 1971).

2.   In McMann v. Richardson, 397 U.S. 759, 90 S.Ct. 1441, (1970), the Court held that a plea of guilty in a state court cannot be attacked on the ground that it was motivated by a coerced confession unless the defendant was incompetently advised by counsel. The Court pointed out that a plea of guilty is usually based on a wide variety of considerations, only one of which may be the question of a confession's admissibility. Furthermore, the Court set a difficult standard for proof of incompetency of counsel:

> "In our view a defendant's plea of guilty based on reasonably competent advice is an intelligent plea not open to attack on the ground that counsel may have misjudged the admissibility of the defendant's confession. Whether a plea of guilty is unintelligent and therefore vulnerable when motivated by a confession erroneously thought admissible in evidence depends as an initial matter not on whether a court would retrospectively consider counsel's advice to be right or wrong, but on whether that advice was within the range of competence demanded of attorneys in criminal cases. On the one hand, uncertainty is inherent in predicting court decisions; but on the other hand defendants facing felony charges are entitled to the effective assistance of competent counsel. Beyond this we think the matter, for the most part, should be left to the good sense and discretion of the trial courts with the admonition that if the right to counsel guaranteed by the Constitution is to serve its purpose, defendants cannot be left to the mercies of incompetent counsel, and that judges should strive to maintain proper standards of performance by attorneys who are representing defendants in criminal cases in their courts. We hold, therefore, that a defendant who alleges that he pleaded guilty because of a prior coerced confession is not, without more, entitled to hearing on his petition for habeas corpus. . . . A plea of guilty in a state court is not subject to collateral attack in a federal court on

the ground that it was motivated by a coerced confession unless the defendant was incompetently advised by his attorney.

In Brady v. United States, 397 U.S. 742, 90 S.Ct. 1463 (1970), the Court held that a plea of guilty was valid although the fear of the death penalty was a prime factor in the decision to plead guilty and the statute providing for the death penalty was later ruled unconstitutional. The Court said:

> "But even if we assume that Brady would not have pleaded guilty except for the death penalty provision . . . , this assumption merely identifies the penalty provision as a 'but for' cause of his plea. That the statute caused the plea in this sense does not necessarily prove that the plea was coerced and invalid as an involuntary act . . . We decline to hold . . . that a guilty plea is compelled and invalid under the Fifth Amendment whenever motivated by the defendant's desire to accept the certainty or probability of a lesser penalty rather than face a wider range of possibilities extending from acquittal to conviction and a higher penalty authorized by law for the crime charged."

The Court reviewed the numerous advantages to both prosecution and defense inherent in the guilty plea procedures and noted that well over three-fourths of all criminal convictions in this country are based on guilty pleas:

> "[A] great many of them no doubt motivated at least in part by the hope or assurance of a lesser penalty than might be imposed if there were a guilty verdict after a trial judge or jury. Of course, that the prevalence of guilty pleas is explainable does not necessarily validate those pleas nor the system which produces them. But we cannot hold that it is unconstitutional for the State to extend a benefit to a defendant who in turn extends a substantial benefit to the State and who demonstrates by his pleas that he is ready and willing to admit his crime and to enter the correctional system in a frame of mind which affords hope for success in rehabilitation over a shorter period of time that might otherwise be necessary. A contrary holding would require the States and Federal Government to forbid guilty pleas altogether, to provide a single invariable penalty for each crime defined by the statutes, or to place the sentencing function in a separate authority having no knowledge of the manner in which the conviction in each case was obtained. In any event, it would be necessary to forbid prosecutors and judges to accept guilty pleas to selected counts, to lesser included offenses, or to reduced charges. The Fifth Amendment does not reach so far. . . ."

3. In Parker v. North Carolina, 397 U.S. 790, 90 S.Ct. 1458 (1970), a plea of guilty was held valid despite allegations that the indictment was invalid because of systematic exclusion of Blacks from the grand jury, that the plea was induced by a coerced confession, and was entered in fear of the death penalty which was provided by an unconstitutional statute. The Court, ruling on the basis of *Brady* and *McCann*, pointed out that there was an interval of one month between confession and plea, that the defendant had the advice of counsel and family before pleading and, therefore, any connection between plea and confession had become attenuated. The Court rejected the contention that the plea was invalid because counsel mistakenly

thought the confession would have been admissible at trial. Even if counsel was in error, there was nothing to indicate that the advice to plead guilty was outside the range of competence required of defense counsel.

4. *McCann, Brady* and *Parker* make it extremely difficult for a defendant to attack his plea of guilty when he is represented by counsel unless counsel was grossly incompetent and the plea almost completely unreasonable. But see People v. Jones, 385 Mich. 288, 188 N.W.2d 536 (1971). The trilogy of cases does not specifically cover situations in which counsel presents a valid motion to suppress and it is denied. Where a defendant wishes to plead after a dubious ruling against him on a key motion, the court should insist on putting off the plea for a couple of weeks to allow defendant time to consider. Further, at the time of the plea, the defendant should be warned that he waives the right to contest the adverse ruling. This warning need not be given in jurisdictions like New York where a plea of guilty does not result in such a waiver.

5. The defendant has the right to challenge the voluntariness of a plea when it is induced by actual threats or physical coercion. See Waley v. Johnston, 316 U.S. 101, 62 S.Ct. 964 (1942); Machibroda v. United States, 368 U.S. 487, 82 S.Ct. 510 (1962); Euziere v. United States, 249 F.2d 560 (10th Cir. 1957); Ryan v. Louisiana, 418 F.2d 560 (5th Cir. 1969). In Fontaine v. United States, 411 U.S. 213, 93 S.Ct. 1461 (1973), the Court, in an abbreviated per curiam, held that an ostensibly voluntary plea could be subject to collateral challenge if, at an evidentiary hearing, the defendant could show that it was the product of coercion. Remanding for a hearing into the claim of coercion, the Court held:

> "We need not take issue with the Government's generalization that when a defendant expressly represents in open court, without counsel, that his plea is voluntary and that he waived counsel voluntarily, he "may not ordinarily" repudiate his statements to the sentencing judge. The objective of Rule 11, Federal Rules of Criminal Procedure, of course, is to flush out and resolve all such issues, but like any procedural mechanism, its exercise is neither always perfect nor uniformly invulnerable to subsequent challenge calling for an opportunity to prove the allegations."

C. PLEA BARGAINING

SANTOBELLO v. NEW YORK

United States Supreme Court, 1971.
404 U.S. 257, 92 S.Ct. 495.

MR. CHIEF JUSTICE BURGER delivered the opinion of the Court.

We granted certiorari in this case to determine whether the State's failure to keep a commitment concerning the sentence recommendation on a guilty plea required a new trial. . . . The State of New York indicted petitioner on two felony counts. . . . Petitioner first entered a plea of not guilty to both counts. After negotiations, the Assistant District Attorney in charge of the case agreed to permit petitioner to plead guilty to a lesser included offense, conviction of which would carry a maximum prison sentence of one year. The prosecutor agreed to make no recommendation as to the sentence.

On June 16, 1969, petitioner accordingly withdrew his plea of not guilty and entered a plea of guilty to the lesser charge. Petitioner represented to the sentencing judge that the plea was voluntary and that the facts of the case, as described by the Assistant District Attorney, were true. The court accepted the plea and set a date for sentencing. A series of delays followed, owing primarily to the absence of a pre-sentence report, so that by September 23, 1969, petitioner had still not been sentenced. By that date petitioner acquired new defense counsel.

Petitioner's new counsel moved immediately to withdraw the guilty plea. In an accompanying affidavit, petitioner alleged that he did not know at the time of his plea that crucial evidence against him had been obtained as a result of an illegal search. The accuracy of this affidavit is subject to challenge since petitioner had filed and withdrawn a motion to suppress, before pleading guilty. In addition to his motion to withdraw his guilty plea, petitioner renewed the motion to suppress and filed a motion to inspect the grand jury minutes.

These three motions in turn caused further delay until November 26, 1969, when the court denied all three and set January 9, 1970, as the date for sentencing. On January 9 petitioner appeared before a different judge, the judge who had presided over the case to this juncture having retired. Petitioner renewed his motions, and the court again rejected them. The court then turned to consideration of the sentence.

At this appearance, another prosecutor had replaced the prosecutor who had negotiated the plea. The new prosecutor recommended the maximum one-year sentence. In making this recommendation, he cited petitioner's criminal record and alleged links with organized crime. Defense counsel immediately objected on the ground that the State had promised petitioner before the plea was entered that there would be no sentence recommendation by the prosecution. He sought to adjourn the sentence hearing in order to have time to prepare proof of the first prosecutor's promise. The second prosecutor, apparently ignorant of his colleague's commitment, argued that there was nothing in the record to support petitioner's claim of a promise, but the State, in subsequent proceedings, has not contested that such a promise was made.

The sentencing judge ended discussion, with the following statement, quoting extensively from the pre-sentence report:

> "Mr. Aronstein [Defense Counsel], I am not at all influenced by what the District Attorney says, so that there is no need to adjourn the sentence, and there is no need to have any testimony. It doesn't make a particle of difference what the District Attorney says he will do, or what he doesn't do.

"I have here, Mr. Aronstein, a probation report. I have here a history of a long, long serious criminal record. I have here a picture of the life history of this man . . .

"He is unamenable to supervision in the community. He is a 'professional criminal.' This is in quotes. 'And a recidivist. Institutionalization—'; that means, in plain language, just putting him away, 'is the only means of halting his anti-social activities,' and protecting you, your family, me, my family, protecting society. 'Institutionalization.' Plain language, put him behind bars.

"Under the plea, I can only send him to the New York City Correctional Institution for men for one year, which I am hereby doing."

The judge then imposed the maximum sentence of one year.

* * *

This record represents another example of an unfortunate lapse in orderly prosecutorial procedures, in part, no doubt, because of the enormous increase in the workload of the often understaffed prosecutor's offices. The heavy workload may well explain these episodes, but it does not excuse them. The disposition of criminal charges by agreement between the prosecutor and the accused, sometimes loosely called "plea bargaining," is an essential component of the administration of justice. Properly administered, it is to be encouraged. If every criminal charge were subjected to a full-scale trial, the States and the Federal Government would need to multiply by many times the number of judges and court facilities.

Disposition of charges after plea discussions is not only an essential part of the process but a highly desirable part for many reasons. It leads to prompt and largely final disposition of most criminal cases; it avoids much of the corrosive impact of enforced idleness during pre-trial confinement for those who are denied release pending trial; it protects the public from those accused persons who are prone to continue criminal conduct even while on pre-trial release; and by shortening the time between charge and disposition, it enhances whatever may be the rehabilitative prospects of the guilty when they are ultimately imprisoned. See Brady v. United States (1970).

However, all of these considerations presuppose fairness in securing agreement between an accused and a prosecutor. It is now clear, for example, that the accused pleading guilty must be counseled absent a waiver. Moore v. Michigan (1957). Rule 11, Fed.Rule Crim.Proc., governing pleas in federal courts, now makes clear that the sentencing judge must develop, *on the record*, the factual basis for the plea, as, for example, by having the accused describe the conduct that gave rise to the charge.[1] The plea must, of course, be vol-

---

1. Rule 11, Fed.Rule Crim.Proc. provides:

"A defendant may plead not guilty, guilty or, with the consent of the court, *nolo contendere*. The court may refuse to accept a plea of guilty, and shall not accept such plea or a plea of *nolo contendere*

untary and knowing and if it was induced by promises, the essence of those promises must in some way be made known. There is, of course, no absolute right to have a guilty plea accepted. Lynch v. Overholser (1962); Rule 11, Fed.Rule Crim.Proc. A court may reject a plea in exercise of sound judicial discretion.

This phase of the process of criminal justice and the adjudicative element inherent in accepting a plea of guilty, must be attended by safeguards to insure the defendant what is reasonably due in the circumstances. Those circumstances will vary, but a constant factor is that when a plea rests in any significant degree on a promise or agreement of the prosecutor, so that it can be said to be part of the inducement or consideration, such promise must be fulfilled.

On this record, petitioner "bargained" and negotiated for a particular plea in order to secure dismissal of more serious charges, but also on condition that no sentence recommendation would be made by the prosecutor. It is now conceded that the promise to abstain from a recommendation was made, and at this stage the prosecution is not in a good position to argue that its inadvertent breach of agreement is immaterial. The staff lawyers in a prosecutor's office have the burden of "letting the left hand know what the right hand is doing" or has done. That the breach of agreement was inadvertent does not lessen its impact.

We need not reach the question whether the sentencing Judge would or would not have been influenced had he known all the details of the negotiations for the plea. He stated that the prosecutor's recommendation did not influence him and we have no reason to doubt that. Nevertheless, we conclude that the interests of justice and appropriate recognition of the duties of the prosecution in relation to promises made in the negotiation of pleas of guilty will be best served by remanding the case to the state courts for further consideration. The ultimate relief to which petitioner is entitled we leave to the discretion of the state court which is in a better position to decide whether the circumstances of this case require only that there be specific performance of the agreement on the plea, in which case petitioner should be resentenced before a different judge, or whether, in the view of the state court, the circumstances require granting the relief sought by petitioner, i. e., the opportunity to withdraw his plea of guilty.[2] We emphasize that this is in no sense to question the fairness of the sentencing judge; the fault here rests on the prosecutor, not on the sentencing judge.

without first addressing the defendant personally and determining that the plea is made voluntarily with understanding of the nature of the charge and the consequences of the plea. If a defendant refuses to plead or if the court refuses to accept a plea of guilty or if a defendant corporation fails to appear, the court shall enter a plea of not guilty. The court shall not enter a judgment upon a plea of guilty unless it is satisfied that there is a factual basis for the plea."

2. If the state court decides to allow withdrawal of the plea, the petitioner will, of course, plead anew to the original charge on two felony counts.

The judgment is vacated and the case is remanded for reconsideration not inconsistent with this opinion.

[MR. JUSTICE DOUGLAS' concurring opinion is omitted.]

MR. JUSTICE MARSHALL, with whom MR. JUSTICE BRENNAN and MR. JUSTICE STEWART join, concurring in part and dissenting in part.

I agree with much of the majority's opinion, but conclude that petitioner must be permitted to withdraw his guilty plea. This is the relief petitioner requested and, on the facts set out by the majority, it is a form of relief to which he is entitled.

There is no need to belabor the fact that the Constitution guarantees to all criminal defendants the right to a trial by judge or jury, or, put another way, the "right not to plead guilty." This and other federal rights may be waived through a guilty plea, but such waivers are not lightly presumed and, in fact, are viewed with the "utmost solicitude." Given this, I believe that where the defendant presents a reason for vacating his plea and the government has not relied on the plea to its disadvantage, the plea may be vacated and the right to trial regained at least where the motion to vacate is made prior to sentence and judgment. In other words, in such circumstances I would not deem the earlier plea to have irrevocably waived the defendant's federal constitutional right to a trial.

Here, petitioner never claimed any automatic right to withdraw a guilty plea before sentencing. Rather, he tendered a specific reason why, in his case, the plea should be vacated. His reason was that the prosecutor had broken a promise made in return for the agreement to plead guilty. When a prosecutor breaks the bargain, he undercuts the basis for the waiver of constitutional rights implicit in the plea. This, it seems to me, provides the defendant ample justification for rescinding the plea. . . . Of course, where the prosecutor has broken the plea agreement, it may be appropriate to permit the defendant to enforce the plea bargain. But that is not the remedy sought here, and it is not a remedy I would require. Rather, it seems to me that a breach of the plea bargain provides ample reason to permit the plea to be vacated.

It is worth noting that in the ordinary case where a motion to vacate is made prior to sentencing, the government has taken no action in reliance on the previously entered guilty plea and would suffer no harm from the plea's withdrawal. More pointedly, here the State claims no such harm beyond disappointed expectations about the plea itself. At least where the government itself has broken the plea bargain, this disappointment cannot bar petitioner from withdrawing his guilty plea and reclaiming his right to a trial.

I would remand the case with instructions that the plea be vacated and petitioner given an opportunity to replead to the original charges in the indictment.

BORDENKIRCHER v. HAYES

Supreme Court of the United States, 1978.
434 U.S. 357, 98 S.Ct. 663.

MR. JUSTICE STEWART delivered the opinion of the Court.

The question in this case is whether the Due Process Clause of the Fourteenth Amendment is violated when a state prosecutor carries out a threat made during plea negotiations to reindict the accused on more serious charges if he does not plead guilty to the offense with which he was originally charged.

I.

The respondent, Paul Lewis Hayes, was indicted by a Fayette County, Ky., grand jury on a charge of uttering a forged instrument in the amount of $88.30, an offense then punishable by a term of two to 10 years in prison. After arrraignment, Hayes, his retained counsel, and the Commonwealth's attorney met in the presence of the clerk of the court to discuss a possible plea agreement. During these conferences the prosecutor offered to recommend a sentence of five years in prison if Hayes would plead guilty to the indictment. He also said that if Hayes did not plead guilty and "save the court the inconvenience and necessity of a trial," he would return to the grand jury to seek an indictment under the Kentucky Habitual Criminal Act, which would subject Hayes to a mandatory sentence of life imprisonment by reason of his two prior felony convictions. Hayes chose not to plead guilty, and the prosecutor did obtain an indictment charging him under the Habitual Criminal Act. It is not disputed that the recidivist charge was fully justified by the evidence, that the prosecutor was in possession of this evidence at the time of the original indictment, and that Hayes' refusal to plead guilty to the original charge was what led to his indictment under the habitual criminal statute.

A jury found Hayes guilty on the principal charge of uttering a forged instrument and, in a separate proceeding, further found that he had twice before been convicted of felonies. As required by the habitual offender statute, he was sentenced to a life term in the penitentiary. The Kentucky Court of Appeals [held] . . . that the prosecutor's decision to indict him as an habitual offender was a legitimate use of available leverage in the plea bargaining process.

On Hayes' petition for a federal writ of habeas corpus, the [Sixth Circuit held] . . . that the prosecutor's conduct during the bargaining negotiations had violated the principles of Blackledge v. Perry, 417 U.S. 21, 94 S.Ct. 2098, which "protect[ed] defendants from the vindictive exercise of a prosecutor's discretion." Accordingly, the court ordered that Hayes be discharged "except for his confinement under a lawful sentence imposed solely for the crime of uttering a forged instrument."

* * *

II.

It may be helpful to clarify at the outset the nature of the issue in this case. While the prosecutor did not actually obtain the recidivist indictment until after the plea conferences had ended, his intention to do so was clearly put forth at the outset of the plea negotiations. Hayes was thus fully informed of the true terms of the offer when he made his decision to plead not guilty. This is not a situation, therefore, where the prosecutor without notice brought an additional and more serious charge after plea negotiations relating only to the original indictment had ended with the defendant's insistence on pleading not guilty. As a practical matter, in short, this case would be no different if the grand jury had indicted Hayes as a recidivist from the outset, and the prosecutor had offered to drop that charge as part of the plea bargain.

* * *

III.

We have recently had occasion to observe that "[w]hatever might be the situation in an ideal world, the fact is that the guilty plea and the often concomitant plea bargain are important components of this country's criminal justice system. Properly administered, they can benefit all concerned." Blackledge v. Allison, 431 U.S. 63, 71, 97 S.Ct. 1621, 1627. The open acknowledgment of this previously clandestine practice has led this Court to recognize the importance of counsel during plea negotiations, Brady v. United States, 397 U.S. 742, 758, 90 S.Ct. 1463, 1474, the need for a public record indicating that a plea was knowingly and voluntarily made, Boykin v. Alabama, 395 U.S. 238, 242, 89 S.Ct. 1709, 1711, and the requirement that a prosecutor's plea bargaining promise must be kept, Santobello v. New York, 404 U.S. 257, 262, 92 S.Ct. 495, 498. The decision of the Court of Appeals in the present case, however, did not deal with considerations such as these, but held that the substance of the plea offer itself violated the limitations imposed by the Due Process Clause of the Fourteenth Amendment. For the reasons that follow, we have concluded that the Court of Appeals was mistaken in so ruling.

IV.

This Court held in North Carolina v. Pearce, 395 U.S. 711, 725, 89 S.Ct. 2072, 2080, that the Due Process Clause of the Fourteenth Amendment "requires that vindictiveness against a defendant for having successfully attacked his first conviction must play no part in the sentence he receives after a new trial." The same principle was later applied to prohibit a prosecutor from reindicting a convicted misdemeanant on a felony charge after the defendant had invoked an appellate remedy, since in this situation there was also a "realistic likelihood of 'vindictiveness.'"

In those cases the Court was dealing with the State's unilateral imposition of a penalty upon a defendant who had chosen to exercise a legal right to attack his original conviction—a situation "very different from the give-and-take negotiation common in plea bargaining between the prosecution and the defense, which arguably possess relatively equal bargaining power." The Court has emphasized that the due process violation in cases such as *Pearce* and *Perry* lay not in the possibility that a defendant might be deterred from the exercise of a legal right, but rather in the danger that the State might be retaliating against the accused for lawfully attacking his conviction.

To punish a person because he has done what the law plainly allows him to do is a due process violation of the most basic sort, and for an agent of the State to pursue a course of action whose objective is to penalize a person's reliance on his legal rights is "patently unconstitutional." . . . But in the "give-and-take" of plea bargaining, there is no such element of punishment or retaliation so long as the accused is free to accept or reject the prosecution's offer.

Plea bargaining flows from "the mutuality of advantage" to defendants and prosecutors, each with his own reasons for wanting to avoid trial. Defendants advised by competent counsel and protected by other procedural safeguards are presumptively capable of intelligent choice in response to prosecutorial persuasion, and unlikely to be driven to false self-condemnation. Indeed, acceptance of the basic legitimacy of plea bargaining necessarily implies rejection of any notion that a guilty plea is involuntary in a constitutional sense simply because it is the end result of the bargaining process. By hypothesis, the plea may have been induced by promises of a recommendation of a lenient sentence or a reduction of charges, and thus by fear of the possibility of a greater penalty upon conviction after a trial.
. . .

While confronting a defendant with the risk of more severe punishment clearly may have a "discouraging effect on the defendant's assertion of his trial rights, the imposition of these difficult choices [is] an inevitable"—and permissible—"attribute of any legitimate system which tolerates and encourages the negotiation of pleas." It follows that, by tolerating and encouraging the negotiation of pleas, this Court has necessarily accepted as constitutionally legitimate the simple reality that the prosecutor's interest at the bargaining table is to persuade the defendant to forego his right to plead not guilty.

It is not disputed here that Hayes was properly chargeable under the recidivist statute, since he had in fact been convicted of two previous felonies. In our systems, so long as the prosecutor has probable cause to believe that the accused committed an offense defined by statute, the decision whether or not to prosecute, and what charge to file or bring before a grand jury, generally rests entirely in his discretion. Within the limits set by the legislature's constitutionally valid definition of chargeable offenses, "the conscious exercise of some selectivity in enforcement is not in itself a federal constitutional violation" so long as "the selection was [not] deliberately based upon an unjustifiable standard such as race, religion, or other arbitrary classification." . . . To hold that the prosecutor's desire to induce a guilty plea is an "unjustifiable standard," which, like race or religion, may play no part in his charging decision, would contradict the very premises that underlie the concept of plea bargaining itself. Moreover, a rigid constitutional rule that would prohibit a prosecutor from acting forthrightly in his dealings with the defense could only invite unhealthy subterfuge that would drive the practice of plea bargaining back into the shadows from which it has so recently emerged.

There is no doubt that the breadth of discretion that our country's legal system vests in prosecuting attorneys carries with it the potential for both individual and institutional abuse. And broad though that discretion may be, there are undoubtedly constitutional limits upon its exercise. We hold only that the course of conduct engaged in by the prosecutor in this case, which no more than openly presented the defendant with the unpleasant alternatives of foregoing trial or facing charges on which he was plainly subject to prosecution, did not violate the Due Process Clause of the Fourteenth Amendment.

Accordingly, the judgment of the Court of Appeals is

Reversed.

MR. JUSTICE BLACKMUN, with whom MR. JUSTICE BRENNAN and MR. JUSTICE MARSHALL join, dissenting.

I feel that the Court, although purporting to rule narrowly . . ., is departing from, or at least restricting, the principles established in North Carolina v. Pearce [supra], and in Blackledge v. Perry [supra]. If those decisions are sound and if those principles are salutary, as I must assume they are, they require, in my view, an affirmance, not a reversal, of the judgment of the Court of Appeals in the present case.

In *Pearce*, . . . it was held that "vindictiveness against a defendant for having successfully attacked his first conviction must play no part in the sentence he receives after a new trial." Accordingly, if on the new trial, the sentence the defendant receives from the court is greater than that imposed after the first trial, it must be explained by reasons "based upon objective information concerning identifiable conduct on the part of the defendant occurring after the time of the original sentencing proceeding," other than his having pursued the appeal or collateral remedy. On the other hand, if the sentence is imposed by the jury and not by the court, if the jury is not aware of the original sentence, and if the second sentence is not otherwise shown to be a product of vindictiveness, *Pearce* has no application. Chaffin v. Stynchcombe, 412 U.S. 17, 93 S.Ct. 1977 (1973).

* * *

The Court now says, however, that this concern with vindictiveness is of no import in the present case, despite the difference between five years in prison and a life sentence, because we are here concerned with plea bargaining where there is give-and-take negotiation. . . .

* * *

Prosecutorial vindictiveness, it seems to me, in the present narrow context, is the fact against which the Due Process Clause ought to protect. I perceive little difference between vindictiveness after what the Court describes, as the exercise of a "legal right to attack his original conviction," and vindictiveness in the "give-and-take negotiation common in plea bargaining." Prosecutorial vindictiveness in any context is still prosecutorial vindictiveness. The Due Process Clause should protect an accused against it, however it asserts itself. The Court of Appeals rightly so held, and I would affirm the judgment.

* * *

MR. JUSTICE POWELL, dissenting.

Although I agree with much of the Court's opinion, I am not satisfied that the result in this case is just or that the conduct of the plea bargaining met the requirements of due process.

* * *

It seems to me that the question to be asked under the circumstances is whether the prosecutor reasonably might have charged respondent under the Habitual Criminal Act in the first place. The deference that courts properly accord the exercise of a prosecutor's discretion perhaps would foreclose judicial criticism if the prosecutor originally had sought an indictment under that act, as unreasonable as it would have seemed. But here the prosecutor evidently made a reasonable, responsible judgment not to subject an individual to a mandatory life sentence when his only new offense had societal implications as limited as those accompanying the uttering of a single $88 forged check and when the circumstances of his prior convictions confirmed the inappropriateness of applying the habitual criminal statute. I think it may be inferred that the prosecutor himself deemed it unreasonable and not in the public interest to put this defendant in jeopardy of a sentence of life imprisonment.

There may be situations in which a prosecutor would be fully justified in seeking a fresh indictment for a more serious offense. The most plausible justification might be that it would have been reasonable and in the public interest initially to have charged the defendant with the greater offense. In most cases a court could not know why the harsher indictment was sought, and an inquiry into the prosecutor's motive would neither be indicated nor likely to be fruitful. In those cases, I would agree with the majority that the situation would not differ materially from one in which the higher charge was brought at the outset.

But this is not such a case. Here, any inquiry into the prosecutor's purpose is made unnecessary by his candid acknowledgement that he threatened to procure and in fact procured the habitual criminal indictment because of respondent's insistence on exercising his constitutional rights.

*   *   *

The plea-bargaining process, as recognized by this Court, is essential to the functioning of the criminal-justice system. It normally affords genuine benefits to defendants as well as to society. And if the system is to work effectively, prosecutors must be accorded the widest discretion, within constitutional limits, in conducting bargaining. This is especially true when a defendant is represented by counsel and presumably is fully advised of his rights. Only in the most exceptional case should a court conclude that the scales of the bargaining are so unevenly balanced as to arouse suspicion. In this case, the prosecutor's actions denied respondent due process because their admitted purpose was to discourage and then to penalize with unique severity his exercise of constitutional rights. Implementation of a strategy calculated solely to deter the exercise of constitutional rights is not a constitutionally permissible exercise of discretion. I would affirm the opinion of the Court of Appeals on the facts of this case.

NOTES

1. Until *Santobello*, plea bargaining was thought to be questionable. The standard approach to admonitions on a plea of guilty required the court to assure itself that no promises had been made; and there was judicial language to support the reluctance to recognize plea bargaining as a valid procedure. Nonetheless, estimates placed the number of cases resolved by plea as high as 95% of all criminal charges, with a substantial number of those the result of plea negotiations. ABA Standards Relating to Pleas of Guilty 1–2 (approved draft 1968). See Note, Guilty Plea Bargaining: Compromises by Prosecutors to Secure Guilty Pleas, 112 U.Pa.L.Rev. 865 (1964). By the time *Santobello* was decided, the criminal justice system had come to depend upon plea negotiations as an important administrative tool. See People v. West, 3 Cal. 3d 595, 91 Cal.Rptr. 385, 477 P.2d 409 (1970). Following the recognition of plea bargaining, the courts began to require that the plea agreement be set forth in the record of the hearing on the plea. See Moody v. United States, 497 F.2d 359 (7th Cir. 1974); Raines v. United States, 423 F.2d 526 (4th Cir. 1970).

2. These developments led to the inclusion of a plea agreement procedure in Fed.R.Crim.P.11. The Rule sanctions plea negotiations and permits the prosecution to move to dismiss other charges, recommend a particular sentence, or agree not to oppose a sentence request by defendant in return for a plea of guilty. The agreement must be stated on the record, and may be accepted or rejected by the court. If the plea is rejected, must the defendant be allowed to withdraw the plea? See text of the Rule.

3. Under the Federal Rule, the court may not participate in plea negotiations. A judge's participation could lead the defendant to believe that he would not receive a fair trial before the judge with whom plea negotiations failed. Moreover, the power of the court may induce a defendant to plead guilty rather than risk going to trial before a judge whose plea recommendation the defendant has rejected. See State v. Cross, 270 S.C. 44, 240 S.E. 2d 514 (1977), where the court held that a plea influenced by a judge's inducements cannot be deemed voluntary.

4. What are the perimeters within which plea negotiations must operate? In essence, what kinds of bargains are fair? See Lesley v. Oklahoma, 407 F.2d 543 (10th Cir. 1969); United States v. Carlino, 400 F.2d 56 (2d Cir. 1968) (dismissal of case against defendant's son); Scott v. United States, 419 F.2d 264 (D.C.Cir. 1969); Mallon v. State, 49 Wis.2d 185, 181 N.W.2d 364 (1970); People v. Smith, 37 Mich.App. 264, 194 N.W. 2d 561 (1971) (improper to promise non-prosecution of accused's wife); People v. Lopez, 28 N.Y.2d 148, 320 N.Y.S.2d 235, 269 N.E.2d 28 (1971) (agreement to impose penalties not authorized by statute); Commonwealth v. Dupree, 442 Pa. 219, 275 A.2d 326 (1971); Patterson v. State, 476 S.W. 2d 608 (Mo.1972) (proper to promise prosecution on all available charges if plea is not entered). See Adelstein, The Negotiated Guilty Plea: A Framework for Analysis, 53 N.Y.U.L.Rev. 783 (1978).

5. What should result when a judge refuses to accept the bargain after the plea has been entered? See State v. Loyd, 291 Minn. 528, 190 N.W. 2d 123 (1971). Where the defendant is given assurances that the judge usually follows the recommendation but the judge does not do so in his case, the plea may be subject to attack. See United States v. Hammerman, 528 F.2d 326 (3d Cir. 1975); Dube v. State, 257 Ind. 398, 275 N.E.2d 7 (1971).

6. Where a defendant is permitted to withdraw a guilty plea or successfully attacks a plea on direct appeal or in a collateral proceeding, can he receive greater punishment after trial than he had received following the plea which was vacated? Does it matter if the plea was "negotiated"? Can charges which were dropped be reinstated? Consider these questions in light of North Carolina v. Pearce, 395 U.S. 711, 89 S.Ct. 2072 (1969), Casebook, Chapter 13, Section A 5, supra. See also Borman, The Chilled Right to Appeal from a Plea Bargain Conviction: A Due Process Cure, 69 Nw.U.L.Rev. 663 (1974); Comment, The Constitutionality of Reindicting Successful Plea-Bargain Appellants on the Original Higher Charges, 62 Cal.L.Rev. 258 (1974). Does Footnote 2, supra, indicate that the *Santobello* court resolved each of these issues?

7. One of the main advantages of a guilty plea (judicial economy) is lost if an evidentiary hearing is later necessary to determine the validity of the plea. How can an evidentiary hearing be avoided if the defendant, sometime after incarceration, claims that he was promised (by defense counsel or prosecutor or judge) that if he entered a plea of guilty he would receive a lesser sentence than he actually received? See Blackledge v. Allison, 431 U.S. 63, 97 S.Ct. 1621 (1977), where a defendant's on-the-record statement, at the time of the plea, that he had received no promises was held *not* to conclusively bar relief under a "broken promise" theory.

8. The defendant ordinarily is not present at plea bargaining conferences. He apparently has no constitutional right to attend. See People v. Pendergraft, 45 Ill.App.3d 954, 360 N.E.2d 489 (1977). Some commentators have argued that "principled" plea bargaining requires that the accused, and perhaps also the victim, be present at plea conferences. See N. Morris & G. Hawkins, The Future of Imprisonment 52–57 (1974).

9. Pleas of guilty are always entered for very practical reasons. Even if the defendant is clearly guilty and the state has overwhelming proof and even where the sentence is perfectly just, the reasons for taking the plea are essentially practical. The plea saves the resources of the legal system. This inherent practicality underlying the plea decision is thought by some to distort the system of justice: ". . . when criminal cases are compromised, the rule of law is invariably sacrificed to the rule of convenience."

Alschuler, The Prosecutor's Role in Plea Bargaining, 36 U.Chi.L.Rev. 50, 85 (1968).

With a few exceptions, however, it is the prosecution that surrenders the most in plea bargaining. Criminal laws may be passed by state legislatures; but the degree of enforcement is determined by the appropriations for courts and prosecutors—appropriations often determined by county boards.

The good prosecutor should be wary of too great a willingness to adopt a plea procedure that fits in easily with the judicial and prosecutorial assets made available to him. He ought to adopt a plea policy that does not quite fit within the budgetary limits. The pressure of an overload may lead to an expansion of facilities; and the less plea bargaining a prosecutor does, the more likely he is to achieve just results in the majority of cases. See generally Note, Plea Bargaining and the Transformation of the Criminal Process, 90 Harv.L.Rev. 564 (1977); Note, Constitutionality of Plea Bargaining, 83 Harv.L.Rev. 1387 (1970); White, A Proposal for Reform of the Plea Bargaining Process, 119 U.Pa.L.Rev. 439 (1971). See also Chapter 21, Section C concerning "penalizing" defendants who refuse to plead guilty.

Chapter 17

TRIAL BY JURY

A. RIGHT TO JURY TRIAL

1. SCOPE OF THE RIGHT

DUNCAN v. LOUISIANA

Supreme Court of the United States, 1968.
391 U.S. 145, 88 S.Ct. 1444.

MR. JUSTICE WHITE delivered the opinion of the Court.

Appellant, Gary Duncan, was convicted of simple battery in the Twenty-fifth Judicial District Court of Louisiana. Under Louisiana law simple battery is a misdemeanor, punishable by a maximum of two years' imprisonment and a $300 fine. Appellant sought trial by jury, but because the Louisiana Constitution grants jury trials only in cases in which capital punishment or imprisonment at hard labor may be imposed, the trial judge denied the request. Appellant was convicted and sentenced to serve 60 days in the parish prison and pay a fine of $150.

* * *

I.

The Fourteenth Amendment denies the States the power to "deprive any person of life, liberty, or property, without due process of law." In resolving conflicting claims concerning the meaning of this spacious language, the Court has looked increasingly to the Bill of Rights for guidance; many of the rights guaranteed by the first eight Amendments to the Constitution have been held to be protected against state action by the Due Process Clause of the Fourteenth Amendment.

* * *

The test for determining whether a right extended by the Fifth and Sixth Amendments with respect to federal criminal proceedings is also protected against state action by the Fourteenth Amendment has been phrased in a variety of ways in the opinions of this Court. The question has been asked whether a right is among those " 'fundamental principles of liberty and justice which lie at the base of all our civil and political institutions,' " Powell v. State of Alabama, 287 U.S. 45, 67, 53 S.Ct. 55, 63 (1932); whether it is "basic in our system of jurisprudence," In re Oliver, 333 U.S. 257, 273, 68 S.Ct. 499, 507 (1948); and whether it is "a fundamental right, essential to a fair trial," Gideon v. Wainwright, 372 U.S. 335, 343–344, 83 S.Ct.

792, 796 (1963); Malloy v. Hogan, 378 U.S. 1, 6, 84 S.Ct. 1489, 1492 (1964); Pointer v. State of Texas, 380 U.S. 400, 403, 85 S.Ct. 1065, 1067 (1965). The claim before us is that the right to trial by jury guaranteed by the Sixth Amendment meets these tests. The position of Louisiana, on the other hand, is that the Constitution imposes upon the States no duty to give a jury trial in any criminal case, regardless of the seriousness of the crime or the size of the punishment which may be imposed. Because we believe that trial by jury in criminal cases is fundamental to the American scheme of justice, we hold that the Fourteenth Amendment guarantees a right of jury trial in all criminal cases which—were they to be tried in a federal court— would come within the Sixth Amendment's guarantee.[1] Since we consider the appeal before us to be such a case, we hold that the Constitution was violated when appellant's demand for jury trial was refused.

The history of trial by jury in criminal cases has been frequently told. It is sufficient for present purposes to say that by the time our Constitution was written, jury trial in criminal cases had been in existence in England for several centuries and carried impressive credentials traced by many to Magna Carta. Its preservation and proper operation as a protection against arbitrary rule were among the major objectives of the revolutionary settlement which was expressed in the Declaration and Bill of Rights of 1689.

* * *

1. In one sense recent cases applying provisions of the first eight Amendments to the States represent a new approach to the "incorporation" debate. Earlier the Court can be seen as having asked, when inquiring into whether some particular procedural safeguard was required of a State, if a civilized system could be imagined that would not accord the particular protection. . . . The recent cases, on the other hand, have proceeded upon the valid assumption that state criminal processes are not imaginary and theoretical schemes but actual systems bearing virtually every characteristic of the common-law system that has been developing contemporaneously in England and in this country. The question thus is whether given this kind of system a particular procedure is fundamental—whether, that is, a procedure is necessary to an Anglo-American regime of ordered liberty. . . . Of immediate relevance for this case are the Court's holdings that the States must comply with certain provisions of the Sixth Amendment, specifically that the States may not refuse a speedy trial, confrontation of witnesses, and the assistance, at state expense if necessary, of counsel. Of each of these determinations that a constitutional provision originally written to bind the Federal Government should bind the States as well it might be said that the limitation in question is not necessarily fundamental to fairness in every criminal system that might be imagined but is fundamental in the context of the criminal processes maintained by the American States. . . . A criminal process which was fair and equitable but used no juries is easy to imagine. It would make use of alternative guarantees and protections which would serve the purposes that the jury serves in the English and American systems. Yet no American State has undertaken to construct such a system. Instead, every American State, including Louisiana, uses the jury extensively, and imposes very serious punishments only after a trial at which the defendant has a right to a jury's verdict. In every State, including Louisiana, the structure and style of the criminal process—the supporting framework and the subsidiary procedures—are of the sort that naturally complement jury trial, and have developed in connection with and in reliance upon jury trial.

Jury trial came to America with English colonists, and received strong support from them. Royal interference with the jury trial was deeply resented. Among the resolutions adopted by the First Congress of the American Colonies (the Stamp Act Congress) on October 19, 1765—resolutions deemed by their authors to state "the most essential rights and liberties of the colonists"—was the declaration:

> "That trial by jury is the inherent and invaluable right of every British subject in these colonies."

The First Continental Congress, in the resolve of October 14, 1774, objected to trials before judges dependent upon the Crown alone for their salaries and to trials in England for alleged crimes committed in the colonies; the Congress therefore declared:

> "That the respective colonies are entitled to the common law of England, and more especially to the great and inestimable privilege of being tried by their peers of the vicinage, according to the course of that law."

The Declaration of Independence stated solemn objections to the King's making "judges dependent on his will alone, for the tenure of their offices, and the amount and payment of their salaries," to his "depriving us in many cases, of the benefits of Trial by Jury," and to his "transporting us beyond Seas to be tried for pretended offenses." The Constitution itself, in Art. III. § 2, commanded:

> "The Trial of all Crimes, except in Cases of Impeachment, shall be by Jury; and such Trial shall be held in the State where the said Crimes shall have been committed."

Objections to the Constitution because of the absence of a bill of rights were met by the immediate submission and adoption of the Bill of Rights. Included was the Sixth Amendment which, among other things, provided:

> "In all criminal prosecutions, the accused shall enjoy the right to a speedy and public trial, by an impartial jury of the State and district wherein the crime shall have been committed." [2]

The constitutions adopted by the original States guaranteed jury trial. Also, the constitution of every State entering the Union thereafter in one form or another protected the right to jury trial in criminal cases.

---

2. Among the proposed amendments adopted by the House of Representatives in 1789 and submitted to the Senate was Article Fourteen:

"No State shall infringe the right of trial by Jury in criminal cases, nor the rights of conscience, nor the freedom of speech, or of the press."

The Senate deleted this article in adopting the amendments which became the Bill of Rights. This relatively clear indication that the framers of the Sixth Amendment did not intend its jury trial requirement to bind the States is, of course, of little relevance to interpreting the Due Process Clause of the Fourteenth Amendment, adopted specifically to place limitations upon the States.

Even such skeletal history is impressive support for considering the right to jury trial in criminal cases to be fundamental to our system of justice, an importance frequently recognized in the opinions of this Court.

* * *

The guarantees of jury trial in the Federal and State Constitutions reflect a profound judgment about the way in which law should be enforced and justice administered. A right to jury trial is granted to criminal defendants in order to prevent oppression by the Government. Those who wrote our constitutions knew from history and experience that it was necessary to protect against unfounded criminal charges brought to eliminate enemies and against judges too responsive to the voice of higher authority. The framers of the constitutions strove to create an independent judiciary but insisted upon further protection against arbitrary action. Providing an accused with the right to be tried by a jury of his peers gave him an inestimable safeguard against the corrupt or overzealous prosecutor and against the compliant, biased, or eccentric judge. If the defendant preferred the common-sense judgment of a jury to the more tutored but perhaps less sympathetic reaction of the single judge, he was to have it. Beyond this, the jury trial provisions in the Federal and State Constitutions reflect a fundamental decision about the exercise of official power—a reluctance to entrust plenary powers over the life and liberty of the citizen to one judge or to a group of judges. Fear of unchecked power, so typical of our State and Federal Governments in other respects, found expression in the criminal law in this insistence upon community participation in the determination of guilt or innocence. The deep commitment of the Nation to the right of jury trial in serious criminal cases as a defense against arbitrary law enforcement qualifies for protection under the Due Process Clause of the Fourteenth Amendment, and must therefore be respected by the States.

Of course jury trial has "its weaknesses and the potential for misuse," Singer v. United States, 380 U.S. 24, 35, 85 S.Ct. 783, 790 (1965). We are aware of the long debate, especially in this century, among those who write about the adminstration of justice, as to the wisdom of permitting untrained laymen to determine the facts in civil and criminal proceedings. Although the debate has been intense, with powerful voices on either side, most of the controversy has centered on the jury in civil cases. Indeed, some of the severest critics of civil juries acknowledge that the arguments for criminal juries are much stronger. In addition, at the heart of the dispute have been express or implicit assertions that juries are incapable of adequately understanding evidence or determining issues of fact, and that they are unpredictable, quixotic, and little better than a roll of dice. Yet, the most recent and exhaustive study of the jury in criminal cases concluded that juries do understand the evidence and come to sound conclusions in most of the cases presented to them and that when juries differ with the result at which the judge would have arrived, it is usually because they are serving some of the very purposes for which they were created and for which they are now employed.[3]

The State of Louisiana urges that holding that the Fourteenth Amendment assures a right to jury trial will cast doubt on the integrity of every trial conducted without a jury. Plainly, this is not the import of our holding. Our conclusion is that in the American States, as in the federal judicial system, a general grant of jury trial for serious offenses is a fundamental right, essential for preventing miscarriages of justice and for assuring that fair trials are provided for all defendants. We would not assert, however, that every criminal trial—or any particular trial—held before a judge alone is unfair or that a defendant may never be as fairly treated by a judge as he would be by a jury. Thus we hold no constitutional doubts about the practices, common in both federal and state courts, of accepting waivers of jury trial and prosecuting petty crimes without extending a right to jury trial. However, the fact is that in most places more trials for serious crimes are to juries than to a court alone; a great many defendants prefer the judgment of a jury to that of a court. Even where defendants are satisfied with bench trials, the right to a jury trial very likely serves its intended purpose of making judicial or prosecutorial unfairness less likely.

II.

Louisiana's final contention is that even if it must grant jury trials in serious criminal cases, the conviction before us is valid and constitutional because here the petitioner was tried for simple battery and was sentenced to only 60 days in the parish prison. We are not persuaded. It is doubtless true that there is a category of petty crimes or offenses which is not subject to the Sixth Amendment jury trial provision and should not be subject to the Fourteenth Amendment jury trial requirement here applied to the States. Crimes carrying possible penalties up to six months do not require a jury trial if they otherwise qualify as petty offenses, Cheff v. Schnackenberg, 384 U.S. 373, 86 S.Ct. 1523 (1966). But the penalty authorized for a particular crime is of major relevance in determining whether it is serious or not and may in itself, if severe enough, subject the trial to the mandates of the Sixth Amendment.

* * *

In the case before us the Legislature of Louisiana has made simple battery a criminal offense punishable by imprisonment for up to two years and a fine. The question, then, is whether a crime carrying such a penalty is an offense which Louisiana may insist on trying without a jury.

We think not. So-called petty offenses were tried without juries both in England and in the Colonies and have always been held to be exempt from the otherwise comprehensive language of the Sixth Amendment's jury trial provisions. There is no substantial evidence

---

3. H. Kalven, Jr. & H. Zeisel, The American Jury (1966).

that the Framers intended to depart from this established common-law practice, and the possible consequences to defendants from convictions for petty offenses have been thought insufficient to outweigh the benefits to efficient law enforcement and simplified judicial administration resulting from the availability of speedy and inexpensive nonjury adjudications. These same considerations compel the same result under the Fourteenth Amendment. Of course the boundaries of the petty offense category have always been ill-defined, if not ambulatory. In the absence of an explicit constitutional provision, the definitional task necessarily falls on the courts, which must either pass upon the validity of legislative attempts to identify those petty offenses which are exempt from jury trial or, where the legislature has not addressed itself to the problem, themselves face the question in the first instance. In either case it is necessary to draw a line in the spectrum of crime, separating petty from serious infractions. This process, although essential, cannot be wholly satisfactory, for it requires attaching different consequences to events which, when they lie near the line, actually differ very little.

In determining whether the length of the authorized prison term or the seriousness of other punishment is enough in itself to require a jury trial, we are counseled . . . to refer to objective criteria, chiefly the existing laws and practices in the Nation. In the federal system, petty offenses are defined as those punishable by no more than six months in prison and a $500 fine. In 49 of the 50 States crimes subject to trial without a jury, which occasionally include simple battery, are punishable by no more than one year in jail. Moreover, in the late 18th century in America crimes triable without a jury were for the most part punishable by no more than a six-month prison term, although there appear to have been exceptions to this rule. We need not, however, settle in this case the exact location of the line between petty offenses and serious crimes. It is sufficient for our purposes to hold that a crime punishable by two years in prison is, based on past and contemporary standards in this country, a serious crime and not a petty offense.[4] Consequently, appellant was entitled to a jury trial and it was error to deny it.

4. It is argued that Cheff v. Schnackenberg, 384 U.S. 373, 86 S.Ct. 1523, (1966), interpreted the Sixth Amendment as meaning that to the extent that the length of punishment is a relevant criterion in distinguishing between serious crimes and petty offenses, the critical factor is not the length of the sentence authorized but the length of the penalty actually imposed. In our view that case does not reach the situation where a legislative judgment as to the seriousness of the crime is imbedded in the statute in the form of an express authorization to impose a heavy penalty for the crime in question. Cheff involved criminal contempt, an offense applied to a wide range of conduct including conduct not so serious as to require jury trial absent a long sentence. In addition criminal contempt is unique in that legislative bodies frequently authorize punishment without stating the extent of the penalty which can be imposed. The contempt statute under which Cheff was prosecuted . . . treated the extent of punishment as a matter to be determined by the forum court. It is therefore understandable that this Court in Cheff seized upon the penalty actually imposed as the best evidence of the seriousness of the offense for which Cheff was tried.

The judgment below is reversed and the case is remanded for proceedings not inconsistent with this opinion.

Reversed and remanded.

MR. JUSTICE BLACK, with whom MR. JUSTICE DOUGLAS joins, concurring.

The Court today holds that the right to trial by jury guaranteed defendants in criminal cases in federal courts by Art. III of the United States Constitution and by the Sixth Amendment is also guaranteed by the Fourteenth Amendment to defendants tried in state courts. With this holding I agree for reasons given by the Court. I also agree because of reasons given in my dissent in Adamson v. People of State of California, 332 U.S. 46, 68, 67 S.Ct. 1672, 1683. In that dissent I took the position that the Fourteenth Amendment made all of the provisions of the Bill of Rights applicable to the States.

* * *

What I wrote there in 1947 was the product of years of study and research. My appraisal of the legislative history followed 10 years of legislative experience as a Senator of the United States, not a bad way, I suspect, to learn the value of what is said in legislative debates, committee discussions, committee reports, and various other steps taken in the course of passage of bills, resolutions, and proposed constitutional amendments.

* * *

[The dissent argues] that "due process of law requires only fundamental fairness." But the "fundamental fairness" test is one on a par with that of shocking the conscience of the Court. Each of such tests depends entirely on the particular judge's idea of ethics and morals instead of requiring him to depend on the boundaries fixed by the written words of the Constitution. Nothing in the history of the phrase "due process of law" suggests that constitutional controls are to depend on any particular judge's sense of values. The origin of the Due Process Clause is Chapter 39 of Magna Carta which declares that "No free man shall be taken, outlawed, banished, or in any way destroyed, nor will We proceed against or prosecute him, except by the lawful judgment of his peers and by the *law of the land*." (Emphasis added.) As early as 1354 the words "due process of law" were used in an English statute interpreting Magna Carta, and by the end of the 14th century "due process of law" and "law of the land" were interchangeable. Thus the origin of this clause was an attempt by those who wrote Magna Carta to do away with the so-called trials of that period where people were liable to sudden arrest and summary conviction in courts and by judicial commissions with no sure and definite procedural protections and under laws that might have been improvised to try their particular cases. Chapter 39 of Magna Carta was a guarantee that the government would take neither life, liberty, nor property without a trial in accord with the law of the land that already existed at the time the alleged offense was committed. This means that the Due Process Clause gives all Americans, whoever they are and wherever they happen to be, the right to be tried by independent and unprejudiced courts using established procedures and applying valid pre-existing laws. There is not one word of legal history that justifies making the term "due process of law" mean a guarantee of a trial free from laws and conduct which the courts deem at the time to be "arbitrary," "unreasonable," "unfair," or "contrary to civilized standards." The due process of law standard for a trial is one in accordance with the Bill of Rights and laws passed pursuant to constitutional power, guaranteeing to all alike a trial under the general law of the land.

Finally I want to add that I am not bothered by the argument that applying the Bill of Rights to the States "according to the same standards that protect those personal rights against federal encroachment," interferes with our concept of federalism in that it may prevent States from trying novel social and economic experiments. I have never believed that under the guise of federalism the States should be able to experiment with the protections afforded our citizens through the Bill of Rights.

*   *   *

No one is more concerned than I that the States be allowed to use the full scope of their powers as their citizens see fit. And that is why I have continually fought against the expansion of this Court's authority over the States through the use of a broad, general interpretation of due process that permits judges to strike down state laws they do not like.

In closing I want to emphasize that I believe as strongly as ever that the Fourteenth Amendment was intended to make the Bill of Rights applicable to the States. I have been willing to support the selective incorporation doctrine, however, as an alternative, although perhaps less historically supportable than complete incorporation. The selective incorporation process, if used properly, does limit the Supreme Court in the Fourteenth Amendment field to specific Bill of Rights' protections only and keeps judges from roaming at will in their own notions of what policies outside the Bill of Rights are desirable and what are not. And, most importantly for me, the selective incorporation process has the virtue of having already worked to make most of the Bill of Rights' protections applicable to the States.

MR. JUSTICE FORTAS, concurring. [Opinion omitted.]

MR. JUSTICE HARLAN, whom MR. JUSTICE STEWART joins, dissenting.

Every American jurisdiction provides for trial by jury in criminal cases. The question before us is not whether jury trial is an ancient institution, which it is; nor whether it plays a significant role in the administration of criminal justice, which it does; nor whether it will endure, which it shall. The question in this case is whether the State of Louisiana, which provides trial by jury for all felonies, is prohibited by the Constitution from trying charges of simple battery to the court alone. In my view, the answer to that question, mandated alike by our constitutional history and by the longer history of trial by jury, is clearly "no."

The States have always borne primary responsibility for operating the machinery of criminal justice within their borders, and adapting it to their particular circumstances. In exercising this responsibility, each State is compelled to conform its procedures to the requirements of the Federal Constitution. The Due Process Clause of the Fourteenth Amendment requires that those procedures be fundamentally fair in all respects. It does not, in my view, impose or encourage nationwide uniformity for its own sake; it does not command adherence to forms that happen to be old; and it does not impose on the States the rules that may be in force in the federal courts except where such rules are also found to be essential to basic fairness.

The Court's approach to this case is an uneasy and illogical compromise among the views of various Justices on how the Due Process Clause should be interpreted. The Court does not say that those who framed the Fourteenth Amendment intended to make the Sixth Amendment applicable to the States. And the Court concedes that it finds nothing unfair about the procedure by which the present appellant was tried. Nevertheless, the Court reverses his conviction: it holds, for some reason not apparent to me that the Due Process Clause incorporates the particular clause of the Sixth Amendment that requires trial by jury in federal criminal cases—including, as I read its opinion, the sometimes trivial accompanying baggage of judicial interpretation in federal contexts.

* * *

The argument that jury trial is not a requisite of due process is quite simple. . . . "due process of law" requires only that criminal trials be fundamentally fair. As stated above, apart from the theory that it was historically intended as a mere shorthand for the Bill of Rights, I do not see what else "due process of law" can intelligibly be thought to mean. If due process of law requires only fundamental fairness, then the inquiry in each case must be whether a state trial process was a fair one. The Court has held, properly I think, that in an adversary process it is a requisite of fairness, for which there is no adequate substitute, that a criminal defendant be afforded a right to counsel and to cross-examine opposing witnesses. But it simply has not been demonstrated, nor, I think, can it be demonstrated, that trial by jury is the only fair means of resolving issues of fact.

The jury is of course not without virtues. It affords ordinary citizens a valuable opportunity to participate in a process of government, an experience fostering, one hopes, a respect for law. It eases the burden on judges by enabling them to share a part of their sometimes awesome responsibility. A jury may, at times, afford a higher justice by refusing to enforce harsh laws (although it necessarily does so haphazardly, raising the questions whether arbitrary enforcement of harsh laws is better than total enforcement, and whether the jury system is to be defended on the ground that jurors sometimes disobey their oaths). And the jury may, or may not, contribute desirably to the willingness of the general public to accept criminal judgments as just.

It can hardly be gainsaid, however, that the principal original virtue of the jury trial—the limitations a jury imposes on a tyrannous judiciary—has largely disappeared. We no longer live in a medieval or colonial society. Judges enforce laws enacted by democratic decision, not by regal fiat. They are elected by the people or appointed by the people's elected officials, and are responsible not to a distant monarch alone but to reviewing courts, including this one.

The jury system can also be said to have some inherent defects, which are multiplied by the emergence of the criminal law from the relative simplicity that existed when the jury system was devised. It is a cumbersome process, not only imposing great cost in time and money on both the State and the jurors themselves, but also contributing to delay in the machinery of justice. Untrained jurors are presumably less adept at reaching accurate conclusions of fact than judges, particularly if the issues are many or complex. And it is argued by some that trial by jury, far from increasing public respect for law, impairs it: the average man, it is said, reacts favorably neither to the notion that matters he knows to be complex are being decided by other average men, nor to the way the jury system distorts the process of adjudication.

That trial by jury is not the only fair way of adjudicating criminal guilt is well attested by the fact that it is not the prevailing way, either in England or in this country. For England, one expert makes the following estimates. Parliament generally provides that new statutory offenses, unless they are of "considerable gravity" shall be tried to judges; consequently, summary offenses now outnumber offenses for which jury trial is afforded by more than six to one. Then, within the latter category, 84% of all cases are in fact tried to the court. Over all, "the ratio of defendants actually tried by jury becomes in some years little more than 1 per cent."

In the United States, where it has not been as generally assumed that jury waiver is permissible, the statistics are only slightly less revealing. Two experts have estimated that, of all prosecutions for crimes triable to a jury, 75% are settled by guilty plea and 40% of the remainder are tried to the court. In one State, Maryland, which has always provided for waiver, the rate of court trial appears in some years to have reached 90%. The Court recognizes the force of these statistics in stating,

"We would not assert, however, that every criminal trial— or any particular trial—held before a judge alone is unfair

> or that a defendant may never be as fairly treated by a judge as he would be by a jury."

I agree. I therefore see no reason why this Court should reverse the conviction of appellant, absent any suggestion that his particular trial was in fact unfair, or compel the State of Louisiana to afford jury trial in an as yet unbounded category of cases that can, without unfairness, be tried to a court.

Indeed, even if I were persuaded that trial by jury is a fundamental right in some criminal cases, I could see nothing fundamental in the rule, not yet formulated by the Court, that places the prosecution of appellant for simple battery within the category of "jury crimes" rather than "petty crimes."

* * *

BALDWIN v. NEW YORK

Supreme Court of the United States, 1970.
399 U.S. 66, 90 S.Ct. 1886.

Mr. Justice White announced the judgment of the Court and delivered an opinion in which Mr. Justice Brennan and Mr. Justice Marshall join.

Appellant was arrested and charged with "jostling"—a Class A misdemeanor in New York, punishable by a maximum term of imprisonment of one year. . . . He was convicted and sentenced to imprisonment for the maximum term. . . .

In Duncan v. Louisiana [preceding casebook case], we held that the Sixth Amendment, as applied to the States through the Fourteenth, requires that defendants accused of serious crimes be afforded the right to trial by jury. We also reaffirmed the long-established view that so-called "petty offenses" may be tried without a jury.

* * *

The question in this case is whether the possibility of a one-year sentence is enough in itself to require the opportunity for a jury trial. We hold that it is. More specifically, we have concluded that no offense can be deemed "petty" for purposes of the right to trial by jury where imprisonment for more than six months is authorized.[1]

New York has urged us to draw the line between "petty" and "serious" to coincide with the line between misdemeanor and felony. As in most States, the maximum sentence of imprisonment for a mis-

---

1. Decisions of this Court have looked to both the nature of the offense itself, District of Columbia v. Colts, 282 U.S. 63, 51 S.Ct. 52 (1930), as well as the maximum potential sentence, Duncan v. Louisiana (1968), in determining whether a particular offense was so serious as to require a jury trial. In this case, we decide only that a potential sentence in excess of six months' imprisonment is sufficiently severe by itself to take the offense out of the category of "petty." None of our decisions involving this issue have ever held such an offense "petty."

demeanor in New York is one year, for a felony considerably longer. It is also true that the collateral consequences attaching to a felony conviction are more severe than those attaching to a conviction for a misdemeanor.[2]   And, like other States, New York distinguishes between misdemeanors and felonies in determining such things as whether confinement shall be in county or regional jails, rather than state prison, and whether prosecution may proceed by information or complaint, rather than by grand jury indictment.   But while these considerations reflect what may readily be admitted—that a felony conviction is more serious than a misdemeanor conviction—they in no way detract from appellant's contention that some misdemeanors are also "serious" offenses.

*   *   *

Of necessity, the task of drawing a line "requires attaching different consequences to events which, when they lie near the line, actually differ very little."   Duncan v. Louisiana, supra.   One who is threatened with the possibility of imprisonment for six months may find little difference between the potential consequences that face him, and the consequences that faced appellant here.   Indeed, the prospect of imprisonment for however short a time will seldom be viewed by the accused as a trivial or "petty" matter and may well result in quite serious repercussions affecting his career and his reputation.   Where the accused cannot possibly face more than six months' imprisonment, we have held that these disadvantages, onerous though they may be, may be outweighed by the benefits that result from speedy and inexpensive nonjury adjudications.   We cannot, however, conclude that these administrative conveniences, in light of the practices that now exist in every one of the 50 States as well as in the federal courts, can similarly justify denying an accused the important right to trial by jury where the possible penalty exceeds six months' imprisonment.   The conviction is

Reversed.

MR. JUSTICE BLACKMUN took no part in the consideration or decision of this case.

MR. JUSTICE BLACK, with whom MR. JUSTICE DOUGLAS joins, concurring in the judgment.

I agree that the appellant here was entitled to a trial by jury in a New York City court for an offense punishable by one year's imprisonment.   I also agree that his right to a trial by jury was governed by the Sixth Amendment to the United States Constitution made applicable to the States by the Fourteenth Amendment.   I disagree, however, with the view that a defendant's right to a jury trial under the Sixth Amendment is determined by whether the offense charged is a "petty" or "serious" one.   The Constitution guarantees a

---

2.   Both the convicted felon and the convicted misdemeanant may be prevented under New York law from engaging in a wide variety of occupa-   tions.   In addition, the convicted felon is deprived of certain civil rights, including the right to vote and to hold public office. . . .

right of trial by jury in two separate places but in neither does it hint of any difference between "petty" offenses and "serious" offenses. .   .   .

* * *

Today three members of the Court would judicially amend that judicial amendment and substitute the phrase "all crimes in which punishment for more than six months is authorized."   This definition of "serious" would be enacted even though those members themselves recognize that imprisonment for less than six months may still have serious consequences.   This decision is reached by weighing the advantages to the defendant against the administrative inconvenience to the State inherent in a jury trial and magically concluding that the scale tips at six months' imprisonment.   Such constitutional adjudication, whether framed in terms of "fundamental fairness," "balancing," or "shocking the conscience," amounts in every case to little more than judicial mutilation of our written Constitution.   Those who wrote and adopted our Constitution and Bill of Rights engaged in all the balancing necessary.   They decided that the value of a jury trial far outweighed its costs for "all crimes" and "[i]n all criminal prosecutions."   Until that language is changed by the constitutionally prescribed method of amendment, I cannot agree that this Court can reassess the balance and substitute its own judgment for that embodied in the Constitution.   Since there can be no doubt in this case that Baldwin was charged with and convicted of a "crime" in any relevant sense of that word—I agree that he was convicted without the benefit of a jury trial.

Mr. Chief Justice Burger, dissenting.

I dissent from today's holding that something in the Sixth and Fourteenth Amendments commands New York City to provide trial by jury for an offense punishable by a confinement of more than six months but less than one year.   Mr. Justice Black has noted correctly that the Constitution guarantees a jury trial "[i]n all criminal prosecutions" (Amendment VI) and for "all Crimes" (Art. III, § 2, cl. 3), but these provisions were not written as a command to the States; they were written at a time when the Federal Government exercised only a limited authority to provide for federal offenses "very grave and few in number."   The limited number of serious acts that were made criminal offenses were against federal authority, and were proscribed in a period when administration of the criminal law was regarded as largely the province of the States.   The Founding Fathers therefore cast the constitutional provisions we deal with here as limitations on federal power, not the power of States.   State administration of criminal justice included a wide range of petty offenses, and as to many of the minor cases, the States often did not require trial by jury.   This state of affairs had not changed appreciably when the Fourteenth Amendment was approved by Congress in 1866 and was ratified by the States in 1868.   In these circumstances, the jury trial guarantees of the Constitution properly have been read as extending only to "serious" crimes.   I find, however, nothing in the "serious" crime coverage of the Sixth or Fourteenth Amendment that would require this Court to invalidate the particular New York City trial scheme at issue here.

I find it somewhat disconcerting that with the constant urging to adjust ourselves to being a "pluralistic society"—and I accept this in its broad sense—we find constant pressure to conform to some uniform pattern on the theory that the Constitution commands it. I see no reason why an infinitely complex entity such as New York City should be barred from deciding that misdemeanants can be punished with up to 365 days' confinement without a jury trial while in less urban areas another body politic would fix a six-month maximum for offenses tried without a jury. That the "near-uniform judgment of the Nation" is otherwise than the judgment in some of its parts affords no basis for me to read into the Constitution something not found there. What may be a serious offense in one setting—*e. g.*, stealing a horse in Cody, Wyoming, where a horse may be an indispensable part of living—may be considered less serious in another area, and the procedures for finding guilt and fixing punishment in the two locales may rationally differ from each other.

[The dissenting opinions of Mr. Justice Harlan and Mr. Justice Stewart are omitted.]

NOTES

1. Although *Baldwin* indicates that no constitutional right to a jury trial exists when the accused could be sentenced to not more than six months, United States v. Sanchez-Meza, 547 F.2d 461 (9th Cir. 1976), found that, in some cases, the very nature of the change may be so grave that the right to trial by jury exists even where the penalty could not exceed six months.

2. In criminal contempt cases, if no maximum sentence is provided by statute or rule, then the *actual* penalty that is imposed provides the benchmark for determining the right to trial by jury. See Taylor v. Hayes, 418 U.S. 488, 94 S.Ct. 2697 (1974). This is why so many "six month" contempt penalties are meted out. Any greater criminal contempt penalty would require that the alleged contemnor be afforded a jury trial on the question of whether his conduct was contemptuous. For one of the rare cases where such a trial was held, see United States v. Patrick, 542 F.2d 381 (7th Cir. 1976). There, after the jury found the alleged contemnor guilty of an improper refusal to testify as a witness in a criminal case, the judge sentenced the contemnor to four years.

3. As a matter of state law, many jurisdictions have afforded the right to trial by jury even when not required by the United States Constitution.

4. What must a defendant do to waive his right to a jury trial? Ordinarily, a defendant and his lawyer will execute a waiver form, and he will be thereafter forclosed from asserting his right. However, in Hawkins v. United States, 385 A.2d 744 (D.C.App.1978), the court held that even though a waiver form was signed, it was incumbent upon the court to conduct a full and complete inquiry on the record:

"To be effective, there must be an oral inquiry of the defendant himself in open court, his replies to which indicate that he understands the nature of his right to a jury trial and that he chooses to waive the right. This oral waiver must accompany a written waiver, signed by the defendant. A written waiver signed by the defendant coupled with an oral waiver by defense counsel is not sufficient."

Is this an example of a hypertechnical theory which requires a new trial for no substantive reason? Is it asking too much to compel trial judges to take a few minutes in order to assure themselves that a defendant understands his right to a jury trial?

5. Does a defendant have a right to a bench trial? In State v. Creech, 99 Idaho 779, 589 P.2d 114 (1979), the trial judge in a murder case refused to permit the defendant to waive a jury. On review, the court held that there was no constitutional right to waive a jury trial. In a highly emotional atmosphere—for example, a multiple murder committed in a small town—should not a defendant, as an aspect of his Sixth Amendment right, have the right to waive a jury trial? In the federal system the case must be tried to a jury unless both the government and the accused assent to a bench trial. See Singer v. United States, 380 U.S. 24, 85 S.Ct. 783 (1965).

2. COMPOSITION OF THE JURY

TAYLOR v. LOUISIANA

Supreme Court of the United States, 1975.
419 U.S. 522, 95 S.Ct. 692.

MR. JUSTICE WHITE delivered the opinion of the Court.

When this case was tried, Art. VII, § 41, of the Louisiana Constitution, and Art. 402 of the Louisiana Code of Criminal Procedure provided that a woman should not be selected for jury service unless she had previously filed a written declaration of her desire to be subject to jury service. The constitutionality of these provisions is the issue in this case.

I.

Appellant, Billy J. Taylor, was indicted by the grand jury of St. Tammany Parish, in the Twenty-second Judicial District of Louisiana, for aggravated kidnapping. On April 12, 1972, appellant moved the trial court to quash the petit jury venire drawn for the special criminal term beginning with his trial the following day. Appellant alleged that women were systematically exluded from the venire and that he would therefore be deprived of what he claimed to be his federal constitutional right to "a fair trial by jury of a representative segment of the community . . . ."

The Twenty-second Judicial District is comprised of the parishes of St. Tammany and Washington. The appellee has stipulated that 53% of the persons eligible for jury service in these parishes were female, and that no more than 10% of the persons on the jury wheel in St. Tammany Parish were women. During the period from December 8, 1971, to November 3, 1972, 12 females were among the 1,800 persons drawn to fill petit jury venires in St. Tammany Parish. It was also stipulated that the discrepancy between females eligible for jury service and those actually included in the venires was the result of the operation of La.Const., Art. VII, § 41, and La.Code Crim.Proc., Art. 402. In the present case, a venire totalling 175 persons was drawn for jury service beginning April 13, 1972. There were no females on the venire.

Appellant's motion to quash the venire was denied that same day. After being tried, convicted, and sentenced to death, appellant sought review in the Supreme Court of Louisiana, where he renewed his claim that the petit jury venire should have been quashed. The Supreme Court of Louisiana, recognizing that this claim drew into question the constitutionality of the provisions of the Louisiana Constitution and Code of Criminal Procedure dealing with the service of women on juries, squarely held, one justice dissenting, that these provisions were valid and not unconstitutional under federal law. . . .

Appellant appealed from that decision to this Court. We noted probable jurisdiction .   .   .   to consider whether the Louisiana jury selection system deprived appellant of his Sixth and Fourteenth Amendment right to an impartial jury trial. We hold that it did and that these amendments were violated in this case by the operation of La.Const., Art. VII, § 41, and La.Code Crim.Proc., Art. 402. In consequence, appellant's conviction must be reversed.

II.

The Louisiana jury selection system does not disqualify women from jury service, but in operation its conceded systematic impact is that only a very few women, grossly disproportionate to the number of eligible women in the community, are called for jury service. In this case, no women were on the venire from which the petit jury was drawn. The issue we have, therefore, is whether a jury selection system which operates to exclude from jury service an identifiable class of citizens constituting 53% of eligible jurors in the community comports with the Sixth and Fourteenth Amendments.

The State first insists that Taylor, a male, has no standing to object to the exclusion of women from his jury. But Taylor's claim is that he was constitutionally entitled to a jury drawn from a venire constituting a fair cross section of the community and that the jury that tried him was not such a jury by reason of the exclusion of women. Taylor was not a member of the excluded class; but there is no rule that claims such as Taylor presents may be made only by those defendants who are members of the group excluded from jury service. In Peters v. Kiff .   .   .   (1972), the defendant, a white man, challenged his conviction on the ground that Negroes had been systematically excluded from jury service. Six Members of the Court agreed that petitioner was entitled to present the issue and concluded that he had been deprived of his federal rights. Taylor, in the case before us, was similarly entitled to tender and have adjudicated the claim that the exclusion of women from jury service deprived him of the kind of fact finder to which he was constitutionally entitled.

III.

The background against which this case must be decided includes our holding in Duncan v. Louisiana . . . (1968), that the Sixth Amendment's provision for jury trial is made binding on the States by virtue of the Fourteenth Amendment. Our inquiry is whether the presence of a fair cross section of the community on venires, panels or lists from which petit juries are drawn is essential to the fulfillment of the Sixth Amendment's guarantee of an impartial jury trial in criminal prosecutions.

The Court's prior cases are instructive. Both in the course of exercising its supervisory powers over trials in federal courts and in the constitutional context, the Court has unambiguously declared that the American concept of the jury trial contemplates a jury drawn from a fair cross section of the community. A unanimous Court stated in Smith v. Texas . . . (1940), that "[i]t is part of the established tradition in the use of juries as instruments of public justice that the jury be a body truly representative of the community." To exclude racial groups from jury service was said to be "at war with our basic concepts of a democratic society and a representative government." A state jury system that resulted in systematic exclusion of Negroes as jurors was therefore held to violate the Equal Protection Clause of the Fourteenth Amendment. Glasser v. United States . . . (1942), in the context of a federal criminal case and the Sixth Amendment's jury trial requirement, stated that "[o]ur notions of what a proper jury is have developed in harmony with our basic concepts of a democratic system and representive government," and repeated the Court's understanding that the jury "be a body truly representative of the community . . . and not the organ of any special group or class."

A federal conviction by a jury from which women had been excluded, although eligible for service under state law, was reviewed in Ballard v. United States . . . (1946). Noting the federal statutory "design to make a jury a 'cross-section of the community'" and the fact that women had been excluded, the Court exercised its supervisory powers over the federal courts and reversed the conviction. In Brown v. Allen . . . (1953), the Court declared that "[o]ur duty to protect the federal constitutional rights of all does not mean we must or should impose on states our conception of the proper source of jury lists, so long as the source reasonably reflects a cross-section of the population suitable in character and intelligence for that civic duty."

Some years later in Carter v. Jury Comm'n . . . (1970), the Court observed that the exclusion of Negroes from jury service because of their race "contravenes the very idea of a jury—'a body truly representative of the community . . . .'" (Quoting from Smith v. Texas, supra.) At about the same time it was contended that the use of six-man juries in noncapital criminal cases violated the Sixth Amendment for failure to provide juries drawn from a cross section of the community, Williams v. Florida   .   .   . (1970).   In the course of rejecting that challenge, we said that the number of persons on the jury should "be large enough to promote group deliberation, free from outside attempts at intimidation, and to provide a fair possibility for obtaining a representative cross-section of the community."   .   .   .   In like vein, in Apodaca v. Oregon   .   .   .   (1970) (plurality opinion), it was said that "a jury will come to such a [commonsense] judgment as long as it consists of a group of laymen representative of a cross section of the community who have the duty and the opportunity to deliberate   .   .   . on the question of a defendant's guilt."   Similarly, three Justices in Peters v. Kiff   .   .   .   observed that the Sixth Amendment comprehended a fair possibility for obtaining a jury constituting a representative cross section of the community.

The unmistakable import of this Court's opinions, at least since 1941, Smith v. Texas, supra, and not repudiated by intervening decisions, is that the selection of a petit jury from a representative cross section of the community is an essential component of the Sixth Amendment right to a jury trial.   Recent federal legislation governing jury selection within the federal court system has a similar thrust.[1]   .   .   .   We accept the fair cross section requirement as fundamental to the jury trial guaranteed by the Sixth Amendment and are convinced that the requirement has solid foundation.   The purpose of a jury is to guard against the exercise of arbitrary power —to make available the commonsense judgment of the community as a hedge against the overzealous or mistaken prosecutor and in preference to the professional or perhaps overconditioned or biased response of a judge.   Duncan v. Louisiana.   .   .   .   This prophylactic vehicle is not provided if the jury pool is made up of only special segments of the populace or if large, distinctive groups are excluded from the pool.   Community participation in the administration of the criminal law, moreover, is not only consistent with our democratic heritage but is also critical to public confidence in the fairness of the criminal justice system.   Restricting jury service to only special groups or excluding identifiable segments playing major roles in the community cannot be squared with the constitutional concept of jury trial.   "Trial by jury presupposes a jury drawn from a pool broadly representative of the community as well as impartial in a specific case.   .   .   .   [T]he broad representative character of the jury should be maintained, partly as assurance of a diffused impartiality and partly because sharing in the administration of justice is a phase of civic responsibility."   Thiel v. Southern Pacific Co.   .   .   . (1946) (Frankfurter, J., dissenting).

---

1.   Federal Jury Selection Act of 1968, Pub.L. No. 90–274, 28 U.S.C.A. § 1861 et seq.

IV.

We are also persuaded that the fair cross section requirement is violated by the systematic exclusion of women, who in the judicial district involved here amounted to 53% of the citizens eligible for jury service. This conclusion necessarily entails the judgment that women are sufficiently numerous and distinct from men that if they are systematically eliminated from jury panels, the Sixth Amendment's fair cross section requirement cannot be satisfied. This very matter was debated in Ballard v. United States, supra. Positing the fair cross-section rule—there said to be a statutory one—the Court concluded that the systematic exclusion of women was unacceptable. The dissenting view that an all-male panel drawn from various groups in the community would be as truly representatve as if women were included, was firmly rejected:

> "The thought is that the factors which tend to influence the action of women are the same as those which influence the action of men—personality, background, economic status —and not sex. Yet it is not enough to say that women when sitting as jurors neither act nor tend to act as a class. Men likewise do not act as a class. But, if the shoe were on the other foot, who would claim that a jury was truly representative of the community if all men were intentionally and systematically excluded from the panel? The truth is that the two sexes are not fungible; a community made up exclusively of one is different from a community composed of both; the subtle interplay of influence one on the other is among the imponderables. To insulate the courtroom from either may not in a given case make an iota of difference. Yet a flavor, a distinct quality is lost if either sex is excluded. The exclusion of one may indeed make the jury less representative of the community than would be true if an economic or racial group were excluded." [2]

In this respect, we agree with the Court in *Ballard*: If the fair cross-section rule is to govern the selection of juries, as we have concluded it must, women cannot be systematically excluded from jury panels from which petit juries are drawn. This conclusion is consistent with the current judgment of the country, now evidenced by legislative or constitutional provisions in every State and at the federal level qualifying women for jury service.

---

2. Compare the opinion of Marshall, J., joined by Douglas and Stewart, JJ., in Peters v. Kiff . . . (1972):
    "These principles compel the conclusion that a State cannot, consistent with due process, subject a defendant to indictment or trial by a jury that has been selected in an arbitrary and discriminatory manner, in violation of the Constitution and laws of the United States. Illegal and unconstitutional jury selection procedures cast doubt on the integrity of the whole judicial process. They create the appearance of bias in the decision of individual cases, and they increase the risk of actual bias as well.

    * * *

    "But the exclusion from jury service of a substantial and identifiable

V.

There remains the argument that women as a class serve a distinctive role in society and that jury service would so substantially interfere with that function that the State has ample justification for excluding women from service unless they volunteer, even though the result is that almost all jurors are men. It is true that Hoyt v. Florida, 368 U.S. 57, 82 S.Ct. 159 (1961), held that such a system did not deny due process of law or equal protection of the laws because there was a sufficiently rational basis for such an exemption.[3] But *Hoyt* did not involve a defendant's Sixth Amendment right to a jury drawn from a fair cross section of the community and the prospect of depriving him of that right if women as a class are systematically excluded. The right to a proper jury cannot be overcome on merely rational grounds.[4] There must be weightier reasons if a distinctive class representing 53% of the eligible jurors is for all practical purposes to be excluded from jury service. No such basis has been tendered here.

The States are free to grant exemptions from jury service to individuals in case of special hardship or incapacity and to those engaged in particular occupations the uninterrupted performance of which is critical to the community's welfare. Rawlins v. Georgia . . . (1906). It would not appear that such exemptions would pose substantial threats that the remaining pool of jurors would not be representative of the community. A system excluding all women,

---

class of citizens has a potential impact that is too subtle and too pervasive to admit of confinement to particular issues or particular cases.

. . .

"Moreover, we are unwilling to make the assumption that the exclusion of Negroes has relevance only for issues involving race. When any large and identifiable segment of the community is excluded from jury service, the effect is to remove from the jury room qualities of human nature and varieties of human experience, the range of which is unknown and perhaps unknowable. It is not necessary to assume that the excluded group will consistently vote as a class in order to conclude, as we do, that its exclusion deprives the jury of a perspective on human events that may have unsuspected importance in any case that may be presented." . . .

Controlled studies of the performance of women as jurors conducted subsequent to the Court's decision in *Ballard* have concluded that women bring to juries their own perspectives and values that influence both jury deliberation and result. See generally Rudolph, Women on Juries—Voluntary or Compulsory?, 44 J.Amer. Jud.Soc. 206 (1961); 55 J. Sociology & Social Research 442 (1971); 3 J.Applied Soc.Phych. 267 (1973); 19 Sociometry 3 (1956).

3. The state interest, as articulated by the Court, was based on the assumption that "woman is still regarded as the center of home and family life." Hoyt v. Florida, 368 U.S. at 62, 82 S. Ct., at 162. Louisiana makes a similar argument here, stating that its grant of an automatic exemption from jury service to females involves only the State's attempt "to regulate and provide stability to the state's own idea of family life." . . .

4. In *Hoyt*, the Court determined both that the underlying classification was rational and that the State's proffered rationale for extending this exemption to females without family responsibilities was justified by administrative convenience. . . .

however, is a wholly different matter. It is untenable to suggest these days that it would be a special hardship for each and every woman to perform jury service or that society cannot spare *any* women from their present duties.[5] This may be the case with many, and it may be burdensome to sort out those who should not be exempted from those who should serve. But that task is performed in the case of men, and the administrative convenience in dealing with women as a class is insufficient justification for diluting the quality of community judgment represented by the jury in criminal trials.

VI.

Although this judgment may appear a foregone conclusion from the pattern of some of the Court's cases over the past 30 years, as well as from legislative developments at both federal and state levels, it is nevertheless true that until today no case had squarely held that the exclusion of women from jury venires deprives a criminal defendant of his Sixth Amendment right to trial by an impartial jury drawn from a fair cross section of the community. It is apparent that the first Congress did not perceive the Sixth Amendment as requiring women on criminal jury panels; for the direction of the First Judiciary Act of 1789 was that federal jurors were to have the qualifications required by the States in which the federal court was sitting and at the time women were disqualified under state law in every State. Necessarily, then, federal juries in criminal cases were all-male, and it was not until the Civil Rights Act of 1957, 71 Stat. 634, 638, 28 U.S.C. § 1861, that Congress itself provided that all citizens, with limited exceptions, were competent to sit on federal juries. Until that time, federal courts were required by statute to exclude women from jury duty in those States where women were disqualified. Utah was the first State to qualify women for juries; it did so in 1898. Moreover, Hoyt v. Florida was decided and has stood for the proposition that, even if women as a group could not be constitution-

---

5. In Hoyt v. Florida, supra, the Court placed some emphasis on the notion, advanced by the State there and by Louisana here in support of the rationality of its statutory scheme, that "woman is still regarded as the center of home and family life." . . . Statistics compiled by the Department of Labor indicate that in October 1974 54.2% of all women between 18 and 64 years of age were in the labor force. United States Dept. of Labor, Women in the Labor Force (Oct. 1974). Additionally, in March 1974, 45.7% of women with children under the age of 18 were in the labor force; with respect to families containing children between the ages of six and 17, 67.3% of mothers who were in widowed, divorced or separated were in the work force, while 51.- 2% of the mothers whose husbands were present in the household were in the work force. Even in family units in which the husband was present and which contained a child under three years old, 31% of the mothers were in the work force. United States Dept. of Labor, Marital and Family Characteristics of the Labor Force, Table F (March 1974). While these statistics perhaps speak more to the evolving nature of the structure of the family unit in American society than to the nature of the role played by women who happen to be members of a family unit, they certainly put to rest the suggestion that all women should be exempt from jury service based solely on their sex and the presumed role in the home.

ally disqualified from jury service, there was ample reason to treat all women differently from men for the purpose of jury service and to exclude them unless they volunteered.

Accepting as we do, however, the view that the Sixth Amendment affords the defendant in a criminal trial the opportunity to have the jury drawn from venires representative of the community, we think it is no longer tenable to hold that women as a class may be excluded or given automatic exemptions based solely on sex if the consequence is that criminal jury venires are almost totally male. To this extent we cannot follow the contrary implications of the prior cases, including Hoyt v. Florida. If it was ever the case that women were unqualified to sit on juries or were so situated that none of them should be required to perform jury service, that time has long since passed. If at one time it could be held that Sixth Amendment juries must be drawn from a fair cross section of the community but that this requirement permitted the almost total exclusion of women, this is not the case today. Communities differ at different times and places. What is a fair cross section at one time or place is not necessarily a fair cross section at another time or a different place. Nothing persuasive has been presented to us in this case suggesting that all-male venires in the parishes involved here are fairly representative of the local population otherwise eligible for jury service.

VII.

Our holding does not augur or authorize the fashioning of detailed jury selection codes by federal courts. The fair cross section principle must have much leeway in application. The States remain free to prescribe relevant qualifications for their jurors and to provide reasonable exemptions so long as it may be fairly said that the jury lists or panels are representative of the community. Carter v. Jury Comm'n, supra, as did Brown v. Allen, supra; Rawlins v. Georgia, supra, and other cases, recognized broad discretion in the States in this respect. We do not depart from the principles enunciated in *Carter*. But, as we have said, Louisiana's special exemption for women operates to exclude them from petit juries, which in our view is contrary to the command of the Sixth and Fourteenth Amendments.

It should also be emphasized that in holding that petit juries must be drawn from a source fairly representative of the community we impose no requirement that petit juries actually chosen must mirror the community and reflect the various distinctive groups in the population. Defendants are not entitled to a jury of any particular composition, Fay v. New York . . . (1947); Apodaca v. Oregon . . . (plurality opinion); but the jury wheels, pools of names, panels or venires from which juries are drawn must not systematically exclude distinctive groups in the community and thereby fail to be reasonably representative thereof.

The judgment of the Louisiana Supreme Court is reversed and the case remanded to that court for further proceedings not inconsistent with this opinion.

So ordered.

Reversed and remanded.

(The dissenting opinion of MR. JUSTICE REHNQUIST is omitted.)

NOTES

1. In Daniel v. Louisiana, 420 U.S. 31, 95 S.Ct. 704 (1975), the Supreme Court, held that *Taylor,* as a matter of federal constitutional law, need not be applied retroactively to void convictions returned by juries which had been empanelled prior to the *Taylor* decision.

2. *Taylor* involved a jury selection system in which women had to file a written declaration of their willingness to serve. But what about a system which exempts any woman who requests not to serve? At the time *Taylor* was decided, five states had just such a system: Georgia, New York, Rhode Island, Tennessee and Missouri. After *Taylor,* Georgia, New York and Rhode Island repealed their statutory exemptions for women; but the remaining two states continued the practice until Duren v. Missouri, 439 U.S. 357, 99 S.Ct. 664 (1979), where the Court, having found that the system created a prima facie violation of the "fair cross-section" requirement, held:

". . . Neither the Missouri Supreme Court nor respondent in its brief have offered any substantial justification for this exemption. In response to questioning at oral argument, counsel for respondent ventured that the only state interest advanced by the exemption is safeguarding the important role played by women in home and family life. But exempting all women because of the preclusive domestic responsibilities of some women is insufficient justification for their disproportionate exclusion on jury venires. What we stated in *Taylor* with respect to the system there challenged under which women could 'opt in' for jury service is equally applicable to Missouri's 'opt out' exemption.

* * *

"We recognize that a State may have an important interest in assuring that those members of the family responsible for the care of children are available to do so. An exemption appropriately tailored to this interest would, we think, survive a fair-cross-section challenge. We stress, however, that the constitutional guarantee to a jury drawn from a fair cross section of the community requires that States exercise proper caution in exempting broad categories of persons from jury service. Although most occupational and other reasonable exemptions may inevitably involve some degree of over- or under-inclusiveness, any category expressly limited to a group in the community of sufficient magnitude and distinctiveness so as to be within the cross-section requirement—such as women—runs the danger of resulting in underrepresentation sufficient to constitute a prima facie violation of that constitutional requirement."

3. Is the right to a representative cross-section violated by a statute which excuses mothers who have children under 18? See McArthur v.

State, 351 So.2d 972 (Fla.1977). It is violated by a statute which excludes convicted felons and resident aliens? See Rubio v. Superior Court, 24 Cal.3d 93, 54 Cal.Rptr. 734, 593 P.2d 595 (1979).

4. In Hamling v. United States, 418 U.S. 87, 94 S.Ct. 2887 (1974), the Court considered a claim by the defendant that the master jury list which provided the jurors in his case had not been changed in almost four years. Thus, because the master list was taken from voter registration records (which were compiled before 18 years olds were permitted to vote through the Twenty-Sixth Amendment), he claimed that he was denied a jury on which young people were represented. Rejecting this argument, the Court said "[I]f the jury wheel is not discriminatory when completely updated at the time of each refilling, a prohibited 'purposeful discrimination' does not arise near the end of the period simply because the young and other persons have belatedly become eligible for jury service by becoming registered voters."

Compare Brown v. State, 239 Ga. 435, 238 S.E.2d 21 (1977), where the court held that a jury list taken from a racially identified tax digest came from an "infected source" and ordered reversal.

5. How do the jury composition cases relate to the grand jury composition cases set in Chapter 11, Section B? Are the principles the same? Should they be? Does the answer depend on the fact that state indictments by grand juries are not constitutionally required, but jury trials are?

3. JURY SIZE

BALLEW v. GEORGIA

Supreme Court of the United States, 1978.
435 U.S. 223, 98 S.Ct. 1029.

MR. JUSTICE BLACKMUN announced the judgment of the Court and delivered an opinion in which MR. JUSTICE STEVENS joined.

This case presents the issue whether a state criminal trial to a jury of only five persons deprives the accused of the right to trial by jury guaranteed to him by the Sixth and Fourteenth Amendments. Our resolution of the issue requires an application of principles enunciated in Williams v. Florida, 399 U.S. 78, 90 S.Ct. 1893 (1970), where the use of a six-person jury in a state criminal trial was upheld against similar constitutional attack.

I.

[Ballew was the manager of an Atlanta movie theater which ran the motion picture, "Behind the Green Door." He was charged with distributing obscene materials, a misdemeanor under Georgia Law. Because state law permitted the trial of misdemeanor cases to proceed before five member juries, Ballew's contention that the size of the jury violated his Sixth Amendment rights was denied, and he was convicted.]

* * *

II.

The Fourteenth Amendment guarantees the right of trial by jury in all state nonpetty criminal cases. Duncan v. Louisiana (1968) [supra this chapter, A1]. The Court in *Duncan* applied this Sixth Amendment right to the States because "trial by jury in criminal cases is fundamental to the American scheme of justice." The right attaches in the present case because the maximum penalty for violating [the statute under which Ballew was convicted] exceeded six months imprisonment. . . .

In Williams v. Florida, 399 U.S., 90 S.Ct., the Court reaffirmed that the "purpose of the jury trial, as we noted in *Duncan*, is to prevent oppression by the Government. 'Providing an accused with the right to be tried by a jury of his peers gave him an inestimable safeguard against the corrupt or overzealous prosecutor and against the compliant, biased, or eccentric judge.'" This purpose is attained by the participation of the community in determinations of guilt and by the application of the common sense of laymen who, as jurors, consider the case.

Williams held that these functions and this purpose could be fulfilled by a jury of six members. As the Court's opinion in that case explained at some length, common-law juries included 12 members by historical accident, "unrelated to the great purposes which gave rise to the jury in the first place." The Court's earlier cases that had *assumed* the number 12 to be constitutionally compelled were set to one side because they had not considered history and the function of the jury. Rather than requiring 12 members, then, the Sixth Amendment mandated a jury only of sufficient size to promote group deliberation, to insulate members from outside intimidation, and to provide a representative cross-section of the community. Although recognizing that by 1970 little empirical research had evaluated jury performance, the Court found no evidence that the reliability of jury verdicts diminished with six-member panels. Nor did the Court anticipate significant differences in result, including the frequency of "hung" juries. Because the reduction in size did not threaten exclusion of any particular class from jury roles, concern that the representative or cross-section character of the jury would suffer with a decrease to six members seemed "an unrealistic one." As a consequence, the six-person jury was held not to violate the Sixth and Fourteenth Amendments.

III.

When the Court in *Williams* permitted the reduction in jury size —or, to put it another way, when it held that a jury of six was not unconstitutional—it expressly reserved ruling on the issue whether a number smaller than six passed constitutional scrutiny. The Court refused to speculate when this so-called "slippery slope" would become too steep. We face now, however, the two-fold question whether a further reduction in the size of the state criminal trial jury does make the grade too dangerous, that is, whether it inhibits the functioning of the jury as an institution to a significant degree, and, if so, whether any state interest counterbalances and justifies the disruption so as to preserve its constitutionality.

Williams v. Florida and Colgrove v. Battin, 413 U.S. 149, 93 S. Ct. 2448 (1973) (where the Court held that a jury of six members did not violate the Seventh Amendment right to a jury trial in a civil case), generated a quantity of scholarly work on jury size. These writings do not draw or identify a bright line below which the number of jurors would not be able to function as required by the standards enunciated in *Williams*. On the other hand, they raise significant questions about the wisdom and constitutionality of a reduction below six. We examine these concerns:

First, recent empirical data suggest that progressively smaller juries are less likely to foster effective group deliberation. At some point, this decline leads to inaccurate fact-finding and incorrect application of the common sense of the community to the facts. Generally, a positive correlation exists between group size and both the quality of group performance and group productivity. A variety of explanations has been offered for this conclusion. Several are particularly applicable in the jury setting. The smaller the group, the less likely are members to make critical contributions necessary for the solution of a given problem. Because most juries are not permitted to take notes, memory is important for accurate jury deliberations. As juries decrease in size, then, they are less likely to have members who remember each of the important pieces of evidence or argument. Furthermore, the smaller the group, the less likely it is to overcome the biases of its members to obtain an accurate result. When individual and group decisionmaking were compared, it was seen that groups performed better because prejudices of individuals were frequently counterbalanced, and objectivity resulted. Groups also exhibited increased motivation and self-criticism. All these advantages, except, perhaps, self-motivation, tend to diminish with group size. Because juries frequently face complex problems laden with value choices, the benefits are important and should be retained. In particular, the counterbalancing of various biases is critical to the accurate application of the common sense of the community to the facts of any given case.

Second, the data now raise doubts about the accuracy of the results achieved by smaller and smaller panels. Statistical studies suggest that the risk of convicting an innocent person (Type I error) rises as the size of the jury diminishes. Because the risk of not convicting a guilty person (Type II error) increases with the size of the panel, an optimal jury size can be selected as a function of the interaction between the two risks. Nagel & Neef concluded that the optimal size, for the purpose of minimizing errors, should vary with the importance attached to the two types of mistakes. After weighing Type I error as 10 times more significant than Type II, perhaps not an unreasonable assumption, they concluded that the optimal jury size was between six and eight. As the size diminished to five and below, the weighted sum of errors increased because of the enlarging risk of the conviction of innocent defendants.[1]

Another doubt about progressively smaller juries arises from the increasing inconsistency that results from the decreases. Saks argued that the "more a jury type fosters consistency, the greater will be the proportion of juries which select the correct (*i. e.*, the same) verdict and the fewer 'errors' will be made." M. Saks, Jury Verdicts, 86–87 (1977). From his mock trials held before undergraduates and former jurors, he computed the percentage of "correct" decisions rendered by 12-person and six-person panels. In the student experiment, 12-person groups reached correct verdicts 83% of the time; six-person panels reached correct verdicts 69% of the time. The results for the former juror study were 71% for the 12-person groups and 57% for the six-person groups.

* * *

. . . [T]hese post-*Williams* studies, therefore, raise significant doubts about the consistency and reliability of the decisions of smaller juries.

Third, the data suggest that the verdicts of jury deliberation in criminal cases will vary as juries become smaller, and that the variance amounts to an imbalance to the detriment of one side, the defense. . . . [Studies have] emphasized that juries in criminal cases generally hang with only one, or more likely two jurors remaining unconvinced of guilt. Also, group theory suggests that a person in the minority will adhere to his position more frequently when he has at least one other person supporting his argument. In the jury setting the significance of this tendency is demonstrated by the following figures: If a minority viewpoint is shared by 10% of the community, 28.2% of 12-member juries may be expected to have no minority representation, but 53.1% of six-member juries would have none. Thirty-four percent of 12-percent panels could be expected to have two minority members, while only 11% of six-member panels would have two. As the numbers diminish below six, even fewer panels would have one member with the minority viewpoint and still fewer would have two. The chance for hung juries would decline accordingly.

Fourth, what has just been said about the presence of minority viewpoint as juries decrease in size foretells problems not only for jury decisionmaking, but also for the representation of minority groups in the community. The Court repeatedly has held that meaningful community participation cannot be attained with the exclusion

---

1. [Nagel & Neef, Deductive Modeling to Determine an Optimum Jury Size and Fraction Required to Convict, 1975 Wash.U.L.Q. 933, 946–48, 956, 957. See also Friedman, Trial by Jury: Criteria for Convictions, Jury Size and Type I and Type II Errors, 26–2 Am.Stat. 21 (April 1972).] Friedman reached a similar conclusion. He varied the appearance of guilt in his statistical study. The more guilty the person appeared, the greater the chance that a six-member panel would convict when a 12-member panel would not. As jury size was reduced, the risk of Type I error would increase, Friedman said, without a significant corresponding advantage in reducing Type II error. . . .

of minorities or other identifiable groups from jury service. "It is part of the established tradition in the use of juries as instruments of public justice that the jury be a body truly representative of the community." Smith v. Texas, 311 U.S. 128, 130, 61 S.Ct. 164, 165 (1940). The exclusion of elements of the community from participation "contravenes the very idea of a jury . . . composed of 'the peers or equals of the person whose rights it is selected or summoned to determine.'" Carter v. Jury Commission, 396 U.S. 320, 330, 90 S. Ct. 518, 524 (1970), quoting Strauder v. West Virginia, 100 U.S. 303, 308 (1879). Although the Court in *Williams* concluded that the six-person jury did not fail to represent adequately a cross-section of the community, the opportunity for meaningful and appropriate representation does decrease with the size of the panels. Thus, if a minority group constitutes 10% of the community, 53.1% of randomly selected six-member juries could be expected to have no minority representative among their members, and 89% not to have two. Further reduction in size will erect additional barriers to representation.

Fifth, several authors have identified in jury research methodological problems tending to mask differences in the operation of smaller and larger juries. For example, because the judicial system handles so many clear cases, decisionmakers will reach similar results through similar analyses most of the time. One study concluded that smaller and larger juries could disagree in their verdicts in no more than 14% of the cases. Disparities, therefore, appear in only small percentages. Nationwide, however, these small percentages will represent a large number of cases. And it is with respect to those cases that the jury trial right has its greatest value. When the case is close, and the guilt or innocence of the defendant is not readily apparent, a properly functioning jury system will insure evaluation by the common sense of the community and will also tend to insure accurate factfinding.

* * *

IV.

While we adhere to, and reaffirm our holding in Williams v. Florida, these studies, most of which have been made since *Williams* was decided in 1970, lead us to conclude that the purpose and functioning of the jury in a criminal trial is seriously impaired, and to a constitutional degree, by a reduction in size to below six members. We readily admit that we do not pretend to discern a clear line between six members and five. But the assembled data raise substantial doubt about the reliability and appropriate representation of panels smaller than six. Because of the fundamental importance of the jury trial to the American system of criminal justice, any further reduction that promotes inaccurate and possibly biased decisionmaking, that causes untoward differences in verdicts, and that prevents juries from truly representing their communities, attains constitutional significance.

* * *

. . . . Georgia argues that its use of five-member juries does not violate the Sixth and Fourteenth Amendments because they are used only in misdemeanor cases. If six persons may constitutionally assess the felony charge in *Williams*, the State reasons, five persons should be a constitutionally adequate number for a misdemeanor trial. The problem with this argument is that the purpose and functions of the jury do not vary significantly with the importance of the crime. In Baldwin v. New York (1970), [this chapter A1], the Court held that the right to a jury trial attached in both felony and misdemeanor cases. Only in cases concerning truly petty crimes, where the deprivation of liberty was minimal, did the defendant have no constitutional right to trial by jury. In the present case the possible deprivation of liberty is substantial. . . . We cannot conclude that there is less need for the imposition and the direction of the common sense of the community in this case than when the State has chosen to label an offense a felony.[2] The need for an effective jury here must be judged by the same standards announced and applied in Williams v. Florida.

* * *

Georgia submits that the five-person jury adequately represents the community because there is no arbitrary exclusion of any particular class. We agree that it has not been demonstrated that the Georgia system violates the Equal Protection Clause by discriminating on the basis of race or some other improper classification. See Carter v. Jury Commission, 396 U.S. 320, 90 S.Ct. 518 (1970); Smith v. Texas, 311 U.S. 128, 61 S.Ct. 164 (1940). But the data outlined above raise substantial doubt about the ability of juries truly to represent the community as membership decreases below six. If the smaller and smaller juries will lack consistency, as the cited studies suggest, then the common sense of the community will not be applied equally in like cases. Not only is the representation of racial minorities threatened in such circumstances, but also majority attitude or various minority positions may be misconstrued or misapplied by the smaller groups. Even though the facts of this case would not establish a jury discrimination claim under the Equal Protection Clause, the question of representation does constitute one factor of several that, when combined, create a problem of constitutional significance under the Sixth and Fourteenth Amendments.

* * *

2. We do not rely on any First Amendment aspect of this case in holding the five-person jury unconstitutional. Nevertheless, the nature of the substance of the misdemeanor charges against petitioner supports the refusal to distinguish between felonies and misdemeanors. The application of the community's standards and common sense is important in obscenity trials where juries must define and apply local standards. See Miller v. California, 413 U.S. 15, 93 S. Ct. 2607 (1973). The opportunity for harassment and overreaching by an overzealous prosecutor or a biased judge is at least as significant in an obscenity trial as in one concerning an armed robbery. This fact does not change merely because the obscenity charge may be labeled a misdemeanor and the robbery a felony.

V.

With the reduction in the number of jurors below six creating a substantial threat to Sixth and Fourteenth Amendment guarantees, we must consider whether any interest of the State justifies the reduction. We find no significant state advantage in reducing the number of jurors from six to five.

The States utilize juries of less than 12 primarily for administrative reasons. Savings in court time and in financial costs are claimed to justify the reductions. The financial benefits of the reduction from 12 to six are substantial; this is mainly because fewer jurors draw daily allowances as they hear cases. On the other hand, the asserted saving in judicial time is not so clear. Pabst in his study found little reduction in the time for voir dire with the six-person jury because many questions were directed at the veniremen as a group. Total trial time did not diminish, and court delays and backlogs improved very little.[3] The point that is to be made, of course, is that a reduction in size from six to five or four or even three would save the States little. They could reduce slightly the daily allowances, but with a reduction from six to five the saving would be minimal. If little time is gained by the reduction from 12 to six, less will be gained with a reduction from six to five. Perhaps this explains why only three States, Georgia, Louisiana, and Virginia, have reduced the size of juries in certain nonpetty criminal cases to five. Other States appear content with six members or more. In short the State has offered little or no justification for its reduction to five members.

Petitioner, therefore, has established that his trial on criminal charges before a five-member jury deprived him of the right to trial by jury guaranteed by the Sixth and Fourteenth Amendments.

VI.

The judgment of the Court of Appeals is reversed, and the case is remanded for further proceedings not inconsistent with this opinion.

It is so ordered.

MR. JUSTICE STEVENS, concurring. [Opinion omitted].

MR. JUSTICE WHITE, concurring in the judgment.

Agreeing that a jury of fewer than six persons would fail to represent the sense of the community and hence not satisfy the fair cross-section requirement of the Sixth and Fourteenth Amendments, I concur in the judgment of reversal.

MR. JUSTICE POWELL, with whom THE CHIEF JUSTICE and MR. JUSTICE REHNQUIST join, concurring in the judgment.

---

3. [Pabst, Statistical Studies of the Costs of Six-Man versus Twelve-Man Juries, 14 Wm. & Mary L.Rev. 326, 328 (1972).]

I concur in the judgment, as I agree that use of a jury as small as five members, with authority to convict for serious offenses, involves grave questions of fairness. As the opinion of Mr. Justice Blackmun indicates, the line between five- and six-member juries is difficult to justify, but a line has to be drawn somewhere if the substance of jury trial is to be preserved.

I do not agree, however, that every feature of jury trial practice must be the same in both federal and state courts. . . .

Because the opinion of Mr. Justice Blackmun today assumes full incorporation of the Sixth Amendment by the Fourteenth Amendment . . . I do not join it. Also, I have reservations as to the wisdom—as well as the necessity—of Mr. Justice Blackmun's heavy reliance on numerology derived from statistical studies. Moreover, neither the validity nor the methodology employed by the studies cited was subjected to the traditional testing mechanisms of the adversary process. The studies relied on merely represent unexamined findings of persons interested in the jury system.

For these reasons I concur only in the judgment.

MR. JUSTICE BRENNAN, with whom MR. JUSTICE STEWART and MR. JUSTICE MARSHALL join.

I join MR. JUSTICE BLACKMUN's opinion insofar as it holds that the Sixth and Fourteenth Amendments require juries in criminal trials to contain more than five persons. However, I cannot agree that petitioner can be subjected to a new trial, since I continue to adhere to my belief that [the Georgia obscenity statute] is overbroad and therefore facially unconstitutional. . . .

NOTES

1. In Williams v. Florida, 399 U.S. 78 (1970), the Supreme Court held that the states were not constitutionally prohibited from using six member juries in criminal cases. As Justice Powell's concurrence in *Ballew* recognized, the practical effects of a reduction in the jury size are difficult to measure with any degree of certainty. However, Professor Hans Zeisel, whose distinction in the field is evidenced by his co-authorship, with Harry Kalven, of the pre-eminent jury study, The American Jury (1966), has made these observations in his article "And Then There Were None: The Diminution Of The Federal Jury", 38 U.Chi.L.Rev. 710, 712–24 (1971):

"History, however, might have embodied more wisdom than the Court would allow. It might be more than an accident that after centuries of trial and error the size of the jury at common law came to be fixed at twelve. A primary function of the jury was to represent the community as broadly as possible; yet at the same time, it had to remain a group of manageable size. Twelve might have been, and might still be, the upper limit beyond which the difficulty of self-management becomes insuperable under the burdensome condition of a trial. On this view, twelve would be the number that optimizes the jury's two conflicting goals—to represent the community and to remain manageable.

* * *

"In addition to the tendency to be less representative and to produce more varied damage verdicts, the six-member jury is likely to yield fewer examples of that treasured, paradoxical phenomenon —the hung jury. Hung juries almost always arise from situations in which there were originally several dissenters. Even if only one holds out, his having once been the member of a group is essential in sustaining him against the majority's efforts to make the verdict unanimous. Fewer hung juries can be expected in six-member juries for two reasons: first, . . . there will be fewer holders of minority positions on the jury; second, if a dissenter appears, he is more likely to be the only one on the jury. Lacking any associate to support his position, he is more likely to abandon it.

* * *

"On grounds of economy, one might welcome any reduction in the number of hung juries. One should understand, however, that such reduction is but the combined result of less representative, more homogeneous juries and of a reduced ability to resist the pressure for unanimity.

* * *

"Both in the short and in the long run our judicial system has many options, but every solution has its own balance sheet of advantages and costs. What is necessary is that we, and with us the United States Supreme Court, see both with equal clarity."

2. For discussion of the principles underlying the Court's decisions in *Williams* and some attempt to ascertain its possible effect on jury deliberations, see Lempert, Uncovering "Nondiscernible" Differences: Empirical Research and the Jury-Size Cases, 73 Mich.L.Rev. 643 (1975); Zeisel & Diamond, "Convincing Empirical Evidence" on the Six Member Jury, 41 U. Chi.L.Rev. 281 (1974); Note, Effect of Jury Size on the Probability of Conviction: An Evaluation of Williams v. Florida, 22 Case W.Res.L.Rev. 529 (1971).

3. Is it easier to convince six people or twelve that your client should prevail? Would one person holding out for your side be more inclined to accede to the majority viewpoint if there are eleven in the majority rather than five?

4. LESS–THAN–UNANIMOUS VERDICTS

JOHNSON v. LOUISIANA

Supreme Court of the United States, 1972.
406 U.S. 356, 92 S.Ct. 1620.

[The defendant was tried for robbery before a 12-man jury and convicted upon a nine to three verdict, as authorized by Louisiana law in cases where the crime is necessarily punishable at hard labor. (Other state law provisions require unanimity for five-man jury trials of offenses in which the punishment may be at hard labor and for 12-man jury trials and capital cases.) The appellant's argument, according to the court, consisted of two parts: first, that nine individual jurors will be unable to vote conscientiously in favor of guilt beyond a reasonable doubt when three of their colleagues are arguing for acquittal, and second, that guilt cannot be said to have been proved beyond a reasonable doubt when one or more of a jury's members at the conclusion of deliberation still possess such a doubt. The majority of the court held that neither argument was persuasive.]

MR. JUSTICE WHITE delivered the opinion of the Court.

* * *

. . . . In considering the first branch of appellant's argument, we can find no basis for holding that the nine jurors who voted for his conviction failed to follow their instructions concerning the need for proof beyond such a doubt or that the vote of any one of the nine failed to reflect an honest belief that guilt had been so proved. Appellant, in effect, asks us to assume that, when minority jurors express sincere doubts about guilt, their fellow jurors will nevertheless ignore them and vote to convict even if deliberation has not been exhausted and minority jurors have grounds for acquittal which, if pursued, might persuade members of the majority to acquit. But the mere fact that three jurors voted to acquit does not in itself demonstrate that, had the nine jurors of the majority attended further to reason and the evidence, all or one of them would have developed a reasonable doubt about guilt. We have no grounds for believing that majority jurors, aware of their responsibility and power over the liberty of the defendant, would simply refuse to listen to arguments presented to them in favor of acquittal, terminate discussion and render a verdict. On the contrary it is far more likely that a juror presenting reasoned argument in favor of acquittal would either have his arguments answered or would carry enough other jurors with him to prevent conviction. A majority will cease discussion and outvote a minority only after reasoned discussion has ceased to have persuasive effect or to serve any other purpose—when a minority, that is, continues to insist upon acquittal without having persuasive reasons in support of its position. At that juncture there is no basis for denigrating the vote of so large a majority of the jury or for refusing to accept their decision as being, at least in their minds, beyond a reasonable doubt. Indeed, at this point, a "dissenting juror should consider whether his doubt was a reasonable one . . . . [when it made] no impression upon the minds of so many men, equally honest, equally intelligent with himself." Allen v. United States, 164 U.S. 492, 501, 17 S.Ct. 154, 157 (1896). Appellant offers no evidence that majority jurors simply ignore the reasonable doubts of their colleagues or otherwise act irresponsibly in casting their votes in favor of conviction, and before we alter our own longstanding perceptions about jury behavior and overturn a considered legislative judgment that unanimity is not essential to reasoned jury verdicts, we must have some basis for doing so other than unsupported assumptions.

We conclude, therefore, that, as to the nine jurors who voted to convict, the State satisfied its burden of proving guilt beyond any reasonable doubt. The remaining question under the Due Process Clause is whether the vote of three jurors for acquittal can be said to impeach the verdict of the other nine and to demonstrate that guilt was not in fact proved beyond such doubt. We hold that it cannot.

Of course, the State's proof could perhaps be regarded as more certain if it had convinced all 12 jurors instead of only nine; it would have been even more compelling if it had been required to convince and had, in fact, convinced 24 or 36 jurors. But the fact remains that nine jurors—a substantial majority of the jury—were convinced by the evidence. In our view disagreement of three jurors does not alone establish reasonable doubt, particularly when such a heavy majority of the jury, after having considered the dissenters' views, remains convinced of guilt. That rational men disagree is not in itself equivalent to a failure of proof by the State, nor does it indicate infidelity to the reasonable doubt standard. Jury verdicts finding guilty beyond a reasonable doubt are regularly sustained even though the evidence was such that the jury would have been justified in having a reasonable doubt; even though the trial judge might not have reached the same conclusion as the jury; and even though appellate judges are closely divided on the issue whether there was sufficient evidence to support a conviction. That want of jury unanimity is not to be equated with the existence of a reasonable doubt emerges even more clearly from the fact that, when a jury in a federal court, which operates under the unanimity rule and is instructed to acquit a defendant if it has a reasonable doubt about his guilt, cannot agree unanimously upon a verdict, the defendant is not acquitted, but is merely given a new trial. If the doubt of a minority of jurors indicates the existence of a reasonable doubt it would appear that a defendant should receive a directed verdict of acquittal rather than a retrial. We conclude, therefore that verdicts rendered by nine out of 12 jurors are not automatically invalidated by the disagreement of the dissenting three. Appellant was not deprived of due process of law.

* * *

The judgment of the Supreme Court of Louisiana is therefore affirmed.

Affirmed.

[The concurring opinions of Justices Blackmun and Powell are omitted.]

MR. JUSTICE STEWART, with whom MR. JUSTICE BRENNAN and MR. JUSTICE MARSHALL join, dissenting.

.   .   .   I think the Fourteenth Amendment alone clearly requires that if a State purports to accord the right of trial by jury in a criminal case, then only a unanimous jury can return a constitutionally valid verdict.

The guarantee against systematic discrimination in the selection of criminal court juries is a fundamental of the Fourteenth Amendment. That has been the insistent message of this Court in a line of decisions extending over nearly a century. The clear purpose of these decisions has been to ensure universal participation of the citizenry in the administration of criminal justice. Yet today's judgment approves the elimination of the one rule that can ensure that such participation will be meaningful—the rule requiring the assent of all jurors before a verdict of conviction or acquittal can be returned. Under today's judgment, nine jurors can simply ignore the views of their fellow panel members of a different race or class.

The constitutional guarantee of an impartial system of jury selection in a state criminal trial rests on the Due Process and Equal Protection Clauses of the Fourteenth Amendment. Only a jury so selected can assure both a fair criminal trial, and public confidence in its result. Today's decision grossly undermines those basic assurances. For only a unanimous jury so selected can serve to minimize the potential bigotry of those who might convict on inadequate evidence, or acquit when evidence of guilt was clear. And community confidence in the administration of criminal justice cannot but be corroded under a system in which a defendant who is conspicuously identified with a particular group can be acquitted or convicted by a jury split along group lines. The requirements of unanimity and impartial selection thus complement each other in ensuring the fair performance of the vital functions of a criminal court jury.

It does not denigrate the system of trial by jury to acknowledge that it is imperfect, nor does it enable that system to drape upon a jury majority the mantle of presumptive reasonableness in all circumstances. The Court has never before been so impervious to reality in this area. Its recognition of the serious risks of jury misbehavior is a theme unifying a series of constitutional decisions that may be in jeopardy if today's facile presumption of regularity becomes the new point of departure. Why, if juries do not sometimes act out of passion and prejudice, does the Constitution require the availability of a change of venue? Why, if juries do not sometimes act improperly, does the Constitution require protection from inflammatory press coverage and *ex parte* influence by court officers? Why, if juries must be presumed to obey all instructions from the bench, does the Constitution require that certain information must not go to the jury no matter how strong a cautionary charge accompanies it? Why, indeed, should we insist that no man can be constitutionally convicted by a jury from which members of an identifiable group to which he belongs have been systematically excluded?

So deeply engrained is the law's tradition of refusal to engage in after-the-fact review of jury deliberations, however, that these and other safeguards provide no more than limited protection. The requirement that the verdict of the jury be unanimous, surely as important as these other constitutional requisites, preserves the jury's function in linking law with contemporary society. It provides the simple and effective method endorsed by centuries of experience and history to combat the injuries to the fair administration of justice that can be inflicted by community passion and prejudice.

I dissent.

[The dissenting opinion of Justice Douglas is omitted.]

NOTES

1. In his concurring opinion in *Johnson*, Mr. Justice Powell expressed the view that the Sixth Amendment requires unanimous verdicts in federal prosecutions. He argued, however, that the Due Process Clause of the Fourteenth Amendment does not incorporate the unanimous verdict provision so as to make it applicable to state prosecutions. Using a generalized "fundamental right, essential to a system of ordered liberty" approach (in the mode of Cardozo and Harlan), Powell concluded that state criminal verdicts of guilt can be sustained even though the vote is less than unanimous. Powell's vote was essential to affirmance in Johnson and in the companion case of Apodaca v. Oregon, 406 U.S. 404, 92 S.Ct. 1628 (1972). The plurality in *Apodaca* said that the essential purpose of jury trial guarantee was to interpose between the accused and the accuser the commonsense judgment of a group of laymen, representative of a cross section of the community, and that this purpose is served even in the absence of a unanimity requirement. It is clear, however, that if the prosecutions under review had been federal, the Court as constituted when *Apodaca* and *Johnson* were decided would, because of Powell's position, mandate a unanimous verdict. The issue is academic now because unanimous verdicts are presently required under federal statutory law and because the Court's composition has changed since 1972.

2. In jurisdictions without statutory provisions for less-than-unanimous verdicts, may a defendant agree to such a verdict while awaiting a conclusion of the jury's deliberation?

Consider Hibdon v. United States, 204 F.2d 834 (6th Cir. 1953), involving a felony prosecution, in which the jury, after twenty-seven minutes of deliberation, reported to the trial judge that they were unable to agree. The judge thereupon inquired of defense counsel and the prosecutor as to whether a majority verdict would be acceptable to them. They (as well as the defendant himself) agreed. The jury convicted the defendant on one count of the indictment by a vote of 9 to 3, and on another count by a vote of 10 to 2. Judgment was entered on the verdict and the defendant appealed. In reversing the conviction the Court of Appeals said:

> "The humanitarian concept that is at the base of criminal prosecutions in Anglo-Saxon countries, and which distinguishes them from those of most continental European nations, is the presumption of innocence which can only be overthrown by proof beyond a reasonable doubt. The unanimity of a verdict in a criminal case is inextricably interwoven with the required measure of proof. To sustain the validity of a verdict by less than all of the jurors is to destroy this test of proof for there cannot be a verdict supported by proof beyond a reasonable doubt if one or more jurors remain reasonably in doubt as to guilt. It would be a contradiction in terms. We are of the view that the right to a unanimous verdict cannot under any circumstances be waived, that it is of the very essence of our traditional concept of due process in criminal cases, and that the verdict in this case is a nullity because it is not the unanimous verdict of the jury as to guilt."

Compare Fournier v. Gonzales, 269 F.2d 26 (1st Cir. 1959).

In the light of *Johnson* and *Apodaca*, should the result be any different than the one reached in the *Hibdon* case?

3. England, with the passage of its 1967 Criminal Justice Bill, inaugurated a procedure for less than unanimous verdicts:

MAJORITY VERDICTS OF JURIES IN CRIMINAL PROCEEDINGS

§ 10.—(1) Subject to the following provisions of this section, the verdict of a jury in criminal proceedings need not be unanimous if—

> (a) in a case where there are not less than eleven jurors, ten of them agree on the verdict; and

> (b) in a case where there are ten jurors, nine of them agree on the verdict; and a verdict authorised by this subsection is hereafter in this section referred to as "a majority verdict".

(2) A court shall not accept a majority verdict unless the foreman of the jury has stated in open court the number of jurors who respectively agreed to and dissented from the verdict.

(3) A court shall not accept a majority verdict unless it appears to the court that the jury have had not less than two hours for deliberation or such longer period as the court thinks reasonable having regard to the nature and complexity of the case.

For an explanation of this English innovation consider the following from Ryan, Less Than Unanimous Verdicts in Criminal Trials, 58 J.Crim. L., C. & P.S. 211 (1967):

> "During the year 1965, forty percent of the defendants who pled not guilty to criminal charges in England were acquitted. 'Quite a lot of them', according to the Home Secretary of England, were known to be guilty 'by everyone connected with the case'; and among those who 'got off', some were the 'centres of networks of criminal activities'.

> "In offering an explanation for England's high percentage of acquittals, the Home Secretary Mr. Roy Jenkins, expressed the view that it was through 'the power to intimidate or corrupt jurors'. He proposed, as a remedy, that less than unanimous jury verdicts be made permissible."

4. Does the unanimity rule apply in jurisdictions which permit bench trials before three judge panels? In State v. Robbins, —— Ohio App. ——, 189 N.E.2d 641 (1963), the court held that unanimous decisions were required:

> "If there is a difference of opinion as to guilt among the three trial judges all of whom are reasonable and experienced, this fact not only suggests that there can be more than one conclusion as to the evidence but it proves it. This fact in and of itself injects reasonable doubt into the case and the State has failed to sustain the burden of proof beyond a reasonable doubt. To say that there was evidently no doubt in the minds of the two concurring judges merely begs the question. The reasonable doubt statute and the statute authorizing a trial by a three judge court in felony cases upon waiver of a jury are in pari materia. The one is equal to the other. The waiver of a trial by jury does not waive the reasonable doubt statute."

Upon appeal by the state from the decision of the Court of Appeals in *Robbins*, the Ohio Supreme Court reversed, for the following reasons, in 176 Ohio St. 362, 199 N.E.2d 742 (1974):

> ". . . two reasonable minds may disagree as to what a reasonable doubt is. Otherwise, the conclusion of one or more dissenters that there had not been proof of a defendant's guilt beyond a reasonable doubt would necessarily require a reversal of his conviction.

> "Proof beyond a reasonable doubt is a subjective individual standard rather than a group standard. If it were otherwise, where any juror has a reasonable doubt, then the 'group mind' has a reasonable doubt, and the group should vote a not guilty. But under the law, the jury is 'hung' and a new trial is necessary."

5. Does it follow from *Johnson* (permitting less than unanimous verdicts) and *Williams* (permitting juries of less than 12 members) that a state may permit less than unanimous verdicts by a 6 member jury in criminal cases? The question was resolved in Burch v. Louisiana, 441 U.S. 130, 99 S.Ct. 1623 (1979), in which the Court held that a 5–1 vote for conviction failed to satisfy the minimum constitutional requirements.

B. SELECTION OF THE JURY

1. CHALLENGES

SWAIN v. ALABAMA

Supreme Court of the United States, 1965.
380 U.S. 202, 85 S.Ct. 824.

MR. JUSTICE WHITE delivered the opinion of the Court.

The petitioner, Robert Swain, a Negro, was indicted and convicted of rape in the Circuit Court of Talladega County, Alabama, and sentenced to death. His motions to quash the indictment, to strike the trial jury venire and to declare void the petit jury chosen in the case, all based on alleged invidious discrimination in the selection of jurors, were denied.

* * *

In providing for jury trial in criminal cases, Alabama adheres to the common-law system of trial by an impartial jury of 12 men who must unanimously agree on a verdict, the system followed in the federal courts by virtue of the Sixth Amendment. As part of this system it provides for challenges for cause and substitutes a system of strikes for the common-law method of peremptory challenge. Alabama contends that its system of peremptory strikes—challenges without cause, without explanation and without judicial scrutiny—affords a suitable and necessary method of securing juries which in fact and in the opinion of the parties are fair and impartial. This system, it is said, in and of itself, provides justification for striking any group of otherwise qualified jurors in any given case, whether they be Negroes, Catholics, accountants or those with blue eyes. Based on the history of this system and its actual use and operation in this country, we think there is merit in this position.

The peremptory challenge has very old credentials. In all trials for felonies at common law, the defendant was allowed to challenge peremptorily 35 jurors, and the prosecutor originally had a right to challenge any number of jurors without cause, a right which was said to tend to "infinite delayes and danger." Coke on Littleton 156 (14th ed. 1791). Thus The Ordinance for Inquests, 33 Edw. 1, Stat. 4 (1305), provided that if "they that sue for the King will challenge any . . . Jurors, they shall assign . . . a Cause certain." So persistent was the view that a proper jury trial required peremptories on both sides, however, that the statute was construed to allow the prosecution to direct any juror after examination to "stand aside" until the entire panel was gone over and the defendant had exercised his challenges; only if there was a deficiency of jurors in the box at that point did the Crown have to show cause in respect to jurors recalled to make up the required number. Peremptories on both sides became the settled law of England, continuing in the above form until after the separation of the Colonies.

This common law provided the starting point for peremptories in this country. In the federal system, Congress early took a part of the subject in hand in establishing that the defendant was entitled to 35 peremptories in trials for treason and 20 in trials for other felonies specified in the 1790 Act as punishable by death, 1 Stat. 119 (1790). In regard to trials for other offenses without the 1790 statute, both the defendant and the Government were thought to have a right of peremptory challenge, although the source of this right was not wholly clear. In 1865, the Government was given by statute five peremptory challenges in capital and treason cases, the defendant being entitled to 20, and two in other cases where the right of the defendant to challenge then existed, he being entitled to 10. Subsequent enactments increased the number of challenges the Government could exercise, the Government now having an equal number with the defendant in capital cases, and six in cases where the crime is punishable by more than one year's imprisonment, the defendant or defendants having ten.

The course in the States apparently paralleled that in the federal system. The defendant's right of challenge was early conferred by statute, the number often corresponding to the English practice, the prosecution was thought to have retained the Crown's common-law right to stand aside, and by 1870, most, if not all, States had enacted statutes conferring on the prosecution a substantial number of peremptory challenges, the number generally being at least half, but often equal to, the number had by the defendant. Although there has been some criticism in the twentieth century leveled at peremptory challenges, on the basis of the delays, expense and elimination of qualified jurors incident to their use, the system has survived these attacks. In every State, except where peremptory strikes are a substitute, peremptory challenges are given by statute to both sides in both criminal and civil cases, the number in criminal cases still being considerably greater. Under these statutes the prosecution generally possesses a substantial number of challenges.

The system of struck juries also has its roots in ancient common-law heritage. Since striking a jury allowed both sides a greater number of challenges and an opportunity to become familiar with the entire venire list, it was deemed an effective means of obtaining more impartial and better qualified jurors. Accordingly, it was used in causes of "great nicety" or "where the sheriff [responsible for the jury list] was suspected of partiality." 3 Bl.Comm. 357. It is available in many States for both civil and criminal cases. The Alabama system adheres to the common-law form, except that the veniremen are drawn from the regular jury list, are summoned to court before striking begins and the striking continues until 12 rather than 24 remain. It was adopted as a fairer system to the defendant and prosecutor and a more efficacious, quicker way to obtain an impartial jury satisfactory to the parties.

In contrast to the course in England, where both peremptory challenge and challenge for cause have fallen into disuse, peremptories were and are freely used and relied upon in this country, perhaps because juries here are drawn from a greater cross-section of a heterogeneous society. The *voir dire* in American trials tends to be extensive and probing, operating as a predicate for the exercise of peremptories, and the process of selecting a jury protracted. The persistence of peremptories and their extensive use demonstrate the long and widely held belief that peremptory challenge is a necessary part of trial by jury. Although "[t]here is nothing in the Constitution of the United States which requires the Congress [or the States] to grant peremptory challenges," Stilson v. United States, 250 U.S. 583, 586, 40 S.Ct. 28, 30, nonetheless the challenge is "one of the most important of the rights secured to the accused."

* * *

The function of the challenge is not only to eliminate extremes of partiality on both sides, but to assure the parties that the jurors before whom they try the case will decide on the basis of the evidence placed before them, and not otherwise. In this way the peremptory satisfies the rule that "to perform its high function in the best way 'justice must satisfy the appearance of justice.'" Indeed the very availability of peremptories allows counsel to ascertain the possibility of bias through probing questions on the *voir dire* and facilitates the exercise of challenges for cause by removing the fear of incurring a juror's hostility through examination and challenge for cause. Although historically the incidence of the prosecutor's challenge has differed from that of the accused, the view in this country has been that the system should guarantee "not only freedom from any bias against the accused, but also from any prejudice against his prosecution. Between him and the state the scales are to be evenly held."

The essential nature of the peremptory challenge is that it is one exercised without a reason stated, without inquiry and without being subject to the court's control. While challenges for cause permit rejection of jurors on a narrowly specified, provable and legally cognizable basis of partiality, the peremptory permits rejection for a real or imagined partiality that is less easily designated or demonstrable. It is often exercised upon the "sudden impressions and unaccountable prejudices we are apt to conceive upon the bare looks and gestures of another," upon a juror's "habits and associations," or upon the feeling that "the bare questioning [a juror's] indifference may sometimes provoke a resentment." It is no less frequently exercised on grounds normally thought irrelevant to legal proceedings or official action, namely, the race, religion, nationality, occupation or affiliations of people summoned for jury duty. For the question a prosecutor or defense counsel must decide is not whether a juror of a particular race or nationality is in fact partial, but whether one from a different group is less likely to be. It is well known that these factors are widely explored during the *voir dire*, by both prosecutor and accused. This Court has held that the fairness of trial by jury requires no less. Hence veniremen are not always judged solely as individuals for the purpose of exercising peremptory challenges. Rather they are challenged in light of the limited knowledge counsel has of them, which may include their group affiliations, in the context of the case to be tried.

With these considerations in mind, we cannot hold that the striking of Negroes in a particular case is a denial of equal protection of the laws. In the quest for an impartial and qualified jury, Negro and white, Protestant and Catholic, are alike subject to being challenged without cause. To subject the prosecutor's challenge in any particular case to the demands and traditional standards of the Equal Protection Clause would entail a radical change, in the nature and operation of the challenge. The challenge, *pro tanto*, would no longer be peremptory, each and every challenge being open to examination, either at the time of the challenge or at a hearing afterwards. The prosecutor's judgment underlying each challenge would be subject to scrutiny for reasonableness and sincerity. And a great many uses of the challenge would be banned.

In the light of the purpose of the peremptory system and the function it serves in a pluralistic society in connection with the institution of jury trial, we cannot hold that the Constitution requires an examination of the prosecutor's reasons for the exercise of his challenges in any given case. The presumption in any particular case must be that the prosecutor is using the State's challenges to obtain a fair and impartial jury to try the case before the court. The presumption is not overcome and the prosecutor therefore subjected to examination by allegations that in the case at hand all Negroes were removed from the jury or that they were removed because they were Negroes. Any other result, we think, would establish a rule wholly at odds with the peremptory challenge system as we know it. Hence the motion to strike the trial jury was properly denied in this case.

Petitioner, however, presses a broader claim in this Court. His argument is that not only were the Negroes removed by the prosecutor in this case but that there never has been a Negro on a petit jury in either a civil or criminal case in Talladega County and that in criminal cases prosecutors have consistently and systematically exercised their strikes to prevent any and all Negroes on petit jury veniries from serving on the petit jury itself. This systematic practice, it is claimed, is invidious discrimination for which the peremptory system is insufficient justification.

We agree that this claim raises a different issue and it may well require a different answer. We have decided that it is permissible to insulate from inquiry the removal of Negroes from a particular jury on the assumption that the prosecutor is acting on acceptable considerations related to the case he is trying, the particular defendant involved and the particular crime charged. But when the prosecutor in a county, in case after case, whatever the circumstances, whatever the crime and whoever the defendant or the victim may be, is responsible for the removal of Negroes who have been selected as qualified jurors by the jury commissioners and who have survived challenges for cause, with the result that no Negroes ever serve on petit juries, the Fourteenth Amendment claim takes on added significance. In these circumstances, giving even the widest leeway to the operation of irrational but trial-related suspicions and antagonisms, it would appear that the purpose of the peremptory challenge are being perverted. If the State has not seen fit to leave a single Negro on any jury in a criminal case, the presumption protecting the prosecutor may well be overcome. Such proof might support a reasonable inference that Negroes are excluded from juries for reasons wholly unrelated to the outcome of the particular case on trial and that the peremptory system is being used to deny the Negro the same right and opportunity to participate in the administration of justice enjoyed by the white population. These ends the peremptory challenge is not designed to facilitate or justify.

We need pursue this matter no further, however, for even if a State's systematic striking of Negroes in the selection of petit juries raises a prima facie case under the Fourteenth Amendment, we think it is readily apparent that the record in this case is not sufficient to demonstrate that the rule has been violated by the peremptory system as it operates in Talladega County.

The difficulty with the record before us, perhaps flowing from the fact that it was made in connection with the motion to quash the indictment, is that it does not with any acceptable degree of clarity, show when, how often, and under what circumstances the prosecutor alone has been responsible for striking those Negroes who have appeared on petit jury panels in Talledega County. The record is absolutely silent as to those instances in which the prosecution participated in striking Negroes, except for the indication that the prosecutor struck the Negroes in this case and except for those occasions when the defendant himself indicated that he did not want Negroes on the jury.   Apparently in some cases, the prosecution agreed with the defense to remove Negroes.   There is no evidence, however, of what the prosecution did or did not do on its own account in any cases other than the one at bar.   In one instance the prosecution offered the defendant an all-Negro jury but the defendant in that case did not want a jury with any Negro members.   There was other testimony that in many cases the Negro defendant preferred an all-white to a mixed jury.   One lawyer, who had represented both white and Negro defendants in criminal cases, could recall no Negro client who wanted Negroes on the jury which was to try him.   The prosecutor himself, who had served since 1953, said that if the Negro defendant wanted Negroes on the jury it would depend "upon the circumstances and the conditions and the case and what I thought justice demanded and what [it] was in that particular case," and that striking is done differently depending on the race of the defendant and the victim of the crime.   These statements do not support an inference that the prosecutor was bent on striking Negroes, regardless of trial-related considerations.   The fact remains, of course, that there has not been a Negro on a jury in Talladega County since about 1950.   But the responsibility of the prosecutor is not illuminated in this record.   There is no allegation or explanation, and hence no opportunity for the State to rebut, as to when, why and under what circumstances in cases previous to this one the prosecutor used his strikes to remove Negroes.   In short, petitioner has not laid the proper predicate for attacking the peremptory strikes as they were used in this case.   Petitioner has the burden of proof and he has failed to carry it.

* * *

We see no reason   .   .   .   why the defendant attacking the prosecutor's systematic use of challenges against Negroes should not be required to establish on the record the prosecutor's conduct in this regard, especially where the same prosecutor for many years is said to be responsible for this practice and is quite available for questioning on this matter.   Accordingly the judgment is affirmed.

Affirmed.

MR. JUSTICE HARLAN, concurring.

In joining the opinion of the Court I deem it appropriate to emphasize my understanding that the Court reserves, and does not decide, the question which   .   .   .   it finds not presented by the record in this case.

MR. JUSTICE BLACK concurs in the result.

MR. JUSTICE GOLDBERG, with whom THE CHIEF JUSTICE and MR. JUSTICE DOUGLAS join, dissenting.

* * *

I agree with the Court that it is a reasonable inference that the State is involved in unconstitutional discrimination where total exclusion of Negroes from all venires is established.   I believe that it is also a reasonable inference that the State is involved where, although some Negroes are on venires, none has ever served on a jury, and the State in the case at bar has excluded from jury service the Negroes on the venire by exercise of its peremptory challenges. . . . it would be unreasonable to assume where Negroes were totally excluded from venires that this came about because all Negroes were unqualified, unwilling, or unable to serve. It would be similarly unreasonable to assume where total exclusion from service has been established and the prosecutor has used peremptory challenges to exclude all Negroes from the jury in the given case that in all previous cases Negroes were excluded solely by defense attorneys without any state involvement. If the instant case is really a unique case, as the Court implies, surely the burden of proof should be on the State to show it.

* * *

The Court departs from the long-established burden of proof rule in this area, and imposes substantial additional burdens upon Negro defendants such as petitioner, because of its view of the importance of retaining inviolate the right of the State to use peremptory challenges. I believe, however, that the preference granted by the Court to the State's use of the peremptory challenge is both unwarranted and unnecessary.

* * *

While peremptory challenges are commonly used in this country both by the prosecution and by the defense, we have long recognized that the right to challenge peremptorily is not a fundamental right, constitutionally guaranteed, even as applied to a defendant, much less to the State. This Court has sanctioned numerous incursions upon the right to challenge peremptorily. Defendants may be tried together even though the exercise by one of his right to challenge peremptorily may deprive his codefendant of a juror he desires or may require that codefendant to use his challenges in a way other than he wishes. A defendant may be required to exercise his challenges prior to the State, so that some may be wasted on jurors whom the State would have challenged. Congress may regulate the number of peremptory challenges available to defendants by statute and may require co-defendants to be treated as a single defendant so that each has only a small portion of the number of peremptories he would have if tried separately. Today this Court [is] in effect holding that "There is nothing in the Constitution of the United States which requires the State to grant trial by an impartial jury so long as the inviolability of the peremptory challenge is secured."

Were it necessary to make an absolute choice between the right of a defendant to have a jury chosen in conformity with the requirements of the Fourteenth Amendment and the right to challenge peremptorily, the Constitution compels a choice of the former. Marbury v. Madison, 1 Cranch 137, 2 L.Ed. 60, settled beyond doubt that when a constitutional claim is opposed by a nonconstitutional one, the former must prevail. But no such choice is compelled in this situation. The holding called for by this case, is that where as here, a Negro defendant proves that Negroes constitute a substantial segment of the population, that Negroes are qualified to serve as jurors, and that none or only a token number has served on juries over an extended period of time, a prima facie case of the exclusion of Negroes from juries is then made out; that the State, under our settled decisions, is then called upon to show that such exclusion has been brought about "for some reason other than racial discrimination"; and that the State wholly fails to meet the prima facie case of systematic and purposeful racial discrimination by showing that it has been accomplished by the use of a peremptory challenge system unless the State also shows that it is not involved in the misuse of such a system to prevent all Negroes from ever sitting on any jury. Such a holding would not interfere with the rights of *defendants* to use peremptories, nor the right of the State to use peremptories as they normally and traditionally have been used.

It would not mean, as the Court's prior decisions, to which I would adhere make clear, that Negroes are entitled to proportionate representation on a jury.

PEOPLE v. WHEELER

Supreme Court of California, 1978.
148 Cal.Rptr. 890, 583 P.2d 748.

MOSK, JUSTICE.

Defendants James Michael Wheeler and Robert Willis appeal from judgments convicting them of murdering Amaury Cedeno, a grocery store owner, in the course of a robbery. . . .

* * *

I.

We begin with a claim of error arising at the very outset of the trial and infecting the entire remainder of the proceedings. Defendants are both black; the man they were accused of murdering was white; a number of blacks were in the venire summoned to hear the case, were called to the jury box, were questioned on voir dire, and were passed for cause; yet the prosecutor proceeded to strike each and every black from the jury by means of his peremptory challenges, and the jury that finally tried and convicted these defendants was all white. The issue is whether in such circumstances defendants were denied their right to trial by an impartial jury guaranteed by the California Constitution. The question is one of first impression in this court.

* * *

We conclude that the use of peremptory challenges to remove prospective jurors on the sole ground of group bias violates the right to trial by a jury drawn from a representative cross-section of the community under article I, section 16, of the California Constitution. This does not mean that the members of such a group are immune from peremptory challenges: individual members thereof may still be struck on grounds of specific bias, as defined herein. Nor does it mean that a party will be entitled to a petit jury that proportionately represents every group in the community: we adhere to the long-settled rule that no litigant has the right to a jury that mirrors the demographic composition of the population, or necessarily includes members of his own group, or indeed is composed of any particular individuals. . . .

What it does mean, however, is that a party is constitutionally entitled to a petit jury that is as near an approximation of the ideal cross-section of the community as the process of random draw permits. Obviously he cannot avoid the effect of that process: the master list must be reduced to a manageable venire, and that venire must in turn be reduced to a 12-person jury. The best the law can do to accomplish those steps with the least risk to the representative nature of the jury pool is to take them by random means, i. e., by drawing lots. We recognize that in a predictable percentage of cases the result will be a wholly unbalanced jury, usually composed exclusively of members of the majority group. This is inevitable, the price we must pay for juries of a workable size. It is no less inevitable, however, that in all other instances—as in the case at bar—the representative nature of the pool or venire will be reflected at least in some degree in the 12 persons called at random to the jury box. It is that degree of representativeness—whatever it may prove to be—that we can and must preserve as essential to trial by an impartial jury. Certainly the prospective jurors are then subject to challenges for cause and peremptory challenges on grounds of specific bias; but for the reasons stated above we cannot countenance the decimation of the surviving jurors by peremptory challenges on the ground of group bias alone.

II.

The question of remedy remains, and we do not underestimate its difficulty. We begin with the proposition that in any given instance the presumption must be that a party exercising a peremptory challenge is doing so on a constitutionally permissible ground. We adopt this presumption for several reasons: in deference to the legislative intent underlying such challenges, in order to encourage their use in all proper cases, and out of respect for counsel as officers of the court.

Yet it is only a presumption, and must be rebuttable if the foregoing constitutional right is not to be nullified even by honest zeal. The issue is what showing is necessary to rebut it. We must define a burden of proof which a party may reasonably be expected to sustain in meritorious cases, but which he cannot abuse to the detriment of the peremptory challenge system.

* * *

If a party believes his opponent is using his peremptory challenges to strike jurors on the ground of group bias alone, he must raise the point in timely fashion and make a prima facie case of such discrimination to the satisfaction of the court. First, as in the case at bar, he should make as complete a record of the circumstances as is feasible. Second, he must establish that the persons excluded are members of a cognizable group within the meaning of the representative cross-section rule. Third, from all the circumstances of the case he must show a strong likelihood that such persons are being challenged because of their group association rather than because of any specific bias.

We shall not attempt a compendium of all the ways in which a party may seek to make such a showing. For illustration, however, we mention certain types of evidence that will be relevant for this purpose. Thus the party may show that his opponent has struck most or all of the members of the identified group from the venire, or has used a disproportionate number of his peremptories against the group. He may also demonstrate that the jurors in question share only this one characteristic—their membership in the group—and that in all other respects they are as heterogeneous as the community as a whole. Next, the showing may be supplemented when appropriate by such circumstances as the failure of his opponent to engage these same jurors in more than desultory voir dire, or indeed to ask them any questions at all. Lastly, .   .   . the defendant need not be a member of the excluded group in order to complain of a violation of the representative cross-section rule; yet if he is, and especially if in addition his alleged victim is a member of the group to which the majority of the remaining jurors belong, these facts may also be called to the court's attention.

Upon presentation of this and similar evidence—in the absence, of course, of the jury—the court must determine whether a reasonable inference arises that peremptory challenges are being used on the ground of group bias alone. We recognize that such a ruling "requires trial judges to make difficult and often close judgments. They are in good position to make such determinations, however, on the basis of their knowledge of local conditions and of local prosecutors." They are also well situated to bring to bear on this question their powers of observation, their understanding of trial techniques, and their broad judicial experience. We are confident of their ability to distinguish a true case of group discrimination by peremptory challenges from a spurious claim interposed simply for purposes of harassment or delay.

If the court finds that a prima facie case has been made, the burden shifts to the other party to show if he can that the peremptory challenges in question were not predicated on group bias alone. The showing need not rise to the level of a challenge for cause. But to sustain his burden of justification, the allegedly offending party must satisfy the court that he exercised such peremptories on grounds that were reasonably relevant to the particular case on trial or its parties or witnesses—i. e., for reasons of specific bias as defined herein. He, too, may support his showing by reference to the totality of the circumstances: for example, it will be relevant if he can demonstrate that in the course of this same voir dire he also challenged similarly situated members of the majority group on identical or comparable grounds. And again we rely on the good judgment of the trial courts to distinguish bona fide reasons for such peremptories from sham excuses belatedly contrived to avoid admitting acts of group discrimination.

If the court finds that the burden of justification is not sustained as to any of the questioned peremptory challenges, the presumption of their validity is rebutted. Accordingly, the court must then conclude that the jury as constituted fails to comply with the representative cross-section requirement, and it must dismiss the jurors thus far selected. So too it must quash any remaining venire, since the complaining party is entitled to a random draw from an entire venire—not one that has been partially or totally stripped of members of a cognizable group by the improper use of peremptory challenges. Upon such dismissal a different venire shall be drawn and the jury selection process may begin anew.

Applying these rules to the record before us, we hold that defendants made a prima facie showing that the prosecutor was exercising peremptory challenges against black jurors on the ground of group bias alone. The trial court therefore erred in ruling that the prosecutor was not required to respond to the allegation, and in denying defendants' motions without a rebuttal showing by the prosecutor that the challenges were each predicated on grounds of specific bias.

* * *

III.

The People nevertheless contend that we are compelled to allow this pernicious practice to continue in our courts by the case of Swain v. Alabama [supra, this chapter, B1.] There a black defendant was convicted of rape and sentenced to death by an all-white jury after the prosecutor had struck each of the six blacks on the venire by the equivalent of peremptory challenges. In an opinion concurred in by only five justices the court rejected the defendant's claim of a violation of the equal protection clause of the Fourteenth Amendment.

* * *

It is apparent that *Swain* provides less protection to California residents than the rule we now adopt. Under *Swain* a defendant is barred from vindicating his right to an impartial jury unless he can prove that over a long period of time the same prosecutor has struck every black from every petit jury "whatever the circumstances, whatever the crime and whoever the defendant or the victim may be."

To begin with, *Swain* obviously furnishes no protection whatever to the first defendant who suffers such discrimination in any given court—or indeed to all his successors, until "enough" such instances have accumulated to show a pattern of prosecutorial abuse. Yet in California each and every defendant—not merely the last in this artificial sequence—is constitutionally entitled to trial by a jury drawn from a representative cross-section of the community.

Moreover, even if we consider only the defendant who believes himself in a position to invoke the exception suggested in *Swain*, we see that his attempt to comply with the federal standard of proof is bound to fail. The defendant is party to only one criminal proceeding, and has no personal experience of racial discrimination in the other trials held in that court. Nor can he easily obtain such information, for several reasons. First, those defendants who are indigent or of limited means cannot afford to pay investigators to develop the necessary data. Second, even if the funds were available—or the public defender's office were willing and able to do the research —the time is not: by definition, abuse of peremptory challenges does not appear until the jury selection process is well under way—as in the case at bar—and few if any trial judges would be willing to interrupt the proceedings at that point by a continuance of unpredictable length to permit the necessary investigation. Third, even if the funds and time were available, the data is not: we know of no central register conveniently listing the names and races of all jurors peremptorily challenged by the prosecution in a given court.

Rather, the defendant would be required to somehow obtain and analyze the records of an undetermined number of individual trials in the hope of finding a pattern of abuse among the many peremptory challenges there exercised by the People. But he would have no practical way of discovering which of the excused jurors were black, or of proving their race even if he could learn of it; nor, for the same reasons, could he discover and prove the race of each of the previous defendants and their victims. And even if he could somehow show such a pattern at the hands of certain prosecutors, what of other prosecutors who had more recently joined the local district attorney's office? Would they be immunized from any inquiry until they had made a "record" of such discrimination? If so, how many "free" unrepresentative juries would each be entitled to?

That these are not fanciful concerns is dramatically demonstrated by the history of attempts by black defendants to meet the *Swain* burden of proof. Those attempts, in both federal and state courts, were recently reviewed in some detail (Annot., Use of Peremptory Challenge to Exclude from Jury Persons Belonging to a Class or Race (1975) 79 A.L.R.3d 14, 56–73), and the author concluded that in the 10 years since *Swain* "in all of the cases involving this issue thus far, all of which have dealt with blacks as the group peremptorily challenged, *no defendant has yet been successful* in proving to the court's satisfaction an invidious discrimination by the use of the peremptory challenge against blacks over a period of time."

* * *

It demeans the Constitution to declare a fundamental personal right under that charter and at the same time make it virtually impossible for an aggrieved citizen to exercise that right. For the reasons stated, the rule of Swain v. Alabama is not to be followed in our courts and the cases applying it are disapproved to that extent.

* * *

The judgments are reversed.

BIRD, CHIEF JUSTICE, concurring.

I agree with the result reached by the majority that the state's use of peremptory challenges to remove prospective jurors on the sole ground of race violates the right to trial by jury drawn from a representative cross-section of the community under article I, section 16 of the California Constitution. I do not believe that the state can systematically exclude blacks from serving on a jury by the selective use of the peremptory challenge by the state's representative, i. e., the prosecutor. However, I do not concur in the dicta in the majority opinion which suggest other restrictions on the use of peremptory challenges. The peremptory challenge is not a challenge for cause. The distinction between the two should not be blurred in our attempt to stop an unconstitutional practice.

RICHARDSON, JUSTICE, dissenting.

I respectfully dissent.

In my opinion when a lawyer during the course of a civil or criminal trial exercises a peremptory challenge he is not accountable for his decision to anyone. This has been axiomatic for many years both in the United States generally and in California.

* * *

The majority's rules place the court in a difficult, indeed precarious, position. It is a fundamental principle of our trial system that it is the litigants who pick and must be satisfied with, the jury. The court can rarely have the intimate knowledge of the case possessed by the parties and a jury with which the court is happy may not be a jury with which either the district attorney or the defense can reasonably be comfortable or satisfied.

* * *

Unlike almost every other area of the criminal justice system in the matter of jury selection there is no inherent or gross disparity between the power and the resources of the People and those of the defense. Each side has an equal opportunity to challenge and the end result is the most satisfactory jury that can be drawn from the venire, for it is not only the fact but the appearance of prejudice which may disqualify a juror. It is the probable rather than the provable fact of prejudice which impairs the legitimacy of the jury. In the matter before us there is no suggestion that the jury was not impartial. On the contrary, the record indicates that defendants did not exhaust their peremptory challenges. Although the defense exercise of peremptory challenges could not replace any jurors theretofore challenged by the prosecution, failure to exhaust their own peremptories suggests to me defense satisfaction with the jury as then comprised. There remained unused several opportunities by which the composition of the jury could have been altered by the defense.

There is a clear salutary effect which peremptory challenges have in assuring an impartial petit jury. The challenge is an important tool for trial lawyers who, bearing heavy responsibilities to their clients, should remain free and unfettered to do their essential job. The legal precedents, notably *Swain*, are compelling. The practical difficulties in administering the majority's scheme are complex.

I would affirm the judgment.

NOTES

1. The constitutional guarantee of trial by jury encompasses the right to an impartial jury. In order to insure impartiality, members of the panel are interrogated to determine their personal predilections or other forms of bias. Jurors who exhibit an inability to judge the facts impartially are excused for "cause".

The ABA standards relating to trial by jury (Tentative Draft 1968), containing a codified modern approach to jury selection buttressed by extensive commentaries, has been looked upon with some degree of favor by the courts. In § 2.5, the procedures relating to challenges for cause are set forth:

> "If the judge after examination of any juror is of the opinion that grounds for challenge for cause are present, the judge should excuse that juror from the trial of the case. If the judge does not excuse the juror, any party may challenge the juror for cause. A challenge to an individual juror should be made before he is sworn to try the case, but the judge may permit it to be made after he is sworn but before jeopardy has attached."

A detailed review of the grounds upon which a challenge for cause may be predicated was inserted into the ALI Code of Criminal Procedure § 277 (1931). The ALI's list includes mental and physical infirmities, prior service on the grand, petit or coroner's jury with respect to the same charge, relationship to a party within the fourth degree and conscientious convictions precluding impartiality.

2. Jurors whom the parties find objectionable for various other reasons may be challenged peremptorily. However, the number of peremptories are limited by statute. For example, in noncapital cases, New York permits 15 challenges for each side, California 13, and Louisiana 12. Maryland allows 10 for the prosecution and 20 for the defense. More states permit 6 challenges than any other number, although some provide more for the defense: Arkansas 8; Alaska 10; Georgia 12. Twenty-two states permit fewer than 6 challenges. How many peremptory challenges represent a "fair" number? Are there legitimate cost savings which would result from a reduction in the number of challenges permitted by statute? Should the defense have more challenges than the prosecution?

3. In Witherspoon v. Illinois, 391 U.S. 510 (1968), the Supreme Court invalidated, on due process grounds, the long-prevailing practice of permitting the prosecution to challenge for cause, in a case where the death penalty was sought, potential jurors who expressed conscientious or religious scruples against the death penalty. When the death penalty had been mandatory, the practice has been thought essential lest a "scrupled" juror might

refuse to vote a guilty verdict which would mean death for the defendant. Later, in return for abolishing mandatory death penalties, because it was thought that "too few" death verdicts would be returned if scrupled jurors participated, legislatures (or sometimes courts) provided challenges for cause in such cases. *Witherspoon* held that "a sentence of death cannot be carried out if the jury that imposed or recommended it was chosen by excluding veniremen for cause simply because they voiced general objections to the death penalty or expressed conscientious or religious scruples against its infliction."

After recent decisions upholding death penalty statutes, *Witherspoon* may have a new importance. In Davis v. Georgia, 429 U.S. 122, 97 S.Ct. 399 (1976), the Court held:

* * *

"The Supreme Court of Georgia found that one prospective juror had been excluded in violation the *Witherspoon* standard. The Court nevertheless affirmed the conviction and death sentence, reasoning that the erroneous exclusion of one death-scrupled juror did not deny the petitioner a jury representing a cross-section of the community since other jurors sharing that attitude were not excused for cause.

* * *

"That, however, is not the test established in *Witherspoon*, and it is not the test that this Court has applied in subsequent cases where a death penalty was imposed after the improper exclusion of one member of the venire. . . .

"Unless a venireman is 'irrevocably committed, before the trial has begun, to vote against the penalty of death regardless of the facts and circumstances that might emerge in the course of the proceedings' he cannot be excluded; if a venireman is improperly excluded even though not so committed, any subsequently imposed death penalty cannot stand."

Because most states provide that only the *same* jury which finds the defendant guilty can sentence a defendant to death or can recommend such a sentence, a *Witherspoon* remand typically means that the defendant will be sentenced to something other than death. The guilty verdict, however, is not invalidated.

4. When a juror makes it clear that his attitude toward capital punishment would prevent him from making an impartial decision on the defendant's *guilt*, *Witherspoon* does not prevent a challenge for cause. See Lockett v. Ohio, 438 U.S. 586, 98 S.Ct. 2954 (1978).

5. When a judge erroneously refuses to excuse a juror for cause and thereby forces the defendant to exercise a peremptory challenge, reversable error may result even though the juror did not sit in the case. See State v. Singletary, 156 N.J.Super. 303, 383 A.2d 1151 (1978) (juror was an armed robbery victim 17 days before armed robbery trial); Commonwealth v. Jones, 477 Pa. 164, 383 A.2d 874 (1978) (juror was a Philadelphia policeman; all police who testified in case were from same force).

Some jurisdictions, however, require that a defendant completely exhaust all peremptory challenges in order to preserve for appeal a claim of error in the overruling of a peremptory challenge.

2.　VOIR DIRE

HAM v. SOUTH CAROLINA

Supreme Court of the United States, 1973.
409 U.S. 524, 93 S.Ct. 848.

MR. JUSTICE REHNQUIST delivered the opinion of the court.

Petitioner was convicted in the South Carolina trial court of the possession of marihuana in violation of state law. . . . We granted certiorari limited to the question of whether the trial judge's refusal to examine jurors on *voir dire* as to possible prejudice against petitioner violated the latter's federal constitutional rights.

Petitioner is a young, bearded Negro who has lived most of his life in Florence County, South Carolina. He appears to have been well known locally for his work in such civil rights activities as the Southern Christian Leadership Conference and the Bi-Racial Committee of the City of Florence. He has never previously been convicted of a crime. His basic defense at the trial was that law enforcement officers were "out to get him" because of his civil rights activities, and that he had been framed on the drug charge.

Prior to the trial judge's *voir dire* examination of prospective jurors, petitioner's counsel requested the judge to ask jurors four questions relating to possible prejudice against petitioner.[1] The first two questions sought to elicit any possible racial prejudice against Negroes; the third question related to possible prejudice against beards; and the fourth dealt with pretrial publicity relating to the drug problem. The trial judge, while putting to the prospective jurors three general questions as to bias, prejudice, or partiality that are specified in the South Carolina statutes,[2] declined to ask any of the four questions posed by petitioner.

1. The four questions sought to be asked are the following:

"1. Would you fairly try this case on the basis of the evidence and disregarding the defendant's race?

"2. You have no prejudice against negroes? Against black people? You would not be influenced by the use of the term 'black'?

"3. Would you disregard the fact that this defendant wears a beard in deciding this case?

"4. Did you watch the television show about the local drug problem a few days ago when a local policeman appeared for a long time? Have you heard about that show? Have you read or heard about recent newspaper articles to the effect that the local drug problem is bad? Would you try this case solely on the basis of the evidence presented in this courtroom? Would you be influenced by the circumstances that the prosecution's witness, a police officer, has publicly spoken on TV about drugs?"

2. The three questions asked of all prospective jurors in this case were, in substance, the following:

"1. Have you formed or expressed any opinion as to the guilt or innocence of the defendant, Gene Ham?

"2. Are you conscious of any bias or prejudice for or against him?

"3. Can you give the State and the defendant a fair and impartial trial?"

The dissenting justices in the Supreme Court of South Carolina thought that this Court's decision in Aldridge v. United States, 283 U.S. 308, 51 S.Ct. 470 (1931), was binding on the State. There a Negro who was being tried for the murder of a white policeman requested that prospective jurors be asked whether they entertained any racial prejudice. This Court reversed the judgment of conviction because of the trial judge's refusal to make such an inquiry. Chief Justice Hughes, writing for the Court, stated that the "essential demands of fairness" required the trial judge under the circumstances of that case to interrogate the veniremen with respect to racial prejudice upon the request of counsel for a Negro criminal defendant.

. . . Since one of the purposes of the Due Process Clause of the Fourteenth Amendment is to insure these "essential demands of fairness," and since a principal purpose of the adoption of the Fourteenth Amendment was to prohibit the States from invidiously discriminating on the basis of race, we think that the Fourteenth Amendment required the judge in this case to interrogate the jurors upon the subject of racial prejudice. South Carolina law permits challenges for cause, and authorizes the trial judge to conduct *voir dire* examination of potential jurors. The State having created this statutory framework for the selection of juries, the essential fairness required by the Due Process Clause of the Fourteenth Amendment requires that under the facts shown by this record the petitioner be permitted to have the jurors interrogated on the issue of racial bias.

. . . [T]he trial judge was not required to put the question in any particular form, or to ask any particular number of questions on the subject, simply because requested to do so by petitioner. The Court in *Aldridge* was at pains to point out, in a context where its authority within the federal system of courts allows a good deal closer supervision than does the Fourteenth Amendment, that the trial court "had a broad discretion as to the questions to be asked." The discretion as to form and number of questions permitted by the Due Process Clause of the Fourteenth Amendment is at least as broad. In this context either of the brief, general questions urged by the petitioner would appear sufficient to focus the attention of prospective jurors to any racial prejudice they might entertain.

The third of petitioner's proposed questions was addresesd to the fact that he wore a beard. While we cannot say that prejudice against people with beards might not have been harbored by one or more of the potential jurors in this case, this is the beginning and not the end of the inquiry as to whether the Fourteenth Amendment required the trial judge to interrogate the prospective jurors about such possible prejudice. Given the traditionally broad discretion accorded to the trial judge in conducting *voir dire*, and our inability to constitutionally distinguish possible prejudice against beards from a host of other possible similar prejudices, we do not believe the petitioner's constitutional rights were violated when the trial judge refused to put this question. The inquiry as to racial prejudice derives its constitutional stature from the firmly established precedent of *Aldridge* and the numerous state cases upon which it relied, and from a principal purpose as well as from the language of those who adopted the Fourteenth Amendment. The trial judge's refusal to inquire as to particular bias against beards, after his inquiries as to bias in general, does not reach the level of a constitutional violation.

* * *

Because of the trial court's refusal to make any inquiry as to racial bias of the prospective jurors after petitioner's timely request therefor, the judgment of the Supreme Court of South Carolina is reversed.

Judgment reversed.

MR. JUSTICE DOUGLAS, concurring in part and dissenting in part.

I, too, concur in that portion of the majority's opinion which holds that the trial judge was constitutionally compelled to inquire into the possibility of racial prejudice on *voir dire*. I think, however, that it was an abuse of discretion for the trial judge to preclude the defendant from an inquiry by which prospective jurors' prejudice to hair growth could have been explored.

* * *

Prejudice to hair growth is unquestionably of a "serious character." Nothing is more indicative of the importance currently being attached to hair growth by the general populace than the barrage of cases reaching the courts evidencing the attempt by one segment of society officially to control the plumage of another. On the issue of a student's right to wear "long-hair" alone there are well over 50 reported cases. In addition the issue of plumage has surfaced in the employment-discrimination context as well as the military area.

The prejudices invoked by the mere sight of "non-conventional" hair growth are deeply felt. Hair growth is symbolic to many of rebellion against traditional society and disapproval of the way the current power structure handles social problems. Taken as an affirmative declaration of an individual's commitment to a change in social values, "non-conventional" hair growth may become a very real personal threat to those who support the *status quo*. For those people, "non-conventional" hair growth symbolizes an undesirable life-style characterized by unreliability, dishonesty, lack of moral values, communial ("communist") tendencies, and the assumption of drug use. If the defendant, especially one being prosecuted for the illegal use of drugs, is not allowed even to make the most minimal inquiry to expose such prejudices, can it be expected that he will receive a fair trial?

Since hair growth is an outward manifestation by which many people determine whether to apply deep-rooted prejudices to an individual, to deny a defendant the right to examine this aspect of a prospective juror's personality is to deny him his most effective means of *voir dire* examination.

MR. JUSTICE MARSHALL, concurring in part and dissenting in part.

* * *

But broad as the judge's discretion is in these matters, I think it clear that it was abused in this case. The defense attorney wished to ask no more than four questions which would have required a scant 15 additional minutes of the court's time. The inquiries, directed *inter alia* to possible prejudice against people with beards, were obviously relevant, since the defendant was in fact bearded. Moreover, the judge afforded petitioner no opportunity to show that there were a significant number of potential jurors who might be prejudiced against people with beards. At minimum, I think such an opportunity should have been provided. I cannot believe that in these circumstances an absolute ban on questions designed to uncover such prejudice represents a proper balance between the competing demands of fairness and expedition.

* * *

NOTES

1. The scope of *Ham* was restricted in Ristaino v. Ross, 424 U.S. 589, 96 S.Ct. 1017 (1976). *Ristaino* held that such questioning must necessarily be permitted only where there is a significant possibility that racial prejudice might affect the jury's decision. Noting that *Ham* was a case in which the accused claimed he was framed because of civil rights activities, the court held that the fact a black is charged with violent crimes against a white is not enough to require the trial judge to permit voir dire concerning racial prejudice.

2. In United States v. Bowles, 574 F.2d 970 (8th Cir. 1978), a black defendant, charged with drug dealing, asked the judge to make a racial prejudice inquiry of prospective jurors. The trial judge refused to do so; but the Eighth Circuit reversed, holding that trial judges must inquire about racial prejudice when the defendant is a member of a racial minority. Is *Bowles* consistent with the *Ristaino* limitation on *Ham*?

UNITED STATES v. DELLINGER

United States Court of Appeals, Seventh Circuit, 1972.
472 F.2d 340.

FAIRCHILD, CIRCUIT JUDGE.

These are appeals from convictions of violation of the 1968 federal Anti-riot Act. The charges arose out of events in Chicago during the last week of August, 1968, during the national convention of the Democratic party. There were several violent encounters between the city police and other persons in the streets and parks. . . .

The appellants are David Dellinger, Rennie Davis, Tom Hayden, Abbie Hoffman, and Jerry Rubin. They, along with Bobby Seale, were charged with making certain speeches for the purposes of inciting, organizing, promoting, and encouraging a riot, after having traveled in interstate commerce to Chicago with intent to do so. Code-fendants Froines and Weiner were charged with teaching the use of an incendiary device in violation of another federal statute, and all eight were charged with conspiracy among themselves and with oth-ers to commit offenses under these statutes. All eight stood trial, ex-cept that a mistrial was declared, during the trial, as to Mr. Seale. The appellants were each convicted on the respective substantive counts. Froines and Weiner were acquitted on the substantive count against them, and they and appellants were acquitted on the conspira-cy count.

* * *

VOIR DIRE EXAMINATION

One of the paths to the impartial jury guaranteed by the sixth amendment is the voir dire examination. Defendants seek reversal on the ground that the voir dire examination was inadequate. [They] claim . . . that the voir dire was so "perfunctory" with respect to attitude that it failed to provide a basis for defendants' challenges, both for cause and peremptory.

The voir dire examination took a little over a day. Pursuant to Rule 24(a), F.R.Cr.P., the district judge conducted the examination, after having solicited proposed questions from the parties. He asked the entire group of veniremen the following questions: whether the prospective jurors were acquainted with employees of the FBI, or of the Justice Department; whether they were acquainted with defend-ants, their counsel or their associates; whether they could agree to follow the law as given to them; whether they could keep an open mind until time to reach a verdict; whether they could treat the testi-mony of a government agent the same as that of any other witness; whether prior jury service would prevent them from being impartial; and whether there was any reason they could not be fair and impar-tial jurors in this case. Fifty-six veniremen stated without explana-tion that they could not be impartial and were excused by agreement of the parties. Two others who said they could not be impartial for a particular reason were also excused.

The jury box was filled and the court questioned the first 12 in-dividually. The court asked standard questions, primarily relating to marital and family status, occupation of prospective juror and spouse, employer and length of employment of prospective juror and spouse, number of children, their schools and occupations.

Two veniremen who said they worked for the federal govern-ment were asked whether being a government employee would influ-ence their judgment. Another was asked, "Do you feel that the fact that your father is a member of the Chicago Police Force and has been for many years would affect your judgment as a juror if you were selected in this case?" All said they could still be impartial.

After interviewing each of these first 12, the court inquired of the group whether any had close relatives or friends who were em-ployed by any law enforcement agency or other agency of the local, state or federal government. When five answered yes, the court asked each whether this would influence his judgment. All answered that it would not. The court did not ask this question of the succeeding veniremen who entered the jury box.

Defense counsel repeated defendants' request that the judge ask the questions they had submitted. The court responded, "I have reached the conclusion that those I haven't asked are not germane to the issues presented here by the indictment and the pleas of not guilty thereto."

The jury was selected after 24 persons had been individually questioned, the defense had exercised 10 of their 17 peremptory challenges,[1] and the government two. Appellants accepted the tendered jury but "under the greatest of protest" because the court had not asked questions they considered necessary for fully exercising their challenges.

In order to sustain their present contention, it is not necessary for defendants to show that members of the jury were in fact prejudiced. The focus is exclusively on whether the procedure used for testing impartiality created a reasonable assurance that prejudice would be discovered if present. We recognize that there is no generally accepted formula for determining the appropriate breadth and depth of the voir dire, except that the court's discretion is "subject to the essential demands of fairness."

We start with the exclusion of jurors for cause, where actual bias is admitted or presumed. The Supreme Court has said that ".　.　. the trial court has a serious duty to determine the question of actual bias," Dennis v. United States, 339 U.S. 162, 70 S.Ct. 519 (1950), and that "[a]ll persons otherwise qualified for jury service are subject to examination as to actual bias." United States v. Wood, 299 U.S. 123, 133, 57 S.Ct. 177, 179 (1936). Jury service by a person with actual bias in a particular case would violate the right to an impartial jury.

Subsidiary to challenge for cause is the peremptory challenge where bias is suspected or implied. It is exercised "on grounds normally thought irrelevant to legal proceedings" such as "the race, religion, nationality, occupation or affiliations of people summoned for jury duty," appearance, association, and the like, and it is "exercised without a reason stated, without inquiry and without being subject to the court's control." Swain v. Alabama, 380 U.S. 202, 220, 85 S.Ct. 824, 836 (1965).

1.　Rule 24(b), F.R.Cr.P., provides the defense with 10 peremptory challenges. In a trial of more than one defendant, the court may allow additional challenges. The trial court in this case allowed one additional challenge for each additional defendant, for a total of 17.

Four alternate jurors were also selected. Rule 24(c) provides two peremptory challenges if 3 or 4 alternates are selected. The defense exercised both. One of the alternates later became a juror when another juror was excused as a result of her expression of inability to be impartial after being shown a letter sent to her home.

The government argues that the court is obligated to inquire only into matters that would disqualify the juror for cause, and that the court's first group of questions were adequate to produce disclosure of any relevant prejudice. We disagree. The government's position must rest upon an assumption that a general question to the group whether there is any reason they could not be fair and impartial can be relied on to produce a disclosure of any disqualifying state of mind. We do not believe that a prospective juror is so alert to his own prejudices. Thus it is essential to explore the backgrounds and attitudes of the jurors to some extent in order to discover actual bias, or cause.

But beyond this, an answer which falls short of an admission of bias may nevertheless aid counsel in deciding to exercise a peremptory challenge. The Supreme Court has stated that the peremptory challenge, although not required in the Constitution, is "one of the most important of the rights secured to the accused," and that "[t]he denial or impairment of the right is reversible error without a showing of prejudice." The peremptory challenge is provided in the federal system by Rule 24(b), F.R.Cr.P.

If this right is not to be an empty one, the defendants must, upon request, be permitted sufficient inquiry into the background and attitudes of the jurors to enable them to exercise intelligently their peremptory challenges.

The government is correct that collateral or unrelated issues should not be raised. But this does not mean that all questions must relate directly to the indictment or pleas in the case. Some questions may appear tangential to the trial but are actually so integral to the citizen juror's view of the case, especially one with publicly controversial issues, that they must be explored. . . . At a minimum, when requested by counsel, inquiry must be made into matters where the likelihood of prejudice is so great that not to inquire would risk failure to assembling an impartial jury.[2]

What these essential inquiries are, of course, varies with each case. Many elements of this case might have aroused the jurors' prejudices. One of the central themes was the protest against this nation's involvement in war in Vietnam. Defendants were leaders in such protest and claimed that their militancy did not go beyond constitutionally protected bounds. There were and are deep divisions in our society resulting from that war, gravely illustrated by this unprecedented confrontation at the convention of a major political party in 1968. Anti-war activists, such as these defendants, have over the last decade challenged the validity of a concept of patriotism that requires young people, sons of people who might be akin to prospec-

---

2. The government suggests that the court's instructions during the voir dire and throughout the trial created an atmosphere of impartiality and reinforced the voir dire. Certainly there are situations where instruc- tions to an impanelled jury would cure weaknesses in the voir dire. But they can never be a substitute for essential inquiries into the areas of seemingly probable prejudice of the veniremen.

tive jurors, to die for country in a war they consider mistaken, and immoral. We do not believe that the court could safely assume, without inquiry, that the veniremen had no serious prejudice on this subject, or could recognize such prejudices and lay them aside.

In evaluating this topic, it is important to recall the time when this trial occurred, and to recognize that the division in public attitudes toward the Vietnam war has changed and is changing still. The extent of unpopularity of the war in 1972, when this opinion is written, is not a fair index of the probable opinions on that subject in a cross section selected in September, 1969. Perspective is important. These defendants' plans for activities in Chicago in August, 1968 were first formed when President Johnson was expected to be a candidate to succeed himself. He withdrew March 31, 1968. The 1968 candidacies of Senators Eugene McCarthy and Robert Kennedy, the latter assassinated in June, 1968, were associated with anti-war sentiment. Further crystallization of anti-war sentiment is associated with the Cambodian venture and the Kent State killings, both in the spring of 1970. These episodes had not yet occurred when the jury was selected for this trial in September, 1969. We have no doubt that defendants brought to trial in 1969 upon charges that their anti-war activities were carried beyond constitutional protection were entitled to a testing of their jurors for biased attitudes on this subject.

Perhaps secondary, but significant, were the conflicts of values represented by the so-called youth culture—hippies, yippies and freaks—in contrast with the more traditional values of the vast majority of the community, presumably including most citizens summoned for jury service. Again, we are not unaware that many otherwise qualified members of the community could not be impartial toward, and in fact are often offended by, persons who wear long hair, beards, and bizarre clothing and who seem to avoid the burdens and responsibilities of regular employment. Several defendants would exemplify this conflict.

* * *

The only question that could be said to relate peculiarly to the case before the court was the one addressed to the first 12 interviewed:

> "I would ask each and every one of the prospective jurors in the jury box . . . whether you have any close relatives or friends who are employed by any law enforcement agency or other agency of the local, State or Federal Government."

Of those who responded affirmatively, the court asked whether that would influence their judgment, and all answered that it would not. But since this was not asked again, only four of those who served on the jury were subjected to this inquiry.

However satisfactory this limited examination might be in some trials, under the circumstances of this case, the court's severe restriction of the voir dire may well have curtailed defendants' challenges for cause and failed to provide them with reasonable guidance in exercising peremptory challenges.

Government counsel submitted a list of requested questions, some of which were asked at least in substance, by the district judge. Other questions requested by the government, but not asked, inquired whether the prospective juror had read about, or was downtown in Chicago during, the Democratic national convention; whether he knew anyone who participated in protest demonstrations then, or at any other time, or whether he himself had participated in a protest demonstration; whether he had ever had an unpleasant experience with law enforcement officers.

Defense counsel submitted a list of 44 questions. Some raised inappropriate subjects of inquiry and few were properly phrased even where the subject was appropriate. Some of the questions, however, would have elicited a prospective juror's attitude toward dissent, and public protest against the Vietnam war; toward long hair, beards, unorthodox clothing, and life styles differing from his own; and toward policemen and law enforcement.

We do not suggest that the court was obligated to ask all the often propagandistic questions in the form submitted by defendants. But their request raised a judicial duty "to do what was reasonably practicable to enable the accused to have the benefit of the right of peremptory challenge or to prevent unfairness in the trial."

[The court considered a great number of other issues and, upon the basis of the *voir dire* and other defects in the trial, reversed and remanded.]

NOTES

1. The efficacy of asking very detailed questions on voir dire to uncover latent juror prejudice was analyzed by Learned Hand in United States v. Dennis, 183 F.2d 201, 227 (2d Cir. 1950), aff'd 341 U.S. 491 (1951):

"It is of course true that any examination on the *voir dire* is a clumsy and imperfect way of detecting suppressed emotional commitments to which all of us are to some extent subject, unconsciously or subconsciously. It is of the nature of our deepest antipathies that often we do not admit them even to ourselves; but when that is so, nothing but an examination, utterly impracticable in a courtroom, will disclose them, an examination extending at times for months, and even then unsuccessful. No such examination is required; indeed, it was exactly the purpose of Criminal Rule 24(a), which allows the judge to frame questions on the *voir dire* if he thinks best, to avoid the interminable examinations sometimes extending for weeks on end that had frequently resulted from the former method. If trial by jury is not to break down by its own weight, it is not feasible to probe more than the upper levels of a juror's mind. The judge's questions . . . were indeed limited to the flat inquiry whether he was aware of any bias, but it is by no means unusual for a juror to admit as much, as anyone accustomed to jury trials knows."

In line with Judge Hand's psychological analysis of the *voir dire*, one might well question whether the propounding of detailed questions concerning the veniremen's life styles would be self-defeating of the primary goal of securing an impartial jury. If the juror's life style, the magazines and newspapers they read, or the music they listen to is relevant to the inquiry on *voir dire*, then the jurors cannot fail to appreciate the implication that the defendant may be tried on some other basis than the evidence submitted in court. It may well be a psychological truth that, if the prospective jurors are treated as if they are expected to decide on the basis of legally impermissible criteria, the jurors who successfully run the *voir dire* gauntlet may be more inclined to decide on the basis of legally irrelevant and impermissible criteria. The *voir dire* may be more effective in securing an impartial jury if this goal is not obscured in the minds of the veniremen by reference to factors which every person knows to be irrelevant to legal guilt.

2. Whatever persuasive qualities Judge Hand's position may have, it represents a waning viewpoint. Although some courts will set aside a trial judge's finding of juror impartiality only where prejudice is "manifest", see Mikus v. United States, 433 F.2d 719 (2d Cir. 1970), the prevailing view seems to favor an elaborate voir dire with penetrating questions seeking to elicit juror attitudes with regard to issues likely to arise in the trial. The rationale underlying the modern judicial conception of the voir dire was well stated in United States v. Lewin, 467 F.2d 1132, 1137 (7th Cir. 1972):

> While trial lawyers devote much cogitation and intraprofessional discussion to the matter of selecting a proper jury—propriety presumably being equated with fairness and disinterestedness —nevertheless, because of the uncertainty of human reactions to often unknown or unanticipated motivating factors, the entire voir dire procedure is fraught with precariousness as to whether the desired resultant jury will be realized. Character qualities derivable from interrogation are often elusive and the answers to questions may frequently be illusory as a firm basis for any type of challenge.
>
> Prejudice and bias are deep running streams more often than not concealed by the calm surface stemming from an awareness of societal distaste for their existence. Extended and trial-delaying interrogation may not pierce the veil, yet a few specific associational questions as a maieutic process may indicate the dormant seeds of prejudice, preconceived and unalterable concepts or other nonfairness disqualifications. The result may not reach the stage of being a basis for cause challenge but could well, because of an abundance of counsel caution, bring about a peremptory challenge which an omniscient eye would have known should have been exercised.
>
> We are told that the British courts quickly secure their juries, and criticism is directed at time-consuming trials within trials in this country when prospective members of the jury may wonder, as their lives are being probed, who is being tried. We think the criticism of too extended voir dire is justified but we are not ready to say that the person who has his liberty or, indeed, his property, at stake must be compelled to accept a jury on a strictly cursory, generality interrogation basis.

At some happy mesne point, there must be permitted sufficient questioning to produce, in the light of the factual situation
involved in the particular trial, some basis for a reasonably knowledgeable exercise of the right of challenge.

3. Pursuant to the modern view, the courts have generally accorded
the defendant a right to seek detailed information from prospective jurors
in four general categories: (1) moral scruples concerning crime charged—
United States v. Napoleone, 349 F.2d 350 (3d Cir. 1965) (questions concerning moral repugnance to lying in impersonating government investigator
case); State v. Barnett, 251 Or. 234, 445 P.2d 124 (1968) (religious affiliations in abortion case); (2) relationship to class of persons to which victim
or witness belongs—Sims v. United States, 405 F.2d 1381 (D.C.Cir. 1968) (relationship to cab drivers in case involving murder of cab driver); United
States v. Johnson, 401 F.2d 746 (2d Cir. 1968) (bank employee in bank robbery case); (3) membership in organizations—United States v. Lewin, 467
F.2d 1132 (7th Cir. 1972) (membership in Better Government Association
in Vote Fraud Case); Smith v. United States, 262 F.2d 50 (4th Cir. 1959)
(Membership in Racist Organizations); (4) past experiences—Jackson v.
United States, 129 U.S.App.D.C. 392, 395 F.2d 615 (1968) (Participant in
Fatal Love Triangle); United States ex rel. De Vita v. McCorkle, 248 F.2d
1 (3d Cir.), cert. denied 355 U.S. 873, 78 S.Ct. 121 (1957) (robbery victim). Thus, with the expanded voir dire in these particular areas, the right
to challenge for cause on account of bias or prejudice has become a more
viable method for knowledgeable jury selection. See generally Note, Community Hostility and the Right to an Impartial Jury, 60 Colum.L.Rev. 349
(1960).

4. Some trial judges, particularly in federal courts, conduct the entire
voir dire themselves, permitting defense counsel to submit suggested questions to the judge, generally in writing. Can the attorneys be wholly deprived of an opportunity to personally question prospective jurors? For
one view, see People v. Jackson, 69 Ill.2d 252, 13 Ill.Dec. 667, 371 N.E.2d 602
(1977).

5. It is clear that a judge need not ask the specific questions submitted by the defense so long as its examination is sufficient to test the qualifications and competency of the prospective jurors. In Hamling v. United
States, 418 U.S. 87, 94 S.Ct. 2887 (1974), the defendants, in an obscenity
case, requested the court to ask specific and detailed questions as to whether the jurors' educational, political and religious beliefs might affect their
views on obscenity. The Court upheld the trial judge's refusal to ask the
specific questions: ". . . the trial judge made a general inquiry into
the jurors' general views concerning obscenity. Failure to ask specific
questions as to the possible effect of educational, political, and religious
biases did 'not reach the level of a constitutional violation,' nor was it error requiring the exercise of our supervisory authority over the administration of justice in the federal courts."

3. THE FOLKLORE OF JURY SELECTION

Where counsel is able to determine juror preconceptions precluding impartiality through the voir dire, his task of jury selection is
simplified. Although a juror's expressed views may not rise to the
level of a challenge for cause, counsel will have enough background
knowledge to make an informed determination with respect to the ex-

ercise of his peremptory challenges. However, where the vior dire is restricted or jurors appear unwilling to communicate freely, counsel must use his own knowledge and background in selecting a jury.

Jury selection technique, although replete with extensive folklore, is an imprecise art. Every general rule has so many exceptions as to totally emasculate the rule itself. But because some attorneys believe cases are won or lost at the time the jury is selected, a few generalized "rules of thumb" are worthy of consideration.

James Bouska, a distinguished County Attorney in Johnson County, Kansas follows these precepts, as set forth in Bouska, Selecting a Jury, in The Prosecutor's Desk Book 372–74 (National District Attorneys Association, 1971):

> "Generally [a prosecutor] will try to pick jurors who are intelligent and conservative, jurors who usually obey the law and expect others to do so and who will enforce the law without being swayed by any emotional appeal or other irrelevant factor.
>
> "In the absence of human capacity to tell the absolute truth in response to a question, and in the absence of a device by which lawyers may read the jurors' conscious and subconscious minds, some lawyers have developed and followed rules in reference to racial, physical and other characteristics of prospective jurors, and in regard to the employment, social and financial status of jurors, to aid in determining which panel members will be the best jurors.
>
> "Such rules are discounted by other successful lawyers, but are worthy of your consideration.
>
> "It has been suggested that those with the certain following national backgrounds will respond more readily to an emotional appeal by a defendant in a criminal case and, if other factors are equal, would not be desirable jurors from a prosecution standpoint: Irish, Jewish, Spanish or other Latin-American, Italian, all Slavic races, and generally, all southern Europeans. [Offhand, the writer can think of an Irish Chief of Police, a Jewish detective, a Mexican businessman (who has been robbed), an Italian prosecutor and a Croatian banker, all of whom I would choose as jurors in a criminal case]. On the other hand, it is said that among those who will less readily respond to an emotional appeal and who will be more responsive to a prosecutor's appeal to enforce the law is the Nordic type: German, Scandinavian or English. A jury selection rule based on racial characteristics has less and less validity as our nation and communities grow more homogeneous, but may be useful to you in your community.
>
> "Personally, I give a lot of weight to the rule and would prefer a German or Scandinavian juror over some other juror, if other factors are consistent with such a choice.

"Women are said to be more responsive to emotional appeals and, at least from a male point of view, are more unpredictable and subject to being deterred from properly voting for conviction by other irrelevant factors ('I can't believe he'd steal anything. He looks like such a nice boy. Besides, there was no evidence he ever stole anything else.') ('How can she say she was raped, when those other boys swore they'd slept with her before? Besides, she was asking for it, waiting in that beer joint to be picked up.').

"Some lawyers believe that women jurors, pretty and otherwise, are a distracting influence to men jurors—and to counsel.

"Employment, financial and social status factors should be given some consideration. It is usually believed that members of the permanent leadership of the community will be most likely to be sympathetic with an appeal to uphold and enforce the law. This would include businessmen, bankers, bank employees, and persons in other responsible positions—members of the 'establishment'.

"Ordinarily, you will not want to take a chance on keeping as a juror one who has been convicted of a crime including a serious traffic offense, but you should determine the fact of conviction by investigation before trial.

"Panelists who you believe cannot identify to some extent with your principal witness *or* be receptive to their testimony should be rejected. A banker, as a juror, may not be able to identify closely with your witness who is a migrant farm worker, but will usually have enough personal security to accept the farm hand's testimony, although the status gap between them is wide. On the other hand, the farm worker, as a juror, may find it difficult to either identify with the banker or be receptive to his testimony as a prosecution witness.

"You may want to consider a panelist's occupation in determining his qualification. Some prosecutors do not like to have as a juror an accountant, an engineer, a cabinetmaker, or a person of any other occupation which requires exact precision, on the theory that he will be too strict in determining whether your case meets the burden of proof. Such a person may expect you to present a perfect case. And, of course, no case, including yours, is perfect.

"Some defense lawyers feel that certain physical characteristics should be considered, believing that the fat, and supposedly jovial, juror will be more preferable from a defense standpoint than the lean and hungry-looking type.

"Many lawyers reject a juror who knows opposing counsel, his lawyer associates, the opposing party, or any of their witnesses, on the theory that you can never know the real nature and extent of the relationship. This may also be true in regard to persons who are acquainted with you and others associated with you in the case, but you can usually count on opposing counsel to use his peremptory challenges on panelists who know you or your witnesses well.

"It is said that most defense attorneys will prefer a juror trying his first case in preference to one who has sat on several cases, while the prosecutor prefers an 'old jury'. It is felt that a new juror will pay more attention to the evidence and will be more responsive to an emotional appeal. Such jurors are said to be more receptive to the instructions on reasonable doubt and burden of proof, while the old jury will have become a bit calloused to such instructions.

"Some prosecutors do not want a person on the jury who is an ego-maniac (*I* am Vice-President; *I* live in Hoxie; *I* have eleven children); other lawyers prefer one 'strong' or aggressive person on the jury, but believe that two such persons may lead to a hung jury.

"You will, of course, want to reject the loudmouth, the smart-aleck and the joker as jurors.

"You will want to consider other factors in picking the jury, including dress, manner of speech and apparent attitude toward jury service. You may vary your requirement and standards to take into account the type of case, and the particular defendant and the particular principal witness involved in the prosecution.

"After considering some of these many and diverse factors and guidelines which might possibly be of use to you in selecting a juror, it is submitted that you will be better able to select the juror you want: the stable, intelligent, openminded juror with a mature and well-developed sense of justice."

For a more defense oriented approach to this subject, see I. Goldstein & F. Lane, I. Goldstein Trial Technique §§ 9.29–9.30 (2d Ed. 1969), where the views expressed for civil plaintiffs are said to apply equally to criminal defendants:

"**Sex.** *Men* are preferred when the [defendant] is a woman. It is considered that they will respond to the emotional aspects of the case and the testimony of pain. They are considered . . . to have the background and experience to follow and analyze the evidence. . . .

"*Women* are preferred when the [defendant] is the breadwinner in the family. They seriously study the evidence and follow the instructions of the court as to the law. They respond to the emotional appeals of the case where youngsters are the [defendants]. Some women seem to have an adverse reaction to spinsters.

"**Marital status.** Both married men and women are preferred when the [defendant] is a minor.

"**Age.** Jurors between the ages of 30 and 55, are considered more favorable to the [defendant].

"**Nationality.** The . . . *defendant* in criminal cases seem to prefer jurors with nationality backgrounds such as Spaniards, Irish, Jews, French, Italians, etc. It is claimed that these nationalities respond well to the emotional appeal in cases.

"**Physical makeup.** Persons with the physical makeup of the round face, friendly manner, jovial temperament, and generally stout (*endomorphs*) are considered more generous and are preferred by [defendants].

"The athletic type, the open face, firm body, square prominent bone person (*mesomorphs*) also are acceptable. . . . .

"**Occupation.** The artist, musician, laborer, carpenter, mechanic, salesman, office worker, union man, actor, or writer are generally considered to be desirable jurors from the viewpoint of the [defendant].

"**New jurors.** Jurors without prior jury experience are considered desirable from the viewpoint of the [defendant]."

Perhaps the best illustration of the exception to the general rule attenuating the rule itself lies in an anecdote told by Justice Louis B. Heller of the New York Supreme Court in L. Heller, Do You Solemnly Swear? 120–21 (Doubleday & Co. 1968):

"Percy Foreman . . . who is considered to be without a peer in the art of selecting jurors, makes it a rule to avoid seating Germans and Scandinavians whenever possible. 'They're too severe and well disciplined,' he maintains. 'They have little understanding of mistakes.' For similar reasons, he tries to eliminate jurors whose occupations demand great precision, like engineers, statisticians, accountants, bookkeepers, and draftsmen, for he finds them too exacting. He prefers Jews, Negroes, Irish Catholics, and others with backgrounds that tend to identify them with those who are persecuted or oppressed.

"Yet, like every master of any art, Foreman knows intuitively just when it is safe to break the 'rules' and make a bold move that seems to defy common sense. In questioning a prospective juror in a murder case, he asked, 'Do you know me by reputation?'

'Oh, yes, I certainly do,' the man replied.

'And would you be prejudiced against my client by what you know about me?' asked Foreman.

'I certainly would,' the venireman promptly answered, 'because I know what a shyster you are. Nobody would hire you unless he was guilty.'

"By all the rules, an answer like that should have immediately disqualified him. But Foreman, to everyone's amazement, declared, 'I'll accept this juror. He's an honest man.'

"Nor did his judgment prove mistaken. As it happened, this was the juror who helped to persuade his colleagues on the panel that Foreman's client should be given the gentle treatment. In the end, the accused received a five-year suspended sentence."

———

The methods used by lawyers to determine whether a particular prospective juror is acceptable are not always based upon a model of logic. The final decision is generally made through a combination of hunches, suppositions, time-honored traditions, questionable generalizations, and a few rule-of-thumb formulas. However, for a discussion of new scientific selection techniques and the role of the computer in the future, see Comment, Computers and Scientific Jury Selection: A Calculated Risk, 55 Det.J.Urb.L. 345 (1978).

In *Roughing It*, Mark Twain said, "We have a criminal jury system which is superior to any in the world, and its efficiency is marred only by the difficulty of finding twelve men every day who don't know anything and can't read." To what extent does the folklore of jury selection support this conclusion?

Chapter 18

QUALITY OF REPRESENTATION BY COUNSEL

A. LIMITS OF PROSECUTORIAL ZEAL

---

1. AMERICAN BAR ASSOCIATION STANDARDS

(Tentative Draft, 2d ed., 1978)

Standard 3–1.1. The function of the prosecutor

(a) The office of prosecutor is charged with responsibility for prosecutions in its jurisdiction.

(b) The prosecutor is both an administrator of justice and an advocate; the prosecutor must exercise sound discretion in the performance of his or her functions.

(c) The duty of the prosecutor is to seek justice, not merely to convict.

(d) It is the duty of the prosecutor to know and be guided by the standards of professional conduct as defined in the codes and canons of the legal profession, and in this chapter. The prosecutor should make use of the guidance afforded by an advisory council . . . .

(e) As used in this chapter, the term "unprofessional conduct" denotes conduct which, in either identical or similar language, is or should be made subject to disciplinary sanctions pursuant to codes of professional responsibility in force in each jurisdiction. Where other terms are used, the standard is intended as a guide to honorable professional conduct and performance. These standards are not intended as criteria for the judicial evaluation of alleged misconduct of the prosecutor to determine the validity of a conviction; they may or may not be relevant in such judicial evaluation, depending upon all the circumstances.

Standard 3–1.2. Conflicts of interest

A prosecutor should avoid the appearance or reality of a conflict of interest with respect to official duties. In some instances, as defined in codes of professional responsibility, failure to do so will constitute unprofessional conduct.

Standard 3–1.3. Public statements

(a) The prosecutor should not exploit the office by means of personal publicity connected with a case before trial, during trial, or thereafter.

(b) The prosecutor should comply with the chapter on fair trial and free press in these standards. In some instances, as defined in codes of professional responsibility, failure to do so will constitute unprofessional conduct.

(c) In order to assure a fair trial for the accused, the prosecutor and police should cooperate in achieving compliance with the chapter on fair trial and free press of these standards and codes of professional responsibility.

* * *

Standard 3–2.8.   Relations with the courts and bar

(a) It is unprofessional conduct for a prosecutor intentionally to misrepresent matters of fact or law to the court.

(b) A prosecutor's duties necessarily involve frequent and regular official contacts with the judge or judges of the prosecutor's jurisdiction. In such contacts the prosecutors should carefully strive to preserve the appearance as well as the reality of the correct relationship which professional traditions and canons require between advocates and judges.

(c) It is unprofessional conduct for a prosecutor to engage in unauthorized ex parte discussions with or submission of material to a judge relating to a particular case which is or may come before the judge.

(d) In the prosecutor's necessarily frequent contacts with other members of the bar, the prosecutor should strive to avoid the appearance as well as the reality of any relationship which would tend to cast doubt on the independence and integrity of the office.

Standard 3–2.9.   Prompt disposition of criminal charges

(a) A prosecutor should not intentionally use procedural devices for delay for which there is no legitimate basis.

(b) The prosecution function should be so organized and supported with staff and facilities as to enable it to dispose of all criminal charges promptly. The prosecutor should be punctual in attendance in court and in the submission of all motions, briefs, and other papers. The prosecutor should emphasize to all witnesses the importance of punctuality in attendance in court.

(c) It is unprofessional conduct intentionally to misrepresent facts or otherwise mislead the court in order to obtain a continuance.

Standard 3–3.1.   Investigative function of prosecutor

(a) A prosecutor ordinarily relies on police and other investigative agencies for investigation of alleged criminal acts, but the prosecutor has an affirmative responsibility to investigate suspected illegal activity when it is not adequately dealt with by other agencies.

(b) It is unprofessional conduct for a prosecutor knowingly to use illegal means to obtain evidence or to employ or instruct or encourage others to use such means.

(c) A prosecutor should not discourage or obstruct communication between prospective witnesses and defense counsel. It is unprofessional conduct for the prosecutor to advise any person or cause any person to be advised to decline to give to the defense information which such person has the right to give.

(d) It is unprofessional conduct for a prosecutor to secure the attendance of persons for interviews by use of any communication which has the appearance or color of a subpoena or similar judicial process unless the prosecutor is authorized by law to do so.

(e) It is unprofessional conduct for a prosecutor to promise not to prosecute for prospective criminal activity, except where such activity is part of an officially supervised investigative and enforcement program.

(f) Unless a prosecutor is prepared to forgo impeachment of a witness by the prosecutor's own testimony as to what the witness stated in an interview or to seek leave to withdraw from the case in order to present the impeaching testimony, a prosecutor should avoid interviewing a prospective witness except in the presence of a third person.

Standard 3–3.2. Relations with prospective witnesses

(a) It is unprofessional conduct to compensate a witness, other than an expert, for giving testimony, but it is not improper to reimburse an ordinary witness for the reasonable expenses of attendance upon court, attendance for depositions pursuant to statute or court rule, or attendance for pretrial interviews. Payments to a witness may be for transportation and loss of income, provided there is no attempt to conceal the fact of reimbursement.

(b) Whenever a prosecutor knows or has reason to believe that the conduct of a witness to be interviewed may be the subject of a criminal prosecution, the prosecutor or the prosecutor's investigator should advise the witness concerning possible self-incrimination and the possible need for counsel.

Standard 3–3.3. Relations with expert witnesses

(a) A prosecutor who engages an expert for an opinion should respect the independence of the expert and should not seek to dictate the formation of the expert's opinion on the subject. To the extent necessary, the prosecutor should explain to the expert his or her role in the trial as an impartial expert called to aid the fact finders and the manner in which the examination of witnesses is conducted.

(b) It is unprofessional conduct for a prosecutor to pay an excessive fee for the purpose of influencing the expert's testimony or to fix the amount of the fee contingent upon the testimony the expert will give or the result in the case.

Standard 3–3.4. Decision to charge

(a) The decision to institute criminal proceedings should be initially and primarily the responsibility of the prosecutor.

(b) Absent exceptional circumstances, no arrest warrant or search warrant should issue without the approval of the prosecutor.

(c) The prosecutor should establish standards and procedures for evaluating complaints to determine whether criminal proceedings should be instituted.

(d) Where the law permits a citizen to complain directly to a judicial officer or the grand jury, the citizen complainant should be required to present the complaint for prior approval to the prosecutor, and the prosecutor's action or recommendation thereon should be communicated to the judicial officer or grand jury.

Standard 3–3.5.   Relations with grand jury

(a) Where the prosecutor is authorized to act as legal adviser to the grand jury, the prosecutor may appropriately explain the law and express an opinion on the legal significance of the evidence but should give due deference to its status as an independent legal body.

(b) The prosecutor should not make statements or arguments in an effort to influence grand jury action in a manner which would be impermissible at trial before a petit jury.

(c) The prosecutor's communications and presentations to the grand jury should be on the record.

Standard 3–3.6.   Quality and scope of evidence before grand jury

(a) A prosecutor should present to the grand jury only evidence which the prosecutor believes would be admissible at trial. However, in appropriate cases, the prosecutor may present witnesses to summarize admissible evidence available to the prosecutor which the prosecutor believes he or she will be able to present at trial.

(b) No prosecutor should knowingly fail to disclose to the grand jury evidence which will tend substantially to negate guilt.

(c) A prosecutor should recommend that the grand jury not indict if it is believed the evidence presented does not warrant an indictment under governing law.

(d) If the prosecutor believes that a witness is a potential defendant, the prosecutor should not seek to compel the witness's testimony before the grand jury without informing the witness that he or she may be charged and that the witness should seek independent legal advice concerning his or her rights.

(e) The prosecutor should not compel the appearance of a witness before the grand jury whose activities are the subject of the inquiry if the witness states in advance that if called he or she will exercise the constitutional privilege not to testify, unless the prosecutor intends to seek a grant of immunity according to the law.

* * *

Standard 3–3.11.   Disclosure of evidence by the prosecutor

(a) It is unprofessional conduct for a prosecutor intentionally to fail to make disclosure to the defense, at the earliest feasible opportunity, of the existence of evidence which tends to negate the guilt of the accused as to the offense charged or which would tend to reduce the punishment of the accused.

(b) The prosecutor should comply in good faith with discovery procedures under the applicable law.

(c) It is unprofessional conduct for a prosecutor intentionally to avoid pursuit of evidence because he or she believes it will damage the prosecution's case or aid the accused.

Standard 3–4.1.   Availability for plea discussions

(a) The prosecutor should make known a general policy or willingness to consult with defense counsel concerning disposition of charges by plea.

(b) It is unprofessional conduct for a prosecutor to engage in plea discussions directly with an accused who is represented by counsel, except with counsel's approval.   Where the defendant has properly waived counsel, the prosecuting attorney may engage in plea discussions with the defendant, although ordinarily a verbatim record of such discussions should be made and preserved.

(c) It is unprofessional conduct for a prosecutor knowingly to make false statements or representations in the course of plea discussions with defense counsel or the accused.

Standard 3–4.2.   Fulfillment of plea discussions

(a) It is unprofessional conduct for a prosecutor to make any promise or commitment concerning the sentence which will be imposed or concerning a suspension of sentence; a prosecutor may properly advise the defense what position will be taken concerning disposition.

(b) It is unprofessional conduct for a prosecutor to imply a greater power to influence the disposition of a case than is actually possessed.

(c) It is unprofessional conduct for a prosecutor to fail to comply with a plea agreement, unless a defendant fails to comply with a plea agreement or other extenuating circumstances are present.

* * *

Standard 3–5.1.   Calendar control

Control over the trial calendar should be vested in the court. The prosecuting attorney should be required to file with the court as a public record periodic reports setting forth the reasons for delay as to each case for which the prosecuting attorney has not requested trial within a prescribed time following charging.   The prosecuting attorney should also advise the court of facts relevant in determining the order of cases on the calendar.

Standard 3–5.2.   Courtroom decorum

(a) The prosecutor should support the authority of the court and the dignity of the trial courtroom by strict adherence to the rules of decorum and by manifesting an attitude of professional respect toward the judge, opposing counsel, witnesses, defendants, jurors, and others in the courtroom.

(b) When court is in session the prosecutor should address the court, not opposing counsel, on all matters relating to the case.

(c) It is unprofessional conduct for a prosecutor to engage in behavior or tactics purposefully calculated to irritate or annoy the court or opposing counsel.

(c) A prosecutor should comply promptly with all orders and directives of the court, but the prosecutor has a duty to have the record reflect adverse rulings or judicial conduct which the prosecutor considers prejudicial. The prosecutor has a right to make respectful requests for reconsideration of adverse rulings.

(e) A prosecutor should be punctual in all court appearances and in the submission of all motions, briefs, and other papers.

(f) Prosecutors should cooperate with courts and the organized bar in developing codes of decorum and professional etiquette for each jurisdiction.

Standard 3–5.3. Selection of jurors

(a) The prosecutor should prepare himself or herself prior to trial to discharge effectively the prosecution function in the selection of the jury and the exercise of challenges for cause and peremptory challenges.

(b) In those cases where it appears necessary to conduct a pre-trial investigation of the background of jurors, investigatory methods of the prosecutor should neither harass nor unduly embarrass potential jurors or invade their privacy and, whenever possible, should be restricted to an investigation of records and sources of information already in existence.

(c) The opportunity to question jurors personally should be used solely to obtain information for the intelligent exercise of challenges. A prosecutor should not intentionally use the voir dire to present factual matter which the prosecutor knows will not be admissible at trial or to argue the prosecution's case to the jury.

Standard 3–5.4. Relations with jury

(a) It is unprofessional conduct for a prosecutor to communicate privately with persons summoned for jury duty or impaneled as jurors concerning a case prior to or during trial. The prosecutor should avoid the reality or appearance of any such improper communications.

(b) The prosecutor should treat jurors with deference and respect, avoiding the reality or appearance of currying favor by a show of undue solicitude for their comfort or convenience.

(c) After discharge of the jury from further consideration of a case, it is unprofessional conduct for the prosecutor to intentionally make comments to or ask questions of a juror for the purpose of harassing or embarrassing the juror in any way which will tend to influence judgment in future jury service.

Standard 3–5.5. Opening statement

The prosecutor's opening statement should be confined to a brief statement of the issues in the case and to remarks on evidence the prosecutor intends to offer which the prosecutor believes in good faith will be available and admissible. It is unprofessional conduct to allude to any evidence unless there is a good faith and reasonable basis for believing that such evidence will be tendered and admitted in evidence.

Standard 3–5.6. Presentation of evidence

(a) It is unprofessional conduct for a prosecutor knowingly to offer false evidence, whether by documents, tangible evidence, or the testimony of witnesses, or fail to seek withdrawal thereof upon discovery of its falsity.

(b) It is unprofessional conduct for a prosecutor knowingly and for the purpose of bringing inadmissible matter to the attention of the judge or jury to offer inadmissible evidence, ask legally objectionable questions, or make other impermissible comments or arguments in the presence of the judge or jury.

(c) It is unprofessional conduct for a prosecutor to permit any tangible evidence to be displayed in the view of the judge or jury which would tend to prejudice fair consideration by the judge or jury until such time as a good faith tender of such evidence is made.

(d) It is unprofessional conduct to tender tangible evidence in the view of the judge or jury if it would tend to prejudice fair consideration by the judge or jury unless there is a reasonable basis for its admission in evidence. When there is any substantial doubt about the admissibility of such evidence, it should be tendered by an offer of proof and a ruling obtained.

Standard 3–5.7. Examination of witnesses

(a) The interrogation of all witnesses should be conducted fairly, objectively, and with due regard for the dignity and legitimate privacy of the witness, and without seeking to intimidate or humiliate the witness unnecessarily. Proper cross-examination can be conducted without violating rules of decorum.

(b) The prosecutor's belief that the witness is telling the truth does not preclude cross-examination, but may affect the method and scope of cross-examination. A prosecutor should not use the power of cross-examination to discredit or undermine a witness if the prosecutor knows the witness is testifying truthfully.

(c) A prosecutor should not call a witness who the prosecutor knows will claim a valid privilege not to testify for the purpose of impressing upon the jury the fact of the claim of privilege. In some instances, as defined in codes of professional responsibility, doing so will constitute unprofessional conduct.

(d) It is unprofessional conduct for a prosecutor to ask a question which implies the existence of a factual predicate for which a good faith belief is lacking.

Standard 3–5.8.   Argument to the jury

(a) The prosecutor may argue all reasonable inferences from evidence in the record. It is unprofessional conduct for the prosecutor intentionally to misstate the evidence or mislead the jury as to the inferences it may draw.

(b) It is unprofessional conduct for the prosecutor to express his or her personal belief or opinion as to the truth or falsity of any testimony or evidence or the guilt of the defendant.

(c) The prosecutor should not use arguments calculated to inflame the passions or prejudices of the jury.

(d) The prosecutor should refrain from argument which would divert the jury from its duty to decide the case on the evidence, by injecting issues broader than the guilt or innocence of the accused under the controlling law, or by making predictions of the consequences of the jury's verdict.

Standard 3–5.9.   Facts outside the record

It is unprofessional conduct for the prosecutor intentionally to refer to or argue on the basis of facts outside the record whether at trial or on appeal, unless such facts are matters of common public knowledge based on ordinary human experience or matters of which the court may take judicial notice.

Standard 3–5.10.   Comments by prosecutor after verdict

The prosecutor should not make public comments critical of a verdict, whether rendered by judge or jury.

* * *

2.   CASE ILLUSTRATION OF PROSECUTORIAL ZEAL

IN RE FRIEDMAN

Supreme Court of Illinois, 1979.
76 Ill.2d 392, 30 Ill.Dec. 288, 392 N.E.2d 1333.

MR. CHIEF JUSTICE GOLDENHERSH delivered the decision of the court and the following opinion in which MR. JUSTICE KLUCZYNSKI joins:

The Review Board of the Attorney Registration and Disciplinary Commission recommended that respondent   . . .   be censured. The two-count complaint filed by the Administrator of the attorney discipline system charged that respondent, while serving as chief of the criminal division of the Cook County State's Attorney's office, was guilty of conduct tending to bring the legal profession into disrepute and violative of four Disciplinary Rules of the Code of Professional Responsibility: Disciplinary Rule 7–102(A)(6) (creation of false evidence), Disciplinary rule 7–102(A)(4) (knowing use of false evidence), Disciplinary Rule 7–109(B) (secreting of a witness), and Disciplinary Rule 1–102(A)(4). The Hearing Board of the Attorney Registration and Disciplinary Commission found that respondent did not violate the Code of Professional Responsibility and recommended that the complaint be dismissed with prejudice. The Administrator filed exceptions with the Review Board.

* * *

[T]he Review Board issued a report and recommendation in which a five-member majority recommended that respondent be censured while three members, with a written dissent, voted that the complaint be dismissed with prejudice.

* * *

Charles Graber was arrested by Officer Jerry Maculitis and charged with driving while under the influence of alcohol. Respondent was informed that Officer Maculitis believed he had been solicited to receive a bribe from Graber's attorney, Lee Howard. Respondent met with Officer Maculitis and directed him to follow Howard's instructions even if those instructions included testifying falsely in favor of Graber. Howard told Maculitis that the defense would not be ready to proceed if the breathalyzer operator were present. Maculitis was instructed by respondent to arrange for the absence of the breathalyzer operator, who, however, on the day of the trial, appeared in court to testify. Following respondent's instructions, Maculitis falsely advised the court that the breathalyzer operator was unavailable. The charges against Graber were dismissed. In a washroom adjacent to the courtroom Maculitis was given $50 by Howard, who was later indicted for bribery.

During the first recess of court after the disposition of the Graber case, an assistant State's Attorney, acting upon the respondent's instructions, advised the associate circuit judge of the circumstances surrounding the case.

The charge contained in count II of the Administrator's complaint arose from [these] facts.   .   .   .   Juanita Guevara was arrested by Chicago police officer Jose Martinez and charged with the aggravated battery of Awilda Torres.   .   .   .   [R]espondent was told that Martinez had been approached by Guevara's attorney, Paul Powell, and was solicited to receive a bribe. Respondent instructed Martinez to give the appearance of cooperating with Powell. After meeting with Powell, Martinez told respondent that Powell had offered to pay him if he would arrest Ms. Torres and use the threat of prosecution to persuade her to drop the charges. Respondent instructed Martinez to tell Powell that the complaining witness had been persuaded to drop the charges. Martinez was also told that if he were called as a witness at the preliminary hearing, he should advise the court that Torres did not wish to appear. Although Torres and her mother appeared in court ready to testify at the preliminary hearing, they were advised of the pending investigation concerning

Powell's conduct and escorted to the State's Attorney's office, where they remained until the preliminary hearing was concluded. The assistant State's Attorney in charge moved that the case be stricken with leave to reinstate. Before ruling on the motion the court asked that Martinez be placed under oath in order to verify the reason for the request, and Martinez testified falsely that he had spoken to Torres and her mother and had been advised that they did not wish to prosecute. The court then granted the State's motion to strike with leave to reinstate. After the preliminary hearing Martinez met Powell in the latter's car and was paid $250. Powell was later indicted and convicted of bribery. Immediately following the preliminary hearing the court was advised of the reasons for Martinez's testimony. The charges against Guevara were later reinstated.

This case presents the questions whether disciplinary action is merited and, if so, the nature of the sanction to be imposed when a prosecutor admittedly engages in conduct violative of the Code of Professional Responsibility for the purpose of developing evidence to be used in a subsequent prosecution. The parties have not been cited nor has our research disclosed any analogous cases previously considered by either a court or disciplinary committee.

Analogizing to the court-tolerated deceit employed in narcotics investigations . . . , respondent argues that "the courtroom is not immunized by the Code of Professional Responsibility from investigation methods otherwise lawful and ethical" and that perjury and the secreting of witnesses are necessary methods for the successful investigation and prosecution of corrupt attorneys, whose stealth makes less deceptive investigatory techniques ineffective. He contends, too, that motive and intent must be considered in judging the ethics of respondent's conduct, and that respondent's lofty motive negates any technical violation of the Code of Professional Responsibility. Any intent to subvert the judicial processes in the two cases, respondent argues, originated not with him, but with attorneys Howard and Powell.

The Administrator contends that deceit and deception, although permissible in drug investigations, may not be employed to mislead or deceive a court while hearing one matter in order to develop evidence to be used in another proceeding, and that motive is not relevant to the question whether there has been professional misconduct and should be considered only in determining the appropriate sanction to be imposed.

ABA Standards, The Prosecution Function, section 1.1(d) (1971), states that "It is the duty of the prosecutor to know and be guided by the standards of professional conduct as defined in codes and canons of the legal profession, and in this report." It provides, too, that it is "unprofessional conduct for a prosecutor knowingly to offer false evidence, whether by documents, tangible evidence, or the testimony of witnesses." (ABA Standards, The Prosecution Function sec. 5.6(a) (1971).) Although this court has not formally approved the Code of Professional Responsibility adopted by the American Bar Association, it frequently serves as a guide for standards of professional conduct. . . . The complaint charged the violation of Disciplinary Rule 1–102(A)(4), which generally proscribes "conduct involving dishonesty, fraud, deceit, or misrepresentation," and violations of Disciplinary Rule 7–102(A)(4), Disciplinary Rule 7–102(A)(6), and Disciplinary Rule 7–109(B), which provide:

> "DR 7–102(A) In his representation of a client a lawyer shall not:
>
> * * *
>
> (4) Knowingly use perjured testimony or false evidence.
>
> * * *
>
> (6) Participate in the creation or preservation of evidence when he knows or it is obvious that the evidence is false."

> "DR 7–109
>
> * * *
>
> (B) A lawyer shall not advise or cause a person to secrete himself or to leave the jurisdiction of a tribunal for the purpose of making him unavailable as a witness therein."

That respondent's conduct has deviated from these rules is apparent; respondent himself admits that were it not for his motives he would be in violation. He argues that to impose discipline for his conduct would give more emphasis to the abstract concept of a courtroom's sanctity than to the substances of an honest legal system. While respondent asserts that he is not arguing that the end justifies the means, we so construe his argument and find it unacceptable. The integrity of the courtroom is so vital to the health of our legal system that no violation of that integrity, no matter what its motivation, can be condoned or ignored. Although arising out of a different context, we find apposite the words of Mr. Justice Brandeis in Olmstead v. United States (1928) (dissenting opinion):

> "Decency, security and liberty alike demand that government officials shall be subjected to the same rules of conduct that are commands to the citizen. In a government of laws, existence of the government will be imperilled if it fails to observe the law scrupulously. Our Government is the potent, the omnipresent teacher. For good or for ill, it teaches the whole people by its example. Crime is contagious. If the Government becomes a law-breaker, it breeds contempt for law; it invites every man to become a law unto himself; it invites anarchy. To declare that in the administration of the criminal law the end justifies the means—to declare that the Government may commit crimes in order to secure the conviction of a private criminal—would bring terrible retribution. Against that pernicious doctrine this Court should resolutely set its face."

Respondent's contention that no alternative methods were available to insure the successful prosecution of corrupt attorneys is also unpersuasive. As the above-quoted language indicates, even if no other ways existed to ferret out bribery, the respondent would still not be privileged to engage in unethical (and perhaps illegal) conduct. Moreover, in the present case alternatives were available to investigate and prosecute the suspected attorneys. They could, for example, have been charged with solicitation of perjury, or attempted bribery. Respondent maintains that as a practical matter convictions are virtually impossible to obtain unless the crime has been consummated and the money has been paid, that even when these circumstances are present conviction is still very difficult. Such factors cannot, however, justify respondent's conduct.

Because respondent acted without the guidance of precedent or settled opinion and because there is apparently considerable belief (as evidenced by the letters and affidavit supporting respondent) that he acted properly in conducting the investigations, we conclude that no sanction should be imposed. It appears that respondent has otherwise served the public diligently and with integrity and acted in the present matter not out of self-interest, but from a sincere, if misguided, desire to bring corrupt attorneys to justice. In light of all these considerations, we hold that no discipline will be imposed.

Respondent discharged.

MR. JUSTICE UNDERWOOD, concurring in the decision:

* * *

[W]hile I do not join in the finding of impropriety contained in the Chief Justice's opinion, I do join in discharging respondent, rather than dismissing the complaint, so that we may have the constitutionally required concurrence of four members in the action to be taken (Ill.Const.1970, art. VI, sec. 3).

The Administrator's case against respondent consisted solely of a statement of facts stipulated to by respondent. In contrast, respondent, after testifying fully and candidly that he accepted full responsibility for the conduct now alleged to be improper, introduced [expert testimony] and some 35 affidavits, statements and letters from both Federal and State judges and prosecutors, the Governor of Illinois, a law school dean and professors, criminal defense attorneys, and others. Many of these, in addition to attesting to respondent's excellent character and impeccable integrity, viewed the undisputed facts as involving no professional impropriety. Notable among them is Dean Monroe H. Freedman of Hofstra University Law School, a former faculty member at Harvard and George Washington law schools who specializes in the field of lawyers' ethics and has written extensively on the subject. His book *Lawyers' Ethics in an Adversary System* has been characterized as the best in the field of legal ethics. Dean Freedman, who was serving as chairman of the Committee on Professional Responsibility of the Society of American Law Teachers, has also served or is serving in many other positions of responsibility in the professional ethics field. He indicated that "[m]otive is, of course, a primary consideration in making judgments regarding the ethical quality of conduct." (M. Freedman, Lawyers' Ethics in an Adversary System 83 (1975).) In his statement in this case, submitted in affidavit form, he indicates his opinion that the proper construction of the ABA-approved Code of Professional Responsibility Rules proscribing the knowing use of false evidence, deceit and misrepresentation restricts the application of those rules to situations in which the responsible attorney engages in such conduct with the intent not to reveal the fraud and deception to the affected person or tribunal. In Dean Freedman's opinion, the complaint in this case should be dismissed for respondent was carrying out his express ethical obligation as a prosecutor to "improve the administration of criminal justice." ABA Standards, The Prosecution Function sec. 1.4 (1971).

* * *

[Based on other affidavits submitted] it is apparent that the pernicious activities of some police officers and some court personnel were either eliminated or substantially reduced by procedural changes suggested by, or inaugurated by, respondent.

* * *

In the *amicus* brief filed in his individual capacity by Thomas P. Sullivan, an able lawyer who formerly argued both criminal and civil cases in this court and now serves the Northern District of Illinois as United States District Attorney, Mr. Sullivan succinctly portrays the difficulty faced by law-enforcement personnel in cases like these. He states:

> "From time to time, prosecutors receive what appear to be reliable allegations that defense attorneys in criminal cases are engaged in suborning perjury, or bribing witnesses, bailiffs, clerks, prosecutors or judges, or the like. The prosecutor to whom such allegations are made has a duty to investigate, and to prosecute those found to be corrupting the criminal process.

> Usually, the hard evidence to prove these crimes is the payment of money by the defense lawyer to the witness, policeman, prosecutor, clerk, bailiff, or judge.

> Usually, to obtain the hard evidence of payment, it is necessary to have one or more of the participants in the case pretend to abet the scheme. Payment usually occurs *after* the policeman, witness, prosecutor, clerk or judge has done whatever he is supposed to do; usually, the payment is made *after* the defendant is acquitted, the evidence is suppressed, the case is dismissed, or the like.

> The Hearing Board's ruling recognizes the practical problems faced by the prosecutor who wishes to investigate these kinds of allegations. Contrariwise, the ruling of the

majority of the Review Board, if sustained by this Court, will seriously impair investigations in cases of this kind in Illinois. The unfortunate result may well be cessation of meaningful investigations of corrupt conduct by defense lawyers, witnesses, clerks, bailiffs, and judges in Illinois.

It is respectfully submitted that this Court should not hold an Illinois prosecutor guilty of unethical conduct when, in good faith, he carefully seeks evidence to ferret out and prosecute lawyers who are engaged in corrupting the criminal process. Surely Mr. Friedman should not be censured for doing that which he honestly believed to be a proper and ethical exercise of his sworn duty."

In an attempt to answer, my colleagues suggest that respondent had alternatives available—the suspect lawyers could have been charged with solicitation of perjury or attempted bribery. The weakness of that naive answer lies in the demonstrated fact that a prosecution of either of those charges, based upon the testimony of a single, uncorroborated witness as to the ambiguous language in which such offers are customarily made, will rarely succeed against the lawyer's vigorous denial of any criminal intent. . . .

The situation before us is analogous to that visualized by section 7–13 of the Criminal Code of 1961.

"Conduct which would otherwise be an offense is justifiable by reason of necessity if the accused was without blame in occasioning or developing the situation and reasonably believed such conduct was necessary to avoid a public or private injury greater than the injury which might reasonably result from his own conduct."

Certainly respondent was without blame in connection with the original bribe offers, and there is no doubt he believed his own conduct necessary to avoid a greater injury—the continued corruption of the judicial process by the two attorneys. That belief was, in my judgment, not only reasonable—it was correct. The fact is that no one, other than the dishonest lawyers, was injured by respondent's conduct. The courts were promptly informed. One case was reinstated, and the other could have been. And respondent created a substantial and obviously needed deterrent to similar misconduct by other attorneys.

I should make clear that I abhor the thought of intentionally deceiving a judge—even temporarily—by the presentation of false testimony. But I abhor even more those members of my profession who seek to prostitute our courts. Since corrupt lawyers will not make payment of the bribe until that which they seek has been done, and payment is, in my judgment, a practical necessity to conviction of the lawyer, some form of misrepresentation to the judge is required if the evidence of payment is to be secured. What was done here, much as I dislike it, seems to me preferable to informing the judge in advance, thereby making him a participant, or immunizing the corrupt lawyer from investigation and prosecution which, I fear, will inevitably result if respondent's conduct is held ethically impermissible.

In short, it is undisputed that respondent was a conscientious prosecutor dedicated to improving the administration of criminal justice. Both defendants and prosecutors benefited from his efforts as Professor Haddad's statement illustrates. At no time did respondent intend to permanently deceive anyone, and the necessary, temporary deception practiced upon the court was corrected immediately after it had served its purpose. No authority is cited by my colleagues indicating that the proscriptions in the disciplinary rules of fraud, misrepresentation, deceit and the use of false evidence were intended to embrace the factual situation involved here, and I agree with Dean Freedman and the hearing panel that they were not so intended.

While I believe respondent's conduct, motivated and circumscribed as it was, did not breach the disciplinary rules, for the reasons earlier noted I concur in respondent's discharge.

MR. JUSTICE RYAN joins in this concurrence.

MR. JUSTICE WARD took no part in the consideration or decision of this case.

MR. JUSTICE CLARK, dissenting:

* * *

Lawyers who cause or permit lies to be told to judges are guilty of conduct which tends to defeat the administration of justice, regardless of the motive of the lawyer and regardless of the immediate impact of the lie. That the respondent's sole apparent motive was to obtain evidence which he considered essential to the effective prosecution of corrupt attorneys therefore is not dispositive of the issues raised by this case. It is not within the province of any attorney, including one who represents the State, to determine whether the public interest requires the temporary deception of the court. That no prior case has addressed the precise form of deception practiced here is hardly exculpatory: If anything, the absence of such authority indicates that prosecutors ordinarily do not consider it within their power to determine whether to deceive judges. Although several distinguished members of the bar have, on behalf of the respondent, sought to explain the necessity and propriety of respondent's conduct, I seriously doubt whether any of them would have, if faced with the choice, acted as did he, particularly as regards his failure to obtain prior judicial sanction for his conduct. Respondent borders on frivolity in arguing that to have sought such prior sanction would have been improper. At the very least, therefore, I find the respondent guilty of incredibly poor ethical judgment and deserving of censure.

We may assume, for the sake of argument, that the respondent in good faith believed that, to persuade a judge or jury to convict an attorney accused of bribery, attempted bribery, or solicitation of perjury, it was necessary to obtain and present evidence of the payment of money by the attorney to the person allegedly bribed or solicited.

.   .   .   We may further assume, for the sake of argument, that the attorneys in question would have been unwilling to make the payments in question until they saw and heard evidence of the perjury and/or suppression of witnesses they had bargained for.

The question remains, however, why did the respondent not inform the court of the foregoing until his agents had played out their strategy and had lied to the court? Respondent's answer apparently is that he believed that to have informed the court beforehand would have been "improper" because (1) it would have, somehow, "involved" the court in a law-enforcement function, and (2) it would have constituted an *"ex parte"* communication in violation of Disciplinary Rule 7–110(B) of the Code of Professional Responsibility. I find that answer incredible. To have been informed before, rather than after, the fact of the falsity of testimony to be offered in his courtroom would not have "involved" the court in a law-enforcement function any more than a judge who reviews the adequacy of a search warrant or the voluntariness of a confession is "involved" in a law-enforcement function. (It is not unheard of, however, for law-enforcement personnel involved in the "competitive enterprise of ferreting out crime" to prefer to avoid the prior scrutiny of their actions that the warrant requirement mandates, although we do not know whether respondent's true motive here was to avoid such prior scrutiny.) Especially here, however, where the rights of a criminal defendant (including the right to avoid unnecessary delay and prejudice to witnesses) also were at stake, it was the court's prerogative to know of this little courtroom drama in advance and to pass upon its propriety. To have made such a determination before the fact would hardly have been anything but a judicial function, i. e., the review of executive decisions in an effort to protect the integrity of the criminal justice process, including the rights of the defendants. The respondent's contention that *he* protected the rights of the defendants is an inadmissible misreading of the proper allocation of responsibilities between the executive and the judiciary. .   .   .   It simply was not sufficient for the respondent to confront the court, after the fact, with the completed deception, stating in effect: "I did it. I'm proud of it. What are you going to do about it?" Respondent apparently had no doubt about the integrity of the trial judges he deceived; he has offered the statements of one of them in his defense. Even if he had such doubts, he was not without alternative fora, as I indicate below.

Respondent's arguments regarding Illinois Code of Professional Responsibility Disciplinary Rule 7–110(B) (1970) also are without merit, in my opinion. Disciplinary Rule 7–110(B) provides as follows:

> "(B) In an adversary proceeding, a lawyer shall not communicate, or cause another to communicate, as to the merits of the cause with a judge or an official before whom the proceeding is pending, except:

> "(1) In the court of official proceedings in the cause.

"(2) In writing if he promptly delivers a copy of the writing to opposing counsel or to the adverse party if he is not represented by a lawyer.

"(3) Orally upon adequate notice to opposing counsel or to the adverse party if he is not represented by a lawyer.

"(4) As otherwise authorized by law."

First, I am not persuaded that the communication in question even falls within the letter of the rule, let alone its intent, because I am not persuaded that advising the court of a proposed strategy for apprehending opposing counsel in the act of bribery is "as to the merits of the cause." Second, paragraph (B)(4) of the rule expressly excepts *ex parte* communications "[a]s otherwise authorized by law." Respondent's statutory duties, which, he so emphatically claims, authorized him temporarily to deceive the court (despite the absence of any such express exemption in Disciplinary Rules 7–102(A) and 7–109), would have provided substantial authority for the communication in question. It is just inconceivable to me that respondent could in good faith have believed that he could not, consistent with the intent of the Code, tell the court the truth, but he could cause the court to be told a lie. The purpose of Disciplinary Rule 7–110(B) is to prevent the "effect or . . . the appearance of granting undue advantage to one party" (ABA Code of Professional Responsibility, Ethical Consideration 7–35 (1970)). Since respondent apparently concedes the need to inform the court of its deception after the fact, it is hard to see how prior warning would have given even the appearance of undue advantage to the State. If anything, it might have helped to preserve the rights of the defendant. It is not inconceivable that the court, thus warned, would have secretly appointed special counsel to represent the defendant's interests in this matter in an emergency, *in camera* hearing. The actions of the respondent effectively foreclosed this possibility too, however.

Finally, even if the respondent had in good faith believed that, for some as yet unarticulated reason, he could not talk to the trial judge, he should not have taken it upon himself to decide whether the temporary deception of the trial judge was appropriate. He should have had the common sense and ethical circumspection to have brought his dilemma to the attention of the presiding judge of the criminal division, or the chief judge of the circuit court, or if the foregoing were for some reason inappropriate, to this court itself, which has supervisory powers over the circuit courts. He did not do so; he thus usurped the role of the courts through deceiving a trial judge, albeit temporarily, and his conduct merits censure.

MR. JUSTICE MORAN, also dissenting:

I agree with the rationale of the lead opinion, dissent from its decision that no discipline should be imposed, and am diametrically opposed to the totality of the joint special concurrence.

Respondent's conduct was, by his own admission, a violation of the disciplinary rules cited. To excuse his conduct because a conviction for bribery would otherwise be impossible would make the court not only a victim of respondent's duplicity but also an advocate of the philosophy that a conviction by any means is the ultimate goal of our system of justice.

That respondent might be excused because his motives were pure is an untenable defense, particularly when intent is not an element of the charge here raised against him.

Without dwelling on my many differences with the concurring decision, it will suffice to say that, in my opinion, it not only condones respondent's conduct but also lauds him for it and encourages it in others. Under the more palatable term "necessary," it avoids stating its assention to the cliche that the end justifies the means. The concurrence finds a cure in respondent's admission after the fact, yet confession does not eradicate the commission. In my view, the concurrence sets an intolerably dangerous precedent.

While we must avoid the temptation of imposing idealistic but unrealistically high expectations on members of the profession merely because of that membership, we cannot content ourselves to expect less of the practitioner than that he be subject to the rules of conduct imposed on all citizens. Even without the criteria of the disciplinary rules, the public, the court and the profession have the right, minimally, to expect a valid, common-sense determination by the practitioner to discern right from wrong, and one need not be trained in the law to know that it is flatly unacceptable to prevaricate to or mislead the court or to be instrumental in encouraging others to do so. The lead opinion finds ameliorating the fact that respondent acted without the guidance of precedent or settled opinion. I am not so persuaded. The canopy of ethics must cover more than black-letter law or we are constrained to excuse all but those infractions so recorded, although it would be impossible to conceive of, much less enumerate, explicitly, every infraction possible.

Respondent's conduct is of the genre which has undermined the public's confidence in the profession, in the courts and, ultimately, in the law. If the public finds it intolerable that a member of the profession can operate without the constraints of law, it can be no less intolerable to the court affronted by the conduct. The court must remain the ultimate forum of truth. Respondent's conduct has disregarded that essential, and, in so critical a consideration, I do not believe that the court can condemn the act but excuse the actor. Under the mitigating circumstances of this case, I feel respondent should be censured.

NOTES

1. If the prosecutor by sanctioning false testimony could have done no harm to the defendant, why was the court so concerned about perjury in *Friedman*? Should prosecutors and law enforcement officers be allowed to violate the letter of the law as long as they do not harm any other individual? Should the test be whether their conduct invades the rights of another which a statute or the Constitution seeks to protect? Would you want to give prosecutors that much power to violate the law? Consider this hypothetical: A prosecutor advises and consents to law enforcement officers'

setting up a "Sting operation." As part of the plan, undercover agents open a tavern. To do so, they obtain a license, a process which, to the knowledge of the prosecutor, leads them to make false statements (concerning their names and the names of the party with the real beneficial interest). Has the prosecutor sanctioned a violation of the law which thereby makes him both criminal and unethical in the eyes of his profession? See Chaney v. Illinois Dept. of Law Enforcement, 74 Ill.App.3d 424, 30 Ill.Dec. 420, 393 N.E.2d 75 (1979), leave to appeal granted where the focus was not the role of the lawyers but rather the legality of the agents' conduct.

2. Federal prosecutors in all of their cases are to be guided by the following principles stated by Mr. Justice Sutherland in Berger v. United States, 295 U.S. 78, 88, 55 S.Ct. 629, 633 (1935).

"The United States Attorney is the representative not of an ordinary party to a controversy, but of a sovereignty whose obligation to govern impartially is as compelling as its obligation to govern at all; and whose interest, therefore, in a criminal prosecution is not that it shall win a case, but that justice shall be done. As such, he is in a peculiar and very definite sense the servant of the law, the twofold aim of which is that guilt shall not escape or innocence suffer. He may prosecute with earnestness and vigor—indeed, he should do so. But, while he may strike hard blows, he is not at liberty to strike foul ones. It is as much his duty to refrain from improper methods calculated to produce a wrongful conviction as it is to use every legitimate means to bring about a just one."

3. Ethical questions touch virtually every facet of the prosecutor's function. Consider the following excerpt from the text in Alderstein, Ethics, Federal Prosecutors: Some Recent Problems, 6 Hofstra L.Rev. 755 (1978):

. . . Almost no aspect of the job of the federal prosecutor has escaped judicial attention: the interviewing of witnesses, conduct of proceedings before the grand jury, applications for arrest and search warrants, statements made in court and during trial, statements made to the press, the giving of information to or the withholding of information from the defendant's attorney, the wording of indictments, as well as the making of agreements with witnesses and defendants.

"Under these conditions, the federal prosecutor has every reason to adhere closely to the standards that the courts set out for the prosecutor's office. As prosecutors on the federal level become increasingly active and aggressive, and cases against persons with stature in the community are brought, there is a strong practical as well as moral motive to adhere to specified ethical standards, however exacting such standards might be. No single prosecution is worth the loss of credibility and status that will attend the dismissal of a case for even an unwitting breach of standards. The idea is therefore enticing that the prosecutor, when faced with an ethical problem, should choose the safest approach from the point of view of ethics. A "safe" approach requires the prosecutor to be open in giving information to the court and to the defendant in a particular case, though not to the press. Such an approach also involves recognizing that agreements with particular witnesses or defendants exist, even when such agreements are nonspecific and adhering to promises, however vague, even when the other party has not completely fulfilled his part of the arrangement.

"The concept of prosecutorial ethics, however, has another side that extends beyond internal job standards. The prosecutor has a duty to the community to assure that perpetrators of crime are convicted and punished. The execution of this responsibility may be thwarted by defendants who, if given too much information about a case before trial, can suborn perjury or endanger and intimidate witnesses, as well as fabricate evidence. The interests of the community are further disserved when a prosecutor grants promised favors to persons who have not genuinely earned such favors. The devaluation of the prosecutor's credibility among those who engage in or witness crime and their attorneys can only weaken the effectiveness of the prosecutor and encourage many to flout the law."

4. In Imbler v. Pachtman, 424 U.S. 409, 96 S.Ct. 984 (1976), the Supreme Court held that for purposes of the federal civil rights statute, 42 U. S.C. § 1983, a state prosecutor is immune from an action for money damages even where the complaint alleges that he knowingly utilized perjured testimony. What policy can possibly justify such a result?

B.   THE DILEMMA OF DEFENSE COUNSEL

1.   AMERICAN BAR ASSOCIATION STANDARDS

(Tentative Draft, 2d ed., 1978)

* * *

Standard 4–1.1.   Role of defense counsel

(a) Counsel for the accused is an essential component of the administration of criminal justice. A court properly constituted to hear a criminal case must be viewed as a tripartite entity consisting of the judge (and jury, where appropriate), counsel for the prosecution, and counsel for the accused.

(b) The basic duty the lawyer for the accused owes to the administration of justice is to serve as the accused's counselor and advocate with courage, devotion, and to the utmost of his or her learning and ability and according to law.

(c) The defense lawyer, in common with all members of the bar, is subject to standards of conduct stated in statutes, rules, decisions of courts, and codes, canons, or other standards of professional conduct. The defense lawyer has no duty to execute any directive of the accused which does not comport with law or such standards; the defense lawyer is the professional representative of the accused, not the accused's alter ego.

(d) It is unprofessional conduct for a lawyer intentionally to misrepresent matters of fact or law to the court.

(e) It is the duty of every lawyer to know the standards of professional conduct as defined in codes and canons of the legal profession and in this chapter. The functions and duties of defense counsel are governed by such standards whether defense counsel is assigned or privately retained.

(f) As used in this chapter, the term "unprofessional conduct" denotes conduct which, in either identical or similar language, is or should be made subject to disciplinary sanctions pursuant to codes of professional responsibility. Where other terms are used, the standard is intended as a guide to honorable professional conduct and performance. These standards are not intended as criteria for the judicial evaluation of alleged misconduct of counsel to determine the validity of a conviction; they may or may not be relevant in such judicial evaluation, depending upon all the circumstances.

Standard 4–1.2. Delays; punctuality

(a) Defense counsel should avoid unnecessary delay in the disposition of cases. Defense counsel should be punctual in attendance upon court and in the submission of all motions, briefs, and other papers. Defense counsel should emphasize to the client and all witnesses the importance of punctuality in attendance in court.

(b) It is unprofessional conduct for defense counsel intentionally to misrepresent facts or otherwise mislead the court in order to obtain a continuance.

(c) Defense counsel should not intentionally use procedural devices for delay for which there is no legitimate basis.

(d) A lawyer should not accept more employment than the lawyer can discharge within the spirit of the constitutional mandate for speedy trial and the limits of the lawyer's capacity to give each client effective representation. It is unprofessional conduct to accept employment for the purpose of delaying trial.

Standard 4–1.3. Public statements

(a) The lawyer representing an accused should avoid personal publicity connected with the case before trial, during trial, and thereafter.

(b) The lawyer should comply with the standards on fair trial and free press herein. In some instances, as defined in codes of professional responsibility, his failure to do so will constitute unprofessional conduct.

* * *

Standard 4–1.5. Trial lawyer's duty to administration of justice

(a) The bar should encourage through every available means the widest possible participation in the defense of criminal cases by experienced trial lawyers. Lawyers active in general trial practice should be encouraged to qualify themselves for participation in criminal cases both by formal training and through experience as associate counsel.

(b) All qualified trial lawyers should stand ready to undertake the defense of an accused regardless of public hostility toward the accused or personal distaste for the offense charged or the person of the defendant.

(c) Qualified trial lawyers should not assert or announce a general unwillingness to appear in criminal cases; law firms should encourage partners and associates to appear in criminal cases.

Standard 4–1.6.   Client interests paramount

The duties of a lawyer to a client are to represent the client's legitimate interests, and considerations of personal and professional advantage should not influence the lawyer's advice or performance.

* * *

Standard 4–2.3.   Prohibited referrals

(a) It is unprofessional conduct for a lawyer to compensate others for referring criminal cases to him or her.

(b) It is unprofessional conduct for a lawyer to accept referrals by agreement or as a regular practice from law enforcement personnel, bondsmen, or court personnel.

(c) It is unprofessional conduct to accept referrals of criminal cases regularly except from an authorized referral agency or a lawyer referring a case in the ordinary course of practice.

(d) Regulations and licensing requirements governing the conduct of law enforcement personnel, bondsmen, court personnel, and others in similar positions should prohibit their referring an accused to any particular lawyer and should require them, when asked to suggest the name of an attorney, to direct the accused to the referral service or to the local bar association if no referral service exists.

* * *

Standard 4–3.3.   Fees

(a) In determining the amount of the fee in a criminal case, it is proper to consider the time and effort required, the responsibility assumed by counsel, the novelty and difficulty of the questions involved, the skill requisite to proper representation, the likelihood that other employment will be precluded, the fee customarily charged in the locality for similar services, the gravity of the charge, the experience, reputation, and ability of the lawyer, and the capacity of the client to pay the fee.

(b) It is unprofessional conduct for a lawyer to imply that compensation of the lawyer is for anything other than professional services rendered by the lawyer or by others for the lawyer.

(c) It is unprofessional conduct for a lawyer to enter into an agreement for, charge, or collect an illegal or clearly excessive fee.

(d) It is unprofessional conduct for a lawyer to divide a fee with a nonlawyer, except as permitted by the Code of Professional Responsibility. A lawyer may share a fee with another lawyer only on the basis of their respective services and responsibility in a case, in accordance with the Code of Professional Responsibility.

(e) It is unprofessional conduct for a lawyer to enter into an arrangement for, charge, or collect a contingent fee for representing a defendant in a criminal case.

Standard 4–3.4. Obtaining publication rights from the accused

It is unprofessional conduct for a lawyer, prior to conclusion of all aspects of the matter giving rise to his or her employment, to enter into any agreement or understanding with a client or a prospective client by which the lawyer acquires an interest in publication rights with respect to the subject matter of the employment or proposed employment.

Standard 4–3.5. Conflict of interest

(a) At the earliest feasible opportunity defense counsel should disclose to the defendant any interest in or connection with the case or any other matter that might be relevant to the defendant's selection of a lawyer to represent him or her.

(b) Except for preliminary matters such as initial hearings or applications for bail, a lawyer or lawyers who are associated in practice should not undertake to defend more than one defendant in the same criminal case if the duty to one of the defendants may conflict with the duty to another. The potential for conflict of interest in representing multiple defendants is so grave that ordinarily a lawyer should decline to act for more than one of several codefendants except in unusual situations when, after careful investigation, it is clear that (i) no conflict is likely to develop; (ii) the several defendants give an informed consent to such multiple representation; and (iii) the consent of the defendants is made a matter of judicial record. In some instances, accepting or continuing employment by more than one defendant in the same criminal case is unprofessional conduct.

(c) In accepting payment of fees by one person for the defense of another, a lawyer should be careful to determine that he or she will not be confronted with a conflict of loyalty since the lawyer's entire loyalty is due the accused. It is unprofessional conduct for the lawyer to accept such compensation except with the consent of the accused after full disclosure. It is unprofessional conduct for a lawyer to permit a person who recommends, employs, or pays the lawyer to render legal services for another to direct or regulate the lawyer's professional judgment in rendering such legal services.

(d) It is unprofessional conduct for a lawyer to defend a criminal case in which the lawyer's partner or other professional associate is or has been the prosecutor.

Standard 4–3.6. Prompt action to protect the accused

* * *

(b) A lawyer should not act as surety on a bail bond either for the accused or for others.

Standard 4–3.7. Advice and service on anticipated unlawful conduct

(a) It is a lawyer's duty to advise a client to comply with the law, but the lawyer may advise concerning the meaning, scope, and validity of a law.

(b) It is unprofessional conduct for a lawyer to counsel a client in or knowingly assist a client to engage in conduct which the lawyer knows to be illegal or fraudulent.

(c) It is unprofessional conduct for a lawyer to agree in advance of the commission of a crime that the lawyer will serve as counsel for the defendant, except as part of a bona fide effort to determine the validity, scope, meaning, or application of the law, or where the defense is incident to a general retainer for legal services to a person or enterprise engaged in legitimate activity.

(d) Except as provided in standard 4–7.7, a lawyer may reveal the expressed intention of a client to commit a crime and the information necessary to prevent the crime, and the lawyer must do so if the contemplated crime is one which would seriously endanger the life or safety of any person or corrupt the processes of the courts and the lawyer believes such action on his or her part is necessary to prevent it.

Standard 4–3.8. Duty to keep client informed

The lawyer has a duty to keep the client informed of the developments in the case and the progress of preparing the defense.

Standard 4–3.9. Obligations to client and duty to court

Once a lawyer has undertaken the representation of an accused, the duties and obligations are the same whether the lawyer is privately retained, appointed, or serving in a legal aid or defender program.

PART 4. INVESTIGATION AND PREPARATION

Standard 4–4.1. Duty to investigate

It is the duty of the lawyer to conduct a prompt investigation of the circumstances of the case and to explore all avenues leading to facts relevant to the merits of the case and the penalty in the event of conviction. The investigation should always include efforts to secure information in the possession of the prosecution and law enforcement authorities. The duty to investigate exists regardless of the accused's admissions or statements to the lawyer of facts constituting guilt or the accused's stated desire to plead guilty.

Standard 4–4.2. Illegal investigation

It is unprofessional conduct for a lawyer knowingly to use illegal means to obtain evidence or information or to employ, instruct, or encourage others to do so.

Standard 4–4.3. Relations with prospective witnesses

(a) It is unprofessional conduct to compensate a witness, other than an expert, for giving testimony, but it is not improper to reimburse a witness for the reasonable expenses of attendance upon court, including transportation and loss of income, attendance for depositions pursuant to statute or court rule, or attendance for pretrial interviews, provided there is no attempt to conceal the fact of reimbursement.

(b) It is not necessary for the lawyer or the lawyer's investigator, in interviewing a prospective witness, to caution the witness concerning possible self-incrimination and the need for counsel.

(c) A lawyer should not discourage or obstruct communication between prospective witnesses and the prosecutor. It is unprofessional conduct to advise any person, other than a client, or cause such person to be advised to decline to give to the prosecutor or counsel for codefendants information which such person has a right to give.

(d) Unless the lawyer for the accused is prepared to forgo impeachment of a witness by the lawyer's own testimony as to what the witness stated in an interview or to seek leave to withdraw from the case in order to present such impeaching testimony, the lawyer should avoid interviewing a prospective witness except in the presence of a third person.

Standard 4–4.4. Relations with expert witnesses

(a) A lawyer who engages an expert for an opinion should respect the independence of the expert and should not seek to dictate the formation of the expert's opinion on the subject. To the extent necessary, the lawyer should explain to the expert his or her role in the trial as an impartial witness called to aid the fact finders and the manner in which the examination of witnesses in conducted.

(b) It is unprofessional conduct for a lawyer to pay an excessive fee for the purpose of influencing the expert's testimony or to fix the amount of the fee contingent upon the testimony the expert will give or the result in the case.

Standard 4–4.5. Compliance with discovery procedure

The lawyer should comply in good faith with discovery procedures under the applicable law.

PART 5. CONTROL AND DIRECTION OF LITIGATION

Standard 4–5.1. Advising the defendant

(a) After informing himself or herself fully on the facts and the law, the lawyer should advise the accused with complete candor concerning all aspects of the case, including a candid estimate of the probable outcome.

(b) It is unprofessional conduct for the lawyer intentionally to understate or overstate the risks, hazards, or prospects of the case to exert undue influence on the accused's decision as to his or her plea.

(c) The lawyer should caution the client to avoid communication about the case with witnesses, except with the approval of the lawyer, to avoid any contact with jurors or prospective jurors, and to avoid either the reality or the appearance of any other improper activity.

Standard 4–5.2.   Control and direction of the case

(a) Certain decisions relating to the conduct of the case are ultimately for the accused and others are ultimately for defense counsel. The decisions which are to be made by the accused after full consultation with counsel are: (i) what pleas to enter; (ii) whether to waive jury trial; and (iii) whether to testify in his or her own behalf.

(b) The decisions on what witnesses to call, whether and how to conduct cross-examination, what jurors to accept or strike, what trial motions should be made, and all other strategic and tactical decisions are the exclusive province of the lawyer after consultation with the client.

(c) If a disagreement on significant matters of tactics or strategy arises between the lawyer and the client, the lawyer should make a record of the circumstances, the lawyer's advice and reasons, and the conclusion reached.   The record should be made in a manner which protects the confidentiality of the lawyer-client relationship.

Standard 4–6.1.   Duty to explore disposition without trial

(a) Whenever the nature and circumstances of the case permit, the lawyer for the accused should explore the possibility of an early diversion of the case from the criminal process through the use of other community agencies.

(b) A lawyer may engage in plea discussions with the prosecutor, although ordinarily the client's consent to engage in such discussions should be obtained in advance.   Under no circumstances should a lawyer recommend to a defendant acceptance of a plea unless a full investigation and study of the case has been completed, including an analysis of controlling law and the evidence likely to be introduced at trial.

Standard 4–6.2.   Conduct of discussions

(a) In conducting discussions with the prosecutor the lawyer should keep the accused advised of developments at all times and all proposals made by the prosecutor should be communicated promptly to the accused.

(b) It is unprofessional conduct for a lawyer knowingly to make false statements concerning the evidence in the course of plea discussions with the prosecutor.

(c) It is unprofessional conduct for a lawyer to seek or accept concessions favorable to one client by any agreement which is detrimental to the legitimate interests of any other client.

Standard 4–7.1.   Courtroom decorum

(a) As an officer of the court the lawyer should support the authority of the court and the dignity of the trial courtroom by strict adherence to the rules of decorum and by manifesting an attitude of professional respect toward the judge, opposing counsel, witnesses, jurors, and others in the courtroom.

(b) When court is in session defense counsel should address the court and should not address the prosecutor directly on any matter relating to the case.

(c) It is unprofessional conduct for a lawyer to engage in behavior or tactics purposefully calculated to irritate or annoy the court or the prosecutor.

(d) The lawyer should comply promptly with all orders and directives of the court, but the lawyer has a duty to have the record reflect adverse rulings or judicial conduct which the lawyer considers prejudicial to his or her client's legitimate interests.   The lawyer has a right to make respectful requests for reconsiderations of adverse rulings.

(e) Lawyers should cooperate with courts and the organized bar in developing codes of decorum and professional etiquette for each jurisdiction.

Standard 4–7.2.   Selection of jurors

(a) The lawyer should prepare himself or herself prior to trial to discharge effectively his or her function in the selection of the jury, including the raising of any appropriate issues concerning the method by which the jury panel was selected and the exercise of both challenges for cause and peremptory challenges.

(b) In those cases where it appears necessary to conduct a pretrial investigation of the background of jurors, investigatory methods of the lawyer should neither harass nor unduly embarrass potential jurors or invade their privacy and, whenever possible, should be restricted to an investigation of records and sources of information already in existence.

(c) The opportunity to question jurors personally, should be used solely to obtain information for the intelligent exercise of challenges.   A lawyer should not intentionally use the voir dire to present factual matter which the lawyer knows will not be admissible at trial or to argue the lawyer's case to the jury.

Standard 4–7.3.   Relations with jury

(a) It is unprofessional conduct for the lawyer to communicate privately with persons summoned for jury duty or impaneled as jurors concerning the case prior to or during the trial.   The lawyer should avoid the reality or appearance of any such improper communications.

(b) The lawyer should treat jurors with deference and respect, avoiding the reality or appearance of currying favor by a show of undue solicitude for their comfort or convenience.

(c) After discharge of the jury from further consideration of a case, it is unprofessional conduct for a lawyer to intentionally make comments to or ask questions of a juror for the purpose of harassing or embarrassing the juror in any way which will tend to influence judgment in future jury service. If the lawyer believes that the verdict may be subject to legal challenge, the lawyer may properly, if no statute or rule prohibits such course, communicate with jurors to determine whether such challenge may be available.

Standard 4–7.4. Opening statement

The lawyer's opening statement should be confined to a brief statement of the issues in the case and evidence the lawyer intends to offer which the lawyer believes in good faith will be available and admissible. It is unprofessional conduct to allude to any evidence unless there is a good faith and reasonable basis for believing such evidence will be tendered and admitted in evidence.

Standard 4–7.5. Presentation of evidence

(a) It is unprofessional conduct for a lawyer knowingly to offer false evidence, whether by documents, tangible evidence, or the testimony of witnesses, or fail to seek withdrawal thereof upon discovery of its falsity.

(b) It is unprofessional conduct for a lawyer knowingly and for the purpose of bringing inadmissible matter to the attention of the judge or jury to offer inadmissible evidence, ask legally objectionable questions, or make other impermissible comments or arguments in the presence of the judge or jury.

(c) It is unprofessional conduct to permit any tangible evidence to be displayed in the view of the judge or jury which would tend to prejudice fair consideration of the case by the judge or jury until such time as a good faith tender of such evidence is made.

(d) It is unprofessional conduct to tender tangible evidence in the presence of the judge or jury if it would tend to prejudice fair consideration of the case unless there is a reasonable basis for its admission in evidence. When there is any substantial doubt about the admissibility of such evidence it should be tendered by an offer of proof and a ruling obtained.

Standard 4–7.6. Examination of witnesses

(a) The interrogation of all witnesses should be conducted fairly, objectively, and with due regard for the dignity and legitimate privacy of the witness, and without seeking to intimidate or humiliate the witness unnecessarily. Proper cross-examination can be conducted without violating rules of decorum.

(b) A lawyer's belief or knowledge that the witness is telling the truth does not preclude cross-examination, but should, if possible, be taken into consideration by counsel in conducting the cross-examination.

(c) A lawyer should not call a witness who he knows will claim a valid privilege not to testify, for the purpose of impressing upon the jury the fact of the claim of privilege. In some instances, doing so will constitute unprofessional conduct.

(d) It is unprofessional conduct for a lawyer to ask a question which implies the existence of a factual predicate for which a good faith belief is lacking.

* * *

Standard 4–7.8.   Argument to the jury

(a) In closing argument to the jury the lawyer may argue all reasonable inferences from the evidence in the record. It is unprofessional conduct for a lawyer intentionally to misstate the evidence or mislead the jury as to the inferences it may draw.

(b) It is unprofessional conduct for a lawyer to express a personal belief or opinion in his or her client's innocence or personal belief or opinion in the truth or falsity of any testimony or evidence, or to attribute the crime to another person unless such an inference is warranted by the evidence.

(c) A lawyer should not make arguments calculated to inflame the passions or prejudices of the jury.

(d) A lawyer should refrain from argument which would divert the jury from its duty to decide the case on the evidence by injecting issues broader than the guilt or innocence of the accused under the controlling law or by making predictions of the consequences of the jury's verdict.

Standard 4–7.9.   Facts outside the record

It is unprofessional conduct for a lawyer intentionally to refer to or argue on the basis of facts outside the record, unless such facts are matters of common public knowledge based on ordinary human experience or matters of which the court can take judicial notice.

Standard 4–7.10.   Posttrial motions

The trial lawyer's responsibility includes presenting appropriate motions, after verdict and before sentence, to protect the defendant's rights.

* * *

2. CASE ILLUSTRATIONS OF DEFENSE COUNSEL'S DILEMMA

IN RE JANUARY 1976 GRAND JURY (GENSON)

United States Court of Appeals, Seventh Circuit, 1976.
534 F.2d 719.

PELL, CIRCUIT JUDGE.

This is an appeal from an order of the district court dated January 15, 1976, adjudging appellant, an attorney, in civil contempt and ordering him to be remanded to the custody of the Attorney General "until such time as he shall purge himself of this contempt or the discharge of the January 1976 Grand Jury, whichever comes first."

* * *

I. Statement of Facts

On December 30, 1975, between 9:00 and 9:30 A.M., the Bellwood Savings and Loan Association of Bellwood, Illinois, was robbed of approximately $6,120.00 by a man and a woman. Investigators from the Federal Bureau of Investigation uncovered information leading to the identification of two suspects, Paul Bijeol and Sharon Kay Holloway, and a complaint and warrant were sworn and issued on December 31, 1975, naming these two suspects.

Investigation and interview disclosed that Bijeol had been in the employ of Edward Genson, attorney at law, prior to the commission of the robbery. Investigation also disclosed that Bijeol and his alleged female accomplice were in the Chicago office of Mr. Genson and one of his associates, Mr. Barry Goodman, between 10:00 A.M. and 12:00 noon on December 30, 1975, approximately one to three hours after the commission of the robbery. Further, Government investigators learned that the male suspect had transferred $200.00 in cash to Mr. Goodman at this time. It was also learned that Bijeol met with Genson at approximately 1:30 P.M. and again at approximately 5:30 P.M. on the day of the robbery.

At approximately 10:00 A.M. on December 31, 1975, Genson was notified by an agent of the FBI that any monies which he had received or would receive as fees for his legal services for the two suspects might constitute proceeds of the robbery. In response to an inquiry of an FBI agent, Genson stated that he received "something" from the male suspect, but he refrained from disclosing what the "something" was. In response to a subsequent inquiry whether he had in fact received any monies or any firearms from either of the two suspects at the time of or subsequent to their meetings on the day of the robbery, Genson asserted the attorney-client privilege as a basis for refusing to respond to the questions.

On January 7, 1976, Genson was served with a subpoena duces tecum requesting the production of

> "[a]ny and all monies paid or delivered to you or into your care, custody, and control by Paul Bijeol or Sharon K. Holloway, . . . or their agents, subsequent to 9:00 A.M. on Tuesday, December 30, 1975."

[Genson's motion to quash the subpoena was denied; and following his refusal to comply with the subpoena before the grand jury, he was held in contempt].

* * *

II. The Fifth Amendment Testimonial Privilege

The major issue in this appeal is whether a subpoena duces tecum requiring an attorney to produce for a grand jury investigation monies turned over to him by his clients and believed to be proceeds of a bank robbery infringes his clients' Fifth Amendment privilege against compelled self-incrimination. . . .

The Fifth Amendment privilege against self-incrimination does not merely encompass evidence which may lead to a criminal conviction, but also includes information which would furnish a "link in the chain of evidence" that could lead to prosecution as well as evidence which an individual reasonably believes could be used against him in a criminal prosecution. . . . One of the important policies underlying the testimonial privilege is the protection of an individual's "private enclave". . . . In order to promote the basic policy objectives which it was believed the framers sought to achieve, the Supreme Court has recognized that the Fifth Amendment privilege respects a private inner sanctum which "necessarily includes an individual's papers and *effects* to the extent that the privilege *bars their compulsory production and authentication.* . . .

A series of recent Supreme Court decisions has established, however, that compulsion which makes a suspect or accused the source of real or physical evidence does not violate the testimonial privilege. . . . The Government relies upon this series of decisions to bolster its contention that Genson's production of the monies, which it characterizes as mere physical evidence, would not be equatable with any self-incriminatory disclosures of a testimonial or communicative nature.

More precisely, the Government contends that Genson's compliance with the subpoena duces tecum would not represent an impermissible authentication of the physical evidence. The only arguable testimonial disclosure which would accompany Genson's production of the subpoenaed monies would be the implied admission that the currency had been transferred to him from one or both of his clients. The appellant meets this argument by observing that the challenged subpoena seeks not just items, but items that were allegedly obtained from the attorney's clients after a specified time on a specified day. Appellant thus argues that because the wording of the subpoena contains references to the "who" and the "when" of the alleged transfer of monies, it necessarily involves assertive conduct which, as such, might well be interpreted to constitute an admission by Genson's clients.

The question of whether the monies constitute mere physical evidence or represent a testimonial utterance is not one to be categorically or easily answered. At oral argument, the appellant insisted that he stood in such a special relationship to his clients that the Government could not enforce a subpoena duces tecum against him. In sum, the Government could demand from Genson only what it might legitimately demand from his clients. Appellant insists that no one could fail to agree that the Government could not enforce a subpoena duces tecum against the robbery suspects demanding production of the monies.

* * *

. . . Here, the subpoena is not being served directly upon the suspects. The clients allegedly transferred monies to Genson, their attorney. He is the witness who has been ordered to appear before the grand jury. His implied admission that he received the monies from his clients on the very day of the bank robbery is not the direct testimony of the suspects themselves. . . .

. . . [It] has been recently established that a lawyer is not subject to the penalty of contempt for *advising* his client to refuse on Fifth Amendment grounds to produce materials demanded by a subpoena duces tecum where the lawyer believes in good faith that the material may tend to incriminate his client. Maness v. Meyers, [419 U.S. 449, 95 S.Ct. 584 (1975)]. In this appeal, however, the court confronts not the situation where the attorney advises his client to refuse production but rather one where the attorney himself, now the alleged possessor of the demanded item, declines to produce.

Unless the relationship of attorney and client is completely *sui generis*, as appellant argues, the author of this opinion finds no precedents supporting Genson's refusal to produce what may possibly be the fruits of a violent crime. . . .

* * *

The attorney-client relationship is not so close or special as to create some form of mystical identity between the two natural persons. No reason exists to obliterate the distinction between the person of the attorney and that of the client. The Fifth Amendment explicitly prohibits compelling an accused to bear witness against himself; it does not proscribe incriminating statements elicited from another. . . . In the present case, the compulsion of the subpoena is directly exerted on Genson and not upon his clients. Unless he has standing to invoke on their behalf the Fifth Amendment privilege, the appellant has shown no just cause for failing to comply with the subpoena or the order of the court.

* * *

In this appeal, the court is concerned not with the compelled production, either by IRS summons or grand jury subpoena, of personal papers or documents but rather with the demand for monies which may have been stolen from a federally insured savings institution. The important testimonial communication in this case is that the suspects have had at a point in time subsequent to the armed robbery possession of the stolen monies. Such an evidentiary fact would appear to the author of this opinion to be an important link in the chain of evidence. .   .   .

.   .   .   The recognition that an attorney need not produce stolen monies in response to a subpoena would provide a mechanism by which a member of a learned profession could become the privileged repository of the fruits of a violent crime. There is no reason for thinking that the policy of respecting the private enclave of individual citizens reaches that far.

.   .   .   [T]he majority of the panel is of the opinion that the money itself is non-testimonial and that its delivery was not assertive conduct. In this situation, the attorney is simply a witness to a criminal act. The fact that the attorney is also a participant in the act is irrelevant since he is not asserting his own privilege against self-incrimination. The author of this opinion rests his opinion upon the lack of standing on the part of the lawyer to assert the Fifth Amendment claim on behalf of his clients. Whatever implied testimony arises from the act of production is that of the lawyer. This remains true even if the wording of the subpoena contains implied questions regarding the "who" and the "when" of the alleged transfer.

III.   The Attorney–Client Privilege

Genson also based his refusal on the attorney-client privilege. Analytically, of course, this privilege is not identical with the Fifth Amendment right, even though closely-related concepts of privacy and confidentiality play an important role in determining the scope of the two privileges. Nor is there a similarity of analysis as regards the issue of standing. The attorney-client privilege arose in the days of Elizabeth I from a consideration of the oath and the honor of the attorney rather than for the apprehensions of his client, and only in the middle of the nineteenth century did the privilege become substantially recognized as that of the client. .   .   .

The basis for the privilege is to afford the client a reasonable expectation of privacy and confidentiality with regard to disclosures made during the course of consultation with his attorney. The general rule is that, barring unusual circumstances, matters involving the receipt of fees from a client are not privileged.

* * *

Assuming that the alleged transfer of monies represented a retainer or a prepayment of fees, the fact of payment and the money itself would fall outside the scope of the privilege. Assuming that the monies were transferred not as a fee payment but as a bailment for the purposes of safekeeping, the appellant finds himself in a position closely analogous to the attorney in the case of In re Ryder, 263 F. Supp. 360 (E.D.Va.) aff'd, 381 F.2d 713 (4th Cir. 1967).

.   .   .   Genson contends that he was under an ethical responsibility not to produce the demanded monies or to answer questions regarding them. The ethical obligation of a lawyer to guard the confidences and secrets of his client is broader than the attorney-client privilege.   See A.B.A. Code of Professional Responsibility, EC 4–4 (1974).*   Accordingly, our focus on the attorney-client privilege proceeds on narrower terms than appellant recognizes as appropriate.

* * *

In *Ryder*, supra, an attorney secreted in his own safety deposit box the greater portion of the proceeds of a bank robbery as well as the sawed-off shotgun used in the crime.   When Ryder asserted the attorney-client privilege in defense of his actions, the Fourth Circuit, in affirming an 18-month suspension from the practice of law, stated:

> "Viewed in any light, the facts furnished no basis for the assertion of an attorney-client privilege.   It is an abuse of a lawyer's professional responsibility knowingly to take possession of and secrete the fruits and instrumentalities of a crime.   Ryder's acts bear no reasonable relation to the privilege and duty to refuse to divulge a client's confidential communication."

We are aware that the *Ryder* case was decided at a time when an earlier formulation of the canons of legal ethics was in force.   The code of conduct then in force did not attempt to distinguish between aspirational provisions labelled as Ethical Considerations and minimum standards of conduct regulated by Disciplinary Rules.   We do not think that the format change initiated in 1969 has any bearing on the scope of the evidentiary privilege.

Ethical Consideration 7–27 states that "[b]ecause it interferes with the proper administration of justice, a lawyer should not suppress evidence that he or his client has a legal obligation to reveal or produce."   Our holding that Genson, under the circumstances of this case, cannot avoid compliance with the subpoena because of a claim of Fifth Amendment protection leads us to conclude that he is under a legal obligation to reveal or produce the monies which we have assumed arguendo that he has.   Failure to comply with the subpoena and the subsequent court order to produce and testify effects the practical suppression of the sought after evidence.

We think that the *Ryder* conclusion is persuasive authority that the appellant cannot assert the privilege.   We hold that Genson's refusal to testify or to produce does not bear a reasonable relation to the privilege and duty to refuse to divulge a client's confidential communications.

---

* Canon 4 of the Code is captioned, "A Lawyer Should Preserve the Confidences and Secrets of a Client."   Each canon is divided into Ethical Considerations (EC) which in the Preamble of the Code are referred to as aspirational in character, representing objectives toward which every member of the profession should strive, and Disciplinary Rules (DR) which, unlike the Ethical Considerations, are mandatory in character.

The first two sentences of EC 4–4 read:
   "The attorney-client privilege is more limited than the ethical obligation of a lawyer to guard the confidences and secrets of his client.   This ethical precept, unlike the evidentiary privilege, exists without regard to the nature or source of information or the fact that others share the knowledge."

We express no opinion as to the extent, if any, to which the conduct of Genson does or does not equate with that of *Ryder* in the aforementioned disciplinary proceedings. The Supreme Court has consistently held that the necessity for expedition in the administration of the criminal law justifies putting one who seeks to resist the production of desired information to a choice between compliance with a court's order to produce prior to any review of that order, and resistance to that order with the concomitant possibility of an adjudication of contempt if his claims are rejected on appeal. . . . We conclude that the appellant's risk of a contempt citation was an appropriate means of achieving pre-compliance review. . . .

IV.   The Sixth Amendment Right to Counsel

A third contention in this appeal is that the subpoena duces tecum violated the clients' Sixth Amendment right to counsel. The appellant argues that the attempt of the Government to subpoena the known attorney of the two suspects and to make him the source of evidence against his clients impermissibly infringes upon their right to counsel. The Government insists that defendants have no right to *particular* counsel and that there is no reason why appellant could not be replaced by equally able counsel. The Government cites several cases from other circuits in support of its assertion that the Sixth Amendment argument is without merit.

It may well be that eventually the appellant's compliance with the subpoena duces tecum and his testimonial response to questions regarding the alleged transfer of monies may place him in the position of being a source of evidence against either or both of his clients. We express no opinion as to whether the suspects having chosen to make the appellant a witness to their crime, if such should subsequently prove to be the fact, may properly invoke the Sixth Amendment to bar his eyewitness testimony at trial. For the purposes of this appeal, we deem any reliance upon a claim of deprivation of right of counsel in violation of the Sixth Amendment is too premature to merit further consideration.

*   *   *

Affirmed.

TONE, CIRCUIT JUDGE (concurring).

I am unable to agree with all that is said in Judge Pell's thoughtful opinion and find it unnecessary to reach some of the questions discussed there. I therefore state my views separately.

We must assume for purposes of this appeal that shortly after robbing a savings and loan association, the robbers delivered money stolen in the robbery to appellant. If that occurred, the money was delivered either for safekeeping, with or without appellant's knowledge that it was stolen, or as an attorney's fee.

If it was the latter, the robbers voluntarily relinquished the money and with it any arguable claim that might have arisen from their possession or constructive possession. As Judge Pell points out, the payment of a fee is not a privileged communication. The money itself is non-testimonial and no plausible argument is left for resisting the subpoena.

If the money was not given as a fee but for safekeeping, the delivery of the money was an act in furtherance of the crime, regardless of whether appellant knew it was stolen. The delivery of the money was not assertive conduct and therefore was not a privileged communication, and, as we just observed, the money itself is non-testimonial. The attorney is simply a witness to a criminal act. The fact that he is also a participant in the act, presumably without knowledge of its criminal quality, is irrelevant since he is not asserting his own privilege against self-incrimination. There is no authority or reason, based on any constitutional provision or the attorney-client privilege, for shielding from judicial inquiry either the fruits of the robbery or the fact of the later criminal act of turning over the money to appellant. Accordingly, it is immaterial that in responding to the subpoena appellant will be making an assertion about who turned over the money and when.

Finally, the proceedings have not yet reached the point at which we must decide whether, when the robbers have chosen to make appellant a witness to their crime, they may invoke the Sixth Amendment to bar his eyewitness testimony at trial, although, for me, to ask that question is almost to answer it.

For these reasons I concur in the judgment of affirmance.

NOTES

1. Was the *Genson* court too concerned with the prospect of an attorney's receipt of the fruits of a crime? See the following excerpts from the text of Seidelson, The Attorney-Client Privilege and Client's Constitutional Rights, 6 Hofstra L.Rev. 693, 713–15 (1978):

> "[T]he considerations affecting the availability of the fifth amendment right against self-incrimination and the attorney-client privilege, after client has retained counsel, are intimately related to client's sixth amendment right to counsel. If the retention of counsel and subsequent intercourse between client and counsel jeopardize client's fifth amendment right against self-incrimination or his privilege of confidentiality, client may be dissuaded from retaining counsel. This dissuasive effect would be in basic opposition to the suspect's right to counsel.
>
> "It would seem, therefore, that to avoid frustrating the fifth amendment right against self-incrimination, the attorney-client privilege, and the sixth amendment right to counsel of a client who may be innocent of the offense under inquiry, courts should accept as a necessary cost of preserving these basic rights the fact that counsel may become 'the privileged repository of the fruits of a violent crime' if, in fact, his client is guilty of the offense being investigated. If in some cases counsel assumes that role, and courts recognize that as a necessary price to pay for preserving basic rights, it seems fair to assume that ultimately the public will become aware of this potential role of counsel. It might well be asserted that such knowledge would diminish the public's view of the

legal profession and its members. Is this an acceptable consequence?

*   *   *

"However unattractive the role of counsel as 'the privileged repository of the fruits of a violent crime' may be to a court, the court should endure that prospect if such toleration is essential to preserving the basic rights of clients. Similarly, whatever adverse impact this potential role of counsel may have on the already tarnished public image of the bar should be endured by lawyers if that toleration is essential to preserving those same basic rights. The public's image of the bar should not be permitted to become of greater concern or significance than the preservation of basic rights of clients. Indeed, it would be difficult to imagine anything which ultimately would be more detrimental to the profession's image—and its character—than eventual recognition by those it purports to serve that the bar is more sensitive to its public image than to the rights of its clients."

2. What should counsel do if, prior to trial, his client advises him that he intends to testify falsely at trial? In a now famous article, Professor Monroe Freedman argued that counsel owes a greater responsibility to his client than to the court, and, therefore, should put the client on the stand and vigorously argue the validity of the false testimony. Freedman, The Three Hardest Questions, 64 Mich.L.Rev. 1469 (1966). This unorthodox view generated heated criticism. See Burger, Standards of Conduct for Prosecution and Defense Personnel: A Judge's Viewpoint, 5 Am.Crim.L.Q. 11 (1966); Braun, Ethical Crisis in Criminal Law, 4 Trial 35 (1967).

In 1971 the ABA adopted the following guidelines:

"ABA Defense Function Standards, § 4–7.7:

"(a) If the defendant has admitted to his lawyer facts which establish guilt and the lawyer's independent investigation establishes that the admissions are true but the defendant insists on his right to trial, the lawyer must advise his client against taking the witness stand to testify falsely.

"(b) If, before trial, the defendant insists that he will take the stand to testify falsely, the lawyer must withdraw from the case, if that is feasible, seeking leave of the court if necessary.

"(c) If withdrawal from the case is not feasible or is not permitted by the court, or if the situation arises during the trial and the defendant insists upon testifying falsely in his own behalf, the lawyer may not lend his aid to the perjury. Before the defendant takes the stand in these circumstances, the lawyer should make a record of the fact that the defendant is taking the stand against the advice of counsel in some appropriate manner without revealing the fact to the court. The lawyer must confine his examination to identifying the witness as the defendant and permitting him to make his statement to the trier or the triers of the facts; the lawyer may not engage in direct examination of the defendant as a witness in the conventional manner and may not later argue the defendant's known false version of facts to the jury as worthy of belief and he may not recite or rely upon the false testimony in his closing argument."

Are these standards workable? Does the attorney-client privilege limit the amount of information which defense counsel can reveal to the court? If so, what happens when the court, based upon a lack of information, denies defense counsel's request to withdraw? What should counsel do if he becomes aware of his client's perjury in the midst of direct examination? What if the court refuses to permit the defendant to testify in narrative form? Since the court may increase the sentence due to a defendant's false testimony, United States v. Grayson, Chapter 21, Section B, infra, must the court, after permitting the false testimony, send the case to another judge for sentencing? Can the court, after conducting a hearing, prohibit the defendant from testifying?

Commentators have suggested a variety of alternatives. See Bowman, Standards of Conduct for Prosecution and Defense Personnel: An Attorney's Viewpoint, 5 Am.Crim.L.Q. 28 (1966); Polster, The Dilemma of the Perjurious Defendant: Resolution, Not Avoidance, 28 Case W.Res.L.Rev. 3 (1977); Wolfram, Client Perjury, 50 S.Cal.L.Rev. 809 (1977).

3. Consider the following example from Waite, How Ethical Are These Lawyers? Readers Digest 56, November, 1957:

> "In a Toledo, Ohio, court a young lawyer admitted to the bar was appointed to defend a penniless man charged with burglary. The evidence was clear. At the trial a police officer testified that he had chased a man from a clothing store at 2 a. m. and arrested him. Another officer swore that the prisoner arrived at the precinct station wearing new clothes with tags from the store still attached, and an assortment of jewelry in the pockets. The merchant identified the clothing and jewelry as his stolen property, and stated that worn-out clothes of a size to fit the arrested man had been found on the counter.

> "No defense was possible. Everyone in the courtroom knew that the defendant was guilty. But no one had taken the important step of getting it into the record that *this was the arrested man.*

> "Realizing this omission, the young defending lawyer could have held his peace and allowed the jury to convict—and thus 'saved' his client. For an appellate court, faced with a stenographic record showing the technical absence of proper identification, would be forced to set aside the conviction. Instead, the young lawyer pointed out the omission. Whereupon the startled prosecutor quickly recalled the first policeman to identify this defendant as the man he had arrested, the jury declared him guilty, and the conviction stood."

What should counsel have done in this situation? Professor Waite responded to criticism of the lawyer in this fashion,

> "This philosophy each year allows countless dangerous men to strut out of court and their lawyers to congratulate themselves. Yet these lawyers are officers of the court, and as such have sworn to be 'true to the court' and to attend to the business of their clients 'with prudence, honesty and skill'."

Is Professor Waite's position correct, or did the lawyer deserve the criticism which he received?

3. EFFECTIVE ASSISTANCE

UNITED STATES v. DECOSTER

United States Court of Appeals for the D.C. Circuit, en banc, 1979.
598 F.2d 311.

LEVENTHAL, CIRCUIT JUDGE, who is joined in this opinion by CIRCUIT JUDGES McGOWAN, TAMM and WILKEY:

This case gives the court en banc the opportunity to present its views on the requirement of effective assistance of counsel in criminal prosecutions, with principal focus on the duty of counsel to make due investigation prior to trial. We conclude that appellant has not made the showing requisite for reversal of his conviction.

A. Proof at Trial

At trial, Roger Crump, a soldier, testified that he was accosted by three men . . . near the parking lot of the Golden Gate Bar. He was yoked from behind by one man, threatened with a razor by another, while a third rifled his pockets and took his wallet which contained over $100 in cash.

Two plainclothes policemen cruising in an unmarked car saw the robbery in progress, alighted and gave chase. One officer followed the man later identified as Fred Eley. Officer Box testified that he followed appellant Decoster—whom he identified as the robber who went through Crump's pockets—from the scene to and into the D.C. Annex Hotel, found him at the lobby desk and arrested him. He testified that the chase lasted two to three minutes, that he did not lose sight of appellant and that Crump, who had been following along, immediately identified Decoster as one of the robbers. Crump was unable to identify Decoster at trial, because in the meanwhile his sight had been impaired in an accident, but he testified that he had been positive of his identification when he made it in the hotel. A search of appellant's pockets did not turn up any money, and the wallet was never recovered.

Appellant testified he had met and had a few drinks with Crump at the Golden Gate Club bar, but had left Crump in the bar, walked back to the hotel about a block away, and was getting his key from the desk clerk when he was arrested.

The defense called Eley. He (as well as the other codefendant, Taylor) had already pleaded guilty at a time when Decoster, having jumped bail, was a fugitive from justice. Eley corroborated that Decoster had met Crump in the bar (a point on which Crump was unsure). However, he also testified that he had seen appellant fighting with Crump in the parking lot across from the bar—and as to this contradicted appellant.

Decoster's conviction for aiding and abetting an armed robbery, which resulted in a 2–8 year sentence, is on appeal to this court.

B. Subsequent Proceedings

When the appeal was first before this court, the panel, while rejecting the contentions presented by appellate counsel, remanded for a hearing on the issue of ineffective assistance of counsel, an issue that it raised *sua sponte* and directed be presented to the district court on motion for a new trial.[1] The panel ruled that a defendant is entitled to the reasonably competent assistance of an attorney acting as his diligent conscientious advocate. Giving content to this standard, the panel adopted duties owed by counsel to his client derived in large part from the guidelines for the defense function promulgated by the American Bar Association Project on Standards for Criminal Justice.[2] The panel then held that once the appellant had shown a substantial violation of a duty owed to him by counsel, the burden was on the government to demonstrate lack of prejudice.

Pursuant to the remand, the motion for new trial was filed . . . . [T]he District Judge . . . held three days of supplementary hearings on the adequacy of trial counsel. [Ultimately] with findings of fact and conclusions of law, he entered an order denying the motion for a new trial.

. . . [T]he panel of this court, one member dissenting, reversed the judgment of conviction, holding that appellant had been denied the effective assistance of counsel. Essentially, the panel opinion (referred to as *Decoster II*) concluded that trial counsel had violated his duty to conduct a factual investigation. . . . [T]he court granted the government's motion for rehearing en banc . . . . .

C. Guiding Principles

The Sixth Amendment guarantees that "in all criminal prosecutions, the accused shall have the Assistance of Counsel for his defense." In giving content to this provision, the courts have recognized the need for differing approaches depending on the nature of the particular claim of denial of assistance in each case. These differences stem from the courts' perceptions of the exactness with which a denial can be identified and remedied, as well as their views of the need for a showing of prejudice.

* * *

Several reflective judges have recognized that differing approaches are pertinent where different aspects of the assistance of counsel are involved. Judge Bright, writing for the Eighth Circuit [in McQueen v. Swenson, 498 F.2d 207 (8th Cir. 1977)] has noted that while the total absence of counsel cannot but be harmful, when a defendant is represented by counsel and the performance of counsel has

---

1. United States v. DeCoster, 487 F.2d 1197 (1973) [hereafter referred to as *DeCoster I*].

2. American Bar Association, Project on Standards for Criminal Justice, Standards Relating to the Defense Function (App. Draft 1971) [hereafter referred to as ABA Standards].

fallen below the accepted standard, "the seriousness of this constitutional violation must be judged in terms of the particular factual circumstances of that case."

Recently, Judge Browning, writing for the Ninth Circuit en banc in Cooper v. Fitzharris, [586 F.2d 1325 (9th Cir. 1978)] pointed out that the rulings that a defendant need not show prejudice involved an absolute denial of counsel or a structural impediment to counsel's effective performance. In a case involving the quality of performance, as reflected in acts or omissions at trial, the accused must prove not mere errors but "serious derelictions" and that counsel's errors prejudiced the defense. Judge Hufstedler's dissent put it that a defendant with a "totally inept counsel" would not also have to show "precisely" how he was affected, but this opinion acknowledged that courts consider "prejudicial impact of attorney behavior" in determining whether the attorney was constitutionally competent, and further recognized that in many cases the outcome would be the same under both majority and dissenting approaches.

The task remains of delineating the non-categorical criteria that are to be applied in evaluating claims of inadequate performance by counsel. It is now clear that the courts will not abstain completely from some oversight of counsel's performance. At one time this court came close to abstention, in [Diggs v. Welch, 148 F.2d 667 (D.C.Cir. 1945)] adopting the "farce and mockery" standard. Even under that standard counsel's performance was on occasion found so delinquent as to prompt judicial correction, but the occasions were rare.

*   *   *

Our [opinion in Bruce v. United States, 379 F.2d 113 (D.C.Cir. 1967)] laid down a standard that recognized the need for more judicial oversight. It was put that "ineffective assistance" was established where "there has been gross incompetence of counsel and . . . this has in effect blotted out the essence of a substantial defense." . . . Although not stated explicitly, the *Bruce* departure was obviously away from Fifth Amendment due process concepts to a Sixth Amendment approach to the problem of ineffective assistance. And *Bruce* went beyond that to state that a less powerful showing of ineffectiveness was required on direct appeal than that necessary to support a collateral attack.

We pause to take note of the formulations adopted by the other circuits. . . . [T]he circuits are in "disarray."

One prominent formulation appears in [Moore v. United States, 432 F.2d 730 (3d Cir. 1970)] as a standard of "normal competency:" "the exercise of the customary skill and knowledge which normally prevails at the time and place." This is essentially a negligence standard. . . . However, . . . the mere fact that performance falls below average does not equal negligence. Thus, the question remains of what departures from a potential "norm" are so egregious as to call for judicial interposition.

Other circuits have adopted variations on a notion of "reasonable" competence,[3] using tests that suffer from the same uncertainties as the Third Circuit's. The Seventh Circuit has held that a defendant is entitled to assistance of counsel that meets a "minimum professional standard." [4] In the last analysis, all the circuits recognize that the performance of counsel must fall below a minimum, not just an abstract "norm." There must be "serious derelictions."

Some circuits have attempted to give content to their standards by adopting, explicitly or by implication, specific duties the violation of which amounts to ineffective assistance. The panel of this court that wrote *DeCoster I* employed—with some embellishment—the standards for the defense function promulgated by the American Bar Association. In *Decoster II* the panel referred to these *DeCoster I* requirements as "the minimal components of 'reasonably competent assistance,' " although in both opinions the panel qualified these duties by requiring a "substantial" violation.

The ABA Standards, however, were not put forward by the ABA as either exclusively "minimum" standards or as "a set of per se rules applicable to post-conviction procedures." Rather, they constitute a "blend of description of function, functional guidelines, ethical guidelines and recommended techniques," a mixture of the aspirational and the obligatory.

* * *

This brief survey underscores that generalized standards may be little more than a "semantic merry-go-round." Our *Bruce* opinion was one formulation and other courts have used others—but in the last analysis they are necessarily limited efforts to describe that courts will condemn only a performance that is egregious and probably prejudicial. As put by Justice Kaplan in [Commonwealth v. Saferian, 366 Mass. 89, 96, 315 N.E.2d 878, 883 (1974)]:

> Whatever the attempted formulation of a standard in general terms, what is required in the actual process of decision

---

3. See, e. g., Cooper v. Fitzharris, 586 F.2d 1325, 1330 (9th Cir. 1978) ("reasonably competent attorney acting as a diligent conscientious advocate"); United States v. Easter, 539 F.2d 663, 666 (8th Cir. 1976) ("customary skills and diligence that a reasonably competent attorney would perform under similar circumstances"); MacKenna v. Ellis, 280 F.2d 592, 599 (5th Cir. 1960) ("counsel reasonably likely to render *and rendering* reasonably effective assistance"). The *MacKenna* test has been adopted by the Sixth Circuit. Beasley v. United States, 491 F.2d at 696.

Three circuits continue to adhere to the "farce and mockery" standard. See, e. g., Gillihan v. Rodriquez, 551 F.2d 1182, 1187 (10th Cir.), cert. denied,

434 U.S. 845 (1977); Rickenbacker v. Warden, 550 F.2d 62 (2d Cir. 1976), cert. denied, 434 U.S. 826 (1977); United States v. Madrid Ramirez, 535 F.2d 125, 129 (1st Cir. 1976). The First and Second Circuits, while formally adhering to the "farce and mockery" standard, have in many recent cases concluded that a reevaluation of that test is not necessary because counsel's alleged deficiencies did not amount to ineffectiveness even under the standard of "reasonable competency." . . .

4. United States ex rel. Williams v. Twomey, 510 F.2d 634, 640 (7th Cir.) (Wyzanski, J.), cert. denied, 423 U.S. 876 (1975).

of claims of ineffective assistance of counsel, and what our own decisions have sought to afford, is a discerning examination and appraisal of the specific circumstances of the given case to see whether there was been serious incompetency, inefficiency, or inattention of counsel—behavior of counsel falling measurably below that which might be expected from an ordinary fallible lawyer—and, if that is found, then, typically, whether it has likely deprived the defendant of an otherwise available, substantial ground of defence.

For the first condition of judicial intervention, *Saferian* speaks of "serious incompetency, inefficiency or inattention—behavior of counsel falling measurably below that which might be expected from an ordinary fallible lawyer." This may fairly be regarded as a refinement of the "gross incompetence" language of *Bruce*. The other condition is more important. *Bruce* required that the accused show that the deficiency "blotted out the essence of a substantial defense." But *Saferian* requires only that the accused show that counsel's deficiency "likely" deprived him "of an otherwise available, substantial ground of defense." This is an appropriate modification of *Bruce*.[5] Overarching concepts of justice tug on the court whenever it is seriously troubled by likelihood of injustice, even though there is no concrete establishment of injustice as a fact.

* * *

The court's appraisal requires a judgmental rather than a categorical approach. It must be wary lest its inquiry and standards undercut the sensitive relationship between attorney and client and tear the fabric of the adversary system. A defense counsel's representation of a client encompasses an almost infinite variety of situations that call for the exercise of professional judgment. A shortfall by defense counsel that is perceptible but is modest rather than egregious is no basis for judicial interposition . . . . This limitation preserves the freedom of counsel to make quick judgments, and avoids the possibility that there will be frequent and wide-ranging inquiries into the information and reasoning that prompted counsel to pursue a given course. The problem is complicated by the fact that these decisions often derive from the information supplied by the client.

For the law to encourage a wide-ranging inquiry, even after trial, into the conduct of defense counsel would undercut the fundamental premises of the trial process and transform its essential nature. The resulting upheaval in the role of the trial judge, widely

---

5. . . . . However, the change is only from a requirement that defendant show actual effect, required by *Bruce*, to the "likelihood" test of *Saferian*, that is in turn subject to prosecution rebuttal to negative prejudice in fact.

As to the content of the effect that defendant must show is likely, whether it be characterized as "blotting out the essence of a substantial defense" or "deprivation of an otherwise available, substantial defense" is a matter of form more than substance.

recognized as a serious difficulty, would in itself call into question any broad doctrine of ineffective assistance. And the prosecution in a criminal case would in turn ask to oversee defense counsel's conduct at trial—to ensure against reversal.

An even more difficult problem would be posed by the supervision of defense counsel's development of the case before trial. Even if we had the authority, it would be unwise to embark upon a doctrine that would open the door to a fundamental reordering of the adversary system into a system more inquisitorial in nature. The adversary system, warts and all, has worked to provide salutary protection for the rights of the accused. Efforts to improve the performance of defense counsel should not imperil that protection.

* * *

D.   The Duty to Investigate

The duty to investigate is a subset of the overall duty of defense counsel. A conscientious defense attorney will naturally investigate possible defenses. As part of this process, witnesses who may have information relevant to the case should be identified and interviewed. However, any claim of ineffectiveness must turn not on abstractions as to duty, but on an appraisal of consequences. And the development of the case before trial is an area of peculiar sensitivity in the attorney/client relationship.

Some failures to investigate may be so egregious as to command judicial correction without more. In McQueen v. Swenson, [498 F.2d 207 (8th Cir. 1974),] the defense counsel had adopted a blanket policy which he adhered to even in the face of requests by the defendant that certain persons be interviewed. This was held "an absurd and dangerous policy which can only be viewed as an abdication—not an exercise—of his professional judgment." Counsel's defect was subject to a simple, workable remedy and thus was a proper subject for judicial intervention.

Most claims of failure to investigate will not involve such clear-cut situations. They must be appraised in light of the information available to the attorney. A claim of failure to interview a witness may sound impressive in the abstract, but it cannot establish ineffective assistance when the person's account is otherwise fairly known to defense counsel.

* * *

Realistically, a defense attorney develops his case in large part from information supplied by his client. . . . [C]hoices based on such information should not later provide the basis for a claim of ineffectiveness even though that basis would have been undercut by inquiry of others. Judicial intervention to require that a lawyer run beyond, or around, his client, would raise ticklish questions of intrusion into the attorney/client relationship, and should be reserved for extreme cases where an effect on the outcome can be demonstrated. And so in Matthews v. United States [518 F.2d 1245 (7th Cir. 1975)] involving a claim that counsel was ineffective in failing to introduce evidence or call witnesses, then Circuit Judge Stevens focused on the failure to allege that such witnesses or evidence existed, adding:

> Petitioners have not told us what was said in their conference with counsel. Perhaps, for all we know, they merely explained that they had indeed forged the 35 ballot applications which were placed in evidence by the government and that they were indeed guilty as charged. Surely, if that were the case, counsel had no duty to search for witnesses, expert or otherwise, who might falsely testify to the contrary.

Our reflections on this point are congruent with the standard applicable when counsel for an indigent defendant seeks funds to obtain investigative services to assist in the preparation of the defense. While in general effective assistance of counsel embraces such an allowance it is far from automatic and "depends on the facts and circumstances of a particular case," with funds provided when counsel makes a showing of necessity, of the specific subjects to be explored and of their likely materiality.

Finally, claims based on a duty to investigate must be considered in light of the strength of the government's case. "When, . . . the prosecution has an overwhelming case based on documents and the testimony of disinterested witnesses, there is not too much the best defense attorney can do." [6] It is all well and good for a millionaire to retain counsel with the instruction to "leave not the smallest stone unturned." But it goes too far to insist that such a course is a general constitutional mandate.

E. Appellant's Claims

We turn from general questions of principle and approach to the matter of application to the case at hand. As focused in the remand proceedings, appellant makes some seven allegations of defective performance by his counsel.[7] Following three days of hearings, [the

---

6. United States v. Katz, 425 F.2d 928, 930 (2d Cir. 1970). Judge Friendly's comment, although directed to the choice of tactics at trial, has more general application. He said:

> Determination of the effectiveness of counsel cannot be divorced from the factual situation with which he is confronted. When, as here, the prosecution has an overwhelming case based on documents and the testimony of disinterested witnesses, there is not too much the best defense attorney can do. If he simply puts the prosecution to its proof and argues its burden to convince the jury beyond a reasonable doubt, the defendant may think him lacking in aggressiveness, and surely will if conviction occurs. If he decides to flail around

and raise a considerable amount of dust, with the inevitable risk that some may settle on his client, the defendant will blame him if the tactic fails, although in the rare event of success the client will rank him with leaders of the bar who have used such methods in some celebrated trials of the past.

7. Listed in order of the proceedings in appellant's case, they are:

(1) Counsel was dilatory in seeking a bond review while appellant was incarcerated for almost five months following his arrest on May 29, 1970;

(2) Counsel failed to obtain a transcript of appellant's prelimi-

trial judge] found that appellant had not been denied the effective assistance of counsel. We affirm. While we do not commend counsel's performance, we have no serious misgivings that would lead us to reverse in the interest of justice.

1.   Failure To Interview Potential Witnesses

We turn first to the claim that defense counsel failed to interview potential witnesses prior to trial. This is the claim that is most vigorously pressed on appeal, and by its nature requires somewhat detailed development.

Admittedly, defense counsel did not attempt prior to trial to interview the three prosecution witnesses—complainant Crump, and Officers Box and Ehler. However, at appellant's preliminary hearing counsel did hear Officer Ehler testify that he and Officer Box were together when they witnessed the crime, and that Box pursued appellant to the hotel where he was apprehended. Ehler further testified that within minutes after the assault, Crump had identified appellant in the hotel lobby—a point appellant has never contested. Defense counsel was aware, therefore, of the main points of the likely testimony of the witnesses at trial.

Appellant attacks defense counsel's failure to interview the desk clerk at the D.C. Annex Hotel, and his failure to make an effort to locate and interview potential eyewitnesses that might have been in the hotel at the time appellant entered and was apprehended. These are abstractions without context. Appellant himself testified at trial that he had just entered the lobby when he was arrested. Counsel was aware that there would be, as indeed there was, testimony of the police officer that he had not lost sight of appellant from the time of the robbery to the time of his apprehension. Appellant makes no claim that he advised counsel of any occurrence that would generate a significant issue as to his entry into the hotel.

If given an unrestricted budget and freed of any constraints as to probable materiality or accountability, a lawyer might have cheerfully logged in many hours looking for the legal equivalent of a needle in a haystack. As already noted, a millionaire might have retained counsel to leave not a single stone unturned. However, a defendant is not entitled to perfection but to basic fairness. In the real

nary hearing and failed to employ that transcript to impeach prosecution witnesses at trial;

(3) Counsel failed to interview any potential witnesses prior to trial;

(4) Counsel announced "ready" for trial at a time when he did not know whether or not he would present alibi witnesses and before he had fully developed his defense;

(5) Counsel offered to waive jury trial and to permit appellant to be tried before the court when the court had heard a part of the evidence in connection with the guilty pleas of the two co-defendants;

(6) Counsel failed to make an opening statement; and

(7) Counsel failed to see that appellant's sentence was properly executed, in that he failed to see that appellant was given credit for time served.

*   *   *

world, expenditure of time and effort is dependent on a reasonable indication of materiality. In the circumstances of this case, appellant has singularly failed to make a meaningful demonstration that counsel's omission probably affected the outcome of the trial. It is argued that potential witnesses might have testified to appellant's demeanor as he entered the lobby. This abstract possibility is not only speculative but remote in the extreme. It cannot fairly be said to undercut materially the positive police testimony.

Appellant goes on to challenge counsel's failure to seek out and interview potential witnesses in the Golden Gate Club. It would be extravagant to require counsel to seek out the anonymous patrons of a bar in order to testify that two persons were having a drink—a point that is, incidentally, undisputed as far as appellant and Crump are concerned. Appellant makes no offer as to what more could have been learned.

We turn next to the failure of defense counsel to interview appellant's co-defendants, Eley and Taylor, prior to trial, and his belated interview of Eley shortly before Eley testified on the second day of trial.

The record reveals that appellant consistently maintained to his attorney that his defense was alibi—that he had not been present at the scene of the crime, but rather had returned directly to the hotel from the bar where he had had a drink with Crump. This was the essence of appellant's eventual testimony at trial.

We may assume for present purposes that appellant's lawyer should have made some timely effort prior to trial to learn of the accounts of the co-defendants, beginning with consultation with their counsel. However, counsel subsequently did interview Eley and called him to the stand. At this time, be it noted, appellant had recently written to his counsel and raised a possible self-defense claim, altering his previous account (that he had left Crump in the bar) to claim that outside the bar Crump had assaulted him, and that Eley and Taylor would testify that they had come to his aid in fighting off Crump.

At the insistence of appellant, Eley was subpoenaed to appear at trial. [Taylor could not be located.] Eley, who was in jail, was brought to the courthouse in the same bus as Decoster and placed in the cellblock behind the courtroom with Decoster. At the remand hearing, defense trial counsel testified that he had interviewed Eley, and that Eley had told him Decoster was not present at the scene of the crime. This narrative was consistent with Decoster's trial testimony, and defense counsel called Eley as a witness. On the stand, however, Eley gave a different account, testifying that he had seen Crump and Decoster fighting. At the remand hearing Decoster and Eley both admitted that counsel had visited the cellblock prior to calling Eley as a witness. Decoster stated that he could not recall whether counsel had interviewed Eley, and Eley denied that he had spoken to counsel. The District Court found Eley's testimony "incredible" and credited the testimony of defense counsel as to his interview of Eley.

As already indicated, we do not approve the belated effort to interview the co-defendants. However, appellant has not demonstrated a likelihood that counsel's omission affected the outcome of trial. Counsel did interview Eley, and at a time when Eley could at least be asked to exculpate appellant without fear of self-injury, for by this time Eley's own fate was set, following the plea of guilty he had made during the period appellant had eloped. Appellant was insisting that Eley be called, and Eley's interview provided a glimmer of hope of corroborating appellant against a phalanx of credible prosecution witnesses. Neither appellant nor his counsel was in an enviable position at any time. Although appellant now claims ineffective assistance of counsel, what this conviction reflects is the clear-cut prosecution evidence, appellant's weak contradiction, and Eley's turnabout.

As a variant on the claim of failure to investigate, appellant points to counsel's apparent confusion at the beginning of the trial. After defense counsel had announced "ready" for trial, the government demanded the names of alibi witnesses. Counsel stated that he might present alibi witnesses, but he sought the full twenty day period permitted by local rules to respond to such a demand. When this was denied, defense counsel announced he would proceed without alibi witnesses.

The effort of defense counsel to keep his options open was hardly unusual, but even if this indicated uncertainty as to theory of defense, some degree of confusion would not be unexpected in view of appellant's shifting accounts and demands. In any event, there is no indication of likely effect on outcome. Counsel's responses came before the jury was impanelled. At the trial, counsel did call Eley as a witness he understood would support defendant's alibi defense.

2.   Other Claims of Ineffective Assistance

As to appellant's other claims, the District Court's findings, while framed in response to the *DeCoster I* mandate, are generally in accord with the principles we have developed in this opinion.

(a) *The Bond Review Motion.* Appellant was arrested on May 29, 1970. A judge of the District of Columbia Court of General Sessions set bond at $5,000. Appellant could not meet that figure and remained incarcerated.

[Due in part to the fact that counsel filed a bond review motion in the wrong court and a two months' lapse before a correct motion was filed, appellant was not released until Jan. 14, 1971.] While lack of diligence in obtaining a criminal defendant's pretrial release cannot be condoned, reversal of a conviction is not the appropriate remedy where the trial itself was not affected by the default.

b. *Failure To Obtain Transcript.* Defense counsel did not obtain a copy of the transcript of the preliminary hearing. At the remand hearing, he testified that it was his normal practice to read the prosecutor's copy. This practice, and their cooperation, was substantiated by the prosecutors' testimony. We cannot say that counsel's practice was impermissible. He had not only access to a transcript, but his own memory of the preliminary hearing that he had attended. Appellant argues that Officer Ehler's testimony at trial differed from his testimony at the preliminary hearing on the exact role of each of the defendants in the robbery. These variations were not "substantial" insofar as the alibi defense was concerned. There is no showing of likely impact on the trial result.

c. *Offer To Waive Jury Trial.* Appellant's effort to condemn defense counsel for the offer to waive jury trial is frivolous. Appellant was in fact tried by a jury. Moreover, as the District Court found, appellant himself demanded that his attorney offer to waive jury trial, and appellant persisted in this demand even after the court advised him of his constitutional rights and explained that the court had heard part of the evidence against him.

*   *   *

d. *Waiver of Opening Statement and Failure To See Sentence Properly Executed.* As the District Court found, there is no merit in the claims of ineffectiveness on the ground of waiver of opening statement and failure to see that appellant's sentence was properly executed. Waiver of an opening statement is a tactical decision. There was no effort to demonstrate that the waiver had, or was likely to have had, a substantial effect on the outcome. As to the sentencing issue, defense trial counsel had withdrawn from the case before the issue had arisen, an appeal had been taken, and appellate counsel had been appointed. And of course an omission would justify at most a reconsideration of sentence, not a reversal of the conviction.

F.   Conclusion

The several claims, both seriatim and in combination, do not raise in our minds serious misgivings as to whether justice was done. We certainly do not commend counsel's performance as ideal. Yet some of the complaints border on the frivolous. And ultimately there was a total failure of appellant to show that it was likely that counsel's deficiencies had any effect on the outcome of this trial. As the District Court found:

> While it may be that defense counsel herein was lax in his duty to conduct as thorough a factual investigation as possible, we find that counsel did raise the only defense available to him, which defense was putting the government to its proof.

In the absence of a governmental impediment to effective assistance of counsel, the court cannot lightly vacate a conviction on the basis of its own appraisal of the performance of defense counsel. The door is open, but only for cases of grievous deficiency and where the court has serious misgivings that justice has not been done. Our adversary system will be tortured out of shape if defense counsel must contemplate from the beginning that the judge will subsequently retrace his conversations with his client, and his evolving perceptions of the problems and possibilities presented by the assignment.

We support efforts to upgrade performance of defense trial counsel. We commend the programs of the last decade in clinical education for law students. We approve the American Bar Association's efforts to clarify the defense and prosecution functions. More should be done. But more is not better if it undercuts the adversary system.

So far as the present case is concerned, ultimately dispositive of the appeal are the strength of the government's case and failure of appellant to demonstrate a likelihood of effect on the outcome.

* * *

As Jan Deutsch has recently noted, it is often in the nature of a dissent to present a political statement.[8]

Judge Bazelon's characteristic eloquence destines his remarks to stand as an oft-quoted expression of aspirations for the legal system. In our view, that eloquence is not matched by tenable standards.

* * *

The judges of this court are emphatically not indifferent to the plight of the poor in the criminal justice system. Certainly there is need for the allocation of additional resources. Certainly there is need to cull out incompetent counsel or to call them to account. Responses are primarily required from the bodies that can supply resources—the legislature and the bar. Judge Bazelon's bold but single-valued approach would tolerate disruption of the administration of justice and a reordering of the adversary system, with little guarantee of improved performance and impassivity as to the uncharted and likely noxious consequences.

Our approach toward the minimum legal obligations of our democratic society to ward off injustice may be more earthbound, but in our view it is more salutary.

Affirmed.

MacKinnon, Circuit Judge, filed the following opinion which is joined by Circuit Judges Tamm and Robb:

* * *

It is hardly an exaggeration to say that under the arguments of the dissent, the [principle] issue in a criminal appeal is whether the accused is poor, rather than whether his guilt was properly determined in a fair trial. Thankfully, this Circuit has now definitively rejected that approach. Neither a rich man nor a poor man has a right to use perjured testimony in his defense. Neither a rich nor a

---

8. Deutsch, Law as Metaphor: A Structural Analysis of Legal Process, 66 Geo.L.J. 1339, 1342 (1978).

poor defendant has a right to compel his counsel to investigate perjured alibis. And no defendant, be he rich or poor, has a right to
have his conviction set aside because his lawyer did not investigate to
obtain witnesses who would support a phony defense.

* * *

While purporting to explore standards for defense counsel in
their representation of criminal defendants, *DeCoster I* was in fact a
bold attempt to shift the burden of proof to the Government. The intolerable results that inevitably follow from such a shift are well illustrated by the position taken by the panel below and the dissent
here.

We now repudiate this misguided attempt to change the law and
reaffirm the well established rule in this Circuit that the burden of
proving prejudice from defense counsel's ineffectiveness rests on the
accused. Counsel in this Circuit need not search for non-existent witnesses who might support perjured alibis conjured up by defendants
on the eve of trial.

Thus fails the attempt of my dissenting colleagues to create a
standard of law that would result in a retrial for an obviously guilty
defendant, supposedly because his lawyer's investigation of the crime
was not thorough enough, despite the defendant's failure to produce a
single witness who would testify to a single truthful exculpatory fact.

* * *

.   .   . It would be unthinkable for this court to reverse such a
conviction because defense counsel failed to investigate every possible
fabricated defense.

ROBINSON, CIRCUIT JUDGE, concurring in the result: I agree
with the majority of my brethren that the conviction in this case
should be affirmed. I am unable, however, to subscribe to one link in
the chain of reasoning they forge in reaching this result. While I applaud the collective action of the full court in now assuring to those
accused of crime a level of legal assistance commensurate with the demands of the Sixth Amendment, I deplore the court's allocation to the
accused of a burden of demonstrating that he was jeopardized by established dereliction of duty on the part of his counsel. Judges Leventhal and MacKinnon, and my colleagues concurring with them,
make prejudice to the defense—likely harm in the one instance and
actual injury in the other—an indispensable prerequisite to any finding of ineffective assistance, and assign the onus of proof on that
score to the defendant. In so holding they stray rather widely, I believe, from established principles of pertinent jurisprudence.

* * *

.   .   . In my view, the claimant before us needed only to show
that his counsel fell substantially short of the standard of reasonable
competence; in theirs, threatened or consummated injury therefrom
is an additional required part of the showing. I believe the majority
err in their approach and denude the constitutional right to effective

assistance of counsel of a great deal of the value it was intended to have.

* * *

I think, then, that in the area of pretrial investigation counsel's performance was substantially deficient and therefore constitutionally ineffective. But I believe, too, that in the circumstances counsel's inadequacies were harmless beyond a reasonable doubt. On that ground, I concur in affirmance of the conviction.

BAZELON, CIRCUIT JUDGE, with whom WRIGHT, CHIEF JUDGE, joins, dissenting: Willie Decoster was denied the effective assistance of counsel guaranteed by the Sixth Amendment because he could not afford to hire a competent and conscientious attorney. His plight is an indictment of our system of criminal justice, which promises "Equal Justice Under Law," but delivers only "Justice for Those Who Can Afford It." Though purporting to address the problem of ineffective assistance, the majority's decision ignores the sordid reality that the kind of slovenly, indifferent representation provided Willie Decoster is uniquely the fate allotted to the poor. Underlying the majority's antiseptic verbal formulations is a disturbing tolerance for a criminal justice system that consistently provides less protection and less dignity for the indigent. I cannot accept a system that conditions a defendant's right to a fair trial on his ability to pay for it. Like Justice Black, I believe that "[t]here can be no equal justice where the kind of trial a man gets depends on the amount of money he has." [1] The Constitution forbids it. Morality condemns it. I dissent.

I.

The evolution of the right to the Assistance of Counsel reflects a growing awareness of the barriers faced by the indigent defendant seeking a fair trial, and of the challenge these obstacles pose to our ideal of justice without regard to wealth. By any reckoning, the barriers are formidable. The "street crime" that clogs our courts is bred by poverty and discrimination. It is committed by the dispossessed, the disadvantaged and the alienated of our society—those who most need the advice of a trained advocate. In the words of Justice Sutherland:

> Even the intelligent and educated layman has small and sometimes no skill in the science of law. . . . He requires the guiding hand of counsel at every step in the proceedings against him. . . . If that be true of men of intelligence, how much more true is it of the ignorant and illiterate, or those of feeble intellect.[2]

1. Griffin v. Illinois, 351 U.S. 12, 19 (1956).

2. Powell v. Alabama, 287 U.S. 45, 69 (1932).

And the cruel irony, of course, is that the indigent are the very people who are least able to obtain competent representation. For the most part, "you get what you pay for" in legal representation.[3]

Only recently have we even recognized that the lack of effective counsel inevitably deprives the poor of the right to a fair trial. For a great many years, the shameful truth was that only the rich could obtain counsel, since only the rich could afford to pay counsel.

* * *

Inevitably there will be disparities in the quality of representation; some lawyers are simply more able or more conscientious than others. What offends the Constitution, however, is not merely that there are variations in the quality of representation, but that the burden of less effective advocacy falls almost exclusively on a single subclass of society—the poor. In constructing standards for assessing the ineffective assistance of counsel, we must therefore consider not only what measures are necessary to assure a fair trial in the case of any particular defendant. We also must structure our approach to eliminate the gross disparities of representation that make a mockery of our commitment to equal justice. We must institutionalize and enforce standards of attorney competence designed to assure adequate representation for *all* defendants.

Because my colleagues in the majority divorce their analysis from the economic and social reality underlying the problem of ineffective assistance of counsel, their decision leaves indigent defendants nothing more than an empty promise in place of the Sixth Amendment's commitment to adequate representation for all defendants, rich and poor. At best, the majority's approach might help to rectify a few cases of blatant injustice. But their standards do nothing to help raise the quality of representation provided the poor to a level anywhere approaching that of the more affluent. On the contrary, my colleagues condone callous, back-of-the-hand representation by dismissing the basic duties of competent lawyering as "aspirational."

3. Despite recent expressions of concern over lawyer incompetence, the problem is not simply that there are too few good attorneys, but that competent legal representation in the United States is grossly maldistributed. There is no dearth of competent counsel for the rich in our society. But no one can say that the same is true for the indigent. The inadequate representation received by the poor is universally recognized and is well documented by the numerous studies and commentary cited below. Nor is the problem of ineffective assistance limited to those who are technically "indigent" and are provided counsel by the court. Those who can scrape together a few dollars to hire their own attorney can retain an attorney who, for a modest fee, will generally provide "modest" services—plea negotiations and *pro forma* representation with little investigation, preparation or concern for their client's cause. Most indigent defendants, of course, must accept whomever the court appoints to represent them. And although the commitment and competence of court-appointed counsel has improved markedly over recent years, particularly with the development of public defender systems, its effectiveness is still handicapped by unmanageable caseloads, insufficient support services, inexperience in criminal trial practice, lack of independence from the judiciary that controls the appointments and fixes compensation, and inadequate levels of funding and fee schedules.

* * *

The majority thus provides no incentive or structure to improve the caliber of defense advocacy. By focusing exclusively on the consequences of counsel's dereliction, their approach encourages an attorney who believes that his client is guilty to "cut corners," with little risk that he will be held accountable for the inadequacies of his representation. The majority opinions may say, "we don't commend this," or "we don't approve of that," but their bottom line is *"Affirmed."*

In its holding, the majority turns its back on the evolution in this circuit of the standard for evaluating claims of ineffective assistance.[4] In the earliest cases, we approached the problem solely from a due process-fundamental fairness viewpoint, requiring a defendant seeking relief to show that the proceedings were a "farce and a mockery of justice." In Bruce v. United States, we reconsidered that standard. We explained that the "farce and mockery" requirement was not to be taken literally, but was meant only to demonstrate that in order to obtain relief the accused bears a heavy burden of showing that "there has been gross incompetence of counsel and that this has in effect blotted out the essence of a substantial defense. . . . ."

* * *

DeCoster I represented a major advance in this court's recognition of the realities of ineffective assistance. In that case, this court shifted the focus of judicial inquiry away from the prejudice to the defendant in any particular case and toward the task of articulating basic duties counsel owes his client. This approach, for the first time, gave content to what previously had been empty verbal formulations. Even more importantly, it recognized that the very lack of effective trial counsel might preclude a defendant from later establishing prejudice. Thus the court concluded that the only way to assure that every defendant receives a fair trial is to promulgate and enforce standards of adequate representation that apply across-the-board. Underlying *DeCoster I*, therefore, was a commitment to the basic principle that every defendant—rich or poor, innocent or guilty—is entitled to the reasonably competent assistance of an attorney acting as his diligent conscientious advocate.

---

4. Despite numerous opportunities, the Supreme Court has never directly confronted the fundamental question of the proper standards and procedures for evaluating challenges to the effectiveness of counsel. See Maryland v. Marzullo, 435 U.S. 1011 (1978) (White, J., with Rehnquist, J., dissenting from denial of certiorari). The Court has come closest to addressing the issue of ineffective assistance in the context of a prisoner's collateral attack on the voluntariness of his guilty plea. In McMann v. Richardson, 397 U.S. 759 (1970), for example, the Court stated that a petitioner seeking relief on that ground must demonstrate that the advice of counsel was not "within the range of competence demanded of attorneys in criminal cases." Accord, Tollett v. Henderson, 411 U.S. 258, 266 (1973). But the Court has yet to determine the minimum standard of attorney competence required by the Sixth Amendment's guarantee of effective assistance of counsel.

II.

*   *   *

[E]vents at the beginning of trial raised serious questions about the adequacy of counsel's pretrial preparation and communication with his client. As the trial was about to start, and after counsel had asserted that he was prepared to proceed, appellant himself stepped forward and asked if the court would subpoena his two codefendants, explaining that he "didn't have a chance" to discuss the matter with his lawyer. Defense counsel then told the court that he had considered the possibility of issuing subpoenas, "except for the fact that we have no address for the other defendants." The prosecutor immediately volunteered that codefendant Eley was in jail with Decoster; an address for Taylor was subsequently provided from the court records.[5] The court thereupon ordered defense counsel to "take care of the situation." [6]

Moments later, after defense counsel again announced that he was ready for trial, the prosecutor informed the court that the Government had not received any response to its alibi-notice demand. Defense Counsel replied that although he might rely on an alibi defense, no response was needed because the Government had not given the twenty days' notice required by the local rules. The trial judge ordered the defense to provide the names of alibi witnesses anyway, whereupon defense counsel relented and stated, "We will proceed without the alibi witnesses."

Defense counsel then informed the court that his client wished to waive jury trial. When asked if he was aware that the trial judge already had heard evidence concerning Decoster's case while presiding over the trial of his codefendants, counsel responded that he was not. After attempting unsuccessfully to find another judge who could hear the case at such a late date, the trial judge ruled that he could not hear the case himself but would instead preside over a jury trial. Appellant's case thereupon proceeded to trial before a jury.

In the midst of all this confusion, Decoster again complained to the court about his attorney's efforts on his behalf.

> The defendant: Your Honor, I feel that this case should be continued because this is, I can't get proper representation that I should be getting and too I think I should have an accurate statement of what happened here when the other two defendants was in court.

---

5. Taylor's address was found from a personal recognizance release form filed with the court 11 months earlier. This address proved to be out of date, however, and the belated effort to locate him was unsuccessful.

6. Despite the trial court's directive, counsel initially was willing to wait until "later in the day" to prepare the subpoenas. Only when the trial judge pointed out that the subpoenas could be processed during the trial preliminaries did counsel move to have them prepared. Even then, however, the subpoenas were not issued until after the first day of the two-day trial.

Defense counsel then requested to withdraw from the case "because apparently I have caused some dissatisfaction to the defendant. . . ." The district judge, however, did not inquire into the basis of the defendant's complaints. Instead, after receiving counsel's assurances that he had prepared the case and was ready to go to trial, the court denied the request for a continuance and refused to appoint new counsel.

In view of the foregoing, in our original opinion we remanded for supplementary hearings on the adequacy of trial counsel's representation and granted leave for appellate counsel to move for a new trial. At the hearings on remand, the district court elicited further information about trial counsel's preparation and his explanations for his actions. Counsel admitted that he had not interviewed the robbery victim or either of the police officers. He also admitted that he had made no attempt to contact or interview the hotel desk clerk, or, for that matter, anyone else at either the D.C. Annex hotel or the Golden Gate bar.

As for the codefendants, counsel conceded that he had not interviewed Taylor, but claimed that he had talked with Eley in the cellblock behind the courtroom on the second day of the trial. Counsel also admitted that he never obtained a transcript of the preliminary hearing, but stated that since he had conducted most of the cross-examination at that hearing, he saw no need for the transcript. Moreover, counsel testified that the U. S. Attorney's office usually makes a copy of the transcript available during discovery. Although he did not specifically remember Decoster's case, counsel said he assumed that the government's copy had been available and that he had read it.

In attempting to defend his actions, counsel testified that he had not interviewed any witnesses because, until shortly before trial, appellant had never mentioned any possible alibi witnesses. Counsel explained that, to the best of his recollection, Decoster had continuously maintained that he had joined Crump for a drink in the bar, had left him there, and had just returned to his hotel when he was arrested. Then, on the eve of trial, counsel received a letter in which appellant changed his story, alleged that he had fought with Crump but did not rob him, and asserted that his codefendants would support this version of the offense. Explaining why he had not interviewed Decoster's codefendants even after receiving this letter, counsel stated that "it was my feeling at that time that any testimony that might be given by either of these defendants might be contradictory to what I had already heard from the Defendant." Counsel claimed that he did interview Eley after appellant insisted at trial that his codefendants be subpoenaed, and that Eley told him that Decoster was not at the scene of the crime.[7] Believing that Eley would

---

7. Counsel was unaccompanied when he interviewed Eley and counsel obtained no written statement from Eley. In fact, counsel testified that he did not even take notes of the conference. Thus, we have only the conflicting testimony of defense counsel, Eley, and Decoster as to what occurred.

say this in court, counsel decided to put him on the stand, but Eley instead testified that he saw Decoster and Crump fighting outside the bar.[8]

Counsel also was asked at the remand hearing to explain the reasons underlying certain "tactical decisions" he had made. He could not recall why the motion for bond review was filed in the wrong court. . . . With respect to the waiver of jury trial, counsel said that although he opposed the idea, he had requested a bench trial at his client's insistence. Finally, counsel stated that he gave no opening statement because he had felt it to be unnecessary, and not because he had no defense theory at the time the trial started. However, counsel could not recall why he had concluded that an opening statement was unnecessary.

* * *

III.

The analysis of this case should be guided by the principles established in *DeCoster I*.[9] We there held that upon showing a substantial violation of any of counsel's specified duties, a defendant establishes that he has been denied effective representation and the burden shifts to the government to demonstrate that the violation did not prejudice the defendant. Thus, *DeCoster I* prescribed a three-step inquiry for determining whether a claim of ineffective assistance of counsel warrants reversing a conviction:

      (1) Did counsel violate one of the articulated duties?

      (2) Was the violation "substantial"?

      (3) Has the government established that no prejudice resulted?

The heart of this approach lies in defining ineffective assistance in terms of the *quality of counsel's performance* rather than looking to the effect of counsel's actions on the outcome of the case. If the

---

8. Ironically, counsel noted at the remand hearing that "[i]t's a cardinal rule with defense counsel that they never put on a witness unless they know what a witness is going to say and I would never have put on Eley unless I knew what he was going to say."

At trial, counsel made no effort to bring to the court's attention the apparent conflict between Eley's proposed and actual testimony. This failure suggests either that, contrary to counsel's claim in the remand hearing, counsel never obtained assurances from Eley as to his testimony, or that counsel negligently failed to impeach Eley's damaging testimony at trial.

9. 487 F.2d 1197 (1973). Although the division of this court in today's deci-

sion places our previous ruling in *DeCoster I* in question, a majority of the court today explicitly reaffirms the standard adopted in that opinion: a defendant is entitled to the reasonably competent assistance of an attorney acting as his diligent conscientious advocate. . . . Where today's decision departs from *DeCoster I* is in the consequences that are held to flow from counsel's violation of a duty to his client. Regardless of the future vitality of *DeCoster I* as precedent within this Circuit, however, I continue to believe that the principles and analysis in that opinion should govern our approach in this and other ineffectiveness claims.

Sixth Amendment is to serve a central role in eliminating second-class justice for the poor, then it must proscribe second-class performances by counsel, whatever the consequences in a particular case. Moreover, by focusing on the quality of representation and providing incentives in all cases for counsel to meet or exceed minimum standards, this approach reduces the likelihood that any particular defendant will be prejudiced by counsel's shortcomings. In this way, courts can safeguard the defendant's rights to a constitutionally adequate trial without engaging in the inherently difficult task of speculating about the precise effect of each error or omission by an attorney. Although the question of prejudice remains part of the court's inquiry, it is distinct from the determination of whether the defendant has received effective assistance. Rather, prejudice is considered only in order to spare defendants, prosecutors and the courts alike a truly futile repetition of the pretrial and trial process.

A. Violation of Articulated Duties

In *DeCoster I*, this court attempted to give substantive content to the Sixth Amendment's mandate by setting forth minimum requirements of competent performance.[10] The obligations were described as "duties owed by counsel to client," and thus were not offered as merely "aspirational" guidelines to which attorneys should strive. Indeed, the duties announced in *DeCoster I* represent the rudiments of competent lawyering guaranteed by the Sixth Amendment to every defendant in a criminal proceeding.

The duties set forth in *DeCoster I* were derived from the American Bar Association's Standards for the Defense Function. These ABA Standards summarize the consensus of the practicing Bar on the crucial elements of defense advocacy in our adversary system. . . . Naturally, given the complexities of each case and the constant call for professional discretion, it would be a misguided endeavor to engrave in stone any rules for attorney performance. Nonetheless, preserving flexibility is not incompatible with establishing mini-

---

10. *DeCoster I* articulated the following duties owed by counsel to a client:

In General. Counsel should be guided by the American Bar Association Standards for the Defense Function. . . .

Specifically. (1) Counsel should confer with his client without delay and as often as necessary to elicit matters of defense, or to ascertain that potential defenses are unavailable. Counsel should discuss fully potential strategies and tactical choices with his client.

(2) Counsel should promptly advise his client of his rights and take all actions necessary to preserve them.

. . . .

(3) Counsel must conduct appropriate investigations, both factual and legal, to determine what matters of defense can be developed. . . . [I]n most cases a defense attorney, or his agent, should interview not only his own witnesses but also those the the government intends to call, when they are accessible. The investigation should always include efforts to secure information in the possession of the prosecution and law enforcement authorities. And, of course, the duty to investigate also requires adequate legal research.

mum components of effective assistance, and the ABA Standards give helpful guidance in pursuing both aims.

* * *

Prominent among the duties of defense counsel is the obligation to "conduct appropriate investigations, both factual and legal, to determine what matter of defense can be developed." As the Commentary of the ABA Standards stresses, "[I]nvestigation and preparation are the keys to effective representation. . . . It is impossible to overemphasize the importance of appropriate investigation to the effective and fair administration of criminal justice."

Investigation is crucial for several reasons. First, the proper functioning of our adversary system demands that both sides prepare and organize their case in advance of trial. There can be no justice where one party to the battle has made no effort to arm itself with the pertinent facts and law. Second, in a very practical sense, cases are won on the facts. Proper investigation is critical not only in turning up leads and witnesses favorable to the defense, but in allowing counsel to take full advantage of trial tactics such as cross-examination and impeachment of adverse witnesses. And of course, adequate legal investigation is necessary to ensure that all available defenses are raised and that the government is put to its proof. "[I]t is axiomatic among trial lawyers and judges that cases are not won in the courtroom but by the long hours of laborious investigation and careful preparation and study of legal points which precede the trial."

Moreover, the necessity for exhaustive investigation is not limited to its value in preparation for trial. As a leading manual for defense lawyers emphasizes:

> "The *facts* are counsel's most important asset not only in arguing before a jury but in every other function counsel performs: seeking advantageous terms of bail, urging the prosecutor to drop or reduce charges, negotiating with him about a plea, urging a favorable sentence recommendation on a probation officer or sentencing disposition on a judge." [11]

At a minimum, the duty to investigate requires counsel (or his investigator) to contact persons whom he has or should have reason to believe were witnesses to the events in question, to seek witnesses in places where he has or should have reason to believe the events occurred, and to conduct these interviews and investigations as promptly as possible, before memories fade or witnesses disappear.

In the present case, Decoster's attorney did none of these things. Although the failure to interview a particular witness, by itself, may not rise to the level of inadequate assistance, defense counsel's investigation and preparation for this case was so perfunctory

---

11. A. Amsterdam, B. Segal & M. Miller, Trial Manual for the Defense of   Criminal Cases § 106 (3d ed. 1976) (emphasis added).

that it clearly violated his duties to his client.[12] The prosecution called three witnesses at trial—Roger Crump and Officers Box and Ehler. Despite the cardinal rule that proper investigation begins with interviews of those witnesses whom the government intends to call, particularly the arresting and investigating officers, defense counsel made no attempt to interview any of these witnesses at any time prior to trial. Nor did he request or obtain a transcript of the preliminary hearing where these witnesses testified.[13] Defense counsel did not even contact and interview Decoster's codefendants, Eley and Taylor, before trial. Nor did he seek or talk to any witnesses at the hotel or bar. In fact, defense counsel made absolutely no effort to discover, contact, or interview *a single witness* prior to trial. Apparently, he was willing to go to trial without having made any real effort to determine what could be elicited by way of defense or to evaluate the strengths and weaknesses of his client's case.

Moreover, defense counsel's violations of the duties owed to his client were not limited to an egregious failure to investigate. There are several indications that counsel did not "confer with his client . . . as often as necessary to elicit matters of defense, or to ascertain that potential defenses are unavailable." Surely, many of the problems that developed at and just prior to trial could have been eliminated had counsel more fully prepared himself and discussed the case with his client.[14] In addition, counsel was derelict in his duty to

* * *

"promptly advise his client of his rights and take all actions necessary to preserve them. . . . Finally, counsel's representation of his client at the sentencing hearing was anything but diligent and conscientious. Despite the critical need for effective advocacy at what "may well be the most important part of the entire proceeding,"

---

12. While the majority properly notes that the Constitution contains no mandate that counsel "leave not the smallest stone unturned, . . . " Decoster's attorney did not turn over even the largest boulder.

13. Despite the obvious value of a transcript of appellant's preliminary hearing for use in impeaching the prosecution's witnesses, counsel ignored his client's requests and did not even take the simple step of obtaining a copy. Yet, acquiring the ability to impeach government witnesses is particularly crucial when, as the district court here observed, "the only defense available . . . was putting the government to its proof."

. . .

14. Counsel's failure to investigate and confer with his client more frequently may have resulted from his inability to devote sufficient time to each of his cases. The records of the Administrative Office of the United States Courts reveal that in 1972, the year that Decoster went to trial, his attorney received payments under the Criminal Justice Act totalling $51,098.47 for handling 284 different cases—more than one case for every working day. This total, of course, does not include any criminal and civil cases that Decoster's attorney may have handled on a retained basis. Compare ABA Standards § 1.2(d) (2d ed. § 4–1.2(d)) ("A lawyer should not accept more employment than he can discharge within . . . the limits of his capacity to give each client effective representation.").

Unfortunately, many court-appointed counsel maintain unmanageable caseloads, in part because a high-volume business is required to compensate for low fee schedules under the CJA.

counsel's total contribution at appellant's hearing consisted of the following "allocution":

> If the Court please, Counsel is aware that Your Honor has a fully comprehensive a [sic] detailed probation report, and Counsel is aware of the report and would submit based on said report.

In sum, counsel violated each of the duties enunciated in *De-Coster I* as the prerequisites of a reasonably competent performance. Appellant's court-appointed attorney provided the kind of shoddy representation that none of us would tolerate for ourselves—a slovenly, slipshod job, almost totally lacking in preparation, characterized by repeated failures to protect his client's rights and an obvious indifference to his client's fate.

B. "Substantial" Violations

Contrary to the intimations of the majority, we do not contend that the slightest departure from a checklist of counsel's duties establishes ineffectiveness and requires reversal. Since counsel's decisions must be adapted to the complexities of a given case, the proper performance of an attorney's obligations necessarily entails considerable discretion. Moreover, the human animal is too fallible and the task of defense counsel too complex to expect that every action taken by an attorney will prove correct on hindsight. We have repeatedly cautioned that "[t]his court does not sit to second guess strategic and tactical choices made by defense counsel." The Sixth Amendment demands that counsel's conduct be conscientious, reasonable, and informed by adequate investigation and preparation; it does not demand that counsel's performance be flawless.

* * *

In this case, the frequency and pervasiveness of defense counsel's omissions and failures certainly belie any notion that these actions were isolated and excusable events. The violation in this case was not simply that counsel failed to interview certain named witnesses. The record reveals that counsel conducted almost no investigation whatsoever in the 17 months preceeding trial. Consequently, he began trial unaware of what the prosecution witnesses would say and as a result was unable to refute their stories, was ignorant of the possible defenses and witnesses he might present, and was even unsure of his own client's version of the events.

Nor do any special circumstances justify counsel's breach of his obligations. In some cases prudential judgments or tactical considerations may be involved in counsel's decision about whom to interview. In the present case, however, there simply is no possible justification for counsel's near-total lack of investigation and preparation.

* * *

In the end, the majority's conclusion that appellant was not denied the effective assistance of counsel rests on their perception that the record contains overwhelming evidence of appellant's guilt.

.   .   .   The logic of their position seems to be as follows: If the accused was probably guilty, then nothing helpful could have been found even through a properly conducted investigation.   Thus, any violation of that duty—no matter how egregious—was inconsequential and hence excusable.

Even on its own terms, such reasoning is faulty.   It assumes that the value of investigation is measured only by information it yields that will exonerate the defendant.   Yet, even if an investigation produces not a scintilla of evidence favorable to the defense—an unlikely hypothesis—appellant still will benefit from a full investigation.   One of the essential responsibilities of the defense attorney is to conduct an independent examination of the law and facts so that he can offer his professional evaluation of the strength of the defendant's case.[15]   If this full investigation reveals that a plea of guilty is in the defendant's best interests, then the attorney should so advise his client and explore the possibility of initiating plea discussions with the prosecutor.[16]   It is no secret that in the majority of criminal prosecutions the accused is in fact guilty, notwithstanding any initial protestations of innocence.   It is also no secret that the vast majority of criminal prosecutions culminating in conviction are settled through plea bargaining.   .   .   .   In many cases   therefore, perhaps the most valuable function that defense counsel can perform is to advise the defendant candidly that a thorough investigation—conducted by his own representative and seeking any glimmer of exonerating evidence—has turned up empty.   Only then can the defendant truly evaluate his position and make an informed decision whether to plead guilty or whether to continue to assert his innocence at trial.

More importantly, the majority's position confuses the defendant's burden of showing that counsel's violation was "substantial" with the government's burden of proving that the violation was not "prejudicial."   The former entails a forward-looking inquiry into whether defense counsel acted in the manner of a diligent and competent attorney; it asks whether, at the time the events occurred, defense counsel's violations of the duties owed to his client were justifiable.   In contrast, the inquiry into "prejudice" requires an after-the-fact determination of whether a violation that was admittedly "substantial," nevertheless did not produce adverse consequences for the defendant.

All that the accused must show to establish a Sixth Amendment violation is that counsel's acts or omissions were substantial enough

---

15.   "Prior to trial an accused is entitled to rely upon his counsel to make an independent examination of the facts, circumstances, pleadings and laws involved and then to offer his informed opinion as to what plea should be entered."   Von Moltke v. Gillies, 332 U.S. 708, 721 (1948).   See ABA Standards § 5.1(a) (2d ed. § 4-5.1(b)) ("After informing himself fully on the facts and the law, the lawyer should advise the accused with complete candor concerning all aspects of the case, including his candid estimate of the probable outcome.").

16.   See ABA Standards § 6.1(b) (2d ed. § 4-6.1(b)) (Duty to Explore Disposition Without Trial).

to have deprived him of the effective assistance of counsel in his defense. He need not prove that counsel's violations were ultimately harmful in affecting the outcome of his trial. Quite simply, the inquiry into the adequacy of counsel is distinct *from the inquiry into guilt or innocence*. The Constitution entitles every defendant to counsel who is "an active advocate in behalf of his client." Where such advocacy is absent, the accused has been denied effective assistance, regardless of his guilt or innocence. The majority opinions nevertheless force the appellant to shoulder the burden of proving that counsel's acts or omissions actually or likely affected the outcome of the trial. To thus condition the right to effective assistance of counsel on the defendant's ability to demonstrate his innocence is to assure that only the constitutional rights of the innocent will be vindicated. Our system of criminal justice does not rest on such a foundation.

* * *

C. Was the Substantial Violation Prejudicial?

Having determined in this case that counsel's violation of his duty to his client was substantial, and that appellant consequently was denied the effective assistance of counsel, we now must consider whether this violation of the Sixth Amendment mandates reversing appellant's conviction.

* * *

It may be that the prejudice to the defendant from the denial of effective assistance of counsel is so great, and the likelihood that the government can prove lack of prejudice so small, that reversal should be required whenever a substantial violation of counsel's duties is shown. Indeed, the Supreme Court has frequently emphasized that "the assistance of counsel is among those 'constitutional rights so basic to a fair trial that their infraction can never be treated as harmless error.'" And it may be that only a rule requiring automatic reversal can provide the deterrent effect necessary to insure that all defendants—innocent or guilty—receive the effective assistance of counsel.

Nevertheless, there may be cases—however few—in which the reviewing court can isolate specific deficiencies in counsel's performance and can accurately gauge the consequences of counsel's acts or omissions.

* * *

On the record before us in the present case, I would conclude that the government has failed to discharge its burden of proving that no adverse consequences resulted from counsel's gross violations of his duties to his client. Several important questions on the matter of prejudice remain unanswered, and in the absence of any evidence on these critical issues, I am unable to find that counsel's violations were "so unimportant and insignificant" that reversing appellant's conviction would be a futile exercise. No inquiry was made, for example, on the relationship between counsel's failure to investigate and Decoster's decision to go to trial rather than to seek and possibly accept a plea bargain comparable to that of his codefendants. Nor was there exploration of whether counsel's failure to offer any allocution at the sentencing hearing had any bearing on the trial judge's decision to sentence Decoster to a prison term of 2–8 years while his codefendants received only probation.

In *DeCoster I*, the court expressly stated that reversal would be required, "unless the government, '*on which is cast the burden of proof once a violation of these precepts is shown*, can establish lack of prejudice thereby.' " Thus, any doubts about the harmlessness of counsel's violations in this case would ordinarily be resolved against the government, and the case would be reversed and remanded for a new trial. Yet, despite our prior remand, it is not clear that the government was ever required to satisfy its burden of proving that the denial of Decoster's right to the effective assistance of counsel was harmless beyond a reasonable doubt. In ruling on several of appellant's contentions, the district court found that counsel had not violated any duty owed to his client. As to these issues, therefore, the question of the prejudicial effect of counsel's conduct was never reached. On several other allegations, the district judge appears to have required appellant to demonstrate that he was prejudiced by counsel's actions in order to establish a constitutional violation. Thus, the government was not put to its proof in establishing harmlessness. Moreover, the initial remand hearing was conducted without benefit of this opinion's elucidation of the principles set forth in *DeCoster I* governing questions of ineffective assistance. I therefore would remand the case to allow the government an opportunity to satisfy its burden of proving harmlessness.

IV.

Of course, even reversing Decoster's conviction would not remedy the pervasive problem of ineffective representation of the indigent. The disparity between representation of the poor and of the well-to-do reflects the larger inequality of riches in our affluent society. The imbalance in the quality of legal assistance provided for the indigent and the wealthy is only one of a host of inequities in our society—inequality of educational opportunity, of jobs, of housing, of health care.

It is not the province of the judiciary to remedy all these inequities. We have neither the means nor the competence to redress all of society's imbalances. We however do have the duty, entrusted to us by the Bill of Rights, to assure that no individual is deprived of liberty by our courts of law without a constitutionally adequate trial. We violate this duty when we place our imprimatur of "Equal Justice Under Law" on the incompetent performance of court-appointed counsel in cases like the one before us.[17]

17. Perhaps some view the goal of equal justice as "utopian" and feel that society's unwillingness to expend the considerable resources required to improve the quality of representa-tion for the poor will doom to failure any efforts in this regard. Perhaps they believe that courts should not promise equality if it cannot be delivered. I cannot agree that the prom-

An appellate court's role is limited. We can promulgate standards that specify the minimum requirements of the constitutionally mandated competent performance. We can closely scrutinize the records of those cases in which effectiveness is at issue, carefully monitoring trial counsel's performance to ensure that the attorney's obligation have been fulfilled. When substantial violations are uncovered, we can enforce the Sixth Amendment's guarantee by vacating the defendant's conviction and remanding for a new trial in which the effective assistance of counsel will be provided.

*   *   *

However vigilant the judge, the problem of inadequate representation of the indigent cannot be solved by the courts alone. The bench, bar and public must jointly renew our commitment to equal justice. The bar certainly must increase its efforts to monitor the performances of its members and to take appropriate disciplinary action against those attorneys who fail to fulfill their obligations to their clients. Additional funding is needed to increase the number of public defender positions and to provide those organizations with better support services. We must increase the compensation of court-appointed counsel to attract high-quality legal talent and to ensure that those who represent the indigent on a regular basis do not have to sacrifice all economic security to perform this vital role. We must reduce the caseloads of both public defenders and court-appointed counsel to manageable levels. And we must establish procedures to insulate appointed counsel from the pressure to curry favor with the judges who appoint them and fix their compensation.

That the ultimate solution does not lie exclusively within the province of the courts does not justify our ignoring the situation nor our accepting it as immutable. The people have bestowed upon the courts a trust: to ensure that the awesome power of the State is not invoked against anyone charged with a crime unless that individual has been afforded all the rights guaranteed by the Constitution. We fail that trust if we sit by silently while countless indigent defendants continue to be deprived of liberty without the effective assistance of counsel.

WRIGHT, CHIEF JUDGE, joined by BAZELON and ROBINSON, CIRCUIT JUDGES: I write only to note that while there is no majority opinion of the court, Judges Bazelon and Robinson and I agree on the two fundamental principles dispositive of this case: (1) The constitutional standard of effective assistance of counsel in a criminal case is the reasonably competent assistance of an attorney acting as the defendant's diligent, conscientious advocate; and (2) where that standard is

ise of equal justice for all is impossible to attain. And I do not believe that the difficulty of attaining that goal justifies stopping short of the mark. Some of my colleagues would relegate fundamental rights to mere "aspirations." Aspirations provide little comfort to those, like the poor, who are powerless to fulfill them. Not just "earthbound," but shackled to an approach that has failed in the past, some of my colleagues find it "salutary" to pursue a course that cannot provide "Equal Justice Under Law."

shown by the defendant not to have been satisfied, the defendant has been denied his constitutional right to counsel and his conviction must be reversed unless the Government proves beyond a reasonable doubt that the ineffective assistance of counsel was harmless. Chapman v. California, 386 U.S. 18 (1967).

NOTES

1. Should the defendant's guilt have any bearing on the question of whether he was effectively represented? What role should the organized bar play in assuring effective assistance of counsel? As DeCoster's counsel, what might you have done differently? How might that have affected the result?

2. Judge Bazelon's dissenting opinion was the culmination of his views on an issue which he has addressed often. See Bazelon, The Realities of Gideon and Argersinger, 64 Geo.L.J. 811 (1976); Bazelon, The Defective Assistance of Counsel, 42 U.Cinn.L.Rev. 1 (1973).

3. See generally Finer, Ineffective Assistance of Counsel, 58 Cornell L.Rev. 1077 (1973); Waltz, Inadequacy of Trial Defense Representation as a Ground for Post-Conviction Relief in Criminal Cases, 59 Nev.L.Rev. 289 (1964).

4. Should the issue of effective assistance of counsel, as commonly happens today, be decided on direct review of a conviction. Would not a post-conviction petition filed in the trial court present a better avenue for reviewing the issue, at least initially? Should the lawyer who is accused of incompetency be given an opportunity to explain his actions? Consider the following hypothetical based upon an actual occurrence. The appellate record reflected that in voir dire examination defense counsel, presumably to lessen the impact, gave jurors advance knowledge that after the accused had testified, the prosecution would be allowed to prove that the defendant had previously been convicted of armed robbery. However, the defendant did not testify, so that the prosecution was not allowed to introduce the "provable" conviction for impeachment purposes. But for the defense lawyer's statements in voir dire the jury never would have known that the accused armed robber had previously been convicted of the same crime. On this record what judgments would you make about the lawyer's competence? Would your view change if you had before you the testimony of the defense lawyer in a post-conviction proceeding to this effect: Although the client had repeatedly been admonished to tell his lawyer the truth before trial, only mid-trial did the client tell the lawyer that he was guilty and that his alibi was fabricated. At that point the lawyer and client agreed that the client would not testify. What would you have done if you were the lawyer? After sentencing would you have explained for the record what had happened? Does a lawyer have a right to protect himself against a charge of incompetency at the risk of diminishing his client's chances on appeal? How would it look to an appellate court if the last statement by defense counsel in the trial court was that the client had privately admitted his guilt to the lawyer? Would ethical principles permit such a disclosure *before* the client has accused the lawyer of incompetency?

4. CONFLICTS OF INTEREST

HOLLOWAY v. ARKANSAS

Supreme Court of the United States, 1978.
435 U.S. 475, 98 S.Ct. 1173.

MR. CHIEF JUSTICE BURGER delivered the opinion of the Court.

Petitioners, codefendants at trial, made timely motions for appointment of separate counsel, based on the representations of their appointed counsel that, because of confidential information received from the codefendants, he was confronted with the risk of representing conflicting interests and could not, therefore, provide effective assistance for each client. We granted certiorari to decide whether petitioners were deprived of the effective assistance of counsel by the denial of those motions.   .   .   .

I.

[Harold Hall, a public defender, was appointed to represent three defendants charged with robbery and rape. Twice prior to trial, Hall moved to have separate counsel appointed because the confidential communications which he had received from individual defendants indicated that a conflict of interest may arise if the defendants elected to testify]

*   *   *

On the second day of trial, after the prosecution had rested its case, Hall advised the court that, against his recommendation, all three defendants had decided to testify. He then stated:

> "Now, since I have been appointed, I had previously filed a motion asking the Court to appoint a separate attorney for each defendant because of a possible conflict of interest. This conflict will probably be now coming up since each one of them wants to testify.

> "THE COURT: That's all right; let them testify. There is no conflict of interest. Every time I try more than one person is this court each one blames it on the other one.

> "MR. HALL: I have talked to each one of these defendants, and I have talked to them individually, not collectively.

> "THE COURT: Now talk to them collectively."

The court then indicated satisfaction that each petitioner understood the nature and consequences of his right to testify on his own behalf, whereupon Hall observed:

> "I am in a position now where I am more or less muzzled as to any cross-examination.

"THE COURT: You have no right to cross-examine your own witness.

"MR. HALL: Or to examine them.

"THE COURT: You have a right to examine them, but have no right to cross-examine them. The prosecuting attorney does that.

"MR. HALL: If one [defendant] takes the stand, somebody needs to protect the other two's interest while that one is testifying, and I can't do that since I have talked to each one individually.

"THE COURT: Well, you have talked to them, I assume, individually and collectively, too. They all say they want to testify. I think it's perfectly alright for them to testify if they want to, or not. It's their business.

* * *

"Each defendant said he wants to testify, and there will be no cross-examination of these witnesses, just a direct examination by you.

"MR. HALL: Your Honor, I can't even put them on direct examination because if I ask them—

"THE COURT: (interposing) You can just put them on the stand and tell the Court that you have advised them of their rights and they want to testify;   then you tell the man to go ahead and relate what he wants to. That's all you need to do." [1]

Holloway then took the stand on his own behalf, testifying that during the time described as the time of the robbery he was at his brother's home. His brother had previously given similar testimony. When Welch took the witness stand, the record shows Hall advised him, as he had Holloway, that "I cannot ask you any questions that might tend to incriminate any one of the three of you . . .. Now, the only thing I can say is tell these ladies and gentlemen of the jury what you know about this case . . .." Welch responded that he did not "have any kind of speech ready for the jury or anything. I thought I was going to be questioned." When Welch denied, from the witness stand, that he was at the restaurant the night of the robbery, Holloway interrupted, asking:

"Your Honor, are we allowed to make an objection?

"THE COURT: No, sir. Your counsel will take care of any objections.

---

1. The record reveals that both the trial court and defense counsel were alert to defense counsel's obligation to avoid assisting in the presentation of what counsel had reason to believe was false testimony, or, at least, testimony contrary to the version of facts given to him earlier and in confidence. Cf. ABA, Standards Relating to the Administration of Criminal Justice—The Defense Function § 7.-7(c), at 133 (1974).

"MR. HALL: Your Honor, that is what I am trying to say. I can't cross-examine them.

"THE COURT: You proceed like I tell you to, Mr. Hall. You have no right to cross-examine your own witnesses anyhow."

Welch proceeded with his unguided direct testimony, denying any involvement in the crime and stating that he was at his home at the time it occurred. Campbell gave similar testimony when he took the stand. He also denied making any confession to the arresting officers.

The jury rejected the versions of events presented by the three defendants and the alibi witness, and returned guilty verdicts on all counts.

* * *

II.

More than 35 years ago, in Glasser v. United States, 315 U.S. 60, 62 S.Ct. 457 (1942), this Court held that by requiring an attorney to represent two codefendants whose interests were in conflict the District Court had denied one of the defendants his Sixth Amendment right to the effective assistance of counsel.

* * *

One principle applicable here emerges from *Glasser* without ambiguity. Requiring or permitting a single attorney to represent codefendants, often referred to as joint representation, is not *per se* violative of constitutional guarantees of effective assistance of counsel. This principle recognizes that in some cases multiple defendants can appropriately be represented by one attorney; indeed, in some cases, certain advantages might accrue from joint representation. In Mr. Justice Frankfurter's view: "Joint representation is a means of insuring against reciprocal recrimination. A common defense often gives strength against a common attack." Glasser v. United States, supra, 315 U.S., at 92, 62 S.Ct., at 475 (dissenting).[2]

* * *

Here trial counsel, by the pretrial motions . . . and by his accompanying representations, made as an officer of the court, focused explicitly on the probable risk of a conflict of interests. The judge then failed either to appoint separate counsel or to take adequate steps to ascertain whether the risk was too remote to warrant separate counsel. We hold that the failure, in the face of the representations made by counsel weeks before trial and again before the jury was empanelled, deprived petitioners of the guarantee of "assistance of counsel."

---

2. By inquiring in *Glasser* whether there had been a waiver, the Court also confirmed that a defendant may waive his right to the assistance of an attorney unhindered by a conflict of interests. 315 U.S., at 70, 62 S.Ct., at 464. In this case, however, Arkansas does not contend that petitioners waived that right.

This conclusion is supported by the Court's reasoning in *Glasser*:

"Upon the trial judge rests the duty of seeing that the trial is conducted with solicitude for the essential rights of the accused. . . . The trial court should protect the right of an accused to have the assistance of counsel. . . .

* * *

"Of equal importance with the duty of the court to see that an accused has the assistance of counsel is its duty to refrain from embarrassing counsel in the defense of an accused *by insisting, or indeed, even suggesting, that counsel undertake to concurrently represent interests which might diverge from those of his first client, when the possibility of that divergence is brought home to the court.*" (Emphasis added).

This reasoning has direct applicability in this case where the "possibility of [petitioners'] inconsistent interests" were "brought home to the court" by formal objections, motions, and defense counsel's representations.

* * *

Additionally, since the decision in *Glasser*, most courts have held that an attorney's request for the appointment of separate counsel, based on his representations as an officer of the court regarding a conflict of interests, should be granted. . . . In so holding, the courts have acknowledged and given effect to several interrelated considerations. An "attorney representing two defendants in a criminal matter is in the best position professionally and ethically to determine when a conflict of interest exists or will probably develop in the course of a trial." Second, defense attorneys have the obligation, upon discovering a conflict of interests, to advise the court at once of the problem.[3] Finally, attorneys are officers of the court, and "'when they address the judge solemnly upon a matter before the court, their declarations are virtually made under oath.'" We find these considerations persuasive.

The State argues, however, that to credit Hall's representations to the trial court would be tantamount to transferring to defense counsel the authority of the trial judge to rule on the existence or

---

3. The American Bar Association in its Standards Relating to the Administration of Criminal Justice—The Defense Function § 3.5(b), at 123 (1974) cautions:

"Except for preliminary matters such as initial hearings or applications for bail, a lawyer or lawyers who are associated in practice should not undertake to defend more than one defendant in the same criminal case if the duty to one of the defendants may conflict with the duty to another. The potential for conflict of interest in representing multiple defendants is so grave that ordinarily a lawyer should decline to act for more than one of several co-defendants except in unusual situations when, after careful investigation, it is clear that no conflict is likely to develop and when the several defendants give an informed consent to such multiple representation."

risk of a conflict and to appoint separate counsel. In the State's view, the ultimate decision on those matters must remain with the trial judge; otherwise unscrupulous defense attorneys might abuse their "authority," presumably for purposes of delay or obstruction of the orderly conduct of the trial.[4]

The State has an obvious interest in avoiding such abuses. But our holding does not undermine that interest. When an untimely motion for separate counsel is made for dilatory purposes, our holding does not impair the trial court's ability to deal with counsel who resort to such tactics. .   .   .   Nor does our holding preclude a trial court from exploring the adequacy of the basis of defense counsel's representations regarding a conflict of interests without improperly requiring disclosure of the confidential communications of the client.[5] In this case the trial court simply failed to take adequate steps in response to the repeated motions, objections and representations made to it, and no prospect of dilatory practices was present to justify that failure.

III.

The issue remains whether the error committed at petitioners' trial requires reversal of their convictions. It has generally been assumed that *Glasser* requires reversal, even in the absence of a showing of specific prejudice to the complaining codefendant, whenever a trial court improperly permits or requires joint presentation. .   .   .   Some courts and commentators have argued, however, that appellate courts should not reverse automatically in such cases but rather should affirm unless the defendant can demonstrate prejudice. .   .   .   This argument rests on two aspects of the Court's decision in *Glasser*. First, although it had concluded that Stewart was forced to represent conflicting interests, the Court did *not* reverse the conviction of Kretske, Stewart's other client, because Kretske failed to "show that the denial of Glasser's consitutional rights *prejudiced* [him] in some manner." (Emphasis added). Second, the Court justified the reversal of Glasser's conviction, in part, by emphasizing the weakness of the Government's evidence against him; with guilt a close question, "error, which under some circumstances *would not be ground for reversal,* cannot be brushed aside as immaterial, since there is a real chance that it might have provided the slight impetus which swung the scales toward guilt." (Emphasis added). Assessing the strength of the prosecution's evidence against the defendant

---

4. Such risks are undoubtedly present; they are inherent in the adversary system. But courts have abundant power to deal with attorneys who misrepresent facts.

5. This case does not require an inquiry into the extent of a court's power to compel an attorney to disclose confidential communications that he concludes would be damaging to his client. Cf. ABA, Code of Professional Responsibility, DR 4–101(C)(2). Such compelled disclosure creates significant risks of unfair prejudice, especially when the disclosure is to a judge who may be called upon later to select sentences for the attorney's clients.

is, of course, one step in applying a harmless error standard.
. . .

We read the Court's opinion in *Glasser*, however, as holding that whenever a trial court improperly requires joint representation over timely objection reversal is automatic. The *Glasser* Court stated:

> "To determine the precise degree of prejudice sustained by Glasser as a result of the [District] Court's appointment of Stewart as counsel for Kretske is at once difficult and unnecessary. The right to have the assistance of counsel is too fundamental and absolute to allow courts to indulge in nice calculations as to the amount of prejudice arising from its denial. . . ."

This language presupposes that the joint representation, over his express objections, prejudiced the accused in some degree. But from the cases cited it is clear that the prejudice is presumed regardless of whether it was independently shown.

* * *

. . . The Court's refusal to reverse Kretske's conviction is not contrary to this interpretation of *Glasser*. Kretske did *not* raise his own Sixth Amendment challenge to the joint representation. As the Court's opinion indicates, some of the codefendants argued that the denial of Glasser's right to the effective assistance of counsel prejudiced them as alleged coconspirators. In that context, the Court required a showing of prejudice; finding none, it affirmed the convictions of the codefendants, including Kretske.

Moreover, this Court has concluded that the assistance of counsel is among those "constitutional rights so basic to a fair trial that their infraction can never be treated as harmless error." . . . Accordingly, when a defendant is deprived of the presence and assistance of his attorney, either throughout the prosecution or during a critical stage in, at least, the prosecution of a capital offense, reversal is automatic. . . .

That an attorney representing multiple defendants with conflicting interests is physically present at pretrial proceedings, during trial, and at sentencing does not warrant departure from this general rule. Joint representation of conflicting interests is suspect because of what it tends to prevent the attorney from doing. For example, in this case it may well have precluded defense counsel for [one defendant] from exploring possible plea negotiations and the possibility of an agreement to testify for the prosecution, provided a lesser charge or a favorable sentencing recommendation would be acceptable. Generally speaking, a conflict may also prevent an attorney from challenging the admission of evidence prejudicial to one client but perhaps favorable to another, or from arguing at the sentencing hearing the relative involvement and culpability of his clients in order to minimize the culpability of one by emphasizing that of another. Examples can be readily multiplied. The mere physical presence of an attorney does not fulfill the Sixth Amendment guarantee when the advocate's conflicting obligations has effectively sealed his lips on crucial matters.

Finally, a rule requiring a defendant to show that a conflict of interests—which he and his counsel tried to avoid by timely objections to the joint representation—prejudiced him in some specific fashion would not be susceptible to intelligent, evenhanded application. In the normal case where a harmless error rule is applied, the error occurs at trial and its scope is readily identifiable. Accordingly, the reviewing court can undertake with some confidence its relatively narrow task of assessing the likelihood that the error materially affected the deliberations of the jury. . . . But in a case of joint representation of conflicting interests the evil—it bears repeating—is in what the advocate finds himself compelled to *refrain* from doing, not only at trial but also as to possible pretrial plea negotiations and in the sentencing process. It may be possible in some cases to identify from the record the prejudice resulting from an attorney's failure to undertake certain trial tasks, but even with a record of the sentencing hearing available it would be difficult to judge intelligently the impact of a conflict on the attorney's representation of a client. And to assess the impact of a conflict of interests on the attorney's options, tactics and decisions in plea negotiations would be virtually impossible. Thus, an inquiry into a claim of harmless error here would require, unlike most cases, unguided speculation.

Accordingly, we reverse and remand for further proceedings not inconsistent with this opinion.

Mr. Justice Powell with whom Mr. Justice Blackmun and Mr. Justice Rehnquist join, dissenting.

While disavowing a *per se* rule of separate representation, the Court holds today that the trial judge's failure in this case "either to appoint separate counsel or take adequate steps to ascertain whether the risk was too remote to warrant separate counsel" worked a violation of the guarantee of "assistance of counsel" embodied in the Sixth and Fourteenth Amendments.

* * *

. . . Because I cannot agree that, in the particular circumstances of this case, the court's failure to inquire requires reversal of petitioners' convictions and because the Court's opinion contains seeds of a *per se* rule of separate representation merely upon the demand of defense counsel, I respectfully dissent.

I.

* * *

The Court's approach in this case is not premised on an ultimate finding of conflict of interest or ineffective assistance of counsel. Rather, it presumes prejudice from the failure to conduct an inquiry, equating that failure with a violation of the Sixth Amendment guarantee. The justification for this approach appears to be the difficulty of a *post-hoc* reconstruction of the record to determine whether a different outcome, or even a different defense strategy, might have obtained had the trial court engaged in the requisite inquiry and ordered separate representation. Although such difficulty may be taken into account in the allocation of the burden of persuasion on the questions of conflict and prejudice, I am not convinced of the need for a prophylactic gloss on the requirements of the Constitution in this area of criminal law. . . .

Several other aspects of the Court opinion suggest a rule of separate representation upon demand of defense counsel. The Court leaves little room for maneuver for a trial judge who seeks to inquire into the substantiality of the defense counsel's representations. Apparently, the trial judge must order separate representation unless the asserted risk of conflict "was too remote to warrant separate counsel," a formulation that suggests a minimal showing on the part of defense counsel. The Court also offers the view that defense counsel in this case could not be expected to make the kind of specific proffer that was present in *Glasser* because of "a risk of violating, by more disclosure, his duty of confidentiality to his clients." Although concededly not necessary to a decision in this case, the Court then states that the trial court's inquiry must be conducted "without improperly requiring disclosure of the confidential communications of the client." When these intimations are coupled with the Court's policy of automatic reversal, the path may have been cleared for potentially disruptive demands for separate counsel predicated solely on the representations of defense counsel.

II.

Recognition of the limits of this Court's role in adding protective layers to the requirements of the Constitution does not detract from the Sixth Amendment obligation to provide separate counsel upon a showing of reasonable probability of need. In my view, a proper accommodation of the interests of defendants in securing effective assistance of counsel and that of the State in avoiding the delay, potential for disruption and costs inherent in the appointment of multiple counsel,[1] can be achieved by means which sweep less broadly than the approach taken by the Court. I would follow the lead of the several Courts of Appeals that have recognized the trial court's duty of inquiry in joint representation cases without minimizing the constitutional predicate of "conflicting interests."

Ordinarily defense counsel has the obligation to raise objections to joint representation as early as possible before the commencement

---

1. Each addition of a lawyer in the trial of multiple defendants presents increased opportunities for delay in setting the trial date, in disposing of pretrial motions, in selecting the jury, and in the conduct of the trial itself. Additional lawyers also may tend to enhance the possibility of trial errors. Moreover, in light of professional canons of ethics, cf. ABA, Code of Professional Responsibility, DR 5-105(D), . . . a rule requiring separate counsel virtually upon demand may disrupt the operation of public defender offices.

of the trial.[2] When such a motion is made, supported by a satisfactory proffer, the trial court is under a duty to conduct "the most careful inquiry to satisfy itself that no conflict of interest would be likely to result and that the parties involved had no valid objection." At that hearing, the burden is on defense counsel, because his clients are in possession of the relevant facts, to make a showing of a reasonable likelihood of conflict or prejudice. Upon such a showing, separate counsel should be appointed. "If the court has carried out this duty of inquiry, then to the extent a defendant later attacks his conviction on grounds of conflict of interest arising from joint representation he will bear a heavy burden indeed of persuading" the reviewing court "that he was, for that reason, deprived of a fair trial." If, however, a proper and timely motion is made, and no hearing is held, "the lack of satisfactory judicial inquiry shifts the burden of proof on the question of prejudice to the Government."

Since the trial judge in this case failed to inquire into the substantiality of defense counsel's representations, . . . the burden shifted to the State to establish the improbability of conflict or prejudice. I agree that the State's burden is not met simply by the assertion that the defenses of petitioners were not mutually inconsistent, for that is not an infrequent consequence of improper joint representation. Nevertheless, the record must offer some basis for a reasonable inference that "conflicting interests" hampered a potentially effective defense. Because the State has demonstrated that such a basis cannot be found in the record of this case,[3] I would affirm the judgment of the Supreme Court of Arkansas.

NOTES

1. What is the trial judge's role in determining whether a conflict of interest will work to a defendant's detriment? See ABA, Standards Relating to the Administration of Criminal Justice—The Function of the Trial Judge § 3.4(b), at 171 (1974):

> "Whenever two or more defendants who have been jointly charged, or whose cases have been consolidated, are represented by the same attorney, the trial judge should inquire into potential conflicts which may jeopardize the right of each defendant to the fidelity of his counsel."

2. Since a proper, timely objection was interposed in this case, there is no occasion to identify the circumstances which might trigger a duty of inquiry in the absence of such a motion.

Of course, a later motion may be appropriate if the conflict is not known or does not become apparent before trial proceeds. To guard against strategic disruption of the trial, however, the court may require a substantial showing of justification for such midtrial motions.

3. It is unlikely that separate counsel would have been able to develop an independent defense in this case because of the degree of overlap in the identification testimony by the State's witnesses and because of the consistency of the alibis advanced by petitioners. . . . Moreover, petitioners do not argue in this Court that joint representation impeded effective cross-examination of the State's witnesses. In sum, this is not a case where an inquiry into the possibility of "conflicting interests" reasonably might have revealed a basis for separate representation.

2.   In United States v. Foster, 469 F.2d 1 (1st Cir. 1972), the court established the following rules:

> "[I]t shall be the duty of the trial court, as early in the litigation as practicable, to comment on some of the risks confronted where defendants are jointly represented to insure that defendants are aware of such risks, and to inquire diligently whether they have discussed the risks with their attorney, and whether they understand that they may retain separate counsel, or if qualified, may have such counsel appointed by the court and paid for by the government. For the time being, at least, we leave to the discretion of the trial court the exact time and form of the inquiry. There may be unusual circumstances where, to avoid the possibility of prejudicial disclosures to the prosecution, the court may exercise its discretion to pursue the inquiry with defendants and their counsel on the record but in chambers."

As this casebook went to press, the Supreme Court decided Cuyler v. Sullivan, —— U.S. —— (1980). The Court held that the Constitution does not require the trial judge to admonish defendants who have the same lawyer as their codefendants of the right to separate representation. The Court noted that such warnings were a good idea and were scheduled to become mandatory in Federal District Courts under amendments to Federal Rule of Criminal Procedure 44(c), effective December 1, 1980. The Court also held that if a defendant has not complained of multiple representation in the trial court, he cannot later obtain relief based upon a claim of conflict unless he can demonstrate an actual conflict which adversely affected his interests. The Court added that once such a showing is made, the defendant need not demonstrate prejudice in order to gain relief.

3.   In People v. Marcerola, 47 N.Y.2d 257, 417 N.Y.S.2d 908, 391 N.E.2d 990 (1979), two defendants, charged with burglary and assault, were jointly represented. In reversing the conviction, the majority held:

> ".   .   .   we have charged the trial court, in cases where codefendants are represented by a single attorney, with the weighty responsibility of determining whether 'the defendant's decision to proceed with his attorney is an informed decision.'   .   .   .   The rationale for imposing such duty is obvious. It is all too apparent that the respective interests of each defendant which must be zealously safeguarded are oftentimes at odds, making crucial decisions by defense counsel during the entire criminal proceeding all the more difficult, and, at times, precluding certain defense strategies. For example, an attorney may be less than willing to engage fervently in plea negotiations to obtain a lesser charge for one defendant if to do so would require that defendant to testify against the other defendants, or to call a defendant to testify on his own behalf when his testimony may be detrimental to other defendants whom the attorney represents.

> *   *   *

> ".   .   .   [T]he record is devoid of any indication that the Trial Judge, by proper inquiry, took the necessary precautions to ensure that the defendants perceived the potential risks inherent in joint representation. Thus, because of this absence of a proper in-

quiry on the record, we are unable to ascertain whether the defendants' decision to proceed with their attorney was knowingly and intelligently made, or whether they merely acquiesced out of ignorance to their joint representation.

* * *

"In this case, the record reveals that there was indeed a conflict of interest which endangered each defendant's right to receive advice and assistance from an attorney whose paramount responsibility is to that defendant alone. Defense counsel found himself in a very awkward position at trial in that by attempting to establish a separate defense for each defendant, he was, by implication, incriminating the other defendant. Thus, to establish [one's] defense to the assault charges, it was necessary for counsel to attribute the responsibility for the physical injuries to [the second defendant]. Further, to establish [the second's] defense to the burglary charge, defense counsel had to stress that only [the other defendant entered the place where the burglary was alleged to have occurred]."

JUDGE GABRIELLI dissented:

"The record in this case does not indicate that either defendant was in any way prejudiced by the joint representation. They merely intimate how their interests *might* have conflicted *if a different theory of defense was used.* This was not a case where a defendant testified and made statements shifting the blame to his codefendant. Nor is it a case where evidence was admissible against only one codefendant but was nevertheless not objected to on behalf of the other. Counsel was not precluded from cross-examining any defense witnesses because he was privy to their secrets. It is, pure and simple, a case where the defendants agreed totally on their story, so access to another attorney would not have changed matters.

* * *

"Mere speculation of what might have been is not enough. Actual, not imagined, conflict of interest must be shown before a defendant may successfully claim that he was denied the right to effective assistance of counsel."

4. With increased frequency prosecutors are filing motions to disqualify defense counsel, alleging a conflict of interest. This often happens while a case is under investigation and the prosecution is hoping to get one of an attorney's clients to testify against another of the same attorney's clients. On occasion it happens just before trial.

Assume that a potential defendant, a defendant, or a witness is fully admonished that his or her attorney may have conflicting obligations to another client. Assume also that the client insists upon keeping the attorney and that the attorney is willing to continue multiple representation. Can the trial judge nevertheless disqualify the attorney upon a determination that the joint representation would violate the Code of Professional Responsibility or the Sixth Amendment right to counsel? Does a client have an absolute right to be represented by the attorney of his choice if the attorney is willing to undertake the representation despite suggestions of a conflict? Compare, Pirillo v. Takiff, 341 A.2d 896 (Pa.1975) (judge may disqualify attorney despite client's waiver of the conflict) with United States v. Armedo-Sarmiento, 524 F.2d 591 (2nd Cir. 1975) (judge may not disqualify attorney where client waives right to conflict-free representation).

5.   See generally Geer, "Representation of Multiple Criminal Defendants: Conflicts of Interest and the Professional Responsibility of the Defense Attorney." 62 Minn.L.Rev. 119 (1978).

Chapter 19

PRESENTING THE CASE—PROBLEMS ENCOUNTERED

A. GETTING THE EVIDENCE BEFORE THE TRIER OF FACTS

---

1. THE TURNCOAT WITNESS

CALIFORNIA v. GREEN

Supreme Court of the United States, 1970.
399 U.S. 149, 90 S.Ct. 1930.

MR. JUSTICE WHITE delivered the opinion of the Court.

Section 1235 of the California Evidence Code, effective as of January 1, 1967, provides that "[e]vidence of a statement made by a witness is not made inadmissible by the hearsay rule if the statement is inconsistent with his testimony at the hearing and is offered in compliance with Section 770." [1] In People v. Johnson the California Supreme Court held that prior statements of a witness that were not subject to cross-examination when originally made, could not be introduced under this section to prove the charges against a defendant without violating the defendant's right of confrontation guaranteed by the Sixth Amendment and made applicable to the States by the Fourteenth Amendment. In the case now before us the California Supreme Court applied the same ban to a prior statement of a witness made at a preliminary hearing, under oath and subject to full cross-examination by an adequately counseled defendant. We cannot agree with the California court for two reasons, one of which involves rejection of the holding in People v. Johnson.

I.

In January 1967, one Melvin Porter, a 16-year-old minor, was arrested for selling marihauna to an undercover police officer. Four days after his arrest, while in the custody of juvenile authorities, Porter named respondent Green as his supplier. As recounted later by one Officer Wade, Porter claimed that Green had called him earlier that month, had asked him to sell some "stuff" or "grass," and

---

1. Cal.Evid.Code, § 1235 (1966). Section 770 merely requires that the witness be given an opportunity to explain or deny the prior statement at some point in the trial. See Cal. Evid.Code, § 770 (1966).

had that same afternoon personally delivered a shopping bag containing 29 "baggies" of marihuana. It was from this supply that Porter had made his sale to the undercover officer. A week later, Porter testified at respondent's preliminary hearing. He again named respondent as his supplier, although he now claimed that instead of personally delivering the marihuana, Green had showed him where to pick up the shopping bag, hidden in the bushes at Green's parents' house. Porter's story at the preliminary hearing was subjected to extensive cross-examination by respondent's counsel—the same counsel who represented respondent at his subsequent trial. At the conclusion of the hearing, respondent was charged with furnishing marihuana to a minor in violation of California law.

Respondent's trial took place some two months later before a court sitting without a jury. The State's chief witness was again young Porter. But this time Porter, in the words of the California Supreme Court, proved to be "markedly evasive and uncooperative on the stand." People v. Green, 75 Cal.Rptr. 782 (1969). He testified that respondent had called him in January 1967, and asked him to sell some unidentified "stuff." He admitted obtaining shortly thereafter 29 plastic "baggies" of marihuana, some of which he sold. But when pressed as to whether respondent had been his supplier, Porter claimed that he was uncertain how he obtained the marihuana, primarily because he was at the time on "acid" (LSD), which he had taken 20 minutes before respondent phoned. Porter claimed that he was unable to remember the events that followed the phone call, and that the drugs he had taken prevented his distinguishing fact from fantasy.

At various points during Porter's direct examination, the prosecutor read excerpts from Porter's preliminary hearing testimony. This evidence was admitted under § 1235 for the truth of the matter contained therein. With his memory "refreshed" by his preliminary hearing testimony, Porter "guessed" that he had indeed obtained the marihuana from the backyard of respondent's parents' home, and had given the money from its sale to respondent. On cross-examination, however, Porter indicated that it was his memory of the preliminary testimony which was "mostly" refreshed, rather than his memory of the events themselves, and he was still unsure of the actual episode. See App. 25. Later in the trial, Officer Wade testified, relating Porter's earlier statement that respondent had personally delivered the marihuana. This statement was also admitted as substantive evidence. Porter admitted making the statement, App. 59, and insisted that he had been telling the truth as he then believed it both to Officer Wade and at the preliminary hearing; but he insisted that he was also telling the truth now in claiming inability to remember the actual events.

Respondent was convicted. The District Court of Appeal reversed, holding that the use of Porter's prior statements for the truth of the matter asserted therein, denied respondent his right of confrontation under the California Supreme Court's recent decision in

People v. Johnson, supra. The California Supreme Court affirmed, finding itself "impelled" by recent decisions of this Court to hold § 1235 unconstitutional insofar as it permitted the substantive use of prior inconsistent statements of a witness, even though the statements were subject to cross-examination at a prior hearing. We granted the State's petition for certiorari.

II.

The California Supreme Court construed the Confrontation Clause of the Sixth Amendment to require the exclusion of Porter's prior testimony offered in evidence to prove the State's case against Green, because in the court's view, neither the right to cross-examine Porter at the trial concerning his current and prior testimony, nor the opportunity to cross-examine Porter at the preliminary hearing satisfied the commands of the Confrontation Clause. We think the California court was wrong on both counts.

Positing that this case posed an instance of a witness who gave trial testimony inconsistent with his prior out-of-court statements, the California court, on the authority of its decision in People v. Johnson, supra, held that belated cross-examination before the trial court, "is not an adequate substitute for the right to cross-examination contemporaneous with the original testimony before a different tribunal." People v. Green, supra. We disagree.

Section 1235 of the California Evidence Code represents a considered choice by the California Legislature between two opposing positions concerning the extent to which a witness' prior statements may be introduced at trial without violating hearsay rules of evidence. The orthodox view, adopted in most jurisdictions,[2] has been that the out-of-court statements are inadmissible for the usual reasons that have led to the exclusion of hearsay statements: the statement may not have been made under oath; the declarant may not have been subjected to cross-examination when he made the statement; and the jury cannot observe the declarant's demeanor at the time he made the statement. Accordingly, under this view, the statement may not be offered to show the truth of the matters asserted therein, but can be introduced under appropriate limiting instructions to impeach the credibility of the witness who has changed his story at trial.

In contrast, the minority view adopted in some jurisdictions and supported by most legal commentators and by recent proposals to codify the law of evidence [3] would permit the substantive use of prior

2. The cases are collected in 3 J. Wigmore, Evidence § 1018 (3d ed. 1940) and Annot., 133 A.L.R. 1454, 1455–1457 (1941).

3. Dean Wigmore was the first noted commentator to adopt this position, abandoning his earlier approval, in the first edition of his Treatise, of the orthodox view. See 3 Wigmore § 1018 n. 2. Both the Model Code and the Uniform Rules have since followed the Wigmore position, see Model Code of Evidence Rule 503(b) (1942); Uniform Rule of Evidence 63(1) (1953), as has the recent preliminary draft of the rules of evidence for the lower federal courts.

inconsistent statements on the theory that the usual dangers of hearsay are largely nonexistent where the witness testifies at trial. "The whole purpose of the Hearsay rule has been already satisfied [because] the witness is present and subject to cross-examination [and] [t]here is ample opportunity to test him as to the basis for his former statement."

Our task in this case is not to decide which of these positions, purely as a matter of the law of evidence, is the sounder. The issue before us is the considerably narrower one of whether a defendant's constitutional right "to be confronted with the witnesses against him" is necessarily inconsistent with a State's decision to change its hearsay rules to reflect the minority view described above. While it may readily be conceded that hearsay rules and the Confrontation Clause are generally designed to protect similar values, it is quite a different thing to suggest that the overlap is complete and that the Confrontation Clause is nothing more or less than a codification of the rules of hearsay and their exceptions as they existed historically at common law. Our decisions have never established such a congruence; indeed, we have more than once found a violation of confrontation values even though the statements in issue were admitted under an arguably recognized hearsay exception. See Barber v. Page, 390 U.S. 719, 88 S.Ct. 1318 (1968); Pointer v. Texas, 380 U.S. 400, 85 S. Ct. 1065 (1965). The converse is equally true: merely because evidence is admitted in violation of a long-established hearsay rule does not lead to the automatic conclusion that confrontation rights have been denied.

Given the similarity of the values protected, however, the modification of a State's hearsay rules to create new exceptions for the admission of evidence against a defendant, will often raise questions of compatibility with the defendant's constitutional right to confrontation. Such questions require attention to the reasons for, and the basic scope of, the protections offered by the Confrontation Clause.

The origin and development of the hearsay rules and of the Confrontation Clause have been traced by others and need not be recounted in detail here. It is sufficient to note that the particular vice that gave impetus to the confrontation claim was the practice of trying defendants on "evidence" which consisted solely of *ex parte* affidavits or depositions secured by the examining magistrates, thus denying the defendant the opportunity to challenge his accuser in a face-to-face encounter in front of the trier of fact. Prosecuting attorneys "would frequently allege matters which the prisoner denied and called upon them to prove. The proof was usually given by reading depositions, confessions of accomplices, letters, and the like; and this occasioned frequent demands by the prisoner to have his 'accusers,' i. e. the witnesses against him, brought before him face to face. . . ."[4]

---

4. 1 J. Stephen, A History of the Criminal Law of England 326 (1883).   See also 9 Holdsworth, supra, n. 9, at 225–228.

But objections occasioned by this practice appear primarily to have been aimed at the failure to call the witness to confront personally the defendant at his trial. So far as appears, in claiming confrontation rights no objection was made against receiving a witness' out-of-court depositions or statements, so long as the witness was present at trial to repeat his story and to explain or repudiate any conflicting prior stories before the trier of fact.

Our own decisions seem to have recognized at an early date that it is this literal right to "confront" the witness at the time of trial that forms the core of the values furthered by the Confrontation Clause:

> "The primary object of the constitutional provision in question was to prevent depositions or *ex parte* affidavits, such as were sometimes admitted in civil cases, being used against the prisoner in lieu of a personal examination and cross-examination of the witness, in which the accused has an opportunity, not only of testing the recollection and sifting the conscience of the witness, but of compelling him to stand face to face with the jury in order that they may look at him, and judge by his demeanor upon the stand and the manner in which he gives his testimony whether he is worthy of belief."

Viewed historically, then, there is good reason to conclude that the Confrontation Clause is not violated by admitting a declarant's out-of-court statements, as long as the declarant is testifying as a witness and subject to full and effective cross-examination.

This conclusion is supported by comparing the purposes of confrontation with the alleged dangers in admitting an out-of-court statement. Confrontation: (1) insures that the witness will give his statements under oath—thus impressing him with the seriousness of the matter and guarding against the lie by the possibility of a penalty for perjury; (2) forces the witness to submit to cross-examination, the "greatest legal engine ever invented for the discovery of truth"; (3) permits the jury that is to decide the defendant's fate to observe the demeanor of the witness in making his statement, thus aiding the jury in assessing his credibility.

It is, of course, true that the out-of-court statement may have been made under circumstances subject to none of these protections. But if the declarant is present and testifying at trial, the out-of-court

---

A famous example is provided by the trial of Sir Walter Raleigh for treason in 1603. A crucial element of the evidence against him consisted of the statements of one Cobham, implicating Raleigh in a plot to seize the throne. Raleigh had since received a written retraction from Cobham, and believed that Cobham would now testify in his favor. After a lengthy dispute over Raleigh's right to have Cobham called as a witness, Cobham was not called, and Raleigh was convicted. See 1 Stephen, supra, at 333–336; 9 Holdsworth, supra, at 216–217, 226–228. At least one author traces the Confrontation Clause to the common-law reaction against these abuses of the Raleigh trial. See F. Heller, The Sixth Amendment 104 (1951).

statement for all practical purposes regains most of the lost protections. If the witness admits the prior statement is his, or if there is other evidence to show the statement is his, the danger of faulty reproduction is negligible and the jury can be confident that it has before it two conflicting statements by the same witness. Thus, as far as the oath is concerned, the witness must now affirm, deny, or qualify the truth of the prior statement under the penalty of perjury; indeed, the very fact that the prior statement was not given under a similar circumstance may become the witness' explanation for its inaccuracy—an explanation a jury may be expected to understand and take into account in deciding which, if either, of the statements represents the truth.

Second, the inability to cross-examine the witness at the time he made his prior statement cannot easily be shown to be of crucial significance as long as the defendant is assured of full and effective cross-examination at the time of trial. The most successful cross-examination at the time the prior statement was made could hardly hope to accomplish more than has already been accomplished by the fact that the witness is now telling a different, inconsistent story, and —in this case—one that is favorable to the defendant. We cannot share the California Supreme Court's view that belated cross-examination can never serve as a constitutionally adequate substitute for cross-examination contemporaneous with the original statement. The main danger in substituting subsequent for timely cross-examination seems to lie in the possibility that the witness' "[f]alse testimony is apt to harden and become unyielding to the blows of truth in proportion as the witness has opportunity for reconsideration and influence by the suggestions of others whose interest may be, and often is, to maintain falsehood rather than truth." State v. Saporen, 205 Minn. 358, 362, 285 N.W. 898, 901 (1939). That danger, however, disappears when the witness has changed his testimony so that, far from "hardening," his prior statement has softened to the point where he now repudiates it.

The defendant's task in cross-examination is, of course, no longer identical to the task that he would have faced if the witness had not changed his story and hence had to be examined as a "hostile" witness giving evidence for the prosecution. This difference, however, far from lessening, may actually enhance the defendant's ability to attack the prior statement. For the witness, favorable to the defendant, should be more than willing to give the usual suggested explanations for the inaccuracy of his prior statement, such as faulty perception or undue haste in recounting the event. Under such circumstances, the defendant is not likely to be hampered in effectively attacking the prior statement, solely because his attack comes later in time.

Similar reasons lead us to discount as a constitutional matter the fact that the jury at trial is foreclosed from viewing the declarant's demeanor when he first made his out-of-court statement. The witness who now relates a different story about the events in question must necessarily assume a position as to the truth value of his prior statement, thus giving the jury a chance to observe and evaluate his demeanor as he either disavows or qualifies his earlier statement. The jury is alerted by the inconsistency in the stories, and its attention is sharply focused on determining either that one of the stories reflects the truth or that the witness who has apparently lied once, is simply too lacking in credibility to warrant its believing either story. The defendant's confrontation rights are not violated, even though some demeanor evidence that would have been relevant in resolving this credibility issue is forever lost.

It may be true that a jury would be in a better position to evaluate the truth of the prior statement if it could somehow be whisked magically back in time to witness a gruelling cross-examination of the declarant as he first gives his statement. But the question as we see it must be not whether one can somehow imagine the jury in "a better position," but whether subsequent cross-examination at the defendant's trial will still afford the trier of fact a satisfactory basis for evaluating the truth of the prior statement. On that issue, neither evidence [5] nor reason convinces us that contemporaneous cross-examination before the ultimate trier of fact is so much more effective than subsequent examination that it must be made the touchstone of the Confrontation Clause.

Finally, we note that none of our decisions interpreting the Confrontation Clause requires excluding the out-of-court statements of a witness who is available and testifying at trial. The concern of most of our cases has been focused on precisely the opposite situation—situations where statements have been admitted in the absence of the declarant and without any chance to cross-examine him at trial. These situations have arisen through application of a number of traditional "exceptions" to the hearsay rule, which permit the introduction of evidence despite the absence of the declarant usually on the theory that the evidence possesses other indicia of "reliability" and is incapable of being admitted, despite good-faith efforts of the State, in any way that will secure confrontation with the declarant. Such exceptions, dispensing altogether with the literal right to "confrontation" and cross-examination, have been subjected on several occasions to careful scrutiny by this Court. In Pointer v. Texas, for example, the State introduced at defendant's trial the transcript of a crucial

---

5. The California Supreme Court in its earlier decision on this issue stated that "[t]his practical truth [the importance of immediate cross-examination] is daily verified by trial lawyers, not one of whom would willingly postpone to both a later date and a different forum his right to cross-examine a witness against his client." People v. Johnson, 68 Cal.2d 646, 655, 68 Cal.Rptr. 599, 606, 441 P.2d 111, 118 (1968), cert. denied 393 U.S. 1051, 89 S.Ct. 679 (1969). The citations that follow this sentence are to books on trial practice that shed little empirical light on the actual comparative effectiveness of subsequent, as opposed to timely, cross-examination. As the text suggests, where the witness has changed his story at trial to favor the defendant he should, if anything, be more rather than less vulnerable to defense counsel's explanations for the inaccuracy of his former statement.

witness' testimony from a prior preliminary hearing. The witness himself, one Phillips, had left the jurisdiction and did not appear at trial. "Because the transcript of Phillips' statement offered against petitioner at his trial had not been taken at a time and under circumstances affording petitioner through counsel an adequate opportunity to cross-examine Phillips," we held that its introduction violated the defendant's confrontation rights. Similarly, in Barber v. Page, the State introduced the preliminary hearing testimony of an absent witness, incarcerated in a federal prison, under an "unavailability" exception to its hearsay rules. We held that that exception would not justify the denial of confrontation where the State had not made a good-faith effort to obtain the presence of the allegedly "unavailable" witness.

We have no occasion in the present case to map out a theory of the Confrontation Clause that would determine the validity of all such hearsay "exceptions" permitting the introduction of an absent declarant's statements. For where the declarant is not absent, but is present to testify and to submit to cross-examination, our cases, if anything, support the conclusion that the admission of his out-of-court statements does not create a confrontation problem. Thus, in Douglas v. Alabama (1965), decided on the same day as *Pointer*, we reversed a conviction in which the prosecution read into the record an alleged confession of the defendant's supposed accomplice, Loyd, who refused to testify on self-incrimination grounds. The confrontation problem arose precisely because Loyd could not be cross-examined as to his prior statement; had such cross-examination taken place, the opinion strongly suggests that the confrontation problem would have been nonexistent:

> "In the circumstances of this case, petitioner's inability to cross-examine Loyd as to the alleged confession plainly denied him the right of cross-examination secured by the Confrontation Clause. . . . Loyd could not be cross-examined on a statement imputed to but not admitted by him. . . . [S]ince [the State's] evidence tended to show only that Loyd made the confession, cross-examination . . . as to its genuineness could not substitute for cross-examination of Loyd to test the truth of the statement itself.
>
> . . .
>
> "Hence, effective confrontation of Loyd was possible only if Loyd affirmed the statement as his."

Again, in Bruton v. United States, 391 U.S. 123, 88 S.Ct. 1620 (1968), the Court found a violation of confrontation rights in the admission of a codefendant's confession, implicating Bruton, where the co-defendant did not take the stand. The Court again emphasized that the error arose because the declarant "does not testify and cannot be tested by cross-examination," suggesting that no confrontation problem would have existed if Bruton had been able to cross-examine his co-defendant. Indeed, *Bruton's* refusal to regard limiting instructions as capable of curing the error, suggests that there is little dif-

ference as far as the Constitution is concerned between permitting
prior inconsistent statements to be used only for impeachment purposes, and permitting them to be used for substantive purposes as
well.

We find nothing, then, in either the history or the purposes of
the Confrontation Clause, or in the prior decisions of this Court, that
compels the conclusion reached by the California Supreme Court concerning the validity of California's § 1235. Contrary to the judgment of that court, the Confrontation Clause does not require excluding from evidence the prior statements of a witness who concedes
making the statements, and who may be asked to defend or otherwise
explain the inconsistency between his prior and his present version of
the events in question, thus opening himself to full cross-examination
at trial as to both stories.

III.

We also think that Porter's preliminary hearing testimony was
admissible as far as the Constitution is concerned wholly apart from
the question of whether respondent had an effective opportunity for
confrontation at the subsequent trial. For Porter's statement at the
preliminary hearing had already been given under circumstances
closely approximating those that surround the typical trial. Porter
was under oath; respondent was represented by counsel—the same
counsel in fact who later represented him at the trial; respondent
had every opportunity to cross-examine Porter as to his statement;
and the proceedings were conducted before a judicial tribunal,
equipped to provide a judicial record of the hearings. Under these
circumstances, Porter's statement would, we think, have been admissible at trial even in Porter's absence if Porter had been actually unavailable, despite good-faith efforts of the State to produce him. That
being the case, we do not think a different result should follow where
the witness is actually produced.

This Court long ago held that admitting the prior testimony of
an unavailable witness does not violate the Confrontation Clause.
Mattox v. United States, 156 U.S. 237, 15 S.Ct. 337 (1895). That
case involved testimony given at the defendant's first trial by a witness who had died by the time of the second trial, but we do not find
the instant preliminary hearing significantly different from an actual
trial to warrant distinguishing the two cases for purposes of the Confrontation Clause. Indeed, we indicated as much in Pointer v. Texas
[supra], where we noted that "[t]he case before us would be quite a
different one had Phillips' statement been taken at a full-fledged
hearing at which petitioner had been represented by counsel who had
been given a complete and adequate opportunity to cross-examine."
And in Barber v. Page [supra], although noting that the preliminary
hearing is ordinarily a less searching exploration into the merits of a
case than a trial, we recognized that "there may be some justification
for holding that the opportunity for cross-examination of a witness
at a preliminary hearing satisfies the demand of the confrontation

clause where the witness is shown to be actually unavailable
. . . ." In the present case respondent's counsel does not appear
to have been significantly limited in any way in the scope or nature
of his cross-examination of the witness Porter at the preliminary
hearing. If Porter had died or was otherwise unavailable, the Confrontation Clause would not have been violated by admitting his testimony given at the preliminary hearing—the right of cross-examination then afforded provides substantial compliance with the purposes
behind the confrontation requirement, as long as the declarant's inability to give live testimony is in no way the fault of the State.

But nothing in Barber v. Page or in or other cases in this Court
indicates that a different result must follow where the State produces
the declarant and swears him as a witness at the trial. It may be
that the rules of evidence applicable in state or federal courts would
restrict resort to prior sworn testimony where the declarant is
present at the trial. But as a constitutional matter, it is untenable to
construe the Confrontation Clause to permit the use of prior testimony to prove the State's case where the declarant never appears, but to
bar that testimony where the declarant is present at the trial, exposed to the defendant and the trier of fact, and subject to cross-
examination.[6] As in the case where the witness is physically unprod-
ucible, the State here has made every effort to introduce its evidence
through the live testimony of the witness; it produced Porter at trial,
swore him as a witness, and tendered him for cross-examination.
Whether Porter then testified in a manner consistent or inconsistent
with his preliminary hearing testimony, claimed a loss of memory,
claimed his privilege against compulsory self-incrimination, or simply
refused to answer, nothing in the Confrontation Clause prohibited the

---

6. The explanation advanced for the contrary conclusion seems to be that where the witness is dead or otherwise unavailable, the State may in good faith assume he would have given the same story at trial, and may introduce the former testimony as reasonably reliable and as prompted by the factor of "necessity." On the contrary, it is argued, where the witness is present to testify but does not relate the same story, "necessity," "reliability," and the assumption that the story would be the same are all destroyed. But the only "necessity" that exists in either case is the State's "need" to introduce relevant evidence that through no fault of its own cannot be introduced in any other way. And the "assumption" that the witness would have given the same story if he had been available at trial, is little more than another way of saying that the testimony was given under circumstances that make it reasonably reliable—there is nothing in a witness' death by itself, for example, which would justify assuming his story would not have changed at trial. Finally, the "reliability" of the statement is based on the circumstances under which it was given—circumstances that remain unaffected regardless of whether the witness is present or absent at the later trial. Surely in terms of protecting the defendant's interests, and the jury's ability to assess the reliability of the evidence it hears, it seems most unlikely that respondent in this case would have been better off, as the dissent seems to suggest, if Porter had died, and his prior testimony were admitted, than he was in the instant case where Porter's conduct on the stand cast substantial doubt on his prior statement. As long as the State has made a good-faith effort to produce the witness, the actual presence or absence of the witness cannot be constitutionally relevant for purposes of the "unavailability" exception.

State from also relying on his prior testimony to prove its case against Green.[7]

IV.

There is a narrow question lurking in this case concerning the admissibility of Porter's statements to Officer Wade. In the typical case to which the California court addressed itself, the witness at trial gives a version of the ultimate events different from that given on a prior occasion. In such a case, as our holding in Part II makes clear, we find little reason to distinguish among prior inconsistent statements on the basis of the circumstances under which the prior statements were given. The subsequent opportunity for cross-examination at trial with respect to both present and past versions of the event, is adequate to make equally admissible, as far as the Confrontation Clause is concerned, both the casual, off-hand remark to a stranger, and the carefully recorded testimony at a prior hearing. Here, however, Porter claimed at trial that he could not remember the events that occurred after respondent telephoned him and hence failed to give any current version of the more important events described in his earlier statement.

Whether Porter's apparent lapse of memory so affected Green's right to cross-examine as to make a critical difference in the application of the Confrontation Clause in this case [8] is an issue which is not ripe for decision at this juncture. The state court did not focus on this precise question, which was irrelevant given its broader and erroneous premise that an out-of-court statement of a witness is inadmissible as substantive evidence, whatever the nature of the opportunity to cross-examine at the trial. Nor has either party addressed itself to the question. Its resolution depends much upon the unique facts in this record, and we are reluctant to proceed without the state court's views of what the record actually discloses relevant to this particular issue. What is more, since we hold that the admission of Porter's preliminary hearing testimony is not barred by the Sixth

7. The hearsay exception itself has generally recognized that a witness is "unavailable" for purposes of the exception where through lapse of memory or a plea of the Fifth Amendment privilege, the State cannot secure his live testimony. See 5 Wigmore §§ 1408, 1409.

8. Even among proponents of the view that prior statements should be admissible as substantive evidence, disagreement appears to exist as to whether to apply this rule to the case of a witness who disclaims all present knowledge of the ultimate event. Commentators have noted that in such a case the opportunities for testing the prior statement through cross-examination at trial may be significantly diminished.

While both the Model Code and the Uniform Rules would apparently admit prior inconsistent statements even where the witness claims to have no present knowledge or recollection of the event, the preliminary draft of proposed rules of evidence for lower federal courts seems to limit admissibility to the case where the witness actually testifies concerning the substance of the event at issue. The latter position accords with the common-law practice of not permitting prior inconsistent statements to be introduced even for impeachment purposes until and unless the witness has actually given "inconsistent" testimony concerning the substance of the event described in the prior statement.

Amendment despite his apparent lapse of memory, the reception into evidence of the Porter statement to Officer Wade may pose a harmless-error question which is more appropriately resolved by the California courts in the first instance. Similarly, faced on remand with our decision that § 1235 is not invalid on its face, the California Supreme Court may choose to dispose of the case on other grounds raised by Green but not passed upon by that court; for example, because of its ruling on § 1235, the California court deliberately put aside the issue of the sufficiency of the evidence to sustain conviction.[9]

We therefore vacate the judgment of the California Supreme Court and remand the case to that court for further proceedings not inconsistent with this opinion. It is so ordered.

Mr. Justice Marshall took no part in the decision of this case.

Mr. Justice Blackmun took no part in the consideration or decision of this case.

[Chief Justice Burger's concurring opinion is omitted.]

Mr. Justice Harlan, concurring.

The California decision that we today reverse demonstrates, however, the need to approach this case more broadly than the Court has seen fit to do, and, to confront squarely the Confrontation Clause because the holding of the California Supreme Court is the result of an understandable misconception, as I see things, of numerous decisions of this Court, old and recent, that have indiscriminately equated "confrontation" with "cross-examination."

* * *

From the scant information available it may tentatively be concluded that the Confrontation Clause was meant to constitutionalize a barrier against flagrant abuses, trials by anonymous accusers, and absentee witnesses. That the Clause was intended to ordain common law rules of evidence with constitutional sanction is doubtful, notwithstanding English decisions that equate confrontation and hearsay. Rather, having established a broad principle, it is far more likely that the Framers anticipated it would be supplemented, as a matter of judge-made common law, by prevailing rules of evidence.

* * *

Notwithstanding language that appears to equate the Confrontation Clause with a right to cross-examine, and, by implication, exclude hearsay, the early holdings and dicta can, I think, only be harmonized by viewing the confrontation guarantee as being confined to an availability rule, one that requires the production of a witness when he is available to testify. This view explains the recognition of the dying declaration exception, which dispenses with any require-

---

9. This issue is not insubstantial. Conviction here rests almost entirely on the evidence in Porter's two prior statements which were themselves inconsistent in some respects.

ment of cross-examination, and the refusal to make an exception for prior recorded statements, taken subject to cross-examination by the accused, when the witness is still available to testify.

* * *

I turn finally to the question of whether this conviction stands on such unreliable evidence that reversal is required. I cannot conclude that the preliminary hearing testimony was obtained under circumstances, as such, so unreliable that its admission requires reversal as a matter of due process, even though it was crucial to the central issue in the case. The statement given to Officer Wade does, however, raise such a possibility. I accordingly would remand the case to the California Supreme Court for consideration of that question and, whether or not it deems the second statement too unreliable to have been admitted, to decide whether this conviction should be reversed under California law for want of sufficient evidence to sustain a conviction beyond a reasonable doubt.

Mr. Justice Brennan, dissenting.

Respondent was convicted of violating California Health and Safety Code, § 11532 which prohibits furnishing narcotics to a minor. The only issue at his trial was whether he had in fact furnished Porter, a minor, with marihuana. On the direct testimony it does not appear that he could have been constitutionally convicted, for it seems that there would have been insufficient evidence to sustain a finding of guilt. The State presented three witnesses to prove respondent's guilt: Porter and Officers Wade and Dominguez. As the Court states, Porter testified at trial that "he was uncertain how he obtained the marihuana, primarily because he was at the time on 'acid' (LSD), which he had taken 20 minutes before respondent phoned. Porter claimed that he was unable to remember the events that followed the phone call, and that the drugs he had taken prevented his distinguishing fact from fantasy." Officer Wade had no personal knowledge of the facts of the alleged offense; he was able only to report the content of an extrajudicial statement that Porter had made to him. Officer Dominguez testified about an incident wholly separate from the alleged offense; his testimony was consistent with the defense account of the facts.

Thus, the evidence on which respondent was found guilty consisted of two pretrial statements by Porter. The first was the account given Officer Wade. It was unsworn and not subject to defense cross-examination. Porter's demeanor while making the statement was not observed by the trial factfinder. The statement was made under unreliable circumstances—it was taken four days after Porter's arrest for selling marihuana to an undercover agent and while he was still in custody. No written transcript of the statement was introduced at trial. Officer Wade recounted it simply as he remembered Porter's words. The second statement was given by Porter during respondent's preliminary hearing. It was sworn and subject to cross-examination. Defense counsel, however, did not engage in a searching examination.[10]   Again, Porter's demeanor while he made this statement was unobserved by the trial factfinder. The statement was put before this factfinder, of course, when at various points during Porter's direct examination at trial the prosecutor read excerpts from his preliminary hearing testimony.

Accordingly, the facts of this case present two questions regarding the application of California Evidence Code, § 1235: first, whether the Confrontation Clause permits a witness' extrajudicial statement to be admitted at trial as substantive evidence when the witness claims to be unable to remember the events with which his prior statement dealt, and, second, whether the clause permits a witness' preliminary hearing statement, made under oath and subject to cross-examination, to be introduced at trial as substantive evidence when the witness claims to be unable to remember the events with which the statement dealt. In my view, neither statement can be introduced without unconstitutionally restricting the right of the accused to challenge incriminating evidence in the presence of the factfinder who will determine his guilt or innocence.

I.

The Court points out that "the particular vice that gave impetus to the confrontation claim was the practice of trying defendants on 'evidence' which consisted solely of *ex parte* affidavits or depositions secured by the examining magistrates, thus denying the defendant the opportunity to challenge his accuser in a face-to-face encounter in front of the trier of fact." A face-to-face encounter, of course, is important, not so that the accused can view at trial his accuser's visage, but so that he can directly challenge the accuser's testimony before the factfinder. See 5 J. Wigmore, Evidence §§ 1364, 1365 (3d ed. 1940). We made this clear in Mattox v. United States (1895), where we stressed the necessity of "a personal examination and cross-examination of the witness, in which the accused has an opportunity, not only of testing the recollection and sifting the conscience of the witness, but of compelling him to stand face to face with the jury in order that they may look at him, and judge by his demeanor upon the stand and the manner in which he gives his testimony whether he is worthy of belief."

There is no way to test the recollection and sift the conscience of a witness regarding the facts of an alleged offense if he is unwilling or unable to be questioned about them;[11] defense counsel cannot probe the story of a silent witness and attempt to expose facts that qualify or discredit it. The impetus to truth inherent in the oath

---

10. No question, for example, was asked Porter by either the defense or prosecution as to whether he was under the influence of drugs at the time of the alleged offense.

11. If, on the other hand, the witness is willing and able to testify at trial about the operative events, the demands of the Confrontation Clause may be met, even though the witness contradicts his pretrial assertions. I see no need on the facts presented here, however, to resolve this issue.

sworn by the witness, in a penalty for perjury, and in the serious purpose of the courtroom have no effect on him so far as the facts of the alleged offense are concerned. Nor, obviously, can the factfinder view his demeanor while he recounts the facts. If the witness claims that he is unable to remember the pertinent events, it is true that this assertion can be challenged, and that in making and defending it the witness will be affected by his oath, the penalty for perjury, and the courtroom atmosphere. It is equally true that the trial factfinder can observe and weigh the witness' demeanor as he makes and defends such a claim. But a decision by the factfinder that the witness is lying sheds no direct light on the accuracy of any pretrial statement made by him; that statement remains without the support or discredit that can come only from the probing of its factual basis while the witness stands face to face with the accused and the factfinder. If the factfinder decides that the witness is honestly unable to remember the events in question, that conclusion may or may not directly guide the factfinder in assessing the reliability of the pretrial statement. If, for example, the witness were unable to remember the pertinent facts because he was under the influence of drugs at the time they occurred, the factfinder might reasonably disregard any pretrial account of these events given by the witness.

This Court has already explicitly held in Douglas v. Alabama (1965), that the Confrontation Clause forbids the substantive use at trial of a prior extrajudicial statement, when the declarant is present at trial but unwilling to testify about the events with which his prior statement dealt. In *Douglas* the prosecution introduced the alleged confession of the accused's supposed accomplice, one Loyd, who was unwilling to testify about the pertinent events for fear of self-incrimination. We held that "petitioner's inability to cross-examine Loyd as to the alleged confession plainly denied him the right of cross-examination secured by the Confrontation Clause. Loyd's alleged statement that the petitioner fired the shotgun constituted the only direct evidence that he had done so .   . . [E]ffective confrontation of Loyd was possible only if Loyd affirmed the statement as his. However, Loyd did not do so, but relied on his privilege to refuse to answer."

For purposes of the Confrontation Clause, there is no significant difference between a witness who fails to testify about an alleged offense because he is unwilling to do so and a witness whose silence is compelled by an inability to remember. Both are called to the stand to testify. The jury may view the demeanor of each as he indicates why he will not discuss the crucial events. But in neither instance are the purposes of the Confrontation Clause satisfied, because the witness cannot be questioned at trial concerning the pertinent facts. In both cases, if a pretrial statement is introduced for the truth of the facts asserted, the witness becomes simply a conduit for the admission of stale evidence, whose reliability can never be tested before the trial factfinder by cross-examination of the declarant about the operative events, and by observation of his demeanor as he testifies about them.

Unlike the Court, I see no reason to leave undecided the inadmissibility of Porter's statements to Officer Wade. We have before us the transcript of Porter's trial testimony. He could not remember the operative events. Whether he feigned loss of memory is irrelevant to respondent's confrontation claim. Under *Douglas* his statement to Officer Wade must be excluded as substantive evidence.[12]

II.

The question remains whether the fact that a pretrial statement was obtained at a preliminary hearing under oath and subject to cross-examination, distinguishes that statement for confrontation purposes from an extrajudicial statement. I thought that our decision in Barber v. Page resolved this issue. In *Barber* we stated that confrontation at a preliminary hearing cannot compensate for the absence of confrontation at trial, because the nature and objectives of the two proceedings differ significantly. In that case, the prosecution argued that the accused had waived his right to cross-examination at the preliminary hearing. Though we rejected that argument, to put beyond doubt the necessity for confrontation *at trial*, we stated:

> "Moreover, we would reach the same result on the facts of this case had petitioner's counsel actually cross-examined [the witness] at the preliminary hearing. . . . The right to confrontation is basically a trial right. It includes both the opportunity to cross-examine and the occasion for the jury to weigh the demeanor of the witness. A preliminary hearing is ordinarily a much less searching exploration into the merits of a case than a trial, simply because its function is the more limited one of determining whether probable cause exists to hold the accused for trial."

We applied *Barber* retroactively in Berger v. California (1969), a case in which defense counsel did have an opportunity to cross-examine the witness at the preliminary hearing. We held, nonetheless, that "[c]learly, petitioner's inability to cross-examine . . . at trial may have had a significant effect on the 'integrity of the fact-finding process.' "

Preliminary hearings in California are not atypical in their nature and objectives:

> "In most California criminal prosecutions the preliminary examination is conducted as a rather perfunctory un-

---

12. The fact that in appropriate circumstances such a statement may be admitted to impeach a witness is not as anomalous as the Court suggests, ante, at 1938. If, for example, Porter's pretrial statements had been admitted at respondent's trial solely for impeachment purposes, they would not have provided substantive proof of his guilt, and, as noted, there would then very likely have been insufficient evidence to sustain his conviction.

> contested proceeding with only one likely denouement—an order holding the defendant for trial. Only television lawyers customarily demolish the prosecution in the magistrate's court. The prosecution need show only 'probable cause,' a burden vastly lighter than proof beyond a reasonable doubt."

It follows that the purposes of the Confrontation Clause cannot be satisfied by a face-to-face encounter at the preliminary hearing. Cross-examination at the hearing pales beside that which takes place at trial. This is so for a number of reasons. First, as noted, the objective of the hearing is to establish the presence or absence of probable cause, not guilt or innocence proved beyond a reasonable doubt; thus, if evidence suffices to establish probable cause, defense counsel has little reason at the preliminary hearing to show that it does not conclusively establish guilt—or, at least, he had little reason before today's decision. Second, neither defense nor prosecution is eager before trial to disclose its case by extensive examination at the preliminary hearing; thorough questioning of a prosecution witness by defense counsel may easily amount to a grant of gratis discovery to the State. Third, the schedules of neither court nor counsel, can easily accommodate lengthy preliminary hearings. Fourth, even were the judge and lawyers not concerned that the proceedings be brief, the defense and prosecution have generally had inadequate time before the hearing to prepare for extensive examination. Finally, though counsel were to engage in extensive questioning, a part of its force would never reach the trial factfinder, who would know the examination only second hand.

* * *

If cross-examination at the preliminary hearing rarely approximates that at trial, observation by the trial factfinder of the witness' demeanor as he gives his prior testimony is virtually nonexistent. Unless the committing magistrate is also the trial factfinder, the demeanor purpose of the Confrontation Clause is wholly negated by substituting confrontation at the preliminary hearing for confrontation at trial. And yet, in the words of the California court, "[i]t is because demeanor—attitude and manner—is a significant factor in weighing testimonial evidence, that it is axiomatic the trier of fact, before whom the witness testified and was cross-examined . . . ., is the sole judge of the credibility of a witness and of the weight to be given his testimony." No such determination of credibility is possible when the witness comes before the trial factfinder by the reading of a cold transcript.

It appears, then, that in terms of the purposes of the Confrontation Clause, an equation of face-to-face encounter at the preliminary hearing with confrontation at trial must rest largely on the fact that the witness testified at the hearing under oath, subject to the penalty for perjury, and in a courtroom atmosphere. These factors are not insignificant, but by themselves they fall far short of satisfying the **demands of constitutional confrontation.** Moreover, the atmosphere and stakes are different in the two proceedings. In the hurried, somewhat *pro forma* context of the average preliminary hearing, a witness may be more careless in his testimony than in the more measured and searching atmosphere of a trial. Similarly, a man willing to perjure himself when the consequences are simply that the accused will stand trial may be less willing to do so when his lies may condemn the defendant to loss of liberty. In short, it ignores reality to assume that the purposes of the Confrontation Clause are met during a preliminary hearing. Accordingly, to introduce preliminary hearing testimony for the truth of the facts asserted, when the witness is in court and either unwilling or unable to testify regarding the pertinent events, denies the accused his Sixth Amendment right to grapple effectively with incriminating evidence.

* * *

In sum, I find that Porter's real or pretended lapse of memory about the pertinent events casts serious doubt upon the reliability of his preliminary hearing testimony. It is clear that so long as a witness, such as Porter, cannot or will not testify about these events at trial, the accused remains unable to challenge effectively that witness' prior assertions about them. The probable unreliability of the prior testimony, coupled with the impossibility of its examination during trial, denies the accused his right to probe and attempt to discredit incriminating evidence. Accordingly, I would hold California Evidence Code, § 1235 in violation of the Confrontation Clause to the extent that it permits the substantive use at trial of prior statements, whether extrajudicial or testimonial, when the declarant is present at trial but unable or unwilling to be questioned about the events with which the prior statements dealt. I would therefore affirm the reversal of respondent's conviction.

CHAMBERS v. MISSISSIPPI

Supreme Court of the United States, 1973.
410 U.S. 284, 93 S.Ct. 1038.

MR. JUSTICE POWELL delivered the opinion of the Court.

Petitioner, Leon Chambers, was tried by a jury in a Mississippi trial court and convicted of murdering a policeman. The jury assessed punishment at life imprisonment and the Mississippi Supreme Court affirmed, one justice dissenting. Chambers v. Mississippi, 252 So.2d 217 (1971). . . . Subsequently the petition for certiorari was granted, to consider whether petitioner's trial was conducted in accord with principles of due process under the Fourteenth Amendment. We conclude that it was not.

I.

The events that led to petitioner's prosecution for murder occurred in the small town of Woodville in southern Mississippi. On Saturday evening, June 14, 1969, two Woodville policemen, James

Forman and Aaron "Sonny" Liberty, entered a local bar and pool hall to execute a warrant for the arrest of a youth named C. C. Jackson. Jackson resisted and a hostile crowd of some 50 or 60 persons gathered. The officers' first attempt to handcuff Jackson was frustrated when 20 or 25 men in the crowd intervened and wrestled him free. Forman then radioed for assistance and Liberty removed his riot gun, a 12-gauge sawed-off shotgun, from the car. Three deputy sheriffs arrived shortly thereafter and the officers again attempted to make their arrest. Once more the officers were attacked by the onlookers and during the commotion five or six pistol shots were fired. Forman was looking in a different direction when the shooting began, but immediately saw that Liberty had been shot several times in the back. Before Liberty died he turned around and fired both barrels of his riot gun into an alley in the area from which the shots appeared to have come. The first shot was wild and high and scattered the crowd standing at the face of the alley. Liberty appeared, however, to take more deliberate aim before the second shot and hit one of the men in the crowd in the back of the head and neck as he ran down the alley. That man was Leon Chambers.

Officer Forman could not see from his vantage point who shot Liberty or whether Liberty's shots hit anyone. One of the deputy sheriffs testified at trial that he was standing several feet from Liberty and that he saw Chambers shoot him. Another deputy sheriff stated that, although he could not see whether Chambers had a gun in his hand, he did see Chambers "break his arm down" shortly before the shots were fired. The officers who saw Chambers fall testified that they thought he was dead but they made no effort at that time either to examine him or to search for the murder weapon. Instead they attended to Liberty, who was placed in the police car and taken to the hospital where he was declared dead on arrival. A subsequent autopsy showed that he had been hit with four bullets from a .22-caliber revolver.

Shortly after the shooting, three of Chambers' friends discovered that he was not yet dead. James Williams, Berkley Turner, and Gable McDonald loaded him into a car and transported him to the same hospital. Later that night, when the county sheriff discovered that Chambers was still alive, a guard was placed outside his room. Chambers was subsequently charged with Liberty's murder. He pleaded not guilty and has asserted his innocence throughout.

The story of Leon Chambers is intertwined with the story of another man, Gable McDonald. McDonald, a lifelong resident of Woodville, was in the crowd on the evening of Liberty's death. Sometime shortly after that day he left his wife in Woodville and moved to Louisiana and found a job at a sugar mill. In November of that same year he returned to Woodville when his wife informed him that an acquaintance of his, known as Reverend Stokes, wanted to see him. Stokes owned a gas station in Natchez, Mississippi, several miles north of Woodville, and upon his return McDonald went to see him. After talking to Stokes, McDonald agreed to make a statement to

Chambers' attorneys, who maintained offices in Natchez. Two days later he appeared at the attorneys' offices and gave a sworn confession that he shot Officer Liberty. He also stated that he had already told a friend of his, James Williams, that he shot Liberty. He said that he used his own pistol, a nine-shot .22-caliber revolver, which he had discarded shortly after the shooting. In response to questions from Chambers' attorneys, McDonald affirmed that his confession was voluntary and that no one had compelled him to come to them. Once the confession had been transcribed, signed and witnessed, McDonald was turned over to the local police authorities and was placed in jail.

One month later, at a preliminary hearing, McDonald repudiated his prior sworn confession. He testified that Stokes had persuaded him to confess that he shot Liberty. He claimed that Stokes had promised that he would not go to jail and that he would share in the proceeds of a lawsuit that Chambers would bring against the town of Woodville. On examination by his own attorney and on cross-examination by the State, McDonald swore that he had not been on the scene when Liberty was shot but had been down the street drinking beer in a cafe with a friend, Berkley Turner. When he and Turner heard the shooting he testified that they walked up the street and found Chambers lying in the alley. He, Turner and Williams took Chambers to the hospital. McDonald further testified at the preliminary hearing that he did not know what had happened, that there was no discussion about the shooting either going to or coming back from the hospital, and that it was not until the next day that he learned that Chambers had been felled by a blast from Liberty's riot gun. In addition, McDonald stated that while he once owned a .22-caliber pistol he had lost it many months before the shooting and did not own or possess a weapon at that time. The local justice of the peace accepted McDonald's repudiation, released him from custody, and the local authorities undertook no further investigation of his possible involvement.

Chambers' case came on for trial in October of the next year. At trial he endeavored to develop two grounds of defense. He first attempted to show that he did not shoot Liberty. Only one officer testified that he actually saw Chambers fire the shots. Although three officers saw Liberty shoot Chambers and testified that they assumed he was shooting his attacker, none of them examined Chambers to see whether he was still alive or whether he possessed a gun. Indeed, no weapon was ever recovered from the scene and there was no proof that Chambers had ever owned a .22-caliber pistol. One witness testified that he was standing in the street near where Liberty was shot, that he was looking at Chambers when the shooting began, and that he was sure that Chambers did not fire the shots.

Petitioner's second defense was that Gable McDonald had shot Officer Liberty. He was only partially successful, however, in his efforts to bring before the jury the testimony supporting this defense. Sam Hardin, a lifelong friend of McDonald's, testified that he saw

McDonald shoot Liberty. A second witness, one of Liberty's cousins, testified that he saw McDonald immediately after the shooting with a pistol in his hand. In addition to the testimony of these two witnesses, Chambers endeavored to show the jury that McDonald had repeatedly confessed to the crime. Chambers attempted to prove that McDonald had admitted responsibility for the murder on four separate occasions, once when he gave the sworn statement to Chambers' counsel and three other times prior to that occasion in private conversations with friends.

In large measure, he was thwarted in his attempt to present this portion of his defense by the strict application of certain Mississippi rules of evidence. Chambers asserts in this Court, as he did unsuccessfully in his motion for new trial and on appeal to the State Supreme Court, that the application of these evidentiary rules rendered his trial fundamentally unfair and deprived him of due process of law. It is necessary, therefore, to examine carefully the rulings made during the trial.

II.

Chambers filed a pretrial motion requesting the court to order McDonald to appear. Chambers also sought a ruling at that time that if the State chose not to call McDonald itself, he be allowed to call him as an adverse witness. Attached to the motion were copies of McDonald's sworn confession and of the transcript of his preliminary hearing at which he repudiated that confession. The trial court granted the motion requiring McDonald to appear but reserved ruling on the adverse witness motion. At trial, after the State failed to put McDonald on the stand, Chambers called McDonald, laid a predicate for the introduction of his sworn out-of-court confession, had it admitted into evidence, and read it to the jury. The State, upon cross-examination, elicited from McDonald the fact that he had rejected his prior confession. McDonald further testified, as he had at the preliminary hearing, that he did not shoot Liberty, and that he confessed to the crime only on the promise of Reverend Stokes that he would not go to jail and would share in a sizeable tort recovery from the town. He also retold his own story of his actions on the evening of the shooting, including his visit to the cafe down the street, his absence from the scene during the critical period, and his subsequent trip to the hospital with Chambers.

At the conclusion of the State's cross-examination, Chambers renewed his motion to examine McDonald as an adverse witness. The trial court denied the motion, stating: "He may be hostile, but he is not adverse in the sense of the word, so your request will be overruled." On appeal, the State Supreme Court upheld the trial court's ruling, finding that "McDonald's testimony was not adverse to appellant" because "[n]owhere did he point the finger at Chambers." 252 So.2d, at 220.

Defeated in his attempt to challenge directly McDonald's renunciation of his prior confession, Chambers sought to introduce the testimony of the three witnesses to whom McDonald had admitted that he shot the officer. The first of these, Sam Hardin, would have testified that, on the night of the shooting, he spent the late evening hours with McDonald at a friend's house after their return from the hospital and that, while driving McDonald home later that night, McDonald stated that he shot Liberty. The State objected to the admission of this testimony on the ground that it was hearsay. The trial court sustained the objection.[1]

Berkley Turner, the friend with whom McDonald said he was drinking beer when the shooting occurred, was then called to testify. In the jury's presence, and without objection, he testified that he had not been in the cafe that Saturday and had not had any beers with McDonald. The jury was then excused. In the absence of the jury, Turner recounted his conversations with McDonald while they were riding with James Williams to take Chambers to the hospital. When asked whether McDonald said anything regarding the shooting of Liberty, Turner testified that McDonald told him that he "shot him." Turner further stated that one week later, when he met McDonald at a friend's house, McDonald reminded him of their prior conversation and urged Turner not to "mess him up." Petitioner argued to the court that, especially where there was other proof in the case that was corroborative of these out-of-court statements, Turner's testimony as to McDonald's self-incriminating remarks should have been admitted as an exception to the hearsay rule. Again, the trial court sustained the State's objection.

The third witness, Albert Carter, was McDonald's neighbor. They had been friends for about 25 years. Although Carter had not been in Woodville on the evening of the shooting, he stated that he learned about it the next morning from McDonald. That same day he and McDonald walked out to a well near McDonald's house and there McDonald told him that he was the one who shot Officer Liberty. Carter testified that McDonald also told him that he had disposed of the .22-caliber revolver later that night. He further testified that several weeks after the shooting he accompanied McDonald to Natchez where McDonald purchased another .22 pistol to replace the one he had discarded.[2] The jury was not allowed to hear Carter's testimony. Chambers urged that these statement were admissible, the State objected, and the court sustained the objection. On appeal, the State Supreme Court approved the lower court's exclusion of these witnesses' testimony on hearsay grounds.

In sum, then, this was Chambers' predicament. As a consequence of the combination of Mississippi's "party witness" or "vouch-

---

1. Hardin's testimony, unlike the testimony of the other two men who stated that McDonald had confessed to them, was actually given in the jury's presence. After the State's objection to Hardin's account of McDonald's statement was sustained, the trial court ordered the jury to disregard it.

2. A gun dealer from Natchez testified that McDonald had made two purchases. The witness' business records indicated that McDonald purchased a nine-shot .22-caliber revolver about a year prior to the murder. He purchased a different style .22 three weeks after Liberty's death.

er" rule and its hearsay rule, he was unable either to cross-examine McDonald or to present witnesses in his own behalf who would have discredited McDonald's repudiation and demonstrated his complicity. Chambers had, however, chipped away at the fringes of McDonald's story by introducing admissible testimony from other sources indicating that he had not been seen in the cafe where he says he was when the shooting started, that he had not been having beer with Turner, and that he possessed a .22 pistol at the time of the crime. But all that remained from McDonald's own testimony was a single written confession countered by an arguably acceptable renunciation. Chambers' defense was far less persuasive than it might have been had he been given an opportunity to subject McDonald's statements to cross-examination or had the other confessions been admitted.

III.

The right of an accused in a criminal trial to due process is, in essence, the right to a fair opportunity to defend against the State's accusations. The rights to confront and cross-examine witnesses and to call witnesses in one's own behalf have long been recognized as essential to due process. Mr. Justice Black, writing for the Court in In re Oliver (1948), identified these rights as among the minimum essentials of a fair trial:

> "A person's right to reasonable notice of a charge against him, and an opportunity to be heard in his defense—a right to his day in court—are basic to our system of jurisprudence; and these rights include, as a minimum, a right to examine the witnesses against him, to offer testimony, and to be represented by counsel."

Both of these elements of a fair trial are implicated in the present case.

A

Chambers was denied an opportunity to subject McDonald's damning repudiation and alibi to cross-examination. He was not allowed to test the witness' recollection, to probe into the details of his alibi, or to "sift" his conscience so that the jury might judge for itself whether McDonald's testimony was worthy of belief. The right of cross-examination is more than a desirable rule of trial procedure. It is implicit in the constitutional right of confrontation, and helps assure the "accuracy of the truth-determining process." It is, indeed, "an essential and fundamental requirement for the kind of fair trial which is this country's constitutional goal." Of course, the right to confront and to cross-examine is not absolute and may, in appropriate cases, bow to accommodate other legitimate interests in the criminal trial process. But its denial or significant diminution calls into question the ultimate "integrity of the fact-finding process" and requires that the competing interest be closely examined.

In this case, petitioner's request to cross-examine McDonald was denied on the basis of a Mississippi common law rule that a party may not impeach his own witness. The rule rests on the presumption—without regard to the circumstances of the particular case—that a party who calls a witness "vouches for his credibility." Although the historical origins of the "voucher" rule are uncertain, it appears to be a remnant of primitive English trial practice in which "oath-takers" or "compurgators" were called to stand behind a particular party's position in any controversy. Their assertions were strictly partisan and, quite unlike witnesses in criminal trials today, their role bore little relation to the impartial ascertainment of the facts.

Whatever validity the "voucher" rule may have once enjoyed, and apart from whatever usefulness it retains today in the civil trial process, it bears little present relationship to the realities of the criminal process. It might have been logical for the early common law to require a party to vouch for the credibility of witnesses he brought before the jury to affirm his veracity. Having selected them especially for that purpose, the party might reasonably be expected to stand firmly behind their testimony. But in modern criminal trials defendants are rarely able to select their witnesses: they must take them where they find them. Moreover, as applied in this case, the "voucher" rule's impact was doubly harmful to Chambers' efforts to develop his defense. Not only was he precluded from cross-examining McDonald, but, as the State conceded at oral argument, he was also restricted in the scope of his direct examination by the rule's corollary requirement that the party calling the witness is bound by anything he might say. He was, therefore, effectively prevented from exploring the circumstances of McDonald's three prior oral confessions and from challenging the renunciation of the written confession.

In this Court Mississippi has not sought to defend the rule or explain its underlying rationale. Nor has it contended that its rule should override the accused's right of confrontation. Instead, it argues that there is no incompatibility between the rule and Chambers' rights because no right of confrontation exists unless the testifying witness is "adverse" to the accused. The State's brief asserts that the "right of confrontation is limited to witnesses *against* the accused." Relying on the trial court's determination that McDonald was not "adverse," and on the State Supreme Court's holding that McDonald "did not point the finger at Chambers," the State contends that Chambers' constitutional right was not involved.

The argument that McDonald's testimony was not "adverse" to, or "against," Chambers is not convincing. The State's proof at trial excluded the theory that more than one person participated in the shooting of Liberty. To the extent that McDonald's sworn confession tended to incriminate him, it tended also to exculpate Chambers. And, in the circumstances of this case, McDonald's retraction inculpated Chambers to the same extent that it exculpated McDonald. It can hardly be disputed that McDonald's testimony was in fact seriously adverse to Chambers. The availability of the right to confront and to cross-examine those who give damaging testimony against the accused has never been held to depend on whether the witness was initially put on the stand by the accused or by the State. We reject the notion that a right of such substance in the criminal process may be governed by that technicality or by any narrow and unrealistic definition of the word "against." The "voucher" rule, as applied in this case, plainly interfered with Chambers' right to defend against the State's charges.

B

We need not decide, however, whether this error alone would occasion reversal since Chambers' claimed denial of due process rests on the ultimate impact of that error when viewed in conjunction with the trial court's refusal to permit him to call other witnesses. The trial court refused to allow him to introduce the testimony of Hardin, Turner and Carter. Each would have testified to the statements purportedly made by McDonald, on three separate occasions shortly after the crime, naming himself as the murderer. The State Supreme Court approved the exclusion of this evidence on the ground that it was hearsay.

The hearsay rule, which has long been recognized and respected by virtually every State, is based on experience and grounded in the notion that untrustworthy evidence should not be presented to the triers of fact. Out-of-court statements are traditionally excluded because they lack the conventional indicia of reliability: they are usually not made under oath or other circumstances that impress the speaker with the solemnity of his statement; the declarant's word is not subject to cross-examination; and he is not available in order that his demeanor and credibility may be assessed by the jury. A number of exceptions have developed over the years to allow admission of hearsay statements made under circumstances that tend to assure reliability and thereby compensate for the absence of the oath and opportunity for cross-examination. Among the most prevalent of these exceptions is the one applicable to declarations against interest —an exception founded on the assumption that a person is unlikely to fabricate a statement against his own interest at the time it is made. Mississippi recognizes this exception but applies it only to declarations against pecuniary interest. It recognizes no exceptions for declarations like McDonald's in this case, that are against the penal interest of the declarant.

This materialistic limitation on the declaration-against-interest hearsay exception appears to be accepted by most States in their criminal trial processes, although a number of States have discarded it. Declarations against penal interest have also been excluded in federal courts under the authority of Donnelly v. United States (1913), although exclusion would not be required under the newly proposed Federal Rules of Evidence. Exclusion, where the limitation prevails, is usually premised on the view that admission would lead to the frequent presentation of perjured testimony to the jury. It is believed that confessions of criminal activity are often motivated by extraneous considerations and, therefore, are not as inherently reliable as statements against pecuniary or proprietary interest. While that rationale has been the subject of considerable scholarly criticism, we need not decide in this case whether, under other circumstances, it might serve some valid state purpose by excluding untrustworthy testimony.

The hearsay statements involved in this case were originally made and subsequently offered at trial under circumstances that provided considerable assurance of their reliability. First, each of McDonald's confessions was made spontaneously to a close acquaintance shortly after the murder had occurred. Second, each one was corroborated by some other evidence in the case—McDonald's sworn confession, the testimony of an eyewitness to the shooting, the testimony that McDonald was seen with a gun immediately after the shooting, and proof of his prior ownership of a .22-caliber revolver and subsequent purchase of a new weapon. The sheer number of independent confessions provided additional corroboration for each. Third, whatever may be the parameters of the penal-interest rationale, each confession here was in a very real sense self-incriminatory and unquestionably against interest. McDonald stood to benefit nothing by disclosing his role in the shooting to any of his three friends and he must have been aware of the possibility that disclosure would lead to criminal prosecution. Indeed, after telling Turner of his involvement, he subsequently urged Turner not to "mess him up." Finally, if there was any question about the truthfulness of the extrajudicial statements, McDonald was present in the courtroom and had been under oath. He could have been cross-examined by the State, and his demeanor and responses weighed by the jury. The availability of McDonald significantly distinguishes this case from the prior Mississippi precedent, Brown v. State, and from the *Donnelly*-type situation, since in both cases the declarant was unavailable at the time of trial.[3]

Few rights are more fundamental than that of an accused to present witnesses in his own defense. In the exercise of this right, the accused, as is required of the State, must comply with established

---

3. McDonald's presence also deprives the State's argument for retention of the penal-interest rule of much of its force. In claiming that "[t]o change the rule would work a travesty of justice," the State posited the following hypothetical:

"If the rule were changed, A could be charged with the crime; B could tell C and D that he committed the crime; *B could go into hiding* and at A's trial C and D would testify as to B's admission of guilt; A could be acquitted and B would return to stand trial; B could then provide several witnesses to testify as to his whereabouts at the time

of the crime. The testimony of those witnesses along with A's statement that he really committed the crime would result in B's acquittal. A would be barred from further prosecution because of the protection against double jeopardy. No one could be convicted of perjury as A did not testify at his first trial, B did not lie under oath, and C and D were truthful in their testimony." Respondent's Brief, at 7 n. 3 (emphasis supplied).

Obviously, "B's" absence at trial is critical to the success of the justice-subverting ploy.

rules of procedure and evidence designed to assure both fairness and reliability in the ascertainment of guilt and innocence. Although perhaps no rule of evidence has been more respected or more frequently applied in jury trials than that applicable to the exclusion of hearsay, exceptions tailored to allow the introduction of evidence which in fact is likely to be trustworthy have long existed. The testimony rejected by the trial court here bore persuasive assurances of trustworthiness and thus was well within the basic rationale of the exception for declarations against interest. That testimony also was critical to Chambers' defense. In these circumstances, where constitutional rights directly affecting the ascertainment of guilt are implicated, the hearsay rule may not be applied mechanistically to defeat the ends of justice.

We conclude that the exclusion of this critical evidence, coupled with the State's refusal to permit Chambers to cross-examine McDonald, denied him a trial in accord with traditional and fundamental standards of due process. In reaching this judgment we establish no new principles of constitutional law. Nor does our holding signal any diminution in the respect traditionally accorded to the States in the establishment and implementation of their own criminal trial rules and procedures. Rather, we hold quite simply that under the facts and circumstances of this case the rulings of the trial court deprived Chambers of a fair trial.

The judgment is reversed and the case is remanded to the Supreme Court of Mississippi for further proceedings not inconsistent with this opinion.

[The concurring opinion of Mr. Justice White is omitted].

Mr. Justice Rehnquist, dissenting.

Were I to reach the merits in this case, I would have considerable difficulty in subscribing to the Court's further constitutionalization of the intricacies of the common law of evidence. I do not reach the merits, since I conclude that petitioner failed to properly raise in the Mississippi courts the constitutional issue that he seeks to have this Court decide.

NOTES

1. Frequently prosecutors in jurisdictions which prohibit the use of prior inconsistent statements as substantive evidence will seek to have the turncoat witness called as a hostile witness, or as a court's witness, and then will try to get the out-of-court statement before the jury under the guise of refreshing his memory, quickening his conscience, or impeaching his testimony. If a court takes seriously its prohibition against the use of prior inconsistent statements as substantive evidence, it will prohibit such tactics. See People v. Bailey, 60 Ill.2d 37, 322 N.E.2d 804 (1975).

2. The Federal Rules of Evidence, as approved by the Supreme Court permitted the use of prior inconsistent statements as substantive evidence. Under the Congressionally approved version, however, which became the law on August 1, 1975, this use is permitted only where the original statement was given under oath at a hearing or in a deposition. Fed.Rule of Evid.

801(d)(1). Congress, however, made no change in Rule 607, which permits a party to impeach his own witness. Will this lead to the tactic discussed in the preceding note? Do you believe that District Judges will permit U. S. Attorneys to call a turncoat witness solely for the purpose of getting before the jury the out-of-court unsworn statement, when the prosecutor seeks to invoke Rule 607?

2. ACCESS TO WITNESSES

PEOPLE v. WILSON

Supreme Court of Illinois, 1962.
24 Ill.2d 425, 182 N.E.2d 203.

MR. JUSTICE SCHAEFER delivered the opinion of the court:

The defendants, Cladie B. Wilson and Louis Washington, were indicted for the unlawful sale of narcotic drugs to Inez Anderson, and they were found guilty after a trial before a judge of the criminal court of Cook County. Cladie Wilson was sentenced to the penitentiary for a term of ten to eleven years and Louis Washington was sentenced to life imprisonment as an habitual criminal. They prosecute this writ of error to review their convictions. The defendant Wilson asserts that the State's failure to produce Ruth Killingsworth, an informer for the Federal bureau of narcotics, deprived her of a fair trial, and that the evidence establishes her defense of entrapment. . . .

* * *

In response to the defendants' inquiries as to the whereabouts of Ruth Killingsworth, the State had replied by giving her address as the local office of the Federal bureau of narcotics. Before the trial the attorney for the defendants moved for the entry of an order directing the prosecution to produce Ruth Killingsworth so that he might interview her in order to prepare his defense, to prepare for cross-examination of the State's witnesses, and to call, or request the court to call, Ruth Killingsworth as a witness. The prosecution resisted the motion, and the court reserved his ruling until the evidence had been heard.

At the trial one of the Federal agents testified that on or about September 14, 1958, he went to Ruth Killingsworth's apartment, and drove her, and a man named Fred Stein whom he described as her "husband," to a railroad station in a government car. There he watched them buy tickets, and put them on a train for Fort Worth, Texas. He further testified that he gave her $60 at this time and had given her $700 a few days earlier. He acknowledged that he was acting in his official capacity and that he used official funds. At the conclusion of the testimony the defendants' motion was renewed, and it was then denied upon the ground that the court did not see "how the production of this witness could help either defendant."

To the defendants' contention that the conduct of the Federal agents deprived her of a fair trial, the State replies that it is not required to call all material witnesses to the commission of a crime. That is true, but there is more here than a determination to call, or not to call, a particular witness. Here a crucial witness was deliberately sent beyond the jurisdiction of the court, and where, as here, all of the evidence is secured by or under the direction of Federal agents, the State can not divorce itself from their conduct when it undertakes a prosecution.

The fact that the prosecution itself brought about the absence of the witness makes it unnecessary to consider the State's contention that the defendant did not show that it could compel her return. We may point out, however, that in a case in which Federal narcotic agents deliberately deferred the prosecution until an informer had voluntarily left the jurisdiction, the Supreme Court of California set aside the conviction, saying: "The record does indicate that the police did not arrange for Stough's absence. The critical question, however, is not necessarily one of improper conduct in bringing about Stough's absence, but rather, whether the defendant's conviction resulted from some form of trial in which his essential rights were disregarded or denied."

* * *

Entrapment is a recognized defense to a criminal prosecution, and the defendant was entitled to a fair hearing on that defense. Moreover, the testimony of Killingsworth as to what was said during the defendants' visits to her apartment was critical.

We hold, therefore, that the conduct of the Federal agents in sending her out of the jurisdiction, and the ruling of the trial court in denying the defendants' motion to compel her production, deprived them of a fair trial. Since this conclusion vitiates the conviction of both defendants, it is unnecessary to discuss any of the other grounds asserted by either of them.

The judgment of the criminal court of Cook County is reversed, and the cause is remanded for a new trial.

NOTES

1. The police must make reasonable efforts to retain or obtain information which can be used to locate informers. See People v. Goliday, 8 Cal.3d 771, 505 P.2d 537 (1973).

2. There is a Uniform Act To Secure The Attendance Of Witnesses From Within Or Without A State In Criminal Proceedings. Relevant portions of the Act are:

§ 1. Definitions

"Witness" as used in this act shall include a person whose testimony is desired in any proceeding or investigation by a grand jury or in a Criminal Action, Prosecution or Proceeding.

The word "State" shall include any Territory of the United States and the District of Columbia.

The word "summons" shall include a subpoena, order or other notice requiring the appearance of a witness.

§ 2. Summoning Witness in This State to Testify in Another State

If a judge of a court of record in any state which by its laws has made provision for commanding persons within that state to attend and testify in this state certifies under the seal of such court that there is a criminal prosecution pending in such court, or that a grand jury investigation has commenced or is about to commence, that a person being within this state is a material witness in such prosecution, or grand jury investigation, and that his presence will be required for a specified number of days, upon presentation of such certificate to any judge of a court of record in the county in which such person is, such judge shall fix a time and place for a hearing, and shall make an order directing the witness to appear at a time and place certain for the hearing.

If at a hearing the judge determines that the witness is material and necessary, that it will not cause undue hardship to the witness to be compelled to attend and testify in the prosecution or a grand jury investigation in the other state, and that the laws of the state in which the prosecution is pending, or grand jury investigation has commenced or is about to commence, [and of any other state through which the witness may be required to pass by ordinary course of travel], will give to him protection from arrest and the service of civil and criminal process, he shall issue a summons, with a copy of the certificate attached, directing the witness to attend and testify in the court where the prosecution is pending, or where a grand jury investigation has commenced or is about to commence at a time and place specified in the summons. In any such hearing the certificate shall be prima facie evidence of all the facts stated therein.

If said certificate recommends that the witness be taken into immediate custody and delivered to an officer of the requesting state to assure his attendance in the requesting state, such judge may, in lieu of notification of the hearing, direct that such witness be forthwith brought before him for said hearing; and the judge at the hearing being satisfied of the desirability of such custody and delivery, for which determination the certificate shall be prima facie proof of such desirability may, in lieu of issuing subpoena or summons, order that said witness be forthwith taken into custody and delivered to an officer of the requesting state.

If the witness, who is summoned as above provided, after being paid or tendered by some properly authorized person the sum of 10 cents a mile for each mile by the ordinary traveled route to and from the court where the prosecution is pending and five dollars for each day, that he is required to travel and attend as a witness, fails without good cause to attend and testify as directed in the summons, he shall be punished in the manner provided for the punishment of any witness who disobeys a summons issued from a court of record in this state.

§ 3. Witness from Another State Summoned to Testify in This State

If a person in any state, which by its laws has made provision for commanding persons within its borders to attend and testify in criminal prosecutions, or grand jury investigations commenced or about to commence, in this state, is a material witness in a prosecution pending in a court of record in this state, or in a grand jury investigation which has commenced or is about to commence, a judge of such court may issue a certificate under the seal of the court stating these facts and specifying the number of days the witness will be required. Such certificate may include a recommendation that the witness be taken into immediate custody and delivered to an officer of this state to assure his attendance in this state. This certificate shall be presented to a judge of a court of record in the county in which the witness is found.

If the witness is summoned to attend and testify in this state he shall be tendered the sum of 10 cents a mile for each mile by the ordinary traveled route to and from the court where the prosecution is pending and five dollars for each day that he is required to travel and attend as a witness. A witness who has appeared in accordance with the provisions of the summons shall not be required to remain within this state a longer period of time than the period mentioned in the certificate, unless otherwise ordered by the court. If such witness, after coming into this state, fails without good cause to attend and testify as directed in the summons, he shall be punished in the manner provided for the punishment of any witness who disobeys a summons issued from a court of record in this state.

§ 4. Exemption from Arrest and Service of Process

If a person comes into this state in obedience to a summons directing him to attend and testify in this state he shall not while in this state pursuant to such summons be subject to arrest or the service of process, civil or criminal, in connection with matters which arose before his entrance into this state under the summons.

If a person passes through this state while going to another state in obedience to a summons to attend and testify in that state or while returning therefrom, he shall not while so passing through this state be subject to arrest or the service of process, civil or criminal, in connection with matters which arose before his entrance into this state under the summons.

[A table of the jurisdictions which have adopted the Uniform Act, along with the statutory citations, appears at the end of the Act itself.]

WEBB v. TEXAS

Supreme Court of the United States, 1972.
409 U.S. 95, 93 S.Ct. 351.

PER CURIAM.

The petitioner was convicted of burglary in the Criminal District Court of Dallas County, Texas, and was sentenced to a term of imprisonment for 12 years. .   .   .

The record shows that, after the prosecution had rested its case, the jury was temporarily excused. During this recess, the petitioner called his only witness, Leslie Max Mills, who had a prior criminal record and was then serving a prison sentence. At this point, the trial judge, on his own initiative, undertook to admonish the witness as follows:

> "Now you have been called down as a witness in this case by the Defendant. It is the Court's duty to admonish you that you don't have to testify, that anything you say can and will be used against you. If you take the witness stand and lie under oath, the Court will personally see that your case goes to the grand jury and you will be indicted for perjury and the liklihood [sic] is that you would get convicted of perjury and that it would be stacked onto what you have already got, so that is the matter you have got to make up your mind on. If you get on the witness stand and lie, it is probably going to mean several years and at least more time that you are going to have to serve. It will also be held against you in the penitentiary when you're up for parole and the Court wants you to thoroughly understand the chances you're taking by getting on that witness stand under oath. You may tell the truth and if you do, that is all right, but if you lie you can get into real trouble. The court wants you to know that. You don't owe anybody anything to testify and it must be done freely and voluntarily and with the thorough understanding that you know the hazard you are taking."

The petitioner's counsel objected to these comments, on the ground that the judge was exerting on the mind of the witness such duress that the witness could not freely and voluntarily decide whether or not to testify in the petitioner's behalf, and was thereby depriving the petitioner of his defense by coercing the only defense witness into refusing to testify. Counsel pointed out that none of the witnesses for the State had been so admonished. When the petitioner's counsel then indicated that he was nonetheless going to ask the witness to take the stand, the judge interrupted: "Counsel, you can state the facts, nobody is going to dispute it. Let him decline to testify." The witness then refused to testify for any purpose and was excused by the court. The petitioner's subsequent motion for a mistrial was overruled.

On appeal, the petitioner argued that the judge's conduct indicated a bias against the petitioner and deprived him of due process of law by driving his sole witness off the witness stand. The Court of Criminal Appeals rejected this contention, stating that, while it did not condone the manner of the admonition, the petitioner had made no objection until the admonition was completed, and there was no showing that the witness had been intimidated by the admonition or had refused to testify because of it.

We cannot agree. The suggestion that the petitioner or his counsel should have interrupted the judge in the middle of his remarks to object is, on this record, not a basis to ground a waiver of the petitioner's rights. The fact that Mills was willing to come to court to testify in the petitioner's behalf, refusing to do so only after the judge's lengthy and intimidating warning, strongly suggests that the judge's comments were the cause of Mills' refusal to testify.

The trial judge gratuitously singled out this one witness for a lengthy admonition on the dangers of perjury. But the judge did not stop at warning the witness of his right to refuse to testify and of the necessity to tell the truth. Instead, the judge implied that he expected Mills to lie, and went on to assure him that if he lied, he would be prosecuted and probably convicted for perjury, that the sentence for that conviction would be added on to his present sentence, and that the result would be to impair his chances for parole. At least some of these threats may have been beyond the power of this judge to carry out. Yet in light of the great disparity between the posture of the presiding judge and that of a witness in these circumstances, the unnecessarily strong terms used by the judge could well have exerted such duress on the witness' mind as to preclude him from making a free and voluntary choice whether or not to testify.

In Washington v. Texas, we stated:

> "The right to offer the testimony of witnesses, and to compel their attendance, if necessary, is in plain terms the right to present a defense, the right to present the defendant's version of the facts as well as the prosecution's to the jury so it may decide where the truth lies. Just as an accused has the right to confront the prosecution's witnesses for the purpose of challenging their testimony, he has the right to present his own witnesses to establish a defense. This right is a fundamental element of due process of law."

In the circumstances of this case, we conclude that the judge's threatening remarks, directed alone at the single witness for the defense, effectively drove that witness off the stand, and thus deprived the petitioner of due process of law under the Fourteenth Amendment. The admonition by the Texas Court of Criminal Appeals might well have given the trial judge guidance for future cases, but it did not serve to repair the infringement of the petitioner's due process rights under the Fourteenth Amendment.

Accordingly, the judgment is reversed.

Reversed.

MR. JUSTICE BLACKMUN, with whom MR. JUSTICE REHNQUIST joins, dissenting.

The facts before us do not, in my opinion, justify the Court's summary disposition. Petitioner Webb (who, on a prior occasion, had been convicted on still another burglary charge) was apprehended by the owner of a lumber business. The owner, armed with his shotgun, had driven to his office at three o'clock in the morning upon the activation of a burglar alarm. When he entered the building, the owner observed a broken window and an assortment of what he regarded as burglary tools on his desk. When men emerged from an adjacent room, a gun fight ensued. Two intruders escaped, but the owner, despite his having been shot twice, succeeded in holding the petitioner at gun point until police arrived.

Although the admonition given by the state trial judge to the sole witness proffered by the defense is obviously improper, sufficient facts have not been presented to this Court to demonstrate the depth of prejudice that requires a summary reversal. The admonition might prove far less offensive, and the conduct of the trial judge understandable, if, for example, as is indicated in petitioner's brief, filed with the Texas Court of Criminal Appeals, the witness were known to have been called for the purpose of presenting an alibi defense. Against the backdrop of being caught on the premises and of apparently overwhelming evidence of guilt, offset only by a bare allegation of prejudice, I would deny the petition for certiorari and, as the Court so often has done, I would remit the petitioner to the relief available to him by way of a post-conviction proceeding with a full evidentiary hearing.

NOTE

Consider People v. Carradine, 52 Ill.2d 231, 287 N.E.2d 670 (1972):

"MR. CHIEF JUSTICE UNDERWOOD delivered the opinion of the court.

The Cook County circuit court found Georgia Carradine to be in direct contempt of court for her refusal to testify [as a witness to a homicide] and sentenced her to imprisonment for six months in the Cook County jail. . .   .

* * *

"The more difficult question is the contemnor's request, predicated upon the extenuating circumstances surrounding her refusal to testify, that her punishment be reduced to the two weeks already spent in jail. Those circumstances include the fact that Mrs. Carradine had been separated from her husband for some four years, had six children aged 5 to 18 at home, and was supported by payments from her husband and supplemental welfare funds; that there seems little reason to doubt her refusal to testify resulted solely from her fear of harm to herself and her children if she testified against the defendants who apparently were members of the Blackstone Rangers, a youth gang; that she believed she had been 'tricked' and lied to by the assistant State's Attorney to whom she had given a statement, because, as she stated, he told her she would not have to appear and testify and that, absent this assurance, she never would have given him the statement; that she did not believe the law enforcement authorities could protect her from the 'Stones' for, as she put it:

'THE WITNESS: Well, look, Judge, I am going to tell you, I live in the middle of the slums, down in the slums. Where I live the police don't even come in there even if we call. I called the police one night about a fight. You'd think they were going to kill one another. But the police don't even come up in there where I live. So, how are they going to protect me and my family when they don't even come up in the building where we live?'

Nor does she believe that relocating her family would solve the problems, for the 'Stones' were 'everywhere.'

"It is completely clear from the record that Mrs. Carradine understood the likely results of her refusal to testify and deliberately chose to incur imprisonment rather than expose herself and her family to what she considered to be the certainty of serious physical harm or death. The conscientious trial judge appointed counsel for her and patiently, clearly and repeatedly explained the situation, urging her to change her mind and reiterating the offers of protection and relocation; the proceedings were continued on several occasions in order that she might have an opportunity to reconsider her decision.

"No useful purpose would be served by prolonged discussion. The reluctance of witnesses to testify is not an uncommon problem, although the circumstances here are particularly distressing. The contempt proceedings were conducted with eminent fairness, and, in our opinion, the judgment and sentence must be affirmed. The fundamental reason therefore was stated by the trial court: '. . . one of the problems that the Court has is that unless we receive the cooperation of the citizens who see certain alleged events take place these events are not going to be rooted out, nor are perpetrators of these acts going to be brought before the bar of justice unless citizens stand up to be counted, and I think this [fear] is not a valid reason for not testifying. If it's a valid reason then we might as well close the doors.'

"The judgment of the Cook County circuit court is affirmed."

WASHINGTON v. TEXAS

Supreme Court of the United States, 1967.
388 U.S. 14, 87 S.Ct. 1920, on remand 417 S.W.2d 278 (Tex.Cr.App.).

MR. CHIEF JUSTICE WARREN delivered the opinion of the Court.

We granted certiorari in this case to determine whether the right of a defendant in a criminal case under the Sixth Amendment to have compulsory process for obtaining witnesses in his favor is applicable to the States through the Fourteenth Amendment, and whether that right was violated by a state procedural statute providing that persons charged as principals, accomplices, or accessories in the same crime cannot be introduced as witnesses for each other.

Petitioner, Jackie Washington, was convicted in Dallas County, Texas, of murder with malice and was sentenced by a jury to 50 years in prison. The prosecution's evidence showed that petitioner, an 18-year-old youth, had dated a girl named Jean Carter until her mother had forbidden her to see him. The girl thereafter began dating another boy, the deceased. Evidently motivated by jealousy, petitioner with several other boys began driving around the City of Dallas on the night of August 29, 1964, looking for a gun. The search eventually led to one Charles Fuller, who joined the group with his shotgun. After obtaining some shells from another source, the group of boys proceeded to Jean Carter's home, where Jean, her family and the deceased were having supper. Some of the boys threw bricks at the house and then ran back to the car, leaving petitioner and Fuller alone in front of the house with the shotgun. At the sound of the bricks the deceased and Jean Carter's mother rushed out on the porch to investigate. The shotgun was fired by either petitioner or Fuller, and the deceased was fatally wounded. Shortly afterward petitioner and Fuller came running back to the car where the other boys waited, with Fuller carrying the shotgun.

Petitioner testified in his own behalf. He claimed that Fuller, who was intoxicated, had taken the gun from him, and that he had unsuccessfully tried to persuade Fuller to leave before the shooting. Fuller had insisted that he was going to shoot someone, and petitioner had run back to the automobile. He saw the girl's mother come out of the door as he began running, and he subsequently heard the shot. At the time, he had thought that Fuller had shot the woman. In support of his version of the facts petitioner offered the testimony of Fuller. The record indicates that Fuller would have testified that petitioner pulled at him and tried to persuade him to leave, and that petitioner ran before Fuller fired the fatal shot.

It is undisputed that Fuller's testimony would have been relevant and material, and that it was vital to the defense. Fuller was the only person other than petitioner who knew exactly who had fired the shotgun and whether petitioner had at the last minute attempted to prevent the shooting. Fuller, however, had been previously convicted of the same murder and sentenced to 50 years in prison, and he was confined in the Dallas County jail. Two Texas statutes provided at the time of the trial in this case that persons charged or convicted as co-participants in the same crime could not testify for one another,[1]

---

1. "Persons charged as principals, accomplices or accessories, whether in the same or by different indictments, can not be introduced as witnesses for one another, but they may claim a severance, and if one or more be

although there was no bar to their testifying for the State. On the basis of these statutes the trial judge sustained the State's objection and refused to allow Fuller to testify. Petitioner's conviction followed, and it was upheld on appeal by the Texas Court of Criminal Appeals. We reverse.

I.

We have not previously been called upon to decide whether the right of an accused to have compulsory process for obtaining witnesses in his favor, guaranteed in federal trials by the Sixth Amendment, is so fundamental and essential to a fair trial that it is incorporated in the Due Process Clause of the Fourteenth Amendment. At one time, it was thought that the Sixth Amendment had no application to state criminal trials. That view no longer prevails, and in recent years we have increasingly looked to the specific guarantees of the Sixth Amendment to determine whether a state criminal trial was conducted with due process of law. We have held that due process requires that the accused have the assistance of counsel for his defense, that he be confronted with the witnesses against him, and that he have the right to a speedy and public trial.

The right of an accused to have compulsory process for obtaining witnesses in his favor stands on no lesser footing than the other Sixth Amendment rights that we have previously held applicable to the States. This Court had occasion in In re Oliver, to describe what it regarded as the most basic ingredients of due process of law. It observed that:

> "A person's right to reasonable notice of a charge against him, and an opportunity to be heard in his defense—a right to his day in court—are basic in our system of jurisprudence; and these rights include, as a minimum, a right to

acquitted they may testify in behalf of the others." Vernon's Ann.Tex. Pen.Code, Art. 82.

"Persons charged as principals, accomplices or accessories, whether in the same or different indictments, cannot be introduced as witnesses for one another, but they may claim a severance; and, if any one or more be acquitted, or the prosecution against them be dismissed, they may testify in behalf of the others." Tex.Code Crim.Proc., Art. 711 (1925).

These statutory provisions were apparently repealed by implication by Art. 36.09 of the Vernon's Ann.Texas Code of Criminal Procedure of 1965, which became effective after petitioner's trial. Article 36.09 provides that "Two or more defendants who are jointly or separately indicated or complained against for the same offense or an offense growing out of the

same transaction may be, in the discretion of the court, tried jointly or separately as to one or more defendants; provided that in any event either defendant may testify for the other or on behalf of the State . . . . ."

Counsel have cited no statutes from other jurisdictions, and we have found none, that flatly disqualify coparticipants in a crime from testifying for each other regardless of whether they are tried jointly or separately. To be distinguished are statutes providing that one of two or more defendants tried jointly may, if the evidence against him is insufficient, be entitled to an immediate acquittal so he may testify for the others. These statutes seem designed to allow such joint defendants to testify without incriminating themselves.

examine the witnesses against him, to offer testimony, and
to be represented by counsel."

The right to offer the testimony of witnesses, and to compel their attendance, if necessary, is in plain terms the right to present a defense, the right to present the defendant's version of the facts as well
as the prosecution's to the jury so it may decide where the truth lies.
Just as an accused has the right to confront the prosecution's witnesses for the purpose of challenging their testimony, he has the
right to present his own witnesses to establish a defense. This right
is a fundamental element of due process of law.

II.

Since the right to compulsory process is applicable in this state
proceeding, the question remains whether it was violated in the circumstances of this case. The testimony of Charles Fuller was denied
to the defense not because the State refused to compel his attendance,
but because a state statute made his testimony inadmissible whether
he was present in the courtroom or not. We are thus called upon to
decide whether the Sixth Amendment guarantees a defendant the
right under any circumstances to put his witnesses on the stand, as
well as the right to compel their attendance in court. The resolution of
this question requires some discussion of the common-law context in
which the Sixth Amendment was adopted.

Joseph Story, in his famous Commentaries on the Constitution of
the United States, observed that the right to compulsory process was
included in the Bill of Rights in reaction to the notorious common-law
rule that in cases of treason or felony the accused was not allowed to
introduce witnesses in his defense at all. Although the absolute prohibition of witnesses for the defense had been abolished in England
by statute before 1787, the Framers of the Constitution felt it necessary specifically to provide that defendants in criminal cases should
be provided the means of obtaining witnesses so that their own evidence, as well as the prosecution's, might be evaluated by the jury.

Despite the abolition of the rule generally disqualifying defense
witnesses, the common law retained a number of restrictions on witnesses who were physically and mentally capable of testifying. To
the extent that they were applicable, they had the same effect of suppressing the truth that the general proscription had had. Defendants
and codefendants were among the large class of witnesses disqualified from testifying on the ground of interest.[2] A party to a civil or
criminal case was not allowed to testify on his own behalf for fear
that he might be tempted to lie. Although originally the disqualification of a codefendant appears to have been based only on his status
as a party to the action, and in some jurisdictions co-indictees were

---

2. See generally 2 Wigmore §§ 575–
576 (3d ed. 1940). We have discussed elsewhere the gradual demise
of the common-law rule prohibiting
defendants from testifying in their
own behalf. See Ferguson v. State
of Georgia, 365 U.S. 570, 81 S.Ct. 756
(1961).

allowed to testify for or against each other if granted separate trials, other jurisdictions came to the view that accomplices or co-indictees were incompetent to testify at least in favor of each other even at separate trials, and in spite of statutes making a defendant competent to testify in his own behalf. It was thought that if two persons charged with the same crime were allowed to testify on behalf of each other, "each would try to swear the other out of the charge." This rule, as well as the other disqualifications for interest, rested on the unstated premises that the right to present witnesses was subordinate to the court's interest in preventing perjury, and that erroneous decisions were best avoided by preventing the jury from hearing any testimony that might be perjured, even if it were the only testimony available on a crucial issue.[3]

The federal courts followed the common-law restrictions for a time, despite the Sixth Amendment. In United States v. Reid, 12 How. 361 (1852), the question was whether one of two defendants jointly indicted for murder on the high seas could call the other as a witness. Although this Court expressly recognized that the Sixth Amendment was designed to abolish some of the harsh rules of the common law, particularly including the refusal to allow the defendant in a serious criminal case to present witnesses in his defense, it held that the rules of evidence in the federal courts were those in force in the various States at the time of the passage of the Judiciary Act of 1789, including the disqualification of defendants indicted together. The holding in United States v. Reid was not satisfactory to later generations, however, and in 1918 this Court expressly overruled it, refusing to be bound by the "the dead hand of the common-law rule of 1789," and taking note of "the conviction of our time that the truth is more likely to be arrived at by hearing the testimony of all persons of competent understanding who may seem to have knowledge of the facts involved in a case, leaving the credit and weight of such testimony to be determined by the jury or by the court . . . ."

Although Rosen v. United States rested on nonconstitutional grounds, we believe that its reasoning was required by the Sixth Amendment. In light of the common-law history, and in view of the recognition in the *Reid* case that the Sixth Amendment was designed in part to make the testimony of a defendant's witnesses admissible on his behalf in court, it could hardly be argued that a State would not violate the clause if it made all defense testimony inadmissible as a matter of procedural law. It is difficult to see how the Constitution is any less violated by arbitrary rules that prevent whole categories of defense witnesses from testifying on the basis of *a priori* categories that presume them unworthy of belief.

---

3. "Indeed, the theory of the common law was to admit to the witness stand only those presumably honest, appreciating the sanctity of an oath, unaffected as a party by the result, and free from any of the temptations of interest. The courts were afraid to trust the intelligence of jurors." Benson v. United States, 146 U.S. 325, 336, 13 S.Ct. 60, 63 (1892).

The rule disqualifying an alleged accomplice from testifying on behalf of the defendant cannot even be defended on the ground that it rationally sets apart a group of persons who are particularly likely to commit perjury. The absurdity of the rule is amply demonstrated by the exceptions that have been made to it. For example, the accused accomplice may be called by the prosecution to testify against the defendant. Common sense would suggest that he often has a greater interest in lying in favor of the prosecution rather than against it, especially if he is still awaiting his own trial or sentencing. To think that criminals will lie to save their fellows but not to obtain favors from the prosecution for themselves is indeed to clothe the criminal class with more nobility than one might expect to find in the public at large. Moreover, under the Texas statutes, the accused accomplice is no longer disqualified if he is acquitted at his own trial. Presumably, he would then be free to testify on behalf on his comrade, secure in the knowledge that he could incriminate himself as freely as he liked in his testimony, since he could not again be prosecuted for the same offense. The Texas law leaves him free to testify when he has a great incentive to perjury, and bars his testimony in situations where he has a lesser motive to lie.

We hold that the petitioner in this case was denied his right to have compulsory process for obtaining witnesses in his favor because the State arbitrarily denied him the right to put on the stand a witness who was physically and mentally capable of testifying to events that he had personally observed, and whose testimony would have been relevant and material to the defense.[4] The Framers of the Constitution did not intend to commit the futile act of giving to a defendant the right to secure the attendance of witnesses whose testimony he had no right to use. The judgment of conviction must be reversed. It is so ordered.

Reversed.

MR. JUSTICE HARLAN, concurring in the result.

. . . I cannot accept the view that the Due Process Clause of the Fourteenth Amendment "incorporates," in its terms, the specific provisions of the Bill of Rights. In my view the Due Process Clause is not reducible to "a series of isolated points," but is rather "a rational continuum which, broadly speaking, includes a freedom from all substantial arbitrary impositions and purposeless restraints . . . . ."

I concur in the result in this case because I believe that the State may not constitutionally forbid the petitioner, a criminal defendant,

4. Nothing in this opinion should be construed as disapproving testimonial privileges, such as the privilege against self-incrimination or the lawyer-client or husband-wife privileges, which are based on entirely different considerations from those underlying the common-law disqualifications for interest. Nor do we deal in this case with nonarbitrary state rules that disqualify as witnesses persons who, because of mental infirmity or infancy, are incapable of observing events or testifying about them.

from introducing on his own behalf the important testimony of one indicted in connection with the same offense, who would not, however, be barred from testifying if called by the prosecution. Texas has put forward no justification for this type of discrimination between the prosecution and the defense in the ability to call the same person as a witness, and I can think of none.

In my opinion this is not, then, really a problem of "compulsory process" at all, although the Court's incorporationist approach leads it to strain this constitutional provision to reach these peculiar statutes. Neither is it a situation in which the State has determined, as a matter of valid state evidentiary law, on the basis of general experience with a particular class of persons, as for example, the mentally incompetent or those previously convicted of perjury, that the pursuit of truth is best served by an across-the-board disqualification as witnesses of persons of that class. This is rather a case in which the State has recognized as relevant and competent the testimony of this type of witness, but has arbitrarily barred its use by the defendant. This, I think, the Due Process Clause forbids.

On this premise I concur in the reversal of the judgment of conviction.

NOTES

1. The concluding footnote of the Court's opinion in Washington v. Texas states that "nothing in this opinion should be construed as disapproving testimonial privileges, such as the privilege against self-incrimination or the lawyer-client or husband-wife privileges. . . ." The Court's examples are not exhaustive. There are numerous statutory privileges and their number has increased in recent years. There is the priest-penitent or clergyman privilege, the physician-patient privilege, and the psychologist-patient privilege. Some jurisdictions have an accountant-client privilege. Recently there has been the use of the news media informant privilege.

The nature and scope of these privileges varies from jurisdiction to jurisdiction, A thorough dissertation of privilege law is found in 8 Wigmore, Evidence (McNaughton Rev. 1961) and a shorter survey in McCormick, Evidence, Chs. 8–13 (2nd Ed. 1972). The privilege against self-incrimination is usually limited to communications, that is, evidence of what the person says as opposed to evidence of what he has done or evidence about his physical characters. This limitation was explored in United States v. Dionisio, supra Chapter 11. Similar forms of limitations usually apply to the husband-wife, psychiatrist-patient and psychologist-patient and clergyman privileges. In most but not all jurisdictions, such privileges preclude only evidence concerning statements made by spouse, patient or penitent. Thus a wife may usually testify as to what her husband did but not what he said, i. e., she may reveal that when he came home his clothes were bloody and that he burned his clothes but she may not reveal that he said "I just killed a child with my hunting knife." Another example is encountered occasionally in modern criminal cases. An attorney may attend a line-up on his client's behalf. What he observes at the line-up is not privileged and the prosecution often is entitled to his testimony if it helps establish their case. See People v. Dozier, 22 Mich.App. 528, 177 N.W.2d 694 (1970). Similarly, counsel may be compelled to testify as to his observations of his client's physical condition at the police station if there is claim that a confession was physically coerced.   State v. Funicello, 49 N.J. 553, 231 A.2d 579 (1967).   But in some jurisdictions, privilege extends to "information" acquired as a result of the privileged relationship as well as communications. The physician-patient, accountant-client, and news media-informant privileges usually cover more than communications.   Generally such privileges apply to all information acquired by virtue of the privileged relationship.

Few jurisdictions have statutes creating all of the aforementioned privileges.   Such a commonly known privilege as physician-patient does not exist in about a third of the states.   There are jurisdictions which have adopted relatively unusual privileges such as the nurse-patient, confidential clerk, or private detective-client privileges.   Except for the self-incrimination privilege, none of the various privileges has been held to be constitutionally required.   Branzburg v. Hayes, 408 U.S. 665, 92 S.Ct. 2646 (1972) ; Felber v. Foote, 321 F.Supp. 85, 87–88 (D.Conn.1970).   An argument can be made that the constitutionally guaranteed right to counsel includes some form of attorney-client privilege.   On the other hand, it can be argued with equal force that the effective assistance of counsel does not require such a privilege.   See McCormick, Evidence, pp. 175–77 (2nd Ed. 1972).

Finally, the various privileges are subject to statutory exceptions.   A court is often given power to disregard privilege in the interests of justice; for instance, physician-patient privileges are sometimes inapplicable in homicide cases.   And state created privileges cannot preclude the production of evidence in any federal trial except in diversity cases.   Wolfle v. United States, 291 U.S. 60, 54 S.Ct. 279; Colton v. United States, 306 F.2d 633, (2nd Cir. 1969) ; Wright, The Law of Federal Courts 414–15 (2nd Ed. 1970).

2.   Is there any way to determine effect of these privileges on criminal cases?   There is simply no way to measure the amount of privileged communication and information that is relevant to criminal cases from the frequency with which the privilege is asserted.   The privilege is asserted when one party to the privileged communication has improperly revealed its contents and the prosecution or defense counsel learns of the contents and attempts to introduce it into evidence.   The attorneys may, of course, guess without knowing that privileged information may be of value, but usually this involves an accomplice or participant in the crime and the privilege against self-incrimination is claimed.   We suspect that some relevant information simply never surfaces at all.   Most legally privileged relationships correspond to relationships which society would generally consider confidential even without sanction of law.   Those who receive confidential communications will often feel a personal compulsion or distaste for public revelation even when they are legally free to do so.   A husband may confess a crime to his wife and she may never repeat his confession to anyone, not because of legal restraint, but rather because she loves her husband and does not wish to damage her own family.

Are we in a position to judge whether privileges or any given privilege should restrict access to evidence when we cannot judge how great a price we pay in terms of the loss of relevant information?

If we cannot judge the price we pay for privilege, is it proper to assume that privileges should exist and place the burden of proof upon those who would abolish privilege or any given privilege?

If privileged information is seldom uncovered because of social rather than legal pressures, would any purpose be served by abolishing socially endorsed privileges?   For example, would repeal of a marital privilege statute really lessen the number of hidden communications? Assume that prosecutors and defense counsel would, after repeal, regularly interview and perhaps subpoena the spouses of the accused, his accomplices, other suspects and key witnesses. Would not the spouse who is willing to keep silent also be willing to commit perjury? If most persons were aware that the privilege had no legal sanction, would they confide in their spouses to the degree they do now? Would the answers be different if a different privilege were involved, e. g., lack of candor with one's physician even where there is no privilege may well have disagreeable or even fatal effects.

3. Consider the effect of privilege on the factual situation presented in Chambers v. Mississippi supra. Assume McDonald confessed not to Chambers' lawyer but to his own lawyer, or to his wife, or to his priest, and Chambers' lawyer learned of the confession. Would the Court adhere to its position in Washington v. Texas and reject Chambers' appeal? From the viewpoint of Chambers himself, does not a ruling sustaining the privilege have precisely the same effect as one sustaining the witness voucher and hearsay arguments that Mississippi offered to defend the conviction? What would the Court say the difference was and would their answer satisfy you?

Suppose that McDonald did not confess to anyone but that Chambers' lawyer suspects (say from physical evidence) that he committed the crime and then he interviews McDonald, but McDonald refuses to answer on grounds of self-incrimination. What can Chambers' lawyer do? McDonald can exonerate his client but the privilege is a barrier. (And cases can be conceived in which the only possible exonerating witness, other than the defendant, may claim the privilege.) Can the prosecution be compelled to grant immunity to McDonald? If this is done, the prosecution will either never be able to prosecute McDonald (if transactional immunity is granted) or will probably be unable to prosecute (if use immunity is granted). It may be said that the policy of the law is to prefer acquittal of the innocent over conviction of the guilty and that it is better to have both McDonald and Chambers escape. But this assumes that McDonald is guilty and Chambers is innocent, an assumption which generally cannot be made in advance of trial. Perhaps McDonald is falsely claiming privilege or he claims privilege because he did not commit murder but was committing robbery or shooting at the other officer at the time of the incident? Perhaps McDonald is operating under a mistaken belief of guilt, i. e., McDonald fires his gun at the officer not knowing the powder was stale and bullet was spent before reaching the target.

In another context, assume a defendant is charged with possessing narcotics and he claims that his mistress, who was the only other person with access to the apartment, planted the narcotics in his overcoat lining. She may be the only witness who can exonerate him but she claims privilege. The prosecution has no intention of prosecuting her, but could a court require the prosecution to grant immunity? Should it? The argument that the government should be compelled to grant immunity was rejected in Earl v. United States, 124 U.S.App.D.C. 77, 361 F.2d 531 (1966) (Burger, J.,) reh. denied 384 F.2d 666 (1966). Compare People v. Sapia, 41 N.Y.2d 160, 319 N.Y.S.2d 93, 359 N.E.2d 688 (1976) (approving the principle that the court may immunize defense witness but holding request properly denied); United States v. Morrison, 535 F.2d 223 (3rd Cir. 1976) (witness for defense must be immunized where the witness had been intimidated by prosecution).

The various foregoing examples disclose another important facet of privilege in a criminal case, namely, that the government has greater access to privileged evidence than does the defense. The privilege against self-incrimination may prevent defense access to a witness but it will not prevent prosecution use of the witness if the government is willing to forego prosecution of the witness. Is this reasonable? If it is unreasonable, is the solution to confer the power of immunity upon defense counsel, or to deprive the prosecution of the power to use immunity statutes. Is it possible to allow the court to grant immunity on the motion of either party?

4. The privileges thus far mentioned belong to private individuals. The state has its own set of privileges, the most common of which is the informer privilege. Law enforcement officers frequently use informers and are entitled generally to keep their names secret. In McCray v. Illinois, 386 U.S. 300, 87 S.Ct. 1056 (1967), the petitioner was arrested, searched, and successfully prosecuted for possession of heroin found in the course of the search. The officers justified the arrest and search on the basis of information from an informer, not present at the arrest, whose reliability was adequately established but whose identity the officers refused to disclose. The Court sustained the informer privilege for the following reasons:

"In permitting the officers to withhold the informant's identity, the court was following well-settled Illinois law. When the issue is not guilt or innocence, but, as here, the question of probable cause for an arrest or search, the Illinois Supreme Court has held that police officers need not invariably be required to disclose an informant's identity 'f the trial judge is convinced, by evidence submitted in open court and subject to cross-examination, that the officers did rely in good faith upon credible information supplied by a reliable informant. This Illinois evidentiary rule is consistent with the law of many other States. .   .   .

*   *   *

"The reasoning of the Supreme Court of New Jersey in judically adopting the same basic evidentiary rule was instructively expressed by Chief Justice Weintraub in State v. Burnett, 42 N.J. 377, 201 A.2d 39:

'If a defendant may insist upon disclosure of the informant in order to test the truth of the officer's statement that there is an informant or as to what the informant related or as to the informant's reliability, we can be sure that every defendant will demand disclosure. He has nothing to lose and the prize may be the suppression of damaging evidence if the State cannot afford to reveal its source, as is so often the case. And since there is no way to test the good faith of a defendant who presses the demand, we must assume the routine demand would have to be routinely granted. The result would be that the State could use the informant's information only as a lead and could search only if it could gather adequate evidence of probable cause apart from the informant's data. Perhaps that approach would sharpen investigatorial techniques, but we doubt that there would be enough talent and time to cope with crime upon that basis. Rather we accept the premise that the informer is a vital part of society's defensive arsenal. The basic rule protecting his identity rests upon that belief. .   .   .

'We must remember also that we are not dealing with the trial of the criminal charge itself. There the need for a truthful verdict outweighs society's need for the informer privilege. Here,

however, the accused seeks to avoid the truth. The very purpose
of a motion to suppress is to escape the inculpatory thrust of evidence in hand, not because its probative force is diluted in the
least by the mode of seizure, but rather as a sanction to compel enforcement officers to respect the constitutional security of all of us
under the Fourth Amendment. . . . If the motion to suppress
is denied, defendant will still be judged upon the untarnished
truth. . . .'

* * *

". . . This Court has the ultimate task of defining the scope to be
accorded to the various common law evidentiary privileges in the trial of
federal criminal cases. . . . In the exercise of this supervisory jurisdiction the Court had occasion 10 years ago, in Roviaro v. United States, to
give thorough consideration to one aspect of the informer's privilege, the
privilege itself having long been recognized in the federal judicial system.

"The *Roviaro* case involved the informer's privilege, not at a preliminary hearing to determine probable cause for an arrest or search, but at the
trial itself where the issue was the fundamental one of innocence or guilt.
The petitioner there had been brought to trial upon a two-count federal indictment charging sale and transportation of narcotics. According to the
prosecution's evidence, the informer had been an active participant in the
crime. He 'had taken a material part in bringing about the possession of
certain drugs by the accused, had been present with the accused at the occurrence of the alleged crime, and might be a material witness as to whether
the accused knowingly transported the drugs as charged.' The trial court
nonetheless denied a defense motion to compel the prosecution to disclose
the informer's identity.

"This Court held that where, in an actual trial of a federal criminal
case,

'the disclosure of an informer's identity . . . is relevant and
helpful to the defense of an accused, or is essential to a fair determination of a cause, the privilege must give way. In these situations the trial court may require disclosure and, if the Government
withholds the information, dismiss the action. . . .

'We believe that no fixed rule with respect to disclosure is justifiable. The problem is one that calls for balancing the public interest in protecting the flow of information against the individual's right to prepare his defense. Whether a proper balance renders nondisclosure erroneous must depend on the particular circumstances of each case, taking into consideration the crime
charged, the possible defenses, the possible significance of the informer's testimony, and other relevant factors.'

"The Court's opinion then carefully reviewed the particular circumstances of Roviaro's trial, pointing out that the informer's 'possible testimony was highly relevant . . . ,' that he 'might have disclosed an entrapment . . . ,' 'might have thrown doubt upon petitioner's identity or on
the identity of the package . . . ,' 'might have testified to petitioner's
possible lack of knowledge of the contents of the package that he "transported" . . . ,' and that the 'informer was the sole participant, other
than the accused, in the transaction charged.' The Court concluded 'that,
under these circumstances, the trial court committed prejudicial error in

permitting the Government to withhold the identity of its undercover employee in the face of repeated demands by the accused for his disclosure.' "

* * *

In *McCray* there is a dichotomy set forth between the assertion of privilege which affects the validity of the acquisition of evidence and the assertion of privilege which affects the trial on the merits. In the first situation, the privilege may be validly asserted; in the second it generally may not.

The premise that the government may not assert its privileges when they preclude defense access to material evidence on the merits is the traditional rule. The courts do not say that the privilege may not be asserted and preserved; the government is given a choice between preserving confidentiality and abandoning the prosecution or pursuing the prosecution and abandoning the privilege. See United States v. Andolschek, 142 F.2d 503, 506 (2nd Cir. 1944).

The government may be entitled to have a court examine the privileged material outside the presence of the defense at least to determine if the material does have any arguable relevance to the case on trial. Palermo v. United States, 360 U.S. 343, 79 S.Ct. 1217 (1959); but see Alderman v. United States, 394 U.S. 165, 89 S.Ct. 961 (1969).

A serious question may arise when a state government institutes prosecution and the defense seeks access to evidence which is in the possession of the federal government and protected by federal privilege. Presumably the state government would have no more right to the evidence than the defendant and the matter would be treated as any case in which a witness (as opposed to a party) asserts the privilege. The nature of the material covered by traditional federal privileges is likely to have relevance to only the rarest of state prosecutions. See Zagel, The State Secrets Privilege, 50 Minn.L. Rev. 875 (1966). (It may be noted that one court has allowed federal prosecution to proceed despite sustaining a claim of the state secrets privilege, but the decision was explicitly based on the fact that the country was fighting a declared war. United States v. Haugen, 58 F.Supp. 436 (E.D.Wash. 1944).)

The government may waive any of its privileges and use the evidence if it so chooses. The government may use the informer or reveal the state secret if it regards the prosecution as sufficiently important. In this regard the defendant is in a similar position when he must decide whether exercising his right to take the stand is worth the sacrifice of his self-incrimination privilege on cross-examination. Brown v. United States, 356 U.S. 148, 78 S.Ct. 662 (1958).

5. There are literally hundreds of other pockets of privilege in American law. These privileges nearly all pertain to government records and are found in either statutes or administrative regulations. Common examples are rules insuring confidentiality of tax returns, accident reports, juvenile delinquency records, unemployment compensation, police reports, and welfare records. Some rules merely prohibit public inspection, while allowing production of records in response to subpoena. These records are sometimes available to the government if it wishes to use them in a prosecution and, if it does so, the defense will presumably be allowed access to them. If the records are not available to the prosecution, the problems which arise

are identical to those occurring when the husband-wife privilege is asserted. These privileges have not created many controversies in the administration of criminal justice, but difficulties have arisen particularly with respect to impeachment of witnesses with their otherwise confidential records of juvenile misconduct. See People v. Franklin, 74 Ill.App.2d 392, 220 N.E.2d 872 (1966) (allowing impeachment). See also People v. Bridgeforth, 51 Ill.2d 52, 281 N.E.2d 617 (1972) (welfare records subject to statutory privilege may not be used to impeach welfare recipients who are prosecution witnesses and the statutory privilege does not deny defendant his constitutional right of access to evidence).

In Davis v. Alaska, 415 U.S. 308, 94 S.Ct. 1105 (1974), the issue was whether the statutory privilege for juvenile court adjudications could preclude cross-examination of a juvenile witness about his current status on probation. The Court said:

> "The claim is made that the State has an important interest in protecting the anonymity of juvenile offenders and that this interest outweighs any competing interest this petitioner might have in cross-examining Green about his being on probation. The State argues that exposure of a juvenile's record of delinquency would likely cause impairment of rehabilitative goals of the juvenile correctional procedures. This exposure, it is argued, might encourage the juvenile offender to commit further acts of delinquency, or cause the juvenile offender to lose employment opportunities or otherwise suffer unnecessarily for his youthful transgression.

> "We do not and need not challenge the State's interest as a matter of its own policy in the administration of criminal justice to seek to preserve the anonymity of a juvenile offender. Here, however, petitioner sought to introduce evidence of Green's probation for the purpose of suggesting that Green was biased and, therefore, that his testimony was either not to be believed in his identification of petitioner or at least very carefully considered in that light. Serious damage to the strength of the State's case would have been a real possibility had petitioner been allowed to pursue this line of inquiry. In this setting we conclude that the right of confrontation is paramount to the State's policy of protecting a juvenile offender. Whatever temporary embarrassment might result to Green or his family by disclosure of his juvenile record—if the prosecution insisted on using him to make its case—is outweighed by petitioner's right to probe into the influence of possible bias in the testimony of a crucial identification witness.

> "In Alford v. United States, we upheld the right of defense counsel to impeach a witness by showing that because of the witness' incarceration in federal prison at the time of trial, the witness' testimony was biased as "given under promise or expectation of immunity, or under the coercive effect of his detention by officers of the United States." 282 U.S., at 693, 51 S.Ct., at 220. In response to the argument that the witness had a right to be protected from exposure of his criminal record, the Court stated:

>> '[N]o obligation is imposed on the court, such as that suggested below, to protect a witness from being discredited on cross-examination, short of an attempted invasion of his constitutional protection from self incrimination, properly invoked. There is a duty to protect him from questions which

go beyond the bounds of proper cross-examination merely to harass, annoy or humiliate him.'

As in *Alford*, we conclude that the State's desire that Green fulfill his public duty to testify free from embarrassment and with his reputation unblemished must fall before the right of petitioner to seek out the truth in the process of defending himself.

"The State's policy interest in protecting the confidentiality of a juvenile offender's record cannot require yielding of so vital a constitutional right as the effective cross-examination for bias of an adverse witness. The State could have protected Green from exposure of his juvenile adjudication in these circumstances by refraining from using him to make out its case; the State cannot, consistent with the right of confrontation, require the petitioner to bear the full burden of vindicating the State's interest in the secrecy of juvenile criminal records."

BOWLES v. UNITED STATES

United States Court of Appeals, D.C.Cir. 1970.
142 U.S.App.D.C. 26, 439 F.2d 536, certiorari denied 1971, 401 U.S. 995, 91 S.Ct. 1240.

ON HEARING EN BANC

LEVENTHAL, CIRCUIT JUDGE.

This is an appeal from a judgment entered on convictions of murder in the first degree (homicide while attempting to perpetrate a robbery) and of assault with intent to rob. . . . .

Appellant gave testimony that on the night of March 13, at around 11:30 p. m. he encountered Raymond Smith, Yvonne Smith and Jerry Neely in the 1300 block of T Street, N.W., and that Raymond Smith said to him, "Man, I just got me one. I just got me a man up the corner. If the police get me, I am going to tell them that Jerry did it."

To buttress appellant's defense that it was Smith and not he who killed Ingham, Neely was called as a witness for the defense. Neely corroborated appellant's account of the conversation with Smith. He testified that Smith had said that he had just got one on R Street. Melvin Royal also testified that Smith had come to him looking for Neely and saying that Neely had been telling people that he had killed a soldier.

The District Court did, however, refuse to permit appellant to call Smith as a witness after it had ascertained, out of the presence of the jury, that Smith intended to invoke his privilege against self-incrimination and would refuse to answer questions put by appellant's trial counsel. Defense trial counsel thereupon requested a missing witness instruction, and the court indicated its view that such an instruction was not appropriate since Smith "was not available to either side." When counsel persisted that he was available, the Court answered, "Not if he invokes his constitutional privilege." Finally defense argued that the fact that Smith had invoked his privilege should be brought to the attention of the jury. The Government objected and the court indicated that it was inclined to agree that no mention should be made as to why Smith was not called as a witness. The court reserved a final ruling, however, to afford defense an opportunity to assemble its authorities. Just before closing argument the court reverted to the problem and ruled, on the authority of Morrison v. United States that counsel should "refrain from any mention of the decision made by Raymond Smith to invoke the Fifth Amendment."

We find no error in these rulings. It is well settled that the jury is not entitled to draw any inferences from the decision of a witness to exercise his constitutional privilege whether those inferences be favorable to the prosecution or the defense. The rule is grounded not only in the constitutional notion that guilt may not be inferred from the exercise of the Fifth Amendment privilege but also in the danger that a witness's invoking the Fifth Amendment in the presence of the jury will have a disproportionate impact on their deliberations. The jury may think it high courtroom drama of probative significance when a witness "takes the Fifth." In reality the probative value of the event is almost entirely undercut by the absence of any requirement that the witness justify his fear of incrimination and by the fact that it is a form of evidence not subject to cross-examination. Fletcher v. United States . . . .

An obvious corollary to these precepts is the rule that a witness should not be put on the stand for the purpose of having him exercise his privilege before the jury. See Fletcher v. United States, supra. This would only invite the jury to make an improper inference. For the same reason no valid purpose can be served by informing the jury that a witness has chosen to exercise his constitutional privilege. That fact is not one the jury is entitled to rely on in reaching its verdict.

The other side of the coin, however, is the rule that the jury is not entitled to draw any inference from a failure to testify that is ascribable to the witness's reliance on his Fifth Amendment privilege. Morrison v. United States, supra. Indeed, this court has held it inappropriate to spark a missing witness inference against the party who would have been called on to produce a witness to incriminate himself.

In the instant case the District Court properly admonished counsel to make no mention in their closing argument of the lack of testimony from a witness counsel knew would have invoked the Fifth Amendment. Certainly the judge was correct in refusing to charge the jury that an inference could be drawn from the absence of such a witness. Morrison v. United States, supra.

However, the trial judge could properly have given a neutralizing instruction, one calculated to reduce the danger that the jury will in fact draw an inference from the absence of such a witness. Morrison v. United States, supra. Had either counsel requested the court to instruct the jury that they should draw no inference from Smith's absence because he was not available to either side, it would have been error to refuse this instruction. Appellant's trial counsel did not request such an instruction. There are meaningful tactical reasons why a defense trial counsel might elect not to seek such an instruction.[1] Had such an instruction been sought in this case, the District Court, which noted in colloquy with counsel that Smith "was not available to either side," would undoubtedly have granted the request. As it is we see no error in the court's handling of the issues presented when Smith decided to invoke his Fifth Amendment privilege.

We have considered other contentions presented by appellant's counsel. We find no reason for reversal.

Affirmed.

BAZELON, CHIEF JUDGE (dissenting) :

The trial court refused to allow appellant to call as a witness one Raymond Smith, who appellant contended was the person who had actually killed the soldier. The court would not allow Smith to take the stand because he said he would not testify for fear of self-incrimination. The court could not, of course, have compelled Smith to testify, once he had asserted his Fifth Amendment privilege to remain silent. Appellant contends, however, that his Sixth Amendment right to compel testimony included the right to have Smith assert his privilege against self-incrimination in the jury's presence. The fact that there were other witnesses who supported Bowles' story that Smith was the one actually responsible for the killing bolsters this position, for it indicates that Bowles was not merely fabricating a story and then buttressing it with Smith's refusal to testify. Yet, in the jury's view, the failure of Smith to appear could not help but make much less credible Bowles' protestations of innocence and his explanation that his "confession" to his mother was only the braggadocio of a poor, unsuccessful man. Furthermore, under the jury's eyes a witness may decide to testify instead.

Fletcher v. United States, relied on by the majority, is not to the contrary. In *Fletcher*, a robbery conviction was reversed where the Government put on the stand a juvenile who had told the grand jury

---

1. The tactical considerations may be elucidated in terms of the facts of the case before us as follows: Defense trial counsel might well conclude that while a jury would readily understand for itself that defendant couldn't be expected to produce as a witness a man (Smith) who would testify that he had killed the deceased, it might have expected—in terms of inquiring whether there was a reasonable doubt of guilt—that the Government would have called Smith to testify that he had not killed the deceased. The possibility for arousal of a reasonable doubt in the minds of

the jurors would have been removed by a neutralizing instruction from the court.

In view of this tactical consideration the case cannot fairly be viewed as involving a failure to seek or provide an instruction that calls for reversal under the plain error doctrine.

The defense might feel more in need of this kind of instruction when there is a danger that the jury will doubt the existence of a person who does not appear as a witness. Here the existence of Smith was corroborated by two witnesses other than appellant.

that Fletcher had participated with him in the robbery. Although the juvenile "had already been subject to the jurisdiction of the Juvenile Court and committed to a training school," at Fletcher's trial he asserted his Fifth Amendment right to refuse to answer any of the Government's numerous questions concerning his knowledge of Fletcher and the crime. Drawing on [another case] this court found two distinct grounds of error in this situation:

> One of these grounds relates to prosecutorial misconduct, and the other "seems to rest upon the conclusion that, in the circumstances of a given case, inferences from a witness' refusal to answer added critical weight to the prosecution's case in a form not subject to cross-examination, and thus unfairly prejudiced the defendant."

This reasoning may not apply to a case, such as the one now before us, in which it is the defense, not the prosecution,[2] which is attempting to obtain his testimony.

> Yet we need not decide whether, by analogy, *all* inferences based on a refusal to testify are improper.[3] In the present case, the entire defense was that Raymond Smith and not appellant was responsible for the murder. Since the jury was not permitted to hear Smith testify (or refuse to do so on grounds of self-incrimination), I believe the trial court's failure to instruct the jury that no inference should be drawn from Smith's absence on the witness stand was plain error. The need for such an instruction was especially great in a first degree murder case where the evidence of guilt was so thin. The record indicates that the court below was aware that no inference unfavorable to the accused should be drawn, but it failed—probably only through inadvertence—to convey this point to the jurors. In my view, this defect is too important for us to overlook.

* * *

[Judge Wright's dissenting opinion is omitted.]

---

2. The position of a defendant asserting his Sixth Amendment right to bring witnesses before the jury is not analogous to that of a prosecutor attempting to insinuate that a defendant is guilty because his confederates refuse to answer incriminating questions. See *Fletcher*, supra. This tactic on the prosecutor's part is equivalent to an outright denial of the defendant's Fifth Amendment right to remain silent, and it is unconstitutional to employ a defendant's silence as an element of the proof needed to convict beyond a reasonable doubt. Griffin v. California, 380 U.S. 609, 85 S.Ct. 1229. By contrast, when the accused suggests that another person is the culpable party, the other's refusal to testify is merely being used as corroboration.

3. There is some danger that a defendant might misuse the inference from another's refusal to testify. This potential abuse is mitigated, however, by jurors' natural skepticism of any "buck passing," and by the prosecutor's right to demonstrate to the jury that the person accused by the defendant is someone on whom he has prevailed (through friendship, or by threats of injury) to come to court and then refuse to testify.

NOTES

1. The propriety of requiring a witness to claim privilege in the presence of the jury was discussed in San Fratello v. United States, 340 F.2d 560 (5th Cir. 1965).

In *San Fratello* the prosecutor called the suspect's wife to the stand despite prior knowledge that she would claim a privilege. Consider the following excerpts from the opinion:

"There is nothing about the government's right to have a witness claim his privilege in response to specific questions while on the stand under oath that requires it to be done in the presence of the jury. As was said in State of Iowa v. Chrismore, where the defendant objected to the action of the prosecution in calling as a witness a woman he had married between the dates of the offense and the trial, '. . . If there was any doubt about the truth of this testimony (about the marriage), investigation of the fact could have been made in the absence of the jury, thereby avoiding the effect which would seem inevitably to follow this sort of examination.' Professor Wigmore says that, 'The layman's natural first suggestion would probably be that the resort to privilege in each instance is a clear confession of crime.' Even in the face of this inevitable inference, it may well be proper in some cases to have the proceeding in the presence of the jury where the government is dealing with what has sometimes been called the 'ordinary' witness; that is, with one not so closely connected with the defendant by the facts of the case, the pleadings, or relationship that the inference of the witness' guilt would likely be imputed to the defendant. The circumstances could be such that the jury would naturally expect the witness to be called. But a defendant's spouse or a co-defendant would not come within that category.

"We are of the opinion that the record shows injury in spite of the Court's [cautionary] instruction. The common law rule is that the *mere fact of calling one spouse* as a witness for the prosecution in a criminal trial of the other for the purpose of forcing the claim of marital privilege against testifying is prejudicial error. It has been generally followed in most jurisdictions where not changed by statute. State v. McGinty, 14 Wash.2d 71, 126 P. 2d 1086, expressed the attitude of most of the courts on this matter when it said that, 'the court has definitely frowned upon the practice of calling as a witness the wife of the defendant in a criminal case for the purpose of compelling him to make an objection to her competency.' The fact that the defendant marries the witness after the commission of the offense and a short time before the trial does not make an exception to the rule, even though it is for the possible purpose of preventing her from testifying. While the wife here based her claim of privilege on possible self-incrimination rather than on the marriage, some cases have considered the effect of the two as being about the same. If there is any difference, the claim against self-incrimination is more prejudicial, because the jury might possibly conclude that a spouse claiming only the marital privilege did not want to be cast in the role of a witness for the prosecution, even though he or she had no connection with or knowledge of the crime. We are of the opinion that the prosecution would have a heavy burden of showing affirmatively that there was no injury where a defendant's spouse is called under circumstances such as those existing in this case. As was said in People v. Trine, 164 Mich. 1, 129 N.W. 3, 6, about the prejudice resulting from requiring the claim of the marital privilege in the presence of the jury, 'Such errors by the prosecuting officer are not easily cured.' The prosecution could have had no purpose in calling this witness and requiring her to claim her privilege in the presence of the jury other than to use her conduct as an incriminating circumstance against her husband; and it is more than reasonably probable that its conduct in so doing prejudiced him."

2. The American Bar Association Minimum Standards Relating To The Prosecution Function and The Defense Function (2nd Ed. 1978) contain clear rules concerning the advocate's use of claims of privilege:

3–5.7 (c) (Prosecution)

(c) A prosecutor *should not* call a witness who the prosecutor knows will claim a valid privilege not to testify, for the purpose of impressing upon the jury the fact of the claim of privilege.
. . . .

4–7.6 (c) (Defense)

(c) A lawyer *should not* call a witness who he knows will claim a valid privilege not to testify, for the purpose of impressing upon the jury the fact of the claim of privilege.

3. The legal issues arising from the silence of the accused in the face of accusation are treated in Chapter 19, Section B.

B. MULTIPLE DEFENDANT TRIALS

-----

1. STATEMENTS OF CO–DEFENDANTS

BRUTON v. UNITED STATES

Supreme Court of the United States, 1968.
391 U.S. 123, 88 S.Ct. 1620, appeal after remand Eighth Circuit, 1969, 416 F.2d 310, certiorari denied 1970, 397 U.S. 1014, 90 S.Ct. 1248.

MR. JUSTICE BRENNAN delivered the opinion of the Court.

This case presents the question, last considered in Delli Paoli v. United States, 352 U.S. 232, whether the conviction of a defendant at a joint trial should be set aside although the jury was instructed that a codefendant's confession inculpating the defendant had to be disregarded in determining his guilt or innocence.

A joint trial of petitioner and one Evans in the District Court for the Eastern District of Missouri resulted in the conviction of both by a jury on a federal charge of armed postal robbery. A postal inspector testified that Evans orally confessed to him that Evans and petitioner committed the armed robbery. The postal inspector obtained the oral confession, and another in which Evans admitted he had an accomplice whom he would not name, in the course of two interrogations of Evans at the city jail in St. Louis, Missouri, where Evans was held in custody on state criminal charges. Both petitioner and Evans appealed their convictions to the Court of Appeals for the Eighth Circuit. That court set aside Evans' conviction on the ground that his oral confessions to the postal inspector should not have been received in evidence against him. However, the court, relying upon *Delli Paoli*, affirmed petitioner's conviction because the trial judge instructed the jury that although Evans' confession was competent evidence against Evans it was inadmissible hearsay against petitioner and therefore had to be disregarded in determining petitioner's guilt or innocence. We granted certiorari to reconsider *Delli Paoli*.

*   *   *

We hold that, because of the substantial risk that the jury, despite instructions to the contrary, looked to the incriminating extrajudicial statements in determining petitioner's guilt, admission of Evans' confession in this joint trial violated petitioner's right of cross-examination secured by the Confrontation Clause of the Sixth Amendment. We therefore overrule *Delli Paoli* and reverse.

The basic premise of *Delli Paoli* was that it is "reasonably possible for the jury to follow" sufficiently clear instructions to disregard the confessor's extrajudicial statement that his codefendant participated with him in committing the crime. If it were true that the jury disregarded the reference to the codefendant no question would arise under the Confrontation Clause, because by hypothesis the case is treated as if the confessor made no statement inculpating the non-confessor. But since *Delli Paoli* was decided this Court has effectively repudiated its basic premise. Before discussing this, we pause to observe that in Pointer v. Texas, 380 U.S. 400, we confirmed "that the right of cross-examination is included in the right of an accused in a criminal case to confront the witnesses against him" secured by the Sixth Amendment; "a major reason underlying the constitutional confrontation rule is to give a defendant charged with crime an opportunity to cross-examine the witnesses against him."

*   *   *

Here Evans' oral confessions were in fact testified to, and were therefore actually in evidence. That testimony was legitimate evidence against Evans and to that extent was properly before the jury during its deliberations. Even greater, then, was the likelihood that the jury would believe Evans made the statements and that they were true—not just the self-incriminating portions but those implicating petitioner as well. Plainly, the introduction of Evans' confession added substantial, perhaps even critical, weight to the Government's case in a form not subject to cross-examination, since Evans did not take the stand. Petitioner thus was denied his constitutional right of confrontation.

Delli Paoli assumed that this encroachment on the right to confrontation could be avoided by the instruction to the jury to disregard the inadmissible hearsay evidence.[1] But, as we have said, that assumption has since been effectively repudiated. True, the repudiation was not in the context of the admission of a confession inculpating a codefendant but in the context of a New York rule which submitted to the jury the question of the voluntariness of the confession itself. Jackson v. Denno, 378 U.S. 368. Nonetheless the message of *Jackson* for *Delli Paoli* was clear. We there held that a defendant is constitutionally entitled at least to have the trial judge first determine whether a confession was made voluntarily before submitting it to the jury for an assessment of its credibility. More specifically, we expressly rejected the proposition that a jury, when determining the confessor's guilt, could be relied on to ignore his confession of guilt should it find the confession involuntary. Significantly, we supported that conclusion in part by reliance upon the dissenting opinion of Mr. Justice Frankfurter for the four Justices who dissented in *Delli Paoli*.

That dissent challenged the basic premise of *Delli Paoli* that a properly instructed jury would ignore the confessor's inculpation of the nonconfessor in determining the latter's guilt. "The fact of the matter is that too often such admonition against misuse is intrinsically ineffective in that the effect of such a nonadmissible declaration cannot be wiped from the brains of the jurors. The admonition therefore becomes a futile collocation of words and fails of its purpose as a legal protection to defendants against whom such a declaration should not tell." "The government should not have the windfall of having the jury be influenced by evidence against a defendant which, as a matter of law, they should not consider but which they cannot put out of their minds." To the same effect is the statement of Mr. Justice Jackson in his concurring opinion in Krulewitch v. United States, 336 U.S. 440, 453: "The naive assumption that prejudicial effects can be overcome by instructions to the jury . . . all practicing lawyers know to be unmitigated fiction. . . ."

* * *

In addition to *Jackson*, our action in 1966 in amending Rule 14 of the Federal Rules of Criminal Procedure also evidences our repudiation of *Delli Paoli*'s basic premise. Rule 14 authorizes a severance where it appears that a defendant might be prejudiced by a joint trial.[2] The Rule was amended in 1966 to provide expressly that

---

1. We emphasize that the hearsay statement inculpating petitioner was clearly inadmissible against him under traditional rules of evidence, the problem arising only because the statement was admissible against the declarant Evans. There is not before us, therefore, any recognized exception to the hearsay rule insofar as petitioner is concerned and we intimate no view whatever that such excep-

tions necessarily raise questions under the Confrontation Clause.

2. Joinder of defendants is governed by Rules 8(b) and 14 of the Federal Rules of Criminal Procedure. "The rules are designed to promote economy and efficiency and to avoid a multiplicity of trials, where these objectives can be achieved without substantial prejudice to the right of

"[i]n ruling on a motion by a defendant for severance the court may order the attorney for the government to deliver to the court for inspection *in camera* any statements or confessions made by the defendants which the government intends to introduce in evidence at the trial." The Advisory Committee on Rules said in explanation of the amendment:

> "A defendant may be prejudiced by the admission in evidence against a co-defendant of a statement or confession made by that co-defendant. This prejudice cannot be dispelled by cross-examination if the co-defendant does not take the stand. Limiting instructions to the jury may not in fact erase the prejudice. . . .
>
> "The purpose of the amendment is to provide a procedure whereby the issue of possible prejudice can be resolved on the motion for severance. . . ."

Those who have defended reliance on the limiting instruction in this area have cited several reasons in support. Judge Learned Hand, a particularly severe critic of the proposition that juries could be counted on to disregard inadmissible hearsay,[3] wrote the opinion for the Second Circuit which affirmed Delli Paoli's conviction, 229 F.2d 319. In Judge Hand's view the limiting instruction, although not really capable of preventing the jury from considering the prejudicial evidence, does as a matter of form provide a way around the exclusionary rules of evidence that is defensible because it "probably furthers, rather than impedes, the search for truth . . . ." Nash v. United States, 54 F.2d 1006, 1007. Insofar as this implies the prosecution ought not to be denied the benefit of the confession to prove the confessor's guilt, however, it overlooks alternative ways of achieving that benefit without at the same time infringing the non-confessor's right of confrontation. Where viable alternatives do exist, it is deceptive to rely on the pursuit of truth to defend a clearly harmful practice.

Another reason cited in defense of *Delli Paoli* is the justification for joint trials in general, the argument being that the benefits of joint proceedings should not have to be sacrificed by requiring sepa-

---

the defendants to a fair trial." An important element of a fair trial is that a jury consider only relevant and competent evidence bearing on the issue of guilt or innocence.

3. Judge Hand addressed the subject several times. The limiting instruction, he said, is a "recommendation to the jury of a mental gymnastic which is beyond, not only their powers, but anybody else's, Nash v. United States, 54 F.2d 1006, 1007: "Nobody can indeed fail to doubt whether the caution is effective, or whether usually the practical result is not to let in hearsay," United States v.

Gottfried, 165 F.2d 360, 367; "it is indeed very hard to believe that a jury will, or for that matter can, in practice observe the admonition," Delli Paoli v. United States, 229 F.2d 319, 321. Judge Hand referred to the instruction as a "placebo," medically defined as "a medicinal lie." Judge Jerome Frank suggested that its legal equivalent "is a kind of 'judicial lie': It undermines a moral relationship between the courts, the jurors, and the public; like any other judicial deception, it damages the decent judicial administration of justice." United States v. Grunewald, 233 F.2d 556, 574.

rate trials in order to use the confession against the declarant. Joint trials do conserve state funds, diminish inconvenience to witnesses and public authorities, and avoid delays in bringing those accused of crime to trial. But the answer to this argument was cogently stated by Judge Lehman of the New York Court of Appeals, dissenting in People v. Fisher, 249 N.Y. 419, 432, 164 N.E. 336, 341:

> "We still adhere to the rule that an accused is entitled to confrontation of the witnesses against him and the right to cross-examine them . . . . We destroy the age-old rule which in the past has been regarded as a fundamental principle of our jurisprudence by a legalistic formula, required of the judge, that the jury may not consider any admissions against any party who did not join in them. We secure greater speed, economy and convenience in the administration of the law at the price of fundamental principles of constitutional liberty. That price is too high."

Finally, the reason advanced by the majority in *Delli Paoli* was to tie the result to maintenance of the jury system. "Unless we proceed on the basis that the jury will follow the court's instructions where those instructions are clear and the circumstances are such that the jury can reasonably be expected to follow them, the jury system makes little sense." We agree that there are many circumstances in which this reliance is justified. Not every admission of inadmissible hearsay or other evidence can be considered to be reversible error unavoidable through limiting instructions; instances occur in almost every trial where inadmissible evidence creeps in, usually inadvertently. "A defendant is entitled to a fair trial but not a perfect one." It is not unreasonable to conclude that in many such cases the jury can and will follow the trial judge's instructions to disregard such information. Nevertheless, as was recognized in *Jackson* there are some contexts in which the risk that the jury will not, or cannot, follow instructions is so great, and the consequences of failure so vital to the defendant, that the practical and human limitations of the jury system cannot be ignored. Such a context is presented here, where the powerfully incriminating extrajudicial statements of a codefendant, who stands accused side-by-side with the defendant, are deliberately spread before the jury in a joint trial. Not only are the incriminations devastating to the defendant but their credibility is inevitably suspect, a fact recognized when accomplices do take the stand and the jury is instructed to weigh their testimony carefully given the recognized motivation to shift blame onto others. The unreliability of such evidence is intolerably compounded when the alleged accomplice, as here, does not testify and cannot be tested by cross-examination. It was against such threats to a fair trial that the Confrontation Clause was directed.

We, of course, acknowledge the impossibility of determining whether in fact the jury did or did not ignore Evans' statement inculpating petitioner in determining petitioner's guilt. But that was also true in the analogous situation in *Jackson* and was not regarded as militating against striking down the New York procedure there involved. It was enough that the procedure posed "substantial threats to a defendant's constitutional rights to have an involuntary confession entirely disregarded and to have the coercion issue fairly and reliably determined. These hazards we cannot ignore." Here the introduction of Evans' confession posed a substantial threat to petitioner's right to confront the witnessses against him, and this is a hazard we cannot ignore. Despite the concededly clear instructions to the jury to disregard Evans' inadmissible hearsay evidence inculpating petitioner, in the context of a joint trial we cannot accept limiting instructions as an adequate substitute for petitioner's constitutional right of cross-examination. The effect is the same as if there had been no instruction at all.

Reversed.

MR. JUSTICE BLACK concurs in the result for the reasons stated in the dissent in Delli Paoli v. United States, 352 U.S. 232, 246.

MR. JUSTICE MARSHALL took no part in the consideration or decision of this case.

[Mr. Justice Stewart's concurring opinion is omitted.]

MR. JUSTICE WHITE, dissenting.

* * *

The rule which the Court announces today will severely limit the circumstances in which defendants may be tried together for a crime which they are both charged with committing. Unquestionably, joint trials are more economical and minimize the burden on witnesses, prosecutors and courts. They also avoid delays in bringing those accused of crime to trial. This much the Court concedes. It is also worth saying that separate trials are apt to have varying consequences for legally indistinguishable defendants. The unfairness of this is confirmed by the common prosecutorial experience of seeing codefendants who are tried separately strenuously jockeying for position with regard to who should be the first to be tried.

In view of the practical difficulties of separate trials and their potential unfairness, I am disappointed that the Court has not spelled out how the federal courts might conduct their business consistent with today's opinion. I would suppose that it will be necessary to exclude all extrajudicial confessions unless all portions of them which implicate defendants other than the declarant are effectively deleted. Effective deletion will probably require not only omission of all direct and indirect inculpations of codefendants but also of any statement that could be employed against those defendants once their identity is otherwise established. Of course, the deletion must not be such that it will distort the statements to the substantial prejudice of either the declarant or the Government. If deletion is not feasible, then the Government will have to choose either not to use the confession at all or to try the defendants separately. To save time, money, and effort, the Government might best seek a ruling at the earliest possible stage of the trial proceedings as to whether the confession is admissible once offending portions are deleted. The failure of the Government to adopt and follow proper procedures for insuring that the inadmissible portions of confessions are excluded will be relevant to the question of whether it was harmless error for them to have gotten before the jury. Oral statements, such as that involved in the present case, will present special problems, for there is a risk that the witness in testifying will inadvertently exceed permissible limits. Except for recommending that caution be used with regard to such oral statements, it is difficult to anticipate the issues which will arise in concrete factual situations.

I would hope, but am not sure, that by using these procedures the federal courts would escape reversal under today's ruling. Even so, I persist in believing that the reversal of *Delli Paoli* unnecessarily burdens the already difficult task of conducting criminal trials, and therefore I dissent in this case.

MR. JUSTICE HARLAN joins this opinion without abandoning his original disagreement with Jackson v. Denno, 378 U.S. 368, 427, expressed in his dissenting opinion in that case.

NOTES ON *POST-BRUTON* DEVELOPMENTS

Frequently *Bruton* issues are treated with severance materials because the *Bruton* "problem" can be solved by severance. Other problems arise, nevertheless. See, generally, Haddad, Post-Bruton Developments: a Reconsideration of the Confrontation Rationale, and a Proposal For a Due Process Evaluation of Limiting Instructions, 18 Am.Cr.L.Rev. 1 (1980).

1. *Burden of Raising Issue.* When the defendant before trial knows that a co-defendant made a statement implicating the defendant, must the defendant make a pre-trial request for severance? United States v. Marks, 585 F.2d 164 (6th Cir. 1978), noted that in *Bruton* neither a severance motion nor a request for redaction had been made by defense counsel. *Marks*, therefore, placed the burden on the prosecution to seek pre-trial solution of *Bruton* problems. Compare People v. McGautha, 70 Cal.2d 770, 76 Cal.Rptr. 434, 452 P.2d 650 (1969). See also Commonwealth v. Johnson, 474 Pa. 410, 378 A.2d 859 (1977); State v. Barnett, 53 N.J. 559, 252 A.2d 33 (1969); Ortiz v. State, 256 Ind. 549, 356 N.E.2d 1188 (1976).

2. *Other Mechanical Solutions.* Severance may not be the only way to prevent the jury in a defendant's case from hearing a co-defendant's out-of-court accusations before deciding the defendant's fate. On probably at least twenty-five occasions trial judges have impanelled separate juries for each defendant, excluded the defendant's jury during testimony about the co-defendant's confession (and during opening and closing statements), but otherwise seated both juries in a single courtroom at the same time. Reviewing courts have avoided flat condemnation or wholehearted approval of such single-trial, multiple-juries solution. See, e. g., United States v. Sidnman, 470 F.2d 1158 (9th Cir. 1972); People v. Hernandez, 163 N.J.Super. 283, 394 A.2d 883 (1979). See also Morris and Savitt, Bruton Revisited: One Trial/Two Juries, 12 Prosecutor 92 (1976). What dangers are there in this procedure? What about allowing a single jury to (1) hear all the evidence except the co-defendant's confession, (2) decide the fate of the

defendant, (3) return to hear the confession of the co-defendant, and (4) retire again to deliberate the fate of the co-defendant? Such a procedure was used in United States v. Crane, 499 F.2d 1385 (6th Cir. 1974). It may originally have been the idea of a Columbia University law student. See 3 Columbia Journal of Law and Social Problems 80 (1967). Is it fair to the co-defendant? Would a prosecutor like the idea?

3. *Inapplicability to Non-Jury Trials.* Most courts view the *Bruton* problem as arising from the ineffectiveness of jury instructions. A trial judge, however, is presumed to be able to hear *C's* confession in a joint trial of *C* and *D* without considering *C's* confession in deciding *D's* fate. Hence most courts have held that severance is not required in bench trials. See, e. g., State v. Gleason, 359 A.2d 808 (Me.1976); People v. Vinson, 49 Ill.App. 3d 602, 7 Ill.Dec. 203, 364 N.E.2d 364 (1977); Cockrell v. Oberhauser, 413 F.2d 256 (9th Cir. 1969). California seemingly disagrees. See In re D. L., 46 Cal.App.3d 65, 120 Cal.Rptr. 276 (1974). If we are worried about a judge making improper use of a co-defendant's confession, would the defendant in a bench trial have to be tried by a judge who did not know that the co-defendant had implicated the defendant? Of course, if in a multiple-defendant bench trial the judge indicates that he has used *C's* confession to convict *D*, he has rebutted the presumption of propriety; in effect, he has made a hearsay blunder by using as evidence an out-of-court statement which, as to *D*, is inadmissible hearsay. See, e. g., In re Appeal No. 977, 22 Md.App. 511, 323 A.2d 663 (1974); United States v. Longee, 603 F.2d 1342 (9th Cir. 1979).

4. *Inapplicable When Statement is Admissible Against Both Defendants.* When the co-defendant's statement is admissible against the defendant (either under a hearsay exception or as relevant non-hearsay evidence), the statement will be admitted at *D's* trial even if he is tried separately from *C*. Hence there is no *Bruton* problem. In a joint trial there would be no limiting instruction as to the evidence being admissible against both *C* and *D*. See, for example, United States v. Appollo, 476 F.2d 156 (5th Cir. 1973) (statement was non-hearsay res gestae evidence, relevant against both defendants); Dutton v. Evans, 400 U.S. 74, 91 S.Ct. 210 (1970) (co-conspirator exception); McLaughlin v. Vinzant, 522 F.2d 448 (1st Cir. 1975) (excited utterance); Miller v. Cardwell, 448 F.2d 186 (4th Cir. 1971), and Commonwealth v. Bethea, 214 Pa.Super. 253, 251 A.2d 727 (1969) (adopted admission). Of course, use of *C's* out-of-court statement as evidence against *D* will not only have to be permissible under local rules of evidence; as in *Dutton*, supra, it may also face an argument that such use violates *D's* right to confront witnesses. This is not a *Bruton* problem, however. The same issue would be presented even if *D* were tried separately. Moreover, *Dutton* indicates that *Bruton* might require severance if local law made a certain statement by *C* inadmissible against *D*; but, also, that if local law were changed to allow use of that same statement against *D*, such use of *C's* out-of-court accusation would not necessarily violate the confrontation clause guarantee. Does it make sense to say that *D's* Sixth Amendment rights are violated if the jury is told not to consider *C's* statement as evidence against *D* whereas his Sixth Amendment rights are not violated if the jury is told that it should consider that statement as evidence against *D*? Would "due process" provide a better rationale than confrontation? At no stage of his case, neither before the Supreme Court nor earlier did George Bruton ever raise a Sixth Amendment claim. Instead, he urged that the procedure was unfair. Why, then, did the Supreme Court use a confrontation analysis?

5. *Inapplicable When Statement Does Not Implicate Co-Defendant.*
Unless the co-defendant's statement implicates the defendant, either as originally given, or as edited, *Bruton* has been held not to require severance.
United States v. Belle, 593 F.2d 487 (3d Cir. 1979); Commonwealth v.
Clark, 5 Mass.App. 673, 369 N.E.2d 468 (1977). Courts vary greatly on
how direct the implication must be and on whether other evidence in the
case must be considered in deciding whether the jury will realize that the
co-defendant's reference to someone else was, in fact, a reference to the defendant. See *Belle*, supra; United States v. Trudo, 449 F.2d 649 (2d Cir.
1971); Fox v. State, —— Ind.App. ——, 384 N.E.2d 1159 (1979).

Consider this situation. *C* and *D* are jointly charged with arson. The
prosecution's theory is that *D* hired *C* to burn a building. *C* has confessed
to setting a fire but all references to his having been hired by anyone have
been edited out of the confession. At trial both *C* and *D* contend that no
arson occurred, contending that the fire was not of human origin. *C*'s
statement (not implicating *D*) is admitted, subject to a limiting instruction
directing the jury not to consider the statement as evidence in deciding *D*'s
fate. Have *D*'s Sixth Amendment rights been violated? Has *D* any less
right to confront *C* concerning the corpus delicti than concerning *D*'s alleged involvement? Is the jury any less likely to misuse the confession in
this case than in *Bruton*?

6. *Possibly Inapplicable When Defendants Have Both Given Similar
Confessions.* In the decade following *Bruton* many courts declared that severance is not required if both defendants have given similar confessions.
United States ex rel. Catanzaro v. Mancusi, 404 F.2d 296 (1968); United
States ex rel. Duff v. Zelker, 452 F.2d 1009 (2d Cir. 1971); People v. Safi-
an, 46 N.Y.2d 181, 413 N.Y.S.2d 118, 385 N.E.2d 1046 (1978). The theory
seemed to be that a co-defendant's confession is not as "powerfully incriminating" if the defendant has also confessed. For the exception to apply,
various courts have said that the two must be "reciprocal," "dovetailing,"
"interlocking," or "substantially similar." The exception has no application
when each defendant has exculpated himself while accusing the other. People
v. Clark, 50 Ill.2d 292, 278 N.E.2d 782 (1972). Some jurisdictions held that
no such exception exists. State v. Edwards, 224 Kan. 226, 579 P.2d 1209
(1978).

In Parker v. Randolph, 442 U.S. 62, 99 S.Ct. 2132 (1979), the four
justices who made up the prevailing plurality recognized the "similar confessions" exception. The other four participating justices, including one
who would have invoked the harmless error doctrine, refused to recognize
an exception. Thus, individual jurisdictions probably remain free to decide
for themselves.

How can it be said that whether *D*'s right to confront *C* has been satisfied depends upon whether the prosecution has utilized *D*'s own confession? Can there be a situation in which, despite *D*'s confession, *C*'s out-
of-court statement, if improperly utilized by the jury, would be very harmful to *D*'s case?

When each defendant has confessed, the confesssion of one remains inadmissible hearsay as to the other even if they are tried together. Thus a
limiting instruction (of the very type deemed ineffective in *Bruton*) must
be utilized. State v. Sullivan, 224 Kan. 110, 578 P.2d 1108 (1978).

7. *Inapplicable When Confessing Co-Defendant Takes the Stand and is
Available for Cross-Examination by Defendant.* In *Bruton* the Supreme

Court said that the procedures utilized by the trial court were constitutionally deficient because the defendant had no opportunity to cross-examine the co-defendant. Subsequently, in California v. Green, Chapter 19, Section A, supra, (a case not concerned with *Bruton* problems) the Court held that use of an earlier out-of-court statement does not violate the confrontation guarantee if the defendant at the time of trial has the opportunity to cross-examine the declarant. From these two premises, the Court concluded in Nelson v. O'Neil, 402 U.S. 622, 91 S.Ct. 1723 (1971), that any *Bruton* error is cured if the confessing co-defendant takes the stand in a joint trial and is available for cross-examination by the defendant. (Presumably, however, the two must be represented by separate attorneys for *Nelson* to apply). Because it is not known before trial whether the accused will testify, *Nelson* may be of little help in avoiding severance. On certain occasions, prosecutors have avoided severance by pledging not to use the co-defendant's confession unless the co-defendant testifies and contradicts what he said in the confession. (The rules of evidence in some jurisdictions might prevent "holding back," for cross-examination and rebuttal, evidence which normally would be offered in the case-in-chief.)

When *Nelson* applies, *C*'s references to *D* need not be edited out of the confession, since *D* has an opportunity to cross-examine *C*. However (except in those jurisdictions such as California which allow prior inconsistent statements as substantive evidence), *C*'s out-of-court statement remains inadmissible hearsay as to *D*. *D* is still entitled to a limiting instruction even though he had an opportunity to cross-examine *C*. State v. Slate, 38 N.C. App. 209, 247 S.E.2d 430 (1978).

2. TRIAL TACTICS OF A CO–DEFENDANT

(a) COMMENTS UPON CO-DEFENDANT'S FAILURE TO TESTIFY

DE LUNA v. UNITED STATES

United States Court of Appeals, Fifth Circuit, 1962.
324 F.2d 375.

WISDOM, CIRCUIT JUDGE.

The conflicting interests of the two co-defendants in this action have generated a narrow but important question relating to the scope of the privilege against self-incrimination: When one of two defendants jointly tried in a criminal proceeding in a federal court exercises his right not to testify, does the Fifth Amendment protect him from prejudicial comments on his silence made to the jury by an attorney for the co-defendant? Pointing to the fact that the United States attorney was free from blame, the Government argues that the general rule against commenting on the exercise of the privilege is inapplicable to the facts of this case. We reject this contention. In a criminal trial in a federal court an accused has a constitutionally guaranteed right of silence free from prejudicial comments, even when they come only from a co-defendant's attorney. If an attorney's duty to his client should require him to draw the jury's attention to the possible inference of guilt from a co-defendant's silence, the trial judge's duty is to order that the defendants be tried separately.

Carlos Garza de Luna and Adolfo Gomez, cousins, were charged jointly in a two-count indictment with receiving and facilitating the transportation and concealment of a narcotic drug and with purchasing and acquiring a narcotic drug in violation of the Narcotic Drug Import and Export Act. Each hired his own attorney. Each attorney defended his client as he saw best, without regard to the interests of the other defendant. Before trial Gomez moved for a severance. The motion was denied. At the trial in San Antonio, Texas, de Luna, a Mexican national, did not take the stand. Gomez, a resident of San Antonio, took the stand and produced members of his family and other witnesses to testify in his behalf. He put all the blame on de Luna. According to Gomez, he was an innocent victim of circumstances; his only connection with the narcotics was when he and de Luna were riding in Gomez's automobile; de Luna saw the police coming, tossed a package (the narcotics) to him and told him to throw it out of the window. The police saw Gomez throw the package. De Luna's attorney argued that the man he represented was being made a scapegoat; that the police officers testified they had not seen de Luna toss the package to Gomez and had seen no movement in the car although they were alongside it; that the sole culprit was Gomez.

In accordance with his theory of the case and impelled by a proper sense of duty to his client, Gomez's attorney, in arguing to the jury, contrasted Gomez's willingness with de Luna's unwillingness to take the stand. He stated plainly that an honest man is not afraid to take the stand and testify. He said:

> "Well, at least one man was honest enough and had courage enough to take the stand and subject himself to cross examination and tell you the whole story, and tell you that, 'Yes, I first colored the story, but when I got back to my senses I told the truth, and that's the whole thing.' You haven't heard a word from this man [de Luna]."

This comment followed on the heels of somewhat similar comment to which de Luna's attorney had objected strenuously as "inflammatory and prejudicial". These were not casual or isolated references; they were integral to Gomez's defense. And considering the case from Gomez's point of view, his attorneys should be free to draw all rational inferences from the failure of a co-defendant to testify, just as an attorney is free to comment on the effect of any interested party's failure to produce material evidence in his possession or to call witnesses who have knowledge of pertinent facts. Gomez has rights as well as de Luna, and they should be no less than if he were prosecuted singly. His right to confrontation allows him to invoke every inference from de Luna's absence from the stand.

The joint trial, the fact situation, and Gomez's defense placed the trial judge in a dilemma. At the time of the prejudicial remarks and

again in his formal charge, he instructed the jury to disregard the
fact that de Luna did not testify. Yet, in justice to Gomez, the trial
judge owed and gave the following instruction:

> "The defendant Adolfo O. Gomez has taken the stand
> and testified in his own behalf in this case. A defendant
> cannot, in a criminal case, be compelled to take the witness
> stand and to testify. Whether he testifies or does not testi-
> fy is a matter of his own choosing.
>
> "When, however, a defendant elects to take the witness
> stand and testify, then you have no right to disregard his
> testimony because he is accused of a crime. When a defend-
> ant does testify, he at once becomes the same as any other
> witness, and his credibility is to be tested by and subjected
> to the same tests as are legally applied to any other witness."

No objection can be taken to such instructions in the ordinary case.
None can be taken in this case, as far as justice to Gomez is concerned. But here, on top of comments prejudicial to de Luna, such
instructions led the jury in the very direction to which the comments
of Gomez's attorney pointed.

Thus, the joint trial of the two defendants put Justice to the task
of simultaneously facing in opposite directions. And Justice is not
Janus-faced.

The jury found Gomez not guilty on both counts of the indictment, de Luna guilty on both counts. The district judge imposed a
sentence of seven years.

*   *   *

In the common law in England until 1898 and in this country until after the Civil War, the incompetency of an accused to testify
made the effect of his silence a metaphysical question. It ceased to
be metaphysical when statutes were enacted giving defendants the
option to testify in their behalf. To make the privilege against self-
incrimination effective and to preserve the presumption of innocence,
almost all of the states adopted laws forbidding comment on a defendant's neglect or refusal to testify and decreeing that no inference
should be drawn from his silence. In 1878 Congress adopted a statute allowing the defendant to testify in federal cases. The pertinent
federal statute, 18 U.S.C. § 3481, on which the appellant relies in addition to relying on the Fifth Amendment, provides that "the person
charged shall, at his own request, be a competent witness" and "[h]is
failure to make such request shall not create any presumption against
him".

*   *   *

If comment on an accused's silence is improper for judge and
prosecutor, it is because of the effect on the jury, not just because the
comment comes from representatives of the State. Indeed, the effect
on the jury of comment by a co-defendant's attorney might be more
harmful than if it comes from judge or prosecutor. A judge, in keeping with his high degree of responsibility to conduct a fair trial,

would be expected to give a balanced, moderate explanation of the inferences to be drawn from silence. Similarly, but to a lesser degree, a prosecutor would be expected to recognize his responsibility for fair comment. But much less restraint can be expected from an attorney to whom no little latitude is allowed when zeal, emotion, eloquence, and the advocate's afflatus take hold of a jury argument.

Even if it were true that reasonable men cannot avoid drawing "natural inferences from an accused's silence," that is quite a different thing from having the silence emphasized by comment. The imputation of guilt from silence, if it does nothing else, may confuse the jury as to the presumption of innocence in favor of the accused.

Here it is by no means certain that the inference Gomez's attorney drew is warranted. De Luna was a Mexican national, in a strange city. He was surrounded by Gomez's family, who came to testify for Gomez. In the "ambiguous circumstances" of this case an innocent man, if he has language difficulties, if he is excessively nervous, if he is placed at a disadvantage as against his co-defendant, or if he has had a previous record of convictions or association with narcotics offenders, might very well decide that his appearance on the stand would subject him to a risk of being misunderstood or convicted of guilt by association, that would be disproportionate to the advantage of testifying truthfully. He is entitled to make that choice.

* * *

This proceeding is one in the federal courts. The Federal Government cannot wash its hands of responsibility for the compulsion to testify resulting from the court's inaction. The exclusive control of the conduct of the trial is in the hands of the presiding federal judge. He is "not a mere moderator, but is the governor of the trial for the purpose of assuring its proper conduct and of determining questions of law." He has the decisive role in assuring an accused a fair trial according to federal standards. "Federal judges are not referees at prize fights but functionaries of justice."

* * *

Here, to meet the requirements of a fair trial as embodied in the Fifth Amendment, the trial judge must protect an accused's right of silence. The trial judge's approval of an improper comment or refusal to disapprove the comment and do whatever is necessary to protect a defendant from being penalized by relying on his constitutional right amounts, in our opinion, to sufficient participation in the comment or sanction of the comment so that it may be properly characterized as a violation of the Fifth Amendment and Section 3481. The narrow view advocated by the Government would lead to complete nullification of the constitutional right whenever one of several co-defendants (one of whom must be guilty) might seek to assert his right of silence.

* * *

The court's instructions were intended, of course, to neutralize the effect of the comments. But considering the head-on collision between the two defendants, the repetition of the comments, and the extended colloquy over the comments between the trial judge and the lawyers, the imputation of guilt to de Luna was magnified to such an extent that it seems unrealistic to think any instruction to the jury could undo the prejudicial effects of the reference to de Luna's silence. The seed of inference was so well planted, it is fair to assume that it germinated.

In short, for each of the defendants to see the face of Justice they must be tried separately.

* * *

The judgment against de Luna is reversed and remanded.

BELL, CIRCUIT JUDGE (concurring specially).

With deference to the majority, I think this matter is controlled over-all by the right to a fair trial under the Sixth Amendment to the Constitution. The right of de Luna under the Fifth Amendment, and Title 18 U.S.C. § 3481, not to have the fact that he failed to testify commented upon is involved primarily. But the right of Gomez to take the stand under § 3481 and to a full and fair defense, and the right of the public to the enforcement of the criminal statutes are also involved. These rights must be balanced by the court whose duty it is to see that a fair trial is afforded while at the same time protecting all rights. And my disagreement with the majority centers around the scope of the right of Gomez.

It was proper in the defense of Gomez for his counsel to comment upon the fact that he had taken the stand, but it was improper for him to comment upon the fact that de Luna had not taken the stand. The inference which plainly would arise against de Luna by comments to the effect that Gomez testified, like the inference that arises in any event from the failure to testify, is one that must be checkmated by admonition of the court in charge.

There is no authority whatever for the proposition that Gomez would in any wise have been deprived of a fair trial if the comments regarding the failure of de Luna to testify had not been made. He had no right to go that far. He did have the right to testify against de Luna as he did. But no presumption or inference of guilt was permissible against de Luna from the fact that he did not testify. All comment in the presence of the jury upon his omission to testify was forbidden.

* * *

The opinion of the majority will create an intolerable procedural problem. If Gomez, or others similarly situated, claims the right which the majority holds that he has to comment on the failure of de Luna to testify, a mistrial will be required at the instance of his co-defendant who did not take the stand. In addition, severance in advance of trial may be required where there is a representation to the court that one co-defendant does not expect to take the stand while another or others do expect to testify, and claim their right to comment upon the failure of the other to testify. This would eliminate joint trials, or vest in a defendant the right to a mistrial during final arguments, or in the alternative create built-in reversible error, all in the discretion of the defendants. The law contemplates no such end.

The Sixth Amendment requires a fair trial. And the facts and circumstances as they arise must be considered. Here counsel for Gomez was allowed to comment, over objection made, on three occasions regarding the failure of de Luna to take the stand. The court overruled the objection on the ground that counsel for the co-defendant, as distinguished from the prosecution, could comment. This was error. When counsel for Gomez first alluded in argument to the fact that de Luna had not taken the stand, the objection should have been sustained, counsel admonished, and the jury instructed as to the rights of de Luna in the premises and to disregard the remark. This would have been the minimum corrective action to insure a fair trial to de Luna. Because it was not done, I join in the opinion of the majority to reverse. I do not agree that Gomez had the right to so comment.

NOTES

1. "The *de Luna* view generally has not found favor with those courts which have considered it, and at least one Court of Appeals has flatly rejected it." United States v. Marquez, 319 F.Supp. 1016, 1020 n. 11 (S.D. N.Y.1970), aff'd 449 F.2d 89 (2d Cir. 1971). Cited for rejecting *de Luna* outright was United States v. McKinney, 379 F.2d 259, 265 (6th Cir. 1967). Moreover, because of the "intolerable procedural problems" anticipated in Judge Bell's opinion, *de Luna* has been specifically limited to situations involving antagonistic defenses evincing "real prejudice". Before being permitted to comment on a codefendant's failure to testify, a defendant must be able to illustrate the manner in which he will receive substantial benefit from such comment. United States v. De La Cruz Bellinger, 422 F.2d 723 (9th Cir. 1970); Hayes v. United States, 329 F.2d 209, 221–22 (8th Cir.), cert. denied 377 U.S. 980, 84 S.Ct. 1883. Consequently, *de Luna* has not created an absolute right to comment on a codefendant's failure to testify without reference to the circumstances of defense at trial. United States v. Kahn, 381 F.2d 824, 840–41 (7th Cir. 1967), cert. denied 389 U.S. 1015, 88 S.Ct. 591; Cook v. State, 374 A.2d 264 (Del.1977) ("impartial and innocuous" comment).

2. When counsel comments on the fact that his client testified without mentioning that the codefendant did not, severance is not required unless the inference is so abiding as to amount to a comment. United States v. Hutul, 416 F.2d 607 (7th Cir. 1969); Parker v. United States, 404 F.2d 1193 (9th Cir. 1968). Essentially, the practical expedient employed by trial judges is to order defense counsel to refrain from commenting on the codefendant's failure to testify unless the separate defenses are so materially antagonistic that a severance is necessary. See United States v. Caci, 401 F.2d 664, 671 (2d Cir. 1968). If counsel contemptuously disobeys the order and comments on circumstances distinguishable from the *de Luna* situation, is the codefendant entitled to relief?

(b) The Need to Call a Co-defendant as a Witness

BYRD v. WAINWRIGHT

United States Court of Appeals, Fifth Circuit, 1970.
428 F.2d 1017.

GODBOLD, CIRCUIT JUDGE.

Byrd was indicted in Florida state court for rape, along with six other defendants. [H]e moved for a severance, stating that his defense would vary from that of the codefendants, that he would require the testimony of certain of the codefendants and could not at any stage of the trial expect or compel any of them to be witnesses in his behalf, and that he could not resolve his dilemma unless the codefendants were tried separately from and earlier than he.

The motion was denied by an order entered immediately before trial. Byrd was convicted, along with three of the other defendants, and was given a life sentence. . . . Following an evidentiary hearing the federal District Court granted habeas on the ground that the denial of a severance was a violation of due process, relying upon United States v. Echeles, 352 F.2d 892 (7th Cir. 1965) and DeLuna v. United States, 308 F.2d 140 (5th Cir. 1962).

We examine the matters known to the trial judge at the time he ruled on the motion to sever, recognizing that a motion for a separate trial is addressed to the discretion of the court, reviewable for abuse of discretion, and bearing in mind that in cases of this nature safeguarding the rights of defendants and the interests of the courts in efficient and expeditious administration of criminal justice is necessarily approached on a case by case basis.

All seven defendants were charged with the mass rape of the same young woman on a single occasion. The other six defendants confessed, some only to presence at the scene, others to actual participation in the rape. Five confessions purported to name all persons present at the commission of the crime; only one of these five named Byrd. Another of the five affirmatively stated that Byrd was not present. The sixth confession implicated Byrd as an active participant in the crime.

* * *

[Prior to trial, counsel for Byrd moved for a severance.] He pointed out that Byrd was the only non-confessing defendant, and that his major defense would be alibi. He noted the possibility that the other defendants might not take the stand, and that he could not require them to testify or even call them to the stand as witnesses.

As to the one confession which incriminated Byrd (that of Parks), Byrd's counsel told the court that he had talked to Parks who had told him there had been confusion in the taking of his confession (arising from the fact that police were also investigating a different incident, near in time, at which some of the defendants had been present) and, in substance, that Byrd had not been present at the rape scene. Byrd's counsel told the court that he had heard conversations among the other defendants to the effect Byrd was not present at the rape, and that the other defendants had told him their testimony would be that Byrd was not with them on the date of the crime.

* * *

This case is similar to *Echeles*, relied on by the court below. There, in the course of a criminal trial, defendant Arrington admitted on the stand that he had engaged in a scheme to present falsified documents and perjured testimony in his defense. In his testimony, and in subsequent statements in open court, he exculpated Echeles, his attorney, of participation. Arrington was indicted for perjury, and Arrington and Echeles (and others) for procuring the perjury, conspiracy, and like offenses.

Echeles faced a prospect, which Byrd did not face, of a trial in which Arrington's incriminating admissions could be introduced into evidence against Arrington and would in some degree prejudice Echeles. But his second problem was the same as Byrd's, inability to get into evidence statements tending to exculpate him made by his codefendant. The 7th Circuit held that the trial court erred in denying a severance, saying:

> At this juncture, we hold merely that, having knowledge of Arrington's record testimony protesting Echeles' innocence, and considering the obvious importance of such testimony to Echeles, it was error to deny the motion for a separate trial. It should have been clear at the outset that a fair trial for Echeles necessitated providing him the *opportunity* of getting the Arrington evidence before the jury, regardless of how we might regard the credibility of that witness or the weight of his testimony. (Emphasis in original.)

When a trial court is presented with a motion to sever based on the desire to offer exculpatory testimony of a codefendant, there are several areas of inquiry, sometimes overlapping, which the court well may pursue for guidance in determining what it should do:

> (1) Does the movant intend or desire to have the codefendant testify? How must his intent be made known to the court, and to what extent must the court be satisfied that it is bona fide?

> (2) Will the projected testimony of the codefendant be exculpatory in nature, and how significant must the effect be? How does the defendant show the nature of the projected testimony and its significance? Must he in some way validate the proposed testimony so as to give it some stamp of verity?

> (3) To what extent, and in what manner, must it be shown that if severance is granted there is likelihood that the codefendant will testify?

(4) What are the demands of effective judicial administration and economy of judicial effort? Related to this is the matter of timeliness in raising the question of severance.

(5) If a joint trial is held, how great is the probability that a codefendant will plead guilty at or immediately before trial and thereby prejudice the defendant, either by cross-defendant prejudice or by surprise as it relates to trial preparation?

There is no duty to sever merely because potentially exculpatory testimony of a codefendant exists. The defendant-movant must desire to use it. The desire of Byrd was plain and was asserted earnestly and repetitiously by his counsel, with full exploration of reasons. We reject the underlying implication of the state that as a matter of law there must be either formal testimony of defense counsel under oath, or an affidavit from him, stating his intent to use the codefendant's testimony. In this instance the transcripts of the hearings reveal not merely argument but extensive dialogue and exchange between attorneys and the court on many aspects of the case, in an atmosphere of apparent candor and trust. It is clear that the court treated as trustworthy the statements of the numerous counsel, as officers of the court.

We turn to the second area of inquiry, the exculpatory nature, and the significance, of the codefendant's testimony and the showing of those factors. This might be restated in terms of the extent of potential prejudice to the defendant if the defendant is tried without the opportunity to elicit the codefendant's testimony.

It must be shown that the testimony would be exculpatory in effect. The movant must make a clear showing of what the codefendant would testify to. Such a showing was made in this case. The confessions were before the court at the hearing and their contents discussed. Again, we reject overly formalistic rules. It is not necessary, as the state implies, that the potential testimony of the codefendant bear the imprimatur of having been given previously in a judicial proceeding under oath. In United States v. Gleason, 259 F. Supp. 282 (S.D.N.Y.1966), severance was granted where "there was no dispute between the government and the moving defendant that a codefendant had in the past made written and oral exculpatory statements concerning the movant." 259 F.Supp. at 283.

In *Echeles* the court considered Arrington's testimony to be of "obvious importance." So it is in the instant case. Perhaps the most critical fact known to the trial judge when acting on Byrd's motion was the inconsistencies of the confessions, which raised strong doubts as to Byrd's guilt. One defendant exculpated him. One (Parks) named him as a participant, but counsel represented that Parks would testify that Byrd was shown as present through error. Four defendants named various persons as being present, but none included Byrd. The state urges that "no one has a constitutional right to be tried last." That is not the problem. Here the one person who had a unique interest in being tried separately and later was Byrd.

Also, this was a shocking crime of violence, committed in the night-time, with at the most two eye witnesses to attempt to identify seven Negro youths. (As it turned out, identification was by one witness, the victim's date—the young woman could identify no one.)

We do not consider the last sentence of the above-quoted language from *Echeles* to establish a principle that the judge presented with a motion to sever may not make inquiry into credibility or weight of the potential testimony of the codefendant but to only refer to the testimony of Arrington under the circumstances of that case. Credibility is for the jury, but the judge is not required to sever on patent fabrications. If the testimony is purely cumulative, or of negligible weight or probative value, the court is not required to sever. The requirement is not a trial which guarantees the defendant every item of evidence he would like to offer but one which meets constitutional standards of due process.

In addition to making the other defendants unavailable, the joint trial affected Byrd adversely in another respect. So long as he was tried with others he had no way to introduce the confessions they had given, since they were taken in violation of *Miranda* and were inadmissible against them. Cf. Bruton v. United States, 391 U.S. 123, 88 S.Ct. 1620 (1968). But at a separate trial he would have at least a possibility of getting the confessions themselves into evidence and enjoying their exculpatory effect even though the codefendants claimed the privilege against self-incrimination.

* * *

A third inquiry may be into the likelihood that the codefendant will be willing to testify if the defendant is tried separately. *Echeles* said this:

> With regard to the question of whether or not Arrington would claim the privilege if he were called as a witness during a trial of Echeles alone—a trial held subsequent to his own—we can only say that such question was not properly the Government's to interpose. Speculation about what Arrington might do at a later Echeles trial undoubtedly would be a matter of some concern to Echeles, but he should not be foreclosed of the possibility that Arrington would testify in his behalf merely because that eventuality was not a certainty. [Citations omitted.] Moreover, it would in fact seem more likely than not that Arrington would have testified for Echeles for the reason that three times previously, in open court, Arrington had voluntarily exculpated Echeles, apparently contrary to his own penal interest.

352 F.2d at 898. We do not agree that likelihood is an inquiry that the government may not even make. The court is not required to sever where the possiblity of the codefendant's testifying is merely colorable or there is no showing that it is anything more than a gleam of possibility in the defendant's eye. "The unsupported possibility that such testimony [exculpatory testimony of a codefendant]

might be forthcoming does not make the denial of a motion for severance erroneous." United States v. Kahn, 381 F.2d 824, 841 (7th Cir. 1967). In United States v. Gleason, 259 F.Supp. 282, 284 (S.D.N.Y. 1966) the court reached this conclusion:

> It is enough to say that Karp [the movant] has shown persuasive ground for the claim that she needs Pitkin's [the codefendant's] evidence; that the need must almost certainly go unsatisfied in a joint trial; and that there is substantially greater likelihood of her using him if they are tried separately.

Byrd asked not only a separate but a later trial, and, as pointed out previously, he was the one defendant with a unique interest in being tried later than the others. This is not a case like Gorin v. United States, 313 F.2d 641 (1st Cir. 1963) in which the court may indulge in an assumption that a codefendant would be no more willing to waive his privilege against self-incrimination when called as a witness in a separate trial than he would be willing to insist upon his privilege as a defendant not to take the stand. The sequence in which trials would be held is in the discretion of the court.[1] Other defense counsel, and the prosecutor, had made known the strong likelihood that at least some of the codefendants would plead guilty.[2]

Bearing on the likelihood issue is the question whether codefendants pleading guilty would lose their right to claim the privilege against self-incrimination at a later trial of the defendant. In this instance the question is complicated by the other incident, known to the judge, at which some of the defendants appeared to have been present, and for which some of them had been charged, and the possibility that one testifying about the rape might tend to incriminate himself as to the other incident. These are questions we need not answer. The inquiry is not as to certainty whether the codefendants will or will not testify but the likelihood.

* * *

Affirmed.

NOTES

1. What kind of evidentiary support does a defendant need to obtain a severance on the ground that his codefendant's testimony is required? It has been uniformly held that a defendant's bare assertion that a joint trial would deprive him of the testimony of his codefendant, without a showing as to the likelihood of testimony being given in separate trials, without a showing that his codefendant would be willing to waive his privilege against self-incrimination and testify, and without a showing that such tes-

1. In a case, such as the present one, where the exculpatory testimony is in such form that it may be independently admissible as an exception to the hearsay rule, inquiry into likelihood that the codefendant will testify may become academic.

2. See United States v. Sanders, 266 F.Supp. 615 (W.D.La.1967), in which the court granted severances to two defendants and established an order of trial consisting of four separate trials, expressly reserving the right to change the sequence and to reconsolidate if appropriate.

timony will tend to exculpate the moving party, is insufficient to support a motion for severance. See, e. g., United States v. Davis, 418 F.2d 59 (9th Cir. 1969); Garnett v. United States, 404 F.2d 26 (5th Cir. 1968), cert. denied 394 U.S. 949, 89 S.Ct. 1288; United States v. Kilgore, 403 F.2d 627 (4th Cir. 1968), cert. denied 394 U.S. 932, 89 S.Ct. 1204; United States v. Caci, 401 F.2d 664, 671–72 (2d Cir. 1968), cert. denied 394 U.S. 917, 89 S. Ct. 1180; Brown v. United States, 126 U.S.App.D.C. 134, 375 F.2d 310, 316–17, cert. denied 388 U.S. 915, 87 S.Ct. 2133; Kolod v. United States, 371 F.2d 983, 990–92 (10th Cir. 1967); Gorin v. United States, 313 F.2d 641, 645–46 (1st Cir. 1963).

Thus, the courts have held that "[t]here is no absolute requirement for severance when a defendant suggests that the testimony of co-defendants is not available to him unless they are tried separately." United States v. Johnson, 426 F.2d 1112, 1116 (7th Cir. 1970). "The unsupported possibility that such testimony might be forthcoming does not make the denial of a motion for severance erroneous." United States v. Kahn, 381 F.2d 824, 841 (7th Cir.), cert. denied 389 U.S. 1015, 88 S.Ct. 591.

2. In light of these decisions, it is apparent that the defendant must demonstrate that his codefendant (1) is willing to testify and (2) can provide exculpatory testimony. The defendant must be able to show that his codefendant is likely to be willing and available to testify, but need not prove these factors to a certainty. United States v. Starr, 584 F.2d 235 (8th Cir. 1978).

3. It is virtually inconceivable that a severance would be denied a defendant who presents a sworn statement of a codefendant demonstrating a willingness to testify in a separate trial and that his evidence would exculpate the movant. See Tifford v. Wainwright, 588 F.2d 954 (5th Cir. 1979); United States v. Shuford, 454 F.2d 772 (4th Cir. 1971). However, the trial judge may ask the codefendant to testify at a hearing on the motion; and, if he refuses to do so, the court may deny the severance. United States v. Becker, 585 F.2d 703 (4th Cir. 1978).

4. May the prosecution elect to try the defendant before his codefendant in order to frustrate the purpose for which a severance is granted? While the issue has never been decided, one court has indicated that it "might well be error for the court to grant a severance in name only while still requiring that the co-defendant witness offering exculpatory testimony be tried after the movant." United States v. Gay, 567 F.2d 916 (9th Cir. 1978).

5. An interesting theory based upon the rationale of *Byrd* and the *Echeles* case referred to in *Byrd* was used to support a motion for a continuance in United States v. Haldeman, 559 F.2d 31 (D.C.Cir.1976). There, defendants argued that they should be able to obtain a continuance because of the unavailability of President Nixon to testify. The court held that the trial judge "must assess the likelihood—again based primarily on defendants' showing—that the evidence will be favorable to the defense and, if so, that it will be significant." It concluded that the trial judge did not abuse his discretion because of the absence of a "verifiable representation" of what the President would say.

3.   CONSPIRACY CASES

UNITED STATES v. JAMES

United States Court of Appeals, Fifth Circuit, 1979.
590 F.2d 575.

CHARLES CLARK, CIRCUIT JUDGE.

The court en banc on its own motion has reconsidered this case following the panel decision reported at 576 F.2d 1121 because of possible conflicts between that decision and prior decisions of this court touching on the admission of out-of-court statements by alleged coconspirators and because of the importance of the question at issue.

* * *

Under a long-recognized exception to the hearsay rule, a statement made by one member of a conspiracy during the course of and in furtherance of the conspiracy may be used against other members of the conspiracy if certain conditions are met. Meeting these conditions is necessary because of the court's recognition of the danger of prejudice to the defendant which would result if the jury were to rely upon coconspirator statements without first addressing and deciding the admissibility question.

(A) JUDGE OR JURY?

Present practice calls for the judge and the jury to share the responsibility for determining whether these conditions have been met. . . . [T]he judge's role is to make a preliminary determination whether the government has presented sufficient evidence, independent of the hearsay itself, to support a finding by the jury that the alleged conspiracy existed and that the declarant and the defendant against whom the statement is offered were members of that conspiracy. This is the "prima facie case" standard . . . . If the judge is satisfied that this test has been met, then under existing law the jury is instructed, both when the hearsay is introduced and at the final charge, that it may consider the hearsay against a particular defendant only if it first finds that the conspiracy existed, that the declarant and the defendant were members of it, and that the statement was made during the course of and in furtherance of the conspiracy. . . .

This case presents the first opportunity for us to consider the effect of the Federal Rules of Evidence upon our present practice. Here, the appellants moved for a pretrial hearing outside the presence of the jury in order to permit the trial judge to determine the admissibility of coconspirator statements. In support of their motion, they argued that Rule 104(a) of the Federal Rules of Evidence allocated to the judge alone the responsibility for deciding the admissibility of such statements and that the complexity of their case called for this to be accomplished at a separate nonjury hearing, as permitted under Rule 104(c). The district court denied the motion, asserting the cautionary . . . instructions would adequately protect the defendants. Faced with this denial of their motion, the defendants requested and received . . . instructions at trial. They now ask us to reverse their convictions on the basis of the denial of their motion. We believe this is an appropriate opportunity to . . . establish a new standard and procedure for handling the admissibility of coconspirator statements in criminal conspiracy trials.

Under the Federal Rules of Evidence, . . . a statement is not hearsay if it is offered against a party and is "a statement by a coconspirator of a party during the course and in furtherance of the conspiracy." Fed.R.Evid. 801(d)(2)(E). While this definitional section of the Rules removes coconspirator statements from the realm of hearsay, admissibility still depends upon the proof of the same facts as required previously. Thus, there must be a conspiracy, the statement must be made during the course of and in furtherance of the conspiracy, and the declarant and the defendant must be members of the conspiracy.[1] However, Rule 801 provides no guidance on whether the judge or the jury is to decide that these conditions have been satisfied.

To resolve that question, we must look to Rule 104, which delineates the functions of judge and jury in the determination of preliminary questions of fact. The relevant portions of Rule 104 provide:

(a) *Questions of Admissibility Generally.* Preliminary questions concerning the qualifications of a person to be a witness, the existence of a privilege, or the admissibility of evidence shall be determined by the court, subject to the provisions of subdivision (b). In making its determination it is not bound by the rules of evidence except those with respect to privileges.

(b) *Relevancy Conditioned on Fact.* When the relevancy of evidence depends upon the fulfillment of a condition of fact, the court shall admit it upon, or subject to, the introduction of evidence sufficient to support a finding of the fulfillment of the condition.

(c) *Hearing of Jury.* Hearings on the admissibility of confessions shall in all cases be conducted out of the hearing of the jury. Hearings on other preliminary matters shall be so conducted when the interests of justice require or, when an accused be a witness, if he so requests.

---

1. The Supreme Court has stated that the rationale behind the coconspirator rule is the notion that coconspirators are partners in crime and the law deems them agents of one another. The "in furtherance of the con- spiracy" requirement is analogous to the agency theory of "in the scope of the agent's authority." Anderson v. United States, 417 U.S. 211, 218 n. 6, 94 S.Ct. 2253, 2259 n. 6, (1974).

The rule thus adopts the orthodox position that the judge alone decides preliminary questions as to the competence of evidence, and the jury decides preliminary questions as to the conditional relevancy of the evidence.

The language of Rule 104 does not conclude our inquiry, however, for neither that rule nor the Advisory Committee's Notes inform us whether coconspirator's statements are to be dealt with under Rule 104(a) as questions of admissibility or under Rule 104(b) as questions of conditional relevancy.

We must look beyond the language of the rule to its underlying policies to determine who should decide the preliminary questions and what standard of proof should control the decision on admissibility. A rule that puts the admissibility of coconspirator statements in the hands of the jury does not avoid the danger that the jury might convict on the basis of these statements without first dealing with the admissibility question. It was this same danger which motivated the Supreme Court to hold in Jackson v. Denno, 378 U.S. 368, 84 S.Ct. 1774 (1964), that a criminal defendant is entitled to have a "reliable and clear-cut determination of the voluntariness of [his] confession, including the resolution of disputed facts upon which the voluntariness issue may depend," made by someone other than the jury which is to determine his guilt or innocence.[2]

We are therefore convinced that the preliminary questions of conditional relevance envisioned by Rule 104(b) are those which present no such danger of prejudice to the defendant. They are questions of probative force rather than evidentiary policy. They involve questions as to the fulfillment of factual conditions which the jury must answer.

The admissibility of a coconspirator's declarations in a conspiracy trial, however, does pose problems precisely because they are relevant. Such evidence endangers the integrity of the trial because the relevancy and apparent probative value of the statements may be so highly prejudicial as to color other evidence even in the mind of a conscientious juror, despite instructions to disregard the statements or to consider them conditionally. As a result, such statements should be evaluated by the trained legal mind of the trial judge.

Rule 104 has now made it clear that we must revise the procedures . . . for testing the trustworthiness of coconspirator statements—that is for determining whether a conspiracy existed and whether the defendant and the declarant were members of it. Because the Rule 104(b) exception is inappropriate to test the admissibility of such declarations, we hold that Rule 104(a) requires that the judge alone make the determination of the admissibility of the evi-

---

2. The Court said that the preliminary determination of the voluntariness of confession could be made by the trial judge, another judge, or another jury. *Jackson,* supra, 378 U.S. at 391 n. 19, 84 S.Ct. at 1788 n. 19. Rule 104(c) now requires that hearings on the admissibility of confessions be conducted out of the hearing of the jury.

dence. The jury is to play no role in determining the admissibility of the statements.

* * *

(B) BY WHAT STANDARD?

Under [the old] rule, the trial judge had to determine whether the prima facie test had been met before permitting the jury to consider the statement.   [W]e described this test as "whether the government, by evidence independent of the hearsay declarations of the coconspirator, has established a prima facie case of the existence of a conspiracy and of the defendant's participation therein, that is whether the other evidence *aliunde* the hearsay would be sufficient to support a finding by the jury that the defendant was himself a conspirator."

It must be borne in mind that the prima facie test was used when the jury also had a part in determining the use of the statements .   . .. This court has not spoken on the standard which the jury was to apply to this determination. Apparently it was not uncommon for the jury to be instructed that it must find the existence of the conspiracy and the defendant's connection to it beyond a reasonable doubt before ever considering the coconspirator statement.

Since we now conclude that the trial court has the responsibility for determining those questions of fact relating to admissibility of the statement, the standard by which the court makes this determination should be high enough to afford adequate protection to the defendant against whom the evidence is offered, yet not so high as to exclude trustworthy, relevant evidence.

* * *

There is some confusion resulting from the use of the terms by the several courts of appeals to describe the quantum of proof necessary for the trial judge to admit a coconspirator's statement. Some courts use the "prima facie" standard; others refer to a "fair preponderance" of the evidence. Still others require "substantial independent evidence."

Because of our conclusion, discussed below, that the trial court's threshold determination of admissibility is normally to be made during the presentation of the government's case in chief and before the evidence is heard by the jury, it is more appropriate to adopt a "substantial" evidence rule rather than one which requires, at that stage of the proceedings, a "preponderance" of the evidence. We conclude that .   .   . a declaration by one defendant is admissible against other defendants only when there is a "sufficient showing, by independent evidence, of a conspiracy among one or more other defendants and the declarant and if the declarations at issue were in furtherance of that conspiracy," and that "as a preliminary matter, there must be *substantial, independent* evidence of a conspiracy at least enough to take the question to the jury." .   .   .

Although Rule 104(a) provides that the court "is not bound by the Rules of Evidence except those with respect to privileges" we do not construe this language as permitting the court to rely upon the content of the very statement whose admissibility is at issue. We adhere to our requirement   .   .   .   that fulfillment of the conditions of admissibility must be established by evidence independent of the coconspirator statement itself. This construction of Rule 104(a) comports with earlier Supreme Court pronouncements that admissibility must depend upon independent evidence in order to prevent this statement from "lift[ing] itself by its own boot straps to the level of competent evidence." *Glasser v. United States*, 315 U.S. 60, 75, 62 S.Ct. 457, 467 (1943).

(C) ORDER OF PROOF

The displacement of [prior law] by the rule we now announce may affect the order of proof at trial in some cases. In our discussion above, we identify the danger to a defendant in a conspiracy trial when the government tenders a coconspirator's statement before laying the foundation for its admission. Courts have on occasion allowed such statements to be heard by the jury upon the promise that the prosecutor will "connect it up." Of course, if it is connected up, the defendant suffers no prejudice in the order of proof. If, however, the judge should conclude at the end of the trial that the proper foundation has not been laid, the defendant will have been prejudiced from the jury's having heard the inadmissible evidence.

While the government here urges that the practice of "connecting up" be permitted to continue at the discretion of the trial judge, it suggests a remedy for failure to make the connection which may be more burdensome and expensive of prosecutorial and judicial effort than a reordering of the proof. The government suggests that "should the trial judge determine that the government has not carried its burden in connecting the previously admitted evidence, the court may 'upon appropriate motion, declare a mistrial, unless a cautionary instruction to disregard the statement would suffice to cure any prejudice.' "

* * *

Both because of the "danger" to the defendant if the statement is not connected and because of the inevitable serious waste of time, energy and efficiency when a mistrial is required in order to obviate such danger, we conclude that the present procedure warrants the statement of a preferred order of proof in such a case. The district court should, whenever reasonably practicable, require the showing of a conspiracy and of the connection of the defendant with it before admitting declarations of a coconspirator. If it determines it is not reasonably practical to require the showing to be made before admitting the evidence, the court may admit the statement subject to being connected up.

(D) AT THE END OF THE TRIAL

Regardless of whether the proof has been made in the preferred order, or the coconspirator's statement has been admitted subject to later connection, on appropriate motion at the conclusion of all the evidence the court must determine as a factual matter whether the prosecution has shown by a preponderance of the evidence independent of the statement itself (1) that a conspiracy existed, (2) that the coconspirator and the defendant against whom the coconspirator's statement is offered were members of the conspiracy, and (3) that the statement was made during the course and in furtherance of the conspiracy.   Rule 801(d)(2)(E).   If the court concludes that the prosecution has not borne its burden of proof on these issues, the statement cannot remain in the evidence to be submitted to the jury. In that event, the judge must decide whether the prejudice arising from the erroneous admission of the coconspirator's statements can be cured by a cautionary instruction to disregard the statement or whether a mistrial is required.   .   .   .

(E) CONCLUSION

This opinion intends to establish minimum standards for the admissibility of coconspirator statements.   Nothing stated here shall prevent a trial judge from requiring more meticulous procedures to assure that such statements (1) are not admitted until properly authenticated by substantial independent evidence and (2) do not remain in the proof to be submitted to the jury unless their admissibility is established by a preponderance of the evidence.

In the case at bar, .   .   .   the trial court did not submit the evidence to the jury for its determination of admissibility until it determined that the prosecution "ha[d] established a prima facie case of the existence of a conspiracy and of the defendant's participation therein, that is [that] the other evidence *aliunde* the hearsay would be sufficient to support a finding by the jury that the defendant was himself a conspirator."   Although the procedures which we now adopt are different from the prima facie rule .   .   .   we do not disturb the conclusion reached by the panel of this Court that the admission of the hearsay statements was fully supported because there was "a preponderance of the independent evidence that the conspiracy existed, that each of the defendants and appellants were members of it, and that the statements were made in the course of and in furtherance of the conspiracy."

Exercising this court's supervisory power over the district courts, .   .   .   we adopt these rules only prospectively.   Accordingly, they are required only as to coconspirator statements which the government seeks to introduce in trials commencing after 30 days from the date of this opinion.

The judgment is affirmed.

TJOFLAT, CIRCUIT JUDGE, with whom AINSWORTH, CIRCUIT JUDGE joins, specially concurring:

The original panel in this case, after concluding that the appellants' drug conspiracy trials contained no reversible error and that their convictions should be affirmed, undertook "to . . . to establish the correct standard and procedure for handling the admissibility of coconspirator statements in criminal conspiracy trials" in this circuit. United States v. James, 576 F.2d 1121, 1127 (5th Cir. 1978). The procedure devised was a "minitrial." Construing Fed.R.Evid. 104 and 611(a), the panel instructed that a district judge may not allow the jury to hear a coconspirator's out-of-court declaration until the judge, following a hearing conducted outside the presence of the jury, has determined by a preponderance of the evidence that the declaration is admissible under Fed.R.Evid. 801(d)(2)(E).

This case was taken en banc because the minitrial procedure fashioned by the panel is obviously unworkable and onerous. Indeed, the panel's approach might well require a district judge, after the jury has been sworn, to try the entire case twice—once at the minitrial on the admissibility question and once before the jury on the issue of guilt.

* * *

In order to understand precisely what the majority has done, I think it useful to recall the practice regarding the admissibility of coconspirator statements before the adoption of the Federal Rules of Evidence. Once this background is set forth, I shall describe what I believe to be the impact of the Federal Rules on prior practice and shall attempt to demonstrate the inappropriateness of the procedures the majority now prescribes.

I.

Prior to the adoption of the Federal Rules of Evidence, a district judge faced with a hearsay objection to an out-of-court statement by a coconspirator made in the absence of the defendant normally made the following inquiries after determining that the statement was relevant to an issue in the case.

First, is there a sufficient predicate to allow the statement to be received for the truth of its contents? In deciding this question, the judge looked to the evidence already presented to the jury to see if it established a prima facie showing that the statement was made by a coconspirator of the defendant during and in furtherance of the conspiracy. . . . If the evidence before the jury met this prima facie test, the statement would have been admitted for the truth of its contents. If the evidence failed the prima facie test, the court, generally in a voir dire hearing, might have entertained the Government's proffer of the predicate necessary to the statement's admissibility. If satisfied that the Government, by the conclusion of its case-in-chief, would have made a prima facie showing, by evidence independent of the statement itself, that a conspiracy involving the defendant existed and that the statement was made by a coconspirator during and in furtherance thereof, the court would have received the statement subject to connection, reserving to the close of the Government's case its ruling on the hearsay objection. Whether the court received the statement after the predicate to admissibility had been demonstrated or beforehand subject to connection, it was required to give the [cautionary] instruction when the statement was received.

Second, if the predicate, in the evidence presented to the jury or in the Government's proffer, were insufficient to admit the statement for the truth of the matter asserted, is the statement otherwise admissible to prove an issue unrelated to the truth of the statement? The statement might have been admissible as bearing on one or more of a variety of other issues; for example, the mere act of making the statement may be probative of the declarant's knowledge of the conspiracy and its objectives, or the words spoken may tend to show the role the declarant played in the conspiracy and may be probative of his intent.

Third, if the statement tends to establish or controvert an issue regardless of its truth, does the probative value of the statement to prove matters other than its contents outweigh the prejudice flowing from the revelation of its contents to the jury and the danger that the jury might accept them as true? If the probative value outweighed the prejudice, the statement was received. Of course, in this instance [the Appolo] instruction was inappropriate.

At the conclusion of the Government's case and, if warranted, at the conclusion of all the evidence, the court might have reconsidered the propriety of admitting the statement to prove the truth of its contents in conjunction with the court's entertainment of a motion for judgment of acquittal. For example, in permitting the statement to come before the jury subject to later connection, the court might have opted to defer ruling on the defendant's hearsay objection until the conclusion of the Government's case, or the court might have received the statement unreservedly, without qualification, subject only to the defendant's right to renew his objection, in the form of a motion to strike, at the close of the Government's proof (and, again, at the close of all the evidence if the defense chose to put on a case). In reconsidering the hearsay objection, the court examined the record to determine whether the Government had established a conspiracy by the evidence, viewed in the light most favorable to the Government, independent of the truth value of the questioned statement. If the court concluded that a conspiracy had not been proven, a ruling on the hearsay objection would be unnecessary since a judgment of acquittal would be in order. However, if the independent evidence justified the submission of the conspiracy charge to the jury, the court's assessment of the statement's admissibility continued. In the event the court found that not all the remaining prerequisites of admissibility, i. e., that the statement was made during the course of *and* in furtherance of the conspiracy, had been established by prima facie evidence, the court could have stricken the statement and admonished the jury not to consider it or it could have granted a mistrial if instructions would have been inadequate to erase the prejudice caused by the erroneous reception of the statement.

The common law developed these procedures to give the trial judge maximum flexibility in ordering the proof at trial to the end that the evidence be presented in an intelligible way.

* * *

II.

Before embarking on a detailed discussion of the new rules of evidence and how the majority largely misconstrues them, I briefly summarize how the new rules alter the preexisting process. As the majority correctly holds, the task for determining the admissibility of coconspirator statements to establish the truth of their contents is now for the judge alone.

* * *

The rules do not disturb the district court's discretion in ordering the proof at trial; that discretion is reaffirmed in rule 611(a). Accordingly, complicated cases should still be tried in a manner that the court judges to be comprehensible to the jury. Thus, I believe, the rules seek to avoid a miscarriage of justice that might result if we straitjacket the district judges of our circuit by requiring them to alter the natural progression of the trial.

A

I read the Federal Rules of Evidence to envision the following procedures for the admissibility of coconspirator statements. I agree with the majority's conclusion that . . . the question of admissibility is one solely for the judge under rule 104(a). I reach this result on somewhat different grounds, however. The requirements of rule 801(d)(2)(E) that the statement be made by a coconspirator during and in furtherance of the conspiracy are not conditions on the statement's *relevancy*, which is the sole concern of rule 104(b). Statements may be highly relevant even though the conditions of rule 801(d)(2)(E) are not met. A classic example of such a statement is a postarrest confession. It is not made during the conspiracy because the declarant has been arrested, and it is hard to imagine a case in which such a confession is made in furtherance of the conspiracy. As this example amply demonstrates, the 801(d)(2)(E) requirements are not conditions on the relevancy of the statement but rather on its admissibility. It is clear, therefore, that the issue whether those requirements have been met is one for the judge under 104(a), because it provides, "Preliminary questions concerning . . . the admissibility of evidence shall be determined by the court, subject to the provisions of [104(b)]."

B

As to the standard that the judge should apply in determining whether the statement is admissible, I believe that logic calls for the employment of the preponderance of the evidence test. The majority's position on this point is, to me, ambiguous at best.

* * *

[T]he burden of resolving factual issues upon which admissibility is predicated is commonplace in the courtroom. The burden under the coconspirator exception is no different and should receive no different treatment—the predicate for the admissibility of a coconspirator declaration should be established by a preponderance of the evidence, not by a standard that measures the sufficiency of a case for the jury.

* * *

I would not deny the trial judge the considerable discretion provided him by the rules to control the "mode and order of interrogating witnesses and presenting evidence so as to (1) make the interrogation and presentation effective for the ascertainment of truth, (2) avoid needless consumption of time, and (3) protect witnesses from harassment or undue embarrassment." Fed.R.Evid. 611(a). The trial judge is given wide latitude by this rule to decide when during the trial and in what manner the predicate for admissibility is developed. Depending upon the circumstances of the case, he may deem it prudent to receive the evidence conditionally on nothing more than the representations of counsel at a routine sidebar conference. At the other extreme, he may think that the potential for mistrial, if the admission of the evidence proves to be erroneous, is so great that nothing less than a full-blown evidentiary hearing is necessary to ensure that the statement is properly admissible.

* * *

I can imagine no more compelling situation in which the judge's discretion in evaluating the predicate to admissibility is necessary and appropriate than in conspiracy-type trials, which are often highly complex and always difficult to present to the jury in a meaningful way. The majority would permit the trial judge to depart from the normal minitrial procedure and to receive the coconspirator's declaration subject to connection only if it determines that "it is not reasonably practical" for the prosecution to establish the predicate to admissibility by substantial independent evidence before eliciting the declaration in the presence of the jury. The majority does not indicate what circumstances might make it "not reasonably practical" for the prosecutor to establish the predicate to admissibility in the preferred order, whether and to what extent findings as to the impracticability must be expressed by the trial judge if he declines to follow the normal procedure, and the standard we shall henceforth employ in reviewing his action.

It should always be borne in mind that however the trial judge exercises his discretion in deciding to admit a hearsay statement or any other evidence to which objection has been voiced, his decision is subject to review before the case is submitted to the jury. If a party persists in its objection, the judge will reassess his earlier ruling on the record as a whole, both at the conclusion of the Government's case-in-chief and at the close of all the evidence, to determine whether the predicate to admissibility has been established by a preponderance of the evidence.[1] If, for example, the predicate to the admissibility of a coconspirator's statement to establish the truth of its contents is not found by a preponderance of the evidence, the judge may instruct the jury to disregard the statement or, if justice so requires, grant a motion for mistrial. At this posture of the case, the trial judge would of course consider whether the statement had any evidentiary value apart from its hearsay aspects and, if so, would determine its admissibility . . . .

C

Contrary to the majority's position, I would allow the trial judge to consider the contents of the proffered statement in determining its admissibility. I think this is the clear mandate of the last sentence of rule 104(a), which states, "In making its determination [the court] is not bound by the rules of evidence except those with respect to privileges."

* * *

As a practical matter, I do not think the determination whether the statement should be received in evidence will in many cases turn on whether the court considers the truth-value of the statement. A decision that the statement is admissible to prove its truth automatically establishes that the statement would be admissible for other purposes, since satisfaction of "[t]he requirement that admissible declarations of coconspirators be in furtherance of the conspiracy virtually insures that the declarations will fall within the category of 'verbal acts,' which are not hearsay." McCormick, Evidence § 53, at 19 (2d ed. Supp.1978) (footnotes omitted). To determine whether this requirement has been met clearly necessitates consideration of the content of the statement.

The majority paints with such a broad brush, however, that it apparently obliterates the possibility of admitting coconspirator

---

1. The majority concedes that at the close of all the evidence, the judge must decide a motion to strike by a preponderance of all the evidence. The anomaly of applying at this point a different standard from the one applied when the statement was offered has already been noted. It is interesting to note that the majority makes no provision for a preponderance of the evidence review at the close of the Government's case-in-chief, as distinguished from the close of all the evidence. The majority either thinks such a review is unnecessary at this juncture or believes that such a review, before the trial is concluded, would be too burdensome.

It seems to me that both the trial judge and the parties would want to know, at the close of the Government's case-in-chief, precisely what evidence is in the record *and* will eventually be considered by the jury in its deliberations. Until this is determined, the court may find it difficult to pass on a motion for judgment of acquittal or for a mistrial. It would be anomalous to decide either motion on the basis of evidence admissible only because "substantial evidence" supported the predicate, but the majority does not say what standard should be used at this point.

statements when relevant to issues apart from the verity of the statements.

* * *

In my judgment this approach amounts to a judicial repeal of rule 402,[2] which makes relevant evidence presumptively admissible. . . . Invariably, a coconspirator's declaration is probative of matters other than the truth of its contents—the declarant's membership in the conspiracy, the character of his intent, the objectives of the conspirators, the identity of members other than the defendant and so on. And as a trial progresses and other issues are raised, such as the credibility of the witnesses, including the declarant, the contents of his out of court statement may well have additional bases of admissibility.

Finally, in addition to restricting, if not altogether foreclosing, the trial judge's authority to admit coconspirator declarations to prove other matters unless the prosecution complies with the substantial independent evidence rule, the majority removes from the trial judge's discretion his authority under rule 403[3] to weigh the probative value of the evidence for other purposes against its prejudice when considered for the truth of its contents. In effect, the majority creates a conclusive presumption that the danger of unfair prejudice substantially outweighs its probative value. Although written in the context of a criminal coconspirator's statement, the logic of the majority's opinion would apply equally to any admissions, if not all out-of-court utterances, as to which a hearsay objection is raised. I find nothing in the rules, common law, or commentary that would justify the majority's special treatment of the narrow evidentiary question before us.

III.

* * *

In sum, perhaps the steps the majority has taken today in laying down a set of rules to control the Government's use of coconspirator statements, are in reality motivated by a concern that criminal cases meriting mistrial because of the erroneous reception of coconspirator declarations will nevertheless result in convictions. This concern may be amplified by the majority's frustration at the inability of an appellate tribunal to retry such cases and to remedy the perceived injustice. . . . We are required to defer to the district judge in

---

2. Rule 402 provides as follows:

   Relevant Evidence Generally Admissible; Irrelevant Evidence Inadmissible

   All relevant evidence is admissible, except as otherwise provided by the Constitution of the United States, by Act of Congress, by these rules, or by other rules prescribed by the Supreme Court pursuant to statutory authority. Evidence which is not relevant is not admissible.

3. Rule 403 provided as follows:

   Exclusion of Relevant Evidence on Grounds of Prejudice, Confusion, or Waste of Time

   Although relevant, evidence may be excluded if its probative value is substantially outweighed by the danger of unfair prejudice, confusion of the issues, or misleading the jury, or by considerations of undue delay, waste of time, or needless presentation of cumulative evidence.

all but the most egregious circumstances. But we are thus limited in every appeal based on the erroneous admission of evidence. Rather than adopt the far reaching measures fashioned by the majority especially for criminal trials (but clearly applicable in all cases involving concerted activity), I would rely upon our district judges to make proper and careful application of the rules of evidence and procedure, to the end that justice may be achieved.

NOTES

1. Any act or declaration by a co-conspirator, committed in furtherance of the conspiracy and during its pendency, is admissible against each member of the conspiracy if, by way of foundation, independent evidence of a conspiracy and an individual defendant's participation in it are shown. See Krulewitch v. United States, 336 U.S. 440, 69 S.Ct. 716 (1949); United States v. Glasser, 315 U.S. 60 (1942). Conspiracy defendants have, for many years, sought to prohibit the introduction of evidence under the co-conspirator's exception until the independent proof required by the exception has been adduced. For example, in Cohen v. United States, 157 F. 651, 655 (2d Cir), cert. denied 207 U.S. 596, 28 S.Ct. 261 (1907), the court stated:

> "[I]t is urged that the evidence of [the co-conspirator's] declarations was received before there was any proof of the conspiracy, and it is claimed that declarations of an alleged conspirator are not admissible to prove the existence of a conspiracy. We are not disposed to question this last claim. But we are of the opinion that there was proof of the conspiracy in this case other than [the co-conspirator's] declarations, and the mere fact that all the evidence thereof was not in at the time the declarations were testified to did not render it erroneous to receive them. It was a question of the order of proof and within the discretion of the trial court."

The procedure of provisionally allowing the introduction of evidence under the co-conspirator's exception subject to later independent proof of the conspiracy represented the general rule: "There is no requirement that the conspiracy be proved at the trial before the declarations [of co-conspirators] are admitted, and the order in which the evidence is received is within the court's discretion." United States v. Halpin, 374 F.2d 493, 495 (7th Cir.), cert. denied 386 U.S. 1032, 87 S.Ct. 1482 (1967). Termed another way, a trial judge, in his discretion, may "permit reception of declarations and acts of alleged co-conspirators subject to later proof of the existence of the conspiracy." United States v. King, 467 F.2d 478, 479 (6th Cir. 1972).

To what extent was this procedure altered in *James*? What are the essential differences between the majority and concurring opinions? Which opinion correctly stated the impact of the Federal Rules of Evidence on conspiracy cases? Compare Kessler, The Treatment of Preliminary Issues of Fact in Conspiracy Litigations: Putting the Conspiracy Back into the Coconspirator Rule, 5 Hofstra L.Rev. 77 (1976), with Bergman, The Coconspirator's Exception: Defining the Standard of the Independent Evidence Test under the New Federal Rules of Evidence, 5 Hofstra L.Rev. 99 (1976).

2. Does *James* require the prosecution to proceed with a particular order of proof in a conspiracy case? Would a requirement that the prosecution prove a conspiracy and each defendant's connection to it before admit-

ting hearsay statements of a co-conspirator as a practical matter, force the prosecution to prove its case in a wholly untenable manner? Witnesses who give testimony provisionally admissible under the co-conspirator's exception ordinarily also testify with respect to independent non-hearsay admissions and other competent evidence. To force them to testify with respect to the latter and wait until a conspiracy is shown before permitting them, most likely on recall, to testify to the former would take the events charged as offenses entirely out of context. United States v. Cerone, 452 F.2d 274 (7th Cir. 1971), cert. denied 405 U.S. 964, 92 S.Ct. 1168 (1972), may serve to exemplify the point.

In *Cerone,* the defendants contended that the record disclosed no evidence, or at most insufficient evidence, connecting them to a conspiracy. These assertions were based upon the claim that the testimony of a government informant, admitted provisionally under the co-conspirator's exception, constituted the only evidence connecting them to a conspiracy. Both the claim of no evidence and that of insufficient evidence were rejected:

> "These arguments miss the mark, for implicit in both is the assumption that all of [the informant's] testimony is admissible, if at all, under the co-conspirators exception to the hearsay rule. Even a casual reading of the record, however, reveals that much of testimony related extra-judicial admissions by word or act of a defendant which were properly admissible against the defendant. Although courts have admitted such evidence on the theory that the declarant's words or acts constituted an admission against interest, the better view is that such admissions are not hearsay at all and are admissible absent other reasons for exclusion. As evidence independent of the hearsay statement of a co-conspirator, such admissions may quite properly constitute corroborative evidence sufficient to justify the admission of a co-conspirator's hearsay declaration."

If the informant in *Cerone* was first required to testify as to the admissions and other competent evidence and, when independent evidence of conspiracy was thereby established, return to the stand to relate extrajudicial declarations under the then cognizable co-conspirator's exception, his testimony would have been disjointed, confusing, and incongruous. Of course, the prosecution could offer evidence with respect to the substantive counts in an indictment without employing the co-conspirator's exception. However, because many of the overt acts in a conspiracy are generally charged as substantive counts, the order of proof would be further skewed. It would be necessary to go through the prosecution's entire case and, if conspiracy were proved, recall each witness, who would necessarily be wholly out of order, to relate testimony under the co-conspirator's exception.

Would a mandated order or proof aid the jury or serve to confuse it in a conspiracy case?

3. To prove that a conspiracy existed, it is incumbent upon the prosecution to show an agreement to violate the law and one overt act, in furtherance of that agreement—"to effect the object of the conspiracy". United States v. Bayer, 331 U.S. 532, 542, 67 S.Ct. 1394, 1399 (1947). See also Ingram v. United States, 360 U.S. 672, 677, 79 S.Ct. 1314, 1318–1319 (1959); Yates v. United States, 354 U.S. 298, 333, 77 S.Ct. 1064, 1084 (1957). The existence of a conspiracy need not be demonstrated by direct evidence, but, rather, a common plan may be inferred from circumstantial

evidence. See Glasser v. United States, 315 U.S. 60, 80, 62 S.Ct. 457, 469–470 (1942). In most cases of its nature, because of the secretiveness and complexity of contemporary conspiracies, proof of an agreement is possible only by circumstantial evidence. Cf. Blumenthal v. United States, 332 U.S. 539, 557, 68 S.Ct. 248, 256–257 (1947).

4. Once the conspiracy is established, it is necessary that the independent evidence in the record show that a defendant, by virtue of his knowledge of the purpose of the conspiracy and intent to further it, was personally connected with the conspiracy charged. See Ingram v. United States, 360 U.S. 672, 678, 79 S.Ct. 1314, 1319 (1958); United States v. Fellabaum, 408 F.2d 220, 224 (7th Cir.), cert. denied 396 U.S. 858, 90 S.Ct. 125 (1969). However, because a defendant need not have knowledge of each and every detail in order to be a member of the conspiracy, the cases uniformly hold that each defendant need not know the identity or number of all of his co-conspirators. See Blumenthal v. United States, 332 U.S. 539, 557, 68 S.Ct. 248, 256–257 (1947); United States v. Crosby, 294 F.2d 928, 945 (2d Cir. 1961), cert. denied 368 U.S. 984, 82 S.Ct. 599 (1962). This showing is not contingent upon proof of a defendant's awareness of every detail of the conspiratorial plan; it is satisfactory if the independent evidence indicates that the defendant knew of the conspiracy's essential objective and acted to further it. See Blumenthal v. United States, 332 U.S. 539, 556–57, 68 S.Ct. 248, 256–257 (1947); United States v. Fellabaum, 408 F.2d 220, 224 (7th Cir.), cert. denied 396 U.S. 858, 90 S.Ct. 125 (1969); United States v. Vittoria, 284 F.2d 451 (7th Cir. 1960). And, as with proof of the conspiratorial agreement itself, an individual defendant's knowledge and intent may be shown by circumstantial evidence.

5. The existence of a conspiracy and a defendant's connection with it must be demonstrated by proof independent of that provisionally admitted under the co-conspirator's exception. But, in assessing precisely what proof can be categorized as "independent", it is important to take into account the distinction betweeen acts and utterances. While extrajudicial *declarations* made by a conspirator out of the presence of his confederates, used to prove the truth of the matter asserted, may not be considered independent evidence, *acts* performed in absence of his co-conspirators are not hearsay and, thus, may be considered as independent proof. See, e. g., Lutwak v. United States, 344 U.S. 604, 617–19, 73 S.Ct. 481, 489–490 (1953). Similarly, independent proof may take the form of admissions made in the presence of other co-conspirators. See United States v. Cerone, 452 F.2d 274, 283–84 (7th Cir. 1971), cert. denied 405 U.S. 964, 92 S.Ct. 1168.

6. Taking into account all cognizable independent evidence, the trial judge must determine whether the prosecution has proved a conspiracy and each defendant's connection with it. In evaluating the evidence of a defendant's participation in a conspiracy, the criterion employed is the slight evidence test:

> "Once the existence of a common scheme is established, very little is required to show that a defendant became a party—'slight evidence may be sufficient to connect the defendant with it'." United States v. Robinson, 470 F.2d 121, 123 (7th Cir. 1972).

See Note, Connecting Defendants to Conspiracies: The Slight Evidence Rule and the Federal Courts, 64 Va.L.Rev. 881 (1978) (criticizing the rule).

Based upon the "slight evidence test" the courts have recognized that a single act may be the foundation for drawing the actor within the ambit of a conspiracy if the act is such that one may reasonably infer from it an intent to participate in an unlawful venture. See United States v. Battaglia, 394 F.2d 304, 311 (7th Cir. 1968), vacated on other grounds 394 U.S. 310, 89 S.Ct. 1163 (defendant made one statement; he said "he liked Lakey and they could use him in other things because he was clean"); United States v. McGann, 431 F.2d 1104, 1107 (5th Cir. 1970) (defendant agreed to purchase television sets); Lopez v. United States, 414 F.2d 909, 911 (5th Cir. 1969) (defendant agreed to haul certain goods). But see United States v. Fiorito, 499 F.2d 106 (7th Cir. 1974) (single ambiguous act—telephone call—held insufficient to connect defendant to conspiracy).

7. What happens when, after all of its evidence has been introduced, the government has failed to prove a conspiracy?

In Schaffer v. United States, 362 U.S. 511, 80 S.Ct. 945 (1962), five defendants were tried on substantive and conspiracy counts of transporting stolen goods in interstate commerce. Before sending the case to the jury the trial judge dismissed the conspiracy count and, in his charge to the jury, meticulously set out the separate evidence against each of the defendants and admonished the jury that they were not to take into consideration any proof against one defendant and apply it by inference to another. After the conviction on the substantive counts was affirmed by the Second Circuit, defendants argued, before the Supreme Court, that, despite the cautionary instructions, prejudice was implicit in the continuation of the joint trial after dismissal of the conspiracy count. The Court, finding joinder to have been originally proper, examined the facts of the case to determine whether any of the defendants were prejudiced by the failure of the trial judge to order a severance after the dismissal of the conspiracy count. The majority of the Court concluded that no prejudice was shown. 362 U.S. at 516.

Under what circumstances are limiting instructions so confusing that a mistrial must be declared on the nonconspiracy counts of an indictment?

8. In Dutton v. Evans, 400 U.S. 74, 91 S.Ct. 210 (1970), the Court acknowledged that the hearsay rules and Confrontation Clause are designed to protect similar interests, but refuse to hold that the constitutional requirement of confrontation paralleled the rules of hearsay as they existed at common law. Finding no inherent tension between the use of hearsay evidence and the Confrontation Clause, the Court approached the issue on the ground of whether the statement was surrounded by the "indicia of reliability which have been widely viewed as determinative of whether a statement may be placed before the jury though there is no confrontation of the declarant".

Does *Dutton* reconcile the apparent antinomy between the probative use of hearsay and the guarantees of the confrontation clause? Does the notion that the declarations of the conspirator made during the pendency and in furtherance of the conspiracy are inherently reliable satisfy confrontation objections? Because criminal conspiracies are frequently clandestine affairs liable to disaster upon discovery, are the participants likely to be cavalier in their statements regarding the enterprise? Does the "community of interest of the conspirators" insure reliability? Dutton v. Evans (Harlan, J., concurring). Is the untrustworthiness of a statement made under coercive circumstances, such as a confession, substantially less than one made in confidence by a co-conspirator?

9. Can a defendant get a fair trial if the jury also has to consider the guilt or innocence of 23 other alleged co-conspirators in a single proceeding? See United States v. Mayes, 512 F.2d 637 (6th Cir. 1975).

C. THE PROBLEM WITNESSES

---

1. ACCOMPLICES, INFORMERS, AND LIARS

PEOPLE v. MILLS

Supreme Court of Illinois, 1968.
40 Ill.2d 4, 237 N.E.2d 697.

MR. JUSTICE UNDERWOOD delivered the opinion of the court:

This is a direct appeal by the defendant, Matthew Mills, from a jury conviction in the circuit court of Cook County for unlawful possession of drugs . . . . He was sentenced to imprisonment for not less than two nor more than seven years, and he now argues . . . that the use of testimony by an informer paid on a contingent fee basis violated due process of law. . . .

A summary of the facts relevant to the defendant's . . . contention is that on February 18, 1965, Nathaniel Clayton, a special employee of the Chicago Police Department, drove with two police officers to a tavern known as the "Corner Club" at the corner of 63rd and Ingleside streets at about 10:30 A.M. Clayton entered the tavern three or four times and each time upon leaving walked directly to report to the officers who waited in an unmarked squad car which was parked near the tavern. On his last entry into the tavern at 2:00 P. M., Clayton observed the defendant who was seated on a stool at one end of the bar. Clayton testified that a man he knew as "Pete" walked up to defendant and engaged him in conversation. During this conversation Clayton stated that he saw defendant place his hand under the plastic covering of the bar stool on which he was sitting and take out a cigarette package which he held in front of him and then replaced under the plastic cover of the stool. After viewing this incident Clayton immediately left the tavern and informed the waiting police officers who thereupon entered the tavern, arrested defendant, and seized the cigarette package from under the plastic cover of his stool. This package contained two small tinfoil packets of heroin.
. . . .

We come now to the defendant's contention that the use of Clayton's testimony "sank far below minimum standards of decency and violated the defendant's right of Due Process" because the informer was paid on a contingent fee basis. Clayton testified that he was paid by the Vice Control Division of the Chicago Police Department according to the number of cases which he "made"; he was paid between $5 and $15 per case and he averaged between $20 to $30 per week while working as an agent for the police. While the phrase "make a case" was not clearly defined during the informer's testimony, it is apparent that the phrase did not mean that Clayton was paid only when his efforts resulted in a conviction, since he testified that he was paid for securing evidence in the instant case before Mills was even brought to trial. Moreover, it seems clear that Clayton was not sent to the Corner Club tavern with the design of securing evidence leading to the conviction of defendant Mills, because Clayton testified that he had never seen the defendant prior to the afternoon in question and that he had to point out the defendant to the arresting officers when they entered the bar. The obvious conclusion to be drawn from this state of facts is that the Corner Club tavern was a place in which the existence of narcotics traffic was suspected by police who staked the informer there to watch for activities commonly performed by persons engaged in such trade. These facts distinguished this case from Williamson v. United States, (5th Cir.), 311 F.2d 441, relied upon by defendant, where the informer was paid a specified contingent fee by government agents for catching certain named suspects. The divided court there held, "Without some . . . justification or explanation, we cannot sanction a contingent fee agreement to produce evidence against particular named defendants as to crimes not yet committed." Actually, the contingent fee payment to Clayton for his activities leading to the arrest of Mills is wholly analogous to contingent fees paid to the informers in United States v. Baxter and United States v. Costner where *Williamson* was distinguished and contingent fee payments condoned. In *Baxter* the court pointed out that the payments to the informers were made prior to trial and were not based on convictions, and we find that the same facts in the present case make the payments to Clayton a permissible procedure. In the present case, the method of compensating Nathaniel Clayton was fully explored during the trial and we find it sufficient that "the informer's interest in the litigation and his status were before the jury . . . ."

We believe that contingent fee payments to informers in narcotics cases are not only permissible, but they may in fact be absolutely necessary to the continued viability of the whole informer system. Various commentaries have indicated that "Particularly in the enforcement of vice, liquor or narcotics laws, it is all but impossible to obtain evidence for prosecution save by the use of decoys." (Model Penal Code, sec. 210, comment, p. 16 (Tent. Draft No. 9, 1959).) "[T]he informer is a vital part of society's defensive arsenal." (State v. Barnett, 42 N.J. 377, 201 A.2d 39, 44.) "Unfortunately for the prosecution, those of blameless lives are rarely chosen as companions by operators of 'dope rings'. Therefore, such persons seldom have opportunity to testify in prosecutions of this sort." "[W]e feel that this right of full cross-examination [on reliability of an undisclosed informer] must give way in face of a compelling policy to protect informants in the stealthy and vicious traffic in narcotics." (People v. McCray, 33 Ill.2d 66, 72, 210 N.E.2d 161, 164.) It is elemental that the narcotics informer is not usually a public spirited citizen who renders his services to improve the conditions of society. He is almost invariably a person who has gained first-hand knowledge of the pernicious activities of those involved in narcotics traffic, and his life is endangered every time he offers the police assistance in bringing the purveyors of illicit drugs to justice. The narcotics informer is frequently motivated by the goal of monetary reward, and if he were paid a uniform wage regardless of results, it would not be indulging in speculation to assume that his effectiveness would decline considerably. We find, therefore, that the type of contingent fee payment used in this case is not only legally permissible but realistically essential, and, at least in the circumstances of this case it must be condoned. . . .

NOTES

1. In United States v. Grimes, 438 F.2d 391 (6th Cir. 1971) the Court rejected outright the decision in Williamson v. United States, 311 F. 2d 441 (5th Cir. 1962) on which defendant relied in People v. Mills, supra. The Court pointed out that *Williamson* had been diluted by other Fifth Circuit cases and strictly construed by three other circuits.

The Court said:

> Appellants also argue that the government violated due process in hiring a paid informer on a contingent fee arrangement. This contention is based on Williamson v. United States, 311 F.2d 441 (5th Cir. 1962), where the Fifth Circuit noted that a contingent fee agreement to produce evidence against particular named defendants as to crimes not yet committed "might tend to a 'frame up,' or to cause an informer to induce or persuade innocent persons to commit crimes which they had no previous intent or purpose to commit. The opportunities for abuse are too obvious to require elaboration." Accordingly, using its supervisory power over the administration of criminal justice in federal courts, the Fifth Circuit held that in the absence of a justification or an explanation for a contingent fee arrangement, a conviction is invalid if based on evidence of informers hired under such an agreement to produce evidence against a particular named defendant as to crimes not yet committed. Concurring, Judge Brown argued that the case did not concern an aspect of entrapment. Rather it merely dealt with means which are essentially revolting to an ordered society. Judge Cameron, in his dissent, noted that the effect of the contingent fee arrangement on the informer's credibility should be left to the jury.

> After a review of the reported cases in which *Williamson* is discussed, we do not find that the *Williamson* rule should be applied in the Sixth Circuit.

* * *

> Our refusal to use our supervisory power over federal criminal proceedings so as to apply the exclusionary rule in this case finds support in observations by the United States Supreme Court. In Lopez v. United States (1963), the Supreme Court stated that "the court's inherent power to refuse to receive material evidence is a

power that must be sparingly exercised." The court observed
that:

> The function of a criminal trial is to seek out and deter-
> mine the truth or falsity of the charges brought against the
> defendant. Proper fulfillment of this function requires that,
> constitutional limitations aside, all relevant, competent evi-
> dence be admissible, unless the manner in which it has been
> obtained—for example, by violating some statute or rule of
> procedure—compels the formulation of a rule excluding its in-
> troduction in a federal court.

No such overriding policy is present when an informer is paid
on a contingent fee agreement for the conviction of specified persons for crimes not yet committed. Although it is true that the
informant working under this type of arrangement *may* be prone
to lie and manufacture crimes, he is no more likely to commit these
wrongs than witnesses acting for other, more common reasons.
Frequently, for example, one co-defendant testifies against another
co-defendant with the expectation of favorable treatment as a reward for his testimony. Like the informant being paid on a contingent fee basis, a co-defendant so testifying may feel it imperative to obtain a conviction of his co-defendant in order to improve
his own position. Similarly, informants paid on bases other than a
contingent arrangement may feel that their employment will be
terminated if they do not bring about a conviction. Therefore, despite admonitions to the contrary, they may believe that their future employment as an informant depends on the manufacture of
crimes in order to prove their worth to the government. Neither
of these methods of "paying" informers has been seriously attacked by the courts; yet the potential for abuse is obvious in each
case. Rather than adopting an exclusionary rule for a particular
factual situation, irrespective of the mode of payment, we prefer
the rule that would leave the entire matter to the jury to consider
in weighing the credibility of the witness-informant. Cf. Heard v.
United States, 414 F.2d 884 (5th Cir. 1969). In our view this approach provides adequate safeguards for the criminal defendant
against possible abuses since the witness must undergo the rigors
of cross-examination.

Congress itself has authorized a form of contingent fee arrangement in certain cases. For example, an informer whose information leads to a conviction for violation of a revenue law may be
awarded up to one-half of any fine levied as a result of that conviction. Internal Rev.Code of 1954, § 7214(a).

It is well-recognized that informers are an important and necessary aspect of our system of criminal justice. Although some
critics view the difficult fight against crime as a game, we take a
different view. "We are not persuaded that the impeccable man-
ners and sportsmanship that would characterize dealings between
members of the Westchester Saddle and Cycle Club must be exhibited by all federal agents when dealing with criminal suspects."

Affirmed.

2. Can the government give a witness a favorable settlement in a civil
tax dispute in return for his testimony? How is this different from de-

fense counsel's paying a witness for "telling the truth"? See United States v. Barrett, 505 F.2d 1091 (7th Cir. 1974).

3. The courts have always considered accomplice testimony with caution but since early common law such testimony has been considered competent evidence. 7 Wigmore, Evidence, §§ 2056–2062 (Chadbourn ed. 1978). One corollary of the judicial attitude toward accomplices is the rule which affords exceptional latitude of cross-examination of such witnesses. United States v. Gordon, 196 F.2d 886 (7th Cir. 1952), rev'd 344 U.S. 414, 73 S.Ct. 369; United States v. Dickens, 417 F.2d 958 (8th Cir. 1969); United States v. Masino, 275 F.2d 129 (2d Cir. 1960); People v. Derrica, 409 Ill. 453, 100 N.E.2d 607 (1951).

In the federal courts and in most state jurisdictions, accomplice testimony alone, if believed by the trier of fact, is sufficient to sustain a conviction. See Caminetti v. United States, 242 U.S. 470, 37 S.Ct. 192 (1917); Toles v. United States, 308 F.2d 590 (9th Cir. 1962); United States v. Fararas, 170 F.2d 968 (7th Cir. 1948); People v. Williams, 19 Ill.2d 171, 166 N.E.2d 568 (1960); Green v. State, 241 Ind. 96, 168 N.E.2d 345 (1960); State v. Zwillman, 112 N.J.Super. 6, 270 A.2d 284 (1970). Several state jurisdictions require independent corroboration. See State v. Howard, 97 Ariz. 399, 400 P.2d 332 (1965); State v. Baker, 161 Minn. 1, 200 N.W. 815 (1924); People v. MacEwing, 45 Cal.2d 218, 288 P.2d 257 (1955); Stein v. New York, 346 U.S. 156, 73 S.Ct. 1077 (1953). See 7 Wigmore, Evidence, § 2059.

The question of what constitutes corroboration is, in those jurisdictions which require it, often an extremely complicated one to resolve. The difficulty of defining what is adequate corroboration as well as the belief that juries and courts will not readily accept uncorroborated accomplice evidence is a significant factor in deterring the majority of jurisdictions from adopting formal corroboration requirements.

4. In many jurisdictions a defendant is entitled to an instruction which urges the jury to evaluate accomplice testimony with special care. As the Court in Williamson v. United States, 332 F.2d 123 (5th Cir. 1964), indicated, the accomplice instruction must usually be requested by the defendant. Failure to make such a request constitutes a waiver. See McMillen v. United States, 386 F.2d 29, 34–35 (1st Cir. 1967); United States v. Kinnard, 465 F.2d 566 (D.C.Cir. 1972).

5. Who is an accomplice and who decides the question? Generally, as defined in the federal courts, the test for determining who is an accomplice is whether the witness who is concerned in the commission of the specific crime with which the defendant is charged could be indicted or convicted for the identical offense for which the defendant is being prosecuted. United States v. De Cicco, 424 F.2d 531 (5th Cir. 1970); Stephenson v. United States, 211 F.2d 702 (9th Cir. 1954).

6. It is permissible to require the defendant to prove that a witness is an accomplice, and several states have recently required such proof by a preponderance of evidence. See People v. Tewksbury, 15 Cal.3d 953, 127 Cal. Rptr. 135, 544 P.2d 1335 (1977), and Bennett v. State, 283 Md. 619, 392 A.2d 76 (1978) where the court stated "Proof by a defendant that a State's witness is an accomplice involves no shifting of the burden to him to disprove any fact essential to the offenses charged since whether or not the witness was an accomplice bears no direct relationship to any element of robbery

with a deadly weapon or the use of a handgun in the commission of a felony. That is, the fact that Fritz was an accomplice *vel non* was not a fact necessary to constitute the crimes with which Bennett was charged. It was not even an affirmative defense or an exculpatory or mitigating circumstance affecting the degree of culpability or the severity of punishment. Nothing was presumed or implied against Bennett. Whether Fritz was an accomplice went only to Fritz's credibility. If he were an accomplice, his credibility is so thought in this State to be in question as to require that the evidence adduced through his testimony be corroborated. We believe it to be fundamental that a party who seeks to attack the credibility of a witness has the burden of going forward. This is indicated by the general principle that a party ordinarily may not sustain the credibility of his own witness absent an attack upon credibility by the other side."

ON LEE v. UNITED STATES

Supreme Court of the United States, 1952.
343 U.S. 747, 72 S.Ct. 967.

MR. JUSTICE JACKSON delivered the opinion of the Court.

Petitioner was convicted on a two-count indictment, one charging the substantive offense of selling a pound of opium . . . the other conspiring to sell the opium.

Petitioner, On Lee, had a laundry in Hoboken. A customers' room opened on the street, back of it was a room for ironing tables, and in the rear were his living quarters. Chin Poy, an old acquaintance and former employee, sauntered in and, while customers came and went, engaged the accused in conversation in the course of which petitioner made incriminating statements. He did not know that Chin Poy was what the Government calls "an undercover agent" and what petitioner calls a "stool pigeon" for the Bureau of Narcotics. Neither did he know that Chin Poy was wired for sound, with a small microphone in his inside overcoat pocket and a small antenna running along his arm. Unbeknownst to petitioner, an agent of the Narcotics Bureau named Lawrence Lee had stationed himself outside with a receiving set properly tuned to pick up any sounds the Chin Poy microphone transmitted. Through the large front window Chin Poy could be seen and through the receiving set his conversation, in Chinese, with petitioner could be heard by agent Lee. A few days later, on the sidewalks of New York, another conversation took place between the two, and damaging admissions were again "audited" by agent Lee.

For reasons left to our imagination, Chin Poy was not called to testify about petitioner's incriminating admissions. Against objection, however, agent Lee was allowed to relate the Conversations as heard with aid of his receiving set. Of this testimony, it is enough to say that it was certainly prejudicial if its admission was improper.

* * *

. . . On Lee's statements to Chin Poy were admissions against interest provable against him as an exception to the hearsay

rule. The normal manner of proof would be to call Chin Poy and
have him relate the conversation. We can only speculate on the reasons why Chin Poy was not called. It seems a not unlikely assumption that the very defects of character and blemishes of record which
made On Lee trust him with confidences would make a jury distrust
his testimony. Chin Poy was close enough to the underworld to serve
as bait, near enough the criminal design so that petitioner would embrace him as a confidante, but too close to it for the Government to
vouch for him as a witness. Instead, the Government called agent
Lee. We should think a jury probably would find the testimony of
agent Lee to have more probative value than the word of Chin Poy.

Society can ill afford to throw away the evidence produced by the
falling out, jealousies, and quarrels of those who live by outwitting
the law. Certainly no one would foreclose the turning of state's evidence by denizens of the underworld. No good reason of public policy occurs to us why the Government should be deprived of the benefit
of On Lee's admissions because he made them to a confidante of
shady character.

The trend of the law in recent years has been to turn away from
rigid rules of incompetence, in favor of admitting testimony and allowing the trier of fact to judge the weight to be given it. As this
Court has pointed out: " 'Indeed, the theory of the common law was
to admit to the witness stand only those presumably honest, appreciating the sanctity of an oath, unaffected as a party by the result,
and free from any of the temptations of interest. The courts were
afraid to trust the intelligence of jurors. But the last 50 years have
wrought a great change in these respects, and today the tendency is
to enlarge the domain of competency, and to submit to the jury for
their consideration as to the credibility of the witness those matters
which heretofore were ruled sufficient to justify his exclusion. This
change has been wrought partially by legislation and partially by judicial construction.' "

The use of informers, accessories, accomplices, false friends, or
any of the other betrayals which are "dirty business" may raise serious questions of credibility. To the extent that they do, a defendant
is entitled to broad latitude to probe credibility by cross-examination
and to have the issues submitted to the jury with careful instructions.
But to the extent that the argument for exclusion departs from such
orthodox evidentiary canons as relevancy and credibility, it rests solely
on the proposition that the Government shall be arbitrarily penalized
for the low morals of its informers. However unwilling we as individuals may be to approve conduct such as that of Chin Poy, such disapproval must not be thought to justify a social policy of the magnitude necessary to arbitrarily exclude otherwise relevant evidence.
We think the administration of justice is better served if stratagems
such as we have here are regarded as raising, not questions of law,
but issues of credibility. We cannot say that testimony such as this
shall, as a matter of law, be refused all hearing.

Judgment affirmed.

[Omitted are the dissenting opinions of JUSTICES BLACK, FRANKFURTER, DOUGLAS, and BURTON.]

NOTES

1. The Court reaffirmed the viability of *On Lee* in United States v. White, 401 U.S. 745, 91 S.Ct. 1122 (1971), Chapter 5, supra.

2. Consider the opinions in United States v. Karnes, 531 F.2d 214 (4th Cir. 1976):

"WINTER, CIRCUIT JUDGE.

I.

"The somewhat complex facts need not be recited because in oral argument the government conceded that it had no case against Karnes without the testimony of the co-defendant, Fred Cassity, and Cassity's wife. At the bench, the government represented that it would not call them as its witnesses because they previously had made conflicting statements and had withheld information and the government could not therefore vouch for their candor. The district court then called the Cassitys as its own witnesses and in accordance with usual practice permitted both sides to cross-examine them. Fred Cassity was also questioned by the court to permit him to identify a witness who testified about an incident which was a crucial part of the chain of proof. The district court made no statement to the jury in explanation of why these two witnesses were called as its own.

II.

"We agree with the parties that ordinarily the utilization of court witnesses is a matter within the discretion of the trial judge. The leading texts, supported by a plethora of precedents, support the rule. See McCormick on Evidence § 8 (1972); 9 Wigmore on Evidence § 2484 (1940). The power to call and to interrogate court witnesses is said to be derived from the judicial system's basic functions of disclosing truth and administering justice. Indeed, the rule is codified in Rule 614 of the new Federal Rules of Evidence, although that rule was not in effect at the time of Karnes' prosecution.

"A trial judge is not captive within the case as made by the parties. He has the authority, if not the duty, to call witnesses who possess relevant information affecting the outcome of the issues when the parties decline to call them. But the due process clause requires that a court be impartial. This impartiality is destroyed when the court assumes the role of prosecutor and undertakes to produce evidence, *essential* to overcome the defendant's presumption of innocence, which the government has declined to present. Further, in this case the jury was never told why the witnesses were called as court witnesses and the jury was not instructed that these witnesses were entitled to no greater credibility because they had been called by the court. The jury, thus, may well have afforded them greater credibility than if they had been called as government witnesses. The jury's determination of credibility of witnesses may therefore have been unfairly, albeit unintentionally, influenced and the government's case thereby strengthened.

"We have no doubt that, failing to appreciate that the government could not prove its case without them, the district court's motive in calling the witnesses was to get at the truth and to enable the government to cross-examine and perhaps to impeach them with regard to any testimony unfavorable to the government which was inconsistent with their prior statements. But the same result could have been achieved by an accepted means. The government must, of course, use its witnesses as it finds them. In many cases the prosecution must depend upon the testimony of persons who are co-defendants, co-conspirators, felons, accomplices, etc., and such witnesses often evidence hostility, are impeachable from their past or current activities, or change or slant their testimony from what, based upon prior statements, the government expects them to say. Under such circumstances, a district judge may afford wide latitude to the government to lead, to cross-examine, and partially to impeach such witnesses. Illustrative of current practice is Rule 607, Fed.R.Ev., which states flatly '[t]he credibility of a witness may be attacked by any party, including the party calling him.'

"Finally, we are not persuaded to a contrary view by United States v. Wilson, 361 F.2d 134 (7 Cir. 1966), and Smith v. United States, 331 F.2d 265 (8 Cir. 1964), on which the government relies for affirmance. In both cases, the propriety of the court's calling a witness in a criminal case who gave testimony unfavorable to the defendant was sustained. But in *Wilson*, the witness was not called until the government had closed its case and made a *prima facie* showing of defendant's guilt. Moreover, the testimony was taken out of the presence of the jury and at the instance of the defendant, it was not revealed to the jury. In *Smith*, although the government had not closed its case before the witness was called, it is clear that the government had proved a case before the witness was called. We disagree with the result in neither case, but we do not think that either is in point here. Our holding is confined to an instance where the government's case would be insufficient as a matter of law without the court witnesses. Neither *Wilson* nor *Smith* arose in that context.

"WIDENER, CIRCUIT JUDGE (concurring):

I.

"I concur in the result reached by Judge Winter in part II of his opinion and in much of that part of the opinion, but in some respects my reasoning differs.

"I decline to base reversal on the already overworked due process clause but rather would base it solely on the too great departure of the trial judge from his historic dispassionate role. After all, the burden of the production of evidence is on the United States, not upon the defendant, and certainly not upon the court. I would classify the error solely as one of federal criminal procedure.

"The dissent of Judge Russell accentuates my thoughts on this matter as he recites that it is no more the duty of a trial judge to permit a guilty defendant to escape because of the reluctance of a prosecutor to call a material and available witness than to stand idly by and let an innocent defendant be convicted because of the hesitancy of defendant's counsel to call a witness. If I thought for even one second that, should a defendant's attorney move the court to call an available witness, explaining that he would not call the witness because the witness had made conflicting statements and he could not vouch for the witness' credibility, and should the motion be denied, this court would hold it reversible error, I would vote to affirm on this point. But I cannot imagine such a result and accordingly vote to reverse, because evenhanded justice is equally or more important than the substance of an applicable rule.

"DONALD RUSSELL, CIRCUIT JUDGE (dissenting):

"I concur fully in all the opinion of Judge Winter herein, except for the finding that the trial court committed error in calling as court's witnesses Fred Cassity and his wife.

"While the opinion freely concedes that all the authorities affirm unequivocally the right of the trial judge to call as a court witness any available person or persons possessing relevant testimony, especially if the government or the defendant is unwilling or hesitant to call the person as a witness, it would justify departure from that rule in this case for two reasons, neither of which finds support either in the authorities or, I respectfully suggest, in reason. The first reason for departing from the rule is that the trial judge assumed 'the role of prosecutor and [undertook] to produce evidence necessary to overcome the defendant's presumption of innocence.' Certainly, the opinion cannot mean that by merely calling a person as a court's witness the trial judge assumes the improper 'role of prosecutor.' If this were true, the trial judge, would be prohibited in all instances from calling a person as a court witness. It is the added qualification that the 'evidence of the witnesses' is necessary to the Government's case and makes it impermissible under this reasoning for the court to call the witnesses as court witnesses.

"I, however, fail to see why the importance of the witness' testimony is determinative of the right of the trial judge to call him or her as a witness. The very importance of the testimony provides its own justification for the action of the trial judge. There is no real warrant for the trial court to call as a court's witness a person whose testimony lacks special relevancy; the power should not be exercised in order merely to add to the record evidence that at best is peripherally pertinent. But when, as here, there are persons whose testimony, if believed by the jury, could either lead to the defendant's conviction or could go far to absolve the defendant, the trial judge has both a right and a duty, if the Government refused to call the persons, to have them sworn as court witnesses. The trial judge does not abandon his role of required impartiality in the case merely by calling as a court witness one whose testimony is vital but whom the Government or the defendant, for some reason, is reluctant to call. This, I am sure, is a rule that the majority would accept if the witness could supply an essential link in the defense. The same rule should follow when the witness is vital to the Government's case. After all, the trial judge has a responsibility to society and the public. Courts must never forget that the function of the criminal court is as much to shield 'the public from criminal behavior' as it is to protect the innocent defendant from undeserved punishment. Cf., United States Ex Rel. Selikoff v. Com. of Corr. (2d Cir. 1975) 524 F.2d 650, 654. Unfortunately, this double obligation is too often forgotten and too frequently courts conceive of their function simply as the guardians of a defendant's rights and not as the protector of the public itself from crime. I do not conceive it any more the duty of a trial judge to permit a guilty defendant to escape because of the reluctance of a prosecutor to call a material witness available to him than to stand idly by and let an innocent defendant be convicted because of the hesitancy of defendant's counsel to call the witness.

"The second reason assigned in the opinion is that the trial judge did not advise the jury 'why the witnesses were called as court witnesses' and that they 'were entitled to no greater credibility because they had been called by the court.' Perhaps in the ordinary case, the rule suggested in the opinion is the proper one. There was no necessity for such advice in this case and the failure to give it, if error, was harmless beyond a reasonable doubt. The prosecutor stated in open court that he was unwilling to call the witnesses because he would not vouch for their credibility. The Government itself thereby cast a heavy shadow over the reliability of their testimony. Anything that the trial judge could have added after that would have been superfluous."

3. The A.B.A. Standards on the Prosecution and Defense Function adopt the following principles which are quoted in full, along with the Commentary:

Section 5.6(a) (Prosecution)

(a) It is unprofessional conduct for a prosecutor knowingly to offer false evidence, whether by documents, tangible evidence, or the testimony of witnesses or fail to seek withdrawal thereof upon discovery of its falsity.

Commentary

a. False evidence

It is so elementary that it hardly calls for comment that a prosecutor, in common with all other advocates, is barred from introducing evidence which he knows to be false. This obligation applies to evidence which bears on the credibility of a witness as well as to evidence on issues going directly to guilt. Napue v. Illinois, 360 U.S. 264 (1950). Even if false testimony is volunteered by the witness and takes the prosecutor by surprise rather than being solicited by him, if he knows it is false his obligation is to see that it is corrected. Ibid; see United States v. Poole, 379 F.2d 645 (7th Cir. 1967). Although some courts have granted new trials to defendants even where the prosecutor was unaware of the falsity of the evidence, see Barbee v. Warden, 331 F.2d 842 (4th Cir. 1964), disciplinary action against prosecutors should be limited to those cases where the falsity of the evidence was known to, or reasonably should have been discovered by, the prosecutor.

Section 7.5(a)   **(Defense)**

(a) It is unprofessional conduct for a lawyer knowingly to offer false evidence, whether by documents, tangible evidence, or the testimony of witnesses or fail to seek withdrawal thereof upon discovery of its falsity.

Commentary

a. Using false evidence or known perjury

The question of the lawyer's duty with respect to false evidence, fabricated documents or perjured testimony by witnesses is touched on by the Code of Professional Responsibility, which states that the duty of the lawyer to his client is to be performed "within the bounds of the law," ABA Code EC 7–1, and which requires that "a lawyer shall not: . . . Knowingly use perjured testimony or false evidence." ABA Code DR 7–102(A)(4). The presentation of false evidence has been considered ample grounds for disbarment. In re Allen, 52 Cal.2d 762, 344 P.2d 609, 612 (1959). See generally Annot., 14 A.L.R. 868 (1921). The lawyer who presents a witness knowing that he intends to perjure himself thereby engages in subornation of perjury. People v. Davis, 48 Cal.2d 241, 309 P.2d 1, 10 (1957) (dictum); see Conn v. Commonwealth, 234 Ky. 153, 27 S.W.2d 702 (1930). Even if the witness does not realize the testimony will be false, the lawyer who knows that it is and nevertheless presents it may be guilty of an attempt to suborn perjury or a like offense. See People v. Mosley, 338 Mich. 559, 61 N.W.2d 785 (1953); People v. Clement, 127 Mich. 130, 86 N.W. 535 (1901).

The second edition of these standards (1978) leaves the foregoing sections unchanged.

Related material is presented in Chapter 15 (Disclosure and Recovery).

---

2. THE ACCUSED AS A WITNESS

BROOKS v. TENNESSEE

Supreme Court of the United States, 1972.
406 U.S. 605, 92 S.Ct. 1891.

MR. JUSTICE BRENNAN delivered the opinion of the Court.

Petitioner was tried and convicted in the Circuit Court of Hamilton County, Tennessee, on charges of armed robbery and unlawful possession of a pistol. During the trial, at the close of the State's case, defense counsel moved to delay petitioner's testimony until after other defense witnesses had testified. The trial court denied this motion on the basis of Tenn.Code Ann. § 40–2403, which requires that a criminal defendant "desiring to testify shall do so before any other testimony for the defense is heard by the court trying the case." Although the prosecutor agreed to waive the statute, the trial court refused, stating that "the law is, as you know it to be, that if a defendant testifies he has to testify first." The defense called two witnesses, but petitioner himself did not take the stand.

I.

The rule that a defendant must testify first is related to the ancient practice of sequestering prospective witnesses in order to prevent their being influenced by other testimony in the case. See 6 Wigmore, Evidence § 1837 (3d ed. 1940). Because the criminal defendant is entitled to be present during trial, and thus cannot be sequestered, the requirement that he precede other defense witnesses was developed by court decision and statute as an alternative means of minimizing this influence as to him. According to Professor Wigmore, "The reason for this rule is the occasional readiness of the interested person to adapt his testimony, when offered later, to victory rather than veracity, so as to meet the necessities as laid open by prior witnesses. . . ." 6 Wigmore, supra, § 1869.

Despite this traditional justification, the validity of the requirement has been questioned in a number of jurisdictions as a limitation upon the defendant's freedom to decide whether or not to take the stand. Two federal courts have rejected the contention, holding that a trial court does not abuse its discretion by requiring the defendant to testify first. . . .

* * *

. . . we are persuaded that the rule embodied in § 40–2403 is an impermissible restriction on the defendant's right against self-incrimination, "to remain silent unless he chooses to speak in the unfettered exercise of his own will, and to suffer no penalty . . . for such silence." Malloy v. Hogan (1964). . . . a defendant's choice to take the stand carries with it serious risks of impeachment and cross-examination; it "may open the door to otherwise inadmissible evidence which is damaging to his case," McGautha v. California (1971), including, now, the use of some confessions for impeachment purposes that would be excluded from the State's case in chief because of constitutional defects. Harris v. New York (1971). Although "it is not thought inconsistent with the enlightened administration of criminal justice to require the defendant to weigh such pros and cons in deciding whether to testify," none would deny that the choice itself may pose serious dangers to the success of an accused's defense.

Although a defendant will usually have some idea of the strength of his evidence, he cannot be absolutely certain that his witnesses will testify as expected or that they will be effective on the stand. They may collapse under skillful and persistent cross-examination, and through no fault of their own they may fail to impress the jury as honest and reliable witnesses. In addition, a defendant is sometimes compelled to call a hostile prosecution witness as his own. Unless the State provides for discovery depositions of prosecution witnesses, which Tennessee apparently does not, the defendant is unlikely to know whether this testimony will prove entirely favorable.

Because of these uncertainties, a defendant may not know at the close of the State's case whether his own testimony will be necessary or even helpful to his cause. Rather than risk the dangers of taking the stand, he might prefer to remain silent at that point, putting off his testimony until its value can be realistically assessed. Yet, under the Tennessee rule, he cannot make that choice "in the unfettered exercise of his own will." Section 40–2403 exacts a price for his silence by keeping him off the stand entirely unless he chooses to testify first. This, we think, casts a heavy burden on a defendant's otherwise unconditional right not to take the stand. The rule, in other words, "cuts down on the privilege [to remain silent] by making its assertion costly."

Although the Tennessee statute does reflect a state interest in preventing testimonial influence, we do not regard that interest as sufficient to override the defendant's right to remain silent at trial. This is not to imply that there may be no risk of a defendant's coloring his testimony to conform to what has gone before. But our adversary system reposes judgment of the credibility of all witnesses in the jury. Pressuring the defendant to take the stand, by foreclosing later testimony if he refuses, is not a constitutionally permissible means of ensuring his honesty. It fails to take into account the very real and legitimate concerns that might motivate a defendant to exercise his right of silence. And it may compel even a wholly truthful defendant, who might otherwise decline to testify for legitimate reasons, to subject himself to impeachment and cross-examination at a time when the strength of his other evidence is not yet clear. For these reasons we hold that § 40–2403 violates an accused's constitutional right to remain silent insofar as it requires him to testify first for the defense or not at all.

II.

For closely related reasons we also regard the Tennessee rule as an infringement on the defendant's right of due process as defined in Ferguson v. Georgia (1961). There the Court reviewed a Georgia statute providing that a criminal defendant, though not competent to testify under oath, could make an unsworn statement at trial. The statute did not permit defense counsel to aid the accused by eliciting his statement through questions. The Court held that this limitation deprived the accused of " 'the guiding hand of counsel at every step in the proceedings against him,' within the requirement of due process in that regard as imposed upon the States by the Fourteenth Amendment." The same may be said of § 40–2403. Whether the defendant is to testify is an important tactical decision as well as a matter of constitutional right. By requiring the accused and his lawyer to make that choice without an opportunity to evaluate the actual worth of their evidence, the statute restricts the defense—particularly counsel—in the planning of its case. Furthermore, the penalty for not testifying first is to keep the defendant off the stand entirely, even though as a matter of professional judgment his lawyer might want to call him later in the trial. The accused is thereby deprived of the "guiding hand of counsel" in the timing of this critical element of his defense. While nothing we say here otherwise curtails in any way the ordinary power of a trial judge to set the order of proof, the accused and his counsel may not be restricted in deciding whether, and when in the course of presenting his defense, the accused should take the stand.

Petitioner, then, was deprived of his constitutional rights when the trial court excluded him from the stand for failing to testify first. The State makes no claim that this was harmless error.

MR. JUSTICE STEWART joins Part II of the opinion, and in the judgment of the Court.

MR. CHIEF JUSTICE BURGER, with whom MR. JUSTICE BLACKMUN and MR. JUSTICE REHNQUIST, join, dissenting.

This case is an example of the Court confusing what it does not approve with the demands of the Constitution. As a matter of choice and policy—if I were a legislator, for example—I would not vote for a statute like that the Court strikes down today. But I cannot accept the idea that the Constitution forbids the States to have such a statute.

Of course it is more convenient for a lawyer to defer the decision to have the accused take the stand until he knows how his other witnesses fare. By the same token it is helpful for an accused to be able to adjust his testimony to what his witnesses have had to say on the matter. No one has seriously challenged the absolute discretion of a trial judge to exclude witnesses, other than the accused, from the courtroom until they are called to the stand. The obvious purpose is to get honest testimony and minimize the prospect that a witness will adjust and "tailor" his version to fit what others have said; it seems somewhat odd to say the Constitution forbids all States to require the accused to give his version before his other witnesses speak, since it is not possible to exclude him from the courtroom, as is the common rule on witnesses who are not parties.

The Court's holding under the Fifth Amendment is admittedly unsupported by any authority and cannot withstand analysis. The Constitution provides only that no person shall "be compelled in any criminal case to be a witness against himself." It is undisputed that petitioner was not in fact compelled to be a witness against himself, as he did not take the stand. Nor was the jury authorized or encouraged to draw perhaps unwarranted inferences from his silence, as in Griffin v. California (1965). Petitioner was clearly not subjected to the obvious compulsion of being held in contempt for his silence, as in Malloy v. Hogan (1964), nor did the Tennessee procedure subject him to any other significant compulsion to testify other than the compulsion faced by every defendant who chooses not to take the stand —the knowledge that in the absence of his testimony the force of the State's evidence may lead the jury to convict. Cases such as Spevack v. Klein (1967), and Gardner v. Broderick (1968), involving loss of employment or disbarment are therefore clearly inapposite. That should end the matter.

However, the Court distorts both the context and content of Malloy v. Hogan, by intimating that the Fifth Amendment may be violated if the defendant is forced to make a difficult choice as to whether to take the stand at some point in time prior to the conclusion of a criminal trial. But, as the Court pointed out only last Term in McGautha v. California (1971), "although a defendant may have a right, even of constitutional dimensions, to follow whichever course he chooses, the Constitution does not by that token always forbid requiring him to choose." Indeed, the "choice" we sustained in *McGautha* was far more difficult than that here, as·the procedure there clearly exerted considerable force to compel the defendant to waive the privilege and take the stand in order to avoid the possible imposition of the death penalty. There is no such pressure here. The majority's rationale would lead to the absurd result that the State could not even require the defendant to finally decide whether he wishes to take the stand prior to the time the jury retires for deliberations, for, even at that point, he "may not know . . . whether his own testimony will be necessary or even helpful to his cause." Even then, he might "prefer to remain silent . . . putting off his testimony until its value can be realistically assessed." In short, even at the close of the defense case, his decision to take the stand is not unfettered by the difficulty to make the hard choice to waive the privilege. Perhaps the defendant's decision will be easier at the close of all the evidence. Perhaps not. The only "burden" cast on the defendant's choice to take the stand by the Tennessee procedure is the burden to make the choice at a given point in time. That the choice might in some cases be easier if made later is hardly a matter of constitutional dimension.

The Court's holding that the Tennessee rule deprives the defendant of the "guiding hand of counsel" at every stage of the proceedings fares no better, as Mr. Justice Rehnquist clearly demonstrates. It amounts to nothing more than the assertion that counsel may not be restricted by ordinary rules of evidence and procedure in presenting an accused's defense if it might be more advantageous to present it in some other way. A rule forbidding defense counsel to ask leading questions of the defendant when he takes the stand may restrict defense counsel in his options and may in many cases bear only remote relationship to the goal of truthful testimony. Yet no one would seriously question that such a universal rule of procedure is prohibited by the Constitution. The rule that the defendant waives the Fifth Amendment privilege as to any and all relevant matters when he decides to take the stand certainly inhibits the choices and options of counsel, yet this Court has never questioned such a rule and reaffirmed its validity only last Term. Countless other rules of evidence and procedure of every State may interfere with the "guiding hand of counsel." The Court does not explain why the rule here differs from those other rules.

Perhaps this reflects what is the true, if unspoken, basis for the Court's decision. That is, that in the majority's view the Tennessee rule is invalid because it is followed presently by only two States in our federal system. But differences in criminal procedures among our States do not provide an occasion for judicial condemnation by this Court.

This is not a case or an issue of great importance, except as it erodes the important policy of allowing diversity of method and procedure to the States to the end that they can experiment and innovate, and retreat if they find they have taken a wrong path. Long ago, Justice Brandeis spoke of the need to let "a single courageous state" try what others have not tried or will not try. In the faltering condition of our machinery of justice this is a singularly inappropriate time to throttle the diversity so essential in the search for improvement.

MR. JUSTICE REHNQUIST, with whom THE CHIEF JUSTICE and MR. JUSTICE BLACKMUN join, dissenting. [Opinion omitted.]

* * *

NOTES

1. In McGautha v. California [Crampton v. Ohio], 402 U.S. 18, 91 S. Ct. 1454 (1971), the accused Crampton challenged the conventional procedure used in capital cases. A jury would hear the evidence of both sides and then return a single verdict on the questions of guilt and punishment. Under that system the accused could testify and offer evidence as to his innocence and evidence to mitigate his punishment. The accused who did not wish to offer evidence on the question of guilt but did wish to offer evidence on the question of punishment could do so but he would be subject to general cross-examination by the prosecution. By taking the stand he waives his customary privilege against self-incrimination. The Court dealt with the issue in these terms:

> . . . The contention is that where guilt and punishment are to be determined by a jury at a single trial the desire to address the jury on punishment unduly encourages waiver of the defendant's privilege to remain silent on the issue of guilt, or, to put the matter another way, that the single-verdict procedure unlawfully compels the defendant to become a witness against himself on the issue of guilt by the threat of sentencing him to death without having heard from him. It is not contended, nor could it be successfully, that the mere force of evidence is compulsion of the sort forbidden by the privilege. It does no violence to the privilege that a person's choice to testify in his own behalf may open the door to otherwise inadmissible evidence which is damaging to his case. The narrow question left open is whether it is consistent with the privilege for the State to provide no means whereby a defendant wishing to present evidence or testimony on the issue of punishment may limit the force of his evidence (and the State's rebuttal) to that issue. We see nothing in the history, policies, or precedents relating to the privilege which requires such means to be available.

> . . . the history of the privilege sheds no light whatever on the subject, unless indeed that which is adverse. Inasmuch as at the time of framing of the Fifth Amendment and for many

years thereafter the accused in criminal cases was not allowed to testify in his own behalf, nothing approaching Crampton's dilemma could arise.

* * *

It is undeniably hard to require a defendant on trial for his life and desirous of testifying on the issue of punishment to make nice calculations of the effect of his testimony on the jury's determination of guilt. The issue of cruelty thus arising, however, is less closely akin to "the cruel trilemma of self-accusation, perjury or contempt," than to the fundamental requirements of fairness and decency embodied in the Due Process Clauses. Whichever label is preferred, appraising such considerations is inevitably a matter of judgement as to which individuals may differ; however, a guide to decision is furnished by the clear validity of analogous choices with which criminal defendants and their attorneys are quite routinely faced.

It has long been held that a defendant who takes the stand in his own behalf cannot then claim the privilege against cross-examination on matters reasonably related to the subject matter of his direct examination. See e. g., Brown v. Walker (1896). It is not thought overly harsh in such situations to require that the determination whether to waive the privilege take into account the matters which may be brought out on cross-examination. It is also generally recognized that a defendant who takes the stand in his own behalf may be impeached by proof of prior convictions or the like. See Spencer v. Texas, 385 U.S., at 561, 87 S.Ct., at 652. Again, it is not thought inconsistent with the enlightened administration of criminal justice to require the defendant to weigh such pros and cons in deciding whether to testify.

Further, a defendant whose motion for acquittal at the close of the Government's case is denied must decide whether to stand on his motion or put on a defense, with the risk that in so doing he will bolster the Government case enough for it to support a verdict of guilty. E. g., United States v. Calderon, 348 U.S. 160, 164 and n. 1, 75 S.Ct. 186, 188 (1954). Finally, only last Term in Williams v. Florida (1970), we had occasion to consider a Florida "notice-of-alibi" rule which put the petitioner in that case to the choice of either abandoning his alibi defense or giving the State both an opportunity to prepare a rebuttal and leads from which to start. We rejected the contention that the rule unconstitutionally compelled the defendant to incriminate himself. The pressures which might lead the defendant to furnish this arguably "testimonial" and "incriminating" information arose simply from

> "the force of historical fact beyond both his and the State's control and the strength of the State's case built on these facts. Response to that kind of pressure by offering evidence or testimony is not compelled self-incrimination transgressing the Fifth and Fourteenth Amendments."

We are thus constrained to reject the suggestion that a desire to speak to one's sentencer unlawfully compels a defendant in a single-verdict capital case to incriminate himself, unless there is something which serves to distinguish sentencing—or at least capital sentencing—from the situations given above. Such a distinguishing factor can only be the peculiar poignancy of the position of a man whose life is at stake, coupled with the imponderables of the decision which the jury is called upon to make. We do not think that the fact that a defendant's sentence, rather than his guilt, is at issue creates a constitutionally sufficient difference from the sorts of situations we have described. While we recognize the peculiar immediacy of a personal plea by the defendant for leniency in sentencing, it is also true that the testimony of an accused denying the case against him has considerably more force than counsel's argument that the prosecution's case has not been proved. The relevant differences between sentencing and determination of guilt or innocence are not so great as to call for a difference in constitutional result. Nor does the fact that capital, as opposed to any other, sentencing is in issue seem to us to distinguish this case. Even in noncapital sentencing the sciences of penology, sociology, and psychology have not advanced to the point that sentencing is wholly a matter of scientific calculation from objectively verifiable facts.

We conclude that the policies of the privilege against compelled self-incrimination are not offended when a defendant in a capital case yields to the pressure to testify on the issue of punishment at the risk of damaging his case on guilt.

Is Brooks v. Tennessee fully consistent with the language of the Court in *McGautha*? What makes the choice in *Brooks* more difficult than the defense choices illustrated in *McGautha*, or more difficult than the choice involved in a plea of guilty? If the choice in *Brooks* is not any more difficult than these other choices, can it be said that the decision in *Brooks* was based upon the relative weight of the state's interest in compelling that choice? If so, how is the state's interest less in the *Brooks* case than it is in the other situations outlined in *McGuatha*?

Consider in this regard the state's interest in the rule which requires that a defendant whose motion for directed verdict is denied must choose between resting on his motion or offering evidence. The defendant who decides to offer evidence waives any future claim (trial or appeal) that his motion should have been granted and he bears the risk that his evidence may supply a missing element of the state's case or strengthen in the jury's eyes a technically sufficient but unpersuasive presentation by the prosecution.

2. There are also ethical problems which arise when the accused takes the stand. The A.B.A. Standards on the Defense Function provides the following guideline:

7.7 Testimony by the Defendant

(a) If the defendant has admitted to his lawyer facts which establish guilt and the lawyer's independent investigation establishes that the admissions are true but the defendant insists on his right to trial, the lawyer must advise his client against taking the witness stand to testify falsely.

(b) If, before trial, the defendant insists that he will take the stand to testify falsely, the lawyer must withdraw from the case, if that is feasible, seeking leave of the court if necessary.

(c) If withdrawal from the case is not feasible or is not permitted by the court, or if the situation arises during the trial and the defendant insists upon testifying falsely in his own behalf, it is unprofessional conduct for the lawyer to lend his aid to the perjury or use the perjured testimony. Before the defendant takes the stand in these circumstances, the lawyer should make a record of the fact that the defendant is taking the stand against the advice of counsel in some appropriate manner without revealing the fact to the court. The lawyer must confine his examination to identifying the witness as the defendant and permitting him to make his statement to the trier or the triers of the facts; the lawyer may not engage in direct examination of the defendant as a witness in the conventional manner and may not later argue the defendant's known false version of facts to the jury as worthy of belief and he may not recite or rely upon the false testimony in his closing argument.

Commentary of Committee:

The absolute prohibition against subornation of perjury, see section 7.5 supra, applies where the defendant himself wishes to testify. Hence, a lawyer should withdraw from the case rather than place himself in the position of offering a perjurious witness. However, often the lawyer confronted by this situation will not be able to withdraw, either because trial has begun or it is so close to trial that withdrawal would leave the client without counsel, or because the court declines to allow withdrawal.

The experienced criminal lawyers consulted at length by the Committee favored the manner of resolving the problem adopted in this standard as the most reasonable accommodation of the competing demands of the lawyer's absolute obligation to refrain from introducing or aiding presentation of false testimony, on the one hand, and the defendant's absolute right on the other hand to testify in his own behalf, however ill-advised that course. These lawyers stated that this problem is not often faced by experienced lawyers in private criminal practice, partly because situations are infrequent when the client having admitted to facts constituting guilt thereafter insisted on testifying falsely; they also pointed to the greater leverage which a privately retained lawyer can exercise over the conduct of the case. The power of the privately retained lawyer to withdraw gives him a stronger posture than that of the court appointed or public defender counsel.

It was the view of these experienced defense counsel that in the unusual situation in which this dilemma presents itself, at a point when withdrawal from the case is not feasible, the lawyer should not participate in a fraud on the court by conducting direct examination in the conventional manner or by referring in any way to his client's perjury in conducting the defense, but simply allow the accused to testify in narrative form and in his own words. See ABA Code DR 7–102(A)(7). Our legal system, permitting the defendant to testify under oath, has not, in their view, completely foreclosed to him the opportunity to speak to the jury or to permit him to do so only at the cost of being abandoned by his lawyer in the midst of trial.

There is a division of opinion among lawyers on the question of what should be said to the client when this juncture is reached. On one hand, some lawyers hold that the lawyer's general obligation to protect the court from fraud in its processes and the exception to the attorney-client privilege for statements of intention to commit a crime may place the lawyer in the position of being required to disclose the fact of perjury. Thus, the lawyer may need to warn the client of that risk. On the other hand, there are lawyers who take the view that the lawyer's obligation of confidentiality does not permit him to disclose the facts he has learned from his client which form the basis for his conclusion that the client intends to perjure himself and that a warning to the client would be inconsistent with the assurances of confidentiality which counsel gave at the outset of the lawyer-client relationship.

This existence of this dilemma is predicated upon the defendant's admitting inculpatory facts to his lawyer which are corroborated by the lawyer's own investigation. So long as the defendant maintains his innocence, the lawyer's realistic appraisal that he is in fact guilty does not preclude a vigorous defense.

Because the lawyer may later have his conduct called into question when his client testifies against the advice of counsel, it is desirable that a record be made of the fact. However, if the trial judge is informed of the situation, the defendant may be unduly prejudiced, especially at sentencing, and the lawyer may feel that he is caught in a dilemma between protecting himself by making such a record and prejudicing his client's case by making it with the court. The dilemma can be avoided in most instances by making the record in some other appropriate manner, for example, by having the defendant subscribe to a file notation, witnessed, if possible, by another lawyer.

3. Considering the difficulties of complying with the A.B.A. Standard when a client wishes to perjure himself, is it likely that lawyers may avoid close questioning of their clients in order to avoid securing dangerous admissions? Are there any countervailing factors which require counsel to question his client rigorously and assume the risk? Is a lawyer wise to ask the ultimate question of his client, i. e., "Are you guilty?", or "Did you do it?"

What about the practice of asking a client a question such as: "If after this fellow called you a queer you flew into a rage and knifed him, then you are guilty; on the other hand, if after he said this, your mind simply went blank and the next thing you remember is the clang of the jail door, you might be considered not guilty by reason of insanity; now tell me, what happened?"

The A.B.A. has not resolved the issue as to the continuing applicability of the foregoing standard. Its continuation was recommended by a committee assigned to update the Standards, but the matter was then referred to the Commission on Evaluation of Professional Standards. No action has been taken as of September 1, 1979.

4. Concerning comments and instructions on the accused's failure to testify at trial, see Griffin v. California, Chapter 19, Section G-2, infra, and Lakeside v. Oregon, Chapter 20, Section C-2, infra. Concerning the accused's post-arrest silence, see Doyle v. Ohio, Chapter 19, Section E-2, infra.

D. OTHER CRIMES EVIDENCE

STATE v. IAUKEA

Supreme Court of Hawaii, 1975.
56 Hawaii 343, 537 P.2d 724.

OGATA, JUSTICE.

Defendant-appellant, Albert Iaukea (hereinafter appellant), was tried for and convicted of rape in the first degree, sodomy in the first degree, robbery in the first degree, and unauthorized operation of a propelled vehicle in a jury trial before the Third Circuit Court. The appellant was sentenced by the court to life imprisonment under the extended term provisions of HRS §§ 706–661 and 706–662(4), as a multiple offender.

He now appeals from the judgment and sentence. He presents for our consideration the following contentions: (1) that the testimony by the complaining witness about appellant's three prior assaults against women and a rape charge pending against him at the time of the alleged rape of the complaining witness deprived appellant of due process; (2) that the court erred when it denied appellant's motion for a mistrial when references were made to prior assaults and alleged prior rape; (3) that the court erred in denying appellant's motion for judgment of acquittal for robbery in the first degree and unauthorized operation of a propelled vehicle at the close of the State's case; (4) that the court erred in giving State's requested instruction No. 22 over appellant's objection; and (5) that the sentence of life imprisonment imposed by the court upon appellant as a multiple offender constitutes cruel or unusual punishment under the Federal and State Constitutions. For reasons hereinafter set forth, we hold that appellant's contentions are without merit.

The appellant was referred for counselling by the public defender to the complaining witness, a thirty-one year old psychiatric social worker at the Hilo Counseling Center. The complaining witness held her first interview with appellant on Wednesday, February 13, 1974. At this session, appellant informed the complaining witness that he would have to appear in court that Friday, February 15, 1974. The complaining witness further learned, at that time, many details of appellant's criminal record and obtained a great deal of information about his family background and social problems. She learned that the upcoming trial involved a rape charge. Appellant returned to the office of the complaining witness unexpectedly the next afternoon, Thursday, February 14, 1974. The complaining witness testified that she could smell liquor on his breath. Appellant told her that he had an argument with his girlfriend that morning. The complaining witness feared that appellant might get himself into more trouble and even fail to appear in court the next day if left alone in a troubled state. She, therefore, inquired if he had any friends or relatives he could stay with. Appellant then stated he thought he could stay with his aunt in Keaukaha. Appellant then feigned a telephone call to his aunt. He spoke as though his aunt agreed to let him stay with her. The complaining witness then offered to drive appellant to his aunt's house, because she believed that he would be less likely to get into trouble and fail to appear in court if she did so. The complaining witness further testified that she and others employed at the Hilo Counseling Center often provide rides for patients.

The complaining witness and the appellant drove from the Hilo Counseling Center to Keaukaha in the complaining witness's 1968 Mustang. Appellant directed the complaining witness to drive along the Escape Road (in Keaukaha), on the pretext that his aunt's home was in that direction. After the 1968 Mustang had reached a deserted stretch of the Escape Road, the appellant grabbed the complaining witness around her neck and held a knife to her stomach. The appellant then proceeded to commit the acts of rape and sodomy which formed the basis of the charges.

The testimony of the complaining witness contained several references to the appellant's use of the knife to threaten her and to his use of his greater size and strength to overcome her will. She also testified that she tried to talk the appellant out of raping or hurting her, but to no avail. She stated that her training as a psychiatric social worker had taught her to cope with crisis situations in a calm manner. Moreover, she did not wish to excite appellant to greater violence because then he might use the knife on her. Her fear was heightened by her knowledge of his past history of assaults and pending rape charge. The victim was further put in fear by appellant's statement to the effect that since he was going to go to jail anyway, it didn't matter what he did to her.

After the commission of rape and sodomy, appellant asked the complaining witness if she had any money. She admitted to him that she had forty dollars in her purse. The appellant dumped out the purse, went through the contents and took the money. The appellant then threw the money back on the car seat, saying he wasn't going to need it because he was going to jail, but he then grabbed the money back.

The complaining witness testified that appellant asked her several times if she was going to "tell." She was afraid to admit that she was going to "tell," "because then, I thought that he wasn't going to let me live." The appellant then told the victim to get out of her car. Thereafter, appellant drove off at a very fast speed. The complaining witness walked for approximately twenty minutes and came to a house. From there, she was able to telephone the police to report the incident.

I.

Appellant contends that references in the testimony of the complaining witness to alleged past crimes, court appearances in regard to a pending rape charge and going to jail were highly prejudicial to him. He asserts that such testimony should not have been admitted and that once the jury heard the testimony the trial judge should have declared a mistrial.

The State contends that the testimony was properly admitted because it was relevant to the elements of the crimes of rape and sodomy.[1]

The admission of evidence which tends to prove the commission of crimes other than the crime charged gives rise to several problems. The jury may believe that the defendant is guilty merely because he is a likely person to do such acts. Territory v. Caminos, 38 Haw. 628 (1950). Furthermore, the defendant may be unprepared to defend himself against the evidence of collateral crimes. State v. Spreigl, 272 Minn. 488, 139 N.W.2d 167 (1965). The responsibility for maintaining the delicate balance between probative value and prejudicial effect lies largely within the discretion of the trial court. Elsbury v. State, Nev., 518 P.2d 599 (1974); State v. Spreigl, supra.

The rule of evidence pertaining to evidence of other crimes has two basic formulations. One is an affirmative statement of the conditions of admissibility and the other is an exclusionary rule with exceptions.[2] Thus with reference to the first formulation, it was stated in People v. Peete, 28 Cal.2d 306, 315–316, 169 P.2d 924, 929–930 (1946), as follows:

> ".   .   .   except when it shows merely criminal disposition [citations omitted], evidence that is relevant is not excluded because it reveals the commission of an offense other than that charged. 'The general tests of the admissibility of evi-

---

1. The language of HRS §§ 707–730 and 707–733, in effect at the time of the incident, read in relevant part as follows:

"§ 707–730 *Rape in the First Degree.* (1) A male commits the offense of rape in the first degree if:
    (a) He intentionally engages in sexual intercourse, by forcible compulsion, with a female and:
        "(i) The female is not, upon the occasion, his voluntary social companion who had within the previous twelve months permitted him sexual contact;

* * *

"(2) Rape in the first degree is a class A felony."

"§ 707–733 *Sodomy in the First Degree.* (1) A person commits the offense of sodomy in the first degree if:

    (a) He intentionally, by forcible compulsion, engages in de-

viate sexual intercourse with another person or causes another person to engage in deviate sexual intercourse, and:
    "(i) The other person was not, upon the occasion, his voluntary social companion who had within the previous twelve months permitted him sexual contact of the kind involved;

* * *

"(2) Sodomy in the first degree is a class A felony."

2. Julius Stone in his law review article discussed and followed in numerous decisions prefers the affirmative formulation of the rule regarding the admissibility of facts tending to show the commission of crimes other than the crime for which defendant is being tried. Stone, "The Rule of Exclusion of Similar Fact Evidence: America," 51 Harvard Law Review 988 (1938).

dence in a criminal case are: .   .   .   does it tend logically,
naturally, and by reasonable inference to establish any fact
material for the people, or to overcome any material matter
sought to be proved by the defense? If it does, then it is admissible, whether it embraces the commission of another
crime or does not, whether the other crime be similar in
kind or not, whether it be part of a single design or not.'
[citations omitted]   'It is true that in trying a person
charged with one offense it is ordinarily inadmissible to offer proof of another and distinct offense, but this is only because the proof of a distinct offense has ordinarily no tendency to establish the offense charged; But, whenever the
case is such that proof of one crime tends to prove any fact
material in the trial of another, such proof is admissible,
and the fact that it may tend to prejudice the defendant in
the minds of jurors is no ground for its exclusion.' "   [cita-
tions omitted]

In accord: United States v. Carney, 461 F.2d 465 (3rd Cir. 1972);
United States v. Stirone, 262 F.2d 571 (3rd Cir. 1958); Nester v.
State, 75 Nev. 41, 334 P.2d 524 (1959); State v. Long, 195 Or. 81,
244 P.2d 1033 (1952).

The alternative formulation of the rule concerning evidence of
collateral crimes, which is structured as an exclusionary rule with
several categories of exceptions, is the form of the rule cited in numerous opinions from numerous jurisdictions. The landmark opinion
from which many such opinions sprang is that of Judge Werner of
the New York Court of Appeals in People v. Molineux, 168 N.Y. 264,
61 N.E. 286 (1901). That opinion stated:

"The general rule of evidence applicable to criminal trials is
that the state cannot prove against a defendant any crime
not alleged in the indictment, either as a foundation for a
separate punishment, or as aiding the proofs that he is
guilty of the crime charged."

The opinion went on to say:

"The exceptions to the rule cannot be stated with categorical
precision. Generally speaking, evidence of other crimes is
competent to prove the specific crime charged when it tends
to establish (1) motive; (2) intent; (3) the absence of mistake or accident; (4) a common scheme or plan embracing
the commission of two or more crimes so related to each other that proof of one tends to establish the others; (5) the
identity of the person charged with the commission of the
crime on trial."

Stating the rule in this manner usually requires the court to enumerate and define the exceptions. The attempt to grapple with the
enumeration and definition of the exceptions to the exclusionary rule
has caused some courts to come almost full circle back to the affirma-

tive statement of the rule, as did the Arizona Supreme Court, in State v. Hill, 104 Ariz. 238, 239, 450 P.2d 696, 697 (1969):

> " '. . . The general rule is that evidence is inadmissible which tends to prove that the accused committed a crime other than the one charged in the indictment. But this rule is subject to certain well-established exceptions "to the end that all relevant facts and circumstances *tending to establish any of the constituent elements of the crime" for which the accused is on trial may be made to appear.*' Witters v. United States, 70 App.D.C. 316, 106 F.2d 837 [Emphasis supplied]."

Both approaches are sometimes used within the same opinion. Stone criticizes this combination of approaches, contending that it is injurious to the effective and fair administration of justice. Careful application, however, should avoid the problem. If the requirements of relevancy to proof of an element of the crime charged, balance of probative value against prejudicial effect, and a flexible use of the exception categories primarily as indices of relevancy are met, then this method should permit the court to make use of both formulations. The case at bar is easily decided under the affirmative, more generally worded formulation of the rule. The testimony in controversy regarding other criminal acts allegedly committed by the defendant is relevant and material to the proof of an element of the crimes charged in the indictment; that element is forcible compulsion. This is, of course, an issue wholly distinct from propensity or bad character.

This case is distinguishable from State v. Kahinu, 53 Haw. 536, 498 P.2d 635 (1972), because the testimony given by a police detective in that case, which was characterized as "the evidential harpoon," was completely irrelevant to the issues at trial. The challenged testimony of the complaining witness in the case at bar is highly relevant to the major issue therein. We observe, further, that in keeping with the spirit of the *Kahinu* decision, the trial court in the instant case gave cautionary instructions regarding the limited use of the controversial testimony.

The testimony of the complaining witness concerning the prior crimes which, to her knowledge, appellant had committed, credibly explained and placed in context many of her statements to and actions toward him. Her fear of the appellant was in part due to his past history of attacks on women. The complaining witness made every effort to remain calm and to refrain from screaming because of her training as a psychiatric social worker. In her judgment she had a better chance of avoiding serious bodily injury if she remained calm. She feared that he would "cut her up" if she "tried to fight him."

It was important that the jury know all of the facts involved so that they would not mistakenly construe the complaining witness's calm manner and lack of screaming as indicative of consent or lack of forcible compulsion. Moreover, the appellant himself was aware of the complaining witness's knowledge of his history. It is highly unlikely that he construed her statements and actions as consent. It was important to apprise the jury of this. Furthermore, it was also essential for the jury to fully understand why the complaining witness offered to drive the defendant to his aunt's house, so as not to draw the erroneous conclusion that she was his voluntary social companion.

The California Court of Appeals in People v. Nazworth, 152 Cal. App.2d 790, 794, 313 P.2d 113, 116 (1957), allowed evidence of other crimes to be admitted to show the state of mind of the prosecutrix, so that the jury could pass upon her conduct at the time in question. In that case the prosecutrix testified that, " 'He (defendant) had beat up two other girls'; that she knew he was wanted by the F.B.I. before; that he had knife fights with his father and that he shot her aunt before." The Court of Appeals held: "Appellant in his cross-examination of the complaining witness attacked the credibility of her testimony and no prejudicial error resulted from the admission of her statement as to why she was afraid of the defendant."

The Oregon Supreme Court in State v. Tracy, 246 Or. 349, 425 P.2d 171 (1967), held that the testimony of the prosecutrix in a rape case was properly admitted where she testified to her knowledge that the defendant had been in an altercation earlier in the evening and she further testified that the defendant had threatened to "beat up" her escort if she did not accompany the defendant. The Oregon Supreme Court held that no error had been committed in the admission of this testimony because of its relevance to the issue of consent. State v. Tracy, supra, and State v. Nazworth, supra, are clearly similar to the case at bar. In each of the three cases the complaining witness had to refer to evidence of other crimes in order to explain why she feared the appellant and to place her own actions in proper context.

In Fields v. State, 235 Ark. 986, 363 S.W.2d 905 (1963), a rape victim testified that the defendant had told her that he "had just killed a man, and what he was going to do now wouldn't be any worse than what he had already done." The Supreme Court of Arkansas affirmed the conviction and observed that such a statement might be made by a rapist to his victim to instill fear in the victim, whether or not the statement were true. In the instant case the complaining witness testified that the appellant told her more than once that he was "going to jail anyway." This testimony is admissible for its probable effect on the complaining witness's state of mind despite the fact that it tends to indicate that the appellant may have committed other crimes.

It is difficult to place this situation into one of the traditional exceptions to the exclusionary form of the rule. However, it could be said that the testimony in controversy could be fitted into the "scheme, plan or design" exception. The appellant, in a sense, capitalized on his own history and the complaining witness's knowledge of it to create the scenario for the crime. He further took advantage of his record to instill an extra measure of fear in his victim. The evidence would, therefore, be admissible under this formulation of the rule as well.

We hold that the testimony in controversy was properly admitted under either approach.

II.

Since we now hold the challenged testimony to have been properly admitted, we, of course, also hold that the trial court did not abuse its discretion in denying appellant's motion for a mistrial. Denial of a motion for a mistrial is generally a matter within the sound discretion of the trial court.

* * *

Affirmed.

NOTE

In United States v. Bradwell, 388 F.2d 619 (2d Cir. 1968), the court held that it was proper to introduce evidence of defendant's indictment concerning promotion of prostitution to show motive for the charged offense of obstruction of justice (i. e., intimidating witnesses on the prostitution charge). The jury was entitled to know the nature of the prior offense and the extent of defendant's involvement in order to assess the intensity of his motive to commit the later offense. The Court further stated:

> Before admitting this testimony the court asked defense counsel if he was willing to have the case submitted to the jury on the simple issue of Bradwell's having made the statement to McElroy or would request a charge that the jury must also find the specific intent required by the statute. Counsel opted for the latter. Near the beginning of Brice's testimony the judge instructed the jury that this was to be considered solely "on the issue of intent on the part of the defendant," and also that any references by her or other witnesses to Bradwell's promoting prostitution have "nothing whatsoever to do with this case." In a painstaking charge he directed that the jury must find, without any reference to Brice's evidence, that McElroy was a witness before the grand jury, that Bradwell knew this, and that Bradwell threatened him on or about December 18; only if they answered all these questions in the affirmative, could they consider Brice's evidence as bearing on Bradwell's "specific intent to influence, intimidate and impede" McElroy as a grand jury witness.

> We cannot conceive how a judge could more carefully comply with the rule, applied by many courts, that evidence of other crimes is admissible only if it serves one of a series of purposes, classically formulated in People v. Molineux. Defendant's true objection must be rather that the ritual so dutifully performed by the trial judge was exactly that; and we must indeed confess a degree of skepticism as to the reality of expecting all twelve jurors to perform a feat of first raising and then lowering a mental bulkhead altogether beyond our capacity. But the *Molineux* rule is not the rule of this circuit. Like several other federal courts of appeals, we hold rather that evidence of another crime may be admit-

ted if it "is substantially relevant for some other purpose than to show a probability" that the defendant "committed the crime on trial because he is a man of criminal character," with admission to depend upon the trial judge's appropriately "balancing, on the one side, the actual need for the other-crimes-evidence in the light of the issues and the other evidence available to the prosecution, the convincingness of the evidence that the other crimes were committed and that the accused was the actor, and the strength or weakness of the other-crimes-evidence in supporting the issue, and on the other, the degree to which the jury will probably be roused by the evidence to overmastering hostility."

The propriety of admitting Brice's testimony under this standard is apparent. This was not a case where the other-crimes-evidence was thrown on scales already heavily tipped against the defendant; the Government had real need to bolster McElroy's testimony against Bradwell's anticipated denial. Evidence that Bradwell had threatened another witness testifying to similar activity before the same grand jury was highly probative, not simply as showing a course of conduct, although that would have sufficed under the circumstances, but, with Brice's elaboration, as confirming that Bradwell did have means of knowing "every word to word" said to the grand jury as McElroy claimed he had asserted. Proof that a defendant has engaged in a second criminal act of the same sort for which he is being tried is not likely to rouse the jury to "overmastering hostility"; that phrase refers to instances "where the minute peg of relevancy will be entirely obscured by the dirty linen hung upon it."

Counsel asserts that, however all this may be, the jury got the impression that Bradwell was a man of bad character. Very likely it did. But what the law rules out is evidence of other crimes directed solely to establishing that. It does not demand exclusion of highly probative evidence simply to prevent noisome odors about the defendant from reaching the jury's nostrils.

Affirmed.

SPENCER v. TEXAS

Supreme Court of the United States, 1967.
385 U.S. 554, 87 S.Ct. 648, rehearing denied 386 U.S. 969, 87 S.Ct. 1015.

MR. JUSTICE HARLAN delivered the opinion of the Court.

Texas, reflecting widely established policies in the criminal law of this country, has long had on its books so-called recidivist or habitual-criminal statutes. Their effect is to enhance the punishment of those found guilty of crime who are also shown to have been convicted of other crimes in the past. The three cases at hand challenge the procedures employed by Texas in the enforcement of such statutes.

Until recently, and at the time of the convictions before us, the essence of those procedures was that, through allegations in the indictment and the introduction of proof respecting a defendant's past convictions, the jury trying the pending criminal charge was fully informed of such previous derelictions, but was also charged by the court that such matters were not to be taken into account in assessing the defendant's guilt or innocence under the current indictment.

The petitioner was indicted for murder, with malice, of his common-law wife. The indictment alleged that the defendant had previously been convicted of murder with malice, a factor which if proved would entitle the jury to sentence the defendant to death or to prison for not less than life, whereas if the prior conviction was not proved the jury could fix the penalty at death or a prison term of not less than two years, see Texas Pen.Code Art. 1257. Spencer made timely objections to the reading to the jury of that portion of the indictment, and objected as well to the introduction of evidence to show his prior conviction. The jury was charged that if it found that Spencer had maliciously killed the victim, and that he had previously been convicted of murder with malice, the jury was to "assess his punishment at death or confinement in the penitentiary for life." The jury was instructed as well that it should not consider the prior conviction as any evidence of the defendant's guilt on the charge on which he was being tried. Spencer was found guilty and sentenced to death.

* * *

The common and sole constitutional claim made in these cases is that Texas' use of prior convictions in the current criminal trial of each petitioner was so egregiously unfair upon the issue of guilt or innocence as to offend the provisions of the Fourteenth Amendment that no State shall "deprive any person of life, liberty, or property, without due process of law . . . ." We took these cases for review because the courts of appeals have divided on the issue. For reasons now to follow we affirm.

The road to decision, it seems to us, is clearly indicated both by what the petitioners in these cases do *not* contend and by the course of the authorities in closely related fields. No claim is made here that recidivist statutes are themselves unconstitutional, nor could there be under our cases. Such statutes and other enhanced-sentence laws, and procedures designed to implement their underlying policies, have been enacted in all the States, and by the Federal Government as well. See e. g., 18 U.S.C. § 2114; Fed.Rule Crim.Proc. 32(c)(2); D.C.Code § 22–104 (1961). Such statutes, though not in the precise procedural circumstances here involved, have been sustained in this Court on several occasions against contentions that they violate constitutional strictures dealing with double jeopardy ex post facto laws, cruel and unusual punishment, due process, equal protection, and privileges and immunities.

Nor is it contended that it is unconstitutional for the jury to assess the punishment to be meted out to a defendant in a capital or other criminal case, or to make findings as to whether there was or was not a prior conviction even though enhanced punishment is left to be imposed by the judge. The States have always been given wide leeway in dividing responsibility between judge and jury in criminal cases.

Petitioners do not even appear to be arguing that the Constitution is infringed if a jury is told of a defendant's prior crimes. The rules concerning evidence of prior offenses are complex, and vary from jurisdiction to jurisdiction, but they can be summarized broadly. Because such evidence is generally recognized to have potentiality for prejudice, it is usually excluded except when it is particularly probative in showing such things as intent; an element in the crime; identity; and motive; a system of criminal activity; or when the defendant has raised the issue of his character; or when the defendant has testified and the State seeks to impeach his credibility.

. . . In all these situations, as under the recidivist statutes, the jury learns of prior crimes committed by the defendant, but the conceded possibility of prejudice is believed to be outweighed by the validity of the State's purpose in permitting introduction of the evidence. The defendants' interests are protected by limiting instructions, and by the discretion residing with the trial judge to limit or forbid the admission of particularly prejudicial evidence even though admissible under an accepted rule of evidence.

This general survey sufficiently indicates that the law of evidence, which has been chiefly developed by the States, has evolved a set of rules designed to reconcile the possibility that this type of information will have some prejudicial effect with the admitted usefulness it has as a factor to be considered by the jury for any one of a large number of valid purposes. The evidence itself is usually, and in recidivist cases almost always, of a documentary kind, and in the cases before us there is no claim that its presentation was in any way inflammatory. To say the United States Constitution is infringed simply because this type of evidence may be prejudicial and limiting instructions inadequate to vitiate prejudicial effects, would make inroads into this entire complex code of state criminal evidentiary law, and would threaten other large areas of trial jurisprudence. For example, all joint trials, whether of several codefendants or of one defendant charged with multiple offenses, furnish inherent opportunities for unfairness when evidence submitted as to one crime (on which there may be an acquittal) may influence the jury as to a totally different charge. See Delli Paoli v. United States, 352 U.S. 232, 77 S.Ct. 294. This type of prejudicial effect is acknowledged to inhere in criminal practice, but it is justified on the grounds that (1) the jury is expected to follow instructions in limiting this evidence to its proper function, and (2) the convenience of trying different crimes against the same person, and connected crimes against different defendants, in the same trial is a valid governmental interest.

* * *

It is contended nonetheless that in this instance the Due Process Clause of the Fourteenth Amendment requires the exclusion of prejudicial evidence of prior convictions even though limiting instructions are given and even though a valid state purpose—enforcement of the habitual-offender statute—is served. We recognize that the use of prior-crime evidence in a one-stage recidivist trial may be thought to represent a less cogent state interest than does its use for other purposes, in that other procedures for applying enhancement-of-sentence statutes may be available to the State that are not suited in the other situations in which such evidence is introduced. We do not think that this distinction should lead to a different constitutional result.

Cases in this Court have long proceeded on the premise that the Due Process Clause guarantees the fundamental elements of fairness in a criminal trial. But it has never been thought that such cases establish this Court as a rule-making organ for the promulgation of state rules of criminal procedure. And none of the specific provisions of the Constitution ordains this Court with such authority. In the face of the legitimate state purpose and the long-standing and widespread use that attend the procedure under attack here, we find it impossible to say that because of the possibility of some collateral prejudice the Texas procedure is rendered unconstitutional under the Due Process Clause as it has been interpreted and applied in our past cases. As Mr. Justice Cardozo had occasion to remark, a state rule of law "does not run foul of the Fourteenth Amendment because another method may seem to our thinking to be fairer or wiser or to give a surer promise of protection to the prisoner at bar." Snyder v. Commonwealth of Massachusetts, 291 U.S. 97, 105, 54 S.Ct. 330, 332.

Petitioners' reliance on Jackson v. Denno, 378 U.S. 368, 84 S.Ct. 1774, is misplaced. There the Court held unconstitutional the New York procedure leaving to the trial jury alone the issue of the voluntariness of a challenged confession, an area of law that has been characterized by the development of particularly stiff constitutional rules. The Court held that a judicial ruling was first required to determine whether as a matter of law—federal constitutional law—the confession could be deemed voluntary. This requirement of a threshold hearing before a judge on the federal question of voluntariness lends no solid support to the argument made here—that a two-stage jury trial is required whenever a State seeks to invoke an habitual-offender statute. It is true that the Court in *Jackson* supported its holding by reasoning that a general jury verdict was not a "reliable" vehicle for determining the issue of voluntariness because jurors might have difficulty in separating the issues of voluntariness from that of guilt or innocence. But the emphasis there was on protection of a specific constitutional right, and the *Jackson* procedure was designed as a specific remedy to ensure that an involuntary confession was not in fact relied upon by the jury. In the procedures before us, in contrast, no specific federal right—such as that dealing with confessions—is involved; reliance is placed solely on a general "fairness" approach. In this area the Court has always moved with caution before striking down state procedures. It would be extravagant in the extreme to take *Jackson* as evincing a general distrust on the part of this Court of the ability of juries to approach their task responsibly and to sort out discrete issues given to them under proper instructions by the judge in a criminal case, or as standing for the proposition that limiting instructions can never purge the erroneous introduction of evidence or limit evidence to its rightful purpose.[1]

It is fair to say that neither the *Jackson* case nor any other due process decision of this Court even remotely supports the proposition that the States are not free to enact habitual-offender statutes of the type Texas has chosen and to admit evidence during trial tending to prove allegations required under the statutory scheme.

Tolerance for a spectrum of state procedures dealing with a common problem of law enforcement is especially appropriate here. The rate of recidivism is acknowledged to be high, a wide variety of methods of dealing with the problem exists, and experimentation is in progress. The common-law procedure for applying recidivist statutes, used by Texas in the cases before us, which requires allegations and proof of past convictions in the current trial, is of course, the simplest and best known procedure. Some jurisdictions deal with the recidivist issue in a totally separate proceeding, Texas to some extent has recently changed to that course. In some States such a proceeding can be instituted even after conviction on the new substantive offense. The method for determining prior convictions varies also between jurisdictions affording a jury trial on this issue, and those leaving that question to the court. Another procedure, used in Great Britain and Connecticut, requires that the indictment allege both the substantive crime and the prior conviction, that both parts be read to the defendant prior to trial, but that only the allegations relating to the substantive crime be read to the jury. If the defendant is convicted, the prior-offense elements are then read to the jury which considers any factual issues raised. Yet another system relies upon the parole authorities to withhold parole in accordance with their findings as to prior convictions. And within each broad approach described, other variations occur.

A determination of the "best" recidivist trial procedure necessarily involves a consideration of a wide variety of criteria, such as which method provides most adequate notice to the defendant and an opportunity to challenge the accuracy and validity of the alleged prior convictions, which method best meets the particular jurisdiction's allocation of responsibility between court and jury, which method is best accommodated to the State's established trial procedures, and of course which method is apt to be the least prejudicial in terms of the effect of prior-crime evidence on the ultimate issue of guilt or innocence. To say that the two-stage jury trial in the English-Connecticut style is probably the fairest, as some commentators and courts have suggested, and with which we might well agree were the matter before us in a legislative or rule-making context, is a far

---

1. Indeed the most recent scholarly study of jury behavior does not sustain the premise that juries are especially prone to prejudice when prior-crime evidence is admitted as to credibility. Kalven & Zeisel, The American Jury (1966). The study contrasts the effect of such evidence on judges and juries and concludes that "Neither the one nor the other can be said to be distinctively gullible or skeptical." Id., at 180.

cry from a constitutional determination that this method of handling the problem is compelled by the Fourteenth Amendment. Two-part jury trials are rare in our jurisprudence; they have never been compelled by this Court as a matter of constitutional law, or even as a matter of federal procedure. With recidivism the major problem that it is, substantial changes in trial procedure in countless local courts around the country would be required were this Court to sustain the contentions made by these petitioners. This we are unwilling to do. To take such a step would be quite beyond the pale of this Court's proper function in our federal system. It would be a wholly unjustifiable encroachment by this Court upon the constitutional power of States to promulgate their own rules of evidence to try their own state-created crimes in their own state courts, so long as their rules are not prohibited by any provision of the United States Constitution, which these rules are not.

Affirmed.

MR. JUSTICE STEWART, concurring.

If the Constitution gave me a roving commission to impose upon the criminal courts of Texas my own notions of enlightened policy, I would not join the Court's opinion. For it is clear to me that the recidivist procedures adopted in recent years by many other States— and by Texas herself since January 1 of last year—are far superior to those utilized in the cases now before us. But the question for decision is not whether we applaud or even whether we personally approve the procedures followed in these recidivist cases. The question is whether those procedures fall below the minimum level the Fourteenth Amendment will tolerate. Upon that question I am constrained to join the opinion and judgment of the Court.

MR. CHIEF JUSTICE WARREN, with whom MR. JUSTICE FORTAS concurs, dissenting.

It seems to me that the only argument made by the Court which might support its disposition of these cases is the amorphous one that this Court should proceed hesitantly in dealing with courtroom procedures which are alleged to violate the Due Process Clause of the Fourteenth Amendment. It attempts to bolster its decision with arguments about the conceded validity of the purpose of recidivist statutes and by pointing to occasions when evidence of prior crimes is traditionally admitted to serve a specific purpose related to finding guilt or innocence. For the reasons which I shall discuss, I do not find in these two arguments support for the decision. Nor am I persuaded by its cautious attitude toward this procedure. I recognize that the criteria for decision in procedural due process cases are necessarily drawn from the traditional jurisprudential attitudes of our legal system rather than from a relatively specific constitutional command. However, this Court has long recognized the central importance of courtroom procedures in maintaining our constitutional liberties. As Mr. Justice Frankfurter often reminded us, the history of individual liberty is largely coincident with the history of observance of procedural safeguards.

It seems to me that the use of prior-convictions evidence in these cases is fundamentally at odds with traditional notions of due process, not because this procedure is not the nicest resolution of conflicting but legitimate interests of the State and the accused, but because it needlessly prejudices the accused without advancing any legitimate interest of the State. If I am wrong in thinking that the introduction of prior-convictions evidence serves no valid purpose I am not alone, for the Court never states what interest of the State is advanced by this procedure. And this failure, in my view, undermines the logic of the Court's opinion.

There is much said about the valid purpose of enhanced punishment for repeating offenders, with which I agree, and about the variety of occasions in criminal trials in which prior-crimes evidence is admitted as having some relevance to the question of guilt or innocence. But I cannot find support for this procedure in either the purposes of recidivist statutes or by analogy to the traditional occasions where prior-crimes evidence is admitted. And the Court never faces up to the problem of trying to justify this recidivist procedure on the ground that the State would not violate due process if it used prior convictions simply as evidence of guilt because it showed criminal propensity.

Recidivist statutes have never been thought to allow the State to show probability of guilt because of prior convictions. Their justification is only that a defendant's prior crimes should lead to enhanced punishment for any subsequent offenses. Recidivist statutes embody four traditional rationales for imposing penal sanctions. A man's prior crimes are thought to aggravate his guilt for subsequent crimes, and thus greater than usual retribution is warranted. Similarly, the policies of insulating society from persons whose past conduct indicates their propensity to criminal behavior, of providing deterrence from future crime, and of rehabilitating criminals are all theoretically served by enhanced punishment according to recidivist statutes. None of these four traditional justifications for recidivist statutes is related in any way to the burden of proof to which the State is put to prove that a crime has currently been committed by the alleged recidivist. The fact of prior convictions is not intended by recidivist statutes to make it any easier for the State to prove the commission of a subsequent crime. The State does not argue in these cases that its statutes are, or constitutionally could be, intended to allow the prosecutor to introduce prior convictions to show the accused's criminal disposition. But the Court's opinion seems to accept, without discussion, that this use of prior-crimes evidence would be consistent with due process.

* * *

Whether or not a State has recidivist statutes on its books, it is well established that evidence of prior convictions may not be used by the State to show that the accused has a criminal disposition and that the probability that he committed the crime currently charged is increased. While this Court has never held that the use of prior convictions to show nothing more than a disposition to commit crime would violate the Due Process Clause of the Fourteenth Amendment, our decisions exercising supervisory power over criminal trials in federal courts, as well as decisions by courts of appeals and of state courts, suggest that evidence of prior crimes introduce for no purpose other than to show criminal disposition would violate the Due Process Clause. Evidence of prior convictions has been forbidden because it jeopardizes the presumption of innocence of the crime currently charged. A jury might punish an acused for being guilty of a previous offense, or feel that incarceration is justified because the accused is a "bad man," without regard to his guilt of the crime currently charged. Of course it flouts human nature to suppose that a jury would not consider a defendant's previous trouble with the law in deciding whether he has committed the crime currently charged against him. As Mr. Justice Jackson put it in a famous phrase, "[t]he naive assumption that prejudicial effects can be overcome by instructions to the jury . . . all practicing lawyers know to be unmitigated fiction." Krulewitch v. United States, 336 U.S. 440, 453, 69 S.Ct. 716, 723 (concurring opinion) (1949). Mr. Justice Jackson's assessment has received support from the most ambitious empirical study of jury behavior that has been attempted, see Kalven & Zeisel, The American Jury 127–130, 177–180.

Recognition of the prejudicial effect of prior-convictions evidence has traditionally been related to the requirement of our criminal law that the State prove beyond a reasonable doubt the commission of a specific criminal act. It is surely engrained in our jurisprudence that an accused's reputation or criminal disposition is no basis for penal sanctions. Because of the possibility that the generality of the jury's verdict might mask a finding of guilt based on an accused's past crimes or unsavory reputation, state and federal courts have consistently refused to admit evidence of past crimes except in circumstances where it tends to prove something other than general criminal disposition.

As I have stated, I do not understand the opinion to assert that this Court would find consistent with due process the admission of prior-crimes evidence for no purpose other than what probative value it has bearing on an accused's disposition to commit a crime currently charged. It ignores this issue, and points out that evidence of prior crimes in other contexts has not been thought so prejudicial that it cannot be admitted to serve a particular valid purpose. Thus, past crimes may be used to show a common design between a past crime and one currently charged, to show the distinctive handiwork of the defendant, or to show that the act presently at issue was probably not unintentional. We need not disagree with the admission of evidence of prior convictions in cases such as these, because past convictions are directly relevant to the question of guilt or innocence of the crime currently charged. It is admitted because its probative value, going to elements of the current charges, is so strong that it outweighs the prejudice inherent in evidence of prior crimes. Also, as the Court further points out, evidence of prior crimes has traditionally been admitted to either impeach the defendant's credibility when he testifies in his own behalf, or to counteract evidence introduced by the defendant as to his good character. In each of these situations, the possibility of prejudice resulting from the evidence of prior convictions is thought to be outweighed by the legitimate purposes served by the evidence. When a defendant attempts to convince the jury of his innocence by showing it that he is a person of such character that it is unlikely that he committed the crime charged, the State has a legitimate interest in counteracting this evidence of good character by showing that the accused has been previously convicted. The defendant has initiated the inquiry into his reputation, and the State should be allowed to respond to this general character evidence as best it can.

Similarly, when prior convictions are introduced to impeach the credibility of a defendant who testifies, a specific purpose is thought to be served. The theory is that the State should be permitted to show that the defendant-witness' credibility is qualified by his past record of delinquent behavior. In other words, the defendant is put to the same credibility test as any other witness. A defendant has some control over the State's opportunity to introduce this evidence in that he may decide whether or not to take the stand. Moreover, the jury hears of the prior convictions following a defendant's testimony, and it may be thought that this trial context combined with the usual limiting instruction results in the jury's actually behaving in accordance with the theory of limiting instructions: that is, that the prior convictions are only taken into account in assessing the defendant's credibility.

Although the theory justifying admission of evidence of prior convictions to impeach a defendant's credibility has been criticized, all that is necessary for purposes of deciding this case is to accept its theoretical justification and to note the basic difference between it and the Texas recidivist procedure. In the case of impeachment, as in all the examples cited by the Court, the prior convictions are considered probative for a limited purpose which is relevant to the jury's finding of guilt or innocence. This purpose is, of course, completely different from the purpose for which prior convictions are admitted in recidivist cases, where there is no connection between the evidence and guilt or innocence.

In all the situations pointed out by the Court, the admission of prior-crimes evidence rests on a conclusion that the probative value of the evidence outweighs the conceded possibility of prejudice. There is no middle position between the alternatives of admission or exclusion because, if the evidence is to serve the purpose for which it is considered probative, it must be admitted before the jury decides whether the defendant is guilty or innocent. The problem thus becomes the delicate one of balancing probative value against the possibility of prejudice, and the result for most state and federal courts (including this Court in the exercise of its supervisory power over proceedings in federal courts) has been that the trial judge is given discretion to draw the balance in the context of the trial. In view of this uniform tradition, it is apparent that prior-convictions evidence introduced for certain specific purposes relating to the determination of guilt or innocence, other than to show a general criminal disposition, would not violate the Due Process Clause.

From these situations where the probative value of prior-convictions evidence is thought to outweigh its prejudicial impact, the Court draws the legitimate conclusion that prior-convictions evidence is not so inherently prejudicial that its admission is invariably prohibited. It combines this premise with the concededly valid purpose of recidivist statutes to produce the following logic: since prior-crimes evidence may be admitted at the guilt phase of a trial where the admission serves a valid purpose and since the purpose of recidivist statutes is valid, prior crimes may be proven in the course of the guilt phase of a trial in order that the jury may also assess whether a defendant, if found guilty, should be sentenced to an enhanced punishment under recidivist statutes. I believe this syllogism is plausible only on the surface, because the Court's premises do not combine to justify its far-reaching result. I believe the Court has fallen into the logical fallacy sometimes known as the fallacy of the undistributed middle, because it has failed to examine the supposedly shared principle between admission of prior crimes related to guilt and admission in connection with recidivist statutes. That the admission in both situations may serve a valid purpose does not demonstrate that the former practice justifies the latter any more than the fact that men and dogs are animals means that men and dogs are the same in all respects.

Unlike the purpose for the admission of prior-convictions evidence in all the examples cited by the Court, the admission in connection with enhancing punishment for repeating offenders has nothing whatever to do with the question of guilt or innocence of the crime currently charged. Because of the complete irrelevance of prior convictions to the question of guilt or innocence, the recidivist situation is not one where the trial courts are called upon to balance the probative value of prior convictions against their prejudicial impact. The purpose of admitting prior-convictions evidence should be served and prejudice completely avoided by the simple expedient of a procedure which reflects the exclusive relevance of recidivist statutes to the issue of proper punishment. Only after a defendant has been found guilty does the question of whether he fits the recidivist category become relevant to the sentence, and any issue of fact as to his prior convictions should then be decided by the jury.

The availability of this procedural alternative, through which the interests of the State as reflected in its recidivist statutes can be fully effectuated while prejudice to the defendant is avoided, means that the only interest the State may offset against the possibility of prejudice to justify introducing evidence of prior crimes in these cases is the inconvenience which would result from postponing a determination that the defendant falls within a recidivist category until after the jury has found him guilty of the crime currently charged. However, for the purpose of deciding these cases, it is not necessary to consider whether the State's convenience in not conducting a two-stage trial justifies the prejudice which ensues when prior convictions are presented to a jury before it has decided whether the defendant is guilty of the crime charged. For the fact is that Texas has not even this matter of convenience in the method used to find facts regarding prior convictions to balance against the prejudice which ensues from the admission of this prior-convictions evidence. Spencer offered to stipulate to the truth of that portion of the indictment which alleged that he had been previously convicted of a crime which put him within the scope of a recidivist statute. The prosecutor refused to accept this stipulation, and the Texas courts allowed proof of the prior conviction to be presented to the jury on the ground that, under the recidivist statute dealing with capital crimes, the jury has a choice between the death penalty and life imprisonment. The courts reasoned that the existence of the prior conviction was information which the jury would find relevant in determining sentence. Of course, the offered stipulation dispensed completely with the need for the State to have the fact of prior crimes found by the jury to determine whether a recidivist statute applied to the defendant. Instead, the State tries to justify the refusal to accept the stipulation on the ground that it was relevant to the jury's discretion in ordering the death penalty. But this rationale would justify letting the jury hear, before determining guilt or innocence, all kinds of evidence which might be relevant to sentencing but which has traditionally been considered extremely prejudicial if admitted during the guilt phase of a trial. Thus, this argument would justify admitting probation reports, all kinds of hearsay evidence about the defendant's past, medical and psychiatric reports, and virtually anything else which might seem relevant to the broad discretion exercised in sentencing. The Court evidently believes that it is consistent with due process for a State to introduce evidence of a kind traditionally considered prejudicial which is relevant only to sentencing discretion in a single-stage trial before a finding of guilt. This seems to me the only possible ground for affirming since it is obvious that the offer of stipulation removes the need for a finding of fact as to the prior conviction in connection with the recidivist statute.

. . . . For me, the State's refusal to accept the stipulation removes any vestige of legitimate interest it might have to balance against the prejudice to the accused.

The decision I propose is consistent with a large body of judicial thought. Two United States Courts of Appeals have adopted the view that recidivist procedures which authorize admission of prior-convictions evidence before the jury determines that the defendant is guilty violate due process. In Lane v. Warden, 320 F.2d 179 (C.A.

4th Cir. 1963), the court reasoned that "it is patent that jurors would be likely to find a man guilty of a narcotics violation more readily if aware that he has had prior illegal association with narcotics. . . . Such a prejudice would clearly violate the standards of impartiality required for a fair trial." In the same vein, the Third Circuit, in United States ex rel. Scoleri v. Banmiller, 310 F.2d 720 (1962), reasoned that a procedure like the one involved in the three cases at bar would cause the jury to have in mind the defendant's previous convictions in determining his guilt of the crime currently charged. . . . In England, the prejudice which results from proof of prior crimes before a finding of guilt has been recognized for more than a century, and the rule has been that a finding as to prior crimes is made in a separate hearing after the finding of guilt.

The majority of States have adopted procedures which cure the prejudice inherent in the procedure in the cases at bar. In all, some 31 States have recidivist procedures which postpone the introduction of prior convictions until after the jury has found the defendant guilty of the crime currently charged. And at least three others have substantially mitigated the prejudice of the single-stage recidivist procedure by affording the defendant the right to stipulate to his prior crimes to prevent their introduction at the trial. Thus, only 16 States still maintain the needlessly prejudicial procedure exemplified in these three cases. The decision I propose would require only a small number of States to make a relatively minor adjustment in their criminal procedure to avoid the manifest unfairness and prejudice which have already been eliminated in England and in 34 of the United States.

[Omitted is the dissenting opinion of JUSTICE BRENNAN, in which JUSTICE DOUGLAS joined.]

NOTE

Since *Spencer*, alleged errors by state courts in admitting evidence of prior unrelated crimes have consistently failed to justify relief in federal habeas corpus. Murphy v. Beto, 416 F.2d 98 (5th Cir. 1969); United States ex rel. Clauson v. Rundle, 396 F.2d 778 (3d Cir. 1968); Parker v. Swenson, 332 F.Supp. 1225 (D.C.Mo.1971), aff'd 459 F.2d 164 (8th Cir.); Echard v. Haskins, 327 F.Supp. 329 (D.C.Ohio 1971); Keener v. State of Tenn., 281 F.Supp. 964 (D.C.Tenn.1968), even when the federal court specifically finds flagrant error. See, also, Jones v. Haskins, 343 F.Supp. 645 (D.C.Ohio 1971).

E.   CROSS EXAMINATION AND IMPEACHMENT

---

1.   THE ORDINARY WITNESS

POINTER v. TEXAS

Supreme Court of the United States, 1965.
380 U.S. 400, 85 S.Ct. 1065, mandate conformed to Tex.Crim.App., 391 S.W.2d 62.

MR. JUSTICE BLACK delivered the opinion of the Court.

* * *

The petitioner Pointer and one Dillard were arrested in Texas and taken before a state judge for a preliminary hearing (in Texas called the "examining trial") on a charge of having robbed Kenneth W. Phillips of $375 "by assault, or violence, or by putting in fear of life or bodily injury," in violation of Texas Penal Code Art. 1408. At this hearing an Assistant District Attorney conducted the prosecution and examined witnesses, but neither of the defendants, both of whom were laymen, had a lawyer. Phillips as chief witness for the State gave his version of the alleged robbery in detail, identifying petitioner as the man who had robbed him at gunpoint. Apparently Dillard tried to cross-examine Phillips but Pointer did not, although Pointer was said to have tried to cross-examine some other witnesses at the hearing. Petitioner was subsequently indicted on a charge of having committed the robbery. Some time before the trial was held, Phillips moved to California. After putting in evidence to show that Phillips had moved and did not intend to return to Texas, the State at the trial offered the transcript of Phillips' testimony given at the preliminary hearing as evidence against petitioner. Petitioner's counsel immediately objected to introduction of the transcript, stating, "Your Honor, we will object to that, as it is a denial of the confrontment of the witnesses against the Defendant." Similar objections were repeatedly made by petitioner's counsel but were overruled by the trial judge, apparently in part because, as the judge viewed it, petitioner had been present at the preliminary hearing and therefore had been "accorded the opportunity of cross examining the witnesses there against him." The Texas Court of Criminal Appeals, the highest state court to which the case could be taken, affirmed petitioner's conviction, rejecting his contention that use of the transcript to convict him denied him rights guaranteed by the Sixth and Fourteenth Amendments. 375 S.W.2d 293. . . .

* * *

. . . . We hold today that the Sixth Amendment's right of an accused to confront the witnesses against him is likewise a fundamental right and is made obligatory on the States by the Fourteenth Amendment.

It cannot seriously be doubted at this late date that the right of cross-examination is included in the right of an accused in a criminal case to confront the witnesses against him. And probably no one, certainly no one experienced in the trial of lawsuits, would deny the value of cross-examination in exposing falsehood and bringing out the truth in the trial of a criminal case. See, e. g., 5 Wigmore, Evidence § 1367 (3d ed. 1940). The fact that this right appears in the Sixth Amendment of our Bill of Rights reflects the belief of the Framers of those liberties and safeguards that confrontation was a fundamental right essential to a fair trial in a criminal prosecution. Moreover, the decisions of this Court and other courts throughout the years have constantly emphasized the necessity for cross-examination as a protection for defendants in criminal cases . .   . .

* * *

. . . This Court has recognized the admissibility against an accused of dying declarations, Mattox v. United States, 146 U.S. 140, 151, 13 S.Ct. 50, 53, and of testimony of a deceased witness who has testified at a former trial, Mattox v. United States, 156 U.S. 237, 240–244, 15 S.Ct. 337, 338–340. Nothing we hold here is to the contrary. The case before us would be quite a different one had Phillips' statement been taken at a full-fledged hearing at which petitioner had been represented by counsel who had been given a complete and adequate opportunity to cross-examine. There are other analogous situations which might not fall within the scope of the constitutional rule requiring confrontation of witnesses. The case before us, however, does not present any situation like those mentioned above or others analogous to them. Because the transcript of Phillips' statement offered against petitioner at his trial had not been taken at a time and under circumstances affording petitioner through counsel an adequate opportunity to cross-examine Phillips, its introduction in a federal court in a criminal case against Pointer would have amounted to denial of the privilege of confrontation guaranteed by the Sixth Amendment. Since we hold that the right of an accused to be confronted with the witnesses against him must be determined by the same standards whether the right is denied in a federal or state proceeding, it follows that use of the transcript to convict petitioner denied him a constitutional right, and that his conviction must be reversed.

Reversed and remanded.

[The concurring opinions of JUSTICES HARLAN, STEWART, and GOLDBERG are omitted.]

MANCUSI v. STUBBS

Supreme Court of the United States, 1972.
408 U.S. 204, 92 S.Ct. 2308.

MR. JUSTICE REHNQUIST delivered the opinion of the Court.

Respondent Stubbs was convicted of a felony in a New York State court and sentenced as a second offender under the laws of that State by reason of a prior Tennessee murder conviction obtained in 1964. He thereafter sought federal habeas corpus, claiming that the Tennessee conviction was had in violation of his Sixth and Fourteenth Amendment right to confront witnesses against him, and thus could not be used by New York as the predicate for a stiffer punishment. The District Court denied habeas corpus, but the Court of Appeals reversed, 442 F.2d 561 (CA 2 1971).

* * *

In July 1954, respondent was convicted in the Tennessee trial court of murder in the first degree, assault with intent to murder, and two counts of kidnapping. The jury empaneled for that trial could have concluded from the evidence presented to it that respondent, a few days after his release from a Texas penitentiary in June 1954, kidnapped Mr. and Mrs. Alex Holm and forced them at gun point to accompany him in their car. Stubbs drove the car and sat in the front seat, while the Holms sat in the back seat. Mr. Holm testified that somewhere east of Blountville, Tennessee, Stubbs, without saying anything, shot him twice in the head and shot and killed Mrs. Holm. Stubbs then left the car, obtained a ride as a hitchhiker, and was ultimately arrested at a roadblock. At the time of his arrest, Stubbs explained the blood on his clothing as having resulted from his having fallen off a cliff while fishing.

Stubbs took the stand in his own defense, admitted that he had kidnapped the Holms at gun point, and that as he drove the Holms' car with them in the back seat he at intervals pointed the gun in Mrs. Holm's face. He testified that during the ride he apologized for forcing a ride; that the Holms then assured him they would let him out at Bristol, Tennessee, and would not cause him any trouble, and that he therefore laid the pistol on the front seat of the car. He also testified that near Bristol, Tennessee:

> "It seems awful strange, but everything just seemed to be
> awful still and I remember a tree and it just seemed to come
> up just like that in a clear focus, but in a reddish haze. I
> mean there was no pain or nothing, . . . I felt a sharp
> pain that seemed to start in my head and go all the way
> down through me and I reached up with both hands and
> heard this loud roar, bang . . . Stuff started down my
> face and down my shirt and all that I could think of is that
> he has got the gun . . . I just went outside through
> the car door . . . ."

After that, Stubbs testified, "everything went black."

Nine years after his state court trial of murder, Stubbs sought release on federal habeas corpus from the United States District Court for the Middle District of Tennessee.

He successfully urged upon that court the contention that he had been denied the effective assistance of counsel in this 1954 trial because counsel had been appointed for him only four days before the trial took place. Stubbs v. Bomar, Civil Action No. 3585 (MD Tenn. 1964). The State of Tennessee then elected to retry him, and did so in 1964. At that time Holm, who had been born in Sweden but had become a naturalized American citizen, had returned to Sweden and taken up permanent residence there. Tennessee issued a subpoena that was sent to Texas authorities in an attempt to serve Holm at his last known United States address. No service having been obtained, the State at trial called Holm's son as a witness and elicited from him the fact that his father now resided in Sweden. Over appropriate objection on constitutional grounds, the Tennessee trial judge then permitted Holm's testimony at the earlier trial to be read to the jury. Stubbs again took the stand, recited his version of the events, and was again convicted. This conviction was in due course affirmed by the Supreme Court of Tennessee. Stubbs v. State, 216 Tenn. 567, 393 S.W.2d 150 (1965).

Respondent has challenged the present second offender sentence that was imposed upon him by the New York courts on the ground that his 1964 conviction upon retrial was constitutionally infirm because he was denied his Sixth and Fourteenth Amendment right to confront the witness Holm .   .   .

*   *   *

.   .   . Upon discovering that Holm resided in a foreign nation, the State of Tennessee so far as this record shows was powerless to compel his attendance at the second trial, either through its own process or through established procedures depending on the voluntary assistance of another government. We therefore hold that the predicate of unavailability was sufficiently strong here that a federal habeas court was not warranted in upsetting the determination of the state trial court as to Holm's unavailability. Before it can be said that Stubbs' constitutional right to confront witnesses was not infringed, however, the adequacy of Holm's examination at the first trial must be taken into consideration.

*   *   *

.   .   . It is clear from numerous prior decisions of this Court, that even though the witness be unavailable his prior testimony must bear some of these "indicia of reliability".

At least since the decision of this Court in Mattox v. United States (1895), prior recorded testimony has been admissible in appropriate cases. The circumstances surrounding the giving of Alex Holm's testimony at the 1954 trial were significantly more conducive to an assurance of reliability than were those obtaining in Barber v.

Page, supra. The 1954 Tennessee proceeding was a trial of a serious felony on the merits, conducted in a court of record before a jury, rather than before a magistrate. Stubbs was represented by counsel who could and did effectively cross-examine prosecution witnesses.

Stubbs urges that because the 1954 conviction was itself overturned by a federal habeas court on a finding of ineffective assistance of counsel, that court must necessarily have concluded that the cross-examination of Holm conducted by such counsel likewise fell short of constitutional standards. The federal habeas judge in Stubbs v. Bomar, supra, however, rested his determination on an apparent *per se* rule of ineffective assistance that was conclusively presumed from the short interval between the time of counsel's appointment and the date of the trial. If the habeas court had rendered its decision after our holding in Chambers v. Maroney, 399 U.S. 42, 90 S.Ct. 1975 (1970), which disapproved any such *per se* rule, it might have addressed itself to the effectiveness of the examination of the witness Holm. But it did not in fact do so. When Stubbs appealed his 1964 conviction to the Supreme Court of Tennessee, that court in affirming the judgment expressly determined that the prior cross-examination of Holm had been adequate. Stubbs v. State, 216 Tenn. 567, 393 S.W. 150 (1965). Whatever might be the case in other circumstances, the State of New York was not bound under any theory of *res judicata* by Stubbs v. Bomar as to the efficacy of the prior cross-examination of the witness Holm.

Stubbs also contends that even though the prior determination may not be binding upon subsequent review, the fact that counsel was appointed only four days before trial necessarily requires a finding that the cross-examination of Holm was constitutionally inadequate. Counsel for Stubbs at the 1964 trial placed in the record a list of 12 questions not asked of Holm in 1954, which he said he would have asked had the witness been present at the second trial. With one exception these were directed to the events leading up to and surrounding the shooting. Though not asked *in haec verba* in 1954, they were nonetheless adverted to in the earlier cross-examination. No one defense counsel will ever develop precisely the same lines of inquiry or frame his questions in exactly the words of another, but from this record counsel at the retrial did not in his proffer show any new and significantly material line of cross-examination that was not at least touched upon in the first trial.

The Court of Appeals concluded that the cross-examination had been inadequate. It reached this conclusion at least in part because it felt that Holm could have been questioned about whether Stubbs, although originally having kidnapped the Holms at gun point, later became in effect their guest. Parts of Stubbs' own testimony presented that version of the events to the jury, and the Second Circuit thought it significant because even if Stubbs fired his pistol accidentally, he might still have been found guilty of felony murder unless the felony of kidnapping had ended. Under this theory if Stubbs had during the trip been transmogrified from a kidnapper into a guest, at least the argument to the jury as to whether the kidnapping had ended before the shooting would have been strengthened by any support Holm's testimony might have given to this notion.

The Tennessee trial court, however, did not charge that the jury could convict Stubbs of felony murder as a result of a death occurring during a kidnapping. Its charge authorized conviction upon a finding of premeditated murder, or upon a finding of murder during the commission of robbery. The failure to elicit from Holm his own views as to whether Stubbs had become a guest in the Holm car prior to the time that he turned from the front seat, shot Mr. Holm, and killed Mrs. Holm—however interesting they might have been to hear —could not have prejudiced Stubbs' case as to any issue that the jury was authorized to deliberate under the trial judge's charge.

Since there was an adequate opportunity to cross-examine Holm at the first trial, and counsel for Stubbs availed himself of that opportunity, the transcript of Holm's testimony in the first trial bore sufficient "indicia of reliability" and afforded "the trier of fact a satisfactory basis for evaluating the truth of the prior statement," Dutton v. Evans, 400 U.S. 74, 89, 91 S.Ct. 210, 220. The witness Holm, consistently with the requirement of the Confrontation Clause, could have been and was found by the trial court to be unavailable at the time of the second trial. There was therefore no constitutional error in permitting his prior recorded testimony to be read to the jury at that trial, and no constitutional infirmity in the judgment of conviction resulting from that trial that would prevent the State of New York from considering that conviction in sentencing Stubbs as a second offender. The judgment of the Court of Appeals is therefore reversed.

Reversed.

MR. JUSTICE MARSHALL, dissenting.

*   *   *

Respondent was convicted of murder in Tennessee after a trial in which the principal prosecution witness, one Axel Holm, did not appear. Instead, Holm's testimony was introduced through a transcript of a previous trial on the same charge. The State made absolutely no effort to secure Holm's presence at the second trial, relying wholly on the claim that Holm was unavailable because he had become a resident of Sweden.

*   *   *

The difficulty with that position is that there never has been any factual inquiry resulting in a determination as to Holm's unavailability. Rather, the courts have consistently presumed his unavailability from the bare fact that he lives in Sweden. The Tennessee Supreme Court thought it was enough that Holm was out of the jurisdiction of the United States, beyond the reach of compulsory process, as did the dissenting judge in the United States Court of Appeals. Apparently this Court takes the same view. But in Barber v. Page we squarely rejected any such presumption of unavailability. In that case, the claim was made that the court had no power to compel the absent witness to appear. We held that nevertheless the State was obliged to make a good faith effort to secure his appearance, for "the possibility of a refusal is not the equivalent of asking and receiving a rebuff."

* * *

I cannot agree, that if neither state nor federal authorities had the power to compel Holm's appearance, that fact relieved the State of its obligation to make a good-faith effort to secure his presence. It simply reduced the likelihood that any effort would succeed. The State's obligation would hardly be framed in terms of "good-faith effort" if that effort were required only in circumstances where success was guaranteed. If, as the Court contends it is more difficult to produce at trial a resident of Sweden than a federal prisoner, that fact might justify a failure to produce the witness; it cannot justify a failure even to try. At a minimum, the State could have notified Mr. Holm that the trial was scheduled, and invited him to come at his own expense. Beyond that, it could have offered to pay his expenses. Finally, it could have sought federal assistance in invoking the cooperation of Swedish authorities, as a matter of international comity.

As in *Barber,* "so far as this record reveals, the sole reason why [the witness] was not present to testify in person was because the State did not attempt to seek his presence. The right of confrontation may not be dispensed with so lightly."

I respectfully dissent.

MR. JUSTICE DOUGLAS joins in this opinion.

NOTE

McCormick offers the following observations on the value of cross-examination in his Handbook of The Law of Evidence at 62–63 (2nd Ed. 1972):

Cross-Examination Revalued

Early Victorian writers on advocacy exaggerated the strategic significance of cross-examination as affecting the outcome of trials. One of them wrote, "There is never a cause contested, the result of which is not mainly dependent upon the skill with which the advocate conducts his cross-examination." This stands in contrast with the view of Scarlett, a great "leader" of a later day, who said, "I learned by much experience that the most useful duty of an advocate is the examination of witnesses, and that much more mischief than benefit generally resulted from cross-examination. I therefore rarely allowed that duty to be performed by my colleagues. I cross-examined in general very little, and more with a view to enforce the facts I meant to rely upon than to affect the witness's credit,—for the most part a vain attempt." Reed, who was one of our most sensible American writers on trial tactics, expresses the modern informed opinion when he says, "Sometimes a great speech bears down the adversary, and sometimes a searching cross-examination turns a witness inside out and shows him up to be a perjured villain. But ordinarily cases are not won by either speaking or cross-examining." At the same time, most lawyers who write concerning the art of cross-examination still believe that failure to use this tool can lose a case. To the advocate of today, it is often a means of gleaning additional facts but it is also still employed as a means of attack upon the credit of the direct testimony of the witness whenever possible. Cross-examination of experts seems particularly important, in many instances. Thus while cross-examination does not loom large as a determinant of victory in many cases, it still may be an important ingredient in other cases.

In the appraisal of policies upon which the modernizing of the existing system of evidence rules must be based, it seems that a similar evaluation of cross-examination as an engine for discovering truth is called for. The present assumption is that the statement of a declarant or witness, if opportunity for cross-examination is not afforded, is so fatally lacking in reliability that it is not even worth hearing in a court of justice, and that the opportunity for cross-examination is indispensable. Now obviously cross-examination is a useful device to secure greater accuracy and completeness for the witness's testimony as a whole, and in the hands of a skillful advocate will often—not always—expose fraud or honest error in the witness. But it has its own hazards of producing errors. It is, in truth, quite doubtful whether it is not the honest but weak or timid witness, rather than the rogue, who most often goes down under the fire of a cross-examination. Certainly every witness in judicial proceedings should in fairness be made available for cross-examination by the opponent wherever possible. But the premise that where cross-examination is not possible, as in the case of out-of-court statements, or as in the case of a witness who dies before cross-examination, the statement or testimony should generally be excluded for that reason alone, seems ill-founded. Cross-examination, it is submitted, should be considered as useful but not indispensable as an agency of discovering truth, and absence of opportunity to cross-examine should only be one factor to be weighed in determining whether the statement or testimony should be received. Such an approach to hearsay problems might lead us to conclude that when opportunity to cross-examine a witness is permanently cut off without fault of either party, the direct testimony should nevertheless be received as suggested in a previous section. It might lead us to further conclude that hearsay statements should be admitted if the statement was made by the declarant on personal knowledge and reported by the witness at first hand, and if the declarant is now dead or unavailable for cross-examination or, on the other hand, if the declarant is alive and still available for cross-examination. Perhaps written statements should be admitted wherever production for cross-examination can fairly be dispensed with.

It should be noted, however, that although these modern viewpoints are supportable, there remains a special problem concerning the criminal defendant's right of cross-examination under the Fifth, Sixth, and Fourteenth Amendments of the federal constitution.

PEOPLE v. NUCCIO

Supreme Court of Illinois, 1969.
43 Ill.2d 375, 253 N.E.2d 353.

MR. CHIEF JUSTICE UNDERWOOD delivered the opinion of the court:

Defendant, Richard Nuccio, was found guilty of murder at the conclusion of a bench trial in the circuit court of Cook County and sentenced to 14–15 years imprisonment. . . .

The testimony is voluminous and conflicting, with few matters undisputed. It is clear, however, that the event in question occurred on the night of June 4, 1968, in an alley near a large parking area opposite Wrigley Field in Chicago. . . . The Franksville Restaurant was located at the southwest corner of this parking area, and a Tastee-Freez Ice Cream stand was at the northeast end surrounded by parking area. . . .

Ben Citron, owner of the Franksville Restaurant, called the police station on June 4 about 9:30 P.M. to report a "disturbance". Defendant Nuccio, then a Chicago police officer, was on duty with Patrolman Rothmund, and the two officers responded to the call in a marked squad car. Officers Hyatt and Sand arrived at the scene in an unmarked police car. This area had apparently been visited by decedent and a group of his friends with some degree of frequency. There had been prior disturbances involving police calls and arrests, and some members of the group, including decedent had been ordered by the court to stay away from the property.

After Officers Nuccio and Rothmund parked their car . . . . , the former went to a group of young people near the Tastee-Freez and the latter went to Franksville where he talked to Ben Citron. Citron pointed to one Steve Austill . . . and said, "There's one", or "there goes one of them". Then Citron pointed to Ronald Nelson, the 19-year-old decedent, who was sitting at a table on the patio outside the restaurant and said, "There's another one that shouldn't be here". Citron testified that he had seen Nelson sitting at the table playing with a knife. While Nelson had had no contact with Citron that evening, Citron was "scared" when he saw Nelson in possession of the knife and called the police because on a previous occasion Nelson had come into his store, created a disturbance and hit him. Officer Rothmund testified that he saw Nelson playing with a pocket knife while Nelson was sitting at the table and immediately before he jumped up and ran. Trena Ciabay, a 16-year-old high school senior, testified that she was present that evening and had been sitting at one of the tables with Nelson for about three minutes before the police arrived. She did not see anything in his hands nor did she see anything on the table. Leonard Noe, another State witness, also testified that he could see Nelson at the table and saw no knife.

After Citron pointed to Nelson and when Officer Rothmund turned toward him, Nelson got up and ran. Citron went back into his place of business. Officer Rothmund testified that he shouted to the other police officer to "grab that man and watch out, he has a knife" (or something similar), and then ran over to where Steve Austill was sitting on an "ad" bench at the corner of Clark and Addison at the southwest tip of the parking area and began to place Austill under arrest.

Officer Nuccio was searching one of the group, John Ahrens, for weapons when he heard Rothmund call from the area of the restaurant, "Stop him and watch out, he's got a knife". Both Officers Hyatt and Sand, the plain clothesmen who arrived in the second car testified that they heard Rothmund yell, "Look out, he's got a knife".

John Ahrens testified that he heard a shout, "Stop him". Six other young persons, who were gathered near the Tastee-Freez and were near the defendant and Ahrens, testified that they heard a shout, "Stop him", or "Get him" coming from the area of the Franksville Restaurant. Only two of them were specifically asked whether they also heard "watch out, he's got a knife" and both of those asked responded they had not.

After hearing the shouted command, Officer Nuccio looked in the direction of the Franksville Restaurant and saw Nelson running in a northwesterly direction toward the juncture of the east-west and north-south alleys.

The testimony is again conflicting as to the defendant's subsequent conduct, although all the witnesses agreed that the defendant immediately ceased searching Ahrens and began to run toward Nelson.

Officer Hyatt . . . was in the area of the parking lot . . . when he heard Officer Rothmund yell. He turned and saw Nelson running from Franksville. He started running toward Nelson, . . . and followed him. As he was running toward the "T" in the alleys, he saw the defendant at a point 15–30 feet east of the "T" and running toward the east-west alley. Nelson was already in the east-west alley and running west on the north side. Officer Hyatt testified that as he and the defendant were entering the alley, he saw something that flashed in Nelson's hand and he presumed it to be a knife. As Nelson was running he looked over his right shoulder and twisted his shoulder to the right. At that time Officer Hyatt screamed, "Look out, he is going to throw the knife". The defendant fell to his knees and fired a shot. Nelson fell forward to the ground.

Officer Hyatt testified that he never drew his gun at any time, and the defendant pulled his out as he was dropping to the ground; that at the time defendant fired the knife was in the air. Officer Hyatt also testified he was slightly behind and to the left of defendant, and estimated that the decedent was approximately 20–25 feet ahead of defendant at the time of the shot. An opened knife, identified by this officer as the one Nelson had, was found in the alley.

Defendant testified that he saw Officer Hyatt trying to apprehend Nelson and defendant started running to cut Nelson off at the entrance to the alley; when Nelson reached the entrance to the alley, the defendant hollered at him to stop, but Nelson turned into the east-west alley and headed west. When Nelson was 40 feet into the alley, and the officers were 20 feet behind him, defendant saw Nelson look back at him, raise his right arm with a knife in his hand and heard Officer Hyatt scream, "Watch out, he's going to throw the knife". Defendant testified, "I dove to the ground and fired, it all happened instantly."

The State's witnesses gave a somewhat different description of the events and differed entirely from the police officers as to the presence of a knife. John Ahrens, whom the defendant had been searching when the shout was heard, testified that the defendant had taken only a few steps when he began to draw his gun. Edward Ryan and Jose Rodriguez, other young men who were near the Tastee-Freez and the spot where the defendant was searching Ahrens, gave similar testimony. Linda Young, who was sitting in a car parked southwest of the Tastee-Freez, testified defendant pulled his gun as he was running. Noel Kitchen, also standing in this area, testified that the defendant drew his gun right before he got to the alley.

Ahrens and Leonard Noe, another young man who was sitting at one of the tables outside Franksville, testified the defendant stopped about 15 feet east of the alley light located at the entrance to the east-west alley, aimed and fired a shot at Nelson. Jose Rodriguez estimated this distance at 30 feet; Edward Ryan at about 20 feet. The estimates given by the State's witnesses of the distance between the defendant and Nelson when the shot was fired ranged from 70 to 90 feet. None of the State's witnesses testified to having seen a knife or object in the hand of Nelson as he ran. Although some of the State's witnesses saw Nelson look over his shoulder or at least turn his head as he entered the east-west alley, none of them saw him turn or look back as he was running west down the alley.

The trial judge accepted the State's version of the distance between defendant and decedent at the time the shot was fired and found that distance to be 70–90 feet. The defendant's claim that the proof does not establish guilt beyond a reasonable doubt is, therefore, not sustainable for the testimony of the State's witnesses, if believed by the trier of fact, is sufficient to justify the verdict.

The argument that defendant was deprived of the opportunity to confront the witnesses against him is interwoven with the argument that improper prosecutorial questioning of defendant and his witnesses deprived him of a fair trial. Both arguments are predicated upon a persistent course of cross-examination by which the State repeatedly insinuated, generally without any supporting testimony, that defendant and his witnesses had engaged in a pattern of reprehensible conduct in their relationships to the youths who frequented Franksville. The impact of the State's unsupported insinuations can only be made clear here by a rather lengthy cataloguing of relevant examples, for it is the totality of the impact which compels our conclusion that the defendant's right to a fair trial, with the attendant's right to cross-examine witnesses against him, was denied.

The impropriety of the cross-examination does not rest simply upon unsupported insinuations of misconduct, but also upon the State's failure to present appropriate rebuttal testimony in response to the defense witnesses' specific denials of misconduct. A fair portrayal of the circumstances requires summarization of the testimony of the two witnesses who did testify to prior misconduct of defendant.

Stephen Austill, while testifying as a State's witness, stated he had been at the police station in February, 1968, when decedent was in custody and that defendant had asked Nelson about his girlfriend, stating that he [defendant] had been making love to her. Defendant allegedly stuck his gun to Nelson's head and asked him if he wanted to play Russian roulette, and ran his [defendant's] knife down decedent's arm, stating that decedent deserved to die and that defendant was going to get him personally. Austill testified that on an earlier occasion, when he had gone to the station while decedent was in custody, "to try and see what I could do for him," defendant stated to the witness, "I'm going to kill you and your punk friend."

On cross-examination Austill testified that the decedent was his best friend. He admitted that he had been arrested in connection with the crimes of shoplifting, car theft, disorderly conduct and possession of marijuana. He admitted that on one occasion when decedent was in police custody, Austill falsely claimed to have access to information on narcotics sales, which he offered to provide in exchange for decedent's release, and that after the release he failed to provide any information.

Another State's witness, Noel Kitchen, testified that on one occasion at Franksville, defendant had "said he would take his badge off any time that I thought that I could do something about it." The following statement was then read to Kitchen, who reluctantly acknowledged having made it on June 5, 1968:

"Q. Did you ever have any contact with Officer Nuccio in the past?

A. Yes, one time I was sitting in front of Franksville, Officer Nuccio came up and grabbed me for no reason at all, he told me he was going to beat the crap out of me if I didn't get out of there. At that time I told him that if he didn't have his badge on, I would fight him."

Thereafter another portion of the same statement was read: "He said, I don't have my badge on and he pulled out his blackjack, at this time Officer Nuccio had his cousin with him and I got into a fight with the cousin but Nuccio didn't participate. Another time Officer Nuccio searched my car, this was about a month ago." Kitchen testified that the alleged altercation had taken place about a year before Nelson's death, but also stated that he had seen defendant on other occasions since the summer of 1967, both on duty and off duty, pull out a gun and a blackjack while at Franksville, often to disperse a crowd of youths. Kitchen also admitted that some weeks prior to the shooting, the owner of Franksville had told him to leave the premises.

Aside from this testimony by Austill and Kitchen, no State witness supported the insinuations of misconduct which were levelled at defendant and other defense witnesses during the State's cross-examination. We turn now to the State's unsupported insinuations of a general pattern of misconduct on the part of defendant and the two main defense witnesses, Officers Kenneth South and Michael Nuccio (unrelated to defendant).

There were three basic inferences which would naturally arise from the State's insinuations: 1) that the State was prepared to show by rebuttal testimony that defendant and his witnesses often intimidated and chastised the youths who congregated at Franksville, and that the defendant may therefore have been pursuing a general pattern of indiscriminate abuse when he shot Ronald Nelson; 2) that the State would show in rebuttal that the defense witnesses, and defendant in particular, had in fact been promiscuously involved with the girls who congregated at Franksville, particularly with Ronald Nelson's girlfriend, and that therefore defendant may have had a specific motive for killing Nelson; and 3) that the State would show in rebuttal that the defendant and his witnesses had been guilty of perjury in the prosecution of a Franksville youth and had intimidated prospective State's witnesses in the instant case.

The following illustrations are taken from the State's cross-examination of the designated defense witnesses:

MICHAEL NUCCIO—

"Q. Isn't it a fact you challenged Mr. Keating to a fight?

"A. No, I did not.

"Q. Didn't you challenge him to come around in the back and 'Let's have it out'?

"A. No, I did not."

KENNETH SOUTH—

"Q. Did you ever take Ronald Nelson, alone with Officer Nuccio, down to Lake Michigan and take his shoes off?

"A. No.

"Q. Did you ever leave Ronald Nelson down at Lake Michigan without any shoes and have him walk home?

"A. No, I didn't."

RICHARD NUCCIO—

"Q. Do you recall the day after St. Patrick's Day, 1968, were you working?

"A.   I don't remember, sir.

"Q.   Do you remember firing at a person by the name of Steven Weinstein and Mr. Darryl on Clyborne Avenue?

"A.   No sir.

"Q.   You never took out your gun on the evening?

"A.   I didn't say that, sir.

"Q.   Did you take out your gun that evening?

"A.   Yes, sir.

"Q.   Did you fire it?

"A.   No, sir.

"Q.   Do you recall ever threatening Mr. Nelson's life in the presence of a Norman Suderski?

"A.   No, sir.

"Q.   Do you recall ever telling John Ahrens, in the presence of Mr. Nelson, that you were going to blow Ronald Nelson's brains out and you were going to blow John Ahrens' brains out?

"A.   Absolutely not, sir.

"Q.   Do you recall or do you know a person by the name of Fillipp?

"A.   What is the name again, sir?

"Q.   Fillipp, do you know somebody by the name of Fillipp?

"A.   I believe that is somebody's first name, but I wish you would give me the last name.

"Q.   How about Stephan Fillipp, F-I-L-L-I-P-P, he lives at 3843, North Hoyne, do you know him?

"A.   I don't recall, sir.

"Q.   Haven't you arrested him in the past?

"Mr. Echeles: What is the name?

"Mr. Tully: Stephan Fillipp, F-I-L-L-I-P-P.

"A.   I don't recall if I had or not.

"Q.   Did you ever recall talking to Mr. Nelson and Mr. Fillipp in which you told both of these men that they usually end up with your head being blown off?

"A.   No, sir. I don't think I even know a Mr. Fillipp.

"Q.   Okay. Do you recall ever telling Mr. Nelson that if he reported any of this to the I.I.D.—

"Mr. Echeles: Object, your Honor, to the preface of his questions: do you recall?

"The Court: Yes, rephrase your question.

"Mr. Tully: All right.

"Did you ever tell Mr. Nelson that if you ever threatened him—strike that—if Mr. Nelson ever told anybody from the I.I.D. about threatening to kill him, that he would kill Mr. Nelson?

"Mr. Echeles: Object, your Honor. How would he know what Nelson would say to somebody else?

"The Court: Well, this is directed not at what Mr. Nelson would say to somebody else, but what he said to Nelson.

"Mr. Echeles: It is my understanding that is not the question, your Honor. If it is, I'll withdraw the objection.

"The Court: Rephrase it.

"Mr. Echeles: Excuse me. May the court reporter read the question?

"The Court: Yes.

(Record read by reporter.)

"Mr. Tully: I'll rephrase the question.

"Did you ever tell Mr. Nelson that you would kill him if he reported any threats to the I.I.D.?

"A.   No, sir.

*   *   *

"Mr. Tully: Now, this evening of March 18th, do you recall talking to a Mr. Weinstein?

"A.   I never talked to a Mr. Weinstein, sir.

"Q.   Do you recall slapping around Mr. Darryl that evening after shooting at him?

"Mr. Echeles: Object to the form of the question about recalling something that no direct question was asked to predicate—

"The Court: Rephrase the question, please.

"Mr. Tully: Do you recall punching Mr. Darryl around after firing at him?

"Mr. Echeles: Object, your Honor, to the form of the question. Just a moment.

"The Court: Rephrase the question, please, Mr. State's Attorney.

"Mr. Tully: Yes, sir, your Honor."

The State then dropped the question without rephrasing or representing it.

The insinuations that a prior pattern of promiscuous involvement may have predicated the shooting of Ronald Nelson were

framed in both general and specific references to the girls who congregated at Franksville:

MICHAEL NUCCIO—

"Q.   Don't you even make caustic or vulgar statements
to young ladies that hang around that Franksville Restaurant?

"Mr. Echeles: I object to the form of the question.

"The Court: The form is improper.

"Mr. Tully: Haven't you intimated to young ladies that
come around there that they are dirty whores?

"Mr. Echeles: Excuse me, your Honor. He should give
time and place and the lady of whom he speaks.

"The Court: Sustained.

"Mr. Tully: Haven't you made caustic remarks to
young ladies up there, all those evenings that you were
hanging around there off duty?

"A.   Will you please define "caustic" for me, please?

"Q.   Did you ever call any of the young ladies up there
whores?

"A.   No, I did not.

"Q.   You're a married man, is that correct, sir?

"A.   That is correct.

"Q.   Do you have a family?

"A.   Yes, I do.

"Q.   You still hang around Franksville, is that right?

"A.   That is right."

RICHARD NUCCIO—

"Q.   In fact, didn't you generally go up there [Franks-
ville] almost every night of the week?

"A.   No, sir.

"Q.   You are a married man?

"A.   Yes, sir.

"Q.   You have a family?

"A.   Yes, sir.

"Q.   You didn't hang around there with Mike Nuccio?

"A.   No, sir.

"Q.   You knew Mike Nuccio hung around there?

"A.   No, sir.

"Q.   Well, on those occasions that you would go up
there did you ever see Mike Nuccio?

"A.   Occasionally.

"Q.   Did you talk to him?

"A.   Yes, sir.

"Q.   Would Mike Nuccio be in uniform or would he be in plain clothes?

"A.   I think he would be in plain clothes, sir.

"Q.   Do you know a girl by the name of Sylvia Londis?

"A.   Yes, sir.

"Q.   She was a girlfriend of Ronald Nelson, is that correct?

"A.   Yes, sir.

"Q.   Did you ever ask Miss Londis out for a date?

"A.   No, sir.

"Q.   Did you ask any of the ladies up in that Franksville area for a date?

"A.   No, sir.

"Q.   Did you ever call those girls up there dirty whores?

"A.   Never.

"Q.   You never called them dirty whores?

"A.   Never, sir.

"Q.   Did you ever use any profanity or vulgarity to them?

"A.   No, sir."

Further insinuations prompted the inference that testimony would be presented in rebuttal to establish perjury in a separate criminal prosecution, and intimidation of opposing witnesses in the prosecution of Officer Nuccio.

Michael Nuccio testified on direct examination to an incident on June 11, 1967, at Franksville:

"I was on the premises over there having lunch or dinner that night, and Mr. Citron, the owner of Franksville, summoned me to talk to some of the youths in back who were throwing stones and creating a disturbance, and I proceeded to go back there and talk to some of the youths.

"I asked them if they would please leave. They began to leave; and, as one of the boys,—It was a James Keating, I believe it was,—as he was walking across the street, he turned and began to use profanity at me. I went across the street and I took him back to Franksville. I was proceeding to bring him into Franksville to call for a wagon, and told him he was under arrest and at that time he turned and lunged at me. Officer Richard Nuccio was at my side at that time. We tried to subdue him and, at the same time, approximately ten other youths came at us.

"Mr. Echeles: Do you know the names of these other youths who came at you?

"A.   There was a Markko,—I don't believe I know his first name—a Futch,—

"Q.   A fudge?

"A.   Futch, F-u-t-c-h, there was a Steve Austill, Ron Nelson, John Ahrens, I believe it is.

"Q.   Will you look around the courtroom and see if you see John Ahrens in this courtroom?

"A.   Yes, I believe he's sitting in the second or third pew back on the left.   (Indicating.).

* * *

"Q.   Did you see Ahrens with anything in his hand?

"A.   Yes, I did.

"Q.   What did he have in his hand?

"A.   A board."

In cross-examining Officer Michael Nuccio in relationship to this incident, the State continued the tactic of making unsubstantiated insinuations:

"Q.   The only one that was brought to a courtroom was James Keating, is that right?

"A.   No.   There were other youths brought to court.

"Q.   Do you recall throwing Phil Futch into that squad car or squadrol that evening just after he drove up?

"A.   No, I don't recall throwing him into the squad car.

"Q.   Isn't it a fact that he wasn't even present at the time of this alleged incident between you and Mr. Keating?

"A.   He was present.

"Q.   He didn't do anything, though, did he?

"A.   Yes.   He was part of the youths that were involved.

"Q.   Part of what youths that were involved?

"A.   That were involved in the disturbance and a gang of youths, as I stated in my case report, that came at us.

"Q.   Ron Nelson wasn't even present when this thing happened?

"A.   Yes, he was.

"Q.   Why did the captain release him?

"Mr. Echeles: Object, your Honor.

"The Court: Sustained.

"Mr. Tully: Did you ever tell Karen Green that you made a mistake, that John Ahrens was never involved in this situation?

"A.   No, I didn't."

Continuing to cross-examine Michael Nuccio, the State pursued the unsupported insinuation that State's witnesses had been threatened in connection with this case:

"Q.   Since the shooting happened, have you threatened people, to break their arms, as they testified in this case?

"Mr. Echeles: I object, your Honor.

"The Court: Sustained.

"Mr. Tully: Have you ever told Steve Austill that you are going to break his arms, if he testifies in this case?

"A.   No.

"Q.   Were you ever with Kenny South, when he threatened Steven Austill he would break his arms if he testified in this case?

"A.   No.

"Q.   Did you ever pull out your gun on your off duty hours, and point it at any of these people.

"A.   No. I have never had an occasion to."

Officer Kenneth South stated during direct examination that he had never threatened Austill in any manner. Thereupon the State began cross-examination, pursuing the matter of threats and also insinuating that Officer South had told the other State's Attorney on the case that he didn't want to testify in defendant's behalf:

"Q.   Officer South, you would tell us, wouldn't you, sir?

"A.   I beg pardon?

"Q.   You would tell us if you had threatened to break his _____.

"Mr. Echeles: Object to the form of the question.

"The Court: Sustained.

"Q.   Do you recall talking to Mr. Walsh [assistant State's Attorney] Friday evening of last week?

"A.   I had occasion to speak to him at Franksville.

"Q.   Did you tell Mr. Walsh you didn't want to get involved in this case?

"A.   No, I didn't say that to Mr. Walsh."

The cross-examination of defendant was again improper, particularly in relationship to the incident, related by Officer Michael Nuccio, involving a group of youths attacking Michael Nuccio and the defendant:

"Mr. Tully: Have you ever pulled out your gun at the Franksville Restaurant on any occasion other than June 4, 1968?

"A.   Yes, sir.

"Q. When?

"A. After I was struck by the board and the offender was going to strike me again.

"Q. Who was the one with the board?

"A. John Ahrens.

"Q. Didn't you testify against a Mr. Keating, that he had the board?

"A. No, sir.

"Q. Isn't it a fact that the warrant which was issued was issued in error as to the wrong person?

"A. No, sir.

"Q. Do you know where Mr. Keating is at right now?

"A. I believe he is in the Army, sir.

"Q. Isn't it a fact that you, in fact, arrested Mr. Futch that evening, who wasn't even present during that altercation?

"Mr. Echeles: Objection, your Honor, unless he goes on the stand to testify—

"The Court: Sustained.

"Mr. Echeles: Object to the form of the question, your Honor.

"The Court: Sustained.

"Mr. Echeles: Will Mr. Tully testify? I have Mr. Walsh's assurance that Mr. Tully will testify. He withdraws the assurance.

"The Court: Proceed.

"A. Would you repeat that? (Pending question read by reporter.)

"A. I arrested him but he was present in the altercation. You were wrong with your question.

"Mr. Tully: I don't know if I was wrong with the question. Your answer might be wrong.

"Mr. Echeles: Object to arguing with the witness.

"The Court: Proceed."

On August 26, 1968, the defense rested its case at 1:00 P.M. The court recessed until 2:00 P.M. at which time the State put in the testimony of one witness in rebuttal. Following this witness's testimony, the State moved for a continuance on the grounds that additional rebuttal witnesses were not present because they had difficulty attending due to the bus and taxi strikes. Counsel for the defense pointed out that a number of the people the State asked questions about—Weinstein, Futch, Austill, Ahrens—were in the courtroom and would be available as rebuttal witnesses. The State, however, did not call any of them, but pressed for the continuance which was granted and the trial recessed until the following morning. At that time the State indicated it did not plan to call any of the witnesses who were in court and available to be put on the stand the previous day.

At the conclusion of all the evidence the defense moved for a mistrial briefly reciting the State's questions, some of which were herein quoted, noting that there was no rebuttal of the denial of the accusations contained within the questions, and alleging that the sole purpose in asking the questions was to prejudice the court. The trial court responded: "The motion for a mistrial will be denied."

It apparently is the State's position that the above questions were legally improper when asked and that the defendant has waived his objection to their prejudicial effect by failing to object at trial. In the words of the defendant he "is in the unusual position of justifying [this conduct of the prosecutor which] the state seeks not to justify". Defendant urges that the prosecutor's questions relating to the alleged prior threats by him against the decedent were proper at the time they were asked provided the State was ready to prove the threats in the event the witnesses denied the accusations implicit in the State's questions. He cites People v. Slaughter, 29 Ill.2d 384, 390, where this court stated: "Prior threats of an accused to do violence to the person eventually slain have consistently been held to be admissible in evidence as showing malice and criminal intent . . .". (People v. Poland, 22 Ill.2d 175; People v. Lion, 10 Ill.2d 208.) Defendant urges that he is entitled to assume the prosecution would not ask such patently prejudicial questions unless proof of the threats was available, and, therefore, he is under no obligation to object thereto, particularly where he moves for a mistrial as soon as the inability or unwillingness of the State to produce such proof is manifested. With this we agree.

We do not intend this opinion to indicate that no objection should have been made by defendant to any of the testimony herein quoted. The admissibility of portions of the testimony unrelated to threats is at least doubtful and might well have been excluded. We have included portions of it here, however, because it seems to demonstrate an intent on the part of the prosecution to prejudice defendant in the eyes of the court.

The vexing question is whether this pattern of prejudicial and unsupported insinuations which would, without question, necessitate a new trial had this case been heard by a jury, requires the same result in a bench trial. The State calls attention to numerous cases, wherein this court has indicated that it will be presumed that a judge considers only competent and proper evidence in reaching his decision.

* * *

. . . The rule as generally applied is a sound one. But there are, it seems to us, limits to the immunity to improper and prejudicial insinuations which judges are presumed to possess. Stripped of the haze created by the innuendoes, the shooting here was either done by an officer who was the target of a knife being thrown at him by decedent from a distance of 20–30 feet as described by defendant and his witnesses, or it was the wanton killing testified to by the State's witnesses. Where, as here, the guilt of the accused is not manifest, but is dependent upon the degree of credibility accorded by the trier of fact to his testimony and that of the witnesses who testify on his behalf, and there appear in the record substantial numbers of unsupported insinuations which, if considered, could have seriously impeached the credibility of the defendant and his witnesses, and there is no indication of the court's awareness of this impropriety even though it is brought to his attention, it is our opinion that justice and fundamental fairness demand that the defendant be afforded a new trial free from such prejudicial misconduct.

The judgment of the Cook County circuit court is accordingly reversed and the cause remanded for a new trial.

Reversed and remanded.

NOTES

1. The A.B.A. Standards assert that, for either prosecutor or defense counsel, "it is unprofessional conduct to ask a question which implies the existence of a factual predicate for which a good faith belief is lacking". Sections 3–5.7(d) and 4–7.6(d). The evil that the rule is designed to prevent is often characterized as proof by insinuation. The attorney inquires "Didn't you tell Mr. Jones that your previous statement was a pack of lies?" The witness answers "no" while the attorney assumes an incredulous expression. Such tactics are generally disapproved when the attorney has no evidence to support the innuendo. See 6 Wigmore, Evidence § 1808(2) (3rd Ed. 1940). The degree of prejudice caused by such questioning varies with the nature of the innuendo and the context of the case. Questions which imply that the accused committed other crimes are thought particularly damaging. State v. Haney, 219 Minn. 518, 18 N.W.2d 315 (1945). See also Barnes v. United States, 124 U.S.App.D.C. 318, 365 F.2d 509 (1966); Boggs v. State, 268 Ala. 358, 106 So.2d 263 (1958); State v. Jacobs, 94 Ariz. 211, 382 P.2d 683 (1963).

In State v. Yoakum, 37 Wash.2d 137, 222 P.2d 181 (1950), the prosecutor repeatedly questioned the accused as to incriminatory statements allegedly made by him and recorded via a wire recorder prior to trial, quoting extensively from the "record" of such statements. The Supreme Court of Washington remanded for new trial when the prosecutor failed to later prove the statements and have the "record" admitted into evidence.

In Lee Won Sing v. United States, 215 F.2d 68 (D.C.Cir. 1954), the government prosecutor asked a severed codefendant testifying for defendant if it were not a fact that the defendant was giving him $20,000 to "take a plea in this case." The Circuit Court reversed and remanded when the prosecutor made no later effort to prove the assertion and stated that he relied solely upon an anonymous letter received by the police.

The rule does not mean that an attorney must be able to disprove every negative answer he receives while cross-examining a witness. A question may imply a factual predicate and yet not be damaging. Compare "Didn't you tell Mr. Jones that your previous statement was a pack of lies?" with "Didn't you discuss your previous statement with Mr. Jones?" The standard by which the question is judged is, assuming the jury accepts the insinuation as a fact, is the fact damaging to the opposition's case.

American Bar Association Standards Relating To The Prosecution Function And The Defense Function

3–5.7 and 4–7.6   Examination of Witnesses

(a) The interrogation of all witnesses should be conducted fairly, objectively and with due regard for the dignity and legitimate privacy of the witness, and without seeking to intimidate or humiliate the witness unnecessarily. Proper cross-examination can be conducted without violating rules of decorum.

3–5.7

(b) The prosecutor's belief that the witness is telling the truth does not preclude cross-examination, but may affect the method and scope of cross-examination. A prosecutor should not use the power of cross-examination to discredit or undermine a witness if the prosecutor knows the witness is testifying truthfully.

4–7.6

(b) A lawyer's belief or knowledge that the witness is telling the truth does not preclude cross-examination, but should, if possible, be taken into consideration by counsel in conducting the cross-examination.

[Editors' note: The Standards are taken from the 1978 second edition where changes of style were made. The following commentaries, however, are from the original edition since the second edition ones are not yet published.]

Commentary on The Prosecution Standard

a.   Avoiding unnecessary embarrassment or humiliation

The scope of examination has always been subject to control in the court's discretion in order to prevent abuse of witnesses. At one time a privilege to refuse to answer degrading questions was recognized. See 3 Wigmore, Evidence § 781 (1940). Some states retain this privilege in statutes protecting witnesses from "irrelevant, improper or insulting questions, and from harsh or insulting demeanor." Utah Code Ann. § 78–24–11 (1953). See also Mont.Rev.Code § 93–2101–3 (1947). Clearly, "a lawyer should never be unfair or abusive or inconsiderate to adverse witnesses or opposing litigants, or ask any question intended only to insult or degrade the witness." American College of Trial Lawyers, Code of Trial Conduct No. 10(d) (1963). The more difficult issue is the lawyer's duty when the question will yield some benefit to his case but at inordinate cost to the reputation of the witness. Highly experienced trial lawyers consulted by the Advisory Committee agreed that in this situation trial counsel must carefully balance the importance of the evidence in question against the humiliation and disgrace to the witness. Especially in the case of impeaching evidence, where the humiliation it will cause the witness is out of proportion in comparison with its impeachment value, the prosecutor should forego the question. For example, if the rules of evidence in force in the jurisdiction permit impeachment by showing convictions for crimes which do not have a direct bearing on the truth-telling propensities of the witness, the prosecutor should not bring to light a long-forgotten criminal conviction of the witness simply to discredit him.

b. Undermining a truthful witness

A question of long standing and not completely resolved is whether in cross-examination of a witness an advocate should be restrained by his belief that the witness has testified truthfully. Numerous experienced defense counsel of the American, Canadian and British bars, consulted by the Advisory Committee, expressed the view that counsel generally is not permitted to substitute his personal opinion for the available fact-finding processes of the trial and may properly invoke the usual cross-examination technique to test the witness's capacity and opportunity for observation and the ability to recall. However, many lawyers expressed the view that the manner and tenor of cross-examination ought to be restricted where examining counsel has knowledge of the truthfulness of the testimony given by the witness.

There was a consensus among the experts consulted, and one shared by the Advisory Committee, that the difficult and delicate decisions presented by the wide range and variety of situations cannot be made the subject of rigid standards. There was general agreement that cross-examination is perhaps the best known human device for ascertaining truth and revealing falsehood. Essentially an "invention" of the common law system, the power to cross-examine adverse witnesses is a monopoly of lawyers and ought not be misused for destroying known truth. The power to cross-examine is a power vested in a lawyer by virtue of his being an officer of the court. It is a power shared by the court itself but not often used. Strong arguments were advanced by highly skilled and experienced trial advocates that if the cross-examiner knows that the testimony of a particular witness is true, he may not properly use this "monopoly power" he possesses as an officer of the court for a purpose alien to its avowed objective by using it to destroy or undermine truth. This is the view shared widely by most British barristers and judges. Some, however, take the view that within limits a cross-examiner may employ conventional cross-examination techniques notwithstanding he knows that the testimony is true. Some also pointed out that the problem rarely arises and that when it does a lawyer is ill-advised to try to undermine a known truth-teller. A large number of trial counsel consulted agreed that no lawyer is under any duty to compromise his conscience or professional honor to use the powerful tool of cross-examination to defeat known truth. All experts, American, British and Canadian, agreed that it is improper to seek to destroy a witness's credibility with an ancient episode or long-forgotten conviction when the injury to the witness heavily outweighs any reasonable relationship to present veracity.

Commentary on Defense Standard

a. Character and scope of direct and cross-examination

The ethic of our legal tradition has long recognized that there are limitations on the manner in which witnesses should be examined beyond those which are contained in the rules of evidence. The Code of Professional Responsibility forbids a lawyer to "[a]sk any question that he has no reasonable basis to believe is relevant to the case and that is intended to degrade a witness or other person." ABA Code DR 7–106(C)(2). See also id., EC 7–25. "A lawyer should never be unfair or abusive or inconsiderate to adverse witnesses or opposing litigants, or ask any question intended only to insult or degrade the witness." American College of Trial Lawyers, Code of Trial Conduct 10(d) (1963). "A lawyer should not ask questions which affect the witness' credibility only by attacking his character, except those encompassed in recognized impeachment procedures." Id., No. 10(e). Some states have by statute guaranteed "the right of a witness to be protected from irrelevant, improper or insulting questions, and from harsh or insulting demeanor. . . . ." Utah Code Ann. § 78–24–11 (1953). See also Mont.Rev.Code 93–2101–3 (1947). Another provides that it is the duty of an attorney "to abstain from offensive personality and to advance no fact prejudicial to the honor or reputation of a witness unless required by the justice of the cause with which he is charged." Ariz.Rev.Stat.Ann. § 32–363 (1956).

An eminent British barrister has spoken on the subject in these terms:

> The right of cross examination is important: it is one of the things which distinguishes the procedures of trial in the common law countries from those derived from Roman law and I think distinguishes it to the advantage of our system. But it is a right easily abused. One has always to remember that its object is not to examine crossly, as Mr. Baron Alderson put it; not to blackguard the witness; not to bring out unhappy or discreditable things there may have been in the witnesses' past unless they have a clear and direct bearing on the witnesses' credibility in the instant case.

Shawcross, The Functions and Responsibilities of an Advocate, 13 Record of N.Y.C.B.A. 483, 493–94 (1958). American lawyers consulted by the Committee concurred generally in this view of the limits of propriety which govern the examination of witnesses. In their opinion, the lawyer must always exercise discretion in determining to what extent the damage done to the reputation of a witness is justified by the contribution which a particular line of questioning may make to the truth-finding function of the trial.

b. Undermining a truthful witness

The mere fact that defense counsel can, by use of impeachment, impair or destroy the credibility of an adverse witness does not impose on him a duty to do so. Cross-examination and impeachment are legal tools which are a monopoly of licensed lawyers, given for the high purpose of exposing falsehood, not to destroy truth or the reputation of a known truthful witness. Rules cannot be formulated to cover every situation but some examples may be useful. A prosecution witness, for example, may testify in a manner which confirms precisely what the defense lawyer has learned from his own client and has substantiated by investigation. But defense counsel may believe that the temperament, personality or inexperience of the witness provide an opportunity, by adroit cross-examination, to confuse the witness and undermine his testimony in the eyes of the jury. A number of leading American and British trial lawyers consulted by the Committee believed that because lawyers are afforded a monopoly of the tools of cross-examination and impeachment in order to expose falsehood it is not proper to use those tools to destroy truth, or to seek to confuse or embarrass the witness under these circumstances.

Another example of a situation where restraint is called for would be where a witness whose testimony the lawyer believes to be truthful is subject to impeachment by revealing to the jury that the witness was convicted of a crime many years earlier. It was agreed that the use of conventional methods of impeachment against a witness who had testified truthfully so undermines the administration of justice that it should be avoided. The reluctance of citizens to testify grows in part from the fear of being humiliated in this manner. Moreover, usually it is tactically unsound as well, since the jury is likely to recognize the undue humiliation and to react adversely to the lawyer for engaging in it and even against the client.

There is added a public policy factor underlying restraint in use of impeachment powers vested in a lawyer. The policy of the law is to encourage witnesses to come forward and give evidence in litigation. If witnesses are subjected to needless humiliation when they testify, the existing human tendency to avoid "becoming involved" will be increased. One of the experienced trial lawyers who consulted with this Committee told of an occasion when a key witness who was under subpoena came to him and asked if the opposing counsel could inquire concerning a prior criminal conviction. Upon being answered in the affirmative, he said he had entered a guilty plea to a non-violent felony committed 30 years before when he was a young man. At the time he was called as a witness, he had become a prosperous and respected business man. He advised the lawyer that in the circumstances his memory concerning the current episode would "fail" him absent agreement from opposing counsel that he would not be impeached by the old conviction. Fortunately such agreement was forthcoming from a lawyer who recognized the limits placed on him and the testimony of the witness was secured.

Since the standards discussed above almost invariably involve matters which are subjective, they are addressed essentially to professional conscience and honor. While largely unenforceable, the limits which the best professional traditions place on an advocate are not wholly beyond reach of a special kind of enforcement at the hands of the lawyer's peers and of judges. Experienced advocates and judges can, over a period of time, identify the lawyer who practices in conformity with high standards as distinguished from those who do not. This is illustrated in the episode just described; it was cited by a trial judge of long experience and related to an event which occurred in his practice 30 or more years before. The lawyer who agreed that he should not and would not impeach the witness with what he considered an irrelevant criminal conviction stands out in the memory of his former adversary. That lawyer was not motivated by reasons of "policy," but the episode tends to suggest that his adherence to principle was indeed a sound policy which earned him a high reputation in the profession. Such a lawyer enters every courtroom with an added dimension which inevitably operates to the benefit of his clients.

[Editors' note: The original defense standard closely resembled the prosecution standard. The rationale for change was expressed in the Tentative Draft, Second Edition:

> Original paragraph (b) provided that defense counsel "should not misuse the power of cross-examination or impeachment by employing it to discredit or undermine a witness if he knows the witness is testifying truthfully." This standard has been changed to make clear that it is permissible, if necessary, for defense counsel to cross-examine vigorously witnesses who are believed or known to be testifying truthfully. There are some cases where, unless counsel challenges the prosecution's known truthful witnesses, there will be no opposition to the prosecution's evidence and the defendant will be denied an effective defense. However, lawyers are encouraged in paragraph (b) to take into consideration in conducting cross-examination the fact that the state's witness is testifying truthfully.

> . . . [T]here unquestionably are many cases where defense counsel cannot provide the accused with a defense at all if counsel is precluded from engaging in vigorous cross-examination of witnesses either believed or known to have testified truthfully. For example, where the defendant has admitted guilt to the lawyer and does not plan to testify, and the lawyer simply intends to put the state to its proof and raise a reasonable doubt, skillful cross-examination of the prosecution's witnesses is essential. Indeed, were counsel in this circumstance to forgo vigorous cross-examination of the prosecution's witnesses, counsel would violate the clear duty of zealous representation that is owed to the client. Justice White, in a 1967 Supreme Court opinion, ad-

dressed the sometimes professional obligation of defense counsel to impeach truthful witnesses:

> [A]bsent a voluntary plea of guilty, we . . . insist that [defense counsel] defend his client whether he is innocent or guilty. The State has the obligation to present the evidence. Defense counsel need present nothing, even if he knows what the truth is. He need not furnish any witnesses to the police, or reveal any confidences of his client, or furnish any other information to help the prosecution's case. If he can confuse a witness, even a truthful one, or make him appear at a disadvantage, unsure or indecisive, that will be his normal course. Our interest in not convicting the innocent permits counsel to put the State to its proof, to put the State's case in the worst possible light, *regardless* of what he thinks or knows to be *the truth*. Undoubtedly there are some limits which defense counsel must observe but more often than not, defense counsel will cross-examine a prosecution witness, and impeach him if he can, even if he thinks the witness is telling the truth, just as he will attempt to destroy a witness who he thinks is lying. In this respect, as part of our modified adversary system and as part of the duty imposed on the most honorable defense counsel, we countenance or require conduct which in many instances has little, if any, relation to the search for truth.

NOTES

1. Are the A.B.A. Standards "practical" in the sense that lawyers may be expected to follow them? Consider the problem of the overworked prosecutor and public defender in a large urban jurisdiction. Neither has much time to prepare cases or to consult with witnesses. Occasionally, such attorneys begin impanelling one jury while the jury in the preceding case is still deliberating on its verdict. Can these lawyers fairly be expected to make delicate judgments about whether cross examination is "unnecessarily" intimidating or humiliating? Public defenders with large caseloads often have cross examination as their only defense tool; can they worry about its overuse? Is the potential penalty of alienating the trier of fact by abusive cross examination a sufficient check on the overly aggressive lawyer?

The A.B.A. Commentary recites the case of a lawyer who agreed not to use an old conviction against a crucial opposition witness even though the use of the conviction would cause the witness's memory to "fail". Did the lawyer fulfil his duty to his client? Does the lawyer have any other duty? The Commentary speaks also of the high reputation of a lawyer who exercises restraint and of the benefit his clients will accrue from his stature. Is it a proper function of an attorney to use his personal reputation to benefit his client? What value does this reputation have when the case is tried before a jury from which, in most cases, people who know the lawyers are excluded?

On the other hand, in revising the defense standard in 1978, the A.B.A. says it is "permissible, if necessary" to use the power of cross-examination against witnesses known to be testifying truthfully. Is this a defensible principle? Is there any tactic whose use could not be defended on the ground that it was "necessary"?

2. When the government calls an informer as a witness, the defense is entitled to cross-examination concerning the informer's true name and address at least where the testimony is uncorroborated. Smith v. Illinois, 390 U.S. 129, 88 S.Ct. 748 (1968). The rationale is that the defense is entitled to the "identification of the witness with his environment". Presumably defense counsel may make investigation into the witness' reputation, character, etc. The rule in *Smith* is not absolute and several courts have upheld the refusal to allow inquiries, particularly as to the witness' present home address, where there is some basis for believing the witness would be endangered if his present whereabouts are learned by the accused. McGrath v. Vinzant, 528 F.2d 681 (1st Cir. 1976). See Comment, "The Informer Privilege: What's In A Name?", 64 J.Crim.L.C. 56 (1973). Of what value to the defense is an informer's address at the time of trial or his new name if the informer has moved from the address where he resided at the time of the crime and assumed a new name? If the witness has moved recently will the defense be able to make meaningful inquiries as to character and reputation in a new neighborhood? Assume defense counsel has no intention of making investigations but knows that pressing for the information may shake the composure of the witness, is it proper for counsel to cross-examine the witness about his present address? If it is proper to do so, will the witness' reluctance to reveal his address or the prosecution's objections to the question lead the jury to believe the prosecution is improperly hiding something or that the accused is a dangerous man?

3. What of the "rape shield" laws precluding cross-examination of a complaining witness about past sexual history? State ex rel. Pope v. Superior Court, 113 Ariz. 22, 545 P.2d 946 (1976); McLean v. United States, 377 A.2d 74 (D.C.Ct.App.1977). About three fourths of the states have enacted some form of "rape shield" law. See 1 Wigmore, Evidence, § 62, n. 2a (3rd Ed. 1940) (1979 Pocket Supp. p. 185–86).

2. CROSS–EXAMINING THE DEFENDANT

DOYLE v. OHIO

Supreme Court of the United States, 1976.
426 U.S. 610, 96 S.Ct. 2240.

MR. JUSTICE POWELL delivered the opinion of the Court.

The question . . . is whether a state prosecutor may seek to impeach a defendant's exculpatory story, told for the first time at trial, by cross-examining the defendant about his failure to have told the story after receiving *Miranda* warnings at the time of his arrest. We conclude that use of the defendant's post-arrest silence in this manner violates due process, and therefore reverse the convictions of both petitioners.

I.

Petitioners Doyle and Wood were arrested together and charged with selling 10 pounds of marihuana to a local narcotics bureau informant. They were convicted in . . . separate trials held about one week apart. The evidence at their trials was identical in all material respects.

The State's witnesses sketched a picture of a routine marihuana transaction. William Bonnell, a well-known "street person" with a long criminal record, offered to assist the local narcotics investigation unit in setting up drug "pushers" in return for support in his efforts to receive lenient treatment in his latest legal problems. The narcotics agents agreed. A short time later, Bonnell advised the unit that he had arranged a "buy" of 10 pounds of marihuana and needed $1,750 to pay for it. Since the banks were closed and time was short, the agents were able to collect only $1,320. Bonnell took this money and left for the rendezvous, under surveillance by four narcotics agents in two cars. As planned, he met petitioners in a bar in Dover, Ohio. From there, he and petitioner Wood drove in Bonnell's pick-up truck to the nearby town of New Philadelphia, Ohio, while petitioner Doyle drove off to obtain the marihuana and then meet them at a prearranged location in New Philadelphia. The narcotics agents followed the Bonnell truck. When Doyle arrived at Bonnell's waiting truck in New Philadelphia, the two vehicles proceeded to a parking lot where the transaction took place. Bonnell left in his truck, and Doyle and Wood departed in Doyle's car. They quickly discovered that they had been paid some $430 less than the agreed-upon price, and began circling the neighborhood looking for Bonnell. They were stopped within minutes by New Phildelphia police acting on radioed instructions from the narcotics agents. One of those agents, Kenneth Beamer, arrived on the scene promptly, arrested petitioners, and gave them *Miranda* warnings. A search of the car, authorized by warrant, uncovered the $1,320.

At both trials, defense counsel's cross-examination of the participating narcotics agents was aimed primarily at establishing that due to a limited view of the parking lot, none of them had seen the actual transaction but had seen only Bonnell standing next to Doyle's car with a package under his arm, presumably after the transaction.[1] Each petitioner took the stand at his trial and admitted practically everything about the State's case except the most crucial point: who was selling marihuana to whom. According to petitioners, Bonnell

---

1. Defense counsel's efforts were not totally successful. One of the four narcotics agents testified at both trials that he had seen the package passed through the window of Doyle's car to Bonnell. In an effort to impeach that testimony, defense counsel played a tape of the preliminary hearing at which the same agent had testified only to seeing the package under Bonnell's arm. The agent did not retract his trial testimony, and both he and the prosecutor explained the apparent inconsistency by noting that the examination at the preliminary hearing had not focused upon whether anyone had seen the package pass to Bonnell.

had framed them. The arrangement had been for Bonnell to sell Doyle 10 pounds of marihuana. Doyle had left the Dover bar for the purpose of borrowing the necessary money, but while driving by himself had decided that he only wanted one or two pounds instead of the agreed-upon 10 pounds. When Bonnell reached Doyle's car in the New Philadelphia parking lot, with the marihuana under his arm, Doyle tried to explain his change of mind. Bonnell grew angry, threw the $1,320 into Doyle's car, and took all 10 pounds of marihuana back to his truck. The ensuing chase was the effort of Wood and Doyle to catch Bonnell to find out what the $1,320 was all about.

Petitioners' explanation of the events presented some difficulty for the prosecution, as it was not entirely implausible and there was little if any direct evidence to contradict it. As part of a wide-ranging cross-examination for impeachment purposes, and in an effort to undercut the explanation the prosecutor asked each petitioner at his respective trial why he had not told the frame-up story to agent Beamer when he arrested petitioners. In the first trial, that of petitioner Wood, the following colloquy occurred:

"Q.   [by the prosecutor] Mr. Beamer did arrive on the scene?

"A: [by Wood] Yes, he did.

"Q: And I assume you told him all about what happened to you?

*   *   *

"A: No.

"Q: You didn't tell Mr. Beamer?

*   *   *

"A: No.

"Q: You didn't tell Mr. Beamer this guy put $1,300 in your car?

*   *   *

"A: No, sir.

"Q: And we can't understand any reason why anyone would put money in your car and you were chasing him around town and trying to give it back?

*   *   *

"A: I didn't understand that.

"Q. You mean you didn't tell him that?

*   *   *

"A: Tell him what?

*   *   *

"Q: Mr. Wood, if that is all you had to do with this and you are innocent, when Mr. Beamer arrived on the scene why didn't you tell him?

*   *   *

"Q: But in any event you didn't bother to tell Mr. Beamer anything about this?

"A: No, sir."

Defense counsel's timely objections to each of the prosecutor's questions were overruled. The cross-examination of petitioner Doyle at his trial contained a similar exchange, and again defense counsel's timely objections were overruled.

* * *

II.

The State pleads necessity as justification for the prosecutor's action in these cases. It argues that the discrepancy between an exculpatory story at trial and silence at time of arrest gives rise to an inference that the story was fabricated somewhere along the way, perhaps to fit within the seams of the State's case as it was developed at pretrial hearings. Noting that the prosecution usually has little else with which to counter such an exculpatory story, the State seeks only the right to cross-examine a defendant as to post-arrest silence for the limited purpose of impeachment. In support of its position the State emphasizes the importance of cross-examination in general . . . and relies upon those cases in which this Court has permitted use for impeachment purposes of post-arrest statements that were inadmissible as evidence of guilt because of an officer's failure to follow *Miranda's* dictates. Harris v. New York, 401 U.S. 221, 91 S.Ct. 643 (1971) . . . .. Thus, although the State does not suggest petitioners' silence could be used as evidence of guilt, it contends that the need to present to the jury all information relevant to the truth of petitioners' exculpatory story fully justifies the cross-examination that is at issue.

Despite the importance of cross-examination,[2] we have concluded that the *Miranda* decision compels rejection of the State's position. The warnings mandated by that case, as a prophylactic means of safeguarding Fifth Amendment rights, . . . require that a person taken into custody be advised immediately that he has the right to remain silent, that anything he says may be used against him, and that he has a right to retained or appointed counsel before submitting to interrogation. Silence in the wake of these warnings may be nothing more than the arrestee's exercise of these *Miranda* rights. Thus, every post-arrest silence is insolubly ambiguous because of what the State is required to advise the person arrested. . . . Moreover, while it is true that the *Miranda* warnings contain no express assurance that silence will carry no penalty, such assurance is implicit to any person who receives the warnings. In such circumstances, it would be fundamentally unfair and a deprivation of due process to al-

---

2. We recognize, of course, that unless prosecutors are allowed wide leeway in the scope of impeachment cross-examination some defendants would be able to frustrate the truth-seeking function of a trial by presenting tailored defenses insulated from effective challenge. . . .

low the arrested person's silence to be used to impeach an explanation subsequently offered at trial. Mr. Justice White, concurring in the judgment in United States v. Hale, 422 U.S., at 182–183, 95 S.Ct., at 2139, put it very well:

> ". . . when a person under arrest is informed as *Mi-randa* requires, that he may remain silent, that anything he says may be used against him, and that he may have an attorney if he wishes, it seems to me that it does not comport with due process to permit the prosecution during the trial to call attention to his silence at the time of arrest and to insist that because he did not speak about the facts of the case at that time, as he was told he need not do, an unfavorable inference might be drawn as to the truth of his trial testimony. . . . Surely Hale was not informed here that his silence, as well as his words, could be used against him at trial. Indeed, anyone would reasonably conclude from *Miranda* warnings that this would not be the case."

We hold that the use for impeachment purposes of petitioners' silence, at the time of arrest and after receiving *Miranda* warnings, violated the Due Process Clause of the Fourteenth Amendment.[3] The State has not claimed that such use in the circumstances of this case might have been harmless error. Accordingly, petitioners' convictions are reversed and their causes remanded to the state courts for further proceedings not inconsistent with this opinion.

* * *

MR. JUSTICE STEVENS, with whom MR. JUSTICE BLACKMUN and MR. JUSTICE REHNQUIST join, dissenting.

* * *

I.

The Court's due process rationale has some of the characteristics of an estoppel theory. If (a) the defendant is advised that he may remain silent, and (b) he does remain silent, then we (c) presume that his decision was made in reliance on the advice, and (d) conclude that it is unfair in certain cases, . . . to use his silence to impeach his trial testimony. The key to the Court's analysis is apparently a concern that the *Miranda* warning, which is intended to increase the probability that a person's response to police questioning will be intelligent and voluntary, will actually be deceptive unless we require the State to honor an unstated promise not to use the accused's silence against him.

---

3. It goes almost without saying that the fact of post-arrest silence could be used by the prosecution to contradict a defendant who testifies to an exculpatory version of events and claims to have told the police the same version upon arrest. In that situation the fact of earlier silence would not be used to impeach the exculpatory story, but rather to challenge the defendant's testimony as to his behavior following arrest. . . .

In my judgment there is nothing deceptive or prejudicial to the defendant in the *Miranda* warning. Nor do I believe that the fact that such advice was given to the defendant lessens the probative value of his silence, or makes the prosecutor's cross-examination about his silence any more unfair than if he had received no such warning.

This is a case in which the defendants' silence at the time of their arrest was graphically inconsistent with their trial testimony that they were the unwitting victims of a "frame" in which the police did not participate. If defendants had been framed, their failure to mention that fact at the time of their arrest is almost inexplicable; for that reason, under accepted rules of evidence, their silence is tantamount to a prior inconsistent statement and admissible for purposes of impeachment.

Indeed, there is irony in the fact that the *Miranda* warning provides the only plausible explanation for their silence. If it were the true explanation, I should think that they would have responded to the questions on cross-examination about why they had remained silent by stating that they relied on their understanding of the advice given by the arresting officers. Instead, however, they gave quite a different jumble of responses.[4] Those responses negate the Court's presumption that their silence was induced by reliance on deceptive advice.

---

4. Petitioner Doyle gave the following testimony on direct and cross-examination at his trial:

"Q. [By defense counsel.] And you were placed under arrest at that time?

"A. [By Doyle.] Yes. I asked what for and he said,—'For the sale of marijuana.' I told him,—I didn't know what he was talking about.

* * *

"Q. [By the prosecutor.] As a matter of fact, if I recall your testimony correctly, you said instead of protesting your innocence, as you do today, you said in response to a question of Mr. Beamer,—'I don't know what you are talking about.'

"A. [By Doyle.] I believe what I said,—'What's this all about?' If I remember, that's the only thing I said.

"Q. You testified on direct.

"A. If I did, then I didn't understand.

"Q. [sic] I was questioning, you know, what it was about. That's what I didn't know. I knew that I was trying to buy, which was wrong, but I didn't know what was going on. I don't know that Bill Bonnell was trying to frame me, or what-have-you.

* * *

At Wood's trial, Doyle gave a somewhat different explanation of his silence at the time of arrest:

* * *

"A. The police officers said they stopped us for a red light. I wanted to get my hands on Bill Bonnell.

* * *

"Q. Why didn't you tell the police that Bill Bonnell just set you up?

"A. Because I would rather have my own hands on him.

* * *

"Q. So on the night of April 29 you felt that you were being framed like you are being framed today?

"A. I was so confused that night, the night of the arrest.

* * *

"Q. You didn't talk to a soul about how rotten it was because you were framed?

* * *

"A. I will answer the question, sir, the best I can. I didn't know what to say. I was stunned about what was going on and I was asked questions and I answered the questions as simply as I could because I didn't have nobody there to help me answer the questions.

* * *

Since the record requires us to put to one side the Court's presumption that the defendants' silence was the product of reliance on the *Miranda* warning, the Court's entire due process rationale collapses. For without reliance on the waiver, the case is no different than if no warning had been given, and nothing in the Court's opinion suggests that there would be any unfairness in using petitioners' prior inconsistent silence for impeachment purposes in such a case.

Indeed, as a general proposition, if we assume the defendant's silence would be admissible for impeachment purposes if no *Miranda* warning had been given, I should think that the warning would have a tendency to salvage the defendant's credibility as a witness. If the defendant is a truthful witness, and if his silence is the consequence of his understanding of the *Miranda* warning, he may explain that fact when he is on the stand. Even if he is untruthful, the availability of that explanation puts him in a better position than if he had received no warning. In my judgment, the risk that a truthful defendant will be deceived by the *Miranda* warning and also will be unable to explain his honest misunderstanding is so much less than the risk that exclusion of the evidence will merely provide a shield for perjury that I cannot accept the Court's due process rationale.

Accordingly, if we assume that the use of a defendant's silence for impeachment purposes would be otherwise unobjectionable, I find no merit in the notion that he is denied due process of law because he received a *Miranda* warning.

II.

Petitioners argue that the State violated their Fifth Amendment privilege against self-incrimination by asking the jury to draw an inference of guilt from their constitutionally protected silence. They challenge both the prosecutor's cross-examination and his closing argument.

Petitioners claim that the cross-examination was improper because it referred to their silence at the time of their arrest, to their failure to testify at the preliminary hearing, and to their failure to reveal the "frame" prior to trial. Their claim applies to the testimony of each defendant at his own trial . . . . .

In support of their objections to the cross-examination about their silence at the time of arrest, petitioners primarily rely on the statement in Miranda v. Arizona, 384 U.S. 436, 86 S.Ct. 1602, that the prosecution may not use at trial the fact that the defendant stood mute or claimed the privilege in the face of accusations during custodial interrogation. There are two reasons why that statement does not adequately support petitioners argument.

First, it is not accurate to say that the petitioners "stood mute or claimed the privilege in the face of accusations." Neither petitioner claimed the privilege and petitioner Doyle did not even remain silent. The case is not one in which a description of the actual conversation between the defendants and the police would give rise to any inference of guilt if it were not so flagrantly inconsistent with their trial testimony. Rather than a claim of privilege, we simply have a failure to advise the police of a "frame" at a time when it most surely would have been mentioned if petitioners' trial testimony were true. That failure gave rise to an inference of guilt only because it belied their trial testimony.

Moreover, Chief Justice Warren, the author of the Court's opinion in *Miranda*, joined the opinion in Walder v. United States, 347 U.S. 62, 74 S.Ct. 354, which squarely held that a valid constitutional objection to the admissibility of evidence as part of the Government's case-in-chief did not bar the use of that evidence to impeach the defendant's trial testimony. The availability of an objection to the affirmative use of improper evidence does not provide the defendant "with a shield against contradiction of his untruths." . . . The need to ensure the integrity of the truth-determining function of the adversary trial process has provided the predicate for an unbroken line of decisions so holding.

Although I have no doubt concerning the propriety of the cross-examination about petitioners' failure to mention the purported "frame" at the time of their arrest, a more difficult question is presented by their objection to the questioning about their failure to testify at the preliminary hearing and their failure generally to mention the "frame" before trial.[5] Unlike the failure to make the kind of spontaneous comment that discovery of a "frame" would be expected to prompt, there is no significant inconsistency between petitioners' trial testimony and their adherence to counsel's advice not to take the stand at the preliminary hearing; moreover, the decision not to divulge their defense prior to trial is probably attributable to counsel rather than to petitioners. Nevertheless, unless and until this Court overrules Raffel v. United States, 271 U.S. 494, 46 S.Ct. 566, I think a state court is [6] free to regard the defendant's decision to take the

---

5. Under Ohio law, the preliminary hearing determines only whether the defendant should be held for trial. The prosecution need establish, at most, that a crime has been committed and that there is "probable and reasonable cause" to hold the defendant for trial, and the court need only find "substantial credible evidence" of the charge against the defendant. Ohio Rev.Code Ann. §§ 2937.12, 2937.-13 (Supp.1973). Indeed, if a defendant has been indicted, no hearing need be held. State v. Morris, 42 Ohio St.2d 307, 326, 329 N.E.2d 85, 97 (1975). Defense counsel thus will have no incentive to divulge the defendant's case at the preliminary hearing if the prosecution has presented substantial evidence of guilt. Since that was the case here, no significant impeaching inference may be drawn from petitioners' silence at that proceeding.

Petitioners' failure to refer to the "frame" at any time between arrest and trial is somewhat more probative; for if the "frame" story were true, one would have expected counsel to try to persuade the prosecution to dismiss the charges in advance of trial.

6. *Raffel* was the last decision of this Court to address the constitutionality of admitting evidence of a defendant's prior silence to impeach his testimony upon direct examination. Raffel had been charged with conspiracy to violate the National Prohibition Act. An agent testified at his first trial that he had admitted ownership of a drinking place; Raffel did not take the stand. The trial ended in a hung jury, and upon retrial, the agent testified as before. Raffel elected to testify and denied making

stand as a waiver of his objection to the use of his failure to testify at an earlier proceeding or his failure to offer his version of the events prior to trial.

NOTES

1. A defendant may, of course, open the door to inquiry about his failure to tell his story the first time he had a chance to do so.

In one case the defendant himself brought out his refusal on direct examination and it was held that the prosecution could then cross-examine as to why he did not turn himself in or assert self defense then. People v. Shaugar, 29 Mich.App. 139, 185 N.W.2d 178 (1970). See also Davis v. State, 501 P.2d 1026 (Alaska 1972) and United States v. Mitchell, 457 F.2d 513 (6th Cir. 1972) (defense asked why there was not further investigation after arrest, explanation was lack of exculpatory statement).

There have been cases in which defendant opened the door to evidence of refusal to speak by claiming that he tried to tell the police his story and was not allowed to do so. See State v. McCaine, 460 S.W.2d 618 (Mo.1970); United States v. Blalock, 564 F.2d 1180 (5th Cir. 1977) (claim by accused that he cooperated with the police opens him to inquiry about prior refusal to speak). Compare People v. Perez, 66 Mich.App. 685, 239 N.W.2d 432 (1976) (accused who claims he can't remember whether or not he gave a statement does not open the door).

2. What if the defendant did make a statement to the police and he testifies in a similar fashion at trial but gives additional, important information he omitted from his police statement. May he be impeached by his omission. The general answer is yes. An omission from a statement is not equated with silence in the face of an accusation. Martin v. United States, 400 F.2d 149 (9th Cir. 1968); United States v. Turner, 551 F.2d 780 (8th Cir. 1977); State v. Osborne, 50 Ohio St.2d 211, 364 N.E.2d 216, 4 O.O.3d 406 (1977). Silence may also be admissible when it is part of a larger occurrence, i. e. failure, as opposed to refusal, to answer one question out of several asked and answered. United States v. Lorenzo, 570 F.2d 294 (9th Cir. 1978); United States v. Ford, 563 F.2d 1366 (9th Cir. 1977). See also United States v. Mitchell, 558 F.2d 1332 (8th Cir. 1977) (proper to admit

the statement, but he was cross-examined on his failure to testify in the first trial. This Court held that the evidence was admissible because Raffel had completely waived the privilege against self-incrimination by deciding to testify.

Subsequent cases, decided in the exercise of this Court's supervisory powers, have diminished the force of *Raffel* in the federal courts. United States v. Hale, 422 U.S. 171, 95 S.Ct. 2133. Stewart v. United States, 366 U.S. 1, 81 S.Ct. 941. Grunewald v. United States, 353 U.S. 391, 77 S.Ct. 963. All three of these cases held that the defendant's prior silence or prior claim of the privilege was inadmissible for purposes of impeachment; all three distinguished *Raffel* on the ground that the Court there assumed that the defendant's prior silence was significantly inconsistent with his testimony on direct examination. Hale, supra, 422 U.S., at 175–176, 95 S.Ct., at 2136–2137; Stewart, supra, 366 U.S., at 5–7, 81 S.Ct., at 943–944; Grunewald, supra, 353 U.S., at 418–424, 77 S.Ct., at 981–984. Two of the three cases relied upon the need to protect the defendant's exercise of the privilege against self-incrimination from unwarranted inferences of guilt, a rationale that is not easily reconciled with the reasoning in *Raffel* that the decision to testify constitutes a complete waiver of the protection afforded by the privilege. Compare Hale, supra, 422 U.S., at 180, 95 S.Ct., at 2138 and n. 7, and Grunewald, supra, 353 U.S., at 423–424, 77 S.Ct., at 983–984, with *Raffel*, 271 U.S., at 499, 46 S.Ct., at 568.

silence in the face of proof that prior statement of accused was false). But see People v. Savala, 10 Cal.App.3d 958, 89 Cal.Rptr. 475 (1970); Younie v. State, 272 Md. 233, 322 A.2d 211 (1974).

3. A troublesome question has been whether certain evidence implies that defendant exercised his right to silence. In State v. Beck, 289 Minn. 287, 183 N.W.2d 781 (1971), an officer testified that after arrest he warned the defendant, the officer then said nothing further on the subject. The court held that despite the absence of any direct testimony concerning refusal, the evidence implied the existence of a refusal to speak and was improper.

In United States v. Cook, 432 F.2d 1093 (7th Cir. 1970), the court rejected an argument that, after completion of a lengthy interrogation, evidence that defendant asked and was allowed to leave constituted a reference to an assertion of the right to silence. In State v. Stark, 459 S.W.2d 249 (Mo.1970), it was held that an officer who testified that he interviewed defendant and that after the interview was over defendant said nothing more did not thereby refer to an exercise of the right to silence. In State v. Finn, 111 Ariz. 271, 528 P.2d 615 (1974), it was held that the phrase "I would be crazy to tell you that" was not an assertion of rights. Also see United States v. Warren, 578 F.2d 1058 (5th Cir. 1978) (proper to show that accused told his companions to be silent) and compare Commonwealth v. Cobb, —— Mass. ——, 373 N.E.2d 1145 (1978) (improper to show accused said "what can I say?" in response to inquiry about location of a weapon).

GORDON v. UNITED STATES

United States Court of Appeals, 1967.
127 U.S.App.D.C. 343, 383 F.2d 936, cert. denied 1968, 390 U.S. 1029, 88 S.Ct. 1421.

BURGER, CIRCUIT JUDGE.

Appellant was convicted of robbery and assault with a dangerous weapon. . . .

On this appeal only one issue raised by Appellant bears comment. Appellant claims that the District Court Judge abused the discretion vested in him by Luck v. United States, 121 U.S.App.D.C. 151, 348 F.2d 763 (1965), when he permitted the government to impeach Appellant's testimony by showing prior convictions. . . .

Because of the direct conflict in the evidence the verdict necessarily turned on how the jury resolved the credibility contest between the complainant and the defendant. Appellant's argument now is that while it was appropriate for him to impeach the complaining witness with a prior criminal record [for larceny] it was improper to allow impeachment of his own credibility by asking him about his criminal convictions. . . .

The rationale of our *Luck* opinion is important; it recognized that a showing of prior convictions can have genuine probative value on the issue of credibility, but that because of the potential for prejudice, the receiving of such convictions as impeachment was discretionary. The defendant who has a criminal record may ask the court to weigh the probative value of the convictions as to the credibility against the degree of prejudice which the revelation of his past crimes would cause; and he may ask the court to consider whether it is more important for the jury to hear his story than to know about prior convictions in relation to his credibility. We contemplated the possibility of allowing some convictions to be shown and some excluded; examples are to be found in those which are remote and those which have no direct bearing on veracity, and those which because of the peculiar circumstances at hand might better be excluded. The *Luck* opinion contemplated an on-the-record consideration by the trial judge whose action would be reviewable only for abuse of discretion, and that once the exercise of discretion appeared, the trial court's action be "accorded a respect appropriately reflective of the inescapable remoteness of appellate review." This is a recognition that the cold record on appeal cannot present all facets and elements which the trial judge must weigh in striking the balance.

Luck also contemplated that it was for the defendant to present to the trial court sufficient reasons for withholding past convictions from the jury in the face of a statute which makes such convictions admissible. The underlying assumption was that prior convictions would ordinarily be admissible unless this burden is met. "The trial court is not *required* to allow impeachment by prior conviction every time a defendant takes the stand in his own defense."

The standard to be applied by the District Judge was stated in terms of whether he "believes the prejudicial effect of impeachment far outweighs the probative relevance of the prior conviction to the issue of credibility." The impact of criminal convictions will often be damaging to an accused and it is admittedly difficult to restrict its impact, by cautionary instructions, to the issue of credibility. The test of *Luck*, however, is that to bar them as impeachment the court must find that the prejudice must "far outweigh" the probative relevance to credibility, or that even if relevant the "cause of truth would be helped more by letting the jury hear the defendant's story than by the defendant's foregoing that opportunity because of the fear of prejudice founded upon a prior conviction."

The burden of persuasion in this regard is on the accused; and, once the issue is raised, the District Court should make an inquiry, allowing the accused an oportunity to show why judicial discretion should be exercised in favor of exclusion of the criminal record.[1]

1. It must be remembered that the prior conviction involved in *Luck* was a guilty plea. The relevance of prior convictions to credibility may well be different as between a case where the conviction of the accused was by admission of guilt by a plea and on the other hand a case where the acused affirmatively contested the charge and testified, for example, that he was not present and did not commit the acts charged. In the latter situation the accused affirmatively puts his own veracity in issue when he testifies so that the jury's verdict amounted to rejection of his testimony; the verdict is in a sense a de facto finding that the accused did not tell the truth when sworn to do so. Exploration of this area risks a diversion which may well be time consuming; hence use of this inquiry should be limited.

This, admittedly, places a very difficult burden on trial judges and some added guidelines are needed even at risk of adding to the burdens of the trial courts.

In considering how the District Court is to exercise the discretionary power we granted, we must look to the legitimate purpose of impeachment which is, of course, not to show that the accused who takes the stand is a "bad" person but rather to show background facts which bear directly on whether jurors ought to believe him rather than other and conflicting witnesses. In common human experience acts of deceit, fraud, cheating, or stealing, for example, are universally regarded as conduct which reflects adversely on a man's honesty and integrity. Acts of violence on the other hand, which may result from a short temper, a combative nature, extreme provocation, or other causes, generally have little or no direct bearing on honesty and veracity. A "rule of thumb" thus should be that convictions which rest on dishonest conduct relate to credibility whereas those of violent or assaultive crimes generally do not; traffic violations, however serious, are in the same category. The nearness or remoteness of the prior conviction is also a factor of no small importance. Even one involving fraud or stealing, for example, if it occurred long before and has been followed by a legally blameless life, should generally be excluded on the ground of remoteness.

A special and even more difficult problem arises when the prior conviction is for the same or substantially the same conduct for which the accused is on trial. Where multiple convictions of various kinds can be shown, strong reasons arise for excluding those which are for the same crime because of the inevitable pressure on lay jurors to believe that "if he did it before he probably did so this time." As a general guide, those convictions which are for the same crime should be admitted sparingly; one solution might well be that discretion be exercised to limit the impeachment by way of a similar crime to a single conviction and then only when the circumstances indicate strong reasons for disclosure, and where the conviction directly relates to veracity.

Of course, there are many other factors that may be relevant in deciding whether or not to exclude prior convictions in a particular case. One important consideration is what the effect will be if the defendant does not testify out of fear of being prejudiced because of impeachment by prior convictions. Even though a judge might find that the prior convictions are relevant to credibility and the risk of prejudice to the defendant does not warrant their exclusion, he may nevertheless conclude that it is more important that the jury have the benefit of the defendant's version of the case than to have the defendant remain silent out of fear of impeachment.[2]

---

2. This weighing process would occur only where it has been determined that the prior convictions are otherwise admissible. Having made that determination, the judge would then consider whether the defendant's testimony is so important that he should not be forced to elect between staying silent—risking prejudice due to the jury's going without one version

We recognize the undesirability of prolonging the trial unduly when the court is already confronted with requirements which work to that end, but in many cases the best way for the District Judge to evaluate the situation is to have the accused take the stand in a non-jury hearing and elicit his testimony and allow cross examination before resolving the *Luck* issue. Not only the trial judge, but both counsel, would then be in a better position to make decisions concerning the impeachment issue. Of course, the defendant could not be compelled to give testimony in the non-jury hearing and his testimony taken at the non-jury hearing would not be admissible in evidence except for impeachment.

We are well aware that these are not firm guidelines which can be applied readily as though they were part of the structure of the Federal Rules of Criminal Procedure; the very nature of judicial discretion precludes rigid standards for its exercise; we seek to give some assistance to the trial judge to whom we have assigned the extremely difficult task of weighing and balancing these elusive concepts. Surely, it would be much simpler if prior convictions of an accused were totally admissible or totally excludable as impeachment; but in the face of an explicit, unambiguous statute allowing use of prior convictions and the holding in *Luck* we have little choice. The lesser step has been taken in *Luck* saying that the statute is to be read as permitting a discretion in the trial judge.

Even though we need not go beyond Appellant's failure to raise the issue he now relies on, we note that the admission of Appellant's criminal record here, along with the criminal record of the complaining witness, was not in a vindictive or "eye for an eye" sense, as Appellant argues. Rather it was received because the case had narrowed to the credibility of two persons—the accused and his accuser —and in those circumstances there was greater, not less, compelling reason for exploring all avenues which would shed light on which of the two witnesses was to be believed. The jurors saw and heard both and we are able to see and hear neither. None of the other contentions urged by Appellant affords a basis for disturbing the judgment.

Affirmed.

NOTES

1. The general rule among the states allowing for impeachment by prior conviction is derived from the ancient common law rule that conviction of a person of treason or any felony, or of a misdemeanor involving dishonesty, or the obstruction of justice rendered the person totally incom-

of the facts—and testifying—risking prejudice through exposure of his criminal past. In this regard, the judge may want to evaluate just how relevant to credibility the prior convictions are; for example, a recent perjury conviction would be difficult to ignore even where the defendant's testimony would be of great importance. This could well be true as to a multiplicity of convictions for crimes of dishonesty referred to earlier. On the other hand, where an instruction relative to inferences arising from unexplained possession of recently stolen property is permissible, the importance of the defendant's testimony becomes more acute. See Smith v. United States, 123 U.S.App. D.C. 259, 359 F.2d 243 (1966).

petent as a witness. McCormick, Evidence, § 43, at 84 (2nd Ed. 1972); 3A
Wigmore, Evidence (Chadbourn rev. 1961) §§ 980, 980a, 985–987. By statutes everywhere, disqualification was eliminated and by specific provision
or decision, conviction for a crime was reduced to grounds for impeachment
of credibility. The definitions of crimes for which a conviction shall be
grounds for impeachment vary widely among the states. People v. Bur-
dette, 22 Ill.2d 577, 177 N.E.2d 170 (1961) (infamous crimes); West's
Ann.Cal.Evid.Code, § 788 (only felonies); Sims v. Callahan, 269 Ala. 216,
112 So.2d 776 (1959) (offenses involving moral turpitude); State v. Hurt,
49 N.J. 114, 228 A.2d 673 (1967) (any felony or misdemeanor). The Uniform Rules of Evidence, Rule 21, limit impeachment to conviction of crimes
"involving dishonesty or false statement."

One court recently reversed its judicially created rule allowing impeachment by prior conviction. In State v. McAboy, —— W.Va. ——, 236 S.E.2d
431 (1977), the Court said:

> "In any inquiry as to admissibility of evidence, the threshold
> question must be its relevancy. The customary answer on the rele-
> vancy of a prior conviction as to credibility is that it bears upon
> the truthfulness of the defendant. This is tenuous at best, since it
> is based on the premise that all persons convicted of a crime are
> disposed not to sell the truth, no matter the nature of the crime or
> the degree of rehabilitation achieved.

> "Even if the relevancy issue were conceded, there are unques-
> tionable prejudicial consequences flowing from the practice of al-
> lowing prior conviction impeachment. One of the most significant
> is that it has a chilling effect as it keeps the defendant with a
> prior conviction from becoming a witness in his own behalf.

> "Statistical evidence supporting the theory that the threat of
> the use of prior convictions operates to keep the defendant from
> taking the witness stand is found in Kalvin & Zeizel, The Ameri-
> can Jury, Table 43, page 160 (1966). The cases sampled were
> ranked in three categories: clear for acquittal, close, and clear for
> conviction. In the average of all categories the defendant with no
> record testified in 91% of the cases, while the defendant with a rec-
> ord testified in 74% of the cases. Of even more significance was
> the category where the case was clear for acquittal. The defend-
> ant without a record testified 90% of the time, while the defend-
> ant with a record testified only 53% of the time.

> "As to the prejudicial effect on the jury, Table 52 in The
> American Jury, supra, at page 160, reveals that in the cases sam-
> pled where the defendant had no record and took the stand, the ac-
> quittal rate was 65%. In contrast with cases sampled of the same
> quality of evidence where the defendant did not take the stand, the
> acquittal rate was 38%.

> "Where the rule arises by statute, at least one court and sever-
> al commentators have suggested that there may be constitutional
> dimension to the prejudicial effect of prior convictions in the due
> process-presumption of innocence area and an equal protection vio-
> lation.

> "This is upon the theory that its chilling effect retards the de-
> fendant from taking the stand, thereby impinging on his due pro-
> cess rights. Concomitantly, the presumption of innocence is im-

paired in the eyes of the jury, which conceives that his failure to testify, notwithstanding instructions to the contrary, is an indication of guilt. The equal protection argument is advanced on the basis that such statute creates an impermissible distinction between criminal defendants, namely, the class with a record and that with no record.

"In State v. Santiago, 53 Haw. 254, 492 P.2d 657 (1971), the court struck down its state statute permitting impeachment of credibility by evidence of prior convictions on the ground that it violated the Due Process Clauses of the state and Federal Constitutions .   .   ..

"We need not reach the constitutional questions in this case, as our rule arises from judicial sources. In returning the law in this area to its status before *Friedman*, we believe that we attain a more harmonious result with the general law as to impeachment of a defendant's character and reputation. This also follows a settled trend in the law to remove the common law restrictions that bar the accused criminal from effectively asserting his defenses.

"Thus far, we have discussed generally the reasons for re-establishing the earlier rule followed by this Court up to the *Friedman* case. We have noted that this rule prohibited the use of evidence of prior criminal convictions to impeach the defendant's credibility. It has been pointed out that under this rule, there was the recognized exception that if the defendant elected to place his good character in issue, evidence of prior convictions could then be introduced along with other relevant evidence bearing on bad character.

"Another exception to the general prohibition against impeachment of the defendant by evidence of his prior convictions which we believe is appropriate is a prior conviction of perjury or false swearing. Conviction of these crimes goes directly to the credibility of the defendant and, in our judgment, their relevancy has a priority over their possible prejudicial effect.

"What has been said about the use of prior criminal convictions to impeach the defendant if he elects to testify is not meant to alter our existing law in regard to other witnesses. As to such other witnesses, the rule is that it rests within the sound discretion of the trial court whether a prior conviction may be shown to impeach his credibility.

"The difference between the two rules is measured by the ultimate penalty arising from the possible prejudice. With a witness, the use of a prior conviction to impeach credibility may result in some loss of credibility in the eyes of the jury and attendant personal embarrassment. With the defendant, the prejudicial effect of a prior conviction may result in an unwarranted conviction."

Some courts have restricted the impeachment of prosecution witnesses by prior conviction. See Mills v. Estelle, 552 F.2d 119 (5th Cir. 1977).

2.   In Loper v. Beto, 405 U.S. 473, 92 S.Ct. 619 (1972), the Court held that prior convictions could not be used for impeachment of defendant if the defendant had not been represented by counsel at the time of prior conviction.

3. *Federal Rule of Evidence 609* became effective on July 1, 1975, which reads:

Impeachment by Evidence of Conviction of Crime

(a) *General Rule.* For the purpose of attacking the credibility of a witness, evidence that he has been convicted of a crime shall be admitted if elicited from him or established by public record during cross-examination but only if the crime (1) was punishable by death or imprisonment in excess of one year under the law under which he was convicted, and the court determines that the probative value of admitting this evidence outweighs its prejudicial effect to the defendant, or (2) involved dishonesty or false statement, regardless of the punishment.

(b) *Time Limit.* Evidence of a conviction under this rule is not admissible if a period of more than ten years has elapsed since the date of the conviction or of the release of the witness from the confinement imposed for that conviction, whichever is the later date, unless the court determines, in the interests of justice, that the probative value of the conviction supported by specific facts and circumstances substantially outweighs its prejudicial effect. However, evidence of a conviction more than 10 years old as calculated herein, is not admissible unless the proponent gives to the adverse party sufficient advance written notice of intent to use such evidence to provide the adverse party with a fair opportunity to contest the use of such evidence.

(c) *Effect of Pardon, Annulment, or Certificate of Rehabilitation.* Evidence of a conviction is not admissible under this rule if (1) the conviction has been the subject of a pardon, annulment, certificate of rehabilitation, or other equivalent procedure based on a finding of the rehabilitation of the person convicted and that person has not been convicted of a subsequent crime which was punishable by death or imprisonment in excess of one year, or (2) the conviction has been the subject of a pardon, annulment, or other equivalent procedure based on a finding of innocence.

(d) *Juvenile Adjudications.* Evidence of juvenile adjudications is generally not admissible under this rule. The court may, however, in a criminal case allow evidence of a juvenile adjudication of a witness other than the accused if conviction of the offense would be admissible to attack the credibility of an adult and the court is satisfied that admission in evidence is necessary for a fair determination of the issue of guilt or innocence.

(e) *Pendency of Appeal.* The pendency of an appeal therefrom does not render evidence of a conviction inadmissible. Evidence of the pendency of an appeal is admissible.

4. In consideration of the problem of "inadvertently" opening the door to impeachment, see United States v. Jansen, 475 F.2d 312 (7th Cir. 1973):

Apparently in an effort to show Jansen's good character, his counsel asked on direct examination: "Have you ever been convicted of a *crime*?" Jansen replied in the negative. At a subsequent conference held outside the presence of the jury, Jansen's lawyer explained that he had made an unfortunate slip of the tongue; he and Jansen had practiced and he had intended to ask the question

"Have you ever been convicted of a *felony?*" The defendant had been convicted of criminal damage to property, a misdemeanor under Illinois law. The Government attorney later elicited testimony from the defendant on cross-examination concerning the prior conviction. The trial court overruled defense counsel's objection.

We find no abuse of discretion in the court's determination not to strike the exchange between Jansen and his attorney, the course of action suggested by the attorney at the conference. Counsel had posed the question at the beginning of the direct examination. The prosecutor was well into his cross-examination of Jansen when the discussion with the court took place. That conference lasted until the end of the court day and was resumed the following morning. Thus, the jury had heard the defendant's denial a substantial period of time before the defense attorney proposed that the exchange be struck. The purported fact had been placed without question before the jury, and we are unaware of any basis for saying that it was error not to strike out the question and answer, particularly in the belated posture here involved. If counsel had listened to his own words and had sought immediately to correct them, the result might have differed. He apparently did neither.

The Government acknowledges that, absent defense counsel's question on direct, the prosecution would have been precluded from cross-examining Jansen about his prior misdemeanor conviction. It argues, however, that once the matter was raised, the prosecutor had a duty to impeach the veracity of defendant's answer. The Government distinguishes this limited use of the misdemeanor conviction from an assault on Jansen's general credibility as a witness. A defendant's general credibility as a witness can be impeached only by a felony conviction.

Because Jansen made his statement on direct examination, the present case falls outside the rule that a witness may not be impeached by contradiction as to collateral or irrelevant matters elicited on cross-examination. Further, although we are aware of Wigmore's argument against allowing contradiction of all extraneous or volunteered assertions made on direct examination, 3A Wigmore, Evidence § 1007 (Chadbourn rev. 1970), decisions by the United States Supreme Court and by several courts of appeals, among them this court, strongly suggest that the impeachment here was permissible. See, e. g., Walder v. United States, 347 U.S. 62 (1954).

On redirect examination, defense counsel attempted to rehabilitate his client. However, the court sustained objections to three of the five questions counsel posed. The result was that Jansen was allowed to respond only to queries whether he had ever been convicted of a felony and what his plea to the misdemeanor charge had been.

.   .   .   Most [Circuits] leave such rehabilitation to the discretion of the trial judge. The cases we have found, however, involve the use of a prior conviction to impeach a witness's general credibility. Here, through an admission elicited from the defendant, the prosecutor in effect corrected misinformation that Jansen had given on his direct examination. The wisdom of limiting discussion about the misstatement is thus much more obvious under these circumstances than when a party has tried to discredit a witness's character. If not disallowed, defense counsel's questions on redirect would have opened a clearly collateral matter. We therefore cannot agree that the trial judge abused his discretion in rejecting the "rehabilitative" questions: how old Jansen had been at the time of the conviction and what sentence he had received.

F.   COURTROOM CONDUCT

ILLINOIS v. ALLEN

Supreme Court of the United States, 1970.
397 U.S. 337, 90 S.Ct. 1057, rehearing denied 398 U.S. 915, 90 S.Ct. 1684.

MR. JUSTICE BLACK delivered the opinion of the Court.

The Confrontation Clause of the Sixth Amendment to the United States Constitution provides that: "In all criminal prosecutions, the accused shall enjoy the right .   .   .   to be confronted with the witnesses against him .   .   . ." We have held that the Fourteenth Amendment makes the guarantees of this clause obligatory upon the States. Pointer v. Texas (1965). One of the most basic of the rights guaranteed by the Confrontation Clause is the accused's right to be present in the courtroom at every stage of his trial. Lewis v. United States (1892). The question presented in this case is whether an accused can claim the benefit of this constitutional right to remain in the courtroom while at the same time he engages in speech and conduct which is so noisy, disorderly, and disruptive that it is exceedingly difficult or wholly impossible to carry on the trial.

The issue arose in the following way. The respondent, Allen, was convicted by an Illinois jury of armed robbery and was sentenced to serve 10 to 30 years in the Illinois State Penitentiary. The evidence against him showed that on August 12, 1956, he entered a tavern in Illinois and, after ordering a drink, took $200 from the bartender at gunpoint. The Supreme Court of Illinois affirmed his conviction. Later Allen filed a petition for a writ of habeas corpus in federal court alleging that he had been wrongfully deprived by the Illinois trial judge of his constitutional right to remain present throughout his trial. Finding no constitutional violation, the District Court declined to issue the writ. The Court of Appeals reversed, Judge Hastings dissenting.

The facts surrounding Allen's expulsion from the courtroom are set out in the Court of Appeals' opinion sustaining Allen's contention:

"After his indictment and during the pretrial stage, the petitioner [Allen] refused court-appointed counsel and indicated to the trial court on several occasions that he wished to conduct his own defense. After considerable argument by the petitioner, the trial judge told him, 'I'll let you be your own lawyer, but I'll ask Mr. Kelly [court-appointed counsel] [to] sit in and protect the record for you, insofar as possible.'

"The trial began on September 9, 1957. After the State's Attorney had accepted the first four jurors following their voir dire examination, the petitioner began examining the first juror and continued at great length. Finally, the trial judge interrupted the petitioner, requesting him to confine his questions solely to matters relating to the prospective juror's qualifications. At that point, the petitioner started to argue with the judge in a most abusive and disrespectful manner. At last, and seemingly in desperation, the judge asked appointed counsel to proceed with the examination of the jurors. The petitioner continued to talk, proclaiming that the appointed attorney was not going to act as his lawyer. He terminated his remarks by saying, 'When I go out for lunchtime, you're [the judge] going to be a corpse here.' At that point he tore the file which his attorney had and threw the papers on the floor. The trial judge thereupon stated to the petitioner, 'One more outbreak of that sort and I'll remove you from the courtroom.' This warning had no affect on the petitioner. He continued to talk back to the judge, saying, 'There's not going to be no trial, either. I'm going to sit here and you're going to talk and you can bring your shackles out and straight jacket and put them on me and tape my mouth, but it will do no good because there's not going to be no trial.' After more abusive remarks by the petitioner, the trial judge ordered the trial to proceed in the petitioner's absence. The petitioner was removed from the courtroom. The voir dire examination then continued and the jury was selected in the absence of the petitioner.

"After a noon recess and before the jury was brought into the courtroom, the petitioner, appearing before the judge, complained about the fairness of the trial and his appointed attorney. He also said he wanted to be present in the court during his trial. In reply, the judge said that the petitioner would be permitted to remain in the courtroom if he 'behaved [himself] and [did] not interfere with the introduction of the case.' The jury was brought in and seated. Counsel for the petitioner then moved to exclude the witnesses from the courtroom. The [petitioner] protested this effort on the part of his attorney, saying: 'There is going to be no proceeding. I'm going to start talking and I'm going to keep on talking all through the trial. There's not going to be no trial like this. I want my sister and my friends here in court to testify for me.' The trial judge thereupon ordered the petitioner removed from the courtroom."

After this second removal, Allen remained out of the courtroom during the presentation of the State's case-in-chief, except that he was brought in on several occasions for purposes of identification. During one of these latter appearances, Allen responded to one of the judge's questions with vile and abusive language. After the prosecution's case had been presented, the trial judge reiterated his promise to Allen that he could return to the courtroom whenever he agreed to conduct himself properly. Allen gave some assurances of proper conduct and was permitted to be present through the remainder of the trial, principally his defense, which was conducted by his appointed counsel.

The Court of Appeals went on to hold that the Supreme Court of Illinois was wrong in ruling that Allen had by his conduct relinquished his constitutional right to be present, declaring that:

> "No conditions may be imposed on the absolute right of a criminal defendant to be present at all stages of the proceeding. The insistence of a defendant that he exercise this right under unreasonable conditions does not amount to a waiver. Such conditions, if insisted upon, should and must be dealt with in a manner that does not compel the relinquishment of his right.
>
> ". . . we are of the view that the defendant should not have been excluded from the courtroom during his trial despite his disruptive and disrespectful conduct. The proper course for the trial judge was to have restrained the defendant by whatever means necessary, even if those means included his being shackled and gagged." 413 F.2d at 235.

The Court of Appeals felt that the defendant's Sixth Amendment right to be present at his own trial was so "absolute" that, no matter how unruly or disruptive the defendant's conduct might be, he could never be held to have lost that right so long as he continued to insist upon it, as Allen clearly did. Therefore the Court of Appeals concluded that a trial judge could never expel a defendant from his own trial and that the judge's ultimate remedy when faced with an obstreperous defendant like Allen who determines to make his trial impossible is to bind and gag him. We accept instead the statement of Mr. Justice Cardozo who, speaking for the Court in Snyder v. Massachusetts (1934), said: "No doubt the privilege [of personally confronting witnesses] may be lost by consent or at times even by misconduct." Although mindful that courts must indulge every reasonable presumption against the loss of constitutional rights, Johnson v. Zerbst (1938), we explicitly hold today that a defendant can lose his right to be present at trial if, after he has been warned by the judge that he will be removed if he continues his disruptive behavior, he nevertheless insists on conducting himself in a manner so disorderly, disruptive, and disrespectful of the court that his trial cannot be carried on with him in the courtroom. Once lost, the right to be present can, of course, be reclaimed as soon as the defendant is willing to conduct himself consistently with the decorum and respect inherent in the concept of courts and judicial proceedings.

It is essential to the proper administration of criminal justice that dignity, order, and decorum be the hallmarks of all court proceedings in our country. The flagrant disregard in the courtroom of elementary standards of proper conduct should not and cannot be tolerated. We believe trial judges confronted with disruptive, contumacious, stubbornly defiant defendants must be given sufficient discretion to meet the circumstances of each case. No one formula for maintaining the appropriate courtroom atmosphere will be best in all situations. We think there are at least three constitutionally permissible ways for a trial judge to handle an obstreperous defendant like Allen: (1) bind and gag him, thereby keeping him present; (2) cite him for contempt; (3) take him out of the courtroom until he promises to conduct himself properly.

I.

Trying a defendant for a crime while he sits bound and gagged before the judge and jury would to an extent comply with that part of the Sixth Amendment's purposes that accords the defendant an opportunity to confront the witnesses at the trial. But even to contemplate such a technique, much less see it, arouses a feeling that no person should be tried while shackled and gagged except as a last resort. Not only is it possible that the sight of shackles and gags might have a significant effect on the jury's feelings about the defendant, but the use of this technique is itself something of an affront to the very dignity and decorum of judicial proceedings that the judge is seeking to uphold. Moreover, one of the defendant's primary advantages of being present at the trial, his ability to communicate with his counsel, is greatly reduced when the defendant is in a condition of total physical restraint. It is in part because of these inherent disadvantages and limitations in this method of dealing with disorderly defendants that we decline to hold with the Court of Appeals that a defendant cannot under any possible circumstances be deprived of his right to be present at trial. However, in some situations which we need not attempt to foresee, binding and gagging might possibly be the fairest and most reasonable way to handle a defendant who acts as Allen did here.

II.

In a footnote the Court of Appeals suggested the possible availability of contempt of court as a remedy to make Allen behave in his robbery trial, and it is true that citing or threatening to cite a contumacious defendant for criminal contempt might in itself be sufficient to make a defendant stop interrupting a trial. If so, the problem would be solved easily, and the defendant could remain in the courtroom. Of course, if the defendant is determined to prevent any trial, then a court in attempting to try the defendant for contempt is still confronted with the identical dilemma that the Illinois court faced in this case. And criminal contempt has obvious limitations as a sanction when the defendant is charged with a crime so serious that a very severe sentence such as death or life imprisonment is likely to be imposed. In such a case the defendant might not be affected by a mere contempt sentence when he ultimately faces a far more serious sanction. Nevertheless, the contempt remedy should be borne in mind by a judge in the circumstances of this case.

Another aspect of the contempt remedy is the judge's power, when exercised consistently with state and federal law, to imprison an unruly defendant such as Allen for civil contempt and discontinue the trial until such time as the defendant promises to behave himself. This procedure is consistent with the defendant's right to be present at trial, and yet it avoids the serious shortcomings of the use of shackles and gags. It must be recognized, however, that a defendant might conceivably, as a matter of calculated strategy, elect to spend a prolonged period in confinement for contempt in the hope that adverse witnesses might be unavailable after a lapse of time. A court must guard against allowing a defendant to profit from his own wrong in this way.

III.

The trial court in this case decided under the circumstances to remove the defendant from the courtroom and to continue his trial in his absence until and unless he promised to conduct himself in a manner befitting an American courtroom. As we said earlier, we find nothing unconstitutional about this procedure. Allen's behavior was clearly of such an extreme and aggravated nature as to justify either his removal from the courtroom or his total physical restraint. Prior to his removal he was repeatedly warned by the trial judge that he would be removed from the courtroom if he persisted in his unruly conduct, and, as Judge Hastings observed in his dissenting opinion, the record demonstrates that Allen would not have been at all dissuaded by the trial judge's use of his criminal contempt powers. Allen was constantly informed that he could return to the trial when he would agree to conduct himself in an orderly manner. Under these circumstances we hold that Allen lost his right guaranteed by the Sixth and Fourteenth Amendments to be present throughout his trial.

IV.

It is not pleasant to hold that the respondent Allen was properly banished from the court for a part of his own trial. But our courts, palladiums of liberty as they are, cannot be treated disrespectfully with impunity. Nor can the accused be permitted by his disruptive conduct indefinitely to avoid being tried on the charges brought against him. It would degrade our country and our judicial system to permit our courts to be bullied, insulted, and humiliated and their orderly progress thwarted and obstructed by defendants brought before them charged with crimes. As guardians of the public welfare, our state and federal judicial systems strive to administer equal justice to the rich and the poor, the good and the bad, the native and foreign born of every race, nationality, and religion. Being manned by humans, the courts are not perfect and are bound to make some errors. But, if our courts are to remain what the Founders intended, the citadels of justice, their proceedings cannot and must not be in-fected with the sort of scurrilous, abusive language and conduct pa-raded before the Illinois trial judge in this case. The record shows that the Illinois judge at all times conducted himself with that digni-ty, decorum, and patience that befit a judge. Even in holding that the trial judge had erred, the Court of Appeals praised his "com-mendable patience under severe provocation."

We do not hold that removing this defendant from his own trial was the only way the Illinois judge could have constitutionally solved the problem he had. We do hold, however, that there is nothing whatever in this record to show that the judge did not act completely within his discretion. Deplorable as it is to remove a man from his own trial, even for a short time, we hold that the judge did not com-mit legal error in doing what he did.

The judgment of the Court of Appeals is reversed.

Reversed.

MR. JUSTICE BRENNAN, concurring. [Opinion omitted.]

MR. JUSTICE DOUGLAS.

I agree with the Court that a criminal trial, in the constitutional sense, cannot take place where the courtroom is a bedlam and either the accused or the judge is hurling epithets at the other. A court-room is a hallowed place where trials must proceed with dignity and not become occasions for entertainment by the participants, by extra-neous persons, by modern mass media, or otherwise.

My difficulty is not with the basic hypothesis of this decision, but with the use of this case to establish the appropriate guidelines for judicial control.

*   *   *

Our real problems of this type lie not with this case but with other kinds of trials. *First* are the political trials. They frequently recur in our history .   .   . and insofar as they take place in fed-eral courts we have broad supervisory powers over them. That is one setting where the question arises whether the accused has rights of confrontation that the law invades at its peril.

In Anglo-American law, great injustices have at times been done to unpopular minorities by judges, as well as by prosecutors. I refer to London in 1670 when William Penn, the gentle Quaker, was tried for causing a riot when all that he did was to preach a sermon on Grace Church Street, his church having been closed under the Con-venticle Act:

*   *   *

The panel of judges who tried William Penn were sincere, law-and-order men of their day. Though Penn was acquitted by the jury, he was jailed by the court for his contemptuous conduct [in repeated-ly asking the court to state by what law he was being charged and where that law could be found]. Would we tolerate removal of a de-fendant from the courtroom during a trial because he was insisting on his constitutional rights, albeit vociferously, no matter how obnoxious his philosophy might have been to the bench that tried him? Would we uphold contempt in that situation?

Problems of political indictments and of political judges raise profound questions going to the heart of the social compact. For that compact is two-sided: majorities undertake to press their grievances within limits of the Constitution and in accord with its procedures; minorities agree to abide by constitutional procedures in resisting those claims.

Does the answer to that problem involve defining the procedure for conducting political trials or does it involve the designing of constitutional methods for putting an end to them? This record is singularly inadequate to answer those questions. It will be time enough to resolve those weighty problems when a political trial reaches this Court for review.

Second are trials used by minorities to destroy the existing constitutional system and bring on repressive measures. Radicals on the left historically have used those tactics to incite the extreme right with the calculated design of fostering a regime of repression from which the radicals on the left hope to emerge as the ultimate victor. The left in that role is the provocateur. The Constitution was not designed as an instrument for that form of rough-and-tumble contest. The social compact has room for tolerance, patience, and restraint, but not for sabotage and violence. Trials involving that spectacle strike at the very heart of constitutional government.

I would not try to provide in this case the guidelines for those two strikingly different types of cases. The case presented here is the classical criminal case without any political or subversive overtones. It involves a defendant who was a sick person and who may or may not have been insane in the classical sense but who apparently had a diseased mind. And, as I have said, the record is so stale that it is now much too late to find out what the true facts really were.

NOTES

1. Consider the following relevant A.B.A. Standards

Section 3–5.2 **Courtroom Decorum**

(a) The prosecutor should support the authority of the court and the dignity of the trial courtroom by strict adherence to the rules of decorum and by manifesting an attitude of professional respect toward the judge, opposing counsel, witnesses, defendants, jurors and others in the courtroom.

(b) When court is in session the prosecutor should address the court, not opposing counsel, on all matters relating to the case.

(c) It is unprofessional conduct for a prosecutor to engage in behavior or tactics purposefully calculated to irritate or annoy the court or opposing counsel.

(d) A prosecutor should comply promptly with all orders and directives of the court, but the prosecutor has a duty to have the record reflect adverse rulings or judicial conduct which the prosecutor considers prejudicial.

He has a right to make respectful requests for reconsideration of adverse rulings.

(e) A prosecutor should be punctual in all court appearances and in the submission of all motions, briefs and other papers.

(f) Prosecutors should cooperate with courts and the organized bar in developing codes of decorum and professional etiquette for each jurisdiction.

Section 4–7.1 Courtroom Decorum

(a) As an officer of the court the lawyer should support the authority of the court and the dignity of the trial courtroom by strict adherence to the rules of decorum and by manifesting an attitude of professional respect toward the judge, opposing counsel, witnesses, jurors, and others in the courtroom.

(b) When court is in session defense counsel should address the court and should not address the prosecutor directly on any matter relating to the case.

(c) It is unprofessional conduct for a lawyer to engage in behavior or tactics purposefully calculated to irritate or annoy the court or the prosecutor.

(d) The lawyer should comply promptly with all orders and directives of the court, but he has a duty to have the record reflect adverse rulings or judicial conduct which he considers prejudicial to his client's legitimate interests. He has a right to make respectful requests for reconsideration of adverse rulings.

(e) Lawyers should cooperate with courts and the organized bar in developing codes of decorum and professional etiquette for each jurisdiction.

Section 3–5.4 [4–7.3] Attitudes Toward the Jury

(b) The prosecutor [the lawyer] should treat jurors with deference and respect, avoiding the reality or appearance of currying favor by a show of undue solicitude for their comfort or convenience.

Section 3–5.6 [4–7.5] Presenting Evidence

(b) It is unprofessional conduct for a prosecutor [lawyer] knowingly and for the purpose of bringing inadmissible matter to the attention of the judge or jury to offer inadmissible evidence, ask legally objectionable questions, or make other impermissible comments or arguments in the presence of the judge or jury.

(c) It is unprofessional conduct for a prosecutor [lawyer] to permit any tangible evidence to be displayed in the view of the judge or jury which would tend to prejudice fair consideration by the judge or jury until such time as a good faith tender of such evidence is made.

(d) It is unprofessional conduct to tender tangible evidence in the view of the judge or jury if it would tend to prejudice fair consideration by the judge or jury unless there is a reasonable basis for its admission in evidence. When there is any substantial doubt about the admissibility of such evidence it should be tendered by an offer of proof and a ruling obtained.

2. What would occur if one attorney followed the rules and the other did not? Should the attorney following the rules continue to do so? Of course, an attorney who is blatant in his violation of the accepted standards of courtroom conduct will alienate both court and jury and his opponent

need not worry. But subtle evasions of the rules may damage the opposition and the court may not be strong enough or determined enough to stop the culpable lawyer.

The most commonly effective but improper tactics are those which are designed to annoy opposing counsel, those which are designed to convey to the jury the unfavorable impression arising from adverse court rulings and from the court's personal bias toward the attorney or his client, and those which are designed to show less than a respectful attitude toward opposing counsel or his witnesses. If these tactics are used by one lawyer, should the other lawyer respond in kind? Further, a lawyer who is too dispassionate in his courtroom practices may run the risk of impressing the jury that he does not care about his case or has no confidence in its merits. One generally accepted principle among criminal lawyers is that counsel must adopt a courtroom demeanor fairly consistent with his out-of-court personality. A volatile man will appear artificial in court if he keeps too tight a rein on himself and so will a methodical man who trys a flamboyant style. Do the A.B.A. Standards ignore these facts of life?

G. ADDRESSING THE JURY

---

1. OPENING STATEMENTS

LEONARD v. UNITED STATES

United States Court of Appeals, Ninth Circuit, 1960.
277 F.2d 834.

JERTBERG, CIRCUIT JUDGE.

. . . appellant was committed to . . . imprisonment for a period of six years, following his conviction by a jury of the offense of transporting in interstate commerce a forged instrument.

Appellant contends that the district court erred . . . in refusing to declare a mistrial because of alleged prejudicial misconduct of the prosecuting attorney in his opening statement; in the giving of an instruction to the jury in relation to the opening statement which appellant claims was inadequate and damaging; . . . .

* * *

It appears that as soon as the jury was empaneled to try the cause the court directed government counsel to make his opening statement, to which counsel replied, "Your Honor, may I have about 5 minutes. We've got the jury faster than I contemplated and I'd like to complete putting something on the board that I want to use in my statement . . . ." Following the recess, the court again directed counsel to make his opening statement . . . .

Counsel proceeded to enumerate the elements of the offense charged in the indictment, and then stated:

* * *

"Now, it has been an ancient and honorable doctrine in the law that the prosecution is not able to show a jury any other crimes committed by the defendant because the law in its wisdom has it that no one shall be convicted because a jury shall conclude from other crimes that he is a bad man and because he is a bad man reasoned that he must have committed this particular crime. And that is a very good rule. However, that rule has about seven classical exceptions and two of the exceptions fit this case and thus enable the Government in this instance to bring to your attention some of the other crimes.

"Now, when I say 'other crimes', I am not talking about previous convictions. I make no intimation whatsoever on the subject of previous convictions. . . . The rule is ordinarily you can't show other crimes, but in this case we are able to do it on two exceptions to that principle of law.

"The first exception is that whenever a defendant denies having the specific intent charged by the Government, . . . the Government may bring in other crimes to show that he did have that intent.

"The other exception to that ancient rule I mentioned is that whenever it is desirable or necessary to identify the defendant . . . the Government may introduce similar crimes, crimes of a similar nature committed by the defendant in order to assist in establishing that identity. Thus it is that the Government brings to you, not alone the one crime charged in the indictment, but a great number of other crimes, all of which will be shown to you as having been confessed to by this defendant, although they have not as yet been the subject of indictment or prosecution, conviction, or penalty. These crimes number 84. They are all felonies. Yes, you heard me correctly. I said 84. Incredible, but true. I should say, to be absolutely accurate, 83 other crimes other than the indictment crime. Thus it is that the presentation of our evidence falls into three parts. Would the bailiff turn around the blackboard. (The bailiff did so.)

"I was just saying that the presentation of our evidence will fall roughly into three parts. And I have put these three parts on the blackboard and I hope that each of you can see. If there is any juror who can't see a raising of the hands will probably permit us to shift this blackboard. Now, I have used a little system that I have seen accountants or bookkeepers use and what I have done here is the subject parts of these various crimes I have put in tabular order here and then I have added them up, you see, and carried that over in that fashion and then in the very last imaginary table of all I have put my grand total.

" . . . The letter 'F' hyphen 'U' I have used as sort of a shorthand to indicate forging and uttering and I must advise you that in the totals out here the subtotals here and of course in the grand total I have counted each forgery as one crime and each uttering as another crime. Ordinarily, when a check is forged and then passed by getting it cashed, you have one unitary transaction, one transaction, but it gives rise to two violations of law, one being forgery and the other being uttering. In the case of William A. Smith, Contracting Company, the evidence of the Government will show that there were 14 felonies committed by this defendant consisting of forgeries and utterings, seven forgeries, seven utterings.

"The second group here in our middle group, 'FWS,' standing for Fish and Wildlife Service. The 'FOS' is my own little abbreviation for false official statement. The evidence on this Fish and Wildlife Service crime will show you that the defendant made out, that is, made an application for a fishing license under a false name. And this last one, 'A.H.A.' stands for Alaska Housing Authority, 12 felonies forging and uttering, six checks here, seven checks up here, a false offical statement here. And subsequent to this conduct or at about the same time the defendant betook himself to Fairbanks and there engaged in a conspiracy and an attempt to commit a gigantic swindle in cooperation and colleague with one Robert Jackson an importation from the States brought into the ring here for certain services that will be in a moment explained to you, a local man.

"Now, these 56 crimes that were committed in the Fairbanks episode occurred in this fashion. They break down as follows: six crimes committed by forging and uttering, there being six checks involved and two crimes on each check. And I have abbreviated this 'C.A. to F.U.' conspiracy and an attempt to forge and utter 50 other checks. That is, 25 other checks which give us a total of 50 crimes because each forgery and uttering constitutes a separate crime giving for the Fairbanks group a total of 56 crimes conspired to or attempted, which includes six crimes actually committed. That is, six checks actually forged and actually passed by this defendant, giving us the astonishing total of 84 crimes including the one for which he is presently being prosecuted.

"Now, will the bailiff assist me, please, in turning around the blackboard. (The bailiff did so.)

"Before I give you the explanation of the crime charged in the indictment I want to recite for you some of the false names used by this man in perpetrating these 84 crimes. In the indictment crime he used the false name, Joe Hill. In the false official statement made to obtain a fishing license he used the false name Don Woods. In the Alaska Housing Authority forging and uttering, 12 offenses, he used the names Eddie Wilson and Bobby Wilson. And with respect to the Fairbanks group of crimes when he registered in a hotel room he registered as James Williams or James Wilson. It is quite impossible to determine absolutely because the manager of that hotel was subpoenaed and telegraphed —I got the telegram this morning—she could not appear due to complete disability. In addition to the names, said James Wilson or James Williams used to register at the Fairbanks hotel, this defendant used on the 50 crimes conspiracy and attempts, the name Willie Lee Andrews. Willie Lee Andrews. A total, I believe, of nine false names that will appear as used by this defendant in the evidence to be presented to you." [Sic.]

Counsel then proceeded to outline the matters he expected to prove in connection with the forged security described in the indictment. Counsel then proceeded:

"Now, I think that it would be, as it were, guilding the lily, if I may use such a term, to describe the middle group of crimes. I am not going to describe them to you any more except merely to say—may we have the board turned around, please, sir, (did so)—except merely to say that the defendant in the middle group of crimes held through to his M.O.—remember, method of operation—and got work for a short time with the—no, I beg your pardon. I think in this particular W. A. Smith thing he broke into, it will show, he burglarized the Smith Company and stole the checks out and, by the way, that reminds me, in my compilation of 84 crimes I have wholly excluded counting the incidental crimes, such as burglary and larceny that were occasionally committed in order to get hold of the instruments or checks that were forged. In the W. A. Smith episode there was breaking and entering. I have described the Fish and Wildlife matter to you. And the Alaska Housing Authority, again he followed his M.O. thereby getting work as a janitor or helping a janitor and got the checks out of the Alaska Housing Authority and forged them and cashed them as a result of access that he had by being a janitor there.

"Now, he departed from his M.O. a little bit in the Fairbanks group of checks, embarking on a colossal scheme here to cheat and defraud. .   .   .   The role played by this defendant was not as active as it would have been, he admits in his confession, were it not be for the fact the police were so hot after him that his role was largely limited to doing the writing in the forgeries. In fact, his confession, which will be read to you, states that he told his confederates, 'Well, now, I can't help you push the checks.' That is the underworld slang for passing. 'I can't help you push them. I am too hot, but I will help you forge them.' Although he wasn't going to pass any according to his original position and his local necessities compelled him to make use of three of them and these three checks, after having forged them, he cashed, with the aid and assistance of a lady named Ruth Lee of Fairbanks. And I have subpoenaed her here and I hope that she will give you available, helpful information. I might say to you in connection with this Fairbanks episode, since this matter was confided to my responsibility only three and a half working days ago, I have been unable to interview the witnesses on the Fairbanks episode. Although they will be, in a sense, questioned cold by me, I think that the presentation will still be adequate to meet your approval.

"If you wonder at the time of introduction why the Government is introducing drivers' licenses, social security numbers on James Berry Hill, on a man named Connelly and on a man named Stone and perhaps on one or two other people, I think perhaps my explanation may have dissipated your inquiry. That would be the purpose of it, to show the possession of the private documents of a great many different people by Jackson, for use by Jackson and Parks and this defendant in this swindle.

"Now, the Fairbanks group of checks were all made out by Mary Andrews. That is the fictitious Mary Andrews. All those checks were signed Mary Andrews and made payable to Willie Lee Andrews. Of course, Willie Lee Andrews was the name under which this gang was going to pass these checks. And, of course, professionals as they were, they had plenty of personal credentials that show Willie Lee Andrews driver's license, social security number, all sorts of things of that kind, on Willie Lee Andrews. And who was Willie Lee Andrews? The Government's inference is—the inference the Government asks you to make with respect to that part of the evidence is that Willie Lee Andrews is undoubtedly some living soul who has been rolled or robbed or has his personal papers stolen, and as long as the description of Willie Lee Andrews on these personal paper fits the description of one of these defendants they then can pass these documents, these checks, and get them cashed. If they are asked for identification they can produce all kinds of personal papers of Willie Lee Andrews proving they are Willie Lee Andrews.

"I think I have concluded my presentation."

At the conclusion of the opening statement, court appointed counsel for the appellant moved the court for a mistrial on the ground that the reference to 83 crimes not charged in the indictment was improper and prejudicial. Then followed conferences between the court and counsel during which proceedings the district court stated:

> "Now Mr. Davis [counsel for appellant], had you objected, as the opening statement was up around 40 minutes and no objection was made, then you would be in much better position to have made your motion for mistrial than you were. . . ."

Counsel for appellant then stated:

> "Our difficulty here, your Honor is this. Had these things come up in what I consider the proper order, had he attempted to prove other similar crimes I could then have gotten up and objected. Your Honor could have ruled. The damage would have not been done. The statement being made that they are going to prove such a thing, there isn't any question but that this jury now believes that the Government thinks that he is guilty of 83 crimes in addition to this, plus the fact that he is a burglar."

> "The court: Well, counsel, of course, if you had timely objected and I felt that there was a number of opportunities. . . .

> "Mr. Davis: I tell you, Your Honor, I certainly considered them, but I figured then in my own best judgment that the time was, that the damage was done had I made any objection at that time. The damage was done and I would have been prejudiced with the jury no matter what would have happened from there on."

Following the conferences between court and counsel at the bench, the court stated:

> "To save the jurors inconvenience the court has heard matters at the bench, as you well know, prior to the lunch recess and again now. . . . I hereby instruct you at this time that you are not to consider the statements made by Mr. Duggar in his opening statement pertaining to the commission of other crimes, that may or may not have been committed by this defendant. I instruct you specifically that we only have one issue before the court and jury at this time and that is whether or not the defendant 'did, on the date here in question, knowingly, wilfully, and feloniously with intent to defraud the Morrison-Knudsen Company, Inc., transport in interstate commerce between Anchorage, Alaska, and Seattle, Washington, a falsely made and altered security, to-wit: A Morrison-Knudsen Company, Inc., Draft No. 2923 in the amount of $285.01 (and then written out figures) payable to the order of Joe Hill, the said Andrew J. Leonard knowing at the time of transporting said security that it was falsely made and altered: Said draft was negotiated in Anchorage and drawn on the First National Bank of

Seattle, Washington.' That is the only issue we have to be concerned with at this time.

"Mr. Davis: If the court please—

"The Court: As the court—just one moment, please, Mr. Davis. As the court instructs you at the close of the trial also an opening statement is like an argument to the jury. It is not evidence. Counsel have the right to make an opening statement both for the plaintiff as well as for the defendant, and likewise to argue the case, but the court specifically instructs you that you cannot consider the arguments and/or the opening statements of counsel as evidence. And your verdict must be determined upon the evidence that is adduced during the course of the trial."

During the course of the trial, which lasted several days, the court ruled that evidence of other crimes alleged to have been committed by the appellant were not admissible in evidence. At the close of the testimony, and prior to the giving of instructions to the jury, the following occurred:

"Now, Mr. Duggar, the court recognizes you.

"Mr. Duggar: Since I have closed the Government's case, and since I did not succeed in introducing the other evidence that I stated in my opening statement, I would introduce, I wish that the court would be good enough to state such fact to the jury that—namely, that it was occasioned by an adverse ruling the Government suffered in its efforts to introduce such material.

"The Court: Very well, Ladies and gentlemen of the jury, you will recall in the opening statement of the Government he stated that they, the Government, would prove that under the exceptions, and he named those two exceptions, he would be allowed to prove incidents of some 83 other crimes. The court has ruled under the rules of evidence that he may not go into those other crimes. As you have now been apprised he has now asked me to instruct you as to the reason why he has not been able to go into these other crimes. Do you understand that (The jury nod in the affirmative.) Thank you."

Apparently the blackboard cataloging the 83 other crimes alleged to have been committed by appellant and referred to by government counsel in his opening statement remained throughout the trial in the view and presence of the jury. . . .

In our view the record hereinbefore set out is more eloquent and convincing than any words of ours in demonstrating that the appellant was denied his constitutional right to a fair trial. For 40 minutes the trial judge sat silently by while the over-zealous prosecutor recounted crimes alleged to have been committed by the appellant, many of which by no stretch of the imagination were admissible to prove intent or identity. The record is clear that the trial judge was aware of the fact that the fair boundaries of an opening statement to the jury were being flagrantly breached, but expected appointed counsel for appellant to object. The court then denied appellant's motion for a mistrial on the ground that appellant had failed to make timely objection. "Plain errors or defects affecting substantial rights may be noticed although they were not brought to the attention of the court." Rule 52(b), Federal Rules of Criminal Procedure, 18 U.S.C. In large measure the statement made by government counsel was an opening statement in name only. An opening statement should be limited to a statement of facts which the government intends or in good faith expects to prove. It should not be argumentative in character, nor should it be designed to destroy the character of the defendant before the introduction of any evidence on the crime charged in the indictment. In our view the prejudice against the appellant which must have been created in the minds of the jurors by government counsel's diatribe was extremely grave. Such prejudice was not removed by subsequent proceedings.

The admonition given by the court to the jury following the motion of appellant for a mistrial was ineffectual. The court simply advised the jury that counsel had the right to make opening statements but that opening statements and arguments of counsel were not to be considered as evidence. The statement clearly implied that the court regarded the opening statement as proper. If at that time the court was of the opinion that the only offense upon which he would admit proof was the one charged in the indictment, he should have admonished the members of the jury to completely erase and put out of their minds all statements made by government counsel concerning other crimes and misconduct attributed to the appellant. . . .

* * *

. . . By the admonition to the jury the minds of the jurors were conditioned to expect and look forward to proof of all of the crimes and misconduct mentioned in the opening statement.

By the admonition of the trial court given to the jury at the close of testimony the jury was expressly told that the only reason for the failure of the government to introduce proof of the crimes described in the opening statement was occasioned by "an adverse ruling the government suffered in its efforts to introduce such material." Here again was presented an opportunity to the trial judge to instruct the jury that while opening statements of counsel should not be considered as evidence, the members of the jury must absolutely and completely disregard and put out of their minds all statements of other crimes and misconduct contained in the opening statement.

The prejudice occasioned to the appellant by the opening statement was heightened by the fact that the cataloging of such crimes on the blackboard remained as a constant reminder to the members of the jury throughout the trial.

The record in this case demonstrates that government counsel "overstepped the bounds of that propriety and fairness which should characterize the conduct of such an officer in the prosecution of a criminal offense." As stated in Berger v. United States:

> "The United States Attorney is the representative not of an ordinary party to a controversy, but of a sovereignty whose obligation to govern impartially is as compelling as its obligation to govern at all; and whose interest, therefore, in a criminal prosecution is not that it shall win a case, but that justice shall be done. As such, he is in a peculiar and very definite sense the servant of the law, the twofold aim of which is that guilt shall not escape or innocence suffer. He may prosecute with earnestness and vigor—indeed, he should do so. But, while he may strike hard blows, he is not at liberty to strike foul ones. It is as much his duty to refrain from improper methods calculated to produce a wrongful conviction as it is to use every legitimate means to bring about a just one.

> "It is fair to say that the average jury, in a greater or less degree, has confidence that these obligations, which so plainly rest upon the prosecuting attorney, will be faithfully observed. Consequently, improper suggestions, insinuations, and, especially, assertions of personal knowledge are apt to carry much weight against the accused when they should properly carry none."

* * *

The judgment is reversed and the cause remanded with instructions to grant appellant a new trial.

NOTES

1. In Commonwealth v. Bearse, 358 Mass. 481, 265 N.E.2d 496 (1970), the defendant was convicted of the murder of his son. The killing was admitted and the issue was whether the act was deliberate (murder) or reckless (involuntary manslaughter). The case was close and on appeal the Court commented on the prosecution's opening statement:

> The prosecutor told the jury that he would prove that the defendant said to Mrs. Bearse on the evening of the fatal event, "I'm going to kill that kid." That proof was never forthcoming. It is of no avail retrospectively to surmise that if made, it was excluded because it was uttered in the course of a private conversation between husband and wife. The statement should never have been included in the opening unless there was no doubt of its admissibility. Having been made, although never proved, it was irretrievably and fatally prejudicial to the defendant in the circumstances, and especially so when the prosecutor in his closing argument repeatedly asserted that the killing was by "design."

Despite the rulings in Leonard v. United States and Commonwealth v. Bearse, reversals based on improper opening statements are not common.

In Government of Virgin Islands v. Rivera Salis, 359 F.2d 518 (3rd Cir. 1966), mere reference by prosecutor in opening statement to "eyewitness testimony", which never later materialized, was held not sufficiently **prejudicial. Nor did the failure of the prosecutor to introduce photographs** referred to in opening statement warrant mistrial in State v. Jones, 233 La. 775, 98 So.2d 185 (1957). Several courts have been less hesitant to find prejudice when the case is close on the question of guilt. People v. Ware, 13 App.Div.2d 1015, 216 N.Y.S.2d 644 (1961); People v. Corn, 163 Cal.App. 2d 568, 329 P.2d 746 (1958); State v. Levy, 262 Mo. 181, 170 S.W. 111 (1914); or when the evidence against the accused is entirely circumstantial, Hilyard v. State, 90 Okla.Crim. 425, 214 P.2d 953 (1950). For collected cases, see 28 A.L.R.2d 961, 972.

Generally, the harmful effect of an opening statement will be cured by court admonition and instruction to the jury to disregard. United States v. Nystrom, 116 F.Supp. 771 (D.C.Penn.1953); People v. Hernandez, 11 Cal. App.3rd 481, 89 Cal.Rptr. 766 (1970); State v. Geiger, 129 N.J.L. 13, 28 A.2d 57 (1942); Commonwealth v. Hartford, 346 Mass. 482, 194 N.E.2d 401 (1963) (where prosecutor disavowed statements in his closing argument and jury was instructed to consider only actual evidence). See collected cases, 28 A.L.R.2d 972.

The general rule that the right to a reversal or a new trial on appeal may be waived by a failure to properly object at trial is equally applicable to opening statements. United States v. Knapfer, 12 F.Supp. 980 (D.C. Penn.1935); Mullins v. Commonwealth, 25 Ky.L.R. 2044, 79 S.W. 258 (1904); Paulson v. State, 118 Wis. 89, 94 N.W. 771 (1903).

2. Apart from the possibility of reversal on appeal (which is meaningful only to the prosecutor), there is a more significant restraint on an advocate tempted to overstate his opening. An advocate who says that he will prove something and then fails to do so may pay a significant tactical penalty of loss of credibility. Most jurisdictions permit opposing counsel to comment on the failure to keep the "promises" made in the opening statement. See State v. McGonigle, 103 Ariz. 267, 440 P.2d 100 (1968); Gathright v. State, 245 Ark. 840, 435 S.W.2d 443 (1968); State v. Marshall, 15 Ohio App.2d 187, 239 N.E.2d 755 (1968). Contra, People v. Levy, 28 Mich. App. 339, 184 N.W.2d 325 (1970).

3. The defense has a particularly difficult dilemma regarding the opening statement. Most jurisdictions require the defense, subject to the court's discretion, to give its opening statement immediately after the prosecution makes its opening statement. If the defense gives a full opening statement, in those jurisdictions denying discovery to the prosecution, it has the effect of giving the prosecution advance discovery of the defense case. Further, in order to make a detailed opening, the defense usually has to commit itself to a particular defense and perhaps to calling the defendant to the stand. On the other hand, a general, vague opening statement may present an unfavorable contrast to a detailed and moving prosecution statement. Then, too, if the defense opening can be delayed until after the prosecution closes its case, the jury may become suspicious about the delay. State law may allow the prosecutor to attack the belated declaration of the defense, although some jurisdictions prohibit such an attack.

4. The applicable A.B.A. Standard follows:

Section 3–5.5 [4–7.4] Opening Statement

The prosecutor's [lawyer's] opening statement should be confined to a brief statement of the issues in the case and to remarks on evidence the prosecutor intends to offer which the prosecutor believes in good faith will be available and admissible. It is unprofessional conduct to allude to any evidence unless there is a

good faith and reasonable basis for believing that such evidence
will be tendered and admitted in evidence.

GLADDEN v. FRAZIER

United States Court of Appeals, Ninth Circuit, 1968.
388 F.2d 777, aff'd 394 U.S. 731, 89 S.Ct. 1420.

MADDEN, JUDGE.

The appellee Frazier was convicted in 1965 of second degree
murder . . . .

Frazier and Rawls, a cousin of Frazier, were jointly indicted by
the Oregon authorities for the murder of one Marleau. Rawls made
a confession to the Oregon authorities, first orally and then in a writing signed by him, which confession deeply implicated Frazier in the
killing. Rawls later pleaded guilty to second degree murder and
when Frazier's trial took place, had not yet been sentenced on his
plea of guilty.

In Frazier's trial, the Oregon prosecutor, in his opening statement to the jury, stated in considerable detail the evidence which he
intended to present, naming the witness or witnesses who would testify to the several items of evidence. He stated that he expected Rawls
to testify to the commission of the crime, and recited what Rawls'
testimony would be. He did not say that Rawls had confessed.
When the prosecutor had completed his opening statement, Frazier's
defense counsel moved for a mistrial. The court denied the motion.
The prosecutor had subpoenaed Rawls, and called him to the witness
stand. When questioned, Rawls claimed the privilege against self-incrimination and refused to answer the prosecutor's questions. The
trial judge sustained Rawls' claim of privilege, and Rawls left the
witness stand. Frazier's defense counsel again moved for a mistrial,
and the motion was again denied. The prosecuting attorney, in the
course of a lengthy trial, made no other reference to any statement
made by Rawls.

The events above recited constituted one of the grounds on which
the district court based his grant of Frazier's application for the writ
of habeas corpus. The court held that the prosecutor's recital, in his
opening statement, of what testimony he expected from Rawls, while
the prosecutor held in his hand several papers, one of which was
Rawls' signed confession, and read several times from that paper,
was, in effect, the introduction before the jury of Rawls' statement,
as to which Frazier's counsel had no opportunity to cross-examine
Rawls.

In any case in which counsel for a litigant elects to make an
opening statement outlining to the jury the substance of what he expects to prove, and naming the witnesses by which he hopes to prove
it, rather than leaving it to the jury to pick up the thread of the continued story from the succession of incidents, each incident testified
to by a separate witness, there is the possibility that the testimony

which counsel has spoken of will never materialize on the witness stand. The expected witness may die or disappear or may effectively claim a privilege not to testify, or some person who has the right to prevent the witness from testifying may assert that right. If it happens that counsel does not get the expected testimony, he has to do the best he can without it. If he can prove his case without it, he may still win. But a rule that a mistrial must be declared because the expected testimony outlined in the opening statement is never given from the witness stand, and consequently the adversary never has a chance to test its truth by cross-examination, would be a wasteful and mischievous rule. The controlling question should be the good faith or lack of good faith of counsel in saying what he said in his opening statement and the likelihood that the opening statement was unfairly prejudicial to the defendant.

In the instant case, at the beginning of the trial and before the jury was selected, Frazier's lawyer, in the presence of the prosecutor, said he had information that Rawls, if called as a witness, would claim his privilege against self-incrimination. He did not say what the source of his information was. Some days before Frazier's trial, the prosecutor had telephoned to Rawls' lawyer, Mr. Jacobs, to get permission to talk to Rawls. Permission was not immediately given, Jacobs saying that he himself had not talked to Rawls yet. The next day the prosecutor's assistant, Thomas, picked up Jacobs and transported him to the jail, where Jacobs talked to Rawls, then told Thomas that Rawls was going to refuse to testify, and gave permission to Thomas to talk to Rawls, saying, "All right, you talk to him. This is what he tells me. This is his own decision." Between that time and the trial, a deputy sheriff had talked to Rawls and had reported to the prosecutor that he felt sure that Rawls would testify and that Rawls' brothers, who had conversed with Rawls, had told the deputy that he wanted to testify and they thought he would testify, in spite of the advice of his lawyer. Rawls' probation officer told the prosecutor that he thought Rawls would testify.

In addition to the foregoing reasons for the prosecutor to believe that Rawls would, if called to the stand, testify, there was of course the fact that Rawls had pleaded guilty and was awaiting sentence, and would feel under strong compulsion not to refuse to cooperate with the prosecutor.

The Oregon trial judge, who was in the best position to determine whether the prosecutor had acted in good faith in calling Rawls to the witness stand, and whether this incident, when coupled with the opening statement, was prejudicial to the defendant, held that the prosecutor had acted in good faith and denied a motion for mistrial. We have before us the same cold record which the United States District Court had before it in this habeas corpus case, and we are in as good a position as was the district court to determine whether the Oregon court's implied findings were supported by the evidence. The district court's position in the habeas corpus case may well have been that good faith and prejudice were not the issues, but that counsel acts subject to the risk that the expected testimony which he recites in his opening statement, if it does not materialize, will require a mistrial. If that was the view of the district court, it was erroneous.

The fact that Rawls' expected testimony, once it became unavailable, was never again mentioned in the extended trial is of some significance on the question of the prosecutor's good faith, and of great significance on the question of the prejudicial effect of the opening statement and the calling of Rawls to the stand.

The Oregon trial judge said, in denying Frazier's second motion for a mistrial, that he would instruct the jury not to give any weight to what the prosecutor had said in his opening statement about Rawls' expected testimony. He did not give a specific instruction on that point. He either forgot his earlier statement or, more probably, thought better of it. Such an instruction, if given, would have recalled the incident to the minds of the jurors. Counsel for Frazier apparently for the same reason did not desire such an instruction or he would have reminded the court of its earlier statement. The court did give a general instruction that statements of counsel are not evidence.

Counsel for Frazier rely heavily upon the Supreme Court's decision in Douglas v. State of Alabama, supra. In Douglas, after the witness had claimed the privilege against self-incrimination, the prosecutor read the confession to him, a few sentences at a time, asking the witness after the reading of each few sentences, "Did you make that statement?" Each time the witness refused to answer, claiming the privilege. Thus the prosecutor, knowing that he was not going to get any testimony from the witness, deliberately placed every word of the inadmissible hearsay before the jury, compelling the witness to repeatedly claim his right to keep silent, and thus impressing the jury with the probable truth of the statement. The prosecutor could not possibly claim that he acted in a good faith expectation that the witness would testify. Douglas was a flagrant case of purposely and in bad faith placing before the jury in the most impressive possible manner inadmissible evidence the truth of which could not be tested by cross-examination. The "evidence" thus offered was the only evidence relating to a crucial element of the prosecution's case. Counsel for Frazier does not cite any case in which an appellate court has reversed a judgment for the reason relied upon by the district court in this phase of the instant case.

In the case before us, there is no problem of lack of opportunity to confront a witness who had given testimony, either directly or, as in Douglas v. State of Alabama, supra, indirectly by having his extra-judicial statements read to him and to the jury while he refused to confirm or deny his having made the statements attributed to him. Rawls was on the witness stand only momentarily, and neither by question nor answer was anything which was contained in his confession brought to the attention of the jury. Our problem then, is whether the references to Rawls in the opening statement, followed by the calling of Rawls to the witness stand, was prosecutorial misconduct. We hold that it was not. We have shown above that it was done in a good faith expectation that Rawls would testify. . . .

* * *

The judgment of the district court is reversed, and the court is directed to dismiss the petition for a writ of habeas corpus.

NOTE

The decision in Gladden v. Frazier was reviewed on certiorari in the United States Supreme Court and the denial of the writ of habeas corpus was affirmed sub nom. Frazier v. Cupp, 394 U.S. 731, 89 S.Ct. 1420 (1969). Similar to *Frazier* is State v. Caffey, 457 S.W.2d 675 (Mo.1970) which held that in the absence of evidence that prosecutor made statement without an intention of calling witnesses to prove it, it must be presumed that at the time of opening statement, the prosecuting attorney in good faith intended to call witnesses to prove the statement. However, several cases have strongly emphasized obvious inadmissibility of proof of opening remarks as indicating bad faith. Pilcher v. State, 90 Okla.Crim. 435, 214 P.2d 953 (1950).

Consider the problem the prosecution faced in Gladden v. Frazier when Rawls refused to testify. If Oregon had a statute like the one discussed in California v. Green, (Chapter 19–A, supra) would the problem have been solved?

2. CLOSING ARGUMENTS

GRIFFIN v. CALIFORNIA

Supreme Court of the United States, 1965.
380 U.S. 609, 85 S.Ct. 1229, rehearing denied 381 U.S. 957, 85 S.Ct. 1797.

MR. JUSTICE DOUGLAS delivered the opinion of the Court.

Petitioner was convicted of murder in the first degree after a jury trial in a California court. He did not testify at the trial on the issue of guilt, though he did testify at the separate trial on the issue of penalty. The trial court instructed the jury on the issue of guilt, stating that a defendant has a constitutional right not to testify. But it told the jury:

> "As to any evidence or facts against him which the defendant can reasonably be expected to deny or explain because of facts within his knowledge, if he does not testify or if, though he does testify, he fails to deny or explain such evidence, the jury may take that failure into consideration as tending to indicate the truth of such evidence and as indicating that among the inferences that may be reasonably drawn therefrom those unfavorable to the defendant are the more probable."

It added, however, that no such inference could be drawn as to evidence respecting which he had no knowledge. It stated that failure of a defendant to deny or explain the evidence of which he had knowledge does not create a presumption of guilt nor by itself warrant an inference of guilt nor relieve the prosecution of any of its burden of proof.

Petitioner had been seen with the deceased the evening of her death, the evidence placing him with her in the alley where her body was found. The prosecutor made much of the failure of petitioner to testify:

> "The defendant certainly knows whether Essie Mae had this beat up appearance at the time he left her apartment and went down the alley with her.

> "What kind of a man is it that would want to have sex with a woman that beat up if she was beat up at the time he left?

> "He would know that. He would know how she got down the alley. He would know how the blood got on the bottom of the concrete steps. He would know how long he was with her in that box. He would know how her wig got off. He would know whether he beat her or mistreated her. He would know whether he walked away from that place cool as a cucumber when he saw Mr. Villasenor because he was conscious of his own guilt and wanted to get away from that damaged or injured woman.

> "These things he has not seen fit to take the stand and deny or explain.

> "And in the whole world, if anybody would know, this defendant would know.

> "Essie Mae is dead, she can't tell you her side of the story. The defendant won't."

The case is here on a writ of certiorari to consider whether comment on the failure to testify violated the Self-Incrimination Clause of the Fifth Amendment.[1]

We think it does. It is in substance a rule of evidence that allows the State the privilege of tendering to the jury for its consideration the failure of the accused to testify. No formal offer of proof is made as in other situations; but the prosecutor's comment and the court's acquiescence are the equivalent of an offer of evidence and its

---

1. The overwhelming consensus of the States is opposed to allowing comment on the defendant's failure to testify. The legislatures or courts of 44 States have recognized that such comment is, in light of the privilege against self-incrimination, "an unwarrantable line of argument." Of the six States which permit comment, two, California and Ohio, give this permission by means of an explicit constitutional qualification of the privilege against self-incrimination. New Jersey permits comment but its constitution contains no provision embodying the privilege against self-incrimination. The absence of an express constitutional privilege against self-incrimination also puts Iowa among the six. Connecticut permits comment by the judge but not by the prosecutor. New Mexico permits comment by the prosecutor but holds that the accused is then entitled to an instruction that "the jury shall indulge no presumption against the accused because of his failure to testify".

acceptance. The Court in Wilson [v. United States, 149 U.S. 60, 13 S.Ct. 765] stated:

> ".   .   . the act was framed with a due regard also to those who might prefer to rely upon the presumption of innocence which the law gives to every one, and not wish to be witnesses. It is not every one who can safely venture on the witness stand, though entirely innocent of the charge against him. Excessive timidity, nervousness when facing others and attempting to explain transactions of a suspicious character, and offenses charged against him, will often confuse and embarrass him to such a degree as to increase rather than remove prejudices against him. It is not every one, however, honest, who would therefore willingly be placed on the witness stand. The statute, in tenderness to the weakness of those who from the causes mentioned might refuse to ask to be witnesses, particularly when they may have been in some degree compromised by their association with others, declares that the failure of a defendant in a criminal action to request to be a witness shall not create any presumption against him."

If the words "Fifth Amendment" are substituted for "act" and for "statute" the spirit of the Self-Incrimination Clause is reflected. For comment on the refusal to testify is a remnant of the "inquisitorial system of criminal justice" which the Fifth Amendment outlaws. It is a penalty imposed by courts for exercising a constitutional privilege. It cuts down on the privilege by making its assertion costly. It is said, however, that the inference of guilt for failure to testify as to facts peculiarly within the accused's knowledge is in any event natural and irresistible, and that comment on the failure does not magnify that inference into a penalty for asserting a constitutional privilege. What the jury may infer, given no help from the court, is one thing. What it may infer when the court solemnizes the silence of the accused into evidence against him is quite another. .   .   .

* * *

.   .   . We .   .   . hold that the Fifth Amendment, .   .   . forbids either comment by the prosecution on the accused's silence or instructions by the court that such silence is evidence of guilt.

Reversed.

THE CHIEF JUSTICE took no part in the decision of this case.

[MR. JUSTICE HARLAN's concurring opinion is omitted.]

MR. JUSTICE STEWART, with whom MR. JUSTICE WHITE joins, dissenting.

* * *

No claim is made that the prosecutor's argument or the trial judge's instructions to the jury in this case deprived the petitioner of due process of law as such. This Court long ago decided that the Due Process Clause of the Fourteenth Amendment does not of its own force forbid this kind of comment on a defendant's failure to testify. The Court holds, however, that the California constitutional provision violates the Fifth Amendment's injunction that no person "shall be compelled in any criminal case to be a witness against himself," an injunction which the Court less than a year ago for the first time found was applicable to trials in the courts of the several States.

With both candor and accuracy, the Court concedes that the question before us is one of first impression here. It is a question which has not arisen before, because until last year the self-incrimination provision of the Fifth Amendment had been held to apply only to federal proceedings, and in the federal judicial system the matter has been covered by a specific Act of Congress which has been in effect ever since defendants have been permitted to testify at all in federal criminal trials.

We must determine whether the petitioner has been "compelled . . . to be a witness against himself." Compulsion is the focus of the inquiry. Certainly, if any compulsion be detected in the California procedure, it is of a dramatically different and less palpable nature than that involved in the procedures which historically gave rise to the Fifth Amendment guarantee. When a suspect was brought before the Court of High Commission or the Star Chamber, he was commanded to answer whatever was asked of him, and subjected to a far-reaching and deeply probing inquiry in an effort to ferret out some unknown and frequently unsuspected crime. He declined to answer on pain of incarceration, banishment, or mutilation. And if he spoke falsely, he was subject to further punishment. Faced with this formidable array of alternatives, his decision to speak was unquestionably coerced.

Those were the lurid realities which lay behind enactment of the Fifth Amendment, a far cry from the subject matter of the case before us. I think that the Court in this case stretches the concept of compulsion beyond all reasonable bounds, and that whatever compulsion may exist derives from the defendant's choice not to testify, not from any comment by court or counsel. In support of its conclusion that the California procedure does compel the accused to testify, the Court has only this to say: "It is a penalty imposed by courts for exercising a constitutional privilege. It cuts down on the privilege by making its assertion costly." Exactly what the penalty imposed consists of is not clear. It is not, as I understand the problem, that the jury becomes aware that the defendant has chosen not to testify in his own defense, for the jury will, of course, realize this quite evident fact, even though the choice goes unmentioned. Since comment by counsel and the court does not compel testimony by creating such a awareness, the Court must be saying that the California constitutional provision places some other compulsion upon the defendant to incriminate himself, some compulsion which the Court does not describe and which I cannot readily perceive.

It is not at all apparent to me, on any realistic view of the trial process, that a defendant will be at more of a disadvantage under the California practice than he would be in a court which permitted no comment at all on his failure to take the witness stand. How can it be said that the inferences drawn by a jury will be more detrimental to a defendant under the limiting and carefully controlling language of the instruction here involved than would result if the jury were left to roam at large with only its untutored instincts to guide it, to draw from the defendant's silence broad inferences of guilt? The instructions in this case expressly cautioned the jury that the defendant's failure to testify "does not create a presumption of guilt or by itself warrant an inference of guilt"; it was further admonished that such failure does not "relieve the prosecution of its burden of proving every essential element of the crime," and finally the trial judge warned that the prosecution's burden remained that of proof "beyond a reasonable doubt." Whether the same limitations would be observed by a jury without the benefit of protective instructions shielding the defendant is certainly open to real doubt.

Moreover, no one can say where the balance of advantage might lie as a result of the attorneys' discussion of the matter. No doubt the prosecution's argument will seek to encourage the drawing of inferences unfavorable to the defendant. However, the defendant's counsel equally has an opportunity to explain the various other reasons why a defendant may not wish to take the stand, and thus rebut the natural if uneducated assumption that it is because the defendant cannot truthfully deny the accusations made.

I think the California comment rule is not a coercive device which impairs the right against self-incrimination, but rather a means of articulating and bringing into the light of rational discussion a fact inescapably impressed on the jury's consciousnes. The California procedure is not only designed to protect the defendant against unwarranted inferences which might be drawn by an uninformed jury; it is also an attempt by the State to recognize and articulate what it believes to be the natural probative force of certain facts. Surely no one would deny that the State has an important interest in throwing the light of rational discussion on that which transpires in the course of a trial, both to protect the defendant from the very real dangers of silence and to shape a legal process designed to ascertain the truth.

The California rule allowing comment by counsel and instruction by the judge on the defendant's failure to take the stand is hardly an idiosyncratic aberration. The Model Code of Evidence, and the Uniform Rules of Evidence both sanction the use of such procedures. The practice has been endorsed by resolution of the American Bar Association and the American Law Institute, and has the support of the weight of scholarly opinion.

The formulation of procedureal rules to govern the administration of criminal justice in the various States is properly a matter of local concern. We are charged with no general supervisory power over such matters; our only legitimate function is to prevent violations of the Constitution's commands. California has honored the constitutional command that no person shall "be compelled in any criminal case to be a witness against himself." The petitioner was not compelled to testify, and he did not do so. But whenever in a jury trial a defendant exercises this constitutional right, the members of the jury are bound to draw inferences from his silence. No constitution can prevent the operation of the human mind. Without limiting instructions, the danger exists that the inferences drawn by the jury may be unfairly broad. Some States have permitted this danger to go unchecked, by forbidding any comment at all upon the defendant's failure to take the witness stand. Other States have dealt with this danger in a variety of ways. Some might differ, as a matter of policy, with the way California has chosen to deal with the problem or even disapprove of the judge's specific instructions in this case. But, so long as the constitutional command is obeyed, such matters of state policy are not for this Court to decide.

I would affirm the judgment.

NOTES

1. The *Griffin* rule is not absolute. If the accused testifies, but refuses to answer certain questions, it is proper for the prosecutor to comment upon the failure to answer these questions. Dyson v. United States, 283 F.2d 636 (9th Cir. 1960), cert. denied 366 U.S. 974, 81 S.Ct. 1944; United States ex rel. Irwin v. Pate, 357 F.2d 911 (7th Cir. 1966); People v. Jackson, 103 Ill.App.2d 209, 243 N.E.2d 551 (1968). See also Chandler v. State, 7 Md.App. 646, 256 A.2d 695 (1969) (vague and evasive testimony amounting to refusal to answer questions of prosecutor on cross-examination justifies argument that such conduct shows guilt). In some cases an accused may be allowed to give testimony on a limited issue, i. e., voluntariness of confession, validity of pre-trial line-up. When that limited testimony is allowed the prosecution may not comment on the failure to testify on other issues. Calloway v. Wainwright, 409 F.2d 59 (5th Cir. 1969); People v. Eaton, 275 Cal.App.2d 584, 80 Cal.Rptr. 192 (1969). Occasionally, an accused wishes to perform some demonstration in court without taking the stand. The extent to which he may do this without waiving his Fifth Amendment privilege (and thus subject himself to adverse comment on his failure to give fuller testimony) is subject to some disagreement. See United States ex rel. Mitchell v. Pinto, 438 F.2d 814 (2nd Cir. 1971) (defendant did not waive privilege by rising and standing next to witness to demonstrate similarity of appearance); State v. Fioravanti, 46 N.J. 109, 215 A.2d 16 (1967), denial of habeas corpus, aff'd 404 F.2d 675 (3d Cir.) (trying on criminal's trousers to show lack of fit is testimonial appearance sufficient to justify comment on failure to deny other evidence). See also People v. Harris, 46 Ill.2d 395, 263 N.E.2d 35 (1970), denial of habeas corpus 457 F.2d 191 (7th Cir. 1972) (accused who wishes to display absence of teeth to jury may not do so without submitting to cross-examination at least as to circumstances and timing of loss of teeth).

2. Violations of the *Griffin* rule may be considered harmless. Chapman v. California, 386 U.S. 18, 87 S.Ct. 824 (1967).

In those jurisdictions strictly adhering to *Chapman*, the courts, in determining if an improper comment had "any reasonable possibility of affecting the verdict", have given primary consideration to the nature and extent of the comment in relation to the strength of the evidence of the defendant's guilt. See People v. Garrison, 252 Cal.App.2d 511, 60 Cal.Rptr. 596 (1967); People v. Rass, 67 Cal.2d 64, 60 Cal.Rptr. 254, 429 P.2d 606 (1967); Anderson v. Nelson, 390 U.S. 523, 88 S.Ct. 1133 (1968); State v. Burrell, 102 Ariz. 136, 426 P.2d 633 (1967); for collected cases see 24 A.L. R.3d 1093.

Several courts have held that *Griffin* violations constitute per se reversible error. State v. Smith, 101 Ariz. 407, 420 P.2d 278 (1966); Flaherty v. State, 183 So.2d 607 (Fla.App.1966); State v. Wright, 251 La. 511, 205 So.2d 381 (1967); Sanders v. State, 216 Tenn. 425, 392 S.W.2d 916 (1965); People v. Alexander, 17 Mich.App. 497, 169 N.W.2d 652 (1969).

There is some authority indicating that the error will be waived by a failure to object. Holden v. United States, 388 F.2d 240 (1st Cir. 1968); People v. Baker, 7 Mich.App. 471, 152 N.W.2d 43 (1967); State v. Thompson, 425 S.W.2d 80 (Mo.1968). But see, People v. Wallenberg, 37 Ill.2d 480, 229 N.E.2d 490 (1967) ("plain error"). The error may be waived by defendant or his attorney inviting the error. Babb v. United States, 351 F.2d 863 (8th Cir. 1965); People v. Hill, 66 Cal.2d 536, 58 Cal.Rptr. 340, 426 P. 2d 908 (1967), cert. denied 390 U.S. 911, 88 S.Ct. 838; Tillford v. State, 437 P.2d 261 (Okla.Crim.1967). Or it may be cured by the conduct of the trial judge. Holden v. United States, 388 F.2d 240 (1st Cir. 1968); People v. Baker, 7 Mich.App. 471, 152 N.W.2d 43 (1967); State v. Gregg, 399 S. W.2d 7 (Mo.1966); State v. Clayton, 272 N.C. 377, 158 S.E.2d 557 (1968).

DESMOND v. UNITED STATES

United States Court of Appeals, Fifth Circuit, 1965.
345 F.2d 225.

Aldrich, Chief Judge.

Appellant was convicted, along with a co-defendant, on narcotic charges, and sentenced to the minimum term of five years.　.　.　.

* * *

At the original trial, in the course of its final argument to the jury the government, referring to the alleged occasion when the two defendants had transferred the heroin to the government agent, said, "Those are the facts, the evidence. Incidentally, may I say to you that the evidence stands unimpeached and uncontradicted." Counsel for appellant immediately objected, stating at the bench that this was a comment upon appellant's failure to testify. The court overruled the objection, saying "Absolutely not," but added that in its charge it would tell the jury that no inference should be drawn against appellant from his failure to take the stand. Subsequently the court did so charge.

Two questions are presented, which we will take in reverse order. If it be assumed that the government's argument constituted comment upon appellant's failure to testify, was it cured by the charge? We think not. Correction of error should be as prompt and timely as possible—particularly where the error involves the infringement of a constitutional right, as this did. The appellant promptly objected. The remedy, to be fully effective, should have been administered equally promptly.

Nor can we doubt that the government's statement that its witness' statement stood "unimpeached and uncontradicted" constituted improper comment. No one but appellant (or his co-defendant, whom appellant could not put on the stand against his will) could have contradicted the government witness. The government's present argument that since the transaction took place in an apartment house perhaps there were other persons around, though its own witness had suggested no one, and on the face of things it would be to a degree unlikely, is sound neither in fact nor in law. Unless it is apparent on the record that there was someone other than himself whom the defendant could have called, the comment of necessity pointed to the only person who could have offered the contradiction, the defendant himself. Hence, in the present case it was clearly improper. This is no new constitutional interpretation. The government made the argument because it thought it would be effective. We can think of no effect other than to invite the jury's attention to the fact the defendants had not taken the stand.

Judgment must be entered   .   .   .   setting aside the verdict and ordering a new trial.

NOTES

1. The *Desmond* case represents the view that if the prosecution evidence characterized as uncontradicted is such that only the defendant himself could contradict it, the comment constitutes an improper reference to the defendant's failure to testify. In accord are United States v. Flannery, 451 F.2d 880 (1st Cir. 1971); Linden v. United States, 296 F. 104 (3rd Cir. 1924); Hood v. United States, 59 F.2d 153 (10th Cir. 1932). For collected state cases see 14 A.L.R.3d 723. There are jurisdictions, however, which approve the argument even when defendant could logically be the only possible witness. People v. Stanbeary, 126 Ill.App.2d 244, 261 N.E.2d 765 (1970).

Most courts hold that if a particular comment that prosecution evidence is uncontradicted refers to testimony which persons other than the defendant could have contradicted, the comment is not an improper reference to defendant's failure to testify. Shea v. United States, 251 F. 440 (6th Cir. 1918), cert. denied 248 U.S. 581, 39 S.Ct. 132; Morrison v. United States, 6 F.2d 809 (8th Cir. 1925). For collected state and federal cases see 14 A.L.R.3d 723. Some courts simply construe such statements as reference to the evidence adduced by the state, as by estimating its weight or persuasiveness, and not as improper comments on defendant's refusal to testify. Barry v. United States, 248 F.2d 201 (10th Cir. 1957); United States v. Parisi, 365 F.2d 601 (6th Cir. 1966); People v. Bloom, 35 Ill.2d 255, 220 N.E.2d 475 (1966).

Courts have approved statements that evidence is uncontradicted—United States v. Heithaus, 377 F.2d 484 (3rd Cir. 1967); uncontroverted—Ruiz v. United States, 365 F.2d 103 (10th Cir. 1966); undenied—State v. Hampton, 430 S.W.2d 160 (Mo.1968); and unrefuted—United States v. Guiliano, 383 F.2d 30 (3rd Cir. 1967). It is usually considered proper to refer directly to the fact that no defense was presented. United States v.

Broadhead, 413 F.2d 1351 (7th Cir. 1969); contra, State v. Murphy, 13 Ohio App.2d 159, 234 N.E.2d 619 (1967).

Many courts hold that the bare statement that evidence is uncontradicted, in the absence of additional facts or circumstances, is not improper. Rinella v. United States, 60 F.2d 216 (7th Cir. 1932); Jardon v. United States, 324 F.2d 178 (5th Cir. 1963); People v. Novak, 370 Ill. 220, 18 N. E.2d 235 (1938). Also see 14 A.L.R.3d 723. Cases upholding the statement generally rely upon the absence of direct reference to the defendant—Edward v. Patterson, 249 F.Supp. 311 (D.C.Cal.1965); Thompson v. State, 41 Ala.App. 353, 132 So.2d 386 (1961); or the absence or paucity of defense evidence—People v. McLeod, 30 Cal.App. 435, 158 P. 506 (1916); People v. Martin, 62 Ill.App.2d 203, 210 N.E.2d 798 (1965), aff'd 35 Ill.2d 289, 220 N.E.2d 170); or the truth and accuracy of the comment—Davis v. United States, 279 F.2d 127 (4th Cir. 1960), cert. denied 364 U.S. 822, 81 S.Ct. 60); or that the comment was confined to prosecution evidence showing only that a crime has been committed—People v. Jones, 33 Ill.2d 357, 211 N.E.2d 261 (1965); Scobey v. State, 145 Tex.Crim. 481, 169 S.W.2d 185 (1943).

2. A particular problem is presented by a defendant who represents himself. If the defendant confines himself to conventional argument, the prosecutor is entitled only to the standard instruction that the arguments of counsel are not evidence. If the accused makes persistent use of his right to address court and jury to make statements amounting to the offering of testimony, the prosecutor may comment on his failure to testify. State v. Schultz, 46 N.J. 254, 216 A.2d 372 (1966).

3. There is one further limited exception to *Griffin*. In cases where inference of guilt arises from some unexplained act, i. e., unexplained possession of recently stolen property, the prosecutor may comment on the absence of explanation (which of course need not, but usually is, given only by defendant). United States v. Davis, 437 F.2d 928 (7th Cir. 1971); State v. DiRienzo, 53 N.J. 360, 251 A.2d 99 (1969).

UNITED STATES v. LATIMER

United States Court of Appeals, Tenth Circuit, 1975.
511 F.2d 498.

JUDGE HOLLOWAY delivered the Court's opinion.

* * *

Second, we turn to appellant's claim of misconduct by Government counsel during final summation in "testifying as to evidence which had not been admitted or proven at trial," thus denying him a fair trial in violation of due process.

At trial two tellers who observed the robbery testified that they had activated the bank's alarm and camera system during the robbery. However, no pictures taken by the camera were introduced by the Government, and no explanation was given as to why the film was not produced. In final argument appellant's counsel pointed to this omission and argued the inference that the film was not produced because it did not identify appellant.

In rebuttal argument Government counsel replied by stating that the film was not offered because the camera mal-functioned; that the films did not show anything; that they didn't show anybody robbing the bank; and that in fact they showed an FBI agent who arrived quite awhile after the incident. Objection by appellant's counsel was made at the outset of such argument, renewed and overruled by the court.

The Government says the argument was responsive to remarks by appellant's counsel; that prohibiting response to the adverse inference would have been improper; and that admissibility of the films was questionable because of the mal-functioning of the camera.

We must disagree with the Government's argument. We start with the fact that appellant's counsel argued a proper inference. The proof had shown operation of the camera and there was no offer of film or explanation for its non-production. Argument of the unfavorable inference was clearly proper. . . . Thus appellant's counsel made *proper* argument, and it cannot serve as any justification for *improper* response by Government counsel on any theory that there is wide latitude for response in argument.[1] We have recently made it clear that even if improper argument is made by defense counsel, the door is not thereby opened to similar conduct by the prosecution. United States v. Ludwig, 508 F.2d 140 (10th Cir. 1974).

The argument by Government counsel violated two fundamental rules. First the argument went outside the record and made statements as to facts not proven as to the malfunctioning of the camera and that the film showed the FBI agent after the incident. This was clearly improper. . . . Second, the statement put the personal knowledge and belief of the prosecuting attorney on the scales, which is also clearly improper. . . . The defense objections were good and should have been sustained. We must hold that the improper and prejudicial argument calls for a new trial. . . .

Accordingly the judgment is reversed and the case remanded for a new trial.

HILL, CIRCUIT JUDGE (dissenting).

I am compelled to respectfully dissent. My distinguished brothers have chosen to upset the conviction for what seems to me to be a trivial error in the trial of the case. Defense counsel in his jury argument invited the occurrence relied upon by the majority. He participated in both the preliminary hearing before the magistrate and the trial under review. On both occasions he heard evidence to the effect one of the witnesses had activated the camera inside the bank.

---

1. It is true that such adverse inferences are open to explanation by circumstances which make some other hypothesis a more natural one than the party's fear of exposure, and that the party is entitled to explain the nonproduction. See II Wigmore, Evidence § 285 (3d ed. 1940); Mc-Cormick, Evidence § 272 at 657 n. 31 (2d ed. 1972). However, such explanation may not be accomplished in the manner attempted here. The nonproduction of evidence which a party would normally be expected to produce may be explained by the testimony of other witnesses, properly sworn and subject to cross-examination, or by the introduction of other evidence at trial.

No photographs from this camera were offered by the prosecution. Certainly the defense counsel knew the reason such evidence was not offered. It is undisputed that the camera malfunctioned. Under these cirumstances defense counsel was clearly "out of bounds" when he referred to the camera and asked the jury to draw an inference favorable to his client. There is ample undisputed eye witness identification testimony in the record together with an admission from the defendant that he was in the vicinity of the bank that was robbed about the same time as the robbery took place. In this setting the prosecutor should be permitted to set the record straight. Even better procedure would have been for the trial judge to advise the jury as to the true facts. In any event I fail to find any error prejudicial to the defendant justifying a new trial. This court has many times reiterated that a criminal defendant is entitled to a fair trial which does not necessarily mean a perfect trial. Viewing all of the evidence I must conclude appellant had a fair trial.

NOTE

Where evidence has been suppressed on defense motion, how far can defense counsel go in urging the jury to draw inferences from the absence of such testimony? Suppose that an out-of-court identification was suppressed because the accused's right to counsel at a lineup was violated. Suppose further that an in-court identification was permitted after a finding that such an identification had origins independent of the lineup. (See Casebook, ch. 3, § A.) Can defense counsel argue that the evidence shows that the first post-crime identification occurred at trial when he knows that is not true? If he did, could the prosecutor respond by telling the jury about the lineup? Should the prosecutor be permitted to re-open his case at this point? Can a prosecutor ever respond to a defense argument by referring to matters not in evidence?

For a case where the defense innuendo occurred during the questioning of the eye-witness rather than in argument, see United States v. Johnson, 502 F.2d 1373 (7th Cir. 1974).

UNITED STATES v. YOUNG

United States Court of Appeals, D.C.Cir. 1972.
463 F.2d 934.

LEVENTHAL, CIRCUIT JUDGE.

Appellant was indicted for first degree murder and convicted of the lesser-included offense of second degree murder. His appeal claims that questions and remarks by the prosecutor in cross-examination and argument to the jury were improper and, in the absence of corrective instructions, deprived him of a fair trial. We affirm.

I.   THE FACTS

The Government's Case

Margaret May related the following events: On Thursday, August 14, 1969, decedent Willie R. Jefferson participated in a card game . . . with appellant James J. Young and others. All the partici-

pants were drinking. The game began around 2:30 p. m. and continued until 6:30 or 6:45 p. m. Shortly thereafter Jefferson, the big
winner, offered to return his winnings to the others because he didn't
need the money. As he started to hand the money back to the players
Mr. Young "snatched" his share. Jefferson then "reached after Mr.
Young, and Mr. Young got back," and Jefferson "told him if he do
that again, he would have to get his gun." Mr. Young said he would
likewise get his gun. Both men then left.

.   .   .   Young returned fifteen minutes later, came into the
hallway, and knocked on Jefferson's apartment door. He had a gun
in his right hand. Mrs. May's account continues:

> He knocked on Mr. Jefferson's door real loud, and the
> door didn't open right then; so he took his foot and kicked
> the man's door in; and at that time, the door flew open;
> Mr. Jefferson at the door; and that is when Mr. Young
> asked, told him, you thought I wouldn't come back, and
> called him a bad word. [M. F.]

She then saw and heard Young shoot Jefferson three times and
run out of the building. Jefferson had said nothing, had made no
movement, and had nothing in his hand. This account was corroborated.

The Alibi Defense

Appellant testified: He, Jefferson, and Mary Young played the
entire game until it ended at 5:00 p. m. He testified that Jefferson
had lost all his money and had to borrow from friends to continue.
At one point Young caught Jefferson cheating, "and so I told him if
you all going to start cheating, I might as well get out the game."
Appellant denied getting angry or arguing with Jefferson; he simply
left the game. On the way over to pick up his car, he was met by
Rudolph Ford, who had previously left the card game and gotten the
car. They went to two bars until 7:00 p. m. and thereafter they went
to Ford's apartment where they spent the rest of the night. Appellant learned of Jefferson's death by shooting on Sunday, August 17,
the day he was arrested.

* * *

Rudolph Ford, the principal alibi witness, testified to the same
effect as appellant Young, with some difference in details. He said
he and Young had left their construction job early on August 14,
cashed their paychecks at a liquor store, and gone to Mrs. Green's
house where they decided to play cards. Ford left the game three
times, first to buy some liquor, second, to check on Young's car which
was being repaired, but was not yet finished, and the third time to
pick the car up. He drove back to the area of the game at about 5:00
p. m. and picked up Young, who had left the game and was waiting
for Ford at a corner.

Ford testified that he was with appellant until the next morning.
They visited two bars and then spent the rest of the night at Ford's

house in the company of Ford's relatives. Ford learned at work the next day that Jefferson had been shot. On Monday, August 18, he learned that Young was charged with shooting someone. When he visited Young in jail, he learned that Young was charged with shooting Jefferson.

*   *   *

Prosecution References to "Missing Witnesses"

Appellant's major attack concerns efforts by the prosecutor to discredit his alibi by inferences to be drawn from the absence of persons mentioned in the alibi account.

On cross-examination, after appellant testified that one Hazel Davis drove him to the card game, the prosecutor asked "Is he here now?" and "Did you make any efforts to get him here?" Referring to Young's testimony that he cashed his paycheck at a liquor store, the prosecutor asked:

"Q: This man that cashed the check at the liquor store, *did you make any efforts to get him here?*

"A: For what reason?

"Q: Can you answer the question, yes or no?

"A: I can't answer."

THE COURT: I think that is a proper answer. What possible reason would he have to have him here? I think the question is quite inappropriate and if an objection was made I would sustain it.

*   *   *

[At bench conference.]

THE COURT: I have indicated to you before, Mr. _____, not only on this trial but on other trials, that I am not favorably disposed toward asking a man who is incarcerated in jail what efforts he has made to get witnesses present. The question of the choice of witnesses is a matter for the tactics and determination of his counsel in connection with the trial. I think it carries to the jury perhaps an implication that he had some obligation to bring these people where, frankly, I can't see where the testimony would be material.

*   *   *

"He doesn't have to corroborate times that are not alibi times. You are talking about what he did in the morning in terms of whether he got two beers or six beers, which has nothing to do with alibi. I think in any event it is counsel's obligation to make those determinations and not an incarcerated man with no particular legal experience."

In cross-examining Rudolph Ford, who had testified that he and appellant went to a bar after leaving the card game, the prosecutor asked if he remembered the name and address of the bar. Ford was not sure. The trial judge sustained defense counsel's objection to the question "You never went back and checked out what address it was?" and observed, "There is no requirement he do that." Later, after Ford said that he had talked briefly with the bar's proprietor, the prosecutor asked, "By the way, sir, that proprietor is not here at this trial, is he?" The trial judge sustained the defense objection, saying "He has no obligation in any regard."

The prosecutor had another occasion to advert to missing witnesses when he focused on Ford's testimony that Young went to Ford's home after they left the bars and stayed there all night. The prosecutor asked Ford who else was at the house that night and Ford gave the names of three witnesses: his cousin, aunt and aunt's boyfriend, and said that they all sat together talking. (Tr. 252–253). No question was raised in advance of summation to the jury concerning the presence or absence of these witnesses. But in closing argument to the jury the prosecutor said:

> "You saw Ford. Are you going to believe him? Ford works with the Defendant, has worked with him, he said, for a couple of years. Are you going to believe him? With the Defendant. Poor recollection of times, places, names, people. He says they talked to people in the two bars. Doesn't recall any of the names. *People not here.* He says that the Defendant went to his house and stayed there that night. Three of his relatives were there that night when they came. *You haven't heard from them, have you?* Are you going to believe Ford?" (Emphasis supplied.)

It is the rule, applicable in criminal as well as civil cases, "if a party has it peculiarly within his power to produce witnesses whose testimony would elucidate the transaction, the fact that he does not do it permits an inference that the testimony, if produced, would have been unfavorable." Both comment by counsel and instruction by the judge as to absent witnesses is prohibited if either of the conditions is lacking, that the witness was peculiarly within the power of the party to produce, and that his testimony would elucidate the transaction.

Plainly the persons referred to by appellant as the man in the liquor store who cashed the paychecks, and the man (Hazel Davis) who drove them earlier in the afternoon, were not "witnesses whose testimony would elucidate the transaction" within the meaning of the missing-witness rule for their testimony would barely have been relevant and certainly could not be considered material. These witnesses encountered Young and Ford well before Young and Ford were admittedly present at the card game. The trial judge was correct in his comments. Their testimony was so remote in time as not to be material, and the Government would not have been entitled to a missing witness instruction. It was not proper for the prosecutor to make a comment during his summation in order to persuade the jury to draw an inference against defendant from the fact that they had not been called by the defense as witnesses.

If a prosecutor engages in prejudicial summation it is not dispositive that defense counsel did not object, especially, since objection cannot always procure a realistic cure for the damage. The question is one of degree, and it counts against this prosecutor that he made his improper comment after having been admonished by the judge to abstain, from this line. Nor is it decisive that part of the prosecutor's argument was justified—such as the comment on the failure of appellant and Ford to remember the names of the persons they met in the bars. The intermesh of the proper may actually escalate the impact of the improper, just as some truth may bait the hook for the impact of a partial lie or libel.

However we do not discern that the references to these relatively remote witnesses wrought the kind of prejudice which warrants reversal. This is not the kind of repetition of references to insignificant absences that "cumulate to the point of distortion." These references, like the prosecutor's questions and comment concerning Ford's failure to contact the police and give a statement, are more fairly condemnable for their weakness than prejudicial impact, a possibility that was further muted by the fact that the trial judge made it clear to the jury that this approach of the prosecutor "is quite inappropriate." This matter is appropriately left by treating it as not ground for reversal but as context wherein more weight may accrue to other objectionable comments of prosecutor.

We now consider the three persons who, Ford said, saw Young at Ford's house. Their testimony would have been material, indeed would have provided important corroboration of the alibi if they had testified in court, and hence would have "elucidated" the issues. Ford's testimony was bolstered by the specific detail provided by his naming his relatives who were present that night, and a desire on the part of the prosecution to comment on their absence is understandable.

We turn to the prosecutor's comments concerning Ford's relatives, for we cannot bypass these on the claim of harmless error. We begin with the fact that he did not follow the specific procedures prescribed by this court to be followed before a party may comment on the absence of witnesses from the trial, in order to avoid the prejudice which can result from improper use of such comment. Surely it should not be put to the jury, as either instruction or argument, that an inference should be drawn from a party's failure to produce witnesses if the judge concludes that the party was powerless to do so, Gass v. United States, 135 U.S.App.D.C. 11, 19, 416 F.2d 767, 775 (1969).

To avoid prejudicial misuse of comment on a party's failure to call witnesses we required in *Gass*, supra, 135 U.S.App.D.C. at 19–20, 416 F.2d at 775–776:

> . . . that for the future when counsel, either for the prosecution or the defense, intends to argue to the jury for an inference to be derived from the absence of a witness, an

advance ruling from the trial court should be sought and obtained.

* * *

The prosecutor's comment would have been improper as to any witnesses defendant would have been powerless to produce at trial, e. g., because he did not know their whereabouts or could not make them amenable to subpoena. We take into account, as the court did in *Gass*, that defense trial counsel did not raise an objection, and that several witnesses were involved. In *Gass* there were eight witnesses, and the court put it as likely that at least one of them was available, a circumstance supporting the prosecutor's comment to that extent. In the case at bar, there are three witnesses, and the overall context is one in which several of the card players could not be found by the marshal.

* * *

In the case at bar, defense trial counsel did not shrink from presenting objections to the prosecutor's summation which he thought appropriate; and indeed he made one shortly prior to these references. If he were concerned lest he emphasize objectionable matters in the mind of the jury, he could have sought a bench conference.

What in the last analysis seems decisive in this case is that defense trial counsel not only failed to object to the prosecutor's references, he tried to use these as a predicate for offering his own comments, in argument, to the absence of Clinton Lee and Johnny Edwards. The fact that his maneuver was properly rejected, since the Government had tried but had been unable to subpoena these men, does not lessen the impact of his earlier silence. In the circumstances, including the fact that although the witnesses were not linked to defendant directly they were relatives of his friend, we think the probability of a substantial claim of defense inability to call or subpoena Ford's relatives, is not sufficient, given the failure to object, the attempt to make tactical use of the reference, the lack of any motion in the trial court or this court, supported by a meaningful affidavit of such defense inability, to result in a reversal or remand in the interest of justice.

Our conclusion that the uncontested comments of the prosecutor should not occasion reversal is fortified by our appraisal that it is most unlikely that the defense could have succeeded in any alternative contention that the prosecutor's comment be hushed on the ground that even assuming the witnesses were available to the defense they were equally available to the prosecution. We are aware that in Brown v. United States, 134 U.S.App.D.C. 269, 414 F.2d 1165 (1969), the court said that a missing witness instruction cannot be given against a defendant unless there is a showing that the witness was not available to be subpoenaed by the Government. But *Brown* is subject to the qualification that "availability" of a witness to the Government, as to any other party, must be judged "practically as well as physically." Stewart v. United States, 135 U.S.App.D.C. 274,

279, 418 F.2d 1110, 1115 (1969). Thus, no inference may arise from the failure to call a witness to give testimony implicating himself. And whether a person is to be regarded as equally available to both sides may depend not only on physical availability but on his "relationship" to the parties. The central question is whether from all the circumstances an inference of unfavorable testimony from an absent witness is a natural and reasonable one.

We are aware that the foregoing does not by any means answer all of the questions that arise with respect to missing witnesses. But it serves to assure us concerning the present case, that it presents a context which makes it improbable that any serious claim of unfairness or prejudice would lie against the prosecutor for comment on the failure of defense to call Ford's relatives, even assuming it could have been established that the Government had opportunity to obtain their attendance by process.

We also take note that this was a case where there was no instruction by the judge. This factor merits some exposition. There is a difference between an instruction, which has the weight of law, and argument of counsel, which is only that. Argument of counsel is limited, however, by requirements such as that it must not be in conflict with the law to be declared by the trial judge and it must not taint the trial with unfairness. As our rulings in *Wynn* and *Pennewell* make clear, when the judge concludes that the witness was not peculiarly available to a party, or that his testimony would not be such as to elucidate the transaction, comment of opposing counsel arguing for an inference from his absence is contrary to law and unfair, and cannot be permitted in argument to the jury. We suggested in *Wynn* and required in *Gass* that a lawyer proposing to comment on absence of a witness first bring the matter to the attention of the trial judge, in order to avoid unnecessary prejudicial error in the case.

We also pointed out in *Gass* that ordinarily a judge permitting argument by counsel should prepare an instruction concerning the inference so as to avoid the risk of prejudicial error and enable the jury to discharge its functions. The judge has the duty to give an instruction if he concludes that the case is clear for a missing witness inference against a party, e. g., the party had the physical ability to locate and produce the witness, and there was such a relationship, in legal status or on the facts as claimed by the party as to make it natural to except the party to have called the witness. But in the in-between case where each side has the physical capacity to locate and produce the witness, and it is debatable which side might more naturally have been expected to call the witness, there may be latitude for the judge to leave the matter to debate without an instruction, simply permitting each counsel to argue to the jury concerning the "natural" inference of fact to be drawn. Permitting the issue to be debated in argument generates a duty to provide an elucidating instruction if one is sought; it is only in the context of lack of request that we contemplate some latitude to omit an instruction.

The basis for omitting the instruction, though ordinarily provided pursuant to *Gass*, would be the conclusion of the judge, first, that even in the absence of instruction the situation is sufficiently clear cut that counsel's argument can be fairly understood and appraised by the jury, without prejudicial impact; and second, that the preparation of a careful instruction to state the ground rules for appraising counsel's argument would be unnecessary and time-consuming; and, possibly, third, that such instruction might even be distracting, conceivably counter-productive, leading a jury, respectful of the court's concerns, to focus unduly on the non-evidence rather than the evidence in the case.

In many cases, perhaps most cases, however, the trial judge may conclude that an instruction would be helpful, and toward that end we have included in the Appendix to this opinion, a specimen instruction which the trial judge may find it useful to use or adapt.

In this case there was argument without an instruction, and the context of the argument was such that we discern no prejudicial error.

Affirmed.

APPENDIX

Specimen Instruction on Absent Witnesses

Counsel have argued that you should draw an inference from the absence of certain witnesses. The court has determined that each side had the ability to produce the witnesses. If you conclude that the testimony of a witness would have cast significant light on the issues, and that it would have been natural for one of the parties to have called that witness in support of his presentation if the facts known by the witness had been favorable to the position of that party, you may infer that if the witness had been called he would have given testimony that would have been unfavorable to that party which failed to call him. But you are not required to draw that inference. And if you think that it would have been equally natural for each of the parties to have called the witness, and that each might equally have been expected to do so, then you may rightly conclude that since an equal inference could be drawn against each party, they cancel each other out. And if the matter seems doubtful, then you may rightly decide that no inference should be drawn from the absence of the witness. In that event, your verdict should be based on the evidence that was presented in court, and should not be affected by the witnesses who were not called.

SPOTTSWOOD W. ROBINSON, III, CIRCUIT JUDGE (concurring):

I join unreservedly in affirmance of appellant's conviction and, in all respects save one, in Judge Leventhal's excellent opinion for the court. My sole difficulty is the holding that in some instances the trial judge has latitude to permit counsel to argue to the jury for an adverse inference from the absence of a trial witness without an instruction by the judge to the jury on that score.

* * *

The whereabouts of the witness may be unknown. He may bear such a relationship with one party as to deter the other from calling him. The witness may be relatively unimportant, able only to offer testimony that is cumulative or inferior. The witness may be biased against the non-calling party, or the testimony anticipated may be privileged. A party may have some other satisfactory explanation for nonproduction. The witness, moreover, may be equally available to both parties, in which event each may be open to an adverse inference depending for strength upon the surrounding circumstances. This catalog is intended to be illustrative rather than exhaustive. And very importantly the missing witness inference is permissive, never mandatory, and even when indulged "exerts [only] impeaching [but] not probative force."

Unlike ordinary evidentiary inferences, then, the missing witness inference is not one that jurors can deal with safely by a process of simple deduction from the fact that the witness did not appear. It is, rather, an inference the accuracy of which depends upon scrupulous observance of the considerations that might serve to give it validity. In sum, it is of a piece with other inferences that are to be indulged only when special conditions have been met, and are to be utilized only for a limited purpose. When lay jurors are not specifically instructed on these topics, counsel's arguments for an inference can be treacherous.

NOTES

1. Prosecution comment on the failure to produce witnesses is logically similar to the comment that the state's evidence is uncontradicted. The comment on missing witnesses is, of course, more specific than the use of the general "uncontradicted". Furthermore, the missing witness is an argument that the defense may have more use for than the prosecution.

Occasionally the courts decide that the defense may use the missing witness argument freely when the absence of the witness is unexplained, because the government has the burden of proof. People v. Gonzales, 125 Ill. App.2d 225, 260 N.E.2d 234 (1970). The prosecutor may usually respond by asserting that the defense did not use its right to subpoena, a right which is as great as the prosecution's. United States v. Panepinto, 430 F. 2d 613 (3rd Cir. 1970).

The more common rule is to apply the general principles announced in United States v. Young to both parties. Many courts adopt the rule that comment by either party is prohibited when the witness is equally available to both parties. United States v. Arendale, 444 F.2d 1260 (5th Cir. 1971); Slater v. State, 43 Ala.App. 513, 194 So.2d 93 (1966); State v. Houston, 451 S.W.2d 37 (Mo.1970). The question of equal accessability depends upon more than mere amenability to subpoena or absence of privilege as United States v. Young points out. Relationships arising from family and business ties as well as friendship are significant factors in determining equality of access.

2. Occasionally, counsel wish to comment on the absence of material evidence. A common defense tactic is to ask, in closing argument, "where are the guns, jewels, fingerprints, bloody shirt, hair samples, fingernail scrapings, etc.?" *If* a prosecutor has established that evidence technicians

made appropriate efforts to secure such evidence but failed to do so, he may argue an inference that the defendant is responsible for the absence of such evidence. People v. Williams, 40 Ill.2d 522, 240 N.E.2d 645 (1968)—accused could not afford to allow weapon to turn up and be submitted to ballistic analysis; State v. Wrose, 463 S.W.2d 792 (Mo.1971)—absence of fingerprints shows professionalism.

An improper commenting on missing witnesses, when promptly admonished by the trial judge, who specifically instructs the jury to disregard prosecutor's comments, does not justify reversal. Dunlap v. United States, 165 U.S. 486, 17 S.Ct. 375; United States v. Socony-Vacuum Oil Co., 310 U.S. 150, 60 S.Ct. 811 (1940); Kawalchuk v. United States, 176 F.2d 873 (6th Cir. 1949); United States v. Haile, 443 F.2d 1295 (9th Cir. 1971). As the Supreme Court said very early in *Dunlap*, supra, at 853: "If every remark made by counsel outside of the testimony were ground for reversal, comparatively few verdicts would stand".

3. An excellent discussion of prosecution argument appears in Vess, "Walking A Tightrope: A Survey of Limitations on the Prosecutor's Closing Argument", 64 J.Crim.L. & Criminology 22 (1973). Portions of this article are reprinted here (the footnotes are omitted, but illustrative examples from the footnotes, without citations, are reprinted in the body of the text in brackets):

Comments On The Scope Of Prosecution Argument

The public prosecutor is responsible for the enforcement of the laws against those who disobey them. Unlike his opposing counsel, whose primary duty is to his client, the prosecutor represents all of the people within his jurisdiction. This creates in the prosecutor's office a position unique to that basic part of our judicial system, the adversary process; for it means that the accused can expect, and indeed must demand, the prosecutor to represent his interests insofar as he, too, is a member of the prosecutor's broad constituency.

* * *

Limitations Upon Prosecutorial Closing Argument

The Relationship of Opening Argument to Rebuttal Argument

The prosecution usually makes the first closing argument and is generally granted rebuttal time in which to respond to the defense closing argument. All essential points must be fairly stated in the opening argument so that the defense has an adequate opportunity to respond. During the rebuttal the prosecutor may in turn only respond to the defense summation. No new line of argument may be introduced. . . .

Commenting on the Law

Since the purpose of argument is to enlighten the jury, the prosecutor may comment on the applicable principles of law during summation, emphasizing the theory of the government's case and the criminal law and perhaps the purposes of the particular statutes involved. However, it is improper for the prosecutor to misstate the law, ...

* * *

Commenting on the Evidence

"A trial is a patchwork of bits and pieces of evidence. A jury may not appreciate the significance of many of these scraps until they have been pieced together by an artful advocate."

The prosecution and defense counsel are likely to take very different, possibly diametrically opposed, approaches to piecing together the evidence in closing argument.　Hence, the court must confer great latitude in the manner, style, and content of summation.

The general rule regarding comment on the evidence is that such comment is proper if it is either proved by direct evidence or is a fair and reasonable inference from the facts and circumstances proved and has bearing on an issue.　The prosecutor is permitted to argue from his own understanding and interpretation of the evidence and the defense cannot be heard to complain merely because the prosecutor's reasoning is faulty or his deductions illogical, though the defense may definitely make such points in its own summation.

An inference is defined as "a process of reasoning by which a fact or proposition sought to be established is deduced as a logical consequence from other facts, or a state of facts, already proved or admitted."　For example, where there was testimony that a fingerprint was found in a red substance, and that the victim was severely beaten, the inference that the print was left in blood was proper.　Similarly, it was within bounds to argue that someone other than the accused punched his time card where there was testimony that there was no way of knowing who punched a particular card.　.　.　.

* * *

.　.　.　Conversely it follows from the general rule that the prosecutor's remarks are improper if not based directly on the evidence, if not reasonably inferred from the evidence, or if they relate to matters outside the issues in the case.　.　.　.

In conformity to the general rule and the enunciated policies, it is naturally improper to misstate the evidence or contradict the record.　These may not be grounds for reversal, however, where the mistake is slight or inadvertent.　.　.　.

There is one recognized exception to the rule that remarks not based in the evidence are improper; such remarks are proper if they concern matters of general knowledge or experience.　Usually such comments are made by the prosecutor for illustrative purposes or dramatic effect and refer to historical facts, public personalities, principles of divine law, biblical teachings, or prominent current events in the community or the nation.　.　.　.

Prosecutorial Conduct During Argument

General Actions.　The considerable latitude permitted the prosecutor in commentary is equally applicable to his conduct during summation. Thus it is generally proper for him to move freely about the courtroom. However, the prosecutor should not sit in the witness chair while delivering his argument since it might give the jury the impression that the argument is testimonial in nature or possibly suggest the truth of the statements made.　Also because of the potential impact on the jurors, addressing individual jurors has been repeatedly disapproved.　Similarly, remarks directed to the defendant are not condoned.　.　.　.

* * *

Use of Real and Demonstrative Evidence.　The use of and reference to admitted real evidence is widely recognized as proper, so long as the action portrayed conforms with that indicated in the record.　For example, it was permissible for the prosecutor, in describing an event, to pick up and swing a two-wheeled hand cart, suggesting the manner in which the wounds were inflicted, where this was in accord with the testimony. It was also proper for the prosecutor, in attempting to demonstrate the manner in which the defendant's fingerprints were left on a door at the scene of the crime, to show how the door had been pushed back and forth, since there was testimony to this effect. Furthermore, the prosecutor was permitted to jump repeatedly for about two minutes in a loud and noisy manner on a piece of paper he had thrown on the floor where such conformed with the description of the defendant's treatment of the victim. On the other hand, it was error for the prosecutor to stand before the jury for three minutes holding a sawed-off shotgun in his hands since the conditions of the crime had not been adequately recreated.

It may also be proper for the prosecutor to demonstrate the government's theory of the crime where there is no affirmative testimony but his action conforms to the state of the evidence. Thus, it was permissible for the prosecutor to rub a pistol with a shirt, both of which were in evidence, to demonstrate his theory supporting the reason why no prints were found on the gun.

*   *   *

Commenting on Witnesses

The examination of witnesses is likely to take up a good part of any trial. Commentary on the testimony, character, and credibility of the witnesses will often require a proportional amount of the prosecutor's summation. Proper remarks by the prosecutor are those which are reasonably justified by the evidence or testimony, and are restricted to presenting an interpretation of the testimony, pointing out conflicts and inconsistencies, and discussing the reliability of the witnesses.

The ultimate issue of credibility is for the jury alone. For the same policy reasons previously discussed, the prosecutor's personal beliefs and opinions as to the truthfulness of the testimony and the character of the witnesses must be avoided; otherwise the veracity of the prosecutor may be placed in issue.

[Within the foregoing limitations the prosecutor may comment favorably, as follows, upon any witness who testifies for either the prosecution or the defense:]

(that government witness has testified truthfully where prosecutor did not say or insinuate that his statement was based upon personal knowledge); (regarding testimony of informers with admitted records, "It takes a thief to catch a thief"); (to acquit defendant jury would have to find witnesses perjurors); ("reputable" officers and "very sweet" complaining witness); (very accurate); (that there was not one bit of conduct on part of witness that rang with anything but truth); (that in any criminal case, witness should be given credit for testifying was proper); (according a citizen credit for doing his civic duty is not the same as an expression of personal opinion that a witness is credible); (witness had nothing to gain by informing police he had committed sodomy with defendant). *But* (that if complaining witness had made any prior inconsistent statement, then defense would have used it to impeach was improper); (that chief government witness was a government employee and therefore eminently credible, improper).

[Or the prosecutor may comment unfavorably on any witness, as follows:]

(that after defendant was caught, the best way for him to get out of his predicament was to hire the best scientists in the country to present their theories that he was psychotic and lost contact with reality during the crime); (defense witnesses members of criminal element); (prosecutor said he was not asking jury to believe that government witnesses were "nice people"); (suggesting defendant's alibi witness had given false testimony); (in prostitution prosecution, that evidence was cluttered with disgusting, shocking, maybe dirty, disrespectful, dishonest testimony and ideas); (evidence justified references to two policemen as the "I don't remember twins" and to police chief as "shifty," and accusation that the three were corrupt); (remark that prosecutor did not consider testimony of government witness reliable could not prejudice defendant); (using phrase "ring around a rosy" to describe situation where defendant had testified for his witness in a witness's case); (discrediting government witness's testimony as to defendant's appearance). *But* (saying government considered defense witness such a scoundrel that he had to be watched, improper); (should not argue personalities, here regarding doctor who testified for defense); (defendant's family "tried to frame up a story" and jury should not let them "come in here with some trumped up perjury defense" improper).

This includes comment upon the inconsistent accounts of the crime, possible sources of bias, and prior convictions, as well as participation in the crime and courtroom conduct. There is some question concerning the propriety of characterizing a witness as liar or perjuror, however, even if accurate.

If justified by the evidence, reference to the fact that a witness was afraid to testify and was given protection may be condoned. However, when a witness does not testify, it is improper to suggest what the testimony would have been since this is clearly beyond the evidence in the case.

Commenting on the Defendant

* * *

Testimony at Trial. The defendant who testifies at trial is subject to cross-examination and impeachment, and the prosecutor may comment on this testimony in accordance with the same rules applicable to comments on the testimony of other witnesses. Remarks should be restricted to the defendant's credibility. Characterizing the testimony is proper if the characterization is based on the evidence and is not an assertion of personal belief.

[A prosecutor, therefore, may use the following expressions:]

("lies"); (defendant's testimony was incredible in view of the evidence); (incredible though expected after a plea of not guilty); ("cock and bull story"); (defendant and his witnesses were "political bosses, dishonest and unworthy of belief"); ("fantastic"); ("would not believe anything defendant said"); (a "bunch of hogwash"). *But* ("a recent fabrication to lure the jury and hoodwink them," improper); ("a lie and fabrication," amounted to a personal opinion of defendant's guilt and was improper); ("If you believe I told him that I hope you will turn him loose," improper).]

* * *

Other Crimes. Prosecutors often attempt three rather subtle methods of calling juror attention to the defendant's prior crimes in cases in which no such evidence was presented. The first is to refer to the accused's "rap sheet" or to the appearance of his picture in police files. Each of these has been condemned repeatedly by the courts. The second method, comment upon testimony that a witness met the defendant during incarceration, is also improper. The third, equally improper in most cases, is suggestion that the defendant is an habitual criminal or professional miscreant.

Even if the evidence is properly in the record the prosecutor must be cautious not to assume facts in connection with the prior crimes beyond those shown by the evidence. Similarly, the prosecutor must confine his remarks to the purposes for which the proof was admitted, which usually restricts his comments to the credibility of the defendant. The only exception in which the remarks may relate more directly to guilt is where the evidence of prior similar convictions is considered probative of intent or motive to commit the present offense.

* * *

Conduct, Character and Appearance of the Defendant. The prosecutor may wish to discuss the defendant's conduct . . . .

The statements may relate to the accused's conduct in the course of or after the crime which is the basis for the prosecution. [Illustrative are these:]

(brutality of defendant's acts and that he had never shown remorse, proper); (flight); (confession); (calling defendant an "expert in furs" proper where evidence showed defendant had advised co-defendant which furs to take during robbery of furrier); ("merchant of murder" where defendant had hired another to kill); (defendant had never shown any remorse, improper).

. . . Whether or not the defendant testifies at the trial, the prosecutor may be able to refer to the defendant's pre-trial statements or to conversations with law enforcement officers. The prosecutor may also comment on the accused's conduct in court, . . . [Following are examples of permissibility:]

(accusation that defendant had sought to disguise his handwriting in giving exemplars); (defendant's conduct during agent's testimony); ("regular smart aleck" proper as a characterization of defendant's conduct during cross-examination).

[Furthermore, prosecutorial comment may be made on conduct at other times and places—for instance:]

(that drinking shown by evidence gave defendant a little extra power to perform rape); (illicit sexual relations with victim); (rhetorical question how many narcotics sales defendant had made in 41 days between the sale charged and his arrest, improper); (where prosecutor went beyond merely asking jury to disbelieve defendant who admitted committing adultery, and turned defendant's admitted acts into equivalence of guilt of violating Ten Commandments, he was using defendant's acts to indicate his propensity to commit murder, not just to impeach his credibility); (references to homosexual tendencies proper where discussed by defense psychiatrist).]

There is some disagreement among the courts concerning whether the use of invective or epithets in characterizing the accused is proper, even when based upon proven conduct. Whatever the view of a particular jurisdiction, . . . disparaging language has been permitted [such as:]

(where defendant plotted to kill wife by putting bomb on plane, proper to refer to him as a subhuman man and a true monster with a rancid, rotten mind); (junk pusher); (big ape and gorilla); ("crooks," "viruses" and "germs" proper); (con artist); (pill peddler and terror to community); (smart thief and parasite on the community); (suede shoe boys and aluminum siding racketeers); (vicious murderous pig); (thug); (where defense counsel compared defendant's conduct and ability to choose between right and wrong with chimpanzee, dog, and trained animal, based on psychiatrist's testimony, proper for prosecutor to reply that defendant had morals of a snake and was a slimy beast); (beast); (under some circumstances, it may be reversible error to characterize defendant as offender; here, it was proper to refer to defendant as robber where witness identified him); (mean punks and vicious men); (goons); (mad dog); (beast); (wolves, in sodomy prosecution); (savage). *But* (big fish, improper); (beast, improper); (referring to defendant as a pervert, weasel, moron, and telling jury that defendant who raped his mother's friend, would rape a dog and would rape each and every member of the jury, there being no evidence in the record to support such remarks); (unpredictable animal, improper); (beastly nature, improper); (junky, rat, and sculptor with a knife, improper); (lower than the bone belly of a cur dog).

Perhaps the reason for the foregoing rulings is the reluctance of the courts to find reversible error on characterization alone. Furthermore, such remarks may be appropriate if based upon the charge which the evidence tends to prove, rather than upon the conduct of the defendant as shown by the evidence. A common example is reference to one charged with armed robbery as a potential murderer. An epithet which lacks a reasonable foundation in the evidence or the charge is improper; it is simply abusive and serves only to inflame and arouse the passions and prejudices of the jury. [Illustrative are the following:]

(where defense was insanity, that defendant should not be turned loose on society because of his homosexual proclivities invited a conviction because defendant was a homosexual); (defendant was doubly vicious because, knowing he was guilty, he demanded his constitutional rights, including right to trial, at which victim of alleged homosexual extortion ring was required to testify); (reference to defendant as a dope peddler where only possession charged).

The prosecutor may comment on the reputation and character of the accused only when the defendant has put such matters in issue, and the comments must be reasonably justified by the evidence.

If the defendant's physical appearance is gross in nature, the physical attributes are certainly obvious to the jury and emphasis should not be added through prosecutorial comment. The exception is where identification is put in issue by the defendant himself or his counsel; under such circumstances it may be appropriate for the prosecutor to comment upon the appearance of the defendant.

Failure to Cooperate Before Trial. The general rule is that the defendant's silence before trial is not a proper subject for comment, at least his silence subsequent to arrest. [Ed. Note: See Doyle v. Ohio, chapter 19–E.]

In those situations in which the courts have held that no privilege to refuse to cooperate exists, comment on such refusal, if properly proved, is permissible. Thus it is proper to point out that the defendant refused to participate in a lineup, or, with the exception of the polygraph, to remark on the failure of the accused to cooperate in the performance of certain experiments or tests.

Guilt. Consistent with the right to comment on the state of the evidence in the case, it is proper for the prosecutor to argue or express the opinion that the accused is guilty, but only where the prosecutor states or it is apparent that the opinion is based solely on the evidence. As in other contexts, the prosecutor must not make the statement one of personal belief, thereby suggesting to the jury that there is other convincing evidence of the defendant's guilt which is not before them.

Commenting on the Defense and Defense Counsel   *   *   *

It is permissible for the prosecutor to characterize the defense presented. However, he has less latitude when the focus of his argument turns from the defense generally to the defendant's counsel.

Consistent with this approach, it has been held improper for the prosecutor to comment in argument on defense counsel's objection to the admission of evidence or testimony or to portions of the prosecutor's summation.

*   *   *

It is also improper to reflect unfavorably on the role of defense counsel, implying the use of improper or unethical tactics, where such remarks are not justified by the evidence. [The following are illustrative:]

(confusing issue and throwing sand in juror's eyes); (cheap trick); (dishonest); (that defense counsel not an officer of court as prosecutor was); (repeatedly asserting that defense counsel was employing tactics designed to confuse jury); (defense was a fiction manufactured by defense counsel); (sandbagging witnesses); (defense lawyer's job is to try to get your eye off the defendant).

[However, where the evidence justifies critical remarks, the prosecutor may make them, as the following will illustrate:]

(proper to state that defense counsel's style of cross-examination deterred people from coming into court to testify, a fair comment on the record); (cross-examination of expert witness was an exhibition to confuse jury, proper); (where defense was that defendant had been involuntarily drugged by his companion, and did not have the requisite mental capacity to commit crime, proper to argue that a defendant who has been advised by a good attorney will not deny his presence at the crime scene but will raise this defense); (throwing dust in jurors' eyes proper).

.   .   . If the defense attorney takes the stand, his testimony is a proper subject for comment under the rules applicable to commenting on witnesses generally.

Commenting on the Duty of the Jury

The prosecutor may not instruct the jury in the law, but may instruct it as to its duty in the case since the prosecutor is responsible for law enforcement in the community. It is proper to dwell upon the evil results of the crime and to urge a fearless administration of the criminal law, and the prosecutor may remind the jury that it is there to protect the life and limb of every citizen, and that the people look to it for the protection against crime. It is proper for the prosecutor to urge the jury to impose severe punishment where it is the province of the jury to assess or recommend punishment. But because the jury verdict is to be reached solely through impartial deliberation on the evidence presented at trial, it is not proper for the prosecutor to suggest that the jury may consider matters outside the record, especially the existence of post-trial procedures, which might encourage the jury to render a guilty verdict.

Appeals to Sympathy and Prejudice

It is obviously improper for the prosecutor to do or say anything in summation the sole effect of which is to inflame the passion of or arouse the prejudice of the jury. Such remarks may encourage the jury to render a verdict based on its emotional response to unadmitted evidence which has no relationship to the guilt or innocence of the accused, rather than a verdict based upon reasoning from the record. The questions for review are to what extent, for what reasons, and with what effect were the arguments advanced. While caution against such comments is always required, it has been said that special care is required in the prosecution of sex offenses.

No attempt should be made to pressure the jury, such as by referring to the actions of other juries or to public sentiment regarding either the particular case or the jury system in general. It has also been deemed improper to refer to the victim of the crime or the victim's family. Furthermore, the prosecutor should not refer to the jurors or their families, hypothesizing the commission of the crime at issue against them. Comments exciting racial, religious, or class prejudice have been repeatedly condemned, as have appeals to the interests of the jurors as taxpayers or as members of a particular community.

While it is generally permissible to argue that a conviction would deter others from the commission of similar crimes, it has been held improper to suggest that if the defendant were acquitted he would commit further crimes or that a verdict of guilty would serve as a good example to young people. On the other hand, the prosecutor may comment on the brutal nature of the crime, point out the number of crimes that go unpunished, and stress the responsibility of the jury for law enforcement.

* * *

Retaliatory Statements and Remarks

When counsel believes that opposing counsel has made an improper comment, it should be called to the attention of the court as soon as possible through an objection. However, it is well established that the prosecutor has the right to make a fair reply to an argument previously made by the defense. Furthermore, the defense has no grounds for objection at trial or complaint on review where the prosecutor's remarks were invited or provoked by the improper comments of the defense, even though the prosecutor's remarks would otherwise be improper. This principle applies generally to all the limitations discussed above.

The courts have recognized, however, that this rule does not convert an improper remark into a proper one; an improper remark is still improper, even in retaliation. But response or invitation is a factor to be considered in evaluating the impact of the remark on the jury and determining possible prejudice to the defendant. Further, this is not to suggest that *any* remark offered in response to an improper defense comment will be considered specially. The prosecutor's statement must be a fair reply in order to avoid the danger of reversible error.

Appellate Review of the Record

Curing and Preserving Improper Argument. The rule generally applicable in the criminal law, that a failure to make a timely objection waives consideration of the alleged defect on review, applies to prosecutorial conduct during argument. The recognized exception to this rule is also applicable; that is, failure to object does not effect a waiver where the error is such that it could not have been cured and a refusal to review would deprive the defendant of a fair trial.

The courts are only slightly receptive to the contention that an objection merely places greater emphasis on the subject matter of the alleged transgression. The defense attorney is thus left in a dilemma, where the choice may be between waiving the error or making the prosecutor's point.

This situation is further complicated by the requirement that an objection be timely, complete and specific.

Assuming an objection is made, the prosecutor's transgression is considered cured where the trial court sustains the objection and either admonishes the jury to disregard, instructs the jury to disregard, or rebukes the prosecutor, or any combination of these which the trial court believes necessary to remove possible prejudice. It is only when the error is so fundamental that it cannot be cured by these methods that the trial court need resort to the more drastic remedy of mistrial.

* * *

In determining whether substantial prejudice to the defendant resulted from the prosecutorial summation, reviewing courts have looked to six other factors besides the law and the exact words used. First, the courts consider the strength of the evidence in the case, applying the standard harmless beyond a reasonable doubt. Thus, if the reviewing court finds overwhelming evidence of guilt, it will probably uphold the conviction, even though it may point to some improprieties which were properly preserved and before the court on review. But if the case is a close one, the court will be more likely to reverse. Some courts consider the punishment imposed in determining whether the jury was improperly influenced by the summation. Where an affirmative answer to this question appears and there is overwhelming evidence of guilt, the conviction will be sustained but the sentence will be modified.

Second, the court will consider the remarks in the context of the entire summation or a large part of it in order to determine the true extent and meaning of the disputed comments. Lengthy and repeated remarks are much more likely to result in reversal than are single or isolated references.

Third, the appellate court will consider whether the trial judge took the proper corrective action on the one hand, or further compounded the error by overruling the defense objection or by insufficiently curing the transgression, on the other.

Fourth, the court may take into account the length of the trial or the length of the argument. It may be that a misstatement in a short trial is not serious error, since the jurors should have an independent recollection of the evidence. On the other hand, a lengthy argument after a long trial is more likely to be imperfect, and minor transgressions in this setting may also be excused.

Fifth, the court may consider the atmosphere of the courtroom throughout the trial, and may be more reluctant to find reversible error where the case was "hotly contested" on both sides.

Finally, where the error in summation alone is not sufficient to require reversal, the court may then examine the cumulative effect of this impropriety in conjunction with other errors which occurred during the rest of the trial.

Conclusion

It is clear that some fine distinctions have been made by the courts in an effort to reconcile the prosecutor's dual roles as impartial representative of the people and vigorous advocate for the state. The prosecutor may fail to meet both obligations in a particular case, performing one task to the exclusion of the other. The appellate court, however, does not sit primarily to enforce ethical or moral standards (though it may frequently speak to the question of what constitutes propriety), but rather to determine whether, all things considered, the defendant did in fact receive a fair trial. The case law of a particular jurisdiction will reveal few if any forms of speech or conduct during summation which are *per se* reversible error. It will suggest many forms which are potentially reversible error and generally improper. It is the combination of these with the particular facts of a case which will dictate the limits of propriety for the prosecutorial closing argument.

Consider in connection with Vess' article, both opinions in United States ex. rel. Perry v. Mulligan, 399 F.Supp. 1285 (D.N.J.1976), rev'd. 544 F.2d 674 (3rd Cir. 1976).

4. With regard to the limitations on defense argument, the A.B.A. Standard for Closing Argument of the defense is similar to the Standard for the prosecution:

4-7.8   Argument to the jury

(a) In closing argument to the jury the lawyer may argue all reasonable inferences from the evidence in the record, it is unprofessional conduct for a lawyer intentionally to misstate the evidence or mislead the jury as to the inferences it may draw.

(b) It is unprofessional conduct for a lawyer to express his personal belief or opinion in his client's innocence or his personal belief or opinion in the truth or falsity of any testimony or evidence, or to attribute the crime to another person unless such an inference is warranted by the evidence.

(c) A lawyer should not make arguments calculated to inflame the passions or prejudices of the jury.

(d) A lawyer should refrain from argument which would divert the jury from its duty to decide the case on the evidence by injecting issues broader than the guilt or innocence of the accused under the controlling law or by making predictions of the consequences of the jury's verdict.

The Commentary to this Standard specifically condemns, under 7.8(c), arguments containing personal attacks on the prosecutor. Presumably defense counsel has some leeway to condemn prosecutorial tactics if justified by the record that the prosecution has when defense tactics are at issue. The value of such an attack, unless based on the evidence, is doubtful. The usual prosecution response is fairly effective i. e., "every lawyer in the criminal court knows that when the facts are against you, tell the jury about the law. If the law is against you, stress the facts to the jury. If both the law and the facts are against you, attack the prosecutor."

5. In Herring v. New York, 422 U.S. 853, 95 S.Ct. 2550 (1975), the Court held that Due Process prohibits the total denial of an opportunity for the defense to make a closing argument in a non-jury trial.

6. In general, the prosecution has effective responses to make to nearly every improper defense tactic either by entering the door opened by the defense and responding in kind, or by pointing out the impropriety of the argument (i. e., appeals to sympathy or prejudice, relies on his personal reputation) and telling the jury why the argument is improper and then stating that no lawyer as able as defense counsel would rely on such desperation tactics if he did not know his case was hopeless. Accordingly, though

the prosecution has no right to appeal even from a grossly improper but effective defense argument (i. e., one causing acquittal), the right of the prosecution to the last word may deter much potential abuse of defense argument. (It should be noted, however, that in some jurisdictions the defense is allowed to close, at least when the defense offers no evidence.) The risk of judicial admonition may also temper extreme defense arguments.

7. The absence of the sanction of appeal from improper defense tactics must leap to mind whenever a study of final argument is made. One can literally read hundreds of cases on jury arguments without ever encountering a discussion of defense arguments except for a handful of cases dealing with prosecutorial responses in kind. For reasons we have suggested, the practical consequences of this lack of sanction are probably not particularly serious. However, at the point of any consideration, it is worthwhile to consider the absence of the appeal sanction in relation to the defense view of the rules discussed in each of the sections of this Chapter. Is it reasonable to expect defense counsel who are often under financial and emotional pressures (resulting from the individual's need to win contests and affection from clients) to gain favorable verdicts, to be punctilious about observing the rules of the game? Reconsider particularly the standards and decisions dealing with perjured testimony, attempting to place probative but inadmissible evidence before the jury, dealing with witnesses who may claim privilege, and putting the defendant on the stand. In these areas are there meaningful sanctions other than appeal (as in the case of closing arguments)?

What are these sanctions and are they effective? Is the appeal sanction itself an adequate and effective check on the one party to whom it does apply, the prosecutor?

In People v. Butler, 58 Ill.2d 45, 317 N.E.2d 35 (1974), the Supreme Court of Illinois stated that a reviewing court should refer to the appropriated disciplinary body instances of improper argument by counsel which come to the court's attention during the course of an appeal. It noted that often prosecutorial misconduct, though great, is properly held harmless error because of the overwhelming nature of the evidence. Accordingly the Illinois high court concluded that some alternative penalty must be exacted. Of course, in a criminal case defense misconduct can never be punished by a reversal because the prosecution cannot appeal from an acquittal.

Rarely does a reviewing court opinion identify by name the attorney who has utilized improper argument. Would identification be a meaningful sanction? Would there be anything wrong with naming the attorney in the appellate opinion?

Chapter 20

SUBMITTING THE CASE TO THE JURY

A. JURY INSTRUCTIONS: AN INTRODUCTION

1. COURT'S CHARGE: PURPOSE AND PROCEDURE

The primary object of the judge's charge to the jury is to explain the law, point out the essential elements that must be proved to sustain the allegations made by each side and bring into perspective the relationship of the evidence to the issues on trial. See White, Some Approaches to the Instructional Problem, 40 Neb.L.Rev. 413 (1961); Soper, The Charge to the Jury, 1 F.R.D. 540 (1941). On a somewhat different level, jury instructions have been viewed as performing the "theoretical" function of enlightening the jury on the law, the function by which appellate courts control judges and juries, the function, from counsel's viewpoint, of trapping the court into reversible error and the function by which trial judges maintain their integrity. Farley, Instruction to Juries—Their Role in the Judicial Process, 42 Yale L.J. 194 (1932).

Nevertheless, since the days of the year books, instructions have been looked upon as the single most important aspect of the trial judge's role. Mr. Justice Frankfurter viewed it thusly in his concurring opinion in Andreas v. United States, 333 U.S. 740, 752, 68 S.Ct. 880 (1948):

> Charging a jury is not a matter of abracadabra. No part of the conduct of a criminal trial lays a heavier task upon the presiding judge. The charge is that part of the whole trial which probably exercises the weightiest influence upon jurors. It should guide their understanding after jurors have been subjected to confusion and deflection from the relevant by the stiff partisanship of counsel.

It is obligatory upon the judge to give instructions that are "clear, concise, accurate and impartial statements of the law written in understandable language and delivered in a conversational tone which will be of helpful guidance to the jurors". Devitt, Ten Practical Suggestions About Federal Jury Instructions, 38 F.R.D. 75 (1966). Because of the difficulties in phrasing unimpeachable statements of law in a comprehensible manner, there is a growing trend toward developing and employing pattern jury instructions. "The reasons given for the adoption of pattern jury instructions vary from state to state, and in order of importance; but generally there are five: accuracy, time savings, impartiality, intelligibility, uniformity". Note, 40 N.Dak.L.Rev. 164 (1964). Variations in standardized in-

structions are closely scrutinized. United States v. McDonald, 455,
F.2d 1259 (1st Cir. 1972).

As a procedural matter, the federal practice, followed in several
states, is governed by Fed.R.Crim.P. 30. Under this rule the parties
are permitted, but not required, to file suggested instructions "at the
close of the evidence or at such earlier time during the trial as the
court reasonably directs". But it has been held unreasonable, though
not erroneous, for the court to require a defendant to file instructions
at the beginning of trial when he is uncertain of the defense theories
that the evidence will support. Bruno v. United States, 259 F.2d 8
(9th Cir. 1958). The instructions tendered must be clear, accurate,
nonpartisan statements of law, for a prolix, imprecise charge that in-
tertwines evidentiary assumptions with a partisan statement of the
law can justifiably be rejected outright by the court. United States
v. Bessesen, 445 F.2d 463 (7th Cir. 1971); United States v. American
Radiator and Standard Sanitary Corp., 433 F.2d 174 (3d Cir. 1970),
cert. denied 401 U.S. 948. Defense counsel is advised to tender a
proper, intelligible charge to avoid total rejection and the loss of a
valuable ground for appeal; and the prosecution should do so to avoid
generating reversible error.

Although the trial judge must rule upon each instruction submitted and advise counsel of his decision, he has no obligation, under
Rule 30, to inform counsel of his intended charge prior to summation.
United States v. Clarke, 468 F.2d 890 (5th Cir. 1972). Martin v.
United States, 404 F.2d 640 (10th Cir. 1968). Professor Moore has
strongly criticized this aspect of the rule because, in his view, counsel
should know the details of the charge in order to make a proper closing argument. 8 Moore's Federal Practice ¶ 30.03, at 30–5–30–8
(Cipes ed. 1972). But the strong interest in giving the judge leeway
to alter his charge up to and during its delivery, and the attendant
practical difficulties that would be caused by permitting counsel to
reopen summation where such a modification occurs, have caused the
courts to reject this criticism. Compare United States v. Bass, 425
F.2d 161 (7th Cir. 1970) (prime example of judicial rule making requiring, in dictum, that counsel be advised of charge) with United
States v. Slaton, 430 F.2d 1109 (7th Cir. 1970), cert. denied 400 U.S.
997, 91 S.Ct. 475 (1971) (rejecting *Bass* dictum absent strong showing of prejudice).

As a predicate to appellate review of a particular instruction, defense counsel must make a specific objection to the instruction involved and briefly state the basis of his complaint. Compare United
States v. Young, 463 F.2d 934 (D.C.Cir.1972) (failure to object) with
United States v. Bennett, 460 F.2d 872 (D.C.Cir.1972) (failure excused where counsel may not have known all requisite facts). This is
generally done after the full charge is given and the jury temporarily
excused in order to permit the court to recall the jury to modify its
charge if counsel's argument proves persuasive. Occasionally, a confident trial judge will permit counsel to have a standing objection to
all instructions and, thereby, subject the entire charge to appellate re-

view. Absent a specific or standing objection, an instruction will be reviewed only where it generates "plain error" under Fed.R.Crim.P. 52(b). See United States v. Wharton, 433 F.2d 451, 456–57 (D.C. Cir.1970):

> Our function does not end with recognition of these instructional miscues; there remains the question whether, in the circumstances presented by this litigation, they warrant reversal. That task, one often fraught with difficulty, is compounded here by the absence of protest to the instructions in the trial court, where possibly the mistakes, upon identification, could have been corrected. Appellant can survive the omission of appropriate objections only if we should exert our authority, which he invokes, to notice "[p]lain errors or defects affecting substantial rights."
>
> * * *
>
> The inquiry here . . . is the probable impact, appraised realistically, of the particular instructional mistakes upon the jury's factfinding function. [We have therefore, examined] the faulty instruction, not in isolation but, as always, against the backdrop of related segments of the trial judge's charge, and concluded that it was unlikely that in context the single misstatement led the jury astray.

Erroneous instructions "are the greatest single source of reversible error". Skidmore v. Baltimore & Ohio R. Co., 167 F.2d 54, 65 (2d Cir. 1948), cert. denied 335 U.S. 816, 69 S.Ct. 34. Because there is rarely a case where technical error cannot be found in a single, isolated instruction, appellate courts focus upon whether the charge as a whole, not a specific instruction, either given or refused, comports with legal requirements. United States v. Bailey, 451 F.2d 181 (3d Cir. 1971).

NOTES

1. The final charge to the jury is not the only point during trial at which the judge issues instructions. Various instructions, often called "cautionary" or "admonitory", are given with respect to the limited admissibility of certain kinds of evidence, events occurring during trial, and the conduct of the jurors. Thus, the judge will normally instruct the jurors not to discuss the case prior to deliberations and to refrain from reading newspaper accounts during trial. Where improper testimony or argument occurs or where, for example, the jury observes the defendant in hand-cuffs as he is brought from the lock-up, the court will instruct the jury to disregard what it saw or heard in its adjudication of guilt or innocence.

As the court held in United States v. Crosby, 294 F.2d 928, 950 (2d Cir. 1961), cert. denied 368 U.S. 984, 82 S.Ct. 599 (1962):

> Whenever information erroneously reaches the ears of the jury in open court, the judge's instruction to disregard it may be disobeyed; yet it is not suggested that in such a case the jury ought to be polled as to whether any of them relied on the forbidden knowledge. Even though presumably the jurors themselves know best,

the question is determined, as is the question whether an error was prejudicial, on the basis of the nature of the matter and its probable effect on a hypothetical average jury.

2.   In multiple defendant cases, the court is often obliged to instruct the jury to consider evidence against only a particular defendant.   While a jury is generally considered capable of following an instruction to provisionally admit hearsay evidence in a conspiracy case subject to disregarding it if a conspiracy is not proven, it has been found incompetent to perform the mental gymnastics necessary to limit a confession, implicating a codefendant, to the declarant.   Bruton v. United States, 391 U.S. 123, 88 S.Ct. 1620 (1968).   Are the "mental gymnastics" involved in these two situations substantially different?   See Chapter 19, Section B.

3.   Admonitory instructions are also given to "consider for impeachment only" prior convictions of the defendant or inadmissible statements designed to show prior inconsistencies.   See United States v. Brown, 453 F. 2d 101 (8th Cir. 1971); United States v. Williams, 445 F.2d 421 (10th Cir. 1971).   Can a jury limit its consideration of this kind of evidence to issues of credibility?   How does the existence of material of this nature affect defense counsel's decision to permit his client to testify?   What force is there in Learned Hand's statement that "trial by jury is a rough scales at best"?   United States v. Brown, 79 F.2d 321, 326 (2d Cir. 1935), cert. denied 296 U.S. 650, 56 S.Ct. 309.

B.   JUDGE'S COMMENT ON THE EVIDENCE

BILLECI v. UNITED STATES

United States Court of Appeals, 1950.
87 U.S.App.D.C. 274, 184 F.2d 394.

PRETTYMAN, CIRCUIT JUDGE.

Appellants were indicted for violation of a statute which provides that, if any person shall within the District of Columbia be concerned in any manner in managing or carrying on a lottery, upon conviction he shall be fined or imprisoned or both.

*   *   *

Appellants were tried before a jury, convicted, and sentenced.

[The convictions were reversed on appeal because the trial judge instructed the jury, in effect, that a government witness' refusal to testify on fifth amendment grounds carries an inference that his testimony would have been adverse to the defendants.   Since the case was remanded for retrial, the court confronted several other issues raised by appellants.]

Appellants say in their brief and argument before us that in instructing the jury the trial judge, by intonations and gestures, emphasized principles beneficial to the prosecution and de-emphasized those things which he said of benefit to the defendants.   They say that he frequently leaned toward the jury, gestured in an emphatic manner with his hand, and raised his voice when he was reciting those principles which tended to produce a verdict of guilty, but that when he told the jurors they could return a verdict of not guilty his remarks were barely audible. When objections to these alleged actions by the trial court were made by the appellants, the judge replied, "Well, of course, all that was dealt with by the Court of Appeals in the Vinci case."

We pointed out in [Vinci v. United States, 159 F.2d 777 (D.C. Cir. 1947)] that the trial court may not do by indirection that which it may not do directly; that it may not coerce, or attempt to coerce, a jury by gesture any more than it may do so by words; that it may not translate by intonation a properly worded charge into an improperly understood one. But we pointed out that an appellate court cannot act upon representations made to it in briefs and upon argument; that if the trial judge conducts himself erroneously to the detriment of the defendants it is incumbent upon counsel to record such action at the time. In the case at bar counsel did raise the point before the trial court. Counsel there said:

"I would like also to take exception—and I say this with all deference to Your Honor—to what I consider certain intonations that were indulged by Your Honor, particularly when you were discussing certain principles of law. I think that they were quite apparent to the jury listening intently as they were to Your Honor's instruction, and I think they were inescapably calculated to carry out the defeat of the ultimate principle of the law that is involved in the case. And on that basis I would like at this time, on behalf of the defendant Lewis, to take an exception to your entire charge."

The description thus given on the conduct of the judge at the time it occurred falls far short of the description now given it by counsel. It was then said merely that certain intonations were thought by counsel to be quite apparent to the jury. Counsel's present description is that the gestures and intonations were so emphatic as to twist the meaning of the charge as worded and to tend to coerce a reluctant jury.

It is our view that if the intonations and gestures of a trial judge are erroneously detrimental to a defendant in a criminal case it is the duty of counsel to record fully and accurately, at the time and on the record, although not in the hearing of the jury, what has transpired. In such a situation it is as much his duty to make that record as it is his duty to record his objections to the charge, as the Rules require, before the jury leaves the room. If the representations then made by counsel are not accurate, the court may say so. But if there is a serious question as to whether the jury may have derived some unintended meaning or have been likely to infer erroneously from the gestures and intonations of the judge, he should emphatically instruct them so as to remove any possible erroneous impression from their minds. If a difference develops between judge and lawyer as to what has happened, the procedure upon exceptions before there were court reporters is available.*

---

* [Ed. note: Where judges have a reputation for structuring their charge by intonation, some defense attorneys tape record the charge for appellate review.]

Since these cases must go back for new trial several features of the present record require us to state again the rule governing a federal trial judge in commenting upon evidence. It has been stated many times by many courts and many judges.

A federal trial judge in a criminal case is not an inert figure. He is not a mere moderator. Besides his own exclusive functions of conducting the trial and declaring the applicable law, he may guide and assist the jury in its consideration of the evidence. The purpose of his comment is to aid, through his experience, the inexperienced laymen in the box in finding the truth in the confusing conflicts of contradictory evidence. In exceptional cases he may even express his opinion upon the evidence or phases of it. But there is a constitutional line across which he cannot go. The accused has a right to a trial by the jury. That means that his guilt or innocence must be decided by twelve laymen and not by the one judge. A judge cannot impinge upon that right any more than he can destroy it. He cannot press upon the jury the weight of his influence any more than he can eliminate the jury altogether. It is for this reason that courts have held time and again that a trial judge cannot be argumentative in his comments; he cannot be an advocate; he cannot urge his own view of the guilt or innocence of the accused. Of course he may direct judgment of acquittal under proper circumstances.

Moreover, other indestructible principles of our criminal law are pertinent to the comment of a judge upon the evidence. An accused is presumed to be innocent. Guilt must be established beyond a reasonable doubt. All twelve jurors must be convinced beyond that doubt; if only one of them fixedly has a reasonable doubt, a verdict of guilty cannot be returned. These principles are not pious platitudes recited to placate the shades of venerated legal ancients. They are working rules of law binding upon the court. Startling though the concept is when fully appreciated, those rules mean that the prosecutor in a criminal case must actually overcome the presumption of innocence, all reasonable doubts as to guilt, and the unanimous verdict requirement.

The public interest requires that persons who have committed crimes be convicted of them. But the responsibility for producing the evidence which will persuade twelve jurors of guilt beyond a reasonable doubt is upon the prosecutor. It is a serious public responsibility, but it is upon the prosecutor and upon him alone. The judge has no part in that task. The prosecutor represents society in the prosecution. The attorney for the defense represents the accused. The judge is a disinterested and objective participant in the proceeding. "Prosecution and judgment are two quite separate functions in the administration of justice; they must not merge." [2]

The difference between assisting the jury, which is a duty of a federal judge, and encroaching upon its responsibilities, which is for-

2. Judge Learned Hand in United States v. Marzano, 2 Cir., 1945, 149 F.2d 923, 926.

bidden, has been developed at great length many times, as we have pointed out. When a federal judge comments upon evidence by expressing his opinion upon phases of it, he is treading close to the line which divides proper judicial action from the field which is exclusively the jury's. Therefore he must make it unequivocally clear to the jurors that conclusions upon such matters are theirs, not his, to make; and he must do so in such manner and at such time that the jury will not be left in doubt; references in some remote or obscure portion of a long charge will not suffice for the purpose.

After a jury has returned a verdict of guilty the defendant is no longer the accused but is the convicted. It is at that point, and not until that point, that punishment becomes a function of the judge.

It is a serious thing for an appellate court to reverse convictions in criminal cases. But the controlling importance is that the law be followed. The rules of law applicable to the function of the judge in a criminal trial by a jury are well settled. No matter what the impulse may be to transgress or evade them under provocative circumstances, they must be observed. This is basic, without exception, and compulsory.

The judgment of the District Court is reversed.

NOTES

1. Compare the view of the trial judge's decision to comment on the evidence taken by the court in United States v. Tourine, 428 F.2d 865, 869–70 (2d Cir. 1970):

> The trial judge in a federal court may summarize and comment upon the evidence and inferences to be drawn therefrom, in his discretion. This does not mean that he must include every scrap of evidence as if the jury were dependent upon the court's summation alone as the basis for its deliberations. United States v. Kahaner, 317 F.2d 459, 479 (2 Cir.), cert. denied 375 U.S. 836, 84 S.Ct. 74 (1963). The purpose of such summation and comment is to assist the jury in winnowing out the truth from the mass of evidence, much of it conflicting, and perhaps placed out of focus by different claims concerning its meaning and interpretation by the arguments of the parties. So long as the trial judge does not by one means or another try to impose his own opinions and conclusions as to the facts on the jury and does not act as an advocate in advancing factual findings of his own, he may in his discretion decide what evidence he will comment upon. His fairness in doing so must be judged in the context of the whole trial record, particularly the evidence and the arguments of the parties. So examined and considered in the present case, we are satisfied that the court did not step outside of its legitimate province in commenting on the evidence. Although most of what he had to say concerned the Government's, rather than the defendants' evidence, there was a great deal more of the former, which ran over three hundred pages, than the latter, which covered less than one hundred pages of the trial transcript.
>
> Although a charge which usurps the function of the jury will not be saved from error by simply repeating in it from time to

time that the jury and not the court is the finder of the facts, such a statement does serve to remind the jury, in the usual case where the court makes no more than fair comment for clarification and to aid the jury in its deliberations, that it must exercise its own judgment and not take what the court has said without further deliberation of its own. In the present case the trial judge, in the course of his comments, amply fulfilled his duty in this regard.

2. While the judge may comment on the evidence in federal cases, he is not obliged to do so. Appellate review of his comments will be dependent upon the facts of the case and the extent to which the judge's commentary impartially reflects the evidence. Some comments are plainly erroneous. For example with respect to a defendant's testimony, one judge charged the jury: "Do you believe that story, gentlemen? To me it is perfectly plain that it is a lie." The appellate court had little difficulty in reversing the conviction. Malaga v. United States, 57 F.2d 822 (1st Cir. 1932). But the type of commentary that is prohibited cannot be generalized into a black letter rule. As Judge Learned Hand said, late in his distinguished career on the bench, in United States v. Allied Stevedoring Corp., 241 F.2d 925 (2d Cir. 1957), cert. denied 358 U.S. 984, 77 S.Ct. 1282:

> It is indeed impossible to lay down any general rule that will help to define the limits beyond which a judge may not stop in his dealing with a jury. That there are such everyone agrees, and we have so held; but the occasion must be one where it is apparent that he has assumed an attitude which goes further than to express his personal opinion. He must give them to suppose that he is more than an impartial observer; and that what he says has the backing of legal authority.

C. PARTICULAR JURY INSTRUCTION PROBLEMS

1. REASONABLE DOUBT AND THE PRESUMPTION OF INNOCENCE

In Commonwealth v. Webster, 59 Mass. 295 (1850), the court viewed "Reasonable Doubt" in the following manner:

> ". . . what is reasonable doubt? It is a term often used, probably pretty well understood, but not easily defined. It is not mere possible doubt; because everything relating to human affairs, and depending on moral evidence, is open to some possible or imaginary doubt. It is that state of the case, which, after the entire comparison and consideration of all the evidence, leaves the minds of the jurors in that condition and they cannot say they feel an abiding conviction, to a moral certainty, of the truth of the charge. The burden of proof is upon the prosecutor. All the presumptions of law independent of evidence are in favor of innocence; and every person is presumed to be innocent until he is proved guilty. If upon such proof there is reasonable doubt remaining, the accused is entitled to the benefit

of it by an acquittal. For it is not sufficient to establish a probability, though a strong one arising from the doctrine of chances, that the fact charged is more likely to be true than the contrary; but the evidence must establish the truth of the fact to a reasonable and moral certainty; a certainty that convinces and directs the understanding, and satisfies the reason and judgment of those who are bound to act conscientiously upon it. This we take to be proof beyond reasonable doubt; because if the law, which mostly depends upon considerations of a moral nature, should go further than this, and require absolute certainty, it would exclude circumstantial evidence altogether. . . ."

In the California Penal Code (§ 1096), the following provision represents that state's attempt at a satisfactory definition and effort to assist juries in understanding the term:

"A defendant in a criminal action is presumed to be innocent until the contrary is proved, and in case of a reasonable doubt whether his guilt is satisfactorily shown, he is entitled to an acquittal, but the effect of this presumption is only to place upon the state the burden of proving him guilty beyond a reasonable doubt. Reasonable doubt is defined as follows: 'It is not a mere possible doubt; because everything relating to human affairs, and depending on moral evidence, is open to some possible or imaginary doubt. It is that state of the case, which, after the entire comparison and consideration of all the evidence, leaves the minds of jurors in that condition that they can not say they feel an abiding conviction, to a moral certainty, of the truth of the charge.'

"In charging a jury, the court may read to the jury section 1096 of this code, and no further instruction on the subject of the presumption of innocence or defining reasonable doubt need be given."

Compare the California Code provision with the viewpoints of the justices of the Supreme Court of Pennsylvania in a 1954 case: [1]

"There are a number of cases which say that 'in order to warrant a conviction [on circumstantial evidence] the facts and circumstances proved must be of such character as to produce a moral certainty of the guilt of the accused beyond any reasonable doubt—'. . . . The inclusion of the words 'moral certainty' has been severely criticized. . . . We are of the opinion that the use of the words 'moral certainty' serves to confuse and befog the jury instead of enlightening and aiding them in determining whether the Commonwealth has convinced them of the guilt

---

1. Commonwealth v. Kloiber, 378 Pa. 412, 106 A.2d 820 (1954).

of the defendant beyond a reasonable doubt and that in the future it would be wiser if the charge did not contain any reference to 'moral certainty.' "

In a dissent from the foregoing, one of the justices said:

"What happens to the time-honored rule that all doubts are to be resolved in favor of the accused if a jury is allowed to return a verdict of guilty when it is not morally certain of the defendant's guilt and the evidence is not incompatible with innocence? . . . I doubt that [a juror] can sleep easily of nights if by his vote he sends a defendant to prison or to his death when he entertains a moral incertainty as to his guilt. . . . Moral certainty means being honest with oneself. Once we allow convictions when the jurors are not honestly certain of the guilt of the accused, a hole beneath the water line has been driven into the ship of criminal law."

A court-martial law officer issued the following instruction, which was approved by the United States Court of Military Appeals:

"Proof beyond a reasonable doubt does not mean proof beyond any doubt whatsoever. . . . *By reasonable doubt, as its name implies, is meant a doubt based on reason; a doubt for which you can give a reason to yourself and not just any whimsical speculation or capricious conjecture. If, after an impartial comparison and consideration of all the evidence you can say to yourself that you are not satisfied of the accused's guilt, then you have a reasonable doubt. . . . The term 'reasonable doubt' means a doubt for which a good reason can be given in the light of all the evidence.*" [2]

2. United States v. Kloh, 10 U.S.C.M. A. 329, 27 C.M.R. 403 (1959), in which the court gave the following reasons in supporting this instruction:

"The . . . appellate defense counsel's argument has been the subject of considerable discussion in Federal and state cases. Most frequently, when objection is taken by appellate courts to a definitive instruction on reasonable doubt which equates it with a doubt for which good reason can be given, the asserted error is said to spring from the possible fear of an inarticulate juror that he may be called upon to express and defend his doubt and the basis therefor. . . . While this reasoning may hold a certain initial appeal, research convinces us that the weight of authority properly rejects this view, particularly when the definition is accompanied by further explanation as it was here. Judge Augustus N. Hand, writing the majority opinion in United States v. Farina [184 F.2d 18 (2d Cir. 1950)] commented:

" ' . . . The appellants argue that the charge given might lead some juryman to suppose that he would be called upon to give his reason. This objection seems fanciful and has already been rejected by this court.' . . .

" . . . In this same connection, as noted above, the law officer here qualified his definition as he used the phrase 'a doubt for which you can give a reason to yourself.' Common experience tells us that

In a 1952 English case an attempt was made by Lord Chief Justice Goddard to resolve the difficulty. He said:

> "Whenever a court attempts to explain what is meant by a reasonable doubt, it . . . tries to explain the term in a way which is often likely to cause more confusion than clarity. It is far better . . . if a jury is told that it is their duty to regard the evidence and see that it satisfies them so that they can feel sure when they return a verdict of guilty. . . . I always tell a jury that . . . they must feel sure and must be satisfied that the prosecution have established the guilt of the prisoner." [3]

Soon thereafter another case arose in which an English trial judge told the jury, while attempting to explain "reasonable doubt", that in order to convict they must be "satisfied" about the defendant's guilt. This was held to be an inadequate explanation. Lord Goddard, in an opinion reversing the trial court conviction, expressed a concern that perhaps his own "feel sure" explanation in the 1952 case may have misled the trial court in the present one. He then offered the following guidance:

> "It is not the particular formula of words that matter. It is the effect of summing up. If the jury are made to understand, whether in one set of words or another, that they must feel sure of his guilt and that the onus all the time is on the prosecution and not the defense, that is enough." [4]

One state supreme court has disposed of the problem thusly:

> "Court and counsel would do well to heed the advice of this court in many cases in which instructions concerning 'reasonable doubt' have been considered. It is a term which needs no definition, and it is erroneous to give instructions resulting in an elaboration of it." [5]

In view of the confusion that he thought was caused by a trial judge's attempt to define "reasonable doubt" to the jury, the late Professor Wigmore made the following comment and recommendation (§ 2497, Wigmore, Evidence, 3d ed. 1940):

> ". . . when anything more than a simple caution and a brief definition is given, the matter tends to become one of mere words, and the actual effect upon the jury, instead of being enlightenment, is likely to be rather confusion, or, at

the average court member is unlikely to suppress doubt in his own mind simply because he must be able to provide himself with a reason for that doubt. And certainly if he personally has no reason to doubt that the Government has established the guilt of the accused, a member honestly performing his duties should convict."

3. R. v. Summers, 36 Cr.App.R. 15, [1952] 1 All Eng.R. 1059.

4. R. v. Hepworth, [1955] 2 All Eng.R. 918.

5. People v. Schuele, 326 Ill. 366, 372, 157 N.E. 215, 217 (1927).

the least, a continued incomprehension. In practice, these detailed amplifications of the doctrine have usually degenerated into a mere tool for counsel who desire to entrap an unwary judge into forgetfulness of some obscure precedent, or to save a cause for a new trial by quibbling, on appeal, over the verbal propriety of a form of words uttered or declined to be uttered by the judge. The effort to perpetuate and develop these elaborate unserviceable definitions is a useless one, and serves today chiefly to aid the purposes of the tacticism. It should be abandoned."

A federal circuit court has held that even where a party tenders a fair instruction on the subject, the district judge need not instruct the jury on the meaning of "reasonable doubt." [6]

NOTES

1. The requirement of "proof of guilt beyond a reasonable doubt" has been held by the Supreme Court of the United States to be of constitutional dimension. In In re Winship, 397 U.S. 358, 90 S.Ct. 1068 (1970), the Court said: ". . . we explicitly hold that the Due Process Clause protects the accused against conviction except upon proof of guilt beyond a reasonable doubt of every fact necessary to constitute the crime with which he is charged". The Court then went on to hold that the reasonable doubt standard was a constitutional requirement in the adjudicatory stage of state juvenile court proceedings where the allegation underlying the delinquency petition is the alleged violation of a criminal statute.

Justice Harlan, in his concurring opinion viewed the reasonable doubt standard as "bottomed on a fundamental value determination of our society that it is far worse to convict an innocent man than to let a guilty man go free". He relied upon two propositions which he thought could not be fairly disputed:

> First, in a judicial proceeding in which there is a dispute about the facts of some earlier event, the factfinder cannot acquire unassailably accurate knowledge of what happened. Instead, all the factfinder can acquire is a belief of what *probably* happened. The intensity of this belief—the degree to which a factfinder is convinced that a given act actually occurred—can, of course, vary. In this regard, a standard of proof represents an attempt to instruct the factfinder concerning the degree of confidence our society thinks he should have in the correctness of factual conclusions for a particular type of adjudication. Although the phrases "preponderance of the evidence" and "proof beyond a reasonable doubt" are quantitatively imprecise, they do communicate to the finder of fact different notions concerning the degree of confidence he is expected to have in the correctness of his factual conclusions.

> A second proposition, which is really nothing more than a corollary of the first, is that the trier of fact will sometimes, despite his best efforts, be wrong in his factual conclusions. In a lawsuit between two parties, a factual error can make a difference in one

6. United States v. Lawson, 507 F.2d 433 (7th Cir. 1974), cert. denied 420 U.S. 1004, 95 S.Ct. 1446.

of two ways. First, it can result in a judgment in favor of the plaintiff when the true facts warrant a judgment for the defendant. The analogue in a criminal case would be the conviction of an innocent man. On the other hand, an erroneous factual determination can result in a judgment for the defendant when the true facts justify a judgment in plaintiff's favor. The criminal analogue would be the acquittal of a guilty man.

The standard of proof influences the relative frequency of these two types of erroneous outcomes. If, for example, the standard of proof for a criminal trial were a preponderance of the evidence rather than proof beyond a reasonable doubt, there would be a smaller risk of factual errors that result in freeing guilty persons, but a far greater risk of factual errors that result in convicting the innocent. Because the standard of proof affects the comparative frequency of these two types of erroneous outcomes, the choice of the standard to be applied in a particular kind of litigation should, in a rational world, reflect an assessment of the comparative social disutility of each.

When one makes such an assessment, the reason for different standards of proof in civil as opposed to criminal litigation becomes apparent. In a civil suit between two private parties for money damages, for example, we view it as no more serious in general for there to be an erroneous verdict in the defendant's favor than for there to be an erroneous verdict in the plaintiff's favor. A preponderance of the evidence standard therefore seems peculiarly appropriate for, as explained most sensibly, it simply requires the trier of fact "to believe that the existence of a fact is more probable than its nonexistence before [he] may find in favor of the party who has the burden to persuade the [judge] of the fact's existence."

In a criminal case, on the other hand, we do not view the social disutility of convicting an innocent man as equivalent to the disutility of acquitting someone who is guilty. As Mr. Justice Brennan wrote for the Court in Speiser v. Randall (1958):

> "There is always in litigation a margin of error, representing error in factfinding, which both parties must take into account. Where one party has at stake an interest of transcending value—as a criminal defendant his liberty—this margin of error is reduced as to him by the process of placing on the other party the burden . . . of persuading the fact-finder at the conclusion of the trial of his guilt beyond a reasonable doubt."

In this context, I view the requirement of proof beyond a reasonable doubt in a criminal case as bottomed on a fundamental value determination of our society that it is far worse to convict an innocent man than to let a guilty man go free. It is only because of the nearly complete and long-standing acceptance of the reasonable-doubt standard by the States in criminal trials that the Court has not before today had to hold explicitly that due process, as an expression of fundamental procedural fairness requires a more stringent standard for criminal trials than for ordinary civil litigation.

Justice Black dissented in *Winship* from the Court's declaration that the reasonable doubt standard is constitutionally mandated in criminal cases. Chief Justice Burger, joined by Justice Stewart, dissented from the requirement as applied to juvenile court proceedings and deplored the transformation of juvenile courts "into criminal courts, which is what we are well on the way to accomplishing".

Compare the statement of the Court in In re Winship in the first paragraph of this note 1 with the following statement of the plurality of the Court in Apodoca v. Oregon, 406 U.S. 404, 92 S.Ct. 1628 (1972):

"We are quite sure, however, that the Sixth Amendment itself has never been held to require proof beyond a reasonable doubt in criminal cases. The reasonable doubt standard developed separately from both the jury trial and the unanimous verdict. . . . the rule requiring proof of crime beyond a reasonable doubt did not crystallize in this country until after the Constitution was adopted."

2. In Holland v. United States, 348 U.S. 121, 75 S.Ct. 121 (1954), defense counsel made the argument that where the government's evidence is circumstantial an instruction should be given which cautions the jury that every reasonable hypothesis other than that of guilt must be excluded before a guilty verdict can be returned. In rejecting that argument the Court said:

". . . where the jury is properly instructed on the standards for reasonable doubt, such an additional instruction on circumstantial evidence is confusing and incorrect . . . .

"Circumstantial evidence in this respect is intrinsically no different from testimonial evidence. Admittedly, circumstantial evidence may in some cases point to a wholly incorrect result. Yet, this is equally true of testimonial evidence. In both instances, a jury is asked to weigh the chances that the evidence correctly points to guilt against the possibility of inaccuracy or ambiguous inference. In both, the jury must use its experience with people and events in weighing the probabilities. If the jury is convinced beyond a reasonable doubt, we can require no more."

MULLANEY v. WILBUR

Supreme Court of the United States, 1975.
421 U.S. 684, 95 S.Ct. 1881.

MR. JUSTICE POWELL delivered the opinion of the Court.

The State of Maine requires a defendant charged with murder to prove that he acted "in the heat of passion on sudden provocation" in order to reduce the homicide to manslaughter. We must decide whether this rule comports with the due process requirement, as defined in In re Winship, 397 U.S. 358, 364, 90 S.Ct. 1068, 1072 (1970), that the prosecution prove beyond a reasonable doubt every fact necessary to constitute the crime charged.

I.

In June 1966 a jury found respondent Stillman E. Wilbur, Jr., guilty of murder. The case against him rested on his own pretrial statement and on circumstantial evidence showing that he fatally assaulted Claude Hebert in the latter's hotel room. Respondent's statement, introduced by the prosecution, claimed that he had attacked Hebert in a frenzy provoked by Hebert's homosexual advance. The defense offered no evidence, but argued that the homicide was not unlawful since respondent lacked criminal intent. Alternatively, Wilbur's counsel asserted that at most the homicide was manslaughter rather than murder, since it occurred in the heat of passion provoked by the homosexual assault.

The trial court instructed the jury that Maine law recognizes only two kinds of homicide, murder and manslaughter, and that these offenses are not subdivided into different degrees. The common elements of both are that the homicide be unlawful—i. e., neither justifiable nor excusable—and that it be intentional. The prosecution is required to prove these elements by proof beyond a reasonable doubt, and only if they are so proved is the jury to consider the distinction between murder and manslaughter.

In view of the evidence the trial court drew particular attention to the difference between murder and manslaughter. After reading the statutory definitions of both offenses,[1] the court charged that "malice aforethought is an essential and indispensable element of the crime of murder," without which the homicide would be manslaughter. The jury was further instructed, however, that if the prosecution established that the homicide was both intentional and unlawful, malice aforethought was to be conclusively implied unless the defendant proved by a fair preponderance of the evidence that he acted in the heat of passion on sudden provocation. The court emphasized that "malice aforethought and heat of passion on sudden provocation are inconsistent things," thus, by proving the latter the defendant would negate the former and reduce the homicide from murder to manslaughter. The court then concluded its charge with elaborate definitions of "heat of passion" and "sudden provocation."

The Maine law of homicide, as it bears on this case, can be stated succinctly: Absent justification or excuse, all intentional or criminally reckless killings are felonious homicides. Felonious homicide is

---

1. The Maine murder statute, Me.Rev. Stat., Tit. 17, § 2651, provides:
   "Whoever unlawfully kills a human being with malice aforethought, either express or implied, is guilty of murder and shall be punished by imprisonment for life."

The manslaughter statute, Tit. 17, § 2551, in relevant part provides:
   "Whoever unlawfully kills a human being in the heat of passion, on sudden provocation, without express or implied malice aforethought . . . shall be punished by a fine of not more than $1,000 or by imprisonment for not more than 20 years . . . ."

punished as murder—i. e., by life imprisonment—unless the defendant proves by a fair preponderance of the evidence that it was committed in the heat of passion on sudden provocation, in which case it is punished as manslaughter—i. e., by a fine not to exceed $1,000 or by imprisonment not to exceed 20 years. The issue is whether the Maine rule requiring the defendant to prove that he acted in the heat of passion on sudden provocation accords with due process.

A

Our analysis may be illuminated if this issue is placed in historical context.

At early common law only those homicides committed in the enforcement of justice were considered justifiable; all others were deemed unlawful and were punished by death. Gradually, however, the severity of the common-law punishment for homicide abated. Between the 13th and 16th centuries the class of justifiable homicides expanded to include, for example, accidental homicides and those committed in self-defense. . . . . It was said that "manslaughter (when voluntary) arises from the sudden heat of passions, murder from the wickedness of the heart." 4 Blackstone's Commentaries 190. Malice aforethought was designated as the element that distinguished the two crimes, but it was recognized that such malice could be implied by law as well as proved by evidence. Absent proof that an unlawful homicide resulted from "sudden and sufficiently violent provocation," the homicide was "presumed to be malicious." In view of this presumption, the early English authorities, relying on the case of The King v. Onerby, 92 Eng.Rep. 465 (KB 1727), held that once the prosecution proved that the accused had committed the homicide, it was "incumbent on the prisoner to make out . . . all . . . circumstances of justification, excuse or alleviation . . . to the satisfaction of the court and jury." 4 Blackstone's Commentaries 201. Thus, at common law the burden of proving heat of passion on sudden provocation appears to have rested on the defendant.

In this country the concept of malice aforethought took on two distinct meanings: in some jurisdictions it came to signify a substantive element of intent, requiring the prosecution to prove that the defendant intended to kill or to inflict great bodily harm; in other jurisdictions it remained a policy presumption, indicating only that absent proof to the contrary a homicide was presumed not to have occurred in the heat of passion. In a landmark case, Commonwealth v. York, 9 Met. (50 Mass.) 93 (1845), Chief Justice Shaw of the Massachusetts Supreme Judicial Court held that the defendant was required to negate malice aforethought by proving a preponderance of the evidence that he acted in the heat of passion. Initially, *York* was adopted in Maine as well as several other jurisdictions. In 1895, however, in the context of deciding a question of federal criminal procedure, this Court explicitly considered and unanimously rejected the general approach articulated in *York*. Davis v. United States, 160 U.S. 469,

16 S.Ct. 353.[2] And, in the past half century, the large majority of States have abandoned *York* and now require the prosecution to prove the absence of the heat of passion on sudden provocation beyond a reasonable doubt. See LaFave & Austin, Criminal Law 539–540 (1972).

This historical review establishes two important points. First, the fact at issue here—the presence or absence of the heat of passion on sudden provocation—has been, almost from the inception of the common law of homicide, the single most important factor in determining the degree of culpability attaching to an unlawful homicide. And, second, the clear trend has been toward requiring the prosecution to bear the ultimate burden of proving this fact.

B

Petitioners, the warden of the Maine Prison and the State of Maine argue that despite these considerations *Winship* should not be extended to the present case. They note that as a formal matter the absence of the heat of passion on sudden provocation is not a "fact necessary to constitute the *crime*" of felonious homicide in Maine. In re Winship (emphasis supplied). This distinction is relevant, according to petitioners, because in *Winship* the facts at issue were essential to establish criminality in the first instance whereas the fact in question here does not come into play until the jury already has determined that the defendant is guilty and may be punished at least for manslaughter. In this situation, petitioners maintain, the defendant's critical interests in liberty and reputation are no longer of paramount concern since, irrespective of the presence or absence of the heat of passion on sudden provocation, he is likely to lose his liberty and certain to be stigmatized. In short, petitioners would limit *Winship* to those facts which, if not proved, would wholly exonerate the defendant.

This analysis fails to recognize that the criminal law of Maine, like that of other jurisdictions, is concerned not only with guilt or innocence in the abstract but also with the degree of criminal culpability. Maine has chosen to distinguish those who kill in the heat of passion from those who kill in the absence of this factor. Because the former are less "blameworth[y]," State v. Lafferty, 309 A.2d, at 671, 673 (concurring opinion), they are subject to substantially less severe penalties. By drawing this distinction, while refusing to require the prosecution to establish beyond a reasonable doubt the fact upon which it turns, Maine denigrates the interests found critical in *Winship*.

The safeguards of due process are not rendered unavailing simply because a determination may already have been reached that would stigmatize the defendant and that might lead to a significant

---

2. In Leland v. Oregon, 343 U.S. 790, 72 S.Ct. 1002 (1952), the Court declined to apply the specific holding of *Davis*—that the prosecution must prove sanity beyond a reasonable doubt—to the States.

impairment of personal liberty. The fact remains that the consequences resulting from a verdict of murder, as compared with a verdict of manslaughter, differ significantly. Indeed, when viewed in terms of the potential difference in restrictions of personal liberty attendant to each conviction, the distinction established by Maine between murder and manslaughter may be of greater importance than the difference between guilt or innocence for many lesser crimes.

Moreover, if *Winship* were limited to those facts that constitute a crime as defined by state law, a State could undermine many of the interests that decision sought to protect without effecting any substantive change in its law. It would only be necessary to redefine the elements that comprise different crimes, characterizing them as factors that bear solely on the extent of punishment. An extreme example of this approach can be fashioned from the law challenged in this case. Maine divides the single generic offense of felonious homicide into three distinct punishment categories—murder, voluntary manslaughter, and involuntary manslaughter. Only the first two of these categories require that the homicidal act either be intentional or the result of criminally reckless conduct. But under Maine law these facts of intent are not general elements of the crime of felonious homicide. Instead, they bear only on the appropriate punishment category. Thus, if petitioners' argument were accepted, Maine could impose a life sentence for any felonious homicide—even those that traditionally might be considered involuntary manslaughter—unless the *defendant* was able to prove that his act was neither intentional nor criminally reckless.

Winship is concerned with substance rather than this kind of formalism. The rationale of that case requires an analysis that looks to the "operation and effect of the law as applied and enforced by the state," and to the interests of both the State and the defendant as affected by the allocation of the burden of proof.

In *Winship* the court emphasized the societal interests in the reliability of jury verdicts:

> "The requirement of proof beyond a reasonable doubt has [a] vital role in our criminal procedure for cogent reasons. The accused during a criminal prosecution has at stake interests of immense importance, both because of the possibility that he may lose his liberty upon conviction and because of the certainty that he would be stigmatized by the conviction.
>
> * * *
>
> "Moreover, use of the reasonable-doubt standard is indispensable to command the respect and confidence of the community in applications of the criminal law. It is critical that the moral force of the criminal law not be diluted by a standard of proof that leaves people in doubt whether innocent men are being condemned."

* * *

.   .   .   In *Winship* the ultimate burden of persuasion remained with the prosecution, although the standard had been reduced to proof by a fair preponderance of the evidence. In this case, by contrast, the State has affirmatively shifted the burden of proof to the defendant. The result, in a case such as this one where the defendant is required to prove the critical fact in dispute, is to increase further the likelihood of an erroneous murder conviction. Such a result directly contravenes the principle articulated in Speiser v. Randall, 357 U.S. 513, 525–526, 78 S.Ct. 1332, 1342 (1958):

> "[W]here one party has at stake an interest of transcending value—as a criminal defendant his liberty—th[e] margin of error is reduced as to him by the process of placing on the [prosecution] the burden   .   .   .   of persuading the factfinder at the conclusion of the trial   .   .   . ."

C

It has been suggested that because of the difficulties in negating an argument that the homicide was committed in the heat of passion the burden of proving this fact should rest on the defendant. No doubt this is often a heavy burden for the prosecution to satisfy. The same may be said of the requirement of proof beyond a reasonable doubt of many controverted facts in a criminal trial. But this is the traditional burden which our system of criminal justice deems essential.

Indeed   .   .   .   most States require the prosecution to prove the absence of passion beyond a reasonable doubt. Moreover, the difficulty of meeting such an exacting burden is mitigated in Maine where the fact at issue is largely an "objective, rather than a subjective, behavioral criterion." State v. Rollins, 295 A.2d, at 920. In this respect, proving that the defendant did not act in the heat of passion on sudden provocation is similar to proving any other element of intent; it may be established by adducing evidence of the factual circumstances surrounding the commission of the homicide. And although intent is typically considered a fact peculiarly within the knowledge of the defendant, this does not, as the Court has long recognized, justify shifting the burden to him.

Nor is the requirement of proving a negative unique in our system of criminal jurisprudence. Maine itself requires the prosecution to prove the absence of self-defense beyond a reasonable doubt. Satisfying this burden imposes an obligation that, in all practical effect, is identical to the burden involved in negating the heat of passion on sudden provocation. Thus, we discern no unique hardship on the prosecution that would justify requiring the defendant to carry the burden of proving a fact so critical to criminal culpability.[3]

---

3. This conclusion is supported by consideration of a related line of cases. Generally in a criminal case the prosecution bears both the production burden and the persuasion burden. In some instances, however, it is aided by a presumption, see Davis v. United States, 160 U.S. 469, 16 S.Ct. 353 (1895) (presumption of sanity), or a permissible inference, see United

Maine law requires a defendant to establish by a preponderance of the evidence that he acted in the heat of passion on sudden provocation in order to reduce murder to manslaughter. Under this burden of proof a defendant can be given a life sentence when the evidence indicates that it is *as likely as not* that he deserves a significantly lesser sentence. This is an intolerable result in a society where, to paraphrase Mr. Justice Harlan, it is far worse to sentence one guilty only of manslaughter as a murderer than to sentence a murderer for the lesser crime of manslaughter. We therefore hold that the Due Process Clause requires the prosecution to prove beyond a reasonable doubt the absence of the heat of passion on sudden provocation when the issue is properly presented in a homicide case.

Mr. Justice Rehnquist, with whom The Chief Justice joins, concurring.

While I join in the Court's opinion, the somewhat peculiar posture of the case as it comes to us leads me to add these observations.

*   *   *

I agree with the Court that In re Winship, does require that the prosecution prove beyond a reasonable doubt every element which constitutes the crime charged against a defendant. I see no inconsistency between that holding and the holding of Leland v. Oregon, 343 U.S. 790, 72 S.Ct. 1002 (1952). In the latter case this Court held that there was no constitutional requirement that the State shoulder the burden of proving the sanity of the defendant.

The Court noted in *Leland* that the issue of insanity as a defense to a criminal charge was considered by the jury only after it had found that all elements of the offense, including the *mens rea* if any required by state law, had been proven beyond a reasonable doubt. Although as the state court's instructions in *Leland* recognized, evidence relevant to insanity as defined by state law may also be relevant to whether the required *mens rea* was present, the existence or nonexistence of legal insanity bears no necessary relationship to the

States v. Gainey, 380 U.S. 63, 85 S. Ct. 754 (1965) (inference of knowledge from presence at an illegal still). These procedural devices require (in the case of a presumption) or permit (in the case of an inference) the trier of fact to conclude that the prosecution has met its burden of proof with respect to the presumed or inferred fact by having satisfactorily established other facts. Thus, in effect they require the defendant to present some evidence contesting the otherwise presumed or inferred fact. See Barnes v. United States, 412 U.S. 837, 846 n. 11, 93 S.Ct. 2357, 2363 (1973). Since they shift the production burden to the defendant, these devices must satisfy certain due process requirements.

In each of these cases, however, the ultimate burden of persuasion by proof beyond a reasonable doubt remained on the prosecution. Shifting the burden of persuasion to the defendant obviously places an even greater strain upon him since he no longer need only present some evidence with respect to the fact at issue; he must affirmatively establish that fact. Accordingly, the Due Process Clause demands more exacting standards before the State may require a defendant to bear this ultimate burden of persuasion. See generally Ashford & Risinger, Presumptions, Assumptions and Due Process in Criminal Cases: A Theoretical Overview, 78 Yale L.J. 165 (1969).

existence or nonexistence of the required mental elements of the crime. For this reason, Oregon's placement of the burden of proof of insanity on Leland, unlike Maine's redefinition of homicide in the instant case, did not effect an unconstitutional shift in the State's traditional burden of proof beyond a reasonable doubt of all necessary elements of the offense. Both the Court's opinion and the concurring opinion of Mr. Justice Harlan in In re Winship, supra, stress the importance of proof beyond a reasonable doubt in a criminal case as "bottomed on a fundamental value determination of our society that it is far worse to convict an innocent man than to let a guilty man go free." Having once met that rigorous burden of proof that, for example, in a case such as this, the defendant not only killed a fellow human being, but did it with malice aforethought, the State could quite consistently with such a constitutional principle conclude that a defendant who sought to establish the defense of insanity, and thereby escape any punishment whatever for a heinous crime, should bear the laboring oar on such an issue.

PATTERSON v. NEW YORK

Supreme Court of the United States, 1977.
432 U.S. 197, 97 S.Ct. 2319.

MR. JUSTICE WHITE delivered the opinion of the Court.

The question here is the constitutionality under the Fourteenth Amendment's Due Process Clause of burdening the defendant in a New York State murder trial with proving the affirmative defense of extreme emotional disturbance as defined by New York law.

After a brief and unstable marriage, the appellant, Gordon Patterson, Jr., became estranged from his wife, Roberta. Roberta resumed an association with John Northrup, a neighbor to whom she had been engaged prior to her marriage to appellant. On December 27, 1970, Patterson borrowed a rifle from an acquaintance and went to the residence of his father-in-law. There, he observed his wife through a window in a state of semiundress in the presence of John Northrup. He entered the house and killed Northup by shooting him twice in the head.

Patterson was charged with second-degree murder. In New York there are two elements of this crime: (1) "intent to cause the death of another person"; and (2) "caus[ing] the death of such person or of a third person." N.Y. Penal Law § 125.25 (McKinney 1975). Malice aforethought is not an element of the crime. In addition, the State permits a person accused of murder to raise an affirmative defense that he "acted under the influence of extreme emotional disturbance for which there was a reasonable explanation or excuse."

New York also recognizes the crime of manslaughter. A person is guilty of manslaughter if he intentionally kills another person "under circumstances which do not constitute murder because he acts under the influence of extreme emotional disturbance." Appellant confessed before trial to killing Northrup, but at trial he raised the defense of extreme emotional disturbance.

The jury was instructed as to the elements of the crime of murder. Focusing on the element of intent, the trial court charged:

> "Before you, considering all of the evidence, can convict this defendant or anyone of murder, you must believe and decide that the People have established beyond a reasonable doubt that he intended, in firing the gun, to kill either the victim himself or some other human being. . . .

> "Always remember that you must not expect or require the defendant to prove to your satisfaction that his acts were done without the intent to kill. Whatever proof he may have attempted, however far he may have gone in an effort to convince you of his innocence or guiltlessness, he is not obliged, he is not obligated to prove anything. It is always the People's burden to prove his guilt, and to prove that he intended to kill in this instance beyond a reasonable doubt."

The jury was further instructed, consistently with New York law, that the defendant had the burden of proving his affirmative defense by a preponderance of the evidence. The jury was told that if it found beyond a reasonable doubt that appellant had intentionally killed Northrup but that appellant had demonstrated by a preponderance of the evidence that he had acted under the influence of extreme emotional disturbance, it had to find appellant guilty of manslaughter instead of murder.

* * *

In determining whether New York's allocation to the defendant of proving the mitigating circumstances of severe emotional disturbance is consistent with due process, it is therefore relevant to note that this defense is a considerably expanded version of the common-law defense of heat of passion on sudden provocation and that at common law the burden of proving the latter, as well as other affirmative defenses—indeed, "all . . . circumstances of justification, excuse or alleviation"—rested on the defendant. 4 W. Blackstone, Commentaries *201; M. Foster, Crown Law 255 (1762). This was the rule when the Fifth Amendment was adopted, and it was the American rule when the Fourteenth Amendment was ratified. Commonwealth v. York, 50 Mass. 93 (1845).

In 1895 the common-law view was abandoned with respect to the insanity defense in federal prosecutions. Davis v. United States, 160 U.S. 469 (1895). This ruling had wide impact on the practice in the federal courts with respect to the burden of proving various affirmative defenses, and the prosecution in a majority of jurisdictions in this country sooner or later came to shoulder the burden of proving the sanity of the accused and of disproving the facts constituting other affirmative defenses, including provocation. Davis was not a constitutional ruling . . . .

* * *

We cannot conclude that Patterson's conviction under the New York law deprived him of due process of law. The crime of murder is defined by the statute, which represents a recent revision of the state criminal code, as causing the death of another person with intent to do so. The death, the intent to kill, and causation are the facts that the State is required to prove beyond a reasonable doubt if a person is to be convicted of murder. No further facts are either presumed or inferred in order to constitute the crime. The statute does provide an affirmative defense—that the defendant acted under the influence of extreme emotional disturbance for which there was a reasonable explanation—which, if proved by a preponderance of the evidence, would reduce the crime to manslaughter, an offense defined in a separate section of the statute. It is plain enough that if the intentional killing is shown, the State intends to deal with the defendant as a murderer unless he demonstrates the mitigating circumstances.

* * *

.   .   .   [I]t seems to us that the State satisfied the mandate of *Winship* [397 U.S. 358 (1970)] that it prove beyond a reasonable doubt "every fact necessary to constitute the crime with which [Patterson was] charged."

.   .   .   [O]nce the facts constituting a crime are established beyond a reasonable doubt, based on all the evidence including the evidence of the defendant's mental state, the State may refuse to sustain the affirmative defense of insanity unless demonstrated by a preponderance of the evidence.

* * *

.   .   .   [E]ven if we were to hold that a State must prove sanity to convict once that fact is put in issue, it would not necessarily follow that a State must prove beyond a reasonable doubt every fact, the existence or nonexistence of which it is willing to recognize as an exculpatory or mitigating circumstance affecting the degree of culpability or the severity of the punishment. Here, in revising its criminal code, New York provided the affirmative defense of extreme emotional disturbance, a substantially expanded version of the older heat-of-passion concept; but it was willing to do so only if the facts making out the defense were established by the defendant with sufficient certainty. The State was itself unwilling to undertake to establish the absence of those facts beyond a reasonable doubt, perhaps fearing that proof would be too difficult and that too many persons deserving treatment as murderers would escape that punishment if the evidence need merely raise a reasonable doubt about the defendant's emotional state. It has been said that the new criminal code of New York contains some 25 affirmative defenses which exculpate or mitigate but which must be established by the defendant to be operative.[1] The Due Process Clause, as we see it, does not put New

1.   The State of New York is not alone in this result:

"Since the Model Penal Code was completed in 1962, some 22 states have codified and reformed their criminal laws. At least 12 of these jurisdictions have used the concept of an 'affirmative defense' by a

York to the choice of abandoning those defenses or undertaking to disprove their existence in order to convict of a crime which otherwise is within its constitutional powers to sanction by substantial punishment.

The requirement of proof beyond a reasonable doubt in a criminal case is "bottomed on a fundamental value determination of our society that it is far worse to convict an innocent man than to let a guilty man go free." *Winship*, 397 U.S. at 372 (Harlan, J., concurring). The social cost of placing the burden on the prosecution to prove guilt beyond a reasonable doubt is thus an increased risk that the guilty will go free. While it is clear that our society has willingly chosen to bear a substantial burden in order to protect the innocent, it is equally clear that the risk it must bear is not without limits; and Mr. Justice Harlan's aphorism provides little guidance for determining what those limits are. Due process does not require that every conceivable step be taken, at whatever cost, to eliminate the possibility of convicting an innocent person. Punishment of those found guilty by a jury, for example, is not forbidden merely because there is a remote possibility in some instances that an innocent person might go to jail.

It is said that the common-law rule permits a State to punish one as a murderer when it is as likely as not that he acted in the heat of passion or under severe emotional distress and when, if he did, he is guilty only of manslaughter. But this has always been the case in those jurisdictions adhering to the traditional rule. It is also very likely true that fewer convictions of murder would occur if New York were required to negative the affirmative defense at issue here. But in each instance of a murder conviction under the present law, New York will have proved beyond a reasonable doubt that the defendant has intentionally killed another person, an act which it is not disputed the State may constitutionally criminalize and punish. If the State nevertheless chooses to recognize a factor that mitigates the degree of criminality or punishment, we think the State may assure itself that the fact has been established with reasonable certainty. To recognize at all a mitigating circumstance does not require the State to prove

preponderance of the evidence. Additionally, at least six proposed state codes and each of the four successive versions of a revised federal code use the same procedural device. Finally, many jurisdictions that do not generally employ this concept of 'affirmative defense' nevertheless shift the burden of proof to the defendant on particular issues." Low & Jeffries, DICTA: Constitutionalizing the Criminal Law?, 29 Va. Law Weekly, No. 18, p. 1 (1977) (footnotes omitted).

Even so, the trend over the years appears to have been to require the prosecution to disprove affirmative defenses beyond a reasonable doubt. See W. LaFave & A. Scott, Criminal Law § 8, p. 50 (1972); C. McCormick, Evidence § 341, pp. 800–802 (2d ed. 1972). The split among the various jurisdictions varies for any given defense. Thus, 22 jurisdictions place the burden of proving the affirmative defense of insanity on the defendant, while 28 jurisdictions place the burden of disproving insanity on the prosecution. Note, Constitutional Limitations on Allocating the Burden of Proof of Insanity to the Defendant in Murder Cases, 56 B.U.L.Rev. 499, 503–505 (1976).

its nonexistence in each case in which the fact is put in issue, if in its judgment this would be too cumbersome, too expensive, and too inaccurate.

* * *

This view may seem to permit state legislatures to reallocate burdens of proof by labeling as affirmative defenses at least some elements of the crimes now defined in their statutes. But there are obviously constitutional limits beyond which the States may not go in this regard. "[I]t is not within the province of a legislature to declare an individual guilty or presumptively guilty of a crime." McFarland v. American Sugar Rfg. Co., 241 U.S. 79, 86 (1916). The legislature cannot "validly command that the finding of an indictment, or mere proof of the identity of the accused, should create a presumption of the existence of all the facts essential to guilt." Tot v. United States, 319 U.S. 463, 469 (1943).

Long before *Winship,* the universal rule in this country was that the prosecution must prove guilt beyond a reasonable doubt. At the same time, the long-accepted rule was that it was constitutionally permissible to provide that various affirmative defenses were to be proved by the defendant. This did not lead to such abuses or to such widespread redefinition of crime and reduction of the prosecution's burden that a new constitutional rule was required. This was not the problem to which *Winship* was addressed. Nor does the fact that a majority of the States have now assumed the burden of disproving affirmative defenses—for whatever reasons—mean that those States that strike a different balance are in violation of the Constitution.

* * *

Mullaney's holding, it is argued, is that the State may not permit the blameworthiness of an act or the severity of punishment authorized for its commission to depend on the presence or absence of an identified fact without assuming the burden of proving the presence or absence of that fact, as the case may be, beyond a reasonable doubt. In our view the Mullaney holding should not be so broadly read. . . .

Mullaney surely held that a State must prove every ingredient of an offense beyond a reasonable doubt, and that it may not shift the burden of proof to the defendant by presuming that ingredient upon proof of the other elements of the offense. This is true even though the State's practice, as in Maine, had been traditionally to the contrary. Such shifting of the burden of persuasion with respect to a fact which the State deems so important that it must be either proved or presumed is impermissible under the Due Process Clause.

It was unnecessary to go further in *Mullaney.* The Maine Supreme Judicial Court made it clear that malice aforethought, which was mentioned in the statutory definition of the crime, was not equivalent to premeditation and that the presumption of malice traditionally arising in intentional homicide cases carried no factual meaning insofar as premeditation was concerned. Even so, a killing became murder in Maine when it resulted from a deliberate, cruel act committed by one person against another, "suddenly without any, or without a considerable provocation." Premeditation was not within the definition of murder; but malice, in the sense of the absence of provocation, was part of the definition of that crime. Yet malice, i. e., lack of provocation, was presumed and could be rebutted by the defendant only by proving by a preponderance of the evidence that he acted with heat of passion upon sudden provocation. In *Mullaney* we held that however traditional this mode of proceeding might have been, it is contrary to the Due Process Clause as construed in *Winship*.

As we have explained, nothing was presumed or implied against Patterson; and his conviction is not invalid under any of our prior cases. The judgment of the New York Court of Appeals is affirmed.

MR. JUSTICE REHNQUIST took no part in the consideration or decision of this case.

MR. JUSTICE POWELL, with whom MR. JUSTICE BRENNAN and MR. JUSTICE MARSHALL join, dissenting.

* * *

. . . The test the Court today establishes allows a legislature to shift, virtually at will, the burden of persuasion with respect to any factor in a criminal case, so long as it is careful not to mention the nonexistence of that factor in the statutory language that defines the crime. The sole requirement is that any references to the factor be confined to those sections that provide for an affirmative defense.

Perhaps the Court's interpretation of *Winship* is consistent with the letter of the holding in that case. But little of the spirit survives. Indeed, the Court scarcely could distinguish this case from *Mullaney* without closing its eyes to the constitutional values for which *Winship* stands. As Mr. Justice Harlan observed in *Winship*, "a standard of proof represents an attempt to instruct the factfinder concerning the degree of confidence our society thinks he should have in the correctness of factual conclusions for a particular type of adjudication." Explaining *Mullaney*, the Court says today, in effect, that society demands full confidence before a Maine factfinder determines that heat of passion is missing—a demand so insistent that this Court invoked the Constitution to enforce it over the contrary decision by the State. But we are told that society is willing to tolerate far less confidence in New York's factual determination of precisely the same functional issue. One must ask what possibly could explain this difference in societal demands. According to the Court, it is because Maine happened to attach a name—"malice aforethought"—to the absence of heat of passion, whereas New York refrained from giving a name to the absence of extreme emotional disturbance.

With all respect, this type of constitutional adjudication is indefensibly formalistic. A limited but significant check on possible abuses in the criminal law now becomes an exercise in arid formalities. What *Winship* and *Mullaney* had sought to teach about the limits a free society places on its procedures to safeguard the liberty of its citizens becomes a rather simplistic lesson in statutory draftsmanship. Nothing in the Court's opinion prevents a legislature from applying this new learning to many of the classical elements of the crimes it punishes.[2] It would be preferable, if the Court has found reason to reject the rationale of *Winship* and *Mullaney*, simply and straightforwardly to overrule those precedents.

The Court understandably manifests some uneasiness that its formalistic approach will give legislatures too much latitude in shifting the burden of persuasion. And so it issues a warning that "there are obviously constitutional limits beyond which the States may not go in this regard." The Court thereby concedes that legislative abuses may occur and that they must be curbed by the judicial branch. But if the State is careful to conform to the drafting formulas articulated today, the constitutional limits are anything but "obvious." This decision simply leaves us without a conceptual framework for distinguishing abuses from legitimate legislative adjustments of the burden of persuasion in criminal cases.

It is unnecessary for the Court to retreat to a formalistic test for applying *Winship*. Careful attention to the *Mullaney* decision reveals the principles that should control in this and like cases. *Winship* held that the prosecution must bear the burden of proving beyond a reasonable doubt " 'the existence of every fact necessary to constitute the crime charged.' " In *Mullaney* we concluded that heat of passion was one of the "facts" described in *Winship*—that is, a factor as to which the prosecution must bear the burden of persuasion beyond a reasonable doubt. We reached that result only after making two careful inquiries. First, we noted that the presence or absence of heat of passion made a substantial difference in punishment of the offender and in the stigma associated with the conviction. Second, we reviewed the history, in England and this country, of the factor at issue. Central to the holding in *Mullaney* was our conclusion that heat of passion "has been, almost from the inception of the common law of homicide, the single most important factor in determining the degree of culpability attaching to an unlawful homicide."

---

2. For example, a state statute could pass muster under the only solid standard that appears in the Court's opinion if it defined murder as mere physical contact between the defendant and the victim leading to the victim's death, but then set up an affirmative defense leaving it to the defendant to prove that he acted without culpable mens rea. The State, in other words, could be relieved altogether of responsibility for proving *anything* regarding the defendant's state of mind, provided only that the face of the statute meets the Court's drafting formulas.

To be sure, it is unlikely that legislatures will rewrite their criminal laws in this extreme form. The Court seems to think this likelihood of restraint is an added reason for limiting review largely to formalistic examination. But it is completely foreign to this Court's responsibility for constitutional adjudication to limit the scope of judicial review because of the expectation—however reasonable—that legislative bodies will exercise appropriate restraint.

Implicit in these two inquiries are the principles that should govern this case. The Due Process Clause requires that the prosecutor bear the burden of persuasion beyond a reasonable doubt only if the factor at issue makes a substantial difference in punishment and stigma. The requirement of course applies *a fortiori* if the factor makes the difference between guilt and innocence. But a substantial difference in punishment alone is not enough. It also must be shown that in the Anglo-American legal tradition the factor in question historically has held that level of importance. If either branch of the test is not met, then the legislature retains its traditional authority over matters of proof. But to permit a shift in the burden of persuasion when both branches of this test are satisfied would invite the undermining of the presumption of innocence, "that bedrock 'axiomatic and elementary' principle whose 'enforcement lies at the foundation of the administration of our criminal law.'" This is not a test that rests on empty form, for "Winship is concerned with substance rather than . . . formalism." Mullaney v. Wilbur.

I hardly need add that New York's provisions allocating the burden of persuasion as to "extreme emotional disturbance" are unconstitutional when judged by these standards. "Extreme emotional disturbance" is, as the Court of Appeals recognized, the direct descendant of the "heat of passion" factor considered at length in *Mullaney*. I recognize, of course, that the differences between Maine and New York law are not unimportant to the defendant; there is a somewhat broader opportunity for mitigation. But none of those distinctions is relevant here. The presence or absence of extreme emotional disturbance makes a critical difference in punishment and stigma, and throughout our history the resolution of this issue of fact, although expressed in somewhat different terms, has distinguished manslaughter from murder.

TAYLOR v. KENTUCKY

Supreme Court of the United States, 1978.
436 U.S. 478, 98 S.Ct. 1930.

MR. JUSTICE POWELL delivered the opinion of the Court.

Only two Terms ago, this Court observed that the "presumption of innocence, although not articulated in the Constitution, is a basic component of a fair trial under our system of criminal justice." Estelle v. Williams, 425 U.S. 501, 503 (1976). In this felony case, the trial court instructed the jury as to the prosecution's burden of proof beyond a reasonable doubt, but refused petitioner's timely request for instructions on the presumption of innocence and the indictment's lack of evidentiary value. We are asked to decide whether the Due Process Clause of the Fourteenth Amendment requires that either or both instructions be given upon timely defense motions.

I.

Petitioner was tried for robbery in 1976, allegedly having forced his way into the home of James Maddox and stolen a house key and a billfold containing $10 to $15. During *voir dire* of the jury, defense counsel questioned the panel about their understanding of the presumption of innocence, the burden of proof beyond a reasonable doubt, and the fact that an indictment is not evidence. The prosecutor then read the indictment to the jury.

* * *

[Following the trial, defense] counsel requested the trial court to instruct the jury that "[t]he law presumes a defendant to be innocent of a crime," [1] and that the indictment, previously read to the jury, was not evidence to be considered against the defendant.[2] The court declined to give either instruction, and did not convey their substance in its charge to the jury. It did instruct the jury as to the Commonwealth's burden of proving petitioner's guilt beyond a reasonable doubt.[3] Petitioner was found guilty and sentenced to five years of imprisonment.

The Kentucky Court of Appeals affirmed, one judge dissenting.

* * *

1. Petitioner's requested instruction on this point read as follows:

"The law presumes a defendant to be innocent of a crime. Thus a defendant, although accused, begins the trial with a 'clean slate.' That is, with no evidence against him. The law permits nothing but legal evidence presented before a jury to be considered in support of any charge against the accused. So the presumption of innocence alone is sufficient to acquit a defendant, unless you are satisfied beyond a reasonable doubt of the defendant's guilt after careful and impartial consideration of all the evidence in the case."

This instruction is nearly identical to one contained in 1 E. Devitt & C. Blackmar, Federal Jury Practice and Instructions § 11.14, p. 310 (3d ed. 1977).

2. Petitioner's proposed instruction on this point read as follows:

"The jury is instructed that an indictment is in no way any evidence against the defendant and no adverse inference can be drawn against the defendant from a finding of the indictment. The indictment is merely a written accusation charging the defendant with the commission of a crime. It has no probative force and carries with it no implication of guilt."

3. The trial court's instructions, in their entirety, were as follows:

"All right. These are your instructions as to the law applicable to the facts you've heard in evidence from the witness stand in this case.

"Number one, you will find the defendant guilty under this instruction if and only if you believe from the evidence beyond a reasonable doubt all of the following: A. That in this county on or about February 16, 1976 and before the finding of the indictment herein, he the defendant stole a sum of money and a house key from James Maddox, 249 Rosewood, Frankfort, Kentucky; and B. in the course of so doing he used physical force on James Maddox. If you find the defendant guilty under this instruction you will fix his punishment at confinement in the penitentiary for not less than five nor more than ten years in your discretion.

"Number two, if upon the whole case you have a reasonable doubt as to the defendant's guilt you will find him not guilty. The term 'reasonable doubt' as used in these in-

II.

"The principle that there is a presumption of innocence in favor of the accused is the undoubted law, axiomatic and elementary, and its enforcement lies at the foundation of the administration of our criminal law." Coffin v. United States, 156 U.S. 432, 453 (1895). The *Coffin* Court traced the venerable history of the presumption from Deuteronomy through Roman law, English common law, and the common law of the United States. While *Coffin* held that the presumption of innocence and the equally fundamental principle that the prosecution bears the burden of proof beyond a reasonable doubt were logically separate and distinct, sharp scholarly criticism demonstrated the error of that view, see, e. g., J. Thayer, A Preliminary Treatise on Evidence 551–576 (1898) (hereafter Thayer); 9 J. Wigmore, Evidence § 2511 (3d ed. 1940) (hereafter Wigmore); C. McCormick, Evidence 805–806 (2d ed. 1972).[4]

Nevertheless, these same scholars advise against abandoning the instruction on the presumption of innocence, even when a complete explanation of the burden of proof beyond a reasonable doubt is provided. This admonition derives from a perceived salutary effect

structions means a substantial doubt, a real doubt, in that you must ask yourself not whether a better case might have been proved but whether after hearing all the evidence you actually doubt that the defendant is guilty.

"Number three, the verdict of the jury must be unanimous and be signed by one of you as foreman. You may use the form provided at the end of these instructions for writing your verdict.

"There is appended to these instructions a form with alternate verdicts, one of which you will use: A. We the jury find the defendant not guilty; B. We the jury find the defendant guilty under instruction number one and fix his punishment at blank years in the penitentiary."

4. The *Coffin* Court viewed the presumption of innocence as "an instrument of proof created by the law in favor of one accused, whereby his innocence is established until sufficient evidence is introduced to overcome the proof which the law has created." As actual "evidence in favor of the accused," it was distinguished from the reasonable-doubt standard, which merely described "the condition of mind produced by the proof resulting from the evidence in the cause." Ibid. Professor Thayer ably demonstrated the error of this distinction, pointing out that the so-called "pre-

sumption" is not evidence—not even an inference drawn from a fact in evidence—but instead is a way of describing the prosecution's duty both to produce evidence on guilt and to convince the jury beyond a reasonable doubt. Thayer 560–563. Shortly after the appearance of Thayer's criticism, the Court, in a case in which the presumption-of-innocence instruction was given, retreated from its conclusion that the presumption of innocence is evidence to be weighed by the jury. See Agnew v. United States, 165 U.S. 36, 51–52 (1897).

It is now generally recognized that the "presumption of innocence" is an inaccurate, shorthand description of the right of the accused to "remain inactive and secure, until the prosecution has taken up its burden and produced evidence and effected persuasion; i. e., to say in this case, as in any other, that the opponent of a claim or charge is presumed not to be guilty is to say in another form that the proponent of the claim or charge must evidence it." Wigmore 407. The principal inaccuracy is the fact that it is not technically a "presumption"—a mandatory inference drawn from a fact in evidence. Instead, it is better characterized as an "assumption" that is indulged in the absence of contrary evidence.

upon lay jurors. While the legal scholar may understand that the presumption of innocence and the prosecution's burden of proof are logically similar, the ordinary citizen well may draw significant additional guidance from an instruction on the presumption of innocence. Wigmore described this effect as follows:

> "[I]n a criminal case the term [presumption of innocence] does convey a special and perhaps useful hint over and above the other form of the rule about the burden of proof, in that it cautions the jury to put away from their minds all the suspicion that arises from the arrest, the indictment, and the arraignment, and to reach their conclusion solely from the legal evidence adduced. In other words, the rule about burden of proof requires the prosecution by evidence to convince the jury of the accused's guilt; while the presumption of innocence, too, requires this, but conveys for the jury a special and additional caution (which is perhaps only an implied corollary to the other) to consider, in the material for their belief, *nothing but the evidence*, i. e., no surmises based on the present situation of the accused. This caution is indeed particularly needed in criminal cases." Wigmore 407.

This Court has declared that one accused of a crime is entitled to have his guilt or innocence determined solely on the basis of the evidence introduced at trial, and not on grounds of official suspicion, indictment, continued custody, or other circumstances not adduced as proof at trial. And it long has been recognized that an instruction on the presumption is one way of impressing upon the jury the importance of that right. While use of the particular phrase "presumption of innocence"—or any other form of words—may not be constitutionally mandated, the Due Process Clause of the Fourteenth Amendment must be held to safeguard "against dilution of the principle that guilt is to be established by probative evidence and beyond a reasonable doubt." The "purging" effect of an instruction on the presumption of innocence simply represents one means of protecting the accused's constitutional right to be judged solely on the basis of proof adduced at trial.

III.

Petitioner argues that in the circumstances of this case, the purging effect of an instruction on the presumption of innocence was essential to a fair trial. He points out that the trial court's instructions were themselves skeletal, placing little emphasis on the prosecution's duty to prove the case beyond a reasonable doubt and none at all on the jury's duty to judge petitioner only on the basis of the testimony heard at trial.

Against the background of the court's rather Spartan instructions, the prosecutor's closing argument ranged far and wide, asking the jury to draw inferences about petitioner's conduct from "facts" not in evidence, but propounded by the prosecutor. For example, he described the reasonable-doubt standard by declaring that petitioner, *"like every other defendant* who's ever been tried who's in the penitentiary or in the reformatory today, has this presumption of innocence until proved guilty beyond a reasonable doubt." (Emphasis added). This statement linked petitioner to every defendant who turned out to be guilty and was sentenced to imprisonment. It could be viewed as an invitation to the jury to consider petitioner's status as a defendant as evidence tending to prove his guilt. Similarly, in responding to defense counsel's rhetorical query as to the whereabouts of the items stolen from Maddox, the prosecutor declared that "[o]ne of the first things *defendants do after they rip someone off,* they get rid of the evidence as fast and as quickly as they can." (Emphasis added). This statement also implied that all defendants are guilty and invited the jury to consider that proposition in determining petitioner's guilt or innocence.[5]

Additionally, the prosecutor observed in his opening statement that Maddox "took out" a warrant against petitioner and that the grand jury had returned an indictment which the prosecutor read to the jury. Thus, the jury not only was invited to consider the petitioner's status as a defendant, but also was permitted to draw inferences of guilt from the fact of arrest and indictment.[6] The prosecutor's description of those events was not necessarily improper, but the combination of the skeletal instructions, the possible harmful inferences from the references to the indictment, and the repeated suggestions that petitioner's status as a defendant tended to establish his guilt created a genuine danger that the jury would convict petitioner on the basis of those extraneous considerations, rather than on the evidence introduced at trial. That risk was heightened because the trial essentially was a swearing contest between victim and accused.[7]

---

5. We do not suggest that such prosecutorial comments, standing alone, would rise to the level of reversible error, an issue not raised in this case. But they are relevant to the need for carefully framed instructions designed to assure that the accused be judged only on the evidence.

6. As noted above, the trial court also refused petitioner's request for an instruction that the indictment was not evidence. This permitted the prosecutor's reference to the indictment to serve as one more extraneous, negative circumstance which may have influenced the jury's deliberations. Because of our conclusion that the cumulative effect of the potentially damaging circumstances of this case violated the due process guarantee of fundamental fairness in the absence of an instruction as to the presumption of innocence, we do not reach petitioner's further claim that the refusal to instruct that an indictment is not evidence independently constituted reversible error.

7. While we do not necessarily approve of the presumption-of-innocence instruction requested by petitioner, it appears to have been well suited to forestalling the jury's consideration of extraneous matters, that is, to performing the purging function described in Part II, above. The requested instruction noted that petitioner, "although accused, [began] the trial with a 'clean slate.'" It emphasized that the law would permit "nothing but legal evidence presented before a jury to be considered in support of any charge against the accused."

IV.

Against the need for a presumption-of-innocence instruction, the Commonwealth argues first that such an instruction is not required where, as here, the jury is instructed as to the burden of proof beyond a reasonable doubt. The trial court's truncated discussion of reasonable doubt, however, was hardly a model of clarity. It defined reasonable doubt as "a substantial doubt, a real doubt." This definition, though perhaps not in itself reversible error, often has been criticized as confusing. And even if the instruction on reasonable doubt had been more clearly stated, the Commonwealth's argument ignores both the special purpose of a presumption-of-innocence instruction and the particular need for such an instruction in this case.

The Commonwealth also contends that no additional instructions were required, because defense counsel argued the presumption of innocence in both his opening and closing statements. But arguments of counsel cannot substitute for instructions by the court. Petitioner's right to have the jury deliberate solely on the basis of the evidence cannot be permitted to hinge upon a hope that defense counsel will be a more effective advocate for that proposition than the prosecutor will be in implying that extraneous circumstances may be considered. It was the duty of the court to safeguard petitioner's rights, a duty only it could have performed reliably.   .   .   .

V.

We hold that on the facts of this case the trial court's refusal to give petitioner's requested instruction on the presumption of innocence resulted in a violation of his right to a fair trial as guaranteed by the Due Process Clause of the Fourteenth Amendment. The judgment of conviction is reversed and the case is remanded for further proceeedings not inconsistent with this opinion.

So ordered.

[MR. JUSTICE BRENNAN's concurring opinion omitted.]

MR. JUSTICE STEVENS, with whom MR. JUSTICE REHNQUIST joins, dissenting.

In a federal court it is reversible error to refuse a request for a proper instruction on the presumption of innocence. That is not, however, a sufficient reason for holding that such an instruction is constitutionally required in every criminal trial.

The function of the instruction is to make it clear that the burden of persuasion rests entirely on the prosecutor. The same function is performed by the instruction requiring proof beyond a reasonable doubt. One standard instruction adds emphasis to the other. Neither should be omitted, but an "omission, or an incomplete instruction, is less likely to be prejudicial than a misstatement of the law." In some cases the omission may be fatal, but the Court wisely avoids a holding that this is always so.

In this case the omission did not violate a specific constitutional guarantee, such as the privilege against compulsory self-incrimination. Nor did it deny the defendant his fundamental right to a fair trial. An instruction on reasonable doubt, admittedly brief, was given. The *voir dire* had made clear to each juror the defendant's right to be presumed innocent despite his indictment. The prosecutor's closing argument did not precipitate any objection from defense counsel who listened to it; it may not, therefore, provide the basis for a reversal. Although the Court's appraisal is not unreasonable, for this was by no means a perfect trial, I do not believe that constitutional error was committed. Accordingly, I respectfully dissent.

NOTES

1. As indicated in *Taylor*, Coffin v. United States requires the court to give a presumption of innocence instruction, upon defendant's request in federal cases. Does *Taylor* impose the same requirement upon state courts? In Kentucky v. Whorton, 441 U.S. 786, 99 S.Ct. 2088 (1979), the Court indicated that *Taylor* does not stand for that proposition:

> "While this Court in *Taylor* reversed a conviction resulting from a trial in which the judge had refused to give a requested instruction on the presumption of innocence, the Court did not there fashion a new rule of constitutional law requiring that such an instruction be given in every criminal case. Rather, the Court's opinion focused on the failure to give the instruction as it related to the overall fairness of the trial considered in its entirety.

> * * *

> "In short, the failure to give a requested instruction on the presumption of innocence does not in and of itself violate the Constitution. Under *Taylor*, such a failure must be evaluated in light of the totality of the circumstances—including all the instructions to the jury, the arguments of counsel, whether the weight of the evidence was overwhelming, and other relevant factors—to determine whether the defendant received a constitutionally fair trial."

JUSTICE STEWART, joined by JUSTICES BRENNAN and MARSHALL, dissented:

> "While an instruction on the presumption of innocence in one sense only serves to remind the jury that the prosecutor has the burden of proof beyond a reasonable doubt, it also has a separate and distinct function. Quite apart from considerations of the burden of proof, the presumption of innocence 'cautions the jury to put away from their minds all the suspicion that arises from the arrest, the indictment, and the arraignment, and to reach their conclusion solely from the evidence adduced.' And because every defendant, regardless of the totality of the circumstances, is entitled to have his guilt determined only on the basis of the evidence properly introduced against him at trial, I would hold that an instruction on the presumption of innocence is constitutionally required in every case where a timely request has been made."

2. In Cupp v. Naughten, 414 U.S. 139, 94 S.Ct. 397 (1973), the jury was instructed as follows:

"Every witness is presumed to speak the truth. This presumption
may be overcome by the manner in which the witness testifies, by
the nature of his or her testimony, by evidence affecting his or her
character, interest, or motives, by contradictory evidence or by a
presumption."

The majority responded to defendant's claim that this instruction diluted
the presumption of innocence by holding:

"Certainly the instruction by its language neither shifts the
burden of proof nor negates the presumption of innocence accorded
under Oregon law. It would be possible perhaps as a matter of abstract logic to contend that any instruction suggesting that the
jury should believe the testimony of a witness might in some tangential respect 'impinge' upon the right of the defendant to have
his guilt proved beyond a reasonable doubt. But instructions bearing on the burden of proof, just as those bearing on the weight to
be accorded different types of testimony and other familiar subjects of jury instructions, are in one way or another designed to
get the jury off dead center and to give it some guidance by which
to evaluate the frequently confusing and conflicting testimony
which it has heard.

* * *

"The jury here was charged fully and explicitly about the presumption of innocence and the State's duty to prove guilt beyond a
reasonable doubt. Whatever tangential undercutting of these
clearly stated propositions may, as a theoretical matter, have resulted from the giving of the instruction on the presumption of
truthfulness is not of constitutional dimension."

JUSTICE BRENNAN, joined by JUSTICES DOUGLAS and MARSHALL, dissented:

"The reduction of the prosecution's burden of persuasion to a
preponderance clearly conflicts with the Due Process Clause guarantee that an accused shall not be convicted "except upon proof beyond a reasonable doubt of every fact necessary to constitute the
crime with which he is charged."

* * *

"In the instant case, common sense does not dictate that a
prosecution witness who has sworn or affirmed to tell the truth
will *inevitably* do so, and there is surely a *reasonable possibility*
that he will fail to do so. Since here no defense witnesses were
called, the practical effect of the presumption of truthfulness was
to permit the jury to find each and every element of the crimes
charged without requiring that the elements be proved beyond a
reasonable doubt."

3. Can a jury presume the innocence of a particularly dangerous or
unruly defendant who appears in court (or even testifies) wearing handcuffs? See United States v. Samuel, 431 F.2d 610, 614–615 (4th Cir.
1970), aff'd 433 F.2d 663. There the court wrote:

"Basic to American jurisprudence is the principle that an accused, despite his previous record or the nature of the pending
charges, is presumed innocent until his guilt is established beyond
a reasonable doubt by competent evidence. It follows that he is

also entitled to the indicia of innocence. In the presence of the jury, he is ordinarily entitled to be relieved of handcuffs, or other unusual restraints, so as not to mark him as an obviously bad man or to suggest that the fact of his guilt is a forgone conclusion.

"However, the right to the indicia of innocence is a relative one. The judge presiding at the trial, the jurors, courtroom personnel and spectators are entitled to security in the performance of their functions or in observing the trial. The members of the public out of the courtroom are entitled to security in the pursuit of their daily activities. The public also has an interest in the expeditious trial of persons accused of crime, and an interest in preventing the guilty from being at large and committing other offenses. Thus, in appropriate circumstances, the accused's right to the indicia of innocence before the jury must bow to the competing rights of participants in the courtroom and society at large."

4. A most unusual, or, as the Court of Appeals said, "inexplicable" incident involving a presumption of innocence problem arose in Armstead v. United States, 347 F.2d 806 (D.C.Cir.1965). The prosecutor, while cross-examining the defendant, referred to him as "Mr. Armstead"; the judge instructed him to discontinue doing so, saying that although he thought witnesses and counsel should be addressed as "Mister", "Mrs.", or "Miss", that should not be done as regards the defendant. In reversing the defendant's conviction the reviewing court said: "When a defendant takes the stand he is a witness; he is entitled to the same form of address, the same courtesies and consideration as all others involved in the proceeding. The presumption of innocence, apart from other factors, requires no less than that nothing be permitted to trench on that presumption."

5. An interesting observation was made in Wainwright, The Presumption of Guilt, 33 Police Journal (England) 104 (1960), to the effect that, in England, because of the efficiency and integrity of the police, there is in effect a *presumption of guilt* at the time of trial. The author, a police official, then cautions his colleagues:

"We must never abuse that presumption . . . to do so would be to play directly into the hands of our critics to bring to naught the work and honesty of those who created the presumption."

6. Consider Sandstrom v. Montana, 442 U.S. 510, 99 S.Ct. 2450 (1979), excerpts of which follow:

"MR. JUSTICE BRENNAN delivered the opinion of the Court.

"On November 22, 1976, 18-year-old David Sandstrom confessed to the slaying of Annie Jessen. Based upon the confession and corroborating evidence, petitioner was charged on December 2nd with 'deliberate homicide,' in that he 'purposely or knowingly caused the death of Annie Jessen.' At trial, Sandstrom's attorney informed the jury that, although his client admitted killing Jessen, he did not do so 'purposely or knowingly,' and was therefore not guilty of 'deliberate homicide' but of a lesser crime. App. 6–8. The basic support for this contention was the testimony of two court-appointed mental health experts, each of whom described for the jury petitioner's mental state at the time of the incident. Sandstrom's attorney argued that this testimony demonstrated that petitioner, due to a personality disorder aggravated by alcohol consumption, did not kill Annie Jessen 'purposely or knowingly.'

"The prosecution requested the trial judge to instruct the jury that '[t]he law presumes that a person intends the ordinary consequences of his voluntary acts.' The instruction was delivered, the jury found petitioner guilty of deliberate homicide, App. 38, and petitioner was sentenced to 100 years in prison.

* * *

". . . [A] reasonable jury could well have interpreted the presumption as 'conclusive,' that is, not technically as a presumption at all, but rather as an irrebuttable direction by the court to find intent once convinced of the facts triggering the presumption. Alternatively, the jury may have interpreted the instruction as a direction to find intent upon proof of the defendant's voluntary actions (and their 'ordinary' consequences), unless *the defendant* proved the contrary by some quantum of proof which may well have been considerably greater than 'some' evidence—thus effectively shifting the burden of persuasion on the element of intent. Numerous federal and state courts have warned that instructions of the type given here can be interpreted in just these ways.
. . .

". . . It is clear that under Montana law, whether the crime was committed purposely or knowingly is a fact necessary to constitute the crime of deliberate homicide. Indeed, it was the lone element of the offense at issue in Sandstrom's trial, as he confessed to causing the death of the victim, told the jury that knowledge and purpose were the only questions he was controverting, and introduced evidence solely on those points. Moreover, it is conceded that proof of defendant's 'intent' would be sufficient to establish this element. Thus, the question before this Court is whether the challenged jury instruction had the effect of relieving the State of the burden of proof enunciated in *Winship* on the critical question of petitioner's state of mind. We conclude that under either of the two possible interpretations of the instruction set out above, precisely that effect would result, and that the instruction therefore represents constitutional error.

"We consider first the validity of a conclusive presumption.
. . .

"Just last Term, in United States v. United States Gypsum, 438 U.S. 422, 98 S.Ct. 2864, (1978), . . . defendants, who were charged with criminal violations of the Sherman Act, challenged the following jury instruction:

'The law presumes that a person intends the necessary and natural consequences of his acts. Therefore, if the effect of the exchanges of pricing information was to raise, fix, maintain and stabilize prices, then the parties to them are presumed, as a matter of law, to have intended that result.'

After again determining that the offense included the element of intent, we held

'[A] defendant's state of mind or *intent is an element of a criminal antitrust offense which* . . . *cannot be taken from the trier of fact through reliance on a legal presumption* of wrongful intent from proof of effect on prices. Cf. Morissette v. United States . . . . .

* * *

'Although an effect on prices may well support an inference that the defendant had knowledge of the probability of such a consequence at the time he acted, the jury must remain free to consider additional evidence before accepting or rejecting the inference. . . . [U]ltimately the decision on the issue of intent must be left to the trier of fact alone. The instruction given invaded this factfinding function.'

. . . [A] conclusive presumption in this case would 'conflict with the overriding presumption of innocence with which the law endows the accused and which extends to every element of the crime,' and would 'invade [the] factfinding function' which in a criminal case the law assigns solely to the jury. The instruction announced to David Sandstrom's jury may well have had exactly these consequences. Upon finding proof of one element of the crime (causing death), and of facts insufficient to establish the second (the voluntariness and 'ordinary consequences' of defendant's action), Sandstrom's jurors could reasonably have concluded that they were directed to find against defendant on the element of intent. The State was thus not forced to prove 'beyond a reasonable doubt . . . every fact necessary to constitute the crime . . . charged.'

"A presumption which, although not conclusive, had the effect of shifting the burden of persuasion to the defendant, would have suffered from similar infirmities. If Sandstrom's jury interpreted the presumption in that manner, it could have concluded that upon proof by the State of the slaying, and of additional facts not themselves establishing the element of intent, the burden was shifted to the defendant to prove that he lacked the requisite mental state. Such a presumption was found constitutionally deficient in Mullaney v. Wilbur. Because David Sandstrom's jury may have interpreted the judge's instruction as constituting either a burden-shifting presumption like that in *Mullaney*, or a conclusive presumption like those in *United States Gypsum*, and because either interpretation would have deprived defendant of his right to the due process of law, we hold the instruction given in this case unconstitutional.

"MR. JUSTICE REHNQUIST, with whom THE CHIEF JUSTICE joins, concurring.

" . . . I am loath to see this Court go into the business of parsing jury instructions given by state trial courts, for as we have consistently recognized, 'a single instruction to a jury may not be judged in artificial isolation, but must be viewed in the context of the overall charge.' Cupp v. Naughten, 414 U.S. 141, 147, 94 S.Ct. 396, 400 (1973). And surely if this charge had, in the words of the Court, 'merely described a permissive inference,' it could not conceivably have run afoul of the constitutional decisions cited by the Court in its opinion. But a majority of my Brethren conclude that 'it is clear that a reasonable juror could have easily viewed such an instruction as mandatory,' and counsel for the State admitted in oral argument 'that "it's possible" that the jury believed they were required to apply the presumption.'

"While I continue to have doubts as to whether this particular jury was so attentively attuned to the instructions of the trial court that it divined the difference recognized by lawyers between 'infer' and 'presume,' I defer to the judgment of the majority of the Court that this difference in meaning may have been critical in its effect on the jury. I therefore concur in the Court's opinion and judgment."

2. DEFENDANT'S FAILURE TO TESTIFY

LAKESIDE v. OREGON

Supreme Court of the United States, 1978.
435 U.S. 333, 98 S.Ct. 1091.

MR. JUSTICE STEWART delivered the opinion of the Court.

* * *

I.

The petitioner was brought to trial in an Oregon court on a charge of escape in the second degree. The evidence showed that he had been an inmate of the Multnomah County Correctional Institution, a minimum security facility in Multnomah County, Ore. On June 16, 1975, he received a special overnight pass requiring him to return by 10 o'clock the following evening. He did not return. The theory of the defense, supported by the testimony of a psychiatrist and three lay witnesses, was that the petitioner was not criminally responsible for his failure to return to the institution.

At the conclusion of the evidence, the trial judge informed counsel in chambers that he intended to include the following instruction in his charge to the jury:

"Under the laws of this State a defendant has the option to take the witness stand to testify in his or her own behalf. If a defendant chooses not to testify, such a circumstance gives rise to no inference or presumption against the defendant, and this must not be considered by you in determining the question of guilt or innocence."

Defense counsel objected to the giving of that instruction, and after it was given, the following colloquy took place in chambers:

"[Defense Counsel]: .   .   . I have one exception.

"I made this in Chambers prior to the closing statement. I told the Court that I did not want an instruction to the effect that the defendant doesn't have to take the stand, because I felt that that's like waving a red flag in front of the jury. .   .   .

"THE COURT: The defendant did orally request the Court just prior to instructing that the Court not give the usual instruction to the effect that there are no inferences to be drawn against the defendant for failing to take the stand in his own behalf.

"The Court felt that it was necessary to give that instruction in order to properly protect the defendant, and
therefore, the defendant may have his exception."

II.

A

The Fifth Amendment commands that no person "shall be compelled in any criminal case to be a witness against himself." This
guarantee was held to be applicable against the States through the
Fourteenth Amendment in Malloy v. Hogan, 378 U.S. 1, 84 S.Ct.
1489. That case, decided in 1964, established that "the same standards" must attach to the privilege "in either a federal or state proceeding." Less than a year later the Court held in Griffin v. California, 380 U.S. 609, 85 S.Ct. 1229 [Casebook Chapter 19, Section G–2,
supra], that it is a violation of this constitutional guarantee to tell a
jury in a state criminal trial that a defendant's failure to testify supports an unfavorable inference against him.

* * *

. . . [T]he petitioner contends that it is an invasion of the
privilege against compulsory self-incrimination, as that privilege was
perceived in the *Griffin* case, for a trial judge to draw the jury's attention in any way to a defendant's failure to testify unless the defendant acquiesces. We cannot accept this argument, either in terms
of the language of the *Griffin* opinion or in terms of the basic postulates of the Fifth and Fourteenth Amendments.

It is clear from even a cursory review of the facts and the square
holding of the *Griffin* case that the Court was there concerned only
with *adverse* comment, whether by the prosecutor or the trial judge
—"comment by the prosecution on the accused's silence or instructions by the court that such silence is evidence of guilt." The Court
reasoned that such adverse comment amounted to "a penalty imposed
by courts for exercising a constitutional privilege. It cuts down on
the privilege by making its assertion costly."

By definition, "a necessary element of compulsory self-incrimination is some kind of compulsion." Hoffa v. United States, 385 U.S.
293, 304, 87 S.Ct. 408, 414. The Court concluded in *Griffin* that unconstitutional compulsion was inherent in a trial where prosecutor
and judge were free to ask the jury to draw adverse inferences from
a defendant's failure to take the witness stand.[1] But a judge's instruction that the jury must draw *no* adverse inferences of any kind

---

1. Compulsion was also found to be
present in Brooks v. Tennessee, 406
U.S. 605, 92 S.Ct. 1891, where the
State required a defendant who chose
to testify to take the witness stand
ahead of any other defense witnesses.

Thus a defendant was compelled to
make his decision—whether or not to
testify—at a point in the trial when
he could not know if his testimony
would be necessary or even helpful
to his case.

from the defendant's exercise of his privilege not to testify is "comment" of an entirely different order. Such an instruction cannot provide the pressure on a defendant found impermissible in *Griffin*. On the contrary, its very purpose is to remove from the jury's deliberations any influence of unspoken adverse inferences. It would be strange indeed to conclude that this cautionary instruction violates the very constitutional provision it is intended to protect.

The petitioner maintains, however, that whatever beneficent effect such an instruction may have in most cases, it may in some cases encourage the jury to draw adverse inferences from a defendant's silence, and, therefore, it cannot constitutionally be given in any case when a defendant objects to it. Specifically, the petitioner contends that in a trial such as this one, where the defense was presented through several witnesses, the defendant can reasonably hope that the jury will not notice that he himself did not testify. In such circumstances, the giving of the cautionary instruction, he says, is like "waving a red flag in front of the jury."

The petitioner's argument would require indulgence in two very doubtful assumptions: First, that the jurors have not noticed that the defendant did not testify and will not, therefore, draw adverse inferences on their own. Second, that the jurors will totally disregard the instruction, and affirmatively give weight to what they have been told not to consider at all. Federal constitutional law cannot rest on speculative assumptions so dubious as these.

Moreover, even if the petitioner's simile be accepted, it does not follow that the cautionary instruction in these circumstances violates the privilege against compulsory self-incrimination. The very purpose of a jury charge is to flag the jurors' attention to concepts that must not be misunderstood, such as reasonable doubt and burden of proof. To instruct them in the meaning of the privilege against compulsory self-incrimination is no different.

It may be wise for a trial judge not to give such a cautionary instruction over a defendant's objection. And each State is, of course, free to forbid its trial judges from doing so as a matter of state law. We hold only that the giving of such an instruction over the defendant's objection does not violate the privilege against compulsory self-incrimination guaranteed by the Fifth and Fourteenth Amendments.

B

The petitioner's second argument is based upon his constitutional right to counsel. That right was violated, he says, when the trial judge refused his lawyer's request not to give the instruction in question, thus interfering with counsel's trial strategy. That strategy assertedly was based upon studious avoidance of any mention of the fact that the defendant had not testified.

The argument is an ingenious one, but, as a matter of federal constitutional law, it falls of its own weight once the petitioner's primary argument has been rejected. In sum, if the instruction was itself constitutionally accurate, and if the giving of it over counsel's objection did not violate the Fifth and Fourteenth Amendments, then the petitioner's right to the assistance of counsel was not denied when the judge gave the instruction. To hold otherwise would mean that the constitutional right to counsel would be implicated in almost every wholly permissible ruling of a trial judge, if it is made over the objection of the defendant's lawyer.

In an adversary system of criminal justice, there is no right more essential than the right to the assistance of counsel. But that right has never been understood to confer upon defense counsel the power to veto the wholly permissible actions of the trial judge. It is the judge, not counsel, who has the ultimate responsibility for the conduct of a fair and lawful trial. " '[T]he judge is not a mere moderator, but is the governor of the trial for the purpose of assuring its proper conduct and of determining questions of law.' " Geders v. United States, 425 U.S. 80, 86, 96 S.Ct. 1330, 1334.

The trial judge in this case determined in the exercise of his duty to give the protective instruction in the defendant's interest. We have held that it was no violation of the defendant's constitutional privilege for him to do so, even over the objection of defense counsel. Yet the petitioner argues that his constitutional right to counsel means that this instruction could constitutionally be given only if his lawyer did not object to it. We cannot accept the proposition that the right to counsel, precious though it be, can operate to prevent a court from instructing a jury in the basic constitutional principles that govern the administration of criminal justice.

[Affirmed.]

Mr. Justice Brennan took no part in the consideration or decision of this case.

Mr. Justice Stevens, dissenting.

Experience teaches us that most people formally charged with crime are guilty; yet we presume innocence until the trial is over. Experience also justifies the inference that most people who remain silent in the face of serious accusation have something to hide and are therefore probably guilty; yet we forbid trial judges or juries to draw that inference. The presumption of innocence and the protections afforded by the Due Process Clause impose a significant cost on the prosecutor who must prove the defendant's guilt beyond a reasonable doubt without the aid of his testimony. That cost is justified by the paramount importance of protecting a small minority of accused persons—those who are actually innocent—from wrongful conviction.

The Fifth Amendment itself is predicated on the assumption that there are innocent persons who might be found guilty if they could be compelled to testify at their own trials. Every trial lawyer knows that some truthful denials of guilt may be considered incredible by a jury—either because of their inherent improbability or because their explanation, under cross-examination, will reveal unfavorable facts about the witness or his associates. The Constitution therefore gives the defendant and his lawyer the absolute right to decide that the accused shall not become a witness against himself. Even if the judge is convinced that the defendant's testimony would exonerate him, and even if he is motivated only by a desire to protect the defendant from the risk of an erroneous conviction, the judge has no power to override counsel's judgment about what is in his client's best interest.

The Constitution wisely commits the critical decision of whether the defendant shall take the stand to the defendant and his lawyer, rather than the judge, for at least two reasons. First, they have greater access to information bearing on the decision than the judge can normally have. Second, they are motivated solely by concern for the defendant's interests; the judge inevitably is concerned with society's interest in convicting the guilty as well as protecting the innocent. The choice, therefore, to testify or not to testify is for the defendant and his lawyer, not the judge, to make. The Constitution commands that the decision be made free of any compulsion by the State.

. . . Of course, a defendant's silence at his own trial is "almost certain to prejudice the defense no matter what else happens in the courtroom;" for the jury will probably draw an unfavorable inference despite instructions to the contrary. Although this "cost" can never be eliminated *Griffin* stands for the proposition that the government may not add unnecessarily to the risk taken by a defendant who stands mute. . . .

In some trials, the defendant's silence will be like "the sun . . . shining with full blaze on the open eye." State v. Cleaves, 59 Me. 298, 301 (1871). But in other trials—perhaps when the whole story has been told by other witnesses or when the prosecutor's case is especially weak—the jury may not focus on the defendant's failure to testify. For the judge or prosecutor to call it to the jury's attention has an undeniably adverse effect on the defendant. Even if jurors try faithfully to obey their instructions, the connection between silence and guilt is often too direct and too natural to be resisted. When the jurors have in fact overlooked it, telling them to ignore the defendant's silence is like telling them not to think of a white bear.

The Court thinks it "would be strange indeed to conclude that this cautionary instruction violates the very constitutional provision it is intended to protect." Unless the same words mean different things in different mouths, this holding also applies to statements made by the prosecutor in his closing argument. Yet I wonder if the Court would find petitioner's argument as strange if the prosecutor, or even the judge, had given the instruction three or four times, in slightly different form, just to make sure the jury knew that silence, like killing Caesar, is consistent with honor.

It is unrealistic to assume that instructions on the right to silence always have a benign effect. At times the instruction will make the defendant's silence costly indeed. So long as *Griffin* is good law, the State must have a strong reason for ignoring the defendant's request that the instruction not be given. Remarkably, the Court fails to identify any reason for overriding the defendant's choice. Eliminating the instruction on request costs the State nothing, other than the advantage of calling attention to the defendant's silence. A defendant may waive his Fifth Amendment right to silence, and a judge who thinks his decision unwise may not overrule it. The defendant should also be able to waive, without leave of court, his lesser right to an instruction about his Fifth Amendment right to silence. Many state courts have accepted this conclusion by ruling that no self-incrimination instruction should be given over the defendant's objection. An ungrudging application of *Griffin* requires that we do the same.

I respectfully dissent.

Mr. Justice Marshall joins this opinion, with the exception of the first paragraph.

3. CREDIBILITY OF WITNESSES

(a) The Defendant

REAGAN v. UNITED STATES

Supreme Court of the United States, 1895.
157 U.S. 301, 15 S.Ct. 610.

Mr. Justice Brewer delivered the opinion of the court.

On April 30, 1894, the defendant was found guilty by the verdict of a jury in the Circuit Court of the United States for the Western District of Texas of a violation of unlawfully, fraudulently, wilfully, knowingly and with intent to defraud the United States, receiving into his possession and concealing forty head of cattle which had been with like intent smuggled and introduced into the United States from the Republic of Mexico.

* * *

[Defendant's principal claim of error is that the court gave this instruction: "You should especially look to the interest which the respective witnesses have in the suit or in its result. Where the witness has a direct personal interest in the result of the suit the temptation is strong to color, pervert, or withhold the facts. The law permits the defendant, at his own request, to testify in his own behalf. The defendant here has availed himself of this privilege. His testimony is before you and you must determine how far it is credible. The deep personal interest which he may have in the result of the suit should be considered by the jury in weighing his evidence and in determining how far or to what extent, if at all, it is worthy of credit."

* * *

[If the defendant testifies in his own behalf] his credibility may be impeached, his testimony may be assailed, and is to be weighed as that of any other witness. Assuming the position of a witness, he is entitled to all its rights and protections, and is subject to all its criticisms and burdens. It is unnecessary to consider whether, when offering himself as a witness as to one matter, he may either, at the will of the government or under the discretion of the court, be called upon to testify as to other matters. That question is not involved in this case, and we notice it simply to exclude it from the scope of our observations. The privileges and limitations to which we refer are those which inhere in the witness as a witness, and which affect the testimony voluntarily given. As to that, he may be fully cross-examined. It may be assailed by contradictory testimony. His credibility may be impeached, and by the same methods as are pursued in the case of any other witness. The jury properly consider his manner of testifying, the inherent probabilities of his story, the amount and character of the contradictory testimony, the nature and extent of his interest in the result of the trial, and the impeaching evidence in determining how much of credence he is entitled to.

It is within the province of the court to call the attention of the jury to any matters which legitimately affect his testimony and his credibility. This does not imply that the court may arbitrarily single out his testimony and denounce it as false. The fact that he is a defendant does not condemn him as unworthy of belief, but at the same time it creates an interest greater than that of any other witness, and to that extent affects the question of credibility. It is, therefore, a matter properly to be suggested by the court to the jury. But the limits of suggestion are the same in respect to him as to others. It is a familiar rule that the relations of a witness to the matter to be deicded are legitimate subjects of consideration in respect to the weight to be given to his testimony. The old law was that interest debarred one from testifying, for fear that such interest might tend to a perversion of the truth. A more enlightened spirit has thrown down this barrier, and now mere interest does not exclude one from the witness stand, but the interest is to be considered as affecting his credibility. This rule is equally potent in criminal as in civil cases, and in neither is it error for the trial court to direct the attention of the jury to the interest which any witness may have in the result of the trial as a circumstance to be considered in weighing his testimony and determining the credence that shall be given to his story.

* * *

[T]he court is not at liberty to charge the jury directly or indirectly that the defendant is to be disbelieved because he is a defendant, for that would practically take away the benefit which the law grants when it gives him the privilege of being a witness. On the other hand, the court may, and sometimes ought, to remind the jury that interest creates a motive for false testimony; that the greater the interest the stronger is the temptation, and that the interest of the defendant in the result of the trial is of a character possessed by no other witness, and is therefore a matter which may seriously affect the credence that shall be given to his testimony. The court should be impartial between the government and the defendant. On behalf of the defendant it is its duty to caution the jury not to convict upon the uncorroborated testimony of an accomplice. Indeed, according to some authorities, it should peremptorily instruct that no verdict of guilty can be founded on such uncorroborated testimony, and this because the inducements to falsehood on the part of an accomplice are so great. And if any other witness for the government is disclosed to have great feeling or large interest against the defendant, the court may, in the interests of justice, call the attention of the jury to the extent of that feeling or interest as affecting his credibility. In the same manner in behalf of the government, the court may charge the jury that the peculiar and deep interest which the defendant has in the result of the trial is a matter affecting his credibility, and to be carefully considered by them.

Tested by these rules we see in the instruction objected to nothing of which complaint can reasonably be made. In the first part it lays down a general rule, applicable to all circumstances, and then in the latter part simply calls attention to the fact that the defendant has a deep personal interest in the result of the suit, and that that should be considered by the jury. There is no declaration nor intimation that the defendant has been untruthful in his testimony. There is only a reference to the jury of the matter of credibility coupled with the declaration that interest in the result is a circumstance to be weighed in its determination. This clearly is unobjectionable.

* * *

The judgment is affirmed.

NOTES

1. In Johnson v. United States, 157 U.S. 320, 15 S.Ct. 614 (1895), a companion to *Reagan*, the Court upheld the following instruction in the context of the overall charge:

> "The defendant goes upon the stand before you and he makes his statement; tells his story. Above all things, in a case of this kind you are to see whether that statement is corroborated substantially and reliably by the proven facts; if so, it is strengthened to the extent of its corroboration. If it is not strengthened in that way, you are to weigh it by its own inherent truthfulness, its own inherent proving power that may belong to it."

2. The *Reagan-Johnson* doctrine remains good law in the federal courts today. The standard instruction reads as follows:

> "A defendant in a criminal trial is permitted to become a witness in his own behalf. His testimony should not be disbelieved merely because he is the defendant. However, in weighing his testimony, you have a right to consider the fact that he does have a vital interest in the outcome of the case. But, again, you should give his testimony such weight as in your very good judgment that testimony is fairly entitled to receive."

See United States v. Jones, 459 F.2d 1225 (D.C.Cir.1972).

3. Several state courts have rejected the foregoing instruction on the ground that it constitutes judicial comment on the evidence, a practice forbidden in some states, and unduly singles out the testimony of a single witness—the defendant. See, e. g., State v. Bester, 167 N.W.2d 705 (Iowa 1969); Anno., 85 A.L.R. 523 (1933).

(b) THE ACCOMPLICE

The subject of the credibility of an accomplice witness has been adequately covered in the preceding materials in Chapter 19, C–1.

(c) THE EYE-WITNESS

UNITED STATES v. HODGES

United States Court of Appeals, Seventh Circuit, 1975.
515 F.2d 650.

GRANT, SENIOR DISTRICT JUDGE.*

Appellant was charged in a one-count indictment with possession of a check stolen from the mail, with knowledge that it was stolen . . . .. After a trial by jury, he was convicted and sentenced to probation for a period of three years. The check in question was an Illinois Public Assistance check payable to the order of one Paul Watkins in the amount of $144.12. With the check, appellant first attempted to purchase a bottle of whisky at Angelo's Liquors, a store in Wilmington, Illinois. However, an employee of the store, Charles Toncrey, refused to cash the check after consulting with the owner, Angelo Aggelopoulous. Appellant then proceeded to go to a Western Auto Store in Coal City, Illinois, where he used the check to purchase a child's bicycle. Clarence A. Rolando, the owner of the store, honored the check but then alerted police after the transaction because of appellant's activities subsequent to the purchase. Shortly thereafter appellant was arrested. The government's case rested almost entirely upon the three eyewitness identifications of Toncrey, Aggelopoulous, and Rolando. Each of these persons positively identified appellant as the man who had attempted to cash the check. At appellant's trial, nevertheless, the court refused to give an identification instruction tendered by appellant's counsel because the court considered the instruction to be argumentative as well as a comment on the evidence. The sole issue in this appeal is whether the trial court erred in refusing to give to the jury appellant's requested instruction regarding eyewitness identifications.

---

* Senior District Judge Robert A. Grant
of the Northern District of Indiana is
sitting by designation.

Appellant contends that an instruction telling the jury that identification was the sole issue in the case was required in the court below because: (1) there was a 15-month delay between the crime and
the in-court identifications; (2) a show-up instead of a line-up was
used at the Coal City police station to identify him; and (3) two of
the witnesses, Toncrey and Aggelopoulous, were not able to identify,
immediately before trial, the picture which showed what appellant
looked like on the day of the arrest. Under these circumstances, appellant argues that the instruction which he tendered was neither argumentative nor a comment on the evidence. Rather, it served to focus the jury's attention on the true issue before them. Further, appellant maintains that an identification instruction must be given
where, as here, it is supported by the evidence and requested by the
defense. Finally, appellant cites the Court to the tendency of many
Circuits to give such an instruction for the reason that "testimony
tending to prove identity is to be scrutinized with extreme care." It
is appellant's position in this appeal, therefore, that based on the circumstances of the present case, an instruction focusing the attention
of the jury on the defense of misidentification was appropriate and
should have been given by the trial court. However, since the instruction was not given, appellant urges this Court to reverse his conviction and remand the cause for a new trial under proper instructions.

In response, appellee maintains that, although there are some
factual situations which would compel an instruction which warns the
jury to closely scrutinize identification testimony, the factual circumstances of the instant case do not require such an instruction. In this
regard, appellee emphasizes that in the present case there is neither
the uncorroborated testimony of a single eyewitness nor a situation
where a conviction has resulted from an identification during a confusing affray of short duration involving a number of participants.
Instead, in the instant case, appellee notes that there were three positive identifications made from direct observation which were, in turn,
corroborated by the identification of the arresting officer . . . . .
Since the witnesses here, argues appellee, had the opportunity to observe the accused, were positive in their identifications, were not
weakened by prior misidentification, and remained unqualified after
cross-examination, an instruction on the dangers of identification testimony was not warranted by the facts. It is appellee's position,
then, that the likelihood of misidentification in the present case was
virtually nonexistent.

In any event, appellee notes that many Circuits have left the
matter of giving an identification instruction to the trial judge's discretion. In this regard, some courts have found such an instruction
to be superfluous in light of adequate cross-examination, summation,
and appropriate burden of proof and credibility instructions. In the
instant case, appellee maintains that cross-examination focused on
the possibility of mistaken identification and that counsel's summation plainly apprised the jury that the identification made by the the

witnesses was the underlying issue in the case. Therefore, appellee argues that the identification issue was fully aired and argued before the jury, and that the jury was clearly aware of its duty to find beyond a reasonable doubt that appellant was properly identified as the person who attempted to cash the check. The trial court's refusal to give appellant's tendered identification instruction, then, was not error, contends appellee. Accordingly, we are urged to affirm the judgment of conviction in the court below.

Although it has been recognized that the giving of instructions on identification is largely within the discretion of the trial judge, . . . and that in certain factual circumstances the failure to give an identification instruction has been determined to be harmless, it has also been stated that trial courts should, as a matter of routine, in cases where identification is a key issue, include an identification instruction which emphasizes to the jury the need for finding that the circumstances of the identification are convincing beyond a reasonable doubt. United States v. Telfaire, 469 F.2d 552, 555 (1972). In *Telfaire*, the District of Columbia Circuit adopted generally for judges within the district a model instruction using material from Judge Aldisert's opinion in United States v. Barber, 442 F.2d 517 (3d Cir. 1971), but permitting variation and adaptation to suit the proof and contentions of a particular case. In this Circuit, although such an instruction or variation thereof, has not been absolutely required in the past, we inferentially, at least, recognized the need for an instruction of the kind that was refused in the instant case in United States v. Dichiarinte, 385 F.2d 333 (7th Cir. 1967). Moreover, we stated in United States v. Napue, 401 F.2d 107, 112 (7th Cir. 1968), that the "better practice" would be to give some instruction on mistaken identity even though the instruction given need not necessarily be in the exact form as offered by the defense. We now adopt what we labeled to be the better practice in *Napue*, as the required practice in this Circuit; and although it is not our intention to require that the *Telfaire* model be given verbatim, we hereby publish notice that we shall in the future view with grave concern the failure to give the substantial equivalent of such an instruction.

This decision which we render today is influenced by many what we believe to be serious considerations relative to the administration of criminal justice. First and foremost, although we realize, on the basis of our careful review of the record herein, that the subject of identification was explored by counsel at appellant's trial on cross-examination as well as in final argument, and that the court's instructions to the jury were indeed accurate as to the burden of proof required in criminal cases and concerning the credibility of witnesses, and that the existence of these circumstances has induced some courts to decline to give a detailed charge on eyewitness identification, we are not persuaded to say that the existence of such circumstances necessarily obviates the giving of such an instruction to the jury. Further, we are not completely satisfied that in the instant case the existence of such circumstances served to focus the jury's attention on the issue of identity. In this regard, we are mindful of what the court stated in United States v. Evans, 484 F.2d 1178 (2d Cir. 1973), with respect to the trial court's failure to give a specific charge to the jury on the dangers of eyewitness identification:

> There is no question that identification testimony is notably fallible, and the result of it can be, and sometimes has been, "the greatest single injustice that can arise out of our system of criminal law," namely the conviction of the wrong man through a mistake in identity. The dangers in this area have been well chronicled, and have been the proper subject of careful attention in this and many other courts . . . .

Since it is our goal to guard against the occurrence of such injustice, we are convinced that neither summation of counsel at the close of the evidence, however prolonged or explicit, nor cross-examination as to the matter of identification by defense counsel adequately protects a defendant against the dangers of misidentification which are inherent in eyewitness testimony. Nor do we believe that such summation and cross-examination by counsel may substitute for proper instructions to the jury by the court. In cases such as the present, where the issue of identification is paramount, we define proper instructions to include an identification instruction, when it is tendered to the court, in addition to accurate instructions as to burden of proof and the credibility of witnesses. As the District of Columbia Circuit stated in Salley v. United States, 353 F.2d 897, 899 (1965): It is the obligation of the trial judge "to instruct the jury that if there was a reasonable doubt as to the identification of the defendant as the person who [committed the crime], then the jury should acquit."

We believe that the *Salley* decision lays down the correct rule of law and that the *Telfaire* case propounds an appropriate model instruction to be applied in cases where, as here, the crucial issue involved is the defendant's identification, and where an instruction specifically bringing the identity issue to the jury's attention is requested by counsel and tendered to the court. Accordingly, since we find that the district court's grounds for refusing to give and its subsequent failure to give to the jury the identification instruction tendered by appellant or an appropriate equivalent thereof based on the facts of the case constituted error, the judgment of conviction in the court below is hereby reversed, and the cause is remanded for a new trial in conformity with this opinion.

NOTES

1. In United States v. Telfaire, 469 F.2d 552 (D.C.Cir. 1972), the principal case cited in *Hodges,* the court affirmed a conviction for a $10 robbery secured through the uncorroborated testimony of the victim who briefly had observed defendant in a dimly lighted hotel hallway. Finding cross-examination of the witness, arguments of counsel, and the standard burden of proof instructions insufficient to focus the jury's attention on the identification issue, the court concluded that the absence of a special identification was not prejudicial. However, under its supervisory powers, the court pro-

mulgated the following, rather elaborate, instruction for use in future cases:

"One of the most important issues in this case is the identification of the defendant as the perpetrator of the crime. The Government has the burden of providing identity, beyond a reasonable doubt. It is not essential that the witness himself be free from doubt as to the correctness of his statement. However, you, the jury, must be satisfied beyond a reasonable doubt of the accuracy of the identification of the defendant before you may convict him. If you are not convinced beyond a reasonable doubt that the defendant was the person who committed the crime, you must find the defendant not guilty.

"Identification testimony is an expression of belief or impression by the witness. Its value depends on the opportunity the witness had to observe the offender at the time of the offense and to make a reliable identification later.

"In appraising the identification testimony of a witness, you should consider the following:

"(1) Are you convinced that the witness had the capacity and an adequate opportunity to observe the offender?

"Whether the witness had an adequate opportunity to observe the offender at the time of the offense will be affected by such matters as how long or short a time was available, how far or close the witness was, how good were lighting conditions, whether the witness had had occasion to see or know the person in the past.

"[In general, a witness bases any identification he makes on his perception through the use of his senses. Usually the witness identifies an offender by the sense of sight—but this is not necessarily so, and he may use other senses.]

"(2) Are you satisfied that the identification made by the witness subsequent to the offense was the product of his own recollection? You may take into account both the strength of the identification, and the circumstances under which the identification was made.

"If the identification by the witness may have been influenced by the circumstances under which the defendant was presented to him for identification, you should scrutinize the identification with great care. You may also consider the length of time that lapsed between the occurrence of the crime and the next opportunity of the witness to see defendant, as a factor bearing on the reliability of the identification.

"[You may also take into account that an identification made by picking the defendant out of a group of similar individuals is generally more reliable than one which results from the presentation of the defendant alone to the witness.]

"[(3) You make take into account any occasions in which the witness failed to make an identification of defendant, or made an identification that was inconsistent with his identification at trial.]

"(4) Finally, you must consider the credibility of each identification witness in the same way as any other witness, consider whether he is truthful, and consider whether he had the capacity and opportunity to make a reliable observation on the matter covered in his testimony.

"I again emphasize that the burden of proof on the prosecutor extends to every element of the crime charged, and this specifically includes the burden of proving beyond a reasonable doubt the identity of the defendant as the perpetrator of the crime with which he stands charged. If after examining the testimony, you have a reasonable doubt as to the accuracy of the identification, you must find the defendant not guilty."

3. In addition to *Hodges* and *Telfaire*, two other courts require that an instruction, similar to the model above, be given in all eye-witness cases. See United States v. Holly, 502 F.2d 273 (4th Cir. 1974); United States v. Barber, 442 F.2d 517 (3d Cir. 1971). In the majority of jurisdictions, trial judges are given broad discretion to determine whether the circumstances require a special identification instruction. See United States v. Dodge, 538 F.2d 770, 784 (8th Cir. 1976); United States v. Masterson, 529 F.2d 30, 32 (9th Cir. 1976); United States v. O'Neal, 496 F.2d 368, 373 (6th Cir. 1974); United States v. Fernandez, 456 F.2d 638, 644 (2d Cir. 1972).

D. SPECIFIC PRESUMPTIONS AND INFERENCES

1. ILLEGAL POSSESSION OF NARCOTICS

LEARY v. UNITED STATES

Supreme Court of the United States, 1969.
395 U.S. 6, 89 S.Ct. 1532, appeal after remand, Fifth Circuit, 431 F.2d 85.

MR. JUSTICE HARLAN delivered the opinion of the Court.

This case presents constitutional questions arising out of the conviction of the petitioner, Dr. Timothy Leary, for violation of two federal statutes governing traffic in marihuana.

The circumstances surrounding petitioner's conviction were as follows. On December 20, 1965, petitioner left New York by automobile, intending a vacation trip to Yucatan, Mexico. He was accompanied by his daughter and son, both teenagers, and two other persons. On December 22, 1965, the party drove across the International Bridge between the United States and Mexico at Laredo, Texas. They stopped at the Mexican customs station and, after apparently being denied entry, drove back across the bridge. They halted at the American secondary inspection area, explained the situation to a customs inspector, and stated that they had nothing from Mexico to declare. The inspector asked them to alight, examined the interior of the car, and saw what appeared to be marihuana seeds on the floor. The inspector then received permission to search the car and passengers. Small amounts of marihuana were found on the car floor and in the glove compartment. A personal search of petitioner's daughter revealed a silver snuff box containing semi-refined marihuana and three partially smoked marihuana cigarettes.

* * *

We granted certiorari to consider . . . whether petitioner was denied due process by the application of the part of 21 U.S.C. § 176a which provides that a defendant's possession of marihuana shall be deemed sufficient evidence that the marihuana was illegally imported or brought into the United States, and that the defendant knew of the illegal importation or bringing in, unless the defendant explains his possession to the satisfaction of the jury. For reasons which follow, we hold in favor of the petitioner . . . and reverse the judgment of the Court of Appeals.

So far as here relevant, the presumption . . . authorizes the jury to infer from a defendant's possession of marihuana two necessary elements of the crime: (1) that the marihuana was imported or brought into the United States illegally; and (2) that the defendant knew of the unlawful importation or bringing in. Petitioner argues that neither inference is valid, citing undisputed testimony at his trial to the effect that marihuana will grow anywhere in the United States, and that some actually is grown here. The Government contends, on the other hand, that both inferences are permissible. For reasons that follow, we hold unconstitutional that part of the presumption which relates to a defendant's knowledge of illegal importation. Consequently, we do not reach the question of the validity of the "illegal importation" inference.

* * *

Once it is established that a significant percentage of domestically consumed marihuana may not have been imported at all, then it can no longer be postulated, without proof, that possessors will be even roughly aware of the proportion actually imported. We conclude that in order to sustain the inference of knowledge we must find on the basis of the available materials that a majority of marihuana possessors either are cognizant of the apparently high rate of importation or otherwise have become aware that *their* marihuana was grown abroad.

We can imagine five ways in which a possessor might acquire such knowledge: (1) he might be aware of the proportion of domestically consumed marihuana which is smuggled from abroad and deduce that his was illegally imported; (2) he might have smuggled the marihuana himself; (3) he might have learned by indirect means that the marihuana consumed in his locality or furnished by his supplier was smuggled from abroad; (4) he might have specified foreign marihuana when making his "buy," or might have been told the course of the marihuana by his supplier; (5) he might be able to tell the source from the appearance, packaging, or taste of the marihuana itself.

* * *

.   .   .   the materials at our disposal leave us at large to estimate even roughly the proportion of marihuana possessors who have
learned in one way or another the origin of their marihuana.   It
must also be recognized that a not inconsiderable proportion of domestically consumed marihuana appears to have been grown in this
country, and that its possessors must be taken to have "known," if
anything, that their marihuana was *not* illegally imported.   In short,
it would be no more than speculation were we to say that even as
much as a majority of possessors "knew" the source of their marihuana.

Nor are these deficiencies in the foundation for the "knowledge"
presumption overcome by paying, as we do, the utmost deference to
the congressional determination that this presumption was warranted.   For Congress, no less than we, is subject to constitutional requirements, and in this instance the legislative record falls even
shorter of furnishing an adequate foundation for the "knowledge"
presumption than do the more extensive materials we have examined.

We thus cannot escape the duty of setting aside petitioner's conviction.   .   .   .

* * *

NOTES

1.   Is the presumption that possession shows knowledge of illegal importation valid with regard to other narcotic substances?   The Supreme
Court in Turner v. United States, 396 U.S. 398, 90 S.Ct. 642 (1970), answered that question in the affirmative for heroin but in the negative for cocaine.   This distinction was drawn because a sizeable quantity of cocaine is
lawfully produced in this country for medicinal purposes, and, consequently,
there is the very real possibility that cocaine in a defendant's possession
may have been stolen from a legal source.   That possibility is sufficient to
negate either the presumption that all cocaine was illegally imported or that
the accused knew of its importation.

For presumption validity purposes, may a distinction be made between
users of the drug and sellers of it?

2.   Does a statutory presumption compel the defendant to testify in order to rebut the presumption?   In Yee Hem v. United States, 268 U.S. 178,
45 S.Ct. 470 (1924), the Court held that the presumption of narcotics importation did not violate the defendant's protection against self-incrimination:

"[The statutory presumption] does no more than to make possession of the prohibited article *prima facie* evidence of guilt.   It
leaves the accused entirely free to testify or not as he chooses.   If
the accused happens to be the only repository of the facts necessary to negative the presumption arising from his possession, that
is a misfortune which the statute under review does not create but
is inherent in the case.   The same situation might present itself if
there were no statutory presumption and a *prima facie* case of concealment with knowledge of unlawful importation were made by
the evidence.   The necessity of an explanation by the accused
would be quite as compelling in that case as in this, but the constraint upon him to give testimony would arise there, as it arises

here, simply from the force of circumstances and not from any form of compulsion forbidden by the Constitution."

3. Under N.Y. Penal Law § 220.25(1): "The presence of a dangerous drug in an automobile, other than a public omnibus, is presumptive evidence of knowing possession thereof by each and every person in the automobile at the time such drug was found".

In People v. Leyva, 38 N.Y.2d 160, 379 N.Y.S.2d 30, 341 N.E.2d 546 (1975), the court construed the statute as creating only a permissive presumption—that is, one authorizing, but not commanding, the jury to reach a certain conclusion from the proof of specified underlying facts. Even in the absence of rebuttal evidence by the defendants, the court held, "A jury is not to be told that it *must* find defendants guilty if the prosecution proves that they and drugs were present in a car together; it is only to be told that it *may* so find."

Although accepting the state court's construction of its own statute, the Second Circuit, on federal habeas corpus, ruled that the manner in which the statute was incorporated into the trial judge's instructions infringed upon defendant's presumption of innocence. In Lopez v. Curry, 583 F.2d 1188 (2d Cir. 1978), the court ruled:

"[The trial judge] charged that 'the Penal Law says in effect that from this evidence [that both the cocaine and the defendants were present in the automobile] each of the defendants possessed the cocaine, knowingly possessed the cocaine.' If the foundation was laid, he added, the state was 'entitled to the presumption . . . charging them with possession.'

"These instructions ran afoul of the guarantee of In re Winship (1970), that 'the Due Process Clause protects the accused against conviction except upon proof beyond a reasonable doubt of every fact necessary to constitute the crime with which he is charged.' Since possession 'is an ingredient of the crime charged, its existence is a question of fact which must be submitted to the jury.' Morissette v. United States, 342 U.S. 246, 274, 72 S.Ct. 240, 255 (1952). It was, accordingly, for the jury in this case to decide not only whether the foundation of presence was properly laid, but also whether the critical leap to a conclusion of possession beyond a reasonable doubt was appropriate. Given the inviolable function of the jury as a trier of fact, *Morissette* instructed, '[i]t follows that the trial court may not withdraw or prejudge the issue by instruction that the law raises a presumption' of an element of the crime from proof of an underlying fact.

"[The trial judge] did precisely that by explaining that upon proof of the defendants' presence in a car with cocaine § 220.25(1) 'says in effect' that each of the defendants knowingly possessed the narcotics. The prosecution, he said, was then 'entitled to the presumption . . . charging them with possession.' And this error was not cured but rather compounded by his additional instruction that the defendants could rebut the presumption. In charging that defendants were required to come forward with evidence that would 'raise a reasonable doubt in your minds that the defendants possessed this cocaine,' the trial judge clearly shifted the burden of proof on the element of knowing possession. This was error—and of manifest constitutional dimension."

2. POSSESSION OF RECENTLY STOLEN GOODS

BARNES v. UNITED STATES

Supreme Court of the United States, 1973.
412 U.S. 847, 93 S.Ct. 2357.

MR. JUSTICE POWELL delivered the opinion of the Court.

Petitioner Barnes was convicted in United States District Court on two counts of possessing United States Treasury checks stolen from the mails, knowing them to be stolen, two counts of forging the checks, and two counts of uttering the checks, knowing the endorsements to be forged. . . .

The evidence at petitioner's trial established that on June 2, 1971, he opened a checking account in the pseudonym "Clarence Smith." On July 1, and July 3, 1971, the United States Disbursing Office at San Francisco mailed four Government checks in the amounts of $269.02, $154.70, $184.00, and $268.80 to Nettie Lewis, Albert Young, Arthur Salazar, and Mary Hernandez, respectively. On July 8, 1971, petitioner deposited these four checks into the "Smith" account. Each check bore the apparent endorsement of the payee and a second endorsement by "Clarence Smith."

At petitioner's trial the four payees testified that they had never received, endorsed, or authorized endorsement of the checks. A Government handwriting expert testified that petitioner had signed the "Clarence Smith" endorsement on all four checks and that he had signed the payees' names on the Lewis and Hernandez checks. Although petitioner did not take the stand, a postal inspector testified to certain statements made by petitioner at a post-arrest interview. Petitioner explained to the inspector that he received the checks in question from people who sold furniture for him door-to-door and that the checks had been signed in the payees' names when he received them. Petitioner further stated that he could not name or identify any of the salespeople. Nor could he substantiate the existence of any furniture orders because the salespeople allegedly wrote their orders on scratch paper that had not been retained. Petitioner admitted that he executed the Clarence Smith endorsements and deposited the checks but denied signing the payees' endorsements.

The District Court instructed the jury that "[p]ossession of recently stolen property, if not satisfactorily explained, is ordinarily a circumstance from which you may reasonably draw the inference and find, in the light of the surrounding circumstances shown by the evidence in the case, that the person in possession knew the property had been stolen."[1]

* * *

1. The full instruction on the inference arising from possession of stolen property stated:

"Possession of recently stolen property, if not satisfactorily ex-

plained, is ordinarily a circumstance from which you may reasonably draw the inference and find, in the light of the surrounding circumstances shown by the evidence

The teaching of Leary v. United States [and other presumption cases] is not altogether clear. To the extent that the "rational connection," "more-likely-than-not," and "reasonable doubt" standards bear ambiguous relationships to one another, the ambiguity is traceable in large part to variations in language and focus rather than to differences of substance. What has been established by the cases, however, is at least this: that if a statutory inference submitted to the jury as sufficient to support conviction satisfies the reasonable doubt standard (that is, the evidence necessary to invoke the inference is sufficient for a rational juror to find the inferred fact beyond a reasonable doubt) as well as the more-likely-than-not standard, then it clearly accords with due process.

In the present case we deal with a traditional common law inference deeply rooted in our law. For centuries courts have instructed juries that an inference of guilty knowledge may be drawn from the fact of unexplained possession of stolen goods. Thayer, writing in his Preliminary Treatise on Evidence (1898), cited this inference as the descendant of a presumption "running through a dozen centuries." Early American cases consistently upheld instructions permitting conviction upon such an inference, and the courts of appeals on numerous occasions have approved instructions essentially identical to the instruction given in this case. This longstanding and consistent judicial approval of the instruction, reflecting accumulated common experience, provides strong indication that the instruction comports with due process.

This impressive historical basis, however, is not in itself sufficient to establish the instruction's constitutionality. Common law inferences, like their statutory counterparts, must satisfy due process

in the case, that the person in possession knew the property had been stolen.

"However, you are never required to make this inference. It is the exclusive province of the jury to determine whether the facts and circumstances shown by the evidence in this case warrant any inference which the law permits the jury to draw from the possession of recently stolen property.

"The term 'recently' is a relative term, and has no fixed meaning. Whether property may be considered as recently stolen depends upon the nature of the property, and all the facts and circumstances shown by the evidence in the case. The longer the period of time since the theft the more doubtful becomes the inference which may reasonably be drawn from unexplained possession.

"If you should find beyond a reasonable doubt from the evidence in the case that the mail described in the indictment was stolen, and that while recently stolen the contents of said mail here, the four United States Treasury checks, were in the possession of the defendant you would ordinarily be justified in drawing from those facts the inference that the contents were possessed by the accused with knowledge that it was stolen property, unless such possession is explained by facts and circumstances in this case which are in some way consistent with the defendant's innocence.

"In considering whether possession of recently stolen property has been satisfactorily explained, you are reminded that in the exercise of constitutional rights the accused need not take the witness stand and testify.

"Possession may be satisfactorily explained through other circumstances, other evidence, independent of any testimony of the accused."

standards in light of present-day experience. In the present case the challenged instruction only permitted the inference of guilt from *unexplained* possession of recently stolen property.[2] The evidence established that petitioner possessed recently stolen Treasury checks payable to persons he did not know, and it provided no plausible explanation for such possession consistent with innocence. On the basis of this evidence alone common sense and experience tell us that petitioner must have known or been aware of the high probability that the checks were stolen. Such evidence was clearly sufficient to enable the jury to find beyond a reasonable doubt that petitioner knew the checks were stolen. Since the inference thus satisfies the reasonable doubt standard, the most stringent standard the Court has applied in judging permissive criminal law inferences, we conclude that it satisfies the requirements of due process.[3]

Petitioner also argues that the permissive inference in question infringes his privilege against self-incrimination. The Court has twice rejected this argument,[4] Turner v. United States, Yee Hem v. United States, 268 U.S. 178, 185, 45 S.Ct. 470, 472 (1925), and we find no reason to re-examine the issue at length. The trial court specifically instructed the jury that petitioner had a constitutional right not to take the witness stand and that possession could be satisfactorily explained by evidence independent of petitioner's testimony. Introduction of any evidence, direct or circumstantial, tending to implicate the defendant in the alleged crime increases the pressure on him to testify. The mere massing of evidence against a defendant cannot be regarded as a violation of his privilege against self-incrimination.

2. Of course, the mere fact that there is some evidence tending to explain a defendant's possession consistent with innocence does not bar instructing the jury on the inference. The jury must weigh the explanation to determine whether it is "satisfactory." The jury is not bound to accept or believe any particular explanation any more than it is bound to accept the correctness of the inference. But the burden of proving beyond a reasonable doubt that the defendant did have knowledge that the property was stolen, an essential element of the crime, remains on the Government.

3. It is true that the practical effect of instructing the jury on the inference arising from unexplained possession of recently stolen property is to shift the burden of going forward with evidence to the defendant. If the Government proves possession and nothing more, this evidence remains unexplained unless the defendant introduces evidence since ordinarily the Government's evidence will not provide an explanation of his possession consistent with innocence. In Tot v. United States, the Court stated that the burden of going forward may not be freely shifted to the defendant. See also Leary v. United States. *Tot* held, however, that where there is a "rational connection" between the facts proved and the fact presumed or inferred, it is permissible to shift the burden of going forward to the defendant. Where an inference satisfies the reasonable doubt standard, as in the present case, there will certainly be a rational connection between the fact presumed or inferred (in this case, knowledge) and the facts the Government must prove in order to shift the burden of going forward (possession of recently stolen property).

We do not decide today whether a judge-formulated inference of lesser age or less widely accepted may properly be emphasized by means of a jury instruction.

4. Nor can the instruction "be fairly understood as a comment on the petitioner's failure to testify." . . .

Petitioner further challenges his conviction on the ground that there was insufficient evidence that he knew the checks were stolen *from the mails.* He contends that 18 U.S.C. § 1708 requires knowledge not only that the checks were stolen, but specifically that they were stolen from the mails. The legislative history of the statute conclusively refutes this argument and the courts of appeals that have addressed the issue have uniformly interpreted the statute to require only knowledge that the property was stolen.

Since we find that the statute was correctly interpreted and that the trial court's instructions on the inference to be drawn from unexplained possession of stolen property were fully consistent with petitioner's constitutional rights, it is unnecessary to consider petitioner's challenges to his conviction on the forging and uttering counts.

[*Affirmed.*]

[JUSTICE DOUGLAS' dissenting opinion is omitted.]

MR. JUSTICE BRENNAN, with whom MR. JUSTICE MARSHALL joins, dissenting.

Petitioner was charged in two counts of a six-count indictment with possession of United States Treasury checks stolen from the mails, knowing them to be stolen. The essential elements of such an offense are (1) that the defendant was in possession of the checks, (2) that the checks were stolen from the mails, and (3) that the defendant knew that the checks were stolen. The Government proved that petitioner had been in possession of the checks and that the checks had been stolen from the mails; and, in addition, the Government introduced some evidence intended to show that petitioner knew or should have known that the checks were stolen. But rather than leaving the jury to determine the element of "knowledge" on the basis of that evidence, the trial court instructed them that they were free to infer the essential element of "knowledge" from petitioner's unexplained possession of the checks. In my view, that instruction violated the Due Process Clause of the Fifth Amendment because it permitted the jury to convict even though the actual evidence bearing on "knowledge" may have been insufficient to establish guilt beyond a reasonable doubt. I therefore dissent.

We held in In re Winship, 397 U.S. 358, 364 (1970), that the Due Process Clause requires "proof beyond a reasonable doubt of every fact necessary to constitute the crime. . . ." Thus, in Turner v. United States we approved the inference of "knowledge" from the fact of possessing smuggled heroin because " '[c]ommon sense' . . . tells us that those who traffic in heroin will *inevitably* become aware that the product they deal in is smuggled. . . ." (Emphasis added.) The basis of that "common sense" judgment was, of course, the indisputable fact that all or virtually all heroin in this country is necessarily smuggled. Here, however, it cannot be said that all or virtually all endorsed United States Treasury checks have been stolen. Indeed, it is neither unlawful nor unusual for people to use such checks as direct payment for goods and services.

Thus, unlike *Turner,* "common sense" simply will not permit the inference that the possessor of stolen Treasury checks *"inevitably"* knew that the checks were stolen.

In short, the practical effect of the challenged instruction was to permit the jury to convict petitioner even if they found insufficient or disbelieved all of the Government's evidence bearing directly on the issue of "knowledge." By authorizing the jury to rely exclusively on the inference in determining the element of "knowledge," the instruction relieved the Government of the burden of proving that element beyond a reasonable doubt. The instruction thereby violated the principle of *Winship* that every essential element of the crime must be proved beyond a reasonable doubt.

3. ILLEGAL POSSESSION OF WEAPONS

COUNTY COURT OF ULSTER COUNTY v. ALLEN

Supreme Court of the United States, 1979.
442 U.S. 142, 99 S.Ct. 2213.

MR. JUSTICE STEVENS delivered the opinion of the Court.

A New York statute provides that, with certain exceptions, the presence of a firearm in an automobile is presumptive evidence of its illegal possession by all persons then occupying the vehicle. The United States Court of Appeals for the Second Circuit held . . . that the statute is "unconstitutional on its face." . . .

Four persons, three adult males (respondents) and a 16-year-old girl (Jane Doe, who is not a respondent here), were jointly tried on charges that they possessed two loaded handguns, a loaded machinegun, and over a pound of heroin found in a Chevrolet in which they were riding when it was stopped for speeding on the New York Thruway shortly after noon on March 28, 1973. The two large-caliber handguns, which together with their ammunition weighed approximately six pounds, were seen through the window of the car by the investigating police officer. They were positioned crosswise in an open handbag on either the front floor or the front seat of the car on the passenger side where Jane Doe was sitting. Jane Doe admitted that the handbag was hers. The machinegun and the heroin were discovered in the trunk after the police pried it open. The car had been borrowed from the driver's brother earlier that day; the key to the trunk could not be found in the car or on the person of any of its occupants, although there was testimony that two of the occupants had placed something in the trunk before embarking in the borrowed car. The jury convicted all four of possession of the handguns and acquitted them of possession of the contents of the trunk.

Counsel for all four defendants objected to the introduction into evidence of the two handguns, the machinegun, and the drugs, arguing that the State had not adequately demonstrated a connection between their clients and the contraband. The trial court overruled the objection, relying on the presumption of possession created by the New York statute. Because that presumption does not apply if a weapon is found "upon the person" of one of the occupants of the car, the three male defendants also moved to dismiss the charges relating to the handguns on the ground that the guns were found on the person of Jane Doe. Respondents made this motion both at the close of the prosecution's case and at the close of all evidence. The trial judge twice denied it, concluding that the applicability of the "on the person" exception was a question of fact for the jury.

At the close of the trial, the judge instructed the jurors that they were entitled to infer possession from the defendants' presence in the car. He did not make any reference to the "upon the person" exception in his explanation of the statutory presumption, nor did any of the defendants object to this omission or request alternative or additional instructions on the subject.

As applied to the facts of this case, the presumption of possession is entirely rational. . . . The argument against possession by any of the respondents was predicated solely on the fact that the guns were in Jane Doe's pocketbook. But several circumstances . . . made it highly improbable that she was the sole custodian of those weapons.

Even if it was reasonable to conclude that she had placed the guns in her purse before the car was stopped by police, the facts strongly suggest that Jane Doe was not the only person able to exercise dominion over them. The two guns were too large to be concealed in her handbag. The bag was consequently open, and part of one of the guns was in plain view, within easy access of the driver of the car and even, perhaps, of the other two respondents who were riding in the rear seat.

Moreover, it is highly improbable that the loaded guns belonged to Jane Doe or that she was solely responsible for their being in her purse. As a 16-year-old girl in the company of three adult men she was the least likely of the four to be carrying one, let alone two, heavy handguns. It is far more probable that she relied on the pocket knife found in her brassiere for any necessary self-protection. Under these circumstances, it was not unreasonable for her counsel to argue and for the jury to infer that when the car was halted for speeding, the other passengers in the car anticipated the risk of a search and attempted to conceal their weapons in a pocketbook in the front seat. The inference is surely more likely than the notion that these weapons were the sole property of the 16-year-old girl.

Under these circumstances, the jury would have been entirely reasonable in rejecting the suggestion—which, incidentally, defense counsel did not even advance in their closing arguments to the jury —that the handguns were in the sole possession of Jane Doe. Assuming that the jury did reject it, the case is tantamount to one in which the guns were lying on the floor or the seat of the car in the plain view of the three other occupants of the automobile. In such a case it is surely rational to infer that each of the respondents was fully aware of the presence of the guns and had both the ability and the intent to exercise dominion and control over the weapons. The application of the statutory presumption in this case therefore comports with the standard [as laid down in *Tot* and *Leary*]. For there is a "rational connection" between the basic facts that the prosecution proved and the ultimate fact presumed, and the latter is "more likely than not to flow from" the former.

Respondents argue, however, that the validity of the New York presumption must be judged by a "reasonable doubt" test rather than the "more likely than not" standard employed in *Leary*. Under the more stringent test, it is argued that a statutory presumption must be rejected unless the evidence necessary to invoke the inference is sufficient for a rational jury to find the inferred fact beyond a reasonable doubt. Respondents' argument again overlooks the distinction between a permissive presumption on which the prosecution is entitled to rely as one not-necessarily-sufficient part of its proof and a mandatory presumption which the jury must accept even if it is the sole evidence of an element of the offense.

In the latter situation, since the prosecution bears the burden of establishing guilt, it may not rest its case entirely on a presumption unless the fact proved is sufficient to support the inference of guilt beyond a reasonable doubt. But in the former situation, the prosecution may rely on all of the evidence in the record to meet the reasonable doubt standard. There is no more reason to require a permissive statutory presumption to meet a reasonable doubt standard before it may be permitted to play any part in a trial than there is to require that degree of probative force for other relevant evidence before it may be admitted. As long as it is clear that the presumption is not the sole and sufficient basis for a finding of guilt, it need only satisfy the test described in *Leary*.

The permissive presumption, as used in this case, satisfied the *Leary* test.   .   .   .

The judgment is reversed.

E.   DELIBERATIONS AND VERDICT OF THE JURY

1.   COMMUNICATIONS WITH DELIBERATING JURY

UNITED STATES v. GLICK

United States Court of Appeals, Second Circuit, 1970.
463 F.2d 491.

IRVING R. KAUFMAN, CIRCUIT JUDGE.

We are asked to reverse a conviction because the trial judge not once, but twice communicated with the jury out of the presence of the defendant (appearing *pro se*) during the course of the jury's deliberations.

John Theodore Glick, the appellant here, and seven other defendants were tried before Judge Burke and a jury on six counts relating to the ransacking of offices in the Federal Building in Rochester, New York. Only defendant Gilchrist was represented by counsel.

The jury retired to commence its deliberations at 12:25 P.M. on Tuesday, December 1, 1970. After their evening meal, the jurors delivered a note to a Deputy Marshal, who in turn handed it to the Deputy Clerk. Because Judge Burke was at home, the Deputy Clerk telephoned the judge and read the jury's question to him: "Must the prosecutor prove in each count that at least one defendant was in a particular office?" Instead of returning to the courthouse to answer the question in open court in the presence of the defendants as required by Rule 43 of the Federal Rules of Criminal Procedure, Judge Burke over the telephone directed the Deputy Clerk to transmit the answer "Yes, except Count 6," to the jury through the Deputy Marshal.

The district judge thereafter returned to his chambers in the courthouse, where he soon received a second note. To the best of Judge Burke's recollection, this note asked: "Can the jury in its verdict recommend leniency?" The judge wrote his one-word answer on the back of the note: "Yes," and returned the note to the jury. None of the defendants nor Gilchrist's counsel was informed of either the first or second series of communications.

At 8:50 P.M. the jury returned its verdict. All eight defendants were found guilty on the six counts, but a recommendation of leniency was included in each of the forty-eight findings. Although we cannot fix the precise time of the questioned communications, it appears that the verdict followed hard on the heels of Judge Burke's instruction that the jury could recommend leniency.

.　.　.　On the morning of the sentencing, the judge was presented with an article which appeared in the Rochester Democrat and Chronicle headlined "One Simple 'Yes' Unlocks a Hung Jury." Written by a reporter named Mark Starr and based upon interviews with jurors, the article revealed that three jurors had changed their votes of "not guilty" to "guilty" after they had been informed by the judge that the jury could recommend leniency. This article disclosed to the defendants and counsel for the first time that the judge and jury had communicated with each other after deliberations had commenced. It was not surprising, therefore, that when court convened that morning, counsel for Gilchrist asked the judge to place all of the communications on the record and at the same time to grant a new trial. Judge Burke denied both motions and proceeded to sentence all the defendants.

A notice of appeal was filed on behalf of Glick, who eventually retained counsel. Thereafter, upon motion of Glick's counsel, this Court remanded the case to Judge Burke with instructions to place the communications on the record to consider a motion for a new trial, and to issue findings of fact and conclusions of law. After recording his recollections, which the parties stipulated were correct,

Judge Burke filed a terse memorandum and order denying a new trial.

* * *

I.

It is clear to us at the outset that the private communications between the judge and jury violated the unequivocal mandate of Rule 43, which requires the defendant to be present "at every stage of the trial."

* * *

Although we recognize that in appropriate circumstances application of the harmless error rule may not require reversal, we are convinced that the judge's bare assertion that the jury could recommend leniency, omitting any limiting or restricting admonitions and given in Glick's absence, was highly prejudicial.

We emphasize at this point, however, that we are not concerned merely with instructions delivered out of the presence of the defendant. The prejudice was compounded here because the volatile instructions on leniency were erroneous. In United States v. Louie Gim Hall, 245 F.2d 338 (2d Cir. 1957), we reversed a conviction where the trial judge, after an inquiry by the jury whether it had the right to recommend leniency, instructed the deadlocked jury that he would be "glad to have that recommendation and you may be sure that it will be acted upon accordingly." Our holding was no more than an application of the familiar rule that a verdict of guilty cannot stand if it has been induced by any intimation from the trial judge that a light sentence might be imposed, thus encouraging a juror to abandon his vote of not guilty. See, e. g., Demetree v. United States, 207 F.2d 892 (5th Cir. 1953) (jury told that the maximum sentence would not be imposed); Lovely v. United States, 169 F.2d 386 (4th Cir. 1948) (jury told that defendant would be eligible for parole after a specified period). In dictum, however, we noted that it would not have been error if the judge merely had instructed the jury that it could recommend leniency and had added that the function of sentencing belonged solely to the judge, that the judge would not be bound by any recommendation from the jury, and that the jury should not concern itself with the question of punishment in arriving at a verdict.

But Judge Burke's over-simplistic "yes" response to the jury's inherently dangerous inquiry opened the way to "unlock" the jury. The response ignored all of the admonitions we considered appropriate in *Louie Gim Hall.* In short, there was a total failure to make clear to the jury that its function was to decide guilt or innocence and that sentencing was the judge's province and his alone. Accordingly, under the circumstances present here, the likelihood existed that "one or more jurors entertaining doubts as to appellants' guilt agreed to vote for conviction because [they believed] they had it in their power to soothe their consciences by causing little or no punishment to be imposed."

II.

Nor can we say that Judge Burke's instructions "did not affect the verdict." Wholly apart from the truthfulness of the newspaper report, we are convinced that the verdict was induced at least in part by Judge Burke's answer. The jury, which had deliberated for approximately eight hours without reaching a verdict, was able to return a verdict soon after being told unconditionally and unequivocally that it could recommend leniency. Moreover, we have a clear indication that the judge's single-word response made an impact on the jury, for its verdict in fact included the recommendation of leniency on each of the forty-eight findings of guilt. This is not a case, therefore, where supplemental instructions on an issue of law delivered out of the presence of the defendant could be considered harmless because they merely repeated instructions previously given in his presence. United States v. Arriagada, 451 F.2d 487 (4th Cir. 1971), or because the jury had reached a verdict on one count before supplemental instructions were requested and delivered on subsequent counts and the defendant was given concurrent sentences on all counts. United States v. Howard, 433 F.2d 1 (5th Cir. 1970), cert. denied 401 U.S. 918, 91 S.Ct. 900 (1971).

Accordingly, the judgment of conviction is reversed.

PARKER v. GLADDEN

United States Supreme Court, 1966.
385 U.S. 363, 87 S.Ct. 468.

PER CURIAM.

Petitioner, after his conviction for second degree murder, filed a petition for post-conviction relief. At a hearing on the petition the trial court found that a court bailiff assigned to shepherd the sequestered jury, which sat for eight days, stated to one of the jurors in the presence of others while the jury was out walking on a public sidewalk: "Oh that wicked fellow [petitioner], he is guilty"; and on another occasion said to another juror under similar circumstances, "If there is anything wrong [in finding petitioner guilty] the Supreme Court will correct it." Both statements were overheard by at least one regular juror or an alternate. The trial court found "that the unauthorized communication was prejudicial and that such conduct materially affected the rights of the [petitioner]." The Supreme Court of Oregon reversed, finding that "the bailiff's misconduct did not deprive [petitioner] of a constitutionally correct trial."

*   *   *

We believe that the statements of the bailiff to the jurors are controlled by the command of the Sixth Amendment, made applicable to the States through the Due Process Clause of the Fourteenth Amendment. It guarantees that "the accused shall enjoy the right to a . . . trial, by an impartial jury . . . [and] be confronted with the witnesses against him   .   .   .." As we said in Turner v. Louisiana, 379 U.S. 466, 472–473, 85 S.Ct. 546, 550 (1965), "the 'evidence developed' against a defendant shall come from the witness stand in a public courtroom where there is full judicial protection of the defendant's right of confrontation, of cross-examination, and of counsel." Here there is dispute neither as to what the bailiff, an officer of the State, said nor that when he said it he was not subjected to confrontation, cross-examination or other safeguards guaranteed to the petitioner. Rather, his expressions were "private talk," tending to reach the jury by "outside influence." Patterson v. People of State of Colorado, 205 U.S. 454, 462, 27 S.Ct. 556, 558, 51 L.Ed. 879 (1907). We have followed the "undeviating rule," that the rights of confrontation and cross-examination are among the fundamental requirements of a constitutionally fair trial.

* * *

The State suggests that no prejudice was shown and that no harm could have resulted because 10 members of the jury testified that they had not heard the bailiff's statements and that Oregon law permits a verdict of guilty by 10 affirmative votes. This overlooks the fact that the official character of the bailiff—as an officer of the court as well as the State—beyond question carries great weight with a jury which he had been shepherding for eight days and nights. Moreover, the jurors deliberated for 26 hours, indicating a difference among them as to the guilt of petitioner. Finally, one of the jurors testified that she *was* prejudiced by the statements, which supports the trial court's finding "that the unauthorized communication was prejudicial and that such conduct materially affected the rights of the defendant." This finding was not upset by Oregon's highest court. Aside from this, we believe that the unauthorized conduct of the bailiff "involves such a probability that prejudice will result that it is deemed inherently lacking in due process," Estes v. State of Texas, 381 U.S. 532, 542–543, 85 S.Ct. 1628, 1633 (1965). As we said in Turner "it would be blinking reality not to recognize the extreme prejudice inherent" in such statements that reached at least three members of the jury and one alternate member. 379 U.S., at 473, 85 S.Ct., at 550. The State says that 10 of the jurors testified that they had not heard the statements of the bailiff.

* * *

In any event, petitioner was entitled to be tried by 12, not 9 or even 10, impartial and unprejudiced jurors. See State v. Murray, 164 La. 883, 888, 114 So. 721, 723.

Reversed.

MR. JUSTICE HARLAN, dissenting.

By not setting forth the background of this proceeding the Court has put seriously out of focus the constitutional issue involved in this case.

Parker was convicted of second degree murder on May 19, 1961, and sentenced to life imprisonment. On September 7, 1961, he addressed a letter to several jurors protesting his innocence, condemning his attorneys for incompetence, intimating that witnesses were coerced into lying, and chiding the jurors for being duped into finding him guilty. After affirmance of his conviction by the Supreme Court of Oregon on September 15, 1963—some two years after the jury verdict—Parker again set out to take his case to the jury. He furnished his wife with a tape recording in which he propounded a series of questions designed to uncover possible improprieties in the jury's deliberations. The jury had deliberated a long time and Parker had been told that their discussion was heated. Although unaware of any irregularities he commenced "shooting in the dark." Mrs. Parker then acquired a jury list and discovered those jurors who had been most sympathetic to her husband. She invited two regular jurors and an alternate to her home to listen to the recording and discuss the case. An attorney was then retained to prepare affidavits detailing the allegations before us and to institute this post-conviction proceeding. The statements before this Court were found to have been made by this apparently Elizabethan-tongued bailiff, but, contrary to this Court's assertion, the trial court found that these statements were only prejudicial in nature and not that they had a prejudicial effect. The Oregon Supreme Court did not find the trial proceedings fundamentally unfair.

This Court finds the bailiff's remarks to be in violation of the Sixth Amendment's confrontation requirement. . . .

As to the confrontation problem here asserted, I know of no case in which this Court has held that jurors must have been absolutely insulated from all expressions of opinion on the merits of the case or the judicial process at the risk of declaration of a new trial. Even where this Court has acted in its supervisory capacity it has refused to hold that jury contact with outside information is always a cause for overthrowing a verdict, wisely preferring to allow "each case [to] turn on its special facts." The Court notes that these remarks were made by a state officer, but does not explain why the bailiff's official capacity would in this instance make him any more a "witness" than any other person able to communicate with the jury. Thus, though I believe unintentionally, the Court's opinion leaves open the possibility of automatically requiring a mistrial on constitutional grounds whenever any juror is exposed to any potentially prejudicial expression of opinion.

* * *

The occurrences before us seem inconsequential to me in light of the eight-day trial and twenty-six-hour jury deliberation. And my feeling is confirmed by the extremely trivial evidence of prejudice amounting to no more than an assertion by one obviously highly emotional and "guilt-ridden" juror that she might have been influenced without realizing it. "[I]t is an impossible standard to require that tribunal [the jury] to be a laboratory, completely sterilized and freed from any external factors." Rideau v. Louisiana, 373 U.S. 723, 733, 83 S.Ct. 1417, 1423, (Clark, J., dissenting).

The potentialities of today's decision may go far beyond what, I am sure, the Court intends. Certainly the Court does not wish to encourage convicted felons to "intimidate, beset and harass," a discharged jury in an effort to establish possible grounds for a new trial. Our courts have always been alert to protect the sanctity of the jury process. But in allowing Parker to overturn his conviction on the basis of what are no more than inconsequential incidents in an otherwise constitutionally flawless proceeding, the Court encourages others to follow his example in pursuing the jury and may be thought by some to commit federal courts in habeas corpus proceedings to interrogate the jury upon the mere allegation that a prejudicial remark has reached the ears of one of its members. To any such result I cannot subscribe.

NOTES

1. A judge's response to a jury's inquiry without the knowledge of counsel is not reversible error per se if the substance of the communication is not prejudicial and the prolongation of the deliberations not an abuse of discretion. See United States v. Di Pietto, 396 F.2d 283, 287 (7th Cir. 1968), vacated on other grounds, 394 U.S. 310, 89 S.Ct. 1163 (1969); United States v. Compagna, 146 F.2d 524, 528 (2d Cir. 1944): ". . . Like other rules for the conduct of trials, [the prevention of improper communications] is not an end in itself; and while lapses should be closely scrutinized, when it appears with certainty that no harm was done, it would be merest pedantry to insist upon procedural regularity."

2. In cases of unauthorized communications to a jury, a presumption of prejudice inures to the benefit of the convicted defendant. Remmer v. United States, 347 U.S. 227, 229, 74 S.Ct. 450, 451 (1956). However, the presumption is rebuttable; and factors which have been held to rebut the presumption of prejudice are numerous. In United States v. Brown, 99 F. Supp. 527 (D.Alas.1951), aff'd 201 F.2d 767 (9th Cir.), a juror asked the bailiff to inform the judge that the jury was unable to reach a verdict. Without authority to do so, the bailiff returned and told the jury that they would not only have to continue their deliberations, but that they would have to reach a verdict. The court held that because it is common knowledge that the members of hung juries are discharged after a reasonable time, it was inconceivable that the jury believed the communication. Was the court's assumption questionable? Would it have been proper for the court to have asked each juror if he believed the communication? On the other hand, in United States ex rel. Tobe v. Bensinger, 492 F.2d 232 (7th Cir. 1974), a bailiff responded to jurors' inquiries, without passing on the questions to the trial judge. The bailiff instructed the jurors that they were required to reach a verdict. Rejecting the state court finding that no such inquiries or instructions took place, in light of the affidavits of seven jurors asserting that they did, the federal court granted habeas corpus relief.

3. Where the judge gives additional substantive instructions to the jury without notice to counsel, reversal is generally mandated. United States v. Schor, 418 F.2d 26 (2d Cir. 1969); Jones v. United States, 113 U. S.App.D.C. 352, 308 F.2d 307 (1962). Compare McClain v. Swenson, 435 F.2d 327 (8th Cir. 1970). Messages to continue deliberations, conveyed through a marshal or bailiff, are generally regarded as harmless absent a strong showing of prejudice. Walsh v. United States, 371 F.2d 135 (9th

Cir. 1967) ; United States v. Grosso, 358 F.2d 154 (3d Cir. 1969). Similarly, innocuous communications with regard to documentary information have been held inconsequential. United States v. Arriagada, 451 F.2d 487 (4th Cir. 1971) (grant of request to rehear testimony). Ferrari v. United States, 244 F.2d 132 (9th Cir. 1957) (denial of request to hear recording).

In United States v. United States Gypsum Co., 438 U.S. 422, 98 S.Ct. 2864 (1978), the jury foreman, after seven days of deliberations, informed the judge that he wanted to discuss the health condition of some jurors. The judge's ex parte meeting with the foreman was held with the parties' consent; but the foreman came away with the impression that the judge wanted a verdict one way or the other. A guilty verdict was returned the following morning. Upholding the reversal of the conviction, the Court said:

> "[I]t is not simply the action of the judge in having the private meeting with the jury foreman, standing alone,—undesirable as that procedure is—which constitutes the error; rather, it is the fact that the *ex parte* discussion was inadvertently allowed to drift into what amounted to a supplemental instruction to the foreman relating to the jury's obligation to return a verdict, coupled with the fact that counsel were denied any chance to correct whatever mistaken impression the foreman might have taken from this conversation, that we find most troubling."

4. However, where contact with the deliberating jury is made by someone other than the trial judge, the courts have been more sensitive to claims of prejudicial error. See Turner v. Louisiana, 379 U.S. 46, 85 S.Ct. 546 (1965) (deliberating jury in custody of sheriffs who had served as key prosecution witnesses) ; United States v. Dellinger, 472 F.2d 340 (7th Cir. 1972) (authorized communication by marshal) ; United States v. Pittman, 449 F.2d 1284 (6th Cir. 1971) (government agent in jury room during deliberations). The question, in each instance, is whether the contact was so inherently prejudicial as to transgress due process rights; and the correlative issue is the extent of the showing that must be made by a defendant before a court must adjudicate the larger question. See Parker v. Gladden, 385 U.S. 363, 87 S.Ct. 468 (1966).

5. Where it is determined that "foreign" objects were present in the jury room during deliberations, the courts assess prejudice by measuring the nature of the object and its likely effect on the jury's deliberations. See United States v. Schaefer, 455 F.2d 1167 (5th Cir. 1972) (documents not admitted into evidence requires reversal) ; United States v. Siragusa, 450 F.2d 592 (2d Cir. 1971) (affirmance despite presence of I.R.S. tax booklet) ; United States v. Boatwright, 446 F.2d 913 (5th Cir. 1971) (affirmance despite presence of two law books).

2. "DEADLOCKED" ("HUNG") JURIES

STATE v. MARSH

Supreme Court of Oregon, 1971.
490 P.2d 491, cert denied 406 U.S. 974, 92 S.Ct. 2420.

TONGUE, JUSTICE.

This is an appeal from a conviction for rape in the front seat of a "Mustang" automobile.

* * *

[Defendant contends] that the trial court erred in giving a so-called "Allen" or "dynamite" instruction to "blast" loose the dead-locked jury.[1] In considering this contention it is necessary to understand not only the terms of the particular instruction as given in this case, but also the circumstances under which it was given, including the failure of defendant's attorney to make any proper exceptions to the instruction at that time.

INSTRUCTION GIVEN AND CIRCUMSTANCES UNDER WHICH GIVEN

At about 4:20 p. m. the trial judge completed his original instructions to the jury and it then retired for deliberation. At 8:45 p. m. (after the jury had been sent out for dinner) the jury sent the following note to the court: "Our discussion is six guilty, six not guilty."

The trial judge then informed counsel that he "propose(d) to call the jury in and instruct them," after which "each side may be permitted to take whatever exception it feels it should." Neither attorney objected to such a procedure. The trial judge then instructed the jury as follows:

"Members of the jury, it is now not quite 9:00 o'clock. You have been at work since about 4:30 this afternoon, omitting the dinner hour. The note you have sent in a moment ago indicates that your number stands six for one side and six for the other.

"It is my duty to urge you to reach a decision on this case. This case has to be tried either now or later. It is unlikely that this case will ever be tried by any jury more competent and more representative of the community than yourselves. It is unlikely that the evidence would be any different before any later trial than it was before this one and so it is important that the matter be resolved. Those of you who stand on one side of the question should give re-

---

1. The name "Allen" charge is taken from the name of the case in which such a charge was approved in Allen   v. United States, 164 U.S. 492, 17 S. Ct. 154 (1896).

spectful attention and consideration to the views of those opposed. And vice-versa.

"None of this, however, should be construed by you as suggesting that I believe that you should not vote any other way than your own conscience based upon the evidence and the instructions in this case. None of us expect you to do anything other than that. But I am sure that you realize along with me that this case should be decided. It ought not to be decided unless it is decided by the appropriate number ten to two and it ought not to be decided unless those ten of you who concur, if you do, each reach your decision honestly base [sic] upon the evidence and the law and your own view of the matter; so nothing I say should be taken as meaning that I want any of you to vote other than what your own good judgment dictates. But for the reasons I have mentioned I urge you to go back and to deliberate further and see if you can reach a verdict. You may now be excused to the jury room."

[The jury then retired again; but two hours later sent the court a note seeking an answer to a legal question. Shortly after midnight, the court reinstructed on the legal point involved and concluded with the following.]

* * *

"Further, I will repeat to you what I told you earlier this evening at about 9:00 o'clock. What we ask of you is the honest, conscientious individual vote of each one of you for any given verdict. We ask each of you on one side to carefully consider the discussions, points of view of those on the other side. And we point out to you that this case ought to be decided. If it is tried again in all likelihood the jury will be no better equipped than yourself, the jury will be similarly selected as you were in all likelihood, the evidence will be the same. And therefore, it is incumbent upon you to reach a verdict. Bearing in mind, however, that we do not expect any of you to vote one way or the other except according to your own conscience based upon the evidence and upon these instructions. I will now ask you to retire to deliberate further."

At 12:28 a. m. the jury . . . returned a verdict of guilty by a vote of ten to two and was then excused.

ORIGIN AND HISTORY OF "ALLEN" CHARGE —RECENT CRITICISM

The "Allen charge," often called the "dynamite charge" is a supplemental instruction given to encourage deadlocked juries to reach agreement. The first reported case of such an instruction was in an

1851 Massachusetts case.[2] In 1896, an almost identical charge was approved by the Supreme Court of the United States in Allen v. United States.

The central idea of the instruction is that although no juror is expected to yield a conscientiously held opinion, the jury has a duty to decide the case if it can conscientiously do so and that if a majority of the jury is for either conviction or acquittal, the minority ought to consider whether a contrary view may be reasonable and correct.

In recent years the "Allen charge" has been the subject of considerable discussion, including increasing criticism upon the ground that it is improperly coercive.

In order to evaluate the use of the "Allen charge," or of any supplemental instructions to deadlocked juries, it is necessary to bear in mind the many variations of the "Allen charge," as well as the fact that the extent to which such an instruction may be coercive depends largely upon the factual context or setting in which the charge is given in a particular case.

VARIATIONS IN TERMS OF "ALLEN" OR "DYNAMITE" INSTRUCTIONS

As might be expected, over the years the various courts have developed many different variations and modifications of the original "Allen charge." These "progeny" have been described as "endless permutations" of the original instruction as approved in *Allen*. They include, however, at least the following variations.

1. The Original "Allen Charge"

The original "Allen charge," as previously described, has been approved in numerous decisions, including subsequent decisions by the Supreme Court of the United States.[3]

In more recent decisions, however, some other courts have been critical of the terms of the original "Allen charge" for its emphasis upon persuading the members of the minority of a jury to reconsider their views and for its potential coercive effect upon such a minority. The original "Allen charge" has also been described as the "limit" beyond which a trial judge cannot go.

2. "Modified" and "Balanced" Allen Charges

As the result of such criticism, some courts have modified the terms of the original "Allen" charge so as to direct its emphasis not only at members of the minority of the jury, but also at members of the majority, or so as to urge all members of the jury, without reference to whether they are members of the minority or majority. On

---

2. Commonwealth v. Tuey, 62 Mass. (8 Cush.) 1, 3 (1851).

3. See cases cited in dissenting opinion by Robb, J., in United States v. Thomas, 449 F.2d 1177, 1188 (D.C. Cir. 1971), including Kawakita v. United States, 343 U.S. 717, 72 S.Ct. 950 (1952).

the contrary, such an attempt has also been described by one court as "an invitation to a frolic with Alice in Wonderland."

Other courts have modified the original "Allen" charge so as to make it a more "balanced" charge by greater emphasis upon the fact that no juror is expected to abandon conscientiously held opinions and that the verdict must represent the verdict of all members of the jury.

3. Reference to Necessity or Expense of Retrial

Some courts have added to the original "Allen charge" a further instruction to the effect that if the jury does not reach a verdict, the case will have to be retired. Some of these instructions also emphasize the backlog of cases to be tried and the cost of retrial to the taxpayers and the parties.

Some also emphasize that on retrial the case will have to be submitted to another jury which will hear the same evidence and be no better qualified to decide the case than this jury. Such additional instructions have also been the subject of further criticism.

4. Instruction That Must Deliberate Until Reach Verdict

Perhaps the most extreme variations or extensions of the original "Allen charge" are those in which the trial judge, by supplemental instructions to a deadlocked jury, informs it that it must continue deliberations until it reaches a verdict or that the trial judge will not declare a mistrial as the result of a deadlocked jury. Such additional instructions have met almost universal condemnation by the appellate courts in recent years.

VARIATIONS IN "FACTUAL SETTING" OF "ALLEN CHARGE"

Almost as important as the terms of the "Allen charge," or its variations, is the factual "setting" or context in which such supplemental instructions are given to deadlocked juries. These variations include the following.

1. Relative Weight of the Evidence

In considering on review whether or not it was error for the trial judge to give an "Allen charge," or variation, to the jury, some appellate courts appear to consider the relative weight of the evidence; i. e., to be less inclined to reverse when such an instruction has been given if the evidence of guilt is overwhelming than if the evidence is otherwise.

According to other authorities, however, the comparative weight of the evidence is not relevant in considering whether it was error to give such an instruction.

2. Knowledge of Trial Judge How Jury Stood

Some authorities also consider the giving of an "Allen charge," or variation, more apt to be improper when the trial judge has either first inquired or has been informed of the numerical split of the deadlocked jury. The rationale of this position is that the giving of such a charge is more clearly coercive in its effect upon the minority of the jury.

It appears, however, that there is a distinct split of authority on this question and that there is good reason to support the contrary contention that the knowledge by the trial judge of such facts is irrelevant in considering the possible coercive effect of such a supplemental instruction upon the minority of the jury.

3. Time Jury Deadlocked Before and After "Allen Charge"

Although it is ordinarily within the discretion of the trial court to determine how long the jury should be allowed to deliberate before giving it supplemental instructions to assist it in breaking the deadlock, that time interval may be so short as to raise the question whether the trial judge abused his discretion in failing to wait for a longer period to elapse before doing so.

Similarly, the time interval in reaching a verdict after the giving of an "Allen charge" may be so short as to raise the question whether the jury was improperly coerced by the charge into returning a verdict without proper and further deliberations.

VARIATIONS IN GROUNDS FOR DECISIONS AND IN RESULTS REACHED

1. Grounds for Decisions Approving "Allen Charge" or Variations

Most decisions approving the giving of an "Allen charge," or variation, to a deadlocked jury do so upon the ground that the terms of the particular charge were not improper or coercive, at least in the factual setting or context in which such a supplemental instruction was given in a particular case.

It has also been held that the giving of a charge that might otherwise be held improper will be affirmed because of failure to make a proper and timely exception.

2. Grounds for Decisions Disapproving "Allen Charge" or Variations

(a) *Constitutionality*

Prior to 1969 no court had held that it was error to give the basic "Allen charge" upon the ground that to do so would violate the constitutional rights of a criminal defendant, although the charge had been criticized as coercive. More recently, however, in Fields v. State, 487 P.2d 831 (Alaska 1971), the Supreme Court of Alaska held that the "dynamite" charge as given in that case violated defendant's constitutional right to a fair trial and to due process. In that case, however, the trial judge directed the jury to "continue your deliberations until you arrive at a unanimous verdict" and this was emphasized as the basis for the decision in that case.

Nevertheless, it has been strongly contended that the basic "Allen charge," with its emphasis directed toward the members of the minority of a jury, not only violates the right of a criminal defendant to conviction by an unanimous jury, but is also contrary to the concepts of reasonable doubt and presumption of innocence.

(b) *Supervisory Power*

Most appellate courts which have disapproved all use of the "Allen charge," or variations, have done so under their supervisory power of control over the trial courts within their respective jurisdictions. This is particularly true of the federal courts.

(c) *Error in Particular Case*

Elsewhere, the usual approach has been to review the cases individually, taking into account both the language of the particular instruction and the factual setting or context in which it was given in each particular case.

3.   Results in Decisions Disapproving "Allen Charge"

Among recent cases there has also been considerable variation in the disposition of cases in which the courts have disapproved the giving of "Allen charge" or variations.

Where a finding of error has been based upon the conclusion that such an instruction was "coercive," after considering the particular terms of the supplemental instruction given to a deadlocked jury or upon the circumstances under which it was given, the usual result has been simply to remand the case for a new trial. Where such a decision has been based upon the supervisory power of the appellate court, some courts have expressly stated that such a holding is not retroactive, but is to be solely prospective in its operation.

Courts have, however, both disapproved the future use of the "Allen charge" under their supervisory power as appellate courts and, at the same time, have affirmed the conviction of the defendant in the case in which it made such a decision. Courts which have disapproved of the "Allen charge" have also been faced with the question whether to disapprove all such supplemental instructions to deadlocked juries or whether to approve some other and different instruction for use in such cases.

Three courts   .   .   .   have approved as a substitute, an instruction prepared and proposed by the American Bar Association Project on Minimum Standards for Criminal Justice.   .   .   .

It has been contended, however, that no supplemental instructions should be approved for use as a means of encouraging deadlocked jurors to make further attempts to agree upon verdicts. Thus, it is contended that any such instruction is "inherently coercive" and that the saving of court time is not worth such a rule, considering the small number of hung juries and the likelihood that most failures to reach a verdict stem from genuine and reasonable differences over the facts.

ANALYSIS OF INSTRUCTIONS GIVEN IN THIS CASE AND OF "FACTUAL SETTING" AND CIRCUMSTANCES OF CASE

1. The Instruction as Given Did Not Violate Defendant's Constitutional Rights

The instruction given by the trial judge in this case was a "modified" charge in that it omitted reference to members of a minority or majority of the jury, but instead urged that ". . . those of you who stand on one side of the question should give respectful attention and consideration to the views of those opposed. And vice versa."

It was also a "balanced" charge in that in the supplemental instructions it was emphasized that ". . . what we ask of you is the honest, conscientious individual vote of each one of you for any given verdict . . ." and that ". . . we do not expect any of you to vote one way or the other except according to your own conscience . . . ."

The supplemental instructions did, however, inform the jury, in effect, that if the case was not decided, the case would have to be retried before another jury no more representative of the community and probably on the same evidence. In the first instruction the trial judge also twice urged the jury to reach a verdict, but also stated that the case "ought not to be decided" unless the ten jurors who concur can ". . . reach your decision honestly base(d) upon the evidence and the law and your own view of the matter . . . ."

The final instruction was somewhat stronger in that it told the jury that ". . . it is incumbent upon you to reach a verdict . . . ," but then immediately added ". . . bearing in mind, however, that we do not expect any of you to vote one way or the other except according to your own conscience . . . ."

Considering these instructions as a whole, we are of the opinion that they were not so extreme or otherwise improper as to deprive defendant of his constitutional right to a fair trial or otherwise to violate any of his constitutional rights. The reference to a retrial if the jury did not reach a verdict was improper, however. Also improper was the statement that "it is incumbent upon you to reach a verdict," but that statement was immediately "followed" by the reminder that no juror was expected to vote other than "according to [his] own conscience." In essence, this charge was quite similar to the ABA approved charge that each juror has the "duty" to "deliberate with a view to reaching an agreement, if you can do so without violence to individual judgment."

2. The "Factual Setting" and Circumstances of the Supplemental Instruction Were Not Such as to Indicate That Defendant's Constitutional Rights Were Violated

In this case the trial judge did not at first inquire as to how the jury stood, but the jury sent out a note stating that it stood "six guilty, six not guilty." Thus, there was no "minority" to be "coerced" by the first supplemental instruction in this case.

Because of this fact, we do not consider that the relative weight of the evidence is a substantial factor in this case in determining whether any of defendant's constitutional rights were violated by that instruction. In any event, the relevance of such a factor has been criticized for reason previously noted. For the same reason we cannot say that the time intervals before and after the giving of the first supplemental instructions in this case were such as to indicate that the jury was improperly coerced by such instructions.

Before the later supplemental instruction was given, however, the trial judge inquired how the jury stood, without indicating whether for conviction or acquittal, and was informed that it stood nine to three. No further supplemental instructions were given, however, until after the jury had responded to a further inquiry by the court asking whether it could arrive at a verdict in thirty minutes. The jury then sent out a second note which, in effect, requested further instructions relating to one of the elements of rape.

This would indicate that upon receiving such instructions the jury expected that it would, in all probability, be able to arrive at a verdict within thirty minutes. Thus, it would also appear that under these circumstances the fact that the jury returned its verdict within a few minutes after receiving the final instructions by the trial court does not demonstrate that it was "coerced" into returning a verdict of guilty by the further instruction urging it to reach a verdict if it could conscientiously do so.

In this "factual context" and under these circumstances, and considering also the "modified" and "balanced" nature of the supplemental instructions as given by the trial judge in this case, we hold that while it was improper to give such instructions, any error in doing so was not so serious or of such a nature as to violate any of defendant's constitutional rights.

3.   Conviction Affirmed in Absence of Exceptions to Instructions

For all of these reasons, we hold that defendant has not sustained his contention on this appeal that his constitutional rights to a fair trial and to due process of law were violated by the supplemental instructions in this case.

* * *

In this case, while we do not approve of the supplemental instructions as given by the court, and expressly disapprove of them, we have examined the entire record and cannot say that any error in the giving of such instructions was "manifest," in view of the many decisions by other courts, including previous decisions by this court, approving the giving of even stronger supplemental instructions.

* * *

FUTURE   USE   OF   "ALLEN   CHARGE"   OR   "DYNAMITE CHARGE" DISAPPROVED

We agree with the statements that "few would maintain that the trial judge should be required immediately to accept a jury's first indication of failure to agree without a fair attempt at encouraging agreement" and that "it is only the method used to induce a verdict that is questionable."

We also agree, however, that the line between proper "guidance" and improper "coercion" is a fine line. We are also concerned whether there is any proper standard or any coherent theory to apply in such cases other than to consider each case separately by looking at the particular terms of the instructions and the particular factual context and circumstances in each case.

* * *

The problem also involves a balancing of such considerations as the need for economy in judicial administration by discouraging hung juries so as to eliminate the time and expense of retrials against the risk that defendants may be convicted as the result of improper coercion by the trial judge in the giving of a "dynamite charge" to a deadlocked jury. In that connection, we are impressed with the apparently accurate statistics to the effect that of the small percentage of persons accused of crime who are actually tried before a jury, only a very small percentage are the subject of mistrials because of deadlocked juries.

We are convinced, however, that the "Allen charge," even when "modified" and "balanced," carries a substantial potential for coercion, even though it may not be possible to demonstrate such coercion in a given case. Indeed, the potential for coercion is greater for the honest and the conscientious juror than for the occasional stubborn and unreasonable juror. Indeed, there is considerable merit to the contention that the majority of a jury is not always right and that the possibility of a hung jury based upon an honest difference in opinion, is part and parcel of our jury system.

For all of these reasons, we agree with the view that the giving of the "Allen charge," even when "modified" and "balanced," involves so many "pitfalls" and is such an invitation to error as to cause more trouble in the administration of justice than it is worth. We thus agree with those courts which have disapproved the future use of such supplemental instructions to deadlocked juries in criminal cases.

In accord with the views as expressed in most of the recent cases on this subject, however, we also approve the supplemental instruction proposed by the ABA Project . . . for use in this state in the event that a trial court may, in its discretion, deem it advisable to give some supplemental instruction to a deadlocked jury.[4] We agree, however, with the view that the terms of that recommended instruction are not to be regarded as "graven in stone."

Affirmed.

4. The approved portions of that instruction are as follows:

"It is your duty, as jurors, to consult with one another, and to

deliberate with a view to reaching an agreement if you can do so without violence to individual judgment. Each of you must decide

NOTES

1.　Although the *Allen* or "dynamite" charge to deadlocked juries has been the subject of intensive criticism from both the courts and commentators alike it has never been overruled by the Supreme Court.

In both United States v. Fioravanti, 412 F.2d 407 (3rd Cir. 1969), cert. denied 396 U.S. 837, 90 S.Ct. 97 and United States v. Thomas, 449 F.2d 1177 (D.C.Cir. 1971) (en banc), the charge, although extensively criticized, was not held to be unconstitutional.　Rather, the courts invoked their supervisory power to prohibit its subsequent use, and specifically directed trial judges in their respective circuits to use particular language in future charges.　Do intermediate federal appellate courts have the power to order trial judges to give a specific instruction?　If they do, should that power be exercised through an adjudicative or rule-making function?　See United States v. Robinson, 560 F.2d 507 (2d Cir. 1977) (en banc).

2.　In United States v. Sawyers, 423 F.2d 1335 (4th Cir. 1970), the trial court gave a lengthy supplemental charge to the jury after 15 hours of deliberation.　The jury retired and deliberated for an additional hour and a half before finding four of the five defendants guilty.　Addressing itself to the propriety of the charge, the court pointed out that:

> "A calmly dispassionate balanced effort on the part of a trial judge to induce a verdict does not seem to us to invade the province of the jury.　What, after all, is the purpose of the judge's initial charge to the jury?　Is it not to induce a verdict based upon the evidence and the law as he has given it to them?　.　.　.　If .　.　. he urges further deliberation in an effort to agree upon a verdict, and in doing so his comments are balanced and not slanted toward conviction, we are unable to perceive harm to the defendant."

Accordingly, the court upheld the giving of the charge but criticized the absence of an instruction which would have placed a duty on the majority to listen and consider any minority viewpoint.　The court concluded by recommending the use of a "modified" version of *Allen* which was approved by the Committee on the Operation of the Jury System of the United States.　This version incorporates the charge recommended by the ABA, but includes an additional admonition to be given to a jury:

> "That each juror who finds himself in the minority shall reconsider his views in light of the opinions of the majority, and each juror who finds himself in the majority shall give equal consideration to the views of the minority."

3.　In People v. Pankey, 58 Ill.App.3d 924, 16 Ill.Dec. 339, 374 N.E.2d 1114 (1978), the trial judge read to a deadlocked jury from the "New Judge's Creed" which stated, in part, "I hope I shall have the strength to make the hard decisions and the composure to stick to them."　Is this language likely to coerce a verdict?

the case for yourself, but do so only after an impartial consideration of the evidence in the case with your fellow jurors.　In the course of your deliberations, do not hesitate to re-examine your own views, and change your opinion, if convinced it is erroneous.　But do not surrender your honest conviction as to the weight or effect of evidence solely because of the opinion of your fellow jurors, or for the mere purpose of returning a verdict."

4.   The commentators abound with suggestions in this area. See Note, Supplemental Jury Charges Urging a Verdict—The Answer Is Yet To Be Found, 56 Minn.L.Rev. 1199, 1210 (1972) ; Comment, The Allen Charge: Recurring Problems and Recent Developments, 47 N.Y.U.L.Rev. 296, 315 (1972) ; Note, Due Process, Judicial Economy and the Hung Jury: A Re-Examination of the Allen Charge, 53 Va.L.Rev. 123, 143 (1967) ; Comment, On Instructing Deadlocked Juries, 78 Yale L.J. 100 (1968).

5.   May the judge ask a deadlocked jury what its numerical division is? In Brasfield v. United States, 272 U.S. 448, 47 S.Ct. 135 (1926), the court held: "We deem it essential to the fair and impartial conduct of the trial, that the inquiry itself should be regarded as grounds for reversal."

6.   Does the *Brasfield* rule apply to state trials? In Ellis v. Reed, 596 F.2d 1195 (4th Cir. 1979), a habeas corpus proceeding arising from a North Carolina trial, the trial judge, upon inquiry, was told that the jury was divided eleven to one. He then gave a modified *Allen* charge; and, eight minutes later, a guilty verdict was returned. The Fourth Circuit majority sustained the verdict, holding that "under the principles of federalism, the decision whether to allow the inquiry is best left to the supervising state court." Judge Winter, dissenting, found the *Brasfield* rule constitutionally mandated, and, therefore, applicable to the states.

3.   INCONSISTENT VERDICTS AND POLLS OF JURORS

1.   What happens when a jury renders a verdict of guilt on one count and acquittal on another where the acquittal logically negates the existence of some fact or element of the crime that the jury must find to convict on the first count? This situation arose in starkest simplicity in Dunn v. United States, 284 U.S. 390, 52 S.Ct. 189 (1932). In *Dunn,* the defendant was indicted on three counts: (1) maintaining a common nuisance by keeping intoxicating liquors for sale at a specified place; (2) unlawful possession of intoxicating liquors; and (3) for the unlawful sale of such liquor. The evidence was the same on all three counts. It showed that two prohibition agents and two unknown men entered the rear room of defendant's store, ordered intoxicating beverages and were served by the defendant without further conversation. They paid for the drinks and the money was placed in a cash register behind the bar. On this evidence, the jury convicted the defendant on the first count and acquitted him on the second and third counts.

Before the Supreme Court, the defendant argued that the verdict was inconsistent and that the conviction must, therefore, be overturned because his possession of liquor was negated by the acquittal on the second count and necessarily affirmed on identical evidence by the conviction on the first count. The Court, in an opinion by Mr. Justice Holmes, bluntly stated that "Consistency in the verdict is not necessary. Each count in an indictment is regarded as if it was a separate indictment." The Court's reason for not disturbing verdicts solely on the grounds of the inconsistency was stated thusly:

> The most that can be said in such cases is that the verdict shows that either in the acquittal or the conviction the

jury did not speak their real conclusions, but that does not show that they were not convinced of the defendant's guilt. We interpret the acquittal as no more than their assumption of a power which they had no right to exercise, but to which they were disposed through lenity.

*   *   *

That the verdict may have been the result of compromise, or of a mistake on the part of the jury, is possible. But verdicts cannot be upset by speculation or inquiry into such matters. 284 U.S. at 294–95.

The principle that inconsistency of verdicts is not grounds for reversal of the conviction has been steadfastly maintained by the Supreme Court. In United States v. Dotterweich, 320 U.S. 277, 64 S.Ct. 134 (1943), a corporation and its president were indicted in three counts for introducing misbranded and adulterated drugs into commerce. The jury acquitted the corporation on all counts and convicted Dotterweich, the president, on all counts. Mr. Justice Frankfurter, in writing for the Court, dismissed Dotterweich's claim that, having failed to find the corporation guilty, the jury could not find him guilty:

> Whether the jury's verdict was the result of carelessness of compromise or a belief that the responsible individual should suffer the penalty instead of merely increasing, as it were, the cost of running the business of the corporation, is immaterial. Juries may indulge in precisely such motives or vagaries.

320 U.S. at 279. See also Fairmount Glass Works v. Coal Co., 287 U.S. 474, 53 S.Ct. 252 (1933); Dealy v. United States, 152 U.S. 539, 14 S.Ct. 680 (1894). Some states, however, hold inconsistent verdicts, if rendered by the same jury, to be reversible error.

Although the principle that consistency of verdicts is not required may seem somewhat unusual, it is in harmony with the historic role of the jury in the Anglo-American system of justice and with the practical functioning of a jury. See United States v. Maybury, 274 F.2d 899, 901–03 (2d Cir. 1960), where the court was forced to consider the reasons for the rule in order to determine whether the rule should be applied in a criminal bench trial as well as a jury trial. There the court referred to the non-rational origins of the jury which was considered the voice of the community and to the requirement of unanimity in jury verdicts and concluded by holding the *Dunn* role inapplicable to bench trials. See Bickel, Judge and Jury—Inconsistent Verdicts in the Federal Courts, 63 Harv.L.Rev. 649 (1950).

2. The ancient practice of "polling the jury", carried over from the common law, exists to determine "before it is too late, whether the jury's verdict reflects the conscience of each of the jurors or whether it was brought about through the coercion or domination of one of them by some of his fellow jurors or resulted from sheer phys-

ical or mental exhaustion of a juror." Commonwealth v. Martin, 379 Pa. 587, 593, 109 A.2d 325, 328 (1954). After the verdict is read, each juror is asked if that verdict "was then and is now" his verdict.

In virtually all jurisdictions, either by statute or decision, the jury must be polled upon the defendant's request. See Fed.R.Crim.P. 31(d); N.Y.Code Crim.P. § 450; Ohio Rev.Code Ann. § 2945.77. However, in some states, notably Connecticut and Rhode Island, a poll is not mandatory, but rests within the discretion of the trial judge. Under what circumstances should a judge be permitted to deny a request to poll the jury? While, in the majority of jurisdictions, the court may conduct a poll *sua sponte*, it is never a requirement absent a specific request. The right to poll is waived if it is not exercised before the jury has "dispersed" and come into contact with outside elements. Compare Miranda v. United States, 255 F.2d 9 (1st Cir. 1958).

The court or the clerk, not counsel, conducts the poll; and jurors are not to be asked for the reasons underlying their verdict. State v. Bounds, 74 Idaho 136, 258 P.2d 751 (1953); State v. Brown, 110 Ohio App. 57, 168 N.E.2d 419 (1953). If counsel consents to a sealed verdict, does he automatically waive the right to have the jury polled? Compare Vaughan v. State, 9 Ga.App. 613, 71 S.E. 945 (1911) (yes) with State v. Callahan, 55 Iowa 364, 7 N.W. 603 (1880) (no).

If a juror during the course of polling indicates that he does not subscribe to the verdict, must the court declare a mistrial or can it direct the jury to retire to continue deliberations? Some statutes compel the court to order continued deliberations while others give the trial judge descretion to do either. Which form of statutory language is preferable? One case State v. Gullette, 3 Conn.Cir. 153, 209 A.2d 529 (1964), has indicated, by way of dictum, that a mistrial must be declared.

For a model statute, see ABA, Standards Relating to Trial by Jury, consider § 5.5. (Tentative Draft 1969):

> When a verdict has been returned and before the jury has dispersed, the jury shall be polled at the request of any party or upon the court's own motion. The poll shall be conducted by the court or clerk of court asking each juror individually whether the verdict announced is his verdict. If upon the poll there is not unanimous concurrence, the jury may be directed to retire for further deliberations or may be discharged.

4. IMPEACHMENT OF JURY VERDICTS

VIRGIN ISLANDS v. GEREAU

United States Court of Appeals, Third Circuit, 1975.
523 F.2d 140.

VAN DUSEN, CIRCUIT JUDGE.

* * *

. . . [D]efendants were found guilty of first degree murder, first degree assault, and robbery. The jury which returned the guilty verdicts had deliberated for nine days.[1] The jurors were polled individually and each acknowledged the verdict as his own. Two days later, defendants filed a motion requesting a new trial on the ground that the verdict had not been freely assented to by all the jurors. The motion was supported by the affidavits of two jurors, Rodgers and Allick, who represented that their verdict was the result of certain "pressures," [2] but the trial judge found that these affidavits were "involuntarily made out of fear" engendered by the President of the Virgin Islands Senate formerly related by marriage to Allick and "friendly with all of the defendants, save Raphael Joseph", Mario Moorhead and John Ross, who were "sympathizers of the defendants." These same two affidavits were presented to Chief District Judge Almeric Christian, who ordered a post-trial hearing to inquire into the allegations that the verdict was influenced by "unauthorized communications with the jury during its sequestration and deliberation." Since neither the trial judge nor Chief Judge Christian was available to conduct the hearing, the parties consented to the

---

1. The case was submitted to the jury at 2 P.M. Saturday, August 4, 1973. A verdict was reached by 2:30 P.M. Sunday, August 12, 1973, but was not announced until the following day.

2. "The affidavit of Mr. Allick states:

'I'm a concerned citizen writing to you on the Verdict of Guilty voted by the twelve jurors. I was one of the twelve, and I have to say that the verdict I turned in was not from my free will. It was involuntary and due to pressure of information being carried in and out of the jury room. Because I am concerned about the justice system in these Virgin Islands that I am writing his letter. Sincerely.'

"That of Mr. Rodgers recites:

'The verdict delivered after nine (9) days of deliberation does not represent my honest judgment. My verdict was not voluntary. It was the end product of pressures

applied by Judge Warren Young, who refused two verdicts and the majority of the jury who, to me seemed to have predetermined verdict. Sincerely.' "

Rodgers testified that the wording of the affidavit was not his, but was dictated by Johnny Ross, who urged Rodgers to aid "civil rights" by signing an affidavit. Rodgers identified his signature on the affidavit, but stated that he had signed "a piece of paper" in the office of one of the defendant's attorneys without looking at the paper he signed.

. . . In this court's previous decision in this case claims that (1) the trial judge was disqualified from conducting the proceedings in the district court (502 F.2d at 931–33), and (2) the trial judge had coerced the jury's verdict through requiring continuing deliberations and through its instructions (502 F.2d at 935–36), were rejected.

appointment of a special master. Upon conclusion of the hearing,[3] the master submitted to the trial judge a report containing both findings of fact and conclusions of law. . . . [T]he trial judge, determining that the special master's findings were not clearly erroneous, entered an order denying the motion for a new trial. The . . . order was appealed, along with the judgments of conviction. Government of the Virgin Islands v. Gereau et al., 502 F.2d 914 (3d Cir. 1974). This court then vacated the order denying a new trial and remanded so that the trial judge could review the record of the hearing *de novo* "and enter findings without reliance on those made by" the special master. Pursuant to the mandate of this court, the trial judge proceeded to make his own findings from the record compiled at the hearing before the special master. No additional hearing was had. On the basis of his *de novo* review, the trial judge entered an opinion and order which set forth his factual findings and again denied defendants' motion for a new trial. This appeal followed.

* * *

IMPEACHMENT OF THE VERDICT

Any attempt to impeach a jury verdict initially encounters two evidentiary obstacles: (1) producing evidence competent to attack the verdict, and (2) establishing the existence of grounds recognized as adequate to overturn the verdict. And even where both obstacles are cleared, there must be a finding that the party seeking to impeach the verdict has suffered prejudice from the misconduct of the jury.

A. The Evidentiary Obstacles: Competency and Sufficiency

1. *Competent Testimony*

It is frequently said to be the rule that a juror may not impeach his own verdict once the jury has been discharged. McDonald v. Pless, 238 U.S. 264, 267, 35 S.Ct. 783 (1915). The rule was formulated to foster several public policies: (1) discouraging harassment of jurors by losing parties eager to have the verdict set aside; (2) encouraging free and open discussion among jurors; (3) reducing incentives for jury tampering; (4) promoting verdict finality; (5) maintaining the viability of the jury as a judicial decision-making body. . . . Courts applying the rule were, however, early aware that any flat prohibition against receiving such testimony contravened another public policy: that of "redressing the injury of the private litigant" where a verdict was reached by a jury not impartial. In order to accommodate these conflicting policies, the courts, often continuing to recite the canon of "no impeachment," evolved a more flexible rubric. This latter rule interdicted reception of a juror's evidence only where it was offered "to show matters which essentially inhere in the verdict itself." . . . Such matters include both

3. The hearing took three days . . . . . Testimony was taken from all jurors, two court attendants and   the President of the Virgin Islands Senate.

"the mental process of any juror or of the jury in arriving at a verdict," and the method by which the verdict is reached.[4] The same accommodation of policies produced the general rule's major exception, which provides that " '[a] juryman may testify to any facts bearing upon the question of the existence of any extraneous influence, although not as to how far that influence operated upon his mind.' " [5] Mattox v. United States, 146 U.S. 140, 149, 13 S.Ct. 50, 53, 36 L.Ed. 917 (1892) "Extraneous influence" has been construed to cover publicity received and discussed in the jury room, consideration by the jury of evidence not admitted in court, and communications or other contact between jurors and third persons, including contacts with the trial judge outside the presence of the defendant and his counsel. By contrast, evidence of discussions among jurors, intimidation or harassment of one juror by another, and other intra-jury influences on the verdict is within the rule, rather than the exception, and is not competent to impeach a verdict.

2. *Grounds Sufficient to Overturn a Verdict*

Those incidents of jury misconduct which may be attested by the jurors and those which furnish a basis for setting aside a verdict overlap extensively. Indeed, courts often seem to treat the two concepts interchangeably in deciding whether a verdict may be successfully impeached. . . . For this reason, it is not possible to abstract from the cases any neat and comprehensive list of grounds upon which a verdict may be overborne. It is possible, however, to categorize roughly common fact patterns which have been held to call a verdict into question. Other than incompetency of a juror during jury service, . . . these are all incidents of "extraneous influence:" (1) exposure of jury to news items "about the matter pending before the jury," (2) consideration by the jury of extra-record facts about the case; (3) communications between third parties and jurors where relevant to the case to be decided; (4) pressures or partiality on the part of the court. The first three types of jury conduct

---

4. Wigmore considers the parol evidence rule as the basis for excluding juror testimony. 8 J. Wigmore, Evidence, § 2346 (McNaughton ed. 1961). See also Note: Impeachment of Jury Verdicts, 53 Marquette L.Rev. 258, 262–63 (1970). A second evidentiary basis for the rule is the privilege accorded communications among deliberating jurors. See Clark v. United States, 289 U.S. 1, 53 S.Ct. 314 (1933).

5. The rule and exception are now embodied in F.R.E. Rule 606(b):

"Upon an inquiry into the validity of a verdict or indictment, a juror may not testify as to any matter or statement occurring during the course of the jury's deliberations or to the effect of anything upon his or any other juror's mind or emotions as influencing him to assent to or dissent from the verdict or indictment or concerning his mental processes in connection therewith, except that a juror may testify on the question whether extraneous prejudicial information was improperly brought to the jury's attention or whether any outside influence was improperly brought to bear upon any juror. Nor may his affidavit or evidence of any statement by him concerning a matter about what he would be precluded from testifying be received for these purposes."

. . . .

render a criminal verdict vulnerable because they are *prima facie* incompatible with the Sixth Amendment. . . .

That Amendment guarantees, *inter alia*, "an impartial jury," the right to confront witnesses, and the assistance of counsel at every critical stage of the trial. Where jurors communicate with outsiders about the merits of the case they are deciding, their impartiality may be compromised unless the communication is tempered by "known rules of the court and the instructions and directions of the court made during the trial . . . ." And where jurors consider evidence, in the form of either fact or opinion, which has not been introduced in court, the confrontation and counsel rights of an accused are obviated as regards the particular evidence received. . . .

The fourth category of cases—those in which an incident impugns the disinterestedness of the court—can also be viewed as turning on Sixth Amendment values. Thus, in Turner v. Louisiana, 379 U.S. 466, 85 S.Ct. 546 (1965), the Court held that a new trial was required because the two principal prosecution witnesses were deputies who also had charge of the sequestered jury. The Court found that in a trial where credibility was a crucial issue, the status of the two witnesses lent a credibility to their testimony which was not developed by evidence at the trial. "In the constitutional sense, trial by jury in a criminal case necessarily implies at the very least that the 'evidence developed' against a defendant shall come from the witness stand in a public courtroom where there is full judicial protection of the defendant's right of confrontation, of cross-examination, and of counsel." . . . .

In addition to the Sixth Amendment, however, the duty of the court "to protect the integrity of its own processes," . . . requires that no verdict be the product of partiality, or its semblance, on the part of the court. This duty is the more binding because of the weight jurors are likely to accord information emanating from court personnel. . . . As normal jury pressures and intra-jury influences may not be impeached by juror evidence, so also they constitute no grounds for overturning a verdict. . . . Nor, indeed, is a verdict invalid merely because the jurors' generalized knowledge about the parties, or some other aspect of the case, is an ingredient of the decision. Though "the specific guarantees of an impartial jury and of confrontation," as well as "the more general one of due process," proscribes consideration of specific extra-record facts about the case on trial, it is not necessary that the jurors be "totally ignorant about a" case.

* * *

B. Misconduct Alleged By Defendants

The trial judge determined that several rumors were circulating among the jurors during their deliberations. He found that at least some of the jurors learned of killings which had occurred on St. Croix during the trial, and concluded that "[t]he news must have come from the outside since it was true." The judge further found that "general rumors of FBI investigations of jurors' families" were circulated among the jurors. Because a similar report was broadcast over a local radio station, the trial judge surmised that the rumor was common throughout the island and had "filtered into the jury room from outside." Neither the actual source of these rumors nor the means by which the jury learned of them was found by the trial judge. Other rumors which he identified concerned the investigation of three jurors regarding specific events in their pasts. None of these specific rumors was credited with an outside source by the trial judge. Rather, he considered that the specific rumors were juror-generated. We find nothing in the record to refute this conclusion.

The defendants characterize all these rumors as threats. They point to the rumors and to the alleged conversations between certain jury attendants and jurors, as instances of impermissible outside influences on the verdict which require that it be set aside. We disagree.

The only rumors that can even qualify as outside influences are those which were assigned an outside source by the trial judge. The rumors about specific jurors are clearly in the category of intra-jury discussions which meet neither the competency nor the sufficiency criteria for overriding the verdict. The rumors concerning other killings on St. Croix and the FBI investigation of persons involved in the case are not so easily categorized. It is clear that they are not "extraneous influences" merely by virtue of having an outside source, however. It is also apparent that the rumors are dissimilar from the types of occurrences which were roughly categorized above as "extraneous influence" cases. Although it may appear, superficially, that they might qualify as communications between jurors and third parties, closer examination establishes that the rumors do not resemble that class of cases either.

The third-party communication cases break down, factually, into three major subclasses: (1) cases where jurors glean from non-jurors facts or opinions concerning the liability or guilt of a defendant; (2) cases involving attempts by outsiders to influence the verdict through intimidation or bribery of jurors; (3) cases where jurors come into personal contact with persons related to one side or another of the controversy before the jury.

The trial judge made no finding that any contact, either direct or indirect, with any non-juror, brought the FBI investigation and murder rumors to the jury's attention. In fact, the trial judge was not able to discover the origin of these rumors. Absent a finding as to the rumors' origin, the element of bias, obvious in the types of third-party communications cases discussed above, is lacking here. Perhaps more importantly, absent such a finding, the rumors themselves are, at most, only tangentially germane to the jury's decision-making. For the rumors are fundamentally unlike the communications typically found objectionable; they are not "pertinent to the disposition of an ultimate issue in the controversy, that is, to the jury's consideration of the guilt or innocence of the defendant." Only if the rumors carried the coercive force of threats or bribery would we be justified in treating them, factually, as "extraneous influences." Unlike a bribe or threat, however, the rumors did not represent either investigation or other killings as contingent upon any particular verdict outcome. Since the rumors were nebulous, had no identified source and since the jurors appeared to regard them as emanating from other jurors, we can discover no coercive or intimidating effect in these rumors.[6] As the Second Circuit observed in United States v. Gersh, 328 F.2d 460, 464 (1964), "[s]omething more than the mere fact of an unknown and here uncompleted contact with a juror is needed . . . ."[7]

In determining that the rumors in this case do not qualify as "extraneous influences," we rely not only upon factual distinctions but upon our analysis of the rationale underlying the "extraneous influence" cases. No Sixth Amendment values are implicated by these rumors. Where no coercive or biasing effect can be attributed to the statements, the impartiality of the jury is not impugned. Where the statements are in no sense "evidence developed" against the defendants, neither confrontation nor counsel rights are abused.

Nor is the integrity of the court put in jeopardy by the spread of such rumors among the jury. The rumors had no official source. Since "a complete sanitizing of the jury room is impossible," as well as unnecessary, the court has not failed in its duty to sequester the jury merely because rumors such as these managed to penetrate to the jury room. . . .

Finally, were we to set aside the jury verdicts because of these rumors, we would be defeating the purposes served by the competency-sufficiency rules in this area of the law. If rumors such as these, filtering into the jury from no known source, were held sufficient to impeach these verdicts, jury tampering and harassment would be encouraged and we "would add unduly to the already fragile state of criminal convictions." Particularly in a locale like the Virgin Islands, where the small area and population are conducive to the rapid

---

6. Defendants argue that *Remmer* [v. United States, 347 U.S. 227, 74 S.Ct. 450 (1954)] establishes that FBI investigation of jurors, if known to the jurors, is inherently coercive. In *Remmer*, however, the juror who was being investigated had previously been offered a "profit" if he voted to acquit. As the Court recognized, such a juror might well feel pressured by an investigation to vote for conviction in order to demonstrate he had not succumbed to bribery. Jurors who had not been similarly importuned would not be subject to this sort of pressure.

Moreover, the linchpin of *Remmer* was the trial court's failure to inform the defendant and his attorney that the juror had been approached. The case was remanded for an adversary hearing to "determine the circumstances,

the impact thereof upon the juror, and whether or not it was prejudicial," since the "trial court should not decide and take final action *ex parte* on information such as was received in this case . . . ." 347 U.S. 229–30, 74 S.Ct. 451. See also Fillippon v. Albion Veiu Slate Co., 250 U.S. 76, 39 S.Ct. 435 (1919). This crucial issue is not raised by the present case.

7. *Gersh* involved anonymous phone calls made to the forewoman of the jury. Each time the caller hung up as soon as the juror answered; nothing was ever said. The Second Circuit considered that these calls, which were not connected to the defendants and which had no articulated objective, raised no issue of jury prejudice.

spread of information about anything that occurs, and "where it might be impossible to find 12 jurors who were totally ignorant about a defendant," we find it difficult to imagine any verdict which would not be subject to challenge on the basis of claims like those raised here. In our view, we cannot allow impeachment by incidents of this type.

Conversations between jurors and jury attendants, however, stand on a different footing than do the rumors just discussed. Numerous cases treat such communications as "extraneous influences." Thus, the occurrence of the conversation between Matron Foye and juror Cappin, would require us to set aside the verdict, if that conversation were prejudicial to the defendants.[8]

C. Prejudice

Even though a party establishes, by competent evidence, an act of jury misconduct sufficient to set aside a verdict, the verdict will stand unless the party has been prejudiced by the misconduct. Although there is normally a presumption that a verdict is valid, certain types of misconduct possess such a high potential of prejudice that they are considered *prima facie* prejudicial. Remarks by jury attendants to jurors, where those remarks relate to the jury's deliberations, are usually of this latter type. Thus, we will assume, as defendants contend, that the government has the burden of proving that Foye's remark to Cappin was not prejudicial. We conclude that the Government carried this burden.

* * *

In the present case, Cappin did not indicate whether she considered herself influenced by the matron's statement. However, the trial judge found that she had voted guilty from the first ballot to the last. Since Cappin did not mention the incident to any of the other jurors, no juror could have been moved by the remark to change his vote. . . .

It thus appearing that no prejudice accrued to the defendants from the only occurrence which was both legally cognizable and sufficient to impeach the jury verdict, we find no abuse of discretion in the trial judge's refusal to order a new trial. The judgment of the district court will be affirmed.

---

8. [Juror Agneta Cappin testified that one of the jury attendants, Matron Foye, spoke to her about the case.

"She just asked me how everything is going and I tell her not so good. And I say two of them that don't understand, they don't come in yet. And she say to me she want them to hurry up so she can get to go home, that is all."

Matron Foye denied the conversation. The trial judge, finding both women to be credible witnesses, chose to believe Foye rather than Cappin because he knew that Foye "was grateful for the opportunity to earn extra income as a jury matron." We do not consider these credibility findings to lack adequate support in the record. However, we do hold that the trial judge's reliance on his personal, subjective belief about the needs and motives of Matron Foye was an improper ground for rejecting Cappin's concededly credible testimony.]

NOTES

1. Can the presence of a newspaper article in the jury room, replete with extrinsic facts, ever be considered harmless error? In United States v. McKinney, 429 F.2d 1019 (5th Cir. 1970), the majority, with one judge dissenting, remanded for a hearing into the prejudicial impact of a newspaper article, indicating that the defendant had escaped from jail while awaiting trial, was discussed by the jury. On petition for rehearing, the court changed its decision. Judge Rives, the pivotal vote, undertook a judicial prerogative rarely exercised and changed his mind. Over the dissent of Judge Goldberg who wrote the original majority opinion, Judge Rives said, at 434 F.2d 831:

> "Upon further consideration, I am convinced that the district judge did not abuse his discretion in denying McKinney's motion for new trial, and, hence, that the judgment of conviction should be affirmed. The most cogent reason for my change of view is that I have become convinced that the evidence does not admit of the slightest doubt of McKinney's guilt.

* * *

> "The most that can possibly be developed from a questioning of the jurors is that there was *some* mention or "discussion" of McKinney's escape during the jury's deliberations.

* * *

> "Such inconclusive inference of guilt as might be drawn from knowledge of McKinney's escape would add practically nothing to the positive and overwhelming evidence of his guilt. This Court, as well as the district court, must necessarily conclude that any mention or 'discussion' of McKinney's escape had practically no effect on the jury's verdict.

> "We simply chose the wrong vehicle to undertake the development of a general rule as to the duty of a district judge in deciding a defendant's motion for new trial when jury misconduct is alleged. Indeed, I do not think that our Court should in any case undertake to promulgate such a general rule. The past literature on the subject is voluminous and shows that the question has arisen under an almost infinite variety of circumstances. Continued development of the jurisprudence can best be accomplished by deciding each case on its own peculiar facts and circumstances."

Compare United States v. Thomas, 463 F.2d 1061 (7th Cir. 1972), where the court upheld a challenge to the sufficiency of the evidence, but reversed the conviction because a juror's affidavit alleged that a newspaper article was in the jury room during deliberations. The article had only one sentence of "extrinsic" evidence:

> "The article was entitled, *Car Insurance Fraud Trial is Nearing End*. The first two paragraphs reported the stage of court proceedings in the Thomas trial and attempted to summarize the testimony of one of the witnesses. In addition, the article stated, "Doctor Pope was indicted with Thomas and five other attorneys in the alleged insurance padding which caused three million dollars in losses to several insurance companies."

The majority elected to draw an extremely nefarious connotation from the items in this sentence, finding that, together, "they suggested that the defendant, was part of a much larger conspiracy than either the evidence at trial had specifically indicated or than the indictment had charged." Rather than remanding for a hearing to determine whether the article was even in the jury room, the court reversed for a new trial:

> "We find that there was a sufficient showing of juror exposure to prejudicial evidence to have prompted further investigation on the part of the trial judge. We find that this failure necessitates a new trial. Remand for the purposes of investigating the jury would be fruitless at this point, over two years after the close of the original proceeding. Moreover, we cannot agree that an error of this gravity, which calls into question the integrity of the jury's deliberations, can be characterized as 'harmless,' . . . ."

Mr. Justice (then Judge) Stevens dissented:

> "The question for us to decide is whether the trial judge abused his discretion in concluding that the article was not sufficiently prejudicial to require a new trial. Since the jury had already arrived at its verdict, it was too late to take remedial steps. The fact that improper matter was considered by the jury was established; hence there was nothing to be accomplished by an investigation unless the judge questioned the veracity of the affidavit. The issue presented to him was whether, on the special facts of this case, a new trial should be held. Necessarily his decision reflected an evaluation of the newspaper story in the context of the entire trial.

> "The record here is cold, but it contains substantial support for the decision made by the trial judge while his recollection of the demeanor of witnesses, the voir dire, and the persuasive impact of testimony and argument, remained vivid.

> * * *

> "Almost every jury trial requires some compromise with standards of absolute perfection; such deviations must be tolerated if the jury system is to function effectively. In my opinion the trial judge did not abuse his discretion in concluding that the deviation reflected by this record was within permissible limits."

Is reversal, rather than remand for a "jury" hearing, the only way to avoid the rule against impeachment of verdicts? If so, is the rule worth retaining where specific acts of interference with the deliberations are alleged? Once a single juror's allegations are put into affidavit form, what harm is there in asking other jurors if those allegations are true and, if so, whether the matter alleged affected their verdict?

2. In order to avoid impeachment of verdict problems, may the court order the jurors not to communicate with the media following return of their verdict? In United States v. Sherman, 581 F.2d 1358 (9th Cir. 1978), following a controversial bank robbery trial, the trial judge forbade the jurors from discussing the case with anyone, and ordered everyone, including the news media, to stay away from the jurors. On a petition for mandamus filed by the *Seattle Times*, the court held that the order operated as a restraint on the media which could not be justified by competing interests. Accordingly, it found that the order, "by depriving the media the opportunity to ask the jurors if they wished to be interviewed, was clearly erroneous as a matter of law."

Chapter 21

SENTENCING ALTERNATIVES

A. SENTENCING PROCEDURES

WILLIAMS v. NEW YORK

United States Supreme Court, 1949.
337 U.S. 241, 69 S.Ct. 1079.

MR. JUSTICE BLACK delivered the opinion of the Court.

A jury in a New York state court found appellant guilty of murder in the first degree. The jury recommended life imprisonment, but the trial judge imposed sentence of death. In giving his reasons for imposing the death sentence the judge discussed in open court the evidence upon which the jury had convicted stating that this evidence had been considered in the light of additional information obtained through the court's "Probation Department, and through other sources."

* * *

About five weeks after the verdict of guilty with recommendation of life imprisonment, and after a statutory pre-sentence investigation report to the judge, the defendant was brought to court to be sentenced. Asked what he had to say, appellant protested his innocence. After each of his three lawyers had appealed to the court to accept the jury's recommendation of a life sentence, the judge gave reasons why he felt that the death sentence should be imposed. He narrated the shocking details of the crime as shown by the trial evidence, expressing his own complete belief in appellant's guilt. He stated that the pre-sentence investigation revealed many material facts concerning appellant's background which though relevant to the question of punishment could not properly have been brought to the attention of the jury in its consideration of the question of guilt. He referred to the experience appellant "had had on thirty other burglaries in and about the same vicinity" where the murder had been committed. The appellant had not been convicted of these burglaries although the judge had information that he had confessed to some and had been identified as the perpetrator of some of the others. The judge also referred to certain activities of appellant as shown by the probation report that indicated appellant possessed "a morbid sexuality" and classified him as a "menace to society." The accuracy of the statements made by the judge as to appellant's background and past practices were not challenged by appellant or his counsel, nor was the judge asked to disregard any of them or to afford appellant a chance to refute or discredit any of them by cross-examination or otherwise.

The case presents a serious and difficult question. The question relates to the rules of evidence applicable to the manner in which a judge may obtain information to guide him in the imposition of sentence upon an already convicted defendant. Within limits fixed by statutes, New York judges are given a broad discretion to decide the type and extent of punishment for convicted defendants. Here, for example, the judge's discretion was to sentence to life imprisonment or death. To aid a judge in exercising this discretion intelligently the New York procedural policy encourages him to consider information about the convicted person's past life, health, habits, conduct, and mental and moral propensities. The sentencing judge may consider such information even though obtained outside the courtroom from persons whom a defendant has not been permitted to confront or cross-examine. It is the consideration of information obtained by a sentencing judge in this manner that is the basis for appellant's broad constitutional challenge to the New York statutory policy.

Appellant urges that the New York statutory policy is in irreconcilable conflict with the underlying philosophy of a second procedural policy grounded in the due process of law clause of the Fourteenth Amendment. That policy . . . is in part that no person shall be tried and convicted of an offense unless he is given reasonable notice of the charges against him and is afforded an opportunity to examine adverse witnesses.

* * *

Tribunals passing on the guilt of a defendant always have been hedged in by strict evidentiary procedural limitations. But both before and since the American colonies became a nation, courts in this country and in England practiced a policy under which a sentencing judge could exercise a wide discretion in the sources and types of evidence used to assist him in determining the kind and extent of punishment to be imposed within limits fixed by law. Out-of-court affidavits have been used frequently, and of course in the smaller communities sentencing judges naturally have in mind their knowledge of the personalities and backgrounds of convicted offenders. A recent manifestation of the historical latitude allowed sentencing judges appears in Rule 32 of the Federal Rules of Criminal Procedure. That rule provides for consideration by federal judges of reports made by probation officers containing information about a convicted defendant, including such information "as may be helpful in imposing sentence or in granting probation or in the correctional treatment of the defendant . . . ."

In addition to the historical basis for different evidentiary rules governing trial and sentencing procedures there are sound practical reasons for the distinction. In a trial before verdict the issue is whether a defendant is guilty of having engaged in certain criminal conduct of which he has been specifically accused. Rules of evidence have been fashioned for criminal trials which narrowly confine the trial contest to evidence that is strictly relevant to the particular offense charged. These rules rest in part on a necessity to prevent a time consuming and confusing trial of collateral issues. They were also designed to prevent tribunals concerned solely with the issue of guilt of a particular offense from being influenced to convict for that offense by evidence that the defendant had habitually engaged in other misconduct. A sentencing judge, however, is not confined to the narrow issue of guilt. His task within fixed statutory or constitutional limits is to determine the type and extent of punishment after the issue of guilt has been determined. Highly relevant—if not essential—to his selection of an appropriate sentence is the possession of the fullest information possible concerning the defendant's life and characteristics. And modern concepts individualizing punishment have made it all the more necessary that a sentencing judge not be denied an opportunity to obtain pertinent information by a requirement of rigid adherence to restrictive rules of evidence properly applicable to the trial.

Undoubtedly the New York statutes emphasize a prevalent modern philosophy of penology that the punishment should fit the offender and not merely the crime. The belief no longer prevails that every offense in a like legal category calls for an identical punishment without regard to the past life and habits of a particular offender. This whole country has traveled far from the period in which the death sentence was an automatic and commonplace result of convictions—even for offenses today deemed trivial. Today's philosophy of individualizing sentences makes sharp distinctions for example between first and repeated offenders. Indeterminate sentences, the ultimate termination of which are sometimes decided by nonjudicial agencies have to a large extent taken the place of the old rigidly fixed punishments. The practice of probation which relies heavily on nonjudicial implementation has been accepted as a wise policy. Execution of the United States parole system rests on the discretion of an administrative parole board. Retribution is no longer the dominant objective of the criminal law. Reformation and rehabilitation of offenders have become important goals of criminal jurisprudence.[1]

Modern changes in the treatment of offenders make it more necessary now than a century ago for observance of the distinctions in the evidential procedure in the trial and sentencing processes. For

---

1. Judge Ulman writing on The Trial Judge's Dilemma discusses the problems that confront the sentencing judge and quotes from one of his court opinions as to the factors that a judge should consider in imposing sentence:

"1st. The protection of society against wrong-doers.

"2nd. The punishment — or much better—the discipline of the wrong-doer.

"3rd. The reformation and rehabilitation of the wrong-doer.

"4th. The deterrence of others from the commission of like offenses.

"It should be obvious that a proper dealing with these factors involves a study of each case upon an individual basis. Was the crime a crime against property only, or did it involve danger to human life? Was it a crime of sudden passion or was it studied and deliberate? Is the criminal a man so constituted and so habituated to war upon society that there is little or no real hope that he ever can be anything other than a menace to society—or is he obviously amenable to reformation?" Glueck, Probation and Criminal Justice 113 (1933).

indeterminate sentences and probation have resulted in an increase in the discretionary powers exercised in fixing punishments. In general, these modern changes have not resulted in making the lot of offenders harder. On the contrary a strong motivating force for the changes has been the belief that by careful study of the lives and personalities of convicted offenders many could be less severely punished and restored sooner to complete freedom and useful citizenship. This belief to a large extent has been justified.

Under the practice of individualizing punishments, investigational techniques have been given an important role. Probation workers making reports of their investigations have not been trained to prosecute but to aid offenders. Their reports have been given a high value by conscientious judges who want to sentence persons on the best available information rather than on guesswork and inadequate information.[2] To deprive sentencing judges of this kind of information would undermine modern penological procedural policies that have been cautiously adopted throughout the nation after careful consideration and experimentation. We must recognize that most of the information now relied upon by judges to guide them in the intelligent imposition of sentences would be unavailable if information were restricted to that given in open court by witnesses subject to cross-examination. And the modern probation report draws on information concerning every aspect of a defendant's life.[3] The type and extent of this information make totally impractical if not impossible open court testimony with cross-examination. Such a procedure could endlessly delay criminal administration in a retrial of collateral issues.

The considerations we have set out admonish us against treating the due-process clause as a uniform command that courts throughout the Nation abandon their age-old practice of seeking information from out-of-court sources to guide their judgment toward a more enlightened and just sentence. Under New York statutes a state judge cannot escape his grave responsibility of fixing sentence. In deter-

---

2. The late Federal Judge Lewis B. Schwellenbach in his article on the difficulties that confront a sentencing judge wrote: "The knowledge of the life of a man, his background and his family, is the only proper basis for the determination as to his treatment. There is, no substitute for information. The sentencing judge in the Federal court has the tools with which to acquire that information. Failure to make full use of those tools cannot be justified." Schwellenbach, Information vs. Intuition in the Imposition of Sentence, 27 J.Am. Jud.Soc. 52 (1943).

3. A publication circulated by the Administrative Office of the United States Courts contains a suggested form for all United States probation reports and serves as an example of the type of information contained in the reports. This form consists of thirteen "marginal headings." (1) Offense; (2) Prior Record; (3) Family History; (4) Home and Neighborhood; (5) Education; (6) Religion; (7) Interests and Activities; (8) Health (physical and mental); (9) Employment; (10) Resources; (11) Summary; (12) Plan; and (13) Agencies Interested. Each of the headings is further broken down into sub-headings. The form represents a framework into which information can be inserted to give the sentencing judge a composite picture of the defendant. Administrative Office of the United States Courts, The Presentence Investigation Report, Pub. No. 101 (1943).

mining whether a defendant shall receive a one-year minimum or a twenty-year maximum sentence, we do not think the Federal Constitution restricts the view of the sentencing judge to the information received in open court. The due-process clause should not be treated as a device for freezing the evidential procedure of sentencing in the mold of trial procedure. So to treat the due-process clause would hinder if not preclude all courts—state and federal—from making progressive efforts to improve the administration of criminal justice.

It is urged, however, that we should draw a constitutional distinction as to the procedure for obtaining information where the death sentence is imposed. We cannot accept the contention. Leaving a sentencing judge free to avail himself of out-of-court information in making such a fateful choice of sentences does secure to him a broad discretionary power, one susceptible of abuse. But in considering whether a rigid constitutional barrier should be created, it must be remembered that there is possibility of abuse wherever a judge must choose between life imprisonment and death. And it is conceded that no federal constitutional objection would have been possible if the judge here had sentenced appellant to death because appellant's trial manner impressed the judge that appellant was a bad risk for society, or if the judge had sentenced him to death giving no reason at all. We cannot say that the due-process clause renders a sentence void merely because a judge gets additional out-of-court information to assist him in the exercise of this awesome power of imposing the death sentence.

Appellant was found guilty after a fairly conducted trial. His sentence followed a hearing conducted by the judge. Upon the judge's inquiry as to why sentence should not be imposed, the defendant made statements. His counsel made extended arguments. The case went to the highest court in the state, and that court had power to reverse for abuse of discretion or legal error in the imposition of the sentence. That court affirmed. We hold that appellant was not denied due process of law.[4]

Affirmed.

Mr. Justice Rutledge dissents.

Mr. Justice Murphy dissenting.

A combination of factors in this case impels me to dissent.

Petitioner was convicted of murder by a jury, and sentenced to death by the judge. The jury which heard the trial unanimously recommended life imprisonment as a suitable punishment for the defendant. They had observed him throughout the trial, had heard all the evidence adduced against him, and in spite of the shocking character of the crime of which they found him guilty, were unwilling to decree that his life should be taken. In our criminal courts the jury

---

4. What we have said is not to be accepted as a holding that the sentencing procedure is immune from scrutiny under the due-process clause. See Townsend v. Burke, 334 U.S. 736, 68 S.Ct. 1252.

sits as the representative of the community; its voice is that of the society against which the crime was committed. A judge even though vested with statutory authority to do so, should hesitate indeed to increase the severity of such a community expression.

He should be willing to increase it, moreover, only with the most scrupulous regard for the rights of the defendant. The record before us indicates that the judge exercised his discretion to deprive a man of his life, in reliance on material made available to him in a probation report, consisting almost entirely of evidence that would have been inadmissible at the trial. Some, such as allegations of prior crimes, was irrelevant. Much was incompetent as hearsay. All was damaging, and none was subject to scrutiny by the defendant.

Due process of law includes at least the idea that a person accused of crime shall be accorded a fair hearing through all the stages of the proceedings against him. I agree with the Court as to the value and humaneness of liberal use of probation reports as developed by modern penologists, but, in a capital case, against the unanimous recommendation of a jury, where the report would concededly not have been admissible at the trial, and was not subject to examination by the defendant, I am forced to conclude that the high commands of due process were not obeyed.

NOTES

1. As *Williams* implies, hearsay is admissible for sentencing purposes. See United States v. Fatico, 579 F.2d 707 (2d Cir. 1979) (information supplied by unidentified informant not improper element of sentence when there is good cause for withholding his identity and information is subject to corroboration by other means). What standards should the court use in determining whether to rely upon hearsay or other disputed information in a presentencing report? See Note, A Hidden Issue of Sentencing: Burdens of Proof for Disputed Allegations in Presentence Reports, 66 Geo.L.J. 1515 (1978).

2. In Gardner v. Florida, 430 U.S. 349, 97 S.Ct. 1197 (1977), a jury had returned a guilty verdict, recommending that the death penalty not be imposed. The judge, as permitted by Florida law, nevertheless decided to sentence the accused to death. Before sentencing the accused, the judge had available to him the results of a pre-sentence investigation, which was not made available to the accused; nor was the report made available to the Florida reviewing court which upheld the death penalty. Under these circumstances the United States Supreme Court held that the death sentence could not stand.

3. A convicted defendant has the right to personally address the court prior to receipt of sentence. This practice, known as allocution, was established at common law so "that the defendant might be identified by the court as the real party adjudged guilty; that he might have a chance to plead a pardon, or move in arrest of judgment; that he might have an opportunity to say why judgment should not be given against him; and that the example of being brought up for the animadversion of the court and the open denunciation of punishment might tend to deter others from the commission of similar offenses." Ball v. United States, 140 U.S. 118, 11 S.Ct. 761 (1891).

In Green v. United States, 365 U.S. 301, 81 S.Ct. 653 (1961), the trial judge asked, "Do you want to say something?" At that point, defense counsel made a detailed argument in mitigation of sentence. In a 5–4 decision, the Court upheld the sentence for the following reason:

"A record, certainly this record, unlike a play, is unaccompanied with stage directions which may tell the significant cast of the eye or the nod of the head. It may well be that the defendant himself was recognized and sufficiently apprised of his right to speak and chose to exercise this right through his counsel. Especially is this conclusion warranted by the fact that the defendant has raised this claim seven years after the occurrence. The defendant has failed to meet his burden of showing that he was not accorded the personal right . . . and we therefore find that his sentence was not illegal.

"However, to avoid litigation arising out of ambiguous records in order to determine whether the trial judge did address himself to the defendant personally, we think that the problem should be, as it readily can be, taken out of the realm of controversy. This is easily accomplished. Trial judges before sentencing should, as a matter of good judicial administration, unambiguously address themselves to the defendant. Hereafter trial judges should leave no room for doubt that the defendant has been issued a personal invitation to speak prior to sentencing."

4. In Hill v. United States, 368 U.S. 424, 82 S.Ct. 468 (1962), the Court held that challenges to the right of allocution may not be maintained collaterally, but must be the subject of direct appeal. Where the judge makes any inquiry of defendant whatsoever with regard to comment before sentence, the right of allocution will generally be deemed satisfied. See Hopkins v. United States, 431 F.2d 429 (5th Cir. 1970); Robins v. United States, 402 F.2d 470 (7th Cir. 1968). What is the substantive effect of the denial of allocution? See Hensley v. United States, 108 U.S.App.D.C. 242, 281 F.2d 605 (1960) (remand for resentencing at which allocution is provided). See generally Barrett, Allocution, 9 Mo.L.Rev. 115 (1944).

5. In Woodson v. North Carolina, 428 U.S. 280, 96 S.Ct. 2978 (1976), the Court held that, in a capital case, a statute which imposed a *mandatory* death sentence—and, thus, preempted the judge's sentencing function—was unconstitutional. Several states had enacted mandatory execution statutes to avoid the effect of Furman v. Georgia, 408 U.S. 238, 92 S.Ct. 2726 (1972), which voided all pending death sentences because, according to the plurality, the imposition of those sentences was "pregnant with discrimination." Nonetheless, *Woodson* concluded that, in a capital case, the respect for humanity underlying the eighth amendment required the court to consider the character and record of the individual and the circumstances of the offense.

6. The Ohio capital punishment statute, enacted in the wake of *Furman*, required the imposition of the death penalty in the absence of a finding that any of three statutory mitigating factors was present: (1) the victim induced or facilitated the offense; (2) the crime was committed under duress or provocation; or (3) the defendant was operating under a mental deficiency that did not rise to the level of an insanity defense. In Lockett v. Ohio, 438 U.S. 586, 98 S.Ct. 2954 (1978), the Court held the statute too restrictive to permit a full consideration of all factors in mitigation before a death sentence was imposed.

B. DETERMINANTS OF SENTENCES

---

1. PRIOR CONVICTIONS

UNITED STATES v. TUCKER

Supreme Court of the United States, 1972.
404 U.S. 443, 92 S.Ct. 589.

MR. JUSTICE STEWART delivered the opinion of the Court.

In 1953 the respondent, Forrest S. Tucker, was brought to trial in a federal district court in California upon a charge of armed bank robbery. He pleaded not guilty. Four female employees of the bank were called as witnesses for the prosecution, and they identified the respondent as the robber. He testified in his own behalf, denying participation in the robbery and offering an alibi defense. To impeach the credibility of his testimony, the prosecution was permitted on cross-examination to ask him whether he had previously been convicted of any felonies. He acknowledged three previous felony convictions, one in Florida in 1938, another in Louisiana in 1946, and a third in Florida in 1950. At the conclusion of the trial the jury returned a verdict of guilty. In the ensuing sentencing proceeding the District Judge conducted an inquiry into the respondent's background, and, the record shows, gave explicit attention to the three previous felony convictions the respondent had acknowledged.[1] The judge then sentenced him to serve 25 years in prison—the maximum term authorized by the applicable federal statute.

Several years later it was conclusively determined that the respondent's 1938 conviction in Florida and his 1946 conviction in Louisiana were constitutionally invalid. This determination was made by the Superior Court of Alameda County, California, upon that court's finding in a collateral proceeding that those convictions had resulted

---

1. An FBI Agent was present at the sentencing proceeding. The District Judge began the proceeding by stating, "I would like to have the Agent's testimony with respect to the prior convictions."

The agent testified, in relevant part, as follows: "As the defendant said, when he was a juvenile, I believe it was in 1938, he received a ten-year sentence in Florida . . . .

* * *

". . . He said there was five years and four months on the chain gang . . . and he said he actually

served two years beyond that . . . .

* * *

"In 1950 Mr. Tucker was sentenced to a five year term in the State of Florida, for, I believe it was burglary, and on January, the 5th, 1951, while in custody in the hospital, he escaped."

* * *

"In 1946 he was convicted in the State of Louisiana on a felony charge and given a term of four years.

* * *

". . . I believe it was a burglary."

from proceedings in which the respondent had been unrepresented by counsel, and that he had been "neither advised of his right to legal assistance nor did he intelligently waive this right to the assistance of counsel." [2]

Thereafter the respondent initiated the present litigation. Proceeding under 28 U.S.C. § 2255, he filed a motion in the Federal District Court in which he had been convicted in 1953, claiming that introduction at the 1953 trial of evidence of his prior invalid convictions had fatally tainted the jury's verdict of guilty. Upon consideration of the motion, the District Judge agreed that "the use of the constitutionally invalid prior convictions on cross-examination for impeachment purposes was error," but found that the error was harmless beyond a reasonable doubt, in view of the overwhelming trial evidence that the respondent had been guilty of the bank robbery.
. . . .

On appeal, the Court of Appeals for the Ninth Circuit agreed that it had been "firmly proved that the evidence of prior convictions did not contribute to the verdict obtained and that, with respect to the verdict of guilty, the error in receiving such evidence was therefore harmless beyond a reasonable doubt." It went on, however, to find that there was "a reasonable probability that the defective prior convictions may have led the trial court to impose a heavier prison sentence than it otherwise would have imposed." Accordingly, the appellate court affirmed the refusal to vacate the conviction, but remanded the case to the District Court for resentencing "without consideration of any prior convictions which are invalid under Gideon v. Wainwright, 372 U.S. 335, 83 S.Ct. 792." Tucker v. United States, 431 F.2d 1292. The government came here with a petition for a writ of certiorari, which we granted.

The government asks us to reverse the judgment of the Court of Appeals insofar as it remanded this case to the District Court for resentencing. It argues that a federal district judge has wide and largely unreviewable discretion in imposing sentence, and that in exercising that discretion his relevant inquiry is not whether the defendant has been formally convicted of past crimes, but whether and to what extent the defendant has in fact engaged in criminal or antisocial conduct. Further, the government argues, in view of other detrimental information about the respondent possessed at the time of sentencing by the trial judge, it is highly unlikely that a different sentence would have been imposed even if the judge had known that two of the respondent's previous convictions were constitutionally invalid. Accordingly, the government concludes that to now remand this case for resentencing would impose an "artificial" and "unrealistic" burden upon the District Court.

---

2. The decision of the Superior Court of Alameda County is unreported, but the accuracy of that court's determination is not questioned. See In re Tucker, 64 Cal.2d 15, 48 Cal.Rptr. 697, 409 P.2d 921; Tucker v. Craven, Cir., 421 F.2d 139.

It is surely true, as the government asserts, that a trial judge in the federal judicial system generally has wide discretion in determining what sentence to impose. It is also true that before making that determination, a judge may appropriately conduct an inquiry broad in scope, largely unlimited either as to the kind of information he may consider, or the source from which it may come. . . .

The government is also on solid ground in asserting that a sentence imposed by a federal district judge, if within statutory limits, is generally not subject to review. . . .

But these general propositions do not decide the case before us. For we deal here not with a sentence imposed in the informed discretion of a trial judge, but with a sentence founded at least in part upon misinformation of constitutional magnitude. As in Townsend v. Burke, 334 U.S. 736, 68 S.Ct. 1252, 92 L.Ed. 1690, "this prisoner was sentenced on the basis of assumptions concerning his criminal record which were materially untrue." The record in the present case makes evident that the sentencing judge gave specific consideration to the respondent's previous convictions before imposing sentence upon him. Yet it is now clear that two of those convictions were wholly unconstitutional under Gideon v. Wainwright, 372 U.S. 335, 83 S.Ct. 792.[3]

We need not speculate about whether the outcome of the respondent's 1938 and 1946 prosecutions would necessarily have been different if he had had the help of a lawyer. Such speculation is not only fruitless, but quite beside the point. For the real question here is not whether the results of the Florida and Louisiana proceedings might have been different if the respondent had had counsel, but whether the sentence in the 1953 federal case might have been different if the sentencing judge had known that at least two of the respondent's previous convictions had been unconstitutionally obtained.

We agree with the Court of Appeals that the answer to this question must be "yes." For if the trial judge in 1953 had been aware of the constitutional infirmity of two of the previous convictions, the factual circumstances of the respondent's background would have appeared in a dramatically different light at the sentencing proceeding. Instead of confronting a defendant who had been legally convicted of three previous felonies, the judge would then have been dealing with a man who, beginning at age 17, had been unconstitutionally imprisoned for more than ten years, including five and one-half years on a chain gang. We cannot agree with the government that a re-evaluation of the respondent's sentence by the District Court even at this late date will be either "artificial" or "unrealistic." [4]

3. The respondent's convictions occurred years before the *Gideon* case was decided, but the impact of that decision was fully retroactive. Pickelsimer v. Wainwright, 375 U.S. 2, 84 S.Ct. 80, 81.

4. As noted above, and emphasized in the dissenting opinion, the trial judge, in ruling upon the respondent's present § 2255 motion, held that the wrongful use of the invalid previous convictions to impeach the respon-

The *Gideon* case established an unequivocal rule "making it unconstitutional to try a person for a felony in a state court unless he had a lawyer or had validly waived one." Burgett v. Texas, 389 U.S. 109, 114, 88 S.Ct. 258, 261. In *Burgett* we said that "[t]o permit a conviction obtained in violation of Gideon v. Wainwright to be used against a person either to support guilt or enhance punishment for another offense . . . is to erode the principle of that case." Erosion of the *Gideon* principle can be prevented here only by affirming the judgment of the Court of Appeals remanding this case to the trial court for reconsideration of the respondent's sentence.

The judgment is affirmed.

MR. JUSTICE POWELL and MR. JUSTICE REHNQUIST took no part in the consideration or decision of this case.

MR. JUSTICE BLACKMUN, with whom THE CHIEF JUSTICE joins, dissenting.

The Court's opinion, of course, is a fine and acceptable exposition of abstract law. If I felt that it fit Tucker's case, I would join it. The Court, however, fails to mention and to give effect to certain facts that, for me, are controlling:

1. At his armed bank robbery trial in May 1953 Tucker was no juvenile. He was 32 years of age and was represented by counsel. A reading of his trial testimony discloses that he was very knowledgeable indeed. Tucker testified on cross-examination at that trial not only as to the fact of three prior state felony convictions, but, as well, as to his engaging in the proscribed conduct underlying two of those convictions. He stated flatly (a) that in 1938 he broke into a garage and took a man's automobile, and (b) that in 1946 he broke into a jewelry store at night. He also acknowledged that, while waiting for transportation to prison in Florida after the third conviction, he escaped and went to California using an assumed name. Thus, wholly apart from formal convictions, Tucker conceded criminal conduct on his part on three separate prior occasions.

2. The judge who presided at Tucker's pre-*Gideon* trial for armed bank robbery in 1953 was the Honorable George B. Harris of the United States District Court for the Northern District of California. After Tucker's conviction by a jury Judge Harris imposed the 25-year maximum sentence. Despite the interim passage of 16 years, Tucker's present petition, filed pursuant to 28 U.S.C. § 2255, also came before the very same Judge Harris, then Chief Judge of the Northern District. The judge denied relief on the ground that

dent's testimony at the 1953 trial was harmless error, in view of the overwhelming evidence that he was guilty of the bank robbery. But the respondent's guilt of that offense hardly "translates" into an "inescapable" assumption that the trial judge would have imposed a maximum 25-year prison sentence if he had known that the respondent had already been unconstitutionally imprisoned for more than 10 years. It would be equally callous to assume now that the constitutional invalidity of the respondent's previous convictions is clear, that the trial judge will upon reconsideration "undoubtedly" impose the same sentence he imposed in 1953.

the error in the use, for impeachment purposes, of two constitutionally invalid prior convictions was harmless beyond a reasonable doubt (a) because the issue of guilt or innocence was not at all close, (b) because Tucker's testimony "had been successfully impeached by prior inconsistent statements made to the Federal Bureau of Investigation agents, and by rebuttal testimony which demonstrated that portions of [his] testimony [were] improbable and untrue," and (c) because his "testimony was successfully impeached, and, in fact, demolished by additional items." Tucker v. United States, 299 F.Supp. 1376, 1378 (ND Cal.1969). As to all of this, on the issue of guilt, the Court of Appeals agreed, 431 F.2d 1292, 1293 (CA9 1970), and this Court today does not rule otherwise.

Chief Judge Harris' § 2255 ruling translates for me into something completely inescapable, namely, that in 1953, wholly apart from the 1938 and 1946 convictions, he would have imposed the 25-year maximum sentence anyway. Surely Judge Harris, of all people, is the best source of knowledge as to the effect, if any, of those two convictions in his determination of the sentence to be imposed. Yet the Court speculates that, despite his identity and despite his obvious disclaimer, Judge Harris might have been influenced in his sentencing by the fact of the two prior convictions, rather than by the three criminal acts that Tucker himself acknowledged.

On remand the case presumably will go once again to Judge Harris, and undoubtedly the same sentence once again will be imposed. Perhaps this is all worthwhile and, if so, I must be content with the Court's disposition of the case on general principles. I entertain more than a mild suspicion, however, that this is an exercise in futility, that the Court is merely marching up the hill only to march right down again, and that it is time we become just a little realistic in the face of a record such as this one.

I would reverse the judgment of the Court of Appeals insofar as it remands the case to the District Court for resentencing.

NOTES

1. When the sentencing judge specifically states that the sentence being imposed is appropriate regardless of the validity of a prior conviction, *Tucker* has no application. See Portillo v. United States, 588 F.2d 714 (9th Cir. 1978) (judge said "when you reach these numbers [of convictions] one more or less is hardly significant"); Farrow v. United States, 580 F.2d 1339 (9th Cir. 1978) (when original sentence would not have been altered, no hearing is necessary on petition for postconviction relief); McAnulty v. United States, 469 F.2d 254 (8th Cir. 1972) ("the sentence would be the same"). However, in Taylor v. United States, 472 F.2d 1178 (8th Cir. 1973), where the judge said that a prior conviction "would be of no consequence" to the sentence at issue, the court remanded for resentencing because the invalid prior conviction placed defendant in a lesser category of recidivists.

2. Would a trial judge be inclined to revise a sentence when he can simply indicate that the prior sentence was appropriate without regard to an invalid previous conviction? Is any other form of relief appropriate? Should a reviewing court simply reduce the sentence on appeal?

3. See Baldasar v. Illinois, —— U.S. ——, 100 S.Ct. 1585 (1980), Chapter 9–B, following *Argersinger,* concerning use of a fine-only uncounseled conviction.

2. MAINTAINING INNOCENCE

(a) DURING TRIAL

UNITED STATES v. GRAYSON

Supreme Court of the United States, 1978.
438 U.S. 41, 98 S.Ct. 2610.

MR. CHIEF JUSTICE BURGER delivered the opinion of the Court.

We granted certiorari to [determine whether] it was improper for a sentencing judge, in fixing the sentence within the statutory limits, to give consideration to the defendant's false testimony observed by the judge during the trial.

I.

In August 1975, respondent Grayson was confined in a federal prison camp under a conviction for distributing a controlled substance. In October, he escaped but was apprehended two days later by FBI agents in New York City. He was indicted for prison escape.

During its case-in-chief, the United States proved the essential elements of the crime, including his lawful confinement and the unlawful escape. In addition, it presented the testimony of the arresting FBI agents that Grayson, upon being apprehended, denied his true identity.

Grayson testified in his own defense. He admitted leaving the camp but asserted that he did so out of fear: "I had just been threatened with a large stick with a nail protruding through it by an inmate that was serving time at Allenwood, and I was scared, and I just ran." He testified that the threat was made in the presence of many inmates by prisoner Barnes who sought to enforce collection of a gambling debt and followed other threats and physical assaults made for the same purpose. Grayson called one inmate, who testified, "I heard [Barnes] talk to Grayson in a loud voice one day, but that's all. I never seen no harm, no hands or no shuffling whatsoever."

Grayson's version of the facts was contradicted by the Government's rebuttal evidence and by cross-examination on crucial aspects of his story. For example, Grayson stated that after crossing the prison fence he left his prison jacket by the side of the road. On re-cross, he stated that he also left his prison shirt but not his trousers. Government testimony showed that on the morning after the escape, a shirt marked with Grayson's number, a jacket and a pair of prison trousers were found outside a hole in the prison fence.[1] Grayson also testified on cross-examination, "I do believe that I phrased the rhetorical question to Captain Kurd, who was in charge of the [prison], and I think I said something if an inmate was being threatened by somebody, what would . . . he do. First of all he said he would want to know who it was." On further cross-examination, however, Grayson modified his description of the conversation. Captain Kurd testified that Grayson had never mentioned in any fashion threats from other inmates. Finally, the alleged assailant, Barnes, by then no longer an inmate, testified that Grayson had never owed him any money and that he had never threatened or physically assaulted Grayson.

The jury returned a guilty verdict, whereupon the District Judge ordered the United States Probation Office to prepare a presentence report. At the sentencing hearing, the judge stated:

> "I'm going to give my reasons for sentencing in this case with clarity, because one of the reasons may well be considered by a Court of Appeals to be impermissible; and although I could come into this Court Room and sentence this Defendant to a five-year prison term without any explanation at all, I think it is fair that I give the reasons so that if the Court of Appeals feels that one of the reasons which I am about to enunciate is an improper consideration for a trial judge, then the Court will be in a position to reverse this court and send the case back for resentencing.
>
> "In my view a prison sentence is indicated, and the sentence that the Court is going to impose is to deter you, Mr. Grayson, and others who are similarly situated. Secondly, *it is my view that your defense was a complete fabrication without the slightest merit whatsoever. I feel it is proper for me to consider that fact in the sentencing, and I will do so.*" (Emphasis added.)

He then sentenced Grayson to a term of two years imprisonment, consecutive to his unexpired sentence.[2]

* * *

II.

In Williams v. New York, 337 U.S. 241, 247, 69 S.Ct. 1079, 1083 (1949, Mr. Justice Black observed that the "prevalent modern phi-

1. The testimony regarding the prison clothing was important for reasons in addition to the light it shed on quality of recollection. Grayson stated that after unpremeditatedly fleeing the prison with no possessions and crossing the fence, he hitch-hiked to New York City—a difficult task for a man with no trousers. The United States suggested that by prearrangement Grayson met someone, possibly a woman friend, on the highway near the break in the fence and that this accomplice provided civilian clothes. It introduced evidence that the friend visited Grayson often at prison, including each of the three days immediately prior to his penultimate day in the camp.

2. The District Court in this Case could have sentenced Grayson for any period up to five years. 18 U.S. C. § 751(a).

losophy of penology [is] that the punishment should fit the offender and not merely the crime," and that, accordingly, sentences should be determined with an eye toward the "[r]eformation and rehabilitation of offenders." But it has not always been so. In the early days of the Republic, when imprisonment had only recently emerged as an alternative to the death penalty, confinement in public stocks and whipping in the town square, the period of incarceration was generally prescribed with specificity by the legislature. Each crime had its defined punishment. The "excessive rigidity of the [mandatory or fixed sentence] system" soon gave way in some jurisdictions, however, to a scheme permitting the sentencing judge—or jury—to consider aggravating and mitigating circumstances surrounding an offense, and, on that basis, to select a sentence within a *range* defined by the legislature. Nevertheless, the focus remained on the crime: each particular offense was to be punished in proportion to the social harm caused by it and according to the offender's culpability. . . . The purpose of incarceration remained, primarily, retribution and punishment.

Approximately a century ago, a reform movement asserting that the purpose of incarceration, and therefore the guiding consideration in sentencing, should be rehabilitation of the offender, dramatically altered the approach to sentencing. A fundamental proposal of this movement was a flexible sentencing system permitting judges and correctional personnel, particularly the latter, to set the release date of prisoners according to informed judgments concerning their potential for or actual rehabilitation and their likely recidivism. Indeed, the most extreme formulations of the emerging rehabilitation model, with its "reformatory sentence," posited "that convicts [regardless of the nature of their crime] can never be rightfully imprisoned except upon proof that it is unsafe for themselves and for society to leave them free, and when confined can never be rightfully released until they show themselves fit for membership in a free community." Lewis, The Indeterminate Sentence, 9 Yale L.J. 17, 27 (1899).

This extreme formulation, although influential, was not adopted unmodified by any jurisdiction. "The influences of legalism and realism were powerful enough . . . to prevent the enactment of this form of indeterminate sentencing. Concern for personal liberty, skepticism concerning administrative decisions about prisoner reformation and readiness for release, insistence upon the preservation of some measure of deterrent emphasis, and other such factors, undoubtedly, led, instead, to a system—indeed, a complex of systems—in which maximum terms were generally employed." Thus it is that today the extent of a federal prisoner's confinement is initially determined by the sentencing judge, who selects a term within an often broad, congressionally prescribed range; release on parole is then available on review by the United States Parole Board, which, as a general rule, may conditionally release a prisoner any time after he serves one-third of the judicially fixed term. To an unspecified degree,[3] the sentencing judge is obligated to make his decision on the basis, among others, of predictions regarding the convicted defendant's potential, or lack of potential, for rehabilitation.[4]

Indeterminate sentencing under the rehabilitation model presented sentencing judges with a serious practical problem: how rationally to make the required predictions so as to avoid capricious and arbitrary sentences, which the newly conferred and broad discretion placed within the realm of possibility. An obvious although only partial, solution was to provide the judge with as much information as reasonably, practical concerning the defendant's "character and propensities[,] . . . his present purposes and tendencies," Pennsylvania ex rel. Sullivan v. Ashe, 302 U.S. 51, 55, 58 S.Ct. 59, 60 (1937), and, indeed, "every aspect of [his] life." Williams v. New York, supra, 337 U.S., at 250, 69 S.Ct., at 1084. Thus, most jurisdictions provided trained probation officers to conduct pre-sentence investigations of the defendant's life and, on that basis, prepare a presentence report for the sentencing judge.

* * *

Of course, a sentencing judge is not limited to the often far-ranging material compiled in a presentence report. "[B]efore making [the sentencing] determination, a judge may appropriately conduct an inquiry broad in scope, largely unlimited either as to the kind of information he may consider or the source from which it may come." United States v. Tucker, 404 U.S. 443, 446, 92 S.Ct. 589, 591 (1972).

* * *

. . . Thus, we have acknowledged that a sentencing authority may legitimately consider the evidence heard during trial, as well as the demeanor of the accused. More to the point presented in this case, one serious study has concluded that the trial judge's "opportunity to observe the defendant, particularly if he chose to take the stand in his defense, can often provide useful insights into an appropriate disposition." ABA, Standards Relating to Sentencing Alternatives and Procedures, § 5.1, at 232 (1971).

---

3. See Task Force on Criminal Sentencing [Fair and Certain Punishment 74 (1976)]:

"In the United States today, rehabilitative assumptions play some role in determining whether and for how long defendants have to be confined, but the precise weight given to such assumptions varies enormously among judges."

But to some of the most thoughtful and experienced correctional authorities, the optimistic predictions of earlier years on the efficacy of rehabilitation are undergoing reappraisal. . . .

4. See Shimm, Foreward, 23 Law & Contemp.Prob. 399 (1958):

"Signalizing on the one hand, the termination of the trial phase, sentencing must accurately reflect the community's attitude toward the misconduct of which the offender has been adjudged guilty, and thereby ratify and reinforce community values. Marking, on the other hand, the threshold of the sanction of treatment phase, however, and largely defining its character and length, sentencing must also look to the offender's rehabilitation, to his restoration as a functioning, productive, responsible member of the community."

A defendant's truthfulness or mendacity while testifying on his own behalf, almost without exception, has been deemed probative of his attitudes toward society and prospects for rehabilitation and hence relevant to sentencing.

* * *

A "universal and persistent" foundation stone in our system of law, and particularly in our approach to punishment, sentencing and incarceration, is the "belief in freedom of the human will and a consequent ability and duty of the normal individual to choose between good and evil." Morissette v. United States, 342 U.S. 246, 250, 72 S. Ct. 240, 243 (1952) . . . . Given that long accepted view of the "ability and duty of the normal individual to choose," we must conclude that the defendant's readiness to lie under oath—especially when, as here, the trial court finds the lie to be flagrant—may be deemed probative of his prospects for rehabilitation.

III.

Against this background we evaluate Grayson's constitutional argument that the District Court's sentence constitutes punishment for the crime of perjury for which he has not been indicted, tried or convicted by due process. A second argument is that permitting consideration of perjury will "chill" defendants from exercising their right to testify on their own behalf.

A

In his due process argument, Grayson does not contend directly that the District Court had an impermissible purpose in considering his perjury and selecting the sentence. Rather, he argues that this Court, in order to preserve due process rights, not only must prohibit the impermissible sentencing practice of incarcerating for the purpose of saving the Government the burden of bringing a separate and subsequent perjury prosecution but also must prohibit the otherwise *permissible* practice of considering a defendant's untruthfulness for the purpose of illuminating his need for rehabilitation and society's need for protection. He presents two interrelated reasons. The effect of both permissible and impermissible sentencing practices may be the same: additional time in prison. Further, it is virtually impossible, he contends, to identify and establish the impermissible practice. We find these reasons insufficient justification for prohibiting what the Court and the Congress have declared appropriate judicial conduct.

First, the evolutionary history of sentencing, demonstrates that it is proper—indeed, even necessary for the rational exercise of discretion—to consider the defendant's whole person and personality, as manifested by his conduct at trial and his testimony under oath, for whatever light those may shed on the sentencing decision. The "parlous" effort to appraise "character," degenerates into a game of chance to the extent that a sentencing judge is deprived of relevant information concerning "every aspect of a defendant's life." The

Government's interest, as well as the offender's, in avoiding irrationality is of the highest order. That interest more than justifies the risk that Grayson asserts is present when a sentencing judge considers a defendant's untruthfulness under oath.

Second, in our view, *Williams* fully supports consideration of such conduct in sentencing. There the Court permitted the sentencing judge to consider the offender's history of prior antisocial conduct, including burglaries for which he had not been duly convicted. This it did despite the risk that the judge might use his knowledge of the offender's prior crimes for an improper purpose.

Third, the efficacy of Grayson's suggested "exclusionary rule" is open to serious doubt. No rule of law, even one garbed in constitutional terms, can prevent improper use of firsthand observations of perjury. The integrity of the judges, and their fidelity to their oaths of office, necessarily provide the only, and in our view, adequate, assurance against that.

B

Grayson's argument that judicial consideration of his conduct at trial impermissibly "chills" a defendant's statutory right, and perhaps a constitutional right to testify on his own behalf is without basis. The right guaranteed by law to a defendant is narrowly the right to testify truthfully in accordance with the oath—unless we are to say that the oath is mere ritual without meaning. This view of the right involved is confirmed by the unquestioned constitutionality of perjury statutes, which punish those who willfully give false testimony. . . . Further support for this is found in an important limitation on a defendant's right to the assistance of counsel: counsel ethically cannot assist his client in presenting what the attorney has reason to believe is false testimony. . . . Assuming, *arguendo*, that the sentencing judge's consideration of defendants' untruthfulness in testifying has any chilling effect on a defendant's decision to testify falsely, that effect is entirely permissible. There is no protected right to commit perjury.

Grayson's further argument that the sentencing practice challenged here will inhibit exercise of the right to testify truthfully is entirely frivolous. That argument misapprehends the nature and scope of the practice we find permissible. Nothing we say today requires a sentencing judge to enhance, in some wooden or reflex fashion, the sentences of all defendants whose testimony is deemed false. Rather, we are reaffirming the authority of a sentencing judge to evaluate carefully a defendant's testimony on the stand, determine— with a consciousness of the frailty of human judgment—whether that testimony contained willful and material falsehoods, and, if so, assess in light of all the other knowledge gained about the defendant the meaning of that conduct with respect to his prospects for rehabilitation and restoration to a useful place in society. Awareness of such a process realistically cannot be deemed to affect the decision of an accused but unconvicted defendant to testify truthfully in his own behalf.

Accordingly, we reverse the judgment of the Court of Appeals and remand for reinstatement of the sentence of the District Court.

Reversed.

MR. JUSTICE STEWART, with whom MR. JUSTICE BRENNAN and MR. JUSTICE MARSHALL join, dissenting.

The Court begins its consideration of this case with the assumption that the respondent gave false testimony at his trial. But there has been no determination that his testimony was false. This respondent was given a greater sentence than he would otherwise have received—how much greater we have no way of knowing—solely because a single judge *thought* that he had not testified truthfully. In essence, the Court holds today that *whenever* a defendant testifies in his own behalf and is found guilty, he opens himself to the possibility of an enhanced sentence. Such a sentence is nothing more nor less than a penalty imposed on the defendant's exercise of his constitutional and statutory rights to plead not guilty and to testify in his own behalf.

It does not change matters to say that the enhanced sentence merely reflects the defendant's "prospects for rehabilitation" rather than an additional punishment for testifying falsely.[1] The fact remains that all defendants who choose to testify, and only those who do so, face the very real prospect of a greater sentence based upon the trial judge's unreviewable perception that the testimony was untruthful. The Court prescribes no limitations or safeguards to minimize a defendant's rational fear that his truthful testimony will be perceived as false. Indeed, encumbrance of the sentencing process with the collateral inquiries necessary to provide such assurance would be both pragmatically unworkable and theoretically inconsistent with the assumption that the trial judge is merely considering one more piece of information in his overall evaluation of the defendant's prospects for rehabilitation. But without such safeguards I fail to see how the Court can dismiss as "frivolous" the argument that this sentencing practice will "inhibit the right to testify truthfully."

A defendant's decision to testify may be inhibited by a number of considerations, such as the possibility that damaging evidence not otherwise admissible will be admitted to impeach his credibility. These constraints arise solely from the fact that the defendant is quite properly treated like any other witness who testifies at trial.

---

1. Indeed, without doubting the sincerity of trial judges one may doubt whether the single incident of a defendant's trial testimony could ever alter the assessment of rehabilitative prospects so drastically as to justify a perceptibly greater sentence. A sentencing judge has before him a presentence report, compiled by trained personnel, that is designed to paint as complete a picture of the defendant's life and character as is possible. If the defendant's suspected perjury is consistent with the evaluation of the report, its impact on the rehabilitative assessment must be minimal. If, on the other hand, it suggests such a markedly different character that different sentencing treatment seems appropriate, the defendant is *effectively* being punished for perjury without even the barest rudiments of due process.

But the practice that the Court approves today actually places the defendant at a disadvantage, as compared with any other witness at trial, simply because he is the defendant. Other witnesses risk punishment for perjury only upon indictment and conviction in accord with the full protections of the Constitution. Only the defendant himself, whose testimony is likely to be of critical importance to his defense, faces the additional risk that the disbelief of a single listener will itself result in time in prison.

The minimal contribution that the defendant's possibly untruthful testimony might make to an overall assessment of his potential for rehabilitation cannot justify imposing this additional burden on his right to testify in his own behalf. I do not believe that a sentencing judge's discretion to consider a wide range of information in arriving at an appropriate sentence allows him to mete out additional punishment to the defendant simply because of his personal belief that the defendant did not testify truthfully at the trial.

Accordingly, I would affirm the judgment of the Court of Appeals.

(b) AFTER TRIAL

ROBERTS v. UNITED STATES

Supreme Court of the United States, 1980.
— U.S. —, 100 S.Ct. 1358.

MR. JUSTICE POWELL delivered the opinion of the Court.

The question is whether the District Court properly considered, as one factor in imposing sentence, the petitioner's refusal to cooperate with officials investigating a criminal conspiracy in which he was a confessed participant.

I

Petitioner Winfield Roberts accompanied Cecilia Payne to the office of the United States Attorney for the District of Columbia one day in June of 1975. Government surveillance previously had revealed that a green Jaguar owned by Payne was used to transport heroin within the District. Payne told investigators that she occasionally lent the Jaguar to petitioner, who was waiting outside in the hall. At Payne's suggestion the investigators asked petitioner if he would answer some questions. Although petitioner was present voluntarily, the investigators gave him the warnings required by Miranda v. Arizona, 384 U.S. 436 (1966). They also told him that he was free to leave. When petitioner indicated that he would stay, the investigators asked whether he knew "Boo" Thornton, then the principle target of the heroin investigation. Petitioner admitted that he had delivered heroin to Thornton on several occasions. Confessing also that he had discussed drug transactions with Thornton in certain intercepted telephone conversations, petitioner explained the meaning of code words used in the conversations. When asked to name suppliers, however, petitioner gave evasive answers. Although the investigators warned petitioner that the extent of his cooperation would bear on the charges brought against him, he provided no further information.

*   *   *

[Roberts eventually pleaded guilty to two counts of using a telephone to facilitate the distribution of heroin]. The District Court imposed consecutive sentences of one to four years on each count and a special parole term of three years, but it declined to impose a fine. The Court explained that these sentences were appropriate because petitioner was on parole from a bank robbery conviction at the time of the offenses, and because he was a dealer who had refused to cooperate with the Government.

*   *   *

II

*   *   * Two Terms ago, we reaffirmed the "fundamental sentencing principle" that " 'a judge may appropriately conduct an inquiry broad in scope, largely unlimited either as to the kind of information he may consider, or the source from which it may come.' " United States v. Grayson [(1978)] . . . We have, however, sustained due process objections to sentences imposed on the basis of "misinformation of constitutional magnitude." . . .

No such misinformation was present in this case. The sentencing court relied upon essentially undisputed facts. There is no question that petitioner rebuffed repeated requests for his cooperation over a period of three years. Nor does petitioner contend that he was unable to provide the requested assistance. . . . Unless a different explanation is provided, a defendant's refusal to assist in the investigation of ongoing crimes gives rise to an inference that these laudable attitudes are lacking.

It hardly could be otherwise. Concealment of crime has been condemned throughout our history. The citizen's duty to "raise the 'hue and cry' and report felonies to the authorities," . . . Although the term "misprision of felony" now has an archaic ring, gross indifference to the duty to report known criminal behavior remains a badge of irresponsible citizenship.

This deeply rooted social obligation is not diminished when the witness to crime is involved in illicit activities himself. Unless his silence is protected by the privilege against self-incrimination, see Part III, infra, the criminal defendant no less than any other citizen is obliged to assist the authorities. The petitioner, for example, was asked to expose the purveyors of heroin in his own community in exchange for a favorable disposition of his case. By declining to cooperate, petitioner rejected an "obligatio[n] of community life" that should be recognized before rehabilitation can begin. Moreover, petitioner's refusal to cooperate protected his former partners in crime, thereby preserving his ability to resume criminal activities upon release.

* * *

III

Petitioner does not seriously contend that disregard for the obligation to assist in a criminal investigation is irrelevant to the determination of an appropriate sentence. He rather contends that his failure to cooperate was justified by legitimate fears of physical retaliation and self-incrimination. In view of these concerns, petitioner asserts that his refusal to act as an informer has no bearing on his prospects for rehabilitation. He also believes that the District Court punished him for exercising his Fifth Amendment privilege against self-incrimination.

These arguments would have merited serious consideration if they had been presented properly to the sentencing judge. But the mere possibility of unarticulated explanations or excuses for antisocial conduct does not make that conduct irrelevant to the sentencing decision. The District Court had no opportunity to consider the theories that petitioner now advances, for each was raised for the first time in petitioner's appellate brief. Although petitioner knew that his intransigency would be used against him, neither he nor his lawyer offered any explanation to the sentencing court. Even after the prosecutor observed that the failure to cooperate could be viewed as evidence of continuing criminal intent, petitioner remained silent.

Petitioner insists that he had a constitutional right to remain silent and that no adverse inferences can be drawn from the exercise of that right. We find this argument singularly unpersuasive. The Fifth Amendment privilege against compelled self-incrimination is not self-executing. At least where the government has no substantial reason to believe that the requested disclosures are likely to be incriminating, the privilege may not be relied upon unless it is invoked in a timely fashion. . . .

* * *

Petitioner would avoid the force of this elementary rule by arguing that *Miranda* warnings supplied additional protection for his right to remain silent. But the right to silence described in those warnings derives from the Fifth Amendment and adds nothing to it. Although *Miranda*'s requirement of specific warnings creates a limited exception to the rule that the privilege must be claimed, the exception does not apply outside the context of the inherently coercive custodial interrogations for which it was designed. The warnings protect persons who, exposed to such interrogation without the assistance of counsel, otherwise might be unable to make a free and informed choice to remain silent.

* * *

Petitioner has identified nothing that might have impaired his " 'free choice to admit, to deny, or to refuse to answer.' " His conduct bears no resemblance to the "insolubly ambiguous" post-arrest silence that may be induced by the assurances contained in *Miranda* warnings. We conclude that the District Court committed no constitutional error. If we were to invalidate petitioner's sentence on the record before us, we would sanction an unwarranted interference with a function traditionally vested in the trial courts. Accordingly, the judgment of the Court of Appeals is

Affirmed.

MR. JUSTICE BRENNAN, concurring.

I join the Court's opinion.

The principal divisive issue in this case is whether petitioner's silence should have been understood to imply continued solicitude for his former criminal enterprise, rather than assertion of the Fifth Amendment right against self-incrimination or fear of retaliation. I agree with the Court that the trial judge cannot be faulted for drawing a negative inference from petitioner's noncooperation when petitioner failed to suggest that other, neutral, inferences were available.

*   *   *

Nevertheless, the problem of drawing inferences from an ambiguous silence is troubling. As a matter of due process, an offender may not be sentenced on the basis of mistaken facts or unfounded assumptions. . . . It is of comparable importance to assure that a defendant is not penalized on the basis of groundless inferences. At the least, sentencing judges should conduct an inquiry into the circumstances of silence where a defendant indicates before sentencing that his refusal to cooperate is prompted by constitutionally protected, or morally defensible, motives. Furthermore, especially where conviction is based upon a guilty plea, it may be advisable for trial judges to raise the question of motive themselves when presented with a prosecutorial recommendation for severity due to an offender's noncooperation. During the allocution before sentencing, the defendant could be asked on the record whether he has a reasonable explanation for his silence; if a justification were proffered, the judge would then proceed to determine its veracity and reasonableness. Such an allocution procedure would reduce the danger of erroneous inference and provide a record to support sentencing against subsequent challenge. . . .

MR. JUSTICE MARSHALL, dissenting.

The Court today permits a term of imprisonment to be increased because of a defendant's refusal to identify others involved in criminal activities—a refusal that was not unlawful and that may have been motivated by a desire to avoid self-incrimination or by a reasonable fear of reprisal. I do not believe that a defendant's failure to inform on others may properly be used to aggravate a sentence of imprisonment, and accordingly, I dissent.

* * *

There can be no doubt that a judge would be barred from increasing the length of a jail sentence because of a defendant's refusal to cooperate based on the constitutional privilege against self-incrimination. In such a case, the threat of a longer sentence of imprisonment would plainly be compulsion within the meaning of the Fifth Amendment. Such an aggravation of sentence would amount to an impermissible penalty imposed solely because of the defendant's assertion of the Fifth Amendment privilege.

I also believe that it would be an abuse of discretion for a judge to use a defendant's refusal to become an informer to increase the length of a sentence when the refusal was motivated by a fear of retaliation. In such a case, the failure to identify other participants in the crime is irrelevant to the defendant's prospects for rehabilitation, and bears no relation to any of the legitimate purposes of sentencing.

* * *

The enhancement of petitioner's sentence, then, was impermissible because it may have burdened petitioner's exercise of his constitutional rights or been based on a factor unrelated to the permissible goals of sentencing. In addition, it represented an improper involvement of the judicial office in the prosecutorial function that should be corrected through our supervisory power over the federal courts.

* * *

I find disturbing the majority's willingness to brush aside these serious objections to the propriety of petitioner's sentence on the strength of "the duty to report known criminal behavior."

* * *

American society has always approved those who own up to their wrongdoing and vow to do better, just as it has admired those who come to the aid of the victims of criminal conduct. But our admiration of those who inform on others has never been as unambiguous as the majority suggests. The countervailing social values of loyalty and personal privacy have prevented us from imposing on the citizenry at large a duty to join in the business of crime detection. If the Court's view of social mores were accurate, it would be hard to understand how terms such as "stoolpigeon," "snitch," "squealer," and "tattletale" have come to be the common description of those who engage in such behavior.

I do not, of course, suggest that those who have engaged in criminal activity should refuse to cooperate with the authorities. The informer plays a vital role in the struggle to check crime, especially the narcotics trade. We could not do without him. In recognition of this role, it is fully appropriate to encourage such behavior by offering leniency in exchange for "cooperation." Cooperation of that sort may be a sign of repentance and the beginning of rehabilitation. But our government has allowed its citizens to decide for themselves whether to enlist in the enterprise of enforcing the criminal laws; it has never imposed a duty to do so, as the Court's opinion suggests. I find no justification for creating such a duty in this case and applying it only to persons about to be sentenced for a crime.

* * *

NOTES

1. Although he should give consideration to the major factors involved in punishment—deterrence, rehabilitation and retribution—a trial judge has monumental discretion in sentencing. See M. Frankel, Criminal Sentences (1972); Wyzanski, A Trial Judge's Freedom and Responsibility, 65 Harv.L.Rev. 1281 (1952). For review of factors that have been approved by the courts in aggravation of sentence, see United States v. Doyle, 348 F. 2d 715 (2d Cir. 1965) (criminal record); Cross v. United States, 122 U.S. App.D.C. 380, 354 F.2d 512 (1965) (intimidation of witnesses). Generally, however, appellate courts circumvent the issue by concluding that the trial judge could not have possibly relied upon an item mentioned at the sentence hearing in reaching its conclusion. See United States v. Lehman, 468 F.2d 93 (7th Cir. 1972) (refusal to plead guilty); United States v. Mitchell, 392 F.2d 314 (2d Cir. 1968) (defendant's agnosticism).

2. Where two or more sentences are imposed either upon separate counts or separate indictments, they are deemed to run concurrent in the absence of an express directive to the contrary. Schultz v. United States, 384 F.2d 374 (5th Cir. 1967); Puccinelli v. United States, 5 F.2d 6 (9th Cir. 1925). However, where a defendant is serving a state sentence at the time of federal disposition, the federal sentence cannot be made concurrent to the existing state sentence. Joslin v. Mosley, 420 F.2d 1204 (10th Cir. 1969); Hash v. Henderson, 385 F.2d 475 (8th Cir. 1967). In the converse situation, where a state sentence is made concurrent to a federal sentence, but federal officials do not take defendant into custody, and he serves his entire state sentence, must he receive credit for the time served against his federal sentence? Compare United States v. Croft, 450 F.2d 1094 (6th Cir. 1971) (yes) with Opela v. United States, 415 F.2d 231 (5th Cir. 1969) (no).

3. Where sentences are worded in a manner susceptible to various interpretations, appellate courts will seek to determine the intent of the trial judge at the time sentence was passed. Ziebart v. Hunter, 177 F.2d 847 (10th Cir. 1949); Hode v. Sanford, 101 F.2d 290 (5th Cir. 1939). If a sentence is ambiguous, the trial judge has the power to recall the defendant to clarify the ambiguity in the original sentence without double jeopardy infringement. United States v. Solomon, 468 F.2d 848 (7th Cir. 1972).

Double jeopardy claims arise with some degree of frequency, however, where a judge imposes consecutive sentences on separate counts. It is undisputed that the trial judge has inherent power to impose consecutive sentences. Harris v. United States, 359 U.S. 19, 79 S.Ct. 560 (1959); Swepston v. United States, 289 F.2d 166 (8th Cir. 1961). However, if one continuous course of conduct is charged in several counts, the imposition of consecutive sentences is violative of the double jeopardy clause. See Ingram v. United States, 122 U.S.App.D.C. 334, 353 F.2d 872 (1965).

4. Several states have followed the ABA's recommendation to develop specific statutory standards for courts to consider in aggravation or mitigation of sentence. Consider Ill.Rev.Stat. Ch. 38, §§ 1005–5–3.1 and 3.2.

1005–5–3.1. Factors in Mitigation

(a) The following grounds shall be accorded weight in favor of withholding or minimizing a sentence of imprisonment:

(1) the defendant's criminal conduct neither caused nor threatened serious physical harm to another;

(2) the defendant did not contemplate that his criminal conduct would cause or threaten serious physical harm to another;

(3) the defendant acted under a strong provocation;

(4) there were substantial grounds tending to excuse or justify the defendant's criminal conduct, though failing to establish a defense;

(5) the defendant's criminal conduct was induced or facilitated by someone other than the defendant;

(6) the defendant has compensated or will compensate the victim of his criminal conduct for the damage or injury that he sustained;

(7) the defendant has no history of prior delinquency or criminal activity or has led a law-abiding life for a substantial period of time before the commission of the present crime;

(8) the defendant's criminal conduct was the result of circumstances unlikely to recur;

(9) the character and attitudes of the defendant indicate that he is unlikely to commit another crime;

(10) the defendant is particularly likely to comply with the terms of a period of probation;

(11) the imprisonment of the defendant would entail excessive hardship to his dependents;

(12) the imprisonment of the defendant would endanger his or her medical condition.

(b) If the court, having due regard for the character of the offender, the nature and circumstances of the offense and the public interest finds that a sentence of imprisonment is the most appropriate disposition of the offender, or where other provisions of this Code mandate the imprisonment of the offender, the grounds listed in paragraph (a) of this subsection shall be considered as factors in mitigation of the term imposed.

1005–5–3.2. Factors in Aggravation

(a) The following factors shall be accorded weight in favor of imposing a term of imprisonment or may be considered by the court as reasons to impose a more severe sentence . . . :

(1) the defendant's conduct caused or threatened serious harm;

(2) the defendant received compensation for committing the offense;

(3) the defendant has a history of prior delinquency or criminal activity;

(4) the defendant, by the duties of his office or by his position, was obliged to prevent the particular offense committed or to bring the offenders committing it to justice;

(5) the defendant held public office at the time of the offense, and the offense related to the conduct of that office;

(6) the defendant utilized his professional reputation or position in the community to commit the offense, or to afford him an easier means of committing it;

(7) the sentence is necessary to deter others from committing the same crime.

(b) The following factors may be considered by the court as reasons to impose [a sentence not to exceed twice the maximum provided] upon any offender who was at least 17 years old on the date the crime was committed:

(1) When a defendant is convicted of any felony, after having been previously convicted in Illinois of the same or greater class felony, within 10 years, excluding time spent in custody, and such charges are separately brought and tried and arise out of different series of acts; or

(2) When a defendant is convicted of any felony and the court finds that the offense was accompanied by exceptionally brutal or heinous behavior indicative of wanton cruelty.

Are there any factors which should be added to these lists? Are there any factors currently in the statutes which should be removed? See Coffee, The Repressed Issue of Sentencing: Accountability, Predictability, and Equality in the Era of the Sentencing Commission, 66 Geo.L.J. 995 (1978).

C. SENTENCE DISPARITIES

JUNG v. STATE

Supreme Court of Wisconsin, 1966.
32 Wis. 541, 145 N.W.2d 684.

HALLOWS, JUSTICE.

[Did] . . . the trial court deny Jung the equal protection of the laws guaranteed by the Fourteenth Amendment to the United States Constitution by the sentences it imposed upon him?

Jung . . . contends his right to equal protection of the laws under the Fourteenth amendment was violated in his sentencing and therefore the trial court abused its discretion. We think a violation of a constitutional right in sentencing, even though the sentence is within the statutory limits for the offense, is error. An objection to a sentence on constitutional grounds is directed not to this court's superintending power over a trial court's administration of criminal justice, but to our appellate review power.

At common law, and until 1907 in England, an appellate court had no power of any kind to review a sentence within the maximum limits and until recently this theory was followed in this state. However, in State v. Tuttle (1963), 21 Wis.2d 147, 124 N.W.2d 9, this court departed from that view and recognized it had appellate power to review sentences. While we did not characterize the nature of the power, we pointed out the power existed, and its exercise would be governed by a strong policy against interference with the discretion of the trial court. In *Tuttle* we cited United States v. Wiley (7th Cir. 1960), 278 F.2d 500, but it is to be noted in that case that the power there exercised was the appellate court's "supervisory control of the district court, in aid of its appellate jurisdiction."

Usually questions involving equal protection of the laws in relation to criminal punishment are in the context of statutes providing for different punishments for different classes of offenders. Rubin, Disparity and Equality of Sentences—A Constitutional Challenge, 40 F.R.D. 55, 64 (1966). In this context it has been held equal protection of the laws requires that in the administration of criminal justice no one shall be subjected for the same offense to a greater or different punishment than that to which other persons of the same class are subjected. 21 Am.Jur.2d Criminal Law, p. 545, sec. 582. However, this does not mean that persons convicted of the same crime cannot be given different sentences depending upon their individual culpability and need for rehabilitation. Rubin, The Law of Criminal Correction, ch. 4, p. 115, sec. 4.

In reviewing a sentence for an abuse of discretion, we start with the presumption that the trial court acted reasonably and with the requirement that the complainant must show some unreasonable or unjustifiable basis in the record for the sentence complained of. Consequently, in the instant case there must be a showing that in determining the sentence of Jung the trial court based its determination upon factors not proper in or irrelevant to sentencing, or was influenced by motives inconsistent with impartiality. We must acknowledge that the standards guiding the imposition of criminal sentences and for testing the propriety of a sentence are not universally agreed upon.

Jung argues his constitutional right to equal protection of the laws was violated, since he was given a more severe sentence because he pleaded not guilty and stood trial, and that the disparity of such sentence with that of Thomas and Venson was not justified by his role in the crime or any indicated need for rehabilitation. Jung, as did Miles and Watkins who stood trial with him, received the maximum sentence of 30 years for armed robbery and consecutively the maximum sentence of 30 years for attempted murder, while Thomas on his plea of guilty received two concurrent 25-year sentences. Venson likewise received 25 years for armed robbery and was never charged with attempted murder.

On the issue of culpability, Jung points out he played a lesser role as the driver of the get-away car than Thomas who helped to plan the robbery and actually entered the supermarket with a sawed-off shotgun. Either Venson or Watkins originated the idea of the robbery and both of them cased the store on the morning of the day of the crime. Venson enlisted Thomas' help in the plot. The guns, furnished by Thomas, were transported from Racine in Venson's car. On this basis it is claimed that Jung's part in the robbery was no greater, and considerably less than, that of Thomas and Venson.

Jung had no prior criminal record and was a married man with five children. The record does not show whether Thomas and Venson had prior criminal records, but at the time of their sentencing Thomas also pleaded guilty to other unrelated counts of robbery and receiving stolen goods for which he received concurrent sentences of 20 and 25 years. Venson pleaded guilty to six other unrelated crimes including armed robbery and received various sentences of 20 years and 15 years, all to run concurrently, as in the case of Thomas, with the sentence on the May 5th armed robbery. Thomas and Venson, after being sentenced, were state witnesses against Jung.

The state argues Thomas and Venson received lighter sentences because they aided in the administration of justice and their guilty pleas and willingness to testify indicated they were willing to accept responsibility and were thus better candidates for rehabilitation. Whether these arguments are factually correct or not they raise the problem of the "bargain plea" or the "negotiated guilty plea" in relation to the Fourteenth amendment respecting codefendants who insist on their right to trial. It is common knowledge there is a wide practice in the courts of this country of accepting pleas of guilty and giving lighter sentences than are generally given for the same crime after a trial. The result of this practice and the problems involved are matters of current concern. . . .

A forceful argument is made that inherent in the practice of awarding reduced sentences following guilty pleas is discrimination against the defendant who pleads not guilty and is more severely punished for the same crime, and who is equally in need of reformation. Unless it can be shown in each case that a guilty plea is in fact evidence of repentance and demonstrates a readiness to accept responsibility for the criminal acts, it is difficult to see how a plea of guilty should be factor in giving a lenient sentence. It is a well-known fact there are more pleas of guilty than not guilty and more second offenders make a compromise or bargain for a guilty plea than do first offenders. These so-called deals may take the form of: (1) Pleading guilty to a reduced charge, (2) pleading guilty to the charge upon the promise or expectation of a recommendation for leniency, (3) concurrent sentences, and (4) dropped charges.

We see little justification for granting leniency to a criminal in exchange for co-operation in becoming a state's witness unless such action in fact is an expression of an incipient salutary character rather than a calculated hide-saving device. While such action on either motivation may assist the district attorney, reduce court backlogs and result in more economical administration of justice, these factors do not seem to have any direct relationship with incarceration as punishment or as a deterrent or for rehabilitation, or for protection of the public.

On the other side of the coin, it is argued that a plea of not guilty followed by conviction may justify additional punishment because: (1) It displays an uncooperative attitude, (2) the defendant presumably committed perjury, (3) the defendant asserted a frivolous defense, (4) the trial revealed circumstances of the crime which might not have been disclosed on a plea of guilty, or (5) the plea did not contribute to an efficient administration of justice. We question the validity of these reasons as a basis for increasing the severity of a sentence; certainly they may be invalid in a given case. See, The Influence of the Defendant's Plea on Judicial Determination of Sentence, 66 Yale Law Journal 204, 209 (1956).

In the instant case, although there is great disparity in the sentences, the present record does not show the trial judge in sentencing Jung after his trial based it upon any of these considerations. In this respect the facts are to be distinguished from those in United States v. Wiley (7th Cir. 1959), 267 F.2d 453 (1960); 278 F.2d 500. The punishment imposed by the district court on Wiley was in part for his plea of not guilty and assertion of his right to a trial, and only in part for the crime of which he was convicted. As stated in the concurring opinion in the second *Wiley* case, "A defendant in a criminal case should not be punished by a heavy sentence merely because he exercises his constitutional right to be tried before an impartial judge or jury."

The statement of the trial court in sentencing Jung shows that his plea was not a factor. The trial judge stated the robbery was carefully planned, dangerous to the public, and performed by a gang. The trial court was intent upon discouraging gang operations, especially gang-executed armed robberies. The trial judge indicated the three defendants were in open warfare with society which could not be tolerated and took calculated risks. He considered they came to the neighborhood of the supermarket as a gang and operated as a gang, and because of their association and of the nature of the crime they were equally culpable regardless of their component roles in the robbery. We cannot say the trial judge was unreasonable in considering all participants, whether they carried a gun or not, as equally guilty of armed robbery. It was an organized adventure with all participants running the calculated risk that the gun a colleague carried might necessarily be used in the perpetration of the crime. Under this theory Jung, even though he did not have a gun in his possession, was also equally culpable of the attempted murder. On this view, Thomas' sentence was too lenient, rather than Jung's being too severe.

The trial judge stated he was not sure what deterrent effect the sentences were going to have, but he imposed the sentences partly for that reason. He did not consider them excessive sentences, because under our parole system the defendant's future was not foreclosed and was in fact "flexible." In this respect we note that Jung will become eligible for parole after two years while Thomas and Venson will be eligible for parole after one year. However, Jung's conditional-release date will be approximately 15 years later than those of Thomas and Venson and for the 60 years Jung will be subject to the sentence even if paroled.

Disparity in sentencing standing alone does not violate due process, nor has it been a basis up to now for relief on other grounds in the federal courts or in this court. Simpson v. United States (7th Cir. 1965), 342 F.2d 643; United States v. De Marie (7th Cir. 1958), 261 F.2d 477. Although the disparity in the sentences is great, we do not find that the reason therefor is because Jung insisted on his right to a trial by jury. In this respect this case is unlike *Tuttle* where the record showed the insistence upon a jury trial was partly the reason for an increased sentence over that which would have been received on a plea of guilty. We do not agree with Jung's argument that because the sentence which followed the plea of guilty of Thomas and Venson is less severe than the sentence given him following his trial and conviction his sentence was necessarily caused by his insistence upon his constitutional right to a trial by jury. This is a *post hoc ergo propter hoc* argument.

Equality of treatment under the Fourteenth amendment in respect to sentencing does not destroy the individualization of sentencing to fit the individual. It requires substantially the same sentence for persons having substantially the same case histories. We find neither error in the disparity of the sentence based upon a denial of a constitutional right nor abuse of discretion based upon the severity of the sentence.

Judgment affirmed.

CURRIE, CHIEF JUSTICE (concurring).

I concur in the result that this is not a proper case in which this court should interfere with the trial court's exercise of discretion in sentencing plaintiff in error Jung. However, I am disturbed by some of the implications of the majority opinion.

If, where a gang of criminals combine to perpetrate a crime, it appears necessary to the state to grant immunity to one of the gang in order to secure his testimony to convict the other defendants, there is no denial of the equal-protection-of-the-laws clause of the Fourteenth amendment in imposing sentences of imprisonment on the remaining members of the gang who are convicted. This being true, it necessarily follows that there would be no denial of equal-protection-of-the-laws to impose a lesser sentence to one of the gang who cooperates with the state without grant of immunity and testifies in favor of the state. While the record before us does not positively establish that this was the basis of the lesser sentences imposed on Thomas and Venson, it strongly suggests that this is the case.

Furthermore, I believe the two *Wiley* cases, should be restricted to their own facts. All those two cases hold is that a different sentence cannot be imposed on two defendants charged with the same crime *solely* on the basis that one pleads guilty and the other not guilty. The court took pains to point out that Wiley, who plead not guilty and had a trial, interposed a legal defense, so there was no possibility of his having committed perjury. In the first *Wiley* case, the court stated:

> ". . . the defense certainly was not frivolous nor does it appear to have been presented in bad faith."

This extract was again quoted with approval in the second *Wiley* case. One who testifies falsely in his own defense certainly acts in "bad faith."

Rehabilitation is conceded to be one of the prime factors to be considered in sentencing a person convicted of crime. Therefore, a trial judge does not abuse his discretion when he metes out a more severe sentence to such a defendant than one who admits his guilt, pleads guilty, and exhibits contrition and a desire to conform his future conduct to the requirements of law. The trial judge can well conclude that such a person needs a lesser term of imprisonment to rehabilitate himself than the defendant who shows no remorse by perjuring himself in an attempt to avoid the infliction of any penalty. As I read the majority opinion it suggests that this may not be a proper basis for imposing a difference in sentence. I wholly disagree.

PEOPLE v. HENNE

Appellate Court of Illinois, 1973.
10 Ill.App.3d 179, 293 N.E.2d 172.

THOMAS J. MORAN, JUSTICE.

A jury found defendant, Willie B. Henne (and co-defendants Tracy Stewart, James DePaolo and John Weisz) guilty of burglary and theft. Henne was sentenced to serve from seven to twenty-one years in the penitentiary.

* * *

Defendant [claims] that his sentence was excessive and grossly disparate from that imposed upon co-defendant Stewart who, despite equal participation, received a one to four year sentence.

Upon sentencing Stewart, the trial judge rejected the State's recommendation of three to five years on the basis of the minimal amount of damage caused during the burglary and the small value of the tools stolen.

In sentencing Henne, the judge stated that he was not taking into consideration the additional crimes of escape and murder pending against defendant but was only considering "all previous convictions, including juvenile proceedings."

Reviewing the records of both Stewart and defendant, we find the gross disparity in sentencing was not justified. Henne, 23 years old, had, while a juvenile, committed some serious offenses such as arson, car theft, hit and run property damage and attempted escape from the Youth Authority. His last offense, however, was committed four years prior to the instant crime; since reaching maturity he has had no convictions. Stewart, 19 years old, had been convicted of two prior thefts, both occurring in the same year as the instant crime. Although the record indicates that defendant apparently escaped from the Sheriff's custody while awaiting sentencing, Stewart, who was on bond, did not appear for his hearing on aggravation and mitigation until a bench warrant had issued for his arrest.

Due to Henne's more serious misconduct, both as a juvenile and while awaiting sentencing, the trial court could have properly imposed a sentence greater than that given Stewart, but the record does not justify the extreme disparity. Fundamental fairness and respect for the law require that defendants similarly situated may not receive grossly disparate sentences. In this interest, we reduce defendant's sentence to a minimum of three to a maximum of nine years in the penitentiary.

Judgment affirmed as modified.

NOTES

1. While *Henne* was decided in a state which, by Supreme Court Rule, authorizes appellate review of sentences, as a general matter, appellate courts have consistently denied their own power to review sentences. See United States v. Rosenberg, 195 F.2d 583 (2d Cir. 1952). However, in exceptional situations there has been a trend moving away from that once completely accepted limitation on appellate review. See United States v. Wiley, 278 F.2d 500 (7th Cir. 1960); Leach v. United States, 334 F.2d 945 (D.C.Cir. 1964); United States v. Holder, 412 F.2d 212 (2d Cir. 1969). See generally Mueller & LaPoole, Appellate Review of Legal but Excessive Sentences: A Comparative Study, 21 Vand.L.Rev. 411 (1968). Should appellate courts, on the basis of the cold record, have the power to revise sentences? See United States v. McCord, 466 F.2d 17 (2d Cir. 1972).

2. What factors give rise to gross sentencing disparities between similarly situated defendants? See Coburn, Disparity in Sentences and Appellate Review of Sentencing, 25 Rutgers L.Rev. 207 (1971) (footnotes omitted):

> "Different social attitudes and conditions which exist in different places of conviction also contribute to disparity in sentencing. Strikingly, these geography-related factors exist not merely on a state-by-state, but also on a county-by-county basis. The least controllable intangible factor precipitating the sentence in any given case, however, is the background and personality of the trial judge. Other factors of varying influence are: the availability and quality of presentence investigations and reports, the existence of duplicate statutes, the use of 'indeterminate sentences,' whether the sentence is determined by the judge or jury, the racial or ethnic characteristics of the offender, and finally, whether the alleged crime was against a person or property."

See also Note, Statutory Structure for Sentencing Felons to Prison, 60 Colum.L.Rev. 1134 (1960).

3. In State v. DeStasio, 49 N.J. 247, 229 A.2d 636 (1967), the court considered a challenge to an administrative directive which it had issued concerning sentencing in gambling cases. The court had ordered the assignment judge in each county to personally impose sentence or designate a single judge to do so in all gambling cases. To defendant's claim that this system violated his constitutional rights, the court responded:

"Uniformity of treatment is an ideal of law enforcement. 'That different judges sentence differently is, and always has been, a major and justified complaint against the courts.' Report by the President's Commission on Law Enforcement and Administration of Justice, 'The Challenge of Crime in a Free Society' (Feb. 1967), p. 145. We have held judicial seminars in the hope that an exchange of views might lead to more uniformity in sentencing. Discussions between the sentencing judge and the probation department tend to assist in this direction. No doubt trial judges consult with one another in difficult cases to benefit from the experiences of each other, and this too can serve to reduce disparity in treatment. See Levin, 'Towards a More Enlightened Sentencing Procedure,' 45 Neb.L.Rev. 499 (1966). To the same end a dozen States have provided for appellate review of sentences, Report by the President's Commission, supra, p. 145, and we have considered such a program. Advocates of the indeterminate sentence find in such sentences a promise of uniformity of treatment.

"Syndicated gambling is an area within which uniformity can be approached. Unlike most crimes, the factual picture is itself quite uniform. A bookmaker is a bookmaker and a runner is a runner. The details of the criminal event are pretty much the same. The demeanor of the defendant on the stand, if he takes it, ordinarily is not critical. The feel of one case is pretty much the feel of most others. The presentence report sums up the crime and the offender.

"Even the circumstances of the individual offenders are more constant than in the case of most other crimes. By and large the defendants who are caught are not vicious and do not menace society in other respects, but they are the hired help of the syndicate without which it could not operate. The difficulty has been that some judges cannot see beyond the individual they are sentencing. If such a judge imposes nothing more painful than a fine, his view is almost certain to become the rule of the county in which he sits. This is so because defendants will wait for that judge, if they can, and plead guilty before him. Moreover, a soft judge can make a sensible one seem harsh and severe, and hence, unhappily, judges tend to abide by the performance of the most unrealistic among them. In other words, the very uniformity of both the offense and the situation of the offenders tends to make disparate treatment unmistakable and thereby to label judges with respect to their attitude toward these offenses.

"For these reasons, we decided as a matter of administrative policy to have all sentencing in these matters handled by a single judge in each county."

Is the procedure chosen by the New Jersey Supreme Court to eliminate disparities in gambling cases a wise course of action? Is it equally applicable to other types of offenses?

D.   SENTENCING ALTERNATIVES

STATE v. CORNWALL

Supreme Court of Idaho, 1974.
95 Idaho 680, 518 P.2d 863.

DONALDSON, JUSTICE.

Herman Ray Cornwall, . . . entered a plea of guilty to the charge of statutory rape. . . . He was subsequently sentenced to a term in the state penitentiary not to exceed fifteen years. From the imposition of that sentence he prosecutes this appeal.

. . . [T]he defendant was drinking in his home in Pocatello in the company of his older brother Phillip Cornwall. The victim, who was thirteen years of age at the time of the offense, was in the home as an overnight guest of defendant's daughter. Defendant and his brother had started drinking that afternoon shortly after work. During the course of the evening, they left the home to go to a local bar. They stayed at the bar until it closed and then returned home to drink some wine which defendant's brother had left there.

Upon returning home, they discovered that the victim and defendant's daughter had consumed the wine. The two men then persuaded the two girls to accompany them to Blackfoot where the brother, Phillip Cornwall, lived. The purpose of this trip was ostensibly to secure some beer which Phillip Cornwall had in his trailer. Upon arriving in Blackfoot, the two men went into the trailer while the two girls stayed in the car. After about ten minutes, defendant's daughter had need of the bathroom facilities so the two girls went into the trailer. The victim stayed in the living room with the two men while the defendant's daughter used the facilities in the bathroom. After some coaxing by the defendant, the victim accompanied him into the bedroom where the act of intercourse occurred. The defendant was not charged with accomplishing the act with force.

. . . The victim reported the incident to her mother who in turn reported it to the police.

. . . The presentence investigation report stated that defendant was of above normal intelligence, that he was not prone to violence, but that when exposed to alcohol his sense of moral values was diminished. The report stated that defendant was a fair risk for probation and recommended some punitive aspect in sentencing. The psychologist's report stated that defendant was above average intelligence, that he was not psychotic or neurotic, but that he did have a serious drinking problem. The report recommended that defendant be granted probation but that the terms of the probation be longer and stricter than usual. In addition, the report recommended continued counseling and a need for treatment of defendant's excessive drinking habits.

* * *

Although there was evidence to the contrary, [defendant's] wife testified that he was a good husband and father and that she would be willing to cooperate with the authorities should probation be granted. The trial court then imposed the sentence from which defendant appeals.

Defendant's first assignment of error is that the trial court abused its discretion in failing to consider probation for the defendant.

* * *

Certain guidelines have . . . been established which delineate what the trial court must consider in reaching its decision of whether to grant probation. The trial court must consider the following in arriving at its decision: (1) all the facts and circumstances surrounding the offense of which the applicant is convicted; (2) whether the applicant is a first offender; (3) the previous actions and character of the applicant; (4) whether the applicant might reasonably be expected to be rehabilitated; (5) whether it reasonably appears that the applicant will abide by the terms of the probation; and (6) the interests of society in being protected from possible future criminal conduct of the applicant. . . .

Defendant argues that the trial court failed to consider the following factors when it imposed a prison term rather than grant probation. (1) Defendant has a history of problems with alcohol, he committed the offense while intoxicated, he pleaded guilty to the charge, and there was no violence used in the attack. (2) Defendant has no prior felony convictions. His prior record consists only of a driving while intoxicated conviction and a reckless driving conviction. (3) Defendant has been steadily employed for six and one half years and his employer expressed a willingness to cooperate with the court. (4) The report of the psychologist recommended probation and the presentence investigation report stated that defendant was a fair probation risk but recommended some punitive aspect in the sentence. (5) Defendant expressed a willingness to conform to any probation program that might be established.

A review of the remarks made by the trial court before passing sentence shows clearly that the court did consider probation and did take those facts which it is required to under consideration in determining the proper sentence. Before imposing sentence upon defendant, the trial court stated:

* * *

"Now I don't know how, in dealing with a man who has done what you have done, I could ever make a finding of absolute certainty at this time that you would not again become involved in such a thing. I guess nobody knows that. We have to make our determination at this point. But, in light of what this record shows, I don't find anything that convinces me that you are a good probation risk at the point. I have to bear in mind that while you come before me with no prior felony, that none has actually occurred.

But I guess I have to accept a record that there is none, and that there have been no convictions.

* * *

"Now, in my opinion, it would demean the crime which you have committed if I were not to impose a sentence upon you to the State Board of Corrections, which would virtually mean that you're going to the penitentiary. We soft pedal the so-called deterrent effect as being not important anymore. Whatever remnants remain there, it still is a fact, in my opinion, that you are not at this point, a good probation risk; that society, at this point, is entitled to some protection against you until such time as the Board of Corrections might feel that you are a good probation risk."

Admittedly, the remarks of the trial court concerning defendant's prior record are open to interpretation, but it cannot be said that they constitute a clear showing of abuse of discretion. The statement of the court, taken as a whole, shows that it did consider the circumstances surrounding the offense, the fact that defendant was a first offender, with no prior felony convictions, whether or not defendant was a good candidate for probation, and the interests of society in being protected from possible future criminal conduct by defendant. Having considered these factors, defendant cannot complain because the court determined that probation should not be granted.

The defendant has no right to probation. The granting or withholding of probation rests entirely within the discretion of the trial court. If the exercise of that discretion is based upon reason rather than emotion, it will not be disturbed by this Court.

* * *

There appearing in the record no error or abuse of the trial court's discretion in imposing a prison term not to exceed fifteen years, that judgment is affirmed.

McQUADE, JUSTICE (concurring in part and dissenting in part).

I agree with the majority that the district court has wide discretion in the imposition of a sentence, but this action should be remanded to the district court for resentencing. The district court has the discretion to impose "probation under such terms and conditions as it deems necessary and expedient . . . ." To properly exercise its discretion, the district court has an obligation to insist that a positive plan for rehabilitation of the defendant be presented in the presentence report. The district court can only exercise its sentencing discretion when it is apprised of all the facts and circumstances concerning the defendant which includes his opportunities for rehabilitation.

The duty of the district court to demand a positive rehabilitation plan from the probation office before imposing a sentence also arises out of our cases holding the district court must consider the following factors in considering a request for probation:

"(1) All the facts and circumstances surrounding the offense of which the defendant is convicted; (2) whether the defendant is a first offender; (3) the previous actions and character of the defendant; (4) whether the defendant might reasonably be expected to be rehabilitated; and (5) whether it reasonably appears that the defendant will abide by the terms of the probation."

In order to evaluate these factors, the district court must have a presentence report that contains a positive rehabilitation plan.

* * *

To be at all useful to the district court, the rehabilitation recommendation must be a positive program for the defendant. It should recommend more than whether probation should or should not be granted, but rather it should set forth what steps need to be taken to prevent a reoccurrence of the defendant's criminal behavior. In formulating a positive plan of rehabilitation, the presentence report should explain the weaknesses and strengths of the defendant and it should explain how the rehabilitation program will rely on the defendant's strengths and correct his weaknesses.

* * *

As an example of what it means to formulate a positive rehabilitation plan, general recommendations will be set forth followed by the detailed information that must be included to make a "tailor-made" plan for the defendant. This list of general proposals is not by any means a complete list of the programs that can be formulated in a positive rehabilitation program.

1. PARTICIPATION IN ALCOHOLICS ANONYMOUS OR OTHER ALCOHOLIC REHABILITATION PROGRAMS

A rehabilitation plan suggesting the use of alcoholic treatment programs must specifically describe the suggested program, establish whether the defendant would qualify for the program, determine whether he can attend the meetings and set specific dates for his attendance, and estimate the duration of treatment and its chances for success. If other members of the defendant's family or his friends contribute to his alcoholism by their own alcoholism, it should be determined whether they are willing to participate in the program. Finally, the recommendation must explain why the alcoholism program will deter future criminal conduct by the defendant.

2. PSYCHOLOGICAL COUNSELING AND/OR GROUP COUNSELING

The availability of psychological counseling and group counseling for the defendant and his willingness to participate in it must be established. The counselor or group session must be named and an appointment schedule set up for the defendant. The probation officer and the counselor or group leader should submit short statements explaining why they believe the counseling will assist the defendant, and estimate the chances of success. The duration of the recommended counseling must be calculated and a means for financing the counseling must be set forth.

3. EDUCATION

The specific educational goals of the defendant, whether academic or vocational, must be set forth and their relevancy to his criminal behavior must be explained. The possibility of waiver of tuition and housing costs at state institutions should be investigated as well as the availability of counseling services on the campuses. The acceptance of the defendant into the named institution must be established, the courses he will attend described, and the means of payment discussed.

4. FAMILY COUNSELING

The possibility of family counseling services for the defendant and his family, and their willingness to participate in them must be determined. A schedule of counseling sessions should be established. A letter from the counselor explaining why his services would be beneficial to the defendant should be included with the recommendation in addition to the presentence investigator's appraisal of the need and benefit to be derived from family counseling.

5. FINANCIAL COUNSELING

In addition to setting forth the financial resources of the defendant, the presentence investigator should determine whether financial counseling is needed by the defendant and the availability of financial counseling should be established. Financial counseling will often be included in family counseling. The defendant's willingness to participate in financial counseling must be set forth as well as a schedule of meetings with the financial counselor.

6. CHURCH RELATED OR OTHER VOLUNTARY PROGRAMS DESIGNED TO ASSIST PERSONS TO DEAL WITH THEIR PROBLEMS

The availability of all community based services must be investigated and the defendant should be informed of these programs. Many of these programs should be considered in the context of assisting the defendant by involving his whole family in the program. If it is determined that specific programs would be helpful to the defendant, then a description of the program and how it relates to the defendant's criminal behavior must be included in the presentence report. A letter from the leader of the program stating how it will assist the defendant should also be included in the report.

In summary, a positive rehabilitation program must be a step by step schedule for the defendant to pursue. It must specifically set forth the needed services which have been investigated to insure that they are available to the defendant. A mere listing of possible programs that the defendant should be urged to participate in is meaningless and gives the district court no real guidance in the imposition of the sentence. If the presentence report fails to set forth a positive rehabilitation program for the defendant, it fails to fulfill the very purpose of recommending a "tailormade" plan of rehabilitation.

Even if the probation officer is unable to formulate a rehabilitation plan, he should prepare an exhaustive list of available community services to aid the court in sentencing.

The district courts have an active role in the formulation of presentence reports. They should request that specific rehabilitation programs be investigated, and if a presentence report does not contain a positive program of rehabilitation, they should require it to be formulated. The importance of the presentence report should also be stressed to the defendant and his attorney, and they should be urged to cooperate with the probation officer preparing the report and encouraged to submit their own plans for rehabilitation.

The district court has continuing jurisdiction over a defendant while he is on probation and can modify the terms of the probation at any time. In accordance with this continuing jurisdiction, the district court should require the probation officer to submit periodic (at least quarterly) follow-up reports which review the progress of the defendant under the court imposed probation plan, and if necessary, the probation plan could then be modified. The follow-up reports would provide the district court with a means of evaluating the reliability of the rehabilitation programs.

The defense counsel must play an active role in the formulation of presentence reports. This role arises out of their overall duty to their client. . . .

* * *

. . . Through the development of more specific rehabilitation plans by the probation officer and the defense attorney, the district court will have a wider range of sentences to choose from to avoid the "dismal failure" of the prison system.

NOTES

1. When a defendant is alleged to have violated the conditions of probation, he is brought before the court for a revocation hearing.

In Mempa v. Rhay, 389 U.S. 128, 88 S.Ct. 254 (1967), the defendant was placed on felony probation after his plea of guilty. Imposition of any other sentence was deferred and made contingent upon a violation of the conditions of probation. The Court held at a subsequent hearing where a violation was found and a mandatory sentence imposed, the defendant was entitled to be represented by counsel.

In Gagnon v. Scarpelli, 411 U.S. 778, 93 S.Ct. 1756 (1973), the defendant pleaded guilty and was sentenced to fifteen years' imprisonment. Sentence was suspended, however, and the defendant was placed on probation. The sentence would be executed only if a probation violation was determined to have occurred. The Court equated this situation to a parole-revocation situation, where the defendant serves a portion of a penitentiary sentence and then is released upon certain conditions. In neither situation, the Court declared, is there an absolute right to counsel. Rather "the decision as to the need for counsel must be made on a case-by-case basis in the exercise of a sound discretion by the state authority charged with responsibility for administering the probation and parole system." The Court said that in some cases but not most a state would be required to provide the indigent with counsel at revocation hearings.

Can probation be revoked upon the basis of evidence presented at a trial at which defendant was acquitted? See Johnson v. State, 242 S.E.2d 53 (Ga.1978) in which the court stated "Before a jury is authorized to convict, evidence must be presented which will establish guilt of the defendant beyond a reasonable doubt. Even when this is done a jury has the power to acquit. This quantum of evidence is not necessary to justify the revocation of a sentence of probation."

Is this consistent with fundamental fairness? What about issues of collateral estoppel? Compare People v. Grayson, 58 Ill.2d 260, 319 N.E.2d 43 (1974).

2. Sentences short of total confinement, such as periodic imprisonment and conditional discharge, are available in most states. Consider ABA Second Edition Tentative Draft of Standards on Sentencing Alternatives and Procedures

Standard 18–2.4. Intermediate sanctions

(a) Attention should be directed to the development of a range of sentencing alternatives which provide an intermediate sanction between supervised probation on the one hand and commitment to a total custody institution on the other. Examples of the types of dispositions which might be authorized are:

(i) commitment on an intermittent basis to a local facility which permits the offender to hold a regular job or to receive education or vocational training while subject to supervision or confinement on nights and weekends;

(ii) commitment to an institution for a short, fixed term, followed by automatic release under supervision;

(iii) a required term of community service, such as in a hospital or other public or charitable facility, or a sentence involving the performance of restitutionary services.

(b) The principles set forth in standard 18–2.3(b)–(f) should also apply to a sentence to partial confinement. Procedures applicable inside the institution of confinement are beyond the scope of these standards.

Under what circumstances should a sentence involving some form of incarceration other than total imprisonment be imposed? Are there any new forms of partial confinement which should be developed?

3. The prospect of imposing a fine in lieu of incarceration provides another sentencing alternative. Under what circumstances should a fine be imposed? In this connection, see ABA Standards on Sentencing Alternatives and Procedures, Second Edition Tentative Draft:

Standard 18–2.7. Fines

(a) The legislature should determine the offenses or categories of offenses for which a fine would be an appropriate sentence, and should state the maximum fine which can be imposed. Although fines should not be routinely imposed on most offenders and seldom should be used in in addition to a substantial period of incarceration, their use is recommended as a less drastic alternative to confinement, as a means of funding restitutionary programs, and as an appropriate deterrent where the defendant has gained money or property through the commission of the offense.

(b) Whether to impose a fine in a particular case, its amount up to the authorized maximum, and the method of payment should remain within the discretion of the sentencing authorities. The sentencing court should be explicitly authorized to permit installment payments of any imposed fine, on conditions tailored to the means of the particular offender.

(c) In determining whether to impose a fine and its amount, the court should consider:

(i) the financial resources of the defendant and the burden that payment of a fine will impose, with due regard to the defendant's other obligations;

(ii) the ability of the defendant to pay a fine on an installment basis or on other conditions to be fixed by the court;

(iii) the extent to which payment of a fine will interfere with the ability of the defendant to make any ordered restitution or reparation to the victim of the crime; and

(iv) whether there are particular reasons which make a fine appropriate as a deterrent to the offense involved or appropriate as an alternative to confinement of the defendant.

Revenue production is not a legitimate basis for imposing a fine.

(d) It would be appropriate for the legislature to endorse standards in the penal code such as those specified in paragraph (c). They are in any event commended to sentencing authorities as guides to the exercise of discretion.

(e) The court should not be authorized to impose alternative sentences, for example, "thirty dollars or thirty days." The effect of non-payment of a fine should be determined after the fine has not been paid and after examination of the reasons for nonpayment. The court's response to nonpayment should be governed by standard 18–7.4.

(f) In fixing the maximum fine for some offenses, the legislature should consider the feasibility of employing an index other than a dollar amount in cases where it might be appropriate. For example, a fine relative to the amount of the gain might be appropriate in cases where the defendant has profited by his or her crime, or a fine relative to sales, profits, or net annual income might be appropriate in some cases, such as business or antitrust offenses, in order to assure a reasonably even impact of the fine on defendants of variant means.

If a defendant is convicted of a $2 million armored car robbery, but the money is never found, what factors should the court rely upon in setting a fine? As to what happens when an indigent defendant cannot pay a fine imposed by the court, see Williams v. Illinois, Chapter 9, Section C.

4. Restitution is an emerging sentencing option in cases in which the defendant is able to pay. In People v. Jacobsohn, 60 A.D.2d 607, 400 N.Y. S.2d 136 (1977), defendant pled guilty to a misdemeanor larceny count and agreed to make restitution as part of a plea bargain in which felony counts would be dismissed and a three year probationary sentence imposed. However, when the court learned that defendant had paid $10,000 of the $68,000 he had embezzled and the insurance company had paid the balance,

a one year jail term was imposed. On appeal, the court modified the sentence to a three year term of probation, for the following reasons:

"It has been stated that a sentence must not only encompass the community's condemnation of the defendant's misconduct, but must also evaluate the possibilities of the defendant as a useful and responsible member of the community. Generally it is the community's gain whenever a family can be kept together as an integrated and emotionally satisfying unit with the head of the family meeting his responsibilities to it instead of unnecessarily marking time in jail. In this case the [Court] in the first instance, obviously was of the mind to follow such guideline when it stated at the taking of the plea, *inter alia,* that subject to reading the probation report, it would consider placing defendant on probation in view of the fact that he had made restitution 'to the satisfaction of the parties concerned.' It had as a firm foundation for such initial intention the fact that defendant was 35 years of age, married, the father of two children, employed by J.C. Penney as an appliance salesman, and had a previously unblemished record.

* * *

"Although the court did indicate that if, after reading the probation report, it was not inclined to go along with its commitment, it would allow the defendant to withdraw his plea and go to trial, it is manifest that the court's change of mind was not founded on any material information contained in the report, but rather on a pique, to wit that insurance premiums generally might somehow be affected by the defendant making restitution of only $10,000 of the amount defalcated, while the surety made good on the $58,000 balance."

Justice Damiani dissented:

"The modification of the sentence in this case to a three-year term of probation constitutes an instance of unwarranted leniency for a 'white collar' crime. The law is clear that even if the sentencing court had made an unconditional promise of probation to defendant, that promise would, 'as a matter of law and strong public policy', be conditioned upon its being lawful and appropriate in the light of the subsequent presentence report or information obtained from other reliable sources. In the case at bar, defendant was not entitled to specific performance of the promise of probation, but rather only to an opportunity to withdraw his plea, which he declined.

"The instant modification allows the defendant to retire to his home in Connecticut, the restoration of which was financed at a cost of some $40,000, without making restitution of the full amount that the available proof shows he stole, and after having served only five days in jail for his crime."

Is restitution alone a sufficient sanction in cases of "white collar" crime?

Chapter 22

POST–TRIAL MOTIONS

UNITED STATES v. MILLER

United States Court of Appeals, Second Circuit, 1969.
411 F.2d 825.

FRIENDLY, CIRCUIT JUDGE.

We have before us appeals from a number of post-trial orders of Judge Blumenfeld in the District Court for Connecticut arising out of the conviction of James Miller for conspiring to import heroin in violation of 21 U.S.C. §§ 173–74. We affirmed the conviction in an opinion noting that the appeal was "rather unusual these days in that Miller claims he was innocent of the crime charged"; in the same opinion we affirmed the denial of Miller's first and somewhat pro forma motion for a new trial. After holding a petition for certiorari for many months, the Supreme Court denied this on the last day of its 1967 Term. Meanwhile the district court had entered an order, denying a second motion for a new trial based on confessions made under highly peculiar circumstances by one Mario Natalizio, who was not brought before the court and had repudiated the confessions. A further order, denied two other motions, one seeking a new trial on grounds relating to the merits, and another based on a supposed threat to one of the jurors. We are constrained to reverse so much of the last order as refused a new trial on the ground of the Government's failure to disclose to the defense the pre-trial hypnosis of its principal witness, in part by the attorney who examined him at trial. This ruling and our concomitant direction of a new trial render the other issues moot.

* * *

In May 1968, at the request of defense counsel, the Government arranged to have Caron attend at the New York City office of Dr. Herbert Walker for a psychiatric interview including hypnosis in the presence of counsel for both sides. Just before being placed under hypnosis, Caron disclosed he had been hypnotized while in custody in Texas.

Caron had been brought to the Southern District of Texas shortly before the trial of Miller's codefendants in September 1965 and had been extensively interviewed by the prosecutors, including Butler. Caron had then gone into some detail about the car used by the recipients of the second Bridgeport delivery that Butler had not previously heard; he identified the car as an old Buick and indicated that he had taken particular note of the license number. Since the identity of the recipients at Bridgeport was of no great importance in the Texas trial, the prosecutors had not pressed him on that point.

After the Texas trial Butler heard that Caron was threatening not to cooperate in the separate Miller trial, the continuance and prospective transfer of which to Connecticut had apparently become known to him. Butler went to see Caron in jail on February 16, 1966, "to assure him I would do the best I could to help him with his problems," and also to revive the question of his memory of the license number of the Buick. The best Caron could do was to recall that the number included 26. Having "a slight knowledge of hypnotism," Butler asked Caron "whether he would be willing to submit to hypnotism to see whether he could recall the license plate." Caron agreed.

Butler was back on February 21 with Edward B. Cushing whom he regarded as an expert in hypnosis. Cushing got the subject into hypnosis quickly. Caron remembered that the car was a green Buick and that the plates were black on yellow. He muttered the letters AM and then some numbers Butler thought were 526 but Cushing identified as 1826, as Caron confirmed. Since Caron was manifesting some distress, Cushing brought him out of hypnosis. After an interval, a second attempt by Cushing failed to produce hypnosis. Butler decided to take over, thinking that despite his "very limited knowledge of hypnotic techniques," he might have more success because of Caron's confidence in him. He asked Caron to reconstruct the early part of his second trip to Bridgeport in his mind and to tell what he recalled. Caron began this recital substantially as in his interviews with the prosecutors but when he reached the point of being in the restaurant for lunch with his family, 381 F.2d at 532, Butler's questions became more searching and Caron gave details Butler had not heard before. He described that the Buick would not start, that Frankie and the other man had to raise the hood, and that one of them complained over the choice of the car. There were six digits on the license plates but, while Caron put forward a considerable number of letters and numbers, he was uncertain about them. After suggesting that Caron dream about the license plates that night, Butler brought Caron out of hypnosis.

Butler and Cushing did not let go that easily. After lunch, Cushing again put Caron into hypnosis, and Butler took over the interrogation, this time proceeding to the license plates rather swiftly; Caron was now quite sure about "AM 1826." Cushing sought a description of the second man and got one consistent with what Caron had previously given.

Once the initial surprise over use of hypnosis has subsided, the incident seems rather colorless. Butler appears to have acted in entire good faith in subjecting Caron to hypnosis. He was endeavoring to revive Caron's memory about the license number, and a correct recollection of this could have tended to lead away from Miller as much as toward him. Neither Butler nor Cushing suggested anything to Caron he had not already said. The Government made no use of Caron's dim recollection of the license number at the trial, and the defense does not assert it would have been assisted by this. To the contrary, the one point on which Caron was clear, namely, the colors of the plates, points away from the defense's current theory.

Naturally the defense did not leave the matter in this stance. It adduced, through affidavit or testimony, the evidence of three psychiatrists expert in hypnosis. They claimed in the first instance that repetition under hypnosis of the story Caron had already told tended to imprint this on his mind; . . . After the hypnosis, they contended, Caron would always behold Miller as Frank and would be immune to defense suggestions that he had picked the wrong man. Still more damage was wrought in their view by Butler's having acted as hypnotist. This, they said, increased the influence Butler already possessed as the man who could help to relieve Caron of the many problems besetting him, and further reduced the reliability of Caron's testimony at the Connecticut trial, where Butler interrogated Caron and acted for the Government during the protracted cross-examination. . . . While the expert called by the Government regarded many of these claims as exaggerated, he conceded on cross-examination that if the hypnosis was not conducted according to expert techniques, what happened "could have had an effect" on Caron's subsequent ability to correct a mistake.

Whatever the rights and wrongs of the expert testimony may be, it is undeniable that disclosure of the hypnosis would have added another arrow to the rather large quiver trial counsel for the defense shot at Caron—limited opportunity for observation; initial alleged misdescription and picking the photograph of another man; a suggestion through the inclusion of three photographs of Miller in the dozen initially exhibited; knowledge that the prosecution was pleased with his identification; a lengthy criminal record; a letter written from jail telling his wife he had lied in identifying Frank; the Government's failure to place any charge against his wife, or any charge against him for the Bridgeport crimes; the Government's maintenance of his family during his incarceration; his fear of deportation; and his hope for pardon or commutation of sentence on the charge of smuggling heroin from Mexico to which he had pleaded guilty. It is not difficult to hear the ringing tones in which defense counsel would have told the jury that, not satisfied with "buying" Caron with money for his family and promises of leniency, the Government had blocked the door to repentance under cross-examination and the sanctity of the oath by hypnotism carried out by none other than the examining prosecutor himself. It is altogether plain that if the defense had known of the hypnosis incident and the court had refused to allow its use at the trial, the amount of other impeaching evidence against Caron would not have avoided a reversal.

The issue here differs since the request is for a new trial on the ground of newly discovered evidence. We have noted, the two classical formulations of the criterion—whether the new evidence "is so material that it would probably produce a different verdict, if the new trial were granted," and whether it might have produced a different verdict, a test that has been stated to be limited to cases of "recantation or where it has been proved that false testimony was given at the trial." In United States v. Johnson, 327 U.S. 106, 111 n. 5, 66 S.Ct. 464 (1946), the Supreme Court also noted the two tests but did not determine their respective areas of application. . . . [which test applies]. For we think developments during the trial placed a duty on the Government to disclose the hypnosis; that, where such a duty has not been discharged, a motion for a new trial must be granted if there is a significant possibility that the undisclosed evidence might have led to an acquittal or a hung jury; and that such a possibility exists here.

* * *

Repeatedly during several days of cross-examination, Caron was questioned about the license number of the green Buick.

Defense counsel had earlier requested notes of all interviews with Caron in the Galveston jail. . . . When the court asked whether "everything that was conceivably Jencks Act material in this case had been furnished to defense counsel or to the Court," Mr. Butler had answered in the affirmative, adding "We made a special effort to search the files." But his special effort had not unearthed his memorandum describing the hypnosis, although admittedly it was there. . . .

After full allowance for the problems confronting counsel in the stress of a long and heated trial which we noted in United States v. Keogh, the prodding furnished by these episodes must be taken to have served the "valuable office" of "flagging" the pretrial hypnosis, see id., thus placing upon Mr. Butler a duty of disclosure he did not discharge. Even if he did not recall the hypnosis or remember or locate his memorandum of it, he should have, and negligence of the prosecutor in failing to make evidence available to the defense reduces the standard of materiality needed to require the granting of a new trial below the formulations applicable where no prosecutorial misconduct exists.

To reduce but not to eliminate it. Negligent or even intentional failure of the prosecutor to disclose an additional item of impeaching evidence would not invariably require that a verdict be set aside. Here, as we have noted, the defense already possessed an abundance of impeaching material, the hypnosis incident seems without much force apart from the elaboration by the defense's psychiatric experts, and we have our own views how seriously a jury of Connecticut Yankees would have been likely to regard that. Still, as the record stands, the hypnosis had arguably placed at least some obstacle in the way of one of the most valuable protections accorded Miller by the Sixth Amendment—the possibility that the sanctity of the oath and effective cross-examination might lead Caron to recant his identification or at least to admit doubt. The defense could and very likely would have made this the capstone of its attack on the crucial witness for the prosecution—with what effect we cannot confidently say. Under all the circumstances, as Judge Swan wrote in Consolidated Laundries, "we are content to rest our decision on our conviction that the denial of a new trial here is inconsistent with the correct administration of criminal justice in the federal courts, which it is our duty as an appellate court to supervise."

We have reached this conclusion with some reluctance, particularly in light of the considered belief of the able and conscientious district judge, who has lived with this case for years, that review of the record in light of all the defense new trial motions left him "convinced of the correctness of the jury's verdict." We, who also have had no small exposure to the facts, are by no means convinced otherwise. The test, however, is not how the newly discovered evidence concerning the hypnosis would affect the trial judge or ourselves but whether, with the Government's case against Miller already subject to serious attack, there was a significant chance that this added item, developed by skilled counsel as it would have been, could have induced a reasonable doubt in the minds of enough jurors to avoid a conviction. We cannot conscientiously say there was not. With the panoply of rules that our legal system has devised to insure fairness in criminal trials, the least appropriate instance for a grudging attitude in applying them would be one where a defendant supposedly leading a blameless life has steadfastly asserted that the prosecution got the wrong man and the proof consisted almost wholly of an identification by an accomplice in the conspiracy and the latter's wife and other testimony by the former. If the price of our decision should be the ultimate escape of a guilty man rather than the vindication of an innocent one, this is the kind of case where that price is worth paying.

Since we hold that a new trial is required because of the failure to disclose Caron's pre-trial hypnosis, in part by Mr. Butler himself, it is unnecessary to consider the many other grounds urged by the defense.

* * *

MOORE, CIRCUIT JUDGE (concurring in the result) :

Although I concur in the result reached by the majority, I cannot adopt the hypotheses or philosophies of the opinion except the one ground on which we place common reliance, namely, disclosure of the hypnosis. . . .

The privilege of dealing with the problem in an abstract way is not afforded us here. We are confronted with actual facts: Caron was a key witness; identification of Miller was all-important; Caron was hypnotized and interrogated by the government in advance of trial (and I assume for purposes of developing the truth); defense counsel were not notified of the hypnosis and had no opportunity by examination or cross-examination to explore whatever might have been found at that time in Caron's subconscious mind or memory; defense counsel were not aware of the pre-trial hypnosis before or during the trial or that the prosecuting attorney had participated therein.

Specifically, I do not join in the majority's reference to the defendant's claim that he had led a blameless life and that because he asserted that "the prosecution got the wrong man," we should be willing to pay the price of "the ultimate escape of a guilty man." Any such philosophy strikes at the heart of our jury system. They saw, heard and convicted. It is what they saw and heard that is crucial. Of course no innocent man should be convicted. And this is no time or place to debate the philosophy, at odds with society's experience in most other fields, that it were better that ninety-nine guilty escape rather than one innocent man be convicted. If mistakes there have been, they have been the mistakes of the judgments of the defendants' fellow men.

Thus the only question open here in my opinion is: did the jury have all the facts before them essential to a fair appraisal of Caron's testimony? With full knowledge of the hypnosis incident, the jury might well have been satisfied with Caron's testimony. But this question is for the jury—not for our speculation. On this subject, I add my complete concurrence with the majority's statement that this "decision is not to be taken as implying any view that Caron's hypnosis disqualifies him from testifying on a new trial."

Lastly a word about Butler's supposed influence over Caron. Naturally, to capitalize on the incident to the maximum, the defense would depict Butler as a modern Svengali and Caron (to up-date the simile) as merely his Charlie McCarthy-like puppet. Here again is a jury question. Very few criminal jury cases are tried by equally-matched counsel. A few highly gifted members of the Bar in that field seem to possess extraordinary talents in eliciting testimony that their less talented brethren, fail to develop. This disparity may be countered—and usually is in jury summation—by comment on this very disparity in counsel's abilities. Many a David has overcome a courtroom Goliath. Whether such an appeal has been the cause or not must be kept securely locked in the jury room. Therefore, despite the interesting statistics and speculations of Messrs. Kalven & Zeisel, I prefer to leave to the future jury here their own appraisal of the effectiveness or influence of such counsel as may appear before them. And with similar thoughts in mind, I would refrain from comment on any evidence adduced on the former trial or on any language in our previous opinions relating thereto.

Thus, because the use of hypnosis as a means of attempting to ascertain the truth is, to say the least, novel and apparently subject to differing medical opinions, I believe that under the circumstances of this particular case, the jury should have had this fact before it in weighing Caron's testimony.

NOTES

1. The *Miller* case is unusual in two regards. It extended over an unusually long period of time and the defendant finally prevailed. The general rule (stated in *Miller*) is that motions for new trial on grounds of newly discovered evidence are generally disfavored and only granted with great caution. See United States v. De Marie, 261 F.2d 477 (7th Cir. 1959); Casias v. United States, 350 F.2d 317 (10th Cir. 1965). As the Illinois Su-

preme Court noted in People v. Holtzman, 1 Ill.2d 562, 116 N.E.2d 338 (1954):

> Applications for a new trial on the ground of newly discovered evidence are not looked upon with favor by the courts, and in order to prevent, so far as possible, fraud and imposition which defeated parties may be tempted to practice, as a last resort, to escape the consequence of an adverse verdict, such application should always be subjected to the closest scrutiny by the court, and the burden is upon the applicant to rebut the presumption that the verdict is correct and to show there has been no lack of diligence. The matter is largely discretionary with the trial court, and the exercise of its discretion will not be disturbed except in case of manifest abuse.

The general principle disapproving new trials for newly discovered evidence has very few exceptions. Motions for new trial based on improper influence of the jury are rarely filed or granted. Jurors are not commonly subjected to improper influence and, if they are, the matter is usually brought to the court's attention before the end of trial (except when a bailiff makes improper remarks to a jury during deliberation, Parker v. Gladden, 385 U.S. 363, 87 S.Ct. 468 (1966)). Finally, because of the strictures against questioning jurors and their reluctance to answer questions and their ignorance of what is improper, the fact of unauthorized contact by some outsider with the jury is not readily uncovered.

2. While traditionally a motion for new trial was necessary to assure review of alleged errors on appeal (See United States v. Pellegrino, 273 F. 2d 570 (2nd Cir. 1960); United States v. Smith, 331 F.2d 145 (6th Cir. 1964); People v. Yetter, 386 Ill. 594, 54 N.E.2d 532 (1944), cert. denied 323 U.S. 743, 65 S.Ct. 56; State v. Davis, 251 S.W.2d 610 (Mo.1952)), in recent years several courts have done away with the requirement if the error was otherwise preserved by timely objection at trial. See United States v. Cook, 432 F.2d 1093 (7th Cir. 1970), cert. denied 401 U.S. 996, 91 S.Ct. 1224: ("Under federal procedure, it is not necessary to file motion for new trial in order to have reviewed on appeal questions properly preserved at trial"); People v. McCabe, 49 Ill.2d 338, 275 N.E.2d 407 (1971). Even in the absence of objection before or at trial, courts will often review the record under the "plain error" doctrine. See United States v. Stamas, 443 F.2d 860 (1st Cir. 1971), cert. denied 404 U.S. 851, 92 S.Ct. 86; United States v. Valez, 431 F.2d 622 (8th Cir. 1970); contra: United States v. Wenner, 417 F.2d 979 (8th Cir. 1969).

If written motions for new trial are or must be filed, several courts deem waived any errors not specifically alleged therein. See People v. Hairston, 46 Ill.2d 348, 263 N.E.2d 840 (1970), cert. denied 402 U.S. 972, 91 S.Ct. 1658; State v. Mallory, 336 S.W.2d 383 (Mo.1960), cert. denied 364 U.S. 852, 81 S.Ct. 99.

Motions for new trial cover both errors of law and sufficiency of the evidence. The scope of evidence review on motions for new trial is, theoretically at least, broader than the motions for a directed verdict of acquittal. The usual standard in directed verdict motions is whether, if believed, the stated case is sufficient. The motion for new trial allows (as the Miller case shows) a certain latitude to the court to act as the thirteenth juror and make credibility judgments.

Along with a motion for new trial, the defense may make a motion in arrest of judgment which is confined to "jurisdictional" errors such as the failure of the indictment to charge an offense or the lack of subject-matter jurisdiction.

Ordinarily, post-trial motions are a very unexciting matter. Defense counsel files form motions raising legal questions or simply states his motions orally. The prosecution seldom replies and the court routinely denies them.

3. In considering the *Miller* case it ought to be noted that motions for new trial based on newly discovered evidence are often, but not always, subject to extended time limits. The Federal Rule (Fed.R.Crim.P. 33) provides a two-year limitation. Few jurisdictions allow such a long period. Consider also what the result in *Miller* would have been if government counsel or the witness Caron had not consented to have Caron examined by a defense psychiatrist? Of course, if a convict discovers strong exculpatory evidence after his conviction is final, he may seek post-conviction relief, i. e. state or federal habeas corpus, if he can establish government suppression of the evidence. If this is not the case, his only official recourse will usually be the pursuit of executive clemency since, without proof of a *Brady* violation (see Chapter 15–A), newly discovered evidence does not provide grounds for federal habeas corpus relief. Unofficially, he may persuade the prosecutor and the court of his innocence and file a motion for new trial, the lateness of which will not be "noticed" by court or prosecutor and which will be granted by agreement.

Chapter 23

APPELLATE AND OTHER POST–TRIAL REMEDIES

A. APPEALS

---

1. APPEALS FROM CONVICTIONS

In jurisdictions in which a defendant's appeal is to an intermediate appellate court, upon affirmance, the defendant may file a petition asking the highest state court, within its discretion, to grant further review.

Once all avenues of direct review are exhausted within the state system, a convicted defendant may petition the United States Supreme Court for certiorari to review any federal constitutional claim which the state reviewing courts rejected. 28 U.S.C. 1257(c). In theory the state court defendant who unsuccessfully challenged a state statute upon federal constitutional grounds has a *right* to have his case heard on appeal by the Supreme Court. 28 U.S.C. 1257(b). In fact, however, most criminal "appeals" to the Supreme Court are dismissed for want of a substantial federal question. As in civil cases, the Supreme Court exercises almost as much discretion in limiting its "appeal" docket as it does its certiorari docket.

NOTES

1. *Rights of Indigent Appellants.* Issues concerning the rights of indigents have been discussed previously in Chapter 9, Section A.

2. *Waiver Principle.* In both federal and state reviewing court, normally an issue will not be considered on direct appeal unless it has been presented to the trial court (in the form of a timely offer of proof, objection, motion to suppress, etc.). This is true even of claims which are of federal constitutional dimension. If a state reviewing court, in accordance with a fairly administered waiver rule, rejects a claim because it had not been properly preserved, an "adequate, independent" state basis for the decision will prevent review by the Supreme Court on appeal or certiorari from the state reviewing court. Henry v. Mississippi, 379 U.S. 443, 85 S.Ct. 564 (1965).

Occasionally an appellate court, in reviewing a conviction, will take notice of a "plain error" even though the defense did not properly preserve the issue in the trial court. Normally such an error must be both blatant and particularly prejudicial. Sometimes such errors are noted to avoid defendant's claim on appeal that defense counsel at trial was incompetent. Although a "plain error" is far more likely to be noticed in an appeal from a criminal conviction than in a civil appeal, even in criminal cases, in the vast majority of situations, a claim of error not properly preserved in the trial court will be deemed waived for appellate purposes.

3. Not every error in a criminal trial requires reversal of a conviction. States remain free to apply their own harmless error rules where the error consists of a violation of state law. However, where the error is of federal constitutional dimension, a federal standard governs. In Chapman v. California, 386 U.S. 18, 87 S.Ct. 824 (1967), the Supreme Court held that reversal was required unless the constitutional error was "harmless beyond a reasonable doubt". Although not expressly disavowing that standard, the Supreme Court has, in the eyes of some observers, deemed error harmless according to a standard more favorable to the prosecution.

In Harrington v. California, 395 U.S. 250, 89 S.Ct. 1726 (1969), the Supreme Court assumed arguendo a violation of the rule announced in Bruton v. United States, 391 U.S. 123, 88 S.Ct. 1620 (1965), in that confessions by two co-defendants apparently implicating Harrington were admitted into evidence at a joint trial. The respondent state of California argued that the erroneous admission of these statements was harmless under the *Chapman* standard. An amicus brief argued that reviewing courts must be "freed from the bonds of the dictum in Chapman which seems to suggest that other overwhelming evidence is not to be an important factor in determining whether a particular constitutional error should be deemed harmless":

> Any rational harmless error rule, whether applied in civil cases or in criminal cases, whether the error is of constitutional or of non-constitutional dimension, must make the weight of the properly admitted evidence a highly relevant factor in making the calculation of whether the error was harmful. This is especially true where the error was committed in good faith reliance upon a then prevailing decision. (Brief of People of State of Illinois, p. 7)

A majority of the Court, asserting that it was not departing from *Chapman*, held the error in question to be harmless, noting that the remaining evidence was "overwhelming." Justice Brennan, joined by Chief Justice Warren and Justice Marshall, dissented, declaring that the Court, purporting to apply *Chapman*, in fact overruled it by holding that "constitutional error in the trial of a criminal offense may be held harmless if there is 'overwhelming' untainted evidence to support the conviction". Note that application of a less stringent harmless error rule is one method of reducing the number of convictions overturned by retroactive application of new constitutional decisions such as *Bruton*. Is this a healthy compromise?

In Chambers v. Maroney, 399 U.S. 42, 90 S.Ct. 1975 (1970), the Supreme Court upheld lower court determinations that the admission into evidence of ammunition allegedly unlawfully seized in a robbery suspect's home, if erroneous, was harmless beyond a reasonable doubt. The Court cited *Harrington* and omitted reference to *Chapman*.

In Schneble v. Florida, 405 U.S. 427, 92 S.Ct. 1056 (1972), another *Bruton* error was found harmless, in a context which suggested that *Chapman* had, indeed, been diluted by *Harrington*.

2. DEFENSE INTERLOCUTORY APPEALS

In many jurisdictions, a defendant who loses a pre-trial ruling (*e.g.*, through the denial of a motion to suppress), has no right to a review of that decision before trial. He or she must go through trial and, if convicted, can present the claim on appeal. One exception in the federal system is that a defendant who loses a motion to dismiss for former jeopardy has a right to interlocutory review. See Chapter 13, Section A8. The same is not true where a speedy trial claim has been rejected. See United States v. MacDonald, 435 U.S. 850, 98 S.Ct. 1547 (1978).

Some state jurisdictions, either through appeal as a matter of right, or through the use of discretionary writs such as mandamus, prohibition, or habeas corpus, more frequently allow a defendant access to a court of review before trial.

3. THE PROSECUTION'S RIGHT TO APPEAL

In many jurisdictions the prosecution has the right to an interlocutory appeal from a pre-trial order suppressing evidence, as was discussed briefly in Chapter 13, Section H. Once jeopardy has attached the prosecution's right to appeal is much more limited. Constitutional limitations upon this right have been treated in various cases and notes found within Chapter 13, Section A.

B. OTHER STATE COLLATERAL REMEDIES

Each state provides a defendant with one or more methods of initiating an attack upon a conviction by filing a petition in the trial court after he has been sentenced.* Some of these remedies were created specifically to permit post-conviction attacks, for example, the Illinois Post Conviction Hearing Act, Ill.Rev.Stat. ch. 38, § 122 (1979). Others, such as coram nobis and state habeas corpus, have come to serve as post-conviction remedies through the evolution of case law or statutory changes. The scope of each post-conviction remedy varies, but some general principles always determine the availability and the limitations of each remedy. The important questions remain the same.

1. What kind of issues can be raised? Can a particular remedy be used to litigate non-jurisdictional issues? Is it designed to remedy wrongs only of a constitutional dimension? Is its use limited to cases where the trial court was under a critical misapprehension of the facts?

2. Is there an exhaustion of remedies requirement? Suppose no direct appeal was taken or suppose a direct appeal is pending; does that mean that a particular collateral remedy is not presently available?

---

* Sometime these remedies are called "collateral" to distinguish them from direct appellate review. The term is something of a misnomer because, if successful, the post-conviction attack voids the conviction just as does a reversal on direct review. Elsewhere in the law the term "collateral attack" refers to efforts in Proceeding *B* to prevent Judgment *A* from being given collateral effect. Thus, for example, a defendant who argues against the use of Conviction *A* in sentencing him in Trial *B* because he was denied counsel in Trial *A* is collaterally attacking Conviction *A*, as that term is usually used outside the criminal law.

3. Is there a statute of limitations? If so, when does it commence and when is it tolled?

4. Is there a custody requirement? If so, what constitutes custody? Does release from custody *pendente lite* moot the proceedings?

5. Is the use of the remedy restricted to certain types of convictions? Does it matter whether the petitioner is a misdemeanant or a felon? Must the sentence under attack have commenced to run before a petitioner serving consecutive sentences is eligible to complain about that sentence?

6. What is the effect of a prior direct appeal or the previous use of the same or a different collateral remedy? How strictly are doctrines of *res judicata* and waiver applied?

State post-conviction proceedings ordinarily are initiated by the filing of a written petition in the trial court. Frequently the warden who has custody is the named respondent. Where matters outside the original trial record are alleged, typically there is a requirement of supporting affidavits. The trial court is required to decide whether sufficient cause is shown to justify an evidentiary hearing. In federal habeas corpus 28 U.S.C. 2254 specifies when a hearing must be held.

Frequently post-conviction proceedings are deemed civil in nature, although just as often ordinary civil discovery rules are held inapplicable. See, e. g., People v. Rose, 48 Ill.2d 300, 268 N.E.2d 700 (1971), and Harris v. Nelson, 394 U.S. 286, 89 S.Ct. 1082 (1969). The United States Supreme Court has not held that the indigent state post-conviction petitioner or the federal habeas corpus petitioner has an absolute right to counsel at the trial level. Thus unless state law provides the right to counsel, appointment of counsel for the post-conviction petitioner is a matter of judicial discretion.

Generally the losing party, whether the petitioner or the respondent, can appeal the trial court's decision in the post-conviction proceedings. A federal habeas corpus petitioner cannot appeal an adverse decision unless either the district judge or the Court of Appeals issues a certificate of probable cause for appeal. The indigent has no absolute constitutional right to appellate counsel in post-conviction proceedings under current decisions. However he does have the right to proceed in *forma pauperis* and the right to a free transcript of the post-conviction proceedings. See Lane v. Brown, 372 U.S. 477, 83 S.Ct. 768 (1963).

The primary post-conviction remedy for attacking a *federal* conviction is 28 U.S.C. 2255, which is sometimes called an analog to federal habeas corpus for state prisoners (28 U.S.C. 2241–2254). As with habeas corpus petitions, 2255 petitions are increasingly numerous.

C. FEDERAL HABEAS CORPUS FOR
STATE PRISONERS

A defendant who has been convicted of a state crime may at some point in time be barred from making effective use of any and all state remedies as a means of raising a particular issue. For example, if the issue was resolved against him on direct appeal, normally the doctrine of *res judicata* will bar relief in any state post-conviction proceeding. In such an instance, if the question is of federal constitutional dimension, he may be entitled to a decision on the merits of his claim from a federal district judge where a federal habeas corpus petition has been filed. Through a series of decisions, of which the most important is Fay v. Noia, 372 U.S. 391, 83 S.Ct. 822 (1963), federal habeas corpus evolved to the point where it could serve as a post-conviction remedy for almost any state prisoner who claims that his conviction is constitutionally infirm and who has exhausted presently available state remedies. In Stone v. Powell, Chapter 6, Section D3, supra, the Supreme Court limited the use of federal habeas corpus as a means of raising Fourth Amendment claims.

"Custody" is a prerequisite for federal habeas corpus, but in recent times the concept has been expanded to permit habeas corpus for individuals on parole, Jones v. Cunningham, 371 U.S. 236, 83 S.Ct. 373 (1963), probation, Benson v. California, 328 F. 2d 159 (9th Cir. 1964), and, in some instances, for convicted defendants free on bond or recognizance before serving their sentences, Hensley v. Municipal Court, 409 U.S. 840, 93 S.Ct. 43 (1972).

If the petition is filed while the petitioner is in custody, as long as "collateral consequences" flow from the conviction, a habeas corpus petition attacking a conviction cannot be dismissed as moot even though the petitioner has been completely discharged *pendente lite.* Carafas v. La Vallee, 391 U.S. 234, 88 S.Ct. 1556 (1968). This may be true even in some misdemeanor cases. United States ex rel. Lawrence v. Woods, 432 F.2d 1072 (7th Cir. 1970). Peculiar problems of consecutive or concurrent sentences and troublesome venue questions have fallen by the wayside, expanding the availability of federal habeas corpus to more and more persons convicted of state crimes. See, e. g., Salker v. Wainwright, 390 U.S. 335, 88 S.Ct. 962 (1968), Peyton v. Rowe, 391 U.S. 54, 88 S.Ct. 1549 (1968), and Braden v. 30th Judicial District Court of Kentucky, 410 U.S. 484, 93 S.Ct. 1123 (1973).

One of the more controversial aspects of federal habeas corpus for state prisoners arose from the "deliberate bypass" rule of Fay v. Noia, supra. Under this concept, even though a state court on direct review had determined that a federal claim had been waived for failure to preserve the issue in the trial court (discussed previously in Section A, note 2), a federal district court might be required to reach the merits of the claim. The "mere" failure to raise the issue in the state court did not bar federal relief. A "deliberate bypass" was required before federal relief was barred. To some federal courts this meant that the state was required to show that the defendant personally participated in the decision not to raise the issue in state court. See, e. g., Henderson v. Heinze, 349 F.2d 67 (9th Cir. 1965). To others this meant that there must have been a tactical advantage to the defendant in not raising the issue in state court. See, e. g., United States ex rel. Williams v. Brantley, 502 F.2d 1383 (7th Cir. 1974). Wainright v. Sykes, 433 U.S. 72, 97 S.Ct. 2497 (1977), overruled *Fay* and in effect, held that normally the mere failure to raise a claim in state court (absent a showing of "cause" for noncompliance with the state procedural rule and a showing of "prejudice") will bar federal habeas corpus relief. The court reasoned, in part, that enforcement of "timely objection" requirements in deciding cases on direct review makes little sense if the defendant will still be entitled to a decision on the merits in subsequent state or federal post conviction proceedings. Together with *Stone*, the *Sykes* decision may be viewed as a major effort of the *Burger* court to undo the Warren court's expansion of federal habeas corpus as an added tier of review for state prisoners.

APPENDIX

Provisions of the Constitution of the United States, and certain Amendments thereto, of particular significance in the administration of criminal justice:

Preamble

We the People of the United States, in Order to form a more perfect Union, establish Justice, insure domestic Tranquility, provide for the common defense, promote the general Welfare, and secure the Blessings of Liberty to ourselves and our Posterity, do ordain and establish this Constitution for the United States of America.

Article I.

* * *

Section 8. The Congress shall have Power To lay and collect Taxes, Duties, Imposts and Excises, to pay the Debts and provide for the common Defence and general Welfare of the United States; but all Duties, Imposts and Excises shall be uniform throughout the United States; . . .

To regulate Commerce with foreign Nations, and among the several States and with the Indian Tribes; . . .

To provide for the Punishment of counterfeiting the Securities and current Coin of the United States; . . .

To constitute Tribunals inferior to the supreme Court;

To define and punish Piracies and Felonies committed on the high Seas, and Offences against the Law of Nations;

To declare War, grant Letters of Marque and Reprisal, and make Rules concerning Captures on Land and Water; . . .;

To make Rules for the Government and Regulation of the land and naval forces;

To provide for calling forth the Militia to execute the Laws of the Union, suppress Insurrections and repel Invasions;

To provide for organizing, arming, and disciplining, the Militia, and for governing such Part of them as may be employed in the Service of the United States, reserving to the States respectively, the Appointment of the Officers, and the Authority of training the Militia according to the discipline prescribed by Congress;

To exercise exclusive Legislation in all Cases whatsoever, over such District (not exceeding ten Miles square) as may, by Cession of particular States, and the Acceptance of Congress, become the Seat of the Government of the United States, and to exercise like Authority over all Places purchased by the Consent of the Legislature of the

State in which the Same shall be, for the Erection of Forts, Magazines, Arsenals, dock-Yards, and other needful Buildings;—And

To make all Laws which shall be necessary and proper for carrying into Execution the foregoing Powers, and all other Powers vested by this Constitution in the Government of the United States, or in any Department or Officer thereof.

Section 9.

* * *

No Bill of Attainder or ex post facto Law shall be passed.

Article III.

Section 1. The judicial Power of the United States, shall be vested in one supreme Court, and in such inferior Courts as the Congress may from time to time ordain and establish. The Judges, both of the supreme and inferior Courts, shall hold their Offices during good Behaviour, and shall, at stated Times, receive for their Services, a Compensation, which shall not be diminished during their Continuance in Office.

Section 2.

.   .   . the supreme Court shall have appellate Jurisdiction, both as to Law and Fact, with such Exceptions, and under such Regulations as the Congress shall make.

The Trial of all Crimes, except in Cases of Impeachment, shall be by Jury; and such Trial shall be held in the State where the said Crimes shall have been committed; but when not committed within any State, the Trial shall be at such Place or Places as the Congress may by Law have directed.

Section 3. Treason against the United States, shall consist only in levying War against them, or in adhering to their Enemies, giving them Aid and Comfort. No Person shall be convicted of Treason unless on the Testimony of two Witnesses to the same overt Act, or on Confession in open Court.

The Congress shall have Power to declare the Punishment of Treason, but no Attainder of Treason shall work Corruption of Blood, or Forfeiture except during the Life of the Person attainted.

Article VI.

* * *

This Constitution, and the Laws of the United States which shall be made in Pursuance thereof; and all Treaties made, or which shall be made, under the Authority of the United States, shall be the supreme Law of the Land; and the Judges in every State shall be bound thereby, any Thing in the Constitution or Laws of any State to the Contrary notwithstanding.

* * *

Amendments

Amendment I.

Congress shall make no law respecting an establishment of religion, or prohibiting the free exercise thereof; or abridging the freedom of speech, or of the press; or the right of the people peaceably to assemble, and to petition the Government for a redress of grievances.

Amendment II.

A well regulated militia, being necessary to the security of a free State, the right of the people to keep and bear arms, shall not be infringed.

Amendment III.

No Soldier shall, in time of peace be quartered in any house, without the consent of the owner, nor in time of war, but in a manner to be prescribed by law.

Amendment IV.

The right of the people to be secure in their persons, houses, papers, and effects, against unreasonable searches and seizures, shall not be violated, and no warrants shall issue, but upon probable cause, supported by oath or affirmation, and particularly describing the place to be searched, and the persons or things to be seized.

Amendment V.

No person shall be held to answer for a capital, or otherwise infamous crime, unless on a presentment or indictment of a Grand Jury, except in cases arising in the land or naval forces, or in the militia, when in actual service in time of war or public danger; nor shall any person be subject for the same offence to be twice put in jeopardy of life or limb; nor shall be compelled in any criminal case to be a witness against himself, nor be deprived of life, liberty, or property, without due process of law; nor shall private property be taken for public use, without just compensation.

Amendment VI.

In all criminal prosecutions, the accused shall enjoy the right to a speedy and public trial, by an impartial jury of the State and district wherein the crime shall have been committed, which district shall have been previously ascertained by law, and to be informed of the nature and cause of the accusation; to be confronted with the witnesses against him; to have compulsory process for obtaining witnesses in his favor, and to have the assistance of Counsel for his defence.

Amendment VII.

In Suits at common law, where the value in controversy shall exceed twenty dollars, the right of trial by jury shall be preserved, and no fact tried by a jury, shall be otherwise re-examined in any Court of the United States, than according to the rules of the common law.

Amendment VIII.

Excessive bail shall not be required, nor excessive fines imposed, nor cruel and unusual punishments inflicted.

Amendment IX.

The enumeration in the Constitution, of certain rights, shall not be construed to deny or disparage others retained by the people.

Amendment X.

The powers not delegated to the United States by the Constitution, nor prohibited by it to the States, are reserved to the States respectively, or to the people.

* * *

Amendment XIII.

Section 1. Neither slavery nor involuntary servitude, except as a punishment for crime whereof the party shall have been duly convicted, shall exist within the United States, or any place subject to their jurisdiction.

Section 2. Congress shall have power to enforce this article by appropriate legislation.

Amendment XIV.

Section 1. All persons born or naturalized in the United States, and subject to the jurisdiction thereof, are citizens of the United States and of the State wherein they reside. No State shall make or enforce any law which shall abridge the privileges or immunities of citizens of the United States; nor shall any State deprive any person of life, liberty, or property, without due process of law; nor deny to any person within its jurisdiction the equal protection of laws.

. . .

Section 5. The Congress shall have power to enforce, by appropriate legislation, the provisions of this article.

Amendment XV.

Section 1. The right of citizens of the United States to vote shall not be denied or abridged by the United States or by any State on account of race, color, or previous condition of servitude.

Section 2. The Congress shall have power to enforce this article by appropriate legislation.

Amendment XVI.

The Congress shall have power to lay and collect taxes on incomes, from whatever source derived, without apportionment among the several States, and without regard to any census or enumeration.

. . .

INDEX

†